"The figure a poem makes. It begins in delight and ends in wisdom."
– Robert Frost

"The historian speaks of what has happened, the poet of the kind of thing that **can** happen. Hence also poetry is a more philosophical and serious business than history; for poetry speaks more of universals, history of particulars."
– Aristotle

"The poem may embody perception so luminous it seems truth, but what keeps it alive is not fixed discovery; what keeps it alive is intelligence."
– Louise Glück

"A poem is the very image of life expressed in its eternal truth."
– Percy Bysshe Shelley

"Poetry is the supreme fiction."
– Wallace Stevens

"The poet's mission on earth is to inspire and to illuminate; and to leave behind to our glorious descendants an intricate and varied map of humanity."
– Marilyn Chin

"If I read a book and it makes my whole body so cold no fire can ever warm me, I know that it is poetry. If I feel physically as if the top of my head were taken off, I know that it is poetry. These are the only ways I know it. Is there any other way?"
– Emily Dickinson

Praise for Previous Editions of
LITERATURE AND ITS WRITERS

"Not only do I find *Literature and Its Writers* to be an excellent instructional text, but I also feel that my students are spending a semester with a literary gold mine. Many of them discover this and read far more selections than are assigned for the course."

— JANE WHORTON, *Pearl River Community College*

"*Literature and Its Writers* presents a wonderful array of authors from a plethora of backgrounds, and it does this in a balanced way so that students walk away from the class having a true understanding of the evolutions that have occurred in literature."

— DONNA PACKER-KINLAW, *University of North Carolina, Wilmington*

"I find the selections tremendously stimulating — the variety is incredible."

— TOM ZANIELLO, *Northern Kentucky University*

"For both my students and me, this collection strikes a good balance between compactness and comprehension: reasonable size, but with plenty of choices. I also appreciate the balance between contemporary and historical texts and the high percentage of women and minority writers."

— CAROLYN SIGLER, *University of Minnesota, Duluth*

"I use the author commentaries to raise issues of intention versus other kinds of meaning, the critical commentaries to provide springboards for arguments, and other kinds of commentaries to provide social, historical, and intellectual contexts. These are wonderfully useful!"

— WES CHAPMAN, *Illinois Wesleyan University*

"I love your commentaries. I've never seen that kind of commitment to hearing what the writers themselves have to say about writing and their own work in a student's text. It's a great idea and one I enjoy using with my classes!"

— ELIZABETH FLORES, *College of Lake County*

LITERATURE AND ITS WRITERS

A Compact Introduction
to Fiction, Poetry,
and Drama

■ **Books Written or Edited by Ann Charters**

The Story and Its Writer: An Introduction to Short Fiction
The American Short Story and Its Writer: An Anthology
Major Writers of Short Fiction: Stories and Commentaries
Beats & Company: Portrait of a Literary Generation
Kerouac: A Biography
The Portable Beat Reader
The Portable Jack Kerouac
The Portable Sixties Reader
Selected Letters of Jack Kerouac, 1940–1956
Selected Letters of Jack Kerouac, 1957–1969
Nobody: The Story of Bert Williams

■ **Books Written by Samuel Charters**

Some Poems/Poets: Studies in American Underground Poetry
Elvis Presley Calls His Mother After the Ed Sullivan Show
Mr. Jabi and Mr. Smythe
Jelly Roll Morton's Last Night at the Jungle Inn: An Imaginary Memoir
Louisiana Black: A Novel
A Country Year: A Chronicle
From a Swedish Notebook
Robert Johnson
Sweet as the Showers of Rain
The Country Blues
The Day Is So Long and the Wages So Small: Music on a Summer Island
The Legacy of the Blues: A Glimpse into the Art and the Lives of Twelve Great Bluesmen
The Roots of the Blues: An African Search
The Bluesmen: The Story and the Music of the Men Who Made the Blues

■ **Books Written by Ann Charters and Samuel Charters**

I Love: The Story of Vladimir Mayakovsky and Lili Brik
Blues Faces

Third Edition

LITERATURE AND ITS WRITERS

A Compact Introduction to Fiction, Poetry, and Drama

Ann Charters

UNIVERSITY OF CONNECTICUT

Samuel Charters

BEDFORD / ST. MARTIN'S
Boston ■ New York

For Bedford/St. Martin's

Developmental Editor: Maura Shea
Production Editor: Arthur Johnson
Senior Production Supervisor: Dennis Conroy
Marketing Manager: Jenna Bookin Barry
Editorial Assistant: Anne Noyes
Production Assistants: Kristen Merrill, Tina Lai, Kerri Cardone
Copyeditor: Lisa Wehrle
Text Design: Anna George
Cover Design: Donna Lee Dennison
Cover Art: "Richard Wright Seated at Typewriter." Copyright © Bettman/CORBIS.
Composition: Stratford Publishing Services
Printing and Binding: Quebecor World Kingsport

President: Joan E. Feinberg
Editorial Director: Denise B. Wydra
Editor in Chief: Karen S. Henry
Director of Marketing: Karen Melton
Director of Editing, Design, and Production: Marcia Cohen
Managing Editor: Elizabeth M. Schaaf

Library of Congress Control Number: 2003101690

Acknowledgments

FICTION

Sherman Alexie. "The Lone Ranger and Tonto Fistfight in Heaven" from *The Lone Ranger and Tonto Fistfight in Heaven* by Sherman Alexie. Copyright © 1993 by Sherman Alexie. Reprinted by permission of Grove/Atlantic, Inc.

Acknowledgments and copyrights are continued at the back of the book on pages 1693–1705, which constitute an extension of the copyright page. It is a violation of the law to reproduce these selections by any means whatsoever without the written permission of the copyright holder.

Preface for Instructors

Introductory literature anthologies are designed to help students explore the many ways to read, think, and write about literature. This is what *Literature and Its Writers* does, but with an important difference: As much as possible, it lets the words of writers themselves—the storytellers, the poets, the dramatists whose works appear in the anthology—lead the exploration. In this third edition, students can more clearly see that the writers are in conversation about literature—its making and its meanings, its purpose and importance—and that they, too, can join the conversation through reading, discussion, and writing.

A DISTINCTIVE EMPHASIS ON WRITERS AND WRITING

Writers, we believe, provide invaluable perspectives on the literature they create. Accordingly, *Literature and Its Writers* is threaded with writer talk: with quotations that clarify, with examples that enlighten, and especially with *commentaries* that show how writers think and write about literature. We have found that students respond readily to these voices in the text. They are more willing to raise their own voices to enter the conversation. They listen more attentively to what is being said. They express themselves more confidently. Having before them examples of writers speaking plainly, or colorfully, or profoundly, or provokingly, they are better able to speak and write that way themselves. Through the weave of literary works and literary voices, students comprehend what a human enterprise literature is—the work of talented individuals like themselves. Not only do students explore *what* and *how* literature means—interpretation and analysis—but also two fundamental questions about it: How is it made, and how is it related to us?

In our anthology, the 60 stories, 268 poems, and 9 plays are complemented by 100 commentaries that discuss specific literary works, literary form and influence, and the creative process. Students encounter not only "A Rose for Emily," but also what William Faulkner had to say about his famous story; not just the poetry of Emily Dickinson, but also Dickinson's remarks about her poetry in letters to Thomas Wentworth Higginson; not just Lorraine Hansberry's *A Raisin in the Sun,* but also Hansberry's admiring tributes to William Shakespeare and Arthur Miller. The commentaries present countless opportunities for discussion and writing, as well as models of how writers think, read, and write about literature. But the focus on writers does not stop with the commentaries. Words of the writers themselves are interwoven throughout the uncommonly full biographical headnotes for individual authors, and in our definitions and discussions of the traditional elements of literary genres. Students hear from Margaret Atwood on a writer's voice, Robert Frost on rhyme, and Edward Albee on playwriting.

Finally, we have shifted all questions and selection-specific writing suggestions from the book itself to the Instructor's Manual (print and online versions) and to the book's companion Web site, which students can access. We do this so that our prompts neither interfere with what the writers have to say about the literature nor influence how students interpret it. The choice of assigning or not assigning our apparatus remains the instructor's.

HOW THE BOOK IS ORGANIZED

After some introductory remarks, *Literature and Its Writers* is divided into four parts. Parts One, Two, and Three are devoted, respectively, to short fiction, poetry, and drama. Within each of these parts, introductory chapters discuss the genre, its elements, and how to read, think about, and write about a work in a particular genre. Then comes the literature. The genre of fiction is represented by the most extensive and diverse selection available in a book of this scope: 60 stories, arranged alphabetically by author. A rich array of 268 poems has been selected and organized to enable a variety of approaches to teaching poetry—through literary elements, themes, and individual poets. The 9 chronologically arranged plays represent essential and widely taught works from the days of ancient Greece to contemporary America.

Following the literature in each part are the commentaries about that literature: 42 commentaries on stories and storytellers, 35 on poetry and poets, and 23 on plays and playwrights. Seven important writers are discussed in depth through multiple commentaries. Although the commentaries mainly present the remarks of the writers themselves, they also include a sampling of contemporary criticism, varieties of which are discussed in detail in Part Four, Writing about Literature.

Part Four is devoted to all aspects of reading and writing and to understanding literary theory. Chapter 24 introduces students to important schools of literary theory and references several commentaries throughout the book as examples of each critical approach. Chapters 25, 26, and 27 walk students through the process of writing an essay about literature, from journal keeping to revising; provide tips on writing basic types of literary papers with model student essays; and include an extensive up-to-date section on writing a research paper with step-by-step guidelines for finding a topic, evaluating online sources, drafting the essay, and documenting sources. Altogether Part Four includes six student papers that provide realistic models for writing different types of essays.

NEW TO THIS EDITION

New Literature and Commentaries   The 16 new stories, 58 new poems, and one new play encompass a greater array of writers than ever before, striking a balance between classic works and less canonical but highly teachable ones. In the fiction section, the new stories include much-anthologized works by Edgar Allan Poe and Kate Chopin, American multicultural stories by Edwidge Danticat and Jhumpa Lahiri, international stories by Nadine Gordimer and Mary Lavin, and contemporary stories by Russell Banks and Annie Proulx. The poetry section continues to provide a balance of familiar and less familiar works on compelling themes by classic and contemporary poets including Billy Collins, Rita Dove, and Seamus Heaney. In the drama section, we include Paula Vogel's recent Pulitzer Prize–winning play, *How I Learned to Drive.* The 12 new commentaries present illuminating essays by Richard Ford on Anton Chekhov, D. H. Lawrence on Edgar Allan Poe, and Sir John Gielgud on playing Hamlet, among others.

New Invitations for Students to Enter the Conversations about Literature   As we mentioned earlier, what sets the third edition of *Literature and Its Writers* apart from its previous editions and from other introductory anthologies is that it aims to help students see literature as a *kind* of conversation—stories tacitly argue a point of view on the human condition; poems are written in response to other poems; dramatic dialogue literally represents conversation, debate, and discussion. Moreover, *Literature and Its Writers* presents literature as a *subject* of spirited, creative, questing conversations—writers' commentaries initiate and contribute to conversations on what literature means, how it comes to be, and why it matters.

In the third edition, we have provided more ways and more help for students to enter those conversations. For example, notice that in the poetry section we have expanded the chapter on "Poets Speaking Out" to present more thematic "poetic conversations." Students sometimes become trapped by the idea that reading poetry means little more than solving linguistic puzzles and finding "hidden meanings." In Chapter 12's five thematic sections on social issues, including new clusters of poems on African American identity and women's experiences, students can discover (or rediscover) that poets have long used their craft to address real-life matters in ways that conventional discourse cannot.

Throughout the book, new Connections references put works in conversation with each other. References at the end of several headnotes indicate related works elsewhere in the book, deepening a student's understanding of a story, poem, or play. For instance, by reading Susan Glaspell's play *Trifles* and her short story on the same topic, "A Jury of Her Peers," a student can see that Glaspell's two works are in conversation with each other, showing us how she treats the same subject in two different genres. Similarly, students see writers in conversation with each other when they read Anton Chekhov's story "The Lady with the Pet Dog" and Joyce Carol Oates's contemporary version of the story.

So students can better understand what is at issue and more readily enter the discussion about it, the casebook-like "author-in-depth" sections have been reframed as "Conversations." These Conversations sections invite students to explore Raymond Carver's writing process and Flannery O'Connor's sources, ideas, and techniques. They also offer new ways of interpreting Emily Dickinson, Robert Frost's poetics, Langston Hughes and the African American poetic tradition, and Shakespeare's *Hamlet* as text and performance (the Shakespeare section includes photographs of *Hamlet* in performance). There is also an entirely new Conversations section that focuses on critical responses to the fiction of Edgar Allan Poe.

To better prepare students to enter the conversation, the first two fiction chapters have been completely revised. They now walk students through a careful reading and analysis of Grace Paley's short story "Samuel" and help them to discover the writing process that works for them. The companion Web site—now fully integrated with the book—also helps students enter the conversation by providing discussion questions and writing suggestions for every selection in the book. The new glossary of literary terms equips students with the essential vocabulary to discuss literature.

INSTRUCTOR'S MANUAL AND WEB SITE

An instructor's manual, *Resources for Teaching* LITERATURE AND ITS WRITERS, Third Edition, presents a wide range of teaching resources, including essays that offer interpretations of individual works to explore in the classroom; selected bibliographies for many writers; questions to prompt student discussion; topics for writing; an extensive list of audiovisual resources; and a thematic table of contents. In addition to the print version, an online version is available through the companion Web site at bedfordstmartins.com/charters. The companion Web site is now fully integrated with the book and includes study and discussion questions and writing assignments for every story, poem, and play in the anthology; LitQuiz (with a comprehension quiz for every story and play in the anthology); LitLinks (with annotated links for almost every writer in the book); and VirtuaLit Interactive Fiction and Poetry Tutorials that introduce students to the elements, criticism, and cultural contexts of literature in an interactive format.

CD AND VIDEOTAPES

Speaking of Literature, a CD with readings of selected poems, stories, scenes from plays, and commentaries from writers, is available to instructors who adopt *Literature and Its Writers,* Third Edition. This rich resource for instructors and students brings literature to life through the compelling voices of celebrated writers and actors. To order the *Literature and Its Writers* book and CD package, use ISBN 0–312–41478–1. A selection of videotapes of stories and plays in the book is also available.

ACKNOWLEDGMENTS

In this third edition, we consider ourselves fortunate to have had the opportunity to work with our most responsive and resourceful editor, Maura Shea, whose dedication to the project has helped us through many bumpy patches. We would also like to acknowledge the steadfast support of the president of Bedford/St. Martin's, Joan Feinberg, and president emeritus Charles Christenson, who originally came to us with the idea for this anthology. In shaping the direction of the book, we worked closely with executive editor Steve Scipione for the first edition, and he has continued to offer useful insights and suggestions throughout the revision process. Our patient production editor, Arthur Johnson, attentively saw the book through its final stages. Also at Bedford/St. Martin's, we would like to thank Anne Noyes for her tireless library research, manuscript preparation, and assistance on the Instructor's Manual and Web site. We are grateful to Herbert Lederer, Emeritus Professor of German at the University of Connecticut in Storrs, for serving as an experienced and knowledgable consultant for the translation of the Kafka stories into American English, and to Kurt Fendt of MIT, for double-checking the translations and offering good advice. In the English Department at the University of Connecticut in Storrs, Professors Tom Roberts and Margaret Higonnet were kind enough to read a draft of the essay on "Translating Kafka" and offer helpful suggestions for revision; Professor Patrick Hogan, a specialist in critical theory, suggested several ways to improve the new Conversations section on Edgar Allan Poe. We thank Janet Gardner of the University of Massachusetts, Dartmouth, and Barbara Fister of Gustavus Adolphus College, who helped write and update the chapter on the research paper in past editions. For assistance with the Instructor's Manual, we are grateful to Susan Abbotson of the University of Connecticut, who wrote many of the entries in the Drama section, and William Sheidley of the University of Southern Colorado, who wrote many of the entries in the Fiction section.

In addition, professors who used the previous edition of the anthology and generously took time to share their ideas about it include: Lawrence Barkley, Mt. San Jacinto College; Chris Beyers, Assumption College; William O. Boggs, Slippery Rock University of Pennsylvania; Yvonne Bruce, The Citadel; Beth Brunk-Chavez, James Madison University; Kevin Cantwell, Macon State College; Wes Chapman, Illinois Wesleyan University; Alice Church, Nashville State Technical Institute; Kelly Crawley, McDowell Community College; Amy DiBello, College of the Desert; Paul Edwards, Northwestern University; Charlene Engleking, Lindenwood University; Patty Fairbanks, Northern Kentucky University; Tyler Farrell, University of Wisconsin–Milwaukee; Andy Fogle, George Mason University; Scott D. Gilbert, Winthrop University; Beth Graham, Campbellsville University; Allen Grove, Alfred University; Paul Gustafson, George Mason University; Thomas Harrison, Macon State College; Linda A. Julian, Furman University; Robert Kelly, Macon State College; Jeff Kosse, Iowa Western Community College; David C. Lowery, Jones County Jr. College; Joyce Morison, Miami University; Patrick Naick, University of Iowa; William Neal, Campbellsville University; Donna Packer-Kinlaw, University of Carolina, Wilmington;

Janice Porth, Northern Kentucky University; Catherine Rogers, Savannah State University; SueAnn Schatz, Lock Haven University; Linda Schmidt, Iowa Western Community College; Michele Sharp, East Carolina University; Carolyn Sigler, University of Minnesota, Duluth; Anthony Turner, George C. Wallace State Community College; Martha Willoughby, Pearl River Community College; Meredith Wilson, Solano Community College; Eleanor Whitaker, Fairfield University.

Ann Charters
University of Connecticut

Samuel Charters

(Photo by Reenie Barrow)

ABOUT THE EDITORS

Ann Charters (Ph.D., Columbia University) is the editor of *The Story and Its Writer,* Sixth Edition (Bedford/St. Martin's, 2003), the best-selling introduction to fiction. She is a professor of English at the University of Connecticut and has taught introduction to literature courses for many years. A preeminent authority on the Beat writers, Charters has written a critically acclaimed biography of Jack Kerouac; compiled *Beats & Company,* a collection of her own photographs of Beat writers; and edited the best-selling *Portable Beat Reader.* Her most recent books are *The Kerouac Reader, Selected Letters of Jack Kerouac, 1957–1969, Beat Down to Your Soul, The Portable Sixties Reader,* and *The American Short Story and Its Writer* (Bedford/St. Martin's, 2000).

Samuel Charters has taught creative writing and published widely in a variety of genres, including eleven books of poetry, four novels, a book of criticism on contemporary American poetry, a biography (coauthored with Ann Charters) of the poet Vladimir Mayakovsky, and translations of the poetry of Tomas Tranströmer and Edith Södergran. An ethnomusicologist, he produces blues and jazz recordings and has published ten books about music, among them histories of New York and New Orleans jazz and a study of Robert Johnson.

Brief Contents

Contents

5. Commentaries on Stories and Storytellers   *547*

Part Two ▪ POETRY 681

9. The Elements of Poetry: A Poet's Meanings   710

10. The Types of Poetry: A Poet's Forms   732

Part Three ■ DRAMA 1047

22. Commentaries on Plays and Playwrights 1528

INTRODUCTION
Connecting with Literature

Writing, for me, is an act of faith, a hope that I will discover what I mean
by "truth." I also think of reading as an act of faith, a hope that I will
discover something remarkable about ordinary life, about myself. And
if the writer and the reader discover the same thing, if they have that
connection, the act of faith has resulted in an act of magic. To me, that's
the mystery and the wonder of both life and fiction—the connection
between two individuals who discover in the end that they are more the
same than they are different.
　　　　　－AMY TAN, "In the Canon, For All the Wrong Reasons"

Why study literature? We read stories, poems, and plays for many reasons. When you allow yourself to become fully immersed in an author's words
and ideas, you can bring to life an imaginary world that can tell you something
about your own everyday reality. As a student of literature, you will find that
the stories, poems, and plays in this anthology will often enable you to view life
with a new clarity as you relate what you have read to your own experience.

The novelist Vladimir Nabokov proposed a quiz for students of literature
that would give ten definitions of a reader and ask them to choose any four definitions that added up to what they considered the necessary qualities of a *good*
reader. In Nabokov's essay "Good Readers and Good Writers," his quiz went
as follows:

1. The reader should belong to a book club.
2. The reader should identify himself or herself with the hero or heroine.
3. The reader should concentrate on the social-economic or historical angle.
4. The reader should prefer a story with action and dialogue to one with
   none.
5. The reader should have seen the book in a movie.
6. The reader should be a budding author.
7. The reader should have imagination.
8. The reader should have memory.
9. The reader should have a dictionary.
10. The reader should have some artistic sense.

Nabokov predicted that most students would choose items 2 and 3 as
essential to being a good reader, but he insisted that only the last four items
were necessary. You don't always have to identify with the hero or heroine of a
literary work, using the text as a mirror to project an image of yourself playing

out different roles. And if you anxiously expect your instructor to teach you that there is only one correct interpretation of a complex poem, story, or play — or if you lazily prefer to approach a text with a preconceived notion of its meaning, which you copy down in the classroom before you read the assignment for yourself — then you will not start out as a good student of literature.

A good reader possesses an active imagination, a retentive memory, a college dictionary, and a rudimentary artistic sense. Furthermore, if you hope to become a great reader, you will also need to bring to the course — along with your imagination and memory — a strong desire to refine and develop your critical sense. This quality will evolve naturally from your close reading and writing about literary texts.

The process of making a close connection with literature and becoming a great reader always helps you to become a better writer. The American poet Robert Frost aptly described this process when he said, "To learn to write is to learn to have ideas." Reading closely and thinking critically about the literature in this anthology will suggest ideas that you can develop in class discussions and in your essays.

At first you may suppose that you have little in common with the distinguished authors gathered here, but bear in mind that each of them was once a beginner. The short story writer Raymond Carver described taking his first college course in "Creative Writing 101." After reading his commentary, one student recognized a connection with Carver's experience in this short essay.

STUDENT ESSAY

Raymond Carver's "Creative Writing 101"

We all have several turning points in our life. These turning points may include getting married, losing loved ones, having children, and changing jobs. However, we can have other turning points which exert more subtle effects on us and are no less significant.

The American writer Raymond Carver married young and had two children. He eked out a living to support his family, but he wanted to go to college because of his desire to be a writer. He felt in his bones that he had to get an education in order to learn more about being a writer. When he finally could enroll in a college writing course, he was fortunate to have John Gardner, a young novelist, as his teacher.

Studying with Gardner was a significant turning point in Carver's life. Gardner became aware of Carver's difficulty in finding a place to work, so he offered his student the key to his office, where Carver could begin what he remembered as his "first serious attempts at writing." Just as important, Gardner read Carver's first stories seriously. Sometimes Carver had to revise a sentence several times to satisfy his teacher. Gardner insisted that a writer must be honest. He couldn't "fake it" by writing about something he didn't believe in.

Carver learned what he called "a writer's values and craft" from his first writing teacher. These were what Gardner taught him in Creative Writing 101, Carver's most important turning point as a writer.

Understanding Carver's experience in Creative Writing 101 as an important turning point is the connection the student makes between her own knowledge of life and Carver's essay. Going on to analyze the "values and craft" exemplified by works of literature will help you to develop your own skills as a reader and writer. For example, you can read about the American playwright Lorraine Hansberry's "Shakespearean Experience" and compare it in an essay with your own response to *Hamlet*. You can analyze the dazzling sparks of ideas about the themes of love and death in the works of Emily Dickinson or Sylvia Plath, or interpret the genius of Langston Hughes as he translates the pain of racism into poetry accessible to everyone.

In the essay "Good Readers and Good Writers," Nabokov understood the complexity of our responses to literature. He believed that every author "may be considered as a storyteller, as a teacher, and as an enchanter. A major writer combines these three—storyteller, teacher, enchanter—but it is the enchanter in him that predominates and makes him a major writer."

Initially we all turn to storytellers for mental and emotional stimulation, the pleasure of entering an alternative universe to our own, evoked in our minds from our connection with the words of a literary text. Not only does great literature entertain us—it also provokes our thought. If we think about what we have read after we have finished a story, poem, or play, we realize that authors are often teachers—their words contribute to the development of our own sense of values and remind us of the inexorable brevity and essential mystery of our everyday lives. Finally, we can return to the story, poem, or play for what many readers consider the most enchanting connection with literature: We can use our artistic sense to study what Nabokov called "the individual magic" of each writer's genius—the beauty resulting from the style, the imagery, and the pattern of the literary text.

READING LITERATURE

Regardless of where you start to read and write about literature—whether you begin with short stories, poems, or plays—the important thing to remember is that you must try to read your assignments slowly and carefully. When you become a student of literature, you do not read in the same casual way that you pick up a newspaper or a magazine, or even in the way that you concentrate on the pages of the assignments for your other courses, trying to find and underline passages in which the author has stated the meaning or main ideas about the subject in words that you then memorize for a quiz or an exam.

The way you read this so-called objective prose in history or science textbooks can be described as linear, in that the objectivity of the text evokes a similar objectivity in your attention to the words on the page. You read along sentence by sentence, following the linear development of the author's thesis or argument. Works of literature, on the other hand, create meaning differently. Literary texts have an additional dimension of *significance* as well as meaning.

Significance is expressed through your personal response to the story, poem, or play. It is how you connect with what the author as storyteller, teacher, and enchanter has created in the text — what *you* make of it. As you read, your comprehension arises from your experience of life, which also includes your study of literature. Reading the author headnotes and commentaries in *Literature and Its Writers* will help you expand your literary background by adding to your knowledge of the writers' lives, historical times, and cultural tradition.

The English critic Cyril Connolly once said, "Literature is the art of writing something that will be read twice." Try to read your assignments twice, the first time enjoying the experience of *arriving* at the end of the text, seeing how the author resolves the plot of a story or play or develops the subject of a poem. The second time you read a text, you can focus on *getting there*, becoming aware of how authors create the world evoked on the page by using the elements of their craft. This is called **close reading**. It is essential for understanding what an author has created in the text. This process will assist you in interpreting accurately what you have read. Close reading will also reveal the writer's creation of design and pattern in the literary work, as distinctive to each author as his or her fingerprints. Through this process of careful reading, you are taking the first steps toward thinking critically about the text and discovering its significance for you.

THINKING AND WRITING ABOUT LITERATURE

With literature, *you* help to create meaning. The way you interpret what you read determines the significance of a story, poem, or play for you. Literature becomes meaningful when you read actively. Slow down. Take the time to think about the text. Relate the author's personal vision to your own experiences of life and literature and the questions you ask of them.

To help you connect with literature so that you can develop your critical thinking and express your ideas effectively in essays, this anthology ends with Part Four on writing about literature. This final part of the book describes the step-by-step process of composing a short essay about literature, and shows how reading an author's commentary on his or her work in the early stages of the writing process can stimulate your critical thinking about the work's significance.

Just as one student understood that there was a parallel between Raymond Carver's commentary "Creative Writing 101" and her experience of life's "turning points," you create the significance that a story, poem, or play has for you as you refine your thoughts about it. Expressing your ideas in an essay will help you to clarify your response for yourself and others. You write to discover what you know, hoping "to find truth at the end of a pencil," as Ernest Hemingway described it.

To facilitate your progress in *Literature and Its Writers,* detailed suggestions to help you think and write about what you read are included in the introductory chapters to each of the literary genres of fiction, poetry, and drama. Part Four, the last section of the textbook, offers strategies for developing your ideas about your reading into essays. Various critical approaches to literature are presented as well as several rhetorical methods useful in writing longer essays, each with an accompanying student paper. The research paper is the topic of the final chapter of the anthology.

WEB *For study and discussion questions and writing suggestions on each author and work in this anthology visit bedfordstmartins.com/charters/litwriters.*

LITERATURE AND ITS WRITERS

A Compact Introduction
to Fiction, Poetry,
and Drama

PART ONE

Fiction

A true work of fiction . . . strikes us, in
the end, not simply as a thing done but
as a shining performance.
—JOHN GARDNER

To plot is to move from asking the
question *and then what happened?* to the
question *why did it happen?*
—JAMES HILLMAN

Surely every written story is, in the final
analysis, a score for voice. These little
black marks on the page mean nothing
without their translation into sound.
—MARGARET ATWOOD

1.

What Is a Short Story?

> Fiction is like the spider's web, attached ever so slightly perhaps, but
> still attached to life at all four corners.
> — VIRGINIA WOOLF, *A Room of One's Own*

People have told stories to each other since before the dawn of history, but the literary genre that we call the **short story** is a relatively recent phenomenon, much younger than the genres of poetry and drama. The terms *story* and *short story* do not necessarily mean the same thing. The word *story* itself has two meanings. It can refer to a literary text (for example, we can say that Grace Paley wrote a story titled "Samuel"), or it can refer to the events themselves that are represented in the text (we can say that the story of "Samuel" is about an accident on a New York subway in which a young boy is killed). In contrast, the term *short story* always means the name of a particular literary genre. It refers to a short fictional prose narrative, usually involving one unified episode, and it is often applied to any work of narrative prose fiction shorter than a novel.

Most of us have spent our lives listening to, telling, watching, and reading stories, and we think we can recognize them. But what are the essential qualities of a short story such as Paley's "Samuel"?

GRACE PALEY

Samuel   1968

Some boys are very tough. They're afraid of nothing. They are the ones who climb a wall and take a bow at the top. Not only are they brave on the roof, but they make a lot of noise in the darkest part of the cellar where even the super hates to go. They also jiggle and hop on the platform between the locked doors of the subway cars.

3

Four boys are jiggling on the swaying platform. Their names are Alfred, Calvin, Samuel, and Tom. The men and the women in the cars on either side watch them. They don't like them to jiggle or jump but don't want to interfere. Of course some of the men in the cars were once brave boys like these. One of them had ridden the tail of a speeding truck from New York to Rockaway Beach without getting off, without his sore fingers losing hold. Nothing happened to him then or later. He had made a compact with other boys who preferred to watch: Starting at Eighth Avenue and Fifteenth Street, he would get to some specified place, maybe Twenty-third and the river, by hopping the tops of the moving trucks. This was hard to do when one truck turned a corner in the wrong direction and the nearest truck was a couple of feet too high. He made three or four starts before succeeding. He had gotten his idea from a film at school called *The Romance of Logging*. He had finished high school, married a good friend, was in a responsible job and going to night school.

These two men and others looked at the four boys jumping and jiggling on the platform and thought, It must be fun to ride that way, especially now the weather is nice and we're out of the tunnel and way high over the Bronx. Then they thought, These kids do seem to be acting sort of stupid. They *are* little. Then they thought of some of the brave things they had done when they were boys and jiggling didn't seem so risky.

The ladies in the car became very angry when they looked at the four boys. Most of them brought their brows together and hoped the boys could see their extreme disapproval. One of the ladies wanted to get up and say, Be careful, you dumb kids, get off that platform or I'll call a cop. But three of the boys were Negroes and the fourth was something else she couldn't tell for sure. She was afraid they'd be fresh and laugh at her and embarrass her. She wasn't afraid they'd hit her, but she was afraid of embarrassment. Another lady thought, Their mothers never know where they are. It wasn't true in this particular case. Their mothers all knew that they had gone to see the missile exhibit on Fourteenth Street.

Out on the platform, whenever the train accelerated, the boys would raise their hands and point them up to the sky to act like rockets going off, then they rat-tat-tatted the shatterproof glass pane like machine guns, although no machine guns had been exhibited.

For some reason known only to the motorman, the train began a sudden slowdown. The lady who was afraid of embarrassment saw the boys jerk forward and backward and grab the swinging guard chains. She had her own boy at home. She stood up with determination and went to the door. She slid it open and said, "You boys will be hurt. You'll be killed. I'm going to call the conductor if you don't just go into the next car and sit down and be quiet."

Two of the boys said, "Yes'm," and acted as though they were about to go. Two of them blinked their eyes a couple of times and pressed their lips together. The train resumed its speed. The door slid shut, parting the lady and the boys. She leaned against the side door because she had to get off at the next stop.

The boys opened their eyes wide at each other and laughed. The lady blushed. The boys looked at her and laughed harder. They began to pound each other's back. Samuel laughed the hardest and pounded Alfred's back until Alfred coughed and the tears came. Alfred held tight to the chain hook. Samuel pounded him even harder when he saw the tears. He said, "Why you bawling? You a baby, huh?" and laughed. One of the men whose boyhood had been more watchful than brave became angry. He stood up straight and looked at the boys for a couple of seconds. Then he walked in a citizenly way to the end of the car, where he pulled the emergency cord. Almost at once, with a terrible hiss, the pressure of air abandoned the brakes and the wheels were caught and held.

People standing in the most secure places fell forward, then backward. Samuel had let go of his hold on the chain so he could pound Tom as well as Alfred. All the passengers in the cars whipped back and forth, but he pitched only forward and fell head first to be crushed and killed between the cars.

The train had stopped hard, halfway into the station, and the conductor called at once for the trainmen who knew about this kind of death and how to take the body from the wheels and brakes. There was silence except for passengers from other cars who asked, What happened! What happened! The ladies waited around wondering if he might be an only child. The men recalled other afternoons with very bad endings. The little boys stayed close to each other, leaning and touching shoulders and arms and legs.

When the policeman knocked at the door and told her about it, Samuel's mother began to scream. She screamed all day and moaned all night, though the doctors tried to quiet her with pills.

Oh, oh, she hopelessly cried. She did not know how she could ever find another boy like that one. However, she was a young woman and she became pregnant. Then for a few months she was hopeful. The child born to her was a boy. They brought him to be seen and nursed. She smiled. But immediately she saw that this baby wasn't Samuel. She and her husband together have had other children, but never again will a boy exactly like Samuel be known.

When you finished reading "Samuel," you probably sensed that it was a short story, different from a newspaper account, but how did you know this? For one thing, the story wasn't simply reporting the facts of a subway accident that had occurred recently. Paley begins and ends her narrative with her subjective response to the death of a young boy. Her first sentence "Some boys are very tough" is not the way a newspaper reporter would open a story, unless perhaps it was meant for the editorial page. Also by the second paragraph of "Samuel," Paley is describing the antics of a group of boys on the swaying platform between two subway cars as they stunt for each other. As a short story writer, she is *showing* you their antics, not *telling* you about their presumed toughness any more.

The way that the writer uses language for showing the events of a narrative, not merely telling about it, is the most important difference between a short story author and a newspaper reporter. In an interview, Paley explained that her decision to write stories was her attempt to "get the world to explain itself to me, to speak to me." She regarded her decision to dramatize the events of the stories as an effort "to reach out to the world and get it to tell me what it was all about." To accomplish this dramatization, this ability to suggest a living world on the page to the reader's imagination, writers of short fiction have various means at their disposal, including plot, characterization, setting, point of view, style, and theme.

With these elements of short fiction, skillful writers such as Paley can create stories that communicate their own unique sense of the mystery of life, the realization that "never again will a boy exactly like Samuel be known." Paley's story is very short, because she wanted to attempt a literary style that was close to poetry. As she described it in an interview,

> I would say that stories are closer to poetry than they are to the novel because first they are shorter, and second they are more concentrated, more economical, and that kind of economy, the pulling together of all the information and making leaps across the information, is really close to poetry. By leaps I mean thought leaps and feeling leaps. Also, when short stories are working right, you pay more attention to language than most novelists do.

The length of "Samuel" is of less importance than what the author succeeds in accomplishing with her few words. Paley believes that the form of the story is very flexible. "It can be just telling a little tale, or writing a complicated philosophical story. It can be a song, almost."

Like poetry, the short story is a concentrated form, dependent for its success on feeling and suggestion. Early in the nineteenth century, the American writer Edgar Allan Poe was one of the first to attempt an analysis of the short story's aesthetic properties. He stressed *unity* of effect as the story's most characteristic feature. Since the flood of events we experience in life is rarely unified by a single impression, in a sense all fiction — whether short story, long story, or novel — is "lies." Paradoxically, however, the measure of success for all fiction is how *true* it is to our emotions, how accurately it reflects the life we all live.

When readers understand the intricate ways an author uses language to create a fictional world, the story's unity has an even greater impact. That's why we read literature closely, unlike the way we skim through a newspaper. Registering every detail of the fictional narrative adds to our enjoyment of the storyteller's achievement. Writers of short stories must forgo the comprehensiveness of the novel, but they often gain a striking compression by using language with the force of poetry. Like poets, short story writers can impress on us the unity of their vision of life by focusing on a single effect.

COMMENTARIES   *Grace Paley, "A Conversation with Ann Charters," page 582; Edgar Allan Poe, "The Importance of the Single Effect in a Prose Tale," page 656.*

2.

The Elements of Fiction: A Storyteller's Means

A true work of fiction is a wonderfully simple thing — so simple that
most so-called serious writers avoid trying it, feeling they ought to do
something more important and ingenious, never guessing how incredibly difficult it is. A true work of fiction does all of the following things,
and does them elegantly, efficiently: it creates a vivid and continuous
dream in the reader's mind; it is implicitly philosophical; it fulfills or
at least deals with all of the expectations it sets up; and it strikes us, in
the end, not simply as a thing done but as a shining performance.
— JOHN GARDNER, "What Writers Do"

Most readers are able to identify short fictional prose narratives as short
stories, whether written by authors in the United States or in countries
throughout the world, because authors in every country employ the same elements of fiction. In the imaginations of gifted storytellers, these basic components are transformed into the texts of short stories as the writers explore the
potentiality of fiction. Literary critics generally agree that these basic elements
comprise six different categories: plot, characterization, setting, point of view,
style, and theme.

PLOT

Since the short story is defined as a prose narrative usually involving one
unified episode or a sequence of related events, plot is basic to this literary
form. **Plot** is the sequence of events in a story and their relation to one another.
Writers usually present the events of the plot in a coherent time frame that the
reader can follow easily. As we read, we sense that the events are related by causation, and their meaning lies in this relation. To the casual reader, causation
(or why something in the plot happened next) seems to result only from the
writer's organization of the events into a chronological sequence. A more
thoughtful reader understands that causation in the plot of a memorable short
story reveals a good deal about the author's use of the other elements of fiction
as well, especially characterization.

As E. M. Forster realized, plot not only answers *what* happened next, but
it also suggests *why*. The psychologist James Hillman has explained in *Healing
Fiction* that plot reveals "human intentions. Plot shows how it all hangs
together and makes sense. Only when a narrative receives inner coherence in

terms of the depths of human nature do we have fiction, and for this fiction we have to have plot. . . . To plot is to move from asking the question *and then what happened?* to the question *why did it happen?"*

A short story can dramatize the events of a brief episode or compress a longer period of time. Analyzing why a short story is short, the critic Norman Friedman suggests that it "may be short not because its action is inherently small, but rather because the author has chosen—in working with an episode or plot—to omit certain of its parts. In other words, an action may be large in size and still be short in the telling because not all of it is there." A short story can describe something that happens in a few minutes or encompass action that takes years to conclude. The narrative possibilities are endless, as the writer may omit or condense complex episodes to intensify their dramatic effect or expand a single incident to make a relatively long story.

Regardless of length, the plot of a short story usually has what critics term an **end orientation**—the outcome of the action or the conclusion of the plot—inherent in its opening paragraphs. As Mark Twain humorously observed, "Fiction is obliged to stick to possibilities. Truth isn't." The novelist may conclude a single episode long before the end of a novel and then pick up the thread of another narrative, or interpret an event from another angle in a different character's point of view, linking episode to episode and character to character so that each illuminates the others. But a story stops earlier. As Edgar Allan Poe recognized in 1842, its narrative dramatizes a single effect complete unto itself.

The events in the plot of a short story usually involve a conflict or struggle between opposing forces. When you analyze a plot, you can often (but not always) see it develop in a pattern during the course of the narration. Typically you find that the first paragraphs of the story or **exposition** give the background or setting of the conflict. The **rising action** dramatizes the specific events that set the conflict in motion. Often there is a turning point in the story midway before further complications prolong the suspense of the conflict's resolution. The **climax** is the emotional high point of the narration. In the **falling action**, the events begin to wind down and point the reader toward the conclusion or dénouement at the end of the story, which resolves the conflict to a greater or lesser degree. Sometimes the conclusion introduces an unexpected turn of events or a surprise ending. In successful stories the writer shapes these stages into a complex structure that may impress you with its balance and proportion.

The plot of Grace Paley's short story "Samuel" (p. 3) is very simple, dramatizing a brief episode on a Manhattan subway train. It relates a sequence of events about four young boys who are fooling around on the platform between two cars of a moving train. A woman watching them tells them they'll get hurt, but the boys only laugh at her. Witnessing their response, a man gets angry and pulls the emergency cord. The train lurches to a stop, causing one of the boys to fall and be crushed to death. The mother of the dead boy grieves, then becomes hopeful after she becomes pregnant again. But after the birth of her baby she realizes that the new child can never replace the son she has lost.

In most stories the beginning sets up the problem or conflict; the middle is where the author introduces various complications that prolong suspense and make the struggle more meaningful; and the end resolves the conflict to a greater or lesser degree. In successful stories the writer shapes these stages into a complex structure that impresses the reader with its balance and proportion, often suggesting an insight into the human condition.

The first part of the plot, or *exposition,* of "Samuel" is the opening paragraph. It introduces the idea that motivates the main characters of Paley's little drama, the idea that boys like to show off for each other. The *rising action* dramatizes the conflict of interest between the young boys and the adults watching them in the subway car. Some of the men in the car sympathize with the kids, remembering the dangerous stunts they pulled when they were young. Most of the women in the car are angry at the boys and want them to behave more responsibly, to take seats and calm down. The *turning point* is when one of the women, with a son at home, summons her courage and admonishes the boys. They make fun of her, and this raises the tension of the story by adding a complicating factor of defiance to their behavior. The *climax* of "Samuel" is when the self-righteous male passenger pulls the emergency cord and Samuel is killed. In the *falling action,* Paley describes the result of the accident. Traffic on the subway is stopped, the passengers who saw the accident are in shock, the others riding the train are curious, and a policeman notifies Samuel's mother of his death. The *conclusion* is the final paragraph of the story, more than a year later, when Samuel's parents understand the full dimensions of their loss.

Paley's story is very short, more of a sketch than a fully developed narrative. The only dialogue is between the lady who warns the boys that they might get hurt and the boys themselves, who find her warning hilarious. Samuel pounds his buddy Alfred's back until the tears come, saying "You a baby, huh?" Paley gives a hint of **foreshadowing** in the opening paragraphs of her story, suggesting the action to come, when some of the men watching the boys think, "These kids do seem to be acting sort of stupid. They *are* little." These words anticipate a turn of events that may or may not go along with our expectations, but when we reread the story, we see that Paley's plot runs along as solidly as a subway train. Not for her are the tricky surprise endings favored in short stories by earlier writers such as Guy de Maupassant, Kate Chopin, and Ambrose Bierce. We sense Paley's emotional involvement in her characters as she chronicles the tragedy of a small boy's senseless death, refusing to play with the fictional events the way that Mary Lavin does in "The Widow's Son" (p. 313), for example. This is another short story about a mother's response to an accidental death, where stretching the limits of the literary form was more important to the author than the emotional content of the story.

Along with her choice of a title, Paley sets up an expectation in the reader early on with her hint of foreshadowing—the story will be about Samuel, and its "single effect" will be the shock of his accidental, senseless death and how it affects the people around him. Paley doesn't go on to tell us about the lives of the three boys who survive the accident, or about the guilty feelings (and subsequent nervous breakdown?) of the man who pulls the emergency cord. That would be another story.

Regardless of the author's method of developing the plot, the goal is the same: The writer of short stories must *show* the reader something about human nature through the dramatic action of the plot and the other elements of the story, and not just *tell* the reader what to think. A good plot arouses our curiosity, engages our emotions, and keeps us in suspense. As the contemporary American writer Eudora Welty understood, "A narrative line is in its deeper sense, of course, the tracing out of a meaning, and the real continuity of a story lies in this probing forward." A storyteller must sustain the illusion of reality until the end of the story, unfolding events with the continuing revelation of an apparently endless silk handkerchief drawn from a skillful magician's coat sleeve.

CHARACTER

If you are like most people, plot is what keeps you going when you first read a story, and character is what stays with you after you have finished reading it. The title of Paley's short narrative is "Samuel," the name of its **protagonist** or central character, the unlucky and foolish young boy (he lacked prudence) whose actions may have prompted her to write the story.

Characters are usually the people who are involved in what happens in a story. Writers can use animals as characters, or giant insects such as Gregor Samsa, the protagonist of Franz Kafka's "The Metamorphosis" (p. 262), or even such inanimate objects as trees, chairs, and shoes. But by the term *character* we usually mean a human being with emotions whose mind works something like our own.

When we ask *why did it happen?* about the plot of a story, we usually find the answer in the characters, who are convincing if we can understand their actions. Paley chooses to keep her story so short that she doesn't give her characters any time to develop. They are *static,* not *dynamic.* We are told their names, but we don't see them change during the narrative or after Samuel's death. They are *flat,* not *round* characters. For characters to emerge as round, the reader must feel the play and pull of their actions and responses to situations. Yet Paley's character types are familiar to all of us. Samuel is a schoolboy clowning for his buddies, and we understand why he acts as he does. The man who pulls the emergency cord in the subway car is a little more complex. We aren't told much about him, except that his "boyhood had been more watchful than brave." Unlike some of the other male spectators, he has no sense of empathy with the boys who are fooling around on the moving platform.

Perhaps part of the anger the man feels toward the boys is prompted by their mockery of the lady who issues the reprimand. Paley tells us only that "he walked in a citizenly way" when he went to pull the emergency cord. Considering the dire results of the man's action, Paley is using *verbal irony* here, meaning the opposite of the literal meaning of the words *good citizen.* No one acting like a good citizen wants to cause a small boy's death. As readers, we instinctively strive to connect the events of a story by more than their simple chronological sequence, because assuming connections between the events and the inner life of the characters makes the story seem coherent.

How are the characters in a short story to be understood? Any discussion of character tends to drift into a value judgment, as our principles of definition and evaluation for fictional characters are based on the ones we use for real people, tentative and unfocused as they may be. We must remember that we are reading about *fictional* characters in a short story, not real ones. The only evidence we have about characters is what the author puts into the story.

We are on firmer ground in literary discussions when we analyze the writer's method of characterization as well as the character's personality. Paley's method is one of economy; the extremely short length of her story mirrors Samuel's brief lifetime. Writing a realistic story, she might be suggesting that characters from modest economic backgrounds have little control over their fates in the big city, underscoring the tragedy of the loss of a young boy who never had the chance to grow up.

Other authors, such as Poe, create a fantasy world in their stories, imagining situations in which their characters have total control. We know that Poe's protagonist Montresor gets away with murder in "The Cask of Amontillado" (p. 473). Pigeonholing his character does not bring us close to understanding the sense of horror that Poe evokes in the story. We can appreciate it more readily by relishing the language Poe uses in dialogue and description to show us Montresor's thoughts and responses as he acts out his obsessive plan to avenge his honor and lure Fortunato to his death. As the literary critic David Reynolds has realized, the two characters in this classic short story, although limited, are not flat.

> They come swiftly alive before our eyes because Poe describes them with acute psychological realism. Montresor is a complex Machiavellian criminal, exhibiting a full range of traits from clever ingratiation to stark sadism. Fortunato, the dupe whose pride leads to his own downfall, nevertheless exhibits . . . admirable qualities. . . . The drama of the story lies in the carefully orchestrated interaction between the two. Poe directs our attention away from the merely sensational and toward the psychological. . . .

Different fictional worlds make different demands on the reader's imagination. What is most important to the reader's enjoyment of the tale is the emotional truth conveyed by the characters, whether they are flat or round, dynamic or static. To avoid **sentimentality** (emotional overindulgence) and **stereotyping** (oversimplified judgment) in creating characters, the writer must be able to suggest enough complexity to engage the reader's emotions, or the story will not succeed.

SETTING

Setting is the place and time of the story. To set the scene and suggest a mood or atmosphere for the events to follow, the writer attempts to create in the reader's visual imagination the illusion of a solid world in which the story takes place. Paley uses only a few words to describe the subway setting of her story, but they create an image of power and danger. The doors are "locked." The platform is "swaying." The cars on either side are full of people, who are watching the boys uneasily. When the cars unexpectedly slow down suddenly for the first time, the boys "grab the swinging guard chains," nearly falling down. Paley's description of the second slowdown, after the man pulls the emergency cord, is more shocking, relying on strong active verbs such as *abandoned, caught, held, fell, whipped, pitched, crushed,* and *killed:*

> Almost at once, with a terrible hiss, the pressure of air abandoned the brakes and the wheels were caught and held.
> People standing in the most secure places fell forward, then backward. Samuel had let go of his hold on the chain so he could pound Tom as well as Alfred. All the passengers in the cars whipped back and forth, but he pitched only forward and fell head first to be crushed and killed between the cars.

When the writer locates the narrative in a physical setting, the reader is moved step by step toward acceptance of the fiction. The *external* reality of the setting is always an illusion, our mental images stimulated by the words that the writer has put on paper. Yet this invented setting is essential if we are to share the *internal* emotional life of the characters involved in the plot. A sense of place engages us in the fictional characters' situations.

In Nathaniel Hawthorne's story "Young Goodman Brown" (p. 219), for example, when the protagonist Goodman Brown enters the dark, tangled world of the forest surrounding the colonial village of Salem to keep his appointment with the devil, the attentive reader may perceive that Brown really enters the troubled world of his own mind. Exercising his own free will, he voluntarily exchanges the companionship of his pretty young wife and her pink ribbons for the attractions of Satan.

The setting of a story furnishes the location for its world of feeling, the different emotional associations awakened in the reader's mind by a gloomy New England forest in a Hawthorne story, a dank burial crypt in a Poe story, or a crowded Manhattan subway train in a Paley story. A sense of place is essential for us to imagine the fictional characters' situations as the author creates the story.

Place helps the characters seem real, but, to be most effective, the setting must also have a dramatic use. It must be shown, or at least felt, to affect character or plot. The emergency brake in the subway car precipitates the disaster of Samuel's death. Exchanging the windy street in Salem village for the dreary, solitary path through the tangled forest leads Young Goodman Brown straight to the devil. The mound of bones piled outside the damp niche where Montresor has planned to entomb his victim Fortunato foreshadows the evil deed to come. Imagining the details of setting in the creation of stories, writers must exert their talents to make the reader see only the fictional world that emerges on the printed page, under the illusion that while the story unfolds, it is the real world itself.

POINT OF VIEW

Point of view refers to the author's choice of a narrator for the story. At the start, the writer must decide whether to employ **first-person narration**, using the pronoun *I*, or **third-person narration**, using the pronouns *he, she,* and *they.* (Second-person narration, *you,* is less common, although the dramatic intimacy of second-person narrative address is often used in poetry and song lyrics.) The writer's choice of a point of view to narrate stories usually falls into two major categories:

FIRST-PERSON NARRATION (NARRATOR APPARENTLY A
PARTICIPANT IN THE STORY)

1. A major character
2. A minor character

THIRD-PERSON NARRATION (NARRATOR A NONPARTICIPANT
IN THE STORY)

1. Omniscient — seeing into the minds of all characters
2. Limited omniscient — seeing into one or, sometimes, two characters' minds
3. Objective — seeing into none of the characters' minds

First-Person Narration

Samuel is the protagonist, but telling his side of the story in a first-person narration by a major character isn't Paley's objective as a writer in "Samuel." The young boy dies before the conclusion of events, before she reaches the point she wants to make as the storyteller. Perhaps we can imagine Samuel telling his story in the first person from his vantage point in heaven, but then Paley is a realistic writer.

Paley might have considered presenting the narrative through the voice of a minor character as a first-person speaker. For example, Samuel's mother, who understands that there will never be another boy like Samuel, could have told the tale, but she wasn't present when the accident on the subway occurred, so she couldn't have described it in close detail. All the women and men in the subway car who witnessed Samuel's death were minor characters in the drama. They could have gone home to their families or friends that evening and told the story of the accident as eye witnesses, using first-person narration. No doubt their stories would have been highly emotional — "I can't believe what happened on the Lexington Avenue express today. I've been riding the subway all my life, and I've never seen anything like it" — but their personal accounts, while dramatic, would lack Paley's compassionate insight into what the loss of the young boy's life really means.

The first-person narrator, whether a major or a minor character, can be *reliable* or *unreliable,* making us aware as we read his or her story that the account is skewed and that we can't quite trust the point of view. In a story such as Herman Melville's "Bartleby, the Scrivener" (p. 352), the garrulous lawyer telling us about his difficult relationship with his eccentric scrivener is actually a minor character in Bartleby's life. Despite his obvious concern for Bartleby and attempts to help him, the lawyer inadvertently serves as a screen between the reader and the protagonist of the story, making it impossible for us to understand Bartleby's point of view. At the beginning of Charlotte Perkins Gilman's "The Yellow Wallpaper" (p. 182), the first-person narrator, who is the major character in the story, says that she is trying to regain her health after a mental breakdown. While she tells her story, an attentive reader notices that her disorientation from the so-called real world becomes much more acute. Both Melville and Gilman choose first-person narrators to heighten the emotional effect of their stories.

Third-Person Narration

Third-person narration means that the author tells the story using the pronouns *he* or *she* instead of the presumably more subjective *I*. Paley uses third-person narration in "Samuel." The narrator isn't a person who participates in the story, but she knows everything about it. She is an *omniscient* narrator, aware that the boys' mothers gave them permission to take the subway downtown and see the missile exhibit on Fourteenth Street in Manhattan. Despite the short length of her tale, Paley communicates her authority as the storyteller because she is so knowledgeable about the incident. We trust her to get the story right and to help us understand what happened. Most people enjoy reading stories told by omniscient narrators, anticipating that they will usually find meaning in the events that they describe.

There can be significant differences in the way authors handle third-person narration. Like Paley, Sherwood Anderson is highly sympathetic to his characters in "Hands" (p. 28), but he uses *limited-omniscient* narration, confining himself to revealing the thoughts of only one character, his protagonist Wing Biddlebaum. Anderson is making an effort to engage our sympathies for this sad character too. Ernest Hemingway uses *objective* third-person narration in "Hills Like White Elephants" (p. 230), relying almost entirely on the dialogue between the two characters to tell the reader about the crisis in their relationship. The author doesn't take sides in the battle between the two lovers over the important decision they face. Hemingway attempts to create a totally detached point of view. Setting and action appear on the page without the narrator's comments or the characters' reflections, heightening the emotion of the desperate struggle going on between the lines of the story.

Narration can be classified further into subcategories (for example, first- and third-person stream-of-consciousness narration), but a writer's handling of different points of view, if successful, always appears to be more flexible than the rigid categories imply. For example, Kafka begins "The Metamorphosis" with a sentence of third-person omniscient narration, but in the second sentence he changes his focus to present his protagonist Gregor Samsa's point of view. Kafka maintains this limited-omniscient narration until Gregor's death. Then, to heighten our sense of Gregor's alienation, Kafka reverts back to his more distant, objective omniscient voice to finish the story.

VOICE AND STYLE

Style is the characteristic way an author uses language to create literature. Style is the result of the writer's habitual use of certain rhetorical patterns, including sentence length and complexity, word choice and placement, and punctuation. Paley's style in "Samuel" is informal, even colloquial in her choice of language. In her story she uses mostly one-syllable words, even slang occasionally ("super" in the first paragraph refers to the superintendent or caretaker of an apartment building).

You might think of the author's prose style as a projection of her or his **voice** as a writer, as if you were hearing the story instead of reading it. Voice, as the Canadian writer Margaret Atwood described it, is "a speaking voice, like the singing voice in music, that moves not across a space, across the page, but through time. Surely every written story is, in the final analysis, a score for voice. These little black marks on the page mean nothing without their retranslation into sound."

Tone is the way the author conveys his or her unstated attitudes toward the story. Paley's tone is serious in "Samuel," despite her use of colloquial language. **Irony** is another means by which writers tell stories. Irony makes the reader aware of a reality that differs from the reality the characters perceive (*dramatic irony*) or from the literal meaning of the author's words (*verbal irony*). Paley uses verbal irony when she says that the man who pulls the emergency cord "walked in a citizenly way." Earlier in the story, Samuel pounds his buddy Alfred's back until the tears come, saying "You a baby, huh?" This is an example of dramatic irony. In only a few minutes Samuel will be crushed between the wheels of the subway car and his life will end while he is still, comparatively, a baby.

The use of **symbolism** can also be an aspect of a writer's style. A literary symbol can be anything in a story's setting, plot, or characterization that suggests an abstract meaning to the reader in addition to its literal significance. Symbols are more eloquent as specific images — visual ideas — than any paraphrase, suggesting infinitely more than they state. They are not always interpreted the same way by all readers. Paley avoids any suggestion of an abstract meaning to her story until its concluding sentence. Then Samuel, for all his foolish high spirits, becomes a symbol for the value of every individual life in its precious uniqueness.

THEME

Theme is a generalization about the meaning of a story. Whereas the plot of a story can be summarized by stating what happens in the action, the theme is the general idea behind the events of the plot that expresses the meaning of the story. At the end of her narrative, Paley makes Samuel's death suggest the larger meaning she had in mind when she told his story.

The stories we encounter daily do much more than entertain us; they also play a central role in our lives. Students of the media tell us that the narratives told to us by parents, friends, teachers, books, audio recordings, radio, film, and television are the real source of what we take to be our "common" sense, helping us arrive at an understanding of ourselves and our place in the world. As James Hillman has explained, our stories provide "dynamic coherence and meaning to the dispersed narratives of our lives." At the same time, fiction has the power to challenge our everyday sense of reality by reminding us of our mortality and suggesting that anything might happen since the future is ultimately beyond our individual control.

Theme comes last in a discussion of the elements of fiction because all the other elements in a story must be accounted for in determining it. The structure and theme of a story are fused like the body and soul of a reader; their interaction creates a living pattern. While the various actions of the plot must strike us as realistic and inevitable, the complete truth that the story reveals is in essence indefinable and untranslatable outside the text. The storyteller says, "Let me tell you how it is," and we pay attention because we want to know what the story can show us about the complexities of human experience. Theme is an abstract formulation of the author's vision of the meaning of life. But the story itself is infinitely more complex than its meaning. To appreciate this truth, try this experiment: In your own words, write a sentence summarizing what you believe to be the theme of "Samuel." Then close your anthology and try to create the story that illustrates this theme.

The summary of a writer's theme is no substitute for the story in its entirety, but our attempt to state it can help us understand the story better. As the southern writer Flannery O'Connor said, "A story is a way to say something that can't be said any other way, and it takes every word in the story to say what the meaning is. . . . When anybody asks what a story is about, the only proper thing is to tell him to read the story."

COMMENTARIES   *Ann Charters, "Translating Kafka," page 551; Anton Chekhov, "Technique in Writing the Short Story," page 554; Flannery O'Connor, "The Element of Suspense in 'A Good Man Is Hard to Find,'" page 639; David S. Reynolds, "Poe's Art of Transformation in 'The Cask of Amontillado,'" page 672; Eudora Welty, "Plot and Character in Chekhov's 'The Darling,'" page 606.*

WEB   *Learn more about the elements of fiction with VirtuaLit Fiction at bedfordstmartins.com/charters/litwriters.*

3.

Reading, Thinking, and Writing about Short Fiction

General rules in art are useful chiefly as a lamp in a mine, or a handrail down a black stairway: they are necessary for the sake of the guidance they give, but it is a mistake, once they are formulated, to be too much in awe of them.

— EDITH WHARTON, *The Writing of Fiction*

READING SHORT FICTION

The great eighteenth-century English critic Samuel Johnson said that the great majority of people need to be reminded more often than instructed. Remember to read each story at least once in its entirety. The best way to give short stories a chance to entertain and enchant you is to sit down and grant them your full attention. Read them carefully straight through from beginning to end.

When you read a story for the first time, you may find it relatively easy to see the elements of plot, character, and setting interact on the page. They stand out because they seem to make the story happen, and—at least for the casual reader—they appear to be what the story is about. Point of view, style, and theme, on the other hand, are less visible elements. Many readers regard them with dread as part of what they call the "hidden meaning" of a story. While it is true that you may have to look for these particular elements deliberately, you will find that this hunt is worth the treasure. The more you read attentively, the easier it will be to appreciate how all the elements operate in short fiction. You will begin to understand more fully that *how* a story is written is an essential part of *what* it is saying.

If you make the effort, you will find that reading literature is an activity that challenges your intellect and emotions to the highest degree. After finishing a story for the first time, you may feel contradictory responses to it, uncertain how to interpret what you have read. A second or third reading may help clarify your impressions, or you may find you have to close your book and think about the story if it doesn't fit easily into your preconceptions about human experience.

The effort is worthwhile. As the critic Ray Carey has explained, the different forms of storytelling can "point a way out of some of the traps of received forms of thinking and feeling. Every artist makes a fresh effort of awareness. He [or she] offers new forms of caring. He [or she] can point out the processed emotions and canned understandings that deceive us. He [or she] can reveal the emotional lies that ensnare us. He [or she] can help us to new and potentially revolutionary understandings of our lives." Because reading a good story is potentially an enlightening experience, you will find that analyzing the means available to the storyteller is one of the best ways to make the story accessible to you.

Stories are shorter than novels, but they're not necessarily easier to read. The editor Charles McGrath cautions that

> stories aren't just *brief,* they're *different;* and they require of the reader something like the degree of concentration they require of the writer. . . . You can't skim or coast or leap ahead, and if you have to put a story down, it's not always easy to pick up — emotionally, that is — where you left off. You have to backtrack a little, or even start over. It's not enough to read a story the way you read a book or a newspaper. Stories ask of us that we surrender ourselves to them.

Guidelines for Reading Short Fiction

1. Make an entry in your notebook for each story assigned in class, writing down the author's name and the story's title and date. As you begin to read, remember T. S. Eliot's advice in his essay "Tradition and the Individual Talent" (p. 972) that "criticism is as inevitable as breathing, and that we should be none the worse for articulating what passes in our minds when we read a book and feel an emotion about it, for criticizing our own minds in their work of criticism."

2. Use a dictionary to look up words in both the headnote and the story that you do not understand.

3. After you have read the story, make notes about the way the author has used the elements of fiction; this will help you remember and review the story later. Note, for example, the names of the characters, the geographical setting, the author's choice of a point of view, and the literary style in which it is written. Try summing up the story's theme in a phrase or sentence.

4. If you have difficulty understanding the story's meaning or how any of the elements of fiction work within it, write down your questions so you can ask them in class.

5. In class, take notes on the important material about the story that you learn from lectures and discussions and ask any questions you have about the assignment. You may be able to develop these notes in your essays.

6. Review technical words about short fiction used in class in the glossary of literary terms (pp. 1679–1692); this will help you to understand them better.

7. If you have particularly enjoyed a story, go to the library to check out other works by its writer. Reading on your own will enrich the class assignments.

CRITICAL THINKING ABOUT SHORT FICTION

You will find that reading a story and discussing it in class are only part of the process of understanding it. Usually your thinking about a story begins with interpreting it, clarifying what the author is saying in the action of the plot, and making sure you understand the characters and have a clear idea of the theme of the story. Critical thinking goes a step beyond interpretation when you discuss how the form of the story is related to its content or when you analyze how the story relates to your own experience.

Reading commentaries about a story for an essay assignment will help you to focus your thoughts. Ideas for writing can come from any number of sources. Sometimes your instructor will give you a specific assignment; other times you will be asked to generate the idea for the paper yourself. Whatever the case, your reading notes and the class discussions will help you prepare for writing about the story.

Before you can start thinking about writing a response to literature, you should feel that you thoroughly understand the story as a whole. When you read it again, notice the passages that strike you with particular force. Underline the words and sentences you consider significant — or, even better, make a list in your notebook of what seems important while you are rereading the story. These can be outstanding descriptions of the characters or settings, passages of meaningful dialogue, details showing the way the author builds toward the story's climax, or hints that foreshadow the conclusion. To stimulate ideas about topics, you may want to jot down answers to the following questions about the elements of the story as you reread it.

Plot. Does the plot depend on chance, or coincidence? Or does it grow out of the personalities of the characters? Are any later incidents foreshadowed early in the story? Are the episodes presented in chronological order? If not, why is this so? Does the climax indicate a change in a situation or a change in a character? How dramatic is this change? Or is there no change at all?

Character. Are the characters believable? Are they stereotypes? Do they suggest real people, or abstract qualities? Is there one protagonist or are there several? Does the story have an antagonist? How does the author tell you about the main character — through description of physical appearance, actions, thoughts, and emotions, or through contrast with a minor character? Does the main character change in the course of the story? If so, how? Why?

Setting. How does the setting influence the plot and the characters? Does it help to suggest or develop the meaning of the story?

Point of view. How does the point of view shape the theme? Would the story change if told from a different viewpoint? In first-person narration, can you trust the narrator?

Style. Is the author's prose style primarily literal or figurative? Can you find examples of irony in dialogue or narrative passages? If dialect or colloquial speech is used, what is its effect? Does the author call attention to the way he or she uses words, or is the literary style inconspicuous?

Theme.   Does the story's title help explain its meaning? Can you find a suggestion of the theme in specific passages of dialogue or description? Are certain symbols or repetitions of images important in revealing the author's intent in the story, what Edgar Allan Poe would call "the single effect"?

Now put the text aside and look over the notes in your journal. Can you see any pattern in them? You may find that you have been most impressed by the way the author developed characterizations, for example. Then you will have a possible topic for your paper. Reading the related commentary for a specific story may also generate ideas. Certainly if you have a choice, you should pick whatever appeals to you the most in the story and concentrate on it.

WRITING ABOUT SHORT FICTION

Your understanding of the elements of fiction can help you to interpret a story, but you can also appreciate that what you are reading is always much more than a self-contained, self-referential text printed on the page before you. When writers create an imaginary world in a story, they are also referring to the world outside the text, what students often call "the real world." Literature's link to the events of human history is as real as the paper it is printed on.

Literary critics point out that history penetrates literature in a variety of ways, and the closer a fictional work is to our own time, the more we take for granted its historical context. For example, the setting of Joyce Carol Oates's "Where Are You Going, Where Have You Been?" (p. 396) includes many details about teen culture in the early 1960s. When fifteen-year-old Connie hangs out with her friends at the drive-in restaurant across the street from the shopping mall, they would listen to "the music that made everything so good: the music was always in the background like music at a church service, it was something to depend upon."

If you research the cultural context of this short story, you will learn that Connie is listening to such jukebox hits as "Kisses Sweeter than Wine," "Chantilly Lace," "Do You Wanna Dance," and "Ten Commandments of Love." The escapist lyrics of romantic songs like these echo in her mind when a menacing visitor, Arnold Friend, turns up unexpectedly in her driveway and psychologically bullies her into submission. Oates dedicated the story to Bob Dylan, who redefined popular music in the mid-1960s when he wrote songs containing a tougher representation of American society — songs like "It Ain't Me, Babe," "The Times They Are A-Changin'," and "Blowin' in the Wind."

Authors themselves sometimes interact with their readers by elucidating their thematic intentions in individual stories, as William Faulkner does in commenting on "A Rose for Emily" (p. 558) and Flannery O'Connor does in her remarks about "A Good Man Is Hard to Find" (p. 639). These explicit statements of authorial intent are part of the historical background of these stories.

From the headnotes to the individual authors and the essays by writers and critics in the Commentaries section (p. 547), you will learn that occasionally storytellers create work based on their personal experience of a specific historic event, as Stephen Crane did in "The Open Boat," when he fictionalized what happened to him as a passenger after the shipwreck of the steamship *Commodore* off the Florida coast in January 1897.

For other writers, the inspiration for their fiction may be a personal story that they tell to communicate their suffering to others in an attempt to expose social injustice, as Charlotte Perkins Gilman did when she wrote "The Yellow Wallpaper" (p. 182). This story emerged from Gilman's own experience of a nervous breakdown, the result of a "rest cure" prescribed by an eminent physician in Philadelphia who, like others of the time, refused to recognize a woman's need for intellectual stimulation.

The headnotes and commentaries on the various authors and stories in this anthology contain a range of topics for you to explore in an essay or a research paper. Different assignments for writing about short fiction may also suggest specific critical approaches to literature. For example, you may be asked to analyze the symbolism in a story as a "reader-response" critic, or you may want to express your ideas about a story as a gender critic or a cultural critic.

Part Four of this textbook contains a description of ten different critical approaches that you may find useful, with accompanying analyses of commentaries in the anthology that illustrate each perspective. This section follows a discussion of the most frequently assigned methods of developing essays about literature: explication, analysis, comparison and contrast, literary contexts, and the research paper, all with examples of student essays. Whatever your assignment, you will find that writing about literature will intensify your involvement with it, clarifying your responses and sharpening your critical thinking.

COMMENTARIES   *Wayne C. Booth, "A Rhetorical Reading of O'Connor's 'Everything That Rises Must Converge,'" page 651; Ralph Ellison, "The Influence of Folklore on 'Battle Royal,'" page 557; Sandra M. Gilbert and Susan Gubar, "A Feminist Reading of Gilman's 'The Yellow Wallpaper,'" page 564; J. Hillis Miller, "Who Is He? Melville's 'Bartleby, the Scrivener,'" page 577.*

RELATED SECTION   *Part Four, Writing about Literature, page 1607.*

WEB   *For writing suggestions on each author in this anthology visit bedfordstmartins.com/charters/litwriters.*

4.

Stories and Storytellers

SHERMAN ALEXIE

Sherman Alexie (b. 1966) was born in Spokane, Washington. A registered member of the Spokane tribe through his mother, he attended grammar school on the Spokane reservation in Wellpinit, Washington. At Washington State University he took a creative writing course with Alex Kuo and began to publish in magazines such as The Beloit Poetry Journal, The Journal of Ethnic Studies, New York Quarterly, Ploughshares, *and* Zyzzyva. *In 1991 he was awarded a poetry fellowship from the Washington State Arts Commission; the following year he received a poetry fellowship from the National Endowment for the Arts.*

In 1992 Alexie published his first two books, I Would Steal Horses *and* The Business of Fancydancing: Stories and Poems. *Several more titles followed in rapid order, including* The Lone Ranger and Tonto Fistfight in Heaven *(1993), which received a PEN/Hemingway Award for best first book of fiction. Alexie also won the American Book Award for his novel* Reservation Blues *(1995), in which he imagined what would happen if the legendary bluesman Robert Johnson were resurrected on the Spokane Indian Reservation. In 1996 Alexie published* Indian Killer, *a novel, and* Summer of Black Widows, *a collection of poetry. A more recent work is the screenplay* Smoke Signals *(1998), based on one of his short stories.*

Alexie has stated, "I am a Spokane/Coeur d'Alene Indian from Wellpinit, Washington, where I live on the Spokane Indian Reservation. Everything I do now, writing and otherwise, has its origin in that." His short fiction, like "The Lone Ranger and Tonto Fistfight in Heaven," reflects his use of the icons of popular culture — radio and television programs, 7-Eleven stores, the neon promise of advertising — to facilitate a rapid crossover between storyteller and reader. As the critic Susan B. Brill has noticed, "Little ever changes in the lives of Alexie's char-

acters. Commodity food, alcoholism, and desperation are constants in the stories."
The Toughest Indian in the World *(2000) is his latest story collection.*

WEB *Research Sherman Alexie and answer questions about his work at*
bedfordstmartins.com/charters/litwriters.

The Lone Ranger and Tonto Fistfight in Heaven   1993

Too hot to sleep so I walked down to the Third Avenue 7-11 for a Cream-sicle and the company of a graveyard-shift cashier. I know that game. I worked graveyard for a Seattle 7-11 and got robbed once too often. The last time the bastard locked me in the cooler. He even took my money and basketball shoes.

The graveyard-shift worker in the Third Avenue 7-11 looked like they all do. Acne scars and a bad haircut, work pants that showed off his white socks, and those cheap black shoes that have no support. My arches still ache from my year at the Seattle 7-11.

"Hello," he asked when I walked into his store. "How you doing?"

I gave him a half-wave as I headed back to the freezer. He looked me over so he could describe me to the police later. I knew the look. One of my old girlfriends said I started to look at her that way, too. She left me not long after that. No, I left her and don't blame her for anything. That's how it happened. When one person starts to look at another like a criminal, then the love is over. It's logical.

"I don't trust you," she said to me. "You get too angry."

She was white and I lived with her in Seattle. Some nights we fought so bad that I would just get in my car and drive all night, only stop to fill up on gas. In fact, I worked the graveyard shift to spend as much time away from her as possible. But I learned all about Seattle that way, driving its back ways and dirty alleys.

Sometimes, though, I would forget where I was and get lost. I'd drive for hours, searching for something familiar. Seems like I'd spent my whole life that way, looking for anything I recognized. Once, I ended up in a nice residential neighborhood and somebody must have been worried because the police showed up and pulled me over.

"What are you doing out here?" the police officer asked me as he looked over my license and registration.

"I'm lost."

"Well, where are you supposed to be?" he asked me, and I knew there were plenty of places I wanted to be, but none where I was supposed to be.

"I got in a fight with my girlfriend," I said. "I was just driving around, blowing off steam, you know?"

"Well, you should be more careful where you drive," the officer said. "You're making people nervous. You don't fit the profile of the neighborhood."

I wanted to tell him that I didn't really fit the profile of the country but I knew it would just get me into trouble.

∙ ∙ ∙

"Can I help you?" the 7-11 clerk asked me loudly, searching for some response that would reassure him that I wasn't an armed robber. He knew this dark skin and long, black hair of mine was dangerous. I had potential.

"Just getting a Creamsicle," I said after a long interval. It was a sick twist to pull on the guy, but it was late and I was bored. I grabbed my Creamsicle and walked back to the counter slowly, scanned the aisles for effect. I wanted to whistle low and menacingly but I never learned to whistle.

"Pretty hot out tonight?" he asked, that old rhetorical weather bullshit question designed to put us both at ease.

"Hot enough to make you go crazy," I said and smiled. He swallowed hard like a white man does in those situations. I looked him over. Same old green, red, and white 7-11 jacket and thick glasses. But he wasn't ugly, just misplaced and marked by loneliness. If he wasn't working there that night, he'd be at home alone, flipping through channels and wishing he could afford HBO or Showtime.

"Will this be all?" he asked me, in that company effort to make me do some impulse shopping. Like adding a clause onto a treaty. *We'll take Washington and Oregon, and you get six pine trees and a brand-new Chrysler Cordoba.* I knew how to make and break promises.

"No," I said and paused. "Give me a Cherry Slushie, too."

"What size?" he asked, relieved.

"Large," I said, and he turned his back to me to make the drink. He realized his mistake but it was too late. He stiffened, ready for the gunshot or the blow behind the ear. When it didn't come, he turned back to me.

"I'm sorry," he said. "What size did you say?"

"Small," I said and changed the story.

"But I thought you said large."

"If you knew I wanted a large, then why did you ask me again?" I asked him and laughed. He looked at me, couldn't decide if I was giving him serious shit or just goofing. There was something about him I liked, even if it was three in the morning and he was white.

"Hey," I said. "Forget the Slushie. What I want to know is if you know all the words to the theme from 'The Brady Bunch'?"

He looked at me, confused at first, then laughed.

"Shit," he said. "I was hoping you weren't crazy. You were scaring me."

"Well, I'm going to get crazy if you don't know the words."

He laughed loudly then, told me to take the Creamsicle for free. He was the graveyard-shift manager and those little demonstrations of power tickled him. All seventy-five cents of it. I knew how much everything cost.

"Thanks," I said to him and walked out the door. I took my time walking home, let the heat of the night melt the Creamsicle all over my hand. At three in the morning I could act just as young as I wanted to act. There was no one around to ask me to grow up.

In Seattle, I broke lamps. She and I would argue and I'd break a lamp, just pick it up and throw it down. At first she'd buy replacement lamps, expensive and beautiful. But after a while she'd buy lamps from Goodwill or garage sales. Then she just gave up the idea entirely and we'd argue in the dark.

"You're just like your brother," she'd yell. "Drunk all the time and stupid."

"My brother don't drink that much."

She and I never tried to hurt each other physically. I did love her, after all, and she loved me. But those arguments were just as damaging as a fist. Words can be like that, you know? Whenever I get into arguments now, I remember her and I also remember Muhammad Ali. He knew the power of his fists but, more importantly, he knew the power of his words, too. Even though he only had an IQ of 80 or so, Ali was a genius. And she was a genius, too. She knew exactly what to say to cause me the most pain.

But don't get me wrong. I walked through that relationship with an executioner's hood. Or more appropriately, with war paint and sharp arrows. She was a kindergarten teacher and I continually insulted her for that.

"Hey, schoolmarm," I asked. "Did your kids teach you anything new today?"

And I always had crazy dreams. I always have had them, but it seemed they became nightmares more often in Seattle.

In one dream, she was a missionary's wife and I was a minor war chief. We fell in love and tried to keep it secret. But the missionary caught us fucking in the barn and shot me. As I lay dying, my tribe learned of the shooting and attacked the whites all across the reservation. I died and my soul drifted above the reservation.

Disembodied, I could see everything that was happening. Whites killing Indians and Indians killing whites. At first it was small, just my tribe and the few whites who lived there. But my dream grew, intensified. Other tribes arrived on horseback to continue the slaughter of whites, and the United States Cavalry rode into battle.

The most vivid image of that dream stays with me. Three mounted soldiers played polo with a dead Indian woman's head. When I first dreamed it, I thought it was just a product of my anger and imagination. But since then, I've read similar accounts of that kind of evil in the old West. Even more terrifying, though, is the fact that those kinds of brutal things are happening today in places like El Salvador.

All I know for sure, though, is that I woke from that dream in terror, packed up all my possessions, and left Seattle in the middle of the night.

"I love you," she said as I left her. "And don't ever come back."

I drove through the night, over the Cascades, down into the plains of central Washington, and back home to the Spokane Indian Reservation.

When I finished the Creamsicle that the 7-11 clerk gave me, I held the wooden stick up into the air and shouted out very loudly. A couple lights flashed on in windows and a police car cruised by me a few minutes later. I waved to the men in blue and they waved back accidentally. When I got home it was still too hot to sleep so I picked up a week-old newspaper from the floor and read.

There was another civil war, another terrorist bomb exploded, and one more plane crashed and all aboard were presumed dead. The crime rate was rising in every city with populations larger than 100,000, and a farmer in Iowa shot his banker after foreclosure on his 1,000 acres.

A kid from Spokane won the local spelling bee by spelling the word *rhinoceros*.

When I got back to the reservation, my family wasn't surprised to see me. They'd been expecting me back since the day I left for Seattle. There's an old Indian poet who said that Indians can reside in the city, but they can never live there. That's as close to truth as any of us can get.

Mostly I watched television. For weeks I flipped through channels, searched for answers in the game shows and soap operas. My mother would circle the want ads in red and hand the paper to me.

"What are you going to do with the rest of your life?" she asked.

"Don't know," I said, and normally, for almost any other Indian in the country, that would have been a perfectly fine answer. But I was special, a former college student, a smart kid. I was one of those Indians who was supposed to make it, to rise above the rest of the reservation like a fucking eagle or something. I was the new kind of warrior.

For a few months I didn't even look at the want ads my mother circled, just left the newspaper where she had set it down. After a while, though, I got tired of television and started to play basketball again. I'd been a good player in high school, nearly great, and almost played at the college I attended for a couple years. But I'd been too out of shape from drinking and sadness to ever be good again. Still, I liked the way the ball felt in my hands and the way my feet felt inside my shoes.

At first I just shot baskets by myself. It was selfish, and I also wanted to learn the game again before I played against anybody else. Since I had been good before and embarrassed fellow tribal members, I knew they would want to take revenge on me. Forget about the cowboys versus Indians business. The most intense competition on any reservation is Indians versus Indians.

But on the night I was ready to play for real, there was this white guy at the gym, playing with all the Indians.

"Who is that?" I asked Jimmy Seyler.

"He's the new BIA° chief's kid."

"Can he play?"

"Oh, yeah."

And he could play. He played Indian ball, fast and loose, better than all the Indians there.

"How long's he been playing here?" I asked.

"Long enough."

I stretched my muscles, and everybody watched me. All these Indians watched one of their old and dusty heroes. Even though I had played most of my ball at the white high school I went to, I was still all Indian, you know? I was

---

BIA: Bureau of Indian Affairs.

Indian when it counted, and this BIA kid needed to be beaten by an Indian, any Indian.

I jumped into the game and played well for a little while. It felt good. I hit a few shots, grabbed a rebound or two, played enough defense to keep the other team honest. Then that white kid took over the game. He was too good. Later, he'd play college ball back East and would nearly make the Knicks team a couple years on. But we didn't know any of that would happen. We just knew he was better that day and every other day.

The next morning I woke up tired and hungry, so I grabbed the want ads, found a job I wanted, and drove to Spokane to get it. I've been working at the high school exchange program ever since, typing and answering phones. Sometimes I wonder if the people on the other end of the line know that I'm Indian and if their voices would change if they did know.

One day I picked up the phone and it was her, calling from Seattle.

"I got your number from your mom," she said. "I'm glad you're working."

"Yeah, nothing like a regular paycheck."

"Are you drinking?"

"No, I've been on the wagon for almost a year."

"Good. "

The connection was good. I could hear her breathing in the spaces between our words. How do you talk to the real person whose ghost has haunted you? How do you tell the difference between the two?

"Listen," I said. "I'm sorry for everything."

"Me, too."

"What's going to happen to us?" I asked her and wished I had the answer for myself.

"I don't know," she said. "I want to change the world."

These days, living alone in Spokane, I wish I lived closer to the river, to the falls where ghosts of salmon jump. I wish I could sleep. I put down my paper or book and turn off all the lights, lie quietly in the dark. It may take hours, even years, for me to sleep again. There's nothing surprising or disappointing in that.

I know how all my dreams end anyway.

SHERWOOD ANDERSON

Sherwood Anderson (1876–1941) was born to a jack-of-all-trades father in Camden, Ohio. He did not publish his first book until he was over forty, after working for many years as a newsboy, farm laborer, stable boy, factory hand, and advertising copywriter. Dissatisfied with the commercial spirit of the advertising business, Anderson made friends with writers in Chicago and began to publish his own poetry and fiction. The poet Carl Sandburg encouraged him, but Anderson's literary style was most influenced by Three Lives *(1909) and* Tender Buttons *(1914), experimental books by the expatriate American writer Gertrude Stein, which he felt revolutionized the language of narrative because Stein did not use conventional plot structure.*

In 1916 Anderson published his first novel, Windy McPherson's Son. *He followed it with another novel and a volume of poetry, but he did not receive wide recognition until 1919, with the book* Winesburg, Ohio. *This collection of related stories, including "Hands," about life in a small town explores the devastating consequences of the repressive conventions of a provincial society. It was followed by other important collections of stories:* The Triumph of the Egg *(1921),* Horses and Men *(1923), and* Death in the Woods and Other Stories *(1933). In his time Anderson was a strong influence on Ernest Hemingway, William Faulkner, Richard Wright, and John Steinbeck. The editor Martha Foley wrote in 1941 that*

> Sherwood Anderson set out on new paths at a time when the American short story seemed doomed to a formula-ridden, conventionalized, mechanized, and commercialized concept. When Winesburg, Ohio appeared in 1919 it was intensely influential on writers who either had lost heart or had not yet found their way. His vision was his own; his characters were people into whose hearts and minds he seemed intuitively to peer; his prose was simple, deceptively simple, sensuous, rich, and evocative.

As literary critics have observed, the characteristic tone of Anderson's short fiction is melancholy reminiscence. In an understated fashion, he wove carefully selected realistic details into such narratives as "Hands," which moves by apparently formless associations of thought and feeling but is actually a controlled progression of fully dramatized situations. Anderson's importance in our literature is suggested by Richard Wright's acknowledgment that Anderson's stories made him see that through the powers of fiction, "America could be shaped nearer to the hearts of those who lived in it."

WEB   *Research Sherwood Anderson and answer questions about his work at bedfordstmartins.com/charters/litwriters.*

Hands   1919

Upon the half decayed veranda of a small frame house that stood near the edge of a ravine near the town of Winesburg, Ohio, a fat little old man walked nervously up and down. Across a long field that had been seeded for clover but that had produced only a dense crop of yellow mustard weeds, he could see the public highway along which went a wagon filled with berry pickers returning from the fields. The berry pickers, youths and maidens, laughed and shouted boisterously. A boy clad in a blue shirt leaped from the wagon and attempted to drag after him one of the maidens who screamed and protested shrilly. The feet of the boy in the road kicked up a cloud of dust that floated across the face of the departing sun. Over the long field came a thin girlish voice. "Oh, you Wing Biddlebaum, comb your hair, it's falling into your eyes," commanded the voice to the man, who was bald and whose nervous little hands fiddled about the bare white forehead as though arranging a mass of tangled locks.

Wing Biddlebaum, forever frightened and beset by a ghostly band of doubts, did not think of himself as in any way a part of the life of the town where he had lived for twenty years. Among all the people of Winesburg but one had come close to him. With George Willard, son of Tom Willard, the proprietor of the new Willard House, he had formed something like a friendship. George Willard was the reporter on the *Winesburg Eagle* and sometimes in the evenings he walked out along the highway to Wing Biddlebaum's house. Now as the old man walked up and down on the veranda, his hands moving nervously about, he was hoping that George Willard would come and spend the evening with him. After the wagon containing the berry pickers had passed, he went across the field through the tall mustard weeds and climbing a rail fence peered anxiously along the road to the town. For a moment he stood thus, rubbing his hands together and looking up and down the road, and then, fear overcoming him, ran back to walk again upon the porch of his own house.

In the presence of George Willard, Wing Biddlebaum, who for twenty years had been the town mystery, lost something of his timidity, and his shadowy personality, submerged in a sea of doubts, came forth to look at the world. With the young reporter at his side, he ventured in the light of day into Main Street or strode up and down on the rickety front porch of his own house, talking excitedly. The voice that had been low and trembling became shrill and loud. The bent figure straightened. With a kind of wriggle, like a fish returned to the brook by the fisherman, Biddlebaum the silent began to talk, striving to put into words the ideas that had been accumulated by his mind during long years of silence.

Wing Biddlebaum talked much with his hands. The slender expressive fingers, forever active, forever striving to conceal themselves in his pockets or behind his back, came forth and became the piston rods of his machinery of expression.

The story of Wing Biddlebaum is a story of hands. Their restless activity, like unto the beating of the wings of an imprisoned bird, had given him his name. Some obscure poet of the town had thought of it. The hands alarmed their owner. He wanted to keep them hidden away and looked with amazement at the quiet inexpressive hands of other men who worked beside him in the fields, or passed, driving sleepy teams on country roads.

When he talked to George Willard, Wing Biddlebaum closed his fists and beat with them upon a table or on the walls of his house. The action made him more comfortable. If the desire to talk came to him when the two were walking in the fields, he sought out a stump or the top board of a fence and with his hands pounding busily talked with renewed ease.

The story of Wing Biddlebaum's hands is worth a book itself. Sympathetically set forth it would tap many strange, beautiful qualities in obscure men. It is a job for a poet. In Winesburg the hands had attracted attention merely because of their activity. With them Wing Biddlebaum had picked as high as a hundred and forty quarts of strawberries in a day. They became his distinguishing feature, the source of his fame. Also they made more grotesque an already grotesque and elusive individuality. Winesburg was proud of the hands of Wing Biddlebaum in the same spirit in which it was proud of Banker White's new stone house and Wesley Moyer's bay stallion, Tony Tip, that had won the two-fifteen trot at the fall races in Cleveland.

As for George Willard, he had many times wanted to ask about the hands. At times an almost overwhelming curiosity had taken hold of him. He felt that there must be a reason for their strange activity and their inclination to keep hidden away and only a growing respect for Wing Biddlebaum kept him from blurting out the questions that were often in his mind.

Once he had been on the point of asking. The two were walking in the fields on a summer afternoon and had stopped to sit upon a grassy bank. All afternoon Wing Biddlebaum had talked as one inspired. By a fence he had stopped and beating like a giant woodpecker upon the top board had shouted at George Willard, condemning his tendency to be too much influenced by the people about him. "You are destroying yourself," he cried.

"You have the inclination to be alone and to dream and you are afraid of dreams. You want to be like others in town here. You hear them talk and you try to imitate them."

On the grassy bank Wing Biddlebaum had tried again to drive his point home. His voice became soft and reminiscent, and with a sigh of contentment he launched into a long rambling talk, speaking as one lost in a dream.

Out of the dream Wing Biddlebaum made a picture for George Willard. In the picture men lived again in a kind of pastoral golden age. Across a green open country came clean-limbed young men, some afoot, some mounted upon horses. In crowds the young men came to gather about the feet of an old man who sat beneath a tree in a tiny garden and who talked to them.

Wing Biddlebaum became wholly inspired. For once he forgot the hands. Slowly they stole forth and lay upon George Willard's shoulders. Something new and bold came into the voice that talked. "You must try to forget all you have learned," said the old man. "You must begin to dream. From this time on you must shut your ears to the roaring of the voices."

Pausing in his speech, Wing Biddlebaum looked long and earnestly at George Willard. His eyes glowed. Again he raised the hands to caress the boy and then a look of horror swept over his face.

With a convulsive movement of his body, Wing Biddlebaum sprang to his feet and thrust his hands deep into his trousers pockets. Tears came to his eyes. "I must be getting along home. I can talk no more with you," he said nervously.

Without looking back, the old man had hurried down the hillside and across a meadow, leaving George Willard perplexed and frightened upon the grassy slope. With a shiver of dread the boy arose and went along the road toward town. "I'll not ask him about his hands," he thought, touched by the memory of the terror he had seen in the man's eyes. "There's something wrong, but I don't want to know what it is. His hands have something to do with his fear of me and of everyone."

And George Willard was right. Let us look briefly into the story of the hands. Perhaps our talking of them will arouse the poet who will tell the hidden wonder story of the influence for which the hands were but fluttering pennants of promise.

In his youth Wing Biddlebaum had been a school teacher in a town in Pennsylvania. He was not then known as Wing Biddlebaum, but went by the less euphonic name of Adolph Myers. As Adolph Myers he was much loved by the boys of his school.

Adolph Myers was meant by nature to be a rare teacher of youth. He was one of those rare, little-understood men who rule by a power so gentle that it passes as a lovable weakness. In their feeling for the boys under their charge such men are not unlike the finer sort of women in their love of men.

And yet that is but crudely stated. It needs the poet there. With the boys of his school, Adolph Myers had walked in the evening or had sat talking until dusk upon the schoolhouse steps lost in a kind of dream. Here and there went his hands, caressing the shoulders of the boys, playing about the tousled heads. As he talked his voice became soft and musical. There was a caress in that also. In a way the voice and the hands, the stroking of the shoulders and the touching of the hair was a part of the schoolmaster's effort to carry a dream into the young minds. By the caress that was in his fingers he expressed himself. He was one of those men in whom the force that creates life is diffused, not centralized. Under the caress of his hands doubt and disbelief went out of the minds of the boys and they began also to dream.

And then the tragedy. A half-witted boy of the school became enamored of the young master. In his bed at night he imagined unspeakable things and in the morning went forth to tell his dreams as facts. Strange, hideous accusations fell from his loose-hung lips. Through the Pennsylvania town went a shiver. Hidden, shadowy doubts that had been in men's minds concerning Adolph Myers were galvanized into beliefs.

The tragedy did not linger. Trembling lads were jerked out of bed and questioned. "He put his arms about me," said one. "His fingers were always playing in my hair," said another.

One afternoon a man of the town, Henry Bradford, who kept a saloon, came to the schoolhouse door. Calling Adolph Myers into the school yard he began to beat him with his fists. As his hard knuckles beat down into the frightened face of the schoolmaster, his wrath became more and more terrible. Screaming with dismay, the children ran here and there like disturbed insects. "I'll teach you to put your hands on my boy, you beast," roared the saloon keeper, who, tired of beating the master, had begun to kick him about the yard.

Adolph Myers was driven from the Pennsylvania town in the night. With lanterns in their hands a dozen men came to the door of the house where he lived alone and commanded that he dress and come forth. It was raining and one of the men had a rope in his hands. They had intended to hang the schoolmaster, but something in his figure, so small, white, and pitiful, touched their hearts and they let him escape. As he ran away into the darkness they repented of their weakness and ran after him, swearing and throwing sticks and great balls of soft mud at the figure that screamed and ran faster and faster into the darkness.

For twenty years Adolph Myers had lived alone in Winesburg. He was but forty but looked sixty-five. The name Biddlebaum he got from a box of goods seen at a freight station as he hurried through an eastern Ohio town. He had an aunt in Winesburg, a black-toothed old woman who raised chickens, and with her he lived until she died. He had been ill for a year after the experience in Pennsylvania, and after his recovery worked as a day laborer in the fields, going timidly about and striving to conceal his hands. Although he did not understand what had happened he felt that the hands must be to blame. Again and again the fathers of the boys had talked of the hands. "Keep your hands to yourself," the saloon keeper had roared, dancing with fury in the schoolhouse yard.

Upon the veranda of his house by the ravine, Wing Biddlebaum continued to walk up and down until the sun had disappeared and the road beyond the field was lost in the grey shadows. Going into his house he cut slices of bread and spread honey upon them. When the rumble of the evening train that took away the express cars loaded with the day's harvest of berries had passed and restored the silence of the summer night, he went again to walk upon the veranda. In the darkness he could not see the hands and they became quiet. Although he still hungered for the presence of the boy, who was the medium through which he expressed his love of man, the hunger became again a part of his loneliness and his waiting. Lighting a lamp, Wing Biddlebaum washed the few dishes soiled by his simple meal and, setting up a folding cot by the screen door that led to the porch, prepared to undress for the night. A few stray white bread crumbs lay on the cleanly washed floor by the table; putting the lamp upon a low stool he began to pick up the crumbs, carrying them to his mouth one by one with unbelievable rapidity. In the dense blotch of light beneath the table, the kneeling figure looked like a priest engaged in some service of his church. The nervous expressive fingers, flashing in and out of the light, might well have been mistaken for the fingers of the devotee going swiftly through decade after decade of his rosary.

MARGARET ATWOOD

Margaret Atwood (b. 1939) is a Canadian writer of poetry and fiction. Born in Ottawa, Ontario, she spent the first eleven years of her life in the sparsely settled "bush" country of northern Ontario and Quebec, where her father, an entomologist, did research. She remembers that

> *I did not spend a full year in school until I was in Grade Eight. I began to write at the age of five—poems, "novels," comic books, and plays—but I had no thought of being a professional writer until I was sixteen. I entered Victoria College, University of Toronto, when I was seventeen and graduated in 1961. I won a Woodrow Wilson Fellowship to Harvard, where I studied Victorian Literature, and spent the next ten years in one place after another: Boston, Montreal, Edmonton, Toronto, Vancouver, England, and Italy, alternately teaching and writing.*

Atwood's first poem was published when she was nineteen. To date she has published two collections of short stories, several novels—including the best-sellers Surfacing *(1972),* The Handmaid's Tale *(1986),* Cat's Eye *(1989),* The Robber

Bride *(1993), and* Bodily Harm *(1999) — and more than a dozen books of poetry. She was encouraged to write as a young woman because Canadians of her generation felt a strong need to develop a national literature.*

Atwood has compared writing stories to telling riddles and jokes, all three requiring "the same mystifying buildup, the same surprising twist, the same impeccable sense of timing." She took pleasure in writing "Happy Endings," but she was puzzled by the form the story took. She has said,

> When I wrote "Happy Endings" — the year was, I think, 1982, and I was writing a number of short fictions then — I did not know what sort of creature it was. It was not a poem, a short story, or a prose poem. It was not quite a condensation, a commentary, a questionnaire, and it missed being a parable, a proverb, a paradox. It was a mutation. Writing it gave me a sense of furtive glee, like scribbling anonymously on a wall with no one looking.
>
> This summer I saw a white frog. It would not have been startling if I didn't know that this species of frog is normally green. This is the way such a mutant literary form unsettles us. We know what is expected, in a given arrangement of words; we know what is supposed to come next. And then it doesn't.
>
> It was a little disappointing to learn that other people had a name for such aberrations [metafiction], and had already made up rules.

"Gertrude Talks Back" was included in Atwood's collection Good Bones and Simple Murders *(1994).*

CONNECTION   *William Shakespeare,* Hamlet, Prince of Denmark, *page 1132.*

WEB   *Research Margaret Atwood and answer questions about her work at bedfordstmartins.com/charters/litwriters.*

Gertrude Talks Back   1994

I always thought it was a mistake, calling you Hamlet. I mean, what kind of a name is that for a young boy? It was your father's idea. Nothing would do but that you had to be called after him. Selfish. The other kids at school used to tease the life out of you. The nicknames! And those terrible jokes about pork.

I wanted to call you George.

I am *not* wringing my hands. I'm drying my nails.

Darling, please stop fidgeting with my mirror. That'll be the third one you've broken.

Yes, I've seen those pictures, thank you very much.

I *know* your father was handsomer than Claudius. High brow, aquiline nose and so on, looked great in uniform. But handsome isn't everything, especially in a man, and far be it from me to speak ill of the dead, but I think it's about time I pointed out to you that your dad just wasn't a whole lot of fun. Noble, sure, I grant you. But Claudius, well, he likes a drink now and then. He appreciates a decent meal. He enjoys a laugh, know what I mean? You don't always have to be tiptoeing around because of some holier-than-thou principle or something.

By the way, darling, I wish you wouldn't call your stepdad *the bloat king*. He does have a slight weight problem, and it hurts his feelings.

The rank sweat of a *what?* My bed is certainly not *enseamed*, whatever that might be! A nasty sty, indeed! Not that it's any of your business, but I change those sheets twice a week, which is more than you do, judging from that student slum pigpen in Wittenberg. I'll certainly never visit you *there* again without prior warning! I see that laundry of yours when you bring it home, and not often enough either, by a long shot! Only when you run out of black socks.

And let me tell you, everyone sweats at a time like that, as you'd find out very soon if you ever gave it a try. A real girlfriend would do you a heap of good. Not like that pasty-faced what's-her-name, all trussed up like a prize turkey in those touch-me-not corsets of hers. If you ask me, there's something off about that girl. Borderline. Any little shock could push her right over the edge.

Go get yourself someone more down-to-earth. Have a nice roll in the hay. Then you can talk to me about nasty sties.

No, darling, I am not *mad* at you. But I must say you're an awful prig sometimes. Just like your Dad. *The Flesh*, he'd say. You'd think it was dog dirt. You can excuse that in a young person, they are always so intolerant, but in someone his age it was getting, well, very hard to live with, and that's the understatement of the year.

Some days I think it would have been better for both of us if you hadn't been an only child. But you realize who you have to thank for *that*. You have no idea what I used to put up with. And every time I felt like a little, you know, just to warm up my aging bones, it was like I'd suggested murder.

You think *what?* You think Claudius murdered your Dad? Well, no wonder you've been so rude to him at the dinner table!

If I'd known *that,* I could have put you straight in no time flat.

It wasn't Claudius, darling.

It was me.

Happy Endings

1983

John and Mary meet.
What happens next?
If you want a happy ending, try A.

A

John and Mary fall in love and get married. They both have worthwhile and remunerative jobs which they find stimulating and challenging. They buy a charming house. Real estate values go up. Eventually, when they can afford live-in help, they have two children, to whom they are devoted. The children turn out well. John and Mary have a stimulating and challenging sex life and worthwhile friends. They go on fun vacations together. They retire. They both have hobbies which they find stimulating and challenging. Eventually they die. This is the end of the story.

B

Mary falls in love with John but John doesn't fall in love with Mary. He merely uses her body for selfish pleasure and ego gratification of a tepid kind. He comes to her apartment twice a week and she cooks him dinner, you'll notice that he doesn't even consider her worth the price of a dinner out, and after he's eaten the dinner he fucks her and after that he falls asleep, while she does the dishes so he won't think she's untidy, having all those dirty dishes lying around, and puts on fresh lipstick so she'll look good when he wakes up, but when he wakes up he doesn't even notice, he puts on his socks and his shorts and his pants and his shirt and his tie and his shoes, the reverse order from the one in which he took them off. He doesn't take off Mary's clothes, she takes them off herself, she acts as if she's dying for it every time, not because she likes sex exactly, she doesn't, but she wants John to think she does because if they do it often enough surely he'll get used to her, he'll come to depend on her and they will get married, but John goes out the door with hardly so much as a good-night and three days later he turns up at six o'clock and they do the whole thing over again.

Mary gets run-down. Crying is bad for your face, everyone knows that and so does Mary but she can't stop. People at work notice. Her friends tell her John is a rat, a pig, a dog, he isn't good enough for her, but she can't believe it. Inside John, she thinks, is another John, who is much nicer. This other John will emerge like a butterfly from a cocoon, a Jack from a box, a pit from a prune, if the first John is only squeezed enough.

One evening John complains about the food. He has never complained about the food before. Mary is hurt.

Her friends tell her they've seen him in a restaurant with another woman, whose name is Madge. It's not even Madge that finally gets to Mary: it's the restaurant. John has never taken Mary to a restaurant. Mary collects all the sleeping pills and aspirins she can find, and takes them and a half a bottle of sherry. You can see what kind of a woman she is by the fact that it's not even whiskey. She leaves a note for John. She hopes he'll discover her and get her to the hospital in time and repent and then they can get married, but this fails to happen and she dies.

John marries Madge and everything continues as in A.

C

John, who is an older man, falls in love with Mary, and Mary, who is only twenty-two, feels sorry for him because he's worried about his hair falling out. She sleeps with him even though she's not in love with him. She met him at work. She's in love with someone called James, who is twenty-two also and not yet ready to settle down.

John on the contrary settled down long ago: this is what is bothering him. John has a steady, respectable job and is getting ahead in his field, but Mary isn't impressed by him, she's impressed by James, who has a motorcycle and a fabulous record collection. But James is often away on his motorcycle, being free. Freedom isn't the same for girls, so in the meantime Mary spends Thursday evenings with John. Thursdays are the only days John can get away.

John is married to a woman called Madge and they have two children, a charming house which they bought just before the real estate values went up, and hobbies which they find stimulating and challenging, when they have the time. John tells Mary how important she is to him, but of course he can't leave his wife because a commitment is a commitment. He goes on about this more than is necessary and Mary finds it boring, but older men can keep it up longer so on the whole she has a fairly good time.

One day James breezes in on his motorcycle with some top-grade California hybrid and James and Mary get higher than you'd believe possible and they climb into bed. Everything becomes very underwater, but along comes John, who has a key to Mary's apartment. He finds them stoned and entwined. He's hardly in any position to be jealous, considering Madge, but nevertheless he's overcome with despair. Finally he's middle-aged, in two years he'll be bald as an egg and he can't stand it. He purchases a handgun, saying he needs it for target practice — this is the thin part of the plot, but it can be dealt with later — and shoots the two of them and himself.

Madge, after a suitable period of mourning, marries an understanding man called Fred and everything continues as in A, but under different names.

D

Fred and Madge have no problems. They get along exceptionally well and are good at working out any little difficulties that may arise. But their charming house is by the seashore and one day a giant tidal wave approaches. Real estate values go down. The rest of the story is about what caused the tidal wave and how they escape from it. They do, though thousands drown, but Fred and Madge are virtuous and lucky. Finally on high ground they clasp each other, wet and dripping and grateful, and continue as in A.

E

Yes, but Fred has a bad heart. The rest of the story is about how kind and understanding they both are until Fred dies. Then Madge devotes herself to charity work until the end of A. If you like, it can be "Madge," "cancer," "guilty and confused," and "bird watching."

F

If you think this is all too bourgeois, make John a revolutionary and Mary a counterespionage agent and see how far that gets you. Remember, this is Canada. You'll still end up with A, though in between you may get a lustful brawling saga of passionate involvement, a chronicle of our times, sort of.

You'll have to face it, the endings are the same however you slice it. Don't be deluded by any other endings, they're all fake, either deliberately fake, with malicious intent to deceive, or just motivated by excessive optimism if not by downright sentimentality.

The only authentic ending is the one provided here:
John and Mary die. John and Mary die. John and Mary die.

So much for endings. Beginnings are always more fun. True connoisseurs, however, are known to favor the stretch in between, since it's the hardest to do anything with.

That's about all that can be said for plots, which anyway are just one thing after another, a what and a what and a what.

Now try How and Why.

JAMES BALDWIN

James Baldwin (1924–1987) was born the son of a clergyman in Harlem, where he attended Public School 24, Frederick Douglass Junior High School, and DeWitt Clinton High School. While still a high school student he preached at the Fireside Pentecostal Assembly, but when he was seventeen he renounced the ministry. Two years later, living in Greenwich Village, he met Richard Wright, who encouraged him to be a writer and helped him win a Eugene Saxton Fellowship. Soon afterward Baldwin moved to France, as Wright had, to escape the stifling racial oppression he found in the United States. Although France was his more or less permanent residence until his death from cancer nearly forty years later, Baldwin regarded himself as a "commuter" rather than an expatriate. He said,

> *Only white Americans can consider themselves to be expatriates. Once I found myself on the other side of the ocean, I could see where I came from very clearly, and I could see that I carried myself, which is my home, with me. You can never escape that. I am the grandson of a slave, and I am a writer. I must deal with both.*

Baldwin began his career by publishing novels and short stories. Go Tell It on the Mountain, *his first novel, was highly acclaimed when it appeared in 1953. It was based on his childhood in Harlem and his fear of his tyrannical father. Baldwin's frank depiction of homosexuality in the novels* Giovanni's Room *(1956) and* Another Country *(1962) drew criticism, but during the civil rights movement a few years later, he established himself as a brilliant essayist. In his lifetime Baldwin published several collections of essays, three more novels, and a book of five short stories,* Going to Meet the Man *(1965).*

"Sonny's Blues," from that collection, is one of Baldwin's strongest psychological dramatizations of the frustrations of African American life in our time. Like Wright's autobiographical books, Baldwin's work is an inspiration to young writers struggling to express their experience of racism. The African writer Chinua Achebe has said that "as long as injustice exists . . . the words of James Baldwin will be there to bear witness and to inspire and elevate the struggle for human freedom."

COMMENTARY   *James Baldwin, "Autobiographical Notes," page 547.*

WEB   *Research James Baldwin and answer questions about his work at* bedfordstmartins.com/charters/litwriters.

Sonny's Blues   1957

I read about it in the paper, in the subway, on my way to work. I read it, and I couldn't believe it, and I read it again. Then perhaps I just stared at it, at the newsprint spelling out his name, spelling out the story. I stared at it in the swinging lights of the subway car, and in the faces and bodies of the people, and in my own face, trapped in the darkness which roared outside.

It was not to be believed and I kept telling myself that, as I walked from the subway station to the high school. And at the same time I couldn't doubt it. I was scared, scared for Sonny. He became real to me again. A great block of ice got settled in my belly and kept melting there slowly all day long, while I taught my classes algebra. It was a special kind of ice. It kept melting, sending trickles of ice water all up and down my veins, but it never got less. Sometimes it hardened and seemed to expand until I felt my guts were going to come spilling out or that I was going to choke or scream. This would always be at a moment when I was remembering some specific thing Sonny had once said or done.

When he was about as old as the boys in my classes his face had been bright and open, there was a lot of copper in it; and he'd had wonderfully direct brown eyes, and great gentleness and privacy. I wondered what he looked like now. He had been picked up, the evening before, in a raid on an apartment downtown, for peddling and using heroin.

I couldn't believe it: but what I mean by that is that I couldn't find any room for it anywhere inside me. I had kept it outside me for a long time. I hadn't wanted to know. I had had suspicions, but I didn't name them, I kept putting them away. I told myself that Sonny was wild, but he wasn't crazy. And he'd always been a good boy, he hadn't ever turned hard or evil or disrespectful, the way kids can, so quick, so quick, especially in Harlem. I didn't want to believe that I'd ever see my brother going down, coming to nothing, all that light in his face gone out, in the condition I'd already seen so many others. Yet it had happened and here I was, talking about algebra to a lot of boys who might, every one of them for all I knew, be popping off needles every time they went to the head. Maybe it did more for them than algebra could.

I was sure that the first time Sonny had ever had horse, he couldn't have been much older than these boys were now. These boys, now, were living as we'd been living then, they were growing up with a rush and their heads bumped abruptly against the low ceiling of their actual possibilities. They were filled with rage. All they really knew were two darknesses, the darkness of their lives, which was now closing in on them, and the darkness of the movies, which had blinded them to that other darkness, and in which they now, vindictively, dreamed, at once more together than they were at any other time, and more alone.

When the last bell rang, the last class ended, I let out my breath. It seemed I'd been holding it for all that time. My clothes were wet — I may have looked as though I'd been sitting in a steam bath, all dressed up, all afternoon. I sat alone in the classroom a long time. I listened to the boys outside, downstairs, shouting and cursing and laughing. Their laughter struck me for perhaps the first time. It was not the joyous laughter which — God knows why — one associates with children. It was mocking and insular, its intent to denigrate. It was disenchanted, and in this, also, lay the authority of their curses. Perhaps I was listening to them because I was thinking about my brother and in them I heard my brother. And myself.

One boy was whistling a tune, at once very complicated and very simple, it seemed to be pouring out of him as though he were a bird, and it sounded very cool and moving through all that harsh, bright air, only just holding its own through all those other sounds.

I stood up and walked over to the window and looked down into the courtyard. It was the beginning of the spring and the sap was rising in the boys. A teacher passed through them every now and again, quickly, as though he or she couldn't wait to get out of that courtyard, to get those boys out of their sight and off their minds. I started collecting my stuff. I thought I'd better get home and talk to Isabel.

The courtyard was almost deserted by the time I got downstairs. I saw this boy standing in the shadow of a doorway, looking just like Sonny. I almost called his name. Then I saw that it wasn't Sonny, but somebody we used to know, a boy from around our block. He'd been Sonny's friend. He'd never been mine, having been too young for me, and, anyway, I'd never liked him. And now, even though he was a grown-up man, he still hung around that block, still spent hours on the street corners, was always high and raggy. I used to run into him from time to time and he'd often work around to asking me for a quarter or fifty cents. He always had some real good excuse, too, and I always gave it to him, I don't know why.

But now, abruptly, I hated him. I couldn't stand the way he looked at me, partly like a dog, partly like a cunning child. I wanted to ask him what the hell he was doing in the school courtyard.

He sort of shuffled over to me, and he said, "I see you got the papers. So you already know about it."

"You mean about Sonny? Yes, I already know about it. How come they didn't get you?"

He grinned. It made him repulsive and it also brought to mind what he'd looked like as a kid. "I wasn't there. I stay away from them people."

"Good for you." I offered him a cigarette and I watched him through the smoke. "You come all the way down here just to tell me about Sonny?"

"That's right." He was sort of shaking his head and his eyes looked strange, as though they were about to cross. The bright sun deadened his damp dark brown skin and it made his eyes look yellow and showed up the dirt in his kinked hair. He smelled funky. I moved a little away from him and I said, "Well, thanks. But I already know about it and I got to get home."

"I'll walk you a little ways," he said. We started walking. There were a couple of kids still loitering in the courtyard and one of them said goodnight to me and looked strangely at the boy beside me.

"What're you going to do?" he asked me. "I mean, about Sonny?"

"Look. I haven't seen Sonny for over a year. I'm not sure I'm going to do anything. Anyway, what the hell *can* I do?"

"That's right," he said quickly, "ain't nothing you can do. Can't much help old Sonny no more, I guess."

It was what I was thinking and so it seemed to me he had no right to say it.

"I'm surprised at Sonny, though," he went on — he had a funny way of talking, he looked straight ahead as though he were talking to himself — "I thought Sonny was a smart boy, I thought he was too smart to get hung."

"I guess he thought so too," I said sharply, "and that's how he got hung. And how about you? You're pretty goddamn smart, I bet."

Then he looked directly at me, just for a minute. "I ain't smart," he said. "If I was smart, I'd have reached for a pistol a long time ago."

"Look. Don't tell *me* your sad story, if it was up to me, I'd give you one." Then I felt guilty — guilty, probably, for never having supposed that the poor bastard *had* a story of his own, much less a sad one, and I asked, quickly, "What's going to happen to him now?"

He didn't answer this. He was off by himself some place. "Funny thing," he said, and from his tone we might have been discussing the quickest way to get to Brooklyn, "when I saw the papers this morning, the first thing I asked myself was if I had anything to do with it. I felt sort of responsible."

I began to listen more carefully. The subway station was on the corner, just before us, and I stopped. He stopped, too. We were in front of a bar and he ducked slightly, peering in, but whoever he was looking for didn't seem to be there. The juke box was blasting away with something black and bouncy and I half watched the barmaid as she danced her way from the juke box to her place behind the bar. And I watched her face as she laughingly responded to something someone said to her, still keeping time to the music. When she smiled one saw the little girl, one sensed the doomed, still-struggling woman beneath the battered face of the semi-whore.

"I never *give* Sonny nothing," the boy said finally, "but a long time ago I come to school high and Sonny asked me how it felt." He paused, I couldn't bear to watch him, I watched the barmaid, and I listened to the music which seemed to be causing the pavement to shake. "I told him it felt great." The music stopped, the barmaid paused and watched the juke box until the music began again. "It did."

All this was carrying me some place I didn't want to go. I certainly didn't want to know how it felt. It filled everything, the people, the houses, the music, the dark, quicksilver barmaid, with menace; and this menace was their reality.

"What's going to happen to him now?" I asked again.

"They'll send him away some place and they'll try to cure him." He shook his head. "Maybe he'll even think he's kicked the habit. Then they'll let him loose" — he gestured, throwing his cigarette into the gutter. "That's all."

"What do you mean, that's *all*?"

But I knew what he meant.

"I *mean,* that's *all*." He turned his head and looked at me, pulling down the corners of his mouth. "Don't you know what I mean?" he asked, softly.

"How the hell *would* I know what you mean?" I almost whispered it, I don't know why.

"That's right," he said to the air, "how would *he* know what I mean?" He turned toward me again, patient and calm, and yet I somehow felt him shaking, shaking as though he were going to fall apart. I felt that ice in my guts again, the dread I'd felt all afternoon; and again I watched the barmaid, moving about the bar, washing glasses, and singing. "Listen. They'll let him out and then it'll just start all over again. That's what I mean."

"You mean — they'll let him out. And then he'll just start working his way back in again. You mean he'll never kick the habit. Is that what you mean?"

"That's right," he said, cheerfully. "*You* see what I mean."

"Tell me," I said at last, "why does he want to die? He must want to die, he's killing himself, why does he want to die?"

He looked at me in surprise. He licked his lips. "He don't want to die. He wants to live. Don't nobody want to die, ever."

Then I wanted to ask him — too many things. He could not have answered, or if he had, I could not have borne the answers. I started walking. "Well, I guess it's none of my business."

"It's going to be rough on old Sonny," he said. We reached the subway station. "This is your station?" he asked. I nodded. I took one step down. "Damn!" he said, suddenly. I looked up at him. He grinned again. "Damn it if I didn't leave all my money home. You ain't got a dollar on you, have you? Just for a couple of days, is all."

All at once something inside gave and threatened to come pouring out of me. I didn't hate him any more. I felt that in another moment I'd start crying like a child.

"Sure," I said. "Don't sweat." I looked in my wallet and didn't have a dollar, I only had a five. "Here," I said. "That hold you?"

He didn't look at it—he didn't want to look at it. A terrible closed look came over his face, as though he were keeping the number on the bill a secret from him and me. "Thanks," he said, and now he was dying to see me go. "Don't worry about Sonny. Maybe I'll write him or something."

"Sure," I said. "You do that. So long."

"Be seeing you," he said. I went on down the steps.

And I didn't write Sonny or send him anything for a long time. When I finally did, it was just after my little girl died, he wrote me back a letter which made me feel like a bastard.

Here's what he said:

> Dear brother,
> You don't know how much I needed to hear from you. I wanted to write you many a time but I dug how much I must have hurt you and so I didn't write. But now I feel like a man who's been trying to climb up out of some deep, real deep and funky hole and just saw the sun up there, outside. I got to get outside.
> I can't tell you much about how I got here. I mean I don't know how to tell you. I guess I was afraid of something or I was trying to escape from something and you know I have never been very strong in the head (smile). I'm glad Mama and Daddy are dead and can't see what's happened to their son and I swear if I'd known what I was doing I would never have hurt you so, you and a lot of other fine people who were nice to me and who believed in me.
> I don't want you to think it had anything to do with me being a musician. It's more than that. Or maybe less than that. I can't get anything straight in my head down here and I try not to think about what's going to happen to me when I get outside again. Sometime I think I'm going to flip and *never* get outside and sometime I think I'll come straight back. I tell you one thing, though, I'd rather blow my brains out than go through this again. But that's what they all say, so they tell me. If I tell you when I'm coming to New York and if you could meet me, I sure would appreciate it. Give my love to Isabel and the kids and I was sure sorry to hear about little Gracie. I wish I could be like Mama and say the Lord's will be done, but I don't know it seems to me that trouble is the one thing that never does get stopped and I don't know what good it does to blame it on the Lord. But maybe it does some good if you believe it.
> Your brother,
> Sonny

Then I kept in constant touch with him and I sent him whatever I could and I went to meet him when he came back to New York. When I saw him many things I thought I had forgotten came flooding back to me. This was because I had begun, finally, to wonder about Sonny, about the life that Sonny lived inside. This life, whatever it was, had made him older and thinner and it had deepened the distant stillness in which he had always moved. He looked very unlike my baby brother. Yet, when he smiled, when we shook hands, the baby brother I'd never known looked out from the depths of his private life, like an animal waiting to be coaxed into the light.

"How you been keeping?" he asked me.

"All right. And you?"

"Just fine." He was smiling all over his face. "It's good to see you again."

"It's good to see you."

The seven years' difference in our ages lay between us like a chasm: I wondered if these years would ever operate between us as a bridge. I was remembering, and it made it hard to catch my breath, that I had been there when he was born; and I had heard the first words he had ever spoken. When he started to walk, he walked from our mother straight to me. I caught him just before he fell when he took the first steps he ever took in this world.

"How's Isabel?"

"Just fine. She's dying to see you."

"And the boys?"

"They're fine, too. They're anxious to see their uncle."

"Oh, come on. You know they don't remember me."

"Are you kidding? Of course they remember you."

He grinned again. We got into a taxi. We had a lot to say to each other, far too much to know how to begin.

As the taxi began to move, I asked, "You still want to go to India?"

He laughed. "You still remember that. Hell, no. This place is Indian enough for me."

"It used to belong to them," I said.

And he laughed again. "They damn sure knew what they were doing when they got rid of it."

Years ago, when he was around fourteen, he'd been all hipped on the idea of going to India. He read books about people sitting on rocks, naked, in all kinds of weather, but mostly bad, naturally, and walking barefoot through hot coals and arriving at wisdom. I used to say that it sounded to me as though they were getting away from wisdom as fast as they could. I think he sort of looked down on me for that.

"Do you mind," he asked, "if we have the driver drive alongside the park? On the west side—I haven't seen the city in so long."

"Of course not," I said. I was afraid that I might sound as though I were humoring him, but I hoped he wouldn't take it that way.

So we drove along, between the green of the park and the stony, lifeless elegance of hotels and apartment buildings, toward the vivid, killing streets of our childhood. These streets hadn't changed, though housing projects jutted up out of them now like rocks in the middle of a boiling sea. Most of the houses in which we had grown up had vanished, as had the stores from which we had stolen, the basements in which we had first tried sex, the rooftops from which we had hurled tin cans and bricks. But houses exactly like the houses of our past yet dominated the landscape, boys exactly like the boys we once had been found themselves smothering in these houses, came down into the streets for light and air and found themselves encircled by disaster. Some escaped the trap, most didn't. Those who got out always left something of themselves behind, as some animals amputate a leg and leave it in the trap. It might be said, perhaps, that I had escaped, after all, I was a school teacher; or that Sonny had, he hadn't lived in Harlem for years. Yet, as the cab moved uptown through streets which seemed, with a rush, to darken with dark people, and as I covertly studied Sonny's face, it came to me that what we both were seeking through our separate cab windows was that part of ourselves which had been left behind. It's always at the hour of trouble and confrontation that the missing member aches.

We hit 110th Street and started rolling up Lenox Avenue. And I'd known this avenue all my life, but it seemed to me again, as it had seemed on the day I'd first heard about Sonny's trouble, filled with a hidden menace which was its very breath of life.

"We almost there," said Sonny.

"Almost." We were both too nervous to say anything more.

We live in a housing project. It hasn't been up long. A few days after it was up it seemed uninhabitably new, now, of course, it's already rundown. It looks like a parody of the good, clean, faceless life—God knows the people who live in it do their best to make it a parody. The beat-looking grass lying around isn't enough to make their lives green, the hedges will never hold out the streets, and they know it. The big windows fool no one, they aren't big enough to make space out of no space. They don't bother with the windows, they watch the TV screen instead. The playground is most popular with the children who don't play at jacks, or skip rope, or roller skate, or swing, and they can be found in it after dark. We moved in partly because it's not too far from where I teach, and partly for the kids; but it's really just like the houses in which Sonny and I grew up. The same things happen, they'll have the same things to remember. The moment Sonny and I started into the house I had the feeling that I was simply bringing him back into the danger he had almost died trying to escape.

Sonny has never been talkative. So I don't know why I was sure he'd be dying to talk to me when supper was over the first night. Everything went fine, the oldest boy remembered him, and the youngest boy liked him, and Sonny had remembered to bring something for each of them; and Isabel, who is really much nicer than I am, more open and giving, had gone to a lot of trouble about dinner and was genuinely glad to see him. And she's always been able to tease Sonny in a way that I haven't. It was nice to see her face so vivid again and to hear her laugh and watch her make Sonny laugh. She wasn't, or, anyway, she didn't seem to be, at all uneasy or embarrassed. She chatted as though there were no subject which had to be avoided and she got Sonny past his first, faint stiffness. And thank God she was there, for I was filled with that icy dread again. Everything I did seemed awkward to me, and everything I said sounded freighted with hidden meaning. I was trying to remember everything I'd heard about dope addiction and I couldn't help watching Sonny for signs. I wasn't doing it out of malice. I was trying to find out something about my brother. I was dying to hear him tell me he was safe.

"Safe!" my father grunted, whenever Mama suggested trying to move to a neighborhood which might be safer for children. "Safe, hell! Ain't no place safe for kids, nor nobody."

He always went on like this, but he wasn't, ever, really as bad as he sounded, not even on weekends, when he got drunk. As a matter of fact, he was always on the lookout for "something a little better," but he died before he found it. He died suddenly, during a drunken weekend in the middle of the war, when Sonny was fifteen. He and Sonny hadn't ever got on too well. And this was partly because Sonny was the apple of his father's eye. It was because he loved Sonny so much and was frightened for him, that he was always fighting with him. It doesn't do any good to fight with Sonny. Sonny just moves back, inside himself, where he can't be reached. But the principal reason that they never hit it off is that they were so much alike. Daddy was big and rough and loud-talking, just the opposite of Sonny, but they both had—that same privacy.

Mama tried to tell me something about this, just after Daddy died. I was home on leave from the army.

This was the last time I ever saw my mother alive. Just the same, this picture gets all mixed up in my mind with pictures I had of her when she was younger. The way I always see her is the way she used to be on a Sunday afternoon, say, when the old folks were talking after the big Sunday dinner. I always see her wearing pale blue. She'd be sitting on the sofa. And my father would be sitting in the easy chair, not far from her. And the living room would be full of church folks and relatives. There they sit, in chairs all around the living room, and the night is creeping up outside, but nobody knows it yet. You can see the darkness growing against the windowpanes and you hear the street noises every now and again, or maybe the jangling beat of a tambourine from one of the churches close by, but it's real quiet in the room. For a moment nobody's talking, but every face looks darkening, like the sky outside. And my mother rocks a little from the waist, and my father's eyes are closed. Everyone is looking at something a child can't see. For a minute they've forgotten the children. Maybe a kid is lying on the rug, half asleep. Maybe somebody's got a kid in his lap and is absent-mindedly stroking the kid's head. Maybe there's a kid, quiet and big-eyed, curled up in a big chair in the corner. The silence, the darkness coming, and the darkness in the faces frightens the child obscurely. He hopes that the hand which strokes his forehead will never stop—will never die. He hopes that there will never come a time when the old folks won't be sitting around the living room, talking about where they've come from, and what they've seen, and what's happened to them and their kinfolk.

But something deep and watchful in the child knows that this is bound to end, is already ending. In a moment someone will get up and turn on the light. Then the old folks will remember the children and they won't talk any more that day. And when light fills the room, the child is filled with darkness. He knows that every time this happens he's moved just a little closer to that darkness outside. The darkness outside is what the old folks have been talking about. It's what they've come from. It's what they endure. The child knows that they won't talk any more because if he knows too much about what's happened to *them*, he'll know too much too soon, about what's going to happen to *him*.

The last time I talked to my mother, I remember I was restless. I wanted to get out and see Isabel. We weren't married then and we had a lot to straighten out between us.

There Mama sat, in black, by the window. She was humming an old church song, *Lord, you brought me from a long ways off.* Sonny was out somewhere. Mama kept watching the streets.

"I don't know," she said, "if I'll ever see you again, after you go off from here. But I hope you'll remember the things I tried to teach you."

"Don't talk like that," I said, and smiled. "You'll be here a long time yet."

She smiled, too, but she said nothing. She was quiet for a long time. And I said, "Mama, don't you worry about nothing. I'll be writing all the time, and you be getting the checks. . . ."

"I want to talk to you about your brother," she said, suddenly. "If anything happens to me he ain't going to have nobody to look out for him."

"Mama," I said, "ain't nothing going to happen to you *or* Sonny. Sonny's all right. He's a good boy and he's got good sense."

"It ain't a question of his being a good boy," Mama said, "nor of his having good sense. It ain't only the bad ones, nor yet the dumb ones that gets sucked under." She stopped, looking at me. "Your Daddy once had a brother," she said, and she smiled in a way that made me feel she was in pain. "You didn't never know that, did you?"

"No," I said, "I never knew that," and I watched her face.

"Oh, yes," she said, "your Daddy had a brother." She looked out of the window again. "I know you never saw your Daddy cry. But *I* did—many a time, through all these years."

I asked her, "What happened to his brother? How come nobody's ever talked about him?"

This was the first time I ever saw my mother look old.

"His brother got killed," she said, "when he was just a little younger than you are now. I knew him. He was a fine boy. He was maybe a little full of the devil, but he didn't mean nobody no harm."

Then she stopped and the room was silent, exactly as it had sometimes been on those Sunday afternoons. Mama kept looking out into the streets.

"He used to have a job in the mill," she said, "and, like all young folks, he just liked to perform on Saturday nights. Saturday nights, him and your father would drift around to different places, go to dances and things like that, or just sit around with people they knew, and your father's brother would sing, he had a fine voice, and play along with himself on his guitar. Well, this particular Saturday night, him and your father was coming home from some place, and they were both a little drunk and there was a moon that night, it was bright like day. Your father's brother was feeling kind of good, and he was whistling to himself, and he had his guitar slung over his shoulder. They was coming down a hill and beneath them was a road that turned off from the highway. Well, your father's brother, being always kind of frisky, decided to run down this hill, and he did, with that guitar banging and clanging behind him, and he ran across the road, and he was making water behind a tree. And your father was sort of amused at him and he was still coming down the hill, kind of slow. Then he heard a car motor and that same minute his brother stepped from behind the tree, into the road, in the moonlight. And he started to cross the road. And your father started to run down the hill, he says he don't know why. This car was full of white men. They was all drunk, and when they seen your father's brother they let out a great whoop and holler and they aimed the car straight at him. They was having fun, they just wanted to scare him, the way they do sometimes, you know. But they was drunk. And I guess the boy, being drunk, too, and scared, kind of lost his head. By the time he jumped it was too late. Your father says he heard his brother scream when the car rolled over him, and he heard the wood of that guitar when it give, and he heard them strings go flying, and he heard them white men shouting, and the car kept on a-going and it ain't stopped till this day. And, time your father got down the hill, his brother weren't nothing but blood and pulp."

Tears were gleaming on my mother's face. There wasn't anything I could say.

"He never mentioned it," she said, "because I never let him mention it before you children. Your Daddy was like a crazy man that night and for many a night thereafter. He says he never in his life seen anything as dark as that road after the lights of that car had gone away. Weren't nothing, weren't nobody on that road, just your Daddy and his brother and that busted guitar. Oh, yes. Your Daddy never did really get right again. Till the day he died he weren't sure but that every white man he saw was the man that killed his brother."

She stopped and took out her handkerchief and dried her eyes and looked at me.

"I ain't telling you all this," she said, "to make you scared or bitter or to make you hate nobody. I'm telling you this because you got a brother. And the world ain't changed."

I guess I didn't want to believe this. I guess she saw this in my face. She turned away from me, toward the window again, searching those streets.

"But I praise my Redeemer," she said at last, "that He called your Daddy home before me. I ain't saying it to throw no flowers at myself, but, I declare, it keeps me from feeling too cast down to know I helped your father get safely through this world. Your father always acted like he was the roughest, strongest man on earth. And everybody took him to be like that. But if he hadn't had *me* there—to see his tears!"

She was crying again. Still, I couldn't move. I said, "Lord, Lord, Mama, I didn't know it was like that."

"Oh, honey," she said, "there's a lot that you don't know. But you are going to find it out." She stood up from the window and came over to me. "You got to hold on to your brother," she said, "and don't let him fall, no matter what it looks like is happening to him and no matter how evil you gets with him. You going to be evil with him many a time. But don't you forget what I told you, you hear?"

"I won't forget," I said. "Don't you worry, I won't forget. I won't let nothing happen to Sonny."

My mother smiled as though she were amused at something she saw in my face. Then, "You may not be able to stop nothing from happening. But you got to let him know you's *there.*"

Two days later I was married, and then I was gone. And I had a lot of things on my mind and I pretty well forgot my promise to Mama until I got shipped home on a special furlough for her funeral.

And, after the funeral, with just Sonny and me alone in the empty kitchen, I tried to find out something about him.

"What do you want to do?" I asked him.

"I'm going to be a musician," he said.

For he had graduated, in the time I had been away, from dancing to the juke box to finding out who was playing what, and what they were doing with it, and he had bought himself a set of drums.

"You mean, you want to be a drummer?" I somehow had the feeling that being a drummer might be all right for other people but not for my brother Sonny.

"I don't think," he said, looking at me very gravely, "that I'll ever be a good drummer. But I think I can play a piano."

I frowned. I'd never played the role of the older brother quite so seriously before, had scarcely ever, in fact, *asked* Sonny a damn thing. I sensed myself in the presence of something I didn't really know how to handle, didn't understand. So I made my frown a little deeper as I asked: "What kind of musician do you want to be?"

He grinned. "How many kinds do you think there are?"

"Be *serious,*" I said.

He laughed, throwing his head back, and then looked at me. "I *am* serious."

"Well, then, for Christ's sake, stop kidding around and answer a serious question. I mean, do you want to be a concert pianist, you want to play classical music and all that, or—or what?" Long before I finished he was laughing again. "For Christ's *sake,* Sonny!"

He sobered, but with difficulty. "I'm sorry. But you sound so—*scared!*" and he was off again.

"Well, you may think it's funny now, baby, but it's not going to be so funny when you have to make your living at it, let me tell you *that.*" I was furious because I knew he was laughing at me and I didn't know why.

"No," he said, very sober now, and afraid, perhaps, that he'd hurt me, "I don't want to be a classical pianist. That isn't what interests me. I mean"—he paused, looking hard at me, as though his eyes would help me to understand, and then gestured helplessly, as though perhaps his hand would help—"I mean, I'll have a lot of studying to do, and I'll have to study *everything,* but, I mean, I want to play *with*—jazz musicians." He stopped. "I want to play jazz," he said.

Well, the word had never before sounded as heavy, as real, as it sounded that afternoon in Sonny's mouth. I just looked at him and I was probably frowning a real frown by this time. I simply couldn't see why on earth he'd

want to spend his time hanging around nightclubs, clowning around on band-
stands, while people pushed each other around a dance floor. It seemed—
beneath him, somehow. I had never thought about it before, had never been
forced to, but I suppose I had always put jazz musicians in a class with what
Daddy called "good-time people."

"Are you *serious?*"

"Hell, *yes,* I'm serious."

He looked more helpless than ever, and annoyed, and deeply hurt.

I suggested, helpfully: "You mean—like Louis Armstrong?"

His face closed as though I'd struck him. "No. I'm not talking about none
of that old-time, down home crap."

"Well, look, Sonny, I'm sorry, don't get mad. I just don't altogether get it,
that's all. Name somebody—you know, a jazz musician you admire."

"Bird."

"Who?"

"Bird! Charlie Parker! Don't they teach you nothing in the goddamn
army?"

I lit a cigarette. I was surprised and then a little amused to discover that I
was trembling. "I've been out of touch," I said. "You'll have to be patient with
me. Now. Who's this Parker character?"

"He's just one of the greatest jazz musicians alive," said Sonny, sullenly,
his hands in his pockets, his back to me. "Maybe *the* greatest," he added, bitterly, "that's probably why *you* never heard of him."

"All right," I said, "I'm ignorant. I'm sorry. I'll go out and buy all the
cat's records right away, all right?"

"It don't," said Sonny, with dignity, "make any difference to me. I don't
care what you listen to. Don't do me no favors."

I was beginning to realize that I'd never seen him so upset before. With
another part of my mind I was thinking that this would probably turn out to be
one of those things kids go through and that I shouldn't make it seem important by pushing it too hard. Still, I didn't think it would do any harm to ask:
"Doesn't all this take a lot of time? Can you make a living at it?"

He turned back to me and half leaned, half sat, on the kitchen table.
"Everything takes time," he said, "and—well, yes, sure, I can make a living at
it. But what I don't seem to be able to make you understand is that it's the only
thing I want to do."

"Well, Sonny," I said, gently, "you know people can't always do exactly
what they *want* to do—"

"*No,* I don't know that," said Sonny, surprising me. "I think people *ought*
to do what they want to do, what else are they alive for?"

"You getting to be a big boy," I said desperately, "it's time you started
thinking about your future."

"I'm thinking about my future," said Sonny, grimly. "I think about it all
the time."

I gave up. I decided, if he didn't change his mind, that we could always
talk about it later. "In the meantime," I said, "you got to finish school." We had
already decided that he'd have to move in with Isabel and her folks. I knew this

wasn't the ideal arrangement because Isabel's folks are inclined to be dicty and they hadn't especially wanted Isabel to marry me. But I didn't know what else to do. "And we have to get you fixed up at Isabel's."

There was a long silence. He moved from the kitchen table to the window. "That's a terrible idea. You know it yourself."

"Do you have a *better* idea?"

He just walked up and down the kitchen for a minute. He was as tall as I was. He had started to shave. I suddenly had the feeling that I didn't know him at all.

He stopped at the kitchen table and picked up my cigarettes. Looking at me with a kind of mocking, amused defiance, he put one between his lips. "You mind?"

"You smoking already?"

He lit the cigarette and nodded, watching me through the smoke. "I just wanted to see if I'd have the courage to smoke in front of you." He grinned and blew a great cloud of smoke to the ceiling. "It was easy." He looked at my face. "Come on, now. I bet you was smoking at my age, tell the truth."

I didn't say anything but the truth was on my face, and he laughed. But now there was something very strained in his laugh. "Sure. And I bet that ain't all you was doing."

He was frightening me a little. "Cut the crap," I said. "We already decided that you was going to go and live at Isabel's. Now what's got into you all of a sudden?"

"*You* decided it," he pointed out. "*I* didn't decide nothing." He stopped in front of me, leaning against the stove, arms loosely folded. "Look, brother. I don't want to stay in Harlem no more, I really don't." He was very earnest. He looked at me, then over toward the kitchen window. There was something in his eyes I'd never seen before, some thoughtfulness, some worry all his own. He rubbed the muscle of one arm. "It's time I was getting out of here."

"Where do you want to *go*, Sonny?"

"I want to join the army. Or the navy, I don't care. If I say I'm old enough, they'll believe me."

Then I got mad. It was because I was so scared. "You must be crazy. You goddamn fool, what the hell do you want to go and join the *army* for?"

"I just told you. To get out of Harlem."

"Sonny, you haven't even finished *school*. And if you really want to be a musician, how do you expect to study if you're in the *army*?"

He looked at me, trapped, and in anguish. "There's ways. I might be able to work out some kind of deal. Anyway, I'll have the G.I. Bill when I come out."

"*If* you come out." We stared at each other. "Sonny, please. Be reasonable. I know the setup is far from perfect. But we got to do the best we can."

"I ain't learning nothing in school," he said. "Even when I go." He turned away from me and opened the window and threw his cigarette out into the narrow alley. I watched his back. "At least, I ain't learning nothing you'd want me to learn." He slammed the window so hard I thought the glass would fly out, and turned back to me. "And I'm sick of the stink of these garbage cans!"

"Sonny," I said, "I know how you feel. But if you don't finish school now, you're going to be sorry later that you didn't." I grabbed him by the shoulders. "And you only got another year. It ain't so bad. And I'll come back and I swear I'll help you do *whatever* you want to do. Just try to put up with it till I come back. Will you please do that? For me?"

He didn't answer and he wouldn't look at me.

"Sonny. You hear me?"

He pulled away. "I hear you. But you never hear anything *I* say."

I didn't know what to say to that. He looked out of the window and then back at me. "OK," he said, and sighed. "I'll try."

Then I said, trying to cheer him up a little, "They got a piano at Isabel's. You can practice on it."

And as a matter of fact, it did cheer him up for a minute. "That's right," he said to himself. "I forgot that." His face relaxed a little. But the worry, the thoughtfulness, played on it still, the way shadows play on a face which is staring into the fire.

But I thought I'd never hear the end of that piano. At first, Isabel would write me, saying how nice it was that Sonny was so serious about his music and how, as soon as he came in from school, or wherever he had been when he was supposed to be at school, he went straight to that piano and stayed there until suppertime. And, after supper, he went back to that piano and stayed there until everybody went to bed. He was at the piano all day Saturday and all day Sunday. Then he bought a record player and started playing records. He'd play one record over and over again, all day long sometimes, and he'd improvise along with it on the piano. Or he'd play one section of the record, one chord, one change, one progression, then he'd do it on the piano. Then back to the record. Then back to the piano.

Well, I really don't know how they stood it. Isabel finally confessed that it wasn't like living with a person at all, it was like living with sound. And the sound didn't make any sense to her, didn't make any sense to any of them — naturally. They began, in a way, to be afflicted by this presence that was living in their home. It was as though Sonny were some sort of god, or monster. He moved in an atmosphere which wasn't like theirs at all. They fed him and he ate, he washed himself, he walked in and out of their door; he certainly wasn't nasty or unpleasant or rude, Sonny isn't any of those things; but it was as though he were all wrapped up in some cloud, some fire, some vision all his own; and there wasn't any way to reach him.

At the same time, he wasn't really a man yet, he was still a child, and they had to watch out for him in all kinds of ways. They certainly couldn't throw him out. Neither did they dare to make a great scene about that piano because even they dimly sensed, as I sensed, from so many thousands of miles away, that Sonny was at that piano playing for his life.

But he hadn't been going to school. One day a letter came from the school board and Isabel's mother got it — there had, apparently, been other letters but Sonny had torn them up. This day, when Sonny came in, Isabel's mother showed him the letter and asked where he'd been spending his time. And she finally got it out of him that he'd been down in Greenwich Village, with musicians and other characters, in a white girl's apartment. And this scared her and she started to scream at him and what came up, once she began—though she denies it to this day—was what sacrifices they were making to give Sonny a decent home and how little he appreciated it.

Sonny didn't play the piano that day. By evening, Isabel's mother had calmed down but then there was the old man to deal with, and Isabel herself. Isabel says she did her best to be calm but she broke down and started crying. She says she just watched Sonny's face. She could tell, by watching him, what was happening with him. And what was happening was that they penetrated his cloud, they had reached him. Even if their fingers had been a thousand times more gentle than human fingers ever are, he could hardly help feeling that they had stripped him naked and were spitting on that nakedness. For he also had to see that his presence, that music, which was life or death to him, had been torture for them and that they had endured it, not at all for his sake, but only for mine. And Sonny couldn't take that. He can take it a little better today than he could then but he's still not very good at it and, frankly, I don't know anybody who is.

The silence of the next few days must have been louder than the sound of all the music ever played since time began. One morning, before she went to work, Isabel was in his room for something and she suddenly realized that all of his records were gone. And she knew for certain that he was gone. And he was. He went as far as the navy would carry him. He finally sent me a postcard from some place in Greece and that was the first I knew that Sonny was still alive. I didn't see him any more until we were both back in New York and the war had long been over.

He was a man by then, of course, but I wasn't willing to see it. He came by the house from time to time, but we fought almost every time we met. I didn't like the way he carried himself, loose and dreamlike all the time, and I didn't like his friends, and his music seemed to be merely an excuse for the life he led. It sounded just that weird and disordered.

Then we had a fight, a pretty awful fight, and I didn't see him for months. By and by I looked him up, where he was living, in a furnished room in the Village, and I tried to make it up. But there were lots of people in the room and Sonny just lay on his bed, and he wouldn't come downstairs with me, and he treated these other people as though they were his family and I weren't. So I got mad and then he got mad, and then I told him that he might just as well be dead as live the way he was living. Then he stood up and he told me not to worry about him any more in life, that he *was* dead as far as I was concerned. Then he pushed me to the door and the other people looked on as though nothing were happening, and he slammed the door behind me. I stood in the hallway, staring at the door. I heard somebody laugh in the room and then the tears came to my eyes. I started down the steps, whistling to keep from crying, I kept whistling to myself, *You going to need me, baby, one of these cold, rainy days.*

I read about Sonny's trouble in the spring. Little Grace died in the fall. She was a beautiful little girl. But she only lived a little over two years. She died of polio and she suffered. She had a slight fever for a couple of days, but it didn't seem like anything and we just kept her in bed. And we would certainly have called the doctor, but the fever dropped, she seemed to be all right. So we thought it had just been a cold. Then, one day, she was up, playing, Isabel was in the kitchen fixing lunch for the two boys when they'd come in from school, and she heard Grace fall down in the living room. When you have a lot of children you don't always start running when one of them falls, unless they start screaming or something. And, this time, Grace was quiet. Yet, Isabel says that when she heard that *thump* and then that silence, something happened in her to make her afraid. And she ran to the living room and there was little Grace on the floor, all twisted up, and the reason she hadn't screamed was that she couldn't get her breath. And when she did scream, it was the worst sound, Isabel says, that she'd ever heard in all her life, and she still hears it sometimes in her dreams. Isabel will sometimes wake me up with a low, moaning, strangled sound and I have to be quick to awaken her and hold her to me and where Isabel is weeping against me seems a mortal wound.

I think I may have written Sonny the very day that little Grace was buried. I was sitting in the living room in the dark, by myself, and I suddenly thought of Sonny. My trouble made his real.

One Saturday afternoon, when Sonny had been living with us, or, anyway, been in our house, for nearly two weeks, I found myself wandering aimlessly about the living room, drinking from a can of beer, and trying to work up the courage to search Sonny's room. He was out, he was usually out whenever I was home, and Isabel had taken the children to see their grandparents. Suddenly I was standing still in front of the living room window, watching Seventh Avenue. The idea of searching Sonny's room made me still. I scarcely dared to admit to myself what I'd be searching for. I didn't know what I'd do if I found it. Or if I didn't.

On the sidewalk across from me, near the entrance to a barbecue joint, some people were holding an old-fashioned revival meeting. The barbecue cook, wearing a dirty white apron, his conked hair reddish and metallic in the pale sun, and a cigarette between his lips, stood in the doorway, watching them. Kids and older people paused in their errands and stood there, along with some older men and a couple of very tough-looking women who watched everything that happened on the avenue, as though they owned it, or were maybe owned by it. Well, they were watching this, too. The revival was being carried on by three sisters in black, and a brother. All they had were their voices and their Bibles and a tambourine. The brother was testifying and while he testified two of the sisters stood together, seeming to say, amen, and the third sister walked around with the tambourine outstretched and a couple of people dropped coins into it. Then the brother's testimony ended and the sister who had been taking up the collection dumped the coins into her palm and transferred them to the pocket of her long black robe. Then she raised both hands, striking the tambourine against the air, and then against one hand, and she started to sing. And the two other sisters and the brother joined in.

It was strange, suddenly, to watch, though I had been seeing these street meetings all my life. So, of course, had everybody else down there. Yet, they paused and watched and listened and I stood still at the window. *"Tis the old ship of Zion,"* they sang, and the sister with the tambourine kept a steady, jangling beat, *"it has rescued many a thousand!"* Not a soul under the sound of their voices was hearing this song for the first time, not one of them had been rescued. Nor had they seen much in the way of rescue work being done around them. Neither did they especially believe in the holiness of the three sisters and the brother, they knew too much about them, knew where they lived, and how. The woman with the tambourine, whose voice dominated the air, whose face was bright with joy, was divided by very little from the woman who stood watching her, a cigarette between her heavy, chapped lips, her hair a cuckoo's nest, her face scarred and swollen from many beatings, and her black eyes glittering like coal. Perhaps they both knew this, which was why, when, as rarely, they addressed each other, they addressed each other as Sister. As the singing filled the air the watching, listening faces underwent a change, the eyes focusing on something within; the music seemed to soothe a poison out of them; and time seemed, nearly, to fall away from the sullen, belligerent, battered faces, as though they were fleeing back to their first condition, while dreaming of their last. The barbecue cook half shook his head and smiled, and dropped his cigarette and disappeared into his joint. A man fumbled in his pockets for change and stood holding it in his hand impatiently, as though he had just remembered a pressing appointment further up the avenue. He looked furious. Then I saw Sonny, standing on the edge of the crowd. He was carrying a wide, flat notebook with a green cover, and it made him look, from where I was standing, almost like a schoolboy. The coppery sun brought out the copper in his skin, he was very faintly smiling, standing very still. Then the singing stopped, the tambourine turned into a collection plate again. The furious man dropped in his coins and vanished, so did a couple of the women, and Sonny dropped some change in the plate, looking directly at the woman with a little smile. He started across the avenue, toward the house. He has a slow, loping walk, something like the way Harlem hipsters walk, only he's imposed on this his own half-beat. I had never really noticed it before.

I stayed at the window, both relieved and apprehensive. As Sonny disappeared from my sight, they began singing again. And they were still singing when his key turned in the lock.

"Hey," he said.

"Hey, yourself. You want some beer?"

"No. Well, maybe." But he came up to the window and stood beside me, looking out. "What a warm voice," he said.

They were singing *If I could only hear my mother pray again!*

"Yes," I said, "and she can sure beat that tambourine."

"But what a terrible song," he said, and laughed. He dropped his notebook on the sofa and disappeared into the kitchen. "Where's Isabel and the kids?"

"I think they went to see their grandparents. You hungry?"

"No." He came back into the living room with his can of beer. "You want to come some place with me tonight?"

I sensed, I don't know how, that I couldn't possibly say no. "Sure. Where?"

He sat down on the sofa and picked up his notebook and started leafing through it. "I'm going to sit in with some fellows in a joint in the Village."

"You mean, you're going to play, tonight?"

"That's right." He took a swallow of his beer and moved back to the window. He gave me a sidelong look. "If you can stand it."

"I'll try," I said.

He smiled to himself and we both watched as the meeting across the way broke up. The three sisters and the brother, heads bowed, were singing *God be with you till we meet again.* The faces around them were very quiet. Then the song ended. The small crowd dispersed. We watched the three women and the lone man walk slowly up the avenue.

"When she was singing before," said Sonny, abruptly, "her voice reminded me for a minute of what heroin feels like sometimes—when it's in your veins. It makes you feel sort of warm and cool at the same time. And distant. And—and sure." He sipped his beer, very deliberately not looking at me. I watched his face. "It makes you feel—in control. Sometimes you've got to have that feeling."

"Do you?" I sat down slowly in the easy chair.

"Sometimes." He went to the sofa and picked up his notebook again. "Some people do."

"In order," I asked, "to play?" And my voice was very ugly, full of contempt and anger.

"Well"—he looked at me with great, troubled eyes, as though, in fact, he hoped his eyes would tell me things he could never otherwise say—"they *think* so. And *if* they think so—!"

"And what do *you* think?" I asked.

He sat on the sofa and put his can of beer on the floor. "I don't know," he said, and I couldn't be sure if he were answering my question or pursuing his thoughts. His face didn't tell me. "It's not so much to *play.* It's to *stand* it, to be able to make it at all. On any level." He frowned and smiled: "In order to keep from shaking to pieces."

"But these friends of yours," I said, "they seem to shake themselves to pieces pretty goddamn fast."

"Maybe." He played with the notebook. And something told me that I should curb my tongue, that Sonny was doing his best to talk, that I should listen. "But of course you only know the ones that've gone to pieces. Some don't—or at least they haven't *yet* and that's just about all *any* of us can say." He paused. "And then there are some who just live, really, in hell, and they know it and they see what's happening and they go right on. I don't know." He sighed, dropped the notebook, folded his arms. "Some guys, you can tell from the way they play, they on something *all* the time. And you can see that, well, it makes something real for them. But of course," he picked up his beer from the floor and sipped it and put the can down again, "they *want* to, too, you've got to see that. Even some of them that say they don't—*some,* not all."

"And what about you?" I asked—I couldn't help it. "What about you? Do *you* want to?"

He stood up and walked to the window and remained silent for a long time. Then he sighed. "Me," he said. Then: "While I was downstairs before, on my way here, listening to that woman sing, it struck me all of a sudden how much suffering she must have had to go through—to sing like that. It's *repulsive* to think you have to suffer that much."

I said: "But there's no way not to suffer—is there, Sonny?"

"I believe not," he said and smiled, "but that's never stopped anyone from trying." He looked at me. "Has it?" I realized, with this mocking look, that there stood between us, forever, beyond the power of time or forgiveness, the fact that I had held silence—so long!—when he had needed human speech to help him. He turned back to the window. "No, there's no way not to suffer. But you try all kinds of ways to keep from drowning in it, to keep on top of it, and to make it seem—well, like *you*. Like you did something, all right, and now you're suffering for it. You know?" I said nothing. "Well you know," he said, impatiently, "why *do* people suffer? Maybe it's better to do something to give it a reason, *any* reason."

"But we just agreed," I said, "that there's no way not to suffer. Isn't it better, then, just to—take it?"

"But nobody just takes it," Sonny cried, "that's what I'm telling you! *Everybody* tries not to. You're just hung up on the *way* some people try—it's not *your* way!"

The hair on my face began to itch, my face felt wet. "That's not true," I said, "that's not true. I don't give a damn what other people do, I don't even care how they suffer. I just care how *you* suffer." And he looked at me. "Please believe me," I said, "I don't want to see you—die—trying not to suffer."

"I won't," he said, flatly, "die trying not to suffer. At least, not any faster than anybody else."

"But there's no need," I said, trying to laugh, "is there? in killing yourself."

I wanted to say more, but I couldn't. I wanted to talk about will power and how life could be—well, beautiful. I wanted to say that it was all within; but was it? or, rather, wasn't that exactly the trouble? And I wanted to promise that I would never fail him again. But it would all have sounded—empty words and lies.

So I made the promise to myself and prayed that I would keep it.

"It's terrible sometimes, inside," he said, "that's what's the trouble. You walk these streets, black and funky and cold, and there's not really a living ass to talk to, and there's nothing shaking, and there's no way of getting it out— that storm inside. You can't talk it and you can't make love with it, and when you finally try to get with it and play it, you realize *nobody's* listening. So *you've* got to listen. You got to find a way to listen."

And then he walked away from the window and sat on the sofa again, as though all the wind had suddenly been knocked out of him. "Sometimes you'll do *anything* to play, even cut your mother's throat." He laughed and looked at me. "Or your brother's." Then he sobered. "Or your own." Then: "Don't worry. I'm all right now and I think I'll *be* all right. But I can't forget—where I've been. I don't mean just the physical place I've been, I mean where I've *been*. And *what* I've been."

"What have you been, Sonny?" I asked.

He smiled—but sat sideways on the sofa, his elbow resting on the back, his fingers playing with his mouth and chin, not looking at me. "I've been something I didn't recognize, didn't know I could be. Didn't know anybody could be." He stopped, looking inward, looking helplessly young, looking old. "I'm not talking about it now because I feel *guilty* or anything like that— maybe it would be better if I did, I don't know. Anyway, I can't really talk about it. Not to you, not to anybody," and now he turned and faced me. "Sometimes, you know, and it was actually when I was most *out* of the world, I felt that I was in it, that I was *with* it, really, and I could play or I didn't really have to *play*, it just came out of me, it was there. And I don't know how I played, thinking about it now, but I know I did awful things, those times, sometimes, to people. Or it wasn't that I *did* anything to them—it was that they weren't real." He picked up the beer can; it was empty; he rolled it between his palms: "And other times—well, I needed a fix, I needed to find a place to lean, I needed to clear a space to *listen*—and I couldn't find it, and I— went crazy, I did terrible things to *me*, I was terrible *for* me." He began pressing the beer can between his hands, I watched the metal begin to give. It glittered, as he played with it, like a knife, and I was afraid he would cut himself, but I said nothing. "Oh well. I can never tell you. I was all by myself at the bottom of something, stinking and sweating and crying and shaking, and I smelled it, you know? *my* stink, and I thought I'd die if I couldn't get away from it and yet, all the same, I knew that everything I was doing was just locking me in with it. And I didn't know," he paused, still flattening the beer can, "I didn't know, I still *don't* know, something kept telling me that maybe it was good to smell your own stink, but I didn't think that *that* was what I'd been trying to do— and—who can stand it?" and he abruptly dropped the ruined beer can, looking at me with a small, still smile, and then rose, walking to the window as though it were the lodestone rock. I watched his face, he watched the avenue. "I couldn't tell you when Mama died—but the reason I wanted to leave Harlem so bad was to get away from drugs. And then, when I ran away, that's what I was running from—really. When I came back, nothing had changed, *I* hadn't changed, I was just—older." And he stopped, drumming with his fingers on the windowpane. The sun had vanished, soon darkness would fall. I watched his face. "It can come again," he said, almost as though speaking to himself. Then he turned to me. "It can come again," he repeated. "I just want you to know that."

"All right," I said, at last. "So it can come again, All right."

He smiled, but the smile was sorrowful. "I had to try to tell you," he said.

"Yes," I said. "I understand that."

"You're my brother," he said, looking straight at me, and not smiling at all.

"Yes," I repeated, "yes. I understand that."

He turned back to the window, looking out. "All that hatred down there," he said, "all that hatred and misery and love. It's a wonder it doesn't blow the avenue apart."

We went to the only nightclub on a short, dark street, downtown. We squeezed through the narrow, chattering, jam-packed bar to the entrance of the big room, where the bandstand was. And we stood there for a moment, for the lights were very dim in this room and we couldn't see. Then, "Hello, boy," said a voice and an enormous black man, much older than Sonny or myself, erupted out of all that atmospheric lighting and put an arm around Sonny's shoulder. "I been sitting right here," he said, "waiting for you."

He had a big voice, too, and heads in the darkness turned toward us.

Sonny grinned and pulled a little away, and said, "Creole, this is my brother. I told you about him."

Creole shook my hand. "I'm glad to meet you, son," he said, and it was clear that he was glad to meet me *there*, for Sonny's sake. And he smiled, "You got a real musician in *your* family," and he took his arm from Sonny's shoulder and slapped him, lightly, affectionately, with the back of his hand.

"Well. Now I've heard it all," said a voice behind us. This was another musician, and a friend of Sonny's, a coal-black, cheerful-looking man, built close to the ground. He immediately began confiding to me, at the top of his lungs, the most terrible things about Sonny, his teeth gleaming like a lighthouse and his laugh coming up out of him like the beginning of an earthquake. And it turned out that everyone at the bar knew Sonny, or almost everyone; some were musicians, working there, or nearby, or not working, some were simply hangers-on, and some were there to hear Sonny play. I was introduced to all of them and they were all very polite to me. Yet, it was clear that, for them, I was only Sonny's brother. Here, I was in Sonny's world. Or, rather: his kingdom. Here, it was not even a question that his veins bore royal blood.

They were going to play soon and Creole installed me, by myself, at a table in a dark corner. Then I watched them, Creole, and the little black man, and Sonny, and the others, while they horsed around, standing just below the bandstand. The light from the bandstand spilled just a little short of them and, watching them laughing and gesturing and moving about, I had the feeling that they, nevertheless, were being most careful not to step into that circle of light too suddenly: that if they moved into the light too suddenly, without thinking, they would perish in flame. Then, while I watched, one of them, the small, black man, moved into the light and crossed the bandstand and started fooling around with his drums. Then—being funny and being, also, extremely ceremonious—Creole took Sonny by the arm and led him to the piano. A woman's voice called Sonny's name and a few hands started clapping. And Sonny, also being funny and being ceremonious, and so touched, I think, that he could have cried, but neither hiding it nor showing it, riding it like a man, grinned, and put both hands to his heart and bowed from the waist.

Creole then went to the bass fiddle and a lean, very bright-skinned brown man jumped up on the bandstand and picked up his horn. So there they were, and the atmosphere on the bandstand and in the room began to change and tighten. Someone stepped up to the microphone and announced them. Then there were all kinds of murmurs. Some people at the bar shushed others. The waitress ran around, frantically getting in the last orders, guys and chicks got closer to each other, and the lights on the bandstand, on the quartet, turned to a kind of indigo. Then they all looked different there. Creole looked about him for the last time, as though he were making certain that all his chickens were in the coop, and then he—jumped and struck the fiddle. And there they were.

All I know about music is that not many people ever really hear it. And even then, on the rare occasions when something opens within, and the music enters, what we mainly hear, or hear corroborated, are personal, private, vanishing evocations. But the man who creates the music is hearing something else, is dealing with the roar rising from the void and imposing order on it as it hits the air. What is evoked in him, then, is of another order, more terrible because it has no words, and triumphant, too, for that same reason. And his triumph, when he triumphs, is ours. I just watched Sonny's face. His face was troubled, he was working hard, but he wasn't with it. And I had the feeling that, in a way, everyone on the bandstand was waiting for him, both waiting for him and pushing him along. But as I began to watch Creole, I realized that it was Creole who held them all back. He had them on a short rein. Up there, keeping the beat with his whole body, wailing on the fiddle, with his eyes half closed, he was listening to everything, but he was listening to Sonny. He was having a dialogue with Sonny. He wanted Sonny to leave the shoreline and strike out for the deep water. He was Sonny's witness that deep water and drowning were not the same thing—he had been there, and he knew. And he wanted Sonny to know. He was waiting for Sonny to do the things on the keys which would let Creole know that Sonny was in the water.

And, while Creole listened, Sonny moved, deep within, exactly like someone in torment. I had never before thought of how awful the relationship must be between the musician and his instrument. He has to fill it, this instrument, with the breath of life, his own. He has to make it do what he wants it to do. And a piano is just a piano. It's made out of so much wood and wires and little hammers and big ones, and ivory. While there's only so much you can do with it, the only way to find this out is to try; to try and make it do everything.

And Sonny hadn't been near a piano for over a year. And he wasn't on much better terms with his life, not the life that stretched before him now. He and the piano stammered, started one way, got scared, stopped; started another way, panicked, marked time, started again; then seemed to have found a direction, panicked again, got stuck. And the face I saw on Sonny I'd never seen before. Everything had been burned out of it, and, at the same time, things usually hidden were being burned in, by the fire and fury of the battle which was occurring in him up there.

Yet, watching Creole's face as they neared the end of the first set, I had the feeling that something had happened, something I hadn't heard. Then they finished, there was scattered applause, and then, without an instant's warning, Creole started into something else, it was almost sardonic, it was *Am I Blue*. And, as though he commanded, Sonny began to play. Something began to happen. And Creole let out the reins. The dry, low, black man said something awful on the drums, Creole answered, and the drums talked back. Then the horn insisted, sweet and high, slightly detached perhaps, and Creole listened, commenting now and then, dry, and driving, beautiful and calm and old. Then they all came together again, and Sonny was part of the family again. I could tell this from his face. He seemed to have found, right there beneath his fingers, a damn brand-new piano. It seemed that he couldn't get over it. Then, for awhile, just being happy with Sonny, they seemed to be agreeing with him that brand-new pianos certainly were a gas.

Then Creole stepped forward to remind them that what they were playing was the blues. He hit something in all of them, he hit something in me, myself, and the music tightened and deepened, apprehension began to beat the air. Creole began to tell us what the blues were all about. They were not about anything very new. He and his boys up there were keeping it new, at the risk of ruin, destruction, madness, and death, in order to find new ways to make us listen. For, while the tale of how we suffer, and how we are delighted, and how we may triumph is never new, it always must be heard. There isn't any other tale to tell, it's the only light we've got in all this darkness.

And this tale, according to that face, that body, those strong hands on those strings, has another aspect in every country, and a new depth in every generation. Listen, Creole seemed to be saying, listen. Now these are Sonny's blues. He made the little black man on the drums know it, and the bright, brown man on the horn. Creole wasn't trying any longer to get Sonny in the water. He was wishing him Godspeed. Then he stepped back, very slowly, filling the air with the immense suggestion that Sonny speak for himself.

Then they all gathered around Sonny and Sonny played. Every now and again one of them seemed to say, amen. Sonny's fingers filled the air with life, his life. But that life contained so many others. And Sonny went all the way back, he really began with the spare, flat statement of the opening phrase of the song. Then he began to make it his. It was very beautiful because it wasn't hurried and it was no longer a lament. I seemed to hear with what burning he had made it his, with what burning we had yet to make it ours, how we could cease lamenting. Freedom lurked around us and I understood, at last, that he could help us to be free if we would listen, that he would never be free until we did. Yet, there was no battle in his face now. I heard what he had gone through, and would continue to go through until he came to rest in earth. He had made it his: that long line, of which we knew only Mama and Daddy. And he was giving it back, as everything must be given back, so that, passing through death, it can live forever. I saw my mother's face again, and felt, for the first time, how the stones of the road she had walked on must have bruised her feet. I saw the moonlit road where my father's brother died. And it brought something else back to me, and carried me past it. I saw my little girl again and felt Isabel's tears again, and I felt my own tears begin to rise. And I was yet aware that this was only a moment, that the world waited outside, as hungry as a tiger, and that trouble stretched above us, longer than the sky.

Then it was over. Creole and Sonny let out their breath, both soaking wet, and grinning. There was a lot of applause and some of it was real. In the dark, the girl came by and I asked her to take drinks to the bandstand. There was a long pause, while they talked up there in the indigo light and after awhile I saw the girl put a Scotch and milk on top of the piano for Sonny. He didn't seem to notice it, but just before they started playing again, he sipped from it and looked toward me, and nodded. Then he put it back on top of the piano. For me, then, as they began to play again, it glowed and shook above my brother's head like the very cup of trembling.

TONI CADE BAMBARA

Toni Cade Bambara (1939–1996) was born in New York City and grew up in Harlem and Bedford-Stuyvesant. As a child she began scribbling stories on the margins of her father's copies of the New York Daily News *and the squares of thin white cardboard her mother's stockings came wrapped around. She has said of herself,*

> I was raised by my family and community to be a combatant. Forays to the Apollo [Theater in Harlem] with my daddy and hanging tough on Speakers Corner with my mama taught me the power of the word, the importance of the resistance tradition, and the high standards our [black] community had regarding verbal performance. While my heart is a laughing gland and my favorite thing to be doing is laughing so hard I have to lower myself on the wall to keep from falling down, near that chamber is a blast furnace where a rifle pokes from the ribs.

In high school and at Queens College, Bambara remembered that she "hogged the lit journal." She took writing courses and wrote novels, stories, plays, film scripts, operas, "you-name-its." After graduating from Queens, she worked various jobs and studied for her M.A. at the City College of New York while she wrote fiction in "the predawn in-betweens." She began to publish her stories, and in 1972 she collected them in her first book, Gorilla, My Love. *It wasn't until Bambara returned from a trip to Cuba in 1973 that she thought of herself as a writer: "There I learned what Langston Hughes and others, most especially my colleagues in the Neo-Black Arts Movement, had been teaching for years—that writing is a legitimate way, an important way, to participate in the empowerment of the community that names me." Her books of stories include* The Black Woman *(1970),* Tales and Stories for Black Folks *(1971), and* The Sea Birds Are Still Alive: Collected Stories *(1977). She also published two novels,* The Salt Eaters *(1980) and* If Blessing Comes *(1987).*

Like Zora Neale Hurston, whom Bambara credited with giving her new ways to consider literary material (folkways as the basis of art) and new categories of perception (women's images), Bambara often used humor in her fiction. She said that "what I enjoy most in my work is the laughter and the outrage and the attention to language." Her stories, like "The Lesson," were often about children, but Bambara tried to avoid sentimentality. She attempted to keep her torrents of language and feeling under control by remembering the premises from which she proceeded as a black writer: "One, we are at war. Two, the natural response to oppression, ignorance, evil, and mystification is wide-awake resistance. Three, the natural response to stress and crisis is not breakdown and capitulation, but transformation and renewal."

WEB   *Research Toni Cade Bambara and answer questions about her work at bedfordstmartins.com/charters/litwriters.*

The Lesson   1972

Back in the days when everyone was old and stupid or young and foolish and me and Sugar were the only ones just right, this lady moved on our block with nappy hair and proper speech and no makeup. And quite naturally we laughed at her, laughed the way we did at the junk man who went about his business like he was some big-time president and his sorry-ass horse his secretary. And we kinda hated her too, hated the way we did the winos who cluttered up our parks and pissed on our handball walls and stank up our hallways and stairs so you couldn't halfway play hide-and-seek without a goddamn gas mask. Miss Moore was her name. The only woman on the block with no first name. And she was black as hell, cept for her feet, which were fish-white and spooky. And she was always planning these boring-ass things for us to do, us being my cousin, mostly, who lived on the block cause we all moved North the same time and to the same apartment then spread out gradual to breathe. And our parents would yank our heads into some kinda shape and crisp up our clothes so we'd be presentable for travel with Miss Moore, who always looked like she was going to church, though she never did. Which is just one of the things the grownups talked about when they talked behind her back like a dog. But when she came calling with some sachet she'd sewed up or some gingerbread she'd made or some book, why then they'd all be too embarrassed to turn her down and we'd get handed over all spruced up. She'd been to college and said it was only right that she should take responsibility for the young ones' education, and she not even related by marriage or blood. So they'd go for it. Specially Aunt Gretchen. She was the main gofer in the family. You got some ole dumb shit foolishness you want somebody to go for, you send for Aunt Gretchen. She been screwed into the go-along for so long, it's a blood-deep natural thing with her. Which is how she got saddled with me and Sugar and Junior in the first place while our mothers were in a la-de-da apartment up the block having a good ole time.

So this one day, Miss Moore rounds us all up at the mailbox and it's puredee hot and she's knockin herself out about arithmetic. And school suppose to let up in summer I heard, but she don't never let up. And the starch in my pinafore scratching the shit outta me and I'm really hating this nappy-head bitch and her goddamn college degree. I'd much rather go to the pool or to the show where it's cool. So me and Sugar leaning on the mailbox being surly, which is a Miss Moore word. And Flyboy checking out what everybody brought for lunch. And Fat Butt already wasting his peanut-butter-and-jelly sandwich like the pig he is. And Junebug punchin on Q.T.'s arm for potato

chips. And Rosie Giraffe shifting from one hip to the other waiting for somebody to step on her foot or ask her if she from Georgia so she can kick ass,
preferably Mercedes'. And Miss Moore asking us do we know what money is,
like we a bunch of retards. I mean real money, she say, like it's only poker chips
or monopoly papers we lay on the grocer. So right away I'm tired of this and say
so. And would much rather snatch Sugar and go to the Sunset and terrorize the
West Indian kids and take their hair ribbons and their money too. And Miss
Moore files that remark away for next week's lesson on brotherhood, I can
tell. And finally I say we oughta get to the subway cause it's cooler and besides
we might meet some cute boys. Sugar done swiped her mama's lipstick, so
we ready.

So we heading down the street and she's boring us silly about what things
cost and what our parents make and how much goes for rent and how money
ain't divided up right in this country. And then she gets to the part about we all
poor and live in the slums, which I don't feature. And I'm ready to speak on
that, but she steps out in the street and hails two cabs just like that. Then she
hustles half the crew in with her and hands me a five-dollar bill and tells me to
calculate 10 percent tip for the driver. And we're off. Me and Sugar and
Junebug and Flyboy hangin out the window and hollering to everybody, putting lipstick on each other cause Flyboy a faggot anyway, and making farts with
our sweaty armpits. But I'm mostly trying to figure how to spend this money.
But they all fascinated with the meter ticking and Junebug starts laying bets as
to how much it'll read when Flyboy can't hold his breath no more. Then Sugar
lays bets as to how much it'll be when we get there. So I'm stuck. Don't nobody
want to go for my plan, which is to jump out at the next light and run off to the
first bar-b-que we can find. Then the driver tells us to get the hell out cause we
there already. And the meter reads eighty-five cents. And I'm stalling to figure
out the tip and Sugar say give him a dime. And I decide he don't need it bad as I
do, so later for him. But then he tries to take off with Junebug foot still in the
door so we talk about his mama something ferocious. Then we check out that
we on Fifth Avenue and everybody dressed up in stockings. One lady in a fur
coat, hot as it is. White folks crazy.

"This is the place," Miss Moore say, presenting it to us in the voice she
uses at the museum. "Let's look in the windows before we go in."

"Can we steal?" Sugar asks very serious like she's getting the ground
rules squared away before she plays. "I beg your pardon," say Miss Moore, and
we fall out. So she leads us around the windows of the toy store and me and
Sugar screamin, "This is mine, that's mine, I gotta have that, that was made for
me, I was born for that," till Big Butt drowns us out.

"Hey, I'm going to buy that there."

"That there? You don't even know what it is, stupid."

"I do so," he say punchin on Rosie Giraffe. "It's a microscope."

"Whatcha gonna do with a microscope, fool?"

"Look at things."

"Like what, Ronald?" ask Miss Moore. And Big Butt ain't got the first
notion. So here go Miss Moore gabbing about the thousands of bacteria in a
drop of water and the somethinorother in a speck of blood and the million and

one living things in the air around us is invisible to the naked eye. And what she say that for? Junebug go to town on that "naked" and we rolling. Then Miss Moore ask what it cost. So we all jam into the window smudgin it up and the price tag say $300. So then she ask how long'd take for Big Butt and Junebug to save up their allowances. "Too long," I say. "Yeh," adds Sugar, "outgrown it by that time." And Miss Moore say no, you never outgrow learning instruments. "Why, even medical students and interns and," blah, blah, blah. And we ready to choke Big Butt for bringing it up in the first damn place.

"This here costs four hundred eighty dollars," say Rosie Giraffe. So we pile up all over her to see what she pointin out. My eyes tell me it's a chunk of glass cracked with something heavy, and different-color inks dripped into the splits, then the whole thing put into a oven or something. But for $480 it don't make sense.

"That's a paperweight made of semi-precious stones fused together under tremendous pressure," she explains slowly, with her hands doing the mining and all the factory work.

"So what's a paperweight?" ask Rosie Giraffe.

"To weigh paper with, dumbbell," say Flyboy, the wise man from the East.

"Not exactly," say Miss Moore, which is what she say when you warm or way off too. "It's to weigh paper down so it won't scatter and make your desk untidy." So right away me and Sugar curtsy to each other and then to Mercedes who is more the tidy type.

"We don't keep paper on top of the desk in my class," say Junebug, figuring Miss Moore crazy or lyin one.

"At home, then," she say. "Don't you have a calendar and a pencil case and a blotter and a letter-opener on your desk at home where you do your homework?" And she know damn well what our homes look like cause she nosys around in them every chance she gets.

"I don't even have a desk," say Junebug. "Do we?"

"No. And I don't get no homework neither," says Big Butt.

"And I don't even have a home," says Flyboy like he do at school to keep the white folks off his back and sorry for him. Send this poor kid to camp posters, is his specialty.

"I do," says Mercedes. "I have a box of stationery on my desk and a picture of my cat. My godmother bought the stationery and the desk. There's a big rose on each sheet and the envelopes smell like roses."

"Who wants to know about your smelly-ass stationery," say Rosie Giraffe fore I can get my two cents in.

"It's important to have a work area all your own so that . . ."

"Will you look at this sailboat, please," say Flyboy, cutting her off and pointin to the thing like it was his. So once again we tumble all over each other to gaze at this magnificent thing in the toy store which is just big enough to maybe sail two kittens across the pond if you strap them to the posts tight. We all start reciting the price tag like we in assembly. "Handcrafted sailboat of fiberglass at one thousand one hundred ninety-five dollars."

"Unbelievable," I hear myself say and am really stunned. I read it again for myself just in case the group recitation put me in a trance. Same thing. For some reason this pisses me off. We look at Miss Moore and she lookin at us, waiting for I dunno what.

"Who'd pay all that when you can buy a sailboat set for a quarter at Pop's, a tube of glue for a dime, and a ball of string for eight cents? It must have a motor and a whole lot else besides," I say. "My sailboat cost me about fifty cents."

"But will it take water?" say Mercedes with her smart ass.

"Took mine to Alley Pond Park once," say Flyboy. "String broke. Lost it. Pity."

"Sailed mine in Central Park and it keeled over and sank. Had to ask my father for another dollar."

"And you got the strap," laugh Big Butt. "The jerk didn't even have a string on it. My old man wailed on his behind."

Little Q.T. was staring hard at the sailboat and you could see he wanted it bad. But he too little and somebody'd just take it from him. So what the hell. "This boat for kids, Miss Moore?"

"Parents silly to buy something like that just to get all broke up," say Rosie Giraffe.

"That much money it should last forever," I figure.

"My father'd buy it for me if I wanted it."

"Your father, my ass," say Rosie Giraffe getting a chance to finally push Mercedes.

"Must be rich people shop here," say Q.T.

"You are a very bright boy," say Flyboy. "What was your first clue?" And he rap him on the head with the back of his knuckles, since Q.T. the only one he could get away with. Though Q.T. liable to come up behind you years later and get his licks in when you half expect it.

"What I want to know is," I says to Miss Moore though I never talk to her, I wouldn't give the bitch that satisfaction, "is how much a real boat costs? I figure a thousand'd get you a yacht any day."

"Why don't you check that out," she says, "and report back to the group?" Which really pains my ass. If you gonna mess up a perfectly good swim day least you could do is have some answers. "Let's go in," she say like she got something up her sleeve. Only she don't lead the way. So me and Sugar turn the corner to where the entrance is, but when we get there I kinda hang back. Not that I'm scared, what's there to be afraid of, just a toy store. But I feel funny, shame. But what I got to be shamed about? Got as much right to go in as anybody. But somehow I can't seem to get hold of the door, so I step away from Sugar to lead. But she hangs back too. And I look at her and she looks at me and this is ridiculous. I mean, damn, I have never been shy about doing nothing or going nowhere. But then Mercedes steps up and then Rosie Giraffe and Big Butt crowd in behind and shove, and next thing we all stuffed into the doorway with only Mercedes squeezing past us, smoothing out her jumper and walking right down the aisle. Then the rest of us tumble in like a glued-together jigsaw done all wrong. And people lookin at us. And it's like the time me and Sugar crashed into the Catholic church on a dare. But once we got in there and everything so hushed and holy and the candles and the bowin and the handkerchiefs on all the drooping heads, I just couldn't go through with the plan. Which was for me to run up to the altar and do a tap dance while Sugar played the nose flute and messed around in the holy water. And Sugar kept givin me the elbow. Then later teased me so bad I tied her up in the shower and turned it on and locked her in. And she'd be there till this day if Aunt Gretchen hadn't finally figured I was lying about the boarder takin a shower.

Same thing in the store. We all walkin on tiptoe and hardly touchin the games and puzzles and things. And I watched Miss Moore who is steady watchin us like she waitin for a sign. Like Mama Drewery watches the sky and sniffs the air and takes note of just how much slant is in the bird formation. Then me and Sugar bump smack into each other, so busy gazing at the toys, 'specially the sailboat. But we don't laugh and go into our fat-lady bump-stomach routine. We just stare at that price tag. Then Sugar run a finger over the whole boat. And I'm jealous and want to hit her. Maybe not her, but I sure want to punch somebody in the mouth.

"Watcha bring us here for, Miss Moore?"

"You sound angry, Sylvia. Are you mad about something?" Givin me one of them grins like she tellin a grown-up joke that never turns out to be funny. And she's lookin very closely at me like maybe she plannin to do my portrait from memory. I'm mad, but I won't give her that satisfaction. So I slouch around the store being very bored and say, "Let's go."

Me and Sugar at the back of the train watchin the tracks whizzin by large then small then getting gobbled up in the dark. I'm thinkin about this tricky toy I saw in the store. A clown that somersaults on a bar then does chin-ups just cause you yank lightly at his leg. Cost $35. I could see me askin my mother for a $35 birthday clown. "You wanna who that costs what?" she'd say, cocking her head to the side to get a better view of the hole in my head. Thirty-five dollars could buy new bunk beds for Junior and Gretchen's boy. Thirty-five dollars and the whole household could go visit Granddaddy Nelson in the country. Thirty-five dollars would pay for the rent and the piano bill too. Who are these people that spend that much for performing clowns and $1000 for toy sailboats? What kinda work they do and how they live and how come we ain't in on it? Where we are is who we are, Miss Moore always pointin out. But it don't necessarily have to be that way, she always adds then waits for somebody to say that poor people have to wake up and demand their share of the pie and don't none of us know what kind of pie she talking about in the first damn place. But she ain't so smart cause I still got her four dollars from the taxi and she sure ain't gettin it. Messin up my day with this shit. Sugar nudges me in my pocket and winks.

Miss Moore lines us up in front of the mailbox where we started from, seem like years ago, and I got a headache for thinkin so hard. And we lean all over each other so we can hold up under the draggy-ass lecture she always finishes us off with at the end before we thank her for borin us to tears. But she just looks at us like she readin tea leaves. Finally she say, "Well, what did you think of F.A.O. Schwarz?"

Rosie Giraffe mumbles, "White folks crazy."

"I'd like to go there again when I get my birthday money," says Mercedes, and we shove her out the pack so she has to lean on the mailbox by herself.

"I'd like a shower. Tiring day," say Flyboy.

Then Sugar surprises me by sayin, "You know, Miss Moore, I don't think all of us here put together eat in a year what that sailboat costs." And Miss Moore lights up like somebody goosed her "And?" she say, urging Sugar on. Only I'm standin on her foot so she don't continue.

"Imagine for a minute what kind of society it is in which some people can spend on a toy what it would cost to feed a family of six or seven. What do you think?"

"I think," say Sugar pushing me off her feet like she never done before, cause I whip her ass in a minute, "that this is not much of a democracy if you ask me. Equal chance to pursue happiness means an equal crack at the dough, don't it?" Miss Moore is besides herself and I am disgusted with Sugar's treachery. So I stand on her foot one more time to see if she'll shove me. She shuts up, and Miss Moore looks at me, sorrowfully I'm thinkin. And somethin weird is goin on, I can feel it in my chest.

"Anybody else learn anything today?" lookin dead at me. I walk away and Sugar has to run to catch up and don't even seem to notice when I shrug her arm off my shoulder.

"Well, we got four dollars anyway," she says.

"Uh, hunh."

"We could go to Hascombs and get half a chocolate layer and then go to the Sunset and still have plenty money for potato chips and ice cream sodas."

"Uh, hunh."

"Race you to Hascombs," she say.

We start down the block and she gets ahead which is O.K. by me cause I'm going to the West End and then over to the Drive to think this day through. She can run if she want to and even run faster. But ain't nobody gonna beat me at nuthin.

RUSSELL BANKS

Russell Banks (b. 1940) was the son of an alcoholic father, the oldest of four children raised in a working-class New Hampshire family. He had what he calls "a turbulent, chaotic, and angry youth." At nineteen, he left his first wife and small child intending to go fight for Fidel Castro, but unable to speak Spanish, he never reached Cuba. Instead he stayed in southern Florida and took jobs as a window dresser and a furniture mover. Five years later, after his mother-in-law helped pay the tuition, Banks earned a B.A. at the University of North Carolina, graduating Phi Beta Kappa. With hindsight, Banks believes that "Writing in some way saved my life. It brought to my life a kind of order and discipline and connection to the world outside myself that I don't see how I could have obtained otherwise." Because he came from a deprived family background, he feels that he earned the right to become a writer "slowly over time, and I have depended heavily on the validation and encouragement of others."

Banks published six books of fiction, which sold modestly, while he sup-ported himself and his family by teaching creative writing at Sarah Lawrence Col-lege, Columbia University, New York University, and Princeton University. In 1985, influenced by the work of several American writers of naturalist fiction, such as Sherwood Anderson and Richard Wright, Banks published Continental Drift, *a novel about immigration. The book sold well and was a finalist for the Pulitzer Prize. Banks told interviewer Paula Deimling that he thought the novel had gained a wider audience because "it was set in a world that mattered to people." Award-winning films were made of his later novels* Affliction *(1989) and* The Sweet Hereafter *(1991). In 1998 Banks retired from teaching to become a full-time writer. His next novel was* Cloudsplitter *(2000), about the nineteenth-century abolitionist and terrorist John Brown, who had been a hero to Banks in the 1960s when he was involved in the civil rights movement as a university student in North Carolina.*

Throughout his career, Banks has written stories in addition to novels, pub-lishing four collections of short fiction and winning O. Henry and Best American Short Story Awards. In 2000, he gathered what he considered his best stories in The Angel on the Roof, *which includes "Black Man and White Woman in Dark Green Rowboat." Banks has said that his aim as a storyteller is to make his readers see, quoting Joseph Conrad: "Conrad meant literally visualize, not understand. That's the ambition for me as a writer too — so that my readers can see the world or themselves or other human beings in the world a little differently, a little more clearly. . . . with more compassion, with more understanding, more patience. I don't stereotype them so easily."*

CONNECTION   *Ernest Hemingway, "Hills Like White Elephants," page 230.*

WEB   *Research Russell Banks and answer questions about his work at bedfordstmartins.com/charters/litwriters.*

Black Man and White Woman in Dark Green Rowboat
1981

It was the third day of an August heat wave. Within an hour of the sun's rising above the spruce and pine trees that grew along the eastern hills, a blue-gray haze had settled over the lake and trailerpark, so that from the short, sandy spit that served as a swimming place for the residents of the trailerpark you couldn't see the far shore of the lake. Around seven, a man in plaid bathing trunks and white bathing cap, in his sixties but still straight and apparently in good physical condition, left one of the trailers and walked along the paved lane to the beach. He draped his white towel over the bow of a flaking, bottle green rowboat that had been dragged onto the sand and walked directly into the water and when the water was up to his waist he began to swim, smoothly, slowly, straight out in the still water for two hundred yards or so, where he turned, treaded water for a few moments, and then started swimming back toward shore. When he reached the shore, he dried himself and walked back to his trailer and went inside. By the time he closed his door the water was smooth again, a dark green plain beneath the thick, gray-blue sky. No birds moved or sang; even the insects were silent.

In the next few hours, people left their trailers to go to their jobs in town, those who had jobs — the nurse, the bank teller, the carpenter, the woman who worked in the office at the tannery, and her little girl, who would spend the day with a baby-sitter in town. They moved slowly, heavily, as if with regret, even the child.

Time passed, and the trailerpark was silent again, while the sun baked the metal roofs and sides of the trailers, heating them up inside, so that by mid-morning it was cooler outside than in, and the people came out and tried to find a shady place to sit. First to appear was a middle-aged woman in large sunglasses and white shorts and halter, her head hidden by a floppy, wide-brimmed, cloth hat. She carried a book and sat on the shaded side of her trailer in an aluminum and plastic-webbing lawn chair and began to read her book. Then from his trailer came the man in the plaid bathing trunks, bareheaded now and shirtless and tanned to a chestnut color, his skin the texture of old leather. He wore rubber sandals and proceeded to hook up a garden hose and water the small, meticulously weeded vegetable garden on the slope behind his trailer. Every now and then he aimed the hose down and sprayed his bony feet. From the first trailer in from the road, where a sign that said MANAGER had been attached over the door, a tall, thick-bodied woman in her forties with cropped, graying hair, wearing faded jeans cut off at midthigh and a floppy T-shirt that had turned pink in the wash, walked slowly out to the main road, a half mile, to get her mail. When she returned she sat on her steps and read the letters and advertisements and the newspaper. About that time a blond boy in his late teens with shoulder-length hair, skinny, tanned, shirtless, and barefoot in jeans, emerged from his trailer, sighed, and sat down on the stoop and smoked a joint. At the last trailer in the park, the one next to the beach, an old man smoking a cob pipe and wearing a sleeveless undershirt and beltless khaki trousers slowly scraped paint from the bottom of an overturned rowboat. He ceased working and watched carefully as, walking slowly past him toward a dark green rowboat on the sand, there came a young black man with a fishing rod in one hand and a tackle box in the other. The man was tall and, though slender, muscular. He wore jeans and a pale blue, unbuttoned, short-sleeved shirt.

The old man said it was too hot for fishing, they wouldn't feed in this weather, and the young man said he didn't care, it had to be cooler on the lake than here on shore. The old man agreed with that, but why bother carrying your fishing rod and tackle box with you when you don't expect to catch any fish?

"Right," the young man said, smiling. "Good question." Placing his box and the rod into the rowboat, he turned to wait for the young woman who was stepping away from the trailer where, earlier, the middle-aged woman in shorts, halter, and floppy hat had come out and sat in the lawn chair to read. The young woman was a girl, actually, twenty or maybe twenty-one. She wore a lime green terry-cloth bikini and carried a large yellow towel in one hand and a fashion magazine and small brown bottle of tanning lotion in the other. Her long, honey blond hair swung from side to side across her tanned shoulders as she walked down the lane to the beach, where both the young man and the old man watched her approach them. She made a brief remark about the heat to the old man, said good morning to the young man, placed her towel, magazine, and tanning lotion into the dark green rowboat, and helped the young man shove the boat off the hot sand into the water. Then she jumped into the boat and sat herself in the stern, and the man, barefoot, with the bottoms of his jeans rolled to his knees, waded out, got into the boat, and began to row.

For a while, as the man rowed and the girl rubbed tanning lotion slowly over her arms and legs and across her shoulders and belly, they said nothing. The man pulled smoothly on the oars and watched the girl, and she examined her light brown skin and stroked it and rubbed the oily, sweet-smelling fluid onto it. After a few moments, holding to the gunwales with her hands so that her entire body got exposed to the powerful sun, she leaned back, closed her eyes, and stretched her legs toward the man, placing her small, white feet over his large, dark feet. The man studied the wedge of her crotch, then her navel, where a puddle of sweat was collecting, then the rise of her small breasts, and finally her long throat glistening in the sunlight. The man was sweating from the effort of rowing and he said he should have brought a hat. He stopped rowing, let the blades of the oars float in the water, and removed his shirt and wrapped it around his head like a turban. The girl, realizing that he had ceased rowing, looked up and smiled at him. "You look like an Arab. A sheik."

"A galley slave, more likely."

"No, really. Honestly." She lay her head back again and closed her eyes, and the man took up the oars and resumed rowing. They were a long ways out now, perhaps a half-mile from the trailerpark. The trailers looked like pastel-colored shoe boxes from here, six of them lined up on one side of the lane, six on the other, with a cleared bit of low ground and marsh off to one side and the outlet of the lake, the Catamount River it was called, on the other. The water was deep there, and below the surface and buried in the mud were blocks of stone and wooden lattices, the remains of fishing weirs the Indians constructed here and used for centuries, until the arrival of the Europeans. In the fall when the lake was low you could see the tops of the huge boulders the Indians placed into the stream to make channels for their nets and traps. There were weirs like this all over northern New England, most of them considerably more elaborate than this, so no one here paid much attention to these, except perhaps to mention the fact of their existence to a visitor from Massachusetts or New York. It gave the place a history and a certain significance when outsiders were present that it did not otherwise seem to have.

The girl lifted her feet away from the man's feet, drawing them back so that her knees pointed straight at his. She turned slightly to one side and stroked her cheekbone and lower jaw with the fingertips and thumb of one hand, leaning her weight on the other forearm and hand. "I'm already putting on weight," she said.

"It doesn't work that way. You're just eating too much."

"I told Mother."

The man stopped rowing and looked at her.

"I told Mother," she repeated. Her eyes were closed and her face was directed toward the sun and she continued to stroke her cheekbone and lower jaw.

"When?"

"Last night."

"And?"

"And nothing. I told her that I love you very much."

"That's all?"

"No. I told her everything."

He started rowing again, faster this time and not as smoothly as before. They were nearing a small, tree-covered island. Large, rounded rocks lay around the island, half-submerged in the shallow water, like the backs of huge, coal-colored hippos. The man peered over his shoulder and observed the distance to the island, then drew in the oars and lifted a broken chunk of cinder block tied to a length of clothesline rope and slid it into the water. The rope went out swiftly and cleanly as the anchor sank and then suddenly stopped. The man opened his tackle box and started poking through it, searching for a deepwater spinner.

The girl was sitting up now, studying the island with her head canted to one side, as if planning a photograph. "Actually, Mother was a lot better than I'd expected her to be. If Daddy were alive, it would be different," she said. "Daddy . . ."

"Hated niggers."

"Jesus Christ!"

"And Mother loves 'em." He located the spinner and attached it to the line.

"My mother likes you. She's a decent woman, and she's tired and lonely. And she's not your enemy, any more than I am."

"You're sure of that." He made a long cast and dropped the spinner between two large rocks and started winding it back in. "No, I know your mamma's okay. I'm sorry. Tell me what she said."

"She thought it was great. She likes you. I'm happy, and that's what is really important to her, and she likes you. She worries about me a lot, you know. She's afraid for me, she thinks I'm fragile. Especially now, because I've had some close calls. At least that's how she sees them."

"Sees what?"

"Oh, you know. Depression."

"Yeah." He cast again, slightly to the left of where he'd put the spinner the first time.

"Listen, I don't know how to tell you this, but I might as well come right out and say it. I'm going to do it. This afternoon. Mother's coming with me. She called and set it up this morning."

He kept reeling in the spinner, slowly, steadily, as if he hadn't heard her, until the spinner clunked against the side of the boat and he lifted it dripping from the water, and he said, "I hate this whole thing. Hate! Just know that much, will you?"

She reached out and placed a hand on his arm. "I know you do. So do I. But it'll be all right again afterwards. I promise. It'll be just like it was."

"You can't promise that. No one can. It won't be all right afterwards. It'll be lousy."

"I suppose you'd rather I just did nothing."

"Yes. That's right."

"Well. We've been through all this before. A hundred times." She sat up straight and peered back at the trailerpark in the distance. "How long do you plan to fish?"

"An hour or so. Why? If you want to swim, I'll row you around to the other side of the island and drop you and come back and get you later."

"No. No. That's all right. There are too many rocks anyhow. I'll go in when we get back to the beach. I have to be ready to go by three-thirty."

"Yeah. I'll make sure you get there on time," he said, and he made a long cast off to his right in deeper water.

"I love to sweat," she said, lying back and showing herself once again to the full sun. "I love to just lie back and sweat."

The man fished, and the girl sunbathed. The water was as slick as oil, the air thick and still. After a while, the man reeled in his line and removed the silvery spinner and went back to poking through his tackle box. "Where the hell is the damn plug?" he mumbled.

The girl sat up and watched him, his long, dark back twisted toward her, the vanilla bottoms of his feet, the fluttering muscles of his shoulders and arms, when suddenly he yelped and yanked his hand free of the box and put the meat of his hand directly into his mouth. He looked up at the girl in rage.

"What? Are you all right?" She slid back in her seat and drew her legs up close to her and wrapped her arms around her knees.

In silence, still sucking on his hand, he reached with the other hand into the tackle box and came back with a pale green and scarlet plug with six double hooks attached to the sides and tail. He held it as if by the head delicately with thumb and forefinger and showed it to her.

The girl grimaced. "Ow! You poor thing."

He took his hand from his mouth and clipped the plug to his line and cast it toward the island, dropping it about twenty feet from the rocky shore, a short ways to the right of a pair of dog-sized boulders. The girl picked up her magazine and began to leaf through the pages, stopping every now and then to examine an advertisement or photograph. Again and again, the man cast the flashing plug into the water and drew it back to the boat, twitching its path from side to side to imitate the motions of an injured, fleeting, pale-colored animal.

Finally, lifting the plug from the water next to the boat, the man said, "Let's go. Old Merle was right, no sense fishing when the fish ain't feeding.

The whole point is catching fish, right?" he said, and he removed the plug from the line and tossed it into his open tackle box.

"I suppose so. I don't like fishing anyhow." Then after a few seconds, as if she were pondering the subject, "But I guess it's relaxing. Even if you don't catch anything."

The man drew up the anchor, pulling in the wet rope hand over hand, and finally he pulled the cinder block free of the water and set it dripping behind him in the bow of the boat. They had drifted closer to the island now and were in the cooling shade of the thicket of oaks and birches that crowded together over the island. The water turned suddenly shallow here, only a few feet deep, and they could see the rocky bottom clearly.

"Be careful," the girl said. "We'll run aground in a minute." She watched the bottom nervously. "Take care."

The man looked over her head and beyond, all the way to the shore and the trailerpark. The shapes of the trailers were blurred together in the distance so that you could not tell where one trailer left off and another began. "I wish I could just leave you here," the man said, still not looking at her.

"What?"

The boat drifted silently in the smooth water between a pair of large rocks, barely disturbing the surface. The man's dark face was somber and ancient beneath the turban that covered his head and the back of his neck. He leaned forward on his seat, his forearms resting wearily on his thighs, his large hands hanging limply between his knees. "I said, I wish I could just leave you here," he said in a soft voice, and he looked down at his hands.

She looked nervously around her, as if for an ally or a witness. "We have to go back."

"You mean, *you* have to go back."

"That's right," she said.

He slipped the oars into the oarlocks and started rowing, turning the boat and shoving it quickly away from the island. Facing the trailerpark, he rowed along the side of the island, then around behind it, out of sight of the trailerpark and the people who lived there, emerging again in a few moments on the far side of the island, rowing steadily, smoothly, powerfully. Now his back was to the trailerpark, and the girl was facing it, looking grimly past the man toward the shore.

He rowed, and they said nothing more. In a while they had returned to shore and life among the people who lived there. A few of them were in the water and on the beach when the dark green rowboat touched land and the black man stepped out and drew the boat onto the sand. The old man in the white bathing cap was standing in waist-deep water, and the woman who was the manager of the trailerpark stood near the edge of the water, cooling her feet and ankles. The old man with the cob pipe was still chipping at the bottom of his rowboat, and next to him, watching and idly chatting, stood the kid with the long blond hair. They all watched silently as the black man turned away from the dark green rowboat and carried his fishing rod and tackle box away, and then they watched the girl, carrying her yellow towel, magazine, and bottle of tanning lotion, step carefully out of the boat and walk to where she lived with her mother.

RAYMOND CARVER

Raymond Carver (1938–1988) grew up in a logging town in Oregon, where his father worked in a sawmill and his mother held odd jobs. After graduating from high school, Carver married at the age of nineteen and had two children. Working hard to support his wife and family, he managed to enroll briefly in 1958 as a student at Chico State College in California, where he took a creative writing course from a then nearly unknown young novelist named John Gardner. Carver remembered that he decided to try to become a writer because he liked to read pulp novels and magazines about hunting and fishing. He credited Gardner for giving him a strong sense of direction as a writer: "A writer's values and craft. This is what the man taught and what he stood for, and this is what I've kept by me in the years since that brief but all-important time."

In 1963 Carver received his B.A. from Humboldt State College in northern California. The following year he studied writing at the University of Iowa. But the 1960s, he said, were difficult for him and his wife:

> I learned a long time ago when my kids were little and we had no money, and we were working our hearts out and weren't getting anywhere, even though we were giving it our best, my wife and I, that there were more important things than writing a poem or a story. That was a very hard realization for me to come to. But it came to me, and I had to accept it or die. Getting milk and food on the table, getting the rent paid, if a choice had to be made, then I had to forgo writing.

Carver's desire to be a writer was so strong that he kept on writing long after the "cold facts" of his life told him he ought to quit. His first collection of stories, Will You Please Be Quiet, Please?, was nominated for the National Book Award in 1976. Four more collections of stories followed, along with five books of poetry, before his death from lung cancer.

Critics have noted that the rapid evolution of Carver's style causes his fiction to fall into three distinct periods. The tentative writing in his first book of stories — many of which he subsequently revised and republished — was followed by a paring down of his prose. This resulted in the hard-edged and detached minimalist style of his middle period, exemplified by the stories in his collection What We Talk About When We Talk About Love (1981), which included "The Bath," later revised as "A Small, Good Thing." In his final period, Carver developed a more expansive style, as in the collection Cathedral (1983) and the new stories in his last collection, Where I'm Calling From: New and Selected Stories (1988).

Influenced by the cadence of Ernest Hemingway's sentences, Carver also believed in simplicity. He wrote,

> It's possible, in a poem or a short story, to write about commonplace things and objects using commonplace but precise language, and to endow those things — a chair, a window curtain, a fork, a stone, a woman's earring — with immense, even startling power. . . . If the words are heavy with the writer's own unbridled emotions, or if they are imprecise and inaccurate for some other reason — if the words are in any way blurred — the reader's eyes will slide right over them and nothing will be achieved. The reader's own artistic sense will simply not be engaged.

CONVERSATIONS   *See pages 610–630, including Raymond Carver, "On Writing,"*
page 610; Raymond Carver, "Creative Writing 101," page 614; Jim Naughton,
"As Raymond Carver Muses, His Stature Grows," page 618; Kathleen Westfall
Shute, "On 'The Bath' and 'A Small, Good Thing,'" page 620; Tom Jenks, "The
Origin of 'Cathedral,'" page 625; A. O. Scott, "Looking for Raymond Carver,"
page 626.

WEB   *Research Raymond Carver and answer questions about his work at*
bedfordstmartins.com/charters/litwriters.

Cathedral   1981

This blind man, an old friend of my wife's, he was on his way to spend the
night. His wife had died. So he was visiting the dead wife's relatives in Connecticut. He called my wife from his in-laws'. Arrangements were made. He
would come by train, a five-hour trip, and my wife would meet him at the station. She hadn't seen him since she worked for him one summer in Seattle ten
years ago. But she and the blind man had kept in touch. They made tapes and
mailed them back and forth. I wasn't enthusiastic about his visit. He was no
one I knew. And his being blind bothered me. My idea of blindness came from
the movies. In the movies, the blind moved slowly and never laughed. Sometimes they were led by seeing-eye dogs. A blind man in my house was not
something I looked forward to.

That summer in Seattle she had needed a job. She didn't have any money.
The man she was going to marry at the end of the summer was in officers' training school. He didn't have any money, either. But she was in love with the guy,
and he was in love with her, etc. She'd seen something in the paper: HELP
WANTED — *Reading to Blind Man,* and a telephone number. She phoned
and went over, was hired on the spot. She'd worked with this blind man all
summer. She read stuff to him, case studies, reports, that sort of thing. She
helped him organize his little office in the county social-service department.
They'd become good friends, my wife and the blind man. How do I know these
things? She told me. And she told me something else. On her last day in the
office, the blind man asked if he could touch her face. She agreed to this. She
told me he touched his fingers to every part of her face, her nose — even her
neck! She never forgot it. She even tried to write a poem about it. She was
always trying to write a poem. She wrote a poem or two every year, usually after
something really important had happened to her.

When we first started going out together, she showed me the poem. In
the poem, she recalled his fingers and the way they had moved around over her
face. In the poem, she talked about what she had felt at the time, about what
went through her mind when the blind man touched her nose and lips. I can
remember I didn't think much of the poem. Of course, I didn't tell her that.
Maybe I just don't understand poetry. I admit it's not the first thing I reach for
when I pick up something to read.

Anyway, this man who'd first enjoyed her favors, the officer-to-be,
he'd been her childhood sweetheart. So okay. I'm saying that at the end of the

summer she let the blind man run his hands over her face, said goodbye to him, married her childhood etc., who was now a commissioned officer, and she moved away from Seattle. But they'd kept in touch, she and the blind man. She made the first contact after a year or so. She called him up one night from an Air Force base in Alabama. She wanted to talk. They talked. He asked her to send him a tape and tell him about her life. She did this. She sent the tape. On the tape, she told the blind man about her husband and about their life together in the military. She told the blind man she loved her husband but she didn't like it where they lived and she didn't like it that he was a part of the military-industrial thing. She told the blind man she'd written a poem and he was in it. She told him that she was writing a poem about what it was like to be an Air Force officer's wife. The poem wasn't finished yet. She was still writing it. The blind man made a tape. He sent her the tape. She made a tape. This went on for years. My wife's officer was posted to one base and then another. She sent tapes from Moody AFB, McGuire, McConnell, and finally Travis, near Sacramento, where one night she got to feeling lonely and cut off from people she kept losing in that moving-around life. She got to feeling she couldn't go it another step. She went in and swallowed all the pills and capsules in the medicine chest and washed them down with a bottle of gin. Then she got into a hot bath and passed out.

But instead of dying, she got sick. She threw up. Her officer—why should he have a name? he was the childhood sweetheart, and what more does he want?—came home from somewhere, found her, and called the ambulance. In time, she put it all on a tape and sent the tape to the blind man. Over the years, she put all kinds of stuff on tapes and sent the tapes off lickety-split. Next to writing a poem every year, I think it was her chief means of recreation. On one tape, she told the blind man she'd decided to live away from her officer for a time. On another tape, she told him about her divorce. She and I began going out, and of course she told her blind man about it. She told him everything, or so it seemed to me. Once she asked me if I'd like to hear the latest tape from the blind man. This was a year ago. I was on the tape, she said. So I said okay, I'd listen to it. I got us drinks and we settled down in the living room. We made ready to listen. First she inserted the tape into the player and adjusted a couple of dials. Then she pushed a lever. The tape squeaked and someone began to talk in this loud voice. She lowered the volume. After a few minutes of harmless chitchat, I heard my own name in the mouth of this stranger, this blind man I didn't even know! And then this: "From all you've said about him, I can only conclude—" But we were interrupted, a knock at the door, something, and we didn't ever get back to the tape. Maybe it was just as well. I'd heard all I wanted to.

Now this same blind man was coming to sleep in my house.

"Maybe I could take him bowling," I said to my wife. She was at the draining board doing scalloped potatoes. She put down the knife she was using and turned around.

"If you love me," she said, "you can do this for me. If you don't love me, okay. But if you had a friend, any friend, and the friend came to visit, I'd make him feel comfortable." She wiped her hands with the dish towel.

"I don't have any blind friends," I said.

"You don't have *any* friends," she said. "Period. Besides," she said, "god-damn it, his wife's just died! Don't you understand that? The man's lost his wife!"

I didn't answer. She'd told me a little about the blind man's wife. Her name was Beulah. Beulah! That's a name for a colored woman.

"Was his wife Negro?" I asked.

"Are you crazy?" my wife said. "Have you just flipped or something?" She picked up a potato. I saw it hit the floor, then roll under the stove. "What's wrong with you?" she said. "Are you drunk?"

"I'm just asking," I said.

Right then my wife filled me in with more detail than I cared to know. I made a drink and sat at the kitchen table to listen. Pieces of the story began to fall into place.

Beulah had gone to work for the blind man the summer after my wife had stopped working for him. Pretty soon Beulah and the blind man had themselves a church wedding. It was a little wedding—who'd want to go to such a wedding in the first place?—just the two of them, plus the minister and the minister's wife. But it was a church wedding just the same. It was what Beulah had wanted, he'd said. But even then Beulah must have been carrying the cancer in her glands. After they had been inseparable for eight years—my wife's word, *inseparable*—Beulah's health went into a rapid decline. She died in a Seattle hospital room, the blind man sitting beside the bed and holding on to her hand. They'd married, lived and worked together, slept together—had sex, sure—and then the blind man had to bury her. All this without his having ever seen what the goddamned woman looked like. It was beyond my understanding. Hearing this, I felt sorry for the blind man for a little bit. And then I found myself thinking what a pitiful life this woman must have led. Imagine a woman who could never see herself as she was seen in the eyes of her loved one. A woman who could go on day after day and never receive the smallest compliment from her beloved. A woman whose husband could never read the expression on her face, be it misery or something better. Someone who could wear makeup or not—what difference to him? She could, if she wanted, wear green eye-shadow around one eye, a straight pin in her nostril, yellow slacks and purple shoes, no matter. And then to slip off into death, the blind man's hand on her hand, his blind eyes streaming tears—I'm imagining now—her last thought maybe this: that he never even knew what she looked like, and she on an express to the grave. Robert was left with a small insurance policy and half of a twenty-peso Mexican coin. The other half of the coin went into the box with her. Pathetic.

So when the time rolled around, my wife went to the depot to pick him up. With nothing to do but wait—sure, I blamed him for that—I was having a drink and watching the TV when I heard the car pull into the drive. I got up from the sofa with my drink and went to the window to have a look.

I saw my wife laughing as she parked the car. I saw her get out of the car and shut the door. She was still wearing a smile. Just amazing. She went around to the other side of the car to where the blind man was already starting to get out. This blind man, feature this, he was wearing a full beard! A beard on a blind man! Too much, I say. The blind man reached into the back seat and dragged out a suitcase. My wife took his arm, shut the car door, and, talking all the way, moved him down the drive and then up the steps to the front porch. I turned off the TV. I finished my drink, rinsed the glass, dried my hands. Then I went to the door.

My wife said, "I want you to meet Robert. Robert, this is my husband. I've told you all about him." She was beaming. She had this blind man by his coat sleeve.

The blind man let go of his suitcase and up came his hand.

I took it. He squeezed hard, held my hand, and then he let it go.

"I feel like we've already met," he boomed.

"Likewise," I said. I didn't know what else to say. Then I said, "Welcome. I've heard a lot about you." We began to move then, a little group, from the porch into the living room, my wife guiding him by the arm. The blind man was carrying his suitcase in his other hand. My wife said things like, "To your left here, Robert. That's right. Now watch it, there's a chair. That's it. Sit down right here. This is the sofa. We just bought this sofa two weeks ago."

I started to say something about the old sofa. I'd liked that old sofa. But I didn't say anything. Then I wanted to say something else, small-talk, about the scenic ride along the Hudson. How going *to* New York, you should sit on the right-hand side of the train, and coming *from* New York, the left-hand side.

"Did you have a good train ride?" I said. "Which side of the train did you sit on, by the way?"

"What a question, which side!" my wife said. "What's it matter which side?" she said.

"I just asked," I said.

"Right side," the blind man said. "I hadn't been on a train in nearly forty years. Not since I was a kid. With my folks. That's been a long time. I'd nearly forgotten the sensation. I have winter in my beard now," he said. "So I've been told, anyway. Do I look distinguished, my dear?" the blind man said to my wife.

"You look distinguished, Robert," she said. "Robert," she said. "Robert, it's just so good to see you."

My wife finally took her eyes off the blind man and looked at me. I had the feeling she didn't like what she saw. I shrugged.

I've never met, or personally known, anyone who was blind. This blind man was late forties, a heavy-set, balding man with stooped shoulders, as if he carried a great weight there. He wore brown slacks, brown shoes, a light-brown shirt, a tie, a sports coat. Spiffy. He also had this full beard. But he didn't use a cane and he didn't wear dark glasses. I'd always thought dark glasses were a must for the blind. Fact was, I wished he had a pair. At first glance, his eyes looked like anyone else's eyes. But if you look close, there was something different about them. Too much white in the iris, for one thing, and the pupils seemed to move around in the sockets without his knowing it or being able to stop it. Creepy. As I stared at his face, I saw the left pupil turn in toward his nose while the other made an effort to keep in one place. But it was only an effort, for that eye was on the roam without his knowing it or wanting it to be.

I said, "Let me get you a drink. What's your pleasure? We have a little of everything. It's one of our pastimes."

"Bub, I'm a Scotch man myself," he said fast enough in this big voice.

"Right," I said. Bub! "Sure you are, I knew it."

He let his fingers touch his suitcase, which was sitting alongside the sofa. He was taking his bearings. I didn't blame him for that.

"I'll move that up to your room," my wife said.

"No, that's fine," the blind man said loudly. "It can go up when I go up."

"A little water with the Scotch?" I said.

"Very little," he said.

"I knew it," I said.

He said, "Just a tad. The Irish actor, Barry Fitzgerald? I'm like that fellow. When I drink water, Fitzgerald said, I drink water. When I drink whiskey, I drink whiskey." My wife laughed. The blind man brought his hand up under his beard. He lifted his beard slowly and let it drop.

I did the drinks, three big glasses of Scotch with a splash of water in each. Then we made ourselves comfortable and talked about Robert's travels. First the long flight from the West Coast to Connecticut, we covered that. Then from Connecticut up here by train. We had another drink concerning that leg of the trip.

I remembered having read somewhere that the blind didn't smoke because, as speculation had it, they couldn't see the smoke they exhaled. I thought I knew that much and that much only about blind people. But this blind man smoked his cigarette down to the nubbin and then lit another one. This blind man filled his ashtray and my wife emptied it.

When we sat down at the table for dinner, we had another drink. My wife heaped Robert's plate with cube steak, scalloped potatoes, green beans. I buttered him up two slices of bread. I said, "Here's bread and butter for you." I swallowed some of my drink. "Now let us pray," I said, and the blind man lowered his head. My wife looked at me, her mouth agape. "Pray the phone won't ring and the food doesn't get cold," I said.

We dug in. We ate everything there was to eat on the table. We ate like there was no tomorrow. We didn't talk. We ate. We scarfed. We grazed that table. We were into serious eating. The blind man had right away located his foods, he knew just where everything was on his plate. I watched with admiration as he used his knife and fork on the meat. He'd cut two pieces of meat, fork the meat into his mouth, and then go all out for the scalloped potatoes, the beans next, and then he'd tear off a hunk of buttered bread and eat that. He'd follow this up with a big drink of milk. It didn't seem to bother him to use his fingers once in a while, either.

We finished everything, including half a strawberry pie. For a few moments, we sat as if stunned. Sweat beaded on our faces. Finally, we got up from the table and left the dirty plates. We didn't look back. We took ourselves into the living room and sank into our places again. Robert and my wife sat on the sofa. I took the big chair. We had us two or three more drinks while they talked about the major things that had come to pass for them in the past ten years. For the most part, I just listened. Now and then I joined in. I didn't want him to think I'd left the room, and I didn't want her to think I was feeling left out. They talked of things that had happened to them — to them! — these past ten years. I waited in vain to hear my name on my wife's sweet lips: "And then my dear husband came into my life" — something like that. But I heard nothing of the sort. More talk of Robert. Robert had done a little of everything, it seemed, a regular blind jack-of-all-trades. But most recently he and his wife had had an Amway distributorship, from which, I gathered, they'd earned their living, such as it was. The blind man was also a ham radio operator. He talked in his loud voice about conversations he'd had with fellow operators in Guam, in the Philippines, in Alaska, and even in Tahiti. He said he'd have a lot of friends there if he ever wanted to go visit those places. From time to time, he'd turn his blind face toward me, put his hand under his beard, ask me something. How long had I been in my present position? (Three years.) Did I like my work? (I didn't.) Was I going to stay with it? (What were the options?) Finally, when I thought he was beginning to run down, I got up and turned on the TV.

My wife looked at me with irritation. She was heading toward a boil. Then she looked at the blind man and said, "Robert, do you have a TV?"

The blind man said, "My dear, I have two TVs. I have a color set and a black-and-white thing, an old relic. It's funny, but if I turn the TV on, and I'm always turning it on, I turn on the color set. It's funny, don't you think?"

I didn't know what to say to that. I had absolutely nothing to say to that. No opinions. So I watched the news program and tried to listen to what the announcer was saying.

"This is a color TV," the blind man said. "Don't ask me how, but I can tell."

"We traded up a while ago," I said.

The blind man had another taste of his drink. He lifted his beard, sniffed it, and let it fall. He leaned forward on the sofa. He positioned his ashtray on the coffee table, then put the lighter to his cigarette. He leaned back on the sofa and crossed his legs at the ankles.

My wife covered her mouth, and then she yawned. She stretched. She said, "I think I'll go upstairs and put on my robe. I think I'll change into something else. Robert, you make yourself comfortable," she said.

"I'm comfortable," the blind man said.

"I want you to feel comfortable in this house," she said.

"I am comfortable," the blind man said.

After she'd left the room, he and I listened to the weather report and then to the sports roundup. By that time, she'd been gone so long I didn't know if she was going to come back. I thought she might have gone to bed. I wished she'd come back downstairs. I didn't want to be left alone with a blind man. I asked him if he wanted another drink, and he said sure. Then I asked if he wanted to smoke some dope with me. I said I'd just rolled a number. I hadn't, but I planned to do so in about two shakes.

"I'll try some with you," he said.

"Damn right," I said. "That's the stuff."

I got our drinks and sat down on the sofa with him. Then I rolled us two fat numbers. I lit one and passed it. I brought it to his fingers. He took it and inhaled.

"Hold it as long as you can," I said. I could tell he didn't know the first thing.

My wife came back downstairs wearing her pink robe and her pink slippers.

"What do I smell?" she said.

"We thought we'd have us some cannabis," I said.

My wife gave me a savage look. Then she looked at the blind man and said, "Robert, I didn't know you smoked."

He said, "I do now, my dear. There's a first time for everything. But I don't feel anything yet."

"This stuff is pretty mellow," I said. "This stuff is mild. It's dope you can reason with," I said. "It doesn't mess you up."

"Not much it doesn't, bub," he said, and laughed.

My wife sat on the sofa between the blind man and me. I passed her the number. She took it and toked and then passed it back to me. "Which way is this going?" she said. Then she said, "I shouldn't be smoking this. I can hardly keep my eyes open as it is. That dinner did me in. I shouldn't have eaten so much."

"It was the strawberry pie," the blind man said. "That's what did it," he said, and he laughed his big laugh. Then he shook his head.

"There's more strawberry pie," I said.

"Do you want some more, Robert?" my wife said.

"Maybe in a little while," he said.

We gave our attention to the TV. My wife yawned again. She said, "Your bed is made up when you feel like going to bed, Robert. I know you must have had a long day. When you're ready to go to bed, say so." She pulled his arm. "Robert?"

He came to and said, "I've had a real nice time. This beats tapes, doesn't it?"

I said, "Coming at you," and I put the number between his fingers. He inhaled, held the smoke, and then let it go. It was like he'd been doing it since he was nine years old.

"Thanks, bub," he said. "But I think this is all for me. I think I'm beginning to feel it," he said. He held the burning roach out for my wife.

"Same here," she said. "Ditto. Me, too." She took the roach and passed it to me. "I may just sit here for a while between you two guys with my eyes closed. But don't let me bother you, okay? Either one of you. If it bothers you, say so. Otherwise, I may just sit here with my eyes closed until you're ready to go to bed," she said. "Your bed's made up, Robert, when you're ready. It's right next to our room at the top of the stairs. We'll show you up when you're ready. You wake me up now, you guys, if I fall asleep." She said that and then she closed her eyes and went to sleep.

The news program ended. I got up and changed the channel. I sat back down on the sofa. I wished my wife hadn't pooped out. Her head lay across the back of the sofa, her mouth open. She'd turned so that her robe had slipped away from her legs, exposing a juicy thigh. I reached to draw her robe back over her, and it was then that I glanced at the blind man. What the hell! I flipped the robe open again.

"You say when you want some strawberry pie," I said.

"I will," he said.

I said, "Are you tired? Do you want me to take you up to your bed? Are you ready to hit the hay?"

"Not yet," he said. "No, I'll stay up with you, bub. If that's all right. I'll stay up until you're ready to turn in. We haven't had a chance to talk. Know what I mean? I feel like me and her monopolized the evening." He lifted his beard and he let it fall. He picked up his cigarettes and his lighter.

"That's all right," I said. Then I said, "I'm glad for the company."

And I guess I was. Every night I smoked dope and stayed up as long as I could before I fell asleep. My wife and I hardly ever went to bed at the same time. When I did go to sleep, I had these dreams. Sometimes I'd wake up from one of them, my heart going crazy.

Something about the church and the Middle Ages was on the TV. Not your run-of-the-mill TV fare. I wanted to watch something else. I turned to the other channels. But there was nothing on them, either. So I turned back to the first channel and apologized.

"Bub, it's all right," the blind man said. "It's fine with me. Whatever you want to watch is okay. I'm always learning something. Learning never ends. It won't hurt me to learn something tonight. I got ears," he said.

We didn't say anything for a time. He was leaning forward with his head turned at me, his right ear aimed in the direction of the set. Very disconcerting. Now and then his eyelids drooped and then they snapped open again. Now and then he put his fingers into his beard and tugged, like he was thinking about something he was hearing on the television.

On the screen, a group of men wearing cowls was being set upon and tormented by men dressed in skeleton costumes and men dressed as devils. The men dressed as devils wore devil masks, horns, and long tails. This pageant was part of a procession. The Englishman who was narrating the thing said it took place in Spain once a year. I tried to explain to the blind man what was happening.

"Skeletons," he said. "I know about skeletons," he said, and he nodded.

The TV showed this one cathedral. Then there was a long, slow look at another one. Finally, the picture switched to the famous one in Paris, with its flying buttresses and its spires reaching up to the clouds. The camera pulled away to show the whole of the cathedral rising above the skyline.

There were times when the Englishman who was telling the thing would shut up, would simply let the camera move around over the cathedrals. Or else the camera would tour the countryside, men in fields walking behind oxen. I waited as long as I could. Then I felt I had to say something. I said, "They're showing the outside of this cathedral now. Gargoyles. Little statues carved to look like monsters. Now I guess they're in Italy. Yeah, they're in Italy. There's paintings on the walls of this one church."

"Are those fresco paintings, bub?" he asked, and he sipped from his drink.

I reached for my glass. But it was empty. I tried to remember what I could remember. "You're asking me are those frescoes?" I said. "That's a good question. I don't know."

The camera moved to a cathedral outside Lisbon. The differences in the Portuguese cathedral compared with the French and Italian were not that great. But they were there. Mostly the interior stuff. Then something occurred to me, and I said, "Something has occurred to me. Do you have any idea what a cathedral is? What they look like, that is? Do you follow me? If somebody says cathedral to you, do you have any notion what they're talking about? Do you know the difference between that and a Baptist church, say?"

He let the smoke dribble from his mouth. "I know they took hundreds of workers fifty or a hundred years to build," he said. "I just heard the man say that, of course. I know generations of the same families worked on a cathedral. I heard him say that too. The men who began their life's work on them, they never lived to see the completion of their work. In that wise, bub, they're no different from the rest of us, right?" He laughed. Then his eyelids drooped again. His head nodded. He seemed to be snoozing. Maybe he was imagining himself in Portugal. The TV was showing another cathedral now. This one was in Germany. The Englishman's voice droned on. "Cathedrals," the blind man said. He sat up and rolled his head back and forth. "If you want the truth, bub, that's about all I know. What I just said. What I heard him say. But maybe you could describe one to me? I wish you'd do it. I'd like that. If you want to know, I really don't have a good idea."

I stared hard at the shot of the cathedral on the TV. How could I even begin to describe it? But say my life depended on it. Say my life was being threatened by an insane guy who said I had to do it or else.

I stared some more at the cathedral before the picture flipped off into the countryside. There was no use. I turned to the blind man and said, "To begin with, they're very tall." I was looking around the room for clues. "They reach way up. Up and up. Toward the sky. They're so big, some of them, they have to have these supports. To help hold them up, so to speak. These supports are called buttresses. They remind me of viaducts, for some reason. But maybe you don't know viaducts, either? Sometimes the cathedrals have devils and such carved into the front. Sometimes lords and ladies. Don't ask me why this is," I said.

He was nodding. The whole upper part of his body seemed to be moving back and forth.

"I'm not doing so good, am I?" I said.

He stopped nodding and leaned forward on the edge of the sofa. As he listened to me, he was running his fingers through his beard. I wasn't getting through to him, I could see that. But he waited for me to go on just the same. He nodded, like he was trying to encourage me. I tried to think what else to say.

"They're really big," I said. "They're massive. They're built of stone. Marble, too, sometimes. In those olden days, when they built cathedrals, men wanted to be close to God. In those olden days, God was an important part of everyone's life. You could tell this from their cathedral-building. I'm sorry," I said, "but it looks like that's the best I can do for you. I'm just no good at it."

"That's all right, bub," the blind man said. "Hey, listen. I hope you don't mind my asking you. Can I ask you something? Let me ask you a simple question, yes or no. I'm just curious and there's no offense. You're my host. But let me ask if you are in any way religious? You don't mind my asking?"

I shook my head. He couldn't see that, though. A wink is the same as a nod to a blind man. "I guess I don't believe in it. In anything. Sometimes it's hard. You know what I'm saying?"

"Sure I do," he said.

"Right," I said.

The Englishman was still holding forth. My wife sighed in her sleep. She drew a long breath and went on with her sleeping.

"You'll have to forgive me," I said. "But I can't tell you what a cathedral looks like. It just isn't in me to do it. I can't do any more than I've done."

The blind man sat very still, his head down, as he listened to me.

I said, "The truth is, cathedrals don't mean anything special to me. Nothing. Cathedrals. They're something to look at on late-night TV. That's all they are."

It was then that the blind man cleared his throat. He brought something up. He took a handkerchief from his back pocket. Then he said, "I get it, bub. It's okay. It happens. Don't worry about it," he said. "Hey, listen to me. Will you do me a favor? I got an idea. Why don't you find us some heavy paper? And a pen. We'll do something. We'll draw one together. Get us a pen and some heavy paper. Go on, bub, get the stuff," he said.

So I went upstairs. My legs felt like they didn't have any strength in them. They felt like they did after I'd done some running. In my wife's room, I looked around. I found some ballpoints in a little basket on her table. And then I tried to think where to look for the kind of paper he was talking about.

Downstairs, in the kitchen, I found a shopping bag with onion skins in the bottom of the bag. I emptied the bag and shook it. I brought it into the living room and sat down with it near his legs. I moved some things, smoothed the wrinkles from the bag, spread it out on the coffee table.

The blind man got down from the sofa and sat next to me on the carpet.

He ran his fingers over the paper. He went up and down the sides of the paper. The edges, even the edges. He fingered the corners.

"All right," he said. "All right, let's do her."

He found my hand, the hand with the pen. He closed his hand over my hand. "Go ahead, bub, draw," he said. "Draw. You'll see. I'll follow along with you. It'll be okay. Just begin now like I'm telling you. You'll see. Draw," the blind man said.

So I began. First I drew a box that looked like a house. It could have been the house I lived in. Then I put a roof on it. At either end of the roof, I drew spires. Crazy.

"Swell," he said. "Terrific. You're doing fine," he said.

"Never thought anything like this could happen in your lifetime, did you, bub? Well, it's a strange life, we all know that. Go on now. Keep it up."

I put in windows with arches. I drew flying buttresses. I hung great doors. I couldn't stop. The TV station went off the air. I put down the pen and closed and opened my fingers. The blind man felt round over the paper. He moved the tips of his fingers over the paper, all over what I had drawn, and he nodded.

"Doing fine," the blind man said.

I took up the pen again, and he found my hand. I kept at it. I'm no artist. But I kept drawing just the same.

My wife opened up her eyes and gazed at us. She sat up on the sofa, her robe hanging open. She said, "What are you doing? Tell me, I want to know."

I didn't answer her.

The blind man said, "We're drawing a cathedral. Me and him are working on it. Press hard," he said to me. "That's right. That's good," he said. "Sure. You got it, bub. I can tell. You didn't think you could. But you can, can't you? You're cooking with gas now. You know what I'm saying? We're going to really have us something here in a minute. How's the old arm?" he said. "Put some people in there now. What's a cathedral without people?"

My wife said, "What's going on? Robert, what are you doing? What's going on?"

"It's all right," he said to her. "Close your eyes now," the blind man said to me.

I did it. I closed them just like he said.

"Are they closed? he said. "Don't fudge."

"They're closed," I said.

"Keep them that way," he said. He said, "Don't stop now. Draw."

So we kept on with it. His fingers rode my fingers as my hand went over the paper. It was like nothing else in my life up to now.

Then he said, "I think that's it. I think you got it," he said. "Take a look. What do you think?"

But I had my eyes closed. I thought I'd keep them that way for a little longer. I thought it was something I ought to do.

"Well?" he said. "Are you looking?"

My eyes were still closed. I was in my house. I knew that. But I didn't feel like I was inside anything.

"It's really something," I said.

The Bath   1981

Saturday afternoon the mother drove to the bakery in the shopping center. After looking through a loose-leaf binder with photographs of cakes taped onto the pages, she ordered chocolate, the child's favorite. The cake she chose was decorated with a spaceship and a launching pad under a sprinkling of white stars. The name SCOTTY would be iced on in green as if it were the name of the spaceship.

The baker listened thoughtfully when the mother told him Scotty would be eight years old. He was an older man, this baker, and he wore a curious apron, a heavy thing with loops that went under his arms and around his back and then crossed in front again where they were tied in a very thick knot. He kept wiping his hands on the front of the apron as he listened to the woman, his wet eyes examining her lips as she studied the samples and talked.

He let her take her time. He was in no hurry.

The mother decided on the spaceship cake, and then she gave the baker her name and her telephone number. The cake would be ready Monday morning, in plenty of time for the party Monday afternoon. This was all the baker was willing to say. No pleasantries, just this small exchange, the barest information, nothing that was not necessary.

Monday morning, the boy was walking to school. He was in the company of another boy, the two boys passing a bag of potato chips back and forth between them. The birthday boy was trying to trick the other boy into telling what he was going to give in the way of a present.

At an intersection, without looking, the birthday boy stepped off the curb, and was promptly knocked down by a car. He fell on his side, his head in the gutter, his legs in the road moving as if he were climbing a wall.

The other boy stood holding the potato chips. He was wondering if he should finish the rest or continue on to school.

The birthday boy did not cry. But neither did he wish to talk anymore. He would not answer when the other boy asked what it felt like to be hit by a car. The birthday boy got up and turned back for home, at which time the other boy waved good-bye and headed off for school.

The birthday boy told his mother what had happened. They sat together on the sofa. She held his hands in her lap. This is what she was doing when the boy pulled his hands away and lay down on his back.

Of course, the birthday party never happened. The birthday boy was in the hospital instead. The mother sat by the bed. She was waiting for the boy to wake up. The father hurried over from his office. He sat next to the mother. So now the both of them waited for the boy to wake up. They waited for hours, and then the father went home to take a bath.

The man drove home from the hospital. He drove the streets faster than he should. It had been a good life till now. There had been work, fatherhood, family. The man had been lucky and happy. But fear made him want a bath.

He pulled into the driveway. He sat in the car trying to make his legs work. The child had been hit by a car and he was in the hospital, but he was going to be all right. The man got out of the car and went up to the door. The dog was barking and the telephone was ringing. It kept ringing while the man unlocked the door and felt the wall for the light switch.

He picked up the receiver. He said, "I just got in the door!"

"There's a cake that wasn't picked up."

This is what the voice on the other end said.

"What are you saying?" the father said.

"The cake," the voice said. "Sixteen dollars."

The husband held the receiver against his ear, trying to understand. He said, "I don't know anything about it."

"Don't hand me that," the voice said.

The husband hung up the telephone. He went into the kitchen and poured himself some whiskey. He called the hospital.

The child's condition remained the same.

While the water ran into the tub, the man lathered his face and shaved. He was in the tub when he heard the telephone again. He got himself out and hurried through the house, saying, "Stupid, stupid," because he wouldn't be doing this if he'd stayed where he was in the hospital. He picked up the receiver and shouted, "Hello!"

The voice said, "It's ready."

The father got back to the hospital after midnight. The wife was sitting in the chair by the bed. She looked up at the husband and then she looked back at the child. From an apparatus over the bed hung a bottle with a tube running from the bottle to the child.

"What's this?" the father said.

"Glucose," the mother said.

The husband put his hand to the back of the woman's head.

"He's going to wake up," the man said.

"I know," the woman said.

In a little while the man said, "Go home and let me take over."

She shook her head. "No," she said.

"Really," he said. "Go home for a while. You don't have to worry. He's sleeping, is all."

A nurse pushed open the door. She nodded to them as she went to the bed. She took the left arm out from under the covers and put her fingers on the wrist. She put the arm back under the covers and wrote on the clipboard attached to the bed.

"How is he?" the mother said.

"Stable," the nurse said. Then she said, "Doctor will be in again shortly."

"I was saying maybe she'd want to go home and get a little rest," the man said. "After the doctor comes."

"She could do that," the nurse said.

The woman said, "We'll see what the doctor says." She brought her hand up to her eyes and leaned her head forward.

The nurse said, "Of course."

The father gazed at his son, the small chest inflating and deflating under the covers. He felt more fear now. He began shaking his head. He talked to himself like this. The child is fine. Instead of sleeping at home, he's doing it here. Sleep is the same wherever you do it.

The doctor came in. He shook hands with the man. The woman got up from the chair.

"Ann," the doctor said and nodded. The doctor said, "Let's just see how he's doing." He moved to the bed and touched the boy's wrist. He peeled back an eyelid and then the other. He turned back the covers and listened to the heart. He pressed his fingers here and there on the body. He went to the end of the bed and studied the chart. He noted the time, scribbled on the chart, and then he considered the mother and the father.

This doctor was a handsome man. His skin was moist and tan. He wore a three-piece suit, a vivid tie, and on his shirt were cufflinks.

The mother was talking to herself like this. He has just come from somewhere with an audience. They gave him a special medal.

The doctor said, "Nothing to shout about, but nothing to worry about. He should wake up pretty soon." The doctor looked at the boy again. "We'll know more after the tests are in."

"Oh, no," the mother said.

The doctor said, "Sometimes you see this."

The father said, "You wouldn't call this a coma, then?"

The father waited and looked at the doctor.

"No, I don't want to call it that," the doctor said. "He's sleeping. It's restorative. The body is doing what it has to do."

"It's a coma," the mother said. "A kind of coma."

The doctor said, "I wouldn't call it that."

He took the woman's hands and patted them. He shook hands with the husband.

The woman put her fingers on the child's forehead and kept them there for a while. "At least he doesn't have a fever," she said. Then she said, "I don't know. Feel his head."

The man put his fingers on the boy's forehead. The man said, "I think he's supposed to feel this way."

The woman stood there awhile longer, working her lip with her teeth. Then she moved to her chair and sat down.

The husband sat in the chair beside her. He wanted to say something else. But there was no saying what it should be. He took her hand and put it in his lap. This made him feel better. It made him feel he was saying something. They sat like that for a while, watching the boy, not talking. From time to time he squeezed her hand until she took it away.

"I've been praying," she said.

"Me too," the father said. "I've been praying too."

A nurse came back in and checked the flow from the bottle.

A doctor came in and said what his name was. This doctor was wearing loafers.

"We're going to take him downstairs for more pictures," he said. "And we want to do a scan."

"A scan?" the mother said. She stood between this new doctor and the bed.

"It's nothing," he said.

"My God," she said.

Two orderlies came in. They wheeled a thing like a bed. They unhooked the boy from the tube and slid him over onto the thing with wheels.

It was after sunup when they brought the birthday boy back out. The mother and father followed the orderlies into the elevator and up to the room. Once more the parents took up their places next to the bed.

They waited all day. The boy did not wake up. The doctor came again and examined the boy again and left after saying the same things again. Nurses came in. Doctors came in. A technician came in and took blood.

"I don't understand this," the mother said to the technician.

"Doctor's orders," the technician said.

The mother went to the window and looked out at the parking lot. Cars with their lights on were driving in and out. She stood at the window with her hands on the sill. She was talking to herself like this. We're into something now, something hard.

She was afraid.

She saw a car stop and a woman in a long coat get into it. She made believe she was that woman. She made believe she was driving away from here to someplace else.

The doctor came in. He looked tanned and healthier than ever. He went to the bed and examined the boy. He said, "His signs are fine. Everything's good."

The mother said, "But he's sleeping."

"Yes," the doctor said.

The husband said, "She's tired. She's starved."

The doctor said, "She should rest. She should eat. Ann," the doctor said.

"Thank you," the husband said.

He shook hands with the doctor and the doctor patted their shoulders and left.

"I suppose one of us should go home and check on things," the man said. "The dog needs to be fed."

"Call the neighbors," the wife said. "Someone will feed him if you ask them to."

She tried to think who. She closed her eyes and tried to think anything at all. After a time she said, "Maybe I'll do it. Maybe if I'm not here watching, he'll wake up. Maybe it's because I'm watching that he won't."

"That could be it," the husband said.

"I'll go home and take a bath and put on something clean," the woman said.

"I think you should do that," the man said.

She picked up her purse. He helped her into her coat. She moved to the door, and looked back. She looked at the child, and then she looked at the father. The husband nodded and smiled.

• • •

She went past the nurses' station and down to the end of the corridor, where she turned and saw a little waiting room, a family in there, all sitting in wicker chairs, a man in a khaki shirt, a baseball cap pushed back on his head, a large woman wearing a housedress, slippers, a girl in jeans, hair in dozens of kinky braids, the table littered with flimsy wrappers and styrofoam and coffee sticks and packets of salt and pepper.

"Nelson," the woman said. "Is it about Nelson?"

The woman's eyes widened.

"Tell me now, lady," the woman said. "Is it about Nelson?"

The woman was trying to get up from her chair. But the man had his hand closed over her arm.

"Here, here," the man said.

"I'm sorry," the mother said. "I'm looking for the elevator. My son is in the hospital. I can't find the elevator."

"Elevator is down that way," the man said, and he aimed a finger in the right direction.

"My son was hit by a car," the mother said. "But he's going to be all right. He's in shock now, but it might be some kind of coma too. That's what worries us, the coma part, I'm going out for a little while. Maybe I'll take a bath. But my husband is with him. He's watching. There's a chance everything will change when I'm gone. My name is Ann Weiss."

The man shifted in his chair. He shook his head.

He said, "Our Nelson."

She pulled into the driveway. The dog ran out from behind the house. He ran in circles on the grass. She closed her eyes and leaned her head against the wheel. She listened to the ticking of the engine.

She got out of the car and went to the door. She turned on lights and put on water for tea. She opened a can and fed the dog. She sat down on the sofa with her tea.

The telephone rang.

"Yes!" she said. "Hello!" she said.

"Mrs. Weiss," a man's voice said.

"Yes," she said. "This is Mrs. Weiss. Is it about Scotty?" she said.

"Scotty," the voice said. "It is about Scotty," the voice said. "It has to do with Scotty, yes."

A Small, Good Thing   1983

Saturday afternoon she drove to the bakery in the shopping center. After looking through a loose-leaf binder with photographs of cakes taped onto the pages, she ordered chocolate, the child's favorite. The cake she chose was decorated with a space ship and launching pad under a sprinkling of white stars, and a planet made of red frosting at the other end. His name, SCOTTY, would be in green letters beneath the planet. The baker, who was an older man with a thick neck, listened without saying anything when she told him the child would be eight years old next Monday. The baker wore a white apron that looked like a smock. Straps cut under his arms, went around in back and then to the front again, where they were secured under his heavy waist. He wiped his hands on his apron as he listened to her. He kept his eyes down on the photographs and let her talk. He let her take her time. He'd just come to work and he'd be there all night, baking, and he was in no real hurry.

She gave the baker her name, Ann Weiss, and her telephone number. The cake would be ready on Monday morning, just out of the oven, in plenty of time for the child's party that afternoon. The baker was not jolly. There were no pleasantries between them, just the minimum exchange of words, the necessary information. He made her feel uncomfortable, and she didn't like that. While he was bent over the counter with the pencil in his hand, she studied his coarse features and wondered if he'd ever done anything else with his life besides be a baker. She was a mother and thirty-three years old, and it seemed to her that everyone, especially someone the baker's age—a man old enough to be her father—must have children who'd gone through this special time of cakes and birthday parties. There must be that between them, she thought. But he was abrupt with her—not rude, just abrupt. She gave up trying to make friends with him. She looked into the back of the bakery and could see a long, heavy wooden table with aluminum pie pans stacked at one end; and beside the table a metal container filled with empty racks. There was an enormous oven. A radio was playing country-Western music.

The baker finished printing the information on the special order card and closed up the binder. He looked at her and said, "Monday morning." She thanked him and drove home.

On Monday morning, the birthday boy was walking to school with another boy. They were passing a bag of potato chips back and forth and the birthday boy was trying to find out what his friend intended to give him for his birthday that afternoon. Without looking, the birthday boy stepped off the curb at an intersection and was immediately knocked down by a car. He fell on his side with his head in the gutter and his legs out in the road. His eyes were closed, but his legs moved back and forth as if he were trying to climb over something. His friend dropped the potato chips and started to cry. The car had gone a hundred feet or so and stopped in the middle of the road. The man in the driver's seat looked back over his shoulder. He waited until the boy got unsteadily to his feet. The boy wobbled a little. He looked dazed, but okay. The driver put the car into gear and drove away.

The birthday boy didn't cry, but he didn't have anything to say about anything either. He wouldn't answer when his friend asked him what it felt like to be hit by a car. He walked home, and his friend went on to school. But after the birthday boy was inside his house and was telling his mother about it—she sitting beside him on the sofa, holding his hands in her lap, saying, "Scotty, honey, are you sure you feel all right, baby?" thinking she would call the doctor anyway—he suddenly lay back on the sofa, closed his eyes, and went limp. When she couldn't wake him up, she hurried to the telephone and called her husband at work. Howard told her to remain calm, remain calm, and then he called an ambulance for the child and left for the hospital himself.

Of course, the birthday party was canceled. The child was in the hospital with a mild concussion and suffering from shock. There'd been vomiting, and his lungs had taken in fluid which needed pumping out that afternoon. Now he simply seemed to be in a very deep sleep—but no coma, Dr. Francis had emphasized, no coma, when he saw the alarm in the parents' eyes. At eleven o'clock that night, when the boy seemed to be resting comfortably enough after the many X-rays and the lab work, and it was just a matter of his waking up and coming around, Howard left the hospital. He and Ann had been at the hospital with the child since that afternoon, and he was going home for a short while to bathe and change clothes. "I'll be back in an hour," he said. She nodded. "It's fine," she said. "I'll be right here." He kissed her on the forehead, and they touched hands. She sat in the chair beside the bed and looked at the child. She was waiting for him to wake up and be all right. Then she could begin to relax.

Howard drove home from the hospital. He took the wet, dark streets very fast, then caught himself and slowed down. Until now, his life had gone smoothly and to his satisfaction—college, marriage, another year of college for the advanced degree in business, a junior partnership in an investment firm. Fatherhood. He was happy and, so far, lucky—he knew that. His parents were still living, his brothers and his sister were established, his friends from college had gone out to take their places in the world. So far, he had kept away from any real harm, from those forces he knew existed and that could cripple or bring down a man if the luck went bad, if things suddenly turned. He pulled into the driveway and parked. His left leg began to tremble. He sat in the car for a minute and tried to deal with the present situation in a rational manner. Scotty had been hit by a car and was in the hospital, but he was going to be all right. Howard closed his eyes and ran his hand over his face. He got out of the car and went up to the front door. The dog was barking inside the house. The telephone rang and rang while he unlocked the door and fumbled for the light switch. He shouldn't have left the hospital, he shouldn't have. "Goddamn it!" he said. He picked up the receiver and said, "I just walked in the door!"

"There's a cake here that wasn't picked up," the voice on the other end of the line said.

"What are you saying?" Howard asked.

"A cake," the voice said. "A sixteen-dollar cake."

Howard held the receiver against his ear, trying to understand. "I don't know anything about a cake," he said. "Jesus, what are you talking about?"

"Don't hand me that," the voice said.

Howard hung up the telephone. He went into the kitchen and poured himself some whiskey. He called the hospital. But the child's condition remained the same; he was still sleeping and nothing had changed there. While water poured into the tub, Howard lathered his face and shaved. He'd just stretched out in the tub and closed his eyes when the telephone rang again. He hauled himself out, grabbed a towel, and hurried through the house, saying, "Stupid, stupid," for having left the hospital. But when he picked up the receiver and shouted, "Hello!" there was no sound at the other end of the line. Then the caller hung up.

He arrived back at the hospital a little after midnight. Ann still sat in the chair beside the bed. She looked up at Howard, and then she looked back at the child. The child's eyes stayed closed, the head was still wrapped in bandages. His breathing was quiet and regular. From an apparatus over the bed hung a bottle of glucose with a tube running from the bottle to the boy's arm.

"How is he?" Howard said. "What's all this?" waving at the glucose and the tube.

"Dr. Francis's orders," she said. "He needs nourishment. He needs to keep up his strength. Why doesn't he wake up, Howard? I don't understand, if he's all right."

Howard put his hand against the back of her head. He ran his fingers through her hair. "He's going to be all right. He'll wake up in a little while. Dr. Francis knows what's what."

After a time, he said, "Maybe you should go home and get some rest. I'll stay here. Just don't put up with this creep who keeps calling. Hang up right away."

"Who's calling?" she asked.

"I don't know who, just somebody with nothing better to do than call up people. You go on now."

She shook her head. "No," she said, "I'm fine."

"Really," he said. "Go home for a while, and then come back and spell me in the morning. It'll be all right. What did Dr. Francis say? He said Scotty's going to be all right. We don't have to worry. He's just sleeping now, that's all."

A nurse pushed the door open. She nodded at them as she went to the bedside. She took the left arm out from under the covers and put her fingers on the wrist, found the pulse, then consulted her watch. In a little while, she put the arm back under the covers and moved to the foot of the bed, where she wrote something on a clipboard attached to the bed.

"How is he?" Ann said. Howard's hand was a weight on her shoulder. She was aware of the pressure from his fingers.

"He's stable," the nurse said. Then she said, "Doctor will be in again shortly. Doctor's back in the hospital. He's making rounds right now."

"I was saying maybe she'd want to go home and get a little rest," Howard said. "After the doctor comes," he said.

"She could do that," the nurse said. "I think you should both feel free to do that, if you wish." The nurse was a big Scandinavian woman with blond hair. There was the trace of an accent in her speech.

"We'll see what the doctor says," Ann said. "I want to talk to the doctor. I don't think he should keep sleeping like this. I don't think that's a good sign." She brought her hand up to her eyes and let her head come forward a little. Howard's grip tightened on her shoulder, and then his hand moved up to her neck, where his fingers began to knead the muscles there.

"Dr. Francis will be here in a few minutes," the nurse said. Then she left the room.

Howard gazed at his son for a time, the small chest quietly rising and falling under the covers. For the first time since the terrible minutes after Ann's telephone call to him at his office, he felt a genuine fear starting in his limbs. He began shaking his head. Scotty was fine, but instead of sleeping at home in his own bed, he was in a hospital bed with bandages around his head and a tube in his arm. But this help was what he needed right now.

Dr. Francis came in and shook hands with Howard, though they'd just seen each other a few hours before. Ann got up from the chair. "Doctor?"

"Ann," he said and nodded. "Let's just first see how he's doing," the doctor said. He moved to the side of the bed and took the boy's pulse. He peeled back one eyelid and then the other. Howard and Ann stood beside the doctor and watched. Then the doctor turned back the covers and listened to the boy's heart and lungs with his stethoscope. He pressed his fingers here and there on the abdomen. When he was finished, he went to the end of the bed and studied the chart. He noted the time, scribbled something on the chart, and then looked at Howard and Ann.

"Doctor, how is he?" Howard said. "What's the matter with him exactly?"

"Why doesn't he wake up?" Ann said.

The doctor was a handsome, big-shouldered man with a tanned face. He wore a three-piece blue suit, a striped tie, and ivory cufflinks. His gray hair was combed along the sides of his head, and he looked as if he had just come from a concert. "He's all right," the doctor said. "Nothing to shout about, he could be better, I think. But he's all right. Still, I wish he'd wake up. He should wake up pretty soon." The doctor looked at the boy again. "We'll know some more in a couple of hours, after the results of a few more tests are in. But he's all right, believe me, except for the hairline fracture of the skull. He does have that."

"Oh, no," Ann said.

"And a bit of a concussion, as I said before. Of course, you know he's in shock," the doctor said. "Sometimes you see this in shock cases. This sleeping."

"But he's out of any real danger?" Howard said. "You said before he's not in a coma. You wouldn't call this a coma, then—would you, doctor?" Howard waited. He looked at the doctor.

"No, I don't want to call it a coma," the doctor said and glanced over at the boy once more. "He's just in a very deep sleep. It's a restorative measure the body is taking on its own. He's out of any real danger, I'd say that for certain, yes. But we'll know more when he wakes up and the other tests are in," the doctor said.

"It's a coma," Ann said. "Of sorts."

"It's not a coma yet, not exactly," the doctor said. "I wouldn't want to call it coma. Not yet, anyway. He's suffered shock. In shock cases, this kind of reaction is common enough; it's a temporary reaction to bodily trauma. Coma. Well, coma is a deep, prolonged unconsciousness, something that could go on for days, or weeks even. Scotty's not in that area, not as far as we can tell. I'm certain his condition will show improvement by morning. I'm betting that it will. We'll know more when he wakes up, which shouldn't be long now. Of course, you may do as you like, stay here or go home for a time. But by all means feel free to leave the hospital for a while if you want. This is not easy, I know." The doctor gazed at the boy again, watching him, and then he turned to Ann and said, "You try not to worry, little mother. Believe me, we're doing all that can be done. It's just a question of a little more time now." He nodded at her, shook hands with Howard again, and then he left the room.

Ann put her hand over the child's forehead. "At least he doesn't have a fever," she said. Then she said, "My God, he feels so cold, though. Howard? Is he supposed to feel like this? Feel his head."

Howard touched the child's temples. His own breathing had slowed. "I think he's supposed to feel this way right now," he said. "He's in shock, remember? That's what the doctor said. The doctor was just in here. He would have said something if Scotty wasn't okay."

Ann stood there a while longer, working her lip with her teeth. Then she moved over to her chair and sat down.

Howard sat in the chair next to her chair. They looked at each other. He wanted to say something else and reassure her, but he was afraid, too. He took her hand and put it in his lap, and this made him feel better, her hand being there. He picked up her hand and squeezed it. Then he just held her hand. They sat like that for a while, watching the boy and not talking. From time to time, he squeezed her hand. Finally, she took her hand away.

"I've been praying," she said.

He nodded.

She said, "I almost thought I'd forgotten how, but it came back to me. All I had to do was close my eyes and say, 'Please God, help us—help Scotty,' and then the rest was easy. The words were right there. Maybe if you prayed, too," she said to him.

"I've already prayed," he said. "I prayed this afternoon—yesterday afternoon, I mean—after you called, while I was driving to the hospital. I've been praying," he said.

"That's good," she said. For the first time, she felt they were together in it, this trouble. She realized with a start that, until now, it had only been happening to her and to Scotty. She hadn't let Howard into it, though he was there and needed all along. She felt glad to be his wife.

The same nurse came in and took the boy's pulse again and checked the flow from the bottle hanging above the bed.

In an hour, another doctor came in. He said his name was Parsons, from Radiology. He had a bushy mustache. He was wearing loafers, a Western shirt, and a pair of jeans.

"We're going to take him downstairs for more pictures," he told them. "We need to do some more pictures, and we want to do a scan."

"What's that?" Ann said. "A scan?" She stood between this new doctor and the bed. "I thought you'd already taken all your X-rays."

"I'm afraid we need some more," he said. "Nothing to be alarmed about. We just need some more pictures, and we want to do a brain scan on him."

"My God," Ann said.

"It's perfectly normal procedure in cases like this," this new doctor said. "We just need to find out for sure why he isn't back awake yet. It's normal medical procedure, and nothing to be alarmed about. We'll be taking him down in a few minutes," this doctor said.

In a little while, two orderlies came into the room with a gurney. They were black-haired, dark-complexioned men in white uniforms, and they said a few words to each other in a foreign tongue as they unhooked the boy from the tube and moved him from his bed to the gurney. Then they wheeled him from the room. Howard and Ann got on the same elevator. Ann gazed at the child. She closed her eyes as the elevator began its descent. The orderlies stood at either end of the gurney without saying anything, though once one of the men made a comment to the other in their own language, and the other man nodded slowly in response.

Later that morning, just as the sun was beginning to lighten the windows in the waiting room outside the X-ray department, they brought the boy out and moved him back up to his room. Howard and Ann rode up on the elevator with him once more, and once more they took up their places beside the bed.

They waited all day, but still the boy did not wake up. Occasionally, one of them would leave the room to go downstairs to the cafeteria to drink coffee and then, as if suddenly remembering and feeling guilty, get up from the table and hurry back to the room. Dr. Francis came again that afternoon and examined the boy once more and then left after telling them he was coming along and could wake up at any minute now. Nurses, different nurses from the night before, came in from time to time. Then a young woman from the lab knocked and entered the room. She wore white slacks and a white blouse and carried a little tray of things which she put on the stand beside the bed. Without a word to them, she took blood from the boy's arm. Howard closed his eyes as the woman found the right place on the boy's arm and pushed the needle in.

"I don't understand this," Ann said to the woman.

"Doctor's orders," the young woman said. "I do what I'm told. They say draw that one, I draw. What's wrong with him, anyway?" she said. "He's a sweetie."

"He was hit by a car," Howard said. "A hit-and-run."

The young woman shook her head and looked again at the boy. Then she took her tray and left the room.

"Why won't he wake up?" Ann said. "Howard? I want some answers from these people."

Howard didn't say anything. He sat down again in the chair and crossed one leg over the other. He rubbed his face. He looked at his son and then he settled back in the chair, closed his eyes, and went to sleep.

Ann walked to the window and looked out at the parking lot. It was night, and cars were driving into and out of the parking lot with their lights on. She stood at the window with her hands gripping the sill, and knew in her heart that they were into something now, something hard. She was afraid, and her teeth began to chatter until she tightened her jaws. She saw a big car stop in front of the hospital and someone, a woman in a long coat, get into the car. She wished she were that woman and somebody, anybody, was driving her away from here to somewhere else, a place where she would find Scotty waiting for her when she stepped out of the car, ready to say *Mom* and let her gather him in her arms.

In a little while, Howard woke up. He looked at the boy again. Then he got up from the chair, stretched, and went over to stand beside her at the window. They both stared out at the parking lot. They didn't say anything. But they seemed to feel each other's insides now, as though the worry had made them transparent in a perfectly natural way.

The door opened and Dr. Francis came in. He was wearing a different suit and tie this time. His gray hair was combed along the sides of his head, and he looked as if he had just shaved. He went straight to the bed and examined the boy. "He ought to have come around by now. There's just no good reason for this," he said. "But I can tell you we're all convinced he's out of any danger. We'll just feel better when he wakes up. There's no reason, absolutely none, why he shouldn't come around. Very soon. Oh, he'll have himself a dilly of a headache when he does, you can count on that. But all of his signs are fine. They're as normal as can be."

"It is a coma, then?" Ann said.

The doctor rubbed his smooth cheek. "We'll call it that for the time being, until he wakes up. But you must be worn out. This is hard. I know this is hard. Feel free to go out for a bite," he said. "It would do you good. I'll put a nurse in here while you're gone if you'll feel better about going. Go and have yourselves something to eat."

"I couldn't eat anything," Ann said.

"Do what you need to do, of course," the doctor said. "Anyway, I wanted to tell you that all the signs are good, the tests are negative, nothing showed up at all, and just as soon as he wakes up he'll be over the hill."

"Thank you, doctor," Howard said. He shook hands with the doctor again. The doctor patted Howard's shoulder and went out.

"I suppose one of us should go home and check on things," Howard said. "Slug needs to be fed, for one thing."

"Call one of the neighbors," Ann said. "Call the Morgans. Anyone will feed a dog if you ask them to."

"All right," Howard said. After a while, he said, "Honey, why don't you do it? Why don't you go home and check on things, and then come back? It'll do you good. I'll be right here with him. Seriously," he said. "We need to keep up our strength on this. We'll want to be here for a while even after he wakes up."

"Why don't *you* go?" she said. "Feed Slug. Feed yourself."

"I already went," he said. "I was gone for exactly an hour and fifteen minutes. You go home for an hour and freshen up. Then come back."

She tried to think about it, but she was too tired. She closed her eyes and tried to think about it again. After a time, she said, "Maybe I will go home for a few minutes. Maybe if I'm not just sitting right here watching him every second, he'll wake up and be all right. You know? Maybe he'll wake up if I'm not here. I'll go home and take a bath and put on clean clothes. I'll feed Slug. Then I'll come back."

"I'll be right here," he said. "You go on home, honey. I'll keep an eye on things here." His eyes were bloodshot and small, as if he'd been drinking for a long time. His clothes were rumpled. His beard had come out again. She touched his face; and then she took her hand back. She understood he wanted to be by himself for a while, not have to talk or share his worry for a time. She picked her purse up from the nightstand, and he helped her into her coat.

"I won't be gone long," she said.

"Just sit and rest for a little while when you get home," he said. "Eat something. Take a bath. After you get out of the bath, just sit for a while and rest. It'll do you a world of good, you'll see. Then come back," he said. "Let's try not to worry. You heard what Dr. Francis said."

She stood in her coat for a minute trying to recall the doctor's exact words, looking for any nuances, any hint of something behind his words other than what he had said. She tried to remember if his expression had changed any when he bent over to examine the child. She remembered the way his features had composed themselves as he rolled back the child's eyelids and then listened to his breathing.

She went to the door, where she turned and looked back. She looked at the child, and then she looked at the father. Howard nodded. She stepped out of the room and pulled the door closed behind her.

She went past the nurses' station and down to the end of the corridor, looking for the elevator. At the end of the corridor, she turned to her right and entered a little waiting room where a Negro family sat in wicker chairs. There was a middle-aged man in a khaki shirt and pants, a baseball cap pushed back on his head. A large woman wearing a housedress and slippers was slumped in one of the chairs. A teenaged girl in jeans, hair done in dozens of little braids, lay stretched out in one of the chairs smoking a cigarette, her legs crossed at the ankles. The family swung their eyes to Ann as she entered the room. The little table was littered with hamburger wrappers and Styrofoam cups.

"Franklin," the large woman said as she roused herself. "Is it about Franklin?" Her eyes widened. "Tell me now, lady," the woman said. "Is it about Franklin?" She was trying to rise from her chair, but the man had closed his hand over her arm.

"Here, here," he said. "Evelyn."

"I'm sorry," Ann said. "I'm looking for the elevator. My son is in the hospital, and now I can't find the elevator."

"Elevator is down that way, turn left," the man said as he aimed a finger.

The girl drew on her cigarette and stared at Ann. Her eyes were narrowed to slits, and her broad lips parted slowly as she let the smoke escape. The Negro woman let her head fall on her shoulder and looked away from Ann, no longer interested.

"My son was hit by a car," Ann said to the man. She seemed to need to explain herself. "He has a concussion and a little skull fracture, but he's going to be all right. He's in shock now, but it might be some kind of coma, too. That's what really worries us, the coma part. I'm going out for a little while, but my husband is with him. Maybe he'll wake up while I'm gone."

"That's too bad," the man said and shifted in the chair. He shook his head. He looked down at the table, and then he looked back at Ann. She was still standing there. He said, "Our Franklin, he's on the operating table. Somebody cut him. Tried to kill him. There was a fight where he was at. At this party. They say he was just standing and watching. Not bothering nobody. But that don't mean nothing these days. Now he's on the operating table. We're just hoping and praying, that's all we can do now." He gazed at her steadily.

Ann looked at the girl again, who was still watching her, and at the older woman, who kept her head down, but whose eyes were now closed. Ann saw the lips moving silently, making words. She had an urge to ask what those words were. She wanted to talk more with these people who were in the same kind of waiting she was in. She was afraid, and they were afraid. They had that in common. She would have liked to have said something else about the accident, told them more about Scotty, that it had happened on the day of his birthday, Monday, and that he was still unconscious. Yet she didn't know how to begin. She stood looking at them without saying anything more.

She went down the corridor the man had indicated and found the elevator. She waited a minute in front of the closed doors, still wondering if she was doing the right thing. Then she put out her finger and touched the button.

She pulled into the driveway and cut the engine. She closed her eyes and leaned her head against the wheel for a minute. She listened to the ticking sounds the engine made as it began to cool. Then she got out of the car. She could hear the dog barking inside the house. She went to the front door, which was unlocked. She went inside and turned on lights and put on a kettle of water for tea. She opened some dogfood and fed Slug on the back porch. The dog ate in hungry little smacks. It kept running into the kitchen to see that she was going to stay. As she sat down on the sofa with her tea, the telephone rang.

"Yes!" she said as she answered. "Hello!"

"Mrs. Weiss," a man's voice said. It was five o'clock in the morning, and she thought she could hear machinery or equipment of some kind in the background.

"Yes, yes! What is it?" she said. "This is Mrs. Weiss. This is she. What is it, please?" She listened to whatever it was in the background. "Is it Scotty, for Christ's sake?"

"Scotty," the man's voice said. "It's about Scotty, yes. It has to do with Scotty, that problem. Have you forgotten about Scotty?" the man said. Then he hung up.

She dialed the hospital's number and asked for the third floor. She demanded information about her son from the nurse who answered the telephone. Then she asked to speak to her husband. It was, she said, an emergency.

She waited, turning the telephone cord in her fingers. She closed her eyes and felt sick at her stomach. She would have to make herself eat. Slug came in from the back porch and lay down near her feet. He wagged his tail. She pulled at his ear while he licked her fingers. Howard was on the line.

"Somebody just called here," she said. She twisted the telephone cord. "He said it was about Scotty," she cried.

"Scotty's fine," Howard told her. "I mean, he's still sleeping. There's been no change. The nurse has been in twice since you've been gone. A nurse or else a doctor. He's all right."

"This man called. He said it was about Scotty," she told him.

"Honey, you rest for a little while, you need the rest. It must be that same caller I had. Just forget it. Come back down here after you've rested. Then we'll have breakfast or something. "

"Breakfast," she said. "I don't want any breakfast."

"You know what I mean," he said. "Juice, something. I don't know. I don't know anything, Ann. Jesus, I'm not hungry, either. Ann, it's hard to talk now. I'm standing here at the desk. Dr. Francis is coming again at eight o'clock this morning. He's going to have something to tell us then, something more definite. That's what one of the nurses said. She didn't know any more than that. Ann? Honey, maybe we'll know something more then. At eight o'clock. Come back here before eight. Meanwhile, I'm right here and Scotty's all right. He's still the same," he added.

"I was drinking a cup of tea," she said, "when the telephone rang. They said it was about Scotty. There was a noise in the background. Was there a noise in the background on that call you had, Howard?"

"I don't remember," he said. "Maybe the driver of the car, maybe he's a psychopath and found out about Scotty somehow. But I'm here with him. Just rest like you were going to do. Take a bath and come back by seven or so, and we'll talk to the doctor together when he gets here. It's going to be all right, honey. I'm here, and there are doctors and nurses around. They say his condition is stable."

"I'm scared to death," she said.

She ran water, undressed, and got into the tub. She washed and dried quickly, not taking the time to wash her hair. She put on clean underwear, wool slacks, and a sweater. She went into the living room, where the dog looked up at her and let its tail thump once against the floor. It was just starting to get light outside when she went out to the car.

She drove into the parking lot of the hospital and found a space close to the front door. She felt she was in some obscure way responsible for what had happened to the child. She let her thoughts move to the Negro family. She remembered the name Franklin and the table that was covered with hamburger papers, and the teenaged girl staring at her as she drew on her cigarette. "Don't have children," she told the girl's image as she entered the front door of the hospital. "For God's sake, don't."

She took the elevator up to the third floor with two nurses who were just going on duty. It was Wednesday morning, a few minutes before seven. There was a page for a Dr. Madison as the elevator doors slid open on the third floor. She got off behind the nurses, who turned in the other direction and continued the conversation she had interrupted when she'd gotten into the elevator. She walked down the corridor to the little alcove where the Negro family had been waiting. They were gone now, but the chairs were scattered in such a way that it looked as if people had just jumped up from them the minute before. The tabletop was cluttered with the same cups and papers, the ashtray was filled with cigarette butts.

She stopped at the nurses' station. A nurse was standing behind the counter, brushing her hair and yawning.

"There was a Negro boy in surgery last night," Ann said. "Franklin was his name. His family was in the waiting room. I'd like to inquire about his condition."

A nurse who was sitting at a desk behind the counter looked up from a chart in front of her. The telephone buzzed and she picked up the receiver, but she kept her eyes on Ann.

"He passed away," said the nurse at the counter. The nurse held the hair-brush and kept looking at her. "Are you a friend of the family or what?"

"I met the family last night," Ann said. "My own son is in the hospital. I guess he's in shock. We don't know for sure what's wrong. I just wondered about Franklin, that's all. Thank you." She moved down the corridor. Elevator doors the same color as the walls slid open and a gaunt, bald man in white pants and white canvas shoes pulled a heavy cart off the elevator. She hadn't noticed these doors last night. The man wheeled the cart out into the corridor and stopped in front of the room nearest the elevator and consulted a clipboard. Then he reached down and slid a tray out of the cart. He rapped lightly on the door and entered the room. She could smell the unpleasant odors of warm food as she passed the cart. She hurried on without looking at any of the nurses and pushed open the door to the child's room.

Howard was standing at the window with his hands behind his back. He turned around as she came in.

"How is he?" she said. She went over to the bed. She dropped her purse on the floor beside the nightstand. It seemed to her she had been gone a long time. She touched the child's face. "Howard?"

"Dr. Francis was here a little while ago," Howard said. She looked at him closely and thought his shoulders were bunched a little.

"I thought he wasn't coming until eight o'clock this morning," she said quickly.

"There was another doctor with him. A neurologist."

"A neurologist," she said.

Howard nodded. His shoulders were bunching, she could see that. "What'd they say, Howard? For Christ's sake, what'd they say? What is it?"

"They said they're going to take him down and run more tests on him, Ann. They think they're going to operate, honey. Honey, they *are* going to operate. They can't figure out why he won't wake up. It's more than just shock or concussion, they know that much now. It's in his skull, the fracture, it has something, something to do with that, they think. So they're going to operate. I tried to call you, but I guess you'd already left the house."

"Oh, God," she said. "Oh, please, Howard, please," she said, taking his arms.

"Look!" Howard said. "Scotty! Look, Ann!" He turned her toward the bed.

The boy had opened his eyes, then closed them. He opened them again now. The eyes stared straight ahead for a minute, then moved slowly in his head until they rested on Howard and Ann, then traveled away again.

"Scotty," his mother said, moving to the bed.

"Hey, Scott," his father said. "Hey, son."

They leaned over the bed. Howard took the child's hand in his hands and began to pat and squeeze the hand. Ann bent over the boy and kissed his forehead again and again. She put her hands on either side of his face. "Scotty, honey, it's Mommy and Daddy," she said. "Scotty?"

The boy looked at them, but without any sign of recognition. Then his mouth opened, his eyes scrunched closed, and he howled until he had no more air in his lungs. His face seemed to relax and soften then. His lips parted as his last breath was puffed through his throat and exhaled gently through the clenched teeth.

The doctors called it a hidden occlusion and said it was a one-in-a-million circumstance. Maybe if it could have been detected somehow and surgery undertaken immediately, they could have saved him. But more than likely not. In any case, what would they have been looking for? Nothing had shown up in the tests or in the X-rays.

Dr. Francis was shaken. "I can't tell you how badly I feel. I'm so very sorry, I can't tell you," he said as he led them into the doctors' lounge. There was a doctor sitting in a chair with his legs hooked over the back of another chair, watching an early-morning TV show. He was wearing a green delivery-room outfit, loose green pants and green blouse, and a green cap that covered his hair. He looked at Howard and Ann and then looked at Dr. Francis. He got to his feet and turned off the set and went out of the room. Dr. Francis guided Ann to the sofa, sat down beside her, and began to talk in a low, consoling voice. At one point, he leaned over and embraced her. She could feel his chest rising and falling evenly against her shoulder. She kept her eyes open and let him hold her. Howard went into the bathroom, but he left the door open. After a violent fit of weeping, he ran water and washed his face. Then he came out and sat down at the little table that held a telephone. He looked at the telephone as though deciding what to do first. He made some calls. After a time, Dr. Francis used the telephone.

"Is there anything else I can do for the moment?" he asked them.

Howard shook his head. Ann stared at Dr. Francis as if unable to comprehend his words.

The doctor walked them to the hospital's front door. People were entering and leaving the hospital. It was eleven o'clock in the morning. Ann was aware of how slowly, almost reluctantly, she moved her feet. It seemed to her that Dr. Francis was making them leave when she felt they should stay, when it would be more the right thing to do to stay. She gazed out into the parking lot and then turned around and looked back at the front of the hospital. She began shaking her head. "No, no," she said. "I can't leave him here, no." She heard herself say that and thought how unfair it was that the only words that came out were the sort of words used on TV shows where people were stunned by violent or sudden deaths. She wanted her words to be her own. "No," she said, and for some reason the memory of the Negro woman's head lolling on the woman's shoulder came to her. "No," she said again.

"I'll be talking to you later in the day," the doctor was saying to Howard. "There are still some things that have to be done, things that have to be cleared up to our satisfaction. Some things that need explaining."

"An autopsy," Howard said.

Dr. Francis nodded.

"I understand," Howard said. Then he said, "Oh, Jesus. No, I don't understand, doctor. I can't, I can't. I just can't."

Dr. Francis put his arm around Howard's shoulders. "I'm sorry. God, how I'm sorry." He let go of Howard's shoulders and held out his hand. Howard looked at the hand, and then he took it. Dr. Francis put his arms around Ann once more. He seemed full of some goodness she didn't understand. She let her head rest on his shoulder, but her eyes stayed open. She kept looking at the hospital. As they drove out of the parking lot, she looked back at the hospital.

At home, she sat on the sofa with her hands in her coat pockets. Howard closed the door to the child's room. He got the coffee-maker going and then he found an empty box. He had thought to pick up some of the child's things that were scattered around the living room. But instead he sat down beside her on the sofa, pushed the box to one side, and leaned forward, arms between his knees. He began to weep. She pulled his head over into her lap and patted his shoulder. "He's gone," she said. She kept patting his shoulder. Over his sobs, she could hear the coffee-maker hissing in the kitchen. "There, there," she said tenderly. "Howard, he's gone. He's gone and now we'll have to get used to that. To being alone."

In a little while, Howard got up and began moving aimlessly around the room with the box, not putting anything into it, but collecting some things together on the floor at one end of the sofa. She continued to sit with her hands in her coat pockets. Howard put the box down and brought coffee into the living room. Later, Ann made calls to relatives. After each call had been placed and the party had answered, Ann would blurt out a few words and cry for a minute. Then she would quietly explain, in a measured voice, what had happened and tell them about arrangements. Howard took the box out to the garage, where he saw the child's bicycle. He dropped the box and sat down on the pavement beside the bicycle. He took hold of the bicycle awkwardly so that it leaned against his chest. He held it, the rubber pedal sticking into his chest. He gave the wheel a turn.

Ann hung up the telephone after talking to her sister. She was looking up another number when the telephone rang. She picked it up on the first ring.

"Hello," she said, and she heard something in the background, a humming noise. "Hello!" she said. "For God's sake," she said. "Who is this? What is it you want?"

"Your Scotty, I got him ready for you," the man's voice said. "Did you forget him?"

"You evil bastard!" she shouted into the receiver. "How can you do this, you evil son of a bitch?"

"Scotty," the man said. "Have you forgotten about Scotty?" Then the man hung up on her.

Howard heard the shouting and came in to find her with her head on her arms over the table, weeping. He picked up the receiver and listened to the dial tone.

Much later, just before midnight, after they had dealt with many things, the telephone rang again.

"You answer it," she said. "Howard, it's him, I know." They were sitting at the kitchen table with coffee in front of them. Howard had a small glass of whiskey beside his cup. He answered on the third ring.

"Hello," he said. "Who is this? Hello! Hello!" The line went dead. "He hung up," Howard said. "Whoever it was."

"It was him," she said. "That bastard. I'd like to kill him," she said. "I'd like to shoot him and watch him kick," she said.

"Ann, my God," he said.

"Could you hear anything?" she said. "In the background? A noise, machinery, something humming?"

"Nothing, really. Nothing like that," he said. "There wasn't much time. I think there was some radio music. Yes, there was a radio going, that's all I could tell. I don't know what in God's name is going on," he said.

She shook her head. "If I could, could get my hands on him." It came to her then. She knew who it was. Scotty, the cake, the telephone number. She pushed the chair away from the table and got up. "Drive me down to the shopping center," she said. "Howard."

"What are you saying?"

"The shopping center. I know who it is who's calling. I know who it is. It's the baker, the son-of-a-bitching baker, Howard. I had him bake a cake for Scotty's birthday. That's who's calling. That's who has the number and keeps calling us. To harass us about that cake. The baker, that bastard."

They drove down to the shopping center. The sky was clear and stars were out. It was cold, and they ran the heater in the car. They parked in front of the bakery. All of the shops and stores were closed, but there were cars at the far end of the lot in front of the movie theater. The bakery windows were dark, but when they looked through the glass they could see a light in the back room and, now and then, a big man in an apron moving in and out of the white, even light. Through the glass, she could see the display cases and some little tables with chairs. She tried the door. She rapped on the glass. But if the baker heard them, he gave no sign. He didn't look in their direction.

They drove around behind the bakery and parked. They got out of the car. There was a lighted window too high up for them to see inside. A sign near the back door said THE PANTRY BAKERY, SPECIAL ORDERS. She could hear faintly a radio playing inside and something creak—an oven door as it was pulled down? She knocked on the door and waited. Then she knocked again, louder. The radio was turned down and there was a scraping sound now, the distinct sound of something, a drawer, being pulled open and then closed.

Someone unlocked the door and opened it. The baker stood in the light and peered out at them. "I'm closed for business," he said. "What do you want at this hour? It's midnight. Are you drunk or something?"

She stepped into the light that fell through the open door. He blinked his heavy eyelids as he recognized her. "It's you," he said.

"It's me," she said. "Scotty's mother. This is Scotty's father. We'd like to come in."

The baker said, "I'm busy now. I have work to do."

She had stepped inside the doorway anyway. Howard came in behind her. The baker moved back. "It smells like a bakery in here. Doesn't it smell like a bakery in here, Howard?"

"What do you want?" the baker said. "Maybe you want your cake? That's it, you decided you want your cake. You ordered a cake, didn't you?"

"You're pretty smart for a baker," she said. "Howard, this is the man who's been calling us." She clenched her fists. She stared at him fiercely. There was a deep burning inside her, an anger that made her feel larger than herself, larger than either of these men.

"Just a minute here," the baker said. "You want to pick up your three-day-old cake? That it? I don't want to argue with you, lady. There it sits over there, getting stale. I'll give it to you for half of what I quoted you. No. You want it? You can have it. It's no good to me, no good to anyone now. It cost me time and money to make that cake. If you want it, okay, if you don't, that's okay, too. I have to get back to work." He looked at them and rolled his tongue behind his teeth.

"More cakes," she said. She knew she was in control of it, of what was increasing in her. She was calm.

"Lady, I work sixteen hours a day in this place to earn a living," the baker said. He wiped his hands on his apron. "I work night and day in here, trying to make ends meet." A look crossed Ann's face that made the baker move back and say, "No trouble, now." He reached to the counter and picked up a rolling pin with his right hand and began to tap it against the palm of his other hand. "You want the cake or not? I have to get back to work. Bakers work at night," he said again. His eyes were small, mean-looking, she thought, nearly lost in the bristly flesh around his cheeks. His neck was thick with fat.

"I know bakers work at night," Ann said. "They make phone calls at night, too. You bastard," she said.

The baker continued to tap the rolling pin against his hand. He glanced at Howard. "Careful, careful," he said to Howard.

"My son's dead," she said with a cold, even finality. "He was hit by a car Monday morning. We've been waiting with him until he died. But, of course, you couldn't be expected to know that, could you? Bakers can't know everything—can they, Mr. Baker? But he's dead. He's dead, you bastard!" Just as suddenly as it had welled in her, the anger dwindled, gave way to something else, a dizzy feeling of nausea. She leaned against the wooden table that was sprinkled with flour, put her hands over her face, and began to cry, her shoulders rocking back and forth. "It isn't fair," she said. "It isn't, isn't fair."

Howard put his hand at the small of her back and looked at the baker. "Shame on you," Howard said to him. "Shame."

The baker put the rolling pin back on the counter. He undid his apron and threw it on the counter. He looked at them, and then he shook his head slowly. He pulled a chair out from under the card table that held papers and receipts, an adding machine, and a telephone directory. "Please sit down," he said. "Let me get you a chair," he said to Howard. "Sit down now, please." The baker went into the front of the shop and returned with two little wrought-iron chairs. "Please sit down, you people."

Ann wiped her eyes and looked at the baker. "I wanted to kill you," she said. "I wanted you dead."

The baker had cleared a space for them at the table. He shoved the adding machine to one side, along with the stacks of notepaper and receipts. He pushed the telephone directory onto the floor, where it landed with a thud. Howard and Ann sat down and pulled their chairs up to the table. The baker sat down, too.

"Let me say how sorry I am," the baker said, putting his elbows on the table. "God alone knows how sorry. Listen to me. I'm just a baker. I don't claim to be anything else. Maybe once, maybe years ago, I was a different kind of human being. I've forgotten, I don't know for sure. But I'm not any longer, if I ever was. Now I'm just a baker. That don't excuse my doing what I did, I know. But I'm deeply sorry. I'm sorry for your son, and sorry for my part in this," the baker said. He spread his hands out on the table and turned them over to reveal his palms. "I don't have any children myself, so I can only imagine what you must be feeling. All I can say to you now is that I'm sorry. Forgive me, if you can," the baker said. "I'm not an evil man, I don't think. Not evil, like you said on the phone. You got to understand what it comes down to is I don't know how to act anymore, it would seem. Please," the man said, "let me ask you if you can find it in your hearts to forgive me?"

It was warm inside the bakery. Howard stood up from the table and took off his coat. He helped Ann from her coat. The baker looked at them for a minute and then nodded and got up from the table. He went to the oven and turned off some switches. He found cups and poured coffee from an electric coffee-maker. He put a carton of cream on the table, and a bowl of sugar.

"You probably need to eat something," the baker said. "I hope you'll eat some of my hot rolls. You have to eat and keep going. Eating is a small, good thing in a time like this," he said.

He served them warm cinnamon rolls just out of the oven, the icing still runny. He put butter on the table and knives to spread the butter. Then the baker sat down at the table with them. He waited. He waited until they each took a roll from the platter and began to eat. "It's good to eat something," he said, watching them. "There's more. Eat up. Eat all you want. There's all the rolls in the world in here."

They ate rolls and drank coffee. Ann was suddenly hungry, and the rolls were warm and sweet. She ate three of them, which pleased the baker. Then he began to talk. They listened carefully. Although they were tired and in anguish, they listened to what the baker had to say. They nodded when the baker began to speak of loneliness, and of the sense of doubt and limitation that had come to him in his middle years. He told them what it was like to be childless all these years. To repeat the days with the ovens endlessly full and endlessly empty. The party food, the celebrations he'd worked over. Icing knuckle-deep. The tiny wedding couples stuck into cakes. Hundreds of them, no, thousands by now. Birthdays. Just imagine all those candies burning. He had a necessary trade. He was a baker. He was glad he wasn't a florist. It was better to be feeding people. This was a better smell anytime than flowers.

"Smell this," the baker said, breaking open a dark loaf. "It's a heavy bread, but rich." They smelled it, then he had them taste it. It had the taste of molasses and coarse grains. They listened to him. They ate what they could. They swallowed the dark bread. It was like daylight under the fluorescent trays of light. They talked on into the early morning, the high, pale cast of light in the windows, and they did not think of leaving.

ANTON CHEKHOV

Anton Chekhov (1860–1904), the Russian short story writer and playwright, wrote his first stories while he was a medical student at Moscow University, to help his family pay off debts. His grandfather had been a serf who had bought his freedom. His father was an unsuccessful grocer in Taganrog, in the southwestern part of the country. After completing medical school, Chekhov became an assistant to the district doctor in a provincial town. His early stories were mostly humorous sketches that he first published in newspapers under various pseudonyms, keeping his own name for his medical articles. But the popularity of these sketches made him decide to become a writer.

Chekhov's first two collections of short stories, published in 1886 and 1887, were acclaimed by readers, and from that time on he was able to devote all his time to writing. He bought a small estate near Moscow, where he lived with his family and treated sick peasants at no charge. Chekhov's kindness and good works were not a matter of any political program or religious impulse but, as Vladimir Nabokov put it, "the natural coloration of his talent." He was extremely modest about his extraordinary ability to empathize with his characters. Once he said to a visitor, "Do you know how I write my stories? Here's how!" And he glanced at his table, took up the first object that he saw — it was an ashtray — and said, "If you want it, you'll have a story tomorrow. It will be called 'The Ashtray.'" And it seemed to the visitor that Chekhov was conjuring up a story in front of his eyes: "Certain indefinite situations, adventures which had not yet found concrete form, were already beginning to crystallize about the ashtray."

Chekhov's story-writing technique appears disarmingly simple. Yet, as Virginia Woolf recognized, "as we read these little stories about nothing at all, the horizon widens; the soul gains an astonishing sense of freedom." Chekhov's remarkable absence of egotism can be seen in masterpieces such as "The Darling" *and "The Lady with the Pet Dog," both of which he wrote toward the end of his life. He once sent a sketch describing himself to the editor who first encouraged him, giving a sense of the depth of his self-knowledge:*

> *Write a story, do, about a young man, the son of a serf, a former grocery boy, a choir singer, a high school pupil and university student, brought up to respect rank, to kiss the hands of priests, to truckle to the ideas of others— a young man who expressed thanks for every piece of bread, who was whipped many times, who went without galoshes to do his tutoring, who used his fists, tortured animals, was fond of dining with rich relatives, was a hypocrite in his dealings with God and men, needlessly, solely out of a real- ization of his own insignificance—write how this young man squeezes the slave out of himself, drop by drop, and how, on awaking one fine morning, he feels that the blood coursing through his veins is no longer that of a slave but that of a real human being.*

Chekhov's more than 800 stories have immensely influenced writers of short fiction. Unconcerned with giving a social or ethical message in his work, he cham- pioned what he called "the holy of holies"— "love and absolute freedom—free- dom from violence and lies, whatever their form."

COMMENTARIES   *Anton Chekhov, "Technique in Writing the Short Story," page 554; Richard Ford, "On Chekhov's 'The Lady with the Pet Dog,'" page 560; Eudora Welty, "Plot and Character in Chekhov's 'The Darling,'" page 606.*

CONNECTION   *Joyce Carol Oates, "The Lady with the Pet Dog," page 384.*

WEB   *Research Anton Chekhov and answer questions about his work at bedfordstmartins.com/charters/litwriters.*

The Darling   1899

TRANSLATED BY CONSTANCE GARNETT

Olenka, the daughter of the retired collegiate assessor, Plemyanniakov, was sitting in her back porch, lost in thought. It was hot, the flies were persist- ent and teasing, and it was pleasant to reflect that it would soon be evening. Dark rainclouds were gathering from the east, and bringing from time to time a breath of moisture in the air.

Kukin, who was the manager of an open-air theatre called the Tivoli, and who lived in the lodge, was standing in the middle of the garden looking at the sky.

"Again!" he observed despairingly. "It's going to rain again! Rain every day, as though to spite me. I might as well hang myself! It's ruin! Fearful losses every day."

He flung up his hands, and went on, addressing Olenka:

"There! that's the life we lead, Olga Semyonovna. It's enough to make one cry. One works and does one's utmost; one wears oneself out, getting no sleep at night, and racks one's brain what to do for the best. And then what happens? To begin with, one's public is ignorant, boorish. I give them the very best operetta, a dainty masque, first rate music-hall artists. But do you suppose that's what they want! They don't understand anything of that sort. They want a clown; what they ask for is vulgarity. And then look at the weather! Almost every evening it rains. It started on the tenth of May, and it's kept it up all May and June. It's simply awful! The public doesn't come, but I've to pay the rent just the same, and pay the artists."

The next evening the clouds would gather again, and Kukin would say with an hysterical laugh:

"Well, rain away, then! Flood the garden, drown me! Damn my luck in this world and the next! Let the artists have me up! Send me to prison! — to Siberia! — the scaffold! Ha, ha, ha!"

And next day the same thing.

Olenka listened to Kukin with silent gravity, and sometimes tears came into her eyes. In the end his misfortunes touched her; she grew to love him. He was a small thin man, with a yellow face, and curls combed forward on his forehead. He spoke in a thin tenor; as he talked his mouth worked on one side, and there was always an expression of despair on his face; yet he aroused a deep and genuine affection in her. She was always fond of some one, and could not exist without loving. In earlier days she had loved her papa, who now sat in a darkened room, breathing with difficulty; she had loved her aunt who used to come every other year from Bryansk; and before that, when she was at school, she had loved her French master. She was a gentle, soft-hearted, compassionate girl, with mild, tender eyes and very good health. At the sight of her full rosy cheeks, her soft white neck with a little dark mole on it, and the kind, naïve smile, which came into her face when she listened to anything pleasant, men thought, "Yes, not half bad," and smiled too, while lady visitors could not refrain from seizing her hand in the middle of a conversation, exclaiming in a gush of delight, "You darling!"

The house in which she had lived from her birth upwards, and which was left her in her father's will, was at the extreme end of the town, not far from the Tivoli. In the evenings and at night she could hear the band playing, and the crackling and banging of fireworks, and it seemed to her that it was Kukin struggling with his destiny, storming the entrenchments of his chief foe, the indifferent public; there was a sweet thrill at her heart, she had no desire to sleep, and when he returned home at daybreak, she tapped softly at her bedroom window, and showing him only her face and one shoulder through the curtain, she gave him a friendly smile. . . .

He proposed to her, and they were married. And when he had a closer view of her neck and her plump, fine shoulders, he threw up his hands, and said:

"You darling!"

He was happy, but as it rained on the day and night of his wedding, his face still retained an expression of despair.

They got on very well together. She used to sit in his office, to look after things in the Tivoli, to put down the accounts and pay the wages. And her rosy cheeks, her sweet, naïve, radiant smile, were to be seen now at the office window, now in the refreshment bar or behind the scenes of the theatre. And already she used to say to her acquaintances that the theatre was the chief and most important thing in life, and that it was only through the drama that one could derive true enjoyment and become cultivated and humane.

"But do you suppose the public understands that?" she used to say. "What they want is a clown. Yesterday we gave 'Faust Inside Out,' and almost all the boxes were empty; but if Vanitchka and I had been producing some vulgar thing, I assure you the theatre would have been packed. Tomorrow Vanitchka and I are doing 'Orpheus in Hell.' Do come."

And what Kukin said about the theatre and the actors she repeated. Like him she despised the public for their ignorance and their indifference to art; she took part in the rehearsals, she corrected the actors, she kept an eye on the behavior of the musicians, and when there was an unfavorable notice in the local paper, she shed tears, and then went to the editor's office to set things right.

The actors were fond of her and used to call her "Vanitchka and I," and "the darling"; she was sorry for them and used to lend them small sums of money, and if they deceived her, she used to shed a few tears in private, but did not complain to her husband.

They got on well in the winter too. They took the theatre in the town for the whole winter, and let it for short terms to a Little Russian company, or to a conjurer, or to a local dramatic society. Olenka grew stouter, and was always beaming with satisfaction, while Kukin grew thinner and yellower, and continually complained of their terrible losses, although he had not done badly all the winter. He used to cough at night, and she used to give him hot raspberry tea or lime-flower water, to rub him with eau-de-Cologne and to wrap him in her warm shawls.

"You're such a sweet pet!" she used to say with perfect sincerity, stroking his hair. "You're such a pretty dear!"

Towards Lent he went to Moscow to collect a new troupe, and without him she could not sleep, but sat all night at her window, looking at the stars, and she compared herself with the hens, who are awake all night and uneasy when the cock is not in the hen-house. Kukin was detained in Moscow, and wrote that he would be back at Easter, adding some instructions about the Tivoli. But on the Sunday before Easter, late in the evening, came a sudden ominous knock at the gate; some one was hammering on the gate as though on a barrel—boom, boom, boom! The drowsy cook went flopping with her bare feet through the puddles, as she ran to open the gate.

"Please open," said some one outside in a thick bass. "There is a telegram for you."

Olenka had received telegrams from her husband before, but this time for some reason she felt numb with terror. With shaking hands she opened the telegram and read as follows:

"Ivan Petrovitch died suddenly to-day. Awaiting immate instructions fufuneral Tuesday."

That was how it was written in the telegram—"fufuneral," and the utterly incomprehensible word "immate." It was signed by the stage manager of the operatic company.

"My darling!" sobbed Olenka. "Vanitchka, my precious, my darling! Why did I ever meet you! Why did I know you and love you! Your poor heart-broken Olenka is all alone without you!"

Kukin's funeral took place on Tuesday in Moscow, Olenka returned home on Wednesday, and as soon as she got indoors she threw herself on her bed and sobbed so loudly that it could be heard next door, and in the street.

"Poor darling!" the neighbors said, as they crossed themselves. "Olga Semyonovna, poor darling! How she does take on!"

Three months later Olenka was coming home from mass, melancholy and in deep mourning. It happened that one of her neighbors, Vassily Andreitch Pustovalov, returning home from church, walked back beside her. He was the manager at Babakayev's, the timber merchant's. He wore a straw hat, a white waistcoat, and a gold watch-chain, and looked more like a country gentleman than a man in trade.

"Everything happens as it is ordained, Olga Semyonovna," he said gravely, with a sympathetic note in his voice; "and if any of our dear ones die, it must be because it is the will of God, so we ought to have fortitude and bear it submissively."

After seeing Olenka to her gate, he said good-bye and went on. All day afterwards she heard his sedately dignified voice, and whenever she shut her eyes she saw his dark beard. She liked him very much. And apparently she had made an impression on him too, for not long afterwards an elderly lady, with whom she was only slightly acquainted, came to drink coffee with her, and as soon as she was seated at table began to talk about Pustovalov, saying that he was an excellent man whom one could thoroughly depend upon, and that any girl would be glad to marry him. Three days later Pustovalov came himself. He did not stay long, only about ten minutes, and he did not say much, but when he left, Olenka loved him—loved him so much that she lay awake all night in a perfect fever, and in the morning she sent for the elderly lady. The match was quickly arranged, and then came the wedding.

Pustovalov and Olenka got on very well together when they were married.

Usually he sat in the office till dinner-time, then he went out on business, while Olenka took his place, and sat in the office till evening, making up accounts and booking orders.

"Timber gets dearer every year; the price rises twenty per cent," she would say to her customers and friends. "Only fancy we used to sell local timber, and now Vassitchka always has to go for wood to the Mogilev district. And the freight!" she would add, covering her cheeks with her hands in horror. "The freight!"

It seemed to her that she had been in the timber trade for ages and ages, and that the most important and necessary thing in life was timber; and there was something intimate and touching to her in the very sound of words such as "baulk," "post," "beam," "pole," "scantling," "batten," "lath," "plank," etc.

At night when she was asleep she dreamed of perfect mountains of planks and boards, and long strings of wagons, carting timber somewhere far away.

She dreamed that a whole regiment of six-inch beams forty feet high, standing on end, was marching upon the timber-yard; that logs, beams, and boards knocked together with the resounding crash of dry wood, kept falling and getting up again, piling themselves on each other. Olenka cried out in her sleep, and Pustovalov said to her tenderly: "Olenka, what's the matter, darling? Cross yourself!"

Her husband's ideas were hers. If he thought the room was too hot, or that business was slack, she thought the same. Her husband did not care for entertainments, and on holidays he stayed at home. She did likewise.

"You are always at home or in the office," her friends said to her. "You should go to the theatre, darling, or to the circus."

"Vassitchka and I have no time to go to theatres," she would answer sedately. "We have no time for nonsense. What's the use of these theatres?"

On Saturdays Pustovalov and she used to go to the evening service; on holidays to early mass, and they walked side by side with softened faces as they came home from church. There was a pleasant fragrance about them both, and her silk dress rustled agreeably. At home they drank tea, with fancy bread and jams of various kinds, and afterwards they ate pie. Every day at twelve o'clock there was a savory smell of beet-root soup and of mutton or duck in their yard, and on fast-days of fish, and no one could pass the gate without feeling hungry. In the office the samovar was always boiling, and customers were regaled with tea and cracknels. Once a week the couple went to the baths and returned side by side, both red in the face.

"Yes, we have nothing to complain of, thank God," Olenka used to say to her acquaintances. "I wish every one were as well off as Vassitchka and I."

When Pustovalov went away to buy wood in the Mogilev district, she missed him dreadfully, lay awake and cried. A young veterinary surgeon in the army, called Smirnin, to whom they had let their lodge, used sometimes to come in in the evening. He used to talk to her and play cards with her, and this entertained her in her husband's absence. She was particularly interested in what he told her of his home life. He was married and had a little boy, but was separated from his wife because she had been unfaithful to him, and now he hated her and used to send her forty rubles a month for the maintenance of their son. And hearing of all this, Olenka sighed and shook her head. She was sorry for him.

"Well, God keep you," she used to say to him at parting, as she lighted him down the stairs with a candle. "Thank you for coming to cheer me up, and may the Mother of God give you health."

And she always expressed herself with the same sedateness and dignity, the same reasonableness, in imitation of her husband. As the veterinary surgeon was disappearing behind the door below, she would say:

"You know, Vladimir Platonitch, you'd better make it up with your wife. You should forgive her for the sake of your son. You may be sure the little fellow understands."

And when Pustovalov came back, she told him in a low voice about the veterinary surgeon and his unhappy home life, and both sighed and shook their heads and talked about the boy, who, no doubt, missed his father, and by some strange connection of ideas, they went up to the holy icons, bowed to the ground before them, and prayed that God would give them children.

And so the Pustovalovs lived for six years quietly and peaceably in love and complete harmony.

But behold! one winter day after drinking hot tea in the office, Vassily Andreitch went out into the yard without his cap on to see about sending off some timber, caught cold, and was taken ill. He had the best doctors, but he grew worse and died after four months' illness. And Olenka was a widow once more.

"I've nobody, now you've left me, my darling," she sobbed, after her husband's funeral. "How can I live without you, in wretchedness and misery! Pity me, good people, all alone in the world!"

She went about dressed in black with long "weepers," and gave up wearing hat and gloves for good. She hardly ever went out, except to church, or to her husband's grave, and led the life of a nun. It was not till six months later that she took off the weepers and opened the shutters of the windows. She was sometimes seen in the mornings, going with her cook to market for provisions, but what went on in her house and how she lived now could only be surmised. People guessed, from seeing her drinking tea in her garden with the veterinary surgeon, who read the newspaper aloud to her, and from the fact that, meeting a lady she knew at the post-office, she said to her:

"There is no proper veterinary inspection in our town, and that's the cause of all sorts of epidemics. One is always hearing of people's getting infection from the milk supply, or catching diseases from horses and cows. The health of domestic animals ought to be as well cared for as the health of human beings."

She repeated the veterinary surgeon's words, and was of the same opinion as he about everything. It was evident that she could not live a year without some attachment, and had found new happiness in the lodge. In any one else this would have been censured, but no one could think ill of Olenka; everything she did was so natural. Neither she nor the veterinary surgeon said anything to other people of the change in their relations, and tried, indeed, to conceal it, but without success, for Olenka could not keep a secret. When he had visitors, men serving in his regiment, and she poured out tea or served the supper, she would begin talking of the cattle plague, of the foot and mouth disease, and of the municipal slaughter-houses. He was dreadfully embarrassed, and when the guests had gone, he would seize her by the hand and hiss angrily:

"I've asked you before not to talk about what you don't understand. When we veterinary surgeons are talking among ourselves, please don't put your word in. It's really annoying."

And she would look at him with astonishment and dismay, and ask him in alarm: "But, Voloditchka, what *am* I to talk about?"

And with tears in her eyes she would embrace him, begging him not to be angry, and they were both happy.

But this happiness did not last long. The veterinary surgeon departed, departed for ever with his regiment, when it was transferred to a distant place—to Siberia, it may be. And Olenka was left alone.

Now she was absolutely alone. Her father had long been dead, and his armchair lay in the attic, covered with dust and lame of one leg. She got thinner and plainer, and when people met her in the street they did not look at her as they used to, and did not smile to her; evidently her best years were over and left behind, and now a new sort of life had begun for her, which did not bear thinking about. In the evening Olenka sat in the porch, and heard the band playing and the fireworks popping in the Tivoli, but now the sound stirred no response. She looked into her yard without interest, thought of nothing, wished for nothing, and afterwards, when night came on she went to bed and dreamed of her empty yard. She ate and drank as it were unwillingly.

And what was worst of all, she had no opinions of any sort. She saw the objects about her and understood what she saw, but could not form any opinion about them, and did not know what to talk about. And how awful it is not to have any opinions! One sees a bottle, for instance, or the rain, or a peasant driving in his cart, but what the bottle is for, or the rain, or the peasant, and what is the meaning of it, one can't say, and could not even for a thousand rubles. When she had Kukin, or Pustovalov, or the veterinary surgeon, Olenka could explain everything, and give her opinion about anything you like, but now there was the same emptiness in her brain and in her heart as there was in her yard outside. And it was as harsh and as bitter as wormwood in the mouth.

Little by little the town grew in all directions. The road became a street, and where the Tivoli and the timber-yard had been, there were new turnings and houses. How rapidly time passes! Olenka's house grew dingy, the roof got rusty, the shed sank on one side, and the whole yard was overgrown with docks and stinging-nettles. Olenka herself had grown plain and elderly; in summer she sat in the porch, and her soul, as before, was empty and dreary and full of bitterness. In winter she sat at her window and looked at the snow. When she caught the scent of spring, or heard the chime of the church bells, a sudden rush of memories from the past came over her, there was a tender ache in her heart, and her eyes brimmed over with tears; but this was only for a minute, and then came emptiness again and the sense of the futility of life. The black kitten, Briska, rubbed against her and purred softly, but Olenka was not touched by these feline caresses. That was not what she needed. She wanted a love that would absorb her whole being, her whole soul and reason—that would give her ideas and an object in life, and would warm her old blood. And she would shake the kitten off her skirt and say with vexation:

"Get along; I don't want you!"

And so it was, day after day and year after year, and no joy, and no opinions. Whatever Mavra, the cook, said she accepted.

One hot July day, towards evening, just as the cattle were being driven away, and the whole yard was full of dust, some one suddenly knocked at the gate. Olenka went to open it herself and was dumbfounded when she looked out; she saw Smirnin, the veterinary surgeon, grey-headed, and dressed as a civilian. She suddenly remembered everything. She could not help crying and letting her head fall on his breast without uttering a word, and in the violence of her feeling she did not notice how they both walked into the house and sat down to tea.

"My dear Vladimir Platonitch! What fate has brought you?" she muttered, trembling with joy.

"I want to settle here for good, Olga Semyonovna," he told her. "I have resigned my post, and have come to settle down and try my luck on my own account. Besides, it's time for my boy to go to school. He's a big boy. I am reconciled with my wife, you know."

"Where is she?" asked Olenka.

"She's at the hotel with the boy, and I'm looking for lodgings."

"Good gracious, my dear soul! Lodgings? Why not have my house? Why shouldn't that suit you? Why, my goodness, I wouldn't take any rent!" cried Olenka in a flutter, beginning to cry again. "You live here, and the lodge will do nicely for me. Oh dear! how glad I am!"

Next day the roof was painted and the walls were whitewashed, and Olenka, with her arms akimbo, walked about the yard giving directions. Her face was beaming with her old smile, and she was brisk and alert as though she had waked from a long sleep. The veterinary's wife arrived—a thin, plain lady, with short hair and a peevish expression. With her was her little Sasha, a boy of ten, small for his age, blue-eyed, chubby, with dimples in his cheeks. And scarcely had the boy walked into the yard when he ran after the cat, and at once there was the sound of his gay, joyous laugh.

"Is that your puss, auntie?" he asked Olenka. "When she has little ones, do give us a kitten. Mamma is awfully afraid of mice."

Olenka talked to him, and gave him tea. Her heart warmed and there was a sweet ache in her bosom, as though the boy had been her own child. And when he sat at the table in the evening, going over his lessons, she looked at him with deep tenderness and pity as murmured to herself:

"You pretty pet! . . . my precious! . . . Such a fair little thing, and so clever."

" 'An island is a piece of land which is entirely surrounded by water,' " he read aloud.

"An island is a piece of land," she repeated, and this was the first opinion to which she gave utterance with positive conviction after so many years of silence and dearth of ideas.

Now she had opinions of her own, and at supper she talked to Sasha's parents, saying how difficult the lessons were at the high schools, but that yet the high school was better than a commercial one, since with a high-school education all careers were open to one, such as being a doctor or an engineer.

Sasha began going to the high school. His mother departed to Harkov to her sister's and did not return; his father used to go off every day to inspect cattle, and would often be away from home for three days together, and it seemed to Olenka as though Sasha was entirely abandoned, that he was not wanted at home, that he was being starved, and she carried him off to her lodge and gave him a little room there.

And for six months Sasha had lived in the lodge with her. Every morning Olenka came into his bedroom and found him fast asleep, sleeping noiselessly with his hand under his cheek. She was sorry to wake him.

"Sashenka," she would say mournfully, "get up, darling. It's time for school."

He would get up, dress and say his prayers, and then sit down to breakfast, drink three glasses of tea, and eat two large cracknels and half a buttered roll. All this time he was hardly awake and a little ill-humored in consequence.

"You don't quite know your fable, Sashenka," Olenka would say, looking at him as though he were about to set off on a long journey. "What a lot of trouble I have with you! You must work and do your best, darling, and obey your teachers."

"Oh, do leave me alone!" Sasha would say.

Then he would go down the street to school, a little figure, wearing a big cap and carrying a satchel on his shoulder. Olenka would follow him noiselessly.

"Sashenka!" she would call after him, and she would pop into his hand a date or a caramel. When he reached the street where the school was, he would feel ashamed of being followed by a tall, stout woman; he would turn round and say:

"You'd better go home, auntie. I can go the rest of the way alone."

She would stand still and look after him fixedly till he had disappeared at the school-gate.

Ah, how she loved him! Of her former attachments not one had been so deep; never had her soul surrendered to any feeling so spontaneously, so disinterestedly, and so joyously as now that her maternal instincts were aroused. For this little boy with the dimple in his cheek and the big school cap, she would have given her whole life, she would have given it with joy and tears of tenderness. Why? Who can tell why?

When she had seen the last of Sasha, she returned home, contented and serene, brimming over with love; her face, which had grown younger during the last six months, smiled and beamed; people meeting her looked at her with pleasure.

"Good-morning, Olga Semyonovna, darling. How are you, darling?"

"The lessons at the high school are very difficult now," she would relate at the market. "It's too much; in the first class yesterday they gave him a fable to learn by heart, and a Latin translation and a problem. You know it's too much for a little chap."

And she would begin talking about the teachers, the lessons, and the school books, saying just what Sasha said.

At three o'clock they had dinner together: in the evening they learned their lessons together and cried. When she put him to bed, she would stay a long time making the Cross over him and murmuring a prayer; then she would go to bed and dream of that far-away misty future when Sasha would finish his studies and become a doctor or an engineer, would have a big house of his own with horses and a carriage, would get married and have children. . . . She would fall asleep still thinking of the same thing, and tears would run down her cheeks from her closed eyes, while the black cat lay purring beside her: "Mrr, mrr, mrr."

Suddenly there would come a loud knock at the gate.

Olenka would wake up breathless with alarm, her heart throbbing. Half a minute later would come another knock.

"It must be a telegram from Harkov," she would think, beginning to tremble from head to foot. "Sasha's mother is sending for him from Harkov. . . . Oh, mercy on us!"

She was in despair. Her head, her hands, and her feet would turn chill, and she would feel that she was the most unhappy woman in the world. But another minute would pass, voices would be heard: it would turn out to be the veterinary surgeon coming home from the club.

"Well, thank God!" she would think.

And gradually the load in her heart would pass off, and she would feel at ease. She would go back to bed thinking of Sasha, who lay sound asleep in the next room, sometimes crying out in his sleep:

"I'll give it you! Get away! Shut up!"

The Lady with the Pet Dog   1899

TRANSLATED BY AVRAHM YARMOLINSKY

I

A new person, it was said, had appeared on the esplanade: a lady with a pet dog. Dmitry Dmitrich Gurov, who had spent a fortnight at Yalta and had got used to the place, had also begun to take an interest in new arrivals. As he sat in Vernet's confectionery shop, he saw, walking on the esplanade, a fair-haired young woman of medium height, wearing a beret; a white Pomeranian was trotting behind her.

And afterwards he met her in the public garden and in the square several times a day. She walked alone, always wearing the same beret and always with the white dog; no one knew who she was and everyone called her simply "the lady with the pet dog."

"If she is here alone without husband or friends," Gurov reflected, "it wouldn't be a bad thing to make her acquaintance."

He was under forty, but he already had a daughter twelve years old, and two sons at school. They had found a wife for him when he was very young, a student in his second year, and by now she seemed half as old again as he. She was a tall, erect woman with dark eyebrows, stately and dignified and, as she said of herself, intellectual. She read a great deal, used simplified spelling in her letters, called her husband, not Dmitry, but Dimitry, while he privately considered her of limited intelligence, narrow-minded, dowdy, was afraid of her, and did not like to be at home. He had begun being unfaithful to her long ago—had been unfaithful to her often and, probably for that reason, almost always spoke ill of women, and when they were talked of in his presence used to call them "the inferior race."

It seemed to him that he had been sufficiently tutored by bitter experience to call them what he pleased, and yet he could not have lived without "the inferior race" for two days together. In the company of men he was bored and ill at ease, he was chilly and uncommunicative with them; but when he was among women he felt free, and knew what to speak to them about and how to comport himself; and even to be silent with them was no strain on him. In his appearance, in his character, in his whole make-up there was something attractive and elusive that disposed women in his favor and allured them. He knew that, and some force seemed to draw him to them, too.

Oft-repeated and really bitter experience had taught him long ago that with decent people—particularly Moscow people—who are irresolute and slow to move, every affair which at first seems a light and charming adventure inevitably grows into a whole problem of extreme complexity, and in the end a painful situation is created. But at every new meeting with an interesting woman this lesson of experience seemed to slip from his memory, and he was eager for life, and everything seemed so simple and diverting.

One evening while he was dining in the public garden the lady in the beret walked up without haste to take the next table. Her expression, her gait, her dress, and the way she did her hair told him that she belonged to the upper class, that she was married, that she was in Yalta for the first time and alone, and that she was bored there. The stories told of the immorality in Yalta are to a great extent untrue; he despised them, and knew that such stories were made up for the most part by persons who would have been glad to sin themselves if they had had the chance; but when the lady sat down at the next table three paces from him, he recalled these stories of easy conquests, of trips to the mountains, and the tempting thought of a swift, fleeting liaison, a romance with an unknown woman of whose very name he was ignorant, suddenly took hold of him.

He beckoned invitingly to the Pomeranian, and when the dog approached him, shook his finger at it. The Pomeranian growled; Gurov threatened it again.

The lady glanced at him and at once dropped her eyes.

"He doesn't bite," she said and blushed.

"May I give him a bone?" he asked; and when she nodded he inquired affably, "Have you been in Yalta long?"

"About five days."

"And I am dragging out the second week here."

There was a short silence.

"Time passes quickly, and yet it is so dull here!" she said, not looking at him.

"It's only the fashion to say it's dull here. A provincial will live in Belyov or Zhizdra and not be bored, but when he comes here it's 'Oh, the dullness! Oh, the dust!' One would think he came from Granada."

She laughed. Then both continued eating in silence, like strangers, but after dinner they walked together and there sprang up between them the light banter of people who are free and contented, to whom it does not matter where they go or what they talk about. They walked and talked of the strange light on the sea: the water was a soft, warm, lilac color, and there was a golden band of moonlight upon it. They talked of how sultry it was after a hot day. Gurov told her that he was a native of Moscow, that he had studied languages and literature at the university, but had a post in a bank; that at one time he had trained to become an opera singer but had given it up, that he owned two houses in Moscow. And he learned from her that she had grown up in Petersburg, but had lived in S—— since her marriage two years previously, that she was going to stay in Yalta for about another month, and that her husband, who needed a rest, too, might perhaps come to fetch her. She was not certain whether her husband was a member of a Government Board or served on a Zemstvo Council,° and this amused her. And Gurov learned too that her name was Anna Sergeyevna.

Afterwards in his room at the hotel he thought about her—and was certain that he would meet her the next day. It was bound to happen. Getting into bed he recalled that she had been a schoolgirl only recently, doing lessons like his own daughter; he thought how much timidity and angularity there was still in her laugh and her manner of talking with a stranger. It must have been the first time in her life that she was alone in a setting in which she was followed, looked at, and spoken to for one secret purpose alone, which she could hardly fail to guess. He thought of her slim, delicate throat, her lovely gray eyes.

"There's something pathetic about her, though," he thought, and dropped off.

II

A week had passed since they had struck up an acquaintance. It was a holiday. It was close indoors, while in the street the wind whirled the dust about and blew people's hats off. One was thirsty all day, and Gurov often went into the restaurant and offered Anna Sergeyevna a soft drink or ice cream. One did not know what to do with oneself.

In the evening when the wind had abated they went out on the pier to watch the steamer come in. There were a great many people walking about the dock; they had come to welcome someone and they were carrying bunches of flowers. And two peculiarities of a festive Yalta crowd stood out: the elderly ladies were dressed like young ones and there were many generals.

Owing to the choppy sea, the steamer arrived late, after sunset, and it was a long time tacking about before it put in at the pier. Anna Sergeyevna peered at the steamer and the passengers through her lorgnette as though looking for acquaintances, and whenever she turned to Gurov her eyes were shining. She talked a great deal and asked questions jerkily, forgetting the next moment what she had asked; then she lost her lorgnette in the crush.

The festive crowd began to disperse; it was now too dark to see people's faces; there was no wind anymore, but Gurov and Anna Sergeyevna still stood as though waiting to see someone else come off the steamer. Anna Sergeyevna was silent now, and sniffed her flowers without looking at Gurov.

"The weather has improved this evening," he said. "Where shall we go now? Shall we drive somewhere?"

She did not reply.

Zemstvo Council: County council.

Then he looked at her intently, and suddenly embraced her and kissed her on the lips, and the moist fragrance of her flowers enveloped him; and at once he looked round him anxiously, wondering if anyone had seen them.

"Let us go to your place," he said softly. And they walked off together rapidly.

The air in her room was close and there was the smell of the perfume she had bought at the Japanese shop. Looking at her, Gurov thought: "What encounters life offers!" From the past he preserved the memory of carefree, good-natured women whom love made gay and who were grateful to him for the happiness he gave them, however brief it might be; and of women like his wife who loved without sincerity, with too many words, affectedly, hysterically, with an expression that it was not love or passion that engaged them but something more significant; and of two or three others, very beautiful, frigid women, across whose faces would suddenly flit a rapacious expression—an obstinate desire to take from life more than it could give, and these were women no longer young, capricious, unreflecting, domineering, unintelligent, and when Gurov grew cold to them their beauty aroused his hatred, and the lace on their lingerie seemed to him to resemble scales.

But here there was the timidity, the angularity of inexperienced youth, a feeling of awkwardness; and there was a sense of embarrassment, as though someone had suddenly knocked at the door. Anna Sergeyevna, "the lady with the pet dog," treated what had happened in a peculiar way, very seriously, as though it were her fall—so it seemed, and this was odd and inappropriate. Her features drooped and faded, and her long hair hung down sadly on either side of her face; she grew pensive and her dejected pose was that of a Magdalene in a picture by an old master.

"It's not right," she said. "You don't respect me now, you first of all."

There was a watermelon on the table. Gurov cut himself a slice and began eating it without haste. They were silent for at least half an hour.

There was something touching about Anna Sergeyevna; she had the purity of a well-bred, naive woman who has seen little of life. The single candle burning on the table barely illumined her face, yet it was clear that she was unhappy.

"Why should I stop respecting you, darling?" asked Gurov. "You don't know what you're saying."

"God forgive me," she said, and her eyes filled with tears. "It's terrible."

"It's as though you were trying to exonerate yourself."

"How can I exonerate myself? No. I am a bad, low woman; I despise myself and I have no thought of exonerating myself. It's not my husband but myself I have deceived. And not only just now; I have been deceiving myself for a long time. My husband may be a good, honest man, but he is a flunkey! I don't know what he does, what his work is, but I know he is a flunkey! I was twenty when I married him. I was tormented by curiosity; I wanted something better. 'There must be a different sort of life,' I said to myself. I wanted to live! To live, to live! Curiosity kept eating at me—you don't understand it, but I swear to God I could no longer control myself; something was going on in me; I could not be held back. I told my husband I was ill, and came here. And here

I have been walking about as though in a daze, as though I were mad; and now I have become a vulgar, vile woman whom anyone may despise."

Gurov was already bored with her; he was irritated by her naive tone, by her repentance, so unexpected and so out of place, but for the tears in her eyes he might have thought she was joking or play-acting.

"I don't understand, my dear," he said softly. "What do you want?"

She hid her face on his breast and pressed close to him.

"Believe me, believe me, I beg you," she said, "I love honesty and purity, and sin is loathsome to me; I don't know what I'm doing. Simple people say, 'The Evil One has led me astray.' And I may say of myself now that the Evil One has led me astray."

"Quiet, quiet," he murmured.

He looked into her fixed, frightened eyes, kissed her, spoke to her softly and affectionately, and by degrees she calmed down, and her gaiety returned; both began laughing.

Afterwards when they went out there was not a soul on the esplanade. The town with its cypresses looked quite dead, but the sea was still sounding as it broke upon the beach; a single launch was rocking on the waves and on it a lantern was blinking sleepily.

They found a cab and drove to Oreanda.

"I found out your surname in the hall just now: it was written on the board—von Dideritz," said Gurov. "Is your husband German?"

"No; I believe his grandfather was German, but he is Greek Orthodox himself."

At Oreanda they sat on a bench not far from the church, looked down at the sea, and were silent. Yalta was barely visible through the morning mist; white clouds rested motionlessly on the mountaintops. The leaves did not stir on the trees, cicadas twanged, and the monotonous muffled sound of the sea that rose from below spoke of the peace, the eternal sleep awaiting us. So it rumbled below when there was no Yalta, no Oreanda here; so it rumbles now, and it will rumble as indifferently and as hollowly when we are no more. And in this constancy, in this complete indifference to the life and death of each of us, there lies, perhaps, a pledge of our eternal salvation, of the unceasing advance of life upon earth, of unceasing movement towards perfection. Sitting beside a young woman who in the dawn seemed so lovely, Gurov, soothed and spellbound by these magical surroundings—the sea, the mountains, the clouds, the wide sky—thought how everything is really beautiful in this world when one reflects: everything except what we think or do ourselves when we forget the higher aims of life and our own human dignity.

A man strolled up to them—probably a guard—looked at them, and walked away. And this detail, too, seemed so mysterious and beautiful. They saw a steamer arrive from Feodosia, its lights extinguished in the glow of dawn.

"There is dew on the grass," said Anna Sergeyevna, after a silence.

"Yes, it's time to go home."

They returned to the city.

Then they met every day at twelve o'clock on the esplanade, lunched and dined together, took walks, admired the sea. She complained that she slept badly, that she had palpitations, asked the same questions, troubled now by jealousy and now by the fear that he did not respect her sufficiently. And often in the square or the public garden, when there was no one near them, he suddenly drew her to him and kissed her passionately. Complete idleness, these kisses in broad daylight exchanged furtively in dread of someone's seeing them, the heat, the smell of the sea, and the continual flitting before his eyes of idle, well-dressed, well-fed people, worked a complete change in him; he kept telling Anna Sergeyevna how beautiful she was, how seductive, was urgently passionate; he would not move a step away from her, while she was often pensive and continually pressed him to confess that he did not respect her, did not love her in the least, and saw in her nothing but a common woman. Almost every evening rather late they drove somewhere out of town, to Oreanda or to the waterfall; and the excursion was always a success, the scenery invariably impressed them as beautiful and magnificent.

They were expecting her husband, but a letter came from him saying that he had eye-trouble, and begging his wife to return home as soon as possible. Anna Sergeyevna made haste to go.

"It's a good thing I am leaving," she said to Gurov. "It's the hand of Fate!"

She took a carriage to the railway station, and he went with her. They were driving the whole day. When she had taken her place in the express, and when the second bell had rung, she said, "Let me look at you once more—let me look at you again. Like this."

She was not crying but was so sad that she seemed ill and her face was quivering.

"I shall be thinking of you—remembering you," she said. "God bless you; be happy. Don't remember evil against me. We are parting forever—it has to be, for we ought never to have met. Well, God bless you."

The train moved off rapidly, its lights soon vanished, and a minute later there was no sound of it, as though everything had conspired to end as quickly as possible that sweet trance, that madness. Left alone on the platform, and gazing into the dark distance, Gurov listened to the twang of the grasshoppers and the hum of the telegraph wires, feeling as though he had just waked up. And he reflected, musing, that there had now been another episode or adventure in his life, and it, too, was at an end, and nothing was left of it but a memory. He was moved, sad, and slightly remorseful: this young woman whom he would never meet again had not been happy with him; he had been warm and affectionate with her, but yet in his manner, his tone, and his caresses there had been a shade of light irony, the slightly coarse arrogance of a happy male who was, besides, almost twice her age. She had constantly called him kind, exceptional, high-minded; obviously he had seemed to her different from what he really was, so he had involuntarily deceived her.

Here at the station there was already a scent of autumn in the air; it was a chilly evening.

"It is time for me to go north, too," thought Gurov as he left the platform. "High time!"

III

At home in Moscow the winter routine was already established; the stoves were heated, and in the morning it was still dark when the children were having breakfast and getting ready for school, and the nurse would light the lamp for a short time. There were frosts already. When the first snow falls, on the first day the sleighs are out, it is pleasant to see the white earth, the white roofs; one draws easy, delicious breaths, and the season brings back the days of one's youth. The old limes and birches, white with hoar-frost, have a good-natured look; they are closer to one's heart than cypresses and palms, and near them one no longer wants to think of mountains and the sea.

Gurov, a native of Moscow, arrived there on a fine frosty day, and when he put on his fur coat and warm gloves and took a walk along Petrovka, and when on Saturday night he heard the bells ringing, his recent trip and the places he had visited lost all charm for him. Little by little he became immersed in Moscow life, greedily read three newspapers a day, and declared that he did not read the Moscow papers on principle. He already felt a longing for restaurants, clubs, formal dinners, anniversary celebrations, and it flattered him to entertain distinguished lawyers and actors, and to play cards with a professor at the physicians' club. He could eat a whole portion of meat stewed with pickled cabbage and served in a pan, Moscow style.

A month or so would pass and the image of Anna Sergeyevna, it seemed to him, would become misty in his memory, and only from time to time he would dream of her with her touching smile as he dreamed of others. But more than a month went by, winter came into its own, and everything was still clear in his memory as though he had parted from Anna Sergeyevna only yesterday. And his memories glowed more and more vividly. When in the evening stillness the voices of his children preparing their lessons reached his study, or when he listened to a song or to an organ playing in a restaurant, or when the storm howled in the chimney, suddenly everything would rise up in his memory; what had happened on the pier and the early morning with the mist on the mountains, and the steamer coming from Feodosia, and the kisses. He would pace about his room a long time, remembering and smiling; then his memories passed into reveries, and in his imagination the past would mingle with what was to come. He did not dream of Anna Sergeyevna, but she followed him about everywhere and watched him. When he shut his eyes he saw her before him as though she were there in the flesh, and she seemed to him lovelier, younger, tenderer than she had been; and he imagined himself a finer man than he had been in Yalta. Of evenings she peered out at him from the bookcase, from the fireplace, from the corner—he heard her breathing, the caressing rustle of her clothes. In the street he followed the women with his eyes, looking for someone who resembled her.

Already he was tormented by a strong desire to share his memories with someone. But in his home it was impossible to talk of his love, and he had no one to talk to outside; certainly he could not confide in his tenants or in anyone at the bank. And what was there to talk about? He hadn't loved her then, had he? Had there been anything beautiful, poetical, edifying, or simply interesting in his relations with Anna Sergeyevna? And he was forced to talk vaguely of love, of women, and no one guessed what he meant; only his wife would twitch her black eyebrows and say, "The part of a philanderer does not suit you at all, Dimitry."

One evening, coming out of the physicians' club with an official with whom he had been playing cards, he could not resist saying:

"If you only knew what a fascinating woman I became acquainted with at Yalta!"

The official got into his sledge and was driving away, but turned suddenly and shouted:

"Dmitry Dmitrich!"

"What is it?"

"You were right this evening: the sturgeon was a bit high."

These words, so commonplace, for some reason moved Gurov to indignation, and struck him as degrading and unclean. What savage manners, what mugs! What stupid nights, what dull, humdrum days! Frenzied gambling, gluttony, drunkenness, continual talk always about the same thing! Futile pursuits and conversations always about the same topics take up the better part of one's time, the better part of one's strength, and in the end there is left a life clipped and wingless, an absurd mess, and there is no escaping or getting away from it—just as though one were in a madhouse or a prison.

Gurov, boiling with indignation, did not sleep all night. And he had a headache all the next day. And the following nights too he slept badly; he sat up in bed, thinking, or paced up and down his room. He was fed up with his children, fed up with the bank; he had no desire to go anywhere or to talk of anything.

In December during the holidays he prepared to take a trip and told his wife he was going to Petersburg to do what he could for a young friend—and he set off for S——. What for? He did not know, himself. He wanted to see Anna Sergeyevna and talk with her, to arrange a rendezvous if possible.

He arrived at S—— in the morning, and at the hotel took the best room, in which the floor was covered with gray army cloth, and on the table there was an inkstand, gray with dust and topped by a figure on horseback, its hat in its raised hand and its head broken off. The porter gave him the necessary information: von Dideritz lived in a house of his own on Staro-Goncharnaya Street, not far from the hotel: he was rich and lived well and kept his own horses; everyone in the town knew him. The porter pronounced the name: "Dridiritz."

Without haste Gurov made his way to Staro-Goncharnaya Street and found the house. Directly opposite the house stretched a long gray fence studded with nails.

"A fence like that would make one run away," thought Gurov, looking now at the fence, now at the windows of the house.

He reflected: this was a holiday, and the husband was apt to be at home. And in any case, it would be tactless to go into the house and disturb her. If he were to send her a note, it might fall into her husband's hands, and that might spoil everything. The best thing was to rely on chance. And he kept walking up and down the street and along the fence, waiting for the chance. He saw a beggar go in at the gate and heard the dogs attack him; then an hour later he heard a piano, and the sound came to him faintly and indistinctly. Probably it was Anna Sergeyevna playing. The front door opened suddenly, and an old woman came out, followed by the familiar white Pomeranian. Gurov was on the point of calling to the dog, but his heart began beating violently, and in his excitement he could not remember the Pomeranian's name.

He kept walking up and down, and hated the gray fence more and more, and by now he thought irritably that Anna Sergeyevna had forgotten him, and was perhaps already diverting herself with another man, and that that was very natural in a young woman who from morning till night had to look at that damn fence. He went back to his hotel room and sat on the couch for a long while, not knowing what to do, then he had dinner and a long nap.

"How stupid and annoying all this is!" he thought when he woke and looked at the dark windows: it was already evening. "Here I've had a good sleep for some reason. What am I going to do at night?"

He sat on the bed, which was covered with a cheap gray blanket of the kind seen in hospitals, and he twitted himself in his vexation:

"So there's your lady with the pet dog. There's your adventure. A nice place to cool your heels in."

That morning at the station a playbill in large letters had caught his eye. *The Geisha* was to be given for the first time. He thought of this and drove to the theater.

"It's quite possible that she goes to first nights," he thought.

The theater was full. As in all provincial theaters, there was a haze above the chandelier, the gallery was noisy and restless; in the front row, before the beginning of the performance the local dandies were standing with their hands clasped behind their backs; in the Governor's box the Governor's daughter, wearing a boa, occupied the front seat, while the Governor himself hid modestly behind the portiere and only his hands were visible; the curtain swayed; the orchestra was a long time tuning up. While the audience was coming in and taking their seats, Gurov scanned the faces eagerly.

Anna Sergeyevna, too, came in. She sat down in the third row, and when Gurov looked at her his heart contracted, and he understood clearly that in the whole world there was no human being so near, so precious, and so important to him; she, this little, undistinguished woman, lost in a provincial crowd, with a vulgar lorgnette in her hand, filled his whole life now, was his sorrow and his joy, the only happiness that he now desired for himself, and to the sounds of the bad orchestra, of the miserable local violins, he thought how lovely she was. He thought and dreamed.

A young man with small side-whiskers, very tall and stooped, came in with Anna Sergeyevna and sat down beside her; he nodded his head at every step and seemed to be bowing continually. Probably this was the husband whom at Yalta, in an access of bitter feeling, she had called a flunkey. And there really was in his lanky figure, his side-whiskers, his small bald patch, something of a flunkey's retiring manner; his smile was mawkish, and in his buttonhole there was an academic badge like a waiter's number.

During the first intermission the husband went out to have a smoke; she remained in her seat. Gurov, who was also sitting in the orchestra, went up to her and said in a shaky voice, with a forced smile:

"Good evening!"

She glanced at him and turned pale, then looked at him again in horror, unable to believe her eyes, and gripped the fan and the lorgnette tightly together in her hands, evidently trying to keep herself from fainting. Both were silent. She was sitting, he was standing, frightened by her distress and not daring to take a seat beside her. The violins and the flute that were being tuned up sang out. He suddenly felt frightened: it seemed as if all the people in the boxes were looking at them. She got up and went hurriedly to the exit; he followed her, and both of them walked blindly along the corridors and up and down stairs, and figures in the uniforms prescribed for magistrates, teachers, and officials of the Department of Crown Lands, all wearing badges, flitted before their eyes, as did also ladies, and fur coats on hangers; they were conscious of drafts and the smell of stale tobacco. And Gurov, whose heart was beating violently, thought:

"Oh, Lord! Why are these people here and this orchestra!"

And at that instant he suddenly recalled how when he had seen Anna Sergeyevna off at the station he had said to himself that all was over between them and that they would never meet again. But how distant the end still was!

On the narrow, gloomy staircase over which it said "To the Amphitheatre," she stopped.

"How you frightened me!" she said, breathing hard, still pale and stunned. "Oh, how you frightened me! I am barely alive. Why did you come? Why?"

"But do understand, Anna, do understand—" he said hurriedly, under his breath. "I implore you, do understand—"

She looked at him with fear, with entreaty, with love; she looked at him intently, to keep his features more distinctly in her memory.

"I suffer so," she went on, not listening to him. "All this time I have been thinking of nothing but you; I live only by the thought of you. And I wanted to forget, to forget; but why, oh, why have you come?"

On the landing above them two high school boys were looking down and smoking, but it was all the same to Gurov; he drew Anna Sergeyevna to him and began kissing her face and hands.

"What are you doing, what are you doing!" she was saying in horror, pushing him away. "We have lost our senses. Go away today; go away at once—I conjure you by all that is sacred, I implore you—People are coming this way!"

Someone was walking up the stairs.

"You must leave," Anna Sergeyevna went on in a whisper. "Do you hear, Dmitry Dmitrich? I will come and see you in Moscow. I have never been happy; I am unhappy now, and I never, never shall be happy, never! So don't make me suffer still more! I swear I'll come to Moscow. But now let us part. My dear, good, precious one, let us part!"

She pressed his hand and walked rapidly downstairs, turning to look round at him, and from her eyes he could see that she really was unhappy. Gurov stood for a while, listening, then when all grew quiet, he found his coat and left the theater.

IV

And Anna Sergeyevna began coming to see him in Moscow. Once every two or three months she left S—— telling her husband that she was going to consult a doctor about a woman's ailment from which she was suffering—and her husband did and did not believe her. When she arrived in Moscow she would stop at the Slavyansky Bazar Hotel, and at once send a man in a red cap to Gurov. Gurov came to see her, and no one in Moscow knew of it.

Once he was going to see her in this way on a winter morning (the messenger had come the evening before and not found him in). With him walked his daughter, whom he wanted to take to school; it was on the way. Snow was coming down in big wet flakes.

"It's three degrees above zero,° and yet it's snowing," Gurov was saying to his daughter. "But this temperature prevails only on the surface of the earth; in the upper layers of the atmosphere there is quite a different temperature."

"And why doesn't it thunder in winter, papa?"

He explained that, too. He talked, thinking all the while that he was on his way to a rendezvous, and no living soul knew of it, and probably no one would ever know. He had two lives, an open one, seen and known by all who needed to know it, full of conventional truth and conventional falsehood, exactly like the lives of his friends and acquaintances; and another life that went on in secret. And through some strange, perhaps accidental, combination of circumstances, everything that was of interest and importance to him, everything that was essential to him, everything about which he felt sincerely and did not deceive himself, everything that constituted the core of his life, was going on concealed from others; while all that was false, the shell in which he hid to cover the truth—his work at the bank, for instance, his discussions at the club, his references to the "inferior race," his appearances at anniversary celebrations with his wife—all that went on in the open. Judging others by himself, he did not believe what he saw, and always fancied that every man led his real, most interesting life under cover of secrecy as under cover of night. The personal life of every individual is based on secrecy, and perhaps it is partly for that reason that civilized man is so nervously anxious that personal privacy should be respected.

Having taken his daughter to school, Gurov went on to the Slavyansky Bazar Hotel. He took off his fur coat in the lobby, went upstairs, and knocked gently at the door. Anna Sergeyevna, wearing his favorite gray dress, exhausted by the journey and by waiting, had been expecting him since the previous

---

three degrees above zero: On the Celsius scale—about thirty-seven degrees Fahrenheit.

evening. She was pale, and looked at him without a smile, and he had hardly entered when she flung herself on his breast. That kiss was a long, lingering one, as though they had not seen one another for two years.

"Well, darling, how are you getting on there?" he asked. "What news?"

"Wait; I'll tell you in a moment—I can't speak."

She could not speak; she was crying. She turned away from him, and pressed her handkerchief to her eyes.

"Let her have her cry; meanwhile I'll sit down," he thought, and he seated himself in an armchair.

Then he rang and ordered tea, and while he was having his tea she remained standing at the window with her back to him. She was crying out of sheer agitation, in the sorrowful consciousness that their life was so sad; that they could only see each other in secret and had to hide from people like thieves! Was it not a broken life?

"Come, stop now, dear!" he said.

It was plain to him that this love of theirs would not be over soon, that the end of it was not in sight. Anna Sergeyevna was growing more and more attached to him. She adored him, and it was unthinkable to tell her that their love was bound to come to an end some day; besides, she would not have believed it!

He went up to her and took her by the shoulders, to fondle her and say something diverting, and at that moment he caught sight of himself in the mirror.

His hair was already beginning to turn gray. And it seemed odd to him that he had grown so much older in the last few years, and lost his looks. The shoulders on which his hands rested were warm and heaving. He felt compassion for this life, still so warm and lovely, but probably already about to begin to fade and wither like his own. Why did she love him so much? He always seemed to women different from what he was, and they loved in him not himself, but the man whom their imagination created and whom they had been eagerly seeking all their lives; and afterwards, when they saw their mistake, they loved him nevertheless. And not one of them had been happy with him. In the past he had met women, come together with them, parted from them, but he had never once loved; it was anything you please, but not love. And only now when his head was gray he had fallen in love, really, truly—for the first time in his life.

Anna Sergeyevna and he loved each other as people do who are very close and intimate, like man and wife, like tender friends; it seemed to them that Fate itself had meant them for one another, and they could not understand why he had a wife and she a husband; and it was as though they were a pair of migratory birds, male and female, caught and forced to live in different cages. They forgave each other what they were ashamed of in their past, they forgave everything in the present, and felt that this love of theirs had altered them both.

Formerly in moments of sadness he had soothed himself with whatever logical arguments came into his head, but now he no longer cared for logic; he felt profound compassion, he wanted to be sincere and tender.

"Give it up now, my darling," he said. "You've had your cry; that's enough. Let us have a talk now, we'll think up something."

Then they spent a long time taking counsel together, they talked of how to avoid the necessity for secrecy, for deception, for living in different cities, and not seeing one another for long stretches of time. How could they free themselves from these intolerable fetters?

"How? How?" he asked, clutching his head. "How?"

And it seemed as though in a little while the solution would be found, and then a new and glorious life would begin; and it was clear to both of them that the end was still far off, and that what was to be most complicated and difficult for them was only just beginning.

KATE CHOPIN

Kate Chopin (1851–1904) was born in St. Louis. Her father died when she was four, and she was raised by her Creole mother's family. In 1870 she married Oscar Chopin, a cotton broker. They lived in Louisiana, first in New Orleans and then on a large plantation among the French-speaking Acadians. When her husband died in 1882, Chopin moved with her six children back to St. Louis. Friends encouraged her to write, and when she was nearly forty years old she published her first novel, At Fault *(1890). Her stories began to appear in* Century *and* Harper's Magazine, *and two collections followed:* Bayou Folk *(1894) and* A Night in Arcadie *(1897). Her last major work, the novel* The Awakening *(1899), is her masterpiece, but its sympathetic treatment of adultery shocked reviewers and readers throughout America. In St. Louis the novel was taken out of the libraries, and Chopin was denied membership in the St. Louis Fine Arts Club. When her third collection of stories was rejected by her publisher at the end of 1899, Chopin felt herself a literary outcast; she wrote very little in the last years of her life.*

What affronted the genteel readers of the 1890s was Chopin's attempt to write frankly about women's emotions in their relations with men, children, and their own sexuality. After her mother's death in 1885, she stopped being a practicing Catholic and accepted the Darwinian view of human evolution. Seeking God in nature rather than through the church, Chopin wrote freely on the subjects of sex and love, but she said she learned to her sorrow that for American authors, "the limitations imposed upon their art by their environment hamper a full and spontaneous expression." Magazine editors turned down her work if it challenged conventional social behavior, as does "The Storm" and "The Story of an Hour," which feminist critics championed more than half a century after Chopin's death.

Chopin adopted Guy de Maupassant as a model after translating his stories from the French. She felt, "Here was life, not fiction; for where were the plots, the old fashioned mechanism and stage trappings that in a vague, unthinking way I had fancied were essential to the art of story making?" If her fiction is sometimes marred by stilted language or improbable coincidence, at her best, as in "Désirée's Baby," Chopin subtly emphasized character rather than plot in her dramatization of the tragic repercussions of racial prejudice.

COMMENTARY *Kate Chopin, "How I Stumbled upon Maupassant," page 556.*

WEB *Research Kate Chopin and answer questions about her work at bedfordstmartins.com/charters/litwriters.*

Désirée's Baby   1892

As the day was pleasant, Madame Valmondé drove over to L'Abri to see Désirée and the baby.

It made her laugh to think of Désirée with a baby. Why, it seemed but yesterday that Désirée was little more than a baby herself; when Monsieur in riding through the gateway of Valmondé had found her lying asleep in the shadow of the big stone pillar.

The little one awoke in his arms and began to cry for "Dada." That was as much as she could do or say. Some people thought she might have strayed there of her own accord, for she was of the toddling age. The prevailing belief was that she had been purposely left by a party of Texans, whose canvas-covered wagon, late in the day, had crossed the ferry that Coton Maïs kept, just below the plantation. In time Madame Valmondé abandoned every speculation but the one that Désirée had been sent to her by a beneficent Providence to be the child of her affection, seeing that she was without child of the flesh. For the girl grew to be beautiful and gentle, affectionate and sincere, — the idol of Valmondé.

It was no wonder, when she stood one day against the stone pillar in whose shadow she had lain asleep, eighteen years before, that Armand Aubigny riding by and seeing her there, had fallen in love with her. That was the way all the Aubignys fell in love, as if struck by a pistol shot. The wonder was that he had not loved her before; for he had known her since his father brought him home from Paris, a boy of eight, after his mother died there. The passion that awoke in him that day, when he saw her at the gate, swept along like an avalanche, or like a prairie fire, or like anything that drives headlong over all obstacles.

Monsieur Valmondé grew practical and wanted things well considered: that is, the girl's obscure origin. Armand looked into her eyes and did not care. He was reminded that she was nameless. What did it matter about a name when he could give her one of the oldest and proudest in Louisiana? He ordered the *corbeille* from Paris, and contained himself with what patience he could until it arrived; then they were married.

Madame Valmondé had not seen Désirée and the baby for four weeks. When she reached L'Abri she shuddered at the first sight of it, as she always did. It was a sad looking place, which for many years had not known the gentle presence of a mistress, old Monsieur Aubigny having married and buried his wife in France, and she having loved her own land too well ever to leave it. The roof came down steep and black like a cowl, reaching out beyond the wide galleries that encircled the yellow stuccoed house. Big, solemn oaks grew close to it, and their thick-leaved, far-reaching branches shadowed it like a pall. Young

Aubigny's rule was a strict one, too, and under it his negroes had forgotten how to be gay, as they had been during the old master's easy-going and indulgent lifetime.

The young mother was recovering slowly, and lay full length, in her soft white muslins and laces, upon a couch. The baby was beside her, upon her arm, where he had fallen asleep, at her breast. The yellow nurse woman sat beside a window fanning herself.

Madame Valmondé bent her portly figure over Désirée and kissed her, holding her an instant tenderly in her arms. Then she turned to the child.

"This is not the baby!" she exclaimed, in startled tones. French was the language spoken at Valmondé in those days.

"I knew you would be astonished," laughed Désirée, "at the way he has grown. The little *cochon de lait!*° Look at his legs, mamma, and his hands and fingernails, — real fingernails. Zandrine had to cut them this morning. Isn't it true, Zandrine?"

The woman bowed her turbaned head majestically, "Mais si, Madame."

"And the way he cries," went on Désirée, "is deafening. Armand heard him the other day as far away as La Blanche's cabin."

Madame Valmondé had never removed her eyes from the child. She lifted it and walked with it over to the window that was lightest. She scanned the baby narrowly, then looked as searchingly at Zandrine, whose face was turned to gaze across the fields.

"Yes, the child has grown, has changed," said Madame Valmondé, slowly, as she replaced it beside its mother. "What does Armand say?"

Désirée's face became suffused with a glow that was happiness itself.

"Oh, Armand is the proudest father in the parish, I believe, chiefly because it is a boy, to bear his name; though he says not, — that he would have loved a girl as well. But I know it isn't true. I know he says that to please me. And mamma," she added, drawing Madame Valmondé's head down to her and speaking in a whisper, "he hasn't punished one of them — not one of them — since baby is born. Even Négrillon, who pretended to have burnt his leg that he might rest from work — he only laughed, and said Négrillon was a great scamp. Oh, mamma, I'm so happy; it frightens me."

What Désirée said was true. Marriage, and later the birth of his son had softened Armand Aubigny's imperious and exacting nature greatly. This was what made the gentle Désirée so happy, for she loved him desperately. When he frowned she trembled, but loved him. When he smiled, she asked no greater blessing of God. But Armand's dark, handsome face had not often been disfigured by frowns since the day he fell in love with her.

When the baby was about three months old, Désirée awoke one day to the conviction that there was something in the air menacing her peace. It was at first too subtle to grasp. It had only been a disquieting suggestion; an air of mystery among the blacks; unexpected visits from far-off neighbors who could hardly account for their coming. Then a strange, an awful change in her

---

cochon de lait: An endearment (literally, "suckling pig" in French).

husband's manner, which she dared not ask him to explain. When he spoke to her, it was with averted eyes, from which the old love-light seemed to have gone out. He absented himself from home; and when there, avoided her presence and that of her child, without excuse. And the very spirit of Satan seemed suddenly to take hold of him in his dealings with the slaves. Désirée was miserable enough to die.

She sat in her room, one hot afternoon, in her *peignoir*, listlessly drawing through her fingers the strands of her long, silky brown hair that hung about her shoulders. The baby, half naked, lay asleep upon her own great mahogany bed, that was like a sumptuous throne, with its satin-lined half-canopy. One of La Blanche's little quadroon boys—half naked too—stood fanning the child slowly with a fan of peacock feathers. Désirée's eyes had been fixed absently and sadly upon the baby, while she was striving to penetrate the threatening mist that she felt closing about her. She looked from her child to the boy who stood beside him, and back again; over and over. "Ah!" It was a cry that she could not help; which she was not conscious of having uttered. The blood turned like ice in her veins, and a clammy moisture gathered upon her face.

She tried to speak to the little quadroon boy; but no sound would come, at first. When he heard his name uttered, he looked up, and his mistress was pointing to the door. He laid aside the great, soft fan, and obediently stole away, over the polished floor, on his bare tiptoes.

She stayed motionless, with gaze riveted upon her child, and her face the picture of fright.

Presently her husband entered the room, and without noticing her, went to a table and began to search among some papers which covered it.

"Armand," she called to him, in a voice which must have stabbed him, if he was human. But he did not notice. "Armand," she said again. Then she rose and tottered towards him. "Armand," she panted once more, clutching his arm, "look at our child. What does it mean? tell me."

He coldly but gently loosened her fingers from about his arm and thrust the hand away from him. "Tell me what it means!" she cried despairingly.

"It means," he answered lightly, "that the child is not white; it means that you are not white."

A quick conception of all that this accusation meant for her nerved her with unwonted courage to deny it. "It is a lie; it is not true, I am white! Look at my hair, it is brown; and my eyes are gray, Armand, you know they are gray. And my skin is fair," seizing his wrist. "Look at my hand; whiter than yours, Armand," she laughed hysterically.

"As white as La Blanche's," he returned cruelly; and went away leaving her alone with their child.

When she could hold a pen in her hand, she sent a despairing letter to Madame Valmondé.

"My mother, they tell me I am not white. Armand has told me I am not white. For God's sake tell them it is not true. You must know it is not true. I shall die. I must die. I cannot be so unhappy, and live."

The answer that came was as brief:

"My own Désirée: Come home to Valmondé; back to your mother who loves you. Come with your child."

When the letter reached Désirée she went with it to her husband's study, and laid it open upon the desk before which he sat. She was like a stone image: silent, white, motionless after she placed it there.

In silence he ran his cold eyes over the written words. He said nothing. "Shall I go, Armand?" she asked in tones sharp with agonized suspense.

"Yes, go."

"Do you want me to go?"

"Yes, I want you to go."

He thought Almighty God had dealt cruelly and unjustly with him; and felt, somehow, that he was paying Him back in kind when he stabbed thus into his wife's soul. Moreover he no longer loved her, because of the unconscious injury she had brought upon his home and his name.

She turned away like one stunned by a blow, and walked slowly towards the door, hoping he would call her back.

"Good-by, Armand," she moaned.

He did not answer her. That was his last blow at fate.

Désirée went in search of her child. Zandrine was pacing the sombre gallery with it. She took the little one from the nurse's arms with no word of explanation, and descending the steps, walked away, under the live-oak branches.

It was an October afternoon; the sun was just sinking. Out in the still fields the negroes were picking cotton.

Désirée had not changed the thin white garment nor the slippers which she wore. Her hair was uncovered and the sun's rays brought a golden gleam from its brown meshes. She did not take the broad, beaten road which led to the far-off plantation of Valmondé. She walked across a deserted field, where the stubble bruised her tender feet, so delicately shod, and tore her thin gown to shreds.

She disappeared among the reeds and willows that grew thick along the banks of the deep, sluggish bayou; and she did not come back again.

Some weeks later there was a curious scene enacted at L'Abri. In the centre of the smoothly swept back yard was a great bonfire. Armand Aubigny sat in the wide hallway that commanded a view of the spectacle; and it was he who dealt out to a half dozen negroes the material which kept this fire ablaze.

A graceful cradle of willow, with all its dainty furbishings, was laid upon the pyre, which had already been fed with the richness of a priceless *layette*. Then there were silk gowns, and velvet and satin ones added to these; laces, too, and embroideries; bonnets and gloves; for the *corbeille* had been of rare quality.

The last thing to go was a tiny bundle of letters; innocent little scribblings that Désirée had sent to him during the days of their espousal. There was the remnant of one back in the drawer from which he took them. But it was not Désirée's; it was part of an old letter from his mother to his father. He read it. She was thanking God for the blessing of her husband's love: —

"But, above all," she wrote, "night and day, I thank the good God for having so arranged our lives that our dear Armand will never know that his mother, who adores him, belongs to the race that is cursed with the brand of slavery."

The Storm   1898

I

The leaves were so still that even Bibi thought it was going to rain. Bobinôt, who was accustomed to converse on terms of perfect equality with his little son, called the child's attention to certain sombre clouds that were rolling with sinister intention from the west, accompanied by a sullen, threatening roar. They were at Friedheimer's store and decided to remain there till the storm had passed. They sat within the door on two empty kegs. Bibi was four years old and looked very wise.

"Mama'll be 'fraid, yes," he suggested with blinking eyes.

"She'll shut the house. Maybe she got Sylvie helpin' her this evenin'," Bobinôt responded reassuringly.

"No; she ent got Sylvie. Sylvie was helpin' her yistiday," piped Bibi.

Bobinôt arose and going across to the counter purchased a can of shrimps, of which Calixta was very fond. Then he returned to his perch on the keg and sat stolidly holding the can of shrimps while the storm burst. It shook the wooden store and seemed to be ripping great furrows in the distant field. Bibi laid his little hand on his father's knee and was not afraid.

II

Calixta, at home, felt no uneasiness for their safety. She sat at a side window sewing furiously on a sewing machine. She was greatly occupied and did not notice the approaching storm. But she felt very warm and often stopped to mop her face on which the perspiration gathered in beads. She unfastened her white sacque at the throat. It began to grow dark, and suddenly realizing the situation she got up hurriedly and went about closing windows and doors.

Out on the small front gallery she had hung Bobinôt's Sunday clothes to air and she hastened out to gather them before the rain fell. As she stepped outside, Alcée Laballière rode in at the gate. She had not seen him very often since her marriage, and never alone. She stood there with Bobinôt's coat in her hands, and the big rain drops began to fall. Alcée rode his horse under the shelter of a side projection where the chickens had huddled and there were plows and a harrow piled up in the corner.

"May I come and wait on your gallery till the storm is over, Calixta?" he asked.

"Come 'long in, M'sieur Alcée."

His voice and her own startled her as if from a trance, and she seized Bobinôt's vest. Alcée, mounting to the porch, grabbed the trousers and snatched Bibi's braided jacket that was about to be carried away by a sudden gust of wind. He expressed an intention to remain outside, but it was soon apparent that he might as well have been out in the open: the water beat in upon the boards in driving sheets, and he went inside, closing the door after him. It was even necessary to put something beneath the door to keep the water out.

"My! what a rain! It's good two years sence it rain' like that," exclaimed Calixta as she rolled up a piece of bagging and Alcée helped her to thrust it beneath the crack.

She was a little fuller of figure than five years before when she married; but she had lost nothing of her vivacity. Her blue eyes still retained their melting quality; and her yellow hair, dishevelled by the wind and rain, kinked more stubbornly than ever about her ears and temples.

The rain beat upon the low, shingled roof with a force and clatter that threatened to break an entrance and deluge them there. They were in the dining room—the sitting room—the general utility room. Adjoining was her bed room, with Bibi's couch along side her own. The door stood open, and the room with its white, monumental bed, its closed shutters, looked dim and mysterious.

Alcée flung himself into a rocker and Calixta nervously began to gather up from the floor the lengths of a cotton sheet which she had been sewing.

"If this keeps up, *Dieu sait*° if the levees goin' to stan' it!" she exclaimed.

"What have you got to do with the levees?"

"I got enough to do! An' there's Bobinôt with Bibi out in that storm— if he only didn't left Friedheimer's!"

"Let us hope, Calixta, that Bobinôt's got sense enough to come in out of a cyclone."

She went and stood at the window with a greatly disturbed look on her face. She wiped the frame that was clouded with moisture. It was stiflingly hot. Alcée got up and joined her at the window, looking over her shoulder. The rain was coming down in sheets obscuring the view of far-off cabins and enveloping the distant wood in a gray mist. The playing of the lightning was incessant. A bolt struck a tall chinaberry tree at the edge of the field. It filled all visible space with a blinding glare and the crash seemed to invade the very boards they stood upon.

Calixta put her hands to her eyes, and with a cry, staggered backward. Alcée's arm encircled her, and for an instant he drew her close and spasmodically to him.

"*Bonté*"° she cried, releasing herself from his encircling arm and retreating from the window, "the house'll go next! If I only knew w'ere Bibi was!" She would not compose herself; she would not be seated. Alcée clasped her shoulders and looked into her face. The contact of her warm, palpitating body when he had unthinkingly drawn her into his arms, had aroused all the old-time infatuation and desire for her flesh.

"Calixta," he said, "don't be frightened. Nothing can happen. The house is too low to be struck, with so many tall trees standing about. There! aren't you going to be quiet? say, aren't you?" He pushed her hair back from her face that

---

Dieu sait: God knows.
Bonté: "Goodness!"

was warm and steaming. Her lips were as red and moist as pomegranate seed. Her white neck and a glimpse of her full, firm bosom disturbed him powerfully. As she glanced up at him the fear in her liquid blue eyes had given place to a drowsy gleam that unconsciously betrayed a sensuous desire. He looked down into her eyes and there was nothing for him to do but to gather her lips in a kiss. It reminded him of Assumption.

"Do you remember—in Assumption, Calixta?" he asked in a low voice broken by passion. Oh! she remembered; for in Assumption he had kissed her and kissed and kissed her; until his senses would well nigh fail, and to save her he would resort to a desperate flight. If she was not an immaculate dove in those days, she was still inviolate; a passionate creature whose very defenselessness had made her defense, against which his honor forbade him to prevail. Now— well, now—her lips seemed in a manner free to be tasted, as well as her round, white throat and her whiter breasts.

They did not heed the crashing torrents, and the roar of the elements made her laugh as she lay in his arms. She was a revelation in that dim, mysterious chamber; as white as the couch she lay upon. Her firm, elastic flesh that was knowing for the first time its birthright, was like a creamy lily that the sun invites to contribute its breath and perfume to the undying life of the world.

The generous abundance of her passion, without guile or trickery, was like a white flame which penetrated and found response in depths of his own sensuous nature that had never yet been reached.

When he touched her breasts they gave themselves up in quivering ecstasy, inviting his lips. Her mouth was a fountain of delight. And when he possessed her, they seemed to swoon together at the very borderland of life's mystery.

He stayed cushioned upon her, breathless, dazed, enervated, with his heart beating like a hammer upon her. With one hand she clasped his head, her lips lightly touching his forehead. The other hand stroked with a soothing rhythm his muscular shoulders.

The growl of the thunder was distant and passing away. The rain beat softly upon the shingles, inviting them to drowsiness and sleep. But they dared not yield.

The rain was over; and the sun was turning the glistening green world into a palace of gems. Calixta, on the gallery, watched Alcée ride away. He turned and smiled at her with a beaming face; and she lifted her pretty chin in the air and laughed aloud.

III

Bobinôt and Bibi, trudging home, stopped without at the cistern to make themselves presentable.

"My! Bibi, w'at will yo' mama say! You ought to be asham'. You oughtn' put on those good pants. Look at 'em! An' that mud on yo' collar! How you got that mud on yo' collar, Bibi? I never saw such a boy!" Bibi was the picture of pathetic resignation. Bobinôt was the embodiment of serious solicitude as he strove to remove from his own person and his son's the signs of their tramp over heavy roads and through wet fields. He scraped the mud off Bibi's bare legs and feet with a stick and carefully removed all traces from his heavy brogans. Then, prepared for the worst—the meeting with an over-scrupulous housewife, they entered cautiously at the back door.

Calixta was preparing supper. She had set the table and was dripping coffee at the hearth. She sprang up as they came in.

"Oh, Bobinôt! You back! My! but I was uneasy. W'ere you been during the rain? An' Bibi? he ain't wet? he ain't hurt?" She had clasped Bibi and was kissing him effusively. Bobinôt's explanations and apologies which he had been composing all along the way, died on his lips as Calixta felt him to see if he were dry, and seemed to express nothing but satisfaction at their safe return.

"I brought you some shrimps, Calixta," offered Bobinôt, hauling the can from his ample side pocket and laying it on the table.

"Shrimps! Oh, Bobinôt! you too good fo' anything!" and she gave him a smacking kiss on the cheek that resounded. "*J'vous réponds,*° we'll have a feas' to-night! umph-umph!"

Bobinôt and Bibi began to relax and enjoy themselves, and when the three seated themselves at table they laughed much and so loud that anyone might have heard them as far away as Laballière's.

IV

Alcée Laballière wrote to his wife, Clarisse, that night. It was a loving letter, full of tender solicitude. He told her not to hurry back, but if she and the babies liked it at Biloxi, to stay a month longer. He was getting on nicely; and though he missed them, he was willing to bear the separation a while longer— realizing that their health and pleasure were the first things to be considered.

V

As for Clarisse, she was charmed upon receiving her husband's letter. She and the babies were doing well. The society was agreeable; many of her old friends and acquaintances were at the bay. And the first free breath since her marriage seemed to restore the pleasant liberty of her maiden days. Devoted as she was to her husband, their intimate conjugal life was something which she was more than willing to forego for a while.

So the storm passed and everyone was happy.

The Story of an Hour   1894

Knowing that Mrs. Mallard was afflicted with a heart trouble, great care was taken to break to her as gently as possible the news of her husband's death.

It was her sister Josephine who told her, in broken sentences; veiled hints that revealed in half concealing. Her husband's friend Richards was there, too, near her. It was he who had been in the newspaper office when intelligence of the railroad disaster was received, with Brently Mallard's name leading the list

---

J'vous réponds: "I give you my word."

of "killed." He had only taken the time to assure himself of its truth by a second telegram, and had hastened to forestall any less careful, less tender friend in bearing the sad message.

She did not hear the story as many women have heard the same, with a paralyzed inability to accept its significance. She wept at once, with sudden, wild abandonment, in her sister's arms. When the storm of grief had spent itself she went away to her room alone. She would have no one follow her.

There stood, facing the open window, a comfortable, roomy armchair. Into this she sank, pressed down by a physical exhaustion that haunted her body and seemed to reach into her soul.

She could see in the open square before her house the tops of trees that were all aquiver with the new spring life. The delicious breath of rain was in the air. In the street below a peddler was crying his wares. The notes of a distant song which some one was singing reached her faintly, and countless sparrows were twittering in the eaves.

There were patches of blue sky showing here and there through the clouds that had met and piled one above the other in the west facing her window.

She sat with her head thrown back upon the cushion of the chair, quite motionless, except when a sob came up into her throat and shook her, as a child who had cried itself to sleep continues to sob in its dreams.

She was young, with a fair, calm face, whose lines bespoke repression and even a certain strength. But now there was a dull stare in her eyes, whose gaze was fixed away off yonder on one of those patches of blue sky. It was not a glance of reflection, but rather indicated a suspension of intelligent thought.

There was something coming to her and she was waiting for it, fearfully. What was it? She did not know; it was too subtle and elusive to name. But she felt it, creeping out of the sky, reaching toward her through the sounds, the scents, the color that filled the air.

Now her bosom rose and fell tumultuously. She was beginning to recognize this thing that was approaching to possess her, and she was striving to beat it back with her will — as powerless as her two white slender hands would have been.

When she abandoned herself a little whispered word escaped her slightly parted lips. She said it over and over under her breath: "free, free, free!" The vacant stare and the look of terror that had followed it went from her eyes. They stayed keen and bright. Her pulses beat fast, and the coursing blood warmed and relaxed every inch of her body.

She did not stop to ask if it were or were not a monstrous joy that held her. A clear and exalted perception enabled her to dismiss the suggestion as trivial.

She knew that she would weep again when she saw the kind, tender hands folded in death; the face that had never looked save with love upon her, fixed and gray and dead. But she saw beyond that bitter moment a long procession of years to come that would belong to her absolutely. And she opened and spread her arms out to them in welcome.

There would be no one to live for her during those coming years: she would live for herself. There would be no powerful will bending hers in that blind persistence with which men and women believe they have a right to impose a private will upon a fellow-creature. A kind intention or a cruel intention made the act seem no less a crime as she looked upon it in that brief moment of illumination.

And yet she had loved him—sometimes. Often she had not. What did it matter! What could love, the unsolved mystery, count for in face of this possession of self-assertion which she suddenly recognized as the strongest impulse of her being!

"Free! Body and soul free!" she kept whispering.

Josephine was kneeling before the closed door with her lips to the keyhole, imploring for admission. "Louise, open the door! I beg; open the door—you will make yourself ill. What are you doing, Louise? For heaven's sake open the door."

"Go away. I am not making myself ill." No; she was drinking in a very elixir of life through that open window.

Her fancy was running riot along those days ahead of her. Spring days, and summer days, and all sorts of days that would be her own. She breathed a quick prayer that life might be long. It was only yesterday she had thought with a shudder that life might be long.

She arose at length and opened the door to her sister's importunities. There was a feverish triumph in her eyes, and she carried herself unwittingly like a goddess of Victory. She clasped her sister's waist, and together they descended the stairs. Richards stood waiting for them at the bottom.

Some one was opening the front door with a latchkey. It was Brently Mallard who entered, a little travel-stained, composedly carrying his gripsack and umbrella. He had been far from the scene of accident, and did not even know there had been one. He stood amazed at Josephine's piercing cry; at Richards' quick motion to screen him from the view of his wife.

But Richards was too late.

When the doctors came they said she had died of heart disease—of joy that kills.

EDWIDGE DANTICAT

Edwidge Danticat (b. 1969) was born in Port-au-Prince, Haiti. When she was two, her father immigrated to the United States to look for work. Two years later her mother followed him, leaving Danticat and her younger brother in the care of their uncle, who was a minister. Danticat remembers her childhood fascination with the ritual of storytelling conducted by her aunt's grandmother in Haiti. When she told a story, her listeners said "Krik?" and she would answer "Krak!"

She told stories when the people would gather—folk tales with her own spin on them, and stories about the family. It was call-and-response— if the audience seemed bored, the story would speed up, and if they were participating, a song would go in. The whole interaction was exciting to me. These cross-generational exchanges didn't happen often, because children were supposed to respect their elders. But when you were telling stories, it was more equal, and fun.

At the age of twelve, Danticat joined her parents in Brooklyn, where she began to learn English (the family still speaks Creole at home). Within a year she was writing articles for her high school newspaper, New Youth Connections. She majored in French literature at Barnard College, graduating in 1990, and went on to study in the MFA program in creative writing at Brown University on a full scholarship. While still a graduate student she sold the manuscript of her first book, Breath, Eyes, Memory, to Soho, a small press she discovered in Writer's Digest. Published in 1994, the novel dramatized a young Haitian woman's coming of age in a troubled mother-daughter relationship and was chosen by Oprah Winfrey for the June 18, 1994, "meeting" of her television book club. With this endorsement, Breath, Eyes, Memory became a paperback best-seller.

The next year Danticat published Krik? Krak!, a collection of stories that was nominated for a National Book Award, and she was chosen as one of the twenty "Best Young American Novelists" by Granta magazine. The Farming of Bones, her third book, published by Soho in 1998 and winner of the 1999 American Book Award, describes the 1937 massacre on the Haitian-Dominican border. As a spokesperson for her community, Danticat insists that she is free to write as she pleases in her fiction: "My characters are not representative of the community as a whole. As a writer, it's the person who is different from everybody else who might be interesting to you." "Seven" is a recent story that first appeared in The New Yorker.

WEB *Research Edwidge Danticat and answer questions about her work at bedfordstmartins.com/charters/litwriters.*

Seven

2001

Next month would make it seven years since he'd last seen his wife. Seven, a number he despised but had discovered was a useful marker. There were seven days between paychecks, seven hours, not counting lunch, spent each day at his day job, seven at his night job. Seven was the last number in his age—thirty-seven. And now there were seven hours left before his wife was due to arrive. Maybe it would be more, with her having to wait for her luggage and then make it through the long immigration line and past customs to look for him in the crowd of welcoming faces on the other side of the sliding doors at JFK. That is, if the flight from Port-au-Prince wasn't delayed, as it often was, or cancelled altogether.

He shared an apartment in the basement of a house in East Flatbush, Brooklyn, with two other men. To prepare for the reunion, he had cleaned his room. He had thrown out some cherry-red rayon shirts that he knew she would hate. And then he had climbed the splintered steps to the first floor to tell the landlady that his wife was coming. His landlady was also Haitian, a self-employed accountant.

"I don't have a problem with your wife coming," she had told him. She was microwaving a frozen dessert. I just hope she is clean."

"She is clean," he said.

The kitchen was the only room in the main part of the house that he'd ever seen. It was spotless, and the dishes were neatly organized in glass cabinets. It smelled of pine-scented air freshener.

"Did you tell the men?" she asked. She opened the microwave and removed two small plastic plates of something that vaguely resembled strawberry cheesecake.

"I told them," he said.

He was waiting for her to announce that she would have to charge him extra. She had agreed to rent the room to one person, not two—a man she'd probably taken for a bachelor.

"I don't know if I can keep this arrangement if everyone's wife starts coming," she said.

He could not speak for the two other men. Michel and Dany had wives, too, but he had no idea if or when those wives would be joining them.

"A woman living down there with three men," the landlady said. "Maybe your wife will be uncomfortable."

He wanted to tell her that it was not up to her to decide whether or not his wife would be comfortable. But he had been prepared for this, too, for some unpleasant remark about his wife. Actually, he was up there as much to give notice that he was looking for an apartment as to announce that his wife was coming. As soon as he found one, he would be moving.

"O.K., then," she said, opening her silverware drawer. "Just remember, you start the month, you pay the whole thing."

"Thank you very much, Madame," he said.

As he walked back downstairs, he scolded himself for calling her Madame. Why had he acted like a servant who had been dismissed? It was one of those class things from home that he couldn't shake. On the other hand, if he had addressed the woman respectfully, it wasn't because she was so-called upper class, or because she spoke French (though never to him), or even because after five years in the same room he was still paying only $350 a month. If he had addressed the woman politely that day, it was because he was making a sacrifice for his wife.

After his conversation with the landlady, he decided to have a more thorough one with the men who occupied the other two rooms in the basement. The day before his wife was to arrive, he went into the kitchen to see them. The fact that they were wearing only white, rather sheer, loose boxers, as they stumbled about bleary-eyed, concerned him.

"You understand, she's a woman," he told them. He wasn't worried that she'd be tempted—they were skin and bones—but if she was still as sensitive as he remembered, their near-nakedness might embarrass her.

The men understood.

"If it were my wife," Michel said, "I would feel the same."

Dany simply nodded.

They had robes, Michel declared after a while. They would wear them.

They didn't have robes—all three men knew this—but Michel would buy some, out of respect for the wife. Michel, at forty, the oldest of the three, had advised him to pretty up his room—to buy some silk roses, some decorative prints for the walls (no naked girls), and some vanilla incense, which would be more pleasing than the air fresheners the woman upstairs liked so much.

Dany told him that he would miss their evenings out together. In the old days, they had often gone dancing at the Rendez-Vous, which was now the Cenegal night club. But they hadn't gone much since the place had become famous—Abner Louima° was arrested there, then beaten and sodomized at a nearby police station.

He told Dany not to mention those nights out again. His wife wasn't to know that he had ever done anything but work his jobs—as a day janitor at Medgar Evers College and as a night janitor at King's County Hospital. And he wasn't going to tell her about those women who had occasionally come home with him in the early-morning hours. Those women, most of whom had husbands, boyfriends, fiancés, and lovers in other parts of the world, had never meant much to him anyway.

Michel, who had become a lay minister at a small Baptist church near the Rendez-Vous and never danced there, laughed as he listened. "The cock can no longer crow," he said. "You might as well give the rest to Jesus."

"Jesus wouldn't know what to do with what's left of this man," Dany said.

Gone were the late-night domino games. Gone was the phone number he'd had for the past five years, ever since he'd had a phone. (He didn't need other women calling him now.) And it was only as he stood in the crowd of people waiting to meet the flights arriving simultaneously from Kingston, Santo Domingo, and Port-au-Prince that he stopped worrying that he might not see any delight or recognition in his wife's face. There, he began to feel some actual joy, even exhilaration, which made him want to leap forward and grab every woman who vaguely resembled the latest pictures she had sent him, all of which he had neatly framed and hung on the walls of his room.

They were searching her suitcase. Why were they searching her suitcase? One meagre bag, which, aside from some gifts for her husband, contained the few things she'd been unable to part with, the things her relatives hadn't nabbed from her, telling her that she could get more, and better, where she was going. She had kept only her undergarments, a nightgown, and two outfits: the green princess dress she was wearing and a red jumper that she'd gift wrapped before packing so that no one would take it. People in her neighborhood who had travelled before had told her to gift wrap everything so that it wouldn't be opened at the airport in New York. Now the customs man was tearing her careful wrapping to shreds as he barked questions at her in mangled Creole.

"*Ki sa l ye?*" He held a package out in front of her before opening it.

What was it? She didn't know anymore. She could only guess by the shapes and sizes.

He unwrapped all her gifts—the mangoes, sugarcane, avocados, the orange- and grapefruit-peel preserves, the peanut, cashew, and coconut confections, the coffee beans, which he threw into a green bin decorated with

---

Abner Louima: Abner Louima is a Haitian immigrant who was brutally tortured by five policemen following an August 1997 disturbance outside a Brooklyn nightclub.

drawings of fruits and vegetables with red lines across them. The only thing that seemed as though it might escape disposal was a small packet of trimmed chicken feathers, which her husband used to enjoy twirling in his ear cavity. In the early days, soon after he'd left, she had spun the tips of the feathers inside her ears, too, and discovered that from them she could get *jwisans*, pleasure, an orgasm. She had thought to herself then that maybe the foreign television programs were right: sex was mostly between the ears.

When the customs man came across the small package of feathers, he stared down at it, then looked up at her, letting his eyes linger on her face, mostly, it seemed to her, on her ears. Obviously, he had seen feathers like these before. Into the trash they went, along with the rest of her offerings.

By the time he was done with her luggage, she had little left. The suitcase was so light now that she could walk very quickly as she carried it in her left hand. She followed a man pushing a cart, which tipped and swerved under the weight of three large boxes. And suddenly she found herself before a door that slid open by itself, parting like a glass sea, and as she was standing there the door closed again, and when she moved a few steps forward it opened, and then she saw him. He charged at her and wrapped both his arms around her. And as he held her she felt her feet leave the ground. It was when he put her back down that she finally believed she was really somewhere else, on another soil, in another country.

He could tell she was happy that so many of her pictures were displayed on the wall facing his bed. During the ride home, he had nearly crashed the car twice. He wasn't sure why he was driving so fast. They dashed through the small talk, the inventory of friends and family members and the state of their health. She had no detailed anecdotes about anyone in particular. Some had died and some were still living; he couldn't even remember which. She was bigger than she had been when he left her, what people here might call chubby. It was obvious that she had been to a professional hairdresser, because she was elegantly coiffed with her short hair gelled down to her scalp and a fake bun bulging in the back. She smelled good—a mixture of lavender and lime. He had simply wanted to get her home, if home it was, to that room, and to reduce the space between them until there was no air for her to breathe that he wasn't breathing, too.

The drive had reminded him of the one they had taken to their one-night honeymoon at the Ifé Hotel, when he had begged the uncle who was driving them to go faster, because the next morning he would be on a plane for New York. That night, he'd had no idea that it would be seven years before he would see her again. He'd had it all planned. He knew that he couldn't send for her right away, since he would be overstaying a tourist visa. But he was going to work hard, to find a lawyer and get himself a green card, and then send for his wife. The green card had taken six years and nine months. But now she was here with him, staring at the pictures on his wall as though they were of someone else.

"Do you remember that one?" he asked, to reassure her. He was pointing at a framed eight-by-twelve of her lying on a red mat by a tiny Christmas tree in a photographer's studio. "You sent it last Noël?"

She remembered, she said. It was just that she looked so desperate, as if she were trying to force *him* to remember *her*.

"I never forgot you for an instant," he said.

She said that she was thirsty.

"What do you want to drink?" He listed the juices he had purchased from the Cuban grocer down the street, the combinations he was sure she'd be craving, papaya and mango, guava and pineapple, cherimoya and passion fruit.

"Just a little water," she said. "Cold."

He didn't want to leave her alone while he went to the kitchen. He would have called through the walls for one of the men to get some water, if they were not doing such a good job of hiding behind the closed doors of their rooms to give him some privacy.

When he came back with the glass, she examined it, as if for dirt, and then gulped it down. It was as though she hadn't drunk anything since the morning he'd got on the plane and left her behind.

"Do you want more?" he asked.

She shook her head.

It's too bad, he thought, that in Creole the word for love, *renmen,* is also the word for like, so that as he told her he loved her he had to embellish it with phrases that illustrated the degree of that love. He loved her more than there were seconds in the years they'd been apart, he babbled. He loved her more than the size of the ocean she had just crossed. To keep himself from saying more insipid things, he jumped on top of her and pinned her down on the bed. She was not as timid as she had been on their wedding night. She tugged at his black tie so fiercely that he was sure his neck was bruised. He yanked a few buttons off her dress and threw them aside as she unbuttoned his starched and ironed white shirt, and though in the rehearsals in past daydreams he had gently placed a cupped hand over her mouth, he didn't think to do it now. He didn't care that the other men could hear her, or him. Only for a moment did he think to feel sorry that it might be years before the others could experience the same thing.

He was exhausted when she grabbed the top sheet from the bed, wrapped it around her, and announced that she was going to the bathroom.

"Let me take you," he said.

"Non non," she said, "I can find it."

He couldn't stand to watch her turn away and disappear.

He heard voices in the kitchen, her talking to the men, introducing herself. He bolted right up from the bed when he remembered that all she had on was the sheet. As he raced to the door, he collided with her coming back.

There were two men playing dominoes in the kitchen, she told him, dressed in identical pink satin robes.

He left early for work the next day, along with the other men, but not before handing her a set of keys and instructing her not to let anyone in. He showed her how to work the stove and how to find all the Haitian stations on the AM/FM dial of his night-table radio. She slept late, reliving the night, their laughter after she'd seen the men, who, he explained, had hurried to buy those robes for her benefit. They had made love again and again, forcing themselves to do so more quietly each time. Seven times, by his count—once for each year they'd been apart—but fewer by hers. He had assured her that there was no need to be embarrassed. They were married, before God and a priest. This was crucial for her to remember. That's why he had seen to it on the night before he left. So that something more judicial and committing than a mere promise would bind them. So that even if their union had become a victim of distance and time, it could not have been easily dissolved. They would have had to sign papers to come apart, write letters, speak on the phone about it. He told her that he didn't want to leave her again, not for one second. But he had asked for the day off and his boss had refused. At least they would have the weekends, Saturdays and Sundays, to do with as they wished—to go dancing, sightseeing, shopping, and apartment hunting. Wouldn't she like to have her own apartment? To make love as much as they wanted and not worry that some men in women's robes had heard them?

At noon, the phone rang. It was him. He asked her what she was doing. She lied and told him that she was cooking, making herself something to eat. He asked what. She said eggs, guessing that there must be eggs in the refrigerator. He asked if she was bored. She said no. She was going to listen to the radio and write letters home.

When she hung up, she turned on the radio. She scrolled between the stations he had pointed out to her and was glad to hear people speaking Creole. There was music playing, too—*konpa*° by a group named Top Vice. She switched to a station with a talk show. She sat up to listen as some callers talked about a Haitian-American named Patrick Dorismond who had been killed. He had been shot by a policeman in a place called Manhattan. She wanted to call her husband back, but he hadn't left a number. Lying back, she raised the sheet over her head and through it listened to the callers, each one angrier than the last.

When he came home, he saw that she had used what she had found in the refrigerator and the kitchen cabinets to cook a large meal for all four of them. She insisted that they wait for the other men to drift in before they ate, even though he had only a few hours before he had to leave for his night job.

The men complimented her enthusiastically on her cooking, and he could tell that this meal made them feel as though they were part of a family, something they had not experienced in years. They seemed to be happy, eating for pleasure as well as sustenance, chewing more slowly than they ever had before. Usually they ate standing up, Chinese or Jamaican takeout from places down the street. Tonight there was little conversation, beyond praise for the food. The men offered to clean the pots and dishes once they were done, and he suspected that they wanted to lick them before washing them.

He and his wife went to the room and lay on their backs on the bed. He explained why he had two jobs. It had been partly to fill the hours away from her, but also partly because he had needed to support both himself here and her in Port-au-Prince. And now he was saving up for an apartment and, ultimately,

---

konpa: A type of music popular in Haiti.

a house. She said that she, too, wanted to work. She had finished a secretarial course; perhaps that would be helpful here. He warned her that, because she didn't speak English, she might have to start as a cook in a restaurant or as a seamstress in a factory. He fell asleep mid-thought. She woke him up at nine o'clock, when he was supposed to start work. He rushed to the bathroom to wash his face, came back, and changed his overalls, all the while cursing himself. He was stupid to have overslept, and now he was late. He kissed her good-bye and ran out. He hated being late, being lectured by the night manager, whose favorite reprimand was "There's tons of people like you in this city. Half of them need a job."

She spent the whole week inside, worried that she'd get lost if she ventured out alone, that she might not be able to retrace her steps. Her days fell into a routine. She'd wake up and listen to the radio for news of what was happening both here and back home. Somewhere, not far from where she was, people were in the streets, marching, protesting Dorismond's death, their outrage made even greater by the fact that the Dorismond boy was the American-born son of a well-known singer, whose voice they had heard on the radio back in Haiti. "No justice, no peace!" she chanted while stewing chicken and frying fish. In the afternoons, she wrote letters home. She wrote of the meals that she had made, of the pictures of her on the wall, of the songs and protest chants on the radio. She wrote to family members, and to childhood girlfriends who had been so happy that she was finally going to be with her husband, and to newer acquaintances from the secretarial school who had been jealous. She also wrote to a male friend, a neighbor who had come to her house three days after her husband had left to see why she had locked herself inside.

He had knocked for so long that she'd had no choice but to open the door. She was still wearing the dress she'd worn to see her husband off. When she collapsed in his arms, he had put a cold compress on her forehead and offered her some water. She had swallowed so much water so quickly that she'd vomited. That night, he had lain down next to her, and in the dark had told her that this was love, if love there was — having the courage to abandon the present for a future that one could only imagine. He had assured her that her husband loved her.

In the afternoons, while she was writing her letters, she would hear someone walking back and forth on the floor above. She took to pacing as well, as she waited for the men to come home. She wanted to tell her husband about that neighbor who had slept next to her for those days after he'd left and in whose bed she had spent many nights after that. Only then would she feel that their future would be true. Someone had said that people lie only at the beginning of relationships. The middle is where the truth resides. But there had been no middle for her husband and herself, just a beginning and many dream-rehearsed endings.

He had first met his wife during carnival in the mountains in Jacmel. His favorite part of the festivities was the finale, on the day before Ash Wednesday, when a crowd of tired revellers would gather on the beach to burn their carnival masks and costumes and feign weeping, symbolically purging themselves of the carousing of the preceding days and nights. She had volunteered to be one of the official weepers—one of those who wailed convincingly as the carnival relics turned to ashes in the bonfire.

"*Papa Kanaval ou ale?*" "Where have you gone, Father Carnival?" she had howled, with real tears running down her face.

If she could grieve so passionately on demand, he thought, perhaps she could love even more. After the other weepers had left, she stayed behind until the last embers of the bonfire had dimmed. It was impossible to distract her, to make her laugh. She could never fake weeping, she told him. Every time she cried for anything, she cried for everything else that had ever hurt her.

He had travelled between Jacmel and Port-au-Prince while he was waiting for his visa to come through. And when he finally had a travel date he had asked her to marry him.

One afternoon, when he came home from work, he found her sitting on the edge of the bed in that small room, staring at the pictures of herself on the opposite wall. She did not move as he kissed the top of her head. He said nothing, simply slipped out of his clothes and lay down on the bed, pressing his face against her back. He did not want to trespass on her secrets. He simply wanted to extinguish the carnivals burning in her head.

She was happy when the weekend finally came. Though he slept until noon, she woke up at dawn, rushed to the bathroom before the men could, put on her red jumper and one of his T-shirts, then sat staring down at him on the bed, waiting for his eyes to open.

"What plan do we have for today?" she asked when they finally did.

The plan, he said, was whatever she wanted.

She wanted to walk down a street with him and see faces. She wanted to eat something, an apple or a chicken leg, out in the open with the sun beating down on her face.

As they were leaving the house, they ran into the woman whose footsteps she had been hearing all week long above her head. The woman smiled coyly and said, "*Bienvenue.*"° She nodded politely, then pulled her husband away by the hand.

They walked down a street filled with people doing their Saturday food shopping at outside stalls stacked with fruits and vegetables.

He asked if she wanted to take the bus.

"Where to?"

"Anywhere," he said.

From the bus, she counted the frame and row houses, beauty-shop signs, church steeples, and gas stations. She pressed her face against the window, and her breath occasionally blocked her view of the streets speeding by. She turned back now and then to look at him, sitting next to her. There was still a trace of sleepiness in his eyes. He watched her as though he were trying to put himself in her place, to see it all as if for the first time, but could not.

Bienvenue: "Welcome."

He took her to a park in the middle of Brooklyn, Prospect Park, a vast stretch of land, trees, and trails. They strolled deep into the park, until they could see only a few of the surrounding buildings, which towered like mountains above the landscape. In all her daydreams, she had never imagined that there would be a place like this here. This immense garden, he told her, was where he came to ponder the passing seasons, lost time, and interminable distances.

It was past seven o'clock when they emerged from the park and headed down Parkside Avenue. She had reached for his hand at 5:10 P.M., he had noted, and had not released it since. And now, as they were walking down a dimly lit side street, she kept her eyes upward, looking into the windows of apartments lit by the indigo glow of television screens. When she said she was hungry, they turned onto Flatbush Avenue in search of something to eat.

Walking hand in hand with her through crowds of strangers made him long for his other favorite piece of carnival theatre. A bride and groom, in their most lavish wedding clothing, would wander the streets. Scanning a crowd of revellers, they would pick the most stony-faced person and ask, "Would you marry us?" Over the course of several days, for variety, they would modify this request. "Would you couple us?" "Would you make us one?" "Would you tie the noose of love around our necks?" The joke was that when the person took the bait and looked closely, he or she might discover that the bride was a man and the groom a woman. The couple's makeup was so skillfully applied that only the most observant could detect this.

On the nearly empty bus on the way home, he sat across the aisle from her, not next to her as he had that morning. She pretended to keep her eyes on the night racing past the window behind him. He was watching her again. This time he seemed to be trying to see *her* as if for the first time, but could not.

She, too, was thinking of carnival, and of how, the year after they'd met, they had dressed as a bride and groom looking for someone to marry them. She had disguised herself as the bride and he as the groom, forgoing the traditional puzzle.

At the end of the celebrations, she had burned her wedding dress in the bonfire and he had burned his suit. She wished now that they had kept them. They could have walked these foreign streets in them, performing their own carnival. Since she didn't know the language, they wouldn't have to speak or ask any questions of the stony-faced people around them. They could perform their public wedding march in silence, a silence like the one that had come over them now.

RALPH ELLISON

Ralph Ellison (1914–1994) was born in Oklahoma City. His father, a small-time vendor of ice and coal, died when Ellison was three, and thereafter his mother worked as a domestic servant to support herself and her son. Ellison later credited his mother, who recruited black votes for the Socialist Party, for turning him into an activist. She also brought home discarded books and phonograph records from the white households where she worked, and as a boy Ellison developed an interest in literature and music. He played trumpet in his high school band, and it was at this time that he began to relate the works of fiction he was reading to real life. "I began to look at my own life through the lives of fictional characters," he observed. "When I read Stendhal, I would search until I began to find patterns of a Stendhalian novel within the Negro communities in which I grew up. I began, in other words, quite early to connect the worlds projected in literature . . . with the life in which I found myself."

In 1933 Ellison entered Tuskegee Institute in Alabama, where he studied music for three years. Then he went to New York City and met the black writers Langston Hughes and Richard Wright, whose encouragement helped him to become a writer. Wright turned Ellison's attention to writing short stories and reading "those works in which writing was discussed as a craft . . . to Henry James's prefaces, to Conrad," and to other authors. In 1939 Ellison's short stories, essays, and reviews began to appear in periodicals. After World War II, he settled down to work on the novel Invisible Man. Published in 1952, it received the National Book Award for fiction and was listed in a 1965 Book Week poll as the most distinguished American novel of the preceding twenty years. As the critic Richard D. Lyons recognized, the novel was "a chronicle of a young black man's awakening to racial discrimination and his battle against the refusal of Americans to see him apart from his ethnic background, which in turn leads to humiliation and disillusionment." "Battle Royal," an excerpt from Invisible Man, is often anthologized. It appears after the prologue describing the underground chamber in which the nameless protagonist has retreated from the chaos of life aboveground.

Insisting that "art by its nature is social," Ellison began Invisible Man with the words "I am an invisible man. No, I am not a spook like those who haunted Edgar Allan Poe; nor am I one of your Hollywood-movie ectoplasms. I am a man of substance, of flesh and bone, fiber and liquids—and I might even be said to possess a mind. I am invisible, understand, simply because people refuse to see me." At the time of his death from cancer, Ellison left an unfinished second novel started in the late 1950s. His initial work on the manuscript was destroyed in a fire, and he never completed the book, which he called his "forty-year work in progress (very long in progress)." Titled Juneteenth (1999), it was edited posthumously by his widow, Fanny, and John Callahan. In addition to Invisible Man, Ellison published a few short stories and two collections of essays, Shadow and Act (1964) and Going to the Territory (1986). He was also Albert Schweitzer Professor of Contemporary Literature and Culture at New York University.

COMMENTARY   Ralph Ellison, "The Influence of Folklore on 'Battle Royal,'" page 557.

WEB   *Research Ralph Ellison and answer questions about his work at bedfordstmartins.com/charters/litwriters.*

Battle Royal   1952

It goes a long way back, some twenty years. All my life I had been looking for something, and everywhere I turned someone tried to tell me what it was. I accepted their answers too, though they were often in contradiction and even self-contradictory. I was naïve. I was looking for myself and asking everyone except myself questions which I, and only I, could answer. It took me a long time and much painful boomeranging of my expectations to achieve a realization everyone else appears to have been born with: That I am nobody but myself. But first I had to discover that I am an invisible man!

And yet I am no freak of nature, nor of history. I was in the cards, other things having been equal (or unequal) eighty-five years ago. I am not ashamed of my grandparents for having been slaves. I am only ashamed of myself for having at one time been ashamed. About eighty-five years ago they were told that they were free, united with others of our country in everything pertaining to the common good, and, in everything social, separate like the fingers of the hand. And they believed it. They exulted in it. They stayed in their place, worked hard, and brought up my father to do the same. But my grandfather is the one. He was an odd old guy, my grandfather, and I am told I take after him. It was he who caused the trouble. On his deathbed he called my father to him and said, "Son, after I'm gone I want you to keep up the good fight. I never told you, but our life is a war and I have been a traitor all my born days, a spy in the enemy's country ever since I give up my gun back in the Reconstruction. Live with your head in the lion's mouth. I want you to overcome 'em with yeses, undermine 'em with grins, agree 'em to death and destruction, let 'em swoller you till they vomit or bust wide open." They thought the old man had gone out of his mind. He had been the meekest of men. The younger children were rushed from the room, the shades drawn, and the flame of the lamp turned so low that it sputtered on the wick like the old man's breathing. "Learn it to the younguns," he whispered fiercely; then he died.

But my folks were more alarmed over his last words than over his dying. It was as though he had not died at all, his words caused so much anxiety. I was warned emphatically to forget what he had said and, indeed, this is the first time it has been mentioned outside the family circle. It had a tremendous effect upon me, however. I could never be sure of what he meant. Grandfather had been a quiet old man who never made any trouble, yet on his deathbed he had called himself a traitor and a spy, and he had spoken of his meekness as a dangerous activity. It became a constant puzzle which lay unanswered in the back of my mind. And whenever things went well for me I remembered my grandfather and felt guilty and uncomfortable. It was as though I was carrying out his advice in spite of myself. And to make it worse, everyone loved me for it. I was praised by the most lily-white men of the town. I was considered an example of desirable conduct—just as my grandfather had been. And what puzzled me was that the old man had defined it as *treachery*. When I was praised for my conduct I felt a guilt that in some way I was doing something that was really against the wishes of the white folks, that if they had understood they would have desired me to act just the opposite, that I should have been sulky and mean, and that that really would have been what they wanted, even though they were fooled and thought they wanted me to act as I did. It made me afraid that some day they would look upon me as a traitor and I would be lost. Still I was more afraid to act any other way because they didn't like that at all. The old man's words were like a curse. On my graduation day I delivered an oration in which I showed that humility was the secret, indeed, the very essence of progress. (Not that I believed this—how could I, remembering my grandfather?—I only believed that it worked.) It was a great success. Everyone praised me and I was invited to give the speech at a gathering of the town's leading white citizens. It was a triumph for our whole community.

It was in the main ballroom of the leading hotel. When I got there I discovered that it was on the occasion of a smoker, and I was told that since I was to be there anyway I might as well take part in the battle royal to be fought by some of my schoolmates as part of the entertainment. The battle royal came first.

All of the town's big shots were there in their tuxedoes, wolfing down the buffet foods, drinking beer and whiskey and smoking black cigars. It was a large room with a high ceiling. Chairs were arranged in neat rows around three sides of a portable boxing ring. The fourth side was clear, revealing a gleaming space of polished floor. I had some misgivings over the battle royal, by the way. Not from a distaste for fighting, but because I didn't care too much for the other fellows who were to take part. They were tough guys who seemed to have no grandfather's curse worrying their minds. No one could mistake their toughness. And besides, I suspected that fighting a battle royal might detract from the dignity of my speech. In those pre-invisible days I visualized myself as a potential Booker T. Washington. But the other fellows didn't care too much for me either, and there were nine of them. I felt superior to them in my way, and I didn't like the manner in which we were all crowded together into the servants' elevator. Nor did they like my being there. In fact, as the warmly lighted floors flashed past the elevator we had words over the fact that I, by taking part in the fight, had knocked one of their friends out of a night's work.

We were led out of the elevator through a rococo hall into an anteroom and told to get into our fighting togs. Each of us was issued a pair of boxing gloves and ushered out into the big mirrored hall, which we entered looking cautiously about us and whispering, lest we might accidentally be heard above the noise of the room. It was foggy with cigar smoke. And already the whiskey was taking effect. I was shocked to see some of the most important men of the town quite tipsy. They were all there—bankers, lawyers, judges, doctors, fire chiefs, teachers, merchants. Even one of the more fashionable pastors. Something we could not see was going on up front. A clarinet was vibrating sensuously and the men were standing up and moving eagerly forward. We were a small tight group, clustered together, our bare upper bodies touching and shining with anticipatory sweat; while up front the big shots were becoming increasingly excited over something we still could not see. Suddenly I heard the school superintendent, who had told me to come, yell, "Bring up the shines, gentlemen! Bring up the little shines!"

We were rushed up to the front of the ballroom, where it smelled even more strongly of tobacco and whiskey. Then we were pushed into place. I almost wet my pants. A sea of faces, some hostile, some amused, ringed around us, and in the center, facing us, stood a magnificent blonde—stark naked. There was dead silence. I felt a blast of cold air chill me. I tried to back away, but they were behind me and around me. Some of the boys stood with lowered heads, trembling. I felt a wave of irrational guilt and fear. My teeth chattered, my skin turned to goose flesh, my knees knocked. Yet I was strongly attracted and looked in spite of myself. Had the price of looking been blindness, I would have looked. The hair was yellow like that of a circus kewpie doll, the face heavily powdered and rouged, as though to form an abstract mask, the eyes hollow and smeared a cool blue, the color of a baboon's butt. I felt a desire to spit upon her as my eyes brushed slowly over her body. Her breasts were firm and round as the domes of East Indian temples, and I stood so close as to see the fine skin texture and beads of pearly perspiration glistening like dew around the pink and erected buds of her nipples. I wanted at one and the same time to run from the room, to sink through the floor, or go to her and cover her from my eyes and the eyes of the others with my body; to feel the soft thighs, to caress her and destroy her, to love her and murder her, to hide from her, and yet to stroke where below the small American flag tattooed upon her belly her thighs formed a capital V. I had a notion that of all in the room she saw only me with her impersonal eyes.

And then she began to dance, a slow sensuous movement; the smoke of a hundred cigars clinging to her like the thinnest of veils. She seemed like a fair bird-girl girdled in veils calling to me from the angry surface of some gray and threatening sea. I was transported. Then I became aware of the clarinet playing and the big shots yelling at us. Some threatened us if we looked and others if we did not. On my right I saw one boy faint. And now a man grabbed a silver pitcher from a table and stepped close as he dashed ice water upon him and stood him up and forced two of us to support him as his head hung and moans issued from his thick bluish lips. Another boy began to plead to go home. He was the largest of the group, wearing dark red fighting trunks much too small to conceal the erection which projected from him as though in answer to the insinuating low-registered moaning of the clarinet. He tried to hide himself with his boxing gloves.

And all the while the blonde continued dancing, smiling faintly at the big shots who watched her with fascination, and faintly smiling at our fear. I noticed a certain merchant who followed her hungrily, his lips loose and drooling. He was a large man who wore diamond studs in a shirtfront which swelled with the ample paunch underneath, and each time the blonde swayed her undulating hips he ran his hand through the thin hair of his bald head and, with his arms upheld, his posture clumsy like that of an intoxicated panda, wound his belly in a slow and obscene grind. This creature was completely hypnotized. The music had quickened. As the dancer flung herself about with a detached expression on her face, the men began reaching out to touch her. I could see their beefy fingers sink into her soft flesh. Some of the others tried to stop them and she began to move around the floor in graceful circles, as they gave chase, slipping and sliding over the polished floor. It was mad. Chairs went crashing, drinks were spilt, as they ran laughing and howling after her. They caught her just as she reached a door, raised her from the floor, and tossed her as college boys are tossed at a hazing, and above her red fixed-smiling lips I saw the terror and disgust in her eyes, almost like my own terror and that which I saw in some of the other boys. As I watched, they tossed her twice and her soft breasts seemed to flatten against the air and her legs flung wildly as she spun. Some of the more sober ones helped her to escape. And I started off the floor, heading for the anteroom with the rest of the boys.

Some were still crying and in hysteria. But as we tried to leave we were stopped and ordered to get into the ring. There was nothing to do but what we were told. All ten of us climbed under the ropes and allowed ourselves to be blindfolded with broad bands of white cloth. One of the men seemed to feel a bit sympathetic and tried to cheer us up as we stood with our backs against the ropes. Some of us tried to grin. "See that boy over there?" one of the men said. "I want you to run across at the bell and give it to him right in the belly. If you don't get him, I'm going to get you. I don't like his looks." Each of us was told the same. The blindfolds were put on. Yet even then I had been going over my speech. In my mind each word was as bright as flame. I felt the cloth pressed into place, and frowned so that it would be loosened when I relaxed.

But now I felt a sudden fit of blind terror. I was unused to darkness. It was as though I had suddenly found myself in a dark room filled with poisonous cottonmouths. I could hear the bleary voices yelling insistently for the battle royal to begin.

"Get going in there!"

"Let me at that big nigger!"

I strained to pick up the school superintendent's voice, as though to squeeze some security out of that slightly more familiar sound.

"Let me at those black sonsabitches!" someone yelled.

"No, Jackson, no!" another voice yelled. "Here, somebody, help me hold Jack."

"I want to get at that ginger-colored nigger. Tear him limb from limb," the first voice yelled.

I stood against the ropes trembling. For in those days I was what they called ginger-colored, and he sounded as though he might crunch me between his teeth like a crisp ginger cookie.

Quite a struggle was going on. Chairs were being kicked about and I could hear voices grunting as with a terrific effort. I wanted to see, to see more desperately than ever before. But the blindfold was as tight as a thick skin-puckering scab and when I raised my gloved hands to push the layers of white aside a voice yelled, "Oh, no you don't, black bastard! Leave that alone!"

"Ring the bell before Jackson kills him a coon!" someone boomed in the sudden silence. And I heard the bell clang and the sound of the feet scuffling forward.

A glove smacked against my head. I pivoted, striking out stiffly as some-one went past, and felt the jar ripple along the length of my arm to my shoulder. Then it seemed as though all nine of the boys had turned upon me at once. Blows pounded me from all sides while I struck out as best I could. So many blows landed upon me that I wondered if I were not the only blindfolded fighter in the ring, or if the man called Jackson hadn't succeeded in getting me after all.

Blindfolded, I could no longer control my motions. I had no dignity. I stumbled about like a baby or a drunken man. The smoke had become thicker and with each new blow it seemed to sear and further restrict my lungs. My saliva became like hot bitter glue. A glove connected with my head, filling my mouth with warm blood. It was everywhere. I could not tell if the mois-ture I felt upon my body was sweat or blood. A blow landed hard against the nape of my neck. I felt myself going over, my head hitting the floor. Streaks of blue light filled the black world behind the blindfold. I lay prone, pretend-ing that I was knocked out, but felt myself seized by hands and yanked to my feet. "Get going, black boy! Mix it up!" My arms were like lead, my head smarting from blows. I managed to feel my way to the ropes and held on, trying to catch my breath. A glove landed in my mid-section and I went over again, feeling as though the smoke had become a knife jabbed into my guts. Pushed this way and that by the legs milling around me, I finally pulled erect and dis-covered that I could see the black, sweat-washed forms weaving in the smoky-blue atmosphere like drunken dancers weaving to the rapid drum-like thuds of blows.

Everyone fought hysterically. It was complete anarchy. Everybody fought everybody else. No group fought together for long. Two, three, four, fought one, then turned to fight each other, were themselves attacked. Blows landed below the belt and in the kidney, with the gloves open as well as closed, and with my eye partly opened now there was not so much terror. I moved carefully, avoiding blows, although not too many to attract attention, fighting from group to group. The boys groped about like blind, cautious crabs crouch-ing to protect their mid-sections, their heads pulled in short against their shoulders, their arms stretched nervously before them, with their fists testing the smoke-filled air like the knobbed feelers of hypersensitive snails. In one corner I glimpsed a boy violently punching the air and heard him scream in pain as he smashed his hand against a ring post. For a second I saw him bent over holding his hand, then going down as a blow caught his unprotected head. I played one group against the other, slipping in and throwing a punch then stepping out of range while pushing the others into the melee to take the blows blindly aimed at me. The smoke was agonizing and there were no rounds, no bells at three minute intervals to relieve our exhaustion. The room spun round me, a swirl of lights, smoke, sweating bodies surrounded by tense white faces. I bled from both nose and mouth, the blood spattering upon my chest.

The men kept yelling, "Slug him, black boy! Knock his guts out!"

"Uppercut him! Kill him! Kill that big boy!"

Taking a fake fall, I saw a boy going down heavily beside me as though we were felled by a single blow, saw a sneaker-clad foot shoot into his groin as the two who had knocked him down stumbled upon him. I rolled out of range, feeling a twinge of nausea.

The harder we fought the more threatening the men became. And yet, I had begun to worry about my speech again. How would it go? Would they recognize my ability? What would they give me?

I was fighting automatically and suddenly I noticed that one after another of the boys was leaving the ring. I was surprised, filled with panic, as though I had been left alone with an unknown danger. Then I understood. The boys had arranged it among themselves. It was the custom for the two men left in the ring to slug it out for the winner's prize. I discovered this too late. When the bell sounded two men in tuxedoes leaped into the ring and removed the blindfold. I found myself facing Tatlock, the biggest of the gang. I felt sick at my stomach. Hardly had the bell stopped ringing in my ears than it clanged again and I saw him moving swiftly toward me. Thinking of nothing else to do I hit him smash on the nose. He kept coming, bringing the rank sharp violence of stale sweat. His face was a black blank of a face, only his eyes alive—with hate of me and aglow with a feverish terror from what had happened to us all. I became anxious. I wanted to deliver my speech and he came at me as though he meant to beat it out of me. I smashed him again and again, taking his blows as they came. Then on a sudden impulse I struck him lightly and as we clinched, I whispered, "Fake like I knocked you out, you can have the prize."

"I'll break your behind," he whispered hoarsely.

"For *them*?"

"For *me*, sonofabitch!"

They were yelling for us to break it up and Tatlock spun me half around with a blow, and as a joggled camera sweeps in a reeling scene, I saw the howling red faces crouching tense beneath the cloud of blue-gray smoke. For a moment the world wavered, unraveled, flowed, then my head cleared and Tatlock bounced before me. That fluttering shadow before my eyes was his jabbing left hand. Then falling forward, my head against his damp shoulder, I whispered, "I'll make it five dollars more."

"Go to hell!"

But his muscles relaxed a trifle beneath my pressure and I breathed, "Seven!"

"Give it to your ma," he said, ripping me beneath the heart.

And while I still held him I butted him and moved away. I felt myself bombarded with punches. I fought back with hopeless desperation. I wanted to deliver my speech more than anything else in the world, because I felt that only these men could judge truly my ability, and now this stupid clown was ruining my chances. I began fighting carefully now, moving in to punch him and out again with my greater speed. A lucky blow to his chin and I had him going too—until I heard a loud voice yell, "I got my money on the big boy."

Hearing this, I almost dropped my guard. I was confused: Should I try to win against the voice out there? Would not this go against my speech, and was not this a moment for humility, for nonresistance? A blow to my head as I danced about sent my right eye popping like a jack-in-the-box and settled my dilemma. The room went red as I fell. It was a dream fall, my body languid and fastidious as to where to land, until the floor became impatient and smashed up to meet me. A moment later I came to. An hypnotic voice said FIVE emphatically. And I lay there, hazily watching a dark red spot of my own blood shaping itself into a butterfly, glistening and soaking into the soiled gray world of the canvas.

When the voice drawled TEN I was lifted up and dragged to a chair. I sat dazed. My eye pained and swelled with each throb of my pounding heart and I wondered if now I would be allowed to speak. I was wringing wet, my mouth still bleeding. We were grouped along the wall now. The other boys ignored me as they congratulated Tatlock and speculated as to how much they would be paid. One boy whimpered over his smashed hand. Looking up front, I saw attendants in white jackets rolling the portable ring away and placing a small square rug in the vacant space surrounded by chairs. Perhaps, I thought, I will stand on the rug to deliver my speech.

Then the M.C. called to us, "Come on up here boys and get your money."

We ran forward to where the men laughed and talked in their chairs, waiting. Everyone seemed friendly now.

"There it is on the rug," the man said. I saw the rug covered with coins of all dimensions and a few crumpled bills. But what excited me, scattered here and there, were the gold pieces.

"Boys, it's all yours," the man said. "You get all you grab."

"That's right, Sambo," a blond man said, winking at me confidentially.

I trembled with excitement, forgetting my pain. I would get the gold and the bills, I thought. I would use both hands. I would throw my body against the boys nearest me to block them from the gold.

"Get down around the rug now," the man commanded, "and don't anyone touch it until I give the signal."

"This ought to be good," I heard.

As told, we got around the square rug on our knees. Slowly the man raised his freckled hand as we followed it upward with our eyes.

I heard, "These niggers look like they're about to pray!"

Then, "Ready," the man said. "Go!"

I lunged for a yellow coin lying on the blue design of the carpet, touching it and sending a surprised shriek to join those rising around me. I tried frantically to remove my hand but could not let go. A hot, violent force tore through my body, shaking me like a wet rat. The rug was electrified. The hair bristled up on my head as I shook myself free. My muscles jumped, my nerves jangled, writhed. But I saw that this was not stopping the other boys. Laughing in fear and embarrassment, some were holding back and scooping up the coins knocked off by the painful contortions of the others. The men roared above us as we struggled.

"Pick it up, goddamnit, pick it up!" someone called like a bass-voiced parrot. "Go on, get it!"

I crawled rapidly around the floor, picking up the coins, trying to avoid the coppers and to get greenbacks and the gold. Ignoring the shock by laughing, as I brushed the coins off quickly, I discovered that I could contain the electricity—a contradiction, but it works. Then the men began to push us onto the rug. Laughing embarrassedly, we struggled out of their hands and kept after the coins. We were all wet and slippery and hard to hold. Suddenly I saw a boy lifted into the air, glistening with sweat like a circus seal, and dropped, his wet back landing flush upon the charged rug, heard him yell and saw him literally dance upon his back, his elbows beating a frenzied tattoo upon the floor, his muscles twitching like the flesh of a horse stung by many flies. When he finally rolled off, his face was gray and no one stopped him when he ran from the floor amid booming laughter.

"Get the money," the M.C. called. "That's good hard American cash!"

And we snatched and grabbed, snatched and grabbed. I was careful not to come too close to the rug now, and when I felt the hot whiskey breath descend upon me like a cloud of foul air I reached out and grabbed the leg of a chair. It was occupied and I held on desperately.

"Leggo, nigger! Leggo!"

The huge face wavered down to mine as he tried to push me free. But my body was slippery and he was too drunk. It was Mr. Colcord, who owned a chain of movie houses and "entertainment palaces." Each time he grabbed me I slipped out of his hands. It became a real struggle. I feared the rug more than I did the drunk, so I held on, surprising myself for a moment by trying to topple *him* upon the rug. It was such an enormous idea that I found myself actually carrying it out. I tried not to be obvious, yet when I grabbed his leg, trying to tumble him out of the chair, he raised up roaring with laughter, and, looking at me with soberness dead in the eye, kicked me viciously in the chest. The chair leg flew out of my hand. I felt myself going and rolled. It was as though I had rolled through a bed of hot coals. It seemed a whole century would pass before I would roll free, a century in which I was seared through the deepest levels of my body to the fearful breath within me and the breath seared and heated to the point of explosion. It'll all be over in a flash, I thought as I rolled clear. It'll all be over in a flash.

But not yet, the men on the other side were waiting, red faces swollen as though from apoplexy as they bent forward in their chairs. Seeing their fingers coming toward me I rolled away as a fumbled football rolls off the receiver's fingertips, back into the coals. That time I luckily sent the rug sliding out of place and heard the coins ringing against the floor and the boys scuffling to pick them up and the M.C. calling, "All right, boys, that's all. Go get dressed and get your money."

I was limp as a dish rag. My back felt as though it had been beaten with wires.

When we had dressed the M.C. came in and gave us each five dollars, except Tatlock, who got ten for being last in the ring. Then he told us to leave. I was not to get a chance to deliver my speech, I thought. I was going out into the dim alley in despair when I was stopped and told to go back. I returned to the ballroom, where the men were pushing back their chairs and gathering in groups to talk.

The M.C. knocked on a table for quiet. "Gentlemen," he said, "we almost forgot an important part of the program. A most serious part, gentlemen.

This boy was brought here to deliver a speech which he made at his graduation yesterday. . . ."

"Bravo!"

"I'm told that he is the smartest boy we've got out there in Greenwood. I'm told that he knows more big words than a pocket-sized dictionary."

Much applause and laughter.

"So now, gentlemen, I want you to give him your attention."

There was still laughter as I faced them, my mouth dry, my eye throbbing. I began slowly, but evidently my throat was tense, because they began shouting, "Louder! Louder!"

"We of the younger generation extol the wisdom of that great leader and educator," I shouted, "who first spoke these flaming words of wisdom: 'A ship lost at sea for many days suddenly sighted a friendly vessel. From the mast of the unfortunate vessel was seen a signal: "Water, water; we die of thirst!" The answer from the friendly vessel came back: "Cast down your bucket where you are." The captain of the distressed vessel, at last heeding the injunction, cast down his bucket, and it came up full of fresh sparkling water from the mouth of the Amazon River.' And like him I say, and in his words, 'To those of my race who depend upon bettering their condition in a foreign land, or who underestimate the importance of cultivating friendly relations with the Southern white man, who is his next-door neighbor, I would say: "Cast down your bucket where you are"—cast it down in making friends in every manly way of the people of all races by whom we are surrounded. . . .' "

I spoke automatically and with such fervor that I did not realize that the men were still talking and laughing until my dry mouth, filling up with blood from the cut, almost strangled me. I coughed, wanting to stop and go to one of the tall brass, sand-filled spittoons to relieve myself, but a few of the men, especially the superintendent, were listening and I was afraid. So I gulped it down, blood, saliva, and all, and continued. (What powers of endurance I had during those days! What enthusiasm! What a belief in the rightness of things!) I spoke even louder in spite of the pain. But still they talked and still they laughed, as though deaf with cotton in dirty ears. So I spoke with greater emotional emphasis. I closed my ears and swallowed blood until I was nauseated. The speech seemed a hundred times as long as before, but I could not leave out a single word. All had to be said, each memorized nuance considered, rendered. Nor was that all. Whenever I uttered a word of three or more syllables a group of voices would yell for me to repeat it. I used the phrase "social responsibility" and they yelled:

"What's the word you say, boy?"

"Social responsibility," I said.

"What?"

"Social . . ."

"Louder."

". . . responsibility."

"More!"

"Respon—"

"Repeat!"

"—sibility."

The room filled with the uproar of laughter until, no doubt, distracted by having to gulp down my blood, I made a mistake and yelled a phrase I had often seen denounced in newspaper editorials, heard debated in private.

"Social . . ."

"What?" they yelled.

". . . equality—"

The laughter hung smokelike in the sudden stillness. I opened my eyes, puzzled. Sounds of displeasure filled the room. The M.C. rushed forward. They shouted hostile phrases at me. But I did not understand.

A small dry mustached man in the front row blared out, "Say that slowly, son!"

"What sir?"

"What you just said!"

"Social responsibility, sir," I said.

"You weren't being smart, were you, boy?" he said, not unkindly.

"No, sir!"

"You sure that about 'equality' was a mistake?"

"Oh, yes, sir," I said. "I was swallowing blood."

"Well, you had better speak more slowly so we can understand. We mean to do right by you, but you've got to know your place at all times. All right, now, go on with your speech."

I was afraid. I wanted to leave but I wanted also to speak and I was afraid they'd snatch me down.

"Thank you, sir," I said, beginning where I had left off, and having them ignore me as before.

Yet when I finished there was a thunderous applause. I was surprised to see the superintendent come forth with a package wrapped in white tissue paper, and, gesturing for quiet, address the men.

"Gentlemen, you see that I did not overpraise this boy. He makes a good speech and some day he'll lead his people in the proper paths. And I don't have to tell you that that is important in these days and times. This is a good, smart boy, and so to encourage him in the right direction, in the name of the Board of Education I wish to present him a prize in the form of this . . ."

He paused, removing the tissue paper and revealing a gleaming calfskin brief case.

". . . in the form of this first-class article from Shad Whitmore's shop."

"Boy," he said, addressing me, "take this prize and keep it well. Consider it a badge of office. Prize it. Keep developing as you are and some day it will be filled with important papers that will help shape the destiny of your people."

I was so moved that I could hardly express my thanks. A rope of bloody saliva forming a shape like an undiscovered continent drooled upon the leather and I wiped it quickly away. I felt an importance that I had never dreamed.

"Open it and see what's inside," I was told.

My fingers a-tremble, I complied, smelling the fresh leather and finding an official-looking document inside. It was a scholarship to the state college for Negroes. My eyes filled with tears and I ran awkwardly off the floor.

I was overjoyed; I did not even mind when I discovered that the gold pieces I had scrambled for were brass pocket tokens advertising a certain make of automobile.

When I reached home everyone was excited. Next day the neighbors came to congratulate me. I even felt safe from grandfather, whose deathbed curse usually spoiled my triumphs. I stood beneath his photograph with my brief case in hand and smiled triumphantly into his stolid black peasant's face. It was a face that fascinated me. The eyes seemed to follow everywhere I went.

That night I dreamed I was at a circus with him and that he refused to laugh at the clowns no matter what they did. Then later he told me to open my brief case and read what was inside and I did, finding an official envelope stamped with the state seal; and inside the envelope I found another and another, endlessly, and I thought I would fall of weariness. "Them's years," he said. "Now open that one." And I did and in it I found an engraved document containing a short message in letters of gold. "Read it," my grandfather said. "Out loud."

"To Whom It May Concern," I intoned. "Keep This Nigger-Boy Running."

I awoke with the old man's laughter ringing in my ears.

(It was a dream I was to remember and dream again for many years after. But at the time I had no insight into its meaning. First I had to attend college.)

LOUISE ERDRICH

Louise Erdrich (b. 1954) is of German and Chippewa Indian descent. She grew up in Wahpeton, North Dakota, as a member of the Turtle Mountain Band of Chippewa. For many years her maternal grandfather was tribal chair of the reservation. At Dartmouth College, Erdrich won several prizes for her fiction and poetry, including the American Academy of Poets Prize. After graduating in 1976, she returned to North Dakota, where she taught in the Poetry in the Schools Program. In 1979 she received her M.A. in creative writing from Johns Hopkins University. During her marriage to the late Michael Dorris, a professor of Native American studies at Dartmouth College, they collaborated on the novel The Crown of Columbus *(1992).*

Erdrich has been an editor of the Boston Indian Council newspaper, The Circle. *Her stories have appeared in* Redbook, *the* New England Review, *the* Mississippi Valley Review, Earth Power Coming, *and* That's What She Said. *In 1984 a collection of her poetry,* Jacklight, *was published and her first work of fiction,* Love Medicine, *won the National Book Critics Circle Award. Her later novels—* The Beet Queen *(1986),* Tracks *(1988),* The Bingo Palace *(1994), and* Tales of Burning Love *(1996)—involve other generations of the families in* Love

Medicine. *The Last Report on the Miracles at Little No Horse (2001) is one of her most recent novels.*

"The Red Convertible" is a chapter from Love Medicine. *Each chapter is a self-enclosed narrative that also functions as a separate short story about the lives of two families, the Kashpaws and the Lamartines, on a North Dakota reservation between 1934 and 1984. "The Red Convertible" takes place in 1974 and is narrated by Lyman Lamartine.*

Erdrich's work has won praise for its psychological depth and its literary excellence; it is a landmark achievement in its depiction of the lives of contemporary Native Americans. As the novelist Peter Matthiessen has observed, Love Medicine *is "quick with agile prose, taut speech, poetry, and power, conveying unflinchingly the funkiness, humor, and great unspoken sadness of the Indian reservations, and a people exiled to a no-man's-land between two worlds."*

WEB *Research Louise Erdrich and answer questions about her work at bedfordstmartins.com/charters/litwriters.*

The Red Convertible   1984

I was the first one to drive a convertible on my reservation. And of course it was red, a red Olds. I owned that car along with my brother Henry Junior. We owned it together until his boots filled with water on a windy night and he bought out my share. Now Henry owns the whole car, and his younger brother Lyman (that's myself), Lyman walks everywhere he goes.

How did I earn enough money to buy my share in the first place? My own talent was I could always make money. I had a touch for it, unusual in a Chippewa. From the first I was different that way, and everyone recognized it. I was the only kid they let in the American Legion Hall to shine shoes, for example, and one Christmas I sold spiritual bouquets for the mission door to door. The nuns let me keep a percentage. Once I started, it seemed the more money I made the easier the money came. Everyone encouraged it. When I was fifteen I got a job washing dishes at the Joliet Café, and that was where my first big break happened.

It wasn't long before I was promoted to busing tables, and then the short-order cook quit and I was hired to take her place. No sooner than you know it I was managing the Joliet. The rest is history. I went on managing. I soon became part owner, and of course there was no stopping me then. It wasn't long before the whole thing was mine.

After I'd owned the Joliet for one year, it blew over in the worst tornado ever seen around here. The whole operation was smashed to bits. A total loss. The fryalator was up in a tree, the grill torn in half like it was paper. I was only sixteen. I had it all in my mother's name, and I lost it quick, but before I lost it I had every one of my relatives, and their relatives, to dinner, and I also bought that red Olds I mentioned, along with Henry.

• • •

The first time we saw it! I'll tell you when we first saw it. We had gotten a ride up to Winnipeg, and both of us had money. Don't ask me why, because we never mentioned a car or anything, we just had all our money. Mine was cash, a big bankroll from the Joliet's insurance. Henry had two checks—a week's extra pay for being laid off, and his regular check from the Jewel Bearing Plant.

We were walking down Portage anyway, seeing the sights, when we saw it. There it was, parked, large as life. Really as *if* it was alive. I thought of the word *repose*, because the car wasn't simply stopped, parked, or whatever. That car reposed, calm and gleaming, a FOR SALE sign in its left front window. Then, before we had thought it over at all, the car belonged to us and our pockets were empty. We had just enough money for gas back home.

We went places in that car, me and Henry. We took off driving all one whole summer. We started off toward the Little Knife River and Mandaree in Fort Berthold and then we found ourselves down in Wakpala somehow, and then suddenly we were over in Montana on the Rocky Boy, and yet the summer was not even half over. Some people hang on to details when they travel, but we didn't let them bother us and just lived our everyday lives here to there.

I do remember this one place with willows. I remember I laid under those trees and it was comfortable. So comfortable. The branches bent down all around me like a tent or a stable. And quiet, it was quiet, even though there was a powwow close enough so I could see it going on. The air was not too still, not too windy either. When the dust rises up and hangs in the air around the dancers like that, I feel good. Henry was asleep with his arms thrown wide. Later on, he woke up and we started driving again. We were somewhere in Montana, or maybe on the Blood Reserve—it could have been anywhere. Anyway it was where we met the girl.

All her hair was in buns around her ears, that's the first thing I noticed about her. She was posed alongside the road with her arm out, so we stopped. That girl was short, so short her lumber shirt looked comical on her, like a nightgown. She had jeans on and fancy moccasins and she carried a little suitcase.

"Hop on in," says Henry. So she climbs in between us.

"We'll take you home," I says. "Where do you live?"

"Chicken," she says.

"Where the hell's that?" I ask her.

"Alaska."

"Okay," says Henry, and we drive.

We got up there and never wanted to leave. The sun doesn't truly set there in summer, and the night is more a soft dusk. You might doze off, sometimes, but before you know it you're up again, like an animal in nature. You never feel like you have to sleep hard or put away the world. And things would grow up there. One day just dirt or moss, the next day flowers and long grass. The girl's name was Susy. Her family really took to us. They fed us and put us up. We had our own tent to live in by their house, and the kids would be in and out of there all day and night. They couldn't get over me and Henry being brothers, we looked so different. We told them we knew we had the same mother, anyway.

One night Susy came in to visit us. We sat around in the tent talking of this and that. The season was changing. It was getting darker by that time, and the cold was even getting just a little mean. I told her it was time for us to go. She stood up on a chair.

"You never seen my hair," Susy said.

That was true. She was standing on a chair, but still, when she unclipped her buns the hair reached all the way to the ground. Our eyes opened. You couldn't tell how much hair she had when it was rolled up so neatly. Then my brother Henry did something funny. He went up to the chair and said, "Jump on my shoulders." So she did that, and her hair reached down past his waist, and he started twirling, this way and that, so her hair was flung out from side to side.

"I always wondered what it was like to have long pretty hair," Henry says. Well we laughed. It was a funny sight, the way he did it. The next morning we got up and took leave of those people.

On to greener pastures, as they say. It was down through Spokane and across Idaho then Montana and very soon we were racing the weather right along under the Canadian border through Columbus, Des Lacs, and then we were in Bottineau County and soon home. We'd made most of the trip, that summer, without putting up the car hood at all. We got home just in time, it turned out, for the army to remember Henry had signed up to join it.

I don't wonder that the army was so glad to get my brother that they turned him into a Marine. He was built like a brick outhouse anyway. We liked to tease him that they really wanted him for his Indian nose. He had a nose big and sharp as a hatchet, like the nose on Red Tomahawk, the Indian who killed Sitting Bull, whose profile is on signs all along the North Dakota highways. Henry went off to training camp, came home once during Christmas, then the next thing you know we got an overseas letter from him. It was 1970, and he said he was stationed up in the northern hill country. Whereabouts I did not know. He wasn't such a hot letter writer, and only got off two before the enemy caught him. I could never keep it straight, which direction those good Vietnam soldiers were from.

I wrote him back several times, even though I didn't know if those letters would get through. I kept him informed all about the car. Most of the time I had it up on blocks in the yard or half taken apart, because that long trip did a hard job on it under the hood.

I always had good luck with numbers, and never worried about the draft myself. I never even had to think about what my number was. But Henry was never lucky in the same way as me. It was at least three years before Henry came home. By then I guess the whole war was solved in the government's mind, but for him it would keep on going. In those years I'd put his car into almost perfect shape. I always thought of it as his car while he was gone, even though when he left he said, "Now it's yours," and threw me his key.

"Thanks for the extra key," I'd said. "I'll put it up in your drawer just in case I need it." He laughed.

When he came home, though, Henry was very different, and I'll say this: the change was no good. You could hardly expect him to change for the better, I know. But he was quiet, so quiet, and never comfortable sitting still anywhere but always up and moving around. I thought back to times we'd sat still for whole afternoons, never moving a muscle, just shifting our weight along the ground, talking to whoever sat with us, watching things. He'd always had a joke, then, too, and now you couldn't get him to laugh, or when he did it was more the sound of a man choking, a sound that stopped up the throats of other people around him. They got to leaving him alone most of the time, and I didn't blame them. It was a fact: Henry was jumpy and mean.

I'd bought a color TV set for my mom and the rest of us while Henry was away. Money still came very easy. I was sorry I'd ever bought it though, because of Henry. I was also sorry I'd bought color, because with black-and-white the pictures seem older and farther away. But what are you going to do? He sat in front of it, watching it, and that was the only time he was completely still. But it was the kind of stillness that you see in a rabbit when it freezes and before it will bolt. He was not easy. He sat in his chair gripping the armrests with all his might, as if the chair itself was moving at a high speed and if he let go at all he would rocket forward and maybe crash right through the set.

Once I was in the room watching TV with Henry and I heard his teeth click at something. I looked over, and he'd bitten through his lip. Blood was going down his chin. I tell you right then I wanted to smash that tube to pieces. I went over to it but Henry must have known what I was up to. He rushed from his chair and shoved me out of the way, against the wall. I told myself he didn't know what he was doing.

My mom came in, turned the set off real quiet, and told us she had made something for supper. So we went and sat down. There was still blood going down Henry's chin, but he didn't notice it and no one said anything, even though every time he took a bit of his bread his blood fell onto it until he was eating his own blood mixed in with the food.

While Henry was not around we talked about what was going to happen to him. There were no Indian doctors on the reservation, and my mom was afraid of trusting the old man, Moses Pillager, because he courted her long ago and was jealous of her husbands. He might take revenge through her son. We were afraid that if we brought Henry to a regular hospital they would keep him.

"They don't fix them in those places," Mom said; "they just give them drugs."

"We wouldn't get him there in the first place," I agreed, "so let's just forget about it."

Then I thought about the car.

Henry had not even looked at the car since he'd gotten home, though like I said, it was in tip-top condition and ready to drive. I thought the car might bring the old Henry back somehow. So I bided my time and waited for my chance to interest him in the vehicle.

One night Henry was off somewhere. I took myself a hammer. I went out to that car and I did a number on its underside. Whacked it up. Bent the tail pipe double. Ripped the muffler loose. By the time I was done with the car it looked worse than any typical Indian car that has been driven all its life on reservation roads, which they always say are like government promises—full of holes. It just about hurt me, I'll tell you that! I threw dirt in the carburetor and I ripped all the electric tape off the seats. I made it look just as beat up as I could. Then I sat back and waited for Henry to find it.

Still, it took him over a month. That was all right, because it was just getting warm enough, not melting, but warm enough to work outside.

"Lyman," he says, walking in one day, "that red car looks like shit."

"Well it's old," I says. "You got to expect that."

"No way!" says Henry. "That car's a classic! But you went and ran the piss right out of it, Lyman, and you know it don't deserve that. I kept that car in A-one shape. You don't remember. You're too young. But when I left, that car was running like a watch. Now I don't even know if I can get it to start again, let alone get it anywhere near its old condition."

"Well you try," I said, like I was getting mad, "but I say it's a piece of junk."

Then I walked out before he could realize I knew he'd strung together more than six words at once.

After that I thought he'd freeze himself to death working on that car. He was out there all day, and at night he rigged up a little lamp, ran a cord out the window, and had himself some light to see by while he worked. He was better than he had been before, but that's still not saying much. It was easier for him to do the things the rest of us did. He ate more slowly and didn't jump up and down during the meal to get this or that or look out the window. I put my hand in the back of the TV set, I admit, and fiddled around with it good, so that it was almost impossible now to get a clear picture. He didn't look at it very often anyway. He was always out with that car or going off to get parts for it. By the time it was really melting outside, he had it fixed.

I had been feeling down in the dumps about Henry around this time. We had always been together before. Henry and Lyman. But he was such a loner now that I didn't know how to take it. So I jumped at the chance one day when Henry seemed friendly. It's not that he smiled or anything. He just said, "Let's take that old shitbox for a spin." Just the way he said it made me think he could be coming around.

We went out to the car. It was spring. The sun was shining very bright. My only sister, Bonita, who was just eleven years old, came out and made us stand together for a picture. Henry leaned his elbow on the red car's windshield, and he took his other arm and put it over my shoulder, very carefully, as though it was heavy for him to lift and he didn't want to bring the weight down all at once.

"Smile," Bonita said, and he did.

· · ·

That picture, I never look at it anymore. A few months ago, I don't know why, I got his picture out and tacked it on the wall. I felt good about Henry at the time, close to him. I felt good having his picture on the wall, until one night when I was looking at television. I was a little drunk and stoned. I looked up at the wall and Henry was staring at me. I don't know what it was, but his smile had changed, or maybe it was gone. All I know is I couldn't stay in the same room with that picture. I was shaking. I got up, closed the door, and went into the kitchen. A little later my friend Ray came over and we both went back into that room. We put the picture in a brown bag, folded the bag over and over tightly, then put it way back in a closet.

I still see that picture now, as if it tugs at me, whenever I pass that closet door. The picture is very clear in my mind. It was so sunny that day Henry had to squint against the glare. Or maybe the camera Bonita held flashed like a mirror, blinding him, before she snapped the picture. My face is right out in the sun, big and round. But he might have drawn back, because the shadows on his face are deep as holes. There are two shadows curved like little hooks around the ends of his smile, as if to frame it and try to keep it there—that one, first smile that looked like it might have hurt his face. He has his field jacket on and the worn-in clothes he'd come back in and kept wearing ever since. After Bonita took the picture, she went into the house and we got into the car. There was a full cooler in the trunk. We started off, east, toward Pembina and the Red River because Henry said he wanted to see the high water.

The trip over there was beautiful. When everything starts changing, drying up, clearing off, you feel like your whole life is starting. Henry felt it, too. The top was down and the car hummed like a top. He'd really put it back in shape, even the tape on the seats was very carefully put down and glued back in layers. It's not that he smiled again or even joked, but his face looked to me as if it was clear, more peaceful. It looked as though he wasn't thinking of anything in particular except the bare fields and windbreaks and houses we were passing.

The river was high and full of winter trash when we got there. The sun was still out, but it was colder by the river. There were still little clumps of dirty snow here and there on the banks. The water hadn't gone over the banks yet, but it would, you could tell. It was just at its limit, hard swollen glossy like an old gray scar. We made ourselves a fire, and we sat down and watched the current go. As I watched it I felt something squeezing inside me and tightening and trying to let go all at the same time. I knew I was not just feeling it myself; I knew I was feeling what Henry was going through at that moment. Except that I couldn't stand it, the closing and opening. I jumped to my feet. I took Henry by the shoulders and I started shaking him. "Wake up," I says, "wake up, wake up, wake up!" I didn't know what had come over me. I sat down beside him again.

His face was totally white and hard. Then it broke, like stones break all of a sudden when water boils up inside them.

"I know it," he says. "I know it. I can't help it. It's no use."

We start talking. He said he knew what I'd done with the car. It was obvious it had been whacked out of shape and not just neglected. He said he wanted to give the car to me for good now, it was no use. He said he'd fixed it just to give it back and I should take it.

"No way," I says, "I don't want it."

"That's okay," he says, "you take it."

"I don't want it, though," I says back to him, and then to emphasize, just to emphasize, you understand, I touch his shoulder. He slaps my hand off.

"Take that car," he says.

"No," I say. "Make me," I say, and then he grabs my jacket and rips the arm loose. That jacket is a class act, suede with tags and zippers. I push Henry backwards, off the log. He jumps up and bowls me over. We go down in a clinch and come up swinging hard, for all we're worth, with our fists. He socks my jaw so hard I feel like it swings loose. Then I'm at his rib cage and land a good one under his chin so his head snaps back. He's dazzled. He looks at me and I look at him and then his eyes are full of tears and blood and at first I think he's crying. But no, he's laughing. "Ha! Ha!" he says. "Ha! Ha! Take good care of it."

"Okay," I says, "okay, no problem. Ha! Ha!"

I can't help it, and I start laughing, too. My face feels fat and strange, and after a while I get a beer from the cooler in the trunk, and when I hand it to Henry he takes his shirt and wipes my germs off. "Hoof-and-mouth disease," he says. For some reason this cracks me up, and so we're really laughing for a while, and then we drink all the rest of the beers one by one and throw them in the river and see how far, how fast, the current takes them before they fill up and sink.

"You want to go on back?" I ask after a while. "Maybe we could snag a couple nice Kashpaw girls."

He says nothing. But I can tell his mood is turning again.

"They're all crazy, the girls up here, every damn one of them."

"You're crazy too," I say, to jolly him up. "Crazy Lamartine boys!"

He looks as though he will take this wrong at first. His face twists, then clears, and he jumps up on his feet. "That's right!" he says. "Crazier 'n hell. Crazy Indians!"

I think it's the old Henry again. He throws off his jacket and starts swinging his legs out from the knees like a fancy dancer. He's down doing something between a grass dance and a bunny hop, no kind of dance I ever saw before, but neither has anyone else on all this green growing earth. He's wild. He wants to pitch whoopee! He's up and at me and all over. All this time I'm laughing so hard, so hard my belly is getting tied up in a knot.

"Got to cool me off!" he shouts all of a sudden. Then he runs over to the river and jumps in.

There's boards and other things in the current. It's so high. No sound comes from the river after the splash he makes, so I run right over. I look around. It's getting dark. I see he's halfway across the water already, and I know he didn't swim there but the current took him. It's far. I hear his voice, though, very clearly across it.

"My boots are filling," he says.

He says this in a normal voice, like he just noticed and he doesn't know what to think of it. Then he's gone. A branch comes by. Another branch. And I go in.

• • •

By the time I get out of the river, off the snag I pulled myself onto, the sun is down. I walk back to the car, turn on the high beams, and drive it up the bank. I put it in first gear and then I take my foot off the clutch. I get out, close the door, and watch it plow softly into the water. The headlights reach in as they go down, searching, still lighted even after the water swirls over the back end. I wait. The wires short out. It is all finally dark. And then there is only the water, the sound of it going and running and going and running and running.

WILLIAM FAULKNER

William Faulkner (1897–1962) was born in New Albany, Mississippi, into an old southern family. When he was a child, his parents moved to the isolated town of Oxford, Mississippi, and except for his service in World War I and some time in New Orleans and Hollywood, he spent the rest of his life there. "I discovered my own little postage stamp of native soil was worth writing about, and that I would never live long enough to exhaust it." His literary career began in New Orleans, where he lived for six months and wrote newspaper sketches and stories for the Times-Picayune. *He met Sherwood Anderson in New Orleans, and Anderson helped him publish his first novel,* Soldier's Pay, *in 1926. Faulkner's major work was written in the late 1920s and the 1930s, when he created an imaginary county adjacent to Oxford, calling it Yoknapatawpha County and chronicling its history in a series of experimental novels. In* The Sound and the Fury *(1929),* As I Lay Dying *(1930),* Sanctuary *(1931),* Light in August *(1932),* Absalom, Absalom! *(1936), and* The Hamlet *(1940), he showed himself to be a writer of genius, although "a willfully and perversely chaotic one," as Jorge Luis Borges noted, whose "labyrinthine world" required a no less labyrinthine prose technique to describe in epic manner the disintegration of the South through many generations. Faulkner was awarded the Nobel Prize for literature in 1952.*

Faulkner rarely included poetic imagery or stream-of-consciousness narration in his stories, which he wrote, he often said, to help him pay his rent. His biographer Frederick Karl has noted that he used short fiction "as a means of working through, or toward, larger ideas." He wrote nearly a hundred stories, often revising them later to fit as sections into a novel. Four books of his stories were published in his lifetime.

Although some readers found symbolism in "A Rose for Emily" that suggested he was implying a battle between the North (the character Homer Barron) and the South (Miss Emily herself), Faulkner denied a schematic interpretation. He said he had intended to write a ghost story, and "I think that the writer is too busy trying to create flesh-and-blood people that will stand up and cast a shadow to have time to be conscious of all the symbolism that he may put into what he does or what people may read into it."

COMMENTARY   *William Faulkner, "The Meaning of 'A Rose for Emily,'" page 558.*

WEB   *Research William Faulkner and answer questions about his work at bedfordstmartins.com/charters/litwriters.*

A Rose for Emily 1931

I

When Miss Emily Grierson died, our whole town went to her funeral: the men through a sort of respectful affection for a fallen monument, the women mostly out of curiosity to see the inside of her house, which no one save an old manservant — a combined gardener and cook — had seen in at least ten years.

It was a big, squarish frame house that had once been white, decorated with cupolas and spires and scrolled balconies in the heavily lightsome style of the seventies, set on what had once been our most select street. But garages and cotton gins had encroached and obliterated even the august names of that neighborhood; only Miss Emily's house was left, lifting its stubborn and coquettish decay above the cotton wagons and the gasoline pumps — an eyesore among eyesores. And now Miss Emily had gone to join the representatives of those august names where they lay in the cedar-bemused cemetery among the ranked and anonymous graves of Union and Confederate soldiers who fell at the battle of Jefferson.

Alive, Miss Emily had been a tradition, a duty, and a care; a sort of hereditary obligation upon the town, dating from that day in 1894 when Colonel Sartoris, the mayor — he who fathered the edict that no Negro woman should appear on the streets without an apron — remitted her taxes, the dispensation dating from the death of her father on into perpetuity. Not that Miss Emily would have accepted charity. Colonel Sartoris invented an involved tale to the effect that Miss Emily's father had loaned money to the town, which the town, as a matter of business, preferred this way of repaying. Only a man of Colonel Sartoris' generation and thought could have invented it, and only a woman could have believed it.

When the next generation, with its more modern ideas, became mayors and aldermen, this arrangement created some little dissatisfaction. On the first of the year they mailed her a tax notice. February came, and there was no reply. They wrote her a formal letter, asking her to call at the sheriff's office at her convenience. A week later the mayor wrote her himself, offering to call or to send his car for her, and received in reply a note on paper of an archaic shape, in a thin, flowing calligraphy in faded ink, to the effect that she no longer went out at all. The tax notice was also enclosed, without comment.

They called a special meeting of the Board of Aldermen. A deputation waited upon her, knocked at the door through which no visitor had passed since she ceased giving china-painting lessons eight or ten years earlier. They were admitted by the old Negro into a dim hall from which a stairway mounted into still more shadow. It smelled of dust and disuse — a close, dank smell. The Negro led them into the parlor. It was furnished in heavy, leather-covered furniture. When the Negro opened the blinds of one window, they could see that the leather was cracked; and when they sat down, a faint dust rose sluggishly about their thighs, spinning with slow motes in the single sun-ray. On a tarnished gilt easel before the fireplace stood a crayon portrait of Miss Emily's father.

They rose when she entered—a small, fat woman in black, with a thin gold chain descending to her waist and vanishing into her belt, leaning on an ebony cane with a tarnished gold head. Her skeleton was small and spare; perhaps that was why what would have been merely plumpness in another was obesity in her. She looked bloated, like a body long submerged in motionless water, and of that pallid hue. Her eyes, lost in the fatty ridges of her face, looked like two small pieces of coal pressed into a lump of dough as they moved from one face to another while the visitors stated their errand.

She did not ask them to sit. She just stood in the door and listened quietly until the spokesman came to a stumbling halt. Then they could hear the invisible watch ticking at the end of the gold chain.

Her voice was dry and cold. "I have no taxes in Jefferson. Colonel Sartoris explained it to me. Perhaps one of you can gain access to the city records and satisfy yourselves."

"But we have. We are the city authorities, Miss Emily. Didn't you get a notice from the sheriff, signed by him?"

"I received a paper, yes," Miss Emily said. "Perhaps he considers himself the sheriff. . . . I have no taxes in Jefferson."

"But there is nothing on the books to show that, you see. We must go by the—"

"See Colonel Sartoris. I have no taxes in Jefferson."

"But, Miss Emily—"

"See Colonel Sartoris." (Colonel Sartoris had been dead almost ten years.) "I have no taxes in Jefferson. Tobe!" The Negro appeared. "Show these gentlemen out."

II

So she vanquished them, horse and foot, just as she had vanquished their fathers thirty years before about the smell. That was two years after her father's death and a short time after her sweetheart—the one we believed would marry her—had deserted her. After her father's death she went out very little; after her sweetheart went away, people hardly saw her at all. A few of the ladies had the temerity to call, but were not received, and the only sign of life about the place was the Negro man—a young man then—going in and out with a market basket.

"Just as if a man—any man—could keep a kitchen properly," the ladies said; so they were not surprised when the smell developed. It was another link between the gross, teeming world and the high and mighty Griersons.

A neighbor, a woman, complained to the mayor, Judge Stevens, eighty years old.

"But what will you have me do about it, madam?" he said.

"Why, send her word to stop it," the woman said. "Isn't there a law?"

"I'm sure that won't be necessary," Judge Stevens said. "It's probably just a snake or a rat that nigger of hers killed in the yard. I'll speak to him about it."

The next day he received two more complaints, one from a man who came in diffident deprecation. "We really must do something about it, Judge.

I'd be the last one in the world to bother Miss Emily, but we've got to do something." That night the Board of Aldermen met — three graybeards and one younger man, a member of the rising generation.

"It's simple enough," he said. "Send her word to have her place cleaned up. Give her a certain time to do it in, and if she don't. . . ."

"Dammit, sir," Judge Stevens said, "will you accuse a lady to her face of smelling bad?"

So the next night, after midnight, four men crossed Miss Emily's lawn and slunk about the house like burglars, sniffing along the base of the brickwork and at the cellar openings while one of them performed a regular sowing motion with his hand out of a sack slung from his shoulder. They broke open the cellar door and sprinkled lime there, and in all the outbuildings. As they recrossed the lawn, a window that had been dark was lighted and Miss Emily sat in it, the light behind her, and her upright torso motionless as that of an idol. They crept quietly across the lawn and into the shadow of the locusts that lined the street. After a week or two the smell went away.

That was when people had begun to feel really sorry for her. People in our town, remembering how old lady Wyatt, her great-aunt, had gone completely crazy at last, believed that the Griersons held themselves a little too high for what they really were. None of the young men were quite good enough for Miss Emily and such. We had long thought of them as a tableau, Miss Emily a slender figure in white in the background, her father a spraddled silhouette in the foreground, his back to her and clutching a horsewhip, the two of them framed by the backflung front door. So when she got to be thirty and was still single, we were not pleased exactly, but vindicated; even with insanity in the family she wouldn't have turned down all of her chances if they had really materialized.

When her father died, it got about that the house was all that was left to her; and in a way, people were glad. At last they could pity Miss Emily. Being left alone, and a pauper, she had become humanized. Now she too would know the old thrill and the old despair of a penny more or less.

The day after his death all the ladies prepared to call at the house and offer condolence and aid, as is our custom. Miss Emily met them at the door, dressed as usual and with no trace of grief on her face. She told them that her father was not dead. She did that for three days, with the ministers calling on her, and the doctors, trying to persuade her to let them dispose of the body. Just as they were about to resort to law and force, she broke down, and they buried her father quickly.

We did not say she was crazy then. We believed she had to do that. We remembered all the young men her father had driven away, and we knew that with nothing left, she would have to cling to that which had robbed her, as people will.

III

She was sick for a long time. When we saw her again, her hair was cut short, making her look like a girl, with a vague resemblance to those angels in colored church windows — sort of tragic and serene.

The town had just let the contracts for paving the sidewalks, and in the summer after her father's death they began the work. The construction company came with niggers and mules and machinery, and a foreman named Homer Barron, a Yankee—a big, dark, ready man, with a big voice and eyes lighter than his face. The little boys would follow in groups to hear him cuss the niggers, and the niggers singing in time to the rise and fall of picks. Pretty soon he knew everybody in town. Whenever you heard a lot of laughing anywhere about the square, Homer Barron would be in the center of the group. Presently, we began to see him and Miss Emily on Sunday afternoons driving in the yellow-wheeled buggy and the matched team of bays from the livery stable.

At first we were glad that Miss Emily would have an interest, because the ladies all said, "Of course a Grierson would not think seriously of a Northerner, a day laborer." But there were still others, older people, who said that even grief could not cause a real lady to forget *noblesse oblige*—without calling it *noblesse oblige*. They just said, "Poor Emily. Her kinsfolk should come to her." She had some kin in Alabama; but years ago her father had fallen out with them over the estate of old lady Wyatt, the crazy woman, and there was no communication between the two families. They had not even been represented at the funeral.

And as soon as the old people said, "Poor Emily," the whispering began. "Do you suppose it's really so?" they said to one another. "Of course it is. What else could. . . ." This behind their hands; rustling of craned silk and satin behind jalousies closed upon the sun of Sunday afternoon as the thin, swift clop-clop-clop of the matched team passed: "Poor Emily."

She carried her head high enough—even when we believed that she was fallen. It was as if she demanded more than ever the recognition of her dignity as the last Grierson; as if it had wanted that touch of earthiness to reaffirm her imperviousness. Like when she bought the rat poison, the arsenic. That was over a year after they had begun to say "Poor Emily," and while the two female cousins were visiting her.

"I want some poison," she said to the druggist. She was over thirty then, still a slight woman, though thinner than usual, with cold, haughty black eyes in a face the flesh of which was strained across the temples and about the eye-sockets as you imagine a lighthouse-keeper's face ought to look. "I want some poison," she said.

"Yes, Miss Emily. What kind? For rats and such? I'd recom——"

"I want the best you have. I don't care what kind."

The druggist named several. "They'll kill anything up to an elephant. But what you want is——"

"Arsenic," Miss Emily said. "Is that a good one?"

"Is . . . arsenic? Yes, ma'am. But what you want——"

"I want arsenic."

The druggist looked down at her. She looked back at him, erect, her face like a strained flag. "Why, of course," the druggist said. "If that's what you want. But the law requires you to tell what you are going to use it for."

Miss Emily just stared at him, her head tilted back in order to look him eye for eye, until he looked away and went and got the arsenic and wrapped it up. The Negro delivery boy brought her the package; the druggist didn't come back. When she opened the package at home there was written on the box, under the skull and bones: "For rats."

IV

So the next day we all said, "She will kill herself"; and we said it would be the best thing. When she had first begun to be seen with Homer Barron, we had said, "She will marry him." Then we said, "She will persuade him yet," because Homer himself had remarked—he liked men, and it was known that he drank with the younger men in the Elks' Club—that he was not a marrying man. Later we said, "Poor Emily" behind the jalousies as they passed on Sunday afternoon in the glittering buggy, Miss Emily with her head high and Homer Barron with his hat cocked and a cigar in his teeth, reins and whip in a yellow glove.

Then some of the ladies began to say that it was a disgrace to the town and a bad example to the young people. The men did not want to interfere, but at last the ladies forced the Baptist minister—Miss Emily's people were Episcopal—to call upon her. He would never divulge what happened during that interview, but he refused to go back again. The next Sunday they again drove about the streets, and the following day the minister's wife wrote to Miss Emily's relations in Alabama.

So she had blood-kin under her roof again and we sat back to watch developments. At first nothing happened. Then we were sure that they were to be married. We learned that Miss Emily had been to the jeweler's and ordered a man's toilet set in silver, with the letters H.B. on each piece. Two days later we learned that she had bought a complete outfit of men's clothing, including a nightshirt, and we said, "They are married." We were really glad. We were glad because the two female cousins were even more Grierson than Miss Emily had ever been.

So we were not surprised when Homer Barron—the streets had been finished some time since—was gone. We were a little disappointed that there was not a public blowing-off, but we believed that he had gone on to prepare for Miss Emily's coming, or to give her a chance to get rid of the cousins. (By that time it was a cabal, and we were all Miss Emily's allies to help circumvent the cousins.) Sure enough, after another week they departed. And, as we had expected all along, within three days Homer Barron was back in town. A neighbor saw the Negro man admit him at the kitchen door at dusk one evening.

And that was the last we saw of Homer Barron. And of Miss Emily for some time. The Negro man went in and out with the market basket, but the front door remained closed. Now and then we would see her at the window for a moment, as the men did that night when they sprinkled the lime, but for almost six months she did not appear on the streets. Then we knew that this was to be expected too; as if that quality of her father which had thwarted her woman's life so many times had been too virulent and too furious to die.

When we next saw Miss Emily, she had grown fat and her hair was turning gray. During the next few years it grew grayer and grayer until it attained an even pepper-and-salt iron-gray, when it ceased turning. Up to the day of her death at seventy-four it was still that vigorous iron-gray, like the hair of an active man.

From that time on her front door remained closed, save during a period of six or seven years, when she was about forty, during which she gave lessons in china-painting. She fitted up a studio in one of the downstairs rooms, where the daughters and granddaughters of Colonel Sartoris' contemporaries were sent to her with the same regularity and in the same spirit that they were sent to church on Sundays with a twenty-five-cent piece for the collection plate. Meanwhile her taxes had been remitted.

Then the newer generation became the backbone and the spirit of the town, and the painting pupils grew up and fell away and did not send their children to her with boxes of color and tedious brushes and pictures cut from the ladies' magazines. The front door closed upon the last one and remained closed for good. When the town got free postal delivery, Miss Emily alone refused to let them fasten the metal numbers above her door and attach a mailbox to it. She would not listen to them.

Daily, monthly, yearly we watched the Negro grow grayer and more stooped, going in and out with the market basket. Each December we sent her a tax notice, which would be returned by the post office a week later, unclaimed. Now and then we would see her in one of the downstairs windows — she had evidently shut up the top floor of the house — like the carven torso of an idol in a niche, looking or not looking at us, we could never tell which. Thus she passed from generation to generation — dear, inescapable, impervious, tranquil, and perverse.

And so she died. Fell ill in the house filled with dust and shadows, with only a doddering Negro man to wait on her. We did not even know she was sick; we had long since given up trying to get any information from the Negro. He talked to no one, probably not even to her, for his voice had grown harsh and rusty, as if from disuse.

She died in one of the downstairs rooms, in a heavy walnut bed with a curtain, her gray head propped on a pillow yellow and moldy with age and lack of sunlight.

V

The Negro met the first of the ladies at the front door and let them in, with their hushed, sibilant voices and their quick, curious glances, and then he disappeared. He walked right through the house and out the back and was not seen again.

The two female cousins came at once. They held the funeral on the second day, with the town coming to look at Miss Emily beneath a mass of bought flowers, with the crayon face of her father musing profoundly above the bier and the ladies sibilant and macabre; and the very old men — some in their brushed Confederate uniforms — on the porch and the lawn, talking of Miss Emily as if she had been a contemporary of theirs, believing that they had danced with her and courted her perhaps, confusing time with its mathematical progression, as the old do, to whom all the past is not a diminishing road but, instead, a huge meadow which no winter ever quite touches, divided from them now by the narrow bottleneck of the most recent decade of years.

Already we knew that there was one room in that region above stairs which no one had seen in forty years, and which would have to be forced. They waited until Miss Emily was decently in the ground before they opened it.

The violence of breaking down the door seemed to fill this room with pervading dust. A thin, acrid pall as of the tomb seemed to lie everywhere upon this room decked and furnished as for a bridal: upon the valance curtains of faded rose color, upon the rose-shaded lights, upon the dressing table, upon the delicate array of crystal and the man's toilet things backed with tarnished silver, silver so tarnished that the monogram was obscured. Among them lay a collar and tie, as if they had just been removed, which, lifted, left upon the surface a pale crescent in the dust. Upon a chair hung the suit, carefully folded; beneath it the two mute shoes and the discarded socks.

The man himself lay in the bed.

For a long while we just stood there, looking down at the profound and fleshless grin. The body had apparently once lain in the attitude of an embrace, but now the long sleep that outlasts love, that conquers even the grimace of love, had cuckolded him. What was left of him, rotted beneath what was left of the nightshirt, had become inextricable from the bed in which he lay; and upon him and upon the pillow beside him lay that even coating of the patient and biding dust.

Then we noticed that in the second pillow was the indentation of a head. One of us lifted something from it, and leaning forward, that faint and invisible dust dry and acrid in the nostrils, we saw a long strand of iron-gray hair.

GABRIEL GARCÍA MÁRQUEZ

Gabriel García Márquez (b. 1928) was born in the remote town of Aracataca in Magdalena province, near the Caribbean coast of Colombia. The oldest of twelve children of a poverty-stricken telegraph operator and his wife, he was raised by his maternal grandparents. When he was eight, he was sent to school near Bogotá, and after his graduation in 1946 he studied law. A writer from childhood, García Márquez published his first book, Leaf Storm and Other Stories, *which includes "A Very Old Man with Enormous Wings," in 1955. He spent the next few years in Paris, where he wrote two short novels. After the Cuban Revolution, he returned to Central America and worked as a journalist and screenwriter. His comic masterpiece, the novel* One Hundred Years of Solitude *(1967), was written while he lived in Mexico City. His other novels include* The Autumn of the Patriarch *(1975), a novel about the life of a Latin American dictator, and the bestseller* Love in the Time of Cholera *(1988). In 1982 he received the Nobel Prize for literature.*

García Márquez mingles realistic and fantastic details in all his fiction, including "A Very Old Man with Enormous Wings." He has said that the origin of his stories is always an image, "not an idea or a concept. The image grows in my head until the whole story takes shape as it might in real life." Leaf Storm *was written after García Márquez returned from visiting the place where he grew up. As he later explained to an interviewer from the* Paris Review,

> The atmosphere, the decadence, the heat in the village were roughly the same as what I had felt in Faulkner. It was a banana plantation region inhabited by a lot of Americans from the fruit companies which gave it the same sort of atmosphere I had found in the writers of the Deep South. Critics have spoken of the literary influence of Faulkner but I see it as a coincidence: I had simply found material that had to be dealt with in the same way that Faulkner had treated similar material. . . .
>
> What really happened to me in that trip to Aracataca was that I realized that everything that had occurred in my childhood had a literary value that I was only now appreciating. From the moment I wrote Leaf Storm I realized I wanted to be a writer and that nobody could stop me and that the only thing left for me to do was to be the best writer in the world.

Other collections of short fiction by García Márquez are No One Writes to the Colonel and Other Stories *(1968),* Innocent Eréndira and Other Stories *(1978),* Collected Stories *(1984), and* Strange Pilgrims *(1993).*

In 1988 García Márquez coauthored (with Fernando Birri) a screenplay of "A Very Old Man with Enormous Wings" for Television Española. In a scene added to the film version of the story, the old man is revealed as a trickster or confidence man who takes off his wings when he is alone. The film also begins with a quotation from Hebrews 13:2: "Be not forgetful to entertain strangers: for thereby some have entertained angels unaware."

WEB   *Research Gabriel García Márquez and answer questions about his work at bedfordstmartins.com/charters/litwriters.*

A Very Old Man with Enormous Wings   1955

TRANSLATED BY GREGORY RABASSA

On the third day of rain they had killed so many crabs inside the house that Pelayo had to cross his drenched courtyard and throw them into the sea, because the newborn child had a temperature all night and they thought it was due to the stench. The world had been sad since Tuesday. Sea and sky were a single ash-gray thing and the sands of the beach, which on March nights glimmered like powdered light, had become a stew of mud and rotten shellfish. The light was so weak at noon that when Pelayo was coming back to the house after throwing away the crabs, it was hard for him to see what it was that was moving and groaning in the rear of the courtyard. He had to go very close to see that it was an old man, a very old man, lying face down in the mud, who, in spite of his tremendous efforts, couldn't get up, impeded by his enormous wings.

Frightened by that nightmare, Pelayo ran to get Elisenda, his wife, who was putting compresses on the sick child, and he took her to the rear of the courtyard. They both looked at the fallen body with mute stupor. He was dressed like a ragpicker. There were only a few faded hairs left on his bald skull and very few teeth in his mouth, and his pitiful condition of a drenched great-grandfather had taken away any sense of grandeur he might have had. His huge buzzard wings, dirty and half-plucked, were forever entangled in the mud. They looked at him so long and so closely that Pelayo and Elisenda very soon overcame their surprise and in the end found him familiar. Then they dared speak to him, and he answered in an incomprehensible dialect with a strong sailor's voice. That was how they skipped over the inconvenience of the wings and quite intelligently concluded that he was a lonely castaway from some foreign ship wrecked by the storm. And yet, they called in a neighbor woman who knew everything about life and death to see him, and all she needed was one look to show them their mistake.

"He's an angel," she told them. "He must have been coming for the child, but the poor fellow is so old that the rain knocked him down."

On the following day everyone knew that a flesh-and-blood angel was held captive in Pelayo's house. Against the judgment of the wise neighbor woman, for whom angels in those times were the fugitive survivors of a celestial conspiracy, they did not have the heart to club him to death. Pelayo watched over him all afternoon from the kitchen, armed with his bailiff's club, and before going to bed he dragged him out of the mud and locked him up with the hens in the wire chicken coop. In the middle of the night, when the rain stopped, Pelayo and Elisenda were still killing crabs. A short time afterward the child woke up without a fever and with a desire to eat. Then they felt magnanimous and decided to put the angel on a raft with fresh water and provisions for three days and leave him to his fate on the high seas. But when they went out into the courtyard with the first light of dawn, they found the whole neighborhood in front of the chicken coop having fun with the angel, without the slightest reverence, tossing him things to eat through the openings in the wire as if he weren't a supernatural creature but a circus animal.

Father Gonzaga arrived before seven o'clock, alarmed at the strange news. By that time onlookers less frivolous than those at dawn had already arrived and they were making all kinds of conjectures concerning the captive's future. The simplest among them thought that he should be named mayor of the world. Others of sterner mind felt that he should be promoted to the rank of five-star general in order to win all wars. Some visionaries hoped that he could be put to stud in order to implant on earth a race of winged wise men who could take charge of the universe. But Father Gonzaga, before becoming a priest, had been a robust woodcutter. Standing by the wire, he reviewed his catechism in an instant and asked them to open the door so that he could take a close look at that pitiful man who looked more like a huge decrepit hen among the fascinated chickens. He was lying in a corner drying his open wings in the sunlight among the fruit peels and breakfast leftovers that the early risers had thrown him. Alien to the impertinences of the world, he only lifted his antiquarian eyes and murmured something in his dialect when Father Gonzaga went into the chicken coop and said good morning to him in Latin. The parish priest had his first suspicion of an impostor when he saw that he did not understand the language of God or know how to greet His ministers. Then he noticed that seen close up he was much too human: he had an unbearable smell of the outdoors, the back side of his wings was strewn with parasites and his main feathers had been mistreated by terrestrial winds, and nothing about him measured up to the proud dignity of angels. Then he came out of the chicken coop and in a brief sermon warned the curious against the risks of being ingenuous. He reminded them that the devil had the bad habit of making use of carnival tricks in order to confuse the unwary. He argued that if wings were not the essential element in determining the difference between a hawk and an airplane, they were even less so in the recognition of angels. Nevertheless, he promised to write a letter to his bishop so that the latter would write to his primate so that the latter would write to the Supreme Pontiff in order to get the final verdict from the highest courts.

His prudence fell on sterile hearts. The news of the captive angel spread with such rapidity that after a few hours the courtyard had the bustle of a marketplace and they had to call in troops with fixed bayonets to disperse the mob that was about to knock the house down. Elisenda, her spine all twisted from sweeping up so much marketplace trash, then got the idea of fencing in the yard and charging five cents admission to see the angel.

The curious came from far away. A traveling carnival arrived with a flying acrobat who buzzed over the crowd several times, but no one paid any attention to him because his wings were not those of an angel but, rather, those of a sidereal° bat. The most unfortunate invalids on earth came in search of health: a poor woman who since childhood had been counting her heartbeats and had run out of numbers; a Portuguese man who couldn't sleep because the noise of the stars disturbed him; a sleep-walker who got up at night to undo the things he had done while awake; and many others with less serious ailments. In the midst of that shipwreck disorder that made the earth tremble, Pelayo and Elisenda were happy with fatigue, for in less than a week they had crammed their rooms with money and the line of pilgrims waiting their turn to enter still reached beyond the horizon.

The angel was the only one who took no part in his own act. He spent his time trying to get comfortable in his borrowed nest, befuddled by the hellish heat of the oil lamps and sacramental candles that had been placed along the wire. At first they tried to make him eat some mothballs, which, according to the wisdom of the wise neighbor woman, were the food prescribed for angels. But he turned them down, just as he turned down the papal lunches that the penitents brought him, and they never found out whether it was because he was an angel or because he was an old man that in the end he ate nothing but eggplant mush. His only supernatural virtue seemed to be patience. Especially during the first days, when the hens pecked at him, searching for the stellar parasites that proliferated in his wings, and the cripples pulled out feathers to touch their defective parts with, and even the most merciful threw stones at him, trying to get him to rise so they could see him standing. The only time they succeeded in arousing him was when they burned his side with an iron for branding steers, for he had been motionless for so many hours that they thought he was dead. He awoke with a start, ranting in his hermetic language

---

sidereal: Coming from the stars.

and with tears in his eyes, and he flapped his wings a couple of times, which brought on a whirlwind of chicken dung and lunar dust and a gale of panic that did not seem to be of this world. Although many thought that his reaction had been one not of rage but of pain, from then on they were careful not to annoy him, because the majority understood that his passivity was not that of a hero taking his ease but that of a cataclysm in repose.

Father Gonzaga held back the crowd's frivolity with formulas of maid-servant inspiration while awaiting the arrival of a final judgment on the nature of the captive. But the mail from Rome showed no sense of urgency. They spent their time finding out if the prisoner had a navel, if his dialect had any connection with Aramaic, how many times he could fit on the head of a pin, or whether he wasn't just a Norwegian with wings. Those meager letters might have come and gone until the end of time if a providential event had not put an end to the priest's tribulations.

It so happened that during those days, among so many other carnival attractions, there arrived in town the traveling show of the woman who had been changed into a spider for having disobeyed her parents. The admission to see her was not only less than the admission to see the angel, but people were permitted to ask her all manner of questions about her absurd state and to examine her up and down so that no one would ever doubt the truth of her hor-ror. She was a frightful tarantula the size of a ram and with the head of a sad maiden. What was most heart-rending, however, was not her outlandish shape but the sincere affliction with which she recounted the details of her misfor-tune. While still practically a child she had sneaked out of her parents' house to go to a dance, and while she was coming back through the woods after having danced all night without permission, a fearful thunderclap rent the sky in two and through the crack came the lightning bolt of brimstone that changed her into a spider. Her only nourishment came from the meatballs that charitable souls chose to toss into her mouth. A spectacle like that, full of so much human truth and with such a fearful lesson, was bound to defeat without even trying that of a haughty angel who scarcely deigned to look at mortals. Besides, the few miracles attributed to the angel showed a certain mental disorder, like the blind man who didn't recover his sight but grew three new teeth, or the para-lytic who didn't get to walk but almost won the lottery, and the leper whose sores sprouted sunflowers. Those consolation miracles, which were more like mocking fun, had already ruined the angel's reputation when the woman who had been changed into a spider finally crushed him completely. That was how Father Gonzaga was cured forever of his insomnia and Pelayo's courtyard went back to being as empty as during the time it had rained for three days and crabs walked through the bedrooms.

The owners of the house had no reason to lament. With the money they saved they built a two-story mansion with balconies and gardens and high net-ting so that crabs wouldn't get in during the winter, and with iron bars on the windows so that angels wouldn't get in. Pelayo also set up a rabbit warren close to town and gave up his job as bailiff for good, and Elisenda bought some satin pumps with high heels and many dresses of iridescent silk, the kind worn on Sunday by the most desirable women in those times. The chicken coop was the only thing that didn't receive any attention. If they washed it down with creolin and burned tears of myrrh inside it every so often, it was not in homage to the angel but to drive away the dungheap stench that still hung everywhere like a ghost and was turning the new house into an old one. At first, when the child learned to walk, they were careful that he not get too close to the chicken coop. But then they began to lose their fears and got used to the smell, and before the child got his second teeth he'd gone inside the chicken coop to play, where the wires were falling apart. The angel was no less standoffish with him than with other mortals, but he tolerated the most ingenious infamies with the patience of a dog who had no illusions. They both came down with chicken pox at the same time. The doctor who took care of the child couldn't resist the temptation to listen to the angel's heart, and he found so much whistling in the heart and so many sounds in his kidneys that it seemed impossible for him to be alive. What surprised him most, however, was the logic of his wings. They seemed so natural on that completely human organism that he couldn't understand why other men didn't have them too.

When the child began school it had been some time since the sun and rain had caused the collapse of the chicken coop. The angel went dragging himself about here and there like a stray dying man. They would drive him out of the bedroom with a broom and a moment later find him in the kitchen. He seemed to be in so many places at the same time that they grew to think that he'd been duplicated, that he was reproducing himself all through the house, and the exasperated and unhinged Elisenda shouted that it was awful living in that hell full of angels. He could scarcely eat and his antiquarian eyes had also become so foggy that he went about bumping into posts. All he had left were the bare cannulae° of his last feathers. Pelayo threw a blanket over him and extended him the charity of letting him sleep in the shed, and only then did they notice that he had a temperature at night, and was delirious with the tongue twisters of an old Norwegian. That was one of the few times they became alarmed, for they thought he was going to die and not even the wise neighbor woman had been able to tell them what to do with dead angels.

And yet he not only survived his worst winter, but seemed improved with the first sunny days. He remained motionless for several days in the farthest corner of the courtyard, where no one would see him, and at the beginning of December some large, stiff feathers began to grow on his wings, the feathers of a scarecrow, which looked more like another misfortune of decrepitude. But he must have known the reason for those changes, for he was quite careful that no one should notice them, that no one should hear the sea chanteys that he sometimes sang under the stars. One morning Elisenda was cutting some bunches of onions for lunch when a wind that seemed to come from the high seas blew into the kitchen. Then she went to the window and caught the angel in his first attempts at flight. They were so clumsy that his fingernails opened a furrow in the vegetable patch and he was on the point of knocking the shed down with the ungainly flapping that slipped on the light and couldn't get a grip on the air. But he did manage to gain altitude. Elisenda

---

cannulae: The tubular pieces by which feathers are attached to a body.

let out a sigh of relief, for herself and for him, when she saw him pass over the last houses, holding himself up in some way with the risky flapping of a senile vulture. She kept watching him even when she was through cutting the onions and she kept on watching until it was no longer possible for her to see him, because then he was no longer an annoyance in her life but an imaginary dot on the horizon of the sea.

CHARLOTTE PERKINS GILMAN

Charlotte Perkins Gilman (1860–1935) was born in Hartford, Connecticut. Her father deserted the family shortly after she was born and provided her mother with only meager support. As a teenager Gilman attended the Rhode Island School of Design for a brief period and worked as a commercial artist and teacher. Like her great-aunt Harriet Beecher Stowe, she was concerned at an early age with social injustice and wrote poetry about the hardship of women's lives.

In 1884 she married the artist Charles Walter Stetson. Suffering extreme depression after the birth of a daughter, she left her husband and moved to California in 1888. They were divorced, and she later married George Houghton Gilman, with whom she lived for thirty-four years. In the 1890s Gilman established her reputation as a lecturer and writer of feminist tracts. Her book Women and Economics *(1898) is considered one of the most important works of the early years of the women's movement in the United States. Gilman's later books—* Concerning Children *(1900),* The Home *(1904), and* Human Work *(1904)— argue that women should be educated to become financially independent; then they could contribute more to the amelioration of systems of justice and the improvement of society. From 1909 to 1917 Gilman published her own journal,* The Forerunner, *for which she wrote voluminously. At the end of her life, suffering from cancer, she committed suicide with chloroform.*

Today Gilman's best-known work is "The Yellow Wallpaper," written around 1890, shortly after her own nervous breakdown. A landmark story in its frank depiction of mental illness, it is part fantasy and part autobiography, an imaginative account of her suffering and treatment by the physician S. Weir Mitchell, who forbade her any activity, especially writing, the thing she most wanted to do. In setting the story Gilman used elements of the conventional gothic romances that were a staple in women's popular fiction—an isolated mansion, a distant but dominating male figure, and a mysterious household—all of which force the heroine into the role of passive victim of circumstances. But Gilman gave her own twist to the form. Using the brief paragraphs and simple sentences of popular fiction, she narrated her story with a clinical precision that avoided the trite language of typical romances.

COMMENTARIES *Sandra M. Gilbert and Susan Gubar, "A Feminist Reading of Gilman's 'The Yellow Wallpaper,'" page 564; Charlotte Perkins Gilman, "Undergoing the Cure for Nervous Prostration," page 567.*

WEB *Research Charlotte Perkins Gilman and answer questions about her work at bedfordstmartins.com/charters/litwriters.*

The Yellow Wallpaper   1892

It is very seldom that mere ordinary people like John and myself secure ancestral halls for the summer.

A colonial mansion, a hereditary estate, I would say a haunted house and reach the height of romantic felicity—but that would be asking too much of fate!

Still I will proudly declare that there is something queer about it.

Else, why should it be let so cheaply? And why have stood so long untenanted?

John laughs at me, of course, but one expects that in marriage.

John is practical in the extreme. He has no patience with faith, an intense horror of superstition, and he scoffs openly at any talk of things not to be felt and seen and put down in figures.

John is a physician, and *perhaps*—(I would not say it to a living soul, of course, but this is dead paper and a great relief to my mind)—*perhaps* that is one reason I do not get well faster.

You see, he does not believe I am sick!

And what can one do?

If a physician of high standing, and one's own husband, assures friends and relatives that there is really nothing the matter with one but temporary nervous depression—a slight hysterical tendency—what is one to do?

My brother is also a physician, and also of high standing, and he says the same thing.

So I take phosphates or phosphites—whichever it is, and tonics, and journeys, and air, and exercise, and am absolutely forbidden to "work" until I am well again.

Personally, I disagree with their ideas.

Personally, I believe that congenial work, with excitement and change, would do me good.

But what is one to do?

I did write for a while in spite of them; but it *does* exhaust me a good deal—having to be so sly about it, or else meet with heavy opposition.

I sometimes fancy that in my condition if I had less opposition and more society and stimulus—but John says the very worst thing I can do is to think about my condition, and I confess it always makes me feel bad.

So I will let it alone and talk about the house.

The most beautiful place! It is quite alone, standing well back from the road, quite three miles from the village. It makes me think of English places that you read about, for there are hedges and walls and gates that lock, and lots of separate little houses for the gardeners and people.

There is a *delicious* garden! I never saw such a garden—large and shady, full of box-bordered paths, and lined with long grape-covered arbors with seats under them.

There were greenhouses, too, but they are all broken now.

There was some legal trouble, I believe, something about the heirs and co-heirs; anyhow, the place has been empty for years.

That spoils my ghostliness, I am afraid, but I don't care—there is something strange about the house—I can feel it.

I even said so to John one moonlight evening, but he said what I felt was a *draught*, and shut the window.

I get unreasonably angry with John sometimes. I'm sure I never used to be so sensitive. I think it is due to this nervous condition.

But John says if I feel so, I shall neglect proper self-control; so I take pains to control myself—before him, at least, and that makes me very tired.

I don't like our room a bit. I wanted one downstairs that opened on the piazza and had roses all over the window, and such pretty old-fashioned chintz hangings! but John would not hear of it.

He said there was only one window and not room for two beds, and no near room for him if he took another.

He is very careful and loving, and hardly lets me stir without special direction.

I have a schedule prescription for each hour in the day; he takes all care from me, and so I feel basely ungrateful not to value it more.

He said we came here solely on my account, that I was to have perfect rest and all the air I could get. "Your exercise depends on your strength, my dear," said he, "and your food somewhat on your appetite; but air you can absorb all the time." So we took the nursery at the top of the house.

It is a big, airy room, the whole floor nearly, with windows that look all ways, and air and sunshine galore. It was nursery first and then playroom and gymnasium, I should judge; for the windows are barred for little children, and there are rings and things in the walls.

The paint and paper look as if a boys' school had used it. It is stripped off—the paper—in great patches all around the head of my bed, about as far as I can reach, and in a great place on the other side of the room low down. I never saw a worse paper in my life.

One of those sprawling flamboyant patterns committing every artistic sin.

It is dull enough to confuse the eye in following, pronounced enough to constantly irritate and provoke study, and when you follow the lame uncertain curves for a little distance they suddenly commit suicide—plunge off at outrageous angles, destroy themselves in unheard of contradictions.

The color is repellant, almost revolting; a smouldering unclean yellow, strangely faded by the slow-turning sunlight.

It is a dull yet lurid orange in some places, a sickly sulphur tint in others.

No wonder the children hated it! I should hate it myself if I had to live in this room long.

There comes John, and I must put this away,—he hates to have me write a word.

We have been here two weeks, and I haven't felt like writing before, since that first day.

I am sitting by the window now, up in this atrocious nursery, and there is nothing to hinder my writing as much as I please, save lack of strength.

John is away all day, and even some nights when his cases are serious.

I am glad my case is not serious!

But these nervous troubles are dreadfully depressing.

John does not know how much I really suffer. He knows there is no *reason* to suffer, and that satisfies him.

Of course it is only nervousness. It does weigh on me so not to do my duty in any way!

I meant to be such a help to John, such a real rest and comfort, and here I am a comparative burden already!

Nobody would believe what an effort it is to do what little I am able, — to dress and entertain, and order things.

It is fortunate Mary is so good with the baby. Such a dear baby!

And yet I *cannot* be with him, it makes me so nervous.

I suppose John never was nervous in his life. He laughs at me so about this wall-paper!

At first he meant to repaper the room, but afterward he said that I was letting it get the better of me, and that nothing was worse for a nervous patient than to give way to such fancies.

He said that after the wall-paper was changed it would be the heavy bedstead, and then the barred windows, and then that gate at the head of the stairs, and so on.

"You know the place is doing you good," he said, "and really, dear, I don't care to renovate the house just for a three months' rental."

"Then do let us go downstairs," I said, "there are such pretty rooms there."

Then he took me in his arms and called me a blessed little goose, and said he would go down cellar, if I wished, and have it whitewashed into the bargain.

But he is right enough about the beds and windows and things.

It is an airy and comfortable room as anyone need wish, and, of course, I would not be so silly as to make him uncomfortable just for a whim.

I'm really getting quite fond of the big room, all but that horrid paper.

Out of one window I can see the garden, those mysterious deep-shaded arbors, the riotous old-fashioned flowers, and bushes and gnarly trees.

Out of another I get a lovely view of the bay and a little private wharf belonging to the estate. There is a beautiful shaded lane that runs down there from the house. I always fancy I see people walking in these numerous paths and arbors, but John has cautioned me not to give way to fancy in the least. He says that with my imaginative power and habit of story-making, a nervous weakness like mine is sure to lead to all manner of excited fancies, and that I ought to use my will and good sense to check the tendency. So I try.

I think sometimes that if I were only well enough to write a little it would relieve the press of ideas and rest me.

But I find I get pretty tired when I try.

It is so discouraging not to have any advice and companionship about my work. When I get really well, John says we will ask Cousin Henry and Julia down for a long visit; but he says he would as soon put fireworks in my pillowcase as to let me have those stimulating people about now.

I wish I could get well faster.

But I must not think about that. This paper looks to me as if it *knew* what a vicious influence it had!

There is a recurrent spot where the pattern lolls like a broken neck and two bulbous eyes stare at you upside down.

I get positively angry with the impertinence of it and the everlastingness. Up and down and sideways they crawl, and those absurd, unblinking eyes are everywhere. There is one place where two breadths didn't match, and the eyes go all up and down the line, one a little higher than the other.

I never saw so much expression in an inanimate thing before, and we all know how much expression they have! I used to lie awake as a child and get more entertainment and terror out of blank walls and plain furniture than most children could find in a toy-store.

I remember what a kindly wink the knobs of our big, old bureau used to have, and there was one chair that always seemed like a strong friend.

I used to feel that if any of the other things looked too fierce I could always hop into that chair and be safe.

The furniture in this room is no worse than inharmonious, however, for we had to bring it all from downstairs. I suppose when this was used as a play-room they had to take the nursery things out, and no wonder! I never saw such ravages as the children have made here.

The wall-paper, as I said before, is torn off in spots, and it sticketh closer than a brother — they must have had perseverance as well as hatred.

Then the floor is scratched and gouged and splintered, the plaster itself is dug out here and there, and this great heavy bed, which is all we found in the room, looks as if it had been through the wars.

But I don't mind it a bit — only the paper.

There comes John's sister. Such a dear girl as she is, and so careful of me! I must not let her find me writing.

She is a perfect and enthusiastic housekeeper, and hopes for no better profession. I verily believe she thinks it is the writing which made me sick!

But I can write when she is out, and see her a long way off from these windows.

There is one that commands the road, a lovely shaded winding road, and one that just looks off over the country. A lovely country, too, full of great elms and velvet meadows.

This wallpaper has a kind of sub-pattern in a different shade, a particularly irritating one, for you can only see it in certain lights, and not clearly then.

But in the places where it isn't faded and where the sun is just so — I can see a strange, provoking, formless sort of figure, that seems to skulk about behind that silly and conspicuous front design.

There's sister on the stairs!

Well, the Fourth of July is over! The people are all gone and I am tired out. John thought it might do me good to see a little company, so we just had mother and Nellie and the children down for a week.

Of course I didn't do a thing. Jennie sees to everything now.

But it tired me all the same.

John says if I don't pick up faster he shall send me to Weir Mitchell° in the fall.

But I don't want to go there at all. I had a friend who was in his hands once, and she says he is just like John and my brother, only more so!

Besides, it is such an undertaking to go so far.

I don't feel as if it was worthwhile to turn my hand over for anything, and I'm getting dreadfully fretful and querulous.

I cry at nothing, and cry most of the time.

Of course I don't when John is here, or anybody else, but when I am alone.

And I am alone a good deal just now. John is kept in town very often by serious cases, and Jennie is good and lets me alone when I want her to.

So I walk a little in the garden or down that lovely lane, sit on the porch under the roses, and lie down up here a good deal.

I'm getting really fond of the room in spite of the wallpaper. Perhaps *because* of the wallpaper.

It dwells in my mind so!

I lie here on this great immovable bed — it is nailed down, I believe — and follow that pattern about by the hour. It is as good as gymnastics, I assure you. I start, we'll say, at the bottom, down in the corner over there where it has not been touched, and I determine for the thousandth time that I *will* follow that pointless pattern to some sort of a conclusion.

I know a little of the principle of design, and I know this thing was not arranged on any laws of radiation, or alternation, or repetition, or symmetry, or anything else that I ever heard of.

It is repeated, of course, by the breadths, but not otherwise.

Looked at in one way each breadth stands alone, the bloated curves and flourishes — a kind of "debased Romanesque" with *delirium tremens* — go waddling up and down in isolated columns of fatuity.

But, on the other hand, they connect diagonally, and the sprawling outlines run off in great slanting waves of optic horror, like a lot of wallowing sea-weeds in full chase.

The whole thing goes horizontally, too, at least it seems so, and I exhaust myself in trying to distinguish the order of its going in that direction.

They have used a horizontal breadth for a frieze, and that adds wonderfully to the confusion.

There is one end of the room where it is almost intact, and there, when the crosslights fade and the low sun shines directly upon it, I can almost fancy radiation after all, — the interminable grotesques seem to form around a common centre and rush off in headlong plunges of equal distraction.

It makes me tired to follow it. I will take a nap I guess.

• • •

Weir Mitchell: Dr. S. Weir Mitchell (1829–1914) was an eminent Philadelphia neurologist who advocated "rest cures" for nervous disorders. He was the author of *Diseases of the Nervous System, Especially of Women* (1881).

I don't know why I should write this.

I don't want to.

I don't feel able.

And I know John would think it absurd. But I *must* say what I feel and think in some way — it is such a relief!

But the effort is getting to be greater than the relief.

Half the time now I am awfully lazy, and lie down ever so much.

John says I mustn't lose my strength, and has me take cod liver oil and lots of tonics and things, to say nothing of ale and wine and rare meat.

Dear John! He loves me very dearly, and hates to have me sick. I tried to have a real earnest reasonable talk with him the other day, and tell him how I wish he would let me go and make a visit to Cousin Henry and Julia.

But he said I wasn't able to go, nor able to stand it after I got there; and I did not make out a very good case for myself, for I was crying before I had finished.

It is getting to be a great effort for me to think straight. Just this nervous weakness I suppose.

And dear John gathered me up in his arms, and just carried me upstairs and laid me on the bed, and sat by me and read to me till it tired my head.

He said I was his darling and his comfort and all he had, and that I must take care of myself for his sake, and keep well.

He says no one but myself can help me out of it, that I must use my will and self-control and not let any silly fancies run away with me.

There's one comfort, the baby is well and happy, and does not have to occupy this nursery with the horrid wallpaper.

If we had not used it, that blessed child would have! What a fortunate escape! Why, I wouldn't have a child of mine, an impressionable little thing, live in such a room for worlds.

I never thought of it before, but it is lucky that John kept me here after all, I can stand it so much easier than a baby, you see.

Of course I never mention it to them any more — I am too wise, but I keep watch of it all the same.

There are things in the wallpaper that nobody knows but me, or ever will.

Behind that outside pattern the dim shapes get clearer every day.

It is always the same shape, only very numerous.

And it is like a woman stooping down and creeping about behind that pattern. I don't like it a bit. I wonder — I begin to think — I wish John would take me away from here!

It is so hard to talk with John about my case, because he is so wise, and because he loves me so.

But I tried it last night.

It was moonlight. The moon shines in all around just as the sun does.

I hate to see it sometimes, it creeps so slowly, and always comes in by one window or another.

John was asleep and I hated to waken him, so I kept still and watched the moonlight on that undulating wallpaper till I felt creepy.

The faint figure behind seemed to shake the pattern, just as if she wanted to get out.

I got up softly and went to feel and see if the paper *did* move, and when I came back John was awake.

"What is it, little girl?" he said. "Don't go walking about like that— you'll get cold."

I thought it was a good time to talk, so I told him that I really was not gaining here, and that I wished he would take me away.

"Why, darling!" said he, "our lease will be up in three weeks, and I can't see how to leave before.

"The repairs are not done at home, and I cannot possibly leave town just now. Of course if you were in any danger, I could and would, but you really are better, dear, whether you can see it or not. I am a doctor, dear, and I know. You are gaining flesh and color, your appetite is better, I feel really much easier about you."

"I don't weigh a bit more," said I, "nor as much; and my appetite may be better in the evening when you are here but it is worse in the morning when you are away!"

"Bless her little heart!" said he with a big hug, "she shall be as sick as she pleases! But now let's improve the shining hours by going to sleep, and talk about it in the morning!"

"And you won't go away?" I asked gloomily.

"Why, how can I, dear? It is only three weeks more and then we will take a nice little trip of a few days while Jennie is getting the house ready. Really dear you are better!"

"Better in body perhaps—" I began, and stopped short, for he sat up straight and looked at me with such a stern, reproachful look that I could not say another word.

"My darling," said he, "I beg you, for my sake and for our child's sake, as well as for your own, that you will never for one instant let that idea enter your mind! There is nothing so dangerous, so fascinating, to a temperament like yours. It is a false and foolish fancy. Can you trust me as a physician when I tell you so?"

So of course I said no more on that score, and we went to sleep before long. He thought I was asleep first, but I wasn't, and lay there for hours trying to decide whether that front pattern and the back pattern really did move together or separately.

On a pattern like this, by daylight, there is a lack of sequence, a defiance of law, that is a constant irritant to a normal mind.

The color is hideous enough, and unreliable enough, and infuriating enough, but the pattern is torturing.

You think you have mastered it, but just as you get well underway in following, it turns a back-somersault and there you are. It slaps you in the face, knocks you down, and tramples upon you. It is like a bad dream.

The outside pattern is a florid arabesque, reminding one of a fungus. If you can imagine a toadstool in joints, an interminable string of toadstools, budding and sprouting in endless convolutions—why, that is something like it.

That is, sometimes!

There is one marked peculiarity about this paper, a thing nobody seems to notice but myself, and that is that it changes as the light changes.

When the sun shoots in through the east window—I always watch for that first long, straight ray—it changes so quickly that I never can quite believe it.

That is why I watch it always.

By moonlight—the moon shines in all night when there is a moon—I wouldn't know it was the same paper.

At night in any kind of light, in twilight, candlelight, lamplight, and worst of all by moonlight, it becomes bars! The outside pattern I mean, and the woman behind it is as plain as can be.

I didn't realize for a long time what the thing was that showed behind, that dim sub-pattern, but now I am quite sure it is a woman.

By daylight she is subdued, quiet. I fancy it is the pattern that keeps her so still. It is so puzzling. It keeps me quiet by the hour.

I lie down ever so much now. John says it is good for me, and to sleep all I can.

Indeed he started the habit by making me lie down for an hour after each meal.

It is a very bad habit I am convinced, for you see I don't sleep.

And that cultivates deceit, for I don't tell them I'm awake—O, no!

The fact is I am getting a little afraid of John.

He seems very queer sometimes, and even Jennie has an inexplicable look.

It strikes me occasionally, just as a scientific hypothesis,—that perhaps it is the paper!

I have watched John when he did not know I was looking, and come into the room suddenly on the most innocent excuses, and I've caught him several times *looking at the paper!* And Jennie too. I caught Jennie with her hand on it once.

She didn't know I was in the room, and when I asked her in a quiet, a very quiet voice, with the most restrained manner possible, what she was doing with the paper—she turned around as if she had been caught stealing, and looked quite angry—asked me why I should frighten her so!

Then she said that the paper stained everything it touched, that she had found yellow smooches on all my clothes and John's, and she wished we would be more careful!

Did not that sound innocent? But I know she was studying that pattern, and I am determined that nobody shall find it out but myself!

Life is very much more exciting now than it used to be. You see I have something more to expect, to look forward to, to watch. I really do eat better, and am more quiet than I was.

John is so pleased to see me improve! He laughed a little the other day, and said I seemed to be flourishing in spite of my wall-paper.

I turned it off with a laugh. I had no intention of telling him it was *because* of the wall-paper—he would make fun of me. He might even want to take me away.

I don't want to leave now until I have found it out. There is a week more, and I think that will be enough.

I'm feeling ever so much better! I don't sleep much at night, for it is so interesting to watch developments; but I sleep a good deal in the daytime.

In the daytime it is tiresome and perplexing.

There are always new shoots on the fungus, and new shades of yellow all over it. I cannot keep count of them, though I have tried conscientiously.

It is the strangest yellow, that wall-paper! It makes me think of all the yellow things I ever saw—not beautiful ones like buttercups, but old foul, bad yellow things.

But there is something else about that paper—the smell! I noticed it the moment we came into the room, but with so much air and sun it was not bad. Now we have had a week of fog and rain, and whether the windows are open or not, the smell is here.

It creeps all over the house.

I find it hovering in the dining-room, skulking in the parlor, hiding in the hall, lying in wait for me on the stairs.

It gets into my hair.

Even when I go to ride, if I turn my head suddenly and surprise it—there is that smell!

Such a peculiar odor, too! I have spent hours in trying to analyze it, to find what it smelled like.

It is not bad—at first, and very gentle, but quite the subtlest, most enduring odor I ever met.

In this damp weather it is awful, I wake up in the night and find it hanging over me.

It used to disturb me at first. I thought seriously of burning the house—to reach the smell.

But now I am used to it. The only thing I can think of that it is like is the *color* of the paper! A yellow smell.

There is a very funny mark on this wall, low down, near the mopboard. A streak that runs round the room. It goes behind every piece of furniture, except the bed, a long, straight, even *smooch*, as if it had been rubbed over and over.

I wonder how it was done and who did it, and what they did it for. Round and round and round—round and round and round—it makes me dizzy!

I really have discovered something at last.

Through watching so much at night, when it changes so, I have finally found out.

The front pattern *does* move—and no wonder! The woman behind shakes it!

Sometimes I think there are a great many women behind, and sometimes only one, and she crawls around fast, and her crawling shakes it all over.

Then in the very bright spots she keeps still, and in the very shady spots she just takes hold of the bars and shakes them hard.

And she is all the time trying to climb through. But nobody could climb through that pattern—it strangles so; I think that is why it has so many heads.

They get through, and then the pattern strangles them off and turns them upside down, and makes their eyes white!

If those heads were covered or taken off it would not be half so bad.

I think that woman gets out in the daytime!

And I'll tell you why—privately—I've seen her!

I can see her out of every one of my windows!

It is the same woman, I know, for she is always creeping, and most women do not creep by daylight.

I see her in that long shaded lane, creeping up and down. I see her in those dark grape arbors, creeping all around the garden.

I see her on that long road under the trees, creeping along, and when a carriage comes she hides under the blackberry vines.

I don't blame her a bit. It must be very humiliating to be caught creeping by daylight!

I always lock the door when I creep by daylight. I can't do it at night, for I know John would suspect something at once.

And John is so queer now, that I don't want to irritate him. I wish he would take another room! Besides, I don't want anybody to get that woman out at night but myself.

I often wonder if I could see her out of all the windows at once.

But, turn as fast as I can, I can only see out of one at one time.

And though I always see her, she *may* be able to creep faster than I can turn!

I have watched her sometimes away off in the open country, creeping as fast as a cloud shadow in a high wind.

If only that top pattern could be gotten off from the under one! I mean to try it, little by little.

I have found out another funny thing, but I shan't tell it this time! It does not do to trust people too much.

There are only two more days to get this paper off, and I believe John is beginning to notice. I don't like the look in his eyes.

And I heard him ask Jennie a lot of professional questions, about me. She had a very good report to give.

She said I slept a good deal in the daytime.

John knows I don't sleep very well at night, for all I'm so quiet!

He asked me all sorts of questions too, and pretended to be very loving and kind.

As if I couldn't see through him!

Still, I don't wonder he acts so, sleeping under this paper for three months.

It only interests me, but I feel sure John and Jennie are secretly affected by it.

• • •

Hurrah! This is the last day, but it is enough. John to stay in town over night, and won't be out until this evening.

Jennie wanted to sleep with me—the sly thing! But I told her I should undoubtedly rest better for a night all alone.

That was clever, for really I wasn't alone a bit! As soon as it was moonlight and that poor thing began to crawl and shake the pattern, I got up and ran to help her.

I pulled and she shook, I shook and she pulled, and before morning we had peeled off yards of that paper.

A strip about as high as my head and half around the room.

And then when the sun came and that awful pattern began to laugh at me, I declared I would finish it to-day!

We go away to-morrow, and they are moving all my furniture down again to leave things as they were before.

Jennie looked at the wall in amazement, but I told her merrily that I did it out of pure spite at the vicious thing.

She laughed and said she wouldn't mind doing it herself, but I must not get tired.

How she betrayed herself that time!

But I am here, and no person touches this paper but me,—not *alive!*

She tried to get me out of the room—it was too patent! But I said it was so quiet and empty and clean now that I believed I would lie down again and sleep all I could, and not to wake me even for dinner—I would call when I woke.

So now she is gone, and the servants are gone, and the things are gone, and there is nothing left but that great bedstead nailed down, with the canvas mattress we found on it.

We shall sleep downstairs to-night, and take the boat home to-morrow.

I quite enjoy the room, now it is bare again.

How those children did tear about here!

This bedstead is fairly gnawed!

But I must get to work.

I have locked the door and thrown the key down into the front path.

I don't want to go out, and I don't want to have anybody come in, till John comes.

I want to astonish him.

I've got a rope up here that even Jennie did not find. If that woman does get out, and tries to get away, I can tie her!

But I forgot I could not reach far without anything to stand on!

This bed will *not* move!

I tried to lift and push it until I was lame, and then I got so angry I bit off a little piece at one corner—but it hurt my teeth.

Then I peeled off all the paper I could reach standing on the floor. It sticks horribly and the pattern just enjoys it! All those strangled heads and bulbous eyes and waddling fungus growths just shriek with derision!

I am getting angry enough to do something desperate. To jump out of the window would be admirable exercise, but the bars are too strong even to try.

Besides I wouldn't do it. Of course not. I know well enough that a step like that is improper and might be misconstrued.

I don't like to *look* out of the windows even—there are so many of those creeping women, and they creep so fast.

I wonder if they all come out of that wall-paper as I did?

But I am securely fastened now by my well-hidden rope—you don't get *me* out in the road there!

I suppose I shall have to get back behind the pattern when it comes night, and that is hard!

It is so pleasant to be out in this great room and creep around as I please!

I don't want to go outside. I won't, even if Jennie asks me to.

For outside you have to creep on the ground, and everything is green instead of yellow.

But here I can creep smoothly on the floor, and my shoulder just fits in that long smooch around the wall, so I cannot lose my way.

Why, there's John at the door!

It is no use, young man, you can't open it!

How he does call and pound!

Now he's crying for an axe.

It would be a shame to break down that beautiful door!

"John dear!" said I in the gentlest voice, "the key is down by the front steps, under a plantain leaf!"

That silenced him for a few moments.

Then he said—very quietly indeed, "Open the door, my darling!"

"I can't," said I. "The key is down by the front door under a plantain leaf!"

And then I said it again, several times, very gently and slowly, and said it so often that he had to go and see, and he got it of course, and came in. He stopped short by the door.

"What is the matter?" he cried. "For God's sake, what are you doing!"

I kept on creeping just the same, but I looked at him over my shoulder.

"I've got out at last," said I, "in spite of you and Jane. And I've pulled off most of the paper, so you can't put me back!"

Now why should that man have fainted? But he did, and right across my path by the wall, so that I had to creep over him every time!

SUSAN GLASPELL

Susan Glaspell (1876–1948) was born in Davenport, Iowa, into a family that had been among the state's first settlers a generation before. After her graduation from high school, she worked as a reporter and society editor for various newspapers before enrolling at Drake University in Des Moines. There she studied literature, philosophy, and history; edited the college newspaper; and began to write short stories. In 1899 she took a job as statehouse reporter for the Des Moines

Daily News. *Years later she claimed that the discipline of newspaper work helped her to become a creative writer.*

At the age of twenty-five, Glaspell returned to Davenport to live with her family, determined, as she said, to "boldly" quit journalism and "give all my time to my own writing. I say 'boldly,' because I had to earn my living." Slowly she began to publish her fiction, mostly sentimental magazine pieces and an undistinguished first novel—work that, as her biographer C. W. E. Bigsby noted, "suggested little of the originality and power which were to mark her work in the theater." In 1909 Glaspell met George Cram Cook, a novelist and utopian socialist from a wealthy family who divorced his second wife and left his two children to marry her. They moved to Greenwich Village and collaborated on a play for the Washington Square Players in 1915, Suppressed Desires. The following year, after the Players had moved to Provincetown on Cape Cod, Cook urged Glaspell to write a new play for the theater company, renamed the Provincetown Players. Her memory of a murder trial in Iowa that she had covered as a newspaper reporter served as the inspiration for the short play Trifles (1916). Glaspell recalled that she "had meant to do it as a short story, but the stage took it for its own."

Trifles *was so successful as an experimental play that Glaspell turned it into a short story a year later, retitling it "A Jury of Her Peers."* Her choice of a limited-omniscient, third-person point of view (via the character Martha Hale's perspective) and her description of the harsh realities of the rural setting in "A Jury of Her Peers" suggest the local-color tradition of such earlier writers as Sarah Orne Jewett, although Glaspell's suffragist sympathies were more radical than the views of nineteenth-century women writers. In 1912 Glaspell published her first book of stories, Lifted Masks, and she continued to write fiction as well as plays for most of her life. In her forty-seven-year career, she published fifty short stories, nine novels, and thirteen plays, including the Pulitzer Prize–winning play Alison's House (1931), based on Genevieve Taggard's biography of Emily Dickinson.

CONNECTION Susan Glaspell, Trifles, page 1290.

COMMENTARY Leonard Mustazza, "Generic Translation and Thematic Shift in Glaspell's Trifles and 'A Jury of Her Peers,'" page 1560.

WEB *Research Susan Glaspell and answer questions about her work at bedfordstmartins.com/charters/litwriters.*

A Jury of Her Peers

1917

When Martha Hale opened the storm-door and got a cut of the north wind, she ran back for her big woolen scarf. As she hurriedly wound that round her head her eye made a scandalized sweep of her kitchen. It was no ordinary thing that called her away—it was probably further from ordinary than anything that had ever happened in Dickson County. But what her eye took in was that her kitchen was in no shape for leaving: her bread all ready for mixing, half the flour sifted and half unsifted.

She hated to see things half done; but she had been at that when the team from town stopped to get Mr. Hale, and then the sheriff came running in to say his wife wished Mrs. Hale would come too—adding, with a grin, that he guessed she was getting scary and wanted another woman along. So she had dropped everything right where it was.

"Martha!" now came her husband's impatient voice. "Don't keep folks waiting out here in the cold."

She again opened the storm-door, and this time joined the three men and the one woman waiting for her in the big two-seated buggy.

After she had the robes tucked around her she took another look at the woman who sat beside her on the back seat. She had met Mrs. Peters the year before at the county fair, and the thing she remembered about her was that she didn't seem like a sheriff's wife. She was small and thin and didn't have a strong voice. Mrs. Gorman, sheriff's wife before Gorman went out and Peters came in, had a voice that somehow seemed to be backing up the law with every word. But if Mrs. Peters didn't look like a sheriff's wife, Peters made it up in looking like a sheriff. He was to a dot the kind of man who could get himself elected sheriff—a heavy man with a big voice, who was particularly genial with the law-abiding, as if to make it plain that he knew the difference between criminals and non-criminals. And right there it came into Mrs. Hale's mind, with a stab, that this man who was so pleasant and lively with all of them was going to the Wrights' now as a sheriff.

"The country's not very pleasant this time of year," Mrs. Peters at last ventured, as if she felt they ought to be talking as well as the men.

Mrs. Hale scarcely finished her reply, for they had gone up a little hill and could see the Wright place now, and seeing it did not make her feel like talking. It looked very lonesome this cold March morning. It had always been a lonesome-looking place. It was down in a hollow, and the poplar trees around it were lonesome-looking trees. The men were looking at it and talking about what had happened. The county attorney was bending to one side of the buggy, and kept looking steadily at the place as they drew up to it.

"I'm glad you came with me," Mrs. Peters said nervously, as the two women were about to follow the men in through the kitchen door.

Even after she had her foot on the door-step, her hand on the knob, Martha Hale had a moment of feeling she could not cross that threshold. And the reason it seemed she couldn't cross it now was simply because she hadn't crossed it before. Time and time again it had been in her mind, "I ought to go over and see Minnie Foster"—she still thought of her as Minnie Foster, though for twenty years she had been Mrs. Wright. And then there was always something to do and Minnie Foster would go from her mind. But *now* she could come.

The men went over to the stove. The women stood close together by the door. Young Henderson, the county attorney, turned around and said, "Come up to the fire, ladies."

Mrs. Peters took a step forward, then stopped. "I'm not—cold," she said.

And so the two women stood by the door, at first not even so much as looking around the kitchen.

The men talked for a minute about what a good thing it was the sheriff had sent his deputy out that morning to make a fire for them, and then Sheriff Peters stepped back from the stove, unbuttoned his outer coat, and leaned his hands on the kitchen table in a way that seemed to mark the beginning of official business. "Now, Mr. Hale," he said in a sort of semi-official voice, "before we move things about, you tell Mr. Henderson just what it was you saw when you came here yesterday morning."

The county attorney was looking around the kitchen.

"By the way," he said, "has anything been moved?" He turned to the sheriff. "Are things just as you left them yesterday?"

Peters looked from cupboard to sink; from that to a small worn rocker a little to one side of the kitchen table.

"It's just the same."

"Somebody should have been left here yesterday," said the county attorney.

"Oh — yesterday," returned the sheriff, with a little gesture as of yesterday having been more than he could bear to think of. "When I had to send Frank to Morris Center for that man who went crazy — let me tell you. I had my hands full *yesterday*. I knew you could get back from Omaha by today, George, and as long as I went over everything here myself—"

"Well, Mr. Hale," said the county attorney, in a way of letting what was past and gone go, "tell just what happened when you came here yesterday morning."

Mrs. Hale, still leaning against the door, had that sinking feeling of the mother whose child is about to speak a piece. Lewis often wandered along and got things mixed up in a story. She hoped he would tell this straight and plain, and not say unnecessary things that would just make things harder for Minnie Foster. He didn't begin at once, and she noticed that he looked queer — as if standing in that kitchen and having to tell what he had seen there yesterday morning made him almost sick.

"Yes, Mr. Hale?" the county attorney reminded.

"Harry and I had started to town with a load of potatoes," Mrs. Hale's husband began.

Harry was Mrs. Hale's oldest boy. He wasn't with them now, for the very good reason that those potatoes never got to town yesterday and he was taking them this morning, so he hadn't been home when the sheriff stopped to say he wanted Mr. Hale to come over to the Wright place and tell the county attorney his story there, where he could point it all out. With all Mrs. Hale's other emotions came the fear now that maybe Harry wasn't dressed warm enough — they hadn't any of them realized how that north wind did bite.

"We come along this road," Hale was going on, with a motion of his hand to the road over which they had just come, "and as we got in sight of the house I says to Harry, 'I'm goin' to see if I can't get John Wright to take a telephone.' You see," he explained to Henderson, "unless I can get somebody to go in with me they won't come out this branch road except for a price *I* can't pay. I'd spoke to Wright about it once before; but he put me off, saying folks talked too much anyway, and all he asked was peace and quiet — guess you know about how much he talked himself. But I thought maybe if I went to the house and talked about it before his wife, and said all the women-folks liked the telephones, and that in this lonesome stretch of road it would be a good thing — well, I said to Harry that that was what I was going to say — though I said at the same time that I didn't know as what his wife wanted made much difference to John —"

Now there he was! — saying things he didn't need to say. Mrs. Hale tried to catch her husband's eye, but fortunately the county attorney interrupted with:

"Let's talk about that a little later, Mr. Hale. I do want to talk about that, but I'm anxious now to get along to just what happened when you got here."

When he began this time, it was very deliberately and carefully:

"I didn't see or hear anything. I knocked at the door. And still it was all quiet inside. I knew they must be up — it was past eight o'clock. So I knocked again, louder, and I thought I heard somebody say, 'Come in.' I wasn't sure — I'm not sure yet. But I opened the door — this door," jerking a hand toward the door by which the two women stood, "and there, in that rocker" — pointing to it — "sat Mrs. Wright."

Everyone in the kitchen looked at the rocker. It came into Mrs. Hale's mind that that rocker didn't look in the least like Minnie Foster — the Minnie Foster of twenty years before. It was a dingy red, with wooden rungs up the back, and the middle rung was gone, and the chair sagged to one side.

"How did she — look?" the county attorney was inquiring.

"Well," said Hale, "she looked — queer."

"How do you mean — queer?"

As he asked it he took out a note-book and pencil. Mrs. Hale did not like the sight of that pencil. She kept her eye fixed on her husband, as if to keep him from saying unnecessary things that would go into that note-book and make trouble.

Hale did speak guardedly, as if the pencil had affected him too.

"Well, as if she didn't know what she was going to do next. And kind of — done up."

"How did she seem to feel about your coming?"

"Why, I don't think she minded — one way or other. She didn't pay much attention. I said, 'Ho' do, Mrs. Wright? It's cold, ain't it?' And she said, 'Is it?' — and went on pleatin' at her apron.

"Well, I was surprised. She didn't ask me to come up to the stove, or to sit down, but just set there, not even lookin' at me. And so I said: 'I want to see John.'

"And then she — laughed. I guess you would call it a laugh.

"I thought of Harry and the team outside, so I said, a little sharp, 'Can I see John?' 'No,' says she — kind of dull like. 'Ain't he home?' says I. Then she looked at me. 'Yes,' says she, 'he's home.' 'Then why can't I see him?' I asked her, out of patience with her now. 'Cause he's dead' says she, just as quiet and dull — and fell to pleatin' her apron. 'Dead?' says I, like you do when you can't take in what you've heard.

"She just nodded her head, not getting a bit excited, but rockin' back and forth.

" 'Why — where is he?' says I, not knowing *what* to say.

"She just pointed upstairs — like this" — pointing to the room above.

"I got up, with the idea of going up there myself. By this time I — didn't know what to do. I walked from there to here; then I says: 'Why, what did he die of?'

" 'He died of a rope around his neck,' says she; and just went on pleatin' at her apron."

Hale stopped speaking, and stood staring at the rocker, as if he were still seeing the woman who had sat there the morning before. Nobody spoke; it was as if every one were seeing the woman who had sat there the morning before.

"And what did you do then?" the county attorney at last broke the silence.

"I went out and called Harry. I thought I might — need help. I got Harry in, and we went upstairs." His voice fell almost to a whisper. "There he was — lying over the —"

"I think I'd rather have you go into that upstairs," the county attorney interrupted, "where you can point it all out. Just go on now with the rest of the story."

"Well, my first thought was to get that rope off. It looked —"

He stopped, his face twitching.

"But Harry, he went up to him, and he said, 'No, he's dead all right, and we'd better not touch anything.' So we went downstairs.

"She was still sitting that same way. 'Has anybody been notified?' I asked. 'No,' says she, unconcerned.

" 'Who did this, Mrs. Wright?' said Harry. He said it businesslike, and she stopped pleatin' at her apron. 'I don't know,' she says. 'You don't *know*?' says Harry. 'Weren't you sleepin' in the bed with him?' 'Yes,' says she, 'but I was on the inside.' 'Somebody slipped a rope round his neck and strangled him, and you didn't wake up?' says Harry. 'I didn't wake up,' she said after him.

"We may have looked as if we didn't see how that could be, for after a minute she said, 'I sleep sound.'

"Harry was going to ask her more questions, but I said maybe that weren't our business; maybe we ought to let her tell her story first to the coroner or the sheriff. So Harry went fast as he could over to High Road — the Rivers' place, where there's a telephone."

"And what did she do when she knew you had gone for the coroner?" The attorney got his pencil in his hand all ready for writing.

"She moved from that chair to this one over here" — Hale pointed to a small chair in the corner — "and just sat there with her hands held together and looking down. I got a feeling that I ought to make some conversation, so I said I had come in to see if John wanted to put in a telephone; and at that she started to laugh, and then she stopped and looked at me — scared."

At the sound of a moving pencil the man who was telling the story looked up.

"I dunno—maybe it wasn't scared," he hastened: "I wouldn't like to say it was. Soon Harry got back, and then Dr. Lloyd came, and you, Mr. Peters, and so I guess that's all I know that you don't."

He said that last with relief, and moved a little, as if relaxing. Everyone moved a little. The county attorney walked toward the stair door.

"I guess we'll go upstairs first—then out to the barn and around there."

He paused and looked around the kitchen.

"You're convinced there was nothing important here?" he asked the sheriff. "Nothing that would—point to any motive?"

The sheriff too looked all around, as if to re-convince himself.

"Nothing here but kitchen things," he said, with a little laugh for the insignificance of kitchen things.

The county attorney was looking at the cupboard—a peculiar, ungainly structure, half closet and half cupboard, the upper part of it being built in the wall, and the lower part just the old-fashioned kitchen cupboard. As if its queerness attracted him, he got a chair and opened the upper part and looked in. After a moment he drew his hand away sticky.

"Here's a nice mess," he said resentfully.

The two women had drawn nearer, and now the sheriff's wife spoke.

"Oh—her fruit," she said, looking to Mrs. Hale for sympathetic understanding. She turned back to the county attorney and explained: "She worried about that when it turned so cold last night. She said the fire would go out and her jars might burst."

Mrs. Peters' husband broke into a laugh.

"Well, can you beat the women! Held for murder, and worrying about her preserves!"

The young attorney set his lips.

"I guess before we're through with her she may have something more serious than preserves to worry about."

"Oh, well," said Mrs. Hale's husband, with good-natured superiority, "women are used to worrying over trifles."

The two women moved a little closer together. Neither of them spoke. The county attorney seemed suddenly to remember his manners—and think of his future.

"And yet," said he, with the gallantry of a young politician, "for all their worries, what would we do without the ladies?"

The women did not speak, did not unbend. He went to the sink and began washing his hands. He turned to wipe them on the roller towel—whirled it for a cleaner place.

"Dirty towels! Not much of a housekeeper, would you say, ladies?"

He kicked his foot against some dirty pans under the sink.

"There's a great deal of work to be done on a farm," said Mrs. Hale stiffly.

"To be sure. And yet"—with a little bow to her—"I know there are some Dickson County farm-houses that do not have such roller towels." He gave it a pull to expose its full length again.

"Those towels get dirty awful quick. Men's hands aren't always as clean as they might be."

"Ah, loyal to your sex, I see," he laughed. He stopped and gave her a keen look. "But you and Mrs. Wright were neighbors. I suppose you were friends, too."

Martha Hale shook her head.

"I've seen little enough of her of late years. I've not been in this house— it's more than a year."

"And why was that? You didn't like her?"

"I liked her well enough," she replied with spirit. "Farmers' wives have their hands full, Mr. Henderson. And then—" She looked around the kitchen.

"Yes?" he encouraged.

"It never seemed a very cheerful place," said she, more to herself than to him.

"No," he agreed; "I don't think anyone would call it cheerful. I shouldn't say she had the home-making instinct."

"Well, I don't know as Wright had, either," she muttered.

"You mean they didn't get on very well?" he was quick to ask.

"No; I don't mean anything," she answered, with decision. As she turned a little away from him, she added: "But I don't think a place would be any the cheerfuller for John Wright's bein' in it."

"I'd like to talk to you about that a little later, Mrs. Hale," he said. "I'm anxious to get the lay of things upstairs now."

He moved toward the stair door, followed by the two men.

"I suppose anything Mrs. Peters does'll be all right?" the sheriff inquired. "She was to take in some clothes for her, you know—and a few little things. We left in such a hurry yesterday."

The county attorney looked at the two women whom they were leaving alone there among the kitchen things.

"Yes—Mrs. Peters," he said, his glance resting on the woman who was not Mrs. Peters, the big farmer woman who stood behind the sheriff's wife. "Of course Mrs. Peters is one of us," he said, in a manner of entrusting responsibility. "And keep your eye out, Mrs. Peters, for anything that might be of use. No telling; you women might come upon a clue to the motive—and that's the thing we need."

Mr. Hale rubbed his face after the fashion of a showman getting ready for a pleasantry.

"But would the women know a clue if they did come upon it?" he said; and, having delivered himself of this, he followed the others through the stair door.

The women stood motionless and silent, listening to the footsteps, first upon the stairs, then in the room above them.

Then, as if releasing herself from something strange, Mrs. Hale began to arrange the dirty pans under the sink, which the county attorney's disdainful push of the foot had deranged.

"I'd hate to have men comin' into my kitchen," she said testily— "snoopin' round and criticizin'."

"Of course it's no more than their duty," said the sheriff's wife, in her manner of timid acquiescence.

"Duty's all right," replied Mrs. Hale bluffly; "but I guess that deputy sheriff that come out to make the fire might have got a little of this on." She gave the roller towel a pull. "Wish I'd thought of that sooner! Seems mean to talk about her for not having things slicked up, when she had to come away in such a hurry."

She looked around the kitchen. Certainly it was not "slicked up." Her eye was held by a bucket of sugar on a low shelf. The cover was off the wooden bucket, and beside it was a paper bag—half full.

Mrs. Hale moved toward it.

"She was putting this in there," she said to herself—slowly.

She thought of the flour in her kitchen at home—half sifted, half not sifted. She had been interrupted, and had left things half done. What had interrupted Minnie Foster? Why had that work been left half done? She made a move as if to finish it,—unfinished things always bothered her,—and then she glanced around and saw that Mrs. Peters was watching her—and she didn't want Mrs. Peters to get that feeling she had got of work begun and then—for some reason—not finished.

"It's a shame about her fruit," she said, and walked toward the cupboard that the county attorney had opened, and got on the chair, murmuring: "I wonder if it's all gone."

It was a sorry enough looking sight, but "Here's one that's all right," she said at last. She held it toward the light. "This is cherries, too." She looked again. "I declare I believe that's the only one."

With a sigh, she got down from the chair, went to the sink, and wiped off the bottle.

"She'll feel awful bad, after all her hard work in the hot weather. I remember the afternoon I put up my cherries last summer."

She set the bottle on the table, and, with another sigh, started to sit down in the rocker. But she did not sit down. Something kept her from sitting down in that chair. She straightened—stepped back, and, half turned away, stood looking at it, seeing the woman who had sat there "pleatin' at her apron."

The thin voice of the sheriff's wife broke in upon her: "I must be getting those things from the front-room closet." She opened the door into the other room, started in, stepped back. "You coming with me, Mrs. Hale?" she asked nervously. "You—you could help me get them."

They were soon back—the stark coldness of that shut-up room was not a thing to linger in.

"My!" said Mrs. Peters, dropping the things on the table and hurrying to the stove.

Mrs. Hale stood examining the clothes the woman who was being detained in town had said she wanted.

"Wright was close!"° she exclaimed, holding up a shabby black skirt that bore the marks of much making over. "I think maybe that's why she kept so

---

close: Frugal, tightfisted.

much to herself. I s'pose she felt she couldn't do her part; and then, you don't enjoy things when you feel shabby. She used to wear pretty clothes and be lively—when she was Minnie Foster, one of the town girls, singing in the choir. But that—oh, that was twenty years ago."

With a carefulness in which there was something tender, she folded the shabby clothes and piled them at one corner of the table. She looked up at Mrs. Peters, and there was something in the other woman's look that irritated her.

"She don't care," she said to herself. "Much difference it makes to her whether Minnie Foster had pretty clothes when she was a girl."

Then she looked again, and she wasn't so sure; in fact, she hadn't at any time been perfectly sure about Mrs. Peters. She had that shrinking manner, and yet her eyes looked as if they could see a long way into things.

"This all you was to take in?" asked Mrs. Hale.

"No," said the sheriff's wife; "she said she wanted an apron. Funny thing to want," she ventured in her nervous little way, "for there's not much to get you dirty in jail, goodness knows. But I suppose just to make her feel more natural. If you're used to wearing an apron—. She said they were in the bottom drawer of this cupboard. Yes—here they are. And then her little shawl that always hung on the stair door."

She took the small gray shawl from behind the door leading upstairs, and stood a minute looking at it.

Suddenly Mrs. Hale took a quick step toward the other woman.

"Mrs. Peters!"

"Yes, Mrs. Hale?"

"Do you think she—did it?"

A frightened look blurred the other thing in Mrs. Peters' eyes.

"Oh, I don't know," she said, in a voice that seemed to shrink away from the subject.

"Well, I don't think she did," affirmed Mrs. Hale stoutly. "Asking for an apron, and her little shawl. Worryin' about her fruit."

"Mr. Peters says—." Footsteps were heard in the room above; she stopped, looked up, then went on in a lowered voice: "Mr. Peters says—it looks bad for her. Mr. Henderson is awful sarcastic in a speech, and he's going to make fun of her saying she didn't—wake up."

For a moment Mrs. Hale had no answer. Then, "Well, I guess John Wright didn't wake up—when they was slippin' that rope under his neck," she muttered.

"No, it's *strange*," breathed Mrs. Peters. "They think it was such a—funny way to kill a man."

She began to laugh; at the sound of the laugh, abruptly stopped.

"That's just what Mr. Hale said," said Mrs. Hale, in a resolutely natural voice. "There was a gun in the house. He says that's what he can't understand."

"Mr. Henderson said, coming out, that what was needed for the case was a motive. Something to show anger—or sudden feeling."

"Well, I don't see any signs of anger around here," said Mrs. Hale, "I don't—" She stopped. It was as if her mind tripped on something. Her eye was caught by a dishtowel in the middle of the kitchen table. Slowly she moved toward the table. One half of it was wiped clean, the other half messy. Her eyes made a slow, almost unwilling turn to the bucket of sugar and the half empty bag beside it. Things begun — and not finished.

After a moment she stepped back, and said, in that manner of releasing herself:

"Wonder how they're finding things upstairs? I hope she had it a little more redd up° up there. You know," — she paused, and feeling gathered, — "it seems kind of *sneaking:* locking her up in town and coming out here to get her own house to turn against her!"

"But, Mrs. Hale," said the sheriff's wife, "the law is the law."

"I s'pose 'tis," answered Mrs. Hale shortly.

She turned to the stove, saying something about that fire not being much to brag of. She worked with it a minute, and when she straightened up she said aggressively:

"The law is the law — and a bad stove is a bad stove. How'd you like to cook on this?" — pointing with the poker to the broken lining. She opened the oven door and started to express her opinion of the oven; but she was swept into her own thoughts, thinking of what it would mean, year after year, to have that stove to wrestle with. The thought of Minnie Foster trying to bake in that oven — and the thought of her never going over to see Minnie Foster —.

She was startled by hearing Mrs. Peters say: "A person gets discouraged — and loses heart."

The sheriff's wife had looked from the stove to the sink — to the pail of water which had been carried in from outside. The two women stood there silent, above them the footsteps of the men who were looking for evidence against the woman who had worked in that kitchen. That look of seeing into things, of seeing through a thing to something else, was in the eyes of the sheriff's wife now. When Mrs. Hale next spoke to her, it was gently:

"Better loosen up your things, Mrs. Peters. We'll not feel them when we go out."

Mrs. Peters went to the back of the room to hang up the fur tippet she was wearing. A moment later she exclaimed, "Why, she was piecing a quilt," and held up a large sewing basket piled high with quilt pieces.

Mrs. Hale spread some of the blocks on the table.

"It's log-cabin pattern," she said, putting several of them together. "Pretty, isn't it?"

They were so engaged with the quilt that they did not hear the footsteps on the stairs. Just as the stair door opened Mrs. Hale was saying:

"Do you suppose she was going to quilt it or just knot it?"

The sheriff threw up his hands.

"They wonder whether she was going to quilt it or just knot it!"

There was a laugh for the ways of women, a warming of hands over the stove, and then the county attorney said briskly:

"Well, let's go right out to the barn and get that cleared up."

---

redd up: Neat.

"I don't see as there's anything so strange," Mrs. Hale said resentfully, after the outside door had closed on the three men—"our taking up our time with little things while we're waiting for them to get the evidence. I don't see as it's anything to laugh about."

"Of course they've got awful important things on their minds," said the sheriff's wife apologetically.

They returned to an inspection of the block for the quilt. Mrs. Hale was looking at the fine, even sewing, and preoccupied with thoughts of the woman who had done that sewing, when she heard the sheriff's wife say, in a queer tone:

"Why, look at this one."

She turned to take the block held out to her.

"The sewing," said Mrs. Peters, in a troubled way. "All the rest of them have been so nice and even—but—this one. Why, it looks as if she didn't know what she was about!"

Their eyes met—something flashed to life, passed between them; then, as if with an effort, they seemed to pull away from each other. A moment Mrs. Hale sat there, her hands folded over that sewing which was so unlike all the rest of the sewing. Then she had pulled a knot and drawn the threads.

"Oh, what are you doing, Mrs. Hale?" asked the sheriff's wife, startled.

"Just pulling out a stitch or two that's not sewed very good," said Mrs. Hale mildly.

"I don't think we ought to touch things," Mrs. Peters said, a little helplessly.

"I'll just finish up this end," answered Mrs. Hale, still in that mild, matter-of-fact fashion.

She threaded a needle and started to replace bad sewing with good. For a little while she sewed in silence. Then, in that thin, timid voice, she heard:

"Mrs. Hale!"

"Yes, Mrs. Peters?"

"What do you suppose she was so—nervous about?"

"Oh, *I* don't know," said Mrs. Hale, as if dismissing a thing not important enough to spend much time on. "I don't know as she was—nervous. I sew awful queer sometimes when I'm just tired."

She cut a thread, and out of the corner of her eye looked up at Mrs. Peters. The small, lean face of the sheriff's wife seemed to have tightened up. Her eyes had that look of peering into something. But next moment she moved, and said in her thin, indecisive way:

"Well, I must get those clothes wrapped. They may be through sooner than we think. I wonder where I could find a piece of paper—and string."

"In that cupboard, maybe," suggested Mrs. Hale, after a glance around.

One piece of the crazy sewing remained unripped. Mrs. Peter's back turned, Martha Hale now scrutinized that piece, compared it with the dainty, accurate sewing of the other blocks. The difference was startling. Holding this block made her feel queer, as if the distracted thoughts of the woman who had perhaps turned to it to try and quiet herself were communicating themselves to her.

Mrs. Peters' voice roused her.

"Here's a bird-cage," she said. "Did she have a bird, Mrs. Hale?"

"Why, I don't know whether she did or not." She turned to look at the cage Mrs. Peters was holding up. "I've not been here in so long." She sighed. "There was a man round last year selling canaries cheap—but I don't know as she took one. Maybe she did. She used to sing real pretty herself."

Mrs. Peters looked around the kitchen.

"Seems kind of funny to think of a bird here." She half laughed—an attempt to put up a barrier. "But she must have had one—or why would she have a cage? I wonder what happened to it."

"I suppose maybe the cat got it," suggested Mrs. Hale, resuming her sewing.

"No; she didn't have a cat. She's got that feeling some people have about cats—being afraid of them. When they brought her to our house yesterday, my cat got in the room, and she was real upset and asked me to take it out."

"My sister Bessie was like that," laughed Mrs. Hale.

The sheriff's wife did not reply. The silence made Mrs. Hale turn round. Mrs. Peters was examining the bird-cage.

"Look at this door," she said slowly. "It's broke. One hinge has been pulled apart."

Mrs. Hale came nearer.

"Looks as if someone must have been—rough with it."

Again their eyes met—startled, questioning, apprehensive. For a moment neither spoke nor stirred. Then Mrs. Hale, turning away, said brusquely:

"If they're going to find any evidence, I wish they'd be about it. I don't like this place."

"But I'm awful glad you came with me, Mrs. Hale." Mrs. Peters put the bird-cage on the table and sat down. "It would be lonesome for me—sitting here alone."

"Yes, it would, wouldn't it?" agreed Mrs. Hale, a certain determined naturalness in her voice. She had picked up the sewing, but now it dropped in her lap, and she murmured in a different voice: "But I tell you what I *do* wish, Mrs. Peters. I wish I had come over sometimes when she was here. I wish—I had."

"But of course you were awful busy, Mrs. Hale. Your house—and your children."

"I could've come," retorted Mrs. Hale shortly. "I stayed away because it weren't cheerful—and that's why I ought to have come. I"—she looked around—"I've never liked this place. Maybe because it's down in a hollow and you don't see the road. I don't know what it is, but it's a lonesome place, and always was. I wish I had come over to see Minnie Foster sometimes. I can see now—" She did not put it into words.

"Well, you mustn't reproach yourself," counseled Mrs. Peters. "Somehow, we just don't see how it is with other folks till—something comes up."

"Not having children makes less work," mused Mrs. Hale, after a silence, "but it makes a quiet house—and Wright out to work all day—and no company when he did come in. Did you know John Wright, Mrs. Peters?"

"Not to know him. I've seen him in town. They say he was a good man."

"Yes—good," conceded John Wright's neighbor grimly. "He didn't drink, and kept his word as well as most, I guess, and paid his debts. But he was a hard man, Mrs. Peters. Just to pass the time of day with him—." She stopped, shivered a little. "Like a raw wind that gets to the bone." Her eye fell upon the cage on the table before her, and she added, almost bitterly: "I should think she would've wanted a bird!"

Suddenly she leaned forward, looking intently at the cage. "But what do you s'pose went wrong with it?"

"I don't know," returned Mrs. Peters; "unless it got sick and died."

But after she said it she reached over and swung the broken door. Both women watched it as if somehow held by it.

"You didn't know—her?" Mrs. Hale asked, a gentler note in her voice.

"Not till they brought her yesterday," said the sheriff's wife.

"She—come to think of it, she was kind of like a bird herself. Real sweet and pretty, but kind of timid and—fluttery. How—she—did—change."

That held her for a long time. Finally, as if struck with a happy thought and relieved to get back to everyday things, she exclaimed:

"Tell you what, Mrs. Peters, why don't you take the quilt in with you? It might take up her mind."

"Why, I think that's a real nice idea, Mrs. Hale," agreed the sheriff's wife, as if she too were glad to come into the atmosphere of a simple kindness. "There couldn't possibly be any objection to that, could there? Now, just what will I take? I wonder if her patches are in here—and her things?"

They turned to the sewing basket.

"Here's some red," said Mrs. Hale, bringing out a roll of cloth. Underneath that was a box. "Here, maybe her scissors are in here—and her things." She held it up. "What a pretty box! I'll warrant that was something she had a long time ago—when she was a girl."

She held it in her hand a moment; then, with a little sigh, opened it.

Instantly her hand went to her nose.

"Why—!"

Mrs. Peters drew nearer—then turned away.

"There's something wrapped up in this piece of silk," faltered Mrs. Hale.

"This isn't her scissors," said Mrs. Peters, in a shrinking voice.

Her hand not steady, Mrs. Hale raised the piece of silk. "Oh, Mrs. Peters!" she cried. "It's—"

Mrs. Peters bent closer.

"It's the bird," she whispered.

"But, Mrs. Peters!" cried Mrs. Hale. "*Look* at it! Its *neck*—look at its neck! It's all—other side *to*."

She held the box away from her.

The sheriff's wife again bent closer.

"Somebody wrung its neck," said she, in a voice that was slow and deep.

And then again the eyes of the two women met—this time clung together in a look of dawning comprehension, of growing horror. Mrs. Peters looked from the dead bird to the broken door of the cage. Again their eyes met. And just then there was a sound at the outside door.

Mrs. Hale slipped the box under the quilt pieces in the basket, and sank into the chair before it. Mrs. Peters stood holding to the table. The county attorney and the sheriff came in from outside.

"Well, ladies," said the county attorney, as one turning from serious things to little pleasantries, "have you decided whether she was going to quilt it or knot it?"

"We think," began the sheriff's wife in a flurried voice, "that she was going to—knot it."

He was too preoccupied to notice the change that came in her voice on that last.

"Well, that's very interesting, I'm sure," he said tolerantly. He caught sight of the bird-cage. "Has the bird flown?"

"We think the cat got it," said Mrs. Hale in a voice curiously even.

He was walking up and down, as if thinking something out.

"Is there a cat?" he asked absently.

Mrs. Hale shot a look up at the sheriff's wife.

"Well, not *now*," said Mrs. Peters. "They're superstitious, you know; they leave."

She sank into her chair.

The county attorney did not heed her. "No sign at all of anyone having come in from the outside," he said to Peters, in the manner of continuing an interrupted conversation. "Their own rope. Now let's go upstairs again and go over it, piece by piece. It would have to have been someone who knew just the—"

The stair door closed behind them and their voices were lost.

The two women sat motionless, not looking at each other, but as if peering into something and at the same time holding back. When they spoke now it was as if they were afraid of what they were saying, but as if they could not help saying it.

"She liked the bird," said Martha Hale, low and slowly. "She was going to bury it."

"When I was a girl," said Mrs. Peters, under her breath, "my kitten—there was a boy took a hatchet, and before my eyes—before I could get there—" She covered her face an instant. "If they hadn't held me back I would have"—she caught herself, looked upstairs where footsteps were heard, and finished weakly—"hurt him."

Then they sat without speaking or moving.

"I wonder how it would seem," Mrs. Hale at last began, as if feeling her way over strange ground—"never to have had any children around?" Her eyes made a slow sweep of the kitchen, as if seeing what that kitchen had meant through all the years. "No, Wright wouldn't like the bird," she said after that—"a thing that sang. She used to sing. He killed that too." Her voice tightened.

Mrs. Peters moved uneasily.

"Of course we don't know who killed the bird."

"I knew John Wright," was Mrs. Hale's answer.

"It was an awful thing was done in this house that night, Mrs. Hale," said the sheriff's wife. "Killing a man while he slept—slipping a thing round his neck that choked the life out of him."

Mrs. Hale's hand went out to the bird-cage.

"His neck. Choked the life out of him."

"We don't *know* who killed him," whispered Mrs. Peters wildly. "We don't *know*."

Mrs. Hale had not moved. "If there had been years and years of—nothing, then a bird to sing to you, it would be awful—still—after the bird was still."

It was as if something within her not herself had spoken, and it found in Mrs. Peters something she did not know as herself.

"I know what stillness is," she said, in a queer, monotonous voice. "When we homesteaded in Dakota, and my first baby died—after he was two years old—and me with no other then—"

Mrs. Hale stirred.

"How soon do you suppose they'll be through looking for the evidence?"

"I know what stillness is," repeated Mrs. Peters, in just the same way. Then she too pulled back. "The law has got to punish crime, Mrs. Hale," she said in her tight little way.

"I wish you'd seen Minnie Foster," was the answer, "when she wore a white dress with blue ribbons, and stood up there in the choir and sang."

The picture of that girl, the fact that she had lived neighbor to that girl for twenty years, and had let her die for lack of life, was suddenly more than she could bear.

"Oh, I *wish* I'd come over here once in a while!" she cried. "That was a crime! Who's going to punish that?"

"We mustn't take on," said Mrs. Peters, with a frightened look toward the stairs.

"I might 'a' *known* she needed help! I tell you, it's *queer,* Mrs. Peters. We live close together, and we live far apart. We all go through the same things—it's all just a different kind of the same thing! If it weren't—why do you and I *understand?* Why do we *know*—what we know this minute?"

She dashed her hand across her eyes. Then, seeing the jar of fruit on the table, she reached for it and choked out:

"If I was you I wouldn't *tell* her her fruit was gone! Tell her it *ain't.* Tell her it's all right—all of it. Here—take this in to prove it to her! She—she may never know whether it was broke or not."

She turned away.

Mrs. Peters reached out for the bottle of fruit as if she were glad to take it—as if touching a familiar thing, having something to do, could keep her from something else. She got up, looked about for something to wrap the fruit in, took a petticoat from the pile of clothes she had brought from the front room, and nervously started winding that round the bottle.

"My!" she began, in a high, false voice, "it's a good thing the men couldn't hear us! Getting all stirred up over a little thing like a—dead canary." She hurried over that. "As if that could have anything to do with—with—My, wouldn't they *laugh?*"

Footsteps were heard on the stairs.

"Maybe they would," muttered Mrs. Hale—"maybe they wouldn't."

"No, Peters," said the county attorney incisively; "it's all perfectly clear, except the reason for doing it. But you know juries when it comes to women. If there was some definite thing — something to show. Something to make a story about. A thing that would connect up with this clumsy way of doing it."

In a covert way Mrs. Hale looked at Mrs. Peters. Mrs. Peters was looking at her. Quickly they looked away from each other. The outer door opened and Mr. Hale came in.

"I've got the team round now," he said. "Pretty cold out there."

"I'm going to stay here awhile by myself," the county attorney suddenly announced. "You can send Frank out for me, can't you?" he asked the sheriff. "I want to go over everything. I'm not satisfied we can't do better."

Again, for one brief moment, the two women's eyes found one another.

The sheriff came up to the table.

"Did you want to see what Mrs. Peters was going to take in?"

The county attorney picked up the apron. He laughed.

"Oh, I guess they're not very dangerous things the ladies have picked out."

Mrs. Hale's hand was on the sewing basket in which the box was concealed. She felt that she ought to take her hand off the basket. She did not seem able to. He picked up one of the quilt blocks which she had piled on to cover the box. Her eyes felt like fire. She had a feeling that if he took up the basket she would snatch it from him.

But he did not take it up. With another little laugh, he turned away, saying:

"No; Mrs. Peters doesn't need supervising. For that matter, a sheriff's wife is married to the law. Ever think of it that way, Mrs. Peters?"

Mrs. Peters was standing beside the table. Mrs. Hale shot a look up at her; but she could not see her face. Mrs. Peters had turned away. When she spoke, her voice was muffled.

"Not — just that way," she said.

"Married to the law!" chuckled Mrs. Peters' husband. He moved toward the door into the front room, and said to the county attorney:

"I just want you to come in here a minute, George. We ought to take a look at these windows."

"Oh — windows," said the county attorney scoffingly.

"We'll be right out, Mr. Hale," said the sheriff to the farmer, who was still waiting by the door.

Hale went to look after the horses. The sheriff followed the county attorney into the other room. Again — for one final moment — the two women were alone in that kitchen.

Martha Hale sprang up, her hands tight together, looking at that other woman, with whom it rested. At first she could not see her eyes, for the sheriff's wife had not turned back since she turned away at that suggestion of being married to the law. But now Mrs. Hale made her turn back. Her eyes made her turn back. Slowly, unwillingly, Mrs. Peters turned her head until her eyes met the eyes of the other woman. There was a moment when they held each other in a steady, burning look in which there was no evasion nor flinching. Then Martha Hale's eyes pointed the way to the basket in which was hidden the thing that would make certain the conviction of the other woman—that woman who was not there and yet who had been there with them all through that hour.

For a moment Mrs. Peters did not move. And then she did it. With a rush forward, she threw back the quilt pieces, got the box, tried to put it in her handbag. It was too big. Desperately she opened it, started to take the bird out. But there she broke—she could not touch the bird. She stood there helpless, foolish.

There was the sound of a knob turning in the inner door. Martha Hale snatched the box from the sheriff's wife, and got it in the pocket of her big coat just as the sheriff and the county attorney came back into the kitchen.

"Well, Henry," said the county attorney facetiously, "at least we found out that she was not going to quilt it. She was going to—what is it you call it, ladies?"

Mrs. Hale's hand was against the pocket of her coat.

"We call it—knot it, Mr. Henderson."

NADINE GORDIMER

*Nadine Gordimer (b. 1923), the recipient of the 1991 Nobel Prize for litera-
ture, was born in the small town of Springs, near Johannesburg, South Africa.
Her mother was English, and her father, a Jewish watchmaker, emigrated to
Africa from the Baltic states. Gordimer attended a convent school and studied at
the University of the Witwatersrand, getting what she has called "a scrappy and
uninspiring minimal education." Growing up in South Africa, she never recognized herself in any of the English books she read until she encountered the stories
of the New Zealand writer Katherine Mansfield. Then, Gordimer says, "I realized here was somebody who was writing about this other world, whose seasons at
least I shared. Then I understood it was possible to be a writer even if you didn't
live in England."*

*Gordimer began to write stories before she attempted a novel. She acknowl-
edges three writers as her guides: D. H. Lawrence, who influenced her way of looking at the natural world; Henry James, who gave her a consciousness of form; and
Ernest Hemingway, who taught her to hear what is essential in dialogue. Her early
stories appeared in The New Yorker, Harper's, and other American magazines,
and were first collected in Face to Face (1949) and The Soft Voice of the Serpent
(1952). Since her first novel, The Lying Days, was published in 1953, she has
continued alternating books of long and short fiction. She rarely experiments
beyond the realistic rendering of her subject in her stories, but her decision to write
in the form of the short story or the novel depends on the shape the material takes
as a narrative.*

*Whether it sprawls or neatly bites its own tail, a short story is a concept that
the writer can "hold" fully realized in his imagination at one time. A novel
is, by comparison, staked out, and must be taken possession of stage by
stage; it is impossible to contain, all at once, the proliferation of concepts it*

ultimately may use. For this reason I cannot understand how people can suppose one makes a conscious choice, after knowing what one wants to write about, between writing a novel or a short story. A short story occurs, in the imaginative sense. To write one is to express from a situation in the exterior or interior world the life-giving drop—sweat, tear, semen, saliva—that will spread an intensity on the page; burn a hole in it.

"The Ultimate Safari" *is from* Crimes of Conscience *(1991). It demonstrates Gordimer's use of fiction over the last forty years to mirror complex social attitudes in her beleaguered country. She feels herself "selected" by her subject as she continues to explore the ramifications of racial strife in South Africa. In 1988 she published an essay collection,* The Essential Gesture: Writing, Politics, and Places. *In 1993 appeared* Why Haven't You Written? Selected Stories 1950–1970. *Gordimer's achievement as a writer is further proof of Flaubert's insight: "One is not at all free to write this or that. One does not choose one's subject. This is what the public and the critics do not understand. The secret of masterpieces lies in the concordance between the subject and the temperament of the author."*

WEB   *Research Nadine Gordimer and answer questions about her work at bedfordstmartins.com/charters/litwriters.*

The Ultimate Safari   1991

"THE AFRICAN ADVENTURE LIVES ON . . . YOU CAN DO IT! THE ULTIMATE
SAFARI OR EXPEDITION WITH LEADERS WHO KNOW AFRICA."
            —Travel advertisement, *Observer,* 27 November 1988

That night our mother went to the shop and she didn't come back. Ever. What happened? I don't know. My father also had gone away one day and never come back; but he was fighting in the war. We were in the war, too, but we were children, we were like our grandmother and grandfather, we didn't have guns. The people my father was fighting—the bandits, they are called by our government—ran all over the place and we ran away from them like chickens chased by dogs. We didn't know where to go. Our mother went to the shop because someone said you could get some oil for cooking. We were happy because we hadn't tasted oil for a long time; perhaps she got the oil and someone knocked her down in the dark and took that oil from her. Perhaps she met the bandits. If you meet them, they will kill you. Twice they came to our village and we ran and hid in the bush and when they'd gone we came back and found they had taken everything; but the third time they came back there was nothing to take, no oil, no food, so they burned the thatch and the roofs of our houses fell in. My mother found some pieces of tin and we put those up over part of the house. We were waiting there for her that night she never came back.

We were frightened to go out, even to do our business, because the bandits did come. Not into our house—without a roof it must have looked as if there was no one in it, everything gone—but all through the village. We heard people screaming and running. We were afraid even to run, without our mother to tell us where. I am the middle one, the girl, and my little brother clung against my stomach with his arms round my neck and his legs round my waist like a baby monkey to its mother. All night my first-born brother kept in his hand a broken piece of wood from one of our burnt house-poles. It was to save himself if the bandits found him.

We stayed there all day. Waiting for her. I don't know what day it was; there was no school, no church any more in our village, so you didn't know whether it was a Sunday or a Monday.

When the sun was going down, our grandmother and grandfather came. Someone from our village had told them we children were alone, our mother had not come back. I say "grandmother" before "grandfather" because it's like that: our grandmother is big and strong, not yet old, and our grandfather is small, you don't know where he is, in his loose trousers, he smiles but he hasn't heard what you're saying, and his hair looks as if he's left it full of soap suds. Our grandmother took us—me, the baby, my first-born brother, our grand-father—back to her house and we were all afraid (except the baby, asleep on our grandmother's back) of meeting the bandits on the way. We waited a long time at our grandmother's place. Perhaps it was a month. We were hungry. Our mother never came. While we were waiting for her to fetch us, our grand-mother had no food for us, no food for our grandfather and herself. A woman with milk in her breasts gave us some for my little brother, although at our house he used to eat porridge, same as we did. Our grandmother took us to look for wild spinach but everyone else in the village did the same and there wasn't a leaf left.

Our grandfather, walking a little behind some young men, went to look for our mother but didn't find her. Our grandmother cried with other women and I sang the hymns with them. They brought a little food—some beans—but after two days there was nothing again. Our grandfather used to have three sheep and a cow and a vegetable garden but the bandits had long ago taken the sheep and the cow, because they were hungry, too; and when planting time came our grandfather had no seed to plant.

So they decided—our grandmother did; our grandfather made little noises and rocked from side to side, but she took no notice—we would go away. We children were pleased. We wanted to go away from where our mother wasn't and where we were hungry. We wanted to go where there were no ban-dits and there was food. We were glad to think there must be such a place; away.

Our grandmother gave her church clothes to someone in exchange for some dried mealies and she boiled them and tied them in a rag. We took them with us when we went and she thought we would get water from the rivers but we didn't come to any river and we got so thirsty we had to turn back. Not all the way to our grandparents' place but to a village where there was a pump. She opened the basket where she carried some clothes and the mealies and she sold her shoes to buy a big plastic container for water. I said, *Gogo*, how will you go to church now even without shoes, but she said we had a long journey and too much to carry. At that village we met other people who were also going away. We joined them because they seemed to know where that was better than we did.

To get there we had to go through the Kruger Park. We knew about the Kruger Park. A kind of whole country of animals—elephants, lions, jackals, hyenas, hippos, crocodiles, all kinds of animals. We had some of them in our own country, before the war (our grandfather remembers; we children weren't born yet) but the bandits kill the elephants and sell their tusks, and the bandits and our soldiers have eaten all the buck. There was a man in our village without legs—a crocodile took them off, in our river; but all the same our country is a country of people, not animals. We knew about the Kruger Park because some of our men used to leave home to work there in the places where white people came to stay and look at the animals.

So we started to go away again. There were women and other children like me who had to carry the small ones on their backs when the women got tired. A man led us into the Kruger Park: are we there yet, are we there yet, I kept asking our grandmother. Not yet, the man said, when she asked him for me. He told us we had to take a long way to get round the fence, which he explained would kill you, roast off your skin the moment you touched it, like the wires high up on poles that give electric light in our towns. I've seen that sign of a head without ears or skin or hair on an iron box at the mission hospital we used to have before it was blown up.

When I asked the next time, they said we'd been walking in the Kruger Park for an hour. But it looked just like the bush we'd been walking through all day, and we hadn't seen any animals except the monkeys and birds which live around us at home, and a tortoise that, of course, couldn't get away from us. My first-born brother and the other boys brought it to the man so it could be killed and we could cook and eat it. He let it go because he told us we could not make a fire; all the time we were in the Park we must not make a fire because the smoke would show we were there. Police, wardens, would come and send us back where we came from. He said we must move like animals among the animals, away from the roads, away from the white people's camps. And at that moment I heard—I'm sure I was the first to hear—cracking branches and the sound of something parting grasses and I almost squealed because I thought it was the police, wardens—the people he was telling us to look out for—who had found us already. And it was an elephant, and another elephant, and more elephants, big blots of dark moved wherever you looked between the trees. They were curling their trunks round the red leaves of the mopane trees and stuffing them into their mouths. The babies leaned against their mothers. The almost grown-up ones wrestled like my first-born brother with his friends—only they used trunks instead of arms. I was so interested I forgot to be afraid. The man said we should just stand still and be quiet while the elephants passed. They passed very slowly because elephants are too big to need to run from anyone.

The buck ran from us. They jumped so high they seemed to fly. The wart-hogs stopped dead, when they heard us, and swerved off the way a boy in our village used to zigzag on the bicycle his father had brought back from the mines. We followed the animals to where they drank. When they had gone, we went to their waterholes. We were never thirsty without finding water, but the animals ate, ate all the time. Whenever you saw them they were eating, grass, trees, roots. And there was nothing for us. The mealies were finished. The only food we could eat was what the baboons ate, dry little figs full of ants, that grow along the branches of the trees at the rivers. It was hard to be like the animals.

When it was very hot during the day we would find lions lying asleep. They were the colour of the grass and we didn't see them at first but the man did, and he led us back and a long way round where they slept. I wanted to lie down like the lions. My little brother was getting thin but he was very heavy. When our grandmother looked for me, to put him on my back, I tried not to see. My first-born brother stopped talking; and when we rested he had to be shaken to get up again, as if he was just like our grandfather, he couldn't hear. I saw flies crawling on our grandmother's face and she didn't brush them off; I was frightened. I picked up a palm leaf and chased them.

We walked at night as well as by day. We could see the fires where the white people were cooking in the camps and we could smell the smoke and the meat. We watched the hyenas with their backs that slope as if they're ashamed, slipping through the bush after the smell. If one turned its head, you saw it had big brown shining eyes like our own, when we looked at each other in the dark. The wind brought voices in our own language from the compounds where the people who work in the camps live. A woman among us wanted to go to them at night and ask them to help us. They can give us the food from the dustbins, she said, she started wailing and our grandmother had to grab her and put a hand over her mouth. The men who led us had told us that we must keep out of the way of our people who worked at the Kruger Park; if they helped us they would lose their work. If they saw us, all they could do was pretend we were not there; they had seen only animals.

Sometimes we stopped to sleep for a little while at night. We slept close together. I don't know which night it was — because we were walking, walking, any time, all the time — we heard the lions very near. Not groaning loudly the way they did far off. Panting, like we do when we run, but it's a different kind of panting: you can hear they're not running, they're waiting, somewhere near. We all rolled closer together, on top of each other, the ones on the edge fighting to get into the middle. I was squashed against a woman who smelled bad because she was afraid but I was glad to hold tight on to her. I prayed to God to make the lions take someone on the edge and go. I shut my eyes not to see the tree from which a lion might jump right into the middle of us, where I was. The man who led us jumped up instead, and beat on the tree with a dead branch. He had taught us never to make a sound but he shouted. He shouted at the lions like a drunk man shouting at nobody in our village. The lions went away. We heard them groaning, shouting back at him from far off.

We were tired, so tired. My first-born brother and the man had to lift our grandfather from stone to stone where we found places to cross the rivers. Our grandmother is strong but her feet were bleeding. We could not carry the basket on our heads any longer, we couldn't carry anything except my little brother. We left our things under a bush. As long as our bodies get there, our grandmother said. Then we ate some wild fruit we didn't know from home and our stomachs ran. We were in the grass called elephant grass because it is nearly as tall as an elephant, that day we had those pains, and our grandfather couldn't just get down in front of people like my little brother, he went off into the grass to be on his own. We had to keep up, the man who led us always kept telling us, we must catch up, but we asked him to wait for our grandfather.

So everyone waited for our grandfather to catch up. But he didn't. It was the middle of the day; insects were singing in our ears and we couldn't hear him moving through the grass. We couldn't see him because the grass was so high and he was so small. But he must have been somewhere there inside his loose trousers and his shirt that was torn and our grandmother couldn't sew because she had no cotton. We knew he couldn't have gone far because he was weak and slow. We all went to look for him, but in groups, so we too wouldn't be hidden from each other in that grass. It got into our eyes and noses; we called him softly but the noise of the insects must have filled the little space left for hearing in his ears. We looked and looked but we couldn't find him. We stayed in that long grass all night. In my sleep I found him curled round in a place he had tramped down for himself, like the places we'd seen where the buck hide their babies.

When I woke up he still wasn't anywhere. So we looked again, and by now there were paths we'd made by going through the grass many times, it would be easy for him to find us if we couldn't find him. All that day we just sat and waited. Everything is very quiet when the sun is on your head, inside your head, even if you lie, like the animals, under the trees. I lay on my back and saw those ugly birds with hooked beaks and plucked necks flying round and round above us. We had passed them often where they were feeding on the bones of dead animals, nothing was ever left there for us to eat. Round and round, high up and then lower down and then high again. I saw their necks poking to this side and that. Flying round and round. I saw our grandmother, who sat up all the time with my little brother on her lap, was seeing them, too.

In the afternoon the man who led us came to our grandmother and told her the other people must move on. He said, If their children don't eat soon they will die.

Our grandmother said nothing.

I'll bring you water before we go, he told her.

Our grandmother looked at us, me, my first-born brother, and my little brother on her lap. We watched the other people getting up to leave. I didn't believe the grass would be empty, all around us, where they had been. That we would be alone in this place, the Kruger Park, the police or the animals would find us. Tears came out of my eyes and nose on to my hands but our grandmother took no notice. She got up, with her feet apart the way she puts them when she is going to lift firewood, at home in our village, she swung my little brother on to her back, tied him in her cloth — the top of her dress was torn and her big breasts were showing but there was nothing in them for him. She said, Come.

So we left the place with the long grass. Left behind. We went with the others and the man who led us. We started to go away, again.

There's a very big tent, bigger than a church or a school, tied down to the ground. I didn't understand that was what it would be, when we got there, away. I saw a thing like that the time our mother took us to the town because she heard our soldiers were there and she wanted to ask them if they knew where our father was. In that tent, people were praying and singing. This one is blue and white like that one but it's not for praying and singing, we live in it with other people who've come from our country. Sister from the clinic says we're 200 without counting the babies, and we have new babies, some were born on the way through the Kruger Park.

Inside, even when the sun is bright it's dark and there's a kind of whole village in there. Instead of houses each family has a little place closed off with sacks or cardboard from boxes—whatever we can find—to show the other families it's yours and they shouldn't come in even though there's no door and no windows and no thatch, so that if you're standing up and you're not a small child you can see into everybody's house. Some people have even made paint from ground rocks and drawn designs on the sacks.

Of course, there really is a roof—the tent is the roof, far, high up. It's like a sky. It's like a mountain and we're inside it; through the cracks paths of dust lead down, so thick you think you could climb them. The tent keeps off the rain overhead but the water comes in at the sides and in the little streets between our places—you can only move along them one person at a time—the small kids like my little brother play in the mud. You have to step over them. My little brother doesn't play. Our grandmother takes him to the clinic when the doctor comes on Mondays. Sister says there's something wrong with his head, she thinks it's because we didn't have enough food at home. Because of the war. Because our father wasn't there. And then because he was so hungry in the Kruger Park. He likes just to lie about on our grandmother all day, on her lap or against her somewhere and he looks at us and looks at us. He wants to ask something but you can see he can't. If I tickle him he may just smile. The clinic gives us special powder to make into porridge for him and perhaps one day he'll be all right.

When we arrived we were like him—my first-born brother and I. I can hardly remember. The people who lived in the village near the tent took us to the clinic, it's where you have to sign that you've come—away, through the Kruger Park. We sat on the grass and everything was muddled. One Sister was pretty with her hair straightened and beautiful high-heeled shoes and she brought us the special powder. She said we must mix it with water and drink it slowly. We tore the packets open with our teeth and licked it all up, it stuck round my mouth and I sucked it from my lips and fingers. Some other children who had walked with us vomited. But I only felt everything in my belly moving, the stuff going down and around like a snake, and hiccups hurt me. Another Sister called us to stand in line on the veranda of the clinic but we couldn't. We sat all over the place there, falling against each other: the Sisters helped each of us up by the arm and then stuck a needle in it. Other needles drew our blood into tiny bottles. This was against sickness, but I didn't understand, every time my eyes dropped closed I thought I was walking, the grass was long. I saw the elephants, I didn't know we were away.

But our grandmother was still strong, she could still stand up, she knows how to write and she signed for us. Our grandmother got us this place in the tent against one of the sides, it's the best kind of place there because although the rain comes in, we can lift the flap when the weather is good and then the sun shines on us, the smells in the tent go out. Our grandmother knows a woman here who showed her where there is good grass for sleeping mats, and our grandmother made some for us. Once every month the food truck comes to the clinic. Our grandmother takes along one of the cards she signed and when it has been punched we get a sack of mealie meal. There are wheelbarrows to take it back to the tent: my first-born brother does this for her and then he and the other boys have races, steering the empty wheelbarrows back to the clinic. Sometimes he's lucky and a man who's bought beer in the village gives him money to deliver it — though that's not allowed, you're supposed to take that wheelbarrow straight back to the Sisters. He buys a cold drink and shares it with me if I catch him. On another day, every month, the church leaves a pile of old clothes in the clinic yard. Our grandmother has another card to get punched, and then we can choose something: I have two dresses, two pants and a jersey, so I can go to school.

The people in the village have let us join their school. I was surprised to find they speak our language; our grandmother told me, That's why they allow us to stay on their land. Long ago, in the time of our fathers, there was no fence that kills you, there was no Kruger Park between them and us, we were the same people under our own king, right from our village we left to this place we've come to.

Now that we've been in the tent so long — I have turned eleven and my little brother is nearly three although he is so small, only his head is big, he's not come right in it yet — some people have dug up the bare ground around the tent and planted beans and mealies and cabbage. The old men weave branches to put up fences round their gardens. No one is allowed to look for work in the towns but some of the women have found work in the village and can buy things. Our grandmother, because she's still strong, finds work where people are building houses — in this village the people build nice houses with bricks and cement, not mud like we used to have at our home. Our grandmother carries bricks for these people and fetches baskets of stones on her head. And so she has money to buy sugar and tea and milk and soap. The store gave her a calendar she has hung up on our flap of the tent. I am clever at school and she collected advertising paper people throw away outside the store and covered my school-books with it. She makes my first-born brother and me do our homework every afternoon before it gets dark because there is no room except to lie down, close together, just as we did in the Kruger Park, in our place in the tent, and candles are expensive. Our grandmother hasn't been able to buy herself a pair of shoes for church yet, but she has bought black school shoes and polish to clean them with for my first-born brother and me. Every morning, when people are getting up in the tent, the babies are crying, people are pushing each other at the taps outside, and some children are already pulling the crusts of porridge off the pots we ate from last night, my first-born brother and I clean our shoes. Our grandmother makes us sit on our mats with our legs straight out so she can look carefully at our shoes to make sure we have done it properly. No other children in the tent have real school shoes. When we three look at them it's as if we are in a real house again, with no war, no away.

Some white people came to take photographs of our people living in the tent — they said they were making a film, I've never seen what that is though I know about it. A white woman squeezed into our space and asked our grandmother questions which were told to us in our language by someone who understands the white woman's.

"How long have you been living like this?"

"She means here?" Our grandmother said. "In this tent, two years and one month."

"And what do you hope for the future?"

"Nothing. I'm here."

"But for your children?"

"I want them to learn so that they can get good jobs and money."

"Do you hope to go back to your own country?"

"I will not go back."

"But when the war is over — you won't be allowed to stay here? Don't you want to go home?"

I didn't think our grandmother wanted to speak again. I didn't think she was going to answer the white woman. The white woman put her head on one side and smiled at us.

Our grandmother looked away from her and spoke. "There is nothing. No home."

Why does our grandmother say that? Why? I'll go back. I'll go back through that Kruger Park. After the war, if there are no bandits any more, our mother may be waiting for us. And maybe when we left our grandfather, he was only left behind, he found his way somehow, slowly, through the Kruger Park, and he'll be there. They'll be home, and I'll remember them.

NATHANIEL HAWTHORNE

Nathaniel Hawthorne (1804–1864), writer of short stories and novels, was born in Salem, Massachusetts, into an eminent family who traced their lineage back to the Puritans. After his graduation from Bowdoin College in 1825, Hawthorne lived at home while he wrote short fiction he called "tales" or "articles" that he tried to sell to periodicals. American magazines of the time were mostly interested in publishing ghost stories, Indian legends, and "village tales" based on historical anecdotes. Hawthorne (like his contemporary Edgar Allan Poe) created stories that transcended the limitations of these conventions; his imagination was stirred by what he called "an inveterate love of allegory."

Hawthorne published his first collection of stories, Twice-Told Tales, *in 1837; a second book of stories,* Mosses from an Old Manse, *appeared in 1846. That year he stopped writing to earn a better living for his family as surveyor of customs for the port of Salem. This was a political appointment, and after the Whigs won the presidency three years later, Hawthorne—a Democrat—was out of a job. He returned to writing fiction, sketching his "official life" at the Custom House in the introduction to his novel* The Scarlet Letter *in 1850. During the last decade of his career as a writer he published three other novels, several books for children, and another collection of tales. In "The Custom House," Hawthorne humorously suggested that his profession would not have impressed his Puritan ancestors:*

> *"What is he?" murmurs one grey shadow of my forefathers to the other. "A writer of story-books! What kind of business in life, what manner of glorifying God, or being serviceable to mankind in his day and generation, may that be? Why, the degenerate fellow might as well have been a fiddler!" Such are the compliments bandied between my great-grandsires and myself across the gulf of time! And yet, let them scorn me as they will, strong traits of their nature have intertwined themselves with mine.*

Despite Hawthorne's portrait of himself as an unappreciated artist, he was recognized by contemporaries such as Herman Melville and Edgar Allan Poe as a "genius of a very lofty order." Hawthorne wrote about 120 short tales and sketches in addition to his novels. His notebooks are filled with ideas for stories, more often jottings of abstract ideas than detailed observations of "real" individuals. "Young Goodman Brown" is one of his moral tales set in colonial New England.

COMMENTARIES *Herman Melville, "Blackness in Hawthorne's 'Young Goodman Brown,'" page 575; Edgar Allan Poe, "The Importance of the Single Effect in a Prose Tale," page 656.*

WEB *Research Nathaniel Hawthorne and answer questions about his work at bedfordstmartins.com/charters/litwriters.*

Young Goodman Brown   1835

Young Goodman Brown came forth at sunset into the street at Salem village; but put his head back, after crossing the threshold, to exchange a parting kiss with his young wife. And Faith, as the wife was aptly named, thrust her own pretty head into the street, letting the wind play with the pink ribbons of her cap while she called to Goodman Brown.

"Dearest heart," whispered she, softly and rather sadly, when her lips were close to his ear, "prithee put off your journey until sunrise and sleep in your own bed to-night. A lone woman is troubled with such dreams and such thoughts that she's afeared of herself sometimes. Pray tarry with me this night, dear husband, of all nights in the year."

"My love and my Faith," replied young Goodman Brown, "of all nights in the year, this one night must I tarry away from thee. My journey, as thou callest it, forth and back again, must needs be done 'twixt now and sunrise.

What, my sweet, pretty wife, dost thou doubt me already, and we but three months married?"

"Then God bless you!" said Faith, with the pink ribbons; "and may you find all well when you come back."

"Amen!" cried Goodman Brown. "Say thy prayers, dear Faith, and go to bed at dusk, and no harm will come to thee."

So they parted; and the young man pursued his way until, being about to turn the corner by the meeting-house, he looked back and saw the head of Faith still peeping after him with a melancholy air, in spite of her pink ribbons.

"Poor little Faith!" thought he, for his heart smote him. "What a wretch am I to leave her on such an errand! She talks of dreams, too. Methought as she spoke there was trouble in her face, as if a dream had warned her what work is to be done to-night. But no, no; 't would kill her to think it. Well, she's a blessed angel on earth, and after this one night I'll cling to her skirts and follow her to heaven."

With this excellent resolve for the future, Goodman Brown felt himself justified in making more haste on his present evil purpose. He had taken a dreary road, darkened by all the gloomiest trees of the forest, which barely stood aside to let the narrow path creep through, and closed immediately behind. It was all as lonely as could be; and there is this peculiarity in such a solitude, that the traveller knows not who may be concealed by the innumerable trunks and the thick boughs overhead; so that with lonely footsteps he may yet be passing through an unseen multitude.

"There may be a devilish Indian behind every tree," said Goodman Brown to himself; and he glanced fearfully behind him as he added, "What if the devil himself should be at my very elbow!"

His head being turned back, he passed a crook of the road, and, looking forward again, beheld the figure of a man, in grave and decent attire, seated at the foot of an old tree. He arose at Goodman Brown's approach and walked onward side by side with him.

"You are late, Goodman Brown," said he. "The clock of the Old South was striking as I came through Boston, and that is full fifteen minutes agone."

"Faith kept me back a while," replied the young man, with a tremor in his voice, caused by the sudden appearance of his companion, though not wholly unexpected.

It was now deep dusk in the forest, and deepest in that part of it where these two were journeying. As nearly as could be discerned, the second traveller was about fifty years old, apparently in the same rank of life as Goodman Brown, and bearing a considerable resemblance to him, though perhaps more in expression than features. Still they might have been taken for father and son. And yet, though the elder person was as simply clad as the younger, and as simple in manner too, he had an indescribable air of one who knew the world, and who would not have felt abashed at the governor's dinner table or in King William's court, were it possible that his affairs should call him thither. But the only thing about him that could be fixed upon as remarkable was his staff, which bore the likeness of a great black snake, so curiously wrought that it might almost be seen to twist and wriggle itself like a living serpent. This, of course, must have been an ocular deception, assisted by the uncertain light.

"Come, Goodman Brown," cried his fellow-traveller, "this is a dull pace for the beginning of a journey. Take my staff, if you are so soon weary."

"Friend," said the other, exchanging his slow pace for a full stop, "having kept covenant by meeting thee here, it is my purpose now to return whence I came. I have scruples touching the matter thou wot'st of."

"Sayest thou so?" replied he of the serpent, smiling apart. "Let us walk on, nevertheless, reasoning as we go; and if I convince thee not thou shalt turn back. We are but a little way in the forest yet."

"Too far! too far!" exclaimed the goodman, unconsciously resuming his walk. "My father never went into the woods on such an errand, nor his father before him. We have been a race of honest men and good Christians since the days of the martyrs; and shall I be the first of the name of Brown that ever took this path and kept" —

"Such company, thou wouldst say," observed the elder person, interpreting his pause. "Well said, Goodman Brown! I have been as well acquainted with your family as with ever a one among the Puritans; and that's no trifle to say. I helped your grandfather, the constable, when he lashed the Quaker woman so smartly through the streets of Salem; and it was I that brought your father a pitch-pine knot, kindled at my own hearth, to set fire to an Indian village, in King Philip's war.° They were my good friends, both; and many a pleasant walk have we had along this path, and returned merrily after midnight. I would fain be friends with you for their sake."

"If it be as thou sayest," replied Goodman Brown, "I marvel they never spoke of these matters; or, verily, I marvel not, seeing that the least rumor of the sort would have driven them from New England. We are a people of prayer, and good works to boot, and abide no such wickedness."

"Wickedness or not," said the traveller with the twisted staff, "I have a very general acquaintance here in New England. The deacons of many a church have drunk the communion wine with me; the selectmen of divers towns make me their chairman; and a majority of the Great and General Court are firm supporters of my interest. The governor and I, too — But these are state secrets."

"Can this be so?" cried Goodman Brown, with a stare of amazement at his undisturbed companion. "Howbeit, I have nothing to do with the governor and council; they have their own ways, and are no rule for a simple husbandman like me. But, were I to go on with thee, how should I meet the eye of that good old man, our minister, at Salem village? Oh, his voice would make me tremble both Sabbath day and lecture day."

Thus far the elder traveller had listened with due gravity; but now burst into a fit of irrepressible mirth, shaking himself so violently that his snake-like staff actually seemed to wriggle in sympathy.

King Philip's war: King Philip, a Wampanoag chief, spearheaded the most destructive Indian war ever waged against the New England colonists (1675–76).

"Ha! ha! ha!" shouted he again and again; then composing himself, "Well, go on, Goodman Brown, go on; but, prithee, don't kill me with laughing."

"Well, then, to end the matter at once," said Goodman Brown, considerably nettled, "there is my wife, Faith. It would break her dear little heart; and I'd rather break my own."

"Nay, if that be the case," answered the other, "e'en go thy ways, Goodman Brown. I would not for twenty old women like the one hobbling before us that Faith should come to any harm."

As he spoke he pointed his staff at a female figure on the path, in whom Goodman Brown recognized a very pious and exemplary dame, who had taught him his catechism in youth, and was still his moral and spiritual adviser, jointly with the minister and Deacon Gookin.

"A marvel, truly that Goody Cloyse should be so far in the wilderness at nightfall," said he. "But with your leave, friend, I shall take a cut through the woods until we have left this Christian woman behind. Being a stranger to you, she might ask whom I was consorting with and whither I was going."

"Be it so," said his fellow-traveller. "Betake you to the woods, and let me keep the path."

Accordingly the young man turned aside, but took care to watch his companion, who advanced softly along the road until he had come within a staff's length of the old dame. She, meanwhile, was making the best of her way, with singular speed for so aged a woman, and mumbling some indistinct words—a prayer, doubtless—as she went. The traveller put forth his staff and touched her withered neck with what seemed the serpent's tail.

"The devil!" screamed the pious old lady.

"Then Goody Cloyse knows her old friend?" observed the traveller, confronting her and leaning on his writhing stick.

"Ah, forsooth, and is it your worship indeed?" cried the good dame. "Yea, truly is it, and in the very image of my old gossip, Goodman Brown, the grandfather of the silly fellow that now is. But—would your worship believe it?—my broomstick hath strangely disappeared, stolen, as I suspect, by that unhanged witch, Goody Cory, and that, too, when I was all anointed with the juice of smallage, and cinquefoil, and wolf's bane"—

"Mingled with fine wheat and the fat of a new-born babe," said the shape of old Goodman Brown.

"Ah, your worship knows the recipe," cried the old lady, cackling aloud. "So, as I was saying, being all ready for the meeting, and no horse to ride on, I made up my mind to foot it; for they tell me there is a nice young man to be taken into communion to-night. But now your good worship will lend me your arm, and we shall be there in a twinkling."

"That can hardly be," answered her friend. "I may not spare you my arm, Goody Cloyse; but here is my staff, if you will."

So saying, he threw it down at her feet, where, perhaps, it assumed life, being one of the rods which its owner had formerly lent to the Egyptian magi. Of this fact, however, Goodman Brown could not take cognizance. He had cast up his eyes in astonishment, and, looking down again, beheld neither Goody

Cloyse nor the serpentine staff, but his fellow-traveller alone, who waited for him as calmly as if nothing had happened.

"That old woman taught me my catechism," said the young man; and there was a world of meaning in this simple comment.

They continued to walk onward, while the elder traveller exhorted his companion to make good speed and persevere in the path, discoursing so aptly that his arguments seemed rather to spring up in the bosom of his auditor than to be suggested by himself. As they went, he plucked a branch of maple to serve for a walking stick, and began to strip it of the twigs and little boughs, which were wet with evening dew. The moment his fingers touched them they became strangely withered and dried up as with a week's sunshine. Thus the pair proceeded, at a good free pace, until suddenly, in a gloomy hollow of the road, Goodman Brown sat himself down on the stump of a tree and refused to go any farther.

"Friend," he said, stubbornly, "my mind is made up. Not another step will I budge on this errand. What if a wretched old woman do choose to go to the devil when I thought she was going to heaven: is that any reason why I should quit my dear Faith and go after her?"

"You will think better of this by and by," said his acquaintance, composedly. "Sit here and rest yourself a while; and when you feel like moving again, there is my staff to help you along."

Without more words, he threw his companion the maple stick, and was as speedily out of sight as if he had vanished into the deepening gloom. The young man sat a few moments by the roadside, applauding himself greatly, and thinking with how clear a conscience he should meet the minister in his morning walk, nor shrink from the eye of good old Deacon Gookin. And what calm sleep would be his that very night, which was to have been spent so wickedly, but so purely and sweetly now, in the arms of Faith! Amidst these pleasant and praiseworthy meditations, Goodman Brown heard the tramp of horses along the road, and deemed it advisable to conceal himself within the verge of the forest, conscious of the guilty purpose that had brought him thither, though now so happily turned from it.

On came the hoof tramps and the voices of the riders, two grave old voices, conversing soberly as they drew near. These mingled sounds appeared to pass along the road, within a few yards of the young man's hiding-place; but, owing doubtless to the depth of the gloom at that particular spot, neither the travellers nor their steeds were visible. Though their figures brushed the small boughs by the wayside, it could not be seen that they intercepted, even for a moment, the faint gleam from the strip of bright sky athwart which they must have passed. Goodman Brown alternately crouched and stood on tiptoe, pulling aside the branches and thrusting forth his head as far as he durst without discerning so much as a shadow. It vexed him the more, because he could have sworn, were such a thing possible, that he recognized the voices of the minister and Deacon Gookin, jogging along quietly, as they were wont to do, when bound to some ordination or ecclesiastical council. While yet within hearing, one of the riders stopped to pluck a switch.

"Of the two, reverend sir," said the voice like the deacon's, "I had rather miss an ordination dinner than to-night's meeting. They tell me that some of our community are to be here from Falmouth and beyond, and others from Connecticut and Rhode Island, besides several of the Indian powwows, who, after their fashion, know almost as much deviltry as the best of us. Moreover, there is a goodly young woman to be taken into communion."

"Mighty well, Deacon Gookin!" replied the solemn old tones of the minister. "Spur up, or we shall be late. Nothing can be done, you know, until I get on the ground."

The hoofs clattered again; and the voices, talking so strangely in the empty air, passed on through the forest, where no church had ever been gathered or solitary Christian prayed. Whither, then, could these holy men be journeying so deep into the heathen wilderness? Young Goodman Brown caught hold of a tree for support, being ready to sink down on the ground, faint and overburdened with the heavy sickness of his heart. He looked up to the sky, doubting whether there really was a heaven above him. Yet there was the blue arch, and the stars brightening in it.

"With heaven above and Faith below, I will yet stand firm against the devil!" cried Goodman Brown.

While he still gazed upward into the deep arch of the firmament and had lifted his hands to pray, a cloud, though no wind was stirring, hurried across the zenith and hid the brightening stars. The blue sky was still visible, except directly overhead, where this black mass of cloud was sweeping swiftly northward. Aloft in the air, as if from the depths of the cloud, came a confused and doubtful sound of voices. Once the listener fancied that he could distinguish the accents of towns-people of his own, men and women, both pious and ungodly, many of whom he had met at the communion table, and had seen others rioting at the tavern. The next moment, so indistinct were the sounds, he doubted whether he had heard aught but the murmur of the old forest, whispering without a wind. Then came a stronger swell of those familiar tones, heard daily in the sunshine at Salem village, but never until now from a cloud of night. There was one voice, of a young woman, uttering lamentations, yet with an uncertain sorrow, and entreating for some favor, which, perhaps, it would grieve her to obtain; and all the unseen multitude, both saints and sinners, seemed to encourage her onward.

"Faith!" shouted Goodman Brown, in a voice of agony and desperation; and the echoes of the forest mocked him, crying, "Faith! Faith!" as if bewildered wretches were seeking her all through the wilderness.

The cry of grief, rage, and terror was yet piercing the night, when the unhappy husband held his breath for a response. There was a scream, drowned immediately in a louder murmur of voices, fading into far-off laughter, as the dark cloud swept away, leaving the clear and silent sky above Goodman Brown. But something fluttered lightly down through the air and caught on the branch of a tree. The young man seized it, and beheld a pink ribbon.

"My Faith is gone!" cried he after one stupefied moment. "There is no good on earth; and sin is but a name. Come, devil; for to thee is this world given."

And, maddened with despair, so that he laughed loud and long, did Goodman Brown grasp his staff and set forth again, at such a rate that he seemed to fly along the forest path rather than to walk or run. The road grew wilder and drearier and more faintly traced, and vanished at length, leaving him in the heart of the dark wilderness, still rushing onward with the instinct that guides mortal man to evil. The whole forest was peopled with frightful sounds—the creaking of the trees, the howling of wild beasts, and the yell of Indians; while sometimes the wind tolled like a distant church bell, and sometimes gave a broad roar around the traveller, as if all Nature were laughing him to scorn. But he was himself the chief horror of the scene, and shrank not from its other horrors.

"Ha! ha! ha!" roared Goodman Brown when the wind laughed at him. "Let us hear which will laugh loudest. Think not to frighten me with your deviltry. Come witch, come wizard, come Indian powwow, come devil himself, and here comes Goodman Brown. You may as well fear him as he fear you."

In truth, all through the haunted forest there could be nothing more frightful than the figure of Goodman Brown. On he flew among the black pines, brandishing his staff with frenzied gestures, now giving vent to an inspiration of horrid blasphemy, and now shouting forth such laughter as set all the echoes of the forest laughing like demons around him. The fiend in his own shape is less hideous than when he rages in the breast of man. Thus sped the demoniac on his course, until, quivering among the trees, he saw a red light before him, as when the felled trunks and branches of a clearing have been set on fire, and throw up their lurid blaze against the sky, at the hour of midnight. He paused, in a lull of the tempest that had driven him onward, and heard the swell of what seemed a hymn, rolling solemnly from a distance with the weight of many voices. He knew the tune; it was a familiar one in the choir of the village meeting-house. The verse died heavily away, and was lengthened by a chorus, not of human voices, but of all the sounds of the benighted wilderness pealing in awful harmony together. Goodman Brown cried out, and his cry was lost to his own ear by its unison with the cry of the desert.

In the interval of silence he stole forward until the light glared full upon his eyes. At one extremity of an open space, hemmed in by the dark wall of the forest, arose a rock, bearing some rude, natural resemblance either to an altar or a pulpit, and surrounded by four blazing pines, their tops aflame, their stems untouched, like candles at an evening meeting. The mass of foliage that had overgrown the summit of the rock was all on fire, blazing high into the night and fitfully illuminating the whole field. Each pendent twig and leafy festoon was in a blaze. As the red light arose and fell, a numerous congregation alternately shone forth, then disappeared in shadow, and again grew, as it were, out of the darkness, peopling the heart of the solitary woods at once.

"A grave and dark-clad company," quoth Goodman Brown.

In truth they were such. Among them, quivering to and fro between gloom and splendor, appeared faces that would be seen next day at the council board of the province, and others which, Sabbath after Sabbath, looked devoutly heavenward, and benignantly over the crowded pews, from the holiest pulpits in the land. Some affirm that the lady of the governor was there. At least there were high dames well known to her, and wives of honored husbands, and widows, a great multitude, and ancient maidens, all of excellent repute, and fair young girls, who trembled lest their mothers should espy them. Either the sudden gleams of light flashing over the obscure field bedazzled Goodman Brown, or he recognized a score of the church members of Salem village famous for their especial sanctity. Good old Deacon Gookin had arrived, and waited at the skirts of that venerable saint, his revered pastor. But, irreverently consorting with these grave, reputable, and pious people, these elders of the church, these chaste dames and dewy virgins, there were men of dissolute lives and women of spotted fame, wretches given over to all mean and filthy vice, and suspected even of horrid crimes. It was strange to see that the good shrank not from the wicked, nor were the sinners abashed by the saints. Scattered also among their pale-faced enemies were the Indian priests, or powwows, who had often scared their native forest with more hideous incantations than any known to English witchcraft.

"But where is Faith?" thought Goodman Brown; and, as hope came into his heart, he trembled.

Another verse of the hymn arose, a slow and mournful strain, such as the pious love, but joined to words which expressed all that our nature can conceive of sin, and darkly hinted at far more. Unfathomable to mere mortals is the lore of fiends. Verse after verse was sung; and still the chorus of the desert swelled between like the deepest tone of a mighty organ; and with the final peal of that dreadful anthem there came a sound, as if the roaring wind, the rushing streams, the howling beasts, and every other voice of the unconcerted wilderness were mingling and according with the voice of guilty man in homage to the prince of all. The four blazing pines threw up a loftier flame, and obscurely discovered shapes and visages of horror on the smoke wreaths above the impious assembly. At the same moment the fire on the rock shot redly forth and formed a flowing arch above its base, where now appeared a figure. With reverence be it spoken, the figure bore no slight similitude, both in garb and manner, to some grave divine of the New England churches.

"Bring forth the converts!" cried a voice that echoed through the field and rolled into the forest.

At the word, Goodman Brown stepped forth from the shadow of the trees and approached the congregation, with whom he felt a loathful brotherhood by the sympathy of all that was wicked in his heart. He could have well-nigh sworn that the shape of his own dead father beckoned him to advance, looking downward from a smoke wreath, while a woman, with dim features of despair, threw out her hand to warn him back. Was it his mother? But he had no power to retreat one step, nor to resist, even in thought, when the minister and good old Deacon Gookin seized his arms and led him to the blazing rock. Thither came also the slender form of a veiled female, led between Goody Cloyse, that pious teacher of the catechism, and Martha Carrier, who had received the devil's promise to be queen of hell. A rampant hag was she. And there stood the proselytes beneath the canopy of fire.

"Welcome, my children," said the dark figure, "to the communion of your race. Ye have found thus young your nature and your destiny. My children, look behind you!"

They turned; and flashing forth, as it were, in a sheet of flame, the fiend worshippers were seen; the smile of welcome gleamed darkly on every visage.

"There," resumed the sable form, "are all whom ye have reverenced from youth. Ye deemed them holier than yourselves and shrank from your own sin, contrasting it with their lives of righteousness and prayerful aspirations heavenward. Yet here are they all in my worshipping assembly. This night it shall be granted you to know their secret deeds: how hoary-bearded elders of the church have whispered wanton words to the young maids of their households; how many a woman, eager for widows' weeds, has given her husband a drink at bedtime and let him sleep his last sleep in her bosom; how beardless youths have made haste to inherit their fathers' wealth; and how fair damsels—blush not, sweet ones—have dug little graves in the garden, and bidden me, the sole guest, to an infant's funeral. By the sympathy of your human hearts for sin ye shall scent out all the places—whether in church, bedchamber, street, field, or forest—where crime has been committed, and shall exult to behold the whole earth one stain of guilt, one mighty blood spot. Far more than this. It shall be yours to penetrate, in every bosom, the deep mystery of sin, the fountain of all wicked arts, and which inexhaustibly supplies more evil impulses than human power—than my power at its utmost—can make manifest in deeds. And now, my children, look upon each other."

They did so; and, by the blaze of the hell-kindled torches, the wretched man beheld his Faith, and the wife her husband, trembling before that unhallowed altar.

"Lo, there ye stand, my children," said the figure, in a deep and solemn tone, almost sad with its despairing awfulness, as if his once angelic nature could yet mourn for our miserable race. "Depending upon one another's hearts, ye had still hoped that virtue were not all a dream. Now are ye undeceived. Evil is the nature of mankind. Evil must be your only happiness. Welcome again, my children, to the communion of your race."

"Welcome," repeated the fiend worshippers, in one cry of despair and triumph.

And there they stood, the only pair, as it seemed, who were yet hesitating on the verge of wickedness in this dark world. A basin was hallowed, naturally, in the rock. Did it contain water, reddened by the lurid light? or was it blood? or, perchance, a liquid flame? Herein did the shape of evil dip his hand and prepare to lay the mark of baptism upon their foreheads, that they might be partakers of the mystery of sin, more conscious of the secret guilt of others, both in deed and thought, than they could now be of their own. The husband cast one look at his pale wife, and Faith at him. What polluted wretches would the next glance show them to each other, shuddering alike at what they disclosed and what they saw!

"Faith! Faith!" cried the husband, "look up to heaven, and resist the wicked one."

Whether Faith obeyed he knew not. Hardly had he spoken when he found himself amid calm night and solitude, listening to a roar of the wind which died heavily away through the forest. He staggered against the rock, and felt it chill and damp; while a hanging twig, that had been all on fire, besprinkled his cheek with the coldest dew.

The next morning young Goodman Brown came slowly into the street of Salem village, staring around him like a bewildered man. The good old minister was taking a walk along the graveyard to get an appetite for breakfast and meditate his sermon, and bestowed a blessing, as he passed, on Goodman Brown. He shrank from the venerable saint as if to avoid an anathema. Old Deacon Gookin was at domestic worship, and the holy words of his prayer were heard through the open window. "What God doth the wizard pray to?" quoth Goodman Brown. Goody Cloyse, that excellent old Christian, stood in the early sunshine at her own lattice, catechizing a little girl who had brought her a pint of morning's milk. Goodman Brown snatched away the child as from the grasp of the fiend himself. Turning the corner by the meeting-house, he spied the head of Faith, with the pink ribbons, gazing anxiously forth, and bursting into such joy at sight of him that she skipped along the street and almost kissed her husband before the whole village. But Goodman Brown looked sternly and sadly into her face, and passed on without a greeting.

Had Goodman Brown fallen asleep in the forest and only dreamed a wild dream of a witch-meeting?

Be it so if you will; but, alas! it was a dream of evil omen for young Goodman Brown. A stern, a sad, a darkly meditative, a distrustful, if not a desperate man did he become from the night of that fearful dream. On the Sabbath day, when the congregation were singing a holy psalm, he could not listen because an anthem of sin rushed loudly upon his ear and drowned all the blessed strain. When the minister spoke from the pulpit with power and fervid eloquence, and, with his hand on the open Bible, of the sacred truths of our religion, and of saint-like lives and triumphant deaths, and of future bliss or misery unutterable, then did Goodman Brown turn pale, dreading lest the roof should thunder down upon the gray blasphemer and his hearers. Often, awaking suddenly at midnight, he shrank from the bosom of Faith; and at morning or eventide, when the family knelt down at prayer, he scowled and muttered to himself, and gazed sternly at his wife, and turned away. And when he had lived long, and was borne to his grave a hoary corpse, followed by Faith, an aged woman, and children and grandchildren, a goodly procession, besides neighbors not a few, they carved no hopeful verse upon his tombstone, for his dying hour was gloom.

ERNEST HEMINGWAY

Ernest Hemingway (1899–1961) was born in Oak Park, Illinois, but he spent most of his boyhood in Michigan, where his father, a doctor, encouraged his enthusiasm for camping and hunting. Active as a reporter for his high school newspaper, Hemingway decided not to go on to college. Instead he worked as a reporter on the Kansas City Star *for a few months before volunteering to serve in an Amer-*

ican ambulance unit in France during World War I. Then he went to Italy, served at the front, and was severely wounded in action just before his nineteenth birthday. After the war he was too restless to settle down in the United States, so he lived in Paris and supported himself and his wife as a newspaper correspondent. He worked hard at learning how to write fiction; as he later said, "I found the greatest difficulty, aside from knowing what you really felt, rather than what you were supposed to feel, or had been taught to feel, was to put down what really happened in action: what the actual things were which produced the emotion that you experienced."

In America Hemingway had admired the work of Sherwood Anderson, especially the colloquial, "unliterary" tone of his stories, and in Paris he came under the influence of Gertrude Stein, telling Anderson in a letter of 1922 that "Gertrude Stein and me are just like brothers." As the critic A. Walton Litz and many others have recognized, Hemingway was receptive to several diverse influences as a young writer forging his literary style, including the work of the experimental poet Ezra Pound, whose advice in essays written in 1913 on the composition of imagist poetry is suggested in the style developed in Hemingway's early fiction:

1. Direct treatment of the "thing," without evasion or cliché.
2. The use of absolutely no word that does not contribute to the general design.
3. Fidelity to the rhythms of natural speech.
4. The natural object is always the adequate symbol.

Hemingway's first book, In Our Time (1925), is a collection of stories and sketches. His early novels, The Sun Also Rises (1926) and A Farewell to Arms (1929), established him as a master stylist, probably the most influential writer of American prose in the first half of the twentieth century. In 1938 he collected what he considered his best short fiction in The Fifth Column and the First Forty-Nine Stories. After publication of The Old Man and the Sea, he was awarded the Nobel Prize for literature in 1954. Seven years later, in poor health and haunted by the memory of the suicide of his father, who had shot himself with a Civil War pistol in 1929, Hemingway killed himself with a shotgun in his Idaho hunting lodge.

Hemingway's concise way of developing a plot through dialogue, as in "Hills Like White Elephants," attracted many imitators. He once explained how he achieved an intense compression by comparing his method to the principle of the iceberg: "There is seven-eighths of it under water for every part that shows. Anything you know you can eliminate and it only strengthens your iceberg. It is the part that doesn't show. If a writer omits something because he does not know it then there is a hole in the story." The most authoritative collection of Hemingway's stories, The Complete Short Stories of Ernest Hemingway: The Finca-Vigia Edition, was published in 1991.

CONNECTION   Russell Banks, "Black Man and White Woman in Dark Green Rowboat," page 68.

WEB   Research Ernest Hemingway and answer questions about his work at bedfordstmartins.com/charters/litwriters.

Hills Like White Elephants

The hills across the valley of the Ebro were long and white. On this side there was no shade and no trees and the station was between two lines of rails in the sun. Close against the side of the station there was the warm shadow of the building and a curtain, made of strings of bamboo beads, hung across the open door into the bar, to keep out flies. The American and the girl with him sat at a table in the shade, outside the building. It was very hot and the express from Barcelona would come in forty minutes. It stopped at this junction for two minutes and went on to Madrid.

"What should we drink?" the girl asked. She had taken off her hat and put it on the table.

"It's pretty hot," the man said.

"Let's drink beer."

"*Dos cervezas,*" the man said into the curtain.

"Big ones?" a woman asked from the doorway.

"Yes. Two big ones."

The woman brought two glasses of beer and two felt pads. She put the felt pads and the beer glasses on the table and looked at the man and the girl. The girl was looking off at the line of hills. They were white in the sun and the country was brown and dry.

"They look like white elephants," she said.

"I've never seen one," the man drank his beer.

"No, you wouldn't have."

"I might have," the man said. "Just because you say I wouldn't have doesn't prove anything."

The girl looked at the bead curtain. "They've painted something on it," she said. "What does it say?"

"Anis del Toro. It's a drink."

"Could we try it?"

The man called "Listen" through the curtain. The woman came out from the bar.

"Four reales."

"We want two Anis del Toro."

"With water?"

"Do you want it with water?"

"I don't know," the girl said. "Is it good with water?"

"It's all right."

"You want them with water?" asked the woman.

"Yes, with water."

"It tastes like licorice," the girl said and put the glass down.

"That's the way with everything."

"Yes," said the girl. "Everything tastes of licorice. Especially all the things you've waited so long for, like absinthe."

"Oh, cut it out."

"You started it," the girl said. "I was being amused. I was having a fine time."

"Well, let's try and have a fine time."

"All right. I was trying. I said the mountains looked like white elephants. Wasn't that bright?"

"That was bright."

"I wanted to try this new drink: That's all we do, isn't it—look at things and try new drinks?"

"I guess so."

The girl looked across at the hills.

"They're lovely hills," she said. "They don't really look like white elephants. I just meant the coloring of their skin through the trees."

"Should we have another drink?"

"All right."

The warm wind blew the bead curtain against the table.

"The beer's nice and cool," the man said.

"It's lovely," the girl said.

"It's really an awfully simple operation, Jig," the man said. "It's not really an operation at all."

The girl looked at the ground the table legs rested on.

"I know you wouldn't mind it, Jig. It's really not anything. It's just to let the air in."

The girl did not say anything.

"I'll go with you and I'll stay with you all the time. They just let the air in and then it's all perfectly natural."

"Then what will we do afterward?"

"We'll be fine afterward. Just like we were before."

"What makes you think so?"

"That's the only thing that bothers us. It's the only thing that's made us unhappy."

The girl looked at the bead curtain, put her hand out, and took hold of two of the strings of beads.

"And you think then we'll be all right and be happy."

"I know we will. You don't have to be afraid. I've known lots of people that have done it."

"So have I," said the girl. "And afterward they were all so happy."

"Well," the man said, "if you don't want to you don't have to. I wouldn't have you do it if you didn't want to. But I know it's perfectly simple."

"And you really want to?"

"I think it's the best thing to do. But I don't want you to do it if you don't really want to."

"And if I do it you'll be happy and things will be like they were and you'll love me?"

"I love you now. You know I love you."

"I know. But if I do it, then it will be nice again if I say things are like white elephants, and you'll like it?"

"I'll love it. I love it now but I just can't think about it. You know how I get when I worry."

"If I do it you won't ever worry?"

"I won't worry about that because it's perfectly simple."

"Then I'll do it. Because I don't care about me."

"What do you mean?"

"I don't care about me."

"Well, I care about you."

"Oh, yes. But I don't care about me. And I'll do it and then everything will be fine."

"I don't want you to do it if you feel that way."

The girl stood up and walked to the end of the station. Across, on the other side, were fields of grain and trees along the banks of the Ebro. Far away, beyond the river, were mountains. The shadow of a cloud moved across the field of grain and she saw the river through the trees.

"And we could have all this," she said. "And we could have everything and every day we make it more impossible."

"What did you say?"

"I said we could have everything."

"We can have everything."

"No, we can't."

"We can have the whole world."

"No, we can't."

"We can go everywhere."

"No, we can't. It isn't ours any more."

"It's ours."

"No, it isn't. And once they take it away, you never get it back."

"But they haven't taken it away."

"We'll wait and see."

"Come on back in the shade," he said. "You mustn't feel that way."

"I don't feel any way," the girl said. "I just know things."

"I don't want you to do anything that you don't want to do——"

"Nor that isn't good for me," she said. "I know. Could we have another beer?"

"All right. But you've got to realize——"

"I realize," the girl said. "Can't we maybe stop talking?"

They sat down at the table and the girl looked across at the hills on the dry side of the valley and the man looked at her and at the table.

"You've got to realize," he said, "that I don't want you to do it if you don't want to. I'm perfectly willing to go through with it if it means anything to you."

"Doesn't it mean anything to you? We could get along."

"Of course it does. But I don't want anybody but you. I don't want any one else. And I know it's perfectly simple."

"Yes, you know it's perfectly simple."

"It's all right for you to say that, but I do know it."

"Would you do something for me now?"

"I'd do anything for you."

"Would you please please please please please please please stop talking?"

He did not say anything but looked at the bags against the wall of the station. There were labels on them from all the hotels where they had spent nights.

"But I don't want you to," he said, "I don't care anything about it."

"I'll scream," the girl said.

The woman came out through the curtains with two glasses of beer and put them down on the damp felt pads. "The train comes in five minutes," she said.

"What did she say?" asked the girl.

"That the train is coming in five minutes."

The girl smiled brightly at the woman, to thank her.

"I'd better take the bags over to the other side of the station," the man said. She smiled at him.

"All right. Then come back and we'll finish the beer."

He picked up the two heavy bags and carried them around the station to the other tracks. He looked up the tracks but could not see the train. Coming back, he walked through the barroom, where people waiting for the train were drinking. He drank an Anis at the bar and looked at the people. They were all waiting reasonably for the train. He went out through the bead curtain. She was sitting at the table and smiled at him.

"Do you feel better?" he asked.

"I feel fine," she said. "There's nothing wrong with me. I feel fine."

ZORA NEALE HURSTON

Zora Neale Hurston (1891–1960) was born to a family of sharecroppers in Notasulga, Alabama. When she was very young she moved to Eatonville, Florida, a town founded by African Americans. After her mother died in 1904, her father, a Baptist minister, could not raise their eight children, so Hurston was forced to move from one relative's home to another. She never finished grade school, but when she was old enough to support herself, she attended Howard University in Washington, D.C. In 1921 she published her first story, "John Redding Goes to Sea," in the student literary magazine.

In 1925 Hurston went to New York City and became active in the cultural renaissance in Harlem, collaborating with Langston Hughes on a folk comedy, Mule Bone. Like Hughes, she was deeply interested in the abiding folk spirit inherent in southern life. With several other writers of that time, she tried to express her cultural heritage by writing short stories. The Eatonville Anthology (1927) was the collection that first brought Hurston's work to national attention. After Hurston studied with the famous anthropologist Franz Boas at Barnard College, she returned to Florida to record the oral traditions of her native community. As critics have noted, from this time to the end of her life she tried to achieve a balance in her literary work expressing the folk culture of her racial background and her individuality as a developing artist. Realizing that many white people used stereotypes to keep African Americans, Asian Americans, Hispanic Americans, and Native Americans in their "place," Hurston insisted it was

> urgent to realize that minorities do think, and think about something other than the race problem. That they are very human and internally, according to natural endowment, are just like everybody else. So long as this is not conceived, there must remain that feeling of unsurmountable difference, and difference to the average man means something bad. If people were made right, they would be just like him.

During the Great Depression of the 1930s, Hurston turned all her energies to writing. "The Gilded Six-Bits" appeared in Story in 1933. She published Mules and Men (1935), based on material from her field trips to Florida, and Their Eyes Were Watching God (1937), a novel about a woman's search for love and personal identity, in addition to several other books, including an autobiography. Although she published more than any other African American woman writer of her time, in the last two decades of her life she earned very little from her writing, and she died penniless in Florida. Fifteen years after Hurston's death, her work was rediscovered by black authors such as Alice Walker, and she is now regarded as one of our most important American writers.

COMMENTARIES *Zora Neale Hurston, "How It Feels to Be Colored Me," page 568; Alice Walker, "Zora Neale Hurston: A Cautionary Tale and a Partisan View," page 602.*

WEB *Research Zora Neale Hurston and answer questions about her work at bedfordstmartins.com/charters/litwriters.*

The Gilded Six-Bits   1933

It was a Negro yard around a Negro house in a Negro settlement that looked to the payroll of the G and G Fertilizer works for its support.

But there was something happy about the place. The front yard was parted in the middle by a sidewalk from gate to doorstep, a sidewalk edged on either side by quart bottles driven neck down to the ground on a slant. A mess of homey flowers planted without a plan but blooming cheerily from their helter-skelter places. The fence and house were whitewashed. The porch and steps scrubbed white.

The front door stood open to the sunshine so that the floor of the front room could finish drying after its weekly scouring. It was Saturday. Everything clean from the front gate to the privy house. Yard raked so that the strokes of the rake would make a pattern. Fresh newspaper cut in fancy-edge on the kitchen shelves.

Missie May was bathing herself in the galvanized washtub in the bedroom. Her dark-brown skin glistened under the soapsuds that skittered down from her wash rag. Her stiff young breasts thrust forward aggressively like broad-based cones with the tips lacquered in black.

She heard men's voices in the distance and glanced at the dollar clock on the dresser.

"Humph! Ah'm way behind time t'day! Joe gointer be heah 'fore Ah git mah clothes on if Ah don't make haste."

She grabbed the clean meal sack at hand and dried herself hurriedly and began to dress. But before she could tie her slippers, there came the ring of singing metal on wood. Nine times.

Missie May grinned with delight. She had not seen the big tall man come stealing in the gate and creep up the walk grinning happily at the joyful mischief he was about to commit. But she knew that it was her husband throwing silver dollars in the door for her to pick up and pile beside her plate at dinner. It was this way every Saturday afternoon. The nine dollars hurled into the open door, he scurried to a hiding place behind the cape jasmine bush and waited.

Missie May promptly appeared at the door in mock alarm.

"Who dat chunkin' money in mah do'way?" she demanded. No answer from the yard. She leaped off the porch and began to search the shrubbery. She peeped under the porch and hung over the gate to look up and down the road. While she did this, the man behind the jasmine darted to the chinaberry tree. She spied him and gave chase.

"Nobody ain't gointer be chunkin' money at me and Ah not do'em nothin'," she shouted in mock anger. He ran around the house with Missie May at his heels. She overtook him at the kitchen door. He ran inside but could not close it after him before she crowded in and locked with him in a rough and tumble. For several minutes the two were a furious mass of male and female energy. Shouting, laughing, twisting, turning, and Joe trying, but not too hard, to get away.

"Missie May, take yo' hand out mah pocket!" Joe shouted out between laughs.

"Ah ain't, Joe, not lessen you gwine gimme whateve' it is good you got in yo' pocket. Turn it go, Joe, do Ah'll tear yo' clothes."

"Go on tear 'em. You de one dat pushes de needles round heah. Move yo' hand Missie May."

"Lemme git dat paper sack out yo' pocket. Ah bet its candy kisses."

"Tain't. Move yo' hand. Woman ain't got no business in a man's clothes nowhow. Go 'way."

Missie May gouged way down and gave an upward jerk and triumphed.

"Unhhunh! Ah got it. It 'tis so candy kisses. Ah knowed you had somethin' for me in yo' clothes. Now Ah got to see whut's in every pocket you got."

Joe smiled indulgently and let his wife go through all of his pockets and take out the things that he had hidden there for her to find. She bore off the chewing gum, the cake of sweet soap, the pocket handkerchief as if she had wrested them from him, as if they had not been bought for the sake of this friendly battle.

"Whew! dat play-fight done got me all warmed up," Joe exclaimed. "Got me some water in de kittle?"

"Yo' water is on de fire and yo' clean things is cross de bed. Hurry up and wash yo'self and git changed so we kin eat. Ah'm hongry." As Missie said this, she bore the steaming kettle into the bedroom.

"You ain't hongry, sugar," Joe contradicted her. "Youse jes's little empty. Ah'm de one whut's hongry. Ah could eat up camp meetin',' back off 'ssociation, and drink Jurdan dry. Have it on de table when Ah git out de tub."

"Don't you mess wid mah business, man. You git in yo' clothes. Ah'm a real wife, not no dress and breath. Ah might not look lak one, but if you burn me, you won't git a thing but wife ashes."

Joe splashed in the bedroom and Missie May fanned around in the kitchen. A fresh red and white checked cloth on the table. Big pitcher of buttermilk beaded with pale drops of butter from the churn. Hot fried mullet, crackling bread, ham hocks atop a mound of string beans and new potatoes, and perched on the window-sill a pone of spicy potato pudding.

Very little talk during the meal but that little consisted of banter that pretended to deny affection but in reality flaunted it. Like when Missie May reached for a second helping of the tater pone. Joe snatched it out of her reach. After Missie May had made two or three unsuccessful grabs at the pan, she begged, "Aw, Joe gimme some mo' dat tater pone."

"Nope, sweetenin' is for us men-folks. Y'all pritty li'l frail eels don't need nothin' lak dis. You too sweet already."

"Please, Joe."

"Naw, naw. Ah don't want you to get no sweeter than whut you is already. We goin' down de road al li'l piece t'night so you go put on yo' Sunday-go-to-meetin' things."

Missie May looked at her husband to see if he was playing some prank. "Sho' nuff, Joe?"

"Yeah. We goin' to de ice cream parlor."

"Where de ice cream parlor at, Joe?"

"A new man done come heah from Chicago and he done got a place and took and opened it up for a ice cream parlor, and bein' as it's real swell, Ah wants you to be one de first ladies to walk in dere and have some set down."

"Do Jesus, Ah ain't knowed nothin' 'bout it. Who de man done it?"

"Mister Otis D. Slemmons, of spots and places—Memphis, Chicago, Jacksonville, Philadelphia, and so on."

"Dat heavy-set man wid his mouth full of gold teethes?"

"Yeah. Where did you see 'im at?"

"Ah went down to de sto' tuh git a box of lye and Ah seen 'im standin' on de corner talkin' to some of de mens, and Ah come on back and went to scrubbin' de floor, and he passed and tipped his hat whilst Ah was scourin' de steps. Ah thought never Ah seen *him* befo'."

Joe smiled pleasantly. "Yeah, he's up to date. He got de finest clothes Ah ever seen on a colored man's back."

"Aw, he don't look no better in his clothes than you do in yourn. He got a puzzlegut on 'im and he so chuckle-headed, he got a pone behind his neck."

Joe looked down at his own abdomen and said wistfully, "Wisht Ah had a build on me lak he got. He ain't puzzle-gutted, honey. He jes' got a corperation. Dat make 'm look lak a rich white man. All rich mens is got some belly on 'em."

"Ah seen de pitchers of Henry Ford and he's a spare-built man and Rockefeller look lak he ain't got but one gut. But Ford and Rockefeller and dis Slemmons and all de rest kin be as many-gutted as dey please, ah'm satisfied wid you jes' lak you is, baby. God took pattern after a pine tree and built you noble. Youse a pritty still man, and if Ah knowed any way to make you mo' pritty still Ah'd take and do it."

Joe reached over gently and toyed with Missie May's ear. "You jes' say dat cause you love me, but Ah know Ah can't hold no light to Otis D. Slemmons. Ah ain't never been nowhere and Ah ain't got nothin' but you."

"How you know dat, Joe."

"He tole us so hisself."

"Dat don't make it so. His mouf is cut cross-ways, ain't it? Well, he kin lie jes' lak anybody els."

"Good Lawd, Missie! You womens sho' is hard to sense into things. He's got a five-dollar gold piece for a stick-pin and he got a ten-dollar gold piece on his watch chain and his mouf is jes' crammed full of gold teethes. Sho' wisht it wuz mine. And whut make it so cool, he got money 'cumulated. And womens give it all to 'im."

"Ah don't see whut de womens see on 'im. Ah wouldn't give 'im a wind if de sherff wuz after 'im."

"Well, he tole us how de white womens in Chicago give 'im all dat gold money. So he don't 'low nobody to touch it at all. Not even put dey finger on it. Dey tole 'im not to. You kin make 'miration at it, but don't tetch it."

"Whyn't he stay up dere where dey so crazy 'bout 'im?"

"Ah reckon dey done made 'im vast-rich and he wants to travel some. He say dey wouldn't leave 'im hit a lick of work. He got mo' lady people crazy 'bout him than he kin shake a stick at."

"Joe, Ah hates to see you so dumb. Dat stray nigger jes' tell y'all anything and y'all b'lieve it."

"Go 'head on now, honey and put on yo' clothes. He talkin' 'bout his pritty womens — Ah want 'im to see *mine*."

Missie May went off to dress and Joe spent the time trying to make his stomach punch out like Slemmons' middle. He tried the rolling swagger of the stranger, but found that his tall bone-and-muscle stride fitted ill with it. He just had time to drop back into his seat before Missie May came in dressed to go.

On the way home that night Joe was exultant. "Didn't Ah say ole Otis was swell? Can't he talk Chicago talk? Wuzn't dat funny whut he said when great big fat ole Ida Armstrong come in? He asted me, 'Who is dat broad wid de forty shake?' Dat's a new word. Us always thought forty was a set of figgers but he showed us where it means a whole heap of things. Sometimes he don't say forty, he jes' say thirty-eight and two and dat mean de same thing. Know whut he tole me when Ah was payin' for our ice cream? He say, 'Ah have to hand it to you, Joe. Dat wife of yours is jes' thirty-eight and two. Yessuh, she's forty!' Ain't he killin?"

"He'll do in case of a rush. But he sho' is got uh heap uh gold on 'im. Dat's de first time Ah ever seed gold money. It looked good on him sho' nuff, but it'd look a whole heap better on you."

"Who, me? Missie May youse crazy! Where would a po' man lak me git gold money from?"

Missie May was silent for a minute, then she said, "Us might find some goin' long de road some time. Us could."

"Who would be losin' gold money 'round heah? We ain't even seen none dese white folks wearin' no gold money on dey watch chain. You must be figgeren' Mister Packard or Mister Cadillac goin' pass through heah . . ."

"You don't know whut been lost 'round heah. Maybe somebody way back in memorial times lost they gold money and went on off and it ain't never been found. And then if we wuz to find it, you could wear some 'thout havin' no gang of womens lak dat Slemmons say he got."

Joe laughed and hugged her. "Don't be so wishful 'bout me. Ah'm satisfied de way Ah is. So long as Ah be yo' husband, Ah don't keer 'bout nothin' else. Ah'd ruther all de other womens in de world to be dead than for you to have de toothache. Less we go to bed and git our night rest."

It was Saturday night once more before Joe could parade his wife in Slemmons' ice cream parlor again. He worked the night shift and Saturday was his only night off. Every other evening around six o'clock he left home, and dying dawn saw him hustling home around the lake where the challenging sun flung a flaming sword from east to west across the trembling water.

That was the best part of life—going home to Missie May. Their whitewashed house, the mock battle on Saturday, the dinner and ice cream parlor afterwards, church on Sunday nights when Missie outdressed any woman in town—all, everything was right.

One night around eleven the acid ran out at the G and G. The foreman knocked off the crew and let the steam die down. As Joe rounded the lake on his way home, a lean moon rode the lake in a silver boat. If anybody had asked Joe about the moon on the lake, he would have said he hadn't paid it any attention. But he saw it with his feelings. It made him yearn painfully for Missie. Creation obsessed him. He thought about children. They had been married for more than a year now. They had money put away. They ought to be making little feet for shoes. A little boy child would be about right.

He saw a dim light in the bedroom and decided to come in through the kitchen door. He could wash the fertilizer dust off himself before presenting himself to Missie May. It would be nice for her not to know that he was there until he slipped into his place in bed and hugged her back. She always liked that.

He eased the kitchen door open slowly and silently, but when he went to set his dinner bucket on the table he bumped it into a pile of dishes, and something crashed to the floor. He heard his wife gasp in fright and hurried to reassure her.

"Iss me, honey. Don't get skeered."

There was a quick, large movement in the bedroom. A rustle, a thud, and a stealthy silence. The light went out.

What? Robbers? Murderers? Some varmint attacking his helpless wife, perhaps. He struck a match, threw himself on guard, and stepped over the door-sill into the bedroom.

The great belt on the wheel of Time slipped and eternity stood still. By the match light he could see the man's legs fighting with his breeches in his frantic desire to get them on. He had both chance and time to kill the intruder in his helpless condition — half-in and half-out of his pants — but he was too weak to take action. The shapeless enemies of humanity that live in the hours of Time had waylaid Joe. He was assaulted in his weakness. Like Samson awakening after his haircut. So he just opened his mouth and laughed.

The match went out and he struck another and lit the lamp. A howling wind raced across his heart, but underneath its fury he heard his wife sobbing and Slemmons pleading for his life. Offering to buy it with all that he had. "Please, suh, don't kill me. Sixty-two dollars at de sto' gold money."

Joe just stood. Slemmons looked at the window, but it was screened. Joe stood out like a rough-backed mountain between him and the door. Barring him from escape, from sunrise, from life.

He considered a surprise attack upon the big clown that stood there laughing like a chessy cat. But before his fist could travel an inch, Joe's own rushed out to crush him like a battering ram. Then Joe stood over him.

"Git into yo' damn rags, Slemmons, and dat quick."

Slemmons scrambled to his feet and into his vest and coat. As he grabbed his hat, Joe's fury overrode his intentions and he grabbed at Slemmons with his left hand and struck at him with his right. The right landed. The left grazed the front of his vest. Slemmons was knocked a somersault into the kitchen and fled through the open door. Joe found himself alone with Missie May, with the golden watch charm clutched in his left fist. A short bit of broken chain dangled between his fingers.

Missie May was sobbing. Wails of weeping without words. Joe stood, and after awhile he found out that he had something in his hand. And then he stood and felt without thinking and without seeing with his natural eyes. Missie May kept on crying and Joe kept on feeling so much and not knowing what to do with all his feelings, he put Slemmons' watch charm in his pants pocket and took a good laugh and went to bed.

"Missie May, whut you crying for?"

"Cause Ah love you so hard and Ah know you don't love *me* no mo'."

Joe sank his face into the pillow for a spell then he said huskily, "You don't know de feelings of dat yet, Missie May."

"Oh Joe, honey, he said he wuz gointer gimme dat gold money and he jes' kept on after me—"

Joe was very still and silent for a long time. Then he said, "Well, don't cry no mo', Missie May. Ah got yo' gold piece for you."

The hours went past on their rusty ankles. Joe still and quiet on one bedrail and Missie May wrung dry of sobs on the other. Finally the sun's tide crept upon the shore of night and drowned all its hours. Missie May with her face stiff and streaked towards the window saw the dawn come into her yard. It was day. Nothing more. Joe wouldn't be coming home as usual. No need to fling open the front door and sweep off the porch, making it nice for Joe. Never no more breakfast to cook; no more washing and starching of Joe's jumper-jackets and pants. No more nothing. So why get up?

With this strange man in her bed, she felt embarrassed to get up and dress. She decided to wait till he had dressed and gone. Then she would get up, dress quickly, and be gone forever beyond reach of Joe's looks and laughs. But he never moved. Red light turned to yellow, then white.

From beyond the no-man's land between them came a voice. A strange voice that yesterday had been Joe's.

"Missie May, ain't you gonna fix me no breakfus'?"

She sprang out of bed. "Yeah, Joe. Ah didn't reckon you wuz hongry."

No need to die today. Joe needed her for a few more minutes anyhow. Soon there was a roaring fire in the cook stove. Water bucket full and two chickens killed. Joe loved fried chicken and rice. She didn't deserve a thing and good Joe was letting her cook him some breakfast. She rushed hot biscuits to the table as Joe took his seat.

He ate with his eyes on his plate. No laughter, no banter.

"Missie May, you ain't eatin' yo' breakfus'."

"Ah don't choose none, Ah thank yuh."

His coffee cup was empty. She sprang to refill it. When she turned from the stove and bent to set the cup beside Joe's plate, she saw the yellow coin on the table between them.

She slumped into her seat and wept into her arms.

Presently Joe said calmly, "Missie May, you cry too much. Don't look back lak Lot's wife and turn to salt."

The sun, the hero of every day, the impersonal old man that beams as brightly on death as on birth, came up every morning and raced across the blue dome and dipped into the sea of fire every evening. Water ran down hill and birds nested.

Missie knew why she didn't leave Joe. She couldn't. She loved him too much. But she couldn't understand why Joe didn't leave her. He was polite, even kind at times, but aloof.

There were no more Saturday romps. No ringing silver dollars to stack beside her plate. No pockets to rifle. In fact the yellow coin in his trousers was like a monster hiding in the cave of his pockets to destroy her.

She often wondered if he still had it, but nothing could have induced her to ask nor yet to explore his pockets to see for herself. Its shadow was in the house whether or no.

One night Joe came home around midnight and complained of pains in the back. He asked Missie to rub him down with liniment. It had been three months since Missie had touched his body and it all seemed strange. But she rubbed him. Grateful for the chance. Before morning, youth triumphed and Missie exulted. But the next day, as she joyfully made up their bed, beneath her pillow she found the piece of money with the bit of chain attached.

Alone to herself, she looked at the thing with loathing, but look she must. She took it into her hands with trembling and saw first thing that it was no gold piece. It was a gilded half-dollar. Then she knew why Slemmons had forbidden anyone to touch his gold. He trusted village eyes at a distance not to recognize his stick-pin as a gilded quarter, and his watch charm as a four-bit piece.

She was glad at first that Joe had left it there. Perhaps he was through with her punishment. They were man and wife again. Then another thought came clawing at her. He had come home to buy from her as if she were any woman in the long house. Fifty cents for her love. As if to say that he could pay as well as Slemmons. She slid the coin into his Sunday pants pocket and dressed herself and left his house.

Halfway between her house and the quarters she met her husband's mother, and after a short talk she turned and went back home. If she had not the substance of marriage, she had the outside show. Joe must leave *her*. She let him see she didn't want his old gold four-bits too.

She saw no more of the coin for some time though she knew that Joe could not help finding it in his pocket. But his health kept poor, and he came home at least every ten days to be rubbed.

The sun swept around the horizon, trailing its robes of weeks and days. One morning as Joe came in from work, he found Missie May chopping wood. Without a word he took the ax and chopped a huge pile before he stopped.

"You ain't got no business choppin' wood, and you know it."

"How come? Ah been choppin' it for de last longest."

"Ah ain't blind. You makin' feet for shoes."

"Won't you be glad to have a li'l baby chile, Joe?"

"You know dat 'thout astin' me."

"Iss gointer be a boy chile and de very spit of you."

"You reckon, Missie May?"

"Who else could it look lak?"

Joe said nothing, but he thrust his hand deep into his pocket and fingered something there.

It was almost six months later Missie May took to bed and Joe went and got his mother to come wait on the house.

Missie May delivered a fine boy. Her travail was over when Joe came in from work one morning. His mother and the old women were drinking great bowls of coffee around the fire in the kitchen.

The minute Joe came into the room his mother called him aside.

"How did Missie May make out?" he asked quickly.

"Who, dat gal? She strong as a ox. She gointer have plenty mo'. We done fixed her wid de sugar and lard to sweeten her for de nex' one."

Joe stood silent awhile.

"You ain't ast 'bout de baby, Joe. You oughter be mighty proud cause he sho' is de spittin' image of yuh, son. Dat's yourn all right, if you never git another one, dat un is yourn. And you know Ah'm mighty proud too, son, cause Ah never thought well of you marryin' Missie May cause her ma used tuh fan her foot 'round right smart and Ah been mighty skeered dat Missie May wuz gointer git misput on her road."

Joe said nothing. He fooled around the house till late in the day then just before he went to work, he went and stood at the foot of the bed and asked his wife how she felt. He did this every day during the week.

On Saturday he went to Orlando to make his market. It had been a long time since he had done that.

Meat and lard, meal and flour, soap and starch. Cans of corn and tomatoes. All the staples. He fooled around town for awhile and bought bananas and apples. Way after while he went around to the candy store.

"Hellow, Joe," the clerk greeted him. "Ain't seen you in a long time."

"Nope, Ah ain't been heah. Been 'round spots and places."

"Want some of them molasses kisses you always buy?"

"Yessuh." He threw the gilded half-dollar on the counter. "Will dat spend?"

"Whut is it, Joe? Well, I'll be doggone! A gold-plated four-bit piece. Where'd you git it, Joe?"

"Offen a stray nigger dat come through Eatonville. He had it on his watch chain for a charm-goin' 'round making out iss gold money. Ha ha! He had a quarter on his tie pin and it wuz all golded up too. Tryin' to fool people. Makin' out he so rich and everything. Ha! Ha! Trying' to tole off folkses wives from home."

"How did you git it, Joe? Did he fool you, too?"

"Who, me? Naw suh! He ain't fooled me none. Know whut Ah done? He come 'round me wid his smart talk. Ah hauled off and knocked 'im down and took his old four-bits 'way from 'im. Gointer buy my wife some good ole 'lasses kisses wid it. Gimme fifty cents worth of dem candy kisses."

"Fifty cents buys a mightly lot of candy kisses, Joe. Why don't you split it up and take some chocolate bars, too. They eat good, too."

"Yessuh, de do, but Ah wants all dat in kisses. Ah got a li'l boy chile home now. Tain't a week old yet, but he kin suck a sugar tit and maybe eat one them kisses hisself."

Joe got his candy and left the store. The clerk turned to the next customer. "Wisht I could be like these darkies. Laughin' all the time. Nothin' worries 'em."

Back in Eatonville, Joe reached his own front door. There was the ring of singing metal on wood. Fifteen times. Missie May couldn't run to the door, but she crept there as quickly as she could.

"Joe Banks, Ah hear you chunkin' money in mah do'way. You wait till Ah got mah strength back and Ah'm gointer fix you for dat."

SHIRLEY JACKSON

Shirley Jackson (1919–1965) was born in San Francisco, her mother a housewife and her father an employee of a lithographing company. Most of her early life was spent in Burlingame, California, which she later used as the setting for her first novel, The Road Through the Wall *(1948). As a child she was interested in writing; she won a poetry prize at age twelve, and in high school she began keeping a diary to record her writing progress. After high school she briefly attended the University of Rochester but left because of an attack of the mental depression that was to recur periodically in her later years. She recovered her health by living quietly at home and writing, conscientiously turning out 1,000 words of prose a day. In 1937 she entered Syracuse University, where she published stories in the student literary magazine. There she met Stanley Edgar Hyman, who was to become a noted literary critic. They were married in 1940, the year she received her degree. They had four children while both continued active literary careers, settling to raise their family in a large Victorian house in Vermont, where Hyman taught literature at Bennington College.*

Jackson's first national publication was a humorous story written after a job at a department store during the Christmas rush: "My Life with R. H. Macy" appeared in The New Republic *in 1941. Her first child was born the next year, but she wrote every day on a disciplined schedule, selling her stories to magazines and publishing three novels. She refused to take herself too seriously as a writer: "I can't persuade myself that writing is honest work. It is a very personal reaction, but 50 percent of my life is spent washing and dressing the children, cooking, washing dishes and clothes, and mending. After I get it all to bed, I turn around to my typewriter and try to — well, to create concrete things again. It's great fun, and I love it. But it doesn't tie any shoes."*

Jackson's best-known work, "The Lottery," is often anthologized, dramatized, and televised. She regarded it as a tale in the sense that Nathaniel Hawthorne used the term — a moral allegory revealing the hidden evil of the human soul. She wrote later that "explaining just what I had hoped the story to say is very difficult. I supposed, I hoped, by setting a particularly brutal ancient rite in the present and in my own village, to shock the story's readers with a graphic dramatization of the pointless violence and general inhumanity in their own lives."

COMMENTARY *Shirley Jackson, "The Morning of June 28, 1948, and 'The Lottery,'" page 571.*

WEB *Research Shirley Jackson and answer questions about her work at bedfordstmartins.com/charters/litwriters.*

The Lottery

1948

The morning of June 27th was clear and sunny, with the fresh warmth of a full-summer day; the flowers were blossoming profusely and the grass was richly green. The people of the village began to gather in the square, between the post office and the bank, around ten o'clock; in some towns there were so many people that the lottery took two days and had to be started on June 26th, but in this village, where there were only about three hundred people, the whole lottery took less than two hours, so it could begin at ten o'clock in the morning and still be through in time to allow the villagers to get home for noon dinner.

The children assembled first, of course. School was recently over for the summer, and the feeling of liberty sat uneasily on most of them; they tended to gather together quietly for a while before they broke into boisterous play, and their talk was still of the classroom and teacher, of books and reprimands. Bobby Martin had already stuffed his pockets full of stones, and the other boys soon followed his example, selecting the smoothest and roundest stones; Bobby and Harry Jones and Dickie Delacroix — the villagers pronounced this name "Dellacroy" — eventually made a great pile of stones in one corner of the square and guarded it against the raids of the other boys. The girls stood aside, talking among themselves, looking over their shoulders at the boys, and the very small children rolled in the dust or clung to the hands of their older brothers or sisters.

Soon the men began to gather, surveying their own children, speaking of planting and rain, tractors and taxes. They stood together, away from the pile of stones in the corner, and their jokes were quiet and they smiled rather than laughed. The women, wearing faded house dresses and sweaters, came shortly after their menfolk. They greeted one another and exchanged bits of gossip as they went to join their husbands. Soon the women, standing by their husbands, began to call to their children, and the children came reluctantly, having to be called four or five times. Bobby Martin ducked under his mother's grasping hand and ran, laughing, back to the pile of stones. His father spoke up sharply, and Bobby came quickly and took his place between his father and his oldest brother.

The lottery was conducted—as were the square dances, the teen-age club, the Halloween program—by Mr. Summers, who had time and energy to devote to civic activities. He was a round-faced, jovial man and he ran the coal business, and people were sorry for him, because he had no children and his wife was a scold. When he arrived in the square, carrying the black wooden box, there was a murmur of conversation among the villagers, and he waved and called, "Little late today, folks." The postmaster, Mr. Graves, followed him, carrying a three-legged stool, and the stool was put in the center of the square and Mr. Summers set the black box down on it. The villagers kept their distance, leaving a space between themselves and the stool, and when Mr. Summers said, "Some of you fellows want to give me a hand?" there was a hesitation before two men, Mr. Martin and his oldest son, Baxter, came forward to hold the box steady on the stool while Mr. Summers stirred up the papers inside it.

The original paraphernalia for the lottery had been lost long ago, and the black box now resting on the stool had been put into use even before Old Man Warner, the oldest man in town, was born. Mr. Summers spoke frequently to the villagers about making a new box, but no one liked to upset even as much tradition as was represented by the black box. There was a story that the present box had been made with some pieces of the box that had preceded it, the one that had been constructed when the first people settled down to make a village here. Every year, after the lottery, Mr. Summers began talking again about a new box, but every year the subject was allowed to fade off without anything's being done. The black box grew shabbier each year; by now it was no longer completely black but splintered badly along one side to show the original wood color, and in some places faded or stained.

Mr. Martin and his oldest son, Baxter, held the black box securely on the stool until Mr. Summers had stirred the papers thoroughly with his hand. Because so much of the ritual had been forgotten or discarded, Mr. Summers had been successful in having slips of paper substituted for the chips of wood that had been used for generations. Chips of wood, Mr. Summers had argued, had been all very well when the village was tiny, but now that the population was more than three hundred and likely to keep on growing, it was necessary to use something that would fit more easily into the black box. The night before the lottery, Mr. Summers and Mr. Graves made up the slips of paper and put them in the box, and it was then taken to the safe of Mr. Summers's coal company and locked up until Mr. Summers was ready to take it to the square next morning. The rest of the year, the box was put away, sometimes one place, sometimes another; it had spent one year in Mr. Graves's barn and another year underfoot in the post office, and sometimes it was set on a shelf in the Martin grocery and left there.

There was a great deal of fussing to be done before Mr. Summers declared the lottery open. There were the lists to make up — of heads of families, heads of households in each family, members of each household in each family. There was the proper swearing-in of Mr. Summers by the postmaster, as the official of the lottery; at one time, some people remembered, there had been a recital of some sort, performed by the official of the lottery, a perfunctory, tuneless chant that had been rattled off duly each year; some people believed that the official of the lottery used to stand just so when he said or sang it, others believed that he was supposed to walk among the people, but years and years ago this part of the ritual had been allowed to lapse. There had been, also, a ritual salute, which the official of the lottery had had to use in addressing each person who came up to draw from the box, but this also had changed with time, until now it was felt necessary only for the official to speak to each person approaching. Mr. Summers was very good at all this; in his clean white shirt and blue jeans, with one hand resting carelessly on the black box, he seemed very proper and important as he talked interminably to Mr. Graves and the Martins.

Just as Mr. Summers finally left off talking and turned to the assembled villagers, Mrs. Hutchinson came hurriedly along the path to the square, her sweater thrown over her shoulders, and slid into place in the back of the crowd. "Clean forgot what day it was," she said to Mrs. Delacroix, who stood next to her, and they both laughed softly. "Thought my old man was out back stacking wood," Mrs. Hutchinson went on, "and then I looked out the window and the kids was gone, and then I remembered it was the twenty-seventh and came a-running." She dried her hands on her apron, and Mrs. Delacroix said, "You're in time, though. They're still talking away up there."

Mrs. Hutchinson craned her neck to see through the crowd and found her husband and children standing near the front. She tapped Mrs. Delacroix on the arm as a farewell and began to make her way through the crowd. The people separated good-humoredly to let her through; two or three people said, in voices just loud enough to be heard across the crowd, "Here comes your Missus, Hutchinson," and "Bill, she made it after all." Mrs. Hutchinson reached her husband, and Mr. Summers, who had been waiting, said cheerfully, "Thought we were going to have to get on without you, Tessie." Mrs. Hutchinson said, grinning, "Wouldn't have me leave m'dishes in the sink, now, would you, Joe?" and soft laughter ran through the crowd as the people stirred back into position after Mrs. Hutchinson's arrival.

"Well, now," Mr. Summers said soberly, "guess we better get started, get this over with, so's we can go back to work. Anybody ain't here?"

"Dunbar," several people said. "Dunbar, Dunbar."

Mr. Summers consulted his list. "Clyde Dunbar," he said. "That's right. He's broke his leg, hasn't he? Who's drawing for him?"

"Me, I guess," a woman said, and Mr. Summers turned to look at her. "Wife draws for her husband," Mr. Summers said. "Don't you have a grown boy to do it for you, Janey?" Although Mr. Summers and everyone else in the village knew the answer perfectly well, it was the business of the official of the lottery to ask such questions formally. Mr. Summers waited with an expression of polite interest while Mrs. Dunbar answered.

"Horace's not but sixteen yet," Mrs. Dunbar said regretfully. "Guess I gotta fill in for the old man this year."

"Right," Mr. Summers said. He made a note on the list he was holding. Then he asked, "Watson boy drawing this year?"

A tall boy in the crowd raised his hand. "Here," he said. "I'm drawing for m'mother and me." He blinked his eyes nervously and ducked his head as several voices in the crowd said things like "Good fellow, Jack," and "Glad to see your mother's got a man to do it."

"Well," Mr. Summers said, "guess that's everyone. Old Man Warner make it?"

"Here," a voice said, and Mr. Summers nodded.

A sudden hush fell on the crowd as Mr. Summers cleared his throat and looked at the list. "All ready?" he called. "Now, I'll read the names — heads of families first — and the men come up and take a paper out of the box. Keep the paper folded in your hand without looking at it until everyone has had a turn. Everything clear?"

The people had done it so many times that they only half listened to the directions; most of them were quiet, wetting their lips, not looking around. Then Mr. Summers raised one hand high and said, "Adams." A man disengaged himself from the crowd and came forward. "Hi, Steve," Mr. Summers said, and Mr. Adams said, "Hi, Joe." They grinned at one another humorlessly and nervously. Then Mr. Adams reached into the black box and took out a folded paper. He held it firmly by one corner as he turned and went hastily back to his place in the crowd, where he stood a little apart from his family, not looking down at his hand.

"Allen," Mr. Summers said, "Anderson. . . . Bentham."

"Seems like there's no time at all between lotteries any more," Mrs. Delacroix said to Mrs. Graves in the back row. "Seems like we got through with the last one only last week."

"Time sure goes fast," Mrs. Graves said.

"Clark. . . . Delacroix."

"There goes my old man," Mrs. Delacroix said. She held her breath while her husband went forward.

"Dunbar," Mr. Summers said, and Mrs. Dunbar went steadily to the box while one of the women said, "Go on, Janey," and another said, "There she goes."

"We're next," Mrs. Graves said. She watched while Mr. Graves came around from the side of the box, greeted Mr. Summers gravely, and selected a slip of paper from the box. By now, all through the crowd there were men holding the small folded papers in their large hands, turning them over and over nervously. Mrs. Dunbar and her two sons stood together, Mrs. Dunbar holding the slip of paper.

"Harburt. . . . Hutchinson."

"Get up there, Bill," Mrs. Hutchinson said, and the people near her laughed.

"Jones."

"They do say," Mr. Adams said to Old Man Warner, who stood next to him, "that over in the north village they're talking of giving up the lottery."

Old Man Warner snorted. "Pack of crazy fools," he said. "Listening to the young folks, nothing's good enough for *them.* Next thing you know, they'll be wanting to go back to living in caves, nobody work any more, live *that* way for a while. Used to be a saying about 'Lottery in June, corn be heavy soon.' First thing you know, we'd all be eating stewed chickweed and acorns. There's *always* been a lottery," he added petulantly. "Bad enough to see young Joe Summers up there joking with everybody."

"Some places have already quit lotteries," Mrs. Adams said.

"Nothing but trouble in *that,*" Old Man Warner said stoutly. "Pack of young fools."

"Martin." And Bobby Martin watched his father go forward. "Over-dyke. . . . Percy."

"I wish they'd hurry," Mrs. Dunbar said to her older son. "I wish they'd hurry."

"They're almost through," her son said.

"You get ready to run tell Dad," Mrs. Dunbar said.

Mr. Summers called his own name and then stepped forward precisely and selected a slip from the box. Then he called, "Warner."

"Seventy-seventh year I been in the lottery," Old Man Warner said as he went through the crowd. "Seventy-seventh time."

"Watson." The tall boy came awkwardly through the crowd. Someone said, "Don't be nervous, Jack," and Mr. Summers said, "Take your time, son."

"Zanini."

After that, there was a long pause, a breathless pause, until Mr. Summers, holding his slip of paper in the air, said, "All right, fellows." For a minute, no one moved, and then all the slips of paper were opened. Suddenly, all the women began to speak at once, saying, "Who is it?" "Who's got it?" "Is it the Dunbars?" "Is it the Watsons?" Then the voices began to say, "It's Hutchinson. It's Bill," "Bill Hutchinson's got it."

"Go tell your father," Mrs. Dunbar said to her older son.

People began to look around to see the Hutchinsons. Bill Hutchinson was standing quiet, staring down at the paper in his hand. Suddenly, Tessie Hutchinson shouted to Mr. Summers, "You didn't give him time enough to take any paper he wanted. I saw you. It wasn't fair!"

"Be a good sport, Tessie," Mrs. Delacroix called, and Mrs. Graves said, "All of us took the same chance."

"Shut up, Tessie," Bill Hutchinson said.

"Well, everyone," Mr. Summers said, "that was done pretty fast, and now we've got to be hurrying a little more to get done in time." He consulted his next list. "Bill," he said, "you draw for the Hutchinson family. You got any other households in the Hutchinsons?"

"There's Don and Eva," Mrs. Hutchinson yelled. "Make *them* take their chance!"

"Daughters drew with their husbands' families, Tessie," Mr. Summers said gently. "You know that as well as anyone else."

"It wasn't *fair*," Tessie said.

"I guess not, Joe," Bill Hutchinson said regretfully. "My daughter draws with her husband's family, that's only fair. And I've got no other family except the kids."

"Then, as far as drawing for families is concerned, it's you," Mr. Summers said in explanation, "and as far as drawing for households is concerned, that's you, too. Right?"

"Right," Bill Hutchinson said.

"How many kids, Bill?" Mr. Summers asked formally.

"Three," Bill Hutchinson said. "There's Bill, Jr., and Nancy, and little Dave. And Tessie and me."

"All right, then," Mr. Summers said. "Harry, you got their tickets back?"

Mr. Graves nodded and held up the slips of paper. "Put them in the box, then," Mr. Summers directed. "Take Bill's and put it in."

"I think we ought to start over," Mrs. Hutchinson said, as quietly as she could. "I tell you it wasn't *fair*. You didn't give him time enough to choose. *Every*body saw that."

Mr. Graves had selected the five slips and put them in the box, and he dropped all the papers but those onto the ground, where the breeze caught them and lifted them off.

"Listen, everybody," Mrs. Hutchinson was saying to the people around her.

"Ready, Bill?" Mr. Summers asked, and Bill Hutchinson, with one quick glance around at his wife and children, nodded.

"Remember," Mr. Summers said, "take the slips and keep them folded until each person has taken one. Harry, you help little Dave." Mr. Graves took the hand of the little boy, who came willingly with him up to the box. "Take a paper out of the box, Davy," Mr. Summers said. Davy put his hand into the box and laughed. "Take just *one* paper," Mr. Summers said. "Harry, you hold it for him." Mr. Graves took the child's hand and removed the folded paper from the tight fist and held it while little Dave stood next to him and looked up at him wonderingly.

"Nancy next," Mr. Summers said. Nancy was twelve, and her school friends breathed heavily as she went forward, switching her skirt, and took a slip daintily from the box. "Bill, Jr.," Mr. Summers said, and Billy, his face red and his feet overlarge, nearly knocked the box over as he got a paper out. "Tessie," Mr. Summers said. She hesitated for a minute, looking around defiantly, and then set her lips and went up to the box. She snatched a paper out and held it behind her.

"Bill," Mr. Summers said, and Bill Hutchinson reached into the box and felt around, bringing his hand out at last with the slip of paper in it.

The crowd was quiet. A girl whispered, "I hope it's not Nancy," and the sound of the whisper reached the edges of the crowd.

"It's not the way it used to be," Old Man Warner said clearly. "People ain't the way they used to be."

"All right," Mr. Summers said. "Open the papers. Harry, you open little Dave's."

Mr. Graves opened the slip of paper and there was a general sigh through the crowd as he held it up and everyone could see that it was blank. Nancy and Bill, Jr., opened theirs at the same time, and both beamed and laughed, turning around to the crowd and holding their slips of paper above their heads.

"Tessie," Mr. Summers said. There was a pause, and then Mr. Summers looked at Bill Hutchinson, and Bill unfolded his paper and showed it. It was blank.

"It's Tessie," Mr. Summers said, and his voice was hushed. "Show us her paper, Bill."

Bill Hutchinson went over to his wife and forced the slip of paper out of her hand. It had a black spot on it, the black spot Mr. Summers had made the night before with the heavy pencil in the coal-company office. Bill Hutchinson held it up and there was a stir in the crowd.

"All right, folks," Mr. Summers said. "Let's finish quickly."

Although the villagers had forgotten the ritual and lost the original black box, they still remembered to use stones. The pile of stones the boys had made earlier was ready; there were stones on the ground with the blowing scraps of paper that had come out of the box. Mrs. Delacroix selected a stone so large she had to pick it up with both hands and turned to Mrs. Dunbar. "Come on," she said. "Hurry up."

Mrs. Dunbar had small stones in both hands, and she said, gasping for breath, "I can't run at all. You'll have to go ahead and I'll catch up with you."

The children had stones already, and someone gave little Davy Hutchinson a few pebbles.

Tessie Hutchinson was in the center of a cleared space by now, and she held her hands out desperately as the villagers moved in on her. "It isn't fair," she said. A stone hit her on the side of the head.

Old Man Warner was saying, "Come on, come on, everyone." Steve Adams was in the front of the crowd of villagers, with Mrs. Graves beside him.

"It isn't fair, it isn't right," Mrs. Hutchinson screamed and then they were upon her.

JAMES JOYCE

James Joyce (1882–1941) was born James Augustine Aloysius Joyce in Rathgar, a suburb of Dublin, during a turbulent era of political change in Ireland. His parents sent him at the age of six to the best Jesuit school, Clongowes Wood College, where he spent three years; but in 1891 his father was no longer able to afford the tuition, and he was withdrawn. During the period of his parents' financial decline, Joyce—a brilliant student—was educated at home and then given free tuition at Belvedere College, where he won prizes for his essays. Shortly after taking his bachelor's degree in 1902 from University College, Dublin, he left Ire-land for Paris, where he attended one class at the Collège de Médecine but dropped out because he could not afford the fees. Nearly starving, he remained in Paris and wrote what he called "Epiphanies." These were notebook jottings of overheard con-versations or passing observations that he later incorporated into his fiction, think-ing that they illuminated in a flash the meaning of a group of apparently unrelated phenomena. In April 1903 Joyce returned to Dublin because his mother was dying. He remained in Ireland for a short time as a teacher, but the following year he went to live abroad again, disillusioned by his home country's political corruption and religious hypocrisy.

Dubliners (1914), a group of fifteen short stories begun in 1904, was Joyce's attempt to "write a chapter of the moral history" of Ireland. He chose Dublin for the setting because that city seemed to him "the center of paralysis," but he also thought of following the book with another titled "Provincials." As if to prove his perception of the extent of stifling moral repression in his country, he had great dif-ficulties getting the book published—a struggle lasting nine years. This so angered and frustrated Joyce that he never again lived in Ireland; he settled in Trieste, Zurich, and Paris and wrote the novels that established him as one of the greatest authors of modern times: A Portrait of the Artist as a Young Man *(1916),* Ulysses *(1922), and* Finnegans Wake *(1939).*

Joyce's stories about the lives of young people, servants, politicians, and the complacent middle class were intended to represent a broad spectrum of Dublin life—not "a collection of tourist impressions" but a penetrating account of the spiritual waste of his times. Today's reader finds it difficult to believe that some sto-ries in Dubliners *could have appeared so scandalous to Joyce's publishers that at one point the plates were destroyed at the printers. As a stylist, Joyce blended a detached sympathy for his subject with a "scrupulous meanness" of observed detail. Instead of dramatic plots, he structured stories such as "Araby" around "epipha-nies"—evanescent moments that reveal "a sudden spiritual manifestation, whether in the vulgarity of speech or of gesture or in a memorable expression of the mind itself."*

WEB   *Research James Joyce and answer questions about his work at bedfordstmartins.com/charters/litwriters.*

Araby   1914

North Richmond Street, being blind, was a quiet street except at the hour when the Christian Brothers' School set the boys free. An uninhabited house of two storeys stood at the blind end, detached from its neighbours in a square ground. The other houses of the street, conscious of decent lives within them, gazed at one another with brown imperturbable faces.

The former tenant of our house, a priest, had died in the back drawing-room. Air, musty from having been long enclosed, hung in all the rooms, and the waste room behind the kitchen was littered with old useless papers. Among these I found a few paper-covered books, the pages of which were curled and damp: *The Abbot*, by Walter Scott, *The Devout Communicant*, and *The Mem-*

oirs of Vidocq. I liked the last best because its leaves were yellow. The wild garden behind the house contained a central apple-tree and a few straggling bushes under one of which I found the late tenant's rusty bicycle-pump. He had been a very charitable priest; in his will he had left all his money to institutions and the furniture of his house to his sister.

When the short days of winter came dusk fell before we had well eaten our dinners. When we met in the street the houses had grown sombre. The space of sky above us was the colour of ever-changing violet and towards it the lamps of the street lifted their feeble lanterns. The cold air stung us and we played till our bodies glowed. Our shouts echoed in the silent street. The career of our play brought us through the dark muddy lanes behind the houses where we ran the gauntlet of the rough tribes from the cottages, to the back doors of the dark dripping gardens where odours arose from the ashpits, to the dark odorous stables where a coachman smoothed and combed the horse or shook music from the buckled harness. When we returned to the street light from the kitchen windows had filled the areas. If my uncle was seen turning the corner we hid in the shadow until we had seen him safely housed. Or if Mangan's sister came out on the doorstep to call her brother in to his tea we watched her from our shadow peer up and down the street. We waited to see whether she would remain or go in and, if she remained, we left our shadow and walked up to Mangan's steps resignedly. She was waiting for us, her figure defined by the light from the half-opened door. Her brother always teased her before he obeyed and I stood by the railings looking at her. Her dress swung as she moved her body and the soft rope of her hair tossed from side to side.

Every morning I lay on the floor in the front parlour watching her door. The blind was pulled down to within an inch of the sash so that I could not be seen. When she came out on the doorstep my heart leaped. I ran to the hall, seized my books, and followed her. I kept her brown figure always in my eye and, when we came near the point at which our ways diverged, I quickened my pace and passed her. This happened morning after morning. I had never spoken to her, except for a few casual words, and yet her name was like a summons to all my foolish blood.

Her image accompanied me even in places the most hostile to romance. On Saturday evenings when my aunt went marketing I had to go to carry some of the parcels. We walked through the flaring streets, jostled by drunken men and bargaining women, amid the curses of labourers, the shrill litanies of shop-boys who stood on guard by the barrel of pigs' cheeks, the nasal chanting of street-singers, who sang a *come-all-you* about O'Donovan Rossa,° or a ballad about the troubles in our native land. These noises converged in a single sensation of life for me: I imagined that I bore my chalice safely through a throng of foes. Her name sprang to my lips at moments in strange prayers and praises which I myself did not understand. My eyes were often full of tears (I could not tell why) and at times a flood from my heart seemed to pour itself out into my

---

O'Donovan Rossa: Jeremiah O'Donovan (1831–1915), born in Ross Carberry of County Cork, was nicknamed "Dynamite Rossa" for championing violent means to achieve Irish independence.

bosom. I thought little of the future. I did not know whether I would ever speak to her or not or, if I spoke to her, how I could tell her of my confused adoration. But my body was like a harp and her words and gestures were like fingers running upon the wires.

One evening I went into the back drawing-room in which the priest had died. It was a dark rainy evening and there was no sound in the house. Through one of the broken panes I heard the rain impinge upon the earth, the fine incessant needles of water playing in the sodden beds. Some distant lamp or lighted window gleamed below me. I was thankful that I could see so little. All my senses seemed to desire to veil themselves and, feeling that I was about to slip from them, I pressed the palms of my hands together until they trembled, murmuring: *"O love! O love!"* many times.

At last she spoke to me. When she addressed the first words to me I was so confused that I did not know what to answer. She asked me was I going to *Araby.* I forgot whether I answered yes or no. It would be a splendid bazaar, she said she would love to go.

"And why can't you?" I asked.

While she spoke she turned a silver bracelet round and round her wrist. She could not go, she said, because there would be a retreat that week in her convent. Her brother and two other boys were fighting for their caps and I was alone at the railings. She held one of the spikes, bowing her head towards me. The light from the lamp opposite our door caught the white curve of her neck, lit up her hair that rested there and, falling, lit up the hand upon the railing. It fell over one side of her dress and caught the white border of a petticoat, just visible as she stood at ease.

"It's well for you," she said.

"If I go," I said, "I will bring you something."

What innumerable follies laid waste my waking and sleeping thoughts after that evening! I wished to annihilate the tedious intervening days. I chafed against the work of school. At night in my bedroom and by day in the classroom her image came between me and the page I strove to read. The syllables of the word *Araby* were called to me through the silence in which my soul luxuriated and cast an Eastern enchantment over me. I asked for leave to go to the bazaar on Saturday night. My aunt was surprised and hoped it was not some Freemason affair. I answered few questions in class. I watched my master's face pass from amiability to sternness; he hoped I was not beginning to idle. I could not call my wandering thoughts together. I had hardly any patience with the serious work of life which, now that it stood between me and my desire, seemed to me child's play, ugly monotonous child's play.

On Saturday morning I reminded my uncle that I wished to go to the bazaar in the evening. He was fussing at the hallstand, looking for the hat-brush, and answered me curtly:

"Yes, boy, I know."

As he was in the hall I could not go into the front parlour and lie at the window. I left the house in bad humour and walked slowly towards the school. The air was pitilessly raw and already my heart misgave me.

When I came home to dinner my uncle had not yet been home. Still it was early. I sat staring at the clock for some time and, when its ticking began to irritate me, I left the room. I mounted the staircase and gained the upper part of the house. The high cold empty gloomy rooms liberated me and I went from room to room singing. From the front window I saw my companions playing below in the street. Their cries reached me weakened and indistinct and, leaning my forehead against the cool glass, I looked over at the dark house where she lived. I may have stood there for an hour, seeing nothing but the brown-clad figure cast by my imagination, touched discreetly by the lamplight at the curved neck, at the hand upon the railings and at the border below the dress.

When I came downstairs again I found Mrs. Mercer sitting at the fire. She was an old garrulous woman, a pawnbroker's widow, who collected used stamps for some pious purpose. I had to endure the gossip of the tea-table. The meal was prolonged beyond an hour and still my uncle did not come. Mrs. Mercer stood up to go: she was sorry she couldn't wait any longer, but it was after eight o'clock and she did not like to be out late, as the night air was bad for her. When she had gone I began to walk up and down the room, clenching my fists. My aunt said:

"I'm afraid you may put off your bazaar for this night of Our Lord."

At nine o'clock I heard my uncle's latchkey in the halldoor. I heard him talking to himself and heard the hallstand rocking when it had received the weight of his overcoat. I could interpret these signs. When he was midway through his dinner I asked him to give me the money to go to the bazaar. He had forgotten.

"The people are in bed and after their first sleep now," he said.

I did not smile. My aunt said to him energetically:

"Can't you give him the money and let him go? You've kept him late enough as it is."

My uncle said he was very sorry he had forgotten. He said he believed in the old saying: "All work and no play makes Jack a dull boy." He asked me where I was going and, when I had told him a second time he asked me did I know *The Arab's Farewell to his Steed.* When I left the kitchen he was about to recite the opening lines of the piece to my aunt.

I held a florin° tightly in my hand as I strode down Buckingham Street towards the station. The sight of the streets thronged with buyers and glaring with gas recalled to me the purpose of my journey. I took my seat in a third-class carriage of a deserted train. After an intolerable delay the train moved out of the station slowly. It crept onward among ruinous houses and over the twinkling river. At Westland Row Station a crowd of people pressed to the carriage doors; but the porters moved them back, saying that it was a special train for the bazaar. I remained alone in the bare carriage. In a few minutes the train drew up beside an improvised wooden platform. I passed out on to the road and saw by the lighted dial of a clock that it was ten minutes to ten. In front of me was a large building which displayed the magical name.

---

florin: A silver coin worth two shillings.

I could not find any sixpenny entrance and, fearing that the bazaar would be closed, I passed in quickly through a turnstile, handing a shilling to a weary-looking man. I found myself in a big hall girdled at half its height by a gallery. Nearly all the stalls were closed and the greater part of the hall was in darkness. I recognised a silence like that which pervades a church after a service. I walked into the centre of the bazaar timidly. A few people were gathered about the stalls which were still open. Before a curtain, over which the words *Café Chantant* were written in coloured lamps, two men were counting money on a salver. I listened to the fall of the coins.

Remembering with difficulty why I had come I went over to one of the stalls and examined porcelain vases and flowered tea-sets. At the door of the stall a young lady was talking and laughing with two young gentlemen. I remarked their English accents and listened vaguely to their conversation.

"O, I never said such a thing!"

"O, but you did!"

"O, but I didn't!"

"Didn't she say that?"

"Yes. I heard her."

"O, there's a . . . fib!"

Observing me the young lady came over and asked me did I wish to buy anything. The tone of her voice was not encouraging; she seemed to have spoken to me out of a sense of duty. I looked humbly at the great jars that stood like eastern guards at either side of the dark entrance to the stall and murmured:

"No, thank you."

The young lady changed the position of one of the vases and went back to the two young men. They began to talk of the same subject. Once or twice the young lady glanced at me over her shoulder.

I lingered before her stall, though I knew my stay was useless, to make my interest in her wares seem the more real. Then I turned away slowly and walked down the middle of the bazaar. I allowed the two pennies to fall against the sixpence in my pocket. I heard a voice call from one end of the gallery that the light was out. The upper part of the hall was now completely dark.

Gazing up into the darkness I saw myself as a creature driven and derided by vanity; and my eyes burned with anguish and anger.

FRANZ KAFKA

Franz Kafka (1883–1924), who said that a book should serve as "an axe to break up the frozen sea within us," led a life whose events are simple and sad. He was born into a Jewish family in Prague, and from youth onward he feared his authoritarian father so much that he stuttered in his presence, although he spoke easily with others. In 1906 he received a doctorate in jurisprudence, and for many years he worked a tedious job as a civil service lawyer investigating claims at the state Worker's Accident Insurance Institute. He never married and lived for the most part with his parents, writing fiction at night (he was an insomniac) and publishing only a few slim volumes of stories during his lifetime. Meditation, a collection of sketches, appeared in 1912; The Stoker: A Fragment in 1913; The Metamorphosis in 1915; The Judgment in 1916; In the Penal Colony in 1919; and A Country Doctor in 1920. Only a few of his friends knew that Kafka was also at work on the great novels that were published after his death from tuberculosis: The Trial (1925), The Castle (1926), and Amerika (1927). (He asked his literary executor, Max Brod, to burn these works in manuscript, but Brod refused.)

Kafka's despair with his writing, his job, his father, and his life was complete. Like Gustave Flaubert—whom he admired—he used his fiction as a "rock" to which he clung in order not to be drowned in the waves of the world around him. With typical irony, however, he saw the effort as futile: "By scribbling I run ahead of myself in order to catch myself up at the finishing post. I cannot run away from myself." In his diaries Kafka recorded his obsession with literature: "What will be my fate as a writer is very simple. My talent for portraying my dreamlike inner life has thrust all other matters into the background." "A Hunger Artist" is one of Kafka's most striking "parables of alienation," as his biographer Ernst Pawel has noted, but the "dreamlike" quality of his imagination is apparent in all his work.

The hero of "The Metamorphosis," Gregor Samsa (pronounced Zamza), is the son of philistine, middle-class parents in Prague, as was Kafka, and literary critics have tended to interpret the story as an autobiographical fiction, in which Kafka projected his sense of inadequacy before his demanding father. Kafka himself considered psychoanalysis "a helpless error," regarding Freud's theories as very rough pictures that do not do justice to either the details or the essence of life. The Russian author Vladimir Nabokov has suggested that the greatest literary influence on Kafka was Flaubert, who also used language with ironic precision and without explicit intrusion of his private sentiments. The visionary, nightmarish quality of Kafka's fiction is in striking contrast to its precise and formal style, the clarity of which intensifies the dark richness of the fantasy.

COMMENTARIES Ann Charters, "Translating Kafka," page 551; John Updike, "Kafka and 'The Metamorphosis,'" page 599.

WEB Research Franz Kafka and answer questions about his work at bedfordstmartins.com/charters/litwriters.

A Hunger Artist   1924

TRANSLATED BY ANN CHARTERS

In recent decades the public's interest in the art of fasting has suffered a marked decline. While formerly it used to pay very well to stage large exhibitions of this kind under private management, today this is quite impossible. Those were different times. Back then the whole town was engaged with the hunger artist; during his fast, the audience's involvement grew from day to day; everyone wanted to see the hunger artist at least once a day; during the later stages subscribers used to sit in specially reserved seats in front of the small barred cage all day long; there were even exhibitions at night by torch-light to heighten the effect; on fine days his cage was carried out into the open, and that was particularly the time when the hunger artist was shown to chil-dren; while for the adults he was often just an entertainment in which they took part because it happened to be in fashion, for the children, who stood open-mouthed, holding each other's hands for safety's sake, watching him as he sat there on the straw spread out for him, even spurning a chair, he was a pale fig-ure in a black leotard with enormously protruding ribs, sometimes nodding politely, answering questions with a forced smile, occasionally even stretching his arm through the bars to let them feel how skinny he was, but then again withdrawing completely into himself, paying attention to no one, not even noticing the striking of the clock, so important for him, the only piece of furni-ture in his cage, but merely staring into space with his eyes almost shut, taking a sip now and then from a tiny glass of water to moisten his lips.

Besides the changing spectators there were also permanent guards selected by the public—strangely enough, usually butchers—who had the job of watching the hunger artist day and night always three at a time to make sure that he didn't consume any nourishment in some secret manner. But this was no more than a formality introduced to reassure the public, because insiders knew well enough that during his fast, the hunger artist would never, under any circumstances, not even under duress, swallow the smallest crumb; his code of honor as an artist forbade it. Not every watchman, of course, was capable of understanding this; often there were groups of night guards who were very lax in carrying out their duties and deliberately congregated in a far corner and absorbed themselves in a game of cards, obviously intending to give the hunger artist the chance to take a little refreshment, which they assumed he could produce from some secret stash. Nothing was more tormenting to the hunger artist than such watchmen; they made him miserable; they made his fasting seem terribly difficult; sometimes he would overcome his physical weakness and sing for as long as he could keep it up during their watch, to show how unfair their suspicions were. But that was of little use; they only marveled at his skill in being able to eat even while singing. He much preferred the guards who sat right up against the bars and who weren't satisfied with the dim night lighting in the hall and so trained on him the beams of the flashlights sup-plied to them by his manager. The harsh light didn't disturb him at all, since he wasn't able to sleep deeply anyway, whereas he could always doze off a little whatever the light or the hour, even in the overcrowded, noisy hall. He was quite prepared to spend the whole night entirely without sleep with such watchmen; he was prepared to swap jokes with them, to tell them stories about his nomadic life and listen to their stories in turn, anything just to keep them awake, to be able to show them again and again that he had nothing to eat in his cage and that he was fasting like no one of them could fast. But he was happiest when morning came and a lavish breakfast was served to them at his expense, on which they threw themselves with the appetites of healthy men after a weary night's vigil. Of course there were even people who would see this breakfast as an attempt to bribe the guards, but that was really going too far, and when these people were asked if they would be willing to take over the night watch without breakfast, just for the sake of the cause, they slunk away, though they stuck to their suspicions all the same.

But suspicions of this nature were really inseparable from fasting. No one, after all, was capable of spending all his days and nights continuously watching the hunger artist, so no one could be absolutely certain from first-hand knowledge that his fasting had truly been an unbroken and faultless performance; only the hunger artist himself could know that, and only he, therefore, could be at the same time both the performer and the satisfied spectator of his own fasting. Yet there was another reason why he was never satisfied; perhaps it wasn't only his fasting that made him so emaciated that many people, much to their regret, couldn't attend his performances because they couldn't bear the sight of him; perhaps he had become so emaciated from dissatisfaction with himself. For he alone knew something that not even other insiders knew: how easy it was to fast. It was the easiest thing in the world. He made no secret of this, either, though no one believed him; at best some thought him modest, but mostly they regarded him as a publicity seeker or even took him for a fraud, a person for whom fasting was easy because he knew how to make it easy and then also even had the audacity more or less to admit it. He was forced to endure all of this, he'd even grown accustomed to it all in the course of time, but inwardly his own dissatisfaction gnawed at him, yet never after a single fasting period — you had to grant him this much — had he voluntarily left his cage. The manager had set forty days as the maximum period of the fasting; he would never allow a fast to run beyond this limit, not even in the major cities, and for good reason. Experience had shown that the public's interest in any town could be stimulated for about forty days by increasing the advertisements, but then the public lost interest, and a substantial drop in attendance was noted; naturally there were small variations in this matter between the different towns and regions, but as a rule forty days was the limit. So then on the fortieth day the gate of the flower-decorated cage was opened, an enthusiastic crowd of spectators filled the hall, a military band played, two doctors entered the cage to take the hunger artist's vital measurements, the results were announced to the audience through a megaphone, and finally two young ladies came forward, pleased that they had won the lottery for the honor of leading the hunger artist out of the cage and down a few steps toward a small table where a carefully prepared invalid's meal was served. And at this point, the hunger artist always resisted. True, he willingly surrendered his bony arms to the outstretched hands of these solicitous ladies as they bent down to him, but he refused to stand up. Why stop now, after just forty days? He could have kept going for much longer, infinitely longer; why stop now when he was at his best — indeed, when he had not yet even reached his best fasting form? Why did they want to rob him of the glory of fasting longer, not only of being the greatest hunger artist of all time, which he probably already was — but also of surpassing himself to achieve the unimaginable, because he felt that his capacity to fast was limitless. Why had this audience, which pretended to admire him so much, had so little patience with him; if he could endure fasting longer, why couldn't they endure it? Besides, he was tired, he was comfortable sitting in straw, and now he was supposed to stand upright and go to a meal; the thought alone nauseated him to such a point that he was prevented from expressing it with great difficulty, only out of regard for the ladies. And he gazed up into the eyes of the ladies, who appeared so friendly but were actually so cruel, and shook his head, which weighed heavily on his feeble neck. But then what happened was always what happened. The manager came forward, silently raised his arms over the hunger artist—the band music made speech impossible—as if he were calling upon heaven to look down on its handiwork there in the straw; on this pathetic martyr, which the hunger artist certainly was, only in an entirely different sense; he grasped the hunger artist around his emaciated waist with exaggerated care as if to suggest what a feeble object he had to deal with here; and giving him a secret shake or two, so that the hunger artist's legs and upper body wobbled to and fro, he handed him over to the care of the ladies, who had turned deathly pale in the meantime. Now the hunger artist submitted to everything; his head lay on his chest, as if it had rolled there by chance and stopped itself inexplicably; his body was hollowed out; his legs were squeezed tightly together at the knees in some instinct of self-preservation, but his feet were scraping at the ground, as if it weren't the real ground—they were still seeking the real ground; and the entire weight of his body, admittedly very modest, lay on one of the ladies, who—looking around for help, with panting breath—this wasn't how she had pictured her position of honor—first craned her neck back as far as possible, at least to keep her face from touching the hunger artist, then finding this impossible, when her more fortunate companion didn't come to her aid, instead contenting herself with carrying before her the small bundle of bones that was the hunger artist's hand, the first lady burst into tears amid the audience's delighted laughter and had to be replaced by an attendant who had been standing by in readiness. Then came the meal, a little of which the manager spooned into the nearly unconscious, comatose hunger artist to the accompaniment of cheerful patter designed to divert attention away from the hunger artist's condition; then came the toast drunk to the audience, which the hunger artist allegedly whispered to the manager; the band concluded everything with a great fanfare; the crowd melted away, and nobody had any cause to feel dissatisfied with the show, no one, only the hunger artist, always just him alone.

So he lived for many years with regular short periods of rest, in apparent glory honored by the world, yet in spite of that mostly in a dark mood that became even darker because no one took it seriously. And indeed, how could anyone have comforted him? What more could he wish for? And if once in awhile some good natured soul came along and felt sorry for him and tried to explain to him that his depression was probably caused by his fasting, it sometimes happened, especially if his fast were well advanced, that the hunger artist responded with a burst of rage and to everyone's alarm began to shake the bars of his cage like a wild beast. But the manager had a method of punishment that he was fond of using in such cases. He would apologize publicly to the assembled audience for the hunger artist, admitting that his behavior could only be excused as an irritable condition brought on by his fasting, something that well-fed people by no means could easily understand; in this connection, he would go on to speak of the hunger artist's claim that he was able to fast for a much longer time than he did fast; the manager praised the high aspirations, the good will, the great measure of self-denial undoubtedly implicit in this claim; but then he would seek to refute this claim simply enough by producing photographs, which were at the same time offered for sale to the public; for these pictures showed the hunger artist on his fortieth day of fasting, in bed, almost dead from exhaustion. This perversion of the truth, which assuredly was familiar to the hunger artist, always unnerved him anew and was too much for him. Here the result of the premature ending of his fast was presented as its cause! To fight against this lack of understanding, against this world of ignorance, was impossible. Up to that point he always stood clinging to the bars of his cage, listening eagerly to the manager in good faith, but as soon as the photographs appeared he would let go and sink back with a groan onto his straw, and the reassured public could come close again and inspect him.

When the witnesses to such scenes recalled them a few years later, they often failed to understand them at all. For in the meantime, the previously mentioned decline of the public's interest in fasting had occurred; it seemed to happen almost overnight; there may have been deeper reasons for it, but who cared about digging them up; in any case, the day came when the hunger artist found himself deserted by the pleasure-seeking crowds, who went streaming past him toward other exhibitions. For one last time his manager dragged him across half Europe to see if the old interest might be revived here and there; all in vain, it was as if a repulsion for exhibition fasting had set in everywhere by secret pact. In reality it couldn't have come about so suddenly, of course, and people now belatedly recalled a number of warning signs that had neither been adequately noted nor adequately dealt with in the flush of success, but now it was too late for countermeasures. Of course fasting would surely make a comeback some day, but that was no comfort to the living. What should the hunger artist do now? He who had been applauded by thousands couldn't appear as a sideshow in village fairs, and as for starting a new profession, the hunger artist was not merely too old, but he was also, above all, too fanatically devoted to his fasting. So he took leave of his manager, his companion throughout an unparalleled career, and found an engagement for himself with a large circus; in order to spare his own feelings, he avoided reading the terms of his contract.

A large circus, with its immense number of personnel and animals and apparatus, all constantly replacing and supplementing one another, can always find a use for anyone at any time, even a hunger artist, provided, of course, that his demands are sufficiently modest, and furthermore in this particular case it wasn't just the hunger artist himself who was being booked, but also his long-famous name; indeed, considering the peculiar nature of his art, which doesn't decrease with advancing age, one couldn't even say that he was a superannuated artist, past his prime, and seeking refuge in a quiet circus job; on the contrary, the hunger artist pledged that he could fast just as well as ever, which was clearly believable; in fact, he even claimed that if they let him have his way, as they readily promised him, he would truly astound the world by setting a new record, a claim that only provoked a smile from the experts, considering the public's current mood, which the hunger artist, in his enthusiasm, was apt to forget.

Basically, however, the hunger artist hadn't lost his sense of the real situation, and he accepted it as self-evident that he and his cage would not be placed as a star attraction in the center ring, but rather would be offered as a sideshow in a readily accessible site near the animal cages. Large, brightly colored posters made a frame for his cage and proclaimed what was to be seen there. When the audience came pouring out during the intermission to look at the animals, they almost inevitably had to pass the hunger artist's cage and stop there for a moment; they would perhaps have stayed longer, if those pressing them from behind in the narrow passageway, who couldn't understand the delay on the path to the animals they were so eager to see, hadn't made a longer, more leisurely contemplation impossible. This was also the reason why the hunger artist, who naturally looked forward to these visiting periods as his purpose in life, trembled at their prospect as well. At first he could hardly wait for the intermissions; he had been delighted watching the crowds come surging toward him, until it was made clear to him only too soon—not even the most obstinate, almost deliberate self-deception could obscure the fact—that most of these people, to judge from their actions, were again and again without exception on their way to the wild animals. And that first sight of them from a distance always remained the best. For as soon as they had reached him, he was immediately deafened by the shouting and cursing from the two contending factions which kept continuously forming—those who wanted to stop and stare at him (and the hunger artist soon found them the more distasteful) out of no real interest but only just as a whim or out of defiance, and those others who only wanted to go straight to the animal cages. Once the first rush was over, then came the stragglers, and these, who had nothing to prevent them from stopping as long as they liked, hurried by with long strides, without hardly even a side glance at him, as they rushed to see the animals in the remaining time. And it was an all too rare stroke of luck when the father of a family came along with his children, pointed to the hunger artist, explained in detail what was happening, told stories about earlier years when he himself had witnessed similar but incomparably more splendid performances, but then the children, since they hadn't been sufficiently prepared by either school or life, remained rather uncomprehending—what was fasting to them?—yet the gleam of their inquisitive eyes suggested something new to come, better and more merciful times. Perhaps, the hunger artist sometimes said to himself, things could become a little better if his cage were located not so close to the animal cages. That made the choice of destination too easy for people, to say nothing of how the stench of the stables, the restlessness of the animals at night, the serving of raw meat to the beasts of prey, and the roars at feeding time constantly offended and depressed him. But he did not dare to complain to the management; after all, he had the animals to thank for the throng of visitors, among them here and there even someone who was there just to see him; and who could tell where they might hide him if he called attention to his existence and thereby to the fact that, strictly speaking, he was no more than an obstacle in the path to the animals.

A small obstacle, to be sure, an obstacle growing smaller all the time. It has become customary nowadays to want to find it strange to call attention to a hunger artist, and in accordance with this custom his fate was sealed. He might fast as much as he could, and indeed he did, but nothing could save him now, people passed him by. Just try to explain the art of fasting to someone! Someone who doesn't feel it cannot be made to understand it. The colorful posters became dirty and illegible, they were torn down and no one thought to replace them; the little signboard tallying the number of days fasted, which at first had been carefully changed every day, had long remained the same, for after the first few weeks the staff had grown tired of even this small task; and so the hunger artist just went on fasting as he had once dreamed of doing, and it was indeed no trouble for him to do so, as he had always predicted, but no one counted the days; no one, not even the hunger artist himself, knew how great his achievement was, and his heart grew heavy. And once in a while, when some casual passer-by stopped, ridiculed the outdated number on the board, and talked about a hoax, that was in its way the stupidest lie ever invented by indifference and inherent malice, since the hunger artist didn't cheat, he was working honestly, but the world was cheating him of his reward.

So again many more days passed and there came an end to that as well. One day a supervisor happened to notice the cage, and he asked the attendants why this perfectly useful cage with the rotten straw in it was left unoccupied; no one knew, until somebody with the help of the signboard remembered the hunger artist. They poked into the straw with sticks and found the hunger artist underneath. "Are you still fasting?" asked the supervisor. "When on earth do you mean to stop?" "Forgive me, everybody," whispered the hunger artist; only the supervisor, who pressed his ear against the bars, understood him. "Certainly," said the supervisor, tapping his finger at the side of his forehead to suggest the hunger artist's condition to the staff, "we forgive you." "I always wanted you to admire my fasting," said the hunger artist. "We do admire it," said the supervisor obligingly. "But you shouldn't admire it," said the hunger artist. "All right, then, we don't admire it," said the supervisor, "but why shouldn't we admire it?" "Because I have to fast, I can't help it," said the hunger artist. "How about that," said the supervisor. "Why can't you help it?" "Because," said the hunger artist, lifting his shriveled head a little, and puckering his lips as if for a kiss, he spoke right into the supervisor's ear, so that nothing would be missed, "because I couldn't find the food I liked. If I had found it, believe me, I shouldn't have made any fuss and stuffed myself just like you and everyone else." These were his last words, but in his dying eyes there remained the firm, if no longer proud, conviction that he was still continuing to fast.

"Now clear this out!" said the supervisor, and they buried the hunger artist, straw and all. Then they put a young panther into the cage. Even the most insensitive felt it was refreshing to see this wild creature leaping about in a cage that had been neglected for so long. He lacked for nothing. The food that he liked was brought to him by his keepers without hesitation; he didn't even appear to miss his freedom; that noble body, full to almost bursting with all he needed, seemed to carry freedom itself around with it; it appeared to be placed somewhere in his jaws; and the joy of life streamed with such ardent passion from his throat, that it wasn't easy for the onlookers to withstand it. But they braced themselves, surrounded the cage, and never wanted to move on.

The Metamorphosis

1915

TRANSLATED BY ANN CHARTERS

I

As Gregor Samsa awoke one morning from troubled dreams, he found himself transformed in his bed into a monstrous insect. He was lying on his hard, armor-plated back, and when he lifted his head a little he could see his dome-like brown belly divided into bow shaped ridges, on top of which the precariously perched bed quilt was about to slide off completely. His numerous legs, pitiably thin compared to the rest of him, fluttered helplessly before his eyes.

"What has happened to me?" he thought. It was no dream. His room — a normal, though rather small, human bedroom — lay quiet within its four familiar walls. Above the table, where a collection of cloth samples was unpacked and laid out — Samsa was a traveling salesman — hung the picture that he had recently cut from an illustrated magazine and put in a pretty gilt frame. It showed a lady wearing a small fur hat and a fur stole, sitting upright, holding out to the viewer a heavy fur muff into which her entire forearm had vanished.

Then Gregor looked toward the window, and the dreary weather — he heard the rain falling on the metal ledge of the window — made him feel quite melancholy. "What if I went back to sleep again for awhile and forgot about all this nonsense?" he thought, but it was absolutely impossible, since he was used to sleeping on his right side, and he was unable to get into that position in his present state. No matter how hard he tried to heave himself over onto his right side, he always rocked onto his back again. He tried a hundred times, closing his eyes so he wouldn't have to look at his wriggly legs, and he didn't give up until he began to feel a faint, dull ache in his side that he had never felt before.

"Oh God," he thought, "what a hard job I picked for myself! Traveling day in and day out. Much more stressful than working in the home office; on top of that, the strain of traveling, the worry about making connections, the bad meals at all hours, meeting new people, no real human contact, no one who ever becomes a friend. The devil take it all!" He felt a slight itch on top of his belly; slowly he pushed himself on his back closer to the bedpost, so he could lift his head better; he found the itchy place, which was covered with little white spots he couldn't identify; he tried to touch the place with one of his legs, but he immediately drew it back, for the contact sent icy shudders through his entire body.

He slid back to his former position. "Getting up so early like this," he thought, "makes you quite stupid. A man has to have his sleep. Other traveling salesmen live like women in a harem. For instance, when I return to the hotel during the morning to write up my orders, I find these gentlemen just sitting down to breakfast. I should try that with my boss; I would be fired on the spot. Anyway, who knows if that wouldn't be a good thing for me after all. If it weren't for my parents, I would have quit long ago, I would have gone to the boss and told him off. That would knock him off his desk! It's a strange thing, too, the way he sits on top of his desk and talks down to his employees from this height, especially since he's hard of hearing and we have to come so close to him. Now, I haven't totally given up hope; as soon as I've saved the money to pay back what my parents owe him — that should take another five or six years — I'll certainly do it. Then I'll take the big step. Right now, though, I have to get up, because my train leaves at five."

He looked over at the alarm clock, which was ticking on the chest of drawers. "Heavenly Father," he thought. It was half past six, and the hands of the clock were quietly moving forward; in fact, it was after half past, it was nearly quarter to seven. Was it possible the alarm hadn't rung? He saw from the bed that it was correctly set at four o'clock; surely it had rung. Yes, but was it possible to sleep peacefully right through that furniture-rattling noise? Well, he hadn't exactly slept peacefully, but probably all the more soundly. What should he do now? The next train left at seven o'clock; to catch it, he would have to rush like mad, and his samples weren't even packed yet, and he definitely didn't feel particularly fresh and rested. And even if he did catch the train, he wouldn't escape a scene with his boss, since the firm's office boy would have been waiting at the five o'clock train and would have reported back to the office long ago that he hadn't turned up. The office boy was the boss's own creature, without backbone or brains. Now, what if he called in sick? But that would be embarrassing, and it would look suspicious, because in the five years he'd been with the company, he'd never been sick before. His boss would be sure to show up with the doctor from the Health Insurance; he'd reproach his parents for their son's laziness, and he'd cut short any excuses by repeating the doctor's argument that people don't get sick, they're just lazy. And in this case, would he be so wrong? The fact was that except for being drowsy, which was certainly unnecessary after his long sleep, Gregor felt quite well, and he was even hungrier than usual.

As he was hurriedly turning all these thoughts over in his mind, still not able to decide to get out of bed — the alarm clock was just striking a quarter to seven — he heard a cautious tap on the door, close by the head of his bed. "Gregor" — someone called — it was his mother — "it's a quarter to seven. Didn't you want to leave?" That gentle voice! Gregor was shocked when he heard his own voice reply; it was unmistakably his old familiar voice, but mixed with it could be heard an irrepressible undertone of painful squeaking, which left the words clear for only a moment, immediately distorting their sound so that you didn't know if you had really heard them right. Gregor would have liked to answer fully and explain everything, but under the circumstances, he contented himself by saying, "Yes, yes, thank you, mother. I'm just getting up." No doubt the wooden door between them must have kept her from noticing the change in Gregor's voice, for his mother was reassured with his announcement and shuffled off. But because of this brief conversation, the other family members had become aware that Gregor unexpectedly was still at home, and soon his father began knocking on a side door softly, but with his fist. "Gregor, Gregor," he called, "what's the matter with you?" And after a little while, in a deeper, warning tone, "Gregor! Gregor!" At the other side door, his sister was asking plaintively, "Gregor, aren't you feeling well? Do you need anything?" To both sides of the room, Gregor answered, "I'm getting ready," and he forced himself to pronounce each syllable carefully and to separate his words by inserting long pauses, so his voice sounded normal. His father went back to his breakfast, but his sister whispered, "Gregor, open the door, please do." But Gregor had no intention of opening the door, and he congratulated himself on having developed the prudent habit during his travels of always locking all doors during the night, even at home.

As a start, he would get up quietly and undisturbed, get dressed, and — what was most important — eat breakfast, and then he would consider what to do next, since he realized that he would never come to a sensible conclusion about the situation if he stayed in bed. He remembered how many times before, perhaps when he was lying in bed in an unusual position, he had felt slight pains that turned out to be imaginary when he got up, and he was looking forward to finding out how this morning's fantasy would fade away. As for the change in his voice, he didn't doubt at all that it was nothing more than the first warning of a serious cold, a traveling salesman's occupational hazard.

It was easy to push off the quilt; all he had to do was to take a deep breath and it fell off by itself. But things got difficult with the next step, especially since he was now much broader. He could have used hands and arms to prop himself up, but all he had were his numerous little legs that never stopped moving in all directions and that he couldn't control at all. Whenever he tried to bend one of his legs, that was the first one to straighten itself out; and when it was finally doing what he wanted it to do, then all the other legs waved uncontrollably, in very painful agitation. "There's simply no use staying idle in bed," said Gregor to himself.

The first thing he meant to do was get the lower part of his body out of bed, but this lower part, which he still hadn't seen, and couldn't imagine either, proved to be too difficult to move, it shifted so slowly; and when finally, growing almost frantic, he gathered his strength and lurched forward, he miscalculated the direction, and banged himself violently into the bottom bedpost, and from the burning pain he felt, he realized that for the moment, it was the lower part of his body that was the most sensitive.

Next he tried to get the upper part of his body out first, and cautiously brought his head to the edge of the bed. This he managed easily, and eventually the rest of his body, despite its width and weight, slowly followed the direction of his head. But when he finally had moved his head off the bed into open space, he became afraid of continuing any further, because if he were to fall in this position, it would be a miracle if he didn't injure his head. And no matter what happened, he must not lose consciousness just now; he would be better off staying in bed.

But when he repeated his efforts and, sighing, found himself stretched out just as before, and again he saw his little legs struggling if possible even more wildly than ever, despairing of finding a way to bring discipline and order to this random movement, he once again realized that it was impossible to stay in bed, and that the wisest course was to make every sacrifice, if there was even the slightest hope of freeing himself from the bed. But at the same time, he continued to remind himself that it was always better to think calmly and cooly than make desperate decisions. In such stressful moments he usually turned his eyes toward the window, but unfortunately the view of the morning fog didn't inspire confidence or comfort; it was so thick that it obscured the other side of the narrow street. "Already seven o'clock," he said as the alarm clock rang again, "already seven o'clock and still such a heavy fog." And for a little while longer he lay quietly, breathing very gently as if expecting perhaps that the silence would restore real and normal circumstances.

But then he told himself, "Before it reaches quarter past seven, I must absolutely be out of bed without fail. Besides, by then someone from the office will be sent here to ask about me, since it opens at seven." And he began to rock the entire length of his body in a steady rhythm to swing it out of bed. If he maneuvered out of bed in this way, then his head, which he intended to lift up as he fell, would presumably escape injury. His back seemed to be hard; it wouldn't be harmed if he fell on the carpet. His biggest worry was the loud crash he was bound to make, which would certainly cause anxiety, perhaps even alarm, behind all the doors. Still, he had to take the risk.

When Gregor was already jutting halfway out of bed—his new approach was more a game than an exertion, for all he needed was to seesaw himself on his back—it occurred to him how easy his task would become if only he had help. Two strong people—he thought of his father and the maid—would have been enough; all they had to do was to slide their arms under his round back, lift him out of bed, bend down with their burden, and then wait patiently while he swung himself onto the ground, where he hoped that his little legs would find some purpose. Well, quite aside from the fact that the doors were locked, should he really have called for help? Despite his misery, he couldn't help smiling at the very thought of it.

By now he had pushed himself so far off the bed with his steady rocking that he could feel himself losing his balance, and he would finally have to decide what he was going to do, because in five minutes it would be quarter after seven—when the front doorbell rang. "That's somebody from the office," he said to himself, and his body became rigid, while his little legs danced in the air even faster. For a moment everything was quiet. "They won't open the door," Gregor told himself, with a surge of irrational hope. But then, as usual, the maid walked to the door with her firm step and opened it. Gregor needed only to hear the first words of greeting from the visitor to know who it was—the office manager himself. Why on earth was Gregor condemned to work for a company where the slightest sign of negligence was seized upon with the gravest suspicion? Were the employees, without exception, all scoundrels? Was no one among them a loyal and dedicated man, who, if he did happen to miss a few hours of work one morning, might drive himself so crazy with remorse that he couldn't get out of bed? Wouldn't it have been enough to send an apprentice to inquire—if inquiries were really necessary—did the manager himself have to come, and make it clear to the whole innocent family that any investigation into this suspicious matter could only be entrusted to a manager? And responding to these irritating thoughts more than to any conscious decision, Gregor swung himself out of bed with all his strength. There was a loud thud, but not really a crash. The carpet softened his fall, and his back was more resilient than Gregor had thought, so the resulting thud wasn't so noticeable. Only he hadn't held his head carefully enough and had banged it; he twisted it and rubbed it against the carpet in pain and annoyance.

"Something fell in there," said the manager in the adjoining room on the left. Gregor tried to imagine whether something similar to what had happened to him today might happen one day to the office manager; one really had to admit this possibility. But, as if in brusque reply, the manager took a few decisive steps in the next room, which made his patent leather boots creak. And in the adjoining room to the right, Gregor's sister whispered, as if warning him, "Gregor, the office manager is here." "I know," said Gregor to himself; but he didn't dare to raise his voice high enough so that his sister could hear.

"Gregor," said his father from the room to his left, "the office manager has come and wants to know why you didn't catch the early train. We don't know what to tell him. Besides, he wants to talk to you in person. So, please, open the door. Surely he will be kind enough to excuse the disorder in your room." "Good morning, Mr. Samsa," the manager was calling in a friendly tone. "He's not well," said his mother to the manager, while his father continued talking through the door. "He's not well, believe me, sir. Why else would Gregor miss a train! That boy doesn't have anything in his head but business. I'm almost upset, as it is, that he never goes out at night; he's been in town for the past week, but he's stayed home every evening. He just sits here with us at the table, quietly reading the newspaper or studying the railroad timetables. His only recreation is when he occupies himself with his fretsaw. For instance, during the past two or three evenings, he's made a small picture frame; you'd be surprised how pretty it is; it's hanging in his room; you'll see it as soon as Gregor opens up. I'm really glad you've come, sir, we haven't been able to persuade Gregor to open the door; he's so obstinate; and he must definitely be feeling unwell, although he denied it earlier this morning." "I'll be right there," said Gregor slowly and deliberately, but he didn't move, so as not to miss a word of the conversation. "Dear madam, I can think of no other explanation, either," said the office manager. "Let us only hope it's nothing serious. Though, on the other hand, I must say, that we business people—fortunately or unfortunately—often very simply must overlook a slight indisposition in order to get on with business." "Well, can the office manager come in now?" asked father impatiently and knocked again on the door. "No," said Gregor. In the room to the left, there was an embarrassed silence; in the room to the right, his sister began sobbing.

Why hadn't she joined the others? Probably she had just gotten out of bed and hadn't yet begun dressing. And why was she crying? Because he hadn't gotten up and let the office manager in, because he was in danger of losing his job, and because his boss would pester his parents again about their old debts? But surely for the moment these were unnecessary worries. Gregor was still here and would never consider abandoning the family. True, at this very moment he was lying on the carpet, and no one who could have seen his condition, could seriously expect him to open his door for the office manager. But Gregor could hardly be fired for this small discourtesy, for which he could easily find a plausible excuse later on. And it seemed to Gregor, that it would be much more sensible, just to leave him in peace for now, instead of pestering him with tears and speeches. But it was just this uncertainty about him that upset the others and excused their behavior.

"Mr. Samsa," the office manager now called out, raising his voice, "what is the matter with you? You are barricading yourself in your room, answering with only Yes and No, causing your parents serious and needless worries, and—I mention this only in passing—now suddenly you neglect your duties to the firm in an absolutely shocking manner. I'm speaking here in the name of your parents and your employer, and I must ask you to give an immediate and satisfactory explanation. I'm amazed, amazed! I took you for a quiet, sensible person, and now suddenly you seem intent on behaving in an absolutely strange manner. Early this morning, the head of the firm did suggest to me a possible explanation for your absence—it concerned the cash payment for sales that you received recently—but I practically gave him my word of honor that this couldn't be true. But now that I'm witness to your unbelievable obstinacy here, I haven't the slightest desire to defend you in any way whatsoever. And your job is by no means secure. I'd originally intended to confide this to you privately, but since you force me to waste my time here needlessly, I see no reason why your parents shouldn't hear it as well. For some time your sales have been quite unsatisfactory; to be sure, it's not the best season for business, we recognize that, but a season for doing no business at all just doesn't exist, Mr. Samsa, it *must* not exist."

"But, sir," Gregor called out, beside himself and forgetting everything in his agitation, "I'll open the door immediately, this very minute. A slight indisposition, a dizzy spell, kept me from getting up. I'm still lying in bed. But I feel completely well again. I'm just climbing out of bed. Please be patient for a moment. It's not going quite so well as I thought. But I'm really all right. How suddenly a thing like this can happen to a person! Just last night I felt fine, my parents know that, or rather last night I already had a slight foreboding. It must have been noticeable. Why didn't I let them know at the office! But you always think that you can recover from an illness without having to stay at home. Please, sir, please spare my parents! Because there are no grounds for all the accusations you just made; no one has ever said a word to me about them. Perhaps you haven't seen the last orders that I sent in. Anyway, I can still catch the eight o'clock train; the last couple hours of rest have made me feel much stronger. Don't delay here any longer, sir; I'll soon be back at work, and please be kind enough to report that to the office, and put in a good word for me with the head of the firm."

And while Gregor was hastily blurting all this out, hardly aware of what he was saying, he had easily reached the chest of drawers, perhaps as a result of his practice in bed, and he was trying to raise himself up against it. He actually wanted to open his door, he actually looked forward to showing himself and speaking with the manager; he was eager to find out what the others, who so wanted to see him, would say when they caught sight of him. If they were frightened, then Gregor was no longer responsible and he could rest in peace. But if they took everything calmly, then he, too, had no grounds for alarm, and could still get to the station in time for the eight o'clock train — if he hurried. At first he kept sliding a few times down the side of the polished chest, but finally, giving one last heave, he stood upright; he no longer paid attention to the pain in his lower abdomen, though it hurt a lot. Then he let himself fall against the back of a nearby chair, clinging to its edges with his little legs. By doing this, he gained control over himself, and he stayed very quiet so he could listen to the office manager.

"Did you understand even a single word?" the manager asked the parents. "Surely he can't be trying to make fools of us?" "For Heaven's sake," cried his mother, already in tears, "perhaps he's seriously ill, and we're torturing him. Grete! Grete!" she then called. "Mother?" answered his sister from the other side — they were communicating across Gregor's room. "You must get the doctor immediately. Gregor is sick. Hurry, run for the doctor. Didn't you hear Gregor talking just now?" "That was an animal voice," said the office manager, in a tone much lower than the mother's shouting. "Anna! Anna!" yelled the father through the hallway into the kitchen, clapping his hands. "Get the locksmith at once!" And already the two young girls were running through the hallway with a rustling of skirts — how had his sister gotten dressed so quickly? — and tearing open the front door to the apartment. There was no sound of the door closing; they must have just left it open, as you sometimes do in homes where a great misfortune had occurred.

But Gregor had grown calmer. Apparently no one understood his words any longer, though they were sufficiently clear to himself, even clearer than before; perhaps his ears were getting adjusted to the sound. But at least people knew now that something was wrong with him and were ready to help him. His parents' first orders had been given with such confidence and dispatch that he already felt comforted. Once more he'd been drawn back into the circle of humanity, and he expected miraculous results from both the doctor and the locksmith, without distinguishing precisely between them. In order to make his voice as clear as possible for the conversations he anticipated in the future, he coughed a little, but as quietly as he could, because it might not sound like a human cough, and he could no longer trust his judgment. Meanwhile, it had become completely quiet in the next room. Perhaps his parents sat at the table whispering with the office manager; perhaps they were all leaning against his door and listening.

Gregor pushed himself along slowly to the door holding onto the chair, then he let go of it and fell against the door, holding himself upright — the balls of his little feet secreted a sticky substance — and rested there a moment from his efforts. Then he attempted to use his mouth to turn the key in the lock. It seemed, unfortunately, that he had no real teeth — then how was he to hold onto the key? — but to compensate for that, his jaws were certainly very powerful; with their help, he succeeded in getting the key to turn, ignoring the fact that he was undoubtedly somehow injuring himself, since a brown fluid was streaming out of his mouth, oozing over the lock and dripping onto the floor. "Listen to that," said the office manager in the next room, "he's turning the key." Gregor felt greatly encouraged; but he felt that all of them, mother and father too, should have been cheering him on. "Keep it up, Gregor," they should have shouted, "Keep going, keep working on that lock!" And imagining that everyone was eagerly following his efforts, he bit down on the key with all the strength he had in his jaws. As the key began to turn, he danced around the lock; hanging on with only his mouth, he used the full weight of his body to either push up on the key or press down on it. The clear click of the lock as it finally snapped open, broke Gregor's concentration. With a sigh of relief, he said to himself, "I didn't need the locksmith after all," and he laid his head down on the handle so the door could open wide.

Since he had to open the door in this manner, it could open out fairly widely while he himself wasn't yet visible. Next he had to turn his body slowly around one half of the double door, moving very carefully so he wouldn't fall flat on his back while crossing over the threshold. He was concentrating on this difficult maneuver, not thinking of anything else, when he heard the manager exclaim a loud "Oh" — it sounded like the wind howling — and then he could see him too, standing closest to the door, pressing his hand against his open mouth and slowly staggering back, as if driven by some invisible and intensely powerful force. His mother — despite the presence of the manager, she was standing in the room with untidy hair sticking out in all directions from the night before — first looked toward his father with her hands clasped; then she took two steps toward Gregor and collapsed on the floor, her skirts billowing out around her and her face hidden on her breast. His father clenched his fist with a menacing air, as if he wanted to knock Gregor back into his room; then he looked uncertainly around the living room, covered his eyes with his hands, and sobbed so hard that his powerful chest heaved.

Now Gregor decided not to enter the room after all; instead he leaned against his side of the firmly bolted wing of the double door, so that only half of his body was visible, his head tilting above it while he peered at the others. Meanwhile, it had become much brighter; across the street a section of an endlessly long, dark gray building was clearly visible — it was a hospital — with its facade starkly broken by regularly placed windows; it was still raining, but now large individual drops were falling, striking the ground one at a time. On the table, the breakfast dishes were set out in a lavish display, since his father considered breakfast the most important meal of the day; he lingered over it for hours, reading various newspapers. Directly on the opposite wall hung a photograph of Gregor, taken during his military service, wearing a lieutenant's uniform, his hand on his sword, with a carefree smile, demanding respect for his bearing and his rank. The door to the entrance hall was open, and since the apartment door also stood open, you could see out to the landing and the top of the descending stairs.

"Well, now," said Gregor, and he was quite aware that he was the only one who had remained calm. "I'll get dressed at once, pack my samples, and be on my way. Will you, will you all let me go catch my train? Now you see, sir, I'm not obstinate, and I'm glad to work; traveling is a hard job, but I couldn't live without it. Where are you going, sir? Back to the office? Yes? Will you give a true account of everything? A man may temporarily seem incapable of working, but that is precisely the moment to remember his past accomplishments and to consider that later on, after overcoming his obstacles, he's sure to work all the harder and more diligently. As you know very well, I'm deeply obligated to the head of the firm. And then I have to take care of my parents and my sister. I'm in a tight spot, but I'll work myself out of it again. Please don't make it harder for me than it already is. I beg you to put in a good word for me at the office. Traveling salesmen aren't regarded highly there, I know. They think we make lots of money and lead easy lives. They have no particular reason to think differently. But you, sir, you have a better idea of what's really going on than the rest of the office, why—speaking just between ourselves—you have an even better idea than the head of the firm himself, who, in his role as our employer, lets his judgment be swayed against his employees. You know very well that a traveling salesman, who's out of the office most of the year, can easily become a victim of gossip, coincidences, and unfounded complaints, against which he can't possibly defend himself, since he almost never hears about them, except perhaps after he returns exhausted from a trip, and then he himself personally suffers the grim consequences without understanding the reasons for them. Sir, please don't leave without having told me that you think I'm at least partly right!"

But at Gregor's very first words the office manager had already turned away, and now with open mouth, he simply stared back at him over a twitching shoulder. And during Gregor's speech, he never stood still for a moment, but—without taking his eyes off Gregor—he kept moving very gradually toward the door, as if there were a secret ban on leaving the room. He was already in the front hall, and from the abrupt way that he pulled his leg out of the living room, you might have thought that he had just scorched the sole of his foot. In the hall, however, he stretched out his right hand as far as he could toward the stairs, as if some supernatural deliverance were awaiting him there.

Gregor realized that he must not let the office manager leave in this frame of mind, or his position in the firm would be seriously compromised. His parents didn't quite understand the situation; over the years they'd convinced themselves that Gregor was set up for life in this firm, and besides, they were now so preoccupied by their immediate worries that they'd lost any sense of the future. But Gregor had more foresight. The office manager must be stopped, calmed down, persuaded, and finally won over; Gregor's future and that of his family depended on it! If only his sister had been here! She had understood, she had even started to cry when Gregor was still lying quietly on his back. And the office manager, a ladies' man, would certainly have listened to her; she would have shut the front door and talked him out of his fright in the hall. But she wasn't there; Gregor would have to handle the situation by himself. And forgetting that he was still completely unfamiliar with his present powers of movement, and also that very possibly, indeed probably once again his words hadn't been understood, he let go of the wing of the door, shoved himself through the opening, and tried to move toward the office manager, who was already on the landing, foolishly clutching the banister with both hands; but instead, groping for support, Gregor fell down with a small cry upon his many little legs. The instant that happened he felt a sense of physical well-being for the first time that morning; his little legs had solid ground under them; he was delighted to discover that they obeyed him perfectly; they even seemed eager to carry him off in whatever direction he chose; and now he felt sure that the end to all his suffering was at hand. But at that same moment, as he lay on the floor rocking with suppressed motion, not far away from his mother, directly opposite her, she — who had seemed so completely self-absorbed — suddenly jumped up, stretched out her arms, spread her fingers out wide, crying "Help, for Heaven's sake, help!" She craned her head forward, as if she wanted to get a better look at Gregor, but then inconsistently, she backed away instead; forgetting that the table laden with breakfast dishes was right behind her, she sat down on it hastily, as if distracted, and then failed to notice that next to her, the coffee was pouring out of the big, overturned pot in a steady stream onto the carpet.

"Mother, mother," Gregor said softly and looked up at her. For a moment, the office manager had completely slipped from his mind; on the other hand, at the sight of the flowing coffee, he couldn't help snapping his jaws a few times. That made his mother scream again; she fled from the table and collapsed into his father's arms as he was rushing towards her. But Gregor had no time now for his parents; the office manager was already on the stairs; his chin on the banister, he was taking a final look back. Gregor leaped forward, moving as fast as he could to catch him; the office manager must have anticipated this, for he jumped down several steps and vanished; but he was still yelling "Aaah!" and the sound echoed through the entire staircase. Unfortunately, the manager's flight seemed to confuse Gregor's father, who had remained relatively calm until now; for instead of running after the office manager himself, or at least not preventing Gregor from going after him, his father seized with his right hand the manager's cane — it had been left behind on a chair along with his hat and overcoat — and with his left hand, he picked up a large newspaper from the table, and stamping his feet, he began to brandish the cane and the newspaper to drive Gregor back to his room. No plea of Gregor's helped; indeed, no plea was understood; no matter how humbly he bent his head, his father only stamped his feet harder. Across the room, his mother had flung open a window despite the cold weather, and she was leaning far out of it with her face buried in her hands. A strong draft was created between the street and the staircase, so that the window curtains billowed up, the newspapers rustled on the table, and a few pages flew across the floor. Relentlessly, his father charged, making hissing noises like a savage. Since Gregor had as yet no practice in moving backwards, it was really slow going. If Gregor had only been able to turn around, he would have returned to his room right away, but he was afraid of making his father impatient by his slow rotation, while at any moment now the cane in his father's hand threatened a deadly blow to his back or his head. Finally, however, Gregor had no other choice when he realized with dismay that while moving backwards he had no control over his direction; and so with constant, fearful glances at his father, he began to turn himself around as quickly as he could, which was in reality very slowly. Perhaps his father sensed Gregor's good intentions, since he didn't interfere—occasionally he even steered the movement from a distance with the tip of the cane. If only his father would stop that unbearable hissing! It made Gregor lose his head completely. He had almost turned totally around, when distracted by the hissing, he made a mistake and briefly shifted the wrong way back again. But when at last he successfully brought his head around to the doorway, he discovered that his body was too wide to squeeze through. Naturally, in his father's present mood it didn't occur to him to open the other wing of the double door and create a passage wide enough for Gregor. He was simply obsessed with the idea that Gregor must return to his room as fast as possible. And he would never have allowed the intricate maneuvers that Gregor needed, in order to pull himself upright and try to fit through the door this way. Instead, as if there were no obstacles, he drove Gregor forward, making a lot of noise; the noise behind Gregor didn't sound any longer like the voice of a single father; now this was really getting serious, and Gregor—regardless of what would happen—jammed into the doorway. One side of his body lifted up, he lay lopsided in the opening, one of his sides was scraped raw, ugly blotches appeared on the white door, soon he was wedged in tightly and unable to move any further by himself; on one side his little legs were trembling in midair, while on the other side they were painfully crushed against the floor—when his father gave him a strong shove from behind that was truly his deliverance, so that he flew far into his room, bleeding profusely. The door was slammed shut with the cane, and at last there was silence.

II

Not until dusk did Gregor awaken from his heavy, torpid sleep. He would certainly have awakened by himself before long, even without being disturbed, for he felt that he had rested and slept long enough, but it seemed to him that a furtive step and a cautious closing of the hall door had aroused him. The light of the electric street lamps were reflected in pale patches here and there on the ceiling and on the upper parts of the furniture, but down below where Gregor lay, it was dark. Slowly, still groping awkwardly with his antennae, which he was just beginning to appreciate, he dragged himself toward the door to see what had been going on there. His left side felt like a single long, unpleasantly tightening scab, and he actually had to limp on his two rows of legs. One little leg, moreover, had been badly hurt during the morning's events—it seemed almost a miracle that only one had been injured—and it dragged along lifelessly.

Only when he reached the door did he discover what had really attracted him: it was the smell of something edible. For there stood a bowl filled with fresh milk in which floated small slices of white bread. He practically laughed with joy, since he was even hungrier now than in the morning, and he immediately plunged his head into the milk almost over his eyes. But he soon pulled it out again in disappointment; not only did he find eating difficult on account of his tender left side—and he could only eat if his whole heaving body joined in—but he also didn't care at all for the milk, which used to be his favorite drink, and that was surely why his sister had placed it there for him; in fact, he turned away from the bowl almost with disgust and crawled back into the middle of the room.

Through the crack in the double door, Gregor could look into the living room where the gas was lit, but while during this time his father was usually in the habit of reading the afternoon newspaper in a loud voice to his mother and sometimes to his sister as well, there wasn't a sound at present. Well, perhaps this practice of reading aloud that his sister was always telling him about and often mentioned in her letters, had recently been dropped altogether. But it was silent in all the other rooms too, though the apartment was certainly not empty. "What a quiet life the family's been leading," Gregor said to himself, and while he sat there staring into the darkness, he felt a great sense of pride that he had been able to provide such a life in so beautiful an apartment for his parents and sister. But what if all the peace, all the comfort, all the contentment were now to come to a terrible end? Rather than lose himself in such thoughts, Gregor decided to start moving and crawled up and down the room.

Once during the long evening, first one of the side doors and then the other was opened a tiny crack and quickly closed again; probably someone had felt the need to come in and then decided against it. Gregor now settled himself directly in front of the living room door, determined to persuade the hesitating visitor to come in or else at least to discover who it might be; but the door wasn't opened again, and Gregor waited in vain. That morning, when the doors had been locked, they all had wanted to come in to see him; now after he had opened one of the doors himself and the others had obviously been unlocked during the day, no one came in, and the keys were even put into the locks on the other side of the doors.

It wasn't until late at night that the light in the living room was turned off, and Gregor could easily tell that his parents and sister had stayed awake until then, because as he could clearly hear, all three of them were tiptoeing away. Certainly now no one would come into Gregor's room until morning; so he had ample time to reflect in peace and quiet about how he should restructure his life. But the high-ceilinged, spacious room in which he had to lie flat on the floor filled him with an anxiety he couldn't explain, since it was his own room and he had lived in it for the past five years; and with a half-unconscious movement—and not without a slight feeling of shame—he scurried under the sofa, where even though his back was slightly squeezed and he couldn't raise his head, he immediately felt quite comfortable, regretting only that his body was too wide to fit completely under the sofa.

There he stayed the entire night, which he spent either dozing and waking up from hunger with a start, or else fretting with vague hopes, but it all led him to the same conclusion, that for now he would have to stay calm and, by exercising patience and trying to be as considerate as possible, help the family to endure the inconveniences he was bound to cause them in his present condition.

Very early in the morning—it was still almost night—Gregor had the opportunity to test the strength of his new resolutions, because his sister, nearly fully dressed, opened the door from the hall and peered in uncertainly. She couldn't locate him immediately, but when she caught sight of him under the sofa—God, he had to be somewhere, he couldn't have flown away, could he?—she was so startled that, unable to control herself, she slammed the door shut again from the outside. But, apparently regretting her behavior, she immediately opened the door again and came in on tiptoe as if she were visiting someone seriously ill or even a complete stranger. Gregor had pushed his head forward just to the edge of the sofa and was watching her. Would she notice that he had left the milk standing, certainly not because he wasn't hungry, and would she bring in some other kind of food he liked better? If she didn't do it on her own, he would rather starve than bring it to her attention, though he felt a tremendous urge to dart out from under the sofa, throw himself at her feet and beg for something good to eat. But, to Gregor's surprise, his sister noticed at once that his bowl was still full, except for a little milk that had spilled around the edges; she immediately picked it up, to be sure not with her bare hands but with an old rag, and carried it out. Gregor was wildly curious to know what she would bring in its place, and he made various guesses about it. But he could never have guessed what his sister, in the goodness of her heart, actually did. To find out what he liked, she brought him a wide selection that she spread out on an old newspaper. There were old, half-rotten vegetables, bones left over from the evening meal covered with a congealed white sauce, a few raisins and almonds, some cheese that Gregor had considered inedible two days ago, a slice of dry bread, a slice of bread and butter, and a slice of bread and butter with some salt. In addition, she set down the bowl, now presumably reserved for Gregor's exclusive use, into which she had poured some water. And from a sense of delicacy, since she understood that Gregor was unlikely to eat in her presence, she quickly left the room and even turned the key in the lock outside so that Gregor would understand that he could indulge himself as freely as he liked. Gregor's little legs whirled as he hurried toward the food. His injuries must have fully healed already; he no longer felt any handicap, which amazed him, and made him think that over a month ago he had nicked his finger with a knife, and that this injury had still been hurting him the day before yesterday. "Could I have become less sensitive?" he wondered, sucking greedily at the cheese, which he was drawn to immediately, more than the other foods. Quickly, one after another, with tears of contentment streaming from his eyes, he devoured the cheese, the vegetables, and the white sauce; on the other hand, the fresh food didn't appeal to him; he couldn't stand the smell, and he even dragged the things he wanted to eat a little distance away. He had finished with everything long ago and was just resting lazily in the same spot, when his sister slowly turned the key in the lock as a signal that he should withdraw. That startled him at once, even though he was almost dozing off, and he scuttled back under the sofa again. But it took a lot of self-control to stay there, even for the brief time that his sister was in the room, because his body was bloated after his heavy meal, and he could hardly breathe in that cramped space. In between brief bouts of near suffocation, he watched with somewhat bulging eyes as his unsuspecting sister swept up with a broom not only the scraps he hadn't eaten, but also the foods that he hadn't touched, as if they were also no longer fit to eat, and then she hastily dumped everything into a bucket which she covered with a wooden lid, and carried it out. She had scarcely turned her back when Gregor came out from under the sofa to stretch himself and let his belly expand.

In this way Gregor was fed each day, once in the morning while his parents and the maid were still sleeping, and the second time in the afternoon after the family's meal, while his parents took a short nap and his sister sent the maid on some errand or other. Certainly they didn't want Gregor to starve either, but perhaps they couldn't stand to know about his feeding arrangements except by hearsay; or perhaps his sister also wished to spare them anything even mildly distressing, since they were already suffering enough as it was.

Gregor couldn't discover what excuses had been made that first morning to get rid of the doctor and the locksmith, for since the others couldn't understand him, no one thought that he could understand them—including his sister—and so whenever she was in his room, he had to content himself with hearing her occasional sighs and appeals to the saints. Not until later on, when she had become a little more used to it all—of course her complete adjustment was out of the question—Gregor sometimes caught a remark that was meant to be friendly or could be interpreted that way. "Today he really liked it," she said, when Gregor had gobbled up his food, or when he hadn't eaten much, as was gradually happening more and more frequently, she would say almost sadly, "Now he hasn't touched anything again."

But while Gregor couldn't get any news directly, he overheard many things from the adjoining rooms, and as soon as he heard the sound of voices, he would immediately run to the corresponding door and press his entire body against it. Especially in the early days, there was no conversation that didn't refer to him somehow, if only indirectly. For two whole days, there were family discussions at every meal about what they should do now; but they also talked about the same subject between meals, because now there were always at least two family members at home, since probably no one wanted to stay alone in the apartment. And yet, on no account could they leave it empty. Besides, on the very first day, the cook—it wasn't entirely clear what or how much she knew of the situation—had begged his mother on bended knees to let her leave at once, and when she departed fifteen minutes later, she thanked them tearfully for her dismissal as if it were the greatest favor they had ever bestowed on her in this house, and without being asked, she swore a solemn oath, promising not to say a word about what had happened to anyone.

So now his sister, together with his mother, had to do the cooking as well; this wasn't much trouble, of course, since they ate almost nothing. Again and again Gregor would hear how one encouraged another to eat, always getting the answer, "Thanks, I've had enough" or something similar. They didn't seem to drink anything either. Often his sister asked his father if he wanted some beer, and she kindly offered to get it herself; and then when his father didn't answer, she suggested that if he didn't want her to bother, she could send the janitor's wife for it, but in the end his father answered with a firm "No," and there wasn't any further discussion.

In the course of the very first day his father explained the family's financial situation and prospects to both the mother and sister. Every now and then he stood up from the table to get some receipt or account book from the small safe that he'd managed to salvage from the collapse of his business five years earlier. He could be heard opening the complicated lock, taking out what he was looking for, and closing it again. The father's explanations, to some extent, were the first encouraging news that Gregor had heard since his captivity. He had always supposed that his father had nothing at all left from his old business, at least his father had never told him anything to the contrary, though Gregor had never actually asked him about it. In those days Gregor's only concern had been to do all that he could to help the family forget as quickly as possible the business catastrophe that had plunged them all into complete despair. And so he had begun to work with exceptional zeal and was promoted almost overnight from a junior clerk to a traveling salesman, who naturally had a much greater earning potential, and his successes were immediately converted by way of commissions into cash that he could bring home and lay on the table for the astonished and delighted family. Those had been happy times, and they had never been repeated, at least not with such splendor, even though Gregor was eventually earning so much money that he was capable of meeting the expenses of the entire family, and in fact did so. They had simply grown used to it, the family as well as Gregor; they accepted the money gratefully and he gave it gladly, but it didn't arouse any especially warm feelings any longer. Only Gregor's sister had stayed close to him, and it was his secret plan that she, who—unlike Gregor—loved music and could play the violin very movingly, should be sent to the conservatory next year despite the considerable expense involved, and which he would certainly have to meet somehow. During Gregor's brief visits home, the conservatory was often mentioned in his conversations with his sister, but it was always only as a beautiful dream that could never come true, and his parents even disliked hearing those innocent allusions; but Gregor had definitely set his mind on it and had intended to announce his plan solemnly on Christmas Eve.

Such were the thoughts, quite futile in his present condition, that passed through his mind as he stood upright, glued to the door, eavesdropping. Sometimes he grew so weary that he could no longer listen and let his head bump carelessly against the door, but then he held it up again immediately, because even the slightest noise that he inadvertently made was enough to be heard next door and to reduce everyone to silence. "Just what's he up to now?" his father would say after a pause, obviously turning toward the door, and only then would the interrupted conversation gradually resume.

Gregor now had ample opportunity to discover—since his father would often repeat his explanations, partly because he hadn't concerned himself with these matters for a long time, and also partly because his mother couldn't always grasp everything the first time—that despite all their misfortune, a sum of money, to be sure a very small one, still remained from the old days and had even increased slightly in the meantime since the interest had never been touched. And besides that, the money Gregor had been bringing home every month—he'd only kept a little for himself—had not been entirely spent and had accumulated into a modest capital. Behind his door, Gregor nodded his head eagerly, delighted at this unexpected foresight and thrift. In fact, he could have used this surplus money to pay off more of his father's debt to the head of the firm, so the day when he could have quit his job would have been a lot closer, but now things were doubtless better the way his father had arranged them.

However, this money was by no means sufficient to allow the family to live off the interest; it might be enough to support them for a year, or for two at the most, but no more than that. It was really just a sum that shouldn't be touched, but instead saved for an emergency; money to live on would have to be earned. Now his father was still certainly healthy, but he was an old man who hadn't done any work for the past five years and couldn't be expected to take on very much; in those five years, which was his first vacation in his hard-working if unsuccessful life, he had put on weight and as a result, had become very sluggish. And as for his old mother, should she really start trying to earn money, when she suffered from asthma and found it a strain just to walk through the apartment, and spent every second day gasping for breath on the couch by the open window? And should his sister go out to work, she who was still a child at seventeen and whose life it would be a pity to disturb, since it consisted of wearing nice clothes, sleeping late, helping out with the housework, enjoying a few modest amusements, and most of all, playing the violin? At first, whenever the conversation turned to the necessity of earning money, Gregor would always let go of the door immediately and then throw himself down on the cool leather sofa beside it, because he felt so flushed with shame and grief.

Often he lay there throughout the long nights, not sleeping a wink and just scrabbling on the leather for hours. Or else, undaunted by the great effort of shoving an armchair to the window, he would crawl to the sill and, propping himself up on the chair, lean against the panes, evidently inspired by some memory of the sense of freedom that he used to experience looking out the window. Because, in fact, from day to day he saw objects only a short distance away becoming more indistinct; the hospital across the street, which he used to curse because he saw it all too often, he now couldn't see at all, and if he weren't certain that he lived on the quiet but decidedly urban Charlotte Street, he might have believed that he was gazing out of his window into a barren wasteland where the gray sky and the gray earth merged indistinguishably. Only twice had his attentive sister needed to see the armchair standing by the window;

from then on whenever she cleaned the room, she carefully pushed the chair back to the window, and now she even left the inside windowpane open.

If Gregor had only been able to speak to his sister and thank her for all she had to do for him, he could have endured her services more easily, but as it was, they oppressed him. To be sure, she tried to ease the embarrassment of the situation as much as possible, and the longer time went on, the better she became at it, but in time Gregor too became more keenly aware of everything. Even the way she came in was terrible for him. Hardly had she entered the room when—not even taking time to close the door, though she was usually so careful to spare everyone the sight of Gregor's room—she'd run straight to the window and tear it open with impatient fingers, almost as if she were suffocating, and then she stayed there for a while, taking deep breaths no matter how cold it was. With this hustle and bustle, she scared Gregor twice a day; he lay quaking under the sofa the entire time, and yet he knew perfectly well that she would surely have spared him if she had only found it possible to stand being in a room with him with the windows closed.

One time—it must have been a month since Gregor's transformation, so there was no particular reason for his sister to be surprised by his appearance any more—she came a little earlier than usual and caught Gregor as he was looking out the window, motionless and terrifyingly upright. It wouldn't have surprised Gregor if she hadn't come in, since his position prevented her from opening the window immediately, but not only did she not enter, she also actually jumped back and shut the door; a stranger might easily have thought that Gregor had been lying in wait for her and meant to bite her. Gregor naturally hid at once under the sofa, but he had to wait until noon before she came back, and she seemed much more uneasy than usual. From this he concluded that the sight of him was still unbearable to her and was bound to remain unbearable in the future, and that she probably was exercising great self-control not to run away at the sight of even the small portion of his body that protruded from under the sofa. To spare her even this sight, he draped the sheet on his back and dragged it over to the sofa one day—he needed four hours for this task—and placed it in such a way so as to conceal himself completely, so that she couldn't see him even if she stooped down. If she considered this sheet unnecessary, then of course she could remove it, because it was clear enough that Gregor was hardly shutting himself off so completely for his own sake; but she left the sheet the way it was, and Gregor believed he caught a grateful look when he once cautiously raised the sheet a little with his head to see how she was reacting to the new arrangement.

During the first two weeks his parents couldn't bring themselves to come in to him, and often he heard them say how much they appreciated his sister's work, whereas previously they'd been annoyed with her because she'd appeared to be a little useless. But often now, both his father and mother waited outside of Gregor's room while his sister was cleaning up inside, and as soon as she emerged, she had to give a detailed report about how the room looked, what Gregor had eaten, how he had behaved this time, and whether perhaps some slight improvement was noticeable. Gregor's mother, incidentally, wanted to visit him relatively soon, but at first his father and sister put her off with sensible arguments, which Gregor listened to most attentively and fully endorsed. But later his mother had to be held back by force, and when she cried out, "Let me go to Gregor; after all, he's my unfortunate son! Don't you understand that I must go to him?" then Gregor thought that perhaps it would be a good idea after all if she did come in; not every day, of course, but perhaps once a week; she surely understood everything much better than his sister, who for all her courage, was still only a child, and had perhaps, in the final analysis, merely taken on this demanding task out of childish recklessness.

Gregor's wish to see his mother was soon fulfilled. During the daytime Gregor didn't want to show himself at the window, if only out of consideration for his parents, but he couldn't crawl very far on his few square yards of floor space, either, nor could he bear to lie still during the night; eating had soon ceased to give him the slightest pleasure, and so as a distraction he got into the habit of crawling crisscross over the walls and ceiling. He especially enjoyed hanging from the ceiling; it was quite different from lying on the floor; he could breathe more freely, and a mild tingle ran through his body; and in the almost blissful oblivion in which Gregor found himself up there, it could happen that, to his surprise, he let himself go and crashed onto the floor. But now of course he had much greater control over his body than before, and he never hurt himself by even this great fall. Gregor's sister immediately noticed the new pastime that he had found for himself—after all, he left some traces of the sticky tracks of his crawling here and there—and she then took it into her head to enable Gregor to crawl around to the greatest possible extent, so she decided to remove the furniture that stood in his way, first of all, the chest of drawers and the desk. But she couldn't do this alone; she didn't dare ask her father for help; and the maid would most certainly not help her, because this girl (about sixteen years old) was bravely staying on since the previous cook had quit, but she'd asked permission to keep the kitchen locked at all times and to open it only when expressly called; so his sister had no other choice than to get her mother one day when her father was out. And indeed, with cries of eager delight, Gregor's mother approached his room, but she fell silent at the door. Of course his sister first looked in to check that everything in the room was in order; only then did she let her mother enter. Gregor had hastily pulled the sheet even lower down in tighter folds; the whole thing really looked like a sheet casually tossed over the sofa. This time Gregor also refrained from peering out from under the sheet; he denied himself the sight of his mother, and was only pleased to know that she had finally come. "Come on in, you can't see him," said his sister, and evidently she was leading her mother by the hand. Now Gregor heard the two weak women shifting the really heavy old chest of drawers from its place, and how his sister obstinately took on the hardest part of the work for herself, ignoring the warnings of her mother, who was afraid she'd strain herself. It took a very long time. After about a quarter of an hour's work, Gregor's mother said that it would be better to leave the chest where it was, because for one thing, it was just too heavy, they would not be finished before the father arrived, and with the chest in the middle of the room, Gregor's path would be blocked; and for the second, it wasn't at all certain that they were doing Gregor a favor to move the furniture. It seemed to her that the opposite was true; the sight of the bare walls made her heart ache; and why shouldn't Gregor also feel the same way, since after all he'd been accustomed to the furniture for so long and might feel abandoned in an empty room. "And doesn't it really look," concluded his mother very softly, in fact she'd been almost whispering the whole time, as if she were anxious that Gregor, whose exact whereabouts she didn't know, couldn't hear even the sound of her voice, for of course she was convinced that he couldn't understand her words, "and doesn't it look as if by moving the furniture we were showing that we'd given up all hope for improvement and were callously abandoning him to his own resources? I think it would be best if we tried to keep the room just as it was, so that when Gregor comes back to us again, everything will be unchanged and it can be easier to forget what happened in the meantime."

Hearing his mother's words, Gregor realized that the lack of all direct human exchange, together with his monotonous life in the midst of the family, must have confused his mind during these past two months, because otherwise he couldn't explain to himself how he could seriously have wanted his room cleared out. Had he really wanted his warm room, with its comfortable old family furniture, to be transformed into a cave in which he could crawl freely around in all directions, no doubt, but only at the cost of swiftly and totally losing his human past? Indeed, he was already on the verge of forgetting it, and only his mother's voice, which he hadn't heard for so long, had brought him to his senses. Nothing should be removed; everything must stay; he couldn't do without the beneficial effects of the furniture on his state of mind; and if the furniture interfered with his mindless crawling about, then it was not a loss but a great gain.

But unfortunately his sister thought differently; she had grown accustomed, to be sure not entirely without reason, to being the great expert on Gregor in any discussion with her parents, and so now her mother's proposal was cause enough for the sister to insist on removing not only the chest of drawers and the desk, as she had originally planned, but also the rest of the furniture in the room except for the indispensable sofa. It was, of course, not only her childish defiance and the self-confidence she had recently and so unexpectedly gained at such cost that led to this determination; but she had also in fact observed that Gregor needed more space to crawl around in, while on the other hand, as far as she could see, he never used the furniture. But, perhaps, what also played some part was the romantic spirit of girls of her age, which seeks satisfaction at every opportunity and tempted Grete to make Gregor's predicament even more frightening so that she might then be able to do even more for him than before. For most likely no one but Grete would ever dare to enter into a room where Gregor ruled the bare walls all by himself.

And so she refused to be dissuaded from her resolve by her mother, who in any case seemed unsure of herself in that room and who soon fell silent out of sheer nervousness, and helped the sister as best she could to move the chest of drawers out of the room. Well, Gregor could do without the chest, if necessary, but the desk had to stay. And no sooner had the two women, groaning and shoving the chest, left the room, when Gregor poked his head out from under the sofa to see how he could intervene as cautiously and tactfully as possible.

Unfortunately, it was his mother who returned first, while Grete kept her arms around the chest in the next room, rocking it back and forth, and naturally unable to move it by herself from its spot. Gregor's mother, however, was not used to the sight of him; it might make her sick, and so Gregor scurried backwards in alarm to the other end of the sofa, though not in time to prevent the front of the sheet from stirring a little. That was enough to catch his mother's attention. She stopped short, stood still a moment, and then went back to Grete.

Although Gregor kept telling himself that nothing out of the ordinary was happening, that just a couple of pieces of furniture were being moved around, all the same he soon had to admit to himself that this walking back and forth by the women, their little cries to each other, the scraping of the furniture along the floor, were affecting him on all sides like a tremendous uproar, and no matter how tightly he tucked in his head and legs and pressed his body against the floor, he was forced to admit that he couldn't endure the fuss much longer. They were emptying out his room, stripping him of everything he loved; they had already removed the chest, which contained his fretsaw and other tools; and now they were prying loose the desk, which was almost embedded in the floor, and at which he'd done his homework when he was in business school, high school, and even as far back as elementary school — at this point he really had no more time to consider the good intentions of the two women, whose existence he had indeed almost forgotten, because by now they were working away in silence from sheer exhaustion, and he heard only the heavy shuffling of their feet.

And so he broke out — just at the moment the women were in the next room, leaning against the desk to catch their breath — and he changed direction four times, not really knowing what he should rescue first, and then he spotted the picture of the lady dressed in nothing but furs, hanging conspicuously on what was otherwise a bare wall opposite him; he crawled rapidly up to it and pressed himself against the glass, which held him fast and soothed his hot belly. At least this picture, which Gregor now completely covered, was definitely not going to be removed by anyone. He twisted his head around toward the door of the living room to observe the women on their return.

They had not given themselves much of a rest and were already coming back; Grete had put her arm around her mother and was almost carrying her. "Well, what should we take now?" said Grete and looked around. Then her eyes met Gregor's on the wall. No doubt it was only due to the presence of her mother that she kept her composure, lowered her head to keep her mother from looking about, and said, although rather shakily and without thinking, "Come on, why don't we go back to the living room for a moment?" Grete's intention was clear to Gregor; she wanted to get her mother to safety and then chase him down from the wall. Well, just let her try! He clung to his picture and wouldn't give it up. He would rather fly in Grete's face.

But Grete's words had made her mother even more anxious; she stepped to one side, caught sight of the huge brown splotch on the flowered wallpaper, and before realizing that what she saw was Gregor, she cried out in a hoarse, shrieking voice, "Oh God, oh God," and collapsed across the sofa with outstretched arms, as if giving up completely, and didn't move. "You, Gregor," cried the sister, raising her fist and glaring at him. These were the first words that she had addressed directly to him since his transformation. She ran into the next room to get some sort of medicine to revive her mother from her fainting fit; Gregor also wanted to help—there was time enough to save his picture later on—but he was stuck fast to the glass and had to wrench himself free; then he also ran into the next room, as if he could give some advice to his sister as in the old days; but once there he had to stand uselessly behind her while she was rummaging among various little bottles; she got frightened when she turned around; one of the bottles fell to the floor and shattered; a splinter of glass sliced Gregor's face, and some kind of burning medicine splashed around him; then without further delay, Grete grabbed as many bottles as she could hold and ran back to her mother with them; she slammed the door closed with her foot. Gregor was now cut off from his mother, who was perhaps nearly dying because of him; he dared not open the door for fear of frightening away his sister, who had to stay with his mother; now he had nothing to do but wait; and so, in an agony of self-reproach and anxiety, he began to crawl, to crawl over everything, walls, furniture, and ceiling; until finally when the entire room was spinning, he dropped in despair onto the middle of the big table.

A little while passed. Gregor lay worn out, all was quiet, perhaps that was a good sign. Then the doorbell rang. The maid, of course, was locked in the kitchen, and Grete had to open the door. Father was back. "What's happened?" were his first words; Grete's face must have told him everything. Grete replied in a muffled voice, evidently with her face pressing against her father's chest. "Mother fainted. But she's better now. Gregor's broken loose." "Just what I expected," said his father. "Just what I've always told you, but you women wouldn't listen." It was clear to Gregor that his father had misinterpreted Grete's all too brief statement and assumed that Gregor was guilty of some act of violence. That meant that he must now try to pacify his father, for he had neither the time nor the means to explain things to him. And so Gregor fled to the door of his room and pressed himself against it, so that as soon as his father came in from the hall, he should see that Gregor had the best intention of returning to his room immediately, and that it was unnecessary to drive him back; but that someone only had to open the door, and he would immediately disappear.

But his father was in no mood to observe such subtlety; "Ah ha!" he cried as soon as he entered, in a tone both furious and elated. Gregor drew his head back from the door and raised it toward his father. He hadn't really pictured his father at all, standing that way; admittedly he had been too preoccupied by the new sensation of crawling around to concern himself with what was going on in the rest of the household as before, and he really ought to have been prepared for some changes. And yet, and yet, was this really his father? The same man who used to lie wearily in bed when Gregor left early on one of his business trips; who always greeted him on his return in the evening wearing a robe and sitting in an armchair; who was actually hardly capable of standing up, but had merely raised his arms to show his pleasure; and who, during the rare family walks on a few Sundays a year and on the high holidays, would always shuffle laboriously along between Gregor and his mother, who walked slowly anyway, walking even a little slower than they walked, bundled in his old overcoat, planting his cane before him for each step he took, and when he wanted to say something, nearly always standing still and gathering his escorts around him? Now, however, he held himself erect, dressed in a tight blue uniform with gold buttons, like that worn by bank messengers; his heavy double chin bulged over the high stiff collar of his jacket; from under his bushy eyebrows, his black eyes flashed alert and observant glances; his previously tousled white hair was combed flat, meticulously parted and gleaming. He tossed his cap, on which was a gold monogram, probably that of some bank, right across the room in a wide arc onto the couch, and started toward Gregor with a grimly set face, the ends of his long uniform jacket thrown back, and his hands in his pockets. Probably he didn't know himself what he intended; nevertheless, he lifted his feet unusually high, and Gregor was astonished at the gigantic size of his boot soles. But Gregor didn't dwell on his reflections; he had known from the very first day of his new life that his father considered only the strictest measures appropriate for dealing with him. And so he fled from his father, pausing only when his father stood still, and immediately hurrying on again when he made any kind of a move. In that way they circled the room several times, without anything decisive happening; in fact, they proceeded in such a slow tempo that it didn't have the appearance of a chase. For this reason, Gregor stayed on the floor for the time being, especially since he feared his father might regard any escape onto the walls or ceiling as a particularly wicked act. At the same time, Gregor had to admit that he couldn't keep up with this kind of running for long; for while his father took a single step, he had to carry out a countless number of movements. Shortness of breath was beginning to appear, and even in his earlier days his lungs had never been entirely reliable. As he went staggering along, saving all his energy for running, hardly keeping his eyes open, in his stupor not even thinking of any other refuge than running, and having almost forgotten that the walls were available, though admittedly here these walls were blocked by elaborately carved furniture full of sharp points and corners— suddenly something came sailing past him, lightly tossed; it landed next to him and rolled away in front of him. It was an apple; immediately a second one came flying after it; Gregor stopped dead in fright; any further running was useless, because his father was determined to bombard him. He had filled his pockets from the fruit bowl on the sideboard and now, without taking careful aim, he was throwing one apple after another. These small red apples rolled around on the floor as if electrified, colliding with one another. One weakly thrown apple grazed Gregor's back and glanced off harmlessly. But another one thrown directly afterwards actually penetrated into Gregor's back; Gregor wanted to drag himself further, as if the surprising and unbelievable pain might pass if he changed his position; but he felt as if nailed to the spot and stretched himself flat out, all his senses in complete confusion. Now with his last conscious sight he saw how the door of his room was flung open, and his mother rushed out in her chemise, ahead of his screaming sister, for his sister had undressed her when she had fainted to make it easier for her to breathe; he saw his mother running to his father, shedding her loosened petticoats one by one on the floor behind her, and stumbling over her petticoats to fling herself upon his father, and embracing him, in complete union with him—but now Gregor's vision failed him—begging him, with her hands clasped around his father's neck, to spare Gregor's life.

III

Gregor suffered from his serious injury for over a month—the apple remained embedded in his flesh as a visible reminder since no one dared to remove it—and it even seemed to bring home to his father that despite Gregor's present deplorable and repulsive shape, he was still a member of the family who ought not to be treated as an enemy, but that on the contrary, family duty required them to swallow their disgust and put up with him, simply put up with him.

And now, although Gregor had probably suffered some permanent loss of mobility as a result of his injury and for the present needed long, long minutes to cross his room like an old invalid—crawling up the walls was out of the question—yet he thought he was granted entirely satisfactory compensation for this deterioration of his condition, since every day toward evening the living room door, which he used to watch intently for an hour or two beforehand, would be opened, so that lying in the darkness of his room and not visible from the living room, he could see the entire family at the lamp-lit table and could listen to the conversation as if by general consent, not at all as he had been obliged earlier to eavesdrop.

Of course, there were no longer the lively discussions of earlier days that Gregor used to recall wistfully in small hotel rooms whenever he had to sink down wearily into the damp bedding. Now it was mostly very quiet. The father fell asleep in his armchair shortly after supper; the mother and sister would caution each other to keep quiet; the mother, hunched forward under the light, stitched away at fine lingerie for a fashion boutique; the sister, who had taken a job as a salesgirl, studied shorthand and French every evening, in the hope of getting a better job some day. Occasionally the father woke up, and as if he didn't know he'd been sleeping, he said to the mother, "How long you've been sewing again today!" and instantly he'd doze off again, while the mother and sister smiled wearily at each other.

With a kind of perverse obstinacy, the father refused to take off his messenger's uniform even in the house, and while his robe hung uselessly on the clothes hook, he slept fully dressed in his chair, as if he were ever ready for duty and waiting for his superior's call even here. As a result, his uniform—not new to begin with—started to look less clean despite all the efforts of the mother and sister, and Gregor would often spend whole evenings staring at the soiled and spotted uniform, with its gleaming, constantly polished gold buttons, in which the old man slept in great discomfort and yet very peacefully.

As soon as the clock struck ten, the mother tried to wake up the father with a few gentle words, trying to persuade him to go to bed, because here he couldn't get any proper rest, which the father sorely needed, since he had to go on duty at six. But with the obstinacy that had possessed him since he'd become a bank messenger, he always insisted on staying at the table a little longer, though he regularly fell asleep, and it was then only with the greatest effort that he could be coaxed into exchanging his armchair for his bed. No matter how much the mother and sister cajoled and admonished him, he would go on shaking his head slowly for a quarter of an hour, keeping his eyes shut and refusing to get up. The mother plucked at his sleeve, whispering sweet words into his ear; the sister would leave her homework to help her mother, but none of this had any effect on the father. He merely sank deeper into his chair. He would open his eyes only when the two women took hold of him under his arms, look back and forth at the mother and sister, and usually say, "What a life. Such is the peace of my old age." And supported by both women, he rose to his feet laboriously, as if he himself were his greatest burden, and allowed the women to lead him to the door, where he waved them away and went on by himself, while the mother hastily dropped her sewing and the sister her pen, to run after the father and provide further assistance.

Who in this overworked and exhausted family had time to worry about Gregor any more than was absolutely necessary? The household was neglected even more; the maid was dismissed after all; a gigantic, bony cleaning woman with white hair fluttering around her head now came every morning and evening to do the heaviest chores; everything else was taken care of by the mother, along with all her sewing. It even came to pass that various pieces of family jewelry, which the mother and sister used to wear with great pleasure at parties and on great occasions, had to be sold, as Gregor learned in the evenings from the family's discussion of the prices they had fetched. But always their greatest complaint was that they couldn't leave this apartment, which was much too large for their present circumstances, since no one could imagine how to move Gregor. But Gregor fully understood that it was not only concern for him that prevented a move, for he could easily have been shipped in a suitable crate with a few air holes; what mostly stopped them was the complete hopelessness of their situation and their sense that they had been struck by a misfortune unlike anyone else in their entire circle of friends and relations. They were suffering to the limit what the world requires of poor people: the father brought in breakfast for junior bank clerks; the mother sacrificed herself sewing underwear for strangers; the sister ran to and fro behind a counter at the bidding of customers, but the family had no more strength beyond that. And the wound in Gregor's back began to hurt again whenever the mother and sister returned after putting the father to bed, dropped their work, drew close together, and sat cheek to cheek; then the mother, pointing to Gregor's room, said "Close the door, Grete," so that Gregor was again left in darkness while in the next room, the women mingled their tears or stared dry eyed at the table.

Gregor spent his nights and days almost entirely without sleep. Sometimes he fancied that the next time the door opened, he would once again take charge of the family affairs just as he had done in the past; in his thoughts there reappeared, as after a long absence, the director and the office manager, the clerks and the trainees, the slow-witted office boy, two or three friends from other firms, a maid in a country hotel (a charming, fleeting memory), a cashier in a hat shop whom he'd courted earnestly but too slowly — they all appeared mixed up with strangers or people he'd forgotten, but instead of helping him and his family, they were all inaccessible, and he was glad when they disappeared. But at other times he was in no mood to worry about his family; he was filled with rage over how badly he was looked after; and even though he couldn't imagine having an appetite for anything, he still invented plans for getting into the pantry so he could help himself to the food that was coming to him, even if he wasn't hungry. No longer considering what might give Gregor some special pleasure, the sister now quickly pushed any old food into Gregor's room with her foot before she rushed off to work both in the morning and at noon; then in the evening, not caring whether the food had only been nibbled at or—most frequently—left completely untouched, she swept it out with a swing of her broom. The cleaning of his room, which she now always took care of in the evening, couldn't have been more perfunctory. Grimy dirt streaked the walls, and balls of dust and filth lay here and there. At first Gregor would stand in particularly offensive corners when the sister came in, as if intending to reproach her. But he could have waited there for weeks without the sister making any improvement; she could see the dirt just as well as he could, of course, but she had simply made up her mind to leave it there. At the same time, with a touchiness that was new to her, and that indeed was felt in the entire family, she made certain that the cleaning of Gregor's room remained her exclusive responsibility. Once Gregor's mother subjected his room to a thorough cleaning, which she managed only by using several buckets of water— the resulting dampness made Gregor sick, of course, and he lay stretched out on the sofa, embittered and immobile—but the mother didn't escape her punishment. Because that evening, the moment Gregor's sister noticed the change in his room, she ran into the living room, deeply insulted, and although the mother raised her hands imploringly, the sister broke out in a fit of weeping, while the parents—the father had of course been frightened out of his armchair—gaped in helpless astonishment, until they too started in; the father reproached the mother on his right for not leaving the cleaning of Gregor's room to the sister, and he shouted at the sister on his left, warning her that she would never again be allowed to clean Gregor's room; meanwhile the mother tried to drag the father, who was beside himself with rage, into the bedroom; the sister, shaking with sobs, beat the table with her small fists; and Gregor hissed loudly in his fury because no one thought of closing the door and sparing him this spectacle and commotion.

But even if Gregor's sister, exhausted by her work at the shop, was fed up with taking care of him as before, it was by no means necessary for the mother to take her place to make sure that Gregor wouldn't be neglected. For now the cleaning woman was there. This old widow, who in her long life must have weathered the worst thanks to her sturdy constitution, wasn't really repelled by Gregor. Without being in the least noisy, she happened one day to open the door to Gregor's room, and at the sight of Gregor, who was completely taken by surprise and began scrambling back and forth though no one was chasing him, she had merely stood still in amazement, her hands folded on her stomach. Since then, she never failed to open his door a crack every morning and night to peep in at Gregor. Initially she would even call him over with words she probably considered friendly, such as "Come on over here, you old dung beetle," or "Just look at that old dung beetle!" Gregor never responded to such calls, but remained motionless where he stood, as if the door had never been opened. If only they had ordered this woman to clean out his room every day, instead of letting her disturb him whenever she pleased! Once, early in the morning—a heavy rain, perhaps a sign of the coming spring, was pelting the windowpanes—Gregor was so annoyed when the cleaning woman again launched into her phrases that he charged toward her as if to attack, but slowly and feebly. Instead of being frightened, the cleaning woman simply raised a chair placed near the door and stood there with her mouth wide open, obviously not intending to close it again until the chair in her hand came crashing down on Gregor's back. "So you're not coming any closer?" she asked, when Gregor turned around again, and she calmly put the chair back in the corner.

By this time Gregor was eating next to nothing. Only when he happened by chance to pass by the food spread out for him, would he take a bite in his mouth just for pleasure, hold it there for hours, and then mostly spit it back out again. At first he thought it was distress at the condition of his room that kept him from eating, but he soon became adjusted to these very changes. The family had gotten into the habit of putting things that had no other place into his room, and now there were plenty of such things, because they had rented a bedroom in the apartment to three boarders. These serious gentlemen—all three had full beards, as Gregor once observed through a crack in the door—were obsessed with order, not only in their room, but also, since they were paying rent there, throughout the apartment, particularly the kitchen. They couldn't stand any kind of useless odds and ends, let alone dirty ones. Furthermore, they had for the most part brought along their own furnishings. For this reason, many things had become superfluous that couldn't be sold but also couldn't be thrown away. All these things ended up in Gregor's room. As did the ash bucket and the garbage pail from the kitchen. Whatever was not being used at the moment was simply flung into Gregor's room by the cleaning woman, who was always in a hurry; Gregor was usually fortunate enough to see only the object in question and the hand that held it. Perhaps the cleaning woman intended to retrieve these objects when she had time and opportunity to do so, or else to throw out everything at once, but in fact they lay wherever they happened to land, unless Gregor waded through the junk pile and set it in motion, at first out of necessity because there was no free space to crawl; but later on with growing pleasure, though after such excursions he would lie still for hours, dead tired and miserable.

Since the boarders also sometimes took their evening meal at home in the common living room, Gregor's door stayed shut on many evenings, but he found it very easy to give up the open door, for when it was left open on many earlier evenings he had already not taken advantage of it, but without the family's notice, he had lain in the darkest corner of his room. Once, however, the cleaning woman had left the door to the living room open a small crack; and it stayed open, even when the boarders entered in the evening and the lamp was lit. They sat at the head of the table where the father, mother, and Gregor had sat in the old days, unfolded their napkins and picked up their knives and forks. Immediately the mother appeared in the doorway with a platter of meat, and right behind her was the sister with a platter piled high with potatoes. The food gave off thick clouds of steam. The boarders bent over the platters placed in front of them as if to examine them before eating, and in fact the man sitting in the middle (whom the other two seemed to regard as an authority) cut up a piece of meat on the platter, obviously in order to determine whether it was tender enough or should perhaps need to be sent back to the kitchen. He was satisfied, and so the mother and sister, who had been watching anxiously, breathed freely again and began to smile.

The family itself ate in the kitchen. Nevertheless, before the father headed for the kitchen, he came into the living room, bowed once, his cap in hand, and walked around the table. The boarders all rose simultaneously and muttered something into their beards. When they were alone again, they ate in almost complete silence. It seemed strange to Gregor that out of the various noises of eating, he could always distinguish the sound of their chomping teeth, as if to demonstrate to Gregor that teeth were necessary for eating, and that even the most wonderful toothless jaws could accomplish nothing. "I do have an appetite," said Gregor mournfully to himself, "but not for these things. How those boarders gorge themselves, and I'm starving to death."

On that very evening—Gregor couldn't remember having once heard the violin during all this time—it was heard from the kitchen. The boarders had already finished their supper, the middle one had taken out a newspaper, handing over a sheet apiece to the two others, and they were now leaning back, reading and smoking. When the violin began to play, they noticed it, stood up, and tiptoed to the hall, where they paused, huddled together. They must have been heard from the kitchen, because the father called, "Are the gentlemen disturbed by the music, perhaps? It can be stopped at once." "On the contrary," said the middle boarder, "wouldn't the young lady like to come in here with us and play in the living room, which is more spacious and comfortable?" "Oh, with pleasure," cried the father, as if he were the violinist. The boarders went back into the living room and waited. Soon the father came with the music stand, the mother with the sheet music, and the sister with the violin. The sister calmly got everything ready to play; the parents, who'd never rented rooms before and therefore were excessively polite to the boarders, didn't dare to sit on their own chairs; the father leaned against the door, his right hand thrust between two buttons of his closed uniform jacket; the mother, however, was offered a chair by one of the boarders and sat down on it just where he happened to put it, off to the side in a corner.

The sister began to play; the father and mother on either side of her followed the movements of her hands attentively. Gregor, attracted by her playing, had ventured out a little further, and his head was already in the living room. He was hardly surprised that he had recently begun to show so little concern for others; previously such thoughtfulness had been his pride. And yet right now he would have had even more reason than ever to stay hidden, because he was completely covered with dust as a result of the particles that lay everywhere in his room and flew about with his slightest movement; bits of fluff, hair, and food remnants also stuck to his back and trailed from his sides; his indifference to everything was much too great for him to lie on his back and rub himself against the carpet, as he had once done several times a day. And in spite of his condition, he felt no shame in edging forward a little onto the immaculate floor of the living room.

To be sure, no one paid any attention to him. The family was completely absorbed by the violin playing; on the other hand, the boarders, with their hands in their pockets, stood at first much too closely behind the sister's music stand so that they all would have been able to read the music, which surely must have distracted the sister, but they soon retreated to the window and stayed there with lowered heads, softly talking with each other, while the father watched them anxiously. Indeed it now appeared all too clearly that they seemed disappointed in their hopes of hearing beautiful or entertaining violin playing, as if they had had enough of the recital and were merely suffering this disturbance of their peace out of politeness. In particular, the way in which they all blew their cigar smoke through their nose and mouth into the air suggested their high degree of irritability. And yet the sister was playing so beautifully. Her face was inclined to one side, her eyes followed the notes of the music with a searching and sorrowful look. Gregor crawled a little bit further forward and kept his head close to the floor so that it might be possible for their eyes to meet. Was he an animal, that music could move him so? It seemed as if he were being shown the way to the unknown nourishment he longed for. He was determined to push his way up to his sister and tug at her skirt, and thus suggest that she should come into his room with her violin, for nobody here was worthy of her playing as he would be worthy of it. He would never let her out of his room again, at least not so long as he lived; his terrible shape would be useful to him for the first time; he would stand guard at all the doors of his room simultaneously, hissing at the intruders; his sister, however, wouldn't be forced to stay with him but should remain of her own free will; she should sit next to him on the sofa, bending her ear down to him, and then he would confide to her that he had made a firm resolve to send her to the Conservatory, and that if misfortune hadn't intervened, he would have announced this to everyone at Christmas — had Christmas passed already? — without listening to any objections. After this declaration his sister would burst into tears of emotion, and Gregor would raise himself up to her shoulder and kiss her on the neck, which — now that she went out to work — she kept free of ribbon or collar.

"Mr. Samsa!" cried the middle boarder to the father, and without wasting another word, he pointed with his forefinger at Gregor, who was slowly crawling forward. The violin fell silent, the middle boarder first smiled at his friends with a shake of his head and then looked at Gregor again. The father seemed to think that it was more urgent to pacify the boarders than to drive Gregor out, though they weren't at all upset, and Gregor seemed to entertain them more than the violin playing. With outstretched arms, the father rushed to them and tried to herd them back to their room, while simultaneously blocking their view of Gregor with his body. Now they really became a bit angry; it wasn't clear whether the father's behavior was to blame or whether the realization was dawning on them that they had unknowingly had a next door neighbor like Gregor. They demanded explanations from the father, waving their arms at him, nervously plucking their beards, and then they backed toward their room very reluctantly. In the meantime, the sister had recovered from the bewildered state she had fallen into with the sudden interruption of her music; after having dangled her violin and bow listlessly for awhile in her slack hands, continuing to gaze at the music as if she were still playing, she had suddenly pulled herself together, placed her instrument in her mother's lap (her mother was still sitting in her chair, gasping for breath with heaving lungs) and run into the next room, which the boarders were approaching more rapidly now under pressure from the father. One could see the blankets and pillows on the beds obeying the sister's skillful hands and arranging themselves neatly. Before the boarders had even reached their room, she finished making the beds and slipped out. Once again the father seemed so overcome by his obstinacy that he was forgetting any respect he still owed his boarders. He kept crowding them and crowding them until, just at the doorway to their room, the middle boarder thunderously stamped his foot and brought the father to a halt. "I hereby declare," he said, raising his hand and looking around for the mother and sister too, "that in view of the disgusting conditions prevailing in this household and family" — here he promptly spit on the floor — "I give immediate notice. I will of course not pay a cent for the days that I have been living here, either; on the contrary, I will think seriously about taking some sort of legal action against you, with claims — believe me — that would be very easy to substantiate." He was silent and looked straight ahead of him, as if he were expecting something. And in fact his two friends immediately chimed in with the words, "We're also leaving tomorrow." Thereupon he seized the door handle and banged the door shut.

Gregor's father staggered with groping hands to his armchair and let himself fall into it; he looked as if he were stretching out for his usual evening nap, but the rapid nodding of his head, as if it were out of control, showed that he was anything but asleep. All this time Gregor had been lying still in the same place where the boarders had caught sight of him. His disappointment over the failure of his plan, and perhaps also the weakness caused by his great hunger, made it impossible for him to move. With a fair degree of certainty, he feared that in the very next moment everything would collapse over him, and he was waiting. He was not even startled when the violin slipped through the mother's trembling fingers, fell off her lap, and gave off a reverberating clang.

"My dear parents," the sister said, striking the table with her hand by way of introduction, "things can't go on like this. Perhaps you don't realize that, but I do. I refuse to utter my brother's name in the presence of this monster, and so I say: we have to try to get rid of it. We've done everything humanly possible to take care of it and put up with it; I think no one could reproach us in the slightest."

"She's right a thousand times over," the father said to himself. Still struggling to catch her breath, a wild look in her eyes, the mother began to cough hollowly into her hand.

The sister rushed to the mother and held her forehead. The father's thoughts seemed to have become clearer as a result of the sister's words; he had sat up straight and was playing with his uniform cap among the dishes that still lay on the table from the boarder's supper, and from time to time he glanced over at Gregor, who remained motionless.

"We must try to get rid of it," said the sister, now only addressing the father, since the mother couldn't hear anything over her coughing. "It'll kill both of you, I can see that coming. When we all have to work as hard as we do, how can we stand this constant torment at home? At least I can't stand it anymore." And she burst out into such violent weeping that her tears flowed down onto her mother's face, where she mechanically wiped them away.

"My child," said the father compassionately and with remarkable comprehension, "but what are we supposed to do?"

The sister just shrugged her shoulders to show the helplessness that had now come over her during her crying fit, in contrast to her former self-confidence.

"If he understood us," said the father, half-questioningly; the sister, still sobbing, waved her hand vehemently to show how unthinkable it was.

"If he understood us," repeated the father, closing his eyes to absorb the sister's conviction that this was impossible, "then perhaps we might be able to come to some sort of agreement with him. But as it is —"

"He's got to go," cried the sister, "that's the only answer, father. You must just try to stop thinking that this is Gregor. The fact that we've believed it for so long is actually our true misfortune. But how can it be Gregor? If it were Gregor, he would long since have understood that it's impossible for people to live together with such a creature, and he would have gone away of his own free will. Then we wouldn't have a brother, but we could go on living and honor his memory. But instead this creature persecutes us, drives away the boarders, obviously wants to take over the entire apartment and let us sleep out in the street. Just look, father," she suddenly shrieked, "he's at it again!" And — in a state of panic that was totally incomprehensible to Gregor — the sister even abandoned her mother, literally bolting away from her chair as if she would rather sacrifice her mother than stay near Gregor, and she rushed behind her father, who got to his feet as well, alarmed at her behavior, and half raised his arms as if to protect her.

But Gregor hadn't the slightest intention of frightening anyone, least of all his sister. He had merely begun to turn himself around so as to return to his room, and that admittedly did attract attention, since in his feeble condition he had to use his head to achieve these difficult turns, raising it and bumping it against the floor several times. He paused and looked around. His good intentions seemed to have been recognized; it had only been a momentary alarm. Now they all watched him, silent and sad. His mother lay back in her chair, her legs stretched out and pressed together, her eyes almost shut from exhaustion; his father and sister were sitting side by side, his sister had placed her hand around her father's neck.

"Perhaps I'm allowed to turn around now," Gregor thought, and he resumed his work. He couldn't suppress his panting from the exertion and also had to stop and rest every once in awhile. Otherwise no one hurried him, it was all left entirely to him. When he had completed the turn, he started to crawl back in a straight line. He was astonished at the great distance separating him from his room and couldn't comprehend how in his weak condition he could have covered the same ground a short time ago almost without noticing it. So intent was he on crawling rapidly, he scarcely noticed that no word or outcry from the family was disturbing his progress. Only when he was already in the doorway did he turn his head, not completely, for he felt his neck stiffening, but enough to see that nothing had changed behind him, except that his sister had stood up. His final gaze fell on his mother, who was now sound asleep.

No sooner was he inside his room than the door was hurriedly slammed shut, firmly bolted, and locked. The sudden noise behind him frightened Gregor so much that his little legs buckled. It was his sister who had been in such a hurry. She had been standing there ready and waiting, then she had swiftly leaped forward, Gregor hadn't even heard her coming, and she had cried "At last!" to her parents as she turned the key in the lock.

"And now?" Gregor asked himself, and peered around in the darkness. He soon made the discovery that he couldn't move at all. It didn't surprise him; rather it seemed unnatural to him that until now he had actually been able to get around on those thin little legs. Otherwise he felt relatively comfortable. He had pains throughout his body, of course, but it seemed to him that they were gradually getting weaker and weaker and would eventually disappear completely. The rotten apple in his back and the inflamed area around it, completely covered over by soft dust, scarcely bothered him. His thoughts went back to his family with tenderness and love. His conviction that he must disappear was, if possible, even stronger than his sister's. He remained in this state of empty, peaceful meditation until the tower clock struck three in the morning. He was just conscious of the beginning of the dawn outside his window. Then his head sank down completely, involuntarily, and his last breath issued faintly from his nostrils.

Early in the morning when the cleaning woman arrived—from sheer energy and impatience she would slam all the doors so loudly, no matter how many times she'd been asked not to do so, that it was impossible to sleep peacefully anywhere in the apartment—she found nothing unusual at first during her customary brief visit to Gregor. She thought that he was deliberately lying motionless like that, acting insulted; she credited him with unlimited intelligence. Since she happened to be holding the long broom in her hand, she tried to tickle Gregor with it from the doorway. When this produced no response, she became annoyed and jabbed Gregor a little, and it was only when she had moved him from his place without his resistance that she began to take notice. When she quickly grasped the fact of the matter, she opened her eyes wide and gave a low whistle, but she didn't stay there long; instead she tore open the bedroom door and shouted at the top of her voice into the darkness, "Come and take a look; it's croaked; it's lying there, completely and totally croaked!"

The Samsa parents sat up in their marriage bed and had to overcome the shock that the cleaning woman had given them before they could finally grasp her message. Then Mr. and Mrs. Samsa quickly climbed out of bed, one from each side; Mr. Samsa wrapped the blanket around his shoulders, Mrs. Samsa came out only in her nightgown; in this way they entered Gregor's room. Meanwhile the living room door had also opened; Grete had been sleeping there since the boarders had moved in; she was fully dressed, as if she'd not slept at all, and her pale face seemed to confirm this. "Dead?" asked Mrs. Samsa, and looked up inquiringly at the cleaning woman, though she could have examined everything herself, and the situation was plain enough without her doing so. "I'll say!" replied the cleaning woman, and to prove it she pushed Gregor's corpse with her broom off to one side. Mrs. Samsa made a movement as if she wanted to hold back the broom, but she didn't do it. "Well," said Mr. Samsa, "now we can thank God." He crossed himself, and the three women followed his example. Grete, who never took her eyes off the corpse, said, "Just look how thin he was. After all, he hadn't been eating anything for so long. The food came out of his room again just the way it went in." As a matter of fact, Gregor's body was completely flat and dry; this was really evident now for the first time when he was no longer lifted up by his little legs and also when nothing else diverted their gaze.

"Come in with us, Grete, for a little while," said Mrs. Samsa with a melancholy smile, and Grete followed her parents into their bedroom, not without looking back at the corpse. The cleaning woman shut Gregor's door and opened his window wide. Although it was early in the morning, the fresh air held a touch of mildness. By now it was nearly the end of March.

The three boarders emerged from their room and looked around in astonishment for their breakfast; they had been forgotten. "Where is breakfast?" the middle one gruffly asked the cleaning woman. But she put her finger to her lips and hastily and silently beckoned them to come into Gregor's room. In they went and stood with their hands in the pockets of their somewhat shabby jackets in a circle around Gregor's corpse in the room that by now was filled with light.

Just then the bedroom door opened, and Mr. Samsa appeared in his uniform with his wife on one arm and his daughter on the other. They all looked as if they had been crying; from time to time Grete pressed her face against her father's sleeve.

"Leave my apartment at once!" said Mr. Samsa and pointed to the door without letting go of the women. "What do you mean?" asked the middle boarder, somewhat dismayed and with a sugary smile. The two others held their hands behind their backs and rubbed them together incessantly, as if in gleeful anticipation of a major quarrel that could only turn out in their favor. "I mean exactly what I say," answered Mr. Samsa, and he marched in a line with his two women companions toward the boarder. At first the boarder quietly stood still and looked at the floor, as if he were rearranging matters in his head. "Well, then, we'll go," he said, and suddenly overcome with humility he looked up at Mr. Samsa as if he were seeking new approval for this decision. Mr. Samsa merely nodded several times, staring at him hard. At that the boarder immediately took long strides into the hall; his two friends, who had been listening for awhile, their hands entirely still, now practically went hopping right after him, as if afraid that Mr. Samsa would reach the hall ahead of them and cut them off from their leader. In the hall, all three took their hats from the coat rack, drew their canes out of the umbrella stand, bowed silently and left the apartment. Impelled by a mistrust that proved to be entirely unfounded, Mr. Samsa and the two women stepped out onto the landing and, leaning over the banister, they watched the three boarders slowly but surely descend the long staircase, disappearing on each floor at a certain turn and then reappearing a few moments later; the lower they got, the more the Samsa family's interest in them dwindled, and when a butcher's boy proudly carrying a tray on his head swung past them on up the stairs, Mr. Samsa and the women left the banister and, as if relieved, all went back to the apartment.

They decided to spend this day resting and going for a walk; they not only deserved a break from their work, they also desperately needed it. And so they sat down at the table to write their letters of excuse, Mr. Samsa to the bank manager, Mrs. Samsa to her employer, and Grete to the store owner. While they were writing, the cleaning woman came in to announce that she was going because her morning work was finished. The three letter writers merely nodded at first without looking up, but as the cleaning woman still kept lingering, they all looked up irritably. "Well?" asked Mr. Samsa. The cleaning woman stood smiling in the doorway as if she had some great news for the family but would only tell it if they questioned her properly. The little ostrich feather sticking up almost straight on her hat, which had annoyed Mr. Samsa during all the time she had been working for them, was fluttering in all directions. "Well, what is it you really want?" asked Mrs. Samsa, for whom the cleaning woman still had the most respect. "Well," answered the cleaning woman, and she couldn't go on immediately for her own good natured chuckling, "well, you don't have to worry about getting rid of the thing next door. It's already been taken care of." Mrs. Samsa and Grete bent their heads down over their letters, as if they intended to resume writing; Mr. Samsa, who realized that the cleaning woman was now eager to start describing everything in detail, cut her short with an outstretched hand. But since she couldn't tell her story, she remembered that she was in a great hurry and cried out, obviously offended, "Goodbye, everyone," then whirled around wildly and left the apartment with a thunderous slamming of the door.

"She'll be fired tonight," said Mr. Samsa, but he received no reply from either his wife or his daughter, because the cleaning woman seemed to have disturbed the peace of mind they had just recently acquired. They got up, went over to the window, and stayed there, their arms around each other. Mr. Samsa turned toward them in his chair and watched them quietly for awhile. Then he called, "Oh, come on over here. Stop brooding over the past. And have a little consideration for me, too." The women obeyed him at once, rushed over to him, caressed him, and hurriedly finished their letters.

Then they all three left the apartment together, which they hadn't done in months, and took the trolley out to the open country on the outskirts of the city. The car, in which they were the only passengers, was flooded with warm sunshine. Leaning back comfortably in their seats, they discussed their prospects for the future and it turned out that, on closer inspection, these weren't bad at all, because all three had positions which—though they hadn't ever really asked one another about them in any detail—were thoroughly advantageous and especially promising for the future. The greatest immediate improvement in their situation would easily result, of course, from a change in apartments; now they would move to a smaller and cheaper apartment, but one better located and in general more practical than their present one, which Gregor had chosen. While they were talking in this way, it occurred almost simultaneously to both Mr. and Mrs. Samsa, as they watched their daughter's increasing liveliness, that despite all the recent cares that had made her cheeks pale, she had blossomed into a good looking and well-developed girl. Growing quieter and almost unconsciously communicating through glances, they thought it would soon be time, too, to find a good husband for her. And it was like a confirmation of their new dreams and good intentions when at the end of their ride, their daughter stood up first and stretched her young body.

JAMAICA KINCAID

Jamaica Kincaid (b. 1949) was born and educated in St. Johns, Antigua, in the West Indies. Her father was a carpenter, and her family doted upon her, the only child. Kincaid remembers:

> My mother did keep everything I ever wore, and basically until I was quite grown up my past was sort of a museum to me. Clearly, the way I became a writer was that my mother wrote my life for me and told it to me. I can't help but think that it made me interested in the idea of myself as an object. I can't account for the reason I became a writer any other way, because I certainly didn't know writers. And not only that. I thought writing was something that people just didn't do anymore, that went out of fashion, like the bustle. I really didn't read a book that was written in the twentieth century until I was about seventeen and away from home.

Kincaid left Antigua to study in the United States, but she found college "a dismal failure," so she educated herself. She began writing and published her stories in Rolling Stone, *the* Paris Review, *and* The New Yorker, *where she became a staff writer in 1978. Six years later she published her first book,* At the Bottom of the River, *a collection of stories, which won the Morton Dauwen Zabel Award of the American Academy and Institute of Arts and Letters. In 1985* Annie John, *her book of interrelated stories about a girl's coming of age in the West Indies, was also much praised. In her autobiographical writing, Kincaid often explores the idea that her deep affection for her family and her native country developed into a conflicting need for separation and independence as she grew up.*

Typically Kincaid writes in a deliberately precise rhythmic style about intense emotions, as in her story "Girl" (1978), which she has described as portraying a mother/daughter "relationship between the powerful and the powerless." Although Kincaid is married to an American and lives in Vermont, she feels that the British West Indies will continue to be the source for her fiction. "What I really feel about America is that it's given me a place to be myself—but myself as I was formed somewhere else." A Small Place *(1988), another book about the West Indies, was described by the novelist Salman Rushdie as "a jeremiad of great clarity and a force that one might have called torrential were the language not so finely controlled." Some recent books are* Lucy *(1990),* The Autobiography of My Mother *(1996), and* My Brother *(1997).*

WEB   *Research Jamaica Kincaid and answer questions about her work at bedfordstmartins.com/charters/litwriters.*

Girl   1978

Wash the white clothes on Monday and put them on the stone heap; wash the color clothes on Tuesday and put them on the clothesline to dry; don't walk barehead in the hot sun; cook pumpkin fritters in very hot sweet oil; soak your little cloths right after you take them off; when buying cotton to make yourself a nice blouse, be sure that it doesn't have gum on it, because that way it won't hold up well after a wash; soak salt fish overnight before you cook it; is it true that you sing benna° in Sunday school?; always eat your food in such a way that it won't turn someone else's stomach; on Sundays try to walk like a lady and not like the slut you are so bent on becoming; don't sing benna in Sunday school; you mustn't speak to wharf-rat boys, not even to give directions; don't eat fruits on the street — flies will follow you; *but I don't sing benna on Sundays at all and never in Sunday school;* this is how to sew on a button; this is how to make a button-hole for the button you have just sewed on; this is how to hem a dress when you see the hem coming down and so to prevent yourself from looking like the slut I know you are so bent on becoming; this is how you iron your father's khaki shirt so that it doesn't have a crease; this is how you iron your father's khaki pants so that they don't have a crease; this is how you grow okra — far from the house, because okra tree harbors red ants; when you are growing dasheen, make sure it gets plenty of water or else it makes your throat itch when you are eating it; this is how you sweep a corner; this is how you sweep a whole house; this is how you sweep a yard; this is how you smile to someone you don't like too much; this is how you smile to someone you don't like at all; this is how you smile to someone you like completely; this is how you set a table for tea; this is how you set a table for dinner; this is how you set a table for dinner with an important guest; this is how you set a table for lunch; this is how you set a table for breakfast; this is how to behave in the presence of men who don't know you very well, and this way they won't recognize immediately the slut I have warned you against becoming; be sure to wash every day, even if it is with your own spit; don't squat down to play marbles — you are not a boy, you know; don't pick people's flowers — you might catch something; don't throw stones at blackbirds, because it might not be a blackbird at all; this is how to make a bread pudding; this is how to make doukona;° this is how to make pepper pot; this is how to make a good medicine for a cold; this is how to make a good medicine to throw away a child before it even becomes a child; this is how to catch a fish; this is how to throw back a fish you don't like, and that

---

benna: Calypso music.
doukona: A spicy plantain pudding.

way something bad won't fall on you; this is how to bully a man; this is how a man bullies you; this is how to love a man, and if this doesn't work there are other ways, and if they don't work don't feel too bad about giving up; this is how to spit up in the air if you feel like it, and this is how to move quick so that it doesn't fall on you; this is how to make ends meet; always squeeze bread to make sure it's fresh; *but what if the baker won't let me feel the bread?;* you mean to say that after all you are really going to be the kind of woman who the baker won't let near the bread?

JHUMPA LAHIRI

Jhumpa Lahiri (b. 1967) was born in London, the daughter of Bengali parents. As a child she often made trips to Calcutta, and she feels that her sense of culture has been influenced by both India and the United States. To Lahiri, India "is the place where my parents are from, a place I visited frequently for extended time and formed relationships with people and with my relatives and felt a tie over time even though it was a sort of parenthesis in my life to be there." Lahiri grew up in Rhode Island and started writing fiction in her grade school notebooks. After graduating with a B.A. from Barnard College, she applied to creative writing programs in several graduate schools, but her applications were rejected by all of them. She began working on her first book of short fiction while in an office job as a research assistant at a nonprofit organization in Cambridge, Massachusetts. She remembers,

> *For the first time I had a computer of my own at my desk, and I started writing fiction again, more seriously. I used to stay late and come in to work on stories. Eventually I had enough material to apply to the creative writing program at Boston University. But once that ended, unsure of what to do next, I went on to graduate school and got my Ph.D. [in Renaissance Studies]. In the process, it became clear to me that I was not meant to be a scholar. It was something I did out of a sense of duty and practicality, but it was never something I loved. I still wrote stories on the side, publishing things here and there. The year I finished my dissertation [1997], I was also accepted to the Fine Arts Work Center in Provincetown, and that changed everything. It was something of a miracle. In seven months I got an agent, sold a book, and had a story published in* The New Yorker. *I've been extremely lucky. It's been the happiest possible ending.*

As a new writer, Lahiri has explained that "the characters I'm drawn to all face some barrier of communication. I like to write about people who think in a way they can't fully express." At first she began to place her stories in Agni, Epoch, The Louisville Review, Harvard Review, *and* Story Quarterly. *In 1993 she was awarded a Transatlantic Review fellowship from the Henfield Foundation, and in 1997 she won a fiction prize from* The Louisville Review. *In 1999 Lahiri published her first collection of short fiction,* Interpreter of Maladies, *a total of nine stories, three of which* The New Yorker *had published. Her book won the Pulitzer Prize for fiction in 2000.*

WEB *Research Jhumpa Lahiri and answer questions about her work at bedfordstmartins.com/charters/litwriters.*

Interpreter of Maladies   1999

At the tea stall Mr. and Mrs. Das bickered about who should take Tina to the toilet. Eventually Mrs. Das relented when Mr. Das pointed out that he had given the girl her bath the night before. In the rearview mirror Mr. Kapasi watched as Mrs. Das emerged slowly from his bulky white Ambassador, dragging her shaved, largely bare legs across the back seat. She did not hold the little girl's hand as they walked to the rest room.

They were on their way to see the Sun Temple at Konarak. It was a dry, bright Saturday, the mid-July heat tempered by a steady ocean breeze, ideal weather for sightseeing. Ordinarily Mr. Kapasi would not have stopped so soon along the way, but less than five minutes after he'd picked up the family that morning in front of Hotel Sandy Villa, the little girl had complained. The first thing Mr. Kapasi had noticed when he saw Mr. and Mrs. Das, standing with their children under the portico of the hotel, was that they were very young, perhaps not even thirty. In addition to Tina they had two boys, Ronny and Bobby, who appeared very close in age and had teeth covered in a network of flashing silver wires. The family looked Indian but dressed as foreigners did, the children in stiff, brightly colored clothing and caps with translucent visors. Mr. Kapasi was accustomed to foreign tourists; he was assigned to them regularly because he could speak English. Yesterday he had driven an elderly couple from Scotland, both with spotted faces and fluffy white hair so thin it exposed their sunburnt scalps. In comparison, the tanned, youthful faces of Mr. and Mrs. Das were all the more striking. When he'd introduced himself, Mr. Kapasi had pressed his palms together in greeting, but Mr. Das squeezed hands like an American so that Mr. Kapasi felt it in his elbow. Mrs. Das, for her part, had flexed one side of her mouth, smiling dutifully at Mr. Kapasi, without displaying any interest in him.

As they waited at the tea stall, Ronny, who looked like the older of the two boys, clambered suddenly out of the back seat, intrigued by a goat tied to a stake in the ground.

"Don't touch it," Mr. Das said. He glanced up from his paperback tour book, which said "INDIA" in yellow letters and looked as if it had been published abroad. His voice, somehow tentative and a little shrill, sounded as though it had not yet settled into maturity.

"I want to give it a piece of gum," the boy called back as he trotted ahead.

Mr. Das stepped out of the car and stretched his legs by squatting briefly to the ground. A clean-shaven man, he looked exactly like a magnified version of Ronny. He had a sapphire blue visor, and was dressed in shorts, sneakers, and a T-shirt. The camera slung around his neck, with an impressive telephoto lens and numerous buttons and markings, was the only complicated thing he wore. He frowned, watching as Ronny rushed toward the goat, but appeared to have no intention of intervening. "Bobby, make sure that your brother doesn't do anything stupid."

"I don't feel like it," Bobby said, not moving. He was sitting in the front seat beside Mr. Kapasi, studying a picture of the elephant god taped to the glove compartment.

"No need to worry," Mr. Kapasi said. "They are quite tame." Mr. Kapasi was forty-six years old, with receding hair that had gone completely silver, but his butterscotch complexion and his unlined brow, which he treated in spare moments to dabs of lotus-oil balm, made it easy to imagine what he must have looked like at an earlier age. He wore gray trousers and a matching jacket-style shirt, tapered at the waist, with short sleeves and a large pointed collar, made of a thin but durable synthetic material. He had specified both the cut and the fabric to his tailor — it was his preferred uniform for giving tours because it did not get crushed during his long hours behind the wheel. Through the wind-shield he watched as Ronny circled around the goat, touched it quickly on its side, then trotted back to the car.

"You left India as a child?" Mr. Kapasi asked when Mr. Das had settled once again into the passenger seat.

"Oh, Mina and I were both born in America," Mr. Das announced with an air of sudden confidence. "Born and raised. Our parents live here now, in Assansol. They retired. We visit them every couple years." He turned to watch as the little girl ran toward the car, the wide purple bows of her sundress flop-ping on her narrow brown shoulders. She was holding to her chest a doll with yellow hair that looked as if it had been chopped, as a punitive measure, with a pair of dull scissors. "This is Tina's first trip to India, isn't it, Tina?"

"I don't have to go to the bathroom anymore," Tina announced.

"Where's Mina?" Mr. Das asked.

Mr. Kapasi found it strange that Mr. Das should refer to his wife by her first name when speaking to the little girl. Tina pointed to where Mrs. Das was purchasing something from one of the shirtless men who worked at the tea stall. Mr. Kapasi heard one of the shirtless men sing a phrase from a popular Hindi love song as Mrs. Das walked back to the car, but she did not appear to understand the words of the song, for she did not express irritation, or embar-rassment, or react in any other way to the man's declarations.

He observed her. She wore a red-and-white-checkered skirt that stopped above her knees, slip-on shoes with a square wooden heel, and a close-fitting blouse styled like a man's undershirt. The blouse was decorated at chest-level with a calico appliqué in the shape of a strawberry. She was a short woman, with small hands like paws, her frosty pink fingernails painted to match her lips, and was slightly plump in her figure. Her hair, shorn only a little longer than her husband's, was parted far to one side. She was wearing large dark brown sunglasses with a pinkish tint to them, and carried a big straw bag, almost as big as her torso, shaped like a bowl, with a water bottle poking out of it. She walked slowly, carrying some puffed rice tossed with peanuts and chili peppers in a large packet made from newspapers. Mr. Kapasi turned to Mr. Das.

"Where in America do you live?"

"New Brunswick, New Jersey."

"Next to New York."

"Exactly. I teach middle school there."

"What subject?"

"Science. In fact, every year I take my students on a trip to the Museum of Natural History in New York City. In a way we have a lot in common, you could say, you and I. How long have you been a tour guide, Mr. Kapasi?"

"Five years."

Mrs. Das reached the car. "How long's the trip?" she asked, shutting the door.

"About two and a half hours," Mr. Kapasi replied.

At this Mrs. Das gave an impatient sigh, as if she had been traveling her whole life without pause. She fanned herself with a folded Bombay film magazine written in English.

"I thought that the Sun Temple is only eighteen miles north of Puri," Mr. Das said, tapping on the tour book.

"The roads to Konarak are poor. Actually it is a distance of fifty-two miles," Mr. Kapasi explained.

Mr. Das nodded, readjusting the camera strap where it had begun to chafe the back of his neck.

Before starting the ignition, Mr. Kapasi reached back to make sure the cranklike locks on the inside of each of the back doors were secured. As soon as the car began to move the little girl began to play with the lock on her side, clicking it with some effort forward and backward, but Mrs. Das said nothing to stop her. She sat a bit slouched at one end of the back seat, not offering her puffed rice to anyone. Ronny and Tina sat on either side of her, both snapping bright green gum.

"Look," Bobby said as the car began to gather speed. He pointed with his finger to the tall trees that lined the road. "Look."

"Monkeys!" Ronny shrieked. "Wow!"

They were seated in groups along the branches, with shining black faces, silver bodies, horizontal eyebrows, and crested heads. Their long gray tails dangled like a series of ropes among the leaves. A few scratched themselves with black leathery hands, or swung their feet, staring as the car passed.

"We call them the hanuman," Mr. Kapasi said. "They are quite common in the area."

As soon as he spoke, one of the monkeys leaped into the middle of the road, causing Mr. Kapasi to brake suddenly. Another bounced onto the hood of the car, then sprang away. Mr. Kapasi beeped his horn. The children began to get excited, sucking in their breath and covering their faces partly with their hands. They had never seen monkeys outside of a zoo, Mr. Das explained. He asked Mr. Kapasi to stop the car so that he could take a picture.

While Mr. Das adjusted his telephoto lens, Mrs. Das reached into her straw bag and pulled out a bottle of colorless nail polish, which she proceeded to stroke on the tip of her index finger.

The little girl stuck out a hand. "Mine too. Mommy, do mine too."

"Leave me alone," Mrs. Das said, blowing on her nail and turning her body slightly. "You're making me mess up."

The little girl occupied herself by buttoning and unbuttoning a pinafore on the doll's plastic body.

"All set," Mr. Das said, replacing the lens cap.

The car rattled considerably as it raced along the dusty road, causing them all to pop up from their seats every now and then, but Mrs. Das continued to polish her nails. Mr. Kapasi eased up on the accelerator, hoping to produce a smoother ride. When he reached for the gearshift the boy in front accommodated him by swinging his hairless knees out of the way. Mr. Kapasi noted that this boy was slightly paler than the other children. "Daddy, why is the driver sitting on the wrong side in this car, too?" the boy asked.

"They all do that here, dummy," Ronny said.

"Don't call your brother a dummy," Mr. Das said. He turned to Mr. Kapasi. "In America, you know . . . it confuses them."

"Oh yes, I am well aware," Mr. Kapasi said. As delicately as he could, he shifted gears again, accelerating as they approached a hill in the road. "I see it on *Dallas,* the steering wheels are on the left-hand side."

"What's *Dallas?*" Tina asked, banging her now naked doll on the seat behind Mr. Kapasi.

"It went off the air," Mr. Das explained. "It's a television show."

They were all like siblings, Mr. Kapasi thought as they passed a row of date trees. Mr. and Mrs. Das behaved like an older brother and sister, not parents. It seemed that they were in charge of the children only for the day; it was hard to believe they were regularly responsible for anything other than themselves. Mr. Das tapped on his lens cap, and his tour book, dragging his thumbnail occasionally across the pages so that they made a scraping sound. Mrs. Das continued to polish her nails. She had still not removed her sunglasses. Every now and then Tina renewed her plea that she wanted her nails done, too, and so at one point Mrs. Das flicked a drop of polish on the little girl's finger before depositing the bottle back inside her straw bag.

"Isn't this an air-conditioned car?" she asked, still blowing on her hand. The window on Tina's side was broken and could not be rolled down.

"Quit complaining," Mr. Das said. "It isn't so hot."

"I told you to get a car with air-conditioning," Mrs. Das continued. "Why do you do this, Raj, just to save a few stupid rupees. What are you saving us, fifty cents?"

Their accents sounded just like the ones Mr. Kapasi heard on American television programs, though not like the ones on *Dallas.*

"Doesn't it get tiresome, Mr. Kapasi, showing people the same thing every day?" Mr. Das asked, rolling down his own window all the way. "Hey, do you mind stopping the car. I just want to get a shot of this guy."

Mr. Kapasi pulled over to the side of the road as Mr. Das took a picture of a barefoot man, his head wrapped in a dirty turban, seated on top of a cart of grain sacks pulled by a pair of bullocks. Both the man and the bullocks were emaciated. In the back seat Mrs. Das gazed out another window, at the sky, where nearly transparent clouds passed quickly in front of one another.

"I look forward to it, actually," Mr. Kapasi said as they continued on their way. "The Sun Temple is one of my favorite places. In that way it is a reward for me. I give tours on Fridays and Saturdays only. I have another job during the week."

"Oh? Where?" Mr. Das asked.

"I work in a doctor's office."

"You're a doctor?"

"I am not a doctor. I work with one. As an interpreter."

"What does a doctor need an interpreter for?"

"He has a number of Gujarati patients. My father was Gujarati, but many people do not speak Gujarati in this area, including the doctor. And so the doctor asked me to work in his office, interpreting what the patients say."

"Interesting. I've never heard of anything like that," Mr. Das said.

Mr. Kapasi shrugged. "It is a job like any other."

"But so romantic," Mrs. Das said dreamily, breaking her extended silence. She lifted her pinkish brown sunglasses and arranged them on top of her head like a tiara. For the first time, her eyes met Mr. Kapasi's in the rearview mirror: pale, a bit small, their gaze fixed but drowsy.

Mr. Das craned to look at her. "What's so romantic about it?"

"I don't know. Something." She shrugged, knitting her brows together for an instant. "Would you like a piece of gum, Mr. Kapasi?" she asked brightly. She reached into her straw bag and handed him a small square wrapped in green-and-white-striped paper. As soon as Mr. Kapasi put the gum in his mouth a thick sweet liquid burst onto his tongue.

"Tell us more about your job, Mr. Kapasi," Mrs. Das said.

"What would you like to know, madame?"

"I don't know," she shrugged, munching on some puffed rice and licking the mustard oil from the corners of her mouth. "Tell us a typical situation." She settled back in her seat, her head tilted in a patch of sun, and closed her eyes. "I want to picture what happens."

"Very well. The other day a man came in with a pain in his throat."

"Did he smoke cigarettes?"

"No. It was very curious. He complained that he felt as if there were long pieces of straw stuck in his throat. When I told the doctor he was able to prescribe the proper medication."

"That's so neat."

"Yes," Mr. Kapasi agreed after some hesitation.

"So these patients are totally dependent on you," Mrs. Das said. She spoke slowly, as if she were thinking aloud. "In a way, more dependent on you than the doctor."

"How do you mean? How could it be?"

"Well, for example, you could tell the doctor that the pain felt like a burning, not straw. The patient would never know what you had told the doctor, and the doctor wouldn't know that you had told the wrong thing. It's a big responsibility."

"Yes, a big responsibility you have there, Mr. Kapasi," Mr. Das agreed.

Mr. Kapasi had never thought of his job in such complimentary terms. To him it was a thankless occupation. He found nothing noble in interpreting people's maladies, assiduously translating the symptoms of so many swollen bones, countless cramps of bellies and bowels, spots on people's palms that changed color, shape, or size. The doctor, nearly half his age, had an affinity for bell-bottom trousers and made humorless jokes about the Congress party. Together they worked in a stale little infirmary where Mr. Kapasi's smartly tailored clothes clung to him in the heat, in spite of the blackened blades of a ceiling fan churning over their heads.

The job was a sign of his failings. In his youth he'd been a devoted scholar of foreign languages, the owner of an impressive collection of dictionaries. He had dreamed of being an interpreter for diplomats and dignitaries, resolving conflicts between people and nations, settling disputes of which he alone could understand both sides. He was a self-educated man. In a series of notebooks, in the evenings before his parents settled his marriage, he had listed the common etymologies of words, and at one point in his life he was confident that he could converse, if given the opportunity, in English, French, Russian, Portuguese, and Italian, not to mention Hindi, Bengali, Orissi, and Gujarati. Now only a handful of European phrases remained in his memory, scattered words for things like saucers and chairs. English was the only non-Indian language he spoke fluently anymore. Mr. Kapasi knew it was not a remarkable talent. Sometimes he feared that his children knew better English than he did, just from watching television. Still, it came in handy for the tours.

He had taken the job as an interpreter after his first son, at the age of seven, contracted typhoid—that was how he had first made the acquaintance of the doctor. At the time Mr. Kapasi had been teaching English in a grammar school, and he bartered his skills as an interpreter to pay the increasingly exorbitant medical bills. In the end the boy had died one evening in his mother's arms, his limbs burning with fever, but then there was the funeral to pay for, and the other children who were born soon enough, and the newer, bigger house, and the good schools and tutors, and the fine shoes and the television, and the countless other ways he tried to console his wife and to keep her from crying in her sleep, and so when the doctor offered to pay him twice as much as he earned at the grammar school, he accepted. Mr. Kapasi knew that his wife had little regard for his career as an interpreter. He knew it reminded her of the son she'd lost, and that she resented the other lives he helped, in his own small way, to save. If ever she referred to his position, she used the phrase "doctor's assistant," as if the process of interpretation were equal to taking someone's temperature, or changing a bedpan. She never asked him about the patients who came to the doctor's office, or said that his job was a big responsibility.

For this reason it flattered Mr. Kapasi that Mrs. Das was so intrigued by his job. Unlike his wife, she had reminded him of its intellectual challenges. She had also used the word "romantic." She did not behave in a romantic way toward her husband, and yet she had used the word to describe him. He wondered if Mr. and Mrs. Das were a bad match, just as he and his wife were. Perhaps they, too, had little in common apart from three children and a decade of their lives. The signs he recognized from his own marriage were there—the bickering, the indifference, the protracted silences. Her sudden interest in him, an interest she did not express in either her husband or her children, was mildly intoxicating. When Mr. Kapasi thought once again about how she had said "romantic," the feeling of intoxication grew.

He began to check his reflection in the rearview mirror as he drove, feeling grateful that he had chosen the gray suit that morning and not the brown one, which tended to sag a little in the knees. From time to time he glanced through the mirror at Mrs. Das. In addition to glancing at her face he glanced at the strawberry between her breasts, and the golden brown hollow in her throat. He decided to tell Mrs. Das about another patient, and another: the young woman who had complained of a sensation of raindrops in her spine, the gentleman whose birthmark had begun to sprout hairs. Mrs. Das listened attentively, stroking her hair with a small plastic brush that resembled an oval bed of nails, asking more questions, for yet another example. The children were quiet, intent on spotting more monkeys in the trees, and Mr. Das was absorbed by his tour book, so it seemed like a private conversation between Mr. Kapasi and Mrs. Das. In this manner the next half hour passed, and when they stopped for lunch at a roadside restaurant that sold fritters and omelette sandwiches, usually something Mr. Kapasi looked forward to on his tours so that he could sit in peace and enjoy some hot tea, he was disappointed. As the Das family settled together under a magenta umbrella fringed with white and orange tassels, and placed their orders with one of the waiters who marched about in tricornered caps, Mr. Kapasi reluctantly headed toward a neighboring table.

"Mr. Kapasi, wait. There's room here," Mrs. Das called out. She gathered Tina onto her lap, insisting that he accompany them. And so, together, they had bottled mango juice and sandwiches and plates of onions and potatoes deep-fried in graham-flour batter. After finishing two omelette sandwiches Mr. Das took more pictures of the group as they ate.

"How much longer?" he asked Mr. Kapasi as he paused to load a new roll of film in the camera.

"About half an hour more."

By now the children had gotten up from the table to look at more monkeys perched in a nearby tree, so there was a considerable space between Mrs. Das and Mr. Kapasi. Mr. Das placed the camera to his face and squeezed one eye shut, his tongue exposed at one corner of his mouth. "This looks funny. Mina, you need to lean in closer to Mr. Kapasi."

She did. He could smell a scent on her skin, like a mixture of whiskey and rosewater. He worried suddenly that she could smell his perspiration, which he knew had collected beneath the synthetic material of his shirt. He polished off his mango juice in one gulp and smoothed his silver hair with his hands. A bit of the juice dripped onto his chin. He wondered if Mrs. Das had noticed.

She had not. "What's your address, Mr. Kapasi?" she inquired, fishing for something inside her straw bag.

"You would like my address?"

"So we can send you copies," she said. "Of the pictures." She handed him a scrap of paper which she had hastily ripped from a page of her film magazine. The blank portion was limited, for the narrow strip was crowded by lines of text and a tiny picture of a hero and heroine embracing under a eucalyptus tree.

The paper curled as Mr. Kapasi wrote his address in clear, careful letters. She would write to him, asking about his days interpreting at the doctor's office, and he would respond eloquently, choosing only the most entertaining anecdotes, ones that would make her laugh out loud as she read them in her house in New Jersey. In time she would reveal the disappointment of her marriage, and he his. In this way their friendship would grow, and flourish. He would possess a picture of the two of them, eating fried onions under a magenta umbrella, which he would keep, he decided, safely tucked between the pages of his Russian grammar. As his mind raced, Mr. Kapasi experienced a mild and pleasant shock. It was similar to a feeling he used to experience long ago when, after months of translating with the aid of a dictionary, he would finally read a passage from a French novel, or an Italian sonnet, and understand the words, one after another, unencumbered by his own efforts. In those moments Mr. Kapasi used to believe that all was right with the world, that all struggles were rewarded, that all of life's mistakes made sense in the end. The promise that he would hear from Mrs. Das now filled him with the same belief.

When he finished writing his address Mr. Kapasi handed her the paper, but as soon as he did so he worried that he had either misspelled his name, or accidentally reversed the numbers of his postal code. He dreaded the possibility of a lost letter, the photograph never reaching him, hovering somewhere in Orissa, close but ultimately unattainable. He thought of asking for the slip of paper again, just to make sure he had written his address accurately, but Mrs. Das had already dropped it into the jumble of her bag.

They reached Konarak at two-thirty. The temple, made of sandstone, was a massive pyramid-like structure in the shape of a chariot. It was dedicated to the great master of life, the sun, which struck three sides of the edifice as it made its journey each day across the sky. Twenty-four giant wheels were carved on the north and south sides of the plinth. The whole thing was drawn by a team of seven horses, speeding as if through the heavens. As they approached, Mr. Kapasi explained that the temple had been built between A.D. 1243 and 1255, with the efforts of twelve hundred artisans, by the great ruler of the Ganga dynasty, King Narasimhadeva the First, to commemorate his victory against the Muslim army.

"It says the temple occupies about a hundred and seventy acres of land," Mr. Das said, reading from his book.

"It's like a desert," Ronny said, his eyes wandering across the sand that stretched on all sides beyond the temple.

"The Chandrabhaga River once flowed one mile north of here. It is dry now," Mr. Kapasi said, turning off the engine.

They got out and walked toward the temple, posing first for pictures by the pair of lions that flanked the steps. Mr. Kapasi led them next to one of the wheels of the chariot, higher than any human being, nine feet in diameter.

" 'The wheels are supposed to symbolize the wheel of life,' ". Mr. Das read. " 'They depict the cycle of creation, preservation, and achievement of realization.' Cool." He turned the page of his book. " 'Each wheel is divided into eight thick and thin spokes, dividing the day into eight equal parts. The rims are carved with designs of birds and animals, whereas the medallions in the spokes are carved with women in luxurious poses, largely erotic in nature.' "

What he referred to were the countless friezes of entwined naked bodies, making love in various positions, women clinging to the necks of men, their knees wrapped eternally around their lovers' thighs. In addition to these were assorted scenes from daily life, of hunting and trading, of deer being killed with bows and arrows and marching warriors holding swords in their hands.

It was no longer possible to enter the temple, for it had filled with rubble years ago, but they admired the exterior, as did all the tourists Mr. Kapasi brought there, slowly strolling along each of its sides. Mr. Das trailed behind, taking pictures. The children ran ahead, pointing to figures of naked people, intrigued in particular by the Nagamithunas, the half-human, half-serpentine couples who were said, Mr. Kapasi told them, to live in the deepest waters of the sea. Mr. Kapasi was pleased that they liked the temple, pleased especially that it appealed to Mrs. Das. She stopped every three or four paces, staring silently at the carved lovers, and the processions of elephants, and the topless female musicians beating on two-sided drums.

Though Mr. Kapasi had been to the temple countless times, it occurred to him, as he, too, gazed at the topless women, that he had never seen his own wife fully naked. Even when they had made love she kept the panels of her blouse hooked together, the string of her petticoat knotted around her waist. He had never admired the backs of his wife's legs the way he now admired those of Mrs. Das, walking as if for his benefit alone. He had, of course, seen plenty of bare limbs before, belonging to the American and European ladies who took his tours. But Mrs. Das was different. Unlike the other women, who had an interest only in the temple, and kept their noses buried in a guidebook, or their eyes behind the lens of a camera, Mrs. Das had taken an interest in him.

Mr. Kapasi was anxious to be alone with her, to continue their private conversation, yet he felt nervous to walk at her side. She was lost behind her sunglasses, ignoring her husband's requests that she pose for another picture, walking past her children as if they were strangers. Worried that he might disturb her, Mr. Kapasi walked ahead, to admire, as he always did, the three life-sized bronze avatars of Surya, the sun god, each emerging from its own niche on the temple facade to greet the sun at dawn, noon, and evening. They wore elaborate headdresses, their languid, elongated eyes closed, their bare chests draped with carved chains and amulets. Hibiscus petals, offerings from previous visitors, were strewn at their gray-green feet. The last statue, on the northern wall of the temple, was Mr. Kapasi's favorite. This Surya had a tired expression, weary after a hard day of work, sitting astride a horse with folded legs. Even his horse's eyes were drowsy. Around his body were smaller sculptures of women in pairs, their hips thrust to one side.

"Who's that?" Mrs. Das asked. He was startled to see that she was standing beside him.

"He is the Astachala-Surya," Mr. Kapasi said. "The setting sun."

"So in a couple of hours the sun will set right here?" She slipped a foot out of one of her square-heeled shoes, rubbed her toes on the back of her other leg.

"That is correct."

She raised her sunglasses for a moment, then put them back on again. "Neat."

Mr. Kapasi was not certain exactly what the word suggested, but he had a feeling it was a favorable response. He hoped that Mrs. Das had understood Surya's beauty, his power. Perhaps they would discuss it further in their letters. He would explain things to her, things about India, and she would explain things to him about America. In its own way this correspondence would fulfill his dream, of serving as an interpreter between nations. He looked at her straw bag, delighted that his address lay nestled among its contents. When he pictured her so many thousands of miles away he plummeted, so much so that he had an overwhelming urge to wrap his arms around her, to freeze with her, even for an instant, in an embrace witnessed by his favorite Surya. But Mrs. Das had already started walking.

"When do you return to America?" he asked, trying to sound placid.

"In ten days."

He calculated: A week to settle in, a week to develop the pictures, a few days to compose her letter, two weeks to get to India by air. According to his schedule, allowing room for delays, he would hear from Mrs. Das in approximately six weeks' time.

The family was silent as Mr. Kapasi drove them back, a little past four-thirty, to Hotel Sandy Villa. The children had bought miniature granite versions of the chariot's wheels at a souvenir stand, and they turned them round in their hands. Mr. Das continued to read his book. Mrs. Das untangled Tina's hair with her brush and divided it into two little ponytails.

Mr. Kapasi was beginning to dread the thought of dropping them off. He was not prepared to begin his six-week wait to hear from Mrs. Das. As he stole glances at her in the rearview mirror, wrapping elastic bands around Tina's hair, he wondered how he might make the tour last a little longer. Ordinarily he sped back to Puri using a shortcut, eager to return home, scrub his feet and hands with sandalwood soap, and enjoy the evening newspaper and a cup of tea that his wife would serve him in silence. The thought of that silence, something to which he'd long been resigned, now oppressed him. It was then that he suggested visiting the hills at Udayagiri and Khandagiri, where a number of monastic dwellings were hewn out of the ground, facing one another across a defile. It was some miles away, but well worth seeing, Mr. Kapasi told them.

"Oh yeah, there's something mentioned about it in this book," Mr. Das said. "Built by a Jain king or something."

"Shall we go then?" Mr. Kapasi asked. He paused at a turn in the road. "It's to the left."

Mr. Das turned to look at Mrs. Das. Both of them shrugged.

"Left, left," the children chanted.

Mr. Kapasi turned the wheel, almost delirious with relief. He did not know what he would do or say to Mrs. Das once they arrived at the hills. Perhaps he would tell her what a pleasing smile she had. Perhaps he would compliment her strawberry shirt, which he found irresistibly becoming. Perhaps, when Mr. Das was busy taking a picture, he would take her hand.

He did not have to worry. When they got to the hills, divided by a steep path thick with trees, Mrs. Das refused to get out of the car. All along the path, dozens of monkeys were seated on stones, as well as on the branches of the trees. Their hind legs were stretched out in front and raised to shoulder level, their arms resting on their knees.

"My legs are tired," she said, sinking low in her seat. "I'll stay here."

"Why did you have to wear those stupid shoes?" Mr. Das said. "You won't be in the pictures."

"Pretend I'm there."

"But we could use one of these pictures for our Christmas card this year. We didn't get one of all five of us at the Sun Temple. Mr. Kapasi could take it."

"I'm not coming. Anyway, those monkeys give me the creeps."

"But they're harmless," Mr. Das said. He turned to Mr. Kapasi. "Aren't they?"

"They are more hungry than dangerous," Mr. Kapasi said. "Do not provoke them with food, and they will not bother you."

Mr. Das headed up the defile with the children, the boys at his side, the little girl on his shoulders. Mr. Kapasi watched as they crossed paths with a Japanese man and woman, the only other tourists there, who paused for a final photograph, then stepped into a nearby car and drove away. As the car disappeared out of view some of the monkeys called out, emitting soft whooping sounds, and then walked on their flat black hands and feet up the path. At one point a group of them formed a little ring around Mr. Das and the children. Tina screamed in delight. Ronny ran in circles around his father. Bobby bent down and picked up a fat stick on the ground. When he extended it, one of the monkeys approached him and snatched it, then briefly beat the ground.

"I'll join them," Mr. Kapasi said, unlocking the door on his side. "There is much to explain about the caves."

"No. Stay a minute," Mrs. Das said. She got out of the back seat and slipped in beside Mr. Kapasi. "Raj has his dumb book anyway." Together, through the windshield, Mrs. Das and Mr. Kapasi watched as Bobby and the monkey passed the stick back and forth between them.

"A brave little boy," Mr. Kapasi commented.

"It's not so surprising," Mrs. Das said.

"No?"

"He's not his."

"I beg your pardon?"

"Raj's. He's not Raj's son."

Mr. Kapasi felt a prickle on his skin. He reached into his shirt pocket for the small tin of lotus-oil balm he carried with him at all times, and applied it to three spots on his forehead. He knew that Mrs. Das was watching him, but he did not turn to face her. Instead he watched as the figures of Mr. Das and the children grew smaller, climbing up the steep path, pausing every now and then for a picture, surrounded by a growing number of monkeys.

"Are you surprised?" The way she put it made him choose his words with care.

"It's not the type of thing one assumes," Mr. Kapasi replied slowly. He put the tin of lotus-oil balm back in his pocket.

"No, of course not. And no one knows, of course. No one at all. I've kept it a secret for eight whole years." She looked at Mr. Kapasi, tilting her chin as if to gain a fresh perspective. "But now I've told you."

Mr. Kapasi nodded. He felt suddenly parched, and his forehead was warm and slightly numb from the balm. He considered asking Mrs. Das for a sip of water, then decided against it.

"We met when we were very young," she said. She reached into her straw bag in search of something, then pulled out a packet of puffed rice. "Want some?"

"No, thank you."

She put a fistful in her mouth, sank into the seat a little, and looked away from Mr. Kapasi, out the window on her side of the car. "We married when we were still in college. We were in high school when he proposed. We went to the same college, of course. Back then we couldn't stand the thought of being separated, not for a day, not for a minute. Our parents were best friends who lived in the same town. My entire life I saw him every weekend, either at our house or theirs. We were sent upstairs to play together while our parents joked about our marriage. Imagine! They never caught us at anything, though in a way I think it was all more or less a setup. The things we did those Friday and Saturday nights, while our parents sat downstairs drinking tea . . . I could tell you stories, Mr. Kapasi."

As a result of spending all her time in college with Raj, she continued, she did not make many close friends. There was no one to confide in about him at the end of a difficult day, or to share a passing thought or a worry. Her parents now lived on the other side of the world, but she had never been very close to them, anyway. After marrying so young she was overwhelmed by it all, having a child so quickly, and nursing, and warming up bottles of milk and testing their temperature against her wrist while Raj was at work, dressed in sweaters and corduroy pants, teaching his students about rocks and dinosaurs. Raj never looked cross or harried, or plump as she had become after the first baby.

Always tired, she declined invitations from her one or two college girlfriends, to have lunch or shop in Manhattan. Eventually the friends stopped calling her, so that she was left at home all day with the baby, surrounded by toys that made her trip when she walked or wince when she sat, always cross and tired. Only occasionally did they go out after Ronny was born, and even more rarely did they entertain. Raj didn't mind; he looked forward to coming home from teaching and watching television and bouncing Ronny on his knee. She had been outraged when Raj told her that a Punjabi friend, someone whom she had once met but did not remember, would be staying with them for a week for some job interviews in the New Brunswick area.

Bobby was conceived in the afternoon, on a sofa littered with rubber teething toys, after the friend learned that a London pharmaceutical company had hired him, while Ronny cried to be freed from his playpen. She made no protest when the friend touched the small of her back as she was about to make a pot of coffee, then pulled her against his crisp navy suit. He made love to her swiftly, in silence, with an expertise she had never known, without the meaningful expressions and smiles Raj always insisted on afterward. The next day Raj drove the friend to JFK. He was married now, to a Punjabi girl, and they lived in London still, and every year they exchanged Christmas cards with Raj and Mina, each couple tucking photos of their families into the envelopes. He did not know that he was Bobby's father. He never would.

"I beg your pardon, Mrs. Das, but why have you told me this information?" Mr. Kapasi asked when she had finally finished speaking, and had turned to face him once again.

"For God's sake, stop calling me Mrs. Das. I'm twenty-eight. You probably have children my age."

"Not quite." It disturbed Mr. Kapasi to learn that she thought of him as a parent. The feeling he had had toward her, that had made him check his reflection in the rearview mirror as they drove, evaporated a little.

"I told you because of your talents." She put the packet of puffed rice back into her bag without folding over the top.

"I don't understand," Mr. Kapasi said.

"Don't you see? For eight years I haven't been able to express this to anybody, not to friends, certainly not to Raj. He doesn't even suspect it. He thinks I'm still in love with him. Well, don't you have anything to say?"

"About what?"

"About what I've just told you. About my secret, and about how terrible it makes me feel. I feel terrible looking at my children, and at Raj, always terrible. I have terrible urges, Mr. Kapasi, to throw things away. One day I had the urge to throw everything I own out the window, the television, the children, everything. Don't you think it's unhealthy?"

He was silent.

"Mr. Kapasi, don't you have anything to say? I thought that was your job."

"My job is to give tours, Mrs. Das."

"Not that. Your other job. As an interpreter."

"But we do not face a language barrier. What need is there for an interpreter?"

"That's not what I mean. I would never have told you otherwise. Don't you realize what it means for me to tell you?"

"What does it mean?"

"It means that I'm tired of feeling so terrible all the time. Eight years, Mr. Kapasi, I've been in pain eight years. I was hoping you could help me feel better, say the right thing. Suggest some kind of remedy."

He looked at her, in her red plaid skirt and strawberry T-shirt, a woman not yet thirty, who loved neither her husband nor her children, who had already fallen out of love with life. Her confession depressed him, depressed him all the more when he thought of Mr. Das at the top of the path, Tina clinging to his shoulders, taking pictures of ancient monastic cells cut into the hills to show his students in America, unsuspecting and unaware that one of his sons was not his own. Mr. Kapasi felt insulted that Mrs. Das should ask him to interpret her common, trivial little secret. She did not resemble the patients in the doctor's office, those who came glassy-eyed and desperate, unable to sleep or breathe or urinate with ease, unable, above all, to give words to their pains. Still, Mr. Kapasi believed it was his duty to assist Mrs. Das. Perhaps he ought to tell her to confess the truth to Mr. Das. He would explain that honesty was the best policy. Honesty, surely, would help her feel better, as she'd put it. Perhaps he would offer to preside over the discussion, as a mediator. He decided to begin with the most obvious question, to get to the heart of the matter, and so he asked, "Is it really pain you feel, Mrs. Das, or is it guilt?"

She turned to him and glared, mustard oil thick on her frosty pink lips. She opened her mouth to say something, but as she glared at Mr. Kapasi some certain knowledge seemed to pass before her eyes, and she stopped. It crushed him; he knew at that moment that he was not even important enough to be properly insulted. She opened the car door and began walking up the path, wobbling a little on her square wooden heels, reaching into her straw bag to eat handfuls of puffed rice. It fell through her fingers, leaving a zigzagging trail, causing a monkey to leap down from a tree and devour the little white grains. In search of more, the monkey began to follow Mrs. Das. Others joined him, so that she was soon being followed by about half a dozen of them, their velvety tails dragging behind.

Mr. Kapasi stepped out of the car. He wanted to holler, to alert her in some way, but he worried that if she knew they were behind her, she would grow nervous. Perhaps she would lose her balance. Perhaps they would pull at her bag or her hair. He began to jog up the path, taking a fallen branch in his hand to scare away the monkeys. Mrs. Das continued walking, oblivious, trailing grains of puffed rice. Near the top of the incline, before a group of cells fronted by a row of squat stone pillars, Mr. Das was kneeling on the ground, focusing the lens of his camera. The children stood under the arcade, now hiding, now emerging from view.

"Wait for me," Mrs. Das called out. "I'm coming."

Tina jumped up and down. "Here comes Mommy!"

"Great," Mr. Das said without looking up. "Just in time. We'll get Mr. Kapasi to take a picture of the five of us."

Mr. Kapasi quickened his pace, waving his branch so that the monkeys scampered away, distracted, in another direction.

"Where's Bobby?" Mrs. Das asked when she stopped.

Mr. Das looked up from the camera. "I don't know. Ronny, where's Bobby?"

Ronny shrugged. "I thought he was right here."

"Where is he?" Mrs. Das repeated sharply. "What's wrong with all of you?"

They began calling his name, wandering up and down the path a bit. Because they were calling, they did not initially hear the boy's screams. When they found him, a little farther down the path under a tree, he was surrounded by a group of monkeys, over a dozen of them, pulling at his T-shirt with their long black fingers. The puffed rice Mrs. Das had spilled was scattered at his feet, raked over by the monkeys' hands. The boy was silent, his body frozen, swift tears running down his startled face. His bare legs were dusty and red with welts from where one of the monkeys struck him repeatedly with the stick he had given to it earlier.

"Daddy, the monkey's hurting Bobby," Tina said.

Mr. Das wiped his palms on the front of his shorts. In his nervousness he accidentally pressed the shutter on his camera; the whirring noise of the advancing film excited the monkeys, and the one with the stick began to beat Bobby more intently. "What are we supposed to do? What if they start attacking?"

"Mr. Kapasi," Mrs. Das shrieked, noticing him standing to one side. "Do something, for God's sake, do something!"

Mr. Kapasi took his branch and shooed them away, hissing at the ones that remained, stomping his feet to scare them. The animals retreated slowly, with a measured gait, obedient but unintimidated. Mr. Kapasi gathered Bobby in his arms and brought him back to where his parents and siblings were standing. As he carried him he was tempted to whisper a secret into the boy's ear. But Bobby was stunned, and shivering with fright, his legs bleeding slightly where the stick had broken the skin. When Mr. Kapasi delivered him to his parents, Mr. Das brushed some dirt off the boy's T-shirt and put the visor on him the right way. Mrs. Das reached into her straw bag to find a bandage which she taped over the cut on his knee. Ronny offered his brother a fresh piece of gum. "He's fine. Just a little scared, right, Bobby?" Mr. Das said, patting the top of his head.

"God, let's get out of here," Mrs. Das said. She folded her arms across the strawberry on her chest. "This place gives me the creeps."

"Yeah. Back to the hotel, definitely," Mr. Das agreed.

"Poor Bobby," Mrs. Das said. "Come here a second. Let Mommy fix your hair." Again she reached into her straw bag, this time for her hairbrush, and began to run it around the edges of the translucent visor. When she whipped out the hairbrush, the slip of paper with Mr. Kapasi's address on it fluttered away in the wind. No one but Mr. Kapasi noticed. He watched as it rose, carried higher and higher by the breeze, into the trees where the monkeys now sat, solemnly observing the scene below. Mr. Kapasi observed it too, knowing that this was the picture of the Das family he would preserve forever in his mind.

MARY LAVIN

Mary Lavin (1912–1996) was born in East Walpole, Massachusetts, the daughter of an Irish couple who had immigrated to the United States. Her father came from Roscommon and her mother was from Galway. In 1921, her mother returned to Ireland with Mary, and they settled in Dublin. Her father followed a year later, taking a job as a trainer of race horses for a wealthy American in

County Meath. Lavin was convent educated and earned a degree at University College Dublin, where she began writing short stories. She acknowledged the stories of Leo Tolstoy and Gustave Flaubert's "A Simple Heart" as early influences on her prose style.

Lavin's first collection of short fiction, Tales from Bective Bridge *(1942), won the James Tait Black Memorial Prize. In her long career she published nineteen books of short stories and two novels in England, Ireland, and the United States. She also contributed regularly to the* Atlantic Monthly, Harper's Bazaar, *and* The New Yorker. *Among her many awards were three Guggenheim Fellowships, the Katherine Mansfield Prize in 1961, and the Irish American Foundation Literary Award (1979). In 1992 she was elected "Saoi" by Aosdana, an organization of Irish artists, for outstanding achievement in literature.*

"The Widow's Son" is from In a Cafe *(1995), a collection assembled by her daughter Elisabeth Walsh Peavoy just before Lavin's death. Lavin said that writing stories gave her the opportunity of "looking deeper than usual into the human heart." Like Alice Munro, she offers the reader a subtle depiction of small-town provincial life under threat "from the forces of life's anarchy," as the English writer Thomas Kilroy realized. Lavin once told Kilroy that "she felt a story often grew out of an opening sentence." Kilroy believed that in Lavin's short fiction,*

> *The hook is in place from the word go. But such sentences are not only beguiling in their promise, they also establish a particular tone, a way of telling that is at least as important as what is being told. That characteristic Lavin tone is at once sympathetic and demanding, highly moral in the way it negotiates human conduct but entirely flexible in its acceptance of the vagaries of experience.*
>
> *I think she is also getting at something else here in her remark about first sentences. She is talking about the way language creates its own world, and its own readers too, in the process. This reverence for the act of writing is exemplified everywhere in her work. She has even written stories about the nature of fiction, stories "with a pattern" like "The Widow's Son."*

WEB *Research Mary Lavin and answer questions about her work at bedfordstmartins.com/charters/litwriters.*

The Widow's Son

1995

This is the story of a widow's son, but it is a story that has two endings.

Once there was a widow, living in a small neglected village at the foot of a steep hill. She had only one son, but he was the meaning of her life. She lived for his sake. She wore herself out working for him. Every day she made sacrifices in order to keep him at school in the town, four miles away, because there was a better teacher there than the village dullard by whom she herself had been taught.

She made great plans for Packy, but she did not tell him about her plans. Instead she threatened him, day and night, that if he didn't turn out well, she would put him to work on the roads, or in the quarry on the other side of the hill.

But as the years went by, everyone in the village, and even Packy himself, could tell by the way she watched him out of sight in the morning, and watched to see him come into sight in the evening, that he was the beat of her heart, and that her gruff words were only a cover for her pride and her joy in him.

It was for Packy's sake that she walked for hours along the road, letting her cow graze the long acre of the wayside grass, in order to spare the few poor blades that pushed up through the stones in her own field. It was for his sake she walked back and forth to the town to sell a few cabbages as soon as ever they were fit. It was for his sake that she got up in the cold dawning hours to gather mushrooms that would replace other foods that had to be bought with money. She bent her back daily to make every penny she could, and as often happens, she made more by industry, out of her few bald acres, than many of the farmers around her made out of their great bearded meadows. By selling eggs alone, she paid for Packy's clothes and for the greater number of his books.

When Packy was fourteen, he was in the last class in the school, and the master had great hopes of his winning a scholarship to a city college. He was getting to be a tall lad, and his features were beginning to take a strong cast. The people of the village were beginning to give him the same respect they gave to the farmers' sons who came home from their fine colleges in the summer, with blue suits and bright ties. And whenever they spoke to the widow they praised him up to the heavens.

One day in June, when the air was so heavy the scent that rose up from the grass was imprisoned under the low clouds and hung in the air, the widow was waiting at the gate for Packy. There had been no rain for some days and the hens and chickens were pecking irritably at the dry ground and wandering up and down the road in bewilderment.

A neighbour passed.

"Waiting for Packy?" said he, pleasantly, and he stood for a minute to take off his hat and wipe the sweat of the day from his face. He was an old man.

"It's a hot day!" he said. "It will be a hard push for Packy on that battered old bike of his. I wouldn't like to have to face into four miles on it on a day like this!"

"Packy would travel three times that distance," said the widow, "if there was a book at the other end," with the pride of those who cannot read more than a line without wearying.

The minutes went by slowly. The widow kept looking up at the sun.

"I suppose the heat is better than the rain!" she said, at last.

Absentmindedly, as he pulled a long blade of grass from between the stones of the wall and began to chew the end of it, the neighbour said, "You could get sunstroke on a day like this!" He looked up at the sun. "The sun is a terror," he said.

The widow strained out farther over the gate. She looked up the hill in the direction of the town.

"He will have a good cool breeze on his face coming down the hill, at any rate," she said.

The man looked up the hill. "That's true. The hottest day of summer you would get a cool breeze coming down that hill on a bicycle. You would feel the air streaming past your cheeks like silk. And in the winter it's like two knives flashing to either side of you, and it could peel off your skin like you'd peel the bark off a sally-rod." He chewed the grass meditatively. "That must be one of the steepest hills in Ireland. That hill is a hill worthy of the name of a hill." He took the grass out of his mouth. "It's my belief," he said, earnestly looking at the widow, "it's my belief that that hill is to be found marked with a name in the Ordnance Survey map!"

"If that's the case," said the widow, "Packy will be able to tell you all about it. When it isn't a book he has in his hand it's a map."

"Is that so?" said the man. "That's interesting. A map is a great thing. A map is not an ordinary thing. It isn't everyone can make out a map."

The widow wasn't listening.

"Here he is. I see Packy!" she said, and she opened the wooden gate and stepped out into the roadway.

At the top of the hill there was a glitter of spokes as the bicycle came into sight. Then there was a flash of blue jersey as Packy came flying downward, gripping the handlebars of the bike, his bright hair blown back from his forehead. The hill was so steep, and he came down so fast, that it seemed to the man and woman at the bottom of the hill that he was not moving at all, but that it was the trees and bushes, the bright ditches and wayside grasses, that were streaming away to either side of him.

The hens and chickens clucked and squawked and ran along the road looking for safe places in the ditch. Packy waved to his mother. He came nearer and nearer. They could see the freckles on his face.

"Shoo!" he cried, at the squawking hens that had not yet left the roadway, but ran with their long necks straining forward.

"Shoo!" Packy's mother lifted her apron and flapped it in the air to frighten the hens out of Packy's way.

It was only afterwards, when the harm was done, that the widow began to think that it might, perhaps, have been the flapping of her own apron that frightened the old clucking hen, and sent her flapping out over the wall into the middle of the road.

The old hen appeared so suddenly above the grassy ditch and looked with a distraught eye at the hens and chickens as they ran to right and left. Her own feathers began to stand out from her. She craned her neck forward and gave a distracted squawk, and fluttered down into the middle of the hot dusty road.

Packy jammed on the brakes. The widow screamed. There was a flurry of white feathers and a spurt of blood. The bicycle swerved and fell. Packy was thrown over the handlebars.

It was such a simple accident that, although the widow screamed, and although the old man looked around to see if there was help near, neither of them thought Packy was badly hurt, but when they ran over and lifted his head, and saw that he could not speak, they wiped the blood from his face and looked at each other desperately, to measure the distance they would have to carry him.

It was only a few yards to the door of the cottage, but Packy was dead before they got him across the threshold.

"It's only a knock on the head," screamed the widow, and she urged the crowd that had gathered outside the door to do something for him. "Get the doctor!" she said, pushing a young labourer towards the door. "Hurry! Hurry! The doctor will bring him around."

But the neighbours that kept coming in the door from all sides were crossing themselves, one after another, and falling on their knees, as soon as they laid eyes on the boy, stretched out flat on the bed, with the dust and dirt and the sweat marks of life on his dead face.

When at last the widow was convinced that her son was dead, the women had to hold her down. She waved her arms and wrestled to get free. She wanted to wring the neck of every hen in the yard.

"I'll kill every one of them. What good are they to me, now? All the hens in the world aren't worth one drop of human blood. That old clucking hen wasn't worth more than six shillings. What is six shillings? Is it worth poor Packy's life?"

But after a time she stopped raving, and looked from one face to another.

"Why didn't he ride over the old hen?" she asked. "Why did he try to save an old hen that wasn't worth more than six shillings? Didn't he know he was worth more to his mother than an old hen that would be going into the pot one of these days? Why did he do it? Why did he put on the brakes going down one of the worst hills in the country? Why? Why?"

The neighbours patted her arm.

"There now!" they said. "There now!" That was all they could think of saying, so they said it over and over again. "There now! There now!"

And years afterwards, whenever the widow spoke of her son to the neighbours who dropped in to keep her company for an hour or two, she always had the same question to ask, the same tireless question. "Why did he put the price of an old clucking hen above the price of his own life?"

And the people always gave the same answer.

"There now! There now!" they said. And after that they sat as silently as the widow herself, looking into the fire.

But surely some of those neighbours must have been stirred to wonder what would have happened had Packy ridden boldly over the clucking hen? And surely some of them must have pictured the scene of the accident again, altering a detail here and there as they did so, and giving the story a different end. For these people knew the widow and they knew Packy, and when you know people well it is as easy to guess what they would say and do in certain circumstances as to remember what they actually did say and do in other circumstances.

So perhaps if I tell you what I think might have happened had Packy killed that cackling old hen, you will not accuse me of abusing my privileges as a writer. Knowing the whole art of storytelling without taking notes, I lean no heavier now on your credulity than I did by telling you what happened in the first instance.

In fact, it is sometimes easier to invent than to remember accurately, and were this not so, the art of the storyteller and the art of the gossip would wither in an instant.

The story begins in the same way. There is the widow, grazing her cow by the wayside, and walking the long road to the town, weighed down with a sack of cabbages to help pay for Packy's schooling. There she is, fussing over Packy in the mornings in case he would be late for class. There she is in the afternoon watching the battered clock on the dresser for the hour when he will appear on the top of the hill at his return. And there, too, on a hot day in June, is the old labouring man coming up the road, and pausing to talk to her as she stood at the door. There he is dragging a blade of grass from between the stones of the wall, and putting it between his teeth, he chews on it before he starts to talk.

"Waiting for Packy?" the old man says, and then he takes off his hat and wipes the sweat from his forehead. "It's a hot day."

"It's very hot," said the widow, looking anxiously up the hill. "It's a hot day to push a bicycle for miles along a bad road with the dust rising to choke you, and the sun striking sparks off the handlebars!"

"The heat is better than the rain, all the same."

"I suppose it is," said the widow. "All the same, there were days Packy came home with the rain dried into his clothes like starch, they stood up stiff."

"Is that so?" said the old man.

"Yes, when he took off his clothes they stood stiff like boards against the wall, for all the world as if he were still standing in them."

"You may be sure he got a good spoiling in those days. There is no son like a widow's son. A ewe lamb!"

"Is it Packy?" The widow turned away in disgust. "Packy never got a day's petting since the day he was born. I made up my mind from the first, that I'd never make a softie out of him."

The widow looked up the hill again, and set herself to raking the gravel outside the gate as if she was out on the road for no other purpose. Then she gave another look up the hill.

"Here he is now!" she said, and she rose such a cloud of dust with the rake they could hardly see the glitter of the bicycle spokes, or the flash of his blue jersey as Packy came down the hill at breakneck speed.

Nearer and nearer he came, faster and faster, waving his hand to the widow, shouting at the hens to leave the way.

The hens ran for the ditches, stretching their necks in gawky terror. And as the last hen squawked into the ditch the way was clear for a moment before the whirling silver spokes. Then, unexpectedly, up from nowhere it seemed, came an old hen who, clucking despairingly, stood for a moment on the top of the wall and then rose into the air with the clumsy flight of a ground fowl.

Packy stopped whistling. The widow screamed. A shower of grit skidded as the wheel braked. Packy swerved the bicycle to bring it to a halt on the hill.

For a minute it could not be seen what exactly had happened, but Packy put his foot down and dragged it along the ground in the dust. Then he threw the bicycle down with a clatter on the hard road and ran back. The widow could not bear to look. She threw her apron over her head.

"He's killed the clucking hen," she said. "He's killed it. He's killed it." She let her apron fall back into place, and ran up the hill. The old man spat out the blade of grass that he had been chewing and ran after the woman.

"Did you kill the hen?" screamed the widow, and as she got near enough to see the blood and feathers she raised her arm over her head, and her fist was clenched till the knuckles shone white. Packy cowered down over the carcass of the speckled fowl and hunched up his shoulders as if to shield himself from a blow. His legs were spattered with blood, and brown speckled feathers were stuck to his hands, and to his clothes, and strewn all over the road. Some of the light white inner feathers were still swirling with the dust in the air.

"I couldn't help it, Mother. I couldn't help it. I didn't see her till it was too late!"

The widow caught up the hen and examined it all over, holding it by the breast bone and letting the long neck dangle. Then, catching it by the leg, she swung it and brought down its bleeding body on the boy's back, in blow after blow, spattering blood all over his face and over his clothes and all over the white dust of the road.

"How dare you lie to me!" she screamed, gaspingly, between the blows. "You saw that hen. I know you saw it. You stopped whistling. You called out. We were watching you. We saw." She turned to the old man. "Isn't that right?" she demanded. "He saw the hen, didn't he? He saw it?"

"It looked that way," said the old man, uncertainly, his eye on the dangling fowl in the widow's hand.

"There you are!" The widow threw the hen down on the road. "You saw the hen in front of you, as plain as you see it now," she accused, "but you wouldn't stop to save it because you were in too big a hurry home to fill your belly! Isn't that so?"

"No, Mother. No! I saw her all right, but it was too late to do anything."

"He admits now that he saw it!" The widow turned and nodded triumphantly at the onlookers who had gathered at the sound of the shouting.

"I never denied seeing it!" said the boy, appealing to the onlookers as to his judges.

"He doesn't deny it!" screamed the widow. "He stands there as brazen as you like, and admits for all the world to hear that he saw the hen as plain as the nose on his face, and he rode over it without a thought!"

"But what else could I do?" said the boy, throwing out his hand, appealing to the crowd now, and now appealing to the widow. "If I'd put on the brakes going down the hill at such a speed I would have been put over the handlebars!"

"And what harm would that have done you?" said the widow. "I often saw you taking a toss when you were wrestling with Jimmy Mack and I heard no complaints afterwards although your elbows and knees would be running blood and your face ridged like a cattlegrid." She turned to the crowd. "That's as true as God. I often saw him come in with his nose spouting blood like a pump, and one eye closed as tight as the eye of a corpse. My hand was often stiff for a week from sopping out wet cloths to put poultices on him and try to bring his face back to rights again." She swung back to Packy. "You're not afraid of a fall when you go climbing trees, are you? You're not afraid to go up on the roof after a cat, are you? Oh, there's more in this than you want me to know. I can see that. You killed that hen on purpose, that's what I believe!

You're tired of going to school. You want to get out of going away to college. That's it! You think if you kill the few poor hens we have there will be no money in the box when the time comes to pay for books and classes. That's it!" Packy began to redden.

"It's late in the day for me to be thinking of things like that," he said. "It's long ago I should have started those tricks if that was the way I felt. But it's not true. I want to go to college. The reason I was coming down the hill so fast was to tell you that I got the scholarship. The teacher told me as I was leaving the schoolhouse. That's why I was pedalling so hard. That's why I was whistling. That's why I was waving my hand. Didn't you see me waving my hand once I came in sight at the top of the hill?"

The widow's hands fell to her sides. The wind of words died down within her and left her flat and limp. She didn't know what to say. She could feel the neighbours staring at her. She wished that they were gone away about their business. She wanted to throw out her arms to the boy, to drag him against her heart and hug him like a small child. But she thought of how the crowd would look at each other and nod and snigger. A ewe lamb! She didn't want to satisfy them. If she gave in to her feelings now they would know how much she had been counting on his getting the scholarship. She wouldn't please them! She wouldn't satisfy them!

She looked at Packy, and when she saw him standing there before her, spattered with the furious feathers and crude blood of the dead hen, she felt a fierce disappointment for the boy's own disappointment, and a fierce resentment against him for killing the hen on this day of all days, and spoiling the great news of his success.

Her mind was in confusion. She stared at the blood on his face, and all at once it seemed as if the spilt blood was a bad omen of the future that was his. Disappointment, fear, resentment, and above all defiance, raised themselves within her like screeching animals. She looked from Packy to the onlookers.

"Scholarship! Scholarship!" she sneered, putting as much derision as she could into her voice and expression.

"I suppose you think you are a great fellow now? I suppose you think you are independent now? I suppose you think you can go off with yourself now, and look down on your poor slave of a mother who scraped and sweated for you with her cabbages and her hens? I suppose you think to yourself that it doesn't matter now whether the hens are alive or dead? Is that the way? Well, let me tell you this! You're not as independent as you think. The scholarship may pay for your books and your teacher's fees but who will pay for your clothes? Ah-ha, you forgot that, didn't you?" She put her hands on her hips. Packy hung his head. He no longer appealed to the gawking neighbours. They might have been able to save him from blows but he knew enough about life to know that no one could save him from shame.

The widow's heart burned at the sight of his shamed face, as her heart burned with grief. But her temper, too, burned fiercer and fiercer, and she came to a point at which nothing could quell the blaze till it had burned itself out. "Who'll buy your suits?" she yelled. "Who'll buy your boots?" She paused to think of more humiliating accusations. "Who'll buy your breeches?" She paused again and her teeth bit against each other. What would wound deepest? What shame could she drag upon him? "Who'll buy your nightshirts or will you sleep in your skin?"

The neighbours laughed at that, and the tension was broken. The widow herself laughed. She held her sides and laughed, and as she laughed everything seemed to take on a newer and simpler significance. Things were not as bad as they seemed a moment before. She wanted Packy to laugh too. She looked at him, but as she looked at Packy her heart turned cold with a strange new fear.

"Get into the house!" she said, giving him a push ahead of her. She wanted him safe under her own roof. She wanted to get him away from the gaping neighbours. She hated them, man, woman and child. She felt that if they had not been there things would have been different. And she wanted to get away from the sight of the blood on the road. She wanted to mash a few potatoes and make a bit of potato cake for Packy. That would comfort him. He loved that.

Packy hardly touched the food. And even after he had washed and scrubbed himself there were stains of blood turning up in the most unexpected places; behind his ears, under his fingernails, inside the cuff of his sleeve.

"Put on your good clothes," said the widow, making a great effort to be gentle, but her manners had become as twisted and as hard as the branches of the trees across the road from her, and the kindly offers she made sounded harsh. The boy sat on the chair in a slumped position that kept her nerves on edge, and set up a further conflict of irritation and love in her heart. She hated to see him slumping there in the chair, not asking to go outside the door, but still she was uneasy whenever he as much as looked in the direction of the door. She felt safe while he was under the roof, under the lintel, under her eyes.

Next day she went in to wake him for school, but his room was empty, his bed had not been slept in, and when she ran out into the yard and called him everywhere, there was no answer. She ran up and down. She called at the houses of the neighbours but he was not in any house. And she thought she could hear sniggering behind her in each house that she left, as she ran to another one. He wasn't in the village. He wasn't in the town. The master of the school said that she should let the police have a description of him. He said he never met a boy as sensitive as Packy. A boy like that took strange notions into his head from time to time.

There was no news of Packy that night. A few days later there was a letter saying that he was well. He asked his mother to notify the master that he would not be coming back, so that some other boy could claim the scholarship. He said that he would send the price of the hen as soon as he made some money.

Another letter in a few weeks said that he had got a job on a trawler and that he would not be able to write very often but that he would put aside some of his pay every week and send it to his mother whenever he got into port. He said that he wanted to pay her back for all she had done for him. He gave no address. He kept his promise about the money but he never gave any address when he wrote.

And so the people may have let their thoughts run on, as they sat by the fire with the widow, many a night, listening to her complaining voice saying the same thing over and over. "Why did he put the price of an old hen above the price of his own life?" And it is possible that their version of the story has a certain element of truth about it too. Perhaps a great many of our actions have this double quality about them, this possibility of alternative, and that it is only by careful watching, and absolute sincerity, that we follow the path that is destined for us, and, no matter how tragic that may be, it is better than the tragedy we bring upon ourselves.

D. H. LAWRENCE

David Herbert Lawrence (1885–1930) was born the son of a coal miner in the industrial town of Eastwood, in Nottinghamshire, England. His mother had been a schoolteacher, and she was frustrated by the hard existence of a coal miner's wife. Through her financial sacrifices, Lawrence was able to complete high school; then he studied to become a teacher. He finished his university studies and was licensed as a teacher at the age of twenty-three. Moving to South London, he allied himself with the young literary rebels there, and his first novel, The White Peacock, *was published in 1910. In 1912 Lawrence fell in love with an older married woman, Frieda von Richthofen, who abandoned her husband and children to run off with him to her native Germany. English society never forgave either of them, although the pair eventually married in 1914 and maintained their exceedingly stormy union, punctuated with frequent affairs, until Lawrence's death. In 1913, Lawrence was established as a major literary figure with the publication of* Sons and Lovers.*

Much of his fiction is about characters caught between their unsatisfactory relationships with others and their struggle to break free. Lawrence sought an ideal balance or, as he wrote in the novel Women in Love *(1920), a "star equilibrium," in which two beings are attracted to each other but never lose their individuality. He felt that "no emotion is supreme, or exclusively worth living for. All emotions go to the achieving of a living relationship between a human being and the other human being or creature or thing he becomes purely related to."*

A prolific writer, Lawrence suffered from tuberculosis and spent years wandering in Italy, Australia, Mexico, New Mexico, and southern France, seeking a warm, sunny climate. He also fled to primitive societies to escape the industrialization and commercialism of Western life. A virulent social critic, he was frequently harassed by censorship because his short stories, novels, and poetry were often explicitly sexual and he always challenged conventional moral attitudes. Literature, for Lawrence, had two great functions: providing an emotional experience, and then, if the reader had the courage of his or her own feelings and could live imaginatively, becoming "a mine of practical truth."

Lawrence wrote stories all his life, publishing a first collection, The Prussian Officer, *in 1914; it was followed by four other collections. In 1961 his stories were compiled in a three-volume paperback edition that has gone through numerous reprintings. The style of the early stories is harshly realistic, but Lawrence's depiction of his characters' emotional situations changed in his later work, where he created fantasies like his famous and chilling story "The Rocking-Horse Winner."*

WEB   *Research D. H. Lawrence and answer questions about his work at*
bedfordstmartins.com/charters/litwriters.

The Rocking-Horse Winner   1926

There was a woman who was beautiful, who started with all the advantages, yet she had no luck. She married for love, and the love turned to dust. She had bonny children, yet she felt they had been thrust upon her, and she could not love them. They looked at her coldly, as if they were finding fault with her. And hurriedly she felt she must cover up some fault in herself. Yet what it was that she must cover up she never knew. Nevertheless, when her children were present, she always felt the center of her heart go hard. This troubled her, and in her manner she was all the more gentle and anxious for her children, as if she loved them very much. Only she herself knew that at the center of her heart was a hard little place that could not feel love, no, not for anybody. Everybody else said of her: "She is such a good mother. She adores her children." Only she herself, and her children themselves, knew it was not so. They read it in each other's eyes.

There were a boy and two little girls. They lived in a pleasant house, with a garden, and they had discreet servants, and felt themselves superior to anyone in the neighborhood.

Although they lived in style, they felt always an anxiety in the house. There was never enough money. The mother had a small income, and the father had a small income, but not nearly enough for the social position which they had to keep up. The father went into town to some office. But though he had good prospects, these prospects never materialized. There was always the grinding sense of the shortage of money, though the style was always kept up.

At last the mother said: "I will see if I can't make something." But she did not know where to begin. She racked her brains, and tried this thing and the other, but could not find anything successful. The failure made deep lines come into her face. Her children were growing up, they would have to go to school. There must be more money, there must be more money. The father, who was always very handsome and expensive in his tastes, seemed as if he never *would* be able to do anything worth doing. And the mother, who had a great belief in herself, did not succeed any better, and her tastes were just as expensive.

And so the house came to be haunted by the unspoken phrase: *There must be more money! There must be more money!* The children could hear it all the time though nobody said it aloud. They heard it at Christmas, when the expensive and splendid toys filled the nursery. Behind the shining modern rocking horse, behind the smart doll's house, a voice would start whispering: "There *must* be more money! There *must* be more money!" And the children would stop playing, to listen for a moment. They would look into each other's eyes, to see if they had all heard. And each one saw in the eyes of the other two that they too had heard. "There *must* be more money! There *must* be more money!"

It came whispering from the springs of the still-swaying rocking horse, and even the horse, bending his wooden, champing head, heard it. The big doll, sitting so pink and smirking in her new pram, could hear it quite plainly, and seemed to be smirking all the more self-consciously because of it. The foolish puppy, too, that took the place of the teddy bear, he was looking so extraordinarily foolish for no other reason but that he heard the secret whisper all over the house: "There *must* be more money!"

Yet nobody ever said it aloud. The whisper was everywhere, and therefore no one spoke it. Just as no one ever says: "We are breathing!" in spite of the fact that breath is coming and going all the time.

"Mother," said the boy Paul one day, "why don't we keep a car of our own? Why do we always use Uncle's, or else a taxi?"

"Because we're the poor members of the family," said the mother.

"But why *are* we, Mother?"

"Well—I suppose," she said slowly and bitterly, "it's because your father has no luck."

The boy was silent for some time.

"Is luck money, Mother?" he asked rather timidly.

"No, Paul. Not quite. It's what causes you to have money."

"Oh!" said Paul vaguely. "I thought when Uncle Oscar said *filthy lucker,* it meant money."

"*Filthy lucre* does mean money," said the mother. "But it's lucre, not luck."

"Oh!" said the boy. "Then what *is* luck, Mother?"

"It's what causes you to have money. If you're lucky you have money. That's why it's better to be born lucky than rich. If you're rich, you may lose your money. But if you're lucky, you will always get more money."

"Oh! Will you? And is Father not lucky?"

"Very unlucky, I should say," she said bitterly.

The boy watched her with unsure eyes.

"Why?" he asked.

"I don't know. Nobody ever knows why one person is lucky and another unlucky."

"Don't they? Nobody at all? Does *nobody* know?"

"Perhaps God. But He never tells."

"He ought to, then. And aren't you lucky either, Mother?"

"I can't be, if I married an unlucky husband."

"But by yourself, aren't you?"

"I used to think I was, before I married. Now I think I am very unlucky indeed."

"Why?"

"Well—never mind! Perhaps I'm not really," she said.

The child looked at her, to see if she meant it. But he saw, by the lines of her mouth, that she was only trying to hide something from him.

"Well, anyhow," he said stoutly, "I'm a lucky person."

"Why?" said his mother, with a sudden laugh.

He stared at her. He didn't even know why he had said it.

"God told me," he asserted, brazening it out.

"I hope He did, dear!" she said, again with a laugh, but rather bitter.

"He did, Mother!"

"Excellent!" said the mother.

The boy saw she did not believe him; or, rather, that she paid no attention to his assertion. This angered him somewhat, and made him want to compel her attention.

He went off by himself, vaguely, in a childish way, seeking for the clue to "luck." Absorbed, taking no heed of other people, he went about with a sort of stealth, seeking inwardly for luck. He wanted luck, he wanted it, he wanted it. When the two girls were playing dolls in the nursery, he would sit on his big rocking horse, charging madly into space, with a frenzy that made the little girls peer at him uneasily. Wildly the horse careered, the waving dark hair of the boy tossed, his eyes had a strange glare in them. The little girls dared not speak to him.

When he had ridden to the end of his mad little journey, he climbed down and stood in front of his rocking horse, staring fixedly into its lowered face. Its red mouth was slightly open, its big eye was wide and glassy-bright.

Now! he could silently command the snorting steed. Now, take me to where there is luck! Now take me!

And he would slash the horse on the neck with the little whip he had asked Uncle Oscar for. He *knew* the horse could take him to where there was luck, if only he forced it. So he would mount again, and start on his furious ride, hoping at last to get there. He knew he could get there.

"You'll break your horse, Paul!" said the nurse.

"He's always riding like that! I wish he'd leave off!" said his elder sister Joan.

But he only glared down on them in silence. Nurse gave him up. She could make nothing of him. Anyhow he was growing beyond her.

One day his mother and his uncle Oscar came in when he was on one of his furious rides. He did not speak to them.

"Hallo, you young jockey! Riding a winner?" said his uncle.

"Aren't you growing too big for a rocking horse? You're not a very little boy any longer, you know," said his mother.

But Paul only gave a blue glare from his big, rather close-set eyes. He would speak to nobody when he was in full tilt. His mother watched him with an anxious expression on her face.

At last he suddenly stopped forcing his horse into the mechanical gallop, and slid down.

"Well, I got there!" he announced fiercely, his blue eyes still flaring, and his sturdy long legs straddling apart.

"Where did you get to?" asked his mother.

"Where I wanted to go," he flared back at her.

"That's right, son!" said Uncle Oscar. "Don't you stop till you get there. What's the horse's name?"

"He doesn't have a name," said the boy.

"Gets on without all right?" asked the uncle.

"Well, he has different names. He was called Sansovino last week."

"Sansovino, eh? Won the Ascot. How did you know his name?"

"He always talks about horse races with Bassett," said Joan.

The uncle was delighted to find that his small nephew was posted with all the racing news. Bassett, the young gardener, who had been wounded in the left foot in the war and had got his present job through Oscar Cresswell, whose batman° he had been, was a perfect blade of the "turf." He lived in the racing events, and the small boy lived with him.

Oscar Cresswell got it all from Bassett.

"Master Paul comes and asks me, so I can't do more than tell him, sir," said Bassett, his face terribly serious, as if he were speaking of religious matters.

"And does he ever put anything on a horse he fancies?"

"Well—I don't want to give him away—he's a young sport, a fine sport, sir. Would you mind asking him himself? He sort of takes a pleasure in it, and perhaps he'd feel I was giving him away, sir, if you don't mind."

Bassett was serious as a church.

The uncle went back to his nephew and took him off for a ride in the car.

"Say, Paul, old man, do you ever put anything on a horse?" the uncle asked.

The boy watched the handsome man closely.

"Why, do you think I oughtn't to?" he parried.

"Not a bit of it! I thought perhaps you might give me a tip for the Lincoln."

The car sped on into the country, going down to Uncle Oscar's place in Hampshire.

"Honor bright?" said the nephew.

"Honor bright, son!" said the uncle.

"Well, then, Daffodil."

"Daffodil! I doubt it, sonny. What about Mirza?"

"I only know the winner," said the boy. "That's Daffodil."

"Daffodil, eh?"

There was a pause. Daffodil was an obscure horse comparatively.

"Uncle!"

"Yes, son?"

"You won't let it go any further, will you? I promised Bassett."

"Bassett be damned, old man! What's he got to do with it?"

"We're partners. We've been partners from the first. Uncle, he lent me my first five shillings, which I lost. I promised him, honor bright, it was only between me and him; only you gave me that ten-shilling note I started winning with, so I thought you were lucky. You won't let it go any further, will you?"

The boy gazed at his uncle from those big, hot, blue eyes, set rather close together. The uncle stirred and laughed uneasily.

"Right you are, son! I'll keep your tip private. Daffodil, eh? How much are you putting on him?"

"All except twenty pounds," said the boy. "I keep that in reserve."

---

batman: An orderly assigned to serve a superior officer in the British military.

The uncle thought it a good joke.

"You keep twenty pounds in reserve, do you, you young romancer? What are you betting, then?"

"I'm betting three hundred," said the boy gravely. "But it's between you and me, Uncle Oscar! Honor bright?"

The uncle burst into a roar of laughter.

"It's between you and me all right, you young Nat Gould,"° he said, laughing. "But where's your three hundred?"

"Bassett keeps it for me. We're partners."

"You are, are you! And what is Bassett putting on Daffodil?"

"He won't go quite as high as I do, I expect. Perhaps he'll go a hundred and fifty."

"What, pennies?" laughed the uncle.

"Pounds," said the child, with a surprised look at his uncle. "Bassett keeps a bigger reserve than I do."

Between wonder and amusement Uncle Oscar was silent. He pursued the matter no further, but he determined to take his nephew with him to the Lincoln races.

"Now, son," he said, "I'm putting twenty on Mirza, and I'll put five for you on any horse you fancy. What's your pick?"

"Daffodil, Uncle."

"No, not the fiver on Daffodil!"

"I should if it was my own fiver," said the child.

"Good! Good! Right you are! A fiver for me and a fiver for you on Daffodil."

The child had never been to a race meeting before, and his eyes were blue fire. He pursed his mouth tight, and watched. A Frenchman just in front had put his money on Lancelot. Wild with excitement, he flailed his arms up and down, yelling *"Lancelot! Lancelot!"* in his French accent.

Daffodil came in first, Lancelot second, Mirza third. The child, flushed and with eyes blazing, was curiously serene. His uncle brought him four five-pound notes, four to one.

"What am I to do with these?" he cried, waving them before the boy's eyes.

"I suppose we'll talk to Bassett," said the boy. "I expect I have fifteen hundred now; and twenty in reserve; and this twenty."

His uncle studied him for some moments.

"Look here, son!" he said. "You're not serious about Bassett and that fifteen hundred, are you?"

"Yes, I am. But it's between you and me, Uncle. Honor bright!"

"Honor bright all right, son! But I must talk to Bassett."

"If you'd like to be a partner, Uncle, with Bassett and me, we could all be partners. Only, you'd have to promise, honor bright, Uncle, not to let it go beyond us three. Bassett and I are lucky, and you must be lucky, because it was your ten shillings I started winning with. . . ."

Nat Gould: Nathaniel Gould (1857–1919) was a British novelist and sports columnist known best for a series of novels about horse racing.

Uncle Oscar took both Bassett and Paul into Richmond Park for an afternoon, and there they talked.

"It's like this, you see, sir," Bassett said. "Master Paul would get me talking about racing events, spinning yarns, you know, sir. And he was always keen on knowing if I'd made or if I'd lost. It's about a year since, now, that I put five shillings on Blush of Dawn for him — and we lost. Then the luck turned, with that ten shillings he had from you, that we put on Singhalese. And since then, it's been pretty steady, all things considering. What do you say, Master Paul?"

"We're all right when we're sure," said Paul. "It's when we're not quite sure that we go down."

"Oh, but we're careful then," said Bassett.

"But when are you *sure?*" Uncle Oscar smiled.

"It's Master Paul, sir," said Bassett, in a secret, religious voice. "It's as if he had it from heaven. Like Daffodil, now, for the Lincoln. That was as sure as eggs."

"Did you put anything on Daffodil?" asked Oscar Cresswell.

"Yes, sir. I made my bit."

"And my nephew?"

Bassett was obstinately silent, looking at Paul.

"I made twelve hundred, didn't I, Bassett? I told Uncle I was putting three hundred on Daffodil."

"That's right," said Bassett, nodding.

"But where's the money?" asked the uncle.

"I keep it safe locked up, sir. Master Paul he can have it any minute he likes to ask for it."

"What, fifteen hundred pounds?"

"And twenty! And *forty,* that is, with the twenty he made on the course."

"It's amazing!" said the uncle.

"If Master Paul offers you to be partners, sir, I would, if I were you; if you'll excuse me," said Bassett.

Oscar Cresswell thought about it.

"I'll see the money," he said.

They drove home again, and sure enough, Bassett came round to the garden house with fifteen hundred pounds in notes. The twenty pounds reserve was left with Joe Glee, in the Turf Commission deposit.

"You see, it's all right, Uncle, when I'm *sure!* Then we go strong, for all we're worth. Don't we, Bassett?"

"We do that, Master Paul."

"And when are you sure?" said the uncle, laughing.

"Oh, well, sometimes I'm *absolutely* sure, like about Daffodil," said the boy; "and sometimes I have an idea; and sometimes I haven't even an idea, have I, Bassett? Then we're careful, because we mostly go down."

"You do, do you! And when you're sure, like about Daffodil, what makes you sure, sonny?"

"Oh, well, I don't know," said the boy uneasily. "I'm sure, you know, Uncle; that's all."

"It's as if he had it from heaven, sir," Bassett reiterated.

"I should say so!" said the uncle.

But he became a partner. And when the Leger was coming on, Paul was "sure" about Lively Spark, which was a quite inconsiderable horse. The boy insisted on putting a thousand on the horse, Bassett went for five hundred, and Oscar Cresswell two hundred. Lively Spark came in first, and the betting had been ten to one against him. Paul had made ten thousand.

"You see," he said, "I was absolutely sure of him."

Even Oscar Cresswell had cleared two thousand.

"Look here, son," he said, "this sort of thing makes me nervous."

"It needn't, Uncle! Perhaps I shan't be sure again for a long time."

"But what are you going to do with your money?" asked the uncle.

"Of course," said the boy. "I started it for Mother. She said she had no luck, because Father is unlucky, so I thought if *I* was lucky, it might stop whispering."

"What might stop whispering?"

"Our house. I *hate* our house for whispering."

"What does it whisper?"

"Why — why" — the boy fidgeted — "why, I don't know. But it's always short of money, you know, Uncle."

"I know it, son, I know it."

"You know people send Mother writs, don't you, Uncle?"

"I'm afraid I do," said the uncle.

"And then the house whispers, like people laughing at you behind your back. It's awful, that is! I thought if I was lucky. . . ."

"You might stop it," added the uncle.

The boy watched him with big blue eyes, that had an uncanny cold fire in them, and he said never a word.

"Well, then!" said the uncle. "What are we doing?"

"I shouldn't like Mother to know I was lucky," said the boy.

"Why not, son?"

"She'd stop me."

"I don't think she would."

"Oh!" — and the boy writhed in an odd way — "I *don't* want her to know, Uncle."

"All right, son! We'll manage it without her knowing."

They managed it very easily. Paul, at the other's suggestion, handed over five thousand pounds to his uncle, who deposited it with the family lawyer, who was then to inform Paul's mother that a relative had put five thousand pounds into his hands, which sum was to be paid out a thousand pounds at a time, on the mother's birthday, for the next five years.

"So she'll have a birthday present of a thousand pounds for five successive years," said Uncle Oscar. "I hope it won't make it all the harder for her later."

Paul's mother had her birthday in November. The house had been "whispering" worse than ever lately, and, even in spite of his luck, Paul could not bear up against it. He was very anxious to see the effect of the birthday letter, telling his mother about the thousand pounds.

When there were no visitors, Paul now took his meals with his parents, as he was beyond the nursery control. His mother went into town nearly every day. She had discovered that she had an odd knack of sketching furs and dress materials, so she worked secretly in the studio of a friend who was the chief artist for the leading drapers. She drew the figures of ladies in furs and ladies in silk and sequins for the newspaper advertisements. This young woman artist earned several thousand pounds a year, but Paul's mother only made several hundreds, and she was again dissatisfied. She so wanted to be first in something, and she did not succeed, even in making sketches for drapery advertisements.

She was down to breakfast on the morning of her birthday. Paul watched her face as she read her letters. He knew the lawyer's letter. As his mother read it, her face hardened and became more expressionless. Then a cold, determined look came on her mouth. She hid the letter under the pile of others, and said not a word about it.

"Didn't you have anything nice in the post for your birthday, Mother?" said Paul.

"Quite moderately nice," she said, her voice cold and absent.

She went away to town without saying more.

But in the afternoon Uncle Oscar appeared. He said Paul's mother had had a long interview with the lawyer, asking if the whole five thousand could not be advanced at once, as she was in debt.

"What do you think, Uncle?" said the boy.

"I leave it to you, son."

"Oh, let her have it, then! We can get some more with the other," said the boy.

"A bird in the hand is worth two in the bush, laddie!" said Uncle Oscar.

"But I'm sure to *know* for the Grand National; or the Lincolnshire; or else the Derby. I'm sure to know for *one* of them," said Paul.

So Uncle Oscar signed the agreement, and Paul's mother touched the whole five thousand. Then something very curious happened. The voices in the house suddenly went mad, like a chorus of frogs on a spring evening. There were certain new furnishings, and Paul had a tutor. He was *really* going to Eton, his father's school, in the following autumn. There were flowers in the winter, and a blossoming of the luxury Paul's mother had been used to. And yet the voices in the house, behind the sprays of mimosa and almond blossom, and from under the piles of iridescent cushions, simply trilled and screamed in a sort of ecstasy: "There *must* be more money! Oh-h-h; there *must* be more money. Oh, now, now-w! Now-w-w—there *must* be more money!—more than ever! More than ever!"

It frightened Paul terribly. He studied away at his Latin and Greek. But his intense hours were spent with Bassett. The Grand National had gone by; he had not "known," and had lost a hundred pounds. Summer was at hand. He was in agony for the Lincoln. But even for the Lincoln he didn't "know," and he lost fifty pounds. He became wild-eyed and strange, as if something were going to explode in him.

"Let it alone, son! Don't you bother about it!" urged Uncle Oscar. But it was as if the boy couldn't really hear what his uncle was saying.

"I've got to know for the Derby! I've got to know for the Derby!" the child reiterated, his big blue eyes blazing with a sort of madness.

His mother noticed how overwrought he was.

"You'd better go to the seaside. Wouldn't you like to go now to the seaside, instead of waiting? I think you'd better," she said, looking down at him anxiously, her heart curiously heavy because of him.

But the child lifted his uncanny blue eyes. "I couldn't possibly go before the Derby, Mother!" he said. "I couldn't possibly!"

"Why not?" she said, her voice becoming heavy when she was opposed. "Why not? You can still go from the seaside to see the Derby with your uncle Oscar, if that's what you wish. No need for you to wait here. Besides, I think you care too much about these races. It's a bad sign. My family has been a gambling family, and you won't know till you grow up how much damage it has done. But it has done damage. I shall have to send Bassett away, and ask Uncle Oscar not to talk racing to you, unless you promise to be reasonable about it; go away to the seaside and forget it. You're all nerves!"

"I'll do what you like, Mother, so long as you don't send me away till after the Derby," the boy said.

"Send you away from where? Just from this house?"

"Yes," he said, gazing at her.

"Why, you curious child, what makes you care about this house so much, suddenly? I never knew you loved it."

He gazed at her without speaking. He had a secret within a secret, something he had not divulged, even to Bassett or to his uncle Oscar.

But his mother, after standing undecided and a little bit sullen for some moments, said:

"Very well, then! Don't go to the seaside till after the Derby, if you don't wish it. But promise me you won't let your nerves go to pieces. Promise you won't think so much about horse racing and *events*, as you call them!"

"Oh, no," said the boy casually. "I won't think much about them, Mother. You needn't worry. I wouldn't worry, Mother, if I were you."

"If you were me and I were you," said his mother, "I wonder what we *should* do!"

"But you know you needn't worry, Mother, don't you?" the boy repeated.

"I should be awfully glad to know it," she said wearily.

"Oh, well you *can*, you know. I mean, you *ought* to know you needn't worry," he insisted.

"Ought I? Then I'll see about it," she said.

Paul's secret of secrets was his wooden horse, that which had no name. Since he was emancipated from a nurse and a nursery governess, he had had his rocking horse removed to his own bedroom at the top of the house.

"Surely, you're too big for a rocking horse!" his mother had remonstrated.

"Well, you see, Mother, till I can have a *real* horse, I like to have *some* sort of animal about," had been his quaint answer.

"Do you feel he keeps you company?" She laughed.

"Oh, yes! He's very good, he always keeps me company, when I'm there," said Paul.

So the horse, rather shabby, stood in an arrested prance in the boy's bedroom.

The Derby was drawing near, and the boy grew more and more tense. He hardly heard what was spoken to him, he was very frail, and his eyes were really uncanny. His mother had sudden strange seizures of uneasiness about him. Sometimes, for half an hour, she would feel a sudden anxiety about him that was almost anguish. She wanted to rush to him at once, and know he was safe.

Two nights before the Derby, she was at a big party in town, when one of her rushes of anxiety about her boy, her firstborn, gripped her heart till she could hardly speak. She fought with the feeling, might and main, for she believed in common sense. But it was too strong. She had to leave the dance and go downstairs to telephone to the country. The children's nursery governess was terribly surprised and startled at being rung up in the night.

"Are the children all right, Miss Wilmot?"

"Oh, yes, they are quite all right."

"Master Paul? Is he all right?"

"He went to bed as right as a trivet. Shall I run up and look at him?"

"No," said Paul's mother reluctantly. "No! Don't trouble. It's all right. Don't sit up. We shall be home fairly soon." She did not want her son's privacy intruded upon.

"Very good," said the governess.

It was about one o'clock when Paul's mother and father drove up to their house. All was still. Paul's mother went to her room and slipped off her white fur cloak. She had told her maid not to wait up for her. She heard her husband downstairs, mixing a whisky and soda.

And then, because of the strange anxiety at her heart, she stole upstairs to her son's room. Noiselessly she went along the upper corridor. Was there a faint noise? What was it?

She stood, with arrested muscles, outside his door, listening. There was a strange, heavy, and yet not loud noise. Her heart stood still. It was a soundless noise, yet rushing and powerful. Something huge, in violent, hushed motion. What was it? What in God's name was it? She ought to know. She felt that she knew the noise. She knew what it was.

Yet she could not place it. She couldn't say what it was. And on and on it went, like a madness.

Softly, frozen with anxiety and fear, she turned the door handle.

The room was dark. Yet in the space near the window, she heard and saw something plunging to and fro. She gazed in fear and amazement.

Then suddenly she switched on the light, and saw her son, in his green pajamas, madly surging on the rocking horse. The blaze of light suddenly lit him up, as he urged the wooden horse, and lit her up, as she stood, blonde, in her dress of pale green and crystal, in the doorway.

"Paul!" she cried. "Whatever are you doing?"

"It's Malabar!" he screamed, in a powerful, strange voice. "It's Malabar!"

His eyes blazed at her for one strange and senseless second, as he ceased urging his wooden horse. Then he fell with a crash to the ground, and she, all her tormented motherhood flooding upon her, rushed to gather him up.

But he was unconscious, and unconscious he remained, with some brain fever. He talked and tossed, and his mother sat stonily by his side.

"Malabar! It's Malabar! Bassett, Bassett, I *know*! It's Malabar!"

So the child cried, trying to get up and urge the rocking horse that gave him his inspiration.

"What does he mean by Malabar?" asked the heart-frozen mother.

"I don't know," said the father stonily.

"What does he mean by Malabar?" she asked her brother Oscar.

"It's one of the horses running for the Derby," was the answer.

And, in spite of himself, Oscar Cresswell spoke to Bassett, and himself put a thousand on Malabar: at fourteen to one.

The third day of the illness was critical: they were waiting for a change. The boy, with his rather long, curly hair, was tossing ceaselessly on the pillow. He never slept nor regained consciousness, and his eyes were like blue stones. His mother sat, feeling her heart had gone, turned actually into a stone.

In the evening, Oscar Cresswell did not come, but Bassett sent a message, saying could he come up for one moment, just one moment? Paul's mother was very angry at the intrusion, but on second thought she agreed. The boy was the same. Perhaps Bassett might bring him to consciousness.

The gardener, a shortish fellow with a little brown mustache, and sharp little brown eyes, tiptoed into the room, touched his imaginary cap to Paul's mother, and stole to the bedside, staring with glittering, smallish eyes at the tossing, dying child.

"Master Paul!" he whispered. "Master Paul! Malabar came in first all right, a clean win. I did as you told me. You've made over seventy thousand pounds, you have; you've got over eighty thousand. Malabar came in all right, Master Paul."

"Malabar! Malabar! Did I say Malabar, Mother? Did I say Malabar? Do you think I'm lucky, Mother? I knew Malabar, didn't I? Over eighty thousand pounds! I call that lucky, don't you, Mother? Over eighty thousand pounds! I knew, didn't I know I knew? Malabar came in all right. If I ride my horse till I'm sure, then I tell you, Bassett, you can go as high as you like. Did you go for all you were worth, Bassett?"

"I went a thousand on it, Master Paul."

"I never told you, Mother, that if I can ride my horse, and *get there*, then I'm absolutely sure — oh, absolutely! Mother, did I ever tell you? I *am* lucky!"

"No, you never did," said the mother.

But the boy died in the night.

And even as he lay dead, his mother heard her brother's voice saying to her: "My God, Hester, you're eighty-odd thousand to the good, and a poor devil of a son to the bad. But, poor devil, poor devil, he's best gone out of a life where he rides his rocking horse to find a winner."

KATHERINE MANSFIELD

Katherine Mansfield (1888–1923) was born Kathleen Mansfield Beauchamp in Wellington, New Zealand. In 1903 she persuaded her father, a banker and industrialist, to send her to London to study the cello. After a brief return to New Zealand, she went back to London with a small allowance from her family. Mansfield decided to become a writer instead of a musician after meeting D. H. Lawrence and Virginia Woolf. Her first book of short stories, In a German Pension, *was published in 1911. In the same year she met the literary critic John Middleton Murry, who became her husband in 1918.* Bliss and Other Stories *(1920) established her reputation and was followed by* The Garden-Party *(1922).*

Mansfield took Anton Chekhov as her model, but after she was stricken with tuberculosis in 1918 she found it difficult to work. In her posthumously published Journal *(1927), she often upbraided herself when she felt too ill to write: "Look at the stories that wait and wait just at the threshold. Why don't I let them in? And their place would be taken by others who are lurking beyond just there—waiting for the chance." Finally she sought a cure for her illness at the Gurdjieff Institute in France, run by the noted Armenian mystic Georges Ivanovitch Gurdjieff, whose methods combined spiritual and physical healing. She died at the institute a few months after her thirty-fourth birthday.*

Eighty-eight of Mansfield's stories have been published (including fifteen left unfinished), and they have had a great influence on the development of the literary form. As did Chekhov and James Joyce, Mansfield simplified plot to intensify its emotional impact, dramatizing small moments to reveal the larger significance in people's lives, or, as Willa Cather observed, approaching "the major forces of life through comparatively trivial incidents." Mansfield developed her own technique of narration in which she transformed a chance incident into a terse psychological drama. As would a symbolist poet, she used point of view and concrete images—such as the sheltered young girl Laura's view of life as a garden party—to convey her characters' feelings, or what she called "the state of the soul." Her stories have affected later writers as powerfully as Chekhov's affected her.

WEB *Research Katherine Mansfield and answer questions about her work at bedfordstmartins.com/charters/litwriters.*

The Garden-Party   1922

And after all the weather was ideal. They could not have had a more perfect day for a garden-party if they had ordered it. Windless, warm, the sky without a cloud. Only the blue was veiled with a haze of light gold, as it is sometimes in early summer. The gardener had been up since dawn, mowing the lawns and sweeping them, until the grass and the dark flat rosettes where the daisy plants had been seemed to shine. As for the roses, you could not help feeling they understood that roses are the only flowers that impress people at garden-parties; the only flowers that everybody is certain of knowing. Hundreds, yes, literally hundreds, had come out in a single night; the green bushes bowed down as though they had been visited by archangels.

Breakfast was not yet over before the men came to put up the marquee.

"Where do you want the marquee put, mother?"

"My dear child, it's no use asking me. I'm determined to leave everything to you children this year. Forget I am your mother. Treat me as an honoured guest."

But Meg could not possibly go and supervise the men. She had washed her hair before breakfast, and she sat drinking her coffee in a green turban, with a dark wet curl stamped on each cheek. Jose, the butterfly, always came down in a silk petticoat and a kimono jacket.

"You'll have to go, Laura; you're the artistic one."

Away Laura flew, still holding her piece of bread-and-butter. It's so delicious to have an excuse for eating out of doors, and besides, she loved having to arrange things; she always felt she could do it so much better than anybody else.

Four men in their shirt-sleeves stood grouped together on the garden path. They carried staves covered with rolls of canvas, and they had big tool-bags slung on their backs. They looked impressive. Laura wished now that she had not got the bread-and-butter, but there was nowhere to put it, and she couldn't possibly throw it away. She blushed and tried to look severe and even a little bit short-sighted as she came up to them.

"Good morning," she said, copying her mother's voice. But that sounded so fearfully affected that she was ashamed, and stammered like a little girl, "Oh—er—have you come—is it about the marquee?"

"That's right, miss," said the tallest of the men, a lanky, freckled fellow, and he shifted his tool-bag, knocked back his straw hat and smiled down at her. "That's about it."

His smile was so easy, so friendly that Laura recovered. What nice eyes he had, small, but such dark blue! And now she looked at the others, they were smiling too. "Cheer up, we won't bite," their smile seemed to say. How very nice workmen were! And what a beautiful morning! She mustn't mention the morning; she must be businesslike. The marquee.

"Well, what about the lily-lawn? Would that do?"

And she pointed to the lily-lawn with the hand that didn't hold the bread-and-butter. They turned, they stared in the direction. A little fat chap thrust out his under-lip, and the tall fellow frowned.

"I don't fancy it," said he. "Not conspicuous enough. You see, with a thing like a marquee," and he turned to Laura in his easy way, "you want to put it somewhere where it'll give you a bang slap in the eye, if you follow me."

Laura's upbringing made her wonder for a moment whether it was quite respectful of a workman to talk to her of bangs slap in the eye. But she did quite follow him.

"A corner of the tennis-court," she suggested. "But the band's going to be in one corner."

"H'm, going to have a band, are you?" said another of the workmen. He was pale. He had a haggard look as his dark eyes scanned the tennis-court. What was he thinking?

"Only a very small band," said Laura gently. Perhaps he wouldn't mind so much if the band was quite small. But the tall fellow interrupted.

"Look here, miss, that's the place. Against those trees. Over there. That'll do fine."

Against the karakas. Then the karaka-trees would be hidden. And they were so lovely, with their broad, gleaming leaves, and their clusters of yellow fruit. They were like trees you imagined growing on a desert island, proud, solitary, lifting their leaves and fruits to the sun in a kind of silent splendour. Must they be hidden by a marquee?

They must. Already the men had shouldered their staves and were making for the place. Only the tall fellow was left. He bent down, pinched a sprig of lavender, put his thumb and forefinger to his nose and snuffed up the smell. When Laura saw that gesture she forgot all about the karakas in her wonder at him caring for things like that — caring for the smell of lavender. How many men that she knew would have done such a thing? Oh, how extraordinarily nice workmen were, she thought. Why couldn't she have workmen for friends rather than the silly boys she danced with and who came to Sunday night supper? She would get on much better with men like these.

It's all the fault, she decided, as the tall fellow drew something on the back of an envelope, something that was to be looped up or left to hang, of these absurd class distinctions. Well, for her part, she didn't feel them. Not a bit, not an atom. . . . And now there came the chock-chock of wooden hammers. Some one whistled, some one sang out, "Are you right there, matey?" "Matey!" The friendliness of it, the — the — Just to prove how happy she was, just to show the tall fellow how at home she felt, and how she despised stupid conventions, Laura took a big bite of her bread-and-butter as she stared at the little drawing. She felt just like a work-girl.

"Laura, Laura, where are you? Telephone, Laura!" a voice cried from the house.

"Coming!" Away she skimmed, over the lawn, up the path, up the steps, across the veranda, and into the porch. In the hall her father and Laurie were brushing their hats ready to go to the office.

"I say, Laura," said Laurie very fast, "you might just give a squiz at my coat before this afternoon. See if it wants pressing."

"I will," said she. Suddenly she couldn't stop herself. She ran at Laurie and gave him a small, quick squeeze. "Oh, I do love parties, don't you?" gasped Laura.

"Ra-ther," said Laurie's warm, boyish voice, and he squeezed his sister too, and gave her a gentle push. "Dash off to the telephone, old girl."

The telephone. "Yes, yes; oh yes. Kitty? Good morning, dear. Come to lunch? Do, dear. Delighted of course. It will only be a very scratch meal — just the sandwich crusts and broken meringue-shells and what's left over. Yes, isn't it a perfect morning? Your white? Oh, I certainly should. One moment — hold the line. Mother's calling." And Laura sat back. "What, mother? Can't hear."

Mrs. Sheridan's voice floated down the stairs. "Tell her to wear that sweet hat she had on last Sunday."

"Mother says you're to wear that *sweet* hat you had on last Sunday. Good. One o'clock. Bye-bye."

Laura put back the receiver, flung her arms over her head, took a deep breath, stretched and let them fall. "Huh," she sighed, and the moment after the sigh she sat up quickly. She was still, listening. All the doors in the house seemed to be open. The house was alive with soft, quick steps and running voices. The green baize door that led to the kitchen regions swung open and shut with a muffled thud. And now there came a long, chuckling absurd sound. It was the heavy piano being moved on its stiff castors. But the air! If you stopped to notice, was the air always like this? Little faint winds were playing chase, in at the tops of the windows, out at the doors. And there were two tiny spots of sun, one on the inkpot, one on a silver photograph frame, playing too. Darling little spots. Especially the one on the inkpot lid. It was quite warm. A warm little silver star. She could have kissed it.

The front door bell pealed, and there sounded the rustle of Sadie's print skirt on the stairs. A man's voice murmured; Sadie answered, careless, "I'm sure I don't know. Wait. I'll ask Mrs. Sheridan."

"What is it, Sadie?" Laura came into the hall.

"It's the florist, Miss Laura."

It was, indeed. There, just inside the door, stood a wide, shallow tray full of pots of pink lilies. No other kind. Nothing but lilies—canna lilies, big pink flowers, wide open, radiant, almost frighteningly alive on bright crimson stems.

"O-oh Sadie!" said Laura, and the sound was like a little moan. She crouched down as if to warm herself at that blaze of lilies; she felt they were in her fingers, on her lips, growing in her breast.

"It's some mistake," she said faintly. "Nobody ever ordered so many. Sadie, go and find mother."

But at that moment Mrs. Sheridan joined them.

"It's quite right," she said calmly. "Yes, I ordered them. Aren't they lovely?" She pressed Laura's arm. "I was passing the shop yesterday, and I saw them in the window. And I suddenly thought for once in my life I shall have enough canna lilies. The garden-party will be a good excuse."

"But I thought you said you didn't mean to interfere," said Laura. Sadie had gone. The florist's man was still outside at his van. She put her arm round her mother's neck and gently, very gently, she bit her mother's ear.

"My darling child, you wouldn't like a logical mother, would you? Don't do that. Here's the man."

He carried more lilies still, another whole tray.

"Bank them up, just inside the door, on both sides of the porch, please," said Mrs. Sheridan. "Don't you agree, Laura?"

"Oh, I *do* mother."

In the drawing-room Meg, Jose, and good little Hans had at last succeeded in moving the piano.

"Now, if we put this chesterfield against the wall and move everything out of the room except the chairs, don't you think?"

"Quite."

"Hans, move these tables into the smoking-room, and bring a sweeper to take these marks off the carpet and — one moment, Hans —" Jose loved giving orders to the servants, and they loved obeying her. She always made them feel they were taking part in some drama. "Tell mother and Miss Laura to come here at once."

"Very good, Miss Jose."

She turned to Meg. "I want to hear what the piano sounds like, just in case I'm asked to sing this afternoon. Let's try over 'This Life Is Weary.'"

Pom! Ta-ta-ta *Tee*-ta! The piano burst out so passionately that Jose's face changed. She clasped her hands. She looked mournfully and enigmatically at her mother and Laura as they came in.

> This Life is *Wee*-ary,
> A Tear — a Sigh.
> A Love that *Chan*-ges,
>   This Life is *Wee*-ary,
> A Tear — a Sigh.
> A Love that *Chan*-ges,
> And then . . . *Good*-bye!

But at the word "Good-bye," and although the piano sounded more desperate than ever, her face broke into a brilliant, dreadfully unsympathetic smile.

"Aren't I in good voice, mummy?" she beamed.

> This Life is *Wee*-ary,
> Hope comes to Die.
> A Dream — a *Wa*-kening.

But now Sadie interrupted them. "What is it, Sadie?"

"If you please, m'm, cook says have you got the flags for the sandwiches?"

"The flags for the sandwiches, Sadie?" echoed Mrs. Sheridan dreamily. And the children knew by her face that she hadn't got them. "Let me see." And she said to Sadie firmly, "Tell cook I'll let her have them in ten minutes."

Sadie went.

"Now, Laura," said her mother quickly. "Come with me into the smoking-room. I've got the names somewhere on the back of an envelope. You'll have to write them out for me. Meg, go upstairs this minute and take that wet thing off your head. Jose, run and finish dressing this instant. Do you hear me, children, or shall I have to tell your father when he comes home to-night? And — and, Jose, pacify cook if you do go into the kitchen, will you? I'm terrified of her this morning."

The envelope was found at last behind the dining-room clock, though how it had got there Mrs. Sheridan could not imagine.

"One of you children must have stolen it out of my bag, because I remember vividly — cream cheese and lemon-curd. Have you done that?"

"Yes."

"Egg and —" Mrs. Sheridan held the envelope away from her. "It looks like mice. It can't be mice, can it?"

"Olive, pet," said Laura, looking over her shoulder.

"Yes, of course, olive. What a horrible combination it sounds. Egg and olive."

They were finished at last, and Laura took them off to the kitchen. She found Jose there pacifying the cook, who did not look at all terrifying.

"I have never seen such exquisite sandwiches," said Jose's rapturous voice. "How many kinds did you say there were, cook? Fifteen?"

"Fifteen, Miss Jose."

"Well, cook, I congratulate you."

Cook swept up crusts with the long sandwich knife, and smiled broadly.

"Godber's has come," announced Sadie, issuing out of the pantry. She had seen the man pass the window.

That meant the cream puffs had come. Godber's were famous for their cream puffs. Nobody ever thought of making them at home.

"Bring them in and put them on the table, my girl," ordered cook.

Sadie brought them in and went back to the door. Of course Laura and Jose were far too grown-up to really care about such things. All the same, they couldn't help agreeing that the puffs looked very attractive. Very. Cook began arranging them, shaking off the extra icing sugar.

"Don't they carry one back to all one's parties?" said Laura.

"I suppose they do," said practical Jose, who never liked to be carried back. "They look beautifully light and feathery, I must say."

"Have one each, my dears," said cook in her comfortable voice. "Yer ma won't know."

Oh, impossible. Fancy cream puffs so soon after breakfast. The very idea made one shudder. All the same, two minutes later Jose and Laura were licking their fingers with that absorbed inward look that only comes from whipped cream.

"Let's go into the garden, out by the back way," suggested Laura. "I want to see how the men are getting on with the marquee. They're such awfully nice men."

But the back door was blocked by cook, Sadie, Godber's man, and Hans. Something had happened.

"Tuk-tuk-tuk," clucked cook like an agitated hen. Sadie had her hand clapped to her cheek as though she had toothache. Hans's face was screwed up in the effort to understand. Only Godber's man seemed to be enjoying himself; it was his story.

"What's the matter? What's happened?"

"There's been a horrible accident," said Cook. "A man killed."

"A man killed! Where? How? When?"

But Godber's man wasn't going to have his story snatched from under his very nose.

"Know those little cottages just below here, miss?" Know them? Of course, she knew them. "Well, there's a young chap living there, name of Scott, a carter. His horse shied at a traction-engine, corner of Hawke Street this morning, and he was thrown out on the back of his head. Killed."

"Dead!" Laura stared at Godber's man.

"Dead when they picked him up," said Godber's man with relish. "They were taking the body home as I come up here." And he said to the cook, "He's left a wife and five little ones."

"Jose, come here." Laura caught hold of her sister's sleeve and dragged her through the kitchen to the other side of the green baize door. There she paused and leaned against it. "Jose!" she said, horrified, "however are we going to stop everything?"

"Stop everything, Laura!" cried Jose in astonishment. "What do you mean?"

"Stop the garden-party, of course." Why did Jose pretend?

But Jose was still more amazed. "Stop the garden-party? My dear Laura, don't be so absurd. Of course we can't do anything of the kind. Nobody expects us to. Don't be so extravagant."

"But we can't possibly have a garden-party with a man dead just outside the front gate."

That really was extravagant, for the little cottages were in a lane to themselves at the very bottom of a steep rise that led up to the house. A broad road ran between. True, they were far too near. They were the greatest possible eyesore, and they had no right to be in that neighbourhood at all. They were little mean dwellings painted a chocolate brown. In the garden patches there was nothing but cabbage stalks, sick hens, and tomato cans. The very smoke coming out of their chimneys was poverty-stricken. Little rags and shreds of smoke, so unlike the great silvery plumes that uncurled from the Sheridans' chimneys. Washerwomen lived in the lane and sweeps and a cobbler, and a man whose house-front was studded all over with minute bird-cages. Children swarmed. When the Sheridans were little they were forbidden to set foot there because of the revolting language and of what they might catch. But since they were grown up, Laura and Laurie on their prowls sometimes walked through. It was disgusting and sordid. They came out with a shudder. But still one must go everywhere; one must see everything. So through they went.

"And just think of what the band would sound like to that poor woman," said Laura.

"Oh, Laura!" Jose began to be seriously annoyed. "If you're going to stop a band playing every time some one has an accident, you'll lead a very strenuous life. I'm every bit as sorry about it as you. I feel just as sympathetic." Her eyes hardened. She looked at her sister just as she used to when they were little and fighting together. "You won't bring a drunken workman back to life by being sentimental," she said softly.

"Drunk! Who said he was drunk?" Laura turned furiously on Jose. She said, just as they had used to say on those occasions, "I'm going straight up to tell mother."

"Do, dear," cooed Jose.

"Mother, can I come in your room?" Laura turned the big glass door-knob.

"Of course, child. Why, what's the matter? What's given you such a colour?" And Mrs. Sheridan turned round from her dressing-table. She was trying on a new hat.

"Mother, a man's been killed," began Laura.

"*Not* in the garden?" interrupted her mother.

"No, no!"

"Oh, what a fright you gave me!" Mrs. Sheridan sighed with relief, and took off the big hat and held it on her knees.

"But listen, mother," said Laura. Breathless, half-choking, she told the dreadful story. "Of course, we can't have our party, can we?" she pleaded. "The band and everybody arriving. They'd hear us, mother; they're nearly neighbors!"

To Laura's astonishment her mother behaved just like Jose, it was harder to bear because she seemed amused. She refused to take Laura seriously.

"But, my dear child, use your common sense. It's only by accident we've heard of it. If some one had died there normally — and I can't understand how they keep alive in those poky little holes — we should still be having our party, shouldn't we?"

Laura had to say "yes" to that, but she felt it was all wrong. She sat down on her mother's sofa and pinched the cushion frill.

"Mother, isn't it really terribly heartless of us?" she asked.

"Darling!" Mrs. Sheridan got up and came over to her, carrying the hat. Before Laura could stop her she had popped it on. "My child!" said her mother, "the hat is yours. It's made for you. It's much too young for me. I have never seen you look such a picture. Look at yourself!" And she held up her hand-mirror.

"But, mother," Laura began again. She couldn't look at herself; she turned aside.

This time Mrs. Sheridan lost patience just as Jose had done.

"You are being very absurd, Laura," she said coldly. "People like that don't expect sacrifices from us. And it's not very sympathetic to spoil everybody's enjoyment as you're doing now."

"I don't understand," said Laura, and she walked quickly out of the room into her own bedroom. There, quite by chance, the first thing she saw was this charming girl in the mirror, in her black hat trimmed with gold daisies, and a long black velvet ribbon. Never had she imagined she could look like that. Is mother right? she thought. And now she hoped her mother was right. Am I being extravagant? Perhaps it was extravagant. Just for a moment she had another glimpse of that poor woman and those little children, and the body being carried into the house. But it all seemed blurred, unreal, like a picture in the newspaper. I'll remember it again after the party's over, she decided. And somehow that seemed quite the best plan. . . .

Lunch was over by half-past one. By half-past two they were all ready for the fray. The green-coated band had arrived and was established in a corner of the tennis-court.

"My dear!" trilled Kitty Maitland, "aren't they too like frogs for words? You ought to have arranged them round the pond with the conductor in the middle on a leaf."

Laurie arrived and hailed them on his way to dress. At the sight of him Laura remembered the accident again. She wanted to tell him. If Laurie agreed with the others, then it was bound to be all right. And she followed him into the hall.

"Laurie!"

"Hallo!" He was half-way upstairs, but when he turned round and saw Laura he suddenly puffed out his cheeks and goggled his eyes at her. "My word, Laura; You do look stunning," said Laurie. "What an absolutely topping hat!"

Laura said faintly, "Is it?" and smiled up at Laurie, and didn't tell him after all.

Soon after that people began coming in streams. The band struck up; the hired waiters ran from the house to the marquee. Wherever you looked there were couples strolling, bending to the flowers, greeting, moving on over the lawn. They were like bright birds that had alighted in the Sheridans' garden for this one afternoon, on their way to — where? Ah, what happiness it is to be with people who all are happy, to press hands, press cheeks, smile into eyes.

"Darling Laura, how well you look!"

"What a becoming hat, child!"

"Laura, you look quite Spanish. I've never seen you look so striking."

And Laura, glowing, answered softly, "Have you had tea? Won't you have an ice? The passion-fruit ices really are rather special." She ran to her father and begged him. "Daddy darling, can't the band have something to drink?"

And the perfect afternoon slowly ripened, slowly faded, slowly its petals closed.

"Never a more delightful garden-party . . ." "The greatest success . . ." "Quite the most . . ."

Laura helped her mother with the good-byes. They stood side by side in the porch till it was all over.

"All over, all over, thank heaven," said Mrs. Sheridan. "Round up the others, Laura. Let's go and have some fresh coffee. I'm exhausted. Yes, it's been very successful. But oh, these parties, these parties! Why will you children insist on giving parties!" And they all of them sat down in the deserted marquee.

"Have a sandwich, daddy dear. I wrote the flag."

"Thanks." Mr. Sheridan took a bite and the sandwich was gone. He took another. "I suppose you didn't hear of a beastly accident that happened to-day?" he said.

"My dear," said Mrs. Sheridan, holding up her hand, "we did. It nearly ruined the party. Laura insisted we should put it off."

"Oh, mother!" Laura didn't want to be teased about it.

"It was a horrible affair all the same," said Mr. Sheridan. "The chap was married too. Lived just below in the lane, and leaves a wife and half a dozen kiddies, so they say."

An awkward little silence fell. Mrs. Sheridan fidgeted with her cup. Really, it was very tactless of father . . .

Suddenly she looked up. There on the table were all those sandwiches, cakes, puffs, all uneaten, all going to be wasted. She had one of her brilliant ideas.

"I know," she said. "Let's make up a basket. Let's send that poor creature some of this perfectly good food. At any rate, it will be the greatest treat for the children. Don't you agree? And she's sure to have neighbours calling in and so on. What a point to have it all ready prepared. Laura!" She jumped up. "Get me the big basket out of the stairs cupboard."

"But, mother, do you really think it's a good idea?" said Laura.

Again, how curious, she seemed to be different from them all. To take scraps from their party. Would the poor woman really like that?

"Of course! What's the matter with you to-day? An hour or two ago you were insisting on us being sympathetic, and now —"

Oh, well! Laura ran for the basket. It was filled, it was heaped by her mother.

"Take it yourself, darling," said she. "Run down just as you are. No, wait, take the arum lilies too. People of that class are so impressed by arum lilies."

"The stems will ruin her lace frock," said practical Jose.

So they would. Just in time. "Only the basket, then. And, Laura!" — her mother followed her out of the marquee — "don't on any account —"

"What, mother?"

No, better not put such ideas into the child's head! "Nothing! Run along."

It was just growing dusky as Laura shut their garden gates. A big dog ran by like a shadow. The road gleamed white, and down below in the hollow the little cottages were in deep shade. How quiet it seemed after the afternoon. Here she was going down the hill to somewhere where a man lay dead, and she couldn't realize it. Why couldn't she? She stopped a minute. And it seemed to her that kisses, voices, tinkling spoons, laughter, the smell of crushed grass were somehow inside her. She had no room for anything else. How strange! She looked up at the pale sky, and all she thought was, "Yes, it was the most successful party."

Now the broad road was crossed. The lane began, smoky and dark. Women in shawls and men's tweed caps hurried by. Men hung over the palings; the children played in the doorways. A low hum came from the mean little cottages. In some of them there was a flicker of light, and a shadow, crab-like, moved across the window. Laura bent her head and hurried on. She wished now she had put on a coat. How her frock shone! And the big hat with the velvet streamer — if only it was another hat! Were the people looking at her? They must be. It was a mistake to have come; she knew all along it was a mistake. Should she go back even now?

No, too late. This was the house. It must be. A dark knot of people stood outside. Beside the gate an old, old woman with a crutch sat in a chair, watching. She had her feet on a newspaper. The voices stopped as Laura drew near. The group parted. It was as though she was expected, as though they had known she was coming here.

Laura was terribly nervous. Tossing the velvet ribbon over her shoulder, she said to a woman standing by, "Is this Mrs. Scott's house?" and the woman, smiling queerly, said, "It is, my lass."

Oh, to be away from this! She actually said, "Help me, God," as she walked up the tiny path and knocked. To be away from those staring eyes, or to be covered up in anything, one of those women's shawls even. I'll just leave the basket and go, she decided. I shan't even wait for it to be emptied.

Then the door opened. A little woman in black showed in the gloom.

Laura said, "Are you Mrs. Scott?" But to her horror the woman answered, "Walk in please, miss," and she was shut in the passage.

"No," said Laura, "I don't want to come in. I only want to leave this basket. Mother sent—"

The little woman in the gloomy passage seemed not to have heard her. "Step this way, please, miss," she said in an oily voice, and Laura followed her.

She found herself in a wretched little low kitchen, lighted by a smoky lamp. There was a woman sitting before the fire.

"Em," said the little creature who had let her in. "Em! It's a young lady." She turned to Laura. She said meaningly, "I'm 'er sister, Miss. You'll excuse 'er, won't you?"

"Oh, but of course!" said Laura. "Please, please don't disturb her. I—I only want to leave—"

But at that moment the woman at the fire turned round. Her face, puffed up, red, with swollen eyes and swollen lips, looked terrible. She seemed as though she couldn't understand why Laura was there. What did it mean? Why was this stranger standing in the kitchen with a basket? What was it all about? And the poor face puckered up again.

"All right, my dear," said the other. "I'll thenk the young lady."

And again she began, "You'll excuse her, miss, I'm sure," and her face, swollen too, tried an oily smile.

Laura only wanted to get out, to get away. She was back in the passage. The door opened. She walked straight through into the bedroom, where the dead man was lying.

"You'd like a look at 'im, wouldn't you?" said Em's sister, and she brushed past Laura over to the bed. "Don't be afraid, my lass,—" and now her voice sounded fond and sly, and fondly she drew down the sheet—"'e looks a picture. There's nothing to show. Come along, my dear."

There lay a young man, fast asleep—sleeping so soundly, so deeply, that he was far, far away from them both. Oh, so remote, so peaceful. He was dreaming. Never wake him up again. His head was sunk in the pillow, his eyes were closed; they were blind under the closed eyelids. He was given up to his dream. What did garden-parties and baskets and lace frocks matter to him? He was far from all those things. He was wonderful, beautiful. While they were laughing and while the band was playing, this marvel had come to the lane. Happy . . . happy. . . . All is well, said that sleeping face. This is just as it should be. I am content.

But all the same you had to cry, and she couldn't go out of the room without saying something to him. Laura gave a loud childish sob.

"Forgive my hat," she said.

And this time she didn't wait for Em's sister. She found her way out of the door, down the path, past all those dark people. At the corner of the lane she met Laurie.

He stepped out of the shadow. "Is that you, Laura?"

"Yes."

"Mother was getting anxious. Was it all right?"

"Yes, quite. Oh, Laurie!" She took his arm, she pressed up against him.

"I say, you're not crying, are you?" asked her brother.

Laura shook her head. She was.

Laurie put his arm round her shoulder. "Don't cry," he said in his warm, loving voice. "Was it awful?"

"No," sobbed Laura. "It was simply marvellous. But, Laurie—" She stopped, she looked at her brother. "Isn't life," she stammered, "isn't life—" But what life was she couldn't explain. No matter. He quite understood.

"*Isn't* it, darling?" said Laurie.

GUY DE MAUPASSANT

Guy de Maupassant (1850–1893) was born in Normandy, the son of a wealthy stockbroker. Unable to accept discipline in school, he joined the army during the Franco-Prussian War of 1870–71. Then for seven years he apprenticed himself to Gustave Flaubert, a distant relative, who attempted to teach him to write. Maupassant remembered, "I wrote verses, short stories, longer stories, even a wretched play. Nothing survived. The master read everything. Then, the following Sunday at lunch, he developed his criticisms." Flaubert taught Maupassant that talent "is nothing other than a long patience. Work."

The essence of Flaubert's now famous teaching is that the writer must look at everything to find some aspect of it that no one has yet seen or expressed. "Everything contains some element of the unexplored because we are accustomed to use our eyes only with the memory of what other people before us have thought about the object we are looking at. The least thing has a bit of the unknown about it. Let us find this."

In 1880 Maupassant caused a sensation with the publication of his story "Boule de Suif" ("Ball of Fat"), a dramatic account of prostitution and bourgeois hypocrisy. During the next decade, before his gradual incapacitation and death from syphilis, he published nearly 300 stories. Characterized by compact and dramatic narrative lines, they read as modern short stories, eliminating the moral judgments and the long digressions used by many earlier writers. Along with his younger contemporary Anton Chekhov, Maupassant is responsible for technical advances that moved the short story toward an austerity that has marked it ever since. These two writers influenced nearly everyone who has written short fiction after them.

As Joseph Conrad recognized, "Facts, and again facts, are his [Maupassant's] unique concern. That is why he is not always properly understood." Maupassant's lack of sentimentality toward his characters, as in his depiction of the wife in "The Necklace," laid him open to charges of cynicism and hardness. Even if Maupassant's stories display a greater distance from his characters and a less sympathetic irony than Chekhov's, both writers were the most accomplished of narrators, equal in their powers of exact observation and independent judgment and in their supple, practiced knowledge of their craft.

COMMENTARY *Kate Chopin, "How I Stumbled upon Maupassant," page 556.*

WEB *Research Guy de Maupassant and answer questions about his work at bedfordstmartins.com/charters/litwriters.*

The Necklace   1884

TRANSLATED BY MARJORIE LAURIE

She was one of those pretty and charming girls who are sometimes, as if by a mistake of destiny, born in a family of clerks. She had no dowry, no expectations, no means of being known, understood, loved, wedded by any rich and distinguished man; and she let herself be married to a little clerk at the Ministry of Public Instructions.

She dressed plainly because she could not dress well, but she was as unhappy as though she had really fallen from her proper station, since with women there is neither caste nor rank: and beauty, grace, and charm act instead of family and birth. Natural fineness, instinct for what is elegant, suppleness of wit, are the sole hierarchy, and make from women of the people the equals of the very greatest ladies.

She suffered ceaselessly, feeling herself born for all the delicacies and all the luxuries. She suffered from the poverty of her dwelling, from the wretched look of the walls, from the worn-out chairs, from the ugliness of the curtains. All those things, of which another woman of her rank would never even have been conscious, tortured her and made her angry. The sight of the little Breton peasant, who did her humble housework aroused in her regrets which were despairing, and distracted dreams. She thought of the silent antechambers hung with Oriental tapestry, lit by tall bronze candelabra, and of the two great footmen in knee breeches who sleep in the big armchairs, made drowsy by the heavy warmth of the hot-air stove. She thought of the long *salons* fitted up with ancient silk, of the delicate furniture carrying priceless curiosities, and of the coquettish perfumed boudoirs made for talks at five o'clock with intimate friends, with men famous and sought after, whom all women envy and whose attention they all desire.

When she sat down to dinner, before the round table covered with a tablecloth three days old, opposite her husband, who uncovered the soup tureen and declared with an enchanted air, "Ah, the good *pot-au-feu*! I don't know anything better than that," she thought of dainty dinners, of shining silverware, of tapestry which peopled the walls with ancient personages and with strange birds flying in the midst of a fairy forest; and she thought of delicious dishes served on marvelous plates, and of the whispered gallantries which you listen to with a sphinxlike smile, while you are eating the pink flesh of a trout or the wings of a quail.

She had no dresses, no jewels, nothing. And she loved nothing but that; she felt made for that. She would so have liked to please, to be envied, to be charming, to be sought after.

She had a friend, a former schoolmate at the convent, who was rich, and whom she did not like to go and see any more, because she suffered so much when she came back.

But one evening, her husband returned home with a triumphant air, and holding a large envelope in his hand.

"There," said he. "Here is something for you."

She tore the paper sharply, and drew out a printed card which bore these words:

"The Minister of Public Instruction and Mme. Georges Ramponneau request the honor of M. and Mme. Loisel's company at the palace of the Ministry on Monday evening, January eighteenth."

Instead of being delighted, as her husband hoped, she threw the invitation on the table with disdain, murmuring:

"What do you want me to do with that?"

"But, my dear, I thought you would be glad. You never go out, and this is such a fine opportunity. I had awful trouble to get it. Everyone wants to go; it is very select, and they are not giving many invitations to clerks. The whole official world will be there."

She looked at him with an irritated glance, and said, impatiently:

"And what do you want me to put on my back?"

He had not thought of that; he stammered:

"Why, the dress you go to the theater in. It looks very well, to me."

He stopped, distracted, seeing his wife was crying. Two great tears descended slowly from the corners of her eyes toward the corners of her mouth. He stuttered:

"What's the matter? What's the matter?"

But, by violent effort, she had conquered her grief, and she replied, with a calm voice, while she wiped her wet cheeks:

"Nothing. Only I have no dress and therefore I can't go to this ball. Give your card to some colleague whose wife is better equipped than I."

He was in despair. He resumed:

"Come, let us see, Mathilde. How much would it cost, a suitable dress, which you could use on other occasions. Something very simple?"

She reflected several seconds, making her calculations and wondering also what sum she could ask without drawing on herself an immediate refusal and a frightened exclamation from the economical clerk.

Finally, she replied, hesitatingly:

"I don't know exactly, but I think I could manage it with four hundred francs."

He had grown a little pale, because he was laying aside just that amount to buy a gun and treat himself to a little shooting next summer on the plain of Nanterre, with several friends who went to shoot larks down there, of a Sunday.

But he said:

"All right. I will give you four hundred francs. And try to have a pretty dress."

The day of the ball drew near, and Mme. Loisel seemed sad, uneasy, anxious. Her dress was ready, however. Her husband said to her one evening:

"What is the matter? Come, you've been so queer these last three days."

And she answered:

"It annoys me not to have a single jewel, not a single stone, nothing to put on. I shall look like distress. I should almost rather not go at all."

He resumed:

"You might wear natural flowers. It's very stylish at this time of the year. For ten francs you can get two or three magnificent roses."

She was not convinced.

"No; there's nothing more humiliating than to look poor among other women who are rich."

But her husband cried:

"How stupid you are! Go look up your friend Mme. Forestier, and ask her to lend you some jewels. You're quite thick enough with her to do that."

She uttered a cry of joy:

"It's true. I never thought of it."

The next day she went to her friend and told of her distress.

Mme. Forestier went to a wardrobe with a glass door, took out a large jewelbox, brought it back, opened it, and said to Mme. Loisel:

"Choose, choose, my dear."

She saw first of all some bracelets, then a pearl necklace, then a Venetian cross, gold and precious stones of admirable workmanship. She tried on the ornaments before the glass, hesitated, could not make up her mind to part with them, to give them back. She kept asking:

"Haven't you any more?"

"Why, yes. Look. I don't know what you like."

All of a sudden she discovered, in a black satin box, a superb necklace of diamonds, and her heart began to beat with an immoderate desire. Her hands trembled as she took it. She fastened it around her throat, outside her high necked dress, and remained lost in ecstasy at the sight of herself.

Then she asked, hesitating, filled with anguish:

"Can you lend me that, only that?"

"Why, yes, certainly."

She sprang upon the neck of her friend, kissed her passionately, then fled with her treasure.

The day of the ball arrived. Mme. Loisel made a great success. She was prettier than them all, elegant, gracious, smiling, and crazy with joy. All the men looked at her, asked her name, endeavored to be introduced. All the attachés of the Cabinet wanted to waltz with her. She was remarked by the minister himself.

She danced with intoxication, with passion, made drunk by pleasure, forgetting all, in the triumph of her beauty, in the glory of her success, in a sort of cloud of happiness composed of all this homage, of all this admiration, of all these awakened desires, and of that sense of complete victory which is so sweet to a woman's heart.

She went away about four o'clock in the morning. Her husband had been sleeping since midnight, in a little deserted anteroom, with three other gentlemen whose wives were having a good time. He threw over her shoulders the wraps which he had brought, modest wraps of common life, whose poverty contrasted with the elegance of the ball dress. She felt this, and wanted to escape so as not to be remarked by the other women, who were enveloping themselves in costly furs.

Loisel held her back.

"Wait a bit. You will catch cold outside. I will go and call a cab."

But she did not listen to him, and rapidly descended the stairs. When they were in the street they did not find a carriage; and they began to look for one, shouting after the cabmen whom they saw passing by at a distance.

They went down toward the Seine, in despair, shivering with cold. At last they found on the quay one of those ancient noctambulant coupés° which, exactly as if they were ashamed to show their misery during the day, are never seen round Paris until after nightfall.

It took them to their door in the Rue des Martyrs, and once more, sadly, they climbed up homeward. All was ended, for her. And as to him, he reflected that he must be at the Ministry at ten o'clock.

She removed the wraps which covered her shoulders before the glass, so as once more to see herself in all her glory. But suddenly she uttered a cry. She no longer had the necklace around her neck!

Her husband, already half undressed, demanded:

"What is the matter with you?"

She turned madly toward him:

"I have—I have—I've lost Mme. Forestier's necklace."

He stood up, distracted.

"What!—how?—impossible!"

And they looked in the folds of her dress, in the folds of her cloak, in her pockets, everywhere. They did not find it.

He asked:

"You're sure you had it on when you left the ball?"

"Yes, I felt it in the vestibule of the palace."

"But if you had lost it in the street we should have heard it fall. It must be in the cab."

"Yes. Probably. Did you take his number?"

"No. And you, didn't you notice it?"

"No."

They looked, thunderstruck, at one another. At last Loisel put on his clothes.

"I shall go back on foot," said he, "over the whole route which we have taken to see if I can find it."

And he went out. She sat waiting on a chair in her ball dress, without strength to go to bed, overwhelmed, without fire, without a thought.

Her husband came back about seven o'clock. He had found nothing.

He went to Police Headquarters, to the newspaper offices, to offer a reward; he went to the cab companies—everywhere, in fact, whither he was urged by the least suspicion of hope.

She waited all day, in the same condition of mad fear before this terrible calamity.

---

coupés: Enclosed four-wheeled carriages.

Loisel returned at night with a hollow, pale face; he had discovered nothing.

"You must write to your friend," said he, "that you have broken the clasp of her necklace and that you are having it mended. That will give us time to turn round."

She wrote at his dictation.

At the end of a week they had lost all hope.

And Loisel, who had aged five years, declared:

"We must consider how to replace that ornament."

The next day they took the box which had contained it, and they went to the jeweler whose name was found within. He consulted his books.

"It was not I, madame, who sold that necklace; I must simply have furnished the case."

Then they went from jeweler to jeweler, searching for a necklace like the other, consulting their memories, sick both of them with chagrin and anguish.

They found, in a shop at the Palais Royal, a string of diamonds which seemed to them exactly like the one they looked for. It was worth forty thousand francs. They could have it for thirty-six.

So they begged the jeweler not to sell it for three days yet. And they made a bargain that he should buy it back for thirty-four thousand francs, in case they found the other one before the end of February.

Loisel possessed eighteen thousand francs which his father had left him. He would borrow the rest.

He did borrow, asking a thousand francs of one, five hundred of another, five louis here, three louis there. He gave notes, took up ruinous obligations, dealt with usurers and all the race of lenders. He compromised all the rest of his life, risked his signature without even knowing if he could meet it; and, frightened by the pains yet to come, by the black misery which was about to fall upon him, by the prospect of all the physical privation and of all the moral tortures which he was to suffer, he went to get the new necklace, putting down upon the merchant's counter thirty-six thousand francs.

When Mme. Loisel took back the necklace, Mme. Forestier said to her, with a chilly manner:

"You should have returned it sooner; I might have needed it."

She did not open the case, as her friend had so much feared. If she had detected the substitution, what would she have thought, what would she have said? Would she not have taken Mme. Loisel for a thief?

Mme. Loisel now knew the horrible existence of the needy. She took her part, moreover, all of a sudden, with heroism. That dreadful debt must be paid. She would pay it. They dismissed their servant; they changed their lodgings; they rented a garret under the roof.

She came to know what heavy housework meant and the odious cares of the kitchen. She washed the dishes, using her rosy nails on the greasy pots and pans. She washed the dirty linen, the shirts, and the dishcloths, which she dried upon a line; she carried the slops down to the street every morning, and carried up the water, stopping for breath at every landing. And, dressed like a woman of the people, she went to the fruiterer, the grocer, the butcher, her basket on her arm, bargaining, insulted, defending her miserable money sou by sou.

Each month they had to meet some notes, renew others, obtain more time.

Her husband worked in the evening making a fair copy of some trades-man's accounts, and late at night he often copied manuscript for five sous a page.

And this life lasted for ten years.

At the end of ten years, they had paid everything, everything, with the rates of usury, and the accumulations of the compound interest.

Mme. Loisel looked old now. She had become the woman of impover-ished households — strong and hard and rough. With frowsy hair, skirts askew, and red hands, she talked loud while washing the floor with great swishes of water. But sometimes, when her husband was at the office, she sat down near the window, and she thought of that gay evening of long ago, of that ball where she had been so beautiful and so fêted.

What would have happened if she had not lost that necklace? Who knows? Who knows? How life is strange and changeful! How little a thing is needed for us to be lost or to be saved!

But, one Sunday, having gone to take a walk in the Champs Elysées to refresh herself from the labor of the week, she suddenly perceived a woman who was leading a child. It was Mme. Forestier, still young, still beautiful, still charming.

Mme. Loisel felt moved. Was she going to speak to her? Yes, certainly. And now that she had paid, she was going to tell her all about it. Why not?

She went up.

"Good-day, Jeanne."

The other, astonished to be familiarly addressed by this plain goodwife, did not recognize her at all, and stammered.

"But — madam! — I do not know — you must be mistaken."

"No. I am Mathilde Loisel."

Her friend uttered a cry.

"Oh, my poor Mathilde! How you are changed!"

"Yes, I have had days hard enough, since I have seen you, days wretched enough — and that because of you!"

"Of me! How so?"

"Do you remember that diamond necklace which you lent me to wear at the ministerial ball?"

"Yes. Well?"

"Well, I lost it."

"What do you mean? You brought it back."

"I brought you back another just like it. And for this we have been ten years paying. You can understand that it was not easy for us, who had nothing. At last it is ended, and I am very glad."

Mme. Forestier had stopped.

"You say that you bought a necklace of diamonds to replace mine?"

"Yes. You never noticed it, then! They were very like."

And she smiled with a joy which was proud and naïve at once.

Mme. Forestier, strongly moved, took her two hands.

"Oh, my poor Mathilde! Why, my necklace was paste. It was worth at most five hundred francs!"

HERMAN MELVILLE

Herman Melville (1819–1891) published his first short story in 1853 as "Bartleby, the Scrivener: A Story of Wall Street." Behind him were seven years of writing novels beginning with the burst of creative energy that produced his early books of sea adventure: Typee *(1846),* Omoo *(1847),* Mardi *(1849),* Redburn *(1849), and* White-Jacket *(1850). All of these were based on his experiences on-board ship. Melville had been left in poverty at the age of fifteen when his father went bankrupt, and in 1839 he went to sea as a cabin boy. Two years later he sailed on a whaler bound for the Pacific, but he deserted in the Marquesas Islands and lived for a time with cannibals. Having little formal education, Melville later boasted that "a whale ship was my Yale College and my Harvard." His most ambitious book was* Moby-Dick *(1851), a work of great allegorical complexity heavily indebted to the influence of Nathaniel Hawthorne, Melville's neighbor in the Berkshires at the time he wrote it.* Moby-Dick *was not a commercial success, however, and the novel that followed it,* Pierre *(1852), was dismissed by critics as incomprehensible trash.*

*It was at this point that Melville turned to the short story. Between 1853 and 1856 he published fifteen sketches and stories and a serialized historical novel, promising the popular magazines that his stories would "contain nothing of any sort to shock the fastidious." But when this work and another novel (*The Confidence Man, *1857) failed to restore his reputation, he ceased trying to support his family by his pen. He moved from his farm in the Berkshires to a house in New York City bought for him by his father-in-law, and worked for more than twenty years as an inspector of customs. He published a few books of poems and wrote a short novel,* Billy Budd, *which critics acclaimed as one of his greatest works when it was published—thirty years after his death.*

Melville stood at the crossroads in the early history of American short fiction. When he began to publish in magazines, Hawthorne and Edgar Allan Poe had already done their best work in the romantic vein of tales and sketches, and the realistic local-color school of short stories had not yet been established. Melville created something new in "Bartleby, the Scrivener," a fully developed, if discursive, short story set in a contemporary social context. It baffled readers of Putnam's Monthly Magazine in 1853, when it was published in two installments. One reviewer called it "a Poeish tale with an infusion of more natural sentiment." For the rest of his stories, Melville used the conventional form of old-fashioned tales mostly set in remote times or places.

COMMENTARIES *Herman Melville, "Blackness in Hawthorne's 'Young Goodman Brown,'" page 575; J. Hillis Miller, "Who Is He? Melville's 'Bartleby, the Scrivener,'" page 577.*

WEB   *Research Herman Melville and answer questions about his work at bedfordstmartins.com/charters/litwriters.*

Bartleby, the Scrivener   1853
A Story of Wall Street

I am a rather elderly man. The nature of my avocations, for the last thirty years, has brought me into more than ordinary contact with what would seem an interesting and somewhat singular set of men, of whom, as yet, nothing, that I know of, has ever been written — I mean, the law-copyists, or scriveners. I have known very many of them, professionally and privately, and, if I pleased, could relate divers histories, at which good-natured gentlemen might smile, and sentimental souls might weep. But I waive the biographies of all other scriveners, for a few passages in the life of Bartleby, who was a scrivener, the strangest I ever saw, or heard of. While, of other law-copyists, I might write the complete life, of Bartleby nothing of that sort can be done. I believe that no materials exist, for a full and satisfactory biography of this man. It is an irreparable loss to literature. Bartleby was one of those beings of whom nothing is ascertainable, except from the original sources, and, in his case, those are very small. What my own astonished eyes saw of Bartleby, *that* is all I know of him, except, indeed, one vague report, which will appear in the sequel.

Ere introducing the scrivener, as he first appeared to me, it is fit I make some mention of myself, my *employés,* my business, my chambers, and general surroundings, because some such description is indispensable to an adequate understanding of the chief character about to be presented. Imprimis:° I am a man who, from his youth upwards, has been filled with a profound conviction that the easiest way of life is the best. Hence, though I belong to a profession proverbially energetic and nervous, even to turbulence, at times, yet nothing of that sort have I ever suffered to invade my peace. I am one of those unambitious lawyers who never address a jury, or in any way draw down public applause; but, in the cool tranquillity of a snug retreat, do a snug business among rich men's bonds, and mortgages, and title-deeds. All who know me, consider me an eminently *safe* man. The late John Jacob Astor, a personage little given to poetic enthusiasm, had no hesitation in pronouncing my first grand point to be prudence; my next, method. I do not speak it in vanity, but simply record the fact, that I was not unemployed in my profession by the late John Jacob Astor; a name which, I admit, I love to repeat; for it hath a rounded and orbicular sound to it, and rings like unto bullion. I will freely add, that I was not insensible to the late John Jacob Astor's good opinion.

Some time prior to the period at which this little history begins, my avocations had been largely increased. The good old office, now extinct in the State of New York, of a Master in Chancery, had been conferred upon me. It was not a very arduous office, but very pleasantly remunerative. I seldom lose my temper; much more seldom indulge in dangerous indignation at wrongs and out-

---

Imprimis: In the first place (Latin).

rages; but I must be permitted to be rash here and declare, that I consider the sudden and violent abrogation of the office of Master in Chancery, by the new Constitution, as a——premature act; inasmuch as I had counted upon a life-lease of the profits, whereas I only received those of a few short years. But this is by the way.

My chambers were up stairs, at No.——Wall Street. At one end, they looked upon the white wall of the interior of a spacious skylight shaft, penetrating the building from top to bottom.

This view might have been considered rather tame than otherwise, deficient in what landscape painters call "life." But, if so, the view from the other end of my chambers offered, at least, a contrast, if nothing more. In that direction, my windows commanded an unobstructed view of a lofty brick wall, black by age and everlasting shade; which wall required no spy-glass to bring out its lurking beauties, but, for the benefit of all near-sighted spectators, was pushed up to within ten feet of my window-panes. Owing to the great height of the surrounding buildings, and my chambers being on the second floor, the interval between this wall and mine not a little resembled a huge square cistern.

At the period just preceding the advent of Bartleby, I had two persons as copyists in my employment, and a promising lad as an office-boy. First, Turkey; second, Nippers; third, Ginger Nut. These may seem names, the like of which are not usually found in the Directory. In truth, they were nicknames, mutually conferred upon each other by my three clerks, and were deemed expressive of their respective persons or characters. Turkey was a short, pursy Englishman, of about my own age—that is, somewhere not far from sixty. In the morning, one might say, his face was of a fine florid hue, but after twelve o'clock, meridian—his dinner hour—it blazed like a grate full of Christmas coals; and continued blazing—but, as it were, with a gradual wane—till six o'clock, P.M., or thereabouts; after which, I saw no more of the proprietor of the face, which, gaining its meridian with the sun, seemed to set with it, to rise, culminate, and decline the following day, with the like regularity and undiminished glory. There are many singular coincidences I have known in the course of my life, not the least among which was the fact, that, exactly when Turkey displayed his fullest beams from his red and radiant countenance, just then, too, at that critical moment, began the daily period when I considered his business capacities as seriously disturbed for the remainder of the twenty-four hours. Not that he was absolutely idle, or averse to business then; far from it. The difficulty was, he was apt to be altogether too energetic. There was a strange, inflamed, flurried, flighty recklessness of activity about him. He would be incautious in dipping his pen into his inkstand. All his blots upon my documents were dropped there after twelve o'clock, meridian. Indeed, not only would he be reckless, and sadly given to making blots in the afternoon, but, some days, he went further, and was rather noisy. At such times, too, his face flamed with augmented blazonry, as if cannel coal had been heaped on anthracite. He made an unpleasant racket with his chair; spilled his sand-box; in mending his pens, impatiently split them all to pieces, and threw them on the floor in a sudden passion; stood up, and leaned over his table, boxing his papers about in a most indecorous manner, very sad to behold in an elderly man like him. Nevertheless, as he was in many ways a most valuable person to me, and all the time before twelve o'clock, meridian, was the quickest, steadiest creature, too, accomplishing a great deal of work in a style not easily to be matched — for these reasons, I was willing to overlook his eccentricities, though, indeed, occasionally, I remonstrated with him. I did this very gently, however, because, though the civilest, nay, the blandest and most reverential of men in the morning, yet, in the afternoon, he was disposed, upon provocation, to be slightly rash with his tongue — in fact, insolent. Now, valuing his morning services as I did, and resolved not to lose them — yet, at the same time, made uncomfortable by his inflamed ways after twelve o'clock — and being a man of peace, unwilling by my admonitions to call forth unseemly retorts from him, I took upon me, one Saturday noon (he was always worse on Saturdays) to hint to him, very kindly, that, perhaps, now that he was growing old, it might be well to abridge his labors; in short, he need not come to my chambers after twelve o'clock, but, dinner over, had best go home to his lodgings, and rest himself till tea-time. But no; he insisted upon his afternoon devotions. His countenance became intolerably fervid, as he oratorically assured me — gesticulating with a long ruler at the other end of the room — that if his services in the morning were useful, how indispensable, then, in the afternoon?

"With submission, sir," said Turkey, on this occasion, "I consider myself your right-hand man. In the morning I but marshal and deploy my columns; but in the afternoon I put myself at their head, and gallantly charge the foe, thus" — and he made a violent thrust with the ruler.

"But the blots, Turkey," intimated I.

"True; but, with submission, sir, behold these hairs! I am getting old. Surely, sir, a blot or two of a warm afternoon is not to be severely urged against gray hairs. Old age — even if it blot the page — is honorable. With submission, sir, we *both* are getting old."

This appeal to my fellow-feeling was hardly to be resisted. At all events, I saw that go he would not. So, I made up my mind to let him stay, resolving, nevertheless, to see to it that, during the afternoon, he had to do with my less important papers.

Nippers, the second on my list, was a whiskered, sallow, and, upon the whole, rather piratical-looking young man, of about five-and-twenty. I always deemed him the victim of two evil powers — ambition and indigestion. The ambition was evinced by a certain impatience of the duties of a mere copyist, an unwarrantable usurpation of strictly professional affairs such as the original drawing up of legal documents. The indigestion seemed betokened in an occasional nervous testiness and grinning irritability, causing the teeth to audibly grind together over mistakes committed in copying; unnecessary maledictions, hissed, rather than spoken, in the heat of business; and especially by a continual discontent with the height of the table where he worked. Though of a very ingenious mechanical turn, Nippers could never get this table to suit him. He put chips under it, blocks of various sorts, bits of pasteboard, and at last went so far as to attempt an exquisite adjustment, by final pieces of folded blotting paper. But no invention would answer. If, for the sake of easing his back, he brought the table-lid at a sharp angle well up towards his chin, and wrote there like a man using the steep roof of a Dutch house for his desk, then he declared that it stopped the circulation in his arms. If now he lowered the table to his waistbands, and stooped over it in writing, then there was a sore aching in his back. In short, the truth of the matter was, Nippers knew not what he wanted. Or, if he wanted anything, it was to be rid of a scrivener's table altogether. Among the manifestations of his diseased ambition was a fondness he had for receiving visits from certain ambiguous-looking fellows in seedy coats, whom he called his clients. Indeed, I was aware that not only was he, at times, considerable of a ward-politician, but he occasionally did a little business at the justices' courts, and was not unknown on the steps of the Tombs.° I have good reason to believe, however, that one individual who called upon him at my chambers, and who, with a grand air, he insisted was his client, was no other than a dun, and the alleged title-deed, a bill. But, with all his failings, and the annoyances he caused me, Nippers, like his compatriot Turkey, was a very useful man to me; wrote a neat, swift hand; and, when he chose, was not deficient in a gentlemanly sort of deportment. Added to this, he always dressed in a gentlemanly sort of way; and so, incidentally, reflected credit upon my chambers. Whereas, with respect to Turkey, I had much ado to keep him from being a reproach to me. His clothes were apt to look oily, and smell of eating-houses. He wore his pantaloons very loose and baggy in summer. His coats were execrable, his hat not to be handled. But while the hat was a thing of indifference to me, inasmuch as his natural civility and deference, as a dependent Englishman, always led him to doff it the moment he entered the room, yet his coat was another matter. Concerning his coats, I reasoned with him; but with no effect. The truth was, I suppose, that a man with so small an income could not afford to sport such a lustrous face and a lustrous coat at one and the same time. As Nippers once observed, Turkey's money went chiefly for red ink. One winter day, I presented Turkey with a highly respectable-looking coat of my own — a padded gray coat, of a most comfortable warmth, and which buttoned straight up from the knee to the neck. I thought Turkey would appreciate the favor, and abate his rashness and obstreperousness of afternoons. But no; I verily believe that buttoning himself up in so downy and blanket-like a coat had a pernicious effect upon him upon the same principle that too much oats are bad for horses. In fact, precisely as a rash, restive horse is said to feel his oats, so Turkey felt his coat. It made him insolent. He was a man whom prosperity harmed.

Though, concerning the self-indulgent habits of Turkey, I had my own private surmises, yet, touching Nippers, I was well persuaded that, whatever might be his faults in other respects, he was, at least, a temperate young man. But, indeed, nature herself seemed to have been his vintner, and, at his birth, charged him so thoroughly with an irritable, brandy-like disposition, that all subsequent potations were needless. When I consider how, amid the stillness of my chambers, Nippers would sometimes impatiently rise from his

---

the Tombs: A prison in New York City.

seat, and stooping over his table, spread his arms wide apart, seize the whole desk, and move it, and jerk it, with a grim, grinding motion on the floor, as if the table were a perverse voluntary agent, intent on thwarting and vexing him, I plainly perceive that, for Nippers, brandy-and-water were altogether superfluous.

It was fortunate for me that, owing to its peculiar cause—indigestion—the irritability and consequent nervousness of Nippers were mainly observable in the morning, while in the afternoon he was comparatively mild. So that, Turkey's paroxysms only coming on about twelve o'clock, I never had to do with their eccentricities at one time. Their fits relieved each other, like guards. When Nippers' was on, Turkey's was off; and *vice versa*. This was a good natural arrangement, under the circumstances.

Ginger Nut, the third on my list, was a lad, some twelve years old. His father was a carman, ambitious of seeing his son on the bench instead of a cart, before he died. So he sent him to my office, as student at law, errand-boy, cleaner, and sweeper, at the rate of one dollar a week. He had a little desk to himself, but he did not use it much. Upon inspection, the drawer exhibited a great array of the shells of various sorts of nuts. Indeed, to this quick-witted youth, the whole noble science of the law was contained in a nutshell. Not the least among the employments of Ginger Nut, as well as one which he discharged with the most alacrity, was his duty as cake and apple purveyor for Turkey and Nippers. Copying lawpapers being proverbially a dry, husky sort of business, my two scriveners were fain to moisten their mouths very often with Spitzenbergs, to be had at the numerous stalls nigh the Custom House and Post Office. Also, they sent Ginger Nut very frequently for that peculiar cake—small, flat, round, and very spicy—after which he had been named by them. Of a cold morning, when business was but dull, Turkey would gobble up scores of these cakes, as if they were mere wafers—indeed, they sell them at the rate of six or eight for a penny—the scrape of his pen blending with the crunching of the crisp particles in his mouth. Of all the fiery afternoon blunders and flurried rashness of Turkey, was his once moistening a ginger-cake between his lips, and clapping it on to a mortgage, for a seal. I came within an ace of dismissing him then. But he mollified me by making an oriental bow, and saying—

"With submission, sir, it was generous of me to find you in stationery on my own account."

Now my original business—that of a conveyancer and title hunter, and drawer-up of recondite documents of all sorts—was considerably increased by receiving the Master's office. There was now great work for scriveners. Not only must I push the clerks already with me, but I must have additional help.

In answer to my advertisement, a motionless young man one morning stood upon my office threshold, the door being open, for it was summer. I can see that figure now—pallidly neat, pitiably respectable, incurably forlorn! It was Bartleby.

After a few words touching his qualifications, I engaged him, glad to have among my corps of copyists a man of so singularly sedate an aspect, which I thought might operate beneficially upon the flighty temper of Turkey, and the fiery one of Nippers.

I should have stated before that ground-glass folding-doors divided my premises into two parts, one of which was occupied by my scriveners, the other by myself. According to my humor, I threw open these doors, or closed them. I resolved to assign Bartleby a corner by the folding-doors, but on my side of them, so as to have this quiet man within easy call, in case any trifling thing was to be done. I placed his desk close up to a small side-window in that part of the room, a window which originally had afforded a lateral view of certain grimy brickyards and bricks, but which, owing to subsequent erections, commanded at present no view at all, though it gave some light. Within three feet of the panes was a wall, and the light came down from far above, between two lofty buildings, as from a very small opening in a dome. Still further to a satisfactory arrangement, I procured a high green folding screen, which might entirely iso- late Bartleby from my sight, though not remove him from my voice. And thus, in a manner, privacy and society were conjoined.

At first, Bartleby did an extraordinary quantity of writing. As if long famishing for something to copy, he seemed to gorge himself on my docu- ments. There was no pause for digestion. He ran a day and night line, copying by sunlight and by candle-light. I should have been quite delighted with his application, had he been cheerfully industrious. But he wrote on silently, palely, mechanically.

It is, of course, an indispensable part of a scrivener's business to verify the accuracy of his copy, word by word. Where there are two or more scriveners in an office, they assist each other in this examination, one reading from the copy, the other holding the original. It is a very dull, wearisome, and lethargic affair. I can readily imagine that, to some sanguine temperaments, it would be altogether intolerable. For example, I cannot credit that the mettlesome poet, Byron, would have contentedly sat down with Bartleby to examine a law docu- ment of, say five hundred pages, closely written in a crimpy hand.

Now and then, in the haste of business, it had been my habit to assist in comparing some brief document myself, calling Turkey or Nippers for this purpose. One object I had, in placing Bartleby so handy to me behind the screen, was, to avail myself of his services on such trivial occasions. It was on the third day, I think, of his being with me, and before any necessity had arisen for having his own writing examined, that, being much hurried to complete a small affair I had in hand, I abruptly called to Bartleby. In my haste and natural expectancy of instant compliance, I sat with my head bent over the original on my desk, and my right hand sideways, and somewhat nervously extended with the copy, so that, immediately upon emerging from his retreat, Bartleby might snatch it and proceed to business without the least delay.

In this very attitude did I sit when I called to him, rapidly stating what it was I wanted him to do — namely, to examine a small paper with me. Imag- ine my surprise, nay, my consternation, when, without moving from his privacy, Bartleby, in a singularly mild, firm voice, replied, "I would prefer not to."

I sat awhile in perfect silence, rallying my stunned faculties. Immediately it occurred to me that my ears had deceived me, or Bartleby had entirely misunderstood my meaning. I repeated my request in the clearest tone I could assume; but in quite as clear a one came the previous reply, "I would prefer not to."

"Prefer not to," echoed I, rising in high excitement, and crossing the room with a stride. "What do you mean? Are you moonstruck? I want you to help me compare this sheet here — take it," and I thrust it towards him.

"I would prefer not to," said he.

I looked at him steadfastly. His face was leanly composed; his gray eye dimly calm. Not a wrinkle of agitation rippled him. Had there been the least uneasiness, anger, impatience, or impertinence in his manner; in other words, had there been anything ordinarily human about him, doubtless I should have violently dismissed him from the premises. But as it was, I should have as soon thought of turning my pale plaster-of-paris bust of Cicero out of doors. I stood gazing at him awhile, as he went on with his own writing, and then reseated myself at my desk. This is very strange, thought I. What had one best do? But my business hurried me. I concluded to forget the matter for the present, reserving it for my future leisure. So, calling Nippers from the other room, the paper was speedily examined.

A few days after this, Bartleby concluded four lengthy documents, being quadruplicates of a week's testimony taken before me in my High Court of Chancery. It became necessary to examine them. It was an important suit, and great accuracy was imperative. Having all things arranged, I called Turkey, Nippers, and Ginger Nut, from the next room, meaning to place the four copies in the hands of my four clerks, while I should read from the original. Accordingly, Turkey, Nippers, and Ginger Nut had taken their seats in a row, each with his document in his hand, when I called to Bartleby to join this interesting group.

"Bartleby! quick, I am waiting."

I heard a slow scrape of his chair legs on the uncarpeted floor, and soon he appeared standing at the entrance of his hermitage.

"What is wanted?" said he, mildly.

"The copies, the copies," said I, hurriedly. "We are going to examine them. There" — and I held towards him the fourth quadruplicate.

"I would prefer not to," he said, and gently disappeared behind the screen.

For a few moments I was turned into a pillar of salt, standing at the head of my seated column of clerks. Recovering myself, I advanced towards the screen, and demanded the reason for such extraordinary conduct.

"*Why* do you refuse?"

"I would prefer not to."

With any other man I should have flown outright into a dreadful passion, scorned all further words, and thrust him ignominiously from my presence. But there was something about Bartleby that not only strangely disarmed me, but, in a wonderful manner, touched and disconcerted me. I began to reason with him.

"These are your own copies we are about to examine. It is labor saving to you, because one examination will answer for your four papers. It is common usage. Every copyist is bound to help examine his copy. Is it not so? Will you not speak? Answer!"

"I prefer not to," he replied in a flute-like tone. It seemed to me that, while I had been addressing him, he carefully revolved every statement that I made; fully comprehended the meaning; could not gainsay the irresistible conclusion; but, at the same time, some paramount consideration prevailed with him to reply as he did.

"You are decided, then, not to comply with my request—a request made according to common usage and common sense?"

He briefly gave me to understand, that on that point my judgment was sound. Yes: his decision was irreversible.

It is not seldom the case that, when a man is browbeaten in some unprecedented and violently unreasonable way, he begins to stagger in his own plainest faith. He begins, as it were, vaguely to surmise that, wonderful as it may be, all the justice and all the reason is on the other side. Accordingly, if any disinterested persons are present, he turns to them for some reinforcement for his own faltering mind.

"Turkey," said I, "what do you think of this? Am I not right?"

"With submission, sir," said Turkey, in his blandest tone, "I think that you are."

"Nippers," said I, "what do *you* think of it?"

"I think I should kick him out of the office."

(The reader of nice perceptions will have perceived that, it being morning, Turkey's answer is couched in polite and tranquil terms, but Nippers replies in ill-tempered ones. Or, to repeat a previous sentence, Nippers' ugly mood was on duty, and Turkey's off.)

"Ginger Nut," said I, willing to enlist the smallest suffrage in my behalf, "what do *you* think of it?"

"I think, sir, he's a little *luny,*" replied Ginger Nut, with a grin.

"You hear what they say," said I, turning towards the screen, "come forth and do your duty."

But he vouchsafed no reply. I pondered a moment in sore perplexity. But once more business hurried me. I determined again to postpone the consideration of this dilemma to my future leisure. With a little trouble we made out to examine the papers without Bartleby, though at every page or two Turkey deferentially dropped his opinion, that this proceeding was quite out of the common; while Nippers, twitching in his chair with a dyspeptic nervousness, ground out, between his set teeth, occasional hissing maledictions against the stubborn oaf behind the screen. And for his (Nippers') part, this was the first and the last time he would do another man's business without pay.

Meanwhile Bartleby sat in his hermitage, oblivious to everything but his own peculiar business there.

Some days passed, the scrivener being employed upon another lengthy work. His late remarkable conduct led me to regard his ways narrowly. I observed that he never went to dinner; indeed, that he never went anywhere.

As yet I had never, of my personal knowledge, known him to be outside of my office. He was a perpetual sentry in the corner. At about eleven o'clock though, in the morning, I noticed that Ginger Nut would advance towards the opening in Bartleby's screen, as if silently beckoned thither by a gesture invisible to me where I sat. The boy would then leave the office, jingling a few pence, and reappear with a handful of ginger-nuts, which he delivered in the hermitage, receiving two of the cakes for his trouble.

He lives, then, on ginger-nuts, thought I; never eats a dinner, properly speaking; he must be a vegetarian, then, but no; he never eats even vegetables, he eats nothing but ginger-nuts. My mind then ran on in reveries concerning the probable effects upon the human constitution of living entirely on ginger-nuts. Ginger-nuts are so called, because they contain ginger as one of their peculiar constituents, and the final flavoring one. Now, what was ginger? A hot, spicy thing. Was Bartleby hot and spicy? Not at all. Ginger, then, had no effect upon Bartleby. Probably he preferred it should have none.

Nothing so aggravates an earnest person as a passive resistance. If the individual so resisted be of a not inhumane temper, and the resisting one perfectly harmless in his passivity, then, in the better moods of the former, he will endeavor charitably to construe to his imagination what proves impossible to be solved by his judgment. Even so, for the most part, I regarded Bartleby and his ways. Poor fellow! thought I, he means no mischief; it is plain he intends no insolence; his aspect sufficiently evinces that his eccentricities are involuntary. He is useful to me. I can get along with him. If I turn him away, the chances are he will fall in with some less indulgent employer, and then he will be rudely treated, and perhaps driven forth miserably to starve. Yes. Here I can cheaply purchase a delicious self-approval. To befriend Bartleby; to humor him in his strange wilfulness, will cost me little or nothing, while I lay up in my soul what will eventually prove a sweet morsel for my conscience. But this mood was not invariable with me. The passiveness of Bartleby sometimes irritated me. I felt strangely goaded on to encounter him in new opposition — to elicit some angry spark from him answerable to my own. But, indeed, I might as well have essayed to strike fire with my knuckles against a bit of Windsor soap. But one afternoon the evil impulse in me mastered me, and the following little scene ensued:

"Bartleby," said I, "when those papers are all copied, I will compare them with you."

"I would prefer not to."

"How? Surely you do not mean to persist in that mulish vagary?"

No answer.

I threw open the folding-doors nearby, and turning upon Turkey and Nippers, exclaimed:

"Bartleby a second time says, he won't examine his papers. What do you think of it, Turkey?"

It was afternoon, be it remembered. Turkey sat glowing like a brass boiler; his bald head steaming; his hands reeling among his blotted papers.

"Think of it?" roared Turkey. "I think I'll just step behind his screen, and black his eyes for him!"

So saying, Turkey rose to his feet and threw his arms into a pugilistic position. He was hurrying away to make good his promise, when I detained him, alarmed at the effect of incautiously rousing Turkey's combativeness after dinner.

"Sit down, Turkey," said I, "and hear what Nippers has to say. What do you think of it, Nippers? Would I not be justified in immediately dismissing Bartleby?"

"Excuse me, that is for you to decide, sir. I think his conduct quite unusual, and, indeed, unjust, as regards Turkey and myself. But it may only be a passing whim."

"Ah," exclaimed I, "you have strangely changed your mind, then — you speak very gently of him now."

"All beer," cried Turkey; "gentleness is effects of beer — Nippers and I dined together to-day. You see how gentle *I* am, sir. Shall I go and black his eyes?"

"You refer to Bartleby, I suppose. No, not to-day, Turkey," I replied; "pray, put up your fists."

I closed the doors, and again advanced towards Bartleby. I felt additional incentives tempting me to my fate. I burned to be rebelled against again. I remembered that Bartleby never left the office.

"Bartleby," said I, "Ginger Nut is away; just step around to the Post Office, won't you?" (it was but a three minutes' walk) "and see if there is anything for me."

"I would prefer not to."

"You *will* not?"

"I *prefer* not."

I staggered to my desk, and sat there in a deep study. My blind inveteracy returned. Was there any other thing in which I could procure myself to be ignominiously repulsed by this lean, penniless wight? my hired clerk? What added thing is there, perfectly reasonable, that he will be sure to refuse to do?

"Bartleby!"

No answer.

"Bartleby," in a louder tone.

No answer.

"Bartleby," I roared.

Like a very ghost, agreeably to the laws of magical invocation, at the third summons, he appeared at the entrance of his hermitage.

"Go to the next room, and tell Nippers to come to me."

"I would prefer not to," he respectfully and slowly said, and mildly disappeared.

"Very good, Bartleby," said I, in a quiet sort of serenely-severe self-possessed tone, intimating the unalterable purpose of some terrible retribution very close at hand. At the moment I half intended something of the kind. But upon the whole, as it was drawing towards my dinner-hour, I thought it best to put on my hat and walk home for the day, suffering much from perplexity and distress of mind.

Shall I acknowledge it? The conclusion of this whole business was, that it soon became a fixed fact of my chambers, that a pale young scrivener, by the name of Bartleby, had a desk there; that he copied for me at the usual rate of four cents a folio (one hundred words); but he was permanently exempt from examining the work done by him, that duty being transferred to Turkey and Nippers, out of compliment, doubtless, to their superior acuteness; moreover, said Bartleby was never, on any account, to be dispatched on the most trivial errand of any sort; and that even if entreated to take upon him such a matter, it was generally understood that he would "prefer not to"—in other words, that he would refuse point blank.

As days passed on, I became considerably reconciled to Bartleby. His steadiness, his freedom from all dissipation, his incessant industry (except when he chose to throw himself into a standing revery behind his screen), his great stillness, his unalterableness of demeanor under all circumstances, made him a valuable acquisition. One prime thing was this—*he was always there*—first in the morning, continually through the day, and the last at night. I had a singular confidence in his honesty. I felt my most precious papers perfectly safe in his hands. Sometimes, to be sure, I could not, for the very soul of me, avoid falling into sudden spasmodic passions with him. For it was exceeding difficult to bear in mind all the time those strange peculiarities, privileges, and unheard-of exemptions, forming the tacit stipulations on Bartleby's part under which he remained in my office. Now and then, in the eagerness of dispatching pressing business, I would inadvertently summon Bartleby, in a short, rapid tone, to put his finger, say, on the incipient tie of a bit of red tape with which I was about compressing some papers. Of course, from behind the screen the usual answer, "I prefer not to," was sure to come; and then, how could a human creature, with the common infirmities of our nature, refrain from bitterly exclaiming upon such perverseness—such unreasonableness? However, every added repulse of this sort which I received only tended to lessen the probability of my repeating the inadvertence.

Here it must be said, that, according to the custom of most legal gentlemen occupying chambers in densely populated law buildings, there were several keys to my door. One was kept by a woman residing in the attic, which person weekly scrubbed and daily swept and dusted my apartments. Another was kept by Turkey for convenience sake. The third I sometimes carried in my own pocket. The fourth I knew not who had.

Now, one Sunday morning I happened to go to Trinity Church, to hear a celebrated preacher, and finding myself rather early on the ground I thought I would walk round to my chambers for a while. Luckily I had my key with me; but upon applying it to the lock, I found it resisted by something inserted from the inside. Quite surprised, I called out; when to my consternation a key was turned from within; and thrusting his lean visage at me, and holding the door ajar, the apparition of Bartleby appeared, in his shirt-sleeves, and otherwise in a strangely tattered *deshabille,* saying quietly that he was sorry, but he was deeply engaged just then, and preferred not admitting me at present. In a brief word or two, he moreover added, that perhaps I had better walk round the block two or three times, and by that time he would probably have concluded his affairs.

Now, the utterly unsurmised appearance of Bartleby, tenanting my law-chambers of a Sunday morning, with his cadaverously gentlemanly *nonchalance*, yet withal firm and self-possessed, had such a strange effect upon me, that incontinently I slunk away from my own door, and did as desired. But not without sundry twinges of impotent rebellion against the mild effrontery of this unaccountable scrivener. Indeed, it was his wonderful mildness chiefly, which not only disarmed me, but unmanned me, as it were. For I consider that one, for the time, is sort of unmanned when he tranquilly permits his hired clerk to dictate to him, and order him away from his own premises. Furthermore, I was full of uneasiness as to what Bartleby could possibly be doing in my office in his shirt-sleeves, and in an otherwise dismantled condition on a Sunday morning. Was anything amiss going on? Nay, that was out of the question. It was not to be thought of for a moment that Bartleby was an immoral person. But what could he be doing there? —copying? Nay again, whatever might be his eccentricities, Bartleby was an eminently decorous person. He would be the last man to sit down to his desk in any state approaching to nudity. Besides, it was Sunday; and there was something about Bartleby that forbade the supposition that he would by any secular occupation violate the proprieties of the day.

Nevertheless, my mind was not pacified; and full of a restless curiosity, at last I returned to the door. Without hindrance I inserted my key, opened it, and entered. Bartleby was not to be seen. I looked round anxiously, peeped behind his screen; but it was very plain that he was gone. Upon more closely examining the place, I surmised that for an indefinite period Bartleby must have ate, dressed, and slept in my office, and that too without plate, mirror, or bed. The cushioned seat of a rickety old sofa in one corner bore the faint impress of a lean, reclining form. Rolled away under his desk, I found a blanket; under the empty grate, a blacking box and brush; on a chair, a tin basin, with soap and a ragged towel; in a newspaper a few crumbs of ginger-nuts and a morsel of cheese. Yes, thought I, it is evident enough that Bartleby has been making his home here, keeping bachelor's hall all by himself. Immediately then the thought came sweeping across me, what miserable friendlessness and loneliness are here revealed! His poverty is great; but his solitude, how horrible! Think of it. Of a Sunday, Wall Street is deserted as Petra;° and every night of every day it is an emptiness. This building, too, which of week-days hums with industry and life, at nightfall echoes with sheer vacancy, and all through Sunday is forlorn. And here Bartleby makes his home; sole spectator of a solitude which he has seen all populous—a sort of innocent and transformed Marius° brooding among the ruins of Carthage!

Petra: A city in what is now Jordan, once the center of an Arab kingdom. It was deserted for more than ten centuries, until its rediscovery by explorers in 1812.
Marius: Gaius Marius (157?–86 B.C.) was a Roman general, several times elected consul. Marius's greatest military successes came in the Jugurthine War, in Africa. Later, when his opponents gained power and he was banished, he fled to Africa. Carthage was a city in North Africa.

For the first time in my life a feeling of overpowering stinging melancholy seized me. Before, I had never experienced aught but a not unpleasing sadness. The bond of a common humanity now drew me irresistibly to gloom. A fraternal melancholy! For both I and Bartleby were sons of Adam. I remembered the bright silks and sparkling faces I had seen that day, in gala trim, swan-like sailing down the Mississippi of Broadway; and I contrasted them with the pallid copyist, and thought to myself, Ah, happiness courts the light, so we deem the world is gay; but misery hides aloof, so we deem that misery there is none. These sad fancyings—chimeras, doubtless, of a sick and silly brain—led on to other and more special thoughts, concerning the eccentricities of Bartleby. Presentiments of strange discoveries hovered round me. The scrivener's pale form appeared to me laid out, among uncaring strangers, in its shivering winding-sheet.

Suddenly I was attracted by Bartleby's closed desk, the key in open sight left in the lock.

I mean no mischief, seek the gratification of no heartless curiosity, thought I; besides, the desk is mine, and its contents, too, so I will make bold to look within. Everything was methodically arranged, the papers smoothly placed. The pigeon-holes were deep, and removing the files of documents, I groped into their recesses. Presently I felt something there, and dragged it out. It was an old bandanna handkerchief, heavy and knotted. I opened it, and saw it was a saving's bank.

I now recalled all the quiet mysteries which I had noted in the man. I remembered that he never spoke but to answer; that, though at intervals he had considerable time to himself, yet I had never seen him reading—no, not even a newspaper; that for long periods he would stand looking out, at his pale window behind the screen, upon the dead brick wall; I was quite sure he never visited any refectory or eating-house; while his pale face clearly indicated that he never drank beer like Turkey; or tea and coffee even, like other men; that he never went anywhere in particular that I could learn; never went out for a walk, unless, indeed, that was the case at present; that he had declined telling who he was, or whence he came, or whether he had any relatives in the world; that though so thin and pale, he never complained of ill-health. And more than all, I remembered a certain unconscious air of pallid—how shall I call it?—of pallid haughtiness, say, or rather an austere reserve about him, which has positively awed me into my tame compliance with his eccentricities, when I had feared to ask him to do the slightest incidental thing for me, even though I might know, from his long-continued motionlessness, that behind his screen he must be standing in one of those dead-wall reveries of his.

Revolving all these things, and coupling them with the recently discovered fact, that he made my office his constant abiding place and home, and not forgetful of his morbid moodiness; revolving all these things, a prudential feeling began to steal over me. My first emotions had been those of pure melancholy and sincerest pity; but just in proportion as the forlornness of Bartleby grew and grew to my imagination, did that same melancholy merge into fear, that pity into repulsion. So true it is, and so terrible, too, that up to a certain point the thought or sight of misery enlists our best affections; but, in certain special cases, beyond that point it does not. They err who would assert that invariably this is owing to the inherent selfishness of the human heart. It rather proceeds from a certain hopelessness of remedying excessive and organic ill. To a sensitive being, pity is not seldom pain. And when at last it is perceived that such pity cannot lead to effectual succor, common sense bids the soul be rid of it. What I saw that morning persuaded me that the scrivener was the victim of innate and incurable disorder. I might give alms to his body; but his body did not pain him; it was his soul that suffered, and his soul I could not reach.

I did not accomplish the purpose of going to Trinity Church that morning. Somehow, the things I had seen disqualified me for the time from church-going. I walked homeward, thinking what I would do with Bartleby. Finally, I resolved upon this — I would put certain calm questions to him the next morning, touching his history, etc., and if he declined to answer them openly and unreservedly (and I supposed he would prefer not), then to give him a twenty dollar bill over and above whatever I might owe him, and tell him his services were no longer required; but that if in any other way I could assist him, I would be happy to do so, especially if he desired to return to his native place, wherever that might be, I would willingly help to defray the expenses. Moreover, if, after reaching home, he found himself at any time in want of aid, a letter from him would be sure of a reply.

The next morning came.

"Bartleby," said I, gently calling to him behind his screen.

No reply.

"Bartleby," said I, in a still gentler tone, "come here; I am not going to ask you to do anything you would prefer not to do — I simply wish to speak to you."

Upon this he noiselessly slid into view.

"Will you tell me, Bartleby, where you were born?"

"I would prefer not to."

"Will you tell me *anything* about yourself?"

"I would prefer not to."

"But what reasonable objection can you have to speak to me? I feel friendly towards you."

He did not look at me while I spoke, but kept his glance fixed upon my bust of Cicero, which, as I then sat, was directly behind me, some six inches above my head.

"What is your answer, Bartleby?" said I, after waiting a considerable time for a reply, during which his countenance remained immovable, only there was the faintest conceivable tremor of the white attenuated mouth.

"At present I prefer to give no answer," he said, and retired into his hermitage.

It was rather weak in me I confess, but his manner, on this occasion, nettled me. Not only did there seem to lurk in it a certain calm disdain, but his perverseness seemed ungrateful, considering the undeniable good usage and indulgence he had received from me.

Again I sat ruminating what I should do. Mortified as I was at his behavior, and resolved as I had been to dismiss him when I entered my office, nevertheless I strangely felt something superstitious knocking at my heart, and forbidding me to carry out my purpose, and denouncing me for a villain if I dared to breathe one bitter word against this forlornest of mankind. At last, familiarly drawing my chair behind his screen, I sat down and said: "Bartleby, never mind, then, about revealing your history; but let me entreat you, as a friend, to comply as far as may be with the usages of this office. Say now, you will help to examine papers tomorrow or next day: in short, say now, that in a day or two you will begin to be a little reasonable:—say so, Bartleby."

"At present I would prefer not to be a little reasonable," was his mildly cadaverous reply.

Just then the folding-doors opened, and Nippers approached. He seemed suffering from an unusually bad night's rest, induced by severer indigestion than common. He overheard those final words of Bartleby.

"*Prefer not*, eh?" gritted Nippers—"I'd *prefer* him, if I were you, sir," addressing me—"I'd *prefer* him; I'd give him preferences, the stubborn mule! What is it, sir, pray, that he *prefers* not to do now?"

Bartleby moved not a limb.

"Mr. Nippers," said I, "I'd prefer that you would withdraw for the present."

Somehow, of late, I had got into the way of involuntarily using this word "prefer" upon all sorts of not exactly suitable occasions. And I trembled to think that my contact with the scrivener had already and seriously affected me in a mental way. And what further and deeper aberration might it not yet produce? This apprehension had not been without efficacy in determining me to summary measures.

As Nippers, looking very sour and sulky, was departing, Turkey blandly and deferentially approached.

"With submission, sir," said he, "yesterday I was thinking about Bartleby here, and I think that if he would but prefer to take a quart of good ale every day, it would do much towards mending him, and enabling him to assist in examining his papers."

"So you have got the word, too," said I, slightly excited.

"With submission, what word, sir?" asked Turkey, respectfully crowding himself into the contracted space behind the screen, and by so doing, making me jostle the scrivener. "What word, sir?"

"I would prefer to be left alone here," said Bartleby, as if offended at being mobbed in his privacy.

"*That's* the word, Turkey," said I—"*that's* it."

"Oh, *prefer*? oh yes—queer word. I never use it myself. But, sir, as I was saying, if he would but prefer—"

"Turkey," interrupted I, "you will please withdraw."

"Oh certainly, sir, if you prefer that I should."

As he opened the folding-door to retire, Nippers at his desk caught a glimpse of me, and asked whether I would prefer to have a certain paper copied on blue paper or white. He did not in the least roguishly accent the word "prefer." It was plain that it involuntarily rolled from his tongue. I thought to myself, surely I must get rid of a demented man, who already has in some degree turned the tongues, if not the heads of myself and clerks. But I thought it prudent not to break the dismission at once.

The next day I noticed that Bartleby did nothing but stand at his window in his dead-wall revery. Upon asking him why he did not write, he said that he had decided upon doing no more writing.

"Why, how now? what next?" exclaimed I, "do no more writing?"

"No more."

"And what is the reason?"

"Do you not see the reason for yourself?" he indifferently replied.

I looked steadfastly at him, and perceived that his eyes looked dull and glazed. Instantly it occurred to me, that his unexampled diligence in copying by his dim window for the first few weeks of his stay with me might have temporarily impaired his vision.

I was touched. I said something in condolence with him. I hinted that of course he did wisely in abstaining from writing for a while; and urged him to embrace that opportunity of taking wholesome exercise in the open air. This, however, he did not do. A few days after this, my other clerks being absent, and being in a great hurry to dispatch certain letters by the mail, I thought that, having nothing else earthly to do, Bartleby would surely be less inflexible than usual, and carry these letters to the Post Office. But he blankly declined. So, much to my inconvenience, I went myself.

Still added days went by. Whether Bartleby's eyes improved or not, I could not say. To all appearance, I thought they did. But when I asked him if they did he vouchsafed no answer. At all events, he would do no copying. At last, in replying to my urgings, he informed me that he had permanently given up copying.

"What!" exclaimed I; "suppose your eyes should get entirely well—better than ever before—would you not copy then?"

"I have given up copying," he answered, and slid aside.

He remained as ever, a fixture in my chamber. Nay—if that were possible—he became still more of a fixture than before. What was to be done? He would do nothing in the office; why should he stay there? In plain fact, he had now become a millstone to me, not only useless as a necklace, but afflictive to bear. Yet I was sorry for him. I speak less than truth when I say that, on his own account, he occasioned me uneasiness. If he would but have named a single relative or friend, I would instantly have written, and urged their taking the poor fellow away to some convenient retreat. But he seemed alone, absolutely alone in the universe. A bit of wreck in the mid-Atlantic. At length, necessities connected with my business tyrannized over all other considerations. Decently as I could, I told Bartleby that in six days' time he must unconditionally leave the office. I warned him to take measures, in the interval, for procuring some other abode. I offered to assist him in this endeavor, if he himself would but take the first step towards a removal. "And when you finally quit me, Bartleby," added I, "I shall see that you go not away entirely unprovided. Six days from this hour, remember."

At the expiration of that period, I peeped behind the screen, and lo! Bartleby was there.

I buttoned up my coat, balanced myself; advanced slowly towards him, touched his shoulder, and said, "The time has come; you must quit this place; I am sorry for you; here is money; but you must go."

"I would prefer not," he replied, with his back still towards me.

"You *must*."

He remained silent.

Now I had an unbounded confidence in this man's common honesty. He had frequently restored to me sixpences and shillings carelessly dropped upon the floor, for I am apt to be very reckless in such shirt-button affairs. The proceeding, then, which followed will not be deemed extraordinary.

"Bartleby," said I, "I owe you twelve dollars on account; here are thirty-two; the odd twenty are yours—Will you take it?" and I handed the bills towards him.

But he made no motion.

"I will leave them here, then," putting them under a weight on the table. Then taking my hat and cane and going to the door, I tranquilly turned and added—" After you have removed your things from these offices, Bartleby, you will of course lock the door—since every one is now gone for the day but you—and if you please, slip your key underneath the mat, so that I may have it in the morning. I shall not see you again; so good-bye to you. If, hereafter, in your new place of abode, I can be of any service to you, do not fail to advise me by letter. Good-bye, Bartleby, and fare you well."

But he answered not a word; like the last column of some ruined temple, he remained standing mute and solitary in the middle of the otherwise deserted room.

As I walked home in a pensive mood, my vanity got the better of my pity. I could not but highly plume myself on my masterly management in getting rid of Bartleby. Masterly I call it, and such it must appear to any dispassionate thinker. The beauty of my procedure seemed to consist in its perfect quietness. There was no vulgar bullying, no bravado of any sort, no choleric hectoring, and striding to and fro across the apartment, jerking out vehement commands for Bartleby to bundle himself off with his beggarly traps. Nothing of the kind. Without loudly bidding Bartleby depart—as an inferior genius might have done—I *assumed* the ground that depart he must; and upon that assumption built all I had to say. The more I thought over my procedure, the more I was charmed with it. Nevertheless, next morning, upon awakening, I had my doubts—I had somehow slept off the fumes of vanity. One of the coolest and wisest hours a man has, is just after he awakes in the morning. My procedure seemed as sagacious as ever—but only in theory. How it would prove in practice—there was the rub. It was truly a beautiful thought to have assumed Bartleby's departure; but, after all, that assumption was simply my own, and none of Bartleby's. The great point was, not whether I had assumed that he would quit me, but whether he would prefer to do so. He was more a man of preferences than assumptions.

After breakfast, I walked down town, arguing the probabilities *pro* and *con*. One moment I thought it would prove a miserable failure, and Bartleby would be found all alive at my office as usual; the next moment it seemed certain that I should find his chair empty. And so I kept veering about. At the corner of Broadway and Canal Street, I saw quite an excited group of people standing in earnest conversation.

"I'll take odds he doesn't," said a voice as I passed.

"Doesn't go? — done!" said I, "put up your money."

I was instinctively putting my hand in my pocket to produce my own, when I remembered that this was an election day. The words I had overheard bore no reference to Bartleby, but to the success or non-success of some candidate for the mayoralty. In my intent frame of mind, I had, as it were, imagined that all Broadway shared in my excitement, and were debating the same question with me. I passed on, very thankful that the uproar of the street screened my momentary absent-mindedness.

As I had intended, I was earlier than usual at my office door. I stood listening for a moment. All was still. He must be gone. I tried the knob. The door was locked. Yes, my procedure had worked to a charm; he indeed must be vanished. Yet a certain melancholy mixed with this: I was almost sorry for my brilliant success. I was fumbling under the door mat for the key, which Bartleby was to have left there for me, when accidentally my knee knocked against a panel, producing a summoning sound, and in response a voice came to me from within — "Not yet; I am occupied."

It was Bartleby.

I was thunderstruck. For an instant I stood like the man who, pipe in mouth, was killed one cloudless afternoon long ago in Virginia, by summer lightning; at his own warm open window he was killed, and remained leaning out there upon the dreamy afternoon, till someone touched him, when he fell.

"Not gone!" I murmured at last. But again obeying that wondrous ascendancy which the inscrutable scrivener had over me, and from which ascendancy, for all my chafing, I could not completely escape, I slowly went down stairs and out into the street, and while walking round the block, considered what I should next do in this unheard-of perplexity. Turn the man out by an actual thrusting I could not; to drive him away by calling him hard names would not do; calling in the police was an unpleasant idea; and yet, permit him to enjoy his cadaverous triumph over me — this, too, I could not think of. What was to be done? or, if nothing could be done, was there anything further that I could *assume* in the matter? Yes, as before I had prospectively assumed that Bartleby would depart, so now I might retrospectively assume that departed he was. In the legitimate carrying out of this assumption, I might enter my office in a great hurry, and pretending not to see Bartleby at all, walk straight against him as if he were air. Such a proceeding would in a singular degree have the appearance of a home-thrust. It was hardly possible that Bartleby could withstand such an application of the doctrine of assumption. But upon second thoughts the success of the plan seemed rather dubious. I resolved to argue the matter over with him again.

"Bartleby," said I, entering the office, with a quietly severe expression, "I am seriously displeased. I am pained, Bartleby. I had thought better of you. I had imagined you of such a gentlemanly organization, that in any delicate dilemma a slight hint would suffice — in short, an assumption. But it appears

I am deceived. Why," I added, unaffectedly starting, "You have not even touched that money yet," pointing to it, just where I had left it the evening previous.

He answered nothing.

"Will you, or will you not, quit me?" I now demanded in a sudden passion, advancing close to him.

"I would prefer *not* to quit you," he replied, gently emphasizing the *not*.

"What earthly right have you to stay here? Do you pay any rent? Do you pay my taxes? Or is this property yours?"

He answered nothing.

"Are you ready to go on and write now? Are your eyes recovered? Could you copy a small paper for me this morning? or help examine a few lines? or step round to the Post Office? In a word, will you do anything at all, to give a coloring to your refusal to depart the premises?"

He silently retired into his hermitage.

I was now in such a state of nervous resentment that I thought it but prudent to check myself at present from further demonstrations. Bartleby and I were alone. I remembered the tragedy of the unfortunate Adams and the still more unfortunate Colt in the solitary office of the latter; and how poor Colt, being dreadfully incensed by Adams, and imprudently permitting himself to get wildly excited, was at unawares hurried into his fatal act—an act which certainly no man could possibly deplore more than the actor himself.° Often it had occurred to me in my ponderings upon the subject that had that altercation taken place in the public street, or at a private residence, it would not have terminated as it did. It was the circumstance of being alone in a solitary office, up stairs, of a building entirely unhallowed by humanizing domestic associations—an uncarpeted office, doubtless, of a dusty, haggard sort of appearance—this it must have been, which greatly helped to enhance the irritable desperation of the hapless Colt.

But when this old Adam of resentment rose in me and tempted me concerning Bartleby, I grappled him and threw him. How? Why, simply by recalling the divine injunction: "A new commandment give I unto you, that ye love one another." Yes, this it was that saved me. Aside from higher considerations, charity often operates as a vastly wise and prudent principle—a great safeguard to its possessor. Men have committed murder for jealousy's sake, and anger's sake, and hatred's sake, and selfishness' sake, and spiritual pride's sake; but no man, that ever I heard of, ever committed a diabolical murder for sweet charity's sake. Mere self-interest, then, if no better motive can be enlisted, should, especially with high-tempered men, prompt all beings to charity and philanthropy. At any rate, upon the occasion in question, I strove to drown my exasperated feelings towards the scrivener by benevolently construing his conduct. Poor fellow, poor fellow! thought I, he don't mean anything; and besides, he has seen hard times, and ought to be indulged.

---

the actor himself: John C. Colt murdered Samuel Adams in January 1842. Later that year, after his conviction, Colt committed suicide a half-hour before he was to be hanged. The case received wide and sensationalistic press coverage at the time.

I endeavored, also, immediately to occupy myself, and at the same time to comfort my despondency. I tried to fancy, that in the course of the morning, at such time as might prove agreeable to him, Bartleby, of his own free accord, would emerge from his hermitage and take up some decided line of march in the direction of the door. But no. Half-past twelve o'clock came; Turkey began to glow in the face, overturn his inkstand, and become generally obstreperous; Nippers abated down into quietude and courtesy; Ginger Nut munched his noon apple; and Bartleby remained standing at his window in one of his profoundest dead-wall reveries. Will it be credited? Ought I to acknowledge it? That afternoon I left the office without saying one further word to him.

Some days now passed, during which, at leisure intervals I looked a little into "Edwards on the Will,"° and "Priestley on Necessity."° Under the circumstances, those books induced a salutary feeling. Gradually I slid into the persuasion that these troubles of mine, touching the scrivener, had been all predestined from eternity, and Bartleby was billeted upon me for some mysterious purpose of an all-wise Providence, which it was not for a mere mortal like me to fathom. Yes, Bartleby, stay there behind your screen, thought I; I shall persecute you no more; you are harmless and noiseless as any of these old chairs; in short, I never feel so private as when I know you are here. At last I see it, I feel it; I penetrate to the predestined purpose of my life. I am content. Others may have loftier parts to enact; but my mission in this world, Bartleby, is to furnish you with office-room for such period as you may see fit to remain.

I believe that this wise and blessed frame of mind would have continued with me, had it not been for the unsolicited and uncharitable remarks obtruded upon me by my professional friends who visited the rooms. But thus it often is, that the constant friction of illiberal minds wears out at last the best resolves of the more generous. Though to be sure, when I reflected upon it, it was not strange that people entering my office should be struck by the peculiar aspect of the unaccountable Bartleby, and so be tempted to throw out some sinister observations concerning him. Sometimes an attorney, having business with me, and calling at my office, and finding no one but the scrivener there, would undertake to obtain some sort of precise information from him touching my whereabouts; but without heeding his idle talk, Bartleby would remain standing immovable in the middle of the room. So after contemplating him in that position for a time, the attorney would depart, no wiser than he came.

Also, when a reference was going on, and the room full of lawyers and witnesses, and business driving fast, some deeply-occupied legal gentleman

---

Edwards on the Will: Jonathan Edwards (1703–1758) was an important American theologian, a rigidly orthodox Calvinist who believed in the doctrine of predestination and a leader of the Great Awakening, the religious revival that swept the North American colonies in the 1740s. The work being alluded to here is *Freedom of the Will* (1754).

Priestley on Necessity: Joseph Priestley (1733–1803) was an English scientist and clergyman who began as a Unitarian but developed his own radical ideas on "natural determinism." As a scientist, he did early experiments with electricity and was one of the first to discover the existence of oxygen. As a political philosopher, he championed the French Revolution—a cause so unpopular in England that he had to flee that country and spend the last decade of his life in the United States.

present, seeing Bartleby wholly unemployed, would request him to run round to his (the legal gentleman's) office and fetch some papers for him. Thereupon, Bartleby would tranquilly decline, and yet remain idle as before. Then the lawyer would give a great stare, and turn to me. And what could I say? At last I was made aware that all through the circle of my professional acquaintance, a whisper of wonder was running round, having reference to the strange creature I kept at my office. This worried me very much. And as the idea came upon me of his possibly turning out a long-lived man, and keeping occupying my chambers, and denying my authority; and perplexing my visitors; and scandalizing my professional reputation; and casting a general gloom over the premises; keeping soul and body together to the last upon his savings (for doubtless he spent but half a dime a day), and in the end perhaps outlive me, and claim possession of my office by right of his perpetual occupancy: as all these dark anticipations crowded upon me more and more, and my friends continually intruded their relentless remarks upon the apparition in my room; a great change was wrought in me. I resolved to gather all my faculties together, and forever rid me of this intolerable incubus.

Ere revolving any complicated project, however, adapted to this end, I first simply suggested to Bartleby the propriety of his permanent departure. In a calm and serious tone, I commended the idea to his careful and mature consideration. But, having taken three days to meditate upon it, he apprised me, that his original determination remained the same; in short, that he still preferred to abide with me.

What shall I do? I now said to myself, buttoning up my coat to the last button. What shall I do? what ought I to do? what does conscience say I *should* do with this man, or, rather, ghost. Rid myself of him, I must; go, he shall. But how? You will not thrust him, the poor, pale, passive mortal you will not thrust such a helpless creature out of your door? you will not dishonor yourself by such cruelty? No, I will not, I cannot do that. Rather would I let him live and die here, and then mason up his remains in the wall. What, then, will you do? For all your coaxing, he will not budge. Bribes he leaves under your own paperweight on your table; in short, it is quite plain that he prefers to cling to you.

Then something severe, something unusual must be done. What! surely you will not have him collared by a constable, and commit his innocent pallor to the common jail? And upon what ground could you procure such a thing to be done? — a vagrant, is he? What! he a vagrant, a wanderer, who refuses to budge? It is because he will not be a vagrant, then, that you seek to count him *as* a vagrant. That is too absurd. No visible means of support: there I have him. Wrong again: for indubitably he *does* support himself, and that is the only unanswerable proof that any man can show of his possessing the means so to do. No more, then. Since he will not quit me, I must quit him. I will change my offices; I will move elsewhere, and give him fair notice, that if I find him on my new premises I will then proceed against him as a common trespasser.

Acting accordingly, next day I thus addressed him: "I find these chambers too far from the City Hall; the air is unwholesome. In a word, I propose to remove my offices next week, and shall no longer require your services. I tell you this now, in order that you may seek another place."

He made no reply, and nothing more was said.

On the appointed day I engaged carts and men, proceeded to my chambers, and, having but little furniture, everything was removed in a few hours. Throughout, the scrivener remained standing behind the screen, which I directed to be removed the last thing. It was withdrawn; and, being folded up like a huge folio, left him the motionless occupant of a naked room. I stood in the entry watching him a moment, while something from within me upbraided me.

I re-entered, with my hand in my pocket — and — and my heart in my mouth.

"Good-bye, Bartleby; I am going — good-bye, and God some way bless you; and take that," slipping something in his hand. But it dropped upon the floor, and then — strange to say — I tore myself from him whom I had so longed to be rid of.

Established in my new quarters, for a day or two I kept the door locked, started at every footfall in the passages. When I returned to my rooms, after any little absence, I would pause at the threshold for an instant, and attentively listen, ere applying my key. But these fears were needless. Bartleby never came nigh me.

I thought all was going well, when a perturbed-looking stranger visited me, inquiring whether I was the person who had recently occupied rooms at No. — Wall Street.

Full of forebodings, I replied that I was.

"Then, sir," said the stranger, who proved a lawyer, "you are responsible for the man you left there. He refuses to do any copying; he refuses to do anything; he says he prefers not to; and he refuses to quit the premises."

"I am very sorry, sir," said I, with assumed tranquillity, but an inward tremor, "but, really, the man you allude to is nothing to me — he is no relation or apprentice of mine, that you should hold me responsible for him."

"In mercy's name, who is he?"

"I certainly cannot inform you. I know nothing about him. Formerly I employed him as a copyist; but he has done nothing for me now for some time past."

"I shall settle him, then — good morning, sir."

Several days passed, and I heard nothing more; and, though I often felt a charitable prompting to call at the place and see poor Bartleby, yet a certain squeamishness, of I know not what, withheld me.

All is over with him, by this time, thought I, at last, when, through another week, no further intelligence reached me. But, coming to my room the day after, I found several persons waiting at my door in a high state of nervous excitement.

"That's the man here — he comes," cried the foremost one, whom I recognized as the lawyer who had previously called upon me alone.

"You must take him away, sir, at once," cried a portly person among them, advancing upon me, and whom I knew to be the landlord of No. — Wall Street. "These gentlemen, my tenants, cannot stand it any longer; Mr. B——" pointing to the lawyer, "has turned him out of his room, and he now persists in haunting the building generally, sitting upon the banisters of the stairs by day, and sleeping in the entry by night. Everybody is concerned; clients are leaving the offices; some fears are entertained of a mob; something you must do, and that without delay."

Aghast at this torrent, I fell back before it, and would fain have locked myself in my new quarters. In vain I persisted that Bartleby was nothing to me—no more than to any one else. In vain—I was the last person known to have anything to do with him, and they held me to the terrible account. Fearful, then, of being exposed in the papers (as one person present obscurely threatened), I considered the matter, and, at length, said that if the lawyer would give me a confidential interview with the scrivener, in his (the lawyer's) own room, I would, that afternoon, strive my best to rid them of the nuisance they complained of.

Going up stairs to my old haunt, there was Bartleby silently sitting upon the banister at the landing.

"What are you doing here, Bartleby?" said I.

"Sitting upon the banister," he mildly replied.

I motioned him into the lawyer's room, who then left us.

"Bartleby," said I, "are you aware that you are the cause of great tribulation to me, by persisting in occupying the entry after being dismissed from the office?"

No answer.

"Now one of two things must take place. Either you must do something, or something must be done to you. Now what sort of business would you like to engage in? Would you like to re-engage in copying for some one?"

"No; I would prefer not to make any change."

"Would you like a clerkship in a dry-goods store?"

"There is too much confinement about that. No, I would not like a clerkship; but I am not particular."

"Too much confinement," I cried, "why, you keep yourself confined all the time!"

"I would prefer not to take a clerkship," he rejoined, as if to settle that little item at once.

"How would a bar-tender's business suit you? There is no trying of the eye-sight in that."

"I would not like it at all; though, as I said before, I am not particular."

His unwonted wordiness inspirited me. I returned to the charge.

"Well, then, would you like to travel through the country collecting bills for the merchants? That would improve your health."

"No, I would prefer to be doing something else."

"How, then, would going as a companion to Europe, to entertain some young gentleman with your conversation—how would that suit you?"

"Not at all. It does not strike me that there is anything definite about that. I like to be stationary. But I am not particular."

"Stationary you shall be, then," I cried, now losing all patience, and, for the first time in all my exasperating connections with him, fairly flying into a passion. "If you do not go away from these premises before night, I shall feel bound—indeed, I *am* bound—to—to—to quit the premises myself!" I rather absurdly concluded, knowing not with what possible threat to try to frighten his immobility into compliance. Despairing of all further efforts, I was precipitately leaving him, when a final thought occurred to me—one which had not been wholly unindulged before.

"Bartleby," said I, in the kindest tone I could assume under such exciting circumstances, "will you go home with me now not to my office, but my dwelling—and remain there till we can conclude upon some convenient arrangement for you at our leisure? Come, let us start now, right away."

"No: at present I would prefer not to make any change at all."

I answered nothing; but, effectually dodging every one by the suddenness and rapidity of my flight, rushed from the building, ran up Wall Street towards Broadway, and, jumping into the first omnibus, was soon removed from pursuit. As soon as tranquillity returned, I distinctly perceived that I had now done all that I possibly could, both in respect to the demands of the landlord and his tenants, and with regard to my own desire and sense of duty, to benefit Bartleby, and shield him from rude persecution. I now strove to be entirely care-free and quiescent; and my conscience justified me in the attempt; though, indeed, it was not so successful as I could have wished. So fearful was I of being again hunted out by the incensed landlord and his exasperated tenants, that, surrendering my business to Nippers, for a few days, I drove about the upper part of the town and through the suburbs, in my rockaway; crossed over to Jersey City and Hoboken, and paid fugitive visits to Manhattanville and Astoria. In fact, I almost lived in my rockaway for the time.

When again I entered my office, lo, a note from the landlord lay upon the desk. I opened it with trembling hands. It informed me that the writer had sent to the police, and had Bartleby removed to the Tombs as a vagrant. Moreover, since I knew more about him than any one else, he wished me to appear at that place, and make a suitable statement of the facts. These tidings had a conflicting effect upon me. At first I was indignant; but, at last, almost approved. The landlord's energetic, summary disposition, had led him to adopt a procedure which I do not think I would have decided upon myself; and yet, as a last resort, under such peculiar circumstances, it seemed the only plan.

As I afterwards learned, the poor scrivener, when told that he must be conducted to the Tombs, offered not the slightest obstacle, but, in his pale, unmoving way, silently acquiesced.

Some of the compassionate and curious by-standers joined the party; and headed by one of the constables arm-in-arm with Bartleby, the silent procession filed its way through all the noise, and heat, and joy of the roaring thoroughfares at noon.

The same day I received the note, I went to the Tombs, or, to speak more properly, the Halls of Justice. Seeking the right officer, I stated the purpose of my call, and was informed that the individual I described was, indeed, within. I then assured the functionary that Bartleby was a perfectly honest man, and greatly to be compassionated, however unaccountably eccentric. I narrated all I knew, and closed by suggesting the idea of letting him remain in as indulgent confinement as possible, till something less harsh might be done—though, indeed, I hardly knew what. At all events, if nothing else could be decided upon, the alms-house must receive him. I then begged to have an interview.

Being under no disgraceful charge, and quite serene and harmless in all his ways, they had permitted him freely to wander about the prison, and, especially, in the inclosed grass-platted yards thereof. And so I found him there, standing all alone in the quietest of the yards, his face towards a high wall, while all around, from the narrow slits of the jail windows, I thought I saw peering out upon him the eyes of murderers and thieves.

"Bartleby!"

"I know you," he said, without looking round — "and I want nothing to say to you."

"It was not I that brought you here, Bartleby," said I, keenly pained at his implied suspicion. "And to you, this should not be so vile a place. Nothing reproachful attaches to you by being here. And see, it is not so sad a place as one might think. Look, there is the sky, and here is the grass."

"I know where I am," he replied, but would say nothing more, and so I left him.

As I entered the corridor again, a broad meat-like man, in an apron, accosted me, and, jerking his thumb over my shoulder, said "Is that your friend?"

"Yes."

"Does he want to starve? If he does, let him live on the prison fare, that's all."

"Who are you?" asked I, not knowing what to make of such an unofficially speaking person in such a place.

"I am the grub-man. Such gentlemen as have friends here, hire me to provide them with something good to eat."

"Is this so?" said I, turning to the turnkey.

He said it was.

"Well, then," said I, slipping some silver into the grub-man's hands (for so they called him), "I want you to give particular attention to my friend there; let him have the best dinner you can get. And you must be as polite to him as possible."

"Introduce me, will you?" said the grub-man, looking at me with an expression which seemed to say he was all impatience for an opportunity to give a specimen of his breeding.

Thinking it would prove of benefit to the scrivener, I acquiesced; and, asking the grub-man his name, went up with him to Bartleby.

"Bartleby, this is a friend; you will find him very useful to you."

"Your sarvant, sir, your sarvant," said the grub-man, making a low salutation behind his apron. "Hope you find it pleasant here, sir; nice grounds — cool apartments — hope you'll stay with us some time — try to make it agreeable. What will you have for dinner to-day?"

"I prefer not to dine to-day," said Bartleby, turning away. "It would disagree with me; I am unused to dinners." So saying, he slowly moved to the other side of the inclosure, and took up a position fronting the dead-wall.

"How's this?" said the grub-man, addressing me with a stare of astonishment. "He's odd, ain't he?"

"I think he is a little deranged," said I, sadly.

"Deranged? deranged is it? Well, now, upon my word, I thought that friend of yourn was a gentleman forger; they are always pale and genteel-like, them forgers. I can't help pity 'em—can't help it, sir. Did you know Monroe Edwards?" he added, touchingly, and paused. Then, laying his hand piteously on my shoulder, sighed, "he died of consumption at Sing-Sing. So you weren't acquainted with Monroe?"

"No, I was never socially acquainted with any forgers. But I cannot stop longer. Look to my friend yonder. You will not lose by it. I will see you again."

Some few days after this, I again obtained admission to the Tombs, and went through the corridors in quest of Bartleby; but without finding him.

"I saw him coming from his cell not long ago," said a turnkey, "may be he's gone to loiter in the yards."

So I went in that direction.

"Are you looking for the silent man?" said another turnkey, passing me. "Yonder he lies—sleeping in the yard there. 'Tis not twenty minutes since I saw him lie down."

The yard was entirely quiet. It was not accessible to the common prisoners. The surrounding walls, of amazing thickness, kept off all sounds behind them. The Egyptian character of the masonry weighed upon me with its gloom. But a soft imprisoned turf grew under foot. The heart of the eternal pyramids, it seemed, wherein, by some strange magic, through the clefts, grass-seed, dropped by birds, had sprung.

Strangely huddled at the base of the wall, his knees drawn up, and lying on his side, his head touching the cold stones, I saw the wasted Bartleby. But nothing stirred. I paused; then went close up to him; stooped over, and saw that his dim eyes were open; otherwise he seemed profoundly sleeping. Something prompted me to touch him. I felt his hand, when a tingling shiver ran up my arm and down my spine to my feet.

The round face of the grub-man peered upon me now. "His dinner is ready. Won't he dine to-day, either? Or does he live without dining?"

"Lives without dining," said I, and closed the eyes.

"Eh!—He's asleep, ain't he?"

"With kings and counselors,"° murmured I.

There would seem little need for proceeding further in this history. Imagination will readily supply the meagre recital of poor Bartleby's interment. But, ere parting with the reader, let me say, that if this little narrative has sufficiently interested him, to awaken curiosity as to who Bartleby was, and

---

With kings and counselors: A reference to Job 3:14. Job, who has lost his family and all his property and has been stricken by a terrible disease, wishes he had never been born: "then had I been at rest with kings and counselors of the earth, which built desolate places for themselves."

what manner of life he led prior to the present narrator's making his acquaintance, I can only reply, that in such curiosity I fully share, but am wholly unable to gratify it. Yet here I hardly know whether I should divulge one little item of rumor, which came to my ear a few months after the scrivener's decease. Upon what basis it rested, I could never ascertain; and hence, how true it is I cannot now tell. But, inasmuch as this vague report has not been without a certain suggestive interest to me, however sad, it may prove the same with some others; and so I will briefly mention it. The report was this: that Bartleby had been a subordinate clerk in the Dead Letter Office at Washington, from which he had been suddenly removed by a change in the administration. When I think over this rumor, hardly can I express the emotions which seize me. Dead letters! does it not sound like dead men? Conceive a man by nature and misfortune prone to a pallid hopelessness, can any business seem more fitted to heighten it than that of continually handling these dead letters, and assorting them for the flames? For by the cart-load they are annually burned. Sometimes from out the folded paper the pale clerk takes a ring the finger it was meant for, perhaps, moulders in the grave; a bank-note sent in swiftest charity he whom it would relieve, nor eats nor hungers any more; pardon for those who died despairing; hope for those who died unhoping; good tidings for those who died stifled by unrelieved calamities. On errands of life, these letters speed to death.

Ah, Bartleby! Ah, humanity!

RICK MOODY

Rick Moody (b. 1961) was born in New York City. His grandfather was the publisher of the New York Daily News, *and his father was a banker. Moody remembers that his parents were "pretty much people who always have a novel they're reading." Encouraged by his family, he was a voracious reader as a child:*

> [My grandfather] used to get first editions all the time. He had a whole set
> of Faulkner and Salinger and all that kind of stuff. So this book reverence
> thing was really central to the people who raised me up, and that's what I
> did first. I sort of was a shy kid and a bit of a storyteller and stuff, but really
> I came to want to write because the first thing I loved was books, the texture
> of them, their physicality, and then also anything that was contained within.

Moody was educated at St. Paul's preparatory school and Brown University, where he took writing workshops with Angela Carter and John Hawkes. He also earned an M.F.A. from Columbia University. For several years he worked as a publisher's assistant at Simon & Schuster and Farrar, Strauss while he wrote his first novel, Garden State *(1993). To date he is the author of two more novels,* The Ice Storm *(1994) and* Purple America *(1997), and two story collections,* The Ring of Brightest Angels around Heaven *(1995) and* Demonology *(2001), which includes "Boys."*

From Moody's experience in writing workshops, he says he learned to enjoy writing stories for specific assignments. For example, he wrote "Drawer" for an editor at Esquire who wanted a story of 650 words, including the title, for the back page of the magazine. "I spent like a week cutting away 23 words and adding 21 back in . . . so it would end up being exactly 650 words." He told interviewer Kristen Lippert-Martin that he holds "no consistent form or idea about form and instead allow[s] form to fluctuate and thereby to reflect tone, theme, and mood." Moody's pleasure experimenting with the writing process is evident in "Boys," a series of variations built on the repeated phrase "Boys enter the house." The critic Eric Lorberer finds the story's theme is a statement about masculinity and culture. Moody has revealed that when he created the story, he was mostly intent upon allowing his narrative total freedom to find its own way:

> I didn't know how "Boys" was going to go . . . all I knew at the beginning was that I was messing around with the sentence and that I really wanted to experience all the possible symbolic and effective interpretations that you could sort of overlay on the sentence "Boys enter the house." What I would do was write about two sentences a day. It only took ten days or two weeks to get the thing into a shapely draft, but I didn't really know that it was going to end up telling the story of the boys from their birth all the way up to when their father dies. I was just messing around with "Boys" and then it kind of acquired its own fate after a while.

WEB *Research Rick Moody and answer questions about his work at bedfordstmartins.com/charters/litwriters.*

Boys   2000

Boys enter the house, boys enter the house. Boys, and with them the ideas of boys (ideas leaden, reductive, inflexible), enter the house. Boys, two of them, wound into hospital packaging, boys with infant pattern baldness, slung in the arms of parents, boys dreaming of breasts, enter the house. Twin boys, kettles on the boil, boys in hideous vinyl knapsacks that young couples from Edison, NJ, wear on their shirt fronts, knapsacks coated with baby saliva and staphylococcus and milk vomit, enter the house. Two boys, one striking the other with a rubberized hot dog, enter the house. Two boys, one of them striking the other with a willow switch about the head and shoulders, the other crying, enter the house. Boys enter the house, speaking nonsense. Boys enter the house, calling for Mother. On a Sunday, in May, a day one might nearly describe as *perfect*, an ice cream truck comes slowly down the lane, chimes inducing salivation, and children run after it, not long after which boys dig a hole in the backyard and bury their younger sister's dolls *two feet down*, so that she will never find these dolls and these dolls will *rot in hell*, after which boys enter the house. Boys, trailing after their father like he is the Second God-damned Coming of Christ Goddamned Almighty, enter the house, repair to the basement to watch baseball. Boys enter the house, site of devastation, and repair immediately to the kitchen, where they mix lighter fluid, vanilla pudding, drain-opening lye, balsamic vinegar, blue food coloring, calamine lotion, cottage cheese, ants, a plastic lizard that one of them received in his Xmas stocking, tacks, leftover mashed potatoes, Spam, frozen lima beans, and chocolate syrup in a medium-sized saucepan and heat over a low flame until thick, afterwards transferring the contents of this saucepan into a Pyrex lasagna dish, baking the Pyrex lasagna dish in the oven for nineteen minutes before attempting to persuade their sister that she should *eat the mixture;* later they smash three family heirlooms (the last, a glass egg, *intentionally*) in a two-and-a-half hour stretch, whereupon they are sent to their bedroom, until freed, in each case thirteen minutes after. Boys enter the house, starchy in pressed shirts and flannel pants that *itch so bad*, fresh from Sunday School instruction, blond and brown locks (respectively) plastered down, but even so with a number of cowlicks protruding at odd angles, disconsolate and humbled, uncertain if boyish things — such as shooting at the neighbor's dog with a pump action bb gun and gagging the fat boy up the street with a bandanna and showing their shriveled boy-penises to their younger sister — are exempted from the commandment to *Love the Lord thy God with all thy heart and with all thy soul, and with all thy might, and thy neighbor as thyself.* Boys enter the house in baseball gear (only one of the boys can hit): in their spikes, in mismatched tube socks that smell like Stilton cheese. Boys enter the house in soccer gear. Boys enter the house carrying skates. Boys enter the house with lacrosse sticks, and, soon after, tossing a lacrosse ball lightly in the living room they destroy a lamp. One boy enters the house sporting basketball clothes, the other wearing jeans and a sweatshirt. One boy enters the house bleeding profusely and is taken out to get stitches, the other watches. Boys enter the house at the end of term carrying report cards, sneak around the house like spies of foreign nationality, looking for a place to hide the report cards for the time being (under the toaster? in a medicine cabinet?). One boy with a black eye enters the house, one boy without. Boys with acne enter the house and squeeze and prod large skin blemishes in front of their sister. Boys with acne treatment products hidden about their persons enter the house. Boys, standing just up the street, sneak cigarettes behind a willow in the Elys' yard, wave smoke away from their natural fibers, hack terribly, experience nausea, then enter the house. Boys call each other *retard, homo, geek,* and, later, *Neckless Thug, Theater Fag,* and enter the house exchanging further epithets. Boys enter the house with nose hair clippers, chase sister around the house threatening to depilate her eyebrows. She cries. Boys attempt to induce girls to whom they would not have spoken only six or eight months prior to enter the house with them. Boys enter the house with girls efflorescent and homely, and attempt to induce girls to sneak into their bedroom, as they still share a single bedroom; girls refuse. Boys enter the house, go to separate bedrooms. Boys, with their father (an arm around each of them), enter the house, but of the monologue preceding and succeeding this entrance, not a syllable is preserved. Boys enter the house having masturbated in a variety of locales. Boys enter the house having masturbated in train station bathrooms, in forests, in beach houses, in football bleachers at night under the stars, in cars (under a blanket), in the shower, backstage, on a plane, the boys masturbate constantly, identically, three times a day in some cases, desire like a madness upon them, at the mere sound of certain words, words that sound like other words, *interrogative* reminding them of *intercourse, beast* reminding them of *breast, sects* reminding them of *sex,* and so forth, the boys are not very smart yet, and, as they enter the house, they feel, as always, immense shame at the scale of this *self-abusive cogitation,* seeing a classmate, seeing a billboard, seeing a fire hydrant, seeing things that should not induce thoughts of masturbation (their sister, e.g.) and then thinking of masturbation anyway. Boys enter the house, go to their rooms, remove sexually explicit magazines from hidden stashes, put on loud music, feel despair. Boys enter the house worried; they argue. The boys are ugly, they are failures, they will never be loved, they enter the house. Boys enter the house and kiss their mother, who feels differently, now they have outgrown her. Boys enter the house, kiss their mother, she explains the seriousness of their sister's difficulty, *her diagnosis.* Boys enter the house, having attempted to locate the spot in their yard where the dolls were buried, eight or nine years prior, without success; they go to their sister's room, sit by her bed. Boys enter the house and tell their completely bald sister jokes about baldness. Boys hold either hand of their sister, laying aside differences, having trudged grimly into the house. Boys skip school, enter house, hold vigil. Boys enter the house after their parents have both gone off to work, sit with their sister and with their sister's nurse. Boys enter the house carrying cases of beer. Boys enter the house, very worried now, didn't know more worry was possible. Boys enter the house carrying controlled substances, neither having told the other that he is carrying a controlled substance, though an intoxicated posture seems appropriate under the circumstances. Boys enter the house *weeping* and hear weeping around them. Boys enter the house, embarrassed, silent, anguished, keening, afflicted, angry, woeful, *griefstricken.* Boys enter the house on vacation, each clasps the hand of the other with genuine warmth, the one wearing dark colors and having shaved a portion of his head, the other having grown his hair out longish and wearing, uncharacteristically, a tie-dyed shirt. Boys enter the house on vacation and argue bitterly about politics (other subjects are no longer discussed), one boy supporting the Maoist insurgency in a certain Southeast Asian country, one believing that *to change the system you need to work inside it;* one boy threatens to *beat the living shit out of the other,* refuses crème brûlée, though it is created by his mother in order to keep the peace. One boy writes home and thereby enters the house only through a mail slot: he argues that the other boy is *crypto-fascist,* believing that *the market can seek its own level on questions of ethics and morals;* boys enter the house on vacation and announce future professions; boys enter the house on vacation and change their minds about professions; boys enter the house on vacation and one boy brings home a *sweetheart,* but throws a tantrum when it is suggested that the *sweetheart* will have to retire on the folding bed in the basement; the other boy, having no *sweetheart,* is distant and withdrawn, preferring to talk late into the night about family members gone from this world. Boys enter the house several weeks apart. Boys enter the house on days of heavy rain. Boys enter the house, in different calendar years, and upon entering, the boys seem to do nothing but compose manifestos, for the benefit of parents; they follow their mother around the place, having fashioned their manifestos in celebration of brand-new independence: *Mom, I like to lie in bed late into the morning watching game shows,* or, *I'm never going to date anyone but artists from now on, mad girls, dreamers, practicers of black magic,* or *A man should eat bologna, sliced meats are important,* or, *An American should bowl at least once a year,* but these manifestos apply only for brief spells, after which they are reversed or discarded. Boys don't enter the house, at all, except as ghostly afterimages of younger selves, fleeting images of sneakers dashing up a staircase; soggy towels on the floor of the bathroom; blue jeans coiled like asps in the basin of the washing machine; boys as an absence of boys, blissful at first, you put a thing down on a spot, put this book down, come back later, *it's still there;* you buy a box of cookies, eat three, later three are missing. Nevertheless, when boys next enter the house, which they ultimately must do, it's a relief, even if it's only in preparation for weddings of acquaintances from boyhood, one boy has a beard, neatly trimmed, the other has rakish sideburns, one boy wears a hat, the other boy thinks hats are ridiculous, one boy wears khakis pleated at the waist, the other wears denim, but each changes into his suit (one suit fits well, one is a little tight), as though suits are *the* liminary marker of adulthood. Boys enter the house after the wedding and they are slapping each other on the back and yelling at anyone who will listen, *It's a party!* One boy enters the house, carried by friends, having been arrested (after the wedding) for driving while intoxicated, complexion ashen; the other boy tries to keep his mouth shut: the car is on its side in a ditch, the car has the top half of a tree broken over its bonnet, the car has struck another car which has in turn struck a third, *Everyone will have seen.* One boy misses his brother horribly, misses the past, misses a time worth being nostalgic over, *a time that never existed,* back when they set their sister's playhouse on fire; the other boy avoids all mention of that time; each of them is once the boy who enters the house alone, missing the other, each is devoted and each callous, and each plays his part on the telephone, over the course of months. Boys enter the house with fishing gear, according to prearranged date and time, arguing about whether to use *lures* or *live bait,* in order to meet their father for the *fishing adventure,* after which boys enter the house again, almost immediately, with live bait, having settled the question; boys boast of having caught fish in the past, though no fish has ever been caught: *Remember when the blues were biting?* Boys enter the house carrying their father, slumped. Happens so fast. Boys rush into the house leading EMTs to the couch in the living room where the body lies, boys enter the house, boys enter the house, boys enter the house. Boys hold open the threshold, awesome threshold that has welcomed them when they haven't even been able to welcome themselves, that threshold which welcomed them when they *had* to be taken in, here is its tarnished knocker, here is its euphonious bell, here's where the boys had to sand the door down because it never would hang right in the frame, here are the scuff-marks from when boys were on the wrong side of the door *demanding,* here's where there were once milk bottles for the milkman, here's where the newspaper always landed, here's the mail slot, here's the light on the front step, illuminated, here's where the boys are standing, as that beloved man is carried out. Boys, no longer boys, exit.

JOYCE CAROL OATES

Joyce Carol Oates (b. 1938) was born in Lockport, New York, one of three children in a Roman Catholic family. She began to put picture stories down on paper even before she could write, and she remembers that her parents "dutifully" supplied her with lined tablets and gave her a typewriter when she was fourteen. In 1956, after Oates graduated from high school, she went on a scholarship to major in English at Syracuse University, but she did not devote most of her time to writing until after she received her M.A. from the University of Wisconsin in 1961. Discovering by chance that one of her stories had been cited in the honor roll of Martha Foley's annual The Best American Short Stories, *Oates assembled the fourteen stories in her first book,* By the North Gate *(1963). Her career was launched, and as John Updike has speculated, she "was perhaps born a hundred years too late; she needs a lustier audience, a race of Victorian word-eaters to be worthy of her astounding productivity, her tireless gift of self-enthrallment."*

One of our most prolific authors, Oates has published almost seventy books and over a hundred stories, including her rewriting of Chekhov's story "The Lady with the Pet Dog." Notable collections of her stories are Raven's Wing *(1986) and* The Assignation *(1988); the same year she published the essays in* (Woman) Writer: Occasions and Opportunities. *Oates also writes poetry and literary criticism.* New Heaven, New Earth *(1974), analyzes the "visionary experience in literature" as exemplified in the work of Henry James, Virginia Woolf, Franz Kafka, D. H. Lawrence, Flannery O'Connor, and others. As a writer, critic, and professor at Princeton University, she dedicates her life to "promoting and exploring literature. . . . I am not conscious of being in any particular literary tradition, though I share with my contemporaries an intense interest in the formal aspects of writing; each of my books is an experiment of a kind, an investigation of the relationship between a certain consciousness and its formal aesthetic expression."*

The story "Where Are You Going, Where Have You Been?" was first published in Epoch *in 1966; it was included in* The Best American Short Stories of 1967 *and* Prize Stories: The O. Henry Awards 1968 *and was made into a film. Oates has said that this story, based on an article in* Life *magazine about a Tucson, Arizona, murderer, has been "constantly misunderstood by one generation, and intuitively understood by another." She sees the story as dealing with a human being "struggling heroically to define personal identity in the face of incredible opposition, even in the face of death itself." Some recent works are* The Collector of Hearts: New Tales of the Grotesque *(1998) and* Broke Heart Blues *(1999), a novel. In 1999 Oates won the O. Henry Prize for Continued Achievement in the Short Story.*

CONNECTION   *Anton Chekhov, "The Lady with the Pet Dog," page 117.*

WEB   *Research Joyce Carol Oates and answer questions about her work at bedfordstmartins.com/charters/litwriters.*

The Lady with the Pet Dog   1972

I

Strangers parted as if to make way for him.

There he stood. He was there in the aisle, a few yards away, watching her.

She leaned forward at once in her seat, her hand jerked up to her face as if to ward off a blow—but then the crowd in the aisle hid him, he was gone. She pressed both hands against her cheeks. He was not here, she had imagined him.

"My God," she whispered.

She was alone. Her husband had gone out to the foyer to make a telephone call; it was intermission at the concert, a Thursday evening.

Now she saw him again, clearly. He was standing there. He was staring at her. Her blood rocked in her body, draining out of her head . . . she was going to faint . . . They stared at each other. They gave no sign of recognition. Only when he took a step forward did she shake her head *no*—*no*—*keep away.* It was not possible.

When her husband returned, she was staring at the place in the aisle where her lover had been standing. Her husband leaned forward to interrupt that stare.

"What's wrong?" he said. "Are you sick?"

Panic rose in her in long shuddering waves. She tried to get to her feet, panicked at the thought of fainting here, and her husband took hold of her. She stood like an aged woman, clutching the seat before her.

At home he helped her up the stairs and she lay down. Her head was like a large piece of crockery that had to be held still, it was so heavy. She was still panicked. She felt it in the shallows of her face, behind her knees, in the pit of her stomach. It sickened her, it made her think of mucus, of something thick and gray congested inside her, stuck to her, that was herself and yet not herself—a poison.

She lay with her knees drawn up toward her chest, her eyes hotly open, while her husband spoke to her. She imagined that other man saying, *Why did you run away from me?* Her husband was saying other words. She tried to listen to them. He was going to call the doctor, he said, and she tried to sit up. "No, I'm all right now," she said quickly. The panic was like lead inside her, so thickly congested. How slow love was to drain out of her, how fluid and sticky it was inside her head!

Her husband believed her. No doctor. No threat. Grateful, she drew her husband down to her. They embraced, not comfortably. For years now they had not been comfortable together, in their intimacy and at a distance, and now they struggled gently as if the paces of this dance were too rigorous for them. It was something they might have known once, but had now outgrown. The panic in her thickened at this double betrayal: she drew her husband to her, she caressed him wildly, she shut her eyes to think about that other man.

A crowd of men and women parting, unexpectedly, and there he stood— there he stood—she kept seeing him, and yet her vision blotched at the memory. It had been finished between them, six months before, but he had come out here . . . and she had escaped him, now she was lying in her husband's arms, in his embrace, her face pressed against his. It was a kind of sleep, this love-making. She felt herself falling asleep, her body falling from her. Her eyes shut.

"I love you," her husband said fiercely, angrily.

She shut her eyes and thought of that other man, as if betraying him would give her life a center.

"Did I hurt you? Are you—?" Her husband whispered.

Always this hot flashing of shame between them, the shame of her husband's near failure, the clumsiness of his love—

"You didn't hurt me," she said.

II

They had said good-by six months before. He drove her from Nantucket, where they had met, to Albany, New York, where she visited her sister. The hours of intimacy in the car had sealed something between them, a vow of silence and impersonality: she recalled the movement of the highways, the passing of other cars, the natural rhythms of the day hypnotizing her toward sleep while he drove. She trusted him, she could sleep in his presence. Yet she could not really fall asleep in spite of her exhaustion, and she kept jerking awake, frightened, to discover that nothing had changed—still the stranger who was driving her to Albany, still the highway, the sky, the antiseptic odor of the rented car, the sense of a rhythm behind the rhythm of the air that might unleash itself at any second. Everywhere on this highway, at this moment, there were men and women driving together, bonded together—what did that mean, to be together? What did it mean to enter into a bond with another person?

No, she did not really trust him; she did not really trust men. He would glance at her with his small cautious smile and she felt a declaration of shame between them.

Shame.

In her head she rehearsed conversations. She said bitterly, "You'll be relieved when we get to Albany. Relieved to get rid of me." They had spent so many days talking, confessing too much, driven to a pitch of childish excitement, laughing together on the beach, breaking into that pose of laughter that seems to eradicate the soul, so many days of this that the silence of the trip was like the silence of a hospital—all these surface noises, these rattles and hums, but an interior silence, a befuddlement. She said to him in her imagination, "One of us should die." Then she leaned over to touch him. She caressed the back of his neck. She said, aloud, "Would you like me to drive for a while?"

They stopped at a picnic area where other cars were stopped—couples, families—and walked together, smiling at their good luck. He put his arm around her shoulders and she sensed how they were in a posture together, a man and a woman forming a posture, a figure, that someone might sketch and show to them. She said slowly, "I don't want to go back. . . ."

Silence. She looked up at him. His face was heavy with her words, as if she had pulled at his skin with her fingers. Children ran nearby and distracted him—yes, he was a father too, his children ran like that, they tugged at his skin with their light, busy fingers.

"Are you so unhappy?" he said.

"I'm not unhappy, back there. I'm nothing. There's nothing to me," she said.

They stared at each other. The sensation between them was intense, exhausting. She thought that this man was her savior, that he had come to her at a time in her life when her life demanded completion, an end, a permanent fixing of all that was troubled and shifting and deadly. And yet it was absurd to think this. No person could save another. So she drew back from him and released him.

A few hours later they stopped at a gas station in a small city. She went to the women's rest room, having to ask the attendant for a key, and when she came back her eye jumped nervously onto the rented car—why? did she think he might have driven off without her?—onto the man, her friend, standing in conversation with the young attendant. Her friend was as old as her husband, over forty, with lanky, sloping shoulders, a full body, his hair thick, a dark, burnished brown, a festive color that made her eye twitch a little—and his hands were always moving, always those rapid conversational circles, going nowhere, gestures that were at once a little aggressive and apologetic.

She put her hand on his arm, a claim. He turned to her and smiled and she felt that she loved him, that everything in her life had forced her to this moment and that she had no choice about it.

They sat in the car for two hours, in Albany, in the parking lot of a Howard Johnson's restaurant, talking, trying to figure out their past. There was no future. They concentrated on the past, the several days behind them, lit up with a hot, dazzling August sun, like explosions that already belonged to other people, to strangers. Her face was faintly reflected in the green-tinted curve of the windshield, but she could not have recognized that face. She began to cry; she told herself: *I am not here, this will pass, this is nothing.* Still, she could not stop crying. The muscles of her face were springy, like a child's, unpredictable muscles. He stroked her arms, her shoulders, trying to comfort her. "This is so hard . . . this is impossible . . ." he said. She felt panic for the world outside this car, all that was not herself and this man, and at the same time she understood that she was free of him, as people are free of other people, she would leave him soon, safely, and within a few days he would have fallen into the past, the impersonal past. . . .

"I'm so ashamed of myself!" she said finally.

She returned to her husband and saw that another woman, a shadow-woman, had taken her place—noiseless and convincing, like a dancer performing certain difficult steps. Her husband folded her in his arms and talked to her of his own loneliness, his worries about his business, his health, his mother, kept tranquilized and mute in a nursing home, and her spirit detached itself from her and drifted about the rooms of the large house she lived in with her husband, a shadow-woman delicate and imprecise. There was no boundary to her, no edge. Alone, she took hot baths and sat exhausted in the steaming water, wondering at her perpetual exhaustion. All that winter she noticed the limp, languid weight of her arms, her veins bulging slightly with the pressure of her extreme weariness. *This is fate,* she thought, to be here and not there, to be one person and not another, a certain man's wife and not the wife of another man. The long, slow pain of this certainty rose in her, but it never became clear, it was baffling and imprecise. She could not be serious about it; she kept congratulating herself on her own good luck, to have escaped so easily, to have freed herself. So much love had gone into the first several years of her marriage that there wasn't much left, now, for another man. . . . She was certain of that. But the bath water made her dizzy, all that perpetual heat, and one day in January she drew a razor blade lightly across the inside of her arm, near the elbow, to see what would happen.

Afterward she wrapped a small towel around it, to stop the bleeding. The towel soaked through. She wrapped a bath towel around that and walked through the empty rooms of her home, lightheaded, hardly aware of the stubborn seeping of blood. There was no boundary to her in this house, no precise limit. She could flow out like her own blood and come to no end.

She sat for a while on a blue love seat, her mind empty. Her husband telephoned her when he would be staying late at the plant. He talked to her always about his plans, his problems, his business friends, his future. It was obvious that he had a future. As he spoke she nodded to encourage him, and her heartbeat quickened with the memory of her own, personal shame, the shame of this man's particular, private wife. One evening at dinner he leaned forward and put his head in his arms and fell asleep, like a child. She sat at the table with him for a while, watching him. His hair had gone gray, almost white, at the temples — no one would guess that he was so quick, so careful a man, still fairly young about the eyes. She put her hand on his head, lightly, as if to prove to herself that he was real. He slept, exhausted.

One evening they went to a concert and she looked up to see her lover there, in the crowded aisle, in this city, watching her. He was standing there, with his overcoat on, watching her. She went cold. That morning the telephone had rung while her husband was still home, and she had heard him answer it, heard him hang up — it must have been a wrong number — and when the telephone rang again, at 9:30, she had been afraid to answer it. She had left home to be out of the range of that ringing, but now, in this public place, in this busy auditorium, she found herself staring at that man, unable to make any sign to him, any gesture of recognition. . . .

He would have come to her but she shook her head. *No. Stay away.*

Her husband helped her out of the row of seats, saying, "Excuse us, please. Excuse us," so that strangers got to their feet, quickly, alarmed, to let them pass. Was that woman about to faint? What was wrong?

At home she felt the blood drain slowly back into her head. Her husband embraced her hips, pressing his face against her, in that silence that belonged to the earliest days of their marriage. She thought, *He will drive it out of me.* He made love to her and she was back in the auditorium again, sitting alone, now that the concert was over. The stage was empty; the heavy velvet curtains had not been drawn; the musicians' chairs were empty, everything was silent and expectant; in the aisle her lover stood and smiled at her — Her husband was impatient. He was apart from her, working on her, operating on her; and then, stricken, he whispered, "Did I hurt you?"

The telephone rang the next morning. Dully, sluggishly, she answered it. She recognized his voice at once—that "Anna?" with its lifting of the second syllable, questioning and apologetic and making its claim—"Yes, what do you want?" she said.

"Just to see you. Please—"

"I can't."

"Anna, I'm sorry, I didn't mean to upset you—"

"I can't see you."

"Just for a few minutes—I have to talk to you—"

"But why, why now? Why now?" she said.

She heard her voice rising, but she could not stop it. He began to talk again, drowning her out. She remembered his rapid conversation. She remembered his gestures, the witty energetic circling of his hands.

"Please don't hang up!" he cried.

"I can't—I don't want to go through it again—"

"I'm not going to hurt you. Just tell me how you are."

"Everything is the same."

"Everything is the same with me."

She looked up at the ceiling, shyly. "Your wife? Your children?"

"The same."

"Your son?"

"He's fine—"

"I'm so glad to hear that. I—"

"Is it still the same with you, your marriage? Tell me what you feel. What are you thinking?"

"I don't know. . . ."

She remembered his intense, eager words, the movement of his hands, that impatient precise fixing of the air by his hands, the jabbing of his fingers.

"Do you love me?" he said.

She could not answer.

"I'll come over to see you," he said.

"No," she said.

What will come next, what will happen?

Flesh hardening on his body, aging. Shrinking. He will grow old, but not soft like her husband. They are two different types: he is nervous, lean, energetic, wise. She will grow thinner, as the tension radiates out from her backbone, wearing down her flesh. Her collarbones will jut out of her skin. Her husband, caressing her in their bed, will discover that she is another woman—she is not there with him—instead she is rising in an elevator in a downtown hotel, carrying a book as a prop, or walking quickly away from that hotel, her head bent and filled with secrets. Love, what to do with it? . . . Useless as moths' wings, as moths' fluttering. . . . She feels the flutterings of silky, crazy wings in her chest.

He flew out to visit her every several weeks, staying at a different hotel each time. He telephoned her, and she drove down to park in an underground garage at the very center of the city.

She lay in his arms while her husband talked to her, miles away, one body fading into another. He will grow old, his body will change, she thought, pressing her cheek against the back of one of these men. If it was her lover, they were in a hotel room: always the propped-up little booklet describing the hotel's many services, with color photographs of its cocktail lounge and dining room and coffee shop. Grow old, leave me, die, go back to your neurotic wife and your sad, ordinary children, she thought, but still her eyes closed gratefully against his skin and she felt how complete their silence was, how they had come to rest in each other.

"Tell me about your life here. The people who love you," he said, as he always did.

One afternoon they lay together for four hours. It was her birthday and she was intoxicated with her good fortune, this prize of the afternoon, this man in her arms! She was a little giddy, she talked too much. She told him about her parents, about her husband. . . . "They were all people I believed in, but it turned out wrong. Now, I believe in you. . . ." He laughed as if shocked by her words. She did not understand. Then she understood. "But I believe truly in you. I can't think of myself without you," she said. . . . He spoke of his wife, her ambitions, her intelligence, her use of the children against him, her use of his younger son's blindness, all of his words gentle and hypnotic and convincing in the late afternoon peace of this hotel room . . . and she felt the terror of laughter, threatening laughter. Their words, like their bodies, were aging.

She dressed quickly in the bathroom, drawing her long hair up around the back of her head, fixing it as always, anxious that everything be the same. Her face was slightly raw, from his face. The rubbing of his skin. Her eyes were too bright, wearily bright. Her hair was blond but not so blond as it had been that summer in the white Nantucket air.

She ran water and splashed it on her face. She blinked at the water. Blind. Drowning. She thought with satisfaction that soon, soon, he would be back home, in that house on Long Island she had never seen, with that woman she had never seen, sitting on the edge of another bed, putting on his shoes. She wanted nothing except to be free of him. Why not be free? *Oh*, she thought suddenly, *I will follow you back and kill you. You and her and the little boy. What is there to stop me?*

She left him. Everyone on the street pitied her, that look of absolute zero.

III

A man and a child, approaching her. The sharp acrid smell of fish. The crashing of waves. Anna pretended not to notice the father with his son — there was something strange about them. That frank, silent intimacy, too gentle, the man's bare feet in the water and the boy a few feet away, leaning away from his father. He was about nine years old and still his father held his hand.

A small yipping dog, a golden dog, bounded near them.

Anna turned shyly back to her reading; she did not want to have to speak to these neighbors. She saw the man's shadow falling over her legs, then over the pages of her book, and she had the idea that he wanted to see what she was reading. The dog nuzzled her; the man called him away.

She watched them walk down the beach. She was relieved that the man had not spoken to her.

She saw them in town later that day, the two of them brown-haired and patient, now wearing sandals, walking with that same look of care. The man's white shorts were soiled and a little baggy. His pullover shirt was a faded green. His face was broad, the cheekbones wide, spaced widely apart, the eyes stark in their sockets, as if they fastened onto objects for no reason, ponderous and edgy. The little boy's face was pale and sharp; his lips were perpetually parted.

Anna realized that the child was blind.

The next morning, early, she caught sight of them again. For some reason she went to the back door of her cottage. She faced the sea breeze eagerly. Her heart hammered. . . . She had been here, in her family's old house, for three days, alone, bitterly satisfied at being alone, and now it was a puzzle to her how her soul strained to fly outward, to meet with another person. She watched the man with his son, his cautious, rather stooped shoulders above the child's small shoulders.

The man was carrying something, it looked like a notebook. He sat on the sand, not far from Anna's spot of the day before, and the dog rushed up to them. The child approached the edge of the ocean, timidly. He moved in short jerky steps, his legs stiff. The dog ran around him. Anna heard the child crying out a word that sounded like "Ty"—it must have been the dog's name—and then the man joined in, his voice heavy and firm.

"Ty—"

Anna tied her hair back with a yellow scarf and went down to the beach. The man glanced around at her. He smiled. She stared past him at the waves. To talk to him or not to talk—she had the freedom of that choice. For a moment she felt that she had made a mistake, that the child and the dog would not protect her, that behind this man's ordinary, friendly face there was a certain arrogant maleness—then she relented, she smiled shyly.

"A nice house you've got there," the man said.

She nodded her thanks.

The man pushed his sunglasses up on his forehead. Yes, she recognized the eyes of the day before—intelligent and nervous, the sockets pale, untanned.

"Is that your telephone ringing?" he said.

She did not bother to listen. "It's a wrong number," she said.

Her husband calling: she had left home for a few days, to be alone.

But the man, settling himself on the sand, seemed to misinterpret this. He smiled in surprise, one corner of his mouth higher than the other. He said nothing. Anna wondered: *What is he thinking?* The dog was leaping about her, panting against her legs, and she laughed in embarrassment. She bent to pet it, grateful for its busyness. "Don't let him jump up on you," the man said. "He's a nuisance."

The dog was a small golden retriever, a young dog. The blind child, standing now in the water, turned to call the dog to him. His voice was shrill and impatient.

"Our house is the third one down—the white one," the man said.

She turned, startled. "Oh, did you buy it from Dr. Patrick? Did he die?"

"Yes, finally. . . ."

Her eyes wandered nervously over the child and the dog. She felt the nervous beat of her heart out to the very tips of her fingers, the fleshy tips of her fingers: little hearts were there, pulsing. *What is he thinking?* The man had opened his notebook. He had a piece of charcoal and he began to sketch something.

Anna looked down at him. She saw the top of his head, his thick brown hair, the freckles on his shoulders, the quick, deft movement of his hand. Upside down, Anna herself being drawn. She smiled in surprise.

"Let me draw you. Sit down," he said.

She knelt awkwardly a few yards away. He turned the page of the sketch pad. The dog ran to her and she sat, straightening out her skirt beneath her, flinching from the dog's tongue. "Ty!" cried the child. Anna sat, and slowly the pleasure of the moment began to glow in her; her skin flushed with gratitude.

She sat there for nearly an hour. The man did not talk much. Back and forth the dog bounded, shaking itself. The child came to sit near them, in silence. Anna felt that she was drifting into a kind of trance while the man sketched her, half a dozen rapid sketches, the surface of her face given up to him. "Where are you from?" the man asked.

"Ohio. My husband lives in Ohio."

She wore no wedding band.

"Your wife—" Anna began.

"Yes?"

"Is she here?"

"Not right now."

She was silent, ashamed. She had asked an improper question. But the man did not seem to notice. He continued drawing her, bent over the sketch pad. When Anna said she had to go, he showed her the drawings—one after another of her, Anna, recognizably Anna, a woman in her early thirties, her hair smooth and flat across the top of her head, tied behind by a scarf. "Take the one you like best," he said, and she picked one of her with the dog in her lap, sitting very straight, her brows and eyes clearly defined, her lips girlishly pursed, the dog and her dress suggested by a few quick irregular lines.

"Lady with pet dog," the man said.

She spent the rest of that day reading, nearer her cottage. It was not really a cottage—it was a two-story house, large and ungainly and weathered. It was mixed up in her mind with her family, her own childhood, and she glanced up from her book, perplexed, as if waiting for one of her parents or her sister to come up to her. Then she thought of that man, the man with the blind child, the man with the dog, and she could not concentrate on her reading. Someone—probably her father—had marked a passage that must be important, but she kept reading and rereading it: *We try to discover in things, endeared to us on that account, the spiritual glamour which we ourselves have cast upon them; we are disillusioned, and learn that they are in themselves barren and devoid of the charm that they owed, in our minds, to the association of certain ideas. . . .*

She thought again of the man on the beach. She lay the book aside and thought of him: his eyes, his aloneness, his drawings of her.

They began seeing each other after that. He came to her front door in the evening, without the child; he drove her into town for dinner. She was shy and extremely pleased. The darkness of the expensive restaurant released her; she heard herself chatter; she leaned forward and seemed to be offering her face up to him, listening to him. He talked about his work on a Long Island newspaper and she seemed to be listening to him, as she stared at his face, arranging her own face into the expression she had seen in that charcoal drawing. Did he see her like that, then? — girlish and withdrawn and patrician? She felt the weight of his interest in her, a force that fell upon her like a blow. A repeated blow. Of course he was married, he had children — of course she was married, permanently married. This flight from her husband was not important. She had left him before, to be alone, it was not important. Everything in her was slender and delicate and not important.

They walked for hours after dinner, looking at the other strollers, the weekend visitors, the tourists, the couples like themselves. Surely they were mistaken for a couple, a married couple. *This is the hour in which everything is decided,* Anna thought. They had both had several drinks and they talked a great deal. Anna found herself saying too much, stopping and starting giddily. She put her hand to her forehead, feeling faint.

"It's from the sun — you've had too much sun —" he said.

At the door to her cottage, on the front porch, she heard herself asking him if he would like to come in. She allowed him to lead her inside, to close the door. *This is not important,* she thought clearly, *he doesn't mean it, he doesn't love me, nothing will come of it.* She was frightened, yet it seemed to her necessary to give in; she had to leave Nantucket with that act completed, an act of adultery, an accomplishment she would take back to Ohio and to her marriage.

Later, incredibly, she heard herself asking: "Do you . . . do you love me?"

"You're so beautiful!" he said, amazed.

She felt this beauty, shy and glowing and centered in her eyes. He stared at her. In this large, drafty house, alone together, they were like accomplices, conspirators. She could not think: how old was she? which year was this? They had done something unforgivable together, and the knowledge of it was tugging at their faces. A cloud seemed to pass over her. She felt herself smiling shrilly.

Afterward, a peculiar raspiness, a dryness of breath. He was silent. She felt a strange, idle fear, a sense of the danger outside this room and this old comfortable bed — a danger that would not recognize her as the lady in that drawing, the lady with the pet dog. There was nothing to say to this man, this stranger. She felt the beauty draining out of her face, her eyes fading.

"I've got to be alone," she told him.

He left, and she understood that she would not see him again. She stood by the window of the room, watching the ocean. A sense of shame overpowered her: it was smeared everywhere on her body, the smell of it, the richness of it. She tried to recall him, and his face was confused in her memory: she would have to shout to him across a jumbled space, she would have to wave her arms wildly. *You love me! You must love me!* But she knew he did not love her, and she did not love him; he was a man who drew everything up into himself, like all men, walking away, free to walk away, free to have his own thoughts, free to envision her body, all the secrets of her body. . . . And she lay down again in the bed, feeling how heavy this body had become, her insides heavy with shame, the very backs of her eyelids coated with shame.

"This is the end of one part of my life," she thought.

But in the morning the telephone rang. She answered it. It was her lover: they talked brightly and happily. She could hear the eagerness in his voice, the love in his voice, that same still, sad amazement—she understood how simple life was, there were no problems.

They spent most of their time on the beach, with the child and the dog. He joked and was serious at the same time. He said, once, "You have defined my soul for me," and she laughed to hide her alarm. In a few days it was time for her to leave. He got a sitter for the boy and took the ferry with her to the mainland, then rented a car to drive her up to Albany. She kept thinking: *Now something will happen. It will come to an end.* But most of the drive was silent and hypnotic. She wanted him to joke with her, to say again that she had defined his soul for him, but he drove fast, he was serious, she distrusted the hawkish look of his profile—she did not know him at all. At a gas station she splashed her face with cold water. Alone in the grubby little rest room, shaky and very much alone. In such places are women totally alone with their bodies. The body grows heavier, more evil, in such silence. . . . On the beach everything had been noisy with sunlight and gulls and waves; here, as if run to earth, everything was cramped and silent and dead.

She went outside, squinting. There he was, talking with the station attendant. She could not think as she returned to him whether she wanted to live or not.

She stayed in Albany for a few days, then flew home to her husband. He met her at the airport, near the luggage counter, where her three pieces of pale-brown luggage were brought to him on a conveyer belt, to be claimed by him. He kissed her on the cheek. They shook hands, a little embarrassed. She had come home again.

"How will I live out the rest of my life?" she wondered.

In January her lover spied on her: she glanced up and saw him, in a public place, in the DeRoy Symphony Hall. She was paralyzed with fear. She nearly fainted. In this faint she felt her husband's body, loving her, working its love upon her, and she shut her eyes harder to keep out the certainty of his love—sometimes he failed at loving her, sometimes he succeeded, it had nothing to do with her or her pity or her ten years of love for him, it had nothing to do with a woman at all. It was a private act accomplished by a man, a husband, or a lover, in communion with his own soul, his manhood.

Her husband was forty-two years old now, growing slowly into middle age, getting heavier, softer. Her lover was about the same age, narrower in the shoulders, with a full, solid chest, yet lean, nervous. She thought, in her paralysis, of men and how they love freely and eagerly so long as their bodies are capable of love, love for a woman; and then, as love fades in their bodies, it fades from their souls and they become immune and immortal and ready to die.

Her husband was a little rough with her, as if impatient with himself. "I love you," he said fiercely, angrily. And then, ashamed, he said, "Did I hurt you? . . ."

"You didn't hurt me," she said.

Her voice was too shrill for their embrace.

While he was in the bathroom she went to her closet and took out that drawing of the summer before. There she was, on the beach at Nantucket, a lady with a pet dog, her eyes large and defined, the dog in her lap hardly more than a few snarls, a few coarse soft lines of charcoal . . . her dress smeared, her arms oddly limp . . . her hands not well drawn at all. . . . She tried to think: did she love the man who had drawn this? did he love her? The fever in her husband's body had touched her and driven her temperature up, and now she stared at the drawing with a kind of lust, fearful of seeing an ugly soul in that woman's face, fearful of seeing the face suddenly through her lover's eyes. She breathed quickly and harshly, staring at the drawing.

And so, the next day, she went to him at his hotel. She wept, pressing against him, demanding of him, "What do you want? Why are you here? Why don't you let me alone?" He told her that he wanted nothing. He expected nothing. He would not cause trouble.

"I want to talk about last August," he said.

"Don't—" she said.

She was hypnotized by his gesturing hands, his nervousness, his obvious agitation. He kept saying, "I understand. I'm making no claims upon you."

They became lovers again.

He called room service for something to drink and they sat side by side on his bed, looking through a copy of *The New Yorker,* laughing at the cartoons. It was so peaceful in this room, so complete. They were on a holiday. It was a secret holiday. Four-thirty in the afternoon, on a Friday, an ordinary Friday: a secret holiday.

"I won't bother you again," he said.

He flew back to see her again in March, and in late April. He telephoned her from his hotel—a different hotel each time—and she came down to him at once. She rose to him in various elevators, she knocked on the doors of various rooms, she stepped into his embrace, breathless and guilty and already angry with him, pleading with him. One morning in May, when he telephoned, she pressed her forehead against the doorframe and could not speak. He kept saying, "What's wrong? Can't you talk? Aren't you alone?" She felt that she was going insane. Her head would burst. Why, why did he love her, why did he pursue her? Why did he want her to die?

She went to him in the hotel room. A familiar room: had they been here before? "Everything is repeating itself. Everything is stuck," she said. He framed her face in his hands and said that she looked thinner—was she sick?—what was wrong? She shook herself free. He, her lover, looked about the same. There was a small, angry pimple on his neck. He stared at her, eagerly and suspiciously. Did she bring bad news?

"So you love me? You love me?" she asked.

"Why are you so angry?"

"I want to be free of you. The two of us free of each other."

"That isn't true—you don't want that—"

He embraced her. She was wild with that old, familiar passion for him, her body clinging to his, her arms not strong enough to hold him. Ah, what despair!—what bitter hatred she felt!—she needed this man for her salvation, he was all she had to live for, and yet she could not believe in him. He embraced her thighs, her hips, kissing her, pressing his warm face against her, and yet she could not believe in him, not really. She needed him in order to live, but he was not worth her love, he was not worth her dying. . . . She promised herself this: when she got back home, when she was alone, she would draw the razor more deeply across her arm.

The telephone rang and he answered it: a wrong number.

"Jesus," he said.

They lay together, still. She imagined their posture like this, the two of them one figure, one substance; and outside this room and this bed there was a universe of disjointed, separate things, blank things, that had nothing to do with them. She would not be Anna out there, the lady in the drawing. He would not be her lover.

"I love you so much . . . ." she whispered.

"Please don't cry! We have only a few hours, please. . . ."

It was absurd, their clinging together like this. She saw them as a single figure in a drawing, their arms and legs entwined, their heads pressing mutely together. Helpless substance, so heavy and warm and doomed. It was absurd that any human being should be so important to another human being. She wanted to laugh: a laugh might free them both.

She could not laugh.

Sometime later he said, as if they had been arguing, "Look. It's you. You're the one who doesn't want to get married. You lie to me—"

"Lie to you?"

"You love me but you won't marry me, because you want something left over—Something not finished—All your life you can attribute your misery to me, to our not being married—you are using me—"

"Stop it! You'll make me hate you!" she cried.

"You can say to yourself that you're miserable because of *me*. We will never be married, you will never be happy, neither one of us will ever be happy—"

"I don't want to hear this!" she said.

She pressed her hands flatly against her face.

She went to the bathroom to get dressed. She washed her face and part of her body, quickly. The fever was in her, in the pit of her belly. She would rush home and strike a razor across the inside of her arm and free that pressure, that fever.

The impatient bulging of the veins: an ordeal over.

The demand of the telephone's ringing: that ordeal over.

The nuisance of getting the car and driving home in all that five o'clock traffic: an ordeal too much for a woman.

The movement of this stranger's body in hers: over, finished.

Now, dressed, a little calmer, they held hands and talked. They had to talk swiftly, to get all their news in: he did not trust the people who worked for him, he had faith in no one, his wife had moved to a textbook publishing company and was doing well, she had inherited a Ben Shahn painting from her father and wanted to "touch it up a little" — she was crazy! — his blind son was at another school, doing fairly well, in fact his children were all doing fairly well in spite of the stupid mistake of their parents' marriage — and what about her? what about her life? She told him in a rush the one thing he wanted to hear: that she lived with her husband lovelessly, the two of them polite strangers, sharing a bed, lying side by side in the night in that bed, bodies out of which souls had fled. There was no longer even any shame between them.

"And what about me? Do you feel shame with me still?" he asked.

She did not answer. She moved away from him and prepared to leave.

Then, a minute later, she happened to catch sight of his reflection in the bureau mirror — he was glancing down at himself, checking himself mechanically, impersonally, preparing also to leave. He too would leave this room: he too was headed somewhere else.

She stared at him. It seemed to her that in this instant he was breaking from her, the image of her lover fell free of her, breaking from her . . . and she realized that he existed in a dimension quite apart from her, a mysterious being. And suddenly, joyfully, she felt a miraculous calm. This man was her husband, truly — they were truly married, here in this room — they had been married haphazardly and accidentally for a long time. In another part of the city she had another husband, a "husband," but she had not betrayed that man, not really. This man, whom she loved above any other person in the world, above even her own self-pitying sorrow and her own life, was her truest lover, her destiny. And she did not hate him, she did not hate herself any longer; she did not wish to die; she was flooded with a strange certainty, a sense of gratitude, of pure selfless energy. It was obvious to her that she had, all along, been behaving correctly; out of instinct.

What triumph, to love like this in any room, anywhere, risking even the craziest of accidents!

"Why are you so happy? What's wrong?" he asked, startled. He stared at her. She felt the abrupt concentration in him, the focusing of his vision on her, almost a bitterness in his face, as if he feared her. What, was it beginning all over again? Their love beginning again, in spite of them? "How can you look so happy?" he asked. "We don't have any right to it. Is it because . . . ?"

"Yes," she said.

Where Are You Going, Where Have You Been?   1966

For Bob Dylan

Her name was Connie. She was fifteen and she had a quick nervous giggling habit of craning her neck to glance into mirrors, or checking other people's faces to make sure her own was all right. Her mother, who noticed everything and knew everything and who hadn't much reason any longer to look at her own face, always scolded Connie about it. "Stop gawking at yourself, who are you? You think you're so pretty?" she would say. Connie would raise her eyebrows at these familiar complaints and look right through her mother, into a shadowy vision of herself as she was right at that moment: she knew she was pretty and that was everything. Her mother had been pretty once too, if you could believe those old snapshots in the album, but now her looks were gone and that was why she was always after Connie.

"Why don't you keep your room clean like your sister? How've you got your hair fixed—what the hell stinks? Hair spray? You don't see your sister using that junk."

Her sister June was twenty-four and still lived at home. She was a secretary in the high school Connie attended, and if that wasn't bad enough—with her in the same building—she was so plain and chunky and steady that Connie had to hear her praised all the time by her mother and her mother's sisters. June did this, June did that, she saved money and helped clean the house and cooked and Connie couldn't do a thing, her mind was all filled with trashy daydreams. Their father was away at work most of the time and when he came home he wanted supper and he read the newspaper at supper and after supper he went to bed. He didn't bother talking much to them, but around his bent head Connie's mother kept picking at her until Connie wished her mother was dead and she herself was dead and it was all over. "She makes me want to throw up sometimes," she complained to her friends. She had a high, breathless, amused voice which made everything she said a little forced, whether it was sincere or not.

There was one good thing: June went places with girl friends of hers, girls who were just as plain and steady as she, and so when Connie wanted to do that her mother had no objections. The father of Connie's best girl friend drove the girls the three miles to town and left them off at a shopping plaza, so that they could walk through the stores or go to a movie, and when he came to pick them up again at eleven he never bothered to ask what they had done.

They must have been familiar sights, walking around that shopping plaza in their shorts and flat ballerina slippers that always scuffed the sidewalk, with charm bracelets jingling on their thin wrists; they would lean together to whisper and laugh secretly if someone passed by who amused or interested them. Connie had long dark blond hair that drew anyone's eye to it, and she wore part of it pulled up on her head and puffed out and the rest of it she let fall down her back. She wore a pullover jersey blouse that looked one way when she was at home and another way when she was away from home. Everything about her had two sides to it, one for home and one for anywhere that was not home: her walk that could be childlike and bobbing, or languid enough to make anyone think she was hearing music in her head, her mouth which was pale and smirking most of the time, but bright and pink on these evenings out, her laugh which was cynical and drawling at home—"Ha, ha, very funny"—but high-pitched and nervous anywhere else, like the jingling of the charms on her bracelet.

Sometimes they did go shopping or to a movie, but sometimes they went across the highway, ducking fast across the busy road, to a drive-in restaurant where older kids hung out. The restaurant was shaped like a big bottle, though squatter than a real bottle, and on its cap was a revolving figure of a grinning boy who held a hamburger aloft. One night in midsummer they ran across, breathless with daring, and right away someone leaned out a car window and invited them over, but it was just a boy from high school they didn't like. It made them feel good to be able to ignore him. They went up through the maze of parked and cruising cars to the bright-lit, fly-infested restaurant, their faces pleased and expectant as if they were entering a sacred building that loomed out of the night to give them what haven and what blessing they yearned for. They sat at the counter and crossed their legs at the ankles, their thin shoulders rigid with excitement and listened to the music that made everything so good: the music was always in the background like music at a church service, it was something to depend upon.

A boy named Eddie came in to talk with them. He sat backwards on his stool, turning himself jerkily around in semi-circles and then stopping and turning again, and after a while he asked Connie if she would like something to eat. She said she did and so she tapped her friend's arm on her way out—her friend pulled her face up into a brave droll look—and Connie said she would meet her at eleven, across the way. "I just hate to leave her like that," Connie said earnestly, but the boy said that she wouldn't be alone for long. So they went out to his car and on the way Connie couldn't help but let her eyes wander over the windshields and faces all around her, her face gleaming with the joy that had nothing to do with Eddie or even this place; it might have been the music. She drew her shoulders up and sucked in her breath with the pure pleasure of being alive, and just at that moment she happened to glance at a face just a few feet from hers. It was a boy with shaggy black hair, in a convertible jalopy painted gold. He stared at her and then his lips widened into a grin. Connie slit her eyes at him and turned away, but she couldn't help glancing back and there he was still watching her. He wagged a finger and laughed and said, "Gonna get you, baby," and Connie turned away again without Eddie noticing anything.

She spent three hours with him, at the restaurant where they ate hamburgers and drank Cokes in wax cups that were always sweating, and then down an alley a mile or so away, and when he left her off at five to eleven only the movie house was still open at the plaza. Her girl friend was there, talking with a boy. When Connie came up the two girls smiled at each other and Connie said, "How was the movie?" and the girl said, "*You* should know." They rode off with the girl's father, sleepy and pleased, and Connie couldn't help but look at the darkened shopping plaza with its big empty parking lot and its signs that were faded and ghostly now, and over at the drive-in restaurant where cars were still circling tirelessly. She couldn't hear the music at this distance.

Next morning June asked her how the movie was and Connie said, "So-so."

She and that girl and occasionally another girl went out several times a week that way, and the rest of the time Connie spent around the house—it was summer vacation—getting in her mother's way and thinking, dreaming, about the boys she met. But all the boys fell back and dissolved into a single face that was not even a face, but an idea, a feeling, mixed up with the urgent insistent pounding of the music and the humid night air of July. Connie's mother kept dragging her back to the daylight by finding things for her to do or saying suddenly, "What's this about the Pettinger girl?"

And Connie would say nervously, "Oh, her. That dope." She always drew thick clear lines between herself and such girls, and her mother was simple and kindly enough to believe her. Her mother was so simple, Connie thought, that it was maybe cruel to fool her so much. Her mother went scuffling around the house in old bedroom slippers and complained over the telephone to one sister about the other, then the other called up and the two of them complained about the third one. If June's name was mentioned her mother's tone was approving, and if Connie's name was mentioned it was disapproving. This did not really mean she disliked Connie and actually Connie thought that her mother preferred her to June because she was prettier, but the two of them kept up a pretense of exasperation, a sense that they were tugging and struggling over something of little value to either of them. Sometimes, over coffee, they were almost friends, but something would come up — some vexation that was like a fly buzzing suddenly around their heads — and their faces went hard with contempt.

One Sunday Connie got up at eleven — none of them bothered with church — and washed her hair so that it could dry all day long, in the sun. Her parents and sister were going to a barbecue at an aunt's house and Connie said no, she wasn't interested, rolling her eyes, to let mother know just what she thought of it. "Stay home alone then," her mother said sharply. Connie sat out back in a lawn chair and watched them drive away, her father quiet and bald, hunched around so that he could back the car out, her mother with a look that was still angry and not at all softened through the windshield, and in the back seat poor old June all dressed up as if she didn't know what a barbecue was, with all the running yelling kids and the flies. Connie sat with her eyes closed in the sun, dreaming and dazed with the warmth about her as if this were a kind of love, the caresses of love, and her mind slipped over onto thoughts of the boy she had been with the night before and how nice he had been, how sweet it always was, not the way someone like June would suppose but sweet, gentle, the way it was in movies and promised in songs; and when she opened her eyes she hardly knew where she was, the back yard ran off into weeds and a fenceline of trees and behind it the sky was perfectly blue and still. The asbestos "ranch house" that was now three years old startled her — it looked small. She shook her head as if to get awake.

It was too hot. She went inside the house and turned on the radio to drown out the quiet. She sat on the edge of her bed, barefoot, and listened for an hour and a half to a program called XYZ Sunday Jamboree, record after record of hard, fast, shrieking songs she sang along with, interspersed by exclamations from "Bobby King": "An' look here you girls at Napoleon's — Son and Charley want you to pay real close attention to this song coming up!"

And Connie paid close attention herself, bathed in a glow of slow-pulsed joy that seemed to rise mysteriously out of the music itself and lay languidly

about the airless little room, breathed in and breathed out with each gentle rise
and fall of her chest.

After a while she heard a car coming up the drive. She sat up at once,
startled, because it couldn't be her father so soon. The gravel kept crunching all
the way in from the road—the driveway was long—and Connie ran to the
window. It was a car she didn't know. It was an open jalopy, painted a bright
gold that caught the sun opaquely. Her heart began to pound and her fingers
snatched at her hair, checking it, and she whispered, "Christ. Christ," wondering how bad she looked. The car came to a stop at the side door and the horn
sounded four short taps as if this were a signal Connie knew.

She went into the kitchen and approached the door slowly, then hung out
the screen door, her bare toes curling down off the step. There were two boys in
the car and now she recognized the driver: he had shaggy, shabby black hair
that looked crazy as a wig and he was grinning at her.

"I ain't late, am I?" he said.

"Who the hell do you think you are?" Connie said.

"Toldja I'd be out, didn't I?"

"I don't even know who you are."

She spoke sullenly, careful to show no interest or pleasure, and he spoke
in a fast bright monotone. Connie looked past him to the other boy, taking her
time. He had fair brown hair, with a lock that fell onto his forehead. His sideburns gave him a fierce, embarrassed look, but so far he hadn't even bothered
to glance at her. Both boys wore sunglasses. The driver's glasses were metallic
and mirrored everything in miniature.

"You wanta come for a ride?" he said.

Connie smirked and let her hair fall loose over one shoulder.

"Don'tcha like my car? New paint job," he said. "Hey."

"What?"

"You're cute."

She pretended to fidget, chasing flies away from the door.

"Don'tcha believe me, or what?" he said.

"Look, I don't even know who you are," Connie said in disgust.

"Hey, Ellie's got a radio, see. Mine's broke down." He lifted his friend's
arm and showed her the little transistor the boy was holding, and now Connie
began to hear the music. It was the same program that was playing inside the
house.

"Bobby King?" she said.

"I listen to him all the time. I think he's great."

"He's kind of great," Connie said reluctantly.

"Listen, that guy's *great*. He knows where the action is."

Connie blushed a little, because the glasses made it impossible for her to
see just what this boy was looking at. She couldn't decide if she liked him or if
he was just a jerk, and so she dawdled in the doorway and wouldn't come down
or go back inside. She said, "What's all that stuff painted on your car?"

"Can'tcha read it?" He opened the door very carefully, as if he was afraid
it might fall off. He slid out just as carefully, planting his feet firmly on the
ground, the tiny metallic world in his glasses slowing down like gelatine hard-

ening and in the midst of it Connie's bright green blouse. "This here is my name, to begin with," he said. ARNOLD FRIEND was written in tar-like black letters on the side, with a drawing of a round grinning face that reminded Connie of a pumpkin, except it wore sunglasses. "I wanta introduce myself, I'm Arnold Friend and that's my real name and I'm gonna be your friend, honey, and inside the car's Ellie Oscar, he's kinda shy." Ellie brought his transistor up to his shoulder and balanced it there. "Now these numbers are a secret code, honey," Arnold Friend explained. He read off the numbers 33, 19, 17 and raised his eyebrows at her to see what she thought of that, but she didn't think much of it. The left rear fender had been smashed and around it was written, on the gleaming gold background: DONE BY CRAZY WOMAN DRIVER. Connie had to laugh at that. Arnold Friend was pleased at her laughter and looked up at her. "Around the other side's a lot more — you wanta come and see them?"

"No."

"Why not?"

"Why should I?"

"Don'tcha wanta see what's on the car? Don'tcha wanta go for a ride?"

"I don't know."

"Why not?"

"I got things to do."

"Like what?"

"Things."

He laughed as if she had said something funny. He slapped his thighs. He was standing in a strange way, leaning back against the car as if he were balancing himself. He wasn't tall, only an inch or so taller than she would be if she came down to him. Connie liked the way he was dressed, which was the way all of them dressed: tight faded jeans stuffed into black, scuffed boots, a belt that pulled his waist in and showed how lean he was, and a white pull-over shirt that was a little soiled and showed the hard small muscles of his arms and shoulders. He looked as if he probably did hard work, lifting and carrying things. Even his neck looked muscular. And his face was a familiar face, somehow: the jaw and chin and cheeks slightly darkened, because he hadn't shaved for a day or two, and the nose long and hawk-like, sniffing as if she were a treat he was going to gobble up and it was all a joke.

"Connie, you ain't telling the truth. This is your day set aside for a ride with me and you know it," he said, still laughing. The way he straightened and recovered from his fit of laughing showed that it had been all fake.

"How do you know what my name is?" she said suspiciously.

"It's Connie."

"Maybe and maybe not."

"I know my Connie," he said, wagging his finger. Now she remembered him even better, back at the restaurant, and her cheeks warmed at the thought of how she sucked in her breath just at the moment she passed him how she must have looked to him. And he had remembered her. "Ellie and I come out here especially for you," he said. "Ellie can sit in back. How about it?"

"Where?"

"Where what?"

"Where're we going?"

He looked at her. He took off the sunglasses and she saw how pale the skin around his eyes was, like holes that were not in shadow but instead in light. His eyes were like chips of broken glass that catch the light in an amiable way. He smiled. It was as if the idea of going for a ride somewhere, to some place, was a new idea to him.

"Just for a ride, Connie sweetheart."

"I never said my name was Connie," she said.

"But I know what it is. I know your name and all about you, lots of things," Arnold Friend said. He had not moved yet but stood still leaning back against the side of his jalopy. "I took a special interest in you, such a pretty girl, and found out all about you like I know your parents and sister are gone somewheres and I know where and how long they're going to be gone, and I know who you were with last night, and your best friend's name is Betty. Right?"

He spoke in a simple lilting voice, exactly as if he were reciting the words to a song. His smile assured her that everything was fine. In the car Ellie turned up the volume on his radio and did not bother to look around at them.

"Ellie can sit in the back seat," Arnold Friend said. He indicated his friend with a casual jerk of his chin, as if Ellie did not count and she could not bother with him.

"How'd you find out all that stuff?" Connie said.

"Listen? Betty Schultz and Tony Fitch and Jimmy Pettinger and Nancy Pettinger," he said, in a chant. "Raymond Stanley and Bob Hutter—"

"Do you know all those kids?"

"I know everybody."

"Look, you're kidding. You're not from around here."

"Sure."

"But—how come we never saw you before?"

"Sure you saw me before," he said. He looked down at his boots, as if he were a little offended. "You just don't remember."

"I guess I'd remember you," Connie said.

"Yeah?" He looked up at this, beaming. He was pleased. He began to mark time with the music from Ellie's radio, tapping his fists lightly together. Connie looked away from his smile to the car, which was painted so bright it almost hurt her eyes to look at it. She looked at that name, ARNOLD FRIEND. And up at the front fender was an expression that was familiar—MAN THE FLYING SAUCERS. It was an expression kids had used the year before, but didn't use this year. She looked at it for a while as if the words meant something to her that she did not yet know.

"What're you thinking about? Huh?" Arnold Friend demanded. "Not worried about your hair blowing around in the car, are you?"

"No."

"Think I maybe can't drive good?"

"How do I know?"

"You're a hard girl to handle. How come?" he said. "Don't you know I'm your friend? Didn't you see me put my sign in the air when you walked by?"

"What sign?"

"My sign." And he drew an X in the air, leaning out toward her. They were maybe ten feet apart. After his hand fell back to his side the X was still in the air, almost visible. Connie let the screen door close and stood perfectly still inside it, listening to the music from her radio and the boy's blend together. She stared at Arnold Friend. He stood there so stiffly relaxed, pretending to be relaxed, with one hand idly on the door handle as if he were keeping himself up that way and had no intention of ever moving again. She recognized most things about him, the tight jeans that showed his thighs and buttocks and the greasy leather boots and the tight shirt, and even that slippery friendly smile of his, that sleepy dreamy smile that all the boys used to get across ideas they didn't want to put into words. She recognized all this and also the singsong way he talked, slightly mocking, kidding, but serious and a little melancholy, and she recognized the way he tapped one fist against the other in homage to the perpetual music behind him. But all these things did not come together.

She said suddenly, "Hey, how old are you?"

His smile faded. She could see then that he wasn't a kid, he was much older—thirty, maybe more. At this knowledge her heart began to pound faster.

"That's a crazy thing to ask. Can'tcha see I'm your own age?"

"Like hell you are."

"Or maybe a coupla years older, I'm eighteen."

"Eighteen?" she said doubtfully.

He grinned to reassure her and lines appeared at the corners of his mouth. His teeth were big and white. He grinned so broadly his eyes became slits and she saw how thick the lashes were, thick and black as if painted with a black tar-like material. Then he seemed to become embarrassed, abruptly, and looked over his shoulder at Ellie. "*Him,* he's crazy," he said. "Ain't he a riot, he's a nut, a real character." Ellie was still listening to the music. His sunglasses told nothing about what he was thinking. He wore a bright orange shirt unbuttoned halfway to show his chest, which was a pale, bluish chest and not muscular like Arnold Friend's. His shirt collar was turned up all around and the very tips of the collar pointed out past his chin as if they were protecting him. He was pressing the transistor radio up against his ear and sat there in a kind of daze, right in the sun.

"He's kinda strange," Connie said.

"Hey, she says you're kinda strange! Kinda strange!" Arnold Friend cried. He pounded on the car to get Ellie's attention. Ellie turned for the first time and Connie saw with shock that he wasn't a kid either—he had a fair, hairless face, cheeks reddened slightly as if the veins grew too close to the surface of his skin, the face of a forty-year-old baby. Connie felt a wave of dizziness rise in her at this sight and she stared at him as if waiting for something to change the shock of the moment, make it all right again. Ellie's lips kept shaping words, mumbling along with the words blasting his ear.

"Maybe you two better go away," Connie said faintly.

"What? How come?" Arnold Friend cried. "We come out here to take you for a ride. It's Sunday." He had the voice of the man on the radio now. It was the same voice, Connie thought. "Don'tcha know it's Sunday all day and honey, no matter who you were with last night today you're with Arnold Friend and don't you forget it! — Maybe you better step out here," he said, and this last was in a different voice. It was a little flatter, as if the heat was finally getting to him.

"No. I got things to do."

"Hey."

"You two better leave."

"We ain't leaving until you come with us."

"Like hell I am —"

"Connie, don't fool around with me. I mean, I mean, don't fool *around*," he said, shaking his head. He laughed incredulously. He placed his sunglasses on top of his head, carefully, as if he were indeed wearing a wig, and brought the stems down behind his ears. Connie stared at him, another wave of dizziness and fear rising in her so that for a moment he wasn't even in focus but was just a blur, standing there against his gold car, and she had the idea that he had driven up the driveway all right but had come from nowhere before that and belonged nowhere and that everything about him and even the music that was so familiar to her was only half real.

"If my father comes and sees you —"

"He ain't coming. He's at a barbecue."

"How do you know that?"

"Aunt Tillie's. Right now they're — uh — they're drinking. Sitting around," he said vaguely, squinting as if he were staring all the way to town and over to Aunt Tillie's back yard. Then the vision seemed to clear and he nodded energetically. "Yeah. Sitting around. There's your sister in a blue dress, huh? And high heels, the poor sad bitch — nothing like you, sweetheart! And your mother's helping some fat woman with the corn, they're cleaning the corn — husking the corn —"

"What fat woman?" Connie cried.

"How do I know what fat woman. I don't know every goddamn fat woman in the world!" Arnold Friend laughed.

"Oh, that's Mrs. Hornby. . . . Who invited her?" Connie said. She felt a little light-headed. Her breath was coming quickly.

"She's too fat. I don't like them fat. I like them the way you are, honey," he said, smiling sleepily at her. They stared at each other for a while, through the screen door. He said softly, "Now what you're going to do is this: you're going to come out that door. You're going to sit up front with me and Ellie's going to sit in the back, the hell with Ellie, right? This isn't Ellie's date. You're my date. I'm your lover, honey."

"What? You're crazy —"

"Yes, I'm your lover. You don't know what that is but you will," he said. "I know that too. I know all about you. But look: it's real nice and you couldn't ask for nobody better than me, or more polite. I always keep my word. I'll tell you how it is, I'm always nice at first, the first time. I'll hold you so tight you won't think you have to try to get away or pretend anything because you'll know you can't. And I'll come inside you where it's all secret and you'll give in to me and you'll love me —"

"Shut up! You're crazy!" Connie said. She backed away from the door. She put her hands against her ears as if she'd heard something terrible, something not meant for her. "People don't talk like that, you're crazy," she muttered. Her heart was almost too big now for her chest and its pumping made sweat break out all over her. She looked out to see Arnold Friend pause and then take a step toward the porch lurching. He almost fell. But, like a clever drunken man, he managed to catch his balance. He wobbled in his high boots and grabbed hold of one of the porch posts.

"Honey?" he said. "You still listening?"

"Get the hell out of here!"

"Be nice, honey. Listen."

"I'm going to call the police —"

He wobbled again and out of the side of his mouth came a fast spat curse, an aside not meant for her to hear. But even this "Christ!" sounded forced. Then he began to smile again. She watched this smile come, awkward as if he were smiling from inside a mask. His whole face was a mask, she thought wildly, tanned down onto his throat but then running out as if he had plastered make-up on his face but had forgotten about his throat.

"Honey —? Listen, here's how it is. I always tell the truth and I promise you this: I ain't coming in that house after you."

"You better not! I'm going to call the police if you — if you don't —"

"Honey," he said, talking right through her voice, "honey, I'm not coming in there but you are coming out here. You know why?"

She was panting. The kitchen looked like a place she had never seen before, some room had run inside but which wasn't good enough, wasn't going to help her. The kitchen window had never had a curtain, after three years, and there were dishes in the sink for her to do — probably — and if you ran your hand across the table you'd probably feel something sticky there.

"You listening, honey? Hey?"

"— going to call the police —"

"Soon as you touch the phone I don't need to keep my promise and can come inside. You won't want that."

She rushed forward and tried to lock the door. Her fingers were shaking. "But why lock it," Arnold Friend said gently, talking right into her face. "It's just a screen door. It's just nothing." One of his boots was at a strange angle, as if his foot wasn't in it. It pointed out to the left, bent at the ankle. "I mean, anybody can break through a screen door and glass and wood and iron or anything else if he needs to, anybody at all and specially Arnold Friend. If the place got lit up with a fire, honey, you'd come running out into my arms, right into my arms and safe at home — like you knew I was your lover and'd stopped fooling around, I don't mind a nice shy girl but I don't like no fooling around." Part of those words were spoken with a slight rhythmic lilt, and Connie somehow recognized them — the echo of a song from last year, about a girl rushing into her boy friend's arms and coming home again —

Connie stood barefoot on the linoleum floor, staring at him. "What do you want?" she whispered.

"I want you," he said.

"What?"

"Seen you that night and thought, that's the one, yes sir. I never needed to look any more."

"But my father's coming back. He's coming to get me. I had to wash my hair first—" She spoke in a dry, rapid voice, hardly raising it for him to hear.

"No, your daddy is not coming and yes, you had to wash your hair and you washed it for me. It's nice and shining and all for me, I thank you, sweetheart," he said, with a mock bow, but again he almost lost his balance. He had to bend and adjust his boots. Evidently his feet did not go all the way down; the boots must have been stuffed with something so that he would seem taller. Connie stared out at him and behind him Ellie in the car, who seemed to be looking off toward Connie's right, into nothing. This Ellie said, pulling the words out of the air one after another as if he were just discovering them, "You want me to pull out the phone?"

"Shut your mouth and keep it shut," Arnold Friend said, his face red from bending over or maybe from embarrassment because Connie had seen his boots. "This ain't none of your business."

"What—what are you doing? What do you want?" Connie said. "If I call the police they'll get you, they'll arrest you—"

"Promise was not to come in unless you touch that phone, and I'll keep that promise," he said. He resumed his erect position and tried to force his shoulders back. He sounded like a hero in a movie, declaring something important. He spoke too loudly and it was as if he were speaking to someone behind Connie. "I ain't made plans for coming in that house where I don't belong but just for you to come out to me, the way you should. Don't you know who I am?"

"You're crazy," she whispered. She backed away from the door but did not want to go into another part of the house, as if this would give him permission to come through the door. "What do you. . . . You're crazy, you. . . ."

"Huh? What're you saying, honey?"

Her eyes darted everywhere in the kitchen. She could not remember what it was, this room.

"This is how it is, honey: you come out and we'll drive away, have a nice ride. But if you don't come out we're gonna wait till your people come home and then they're all going to get it."

"You want that telephone pulled out?" Ellie said. He held the radio away from his ear and grimaced, as if without the radio the air was too much for him.

"I toldja shut up, Ellie." Arnold Friend said, "You're deaf, get a hearing aid, right? Fix yourself up. This little girl's no trouble and's gonna be nice to me, so Ellie keep to yourself, this ain't your date—right? Don't hem in on me. Don't hog. Don't crush. Don't bird dog. Don't trail me," he said in a rapid meaningless voice, as if he were running through all the expressions he'd learned but was no longer sure which one of them was in style, then rushing on to new ones, making them up with his eyes closed, "Don't crawl under my fence, don't squeeze in my chipmunk hole, don't sniff my glue, suck my popsicle, keep your own greasy fingers on yourself!" He shaded his eyes and peered in at Connie, who was backed against the kitchen table. "Don't mind him, honey, he's just a creep. He's a dope. Right? I'm the boy for you and like I said you come out here nice like a lady and give me your hand, and nobody else gets hurt, I mean, your nice old bald-headed daddy and your mummy and your sister in her high heels. Because listen: why bring them in this?"

"Leave me alone," Connie whispered.

"Hey, you know that old woman down the road, the one with the chickens and stuff—you know her?"

"She's dead!"

"Dead? What? You know her?" Arnold Friend said.

"She's dead—"

"Don't you like her?"

"She's dead—she's—she isn't here any more—"

"But don't you like her, I mean, you got something against her? Some grudge or something?" Then his voice dipped as if he were conscious of rudeness. He touched the sunglasses on top of his head as if to make sure they were still there. "Now you be a good girl."

"What are you going to do?"

"Just two things, or maybe three," Arnold Friend said. "But I promise it won't last long and you'll like me that way you get to like people you're close to. You will. It's all over for you here, so come on out. You don't want your people in any trouble, do you?"

She turned and bumped against a chair or something, hurting her leg, but she ran into the back room and picked up the telephone. Something roared in her ear, a tiny roaring, and she was so sick with fear that she could do nothing but listen to it—the telephone was clammy and very heavy and her fingers groped down to the dial but were too weak to touch it. She began to scream into the phone, into the roaring. She cried out, she cried for her mother, she felt her breath start jerking back and forth in her lungs as if it were something Arnold Friend were stabbing her with again and again with no tenderness. A noisy sorrowful wailing rose all about her and she was locked inside it the way she was locked inside this house.

After a while she could hear again. She was sitting on the floor, with her wet back against the wall.

Arnold Friend was saying from the door, "That's a good girl. Put the phone back."

She kicked the phone away from her.

"No, honey. Pick it up. Put it back right."

She picked it up and put it back. The dial tone stopped.

"That's a good girl. Now you come outside."

She was hollow with what had been fear, but what was now just an emptiness. All that screaming had blasted it out of her. She sat, one leg cramped under her, and deep inside her brain was something like a pinpoint of light that kept going and would not let her relax. She thought, I'm not going to see my mother again. She thought, I'm not going to sleep in my bed again. Her bright green blouse was all wet.

Arnold Friend said, in a gentle-loud voice that was like a stage voice. "The place where you came from ain't there any more, and where you had in mind to go is cancelled out. This place you are now — inside your daddy's house — is nothing but a cardboard box I can knock down any time. You know that and always did know it. You hear me?"

She thought, I have got to think. I have to know what to do.

"We'll go out to a nice field, out in the country here where it smells so nice and it's sunny," Arnold Friend said. "I'll have my arms tight around you so you won't need to try to get away and I'll show you what love is like, what it does. The hell with this house! It looks solid all right," he said. He ran a finger-nail down the screen and the noise did not make Connie shiver, as it would have the day before. "Now put your hand on your heart, honey. Feel that? That feels solid too but we know better, be nice to me, be sweet like you can because what else is there for a girl like you but to be sweet and pretty and give in? — and get away before her people come back?"

She felt her pounding heart. Her hands seemed to enclose it. She thought for the first time in her life that it was nothing that was hers, that belonged to her, but just a pounding, living thing inside this body that wasn't hers either.

"You don't want them to get hurt," Arnold Friend went on. "Now get up, honey. Get up all by yourself."

She stood.

"Now turn this way. That's right. Come over to me — Ellie, put that away, didn't I tell you? You dope. You miserable creepy dope," Arnold Friend said. His words were not angry but only part of an incantation. The incantation was kindly. "Now come out through the kitchen to me honey and let's see a smile, try it, you're a brave sweet little girl and now they're eating corn and hot-dogs cooked to bursting over an outdoor fire, and they don't know one thing about you and never did and honey you're better than them because not one of them would have done this for you."

Connie felt the linoleum under her feet; it was cool. She brushed her hair back out of her eyes. Arnold Friend let go of the post tentatively and opened his arms for her, his elbows pointing up toward each other and his wrist limp, to show that this was an embarrassed embrace and a little mocking, he didn't want to make her self-conscious.

She put out her hand against the screen. She watched herself push the door slowly open as if she were safe back somewhere in the other doorway, watching this body and this head of long hair moving out into the sunlight where Arnold Friend waited.

"My sweet little blue-eyed girl," he said, in a half-sung sigh that had nothing to do with her brown eyes but was taken up just the same by the vast sunlit reaches of the land behind him and on all sides of him, so much land that Connie had never seen before and did not recognize except to know that she was going to it.

TIM O'BRIEN

Tim O'Brien (b. 1946) was born in Austin, Minnesota, and educated at Macalester College and Harvard University. Drafted into the army during the Vietnam War, he attained the rank of sergeant and received the Purple Heart.

O'Brien's first book, If I Die in a Combat Zone, Box Me Up and Ship Me Home *(1973), is an account of his combat experience presented as "autofiction," a mixture of autobiography and fiction. His next book,* Northern Lights *(1974), depicts a conflict between two brothers. But O'Brien produced his finest novel to date in* Going after Cacciato *(1978), which won the National Book Award and was judged by many critics to be the best book by an American about the Vietnam War. This was followed by* The Nuclear Age *(1985), a novel set in 1995 about the ominous future of the human race.*

"Soldiers are dreamers," a line by the English poet Siegfried Sassoon, who survived a sniper's bullet during World War I, is the epigraph for Going after Cacciato. *Dreams play an important role in all O'Brien's fiction, yet the note they sound in a story such as "The Things They Carried" is not surrealistic. The dream is always rooted so firmly in reality that it survives, paradoxically, as perhaps the most vital element in an O'Brien story. "The Things They Carried" first appeared in* Esquire *magazine and was included in* The Best American Short Stories *when Ann Beattie edited the volume in 1987. It is also included in O'Brien's collection* The Things They Carried *(1990).*

COMMENTARY   Bobbie Ann Mason, *"On Tim O'Brien's 'The Things They Carried,'"* page 574.

WEB   *Research Tim O'Brien and answer questions about his work at* bedfordstmartins.com/charters/litwriters.

The Things They Carried   1986

First Lieutenant Jimmy Cross carried letters from a girl named Martha, a junior at Mount Sebastian College in New Jersey. They were not love letters, but Lieutenant Cross was hoping, so he kept them folded in plastic at the bottom of his rucksack. In the late afternoon, after a day's march, he would dig his foxhole, wash his hands under a canteen, unwrap the letters, hold them with the tips of his fingers, and spend the last hour of light pretending. He would imagine romantic camping trips into the White Mountains in New Hampshire. He would sometimes taste the envelope flaps, knowing her tongue had been there. More than anything, he wanted Martha to love him as he loved her, but the letters were mostly chatty, elusive on the matter of love. She was a virgin, he was almost sure. She was an English major at Mount Sebastian, and she wrote beautifully about her professors and roommates and midterm exams, about her respect for Chaucer and her great affection for Virginia Woolf. She often quoted lines of poetry; she never mentioned the war, except to say, Jimmy, take care of yourself. The letters weighed ten ounces. They were signed "Love, Martha," but Lieutenant Cross understood that "Love" was only a way of signing and did not mean what he sometimes pretended it meant. At dusk, he would carefully return the letters to his rucksack. Slowly, a bit distracted, he would get up and move among his men, checking the perimeter, then at full dark he would return to his hole and watch the night and wonder if Martha was a virgin.

The things they carried were largely determined by necessity. Among the necessities or near necessities were P-38 can openers, pocket knives, heat tabs, wrist watches, dog tags, mosquito repellant, chewing gum, candy, cigarettes, salt tablets, packets of Kool-Aid, lighters, matches, sewing kits, Military Payment Certificates, C rations, and two or three canteens of water. Together, these items weighed between fifteen and twenty pounds, depending upon a man's habits or rate of metabolism. Henry Dobbins, who was a big man, carried extra rations; he was especially fond of canned peaches in heavy syrup over pound cake. Dave Jensen, who practiced field hygiene, carried a toothbrush, dental floss, and several hotel-size bars of soap he'd stolen on R&R in Sydney, Australia. Ted Lavender, who was scared, carried tranquilizers until he was shot in the head outside the village of Than Khe in mid-April. By necessity, and because it was SOP,° they all carried steel helmets that weighed five pounds including the liner and camouflage cover. They carried the standard fatigue jackets and trousers. Very few carried underwear. On their feet they carried jungle boots—2.1 pounds—and Dave Jensen carried three pairs of socks and a can of Dr. Scholl's foot powder as a precaution against trench foot. Until he was shot, Ted Lavender carried six or seven ounces of premium dope, which for him was a necessity. Mitchell Sanders, the RTO,° carried condoms. Norman Bowker carried a diary. Rat Kiley carried comic books. Kiowa, a devout Baptist, carried an illustrated New Testament that had been presented to him by his father, who taught Sunday school in Oklahoma City, Oklahoma. As a hedge against bad times, however, Kiowa also carried his grandmother's distrust of the white man, his grandfather's old hunting hatchet. Necessity dictated. Because the land was mined and booby-trapped, it was SOP for each man to carry a steel-centered, nylon-covered flak jacket, which weighed 6.7 pounds, but which on hot days seemed much heavier. Because you could die so quickly, each man carried at least one large compress bandage, usually in the helmet band for easy access. Because the nights were cold, and because the monsoons were wet, each carried a green plastic poncho that could be used as a raincoat or ground sheet or makeshift tent. With its quilted liner, the poncho weighed almost two pounds, but it was worth every ounce. In April, for instance, when Ted Lavender was shot, they used his poncho to wrap him up, then to carry him across the paddy, then to lift him into the chopper that took him away.

They were called legs or grunts.

To carry something was to "hump" it, as when Lieutenant Jimmy Cross humped his love for Martha up the hills and through the swamps. In its intran-

---

SOP: Standard operating procedure.
RTO: Radiotelephone operator.

sitive form, "to hump" meant "to walk," or "to march," but it implied burdens far beyond the intransitive.

Almost everyone humped photographs. In his wallet, Lieutenant Cross carried two photographs of Martha. The first was a Kodachrome snapshot signed "Love," though he knew better. She stood against a brick wall. Her eyes were gray and neutral, her lips slightly open as she stared straight-on at the camera. At night, sometimes, Lieutenant Cross wondered who had taken the picture, because he knew she had boyfriends, because he loved her so much, and because he could see the shadow of the picture taker spreading out against the brick wall. The second photograph had been clipped from the 1968 Mount Sebastian yearbook. It was an action shot—women's volleyball—and Martha was bent horizontal to the floor, reaching, the palms of her hands in sharp focus, the tongue taut, the expression frank and competitive. There was no visible sweat. She wore white gym shorts. Her legs, he thought, were almost certainly the legs of a virgin, dry and without hair, the left knee cocked and carrying her entire weight, which was just over one hundred pounds. Lieutenant Cross remembered touching that left knee. A dark theater, he remembered, and the movie was *Bonnie and Clyde,* and Martha wore a tweed skirt, and during the final scene, when he touched her knee, she turned and looked at him in a sad, sober way that made him pull his hand back, but he would always remember the feel of the tweed skirt and the knee beneath it and the sound of the gunfire that killed Bonnie and Clyde, how embarrassing it was, how slow and oppressive. He remembered kissing her good night at the dorm door. Right then, he thought, he should've done something brave. He should've carried her up the stairs to her room and tied her to the bed and touched that left knee all night long. He should've risked it. Whenever he looked at the photographs, he thought of new things he should've done.

What they carried was partly a function of rank, partly of field specialty.

As a first lieutenant and platoon leader, Jimmy Cross carried a compass, maps, code books, binoculars, and a .45-caliber pistol that weighed 2.9 pounds fully loaded. He carried a strobe light and the responsibility for the lives of his men.

As an RTO, Mitchell Sanders carried the PRC-25 radio, a killer, twenty-six pounds with its battery.

As a medic, Rat Kiley carried a canvas satchel filled with morphine and plasma and malaria tablets and surgical tape and comic books and all the things a medic must carry, including M&M's for especially bad wounds, for a total weight of nearly twenty pounds.

As a big man, therefore a machine gunner, Henry Dobbins carried the M-60, which weighed twenty-three pounds unloaded, but which was almost always loaded. In addition, Dobbins carried between ten and fifteen pounds of ammunition draped in belts across his chest and shoulders.

As PFCs or Spec 4s, most of them were common grunts and carried the standard M-16 gas-operated assault rifle. The weapon weighed 7.5 pounds unloaded, 8.2 pounds with its full twenty-round magazine. Depending on numerous factors, such as topography and psychology, the riflemen carried anywhere from twelve to twenty magazines, usually in cloth bandoliers, adding on another 8.4 pounds at minimum, fourteen pounds at maximum. When it was available, they also carried M-16 maintenance gear—rods and steel brushes and swabs and tubes of LSA oil—all of which weighed about a pound. Among the grunts, some carried the M-79 grenade launcher, 5.9 pounds unloaded, a reasonably light weapon except for the ammunition, which was heavy. A single round weighed ten ounces. The typical load was twenty-five rounds. But Ted Lavender, who was scared, carried thirty-four rounds when he was shot and killed outside Than Khe, and he went down under an exceptional burden, more than twenty pounds of ammunition, plus the flak jacket and helmet and rations and water and toilet paper and tranquilizers and all the rest, plus the unweighed fear. He was dead weight. There was no twitching or flopping. Kiowa, who saw it happen, said it was like watching a rock fall, or a big sandbag or something—just boom, then down—not like the movies where the dead guy rolls around and does fancy spins and goes ass over tea-kettle—not like that, Kiowa said, the poor bastard just flat-fuck fell. Boom. Down. Nothing else. It was a bright morning in mid-April. Lieutenant Cross felt the pain. He blamed himself. They stripped off Lavender's canteens and ammo, all the heavy things, and Rat Kiley said the obvious, the guy's dead, and Mitchell Sanders used his radio to report one U.S. KIA° and to request a chopper. Then they wrapped Lavender in his poncho. They carried him out to a dry paddy, established security, and sat smoking the dead man's dope until the chopper came. Lieutenant Cross kept to himself. He pictured Martha's smooth young face, thinking he loved her more than anything, more than his men, and now Ted Lavender was dead because he loved her so much and could not stop thinking about her. When the dust-off arrived, they carried Lavender aboard. Afterward they burned Than Khe. They marched until dusk, then dug their holes, and that night Kiowa kept explaining how you had to be there, how fast it was, how the poor guy just dropped like so much concrete. Boom-down, he said. Like cement.

In addition to the three standard weapons—the M-60, M-16, and M-79—they carried whatever presented itself, or whatever seemed appropriate as a means of killing or staying alive. They carried catch-as-catch-can. At various times, in various situations, they carried M-14s and CAR-15s and Swedish Ks and grease guns and captured AK-47s and Chi-Coms and RPGs and Simonov carbines and black-market Uzis and .38-caliber Smith & Wesson handguns and 66 mm LAWs and shotguns and silencers and blackjacks and bayonets and C-4 plastic explosives. Lee Strunk carried a slingshot; a weapon of last resort, he called it. Mitchell Sanders carried brass knuckles. Kiowa carried his grandfather's feathered hatchet. Every third or fourth man carried a Claymore antipersonnel mine—3.5 pounds with its firing device. They all carried fragmentation grenades—fourteen ounces each. They all carried at least one M-18 colored smoke grenade—twenty-four ounces. Some carried CS or tear-gas grenades. Some carried white-phosphorus grenades. They carried all

---

KIA: Killed in action.

they could bear, and then some, including a silent awe for the terrible power of the things they carried.

In the first week of April, before Lavender died, Lieutenant Jimmy Cross received a good-luck charm from Martha. It was a simple pebble, an ounce at most. Smooth to the touch, it was a milky-white color with flecks of orange and violet, oval-shaped, like a miniature egg. In the accompanying letter, Martha wrote that she had found the pebble on the Jersey shoreline, precisely where the land touched water at high tide, where things came together but also separated. It was this separate-but-together quality, she wrote, that had inspired her to pick up the pebble and to carry it in her breast pocket for several days, where it seemed weightless, and then to send it through the mail, by air, as a token of her truest feelings for him. Lieutenant Cross found this romantic. But he wondered what her truest feelings were, exactly, and what she meant by separate-but-together. He wondered how the tides and waves had come into play on that afternoon along the Jersey shoreline when Martha saw the pebble and bent down to rescue it from geology. He imagined bare feet. Martha was a poet, with the poet's sensibilities, and her feet would be brown and bare, the toenails unpainted, the eyes chilly and somber like the ocean in March, and though it was painful, he wondered who had been with her that afternoon. He imagined a pair of shadows moving along the strip of sand where things came together but also separated. It was phantom jealousy, he knew, but he couldn't help himself. He loved her so much. On the march, through the hot days of early April, he carried the pebble in his mouth, turning it with his tongue, tasting sea salts and moisture. His mind wandered. He had difficulty keeping his attention on the war. On occasion he would yell at his men to spread out the column, to keep their eyes open, but then he would slip away into daydreams, just pretending, walking barefoot along the Jersey shore, with Martha, carrying nothing. He would feel himself rising. Sun and waves and gentle winds, all love and lightness.

What they carried varied by mission.

When a mission took them to the mountains, they carried mosquito netting, machetes, canvas tarps, and extra bug juice.

If a mission seemed especially hazardous, or if it involved a place they knew to be bad, they carried everything they could. In certain heavily mined AOs,° where the land was dense with Toe Poppers and Bouncing Betties, they took turns humping a twenty-eight-pound mine detector. With its headphones and big sensing plate, the equipment was a stress on the lower back and shoulders, awkward to handle, often useless because of the shrapnel in the earth, but they carried it anyway, partly for safety, partly for the illusion of safety.

On ambush, or other night missions, they carried peculiar little odds and ends. Kiowa always took along his New Testament and a pair of moccasins for silence. Dave Jensen carried night-sight vitamins high in carotin. Lee Strunk carried his slingshot; ammo, he claimed, would never be a problem. Rat Kiley carried brandy and M&M's. Until he was shot, Ted Lavender carried the

---

AOs: Areas of operations.

starlight scope, which weighed 6.3 pounds with its aluminum carrying case. Henry Dobbins carried his girlfriend's pantyhose wrapped around his neck as a comforter. They all carried ghosts. When dark came, they would move out single file across the meadows and paddies to their ambush coordinates, where they would quietly set up the Claymores and lie down and spend the night waiting.

Other missions were more complicated and required special equipment. In mid-April, it was their mission to search out and destroy the elaborate tunnel complexes in the Than Khe area south of Chu Lai. To blow the tunnels, they carried one-pound blocks of pentrite high explosives, four blocks to a man, sixty-eight pounds in all. They carried wiring, detonators, and battery-powered clackers. Dave Jensen carried earplugs. Most often, before blowing the tunnels, they were ordered by higher command to search them, which was considered bad news, but by and large they just shrugged and carried out orders. Because he was a big man, Henry Dobbins was excused from tunnel duty. The others would draw numbers. Before Lavender died there were seventeen men in the platoon, and whoever drew the number seventeen would strip off his gear and crawl in head first with a flashlight and Lieutenant Cross's .45-caliber pistol. The rest of them would fan out as security. They would sit down or kneel, not facing the hole, listening to the ground beneath them, imagining cobwebs and ghosts, whatever was down there—the tunnel walls squeezing in—how the flashlight seemed impossibly heavy in the hand and how it was tunnel vision in the very strictest sense, compression in all ways, even time, and how you had to wiggle in—ass and elbows—a swallowed-up feeling—and how you found yourself worrying about odd things—will your flashlight go dead? Do rats carry rabies? If you screamed, how far would the sound carry? Would your buddies hear it? Would they have the courage to drag you out? In some respects, though not many, the waiting was worse than the tunnel itself. Imagination was a killer.

On April 16, when Lee Strunk drew the number seventeen, he laughed and muttered something and went down quickly. The morning was hot and very still. Not good, Kiowa said. He looked at the tunnel opening, then out across a dry paddy toward the village of Than Khe. Nothing moved. No clouds or birds or people. As they waited, the men smoked and drank Kool-Aid, not talking much, feeling sympathy for Lee Strunk but also feeling the luck of the draw. You win some, you lose some, said Mitchell Sanders, and sometimes you settle for a rain check. It was a tired line and no one laughed.

Henry Dobbins ate a tropical chocolate bar. Ted Lavender popped a tranquilizer and went off to pee.

After five minutes, Lieutenant Jimmy Cross moved to the tunnel, leaned down, and examined the darkness. Trouble, he thought—a cave-in maybe. And then suddenly, without willing it, he was thinking about Martha. The stresses and fractures, the quick collapse, the two of them buried alive under all that weight. Dense, crushing love. Kneeling, watching the hole, he tried to concentrate on Lee Strunk and the war, all the dangers, but his love was too much for him, he felt paralyzed, he wanted to sleep inside her lungs and breathe her blood and be smothered. He wanted her to be a virgin and not a virgin, all at once. He wanted to know her. Intimate secrets—why poetry? Why so sad? Why the grayness in her eyes? Why so alone? Not lonely, just alone— riding her bike across campus or sitting off by herself in the cafeteria. Even dancing, she danced alone—and it was the aloneness that filled him with love. He remembered telling her that one evening. How she nodded and looked away. And how, later, when he kissed her, she received the kiss without returning it, her eyes wide open, not afraid, not a virgin's eyes, just flat and uninvolved.

Lieutenant Cross gazed at the tunnel. But he was not there. He was buried with Martha under the white sand at the Jersey shore. They were pressed together, and the pebble in his mouth was her tongue. He was smiling. Vaguely, he was aware of how quiet the day was, the sullen paddies, yet he could not bring himself to worry about matters of security. He was beyond that. He was just a kid at war, in love. He was twenty-two years old. He couldn't help it.

A few moments later Lee Strunk crawled out of the tunnel. He came up grinning, filthy but alive. Lieutenant Cross nodded and closed his eyes while the others clapped Strunk on the back and made jokes about rising from the dead.

Worms, Rat Kiley said. Right out of the grave. Fuckin' zombie.

The men laughed. They all felt great relief.

Spook City, said Mitchell Sanders.

Lee Strunk made a funny ghost sound, a kind of moaning, yet very happy, and right then, when Strunk made that high happy moaning sound, when he went *Ahhooooo,* right then Ted Lavender was shot in the head on his way back from peeing. He lay with his mouth open. The teeth were broken. There was a swollen black bruise under his left eye. The cheekbone was gone. Oh shit, Rat Kiley said, the guy's dead. The guy's dead, he kept saying, which seemed profound—the guy's dead. I mean really.

The things they carried were determined to some extent by superstition. Lieutenant Cross carried his good-luck pebble. Dave Jensen carried a rabbit's foot. Norman Bowker, otherwise a very gentle person, carried a thumb that had been presented to him as a gift by Mitchell Sanders. The thumb was dark brown, rubbery to the touch, and weighed four ounces at most. It had been cut from a VC corpse, a boy of fifteen or sixteen. They'd found him at the bottom of an irrigation ditch, badly burned, flies in his mouth and eyes. The boy wore black shorts and sandals. At the time of his death he had been carrying a pouch of rice, a rifle, and three magazines of ammunition.

You want my opinion, Mitchell Sanders said, there's a definite moral here.

He put his hand on the dead boy's wrist. He was quiet for a time, as if counting a pulse, then he patted the stomach, almost affectionately, and used Kiowa's hunting hatchet to remove the thumb.

Henry Dobbins asked what the moral was.

Moral?

You know. *Moral.*

Sanders wrapped the thumb in toilet paper and handed it across to Norman Bowker. There was no blood. Smiling, he kicked the boy's head, watched the flies scatter, and said, It's like with that old TV show—Paladin. Have gun, will travel.

Henry Dobbins thought about it.

Yeah, well, he finally said. I don't see no moral.

There it *is*, man.

Fuck off.

They carried USO stationery and pencils and pens. They carried Sterno, safety pins, trip flares, signal flares, spools of wire, razor blades, chewing tobacco, liberated joss sticks and statuettes of the smiling Buddha, candles, grease pencils, *The Stars and Stripes*, fingernail clippers, Psy Ops° leaflets, bush hats, bolos, and much more. Twice a week, when the resupply choppers came in, they carried hot chow in green Mermite cans and large canvas bags filled with iced beer and soda pop. They carried plastic water containers, each with a two-gallon capacity. Mitchell Sanders carried a set of starched tiger fatigues for special occasions. Henry Dobbins carried Black Flag insecticide. Dave Jensen carried empty sandbags that could be filled at night for added protection. Lee Strunk carried tanning lotion. Some things they carried in common. Taking turns, they carried the big PRC-77 scrambler radio, which weighed thirty pounds with its battery. They shared the weight of memory. They took up what others could no longer bear. Often, they carried each other, the wounded or weak. They carried infections. They carried chess sets, basketballs, Vietnamese-English dictionaries, insignia of rank, Bronze Stars and Purple Hearts, plastic cards imprinted with the Code of Conduct. They carried diseases, among them malaria and dysentery. They carried lice and ringworm and leeches and paddy algae and various rots and molds. They carried the land itself—Vietnam, the place, the soil—a powdery orange-red dust that covered their boots and fatigues and faces. They carried the sky. The whole atmosphere, they carried it, the humidity, the monsoons, the stink of fungus and decay, all of it, they carried gravity. They moved like mules. By daylight they took sniper fire, at night they were mortared, but it was not battle, it was just the endless march, village to village, without purpose, nothing won or lost. They marched for the sake of the march. They plodded along slowly, dumbly, leaning forward against the heat, unthinking, all blood and bone, simple grunts, soldiering with their legs, toiling up the hills and down into the paddies and across the rivers and up again and down, just humping, one step and then the next and then another, but no volition, no will, because it was automatic, it was anatomy, and the war was entirely a matter of posture and carriage, the hump was everything, a kind of inertia, a kind of emptiness, a dullness of desire and intellect and conscience and hope and human sensibility. Their principles were in their feet. Their calculations were biological. They had no sense of strategy or mission. They searched the villages without knowing what to look for, not caring, kicking over jars of rice, frisking children and old men, blowing tunnels, sometimes setting fires and sometimes not, then forming up and mov-

---

Psy Ops: Psychological operations.

ing on to the next village, then other villages, where it would always be the same. They carried their own lives. The pressures were enormous. In the heat of early afternoon, they would remove their helmets and flak jackets, walking bare, which was dangerous but which helped ease the strain. They would often discard things along the route of march. Purely for comfort, they would throw away rations, blow their Claymores and grenades, no matter, because by nightfall the resupply choppers would arrive with more of the same, then a day or two later still more, fresh watermelons and crates of ammunition and sunglasses and woolen sweaters — the resources were stunning — sparklers for the Fourth of July, colored eggs for Easter. It was the great American war chest — the fruits of science, the smokestacks, the canneries, the arsenals at Hartford, the Minnesota forests, the machine shops, the vast fields of corn and wheat — they carried like freight trains; they carried it on their backs and shoulders — and for all the ambiguities of Vietnam, all the mysteries and unknowns, there was at least the single abiding certainty that they would never be at a loss for things to carry.

After the chopper took Lavender away, Lieutenant Jimmy Cross led his men into the village of Than Khe. They burned everything. They shot chickens and dogs, they trashed the village well, they called in artillery and watched the wreckage, then they marched for several hours through the hot afternoon, and then at dusk, while Kiowa explained how Lavender died, Lieutenant Cross found himself trembling.

He tried not to cry. With his entrenching tool, which weighed five pounds, he began digging a hole in the earth.

He felt shame. He hated himself. He had loved Martha more than his men, and as a consequence Lavender was now dead, and this was something he would have to carry like a stone in his stomach for the rest of the war.

All he could do was dig. He used his entrenching tool like an ax, slashing, feeling both love and hate, and then later, when it was full dark, he sat at the bottom of his foxhole and wept. It went on for a long while. In part, he was grieving for Ted Lavender, but mostly it was for Martha, and for himself, because she belonged to another world, which was not quite real, and because she was a junior at Mount Sebastian College in New Jersey, a poet and a virgin and uninvolved, and because he realized she did not love him and never would.

Like cement, Kiowa whispered in the dark. I swear to God — boom-down. Not a word.

I've heard this, said Norman Bowker.

A pisser, you know? Still zipping himself up. Zapped while zipping.

All right, fine. That's enough.

Yeah, but you had to see it, the guy just —

I *heard,* man. Cement. So why not shut the fuck *up?*

Kiowa shook his head sadly and glanced over at the hole where Lieutenant Jimmy Cross sat watching the night. The air was thick and wet. A warm, dense fog had settled over the paddies and there was the stillness that precedes rain.

After a time Kiowa sighed.

One thing for sure, he said. The Lieutenant's in some deep hurt. I mean that crying jag—the way he was carrying on—it wasn't fake or anything, it was real heavy-duty hurt. The man cares.

Sure, Norman Bowker said.

Say what you want, the man does care.

We all got problems.

Not Lavender.

No, I guess not, Bowker said. Do me a favor, though.

Shut up?

That's a smart Indian. Shut up.

Shrugging, Kiowa pulled off his boots. He wanted to say more, just to lighten up his sleep, but instead he opened his New Testament and arranged it beneath his head as a pillow. The fog made things seem hollow and unattached. He tried not to think about Ted Lavender, but then he was thinking how fast it was, no drama, down and dead, and how it was hard to feel anything except surprise. It seemed un-Christian. He wished he could find some great sadness, or even anger, but the emotion wasn't there and he couldn't make it happen. Mostly he felt pleased to be alive. He liked the smell of the New Testament under his cheek, the leather and ink and paper and glue, whatever the chemicals were. He liked hearing the sounds of night. Even his fatigue, it felt fine, the stiff muscles and the prickly awareness of his own body, a floating feeling. He enjoyed not being dead. Lying there, Kiowa admired Lieutenant Jimmy Cross's capacity for grief. He wanted to share the man's pain, he wanted to care as Jimmy Cross cared. And yet when he closed his eyes, all he could think was Boom-down, and all he could feel was the pleasure of having his boots off and the fog curling in around him and the damp soil and the Bible smells and the plush comfort of night.

After a moment Norman Bowker sat up in the dark.

What the hell, he said. You want to talk, *talk*. Tell it to me.

Forget it.

No, man, go on. One thing I hate, it's a silent Indian.

For the most part they carried themselves with poise, a kind of dignity. Now and then, however, there were times of panic, when they squealed or wanted to squeal but couldn't, when they twitched and made moaning sounds and covered their heads and said Dear Jesus and flopped around on the earth and fired their weapons blindly and cringed and sobbed and begged for the noise to stop and went wild and made stupid promises to themselves and to God and to their mothers and fathers, hoping not to die. In different ways, it happened to all of them. Afterward, when the firing ended, they would blink and peek up. They would touch their bodies, feeling shame, then quickly hiding it. They would force themselves to stand. As if in slow motion, frame by frame, the world would take on the old logic—absolute silence, then the wind, then sunlight, then voices. It was the burden of being alive. Awkwardly, the men would reassemble themselves, first in private, then in groups, becoming soldiers again. They would repair the leaks in their eyes. They would check for casualties, call in dust-offs, light cigarettes, try to smile, clear their throats and spit and begin cleaning their weapons. After a time someone would shake his head and say, No lie, I almost shit my pants, and someone else would laugh, which meant it was bad, yes, but the guy had obviously not shit his pants, it wasn't that bad, and in any case nobody would ever do such a thing and then go ahead and talk about it. They would squint into the dense, oppressive sunlight. For a few moments, perhaps, they would fall silent, lighting a joint and tracking its passage from man to man, inhaling, holding in the humiliation. Scary stuff, one of them might say. But then someone else would grin or flick his eyebrows and say, Roger-dodger, almost cut me a new asshole, *almost*.

There were numerous such poses. Some carried themselves with a sort of wistful resignation, others with pride or stiff soldierly discipline or good humor or macho zeal. They were afraid of dying but they were even more afraid to show it.

They found jokes to tell.

They used a hard vocabulary to contain the terrible softness. *Greased*, they'd say. *Offed, lit up, zapped while zipping.* It wasn't cruelty, just stage presence. They were actors and the war came at them in 3-D. When someone died, it wasn't quite dying, because in a curious way it seemed scripted, and because they had their lines mostly memorized, irony mixed with tragedy, and because they called it by other names, as if to encyst and destroy the reality of death itself. They kicked corpses. They cut off thumbs. They talked grunt lingo. They told stories about Ted Lavender's supply of tranquilizers, how the poor guy didn't feel a thing, how incredibly tranquil he was.

There's a moral here, said Mitchell Sanders.

They were waiting for Lavender's chopper, smoking the dead man's dope. The moral's pretty obvious, Sanders said, and winked. Stay away from drugs. No joke, they'll ruin your day every time.

Cute, said Henry Dobbins.

Mind-blower, get it? Talk about wiggy—nothing left, just blood and brains.

They made themselves laugh.

There it is, they'd say, over and over, as if the repetition itself were an act of poise, a balance between crazy and almost crazy, knowing without going. There it is, which meant be cool, let it ride, because oh yeah, man, you can't change what can't be changed, there it is, there it absolutely and positively and fucking well *is*.

They were tough.

They carried all the emotional baggage of men who might die. Grief, terror, love, longing—these were intangibles, but the intangibles had their own mass and specific gravity, they had tangible weight. They carried shameful memories. They carried the common secret of cowardice barely restrained, the instinct to run or freeze or hide, and in many respects this was the heaviest burden of all, for it could never be put down, it required perfect balance and perfect posture. They carried their reputations. They carried the soldier's greatest fear, which was the fear of blushing. Men killed, and died, because they were embarrassed not to. It was what had brought them to the war in the first place, nothing positive, no dreams of glory or honor, just to avoid the blush of dishonor. They died so as not to die of embarrassment. They crawled into tunnels and walked point and advanced under fire. Each morning, despite the unknowns, they made their legs move. They endured. They kept humping. They did not submit to the obvious alternative, which was simply to close the eyes and fall. So easy, really. Go limp and tumble to the ground and let the muscles unwind and not speak and not budge until your buddies picked you up and lifted you into the chopper that would roar and dip its nose and carry you off to the world. A mere matter of falling, yet no one ever fell. It was not courage, exactly; the object was not valor. Rather, they were too frightened to be cowards.

By and large they carried these things inside, maintaining the masks of composure. They sneered at sick call. They spoke bitterly about guys who had found release by shooting off their own toes or fingers. Pussies, they'd say. Candyasses. It was fierce, mocking talk, with only a trace of envy or awe, but even so, the image played itself out behind their eyes.

They imagined the muzzle against flesh. They imagined the quick, sweet pain, then the evacuation to Japan, then a hospital with warm beds and cute geisha nurses.

They dreamed of freedom birds.

At night, on guard, staring into the dark, they were carried away by jumbo jets. They felt the rush of takeoff. *Gone!* they yelled. And then velocity, wings and engines, a smiling stewardess—but it was more than a plane, it was a real bird, a big sleek silver bird with feathers and talons and high screeching. They were flying. The weights fell off, there was nothing to bear. They laughed and held on tight, feeling the cold slap of wind and altitude, soaring, thinking *It's over, I'm gone!*—they were naked, they were light and free—it was all lightness, bright and fast and buoyant, light as light, a helium buzz in the brain, a giddy bubbling in the lungs as they were taken up over the clouds and the war, beyond duty, beyond gravity and mortification and global entanglements—*Sin loi!*° they yelled, *I'm sorry, motherfuckers, but I'm out of it, I'm goofed, I'm on a space cruise, I'm gone!*—and it was a restful, disencumbered sensation, just riding the light waves, sailing that big silver freedom bird over the mountains and oceans, over America, over the farms and great sleeping cities and cemeteries and highways and the golden arches of McDonald's. It was flight, a kind of fleeing, a kind of falling, falling higher and higher, spinning off the edge of the earth and beyond the sun and through the vast, silent vacuum where there were no burdens and where everything weighed exactly nothing. *Gone!* they screamed, *I'm sorry but I'm gone!* And so at night, not quite dreaming, they gave themselves over to lightness, they were carried, they were purely borne.

On the morning after Ted Lavender died, First Lieutenant Jimmy Cross crouched at the bottom of his foxhole and burned Martha's letters. Then he burned the two photographs. There was a steady rain falling, which made it

---

Sin loi!: "Sorry about that!"

difficult, but he used heat tabs and Sterno to build a small fire, screening it with his body, holding the photographs over the tight blue flame with the tips of his fingers.

He realized it was only a gesture. Stupid, he thought. Sentimental, too, but mostly just stupid.

Lavender was dead. You couldn't burn the blame.

Besides, the letters were in his head. And even now, without photographs, Lieutenant Cross could see Martha playing volleyball in her white gym shorts and yellow T-shirt. He could see her moving in the rain.

When the fire died out, Lieutenant Cross pulled his poncho over his shoulders and ate breakfast from a can.

There was no great mystery, he decided.

In those burned letters Martha had never mentioned the war, except to say, Jimmy, take care of yourself. She wasn't involved. She signed the letters "Love," but it wasn't love, and all the fine lines and technicalities did not matter.

The morning came up wet and blurry. Everything seemed part of everything else, the fog and Martha and the deepening rain.

It was a war, after all.

Half smiling, Lieutenant Jimmy Cross took out his maps. He shook his head hard, as if to clear it, then bent forward and began planning the day's march. In ten minutes, or maybe twenty, he would rouse the men and they would pack up and head west, where the maps showed the country to be green and inviting. They would do what they had always done. The rain might add some weight, but otherwise it would be one more day layered upon all the other days.

He was realistic about it. There was that new hardness in his stomach.

No more fantasies, he told himself.

Henceforth, when he thought about Martha, it would be only to think that she belonged elsewhere. He would shut down the daydreams. This was not Mount Sebastian, it was another world, where there were no pretty poems or midterm exams, a place where men died because of carelessness and gross stupidity. Kiowa was right. Boom-down, and you were dead, never partly dead.

Briefly, in the rain, Lieutenant Cross saw Martha's gray eyes gazing back at him.

He understood.

It was very sad, he thought. The things men carried inside. The things men did or felt they had to do.

He almost nodded at her, but didn't.

Instead he went back to his maps. He was now determined to perform his duties firmly and without negligence. It wouldn't help Lavender, he knew that, but from this point on he would comport himself as a soldier. He would dispose of his good-luck pebble. Swallow it, maybe, or use Lee Strunk's slingshot, or just drop it along the trail. On the march he would impose strict field discipline. He would be careful to send out flank security, to prevent straggling or bunching up, to keep his troops moving at the proper pace and at the proper interval. He would insist on clean weapons. He would confiscate the remainder of Lavender's dope. Later in the day, perhaps, he would call the men together and speak to them plainly. He would accept the blame for what had happened to Ted Lavender. He would be a man about it. He would look them in the eyes, keeping his chin level, and he would issue the new SOPs in a calm, impersonal tone of voice, an officer's voice, leaving no room for argument or discussion. Commencing immediately, he'd tell them, they would no longer abandon equipment along the route of march. They would police up their acts. They would get their shit together, and keep it together, and maintain it neatly and in good working order.

He would not tolerate laxity. He would show strength, distancing himself.

Among the men there would be grumbling, of course, and maybe worse, because their days would seem longer and their loads heavier, but Lieutenant Cross reminded himself that his obligation was not to be loved but to lead. He would dispense with love; it was not now a factor. And if anyone quarreled or complained, he would simply tighten his lips and arrange his shoulders in the correct command posture. He might give a curt little nod. Or he might not. He might just shrug and say Carry on, then they would saddle up and form into a column and move out toward the villages of Than Khe.

FLANNERY O'CONNOR

Flannery O'Connor (1925–1964) was born in Savannah, Georgia, the only child of Roman Catholic parents. When she was thirteen her father was found to have disseminated lupus, an incurable disease in which antibodies in the immune system attack the body's own substances. After her father's death in 1941, O'Connor attended Georgia State College for Women in Milledgeville, where she also published stories and edited the literary magazine. On the strength of these stories, she was awarded a fellowship at the Writers Workshop at the University of Iowa and earned her M.F.A. degree there. Late in 1950 she became ill with what was diagnosed as lupus, and she returned to Milledgeville to start a series of treatments that temporarily arrested the disease. Living with her mother on the family's 500-acre dairy farm, O'Connor began to work again, writing from nine to twelve in the morning and spending the rest of the day resting, reading, writing letters, and raising peacocks.

O'Connor's first book, Wise Blood, *a complex comic novel attacking the contemporary secularization of religion, was published in 1952. It was followed in 1955 by a collection of stories,* A Good Man Is Hard to Find. *O'Connor was able to see a second novel,* The Violent Bear It Away, *through to publication in 1960, but she died of lupus in 1964, having completed enough stories for a second collection,* Everything That Rises Must Converge *(1965). Her total output of just thirty-one stories, collected in her* Complete Stories, *won the National Book Award for fiction in 1972.*

Despite her illness, O'Connor was never a recluse; she accepted as many lecture invitations as her health would permit. A volume of her lectures and occa-

sional pieces was published in 1969 as Mystery and Manners. *It is a valuable companion to her stories and novels, because she often reflected on her writing and interpreted her fiction. As a devout Roman Catholic, O'Connor was uncompromising in her religious views: "For I am no disbeliever in spiritual purpose and no vague believer. This means that for me the meaning of life is centered in our Redemption by Christ and what I see in the world I see in relation to that." As Joyce Carol Oates recognized in her essay "The Visionary Art of Flannery O'Connor," O'Connor is a great modern religious writer, thoroughly unique "in her celebration of the necessity of succumbing to the divine through violence that is immediate and irreparable. There is no mysticism in her work that is only spiritual; it is physical as well." O'Connor's stories, like the three included here, frequently involve family relationships but are not meant to be read as realistic fiction, despite her remarkable ear for dialogue. O'Connor said she wrote them as parables, as the epigraph to* A Good Man Is Hard to Find *attests.*

CONVERSATIONS   *See pages 630–654, including Flannery O'Connor, "From Letters, 1954–55," page 630, "Writing Short Stories," page 633, "The Element of Suspense in 'A Good Man Is Hard to Find,'" page 639; Sally Fitzgerald, "Southern Sources of 'A Good Man Is Hard to Find,'" page 641; Robert H. Brinkmeyer Jr., "Flannery O'Connor and Her Readers," page 642; Dorothy Tuck McFarland, "On 'Good Country People,'" page 647; Wayne C. Booth, "A Rhetorical Reading of O'Connor's 'Everything That Rises Must Converge,'" page 651.*

WEB   *Research Flannery O'Connor and answer questions about her work at bedfordstmartins.com/charters/litwriters.*

Everything That Rises Must Converge   1961

Her doctor had told Julian's mother that she must lose twenty pounds on account of her blood pressure, so on Wednesday nights Julian had to take her downtown on the bus for a reducing class at the Y. The reducing class was designed for working girls over fifty, who weighed from 165 to 200 pounds. His mother was one of the slimmer ones, but she said ladies did not tell their age or weight. She would not ride the buses by herself at night since they had been integrated, and because the reducing class was one of her few pleasures, necessary for her health, and *free*, she said Julian could at least put himself out to take her, considering all she did for him. Julian did not like to consider all she did for him, but every Wednesday night he braced himself and took her.

She was almost ready to go, standing before the hall mirror, putting on her hat, while he, his hands behind him, appeared pinned to the door frame, waiting like Saint Sebastian for the arrows to begin piercing him. The hat was new and had cost her seven dollars and a half. She kept saying, "Maybe I shouldn't have paid that for it. No, I shouldn't have. I'll take it off and return it tomorrow. I shouldn't have bought it."

Julian raised his eyes to heaven. "Yes, you should have bought it," he said. "Put it on and let's go." It was a hideous hat. A purple velvet flap came down on one side of it and stood up on the other; the rest of it was green and looked like a cushion with the stuffing out. He decided it was less comical than jaunty and pathetic. Everything that gave her pleasure was small and depressed him.

She lifted the hat one more time and set it down slowly on top of her head. Two wings of gray hair protruded on either side of her florid face, but her eyes, sky-blue, were as innocent and untouched by experience as they must have been when she was ten. Were it not that she was a widow who had struggled fiercely to feed and clothe and put him through school and who was supporting him still, "until he got on his feet," she might have been a little girl that he had to take to town.

"It's all right, it's all right," he said. "Let's go." He opened the door himself and started down the walk to get her going. The sky was a dying violet and the houses stood out darkly against it, bulbous liver-colored monstrosities of a uniform ugliness though no two were alike. Since this had been a fashionable neighborhood forty years ago, his mother persisted in thinking they did well to have an apartment in it. Each house had a narrow collar of dirt around it in which sat, usually, a grubby child. Julian walked with his hands in his pockets, his head down and thrust forward, and his eyes glazed with the determination to make himself completely numb during the time he would be sacrificed to her pleasure.

The door closed and he turned to find the dumpy figure, surmounted by the atrocious hat, coming toward him. "Well," she said, "you only live once and paying a little more for it, I at least won't meet myself coming and going."

"Some day I'll start making money," Julian said gloomily — he knew he never would — "and you can have one of those jokes whenever you take the fit." But first they would move. He visualized a place where the nearest neighbor would be three miles away on either side.

"I think you're doing fine," she said, drawing on her gloves. "You've only been out of school a year. Rome wasn't built in a day."

She was one of the few members of the Y reducing class who arrived in hat and gloves and who had a son who had been to college. "It takes time," she said, "and the world is in such a mess. This hat looked better on me than any of the others, though when she brought it out I said, 'Take that thing back. I wouldn't have it on my head,' and she said, 'Now wait till you see it on,' and when she put it on me, I said, 'We-ull,' and she said, 'If you ask me, that hat does something for you and you do something for the hat, and besides,' she said, 'with that hat, you won't meet yourself coming and going.'"

Julian thought he could have stood his lot better if she had been selfish, if she had been an old hag who drank and screamed at him. He walked along, saturated in depression, as if in the midst of his martyrdom he had lost his faith. Catching sight of his long, hopeless, irritated face, she stopped suddenly with a grief-stricken look, and pulled back on his arm. "Wait on me," she said. "I'm going back to the house and take this thing off and tomorrow I'm going to return it. I was out of my head. I can pay the gas bill with the seven-fifty."

He caught her arm in a vicious grip. "You are not going to take it back," he said. "I like it."

"Well," she said, "I don't think I ought . . ."

"Shut up and enjoy it," he muttered, more depressed than ever.

"With the world in the mess it's in," she said, "it's a wonder we can enjoy anything. I tell you, the bottom rail is on the top."

Julian sighed.

"Of course," she said, "if you know who you are, you can go anywhere." She said this every time he took her to the reducing class. "Most of them in it are not our kind of people," she said, "but I can be gracious to anybody. I know who I am."

"They don't give a damn for your graciousness," Julian said savagely. "Knowing who you are is good for one generation only. You haven't the foggiest idea where you stand now or who you are."

She stopped and allowed her eyes to flash at him. "I most certainly do know who I am," she said, "and if you don't know who you are, I'm ashamed of you."

"Oh hell," Julian said.

"Your great-grandfather was a former governor of this state," she said. "Your grandfather was a prosperous landowner. Your grandmother was a Godhigh."

"Will you look around you," he said tensely, "and see where you are now?" and he swept his arm jerkily out to indicate the neighborhood, which the growing darkness at least made less dingy.

"You remain what you are," she said. "Your great-grandfather had a plantation and two hundred slaves."

"There are no more slaves," he said irritably.

"They were better off when they were," she said. He groaned to see that she was off on that topic. She rolled onto it every few days like a train on an open track. He knew every stop, every junction, every swamp along the way, and knew the exact point at which her conclusion would roll majestically into the station: "It's ridiculous. It's simply not realistic. They should rise, yes, but on their own side of the fence."

"Let's skip it," Julian said.

"The ones I feel sorry for," she said, "are the ones that are half white. They're tragic."

"Will you skip it?"

"Suppose we were half white. We would certainly have mixed feelings."

"I have mixed feelings now," he groaned.

"Well let's talk about something pleasant," she said. "I remember going to Grandpa's when I was a little girl. Then the house had double stairways that went up to what was really the second floor—all the cooking was done on the first. I used to like to stay down in the kitchen on account of the way the walls smelled. I would sit with my nose pressed against the plaster and take deep breaths. Actually the place belonged to the Godhighs but your grandfather Chestny paid the mortgage and saved it for them. They were in reduced circumstances," she said, "but reduced or not, they never forgot who they were."

"Doubtless that decayed mansion reminded them," Julian muttered. He never spoke of it without contempt or thought of it without longing. He had seen it once when he was a child before it had been sold. The double stairways had rotted and had been torn down. Negroes were living in it. But it remained in his mind as his mother had known it. It appeared in his dreams regularly. He would stand on the wide porch, listening to the rustle of oak leaves, then wander through the high-ceilinged hall into the parlor that opened onto it and gaze at the worn rugs and faded draperies. It occurred to him that it was he, not she, who could have appreciated it. He preferred its threadbare elegance to anything he could name and it was because of it that all the neighborhoods they had lived in had been a torment to him — whereas she had hardly known the difference. She called her insensitivity "being adjustable."

"And I remember the old darky who was my nurse, Caroline. There was no better person in the world. I've always had a great respect for my colored friends," she said. "I'd do anything in the world for them and they'd . . ."

"Will you for God's sake get off that subject?" Julian said. When he got on a bus by himself, he made it a point to sit down beside a Negro, in reparation as it were for his mother's sins.

"You're mighty touchy tonight," she said. "Do you feel all right?"

"Yes I feel all right," he said. "Now lay off."

She pursed her lips. "Well, you certainly are in a vile humor," she observed. "I just won't speak to you at all."

They had reached the bus stop. There was no bus in sight and Julian, his hands still jammed in his pockets and his head thrust forward, scowled down the empty street. The frustration of having to wait on the bus as well as ride on it began to creep up his neck like a hot hand. The presence of his mother was borne in upon him as she gave a pained sigh. He looked at her bleakly. She was holding herself very erect under the preposterous hat, wearing it like a banner of her imaginary dignity. There was in him an evil urge to break her spirit. He suddenly unloosened his tie and pulled it off and put it in his pocket.

She stiffened. "Why must you look like *that* when you take me to town?" she said. "Why must you deliberately embarrass me?"

"If you'll never learn where you are," he said, "you can at least learn where I am."

"You look like a — thug," she said.

"Then I must be one," he murmured.

"I'll just go home," she said. "I will not bother you. If you can't do a little thing like that for me . . ."

Rolling his eyes upward, he put his tie back on. "Restored to my class," he muttered. He thrust his face toward her and hissed, "True culture is in the mind, the *mind*," he said, and tapped his head, "the mind."

"It's in the heart," she said, "and in how you do things and how you do things is because of who you *are*."

"Nobody in the damn bus cares who you are."

"I care who I am," she said icily.

The lighted bus appeared on top of the next hill and as it approached, they moved out into the street to meet it. He put his hand under her elbow and hoisted her up on the creaking step. She entered with a little smile, as if she were going into a drawing room where everyone had been waiting for her. While he put in the tokens, she sat down on one of the broad front seats for three which faced the aisle. A thin woman with protruding teeth and long yellow hair was sitting on the end of it. His mother moved up beside her and left room for Julian beside herself. He sat down and looked at the floor across the aisle where a pair of thin feet in red and white canvas sandals were planted.

His mother immediately began a general conversation meant to attract anyone who felt like talking. "Can it get any hotter?" she said and removed from her purse a folding fan, black with a Japanese scene on it, which she began to flutter before her.

"I reckon it might could," the woman with the protruding teeth said, "but I know for a fact my apartment couldn't get no hotter."

"It must get the afternoon sun," his mother said. She sat forward and looked up and down the bus. It was half filled. Everybody was white. "I see we have the bus to ourselves," she said. Julian cringed.

"For a change," said the woman across the aisle, the owner of the red and white canvas sandals. "I come on one the other day and they were thick as fleas—up front and all through."

"The world is in a mess everywhere," his mother said. "I don't know how we've let it get in this fix."

"What gets my goat is all those boys from good families stealing automobile tires," the woman with the protruding teeth said. "I told my boy, I said you may not be rich but you been raised right and if I ever catch you in any such mess, they can send you on to the reformatory. Be exactly where you belong."

"Training tells," his mother said. "Is your boy in high school?"

"Ninth grade," the woman said.

"My son just finished college last year. He wants to write but he's selling typewriters until he gets started," his mother said.

The woman leaned forward and peered at Julian. He threw her such a malevolent look that she subsided against the seat. On the floor across the aisle there was an abandoned newspaper. He got up and got it and opened it out in front of him. His mother discreetly continued the conversation in a lower tone but the woman across the aisle said in a loud voice, "Well that's nice. Selling typewriters is close to writing. He can go right from one to the other."

"I tell him," his mother said, "that Rome wasn't built in a day."

Behind the newspaper Julian was withdrawing into the inner compartment of his mind where he spent most of his time. This was a kind of mental bubble in which he established himself when he could not bear to be part of what was going on around him. From it he could see out and judge but in it he was safe from any kind of penetration from without. It was the only place where he felt free of the general idiocy of his fellows. His mother had never entered it but from it he could see her with absolute clarity.

The old lady was clever enough and he thought that if she had started from any of the right premises, more might have been expected of her. She lived according to the laws of her own fantasy world, outside of which he had never seen her set foot. The law of it was to sacrifice herself for him after she had first created the necessity to do so by making a mess of things. If he had permitted her sacrifices, it was only because her lack of foresight had made them necessary. All of her life had been a struggle to act like a Chestny without the Chestny goods, and to give him everything she thought a Chestny ought to have; but since, said she, it was fun to struggle, why complain? And when you had won, as she had won, what fun to look back on the hard times! He could not forgive her that she had enjoyed the struggle and that she thought *she* had won.

What she meant when she said she had won was that she had brought him up successfully and had sent him to college and that he had turned out so well — good looking (her teeth had gone unfilled, so that his could be straightened), intelligent (he realized he was too intelligent to be a success), and with a future ahead of him (there was of course no future ahead of him). She excused his gloominess on the grounds that he was still growing up and his radical ideas on his lack of practical experience. She said he didn't yet know a thing about "life," that he hadn't even entered the real world — when already he was as disenchanted with it as a man of fifty.

The further irony of all this was that in spite of her, he had turned out so well. In spite of going to only a third-rate college, he had, on his own initiative, come out with a first-rate education; in spite of growing up dominated by a small mind, he had ended up with a large one; in spite of all her foolish views, he was free of prejudice and unafraid to face facts. Most miraculous of all, instead of being blinded by love for her as she was for him, he had cut himself emotionally free of her and could see her with complete objectivity. He was not dominated by his mother.

The bus stopped with a sudden jerk and shook him from his meditation. A woman from the back lurched forward with little steps and barely escaped falling in his newspaper as she righted herself. She got off and a large Negro got on. Julian kept his paper lowered to watch. It gave him a certain satisfaction to see injustice in daily operation. It confirmed his view that with a few exceptions there was no one worth knowing within a radius of three hundred miles. The Negro was well dressed and carried a briefcase. He looked round and then sat down on the other end of the seat where the woman with the red and white canvas sandals was sitting. He immediately unfolded a newspaper and obscured himself behind it. Julian's mother's elbow at once prodded insistently into his ribs. "Now you see why I won't ride on these buses by myself," she whispered.

The woman with the red and white canvas sandals had risen at the same time the Negro sat down and had gone further back in the bus and taken the seat of the woman who had got off. His mother leaned forward and cast her an approving look.

Julian rose, crossed the aisle, and sat down in the place of the woman with the canvas sandals. From this position, he looked serenely across at his mother. Her face had turned an angry red. He stared at her, making his eyes the eyes of a stranger. He felt his tension suddenly lift as if he had openly declared war on her.

He would have liked to get in conversation with the Negro and to talk with him about art or politics or any subject that would be above the comprehension of those around them, but the man remained entrenched behind his paper. He was either ignoring the change of seating or had never noticed it. There was no way for Julian to convey his sympathy.

His mother kept her eyes fixed reproachfully on his face. The woman with the protruding teeth was looking at him avidly as if he were a type of monster new to her.

"Do you have a light?" he asked the Negro.

Without looking away from his paper, the man reached in his pocket and handed him a packet of matches.

"Thanks," Julian said. For a moment he held the matches foolishly. A NO SMOKING sign looked down upon him from over the door. This alone would not have deterred him; he had no cigarettes. He had quit smoking some months before because he could not afford it. "Sorry," he muttered and handed back the matches. The Negro lowered the paper and gave him an annoyed look. He took the matches and raised the paper again.

His mother continued to gaze at him but she did not take the advantage of his momentary discomfort. Her eyes retained their battered look. Her face seemed to be unnaturally red, as if her blood pressure had risen. Julian allowed no glimmer of sympathy to show on his face. Having got the advantage, he wanted desperately to keep it and carry it through. He would have liked to teach her a lesson that would last her a while, but there seemed no way to continue the point. The Negro refused to come out from behind his paper.

Julian folded his arms and looked stolidly before him, facing her but as if he did not see her, as if he had ceased to recognize her existence. He visualized a scene in which, the bus having reached their stop, he would remain in his seat and when she said, "Aren't you going to get off?" he would look at her as a stranger who had rashly addressed him. The corner they got off on was usually deserted, but it was well lighted and it would not hurt her to walk by herself the four blocks to the Y. He decided to wait until the time came and then decide whether or not he would let her get off by herself. He would have to be at the Y at ten to bring her back, but he could leave her wondering if he was going to show up. There was no reason for her to think she could always depend on him.

He retired again into the high-ceilinged room sparsely settled with large pieces of antique furniture. His soul expanded momentarily but then he became aware of his mother across from him and the vision shriveled. He studied her coldly. Her feet in little pumps dangled like a child's and did not quite reach the floor. She was training on him an exaggerated look of reproach. He felt completely detached from her. At that moment he could with pleasure have slapped her as he would have slapped a particularly obnoxious child in his charge.

He began to imagine various unlikely ways by which he could teach her a lesson. He might make friends with some distinguished Negro professor or lawyer and bring him home to spend the evening. He would be entirely justified but her blood pressure would rise to 300. He could not push her to the extent of making her have a stroke, and moreover, he had never been successful at making any Negro friends. He had tried to strike up an acquaintance on the bus with some of the better types, with ones that looked like professors or ministers or lawyers. One morning he had sat down next to a distinguished-looking dark brown man who had answered his questions with a sonorous solemnity but who had turned out to be an undertaker. Another day he had sat down beside a cigar-smoking Negro with a diamond ring on his finger, but after a few stilted pleasantries, the Negro had rung the buzzer and risen, slipping two lottery tickets into Julian's hand as he climbed over him to leave.

He imagined his mother lying desperately ill and his being able to secure only a Negro doctor for her. He toyed with that idea for a few minutes and then dropped it for a momentary vision of himself participating as a sympathizer in a sit-in demonstration. This was possible but he did not linger with it. Instead, he approached the ultimate horror. He brought home a beautiful suspiciously Negroid woman. Prepare yourself, he said. There is nothing you can do about it. This is the woman I've chosen. She's intelligent, dignified, even good, and she's suffered and she hasn't thought it *fun*. Now persecute us, go ahead and persecute us. Drive her out of here, but remember, you're driving me too. His eyes were narrowed and through the indignation he had generated, he saw his mother across the aisle, purplefaced, shrunken to the dwarf-like proportions of her moral nature, sitting like a mummy beneath the ridiculous banner of her hat.

He was tilted out of his fantasy again as the bus stopped. The door opened with a sucking hiss and out of the dark a large, gaily dressed, sullen-looking colored woman got on with a little boy. The child, who might have been four, had on a short plaid suit and a Tyrolean hat with a blue feather in it. Julian hoped that he would sit down beside him and that the woman would push in beside his mother. He could think of no better arrangement.

As she waited for her tokens, the woman was surveying the seating possibilities — he hoped with the idea of sitting where she was least wanted. There was something familiar-looking about her but Julian could not place what it was. She was a giant of a woman. Her face was set not only to meet opposition but to seek it out. The downward tilt of her large lower lip was like a warning sign: DON'T TAMPER WITH ME. Her bulging figure was encased in a green crepe dress and her feet overflowed in red shoes. She had on a hideous hat. A purple velvet flap came down on one side of it and stood up on the other; the rest of it was green and looked like a cushion with the stuffing out. She carried a mammoth red pocketbook that bulged throughout as if it were stuffed with rocks.

To Julian's disappointment, the little boy climbed up on the empty seat beside his mother. His mother lumped all children, black and white, into the common category, "cute," and she thought little Negroes were on the whole cuter than little white children. She smiled at the little boy as he climbed on the seat.

Meanwhile the woman was bearing down upon the empty seat beside Julian. To his annoyance, she squeezed herself into it. He saw his mother's face change as the woman settled herself next to him and he realized with satisfaction that this was more objectionable to her than it was to him. Her face seemed almost gray and there was a look of dull recognition in her eyes, as if suddenly she had sickened at some awful confrontation. Julian saw that it was because she and the woman had, in a sense, swapped sons. Though his mother would not realize the symbolic significance of this, she would feel it. His amusement showed plainly on his face.

The woman next to him muttered something unintelligible to herself. He was conscious of a kind of bristling next to him, muted growling like that of an angry cat. He could not see anything but the red pocketbook upright on the bulging green thighs. He visualized the woman as she had stood waiting for her tokens—the ponderous figure, rising from the red shoes upward over the solid hips, the mammoth bosom, the haughty face, to the green and purple hat.

His eyes widened.

The vision of the two hats, identical, broke upon him with the radiance of a brilliant sunrise. His face was suddenly lit with joy. He could not believe that Fate had thrust upon his mother such a lesson. He gave a loud chuckle so that she would look at him and see that he saw. She turned her eyes on him slowly. The blue in them seemed to have turned a bruised purple. For a moment he had an uncomfortable sense of her innocence, but it lasted only a second before principle rescued him. Justice entitled him to laugh. His grin hardened until it said to her as plainly as if he were saying aloud: Your punishment exactly fits your pettiness. This should teach you a permanent lesson.

Her eyes shifted to the woman. She seemed unable to bear looking at him and to find the woman preferable. He became conscious again of the bristling presence at his side. The woman was rumbling like a volcano about to become active. His mother's mouth began to twitch slightly at one corner. With a sinking heart, he saw incipient signs of recovery on her face and realized that this was going to strike her suddenly as funny and was going to be no lesson at all. She kept her eyes on the woman and an amused smile came over her face as if the woman were a monkey that had stolen her hat. The little Negro was looking up at her with large fascinated eyes. He had been trying to attract her attention for some time.

"Carver," the woman said suddenly. "Come heah!"

When he saw that the spotlight was on him at last, Carver drew his feet up and turned himself toward Julian's mother and giggled.

"Carver!" the woman said. "You heah me? Come Heah!"

Carver slid down from the seat but remained squatting with his back against the base of it, his head turned slowly around toward Julian's mother, who was smiling at him. The woman reached a hand across the aisle and snatched him to her. He righted himself and hung backwards on her knees, grinning at Julian's mother. "Isn't he cute?" Julian's mother said to the woman with the protruding teeth.

"I reckon he is," the woman said without conviction.

The Negress yanked him upright but he eased out of her grip and shot across the aisle and scrambled, giggling wildly, onto the seat beside his love.

"I think he likes me," Julian's mother said, and smiled at the woman. It was the smile she used when she was being particularly gracious to an inferior. Julian saw everything lost. The lesson had rolled off her like rain on a roof.

The woman stood up and yanked the little boy off the seat as if she were snatching him from contagion. Julian could feel the rage in her at having no weapon like his mother's smile. She gave the child a sharp slap across his leg. He howled once and then thrust his head into her stomach and kicked his feet against her shins. "Behave," she said vehemently.

The bus stopped and the Negro who had been reading the newspaper got off. The woman moved over and set the little boy down with a thump between herself and Julian. She held him firmly by the knee. In a moment he put his hands in front of his face and peeped at Julian's mother through his fingers.

"I see yoooooooo!" she said and put her hand in front of her face and peeped at him.

The woman slapped his hand down. "Quit yo' foolishness," she said, "before I knock the living Jesus out of you!"

Julian was thankful that the next stop was theirs. He reached up and pulled the cord. The woman reached up and pulled it at the same time. Oh my God, he thought. He had the terrible intuition that when they got off the bus together, his mother would open her purse and give the little boy a nickel. The gesture would be as natural to her as breathing. The bus stopped and the woman got up and lunged to the front, dragging the child, who wished to stay on, after her. Julian and his mother got up and followed. As they neared the door, Julian tried to relieve her of her pocketbook.

"No," she murmured, "I want to give the little boy a nickel."

"No!" Julian hissed. "No!"

She smiled down at the child and opened her bag. The bus door opened and the woman picked him up by the arm and descended with him, hanging at her hip. Once in the street she set him down and shook him.

Julian's mother had to close her purse while she got down the bus step but as soon as her feet were on the ground, she opened it again and began to rummage inside. "I can't find but a penny," she whispered, "but it looks like a new one."

"Don't do it!" Julian said fiercely between his teeth. There was a streetlight on the corner and she hurried to get under it so that she could better see into her pocketbook. The woman was heading off rapidly down the street with the child still hanging backward on her hand.

"Oh little boy!" Julian's mother called and took a few quick steps and caught up with them just beyond the lamppost. "Here's a bright new penny for you," and she held out the coin, which shone bronze in the dim light.

The huge woman turned and for a moment stood, her shoulders lifted and her face frozen with frustrated rage, and stared at Julian's mother. Then all at once she seemed to explode like a piece of machinery that had been given one ounce of pressure too much. Julian saw the black fist swing out with the red pocketbook. He shut his eyes and cringed as he heard the woman shout, "He don't take nobody's pennies!" When he opened his eyes, the woman was disappearing down the street with the little boy staring wide-eyed over her shoulder. Julian's mother was sitting on the sidewalk.

"I told you not to do that," Julian said angrily. "I told you not to do that!"

He stood over her for a minute, gritting his teeth. Her legs were stretched out in front of her and her hat was on her lap. He squatted down and looked her in the face. It was totally expressionless. "You got exactly what you deserved," he said. "Now get up."

He picked up her pocketbook and put what had fallen out back in it. He picked the hat up off her lap. The penny caught his eye on the sidewalk and he picked that up and let it drop before her eyes into the purse. Then he stood up and leaned over and held his hands out to pull her up. She remained immobile. He sighed. Rising above them on either side were black apartment buildings, marked with irregular rectangles of light. At the end of the block a man came out of a door and walked off in the opposite direction. "All right," he said, "suppose somebody happens by and wants to know why you're sitting on the sidewalk?"

She took the hand and, breathing hard, pulled heavily up on it and then stood for a moment, swaying slightly as if the spots of light in the darkness were circling around her. Her eyes, shadowed and confused, finally settled on his face. He did not try to conceal his irritation. "I hope this teaches you a lesson," he said. She leaned forward and her eyes raked his face. She seemed trying to determine his identity. Then, as if she found nothing familiar about him, she started off with a headlong movement in the wrong direction.

"Aren't you going to the Y?" he asked.

"Home," she muttered.

"Well, are we walking?"

For answer she kept going. Julian followed along, his hands behind him. He saw no reason to let the lesson she had had go without backing it up with an explanation of its meaning. She might as well be made to understand what had happened to her. "Don't think that was just an uppity Negro woman," he said. "That was the whole colored race which will no longer take your condescending pennies. That was your black double. She can wear the same hat as you, and to be sure," he added gratuitously (because he thought it was funny), "it looked better on her than it did on you. What all this means," he said, "is that the old world is gone. The old manners are obsolete and your graciousness is not worth a damn." He thought bitterly of the house that had been lost for him. "You aren't who you think you are," he said.

She continued to plow ahead, paying no attention to him. Her hair had come undone on one side. She dropped her pocketbook and took no notice. He stopped and picked it up and handed it to her but she did not take it.

"You needn't act as if the world had come to an end," he said, "because it hasn't. From now on you've got to live in a new world and face a few realities for a change. Buck up," he said, "it won't kill you."

She was breathing fast.

"Let's wait on the bus," he said.

"Home," she said thickly.

"I hate to see you behave like this," he said. "Just like a child. I should be able to expect more of you." He decided to stop where he was and make her stop and wait for a bus. "I'm not going any farther," he said, stopping. "We're going on the bus."

She continued to go on as if she had not heard him. He took a few steps and caught her arm and stopped her. He looked into her face and caught his breath. He was looking into a face he had never seen before. "Tell Grandpa to come get me," she said.

He stared, stricken.

"Tell Caroline to come get me," she said.

Stunned, he let her go and she lurched forward again, walking as if one leg were shorter than the other. A tide of darkness seemed to be sweeping her from him. "Mother!" he cried. "Darling, sweetheart, wait!" Crumpling, she fell to the pavement. He dashed forward and fell at her side, crying, "Mamma, Mamma!" He turned her over. Her face was fiercely distorted. One eye, large and staring, moved slightly to the left as if it had become unmoored. The other remained fixed on him, raked his face again, found nothing, and closed.

"Wait here, wait here!" he cried and jumped up and began to run for help toward a cluster of lights he saw in the distance ahead of him. "Help, help!" he shouted, but his voice was thin, scarcely a thread of sound. The lights drifted farther away the faster he ran and his feet moved numbly as if they carried him nowhere. The tide of darkness seemed to sweep him back to her, postponing from moment to moment his entry into the world of guilt and sorrow.

Good Country People   1955

Besides the neutral expression that she wore when she was alone, Mrs. Freeman had two others, forward and reverse, that she used for all her human dealings. Her forward expression was steady and driving like the advance of a heavy truck. Her eyes never swerved to left or right but turned as the story turned as if they followed a yellow line down the center of it. She seldom used the other expression because it was not often necessary for her to retract a statement, but when she did, her face came to a complete stop, there was an almost imperceptible movement of her black eyes, during which they seemed to be receding, and then the observer would see that Mrs. Freeman, though she might stand there as real as several grain sacks thrown on top of each other, was no longer there in spirit. As for getting anything across to her when this was the case, Mrs. Hopewell had given it up. She might talk her head off. Mrs. Freeman could never be brought to admit herself wrong on any point. She would stand there and if she could be brought to say anything, it was something like, "Well, I wouldn't of said it was and I wouldn't of said it wasn't," or letting her gaze range over the top kitchen shelf where there was an assortment of dusty bottles, she might remark, "I see you ain't ate many of them figs you put up last summer."

They carried on their most important business in the kitchen at breakfast. Every morning Mrs. Hopewell got up at seven o'clock and lit her gas heater and Joy's. Joy was her daughter, a large blonde girl who had an artificial leg. Mrs. Hopewell thought of her as a child though she was thirty-two years old and highly educated. Joy would get up while her mother was eating and lumber into the bathroom and slam the door, and before long, Mrs. Freeman would arrive at the back door. Joy would hear her mother call, "Come on in," and then they would talk a while in low voices that were indistinguishable in the bathroom. By the time Joy came in, they had usually finished the weather report and were on one or the other of Mrs. Freeman's daughters, Glynese or Carramae, Joy called them Glycerin and Caramel. Glynese, a redhead, was eighteen and had many admirers; Carramae, a blonde, was only fifteen but already married and pregnant. She could not keep anything on her stomach. Every morning Mrs. Freeman told Mrs. Hopewell how many times she had vomited since the last report.

Mrs. Hopewell liked to tell people that Glynese and Carramae were two of the finest girls she knew and that Mrs. Freeman was a *lady* and that she was never ashamed to take her anywhere or introduce her to anybody they might meet. Then she would tell how she had happened to hire the Freemans in the first place and how they were a godsend to her and how she had had them four years. The reason for her keeping them so long was that they were not trash. They were good country people. She had telephoned the man whose name they had given as a reference and he had told her that Mr. Freeman was a good farmer but that his wife was the nosiest woman ever to walk the earth. "She's got to be into everything," the man said. "If she don't get there before the dust settles, you can bet she's dead, that's all. She'll want to know all your business. I can stand him real good," he had said, "but me nor my wife neither could have stood that woman one more minute on this place." That had put Mrs. Hopewell off for a few days.

She had hired them in the end because there were no other applicants but she had made up her mind beforehand exactly how she would handle the woman. Since she was the type who had to be into everything, then, Mrs. Hopewell had decided, she would not only let her be into everything, she would *see to it* that she was into everything—she would give her the responsibility of everything, she would put her in charge. Mrs. Hopewell had no bad qualities of her own but she was able to use other people's in such a constructive way that she never felt the lack. She had hired the Freemans and she had kept them four years.

Nothing is perfect. This was one of Mrs. Hopewell's favorite sayings. Another was: that is life! And still another, the most important, was: well, other people have their opinions too. She would make these statements, usually at the table, in a tone of gentle insistence as if no one held them but her, and the large hulking Joy, whose constant outrage had obliterated every expression from her face, would stare just a little to the side of her, her eyes icy blue, with the look of someone who has achieved blindness by an act of will and means to keep it.

When Mrs. Hopewell said to Mrs. Freeman that life was like that, Mrs. Freeman would say, "I always said so myself." Nothing had been arrived at by anyone that had not first been arrived at by her. She was quicker than Mr. Freeman. When Mrs. Hopewell said to her after they had been on the place a while, "You know, you're the wheel behind the wheel," and winked, Mrs. Freeman had said, "I know it. I've always been quick. It's some that are quicker than others."

"Everybody is different," Mrs. Hopewell said.

"Yes, most people is," Mrs. Freeman said.

"It takes all kinds to make the world."

"I always said it did myself."

The girl was used to this kind of dialogue for breakfast and more of it for dinner; sometimes they had it for supper too. When they had no guest they ate in the kitchen because that was easier. Mrs. Freeman always managed to arrive at some point during the meal and to watch them finish it. She would stand in the doorway if it were summer but in the winter she would stand with one elbow on top of the refrigerator and look down on them, or she would stand by the gas heater, lifting the back of her skirt slightly. Occasionally she would stand against the wall and roll her head from side to side. At no time was she in any hurry to leave. All this was very trying on Mrs. Hopewell but she was a woman of great patience. She realized that nothing is perfect and that in the Freemans she had good country people and that if, in this day and age, you get good country people, you had better hang onto them.

She had had plenty of experience with trash. Before the Freemans she had averaged one tenant family a year. The wives of these farmers were not the kind you would want to be around you for very long. Mrs. Hopewell, who had divorced her husband long ago, needed someone to walk over the fields with her; and when Joy had to be impressed for these services, her remarks were usually so ugly and her face so glum that Mrs. Hopewell would say, "If you can't come pleasantly, I don't want you at all," to which the girl, standing square and rigid-shouldered with her neck thrust slightly forward, would reply, "If you want me, here I am—LIKE I AM."

Mrs. Hopewell excused this attitude because of the leg (which had been shot off in a hunting accident when Joy was ten). It was hard for Mrs. Hopewell to realize that her child was thirty-two now and that for more than twenty years she had had only one leg. She thought of her still as a child because it tore her heart to think instead of the poor stout girl in her thirties who had never danced a step or had any *normal* good times. Her name was really Joy but as soon as she was twenty-one and away from home, she had had it legally changed. Mrs. Hopewell was certain that she had thought and thought until she had hit upon the ugliest name in any language. Then she had gone and had the beautiful name, Joy, changed without telling her mother until after she had done it. Her legal name was Hulga.

When Mrs. Hopewell thought the name Hulga, she thought of the broad blank hull of a battleship. She would not use it. She continued to call her Joy to which the girl responded but in a purely mechanical way.

Hulga had learned to tolerate Mrs. Freeman who saved her from taking walks with her mother. Even Glynese and Carramae were useful when they occupied attention that might otherwise have been directed at her. At first she had thought she could not stand Mrs. Freeman for she had found that it was not possible to be rude to her. Mrs. Freeman would take on strange resentments and for days together she would be sullen but the source of her displeasure was always obscure; a direct attack, a positive leer, blatant ugliness to her face—these never touched her. And without warning one day, she began calling her Hulga.

She did not call her that in front of Mrs. Hopewell who would have been incensed but when she and the girl happened to be out of the house together, she would say something and add the name Hulga to the end of it, and the big spectacled Joy-Hulga would scowl and redden as if her privacy had been intruded upon. She considered the name her personal affair. She had arrived at it first purely on the basis of its ugly sound and then the full genius of its fitness had struck her. She had a vision of the name working like the ugly sweating Vulcan who stayed in the furnace and to whom, presumably, the goddess had to come when called. She saw it as the name of her highest creative act. One of her major triumphs was that her mother had not been able to turn her dust into Joy, but the greater one was that she had been able to turn it herself into Hulga. However, Mrs. Freeman's relish for using the name only irritated her. It was as if Mrs. Freeman's beady steel-pointed eyes had penetrated far enough behind her face to reach some secret fact. Something about her seemed to fascinate Mrs. Freeman and then one day Hulga realized that it was the artificial leg. Mrs. Freeman had a special fondness for the details of secret infections, hidden deformities, assaults upon children. Of diseases, she preferred the lingering or incurable. Hulga had heard Mrs. Hopewell give her the details of the hunting accident, how the leg had been literally blasted off, how she had never lost consciousness. Mrs. Freeman could listen to it any time as if it had happened an hour ago.

When Hulga stumped into the kitchen in the morning (she could walk without making the awful noise but she made it—Mrs. Hopewell was certain—because it was ugly-sounding), she glanced at them and did not speak. Mrs. Hopewell would be in her red kimono with her hair tied around her head in rags. She would be sitting at the table, finishing her breakfast and Mrs. Freeman would be hanging by her elbow outward from the refrigerator, looking down at the table. Hulga always put her eggs on the stove to boil and then stood over them with her arms folded, and Mrs. Hopewell would look at her—a kind of indirect gaze divided between her and Mrs. Freeman—and would think that if she would only keep herself up a little, she wouldn't be so bad looking. There was nothing wrong with her face that a pleasant expression wouldn't help. Mrs. Hopewell said that people who looked on the bright side of things would be beautiful even if they were not.

Whenever she looked at Joy this way, she could not help but feel that it would have been better if the child had not taken the Ph.D. It had certainly not brought her out any and now that she had it, there was no more excuse for her to go to school again. Mrs. Hopewell thought it was nice for girls to go to school to have a good time but Joy had "gone through." Anyhow, she would not have been strong enough to go again. The doctors had told Mrs. Hopewell that with the best of care, Joy might see forty-five. She had a weak heart. Joy had made it plain that if it had not been for this condition, she would be far from these red hills and good country people. She would be in a university lecturing to people who knew what she was talking about. And Mrs. Hopewell could very well picture her there, looking like a scarecrow and lecturing to more of the same. Here she went about all day in a six-year-old skirt and a yellow sweat shirt with a faded cowboy on a horse embossed on it. She thought this was funny; Mrs. Hopewell thought it was idiotic and showed simply that she was still a child. She was brilliant but she didn't have a grain of sense. It seemed to Mrs. Hopewell that every year she grew less like other people and more like herself—bloated, rude, and squint-eyed. And she said such strange things! To her own mother she had said—without warning, without excuse, standing up

in the middle of a meal with her face purple and her mouth half full—
"Woman! do you ever look inside? Do you ever look inside and see what you
are *not*? God!" she had cried sinking down again and staring at her plate,
"Malebranche was right: we are not our own light. We are not our own light!"
Mrs. Hopewell had no idea to this day what brought that on. She had only
made the remark, hoping Joy would take it in, that a smile never hurt anyone.

The girl had taken the Ph.D. in philosophy and this left Mrs. Hopewell
at a complete loss. You could say, "My daughter is a nurse," or "My daughter is
a schoolteacher," or even, "My daughter is a chemical engineer." You could not
say, "My daughter is a philosopher." That was something that had ended with
the Greeks and Romans. All day Joy sat on her neck in a deep chair, reading.
Sometimes she went for walks but she didn't like dogs or cats or birds or flowers
or nature or nice young men. She looked at nice young men as if she could smell
their stupidity.

One day Mrs. Hopewell had picked up one of the books the girl had just
put down and opening it at random, she read, "Science, on the other hand, has
to assert its soberness and seriousness afresh and declare that it is concerned
solely with what-is. Nothing—how can it be for science anything but a horror
and a phantasm? If science is right, then one thing stands firm: science wishes
to know nothing of nothing. Such is after all the strictly scientific approach to
Nothing. We know it by wishing to know nothing of Nothing." These words
had been underlined with a blue pencil and they worked on Mrs. Hopewell like
some evil incantation in gibberish. She shut the book quickly and went out of
the room as if she were having a chill.

This morning when the girl came in, Mrs. Freeman was on Carramae.
"She thrown up four times after supper," she said, "and was up twict in the
night after three o'clock. Yesterday she didn't do nothing but ramble in the
bureau drawer. All she did. Stand up there and see what she could run up on."

"She's got to eat," Mrs. Hopewell muttered, sipping her coffee, while she
watched Joy's back at the stove. She was wondering what the child had said to
the Bible salesman. She could not imagine what kind of a conversation she
could possibly have had with him.

He was a tall gaunt hatless youth who had called yesterday to sell them a
Bible. He had appeared at the door, carrying a large black suitcase that
weighted him so heavily on one side that he had to brace himself against the
door facing. He seemed on the point of collapse but he said in a cheerful voice,
"Good morning, Mrs. Cedars!" and set the suitcase down on the mat. He was
not a bad-looking young man though he had on a bright blue suit and yellow
socks that were not pulled up far enough. He had prominent face bones and a
streak of sticky-looking brown hair falling across his forehead.

"I'm Mrs. Hopewell," she said.

"Oh!" he said, pretending to look puzzled but with his eyes sparkling, "I
saw it said 'The Cedars' on the mailbox so I thought you was Mrs. Cedars!"
and he burst out in a pleasant laugh. He picked up the satchel and under cover
of a pant, he fell forward into her hall. It was rather as if the suitcase had moved
first, jerking him after it. "Mrs. Hopewell!" he said and grabbed her hand. "I

hope you are well!" and he laughed again and then all at once his face sobered completely. He paused and gave her a straight earnest look and said, "Lady, I've come to speak of serious things."

"Well, come in," she muttered, none too pleased because her dinner was almost ready. He came into the parlor and sat down on the edge of a straight chair and put the suitcase between his feet and glanced around the room as if he were sizing her up by it. Her silver gleamed on the two sideboards; she decided he had never been in a room as elegant as this.

"Mrs. Hopewell," he began, using her name in a way that sounded almost intimate, "I know you believe in Chrustian service."

"Well yes," she murmured.

"I know," he said and paused, looking very wise with his head cocked on one side, "that you're a good woman. Friends have told me."

Mrs. Hopewell never liked to be taken for a fool. "What are you selling?" she asked.

"Bibles," the young man said and his eye raced around the room before he added, "I see you have no family Bible in your parlor, I see that is the one lack you got!"

Mrs. Hopewell could not say, "My daughter is an atheist and won't let me keep the Bible in the parlor." She said, stiffening slightly, "I keep my Bible by my bedside." This was not the truth. It was in the attic somewhere.

"Lady," he said, "the word of God ought to be in the parlor."

"Well, I think that's a matter of taste," she began. "I think . . . ."

"Lady," he said, "for a Chrustian, the word of God ought to be in every room in the house besides in his heart. I know, you're a Chrustian because I can see it in every line of your face."

She stood up and said, "Well, young man, I don't want to buy a Bible and I smell my dinner burning."

He didn't get up. He began to twist his hands and looking down at them he said softly, "Well lady, I'll tell you the truth — not many people want to buy one nowadays and besides, I know I'm real simple. I don't know how to say a thing but to say it. I'm just a country boy." He glanced up into her unfriendly face. "People like you don't like to fool with country people like me!"

"Why!" she cried, "good country people are the salt of the earth! Besides, we all have different ways of doing, it takes all kinds to make the world go 'round. That's life!"

"You said a mouthful," he said.

"Why, I think there aren't enough good country people in the world!" she said, stirred. "I think that's what's wrong with it!"

His face had brightened. "I didn't inraduce myself," he said. "I'm Manley Pointer from out in the country around Willohobie, not even from a place, just from near a place."

"You wait a minute," she said. "I have to see about my dinner." She went out to the kitchen and found Joy standing near the door where she had been listening.

"Get rid of the salt of the earth," she said, "and let's eat."

Mrs. Hopewell gave her a pained look and turned the heat down under the vegetables. "*I* can't be rude to anybody," she murmured and went back into the parlor.

He had opened the suitcase and was sitting with a Bible on each knee.

"You might as well put those up," she told him. "I don't want one."

"I appreciate your honesty," he said. "You don't see any more real honest people unless you go way out in the country."

"I know," she said, "real genuine folks!" Through the crack in the door she heard a groan.

"I guess a lot of boys come telling you they're working their way through college," he said, "but I'm not going to tell you that. Somehow," he said, "I don't want to go to college. I want to devote my life to Chrustian service. See," he said, lowering his voice, "I got this heart condition. I may not live long. When you know it's something wrong with you and you may not live long, well then, lady . . ." He paused, with his mouth open, and stared at her.

He and Joy had the same condition! She knew that her eyes were filling with tears but she collected herself quickly and murmured, "Won't you stay for dinner? We'd love to have you!" and was sorry the instant she heard herself say it.

"Yes mam," he said in an abashed voice, "I would sher love to do that!"

Joy had given him one look on being introduced to him and then throughout the meal had not glanced at him again. He had addressed several remarks to her, which she had pretended not to hear. Mrs. Hopewell could not understand deliberate rudeness, although she lived with it, and she felt she had always to overflow with hospitality to make up for Joy's lack of courtesy. She urged him to talk about himself and he did. He said he was the seventh child of twelve and that his father had been crushed under a tree when he himself was eight years old. He had been crushed very badly, in fact, almost cut in two and was practically not recognizable. His mother had got along the best she could by hard working and she had always seen that her children went to Sunday School and that they read the Bible every evening. He was now nineteen years old and he had been selling Bibles for four months. In that time he had sold seventy-seven Bibles and had the promise of two more sales. He wanted to become a missionary because he thought that was the way you could do most for people. "He who losest his life shall find it," he said simply and he was so sincere, so genuine and earnest that Mrs. Hopewell would not for the world have smiled. He prevented his peas from sliding onto the table by blocking them with a piece of bread which he later cleaned his plate with. She could see Joy observing sidewise how he handled his knife and fork and she saw too that every few minutes, the boy would dart a keen appraising glance at the girl as if he were trying to attract her attention.

After dinner Joy cleared the dishes off the table and disappeared and Mrs. Hopewell was left to talk with him. He told her again about his childhood and his father's accident and about various things that had happened to him. Every five minutes or so she would stifle a yawn. He sat for two hours until finally she told him she must go because she had an appointment in town. He packed his Bibles and thanked her and prepared to leave, but in the doorway he stopped and wrung her hand and said that not on any of his trips had he met a lady as nice as her and he asked if he could come again. She had said she would always be happy to see him.

Joy had been standing in the road, apparently looking at something in the distance, when he came down the steps toward her, bent to the side with his heavy valise. He stopped where she was standing and confronted her directly. Mrs. Hopewell could not hear what he said but she trembled to think what Joy would say to him. She could see that after a minute Joy said something and that then the boy began to speak again, making an excited gesture with his free hand. After a minute Joy said something else at which the boy began to speak once more. Then to her amazement, Mrs. Hopewell saw the two of them walk off together, toward the gate. Joy had walked all the way to the gate with him and Mrs. Hopewell could not imagine what they had said to each other, and she had not yet dared to ask.

Mrs. Freeman was insisting upon her attention. She had moved from the refrigerator to the heater so that Mrs. Hopewell had to turn and face her in order to seem to be listening. "Glynese gone out with Harvey Hill again last night," she said. "She had this sty."

"Hill," Mrs. Hopewell said absently, "is that the one who works in the garage?"

"Nome, he's the one that goes to chiropracter school," Mrs. Freeman said. "She had this sty. Been had it two days. So she says when he brought her in the other night he says, 'Lemme get rid of that sty for you,' and she says, 'How?' and he says, 'You just lay yourself down acrost the seat of that car and I'll show you.' So she done it and he popped her neck. Kept on a-popping it several times until she made him quit. This morning," Mrs. Freeman said, "she ain't got no sty. She ain't got no traces of a sty."

"I never heard of that before," Mrs. Hopewell said.

"He ast her to marry him before the Ordinary," Mrs. Freeman went on, "and she told him she wasn't going to be married in no *office*."

"Well, Glynese is a fine girl," Mrs. Hopewell said. "Glynese and Carramae are both fine girls."

"Carramae said when her and Lyman was married Lyman said it sure felt sacred to him. She said he said he wouldn't take five hundred dollars for being married by a preacher."

"How much would he take?" the girl asked from the stove.

"He said he wouldn't take five hundred dollars," Mrs. Freeman repeated.

"Well we all have work to do," Mrs. Hopewell said.

"Lyman said it just felt more sacred to him," Mrs. Freeman said. "The doctor wants Carramae to eat prunes. Says instead of medicine. Says them cramps is coming from pressure. You know where I think it is?"

"She'll be better in a few weeks," Mrs. Hopewell said.

"In the tube," Mrs. Freeman said. "Else she wouldn't be as sick as she is."

Hulga had cracked her two eggs into a saucer and was bringing them to the table along with a cup of coffee that she had filled too full. She sat down carefully and began to eat, meaning to keep Mrs. Freeman there by questions if for any reason she showed an inclination to leave. She could perceive her mother's eye on her. The first round-about question would be about the Bible salesman and she did not wish to bring it on. "How did he pop her neck?" she asked.

Mrs. Freeman went into a description of how he had popped her neck. She said he owned a '55 Mercury but that Glynese said she would rather marry a man with only a '36 Plymouth who would be married by a preacher. The girl asked what if he had a '32 Plymouth and Mrs. Freeman said what Glynese had said was a '36 Plymouth.

Mrs. Hopewell said there were not many girls with Glynese's common sense. She said what she admired in those girls was their common sense. She said that reminded her that they had had a nice visitor yesterday, a young man selling Bibles. "Lord," she said, "he bored me to death but he was so sincere and genuine I couldn't be rude to him. He was just good country people, you know," she said, "—just the salt of the earth."

"I seen him walk up," Mrs. Freeman said, "and then later—I seen him walk off," and Hulga could feel the slight shift in her voice, the slight insinuation, that he had not walked off alone, had he? Her face remained expressionless but the color rose into her neck and she seemed to swallow it down with the next spoonful of egg. Mrs. Freeman was looking at her as if they had a secret together.

"Well, it takes all kinds of people to make the world go 'round," Mrs. Hopewell said. "It's very good we aren't all alike."

"Some people are more alike than others," Mrs. Freeman said.

Hulga got up and stumped, with about twice the noise that was necessary, into her room and locked the door. She was to meet the Bible salesman at ten o'clock at the gate. She had thought about it half the night. She had started thinking of it as a great joke and then she had begun to see profound implications in it. She had lain in bed imagining dialogues for them that were insane on the surface but that reached below to depths that no Bible salesman would be aware of. Their conversation yesterday had been of this kind.

He had stopped in front of her and had simply stood there. His face was bony and sweaty and bright, with a little pointed nose in the center of it, and his look was different from what it had been at the dinner table. He was gazing at her with open curiosity, with fascination, like a child watching a new fantastic animal at the zoo, and he was breathing as if he had run a great distance to reach her. His gaze seemed somehow familiar but she could not think where she had been regarded with it before. For almost a minute he didn't say anything. Then on what seemed an insuck of breath, he whispered, "You ever ate a chicken that was two days old?"

The girl looked at him stonily. He might have just put this question up for consideration at the meeting of a philosophical association. "Yes," she presently replied as if she had considered it from all angles.

"It must have been mighty small!" he said triumphantly and shook all over with little nervous giggles, getting very red in the face, and subsiding finally into his gaze of complete admiration, while the girl's expression remained exactly the same.

"How old are you?" he asked softly.

She waited some time before she answered. Then in a flat voice she said, "Seventeen."

His smiles came in succession like waves breaking on the surface of a little lake. "I see you got a wooden leg," he said. "I think you're brave. I think you're real sweet."

The girl stood blank and solid and silent.

"Walk to the gate with me," he said. "You're a brave sweet little thing and I liked you the minute I seen you walk in the door."

Hulga began to move forward.

"What's your name?" he asked, smiling down on the top of her head.

"Hulga," she said.

"Hulga," he murmured, "Hulga. Hulga. I never heard of anybody name Hulga before. You're shy, aren't you, Hulga?" he asked.

She nodded, watching his large red hand on the handle of the giant valise.

"I like girls that wear glasses," he said. "I think a lot. I'm not like these people that a serious thought don't ever enter their heads. It's because I may die."

"I may die too," she said suddenly and looked up at him. His eyes were very small and brown, glittering feverishly.

"Listen," he said, "don't you think some people was meant to meet on account of what all they got in common and all? Like they both think serious thoughts and all?" He shifted the valise to his other hand so that the hand nearest her was free. He caught hold of her elbow and shook it a little. "I don't work on Saturday," he said. "I like to walk in the woods and see what Mother Nature is wearing. O'er the hills and far away. Pic-nics and things. Couldn't we go on a pic-nic tomorrow? Say yes, Hulga," he said and gave her a dying look as if he felt his insides about to drop out of him. He had even seemed to sway slightly toward her.

During the night she had imagined that she seduced him. She imagined that the two of them walked on the place until they came to the storage barn beyond the two back fields and there, she imagined, that things came to such a pass that she very easily seduced him and that then, of course, she had to reckon with his remorse. True genius can get an idea across even to an inferior mind. She imagined that she took his remorse in hand and changed it into a deeper understanding of life. She took all his shame away and turned it into something useful.

She set off for the gate at exactly ten o'clock, escaping without drawing Mrs. Hopewell's attention. She didn't take anything to eat, forgetting that food is usually taken on a pic-nic. She wore a pair of slacks and a dirty white shirt, and as an afterthought, she had put some Vapex on the collar of it since she did not own any perfume. When she reached the gate no one was there.

She looked up and down the empty highway and had the furious feeling that she had been tricked, that he had only meant to make her walk to the gate after the idea of him. Then suddenly he stood up, very tall, from behind a bush on the opposite embankment. Smiling, he lifted his hat which was new and wide-brimmed. He had not worn it yesterday and she wondered if he had bought it for the occasion. It was toast-colored with a red and white band around it and was slightly too large for him. He stepped from behind the bush still carrying the black valise. He had on the same suit and the same yellow socks sucked down in his shoes from walking. He crossed the highway and said, "I knew you'd come!"

The girl wondered acidly how he had known this. She pointed to the valise and asked, "Why did you bring your Bibles?"

He took her elbow, smiling down on her as if he could not stop. "You can never tell when you'll need the word of God, Hulga," he said. She had a moment in which she doubted that this was actually happening and then they began to climb the embankment. They went down into the pasture toward the woods. The boy walked lightly by her side, bouncing on his toes. The valise did not seem to be heavy today; he even swung it. They crossed half the pasture without saying anything and then, putting his hand easily on the small of her back, he asked softly, "Where does your wooden leg join on?"

She turned an ugly red and glared at him and for an instant the boy looked abashed. "I didn't mean you no harm," he said. "I only meant you're so brave and all. I guess God takes care of you."

"No," she said, looking forward and walking fast, "I don't even believe in God."

At this he stopped and whistled. "No!" he exclaimed as if he were too astonished to say anything else.

She walked on and in a second he was bouncing at her side, fanning with his hat. "That's very unusual for a girl," he remarked, watching her out of the corner of his eye. When they reached the edge of the wood, he put his hand on her back again and drew her against him without a word and kissed her heavily.

The kiss, which had more pressure than feeling behind it, produced that extra surge of adrenalin in the girl that enables one to carry a packed trunk out of a burning house, but in her, the power went at once to the brain. Even before he released her, her mind, clear and detached and ironic anyway, was regarding him from a great distance, with amusement but with pity. She had never been kissed before and she was pleased to discover that it was an unexceptional experience and all a matter of the mind's control. Some people might enjoy drain water if they were told it was vodka. When the boy, looking expectant but uncertain, pushed her gently away, she turned and walked on, saying nothing as if such business, for her, were common enough.

He came along panting at her side, trying to help her when he saw a root that she might trip over. He caught and held back the long swaying blades of thorn vine until she had passed beyond them. She led the way and he came breathing heavily behind her. Then they came out on a sunlit hillside, sloping softly into another one a little smaller. Beyond, they could see the rusted top of the old barn where the extra hay was stored.

The hill was sprinkled with small pink weeds. "Then you ain't saved?" he asked suddenly, stopping.

The girl smiled. It was the first time she had smiled at him at all. "In my economy," she said, "I'm saved and you are damned but I told you I didn't believe in God."

Nothing seemed to destroy the boy's look of admiration. He gazed at her now as if the fantastic animal at the zoo had put its paw through the bars and given him a loving poke. She thought he looked as if he wanted to kiss her again and she walked on before he had the chance.

"Ain't there somewheres we can sit down sometime?" he murmured, his voice softening toward the end of the sentence.

"In that barn," she said.

They made for it rapidly as if it might slide away like a train. It was a large two-story barn, cool and dark inside. The boy pointed up the ladder that led into the loft and said, "It's too bad we can't go up there."

"Why can't we?" she asked.

"Yer leg," he said reverently.

The girl gave him a contemptuous look and putting both hands on the ladder, she climbed it while he stood below, apparently awestruck. She pulled herself expertly through the opening and then looked down at him and said, "Well, come on if you're coming," and he began to climb the ladder, awkwardly bringing the suitcase with him.

"We won't need the Bible," she observed.

"You never can tell," he said, panting. After he had got into the loft, he was a few seconds catching his breath. She had sat down in a pile of straw. A wide sheath of sunlight, filled with dust particles, slanted over her. She lay back against a bale, her face turned away, looking out the front opening of the barn where hay was thrown from a wagon into the loft. The two pink-speckled hillsides lay back against a dark ridge of woods. The sky was cloudless and cold blue. The boy dropped down by her side and put one arm under her and the other over her and began methodically kissing her face, making little noises like a fish. He did not remove his hat but it was pushed far enough back not to interfere. When her glasses got in his way, he took them off of her and slipped them into his pocket.

The girl at first did not return any of the kisses but presently she began to and after she had put several on his cheek, she reached his lips and remained there, kissing him again and again as if she were trying to draw all the breath out of him. His breath was clear and sweet like a child's and the kisses were sticky like a child's. He mumbled about loving her and about knowing when he first seen her that he loved her, but the mumbling was like the sleepy fretting of a child being put to sleep by his mother. Her mind, throughout this, never stopped or lost itself for a second to her feelings. "You ain't said you loved me none," he whispered finally, pulling back from her. "You got to say that."

She looked away from him off into the hollow sky and then down at a black ridge and then down farther into what appeared to be two green swelling lakes. She didn't realize he had taken her glasses but this landscape could not seem exceptional to her for she seldom paid any close attention to her surroundings.

"You got to say it," he repeated. "You got to say you love me."

She was always careful how she committed herself. "In a sense," she began, "if you use the word loosely, you might say that. But it's not a word I use. I don't have illusions. I'm one of those people who see *through* to nothing."

The boy was frowning. "You got to say it. I said it and you got to say it," he said.

The girl looked at him almost tenderly. "You poor baby," she murmured. "It's just as well you don't understand," and she pulled him by the neck, face-down, against her. "We are all damned," she said, "but some of us have taken off our blindfolds and see that there's nothing to see. It's a kind of salvation."

The boy's astonished eyes looked blankly through the ends of her hair. "Okay," he almost whined, "but do you love me or don'tcher?"

"Yes," she said and added, "in a sense. But I must tell you something. There mustn't be anything dishonest between us." She lifted his head and looked him in the eye. "I am thirty years old," she said. "I have a number of degrees."

The boy's look was irritated but dogged. "I don't care," he said. "I don't care a thing about what all you done. I just want to know if you love me or don'tcher?" and he caught her to him and wildly planted her face with kisses until she said, "Yes, yes."

"Okay then," he said, letting her go. "Prove it."

She smiled, looking dreamily out on the shifty landscape. She had seduced him without even making up her mind to try. "How?" she asked, feeling that he should be delayed a little.

He leaned over and put his lips to her ear. "Show me where your wooden leg joins on," he whispered.

The girl uttered a sharp little cry and her face instantly drained of color. The obscenity of the suggestion was not what shocked her. As a child she had sometimes been subject to feelings of shame but education had removed the last traces of that as a good surgeon scrapes for cancer; she would no more have felt it over what he was asking than she would have believed in his Bible. But she was as sensitive about the artificial leg as a peacock about his tail. No one ever touched it but her. She took care of it as someone else would his soul, in private and almost with her own eyes turned away. "No," she said.

"I known it," he muttered, sitting up. "You're just playing me for a sucker."

"Oh no no!" she cried. "It joins on at the knee. Only at the knee. Why do you want to see it?"

The boy gave her a long penetrating look. "Because," he said, "it's what makes you different. You ain't like anybody else."

She sat staring at him. There was nothing about her face or her round freezing-blue eyes to indicate that this had moved her; but she felt as if her heart had stopped and left her mind to pump her blood. She decided that for the first time in her life she was face to face with real innocence. This boy, with an instinct that came from beyond wisdom, had touched the truth about her. When after a minute, she said in a hoarse high voice, "All right," it was like surrendering to him completely. It was like losing her own life and finding it again, miraculously, in his.

Very gently he began to roll the slack leg up. The artificial limb, in a white sock and brown flat shoe, was bound in a heavy material like canvas and ended in an ugly jointure where it was attached to the stump. The boy's face and his voice were entirely reverent as he uncovered it and said, "Now show me how to take it off and on."

She took it off for him and put it back on again and then he took it off himself, handling it as tenderly as if it were a real one. "See!" he said with a delighted child's face. "Now I can do it myself!"

"Put it back on," she said. She was thinking that she would run away with him and that every night he would take the leg off and every morning put it back on again. "Put it back on," she said.

"Not yet," he murmured, setting it on its foot out of her reach. "Leave it off for a while. You got me instead."

She gave a little cry of alarm but he pushed her down and began to kiss her again. Without the leg she felt entirely dependent on him. Her brain seemed to have stopped thinking altogether and to be about some other function that it was not very good at. Different expressions raced back and forth over her face. Every now and then the boy, his eyes like two steel spikes, would glance behind him where the leg stood. Finally she pushed him off and said, "Put it back on me now."

"Wait," he said. He leaned the other way and pulled the valise toward him and opened it. It had a pale blue spotted lining and there were only two Bibles in it. He took one of these out and opened the cover of it. It was hollow and contained a pocket flask of whiskey, a pack of cards, and a small blue box with printing on it. He laid these out in front of her one at a time in an evenly-spaced row, like one presenting offerings at the shrine of a goddess. He put the blue box in her hand. THIS PRODUCT TO BE USED ONLY FOR THE PREVENTION OF DISEASE, she read, and dropped it. The boy was unscrewing the top of the flask. He stopped and pointed, with a smile, to the deck of cards. It was not an ordinary deck but one with an obscene picture on the back of each card. "Take a swig," he said, offering her the bottle first. He held it in front of her, but like one mesmerized, she did not move.

Her voice when she spoke had an almost pleading sound. "Aren't you," she murmured, "aren't you just good country people?"

The boy cocked his head. He looked as if he were just beginning to understand that she might be trying to insult him. "Yeah," he said, curling his lip slightly, "but it ain't held me back none. I'm as good as you any day in the week."

"Give me my leg," she said.

He pushed it farther away with his foot. "Come on now, let's begin to have us a good time," he said coaxingly. "We ain't got to know one another good yet."

"Give me my leg!" she screamed and tried to lunge for it but he pushed her down easily.

"What's the matter with you all of a sudden?" he asked, frowning as he screwed the top on the flask and put it quickly back inside the Bible. "You just a while ago said you didn't believe in nothing. I thought you was some girl!"

Her face was almost purple. "You're a Christian!" she hissed. "You're a fine Christian! You're just like them all — say one thing and do another. You're a perfect Christian, you're . . ."

The boy's mouth was set angrily. "I hope you don't think," he said in a lofty indignant tone, "that I believe in that crap! I may sell Bibles but I know which end is up and I wasn't born yesterday and I know where I'm going!"

"Give me my leg!" she screeched. He jumped up so quickly that she barely saw him sweep the cards and the blue box into the Bible and throw the Bible into the valise. She saw him grab the leg and then she saw it for an instant slanted forlornly across the inside of the suitcase with a Bible at either side of its opposite ends. He slammed the lid shut and snatched up the valise and swung it down the hole and then stepped through himself.

When all of him had passed but his head, he turned and regarded her with a look that no longer had any admiration in it. "I've gotten a lot of interesting things," he said. "One time I got a woman's glass eye this way. And you needn't to think you'll catch me because Pointer ain't really my name. I use a different name at every house I call at and don't stay nowhere long. And I'll tell you another thing, Hulga," he said, using the name as if he didn't think much of it, "you ain't so smart. I been believing in nothing ever since I was born!" and then the toast-colored hat disappeared down the hole and the girl was left, sitting on the straw in the dusty sunlight. When she turned her churning face toward the opening, she saw his blue figure struggling successfully over the green speckled lake.

Mrs. Hopewell and Mrs. Freeman, who were in the back pasture, digging up onions, saw him emerge a little later from the woods and head across the meadow toward the highway. "Why, that looks like that nice dull young man that tried to sell me a Bible yesterday," Mrs. Hopewell said, squinting. "He must have been selling them to the Negroes back in there. He was so simple," she said, "but I guess the world would be better off if we were all that simple."

Mrs. Freeman's gaze drove forward and just touched him before he disappeared under the hill. Then she returned her attention to the evil-smelling onion shoot she was lifting from the ground. "Some can't be that simple," she said. "I know I never could."

A Good Man Is Hard to Find   1955

> The dragon is by the side of the road, watching those who pass. Beware
> lest he devour you. We go to the Father of Souls, but it is necessary to
> pass by the dragon.
>
> —St. Cyril of Jerusalem

The grandmother didn't want to go to Florida. She wanted to visit some of her connections in east Tennessee and she was seizing at every chance to change Bailey's mind. Bailey was the son she lived with, her only boy. He was sitting on the edge of his chair at the table, bent over the orange sports section of the *Journal*. "Now look here, Bailey," she said, "see here, read this," and she stood with one hand on her thin hip and the other rattling the newspaper at his bald head. "Here this fellow that calls himself The Misfit is aloose from the Federal Pen and headed toward Florida and you read here what it says he did to these people. Just you read it. I wouldn't take my children in any direction with a criminal like that aloose in it. I couldn't answer to my conscience if I did."

Bailey didn't look up from his reading so she wheeled around then and faced the children's mother, a young woman in slacks, whose face was as broad and innocent as a cabbage and was tied around with a green headkerchief that had two points on the top like a rabbit's ears. She was sitting on the sofa, feeding the baby his apricots out of a jar. "The children have been to Florida before," the old lady said. "You all ought to take them somewhere else for a change so they would see different parts of the world and be broad. They never have been to east Tennessee."

The children's mother didn't seem to hear her but the eight-year-old boy, John Wesley, a stocky child with glasses, said, "If you don't want to go to Florida, why dontcha stay at home?" He and the little girl, June Star, were reading the funny papers on the floor.

"She wouldn't stay at home to be queen for a day," June Star said without raising her yellow head.

"Yes and what would you do if this fellow, The Misfit, caught you?" the grandmother asked.

"I'd smack his face," John Wesley said.

"She wouldn't stay at home for a million bucks," June Star said. "Afraid she'd miss something. She has to go everywhere we go."

"All right, Miss," the grandmother said. "Just remember that the next time you want me to curl your hair."

June Star said her hair was naturally curly.

The next morning the grandmother was the first one in the car, ready to go. She had her big black valise that looked like the head of a hippopotamus in one corner, and underneath it she was hiding a basket with Pitty Sing, the cat, in it. She didn't intend for the cat to be left alone in the house for three days because he would miss her too much and she was afraid he might brush against one of the gas burners and accidentally asphyxiate himself. Her son, Bailey, didn't like to arrive at a motel with a cat.

She sat in the middle of the back seat with John Wesley and June Star on either side of her. Bailey and the children's mother and the baby sat in front and they left Atlanta at eight forty-five with the mileage on the car at 55890. The grandmother wrote this down because she thought it would be interesting to say how many miles they had been when they got back. It took them twenty minutes to reach the outskirts of the city.

The old lady settled herself comfortably, removing her white cotton gloves and putting them up with her purse on the shelf in front of the back window. The children's mother still had on slacks and still had her head tied up in a green kerchief, but the grandmother had on a navy blue straw sailor hat with a bunch of white violets on the brim and a navy blue dress with a small white dot in the print. Her collars and cuffs were white organdy trimmed with lace and at her neckline she had pinned a purple spray of cloth violets containing a sachet. In case of an accident, anyone seeing her dead on the highway would know at once that she was a lady.

She said she thought it was going to be a good day for driving, neither too hot nor too cold, and she cautioned Bailey that the speed limit was fifty-five miles an hour and that the patrolmen hid themselves behind billboards and small clumps of trees and sped out after you before you had a chance to slow down. She pointed out interesting details of the scenery: Stone Mountain; the blue granite that in some places came up to both sides of the highway; the brilliant red clay banks slightly streaked with purple; and the various crops that made rows of green lace-work on the ground. The trees were full of silver-white sunlight and the meanest of them sparkled. The children were reading comic magazines and their mother had gone back to sleep.

"Let's go through Georgia fast so we won't have to look at it much," John Wesley said.

"If I were a little boy," said the grandmother, "I wouldn't talk about my native state that way. Tennessee has the mountains and Georgia has the hills."

"Tennessee is just a hillbilly dumping ground," John Wesley said, "and Georgia is a lousy state too."

"You said it," June Star said.

"In my time," said the grandmother, folding her thin veined fingers, "children were more respectful of their native states and their parents and everything else. People did right then. Oh look at the cute little pickaninny!" she said and pointed to a Negro child standing in the door of a shack. "Wouldn't that make a picture, now?" she asked and they all turned and looked at the little Negro out of the back window. He waved.

"He didn't have any britches on," June Star said.

"He probably didn't have any," the grandmother explained. "Little niggers in the country don't have things like we do. If I could paint, I'd paint that picture," she said.

The children exchanged comic books.

The grandmother offered to hold the baby and the children's mother passed him over the front seat to her. She set him on her knee and bounced him and told him about the things they were passing. She rolled her eyes and screwed up her mouth and stuck her leathery thin face into his smooth bland one. Occasionally he gave her a faraway smile. They passed a large cotton field with five or six graves fenced in the middle of it, like a small island. "Look at the graveyard!" the grandmother said, pointing it out. "That was the old family burying ground. That belonged to the plantation."

"Where's the plantation?" John Wesley asked.

"Gone with the Wind," said the grandmother. "Ha. Ha."

When the children finished all the comic books they had brought, they opened the lunch and ate it. The grandmother ate a peanut butter sandwich and an olive and would not let the children throw the box and the paper napkins out the window. When there was nothing else to do they played a game by choosing a cloud and making the other two guess what shape it suggested. John Wesley took one the shape of a cow and June Star guessed a cow and John Wesley said, no, an automobile, and June Star said he didn't play fair, and they began to slap each other over the grandmother.

The grandmother said she would tell them a story if they would keep quiet. When she told a story, she rolled her eyes and waved her head and was very dramatic. She said once when she was a maiden lady she had been courted by a Mr. Edgar Atkins Teagarden from Jasper, Georgia. She said he was a very good-looking man and a gentleman and that he brought her a watermelon every Saturday afternoon with his initials cut in it, E. A. T. Well, one Saturday, she said, Mr. Teagarden brought the watermelon and there was nobody at home and he left it on the front porch and returned in his buggy to Jasper, but she never got the watermelon, she said, because a nigger boy ate it when he saw the initials, E. A. T.! This story tickled John Wesley's funny bone and he giggled and giggled but June Star didn't think it was any good. She said she wouldn't marry a man that just brought her a watermelon on Saturday. The grandmother said she would have done well to marry Mr. Teagarden because he was a gentleman and had bought Coca-Cola stock when it first came out and that he had died only a few years ago, a very wealthy man.

They stopped at The Tower for barbecued sandwiches. The Tower was a part stucco and part wood filling station and dance hall set in a clearing outside of Timothy. A fat man named Red Sammy Butts ran it and there were signs stuck here and there on the building and for miles up and down the high-way saying, TRY RED SAMMY'S FAMOUS BARBECUE. NONE LIKE FAMOUS RED SAMMY'S! RED SAM! THE FAT BOY WITH THE HAPPY LAUGH. A VETERAN! RED SAMMY'S YOUR MAN!

Red Sammy was lying on the bare ground outside The Tower with his head under a truck while a gray monkey about a foot high, chained to a small chinaberry tree, chattered nearby. The monkey sprang back into the tree and got on the highest limb as soon as he saw the children jump out of the car and run toward him.

Inside, The Tower was a long dark room with a counter at one end and tables at the other and dancing space in the middle. They all sat down at a board table next to the nickelodeon and Red Sam's wife, a tall burnt-brown woman with hair and eyes lighter than her skin, came and took their order. The children's mother put a dime in the machine and played "The Tennessee Waltz," and the grandmother said that tune always made her want to dance. She asked Bailey if he would like to dance but he only glared at her. He didn't have a naturally sunny disposition like she did and trips made him nervous. The grandmother's brown eyes were very bright. She swayed her head from side to side and pretended she was dancing in her chair. June Star said play something she could tap to so the children's mother put in another dime and played a fast number and June Star stepped out onto the dance floor and did her tap routine.

"Ain't she cute?" Red Sam's wife said, leaning over the counter. "Would you like to come be my little girl?"

"No I certainly wouldn't," June Star said. "I wouldn't live in a broken-down place like this for a million bucks!" and she ran back to the table.

"Ain't she cute?" the woman repeated, stretching her mouth politely.

"Aren't you ashamed?" hissed the grandmother.

Red Sam came in and told his wife to quit lounging on the counter and hurry up with these people's order. His khaki trousers reached just to his hip bones and his stomach hung over them like a sack of meal swaying under his shirt. He came over and sat down at a table nearby and let out a combination sigh and yodel. "You can't win," he said. "You can't win," and he wiped his sweating red face off with a gray handkerchief. "These days you don't know who to trust," he said. "Ain't that the truth?"

"People are certainly not nice like they used to be," said the grandmother.

"Two fellers come in here last week," Red Sammy said, "driving a Chrysler. It was a old beat-up car but it was a good one and these boys looked all right to me. Said they worked at the mill and you know I let them fellers charge the gas they bought? Now why did I do that?"

"Because you're a good man!" the grandmother said at once.

"Yes'm, I suppose so," Red Sam said as if he were struck with this answer.

His wife brought the orders, carrying the five plates all at once without a tray, two in each hand and one balanced on her arm. "It isn't a soul in this green world of God's that you can trust," she said. "And I don't count nobody out of that, not nobody," she repeated, looking at Red Sammy.

"Did you read about that criminal, The Misfit, that's escaped?" asked the grandmother.

"I wouldn't be a bit surprised if he didn't attack this place right here," said the woman. "If he hears about it being here, I wouldn't be none surprised to see him. If he hears it's two cent in the cash register, I wouldn't be a tall surprised if he. . . ."

"That'll do," Red Sam said. "Go bring these people their Co'-Colas," and the woman went off to get the rest of the order.

"A good man is hard to find," Red Sammy said. "Everything is getting terrible. I remember the day you could go off and leave your screen door unlatched. Not no more."

He and the grandmother discussed better times. The old lady said that in her opinion Europe was entirely to blame for the way things were now. She said the way Europe acted you would think we were made of money and Red Sam said it was no use talking about it, she was exactly right. The children ran outside into the white sunlight and looked at the monkey in the lacy chinaberry tree. He was busy catching fleas on himself and biting each one carefully between his teeth as if it were a delicacy.

They drove off again into the hot afternoon. The grandmother took cat naps and woke up every few minutes with her own snoring. Outside of Toombsboro she woke up and recalled an old plantation that she had visited in this neighborhood once when she was a young lady. She said the house had six white columns across the front and that there was an avenue of oaks leading up to it and two little wooden trellis arbors on either side in front where you sat down with your suitor after a stroll in the garden. She recalled exactly which road to turn off to get to it. She knew that Bailey would not be willing to lose any time looking at an old house, but the more she talked about it, the more she wanted to see it once again and find out if the little twin arbors were still stand-ing. "There was a secret panel in this house," she said craftily, not telling the truth but wishing that she were, "and the story went that all the family silver was hidden in it when Sherman came through but it was never found. . . ."

"Hey!" John Wesley said. "Let's go see it! We'll find it! We'll poke all the woodwork and find it! Who lives there? Where do you turn off at? Hey Pop, can't we turn off there?"

"We never have seen a house with a secret panel!" June Star shrieked. "Let's go to the house with the secret panel! Hey Pop, can't we go see the house with the secret panel!"

"It's not far from here, I know," the grandmother said. "It won't take over twenty minutes."

Bailey was looking straight ahead. His jaw was as rigid as a horseshoe. "No," he said.

The children began to yell and scream that they wanted to see the house with the secret panel. John Wesley kicked the back of the front seat and June Star hung over her mother's shoulder and whined desperately into her ear that they never had any fun even on their vacation, that they could never do what THEY wanted to do. The baby began to scream and John Wesley kicked the back of the seat so hard that his father could feel the blows in his kidney.

"All right!" he shouted and drew the car to a stop at the side of the road. "Will you all shut up? Will you all just shut up for one second? If you don't shut up, we won't go anywhere."

"It would be very educational for them," the grandmother murmured.

"All right," Bailey said, "but get this: this is the only time we're going to stop for anything like this. This is the one and only time."

"The dirt road that you have to turn down is about a mile back," the grandmother directed. "I marked it when we passed."

"A dirt road," Bailey groaned.

After they had turned around and were headed toward the dirt road, the grandmother recalled other points about the house, the beautiful glass over the front doorway and the candle-lamp in the hall. John Wesley said that the secret panel was probably in the fireplace.

"You can't go inside this house," Bailey said. "You don't know who lives there."

"While you all talk to the people in front, I'll run around behind and get in a window," John Wesley suggested.

"We'll all stay in the car," his mother said.

They turned onto the dirt road and the car raced roughly along in a swirl of pink dust. The grandmother recalled the times when there were no paved roads and thirty miles was a day's journey. The dirt road was hilly and there were sudden washes in it and sharp curves on dangerous embankments. All at once they would be on a hill, looking down over the blue tops of trees for miles around, then the next minute, they would be in a red depression with the dust-coated trees looking down on them.

"This place had better turn up in a minute," Bailey said, "or I'm going to turn around."

The road looked as if no one had traveled on it for months.

"It's not much farther," the grandmother said and just as she said it, a horrible thought came to her. The thought was so embarrassing that she turned red in the face and her eyes dilated and her feet jumped up, upsetting her valise in the corner. The instant the valise moved, the newspaper top she had over the basket under it rose with a snarl and Pitty Sing, the cat, sprang onto Bailey's shoulder.

The children were thrown to the floor and their mother, clutching the baby, was thrown out the door onto the ground, the old lady was thrown into the front seat. The car turned over once and landed right-side-up in a gulch off the side of the road. Bailey remained in the driver's seat with the cat gray-striped with a broad white face and an orange nose clinging to his neck like a caterpillar.

As soon as the children saw they could move their arms and legs, they scrambled out of the car, shouting, "We've had an ACCIDENT!" The grandmother was curled up under the dashboard, hoping she was injured so that Bailey's wrath would not come down on her all at once. The horrible thought she had before the accident was that the house she had remembered so vividly was not in Georgia but in Tennessee.

Bailey removed the cat from his neck with both hands and flung it out the window against the side of a pine tree. Then he got out of the car and started looking for the children's mother. She was sitting against the side of the red gutted ditch, holding the screaming baby, but she only had a cut down her face and a broken shoulder. "We've had an ACCIDENT!" the children screamed in a frenzy of delight.

"But nobody's killed," June Star said with disappointment as the grandmother limped out of the car, her hat still pinned to her head but the broken front brim standing up at a jaunty angle and the violet spray hanging off the side. They all sat down in the ditch, except the children, to recover from the shock. They were all shaking.

"Maybe a car will come along," said the children's mother hoarsely.

"I believe I have injured an organ," said the grandmother, pressing her side, but no one answered her. Bailey's teeth were clattering. He had on a yellow sport shirt with bright blue parrots designed in it and his face was as yellow as the shirt. The grandmother decided that she would not mention that the house was in Tennessee.

The road was about ten feet above and they could only see the tops of the trees on the other side of it. Behind the ditch they were sitting in there were more woods, tall and dark and deep. In a few minutes they saw a car some distance away on top of a hill, coming slowly as if the occupants were watching them. The grandmother stood up and waved both arms dramatically to attract their attention. The car continued to come on slowly, disappeared around a bend and appeared again, moving even slower, on top of the hill they had gone over. It was a big black battered hearse-like automobile. There were three men in it.

It came to a stop just over them and for some minutes, the driver looked down with a steady expressionless gaze to where they were sitting, and didn't speak. Then he turned his head and muttered something to the other two and they got out. One was a fat boy in black trousers and a red sweat shirt with a silver stallion embossed on the front of it. He moved around on the right side of them and stood staring, his mouth partly open in a kind of loose grin. The other had on khaki pants and a blue striped coat and a gray hat pulled very low, hiding most of his face. He came around slowly on the left side. Neither spoke.

The driver got out of the car and stood by the side of it, looking down at them. He was an older man than the other two. His hair was just beginning to gray and he wore silver-rimmed spectacles that gave him a scholarly look. He had a long creased face and didn't have on any shirt or undershirt. He had on blue jeans that were too tight for him and was holding a black hat and a gun. The two boys also had guns.

"We've had an ACCIDENT!" the children screamed.

The grandmother had the peculiar feeling that the bespectacled man was someone she knew. His face was as familiar to her as if she had known him all her life but she could not recall who he was. He moved away from the car and began to come down the embankment, placing his feet carefully so that he wouldn't slip. He had on tan and white shoes and no socks, and his ankles were red and thin. "Good afternoon," he said. "I see you all had you a little spill."

"We turned over twice!" said the grandmother.

"Oncet," he corrected. "We seen it happen. Try their car and see will it run, Hiram," he said quietly to the boy with the gray hat.

"What you got that gun for?" John Wesley asked. "Whatcha gonna do with that gun?"

"Lady," the man said to the children's mother, "would you mind calling them children to sit down by you? Children make me nervous. I want all you all to sit down right together there where you're at."

"What are you telling US what to do for?" June Star asked.

Behind them the line of woods gaped like a dark open mouth. "Come here," said the mother.

"Look here now," Bailey said suddenly, "we're in a predicament! We're in . . ."

The grandmother shrieked. She scrambled to her feet and stood staring. "You're The Misfit!" she said. "I recognized you at once!"

"Yes'm," the man said, smiling slightly as if he were pleased in spite of himself to be known, "but it would have been better for all of you, lady, if you hadn't of reckernized me."

Bailey turned his head sharply and said something to his mother that shocked even the children. The old lady began to cry and The Misfit reddened.

"Lady," he said, "don't you get upset. Sometimes a man says things he don't mean. I don't reckon he meant to talk to you thataway."

"You wouldn't shoot a lady, would you?" the grandmother said and removed a clean handkerchief from her cuff and began to slap at her eyes with it.

The Misfit pointed the toe of his shoe into the ground and made a little hole and then covered it up again. "I would hate to have to," he said.

"Listen," the grandmother almost screamed, "I know you're a good man. You don't look a bit like you have common blood. I know you must come from nice people!"

"Yes mam," he said, "finest people in the world." When he smiled he showed a row of strong white teeth. "God never made a finer woman than my mother and my daddy's heart was pure gold," he said. The boy with the red sweat shirt had come around behind them and was standing with his gun at his hip. The Misfit squatted down on the ground. "Watch them children, Bobby Lee," he said. "You know they make me nervous." He looked at the six of them huddled together in front of him and he seemed to be embarrassed as if he couldn't think of anything to say. "Ain't a cloud in the sky," he remarked, looking up at it. "Don't see no sun but don't see no cloud neither."

"Yes, it's a beautiful day," said the grandmother. "Listen," she said, "you shouldn't call yourself The Misfit because I know you're a good man at heart. I can just look at you and tell."

"Hush!" Bailey yelled. "Hush! Everybody shut up and let me handle this!" He was squatting in the position of a runner about to sprint forward but he didn't move.

"I pre-chate that, lady," The Misfit said and drew a little circle in the ground with the butt of his gun.

"It'll take a half a hour to fix this here car," Hiram called, looking over the raised hood of it.

"Well, first you and Bobby Lee get him and that little boy to step over yonder with you," The Misfit said, pointing to Bailey and John Wesley. "The boys want to ast you something," he said to Bailey. "Would you mind stepping back in them woods there with them?"

"Listen," Bailey began, "we're in a terrible predicament! Nobody realizes what this is," and his voice cracked. His eyes were as blue and intense as the parrots in his shirt and he remained perfectly still.

The grandmother reached up to adjust her hat brim as if she were going to the woods with him but it came off in her hand. She stood staring at it and after a second she let it fall to the ground. Hiram pulled Bailey up by the arm as if he were assisting an old man. John Wesley caught hold of his father's hand and Bobby Lee followed. They went off toward the woods and just as they reached the dark edge, Bailey turned and supporting himself against a gray naked pine trunk, he shouted, "I'll be back in a minute, Mamma, wait on me!"

"Come back this instant!" his mother shrilled but they all disappeared into the woods.

"Bailey Boy!" the grandmother called in a tragic voice but she found she was looking at The Misfit squatting on the ground in front of her. "I just know you're a good man," she said desperately. "You're not a bit common!"

"Nome, I ain't a good man," The Misfit said after a second as if he had considered her statement carefully, "but I ain't the worst in the world neither. My daddy said I was a different breed of dog from my brothers and sisters. 'You know,' Daddy said, 'it's some that can live their whole life out without asking about it and it's others has to know why it is, and this boy is one of the latters. He's going to be into everything!'" He put on his black hat and looked up suddenly and then away deep into the woods as if he were embarrassed again. "I'm sorry I don't have on a shirt before you ladies," he said, hunching his shoulders slightly. "We buried our clothes that we had on when we escaped and we're just making do until we can get better. We borrowed these from some folks we met," he explained.

"That's perfectly all right," the grandmother said. "Maybe Bailey has an extra shirt in his suitcase."

"I'll look and see terrectly," The Misfit said.

"Where are they taking him?" the children's mother screamed.

"Daddy was a card himself," The Misfit said. "You couldn't put anything over on him. He never got in trouble with the Authorities though. Just had the knack of handling them."

"You could be honest too if you'd only try," said the grandmother. "Think how wonderful it would be to settle down and live a comfortable life and not have to think about somebody chasing you all the time."

The Misfit kept scratching in the ground with the butt of his gun as if he were thinking about it. "Yes'm, somebody is always after you," he murmured.

The grandmother noticed how thin his shoulder blades were just behind his hat because she was standing up looking down at him. "Do you ever pray?" she asked.

He shook his head. All she saw was the black hat wiggle between his shoulder blades. "Nome," he said.

There was a pistol shot from the woods, followed closely by another. Then silence. The old lady's head jerked around. She could hear the wind move through the tree tops like a long satisfied insuck of breath. "Bailey Boy!" she called.

"I was a gospel singer for a while," The Misfit said. "I been most everything. Been in the arm service, both land and sea, at home and abroad, been twict married, been an undertaker, been with the railroads, plowed Mother Earth, been in a tornado, seen a man burnt alive oncet," and he looked up at the children's mother and the little girl who were sitting close together, their faces white and their eyes glassy; "I even seen a woman flogged," he said.

"Pray, pray," the grandmother began, "pray, pray. . . ."

"I never was a bad boy that I remember of," The Misfit said in an almost dreamy voice, "but somewheres along the line I done something wrong and got sent to the penitentiary. I was buried alive," and he looked up and held her attention to him by a steady stare.

"That's when you should have started to pray," she said. "What did you do to get sent to the penitentiary, that first time?"

"Turn to the right, it was a wall," The Misfit said, looking up again at the cloudless sky. "Turn to the left, it was a wall. Look up it was a ceiling, look down it was a floor. I forgot what I done, lady. I set there and set there, trying to remember what it was I done and I ain't recalled it to this day. Oncet in a while, I would think it was coming to me, but it never come."

"Maybe they put you in by mistake," the old lady said vaguely.

"Nome," he said. "It wasn't no mistake. They had the papers on me."

"You must have stolen something," she said.

The Misfit sneered slightly. "Nobody had nothing I wanted," he said. "It was a head-doctor at the penitentiary said what I had done was kill my daddy but I known that for a lie. My daddy died in nineteen ought nineteen of the epidemic flu and I never had a thing to do with it. He was buried in the Mount Hopewell Baptist churchyard and you can see for yourself."

"If you would pray," the old lady said, "Jesus would help you."

"That's right," The Misfit said.

"Well then, why don't you pray?" she asked trembling with delight suddenly.

"I don't want no hep," he said. "I'm doing all right by myself."

Bobby Lee and Hiram came ambling back from the woods. Bobby Lee was dragging a yellow shirt with bright blue parrots in it.

"Throw me that shirt, Bobby Lee," The Misfit said. The shirt came flying at him and landed on his shoulder and he put it on. The grandmother couldn't name what the shirt reminded her of. "No, lady," The Misfit said while he was buttoning it up, "I found out the crime don't matter. You can do one thing or you can do another, kill a man or take a tire off his car, because sooner or later you're going to forget what it was you done and just be punished for it."

The children's mother had begun to make heaving noises as if she couldn't get her breath. "Lady," he asked, "would you and that little girl like to step off yonder with Bobby Lee and Hiram and join your husband?"

"Yes, thank you," the mother said faintly. Her left arm dangled helplessly and she was holding the baby, who had gone to sleep, in the other. "Hep that lady up, Hiram," The Misfit said as she struggled to climb out of the ditch, "and Bobby Lee, you hold onto that little girl's hand."

"I don't want to hold hands with him," June Star said. "He reminds me of a pig."

The fat boy blushed and laughed and caught her by the arm and pulled her off into the woods after Hiram and her mother.

Alone with The Misfit, the grandmother found that she had lost her voice. There was not a cloud in the sky nor any sun. There was nothing around her but woods. She wanted to tell him that he must pray. She opened and closed her mouth several times before anything came out. Finally she found herself saying, "Jesus, Jesus," meaning, Jesus will help you, but the way she was saying it, it sounded as if she might be cursing.

"Yes'm," The Misfit said as if he agreed. "Jesus thrown everything off balance. It was the same case with Him as with me except He hadn't committed any crime and they could prove I had committed one because they had the papers on me. Of course," he said, "they never shown me my papers. That's why I sign myself now. I said long ago, you get your signature and sign everything you do and keep a copy of it. Then you'll know what you done and you can hold up the crime to the punishment and see do they match and in the end you'll have something to prove you ain't been treated right. I call myself The Misfit," he said, "because I can't make what all I done wrong fit what all I gone through in punishment."

There was a piercing scream from the woods, followed closely by a pistol report. "Does it seem right to you, lady, that one is punished a heap and another ain't punished at all?"

"Jesus!" the old lady cried. "You've got good blood! I know you wouldn't shoot a lady! I know you come from nice people! Pray! Jesus, you ought not to shoot a lady. I'll give you all the money I've got!"

"Lady," The Misfit said, looking beyond her far into the woods, "there never was a body that give the undertaker a tip."

There were two more pistol reports and the grandmother raised her head like a parched old turkey hen crying for water and called, "Bailey Boy, Bailey Boy!" as if her heart would break.

"Jesus was the only One that ever raised the dead," The Misfit continued, "and He shouldn't have done it. He thrown everything off balance. If He did what He said, then it's nothing for you to do but throw away everything and follow Him, and if He didn't, then it's nothing for you to do but enjoy the few minutes you got left the best you can by killing somebody or burning down his house or doing some other meanness to him. No pleasure but meanness," he said and his voice had become almost a snarl.

"Maybe He didn't raise the dead," the old lady mumbled, not knowing what she was saying and feeling so dizzy that she sank down in the ditch with her legs twisted under her.

"I wasn't there so I can't say He didn't," The Misfit said. "I wisht I had of been there," he said, hitting the ground with his fist. "It ain't right I wasn't there because if I had of been there I would of known. Listen lady," he said in a high voice, "if I had of been there I would of known and I wouldn't be like I am now." His voice seemed about to crack and the grandmother's head cleared for an instant. She saw the man's face twisted close to her own as if he were going to cry and she murmured, "Why you're one of my babies. You're one of my own children!" She reached out and touched him on the shoulder. The Misfit sprang back as if a snake had bitten him and shot her three times through the chest. Then he put his gun down on the ground and took off his glasses and began to clean them.

Hiram and Bobby Lee returned from the woods and stood over the ditch, looking down at the grandmother who half sat and half lay in a puddle of blood with her legs crossed under her like a child's and her face smiling up at the cloudless sky.

Without his glasses, The Misfit's eyes were red-rimmed and pale and defenseless-looking. "Take her off and throw her where you thrown the others," he said, picking up the cat that was rubbing itself against his leg.

"She was a talker, wasn't she?" Bobby Lee said, sliding down the ditch with a yodel.

"She would of been a good woman," The Misfit said, "if it had been somebody there to shoot her every minute of her life."

"Some fun!" Bobby Lee said.

"Shut up, Bobby Lee," The Misfit said. "It's no real pleasure in life."

TILLIE OLSEN

*Tillie Olsen (b. 1913) was born in Omaha, Nebraska, the daughter of polit-
ical refugees from the Russian Czarist repression after the revolution of 1905. Her
father was a farmer, packing-house worker, house painter, and jack-of-all-
trades; her mother was a factory worker. At the age of sixteen Olsen dropped out of
high school to help support her family during the Depression. She was a member of
the Young Communist League, involved in the Warehouse Union's labor disputes
in Kansas City. At age nineteen she began her first novel,* Yonnondio. *Four chapters of this book about a poverty-stricken working-class family were completed in
the next four years, during which time she married, gave birth to her first child,
and was left with the baby by her husband because, as she later wrote in her autobiographical story "I Stand Here Ironing," he "could no longer endure sharing
want" with them. In 1934 a section of the first chapter of her novel was published
in* Partisan Review, *but she abandoned the unfinished book in 1937. The year
before she had married Jack Olsen, with whom she had three more children; raising
the children and working for political causes took up all her time. In the 1940s she
was a factory worker; in the 1950s, a secretary. It was not until 1953, when her
youngest daughter started school, that she was able to begin writing again.*

*That year Olsen enrolled in a class in fiction writing at San Francisco State
College. She was awarded a Stanford University creative writing fellowship for
1955 and 1956. During the 1950s she wrote the four stories collected in* Tell Me a
Riddle, *which established her reputation when the book was published as a paperback in 1961. Identified as a champion of the reemerging feminist movement,
Olsen wrote a biographical introduction to Rebecca Harding Davis's nineteenth-
century proletarian story,* Life in the Iron Mills, *published by the Feminist Press in
1972. Two years later, after several grants and creative writing fellowships, she published the still-unfinished* Yonnondio. Silences, *a collection of essays exploring the
different circumstances that obstruct or silence literary creation, appeared in 1978.*

As the Canadian author Margaret Atwood has understood about Olsen,

> *Few writers have gained such wide respect on such a small body of published
> work. . . . Among women writers in the United States, "respect" is too pale
> a word: "reverence" is more like it. This is presumably because women writ-
> ers, even more than their male counterparts, recognize what a heroic feat it
> is to have held down a job, raised four children, and still somehow managed
> to become and to remain a writer.*

*A radical feminist, Olsen has said that she felt no personal guilt as a single par-
ent over her daughter's predicament, as described in her confessional narrative
"I Stand Here Ironing," since "guilt is a word used far too sloppily, to cover up
harmful situations in society that must be changed." Her four stories have appeared in more than fifty anthologies and have been translated into many languages. In 1994 she received the Rea Award for the Short Story, a literary prize
that honors a living American author who has made "a significant contribution to
the short story as an art form."*

WEB   *Research Tillie Olsen and answer questions about her work at
bedfordstmartins.com/charters/litwriters.*

I Stand Here Ironing 1961

I stand here ironing, and what you asked me moves tormented back and forth with the iron.

"I wish you would manage the time to come in and talk with me about your daughter. I'm sure you can help me understand her. She's a youngster who needs help and whom I'm deeply interested in helping."

"Who needs help." . . . Even if I came, what good would it do? You think because I am her mother I have a key, or that in some way you could use me as a key? She has lived for nineteen years. There is all that life that has happened outside of me, beyond me.

And when is there time to remember, to sift, to weigh, to estimate, to total? I will start and there will be an interruption and I will have to gather it all together again. Or I will become engulfed with all I did or did not do, with what should have been and what cannot be helped.

She was a beautiful baby. The first and only one of our five that was beautiful at birth. You do not guess how new and uneasy her tenancy in her now-loveliness. You did not know her all those years she was thought homely, or see her poring over her baby pictures, making me tell her over and over how beautiful she had been—and would be, I would tell her—and was now, to the seeing eye. But the seeing eyes were few or nonexistent. Including mine.

I nursed her. They feel that's important nowadays, I nursed all the children, but with her, with all the fierce rigidity of first motherhood, I did like the books then said. Though her cries battered me to trembling and my breasts ached with swollenness, I waited till the clock decreed.

Why do I put that first? I do not even know if it matters, or if it explains anything.

She was a beautiful baby. She blew shining bubbles of sound. She loved motion, loved light, loved color and music and textures. She would lie on the floor in her blue overalls patting the surface so hard in ecstasy her hands and feet would blur. She was a miracle to me, but when she was eight months old I had to leave her daytimes with the woman downstairs to whom she was no miracle at all, for I worked or looked for work and for Emily's father, who "could no longer endure" (he wrote in his good-bye note) "sharing want with us."

I was nineteen. It was the pre-relief, pre-WPA world of the depression. I would start running as soon as I got off the streetcar, running up the stairs, the place smelling sour, and awake or asleep to startle awake, when she saw me she would break into a clogged weeping that could not be comforted, a weeping I can hear yet.

After a while I found a job hashing at night so I could be with her days, and it was better. But it came to where I had to bring her to his family and leave her.

It took a long time to raise the money for her fare back. Then she got chicken pox and I had to wait longer. When she finally came, I hardly knew her, walking quick and nervous like her father, looking like her father, thin, and dressed in a shoddy red that yellowed her skin and glared at the pockmarks. All the baby loveliness gone.

She was two. Old enough for nursery school they said, and I did not know then what I know now—the fatigue of the long day, and the lacerations of group life in the kinds of nurseries that are only parking places for children.

Except that it would have made no difference if I had known. It was the only place there was. It was the only way we could be together, the only way I could hold a job.

And even without knowing, I knew. I knew the teacher that was evil because all these years it has curdled into my memory, the little boy hunched in the corner, her rasp, "why aren't you outside, because Alvin hits you? that's no reason, go out, scaredy." I knew Emily hated it even if she did not clutch and implore "don't go Mommy" like the other children, mornings.

She always had a reason why we should stay home. Momma, you look sick. Momma, I feel sick. Momma, the teachers aren't there today, they're sick. Momma, we can't go, there was a fire there last night. Momma, it's a holiday today, no school, they told me.

But never a direct protest, never rebellion. I think of our others in their three-, four-year-oldness—the explosions, the tempers, the denunciations, the demands—and I feel suddenly ill. I put the iron down. What in me demanded that goodness in her? And what was the cost, the cost to her of such goodness?

The old man living in the back once said in his gentle way: "You should smile at Emily more when you look at her." What *was* in my face when I looked at her? I loved her. There were all the acts of love.

It was only with the others I remembered what he said, and it was the face of joy, and not of care or tightness or worry I turned to them—too late for Emily. She does not smile easily, let alone almost always as her brothers and sisters do. Her face is closed and sombre, but when she wants, how fluid. You must have seen it in her pantomimes, you spoke of her rare gift for comedy on the stage that rouses laughter out of the audience so dear they applaud and applaud and do not want to let her go.

Where does it come from, that comedy? There was none of it in her when she came back to me that second time, after I had to send her away again. She had a new daddy now to learn to love, and I think perhaps it was a better time.

Except when we left her alone nights, telling ourselves she was old enough.

"Can't you go some other time, Mommy, like tomorrow?" she would ask. "Will it be just a little while you'll be gone? Do you promise?"

The time we came back, the front door open, the clock on the floor in the hall. She rigid awake. "It wasn't just a little while. I didn't cry. Three times I called you, just three times, and then I ran downstairs to open the door so you could come faster. The clock talked loud. I threw it away, it scared me what it talked."

She said the clock talked loud again that night I went to the hospital to have Susan. She was delirious with the fever that comes before red measles, but she was fully conscious all the week I was gone and the week after we were home when she could not come near the new baby or me.

She did not get well. She stayed skeleton thin, not wanting to eat, and night after night she had nightmares. She would call for me, and I would rouse from exhaustion to sleepily call back: "You're all right, darling, go to sleep, it's just a dream," and if she still called, in a sterner voice, "now go to sleep, Emily, there's nothing to hurt you." Twice, only twice, when I had to get up for Susan anyhow, I went in to sit with her.

Now when it is too late (as if she would let me hold her and comfort her like I do the others) I get up and go to her at once at her moan or restless stirring. "Are you awake, Emily? Can I get you something?" And the answer is always the same: "No, I'm all right, go back to sleep, Mother."

They persuaded me at the clinic to send her away to a convalescent home in the country where "she can have the kind of food and care you can't manage for her, and you'll be free to concentrate on the new baby." They still send children to that place. I see pictures on the society page of sleek young women planning affairs to raise money for it, or dancing at the affairs, or decorating Easter eggs or filling Christmas stockings for the children.

They never have a picture of the children so I do not know if the girls still wear those gigantic red bows and the ravaged looks on the every other Sunday when parents can come to visit "unless otherwise notified"—as we were notified the first six weeks.

Oh it is a handsome place, green lawns and tall trees and fluted flower beds. High up on the balconies of each cottage the children stand, the girls in their red bows and white dresses, the boys in white suits and giant red ties. The parents stand below shrieking up to be heard and the children shriek down to be heard, and between them the invisible wall "Not To Be Contaminated by Parental Germs or Physical Affection."

There was a tiny girl who always stood hand in hand with Emily. Her parents never came. One visit she was gone. "They moved her to Rose Cottage," Emily shouted in explanation. "They don't like you to love anybody here."

She wrote once a week, the labored writing of a seven-year-old. "I am fine. How is the baby. If I write my leter nicly I will have a star. Love." There never was a star. We wrote every other day, letters she could never hold or keep but only hear read—once. "We simply do not have room for children to keep any personal possessions," they patiently explained when we pieced one Sunday's shrieking together to plead how much it would mean to Emily, who loved so to keep things, to be allowed to keep her letters and cards.

Each visit she looked frailer. "She isn't eating," they told us.

(They had runny eggs for breakfast or mush with lumps, Emily said later, I'd hold it in my mouth and not swallow. Nothing ever tasted good, just when they had chicken.)

It took us eight months to get her released home, and only the fact that she gained back so little of her seven lost pounds convinced the social worker.

I used to try to hold and love her after she came back, but her body would stay stiff, and after a while she'd push away. She ate little. Food sickened her, and I think much of life too. Oh she had physical lightness and brightness, twinkling by on skates, bouncing like a ball up and down up and down over the jump rope, skimming over the hill; but these were momentary.

She fretted about her appearance, thin and dark and foreign-looking at a time when every little girl was supposed to look or thought she should look a chubby blonde replica of Shirley Temple. The doorbell sometimes rang for her, but no one seemed to come and play in the house or to be a best friend. Maybe because we moved so much.

There was a boy she loved painfully through two school semesters. Months later she told me how she had taken pennies from my purse to buy him candy. "Licorice was his favorite and I brought him some every day, but he still liked Jennifer better'n me. Why, Mommy?" The kind of question for which there is no answer.

School was a worry for her. She was not glib or quick in a world where glibness and quickness were easily confused with ability to learn. To her over-worked and exasperated teachers she was an overconscientious "slow learner" who kept trying to catch up and was absent entirely too often.

I let her be absent, though sometimes the illness was imaginary. How different from my now-strictness about attendance with the others. I wasn't working. We had a new baby. I was home anyhow. Sometimes, after Susan grew old enough, I would keep her home from school, too, to have them all together.

Mostly Emily had asthma, and her breathing, harsh and labored, would fill the house with a curiously tranquil sound. I would bring the two old dresser mirrors and her boxes of collections to her bed. She would select beads and single earrings, bottle tops and shells, dried flowers and pebbles, old postcards and scraps, all sorts of oddments; then she and Susan would play Kingdom, setting up landscapes and furniture, peopling them with action.

Those were the only times of peaceful companionship between her and Susan. I have edged away from it, that poisonous feeling between them, that terrible balancing of hurts and needs I had to do between the two, and did so badly, those earlier years.

Oh there were conflicts between the others too, each one human, need-ing, demanding, hurting, taking—but only between Emily and Susan, no, Emily toward Susan that corroding resentment. It seems so obvious on the sur-face, yet it is not obvious; Susan, the second child, Susan, golden- and curly-haired and chubby, quick and articulate and assured, everything in appearance and manner Emily was not; Susan, not able to resist Emily's precious things, losing or sometimes clumsily breaking them; Susan telling jokes and riddles to company for applause while Emily sat silent (to say to me later: that was *my* riddle, Mother, I told it to Susan); Susan, who for all the five years' difference in age was just a year behind Emily in developing physically.

I am glad for that slow physical development that widened the difference between her and her contemporaries, though she suffered over it. She was too vulnerable for that terrible world of youthful competition, of preening and parading, of constant measuring of yourself against every other, of envy,

"If I had that copper hair," "If I had that skin. . . ." She tormented herself enough about not looking like the others, there was enough of unsureness, the having to be conscious of words before you speak, the constant caring—what are they thinking of me? without having it all magnified by the merciless physical drives.

Ronnie is calling. He is wet and I change him. It is rare there is such a cry now. That time of motherhood is almost behind me when the ear is not one's own but must always be racked and listening for the child cry, the child call. We sit for a while and I hold him, looking out over the city spread in charcoal with its soft aisles of light. "*Shoogily,*" he breathes and curls closer. I carry him back to bed, asleep. *Shoogily.* A funny word, a family word, inherited from Emily, invented by her to say: *comfort.*

In this and other ways she leaves her seal, I say aloud. And startle at my saying it. What do I mean? What did I start to gather together, to try and make coherent? I was at the terrible, growing years. War years. I do not remember them well. I was working, there were four smaller ones now, there was not time for her. She had to help be a mother, and housekeeper, and shopper. She had to get her seal. Mornings of crisis and near hysteria trying to get lunches packed, hair combed, coats and shoes found, everyone to school or Child Care on time, the baby ready for transportation. And always the paper scribbled on by a smaller one, the book looked at by Susan then mislaid, the homework not done. Running out to that huge school where she was one, she was lost, she was a drop; suffering over the unpreparedness, stammering and unsure in her classes.

There was so little time left at night after the kids were bedded down. She would struggle over books, always eating (it was in those years she developed her enormous appetite that is legendary in our family) and I would be ironing, or preparing food for the next day, or writing V-mail to Bill, or tending the baby. Sometimes, to make me laugh, or out of her despair, she would imitate happenings or types at school.

I think I said once: "Why don't you do something like this in the school amateur show?" One morning she phoned me at work, hardly understandable through the weeping: "Mother, I did it. I won, I won; they gave me first prize; they clapped and clapped and wouldn't let me go."

Now suddenly she was Somebody, and as imprisoned in her difference as she had been in anonymity.

She began to be asked to perform at other high schools, even in colleges, then at city and statewide affairs. The first one we went to, I only recognized her that first moment when thin, shy, she almost drowned herself into the curtains. Then: Was this Emily? The control, the command, the convulsing and deadly clowning, the spell, then the roaring, stamping audience, unwilling to let this rare and precious laughter out of their lives.

Afterwards: You ought to do something about her with a gift like that— but without money or knowing how, what does one do? We have left it all to her, and the gift has so often eddied inside, clogged and clotted, as been used and growing.

She is coming. She runs up the stairs two at a time with her light graceful step, and I know she is happy tonight. Whatever it was that occasioned your call did not happen today.

"Aren't you ever going to finish the ironing, Mother? Whistler painted his mother in a rocker. I'd have to paint mine standing over an ironing board." This is one of her communicative nights and she tells me everything and nothing as she fixes herself a plate of food out of the icebox.

She is so lovely. Why did you want me to come in at all? Why were you concerned? She will find her way.

She starts up the stairs to bed. "Don't get me up with the rest in the morning." "But I thought you were having midterms." "Oh, those," she comes back in, kisses me, and says quite lightly, "in a couple of years when we'll all be atom-dead they won't matter a bit."

She has said it before. She *believes* it. But because I have been dredging the past, and all that compounds a human being is so heavy and meaningful in me, I cannot endure it tonight.

I will never total it all. I will never come in to say: She was a child seldom smiled at. Her father left me before she was a year old. I had to work her first six years when there was work, or I sent her home and to his relatives. There were years she had care she hated. She was dark and thin and foreign-looking in a world where the prestige went to blondeness and curly hair and dimples, she was slow where glibness was prized. She was a child of anxious, not proud, love. We were poor and could not afford for her the soil of easy growth. I was a young mother, I was a distracted mother. There were other children pushing up, demanding. Her younger sister seemed all that she was not. There were years she did not want me to touch her. She kept too much in herself, her life was such she had to keep too much in herself. My wisdom came too late. She has much to her and probably little will come of it. She is a child of her age, of depression, of war, of fear.

Let her be. So all that is in her will not bloom—but in how many does it? There is still enough left to live by. Only help her to know—help make it so there is cause for her to know—that she is more than this dress on the ironing board, helpless before the iron.

GRACE PALEY

Grace Paley (b. 1922) was born in New York City. She studied at Hunter College and New York University, and in 1942 she married for the first time. She had two children from that marriage. In the 1950s she turned from writing poetry to short fiction. Her first book of stories, The Little Disturbances of Man *(1959), established her reputation as a writer with a remarkably supple gift for language. As Susan Sontag has noted, "She is that rare kind of writer, a natural with a voice like no one else's—funny, sad, lean, modest, energetic, acute." When this book went out of print in 1965, its reputation survived, strengthened by the infre-*

quent appearances of Paley's new stories in magazines such as the Atlantic Monthly, Esquire, the Noble Savage, Genesis West, the New American Review, Ararat, and Fiction.

During the 1960s and 1970s Paley was prominent as a nonviolent activist protesting the Vietnam War. She was secretary of the Greenwich Village Peace Center, spent time in jail for her antiwar activities, and visited Hanoi and Moscow as a member of peace delegations, defining herself as a "somewhat combative pacifist and cooperative anarchist." During the World Peace Congress in Moscow in 1973, she condemned the Soviet Union for silencing political dissidents; the congress disassociated itself from her statement. Paley has long been a feminist and active in the antinuclear movement. In 1974 her second volume of stories, Enormous Changes at the Last Minute, was published — it is a quieter, more openly personal collection of seventeen stories, many of them, such as "A Conversation with My Father," autobiographical. Her third book of stories, Later the Same Day, appeared in 1985. In 1988 Paley was designated the first official New York State Author by an act of the state legislature.

Paley refuses to blame her teaching jobs or her involvements as an activist for her relatively low productivity as a writer. She says she writes "from distress." What she tries to get at in her stories is "a history of everyday life," and her subject matter and prose style are unmistakable. Living in a Manhattan apartment close to the Greenwich Village School (P.S. 41), Little Tony's Unisex Haircutters, the Famous Ray's Pizza, the H & H Fruit and Vegetable Market, and the Jefferson Market Branch of the New York Public Library, Paley observes her neighbors, friends, and family with compassion, humor, and hope. Her spare dissection of her characters is never performed at the expense of sympathy for the human condition. The Collected Stories of Grace Paley was published in 1994. (See also Paley's "Samuel" on p. 3.)

COMMENTARY   Grace Paley, "A Conversation with Ann Charters," page 582.

WEB   Research Grace Paley and answer questions about her work at bedfordstmartins.com/charters/litwriters.

A Conversation with My Father   1974

My father is eighty-six years old and in bed. His heart, that bloody motor, is equally old and will not do certain jobs any more. It still floods his head with brainy light. But it won't let his legs carry the weight of his body around the house. Despite my metaphors, this muscle failure is not due to his old heart, he says, but to a potassium shortage. Sitting on one pillow, leaning on three, he offers last-minute advice and makes a request.

"I would like you to write a simple story just once more," he says, "the kind de Maupassant wrote, or Chekhov, the kind you used to write. Just recognizable people and then write down what happened to them next."

I say, "Yes, why not? That's possible." I want to please him, though I don't remember writing that way. I *would* like to try to tell such a story, if he means the kind that begins: "There was a woman . . ." followed by plot, the absolute line between two points which I've always despised. Not for literary reasons, but because it takes all hope away. Everyone, real or invented, deserves the open destiny of life.

Finally I thought of a story that had been happening for a couple of years right across the street. I wrote it down, then read it aloud. "Pa," I said, "how about this? Do you mean something like this?"

> Once in my time there was a woman and she had a son. They lived nicely, in a small apartment in Manhattan. This boy at about fifteen became a junkie, which is not unusual in our neighborhood. In order to maintain her close friendship with him, she became a junkie too. She said it was part of the youth culture, with which she felt very much at home. After a while, for a number of reasons, the boy gave it all up and left the city and his mother in disgust. Hopeless and alone, she grieved. We all visit her.

"O.K., Pa, that's it," I said, "an unadorned and miserable tale."

"But that's not what I mean," my father said. "You misunderstood me on purpose. You know there's a lot more to it. You know that. You left everything out. Turgenev wouldn't do that. Chekhov wouldn't do that. There are in fact Russian writers you never heard of, you don't have an inkling of, as good as anyone, who can write a plain ordinary story, who would not leave out what you have left out. I object not to facts but to people sitting in trees talking senselessly, voices from who knows where. . . ."

"Forget that one, Pa, what have I left out now? In this one?"

"Her looks, for instance."

"Oh. Quite handsome, I think. Yes."

"Her hair?"

"Dark, with heavy braids, as though she were a girl or a foreigner."

"What were her parents like, her stock? That she became such a person. It's interesting, you know."

"From out of town. Professional people. The first to be divorced in their county. How's that? Enough?" I asked.

"With you, it's all a joke," he said. "What about the boy's father? Why didn't you mention him? Who was he? Or was the boy born out of wedlock?"

"Yes," I said. "He was born out of wedlock."

"For Godsakes, doesn't anyone in your stories get married? Doesn't anyone have the time to run down to City Hall before they jump into bed?"

"No," I said. "In real life, yes. But in my stories, no."

"Why do you answer me like that?"

"Oh, Pa, this is a simple story about a smart woman who came to N.Y.C. full of interest love trust excitement very up to date, and about her son, what a hard time she had in this world. Married or not, it's of small consequence."

"It is of great consequence," he said.

"O.K.," I said.

"O.K. O.K. yourself," he said, "but listen. I believe you that she's good-looking, but I don't think she was so smart."

"That's true," I said. "Actually that's the trouble with stories. People start out fantastic. You think they're extraordinary, but it turns out as the work goes along, they're just average with a good education. Sometimes the other way around, the person's a kind of dumb innocent, but he outwits you and you can't even think of an ending good enough."

"What do you do then?" he asked. He had been a doctor for a couple of decades and then an artist for a couple of decades and he's still interested in details, craft, technique.

"Well, you just have to let the story lie around till some agreement can be reached between you and the stubborn hero."

"Aren't you talking silly now?" he asked. "Start again," he said. "It so happens I'm not going out this evening. Tell the story again. See what you can do this time."

"O.K.," I said. "But it's not a five-minute job." Second attempt:

> Once, across the street from us, there was a fine handsome woman, our neighbor. She had a son whom she loved because she'd known him since birth (in helpless chubby infancy, and in the wrestling, hugging ages, seven to ten, as well as earlier and later). This boy, when he fell into the fist of adolescence, became a junkie. He was not a hopeless one. He was in fact hopeful, an ideologue and successful converter. With his busy brilliance, he wrote persuasive articles for his high-school newspaper. Seeking a wider audience, using important connections, he drummed into Lower Manhattan newsstand distribution a periodical called *Oh! Golden Horse!*
>
> In order to keep him from feeling guilty (because guilt is the stony heart of nine tenths of all clinically diagnosed cancers in America today, she said), and because she had always believed in giving bad habits room at home where one could keep an eye on them, she too became a junkie. Her kitchen was famous for a while—a center for intellectual addicts who knew what they were doing. A few felt artistic like Coleridge° and others were scientific and revolutionary like Leary.° Although she was often high herself, certain good mothering reflexes remained, and she saw to it that there was lots of orange juice around and honey and milk and vitamin pills. However, she never cooked anything but chili, and that no more than once a week. She explained, when we talked to her, seriously, with neighborly concern, that it was her part in the youth culture and she would rather be with the young, it was an honor, than with her own generation.
>
> One week, while nodding through an Antonioni film, this boy was severely jabbed by the elbow of a stern and proselytizing girl, sitting beside him. She offered immediate apricots and nuts for his sugar level, spoke to him sharply, and took him home.

Coleridge: Samuel Taylor Coleridge (1772–1834), the English Romantic poet, was an opium addict.
Leary: Timothy Leary (1920–1996) was a former Harvard professor of psychology and early advocate of the use of LSD.

She had heard of him and his work and she herself published, edited, and wrote a competitive journal called *Man Does Live by Bread Alone.* In the organic heat of her continuous presence he could not help but become interested once more in his muscles, his arteries, and nerve connections. In fact he began to love them, treasure them, praise them with funny little songs in *Man Does Live.* . . .

> the fingers of my flesh transcend
> my transcendental soul
> the tightness in my shoulders end
> my teeth have made me whole

To the mouth of his head (that glory of will and determination) he brought hard apples, nuts, wheat germ, and soybean oil. He said to his old friends, From now on, I guess I'll keep my wits about me. I'm going on the natch. He said he was about to begin a spiritual deep-breathing journey. How about you too, Mom? he asked kindly.

His conversion was so radiant, splendid, that neighborhood kids his age began to say that he had never been a real addict at all, only a journalist along for the smell of the story. The mother tried several times to give up what had become without her son and his friends a lonely habit. This effort only brought it to supportable levels. The boy and his girl took their electronic mimeograph and moved to the bushy edge of another borough. They were very strict. They said they would not see her again until she had been off drugs for sixty days.

At home alone in the evening, weeping, the mother read and reread the seven issues of *Oh! Golden Horse!* They seemed to her as truthful as ever. We often crossed the street to visit and console. But if we mentioned any of our children who were at college or in the hospital or dropouts at home, she would cry out, My baby! My baby! and burst into terrible, face-scarring, time-consuming tears. The End.

First my father was silent, then he said, "Number One: You have a nice sense of humor. Number Two: I see you can't tell a plain story. So don't waste time." Then he said sadly, "Number Three: I suppose that means she was alone, she was left like that, his mother. Alone. Probably sick?"

I said, "Yes."

"Poor woman. Poor girl, to be born in a time of fools, to live among fools. The end. The end. You were right to put that down. The end."

I didn't want to argue, but I had to say, "Well, it is not necessarily the end, Pa."

"Yes," he said, "what a tragedy. The end of a person."

"No, Pa," I begged him. "It doesn't have to be. She's only about forty. She could be a hundred different things in this world as time goes on. A teacher or a social worker. An ex-junkie! Sometimes it's better than having a master's in education."

"Jokes," he said. "As a writer that's your main trouble. You don't want to recognize it. Tragedy! Plain tragedy! Historical tragedy! No hope. The end."

"Oh, Pa," I said. "She could change."

"In your own life, too, you have to look it in the face." He took a couple of nitroglycerin. "Turn to five," he said, pointing to the dial on the oxygen tank.

He inserted the tubes into his nostrils and breathed deep. He closed his eyes and said, "No."

I had promised the family to always let him have the last word when arguing, but in this case I had a different responsibility. That woman lives across the street. She's my knowledge and my invention. I'm sorry for her. I'm not going to leave her there in that house crying. (Actually neither would Life, which unlike me has no pity.)

Therefore: She did change. Of course her son never came home again. But right now, she's the receptionist in a storefront community clinic in the East Village. Most of the customers are young people, some old friends. The head doctor has said to her, "If we only had three people in this clinic with your experiences. . . ."

"The doctor said that?" My father took the oxygen tubes out of his nostrils and said, "Jokes. Jokes again."

"No, Pa, it could really happen that way, it's a funny world nowadays."

"No," he said. "Truth first. She will slide back. A person must have character. She does not."

"No, Pa," I said. "That's it. She's got a job. Forget it. She's in that storefront working."

"How long will it be?" he asked. "Tragedy! You too. When will you look it in the face?"

EDGAR ALLAN POE

Edgar Allan Poe (1809–1849), the son of poor traveling actors, was adopted by the merchant John Allan of Richmond, Virginia, after the death of Poe's mother when Poe was three years old. He was educated in England and Virginia, enlisted and served two years in the army, then entered the military academy at West Point, from which he was expelled for absenteeism after a year. When John Allan disinherited him, Poe became a writer to earn his living.

In 1833 Poe's story "A MS. Found in a Bottle" won a fifty-dollar prize for the best story in a popular Baltimore periodical, and soon afterward he assumed editorship of the Southern Literary Messenger. *In 1836 he married his cousin Virginia Clemm, shortly before her fourteenth birthday. Poe's brilliant reviews, poems, and stories attracted wide attention, but in 1837 he quarreled with the owner of the* Messenger *over his salary and the degree of his independence as an editor, and he resigned from the magazine.*

In 1841 he became an editor of Graham's Magazine, *and during his year-long tenure he quadrupled subscriptions by publishing his own stories and articles. He left* Graham's *to start his own magazine, which failed. His remaining years as a freelance writer were a struggle with poverty, depression, poor health aggravated by addiction to drugs and alcohol, and—after 1847—grief over the death of his wife. The writer Jorge Luis Borges observed that Poe's life "was short and unhappy, if unhappiness can be short."*

Poe's first collection of twenty-five short stories appeared in two volumes in 1840, Tales of the Grotesque and Arabesque. *His second collection of twelve stories,* Tales, *published in 1845, was so successful that it was followed by* The Raven and Other Poems *the same year. Poe was industrious, and his books of short fiction and poetry sold well, but his total income from them in his lifetime was less than three hundred dollars.*

Most of Poe's best stories can be divided into two categories: melodramatic tales of gothic terror, symbolic psychological fiction that became the source of the modern horror story, such as "The Cask of Amontillado," "The Fall of the House of Usher," and "The Tell-Tale Heart"; and stories of intellect or reason, analytic tales that were precursors of the modern detective story. After critics accused Poe of imitating the extravagant "mysticism" of German romantic writers in his monologues of inspired madness, Poe asserted his originality in the preface to his first story collection: "If in many of my productions terror has been the thesis, I maintain that terror is not of Germany, but of the soul."

Known as a literary critic as well as a poet and writer of short fiction, Poe published more than seventy tales. He is important as one of the earliest writers to attempt to formulate an aesthetic theory about the short story form, or "prose tale" as it was called in his time. Some of his most extensive comments on this subject are found in his reviews of Hawthorne's Twice-Told Tales *for* Graham's Magazine *in 1842 and* Godey's Lady's Book *in 1847. In these essays he also described his own philosophy of composition. Poe believed that unity of a "single effect" was the most essential quality of all successful short fiction. He praised Hawthorne for his "invention, creation, imagination, originality"—qualities Poe himself possessed in abundance. In June 1846, Hawthorne returned the compliment by sending Poe a graceful letter with a copy of his second collection,* Mosses from an Old Manse, *saying that he would never fail to recognize Poe's "force and originality" as a writer of tales even if he sometimes disagreed with Poe's opinions as a critic.*

Poe's stories were widely translated, and he became the first American writer of short fiction to be internationally celebrated. Interpretations of his creative work by writers living abroad usually focused on aspects of his genius that supported their views of America. The Russian novelist Fyodor Dostoevsky admired Poe's "strangely material" imagination and recognized that Poe, unlike the German romantic writers, did not give a large role to supernatural agents in his gothic tales. Instead, Dostoevsky felt that the "power of details" in Poe's descriptions was presented "with such stupendous plasticity that you cannot but believe in the reality or possibility of a fact which actually never has occurred."

The French poet Charles Baudelaire, who translated Poe's tales and championed his genius, regarded Poe from a completely different perspective when he identified him as an alienated artist—"le poète maudit"—a writer outside his society who reflected the derangement of a hypocritical country that professed individual freedom yet permitted slavery in the southern states and bigamy among the Mormons in Utah.

Other readers were more critical—for instance, the transcendentalist writer Margaret Fuller, who took Poe to task for what she considered his careless use of language. Perhaps the most sweeping dismissal of Poe's writing originated with

Henry James, who—despite his interest in the psychological presentation of fictional characters—declared that *"an enthusiasm for Poe is the mark of a decidedly primitive stage of reflection."* Later critics are more appreciative and continue to engage in a lively conversation about Poe's work.

CONVERSATIONS See pages 654–679, including Edgar Allan Poe, "The Importance of the Single Effect in a Prose Tale," page 656; D. H. Lawrence, "On 'The Fall of the House of Usher' and 'The Cask of Amontillado,'" page 659; Cleanth Brooks and Robert Penn Warren, "A New Critical Reading of 'The Fall of the House of Usher,'" page 662; James W. Gargano, "The Question of Poe's Narrators in 'The Tell-Tale Heart' and 'The Cask of Amontillado,'" page 665; J. Gerald Kennedy, "On 'The Fall of the House of Usher,'" page 668; David S. Reynolds, "Poe's Art of Transformation in 'The Cask of Amontillado,'" page 672; Joan Dayan, "Amorous Bondage: Poe, Ladies, and Slaves," page 676.

WEB Research Edgar Allan Poe and answer questions about his work at *bedfordstmartins.com/charters/litwriters.*

The Cask of Amontillado   1846

The thousand injuries of Fortunato I had borne as I best could; but when he ventured upon insult, I vowed revenge. You, who so well know the nature of my soul, will not suppose, however, that I gave utterance to a threat. *At length* I would be avenged; this was a point definitely settled—but the very definitiveness with which it was resolved precluded the idea of risk. I must not only punish, but punish with impunity. A wrong is unredressed when retribution overtakes its redresser. It is equally unredressed when the avenger fails to make himself felt as such to him who has done the wrong.

It must be understood, that neither by word nor deed had I given Fortunato cause to doubt my good-will. I continued, as was my wont, to smile in his face, and he did not perceive that my smile *now* was at the thought of his immolation.

He had a weak point—this Fortunato—although in other regards he was a man to be respected and even feared. He prided himself on his connoisseurship in wine. Few Italians have the true virtuoso spirit. For the most part their enthusiasm is adopted to suit the time and opportunity—to practise imposture upon the British and Austrian *millionnaires*. In painting and gemmary Fortunato, like his countrymen, was a quack—but in the matter of old wines he was sincere. In this respect I did not differ from him materially: I was skilful in the Italian vintages myself, and bought largely whenever I could.

It was about dusk, one evening during the supreme madness of the carnival season, that I encountered my friend. He accosted me with excessive warmth, for he had been drinking much. The man wore motley. He had on a tight-fitting parti-striped dress, and his head was surmounted by the conical cap and bells. I was so pleased to see him, that I thought I should never have done wringing his hand.

I said to him: "My dear Fortunato, you are luckily met. How remarkably well you are looking to-day! But I have received a pipe° of what passes for Amontillado, and I have my doubts."

"How?" said he. "Amontillado? A pipe? Impossible! And in the middle of the carnival!"

"I have my doubts," I replied; "and I was silly enough to pay the full Amontillado price without consulting you in the matter. You were not to be found, and I was fearful of losing a bargain."

"Amontillado!"

"I have my doubts."

"Amontillado!"

"And I must satisfy them."

"Amontillado!"

"As you are engaged, I am on my way to Luchesi. If any one has a critical turn, it is he. He will tell me——"

"Luchesi cannot tell Amontillado from Sherry."

"And yet some fools will have it that his taste is a match for your own."

"Come, let us go."

"Whither?"

"To your vaults."

"My friend, no; I will not impose upon your good nature. I perceive you have an engagement. Luchesi——"

"I have no engagement;—come."

"My friend, no. It is not the engagement, but the severe cold with which I perceive you are afflicted. The vaults are insufferably damp. They are encrusted with nitre."

"Let us go, nevertheless. The cold is merely nothing. Amontillado! You have been imposed upon. And as for Luchesi, he cannot distinguish Sherry from Amontillado."

Thus speaking, Fortunato possessed himself of my arm. Putting on a mask of black silk, and drawing a *roquelaire*° closely about my person, I suffered him to hurry me to my palazzo.

There were no attendants at home; they had absconded to make merry in honor of the time. I had told them that I should not return until the morning, and had given them explicit orders not to stir from the house. These orders were sufficient, I well knew, to insure their immediate disappearance, one and all, as soon as my back was turned.

I took from their sconces two flambeaux, and giving one to Fortunato, bowed him through several suites of rooms to the archway that led into the vaults. I passed down a long and winding staircase, requesting him to be cautious as he followed. We came at length to the foot of the descent, and stood together on the damp ground of the catacombs of the Montresors.

---

pipe: A large cask or keg.
roquelaire: A short cloak.

The gait of my friend was unsteady, and the bells upon his cap jingled as he strode.

"The pipe?" said he.

"It is farther on," said I; "but observe the white web-work which gleams from these cavern walls."

He turned toward me, and looked into my eyes with two filmy orbs that distilled the rheum of intoxication.

"Nitre?" he asked, at length.

"Nitre," I replied. "How long have you had that cough?"

"Ugh! ugh! ugh! — ugh! ugh! ugh! — ugh! ugh! ugh! — ugh! ugh! ugh! — ugh! ugh! ugh!"

My poor friend found it impossible to reply for many minutes.

"It is nothing," he said, at last.

"Come," I said, with decision, "we will go back; your health is precious. You are rich, respected, admired, beloved; you are happy, as once I was. You are a man to be missed. For me it is no matter. We will go back; you will be ill, and I cannot be responsible. Besides, there is Luchesi——"

"Enough," he said; "the cough is a mere nothing; it will not kill me. I shall not die of a cough."

"True—true," I replied; "and, indeed, I had no intention of alarming you unnecessarily; but you should use all proper caution. A draught of this Medoc will defend us from the damps."

Here I knocked off the neck of a bottle which I drew from a long row of its fellows that lay upon the mould.

"Drink," I said, presenting him the wine.

He raised it to his lips with a leer. He paused and nodded to me familiarly, while his bells jingled.

"I drink," he said, "to the buried that repose around us."

"And I to your long life."

He again took my arm, and we proceeded.

"These vaults," he said, "are extensive."

"The Montresors," I replied, "were a great and numerous family."

"I forget your arms."

"A huge human foot d'or,° in a field azure; the foot crushes a serpent rampant whose fangs are imbedded in the heel."

"And the motto?"

"*Nemo me impune lacessit.*"°

"Good!" he said.

The wine sparkled in his eyes and the bells jingled. My own fancy grew warm with the Medoc. We had passed through walls of piled bones, with casks and puncheons intermingling into the inmost recesses of the catacombs. I paused again, and this time I made bold to seize Fortunato by an arm above the elbow.

---

d'or: Of gold.
Nemo me impune lacessit: "No one wounds me with impunity"; the motto of the royal arms of Scotland.

"The nitre!" I said; "see, it increases. It hangs like moss upon the vaults. We are below the river's bed. The drops of moisture trickle among the bones. Come, we will go back ere it is too late. Your cough——"

"It is nothing," he said; "let us go on. But first, another draught of the Medoc."

I broke and reached him a flagon of De Grâve. He emptied it at a breath. His eyes flashed with a fierce light. He laughed and threw the bottle upward with a gesticulation I did not understand.

I looked at him in surprise. He repeated the movement—a grotesque one.

"You do not comprehend?" he said.

"Not I," I replied.

"Then you are not of the brotherhood."

"How?"

"You are not of the masons."

"Yes, yes," I said; "yes, yes."

"You? Impossible! A mason?"

"A mason," I replied.

"A sign," he said.

"It is this," I answered, producing a trowel from beneath the folds of my *roquelaire*.

"You jest," he exclaimed, recoiling a few paces. "But let us proceed to the Amontillado."

"Be it so," I said, replacing the tool beneath the cloak, and again offering him my arm. He leaned upon it heavily. We continued our route in search of the Amontillado. We passed through a range of low arches, descended, passed on, and descending again, arrived at a deep crypt, in which the foulness of the air caused our flambeaux rather to glow than flame.

At the most remote end of the crypt there appeared another less spacious. Its walls had been lined with human remains, piled to the vault overhead, in the fashion of the great catacombs of Paris. Three sides of this interior crypt were still ornamented in this manner. From the fourth the bones had been thrown down, and lay promiscuously upon the earth, forming at one point a mound of some size. Within the wall thus exposed by the displacing of the bones, we perceived a still interior recess, in depth about four feet, in width three, in height six or seven. It seemed to have been constructed for no especial use within itself, but formed merely the interval between two of the colossal supports of the roof of the catacombs, and was backed by one of their circumscribing walls of solid granite.

It was in vain that Fortunato, uplifting his dull torch, endeavored to pry into the depth of the recess. Its termination the feeble light did not enable us to see.

"Proceed," I said; "herein is the Amontillado. As for Luchesi——"

"He is an ignoramus," interrupted my friend, as he stepped unsteadily forward, while I followed immediately at his heels. In an instant he had reached the extremity of the niche, and finding his progress arrested by the rock, stood stupidly bewildered. A moment more and I had fettered him to the granite. In its surface were two iron staples, distant from each other about two feet, horizontally. From one of these depended a short chain, from the other a padlock. Throwing the links about his waist, it was but the work of a few seconds to secure it. He was too much astounded to resist. Withdrawing the key I stepped back from the recess.

"Pass your hand," I said, "over the wall; you cannot help feeling the nitre. Indeed it is *very* damp. Once more let me *implore* you to return. No? Then I must positively leave you. But I must first render you all the little attentions in my power."

"The Amontillado!" ejaculated my friend, not yet recovered from his astonishment.

"True," I replied; "the Amontillado."

As I said these words I busied myself among the pile of bones of which I have before spoken. Throwing them aside, I soon uncovered a quantity of building stone and mortar. With these materials and with the aid of my trowel, I began vigorously to wall up the entrance of the niche.

I had scarcely laid the first tier of the masonry when I discovered that the intoxication of Fortunato had in a great measure worn off. The earliest indication I had of this was a low moaning cry from the depth of the recess. It was *not* the cry of a drunken man. There was then a long and obstinate silence. I laid the second tier, and the third, and the fourth; and then I heard the furious vibrations of the chain. The noise lasted for several minutes, during which, that I might hearken to it with the more satisfaction, I ceased my labors and sat down upon the bones. When at last the clanking subsided, I resumed the trowel, and finished without interruption the fifth, the sixth, and the seventh tier. The wall was now nearly upon a level with my breast. I again paused, and holding the flambeaux over the masonwork, threw a few feeble rays upon the figure within.

A succession of loud and shrill screams, bursting suddenly from the throat of the chained form, seemed to thrust me violently back. For a brief moment I hesitated—I trembled. Unsheathing my rapier, I began to grope with it about the recess; but the thought of an instant reassured me. I placed my hand upon the solid fabric of the catacombs, and felt satisfied. I reapproached the wall. I replied to the yells of him who clamored. I reechoed—I aided—I surpassed them in volume and in strength. I did this, and the clamorer grew still.

It was now midnight, and my task was drawing to a close. I had completed the eighth, the ninth, and the tenth tier. I had finished a portion of the last and the eleventh; there remained but a single stone to be fitted and plastered in. I struggled with its weight; I placed it partially in its destined position. But now there came from out the niche a low laugh that erected the hairs upon my head. It was succeeded by a sad voice, which I had difficulty in recognizing as that of the noble Fortunato. The voice said—

"Ha! ha! ha!—he! he!—a very good joke indeed—an excellent jest. We will have many a rich laugh about it at the palazzo—he! he! he!—over our wine—he! he! he!"

"The Amontillado!" I said.

"He! he! he! — he! he! he! — yes, the Amontillado. But is it not getting late? Will not they be awaiting us at the palazzo, the Lady Fortunato and the rest? Let us be gone."

"Yes," I said, "let us be gone."

"For the love of God, Montresor!"

"Yes," I said, "for the love of God!"

But to these words I hearkened in vain for a reply. I grew impatient. I called aloud:

"Fortunato!"

No answer. I called again:

"Fortunato!"

No answer still, I thrust a torch through the remaining aperture and let it fall within. There came forth in return only a jingling of the bells. My heart grew sick — on account of the dampness of the catacombs. I hastened to make an end of my labor. I forced the last stone into its position; I plastered it up. Against the new masonry I re-erected the old rampart of bones. For the half of a century no mortal has disturbed them. *In pace requiescat!*

The Fall of the House of Usher   1839

Son cœur est un luth suspendu;
Sitôt qu'on le touche il résonne.[1]

—De Béranger

During the whole of a dull, dark, and soundless day in the autumn of the year, when the clouds hung oppressively low in the heavens, I had been passing alone, on horseback, through a singularly dreary tract of country, and at length found myself, as the shades of the evening drew on, within view of the melancholy House of Usher. I know not how it was — but, with the first glimpse of the building, a sense of insufferable gloom pervaded my spirit. I say insufferable; for the feeling was unrelieved by any of that half-pleasurable, because poetic, sentiment, with which the mind usually receives even the sternest natural images of the desolate or terrible. I looked upon the scene before me — upon the mere house, and the simple landscape features of the domain — upon the bleak walls — upon the vacant eye-like windows — upon a few rank sedges — and upon a few white trunks of decayed trees — with an utter depression of soul which I can compare to no earthly sensation more properly than to the after-dream of the reveller upon opium — the bitter lapse into every-day life — the hideous dropping off of the veil. There was an iciness, a sinking, a sickening of the heart — an unredeemed dreariness of thought which no goading of the imagination could torture into aught of the sublime. What was it — I paused to think — what was it that so unnerved me in the contemplation of the House of Usher? It was a mystery all insoluble; nor could I grapple with the shadowy fancies that crowded upon me as I pondered. I was forced to fall back upon the

---

[1]His heart is a suspended lute; / Which resonates as soon as touched.

unsatisfactory conclusion, that while, beyond doubt, there *are* combinations of very simple natural objects which have the power of thus affecting us, still the analysis of this power lies among considerations beyond our depth. It was possible, I reflected, that a mere different arrangement of the particulars of the scene, of the details of the picture, would be sufficient to modify, or perhaps to annihilate its capacity for sorrowful impression; and, acting upon this idea, I reined my horse to the precipitous brink of a black and lurid tarn that lay in unruffled lustre by the dwelling, and gazed down — but with a shudder even more thrilling than before — upon the remodelled and inverted images of the gray sedge, and the ghastly tree-stems, and the vacant and eye-like windows.

Nevertheless, in this mansion of gloom I now proposed to myself a sojourn of some weeks. Its proprietor, Roderick Usher, had been one of my boon companions in boyhood; but many years had elapsed since our last meeting. A letter, however, had lately reached me in a distant part of the country — a letter from him — which, in its wildly importunate nature, had admitted of no other than a personal reply. The MS. gave evidence of nervous agitation. The writer spoke of acute bodily illness — of a mental disorder which oppressed him — and of an earnest desire to see me, as his best, and indeed his only personal friend, with a view of attempting, by the cheerfulness of my society, some alleviation of his malady. It was the manner in which all this, and much more, was said — it was the apparent *heart* that went with his request — which allowed me no room for hesitation; and I accordingly obeyed forthwith what I still considered a very singular summons.

Although, as boys, we had been even intimate associates, yet I really knew little of my friend. His reserve had been always excessive and habitual. I was aware, however, that his very ancient family had been noted, time out of mind, for a peculiar sensibility of temperament, displaying itself, through long ages, in many works of exalted art, and manifested, of late, in repeated deeds of munificent yet unobtrusive charity, as well as in a passionate devotion to the intricacies, perhaps even more than to the orthodox and easily recognizable beauties, of musical science. I had learned, too, the very remarkable fact, that the stem of the Usher race, all time-honoured as it was, had put forth, at no period, any enduring branch; in other words, that the entire family lay in the direct line of descent, and had always, with very trifling and very temporary variation, so lain. It was this deficiency, I considered, while running over in thought the perfect keeping of the character of the premises with the accredited character of the people, and while speculating upon the possible influence which the one, in the long lapse of centuries, might have exercised upon the other — it was this deficiency, perhaps of collateral issue, and the consequent undeviating transmission, from sire to son, of the patrimony with the name, which had, at length, so identified the two as to merge the original title of the estate in the quaint and equivocal apellation of the "House of Usher" — an apellation which seemed to include, in the minds of the peasantry who used it, both the family and the family mansion.

I have said that the sole effect of my somewhat childish experiment — that of looking down within the tarn — had been to deepen the first singular impression. There can be no doubt that the consciousness of the rapid increase of my superstition — for why should I not so term it? — served mainly to accelerate the increase itself. Such, I have long known, is the paradoxical law of all sentiments having terror as a basis. And it might have been for this reason only, that, when I again uplifted my eyes to the house itself, from its image in the pool, there grew in my mind a strange fancy — a fancy so ridiculous, indeed, that I but mention it to show the vivid force of the sensations which oppressed me. I had so worked upon my imagination as really to believe that about the whole mansion and domain there hung an atmosphere peculiar to themselves and their immediate vicinity — an atmosphere which had no affinity with the air of heaven, but which had reeked up from the decayed trees, and the gray wall, and the silent tarn — a pestilent and mystic vapour, dull, sluggish, faintly discernible, and leaden-hued.

Shaking off from my spirit what *must* have been a dream, I scanned more narrowly the real aspect of the building. Its principal feature seemed to be that of an excessive antiquity. The discoloration of ages had been great. Minute fungi overspread the whole exterior, hanging in a fine tangled web-work from the eaves. Yet all this was apart from an extraordinary dilapidation. No portion of the masonry had fallen; and there appeared to be a wild inconsistency between its still perfect adaptation of parts, and the crumbling condition of the individual stones. In this there was much that reminded me of the specious totality of the old woodwork which has rotted for long years in some neglected vault, with no disturbance from the breath of the external air. Beyond this indication of extensive decay, however, the fabric gave little token of instability. Perhaps the eye of a scrutinizing observer might have discovered a barely perceptible fissure, which, extending from the roof of the building in front, made its way down the wall in a zigzag direction, until it became lost in the sullen waters of the tarn.

Noticing these things, I rode over a short causeway to the house. A servant in waiting took my horse, and I entered the Gothic archway of the hall. A valet, of stealthy step, thence conducted me, in silence, through many dark and intricate passages in my progress to the *studio* of his master. Much that I encountered on the way contributed, I know not how, to heighten the vague sentiments of which I have already spoken. While the objects around me — while the carvings of the ceilings, the sombre tapestries of the walls, the ebon blackness of the floors, and the phantasmagoric armorial trophies which rattled as I strode, were but matters to which, or to such as which, I had been accustomed from my infancy — while I hesitated not to acknowledge how familiar was all this — I still wondered to find how unfamiliar were the fancies which ordinary images were stirring up. On one of the staircases, I met the physician of the family. His countenance, I thought, wore a mingled expression of low cunning and perplexity. He accosted me with trepidation and passed on. The valet now threw open a door and ushered me into the presence of his master.

The room in which I found myself was very large and lofty. The windows were long, narrow, and pointed, and at so vast a distance from the black oaken floor as to be altogether inaccessible from within. Feeble gleams of encrimsoned light made their way through the trellised panes, and served to render sufficiently distinct the more prominent objects around; the eye, however, struggled in vain to reach the remoter angles of the chamber, or the recesses of the vaulted and fretted ceiling. Dark draperies hung upon the walls. The general furniture was profuse, comfortless, antique, and tattered. Many books and musical instruments lay scattered about, but failed to give any vitality to the scene. I felt that I breathed an atmosphere of sorrow. An air of stern, deep, and irredeemable gloom hung over and pervaded all.

Upon my entrance, Usher arose from a sofa on which he had been lying at full length, and greeted me with a vivacious warmth which had much in it, I at first thought, of an overdone cordiality—of the constrained effort of the *ennuyé* man of the world. A glance, however, at his countenance convinced me of his perfect sincerity. We sat down; and for some moments, while he spoke not, I gazed upon him with a feeling half of pity, half of awe. Surely, man had never before so terribly altered, in so brief a period, as had Roderick Usher! It was with difficulty that I could bring myself to admit the identity of the wan being before me with the companion of my early boyhood. Yet the character of his face had been at all times remarkable. A cadaverousness of complexion; an eye large, liquid, and luminous beyond comparison; lips somewhat thin and very pallid, but of a surpassingly beautiful curve; a nose of a delicate Hebrew model, but with a breadth of nostril unusual in similar formations; a finely moulded chin, speaking, in its want of prominence, of a want of moral energy; hair of a more than web-like softness and tenuity; these features, with an inordinate expansion above the regions of the temple, made up altogether a countenance not easily to be forgotten. And now in the mere exaggeration of the prevailing character of these features, and of the expression they were wont to convey, lay so much of change that I doubted to whom I spoke. The now ghastly pallor of the skin, and the now miraculous lustre of the eye, above all things startled and even awed me. The silken hair, too, had been suffered to grow all unheeded, and as, in its wild gossamer texture, it floated rather than fell about the face, I could not, even with effort, connect its Arabesque expression with any idea of simple humanity.

In the manner of my friend I was at once struck with an incoherence—an inconsistency; and I soon found this to arise from a series of feeble and futile struggles to overcome an habitual trepidancy—an excessive nervous agitation. For something of this nature I had indeed been prepared, no less by his letter, than by reminiscences of certain boyish traits, and by conclusions deduced from his peculiar physical conformation and temperament. His action was alternately vivacious and sullen. His voice varied rapidly from a tremulous indecision (when the animal spirits seemed utterly in abeyance) to that species of energetic concision—that abrupt, weighty, unhurried, and hollow-sounding enunciation—that leaden, self-balanced, and perfectly modulated guttural utterance, which may be observed in the lost drunkard, or the irreclaimable eater of opium, during the periods of his most intense excitement.

It was thus that he spoke of the object of my visit, of his earnest desire to see me, and of the solace he expected me to afford him. He entered, at some length, into what he conceived to be the nature of his malady. It was, he said, a constitutional and a family evil, and one for which he despaired to find a remedy—a mere nervous affection, he immediately added, which would undoubtedly soon pass off. It displayed itself in a host of unnatural sensations. Some of these, as he detailed them, interested and bewildered me; although, perhaps, the terms and the general manner of their narration had their weight. He suffered much from a morbid acuteness of the senses; the most insipid food was alone endurable; he could wear only garments of certain texture; the odours of all flowers were oppressive; his eyes were tortured by even a faint light; and there were but peculiar sounds, and these from stringed instruments, which did not inspire him with horror.

To an anomalous species of terror I found him a bounden slave. "I shall perish," said he, "I *must* perish in this deplorable folly. Thus, thus, and not otherwise, shall I be lost. I dread the events of the future, not in themselves, but in their results. I shudder at the thought of any, even the most trivial, incident, which may operate upon this intolerable agitation of soul. I have, indeed, no abhorrence of danger, except in its absolute effect—in terror. In this unnerved—in this pitiable condition—I feel that the period will sooner or later arrive when I must abandon life and reason together, in some struggle with the grim phantasm, FEAR."

I learned, moreover, at intervals, and through broken and equivocal hints, another singular feature of his mental condition. He was enchained by certain superstitious impressions in regard to the dwelling which he tenanted, and whence, for many years, he had never ventured forth—in regard to an influence whose supposititious force was conveyed in terms too shadowy here to be re-stated—an influence which some peculiarities in the mere form and substance of his family mansion had, by dint of long sufferance, he said, obtained over his spirit—an effect which the *physique* of the gray wall and turrets, and of the dim tarn into which they all looked down, had, at length, brought about upon the *morale* of his existence.

He admitted, however, although with hesitation, that much of the peculiar gloom which thus afflicted him could be traced to a more natural and far more palpable origin—to the severe and long-continued illness—indeed to the evidently approaching dissolution—of a tenderly beloved sister, his sole companion for long years, his last and only relative on earth. "Her decease," he said, with a bitterness which I can never forget, "would leave him (him the hopeless and the frail) the last of the ancient race of the Ushers." While he spoke, the lady Madeline (for so was she called) passed slowly through a remote portion of the apartment, and, without having noticed my presence, disappeared. I regarded her with an utter astonishment not unmingled with dread—and yet I found it impossible to account for such feelings. A sensation of stupor oppressed me, as my eyes followed her retreating steps. When a door, at length, closed upon her, my glance sought instinctively and eagerly the countenance of the brother—but he had buried his face in his hands, and I could only perceive that a far more than ordinary wanness had overspread the emaciated fingers through which trickled many passionate tears.

The disease of the lady Madeline had long baffled the skill of her physicians. A settled apathy, a gradual wasting away of the person, and frequent although transient affections of a partially cataleptical character were the unusual diagnosis. Hitherto she had steadily borne up against the pressure of her malady, and had not betaken herself finally to bed; but on the closing in of the evening of my arrival at the house, she succumbed (as her brother told me at night with inexpressible agitation) to the prostrating power of the destroyer; and I learned that the glimpse I had obtained of her person would thus proba- bly be the last I should obtain—that the lady, at least while living, would be seen by me no more.

For several days ensuing, her name was unmentioned by either Usher or myself: and during this period I was busied in earnest endeavours to alleviate the melancholy of my friend. We painted and read together, or I listened, as if in a dream, to the wild improvisations of his speaking guitar. And thus, as a closer and still closer intimacy admitted me more unreservedly into the recesses of his spirit, the more bitterly did I perceive the futility of all attempt at cheering a mind from which darkness, as if an inherent positive quality, poured forth upon all objects of the moral and physical universe in one unceasing radi- ation of gloom.

I shall ever bear about me a memory of the many solemn hours I thus spent alone with the master of the House of Usher. Yet I should fail in any attempt to convey an idea of the exact character of the studies, or of the occupations, in which he involved me, or led me the way. An excited and highly distempered ideality threw a sulphureous lustre over all. His long improvised dirges will ring forever in my ears. Among other things, I hold painfully in mind a certain singular perversion and amplification of the wild air of the last waltz of Von Weber. From the paintings over which his elaborate fancy brooded, and which grew, touch by touch, into vagueness at which I shuddered the more thrillingly, because I shuddered knowing not why;—from these paintings (vivid as their images now are before me) I would in vain endeavour to educe more than a small portion which should lie within the compass of merely written words. By the utter simplicity, by the nakedness of his designs, he arrested and overawed attention. If ever mortal painted an idea, that mortal was Roderick Usher. For me at least—in the circumstances then surrounding me—there arose out of the pure abstractions which the hypochondriac contrived to throw upon his canvas, an intensity of intolerable awe, no shadow of which I felt ever yet in the contemplation of the certainly glowing yet too concrete reveries of Fuseli.

One of the phantasmagoric conceptions of my friend, partaking not so rigidly of the spirit of abstraction, may be shadowed forth, although feebly, in words. A small picture presented the interior of an immensely long and rec- tangular vault or tunnel, with low walls, smooth, white, and without interrup- tion or device. Certain accessory points of the design served well to convey the idea that this excavation lay at an exceeding depth below the surface of the earth. No outlet was observed in any portion of its vast extent, and no torch or other artificial source of light was discernible; yet a flood of intense rays rolled throughout, and bathed the whole in a ghastly and inappropriate splendour.

I have just spoken of that morbid condition of the auditory nerve which rendered all music intolerable to the sufferer, with the exception of certain effects of stringed instruments. It was, perhaps, the narrow limits to which he thus confined himself upon the guitar, which gave birth, in great measure, to the fantastic character of his performances. But the fervid *facility* of his *impromptus* could not be so accounted for. They must have been, and were, in the notes, as well as in the words of his wild fantasias (for he not unfrequently accompanied himself with rhymed verbal improvisations), the result of that intense mental collectedness and concentration to which I have previously alluded as observable only in particular moments of the highest artificial excitement. The words of one of these rhapsodies I have easily remembered. I was, perhaps, the more forcibly impressed with it, as he gave it, because, in the under or mystic current of its meaning, I fancied that I perceived, and for the first time, a full consciousness on the part of Usher, of the tottering of his lofty reason upon her throne. The verses, which were entitled "The Haunted Palace," ran very nearly, if not accurately, thus:

I

In the greenest of our valleys,
   By good angels tenanted,
Once a fair and stately palace—
   Radiant palace—reared its head.
In the monarch Thought's dominion—
   It stood there!
Never seraph spread a pinion
   Over fabric half so fair.

II

Banners yellow, glorious, golden,
   On its roof did float and flow;
(This—all this—was in the olden
   Time long ago)
And every gentle air that dallied,
   In that sweet day,
Along the ramparts plumed and pallid,
   A winged odour went away.

III

Wanderers in that happy valley
   Through two luminous windows saw
Spirits moving musically
   To a lute's well-tunèd law,
Round about a throne, where sitting
   (Porphyrogene!)
In state his glory well befitting,
   The ruler of the realm was seen.

IV

And all with pearl and ruby glowing
   Was the fair palace door,
Through which came flowing, flowing, flowing
   And sparkling evermore,
A troop of Echoes whose sweet duty
   Was but to sing,
In voices of surpassing beauty,
   The wit and wisdom of their king.

V

But evil things, in robes of sorrow,
    Assailed the monarch's high estate;
(Ah, let us mourn, for never morrow
    Shall dawn upon him, desolate!)
And, round about his home, the glory
    That blushed and bloomed
Is but a dim-remembered story
    Of the old time entombed.

VI

And travellers now within that valley,
    Through the red-litten windows see
Vast forms that move fantastically
    To a discordant melody;
While, like a rapid ghastly river,
    Through the pale door,
A hideous throng rush out forever,
    And laugh—but smile no more.

I well remember that suggestions arising from this ballad led us into a train of thought wherein there became manifest an opinion of Usher's which I mention not so much on account of its novelty (for other men[2] have thought thus), as on account of the pertinacity with which he maintained it. This opinion, in its general form, was that of the sentience of all vegetable things. But, in his disordered fancy, the idea had assumed a more daring character, and trespassed, under certain conditions, upon the kingdom of inorganization. I lack words to express the full extent, or the earnest *abandon* of his persuasion. The belief, however, was connected (as I have previously hinted) with the gray stones of the home of his forefathers. The conditions of the sentience had been here, he imagined, fulfilled in the method of collocation of these stones—in the order of their arrangement, as well as in that of the many *fungi* which overspread them, and of the decayed trees which stood around—above all, in the long undisturbed endurance of this arrangement, and in its reduplication in the still waters of the tarn. Its evidence—the evidence of the sentience—was to be seen, he said (and I here started as he spoke), in the gradual yet certain condensation of an atmosphere of their own about the waters and the walls. The result was discoverable, he added, in that silent yet importunate and terrible influence which for centuries had moulded the destinies of his family, and which made *him* what I now saw him—what he was. Such opinions need no comment, and I will make none.

Our books—the books which, for years, had formed no small portion of the mental existence of the invalid—were, as might be supposed, in strict keeping with his character of phantasm. We pored together over such works as the Ververt et Chartreuse of Gresset; the Belphegor of Machiavelli; the Heaven and Hell of Swedenborg; the Subterranean Voyage of Nicholas Klimm

---

[2]Watson, Dr. Percival, Spallanzani, and especially the Bishop of Landaff.—See *Chemical Essays*, vol. v. [Poe's note.]

of Holberg; the Chiromancy of Robert Flud, of Jean D'Indaginé, and of De la Chambre; the Journey into the Blue Distance of Tieck; and the City of the Sun of Campanella. One favourite volume was a small octavo edition of the *Directorium Inquisitorum*, by the Dominican Eymeric de Gironne; and there were passages in Pomponius Mela, about the old African Satyrs and Ægipans, over which Usher would sit dreaming for hours. His chief delight, however, was found in the perusal of an exceedingly rare and curious book in quarto Gothic—the manual of a forgotten church—the *Vigiliæ Mortuorum secundum Chorum Ecclesiæ Maguntinæ*.

I could not help thinking of the wild ritual of this work, and of its probable influence upon the hypochondriac, when, one evening, having informed me abruptly that the lady Madeline was no more, he stated his intention of preserving her corpse for a fortnight, (previously to its final interment), in one of the numerous vaults within the main walls of the building. The worldly reason, however, assigned for this singular proceeding, was one which I did not feel at liberty to dispute. The brother had been led to his resolution (so he told me) by consideration of the unusual character of the malady of the deceased, of certain obtrusive and eager inquiries on the part of her medical men, and of the remote and exposed situation of the burial-ground of the family. I will not deny that when I called to mind the sinister countenance of the person whom I met upon the staircase, on the day of my arrival at the house, I had no desire to oppose what I regarded as at best but a harmless, and by no means an unnatural, precaution.

At the request of Usher, I personally aided him in the arrangements for the temporary entombment. The body having been encoffined, we two alone bore it to its rest. The vault in which we placed it (and which had been so long unopened that our torches, half smothered in its oppressive atmosphere, gave us little opportunity for investigation) was small, damp, and entirely without means of admission for light; lying, at great depth, immediately beneath that portion of the building in which was my own sleeping apartment. It had been used, apparently, in remote feudal times, for the worst purposes of a donjon-keep, and, in later days, as a place of deposit for powder, or some other highly combustible substance, as a portion of its floor, and the whole interior of a long archway through which we reached it, were carefully sheathed with copper. The door, of massive iron, had been, also, similarly protected. Its immense weight caused an unusually sharp grating sound, as it moved upon its hinges.

Having deposited our mournful burden upon tressels within this region of horror, we partially turned aside the yet unscrewed lid of the coffin, and looked upon the face of the tenant. A striking similitude between the brother and sister now first arrested my attention; and Usher, divining, perhaps, my thoughts, murmured out some few words from which I learned that the deceased and himself had been twins, and that sympathies of a scarcely intelligible nature had always existed between them. Our glances, however, rested not long upon the dead—for we could not regard her unawed. The disease which had thus entombed the lady in the maturity of youth, had left, as usual in all maladies of a strictly cataleptical character, the mockery of a faint blush upon the bosom and the face, and that suspiciously lingering smile upon the lip which is so terrible in death. We replaced and screwed down the lid, and, having secured the door of iron, made our way, with toil, into the scarcely less gloomy apartments of the upper portion of the house.

And now, some days of bitter grief having elapsed, an observable change came over the features of the mental disorder of my friend. His ordinary manner had vanished. His ordinary occupations were neglected or forgotten. He roamed from chamber to chamber with hurried, unequal, and objectless step. The pallor of his countenance had assumed, if possible, a more ghastly hue — but the luminousness of his eye had utterly gone out. The once occasional huskiness of his tone was heard no more; and a tremulous quaver, as if of extreme terror, habitually characterized his utterance. There were times, indeed, when I thought his unceasingly agitated mind was labouring with some oppressive secret, to divulge which he struggled for the necessary courage. At times, again, I was obliged to resolve all into the mere inexplicable vagaries of madness, for I beheld him gazing upon vacancy for long hours, in an attitude of the profoundest attention, as if listening to some imaginary sound. It was no wonder that his condition terrified — that it infected me. I felt creeping upon me, by slow yet certain degrees, the wild influences of his own fantastic yet impressive superstitions.

It was, especially, upon retiring to bed late in the night of the seventh or eighth day after the placing of the lady Madeline within the donjon, that I experienced the full power of such feelings. Sleep came not near my couch — while the hours waned and waned away. I struggled to reason off the nervousness which had dominion over me. I endeavoured to believe that much, if not all of what I felt, was due to the bewildering influence of the gloomy furniture of the room — of the dark and tattered draperies, which, tortured into motion by the breath of a rising tempest, swayed fitfully to and fro upon the walls, and rustled uneasily about the decorations of the bed. But my efforts were fruitless. An irrepressible tremour gradually pervaded my frame; and, at length, there sat upon my very heart an incubus of utterly causeless alarm. Shaking this off with a gasp and a struggle, I uplifted myself upon the pillows, and, peering earnestly within the intense darkness of the chamber, hearkened — I know not why, except that an instinctive spirit prompted me — to certain low and indefinite sounds which came, through the pauses of the storm, at long intervals, I knew not whence. Overpowered by an intense sentiment of horror, unaccountable yet unendurable, I threw on my clothes with haste (for I felt that I should sleep no more during the night), and endeavoured to arouse myself from the pitiable condition into which I had fallen, by pacing rapidly to and fro through the apartment.

I had taken but few turns in this manner, when a light step on an adjoining staircase arrested my attention. I presently recognised it as that of Usher. In an instant afterward he rapped, with a gentle touch, at my door, and entered, bearing a lamp. His countenance was, as usual, cadaverously wan — but, moreover, there was a species of mad hilarity in his eyes — an evidently restrained *hysteria* in his whole demeanour. His air appalled me—but anything was preferable to the solitude which I had so long endured, and I even welcomed his presence as a relief.

"And you have not seen it?" he said abruptly, after having stared about him for some moments in silence—"you have not then seen it?—but, stay! you shall." Thus speaking, and having carefully shaded his lamp, he hurried to one of the casements, and threw it freely open to the storm.

The impetuous fury of the entering gust nearly lifted us from our feet. It was, indeed, a tempestuous yet sternly beautiful night, and one wildly singular in its terror and its beauty. A whirlwind had apparently collected its force in our vicinity; for there were frequent and violent alterations in the direction of the wind; and the exceeding density of the clouds (which hung so low as to press upon the turrets of the house) did not prevent our perceiving the life-like velocity with which they flew careering from all points against each other, without passing away into the distance. I say that even their exceeding density did not prevent our perceiving this—yet we had no glimpse of the moon or stars—nor was there any flashing forth of the lightning. But the under surfaces of the huge masses of agitated vapour, as well as all terrestrial objects immediately around us, were glowing in the unnatural light of a faintly luminous and distinctly visible gaseous exhalation which hung about and enshrouded the mansion.

"You must not—you shall not behold this!" said I, shudderingly, to Usher, as I led him, with a gentle violence, from the window to a seat. "These appearances, which bewilder you, are merely electrical phenomena not uncommon—or it may be that they have their ghastly origin in the rank miasma of the tarn. Let us close this casement;—the air is chilling and dangerous to your frame. Here is one of your favourite romances. I will read, and you shall listen;—and so we will pass away this terrible night together."

The antique volume which I had taken up was the "Mad Trist" of Sir Launcelot Canning; but I had called it a favourite of Usher's more in sad jest than in earnest; for, in truth, there is little in its uncouth and unimaginative prolixity which could have had interest for the lofty and spiritual ideality of my friend. It was, however, the only book immediately at hand; and I indulged a vague hope that the excitement which now agitated the hypochondriac might find relief (for the history of mental disorder is full of similar anomalies) even in the extremeness of the folly which I could read. Could I have judged, indeed, by the wild overstrained air of vivacity with which he hearkened, or apparently hearkened, to the words of the tale, I might well have congratulated myself upon the success of my design.

I had arrived at that well-known portion of the story where Ethelred, the hero of the Trist, having sought in vain for peaceable admission into the dwelling of the hermit, proceeds to make good an entrance by force. Here, it will be remembered, the words of the narrative run thus:

"And Ethelred, who was by nature of a doughty heart, and who was now mighty withal, on account of the powerfulness of the wine which he had drunken, waited no longer to hold parley with the hermit, who, in sooth, was of an obstinate and maliceful turn, but, feeling the rain upon his shoulders, and fearing the rising of the tempest, uplifted his mace outright, and, with blows, made quickly room in the plankings of the door for his gauntleted hand; and now pulling therewith sturdily, he so cracked, and ripped, and tore all asunder, that the noise of the dry and hollow-sounding wood alarmed and reverberated throughout the forest."

At the termination of this sentence I started and, for a moment, paused; for it appeared to me (although I at once concluded that my excited fancy had deceived me)—it appeared to me that, from some very remote portion of the mansion, there came, indistinctly, to my ears, what might have been, in its exact similarity of character, the echo (but a stifled and dull one certainly) of the very cracking and ripping sound which Sir Launcelot had so particularly described. It was, beyond doubt, the coincidence alone which had arrested my attention; for, amid the rattling of the sashes of the casements, and the ordinary commingled noises of the still increasing storm, the sound, in itself, had nothing, surely, which should have interested or disturbed me. I continued the story:

"But the good champion Ethelred, now entering within the door, was sore enraged and amazed to perceive no signal of the maliceful hermit; but, in the stead thereof, a dragon of a scaly and prodigious demeanour, and of a fiery tongue, which sate in guard before a palace of gold, with a floor of silver; and upon the wall there hung a shield of shining brass with this legend enwritten—

Who entereth herein, a conqueror hath bin;
Who slayeth the dragon, the shield he shall win.

And Ethelred uplifted his mace, and struck upon the head of the dragon, which fell before him, and gave up his pesty breath, with a shriek so horrid and harsh, and withal so piercing, that Ethelred had fain to close his ears with his hands against the dreadful noise of it, the like whereof was never before heard."

Here again I paused abruptly, and now with a feeling of wild amaze-ment—for there could be no doubt whatever that, in this instance, I did actu-ally hear (although from what direction it proceeded I found it impossible to say) a low and apparently distant, but harsh, protracted, and most unusual screaming or grating sound—the exact counterpart of what my fancy had already conjured up for the dragon's unnatural shriek as described by the romancer.

Oppressed, as I certainly was, upon the occurrence of the second and most extraordinary coincidence, by a thousand conflicting sensations, in which wonder and extreme terror were predominant, I still retained sufficient pres-ence of mind to avoid exciting, by any observation, the sensitive nervousness of my companion. I was by no means certain that he had noticed the sounds in question; although, assuredly, a strange alteration had, during the last few minutes, taken place in his demeanour. From a position fronting my own, he had gradually brought round his chair, so as to sit with his face to the door of the chamber; and thus I could but partially perceive his features, although I saw that his lips trembled as if he were murmuring inaudibly. His head had dropped upon his breast—yet I knew that he was not asleep, from the wide and rigid opening of the eye as I caught a glance of it in profile. The motion of his body, too, was at variance with this idea—for he rocked from side to side with a gentle yet constant and uniform sway. Having rapidly taken notice of all this, I resumed the narrative of Sir Launcelot, which thus proceeded:

"And now, the champion, having escaped from the terrible fury of the dragon, bethinking himself of the brazen shield, and of the breaking up of the enchantment which was upon it, removed the carcass from out of the way before him, and approached valorously over the silver pavement of the castle to where the shield was upon the wall; which in sooth tarried not for his full coming, but fell down at his feet upon the silver floor, with a mighty great and terrible ringing sound."

No sooner had these syllables passed my lips, than—as if a shield of brass had indeed, at the moment, fallen heavily upon a floor of silver—I became aware of a distinct, hollow, metallic, and clangorous, yet apparently muffled reverberation. Completely unnerved, I leaped to my feet; but the measured rocking movement of Usher was undisturbed. I rushed to the chair in which he sat. His eyes were bent fixedly before him, and throughout his whole countenance there reigned a stony rigidity. But, as I placed my hand upon his shoulder, there came a strong shudder over his whole person; a sickly smile quivered about his lips; and I saw that he spoke in a low, hurried, and gibbering murmur, as if unconscious of my presence. Bending closely over him, I at length drank in the hideous import of his words.

"Not hear it?—yes, I hear it, and *have* heard it. Long—long—long— many minutes, many hours, many days, have I heard it—yet I dared not—oh, pity me, miserable wretch that I am!—I dared not—I *dared* not speak! *We have put her living in the tomb!* Said I not that my senses were acute? I *now* tell you that I heard her first feeble movements in the hollow coffin. I heard them—many, many days ago—yet I dared not—I *dared not speak!* And now—to-night—Ethelred—ha! ha!—the breaking of the hermit's door, and the death-cry of the dragon, and the clangour of the shield!—say, rather, the rending of her coffin, and the grating of the iron hinges of her prison, and her struggles within the coppered archway of the vault! Oh whither shall I fly? Will she not be here anon? Is she not hurrying to upbraid me for my haste? Have I not heard her footsteps on the stair? Do I not distinguish that heavy and horrible beating of her heart? MADMAN!"—here he sprang furiously to his feet, and shrieked out his syllables, as if in the effort he were giving up his soul— "MADMAN! I TELL YOU THAT SHE NOW STANDS WITHOUT THE DOOR!"

As if in the superhuman energy of his utterance there had been found the potency of a spell—the huge antique panels to which the speaker pointed threw slowly back, upon the instant, their ponderous and ebony jaws. It was the work of the rushing gust—but then without those doors there *did* stand the lofty and enshrouded figure of the lady Madeline of Usher. There was blood upon her white robes, and the evidence of some bitter struggle upon every portion of her emaciated frame. For a moment she remained trembling and reeling to and fro upon the threshold, then, with a low moaning cry, fell heavily inward upon the person of her brother, and in her violent and now final death-agonies, bore him to the floor a corpse, and a victim to the terrors he had anticipated.

From that chamber, and from that mansion, I fled aghast. The storm was still abroad in all its wrath as I found myself crossing the old causeway. Suddenly there shot along the path a wild light, and I turned to see whence a gleam so unusual could have issued; for the vast house and its shadows were alone behind me. The radiance was that of the full, setting, and blood-red moon, which now shone vividly through that once barely discernible fissure, of which I have before spoken as extending from the roof of the building, in a zigzag direction, to the base. While I gazed, this fissure rapidly widened—there came a fierce breath of the whirlwind—the entire orb of the satellite burst at once upon my sight—my brain reeled as I saw the mighty walls rushing asunder—there was a long tumultuous shouting sound like the voice of a thousand waters—and the deep and dank tarn at my feet closed sullenly and silently over the fragments of the "HOUSE OF USHER."

The Tell-Tale Heart   1843

True!—nervous—very, very dreadfully nervous I had been and am; but why *will* you say that I am mad? The disease had sharpened my senses—not destroyed—not dulled them. Above all was the sense of hearing acute. I heard all things in the heaven and in the earth. I heard many things in hell. How, then, am I mad? Hearken! and observe how healthily—how calmly I can tell you the whole story.

It is impossible to say how first the idea entered my brain; but once conceived, it haunted me day and night. Object there was none. Passion there was none. I loved the old man. He had never wronged me. He had never given me insult. For his gold I had no desire. I think it was his eye! yes, it was this! One of his eyes resembled that of a vulture—a pale blue eye, with a film over it. Whenever it fell upon me, my blood ran cold; and so by degrees—very gradually—I made up my mind to take the life of the old man, and thus rid myself of the eye for ever.

Now this is the point. You fancy me mad. Madmen know nothing. But you should have seen *me*. You should have seen how wisely I proceeded—with what caution—with what foresight—with what dissimulation I went to work! I was never kinder to the old man than during the whole week before I killed him. And every night, about midnight, I turned the latch of his door and opened it—oh, so gently! And then, when I had made an opening sufficient for my head, I put in a dark lantern, all closed, closed, so that no light shone out, and then I thrust in my head. Oh, you would have laughed to see how cunningly I thrust it in! I moved it slowly—very, very slowly, so that I might not disturb the old man's sleep. It took me an hour to place my whole head within the opening so far that I could see him as he lay upon his bed. Ha—would a madman have been so wise as this? And then, when my head was well in the room, I undid the lantern cautiously—oh, so cautiously—cautiously (for the hinges creaked)—I undid it just so much that a single thin ray fell upon the vulture eye. And this I did for seven long nights—every night just after midnight—but I found the eye always closed; and so it was impossible to do the work; for it was not the old man who vexed me, but his Evil Eye. And every morning, when the day broke, I went boldly into the chamber, and spoke courageously to him, calling him by name in a hearty tone, and inquiring how he had passed the night. So you see he would have been a very profound old man, indeed, to suspect that every night, just at twelve, I looked in upon him while he slept.

Upon the eighth night I was more than usually cautious in opening the door. A watch's minute hand moves more quickly than did mine. Never before that night had I *felt* the extent of my own powers—of my sagacity. I could scarcely contain my feelings of triumph. To think that there I was, opening the door, little by little, and he not even to dream of my secret deeds or thoughts. I fairly chuckled at the idea; and perhaps he heard me; for he moved on the bed suddenly, as if startled. Now you may think that I drew back—but no. His room was as black as pitch with the thick darkness (for the shutters were close fastened, through fear of robbers), and so I knew that he could not see the opening of the door, and I kept pushing it on steadily, steadily.

I had my head in, and was about to open the lantern, when my thumb slipped upon the tin fastening, and the old man sprang up in the bed, crying out—"Who's there?"

I kept quite still and said nothing. For a whole hour I did not move a muscle, and in the meantime I did not hear him lie down. He was still sitting up in the bed listening;—just as I have done, night after night, hearkening to the death watches in the wall.

Presently I heard a slight groan, and I knew it was the groan of mortal terror. It was not a groan of pain or of grief—oh, no!—it was the low stifled sound that arises from the bottom of the soul when overcharged with awe. I knew the sound well. Many a night, just at midnight, when all the world slept, it has welled up from my own bosom, deepening with its dreadful echo, the terrors that distracted me. I say I knew it well. I knew what the old man felt, and pitied him, although I chuckled at heart. I knew that he had been lying awake ever since the first slight noise, when he had turned in the bed. His fears had been ever since growing upon him. He had been trying to fancy them causeless, but could not. He had been saying to himself—"It is nothing but the wind in the chimney—it is only a mouse crossing the floor," or "it is merely a cricket which has made a single chirp." Yes, he has been trying to comfort himself with these suppositions; but he had found all in vain. *All in vain;* because Death, in approaching him, had stalked with his black shadow before him, and enveloped the victim. And it was the mournful influence of the unperceived shadow that caused him to feel—although he neither saw nor heard—to *feel* the presence of my head within the room.

When I had waited a long time, very patiently, without hearing him lie down, I resolved to open a little—a very, very little crevice in the lantern. So I opened it—you cannot imagine how stealthily, stealthily—until, at length, a single dim ray, like the thread of the spider, shot from out the crevice and full upon the vulture eye.

It was open—wide, wide open—and I grew furious as I gazed upon it. I saw it with perfect distinctness—all a dull blue, with a hideous veil over it that chilled the very marrow in my bones, but I could see nothing else of the old man's face or person: for I had directed the ray as if by instinct, precisely upon the damned spot.

And now have I not told you that what you mistake for madness is but over-acuteness of the senses? — now, I say, there came to my ears a low, dull, quick sound, such as a watch makes when enveloped in cotton. I knew *that* sound well too. It was the beating of the old man's heart. It increased my fury, as the beating of a drum stimulates the soldier into courage.

But even yet I refrained and kept still. I scarcely breathed. I held the lantern motionless. I tried how steadily I could maintain the ray upon the eye. Meantime the hellish tattoo of the heart increased. It grew quicker and quicker, and louder and louder every instant. The old man's terror *must* have been extreme! It grew louder, I say, louder every moment! — do you mark me well? I have told you that I am nervous: so I am. And now at the dead hour of the night, amid the dreadful silence of that old house, so strange a noise as this excited me to uncontrollable terror. Yet, for some minutes longer I refrained and stood still. But the beating grew louder, louder! I thought the heart must burst. And now a new anxiety seized me — the sound would be heard by a neighbor! The old man's hour had come! With a loud yell, I threw open the lantern and leaped into the room. He shrieked once — once only. In an instant I dragged him to the floor, and pulled the heavy bed over him. I then smiled gaily, to find the deed so far done. But, for many minutes, the heart beat on with a muffled sound. This, however, did not vex me; it would not be heard through the wall. At length it ceased. The old man was dead. I removed the bed and examined the corpse. Yes, he was stone, stone dead. I placed my hand upon the heart and held it there many minutes. There was no pulsation. He was stone dead. His eye would trouble me no more.

If still you think me mad, you will think so no longer when I describe the wise precautions I took for the concealment of the body. The night waned, and I worked hastily, but in silence. First of all I dismembered the corpse. I cut off the head and the arms and the legs.

I then took up three planks from the flooring of the chamber, and deposited all between the scantlings. I then replaced the boards so cleverly, so cunningly, that no human eye — not even *his* — could have detected anything wrong. There was nothing to wash out — no stain of any kind — no blood-spot whatever. I had been too wary for that. A tub had caught all — ha! ha!

When I had made an end of these labors, it was four o'clock — still dark as midnight. As the bell sounded the hour, there came a knocking at the street door. I went down to open it with a light heart — for what had I *now* to fear? There entered three men, who introduced themselves, with perfect suavity, as officers of the police. A shriek had been heard by a neighbor during the night; suspicion of foul play had been aroused; information had been lodged at the police office, and they (the officers) had been deputed to search the premises.

I smiled — for *what* had I to fear? I bade the gentlemen welcome. The shriek, I said, was my own in a dream. The old man, I mentioned, was absent in the country. I took my visitors all over the house. I bade them search — search *well*. I led them, at length, to *his* chamber. I showed them his treasures, secure, undisturbed. In the enthusiasm of my confidence, I brought chairs into the room, and desired them *here* to rest from their fatigues, while I myself, in the wild audacity of my perfect triumph, placed my own seat upon the very spot beneath which reposed the corpse of the victim.

The officers were satisfied. My *manner* had convinced them. I was singularly at ease. They sat, and while I answered cheerily, they chatted familiar things. But, ere long, I felt myself getting pale and wished them gone. My head ached, and I fancied a ringing in my ears: but still they sat and still chatted. The ringing became more distinct: — it continued and became more distinct: I talked more freely to get rid of the feeling: but it continued and gained definitiveness — until, at length, I found that the noise was *not* within my ears.

No doubt I now grew *very* pale; — but I talked more fluently, and with a heightened voice. Yet the sound increased — and what could I do? It was *a low, dull, quick sound — much such a sound as a watch makes when enveloped in cotton.* I gasped for breath — and yet the officers heard it not. I talked more quickly — more vehemently; but the noise steadily increased. I arose and argued about trifles, in a high key and with violent gesticulations, but the noise steadily increased. Why *would* they not be gone? I paced the floor to and fro with heavy strides, as if excited to fury by the observation of the men — but the noise steadily increased. Oh God! what *could* I do? I foamed — I raved — I swore! I swung the chair upon which I had been sitting, and grated it upon the boards, but the noise arose over all and continually increased. It grew louder — louder — *louder!* And still the men chatted pleasantly, and smiled. Was it possible they heard not? Almighty God! — no, no! They heard! — they suspected! — they *knew!* — they were making a mockery of my horror! — this I thought, and this I think. But any thing was better than this agony! Any thing was more tolerable than this derision! I could bear those hypocritical smiles no longer! I felt that I must scream or die! — and now — again! — hark! louder! louder! louder! *louder!* —

"Villains!" I shrieked, "dissemble no more! I admit the deed! — tear up the planks! — here, here! — it is the beating of his hideous heart!"

ANNIE PROULX

Annie Proulx (b. 1935) was born in Norwich, Connecticut, the oldest of five sisters. Her mother was a painter and amateur naturalist whose family had lived in Connecticut since 1635 as farmers, millworkers, inventors, and artists. Her father was the vice president of a textile company, and Proulx remembers that "we moved frequently when I was a child, North Carolina, Vermont, Maine, Rhode Island, town after town." She credits her mother for encouraging her to observe the environment closely. "From the time I was extremely small, I was told, 'Look at that.' . . . everything — from the wale of corduroy to the broken button to the loose thread to the disheveled mustache to the clouded eye." Proulx attended Colby College, the University of Vermont, and Concordia University, earning a B.A. and an M.A., as well as passing her doctoral oral examinations in history. In 1975, with

few teaching jobs available, she abandoned work on her Ph.D. and began a per-
ilous career in freelance journalism. In the 1980s she published six "how-to" books
on a variety of subjects, including Plan and Make Your Own Fences and Gates,
Walkways, Walls and Drives *(1983). During this time she also raised her three*
sons from her third marriage while living in an isolated cabin in a rural town in
Vermont. Later she said that this life made her "very alert and aware of every-
thing, from tree branches and wild mushrooms to animal tracks. It's an excellent
training for the eye. Most of us stagger around deaf and dumb."

Supporting herself and her sons on her meager income as a journalist,
Proulx began to write stories for fun, creating one or two a year. "It was my pleas-
ure, my indulgence, when I wanted to do something that wasn't fishing or canoe-
ing." Most of these early stories were written for a men's magazine about hunting
and fishing, where her first editor told her that she had to publish under a mascu-
line name, "something like Joe or Zack, retrievers' names," she complained. They
compromised on using her initials, E. A. Proulx, the E standing for her first name,
Edna. In 1983 and 1987, two of her stories were listed among the "Distinguished
Short Stories" in Best American Short Stories. *In 1988, Proulx published her*
first book of fiction, the nine stories set in northern Vermont constituting Heart
Songs and Other Stories.

Proulx's contract with her publisher Charles Scribner's Sons for Heart
Songs *also required her to produce a novel. She felt she "had not a clue about writ-*
ing a novel, or even the faintest desire. I thought of myself as a short story writer.
Period, period, period." Proulx found the inspiration for her first work of long fic-
tion in a group of old postcards, and after her novel Postcards *appeared in 1992,*
she told interviewer Esther Fein, "It was astonishing how easy writing a novel was
compared to writing a short story. I was so used to cramping thoughts and sections
and cutting, and suddenly I had room to expand." In 1993 Proulx was the recipi-
ent of the PEN/Faulkner Award for Postcards. *The following year her second*
novel, The Shipping News, *won the National Book Award and the Pulitzer*
Prize. This was followed by the novel Accordion Crimes *in 1996. Proulx has*
moved from Vermont to Wyoming, the location of her story "The Blood Bay,"
included in Close Range *(2000).*

WEB   *Research Annie Proulx and answer questions about her work at*
bedfordstmartins.com/charters/litwriters.

The Blood Bay   2000

For Buzzy Malli

The winter of 1886–87 was terrible. Every goddamn history of the high
plains says so. There were great stocks of cattle on overgrazed land during the
droughty summer. Early wet snow froze hard so the cattle could not break
through the crust to the grass. Blizzards and freeze-eye cold followed, the gant
bodies of cattle piling up in draws and coulees.

A young Montana cowboy, somewhat vain, had skimped on coat and
mittens and put all his wages into a fine pair of handmade boots. He crossed

into Wyoming Territory thinking it would be warmer, for it was south of where he was. That night he froze to death on Powder River's bitter west bank, that stream of famous dimensions and direction — an inch deep, a mile wide, and she flows uphill from Texas.

The next afternoon three cowpunchers from the Box Spring outfit near Suggs rode past his corpse, blue as a whetstone and half-buried in snow. They were savvy and salty. They wore blanket coats, woolly chaps, grease-wool scarves tied over their hats and under their bristled chins, sheepskin mitts, and two of them were fortunate enough to park their feet in good boots and heavy socks. The third, Dirt Sheets, a cross-eyed drinker of hair-oil, was all right on top but his luck was running muddy near the bottom, no socks and curl-toe boots cracked and holed.

"That can a corn beef's wearin my size boots," Sheets said and got off his horse for the first time that day. He pulled at the Montana cowboy's left boot but it was frozen on. The right one didn't come off any easier.

"Son of a sick steer in a snowbank," he said, "I'll cut em off and thaw em after supper." Sheets pulled out a Bowie knife and sawed through Montana's shins just above the boot tops, put the booted feet in his saddlebags, admiring the tooled leather and topstitched hearts and clubs. They rode on down the river looking for strays, found a dozen bogged in deep drifts and lost most of the daylight getting them out.

"Too late to try for the bunkhouse. Old man Grice's shack is somewheres up along. He's bound a have dried prunes or other dainties or at least a hot stove." The temperature was dropping, so cold that spit crackled in the air and a man didn't dare to piss for fear he'd be rooted fast until spring. They agreed it must be forty below and more, the wind scything up a nice Wyoming howler.

They found the shack four miles north. Old man Grice opened the door a crack.

"Come on in, puncher or rustler, I don't care."

"We'll put our horses up. Where's the barn."

"Barn. Never had one. There's a lean-to out there behind the woodpile should keep em from blowin away or maybe freezin. I got my two horses in here beside the dish cupboard. I pamper them babies somethin terrible. Sleep where you can find a space, but I'm tellin you don't bother that blood bay none, he will mull you up and spit you out. He's a spirited steed. Pull up a chair and have some a this son-of-a-bitch stew. And I got plenty conversation juice a wash it down. Hot biscuits just comin out a the oven."

It was a fine evening, eating, drinking, and playing cards, swapping lies, the stove kicking out heat, old man Grice's spoiled horses sighing in comfort. The only disagreeable tone to the evening from the waddies'° point of view was the fact that their host cleaned them out, took them for three dollars and four bits. Around midnight Grice blew out the lamp and got in his bunk and the three punchers stretched out on the floor. Sheets set his trophies behind the stove, laid his head on his saddle, and went to sleep.

---

waddies: Cowboys.

He woke half an hour before daylight, recalled it was his mother's birthday and if he wanted to telegraph a filial sentiment to her he would have to ride faster than chain lightning with the links snapped, for the Overland office closed at noon. He checked his grisly trophies, found them thawed and pulled the boots and socks off the originals, drew them onto his own pedal extremities. He threw the bare Montana feet and his old boots in the corner near the dish cupboard, slipped out like a falling feather, saddled his horse, and rode away. The wind was low and the fine cold air refreshed him.

Old man Grice was up with the sun grinding coffee beans and frying bacon. He glanced down at his rolled-up guests and said, "Coffee's ready." The blood bay stamped and kicked at something that looked like a man's foot. Old man Grice took a closer look.

"There's a bad start to the day," he said, "it is a man's foot and there's the other." He counted the sleeping guests. There were only two of them.

"Wake up, survivors, for god's sake wake up and get up."

The two punchers rolled out, stared wild-eyed at the old man who was fairly frothing, pointing at the feet on the floor behind the blood bay.

"He's ate Sheets. Ah, I knew he was a hard horse, but to eat a man whole. You savage bugger," he screamed at the blood bay and drove him out into the scorching cold. "You'll never eat human meat again. You'll sleep out with the blizzards and wolves, you hell-bound fiend." Secretly he was pleased to own a horse with the sand to eat a raw cowboy.

The leftover Box Spring riders were up and drinking coffee. They squinted at old man Grice, hitched at their gun belts.

"Ah, boys, for god's sake, it was a terrible accident. I didn't know what a brute of a animal was that blood bay. Let's keep this to ourselves. Sheets was no prize and I've got forty gold dollars says so and the three and four bits I took off a you last night. Eat your bacon, don't make no trouble. There's enough trouble in the world without no more."

No, they wouldn't make trouble and they put the heavy money in their saddlebags, drank a last cup of hot coffee, saddled up, and rode out into the grinning morning.

When they saw Sheets that night at the bunkhouse they nodded, congratulated him on his mother's birthday but said nothing about blood bays or forty-three dollars and four bits. The arithmetic stood comfortable.

LESLIE MARMON SILKO

Leslie Marmon Silko (b. 1948), a Laguna Pueblo, was born and grew up in New Mexico. She was educated at Board of Indian Affairs schools in Laguna, a Catholic school in Albuquerque, and the University of New Mexico, where she received her B.A. in English in 1969. After teaching at various colleges, she became a professor of English at the University of Arizona at Tucson. Silko's first novel, Ceremony *(1977), is regarded as one of the most important books in modern Native American literature. In it she forged a connection between the shared past of the tribe and the individual life of a Native American returning home after World War II. Silko has received a National Endowment for the Arts fellowship, a Pushcart Prize, and a three-year grant from the MacArthur Foundation, which enabled her to take time off from teaching and become "a little less beholden to the everyday world."*

Storyteller (1981), a collection of tribal folktales, family anecdotes, photographs by her grandfather, and her own poems and stories, is Silko's personal anthology of the Laguna Pueblo culture. "The Man to Send Rain Clouds" is from that collection.

Silko has said that she writes "because I like seeing how I can translate [a] sort of feeling or flavor or sense of a story that's told and heard onto the page." Some recent books are The Almanac of the Dead *(1991),* Sacred Water *(1993), and* Garden in the Dunes *(1999).*

COMMENTARY   *Leslie Marmon Silko, "Language and Literature from a Pueblo Indian Perspective," page 586.*

WEB   *Research Leslie Marmon Silko and answer questions about her work at bedfordstmartins.com/charters/litwriters.*

The Man to Send Rain Clouds   1981

They found him under a big cottonwood tree. His Levi jacket and pants were faded light blue so that he had been easy to find. The big cottonwood tree stood apart from a small grove of winterbare cottonwoods which grew in the wide, sandy arroyo. He had been dead for a day or more, and the sheep had wandered and scattered up and down the arroyo. Leon and his brother-in-law, Ken, gathered the sheep and left them in the pen at the sheep camp before they returned to the cottonwood tree. Leon waited under the tree while Ken drove the truck through the deep sand to the edge of the arroyo. He squinted up at the sun and unzipped his jacket—it sure was hot for this time of year. But high and northwest the blue mountains were still in snow. Ken came sliding down the low, crumbling bank about fifty yards down, and he was bringing the red blanket.

Before they wrapped the old man, Leon took a piece of string out of his pocket and tied a small gray feather in the old man's long white hair. Ken gave him the paint. Across the brown wrinkled forehead he drew a streak of white and along the high cheekbones he drew a strip of blue paint. He paused and watched Ken throw pinches of corn meal and pollen into the wind that fluttered the small gray feather. Then Leon painted with yellow under the old man's broad nose, and finally, when he had painted green across the chin, he smiled.

"Send us rain clouds, Grandfather." They laid the bundle in the back of the pickup and covered it with a heavy tarp before they started back to the pueblo.

They turned off the highway onto the sandy pueblo road. Not long after they passed the store and post office they saw Father Paul's car coming toward them. When he recognized their faces he slowed his car and waved for them to stop. The young priest rolled down the car window.

"Did you find old Teofilo?" he asked loudly.

Leon stopped the truck. "Good morning, Father. We were just out to the sheep camp. Everything is O.K. now."

"Thank God for that. Teofilo is a very old man. You really shouldn't allow him to stay at the sheep camp alone."

"No, he won't do that any more now."

"Well, I'm glad you understand. I hope I'll be seeing you at Mass this week—we missed you last Sunday. See if you can get old Teofilo to come with you." The priest smiled and waved at them as they drove away.

Louise and Teresa were waiting. The table was set for lunch, and the coffee was boiling on the black iron stove. Leon looked at Louise and then at Teresa.

"We found him under a cottonwood tree in the big arroyo near sheep camp. I guess he sat down to rest in the shade and never got up again." Leon walked toward the old man's bed. The red plaid shawl had been shaken and spread carefully over the bed, and a new brown flannel shirt and pair of stiff new Levi's were arranged neatly beside the pillow. Louise held the screen door open while Leon and Ken carried in the red blanket. He looked small and shriveled, and after they dressed him in the new shirt and pants he seemed more shrunken.

It was noontime now because the church bells rang the Angelus. They ate the beans with hot bread, and nobody said anything until after Teresa poured the coffee.

Ken stood up and put on his jacket. "I'll see about the gravediggers. Only the top layer of soil is frozen. I think it can be ready before dark."

Leon nodded his head and finished his coffee. After Ken had been gone for a while, the neighbors and clanspeople came quietly to embrace Teofilo's family and to leave food on the table because the gravediggers would come to eat when they were finished.

The sky in the west was full of pale yellow light. Louise stood outside with her hands in the pockets of Leon's green army jacket that was too big for her. The funeral was over, and the old men had taken their candles and medicine bags and were gone. She waited until the body was laid into the pickup before she said anything to Leon. She touched his arm, and he noticed that her hands were still dusty from the corn meal that she had sprinkled around the old man. When she spoke, Leon could not hear her.

"What did you say? I didn't hear you."

"I said that I had been thinking about something."

"About what?"

"About the priest sprinkling holy water for Grandpa. So he won't be thirsty."

Leon stared at the new moccasins that Teofilo had made for the ceremonial dances in the summer. They were nearly hidden by the red blanket. It was getting colder, and the wind pushed gray dust down the narrow pueblo road. The sun was approaching the long mesa where it disappeared during the winter. Louise stood there shivering and watching his face. Then he zipped up his jacket and opened the truck door. "I'll see if he's there."

Ken stopped the pickup at the church, and Leon got out; and then Ken drove down the hill to the graveyard where people were waiting. Leon knocked at the old carved door with its symbols of the Lamb. While he waited he looked up at the twin bells from the king of Spain with the last sunlight pouring around them in their tower.

The priest opened the door and smiled when he saw who it was. "Come in! What brings you here this evening?"

The priest walked toward the kitchen, and Leon stood with his cap in his hand, playing with the earflaps and examining the living room—the brown sofa, the green armchair, and the brass lamp that hung down from the ceiling by links of chain. The priest dragged a chair out of the kitchen and offered it to Leon.

"No thank you, Father. I only came to ask you if you would bring your holy water to the graveyard."

The priest turned away from Leon and looked out the window at the patio full of shadows and the dining-room windows of the nuns' cloister across the patio. The curtains were heavy, and the light from within faintly penetrated; it was impossible to see the nuns inside eating supper. "Why didn't you tell me he was dead? I could have brought the Last Rites anyway."

Leon smiled. "It wasn't necessary, Father."

The priest stared down at his scuffed brown loafers and the worn hem of his cassock. "For a Christian burial it was necessary."

His voice was distant, and Leon thought that his blue eyes looked tired. "It's O.K., Father, we just want him to have plenty of water."

The priest sank down into the green chair and picked up a glossy missionary magazine. He turned the colored pages full of lepers and pagans without looking at them.

"You know I can't do that, Leon. There should have been the Last Rites and a funeral Mass at the very least."

Leon put on his green cap and pulled the flaps down over his ears. "It's getting late, Father. I've got to go."

When Leon opened the door Father Paul stood up and said, "Wait." He left the room and came back wearing a long brown overcoat. He followed Leon out the door and across the dim churchyard to the adobe steps in front of the church. They both stooped to fit through the low adobe entrance. And when they started down the hill to the graveyard only half of the sun was visible above the mesa.

The priest approached the grave slowly, wondering how they had managed to dig into the frozen ground; and then he remembered that this was New Mexico, and saw the pile of cold loose sand beside the hole. The people stood close to each other with little clouds of steam puffing from their faces. The priest looked at them and saw a pile of jackets, gloves, and scarves in the yellow, dry tumbleweeds that grew in the graveyard. He looked at the red blanket, not sure that Teofilo was so small, wondering if it wasn't some perverse Indian trick—something they did in March to ensure a good harvest—wondering if maybe old Teofilo was actually at sheep camp corralling the sheep for the night. But there he was, facing into a cold dry wind and squinting at the last sunlight, ready to bury a red wool blanket while the faces of his parishioners were in shadow with the last warmth of the sun on their backs.

His fingers were stiff, and it took him a long time to twist the lid off the holy water. Drops of water fell on the red blanket and soaked into dark icy spots. He sprinkled the grave and the water disappeared almost before it touched the dim, cold sand; it reminded him of something—he tried to remember what it was, because he thought if he could remember he might understand this. He sprinkled more water; he shook the container until it was empty, and the water fell through the light from sundown like August rain that fell while the sun was still shining, almost evaporating before it touched the wilted squash flowers.

The wind pulled at the priest's brown Franciscan robe and swirled away the corn meal and pollen that had been sprinkled on the blanket. They lowered the bundle into the ground, and they didn't bother to untie the stiff pieces of new rope that were tied around the ends of the blanket. The sun was gone, and over on the highway the eastbound lane was full of headlights. The priest walked away slowly. Leon watched him climb the hill, and when he had disappeared within the tall, thick walls, Leon turned to look up at the high blue mountains in the deep snow that reflected a faint red light from the west. He felt good because it was finished, and he was happy about the sprinkling of the holy water; now the old man could send them big thunderclouds for sure.

JOHN STEINBECK

John Steinbeck (1902–1968) was born in Salinas and raised near Monterey in the fertile farm country of the Salinas Valley in California, the locale for his story "The Chrysanthemums." His mother was a former schoolteacher; his father was the county treasurer. In high school Steinbeck wrote for the school newspaper and was president of his class. He enjoyed literature from an early age and read novels by Gustave Flaubert, Fyodor Dostoevsky, and Thomas Hardy in the family library. Enrolled at Stanford University as an English major, Steinbeck dropped out before graduating and worked at odd jobs—fruit picker, caretaker, laboratory assistant—while he practiced writing fiction. Several times he took short-term jobs with the Spreckels Sugar Company and gained a perspective on labor problems, which he would later describe in his novels.

In 1929 Steinbeck began his literary career by publishing Cup of Gold, *a fictionalized biography of Henry Morgan, the seventeenth-century Welsh pirate. His next book,* The Pastures of Heaven (1932), *is a collection of short stories about the people in a farm community in California. The critic Brian Barbour has stated that Steinbeck realized early in his career that the short story form was not congenial to his talents. He needed the more expansive form of the novel to give his characters the room for what he considered real growth. In 1936 Steinbeck wrote* In Dubious Battle, *his first major political novel. He then published four more novels and another book of short fiction before his greatest work,* The Grapes of Wrath *(1939). This book, about a family from the Dust Bowl that emigrates to California and struggles to make a living despite agricultural exploitation, won Steinbeck the Pulitzer Prize. Among his many other successful novels are* East of Eden *(1952) and* The Winter of Our Discontent *(1961). He received the Nobel Prize for literature in 1962.*

One of the most accomplished popular novelists in the United States, Steinbeck excelled — as did Ernest Hemingway — in the creation of exciting conflicts, convincing dialogue, and recognizable characters to dramatize his philosophy of life. Although his production of short stories was relatively slight, his work is often anthologized because of his clear, realistic treatment of social themes as his characters struggle to forge meaningful lives. "The Chrysanthemums" echoes the D. H. Lawrence story "Odour of Chrysanthemums" in its concerns with sexual roles and the difficulty of striking a balance between self-interest and the needs of others. Steinbeck's biographer, Jackson J. Benson, also commented that the excellence of "The Chrysanthemums" lies in "its delicate, indirect handling of a woman's emotions . . . [especially] the difficulty of the woman in finding a creative significant role in a male-dominated society."

WEB   *Research John Steinbeck and answer questions about his work at bedfordstmartins.com/charters/litwriters.*

The Chrysanthemums   1938

The high grey-flannel fog of winter closed off the Salinas Valley from the sky and from all the rest of the world. On every side it sat like a lid on the mountains and made of the great valley a closed pot. On the broad, level land floor the gang plows bit deep and left the black earth shining like metal where the shares had cut. On the foothill ranches across the Salinas River, the yellow stubble fields seemed to be bathed in pale cold sunshine, but there was no sunshine in the valley now in December. The thick willow scrub along the river flamed with sharp and positive yellow leaves.

It was a time of quiet and of waiting. The air was cold and tender. A light wind blew up from the southwest so that the farmers were mildly hopeful of a good rain before long; but fog and rain do not go together.

Across the river, on Henry Allen's foothill ranch there was little work to be done, for the hay was cut and stored and the orchards were plowed up to receive the rain deeply when it should come. The cattle on the higher slopes were becoming shaggy and rough-coated.

Elisa Allen, working in her flower garden, looked down across the yard and saw Henry, her husband, talking to two men in business suits. The three of them stood by the tractor shed, each man with one foot on the side of the little Fordson. They smoked cigarettes and studied the machine as they talked.

Elisa watched them for a moment and then went back to her work. She was thirty-five. Her face was lean and strong and her eyes were as clear as water. Her figure looked blocked and heavy in her gardening costume, a man's black hat pulled low down over her eyes, clod-hopper shoes, a figured print dress almost completely covered by a big corduroy apron with four big pockets to hold the snips, the trowel and scratcher, the seeds, and the knife she worked with. She wore heavy leather gloves to protect her hands while she worked.

She was cutting down the old year's chrysanthemum stalks with a pair of short and powerful scissors. She looked down toward the men by the tractor shed now and then. Her face was eager and mature and handsome; even her work with the scissors was overeager, overpowerful. The chrysanthemum stems seemed too small and easy for her energy.

She brushed a cloud of hair out of her eyes with the back of her glove, and left a smudge of earth on her cheek in doing it. Behind her stood the neat white farm house with red geraniums close-banked around it as high as the windows. It was a hard-swept looking little house with hard-polished windows, and a clean mud-mat on the front steps.

Elisa cast another glance toward the tractor shed. The strangers were getting into their Ford coupe. She took off a glove and put her strong fingers down into the forest of new green chrysanthemum sprouts that were growing around the old roots. She spread the leaves and looked down among the close-growing stems. No aphids were there, no sowbugs or snails or cutworms. Her terrier fingers destroyed such pests before they could get started.

Elisa started at the sound of her husband's voice. He had come near quietly, and he leaned over the wire fence that protected her flower garden from cattle and dogs and chickens.

"At it again," he said. "You've got a strong new crop coming."

Elisa straightened her back and pulled on the gardening glove again. "Yes. They'll be strong this coming year." In her tone and on her face there was a little smugness.

"You've got a gift with things," Henry observed. "Some of those yellow chrysanthemums you had this year were ten inches across. I wish you'd work out in the orchard and raise some apples that big."

Her eyes sharpened. "Maybe I could do it, too. I've a gift with things, all right. My mother had it. She could stick anything in the ground and make it grow. She said it was having planters' hands that knew how to do it."

"Well, it sure works with flowers," he said.

"Henry, who were those men you were talking to?"

"Why, sure, that's what I came to tell you. They were from the Western Meat Company. I sold thirty head of three-year-old steers. Got nearly my own price, too."

"Good," she said. "Good for you."

"And I thought," he continued, "I thought how it's Saturday afternoon, and we might go into Salinas for dinner at a restaurant, and then to a picture show—to celebrate, you see."

"Good," she repeated. "Oh, yes. That will be good."

Henry put on his joking tone. "There's fights tonight. How'd you like to go to the fights?"

"Oh, no," she said breathlessly. "No, I wouldn't like fights."

"Just fooling, Elisa. We'll go to a movie. Let's see. It's two now. I'm going to take Scotty and bring down those steers from the hill. It'll take us maybe two hours. We'll go in town about five and have dinner at the Cominos Hotel. Like that?"

"Of course I'll like it. It's good to eat away from home."

"All right, then. I'll go get up a couple of horses."

She said, "I'll have plenty of time to transplant some of these sets, I guess."

She heard her husband calling Scotty down by the barn. And a little later she saw the two men ride up the pale yellow hillside in search of the steers.

There was a little square sandy bed kept for rooting the chrysanthemums. With her trowel she turned the soil over and over, and smoothed it and patted it firm. Then she dug ten parallel trenches to receive the sets. Back at the chrysanthemum bed she pulled out the little crisp shoots, trimmed off the leaves at each one with her scissors, and laid it on a small orderly pile.

A squeak of wheels and plod of hoofs came from the road. Elisa looked up. The country road ran along the dense bank of willows and cottonwoods that bordered the river, and up this road came a curious vehicle, curiously drawn. It was an old spring-wagon, with a round canvas top on it like the corner of a prairie schooner. It was drawn by an old bay horse and a little grey-and-white burro. A big stubble-bearded man sat between the cover flaps and drove the crawling team. Underneath the wagon, between the hind wheels, a lean and rangy mongrel dog walked sedately. Words were painted on the canvas, in clumsy, crooked letters. "Pots, pans, knives, sisors, lawn mores, Fixed." Two rows of articles, and the triumphantly definitive "Fixed" below. The black paint had run down in little sharp points beneath each letter.

Elisa, squatting on the ground, watched to see the crazy, loose-jointed wagon pass by. But it didn't pass. It turned into the farm road in front of her house, crooked old wheels skirling and squeaking. The rangy dog darted from between the wheels and ran ahead. Instantly the two ranch shepherds flew out at him. Then all three stopped, and with stiff and quivering tails, with taut straight legs, with ambassadorial dignity, they slowly circled, sniffing daintily. The caravan pulled up to Elisa's wire fence and stopped. Now the newcomer dog, feeling outnumbered, lowered his tail and retired under the wagon with raised hackles and bared teeth.

The man on the seat called out, "That's a bad dog in a fight when he gets started."

Elisa laughed. "I see he is. How soon does he generally get started?"

The man caught up her laughter and echoed it heartily. "Sometimes not for weeks and weeks," he said. He climbed stiffly down, over the wheel. The horse and the donkey dropped like unwatered flowers.

Elisa saw that he was a very big man. Although his hair and beard were greying, he did not look old. His worn black suit was wrinkled and spotted with grease. The laughter had disappeared from his face and eyes the moment his laughing voice ceased. His eyes were dark, and they were full of the brooding that gets in the eyes of teamsters and of sailors. The calloused hands he rested on the wire fence were cracked, and every crack was a black line. He took off his battered hat.

"I'm off my general road, ma'am," he said. "Does this dirt road cut over across the river to the Los Angeles highway?"

Elisa stood up and shoved the thick scissors in her apron pocket. "Well, yes, it does, but it winds around and then fords the river. I don't think your team could pull through the sand."

He replied with some asperity, "It might surprise you what them beasts can pull through."

"When they get started?" she asked.

He smiled for a second. "Yes. When they get started."

"Well," said Elisa, "I think you'll save time if you go back to the Salinas road and pick up the highway there."

He drew a big finger down the chicken wire and made it sing. "I ain't in any hurry, ma'am. I go from Seattle to San Diego and back every year. Takes all my time. About six months each way. I aim to follow nice weather."

Elisa took off her gloves and stuffed them in the apron pocket with the scissors. She touched the under edge of her man's hat, searching for fugitive hairs. "That sounds like a nice kind of a way to live," she said.

He leaned confidentially over the fence. "Maybe you noticed the writing on my wagon. I mend pots and sharpen knives and scissors. You got any of them things to do?"

"Oh, no," she said, quickly. "Nothing like that." Her eyes hardened with resistance.

"Scissors is the worst thing," he explained. "Most people just ruin scissors trying to sharpen 'em, but I know how. I got a special tool. It's a little bobbit kind of thing, and patented. But it sure does the trick."

"No. My scissors are all sharp."

"All right, then. Take a pot," he continued earnestly, "a bent pot, or a pot with a hole. I can make it like new so you don't have to buy no new ones. That's a savings for you."

"No," she said shortly. "I tell you I have nothing like that for you to do."

His face fell to an exaggerated sadness. His voice took on a whining undertone. "I ain't had a thing to do today. Maybe I won't have no supper tonight. You see I'm off my regular road. I know folks on the highway clear from Seattle to San Diego. They save their things for me to sharpen up because they know I do it so good and save them money."

"I'm sorry," Elisa said irritably. "I haven't anything for you to do."

His eyes left her face and fell to searching the ground. They roamed about until they came to the chrysanthemum bed where she had been working. "What's them plants, ma'am?"

The irritation and resistance melted from Elisa's face. "Oh, those are chrysanthemums, giant whites and yellows. I raise them every year, bigger than anybody around here."

"Kind of a long-stemmed flower? Looks like a quick puff of colored smoke?" he asked.

"That's it. What a nice way to describe them."

"They smell kind of nasty till you get used to them," he said.

"It's a good bitter smell," she retorted, "not nasty at all."

He changed his tone quickly, "I like the smell myself."

"I had ten-inch-blooms this year," she said.

The man leaned farther over the fence. "Look, I know a lady down the road a piece, has got the nicest garden you ever seen. Got nearly every kind of flower but no chrysanthemums. Last time I was mending a copper-bottom washtub for her (that's a hard job but I do it good), she said to me, 'If you ever run acrost some nice chrysanthemums I wish you'd try to get me a few seeds.' That's what she told me."

Elisa's eyes grew alert and eager. "She couldn't have known much about chrysanthemums. You *can* raise them from seed, but it's much easier to root the little sprouts you see there."

"Oh," he said. "I s'pose I can't take none to her, then."

"Why yes you can," Elisa cried. "I can put some in damp sand, and you can carry them right along with you. They'll take root in the pot if you keep them damp. And then she can transplant them."

"She'd sure like to have some, ma'am. You say they're nice ones?"

"Beautiful," she said. "Oh, beautiful." Her eyes shone. She tore off the battered hat and shook out her dark pretty hair. "I'll put them in a flower pot, and you can take them right with you. Come into the yard."

While the man came through the picket gate Elisa ran excitedly along the geranium-bordered path to the back of the house. And she returned carrying a big red flower pot. The gloves were forgotten now. She kneeled on the ground by the starting bed and dug up the sandy soil with her fingers and scooped it into the bright new flower pot. Then she picked up the little pile of shoots she had prepared. With her strong fingers she pressed them into the sand and tamped around them with her knuckles. The man stood over her. "I'll tell you what to do," she said. "You remember so you can tell the lady."

"Yes, I'll try to remember."

"Well, look. These will take root in about a month. Then she must set them out, about a foot apart in good rich earth like this, see?" She lifted a handful of dark soil for him to look at. "They'll grow fast and tall. Now remember this: In July tell her to cut them down, about eight inches from the ground."

"Before they bloom?" he asked.

"Yes, before they bloom." Her face was tight with eagerness. "They'll grow right up again. About the last of September the buds will start."

She stopped and seemed perplexed. "It's the budding that takes the most care," she said hesitantly. "I don't know how to tell you." She looked deep into his eyes, searchingly. Her mouth opened a little, and she seemed to be listening. "I'll try to tell you," she said. "Did you ever hear of planting hands?"

"Can't say I have, ma'am."

"Well, I can only tell you what it feels like. It's when you're picking off the buds you don't want. Everything goes right down into your fingertips. You watch your fingers work. They do it themselves. You can feel how it is. They pick and pick the buds. They never make a mistake. They're with the plant. Do you see? Your fingers and the plant. You can feel that, right up your arm. They know. They never make a mistake. You can feel it. When you're like that you can't do anything wrong. Do you see that? Can you understand that?"

She was kneeling on the ground looking up at him. Her breast swelled passionately.

The man's eyes narrowed. He looked away self-consciously. "Maybe I know," he said. "Sometimes in the night in the wagon there—"

Elisa's voice grew husky. She broke in on him, "I've never lived as you do, but I know what you mean. When the night is dark—why, the stars are sharp-pointed, and there's quiet. Why, you rise up and up! Every pointed star gets driven into your body. It's like that. Hot and sharp and—lovely."

Kneeling there, her hand went out toward his legs in the greasy black trousers. Her hesitant fingers almost touched the cloth. Then her hand dropped to the ground. She crouched low like a fawning dog.

He said, "It's nice, just like you say. Only when you don't have no dinner, it ain't."

She stood up then, very straight, and her face was ashamed. She held the flower pot out to him and placed it gently in his arms. "Here. Put it in your wagon, on the seat, where you can watch it. Maybe I can find something for you to do."

At the back of the house she dug in the can pile and found two old and battered aluminum saucepans. She carried them back and gave them to him. "Here, maybe you can fix these."

His manner changed. He became professional. "Good as new I can fix them." At the back of his wagon he set a little anvil, and out of an oily tool box dug a small machine hammer. Elisa came through the gate to watch him while he pounded out the dents in the kettles. His mouth grew sure and knowing. At a difficult part of the work he sucked his underlip.

"You sleep right in the wagon?" Elisa asked.

"Right in the wagon, ma'am. Rain or shine I'm dry as a cow in there."

"It must be nice," she said. "It must be very nice. I wish women could do such things."

"It ain't the right kind of a life for a woman."

Her upper lip raised a little, showing her teeth. "How do you know? How can you tell?" she said.

"I don't know, ma'am," he protested. "Of course I don't know. Now here's your kettles, done. You don't have to buy no new ones."

"How much?"

"Oh, fifty cents'll do. I keep my prices down and my work good. That's why I have all them satisfied customers up and down the highway."

Elisa brought him a fifty-cent piece from the house and dropped it in his hand. "You might be surprised to have a rival some time. I can sharpen scissors, too. And I can beat the dents out of little pots. I could show you what a woman might do."

He put his hammer back in the oily box and shoved the little anvil out of sight. "It would be a lonely life for a woman, ma'am, and a scarey life, too, with animals creeping under the wagon all night." He climbed over the singletree, steadying himself with a hand on the burro's white rump. He settled himself in the seat, picked up the lines. "Thank you kindly, ma'am," he said. "I'll do like you told me; I'll go back and catch the Salinas road."

"Mind," she called, "if you're long in getting there, keep the sand damp."

"Sand, ma'am? . . . Sand? Oh, sure. You mean around the chrysanthemums. Sure I will." He clucked his tongue. The beasts leaned luxuriously into their collars. The mongrel dog took his place between the back wheels. The wagon turned and crawled out the entrance road and back the way it had come, along the river.

Elisa stood in front of her wire fence watching the slow progress of the caravan. Her shoulders were straight, her head thrown back, her eyes half-closed, so that the scene came vaguely into them. Her lips moved silently, forming the words "Good-bye—good-bye." Then she whispered, "That's a bright direction. There's a glowing there." The sound of her whisper startled her. She shook herself free and looked about to see whether anyone had been listening. Only the dogs had heard. They lifted their heads toward her from their sleeping in the dust, and then stretched out their chins and settled asleep again. Elisa turned and ran hurriedly into the house.

In the kitchen she reached behind the stove and felt the water tank. It was full of hot water from the noonday cooking. In the bathroom she tore off her soiled clothes and flung them into the corner. And then she scrubbed herself with a little block of pumice, legs and thighs, loins and chest and arms, until her skin was scratched and red. When she had dried herself she stood in front of a mirror in her bedroom and looked at her body. She tightened her stomach and threw out her chest. She turned and looked over her shoulder at her back.

After a while she began to dress, slowly. She put on her newest underclothing and her nicest stockings and the dress which was the symbol of her prettiness. She worked carefully on her hair, penciled her eyebrows and rouged her lips.

Before she was finished she heard the little thunder of hoofs and the shouts of Henry and his helper as they drove the red steers into the corral. She heard the gate bang shut and set herself for Henry's arrival.

His step sounded on the porch. He entered the house calling, "Elisa, where are you?"

"In my room, dressing. I'm not ready. There's hot water for your bath. Hurry up. It's getting late."

When she heard him splashing in the tub, Elisa laid his dark suit on the bed, and shirt and socks and tie beside it. She stood his polished shoes on the floor beside the bed. Then she went to the porch and sat primly and stiffly down. She looked toward the river road where the willow-line was still yellow with frosted leaves so that under the high grey fog they seemed a thin band of sunshine. This was the only color in the grey afternoon. She sat unmoving for a long time. Her eyes blinked rarely.

Henry came banging out of the door, shoving his tie inside his vest as he came. Elisa stiffened and her face grew tight. Henry stopped short and looked at her. "Why — why, Elisa. You look so nice!"

"Nice? You think I look nice? What do you mean by 'nice'?"

Henry blundered on. "I don't know. I mean you look different, strong and happy."

"I am strong? Yes, strong. What do you mean 'strong'?"

He looked bewildered. "You're playing some kind of a game," he said helplessly. "It's a kind of a play. You look strong enough to break a calf over your knee, happy enough to eat it like a watermelon."

For a second she lost her rigidity. "Henry! Don't talk like that. You didn't know what you said." She grew complete again. "I'm strong," she boasted, "I never knew before how strong."

Henry looked down toward the tractor shed, and when he brought his eyes back to her, they were his own again. "I'll get out the car. You can put on your coat while I'm starting."

Elisa went into the house. She heard him drive to the gate and idle down his motor, and then she took a long time to put on her hat. She pulled it here and pressed it there. When Henry turned the motor off she slipped into her coat and went out.

The little roadster bounced along on the dirt road by the river, raising the birds and driving the rabbits into the brush. Two cranes flapped heavily over the willow-line and dropped into the river-bed.

Far ahead on the road Elisa saw a dark speck. She knew.

She tried not to look as they passed it, but her eyes would not obey. She whispered to herself sadly, "He might have thrown them off the road. That wouldn't have been much trouble, not very much. But he kept the pot," she explained. "He had to keep the pot. That's why he couldn't get them off the road."

The roadster turned a bend and she saw the caravan ahead. She swung full around toward her husband so she could not see the little covered wagon and the mismatched team as the car passed them.

In a moment it was over. The thing was done. She did not look back.

She said loudly, to be heard above the motor. "It will be good, tonight, a good dinner."

"Now you're changed again," Henry complained. He took one hand from the wheel and patted her knee. "I ought to take you in to dinner oftener. It would be good for both of us. We get so heavy out on the ranch."

"Henry," she asked, "could we have wine at dinner?"

"Sure we could. Say! That will be fine."

She was silent for a while; then she said, "Henry, at those prize fights, do the men hurt each other very much?"

"Sometimes a little, not often. Why?"

"Well, I've read how they break noses, and blood runs down their chests. I've read how the fighting gloves get heavy and soggy with blood."

He looked around at her. "What's the matter, Elisa? I didn't know you read things like that." He brought the car to a stop, then turned to the right over the Salinas River bridge.

"Do any women ever go to the fights?" she asked.

"Oh, sure, some. What's the matter Elisa? Do you want to go? I don't think you'd like it, but I'll take you if you really want to go."

She relaxed limply in the seat. "Oh, no. No. I don't want to go. I'm sure I don't." Her face was turned away from him. "It will be enough if we can have wine. It will be plenty." She turned up her coat collar so he could not see that she was crying weakly—like an old woman.

AMY TAN

Amy Tan (b. 1952) was born in Oakland, California. Her father was educated as an engineer in Beijing; her mother left China in 1949, just before the Communist revolution. Tan remembers that as a child she felt like an American girl trapped in a Chinese body: "There was shame and self-hate. There is this myth that America is a melting pot, but what happens in assimilation is that we end up deliberately choosing the American things—hot dogs and apple pie—and ignoring the Chinese offerings."

After her father's death, Tan and her mother lived in Switzerland, where she attended high school. "I was a novelty," she recalls. "There were so few Asians in Europe that everywhere I went people stared. Europeans asked me out. I had never been asked out in America." After attending a small college in Oregon, she worked for IBM as a writer of computer manuals. In 1984 Tan and her mother visited China and met her relatives; there she made the important discovery, as she has said, that "I belonged to my family and my family belonged to China." A year later, back in San Francisco, Tan read Louise Erdrich's Love Medicine *and was so impressed by the power of its interlocking stories about another cultural minority, American Indians, that she began to write short stories herself. One of them was published in a little magazine read by a literary agent in San Diego, who urged Tan to outline a book about the conflicts between different cultures and generations of Chinese mothers and daughters in the United States. After her agent negotiated a $50,000 advance from Putnam, Tan worked full-time on the first draft of her book* The Joy Luck Club *(1989) and finished it in four months.*

"Two Kinds" is an excerpt from that novel. At first Tan thought her book contract was "all a token minority thing. I thought they had to fill a quota since there weren't many Chinese Americans writing." But her book was a best-seller and was nominated for a National Book Award. As the novelist Valerie Miner has recognized, Tan's special gifts are her storytelling ability and her "remarkable ear for dialogue and dialect, representing the choppy English of the mother and the sloppy California vernacular of the daughter with a sensitive authenticity." At the heart of Tan's book is the tough bond between mother and daughter. "I'm my own

person," the daughter says. "How can she be her own person," the mother answers. "When did I give her up?"

COMMENTARY *Amy Tan, "In the Canon, For All the Wrong Reasons," page 591.*

WEB *Research Amy Tan and answer questions about her work at bedfordstmartins.com/charters/litwriters.*

Two Kinds   1989

My mother believed you could be anything you wanted to be in America. You could open a restaurant. You could work for the government and get good retirement. You could buy a house with almost no money down. You could become rich. You could become instantly famous.

"Of course you can be prodigy, too," my mother told me when I was nine. "You can be best anything. What does Auntie Lindo know? Her daughter, she is only best tricky."

America was where all my mother's hopes lay. She had come here in 1949 after losing everything in China: her mother and father, her family home, her first husband, and two daughters, twin baby girls. But she never looked back with regret. There were so many ways for things to get better.

We didn't immediately pick the right kind of prodigy. At first my mother thought I could be a Chinese Shirley Temple. We'd watch Shirley's old movies on TV as though they were training films. My mother would poke my arm and say, *"Ni kan"*—You watch. And I would see Shirley tapping her feet, or singing a sailor song, or pursing her lips into a very round O while saying, "Oh my goodness."

"Ni kan," said my mother as Shirley's eyes flooded with tears. "You already know how. Don't need talent for crying!"

Soon after my mother got this idea about Shirley Temple, she took me to a beauty training school in the Mission district and put me in the hands of a student who could barely hold the scissors without shaking. Instead of getting big fat curls, I emerged with an uneven mass of crinkly black fuzz. My mother dragged me off to the bathroom and tried to wet down my hair.

"You look like Negro Chinese," she lamented, as if I had done this on purpose.

The instructor of the beauty training school had to lop off these soggy clumps to make my hair even again. "Peter Pan is very popular these days," the instructor assured my mother. I now had hair the length of a boy's, with straight-across bangs that hung at a slant two inches above my eyebrows. I liked the haircut and it made me actually look forward to my future fame.

In fact, in the beginning, I was just as excited as my mother, maybe even more so. I pictured this prodigy part of me as many different images, trying each one on for size. I was a dainty ballerina girl standing by the curtains, waiting to hear the right music that would send me floating on my tiptoes. I was like the Christ child lifted out of the straw manger, crying with holy indignity. I was

Cinderella stepping from her pumpkin carriage with sparkly cartoon music filling the air.

In all of my imaginings, I was filled with a sense that I would soon become *perfect*. My mother and father would adore me. I would be beyond reproach. I would never feel the need to sulk for anything.

But sometimes the prodigy in me became impatient. "If you don't hurry up and get me out of here, I'm disappearing for good," it warned. "And then you'll always be nothing."

Every night after dinner, my mother and I would sit at the Formica kitchen table. She would present new tests, taking her examples from stories of amazing children she had read in *Ripley's Believe It or Not,* or *Good Housekeeping, Reader's Digest,* and a dozen other magazines she kept in a pile in our bathroom. My mother got these magazines from people whose houses she cleaned. And since she cleaned many houses each week, we had a great assortment. She would look through them all, searching for stories about remarkable children.

The first night she brought out a story about a three-year-old boy who knew the capitals of all the states and even most of the European countries. A teacher was quoted as saying the little boy could also pronounce the names of the foreign cities correctly.

"What's the capital of Finland?" my mother asked me, looking at the magazine story.

All I knew was the capital of California, because Sacramento was the name of the street we lived on in Chinatown. "Nairobi!" I guessed, saying the most foreign word I could think of. She checked to see if that was possibly one way to pronounce "Helsinki" before showing me the answer.

The tests got harder — multiplying numbers in my head, finding the queen of hearts in a deck of cards, trying to stand on my head without using my hands, predicting the daily temperatures in Los Angeles, New York, and London.

One night I had to look at a page from the Bible for three minutes and then report everything I could remember. "Now Jehoshaphat had riches and honor in abundance and . . . that's all I remember, Ma," I said.

And after seeing my mother's disappointed face once again, something inside of me began to die. I hated the tests, the raised hopes and failed expectations. Before going to bed that night, I looked in the mirror above the bathroom sink and when I saw only my face staring back — and that it would always be this ordinary face — I began to cry. Such a sad, ugly girl! I made high-pitched noises like a crazed animal, trying to scratch out the face in the mirror.

And then I saw what seemed to be the prodigy side of me — because I had never seen that face before. I looked at my reflection, blinking so I could see more clearly. The girl staring back at me was angry, powerful. This girl and I were the same. I had new thoughts, willful thoughts, or rather thoughts filled with lots of won'ts. I won't let her change me, I promised myself. I won't be what I'm not.

So now on nights when my mother presented her tests, I performed listlessly, my head propped on one arm. I pretended to be bored. And I was. I got so bored I started counting the bellows of the foghorns out on the bay while my mother drilled me in other areas. The sound was comforting and reminded me of the cow jumping over the moon. And the next day, I played a game with myself, seeing if my mother would give up on me before eight bellows. After a while I usually counted only one, maybe two bellows at most. At last she was beginning to give up hope.

Two or three months had gone by without any mention of my being a prodigy again. And then one day my mother was watching *The Ed Sullivan Show* on TV. The TV was old and the sound kept shorting out. Every time my mother got halfway up from the sofa to adjust the set, the sound would go back on and Ed would be talking. As soon as she sat down, Ed would go silent again. She got up, the TV broke into loud piano music. She sat down. Silence. Up and down, back and forth, quiet and loud. It was like a stiff embraceless dance between her and the TV set. Finally she stood by the set with her hand on the sound dial.

She seemed entranced by the music, a little frenzied piano piece with this mesmerizing quality, sort of quick passages and then teasing lilting ones before it returned to the quick playful parts.

"*Ni kan*," my mother said, calling me over with hurried hand gestures. "Look here."

I could see why my mother was fascinated by the music. It was being pounded out by a little Chinese girl, about nine years old, with a Peter Pan haircut. The girl had the sauciness of a Shirley Temple. She was proudly modest like a proper Chinese child. And she also did this fancy sweep of a curtsy, so that the fluffy skirt of her white dress cascaded slowly to the floor like the petals of a large carnation.

In spite of these warning signs, I wasn't worried. Our family had no piano and we couldn't afford to buy one, let alone reams of sheet music and piano lessons. So I could be generous in my comments when my mother badmouthed the little girl on TV.

"Play note right, but doesn't sound good! No singing sound," complained my mother.

"What are you picking on her for?" I said carelessly. "She's pretty good. Maybe she's not the best, but she's trying hard." I knew almost immediately I would be sorry I said that.

"Just like you," she said. "Not the best. Because you not trying." She gave a little huff as she let go of the sound dial and sat down on the sofa.

The little Chinese girl sat down also to play an encore of "Anitra's Dance" by Grieg. I remember the song, because later on I had to learn how to play it.

Three days after watching *The Ed Sullivan Show*, my mother told me what my schedule would be for piano lessons and piano practice. She had talked to Mr. Chong, who lived on the first floor of our apartment building. Mr. Chong was a retired piano teacher and my mother had traded housecleaning services for weekly lessons and a piano for me to practice on every day, two hours a day, from four until six.

When my mother told me this, I felt as though I had been sent to hell. I whined and then kicked my foot a little when I couldn't stand it anymore.

"Why don't you like me the way I am? I'm *not* a genius! I can't play the piano. And even if I could, I wouldn't go on TV if you paid me a million dollars!" I cried.

My mother slapped me. "Who ask you be genius?" she shouted. "Only ask you be your best. For you sake. You think I want you be genius? Hnnh! What for! Who ask you!"

"So ungrateful," I heard her mutter in Chinese. "If she had as much talent as she has temper, she would be famous now."

Mr. Chong, whom I secretly nicknamed Old Chong, was very strange, always tapping his fingers to the silent music of an invisible orchestra. He looked ancient in my eyes. He had lost most of the hair on top of his head and he wore thick glasses and had eyes that always looked tired and sleepy. But he must have been younger than I thought, since he lived with his mother and was not yet married.

I met Old Lady Chong once and that was enough. She had this peculiar smell like a baby that had done something in its pants. And her fingers felt like a dead person's, like an old peach I once found in the back of the refrigerator; the skin just slid off the meat when I picked it up.

I soon found out why Old Chong had retired from teaching piano. He was deaf. "Like Beethoven!" he shouted to me. "We're both listening only in our head!" And he would start to conduct his frantic silent sonatas.

Our lessons went like this. He would open the book and point to different things, explaining their purpose: "Key! Treble! Bass! No sharps or flats! So this is C major! Listen now and play after me!"

And then he would play the C scale a few times, a simple chord, and then, as if inspired by an old, unreachable itch, he gradually added more notes and running trills and a pounding bass until the music was really something quite grand.

I would play after him, the simple scale, the simple chord, and then I just played some nonsense that sounded like a cat running up and down on top of garbage cans. Old Chong smiled and applauded and then said, "Very good! But now you must learn to keep time!"

So that's how I discovered that Old Chong's eyes were too slow to keep up with the wrong notes I was playing. He went through the motions in half-time. To help me keep rhythm, he stood behind me, pushing down on my right shoulder for every beat. He balanced pennies on top of my wrists so I would keep them still as I slowly played scales and arpeggios. He had me curve my hand around an apple and keep that shape when playing chords. He marched stiffly to show me how to make each finger dance up and down, staccato like an obedient little soldier.

He taught me all these things, and that was how I also learned I could be lazy and get away with mistakes, lots of mistakes. If I hit the wrong notes because I hadn't practiced enough, I never corrected myself. I just kept playing in rhythm. And Old Chong kept conducting his own private reverie.

So maybe I never really gave myself a fair chance. I did pick up the basics pretty quickly, and I might have become a good pianist at that young age. But I was so determined not to try, not to be anybody different that I learned to play only the most ear-splitting preludes, the most discordant hymns.

Over the next year, I practiced like this, dutifully in my own way. And then one day I heard my mother and her friend Lindo Jong both talking in a loud bragging tone of voice so others could hear. It was after church, and I was leaning against the brick wall wearing a dress with stiff white petticoats. Auntie Lindo's daughter, Waverly, who was about my age, was standing farther down the wall about five feet away. We had grown up together and shared all the closeness of two sisters squabbling over crayons and dolls. In other words, for the most part, we hated each other. I thought she was snotty. Waverly Jong had gained a certain amount of fame as "Chinatown's Littlest Chinese Chess Champion."

"She bring home too many trophy," lamented Auntie Lindo that Sunday. "All day she play chess. All day I have no time do nothing but dust off her winnings." She threw a scolding look at Waverly, who pretended not to see her.

"You lucky you don't have this problem," said Auntie Lindo with a sigh to my mother.

And my mother squared her shoulders and bragged: "Our problem worser than yours. If we ask Jing-mei wash dish, she hear nothing but music. It's like you can't stop this natural talent."

And right then, I was determined to put a stop to her foolish pride.

A few weeks later, Old Chong and my mother conspired to have me play in a talent show which would be held in the church hall. By then, my parents had saved up enough to buy me a secondhand piano, a black Wurlitzer spinet with a scarred bench. It was the showpiece of our living room.

For the talent show, I was to play a piece called "Pleading Child" from Schumann's *Scenes from Childhood*. It was a simple, moody piece that sounded more difficult than it was. I was supposed to memorize the whole thing, playing the repeat parts twice to make the piece sound longer. But I dawdled over it, playing a few bars and then cheating, looking up to see what notes followed. I never really listened to what I was playing. I daydreamed about being somewhere else, about being someone else.

The part I liked to practice best was the fancy curtsy: right foot out, touch the rose on the carpet with a pointed foot, sweep to the side, left leg bends, look up and smile.

My parents invited all the couples from the Joy Luck Club to witness my debut. Auntie Lindo and Uncle Tin were there. Waverly and her two older brothers had also come. The first two rows were filled with children both younger and older than I was. The littlest ones got to go first. They recited simple nursery rhymes, squawked out tunes on miniature violins, twirled Hula Hoops, pranced in pink ballet tutus, and when they bowed or curtsied, the audience would sigh in unison, "Awww," and then clap enthusiastically.

When my turn came, I was very confident. I remember my childish excitement. It was as if I knew, without a doubt, that the prodigy side of me really did exist. I had no fear whatsoever, no nervousness. I remember thinking to myself, This is it! This is it! I looked out over the audience, at my mother's blank face, my father's yawn, Auntie Lindo's stiff-lipped smile, Waverly's sulky expression. I had on a white dress layered with sheets of lace, and a pink bow in my Peter Pan haircut. As I sat down I envisioned people jumping to their feet and Ed Sullivan rushing up to introduce me to everyone on TV.

And I started to play. It was so beautiful. I was so caught up in how lovely I looked that at first I didn't worry how I would sound. So it was a surprise to me when I hit the first wrong note and I realized something didn't sound quite right. And then I hit another and another followed that. A chill started at the top of my head and began to trickle down. Yet I couldn't stop playing, as though my hands were bewitched. I kept thinking my fingers would adjust themselves back, like a train switching to the right track. I played this strange jumble through two repeats, the sour notes staying with me all the way to the end.

When I stood up, I discovered my legs were shaking. Maybe I had just been nervous and the audience, like Old Chong, had seen me go through the right motions and had not heard anything wrong at all. I swept my right foot out, went down on my knee, looked up and smiled. The room was quiet, except for Old Chong, who was beaming and shouting, "Bravo! Bravo! Well done!" But then I saw my mother's face, her stricken face. The audience clapped weakly, and as I walked back to my chair, with my whole face quivering as I tried not to cry, I heard a little boy whisper loudly to his mother, "That was awful," and the mother whispered back, "Well, she certainly tried."

And now I realized how many people were in the audience, the whole world it seemed. I was aware of eyes burning into my back. I felt the shame of my mother and father as they sat stiffly throughout the rest of the show.

We could have escaped during intermission. Pride and some strange sense of honor must have anchored my parents to their chairs. And so we watched it all: the eighteen-year-old boy with a fake mustache who did a magic show and juggled flaming hoops while riding a unicycle. The breasted girl with white makeup who sang from *Madama Butterfly* and got honorable mention. And the eleven-year-old boy who won first prize playing a tricky violin song that sounded like a busy bee.

After the show, the Hsus, the Jongs, and the St. Clairs from the Joy Luck Club came up to my mother and father.

"Lots of talented kids," Auntie Lindo said vaguely, smiling broadly.

"That was somethin' else," said my father, and I wondered if he was referring to me in a humorous way, or whether he even remembered what I had done.

Waverly looked at me and shrugged her shoulders. "You aren't a genius like me," she said matter-of-factly. And if I hadn't felt so bad, I would have pulled her braids and punched her stomach.

But my mother's expression was what devastated me: a quiet, blank look that said she had lost everything. I felt the same way, and it seemed as if every-body were now coming up, like gawkers at the scene of an accident, to see what parts were actually missing. When we got on the bus to go home, my father was humming the busy-bee tune and my mother was silent. I kept thinking she wanted to wait until we got home before shouting at me. But when my father unlocked the door to our apartment, my mother walked in and then went to the back, into the bedroom. No accusations. No blame. And in a way, I felt disappointed. I had been waiting for her to start shouting, so I could shout back and cry and blame her for all my misery.

I assumed my talent-show fiasco meant I never had to play the piano again. But two days later, after school, my mother came out of the kitchen and saw me watching TV.

"Four clock," she reminded me as if it were any other day. I was stunned, as though she were asking me to go through the talent-show torture again. I wedged myself more tightly in front of the TV.

"Turn off TV," she called from the kitchen five minutes later.

I didn't budge. And then I decided. I didn't have to do what my mother said anymore. I wasn't her slave. This wasn't China. I had listened to her before and look what happened. She was the stupid one.

She came out from the kitchen and stood in the arched entryway of the living room. "Four clock," she said once again, louder.

"I'm not going to play anymore," I said nonchalantly. "Why should I? I'm not a genius."

She walked over and stood in front of the TV. I saw her chest was heaving up and down in an angry way.

"No!" I said, and I now felt stronger, as if my true self had finally emerged. So this was what had been inside me all along.

"No! I won't!" I screamed.

She yanked me by the arm, pulled me off the floor, snapped off the TV. She was frighteningly strong, half pulling, half carrying me toward the piano as I kicked the throw rugs under my feet. She lifted me up and onto the hard bench. I was sobbing by now, looking at her bitterly. Her chest was heaving even more and her mouth was open, smiling crazily as if she were pleased I was crying.

"You want me to be someone that I'm not!" I sobbed. "I'll never be the kind of daughter you want me to be!"

"Only two kinds of daughters," she shouted in Chinese. "Those who are obedient and those who follow their own mind! Only one kind of daughter can live in this house. Obedient daughter!"

"Then I wish I wasn't your daughter. I wish you weren't my mother," I shouted. As I said these things I got scared. I felt like worms and toads and slimy things were crawling out of my chest, but it also felt good, as if this awful side of me had surfaced, at last.

"Too late change this," said my mother shrilly.

And I could sense her anger rising to its breaking point. I wanted to see it spill over. And that's when I remembered the babies she had lost in China, the ones we never talked about. "Then I wish I'd never been born!" I shouted. "I wish I were dead! Like them."

It was as if I had said the magic words, Alakazam!—and her face went blank, her mouth closed, her arms went slack, and she backed out of the room, stunned, as if she were blowing away like a small brown leaf, thin, brittle, lifeless.

It was not the only disappointment my mother felt in me. In the years that followed, I failed her so many times, each time asserting my own will, my right to fall short of expectations. I didn't get straight As. I didn't become class president. I didn't get into Stanford. I dropped out of college.

For unlike my mother, I did not believe I could be anything I wanted to be. I could only be me.

And for all those years, we never talked about the disaster at the recital or my terrible accusations afterward at the piano bench. All that remained unchecked, like a betrayal that was now unspeakable. So I never found a way to ask her why she had hoped for something so large that failure was inevitable.

And even worse, I never asked her what frightened me the most: Why had she given up hope?

For after our struggle at the piano, she never mentioned my playing again. The lessons stopped, the lid to the piano was closed, shutting out the dust, my misery, and her dreams.

So she surprised me. A few years ago, she offered to give me the piano, for my thirtieth birthday. I had not played in all those years. I saw the offer as a sign of forgiveness, a tremendous burden removed.

"Are you sure?" I asked shyly. "I mean, won't you and Dad miss it?"

"No, this your piano," she said firmly. "Always your piano. You only one can play."

"Well, I probably can't play anymore," I said. "It's been years."

"You pick up fast," said my mother, as if she knew this was certain. "You have natural talent. You could been genius if you want to."

"No I couldn't."

"You just not trying," said my mother. And she was neither angry nor sad. She said it as if to announce a fact that could never be disproved. "Take it," she said.

But I didn't at first. It was enough that she had offered it to me. And after that, every time I saw it in my parents' living room, standing in front of the bay windows, it made me feel proud, as if it were a shiny trophy I had won back.

Last week I sent a tuner over to my parents' apartment and had the piano reconditioned, for purely sentimental reasons. My mother had died a few months before and I had been getting things in order for my father, a little bit at a time. I put the jewelry in special silk pouches. The sweaters she had knitted in yellow, pink, bright orange—all the colors I hated—I put those in moth-proof boxes. I found some old Chinese silk dresses, the kind with little slits up the sides. I rubbed the old silk against my skin, then wrapped them in tissue and decided to take them home with me.

After I had the piano tuned, I opened the lid and touched the keys. It sounded even richer than I remembered. Really, it was a very good piano. Inside the bench were the same exercise notes with handwritten scales, the same secondhand music books with their covers held together with yellow tape.

I opened up the Schumann book to the dark little piece I had played at the recital. It was on the left-hand side of the page, "Pleading Child." It looked more difficult than I remembered. I played a few bars, surprised at how easily the notes came back to me.

And for the first time, or so it seemed, I noticed the piece on the right-hand side. It was called "Perfectly Contented." I tried to play this one as well. It had a lighter melody but the same flowing rhythm and turned out to be quite easy. "Pleading Child" was shorter but slower; "Perfectly Contented" was longer but faster. And after I played them both a few times, I realized they were two halves of the same song.

JOHN UPDIKE

John Updike (b. 1932) was born in Shillington, Pennsylvania, an only child. His father taught algebra in a local high school, and his mother wrote short stories and novels. His mother's consciousness of a special destiny, combined with his family's meager income—they lived with his mother's parents for the first thirteen years of Updike's life—made him "both arrogant and shy" as a teenager. He wrote stories, drew cartoons, and clowned for the approval of his peers. After getting straight A's in high school, he went to Harvard University on a full scholarship, studying English and graduating summa cum laude in 1954. He spent a year at Oxford on a fellowship, then joined the staff of The New Yorker. *In 1959 Updike published both his first book of short fiction,* The Same Door, *and his first novel,* The Poorhouse Fair. *That year he also moved from New York City to a coastal town in Massachusetts, where he has lived most of the time since.*

In the 1960s, 1970s, and early 1980s, Updike continued to alternate novels and collections of stories, adding occasional volumes of verse, collections of essays, and one play. His novels include Rabbit, Run *(1960),* Couples *(1968),* Rabbit Redux *(1971), and* Marry Me *(1976).* Rabbit Is Rich *(1981), continuing the story of Harry "Rabbit" Angstrom, a suburban Pennsylvanian whom Updike has traced through adolescence, marriage, fatherhood, and middle age, won virtually every major American literary award for the year it appeared; Updike concluded the series with* Rabbit at Rest *(1991). Updike's collections of stories include* Pigeon Feathers *(1962),* Museums and Women *(1972), and* Problems and Other Stories *(1981). In 1983 Updike won the National Book Critics Circle Award for his collection of essays and criticism* Hugging the Shore. *In 1989 he published his memoirs,* Self-Consciousness. *Among his many recent books is another collection,* Philadelphia and Other Stories *(1995).*

Updike has said he is indebted to J. D. Salinger's stories for the literary form he adopted to describe the painful experience of adolescence: "I learned a lot from Salinger's short stories; he did remove the short narrative from the wise-guy, slice-of-life stories of the thirties and forties. Like most innovative artists, he made new room for shapelessness, for life as it is lived." Updike writes realistic narrative,

believing that "fiction is a tissue of lies that refreshes and informs our sense of actu-
ality. Reality is—chemically, atomically, biologically—a fabric of microscopic
accuracies." His fiction, such as the story "A & P," concentrates on these "micro-
scopic accuracies," tiny details of characterization and setting brilliantly described.

COMMENTARY *John Updike, "Kafka and 'The Metamorphosis,'" page 599.*

WEB *Research John Updike and answer questions about his work at*
bedfordstmartins.com/charters/litwriters.

A & P   1961

In walks these three girls in nothing but bathing suits. I'm in the third
checkout slot, with my back to the door, so I don't see them until they're over by
the bread. The one that caught my eye first was the one in the plaid green two-
piece. She was a chunky kid, with a good tan and a sweet broad soft-looking can
with those two crescents of white just under it, where the sun never seems to
hit, at the top of the backs of her legs. I stood there with my hand on a box of
HiHo crackers trying to remember if I rang it up or not. I ring it up again and
the customer starts giving me hell. She's one of these cash-register-watchers, a
witch about fifty with rouge on her cheekbones and no eyebrows, and I know it
made her day to trip me up. She'd been watching cash registers for fifty years
and probably never seen a mistake before.

By the time I got her feathers smoothed and her goodies into a bag—she
gives me a little snort in passing, if she'd been born at the right time they would
have burned her over in Salem—by the time I get her on her way the girls had
circled around the bread and were coming back, without a pushcart, back my
way along the counters, in the aisle between the checkouts and the Special bins.
They didn't even have shoes on. There was this chunky one, with the two-
piece—it was bright green and the seams on the bra were still sharp and her
belly was still pretty pale so I guessed she just got it (the suit)—there was this
one, with one of those chubby berry-faces, the lips all bunched together under
her nose, this one, and a tall one, with black hair that hadn't quite frizzed right,
and one of these sunburns right across under the eyes, and a chin that was too
long—you know, the kind of girl other girls think is very "striking" and
"attractive" but never quite makes it, as they very well know, which is why they
like her so much—and then the third one, that wasn't quite so tall. She was the
queen. She kind of led them, the other two peeking around and making their
shoulders round. She didn't look around, not this queen, she just walked
straight on slowly, on these long white prima-donna legs. She came down a
little hard on her heels, as if she didn't walk in her bare feet that much, putting
down her heels and then letting the weight move along to her toes as if she was
testing the floor with every step, putting a little deliberate extra action into it.
You never know for sure how girls' minds work (do you really think it's a mind
in there or just a little buzz like a bee in a glass jar?) but you got the idea she had
talked the other two into coming in here with her, and now she was showing
them how to do it, walk slow and hold yourself straight.

She had on a kind of dirty-pink — beige maybe, I don't know — bathing suit with a little nubble all over it, and what got me, the straps were down. They were off her shoulders looped loose around the cool tops of her arms, and I guess as a result the suit had slipped a little on her, so all around the top of the cloth there was this shining rim. If it hadn't been there you wouldn't have known there could have been anything whiter than those shoulders. With the straps pushed off, there was nothing between the top of the suit and the top of her head except just *her,* this clean bare plane of the top of her chest down from the shoulder bones like a dented sheet of metal tilted in the light. I mean, it was more than pretty.

She had sort of oaky hair that the sun and salt had bleached, done up in a bun that was unravelling, and a kind of prim face. Walking into the A & P with your straps down, I suppose it's the only kind of face you *can* have. She held her head so high her neck, coming up out of those white shoulders, looked kind of stretched, but I didn't mind. The longer her neck was, the more of her there was.

She must have felt in the corner of her eye me and over my shoulder Stokesie in the second slot watching, but she didn't tip. Not this queen. She kept her eyes moving across the racks, and stopped, and turned so slow it made my stomach rub the inside of my apron, and buzzed to the other two, who kind of huddled against her for relief, and then they all three of them went up the cat-and-dog-food-breakfast-cereal-macaroni-rice-raisins-seasonings-spreads-spaghetti-soft-drinks-crackers-and-cookies aisle. From the third slot I look straight up this aisle to the meat counter, and I watched them all the way. The fat one with the tan sort of fumbled with the cookies, but on second thought she put the package back. The sheep pushing their carts down the aisle — the girls were walking against the usual traffic (not that we have one-way signs or anything) — were pretty hilarious. You could see them, when Queenie's white shoulders dawned on them, kind of jerk, or hop, or hiccup, but their eyes snapped back to their own baskets and on they pushed. I bet you could set off dynamite in an A & P and the people would by and large keep reaching and checking oatmeal off their lists and muttering "Let me see, there was a third thing, began with A, asparagus, no, ah, yes, applesauce!" or whatever it is they do mutter. But there was no doubt, this jiggled them. A few houseslaves in pin curlers even looked around after pushing their carts past to make sure what they had seen was correct.

You know, it's one thing to have a girl in a bathing suit down on the beach, where what with the glare nobody can look at each other much anyway, and another thing in the cool of the A & P, under the fluorescent lights, against all those stacked packages, with her feet paddling along naked over our checkboard green-and-cream rubber-tile floor.

"Oh Daddy," Stokesie said beside me. "I feel so faint."

"Darling," I said. "Hold me tight." Stokesie's married, with two babies chalked up on his fuselage already, but as far as I can tell that's the only difference. He's twenty-two, and I was nineteen this April.

"Is it done?" he asks, the responsible married man finding his voice. I forgot to say he thinks he's going to be manager some sunny day, maybe in

1990 when it's called the Great Alexandrov and Petrooshki Tea Company or something.

What he meant was, our town is five miles from a beach, with a big summer colony out on the Point, but we're right in the middle of town, and the women generally put on a shirt or shorts or something before they get out of the car into the street. And anyway these are usually women with six children and varicose veins mapping their legs and nobody, including them, could care less. As I say, we're right in the middle of town, and if you stand at our front doors you can see two banks and the Congregational church and the newspaper store and three real-estate offices and about twenty-seven old freeloaders tearing up Central Street because the sewer broke again. It's not as if we're on the Cape; we're north of Boston and there's people in this town haven't seen the ocean for twenty years.

The girls had reached the meat counter and were asking McMahon something. He pointed, they pointed, and they shuffled out of sight behind a pyramid of Diet Delight peaches. All that was left for us to see was old McMahon patting his mouth and looking after them sizing up their joints. Poor kids, I began to feel sorry for them, they couldn't help it.

Now here comes the sad part of the story, at least my family says it's sad, but I don't think it's so sad myself. The store's pretty empty, it being Thursday afternoon, so there was nothing much to do except lean on the register and wait for the girls to show up again. The whole store was like a pinball machine and I didn't know which tunnel they'd come out of. After a while they come around out of the far aisle, around the light bulbs, records at discount of the Caribbean Six or Tony Martin Sings or some such gunk you wonder they waste the wax on, sixpacks of candy bars, and plastic toys done up in cellophane that fall apart when a kid looks at them anyway. Around they come, Queenie still leading the way, and holding a little gray jar in her hand. Slots Three through Seven are unmanned and I could see her wondering between Stokes and me, but Stokesie with his usual luck draws an old party in baggy gray pants who stumbles up with four giant cans of pineapple juice (what do these bums *do* with all that pineapple juice? I've often asked myself) so the girls come to me. Queenie puts down the jar and I take it into my fingers icy cold. Kingfish Fancy Herring Snacks in Pure Sour Cream: 49¢. Now her hands are empty, not a ring or a bracelet, bare as God made them, and I wonder where the money's coming from. Still with that prim look she lifts a folded dollar bill out of the hollow at the center of her nubbled pink top. The jar went heavy in my hand. Really, I thought that was so cute.

Then everybody's luck begins to run out. Lengel comes in from haggling with a truck full of cabbages on the lot and is about to scuttle into that door marked MANAGER behind which he hides all day when the girls touch his eye. Lengel's pretty dreary, teaches Sunday school and the rest, but he doesn't miss that much. He comes over and says, "Girls, this isn't the beach."

Queenie blushes, though maybe it's just a brush of sunburn I was noticing for the first time, now that she was so close. "My mother asked me to pick up a jar of herring snacks." Her voice kind of startled me, the way voices do when you see the people first, coming out so flat and dumb yet kind of tony, too, the way it ticked over "pick up" and "snacks." All of a sudden I slid right down her voice into her living room. Her father and the other men were standing around in ice-cream coats and bow ties and the women were in sandals picking up herring snacks on toothpicks off a big glass plate and they were all holding drinks the color of water with olives and sprigs of mint in them. When my parents have somebody over they get lemonade and if it's a real racy affair Schlitz in tall glasses with "They'll Do It Every Time" cartoons stencilled on.

"That's all right," Lengel said. "But this isn't the beach." His repeating this struck me as funny, as if it had just occurred to him, and he had been thinking all these years the A & P was a great big sand dune and he was the head lifeguard. He didn't like my smiling — as I say he doesn't miss much — but he concentrates on giving the girls that sad Sunday-school-superintendent stare.

Queenie's blush is no sunburn now, and the plump one in plaid, that I liked better from the back — a really sweet can — pipes up, "We weren't doing any shopping. We just came in for the one thing."

"That makes no difference," Lengel tells her, and I could see from the way his eyes went that he hadn't noticed she was wearing a two-piece before. "We want you decently dressed when you come in here."

"We *are* decent," Queenie says suddenly, her lower lip pushing, getting sore now that she remembers her place, a place from which the crowd that runs the A & P must look pretty crummy. Fancy Herring Snacks flashed in her very blue eyes.

"Girls, I don't want to argue with you. After this come in here with your shoulders covered. It's our policy." He turns his back. That's policy for you. Policy is what the kingpins want. What the others want is juvenile delinquency.

All this while, the customers had been showing up with their carts but, you know, sheep, seeing a scene, they had all bunched up on Stokesie, who shook open a paper bag as gently as peeling a peach, not wanting to miss a word. I could feel in the silence everybody getting nervous, most of all Lengel, who asks me, "Sammy, have you rung up their purchase?"

I thought and said "No" but it wasn't about that I was thinking. I go through the punches, 4, 9, GROC, TOT — it's more complicated than you think, and after you do it often enough, it begins to make a little song, that you hear words to, in my case "Hello (*bing*) there, you (*gung*) hap-py *pee*-pul (*splat*)!" — the *splat* being the drawer flying out. I uncrease the bill, tenderly as you may imagine, it just having come from between the two smoothest scoops of vanilla I had ever known were there, and pass a half and a penny into her narrow pink palm, and nestle the herrings in a bag and twist its neck and hand it over, all the time thinking.

The girls, and who'd blame them, are in a hurry to get out, so I say "I quit" to Lengel enough for them to hear, hoping they'll stop and watch me, their unsuspected hero. They keep right on going, into the electric eye; the door flies open and they flicker across the lot to their car, Queenie and Plaid and Big Tall Goony-Goony (not that as raw material she was so bad), leaving me with Lengel and a kink in his eyebrow.

"Did you say something, Sammy?"

"I said I quit."

"I thought you did."

"You didn't have to embarrass them."

"It was they who were embarrassing us."

I started to say something that came out "Fiddle-de-doo." It's a saying of my grandmother's, and I know she would have been pleased.

"I don't think you know what you're saying," Lengel said.

"I know you don't," I said. "But I do." I pull the bow at the back of my apron and start shrugging it off my shoulders. A couple customers that had been heading for my slot begin to knock against each other, like scared pigs in a chute.

Lengel sighs and begins to look very patient and old and gray. He's been a friend of my parents for years. "Sammy, you don't want to do this to your Mom and Dad," he tells me. It's true, I don't. But it seems to me that once you begin a gesture it's fatal not to go through with it. I fold the apron, "Sammy" stitched in red on the pocket, and put it on the counter, and drop the bow tie on top of it. The bow tie is theirs, if you've ever wondered. "You'll feel this for the rest of your life," Lengel says, and I know that's true, too, but remembering how he made that pretty girl blush makes me so scrunchy inside I punch the No Sale tab and the machine whirs "pee-pul" and the drawer splats out. One advantage to this scene taking place in summer, I can follow this up with a clean exit, there's no fumbling around getting your coat and galoshes, I just saunter into the electric eye in my white shirt that my mother ironed the night before, and the door heaves itself open, and outside the sunshine is skating around on the asphalt.

I look around for my girls, but they're gone, of course. There wasn't anybody but some young married screaming with her children about some candy they didn't get by the door of a powder-blue Falcon station wagon. Looking back in the big windows, over the bags of peat moss and aluminum lawn furniture stacked on the pavement, I could see Lengel in my place in the slot, checking the sheep through. His face was dark gray and his back stiff, as if he'd just had an injection of iron, and my stomach kind of fell as I felt how hard the world was going to be to me hereafter.

HELENA MARÍA VIRAMONTES

Helena María Viramontes (b. 1954) was born in East Los Angeles, the daughter of a construction worker and a housewife who raised six daughters and three sons in a community that offered refuge for relatives and friends crossing the border from Mexico into California. As a child Viramontes witnessed "late night kitchen meetings where everyone talked and laughed in low voices" about having reached the United States, el otro lado ("the other side"). After graduation from Garfield High School, Viramontes worked twenty hours a week while earning her B.A. from Immaculate Heart College, one of five Chicanas in her class. She then entered the graduate program at the University of California at Irvine as a cre-

ative writing student, but she left in 1981 and completed the requirements for the M.F.A. degree after the publication of her stories.

As the critic Maria Herrera-Sobek has observed, the 1980s decade "witnessed an explosion in the literary output of Chicana authors," when Chicano-oriented publishers began to "risk investing in Mexican American women writers." Viramontes began to place her stories in small magazines such as Maize *and* XhismArte Magazine *as well as the anthology* Cuentos: Stories by Latinas *(1983). Her first book,* The Moths and Other Stories, *was published in 1985 by Arte Publico Press in Houston, Texas. The same year the University of California at Irvine sponsored the first national conference on Mexican American women writers, resulting in the volume* Beyond Stereotypes: A Critical Analysis of Chicana Literature *(1985). Three years later Viramontes helped organize a second Chicana writers conference at Irvine and coedited the anthology* Chicana Creativity and Criticism *(1988), in which "Miss Clairol" was first published. In 1989 Viramontes received a National Endowment for the Arts Fellowship grant; she was also selected by Gabriel García Márquez to participate in a ten-day storytelling workshop sponsored by the Sundance Institute in Utah. After this experience she began adapting one of her short stories into a film script. In 1993 she published her second book of short stories,* Paris Rats in E.L.A. *Her first novel,* Under the Feet of Jesus, *followed in 1995.*

As a woman of color, Viramontes believes that language is her most powerful tool for survival. She explains in "Why I Write" (1993) that "through writing, I have learned to protect the soles of my feet from the broken glass. . . . Writing is the only way I know how to pray."

WEB *Research Helena María Viramontes and answer questions about her work at bedfordstmartins.com/charters/litwriters.*

Miss Clairol

1988

Arlene and Champ walk to K-Mart. The store is full of bins mounted with bargain buys from T-shirts to rubber sandals. They go to aisle 23, Cosmetics. Arlene, wearing bell bottom jeans two sizes too small, can't bend down to the Miss Clairol boxes, asks Champ.

—Which one mamá—asks Champ, chewing her thumb nail.

—Shit, mija,° I dunno.—Arlene smacks her gum, contemplating the decision.—Maybe I need a change, tú sabes.° What do you think?—She holds up a few blond strands with black roots. Arlene has burned the softness of her hair with peroxide; her hair is stiff, breaks at the ends and she needs plenty of Aqua Net hairspray to tease and tame her ratted hair, then folds it back into a high lump behind her head. For the last few months she has been a platinum "Light Ash" blond, before that a Miss Clairol "Flame" redhead, before that Champ couldn't even identify the color—somewhere between

---

mija: Spanish slang short for "mi hija," or "my daughter."
tú sabes: Spanish for "you know."

orange and brown, a "Sun Bronze." The only way Champ knows her mother's true hair color is by her roots which, like death, inevitably rise to the truth.

—I hate it, tú sabes, when I can't decide.—Arlene is wearing a pink, strapless tube top. Her stomach spills over the hip hugger jeans. Spits the gum onto the floor.—Fuck it.—And Champ follows her to the rows of nailpolish, next to the Maybelline rack of make-up, across the false eyelashes that look like insects on display in clear, plastic boxes. Arlene pulls out a particular color of nailpolish, looks at the bottom of the bottle for the price, puts it back, gets another. She has a tattoo of purple XXX's on her left finger like a ring. She finally settles for a purple-blackish color, Ripe Plum, that Champ thinks looks like the color of Frankenstein's nails. She looks at her own stubby nails, chewed and gnawed.

Walking over to the eyeshadows, Arlene slowly slinks out another stick of gum from her back pocket, unwraps and crumbles the wrapper into a little ball, lets it drop on the floor. Smacks the gum.

—Grandpa Ham used to make chains with these gum wrappers—she says, toeing the wrapper on the floor with her rubber sandals, her toes dotted with old nailpolish.—He started one, tú sabes, that went from room to room. That was before he went nuts—she says, looking at the price of magenta eyeshadow.—Sabes que?° What do you think?—lifting the eyeshadow to Champ.

—I dunno know—responds Champ, shrugging her shoulders the way she always does when she is listening to something else, her own heartbeat, what Gregorio said on the phone yesterday, shrugs her shoulders when Miss Smith says OFELIA, answer my question. She is too busy thinking of things people otherwise dismiss like parentheses, but sticks to her like gum, like a hole on a shirt, like a tattoo, and sometimes she wishes she weren't born with such adhesiveness. The chain went from room to room, round and round like a web, she remembers. That was before he went nuts.

—Champ. You listening? Or in lala land again?—Arlene has her arms akimbo on a fold of flesh, pissed.

—I said, I dunno know.—Champ whines back, still looking at the wrapper on the floor.

—Well you better learn, tú sabes, and fast too. Now think, will this color go good with Pancha's blue dress?—Pancha is Arlene's comadre. Since Arlene has a special date tonight, she lent Arlene her royal blue dress that she keeps in a plastic bag at the end of her closet. The dress is made of chiffon, with satin-like material underlining, so that when Arlene first tried it on and strutted about, it crinkled sounds of elegance. The dress fits too tight. Her plump arms squeeze through, her hips breathe in and hold their breath, the seams do all they can to keep the body contained. But Arlene doesn't care as long as it sounds right.

—I think it will—Champ says, and Arlene is very pleased.

—Think so? So do I mija.—

Sabes que?: Spanish for "You know what?"

They walk out the double doors and Champ never remembers her mother paying.

It is four in the afternoon, but already Arlene is preparing for the date. She scrubs the tub, Art Labo on the radio, drops crystals of Jean Naté into the running water, lemon scent rises with the steam. The bathroom door ajar, she removes her top and her breasts flop and sag, pushes her jeans down with some difficulty, kicks them off, and steps in the tub.

—Mija. MIJA—she yells.—Mija, give me a few bobby pins.—She is worried about her hair frizzing and so wants to pin it up.

Her mother's voice is faint because Champ is in the closet. There are piles of clothes on the floor, hangers thrown askew and tangled, shoes all piled up or thrown on the top shelf. Champ is looking for her mother's special dress. Pancha says every girl has one at the end of her closet.

—Goddamn it Champ.—

Amidst the dirty laundry, the black hole of the closet, she finds nothing.

—NOW—

—Alright, ALRIGHT. Cheeze amá, stop yelling—says Champ, and goes in the steamy bathroom, checks the drawers, hairbrushes jump out, rollers, strands of hair, rummages through bars of soap, combs, eyeshadows, finds nothing; pulls open another drawer, powder, empty bottles of oil, manicure scissors, Kotex, dye instructions crinkled and botched, finally, a few bobby pins.

After Arlene pins up her hair, she asks Champ,—Sabes que? Should I wear my hair up? Do I look good with it up?—Champ is sitting on the toilet.

—Yea, amá, you look real pretty.—

—Thanks mija—says Arlene, Sabes que? When you get older I'll show you how you can look just as pretty—and she puts her head back, relaxes, like the Calgon commercials.

Champ lays on her stomach, T.V. on to some variety show with pogo stick dancers dressed in outfits of stretchy material and glitter. She is wearing one of Gregorio's white T-shirts, the ones he washes and bleaches himself so that the whiteness is impeccable. It drapes over her deflated ten-year-old body like a dress. She is busy cutting out Miss Breck models from the stacks of old magazines Pancha found in the back of her mother's garage. Champ collects the array of honey colored haired women, puts them in a shoe box with all her other special things.

Arlene is in the bathroom, wrapped in a towel. She has painted her eyebrows so that the two are arched and even, penciled thin and high. The magenta shades her eyelids. The towel slips, reveals one nipple blind from a cigarette burn, a date to forget. She rewraps the towel, likes her reflection, turns to her profile for additional inspection. She feels good, turns up the radio to . . . your love. For your loveeeee, I will do anything, I will do anything, forrr your love. For your kiss . . .

Champ looks on. From the open bathroom door, she can see Arlene, anticipation burning like a cigarette from her lips, sliding her shoulders to the ahhhh ahhhhh, and pouting her lips until the song ends. And Champ likes her mother that way.

Arlene carefully stretches black eyeliner, like a fallen question mark, outlines each eye. The work is delicate, her hand trembles cautiously, stops the process to review the face with each line. Arlene the mirror is not Arlene the face who has worn too many relationships, gotten too little sleep. The last touch is the chalky, beige lipstick.

By the time she is finished, her ashtray is full of cigarette butts, Champ's variety show is over, and Jackie Gleason's dancing girls come on to make kaleidoscope patterns with their long legs and arms. Gregorio is still not home, and Champ goes over to the window, checks the houses, the streets, corners, roams the sky with her eyes.

Arlene sits on the toilet, stretches up her nylons, clips them to her girdle. She feels good thinking about the way he will unsnap her nylons, and she will unroll them slowly, point her toes when she does.

Champ opens a can of Campbell soup, finds a perfect pot in the middle of a stack of dishes, pulls it out to the threatening rumble of the tower. She washes it out, pours the contents of the red can, turns the knob. After it boils, she puts the pot on the sink for it to cool down. She searches for a spoon.

Arlene is romantic. When Champ begins her period, she will tell her things that only women can know. She will tell her about the first time she made love with a boy, her awkwardness and shyness forcing them to go under the house, where the cool, refined soil made a soft mattress. How she closed her eyes and wondered what to expect, or how the penis was the softest skin she had ever felt against her, how it tickled her, searched for a place to connect. She was eleven and his name was Harry.

She will not not tell Champ that her first fuck was a guy named Puppet who ejaculated prematurely, at the sight of her apricot vagina, so plump and fuzzy. — Pendejo° — she said — you got it all over me. — She rubbed the gooey substance off her legs, her belly in disgust. Ran home to tell Rat and Pancha, her mouth open with laughter.

Arlene powder puffs under her arms, between her breasts, tilts a bottle of *Love Cries* perfume and dabs behind her ears, neck and breasts for those tight caressing songs which permit them to grind their bodies together until she can feel a bulge in his pants and she knows she's in for the night.

Jackie Gleason is a bartender in a saloon. He wears a black bow tie, a white apron, and is polishing a glass. Champ is watching him, sitting in the radius of the gray light, eating her soup from the pot.

Arlene is a romantic. She will dance until Pancha's dress turns a different color, dance until her hair becomes undone, her hips jiggering and quaking beneath a new pair of hosiery, her mascara shadowing under her eyes from the perspiration of the ritual, dance spinning herself into Miss Clairol, and stopping only when it is time to return to the sewing factory, time to wait out the next date, time to change hair color. Time to remember or to forget.

Pendejo: Spanish for "idiot" (used as an insult).

Champ sees Arlene from the window. She can almost hear Arlene's nylons rubbing against one another, hear the crinkling sound of satin when she gets in the blue and white shark-finned Dodge. Champ yells goodbye. It all sounds so right to Arlene who is too busy cranking up the window to hear her daughter.

ALICE WALKER

Alice Walker (b. 1944) was the eighth and youngest child of Willie Lee and Minnie Lou Grant Walker, sharecroppers in Eatonton, Georgia. Walker did well in school, encouraged by her teachers and her mother, whose stories she loved as "a walking history of our community." For two years, Walker attended Spelman College in Atlanta, the oldest college for black women in the United States. Then she studied at Sarah Lawrence College in New York, where she began her writing career by publishing a book of poetry, Once *(1968). Since that time Walker has published several collections of poetry, novels, volumes of short stories, and* Living by the Word *(1988), a book of essays. Her best-known novel,* The Color Purple *(1982), won the American Book Award and the Pulitzer Prize and was made into a motion picture. Later books include* The Temple of My Familiar *(1989),* Possessing the Secret of Joy *(1992),* Anything We Love Can Be Saved: A Writer's Activism *(1997), and* By the Light of My Father's Smile *(1999).*

Walker's works show her commitment to the idea of radical social change. She was active in the civil rights movement in Mississippi, where she met and married a civil rights lawyer from whom she separated after the birth of their daughter. In confronting the painful struggle of black people's history, Walker asserts that the creativity of black women—the extent to which they are permitted to express themselves—is a measure of the health of the entire American society. She calls herself a "womanist," her term for a black feminist. In her definition, "womanism" is preferable to "feminism" because, as she has said,

> part of our tradition as black women is that we are universalists. Black children, yellow children, red children, brown children, that is the black woman's normal, day-to-day relationship. In my family alone, we are about four different colors. When a black woman looks at the world, it is so different . . . when I look at the people in Iran they look like kinfolk. When I look at the people in Cuba, they look like my uncles and nieces.

Walker credits many writers for influencing her prose style in her short fiction. Virginia Woolf, Zora Neale Hurston, and Gabriel García Márquez seem to Walker to be "like musicians; at one with their cultures and their historical subconscious." Her two books of stories show a clear progression of theme. The women of In Love and Trouble *(1973) struggle against injustice almost in spite of themselves, as does the protagonist in "Everyday Use" from that collection; the heroines of* You Can't Keep a Good Woman Down *(1981) consciously challenge conventions. Walker has said, "Writing really helps you heal yourself. I think if you write long enough, you will be a healthy person. That is, if you write what you need to write, as opposed to what will make money, or what will make fame."* "Everyday Use" was first published in Harper's Magazine in 1973.

COMMENTARIES *Cheryl B. Torsney, "'Everyday Use': My Sojourn at Parchman Farm," page 595; Alice Walker, "Zora Neale Hurston: A Cautionary Tale and a Partisan View," page 602.*

WEB *Research Alice Walker and answer questions about her work at bedfordstmartins.com/charters/litwriters.*

Everyday Use   1973

I will wait for her in the yard that Maggie and I made so clean and wavy yesterday afternoon. A yard like this is more comfortable than most people know. It is not just a yard. It is like an extended living room. When the hard clay is swept clean as a floor and the fine sand around the edges lined with tiny, irregular grooves, anyone can come and sit and look up into the elm tree and wait for the breezes that never come inside the house.

Maggie will be nervous until after her sister goes: she will stand hopelessly in corners, homely and ashamed of the burn scars down her arms and legs, eyeing her sister with a mixture of envy and awe. She thinks her sister has held life always in the palm of one hand, that "no" is a word the world never learned to say to her.

You've no doubt seen those TV shows where the child who has "made it" is confronted, as a surprise, by her own mother and father, tottering in weakly from backstage. (A pleasant surprise, of course: What would they do if parent and child came on the show only to curse out and insult each other?) On TV mother and child embrace and smile into each other's faces. Sometimes the mother and father weep, the child wraps them in her arms and leans across the table to tell how she would not have made it without their help. I have seen these programs.

Sometimes I dream a dream in which Dee and I are suddenly brought together on a TV program of this sort. Out of a dark and soft-seated limousine I am ushered into a bright room filled with many people. There I meet a smiling, gray, sporty man like Johnny Carson who shakes my hand and tells me what a fine girl I have. Then we are on the stage and Dee is embracing me with tears in her eyes. She pins on my dress a large orchid, even though she has told me once that she thinks orchids are tacky flowers.

In real life I am a large, big-boned woman with rough, man-working hands. In the winter I wear flannel nightgowns to bed and overalls during the day. I can kill and clean a hog as mercilessly as a man. My fat keeps me hot in zero weather. I can work outside all day, breaking ice to get water for washing; I can eat pork liver cooked over the open fire minutes after it comes steaming from the hog. One winter I knocked a bull calf straight in the brain between the eyes with a sledge hammer and had the meat hung up to chill before nightfall. But of course all this does not show on television. I am the way my daughter would want me to be: a hundred pounds lighter, my skin like an uncooked barley pancake. My hair glistens in the hot bright lights. Johnny Carson has much to do to keep up with my quick and witty tongue.

But that is a mistake. I know even before I wake up. Who ever knew a Johnson with a quick tongue? Who can even imagine me looking a strange white man in the eye? It seems to me I have talked to them always with one foot raised in flight, with my head turned in whichever way is farthest from them. Dee, though. She would always look anyone in the eye. Hesitation was no part of her nature.

"How do I look, Mama?" Maggie says, showing just enough of her thin body enveloped in pink skirt and red blouse for me to know she's there, almost hidden by the door.

"Come out into the yard," I say.

Have you ever seen a lame animal, perhaps a dog run over by some careless person rich enough to own a car, sidle up to someone who is ignorant enough to be kind to him? That is the way my Maggie walks. She has been like this, chin on chest, eyes on ground, feet in shuffle, ever since the fire that burned the other house to the ground.

Dee is lighter than Maggie, with nicer hair and a fuller figure. She's a woman now, though sometimes I forget. How long ago was it that the other house burned? Ten, twelve years? Sometimes I can still hear the flames and feel Maggie's arms sticking to me, her hair smoking and her dress falling off her in little black papery flakes. Her eyes seemed stretched open, blazed open by the flames reflected in them. And Dee. I see her standing off under the sweet gum tree she used to dig gum out of; a look of concentration on her face as she watched the last dingy gray board of the house fall in toward the red-hot brick chimney. Why don't you do a dance around the ashes? I'd wanted to ask her. She had hated the house that much.

I used to think she hated Maggie, too. But that was before we raised the money, the church and me, to send her to Augusta to school. She used to read to us without pity; forcing words, lies, other folks' habits, whole lives upon us two, sitting trapped and ignorant underneath her voice. She washed us in a river of make-believe, burned us with a lot of knowledge we didn't necessarily need to know. Pressed us to her with the serious way she read, to shove us away at just the moment, like dimwits, we seemed about to understand.

Dee wanted nice things. A yellow organdy dress to wear to her graduation from high school; black pumps to match a green suit she'd made from an old suit somebody gave me. She was determined to stare down any disaster in her efforts. Her eyelids would not flicker for minutes at a time. Often I fought off the temptation to shake her. At sixteen she had a style of her own: and knew what style was.

I never had an education myself. After second grade the school was closed down. Don't ask me why: in 1927 colored asked fewer questions than they do now. Sometimes Maggie reads to me. She stumbles along good-naturedly but can't see well. She knows she is not bright. Like good looks and money, quickness passed her by. She will marry John Thomas (who has mossy teeth in an earnest face) and then I'll be free to sit here and I guess just sing church songs to myself. Although I never was a good singer. Never could carry a tune. I was always better at a man's job. I used to love to milk till I was hooked in the side in '49. Cows are soothing and slow and don't bother you, unless you try to milk them the wrong way.

I have deliberately turned my back on the house. It is three rooms, just like the one that burned, except the roof is tin; they don't make shingle roofs any more. There are no real windows, just some holes cut in the sides, like the portholes in a ship, but not round and not square, with rawhide holding the shutters up on the outside. This house is in a pasture, too, like the other one. No doubt when Dee sees it she will want to tear it down. She wrote me once that no matter where we "choose" to live, she will manage to come see us. But she will never bring her friends. Maggie and I thought about this and Maggie asked me, "Mama, when did Dee ever *have* any friends?"

She had a few. Furtive boys in pink shirts hanging about on washday after school. Nervous girls who never laughed. Impressed with her they worshiped the well-turned phrase, the cute shape, the scalding humor that erupted like bubbles in lye. She read to them.

When she was courting Jimmy T she didn't have much time to pay to us, but turned all her faultfinding power on him. He *flew* to marry a cheap city gal from a family of ignorant flashy people. She hardly had time to recompose herself.

When she comes I will meet—but there they are!

Maggie attempts to make a dash for the house, in her shuffling way, but I stay her with my hand. "Come back here," I say. And she stops and tries to dig a well in the sand with her toe.

It is hard to see them clearly through the strong sun. But even the first glimpse of leg out of the car tells me it is Dee. Her feet were always neat-looking, as if God himself had shaped them with a certain style. From the other side of the car comes a short, stocky man. Hair is all over his head a foot long and hanging from his chin like a kinky mule tail. I hear Maggie suck in her breath. "Uhnnnh," is what it sounds like. Like when you see the wriggling end of a snake just in front of your foot on the road. "Uhnnnh."

Dee next. A dress down to the ground, in this hot weather. A dress so loud it hurts my eyes. There are yellows and oranges enough to throw back the light of the sun. I feel my whole face warming from the heat waves it throws out. Earrings gold, too, and hanging down to her shoulders. Bracelets dangling and making noises when she moves her arm up to shake the folds of the dress out of her armpits. The dress is loose and flows, and as she walks closer, I like it. I hear Maggie go "Uhnnnh" again. It is her sister's hair. It stands straight up like the wool on a sheep. It is black as night and around the edges are two long pigtails that rope about like small lizards disappearing behind her ears.

"Wa-su-zo-Tean-o!" she says, coming on in that gliding way the dress makes her move. The short stocky fellow with the hair to his navel is all grinning and he follows up with "Asalamalakim, my mother and sister!" He moves to hug Maggie but she falls back, right up against the back of my chair. I feel her trembling there and when I look up I see the perspiration falling off her chin.

"Don't get up," says Dee. Since I am stout it takes something of a push. You can see me trying to move a second or two before I make it. She turns, showing white heels through her sandals, and goes back to the car. Out she peeks next with a Polaroid. She stoops down quickly and lines up picture after picture of me sitting there in front of the house with Maggie cowering behind me. She never takes a shot without making sure the house is included. When a cow comes nibbling around the edge of the yard she snaps it and me *and* the house. Then she puts the Polaroid in the back seat of the car, and comes up and kisses me on the forehead.

Meanwhile Asalamalakim is going through the motions with Maggie's hand. Maggie's hand is as limp as a fish, and probably as cold, despite the sweat, and she keeps trying to pull it back. It looks like Asalamalakim wants to shake hands but wants to do it fancy. Or maybe he don't know how people shake hands. Anyhow, he soon gives up on Maggie.

"Well," I say. "Dee."

"No, Mama," she says. "Not 'Dee,' Wangero Leewanika Kemanjo!"

"What happened to 'Dee'?" I wanted to know.

"She's dead," Wangero said. "I couldn't bear it any longer being named after the people who oppress me."

"You know as well as me you was named after your aunt Dicie," I said. Dicie is my sister. She named Dee. We called her "Big Dee" after Dee was born.

"But who was *she* named after?" asked Wangero.

"I guess after Grandma Dee," I said.

"And who was she named after?" asked Wangero.

"Her mother," I said, and saw Wangero was getting tired. "That's about as far back as I can trace it," I said. Though, in fact, I probably could have carried it back beyond the Civil War through the branches.

"Well," said Asalamalakim, "there you are."

"Uhnnnh," I heard Maggie say.

"There I was not," I said, "before 'Dicie' cropped up in our family, so why should I try to trace it that far back?"

He just stood there grinning, looking down on me like somebody inspecting a Model A car. Every once in a while he and Wangero sent eye signals over my head.

"How do you pronounce this name?" I asked.

"You don't have to call me by it if you don't want to," said Wangero.

"Why shouldn't I?" I asked. "If that's what you want us to call you, we'll call you."

"I know it might sound awkward at first," said Wangero.

"I'll get used to it," I said. "Ream it out again."

Well, soon we got the name out of the way. Asalamalakim had a name twice as long and three times as hard. After I tripped over it two or three times he told me to just call him Hakim-a-barber. I wanted to ask him was he a barber, but I didn't really think he was, so I didn't ask.

"You must belong to those beef-cattle peoples down the road," I said. They said "Asalamalakim" when they met you, too, but they didn't shake hands. Always too busy: feeding the cattle, fixing the fences, putting up salt-lick shelters, throwing down hay. When the white folks poisoned some of the herd the men stayed up all night with rifles in their hands. I walked a mile and a half just to see the sight.

Hakim-a-barber said, "I accept some of their doctrines, but farming and raising cattle is not my style." (They didn't tell me, and I didn't ask, whether Wangero [Dee] had really gone and married him.)

We sat down to eat and right away he said he didn't eat collards and pork was unclean. Wangero, though, went on through the chitlins and corn bread, the greens and everything else. She talked a blue streak over the sweet potatoes. Everything delighted her. Even the fact that we still used the benches her daddy made for the table when we couldn't afford to buy chairs.

"Oh, Mama!" she cried. Then turned to Hakim-a-barber. "I never knew how lovely these benches are. You can feel the rump prints," she said, running her hands underneath her and along the bench. Then she gave a sigh and her hand closed over Grandma Dee's butter dish. "That's it!" she said. "I knew there was something I wanted to ask you if I could have." She jumped up from the table and went over in the corner where the churn stood, the milk in it clabber by now. She looked at the churn and looked at it.

"This churn top is what I need," she said. "Didn't Uncle Buddy whittle it out of a tree you all used to have?"

"Yes," I said.

"Uh-huh," she said happily. "And I want the dasher, too."

"Uncle Buddy whittle that, too?" asked the barber.

Dee (Wangero) looked up at me.

"Aunt Dee's first husband whittled the dash," said Maggie so low you almost couldn't hear her. "His name was Henry, but they called him Stash."

"Maggie's brain is like an elephant's," Wangero said, laughing. "I can use the churn top as a centerpiece for the alcove table," she said, sliding a plate over the churn, "and I'll think of something artistic to do with the dasher."

When she finished wrapping the dasher the handle stuck out. I took it for a moment in my hands. You didn't even have to look close to see where hands pushing the dasher up and down to make butter had left a kind of sink in the wood. In fact, there were a lot of small sinks; you could see where thumbs and fingers had sunk into the wood. It was beautiful light yellow wood, from a tree that grew in the yard where Big Dee and Stash had lived.

After dinner Dee (Wangero) went to the trunk at the foot of my bed and started rifling through it. Maggie hung back in the kitchen over the dish-pan. Out came Wangero with two quilts. They had been pieced by Grandma Dee and then Big Dee and me had hung them on the quilt frames on the front porch and quilted them. One was in the Lone Star pattern. The other was Walk Around the Mountain. In both of them were scraps of dresses Grandma Dee had worn fifty and more years ago. Bits and pieces of Grandpa Jarrell's

Paisley shirts. And one teeny faded blue piece, about the size of a penny matchbox, that was from Great Grandpa Ezra's uniform that he wore in the Civil War.

"Mama," Wangero said sweet as a bird. "Can I have these old quilts?"

I heard something fall in the kitchen, and a minute later the kitchen door slammed.

"Why don't you take one or two of the others?" I asked. "These old things was just done by me and Big Dee from some tops your grandma pieced before she died."

"No," said Wangero. "I don't want those. They are stitched around the borders by machine."

"That'll make them last better," I said.

"That's not the point," said Wangero. "These are all pieces of dresses Grandma used to wear. She did all this stitching by hand. Imagine!" She held the quilts securely in her arms, stroking them.

"Some of the pieces, like those lavender ones, come from old clothes her mother handed down to her," I said, moving up to touch the quilts. Dee (Wangero) moved back just enough so that I couldn't reach the quilts. They already belonged to her.

"Imagine!" she breathed again, clutching them closely to her bosom.

"The truth is," I said, "I promised to give them quilts to Maggie, for when she marries John Thomas."

She gasped like a bee had stung her.

"Maggie can't appreciate these quilts!" she said. "She'd probably be backward enough to put them to everyday use."

"I reckon she would," I said. "God knows I been saving 'em for long enough with nobody using 'em. I hope she will!" I didn't want to bring up how I had offered Dee (Wangero) a quilt when she went away to college. Then she had told me they were old-fashioned, out of style.

"But they're *priceless*!" she was saying now, furiously; for she has a temper. "Maggie would put them on the bed and in five years they'd be in rags. Less than that!"

"She can always make some more," I said. "Maggie knows how to quilt."

Dee (Wangero) looked at me with hatred. "You just will not understand. The point is these quilts, *these* quilts!"

"Well," I said, stumped. "What would *you* do with them?"

"Hang them," she said. As if that was the only thing you *could* do with quilts.

Maggie by now was standing in the door. I could almost hear the sound her feet made as they scraped over each other.

"She can have them, Mama," she said, like somebody used to never winning anything, or having anything reserved for her. "I can 'member Grandma Dee without the quilts."

I looked at her hard. She had filled her bottom lip with checkerberry snuff and it gave her face a kind of dopey, hangdog look. It was Grandma Dee and Big Dee who taught her how to quilt herself. She stood there with her scarred hands hidden in the folds of her skirt. She looked at her sister with something like fear but she wasn't mad at her. This was Maggie's portion. This was the way she knew God to work.

When I looked at her like that something hit me in the top of my head and ran down to the soles of my feet. Just like when I'm in church and the spirit of God touches me and I get happy and shout. I did something I never had done before: hugged Maggie to me, then dragged her on into the room, snatched the quilts out of Miss Wangero's hands and dumped them into Maggie's lap. Maggie just sat there on my bed with her mouth open.

"Take one or two of the others," I said to Dee.

But she turned without a word and went out to Hakim-a-barber.

"You just don't understand," she said, as Maggie and I came out to the car.

"What don't I understand?" I wanted to know.

"Your heritage," she said. And then she turned to Maggie, kissed her, and said, "You ought to try to make something of yourself, too, Maggie. It's really a new day for us. But from the way you and Mama still live you'd never know it."

She put on some sunglasses that hid everything above the tip of her nose and her chin.

Maggie smiled; maybe at the sunglasses. But a real smile, not scared. After we watched the car dust settle I asked Maggie to bring me a dip of snuff. And then the two of us sat there just enjoying, until it was time to go in the house and go to bed.

EUDORA WELTY

Eudora Welty (1909–2001) was born in Jackson, Mississippi, where she spent nearly her whole life. She had a predominately tranquil view of the South, so her stories and novels provide a strong contrast to the turbulent fiction of William Faulkner and Richard Wright, who also wrote about Mississippi. Welty grew up as one of three children in a close-knit family living two blocks from the state capitol. Her father was the president of an insurance company, and her mother was a thrifty housewife who kept a Jersey cow in a little pasture behind the backyard. An insatiable reader as a child, Welty began writing spontaneously and continued, without any particular encouragement or any plan to be a writer, during her years in college. In her midtwenties she started to publish stories in the Southern Review, *but she credited the persistence of her New York literary agent with helping her get a story published in the* Atlantic Monthly *in 1941. This event led directly to the publication of her first book of stories,* A Curtain of Green, *the same year.*

During World War II Welty was a staff member of the New York Times Book Review *while she lived at home with her mother and continued to write short fiction. Another collection was published in 1943 as* The Wide Net and Other Stories. *After leaving her newspaper work, she turned a short story into her first novel,* Delta Wedding *(1946), on the advice of her agent. She produced several other story collections over the years. Her novel* The Optimist's Daughter won the Pulitzer Prize in 1972. In 1980 The Collected Stories of Eudora Welty *appeared, forty-one stories in all. Welty was also a fine critic of the short story. Her essays and reviews of the work of writers such as Anton Chekhov, Willa Cather, Katherine Anne Porter, Virginia Woolf, and Isak Dinesen, as well as some comments on her own work, were collected in* The Eye of the Story *(1977). Eight years later the book* Conversations with Eudora Welty *was a best-seller.*

In the preface to her collected stories, Welty stated,

> I have been told, both in approval and in accusation, that I seem to love all my characters. What I do in writing of any character is to try to enter into the mind, heart, and skin of a human being who is not myself. Whether this happens to be a man or a woman, old or young, with skin black or white, the primary challenge lies in making the jump itself. It is the act of a writer's imagination that I set most high.

Welty's usual manner was a calm celebration of her characters' minor victories, as in "A Worn Path." The e-mail software used by millions of people was named after her and her story "Why I Live at the P.O." According to inventor Steve Dorner, he felt as if he "lived at the post office" while developing e-mail, so he transposed the short story title into his slogan, "Bringing the P.O. to Where You Live." Later Dorner publicly apologized for being "presumptuous" enough to name his e-mail program Eudora, after a living person, but Welty's literary agent said the writer had been "pleased and amused" to hear of the tribute.

COMMENTARIES *Eudora Welty, "Is Phoenix Jackson's Grandson Really Dead?," page 604; Eudora Welty, "Plot and Character in Chekhov's 'The Darling,'" page 606.*

WEB *Research Eudora Welty and answer questions about her work at bedfordstmartins.com/charters/litwriters.*

A Worn Path   1941

It was December — a bright frozen day in the early morning. Far out in the country there was an old Negro woman with her head tied in a red rag, coming along a path through the pinewoods. Her name was Phoenix Jackson. She was very old and small and she walked slowly in the dark pine shadows, moving a little from side to side in her steps, with the balanced heaviness and lightness of a pendulum in a grandfather clock. She carried a thin, small cane made from an umbrella, and with this she kept tapping the frozen earth in front of her. This made a grave and persistent noise in the still air, that seemed meditative like the chirping of a solitary little bird.

She wore a dark striped dress reaching down to her shoe tops, and an equally long apron of bleached sugar sacks, with a full pocket: all neat and tidy, but every time she took a step she might have fallen over her shoelaces, which dragged from her unlaced shoes. She looked straight ahead. Her eyes were blue with age. Her skin had a pattern all its own of numberless branching wrinkles and as though a whole little tree stood in the middle of her forehead, but a golden color ran underneath, and the two knobs of her cheeks were illumined by a yellow burning under the dark. Under the red rag her hair came down on her neck in the frailest of ringlets, still black, and with an odor like copper.

Now and then there was a quivering in the thicket. Old Phoenix said, "Out of my way, all you foxes, owls, beetles, jack rabbits, coons and wild animals! . . . Keep out from under these feet, little bobwhites. . . . Keep the big wild hogs out of my path. Don't let none of those come running my direction. I got a long way." Under her small black-freckled hand her cane, limber as a buggy whip, would switch at the brush as if to rouse up any hiding things.

On she went. The woods were deep and still. The sun made the pine needles almost too bright to look at, up where the wind rocked. The cones dropped as light as feathers. Down in the hollow was the mourning dove—it was not too late for him.

The path ran up a hill. "Seem like there is chains about my feet, time I get this far," she said, in the voice of argument old people keep to use with themselves. "Something always take a hold of me on this hill—pleads I should stay."

After she got to the top she turned and gave a full, severe look behind her where she had come. "Up through pines," she said at length. "Now down through oaks."

Her eyes opened their widest, and she started down gently. But before she got to the bottom of the hill a bush caught her dress.

Her fingers were busy and intent, but her skirts were full and long, so that before she could pull them free in one place they were caught in another. It was not possible to allow the dress to tear. "I in the thorny bush," she said. "Thorns, you doing your appointed work. Never want to let folks pass, no sir. Old eyes thought you was a pretty little *green* bush."

Finally, trembling all over, she stood free, and after a moment dared to stoop for her cane.

"Sun so high!" she cried, leaning back and looking, while the thick tears went over her eyes. "The time getting all gone here."

At the foot of this hill was a place where a log was laid across the creek.

"Now comes the trial," said Phoenix.

Putting her right foot out, she mounted the log and shut her eyes. Lifting her skirt, leveling her cane fiercely before her, like a festival figure in some parade, she began to march across. Then she opened her eyes and she was safe on the other side.

"I wasn't as old as I thought," she said.

But she sat down to rest. She spread her skirts on the bank around her and folded her hands over her knees. Up above her was a tree in a pearly cloud of mistletoe. She did not dare to close her eyes, and when a little boy brought her a plate with a slice of marble-cake on it she spoke to him. "That would be acceptable," she said. But when she went to take it there was just her own hand in the air.

So she left that tree, and had to go through a barbed-wire fence. There she had to creep and crawl, spreading her knees and stretching her fingers like a baby trying to climb the steps. But she talked loudly to herself: she could not let her dress be torn now, so late in the day, and she could not pay for having her arm or her leg sawed off if she got caught fast where she was.

At last she was safe through the fence and risen up out in the clearing. Big dead trees, like black men with one arm, were standing in the purple stalks of the withered cotton field. There sat a buzzard.

"Who you watching?"

In the furrow she made her way along.

"Glad this not the season for bulls," she said, looking sideways, "and the good Lord made his snakes to curl up and sleep in the winter. A pleasure I don't see no two-headed snake coming around that tree, where it come once. It took a while to get by him, back in the summer."

She passed through the old cotton and went into a field of dead corn. It whispered and shook and was taller than her head. "Through the maze now," she said, for there was no path.

Then there was something tall, black, and skinny there, moving before her.

At first she took it for a man. It could have been a man dancing in the field. But she stood still and listened, and it did not make a sound. It was as silent as a ghost.

"Ghost," she said sharply, "who be you the ghost of? For I have heard of nary death close by."

But there was no answer — only the ragged dancing in the wind.

She shut her eyes, reached out her hand, and touched a sleeve. She found a coat and inside that an emptiness, cold as ice.

"You scarecrow," she said. Her face lighted. "I ought to be shut up for good," she said with laughter. "My senses is gone. I too old. I the oldest people I ever know. Dance, old scarecrow," she said, "while I dancing with you."

She kicked her foot over the furrow, and with mouth drawn down, shook her head once or twice in a little strutting way. Some husks blew down and whirled in streamers about her skirts.

Then she went on, parting her way from side to side with the cane, through the whispering field. At last she came to the end, to a wagon track where the silver grass blew between the red ruts. The quail were walking around like pullets, seeming all dainty and unseen.

"Walk pretty," she said. "This the easy place. This the easy going."

She followed the track, swaying through the quiet bare fields, through the little strings of trees silver in their dead leaves, past cabins silver from weather, with the doors and windows boarded shut, all like old women under a spell sitting there. "I walking in their sleep," she said, nodding her head vigorously.

In a ravine she went where a spring was silently flowing through a hollow log. Old Phoenix bent and drank. "Sweet-gum makes the water sweet," she said, and drank more. "Nobody know who made this well, for it was here when I was born."

The track crossed a swampy part where the moss hung as white as lace from every limb. "Sleep on, alligators, and blow your bubbles." Then the track went into the road.

Deep, deep the road went down between the high green-colored banks. Overhead the live-oaks met, and it was as dark as a cave.

A black dog with a lolling tongue came up out of the weeds by the ditch. She was meditating, and not ready, and when he came at her she only hit him a little with her cane. Over she went in the ditch, like a little puff of milkweed.

Down there, her senses drifted away. A dream visited her, and she reached her hand up, but nothing reached down and gave her a pull. So she lay there and presently went to talking. "Old woman," she said to herself, "that black dog come up out of the weeds to stall you off, and now there he sitting on his fine tail, smiling at you."

A white man finally came along and found her—a hunter, a young man, with his dog on a chain.

"Well, Granny!" he laughed. "What are you doing there?"

"Lying on my back like a June-bug waiting to be turned over, mister," she said, reaching up her hand.

He lifted her up, gave her a swing in the air, and set her down. "Anything broken, Granny?"

"No sir, them old dead weeds is springy enough," said Phoenix, when she had got her breath. "I thank you for your trouble."

"Where do you live, Granny?" he asked, while the two dogs were growling at each other.

"Away back yonder, sir, behind the ridge. You can't even see it from here."

"On your way home?"

"No sir, I going to town."

"Why, that's too far! That's as far as I walk when I come out myself, and I get something for my trouble." He patted the stuffed bag he carried, and there hung down a little closed claw. It was one of the bobwhites, with its beak hooked bitterly to show it was dead. "Now you go on home, Granny!"

"I bound to go to town, mister," said Phoenix. "The time come around."

He gave another laugh, filling the whole landscape. "I know you old colored people! Wouldn't miss going to town to see Santa Claus!"

But something held old Phoenix very still. The deep lines in her face went into a fierce and different radiation. Without warning, she had seen with her own eyes a flashing nickel fall out of the man's pocket onto the ground.

"How old are you, Granny?" he was saying.

"There is no telling, mister," she said, "no telling."

Then she gave a little cry and clapped her hands and said, "Git on away from here, dog! Look! Look at that dog!" She laughed as if in admiration. "He ain't scared of nobody. He a big black dog." She whispered, "Sic him!"

"Watch me get rid of that cur," said the man. "Sic him, Pete! Sic him!"

Phoenix heard the dogs fighting, and heard the man running and throwing sticks. She even heard a gunshot. But she was slowly bending forward by that time, further and further forward, the lid stretched down over her eyes, as if she were doing this in her sleep. Her chin was lowered almost to her knees. The yellow palm of her hand came out from the fold of her apron. Her fingers slid down and along the ground under the piece of money with the grace and care they would have in lifting an egg from under a setting hen. Then she slowly straightened up, she stood erect, and the nickel was in her apron pocket.

A bird flew by. Her lips moved. "God watching me the whole time. I come to stealing."

The man came back, and his own dog panted about them. "Well, I scared him off that time," he said, and then he laughed and lifted his gun and pointed it at Phoenix.

She stood straight and faced him.

"Doesn't the gun scare you?" he said, still pointing it.

"No, sir, I seen plenty go off closer by, in my day, and for less than what I done," she said, holding utterly still.

He smiled, and shouldered the gun. "Well, Granny," he said, "you must be a hundred years old, and scared of nothing. I'd give you a dime if I had any money with me. But you take my advice and stay home, and nothing will happen to you."

"I bound to go on my way, mister," said Phoenix. She inclined her head in the red rag. Then they went in different directions, but she could hear the gun shooting again and again over the hill.

She walked on. The shadows hung from the oak trees to the road like curtains. Then she smelled wood-smoke, and smelled the river, and she saw a steeple and the cabins on their steep steps. Dozens of little black children whirled around her. There ahead was Natchez shining. Bells were ringing. She walked on.

In the paved city it was Christmas time. There were red and green electric lights strung and crisscrossed everywhere, and all turned on in the daytime. Old Phoenix would have been lost if she had not distrusted her eyesight and depended on her feet to know where to take her.

She paused quietly on the sidewalk where people were passing by. A lady came along in the crowd, carrying an armful of red-, green-, and silver-wrapped presents; she gave off perfume like the red roses in hot summer, and Phoenix stopped her.

"Please, missy, will you lace up my shoe?" She held up her foot.

"What do you want, Grandma?"

"See my shoe," said Phoenix. "Do all right for out in the country, but wouldn't look right to go in a big building."

"Stand still then, Grandma," said the lady. She put her packages down on the sidewalk beside her and laced and tied both shoes tightly.

"Can't lace 'em with a cane," said Phoenix. "Thank you, missy. I doesn't mind asking a nice lady to tie up my shoe, when I gets out on the street."

Moving slowly and from side to side, she went into the big building, and into a tower of steps, where she walked up and around and around until her feet knew to stop.

She entered a door, and there she saw nailed up on the wall the document that had been stamped with the gold seal and framed in the gold frame, which matched the dream that was hung up in her head.

"Here I be," she said. There was a fixed and ceremonial stiffness over her body.

"A charity case, I suppose," said an attendant who sat at the desk before her.

But Phoenix only looked above her head. There was sweat on her face, the wrinkles in her skin shone like a bright net.

"Speak up, Grandma," the woman said. "What's your name? We must have your history, you know. Have you been here before? What seems to be the trouble with you?"

Old Phoenix only gave a twitch to her face as if a fly were bothering her.

"Are you deaf?" cried the attendant.

But then the nurse came in.

"Oh, that's just old Aunt Phoenix," she said. "She doesn't come for herself—she has a little grandson. She makes these trips just as regular as clockwork. She lives away back off the Old Natchez Trace." She bent down. "Well, Aunt Phoenix, why don't you just take a seat? We won't keep you standing after your long trip." She pointed.

The old woman sat down, bolt upright in the chair.

"Now, how is the boy?" asked the nurse.

Old Phoenix did not speak.

"I said, how is the boy?"

But Phoenix only waited and stared straight ahead, her face very solemn and withdrawn into rigidity.

"Is his throat any better?" asked the nurse. "Aunt Phoenix, don't you hear me? Is your grandson's throat any better since the last time you came for the medicine?"

With her hands on her knees, the old woman waited, silent, erect and motionless, just as if she were in armor.

"You mustn't take up our time this way, Aunt Phoenix," the nurse said. "Tell us quickly about your grandson, and get it over. He isn't dead, is he?"

At last there came a flicker and then a flame of comprehension across her face, and she spoke.

"My grandson. It was my memory had left me. There I sat and forgot why I made my long trip."

"Forgot?" The nurse frowned. "After you came so far?"

Then Phoenix was like an old woman begging a dignified forgiveness for waking up frightened in the night. "I never did go to school, I was too old at the Surrender," she said in a soft voice. "I'm an old woman without an education. It was my memory fail me. My little grandson, he is just the same, and I forgot it in the coming."

"Throat never heals, does it?" said the nurse, speaking in a loud, sure voice to old Phoenix. By now she had a card with something written on it, a little list. "Yes. Swallowed lye. When was it?—January—two, three years ago—"

Phoenix spoke unasked now. "No, missy, he not dead, he just the same. Every little while his throat began to close up again, and he not able to swallow. He not get his breath. He not able to help himself. So the time come around, and I go on another trip for the soothing medicine."

"All right. The doctor said as long as you came to get it, you could have it," said the nurse. "But it's an obstinate case."

"My little grandson, he sit up there in the house all wrapped up, waiting by himself," Phoenix went on. "We is the only two left in the world. He suffer and it don't seem to put him back at all. He got a sweet look. He going to last. He wear a little patch quilt and peep out holding his mouth open like a little bird. I remembers so plain now. I not going to forget him again, no, the whole enduring time. I could tell him from all the others in creation."

"All right." The nurse was trying to hush her now. She brought her a bottle of medicine. "Charity," she said, making a check mark in a book.

Old Phoenix held the bottle close to her eyes, and then carefully put it into her pocket.

"I thank you," she said.

"It's Christmas time, Grandma," said the attendant. "Could I give you a few pennies out of my purse?"

"Five pennies is a nickel," said Phoenix stiffly.

"Here's a nickel," said the attendant.

Phoenix rose carefully and held out her hand. She received the nickel and then fished the other nickel out of her pocket and laid it beside the new one. She stared at her palm closely, with her head on one side.

Then she gave a tap with her cane on the floor.

"This is what come to me to do," she said. "I going to the store and buy my child a little windmill they sells, made out of paper. He going to find it hard to believe there such a thing in the world. I'll march myself back where he waiting, holding it straight up in this hand."

She lifted her free hand, gave a little nod, turned around, and walked out of the doctor's office. Then her slow step began on the stairs, going down.

WILLIAM CARLOS WILLIAMS

William Carlos Williams (1883–1963), the poet, novelist, playwright, and short story writer, was born in Rutherford, New Jersey. After graduating from the University of Pennsylvania Medical School, he returned to Rutherford, where he practiced medicine as a pediatrician for the rest of his life. While still an undergraduate, he began to write poetry, influenced by his friends the poets Ezra Pound and Hilda Doolittle. Williams published his first book, Poems, *in 1909. Initially he devoted himself to poetry, but his experimental writing in the 1920s led him to the novel and the short story. The story became for him a way to emphasize his social and humanitarian concerns, which influenced the gritty, down-to-earth realism of his literary style.*

Williams wrote most of his stories during the Depression, when his patients in Rutherford were the poor people characterized by President Franklin Delano Roosevelt in 1933 as "ill-fed, ill-housed, and ill-clothed." Williams's patients were often down and out, but he saw them as splendidly vital people. When asked how he managed the two careers of medicine and writing, Williams answered, "It's no strain. In fact, the one [medicine] nourishes the other [writing], even if at times I've groaned to the contrary."

Like the doctor-writer Anton Chekhov before him, Williams understood the moral responsibility of his calling, and he was vigilant against his feelings of arrogance and self-importance. "*There's nothing like a difficult patient to show us ourselves,*" *he once told a medical student.* "*I would learn so much on my rounds, or making home visits. At times I felt like a thief because I heard words, lines, saw people and places—and used it all in my writing. I guess I've told people that, and no one's so surprised! There was something deeper going on, though—the force of all those encounters. I was put off guard again and again, and the result was—well, a descent into myself.*"

Williams collected his stories in four volumes: The Knife of the Times *(1932),* Life along the Passaic River *(1938),* Make Light of It *(1950), and* The Farmers' Daughters *(1961). More recently Robert Coles compiled* The Doctor Stories *(1984). As Coles understands, in* "*The Use of Force,*" *Williams* "*extends to us, really, moments of a doctor's self-recognition—rendered in such a way that the particular becomes the universal.*" *Williams used vernacular American speech and direct observation in all his writing. His work includes twenty books of poetry, four novels, several books of nonfiction, a collection of plays, and an autobiography.*

WEB *Research William Carlos Williams and answer questions about his work at bedfordstmartins.com/charters/litwriters.*

The Use of Force   1938

They were new patients to me, all I had was the name, Olson. Please come down as soon as you can, my daughter is very sick. When I arrived I was met by the mother, a big startled looking woman, very clean and apologetic who merely said, Is this the doctor? and let me in. In the back, she added. You must excuse us, doctor, we have her in the kitchen where it is warm. It is very damp here sometimes.

The child was fully dressed and sitting on her father's lap near the kitchen table. He tried to get up, but I motioned for him not to bother, took off my overcoat and started to look things over. I could see that they were all very nervous, eyeing me up and down distrustfully. As often, in such cases, they weren't telling me more than they had to, it was up to me to tell them; that's why they were spending three dollars on me.

The child was fairly eating me up with her cold, steady eyes, and no expression to her face whatever. She did not move and seemed, inwardly, quiet; an unusually attractive little thing, and as strong as a heifer in appearance. But her face was flushed, she was breathing rapidly, and I realized that she had a high fever. She had magnificent blonde hair, in profusion. One of those picture children often reproduced in advertising leaflets and the photogravure sections of the Sunday papers.

She's had a fever for three days, began the father and we don't know what it comes from. My wife has given her things, you know, like people do, but it don't do no good. And there's been a lot of sickness around. So we tho't you'd better look her over and tell us what is the matter.

As doctors often do I took a trial shot at it as a point of departure. Has she had a sore throat?

Both parents answered me together, No . . . No, she says her throat don't hurt her.

Does your throat hurt you? added the mother to the child. But the little girl's expression didn't change nor did she move her eyes from my face.

Have you looked?

I tried to, said the mother, but I couldn't see.

As it happens we had been having a number of cases of diphtheria in the school to which this child went during that month and we were all, quite apparently, thinking of that, though no one had as yet spoken of the thing.

Well, I said, suppose we take a look at the throat first. I smiled in my best professional manner and asking for the child's first name I said, come on, Mathilda, open your mouth and let's take a look at your throat.

Nothing doing.

Aw, come on, I coaxed, just open your mouth wide and let me take a look. Look, I said opening both hands wide, I haven't anything in my hands. Just open up and let me see.

Such a nice man, put in the mother. Look how kind he is to you. Come on, do what he tells you to. He won't hurt you.

At that I ground my teeth in disgust. If only they wouldn't use the word "hurt" I might be able to get somewhere. But I did not allow myself to be hurried or disturbed but speaking quietly and slowly I approached the child again.

As I moved my chair a little nearer suddenly with one catlike movement both her hands clawed instinctively for my eyes and she almost reached them too. In fact she knocked my glasses flying and they fell, though unbroken, several feet away from me on the kitchen floor.

Both the mother and father almost turned themselves inside out in embarrassment and apology. You bad girl, said the mother, taking her and shaking her by one arm. Look what you've done. The nice man . . .

For heaven's sake, I broke in. Don't call me a nice man to her. I'm here to look at her throat on the chance that she might have diphtheria and possibly die of it. But that's nothing to her. Look here, I said to the child, we're going to look at your throat. You're old enough to understand what I'm saying. Will you open it now by yourself or shall we have to open it for you?

Not a move. Even her expression hadn't changed. Her breaths however were coming faster and faster. Then the battle began. I had to do it. I had to have a throat culture for her own protection. But first I told the parents that it was entirely up to them. I explained the danger but said that I would not insist on a throat examination so long as they would take the responsibility.

If you don't do what the doctor says you'll have to go to the hospital, the mother admonished her severely.

Oh yeah? I had to smile to myself. After all, I had already fallen in love with the savage brat, the parents were contemptible to me. In the ensuing struggle they grew more and more abject, crushed, exhausted while she surely rose to magnificent heights of insane fury of effort bred of her terror of me.

The father tried his best, and he was a big man but the fact that she was his daughter, his shame at her behavior and his dread of hurting her made him release her just at the critical times when I had almost achieved success, till I wanted to kill him. But his dread also that she might have diphtheria made him tell me to go on, go on though he himself was almost fainting, while the mother moved back and forth behind us raising and lowering her hands in an agony of apprehension.

Put her in front of you on your lap, I ordered, and hold both her wrists.

But as soon as he did the child let out a scream. Don't, you're hurting me. Let go of my hands. Let them go I tell you. Then she shrieked terrifyingly, hysterically. Stop it! Stop it! You're killing me!

Do you think she can stand it, doctor! said the mother.

You get out, said the husband to his wife. Do you want her to die of diphtheria?

Come on now, hold her, I said.

Then I grasped the child's head with my left hand and tried to get the wooden tongue depressor between her teeth. She fought, with clenched teeth, desperately! But now I also had grown furious—at a child. I tried to hold myself down but I couldn't. I know how to expose a throat for inspection. And I did my best. When finally I got the wooden spatula behind the last teeth and just the point of it into the mouth cavity, she opened up for an instant but before I could see anything she came down again and gripped the wooden blade between her molars. She reduced it to splinters before I could get it out again.

Aren't you ashamed, the mother yelled at her. Aren't you ashamed to act like that in front of the doctor?

Get me a smooth-handled spoon of some sort, I told the mother. We're going through with this. The child's mouth was already bleeding. Her tongue was cut and she was screaming in wild hysterical shrieks. Perhaps I should have desisted and come back in an hour or more. No doubt it would have been better. But I have seen at least two children lying dead in bed of neglect in such cases, and feeling that I must get a diagnosis now or never I went at it again. But the worst of it was that I too had got beyond reason. I could have torn the child apart in my own fury and enjoyed it. It was a pleasure to attack her. My face was burning with it.

The damned little brat must be protected against her own idiocy, one says to one's self at such times. Others must be protected against her. It is a social necessity. And all these things are true. But a blind fury, a feeling of adult shame, bred of a longing for muscular release are the operatives. One goes on to the end.

In the final unreasoning assault I overpowered the child's neck and jaws. I forced the heavy silver spoon back of her teeth and down her throat till she gagged. And there it was—both tonsils covered with membrane. She had fought valiantly to keep me from knowing her secret. She had been hiding that sore throat for three days at least and lying to her parents in order to escape just such an outcome as this.

Now truly she was furious. She had been on the defensive before but now she attacked. Tried to get off her father's lap and fly at me while tears of defeat blinded her eyes.

5.

Commentaries on Stories and Storytellers

JAMES BALDWIN

James Baldwin wrote this account of how he became a writer in his book Notes of a Native Son *(1955). He admitted that "the most difficult (and most rewarding) thing in my life has been the fact that I was born a Negro and was forced, therefore, to effect some kind of truce with this reality." As his biographer Louis H. Pratt has understood, this "truce" forced Baldwin "into an open confrontation with his experience, enabling him to make an honest assessment of his past. . . . Baldwin the artist has been liberated because he has found a way to use his past and to transform those experiences resulting therefrom into art."*

Autobiographical Notes   1955

I was born in Harlem thirty-one years ago. I began plotting novels at about the time I learned to read. The story of my childhood is the usual bleak fantasy, and we can dismiss it with the unrestrained observation that I certainly would not consider living it again. In those days my mother was given to the exasperating and mysterious habit of having babies. As they were born, I took them over with one hand and held a book with the other. The children probably suffered, though they have since been kind enough to deny it, and in this way I read *Uncle Tom's Cabin* and *A Tale of Two Cities* over and over and over again; in this way, in fact, I read just about everything I could get my hands on — except the Bible, probably because it was the only book I was encouraged to read. I must also confess that I wrote — a great deal — and my first professional triumph, in any case, the first effort of mine to be seen in print, occurred at the age of twelve or thereabouts, when a short story I had written about the

Spanish revolution won some sort of prize in an extremely short-lived church newspaper. I remember the story was censored by the lady editor, though I don't remember why, and I was outraged.

Also wrote plays, and songs, for one of which I received a letter of congratulations from Mayor La Guardia, and poetry, about which the less said, the better. My mother was delighted by all these goings-on, but my father wasn't; he wanted me to be a preacher. When I was fourteen I became a preacher, and when I was seventeen I stopped. Very shortly thereafter I left home. For God knows how long I struggled with the world of commerce and industry—I guess they would say they struggled with *me*—and when I was about twenty-one I had enough done of a novel to get a Saxton Fellowship. When I was twenty-two the fellowship was over, the novel turned out to be unsalable, and I started waiting on tables in a Village° restaurant and writing book reviews—mostly, as it turned out, about the Negro problem, concerning which the color of my skin made me automatically an expert. Did another book, in company with photographer Theodore Pelatowski, about the storefront churches in Harlem. This book met exactly the same fate as my first—fellowship, but no sale. (It was a Rosenwald Fellowship.) By the time I was twenty-four I had decided to stop reviewing books about the Negro problem—which, by this time, was only slightly less horrible in print than it was in life—and I packed my bags and went to France, where I finished, God knows how, *Go Tell It on the Mountain.*

Any writer, I suppose, feels that the world into which he was born is nothing less than a conspiracy against the cultivation of his talent—which attitude certainly has a great deal to support it. On the other hand, it is only because the world looks on his talent with such a frightening indifference that the artist is compelled to make his talent important. So that any writer, looking back over even so short a span of time as I am here forced to assess, finds that the things which hurt him and the things which helped him cannot be divorced from each other; he could be helped in a certain way only because he was hurt in a certain way; and his help is simply to be enabled to move from one conundrum to the next—one is tempted to say that he moves from one disaster to the next. When one begins looking for influences one finds them by the score. I haven't thought much about my own, not enough anyway; I hazard that the King James Bible, the rhetoric of the store-front church, something ironic and violent and perpetually understated in Negro speech—and something of Dickens' love for bravura—have something to do with me today; but I wouldn't stake my life on it. Likewise, innumerable people have helped me in many ways; but finally, I suppose, the most difficult (and most rewarding) thing in my life has been the fact that I was born a Negro and was forced, therefore, to effect some kind of truce with this reality. (Truce, by the way, is the best one can hope for.)

One of the difficulties about being a Negro writer (and this is not special pleading, since I don't mean to suggest that he has it worse than anybody else) is that the Negro problem is written about so widely. The bookshelves groan under the weight of information, and everyone therefore considers himself

---

Village: Greenwich Village, New York City.

informed. And this information, furthermore, operates usually (generally, popularly) to reinforce traditional attitudes. Of traditional attitudes there are only two—For or Against—and I, personally, find it difficult to say which attitude has caused me the most pain. I am perfectly aware that the change from ill-will to good-will, however motivated, however imperfect, however expressed, is better than no change at all.

But it is part of the business of the writer—as I see it—to examine attitudes, to go beneath the surface, to tap the source. From this point of view the Negro problem is nearly inaccessible. It is not only written about so widely; it is written about so badly. It is quite possible to say that the price a Negro pays for becoming articulate is to find himself, at length, with nothing to be articulate about. ("You taught me the language," says Caliban to Prospero,° "and my profit on't is I know how to curse.") Consider: The tremendous social activity that this problem generates imposes on whites and Negroes alike the necessity of looking forward, of working to bring about a better day. This is fine, it keeps the waters troubled; it is all, indeed, that has made possible the Negro's progress. Nevertheless, social affairs are not generally speaking the writer's prime concern, whether they ought to be or not; it is absolutely necessary that he establish between himself and these affairs a distance that will allow, at least, for clarity, so that before he can look forward in any meaningful sense, he must first be allowed to take a long look back. In the context of the Negro problem neither whites nor blacks, for excellent reasons of their own, have the faintest desire to look back; but I think that the past is all that makes the present coherent, and further, that the past will remain horrible for exactly as long as we refuse to assess it honestly.

I know, in any case, that the most crucial time in my own development came when I was forced to recognize that I was a kind of bastard of the West; when I followed the line of my past I did not find myself in Europe but in Africa. And this meant that in some subtle way, in a really profound way, I brought to Shakespeare, Bach, Rembrandt, to the stones of Paris, to the cathedral at Chartres, and to the Empire State Building, a special attitude. These were not really my creations, they did not contain my history; I might search in them in vain forever for any reflection of myself. I was an interloper; this was not my heritage. At the same time I had no other heritage which I could possibly hope to use—I had certainly been unfitted for the jungle or the tribe. I would have to appropriate these white centuries, I would have to make them mine—I would have to accept my special attitude, my special place in this scheme—otherwise I would have no place in *any* scheme. What was the most difficult was the fact that I was forced to admit something I had always hidden from myself, which the American Negro has had to hide from himself as the price of his public progress; that I hated and feared white people. This did not mean that I loved black people; on the contrary, I despised them, possibly because they failed to produce Rembrandt. In effect, I hated and feared the world. And this meant, not only that I thus gave the world an altogether

---

Caliban ... Prospero: In Shakespeare's *The Tempest,* the monster Caliban is a servant of the magician Prospero.

murderous power over me, but also that in such a self-destroying limbo I could never hope to write.

One writes out of one thing only—one's own experience. Everything depends on how relentlessly one forces from this experience the last drop, sweet or bitter, it can possibly give. This is the only real concern of the artist, to recreate out of the disorder of life that order which is art. The difficulty then, for me, of being a Negro writer was the fact that I was, in effect, prohibited from examining my own experience too closely by the tremendous demands and the very real dangers of my social situation.

I don't think the dilemma outlined above is uncommon. I do think, since writers work in the disastrously explicit medium of language, that it goes a little way towards explaining why, out of the enormous resources of Negro speech and life, and despite the example of Negro music, prose written by Negroes has been generally speaking so pallid and so harsh. I have not written about being a Negro at such length because I expect that to be my only subject, but only because it was the gate I had to unlock before I could hope to write about anything else. I don't think that the Negro problem in America can be even discussed coherently without bearing in mind its context; its context being the history, traditions, customs, the moral assumptions and preoccupations of the country; in short, the general social fabric. Appearances to the contrary, no one in America escapes its effects and everyone in America bears some responsibility for it. I believe this the more firmly because it is the overwhelming tendency to speak of this problem as though it were a thing apart. But in the work of Faulkner, in the general attitude and certain specific passages in Robert Penn Warren,° and, most significantly, in the advent of Ralph Ellison, one sees the beginnings—at least—of a more genuinely penetrating search. Mr. Ellison, by the way, is the first Negro novelist I have ever read to utilize in language, and brilliantly, some of the ambiguity and irony of Negro life.

About my interests: I don't know if I have any, unless the morbid desire to own a sixteen-millimeter camera and make experimental movies can be so classified. Otherwise, I love to eat and drink—it's my melancholy conviction that I've scarcely ever had enough to eat (this is because it's *impossible* to eat enough if you're worried about the next meal)—and I love to argue with people who do not disagree with me too profoundly, and I love to laugh. I do *not* like bohemia, or bohemians, I do not like people whose principal aim is pleasure, and I do not like people who are *earnest* about anything. I don't like people who like me because I'm a Negro; neither do I like people who find in the same accident grounds for contempt. I love America more than any other country in the world, and, exactly for this reason, I insist on the right to criticize her perpetually. I think all theories are suspect, that the finest principles may have to be modified, or may even be pulverized by the demands of life, and that one must find, therefore, one's own moral center and move through the world hoping that this center will guide one aright. I consider that I have many responsibilities, but none greater than this: to last, as Hemingway says, and get my work done.

I want to be an honest man and a good writer.

Robert Penn Warren: An American novelist, poet, and critic (1905–1989).

ANN CHARTERS

Ann Charters studied German as an undergraduate and graduate student at Los Angeles City College, the University of California at Berkeley, and Columbia University.

Translating Kafka   2002

Why another translation of Franz Kafka's most famous story, "Die Ver-wandlung" (1915), from its original German into English? Several English translations of "The Metamorphosis" are available to the twenty-first century reader of Kafka's short fiction. In my translation I wanted to tell the story as well as I could in American English, not British English, the language used in the most widely available English versions by the early Kafka translators Willa Muir and Edwin Muir, who began to publish translations of Kafka's fiction only a few years after his death in 1924.

After years of reading Kafka's short fiction, I became dissatisfied with the older translations, especially when I considered them in the context of contem-porary usage and literature. The Muirs' vocabulary seemed dated, especially their occasional use of old-fashioned terms in British English. In the second paragraph of their 1936 translation of "The Metamorphosis," for example, they call Gregor Samsa "a commercial traveler" instead of "a traveling sales-man." In the middle of the first section, the Muirs use "chief clerk" as the title of the man from Gregor's office who visits the Samsa household to find out why Gregor hadn't shown up for work that morning. The modern equivalent of the job title is "office manager." In other stories, such as "A Hunger Artist," I felt it was possible to translate from German to English more clearly than the Muirs' translations. In the final paragraph of this story, for example, they wrote, "The panther was all right." Closer to Kafka's intention are the words, "He lacked for nothing."

So in the spring of 2002, I sat down with the German text of "Die Ver-wandlung" and *The New Cassell's German Dictionary* and attempted to create a fresh version of the story that I hoped would bring it more vividly to life for American readers. Like all the other translators before me, I found that the opening sentence of "Die Verwandlung" posed my greatest challenge. In the original German, Kafka wrote, "As Gregor Samsa eines Morgens aus unruhi-gen Träumen erwachte, fand er sich in seinem Bett zu einem ungeheueren Ungeziefer verwandelt." English translators have no problem with eighteen words of the twenty-word sentence, usually translating them: "As Gregor Samsa awoke one morning from troubled dreams, he found himself trans-formed in his bed into a ——"

The Muirs translated "ungeheueren Ungeziefer" as "a gigantic insect." When I checked the definition of the two words in my German dictionary, I found that the adjective *ungeheueren* literally means "monstrous, gigantic, large," and the noun *Ungeziefer* means "vermin" or "verminous insect." Translators Stanley Corngold (1972), Joachim Neugroschel (1992), and Donna Freed (1996) translated the noun and adjective literally as "a monstrous vermin" in their versions of the story. Vladimir Nabokov (who translated parts of the story) and Malcolm Pasley (who translated it into British English in 1992) preferred "a monstrous insect"; Stanley Appelbaum (1996) chose the words "an enormous bug."

Working with Kafka's text, I couldn't accept the literal translation of "a monstrous vermin," because German and English usages are different for the word *vermin*. In English, *vermin* is rarely used as a singular noun. It means "small common harmful or objectionable animals (as lice or fleas) that are difficult to control." The plural implications of the word *vermin* bothered me. There had to be a better way in English to complete the most extraordinary opening sentence in short story literature.

Nowhere in the text does Kafka specify the type of insect that Gregor has become, so I couldn't consider translating "ungeheueren Ungeziefer" as "a monstrous louse" or "a monstrous cockroach." As Nabokov noted in his Cornell University lecture on Kafka's story, the vermin

> obviously belongs to the branch of "jointed leggers" (*Arthropoda*) to which insects, and spiders, and crustaceans belong. . . . Next question: what insect? Commentators say *cockroach*, which of course does not make sense. A cockroach is an insect that is flat in shape with large legs, and Gregor is anything but flat: he is convex on both sides, belly, and back, and his legs are small. He approaches a cockroach in only one aspect: his coloration is brown. That is all.

Initially when I completed my opening sentence of "The Metamorphosis," I chose the words "a giant insect." A giant was a monster, after all. I felt that as a one-syllable adjective, *giant* also possessed the palpable impact and solidity of a noun. On second thought, I realized that "a giant insect" seemed too simple a way to start the story, almost as if I were trying to turn Kafka's subtle, darkly humorous narrative into a comic book.

I also found that I couldn't disregard the troublesome presence of the two syllables *unge-* in the original German that started both the adjective and noun "ungeheueren Ungeziefer." They suggested the double negative (*un-*), something unspecified that had occurred in the past (*ge-*) that definitely did not leave a positive impression on the narrator. These two words implied that Kafka *was* making a judgment: something really bad *had* happened. "Giant insect" didn't carry enough emotional weight. So I decided to use the words "a monstrous insect" as being closer to his original intention.

I rejected the words "an enormous bug" as being too colloquial. Born into an assimilated Jewish family in Prague, Kafka spoke Yiddish, German, and Czech. He chose to write in what is called "Prague German," a much blander version of the language found in Germany and Austria, lacking the coloring of slang, colloquialisms, and dialectical influences found in High German. Kafka was aware that his Prague German language was regarded as simple and "juiceless." Writing a letter to his friend Max Brod in June 1921, he said that he felt Prague German was "nothing but embers which can be brought to a semblance of life only when excessively lively Jewish hands rummage through them."

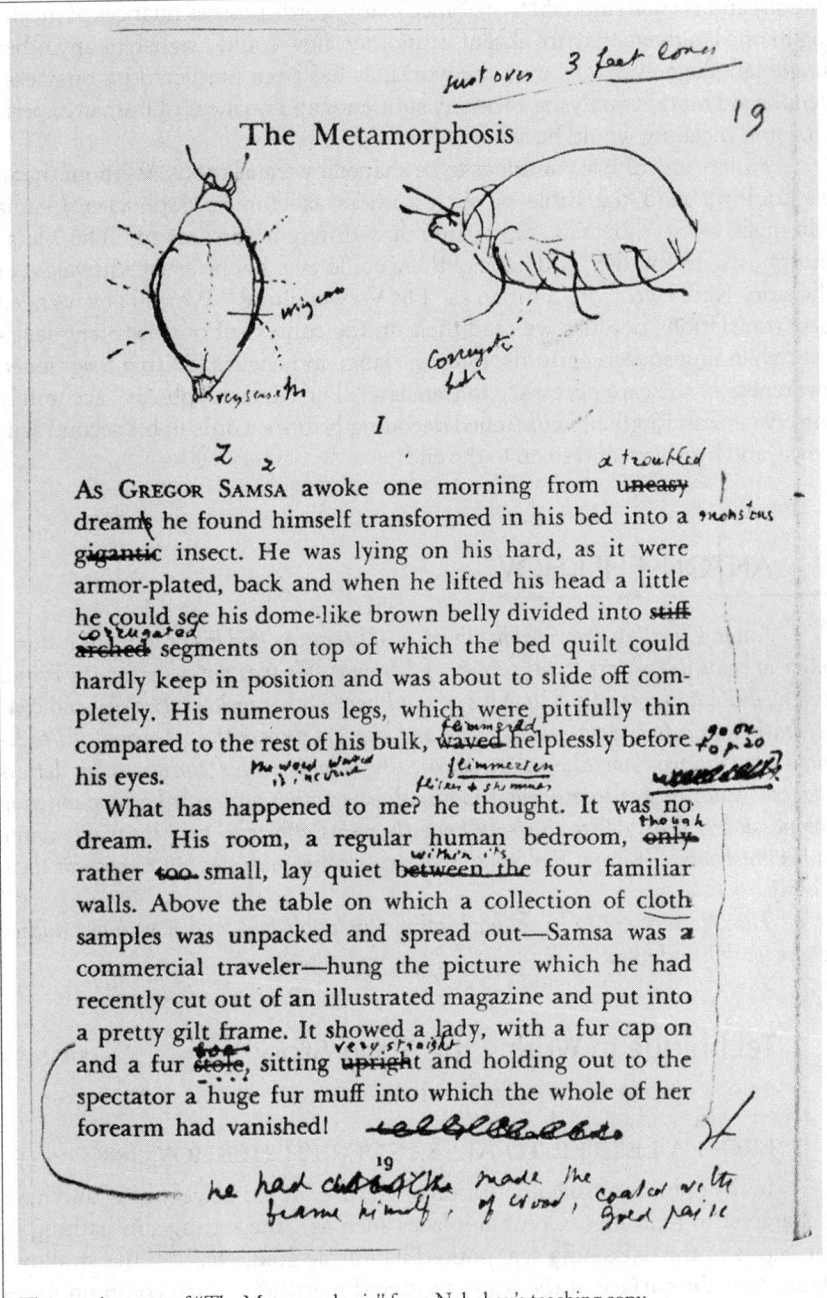

The opening page of "The Metamorphosis" from Nabokov's teaching copy.

Translating the two words "ungeheueren Ungeziefer" from German into English had been a daunting task. My problem was similar to those faced by all translators from one language to another: Do I translate literally or imaginatively? There are even two different words to describe this process: *translation* (literal) and *version* (imaginative). Since many words possess nuances of meaning in one language that are absent in another, how could English or any other single language ever take over the world, as has been predicted by business-people and market analysts? So many subtleties and nuances of human experience and meaning would be lost!

American culture continues to be shaped by translations. Without them, we couldn't read the Bible or such authors as Homer, Sophocles, García Márquez, or Szymborska. There are many different versions of "The Metamorphosis" in English, and none of them could ever be the exact equivalent of the story Kafka wrote in German as "Die Verwandlung." We will always need new translations because we read them in the context of our own language's ever-changing speech patterns, idioms, slang, and clichés. With a heightened awareness of the care necessary to translate "The Metamorphosis" accurately into American English, I continued decoding Kafka's words in his second sentence, and his third, and so on to the end.

ANTON CHEKHOV

Anton Chekhov described his theories of literature and his practice as a story-teller in countless letters to his family and friends. He was not a systematic critic, and he did not necessarily follow his own advice to other writers. Brevity and concentration on a few essentials of scene and character were the essence of his technique, but he was not always as drastically laconic in his stories as his letters suggest. What is consistently clear in his advice to other writers is his own untiring compassion and his desire to speak honestly in his efforts to help them. He wrote in his notebook, "It is not the function of art to solve problems but to present them clearly."

These letters are to his older brother, his publisher, and a younger author whose work he admired.

Technique in Writing the Short Story   1886–99

TRANSLATED BY CONSTANCE GARNETT

FROM A LETTER TO ALEXANDER P. CHEKHOV, 1886

In my opinion a true description of Nature should be very brief and have a character of relevance. Commonplaces such as, "the setting sun bathing in the waves of the darkening sea, poured its purple gold, etc." — "the swallows flying over the surface of the water twittered merrily" — such commonplaces one ought to abandon. In descriptions of Nature one ought to seize upon the little particulars, grouping them in such a way that, in reading, when you shut your eyes, you get a picture.

For instance, you will get the full effect of a moonlight night if you write that on the mill-dam a little glowing star-point flashed from the neck of a broken bottle, and the round, black shadow of a dog, or a wolf, emerged and ran, etc. Nature becomes animated if you are not squeamish about employing comparisons of her phenomena with ordinary human activities, etc.

In the sphere of psychology, details are also the thing. God preserve us from commonplaces. Best of all is it to avoid depicting the hero's state of mind; you ought to try to make it clear from the hero's actions. It is not necessary to portray many characters. The center of gravity should be in two persons: him and her.

FROM A LETTER TO ALEKSEY S. SUVORIN, 1890

You abuse me for objectivity, calling it indifference to good and evil, lack of ideals and ideas, and so on. You would have me, when I describe horse-thieves, say: "Stealing horses is an evil." But that has been known for ages without my saying so. Let the jury judge them; it's my job simply to show what sort of people they are. I write: You are dealing with horse-thieves, so let me tell you that they are not beggars but well-fed people, that they are people of a special cult, and that horse-stealing is not simply theft but a passion. Of course it would be pleasant to combine art with a sermon, but for me personally it is extremely difficult and almost impossible, owing to the conditions of technique. You see, to depict horse-thieves in seven hundred lines I must all the time speak and think in their tone and feel in their spirit, otherwise, if I introduce subjectivity, the image becomes blurred and the story will not be as compact as all short stories ought to be. When I write, I reckon entirely upon the reader to add for himself the subjective elements that are lacking in the story.

FROM A LETTER TO MAXIM GORKY, 1899

More advice: when reading the proofs, cross out a host of terms qualifying nouns and verbs. You have so many such terms that the reader's mind finds it a task to concentrate on them, and he soon grows tired. You understand it at once when I say, "The man sat on the grass"; you understand it because it is clear and makes no demands on the attention. On the other hand, it is not easily understood, and it is difficult for the mind, if I write, "A tall, narrow-chested, middle-sized man, with a red beard, sat on the green grass, already trampled by pedestrians, sat silently, shyly, and timidly looked about him." That is not immediately grasped by the mind, whereas good writing should be grasped at once — in a second.

KATE CHOPIN

Kate Chopin made a number of translations, mostly of stories by Guy de Maupassant, and she published several essays on literature in St. Louis periodicals. She wrote about the influence of Maupassant on her fiction in response to an invitation from the editor of the Atlantic Monthly *in 1896. He returned her first version of the essay, however, advising her to "set forth the matter directly." Her revised version was later included in the magazine with the title "In the*

Confidence of a Story-Teller," but the section describing how she first encountered Maupassant's tales and the impression they made on her was dropped, perhaps because she spoke so enthusiastically about the French writer's escape "from tradition and authority." This portion of the essay is reprinted from the manuscript included in Volume 2 of The Complete Works of Kate Chopin *(1969).*

How I Stumbled upon Maupassant 1896

About eight years ago there fell accidentally into my hands a volume of Maupassant's tales. These were new to me. I had been in the woods, in the fields, groping around; looking for something big, satisfying, convincing, and finding nothing but—myself; a something neither big nor satisfying but wholly convincing. It was at this period of my emerging from the vast solitude in which I had been making my own acquaintance, that I stumbled upon Maupassant. I read his stories and marvelled at them. Here was life, not fiction; for where were the plots, the old fashioned mechanism and stage trapping that in a vague, unthinking way I had fancied were essential to the art of story making? Here was a man who had escaped from tradition and authority, who had entered into himself and looked out upon life through his own being and with his own eyes; and who, in a direct and simple way, told us what he saw. When a man does this, he gives us the best that he can; something valuable for it is genuine and spontaneous. He gives us his impressions. Someone told me the other day that Maupassant had gone out of fashion. I was not grieved to hear it. He has never seemed to me to belong to the multitude, but rather to the individual. He is not one whom we gather in crowds to listen to—whom we follow in procession—with beating of brass instruments. He does not move us to throw ourselves into the throng—having the integral of an unthinking whole to shout his praise. I even like to think that he appeals to me alone. You probably like to think that he reaches you exclusively. A whole multitude may be secretly nourishing the belief in regard to him for all I know. Someway I like to cherish the delusion that he has spoken to no one else so directly, so intimately as he does to me. He did not say, as another might have done, "do you see these are charming stories of mine? take them into your closet—study them closely—mark their combination—observe the method, the manner of their putting together—and if ever you are moved to write stories you can do no better than to imitate."

RALPH ELLISON

Ralph Ellison gave an interview for the "Art of Fiction" series of the Paris Review *that was reprinted in his volume of essays,* Shadow and Act *(1964). In the introduction to that book he said that what is basic to the fiction writer's confrontation with the world is "converting experience into symbolic action. Good fiction is made of that which is real, and reality is difficult to come by. So much of it depends*

upon the individual's willingness to discover his true self, upon his defining him-
self—for the time being at least—against his background."

The Influence of Folklore on "Battle Royal" 1964

Interviewer: Can you give us an example of the use of folklore in your
own novel?

Ellison: Well, there are certain themes, symbols, and images which are
based on folk material. For example, there is the old saying amongst Negroes:
If you're black, stay back; if you're brown, stick around; if you're white, you're
right. And there is the joke Negroes tell on themselves about their being so
black they can't be seen in the dark. In my book this sort of thing was merged
with the meanings which blackness and light have long had in Western
mythology: evil and goodness, ignorance and knowledge, and so on. In my
novel the narrator's development is one through blackness to light; that is,
from ignorance to enlightenment: invisibility to visibility. He leaves the South
and goes North; this, as you will notice in reading Negro folktales, is always the
road to freedom—the movement upward. You have the same thing again when
he leaves his underground cave for the open.

It took me a long time to learn how to adapt such examples of myth into
my work—also ritual. The use of ritual is equally a vital part of the creative
process. I learned a few things from Eliot, Joyce, and Hemingway, but not how
to adapt them. When I started writing, I knew that in both *The Waste Land*°
and *Ulysses*° ancient myth and ritual were used to give form and significance to
the material; but it took me a few years to realize that the myths and rites which
we find functioning in our everyday lives could be used in the same way. In my
first attempt at a novel—which I was unable to complete—I began by trying
to manipulate the simple structural unities of *beginning, middle,* and *end,* but
when I attempted to deal with the psychological strata—the images, symbols,
and emotional configurations—of the experience at hand, I discovered that the
unities were simply cool points of stability on which one could suspend the
narrative line—but beneath the surface of apparently rational human relationships there seethed a chaos before which I was helpless. People rationalize what
they shun or are incapable of dealing with; these superstitions and their rationalizations become ritual as they govern behavior. The rituals become social
forms, and it is one of the functions of the artist to recognize them and raise
them to the level of art.

I don't know whether I'm getting this over or not. Let's put it this way:
Take the "Battle Royal" passage in my novel, where the boys are blindfolded
and forced to fight each other for the amusement of the white observers. This is
a vital part of behavior pattern in the South, which both Negroes and whites
thoughtlessly accept. It is a ritual in preservation of caste lines, a keeping of
taboo to appease the gods and ward off bad luck. It is also the initiation ritual to

---

The Waste Land: A long, extremely influential poem (1922) by T. S. Eliot (1888–1965).
Ulysses: An experimental novel (1922) by James Joyce (1882–1941).

which all greenhorns are subjected. This passage which states what Negroes will see I did not have to invent; the patterns were already there in society, so that all I had to do was present them in a broader context of meaning. In any society there are many rituals of situation which, for the most part, go unquestioned. They can be simple or elaborate, but they are the connective tissue between the work of art and the audience.

Interviewer: Do you think a reader unacquainted with this folklore can properly understand your work?

Ellison: Yes, I think so. It's like jazz; there's no inherent problem which prohibits understanding but the assumptions brought to it. We don't all dig Shakespeare uniformly, or even *Little Red Riding Hood.* The understanding of art depends finally upon one's willingness to extend one's humanity and one's knowledge of human life. I noticed, incidentally, that the Germans, having no special caste assumptions concerning American Negroes, dealt with my work simply as a novel. I think Americans will come to view it that way in twenty years — if it's around that long.

Interviewer: Don't you think it will be?

Ellison: I doubt it. It's not an important novel. I failed of eloquence, and many of the immediate issues are rapidly fading away. If it does last, it will be simply because there are things going on in its depth that are of more permanent interest than on its surface. I hope so, anyway.

WILLIAM FAULKNER

William Faulkner was writer-in-residence at the University of Virginia in 1957 and 1958. During that time he encouraged students to ask questions about his writing. He answered more than 2,000 queries on everything from spelling to the nature of man, including a series of questions about "A Rose for Emily" addressed to him at different interviews by students of Frederick Gwynn and Joseph Blotner. These professors later edited the book Faulkner in the University *(1959), in which the following excerpt first appeared.*

The Meaning of "A Rose for Emily"   1959

Interviewer: What is the meaning of the title "A Rose for Emily"?

Faulkner: Oh, it's simply the poor woman had had no life at all. Her father had kept her more or less locked up and then she had a lover who was about to quit her, she had to murder him. It was just "A Rose for Emily" — that's all.

Interviewer: I was wondering, one of your short stories, "A Rose for Emily," what ever inspired you to write this story . . . ?

Faulkner: That to me was another sad and tragic manifestation of man's condition in which he dreams and hopes, in which he is in conflict with himself or with his environment or with others. In this case there was the young girl with a young girl's normal aspirations to find love and then a husband and a family, who was brow-beaten and kept down by her father, a selfish man who didn't want her to leave home because he wanted a housekeeper, and it was a natural instinct of—repressed which—you can't repress it—you can mash it down but it comes up somewhere else and very likely in a tragic form, and that was simply another manifestation of man's injustice to man, of the poor tragic human being struggling with its own heart, with others, with its environment, for the simple things which all human beings want. In that case it was a young girl that just wanted to be loved and to love and to have a husband and a family.

Interviewer: And that purely came from your imagination?

Faulkner: Well, the story did but the condition is there. It exists. I didn't invent that condition, I didn't invent the fact that young girls dream of someone to love and children and a home, but the story of what her own particular tragedy was was invented, yes. . . .

Interviewer: Sir, it has been argued that "A Rose for Emily" is a criticism of the North, and others have argued saying that it is a criticism of the South. Now, could this story, shall we say, be more properly classified as a criticism of the times?

Faulkner: Now that I don't know, because I was simply trying to write about people. The writer uses environment—what he knows—and if there's a symbolism in which the lover represented the North and the woman who murdered him represents the South, I don't say that's not valid and not there, but it was no intention of the writer to say, Now let's see, I'm going to write a piece in which I will use a symbolism for the North and another symbol for the South, that he was simply writing about people, a story which he thought was tragic and true, because it came out of the human heart, the human aspiration, the human—the conflict of conscience with glands, with the Old Adam. It was a conflict not between the North and the South so much as between, well you might say, God and Satan.

Interviewer: Sir, just a little more on that thing. You say it's a conflict between God and Satan. Well, I don't quite understand what you mean. Who is—did one represent the——

Faulkner: The conflict was in Miss Emily, that she knew that you do not murder people. She had been trained that you do not take a lover. You marry, you don't take a lover. She had broken all the laws of her tradition, her background, and she had finally broken the law of God too, which says you do not take human life. And she knew she was doing wrong, and that's why her own life was wrecked. Instead of murdering one lover, and then to go and take another and when she used him up to murder him, she was expiating her crime.

Interviewer: Was the "Rose for Emily" an idea or a character? Just how did you go about it?

Faulkner: That came from a picture of the strand of hair on the pillow. It was a ghost story. Simply a picture of a strand of hair on the pillow in the abandoned house.

RICHARD FORD

Richard Ford edited The Essential Tales of Chekhov *(1998). In his introduction to the volume, "Why We Like Chekhov," Ford discussed his earliest encounter with "The Lady with the Pet Dog" as a college student.*

On Chekhov's "The Lady with the Pet Dog"   1998

As is true of many American readers who encountered Chekhov first in college, my experience with his stories was both abrupt and brief, and came too early. When I read him at age twenty, I had no idea of his prestige and importance or why I should be reading him—one of those gaps of ignorance for which a liberal education tries to be a bridge. But typical of my attentiveness then, I remember no one telling me anything more than that Chekhov was great, and that he was Russian.

And for all their surface plainness, their apparent accessibility and clarity, Chekhov's stories—especially the greatest ones—still do not seem so easily penetrable by the unexceptional young. Rather, Chekhov seems to me a writer for adults, his work becoming useful and also beautiful by attracting attention to mature feelings, to complicated human responses and small issues of moral choice within large, overarching dilemmas, any part of which, were we to encounter them in our complex, headlong life with others, might evade even sophisticated notice. Chekhov's wish is to complicate and compromise our view of characters we might mistakenly suppose we could understand with only a glance. He almost always approaches us with a great deal of focussed seriousness which he means to make irreducible and accessible, and by this concentration to insist that we take life to heart. Such instruction, of course, is not always easy to comply with when one is young.

My own college experience was to read the great anthology standard, "The Lady with the Dog" (published in 1899 and included here), and basically to be baffled by it, although the story's fundamental directness and authority made me highly respectful of something I can only describe as a profound-feeling gray light emanating from the story's austere interior.

"The Lady with the Dog" concerns the chance amorous meeting of two people married to two other people. One lover is a bored, middle-aged businessman from Moscow, and the other an idle young bride in her twenties—both on marital furlough in the Black Spa of Yalta. The two engage in a brief, fervid tryst that seems—at least to the story's principal character Dmitri Gurov, the Muscovite businessman—not very different from other trysts in his life. And after their short, breathless time together, their holiday predictably ends. The young wife, Anna Sergeyevna, departs for her home and husband in Petersburg, while Gurov, with no specific plans for Anna, travels back to his coolly intellectual wife and the tiresome business connections of Moscow.

But the effect of his affair and of Anna (the very lady with the dog—a Pomeranian) soon begin to infect and devil Gurov's daily life and torment him with desire, so that eventually he thinks up a lie, leaves home and travels to Petersburg where he reunites (more or less) with the pining Anna, whom he encounters between the acts of a play expressively titled *The Geisha*. In the weeks following this passionate lovers' meeting, Anna begins a routine of visiting Gurov in Moscow where, the omniscient narrator observes, they "loved each other like people very close and akin, like husband and wife, like tender friends; it seemed to them that fate itself had meant them for one another, and they could not understand why he had a wife and she a husband; and it was as though they were a pair of birds of passage, caught and forced to live in different cages."

Their union, while hot-burning, soon seems to them destined to stay furtive and intermittent. And in their secret lovers' room in the Slaviansky Bazaar, Anna cries bitterly over the predicament, while Gurov troubles himself in a slightly imperious manner to console her. The story ends with the narrator concluding with something of a knowing poker face, that . . . "it seemed as though in a little while the solution would be found, and then a new and splendid life would begin; and it was clear to both of them that they had still a long, long road before them, and that the most complicated and difficult part of it was only just beginning."

What I didn't understand back in 1964, when I was twenty, was: what made this drab set of nonevents a great short story—reputedly one of the greatest ever written. It was, I knew, a story about passion, and that passion was a capital subject; and that although Chekhov didn't describe any of it, sex took place, adulterous sex no less. I could also see that the effect of passion was calculated to be loss, loneliness, and indeterminacy, and that the institution of marriage came in for a beating. Clearly these were important matters.

But it seemed to me at the story's end, when Gurov and Anna meet in the hotel, away from spousal eyes, that far too little happened, or at least too little that *I* could detect. They make love (albeit offstage); Anna weeps; Gurov fussily says "Don't cry, my darling . . . that's enough. . . . Let us talk now, let us think of some plan." And then the story is over, with Gurov and Anna wandering off to who knows where—probably, I thought, no place very exciting were we to accompany them. Which we don't.

Back in 1964, I didn't dare to say, "I don't like this," because in truth I didn't *not* like "The Lady with the Dog." I merely didn't sense what in it was *so* to be liked. In class, much was made of its opening paragraph, containing the famously brief, complex, yet direct setting out of significant information, issues and strategies of telling which the story would eventually develop. For this reason—economy—it was deemed good. The ending was also said to be admirable *because* it wasn't very dramatic and wasn't conclusive. But beyond that, if anybody said something more specific about how the story made itself excellent I don't remember it. Although I distinctly remember thinking the story was over my head, and that Gurov and Anna were adults (read: enigmatic, impenetrable) in a way I wasn't one, and what they did and said to each other must reveal heretofore unheard of truths about love and passion, only I wasn't a good enough reader or mature enough human to recognize these truths. I'm certain that I eventually advertised actually *liking* the story, though only because I thought I should. And not long afterward I began maintaining the position that Chekhov was a story writer of near mythical—and certainly mysterious—importance, one who seemed to tell rather ordinary stories but who was really unearthing the most subtle, and for that reason, unobvious and important truth. (It is of course still a useful habit of inquiry to wonder, when the surface of reputedly great literature—and life—seem plain and equable, if something important might not be revealed upon closer notice; and also to realize that a story's ending may not always be the place to locate that something.)

In 1998, what I would say is good about "The Lady with the Dog" (and maybe you should stop here, read the story, then come back and compare notes) and indeed why I like it is primarily that it concentrates its narrative attentions *not* on the conventional hot spots—sex, deceit, and what happens at the end—but rather, by its precision, pacing, and decisions about what to tell, it directs our interest toward those flatter terrains of a love affair where we, being conventional souls, might overlook something important. "The Lady with the Dog" demonstrates by its scrupulous notice and detail that ordinary goings-on contain moments of significant moral choice—willed human acts judgeable as good or bad—and as such they have consequences in life which we need to pay heed to, whereas before reading the story we might've supposed they didn't. I'm referring specifically to Gurov's rather prosaic feelings of "torment" at home in Moscow, followed by his decision to visit Anna; his wife's reasonable dismissal of his suffering, the repetitiveness of trysts, the relative brevity of desire's satiation, and the necessity for self-deception to keep a small passion inflamed. These are matters the story wants us *not* to skip over, but to believe are important and that paying attention to them is good.

In a purely writerly way, I also find interest and take pleasure in Chekhov's choosing *these* characters and this seemingly unspectacular liaison upon which to stake a claim of significance and to treat with intelligence, amusement, and some compassion. And superintending all there is Chekhov's surgical deployment of his probing narrator as inventor and mediator of Gurov's bland but still provocative interior life with women: "It seemed to him," the narrator says of the stolid Dmitri, "that he had been so schooled by bitter experience that he might call them [women, of course] what he liked, and yet he could not get on for two days together without 'the lower race.' In the society of men he was bored and not himself, with them he was cool and uncommunicative; but when he was in the company of women he felt free. . . ."

Finally, in "The Lady with the Dog," what seems good is Chekhov the fastidious and amused ironist who finds the right exalted language to accompany staid Gurov and pliant Anna's most unexalted amours, and in so doing discloses their love's frothy mundaneness. High on a hill overlooking Yalta and the sea, the two lovers sit and moon off, while the narrator archly muses over the landscape.

> The leaves did not stir on the trees, grasshoppers chirruped, and the monotonous hollow sound of the sea rising up from below, spoke of peace, of the eternal sleep awaiting us. So it must have sounded when there was no Yalta, no Oreanda here; so it sounds now, and it will sound

as indifferently and monotonously when we are all no more. And in this constancy, in this complete indifference to the life and death of each of us, there lies hid, perhaps, a pledge of our eternal salvation, of the unceasing movement of life upon earth, of unceasing progress towards perfection.

Over the years, "The Lady with the Dog" has come to stand high in my esteem as the story by whose subtleties I not only began to know how and why to like Chekhov, but also by its exemplary fullness I came to experience literature as F. R. Leavis portrays it in his famous essay on Lawrence, as the supreme means by which we "undergo a renewal of sensuous and emotional life, and learn a new awareness." Chekhov's representation of this minor-key love affair committed by respectable nonentities more than renewed, it helped give early form to my awareness of what the words "emotional life" might entail, but also conceal and importantly leave out. . . .

As readers of imaginative literature, we are always seeking clues, warnings: where in life to search more assiduously; what not to overlook; what's the origin of this sort of human calamity, that sort of joy and pleasure; how can we live nearer to the latter, further off from the former? And to such seekers as we are, Chekhov is guide, perhaps *the* guide.

To twentieth-century writers, of course, his presence has affected all of our assumptions about what's a fit subject for imaginative writing; about which moments in life are too crucial or precious to relegate to conventional language; about how stories should begin, and the variety of ways a writer may choose to end them; and importantly about how final life is, and therefore how tenacious must be our representations of it.

More than anything else, though, it is Chekhov's great sufficiency that moves us and makes us admire; our reader's awareness that story to story, degree by degree around the sphere of observable human existence, Chekhov's measure is perfect. Given the subjects, the characters, the actions he brings into play, we routinely feel that everything of importance is always there in Chekhov. And our imaginations are for that reason ignited to know exactly what that great sufficiency is a reply to; what is the underlying urgency such that almost any story of Chekhov's can cause us to feel, either joyfully or pitifully, confirmed in life? As adults, we usually like what makes us want to know more, and are flattered by an assertive authority which makes us trust and then provides good counsel. It is indeed as though Chekhov knew us.

Finally, the stories found here are never difficult but often demanding; always dense but never turgid; sometimes dour, but rarely hopeless. Yet occasionally, reading through the great body of Chekhov's stories (220 plus), I have experienced secret relief when a story, here or there, seemed somehow *lesser*, was possibly tossed off in a way that allows me to imagine this most humane of writers in a new light—as a man agreeably unburdened by some demonic masterpiece-only obsession, a man I could've known, as a writer indeed willing to take us unblinkingly into the musing consciousness of kittens(!) and offer us assurance that nothing very important goes on there: "The kitten lay awake thinking. Of what? . . . The soul of another is darkness, and a cat's soul more than most. . . . Fate had destined him to be the terror of cellars, store-rooms and corn bins, and had it not been for education . . . we will not anticipate, however" ("Who Was to Blame").

And so, no more anticipation. Just read these wonderful stories for pleasure, first, and do not read them fast. The more you linger, the more you reread, the more you'll experience and feel addressed by this great genius who, surprisingly, in spite of distance and time, shared a world we know and saw as his great privilege the chance to redeem it with language.

SANDRA M. GILBERT AND SUSAN GUBAR

Sandra M. Gilbert and Susan Gubar presented a feminist reading of Charlotte Perkins Gilman's "The Yellow Wallpaper" in The Madwoman in the Attic: The Woman Writer and the Nineteenth-Century Literary Imagination *(1979). In this book they argued that a recognizable literary tradition existed in English and American literature in which the female imagination had demonstrated "the anxiety of authorship." According to Gilbert and Gubar, "Images of enclosure and escape, fantasies in which maddened doubles functioned as asocial surrogates for docile selves . . . such patterns reoccurred throughout this tradition, along with obsessive depictions of diseases like anorexia, agoraphobia, and claustrophobia." Gilman's story is securely within this tradition of the "literature of confinement," in which a woman writer, trapped by the patriarchal society, tries to struggle free "through strategic redefinitions of self, art, and society."*

A Feminist Reading of Gilman's "The Yellow Wallpaper"

1979

As if to comment on the unity of all these points—on, that is, the anxiety-inducing connections between what women writers tend to see as their parallel confinements in texts, houses, and maternal female bodies—Charlotte Perkins Gilman brought them all together in 1890 in a striking story of female confinement and escape, a paradigmatic tale which (like *Jane Eyre*°) seems to tell *the* story that all literary women would tell if they could speak their "speechless woe." "The Yellow Wallpaper," which Gilman herself called "a description of a case of nervous breakdown," recounts in the first person the experiences of a woman who is evidently suffering from a severe postpartum psychosis. Her husband, a censorious and paternalistic physician, is treating her according to methods by which S. Weir Mitchell, a famous "nerve specialist," treated Gilman herself for a similar problem. He has confined her to a large garret room in an "ancestral hall" he has rented, and he has forbidden her

---

Jane Eyre: The classic Victorian novel (1847) by Charlotte Brontë (1816–1855) is considered an important feminist work.

to touch pen to paper until she is well again, for he feels, says the narrator, "that with my imaginative power and habit of story-making, a nervous weakness like mine is sure to lead to all manner of excited fancies, and that I ought to use my will and good sense to check the tendency."

The cure, of course, is worse than the disease, for the sick woman's mental condition deteriorates rapidly. "I think sometimes that if I were only well enough to write a little it would relieve the press of ideas and rest me," she remarks, but literally confined in a room she thinks is a one-time nursery because it has "rings and things" in the walls, she is literally locked away from creativity. The "rings and things," although reminiscent of children's gymnastic equipment, are really the paraphernalia of confinement, like the gate at the head of the stairs, instruments that definitively indicate her imprisonment. Even more tormenting, however, is the room's wallpaper: a sulphurous yellow paper, torn off in spots, and patterned with "lame uncertain curves" that "plunge off at outrageous angles" and "destroy themselves in unheard of contradictions." Ancient, smoldering, "unclean" as the oppressive structures of the society in which she finds herself, this paper surrounds the narrator like an inexplicable text, censorious and overwhelming as her physician husband, haunting as the "hereditary estate" in which she is trying to survive. Inevitably she studies its suicidal implications—and inevitably, because of her "imaginative power and habit of story-making," she revises it, projecting her own passion for escape into its otherwise incomprehensible hieroglyphics. "This wallpaper," she decides, at a key point in her story,

> has a kind of subpattern in a different shade, a particularly irritating one, for you can only see it in certain lights, and not clearly then.
> But in the places where it isn't faded and where the sun is just so—I can see a strange, provoking, formless sort of figure, that seems to skulk about behind that silly and conspicuous front design.

As time passes, this figure concealed behind what corresponds (in terms of what we have been discussing) to the facade of the patriarchal text becomes clearer and clearer. By moonlight the pattern of the wallpaper "becomes bars! The outside pattern I mean, and the woman behind it is as plain as can be." And eventually, as the narrator sinks more deeply into what the world calls madness, the terrifying implications of both the paper and the figure imprisoned behind the paper begin to permeate—that is, to *haunt*—the rented ancestral mansion in which she and her husband are immured. The "yellow smell" of the paper "creeps all over the house," drenching every room in its subtle aroma of decay. And the woman creeps too—through the house, in the house, and out of the house, in the garden and "on that long road under the trees." Sometimes, indeed, the narrator confesses, "I think there are a great many women" both behind the paper and creeping in the garden, "and sometimes only one, and she crawls around fast, and her crawling shakes [the paper] all over. . . . And she is all the time trying to climb through. But nobody could climb through that pattern—it strangles so; I think that is why it has so many heads."

Eventually it becomes obvious to both reader and narrator that the figure creeping through and behind the wallpaper is both the narrator and the narrator's double. By the end of the story, moreover, the narrator has enabled this double to escape from her textual/architectural confinement: "I pulled and she shook, I shook and she pulled, and before morning we had peeled off yards of that paper." Is the message of the tale's conclusion mere madness? Certainly the righteous Doctor John—whose name links him to the anti-hero of Charlotte Brontë's *Villette*—has been temporarily defeated, or at least momentarily stunned. "Now why should that man have fainted?" the narrator ironically asks as she creeps around her attic. But John's unmasculine swoon of surprise is the least of the triumphs Gilman imagines for her madwoman. More significant are the madwoman's own imaginings and creations, mirages of health and freedom with which her author endows her like a fairy godmother showering gold on a sleeping heroine. The woman from behind the wallpaper creeps away, for instance, creeps fast and far on the long road, in broad daylight. "I have watched her sometimes away off in the open country," says the narrator, "creeping as fast as a cloud shadow in a high wind."

Indistinct and yet rapid, barely perceptible but inexorable, the progress of that cloud shadow is not unlike the progress of nineteenth-century literary women out of the texts defined by patriarchal poetics into the open spaces of their own authority. That such an escape from the numb world behind the patterned walls of the text was a flight from disease into health was quite clear to Gilman herself. When "The Yellow Wallpaper" was published she sent it to Weir Mitchell whose strictures had kept her from attempting the pen during her own breakdown, thereby aggravating her illness, and she was delighted to learn, years later, that "he had changed his treatment of nervous prostration since reading" her story. "If that is a fact," she declared, "I have not lived in vain." Because she was a rebellious feminist besides being a medical iconoclast, we can be sure that Gilman did not think of this triumph of hers in narrowly therapeutic terms. Because she knew, with Emily Dickinson, that "Infection in the sentence breeds," she knew that the cure for female despair must be spiritual as well as physical, aesthetic as well as social. What "The Yellow Wallpaper" shows she knew, too, is that even when a supposedly "mad" woman has been sentenced to imprisonment in the "infected" house of her own body, she may discover that, as Sylvia Plath° was to put it seventy years later, she has "a self to recover, a queen."

CHARLOTTE PERKINS GILMAN

Charlotte Perkins Gilman wrote her autobiography, The Living of Charlotte Perkins Gilman *(1935), in the last years of her life. Her intelligence and strength of character are evident in this work, as is her modesty after a long career as an eminent American feminist. Her straightforward description of her mental breakdown nearly fifty years earlier is in marked contrast to the obsessive fantasy of her story "The Yellow Wallpaper," written shortly after her illness.*

Sylvia Plath: American poet (1932–1963). See p. 931.

Undergoing the Cure for Nervous Prostration   1935

This was a worse horror than before, for now I saw the stark fact—that I was well while away and sick while at home—a heartening prospect! Soon ensued the same utter prostration, the unbearable inner misery, the ceaseless tears. A new tonic had been invented, Essence of Oats, which was given me, and did some good for a time. I pulled up enough to do a little painting that fall, but soon slipped down again and stayed down. An old friend of my mother's, dear Mrs. Diman, was so grieved at this condition that she gave me a hundred dollars and urged me to go away somewhere and get cured.

At that time the greatest nerve specialist in the country was Dr. S. W. Mitchell of Philadelphia. Through the kindness of a friend of Mr. Stetson's living in that city, I went to him and took "the rest cure"; went with the utmost confidence, prefacing the visit with a long letter giving "the history of the case" in a way a modern psychologist would have appreciated. Dr. Mitchell only thought it proved self-conceit. He had a prejudice against the Beechers. "I've had two women of your blood here already," he told me scornfully. This eminent physician was well versed in two kinds of nervous prostration; that of the business man exhausted from too much work, and the society woman exhausted from too much play. The kind I had was evidently behind him. But he did reassure me on one point—there was no dementia, he said, only hysteria.

I was put to bed and kept there. I was fed, bathed, rubbed, and responded with the vigorous body of twenty-six. As far as he could see there was nothing the matter with me, so after a month of this agreeable treatment he sent me home, with this prescription:

> Live as domestic a life as possible. Have your child with you all the time. (Be it remarked that if I did but dress the baby it left me shaking and crying—certainly far from a healthy companionship for her, to say nothing of the effect on me.) Lie down an hour after each meal. Have but two hours' intellectual life a day. And never touch pen, brush, or pencil as long as you live.

I went home, followed those directions rigidly for months, and came perilously near to losing my mind. The mental agony grew so unbearable that I would sit blankly moving my head from side to side—to get out from under the pain. Not physical pain, not the least "headache" even, just mental torment, and so heavy in its nightmare gloom that it seemed real enough to dodge.

I made a rag baby, hung it on a doorknob, and played with it. I would crawl into remote closets and under beds—to hide from the grinding pressure of that profound distress. . . .

Finally, in the fall of '87, in a moment of clear vision, we agreed to separate, to get a divorce. There was no quarrel, no blame for either one, never an unkind word between us, unbroken mutual affection—but it seemed plain that if I went crazy, it would do my husband no good, and be a deadly injury to my child.

What this meant to the young artist, the devoted husband, the loving father, was so bitter a grief and loss that nothing would have justified breaking the marriage save this worse loss which threatened. It was not a choice between going and staying, but between going, sane, and staying, insane. If I had been of the slightest use to him or to the child, I would have "stuck it," as the English say. But this progressive weakening of the mind made a horror unnecessary to face; better for that dear child to have separated parents than a lunatic mother.

We had been married four years and more. This miserable condition of mind, this darkness, feebleness, and gloom, had begun in those difficult years of courtship, had grown rapidly worse after marriage, and was now threatening utter loss; whereas I had repeated proof that the moment I left home I began to recover. It seemed right to give up a mistaken marriage.

Our mistake was mutual. If I had been stronger and wiser I should never have been persuaded into it. Our suffering was mutual too, his unbroken devotion, his manifold cares and labors in tending a sick wife, his adoring pride in the best of babies, all coming to naught, ending in utter failure — we sympathized with each other but faced a bitter necessity. The separation must come as soon as possible, the divorce must wait for conditions.

If this decision could have been reached sooner it would have been much better for me, the lasting mental injury would have been less. Such recovery as I have made in forty years, and the work accomplished, seem to show that the fear of insanity was not fulfilled, but the effects of nerve bankruptcy remain to this day. So much of my many failures, of misplay and misunderstanding and "queerness" is due to this lasting weakness, and kind friends so unfailingly refuse to allow for it, to believe it, that I am now going to some length in stating the case.

ZORA NEALE HURSTON

Zora Neale Hurston continued throughout her life to make what the critic Mary Helen Washington called "unorthodox and paradoxical assertions on racial issues." Often conveyed with great wit and style, Hurston's views were always passionately held, as in her essay "How It Feels to Be Colored Me," first published in 1928.

How It Feels to Be Colored Me   1928

I am colored but I offer nothing in the way of extenuating circumstances except the fact that I am the only Negro in the United States whose grandfather on the mother's side was *not* an Indian chief.

I remember the very day that I became colored. Up to my thirteenth year I lived in the little Negro town of Eatonville, Florida. It is exclusively a colored town. The only white people I knew passed through the town going to or coming from Orlando. The native whites rode dusty horses, the Northern tourists chugged down the sandy village road in automobiles. The town knew the Southerners and never stopped cane chewing when they passed. But the Northerners were something else again. They were peered at cautiously from behind curtains by the timid. The more venturesome would come out on the porch to watch them go past and got just as much pleasure out of the tourists as the tourists got out of the village.

The front porch might seem a daring place for the rest of the town, but it was a gallery seat for me. My favorite place was atop the gate-post. Proscenium box for a born first-nighter. Not only did I enjoy the show, but I didn't mind the actors knowing that I liked it. I usually spoke to them in passing. I'd wave at them and when they returned my salute, I would say something like this: "Howdy-do-well-I-thank-you-where-you-goin'?" Usually automobile or the horse paused at this, and after a queer exchange of compliments, I would probably "go a piece of the way" with them, as we say in farthest Florida. If one of my family happened to come to the front in time to see me, of course negotiations would be rudely broken off. But even so, it is clear that I was the first "welcome-to-our-state" Floridian, and I hope the Miami Chamber of Commerce will please take notice.

During this period, white people differed from colored to me only in that they rode through town and never lived there. They liked to hear me "speak pieces" and sing and wanted to see me dance the parse-me-la, and gave me generously of their small silver for doing these things, which seemed strange to me for I wanted to do them so much that I needed bribing to stop. Only they didn't know it. The colored people gave no dimes. They deplored any joyful tendencies in me, but I was their Zora nevertheless. I belonged to them, to the nearby hotels, to the county — everybody's Zora.

But changes came in the family when I was thirteen, and I was sent to school in Jacksonville. I left Eatonville, the town of the oleanders, as Zora. When I disembarked from the river-boat at Jacksonville, she was no more. It seemed that I had suffered a sea change. I was not Zora of Orange County any more, I was now a little colored girl. I found it out in certain ways. In my heart as well as in the mirror, I became a fast brown — warranted not to rub nor run.

But I am not tragically colored. There is no great sorrow dammed up in my soul, nor lurking behind my eyes. I do not mind at all. I do not belong to the sobbing school of Negrohood who hold that nature somehow has given them a lowdown dirty deal and whose feelings are all hurt about it. Even in the helter-skelter skirmish that is my life, I have seen that the world is to the strong regardless of a little pigmentation more or less. No, I do not weep at the world — I am too busy sharpening my oyster knife.

Someone is always at my elbow reminding me that I am the granddaughter of slaves. It fails to register depression with me. Slavery is sixty years in the past. The operation was successful and the patient is doing well, thank you. The terrible struggle that made me an American out of a potential slave said "On the line!" The Reconstruction said "Get set!"; and the generation before said "Go!" I am off to a flying start and I must not halt in the stretch to look behind and weep. Slavery is the price I paid for civilization, and the choice was not with me. It is a bully adventure and worth all that I have paid through my ancestors for it. No one on earth ever had a greater chance for glory. The world to be won and nothing to be lost. It is thrilling to think — to know that for any act of mine, I shall get twice as much praise or twice as much blame. It is quite exciting to hold the center of the national stage, with the spectators not knowing whether to laugh or to weep.

The position of my white neighbor is much more difficult. No brown specter pulls up a chair beside me when I sit down to eat. No dark ghost thrusts its leg against mine in bed. The game of keeping what one has is never so exciting as the game of getting.

I do not always feel colored. Even now I often achieve the unconscious Zora of Eatonville before the Hegira. I feel most colored when I am thrown against a sharp white background.

For instance at Barnard. "Beside the waters of the Hudson" I feel my race. Among the thousand white persons, I am a dark rock surged upon, and overswept, but through it all, I remain myself. When covered by the waters, I am; and the ebb but reveals me again.

Sometimes it is the other way around. A white person is set down in our midst, but the contrast is just as sharp for me. For instance, when I sit in the drafty basement that is The New World Cabaret with a white person, my color comes. We enter chatting about any little nothing that we have in common and are seated by the jazz waiters. In the abrupt way that jazz orchestras have, this one plunges into a number. It loses no time in circumlocutions, but gets right down to business. It constricts the thorax and splits the heart with its tempo and narcotic harmonies. This orchestra grows rambunctious, rears on its hind legs and attacks the tonal veil with primitive fury, rending it, clawing it until it breaks through to the jungle beyond. I follow those heathen—follow them exultingly. I dance wildly inside myself; I yell within, I whoop; I shake my assegai above my head, I hurl it true to the mark *yeeeeoooww!* I am in the jungle and living in the jungle way. My face is painted red and yellow and my body is painted blue. My pulse is throbbing like a war drum. I want to slaughter something—give pain, give death to what, I do not know. But the piece ends. The men of the orchestra wipe their lips and rest their fingers. I creep back slowly to the veneer we call civilization with the last tone and find the white friend sitting motionless in his seat, smoking calmly.

"Good music they have here," he remarks, drumming the table with his fingertips.

Music. The great blobs of purple and red emotion have not touched him. He has only heard what I felt. He is far away and I see him but dimly across the ocean and the continent that have fallen between us. He is so pale with his whiteness then and I am *so* colored.

At certain times I have no race, I am *me*. When I set my hat at a certain angle and saunter down Seventh Avenue, Harlem City, feeling as snooty as the lions in front of the Forty-Second Street Library, for instance. So far as my feelings are concerned, Peggy Hopkins Joyce on the Boule Mich with her gorgeous raiment, stately carriage, knees knocking together in a most aristocratic manner, has nothing on me. The cosmic Zora emerges. I belong to no race nor time. I am the eternal feminine with its string of beads.

I have no separate feeling about being an American citizen and colored. I am merely a fragment of the Great Soul that surges within the boundaries. My country, right or wrong.

Sometimes, I feel discriminated against, but it does not make me angry. It merely astonishes me. How *can* any deny themselves the pleasure of my company? It's beyond me.

But in the main, I feel like a brown bag of miscellany propped against a wall. Against a wall in company with other bags, white, red and yellow. Pour out the contents, and there is discovered a jumble of small things priceless and worthless. A first-water diamond, an empty spool, bits of broken glass, lengths of string, a key to a door long since crumbled away, a rusty knife-blade, old shoes saved for a road that never was and never will be, a nail bent under the weight of things too heavy for any nail, a dried flower or two still a little fragrant. In your hand is the brown bag. On the ground before you is the jumble it held — so much like the jumble in the bags, could they be emptied, that all might be dumped in a single heap and the bags refilled without altering the content of any greatly. A bit of colored glass more or less would not matter. Perhaps that is how the Great Stuffer of Bags filled them in the first place — who knows?

SHIRLEY JACKSON

Shirley Jackson wrote this "biography of a story" in 1960 as a lecture to be delivered before reading "The Lottery" to college audiences. After her death it was included in Come Along with Me *(1968), edited by her husband, Stanley Edgar Hyman. The lecture also contained extensive quotations from letters she had received from readers who took the story literally. These so disgusted Jackson that she promised her listeners at the conclusion of her talk, "I am out of the lottery business for good."*

The Morning of June 28, 1948, and "The Lottery" 1968

On the morning of June 28, 1948, I walked down to the post office in our little Vermont town to pick up the mail. I was quite casual about it, as I recall — I opened the box, took out a couple of bills and a letter or two, talked to the postmaster for a few minutes, and left, never supposing that it was the last time for months that I was to pick up the mail without an active feeling of panic. By the next week I had had to change my mailbox to the largest one in the post office, and casual conversation with the postmaster was out of the question, because he wasn't speaking to me. June 28, 1948, was the day *The New Yorker* came out with a story of mine in it. It was not my first published story, nor my last, but I have been assured over and over that if it had been the only story I ever wrote or published, there would be people who would not forget my name.

I had written the story three weeks before, on a bright June morning when summer seemed to have come at last, with blue skies and warm sun and no heavenly signs to warn me that my morning's work was anything but just another story. The idea had come to me while I was pushing my daughter up the hill in her stroller — it was, as I say, a warm morning, and the hill was steep, and beside my daughter the stroller held the day's groceries — and perhaps the effort of that last fifty yards up the hill put an edge to the story; at any rate, I had the idea fairly clearly in my mind when I put my daughter in her playpen and the frozen vegetables in the refrigerator, and, writing the story, I found that it went quickly and easily, moving from beginning to end without pause. As a matter of fact, when I read it over later I decided that except for one or two minor corrections, it needed no changes, and the story I finally typed up and sent off to my agent the next day was almost word for word the original draft. This, as any writer of stories can tell you, is not a usual thing. All I know is that when I came to read the story over I felt strongly that I didn't want to fuss with it. I didn't think it was perfect, but I didn't want to fuss with it. It was, I thought, a serious, straightforward story, and I was pleased and a little surprised at the ease with which it had been written; I was reasonably proud of it, and hoped that my agent would sell it to some magazine and I would have the gratification of seeing it in print.

My agent did not care for the story, but — as she said in her note at the time — her job was to sell it, not to like it. She sent it at once to *The New Yorker,* and about a week after the story had been written I received a telephone call from the fiction editor of *The New Yorker;* it was quite clear that he did not really care for the story, either, but *The New Yorker* was going to buy it. He asked for one change — that the date mentioned in the story be changed to coincide with the date of the issue of the magazine in which the story would appear, and I said of course. He then asked, hesitantly, if I had any particular interpretation of my own for the story; Mr. Harold Ross, then the editor of *The New Yorker,* was not altogether sure that he understood the story, and wondered if I cared to enlarge upon its meaning. I said no. Mr. Ross, he said, thought that the story might be puzzling to some people, and in case anyone telephoned the magazine, as sometimes happened, or wrote in asking about the story, was there anything in particular I wanted them to say? No, I said, nothing in particular; it was just a story I wrote.

I had no more preparation than that. I went on picking up the mail every morning, pushing my daughter up and down the hill in her stroller, anticipating pleasurably the check from *The New Yorker,* and shopping for groceries. The weather stayed nice and it looked as though it was going to be a good summer. Then, on June 28, *The New Yorker* came out with my story.

Things began mildly enough with a note from a friend at *The New Yorker:* "Your story has kicked up quite a fuss around the office," he wrote. I was flattered; it's nice to think that your friends notice what you write. Later that day there was a call from one of the magazine's editors; they had had a couple of people phone in about my story, he said, and was there anything I particularly wanted him to say if there were any more calls? No, I said, nothing particular; anything he chose to say was perfectly all right with me; it was just a story.

I was further puzzled by a cryptic note from another friend: "Heard a man talking about a story of yours on the bus this morning," she wrote. "Very exciting. I wanted to tell him I knew the author, but after I heard what he was saying I decided I'd better not."

One of the most terrifying aspects of publishing stories and books is the realization that they are going to be read, and read by strangers. I had never fully realized this before, although I had of course in my imagination dwelt lovingly upon the thought of the millions and millions of people who were going to be uplifted and enriched and delighted by the stories I wrote. It had simply never occurred to me that these millions and millions of people might be so far from being uplifted that they would sit down and write me letters I was downright scared to open; of the three-hundred-odd letters that I received that summer I can count only thirteen that spoke kindly to me, and they were mostly from friends. Even my mother scolded me: "Dad and I did not care at all for your story in *The New Yorker*," she wrote sternly, "it does seem, dear, that this gloomy kind of story is what all you young people think about these days. Why don't you write something to cheer people up?"

By mid-July I had begun to perceive that I was very lucky indeed to be safely in Vermont, where no one in our small town had ever heard of *The New Yorker*, much less read my story. Millions of people, and my mother, had taken a pronounced dislike to me.

The magazine kept no track of telephone calls, but all letters addressed to me care of the magazine were forwarded directly to me for answering, and all letters addressed to the magazine — some of them addressed to Harold Ross personally; these were the most vehement — were answered at the magazine and then the letters were sent me in great batches, along with carbons of the answers written at the magazine. I have all the letters still, and if they could be considered to give any accurate cross section of the reading public, or the reading public of *The New Yorker*, or even the reading public of one issue of *The New Yorker*, I would stop writing now.

Judging from these letters, people who read stories are gullible, rude, frequently illiterate, and horribly afraid of being laughed at. Many of the writers were positive that *The New Yorker* was going to ridicule them in print, and the most cautious letters were headed, in capital letters: NOT FOR PUBLICATION or PLEASE DO NOT PRINT THIS LETTER, or, at best, THIS LETTER MAY BE PUBLISHED AT YOUR USUAL RATES OF PAYMENT. Anonymous letters, of which there were a few, were destroyed. *The New Yorker* never published any comment of any kind about the story in the magazine, but did issue one publicity release saying that the story had received more mail than any piece of fiction they had ever published; this was after the newspapers had gotten into the act, in midsummer, with a front-page story in the San Francisco *Chronicle* begging to know what the story meant, and a series of columns in New York and Chicago papers pointing out that *New Yorker* subscriptions were being canceled right and left.

Curiously, there are three main themes which dominate the letters of that first summer — three themes which might be identified as bewilderment, speculation, and plain old-fashioned abuse. In the years since then, during which the story has been anthologized, dramatized, televised, and even—in one completely mystifying transformation—made into a ballet, the tenor of letters I receive has changed. I am addressed more politely, as a rule, and the letters largely confine themselves to questions like what does this story mean? The general tone of the early letters, however, was a kind of wide-eyed, shocked innocence. People at first were not so much concerned with what the story meant; what they wanted to know was where these lotteries were held, and whether they could go there and watch.

BOBBIE ANN MASON

Bobbie Ann Mason described her response to Tim O'Brien's story "The Things They Carried" in Ron Hansen and Jim Shepard's collection You've Got to Read This *(1994).*

On Tim O'Brien's "The Things They Carried"   1994

Of all the stories I've read in the last decade, Tim O'Brien's "The Things They Carried" hit me hardest. It knocked me down, just as if a hundred-pound rucksack had been thrown right at me. The weight of the things the American soldiers carried on their interminable journey through the jungle in Vietnam sets the tone for this story. But the power of it is not just the poundage they were humping on their backs. The story's list of "things they carried" extends to the burden of memory and desire and confusion and grief. It's the weight of America's involvement in the war. You can hardly bear to contemplate all that this story evokes with its matter-of-fact yet electrifying details.

The way this story works makes me think of the Vietnam Veterans Memorial in Washington. The memorial is just a list of names, in a simple, dark—yet soaring—design. Its power is in the simplicity of presentation and in what lies behind each of those names.

In the story, there is a central incident, the company's first casualty on its march through the jungle. But the immediate drama is the effort—by the main character, by the narrator, by the writer himself—to contain the emotion, to carry it. When faced with a subject almost too great to manage or confront, the mind wants to organize, to categorize, to simplify. Restraint and matter-of-factness are appropriate deflective techniques for dealing with pain, and they work on several levels in the story. Sometimes it is more affecting to see someone dealing with pain than it is to know about the pain itself. That's what's happening here.

By using the simplicity of a list and trying to categorize the simple items the soldiers carried, O'Brien reveals the real terror of the war itself. And the categories go from the tangible—foot powder, photographs, chewing gum—to the intangible. They carried disease; memory. When it rained, they carried the sky. The weight of what they carried moves expansively, opens out, grows from the stuff in the rucksack to the whole weight of the American war chest, with its litter of ammo and packaging through the landscape of Vietnam. And then it moves back, away from the huge outer world, back into the interior of the self. The story details the way they carried themselves (dignity, laughter, words) as well as what they carried inside (fear, "emotional baggage").

And within the solemn effort to list and categorize, a story unfolds. PFC Ted Lavender, a grunt who carries tranquilizers, is on his way back from relieving himself in the jungle when he is shot by a sniper. The irony and horror of it are unbearable. Almost instantaneously, it seems, the central character, Lieutenant Cross, changes from a romantic youth to a man of action and duty. With his new, hard clarity, he is carried forward by his determination not to be caught unprepared again. And the way he prepares to lead his group is to list his resolves. He has to assert power over the event by detaching himself. It is a life-and-death matter.

So this effort to detach and control becomes both the drama and the technique of the story. For it is our impulse to deal with unspeakable horror and sadness by fashioning some kind of order, a story, to clarify and contain our emotions. As the writer, Tim O'Brien stands back far enough not to be seen but not so far that he isn't in charge.

"They carried all they could bear, and then some, including a silent awe for the terrible power of the things they carried."

HERMAN MELVILLE

Herman Melville wrote an eloquent essay on Nathaniel Hawthorne's volume of short stories, Mosses from an Old Manse, *for the New York periodical the* Literary World *in August 1850. Unlike Edgar Allan Poe in his review of Hawthorne's short fiction, Melville did not use the opportunity to theorize about the form of the short story. Instead, he conveyed his enthusiasm for Hawthorne's tragic vision, what Melville saw as the "great power of blackness" in Hawthorne's writing that derived "its force from its appeals to that Calvinistic sense of Innate Depravity and Original Sin." This was the aspect of Hawthorne's work that seemed most congenial to Melville's own genius while he continued work that summer on his novel-in-progress,* Moby-Dick.

Blackness in Hawthorne's "Young Goodman Brown"

1850

It is curious, how a man may travel along a country road, and yet miss the grandest or sweetest of prospects, by reason of an intervening hedge so like all other hedges as in no way to hint of the wide landscape beyond. So has it been with me concerning the enchanting landscape in the soul of this Hawthorne, this most excellent Man of Mosses. His Old Manse has been written now four years, but I never read it till a day or two since. I had seen it in the bookstores— heard of it often—even had it recommended to me by a tasteful friend, as a rare, quiet book, perhaps too deserving of popularity to be popular. But there are so many books called "excellent" and so much unpopular merit, that amid the thick stir of other things, the hint of my tasteful friend was disregarded; and for four years the Mosses on the Old Manse never refreshed me with their perennial green. It may be, however, that all this while, the book, like wine, was only improving in flavor and body. . . .

But it is the least part of genius that attracts admiration. Where Hawthorne is known, he seems to be deemed a pleasant writer, with a pleasant style—a sequestered, harmless man, from whom any deep and weighty thing would hardly be anticipated: a man who means no meanings. But there is no man, in whom humor and love, like mountain peaks, soar to such a rapt height, as to receive the irradiations of the upper skies; there is no man in whom humor and love are developed in that high form called genius—no such man can exist without also possessing, as the indispensable complement of these, a great, deep intellect, which drops down into the universe like a plummet. Or, love and humor are only the eyes, through which such an intellect views this world. The great beauty in such a mind is but the product of its strength. . . .

For spite of all the Indian-summer sunlight on the hither side of Hawthorne's soul, the other side—like the dark half of the physical sphere—is shrouded in a blackness, ten times black. But this darkness but gives more effect to the ever-moving dawn, that forever advances through it, and circumnavigates his world. Whether Hawthorne has simply availed himself of this mystical blackness as a means to the wondrous effects he makes it to produce in his lights and shades; or whether there really lurks in him, perhaps unknown to himself, a touch of Puritanic gloom—this I cannot altogether tell. Certain it is, however, that this great power of blackness in him derives its force from its appeals to that Calvinistic sense of Innate Depravity and Original Sin, from whose visitations, in some shape or other, no deeply thinking mind is always and wholly free. For, in certain moods, no man can weigh this world, without throwing in something, somehow like Original Sin, to strike the uneven balance. . . .

But with whatever motive, playful or profound, Nathaniel Hawthorne has chosen to entitle his pieces in the manner he has, it is certain that some of them are directly calculated to deceive—egregiously deceive—the superficial skimmer of pages. To be downright and candid once more, let me cheerfully say that two of these titles did dolefully dupe no less an eagle-eyed reader than myself; and that, too, after I had been impressed with a sense of the great depth and breadth of this American man. "Who in the name of thunder" (as the country people say in this neighborhood), "who in the name of thunder," would anticipate any marvel in a piece entitled "Young Goodman Brown"? You would of course suppose that it was a simple little tale, intended as a supplement to "Goody Two-Shoes." Whereas it is deep as Dante; nor can you finish it, without addressing the author in his own words: "It is yours to penetrate, in every bosom, the deep mystery of sin." And with Young Goodman, too, in allegorical pursuit of his Puritan wife, you cry out in your anguish,

> "Faith!" shouted Goodman Brown, in a voice of agony and desperation; and the echoes of the forest mocked him, crying — "Faith! Faith!" as if bewildered wretches were seeking her, all through the wilderness.

Now this same piece, entitled "Young Goodman Brown," is one of the two that I had not at all read yesterday; and I allude to it now, because it is, in itself, such a strong positive illustration of that blackness in Hawthorne which I had assumed from the mere occasional shadows of it, as revealed in several of the other sketches. But had I previously perused "Young Goodman Brown," I should have been at no pains to draw the conclusion which I came to at a time when I was ignorant that the book contained one such direct and unqualified manifestation of it.

J. HILLIS MILLER

J. Hillis Miller analyzed the effect of what he called "Bartleby's celebrated immobility" in the critical study Versions of Pygmalion *(1990). Miller was intent on examining "strange and unaccountable" versions of the Pygmalion myth in European literature; each story he discussed "contains a character who does something like falling in love with a statue." In Miller's view, a story like "Bartleby, the Scrivener" was an occasion for "the act of personification essential to all story-telling and story-reading."*

Who Is He? Melville's "Bartleby, the Scrivener" 1990

After the failure of all these strategies for getting rid of Bartleby, the narrator tries another. In part through charity but in part through the notion that it is his fate to have Bartleby permanently in his chambers, he decides to try to live with Bartleby, to take him as a permanent fixture in his office. The narrator looks into two quite different books that deny man free will in determining his life, "Edwards on the Will" and "Priestly on Necessity." For Jonathan Edwards man does not have free will because everything he does is predestined by God. For Joseph Priestly, on the other hand, man is bound within the chains of a universal material necessity. Everything happens through physical causality, and therefore everything happens as it must happen, as it has been certain through all time to happen. In either case Bartleby's presence in the narrator's rooms is something predestined:

> Gradually I slid into the persuasion that these troubles of mine touching the scrivener, had been all predestinated from eternity, and Bartleby was billeted upon me for some mysterious purpose of an all-wise Providence,

which it was not for a mere mortal like me to fathom. Yes, Bartleby, stay there behind your screen, thought I; I shall persecute you no more; you are harmless and noiseless as any of these old chairs; in short, I never feel so private as when I know you are here. At last I see it, I feel it; I penetrate to the predestinated purpose of my life. I am content. Others may have loftier parts to enact; but my mission in this world, Bartleby, is to furnish you with office-room for such period as you may see fit to remain.

This strategy fails too, when the narrator's clients and associates let him know that Bartleby's presence in his offices is scandalizing his professional reputation. It is then that the narrator, who is nothing if not logical, conceives his strangest way of dealing with Bartleby. Since Bartleby will not budge, he himself will leave. The immobility of Bartleby turns the narrator into a nomad: "No more then. Since he will not quit me, I must quit him. I will change my offices; I will move elsewhere."

When the new tenants and the landlord of his old premises come to charge the narrator with responsibility for the nuisance Bartleby is causing, "haunting the building generally, sitting upon the banisters of the stairs by day, and sleeping in the entry by night," the narrator tries first a new strategy of saying he is in no way related to Bartleby or responsible for him. But it is no use: "I was the last person known to have anything to do with him, and they held me to the terrible account."

The narrator then meets Bartleby once more face to face. He offers to set him up in a respectable position, as a clerk in a dry-goods store, a bartender, a bill collector, or a companion for young gentlemen traveling to Europe. To all these ludicrous suggestions Bartleby replies that he is not particular, but he would prefer to remain "stationary." The narrator then, and finally, offers to take Bartleby home with him, like a stray cat, and give him refuge there. This meets with the same reply. The narrator flees the building and becomes truly a vagrant, wandering for days here and there in his rockaway.

The narrator's life and work seem to have been permanently broken by the irruption of Bartleby. It is not he but his old landlord who deals effectively with the situation. He has Bartleby "removed to the Tombs as a vagrant." This is just what the more intellectually consequent narrator has not been able to bring himself to do, not just because Bartleby is not, strictly speaking, a vagrant and not just because doing such violence to Bartleby would disobey the law of charity, but because he cannot respond with violence to a resistance that has been purely passive and has thereby "disarmed" or "unmanned" any decisive action: "Turn the man out by an actual thrusting I could not; to drive him away by calling him hard names would not do; calling in the police was an unpleasant idea. . . . You will not thrust him, the poor, pale, passive mortal,—you will not thrust such a helpless creature out of your door? you will not dishonor yourself by such cruelty? No, I will not, I cannot do that."

Even after the police have been called in and society has placed Bartleby where he belongs, the narrator continues to be haunted by a sense of unfulfilled responsibility. He visits him in the Tombs, the prison so called because it was in the Egyptian Revival style of architecture, but also no doubt in response to a deeper sense of kinship between incarceration and death: "The Egyptian character of the masonry weighed upon me with its gloom. But a soft imprisoned turf grew under foot. The heart of the eternal pyramids, it seemed, wherein, by some strange magic, through the clefts, grass-seed, dropped by birds, had sprung." Bartleby is appropriately placed in the Tombs since, if the prison courtyard where Bartleby dies is green life in the midst of death, Bartleby has been death in the midst of life. In the Tombs the narrator makes his last unsuccessful attempt to deal with Bartleby in a rational manner, to reincorporate him into ordinary life. He "narrates" to the prison authorities, as he says, "all I knew" about Bartleby, telling them Bartleby does not really belong there but must stay "till something less harsh might be done—though indeed I hardly knew what." He yields at last to the accounting for Bartleby that had been used by Ginger Nut: "I think, sir, he's a little *luny*." The narrator now tells the "grub-man" in the prison, Mr. Cutlets, "I think he is a little deranged." One powerful means society has for dealing with someone who does not fit any ordinary social category is to declare him insane.

Mr. Cutlets has his own curious and by no means insignificant way of placing Bartleby. He thinks Bartleby must be a forger. "Deranged? deranged is it? Well now, upon my word, I thought that friend of yourn was a gentleman forger; they are always pale and genteel-like, them forgers. I can't help pity 'em—can't help it, sir. Did you know Monroe Edwards?" To which the narrator answers, "No, I was never socially acquainted with any forgers." In a way Mr. Cutlets has got Bartleby right, since forgery involves the exact copying of someone else's handwriting in order to make a false document that functions performatively as if it were genuine. Bartleby is a species of forger in reverse. He copies documents all right, but he does this in such a way as to deprive them of their power to make anything happen. On the other hand, when the narrator has copied documents checked, corrected, and made functional, he is himself performing an act of forgery. He may not be socially acquainted with any forgers, but he is in a manner of speaking one himself.

The arrangement he makes with Mr. Cutlets to feed Bartleby in prison is the narrator's last attempt to reincorporate Bartleby into society. There is much emphasis on eating in the story, on what the narrator's different employees eat and drink and on how little Bartleby eats, apparently nothing at all in prison: " 'I prefer not to dine to-day,' said Bartleby, turning away. 'It would disagree with me; I am unused to dinners.' So saying he slowly moved to the other side of the inclosure, and took up a position fronting the dead-wall." Eating is one of the basic ways to share our common humanity. This Bartleby refuses, or rather he says he would prefer not to share in the ritual of eating. To refuse that is in the end deadly. Bartleby's death makes him what he has been all along, a bit of death in the midst of life.

It is entirely appropriate that the narrator's account of Bartleby should end with Bartleby's death, not because any biography should end with the death of the biographee but because in death Bartleby becomes what he has always already been. As I have said, his "I would prefer not to" is strangely oriented toward the future. It opens the future, but a future of perpetual not-yet. It can only come as death, and death is that which can never be present. There, at the end, the narrator finds the corpse of Bartleby, "strangely huddled at the base of the wall, his knees drawn up, and lying on his side, his head touching the cold stones." In an earlier version, the "Bartleby" fragment in the Melville family papers in the Gansevoort-Lansing Collection at the New York Public Library, Bartleby is found by the narrator lying in a white-washed room with his head against a tombstone: "It was clean, well-lighted and scrupulously white washed. The head-stone was standing up against the wall, and stretched on a blanket at its base, his head touching the cold marble and his feet upon the threshold lay the wasted form of Bartleby."

The corpse of Bartleby is not the presence of Bartleby. It is his eternal absence. In death he becomes what he has always been, a cadaver who "lives without dining," as the narrator says to the grub-man. Bartleby returns at death, in the final version of the story, to a fetal position. He is the incursion into life of that unattainable realm somewhere before birth and after death. But the word "realm" is misleading. What Bartleby brings is not a realm in the sense of place we might go. It is the otherness that all along haunts or inhabits life from the inside. This otherness can by no method, such as the long series of techniques the narrator tries, be accounted for, narrated, rationalized, or in any other way reassimilated into ordinary life, though it is a permanent part of that ordinary life. Bartleby is the alien that may neither be thrust out the door nor domesticated, brought into the family, given citizenship papers. Bartleby is the invasion of death into life, but not death as something from outside life. He is death as the other side of life or the cohabitant with life. "Death," nevertheless, is not the proper name for this ghostly companion of life, as if it were an allegorical meaning identified at last. Nor is "Death" its generic or common name. "Death" is a catachresis for what can never be named properly.

The narrator's last method of attempting to deal with Bartleby is his narration, going all the way from "I am a rather elderly man" to "Ah Bartleby! Ah humanity!" This narration is explicitly said to be written down and addressed to a "reader." It repeats for a more indeterminate reader, that is, for whoever happens to read it, the quasi-legal deposition he has made before the proper officer of "the Tombs, or to speak more properly, the Halls of Justice." If the narrator can encompass Bartleby with words, if he can do justice to him, he may simultaneously have accounted for him, naturalized him after all, and freed himself from his unfulfilled obligation. He will have made an adequate response to the demand Bartleby has made on him. The narrator, that is, may have justified himself while doing justice to Bartleby.

This is impossible because Bartleby cannot be identified. His story cannot be told. But the reader at the end knows better just why this is so, since we have watched the narrator try one by one a whole series of strategies for accounting for someone and has seen them one by one fail. This failure leaves Bartleby still imperturbably bringing everything to a halt or indefinitely postponing everything with his "I would prefer not to." The narrator's account is not so much an account as an apology for his failure to give an adequate account.

The narrator's writing is also an attempt at a reading, a failed attempt to read Bartleby. In this sense it is the first in a long line of attempts to read Bartleby the scrivener, though the narrator's successors do this by trying to read the text written by Melville, "Bartleby, the Scrivener." Just as Bartleby by his immovable presence in the narrator's office has demanded to be read and accounted for by him, so Melville's strange story demands to be read and accounted for. Nor have readers failed to respond to the demand. A large secondary literature has grown up around "Bartleby," remarkable for its multiplicity and diversity. All claim in one way or another to have identified Bartleby and to have accounted for him, to have done him justice. They tend to exemplify that function of policing or putting things in their place which is entrusted by our society to literary studies as one realm among many of the academic forms of accounting or accounting for. In the case of the essays on "Bartleby" this accounting often takes one or the other of two main forms, as Warminski has observed. These forms could be put under the aegis of the two-pronged last paragraph of the story—"Ah Bartleby! Ah humanity!"—or they might be said to fly in the face either of Bartleby's "But I am not particular" or of the manifest failure of the narrator's attempt to draw close to Bartleby by way of "the bond of a common humanity." Many of the essays try to explain Bartleby either by making him an example of some universal type, for example "existential man," or by finding some particular original or explanatory context for him, for example one of Melville's acquaintances who worked in a law office, or some aspect of nineteenth-century capitalism in America. But Bartleby is neither general nor particular: he is neutral. As such, he disables reading by any of these strategies, any attempt to put "Bartleby, the Scrivener" in its place by answering the question, "In mercy's name, who is he?"

No doubt my own reading also claims to have identified Bartleby, in this case by defining him as the neutral in-between that haunts all thinking and living by dialectical opposition. All readings of the story, including my own, are more ways to call in the police. They are ways of trying to put Bartleby in his place, to convey him where we want to put him, to make sense of him, even if it is an accounting that defines him as the nonsense that inhabits all sense-making. All readings attempt in one way or another to fulfill what the narrator has tried and failed to do: to tell Bartleby's story in a way that will allow us to assimilate him and the story into the vast archives of rationalization that make up the secondary literature of our profession. We are institutionalized to do that work of policing for our society. None of these techniques of assimilation works any better than any of the narrator's methods, and we remain haunted by Bartleby, but haunted also by "Bartleby, the Scrivener: A Story of Wall-Street." I claim, however, that my accounting succeeds where the others fail by showing (though that is not quite the right word) why it is that "accounting for" in any of its usual senses cannot work, either for the story or for the character the story poses.

GRACE PALEY

Grace Paley talked with Ann Charters about her experiences as a short story writer during lunch in her Greenwich Village apartment on a snowy day in February 1986. On the wall above the kitchen table hung an oil painting, a still life of vegetables painted by her father after his retirement from the practice of medicine. Paley mentions her father's interest in art in her story "A Conversation with My Father."

A Conversation with Ann Charters   1986

Charters: Some literary critics think that short stories are more closely related to poetry than to the novel. Would you agree?

Paley: I would say that stories are closer to poetry than they are to the novel because first they are shorter, and second they are more concentrated, more economical, and that kind of economy, the pulling together of all the information and making leaps across the information, is really close to poetry. By leaps I mean thought leaps and feeling leaps. Also, when short stories are working right, you pay more attention to language than most novelists do.

Charters: Poe said unity was an essential factor of short stories. Do you have any ideas about this in your own work?

Paley: I suppose there has to be some kind of unity, but that's true in a novel too. It seems to me that unity is form. Form is really the vessel in which the story or poem or novel exists. The reason I don't have an answer for you is that there's really no telling—sometimes I like to start a story with one thing and end it with another. I don't know where the unity is in that case. I see the word *unity* meaning that something has to be whole, even if it ends in an open way.

Charters: You mean, as you wrote in "A Conversation with My Father," that "everyone, real or invented, deserves the open destiny of life."

Paley: Yes.

Charters: You started writing poetry before short stories, and the language of your fiction is often as compressed and metaphorical as the language of poetry. Can you describe the process of how you learned to write?

Paley: Let me put it this way: I went to school to poetry—that was where I learned how to write. People learn to write by doing various things. I suppose I also wrote a lot of letters, since it was the time of the Second World War. But apart from that I wrote poems, that's what I wrote. I thought about language a lot. That was important to me. That was my teacher. My fiction teacher was poetry.

Charters: What poets did you read when you were learning how to write?

Paley: I just read all the poets. If there was an anthology of poets, I read every single one. I knew all the Victorians. I read the Imagists. At a certain point I fell in love with the Englishmen who came to America—Christopher Isherwood, Stephen Spender, and W. H. Auden. I thought Auden was the greatest. And I loved the poetry of Dylan Thomas. Yeats meant a lot to me. I paid attention to all of them and listened to all of them. Some of them must have gotten into my ear. That's not up to me to say. That's for the reader to say. The reader of my stories will tell me, "This is whom you're influenced by," but I can't say that. I feel I was influenced by everybody.

Charters: Why did you stop writing poetry and start writing stories? What did the form of the short story offer you that the poem didn't?

Paley: First of all, I began to think of certain subject matter, women's lives specifically, and what was happening around me. I was in my thirties, which I guess is the time people start to notice these things, women's and men's lives and what their relationship is. I knew lots of women with small kids, and I was developing very close relationships with a variety of women. All sorts of things began to worry me, and I began to think about them a lot. I couldn't deal with any of this subject matter in poetry; I just didn't know how. I didn't have the technique. Other people can, but I didn't want to write poems saying "I feel this" and "I feel that." That was the last thing I wanted to do.

I can give you a definition that can be proven wrong in many ways, but for me it was that in writing poetry I wanted to talk to the world, I wanted to address the world, so to speak. But writing stories, I wanted to get the world to explain itself to me, to speak to me. And for me that was the essential difference between writing poetry and stories, and it still is, in many ways. So I had to get that world to talk to me. I had to reach out to it, a very different thing than writing poems. I had to reach out to the world and get it to tell me what it was all about, because I didn't understand it. I just didn't understand. Also, I'd always been very interested in people and told funny stories, and I didn't have any room for doing that in poems, again because of my own self. My poems were too literary, that's the real reason.

Charters: What do you mean, you had to get the world to tell you what it was all about?

Paley: In the first story I ever wrote, "The Contest," I did exactly what I just told you—I got this guy to talk. That's what I did. I had a certain guy in mind. In fact, I stuck pretty close to my notion of what he was, and the story was about a contest he had told me about. The second story I wrote was about Aunt Rose in "Goodbye and Good Luck." That began with my husband's aunt visiting us, and saying exactly the sentence I used to start the story: "I was popular in certain circles." But the rest has nothing to do with her life at all. She looked at us, this aunt of his, and she felt we didn't appreciate her, so she looked at us and she said to us, "Listen," she said. "I was popular in certain circles." That statement really began that particular story. That story was about lots of older women I knew who didn't get married, and I was thinking about them. These are two examples of how I began, how I got to my own voice by hearing and using all these other voices.

Charters: I suppose "A Conversation with My Father" isn't typical of your work, because the story you make up for him isn't what he wants, the old-fashioned Chekhov or Maupassant story, and it's not really one of your "voice" stories either, is it?

Paley: No. I'm just trying to oblige him.

Charters: So that may be one of the jokes of the story?

Paley: It could be, but I never thought of it that way. I think it's a good story. People have found it useful in literature classes, which I think is funny, but nice.

Charters: Did you make up the plot of "A Conversation with My Father," or did it actually happen when you were visiting him before he died?

Paley: My father was eighty-six years old and in bed. I spent a lot of time with him. He was an artist, and he painted pictures after he retired from being a doctor. I visited him at least once a week, and we were very close. We would have discussions. I never wrote a story for him about this neighbor, but he did say to me once, "Why can't you write a regular story, for God's sake?" something like that. So that particular story is both about literature and about that particular discussion, but it's also about generational differences, about different ways of looking at life. What my father thought could be done in the world was due to his own history. What I thought could be done in the world was different, not because I was a more open person, because he was also a very open person, but because I lived in a particularly open time, the late 1960s. The story I wrote for him was about all these druggies. It was made up, but it was certainly true. I could point out people on my block whose kids became junkies. Many of them have recovered from being junkies and are in good shape now.

Charters: Did you know any mothers in Greenwich Village who became junkies to keep their kids company?

Paley: Sure. It was a very open neighborhood then, with lots of freedom. But my father was born into a very different time. He was born in Czarist Russia and came over to America when he was twenty and worked hard and studied medicine and had a profession.

Charters: When you were growing up did you read the writers your father admired — Maupassant and Chekhov?

Paley: Actually, he had never mentioned Maupassant to me before. He did mention him in that conversation. He did read a lot, he loved Chekhov. And when he came to this country, he taught himself English by reading Dickens.

Charters: So the idea for the story came to you when he mentioned Maupassant?

Paley: Well, not really. He had just read my story "Faith in a Tree," and there are a lot of voices coming from all over in that story. And so he asked me, "What is this? All those voices? Voices from who knows where?" He wasn't actually that heavy. But when I wrote about our conversation it became a fiction, and it's different from what really happened.

Charters: It must have been fun for you to make up the two versions of the story about your neighbor in "A Conversation with My Father."

Paley: I enjoyed writing that story. Some stories you don't enjoy, because they're very hard. I didn't write it right off, but I enjoyed it.

Charters: How many days did it take you to write?

Paley: There's no such thing as days with me when I write a story. More like months. I write it and I write slow, and then I rewrite, and then I put it away, and then I take it out again. It's tedious in some respects. But that's the way it works.

Charters: When do you decide it's finished?

Paley: When I've gone over it and I can't think of another thing to change.

Charters: I was looking over your book *Enormous Changes at the Last Minute,* which is where "A Conversation with My Father" appears, and I noticed you've placed it between two very dark stories, "The Little Girl," about a runaway in the Village who commits suicide after she's raped, and "The Immigrant Story," about the starvation of the young children in a Jewish family in Poland before the mother emigrates to America. I assume you did this for a reason. When you put a collection of short fiction together, how do you order the stories?

Paley: I always have something in mind. I like to put one or two at the beginning that will be readable immediately, and then I just work it out. I like to mix the long and the short, and the serious and the funny ones. But I did put those two dark stories around "A Conversation with My Father" to show him I could look tragedy in the face. Remember he asks me at the end of the story, "When will you look it in the face?"

Charters: Was that one of the things he actually said to you when you visited him?

Paley: Well, he did tend to say that I wouldn't look things in the face. That things were hard, and I wasn't looking at it. I didn't see certain problems with my kids when they were small, and he was in some degree right. In "The Immigrant Story" a man tells me, "You have a rotten rosy temperament." But then she says, "Rosiness is not a worse windowpane than gloomy gray when viewing the world." They're both just prisms to look through.

Charters: Is that what you still believe?

Paley: Well, I do believe it, but I also believe that things are bad.

Charters: A theme that some students find when reading "A Conversation with My Father" is that one of the things you don't want to look in the face that your father is trying to prepare you for is his own death. Were you conscious of that when you wrote the story?

Paley: No.

Charters: Can you see that theme in it now?

Paley: No. But maybe you're right. As I said, that's not up to me to say. Maybe the reader of a particular story knows better than the writer what it means. But I know I wasn't thinking about that when I wrote it. I wasn't thinking of his death at all. I was thinking of him being sick and trying not to get him excited.

LESLIE MARMON SILKO

Leslie Marmon Silko discussed her view of her audience and her background growing up in a matriarchal society in a lecture titled "Language and Literature from a Pueblo Indian Perspective." It was originally published in English Literature: Opening Up the Canon *(1979).*

Language and Literature from a
Pueblo Indian Perspective
1979

Where I come from, the words that are most highly valued are those which are spoken from the heart, unpremeditated and unrehearsed. Among the Pueblo people, a written speech or statement is highly suspect because the true feelings of the speaker remain hidden as he reads words that are detached from the occasion and the audience. I have intentionally not written a formal paper to read to this session because of this and because I want you to hear and to experience English in a nontraditional structure, a structure that follows patterns from the oral tradition. For those of you accustomed to a structure that moves from point A to point B to point C, this presentation may be somewhat difficult to follow because the structure of Pueblo expression resembles something like a spider's web—with many little threads radiating from a center, crisscrossing each other. As with the web, the structure will emerge as it is made and you must simply listen and trust, as the Pueblo people do, that meaning will be made.

I suppose the task that I have today is a formidable one because basically I come here to ask you, at least for a while, to set aside a number of basic approaches that you have been using and probably will continue to use in approaching the study of English or the study of language; first of all, I come to ask you to see language from the Pueblo perspective, which is a perspective that is very much concerned with including the whole of creation and the whole of history and time. And so we very seldom talk about breaking language down into words. As I will continue to relate to you, even the use of a specific language is less important than the one thing—which is the "telling," or the storytelling. And so, as Simon Ortiz has written, if you approach a Pueblo person and want to talk words or, worse than that, to break down an individual word into its components, ofttimes you will just get a blank stare, because we don't think of words as being isolated from the speaker, which, of course, is one element of the oral tradition. Moreover, we don't think of words as being alone: Words are always with other words, and the other words are almost always in a story of some sort.

Today I have brought a number of examples of stories in English because I would like to get around to the question that has been raised, or the topic that has come along here, which is what changes we Pueblo writers might make with English as a language for literature. But at the same time I would like to explain the importance of storytelling and how it relates to a Pueblo theory of language.

So first I would like to go back to the Pueblo Creation story. The reason I go back to that story is because it is an all-inclusive story of creation and how life began. Tséitsínako, Thought Woman, by thinking of her sisters, and

---

This "essay" is an edited transcript of an oral presentation. The "author" deliberately did not read from a prepared paper so that the audience could experience firsthand one dimension of the oral tradition—nonlinear structure. Her remarks were intended to be heard, not read.

together with her sisters, thought of everything which is, and this world was created. And the belief was that everything in this world was a part of the original creation, and that the people at home realized that far away there were others—other human beings. There is even a section of the story which is a prophesy—which describes the origin of the European race, the African, and also remembers the Asian origins.

Starting out with this story, with this attitude which includes all things, I would like to point out that the reason the people are more concerned with story and communication and less with a particular language is in part an outgrowth of the area [pointing to a map] where we find ourselves. Among the twenty Pueblos there are at least six distinct languages, and possibly seven. Some of the linguists argue—and I don't set myself up to be a linguist at all—about the number of distinct languages. But certainly Zuni is all alone, and Hopi is all alone, and from mesa to mesa there are subtle differences in language—very great differences. I think that this might be the reason that what particular language was being used wasn't as important as what a speaker was trying to say. And this, I think, is reflected and stems or grows out of a particular view of the story—that is, that language *is* story. At Laguna many words have stories which make them. So when one is telling a story, and one is using words to tell the story, each word that one is speaking has a story of its own too. Often the speakers or tellers go into the stories of the words they are using to tell one story so that you get stories within stories, so to speak. This structure becomes very apparent in the storytelling, and what I would like to show you later on by reading some pieces that I brought is that this structure also informs the writing and the stories which are currently coming from Pueblo people. I think what is essential is this sense of story, and story within story, and the idea that one story is only the beginning of many stories, and the sense that stories never truly end. I would like to propose that these views of structure and the dynamics of storytelling are some of the contributions which Native American cultures bring to the English language or at least to literature in the English language.

First of all, a lot of people think of storytelling as something that is done at bedtime—that it is something that is done for small children. When I use the term "storytelling," I include a far wider range of telling activity. I also do not limit storytelling to simply old stories, but to again go back to the original view of creation, which sees that it is all part of a whole; we do not differentiate or fragment stories and experiences. In the beginning, Tséitsínako, Thought Woman, thought of all these things, and all of these things are held together as one holds many things together in a single thought.

So in the telling (and today you will hear a few of the dimensions of this telling) first of all, as was pointed out earlier, the storytelling always includes the audience and the listeners, and, in fact, a great deal of the story is believed to be inside the listener, and the storyteller's role is to draw the story out of the listeners. This kind of shared experience grows out of a strong community base. The storytelling goes on and continues from generation to generation.

The Origin story functions basically as a maker of our identity—with the story we know who we are. We are the Lagunas. This is where we came from. We came this way. We came by this place. And so from the time you are very young, you hear these stories, so that when you go out into the wider world, when one asks who you are, or where are you from, you immediately know: We are the people who came down from the north. We are the people of these stories. It continues down into clans so that you are not just talking about Laguna Pueblo people, you are talking about your own clan. Within the clans there are stories which identify the clan.

In the Creation story, Antelope says that he will help knock a hole in the earth so that the people can come up, out into the next world. Antelope tries and tries, and he uses his hooves and is unable to break through; and it is then that Badger says, "Let me help you." And Badger very patiently uses his claws and digs a way through, bringing the people into the world. When the Badger clan people think of themselves, or when the Antelope people think of themselves, it is as people who are of *this* story, and this is *our* place, and we fit into the very beginning when the people first came, before we began our journey south.

So you can move, then, from the idea of one's identity as a tribal person into clan identity. Then we begin to get to the extended family, and this is where we begin to get a kind of story coming into play which some people might see as a different kind of story, though Pueblo people do not. Anthropologists and ethnologists have, for a long time, differentiated the types of oral language they find in the Pueblos. They tended to rule out all but the old and sacred and traditional stories and were not interested in family stories and the family's account of itself. But these family stories are just as important as the other stories—the older stories. These family stories are given equal recognition. There is no definite, pre-set pattern for the way one will hear the stories of one's own family, but it is a very critical part of one's childhood, and it continues on throughout one's life. You will hear stories of importance to the family—sometimes wonderful stories—stories about the time a maternal uncle got the biggest deer that was ever seen and brought back from the mountains. And so one's sense of who the family is, and who you are, will then extend from that—"I am from the family of my uncle who brought in this wonderful deer, and it was a wonderful hunt"—so you have this sort of building or sense of identity.

There are also other stories, stories about the time when another uncle, perhaps, did something that wasn't really acceptable. In other words, this process of keeping track, of telling, is an all-inclusive process which begins to create a total picture. So it is very important that you know all of the stories—both positive and not so positive—about one's own family. The reason that it is very important to keep track of all the stories in one's own family is because you are liable to hear a story from somebody else who is perhaps an enemy of the family, and you are liable to hear a version which has been changed, a version which makes your family sound disreputable—something that will taint the honor of the family. But if you have already heard the story, you know your family's version of what *really* happened that night, so when somebody else is mentioning it, you will have a version of the story to counterbalance it. Even when there is no way around it—old Uncle Pete did a terrible thing—by knowing the stories that come out of other families, by keeping very close watch, listening constantly to learn the stories about other families, one is in a sense able to deal with terrible sorts of things that might happen within one's own family. When a member of one's own family does something that cannot be excused, one always knows stories about similar things which happened in other families. And it is not done maliciously. I think it is very important to realize this. Keeping track of all the stories within the community gives a certain distance, a useful perspective which brings incidents down to a level we can deal with. If others have done it before, it cannot be so terrible. If others have endured, so can we.

The stories are always bringing us together, keeping this whole together, keeping this family together, keeping this clan together. "Don't go away, don't isolate yourself, but come here, because we have all had these kinds of experiences"—this is what the people are saying to you when they tell you these other stories. And so there is this constant pulling together to resist what seems to me to be a basic part of human nature: When some violent emotional experience takes place, people get the urge to run off and hide or separate themselves from others. And of course, if we do that, we are not only talking about endangering the group, we are also talking about the individual or the individual family never being able to recover or to survive. Inherent in this belief is the feeling that one does not recover or get well by one's self, but it is together that we look after each other and take care of each other.

In the storytelling, then, we see this process of bringing people together, and it works not only on the family level, but also on the level of the individual. Of course, the whole Pueblo concept of the individual is a little bit different from the usual Western concept of the individual. But one of the beauties of the storytelling is that when something happens to an individual, many people will come to you and take you aside, or maybe a couple of people will come and talk to you. These are occasions of storytelling. These occasions of storytelling are continuous; they are a way of life.

Storytelling lies at the heart of the Pueblo people, and so when someone comes in and says, "When did they tell the stories, or what time of day does the storytelling take place?" that is a ridiculous question. The storytelling goes on constantly—as some old grandmother puts on the shoes of a little child and tells the child the story of a little girl who didn't wear her shoes. At the same time somebody comes into the house for coffee to talk with an adolescent boy who has just been into a lot of trouble, to reassure him that *he* got into that kind of trouble, or somebody else's son got into that kind of trouble too. You have this constant ongoing process, working on many different levels.

One of the stories I like to bring up about helping the individual in crisis is a recent story, and I want to remind you that we make no distinctions between the stories—whether they are history, whether they are fact, whether they are gossip—these distinctions are not useful when we are talking about this particular experience with language. Anyway, there was a young man who, when he came back from the war in Vietnam, had saved up his Army pay and bought a beautiful red Volkswagen Beetle. He was very proud of it, and one night drove up to a place right across the reservation line. It is a very notorious place for many reasons, but one of the more notorious things about the place is a deep arroyo behind the place. This is the King's Bar. So he ran in to pick up a cold six-pack to take home, but he didn't put on his emergency brake. And his little red Volkswagen rolled back into the arroyo and was all smashed up. He felt very bad about it, but within a few days everybody had come to him and told him stories about other people who had lost cars to that arroyo. And probably the story that made him feel the best was about the time that George Day's station wagon, with his mother-in-law and kids in the back, rolled into that arroyo. So everybody was saying, "Well, at least your mother-in-law and kids weren't in the car when it rolled in," and you can't argue with that kind of story. He felt better then because he wasn't alone anymore. He and his smashed-up Volkswagen were now joined with all the other stories of cars that fell into that arroyo.

There are a great many parallels between Pueblo experiences and the remarks that have been made about South Africa and the Caribbean countries—similarities in experiences so far as language is concerned. More specifically, with the experience of English being imposed upon the people. The Pueblo people, of course, have seen intruders come and intruders go. The first they watched come were the Spaniards; while the Spaniards were there, things had to be conducted in Spanish. But as the old stories say, if you wait long enough, they'll go. And sure enough, they went. Then another bunch came in. And old stories say, well, if you wait around long enough, not so much that they'll go, but at least their ways will go. One wonders now, when you see what's happening to technocratic-industrial culture, now that we've used up most of the sources of energy, you think perhaps the old people are right.

But anyhow, our experience with English has been different because the Bureau of Indian Affairs schools were so terrible that we never heard of Shakespeare. There was Dick and Jane, and I can remember reading that the robins were heading south for winter, but I knew that all winter the robins were around Laguna. It took me a long time to figure out what was going on. I worried for quite a while about the robins because they didn't leave in the winter, not realizing that the textbooks were written in Boston. The big textbook companies are up here in Boston and *their* robins do go south in the winter. But this freed us and encouraged us to stay with our narratives. Whatever literature we received at school (which was damn little), at home the storytelling, the special regard for telling and bringing together through the telling, was going on constantly. It has continued, and so we have a great body of classical oral literature, both in the narratives and in the chants and songs.

As the old people say, "If you can remember the stories, you will be all right. Just remember the stories." And, of course, usually when they say that to you, when you are young, you wonder what in the world they mean. But when I returned—I had been away from Laguna Pueblo for a couple of years, well more than a couple of years after college and so forth—I returned to Laguna and I went to Laguna-Acoma high school to visit an English class, and I was wondering how the telling was continuing, because Laguna Pueblo, as the anthropologists have said, is one of the more acculturated pueblos. So I walked into this high school English class and there they were sitting, these very beautiful Laguna and Acoma kids. But I knew that out in their lockers they had cassette tape recorders, and I knew that at home they had stereos, and they were listening to Kiss and Led Zeppelin and all those other things. I was almost afraid, but I had to ask—I had with me a book of short fiction (it's called *The Man to Send Rain Clouds* [New York: Viking Press, 1974]), and among the stories of other Native American writers, it has stories that I have written and Simon Ortiz has written. And there is one particular story in the book about the killing of a state policeman in New Mexico by three Acoma Pueblo men. It was an act that was committed in the early fifties. I was afraid to ask, but I had to. I looked at the class and I said, "How many of you heard this story before you read it in the book?" And I was prepared to hear this crushing truth that indeed the anthropologists were right about the old traditions dying out. But it was amazing, you know, almost all but one or two students raised their hands. They had heard that story, just as Simon and I had heard it, when we were young. That was my first indication that storytelling continues on. About half of them had heard it in English, about half of them had heard it in Laguna. I think again, getting back to one of the original statements, that if you begin to look at the core of the importance of the language and how it fits in with the culture, it is the *story* and the feeling of the story which matters more than what language it's told in.

AMY TAN

Amy Tan discussed the subject of multicultural literature in an essay written for The Threepenny Review *in 1996. There she admitted that she was proud to find her name on the reading lists for many college courses ("What writer wouldn't want her work to be read?"), and then went on to explain why she was "not altogether comfortable" about the use of her book as required reading.*

In the Canon, For All the Wrong Reasons   1996

Several years ago I learned that I had passed a new literary milestone. I had made it to the Halls of Education under the rubric of "Multicultural Literature," also known in many schools as "Required Reading."

Thanks to this development, I now meet students who proudly tell me they're doing their essays, term papers, or master's theses on me. By that they mean that they are analyzing not just my books but me—my grade-school achievements, youthful indiscretions, marital status, as well as the movies I watched as a child, the slings and arrows I suffered as a minority, and so forth—all of which, with the hindsight of classroom literary investigation, prove to contain many Chinese omens that made it inevitable that I would become a writer.

Once I read a master's thesis on feminist writings, which included examples from *The Joy Luck Club*. The student noted that I had often used the number four, something on the order of thirty-two or thirty-six times—in any case, a number divisible by four. She pointed out that there were four mothers, four daughters, four sections of the book, four stories per section. Furthermore, there were four sides to a mah jong table, four directions of the wind, four players. More important, she postulated, my use of the number four was a symbol for the four stages of psychological development, which corresponded in uncanny ways to the four stages of some type of Buddhist philosophy I had never heard of before. The student recalled that the story contained a character called Fourth Wife, symbolizing death, and a four-year-old girl with a feisty spirit, symbolizing regeneration.

In short, her literary sleuthing went on to reveal a mystical and rather Byzantine puzzle, which, once explained, proved to be completely brilliant and precisely logical. She wrote me a letter and asked if her analysis had been correct. How I longed to say "absolutely."

The truth is, if there are symbols in my work they exist largely by accident or through someone else's interpretive design. If I wrote of "an orange moon rising on a dark night," I would more likely ask myself later if the image was a cliché, not whether it was a symbol for the feminine force rising in anger, as one master's thesis postulated. To plant symbols like that, you need a plan, good organizational skills, and a prescient understanding of the story you are about to write. Sadly, I lack those traits.

All this is by way of saying that I don't claim my use of the number four to be a brilliant symbolic device. In fact, now that it's been pointed out to me in rather astonishing ways, I consider my overuse of the number to be a flaw.

Reviewers and students have enlightened me about not only how I write but why I write. Apparently, I am driven to capture the immigrant experience, to demystify Chinese culture, to point out the differences between Chinese and American culture, even to pave the way for other Asian American writers.

If only I were that noble. Contrary to what is assumed by some students, reporters, and community organizations wishing to bestow honors on me, I am not an expert on China, Chinese culture, mah jong, the psychology of mothers and daughters, generation gaps, immigration, illegal aliens, assimilation, acculturation, racial tension, Tiananmen Square, the Most Favored Nation trade agreements, human rights, Pacific Rim economics, the purported one million missing baby girls of China, the future of Hong Kong after 1997, or, I am sorry to say, Chinese cooking. Certainly I have personal opinions on many of these topics, but by no means do my sentiments and my world of make-believe make me an expert.

So I am alarmed when reviewers and educators assume that my very personal, specific, and fictional stories are meant to be representative down to the nth detail not just of Chinese Americans but, sometimes, of all Asian culture. Is Jane Smiley's *A Thousand Acres* supposed to be taken as representative of all of American culture? If so, in what ways? Are all American fathers tyrannical? Do all American sisters betray one another? Are all American conscientious objectors flaky in love relationships?

Over the years my editor has received hundreds of permissions requests from publishers of college textbooks and multicultural anthologies, all of them wishing to reprint my work for "educational purposes." One publisher wanted to include an excerpt from *The Joy Luck Club*, a scene in which a Chinese woman invites her non-Chinese boyfriend to her parents' house for dinner. The boyfriend brings a bottle of wine as a gift and commits a number of social gaffes at the dinner table. Students were supposed to read this excerpt, then answer the following question: "If you are invited to a Chinese family's house for dinner, should you bring a bottle of wine?"

In many respects, I am proud to be on the reading lists for courses such as Ethnic Studies, Asian American Studies, Asian American Literature, Asian American History, Women's Literature, Feminist Studies, Feminist Writers of Color, and so forth. What writer wouldn't want her work to be read? I also take a certain perverse glee in imagining countless students, sleepless at three in the morning, trying to read *The Joy Luck Club* for the next day's midterm. Yet I'm also not altogether comfortable about my book's status as required reading.

Let me relate a conversation I had with a professor at a school in southern California. He told me he uses my books in his literature class but he makes it a point to lambast those passages that depict China as backward or unattractive. He objects to any descriptions that have to do with spitting, filth, poverty, or superstitions. I asked him if China in the 1930s and 1940s was free of these elements. He said, No, such descriptions are true; but he still believes it is "the obligation of the writer of ethnic literature to create positive, progressive images."

I secretly shuddered and thought, Oh well, that's southern California for you. But then, a short time later, I met a student from UC Berkeley, a school that I myself attended. The student was standing in line at a book signing. When his turn came, he swaggered up to me, then took two steps back and said in a loud voice, "Don't you think you have a responsibility to write about Chinese men as positive role models?"

In the past, I've tried to ignore the potshots. A *Washington Post* reporter once asked me what I thought of another Asian American writer calling me something on the order of "a running dog whore sucking on the tit of the imperialist white pigs."

"Well," I said, "You can't please everyone, can you?" I pointed out that readers are free to interpret a book as they please, and that they are free to appreciate or not appreciate the result. Besides, reacting to your critics makes a writer look defensive, petulant, and like an all-around bad sport.

But lately I've started thinking it's wrong to take such a laissez-faire attitude. Lately I've come to think that I must say something, not so much to defend myself and my work but to express my hopes for American literature, for what it has the potential to become in the twenty-first century—that is, a truly American literature, democratic in the way it includes many colorful voices.

Until recently, I didn't think it was important for writers to express their private intentions in order for their work to be appreciated; I believed that any analysis of my intentions belonged behind the closed doors of literature classes. But I've come to realize that the study of literature does have its effect on how books are being read, and thus on what might be read, published, and written in the future. For that reason, I do believe writers today must talk about their intentions—if for no other reason than to serve as an antidote to what others say our intentions should be.

For the record, I don't write to dig a hole and fill it with symbols. I don't write stories as ethnic themes. I don't write to represent life in general. And I certainly don't write because I have answers. If I knew everything there is to know about mothers and daughters, Chinese and Americans, I wouldn't have any stories left to imagine. If I had to write about only positive role models, I wouldn't have enough imagination left to finish the first story. If I knew what to do about immigration, I would be a sociologist or a politician and not a long-winded storyteller.

So why do I write?

Because my childhood disturbed me, pained me, made me ask foolish questions. And the questions still echo. Why does my mother always talk about killing herself? Why did my father and brother have to die? If I die, can I be reborn into a happy family? Those early obsessions led to a belief that writing could be my salvation, providing me with the sort of freedom and danger, satisfaction and discomfort, truth and contradiction I can't find in anything else in life.

I write to discover the past for myself. I don't write to change the future for others. And if others are moved by my work—if they love their mothers more, scold their daughters less, or divorce their husbands who were not positive role models—I'm often surprised, usually grateful to hear from kind readers. But I don't take either credit or blame for changing their lives for better or for worse.

Writing, for me, is an act of faith, a hope that I will discover what I mean by "truth." I also think of reading as an act of faith, a hope that I will discover something remarkable about ordinary life, about myself. And if the writer and the reader discover the same thing, if they have that connection, the act of faith has resulted in an act of magic. To me, that's the mystery and the wonder of both life and fiction—the connection between two individuals who discover in the end that they are more the same than they are different.

And if that doesn't happen, it's nobody's fault. There are still plenty of other books on the shelf. Choose what you like.

CHERYL B. TORSNEY

Cheryl B. Torsney wrote an essay about Alice Walker's "Everyday Use" as a reader-response or autobiographical literary critic. Her essay was included in the collection The Intimate Critique *(1993), edited by Diane P. Freedman, Olivia Frey, and Frances Murphy Zauhar.*

"Everyday Use": My Sojourn at Parchman Farm   1993

Today, when autumn colors camouflage the existence of the strip mines in the vertical West Virginia landscape of mountain and hollow, it's hard to remember actually having lived in the Mississippi Delta. What I do recall is that although the area lacks coal, it is rich in other things — soybeans, rice, and cotton — and flat as a quilt pulled tight over an old bed. From my backyard, I could see the water towers of six neighboring towns, not including the cotton boll affair in Minter City, Sunflower County.

In 1983, during the height of the job crunch in literary studies, I, a white Northern Jew — an alien by the standards of nearly everyone in Bolivar County, Mississippi — was delighted to be teaching in a tenure-line position at a small university in the state where Goodman's, Schwerner's, and Chaney's bodies had been found buried in an earthen dam near the ironically named city of Philadelphia. With the enthusiasm of a recent-vintage Ph.D., I brazenly challenged my mostly white students to reconsider their understandings of Southern history and traditions, to revise their notions of what constitutes sense of place, political agenda, race, and class. I remember talking about Eudora Welty, Fannie Lou Hamer, Alice Walker. I figured, presumptuously I now see, that if no one else was doing it, then I was responsible for telling my students what I thought they should know about their past, not to mention their present.

My teaching of Alice Walker's short story "Everyday Use" and my continuing research on quilting as a metaphor in women's writing led me to ask my husband to take me to work with him, to meet a quilter he had heard about. At that time, Jack was employed in the psychiatric hospital at the Mississippi State Penitentiary, the Parchman Farm of so many blues songs. He arranged for me to meet a female inmate who had pieced a quilt for another one of the psychologists at the prison hospital. . . .

I let Lucille Sojourner tell her story.

She had been quilting since 1980, when she was sentenced to life in prison. A quiet woman, Lucille had been approached by a white prisoner, who got her started. At that time she'd had no means of support. Soon after completing her first quilt, however, a big freeze hit northern Mississippi, and when another inmate offered to buy the cover to keep herself warm, Lucille sold it right from her bed.

Financially strapped, Lucille was emotionally depressed as well. Her family of many brothers and sisters and her own seven children did not visit her on the Farm. Her husband was in one of the men's camps. Soon she began to contract quilts with several women from Jackson, who would provide her with good material and pay her $150 a quilt. She'd recently made "an old nine-patch" for them, and those Jackson women sold it, not even a fancy patterned top, for $90. Ecstatic, she could send this money to her several sisters who were caring for her many children. At that time she was piecing for one of the counselors in the psychiatric unit a churn dash crib quilt in muted Laura Ashley tones of brick and blue. When Lucille Sojourner modestly offered "Round the World" as her favorite pattern, given the quilter's name, I was not surprised.

Parchman is a violent place. Lucille told me of one of her "friend girls" who had succumbed to gossip and gotten severely beaten. On another occasion two inmates had grabbed the freestanding quilting frame the Jackson women had bought her, destroyed it, and used the legs as clubs. As a result, she switched to a lap frame, quilting all day every day, taking time out only for trips to the bathroom. Wisely, as it turns out, she did not eat prison food: the week before I visited, seventy men in one of the camps got food poisoning, and one of them had died. Lucille told me that she got canned goods at the canteen, figuring she could survive on those and candy bars until she came up for parole. Constantly working—to make the time pass—she could piece a top in a week and quilt it in three days.

About thirty other women in the unit quilted, and Lucille spoke admiringly of a woman who worked more complicated patterns, like the lily of the valley and the double wedding ring. Yet she displayed real pride in her own skill. Some of the prison's quilters used a sewing machine to piece their tops, but she found that sometimes their seams didn't hold. Thus, she preferred, as she said, "to sew on my hands." And then she showed me her bruised fingers, swearing that they were better and had been much worse.

Why do it, I had asked. "It gives me constellation," she responded unhesitatingly, offering me an image of cosmic order.

She continued, telling of the guard who had asked her to quilt an already-pieced cover for free, since she was a convict with time on her hands. Clearly insulted by the guard's assumption that her time was of no value, Lucille noted that she was studying for her Graduation Equivalency Diploma.

This meeting with Lucille Sojourner forced me to revise my entire understanding of Alice Walker's short story, not to mention to examine my own position in the new narrative featuring the Yankee English professor's encounter with the convicted murderess. If Walker's Maggie, the stay-at-home sister of the story, was the type of meek, hard-working devoted daughter, Lucille (never mind the crime that had put her in Parchman) was the antitype, sewing for her place in the world, for her sanity. And if Dee/Wangero was the type of culturally hip daughter who desired tangible evidence of her heritage while rejecting her family, I was the antitype.

Both Dee and I had been named for family matriarchs: she had been originally named after her grandmother, and I, in the tradition of assimilated American Jews, was given a Hebrew name, Chaya—Life—after my maternal grandmother's mother. Our name changes reveal us to be cultural cross-dressers: Dee had been renamed Wangero, and I go by the English Cheryl. Lucille, too, had been renamed: #46496. Although Lucille was the only one of us to be literally incarcerated, from the perspective of Dee/Wangero's mother, Mrs. Johnson, Dee was as truly imprisoned by some institutionalized movement that had stripped her of her familial identity. And although I was privileged by education and race, I nonetheless felt a curious kinship with both Lucille/Maggie and Dee/Wangero. For in the foreign Delta culture, I felt constrained if not in many senses imprisoned as a result of my past, like Lucille; both of us, as it were, had been given "Life." But like Dee/Wangero, I was also estranged from my personal history, wanting it to confer identity, yet rejecting it at the same time. My double-bind hit home in the small synagogue in my Delta town during a Rosh Hashanah service, to which I had gone, I reasoned, to please my mother. Here the High Holy Days liturgy, sung in transliterated Hebrew, in major modes by the members of the First Baptist Church choir, only heightened my alienation.

In Walker's story, Dee has ironically been given a sort of work-release in order to return home to appropriate the family quilts, which contain pieces of people's lives: scraps from a wedding dress and a Civil War uniform, for example. Dee/Wangero wants to hang them like museum pieces on her wall, a motive that declares with additional irony that this newly liberated dashiki-ed black woman is both a prisoner to trends in interior design and a woman bent on larceny. Seeing her reentry into the dull life of her mother and sister as a diversion from her fashionable pursuit of her black heritage, Dee/Wangero plots to take what she wants and retreat once again from her past into a world that does not validate her familial history, into a social set whose project is to write a new narrative of African-American power. Mrs. Johnson and Maggie, then, are the ones who, in Dee/Wangero's fiction, are imprisoned in their rural lives and in their "ignorance," just like the students whom I had made it my business to enlighten.

In "Everyday Use" Maggie, the plain sister, who has remained at home with Mrs. Johnson, the focus of strength in the story, is, we remember, scarred, a description that gained a metaphoric import it never had before my trip to camp 25, before my examination of Lucille Sojourner's fingers. In fact, the whole notion of "everyday use" was transformed by my own sojourn at Parchman Farm. Originally, I had understood that, like the woman to whom Lucille made her first sale, Maggie would put the quilts to everyday use—she would use them to keep her and her family warm, to preserve their bodies as well as their souls—and in that fashion perpetuate the family's heritage in a way that displaying the quilts in a museum could never accomplish. She would use them *freely,* as a woman who gains strength from the narrative of her past, which she embodies. From the quilts Maggie would derive, as Lucille would say, constellation. Most interpretations of Walker's short story follow this line of reasoning, reading Maggie as the Cinderella—good sister, and Dee/Wangero as the evil sister in the flashy clothes. But Dee/Wangero doesn't want the quilts to destroy them. True, she wants to remove them from everyday use, but her motive is, after all, preservation, of personal family history in the context of larger cultural history, and preservation, as many recent feminist readers understand, of a valid text(ile) of women's tradition.

I am similarly engaged in making my own way through both family tradition and male and female literary traditions, taking what I want: for example, the copy of *Anna Karenina* that my grandmother brought with her on the boat from her Anatevka-like village (even though I can't read a word of Russian); her volumes of the works of Sholem Aleichem (even though I can't read a word of Yiddish). Many critics have faulted Dee/Wangero for trying to "preserve" her past in the sterile, academic hanging out of the family linen as though it is the formal blazon that people like me make it out to be in our scholarship. I used to fault her, too.

But after my meeting with Lucille, who so reminds me of Maggie though her visible scars are limited to her fingertips, I feel a strong kinship with Dee/Wangero, who, had she been in my shoes, would have been called upon Passover Seder after Passover Seder to read the part of The Wicked Son, who does not believe. Like Dee/Wangero, I am trying to negotiate the old by casting my lot with the new. But whereas Walker presents no evidence that Dee/Wangero questions her own motivations, I do: call it Jewish guilt; a habit of self-reflexively examining my assumptions borne of graduate courses in literature and theory; or a rhetorical strategy to fend off an imagined reader's criticism. Why did I ask to meet Lucille Sojourner in the first place? To talk with her about quilting and do serious scholarship, or to commission a quilt for my bed? An even more fundamental question, however, is why I'm so interested in quilting, I don't quilt myself, I don't collect quilts (although I have a few), no members of my family, immediate or extended, quilt. The tradition is foreign to my family. Is it, then, that to give me some identity—cultural, professional, ultimately personal—I have wrapped myself in the critical quilt of literary theory and feminist criticism, which created the academic interest in quilting in the first place? If Lucille, Maggie, and Dee/Wangero are each imprisoned in ways both literal and metaphoric, am I a prisoner not only of literary trends but also of capitalist production and consumption, the system that, according to Michel Foucault, necessitated the existence of prisons in the first place? Admittedly, I did end up paying Lucille to make me a quilt of my own. . . .

It's been over six years since I interviewed Lucille. Although I wrote to her several times, sending her at one point a photocopy of "Everyday Use," I never heard from her. Perhaps she had been offended by my offer of the story, thinking that I was condescending to enlighten her. I hadn't thought I was, but my naive motive, thinking that it might "brighten her day," might have been condescension after all. A few years ago Parchman Farm closed camp 25 to women inmates, who were moved to Jackson, where, for what it's worth, the chief proponent of "sense of place," Eudora Welty, whose mother was a West Virginian, lives.

I wonder if Lucille was ever granted parole. I wouldn't be surprised: she was an ideal prisoner, never causing trouble, doing little other than plying her needle. In abstract terms, terms admittedly lacking any immediate meaning for a prisoner, in her quilting she established her own *parole* from the general *langue* of art and humanity. The cover she quilted for me, patched in primary colors and backed in the bright red of Isis, the goddess of creativity, is that narrative that now gives me *parole*, passing down to me, as it were, like Maggie's quilts, her stories for everyday use. Even as I write this last sentence, however, I recognize that its allusions derive from scholarship and from a culture not originally my own; that this paper, if quiltlike in its narrative, is hardly for everyday use. Rather, it is a narrative designed to be metaphorically hung, to establish an identity for myself as scholar, teacher, writer, feminist, to be used as a blazon. . . .

JOHN UPDIKE

John Updike wrote a foreword to The Complete Stories of Franz Kafka *in 1983. Updike begins his essay by quoting "He," one of Kafka's aphorisms: "All that he does seems to him, it is true, extraordinarily new, but also, because of the incredible spate of new things, extraordinarily amateurish, indeed scarcely tolerable, incapable of becoming history, breaking short the chain of the generations, cutting off for the first time at its most profound source the music of the world, which before him could at least be divined. Sometimes in his arrogance he has more anxiety for the world than for himself." Updike has great sympathy for Kafka and has written about him with considerable perception.*

Kafka and "The Metamorphosis"   1983

The century since Franz Kafka was born has been marked by the idea of "modernism"—a self-consciousness new among centuries, a consciousness of being new. Sixty years after his death, Kafka epitomizes one aspect of this modern mind-set: a sensation of anxiety and shame whose center cannot be located and therefore cannot be placated; a sense of an infinite difficulty within things, impeding every step; a sensitivity acute beyond usefulness, as if the nervous system, flayed of its old hide of social usage and religious belief, must record every touch as pain. In Kafka's peculiar and highly original case this dreadful quality is mixed with immense tenderness, oddly good humor, and a certain severe and reassuring formality. The combination makes him an artist; but rarely can an artist have struggled against greater inner resistance and more sincere diffidence as to the worth of his art. . . .

Kafka dated his own maturity as a writer from the long night of September 22nd–23rd, 1912, in which he wrote "The Judgment" at a single eight-hour sitting. He confided to his diary that morning, "Only *in this way* can writing be done, only with such coherence, with such a complete opening out of the body and the soul." Yet the story is not quite free of the undeclared neurotic elements that twist the earlier work; the connection between the engagement and the father seems obscure, and the old man's fury illogical. But in staring at, with his hero Georg, "the bogey conjured up by his father," Kafka broke through to a great cavern of stored emotion. He loved this story, and among friends praised—he who deprecated almost everything from his own pen—its *Zweifellosigkeit*, its "indubitableness." Soon after its composition, he wrote, in a few weeks, "The Metamorphosis," an indubitable masterpiece. It begins with a fantastic premise, whereas in "The Judgment" events become fantastic. This premise—the gigantic insect—established in the first sentence, "The Metamorphosis" unfolds with a beautiful naturalness and a classic economy. It takes place in three acts: three times the metamorphosed Gregor Samsa ventures out of his room, with tumultuous results. The members of his family—rather simpler than Kafka's own, which had three sisters—dispose themselves around the central horror with a touching, as well as an amusing, plausibility. The father's fury, roused in defense of the fragile mother, stems directly from the action and inflicts a psychic wound gruesomely objectified in the rotting apple Gregor carries in his back; the evolutions of the sister, Grete, from shock to distasteful ministration to a certain sulky possessiveness and finally to exasperated indifference are beautifully sketched, with not a stroke too much. The terrible but terribly human tale ends with Grete's own metamorphosis, into a comely young woman. This great story resembles a great story of the nineteenth century, Tolstoy's "The Death of Ivan Ilych"; in both, a hitherto normal man lies hideously, suddenly stricken in the midst of a family whose irritated, banal daily existence flows around him. The abyss within life is revealed, but also life itself.

What kind of insect is Gregor? Popular belief has him a cockroach, which would be appropriate for a city apartment; and the creature's retiring nature and sleazy dietary preferences would seem to conform. But, as Vladimir Nabokov, who knew his entomology, pointed out in his lectures upon "The Metamorphosis" at Cornell University, Gregor is too broad and convex to be a cockroach. The charwoman calls him a "dung beetle" (*Mistkäfer*) but, Nabokov said, "it is obvious that the good woman is adding the epithet only to be friendly." Kafka's Eduard Raban of "Wedding Preparations" daydreams, walking along, "As I lie in bed I assume the shape of a big beetle, a stag beetle or a cockchafer, I think." Gregor Samsa, awaking, sees "numerous legs, which were pitifully thin compared to the rest of his bulk." If "numerous" is more than six, he must be a centipede—not an insect at all. From evidence in the story he is brown in color and about as long as the distance between a doorknob and the floor; he is broader than half a door. He has a voice at first, "but with a persistent horrible twittering squeak behind it like an undertone," which disappears as the story progresses. His jaws don't work as ours do but he has eyelids, nostrils, and a neck. He is, in short, impossible to picture except when the author wants to evoke his appearance, to bump the reader up against some astounding, poignant new aspect of Gregor's embodiment. The strange physical discomfort noted in the earlier work is here given its perfect allegorical envelope. A wonderful moment comes when Gregor, having been painfully striving to achieve human postures, drops to his feet:

> Hardly was he down when he experienced for the first time this morning a sense of physical comfort; his legs had firm ground under them; they were completely obedient, as he noted with joy; they even strove to carry him forward in whatever direction he chose; and he was inclined to believe that a final relief from all his sufferings was at hand.

When "The Metamorphosis" was to be published as a book in 1915, Kafka, fearful that the cover illustrator "might want to draw the insect itself," wrote the publisher, "Not that, please not that! . . . The insect itself cannot be depicted. It cannot even be shown from a distance." He suggested instead a scene of the family in the apartment with a locked door, or a door open and giving on darkness. Any theatrical or cinematic version of the story must founder on this point of external representation: A concrete image of the insect would be too distracting and shut off sympathy; such a version would lack the very heart of comedy and pathos which beats in the unsteady area between objective and subjective, where Gregor's insect and human selves swayingly struggle. Still half-asleep, he notes his extraordinary condition yet persists in remembering and trying to fulfill his duties as a travelling salesman and the mainstay of this household. Later, relegated by the family to the shadows of a room turned storage closet, he responds to violin music and creeps forward, covered with dust and trailing remnants of food, to claim his sister's love. Such scenes could not be done except with words. In this age that lives and dies by the visual, "The Metamorphosis" stands as a narrative absolutely literary, able to exist only where language and the mind's hazy wealth of imagery intersect.

"The Metamorphosis" stands also as a gateway to the world Kafka created after it. His themes and manner were now all in place. His mastery of official pomposity—the dialect of documents and men talking business—shows itself here for the first time, in the speeches of the chief clerk. Music will again be felt, by mice and dogs, as an overwhelming emanation in Kafka's later fables—a theme whose other side is the extreme sensitivity to noise, and the longing for unblemished silence, that Kafka shared with his hero in "The Burrow." Gregor's death scene, and Kafka's death wish, return in "A Hunger Artist"—the saddest, I think, of Kafka's stories, written by a dying man who was increasingly less sanguine (his correspondence reveals) about dying. The sweeping nature of the hunger artist's abstention is made plain by the opposing symbol of the panther who replaces him in his cage: "the joy of life streamed with such ardent passion from his throat that for the onlookers it was not easy to stand the shock of it." In 1920 Milena Jesenská wrote to Brod: "Frank cannot live. Frank does not have the capacity for living. . . . He is absolutely incapable of living, just as he is incapable of getting drunk. He possesses not the slightest refuge. For that reason he is exposed to all those things against which we are protected. He is like a naked man among a multitude who are dressed." After Gregor Samsa's incarnation, Kafka showed a fondness for naked heroes—animals who have complicated and even pedantic confessions to make but who also are distinguished by some keenly observed bestial traits—the ape of "A Report to an Academy" befouls himself and his fur jumps with fleas; the dog of "Investigations" recalls his young days when, very puppylike, "I believed that great things were going on around me of which I was the leader and to which I must lend my voice, things which must be wretchedly thrown aside if I did not run for them and wag my tail for them"; the mouse folk of "Josephine the Singer" pipe and multiply and are pervaded by an "unexpended, ineradicable childishness"; and the untaxonomic inhabitant of "The Burrow" represents the animal in all of us, his cheerful consumption of "small fry" existentially yoked to a terror of being consumed himself. An uncanny empathy broods above these zoömorphs, and invests them with more of their creator's soul than all but a few human characters receive. So a child, cowed and bored by the world of human adults, makes companions of pets and toy animals.

ALICE WALKER

Alice Walker wrote about Zora Neale Hurston in her collection In Search of Our Mothers' Gardens: Womanist Prose *(1983). There she also looked at Flannery O'Connor, Langston Hughes, Jean Toomer, and other writers from what she called her "womanist" perspective as a radical black woman. To clarify the meaning of her term, Walker added that "womanist is to feminist as purple is to lavender."*

Zora Neale Hurston: A Cautionary Tale and a Partisan View   1979

During the early and middle years of her career Zora was a cultural revolutionary simply because she was always herself. Her work, so vigorous among the rather pallid productions of many of her contemporaries, comes from the essence of black folk life. During her later life she became frightened of the life she had always dared bravely before. Her work too became reactionary, static, shockingly misguided and timid. (This is especially true of her last novel, *Seraphs on the Sewannee,* which is not even about black people, which is no crime, but *is* about white people for whom it is impossible to care, which is.)

A series of misfortunes battered Zora's spirit and her health. And she was broke.

Being broke made all the difference.

Without money of one's own in a capitalist society, there is no such thing as independence. This is one of the clearest lessons of Zora's life, and why I consider the telling of her life "a cautionary tale." We must learn from it what we can.

Without money, an illness, even a simple one, can undermine the will. Without money, getting into a hospital is problematic and getting out without money to pay for the treatment is nearly impossible. Without money, one becomes dependent on other people, who are likely to be—even in their kindness—erratic in their support and despotic in their expectations of return. Zora was forced to rely, like Tennessee Williams's Blanche,° "on the kindness of strangers." Can anything be more dangerous, if the strangers are forever in control? Zora, who worked so hard, was never able to make a living from her work.

She did not complain about not having money. She was not the type. (Several months ago I received a long letter from one of Zora's nieces, a bright ten-year-old, who explained to me that her aunt was so proud that the only way the family could guess she was ill or without funds was by realizing they had no idea where she was. Therefore, none of the family attended either Zora's sickbed or her funeral.) Those of us who have had "grants and fellowships from 'white folks'" know this aid is extended in precisely the way welfare is ex-

---

Tennessee Williams's Blanche: Main character in Williams's play *A Streetcar Named Desire* (1947).

tended in Mississippi. One is asked, *curtly,* more often than not: How much do you need *just to survive?* Then one is—if fortunate—given a third of that. What is amazing is that Zora, who became an orphan at nine, a runaway at fourteen, a maid and manicurist (because of necessity and not from love of the work) before she was twenty—with one dress—managed to become Zora Neale Hurston, author and anthropologist, at all.

For me, the most unfortunate thing Zora ever wrote is her autobiography. After the first several chapters, it rings false. One begins to hear the voice of someone whose life required the assistance of too many transitory "friends." A Taoist proverb states that *to act sincerely with the insincere is dangerous.* (A mistake blacks as a group have tended to make in America.) And so we have Zora sincerely offering gratitude and kind words to people one knows she could not have respected. But this unctuousness, so out of character for Zora, is also a result of dependency, a sign of her powerlessness, her inability to pay back her debts with anything but words. They must have been bitter ones for her. In her dependency, it should be remembered, Zora was not alone—because it is quite true that America does not support or honor us as human beings, let alone as blacks, women, and artists. We have taken help where it was offered because we are committed to what we do and to the survival of our work. Zora was committed to the survival of her people's cultural heritage as well.

In my mind, Zora Neale Hurston, Billie Holiday,° and Bessie Smith° form a sort of unholy trinity. Zora *belongs* in the tradition of black women singers, rather than among "the literati," at least to me. There were the extreme highs and lows of her life, her undaunted pursuit of adventure, passionate emotional and sexual experience, and her love of freedom. Like Billie and Bessie she followed her own road, believed in her own gods, pursued her own dreams, and refused to separate herself from "common" people. It would have been nice if the three of them had had one another to turn to, in times of need. I close my eyes and imagine them: Bessie would be in charge of all the money; Zora would keep Billie's masochistic tendencies in check and prevent her from singing embarrassing anything-for-a-man songs, thereby preventing Billie's heroin addiction. In return, Billie could be, along with Bessie, the family that Zora felt she never had.

We are a people. A people do not throw their geniuses away. And if they are thrown away, it is our duty *as artists and as witnesses for the future* to collect them again for the sake of our children, and, if necessary, bone by bone.

Billie Holiday: African American jazz singer (1915–1959) known for her pioneering vocal style and tragic life.
Bessie Smith: Prominent African American blues singer and song writer (1898–1937), the highest paid black artist in the United States in the 1920s.

EUDORA WELTY

Eudora Welty included this discussion of her story "The Worn Path" in her book The Eye of the Story *(1977). It appeared in the section "On Writing," along with her most extensive essays on the art of short fiction—essays that take up general topics such as place and time in fiction, and the art of reading and writing stories. Her reviews of the work of Isak Dinesen, Ralph Ellison, William Faulkner, and Virginia Woolf from the* New York Times *are also included in this collection.*

Is Phoenix Jackson's Grandson Really Dead? 1977

A story writer is more than happy to be read by students; the fact that these serious readers think and feel something in response to his work he finds life-giving. At the same time he may not always be able to reply to their specific questions in kind. I wondered if it might clarify something, for both the questioners and myself, if I set down a general reply to the question that comes to me most often in the mail, from both students and their teachers, after some classroom discussion. The unrivaled favorite is this: "Is Phoenix Jackson's grandson really *dead?*"

It refers to a short story I wrote years ago called "A Worn Path," which tells of a day's journey an old woman makes on foot from deep in the country into town and into a doctor's office on behalf of her little grandson; he is at home, periodically ill, and periodically she comes for his medicine; they give it to her as usual, she receives it and starts the journey back.

I had not meant to mystify readers by withholding any fact; it is not a writer's business to tease. The story is told through Phoenix's mind as she undertakes her errand. As the author at one with the character as I tell it, I must assume that the boy is alive. As the reader, you are free to think as you like, of course: The story invites you to believe that no matter what happens, Phoenix for as long as she is able to walk and can hold to her purpose will make her journey. The *possibility* that she would keep on even if he were dead is there in her devotion and its single-minded, single-track errand. Certainly the *artistic* truth, which should be good enough for the fact, lies in Phoenix's own answer to that question. When the nurse asks, "He isn't dead, is he?" she speaks for herself: "He still the same. He going to last."

The grandchild is the incentive. But it is the journey, the going of the errand, that is the story, and the question is not whether the grandchild is in reality alive or dead. It doesn't affect the outcome of the story or its meaning from start to finish. But it is not the question itself that has struck me as much as the idea, almost without exception implied in the asking, that for Phoenix's grandson to be dead would somehow make the story "better."

It's *all right*, I want to say to the students who write to me, for things to be what they appear to be, and for words to mean what they say. It's all right, too, for words and appearances to mean more than one thing—ambiguity is a fact of life. A fiction writer's responsibility covers not only what he presents as the facts of a given story but what he chooses to stir up as their implications; in the end, these implications, too, become facts, in the larger, fictional sense. But it is not all right, not in good faith, for things *not* to mean what they say.

The grandson's plight was real and it made the truth of the story, which is the story of an errand of love carried out. If the child no longer lived, the truth would persist in the "wornness" of the path. But his being dead can't increase the truth of the story, can't affect it one way or the other. I think I signal this, because the end of the story has been reached before old Phoenix gets home again: she simply starts back. To the question "Is the grandson really dead?" I could reply that it doesn't make any difference. I could also say that I did not make him up in order to let him play a trick on Phoenix. But my best answer would be: "*Phoenix* is alive."

The origin of a story is sometimes a trustworthy clue to the author—or can provide him with the clue—to its key image; maybe in this case it will do the same for the reader. One day I saw a solitary old woman like Phoenix. She was walking; I saw her, at middle distance, in a winter country landscape, and watched her slowly make her way across my line of vision. That sight of her made me write the story. I invented an errand for her, but that only seemed a living part of the figure she was herself: What errand other than for someone else could be making her go? And her going was the first thing, her persisting in her landscape was the real thing, and the first and the real were what I wanted and worked to keep. I brought her up close enough, by imagination, to describe her face, make her present to the eyes, but the full-length figure moving across the winter fields was the indelible one and the image to keep, and the perspective extending into the vanishing distance the true one to hold in mind.

I invented for my character, as I wrote, some passing adventures—some dreams and harassments and a small triumph or two, some jolts to her pride, some flights of fancy to console her, one or two encounters to scare her, a moment that gave her cause to feel ashamed, a moment to dance and preen— for it had to be a *journey,* and all these things belonged to that, parts of life's uncertainty.

A narrative line is in its deeper sense, of course, the tracing out of a meaning, and the real continuity of a story lies in this probing forward. The real dramatic force of a story depends on the strength of the emotion that has set it going. The emotional value is the measure of the reach of the story. What gives any such content to "A Worn Path" is not its circumstances but its *subject:* the deep-grained habit of love.

What I hoped would come clear was that in the whole surround of this story, the world it threads through, the only certain thing at all is the worn path. The habit of love cuts through confusion and stumbles or contrives its way out of difficulty, it remembers the way even when it forgets, for a dumfounded moment, its reason for being. The path is the thing that matters.

Her victory—old Phoenix's—is when she sees the diploma in the doctor's office, when she finds "nailed up on the wall the document that had been stamped with the gold seal and framed in the gold frame, which matched the dream that was hung up in her head." The return with the medicine is just a matter of retracing her own footsteps. It is the part of the journey, and of the story, that can now go without saying.

In the matter of function, old Phoenix's way might even do as a sort of parallel to your way of work if you are a writer of stories. The way to get there is the all-important, all-absorbing problem, and this problem is your reason for undertaking the story. Your only guide, too, is your sureness about your subject, about what this subject is. Like Phoenix, you work all your life to find your way, through all the obstructions and the false appearances and the upsets you may have brought on yourself, to reach a meaning — using inventions of your imagination, perhaps helped out by your dreams and bits of good luck. And finally too, like Phoenix, you have to assume that what you are working in aid of is life, not death.

But you would make the trip anyway — wouldn't you? — just on hope.

Eudora Welty included her statement on Anton Chekhov's "The Darling" in her book The Eye of the Story (1977). *In her brief reading she analyzes the elements of plot ("aware of its clear open stress, the variations all springing from Chekhov's boundless and minute perception of character"), character motivation ("maternalism: for there it is most naturally innocent of anything but formless, thoughtless, blameless embracing; the true innocence is in never perceiving"), and theme ("Protest to the darlings of this world will always be [delivered] — out of inward and silent rebellion alone").*

Plot and Character in Chekhov's "The Darling"   1977

Clearly, the fact that stories have plots in common is of no more account than that many people have blue eyes. Plots are, indeed, what the story writer sees with, and so do we as we read. The plot is the Why. Why? is asked and replied to at various depths; the fishes in the sea are bigger the deeper we go. To learn that character is a more awe-inspiring fish and (in a short story, though not, I think, in a novel) one some degrees deeper down than situation, we have only to read Chekhov. What constitutes the reality of his characters is what they reveal to us. And the possibility that they may indeed reveal everything is what makes fictional characters differ so greatly from us in real life; yet isn't it strange that they don't really *seem* to differ? This is one clue to the extraordinary magnitude of character in fiction. Characters in the plot connect us with the vastness of our secret life, which is endlessly explorable. This is their role. What happens to them is what they have been put here to show.

In his story "The Darling," the darling's first husband, the theater manager, dies suddenly *because* of the darling's sweet passivity; this is the causality of fiction. In everyday or real life he might have held on to his health for years. But under Chekhov's hand he is living and dying in dependence on, and in revelation of, Olenka's character. He can only last a page and a half. Only by force of the story's circumstance is he here at all; Olenka took him up to begin with because he lived next door. . . . Kukin proposes and they are married. . . . And when Kukin dies, Olenka's cry of heartbreak is this: "Vanitchka, my precious, my darling! Why did I ever meet you! Why did I know you and love you! Your poor brokenhearted Olenka is all alone without you!"

With variations the pattern is repeated, and we are made to feel it as plot, aware of its clear open stress, the variations all springing from Chekhov's boundless and minute perception of character. The timber-merchant, another neighbor, is the one who walks home from the funeral with Olenka. The outcome follows tenderly, is only natural. After three days, he calls. "He did not stay long, only about ten minutes, and he did not say much, but when he left, Olenka loved him — loved him so much that she lay awake all night in a perfect fever."

Olenka and Pustovalov get along very well together when they are married. . . . Even in her dreams Olenka is in the timber business, dreaming of "perfect mountains of planks and boards," and cries out in her sleep, so that Pustovalov says to her tenderly, "Olenka, what's the matter, darling? Cross yourself!" But the timber merchant inevitably goes out in the timber yard one day without his cap on; he catches cold and dies, to leave Olenka a widow once more. "I've nobody, now you've left me, my darling," she sobs after the funeral. "How can I live without you?"

And the timber merchant is succeeded by a veterinary surgeon — who gets transferred to Siberia. But the plot is not repetition — it is direction. The love which Olenka bears to whatever is nearest her reaches its final and, we discover, its truest mold in maternalism: For there it is most naturally innocent of anything but formless, thoughtless, blameless *embracing*; the true innocence is in never perceiving. Only mother love could endure in a pursuit of such blind regard, caring so little for the reality of either life involved so long as love wraps them together, Chekhov tells us — unpretentiously, as he tells everything, and with the simplest of concluding episodes. Olenka's character is seen purely then for what it is: limpid reflection, mindless and purposeless regard, love that falls like the sun and rain on all alike, vacant when there is nothing to reflect.

We know this because, before her final chance to love, Olenka is shown to us truly alone:

> [She] got thinner and plainer; and when people met her in the street they did not look at her as they used to, and did not smile to her; evidently her best years were over and left behind, and now a new sort of life had begun for her, which did not bear thinking about. . . . And what was worst of all, she had no opinions of any sort. She saw the objects about her and understood what she saw, but could not form any opinions about them, and did not know what to talk about. And how awful it is not to have any opinions! She wanted a love that would absorb her whole being, her whole soul and reason — that would give her ideas and an object in her life, and would warm her old blood.

The answer is Sasha, the ten-year-old son of the veterinary surgeon, an unexpected blessing from Siberia — a schoolchild. The veterinarian has another wife now, but this no longer matters. "Olenka, with arms akimbo, walked about the yard giving directions. Her face was beaming, and she was brisk and alert, as though she had waked from a long sleep. . . ." "An island is a piece of land entirely surrounded by water," Sasha reads aloud. " 'An island is a piece of land,' she repeated, and this was the first opinion to which she gave utterance with positive conviction, after so many years of silence and dearth of ideas." She would follow Sasha halfway to school, until he told her to go back. She would go to bed thinking blissfully of Sasha, "who lay sound asleep in the next room, sometimes crying out in his sleep, 'I'll give it to you! Get away! Shut up!' "

The darling herself *is* the story; all else is sacrificed to her; deaths and departures are perfunctory and to be expected. The last words of the story are the child's and a protest, but they are delivered in his sleep, as indeed protest to the darlings of this world will always be—out of inward and silent rebellion alone, as this master makes plain.

6.

Conversations on Stories and Storytellers

RAYMOND CARVER

EDGAR ALLAN POE

FLANNERY O'CONNOR

Conversations on Raymond Carver's Writing Process

Raymond Carver offers a clear example of how a contemporary author has responded to the work of earlier short story writers by following a line of thought that links him with his predecessors. Carver acknowledged the influence of Ernest Hemingway and Flannery O'Connor in his essay "On Writing." He also described his class with the young novelist John Gardner at Chico State College in California in "Creative Writing 101." In 1982 Carver discussed the origin of "The Bath" (p. 85) and "A Small, Good Thing" (p. 90) with the reporter Jim Naughton for the Syracuse Post-Standard. *Five years later, the academic critic Kathleen Westfall Shute wrote an extended analysis of the two stories for the* Hollins Critic. *Finally, Carver's editor Tom Jenks recalled Carver's explanation of the origin of "Cathedral" (p. 75), and A. O. Scott gave an overview of Carver's career.*

RAYMOND CARVER

On Writing   1981

Back in the mid-1960s, I found I was having trouble concentrating my attention on long narrative fiction. For a time I experienced difficulty in trying to read it as well as in attempting to write it. My attention span had gone out on me; I no longer had the patience to try to write novels. It's an involved story, too tedious to talk about here. But I know it has much to do now with why I write poems and short stories. Get in, get out. Don't linger. Go on. It could be that I lost any great ambitions at about the same time, in my late twenties. If I did, I think it was good it happened. Ambition and a little luck are good things for a writer to have going for him. Too much ambition and bad luck, or no luck at all, can be killing. There has to be talent.

Some writers have a bunch of talent; I don't know any writers who are without it. But a unique and exact way of looking at things, and finding the right context for expressing that way of looking, that's something else. *The World According to Garp* is, of course, the marvelous world according to John Irving. There is another world according to Flannery O'Connor, and others according to William Faulkner and Ernest Hemingway. There are worlds according to Cheever, Updike, Singer, Stanley Elkin, Ann Beattie, Cynthia Ozick, Donald Barthelme, Mary Robison, William Kittredge, Barry Hannah, Ursula K. Le Guin. Every great or even every very good writer makes the world over according to his own specifications.

It's akin to style, what I'm talking about, but it isn't style alone. It is the writer's particular and unmistakable signature on everything he writes. It is his world and no other. This is one of the things that distinguishes one writer from another. Not talent. There's plenty of that around. But a writer who has some

Raymond Carver. (© Marion Ettlinger.)

special way of looking at things and who gives artistic expression to that way of looking: that writer may be around for a time.

Isak Dinesen said that she wrote a little every day, without hope and without despair. Someday I'll put that on a three-by-five card and tape it to the wall beside my desk. I have some three-by-five cards on the wall now.

"Fundamental accuracy of statement is the ONE sole morality of writing." Ezra Pound. It is not everything by ANY means, but if a writer has "fundamental accuracy of statement" going for him, he's at least on the right track.

I have a three-by-five up there with this fragment of a sentence from a story by Chekhov: ". . . and suddenly everything became clear to him." I find these words filled with wonder and possibility. I love their simple clarity, and the hint of revelation that's implied. There is mystery, too. What has been unclear before? Why is it just now becoming clear? What's happened? Most of all — what now? There are consequences as a result of such sudden awakenings. I feel a sharp sense of relief — and anticipation.

I overheard the writer Geoffrey Wolff say "No cheap tricks" to a group of writing students. That should go on a three-by-five card. I'd amend it a little to "No tricks." Period. I hate tricks. At the first sign of a trick or a gimmick in a piece of fiction, a cheap trick or even an elaborate trick, I tend to look for cover. Tricks are ultimately boring, and I get bored easily, which may go along with my not having much of an attention span. But extremely clever chi-chi writing, or just plain tomfoolery writing, puts me to sleep. Writers don't need tricks or gimmicks or even necessarily need to be the smartest fellows on the block. At the risk of appearing foolish, a writer sometimes needs to be able to just stand and gape at this or that thing — a sunset or an old shoe — in absolute and simple amazement.

Some months back, in the *New York Times Book Review*, John Barth said that ten years ago most of the students in his fiction writing seminar were interested in "formal innovation," and this no longer seems to be the case. He's a little worried that writers are going to start writing mom-and-pop novels in the 1980s. He worries that experimentation may be on the way out, along with liberalism. I get a little nervous if I find myself within earshot of somber discussions about "formal innovation" in fiction writing. Too often "experimentation" is a license to be careless, silly, or imitative in the writing. Even worse, a license to try to brutalize or alienate the reader. Too often such writing gives us no news of the world, or else describes a desert landscape and that's all — a few dunes and lizards here and there, but no people; a place uninhabited by anything recognizably human, a place of interest only to a few scientific specialists.

It should be noted that real experiment in fiction is original, hard-earned and cause for rejoicing. But someone else's way of looking at things — Barthelme's, for instance — should not be chased after by other writers. It won't work. There is only one Barthelme, and for another writer to try to appropriate Barthelme's peculiar sensibility or mise en scène under the rubric of innovation is for that writer to mess around with chaos and disaster and, worse, self-deception. The real experimenters have to Make It New, as Pound urged, and in the process have to find things out for themselves. But if writers haven't taken leave of their senses, they also want to stay in touch with us, they want to carry news from their world to ours.

It's possible, in a poem or a short story, to write about commonplace things and objects using commonplace but precise language, and to endow those things — a chair, a window curtain, a fork, a stone, a woman's earring —

with immense, even startling power. It is possible to write a line of seemingly innocuous dialogue and have it send a chill along the reader's spine—the source of artistic delight, as Nabokov would have it. That's the kind of writing that most interests me. I hate sloppy or haphazard writing whether it flies under the banner of experimentation or else is just clumsily rendered realism. In Isaac Babel's wonderful short story, "Guy de Maupassant," the narrator has this to say about the writing of fiction: "No iron can pierce the heart with such force as a period put just at the right place." This too ought to go on a three-by-five.

Evan Connell said once that he knew he was finished with a short story when he found himself going through it and taking out commas and then going through the story again and putting commas back in the same places. I like that way of working on something. I respect that kind of care for what is being done. That's all we have, finally, the words, and they had better be the right ones, with the punctuation in the right places so that they can best say what they are meant to say. If the words are heavy with the writer's own unbridled emotions, or if they are imprecise and inaccurate for some other reason—if the words are in any way blurred—the reader's eyes will slide right over them and nothing will be achieved. The reader's own artistic sense will simply not be engaged. Henry James called this sort of hapless writing "weak specification."

I have friends who've told me they had to hurry a book because they needed the money, their editor or their wife was leaning on them or leaving them—something, some apology for the writing not being very good. "It would have been better if I'd taken the time." I was dumbfounded when I heard a novelist friend say this. I still am, if I think about it, which I don't. It's none of my business. But if the writing can't be made as good as it is within us to make it, then why do it? In the end, the satisfaction of having done our best, and the proof of that labor, is the one thing we can take into the grave. I wanted to say to my friend, for heaven's sake go do something else. There have to be easier and maybe more honest ways to try and earn a living. Or else just do it to the best of your abilities, your talents, and then don't justify or make excuses. Don't complain, don't explain.

In an essay called, simply enough, "Writing Short Stories," Flannery O'Connor talks about writing as an act of discovery. O'Connor says she most often did not know where she was going when she sat down to work on a short story. She says she doubts that many writers know where they are going when they begin something. She uses "Good Country People" as an example of how she put together a short story whose ending she could not even guess at until she was nearly there:

> When I started writing that story, I didn't know there was going to be a Ph.D. with a wooden leg in it. I merely found myself one morning writing a description of two women I knew something about, and before I realized it, I had equipped one of them with a daughter with a wooden leg. I brought in the Bible salesman, but I had no idea what I was going to do with him. I didn't know he was going to steal that wooden leg until ten or twelve lines before he did it, but when I found out that this was what was going to happen, I realized it was inevitable.

When I read this some years ago it came as a shock that she, or anyone for that matter, wrote stories in this fashion. I thought this was my uncomfortable secret, and I was a little uneasy with it. For sure I thought this way of working on a short story somehow revealed my own shortcomings. I remember being tremendously heartened by reading what she had to say on the subject.

I once sat down to write what turned out to be a pretty good story, though only the first sentence of the story had offered itself to me when I began it. For several days I'd been going around with this sentence in my head: "He was running the vacuum cleaner when the telephone rang." I knew a story was there and that it wanted telling. I felt it in my bones, that a story belonged with that beginning, if I could just have the time to write it. I found the time, an entire day — twelve, fifteen hours even — if I wanted to make use of it. I did, and I sat down in the morning and wrote the first sentence, and other sentences promptly began to attach themselves. I made the story just as I'd make a poem; one line and then the next, and the next. Pretty soon I could see a story, and I knew it was my story, the one I'd been wanting to write.

I like it when there is some feeling of threat or sense of menace in short stories. I think a little menace is fine to have in a story. For one thing, it's good for the circulation. There has to be tension, a sense that something is imminent, that certain things are in relentless motion, or else, most often, there simply won't be a story. What creates tension in a piece of fiction is partly the way the concrete words are linked together to make up the visible action of the story. But it's also the things that are left out, that are implied, the landscape just under the smooth (but sometimes broken and unsettled) surface of things.

V. S. Pritchett's° definition of a short story is "something glimpsed from the corner of the eye, in passing." Notice the "glimpse" part of this. First the glimpse. Then the glimpse given life, turned into something that illuminates the moment and may, if we're lucky — that word again — have even further-ranging consequences and meaning. The short story writer's task is to invest the glimpse with all that is in his power. He'll bring his intelligence and literary skill to bear (his talent), his sense of proportion and sense of the fitness of things: of how things out there really are and how he sees those things — like no one else sees them. And this is done through the use of clear and specific language, language used so as to bring to life the details that will light up the story for the reader. For the details to be concrete and convey meaning, the language must be accurate and precisely given. The words can be so precise they may even sound flat, but they can still carry; if used right, they can hit all the notes.

Creative Writing 101   1983

A long time ago — it was the summer of 1958 — my wife and I and our two baby children moved from Yakima, Washington, to a little town outside of Chico, California. There we found an old house and paid twenty-five dollars a

---

V. S. Pritchett: British master of the short story and literary critic (1900–1997).

month rent. In order to finance this move, I'd had to borrow a hundred and twenty-five dollars from a druggist I'd delivered prescriptions for, a man named Bill Barton.

This is by way of saying that in those days my wife and I were stone broke. We had to eke out a living, but the plan was that I would take classes at what was then called Chico State College. But for as far back as I can remember, long before we moved to California in search of a different life and our slice of the American pie, I'd wanted to be a writer. I wanted to write, and I wanted to write anything — fiction, of course, but also poetry, plays, scripts, articles for *Sports Afield*, *True*, *Argosy*, and *Rogue* (some of the magazines I was then reading), pieces for the local newspaper — anything that involved putting words together to make something coherent and of interest to someone besides myself. But at the time of our move, I felt in my bones I had to get some education in order to go along with being a writer. I put a very high premium on education then — much higher in those days than now, I'm sure, but that's because I'm older and have an education. Understand that nobody in my family had ever gone to college or for that matter had got beyond the mandatory eighth grade in high school. I didn't know *anything*, but I knew I didn't know anything.

So along with this desire to get an education, I had this very strong desire to write; it was a desire so strong that, with the encouragement I was given in college, and the insight acquired, I kept on writing long after "good sense" and the "cold facts" — the "realities" of my life told me, time and again, that I ought to quit, stop the dreaming, quietly go ahead and do something else.

That fall at Chico State I enrolled in classes that most freshman students have to take, but I enrolled as well for something called Creative Writing 101. This course was going to be taught by a new faculty member named John Gardner, who was already surrounded by a bit of mystery and romance. It was said that he'd taught previously at Oberlin College but had left there for some reason that wasn't made clear. One student said Gardner had been fired — students, like everyone else, thrive on rumor and intrigue — and another student said Gardner had simply quit after some kind of flap. Someone else said his teaching load at Oberlin, four or five classes of freshman English each semester, had been too heavy and that he couldn't find time to write. For it was said that Gardner was a real, that is to say a practicing, writer — someone who had written novels and short stories. In any case, he was going to teach CW 101 at Chico State, and I signed up.

I was excited about taking a course from a real writer. I'd never laid eyes on a writer before, and I was in awe. But where were these novels and short stories, I wanted to know. Well, nothing had been published yet. It was said that he couldn't get his work published and that he carried it around with him in boxes. (After I became his student, I was to see those boxes of manuscript. Gardner had become aware of my difficulty in finding a place to work. He knew I had a young family and cramped quarters at home. He offered me the key to his office. I see that gift now as a turning point. It was a gift not made casually, and I took it, I think, as a kind of mandate — for that's what it was. I spent part of every Saturday and Sunday in his office, which is where he kept the boxes of manuscript. The boxes were stacked up on the floor beside the desk. *Nickel Mountain,* grease-pencilled on one of the boxes, is the only title I recall. But it was in his office, within sight of his unpublished books, that I undertook my first serious attempts at writing.) . . .

For short story writers in his class, the requirement was one story, ten to fifteen pages in length. For people who wanted to write a novel—I think there must have been one or two of these souls—a chapter of around twenty pages, along with an outline of the rest. The kicker was that this one short story, or the chapter of the novel, might have to be revised ten times in the course of the semester for Gardner to be satisfied with it. It was a basic tenet of his that a writer found what he wanted to say in the ongoing process of seeing what he'd said. And this seeing, or seeing more clearly, came about through revision. He *believed* in revision, endless revision; it was something very close to his heart and something he felt was vital for writers, at whatever stage of their development. And he never seemed to lose patience rereading a student story, even though he might have seen it in five previous incarnations.

I think his idea of a short story in 1958 was still pretty much his idea of a short story in 1982; it was something that had a recognizable beginning, middle, and an end to it. Once in a while he'd go to the blackboard and draw a diagram to illustrate a point he wanted to make about rising or falling emotion in a story—peaks, valleys, plateaus, resolution, *denouement,* things like that. Try as I might, I couldn't muster a great deal of interest or really understand this side of things, the stuff he put on the blackboard. But what I did understand was the way he would comment on a student story that was undergoing class discussion. Gardner might wonder aloud about the author's reasons for writing a story about a crippled person, say, and leaving out the fact of the character's crippledness until the very end of the story. "So you think it's a good idea not to let the reader know this man is crippled until the last sentence?" His tone of voice conveyed his disapproval, and it didn't take more than an instant for everyone in class, including the author of the story, to see that it wasn't a good strategy to use. Any strategy that kept important and necessary information away from the reader in the hope of overcoming him by surprise at the end of the story was cheating.

In class he was always referring to writers whose names I was not familiar with. Or if I knew their names, I'd never read the work. . . . He talked about James Joyce and Flaubert and Isak Dinesen as if they lived just down the road, in Yuba City. He said, "I'm here to tell you who to read as well as teach you how to write." I'd leave class in a daze and make straight for the library to find books by these writers he was talking about.

Hemingway and Faulkner were the reigning authors in those days. But altogether I'd probably read at the most two or three books by these fellows. Anyway, they were so well-known and so much talked about, they couldn't be all that good, could they? I remember Gardner telling me, "Read all the Faulkner you can get your hands on, and then read all of Hemingway to clean the Faulkner out of your system."

He introduced us to the "little" or literary periodicals by bringing a box of these magazines to class one day and passing them around so that we could acquaint ourselves with their names, see what they looked like and what they felt like to hold in the hand. He told us that this was where most of the best fiction in the country and just about all of the poetry was appearing. Fiction, poetry, literary essays, book reviews of recent books, criticism of *living* authors *by* living authors. I felt wild with discovery in those days.

For the seven or eight of us who were in his class, he ordered heavy black binders and told us we should keep our written work in these. He kept his own work in such binders, he said, and of course that settled it for us. We carried our stories in those binders and felt we were special, exclusive, singled out from others. And so we were.

I don't know how Gardner might have been with other students when it came time to have conferences with them about their work. I suspect he gave everybody a good amount of attention. But it was and still is my impression that during that period he took my stories more seriously, read them closer and more carefully, than I had any right to expect. I was completely unprepared for the kind of criticism I received from him. Before our conference he would have marked up my story, crossing out unacceptable sentences, phrases, individual words, even some of the punctuation; and he gave me to understand that these deletions were not negotiable. In other cases he would bracket sentences, phrases, or individual words, and these were items we'd talk about, these cases were negotiable. And he wouldn't hesitate to add something to what I'd written — a word here and there, or else a few words, maybe a sentence that would make clear what I was trying to say. We'd discuss commas in my story as if nothing else in the world mattered more at that moment — and, indeed, it did not. He was always looking to find something to praise. When there was a sentence, a line of dialogue, or a narrative passage that he liked, something that he thought "worked" and moved the story along in some pleasant or unexpected way, he'd write "Nice" in the margin, or else "Good!" And seeing these comments, my heart would lift.

It was close, line-by-line criticism he was giving me, and the reasons behind the criticism, why something ought to be this way instead of that; and it was invaluable to me in my development as a writer. After this kind of detailed talk about the text, we'd talk about the larger concerns of the story, the "problem" it was trying to throw light on, the conflict it was trying to grapple with, and how the story might or might not fit into the grand scheme of story writing. It was his conviction that if the words in the story were blurred because of the author's insensitivity, carelessness, or sentimentality, then the story suffered from a tremendous handicap. But there was something even worse and something that must be avoided at all costs: if the words and the sentiments were dishonest, the author was faking it, writing about things he didn't care about or believe in, then nobody could ever care anything about it.

A writer's values and craft. This is what the man taught and what he stood for, and this is what I've kept by me in the years since that brief but all-important time.

JIM NAUGHTON

As Raymond Carver Muses, His Stature Grows   1982

When Raymond Carver was a boy he was walking to school with a friend who got hit by a car. The boy wasn't hurt, but years later, Carver wondered what if?

Several years ago Carver's telephone rang late at night. When he answered, the caller hung up. Carver was not disturbed by the call, but he wondered what if the call had come when he was upset about something else?

Two years ago Carver turned the fruits of his wonderings into a short story called "The Bath," which was published in *What We Talk About When We Talk About Love,* a critically acclaimed collection that was featured on the front page of *The New York Times Book Review.*

Still, when he thought about the story, Carver wondered what if he had written it differently?

During his Christmas vacation last year in early January, he sat down to answer the question. When he finished the new version, Carver remembers feeling "a rush" because he had written something special.

The story that emerged, "A Small, Good Thing," was recently awarded first prize by the editor of *Prize Stories 1983: The O. Henry Awards,* which will be published in April by Doubleday. The prize-winning story is generally recognized as the best short story published in the country in the previous year.

"A Small, Good Thing," which was published in the literary magazine *Ploughshares* in the summer of 1982, deals with parents' anguish after their child is hit by a car and later, mysteriously, dies.

Carver went back to the story because it was "unfinished business."

"I wrote the story and I didn't go far enough with it," he said in his office at Syracuse University Monday.

"I saw a place to stop it and I stopped it . . . but the notion of what could have happened stayed with me."

William Abrahams, who edited the collection and made the choice, said he feels the story marks a new direction in Carver's career.

"I think it's a magnificent story, deeply moving. I think it's one of the most impressive he's ever written.

"The original can't compare to this," he said. "The original seemed like the bare bones of a story he could have done.

"In this new version which must be at least twice the length, he's able to develop the people as people. All this has a terrific intensity."

Carver too feels his writing has taken a new turn. "I feel it is [a departure]," he said. "All those stories I wrote last winter are different.

"There is definitely a change going on in my writing and I'm glad of it. It happened when I wrote the story 'Cathedral.' I date the change from that story."

"Cathedral" has won a distinction of its own. It is the first story in *The Best American Short Stories 1982,* which was edited by Carver's friend, the late John Gardner.

"These stories are fuller, more generous somehow," Carver said of his recent work. "I hope without losing any of the other virtues."

He said the change occurred because: "I went as far as I wanted to go with reducing the stories to bare bones minimums."

Reducing stories to bare bones minimums is how Carver made his name as a fiction writer. His collection of stories *Will You Please Be Quiet, Please?* was nominated for the National Book Award in 1977.

"That put him on the map in terms of the general public," said Tobias Wolff, Carver's colleague in Syracuse University's Creative Writing Program. Wolff has had two of his own stories included in previous editions of the O. Henry collection.

"He has for at least ten years now been considered one of its best practitioners by anyone who is aware of the state of the short story," he said.

Carver did not come easily to this eminence. He grew up in a working-class family in Yakima, Washington, married young and worked as a laborer. He was nineteen when he met Gardner, then an unpublished writer teaching at Chico State College in California. Carver was sweeping floors to feed his young wife and their two children and writing on the side. In the early '60s Gardner gave him encouragement and the key to his office so he would have a place to write.

Carver published books of poetry in 1968 and 1970, struggling to support his family all the while. His marriage broke up after a trip to the Middle East in the early '70s, but it was around that point that his stories began to be noticed. *Esquire* bought a story called "Neighbors" and several others. He published another book of poetry and the critically acclaimed *Will You Please Be Quiet, Please?* in 1976. In the six years since then his popularity has increased dramatically.

The style that made Carver famous is best characterized by some words of his own taken from "The Bath." "No pleasantries, just this small exchange, the barest information, nothing that was not necessary."

This sparsely eloquent style became so well known in literary circles that Abrahams says he reads ten to fifteen stories a year by people who are trying to write like Raymond Carver.

Some critics have charged that Carver's work is too bare, that it is minimalistic. Wolff disagrees. "There is a tremendous richness, a music to his work. His work has the kind of music that Hemingway's had."

Abrahams, who felt things were "deliberately flattened out" in some of Carver's early work, said his recent stories have "taken him to a higher level of art."

For his efforts Carver joins writers like Hemingway, Fitzgerald, Faulkner, Sherwood Anderson, Ring Lardner, Katherine Anne Porter, Flannery O'Connor, Isaac Bashevis Singer, and Joyce Carol Oates, as first-prize winners.

Abrahams makes an even headier comparison. "It reminds me of Chekhov, to tell you the truth," he said.

Success has changed Raymond Carver's life, but not fundamentally. He still lives quietly on Maryland Avenue and teaches his writing classes at the university. He is on the road a bit more often.

"I'm busier at every level," he said. "But it hasn't changed the way I feel about myself or my family or my loved ones.

"I feel comfortable with my life. Not comfortable like a fat lazy cat, but comfortable, you know what I mean, comfortable being in my own skin."

KATHLEEN WESTFALL SHUTE

On "The Bath" and "A Small, Good Thing"   1987

. . . Clearly, Raymond Carver's fiction is in flux. The stories in *Fires* and *Cathedral* seem to me richer, more emotionally and artistically complex than the earlier works. Permeated now by subtle shades of choice and option, Carver's "landscape of characters," as Robert Houston has fittingly called it in *The Nation*, resonates with an authenticity, a sense of the "real America," that was unrealized heretofore. How great this philosophic and creative transformation is can be readily appreciated by a comparative detailing of the structures and "obsessions" (as Carver dislikes the term "themes") in stories like "The Bath" and its new version "A Small, Good Thing" and in the two variations of "So Much Water So Close to Home." In light of Carver's new, more optimistic version, these are fictions that, as he explained to Larry McCaffery and Sinda Gregory (*Alive and Writing*, University of Illinois Press, 1987), were in clear need of being "enhanced, redrawn, reimagined" (69).

Like so many of the tales in *What We Talk About When We Talk About Love* and the other collections, "The Bath" focuses on the dilemmas engendered when, as Thomas R. Edwards has written in the *New York Review of Books*, "marginal lives are intruded upon by mystery, a sense of something larger or more elemental" than what has been previously experienced. In "The Bath," with a stroke that is typically Carverian, this "mystery" is death—or, at least, the real possibility of it when a young boy, on his birthday, is struck by a hit-and-run car. Lapsing into a "sleep-like" state, the child lingers in the hospital, his terrified and confused parents hovering near. Their vigil, which would be horrifying enough, is further menaced when, on brief trips home to bathe and feed the dog, they are subjected to ominous calls "about Scotty" from a baker enraged about "the Birthday Boy's" expensive and now-forgotten cake.

Despite evidence of a genuinely loving domesticity and a somewhat affluent (at least, solidly middle-class) lifestyle, the characters in "The Bath" are nonetheless typical of Carver's "down-and-outers," his people on the verge. Like the rock-throwing protagonist in "Viewfinder" or the battling young parents in "Popular Mechanics," these folks are totems, faceless, nearly nameless emblems of a class. While the baker is deftly particularized by his "watery eyes" and the "curious apron," which loops about him in the fashion of a straight-jacket to end in a "very thick knot," the parents and child go without description. Two thirds of the way through the story, and then almost grudgingly, we are finally given a name for the family—Weiss. And while the mother's Christian name does manage to slip out in conversation, we are never told the father's.

Skeletally drawn, the Weisses reveal little of themselves. Though they no doubt entertain vague, unspoken dreams—symbolically evidenced by the futuristic cake for Scotty with its rocketship and stars—they, and all the other characters here, are clearly enmeshed in the unexamined life. This is Carver's "real America": a netherland of work-place, home, and shopping centers. With junk food for the body (characteristically, Scotty is munching potato chips as he is struck) and even junkier sentiments for the soul (Scotty's young companion, holding the bag after his friend has crumpled in the gutter, actually wonders "if he should finish the rest or continue on to school"), perhaps it is easier not to think, not to question, to take the bad curves and good in life for granted. In "The Bath," it is the unnamed father who senses this. Driving home from the hospital "faster than he should," he dimly realizes that "It had been a good life till now. There had been work, fatherhood, family. He had been lucky and happy." But beyond this vaguely articulable grocery-list of good things, he seems unable to go. In the shadow of this overwhelming mystery, "Fear made him want to take a bath." And with this act, he tries, unsuccessfully, to wash all thought from him as though it were sin.

In "The Bath," this moment is the closest we come to insight, epiphany. But, true to the harsh parameters Carver has already drawn, it is brushed aside by the ritual cleansing and, of even greater import, the increasing menace from the outside world: that ringing phone, the unrecognized voice with its torturing accusations.

In a world where ordinary kindness seems so often proscribed, where the larger community seems simply not to exist, we are not surprised that understanding of the self and others is limited, communication negligible or, worse, mere "human noise" ("What We Talk About When We Talk About Love"). As the tale progresses towards its final horror, we witness growing confusion, an increasing inability to define and name. When the father suggests that the dog might need to be fed, the mother makes a counterproposal of calling the neighbors: "Someone will feed him if you ask them to." Trying to conjure a name, she cannot come up with one. Even the doctors shilly-shally with words, refusing to define the boy's condition, to say if it is "coma" or not. The parents admit to prayer about their son, but it seems clear that no one is listening. In the end, they are left in limbo: their child hovering in some unnameable state, caught between existence and extinction, while the phone rings a final time. "It's about Scotty," the voice tells them. "Yes, it's about Scotty."

Winner of the Carlos Fuentes Award for Fiction, "The Bath" is obviously a masterwork of American minimalism and a product of Carver's own early aesthetic: "Get in, get out. Don't linger. Go On." Typical of the other stories in *What We Talk About,* the style admits "nothing vague, or blurred, no smoked-glass prose" (*Fires* 28). Indeed, its language is so attenuated, so pared of ornament and intentional ambiguity, so stunningly bare, it is almost, as David Boxer and Cassandra Phillips have claimed, "photorealistic." But however successful "The Bath" may be on its own minimalist terms—however mimetic, as Michael Gorra observes, its "intentional poverty [and] anorexia" of style is of "the spiritual poverty of [the] characters' lives"—this story clearly represents for Carver an avenue now exhausted.

Halfway through the writing of *Cathedral,* in the bloom of his "second life," Carver revised the tale, a process which finally took him "into the heart of what the story is *about*" (*Fires* 218). Three times the length of its parent-story, "A Small, Good Thing" concerns many of the same "obsessions" as "The Bath," but told by a richer, more generous voice, these "obsessions" are transfigured, mediated and tempered by genuine compassion.

In "A Small, Good Thing," Carver's "submerged population" begins to surface, moving out from the preoccupations of self to become aware of and even feel kinship to the larger community. Instead of ignoring the surly baker as she did in "The Bath," her attention then focused squarely upon the material object of the cake, this "reimagined" mother now searches for some common denominator. She studies his "coarse features." She wonders "if he's ever done anything else with his life besides being a baker." Trying to diminish the "uncomfortable" feeling his presence causes her, she examines her own life, as well as her own perception of his, looking for a mutual base: "She was a mother and thirty-three years old, and it seemed to her that everyone, especially someone the baker's age—a man old enough to be her father—must have children who'd gone through this special time of cakes and birthday parties. There must be that between them, she thought." Equally revealing are the changes in the scene that immediately follows this encounter. When Scotty is struck, his friend now drops the potato chips and begins "to cry." Even the driver of the car evidences a certain moral awareness, stopping now "in the middle of the road," waiting, before he drives off, "until the boy got unsteadily to his feet . . . dazed, but [apparently] okay" (*Where* [*I'm Calling From,* Atlantic Monthly, 1988,] 281).

As one would expect, the introduction into Carver's world of compassion, however shaky or seedling, proves to be a mixed blessing. While this new-found empathy considerably deepens the emotional scope of the characters, it also brings into their now less-marginal lives a greater share of pain. This becomes achingly clear in Carver's revision of the mother's encounter with the black family. Their loved one, Nelson, in surgery—victim of a senseless knifing—they, like the Weisses, are awaiting news. Accidentally stumbling upon them in a littered waiting room, the mother apologizes, then asks for directions to the elevator. This given, she suddenly blurts out the painful details of her story. In "The Bath," with a brush-stroke that is typical of the early Carver, the response to her agony is an impotent shake of the father's head, the self-enclosed utterance, "Our Nelson." In this one, almost perfunctorily sketched scene, Carver, while acknowledging the universality of tragedy, dismisses the possibility of connection between the aggrieved, a sentiment which is reversed in "A Small, Good Thing." Here, in a scene that is greatly expanded, the characters engage in a mutually felt sympathy, their discourse characterized by the give-and-take of genuine conversation. The grief briefly shared reverberates as the mother, returning to the hospital later, recreates the young girl she encountered in that room, silently warning her not to have children: "For God's sake, don't" (*Where* 293).

If empathy pains, it also transfigures, creating in Carver's new world a contemporary *via dolorosa* by which the characters may trudge toward salvation. Once the imagination succeeds, as the mother's has, in breaking through the crust of self toward an honest realization of others, a host of options and possibilities suddenly arise. In Carver's recent work, this process of personal redemption begins — much like the Christian theology which seems increasingly, if eclectically, to inform it — with the word.

Their despairing, blue-collar mediocrity aside, if Carver's early protagonists have anything in common, it is, as Robert Houston has remarked, their "stunning inarticulateness." From the teenaged girl in "Why Don't You Dance?" — who, faced with the mystery of domestic dissolution, tries to "get it talked out" and eventually "quit[s] trying" — to the alcoholic L.D. in "One More Thing" — who, upon leaving his wife and daughter, wants to spit out *the* parting shot, but cannot for the life of him think "what it could possibly be" — the characters in *What We Talk About* display a remarkable, if sometimes gratuitous, aphasia. In "The Bath" this is exemplified by the baker's elliptical calls, by the physicians' inability to name the boy's condition, by perhaps even the narrator himself who, so masterfully effaced in Carver's stories, often flounders with the simplest words, describing, for example, a gurney (properly named in "A Small, Good Thing") as "a thing like a bed . . . a thing with wheels."

In the new version, this poverty of language diminishes. With the artful exception of the baker, every major character is now named, an act which signals a critical turn in Carver's work, for by creating a world in which things *can* be named — explored and objectified by the communal activity of language — Carver allows and, in fact, demands of his characters a truer engagement. In "A Small, Good Thing," Dr. Francis can no longer hedge about Scotty's unnatural sleep; he must confront it and call it by its name: "coma." By the same token, the irrational guilt of the parents (beautifully symbolized in "The Bath," but unacknowledged by the protagonists) must also be tackled, with Ann now admitting to herself that "she felt she was in some obscure way responsible for what had happened to the child" (*Where* 293). Indeed, even the "mystery" itself can be broached; eyed squarely and investigated with words, as Carver now, courageously, releases Scotty from his hellish half-existence.

Carver's rendering of the child's death and its ramifications points in a way few other scenes can, to the depth of change in his aesthetic and philosophic perspective. In the earlier stories, death is generally portrayed as a malign and ultimately unknowable force; like a bolt from the natural world, it blasts in at the finale to shatter the artificial parameters constructed around unexamined lives. Faced with this powerful, ill-defined specter, Carver's characters could manage little beyond a mute, uncomprehending horror. . . .

With "A Small, Good Thing," this paradigm of helpless resignation is abandoned as Carver not only confronts death here — a victory in itself — but goes on to record the life after, the agony and resulting growth of those who survive. Given Carver's "obsession" for equating the masked and inarticulate life with spiritual death, one would be hard pressed to conjure a more symbolically fitting demise than Scotty's, as the child rouses briefly from his coma, emits a harrowing and incomprehensible howl, then dies, victim of "a hidden occlusion" of the brain. That this death is, as the bewildered doctors report, "a one in a million circumstance" only serves to intensify the parents' horror (and our own), for by this detail Carver reiterates his belief that, even in this more optimistic universe, a blind and inexplicable randomness still lurks, shaping and destroying at will.

If, in human affairs, contingency plays a major role, it is no longer necessarily a decisive one. There are choices of response, Carver now makes clear, options, even the opportunity to fight back. And this is what Scotty's parents do. After a brief and expected period of stunned denial, the Weisses return home. Rejecting the impulse to box Scotty's toys, thus prolonging his denial of the child's death, Howard finds himself drawn to Ann. Sitting on the couch, he weeps; they embrace; she struggles to find the words that, in elucidating their new and horrible reality, will console. Finally, she tells him, "He's gone . . . Howard, he's gone. He's gone and now we'll have to get used to that. To being alone" (*Where* 296). Later, phoning relatives, she seems to find some relief in the act of articulation, only to have this shattered when the phone rings, its disembodied voice demanding to know, "Have you forgotten Scotty?" (*Where* 297).

Just before midnight, the torture resumes with yet another call to the Weisses; but this time, by virtue of her engagement with the old man in the story's opening scene, Ann is able to identify the menacing source without. "I know who it is!" she exclaims to Howard. "It's the baker, the son-of-a-bitching baker!" (*Where* 298). With this knowledge, the stage is set for the final encounter.

In the middle of the night, the fake-icing stars of Scotty's cake now aptly transfigured into the real thing, the Weisses drive to the shopping center. In a tense scene, reminiscent of the repressed violence ubiquitous in Carver's early tales, the angry parents confront the baker, who in turn arms himself with his rolling pin. Feeling "a deep burning inside her, an anger that made her feel larger than herself, larger than either of these men" (*Where* 299), the mother spits out the reason for the abandoned cake, the story of Scotty's death. By articulating her pain, she is released from her murderous rage; amid tears and a growing nausea, she cries out for response, saying, "It isn't fair!" (*Where* 300).

While God or the Fates may be unmoved by the Weisses' private disaster, the baker clearly is not. In the stark radiance of another's grief, his own "hidden occlusion"—a mask erected by years of loneliness and failure—is brought to light, begins dissolving as he discards the pin, unties the heavy apron. Drawn into this mode of confession, he apologizes for his boorish behavior, even seeks to understand it as, in a monologue reminiscent of the mother's frantic speech to the black family, he unburdens himself, recounting to the Weisses the pain of his solitary life. Finally, he invites the couple to sit down and eat, for "Eating is a small, good thing in a time like this" (*Where* 301).

If Carver's titles are intended to suggest the essence of his fictions, it is apparent that the major "obsessions" of "A Small, Good Thing" are vastly different from those of "The Bath." While the earlier story, with its Old Testament image of *mikvah*, or ritual cleansing, hinges upon the despair of a guilt which cannot be washed away, a grief that stands no chance of utterance and resolution, the revised version, like Scripture itself, strives for something better, a new covenant between the players: the chance for salvation through communion. Surely, this is the "message" of the final scene with the baker offering the suffering couple "cinnamon rolls just out of the oven," coffee, conversation, then a dark, heavy bread which he "break[s] open" like the Eucharist. As the boundaries between them are chipped away through this sharing of bread and pain, the characters find, even in a world that seems fundamentally artificial, transcendence of a sort, for "It was like daylight under the fluorescent trays of light. They talked on into the early morning, the high, pale cast of light in the windows, and they did not think of leaving" (*Where* 301). . . .

TOM JENKS

The Origin of "Cathedral" 1993

I first met Ray Carver in New York in early September 1984 at a publishing dinner to launch Gary Fisketjon's Vintage Contemporary paperback series. Many of the new VC authors and their friends were there: Richard Ford, Toby Wolff, Jay McInerney, Tom McGuane, Jim Crumley, and Ralph Beer — a distinctly male crowd, and what struck me most was that, as we geared up to move to a nightclub, Ray, amid teasing about running off somewhere to see a woman, put himself in a taxi and headed for his hotel room alone. By the ginger way he got himself into the cab and laughingly ducked the barbs all around him, there was no doubt he meant to keep himself out of trouble.

But he was fair game for the friendly taunts that followed him into the cab. We were witnessing the Good Ray, but we all knew about the Bad Ray, the one who used to be Lord Misrule himself.

Reformed, Ray was fast becoming the most famous short story writer in the world, and the facts of his life were well known, partly because they were often the stuff of his writing and because fame brings a peculiar public intimacy.

At the time, I was an editor of *Esquire* and had made Ray's acquaintance through the mail and on the phone. I had published some of his work and knew him somewhat, and as I watched him slip away in the cab, I imagined him going back to his hotel room (it was early yet — ten o'clock) and telephoning Tess Gallagher [Carver's wife] at their home in Syracuse. Each evening they set aside the hours beyond ten o'clock to spend with each other. He *was,* in a sense, running off to see a woman.

A year and a half later, I visited them in Syracuse. During the days, Ray and I read stories for a book we were working on and at night we watched TV. One night, we were watching a PBS version of *Wuthering Heights,* ° and Ray

---

Wuthering Heights: Classic Victorian gothic romance (1847) by Emily Brontë (1818–1848).

began to tell about another night of TV: the night the blind man for whom Tess once worked had come to visit. Tess told her side, too — how Ray was uneasy about the man's visit, uncomfortable with his blindness and his familiarity with Tess, a mild jealousy rising in Ray. Their evening was slow and tedious, and ended with the three of them watching PBS, just as we were. But on the night the blind man was visiting, Tess had fallen asleep, and then a program about cathedrals came on. The blind man had no idea what a cathedral looked like, and, in the end, Ray sat on the floor with him, holding his hands, drawing a cathedral so the blind man could sense the miracle of the shape.

Ray had written this story and titled it "Cathedral." Tess, who with Ray's encouragement had recently begun writing stories, had her own version, titled "The Harvest."° She gave me a copy, humorously telling Ray, "Watch out, I'm nipping at your heels." Their good-natured competition and openness was rare in my experience of writers, many of whom are cagey about the intimate, personal connections in their work.

A. O. SCOTT

Looking for Raymond Carver   1999

> "And did you get what
> you wanted from this life, even so?
> I did.
> And what did you want?
> To call myself beloved, to feel myself
> beloved on the earth."

Plenty of writers are admired, celebrated, imitated, and hyped. Very few writers can, as Raymond Carver does in his poem "Late Fragment," call themselves beloved. In the years since his death in 1988, at fifty, from lung cancer, Carver's reputation has blossomed. He has gone from being an influential — and controversial — member of a briefly fashionable school of experimental fiction to being an international icon of traditional American literary values. His genius — but more his honesty, his decency, his commitment to the exigencies of craft — is praised by an extraordinarily diverse cross section of his peers. . . .

Through the ministrations of his friends and the tireless efforts of his widow, the poet and short-story writer Tess Gallagher, to keep his memory alive, Carver has begun to approach something like literary sainthood. Certain facts about his life and death — his stoicism in the face of terminal illness, his generosity as a friend and teacher, his successful battle with alcoholism, the happy and productive life he made in Port Angeles, Washington, with Gallagher after the collapse of his first marriage — have added luster to his image. The best of Carver's writing now seems, in retrospect, to be suffused with the best of his personality — affable, humble, battered, wise. But to say this may

---

"The Harvest": Gallagher eventually retitled the story "Rain Flooding Your Campfire."

also be to note that the adversities and triumphs of Carver's life have obscured his work, that we now read that work through the screen of biography, and that his identity as a writer is, in consequence, blurred. What kind of a writer was he, and how are we to assess his achievement? Was he a hard-boiled cynic or an open-hearted sentimentalist? A regionalist rooted in his native Pacific North-west or the chronicler of an America whose trailer parks and subdivisions had become indistinguishable? Did he help to revive American fiction or con-tribute to its ruin? Is he, as the London *Times* once declared, "America's Chekhov," or merely the O. Henry of America's graduate writing programs?

If anything, the current state of Carver's published work makes these questions, which have lingered for some time, more difficult than ever to address. More than a decade after his death, Carver's *oeuvre* is still taking shape. Last autumn Knopf brought out his collected poems, and the Atlantic Monthly Press issued a tenth-anniversary hardcover edition of *Where I'm Calling From*, which Carver viewed as the definitive collection of his stories. Around the same time, a *New York Times Magazine* article raised questions about the extent to which Carver was the sole, or even the primary, begetter of his own work, pointing to evidence that Gordon Lish, the editor of Carver's first two books, had drastically cut, rearranged, and even rewritten many of the sto-ries which established Carver's fame.[1] And then there is the question of Gal-lagher's role, which seems to have been that of soulmate, sounding board, first reader—and collaborator. The journal *Philosophy and Literature* recently printed some short plays Carver and Gallagher wrote together. The journal also ran a photograph of the manuscript of the final page of "Errand," Carver's last published story; the concluding paragraph is in Gallagher's handwriting. . . .

To his admirers, Carver's taciturnity becomes its own kind of eloquence. But critics, especially those who are bothered by Carver's disproportionate influence on other writers, have complained about how much he leaves out. For Sven Birkerts, writing in 1986, the fiction of Carver and his followers is marked by "a total refusal of any vision of larger social connection." And it is true that the inhabitants of Carver's world appear to exist not only in states of isolation and impermanence, but, to borrow a phrase from George W. S. Trow, in a con-text of no context, without geographical, social, or historical coordinates. We seldom learn the name of the town, or even the state, in which a given story takes place. The stories tend to be devoid of the cultural and commercial refer-ences—popular songs, brand names, movies—that so many contemporary writers use to fix their narratives in time and space. And though Carver began writing in the early 1960s, and came to prominence over the next two decades, his stories, at first glance, take no notice of the social and political tumult of the era. We never know who the president is, or whether men have walked on the moon; the characters never read newspapers; and nobody expresses any political interests or opinions. As far as I can tell, Vietnam is mentioned exactly

---

[1] D. T. Max, "The Carver Chronicles," *The New York Times Magazine*, August 9, 1998. [Scott's note]

once: in "Vitamins" the leering, predatory behavior of a black man named Nelson—one of the very few nonwhite characters who appear in Carver's work—is ascribed to the fact that he is a veteran just returned from combat in Southeast Asia.

Carver's people often exist not only outside history and politics, but beyond psychology, unless the psychology in question is Skinnerian behaviorism. Their thoughts are typically left unreported; they are creatures of simple speech and sudden action:

> She unbuttoned her coat and put her purse down on the counter. She looked at L.D. and said, "L.D., I've had it. So has Rae. So has everyone who knows you. I've been thinking it over. I want you out of here. Tonight. This minute. Now. Get the hell out of here right now."
>
> L.D. had no intention of going anywhere. He looked from Maxine to the jar of pickles that had been on the table since lunch. He picked up the jar and pitched it through the kitchen window.

The jaggedness, the deadpan narration, the rigorous refusal of any inflection of language that would suggest interpretation, judgment, or inwardness—these are the aspects of Carver's style that inspired people to think of him as a minimalist. The passage above is from "One More Thing," which, like "Why Don't You Dance?," appears both in *What We Talk About When We Talk About Love* and in *Where I'm Calling From*. The earlier book, which did a great deal to solidify Carver's reputation as an important voice in American fiction in the 1980s, has also done him lasting damage. It was on this book that the editorial hand of Gordon Lish fell most heavily, as Lish cut, rearranged, and rewrote freely, without regard for Carver's wishes or feelings. According to Tess Gallagher, "Ray felt the book, even at the time of its publication, did not represent the main thrust of his writing, nor his true pulse and instinct in the work. He had, in fact, even begged Gordon Lish, to no avail, not to publish the book in this misbegotten version."

Carver, it seems to me, was well within his rights. He was also, as a matter of literary judgment, right. There has been much discussion of the changes Lish imposed on two stories in particular, "The Bath" (which Carver had originally and would subsequently title "A Small, Good Thing") and "So Much Water So Close to Home." The Lish versions are jarring and, briefly, horrifying: the stories, like the people who inhabit them, seem violently discombobulated. In "The Bath," events happen almost at random, and crucial information—for instance, whether a child is alive or dead—is cruelly, capriciously, withheld. . . .

For Lish, the paring of a story down to its verbal and narrative skeleton was a mode of formal experimentation—a trick, if you will. The kind of writing he championed in the 1980s was not an antidote to the antirealist, avant-garde impulse of the 1960s and 1970s, of writers like John Barth and Donald Barthelme, but rather its most extreme expression. The refusal of explanation, the resistance to psychology, and the deliberate impoverishment of language reflect, on Lish's part, an aesthetic choice, and it is clear that he saw affinities between Carver's plain manner and his own stark vision. But the aesthetic principles that Carver discovered in the course of his literary education — from his readings in the modernist tradition, from his first teacher, the novelist John Gardner, and from Lish himself — were ultimately less important than the ethical commitments that are the deepest source of his work. . . .

To read *Where I'm Calling From* from beginning to end, supplemented by some of the stories from earlier collections that Carver chose not to reprint, is to discover that a great deal of what is supposed to be missing — in particular, the changing social landscape of the United States — has been there all along, but that it has been witnessed from a perspective almost without precedent in American literature. Stories like "What Do You Do in San Francisco?" and "After the Denim" record the curious, suspicious, and disgusted reactions of the small-town working class to interlopers from the urban, well-to-do counterculture. "Jerry and Molly and Sam," "Nobody Said Anything," and "Bicycles, Muscles, Cigarettes," among others, are ultimately about how the spread of the suburbs transformed family life, and about the crisis of masculinity that resulted. Carver's work, read closely and in the aggregate, also carries a lot of news about feminism, working conditions, and substance abuse in late-twentieth-century provincial America.

To generalize in this way is, of course, to engage in a kind of analytical discourse Carver resolutely mistrusted. More often than not, the big talkers in Carver's stories are in possession of a degree of class privilege. "My friend Mel McGinnis was talking," goes the famous opening of "What We Talk About When We Talk About Love." "Mel McGinnis is a cardiologist, and sometimes that gives him the right." The imperious homeowner in "Put Yourself in My Shoes" and the jealous college teacher in "Will You Please Be Quiet, Please?" also come to mind. People who carry on as if they know what they're talking about are regarded with suspicion. Carver's greatest sympathy is reserved for those characters who struggle to use language to make sense of things, but who founder or fail in the attempt.

It is striking how many of his stories turn on the inability or refusal of people to say what happened. Think of the girl at the end of "Why Don't You Dance?," unable to convey the fullness of what she has seen on the strange man's lawn, or the narrator of "Where Is Everyone?," clamming up at his AA meetings. And there are many more examples. "Why, Honey?" is a mother's desperate, almost incoherent, and yet strangely formal effort ("Dear Sir," it begins) to explain to a nameless, prying stranger how her darling son went wrong. In "Distance" (also published as "Everything Stuck to Him"), a father, asked by his grown daughter to tell her "what it was like when she was a kid," produces a fairy tale of young parenthood (the main characters in which are referred to only as "the boy" and "the girl") that leaves both teller and listener unsettled, unenlightened, and remote from each other.

And then there is "Cathedral," one of Carver's most beloved stories and the closest thing he produced to an allegory of his own method. The narrator is visited by a garrulous blind man, an old friend of his wife's, whose arrival he anticipates with apprehension. The two men end up smoking marijuana together, while the television airs a documentary about the cathedrals of Europe.

It starts to bother the narrator that his new acquaintance, while he knows something about the history of church-building, has no idea of what cathedrals really are, and he tries to tell him about them:

> "They're really big," I said. "They're massive. They're built of stone. Marble, too, sometimes. In those olden days, when they built cathedrals, men wanted to be close to God. In those olden days, God was an important part of everyone's life. You could tell this from their cathedral-building. I'm sorry," I said, "but it looks like that's the best I can do for you. I'm just no good at it."

The blind man proposes that they draw a cathedral instead, and they do—the narrator's eyes closed, the blind man's hand guiding his. The narrator undergoes an epiphany: "It was like nothing else in my life up to now."

The reader is left out: the men's shared experience, visual and tactile, is beyond the reach of words. But the frustrating vicariousness of the story is also the source of its power. Art, according to Carver, is a matter of the blind leading the tongue-tied. Carver was an artist of a rare and valuable kind: he told simple stories, and made it look hard.

Conversations on Flannery O'Connor's Sources, Ideas, and Techniques

Flannery O'Connor is unusual among writers in that she shared with readers her own interpretations of her stories. While acknowledging that there is usually more than one way to read a story, she also stated that there was only one way she could possibly have written it. O'Connor's discussion of "A Good Man Is Hard to Find" (p. 448) can be read alongside the interpretations of "Good Country People" (p. 434) and "Everything That Rises Must Converge" (p. 423) by academic critics Dorothy Tuck McFarland and Wayne C. Booth. Sally Fitzgerald reveals the newspaper sources of "A Good Man Is Hard to Find," and Robert H. Brinkmeyer Jr. considers the relationship between O'Connor and her readers.

FLANNERY O'CONNOR

From Letters, 1954–55   1955

TO SALLY FITZGERALD

26 Dec 54

. . . I have finally got off the ms. for my collection [*A Good Man Is Hard to Find*] and it is scheduled to appear in May. Without yr kind permission I have taken the liberty of dedicating (grand verb) it to you and Robert. This is

Flannery O'Connor in the summer of 1962 at Andalusia, her family farm and home outside Milledgeville, Georgia. (© Joe McTyre. Reprinted by permission of Joe McTyre Photo / Atlanta Constitution.)

because you all are my adopted kin and if I dedicated it to any of my blood kin they would think they had to go into hiding. Nine stories about original sin, with my compliments.

I have been invited to go to Greensboro to the Women's College in March to be on an arts panel. That is where Brother Randall Jarrell° holds forth. I accepted but I am not looking forward to it. Can you fancy me hung in conversation with the likes of him?

When I had lunch with Giroux [O'Connor's editor] in Atlanta he told me about Cal's escapade in Cincinnati. It seems [Cal] convinced everybody it

---

Randall Jarrell: American poet and influential critic (1914–1965).

was Elizabeth who was going crazy. . . . Toward the end he gave a lecture at the university that was almost pure gibberish. I guess nobody noticed, thinking it was the new criticism. . . .

I just got a check for $200 for the 2nd prize in the O. Henry book° this year. My ex-mentor Paul Engle does the selecting. Jean Stafford° got the first one.

I am walking with a cane these days which gives me a great air of distinction. The scientist tells me this has nothing to do with the lupus but is rheumatism. I would not believe it except that the dose of ACTH has not been increased. Besides which I now feel it makes very little difference what you call it. As the niggers say, I have the misery.

I am reading everything I can of Romano Guardini's [Italian priest and theologian]. Have you become acquainted with his work? A book called *The Lord* of his is very fine.

TO ELIZABETH MCKEE

13 January 1955

The carbon of "An Exile in the East" is enclosed, but I don't know if you realize or not that this is a rewritten version of "The Geranium" originally printed in *Accent*. *Accent* didn't pay me for it and it is rather much changed, but I enclose both stories so [the editor] can see what she's doing. I don't want to go to the penitentiary for selling a story twice (but if I do I would like to get a good price for the story).

TO ROBERT GIROUX

22 January 55

Nothing has been said about a picture for the jacket of this collection *but if you have to have one,* I would be much obliged if you could use the enclosed so that I won't have to have a new picture made. This is a self-portrait with a pheasant cock, that I painted in 1953; however, I think it will do justice to the subject for some time to come.

26 February 55

I have just written a story called "Good Country People" that Allen and Caroline [Tate?] both say is the best thing I have written and should be in this collection. I told them I thought it was too late, but anyhow I am writing now to ask if it is. It is really a story that would set the whole collection on its feet. It is 27 pages and if you can eliminate the one called "A Stroke of Good Fortune," and the other called "An Afternoon in the Woods," this one would fit the available space nicely. Also I remember you said it would be good to have one that had never been published before. I could send it to you at once *on being wired.* Please let me know.

O. Henry book: The O. Henry Prizes are awarded annually to outstanding American short stories, which are collected each year in a book. O. Henry was the pen name of the popular American short story writer William Sydney Porter (1862–1910).
Jean Stafford: American short story writer and novelist (1915–1979).

Giroux wired O'Connor that every effort would be made to include the story. After he had read it, he wrote suggesting that an appearance by the mother and Mrs. Freeman at the end might improve it. Flannery recognized the value of the suggestion and added the sentences that are now a part of the story.

7 March 55

I like the suggestion about the ending of "Good Country People" and enclose a dozen or so lines that can be added on to *the present end.* I enclose them in case you can get them put on before I get the proofs. I am mighty wary of making changes on proofs. . . .

TO SALLY AND ROBERT FITZGERALD

1 April 55

We are wondering if #6 is here yet or due to arrive momentarily. Let us hear and if you need any names, I'll be glad to cable you a rich collection. I have just got back from Greensboro where I said nothing intelligent the whole time, but enjoyed myself. Mr. Randall Jarrell, wife and stepdaughters I met and et dinner with. I must say I was shocked at what a very kind man he is—that is the last impression I expected to have of him. I also met Peter Taylor,° who is more like folks. Mrs. Jarrell is writing a novel. You get the impression the two stepdaughters may be at it too and maybe the dog. Mr. Jarrell has a beard and looks like Mephistopheles (sp?) only fatter. Mrs. Jarrell is very friendly & sunkist.

The Easter rabbit is bringing my mother a three-quarter ton truck.

I trust Giroux will be sending you a copy of the book soon. I wrote a very hot story at the last minute called "Good Country People": so now there are ten.

While I was in NC I heard somebody recite a barroom ballad. I don't remember anything but the end but beinst you all are poets I will give it to you as it is mighty deathless:

"They stacked the stiffs outside the door.
They made, I reckon, a cord or more."

I call that real poetry.

I have put the cane up and am walking on my own very well. Let us hear. Regards to children.

Writing Short Stories   1961

. . . Perhaps the central question to be considered in any discussion of the short story is what do we mean by short. Being short does not mean being slight. A short story should be long in depth and should give us an experience of meaning. I have an aunt who thinks that nothing happens in a story unless somebody gets married or shot at the end of it. I wrote a story about a tramp who marries an old woman's idiot daughter in order to acquire the old

---

Peter Taylor: Tennessee-born-and-bred novelist and short story writer (1917–1994).

634 Conversations on Stories and Storytellers

woman's automobile. After the marriage, he takes the daughter off on a wedding trip in the automobile and abandons her in an eating place and drives on by himself. Now that is a complete story. There is nothing more relating to the mystery of that man's personality that could be shown through that particular dramatization. But I've never been able to convince my aunt that it's a complete story. She wants to know what happened to the idiot daughter after that.

Not long ago that story was adapted for a television play, and the adapter, knowing his business, had the tramp have a change of heart and go back and pick up the idiot daughter and the two of them ride away, grinning madly. My aunt believes that the story is complete at last, but I have other sentiments about it—which are not suitable for public utterance. When you write a story, you only have to write one story, but there will always be people who will refuse to read the story you have written.

And this naturally brings up the awful question of what kind of a reader you are writing for when you write fiction. Perhaps we each think we have a personal solution for this problem. For my own part, I have a very high opinion of the art of fiction and a very low opinion of what is called the "average" reader. I tell myself that I can't escape him, that this is the personality I am supposed to keep awake, but that at the same time, I am also supposed to provide the intelligent reader with the deeper experience that he looks for in fiction. Now actually, both of these readers are just aspects of the writer's own personality, and in the last analysis, the only reader he can know anything about is himself. We all write at our own level of understanding, but it is the peculiar characteristic of fiction that its literal surface can be made to yield entertainment on an obvious physical plane to one sort of reader while the selfsame surface can be made to yield meaning to the person equipped to experience it there.

Meaning is what keeps the short story from being short. I prefer to talk about the meaning in a story rather than the theme of a story. People talk about the theme of a story as if the theme were like the string that a sack of chicken feed is tied with. They think that if you can pick out the theme, the way you pick the right thread in the chicken-feed sack, you can rip the story open and feed the chickens. But this is not the way meaning works in fiction.

When you can state the theme of a story, when you can separate it from the story itself, then you can be sure the story is not a very good one. The meaning of a story has to be embodied in it, has to be made concrete in it. A story is a way to say something that can't be said any other way, and it takes every word in the story to say what the meaning is. You tell a story because a statement would be inadequate. When anybody asks what a story is about, the only proper thing is to tell him to read the story. The meaning of fiction is not abstract meaning but experienced meaning, and the purpose of making statements about the meaning of a story is only to help you to experience that meaning more fully.

Fiction is an art that calls for the strictest attention to the real—whether the writer is writing a naturalistic story or a fantasy. I mean that we always begin with what is or with what has an eminent possibility of truth about it.

Even when one writes a fantasy, reality is the proper basis of it. A thing is fantastic because it is so real, so real that it is fantastic. Graham Greene° has said that he can't write, "I stood over a bottomless pit," because that couldn't be true, or "Running down the stairs I jumped into a taxi," because that couldn't be true either. But Elizabeth Bowen° can write about one of her characters that "she snatched at her hair as if she heard something in it," because that is eminently possible.

I would even go so far as to say that the person writing a fantasy has to be even more strictly attentive to the concrete detail than someone writing in a naturalistic vein — because the greater the story's strain on the credulity, the more convincing the properties in it have to be.

A good example of this is a story called "The Metamorphosis" by Franz Kafka. This is a story about a man who wakes up one morning to find that he has turned into a cockroach overnight, while not discarding his human nature. The rest of the story concerns his life and feelings and eventual death as an insect with human nature, and this situation is accepted by the reader because the concrete detail of the story is absolutely convincing. The fact is that this story describes the dual nature of man in such a realistic fashion that it is almost unbearable. The truth is not distorted here, but rather, a certain distortion is used to get at the truth. If we admit, as we must, that appearance is not the same thing as reality, then we must give the artist the liberty to make certain rearrangements of nature if these will lead to greater depths of vision. The artist himself always has to remember that what he is rearranging *is* nature, and that he has to know it and be able to describe it accurately in order to have the authority to rearrange it at all.

The peculiar problem of the short-story writer is how to make the action he describes reveal as much of the mystery of existence as possible. He has only a short space to do it in and he can't do it by statement. He has to do it by showing, not by saying, and by showing the concrete — so that his problem is really how to make the concrete work double time for him.

In good fiction, certain of the details will tend to accumulate meaning from the action of the story itself, and when this happens they become symbolic in the way they work. I once wrote a story called "Good Country People," in which a lady Ph.D. has her wooden leg stolen by a Bible salesman whom she has tried to seduce. Now I'll admit that, paraphrased in this way, the situation is simply a low joke. The average reader is pleased to observe anybody's wooden leg being stolen. But without ceasing to appeal to him and without making any statements of high intention, this story does manage to operate at another level of experience, by letting the wooden leg accumulate meaning. Early in the story, we're presented with the fact that the Ph.D. is spiritually as well as physically crippled. She believes in nothing but her own belief in nothing, and we perceive that there is a wooden part of her soul that corresponds to her wooden leg. Now of course this is never stated. The fiction writer states as little as possible. The reader makes this connection from things he is

---

Graham Greene: English writer (1904–1991).
Elizabeth Bowen: British novelist and short story writer (1899–1973).

shown. He may not even know that he makes the connection, but the connection is there nevertheless and it has its effect on him. As the story goes on, the wooden leg continues to accumulate meaning. The reader learns how the girl feels about her leg, how her mother feels about it, and how the country woman on the place feels about it; and finally, by the time the Bible salesman comes along, the leg has accumulated so much meaning that it is, as the saying goes, loaded. And when the Bible salesman steals it, the reader realizes that he has taken away part of the girl's personality and has revealed her deeper affliction to her for the first time.

If you want to say that the wooden leg is a symbol, you can say that. But it is a wooden leg first, and as a wooden leg it is absolutely necessary to the story. It has its place on the literal level of the story, but it operates in depth as well as on the surface. It increases the story in every direction, and this is essentially the way a story escapes being short.

Now a little might be said about the way in which this happens. I wouldn't want you to think that in that story I sat down and said, "I am now going to write a story about a Ph.D. with a wooden leg, using the wooden leg as a symbol for another kind of affliction." I doubt myself if many writers know what they are going to do when they start out. When I started writing that story, I didn't know there was going to be a Ph.D. with a wooden leg in it. I merely found myself one morning writing a description of two women that I knew something about, and before I realized it, I had equipped one of them with a daughter with a wooden leg. As the story progressed, I brought in the Bible salesman, but I had no idea what I was going to do with him. I didn't know he was going to steal that wooden leg until ten or twelve lines before he did it, but when I found out that this was what was going to happen, I realized that it was inevitable. This is a story that produces a shock for the reader, and I think one reason for this is that it produced a shock for the writer.

Now despite the fact that this story came about in this seemingly mindless fashion, it is a story that almost no rewriting was done on. It is a story that was under control throughout the writing of it, and it might be asked how this kind of control comes about, since it is not entirely conscious.

I think the answer to this is what Maritain° calls "the habit of art." It is a fact that fiction writing is something in which the whole personality takes part—the conscious as well as the unconscious mind. Art is the habit of the artist; and habits have to be rooted deep in the whole personality. They have to be cultivated like any other habit, over a long period of time, by experience; and teaching any kind of writing is largely a matter of helping the student develop the habit of art. I think this is more than just a discipline, although it is that; I think it is a way of looking at the created world and of using the senses so as to make them find as much meaning as possible in things.

Now I am not so naïve as to suppose that most people come to writers' conferences in order to hear what kind of vision is necessary to write stories that will become a permanent part of our literature. Even if you do wish to hear this,

---

Maritain: Jacques Maritain (1882–1973) was a French philosopher and critic.

your greatest concerns are immediately practical. You want to know how you can actually write a good story, and further, how you can tell when you've done it; and so you want to know what the form of a short story is, as if the form were something that existed outside of each story and could be applied or imposed on the material. Of course, the more you write, the more you will realize that the form is organic, that it is something that grows out of the material, that the form of each story is unique. A story that is any good can't be reduced, it can only be expanded. A story is good when you continue to see more and more in it, and when it continues to escape you. In fiction two and two is always more than four.

The only way, I think, to learn to write short stories is to write them, and then to try to discover what you have done. The time to think of technique is when you've actually got the story in front of you. The teacher can help the student by looking at his individual work and trying to help him decide if he has written a complete story, one in which the action fully illuminates the meaning.

Perhaps the most profitable thing I can do is to tell you about some of the general observations I made about these seven stories I read of yours. All of these observations will not fit any one of the stories exactly, but they are points nevertheless that it won't hurt anyone interested in writing to think about.

The first thing that any professional writer is conscious of in reading anything is, naturally, the use of language. Now the use of language in these stories was such that, with one exception, it would be difficult to distinguish one story from another. While I can recall running into several clichés, I can't remember one image or one metaphor from the seven stories. I don't mean there weren't images in them; I just mean that there weren't any that were effective enough to take away with you.

In connection with this, I made another observation that startled me considerably. With the exception of one story, there was practically no use made of the local idiom. Now this is a Southern Writers' Conference. All the addresses on these stories were from Georgia or Tennessee, yet there was no distinctive sense of Southern life in them. A few place-names were dropped, Savannah or Atlanta or Jacksonville, but these could just as easily have been changed to Pittsburgh or Passaic without calling for any other alteration in the story. The characters spoke as if they had never heard any kind of language except what came out of a television set. This indicates that something is way out of focus.

There are two qualities that make fiction. One is the sense of mystery and the other is the sense of manners. You get the manners from the texture of existence that surrounds you. The great advantage of being a Southern writer is that we don't have to go anywhere to look for manners; bad or good, we've got them in abundance. We in the South live in a society that is rich in contradiction, rich in irony, rich in contrast, and particularly rich in its speech. And yet here are six stories by Southerners in which almost no use is made of the gifts of the region.

Of course the reason for this may be that you have seen these gifts abused so often that you have become self-conscious about using them. There is nothing worse than the writer who doesn't *use* the gifts of the region, but wallows in them. Everything becomes so Southern that it's sickening, so local that it is unintelligible, so literally reproduced that it conveys nothing. The general gets lost in the particular instead of being shown through it.

However, when the life that actually surrounds us is totally ignored, when our patterns of speech are absolutely overlooked, then something is out of kilter. The writer should then ask himself if he is not reaching out for a kind of life that is artificial to him.

An idiom characterizes a society, and when you ignore the idiom, you are very likely ignoring the whole social fabric that could make a meaningful character. You can't cut characters off from their society and say much about them as individuals. You can't say anything meaningful about the mystery of a personality unless you put that personality in a believable and significant social context. And the best way to do this is through the character's own language. When the old lady in one of Andrew Lytle's stories says contemptuously that she has a mule that is older than Birmingham, we get in that one sentence a sense of a society and its history. A great deal of the Southern writers' work is done for him before he begins, because our history lives in our talk. In one of Eudora Welty's stories a character says, "Where I come from, we use fox for yard dogs and owls for chickens, but we sing true." Now there is a whole book in that one sentence; and when the people of your section can talk like that, and you ignore it, you're just not taking advantage of what's yours. The sound of our talk is too definite to be discarded with impunity, and if the writer tries to get rid of it, he is liable to destroy the better part of his creative power.

Another thing I observed about these stories is that most of them don't go very far inside a character, don't reveal very much of the character. I don't mean that they don't enter the character's mind, but they simply don't show that he has a personality. Again this goes back partly to speech. These characters have no distinctive speech to reveal themselves with; and sometimes they have no really distinctive features. You feel in the end that no personality is revealed because no personality is there. In most good stories it is the character's personality that creates the action of the story. In most of these stories, I feel that the writer has thought of some action and then scrounged up a character to perform it. You will usually be more successful if you start the other way around. If you start with a real personality, a real character, then something is bound to happen; and you don't have to know what before you begin. In fact it may be better if you don't know what before you begin. You ought to be able to discover something from your stories. If you don't, probably nobody else will.

The Element of Suspense in "A Good Man Is Hard to Find" 1969

A story really isn't any good unless it successfully resists paraphrase, unless it hangs on and expands in the mind. Properly, you analyze to enjoy, but it's equally true that to analyze with any discrimination, you have to have enjoyed already, and I think that the best reason to hear a story read is that it should stimulate that primary enjoyment.

I don't have any pretensions to being an Aeschylus or Sophocles and providing you in this story with a cathartic experience out of your mythic background, though this story I'm going to read certainly calls up a good deal of the South's mythic background, and it should elicit from you a degree of pity and terror, even though its way of being serious is a comic one. I do think, though, that like the Greeks you should know what is going to happen in this story so that any element of suspense in it will be transferred from its surface to its interior.

I would be most happy if you had already read it, happier still if you knew it well, but since experience has taught me to keep my expectations along these lines modest, I'll tell you that this is the story of a family of six which, on its way driving to Florida, gets wiped out by an escaped convict who calls himself the Misfit. The family is made up of the Grandmother and her son, Bailey, and his children, John Wesley and June Star and the baby, and there is also the cat and the children's mother. The cat is named Pitty Sing, and the Grandmother is taking him with them, hidden in a basket.

Now I think it behooves me to try to establish with you the basis on which reason operates in this story. Much of my fiction takes its character from a reasonable use of the unreasonable, though the reasonableness of my use of it may not always be apparent. The assumptions that underlie this use of it, however, are those of the central Christian mysteries. These are assumptions to which a large part of the modern audience takes exception. About this I can only say that there are perhaps other ways than my own in which this story could be read, but none other by which it could have been written. Belief, in my own case anyway, is the engine that makes perception operate.

The heroine of this story, the Grandmother, is in the most significant position life offers the Christian. She is facing death. And to all appearances she, like the rest of us, is not too well prepared for it. She would like to see the event postponed. Indefinitely.

I've talked to a number of teachers who use this story in class and who tell their students that the Grandmother is evil, that in fact, she's a witch, even down to the cat. One of these teachers told me that his students, and particularly his southern students, resisted this interpretation with a certain bemused vigor, and he didn't understand why. I had to tell him that they resisted it because they all had grandmothers or great-aunts just like her at home, and they knew, from personal experience, that the old lady lacked comprehension, but that she had a good heart. The southerner is usually tolerant of those weaknesses that proceed from innocence, and he knows that a taste for self-preservation can be readily combined with the missionary spirit.

This same teacher was telling his students that morally the Misfit was several cuts above the Grandmother. He had a really sentimental attachment to the Misfit. But then a prophet gone wrong is almost always more interesting than your grandmother, and you have to let people take their pleasures where they find them.

It is true that the old lady is a hypocritical old soul; her wits are no match for the Misfit's, nor is her capacity for grace equal to his; yet I think the unprejudiced reader will feel that the Grandmother has a special kind of triumph in this story which instinctively we do not allow to someone altogether bad.

I often ask myself what makes a story work, and what makes it hold up as a story, and I have decided that it is probably some action, some gesture of a character that is unlike any other in the story, one which indicates where the real heart of the story lies. This would have to be an action or a gesture which was both totally right and totally unexpected; it would have to be one that was both in character and beyond character; it would have to suggest both the world and eternity. The action or gesture I'm talking about would have to be on the anagogical level, that is, the level which has to do with the Divine life and our participation in it. It would be a gesture that transcended any neat allegory that might have been intended or any pat moral categories a reader could make. It would be a gesture which somehow made contact with mystery.

There is a point in this story where such a gesture occurs. The Grandmother is at last alone, facing the Misfit. Her head clears for an instant and she realizes, even in her limited way, that she is responsible for the man before her and joined to him by ties of kinship which have their roots deep in the mystery she has been merely prattling about so far. And at this point, she does the right thing, she makes the right gesture.

I find that students are often puzzled by what she says and does here, but I think myself that if I took out this gesture and what she says with it, I would have no story. What was left would not be worth your attention. Our age not only does not have a very sharp eye for the almost imperceptible intrusions of grace, it no longer has much feeling for the nature of the violences which precede and follow them. The devil's greatest wile, Baudelaire has said, is to convince us that he does not exist.

I suppose the reasons for the use of so much violence in modern fiction will differ with each writer who uses it, but in my own stories I have found that violence is strangely capable of returning my characters to reality and preparing them to accept their moment of grace. Their heads are so hard that almost nothing else will do the work. This idea, that reality is something to which we must be returned at considerable cost, is one which is seldom understood by the casual reader, but it is one which is implicit in the Christian view of the world.

I don't want to equate the Misfit with the devil. I prefer to think that, however unlikely this may seem, the old lady's gesture, like the mustard-seed, will grow to be a great crow-filled tree in the Misfit's heart, and will be enough of a pain to him there to turn him into the prophet he was meant to become. But that's another story.

This story has been called grotesque, but I prefer to call it literal. A good story is literal in the same sense that a child's drawing is literal. When a child draws, he doesn't intend to distort but to set down exactly what he sees, and as his gaze is direct, he sees the lines that create motion. Now the lines of motion that interest the writer are usually invisible. They are lines of spiritual motion. And in this story you should be on the lookout for such things as the action of grace in the Grandmother's soul, and not for the dead bodies.

We hear many complaints about the prevalence of violence in modern fiction, and it is always assumed that this violence is a bad thing and meant to be an end in itself. With the serious writer, violence is never an end in itself. It is the extreme situation that best reveals what we are essentially, and I believe these are times when writers are more interested in what we are essentially than in the tenor of our daily lives. Violence is a force which can be used for good or evil, and among other things taken by it is the kingdom of heaven. But regardless of what can be taken by it, the man in the violent situation reveals those qualities least dispensable in his personality, those qualities which are all he will have to take into eternity with him; and since the characters in this story are all on the verge of eternity, it is appropriate to think of what they take with them. In any case, I hope that if you consider these points in connection with the story, you will come to see it as something more than an account of a family murdered on the way to Florida.

SALLY FITZGERALD

Southern Sources of "A Good Man Is Hard to Find"   1997

The germ of the story, like a number of others, came from the newspapers close to home — in this instance from several newspaper accounts of unrelated matters shortly before she wrote the story, in 1953. The title she found in a local item — with photograph — concerning a prize-winning performance by a hideously painted-up little girl still in kitten teeth, decked out in ribbons and tutu and sausage curls, singing "A Good Man Is Hard to Find." Beyond the title, there is no connection between the photograph and the events of the short story, but possibly this child served to inspire the awful little granddaughter, June Star, who sasses her way through the action, and does her tap-routine at the barbecue stand of Red Sammy Butts, the fat veteran "with the happy laugh," who is so thoroughly nasty to his wife. Flannery thought well enough of this newspaper photograph and caption to pass them along for my delectation, together with various ads and testimonials for patent medicines and inspirational columns from the local press, and I remember the clipping very clearly. So did she, and she took the nectar from it to make her fictional honey.

About the same time, an article appeared in the Atlanta paper about a small-time robber who called himself "The Misfit," in a self-pitying explanation or excuse for his crimes. A clipping about him and his honorary title turned up among her papers. Obviously, the name he gave himself was the only thing about this man that much interested the author, and certainly he was no match for the towering figure she turned him into. Incidentally, his excuse for his peccadilloes was taken rather literally in the judicial system: he was judged to be of unsound mind and committed to the lunatic asylum—in Milledgeville, the town in which Flannery lived. This news cannot have escaped her notice. By the way, the mental hospital there was once the largest in the world under one roof. Flannery once described Milledgeville as a town of 8,000, of whom 4,000 were locked up.

There was a third element in the inspirational mix for the story, and this was also to be found in the newspapers, in a series of accounts of another criminal "aloose" in the region. The subject was the person of Mr. James Francis ("Three-Gun") Hill, who amassed a record of twenty-six kidnappings in four states, an equal number of robberies, ten car thefts, and a daring rescue of four Florida convicts from a prison gang—all brought off in two fun-filled weeks. The papers at the time were full of these accounts, and the lurid headlines of the day might well have excited a grandmother like the one who is shaking a newspaper at Bailey Boy's bald head and lecturing him on the dangers to be feared on the road to Florida, when the O'Connor story opens.

Mr. Hill was a far more formidable figure than the original self-styled Misfit, and a more vivid one. Newspaper photographs show him to have looked almost exactly as she described the character in her story, complete with metal-rimmed spectacles. There were other details evidently appropriated by Flannery from life, or life as strained through the *Atlanta Journal* and the *Atlanta Constitution:* Mr. Hill was proud of his courtly manners, and in one press account called himself a "gentleman-bandit," explaining that he never cussed before ladies. (Readers will remember that Flannery's mass-murderer blushes when Bailey curses his mother for her incautious tongue.) In some accounts, "Three-Gun" Hill had two accomplices, although the fictional Hiram and Bobby Lee seem entirely imagined by O'Connor in their physical aspects and rather subhuman personalities.

The Misfit in O'Connor's story recounts a brush with a "head-doctor," which accords with the fate of both these actual criminals who initially inspired her. "Three-Gun" Hill, too, was committed to an insane asylum in the end, when he pled guilty to the charges against him. He was sent to a hospital in Tennessee, however, and not to Milledgeville, but the author no doubt read about the sentencing, and it may be that the eventual guilty plea suggested to her the beginnings of capitulation, the stirring of life in the Misfit, whom she conceived as a spoiled prophet, on which note her story ends.

ROBERT H. BRINKMEYER JR.

Flannery O'Connor and Her Readers   1989

As her letters and essays clearly indicate, O'Connor was very much concerned with her reading audience. Her comments on her audience and how it affected her as an artist, however, were not entirely consistent, and it seems clear that O'Connor was of two minds on the subject.[1] One part of O'Connor downplayed the significance of the audience, saying that artists should be concerned with one thing—their art—and that they bear no responsibility to the audience. By this line of thinking writers concentrate on making their fiction—the characters and their worlds—come alive, and they make sure that the story works as a story and not as a medium for expressing an abstract statement. The meaning of a piece of fiction, O'Connor insisted, was the entire experience one has with it and was not a statement imposed on it that could then later be extracted and held up as its "message." Such thinking was central to the advice she wrote (December 11, 1956) to A. about writing fiction. O'Connor wrote that a writer should merely "start simply with a character or anything that you can make come alive." She continued, "When you have a character he will create his own situation and his situation will suggest some kind of resolution as you get into it. Wouldn't it be better to discover a meaning in what you write than to impose one?" (*HB*, 188).

Behind O'Connor's thinking is the thought of Saint Thomas Aquinas, whom O'Connor frequently cites. For Aquinas a work of art is, as O'Connor points out in "Catholic Novelists and Their Readers," "a good in itself," being "wholly concerned with the good of that which is made." As such, it "glorifies God because it reflects God," and writers have no cause to put their work to any other end; such endeavors only undermine the integrity of the vision and sully the purity of the art. Modern writers, O'Connor says in this same essay, by and large fail to heed Aquinas's lesson and instead wrench their art to make it fit utilitarian ends. For her, in contrast, "the artist has his hands full and does his duty if he attends to his art. He can safely leave the evangelizing to the evangelists" (*MM*, 171, 173, 171).

Catholic writers, in O'Connor's eyes, were particularly prone to distort their fiction for utilitarian purposes—to make it do something rather than be something. Particularly disturbing to her were those writers, in part goaded by the Catholic press, who wrote in pious language about the pieties of the Church. O'Connor's attitude toward this type of fiction was sharp: "As for the fiction," she wrote (February 19, 1956) to John Lynch, "the motto of the Catholic press should be: We guarantee to corrupt nothing but your taste" (*HB*, 138). In ignoring the realities of the here and now outside the Church, such fiction was for O'Connor little more than religious propaganda, the stuff one expects to find in the vestibules of churches but not in bookstores. These writers, she believed, were too concerned with presenting the Church in a favorable light and tending to their readership's spiritual needs; O'Connor's answer to them was that in writing fiction the Catholic writer "does not decide what would be good for the Christian body and proceed to deliver it" (*MM*, 183). Instead, as we have seen O'Connor stressing, writers must work within the limitations of their vocation to create the best story—not tract—possible. "The writer is only free when he can tell the reader to go jump in the lake,"

---

[1]The most extensive discussion of O'Connor's interpretation of her audience is in Carol Shloss, *Flannery O'Connor's Dark Comedies: The Limits of Inference* (Baton Rouge, 1980). [Brinkmeyer's note]

O'Connor said in one of her interviews, stressing the artist's independence from the audience. She added that though the writer of course wants to communicate a personal vision, "whether [the reader] likes it or not is no concern of the writer" (*CFO*, 39).

If in this way O'Connor downplayed the significance of the audience, she also frequently said something quite different. She argued that the audience played a crucial role in artistic creation and that writers always had to be aware of, and to take account of, their audience. She spoke of this connection in "Catholic Novelists and Their Readers," saying that "it takes readers as well as writers to make literature," and she added in "The Catholic Novelist in the Protestant South" that "it is what writer, character, and reader share that makes it possible to write fiction at all." Elsewhere (in "Novelist and Believer") O'Connor wrote that fiction was ultimately an attempt at communication; successful writing, she added, was not merely a rendering of the artist's vision but a rendering of it in such a way that the reader could understand it. "The novelist doesn't write to express himself, he doesn't write simply to render a vision he believes true, rather he renders his vision so it can be transferred, as nearly whole as possible, to his reader," she wrote. "You can safely ignore the reader's taste, but you can't ignore his nature, you can't ignore his limited patience. Your problem is going to be difficult in direct proportion as your beliefs depart from his." She echoes this observation in "Some Aspects of the Grotesque in Southern Fiction," saying that the writer's vision "has to be transmitted and that the limitations and blind spots of his audience will very definitely affect the way he is able to show what he sees" (*MM*, 182, 204–205, 162, 47).

When speaking of her own audience, O'Connor almost always stressed the great distance she felt between herself and her readers and pointed to the ways this gulf pressured and limited her as a writer. She believed that she and other American Catholic writers lacked a significant and responsive audience, and that this situation stifled imaginative growth and artistic expression. O'Connor found several reasons for this development. Central to the Catholic writer's plight, O'Connor believed, was the fact that in America Catholic writers lacked a distinctive social and cultural heritage based on religious identity. In "The Catholic Novelist in the Protestant South" she asserts that "the writer whose themes are religious particularly needs a region where these themes find a response in the life of the people." She then adds: "The American Catholic is short on places that reflect his particular religious life and his particular problems. This country isn't exactly cut in his image." She goes on to say that even in areas where there are large numbers of Catholics, Catholic life there lacks "the significant features that result in a high degree of regional self-consciousness" and so offers the Catholic writer few "exploitable benefits." O'Connor's analysis of Catholic writers continues: "They have no great geographical extent, they have no particularly significant history, certainly no history of defeat; they have no real peasant class, and no cultural unity of the kind you find in the South." She adds that Catholics usually "blend almost imperceptively into the general materialistic background." This lack of a strong cultural tradition and a supportive audience greatly burdens Catholic writers, impoverishing their imaginative life and art. "If the Catholic faith were central to life in America, Catholic fiction would fare better, but the Church is not central to this society." O'Connor continues: "The things that bind us together as Catholics are known only to ourselves. A secular society understands us less and less. It becomes more and more difficult in America to make belief believable" (*MM,* 200, 201).

These final words point to the second reason American Catholics lack a supportive audience: The larger society they write from and to is overwhelmingly secular and materialistic, money based rather than religious based. O'Connor, as we saw in the first chapter, was well aware of the trends in modern social and intellectual thought that since the Enlightenment have been validating and valorizing the human consciousness and rationality while undermining and reducing the significance of the religious. In a letter (October 19, 1958) to T. R. Spivey, O'Connor wrote that by and large people in today's society have "no sense of the power of God that could produce the Incarnation and the Resurrection. They are all so busy explaining away the virgin birth and such things, reducing everything to human proportions that in time they lose even the sense of the human itself, what they were aiming to reduce everything to" (*HB,* 300). Because moderns lacked a faith in transcendent values and order, O'Connor, as she said in "Some Aspects of the Grotesque in Southern Fiction," saw the age as one "which doubts both fact and value, which is swept this way and that by momentary convictions" (*MM,* 49). O'Connor found such relativism particularly disturbing, and this in part explains her strong attraction to the fundamentalist imperative that defines all values according to the simple — but total — choice of being for either Christ or the Devil.

Given these trends and developments, O'Connor saw her own position, as well as that of almost all American Catholic writers, as being particularly precarious in terms of communicating with her readership. O'Connor frequently asserted in her letters that she could consistently count on only a handful of informed readers — an assertion largely borne out by the number of vicious and misinformed readings her work received, particularly early on — and that she had to make these readers go a long way in her life as an author. O'Connor knew hers was not the type of fiction that most Catholic readers yearned to read — not, in other words, fiction that was thoroughly positive and that went out of its way to celebrate the life of the Church. She characterized the general Catholic reader as unthinking, and she said that this reader "is so busy looking for something that fits his needs, and shows him in the best possible light, that he will find suspect anything that doesn't serve such purpose" (*MM,* 182). Elsewhere, in a letter (May 4, 1963) to Sister Mariella Gable, she wrote that those Catholic readers who demand that the writer make Christianity look desirable are asking the writer to describe Christianity's essence and not what the writer actually sees. "Ideal Christianity doesn't exist, because anything the human being touches, even Christian truth, he deforms slightly in his own image," she wrote, adding a bit later that the tendency of the Catholic readers she had been discussing "is always toward the abstract and therefore toward allegory, thinness, and ultimately what they are looking for is apologetic fiction. The best of them think: make it look desirable because it is desirable. And the rest of them think: make it look desirable so I won't look like a fool for holding it" (*HB*, 516). Such readers would find little to like in O'Connor's fiction and in all likelihood would see it as a good deal more than suspect—subversive, probably.

O'Connor of course felt an even greater distance from what she saw as the thoroughly secular and unbelieving general reader, the reader to whom she claimed she primarily wrote. In "The Catholic Novelists and Their Readers" she said that Catholic readers make a great mistake in supposing that Catholic writers write exclusively for them. "Occasionally this may happen," she wrote, "but generally it is not happening today" (*MM*, 185), and O'Connor made it clear elsewhere that it was not happening in her fiction. To A., O'Connor wrote (August 2, 1955) of the audience she perceived, saying that "one of the awful things about writing when you are a Christian is that for you the ultimate reality is the Incarnation, the present reality is the Incarnation, and nobody believes in the Incarnation; that is, nobody in your audience. My audience are the people who think God is dead. At least these are the people I am conscious of writing for" (*HB*, 92). Trying to bridge this gap between believing author and unbelieving audience was a terrible burden for O'Connor, and one that haunted her throughout her career. In a review of Caroline Gordon's *The Male-factors*, O'Connor wrote that "making grace believable to the contemporary reader is the almost insurmountable problem of the novelist who writes from the standpoint of Christian orthodoxy," an observation that speaks crucially to O'Connor's own situation in communicating with her audience (*PG*, 16).

O'Connor further perceived her audience as making demands that she was not prepared to meet—ever. She complained in "Some Aspects of the Grotesque in Southern Fiction" that her freedom as a writer was always under pressure, since everywhere "the novelist is asked to be the handmaid of his age." She wrote, "Whenever the public is heard from, it is heard demanding a literature which is balanced and which will somehow heal the ravages of our time." This literature, she said elsewhere in this essay, was based on what she called "a realism of fact"—a realism that associated "the only legitimate material for long fiction with the movement of social forces, with the typical, with the fidelity to the way things look and happen in normal life." Such realism, she added, limited both the scope of the imaginative vision of artists and their fiction. As O'Connor noted here and elsewhere, her own fiction was written with a realism of an altogether different sort—a realism that sought not to mirror the typical but to reveal the spiritual. To this end, she says in "Novelist and Believer," the writer "is bound by the reasonable possibilities, not the probabilities of his culture" (*MM*, 46, 39, 165).

If the overall critical environment established its own orthodoxy for fiction, O'Connor also saw general readers establishing their own expectations and demands for what they should experience in the act of reading. She characterized the general readers as being "tired," of wanting what she called at one point "Instant Uplift"—that is, wanting to have their spirits raised in an act of easy compassion and sentiment. This demand for uplift and the redemptive act, O'Connor notes in "Some Aspects of the Grotesque in Southern Fiction," is a characteristic human need, and one that both the storyteller and the listener find particularly compelling in narrative. What bothers O'Connor is not that the reader seeks this motion in fiction but that the reader "has forgotten the cost of it." She explains that the modern reader's "sense of evil is diluted or lacking altogether, and so he has forgotten the price of restoration. When he reads a novel, he wants either his senses tormented or his spirits raised. He wants to be transported, instantly, either to mock damnation or a mock innocence." To underscore the risks the writer takes in ignoring such readers, O'Connor writes in this same essay that there are those who "say that the serious writer doesn't have to bother about the tired reader, but he does, because they are all tired. One old lady who wants her heart uplifted wouldn't be so bad, but you multiply her two hundred and fifty thousand times and what you get is a book club" (*MM*, 165, 48–49).

ABBREVIATIONS

Abbreviations of works by Flannery O'Connor commonly cited in the text refer to the following editions:

CFO   *Conversations with Flannery O'Connor.* Edited by Rosemary M. Magee. Jackson, Miss., 1987.

HB   *The Habit of Being: Letters.* Edited by Sally Fitzgerald. New York, 1969.

MM   *Mystery and Manners: Occasional Prose.* Edited by Sally Fitzgerald and Robert Fitzgerald. New York, 1969.

PG   *The Presence of Grace and Other Book Reviews by Flannery O'Connor.* Compiled by Leo J. Zuber. Edited by Carter W. Martin. Athens, Ga., 1983.

DOROTHY TUCK McFARLAND

On "Good Country People"   1976

"Good Country People," the penultimate story in the collection, is something of a comic variation on "A Good Man Is Hard to Find." As the grandmother of the title story thinks of herself as a good Christian woman who believes in all the conventional platitudes, Hulga Hopewell, the Ph.D. in philosophy who is the protagonist of "Good Country People," thinks of herself as a good nihilist who energetically disbelieves in all the conventional platitudes. In their titles both stories implicitly ask the reader to consider what are good men or good people. And in both stories O'Connor uses conventional language for comic and ironic purposes, emphasizing the meaninglessness of the platitudes in the mouths of her characters, and at the same time using their words to sound the main themes of the story. For instance, Hulga's mother, Mrs. Hopewell, characteristically strings together remarks like "Everybody is different. . . . It takes all kinds to make the world. . . . Nothing is perfect." Nevertheless, she actually tolerates differences and imperfections very poorly. Two of the themes in the story grow out of the characters' attitudes toward uniqueness ("everybody is different") and imperfection.

Mrs. Hopewell and her tenant's wife, Mrs. Freeman, embody contrasting ways of looking at the world that provide the frame for the story. Whereas Mrs. Hopewell is determined always to put a smiling face on things and never look beneath the surface, the gimlet-eyed Mrs. Freeman has a fondness for hidden things: "the details of secret infections, hidden deformities, assaults upon children." She is obsessed with the physical demands and ills of the body, and in her conversation about her two daughters she dwells on the details of two major aspects of their physical being: their sexuality and their ailments. One daughter, Glynese, is being courted by several admirers, one of whom is going to chiropractor school and who cures her of a sty by popping her neck. The other daughter, Carramae, is pregnant and unable to "keep anything on her stomach."

Mrs. Hopewell's daughter, Hulga, is antagonized by her mother's platitudinous optimism to the extent that her face has come to wear a look of constant outrage that "obliterated every other expression." She finds Mrs. Freeman tolerable only on the ground that Mrs. Freeman diverts some of her mother's attention from her; otherwise, she is uncomfortable with Mrs. Freeman's fascination with the secrets of the body.

Hulga has rejected the physical world and the life of the body in preference for the life of the mind: "She didn't like dogs or cats or birds or flowers or nature or nice young men. She looked at nice young men as if she could smell their stupidity." Her rejection of the physical world stems from her awareness of its liability to imperfection. Hulga's own imperfection is gross—she lost a leg when she was ten—but O'Connor obviously intended her to be a figure of all mankind, which suffers from the imperfections of the human condition. Hulga insists on calling attention to her physical imperfection and refuses to try to improve her appearance. However, this defensive insistence that she be accepted "LIKE I AM" does not indicate that *she* has really accepted what she is; rather, it suggests that she is trying to insulate herself against the pain of difference and imperfection.

Hulga's choice of her name reflects her response to her condition. Named Joy by her mother, she could not tolerate the incongruity between the idea of joy and her knowledge that she was "dust." She therefore chose to emphasize her deformity and ugliness by assuming an ugly name—Hulga—and a rude manner, and closed herself to joy for the sake of affirming the truth about herself. The persona she creates with the name Hulga is a blind, stony, armored creature. To her mother, the name Hulga suggests the "broad blank hull of a battleship." Hulga herself is described as being "square and rigid-shouldered," and as standing "blank and solid and silent." Her face is characteristically expressionless, and her "icy blue" eyes have the "look of someone who has achieved blindness by an act of will and means to keep it." Though she believes the self she has created is her true self, this imagery suggests that her willful blindness prevents her from seeing the true nature of the human condition as much as does her mother's insistence on always looking "at the bright side of things."

Though she has rejected joy for herself, Hulga has not given up on the possibility of love, and this secret desire is her one area of vulnerability. However, she thinks the persona she has created through her name is a means of making herself invulnerable, so that she can command and control love from a position of strength. She envisions her name working "like the ugly sweating Vulcan who stayed in the furnace and to whom the goddess [of love] had to come when called."

When an apparently naive country boy appears selling Bibles, Hulga feels that he offers no threat to her and allows herself to respond to his open admiration. Despite her utter inexperience (she has never been kissed) she decides to demonstrate her command of love by seducing him. She reinforces her image of herself as a woman of intellectual superiority and worldly wisdom by imagining that the simple Bible salesman, once seduced, will suffer from remorse, whereupon she will take away his shame and "transform it into something useful."

However, the Bible salesman's simplicity seduces her. Having climbed with her into the loft of an isolated barn, the Bible salesman gets Hulga to declare (with some reservations) that she loves him. He then demands that she prove it by showing him where her wooden leg joins on. At first shocked by his proposal, Hulga resists until he tells her why: "because [the wooden leg is] what makes you different." She feels that the Bible salesman, "with an instinct that came from beyond wisdom, had touched the truth about her." She comes to the conclusion that for the first time in her life she has encountered true innocence. She is so moved by her perception of his innocence that she lets down her defenses and allows her hidden vulnerability to emerge.

This area of vulnerability O'Connor equates with Hulga's soul and symbolizes it by her wooden leg: "she was as sensitive about the artificial leg as a peacock about his tail. No one ever touched it but her. She took care of it as someone else would his soul, in private and almost with her own eyes turned away." The leg is also, as the Bible salesman cannily recognized, what makes her different—a difference which, up to now, she has worn defensively and defiantly. Now, for the first time in the story, she accepts her difference, and allows herself to be touched in what is symbolically her soul. Accepting herself, she can surrender herself, and having surrendered herself she finds herself again, in the classic progression of love. When she allows the Bible salesman to remove her leg, "it was like surrendering to him completely. It was like losing her own life and finding it again, miraculously, in his."

Significantly, she surrenders to love in a scene in which her physical grotesqueness is not only emphasized but becomes the very means of love's expression and fulfillment. Though this scene of the Bible salesman removing Hulga's wooden leg is objectively ludicrous (and O'Connor's handling of it is full of irony), Hulga herself is, for the first time, completely without irony. The boy seems to her to be "entirely reverent" as he approaches the leg, and his removal of it is clearly the psychological and emotional equivalent to Hulga of the act of love: "She was thinking that she would run away with him and that every night he would take the leg off and every morning put it back on again."

Hulga's surrender to love also makes her vulnerable to a revelation of her own blindness. She had been convinced that she can see and that others cannot, and that she knows the truth. "Woman!" she had once shouted at her mother, enraged at Mrs. Hopewell's habit of blandly papering over ugliness with smiles. "Do you ever look inside . . . and see what you are *not*?" As a philosopher, Hulga is professionally concerned with truth. She is convinced that she has no illusions, that she has seen through appearances to the nothing that is beneath. "Some of us," she informs the Bible salesman, "have taken off our blindfolds and see that there's nothing to see." And she is utterly convinced of the truth of her assessment of the Bible salesman's innocence.

The Bible salesman, however, is anything but an innocent. Having put Hulga's leg out of her reach, he takes out of his suitcase a hollowed-out Bible containing a flask of whiskey, a deck of pornographic playing cards, and a packet of contraceptives. In response to Hulga's evident dismay, he replies, "What's the matter with you all of a sudden? . . . You just a while ago said you didn't believe in nothing. I thought you was some girl!" When he sees that he will get no farther with her, he snatches up her wooden leg, thrusts it into his suitcase, and disappears down the ladder of the barn loft.

The Bible salesman's thoroughgoing nihilism shows up Hulga's claim to believe in nothing as a superficial intellectual posture. Both his actions and his words devastate her assumption of intellectual superiority: "he turned and regarded her with a look that no longer had any admiration in it. . . . 'And I'll tell you another thing, Hulga,' he said, using the name as if he didn't think much of it, 'you ain't so smart. I been believing in nothing ever since I was born!' "

Hulga is left stranded, her previously stony face "churning" with emotion. But the Bible salesman's destruction of her illusions and her defenses (like the destruction of conventional order that resulted from the grandmother's encounter with The Misfit) may be, for Hulga, the means of her salvation. That the Bible salesman might be a kind of savior is suggested in the description of Hulga's final glimpse of him. Looking out the window of the barn loft, she sees him making his way across the pasture. O'Connor implicitly compares him to Christ walking on the water; to Hulga's blurred vision (the Bible salesman has also taken her glasses), he seems to be "struggling successfully over the green speckled lake."

The actual or implied references to Christ in *A Good Man Is Hard to Find* are numerous. The climactic moment in the title story comes about after The Misfit expresses his intense concern over the question of whether or not Jesus raised the dead. . . . The Bible salesman in "Good Country People" is implicitly compared to Christ.

Christ, as Simeon prophesied in St. Luke's gospel, is a "sign that will be contradicted," a sign of the presence of God in the world that, to many, will not seem to be a sign of God at all — will seem, rather, its opposite. The unexpected and often grotesque and incongruous ways in which O'Connor felt Christ to be present in the world is, I think, the real subject of this collection. Not only is the image of Christ suggested in unlikely places or associated with unlikely characters; but in style as well the stories embody contradiction and incongruity — in the double point of view, in the mixture of comedy and horror, in the pervasive tone of emotional flatness and irony, on the one hand, and the intimations of depth and serious meaning on the other. Thematically and stylistically, the centrality of Christ—of that which we experience as contradictory—provides *A Good Man Is Hard to Find* with a unity that makes it more than simply a random collection of stories. . . . I would add another gloss on the meaning of the title: the good man is so hard to find because he appears in such unlikely guises, because he is hidden in irony and contradiction.

WAYNE C. BOOTH

A Rhetorical Reading of O'Connor's "Everything That Rises Must Converge"   1974

This is an extremely complex story, not only in its ironic undercuttings but in its affirmations. No reading of it can be considered adequate unless it somehow relates the curious title to the various attempts to "rise" and to the failures to "converge." In the web of inference that we must create to see the story whole, our running translation of Julian's judgments into alternative judgments is only one strand. But once we have discerned that strand clearly, the rest of the story gives few difficulties.

Since Julian's is the only mind offering us opinions (except for a few observations and metaphors from the narrator, most notably the final sentence), we must sooner or later decide how far we can trust him. It is not hard to see that he is unreliable about many things. "He never spoke of it without contempt or thought of it without longing"—what kind of man is it, we ask, who always belies his true feelings? His life is full of such contradictions, showing that in his own way he is as far out of touch with reality as he takes his mother to be. His radical self-deception is perhaps clearest in the long fantasy that begins when he "withdraws into the inner compartment of his mind where he spent most of his time." No one could misread his own character more thoroughly than Julian does in thinking that he has "turned out so well," that he has a "first rate education," that he has a "large" mind, that he is "free of prejudice and unafraid to face facts"—remember, this is the boy who "did not like to consider all she did for him" and who can take pride in having "cut himself emotionally free of her." The closer we look at the disharmonies among his various opinions and actions, the more vigorously we must work in reconstructing the terrible lost young man we see behind his self-defensive rhetoric. His childish efforts to hurt his mother begin in a comic light, as he poses like a martyr and does everything he possibly can to spoil her one pleasant time of the week. But the comedy slowly gives place to pathos and horror as he runs over in his mind the possible tortures he might subject her to, then enjoys her humiliation about the duplicate hat, and finally—so wrapped up in his own petty bitterness and futility that he cannot see what is in front of his eyes—shouts irony-laden insults at the stricken woman. "You aren't who you think you are," he says, summarizing himself as much as his mother. "You've got to live in the new world and face a few realities for a change. Buck up, it won't kill you." It *is* killing her, and *he* is the one who must now begin to "face a few realities for a change."

These disharmonies are simple and clear. But the reconstruction of what "the realities" are—of what Julian must face—is not so easy. It is obviously not to be found in the "unreal," absurdly "innocent" world of the class-bound mother, nor in the equally unreal and absurd but vicious world of Julian. One kind of unmistakable reality is found in the irreducible, often harsh details of the life that Julian and his mother encounter but cannot see because of the abstractions that blur their vision. The mother does not see real "Negroes," for example, only the stereotypes that her childhood has provided her with. But Julian does not see real people either; instead he sees only the stereotypes that his liberal opinions dictate. Similarly, neither of them can see the other: Julian cannot see his mother for what she is; she cannot see what a miserable failure she has helped to create in him.

Our question then becomes: is there some ordering of values that for this story constitutes an alternative reality, one that in a sense judges everything the characters do? Our knowledge that Flannery O'Connor was known as a devout Catholic, or even that she herself talked about her stories in religious terms, can only alert us to one possible direction of interpretation. She might, after all, write one story that was entirely different from the others; for all I know, independently of my reading, she could have written this one before being converted, or after losing her faith. Even the most detailed knowledge about the author's life and statements of purpose can only alert me to certain possibilities; I must finally ask what kinds of clues the story itself provides to aid in the task of reconstructing a world of values that contrast with Julian's inanities.

The curious title is itself a kind of warning that seems to be spoken, as it were, in a special tone of voice. It simply does not harmonize easily with most of the surface, and indeed at first hardly makes sense at all. Does everything that "rises" in the story "converge"? Hardly. The black characters are "rising," but in spite of the liberal platitudes of Julian, there is no sign in the story that in their rising they will converge with the whites or with each other; one must thus ask whether or in what limited sense they are rising at all. Julian's liberal abstractions lead him to expect all Negroes to want his sympathy and interest, and to conform to his stereotyped demand that they "rise" to "talk on subjects that would be *above* the comprehension of those around him." But they insist on dwelling in a totally inaccessible world.

Julian has been "rising," too, as he obtains what he likes to think was a "first-class education." But his sense of elevation has, obviously, separated him not only from his mother but from all of his roots, without providing him with any other allegiances that could possibly support the claim of the title. What, then, can the title mean? It does not help us much to learn that it comes from the works of Teilhard de Chardin, the Catholic priest whose scientific and theological speculations earned him the accusation of heresy.

Is there any genuine change in the story that could be considered a "rising"? There is one, indeed, if we take seriously the change in Julian produced by the catastrophe. Julian is not just nasty and petty throughout the story; he is totally absorbed in his own ego. In contrast to his mother, who is "innocent," he is corrupt. Her desire is not to do ill in the world, but good, and only the limitations of what Julian calls her "fantasy world" betray her. But Julian, as we discover him behind his rationalizations, is actually malevolent, totally incapable of "converging" with the interests of any other person. His thoughts run constantly on his hatred of the world and his desire to "justify" himself in ways that he knows will hurt his mother deeply. "He would be entirely justified [in bringing home a Negro wife] but her blood pressure would rise to 300. He could not push her to the extent of making her have a stroke, and moreover, he had never been successful at making any Negro friends."

Throughout his absurd but vicious fantasies there thus run clues that prepare us for his discovery at the end. "For a moment he had an uncomfortable sense of her *innocence,* but it lasted only a second before *principle* rescued him. *Justice* entitled him to laugh." Dimly aware of her "innocence," passionately devoted to proving his own "principles" and obtaining "justice," he can be touched only by the greatest of disasters. Having never once been genuinely touched by any trouble, having in fact used his mother and her innocence as a shield against knowledge of himself, he is at last "stricken," "stunned." The change in him is as startling as the physical change produced in her by the stroke which he has helped to induce: "Darling, sweetheart, wait!" He is "crumpled," crushed into letting his defenses down and trying, too late, to call to his mother in love.

It would probably be a mistake to see anything strongly affirmative in this final dropping of all his egotistical defenses and crying "Mamma, mamma." He has not risen very far, but as he watches her destruction, falls at her side, and then runs for help, there has been, at last, a "convergence," a meeting of two human wills, that *might* presage his genuine "entry into the world of guilt and sorrow." For the Julian we have known throughout the story to experience either genuine guilt or sorrow would be a "rise" indeed, a rise based on the final convergence. The honest nightmare of his nothingness moving into "nowhere" in the final paragraph is thus a great improvement — in the light of this view of reality we now share with the implied author — over the "mental bubble" in which he established himself, where "he was safe from any kind of penetration from without." In his bubble he had been able to "see her with absolute clarity," or so he thought. Now, at the end, his bubble has been penetrated; he is swept by a "tide of darkness," and we are led to feel that he is for the first time in a position from which some sort of genuine human life is conceivable.

Whether this interpretation is sound or not, it certainly is never stated. Except for the ending, most of the words report Julian's misguided thoughts without open correction, and they must consequently be reconstructed. But they are not translated into a message.

There is perhaps no absolute need to go further than this. Readers of many different faiths and anti-faiths can presumably participate in this story of punishment and discovery, without pushing toward any special meaning for words like sin, innocence, faith, realities, guilt, and sorrow. But those of us who have read many of Flannery O'Connor's stories and studied her life will be unable to resist seeing Julian's final problematic redemption as presented in a religious light, even a specifically Roman Catholic light. Once the story is reread from this point of view, many additional ironies accumulate, ranging from Julian's name and his saintly posings at the beginning to the gratuitousness of grace at the end. But Flannery O'Connor was eager to write stories that were not mere allegories; as she intended, this story can be experienced by anyone who catches the essential contrast among the three systems of norms, Julian's, his mother's, and the cluster of traditional, conventional values we share with the author. Though it may seem thinner to those for whom Julian's self-absorption and cruelty are judged in secular terms than for a Catholic who sees him as in mortal sin, the structure of experience will be the same for both: Everyone will be forced to reject all or most of what the words seem to say. At every point we must decide on one out of many possible reconstructions, on the basis of a set of unshakable but silent beliefs that we are expected to share (however fleetingly) with the author. No one who fails to discern and feel some sympathy for these beliefs—only a few of them specifically Roman Catholic—is likely to make very much of the story.

For readers who do see behind Julian's absurd and egotistical words, the energy devoted to the act of seeing will of course increase the emotional effect and thus their estimate of the story's worth. This will not necessarily lead them to agree with me that it is a first-class story. But if they like it at all, the force of their liking will have been strengthened by their active engagement with the ironies.

Critical Conversations on Edgar Allan Poe's Stories

Edgar Allan Poe offers a valuable opportunity to trace the evolution of some different methods that critics have used to read short stories over an extended period of time. In the essays that follow, you will find examples of early psychological criticism, New Criticism, narrative theory, deconstruction, cultural criticism, and New Historical criticism. These excerpts by various critics responding over the years to three of Poe's stories will suggest the wealth of different approaches available to the contemporary reader.

Poe himself was not a systematic critic, and his writing on the short story does not fall into any academic category. He was one of the earliest writers to discuss the aesthetic qualities of the short story—what he called "the prose tale"—in his two long reviews praising the tales of Nathaniel Hawthorne. These articles, published in Graham's Magazine *in 1842 and* Godey's Lady's Book *in 1847, are pioneering examples of the analytic literary essay in America. This section begins with an excerpt from Poe's 1842 review, in which he introduces his theory of the short story and emphasizes the importance of unity of effect in a well-written tale.*

Edgar Allan Poe, photographed in Lowell, Massachusetts, in the last year of his life. (© Hulton-Deutsch Collection/CORBIS.)

In Poe's time, criticism of the short story, like the short story itself, was still a new field, but twentieth-century literary critics and scholars have developed many different approaches that enhance our understanding of short fiction, including Poe's mastery of this genre. Critics have been commenting on and analyzing Poe's tales for over a century. The field of literary theory investigating how authors *tell their stories expanded greatly due to a variety of cultural changes following the disruptions of World War II, and although early critics in the United States were reluctant to recognize Poe's achievement, Poe's genius was widely recognized by the end of the 1950s. In a 1959 lecture on "The House of Poe" at the Library of Congress, the American poet Richard Wilbur concluded that "Poe is a great artist, and I would rest my case for him on his prose allegories of psychic conflict. In them, Poe broke new ground, and they remain the best things of their kind in our literature."*

Most contemporary critics group the different ways of writing about literature into four broad categories: approaches that focus on either the author, the reader, the text, or the social and historical background of the text. Often critics combine two or more of these approaches when they develop their analyses of a short story. In this section, examples of some of the ways that critics have written about the texts and the backgrounds of "The Cask of Amontillado" (p. 473), "The Fall of the House of Usher" (p. 478), and "The Tell-Tale Heart" (p. 491) follow Poe's pioneering 1842 review of Hawthorne's Twice-Told Tales. *In addition to suggesting new ways to read Poe's short fiction, these essays show how different critics use different approaches to write about the same author, and how these approaches have developed in recent years. Since Poe is one of the most controversial American authors, these excerpts also suggest the continuing debate among academics over his place in the literary canon.*

EDGAR ALLAN POE

The Importance of the Single Effect in a Prose Tale
1842

But it is of [Hawthorne's] tales that we desire principally to speak. The tale proper, in our opinion, affords unquestionably the fairest field for the exercise of the loftiest talent, which can be afforded by the wide domains of mere prose. Were we bidden to say how the highest genius could be most advantageously employed for the best display of its own powers, we should answer, without hesitation — in the composition of a rhymed poem, not to exceed in length what might be perused in an hour. Within this limit alone can the highest order of true poetry exist. We need only here say, upon this topic, that, in almost all classes of composition, the unity of effect or impression is a point of the greatest importance. It is clear, moreover, that this unity cannot be thoroughly preserved in productions whose perusal cannot be completed at one sitting. We may continue the reading of a prose composition, from the very nature of prose itself, much longer than we can persevere, to any good purpose, in the perusal of a poem. This latter, if truly fulfilling the demands of the poetic sentiment, induces an exaltation of the soul which cannot be long sustained. All high excitements are necessarily transient. Thus a long poem is a paradox. And, without unity of impression, the deepest effects cannot be brought about.

Epics were the offspring of an imperfect sense of Art, and their reign is no more. A poem *too* brief may produce a vivid, but never an intense or enduring impression. Without a certain continuity of effort—without a certain duration or repetition of purpose—the soul is never deeply moved. There must be the dropping of the water upon the rock. . . .

Were we called upon, however, to designate that class of composition which, next to such a poem as we have suggested, should best fulfill the demands of high genius—should offer it the most advantageous field of exertion—we should unhesitatingly speak of the prose tale, as Mr. Hawthorne has here exemplified it. We allude to the short prose narrative, requiring from a half-hour to one or two hours in its perusal. The ordinary novel is objectionable, from its length, for reasons already stated in substance. As it cannot be read at one sitting, it deprives itself, of course, of the immense force derivable from *totality*. Worldly interests intervening during the pauses of perusal, modify, annul, or counteract, in a greater or less degree, the impressions of the book. But simple cessation in reading would, of itself, be sufficient to destroy the true unity. In the brief tale, however, the author is enabled to carry out the fullness of his intention, be it what it may. During the hour of perusal the soul of the reader is at the writer's control. There are no external or extrinsic influences—resulting from weariness or interruption.

A skillful literary artist has constructed a tale. If wise, he has not fashioned his thoughts to accommodate his incidents; but having conceived, with deliberate care, a certain unique or single *effect* to be wrought out, he then invents such incidents—he then combines such events as may best aid him in establishing this preconceived effect. If his very initial sentence tend not to the outbringing of this effect, then he has failed in his first step. In the whole composition there should be no word written, of which the tendency, direct or indirect, is not to the one pre-established design. And by such means, with such care and skill, a picture is at length painted which leaves in the mind of him who contemplates it with a kindred art, a sense of the fullest satisfaction. The idea of the tale has been presented unblemished, because undisturbed; and this is an end unattainable by the novel. Undue brevity is just as exceptionable here as in the poem; but undue length is yet more to be avoided.

We have said that the tale has a point of superiority even over the poem. In fact, while the *rhythm* of this latter is an essential aid in the development of the poem's highest idea—the idea of the Beautiful—the artificialities of this rhythm are an inseparable bar to the development of all points of thought or expression which have their basis in *Truth*. But Truth is often, and in very great degree, the aim of the tale. Some of the finest tales are tales of ratiocination. Thus the field of this species of composition, if not in so elevated a region of the mountain of Mind, is a tableland of far vaster extent than the domain of the mere poem. Its products are never so rich, but infinitely more numerous, and more appreciable by the mass of mankind. The writer of the prose tale, in short, may bring to his theme a vast variety of modes or reflections of thought and expression—(the ratiocinative, for example, the sarcastic, or the humorous) which are not only antagonistical to the nature of the poem, but absolutely forbidden by one of its most peculiar and indispensable adjuncts; we allude, of course, to rhythm. It may be added, here, *par parenthèse*, that the author who aims at the purely beautiful in a prose tale is laboring at a great disadvantage. For Beauty can be better treated in the poem. Not so with terror, or passion, or horror, or a multitude of such other points. . . .

Of Mr. Hawthorne's "Tales" we would say, emphatically, that they belong to the highest region of Art—an Art subservient to genius of a very lofty order. We have supposed, with good reason for so supposing, that he had been thrust into his present position by one of the impudent cliques which beset our literature, and whose pretensions it is our full purpose to expose at the earliest opportunity; but we have been most agreeably mistaken. We know of few compositions which the critic can more honestly commend than these "Twice-Told Tales." As Americans, we feel proud of the book.

Mr. Hawthorne's distinctive trait is invention, creation, imagination, originality—a trait which, in the literature of fiction, is positively worth all the rest. But the nature of the originality, so far as regards its manifestation in letters, is but imperfectly understood. The inventive or original mind as frequently displays itself in novelty of *tone* as in novelty of matter. Mr. Hawthorne is original in *all* points.

It would be a matter of some difficulty to designate the best of these tales; we repeat that, without exception, they are beautiful. . . . In the way of objection we have scarcely a word to say of these tales. There is, perhaps, a somewhat too general or prevalent *tone*—a tone of melancholy and mysticism. The subjects are insufficiently varied. There is not so much of *versatility* evinced as we might well be warranted in expecting from the high powers of Mr. Hawthorne. But beyond these trivial exceptions we have really none to make. The style is purity itself. Force abounds. High imagination gleams from every page. Mr. Hawthorne is a man of the truest genius.

D. H. LAWRENCE

D. H. Lawrence, the English novelist, poet, and critic, was fascinated by Poe's genius in his tales. Lawrence wrote an early form of psychological criticism of Poe's texts. Lawrence's approach was indebted to but often differed from the theories of the Austrian psychoanalyst Sigmund Freud (1856–1939). Freud's writing about human psychology, along with books by his disciples including Carl Jung, Marie Bonaparte, and Bruno Bettelheim, modified our understanding of human behavior, introducing such concepts as the unconscious forces of the id and the superego active within every individual.

Most literary criticism involves psychology to some degree, since we instinctively understand the human beings who are the creators or the subjects of short fiction in psychological terms. The way a text is interpreted also depends on the psychological assumptions of its reader. Lawrence, for example, projected his personal obsession about the potential of human relationships to become destructive into his interpretations of "The Fall of the House of Usher" and "The Cask of Amontillado."

Lawrence's chapter on Poe originally appeared in the English Review in 1919. It was later revised and reprinted in Lawrence's pioneering volume Studies in Classic American Literature (1923). In this book, Lawrence explored what he considered "the crisis of winterdeath," the disintegration of the soul of "the great white race in America." Lawrence believed that Poe's tales needed to be written "because old things need to die and disintegrate, because the old white psyche has to be gradually broken down before anything else can come to pass."

On "The Fall of the House of Usher" and "The Cask of Amontillado" 1919

[In "The Fall of the House of Usher,"] the love is between brother and sister. When the self is broken, and the mystery of the recognition of otherness fails, then the longing for identification with the beloved becomes a lust. And it is this longing for identification, utter merging, which is at the base of the incest problem. In psychoanalysis almost every trouble in the psyche is traced to an incest-desire. But this will not do. The incest-desire is only one of the manifestations of the self-less desire for merging. It is obvious that this desire for merging, or unification, or identification of the man with the woman, or the woman with the man, finds its gratification most readily in the merging of those things which are already near—mother with son, brother with sister, father with daughter. But it is not enough to say, as Jung does, that all life is a matter of lapsing towards, or struggling away from, mother-incest. It is necessary to see what lies at the back of this helpless craving for utter merging or identification with a beloved.

The motto to "The Fall of the House of Usher" is a couple of lines from De Béranger.

> "Son coeur est un luth suspendu;
> Sitôt qu'on le touche il résonne."

We have all the trappings of Poe's rather overdone vulgar fantasy. "I reined my horse to the precipitous brink of a black and lurid tarn that lay in unruffled lustre by the dwelling, and gazed down—but with a shudder even more thrilling than before—upon the remodelled and inverted images of the grey sedge, and the ghastly tree-stems, and the vacant and eye-like windows." The House of Usher, both dwelling and family, was very old. Minute fungi overspread the exterior of the house, hanging in festoons from the eaves. Gothic archways, a valet of stealthy step, sombre tapestries, ebon black floors, a profusion of tattered and antique furniture, feeble gleams of encrimsoned light through latticed panes, and over all "an air of stern, deep, irredeemable gloom"—this makes up the interior.

The inmates of the house, Roderick and Madeline Usher, are the last remnants of their incomparably ancient and decayed race. Roderick has the same large, luminous eye, the same slightly arched nose of delicate Hebrew model, as characterised Ligeia.[1] He is ill with the nervous malady of his family. It is he whose nerves are so strung that they vibrate to the unknown quiverings of the ether. He, too, has lost his self, his living soul, and become a sensitised instrument of the external influences; his nerves are verily like an aeolian harp which must vibrate. He lives in "some struggle with the grim phantasm, Fear," for he is only the physical, post-mortem reality of a living being.

It is a question how much, once the rich centrality of the self is broken, the instrumental consciousness of man can register. When man becomes self-less, wafting instrumental like a harp in an open window, how much can his elemental consciousness express? It is probable that even the blood as it runs has its own sympathies and responses to the material world, quite apart from seeing. And the nerves we know vibrate all the while to unseen presences, unseen forces. So Roderick Usher quivers on the edge of dissolution.

It is this mechanical consciousness which gives "the fervid facility of his impromptus." It is the same thing that gives Poe his extraordinary facility in versification. The absence of real central or impulsive being in himself leaves him inordinately mechanically sensitive to sounds and effects, associations of sounds, association of rhyme, for example—mechanical, facile, having no root in any passion. It is all a secondary, meretricious process. So we get Roderick Usher's poem, "The Haunted Palace," with its swift yet mechanical subtleties of rhyme and rhythm, its vulgarity of epithet. It is all a sort of dream-process, where the association between parts is mechanical, accidental as far as passional meaning goes.

Usher thought that all vegetable things had sentience. Surely all material things have a form of sentience, even the inorganic: surely they all exist in some subtle and complicated tension of vibration which makes them sensitive to external influence and causes them to have an influence on other external objects, irrespective of contact. It is of this vibrational or inorganic conscious-ness that Poe is master: the sleep-consciousness. Thus Roderick Usher was convinced that his whole surroundings, the stones of the house, the fungi, the water in the tarn, the very reflected image of the whole, was woven into a phys-ical oneness with the family, condensed, as it were, into one atmosphere—the special atmosphere in which alone the Ushers could live. And it was this atmosphere which had moulded the destinies of his family.

In the human realm, Roderick had one connection: his sister Madeline. She, too, was dying of a mysterious disorder, nervous, cataleptic. The brother and sister loved each other passionately and exclusively. They were twins, almost identical in looks. It was the same absorbing love between them, where human creatures are absorbed away from themselves, into a unification in death. So Madeline was gradually absorbed into her brother; the one life absorbed the other in a long anguish of love.

Madeline died and was carried down by her brother into the deep vaults of the house. But she was not dead. Her brother roamed about in incipient madness—a madness of unspeakable terror and guilt. After eight days they

---

[1]A reference to the heroine of Poe's short story "Ligeia."

were suddenly startled by a clash of metal, then a distinct, hollow, metallic, and clangorous, yet apparently muffled, reverberation. Then Roderick Usher, gibbering, began to express himself: *"We have put her living into the tomb! Said I not that my senses were acute? I now tell you that I heard her first feeble movements in the hollow coffin. I heard them—many, many days ago—yet I dared not—I dared not speak."*

It is again the old theme of "each man kills the thing he loves." He knew his love had killed her. He knew she died at last, like Ligeia, unwilling and unappeased. So, she rose again upon him. "But then without those doors there *did* stand the lofty and enshrouded figure of the Lady Madeline of Usher. There was blood upon her white robes, and the evidence of some bitter struggle upon every portion of her emaciated frame. For a moment she remained trembling and reeling to and fro upon the threshold, then, with a low moaning cry, fell heavily inward upon the person of her brother, and in her violent and now final death-agonies bore him to the floor a corpse, and a victim to the terrors he had anticipated."

It is lurid and melodramatic, but it really is a symbolic truth of what happens in the last stages of this inordinate love, which can recognise none of the sacred mystery of *otherness,* but must unite into unspeakable identification, oneness in death. Brother and sister go down together, made one in the unspeakable mystery of death. It is the world-long incest problem, arising inevitably when man, through insistence of his will in one passion or aspiration, breaks the polarity of himself.

The best tales all have the same burden. Hate is as love, and as slowly consuming, as secret, as underground, as subtle. All this underground vault business in Poe only symbolises that which takes place *beneath* the consciousness. On top, all is fair-spoken. Beneath, there is the awful murderous extremity of burying alive. Fortunato, in "The Cask of Amontillado," is buried alive out of perfect hatred, as the Lady Madeline of Usher is buried alive out of love. The lust of hate is the inordinate desire to consume and unspeakably possess the soul of the hated one, just as the lust of love is the desire to possess, or to be possessed by, the beloved, utterly. But in either case the result is the dissolution of both souls, each losing itself in transgressing its own bounds.

The lust of Montresor is to devour utterly the soul of Fortunato. It would be no use killing him outright. If a man is killed outright his soul remains integral, free to return into the bosom of some beloved, where it can enact itself. In walling-up his enemy in the vault, Montresor seeks to bring about the indescribable capitulation of the man's soul, so that he, the victor, can possess himself of the very being of the vanquished. Perhaps this can actually be done. Perhaps, in the attempt, the victor breaks the bounds of his own identity, and collapses into nothingness, or into the infinite.

What holds good for inordinate hate holds good for inordinate love. The motto, *Nemo me impune lacessit,*[2] might just as well be *Nemo me impune amat.*[3] . . .

---

[2]No one hates me with impunity.
[3]No one loves me with impunity.

As long as man lives he will be subject to the incalculable influence of love or of hate, which is only inverted love. The necessity to love is probably the source of all our unhappiness; but since it is the source of everything it is foolish to particularise. Probably even gravitation is only one of the lowest manifestations of the mystic force of love. But the triumph of love, which is the triumph of life and creation, does not lie in merging, mingling, in absolute identification of the lover with the beloved. It lies in the communion of beings, who, in the very perfection of communion, recognise and allow the mutual otherness. There is no desire to transgress the bounds of being. Each self remains utterly itself—becomes, indeed, most burningly and transcendently itself in the uttermost embrace or communion with the other. One self may yield honourable precedence to the other, may pledge itself to undying service, and in so doing become fulfilled in its own nature. For the highest achievement of some souls lies in perfect service. But the giving and the taking of service does not obliterate the mystery of otherness, the being-in-singleness, either in master or servant. On the other hand, slavery is an avowed obliteration of the singleness of being.

CLEANTH BROOKS AND
ROBERT PENN WARREN

Cleanth Brooks and Robert Penn Warren wrote what they termed New Criticism when they analyzed "The Fall of the House of Usher" in their book Understanding Fiction *(1943). Their work influenced generations of academics who taught the New Critical method of analyzing texts in college literature classes.*

In Brooks and Warren's analysis of "The Fall of the House of Usher," they practiced "close reading": They concentrated on showing how the various elements of the tale were integrated into a unique aesthetic structure. Avoiding biographical or psychological analysis, they examined the structure of the tale, concerned primarily with the text itself, not its author. As critics, they looked for qualities of textual complexity in works of literature, placing a high value on the presence of irony. With little imaginative sympathy for the protagonist Roderick Usher, Brooks and Warren were also unsympathetic to what they considered the excesses of Poe's romantic style. Later critics trained in the New Critical method admired Poe's tales and found much to praise in them by taking different approaches to the texts.

A New Critical Reading of
"The Fall of the House of Usher"   1943

This is a story of horror, and the author has used nearly every kind of device at his disposal in order to stimulate a sense of horror in the reader: not only is the action itself horrible but the descriptions of the decayed house, the gloomy landscape in which it is located, the furnishings of its shadowy interior, the ghastly and unnatural storm—all of these are used to build up in the reader the sense of something mysterious and unnatural. Within its limits, the story is rather successful in inducing in the reader the sense of nightmare; that is, if the reader allows himself to enter into the mood of the story, the mood infects him rather successfully.

But one usually does not find nightmares pleasant, and though there is an element of horror in many of the great works of literature—Dante's *Inferno*, Shakespeare's tragedies—still, we do not value the sense of horror for its own sake. What is the meaning, the justification of the horror in this story? Does the story have a meaning, or is the horror essentially meaningless, horror aroused for its own sake?

In the beginning of the story, the narrator says of the House of Usher that he experienced "a sense of insufferable gloom," a feeling which had nothing of that "half-pleasurable, because poetic, sentiment with which the mind usually receives even the sternest natural images of the desolate or terrible. . . . It was a mystery all insoluble. . . ." Does the reader feel, with regard to the story as a whole, what the narrator in the story feels toward the house in the story?

One point to determine is the quality of the horror—whether it is merely vague and nameless, or an effect of a much more precise and special imaginative perception. Here, the description which fills the story will be helpful: the horror apparently springs from a perception of decay, a decay which constitutes a kind of life-in-death, monstrous because it represents death and yet pulsates with a special vitality of its own. For example, the house itself gets its peculiar *atmosphere* . . . from its ability apparently to defy reality: to remain intact and yet seem to be completely decayed in every detail. By the same token, Roderick Usher has a wild vitality, a preternatural acuteness and sensitiveness which itself springs from the fact that he is sick unto death. Indeed, Roderick Usher is more than once in the story compared to the house, and by more subtle hints, by implications of descriptive detail, throughout the story, the house is identified with its heir and owner. For example, the house is twice described as having "vacant eye-like windows"—the house, it is suggested, is like a man. Or, again, the mad song, which Roderick Usher sings with evident reference to himself, describes a man under the *allegory* . . . of a house. To repeat, the action of the story, the description, and the symbolism, consistently insist upon the horror as that which springs from the unnatural and monstrous. One might reasonably conclude that the "meaning" of the story lies in its perception of the dangers of divorcement from reality and the attempt to live in an unreal world of the past, or in any private and abstract world of thought. Certainly, elements of such a critique are to be found in the story. But their mere presence there does not in itself justify the pertinacious and almost loving care with which Poe conjures up for us the sense of the horrors of the dying House of Usher.

One may penetrate perhaps further into the question by considering the relation of the horror to Roderick Usher himself. The story is obviously his story. It is not Madeline's—in the story she hardly exists for us as a human being—nor is it the narrator's story, though his relation to the occupants of the doomed House of Usher becomes most important when we attempt to judge the ultimate success or failure of the story.

Roderick Usher, it is important to notice, recognizes the morbidity of the life which he is leading. Indeed, he even calls his persistence in carrying on his mode of living in the house a deplorable "folly." And yet one has little or no sense in the story that Roderick Usher is actually making any attempt to get away from the haunting and oppressive gloom of the place. Actually, there is abundant evidence that he is in love with "the morbid acuteness of the senses" which he has cultivated in the gloomy mansion, and that in choosing between this and the honest daylight of the outside world, there is but one choice for him. But, in stating what might be called the moral issue of the story in such terms as these, we have perhaps already overstated it. The reader gets no sense of struggle, no sense of real choice at all. Rather, Roderick Usher impresses the reader as being as thoroughly doomed as the decaying house in which he lives.

One may go further with this point: we hardly take Roderick Usher seriously as a real human being at all. Even on the part of the narrator who tells us that Usher has been one of his intimate companions in boyhood, there is little imaginative identification of his interests and feelings with those of Usher. At the beginning of the story, the narrator admits that he "really knew little" of his friend. Even his interest in Usher's character tends to be what may be called a "clinical" interest. Now, baffled by the vague terrors and superstitions that beset Roderick Usher, he is able to furnish us, not so much a reading of his friend's character as a list of symptoms and aberrations. Usher is a medical case, a fascinating case to be sure, a titillatingly horrible case, but merely another case after all.

In making these points, we are really raising questions that have to do with the limits of tragedy. The tragic protagonist must be a man who engages our own interests and hopes and fears as a Macbeth or a Lear, of superhuman stature though these be, engages them. We must not merely look on from without. . . .

In the case of Roderick Usher, then, there is on our part little imaginative sympathy and there is, on his own part, very little struggle. The story lacks tragic quality. One can go farther: the story lacks even pathos—that is, a feeling of pity, as for the misfortune of a weak person, or the death of a child. To sum up, Poe has narrowed the fate of his protagonist from a universal thing into something special and even peculiar, and he has played up the sense of gloom and monstrous derangement so heavily that free will and rational decision hardly exist in the nightmare world which he describes. The horror is relatively meaningless—it is generated for its own sake; and one is inclined to feel that Poe's own interest in the story was a morbid interest.

JAMES W. GARGANO

James W. Gargano took the approach of a narrative theorist in his analysis of "The Tell-Tale Heart" and "The Cask of Amontillado." Narrative theory focuses on the difference between story and discourse. Story in this sense refers to the series of real or fictitious events, connected by chronology, that happen to cer-

tain characters; discourse refers to the ways that authors dramatize this series of events with their creation of plot, characters, settings, and point of view.

Gargano's essay, "The Question of Poe's Narrators," first appeared in Col-lege English (December 1963) and then was reprinted in The Naiad Voice: Essays on Poe's Satiric Hoaxing, *edited by Dennis W. Eddings and published by Associated Faculty Press in 1983. In Gargano's introduction to his essay, he sum-marized some earlier attacks on Poe's writing by notable American and English authors such as James Russell Lowell, Henry James, T. S. Eliot, Ivor Winters, and Aldous Huxley. Then Gargano went on to defend Poe's method of storytelling, analyzing how Poe created different fictional narrators to tell his tales and sug-gesting how a good reader can sustain what Gargano called "a thoughtful perspec-tive" on the stories.*

The Question of Poe's Narrators
in "The Tell-Tale Heart" and
"The Cask of Amontillado"   1963

Part of the widespread critical condescension toward Edgar Allan Poe's short stories undoubtedly stems from impatience with what is taken to be his "cheap" or embarrassing Gothic style. Finding turgidity, hysteria, and crudely poetic overemphasis in Poe's works, many critics refuse to accept him as a really serious writer. [James Russell] Lowell's flashy indictment of Poe as "two-fifths sheer fudge" agrees essentially with Henry James's magisterial dec-laration that an "enthusiasm for Poe is the mark of a decidedly primitive stage of reflection." T. S. Eliot seems to be echoing James when he attributes to Poe "the intellect of a highly gifted young person before puberty." Discovering in Poe one of the fountainheads of American obscurantism, Yvor Winters con-demns the incoherence, puerility, and histrionics of his style. Moreover, [Aldous] Huxley's charge that Poe's poetry suffers from "vulgarity" of spirit, has colored the views of critics of Poe's prose style.[1]

Certainly, Poe has always had his defenders. One of the most brilliant of modern critics, Allen Tate, finds a variety of styles in Poe's works; although Tate makes no high claims for Poe as stylist, he nevertheless points out that Poe could, and often did, write with lucidity and without Gothic mannerisms.[2] Floyd Stovall, a long-time and more enthusiastic admirer of Poe, has recently paid his critical respects to "the conscious art of Edgar Allan Poe." Though he says little about Poe's style, he seems to me to suggest that the elements of Poe's stories, style for example, should be analyzed in terms of Poe's larger artistic

---

[1]Lowell's comment appears in "A Fable for Critics"; Henry James, "Charles Baudelaire," *French Poets and Novelists* (London: MacMillan, 1878), p. 76; T. S. Eliot, *From Poe to Valéry* (New York: Harcourt, Brace, 1948), p. 28; Yvor Winters, "Edgar Allan Poe: A Crisis in the History of American Obscurantism," in *In Defense of Reason* (New York: Swallow Press, 1947); Aldous Huxley, "Vulgarity in Literature," in *Music at Night and Other Essays* (London: Chatto & Windus, 1949), pp. 297–309.

[2]Allen Tate, "Our Cousin, Mr. Poe," in *The Man of Letters in the Modern World: Selected Essays, 1928–1955* (New York: Meridian Books, 1955), pp. 132–45.

intentions. Of course, other writers, notably Edward H. Davidson, have done much to demonstrate that an intelligible rationale informs Poe's best work.

It goes without saying that Poe, like other creative men, is sometimes at the mercy of his own worst qualities. Yet the contention that he is fundamentally a bad or tawdry stylist appears to me to be rather facile and sophistical. It is based, ultimately, on the untenable and often unanalyzed assumption that Poe and his narrators are identical literary twins and that he must be held responsible for all their wild or perfervid utterances; their shrieks and groans are too often conceived as emanating from Poe himself. I believe, on the contrary, that Poe's narrators possess a character and consciousness distinct from those of their creator. These protagonists, I am convinced, speak their own thoughts and are the dupes of their own passions. In short, Poe understands them far better than they can possibly understand themselves. Indeed, he often so designs his tales as to show his narrators' limited comprehension of their own problems and states of mind; the structure of many of Poe's stories clearly reveals an ironical and comprehensive intelligence critically and artistically ordering events so as to establish a vision of life and character which the narrator's very inadequacies help to "prove."

What I am saying is simply that the total organization or completed form of a work of art tells more about the author's sensibility than does the report or confession of one of its characters. Only the most naive reader, for example, will credit as the "whole truth" what the narrators of *Barry Lyndon, Huckleberry Finn,* and *The Aspern Papers* will divulge about themselves and their experiences. In other words, the "meaning" of a literary work (even when it has no narrator) is to be found in its fully realized form; for only the entire work achieves the resolution of the tensions, heterogeneities, and individual visions which make up the parts. The Romantic apologists for Milton's Satan afford a notorious example of the fallacy of interpreting a brilliantly integrated poem from the point of view of its most brilliant character.

The structure of Poe's stories compels realization that they are more than the effusions of their narrators' often disordered mentalities. Through the irony of his characters' self-betrayal and through the development and arrangement of his dramatic actions, Poe suggests to his readers ideas never entertained by the narrators. Poe intends his readers to keep their powers of analysis and judgment ever alert; he does not require or desire complete surrender to the experience of the sensations being felt by his characters. The point of Poe's technique, then, is not to enable us to lose ourselves in strange or outrageous emotions, but to see these emotions and those obsessed by them from a rich and thoughtful perspective. I do not mean to advocate that, while reading Poe, we should cease to feel; but feeling should be "simultaneous" with an analysis carried on with the composure and logic of Poe's great detective, Dupin. For Poe is not merely a Romanticist; he is also a chronicler of the consequences of the Romantic excesses which lead to psychic disorder, pain, and disintegration.

Once Poe's narrative method is understood, the question of Poe's style and serious artistry returns in a new guise. Clearly, there is often an aesthetic compatibility between his narrators' hypertrophic language and their psychic derangement. . . .

In "The Tell-Tale Heart" the cleavage between author and narrator is perfectly apparent. The sharp exclamations, nervous questions, and broken sentences almost too blatantly advertise Poe's conscious intention; the protagonist's painful insistence in "proving" himself sane only serves to intensify the idea of his madness. Once again Poe presides with precision of perception at the psychological drama he describes. He makes us understand that the voluble murderer has been tortured by the nightmarish terrors he attributes to his victim: "He was still sitting up in bed, listening;—just as I have done, night after night, hearkening to the death watches in the wall"; further, the narrator interprets the old man's groan in terms of his own persistent anguish: "Many a night, just at midnight, when all the world slept, it has welled up from my own bosom, deepening, with its dreadful echo, the terrors that distracted me." Thus, Poe, in allowing his narrator to disburden himself of his tale, skillfully contrives to show also that he lives in a haunted and eerie world of his own demented making.

Poe assuredly knows what the narrator never suspects and what, by the controlled conditions of the tale, he is not meant to suspect—that the narrator is a victim of his own self-torturing obsessions. Poe so manipulates the action that the murder, instead of freeing the narrator, is shown to heighten his agony and intensify his delusions. The watches in the wall become the ominously beating heart of the old man, and the narrator's vaunted self-control explodes into a frenzy that leads to self-betrayal. I find it almost impossible to believe that Poe has no serious artistic motive in "The Tell-Tale Heart," that he merely revels in horror and only inadvertently illuminates the depths of the human soul. I find it equally difficult to accept the view that Poe's style should be assailed because of the ejaculatory and crazy confession of his narrator. . . .

Evidence of Poe's "seriousness" seems to me indisputable in "The Cask of Amontillado," a tale which W. H. Auden has belittled.[3] Far from being his author's mouthpiece, the narrator, Montresor, is one of the supreme examples in fiction of a deluded rationalist who cannot glimpse the moral implications of his planned folly. Poe's fine ironic sense makes clear that Montresor, the stalker of Fortunato, is both a compulsive and pursued man; for in committing a flawless crime against another human being, he really (like . . . the protagonist in "The Tell-Tale Heart") commits the worst of crimes against himself. His reasoned, "cool" intelligence weaves an intricate plot which, while ostensibly satisfying his revenge, despoils him of humanity. His impeccably contrived murder, his weird mask of goodness in an enterprise of evil, and his abandonment of all his life-energies in one pet project of hate convict him of a madness which he mistakes for the inspiration of genius. The brilliant masquerade setting of Poe's tale intensifies the theme of Montresor's apparently successful duplicity; Montresor's ironic appreciation of his own deviousness seems

[3]W. H. Auden, introduction, *Edgar Allan Poe: Selected Prose and Poetry* (New York: Holt, Rinehart & Winston, 1950), p. v.

further to justify his arrogance of intellect. But the greatest irony of all, to which Montresor is never sensitive, is that the "injuries" supposedly perpetrated by Fortunato are illusory and that the vengeance meant for the victim recoils upon Montresor himself. In immolating Fortunato, the narrator unconsciously calls him the "noble" Fortunato and confesses that his own "heart grew sick." Though Montresor attributes this sickness to "the dampness of the catacombs," it is clear that his crime has begun to "possess" him. We see that, after fifty years, it remains the obsession of his life; the meaning of his existence resides in the tomb in which he has, symbolically, buried himself. In other words, Poe leaves little doubt that the narrator has violated his own mind and humanity, that the external act has had its destructive inner consequences. . . .

If my thesis is correct, Poe's narrators should not be construed as his mouthpieces; instead, they should be regarded as expressing, in "charged" language indicative of their internal disturbances, their own peculiarly nightmarish visions. Poe, I contend, is conscious of the abnormalities of his narrators and does not condone the intellectual ruses through which they strive, only too earnestly, to justify themselves. In short, though his narrators are often febrile or demented, Poe is conspicuously "sane." They may be "decidedly primitive" or "wildly incoherent," but Poe, in his stories at least, is mature and lucid.

J. GERALD KENNEDY

J. Gerald Kennedy used deconstruction to analyze the function of the story of "the 'Mad Trist' of Sir Launcelot Canning" included in Poe's "The Fall of the House of Usher." Deconstruction *emphasizes a close reading of literature guided not so much by a search for surface meaning as by an exploration of the text's internal contradictions, the places where meaning does not remain stable.*

In his book Poe, Death, and the Life of Writing, *published by Yale University Press in 1987, Kennedy attempted to show that "the 'Mad Trist'" was linked to what he called a "deep structure" in "The Fall of the House of Usher" that signified Poe's larger theme of his ultimate survival through his writing. Kennedy felt that "Poe's responsiveness to the problem of death led to self-conscious reflection upon writing and the power of words," and that "the rupture between word and world, signifier and signified, finds its origin in the semiotic impasse of mortality located by Poe."*

On "The Fall of the House of Usher" 1987

What Poe reveals, in the succession of tales and poems which constitute his literary corpus, is the enormous complexity, the imaginative fecundity, of this elemental insight [—that by creating works of literature, he could defy his own physical death]. This is the problem to which he returns obsessively in his most striking enactments of the encounter with death. Hence, for example, the fatality of "The Fall of the House of Usher": at a crucial moment, the narrator attempts to calm his host by reading "the 'Mad Trist' of Sir Launcelot Canning" and in the correspondence between that narrative and underground noises, Poe suggests that the romance holds a clue to the curse upon the Ushers. At three separate points, events in the "Mad Trist" seem to evoke sounds within the mansion, as if the text possessed some preternatural agency which ultimately called forth Madeline from the burial vault. Although this "coincidence" may be dismissed as anticipatory anxiety—one can argue that the narrator unconsciously chooses a text which describes sounds like those he hears beneath the house—the details of the story indeed furnish a coded version of the problem of dread figured by Usher's relationship to his sister's corpse. And in a more important sense the "Mad Trist" exemplifies the way in which writing corresponds to the mortal condition which determines and authorizes it.

The episode supposedly read by the narrator (and then reproduced in the text of "Usher") depicts Ethelred's forcible entry into the dwelling of a "maliceful" hermit. Having battered down the door, the hero discovers no sign of the hermit; instead he confronts a scaly dragon which guards a golden palace ornamented by a brass shield bearing the inscription: "Who entereth herein, a conqueror hath bin; / Who slayeth the dragon, the shield he shall win." Ethelred promptly dispatches the dragon, which dies hideously, "[giving] up his pesty breath, with a shriek so horrid and harsh, and withal so piercing, that Ethelred had fain to close his ears with his hands against the dreadful noise of it, the like whereof was never before heard." Wishing to complete "the breaking up of the enchantment," Ethelred "[removes] the carcass from out of the way before him" and approaches the shield. But as if unfastened by the removal of the carcass, the shield falls to the silver floor with a "great and terrible ringing sound." At this juncture the reading of the "Mad Trist" is interrupted by a "clangorous" reverberation within the House of Usher, followed by Roderick's hysterical interpretation of the romance as a figuring of Madeline's return: "And now—tonight—Ethelred—ha! ha!—the breaking of the hermit's door, and the death-cry of the dragon, and the clangor of the shield!—say, rather, the rending of her coffin, and the grating of the iron hinges of her prison, and her struggles within the coppered archway of the vault." And indeed, the appearance of "the lofty and enshrouded figure of the lady Madeline of Usher" seems to validate this reading and imply an occult relationship between the "Mad Trist" and the fall of the Ushers.

But like the image of the house in the tarn, the analogy is reversed and inverted. For the ancient tale of Sir Launcelot Canning represents the dispelling of an enchantment, whereas the extinction of the Ushers marks the completion of a curse. And so the meaning of the last, horrific scene—the deadly embrace of Roderick by Madeline—becomes intelligible only through a consideration of the way in which it effects a reversal of the "Mad Trist." Reduced to constituent terms (the dragon, the palace, and the shield), the romance may be understood as a fantasy of psychic liberation; as such it corresponds closely to Poe's earlier insertion, "The Haunted Palace," and in some sense answers the despairing poem with a narrative of reclamation and recovery. Insofar as "The Haunted Palace" allegorizes the usurpation of reason by griefs and fears, the verses summarize the anxieties of Usher, who anticipates that he will "abandon life and reason together in some struggle with the grim phantasm, FEAR." Significantly, Ethelred too encounters a haunted palace and a frightening embodiment of that which holds the edifice in thrall; but he slays the monster, endures its dying shriek, disposes of the body, and shield, which signifies both victory over the beast and entitlement to the palace. If we understand the palace in both texts as a metaphor for mind, we must then construe both the "evil things, in robes of sorrow" and the scaly dragon as versions of that phantasm which threatens life and reason together—that is, as figurations of the fate which Roderick dreads, the fate prefigured by the transformation of his twin sister. Poe underscores the analogy through the "death-cry" of the dragon, which anticipates Madeline's "moaning cry" as she falls upon her brother "in her violent and now final death-agonies." But whereas Ethelred destroys the dragon and lifts the enchantment, Usher falls to the floor "a corpse, and a victim to the terrors he had anticipated."

In the difference between Ethelred's story and Usher's, Poe inscribes the dilemma of the new death within the metaphysical void of the modern age. One key distinction lies in the relation of the hero to the body of death: whereas the knight removes "the carcass from out of the way before him" and so figuratively confronts and resolves the fear of mortality, Usher experiences a paralysis of will, cannot bring himself to bury his sister's body, and is at last driven mad by the uncertainty signaled by her "temporary entombment." His indecision derives not simply from the ambiguity of her demise (with the attendant symptoms of catalepsy) but from the tension between that which bonds him to Madeline—the "striking similitude" of the twins and the "sympathies of a scarcely intelligible nature"—and that which horrifies him, the signs of her moribund condition. With the apparent death of Madeline (she is said to be "no more"), Usher is caught between the desire to preserve the possibly still-living body and the need to protect himself from the contagion of death. In the decline of Madeline, the cadaverous Usher has perceived the image of his own disintegration; but in his desolate world, it is a fate too ghastly to be contemplated. Ultimately, his anxiety about the physical condition of Madeline betrays an unarticulated despair about her spiritual destiny. By refusing to consign his sister to the earth, Usher simultaneously denies death and condemns himself to a life of horror.

For, as the story of Ethelred suggests, it is only by confronting the dragon and disposing of the carcass—that is, by recognizing that death is paradoxically the end of the monster of death—that one can liberate the palace and live one's life. What Usher fears—what we all fear—is not so much death itself but the experience of dying, the last agony. Though he claims to have heard his sister's "first feeble movements in the hollow coffin," Usher has been unable to summon the moral energy to face the possible image of decay; in psychic terms, his velleity is itself the product of a refusal to confront death. . . . And so when Usher deposits the body of Madeline in the vault beneath the house, figuratively pushing into the unconscious that overwhelming reality which she incarnates, he condemns himself to a death-in-life. He has not faced the shadow; he has evaded it. And so its eruption, in the form of Madeline's enshrouded figure, marks the inevitable—and fatal—return of the repressed.

In this complex metaphorizing of the problem of death, Poe articulates both the nature of the crisis and a figurative solution to the paralysis of death anxiety. But that solution seems as remote as the world of the romance; our spiritual contemporary, Usher dwells literally and figuratively on the brink of the abyss and cannot escape the fatality of his situation. Nor in fact does the putative narrator, who flees "aghast" from the crumbling mansion to record his tale and thus (like the Ancient Mariner) to signify the continuing hold of the experience upon his consciousness. But the writing of "Usher" may be construed as a modern effort to confront the dragon, to extract from the romance a principle of survival. In this sense the text of the "Mad Trist" presents a model of the complicity between inscription and mortality, for the surface action replicates the resistance to death which is the agony of writing. Poe attributes the romance to Canning, the same imaginary author to whom he later ascribed the motto for the *Stylus:* "—unbending that all men / Of thy firm TRUTH may say—'Lo! this is writ / With the antique *iron pen.'*" The idea of a writing whose truth outlasts death occurs in the "Mad Trist" as the legend "enwritten" on the magical brass shield: one who enters into writing "a conqueror hath bin." Ethelred's adventure enacts the ordeal undergone by both Canning and the narrator: that confrontation with death which impels writing by foreshadowing the silence of nonbeing.

To perceive "Usher" as a fable of dread and avoidance is to understand more clearly its centrality within the Poe canon. If the text signifies the survival of the writer, it also implies the impossibility of writing within the house of Usher—that is, in a condition of paralyzing denial. The narrator inscribes his account from an unspecified place on the opposite side of "the old causeway," at some geographical and psychic distance from the tarn into which the house disappears. Only elsewhere can he record Usher's struggle to preserve life and reason against the consciousness of impending annihilation. That struggle, objectified in the relationship of Usher to his dying sister, defines a fundamental opposition, a quintessential version of the deep structure which may be said to inform most of those texts Poe described as tales of effect.

DAVID S. REYNOLDS

David S. Reynolds practiced cultural criticism *in his investigation of "Poe's Art of Transformation in 'The Cask of Amontillado.'" Culture critics analyze aspects of social forms such as religion and popular literature in a writer's background that might have influenced the creation of a specific literary work.*

Reynolds's essay was commissioned for the volume New Essays on Poe's Major Tales, *edited by Kenneth Silverman for Cambridge University Press in 1993. In the first half of the essay, Reynolds discussed Poe's ability to recycle materials from popular literature in his own tales, quoting Poe's statement that "the truest and surest test of originality is the manner of handling a hackneyed subject." In the second half, Reynolds focused on "The Cask of Amontillado" in an attempt to explain how the story transcended the specific cultural references of its time and place to attain its stature as an American masterpiece that continues to evoke emotions of pity and terror in new generations of readers.*

Poe's Art of Transformation in "The Cask of Amontillado"   1993

Though grounded in nineteenth-century American culture, "The Cask of Amontillado" transcends its time-specific referents because it is crafted in such a way that it remains accessible to generations of readers unfamiliar with such sources as anti-Catholicism, temperance, and live-burial literature. The special power of the tale can be understood if we take into account Poe's theories about fiction writing, developed largely in response to emerging forms of popular literature that aroused both his interest and his concern. On the one hand, as a literary professional writing for popular periodicals ("Cask" appeared in the most popular of all, *Godey's Lady's Book*) Poe had to keep in mind the demands of an American public increasingly hungry for sensation. On the other hand, as a scrupulous craftsman he was profoundly dissatisfied with the way in which other writers handled sensational topics. John Neal's volcanic, intentionally disruptive fiction seemed energetic but formless to Poe, who saw in it "no precision, no finish . . . —always an excessive *force* but little of refined art."[1] Similarly, he wrote of the blackly humorous stories in Washington Irving's *Tales of a Traveller* that "the interest is subdivided and frittered away, and their conclusions are insufficiently *climacic* [sic]" (*ER*, 586–7). George Lippard's *The Ladye Annabel*, a dizzying novel involving medieval torture and necrophilic visions, struck him as indicative of genius yet chaotic. A serial novel by Edward Bulwer-Lytton wearied him with its "continual and vexatious shifting of scene," while N. P. Willis's sensational play *Tortesa* exhibited "the great error" of "*inconsequence*. Underplot is piled on underplot," as Willis gives us "vast designs that terminate in nothing" (*ER*, 153, 367).

In his own fiction Poe tried to correct the mistakes he saw in other writers. The good plot, he argued, was that from which nothing can be taken without detriment to the whole. If, as he rightly pointed out, much sensational fiction of the day was digressive and directionless, his best tales were tightly unified. Of them all, "The Cask of Amontillado" perhaps most clearly exemplifies the unity he aimed for.

The tale's compactness becomes instantly apparent when we compare it with the popular live-burial works mentioned earlier. Headley's journalistic "A Man Built in a Wall" begins with a long passage about a lonely Italian inn and ends with an account of the countryside around Florence; the interpolated story about the entombed man dwells as much on the gruesome skeleton as on the vindictive crime. Balzac's "La Grande Bretêche" is a slowly developing tale in which the narrator gets mixed accounts about an old abandoned mansion near the Loire; only in the second half of the story does he learn from his land-

---

[1]Poe, *Essays and Reviews* (New York: Library of America, 1984), p. 1151. This volume is hereafter cited parenthetically in the text as *ER*.

lady that the mansion had been the scene of a live burial involving a husband's jealous revenge. The entombment in "Apropos of Bores" is purely accidental (two unlucky men find themselves trapped in a wine vault) and is reduced to frivolous chatter when the narrator breaks off at the climactic moment and his listeners crack jokes and disperse to tea. Closest in spirit to Poe, perhaps, is the "dead-vault" scene in Lippard's *The Quaker City:* There is the same ritualistic descent into an immense cellar by a sadistic murderer intent on burying his victim alive. Lippard, however, constantly interrupts the scene with extraneous descriptions (he's especially fascinated by the skeletons and caskets strewn around the cellar). In addition, this is just one of countless bloodcurdling scenes in a meandering novel light-years distant, structurally, from Poe's carefully honed tale.

So tightly woven is "The Cask" that it may be seen as an effort at literary one-upsmanship on Poe's part, designed pointedly as a contrast to other, more casually constructed live-burial pieces. In his essays on popular literature, Poe expressed particular impatience with irrelevancies of plot or character. For instance, commenting on J. H. Ingraham's perfervid best-seller *Lafitte, the Pirate of the Gulf,* he wrote: "We are surfeited with unnecessary details. . . . Of outlines there are none. Not a dog yelps, unsung" (*ER*, 611).

There is absolutely no excess in "The Cask of Amontillado." Every sentence points inexorably to the horrifying climax. In the interest of achieving unity, Poe purposely leaves several questions unanswered. The tale is remarkable for what it leaves out. What are the "thousand injuries" Montresor has suffered at the hands of Fortunato? In particular, what was the "insult" that has driven Montresor to the grisly extreme of murder by live burial? What personal misfortune is he referring to when he tells his foe, "you are happy, as I once was"? Like a painter who leaves a lot of suggestive white canvas, Poe sketches character and setting lightly, excluding excess material. Even so simple a detail as the location of the action is unknown. Most assume the setting is Italy, but one commentator makes a good case for France.[2] What do we know about the main characters? As discussed, both are bibulous and proud of their connoisseurship in wines. Fortunato, besides being a Mason, is "rich, respected, admired, beloved," and there is a Lady Fortunato who will miss him. Montresor is descended from "a great and numerous family" and is wealthy enough to sustain a palazzo, servants, and extensive wine vaults.

Other than that, Poe tells very little about the two. Both exist solely to fulfill the imperatives of the plot Poe has designed. Everything Montresor does and says furthers his strategy of luring his enemy to his death. Everything Fortunato does and says reveals the fatuous extremes his vanity about wines will lead him to. Though limited, these characters are not what E. M. Forster would

---

[2]Pollin, *Discoveries in Poe*, pp. 29–33. Pollin points out that when Poe compares Montresor's crypts with "the great catacombs of Paris" he is revealing his awareness of contemporary accounts of the great necropolis under the Faubourg St. Jacques, in which the skeletal remains of some three million former denizens of Paris were piled along the walls. One such account had appeared in the "Editor's Table" of the *Knickerbocker Magazine* for March 1838. Pollin also develops parallels between "The Cask" and Victor Hugo's *Notre-Dame de Paris*, a novel Poe knew well.

call flat. They swiftly come alive before our eyes because Poe describes them with acute psychological realism. Montresor is a complex Machiavellian criminal, exhibiting a full range of traits from clever ingratiation to stark sadism. Fortunato, the dupe whose pride leads to his own downfall, nevertheless exhibits enough admirable qualities that one critic has seen him as a wronged man of courtesy and good will.[3] The drama of the story lies in the carefully orchestrated interaction between the two. Poe directs our attention away from the merely sensational and toward the psychological. . . .

Is "The Cask of Amontillado" intensely moralistic or frighteningly amoral? These questions, I would say, are finally unresolvable, and their very unresolvability reflects profound paradoxes within the antebellum cultural phenomena that lie behind the tale. A fundamental feature of anti-Catholic novels, dark temperance literature, and reform novels like Lippard's *The Quaker City* is that they invariably proclaimed themselves pure and moralistic but were criticized, with justification, for being violent and perverse. Many popular American writers of Poe's day wallowed in foul moral sewers with the announced intent of scouring them clean, but their seamy texts prove that they were more interested in wallowing than in cleaning. This paradox of immoral didacticism, as I have called it elsewhere,[4] helps account for the hermeneutic circularities of "The Cask of Amontillado." On the one hand, there is evidence for a moral or even religious reading: The second sentence, "You, who know so well the nature of my soul," may be addressed to a priest to whom Montresor, now an old man, is confessing in an effort to gain deathbed expiation. On the other hand, there is no explicit moralizing, and the tale reveals an undeniable fascination with the details of cunning crime. Transforming the cultural phenomenon of immoral didacticism into a polyvalent dramatization of pathological behavior, Poe has it both ways: He satisfies the most fiendish fantasies of sensation lovers (including himself, at a time when revenge was on his mind), still retaining an aura of moral purpose. He thus serves two types of readers

---

[3]Joy Rea, "In Defense of Fortunato's Courtesy," *Studies in Short Fiction*, 4 (1967): 57–69. I agree, however, with William S. Doxey, who in his rebuttal to Rea emphasizes Fortunato's vanity and doltishness; see Doxey, "Concerning Fortunato's 'Courtesy,'" *Studies in Short Fiction*, 4 (1967): 266. Others have pointed out that there may be an economic motive behind the revenge scheme. Montresor, who calls the wealthy Fortunato happy "as I once was," seems to feel as though he has fallen into social insignificance and to think delusively he can regain his "fortune" by the violent destruction of his supposed nemesis, who represents his former socially prominent self. See James Gargano, " 'The Cask of Amontillado': A Masquerade of Motive and Identity," *Studies in Short Fiction*, 4 (1967): 119–26. That economic matters would be featured in this tale is not surprising, since Poe was impoverished and sickly during the period it was written. His preoccupation with money is reflected in the names Montresor, Fortunato, Luchesi ("Luchresi" in the original version)—"treasure," "fortune," and "lucre"—which, as David Ketterer points out, all add up to much the same thing (*The Rationale of Deception* [Baton Rouge: Louisiana State University Press], p. 110).

[4]David S. Reynolds, *Beneath the American Renaissance* (Boston: Harvard U.P., 1989), Chapter 2.

simultaneously: the sensationally inclined, curious about this cleverest of killers, and the religiously inclined, expectant that such a killer will eventually get his due. In the final analysis, he is pointing to the possibility that these ostensibly different kinds of readers are one and the same. Even the most devoutly religious reader, ready to grab at a moral lesson, could not help being intrigued by, and on some level moved by, this deftly told record of shrewd criminality.

Poe had famously objected to fiction that struck him as too allegorical, fiction in which imagery pointed too obviously to some exterior meaning, and had stressed that the province of literary art was not meaning but effect, not truth but pleasure. Effect is what a tale like "The Cask of Amontillado" is about. An overwhelming effect of terror is produced by this tightly knit tale that reverberates with psychological and moral implications. Curiosity and an odd kind of pleasure are stimulated by the interlocking images, by the puns and double meanings, and, surprisingly, by the ultimate humanity of the seemingly inhuman characters. Fortunato's emotional contortions as he is chained to the wall are truly frightening; they reveal depths in his character his previous cockiness had concealed. Montresor's moments of wavering suggest that Poe is delving beneath the surface of the stock revenge figure to reveal inchoate feelings of self-doubt and guilt. Unlike his many precursors in popular culture, Poe doesn't just entertain us with skeletons in the cellar. He makes us contemplate ghosts in the soul.

JOAN DAYAN

Joan Dayan, author of Fables of Mind: An Inquiry into Poe's Fiction *(1987), drew on New Historical criticism, addressing issues of gender and race in her essay "Amorous Bondage: Poe, Ladies, and Slaves." New Historicism uses recent theoretical work, such as deconstruction, to approach historical literary study in new and complex ways. Closely related to cultural criticism in its scrutiny of the background of important texts, New Historicism often focuses on the struggles of dominated groups.*

Dayan's essay was included in The American Face of Edgar Allan Poe, *edited by Shawn Rosenheim and Stephen Rachman for the Johns Hopkins University Press in 1995. Dayan was familiar with the traditional approach to Poe, which emphasized his indebtedness to German and English philosophy and literature. In her 1987 book, she discussed the influence of John Locke, John Calvin, and Jonathan Edwards on his writing. As a New Historical critic, she took a different approach because she was concerned about "the institutional erasure of Poe, slavery, and the South" in academic scholarship. Insisting that critics must recognize the complexities of the historical record, Dayan argued that since Poe was a southern writer, brought up by slaves in his guardians' home, he probably heard African American stories in the oral tradition, which could have exerted a powerful and lasting effect on his extraordinary imagination.*

Amorous Bondage:
Poe, Ladies, and Slaves   1995

> The *order of nature* has, in the end, vindicated itself, and the dependence
> between master and slave has scarcely for a moment ceased.
> — Thomas R. Dew, *Review of the Debate*
> *in the Virginia Legislature* (1832)

IT DOTH HAUNT ME STILL

In October 1989 I presented the annual Poe Lecture at the Enoch Pratt
Free Library in Baltimore. As part of the memorial to Poe's death, we walked to
the grave, put flowers on the ground, wondering if Poe was really there—for
some say the body has been removed—and then proceeded to the library,
where I was to deliver the sixty-ninth lecture on Poe. I had titled the talk "Poe's
Love Poems." In writing it, in thinking about those difficult last poems of
Poe—unique in the history of American poetry—I turned to what I called
"his greatest love poem," the much-contested review of Paulding's *Slavery in
the United States,* published in the *Southern Literary Messenger* in April 1836,
the same year as Lydia Maria Child's *Anti-Slavery Catechism.*[1] Traditionally
these talks are published as monographs by the Poe Society of Baltimore. A
month after my talk, I received a letter saying that the society wanted to publish the proceedings, but advised that I limit the paper to the "fine analysis of
the love poems" and cut out the dubious part on slavery.

I realized then that the process of how we come to read or understand our
fondest fictions results from a sometimes vicious cutting or decorous forgetting. I have not been allowed to forget my attempt to talk about the "peculiar
institution" behind Poe's most popular fantasies. I received letters from male
members of the Poe Society arguing that Poe did not write the proslavery
review. Three years ago, after I spoke on Poe at the Boston Athenaeum, an
unidentified man appeared before me, saying: "I enjoyed your talk, but Poe
had nothing to do with such social issues as slavery." He then referred to an
ongoing communication he had had with another Poe critic following my talk
in Baltimore, adding that I had "overstepped the bounds of good taste and discretion, by contaminating the purest love poems in the English language."[2]

---

[1]Poe, "Review of J. K. Paulding's *Slavery in the United States* and *The South Vindicated from the Treason and Fanaticism of the Northern Abolitionists,*" T. C. Mabbott, ed.,
The Collected Works of Edgar Allan Poe (Cambridge: Harvard UP, 1979), 8:265–75.
Although the review is often referred to as the "Paulding review," Bernard Rosenthal
argues that it is more accurate to refer to it as the "Paulding-Drayton review," since the
other book under review, *The South Vindicated from the Treason and Fanaticism of the
Northern Abolitionists,* once thought to be anonymous, is known to be by William Dray-
ton, to whom Poe dedicated his *Tales of the Grotesque and Arabesque.* . . .

[2]Until 1941, with William Doyle Hull's claim that Beverly Tucker wrote this
review, scholars did not question Poe's authorship. The review was included in Harrison's
Virginia edition of Poe's work, and both Hervey Allen in *Israfel* in 1927 and Arthur Hob-
son Quinn in his critical biography in 1941 discuss Poe's review on slavery. The institutional erasure of Poe, slavery, and the South continues in the Library of America edition of
Poe's *Essays and Reviews* (New York: Library of America, 1984), which omits the review. . . .

What matters in these continuing altercations is the way in which the very questioning of authorship prods us to ask questions about Poe, property, status, superstition, and gentrification that put Poe quite squarely in dialogue with the romance of the South and the realities of race. Just as the ideology of southern honor depended on fantasies of black degradation, racist discourse needed the rhetoric of natural servility to confirm absolute privilege. As I will argue, the cultivation of romance and the facts of slavery are inextricably linked.

I do not want to sound like Poe in his protracted discussion of his infamous performance at the Boston Lyceum in the *Broadway Journal* for two years, but I do want to draw attention to the coercive monumentalization of certain writers — specifically, how necessary Poe and his "ladies" remain as an icon to the most cherished and necessary ideals of some men. Here is Floyd Stovall in "The Women of Poe's Poems and Tales": "They are all noble and good, and naturally very beautiful. . . . Most remarkable of all is their passionate and enduring love for the hero."[3] It is perhaps not surprising that some Poe critics — the founding fathers of the Poe Society, for example — sound rather like the proslavery ideologues who promoted the ideals of the lady, elegant, white, and delicate.

Poe's ladies, those dream-dimmed, ethereal living dead of his poems, have been taken straight as exemplars of what Poe called "supernal Beauty" — an entitlement that he would degrade again and again. Think about the idea that was "Lady Madeline Usher" returning from the grave as a brute and bloodied thing, the frenziedly iterated *"it"* of her brother Roderick. Many of the dissolutions and decays so marked in Poe's tales about women subvert the status of women as a saving ideal, thus undermining his own [essay] "Philosophy of Composition": the "death of a beautiful woman is, unquestionably, the most poetical topic in the world." No longer pure or passive, she returns as an earthy — and very unpoetical — subject.

Let us take my experience as prelude to a rereading of Poe that depends absolutely on what has so often been cut out of his work: the institution of slavery, Poe's troubled sense of himself as a southern aristocrat, and finally, the precise and methodical transactions in which he revealed the threshold separating humanity from animality in an unsettling way. His most unnatural fictions are bound to the natural histories that are so much a part of their origination. Read in this way, Poe's sometimes inexplicable fantasies — for example, a general's artificial body parts named, claimed, and screwed on by a black valet in "The Man That Was Used Up" — become intelligible. Poe's Gothicism is crucial to our understanding of the entangled metaphysics of romance and servitude. What might have remained local historiography becomes a harrowing myth of the Americas. . . .

Perhaps all of Poe's work is finally about radical dehumanization: one can dematerialize — idealize — by turning humans into animals or by turning them into angels. As Poe proves throughout *Eureka* and in his angelic colloquies, matter and not-matter are convertible. Further, both processes, etherealization

---

[3]Floyd Stovall, "The Women of Poe's Poems and Tales," *Texas Studies in English* (1925) 5:197.

and brutalization (turning into angel or brute), involve displacement of the human element. We are dealing with a process of sublimation, either up or down. Animality, after all, emerges for most nineteenth-century phrenologists, theologians, and anthropologists in those beings who are at once man and beast: lunatics, women, primates, black men, and children. What remains unmentioned, and unencoded, is the *manhood* at the center of these operations. It is this powerfully absent construction that Poe intentionally probes. He, the white epistemologist of the sublime, the Enlightenment "universal man," haunts Poe's writings. It is his divisions, as well as his projections, that Poe confounds.

Thus the unbelievable overturning of the *law of identity and contradiction* that I have argued to be central to Poe's work can now be considered as more than a fable of mind. Poe's reconstructions depend on experiences that trade on unspeakable slippages between men and women, humans and animals, life and death. Poe deliberately undermines the taxonomic vocations of male supremacy, and thus attributes to it a troubling, ambiguous vitality.

MY TANTALIZED SPIRIT

The tales about women, "Morella," "Ligeia," "Berenice," "The Fall of the House of Usher," and "Eleonora," are about men who narrate the unspeakable remembrance: not the gun-toting, masterful cavaliers or gentlemen of southern fictions of the gentry, but the delicate acolytes of erudite ladies or the terrified victims of the lady revenants. In these tales, possession, multiple hauntings, and identity dissolutions suspend gender difference as a component of identity. The memorial act demands a willing surrender to an anomalous atmosphere where one thing remains certain: the dead do not die. They will not stay buried. In Poe's tales, these awfully corporeal ghosts are always women. As we read the compelling narratives of the men who wait and watch for the inevitable return, we sense how much the terror depends on the men's will to remember, their sorcererlike ability to name and to conjure the beloved, who is, of course, the exemplar for later "white zombies." . . .

We have evidence of Poe's relationships with the leading proslavery advocates in Virginia, but what about those variously represented in the Virginia slavery debate of 1831–32 as "pets," "playmates of the white children," "the merriest people in the world," "valuable property," or "monsters"? How can we begin to think about those who left no written records but were a constant presence, whose existence, though distorted or erased, informed Poe's unique brand of Gothic narrative in ways that have been ignored?

Poe's guardians, the Allans, had at least three household servants (all slaves, but at least one of these was owned by someone else and bonded to Mr. Allan). On 1 January 1811, Mr. Allan hired a woman named Judith from Master Cheatham for twenty-five pounds, "to be retained and clothed as usual under a bond of 50 [fifty pounds sterling]."[4] According to some accounts, Judith was Edgar's "Mammy"; other accounts note the names "Juliet" and "Eudocia" mentioned in receipts and bills of sale as being in John Allan's

---

[4] I am grateful to Jean M. Mudge for this information.

household. Whatever her name, she sometimes took Edgar to the "Old Church on the Hill" grounds, where he spent many late afternoons. His foster mother Fanny Allan was often too ill to attend to Poe. Though we hear about Poe's dead mother Eliza and all those subsequent, surrogate pale mothers (especially Jane Stannard and Fanny Allan in Richmond), we are never reminded of the black woman in the house. When Poe was awaiting entry into West Point in 1829, living with Maria Clemm in Baltimore, he sold a slave. In April 1940, the *Baltimore Sun* published the record of the bill of sale of "a negro man named Edwin," calling it an "Item for Biographers." The article begins: "While examining some entries in an underground record room at the Courthouse a few days ago a Baltimore man who wishes his name withheld quite by chance came across an old document relating to Edgar Allan Poe, which seems thus far to have entirely escaped the poet's biographers."[5]

Many Virginia accounts of the Nat Turner rebellion blamed its occurrence on superstition and religious fanaticism. But these written accounts of the "extraordinary" beliefs of Negroes, shared by many whites, probably mattered less to Poe than his daily encounters with slaves in his own house or on the plantations he visited. Poe's Gothicism and his unique tools of terror finally have less to do with "Germany" or the "soul," as he proclaimed in the preface to his "Tales of the Grotesque and Arabesque," than with African American stories of the angry dead, sightings of teeth, the bones and matter of charms, and the power of conjuring. Such stories, merging with early Christian folk beliefs transplanted to the South, as well as the frenzy of revivals with whites and slaves caught up in the Holy Spirit, might also have encouraged the strangely sentient landscapes of Poe, his obsession with the reciprocities between living and dead, human and animal, and the possessions and demonic visitations of his best-known tales.[6]

. . . In "Unspeakable Things Unspoken," Toni Morrison notes the presence, the shadow, the ghost from which most critics have fled.[7] In a world where identities wavered between colors, where signs of whitening and darkening were quickly apprehended by all inhabitants, enlightenment depended on shadows. The gods, monsters, and ghosts spawned by racist discourse redefined the supernatural. What the white masters called sorcery was rather an alternative philosophy, a set of spiritual experiences shared by blacks and whites. The most horrific spirits of the Americas were produced by the logic of the master filtered through the thought and memory of slaves.

---

[5]I thank Jeffrey Savoy of the Poe Society of Baltimore for sending me this article.
[6]The biography that deals most with the contact between the young Poe and slaves is Hervey Allen's *Israfel* (1927). Note that the revised, one-volume edition of *Israfel* issued in 1934 excludes these discussions of Poe and his African American surroundings.
[7]Toni Morrison, "Unspeakable Things Unspoken: The Afro-American Presence in American Literature." *Michigan Quarterly Review* 28, no. 1 (Winter 1989), 12.

Poetry

For the sake of a single poem, you must
see many cities, many people and
Things, you must understand animals,
must feel how birds fly, and know the
gesture which small flowers make when
they open in the morning.
                    —Rainer Maria Rilke

7.

What Is a Poem?

The universe of poetry is the universe of emotional truth.
—MURIEL RUKEYSER, from *The Life of Poetry*

Just as it is important to begin reading short stories with some idea of what a short story is, we should begin reading poetry with some idea of what we mean by poetry. What is poetry and what is a poem? The poet Emily Dickinson, when she was asked in a letter how she knew something she had read was poetry, answered,

> If I read a book and it makes my whole body so cold no fire can ever warm me, I know that it is poetry. If I feel physically as if the top of my head were taken off, I know that it is poetry. These are the only ways I know it. Is there any other way?

It is not necessary for you as a reader to have such a strong emotional response to a poem in order to enjoy it, but as you begin to know more about poetry, you will also understand some of what she felt.

You will find, as you begin your study of poetry, that it is not so simple to say just what a poem is, but this is also true of other things that can give us the feeling that the tops of our heads have been taken off. Often when rock musicians are asked by interviewers to define rock and roll, they answer, without hesitation, "That's the kind of music I play." Their answer echoes the response of the American poet Robert Frost, who, when he was asked what poetry was, shrugged, "Poetry is the kind of thing that poets write."

Part of the difficulty of finding a simple definition of poetry is that there has been so much of it. Poetry is our oldest language art. Only drama, which probably emerged two centuries later, takes us as far back into antiquity. The novel, with its history of only three or four hundred years, and the short story, with its history of less than two hundred years, are newcomers compared with poetry. In Asia and in the eastern Mediterranean and Europe, poetry has had an unbroken line of expression for almost three thousand years, and the way we define poetry would have changed as societies and poetry itself changed during these millennia.

Many poets have felt the need to define poetry, and often they use the medium of poetry to describe what it is they create. In the famous poem "Ars Poetica," the American writer Archibald MacLeish tells us that poetry is not something to be explained or analyzed, that a poem can tell the story of grief simply by showing us "An empty doorway and a maple leaf."

ARCHIBALD MACLEISH

Ars Poetica   1926

A poem should be palpable and mute
As a globed fruit

Dumb
As old medallions to the thumb

Silent as the sleeve-worn stone   5
Of casement ledges where the moss has grown —

  •

A poem should be wordless
As the flight of birds

A poem should be motionless in time
As the moon climbs   10

Leaving, as the moon releases
Twig by twig the night-entangled trees,

Leaving, as the moon behind the winter leaves,
Memory by memory the mind —

A poem should be motionless in time   15
As the moon climbs

  •

A poem should be equal to:
Not true

For all the history of grief
An empty doorway and a maple leaf   20

For love
The leaning grasses and two lights above the sea —

A poem should not mean
But be.

In a poem titled simply "Poetry," Marianne Moore attempts to state her idea of what a poem should be. A poem, as she says, is "a place for the genuine," and she scolds writers who let themselves forget that it is a direct, real experience that must go into a poem. To her, the greatness of poetry is that it can cross the boundary between our inner emotions and something outside ourselves that can reawaken these emotions. In her unforgettable phrase, a poem "can present / for inspection, 'imaginary gardens with real toads in them.' . . ."

MARIANNE MOORE

Poetry   1921, 1935

I, too, dislike it: there are things that are important beyond all this fiddle.
   Reading it, however, with a perfect contempt for it, one discovers in
      it after all, a place for the genuine.
         Hands that can grasp, eyes
           that can dilate, hair that can rise   5
              if it must, these things are important not because a
high-sounding interpretation can be put upon them but because they are
   useful. When they become so derivative as to become unintelligible,
      the same thing may be said for all of us, that we
         do not admire what   10
           we cannot understand: the bat
              holding on upside down or in quest of something to
eat, elephants pushing, a wild horse taking a roll, a tireless wolf under
   a tree, the immovable critic twitching his skin like a horse that feels a
            flea, the base-
      ball fan, the statistician —   15
         nor is it valid
            to discriminate against "business documents and
school-books";[1] all these phenomena are important. One must make a
           distinction
   however: when dragged into prominence by half poets, the result is
           not poetry,
        nor till the poets among us can be   20
          "literalists of
            the imagination"[2] — above
              insolence and triviality and can present

---

[1]Diary of Tolstoy (Dutton), p. 84. "Where the boundary between prose and poetry lies, I shall never be able to understand. The question is raised in manuals of style, yet the answer to it lies beyond me. Poetry is verse; prose is not verse. Or else poetry is everything with the exception of business documents and school books." [Moore's note]

[2]Yeats's *Ideas of Good and Evil* (A. H. Bullen), p. 182. "The limitation of his view was from the very intensity of his vision; he was a too literal realist of imagination, as others are of nature; and because he believed that the figures seen by the mind's eye, when exalted by inspiration, were 'eternal existences,' symbols of divine essences, he hated every grace of style that might obscure their lineaments." [Moore's note]

for inspection, "imaginary gardens with real toads in them," shall we have
  it. In the meantime, if you demand on the one hand,   25
     the raw material of poetry in
        all its rawness and
        that which is on the other hand
            genuine, then you are interested in poetry.

In this version of her poem, however, Moore may have felt that she had
given away too many of a poet's secrets, or that she might have been stating
something that was too obvious to need explaining. For whatever reason, when
she printed it again several years later in her *Collected Poems,* she trimmed it
down to the lines she felt were essential. The poem as she published it then
reads simply,

  I, too, dislike it.
     Reading it, however, with a perfect contempt for it, one discovers in
      it, after all, a place for the genuine.

As Moore made very clear (and you should remember this as you study
poetry), poets have their own reasons for whatever they do.

Even if they haven't written a poem in their concern with defining
their art, poets often attempt a definition that is as lyric and as distinctive as
their poetry. For Carl Sandburg poetry is "a series of explanations of life, fading
off into horizons too swift for explanations." Robert Frost's well-known, no-
nonsense description of poetry is "a momentary stay against confusion." To
William Carlos Williams, a poet concerned with the "things" named in a
poem, a poem is "a machine made out of words." The contemporary poet Louise
Glück tells us, "The poem may embody perception so luminous it seems truth,
but what keeps it alive is not fixed discovery but the means of discovery; what
keeps it alive is intelligence," while for Wallace Stevens, "Poetry is the supreme
fiction."

Descriptions like these tell us a great deal about the poet, and the poems
by Archibald MacLeish and Marianne Moore suggest many things about
poetry itself, but we still don't have a definition. Perhaps a useful way to begin
is to turn to a dictionary, where we find definitions that tell us something very
specific about what a poem is. A dictionary will tell us that "a poem is a metrical composition of elevated tone depicting an emotional or philosophical
truth." If you keep a definition like this in mind when you begin reading
poetry, you will find it is a useful tool. The term *metrical composition* tells us to
expect a poem's formal structure to be based on a rhythmic pattern of words
and syllables that we can hear and anticipate. The term *elevated tone* tells us
that a poem can use a different kind of language, or if it uses everyday speech it
can use these words in ways that give them a special — "elevated" — significance. The term *emotional or philosophical truth* tells us that poetry can touch
our deepest emotions.

As you begin studying poetry you will find it helpful to separate a poem
into two parts. The first part is the emotion or the insight at the heart of the
poem. This is called the **theme.** You should remember, however, that the

theme of the poem is not necessarily the subject of the poem. The subject of the poem may be the writer's pet cat, but the theme of the poem is the writer's pleasure in everyday things that the cat symbolizes.

The second part of what you should think of as you read poetry consists of the elements of formal structure and "poetic" language, what we can call the *means* of the poem. A poet's means are the rhythms and verbal wordplay, the kind of language, the poetic form, the suggestions of the other poems or paintings or music that are there for poets to use as they write. These resources are sometimes called the *elements* of poetry, but if we use the term *means,* it also suggests that these elements are what poets *use* as they write.

With these tools, the theme and the means, you will find that you can enjoy more fully any of the poems you will be reading. Remember that these two aspects of a poem work each in different ways. The themes of poems come from within the poet's own personality. They can be the poet's thoughts, dreams, disappointments, or joys, or responses to someone else's thoughts, dreams, disappointments, or joys. The themes of a poem are also our shared experience of life. Because they come from our common humanity, they are continually renewed.

The means of poetry, however, are bound into the moment in time when each poem is written. They draw from the language and the social attitudes, the poetic traditions, and the background of the poets' lives and the moments in history when they lived. This is why you will find that poems from different times with the same themes — perhaps the poet's disappointment at the end of a love affair or the definition of poetry itself — will be expressed in different languages and forms, each a reflection of its own time and place.

As we have seen, poets often turn their thoughts about poetry into poems. This poem by San Francisco writer Lawrence Ferlinghetti describes the emotions that some poets feel as they write.

LAWRENCE FERLINGHETTI

Constantly Risking Absurdity   1955–58

Constantly risking absurdity
                 and death
    whenever he performs
         above the heads
               of his audience   5
    the poet like an acrobat
        climbs on rime
            to a high wire of his own making
   and balancing on eyebeams
         above a sea of faces   10
    paces his way
       to the other side of day

> performing entrechats
> and sleight-of-foot tricks
> and other high theatrics   15
> and all without mistaking
> any thing
> for what it may not be
> For he's the super realist
> who must perforce perceive   20
> taut truth
> before the taking of each stance or step
> in his supposed advance
> toward that still higher perch
> where Beauty stands and waits   25
> with gravity
> to start her death-defying leap
> And he
> a little charleychaplin man
> who may or may not catch   30
> her fair eternal form
> spreadeagled in the empty air
> of existence

It is the painstaking work of creating her poems that American poet Lorine Niedecker describes in her poem about a poet's dedication to the craft of writing. The word *condensery* was her own bemused invention to characterize what she did.

LORINE NIEDECKER

Poet's work   1960

> Grandfather
> advised me:
> Learn a trade
> I learned
> to sit at a desk
> and condense
> No layoff
> from this
> condensery

Sometimes poets describe what they do in phrases that are poems in themselves. The English poet Percy Bysshe Shelley wrote, "A poet is a nightingale, who sits in darkness and sings to cheer its own solitude with sweet sounds." Robert Frost tells us, "The figure a poem makes. It begins in delight and ends in wisdom." When poets write about their art they usually are serious. If they are in the mood, however, they can be half-serious. Tobey Hiller, who lives and works in Oakland, California, pretends in "The Poem" that she cannot find anything useful about poems—until the last lines, in which she tells us that with a poem we can fly above the ordinary experience of everyday life. The Alice she refers to in the title is the main character in Lewis Carroll's *Alice in Wonderland.*

TOBEY HILLER

The Poem   1987

(or, Alice's Remarks on Reading
the Fine Print on the Bottle's Label)

Can it walk, or talk,
or do the mambo?

Will it set off, sleek,
and neigh its way to Mexico?

Provide a shade against the sun?   5
Cure freckles? Siphon sadness?

Recited right, won't it turn the curl of waves acrylic,
cast sunsets into glass,

make grass grow green
upon a desert page?   10

Perhaps you're hoping
it will turn the t.v. off.

Or make the kids grow up un-mumbling
and acquainted with the phases of the moon.

Perhaps it does a trick   15
with eyes, closing them, or opening.

But don't confuse it with a pear.
You wouldn't try to eat it, would you?

Remember that only angels can make hair and wings
and finger-nails out of the alphabet.   20

What we make is all flight.

Finally, in her poem "I Said to Poetry," Alice Walker, author of the novel *The Color Purple,* protests against the power that poetry has over her life, with its insistence on waking her in the night with lines that demand to be written and emotions that must be expressed. In the end, as she wryly admits, it is poetry that has the upper hand.

ALICE WALKER

I Said to Poetry   1984

I said to Poetry: 'I'm finished
with you.'
Having to almost die
before some weird light
comes creeping through   5
is no fun.
'No thank you, Creation,
no muse need apply.
I'm out for good times—
at the very least,   10
some painless convention.'

Poetry laid back
and played dead
until this morning.
I wasn't sad or anything,   15
only restless.

Poetry said: 'You remember
the desert, and how glad you were
that you have an eye
to see it with? You remember   20
that, if ever so slightly?'
I said: 'I didn't hear that.
Besides, it's five o'clock in the a.m.
I'm not getting up
in the dark   25
to talk to you.'

Poetry said: 'But think about the time
you saw the moon
over that small canyon
that you liked much better   30
than the grand one—and how surprised you were
that the moonlight was green
and you still had
one good eye
to see it with.   35
Think of that!'

'I'll join the church!' I said,
huffily, turning my face to the wall.
'I'll learn how to pray again!'

'Let me ask you,' said Poetry.   40
'When you pray, what do you think
you'll see?'

Poetry had me.

'There's no paper
in this room,' I said.
'And that new pen I bought
makes a funny noise.'

'Bullshit,' said Poetry.

'Bullshit,' said I.

45

COMMENTARY   *Louise Glück, "Poems Are Autobiography," page 979.*

8.

The Elements of Poetry:
A Poet's Means

A word is dead
When it is said,
Some say.
I say it just
Begins to live
That day.
            — EMILY DICKINSON

WORDS AND THEIR SOUND

When we first read a poem it is almost always its subject and theme that stir our interest. We ask ourselves, "What is the poem about?" If the poem is about something that concerns us, then we will read it. There are, however, many poems that deal with the same basic themes, since poetry draws up its materials from the well of our deepest emotions. What is it that makes us say one poem is beautiful and another poem is not, even if each poem describes the same feeling or emotional mood? The pleasure is in the *means* the poet has used to present the theme: the sound of the words, the rhythms of the lines, the vividness of the images. If we have some familiarity with these means, or formal elements of poetry, our understanding and enjoyment of the poem will be greatly increased.

Alliteration and Assonance

One of the simplest — and earliest — ways poets use the sound of words to structure their writing is what is called **alliteration.** Alliteration is the repetition of the same sounding letters. If it is the first letter that is repeated, and the letter is a consonant, it is called **initial alliteration.** This is the easiest form of alliteration to recognize, and people often use it for a humorous effect. "Little Lyle lies longingly on the lawn," is one example, or "Susan sat sewing sister's smock." Poets have generally used it more subtly, but alliteration was a common effect in the earliest poetry in English. *Beowulf,* from the beginning of the eighth century, is the first poem composed in what was to become the English language, and it uses a style based on alliteration.

Closely related to alliteration is **assonance,** the repetition of vowel sounds within a phrase. It can be an elusive effect, sometimes difficult to recognize. Its most obvious form is a phrase like "Opacity opens up rooms," with its repetition of *o* sounds, from Amy Clampitt's poem "Fog." In the hands of a skilled poet, assonance can be an effective means to shade the meaning of the poem. In the opening lines of the poem listen to the sound of the letter *o* as it is repeated several times:

> A vagueness comes over everything,
> as though proving color and contour
> alike dispensable. . . .

If you read the lines carefully, you also can hear the alliteration of the *c* consonants of "color and contour." Clampitt has used both alliteration and assonance so skillfully that you can enjoy her use of words as you read the entire poem. In the second verse, which begins "Tactile / definition, however, has not been / totally banished," she is saying that even though the fog has made everything vague, objects still can be felt, that they are "tactile." Clampitt loved to use unfamiliar words in her poetry, and here she has given us "panicled," which is a botanical term to describe the way the kernels of blossom and seed are distributed irregularly on the stem of certain grasses and grains, like oats. Georgia O'Keeffe, mentioned in the last verse, was an American painter who in some of her canvases caught the effect of a "hueless moonflower / corolla."

AMY CLAMPITT

Fog

1985

A vagueness comes over everything,
as though proving color and contour
alike dispensable: the lighthouse
extinct, the islands' spruce-tips
drunk up like milk in the   5
universal emulsion; houses
reverting into the lost
and forgotten; granite
subsumed, a rumor
in a mumble of ocean.   10
                          Tactile
definition, however, has not been
totally banished: hanging

tassel by tassel, panicled
foxtail and needlegrass,   15
dropseed, furred hawkweed,

and last season's rose-hips
are vested in silenced
chimes of the finest,
clearest sea-crystal.   20
                    Opacity
opens up rooms, a showcase
for the hueless moonflower
corolla, as Georgia
O'Keeffe might have seen it,   25
of foghorns; the nodding
campanula of bell buoys;
the ticking, linear
filigree of bird voices.

Onomatopoeia

Another effect that a writer can employ using the sound of words is called
onomatopoeia. The word is derived from Greek roots, meaning "to make
names," which implies that the word is made up to describe the sound. Onomatopoeia means that a word can "sound" like the noise it describes. *Bang!* is
an easy example, or if you want a bigger sound, *Boom!* Comic books are a treasure trove of onomatopoeia. How about *Pow!, Splat!, Zap!, RaTaTat!, Ping!,*
and *Who-o-o-sh?* One American poet who used onomatopoeia effectively was
Vachel Lindsay, who performed his poetry in informal readings across the
United States in the early years of the century. Read aloud the opening line of
his poem about the founder of the Salvation Army, William S. Booth:

> Booth led boldly with his big bass drum. . . .

Using alliteration and onomatopoeia, Lindsay catches the sound of a Salvation
Army drum with the clamorous tone of the words. In a very different example,
Amy Clampitt, in the last lines of "Fog," suggests the delicate sound of "the
ticking, linear / filigree of bird voices."

In an unexpected use of the possibilities of word sounds, Edwin Morgan
created an entire poem that brilliantly and humorously presents us with a vivid
example of onomatopoeia.

EDWIN MORGAN

Siesta of a Hungarian Snake   1985

s sz sz SZ sz SZ sz ZS zs ZS zs zs z

Rhyme

Of all the means the poet has to work with that come out of the sound of
words, none of them is more familiar to us than **rhyme.** For hundreds of years

part of the definition of poetry was that it rhymed. When other poets began to break away from rhyme in the early part of this century, the American poet Robert Frost, who wrote in traditional rhymed styles, growled that writing poetry without rhyme was like "playing tennis with the net down." Although there is a kind of rhyme called **eye rhyme,** which means that two words look as though they would sound alike, but the sound, if spoken aloud, is different (for example, *house* and *rouse* or *tough* and *though*), the essence of rhyme is a similarity of sound.

Two kinds of rhyme — perfect rhyme and near or slant rhyme — define most of what we mean by the term. The type of rhyme you recognize most in your reading is **perfect rhyme.** Some of the most common perfect rhymes have been used so often that they have become clichés: *moon* and *June, sigh* and *cry, dream* and *scheme.* In perfect rhyme the sound of the two words is exactly alike, and if the poet can avoid the expected or the commonplace rhyme, the effect can be exciting in itself. The most familiar use of rhyme is called **end rhyme,** in which the words at the end of the line rhyme.

One of the masters of rhymed verse in English was A. E. Housman. Here are two of his best-known poems, each of which is an excellent example of the use of perfect rhyme.

A. E. HOUSMAN

Loveliest of trees, the cherry now   1896

Loveliest of trees, the cherry now
Is hung with bloom along the bough,
And stands about the woodland ride
Wearing white for Eastertide.

Now, of my three score years and ten,   5
Twenty will not come again,
And take from seventy springs a score,
It only leaves me fifty more.

And since to look at things in bloom
Fifty springs are little room,   10
About the woodlands I will go
To see the cherry hung with snow.

When I was one-and-twenty   1896

When I was one-and-twenty
    I heard a wise man say,
"Give crowns and pounds and guineas
    But not your heart away;
Give pearls away and rubies   5
    But keep your fancy free."

> But I was one-and-twenty,
>   No use to talk to me.
> When I was one-and-twenty
>   I heard him say again,   10
> "The heart out of the bosom
>   Was never given in vain;
> 'Tis paid with sighs a-plenty
>   And sold for endless rue."
> And I am two-and-twenty,   15
>   And oh, 'tis true, 'tis true.

Poets who write rhymed verse can benefit from pleasure that readers feel as they anticipate the sound of the rhyme, but this way of writing also has disadvantages. Because each line closes with a rhyme, the repeated pattern can begin to leave the reader feeling that the rhyme is interrupting the poem's flow of ideas and imagery. Perfect rhyme can become monotonous, and the need to find a rhyme can force the poet into an awkward word order or sentences that are muddy and unclear.

Poets have devised many strategies to deal with this problem, such as working with subtle differences in the sound of the rhyming words. They discovered they could vary the sound and have a little more flexibility to shape their lines if they used **near rhymes** or **slant rhymes.** With this kind of rhyme the sound of the two words is close but not exact. Examples of near rhyme are pairs of words like *read* and *red, seal* and *sail, ball* and *bell.*

In her well-known poem "Not Waving but Drowning," Stevie Smith, a modern English poet, consciously used near rhyme to mirror the pathos of a drowning man whose waving people thought was only "larking," or showing his high spirits. The truth is that his waving was a desperate signal for help.

STEVIE SMITH

Not Waving but Drowning   1957

> Nobody heard him, the dead man,
> But still he lay moaning:
> I was much further out than you thought
> And not waving but drowning.
>
> Poor chap, he always loved larking   5
> And now he's dead
> It must have been too cold for him his heart gave way,
> They said.
>
> Oh, no, no, no, it was too cold always
> (Still the dead one lay moaning)   10
> I was much too far out all my life
> And not waving but drowning.

Smith was a skilled poet, and she certainly could have found a perfect rhyme for the first and last stanzas of the poem, but instead she gives us "moaning," to rhyme with "drowning," a half rhyme that suggests everything that was half successful about the man's life.

In her poem "Real Estate," Amy Clampitt presents us with a rich variety of near or slant rhymes. As the opening lines make clear, with their allusion to the famous opening lines of Robert Frost's "Mending Wall," the poet is enjoying herself, and for the reader there is a pleasant surprise at rhymes like "pathos / umbrellas," or "wraith / dustcloth."

AMY CLAMPITT

Real Estate   1985

Something there is that doesn't
love a Third Avenue tenement,

that wants it gone the way the El
went. Façade a typical example

of red-brick eclectic, its five dozen   5
windows half now behind blank tin,

scrollwork lintels of strange parentage,
fire escapes' curling-iron birdcage,

are an anomaly among high-rise elevators,
besieged by Urban Relocation (Not A   10

Governmental Agency). Holdout tenants
confer, gesticulating, by storefronts

adapted only to an anxious present — Le
Boudoir, Le Shampoo, Le Retro (if passé

is chic, is chic passé?). One gelded   15
pawnshop, until last week, still brooded,

harboring, among tag ends of pathos,
several thirty-year-old umbrellas.

Regularly twice a day, the lingering wraith
within stepped out to shake her dustcloth.   20

That's done now. She advertised a sale.
Still nothing moved. Finally, a U-Haul

truck carted everything off somewhere.
Hail, real estate! Bravo, entrepreneur!

Two other terms are also used in discussing rhyme: masculine rhyme and feminine rhyme. Words are pronounced in syllables, and some syllables are given more emphasis than others. The strong syllable is called an **accent,** and we will be talking more about accents when we discuss the rhythms of poetry.

Masculine rhyme means that the accent on the rhyming words is on a final strong syllable. *Stay* and *away, bells* and *foretells, otherwise* and *guise* are masculine rhymes. In a **feminine rhyme,** the accent on the rhyming words is on a weak syllable. *Season* and *reason, tower* and *flower, thunder* and *wonder* are feminine rhymes.

You will sometimes notice that a poet uses rhyme in the middle of the line as well as the end. This is called **internal rhyme.** This example is from "Blow, Bugle, Blow" by the nineteenth-century English poet Alfred, Lord Tennyson. The internal rhyme occurs in the first and third lines:

> The splendor *falls* on castle *walls*
> And snowy summits old in story:
> The long light *shakes* across the *lakes*
> And the wild cataract leaps in glory.

There are two other terms that help describe what happens at the ends of the lines in a poem. If the meaning of the line comes to a definite end, it is called **end-stopped;** if the meaning does not end but continues on to the next line, it is called **enjambed.** The noun for this running of one line into another line is **enjambment.** Here is an example of end-stopped lines:

> I long to hear love's gentle tune.
> I only mourn it ends so soon.

Here is an example of enjambed lines:

> Oh, to feel the soft, soft touch of spring
> again, and the April softness it will bring!

Usually the poet tries only for a rhyme with one syllable, but many multi-syllabic words are also useful as rhymes, like *September* and *remember, despair* and *aware.* During the centuries when most poets were concerned with rhyme they often looked for complicated rhymes to show off their skill with language. A famous example is the two-line poem the English poet John Dryden sent to a patron whose family name was Cadwallader. His patron had promised to send him a rabbit for supper, and when it did not appear, Dryden sent him a note in rhyme:

> Oh thou son of great Cadwallader
> Hast thou my hare, or hast thou swallowed her?

Although most poetry today is written without rhyme, many poets still turn to this most basic of poetic means to strengthen a poem's structure or to add another level of verbal dexterity to the poem's pleasures. This poem by Marianne Moore mixes rhyming lines with lines that are not rhymed. The first and third lines of each verse rhyme, as do each verse's final two lines. The final rhymes are a good example of a skilled poet's use of unexpected word combinations—*others / stirs, surrendering / continuing, mortality / eternity.* As you read the poem you will find many examples of enjambed lines, and you should also note the remarkable sentence that begins at the end of the third line with *And whence* and doesn't end until eight lines later, when it finally winds down in the opening line of the second verse, *the soul to be strong.*

MARIANNE MOORE

What Are Years?   1939

What is our innocence,
what is our guilt? All are
   naked, none is safe. And whence
is courage: the unanswered question,
the resolute doubt—   5
dumbly calling, deafly listening—that
in misfortune, even death,
     encourages others
     and in its defeat, stirs

   the soul to be strong? He   10
sees deep and is glad, who
   accedes to mortality
and in his imprisonment rises
upon himself as
the sea in a chasm, struggling to be   15
free and unable to be,
     in its surrendering
     finds its continuing.

   So he who strongly feels,
behaves. The very bird,   20
   grown taller as he sings, steels
his form straight up. Though he is captive,
his mighty singing
says, satisfaction is a lowly
thing, how pure a thing is joy.   25
     This is mortality,
     this is eternity.

Poems for Further Reading

SIR THOMAS WYATT

They Flee from Me   1557

They flee from me, that sometime did me seek,
With naked foot stalking in my chamber.
I have seen them, gentle, tame, and meek,
That now are wild, and do not remember
That sometime they put themselves in danger   5
To take bread at my hand; and now they range,
Busily seeking with a continual change.

Thanked be Fortune it hath been otherwise,
Twenty times better; but once in special,
In thin array, after a pleasant guise,   10
When her loose gown from her shoulders did fall,
And she me caught in her arms long and small,
And therewith all sweetly did me kiss
And softly said, "Dear heart, how like you this?"

It was no dream, I lay broad waking.   15
But all is turned, thorough° my gentleness,   *through*
Into a strange fashion of forsaking;
And I have leave to go, of her goodness,
And she also to use newfangleness.
But since that I so kindely am served,   20
I fain would know what she hath deserved.

BEN JONSON

On My First Son   1616

Farewell, thou child of my right hand,° and joy;
My sin was too much hope of thee, loved boy:
Seven years thou'wert lent to me, and I thee pay,
Exacted by thy fate, on the just day.°
Oh, could I lose all father now! for why   5
Will man lament the state he should envy,
To have so soon 'scaped world's and flesh's rage,
And, if no other misery, yet age?
Rest in soft peace, and asked, say, "Here doth lie
Ben Jonson his best piece of poetry."   10
For whose sake henceforth all his vows be such
As what he loves may never like too much.

ROBERT HERRICK

To the Virgins, to Make Much of Time   1648

Gather ye rosebuds while ye may,
    Old time is still a-flying;

---

1. child of my right hand: The literal translation of the Hebrew name *Benjamin;* Jonson's first son.   **4. the just day:** A reference to Benjamin's death on his seventh birthday.

And this same flower that smiles today
   Tomorrow will be dying.

The glorious lamp of heaven, the sun,   5
   The higher he's a-getting,
The sooner will his race be run,
   And nearer he's to setting.

That age is best which is the first,
   When youth and blood are warmer;   10
But being spent, the worse, and worst
   Times still succeed the former.

Then be not coy, but use your time,
   And, while ye may, go marry;
For, having lost but once your prime,   15
   You may forever tarry.

GEORGE HERBERT

Easter Wings   1633

Lord, who createdst man in wealth and store,°
   Though foolishly he lost the same,
      Decaying more and more
         Till he became
           Most poor: 5
           With thee
         O let me rise
      As larks, harmoniously,
   And sing this day thy victories:
Then shall the fall further the flight in me.   10

My tender age in sorrow did begin:
   And still with sicknesses and shame
      Thou didst so punish sin,
         That I became
           Most thin.   15
           With thee
         Let me combine,
      And feel this day thy victory;
   For, if I imp° my wing on thine,
Affliction shall advance the flight in me.   20

---

1. wealth and store: Abundance.   **19. imp:** Graft, a term used in falconry.

CHRISTINA ROSSETTI

Song   1848

When I am dead, my dearest,
    Sing no sad songs for me;
Plant thou no roses at my head,
    Nor shady cypress tree:
Be the green grass above me   5
    With showers and dewdrops wet:
And if thou wilt, remember,
    And if thou wilt, forget.

I shall not see the shadows,
    I shall not feel the rain;   10
I shall not hear the nightingale
    Sing on as if in pain:
And dreaming through the twilight
    That doth not rise nor set,
Haply I may remember,   15
    And haply may forget.

DOROTHY PARKER

Indian Summer   1926

In youth, it was a way I had
    To do my best to please,
And change, with every passing lad,
    To suit his theories.

But now I know the things I know,
    And do the things I do;
And if you do not like me so,
    To hell, my love, with you!

ROBERT PENN WARREN

What Voice at Moth-Hour   1985

What voice at moth-hour did I hear calling
As I stood in the orchard while the white
Petals of apple blossoms were falling,
Whiter than moth-wing in that twilight?

What voice did I hear as I stood by the stream, 5
Bemused in the murmurous wisdom there uttered,
While ripples at stone, in their steely gleam,
Caught last light before it was shuttered?

What voice did I hear as I wandered alone
In a premature night of cedar, beech, oak, 10
Each foot set soft, then still as stone
Standing to wait while the first owl spoke?

The voice that I heard once at dew-fall, I now
Can hear by a simple trick. If I close
My eyes, in that dusk I again know 15
The feel of damp grass between bare toes,

Can see the last zigzag, sky-skittering, high,
Of a bullbat, and even hear, far off, from
Swamp-cover, the whip-o-will, and as I
Once heard, hear the voice: *It's late! Come home.* 20

Song and Rhyme

Although rhyme is no longer considered to be an essential element in poetry, rhyme has never given up its place in song lyrics. Since it isn't possible for us to glance back to reread a line as we're listening, the rhymes in a song work as guidelines that help us follow the song's text. One of the most popular of today's song styles, rap, is built around rhyme and verbal play, and one of the characteristics of the blues, a basic building block of much rock music, is its distinctive rhyme scheme. Like Mississippi singer Big Joe Williams's "Levee Break Blues," each verse of a blues song has three rhyming lines. The first line begins a statement that the second line repeats, using a different harmony and a variation of the melody. The third line rhymes with the first two and completes the statement that the first two have initiated.

BIG JOE WILLIAMS

Levee Break Blues 1975

Woman I'm lovin' sleepin' in her grave
Woman I'm lovin' sleepin' in her grave
Well, the fool I hate, meet her every day.

Please, don't give my woman no job
Please, don't give my baby no job 5
She's a married woman, and I don't 'low her to work too hard.

Oh, early in the morning 'bout the break of day
Early in the morning, baby, about the break of day
I'm goin' to grab the pillow where my baby used to lay.

Take me out of the bottom before the water rise   10
Take me out of the bottom, baby, before the water rise
Don't want to be buried down on the levee side.

Lou Reed is one of a generation of rock musicians who have brought a
sense of poetic sensitivity and social engagement to their lyrics. This song
describes the young women waiting in rooms at New York's Chelsea Hotel,
hoping to be with the musicians who often stayed there. The song was written
for a film by Andy Warhol with the same name, but it was written after the
movie was released and was not included in the film score.

LOU REED

Chelsea Girls   1967

Here's Room 506
It's enough to make you sick
Bridget's all wrapped in foil
You wonder if she can uncoil
Here they come now   5
See them run now
Here they come now
Chelsea Girls

Here's Room 115
Filled with S & M queens   10
Magic marker row
You wonder just how high they go
Here's Pope dear Ondine
Rona's treated him so mean
She wants another scene   15
She wants to be a human being

Pepper she's having fun
She thinks she's some man's son
Her perfect loves don't last
Her future died in someone's past   20
Here they come
See them run now
Here they come now
Chelsea Girls

Dear Ingrid's found her lick   25
She's turned another trick
Her treats and times revolve
She's got problems to be solved

Poor Mary, she's uptight
She can't turn out her light   30
She rolled Susan in a ball
and now she can't see her at all

Dropout, she's in a fix
amphetamine has made her sick
white powder in the air   35
She's got no bones and can't be scared

Here comes Johnny Bore
He collapsed on the floor
They shot him up with milk
And when he died sold him for silk   40
Here they come now
See them run now
Here they come now
Chelsea Girls

Rhythm

If the only poetry you read is written by contemporary poets, then it might seem that you will not need to learn about the kinds of rhythm that went into the writing of verse a hundred years ago. In the politically turbulent years at the beginning of the twentieth century, many young poets in Europe and the United States felt that they had to break free of old poetic forms to find a new language that could reflect the enormous social changes they could see around them. What they chose to write was called **free verse,** because it looked on the page as if it were free of the restrictions of traditional poetry. Now we realize that writing poetry this way requires the same concentration and skill needed to write in traditional forms, so often we use the term *open form* instead. (Open form is discussed further in Chapter 11.) We call the traditional verse techniques **closed form.**

Accent and Meter

Like the other poetic means we have considered so far, the rhythm of a poem is built on the sound of words. When we discussed the difference between masculine and feminine rhyme we defined the term *accent,* which is the strong syllable, or syllables, in a word. This is the part of the word we emphasize with breath and tone as we say it out loud. The accents in the words give the poem its rhythm. All words with more than one syllable will have at least one strong accent. The other syllables are called weak accents. Sometimes the terms used are **stressed** and **unstressed** instead of strong and weak, but they refer to the same pattern of emphasized and unemphasized sounds.

A technical note: you should remember that one-syllable words like *a,* *the,* and *an,* which are called articles, generally are weak, unless we want to emphasize them for a special effect. One of the most common of these effects is a phrase like "There was THE Elvis Presley, standing in our own supermarket checkout line!" This same rule applies to one-syllable prepositions like *at, from, to, by, with,* and *of* and the conjunctions *and* and *but*.

One-syllable words like *I* and *me* are more complicated in their usage. You will find that all of these words can have strong or weak accents, depending on the words around them. Some short words have two strong accents: *uptight* is an example. Longer words can have complex patterns of strong and weak accents. Some, like *disenchanted,* stride briskly on with alternating strong and weak accents; others, like *encyclopedia,* dance to a rhythm all their own.

Two symbols are commonly used to indicate strong and weak accents: ´ (strong) and ˘ (weak). We would indicate the pattern of accents for *disenchanted* as

dis en chant ed.

The indications for *encyclopedia* would be

en cy clo pe di a.

Marking the pattern of accents or stresses in a line of poetry will help you understand how the line achieves its effect, and it is a skill you should practice. You should, however, practice it by copying the poem into a notebook or into your word processor. If you mark a poem on the page of your text you will never be able to see the poem without the markings, and they will become small pricks that catch at your eye when you should be thinking only of the meaning and the language of the poem. The term for this kind of analysis is **scansion,** and what you are doing is scanning the poem.

The pattern set up by the regular rhythm of words in a poem is called **meter.** To have a meter we have to have more than one or two accents; this means we have to have at least three or four words to hear the meter. In some poems it is almost necessary to follow the pattern all the way to the end of the poem to decide what the meter is.

The meters you will be studying all have names, based on what is called a **foot,** one unit of the rhythmic pattern that makes up the meter. This may sound as if we have simply gone around in a circle, but it is not difficult to understand if you write down a line of the poem and mark it with the symbols for stressed and unstressed or accented and unaccented syllables. Here is an example from a sonnet by William Shakespeare:

So oft | have I | invok'd | thee for | my muse

If you read the line out loud, the first syllable, *So,* is unaccented, so the pattern of weak and strong accents is weak-strong, weak-strong, weak-strong, weak-strong, weak-strong. The foot is the unit of the two syllables—a weak one and a strong one—and as you can see we marked the foot with the symbol |. A rhythm based on a foot of one weak and one strong syllable, which has the name **iamb,** is called **iambic meter,** and it is one of the basic building blocks of English poetry.

What happens if we reverse the pattern of accents, and we have a line with a stress on the first syllable?

Does he | ever | wonder | where I | am?

Here the pattern is strong-weak, strong-weak, strong-weak, strong-weak, strong. This metrical foot is called a **trochee,** and the name for its meter is **trochaic meter.**

Two other rhythmic patterns are commonly found in poetry in English. One is a rhythmic foot of two unaccented syllables followed by a strong syllable. An example would be

By the sea, | by the sea, | by the beau | tiful sea.

The foot is called an **anapest,** and the line produces **anapestic meter.** The other foot reverses this pattern and we have a strong syllable followed by two weak syllables:

Down by the | sea, by the | beautiful | sea.

The foot is called a **dactyl** and its meter is **dactylic.**

As you begin using these terms and reading poems with them in mind, you should remember that poets usually do not follow the meters consistently through the poem. When the meter never varies, the poem may be considered too "sing-song." If you read through a poem and find that most of its lines are in one meter, then you will say that the poem is iambic or dactylic, trochaic or anapestic, depending on whichever foot is used most often in the poem. We call any foot that is not part of the overall meter by its own name. If you read a line like

She watched | him walk | in the sum | mer's light

you see that the rhythm is weak-strong, weak-strong, weak-weak-strong, weak-strong. You would say that this line is iambic, with an anapestic third foot. You will also find when you analyze the meter of some lines that there is a break in the meter. It stops and starts somewhere within the line. This is called a **caesura,** and it is an important term to remember, because it will help you to sort through some of the meters in more complex lines. The symbol for a caesura is | |. In this line from another of Shakespeare's sonnets the caesura occurs between *cruel* and *do:*

Be wise | as thou | art cruel, | | do | not press

You will usually have some help in recognizing the caesura. There will often be punctuation at that point — a period, a colon, or semicolon. Even a comma can be enough to tell you that there is a break in the rhythm. Sometimes there is an unstressed syllable at the beginning of a line that does not affect the overall meter. The term for this is an **anacrusis.** In this example the meter of the line is dactylic, with the opening word *I* as an anacrusis:

I | went to the | river to | see the sun | fade

If you have ever studied a play by Shakespeare, you've heard the term **iambic pentameter.** We already discussed the word *iambic. Pentameter* is derived from the Greek word *penta,* which means "five." Combined with the word *meter,* it means a meter with five units, or feet. If you consider the first line we analyzed from a sonnet by Shakespeare—"So oft have I invok'd thee for my muse"—you see that it has five strong accents. We say the line is written in iambic pentameter, as it is made up of a foot with weak-strong syllables, and it has five of them. There are terms derived from the Greek for almost all of the conceivable line lengths, and we can list them here:

> *monometer* is a line of one foot
> *dimeter,* a line of two feet
> *trimeter,* a line of three feet
> *tetrameter,* four feet
> *pentameter,* five feet
> *hexameter,* six feet
> *heptameter,* seven feet
> *octameter,* eight feet

Most poetry written in regular meter uses one of the shorter line lengths—three, four, or five strong syllables. Poems have been written, however, in all of these meters. One of the most famous American poems from the nineteenth century, "The Raven" by Edgar Allan Poe is an example of composition using an eight-syllable line. It is written with a strong-weak pattern of syllables, which means the technical term for the meter of the poem is *trochaic octameter.* This is the poem's opening line:

Once up | on a | midnight | dreary, | while I | pondered | weak and | weary

Two strong accents together are called a **spondee** and two weak accents together are called a **pyrrhus.** There are some further refinements of the terms for poetic meter. We use the term **rising meter** for the two feet that begin with a weak syllable, iambic and anapestic, and the term **falling meter** for the two feet that begin with a strong syllable, trochaic and dactylic.

Blank Verse

In your studies of a play by Shakespeare, you would also have encountered the term **blank verse.** Blank verse is a form that utilizes the oratorical style of a long line in regular meter, but without the confines of rhyme. The meter is iambic pentameter, although writers generally allow themselves considerable metric freedom. Blank verse was the basic language of Elizabethan drama. Here is an example from Shakespeare's *King Henry the Fourth, Part I:*

> So shaken as we are, so wan with care,
> Find we a time for frighted peace to pant,
> And breathe short-winded accents of new broils
> To be commenced in stronds° afar remote.   *strands*

In the long centuries that poets have used the sound of words to create rhyme and meter they have become increasingly dexterous in the effects that they can achieve with these poetic means. Before we move on to the elements of a poem that build on the meaning of words, we close with an example by a modern writer whose poetry exemplifies this tradition, the American poet Richard Wilbur. His "My Father Paints the Summer" confirms the vitality of these poetic traditions in writing that is a reflection of our own everyday experience.

RICHARD WILBUR

My Father Paints the Summer   1947

A smoky rain riddles the ocean plains,
Rings on the beaches' stones, stomps in the swales,
Batters the panes
Of the shore hotel, and the hoped-for summer chills and fails.
The summer people sigh,   5
"Is this July?"

They talk by the lobby fire but no one hears
For the thrum of the rain. In the dim and sounding halls,
Din at the ears,
Dark at the eyes well in the head, and the ping-pong balls   10
Scatter their hollow knocks
Like crazy clocks.

But up in his room by artificial light
My father paints the summer, and his brush
Tricks into sight   15
The prosperous sleep, the girdling stir and clear steep hush
Of a summer never seen,
A granted green.

Summer, luxuriant Sahara, the orchard spray
Gales in the Eden trees, the knight again   20
Can cast away
His burning mail, Rome is at Anzio: but the rain
For the ping-pong's optative bop
Will never stop.

Caught Summer is always an imagined time.   25
Time gave it, yes, but time out of any mind.
There must be prime
In the heart to beget that season, to reach past rain and find
Riding the palest days
Its perfect blaze.   30

COMMENTARY   T. S. Eliot, *"From 'Tradition and the Individual Talent,'"* page 972.

WEB   *For exercises and activities on the elements of poetry, see VirtuaLit Poetry at bedfordstmartins.com/charters/litwriters.*

9.

The Elements of Poetry:
A Poet's Meanings

No tears in the writer, no tears in the reader. No surprise for the writer, no surprise for the reader.

—ROBERT FROST, from the introduction
to *Collected Poems*, 1939

What we have been studying so far is how poets use the sound of words as part of the work they do in writing a poem. You may, however, also have heard the term *tone* used as a way to characterize a poem, and it will help you if you remember that the terms *sound* and *tone* mean different things. Before we begin to discuss those elements of a poem that depend on what a word means we should consider tone, and how it is used to describe a poem.

Tone

We are all familiar with the differences in tone in the things we say to each other in our everyday speech. The same words will mean entirely different things, depending on the tone of our voice when we say them. When a mother or father says admiringly to a young child, "You're so smart!" they will use an entirely different tone from the derisive cry of an angry classmate's voice when he or she says the same words, "You're so smart." So much of what we say to each other is shaded by our tone of voice and expression that we become accustomed to reading each other's intentions by responding to the tone of how something is said.

A poem presents us with a wide range of choices, but unless we are hearing the poem read aloud, we will have to look for the poem's meaning in the tone of its language. The words on the page will have to suggest enough for us to understand what the poet is trying to express. When we read these lines,

What high, bright hopes
  her shining spirit brings!

we know from the words *high, bright,* and *shining* that the tone of the poem is positive and admiring. We would read the poem aloud with a strong, respectful tone. When we read these next lines, however, we immediately respond to a different tone.

> Whatever you thought you were doing,
> my love, it wasn't enough for me,
> Whatever you thought you were feeling,
>   it wasn't, it wasn't,
>   oh lord,
>   it wasn't enough for me.

In the querulous phrase "whatever you thought you were doing," we hear a tone of exasperation and impatience, and if we read the lines aloud we find ourselves, almost without thinking, shaking our heads.

As you read the next three poems, think of how the tone of the writing helps you experience the emotions the poet wants to express. Two of the poems, "Miniver Cheevy" and "Richard Cory" by the American poet Edwin Arlington Robinson, achieve much of their effect through skillful irony. In the third, "Bells for John Whiteside's Daughter" written in the 1930s after the death of a friend's daughter, John Crowe Ransom weaves the tones of melancholy and loss into a moving elegy for a young girl.

EDWIN ARLINGTON ROBINSON

Miniver Cheevy   1910

> Miniver Cheevy, child of scorn,
>   Grew lean while he assailed the seasons;
> He wept that he was ever born,
>   And he had reasons.
>
> Miniver loved the days of old   5
>   When swords were bright and steeds were prancing;
> The vision of a warrior bold
>   Would set him dancing.
>
> Miniver sighed for what was not,
>   And dreamed, and rested from his labors;   10
> He dreamed of Thebes° and Camelot,°
>   And Priam's° neighbors.

---

11. Thebes: Ancient city of Greece; also, ancient city on the Nile River in Egypt. **Camelot:** The kingdom of King Arthur and legendary seat of the Knights of the Round Table in Britain. **12. Priam's:** Priam was the father of Hector and Paris and king of Troy during the Trojan War.

Miniver mourned the ripe renown
    That made so many a name so fragrant;
He mourned Romance, now on the town,   15
    And Art, a vagrant.

Miniver loved the Medici,°
    Albeit he had never seen one;
He would have sinned incessantly
    Could he have been one.   20

Miniver cursed the commonplace
    And eyed a khaki suit with loathing;
He missed the medieval grace
    Of iron clothing.

Miniver scorned the gold he sought,   25
    But sore annoyed was he without it;
Miniver thought, and thought, and thought,
    And thought about it.

Miniver Cheevy, born too late,
    Scratched his head and kept on thinking;   30
Miniver coughed, and called it fate,
    And kept on drinking.

Richard Cory   1897

Whenever Richard Cory went down town,
We people on the pavement looked at him:
He was a gentleman from sole to crown,
Clean favored, and imperially slim.

And he was always quietly arrayed,   5
And he was always human when he talked;
But still he fluttered pulses when he said,
'Good-morning,' and he glittered when he walked.

And he was rich — yes, richer than a king —
And admirably schooled in every grace: 10
In fine, we thought that he was everything
To make us wish that we were in his place.

So on we worked, and waited for the light,
And went without the meat, and cursed the bread;
And Richard Cory, one calm summer night,   15
Went home and put a bullet through his head.

---

17. **Medici:** The ruling family of Florence, Italy, from the fifteenth to the eighteenth century.

JOHN CROWE RANSOM

Bells for John Whiteside's Daughter   1924

There was such speed in her little body,
And such lightness in her footfall,
It is no wonder her brown study
Astonishes us all.

Her wars were bruited in our high window.   5
We looked among orchard trees and beyond
Where she took arms against her shadow,
Or harried unto the pond

The lazy geese, like a snow cloud
Dripping their snow on the green grass,   10
Tricking and stopping, sleepy and proud,
Who cried in goose, Alas,

For the tireless heart within the little
Lady with rod that made them rise
From their noon apple-dreams and scuttle   15
Goose-fashion under the skies!

But now go the bells, and we are ready,
In one house we are sternly stopped
To say we are vexed at her brown study,
Lying so primly propped.   20

WORDS AND THEIR MEANING

Keeping in mind the difference between the *sound* of a poem and the *tone* of a poem, we will begin to discuss those elements of a poem that depend on what a word *means*. Any writer is sensitive to the meanings of words, and poets, who must also think of the sound and the rhythm of each word they use, are even more conscious of the subtleties of meaning in every phrase they write, and they continually look for new and unexpected words to express their ideas. One of the popular poems from the nineteenth century is this "nonsense" verse by Lewis Carroll, which seems to make fun of this concern by poets to find new and unusual ways of saying things. Carroll simply invented words to create a poem that may mean many things, though readers have never been entirely certain just what those meanings might be. It is ironic that one of the nonsense words he made up, *chortled,* quickly became part of the English language.

LEWIS CARROLL

Jabberwocky°   1871

'Twas brillig, and the slithy toves
    Did gyre and gimble in the wabe;
All mimsy were the borogoves,
    And the mome raths outgrabe.

"Beware the Jabberwock, my son!   5
    The jaws that bite, the claws that catch!
Beware the Jubjub bird, and shun
    The frumious Bandersnatch!"

He took his vorpal sword in hand;
    Long time the manxome foe he sought—   10
So rested he by the Tumtum tree,
    And stood awhile in thought.

And, as in uffish thought he stood,
    The Jabberwock, with eyes of flame,
Came whiffling through the tulgey wood,   15
    And burbled as it came!

One, two! One, two! And through and through
    The vorpal blade went snicker-snack!
He left it dead, and with its head
    He went galumphing back.   20

"And hast thou slain the Jabberwock?
    Come to my arms, my beamish boy!
O frabjous day! Callooh! Callay!"
    He chortled in his joy.

'Twas brillig, and the slithy toves   25
    Did gyre and gimble in the wabe;
All mimsy were the borogoves,
    And the mome raths outgrabe.

Denotative and Connotative Meaning

The meanings of many words we use may seem to be simple and straight-forward, but other words have many associations that alter the way we understand them. To describe this we use two terms. The first is **denotative,** or what a word denotes. This is the dictionary meaning of the word. The second term is **connotative.** This is the associated meanings that have built up around the word, or what the word connotes. As an example, let's take the word *sweat:*

Jabberwocky: Meaningless speech or writing. This poem is from the first chapter of Carroll's *Through the Looking Glass.*

The *denotative meaning*, which we find in the dictionary: "Moisture exuded from the skin, perspiration."

The *connotative meaning*, which we understand from common usage: hard work.

Someone asks you if you can do something for them, and you answer, "No sweat." What you have said, in the denotative meaning of the word, though you have shortened it considerably, is "Doing what you have asked me to do will be so easy for me that I won't even perspire while I do it." What you have said in its connotative meaning is that for you it's an easy job. Why did you use the connotations of the word *sweat*? For the same reason a writer uses connotations. These suggested or implied meanings make our language more rich and varied, and more vivid in its expression.

Many words that you can think of also have multiple meanings in their denotative sense. *Sweet* is an adjective in the United States; it can also be a term of endearment. In Britain it is a noun meaning "dessert." *Fall* can be a verb or a noun, with its denotative meaning "to descend freely." It can also mean a season of the year, autumn. You will have to be careful in your reading to recognize which meaning the writer wants.

Fall also has connotative meanings. We often use it in a phrase like "He's heading for a fall." The denotative meaning is that if he continues in the direction he is going he will fall down. The connotation of the phrase is that he is going to get into serious trouble. Sometimes the connotation of the word will be immediately obvious; sometimes you have to study the whole poem to see what the writer intended to say. For this way of reading the poem we'll be concerning ourselves with diction and syntax.

Diction

When we speak of **diction** we are describing the language that a writer has chosen to use in a poem. For us today this means looking at the poem and deciding why one word was chosen and not another one that means the same thing and that in most ways would have done just as well as the word the poet selected. For hundreds of years, however, when people used the term *diction* in discussing a poem, they meant a special kind of language for poetry that they called **poetic diction.** Poetry was considered to be such a refined art that you could only use refined words when you wrote it. In the words of Samuel Johnson, the poet and critic of the late eighteenth century who also compiled the first dictionary of the English language, poetic diction was "a system of words refined from the grossness of domestic use."

Sometimes readers make the mistake of thinking that people in the eighteenth century talked the way their poetry sounds. Except for the occasional person of conscious literary wit such as Johnson, you can be sure that ordinary conversation did not sound that way. This idea of poetic diction, which had grown out of the classical education of that time, was grounded in the study of Latin and Greek. The poets took the classic poets and the myths and legends of the older languages as models for their own poetry. As they worked with these models, their poetry almost developed a language of its own. The term *neoclassical* (or *Augustan*) is used to describe poetry written in this style. You will get an idea of this language from these lines from "Sound and Sense" by one of the most celebrated English poets of the eighteenth century, Alexander Pope:

> True ease in writing comes from art, not chance,
> As those move easiest who have learned to dance.
> 'Tis not enough no harshness gives offense,
> The sound must seem an echo to the sense:
> Soft is the strain when Zephyr° gently blows,   5
> And the smooth stream in smoother numbers flows;
> But when loud surges lash the sounding shore,
> The hoarse, rough verse should like the torrent roar.
> When Ajax° strives, some rock's vast weight to throw,
> The line too labors, and the words move slow;   10
> Not so, when swift Camilla° scours the plain,
> Flies o'er th' unbending corn, and skims along the main.

If you had said to Pope that these lines sound artificial, not at all like the way people talk, he would have bowed his head and thanked you for the compliment. What he is telling us, in his seemingly effortless iambic pentameter and perfect rhyme, is that writing poetry does not depend on spontaneity, or "chance." The best poets will use artifice or be the ones "who have learned to dance." This is almost the opposite of our own concern with spontaneity and sincerity, but we must remember that the conventions of language reflect different historical periods.

The revolution against the limitations and artificialities that began to dominate neoclassical poetry came at the end of the eighteenth century, with the group of poets we call the *romantics*. Led by the English writers William Wordsworth and Samuel Taylor Coleridge, they broke away from the old style and tried to use language closer to ordinary ways of speaking. As Wordsworth expressed it in his introduction to the first collection of poems written in the new style, he wanted to write in "the language of the middle and lower classes of society."

The poets who are associated with the first romantics—among them William Blake, Robert Burns, Percy Bysshe Shelley, John Keats, and Lord Byron—continued to open up the poetic language to new possibilities in diction and emotional directness. Their poetry was the most important influence on the kind of immediate, personal writing that we value today.

Syntax

Syntax is derived from the Greek word "to arrange together." It refers to the order of the words in writing of any kind, not only poetry. A change in natural word order can affect the way we hear or read any kind of phrase or sentence. In poetry, where each word bears so much weight, any change becomes

---

5. Zephyr: The west wind.   **9. Ajax:** Mighty warrior in Homer's *Iliad.*   **11. Camilla:** Female warrior in Virgil's *Aeneid.*

significant. Poets will sometimes spend as much time deciding the order of the words as they do deciding on what words to use in the first place. For anyone using traditional poetic forms, which meant rhyme and meter, the most common decision about word order was often forced on the writer by the need to find a rhyme.

If you look again at the lines from Alexander Pope's "Sound and Sense," you will see that the natural word order is altered at the ends of line 8 and line 9 because of the necessities of the rhyme. Line 8 would end, in a natural word order, as "should roar like the current," but line 7 ends with "shore." The change of order to bring "roar" at the end of the line solves the problem. Line 9 presents the same difficulty. The natural word order would be "to throw some rock's vast weight," but the rhyme at the end of line 10 is "slow," and here also the change in order gives us the rhyme. You might also have noticed that there is a change in word order at the beginning of line 5. Instead of "The strain is soft," we have "Soft is the strain." Here the change has been made for the sound. If you read line 4 and then follow it with "The strain is soft," you will feel that the meter of the lines is clumsy. The change in order gives us a much smoother line, and this smoothness was one of the qualities that writers such as Pope prized most in a poem.

Imagery

We are all familiar with the literal, denotative meaning of the word *image* as a picture of something. If we say that a girl is the image of her mother, we mean that she looks just like her. If we are talking about an image in a poem, however, the word has different connotations. We do not, in a literal sense, *see* anything in a poem; we just read about it. What we call an image in poetry is a concrete description of something. It can also be a description of something we hear, touch, or feel in a physical sense. There are terms to describe each of these three kinds of images: *visual images* (things we see), *aural images* (things we hear), and *tactile images* (things we touch). If we write "an old, dark green convertible," that is a visual image. If we go on to describe the convertible's "noisy, rattling roar," that is an aural image. If we imagine sitting behind the wheel and feel "the prickly upholstery" on the seat, that is a tactile image.

Being even more precise in defining images, we have two more names for different types of tactile images. One is *gustatory* (things we taste), and the other is *olfactory* (things we smell). Describing the convertible's "lingering gas fumes" is an olfactory image, and if we drive it to a fast-food restaurant and eat a hamburger that has "a greasy, half-cooked taste," that is a gustatory image.

These kinds of physical descriptions have always been part of the poet's means, because a writer's description of specific and concrete objects in a poem strengthens our sense that what we are being told is real. This is, after all, the way we perceive the world. Our information comes to us through the perceptions of our senses, which gather in the raw material that we use to decide what we are experiencing. A poem can also include words like *beauty* and *truth*, but these are not images. They have no concrete reality, however intensely we may feel them. The word we use for them is **abstractions.**

The poems you are reading may have many images, or they may have only a single image. If we are talking about all of the images within a poem, we use the term **imagery.** The connotation of the term is that the poem presents us with a series of images that relate to one another in a way that helps to shape the poem's meaning. As you read "To Autumn" by the English romantic poet John Keats, you will see that the description of autumn is filled with visual images. Although we may find the language of the poem old-fashioned, Keats's poetry seemed revolutionary to the readers of his day.

JOHN KEATS

To Autumn   1819

Season of mists and mellow fruitfulness,
   Close bosom friend of the maturing sun:
Conspiring with him how to load and bless
   With fruit the vines that round the thatch-eaves run;
To bend with apples the mossed cottage-trees,   5
   And fill all fruit with ripeness to the core;
      To swell the gourd, and plump the hazel shells
With a sweet kernel; to set budding more,
   And still more, later flowers for the bees,
      Until they think warm days will never cease,   10
      For summer has o'er-brimmed their clammy cells.

Who hath not seen thee oft amid thy store?
   Sometimes whoever seeks abroad may find
Thee sitting careless on a granary floor,
   Thy hair soft-lifted by the winnowing wind;   15
Or on a half-reaped furrow sound asleep,
   Drowsed with the fume of poppies, while thy hook
      Spares the next swath and all its twined flowers:
And sometimes like a gleaner thou dost keep,
   Steady thy laden head across a brook;   20
   Or by a cider-press, with patient look,
      Thou watchest the last oozings hours by hours.

Where are the songs of Spring? Ay, where are they?
   Think not of them, thou hast thy music too,—
While barred clouds bloom the soft-dying day,   25
   And touch the stubble-plains with rosy hue;
Then in a wailful choir the small gnats mourn
   Among the river sallows, borne aloft
      Or sinking as the light wind lives or dies;
And full-grown lambs loud bleat from hilly bourn;   30
   Hedge-crickets sing: and now with treble soft
   The red-breast whistles from a garden-croft;
      and gathering swallows twitter in the skies.

Keats is writing here about an everyday subject, the coming of autumn to a country farm, and although his language is still too elevated to be mistaken for the way ordinary people spoke, he does not break up the poem's imagery with the continual references to classical learning that writers such as Pope considered an essential element of their poetry.

The first line is an image in itself, the autumn as a "season of mists and mellow fruitfulness." Then, almost as if we are standing in the center of the farmyard, we see the vines on the cottage eaves, the "mossed cottage-trees," the flowers for the bees, and the bees, which have gathered so much honey that they've "o'er-brimmed their clammy cells," in their hives. The figure that the poet addresses as "thee" in the second verse is autumn. The term for this way of speaking to something that is inanimate is the figure of speech called **apostrophe.**

At the end of the poem, Keats does not make any larger statement about the scene in the farmyard. He does not draw any moral or lesson from it. This was also part of the revolutionary quality of his poetry. Simply to be there, at that moment, and hear the red-breast whistling from the croft and the swallows twittering in the sky was enough for him. The sallows he notices in line 28 are low willows that grow along riverbanks, and one of the poet's strongest aural images is the description of the gnats "mourning" above the brushy willows.

Many modern poets write with the same open and direct response to a natural scene as Keats wrote. In the following poem the American writer Elizabeth Bishop is also satisfied simply to look at what is before her. She is seeing it so intensely that the poem is constructed entirely around its visual images. What she is describing is a *bight,* a small bay, usually by the ocean. *Marl* is the rich deposit of soil that streams have left on the bottom of the bight, and *claves* are wooden percussion instruments used in Caribbean and South American dance music. Charles Baudelaire, who is named in line 7, was a nineteenth-century French poet who shocked many people with the frank sensuality of his writing. He also puzzled people with his theories that poetry could find the associations between the world of the sense — the physical world — and the world of the spirit. In her line about marimba music (line 8), Bishop is humorously suggesting that this is the kind of association Baudelaire would have made when he was experimenting with substances such as the gas she can smell coming out of the muck at the bottom of the bay.

ELIZABETH BISHOP

The Bight   1955

(On My Birthday)

At low tide like this how sheer the water is.
White, crumbling ribs of marl protrude and glare
and the boats are dry, the pilings dry as matches.

Absorbing, rather than being absorbed,
the water in the bight doesn't wet anything,   5
the color of the gas flame turned as low as possible.
One can smell it turning to gas; if one were Baudelaire
one could probably hear it turning into marimba music.
The little ochre dredge at work off the end of the dock
already plays the dry perfectly off-beat claves.   10
The birds are outsize. Pelicans crash
into this peculiar gas unnecessarily hard,
it seems to me, like pickaxes,
rarely coming up with anything to show for it,
and going off with humorous elbowings.   15
Black-and-white man-of-war birds soar
on impalpable drifts
and open their tails like scissors on the curves
or tense them like wishbones, till they tremble.
The frowsy sponge boats keep coming in   20
with the obliging air of retrievers,
bristling with jackstraw gaffs and hooks
and decorated with bobbles of sponges.
There is a fence of chicken wire along the dock
where, glinting like little plowshares,   25
the blue-gray shark tails are hung up to dry
for the Chinese-restaurant trade.
Some of the little white boats are still piled up
against each other, or lie on their sides, stove in,
and not yet salvaged, if they ever will be, from the last bad storm,   30
like torn-open, unanswered letters.
The bight is littered with old correspondences.
Click. Click. Goes the dredge,
and brings up a dripping jawful of marl.
All the untidy activity continues,   35
awful but cheerful.

As you read the poem you may have noticed some of the poetic means
that Bishop uses to bring her description of the harbor to life. In the first line
she has changed the *syntax* to tell us the most important thing about the scene.
The line in customary order would be, "How sheer the water is like this at low
tide." Instead, the first thing she tells us is that it is low tide, so we will have that
as our immediate visual image.

Sheer is not an obvious choice to describe the gleam of the water on the
mud flats, but Bishop has made a choice in the *diction* of the poem to use *sheer*
instead of another possible word, like *shiny. Sheer* has the connotations of silk,
and it also has an *r* sound, which relates to the *r* of water, and gives the line a
subtle *assonance. Sheer* also has one syllable, which smooths out the rhythm of
the last half of the line to three iambic feet.

We can see several other phrases in which Bishop has made choices in the diction to create an even more vivid image: *ochre* instead of yellow-brown for the color of the dredge, "dry perfectly off-beat" for the sound of the claves, the adjective *outsize* instead of *big* for the size of the birds, *frowsy* for the sponge boats instead of *tattered*. The poem is written without regular meter or rhyme, but certainly, with Bishop's brilliant skill with words, she intended to use the near rhyme of *marl* and *cheerful* that helps to bring the poem to a close.

Simile and Metaphor

As we looked closely at Bishop's poem, we realized that she had other means of showing us the harbor. Several times she used comparisons — phrases that began with the word *like*. The term for this is **simile.** For an image of the pelicans flapping out of the water she used the phrase "humorous elbowings," which is an indirect comparison. The term for this is **metaphor.** Both of these terms are important in understanding how poems are written.

Writers have always used simile and metaphor because language without simile is as flat as chili without chili powder. If you have studied literature, you recognized that "as flat as chili without chili powder" is a simile. Simile and metaphor are both comparisons, but a simile tells us to watch out for the comparison with the words *like, as, as if,* or *as though,* while a metaphor does not.

Writers use comparisons for several reasons. It is often easier to describe something that is not familiar by comparing it to something that is, as in the sentence "The wing of a Morpha butterfly looks like a large blue leaf." Another use of a simile is to give a tangible reality to something that is intangible. An example: "Our love is like the shine of the sun on the sea."

The use of metaphor has long been considered one of the measures of a poet's skill. The Greek philosopher Aristotle defined metaphor as "an intuitive perception of the similarity in dissimilars." A simple metaphor would be a phrase like "You are my sunshine." Most poets, however, try to find comparisons that are more unexpected, that make the reader think about what is similar in the two objects that are being drawn together in a comparison.

The Anglo-Saxon church historian the Venerable Bede included one of the first memorable extended similes in English literature (it was derived from Psalm 84) in his eighth-century *Ecclesiastical History of the English People.* Bede wrote that the brief span of our lifetime between birth and death is "as if a sparrow beaten with wind and weather" flies into a warm, lighted hall and then, after "a short space of this fair weather," departs back outside "to return from winter to winter again."

In Elizabeth Bishop's poem we identified both similes and a metaphor. The similes are strong word pictures. The pelicans crash into the water "like pickaxes," the man-of-war birds open their tails "like scissors," "glinting like little plowshares, / the blue-gray shark tails are hung up to dry," the little white boats lie damaged on the mud "like torn-open, unanswered letters." The metaphor is a description of pelicans struggling to fly up from the water. Bishop describes them as "going off with humorous elbowings," which compares them with people using their elbows to get through a crowd.

Here are some examples of similes:

Like as the waves make towards the pebbled shore,
So do our minutes hasten to their end.
　　　　　　　　　　　—WILLIAM SHAKESPEARE, from "Sonnet 61"

Oh, my luve is like a red, red rose,
　　That's newly sprung in June.
　　—ROBERT BURNS, from "A Red, Red Rose"

I love smooth words, like gold-enameled fish
which circle slowly with a golden swish.
　　　　　—ELINOR WYLIE, from "Pretty Words"

Let us go then, you and I
When the evening is spread out against the sky
Like a patient etherized upon a table.
　　　　　—T. S. ELIOT, from "The Love Song of J. Alfred Prufrock"

I am scattered like
the hot shriveled seeds.
　　　　　　　　—H.D., from "Mid-day"

Love set you going like a fat gold watch.
　　—SYLVIA PLATH, from "Morning Song"

What happens to a dream deferred?
　　Does it dry up
　　like a raisin in the sun?
　　　　—LANGSTON HUGHES, from "Harlem"

I like small kindnesses.
In fact I actually prefer them to the more
substantial kindness that is always eyeing you,
like a large animal on a rug.
　　　　　—LOUISE GLÜCK, from "Gratitude"

Here are some examples of metaphors:

My Rosalind, my Rosalind,
My frolic falcon, with bright eyes.
　　　　　　　　—ALFRED, LORD TENNYSON, from "Rosalind"

Your mind and you are our Sargasso Sea.
　　　　　　　—EZRA POUND, from "Portrait d'une Femme"

Now that I have your voice by heart, I read
In the black chords upon a dulling page
Music that is not meant for music's cage,
Whose emblems mix with words that shake and bleed.
　　　　　　　—LOUISE BOGAN, from "Song for the Last Act"

> . . . your knees
> are a southern breeze.
> —WILLIAM CARLOS WILLIAMS, from "Portrait of a Lady"

> The corpse was bloodless. . . .
> Its open staring eyes were lustreless dead-lights.
> —ROBERT LOWELL, from "The Quaker Graveyard in Nantucket"

> Marriage is not
> a house or even a tent
> it is before that, and colder.
> —MARGARET ATWOOD, from "Habitation"

Poets often work consciously with the possibilities that simile and metaphor present. In this poem by Hart Crane, we encounter a simile in the first line, and then the same technique is used again in the second verse, this time to present a metaphor. You will also notice that the poem ends with a contradiction that is called a *paradox.*

HART CRANE

Forgetfulness   1918

Forgetfulness is like a song
That, freed from beat and measure, wanders.
Forgetfulness is like a bird whose wings are reconciled,
Outspread and motionless, —
A bird that coasts the wind unwearyingly.   5
Forgetfulness is rain at night,
Or an old house in a forest, — or a child.
Forgetfulness is white, — white as a blasted tree,
And it may stun the sybil into prophecy,
Or bury the Gods.   10

I can remember much forgetfulness.

One of the classic American poems from the first years of modernist experimentation is Carl Sandburg's "Fog." It compares the fog's drift over the city to a cat entering silently to sit for a moment and look down at the scene. Sandburg doesn't use the words *like* or *as,* so we are aware that the poem is a metaphor.

CARL SANDBURG

Fog

1916

The fog comes
on little cat feet.

It sits looking
over harbor and city
on silent haunches
and then moves on.

Figurative and Literal Language

The term **figurative language** means that the poem uses simile or metaphor, or any of the figures of speech we will study in the next pages. The opposite of figurative language is **literal language,** which means that each word is being used in its denotative sense.

Symbol

We've already seen how words and phrases have connotations and associations. A word becomes a **symbol** when it has so much meaning attached to it that we cannot hear it spoken without immediately thinking of something else at the same time. Mention of "the flag" brings up thoughts of patriotism and America. "Wall Street" could be a reference to the structure of American capitalism. In the 1920s the poet T. S. Eliot became the center of a lengthy discussion about symbols and symbolism, because several of his most influential poems used objects like roses or yew trees as symbols for his beliefs in tradition and his religious faith. In our own period poets more often write directly what they mean, but words like *Hollywood* or *Barbie* in a poem come loaded with associations.

Figures of Speech

There are more than two hundred ways that words can be used as figures of speech, but you need to familiarize yourself with only a few that you will meet most often. If you say "The sky is crying," you are using **personification,** which is giving human characteristics to something inanimate, animal, or abstract. In this poem the Swedish poet Rolf Aggestam personifies ordinary lightning as a difficult and unpredictable barefoot companion.

ROLF AGGESTAM

Lightning Bolt   1997

TRANSLATED BY SAMUEL CHARTERS

A lightning bolt
is in heat most of the time and doesn't
believe in anything. Unfaithful to any
system. Doesn't measure things. Doesn't make
comparisons.   5
Doesn't have any hair.

A lightning bolt
is unsure of itself, incomprehensible and curious.
If you understand a lightning bolt it's too late.

You can stuff   10
a lightning bolt. Stand it up there staring from a
book shelf, seeing everything so clearly.
It hurls itself out of the bare sky and
immediately begins to look for earth.

Challenge the lightning bolt to perform   15
your deepest and most secret commission
and walk around it wearing heavy boots.
A lightning bolt wants earth under the soles of its feet.

The term *apostrophe* means to address something intangible or someone not commonly spoken to. The opening line of this sonnet by John Donne (see p. 753) is an example of apostrophe, as the intangible presence he is crying out to is Death:

> Death, be not proud, though some have callèd thee
> Mighty and dreadful, for thou art not so;
> For those whom thou think'st thou dost overthrow
> Die not, poor Death. . . .

Metonymy and a type of figurative speech closely related to it, **synecdoche,** are similar to metaphor. In using metonymy the writer uses the name of one thing in place of the name of something closely related to it. Instead of saying "I knew him when he was young," the line could be "I knew him in his cradle." Synecdoche is the use of part of something to stand for the whole thing. If we say someone playing baseball or softball "has a heavy bat," we are using the bat as a substitute for the whole concept, which is that the batter hits the ball well.

There are other figures of speech that you will find in your reading, but most of these concepts are used by all writers, and you are probably already familiar with them. Some of these are *paradox, oxymoron, hyperbole,* and *understatement.* By **paradox** we mean a statement that on the surface seems that it cannot possibly be true but is true after all. In the last lines of the sonnet

"Death, be not proud," John Donne uses a paradox when he suggests that because of the miracle of eternal life, it is Death itself that dies at the moment of mortality:

> One short sleep past, we wake eternally
> And death shall be no more; Death, thou shalt die.

An **oxymoron** is a statement that contradicts itself. Probably the best-known modern example is the phrase "jumbo shrimp." A more literary example is "darkness visible," Milton's phrase describing hell in *Paradise Lost*. By **hyperbole** we mean exaggerated statements that we do not really intend to be taken for the truth. When the seventeenth-century American poet Anne Bradstreet writes, in "To My Dear and Loving Husband" (p. 847), "I prize thy love more than whole mines of gold / Or all the riches that the East doth hold," she is using hyperbole. **Understatement** is the opposite of hyperbole. Here something is deliberately described in terms that suggest it is much smaller or less important than we know it really is. The line "Life for me ain't been no crystal stair" from Langston Hughes's poem "Mother to Son" (p. 908) is an example of understatement.

Poems for Further Reading

ANDREW MARVELL

To His Coy Mistress   1681

    Had we but world enough, and time,
This coyness, lady, were no crime.
We would sit down, and think which way
To walk, and pass our long love's day.
Thou by the Indian Ganges' side   5
Shouldst rubies find; I by the tide
Of Humber would complain. I would
Love you ten years before the flood,
And you should, if you please, refuse
Till the conversion of the Jews.   10
My vegetable love should grow
Vaster than empires and more slow;
An hundred years should go to praise
Thine eyes, and on thy forehead gaze;
Two hundred to adore each breast,   15
But thirty thousand to the rest;
An age at least to every part,
And the last age should show your heart.
For, lady, you deserve this state,
Nor would I love at lower rate.   20

But at my back I always hear
Time's wingéd chariot hurrying near;
And yonder all before us lie
Deserts of vast eternity.
Thy beauty shall no more be found,   25
Nor, in thy marble vault, shall sound
My echoing song; then worms shall try
That long-preserved virginity,
And your quaint honor turn to dust,
And into ashes all my lust: 30
The grave's a fine and private place,
But none, I think, do there embrace.
   Now therefore, while the youthful hue
Sits on thy skin like morning dew,
And while thy willing soul transpires°   *breathes forth* 35
At every pore with instant fires,
Now let us sport us while we may,
And now, like amorous birds of prey,
Rather at once our time devour
Than languish in his slow-chapped° power.   *slow-jawed* 40
Let us roll all our strength and all
Our sweetness up into one ball,
And tear our pleasures with rough strife
Thorough the iron gates of life:
Thus, though we cannot make our sun   45
Stand still, yet we will make him run.

WILLIAM WORDSWORTH

I Wandered Lonely as a Cloud   1804

I wandered lonely as a cloud
That floats on high o'er vales and hills,
When all at once I saw a crowd,
A host, of golden daffodils;
Beside the lake, beneath the trees,   5
Fluttering and dancing in the breeze.

Continuous as the stars that shine
And twinkle on the milky way,
They stretched in never-ending line
Along the margin of a bay: 10
Ten thousand saw I at a glance,
Tossing their heads in sprightly dance.

The waves beside them danced; but they
Outdid the sparkling waves in glee;

A poet could not but be gay,   15
In such a jocund company;
I gazed — and gazed — but little thought
What wealth the show to me had brought:

For oft, when on my couch I lie
In vacant or in pensive mood,   20
They flash upon that inward eye
Which is the bliss of solitude;
And then my heart with pleasure fills,
And dances with the daffodils.

GEORGE GORDON, LORD BYRON

She Walks in Beauty   1814

1

She walks in beauty, like the night
  Of cloudless climes and starry skies;
And all that's best of dark and bright
  Meet in her aspect and her eyes:
Thus mellowed to that tender light   5
  Which heaven to gaudy day denies.

2

One shade the more, one ray the less,
  Had half impaired the nameless grace
Which waves in every raven tress,
  Or softly lightens o'er her face;   10
Where thoughts serenely sweet express
  How pure, how dear their dwelling place.

3

And on that cheek, and o'er that brow,
  So soft, so calm, yet eloquent,
The smiles that win, the tints that glow,   15
  But tell of days in goodness spent,
A mind at peace with all below,
  A heart whose love is innocent!

EMILY BRONTË

If grief for grief

1840

If grief for grief can touch thee,
If answering woe for woe,
If any ruth can melt thee,
Come to me now!

I cannot be more lonely,   5
More drear I cannot be!
My worn heart throbs so wildly
'Twil break for thee.

And when the world despises,
When heaven repels my prayer,   10
Will not mine angel comfort?
Mine idol hear?

Yes, by the tears I've poured [thee],
By all my hours of pain,
O I shall surely win thee,   15
Beloved, again!

ALFRED, LORD TENNYSON

Ulysses

1833

It little profits that an idle king,
By this still hearth, among these barren crags,
Matched with an aged wife, I mete and dole
Unequal laws unto a savage race
That hoard, and sleep, and feed, and know not me.   5
I cannot rest from travel: I will drink
Life to the lees: all times I have enjoyed
Greatly, have suffered greatly, both with those
That loved me, and alone; on shore, and when
Through scudding drifts the rainy Hyades°   10
Vexed the dim sea: I am become a name;
For always roaming with a hungry heart
Much have I seen and known; cities of men
And manners, climates, councils, governments,
Myself not least, but honored of them all;   15
And drunk delight of battle with my peers,
Far on the ringing plains of windy Troy.

---

10. Hyades: A cluster of stars whose rising was thought to be a sign of rain.

I am a part of all that I have met;
Yet all experience is an arch wherethrough
Gleams that untravelled world, whose margin fades   20
For ever and for ever when I move.
How dull it is to pause, to make an end,
To rust unburnished, not to shine in use!
As though to breathe were life. Life piled on life
Were all too little, and of one to me   25
Little remains: but every hour is saved
From that eternal silence, something more,
A bringer of new things; and vile it were
For some three suns to store and hoard myself,
And this gray spirit yearning in desire   30
To follow knowledge like a sinking star,
Beyond the utmost bound of human thought.
    This is my son, mine own Telemachus,°
To whom I leave the scepter and the isle —
Well-loved of me, discerning to fulfil   35
This labor, by slow prudence to make mild
A rugged people, and through soft degrees
Subdue them to the useful and the good.
Most blameless is he, centered in the sphere
Of common duties, decent not to fail   40
In offices of tenderness, and pay
Meet° adoration to my household gods   *proper*
When I am gone. He works his work, I mine.
    There lies the port: the vessel puffs her sail;
There gloom the dark broad seas. My mariners,   45
Souls that have toiled, and wrought, and thought with me —
That ever with a frolic welcome took
The thunder and the sunshine, and opposed
Free hearts, free foreheads — you and I are old;
Old age hath yet his honor and his toil;   50
Death closes all: but something ere the end,
Some work of noble note, may yet be done,
Not unbecoming men that strove with gods.
The lights begin to twinkle from the rocks:
The long day wanes: the slow moon climbs: the deep   55
Moans round with many voices. Come, my friends,
'Tis not too late to seek a newer world.
Push off, and sitting well in order smite
The sounding furrows; for my purpose holds
To sail beyond the sunset and the baths   60
Of all the western stars, until I die.

---

33. Telemachus: The son of Odysseus and Penelope who plots with his father to murder his mother's suitors.

It may be that the gulfs will wash us down:
It may be we shall touch the Happy Isles°
And see the great Achilles, whom we knew.
Though much is taken, much abides; and though   65
We are not now that strength which in old days
Moved earth and heaven, that which we are, we are;
One equal temper of heroic hearts,
Made weak by time and fate but strong in will
To strive, to seek, to find, and not to yield.   70

COMMENTARIES   *Percy Bysshe Shelley, "From 'A Defence of Poetry,'" page 1002; William Wordsworth, "From the Introduction to* Lyrical Ballads,*" page 1006.*

WEB   *For exercises and activities on the elements of poetry, see VirtuaLit Poetry at bedfordstmartins.com/charters/litwriters.*

---

63. touch the Happy Isles: In Greek mythology the Happy Isles were the home of dead warriors. In line 64, Ulysses speaks of his old comrade Achilles, who fought alongside him at Troy and was killed there.

10.

The Types of Poetry:
A Poet's Forms

one loves only form
and form only comes
into existence when
the thing is born

        —CHARLES OLSON, from "I, Maximus of Gloucester"

TYPES OF VERSE

Meter and rhyme, and their complex intertwining, are at the core of all of the forms of traditional verse. For much English poetry the basic building block is a unit of two lines that end in perfect rhyme. The term for this unit is a **couplet.** The couplet appears in English poetry as early as the twelfth century. In this poem, "Hymn to Godric," two couplets are joined together to make a four-line unit called a **stanza,** or a **verse:**

Sainte Marye, Christes bur°	*shelter*
Maidenes clenhad,° moderes flur°	*purity; flower*
Dilie° min sinne, rix° in min mod°	*remove; merge; heart*
Bring me to winne° with the self God	*joy*

We do not recognize all of the words, since language and its meanings are continually changing, but the four-line stanza, written in the four-stress line called *tetrameter* or *quadrameter,* continued to be one of the most widely used poetic means in English and American poetry for hundreds of years. One of the best-known examples of perfect rhyme, A. E. Housman's "Loveliest of trees, the cherry now" (p. 695), is written in this same stanza:

Loveliest of trees, the cherry now
Is hung with bloom along the bough,
And stands about the woodland ride
Wearing white for Eastertide.

We mark the sequence of rhymes in a poem with a tool like the accent symbols that we used to study the meter of a line. Instead of symbols, however, each rhyme is given a letter of the alphabet. Here is an example of how we mark the rhyme pattern of a poem using the same Housman stanza:

Loveliest of trees, the cherry now	a
Is hung with bloom along the bough,	a
And stands about the woodland ride	b
Wearing white for Eastertide.	b

Another form of this same stanza has been used almost as often by many poets. The stanza also has four lines and it is written in alternating lines of tetrameter and trimeter, but instead of *aabb*, the rhyme scheme is *abab*. Here is an example.

A. E. HOUSMAN

Oh, when I was in love with you   1896

Oh, when I was in love with you,	a
Then I was clean and brave,	b
And miles around the wonder grew	a
How well I did behave.	b
And now the fancy passes by,	c
And nothing will remain,	d
And miles around they'll say that I	c
Am quite myself again.	d

A term that is also used for a group of four rhymed lines is a **quatrain,** especially when it is part of a longer unit in a poem. A group of six lines with a recurring rhyme scheme is called a **sestet,** and the term for an eight-line group is an **octave.**

Although the couplet is the basic unit for so much poetry, occasionally the writer will also use a unit of three lines, which is called a **tercet.** Tennyson, who was ingenious in his use of rhyme, included a tercet in each stanza of his long ballad poem *The Lady of Shalott.*

> A red-cross knight forever kneeled
> To a lady in his shield,
> That sparkled on the yellow field.

With these basic terms to help us, we can begin to look at some types of poetry. Whether they are written in traditional—closed—forms or in free— open—forms, poems can generally be sorted into three main types: narrative, lyric, and dramatic.

NARRATIVE POETRY

Narrative poetry is simply poetry that tells a story, such as the poem that begins " 'Twas the night before Christmas, and all through the house . . ." The oldest form of narrative poetry is the **epic,** which is probably best known today for the two epic poems, the *Iliad* and the *Odyssey,* composed by the poet Homer. The large scale of these narratives and their sweeping depiction of the lives and events of another time have given us the adjective *epic.*

The Ballad

Ballads, which are also narrative poems, are part of the folk tradition of every culture. Even though we know them as printed compositions, traditional ballads come from an earlier period, when they were part of an oral tradition. They tell of a death in a family, of women who were taken by spirits, of bloody quarrels where families are broken or reunited. Most ballads were probably composed by a single individual, but when they come down to us they are usually anonymous. The name of the original writer has been lost as the ballads were passed on from singer to singer. Ballads were meant to be sung, and they are composed in simple quatrains with meters that are easily followed, sometimes with a repeated line that ends every verse, which is called a **refrain.**

In the well-known folk ballad "Barbara Allan," the stanza form uses alternating lines of four and three stressed beats. As is usual in poems that are meant to be sung, there is considerable looseness in the scansion of the beats. Another characteristic of ballads like these is that rhyme is used only for the second and fourth lines of the stanza.

Barbara Allan   date unknown

It was in and about the Martinmas° time,   *November 11*
    When the green leaves were a-fallin',
That Sir John Graeme in the West Country
    Fell in love with Barbara Allan.

He sent his man down through the town   5
    To the place where she was dwellin':
"O haste and come to my master dear,
    Gin° ye be Barbara Allan."   *if*

O slowly, slowly rase° she up,   *rose*
    To the place where he was lyin',   10
And when she drew the curtain by:
    "Young man, I think you're dyin'."

"O it's I'm sick, and very, very sick,
    And 'tis a' for Barbara Allan."
"O the better for me ye sal° never be   *shall* 15
    Though your heart's blood were a-spillin'.

"O dinna ye mind, young man," said she,
    "When ye the cups were fillin',
That ye made the healths gae round and round,
    And slighted Barbara Allan?"   20

He turned his face unto the wall,
　　And death with him was dealin':
"Adieu, adieu, my dear friends all,
　　And be kind to Barbara Allan."

And slowly, slowly, rase she up,　　　　　　　　　　　　　25
　　And slowly, slowly left him;
And sighing said she could not stay,
　　Since death of life had reft him.

She had not gane a mile but twa,
　　When she heard the dead-bell knellin',　　　　　　　30
And every jow° that the dead-bell ga'ed　　　　　*stroke*
　　It cried, "Woe to Barbara Allan."

"O mother, mother, make my bed,
　　O make it soft and narrow:
Since my love died for me today,　　　　　　　　　　　35
　　I'll die for him tomorrow."

When we read a folk ballad it is easy to forget that the words are a transcription of what someone was singing. Although the ballads of the African American culture have not often made their way into literary anthologies, they are a vital expression that tells us much about the social background that created them. The song "Gray Goose," which is sung by black work gangs in Texas prisons, is a ballad with a sly double meaning. The "gray goose" is understood by the singers to be a veiled reference to the black American who is too tough to be destroyed, despite the tragedies of slavery and segregation.

Gray Goose　　　　　　　　　　　　　　　　　date unknown

Well, my papa went a-hunting,
　　　　Well, well, well . . .
You know he took along his shotgun,
　　　　Well, well, well . . .
You know he rared the hammer 'way back,　　　　　　5
　　　　Well, well, well . . .
You know he shot at the gray goose,
　　　　Well, well, well . . .
Well down came the gray goose,
　　　　Well, well, well . . .　　　　　　　　　　　　10
After six weeks a falling,
　　　　Well, well, well . . .
Well we gave a feather picking,
　　　　Well, well, well . . .
Was a six weeks a pickin' him,　　　　　　　　　　　15
　　　　Well, well, well . . .

Well we put him on to parboil,
   Well, well, well . . .
Well we put him in the oven,
   Well, well, well . . .   20
Was a six weeks a bakin' him,
   Well, well, well . . .
Well we put him on the table,
   Well, well, well . . .
Well the knife couldn't cut him,
   Well, well, well . . .   25
Well the last time I seen him,
   Well, well, well . . .
He was flyin' across the ocean,
   Well, well, well . . .   30

The song is started by a leader, who sings the opening phrase; then the work gang answers with the refrain, "Well, well, well . . ." This version was sung by two convicts, Louis Houston and D. J. Miller, with other prisoners at Ramsey State Prison. It was recorded in 1964 by folklorist Bruce Jackson. As they performed it, each line was repeated, but it is more interesting to read it with each line sung only once. Like most songs from the folk tradition, the rhythm is counted in accents. Here there are two strong accents in each line of the verse, and the other words and syllables are given less emphasis. The strong accents in the opening lines, as the singer performs them, are "well my PA-pa went a-HUNT-ing" and "you know he TOOK along his SHOT-gun."

Ballads for Further Reading

The Three Ravens   date unknown

There were three ravens sat on a tree,
 Down a down, hay down, hay down,
There were three ravens sat on a tree,
 With a down,
There were three ravens sat on a tree,   5
They were as black as they might be,
 With a down, derry, derry, derry, down, down.

The one of them said to his mate,
"Where shall we our breakfast take?"

"Down in yonder green field   10
There lies a knight slain under his shield.

"His hounds they lie down at his feet,
So well they can their master keep.

"His hawks they fly so eagerly,
There's no fowl dare him come nigh."   15

Down there comes a fallow doe,
As great with young as she might go.

She lifted up his bloody head,
And kissed his wounds that were so red.

She got him up upon her back,   20
And carried him to earthen lake.°   *pit*

She buried him before the prime;°   *sunrise*
She was dead herself ere evensong time.

God send every gentleman
Such hawks, such hounds, and such a lemman.°   *lover* 25

Lord Randall   date unknown

"Oh where ha'e ye been, Lord Randall my son?
O where ha'e ye been, my handsome young man?"
　　"I ha'e been to the wild wood: mother, make my bed soon,
　　For I'm weary wi' hunting, and fain wald° lie down."   *would gladly*

"Where gat ye your dinner, Lord Randall my son?   5
Where gat ye your dinner, my handsome young man?"
　　"I dined wi' my true love: mother, make my bed soon,
　　For I'm weary wi' hunting, and fain wald lie down."

"What gat ye to your dinner, Lord Randall my son?
What gat ye to your dinner, my handsome young man?"   10
　　"I gat eels boiled in broo:° mother, make my bed soon,   *broth*
　　For I'm weary wi' hunting, and fain wald lie down."

"What became of your bloodhounds, Lord Randall my son?
What became of your bloodhounds, my handsome young man?"
　　"O they swelled and they died: mother, make my bed soon,   15
　　For I'm weary wi' hunting, and fain wald lie down."

"O I fear ye are poisoned, Lord Randall my son!
O I fear ye are poisoned, my handsome young man!"
　　"Oh yes, I am poisoned: mother, make my bed soon,
　　For I'm sick at the heart, and I fain wald lie down."   20

STERLING A. BROWN

Frankie and Johnny   1932

Oh Frankie and Johnny were lovers
Oh Lordy how they did love!
　　　　　　　　　—Old Ballad

Frankie was a halfwit, Johnny was a nigger,
　　Frankie liked to pain poor creatures as a little 'un,

Kept a crazy love of torment when she got bigger,
    Johnny had to slave it and never had much fun.

Frankie liked to pull wings off of living butterflies,   5
    Frankie liked to cut long angleworms in half,
Frankie liked to whip curs and listen to their drawn out cries,
    Frankie liked to shy stones at the brindle calf.

Frankie took her pappy's lunch week-days to the sawmill,
    Her pappy, red-faced cracker, with a cracker's thirst,   10
Beat her skinny body and reviled the hateful imbecile,
    She screamed at every blow he struck, but tittered when he curst.

Frankie had to cut through Johnny's field of sugar corn
    Used to wave at Johnny, who didn't *'pay no min'*—
Had had to work like fifty from the day that he was born,   15
    And wan't no cracker hussy gonna put his work behind—.

But everyday Frankie swung along the cornfield lane,
    And one day Johnny helped her partly through the wood,
Once he had dropped his plow lines, he dropped them many times
    again—
    Though his mother didn't know it, else she'd have whipped him good.   20

Frankie and Johnny were lovers; oh Lordy how they did love!
    But one day Frankie's pappy by a big log laid him low,
To find out what his crazy Frankie had been speaking of;
    He found that what his gal had muttered was exactly so.

Frankie, she was spindly limbed with corn silk on her crazy head,   25
    Johnny was a nigger, who never had much fun—
They swung up Johnny on a tree, and filled his swinging hide with lead,
    And Frankie yowled hilariously when the thing was done.

ROBERT DUNCAN

The Ballad of Mrs Noah   1957

    Mrs Noah in the Ark
      wove a great nightgown out of the dark,
      did Mrs Noah,
had her own hearth in the Holy Boat,
two cats, two books, two cooking pots,   5
had Mrs Noah,
two pints of porter, two pecks of peas,
and a stir in her stew of memories.

Oh, that was a town, said Mrs Noah,
that the Lord in His wrath   10
did up and drown!

I liked its windows and I liked its trees.
Save me a little, Lord, I prayd on my knees.
And now, Lord save me, I've two of each!
apple, apricot, cherry and peach.   15

How shall I manage it? I've two of them all—
hairy, scaly, leathery, slick,
fluttery, buttery, thin and thick,
shaped like a stick, shaped like a ball,
too tiny to see, and much too tall.   20

I've all that I askd for and more and more,
windows and chimneys, and a great store
of needles and pins, of outs and ins,
and a regular forgive-us for some of my sins.

> She wove a great nightgown out of the dark   25
> decorated like a Sunday Park
> with clouds of black thread to remember her grief
> sewn about with bright flowers to give relief,

and, in a grim humor, a border all round
with the little white bones of the wicked drownd.   30

> Tell me, Brother, what do you see?
> said Mrs Noah to the Lowly Worm.

O Mother, the Earth is black, black.
To my crawlly bride and lowly me
the Earth is bitter as can be   35
where the Dead lie down and never come back,
said the blind Worm.

Tell me, Brother, what do *you* see?
Said Mrs Noah to the sleeping Cat.

O Mother, the weather is dreadful wet.   40
I'll keep house for you wherever you'll be.
I'll sit by the fireside and be your pet.
And as long as I'm dry I'll purr for free,
said snug-loving Cat.

Tell me, Brother, has the Flood gone?   45
said Mrs Noah to the searching Crow.

No. No. No home in sight.
I fly thru the frightful waste alone,
said the carrion Crow.
The World is an everlasting Night.   50

Now that can't be true, Noah, Old Noah,
said the good Housewife to her good Spouse.
How long must we go in this floating House?
growing old and hope cold,
Husband, without new land?   55

And then Glory-Be with a Rainbow to-boot!
the Dove returnd with an Olive Shoot.

Tell me, Brother, what have we here,
my Love? to the Dove said Mrs Noah.

It's a Branch of All-Cheer   60
you may wear on your nightgown all the long year
as a boa, Mrs Noah, said the Dove,
with God's love!

> Then out from the Ark
> in her nightgown all dark   65
> with only her smile to betoken the Day
> and a wreath-round of olive leaves

Mrs Noah stepped down
into the same old wicked repenting
Lord-Will-We-Ever recently recoverd   70
comfortable World-Town.

O where have you been, Mother Noah, Mother Noah?

I've had a great Promise for only Tomorrow.
In the Ark of Sleep I've been on a sail
over the wastes of the world's sorrow.   75

And the Promise? the Tomorrow? Mother Noah, Mother Noah?

Ah! the Rainbow's awake
and we will not fail!

LYRIC POETRY

Just as my fingers on these keys
Make music, so the selfsame sounds
On my spirit make a music, too. . . .
  – WALLACE STEVENS, from "Peter Quince at the Clavier"

The word *lyric* comes from *lyre,* the small harp that the Greek poets
played to accompany their songs, and for many centuries **lyric poetry** was
written in the stanza forms and the rhyme schemes of a song. Now a lyric poem
is defined as a short poem that expresses the emotions and thoughts of the poet.
Often lyric poems are written in the first person, though the "I" of the poem
may be a **persona,** which is another person through whom the poet is speaking. The term *lyrics* is still used today, but its meaning is more specifically the
text of a song. Lyric poetry is highly subjective, deeply personal, and usually
intensely emotional.

In the nineteenth century, when the lyric poem was first taking on its
present form, the poem generally had a subject that drew an emotional response from the writer. The lines were intended to create in the reader the same
emotions that the writer felt, as in Edgar Allan Poe's classic lines about the

imagined beauty of Helen of Troy. In the modern period it is enough for a poet to look into her own soul for the storms and joys of poetry, as in H.D.'s response to the light and the winds of a late summer day.

EDGAR ALLAN POE

To Helen   1831

Helen, thy beauty is to me
  Like those Nicean° barks of yore,
That gently, o'er a perfumed sea
  The weary, way-worn wanderer bore
    To his own native shore.   5

On desperate seas long wont to roam,
  Thy hyacinth° hair, thy classic face
Thy Naiad° airs have brought me home
  To the glory that was Greece
And the grandeur that was Rome.   10

Lo! in yon brilliant window-niche
  How statue-like I see thee stand!
  The agate lamp within thy hand,
Ah! Psyche,° from the regions which
  Are Holy Land!   15

H.D.

Mid-day   1916

The light beats upon me.
I am startled—
a split leaf crackles on the paved floor—
I am anguished—defeated.

A slight wind shakes the seed-pods—   5
my thoughts are spent
as the black seeds.

---

2. **Nicean:** Of Nicaea, an ancient city of the Byzantine Empire near the modern village of Iznik in Turkey; or possibly of Nice (in southern France).   7. **hyacinth:** The red of the flower in Greek mythology.   8. **Naiad:** A water nymph in classical mythology.   14. **Psyche:** In Greek mythology, a princess loved by Cupid; also, the soul or self.

My thoughts tear me,
I dread their fever.
I am scattered in its whirl.
I am scattered like   10
the hot shrivelled seeds.

The shrivelled seeds
are split on the path —
the grass bends with dust,   15
the grape slips
under its crackled leaf:
Yet far beyond the spent seed-pods,
and the blackened stalks of mint,
the poplar is bright on the hill,   20
the poplar spreads out,
deep-rooted among trees.

O poplar, you are great
among the hill-stones,
while I perish on the path   25
among the crevices of the rocks.

The subjectivity that is one of the characteristics of a lyric poem is much more strongly expressed if the poem is written in a style that is closer to the writer's own way of speaking. As we have already discussed in our study of rhyme and meter, certain elements of style and language are won or lost with any changes in the way poets use the means to create their poem. What the lyric poem by H.D. has lost is the musical experience of meter and rhyme. What has been gained is a directness and immediacy of expression.

The Ode

Among the oldest forms of lyric poetry is the **ode.** As a poem of praise, it is found in nearly every language and culture. For European poets, the style had a classical model, the odes written by the Greek poet Pindar to honor the victorious athletes of the Olympic Games of fifth-century Athens. His poems are often called the "Great Odes" to separate them from the imitations that followed. Pindar intended them to be performed in public ceremonies by choruses that sang or chanted the lines.

An ode is a long, serious lyric poem, addressed to a person or to an object, that presents philosophic ideas and moral concerns. Often odes were addressed to inanimate concepts, as in Percy Bysshe Shelley's "Ode to the West Wind" or objects, as in John Keats's "Ode on a Grecian Urn." In Keats's ode he looks at a half-imagined Greek vase covered with painted scenes and decorations. When he asks, in the first stanza, "What men or gods are these? What maidens loth?," he is asking about the figures painted on the sides of the urn. In the turmoil and riot of the life that he sees there, he imagines an eternal reality.

JOHN KEATS

Ode on a Grecian Urn 1820

Thou still unravished bride of quietness,
  Thou foster-child of silence and slow time,
Sylvan historian, who canst thus express
  A flowery tale more sweetly than our rhyme:
What leaf-fringed legend haunts about thy shape 5
  Of deities or mortals, or of both,
    In Tempe or the dales of Arcady?°
  What men or gods are these? What maidens loth?
What mad pursuit? What struggle to escape?
    What pipes and timbrels? What wild ecstasy? 10

Heard melodies are sweet, but those unheard
  Are sweeter; therefore, ye soft pipes, play on;
Not to the sensual° ear, but, more endeared,   *physical*
  Pipe to the spirit ditties of no tone:
Fair youth, beneath the trees, thou canst not leave 15
  Thy song, nor ever can those trees be bare;
    Bold Lover, never, never canst thou kiss,
Though winning near the goal — yet, do not grieve;
    She cannot fade, though thou hast not thy bliss,
  For ever wilt thou love, and she be fair! 20

Ah, happy, happy boughs! that cannot shed
  Your leaves, nor ever bid the Spring adieu;
And, happy melodist, unwearièd,
  For ever piping songs for ever new;
More happy love! more happy, happy love! 25
  For ever warm and still to be enjoyed,
    For ever panting, and for ever young;
All breathing human passion far above,
  That leaves a heart high-sorrowful and cloyed,
    A burning forehead, and a parching tongue. 30

Who are these coming to the sacrifice?
  To what green altar, O mysterious priest,
Lead'st thou that heifer lowing at the skies,
  And all her silken flanks with garlands drest?
What little town by river or sea shore, 35
  Or mountain-built with peaceful citadel,
    Is emptied of this folk, this pious morn?

---

7. Tempe . . . Arcady: Rural places in Greece.

And, little town, thy streets for evermore
   Will silent be; and not a soul to tell
     Why thou art desolate, can e'er return.   40

O Attic° shape! Fair attitude! with brede°   *Greek; design*
   Of marble men and maidens overwrought,
With forest branches and the trodden weed;
   Thou, silent form, dost tease us out of thought
As doth Eternity: Cold Pastoral!   45
   When old age shall this generation waste,
     Thou shalt remain, in midst of other woe
Than ours, a friend to man, to whom thou say'st,
Beauty is truth, truth beauty, — that is all
   Ye know on earth, and all ye need to know.   50

"Ode to the West Wind" has none of the philosophic calm of Keats's ode. Shelley's poem is a tumultuous reflection of the personal difficulties that had almost overwhelmed him. The autumn wind is an appropriate image for his emotions, driving before it the falling leaves that mark the approach of winter. Although it is a turbulent poem with many currents of feeling, it is written with great care and subtlety. Shelley allows himself more freedom with the meter than is usual in a formal poem, but each line has five stressed beats.

The complexity lies in the rhyme scheme. The poem is written in **terza rima.** The form is a tercet in iambic pentameter, with a sequence of rhymes that crosses from one stanza to the next, binding them together. The rhyme scheme is *aba, bcb, cdc,* continuing with the same pattern. The middle line becomes the rhyme for the outer lines of the next tercet.

Terza rima is especially effective for narrative poems and for poems, like this one, with a restless, unsettled mood. To strengthen the poem's overall structure, Shelley constructs the tercets in groups of four with an added couplet that rhymes with the middle line of the fourth tercet. This is the rhyme scheme for each stanza: *aba, bcb, cdc, ded, ee.*

PERCY BYSSHE SHELLEY

Ode to the West Wind   1819

I

O wild West Wind, thou breath of Autumn's being,
Thou, from whose unseen presence the leaves dead
Are driven, like ghosts from an enchanter fleeing,

Yellow, and black, and pale, and hectic red,
Pestilence-stricken multitudes: O Thou,   5
Who chariotest to their dark wintry bed

The winged seeds, where they lie cold and low,
Each like a corpse within its grave, until
Thine azure sister of the Spring shall blow

Her clarion° o'er the dreaming earth, and fill   *trumpet call* 10
(Driving sweet buds like flocks to feed in air)
With living hues and odours plain and hill:

Wild Spirit, which art moving everywhere;
Destroyer and Preserver; hear, O hear!

II
Thou on whose stream, 'mid the steep sky's commotion,   15
Loose clouds like Earth's decaying leaves are shed,
Shook from the tangled boughs of Heaven and Ocean,

Angels of rain and lightning: there are spread
On the blue surface of thine aery surge,
Like the bright hair uplifted from the head   20

Of some fierce Mænad,° even from the dim verge
Of the horizon to the zenith's height,
The locks of the approaching storm. Thou Dirge

Of the dying year, to which this closing night
Will be the dome of a vast sepulchre,   25
Vaulted with all thy congregated might

Of vapours, from whose solid atmosphere
Black rain and fire and hail will burst: O hear!

III
Thou who didst waken from his summer dreams
The blue Mediterranean, where he lay,   30
Lulled by the coil of his chrystalline streams,

Beside a pumice isle in Baiæ's bay,°
And saw in sleep old palaces and towers
Quivering within the wave's intenser day,

All overgrown with azure moss and flowers   35
So sweet, the sense faints picturing them! Thou
For whose path the Atlantic's level powers

Cleave themselves into chasms, while far below
The sea-blooms and the oozy woods which wear
The sapless foliage of the ocean, know   40

Thy voice, and suddenly grow grey with fear,
And tremble and despoil themselves: O hear!

---

21. Mænad: Female worshiper of Bacchus, the Greek god of wine and revelry. **32. Baiæ's bay:** A bay near Naples, Italy.

IV

If I were a dead leaf thou mightest bear;
If I were a swift cloud to fly with thee;
A wave to pant beneath thy power, and share   45

The impulse of thy strength, only less free
Than thou, O Uncontrollable! If even
I were as in my boyhood, and could be

The comrade of thy wanderings over Heaven,
As then, when to outstrip thy skiey speed   50
Scarce seemed a vision; I would ne'er have striven

As thus with thee in prayer in my sore need.
Oh! lift me as a wave, a leaf, a cloud!
I fall upon the thorns of life! I bleed!

A heavy weight of hours has chained and bowed   55
One too like thee: tameless, and swift, and proud.

V

Make me thy lyre, even as the forest is:
What if my leaves are falling like its own!
The tumult of thy mighty harmonies

Will take from both a deep, autumnal tone,   60
Sweet though in sadness. Be thou, Spirit fierce,
My spirit! Be thou me, impetuous one!

Drive my dead thoughts over the universe
Like withered leaves to quicken a new birth!
And, by the incantation of this verse,   65

Scatter, as from an unextinguished hearth
Ashes and sparks, my words among mankind!
Be through my lips to unawakened Earth

The trumpet of a prophecy! O Wind,
If Winter comes, can Spring be far behind?   70

The Elegy

An **elegy**, like an ode, is a serious poem. In its usual form it is a long lyric
poem written to lament someone's death and memorialize their life. The most
widely read elegy in traditional English poetry is Thomas Gray's "Elegy Written in a Country Churchyard," published in 1751.

THOMAS GRAY

Elegy Written in a Country Churchyard   1751

The curfew tolls the knell of parting day,
   The lowing herd wind slowly o'er the lea,°   *pasture*
The plowman homeward plods his weary way,
   And leaves the world to darkness and to me.

Now fades the glimmering landscape on the sight,   5
   And all the air a solemn stillness holds,
Save where the beetle wheels his droning flight,
   And drowsy tinklings lull the distant folds;

Save that from yonder ivy-mantled tower
   The moping owl does to the moon complain   10
Of such, as wand'ring near her secret bower,
   Molest her ancient solitary reign.

Beneath those rugged elms, that yew tree's shade,
   Where heaves the turf in many a mold'ring heap,
Each in his narrow cell forever laid,   15
   The rude forefathers of the hamlet sleep.

The breezy call of incense-breathing morn,
   The swallow twitt'ring from the straw-built shed,
The cock's shrill clarion, or the echoing horn,°   *hunting horn*
   No more shall rouse them from their lowly bed.   20

For them no more the blazing hearth shall burn,
   Or busy housewife ply her evening care;
No children run to lisp their sire's return,
   Or climb his knees the envied kiss to share.

Oft did the harvest to their sickle yield,   25
   Their furrow oft the stubborn glebe° has broke;   *turf*
How jocund did they drive their team afield!
   How bowed the woods beneath their sturdy stroke!

Let not Ambition mock their useful toil,
   Their homely joys, and destiny obscure;   30
Nor Grandeur hear with a disdainful smile
   The short and simple annals of the poor.

The boast of heraldry, the pomp of pow'r,
   And all that beauty, all that wealth e'er gave,
Awaits alike th' inevitable hour.   35
   The paths of glory lead but to the grave.

Nor you, ye proud, impute to these the fault,
   If Mem'ry o'er their tomb no trophies raise,
Where through the long-drawn aisle and fretted vault
   The pealing anthem swells the note of praise.   40

Can storied urn or animated bust
    Back to its mansion call the fleeting breath?
Can Honor's voice provoke the silent dust,
    Or Flatt'ry soothe the dull cold ear of Death?

Perhaps in this neglected spot is laid   45
    Some heart once pregnant with celestial fire;
Hands that the rod of empire might have swayed,
    Or waked to ecstasy the living lyre.

But knowledge to their eyes her ample page
    Rich with the spoils of time did ne'er unroll;   50
Chill Penury repressed their noble rage,
    And froze the genial current of the soul.

Full many a gem of purest ray serene,
    The dark unfathomed caves of ocean bear:
Full many a flower is born to blush unseen,   55
    And waste its sweetness on the desert air.

Some village Hampden,° that with dauntless breast
    The little tyrant of his field withstood;
Some mute inglorious Milton° here may rest,
    Some Cromwell,° guiltless of his country's blood.   60

Th' applause of list'ning senates to command,
    The threats of pain and ruin to despise,
To scatter plenty o'er a smiling land,
    And read their hist'ry in a nation's eyes,

Their lot forbade; nor circumscribed alone   65
    Their growing virtues, but their crimes confined;
Forbade to wade through slaughter to a throne,
    And shut the gates of mercy on mankind,

The struggling pangs of conscious truth to hide,
    To quench the blushes of ingenuous shame,   70
Or heap the shrine of Luxury and Pride
    With incense kindled at the Muse's flame.°

Far from the madding crowd's ignoble strife,
    Their sober wishes never learned to stray;
Along the cool sequestered vale of life   75
    They kept the noiseless tenor° of their way.   *continual movement*

---

57. Hampden: John Hampden (1594–1643) was a member of Parliament who resisted
the illegal taxes on his lands that were imposed by Charles I.   **59. Milton:** John Milton
(1608–1674), the English poet.   **60. Cromwell:** Oliver Cromwell (1599–1658) served
as Lord Protector of England from 1653 until his death.   **71–72. heap the shrine . . .
Muse's flame:** Gray is criticizing poets who write to please wealthy patrons.

Yet ev'n these bones from insult to protect
    Some frail memorial still erected nigh,
With uncouth rhymes and shapeless sculpture decked,
    Implores the passing tribute of a sigh.   80

Their name, their years, spelt by th' unlettered Muse,
    The place of fame and elegy supply:
And many a holy text around she strews,
    That teach the rustic moralist to die.   85

For who to dumb Forgetfulness a prey,
    This pleasing anxious being e'er resigned,
Left the warm precincts of the cheerful day,
    Nor cast one longing ling'ring look behind?

On some fond breast the parting soul relies,
    Some pious drops the closing eye requires;   90
Ev'n from the tomb the voice of Nature cries,
    Ev'n in our ashes live their wonted fires.

For thee, who mindful of th' unhonored dead
    Dost in these lines their artless tale relate;
If chance, by lonely contemplation led,   95
    Some kindred spirit shall inquire thy fate,

Haply° some hoary-headed swain° may say,   *perchance; shepherd*
    "Oft have we seen him at the peep of dawn
Brushing with hasty steps the dews away
    To meet the sun upon the upland lawn.   100

"There at the foot of yonder nodding beech
    That wreathes its old fantastic roots so high,
His listless length at noontide would he stretch,
    And pore upon the brook that babbles by.

"Hard by yon wood, now smiling as in scorn,   105
    Mutt'ring his wayward fancies he would rove,
Now drooping, woeful wan, like one forlorn,
    Or crazed with care, or crossed in hopeless love.

"One morn I missed him, on the customed hill,
    Along the heath and near his fav'rite tree;   110
Another came; nor yet beside the rill,
    Nor up the lawn, nor at the wood was he;

"The next with dirges due in sad array
    Slow through the churchway path we saw him borne.
Approach and read (for thou canst read) the lay,°   *song or poem* 115
    Graved on the stone beneath yon aged thorn."

THE EPITAPH

Here rests his head upon the lap of Earth
    A youth to Fortune and to Fame unknown.

Fair Science frowned not on his humble birth,
  And Melancholy marked him for her own.   120

Large was his bounty, and his soul sincere,
  Heav'n did a recompense as largely send:
He gave to Mis'ry all he had, a tear,
  He gained from Heav'n ('twas all he wished) a friend.

No farther seek his merits to disclose,
  Or draw his frailties from their dread abode,   125
(There they alike in trembling hope repose),
  The bosom of His Father and his God.

The poem can seem placid and uneventful to modern readers, but at the time it was written it made a strong and disturbing political statement. The poem was unlike other elegies that had been written before it because the individual for whom the elegy was written was an ordinary person. He was simply someone who had been buried in this village's churchyard. As Gray wrote in the epitaph that ends the poem,

> Here rests his head upon the lap of Earth
> A youth to Fortune and to Fame unknown.

The person buried in the churchyard is never named. What Gray is insisting is that under other circumstances this ordinary person could have been the equal of any other person in their society. In the years leading up to the revolutions in the American colonies and in France—revolutions that overthrew the rigid class lines of the old social order—these were fiery sentiments. Another stanza from the poem, the twelfth, burned itself into the consciousness of its time, with its bold idea that in the grave might lie someone who could have ruled a nation or could have written immortal poetry. The phrases were echoed again and again by poets, politicians, and writers everywhere:

> Perhaps in this neglected spot is laid
>   Some heart once pregnant with celestial fire;
> Hands that the rod of empire might have swayed,
>   Or waked to ecstasy the living lyre.

The final line of the ninth stanza of his poem has been quoted in more speeches, books, and plays than Gray could ever have imagined: "The paths of glory lead but to the grave."

The Sonnet

Although a **sonnet** is short—generally fourteen lines—and is written in a regular rhyme sequence, it is one of the richest and most durable forms of lyric poetry. The difference between a sonnet and other lyric poetry is in the way the poet works with its theme. At the heart of most traditional sonnets is an implied argument that muses on the philosophic implications of the sonnet's main idea. The form has been so useful to poets for so many centuries that authors today continue to write sonnets, even if they don't feel they have to restrict themselves to traditional rhyme schemes and meter. What they want to tell the reader, when they use the term *sonnet* or write in a variant of the sonnet form, is that the poem will have a seriousness that may not be characteristic of their other short lyrics.

The sonnet was perfected in Italy in the early fourteenth century. The name comes from the Italian word *sonnetto,* which means "little song." Several poets helped develop the form, but the one whose work was most influential with English poets was Francesco Petrarca, an Italian nobleman known in English as Petrarch, who lived from 1304 to 1374. His sonnets were personal poems, written to express his unhappiness over his love for a woman who did not return his affection. In structure, the individual sonnets presented a kind of short philosophical discussion, with a presentation of the theme of the poem in the opening lines, a consideration of the theme in the next lines, then a conclusion summed up in a final couplet.

The sonnet was brought to England by a courtier and diplomat named Sir Thomas Wyatt, who was sent by Henry VIII on diplomatic missions to France and Italy. Wyatt encountered the writing of Petrarch on his travels, and before his death in 1542 he translated more than a hundred Italian sonnets. The translations were circulated in manuscript through court circles, and a younger poet, also a courtier and nobleman named Henry Howard, Earl of Surrey, who often caroused through the streets of London with Wyatt's son, translated many of the same sonnets. It was Surrey who established the rhyme scheme used by William Shakespeare.

A great playwright, Shakespeare was also an accomplished sonneteer, and one of his enduring works is a collection of 154 sonnets published in 1609. This famous example, untitled but numbered 73, takes as its theme the poet's old age. In the development of its theme and the rich use of imagery and rhyme, the poem shows all the characteristics of the classic sonnet form.

WILLIAM SHAKESPEARE

That time of year thou mayst in me behold   1609

That time of year thou mayst in me behold
When yellow leaves, or none, or few, do hang
Upon those boughs which shake against the cold,
Bare ruined choirs, where late the sweet birds sang.
In me thou seest the twilight of such day   5
As after sunset fadeth in the west;
Which by and by black night doth take away,
Death's second self that seals up all in rest.

In me thou seest the glowing of such fire,
That on the ashes of his youth doth lie,   10
As the deathbed whereon it must expire,
Consumed with that which it was nourished by.
  This thou perceiv'st, which makes thy love more strong,
    To love that well, which thou must leave ere long.

If we look at the meter of the poem we can see that it is in iambic pentameter. The five-foot line, which is also the line of dramatic blank verse, has a feeling of weight and substance that the more common four-foot line of other short lyric poems does not. The fourteen lines consist of three quatrains with the rhyme scheme of *abab, cdcd, efef*, and a concluding couplet, *gg*. This way of structuring the rhyme is called the *English*, or Shakespearean, sonnet. The rhyme scheme for the *Italian*, or Petrarchan sonnet, is an octave of two quatrains that rhyme *abba*, followed by a sextet with a rhyme scheme that may have some variation but is usually either *cdecde* or *cdcdcd*.

Shakespeare was so skillful that he was able to work the sonnet form into the dialogue of one of his plays. In scene 5 of the first act of *Romeo and Juliet*, the lines of dialogue between the two lovers are written as a sonnet.

ROMEO: If I profane with my unworthiest hand
         This holy shrine, the gentle fine is this,
         My lips, two blushing pilgrims, ready stand
         To smooth that rough touch with a tender kiss.
JULIET: Good pilgrim, you do wrong your hand too much,
         Which mannerly devotion shows in this;
         For saints have hands that pilgrims' hands do touch,
         And palm to palm is holy palmers' kiss.
ROMEO: Have not saints lips, and holy palmers too?
JULIET: Aye, pilgrim, lips that they must use in prayer.
ROMEO: Oh then, dear saint, let lips do what hands do.
         Then pray. Grant thou, lest faith turn to despair.
JULIET: Saints do not move, though grant for prayers' sake.
ROMEO: Then move not while my prayer's effect I take.

Several of Shakespeare's sonnets are gathered in Chapter 15, "Poems and Poets."

Sonnets for Further Reading

Because of the variety of subjects and themes in the sonnet, the best way to experience these poems is to read as many of them as you can. Try to follow their rhyme schemes and the way each sonnet develops its theme. This gathering of sonnets will introduce you to some of the important writers from Petrarca's time to our own. Contemporary poets use the form more freely, but the same concentration of ideas and imagery is still what makes the sonnet unique.

FRANCESCO PETRARCA

Love's Inconsistency

1557

TRANSLATED BY SIR THOMAS WYATT

I find no peace, and all my war is done;
  I fear and hope, I burn and freeze likewise;
  I fly above the wind, yet cannot rise;
  And nought I have, yet all the world I seize on;
That looseth, nor locketh, holdeth me in prison,   5
  And holds me not, yet can I 'scape no wise;
  Nor lets me live, nor die, at my devise,
  And yet of death it giveth none occasion.
Without eyes I see, and without tongue I plain;
  I wish to perish, yet I ask for health;   10
  I love another, and yet I hate myself;
I feed in sorrow, and laugh in all my pain;
  Lo, thus displeaseth me both death and life,
  And my delight is causer of my grief.

JOHN DONNE

Death, be not proud

1633

Death, be not proud, though some have calléd thee
Mighty and dreadful, for thou art not so;
For those whom thou think'st thou dost overthrow
Die not, poor Death, nor yet canst thou kill me.
From rest and sleep, which but thy pictures be,   5
Much pleasure; then from thee much more must flow,
And soonest our best men with thee do go,
Rest of their bones, and soul's delivery.
Thou art slave to fate, chance, kings, and desperate men,
And dost with poison, war, and sickness dwell,   10
And poppy° or charms can make us sleep as well   *opium*
And better than thy stroke; why swell'st thou then?
One short sleep past, we wake eternally
And death shall be no more; Death, thou shalt die.

PERCY BYSSHE SHELLEY

Ozymandias°   1818

I met a traveler from an antique land
Who said: Two vast and trunkless legs of stone
Stand in the desert . . . Near them, on the sand,
Half sunk, a shattered visage lies, whose frown,
And wrinkled lip, and sneer of cold command,   5
Tell that its sculptor well those passions read
Which yet survive, stamped on these lifeless things,
The hand that mocked them, and the heart that fed:
And on the pedestal these words appear:
"My name is Ozymandias, king of kings: 10
Look on my works, ye Mighty, and despair!"
Nothing beside remains. Round the decay
Of that colossal wreck, boundless and bare
The lone and level sands stretch far away.

ELIZABETH BARRETT BROWNING

How Do I Love Thee?   1850

How do I love thee? Let me count the ways.
I love thee to the depth and breadth and height
My soul can reach, when feeling out of sight
For the ends of Being and ideal Grace.
I love thee to the level of every day's   5
Most quiet need, by sun and candlelight.
I love thee freely, as men strive for Right;
I love thee purely, as they turn from Praise;
I love thee with the passion put to use
In my old griefs, and with my childhood's faith.   10
I love thee with a love I seemed to lose
With my lost saints—I love thee with the breath,
Smiles, tears of all my life!—and, if God choose,
I shall but love thee better after death.

Ozymandias: Greek name for the thirteenth-century B.C. Egyptian pharaoh Ramses II.

COUNTEE CULLEN

Yet Do I Marvel   1925

I doubt not God is good, well-meaning, kind,
And did He stoop to quibble could tell why
The little buried mole continues blind,
Why flesh that mirrors Him must some day die,
Make plain the reason tortured Tantalus°   5
Is baited by the fickle fruit, declare
If merely brute caprice dooms Sisyphus°
To struggle up a never-ending stair.
Inscrutable His ways are, and immune
To catechism by a mind too strewn   10
With petty cares to slightly understand
What awful brain compels His awful hand.
Yet do I marvel at this curious thing:
To make a poet black, and bid him sing!

RITA DOVE

Sonnet in Primary Colors   1995

This is for the woman with one black wing
perched over her eyes: lovely Frida,° erect
among parrots, in the stern petticoats of the peasant,
who painted herself a present—
wildflowers entwining the plaster corset   5
her spine resides in, that flaming pillar—
this priestess in the romance of mirrors.

Each night she lay down in pain and rose
to the celluloid butterflies of her Beloved Dead,
Lenin and Marx and Stalin arrayed at the footstead.   10
And rose to her easel, the hundred dogs panting
like children along the graveled walls of the garden, Diego's°

---

5. Tantalus: In Hades, the Greek underworld, Tantalus was prevented from assuaging his hunger as he reached for fruit just beyond his grasp.   **7. Sisyphus:** In Greek myth, Sisyphus was condemned to roll a huge stone uphill that always rolled back down just before he reached the top.
2. Frida: Refers to Frida Kahlo (1907–1954), Mexican surrealist artist famous for her self-portraits revealing her tumultuous life—which included her marriage to muralist Diego Rivera.   **12. Diego's:** Refers to Diego Rivera (1886–1957), Mexican artist whose bold, leftist-oriented murals captured significant moments in Mexican history and inspired a revival of fresco painting in Latin America and the United States.

love a skull in the circular window
of the thumbprint searing her inimitable brow.

BILLY COLLINS

American Sonnet   1991

We do not speak like Petrarch or wear a hat like Spenser
and it is not fourteen lines
like furrows in a small, carefully plowed field

but the picture postcard, a poem on vacation,
that forces us to sing our songs in little rooms   5
or pour our sentiments into measuring cups.

We write on the back of a waterfall or lake,
adding to the view a caption as conventional
as an Elizabethan woman's heliocentric eyes.

We locate an adjective for the weather.   10
We announce that we are having a wonderful time.
We express the wish that you were here

and hide the wish that we were where you are,
walking back from the mailbox, your head lowered,
as you read and turn the thin message in your hands.   15

A slice of this place, a length of white beach,
a piazza or carved spires of a cathedral
will pierce the familiar place where you remain,

and you will toss on the table this reversible display:
a few square inches of where we have strayed   20
and a compression of what we feel.

The Epigram and the Aphorism

Lyric poetry, by its nature, has very loosely defined boundaries or limitations, and it also has room for many forms of humorous short poetry. One of
these is the **epigram.** Epigrams are short poems, never more than a few lines
long, often rhymed, and usually funny or wryly satirical. They are intended to
make a sharp comment or witty observation. The epigram has also been popular with humorous writers of what used to be called *light verse,* short poems
usually written for magazines that dressed down-to-earth truths in funny
poetic language. The American writer of light verse Ogden Nash was particularly skilled at the art of the epigram.

OGDEN NASH

Reflection on Ice-Breaking   1931

Candy
Is Dandy,
But liquor
Is Quicker.

The English poet W. H. Auden turned often to the epigram, and he used the short, trenchant form as a kind of diary of his responses to the day's political situation.

W. H. AUDEN

Five Epigrams   1965–71

The palm extended in welcome:
Look! for you
I have unclenched my fist.

.   .   .

Everyone thinks:
"I am the most important
Person at present."
The sane remember to add:
"important, I mean, to me."

.   .   .

In States unable
to alleviate Distress,
Discontent is hanged.

.   .   .

Only bad rhetoric
can improve this world:
to true Speech it is deaf.

.   .   .

Virtue is always
more expensive than Vice, but
cheaper than Madness.

Another kind of short, usually humorous poem is the **aphorism.** Epigrams and aphorisms are so close in style and mood that it is difficult sometimes to decide where a particular poem belongs. The usual definition of an aphorism is that it is a short, concise statement of a principle or a sentiment. This short poem fits the definition very well.

WENDY COPE

Two Cures for Love

1992

1 Don't see him. Don't phone or write a letter.
2 The easy way: get to know him better.

The Limerick

The **limerick** is a short, humorous poem that is defined by its verse form. It has become one of the most widespread types of folk poetry, usually in the scatalogical and obscene forms that everyone has read or heard at some time in their lives. The form is a fixed five-line verse, and there is only a single stanza, rhyming *aabba*. It is the characteristic meter of limericks that makes them so easy to remember. Their rhythmic pattern is two rhyming lines of three strong accents, followed by two lines of two strong accents—with a different rhyme—then a final line that returns to the three accents of the first two lines and rhymes with them. The meter is an anapest, but the form allows for some variation.

Whatever a reader may think of limericks, there is no other kind of poetry quite like them. They are a good example of what we mean when we talk about freedom within limits. Often writers who are known for more serious work have used the form to write poems that are more lighthearted than their usual poetry. Here is an example by the well-known poet Dylan Thomas.

> The last time I slept with the Queen
> She said, as I whistled "Ich Dien":°
>   "It's royalty's night out,
>   But please put the light out,
> The Queen may be had, but not seen."
>   –DYLAN THOMAS

Although it may seem a contradiction in terms, limericks are also very useful as literary criticism. Although these limericks, all by English writers, are meant to be laughed at, each of them is also a skillfully presented comment on the poem or the play that is the limerick's subject. It would be hard to think of a better short description of the central figure of T. S. Eliot's "The Love Song of J. Alfred Prufrock" (p. 882) than J. Walker's opening line, "An angst-ridden amorist, Fred. . . ." A. Cinna, in a limerick's small dimensions, manages to present some of the questions that have often bothered students trying to make sense out of Shakespeare's *Hamlet*.

"Ich Dien": "I serve"—the official motto of the Prince of Wales.

The fine English poet, John Donne,
Was wont to admonish the Sunne:
   "You busie old foole
   Lie still and keep coole,
For I am in bed having funne."
                  –WENDY COPE

(ON T. S. ELIOT'S "PRUFROCK")

An angst-ridden amorist, Fred,
Saw sartorial changes ahead.
   His mind kept on ringing
   With fishy girls singing.
Soft fruit also filled him with dread.
                  –J. WALKER

(APROPOS COLERIDGE'S "KUBLA KHAN")

When approached by a person from Porlock
It's best to take time by the forelock.
   Shout, "I'm not at home
   'Till I've finished this pome!"
And refuse to unfasten the door-lock.
          –RICHARD LEIGHTON GREEN

Did Ophelia ask Hamlet to bed?
Was Gertrude incestuously wed?
   Is there anything certain?
   By the fall of the curtain
Almost everyone's certainly dead.
              –A. CINNA

COMMENTARIES *Rita Dove, "An Intact World," page 971; Erica Jong, "Devouring Time: Shakespeare's Sonnets," page 984.*

WEB *For study and discussion questions and writing suggestions on each poet in this anthology, visit bedfordstmartins.com/charters/litwriters.*

11.

The Types of Poetry: Other Poetic Forms

Many other forms of lyric poetry have been popular in the past, and you might encounter some of their names in your reading. **Rhyme royal** is a form that, like the sonnet, also developed from Italian models. It is a seven-line stanza in iambic pentameter with a rhyme scheme of *ababbcc*. The English medieval poet Geoffrey Chaucer used it for his long poem *Troilus and Criseyde*, and Sir Thomas Wyatt's great love poem, "They Flee from Me" (p. 699), is written in rhyme royal. Another form that Wyatt first used in English was an eight-line stanza called **ottava rima.** It has a rhyme scheme of *abababcc*.

Although terza rima, another of the forms taken from Italian models, has been used only occasionally by poets writing in English since the fifteenth century, it is the form for Percy Bysshe Shelley's "Ode to the West Wind" (p. 744), which we discussed earlier in the previous chapter. The most complex stanza form in English that continued to be used by later writers was created by Edmund Spenser at the end of the sixteenth century for his epic poem *The Faerie Queen*. The **Spenserian stanza** uses eight lines of iambic pentameter and a last line of six stressed feet, which is called an **alexandrine.** The rhyme scheme is *ababbcbcc*. Here is a stanza from Spenser's epic.

> A Gentle Knight was pricking° on the plaine,   *cantering*
> Y cladd in mightie arms and silver shielde,
> Wherein old dints of deepe wounds did remaine,
> The cruell markes of many a bloudy fielde;
> Yet armes till that time did he never wield.
> His angry steede did chide his foaming bitt,
> As much disdayning to the curbe to yield:
> Full jolly° knight he seemd, and faire did sitt,   *gallant*
> As one for knightly giusts° and fierce encounters fitt.   *jousts*

Despite its daunting complexity, John Keats used the Spenserian stanza for his ballad "Eve of St. Agnes," and Shelley wrote "Adonais," his elegy on the death of Keats, in the same form.

There are several shorter forms of lyric poetry that have been used by modern poets looking for a form of verse that would have some of the usefulness of the sonnet but would have more of a songlike quality. All of these types of lyric are characterized by complicated rhyme schemes and concise patterns of meter. The rules for writing each of them seem to contradict the idea of spontaneity, which is also considered one of the essentials of lyric poetry, but poets respond to challenges from other poets. Nearly everyone who writes in traditional closed forms tries one of these rich hybrids at one time or another. Here are two of the best-known forms, the sestina and the villanelle.

The **sestina** is composed of six stanzas, each six lines long, with a concluding verse of three lines called the envoy. The form, which is called the "song of sixes," is from France, where it is said to have been introduced into Provençal love poetry in the thirteenth century. It is a complicated word game where the last words of the first six lines are repeated as end words of the lines of the other five stanzas, changing places in a carefully ordered procession. The final three lines must include the words, but in any order. One of the best-known modern examples of a sestina is this poem by Elizabeth Bishop.

ELIZABETH BISHOP

Sestina   1965

September rain falls on the house.
In the failing light, the old grandmother
sits in the kitchen with the child
beside the Little Marvel Stove,
reading the jokes from the almanac,   5
laughing and talking to hide her tears.

She thinks that her equinoctial tears
and the rain that beats on the roof of the house
were both foretold by the almanac,
but only known to a grandmother.   10
The iron kettle sings on the stove.
She cuts some bread and says to the child,

It's time for tea now; but the child
is watching the teakettle's small hard tears
dance like mad on the hot black stove,   15
the way the rain must dance on the house.
Tidying up, the old grandmother
hangs up the clever almanac

on its string. Birdlike, the almanac
hovers half open above the child,   20
hovers above the old grandmother
and her teacup full of dark brown tears.
She shivers and says she thinks the house
feels chilly, and puts more wood in the stove.

It was to be, says the Marvel Stove.   25
I know what I know, says the almanac.
With crayons the child draws a rigid house
and a winding pathway. Then the child
puts in a man with buttons like tears
and shows it proudly to the grandmother.   30

But secretly, while the grandmother
busies herself about the stove,
the little moons fall down like tears
from between the pages of the almanac
into the flower bed the child   35
has carefully placed in the front of the house.

Time to plant tears, says the almanac.
The grandmother sings to the marvellous stove
and the child draws another inscrutable house.

The **villanelle** is composed of five tercets and a final quatrain, written in iambic pentameter. The rhyme scheme for the tercets is *aba,* and the quatrain repeats the final rhyme, *abaa.* Like the sestina, the poem is an elaborate game in which entire lines appear again and again. The first line of the poem is used as the final line of the second and fourth tercets, and it also becomes the next to last line of the quatrain. The last line of the first tercet becomes the last line (with slight variations in this example) of the third and fifth tercets and finally ends the poem. This is an example by the modern American poet Theodore Roethke.

THEODORE ROETHKE

The Waking   1953

I wake to sleep, and take my waking slow.
I feel my fate in what I cannot fear.
I learn by going where I have to go.

We think by feeling. What is there to know?
I hear my being dance from ear to ear.   5
I wake to sleep and take my waking slow.

Of those so close beside me, which are you?
God bless the Ground! I shall walk softly there,
And learn by where I have to go.
Light takes the Tree, but who can tell us how? 10
The lowly worm climbs up a winding stair;
I wake to sleep, and take my waking slow.

Great Nature has another thing to do
To you and me; so take the lively air,
And, lovely, learn by going where to go. 15

This shaking keeps me steady, I should know.
What falls away is always. This is near.
I wake to sleep, and take my waking slow.
I learn by going where I have to go.

One of the best-known examples of the modern villanelle is "Do Not Go Gentle into That Good Night," the Welsh poet Dylan Thomas's moving tribute to his father. In a note to his publisher when he sent him the poem Thomas wrote, "The only person I can't show the little enclosed poem to is my father, who doesn't know he's dying."

DYLAN THOMAS

Do Not Go Gentle into That Good Night 1951

Do not go gentle into that good night,
Old age should burn and rave at close of day;
Rage, rage against the dying of the light.

Though wise men at their end know dark is right,
Because their words had forked no lightning they 5
Do not go gentle into that good night.

Good men, the last wave by, crying how bright
Their frail deeds might have danced in a green bay,
Rage, rage against the dying of the light.

Wild men who caught and sang the sun in flight, 10
And learn, too late, they grieved it on its way,
Do not go gentle into that good night.

Grave men, near death, who see with blinding sight
Blind eyes could blaze like meteors and be gay,
Rage, rage against the dying of the light. 15

And you, my father, there on the sad height,
Curse, bless, me now with your fierce tears, I pray.
Do not go gentle into that good night.
Rage, rage against the dying of the light.

Open Form

Like the nineteenth-century photographer Louis Daguerre, who was supposed to have cried out, when he managed to capture an image on a silver-coated plate, "From this moment, painting is dead!," many people were certain that when poetry lost its centuries-old anchors of rhyme and meter there would be no more poetry. As we know, poetry is still with us, even though we do not usually look for rhyme schemes or count the meter when we read a poem today. In the first years of the "free verse" movement, as **open form** was called then, there was some feeling that poetry could be as "free" as the wind and that a poem could take any form the writer chose. The writers found, however, that although the way they wrote had changed, the means they worked with to create a poem were still the same. Poetry written in open form had to have the concentration and the technical virtuosity of poetry written in traditional closed forms.

This poem by the American poet Galway Kinnell has the tone of ordinary conversation, but, although the poem is not rhymed, he has used many of the traditional technical means to create it.

GALWAY KINNELL

The Man Splitting Wood in the Daybreak   1985

The man splitting wood in the daybreak
looks strong, as though, if one weakened,
one could turn to him and he would help.
Gus Newland was strong. When he split wood
he struck hard, flashing the bright steel   5
through air of daybreak so fast rock maple
leapt apart — as they think marriages will
in countries about to institute divorce —
and even willow, which, though stacked
to dry a full year, on separating   10
actually weeps — totem wood, therefore,
to the married-until-death — miseried asunder
with many small lip-smacking gasp-noises.
But Gus is dead. We could turn to our fathers,
but they protect us only through the unperplexed   15
looking-back of the numerals cut into their headstones.
Or to our mothers, whose love, so devastated,
can't, even in spring, break through the hard earth.
Our spouses weaken at the same rate we do.
We have to hold our children up to lean on them.   20
What about the man splitting wood in the daybreak,
who looked strong? That was years ago. That was me.

Kinnell develops an extended metaphor of splitting wood as a symbol of young strength; he uses a shift of syntax in lines like "Or to our mothers, whose love, so devastated, / can't, even in spring, break through the hard earth"; he employs the conscious awkwardness of the constructed word *miseried* set beside the more elegant-sounding *asunder.* The meter is irregular, but if you scan the opening line, "The man splitting wood in the daybreak," you are already conscious of a strong metric pulse, which Kinnell interrupts with the phrase "Gus Newland was strong" for dramatic effect at the beginning of the fourth line. You can find alliteration in the phrase "air of daybreak." Kinnell even uses an adjective that causes a problem of interpretation, "totem wood," suggesting perhaps that the wood is an emblem or symbol for a marriage that lasts "until-death."

The Prose Poem

As readers have become more used to open form, poets have continued to explore its possibilities. A form that was first developed in France but which has now spread to every other language is the **prose poem.** The term contradicts itself by telling us that this is both prose and poetry, two forms of writing we have always been told are separate, but the term also is a good description of what writers do with the form. A prose poem is a lyric poem that has all the characteristics of a lyric but is written in prose. It presents one image or, like a lyric poem in open form, a response to a single emotion.

A prose poem can have some kind of narrative, but the story line is one of the means the poet uses to illustrate the theme of the poem. Some prose poems have the effect of a **parable,** a short narrative used to point out a moral. Others have the effect of opening the mind to the possibilities of the unconscious. Even if they present us with a single, condensed image, they often leave us with the sense that what we have just read has made us conscious of something *else.* We call poetry like this associative. Here are two contemporary prose poems by American writers that show some of the range of the form.

ROBERT BLY

August Rain   1975

After a month and a half without rain, at last, in late August, darkness comes at three in the afternoon. A cheerful thunder begins, and then the rain. I set a glass out on a table to measure the rain and, suddenly buoyant and affectionate, go indoors to find my children. They are upstairs, playing quietly alone in their doll-filled rooms, hanging pictures, thought- 5 fully moving "the small things that make them happy" from one side of the room to another. I feel triumphant, without need of money, far from the grave. I walk over the grass, watching the soaked chairs, and the cooled towels, and sit down on my stoop, pulling a chair out with me. The

rain deepens. It rolls off the porch roof, making a great puddle near me. 10
The bubbles slide toward the puddle edge, become crowded, and disappear. The black earth turns blacker; it absorbs the rain needles without
a sound. The sky is low, everything silent, as when parents are angry. . . .
What has failed and been forgiven — the leaves from last year unable to
go on, lying near the foundation, dry under the porch, retreat farther into 15
the shadow; they give off a faint hum, as of birds' eggs, or the tail of a dog.

      The older we get the more we fail, but the more we fail the more we
feel a part of the dead straw of the universe, the corner of a barn with cow-
dung twenty years old, the chair fallen back on its head in a deserted
farmhouse, the belt left hanging over the chairback after the bachelor has 20
died in the ambulance on the way to the city. These objects belong to us;
they ride us as the child holds on to the dog's fur; they appear in our
dreams; they approach nearer and nearer, coming in slowly from the
wainscoting. They make our trunks heavy, accumulating between trips.
These objects lie against the ship's side, and will nudge the hole open that 25
lets the water in at last.

ROBERT HASS

A Story about the Body   1989

The young composer, working that summer at an artist's colony, had
watched her for a week. She was Japanese, a painter, almost sixty, and he
thought he was in love with her. He loved her work, and her work was
like the way she moved her body, used her hands, looked at him directly
when she made amused and considered answers to his questions. One 5
night, walking back from a concert, they came to her door and she turned
to him and said, "I think you would like to have me. I would like that too,
but I must tell you that I have had a double mastectomy," and when he
didn't understand, "I've lost both my breasts." The radiance that he had
carried around in his belly and chest cavity — like music — withered very 10
quickly, and he made himself look at her when he said, "I'm sorry. I don't
think I could." He walked back to his own cabin through the pines, and
in the morning he found a small blue bowl on the porch outside his door.
It looked to be full of rose petals, but he found when he picked it up that
the rose petals were on top; the rest of the bowl — she must have swept 15
them from the corners of her studio — was full of dead bees.

Haiku

An easy definition of **haiku** might be,

    A HAIKU
Seventeen syllable
    Japanese poem
popular with students.

Most dictionaries insist on two syllables for the word *poem;* so our definition can claim to have the required seventeen syllables. The haiku is so well known in Japan that most of the members of an educated Japanese family would be skilled enough in writing haiku to present verses to one another. Among experienced poets the poems were usually written in a linked sequence, each poet writing a new haiku in response to the haiku that had just been written, or that he had just read.

Most haiku are written in three lines, with five syllables in the two outer lines and seven in the middle line. As with so many other things between the two languages, Japanese and English, the similarity between our syllable and the Japanese ideogram—the system of writing using pictures to represent a thing or idea—is not as close as our precise definition suggests. An ideogram can have the connotations of one or more of our words and even an entire phrase. A direct translation from a Japanese haiku sometimes means that when you read the poem in English, you are getting considerably less from it than a Japanese reader would.

Since an ideogram may be written in different ways, the poet can also allude to other haiku or to another poet by the way the ideogram is set down on the paper. Specific places or certain seasons of the year are identified with the best-known writers. With all of these possibilities, a haiku that can seem like a small, simple poem to an English reader can present a Japanese reader with a world of allusion and response. This allusion and response are the essence of a haiku. The small glimpse of a real instant should recall in the reader some moment of life, some half-forgotten memory.

There have been thousands of writers of haiku since the form was first created, but four poets are considered to be the most important. The first is Bashō, who was born in 1644 into a samurai family. Before his death in 1694, he had turned to a simple life and spent much of his time making long journeys over the Japanese countryside, traveling by foot or on horseback. The spare simplicity of his poems reflects his Zen Buddhist beliefs. Many of his haiku were written on his travels. This is a typical Bashō poem:

> A crow is perched
> Upon a leafless withered bough—
> The evening dusk.

Here are three of Bashō's linked haiku, freely interpreted by Robert Hass:

> Ripening barley—
> does it get that color
> from the skylark's tears?

> Day by day
> the barley ripens,
> the skylarks sing.

> Having no talent,
> I just want to sleep,
> you noisy birds.

Two generations after Bashō's death, his poetry was taken up by a well-educated writer and painter named Buson, who lived from 1716 to 1783.

Buson revered Bashō's poetry and at the same time brought his own sensitivity to the haiku:

> The sea in springtime
> All the warm day in breathing swells—
> In breathing swells.

Although Issa lived at almost the same time as Buson, from 1763 to 1827, his poetry had a distinctive tone that came as much from his country background as it did from his poetic studies:

> Children imitating cormorants—
> more wonderful
> than cormorants.

In the century that followed Buson's death, the haiku was neglected and the form lost some of its purity, but it was once again taken up by a younger poet, Shiki, who lived from 1872 to 1923. Shiki set the tone of the modern haiku:

> The ocean freshly green
> Mountain on mountain peaked with snow
> Birds homing to the north.

The haiku has been adopted by many American poets, particularly the Beat poets of the 1950s and the 1960s, who had become Buddhists and who tried to match the severity of the Japanese poems with their own rigor and restraint. The best known of the Beat writers, Jack Kerouac, wrote dozens of haiku, sometimes jotting them down in pencil on the back pages of the paperback books he carried in his pocket when he worked on the railroad. He called what he was writing "Western Haikus."

> Birds singing
> in the dark
> — Rainy dawn

> The summer chair
> rocking by itself
> In the blizzard

> In my medicine cabinet
> the winter fly
> has died of old age

The American writer who has perhaps best caught the essence of the haiku is the African American novelist and author of short stories Richard Wright. Wright discovered the haiku in 1959, shortly before his death. As he wrote a friend, "Maybe I'm fooling around with these little poems, but I could not let them go. I was possessed by them" (quoted in *American Poetry and Japanese Culture*, Kodama, Archon Books, 1994, p. 158). Within a few months he wrote 4,000 haiku and then spent almost as much time winnowing them down into a collection describing the seasons of the year.

I would like a bell
Tolling in this soft twilight
Over willow trees

A freezing morning
I left a bit of my skin
On the broomstick handle

A soft wind at dawn
Lifts one dry leaf and lays it
Upon another

An empty sickbed
An indented white pillow
In weak winter sun

Imagism

The term **imagism** was invented by an American poet, Ezra Pound, who was living in London and closely associated with a small group of friends who were the first imagists. As a literary movement, imagism lasted only a few years, but it was widely discussed, ridiculed, and parodied, and it had an important role in the development of open form poetry. Even poets who would not think of themselves as imagists used the methods of the imagists for their own work. The imagists were trying to create poetry that was, as it was expressed by another of their founders, T. E. Hulme, "a moment of discovery or awareness, created by effective metaphor which provides the sharp, intuitive insight that is the essence of life." In the credo that opened the 1915 imagist anthology, the first point was "To use the language of common speech, but the exact word, not the nearly exact, nor the merely decorative." The fourth point was that imagist poems should "Present an image. Poetry should render particulars exactly, and not deal in vague generalities, however magnificent and sonorous."

It was the lean, hard diction of imagist poetry that was to have a lasting effect on modern poetry. Poets found that they did not have to round every poem into a generality. As William Carlos Williams, a friend of Pound's who stayed in New Jersey and wrote his poetry with his own American voice, expressed the imagist ideal, "No ideas, but in things."

This poem by Ezra Pound is perhaps the most famous of the imagist poems. Pound used it as an example of what he meant by imagism in his introduction to the first collection of his friends' poems. It is a description of people in the Paris subway on a rainy, dark night.

EZRA POUND

In a Station of the Metro   1913

The apparition of these faces in the crowd
Petals on a wet, black bough.

T. E. Hulme's role in the early years of imagism is well known, and he contributed several imagist poems, like this description of a scene in London, to the movement's early anthologies.

T. E. HULME

Images

1914

Old houses were scaffolding once
　　　　and workmen whistling.

For a few months, when they both were students at the University of Pennsylvania, Pound had been engaged to Hilda Doolittle. When she came to London he persuaded her to use her initials, H.D., for her poetry. She and her husband, Richard Aldington, were part of the original imagist group.

H.D.

Oread°

1914

Whirl up, sea—
whirl your pointed pines,
splash your great pines
on our rocks,
hurl your green over us,
cover us with your pools of fir.

In the imagist poems of American poet Adelaide Crapsey, the strong underpinning of the Japanese haiku in imagist writing can be clearly seen.

ADELAIDE CRAPSEY

November Night

1913

Listen . . .
With faint dry sound,
Like steps of passing ghosts,
The leaves, frost-crisp'd, break from the tree
And fall.

Oread: Mountain nymph.

Although William Carlos Williams never considered himself an imagist, the poetry he wrote after the group began to publish reflected their aims. The best way to describe the effect of the imagist credo on his work is to say that he wrote poems that were made possible by imagism. His poem "The Red Wheelbarrow" would be a classic imagist description of a wheelbarrow left out in the rain close to the chickens, except for his enigmatic phrase, "so much depends." What Williams seems to be suggesting in his eight short lines is that he finds something very important in this image of rain and chickens and a wheelbarrow in his backyard. Although we know now that the inspiration for the poem came to Dr. Williams when he was waiting for news of a patient as he stared out of the family's window into their backyard, the basic image of the poem has never given away all of its secrets.

WILLIAM CARLOS WILLIAMS

The Red Wheelbarrow 1923

so much depends
upon

a red wheel
barrow

glazed with rain
water

beside the white
chickens

Although Wallace Stevens was an insurance executive who lived in Hartford, Connecticut, he had many associations with Williams and other young poets who were experimenting with the new style. The first and last verses of his poem "Thirteen Ways of Looking at a Blackbird" have all the characteristics of an imagist poem. The first verse also suggests the tone of a haiku, although it has too many syllables. Other verses, like the seventh, with its admonition to the men of Haddam, a small city in Connecticut, to stop thinking about imagined exotic birds and see the blackbirds walking around the ground, are more didactic.

Like Williams's poem about the red wheelbarrow, this poem has also defied easy access to its meanings. Perhaps one way to understand it is to think of it as a series of imagist poems and short enigmatic lyrics, with blackbirds suddenly flying through. It is a poem that reminds us of Marianne Moore's description of poetry as something that can present us with "imaginary gardens with real toads in them."

WALLACE STEVENS

Thirteen Ways of Looking at a Blackbird   1931

I

Among twenty snowy mountains
The only moving thing
Was the eye of the blackbird.

II

I was of three minds,
Like a tree
In which there are three blackbirds.   5

III

The blackbird whistled in the autumn winds.
It was a small part of the pantomime.

IV

A man and a woman
Are one.   10
A man and a woman and a blackbird
Are one.

V

I do not know which to prefer,
The beauty of inflections
Or the beauty of innuendoes,   15
The blackbird whistling
Or just after.

VI

Icicles filled the long window
With barbaric glass.
The shadow of the blackbird   20
Crossed it, to and fro.
The mood
Traced in the shadow
An indecipherable cause.

VII

O thin men of Haddam,   25
Why do you imagine golden birds?
Do you not see how the blackbird
Walks around the feet
Of the women about you?

VIII

I know noble accents   30
And lucid, inescapable rhythms;
But I know, too,
That the blackbird is involved
In what I know.

IX

When the blackbird flew out of sight,   35
It marked the edge
Of one of many circles.

X

At the sight of blackbirds
Flying in a green light,
Even the bawds of euphony   40
Would cry out sharply.

XI

He rode over Connecticut
In a glass coach.
Once, a fear pierced him,
In that he mistook   45
The shadow of his equipage
For blackbirds.

XII

The river is moving.
The blackbird must be flying.

XIII

It was evening all afternoon.   50
It was snowing
And it was going to snow.
The blackbird sat
In the cedar-limbs.

DRAMATIC POETRY

The term **dramatic poetry,** in its denotative sense, means the use of poetry in the writing of drama. If we have grown up with English as our language, when we think of poetry as dramatic dialogue we usually are hearing, in our memory, the blank-verse cadences of Shakespeare and the other Elizabethan dramatists.

Many poets have looked for a form that would combine the power of the spoken poem from the stage and the more intimate expression of a poem on the page. One of the most popular of these forms is the dramatic monologue, and a student will come much closer to understanding poems like these by reading them out loud.

The Dramatic Monologue

A **dramatic monologue** is usually defined as a poem written in the form of a speech or extended narration that the person who is the subject of the poem delivers to someone else. In the nineteenth century, when the form was very popular, a dramatic monologue had a definite speaker who was talking to an imaginary person; there was some implied action; and the action took place in the present. Often the subject of the more lurid monologues was someone, often a woman, who related a story about something terrible that had happened to them, and then ended the poem by hurling themselves off a cliff or into the ocean.

The dramatic monologues written by the English poet Robert Browning, however, are character studies of people who reveal themselves as they speak. One of the best known is "My Last Duchess." If you read the poem aloud, you will hear the subtlety and ease of its language. The poem perfectly fits the nineteenth-century idea of the dramatic monologue. It includes a definite speaker, the action of the duke showing his art collection, and the moment in the present when he is talking to the emissary.

ROBERT BROWNING

My Last Duchess   1842

Ferrara

That's my last Duchess painted on the wall,
Looking as if she were alive. I call
That piece a wonder, now: Frà Pandolf's° hands
Worked busily a day, and there she stands.
Will't please you sit and look at her? I said   5
"Frà Pandolf" by design, for never read
Strangers like you that pictured countenance,
The depth and passion of its earnest glance,
But to myself they turned (since none puts by
The curtain I have drawn for you, but I)   10
And seemed as they would ask me, if they durst,
How such a glance came there; so, not the first
Are you to turn and ask thus. Sir, 'twas not
Her husband's presence only, called that spot

---

3. Frà Pandolf's: Brother Pandolf, a fictional painter.

Of joy into the Duchess' cheek: perhaps 15
Frà Pandolf chanced to say "Her mantle laps
Over my lady's wrist too much," or "Paint
Must never hope to reproduce the faint
Half-flush that dies along her throat": such stuff
Was courtesy, she thought, and cause enough 20
For calling up that spot of joy. She had
A heart—how shall I say?—too soon made glad,
Too easily impressed; she liked whate'er
She looked on, and her looks went everywhere.
Sir, 'twas all one! My favor at her breast, 25
The dropping of the daylight in the West,
The bough of cherries some officious fool
Broke in the orchard for her, the white mule
She rode with round the terrace—all and each
Would draw from her alike the approving speech, 30
Or blush, at least. She thanked men,—good! but thanked
Somehow—I know not how—as if she ranked
My gift of a nine-hundred-years-old name
With anybody's gift. Who'd stoop to blame
This sort of trifling? Even had you skill 35
In speech—which I have not—to make your will
Quite clear to such an one, and say, "Just this
Or that in you disgusts me; here you miss,
Or there exceed the mark"—and if she let
Herself be lessoned so, nor plainly set 40
Her wits to yours, forsooth, and made excuse,
—E'en then would be some stooping; and I choose
Never to stoop. Oh sir, she smiled, no doubt,
Whene'er I passed her; but who passed without
Much the same smile? This grew; I gave commands; 45
Then all smiles stopped together. There she stands
As if alive. Will't please you rise? We'll meet
The company below, then. I repeat,
The Count your master's known munificence
Is ample warrant that no just pretense 50
Of mine for dowry will be disallowed;
Though his fair daughter's self, as I avowed
At starting, is my object. Nay, we'll go
Together down, sir. Notice Neptune, though,
Taming a sea-horse, thought a rarity, 55
Which Claus of Innsbruck° cast in bronze for me!

---

56. Claus of Innsbruck: Unidentified; probably a fictional sculptor.

Poems for the Ear

Many students today, whether or not they read poetry, *hear* poetry. Poetry slams, readings, recorded cassettes, and television appearances by poets performing in every style are part of today's world. Poets have always read their work aloud, but with the Beat poets of the 1950s, led by Allen Ginsberg, the spoken poem became one of the most popular ways for poets to reach their audience. Their poems, like dramatic monologues, were written to be performed. Reading their poems to a live audience, the poets used everyday language; they expressed their audience's problems and enthusiasm, and their language was immediately understandable. Ginsberg introduced his most famous poem, *Howl,* in excited readings to California audiences even before it was published. The poem went on to sell nearly a million copies in a small paperback, and Ginsberg read it for audiences around the world. Part tribal shamans and part theatrical performers, the poets writing for the ear have given contemporary poetry a new and exciting dimension.

ALLEN GINSBERG

America   1956

America I've given you all and now I'm nothing.
America two dollars and twentyseven cents January 17, 1956.
I can't stand my own mind.
America when will we end the human war?
Go fuck yourself with your atom bomb.   5
I don't feel good don't bother me.
I won't write my poem till I'm in my right mind.
America when will you be angelic?
When will you take off your clothes?
When will you look at yourself through the grave?   10
When will you be worthy of your million Trotskyites?°
America why are your libraries full of tears?
America when will you send your eggs to India?
I'm sick of your insane demands.
When can I go into the supermarket and buy what I need with my good
      looks?   15
America after all it is you and I who are perfect not the next world.
Your machinery is too much for me.
You made me want to be a saint.
There must be some other way to settle this argument.
Burroughs° is in Tangiers I don't think he'll come back it's sinister.   20

---

11. Trotskyites: Communists who continued to consider Leon Trotsky a legitimate leader.
20. Burroughs: William S. Burroughs (1914–1997), an American author whose harrowing works about life as a drug addict were written when he was an expatriate living abroad in Mexico and Tangiers.

Are you being sinister or is this some form of practical joke?
I'm trying to come to the point.
I refuse to give up my obsession.
America stop pushing I know what I'm doing.
America the plum blossoms are falling.   25
I haven't read the newspapers for months, everyday somebody goes on
    trial for murder.
America I feel sentimental about the Wobblies.°
America I used to be a communist when I was a kid I'm not sorry.
I smoke marijuana every chance I get.
I sit in my house for days on end and stare at the roses in the closet.   30
When I go to Chinatown I get drunk and never get laid.
My mind is made up there's going to be trouble.
You should have seen me reading Marx.
My psychoanalyst thinks I'm perfectly right.
I won't say the Lord's Prayer.   35
I have mystical visions and cosmic vibrations.
America I still haven't told you what you did to Uncle Max after he came
    over from Russia.
I'm addressing you.
Are you going to let your emotional life be run by Time Magazine?
I'm obsessed by Time Magazine.   40
I read it every week.
Its cover stares at me every time I slink past the corner candystore.
I read it in the basement of the Berkeley Public Library.
It's always telling me about responsibility. Businessmen are serious.
    Movie producers are serious. Everybody's serious but me.
It occurs to me that I am America.   45
I am talking to myself again.

Asia is rising against me.
I haven't got a chinaman's chance.
I'd better consider my national resources.
My national resources consist of two joints of marijuana millions of
    genitals an unpublishable private literature that jetplanes 1400 miles
    an hour and twentyfive-thousand mental institutions.   50
I say nothing about my prisons nor the millions of underprivileged who
    live in my flowerpots under the light of five hundred suns.
I have abolished the whorehouses of France, Tangiers is the next to go.
My ambition is to be President despite the fact that I'm a Catholic.
America how can I write a holy litany in your silly mood?
I will continue like Henry Ford my strophes are as individual as his
    automobiles more so they're all different sexes.   55
America I will send you strophes $2500 apiece $500 down on your old
    strophe

---

27. **Wobblies:** Members of the radical International Workers of the World.

America free Tom Mooney°
America save the Spanish Loyalists
America Sacco & Vanzetti must not die
America I am the Scottsboro boys. 60
America when I was seven momma took me to Communist Cell meet-
    ings they sold us garbanzos a handful per ticket a ticket costs a nickel
    and the speeches were free everybody was angelic and sentimental
    about the workers it was all so sincere you have no idea what a good
    thing the party was in 1935 Scott Nearing° was a grand old man a
    real mensch Mother Bloor the Silk-strikers' Ewig-Weibliche made
    me cry I once saw the Yiddish orator Israel Amter° plain. Everybody
    must have been a spy.
America you don't really want to go to war.
America it's them bad Russians.
Them Russians them Russians and them Chinamen. And them Russians.
The Russia wants to eat us alive. The Russia's power mad. She wants to
    take our cars from out our garages. 65
Her wants to grab Chicago. Her needs a Red *Reader's Digest.* Her wants
    our auto plants in Siberia. Him big bureaucracy running our filling-
    stations.
That no good. Ugh. Him make Indians learn read. Him need big black
    niggers. Hah. Her make us all work sixteen hours a day. Help.
America this is quite serious.
America this is the impression I get from looking in the television set.
America is this correct? 70
I'd better get right down to the job.
It's true I don't want to join the Army or turn lathes in precision parts
    factories, I'm nearsighted and psychopathic anyway.
America I'm putting my queer shoulder to the wheel.

Poems for Further Reading

WALLACE STEVENS

The Emperor of Ice-Cream   1923

Call the roller of big cigars,
The muscular one, and bid him whip
In kitchen cups concupiscent curds.°

---

57. Tom Mooney: Labor organizer convicted of a bombing based on perjured evidence.
61. Scott Nearing: A radical economist; **Mother Bloor . . . Israel Amter:** New York–
based leaders of the American Communist Party.
3. concupiscent curds: "The words 'concupiscent curds' have no genealogy; they are
merely expressive: at least, I hope they are expressive. They express the concupiscence of
life, but, by contrast with the things in relation in the poem, they express or accentuate

Let the wenches dawdle in such dress
As they are used to wear, and let the boys   5
Bring flowers in last month's newspapers.
Let be be finale of seem.°
The only emperor is the emperor of ice-cream.

Take from the dresser of deal,
Lacking the three glass knobs, that sheet   10
On which she embroidered fantails once
And spread it so as to cover her face.
If her horny feet protrude, they come
To show how cold she is, and dumb.
Let the lamp affix its beam.   15
The only emperor is the emperor of ice-cream.

MARGARET ATWOOD

Siren° Song   1974

This is the one song everyone
would like to learn: the song
that is irresistible:

the song that forces men
to leap overboard in squadrons   5
even though they see the beached skulls

the song nobody knows
because anyone who has heard it
is dead, and the others can't remember.

Shall I tell you the secret   10
and if I do, will you get me
out of this bird suit?

I don't enjoy it here
squatting on this island
looking picturesque and mythical   15

with these two feathery maniacs,
I don't enjoy singing
this trio, fatal and valuable.

---

life's destitution, and it is this that gives them something more than a cheap lustre" (Wallace Stevens, *Letters* [New York: Knopf, 1960], p. 500). **7. Let ... seem:** "The true sense of 'Let be be finale of seem' is let being become the conclusion or denouement of appearing to be: in short, ice cream is an absolute good. The poem is obviously not about ice cream, but about being as distinguished from seeming to be" (*Letters*, p. 341).
Siren: In Greek mythology, a creature who could assume the shape of a beautiful woman; its song lured passing mariners to their deaths.

I will tell the secret to you,
to you, only to you.   20
Come closer. This song

is a cry for help: Help me!
Only you, only you can,
you are unique

at last. Alas   25
it is a boring song
but it works every time.

ANNE STEVENSON

The Spirit is too Blunt an Instrument   1970

The spirit is too blunt an instrument
to have made this baby.
Nothing so unskilful as human passions
could have managed the intricate
exacting particulars: the tiny   5
blind bones with their manipulating tendons,
the knee and the knucklebones, the resilient
fine meshings of ganglia and vertebrae,
the chain of the difficult spine.

Observe the distinct eyelashes and sharp crescent   10
fingernails, the shell-like complexity
of the ear, with its firm involutions
concentric in miniature to minute
ossicles. Imagine the
infinitesimal capillaries, the flawless connections   15
of the lungs, the invisible neural filaments
through which the completed body
already answers to the brain.

Then name any passion or sentiment
possessed of the simplest accuracy.   20
No, no desire or affection could have done
with practice what habit
has done perfectly, indifferently,
through the body's ignorant precision.
It is left to the vagaries of the mind to invent   25
love and despair and anxiety
and their pain.

WISLAWA SZYMBORSKA

True Love   1972

TRANSLATED BY STANISLAW BARÁNCZAK AND CLARE CAVANAGH

True love. Is it normal,
is it serious, is it practical?
What does the world get from two people
who exist in a world of their own?

Placed on the same pedestal for no good reason,   5
drawn randomly from millions, but convinced
it had to happen this way—in reward for what?
    For nothing.
The light descends from nowhere.
Why on these two and not on others?   10
Doesn't this outrage justice? Yes it does.
Doesn't it disrupt our painstakingly erected principles,
and cast the moral from the peak? Yes on both accounts.

Look at the happy couple.
Couldn't they at least try to hide it,   15
fake a little depression for their friends' sake!
Listen to them laughing—it's an insult.
The language they use—deceptively clear.
And their little celebrations, rituals,
the elaborate mutual routines—   20
it's obviously a plot behind the human race's back!

It's hard even to guess how far things might go
if people start to follow their example.
What could religion and poetry count on?
What would be remembered? What renounced?   25
Who'd want to stay within bounds?

True love. Is it really necessary?
Tact and common sense tell us to pass over it in silence,
like a scandal in Life's highest circles.
Perfectly good children are born without its help.   30
It couldn't populate the planet in a million years,
it comes along so rarely.

Let the people who never find true love
keep saying that there's no such thing.

Their faith will make it easier for them to live and die.   35

COMMENTARIES *Marge Piercy, "Imagery Can't Really Be Taught," page 997;
Ezra Pound, "On the Principles of Imagism," page 998.*

WEB *For study and discussion questions and writing suggestions on each poet in
this anthology, visit bedfordstmartins.com/charters/litwriters.*

12.

Poets Speaking Out: Poems about Politics, Society, and the Environment

No single poet—Dante, Goethe, or even Shakespeare—has had a more pervasive influence on the cultural foundation of the West than the shadowy figure we call Homer. His name is so familiar that it is easy to overlook just how long his work has been our heritage. Homer described events that took place, as far as we can tell, at roughly the same time as the Exodus. Before the Old Testament was complete, his works were already the basic scrolls in a cultured man's library. By the time Jesus was born, so much had been written about Homer and his work that it would be a very long time before any of the Apostles could challenge his leading position as the most intensely studied author in Western Civilization. All this Homer accomplished with just two poems—the *Iliad* and the *Odyssey*.

—TIM SEVERIN, *The Ulysses Voyage*

As Muriel Rukeyser told us in the epigraph that began our study of poetry and poets, "the universe of poetry is the universe of emotional truth," and what you have found in your reading is that poets write about the things that set off their emotional triggers. Poets, like everyone else, are passionately engaged in the issues that divide their times, and the world around them is mirrored in their writing. Often the poetry inspired by social upheaval loses its immediacy once the dust has settled, and poems written in these moments of emotion are forgotten later. Edna St. Vincent Millay is still read for her early poetry about the physical world and for her sonnets, but in the late 1920s it was her angry poetry protesting the execution of the falsely accused anarchists Sacco and Vanzetti that attracted many readers. In the excitement of the first years of the social experiment in the Soviet Union, Langston Hughes wrote several long, fervent poems calling for revolution in the United States, but he left them out of later collections of his work.

POETRY OF PROTEST AND SOCIAL CONCERN

Poets writing today reflect many of the themes and the attitudes that concerned writers of a generation ago. Although some of the strident rhetoric of the 1960s has been muted, they are still deeply engaged in their own moment of history. In the 1970s and 1980s, young African American writers began to voice their anger at the racism that they encountered in American society, and at the same time new women writers were giving vent to their impatience with the limited role that society's customs were forcing on them. For these writers, the voice of their protest often was poetry. They wrote poems to convince us, to shock us, or to inform us, and they were more concerned with the message of their poetry than with traditional conventions of language, style, or form. Their poems were political, and political poetry has been used to open prayer meetings and to lead revolutions.

In much contemporary poetry, we find ourselves and our concerns reflected back to us. Yusef Komunyakaa served in Vietnam and many of his poems have the harrowing emotional experience of the war as their source. In "Facing It," he is writing several years after the war's end, but his emotions still reverberate in its aftermath.

YUSEF KOMUNYAKAA

Facing It   1988

5

My black face fades,
hiding inside the black granite.
I said I wouldn't,
dammit: No tears.
I'm stone. I'm flesh.   5
My clouded reflection eyes me
like a bird of prey, the profile of night
slanted against morning. I turn
this way — the stone lets me go.
I turn that way — I'm inside   10
the Vietnam Veterans Memorial
again, depending on the light
to make a difference.
I go down the 58,022 names,
half-expecting to find   15
my own in letters like smoke.
I touch the name Andrew Johnson;
I see the booby trap's white flash.
Names shimmer on a woman's blouse
but when she walks away   20
the names stay on the wall.
Brushstrokes flash, a red bird's
wings cutting across my stare.
The sky. A plane in the sky.
A white vet's image floats   25
closer to me, then his pale eyes
look through mine. I'm a window.
He's lost his right arm
inside the stone. In the black mirror

a woman's trying to erase names: 30
No, she's brushing a boy's hair.

Although a poem like "The Day Lady Died," by New York poet Frank
O'Hara, is not specifically political, in its *topicality* it is related to a poem like
"Facing It." It reflects our social concerns, and it is written with the direct emotional response of the political poets. O'Hara is writing about an ordinary day
in New York City, but it is a day that abruptly changes for him when he glances
at a headline and reads that the singer Billie Holiday, who was for O'Hara's
generation what John Lennon or Kurt Cobain is for ours, has just died.

FRANK O'HARA

The Day Lady° Died   1964

It is 12:20 in New York a Friday
three days after Bastille day, yes
it is 1959 and I go get a shoeshine
because I will get off the 4:19 in Easthampton
at 7:15 and then go straight to dinner   5
and I don't know the people who will feed me

I walk up the muggy street beginning to sun
and have a hamburger and a malted and buy
an ugly NEW WORLD WRITING to see what the poets
in Ghana are doing these days   10
            I go on to the bank
and Miss Stillwagon (first name Linda I once heard)
doesn't even look up my balance for once in her life
and in the GOLDEN GRIFFIN I get a little Verlaine
for Patsy with drawings by Bonnard° although I do   15
think of Hesiod,° trans. Richmond Lattimore or
Brendan Behan's new play° or *Le Balcon* or *Les Nègres*
of Genet,° but I don't, I stick with Verlaine
after practically going to sleep with quandariness

and for Mike I just stroll into the PARK LANE   20
Liquor Store and ask for a bottle of Strega and

Lady: Billie Holiday (1915–1959), known as "Lady Day," a popular African American
singer of the 1930s, who struggled at the end of her career against alcohol and drug abuse.
14–15. Verlaine . . . Bonnard: Paul Verlaine (1844–1896), the French poet; the reference
is to an edition of Verlaine's poems with illustrations by Pierre Bonnard (1867–1947).
16. Hesiod: Greek poet (eighth century B.C.).   **17. Brendan Behan's new play:** Possibly *The Quare Fellow* (1956) or *The Hostage* (1958).   **18. Genet:** Jean Genet (1910–
1986), French novelist and playwright whose plays included *The Balcony* (1956) and *The
Blacks* (1958).

then I go back where I came from to 6th Avenue
and the tobacconist in the Ziegfeld Theatre and
casually ask for a carton of Gauloises and a carton
of Picayunes, and a NEW YORK POST with her face on it   25

and I am sweating a lot by now and thinking of
leaning on the john door in the 5 SPOT
while she whispered a song along the keyboard
to Mal Waldron° and everyone and I stopped breathing

Norman Rosten's poem about the death of Marilyn Monroe is much
more specific in its indictment of the social forces that he felt led to her suicide.

NORMAN ROSTEN

Who Killed Norma Jean?   1962

Who killed Norma Jean?
I, said the city
As a civic duty
I killed Norma Jean

Who saw her die?   5
I, said the night
And a bedroom light
We saw her die

Who'll catch her blood?
I, said the fan   10
With my little pan
I'll catch her blood

Who'll make her shroud?
I, said the lover
My guilt to cover   15
I'll make her shroud

Who'll dig her grave?
A tourist will come
And join in the fun
He'll dig her grave   20

Who'll be chief mourners?
We, who represent
And lose our ten percent
We'll be the chief mourners

---

29. Mal Waldron: A jazz pianist who sometimes accompanied Holiday in her club
engagements.

Who'll bear her pall?   25
We, said the Press
In pain and distress
We'll bear the pall

Who'll toll the bell?
I, screamed the mother   30
Locked in her tower
I'll ring the bell

Who'll soon forget?
I, said the page
Beginning to fade   35
I'll be first to forget

Although more than a half-century has passed since the world first
became aware of the totality of the Holocaust, there are still poems being written that struggle to deal with its story. This poem, by England's poet laureate,
Andrew Motion, describes his feelings after visiting the hiding place of Anne
Frank in Amsterdam, Holland. *Huis* is the Dutch word for "house."

ANDREW MOTION

Anne Frank Huis   1978

Even now, after twice her lifetime of grief
and anger in the very place, whoever comes
to climb these narrow stairs, discovers how
the bookcase slides aside, then walks through
shadow into sunlit rooms, can never help   5
but break her secrecy again. Just listening
is a kind of guilt: the Westerkirk° repeats
itself outside, as if all time worked round
towards her fear, and made each stroke
die down on guarded streets. Imagine it—   10
three years of whispering and loneliness
and plotting, day by day, the Allied line
in Europe with a yellow chalk. What hope
she had for ordinary love and interest
survives her here, displayed above the bed   15

---

7. **Westerkirk:** A church in Amsterdam. Built in 1620, it is famous for its carillon and
tower, the highest in the city.

as pictures of her family; some actors;
fashions chosen by Princess Elizabeth.
And those who stoop to see them find
not only patience missing its reward,
but one enduring wish for chances   20

like my own: to leave as simply
as I do, and walk at ease
up dusty tree-lined avenues, or watch
a silent barge come clear of bridges
settling their reflections in the blue canals.   25

One of the tragedies still on our horizons today is the AIDS epidemic,
and there has been an outpouring of art and poetry struggling with the ravages
of the disease. In this poem, the American writer Miller Williams describes a
hospital visit to a dying friend.

MILLER WILLIAMS

Thinking about Bill, Dead of AIDS   1989

We did not know the first thing about
how blood surrenders to even the smallest threat
when old allergies turn inside out,

the body rescinding all its normal orders
to all defenders of flesh, betraying the head,   5
pulling its guards back from all its borders.

Thinking of friends afraid to shake your hand,
we think of your hand shaking, your mouth set,
your eyes drained of any reprimand.

Loving, we kissed you, partly to persuade   10
both you and us, seeing what eyes had said,
that we were loving and we were not afraid.

If we had had more, we would have given more.
As it was we stood next to your bed,
stopping, though, to set our smiles at the door.   15

Not because we were less sure at the last.
Only because, not knowing anything yet,
we didn't know what look would hurt you least.

The brutal prose poem "The Colonel," by American poet and activist
Carolyn Forché, is an angry response to the oppression of native rights movements in Central and South America.

CAROLYN FORCHÉ

The Colonel   1978

What you have heard is true. I was in his house. His wife carried a tray of
coffee and sugar. His daughter filed her nails, his son went out for the
night. There were daily papers, pet dogs, a pistol on the cushion beside
him. The moon swung bare on its black cord over the house. On the television was a cop show. It was in English. Broken bottles were embedded   5
in the walls around the house to scoop the kneecaps from a man's legs or
cut his hands to lace. On the windows there were gratings like those in
liquor stores. We had dinner, rack of lamb, good wine, a gold bell was on
the table for calling the maid. The maid brought green mangoes, salt, a
type of bread. I was asked how I enjoyed the country. There was a brief   10
commercial in Spanish. His wife took everything away. There was some
talk then of how difficult it had become to govern. The parrot said hello
on the terrace. The colonel told it to shut up, and pushed himself from
the table. My friend said to me with his eyes: say nothing. The colonel
returned with a sack used to bring groceries home. He spilled many   15
human ears on the table. They were like dried peach halves. There is no
other way to say this. He took one of them in his hands, shook it in our
faces, dropped it into a water glass. It came alive there. I am tired of fooling around he said. As for the rights of anyone, tell your people they can
go fuck themselves. He swept the ears to the floor with his arm and held 20
the last of his wine in the air. Something for your poetry, no? he said.
Some of the ears on the floor caught this scrap of his voice. Some of the
ears on the floor were pressed to the ground.

Although our century has seen remarkable advances in our daily
lives, it has also been darkened by political oppression. This poem by a
Russian poet poignantly describes not only her own protest against the
imprisonment of her son, but also tells us what the poet's role can be in
telling of injustice.

ANNA AKHMATOVA

Instead of a Preface   1917

TRANSLATED BY RICHARD MCKANE

In the terrible years of the Yezhov terror I spent seventeen months
waiting in line outside the prison in Leningrad. One day somebody in the
crowd identified me. Standing behind me was a woman, with lips blue
from the cold, who had, of course, never heard me called by name before.
Now she started out of the torpor common to us all and asked me in a   5
whisper (everyone whispered there):

"Can you describe this?"
And I said: "I can."
Then something like a smile passed fleetingly over what had once
been her face.   10

FACES OF WAR

A subject that has continued to engage the emotions of poets is war. The
earliest literary classic of European culture is the *Iliad,* an epic poem written
several hundred years before the Christian era by the blind Greek poet Homer.
The poem tells the story of the ten-year-long war between the Greeks and the
Trojans. The following group of poems reflect a shared theme: the brutality
and inhumanity of war. Stephen Crane wrote "War Is Kind" about the Ameri-
can Civil War. Thomas Hardy's poem "The Man He Killed" is about the Boer
War between England and the Dutch settlers in South Africa from 1899 to
1902. "Dulce et Decorum Est," by Wilfred Owen, was written in the midst of
World War I, shortly before Owen was killed in the fighting. Randall Jarrell's
"The Death of the Ball Turret Gunner" was written while he was serving in the
U.S. Air Force in England during World War II.

STEPHEN CRANE

War Is Kind   1896

Do not weep, maiden, for war is kind.
Because your lover threw wild hands toward the sky
And the affrighted steed ran on alone,
Do not weep.
War is kind.   5

    Hoarse, booming drums of the regiment,
    Little souls who thirst for fight,
    These men were born to drill and die.
    The unexplained glory flies above them,
    Great is the battle-god, great, and his kingdom—   10
    A field where a thousand corpses lie.

Do not weep, babe, for war is kind
Because your father tumbled in the yellow trenches,
Raged at his breast, gulped and died,
Do not weep.   15
War is kind.

    Swift blazing flag of the regiment,
    Eagle with crest of red and gold,
    These men were born to drill and die.
    Point for them the virtue of slaughter,   20

Make plain to them the excellence of killing
And a field where a thousand corpses lie.

Mother whose heart hung humble as a button
On the bright splendid shroud of your son,
Do not weep.   25
War is kind.

THOMAS HARDY

The Man He Killed   1902

"Had he and I but met
    By some old ancient inn,
We should have sat us down to wet
    Right many a nipperkin!°

"But ranged as infantry,   5
    And staring face to face,
I shot at him as he at me,
    And killed him in his place.

"I shot him dead because—
    Because he was my foe,   10
Just so: my foe of course he was:
    That's clear enough; although

"He thought he'd 'list, perhaps,
    Off-hand-like—just as I—
Was out of work—had sold his traps—   15
    No other reason why.

"Yes; quaint and curious war is!
    You shoot a fellow down
You'd treat, if met where any bar is,
    Or help to half-a-crown."   20

WILFRED OWEN

Dulce et Decorum Est°   1920

Bent double, like old beggars under sacks,
Knock-kneed, coughing like hags, we cursed through sludge,
Till on the haunting flares we turned our backs

---

4. nipperkin: A measure of alcohol less than a half pint.
Dulce et Decorum Est: The Latin phrase in lines 27–28 reads, "It is sweet and proper to die for one's country" (from the Roman poet Horace).

And towards our distant rest began to trudge.
Men marched asleep. Many had lost their boots   5
But limped on, blood-shod. All went lame; all blind;
Drunk with fatigue; deaf even to the hoots
Of tired, outstripped Five-Nines° that dropped behind.

Gas! Gas! Quick, boys!—An ecstasy of fumbling
Fitting the clumsy helmets just in time;   10
But someone still was yelling out and stumbling
And flound'ring like a man in fire or lime . . .
Dim, through the misty panes and thick green light,°
As under a green sea, I saw him drowning.

In all my dreams, before my helpless sight,   15
He plunges at me, guttering, choking, drowning.

If in some smothering dreams you too could pace
Behind the wagon that we flung him in,
And watch the white eyes writhing in his face,
His hanging face, like a devil's sick of sin;   20
If you could hear, at every jolt, the blood
Come gargling from the froth-corrupted lungs,
Obscene as cancer, bitter as the cud
Of vile, incurable sores on innocent tongues,—
My friend,° you would not tell with such high zest   25
To children ardent for some desperate glory,
The old Lie: Dulce et decorum est
Pro patria mori.

RANDALL JARRELL

The Death of the Ball Turret Gunner   1945

From my mother's sleep I fell into the state
And I hunched in its belly till my wet fur froze.
Six miles from earth, loosed from its dream of life,
I woke to black flak and the nightmare fighters.
When I died they washed me out of the turret with a hose.

BLACK CONSCIOUSNESS, BLACK VOICES

Although the poetry written today by a talented generation of African Americans is now a vigorous and vital part of the American cultural mainstream, for long, tragic years black Americans have been the victims of prejudice and

---

8. Five-Nines: German 59 mm artillery shells.   **13. misty . . . light:** Through a gas mask.
25. My friend: The poem is addressed to a poet known for patriotic verse, Jessie Pope (1868–1941).

discrimination. Black writing, beginning with the early poetry of Phillis Wheatley, has reflected the racial situation in the country, and it has also reflected the obvious reality that there have emerged two Americas, one white and one black, with different, though intertwined, histories.

PHILLIS WHEATLEY

On Being Brought from Africa to America   1773

'Twas mercy brought me from my *Pagan* land,
Taught my benighted soul to understand
That there's a God, that there's a *Saviour* too:
Once I redemption neither sought nor knew.

Some view our sable race with scornful eye,
"Their colour is a diabolic die."
Remember, *Christians*, *Negros*, black as *Cain*,°
May be refin'd, and join th'angelic train.

PAUL LAWRENCE DUNBAR

Sympathy   1903

I know what the caged bird feels, alas!
When the sun is bright on the upland slopes;
When the wind stirs soft through the springing grass,
And the river flows like a stream of glass;
When the first bird sings and the first bud opes,   5
And the faint perfume from its chalice steals—
I know what the caged bird feels!

I know why the caged bird beats his wing
Till its blood is red on the cruel bars;
For he must fly back to his perch and cling   10
When he fain would be on the bough a-swing;
And a pain still throbs in the old, old scars
And they pulse again with a keener sting—
I know why he beats his wing!

I know why the caged bird sings, ah me,   15
When his wing is bruised and his bosom sore,
When he beats his bars and would be free;
It is not a carol of joy or glee,

---

7. **black as *Cain*:** In Genesis 4:14, God puts a mark on Cain for having murdered his brother Abel. Some traditions hold that this "mark" is black skin.

But a prayer that he sends from his heart's deep core,
But a plea, that upward to Heaven he flings —   20
I know why the caged bird sings!

ETHERIDGE KNIGHT

The Idea of Ancestry   1968

I

Taped to the wall of my cell are 47 pictures: 47 black
faces: my father, mother, grandmothers (1 dead), grand
fathers (both dead), brothers, sisters, uncles, aunts,
cousins (1st & 2nd), nieces, and nephews. They stare
across the space at me sprawling on my bunk. I know   5
their dark eyes, they know mine. I know their style,
they know mine. I am all of them, they are all of me;
they are farmers, I am a thief, I am me, they are thee.

I have at one time or another been in love with my mother,
1 grandmother, 2 sisters, 2 aunts (I went to the asylum),   10
and 5 cousins. I am now in love with a 7 yr old niece
(she sends me letters written in large block print, and
her picture is the only one that smiles at me).

I have the same name as 1 grandfather, 3 cousins, 3 nephews,
and 1 uncle. The uncle disappeared when he was 15, just took 15
off and caught a freight (they say). He's discussed each year
when the family has a reunion, he causes uneasiness in
the clan, he is an empty space. My father's mother, who is 93
and who keeps the Family Bible with everybody's birth dates
(and death dates) in it, always mentions him. There is no   20
place in her Bible for "whereabouts unknown."

II

Each Fall the graves of my grandfathers call me, the brown
hills and red gullies of mississippi send our their electric
messages, galvanizing my genes. Last yr/ like a salmon quitting
the cold ocean — leaping and bucking up his birthstream/ I   25
hitchhiked my way from L.A. with 16 caps in my pocket and a
monkey on my back, and I almost kicked it with the kinfolks.
I walked barefoot in my grandmother's backyard/ I smelled the old
land and the woods /I sipped cornwhiskey from fruit jars with the men/
I flirted with the women/ I had a ball till the caps ran out   30
and my habit came down. That night I looked at my grandmother
and split/ my guts were screaming for junk/ but I was almost
contented/ I had almost caught up with me.
 The next day in Memphis I cracked a croaker's crib for a fix.

This yr there is a gray stone wall damming my stream, and when   35
the falling leaves stir my genes, I pace my cell or flop on my bunk
and stare at 47 black faces across the space. I am all of them,
they are all of me, I am me, they are thee, and I have no sons
to float in the space between.

ALLEN POLITE

Song   1958

When I sing this song without accompaniment
        I can hear the silence the emptiness
When I sing this song in which the only instrument
        is my voice
                        my voice which comes over the lips   5
            as a man comes out of a desert
                    just near death then near life
        I know why man sang before he talked
            Why he sings before he walks
            Why he hates to be a slave   10
            Why he is singing in the grave
I know what it is to long for
        that which we have never known
            I know why man sang before he talked
            Why he sings before he walks
            Why he hates to be a slave   15
            Why he is singing in the grave
When your voice joins mine, as something coming
        to meet the dead
See we then the genius of man? See him strike the first
instrument?   20
See him paint paradise as bird song?
See him paint wings on loaves of bread?
I know why man sang before he talked
            Why he sings before he walks
            Why he hates to be a slave   25
            Why he is singing in the grave
And when we sing together without effort
        the stops in the greatest organ are like child's play
When we are singing into each others mouths and
hearing   30
        songs
Unison is night changing to day —

I know why man sang before he talked
    Why he sings before he walks
    Why he hates to be a slave
    Why he is singing in the grave

35

AMIRI BARAKA

Legacy

1969

(For Blues People)

In the south, sleeping against
the drugstore, growling under
the trucks and stoves, stumbling
through and over the cluttered eyes
of early mysterious night. Frowning
drunk waving moving a hand or lash.
Dancing kneeling reaching out, letting
a hand rest in shadows. Squatting
to drink or pee. Stretching to climb
pulling themselves onto horses near
where there was sea (the old songs
lead you to believe). Riding out
from this town, to another, where
it is also black. Down a road
where people are asleep. Towards
the moon or the shadows of houses.
Towards the song's pretended sea.

5
10
15

AUDRE LORDE

Hanging Fire

1978

I am fourteen
and my skin has betrayed me
the boy I cannot live without
still sucks his thumb
in secret
how come my knees are
always so ashy
what if I die
before morning
and momma's in the bedroom
with the door closed.

5
10

I have to learn how to dance
in time for the next party
my room is too small for me
suppose I die before graduation   15
they will sing sad melodies
but finally
tell the truth about me
There is nothing I want to do
and too much   20
that has to be done
and momma's in the bedroom
with the door closed.

Nobody even stops to think
about my side of it   25
I should have been on Math Team
my marks were better than his
why do I have to be
the one
wearing braces   30
I have nothing to wear tomorrow
will I live long enough
to grow up
and momma's in the bedroom
with the door closed.   35

DUDLEY RANDALL

Ballad of Birmingham°   1966

(On the bombing of a church in Birmingham, Alabama, 1963)

"Mother dear, may I go downtown
Instead of out to play,
And march the streets of Birmingham
In a Freedom March today?"

"No, baby, no, you may not go,   5
For the dogs are fierce and wild,
And clubs and hoses, guns and jails
Aren't good for a little child."

Birmingham: This poem was written in response to the 1963 bombing of the 16th Street
Baptist Church in Birmingham, Alabama. Four black children perished in the explosion.

"But, mother, I won't be alone.
Other children will go with me,   10
And march the streets of Birmingham
To make our country free."

"No, baby, no, you may not go,
For I fear those guns will fire.
But you may go to church instead   15
And sing in the children's choir."

She has combed and brushed her night-dark hair,
And bathed rose petal sweet,
And drawn white gloves on her small brown hands,
And white shoes on her feet.   20

The mother smiled to know her child
Was in the sacred place,
But that smile was the last smile
To come upon her face.

For when she heard the explosion,   25
Her eyes grew wet and wild.
She raced through the streets of Birmingham
Calling for her child.

She clawed through bits of glass and brick,
Then lifted out a shoe   30
"Oh, here's the shoe my baby wore,
But, baby, where are you?"

LUCILLE CLIFTON

to ms. ann   1994

i will have to forget
your face
when you watched me breaking
in the fields,
missing my children.   5

i will have to forget
your face
when you watched me carry
your husband's
stagnant water.   10

i will have to forget
your face
when you handed me
your house
to make a home,   15

and you never called me sister
then, you never called me sister
and it has only been forever and
i will have to forget your face.

why some people be mad at me sometimes   1987

they ask me to remember
but they want me to remember
their memories
and i keep on remembering
mine.

ISHMAEL REED

The Reactionary Poet   1973

If you are a revolutionary
Then I must be a reactionary
For if you stand for the future
I have no choice but to
Be with the past   5

Bring back suspenders!
Bring back Mom!
Homemade ice cream
Picnics in the park
Flagpole sitting   10
Straw hats
Rent parties
Corn liquor
The banjo
Georgia quilts   15
Krazy Kat
Restock

The syncopation of
Fletcher Henderson
The Kiplingesque lines   20
of James Weldon Johnson
Black Eagle
Mickey Mouse
The Bach Family
Sunday School   25
Even Mayor La Guardia
Who read the comics

Is more appealing than
Your version of
What Lies Ahead   30

In your world of
Tomorrow Humor
Will be locked up and
The key thrown away
The public address system   35
Will pound out headaches
All day
Everybody will wear the same
Funny caps
And the same funny jackets   40
Enchantment will be found
Expendable, charm, a
Luxury
Love and kisses
A crime against the state   45
Duke Ellington will be
Ordered to write more marches
"For the people," naturally

If you are what's coming
I must be what's going.   50

Make it by steamboat
I likes to take it real slow

WOMEN'S CONSCIOUSNESS, WOMEN'S VOICES

It has been characteristic of our long human history that the roles of men
and women, both in the family and in society, have been defined differently,
and there is a tradition of art and writing that has been defined by gender. We
are all familiar with the designation of a story or a poem as "women's writing."
In our modern period women writers have reacted against this categorizing,
and at the same time they have examined it more closely to celebrate its consciousness of the different experience of men and women in so many crucial
aspects of our lives.

MINA LOY

One O'Clock at Night   1931

Though you have never possessed me
I have belonged to you since the beginning of time
And sleepily I sit on your chair beside you
Leaning against your shoulder

And your careless arm across my back gesticulates   5
As your indisputable male voice   roars
Through my brain and my body
Arguing "Dynamic Decomposition"
Of which I understand nothing
Sleepily   10
And the only less male voice of your brother pugilist of the intellect
Booms   as it seems to me   so sleepy
Across an interval of a thousand miles
An interim of a thousand years
But you who make more noise than any man in the world when you clear
    your throat   15
Deafening   wake me
And I catch the thread of the argument
Immediately assuming my personal mental attitude
And cease to be a woman

Beautiful halfhour of being a mere woman   20
The animal woman
Understanding nothing of man
But mastery   and the security of imparted physical heat
Indifferent to cerebral gymnastics
Or regarding them as the self-indulgent play of children   25
Or the thunder of alien gods
But you wake me up
Anyhow   who am I that I should criticize your theories of "Plastic
    Velocity"

"Let us go home   she is tired   and wants to go to bed."

DENISE LEVERTOV

The Mutes   1966

Those groans men use
passing a woman on the street
or on the steps of the subway

to tell her she is a female
and their flesh knows it,   5

are they a sort of tune,
an ugly enough song, sung
by a bird with a slit tongue

but meant for music?

Or are they the muffled roaring   10
of deafmutes trapped in a building that is
slowly filling with smoke?

Perhaps both.

Such men most often
look as if groan were all they could do,   15
yet a woman, in spite of herself,

knows it's a tribute:
if she were lacking all grace
they'd pass her in silence:

so it's not only to say she's   20
a warm hole. It's a word

in grief-language, nothing to do with
primitive, not an ur-language;
language stricken, sickened, cast down

in decrepitude. She wants to   25
throw the tribute away, dis-
gusted, and can't,

it goes on buzzing in her ear,
it changes the pace of her walk,
the torn posters in echoing corridors   30

spell it out, it
quakes and gnashes as the train comes in.
Her pulse sullenly

had picked up speed,
but the cars slow down and   35
jar to a stop while her understanding

keeps on translating:
"Life after life after life goes by

without poetry,
without seemliness,   40
without love."

LOUISE GLÜCK

First Memory   1990

Long ago, I was wounded. I lived
to revenge myself
against my father, not
for what he was —
for what I was: from the beginning of time,
in childhood, I thought
that pain meant
I was not loved.
It meant I loved.

ALICIA SUSKIN OSTRIKER

Wrinkly Lady Dancer   1974

Going to be an old wrinkly lady
Going to be one of those frail rag people
Going to have withered hands and be
Puzzled to tears crossing the street

Hobble cautiously onto buses   5
Like a withery fruit
And quite silently sitting in this lurching bus
The avenues coming by

Some other passengers gaze at me
Clutching my cane and my newspaper   10
Seemingly protectively, but I will really be thinking about
The afternoon I danced naked with you
The afternoon I danced naked with you
The afternoon! I danced! Naked with you!

The Change   1980

Happening now! it is happening
now! even while, after these
gray March weeks—
when every Saturday you drive
out of town into the country   5
to take your daughter to her riding lesson
and along the thin curving road you peer
into the brown stuff—
still tangled, bare, nothing
beginning   10

Nothing beginning, the mud,
the vines, the corpse-like trees
and their floor of sodden leaves unaltered,
oh, you would like to heave
the steering wheel from its socket   15
or tear your own heart out, exasperated—
that it should freeze and thaw,
then freeze again, and that
no buds have burst, sticky,
deep red, from their twigs—   20

You want to say it to your daughter.
You want to tell her also how the gray
beeches, ashes and oaks here on Cherry Hill Road
on the way to her riding school
feel the same, although they cannot   25

rip themselves up by the roots, or run about raving,
or take any action whatever, and are almost dead
with their wish to be alive,
to suck water, to send force through their fibers,
and to change! to change!   30

Your daughter, surly, unconversational,
a house locking its doors against you,
pulls away
when you touch her shoulder, looks out the window.

You are too old. You remind her of frozen mud.   35
Nevertheless it is happening, the planet
is swimming toward the sun
like a woman with naked breasts. She cannot help it.
Can you sense, under the ground, the great melting?

MARILYN CHIN

How I Got That Name   1994

an essay on assimilation

I am Marilyn Mei Ling Chin.
Oh, how I love the resoluteness
of that first person singular
followed by that stalwart indicative
of "be," without the uncertain i-n-g   5
of "becoming." Of course,
the name had been changed
somewhere between Angel Island and the sea,
when my father the paperson
in the late 1950s   10
obsessed with a bombshell blonde
transliterated "Mei Ling" to "Marilyn."
And nobody dared question
his initial impulse — for we all know
lust drove men to greatness,   15
not goodness, not decency.
And there I was, a wayward pink baby,
named after some tragic white woman
swollen with gin and Nembutal.
My mother couldn't pronounce the "r."   20
She dubbed me "Numba one female offshoot"
for brevity: henceforth, she will live and die
in sublime ignorance, flanked
by loving children and the "kitchen deity."

While my father dithers,   25
a tomcat in Hong Kong trash—
a gambler, a petty thug,
who bought a chain of chopsuey joints
in Piss River, Oregon,
with bootlegged Gucci cash.   30
Nobody dared question his integrity given
his nice, devout daughters
and his bright, industrious sons
as if filial piety were the standard
by which all earthly men were measured.   35

Oh, how trustworthy our daughters,
how thrifty our sons!
How we've managed to fool the experts
in education, statistics and demography—
We're not very creative but not adverse to rote-learning.   40
Indeed, they can *use* us.
But the "Model Minority"° is a tease.
We know you are watching now,
so we refuse to give you any!
Oh, bamboo shoots, bamboo shoots!   45
The further west we go, we'll hit east;
the deeper down we dig, we'll find China.
History has turned its stomach
on a black polluted beach—
where life doesn't hinge   50
on that red, red wheelbarrow,°
but whether or not our new lover
in the final episode of "Santa Barbara"°
will lean over a scented candle
and call us a "bitch."   55
Oh God, where have we gone wrong?
We have no inner resources!

Then, one redolent spring morning
the Great Patriarch Chin
peered down from his kiosk in heaven   60
and saw that his descendants were ugly.
One had a squarish head and a nose without a bridge.
Another's profile—long and knobbed as a gourd.
A third, the sad, brutish one

---

42. **Model Minority:** Asian Americans have been stereotyped as a well-behaved, industrious "model minority."   51. **red, red wheelbarrow:** A reference to William Carlos Williams's brief modernist poem "The Red Wheelbarrow" (see p. 771 in this text).
53. **Santa Barbara:** Prime-time television "soap opera" about wealthy, glamorous characters living in the California seaside city.

may never, never marry.   65
And I, his least favorite—
"not quite boiled, not quite cooked,"
a plump pomfret° simmering in my juices—
too listless to fight for my people's destiny.
"To kill without resistance is not slaughter"   70
says the proverb. So, I wait for imminent death.
The fact that this death is also metaphorical
is testament to my lethargy.

So here lies Marilyn Mei Ling Chin,
married once, twice to so-and-so, a Lee and a Wong,   75
granddaughter of Jack "the patriarch"
and the brooding Suilin Fong,
daughter of the virtuous Yuet Kuen Wong
and G. G. Chin the infamous,
sister of a dozen, cousin of a million,   80
survived by everybody and forgotten by all.
She was neither black nor white,
neither cherished nor vanquished,
just another squatter in her own bamboo grove
minding her poetry—   85
when one day heaven was unmerciful,
and a chasm opened where she stood.
Like the jowls of a mighty white whale,
or the jaws of a metaphysical Godzilla,
it swallowed her whole.   90
She did not flinch nor writhe,
nor fret about the afterlife,
but stayed! Solid as wood, happily
a little gnawed, tattered, mesmerized
by all that was lavished upon her   95
and all that was taken away!

SUSAN YUZNA

On the Way to Lolo Hot Springs   1995

If I wrapped myself in some animal's skin,
wore one silver earring
and smoked opium,
it would embarrass him. If I wandered
over the desert, whirling   5

---

68. pomfret: A spiny, edible fish.

and whirling until my spirit broke through
the veil of the actual, he would say
he wants a *traditional* mother, lingering
over the word with a nostalgia
incredible for his ten years.   10

He finds the trees boring.
The mountains don't move him,
nor does my account of Lewis and Clark
threading their way through this canyon.
He is thoroughly engaged   15
in moving a minuscule blue hedgehog
over a two-inch screen
by pushing buttons, collecting
rings of power, exploding boxes.
The desert would be quiet.   20

In the photograph
I keep thinking of, a Pakistani woman
leans against the brick wall
opposite a saint's tomb, her long, black hair
splayed over the crumbling surface   25
as if electrified. Thin as sin, and deep
into the trance, while a child
beside her sleeps, his round rump
barely covered. I could live
on locusts and honey.   30

THE LIVING EARTH

For the thousands of years that poetry has been part of our human expression, writers have taken nature as one of their subjects. In recent decades,
however, it has become increasingly evident that the beauty and the bounty of
nature, which we have for so long taken for granted, is seriously threatened by
exploitation and ever-expanding human populations. In recent poetry written
in response to the natural world, there is a consciousness that what the poet sees
today perhaps will be the last we will experience of this vision.

PRIMO LEVI

Almanac   1987

TRANSLATED FROM THE ITALIAN BY RUTH FELDMAN

The indifferent rivers
Will keep on flowing to the sea
Or ruinously overflowing dikes,
Ancient handiwork of determined men.

The glaciers will continue to grate,   5
Smoothing what's under them
Or suddenly fall headlong,
Cutting short fir trees' lives.
The sea, captive between
Two continents, will go on struggling,   10
Always miserly with its riches.
Sun stars planets and comets
Will continue on their course.
Earth too will fear the immutable
Laws of the universe.   15
Not us. We, rebellious progeny
With great brainpower, little sense,
Will destroy, defile
Always more feverishly.
Very soon we'll extend the desert   20
Into the Amazon forests,
Into the living heart of our cities,
Into our very hearts.

JAMES DICKEY

The Dusk of Horses   1962

Right under their noses, the green
Of the field is paling away
Because of something fallen from the sky.

They see this, and put down
Their long heads deeper in grass   5
That only just escapes reflecting them

As the dream of a millpond would.
The color green flees over the grass
Like an insect, following the red sun over

The next hill. The grass is white.   10
There is no cloud so dark and white at once;
There is no pool at dawn that deepens

Their faces and thirsts as this does.
Now they are feeding on solid
Cloud, and, one by one,   15

With nails as silent as stars among the wood
Hewed down years ago and now rotten,

Now if they lean, they come
On wood on any side. Not touching it, they sleep.
No beast ever lived who understood   20

What happened among the sun's fields,
Or cared why the color of grass
Fled over the hill while he stumbled,

Led by the halter to sleep
On his four taxed, worthy legs.   25
Each thinks he awakens where

The sun is black on the rooftop,
That the green is dancing in the next pasture,
And that the way to sleep

In a cloud, or in a risen lake,   30
Is to walk as though he were still
In the drained field standing, head down,

To pretend to sleep when led,
And thus to go under the ancient white
Of the meadow, as green goes   35

And whiteness comes up through his face
Holding stars and rotten rafters,
Quiet, fragrant, and relieved.

JIM HARRISON

Northern Michigan   1965

On this back road the land
has the juice taken out of it:

stump fences surround nothing
worth their tearing down

by a deserted filling station   5
a Veedol sign, the rusted hulk

of a Frazer, "live bait"
on battered tin.

        A barn
with half a tobacco ad   10
owns the greenness of a manure
pile

a half-moon on a privy door
a rope swinging from an elm. A

collapsed henhouse, a pump   15
with the handle up

the orchard with wild tangled branches.

In the far corner of the pasture,
in the shadow of the woodlot

a herd of twenty deer: 20
             three bucks
are showing off—
they jump in turn across the fence,
flanks arch and twist to get higher
in the twilight   25
as the last light filters
through the woods.

SAMUEL CHARTERS

Hopi Corn at Walpi Mesa   1969

I wouldn't have planted the corn
               like that—
in crumbling holes dug into
the tan hillside,
        among stones dusty with their   5
rough handling by the
           sand's fingers.
I wouldn't have heaped the sticks
          and bits of leaf like that—
around the slight green shoots   10
of corn as they warily split up
        through the rind of softening
kernel left to mould
        in the heated earth.
I wouldn't have shielded the corn   15
        with those flapping shreds
of cloth whose shadows toss in a
nervous dance in the bare breath
        of the sunset
on the dried, hard earth.   20
The corn I planted
        wouldn't have grown.

W. S. MERWIN

Birds Waking   1956

I went out at daybreak and stood on Primrose Hill.
It was April: a white haze over the hills of Surrey
Over the green haze of the hills above the dark green

Of the park trees, and over it all the light came up clear,
The sky like deep porcelain paling and paling,   5
With everywhere under it the faces of the buildings
Where the city slept, gleaming white and quiet,
St Paul's and the water tower taking the gentle gold.
And from the hill chestnuts and the park trees
There was such a clamour rose as the birds woke,   10
Such uncontainable tempest of whirled
Singing flung upward and upward into the new light,
Increasing still as the birds themselves rose
From the black trees and whirled in a rising cloud,
Flakes and water-spouts and hurled seas and continents of them   15
Rising, dissolving, streamering out, always
Louder and louder singing, shrieking, laughing.
Sometimes one would break from the cloud but from the song never,
And would beat past my ear dinning his deafening note.
I thought I had never known the wind   20
Of joy to be so shrill, so unanswerable,
With such clouds of winged song at its disposal, and I thought
Oh Voice that my demand is the newest name for,
There are many ways we may end, and one we must,
Whether burning, or the utter cold descending in darkness,   25
Explosion of our own devising, collision of planets, all
Violent, however silent they at last may seem;
Oh let it be by this violence, then, let it be now,
Now when in their sleep, unhearing, unknowing,
Most faces must be closest to innocence,   30
When the light moves unhesitating to fill the sky with clearness
And no dissent could be heard above the din of its welcome,
Let the great globe well up and dissolve like its last birds,
With the bursting roar and uprush of song!

GARY SNYDER

Ripples on the Surface   1992

"Ripples on the surface of the water
were silver salmon passing under — different
from the sorts of ripples caused by breezes"

A scudding plume on the wave —
a humpback whale is   5
breaking out in air up
gulping herring
     —Nature not a book, but a *performance*, a
high old culture

Ever-fresh events   10
scraped out, rubbed out, and used, used, again —
the braided channels of the rivers
hidden under fields of grass —

The vast wild.
    the house, alone.   15
the little house in the wild,
    the wild in the house.

both forgotten.

    No nature.

Both together, one big empty house.   20

13.

Poet to Poet

We're all writing the same poem.
— ROBERT DUNCAN

Perhaps because poetry is written from emotions that lie so close to the surface of the skin, poets are very conscious of each other's work, and they respond strongly to other poetry. Poets are their own best audience. Adrienne Rich has described her own experience of poetry as a child:

> I thought that the poets in the anthologies were the only real poets, that their being in the anthologies was proof of this, though some were classified as "great" and others as "minor." I owed much to these anthologies: *Silver Pennies;* the constant outflow of volumes edited by Louis Untermeyer; *The Cambridge Book of Poetry for Children;* Palgrave's *Golden Treasury;* the *Oxford Book of English Verse.* . . . I still believed that poets were inspired by some transcendental authority and spoke from some extraordinary height.

Margaret Atwood has described her emotions when she heard Rich read from her book *Diving into the Wreck* (1973): "When I first heard the author read from it, I felt as though the top of my head was being attacked, sometimes with an ice pick, sometimes with a blunter instrument: a hatchet or a hammer." Atwood, in *her* turn, reminds the reader of Emily Dickinson's description of how she knew something she read was poetry: "If I feel physically as if the top of my head were taken off, I know that it is poetry."

You will find in your reading that it is not only modern poets who are so excited by the words of another poet. When a friend introduced John Keats to the translation of Homer by the Elizabethan poet George Chapman, they stayed up all night reading to each other. As Keats walked home at dawn he was already composing his sonnet, "On First Looking into Chapman's Homer." The poem was finished and reached his friend by the first mail, only a few hours later.

JOHN KEATS

On First Looking into Chapman's Homer   1816

Much have I travell'd in the realms of gold,
   And many goodly states and kingdoms seen;
   Round many western islands have I been
Which bards in fealty to Apollo° hold.
Oft of one wide expanse had I been told   5
   That deep-browed Homer ruled as his demesne;°
   Yet never did I breathe its pure serene°
Till I heard Chapman° speak out loud and bold:
Then felt I like some watcher of the skies
   When a new planet swims into his ken;   10
Or like stout Cortez° when with eagle eyes
   He star'd at the Pacific — and all his men
Look'd at each other with a wild surmise —
   Silent upon a peak in Darien.

In his mood of exhilaration, Keats made a mistake in the name of the Spanish explorer who first saw the Pacific (it was Balboa and not "Cortez"), but critics have never felt that this diminishes the effect of his poem.

Many poets also have poets as friends, they translate one another's poems from other languages, they read their poems to each other, they send each other copies of new manuscripts, they publish magazines of each other's poetry. In the sense that living writers are part of a community, they also are an important influence on each other. To speak of a poem from an earlier generation "influencing" a younger writer, however, is more complicated. In a discussion of young painters that applies equally well to young poets, art critic Michael Baxadall has pointed out that to say a writer or a text from an earlier generation "influences" a younger writer is misleading, since a poem written by a poet who is no longer living cannot "do" anything. It is the younger writer who *does* something. Baxadall drew up a list of the things that the younger writer can do. If the young writer is moved to respond to something by an older writer, the younger — in just the same way that a young painter responds to the work of an older artist — can

> draw on, resort to, avail oneself of, appropriate from, have recourse to, adapt, misunderstand, refer to, pick up, take on, engage with, react to, quote, differentiate oneself from, assimilate oneself to, assimilate, align oneself with, copy, address, paraphrase, absorb, make a variation on,

---

4. Apollo: Greek god of poetry. **6. demesne:** Domain. **7. serene:** Atmosphere.
8. Chapman: George Chapman (c. 1560–1634), Elizabethan poet whose translations of Homer's Greek epics *Iliad* and *Odyssey* Keats found superior to the eighteenth-century translations with which he was familiar. **11. Cortez:** Keats mistakenly identifies Hernando Cortés, not Vasco Núñez de Balboa, as the first European to view the Pacific Ocean from Darien, a peak in Panama.

revive, continue, remodel, ape, emulate, travesty, parody, extract from, distort, attend to, resist, simplify, reconstitute, elaborate on, develop, face up to, master, subvert, perpetuate, reduce, promote, respond to, transform, tackle. . . . [E]veryone will be able to think of others.

As we have seen in Keats's response to Homer, whichever way a young poet responds to the work of another poet, the result will be poetry.

For women readers today, the early centuries of poetry in English can present a difficult hurdle. Because of social attitudes, it is not until the nineteenth century that poetry written by women begins to play an important role in the poetic tradition. However, as critic Jan Montefiore shows us in her analysis of a sonnet by Edna St. Vincent Millay, an American poet of the 1920s, women poets did not feel that they were entirely excluded from this tradition, and they did not hesitate to take it and mold it for their own work. Montefiore writes,

> Millay's best-known sequence of love sonnets, *Fatal Interview*, depends on an individual voice speaking with a poetic vocabulary (thematic as well as lexical) which is drawn from Elizabethan poetry as reread by the Romantics, as in this excerpt from sonnet VIII:
>
> > Yet in an hour to come, disdainful dust,
> > You shall be bowed and brought to bed with me.
> > While the blood roars, or when the blood is rust
> > About a broken engine, this shall be.
> > If not today, then later; if not here,
> > On the green grass, with sighing and delight,
> > Then under it, all in good time, my dear,
> > We shall be laid together in the night.
>
> The poet's confidence and ease in handling the sonnet form are immediately apparent; she slides effortlessly from the twentieth-century image of "rust / About a broken engine" to the "timeless" line "On the green grass, with sighing and delight," using the associative rhymes "rust" and "dust" and the emphatic alliteration of "bowed and brought to bed" with an effect of relish, not cliché. Her appropriation of literary tradition is equally apparent in the way that the counterposing of love and death, the brevity of human life and the sleep of the grave, recalls Shakespeare, Marvell, and Catullus in a *cantabile* lyricism formed on Yeats. This is not an allusive poem; rather its themes are smoothed with poetic handling, and it is written in a style which assumes that poetry is timeless.

The term *allusive* that Montefiore uses, which means to allude or refer to some other writing, suggests one of the ways in which a poet responds to another poem. It is one of several ways that are part of the poet's means, the tools a poet uses to make a poem. Here are some of the most common you will find in your reading.

QUOTATION

Many poets quote directly or indirectly from other poems. Sometimes the use of someone else's words is indicated by quotation marks, but more often the quotation is left without any marks to indicate it. The writer wants to leave it to the reader, whether or not the different voice in the poem is heard. One of the uses of quotation that you will find is to give the poem a more general meaning or to present the poem in a clearer historical perspective. The California poet Robert Duncan used a quote from the Greek poet Pindar as the title and the source of ideas for one of his major poems, *A Poem Beginning with a Line by Pindar*. The line from Pindar that begins the poem is "The light foot hears you and the brightness begins." In the poem, Duncan alludes to Walt Whitman's elegy on the death of Lincoln, *When Lilacs Last in the Dooryard Bloom'd:*

> What
> if lilacs last in *this* dooryard bloomd?

A few lines later he quotes directly from Whitman, using quotation marks:

> How sad "amid lanes and through old woods"
> echoes Whitman's love for Lincoln!

Marianne Moore used many quotations in her poetry. Often it was material from magazine articles or books she was reading, or phrases that she took from other poets or writers, sometimes slightly altering them. Consider these lines from the poem "The Student":

> . . . With us, a
> school—like the singing tree of which
> the leaves were mouths singing in concert
> is both a tree of knowledge
> and of liberty. . . .

Moore tells us in a note to the poem that she adapted the sentence "Each leaf was a mouth, and every leaf joined in concert" from the book *The Arabian Nights*.

A poet who was influenced by Moore, Amy Clampitt includes a note on the line in her poem "The Outer Bar" that describes the waves striking the sandbar:

> chain-gang archangels that in their prismatic
> frenzy fall, gall and gash the daylight. . . .

Clampitt's note points out that " 'fall, gall and gash the daylight' . . . derives, of course, from 'The Windhover' by Gerard Manley Hopkins."

Quotation is also used to "engage with," if we use another of the ways younger writers respond to other poems that we listed a few paragraphs ago. In the opening lines of her poem "the closing of the south park road," Tobey Hiller uses a quotation from Emily Dickinson:

> the closing of the south park road
>
> happens every year between Thanksgiving and Christmas
> just when the light grows lucid, forgiving nothing and
> disappearing *into beauty,*
> as Emily says

on these days the air over the water opens into a hard wise body
lying low and immortal over everything it loves.

In the same way, Langston Hughes uses the last line from the song "Dixie"
for a bitter, ironic comment on racism in "Song for a Dark Girl" (p. 909):

> Way Down South in Dixie
> (Break the heart of me)
> They hung my black young lover
> To a cross roads tree.

> Way Down South in Dixie
> (Bruised body high in air)
> I asked the white Lord Jesus
> What was the use of prayer.

As the critic Helen Vendler writes, "All cultural production comes about
from constant interchanges of past works and ideas with current ones."

PARAPHRASE

Another way that a poet may use another poet's words is to **paraphrase** a
line or a stanza. The denotative meaning of paraphrase is "to render freely, or
amplify, a passage, or express its sense in other words." In his poem "Journey
of the Magi," T. S. Eliot paraphrased a section from a sermon by the early English religious writer Lancelot Andrewes. This is the section from Andrewes's
"Nativity Sermon" XV:

> It was no summer progress. A cold coming they had of it at this time of
> the year, just the worst time of the year to take a journey, and specially a
> long journey in. The ways deep, the weather sharp, the days short, the
> sun furthest off, *in solstitio brumali,* "the very dead of winter."

This is Eliot's paraphrase, which he sets off with quotation marks to show that
there is a source for the lines:

> "A cold coming we had of it,
> Just the worst time of the year
> For a journey, and such a long journey:
> The ways deep and the weather sharp,
> The very dead of winter."

Eliot's poems were often a maze of unidentified paraphrases and translations.
He felt that this was one way to respond to the traditions behind his poetry.
As he wrote in an essay on Elizabethan drama, "One of the surest tests is the
way in which a poet borrows. Immature poets imitate; mature poets steal; bad
poets deface what they take; and good poets make it into something better, or at
least something different." You should also read the excerpt from Eliot's essay
"Tradition and the Individual Talent" in Chapter 16, Commentaries on Poetry
and Poets.

IMITATION

At some point in their struggle to find their own voice, young writers usually try every form of traditional poetry. Sometimes in their mature work they will casually begin to imitate the work of another poet or another poetic style. The American poet James Merrill was very skillful at slipping in and out of a wide range of poetic voices. Often he used rhyme and near rhyme for groups of lines within his poems. As an example, in his long poem *Coda: The Higher Keys,* in addition to a crowd of allusions to other writers and other poems, his elegant diction and perfect rhyme in lines 120–28 suggest that the setting of the poem is an eighteenth-century English ballroom:

> . . . A splendor
> Across lawns meets, in Sandover's tall time —
> Dappled mirrors, its own eye. Should rhyme
> Calling to rhyme awaken the odd snore,
> No harm done. I shall study to ignore
> Looks that more boldly with each session yearn
> Toward the buffet where steaming silver urn,
> Cucumber sandwiches, rum punch, fudge laced
> With hashish cater to whatever taste.

PARODY

There is a saying that "imitation is the sincerest form of flattery," and **parody** achieves the same result, by paying an indirect tribute to the popularity of the poet whose work is the subject of the parody. The denotative meaning of parody is "a composition in which an author's characteristics are humorously imitated." Parodies have been written of almost every well-known writer, though they often are more malicious than humorous. Here is one written in the 1920s by Hugh Kingsmill that is humorous. The writer being parodied is A. E. Housman.

HUGH KINGSMILL

What, Still Alive at Twenty-Two?   1920

> What, still alive at twenty-two,
> A clean, upstanding chap like you?
> Sure, if your throat 'tis hard to slit,
> Slit your girl's, and swing for it.
>
> Like enough, you won't be glad   5
> When they come to hang you, lad:
> But bacon's not the only thing
> That's cured by hanging from a string.

So, when the spilt ink of the night
Spreads o'er the blotting-pad of light,
Lads whose job is still to do
Shall whet their knives, and think of you.

10

ALLUSION

The denotative meaning of **allusion**—"to allude to"—means to "refer indirectly to something presumably known to the listener or reader." It is different from quotation because it is indirect. If you allude to something, you name it, or suggest it, and readers add their own understanding of the context. In his poem "The Love Song of J. Alfred Prufrock," T. S. Eliot alludes to Shakespeare with the line "I know the voices dying with a dying fall." Shakespeare's phrase, from *Twelfth Night,* is "If music be the food of love, play on. . . . That strain again! It had a dying fall." In act 2, scene 2 of *Hamlet,* Shakespeare alludes to the *Iliad* in Hamlet's soliloquy. After listening to one of the players begin to weep as he described the grief of Hecuba, Queen of Troy, at the death of her husband, Priam, Hamlet bursts out,

> For Hecuba!
> What's Hecuba to him, or he to Hecuba,
> That he should weep for her?

Matthew Arnold, in his poem "Dover Beach" (p. 831), alludes to the Greek dramatist Sophocles when he describes the eternal note of sadness he hears in the sea:

> Sophocles long ago
> Heard it on the Aegean . . .

In the titles of her poems, Adrienne Rich often alludes to other poems and writers. The title "The Demon Lover" is a phrase from Samuel Taylor Coleridge's "Kubla Khan." "A Valediction Forbidding Mourning" is also the title of a poem by John Donne, and "When We Dead Awaken" is the title of the last play by the Norwegian playwright Henrik Ibsen.

In our discussion of quotation, we have already read some examples of allusion. In your reading you will find many other poets who use allusion to develop the themes or the language of their poetry.

ADDRESS AND TRIBUTE

Another of the ways poets respond to other poets is to address them directly, and there is a long tradition of poetry written as a tribute from one writer to another. A good example is the poem "A Pact," by the then-young American poet Ezra Pound, addressing the classic older American poet Walt Whitman.

EZRA POUND

A Pact 1913

I made a pact with you, Walt Whitman—
I have detested you long enough.
I come to you as a grown child
who has had a pig-headed father;
I am old enough now to make friends.
It was you that broke the new wood,
Now is the time for carving.
We have one sap and one root—
Let there be commerce between us.

Often the response to the other poet is a way of paying tribute to the other writer's work. In his poem "A Supermarket in California," Allen Ginsberg also addresses Walt Whitman, paying him an affectionate tribute.

ALLEN GINSBERG

A Supermarket in California 1956

What thoughts I have of you tonight, Walt Whitman, for I walked down the sidestreets under the trees with a headache self-conscious looking at the full moon.

In my hungry fatigue, and shopping for images, I went into the neon fruit supermarket, dreaming of your enumerations! 5

What peaches and what penumbras! Whole families shopping at night! Aisles full of husbands! Wives in the avocados, babies in the tomatoes!—and you, García Lorca, what were you doing down by the watermelons!

I saw you, Walt Whitman, childless, lonely old grubber, poking among the meats in the refrigerator and eyeing the grocery boys. 10

I heard you asking questions of each: Who killed the pork chops? What price bananas? Are you my Angel?

I wandered in and out of the brilliant stacks of cans following you, and followed in my imagination by the store detective.

We strode down the open corridors together in our solitary fancy tasting 15 artichokes, possessing every frozen delicacy, and never passing the cashier.

Where are we going, Walt Whitman? The doors close in an hour. Which way does your beard point tonight?

(I touch your book and dream of our odyssey in the supermarket and feel absurd.) 20

Will we walk all night through solitary streets? The trees add shade to shade, lights out in the houses, we'll both be lonely.

Will we stroll dreaming of the lost America of love past blue automobiles in driveways, home to our silent cottage?

Ah, dear father, graybeard, lonely old courage-teacher, what America did   25
you have when Charon° quit poling his ferry and you got out on a smoking bank and stood watching the boat disappear on the black waters of Lethe°?

Berkeley, 1955

The García Lorca alluded to in the poem is the Spanish poet who was murdered by the Fascists during the Spanish Civil War.

A tribute to another poet can also be casual and amusing. In his poem "Oatmeal," Galway Kinnell imagines that he is eating oatmeal with John Keats, and this gives him a chance to talk about a problem with the text of one of Keats's best-known poems. Kinnell's reference to Patrick Kavanagh in the final line is an inside joke for readers who may recognize the Irish writer whose best-known poem is titled "The Great Hunger."

GALWAY KINNELL

Oatmeal   1990

I eat oatmeal for breakfast.
I make it on the hot plate and put skimmed milk on it.
I eat it alone.
I am aware it is not good to eat oatmeal alone.
Its consistency is such that it is better for your mental health if somebody
    eats it with you.   5
That is why I often think up an imaginary companion to have breakfast
    with.
Possibly it is even worse to eat oatmeal with an imaginary companion.
Nevertheless, yesterday morning, I ate my oatmeal — porridge, as he
    called it — with John Keats.
Keats said I was absolutely right to invite him: due to its glutinous tex-
    ture, gluey lumpishness, hint of slime, and unusual willingness to dis-
    integrate, oatmeal must never be eaten alone.
He said that in his opinion, however, it is perfectly OK to eat it with an
    imaginary companion,   10
and he himself had enjoyed memorable porridges with Edmund Spenser
    and John Milton.
Even if eating oatmeal with an imaginary companion is not as wholesome
    as Keats claims, still, you can learn something from it.

---

26. Charon: Greek mythological figure who ferries the souls of the dead over the Styx
River.   **27. Lethe:** River in Hades whose waters cause drinkers to forget their pasts.

Yesterday morning, for instance, Keats told me about writing the "Ode
  to a Nightingale."
He had a heck of a time finishing it—those were his words—"Oi 'ad a
  'eck of a toime," he said, more or less, speaking through his porridge.
He wrote it quickly, on scraps of paper, which he then stuck in his pocket, 15
but when he got home he couldn't figure out the order of the stanzas, and
  he and a friend spread the papers on a table, and they made some sense
  of them, but he isn't sure to this day if they got it right.
An entire stanza may have slipped into the lining of his jacket through a
  hole in the pocket.
He still wonders about the occasional sense of drift between stanzas,
and the way here and there a line will go into the configuration of a
  Moslem at prayer, then raise itself up and peer about, and then lay
  itself down slightly off the mark, causing the poem to move forward
  with God's reckless wobble.
He said someone told him that later in life Wordsworth heard about the
  scraps of paper on the table, and tried shuffling some stanzas of his
  own, but only made matters worse.   20
I would not have known about any of this but for my reluctance to eat
  oatmeal alone.
When breakfast was over, John recited "To Autumn."
He recited it slowly, with much feeling, and he articulated the words
  lovingly, and his odd accent sounded sweet.
He didn't offer the story of writing "To Autumn," I doubt if there is
  much of one.
But he did say the sight of a just-harvested oat field got him started on it, 25
and two of the lines, "For Summer has o'er-brimmed their clammy cells"
  and "Thou watchest the last oozings hours by hours," came to him
  while eating oatmeal alone.
I can see him—drawing a spoon through the stuff, gazing into the glimmering furrows, muttering—and it occurs to me:
maybe there is no sublime; only the shining of the amnion's tatters.
For supper tonight I am going to have a baked potato left over from
  lunch.
I am aware that a leftover baked potato is damp, slippery, and simultaneously gummy and crumbly,   30
and therefore I'm going to invite Patrick Kavanagh to join me.

COMMENTARIES *Marilyn Chin, "On the Canon," page 970; T. S. Eliot, From
"Tradition and the Individual Talent," page 972.*

14.

Reading, Thinking, and Writing about Poetry

> It is difficult
> to get the news from poems
> yet men die miserably every day
> for lack
> of what is found there.
> — WILLIAM CARLOS WILLIAMS, from
> "Asphodel, That Greeny Flower"

READING POETRY

Perhaps it is because poetry *looks* different on the page, or perhaps it is because poetry sometimes wears its heart on its sleeve, but for many readers the experience of reading a poem seems different from reading a short story or a play. It is easy to be put off by the formal arrangement of lines and verses and by language that describes private emotions and hidden dreams. Reading poetry, however, is an experience very similar to reading anything else. You read a poem for what you will find there, for what it tells you about yourself, your life, your world. Then you read it a second time for the pleasure you find in the way the poet uses words.

In Chapter 7, "What Is a Poem?," you learned that it will help you to understand a poem if you can separate it into two parts as you read it over. First read the poem for what it is about, its subject and its theme; then read it to appreciate further the skill and imagination the poet has used in presenting you with this theme.

Even if you are not entirely sure that you understand everything in the poem in your first reading, you can be struck by the writer's skill. If we take a very short poem as an example, you can see that it is often the poet's ability to choose one thing out of the mass of small details that brings a poem to life. Here is a haiku by the Japanese poet Buson quoted by the American writer Jack Kerouac in his introduction to his own "Western Haikus":

> The nightingale is singing,
> Its small mouth
> open.

The description "Its small mouth / open" suggests the nightingale's song so simply and yet so vividly that the group of three short lines surrounded by the white space on the page seems to reverberate like the nightingale song itself in your imagination. Other poems can suggest an emotional situation so clearly and with such intensity that you find the words stay in your memory, even if you could not write them down exactly if you were asked. This short English medieval lyric has been part of our emotional storehouse for more than four hundred years:

> Western wind, when wilt thou blow,
> The small rain down can rain?
> Christ, if my love were in my arms,
> And I in my bed again!

You do not have to be told to read poems like these more than once. Their appeal to your feelings is immediate and unforgettable. The skill of the author has been in finding the small moment that suggests the poem's theme—the wonder of experiencing nature in Buson's haiku, and the joy of love in the medieval lyric.

Longer poems can be more difficult for the reader. Sometimes the language is unfamiliar; sometimes the theme is not clear at first reading. The general rule is to read the poem straight through to the end, even if you are unsure of the meaning of all the words or phrases the first time around. Inexperienced readers often stop after just a few lines if they begin to feel confused by what the poet appears to be saying.

If this happens, you should disregard your sense that you have lost your bearings in the poem and continue reading until you have finished it. Often the whole poem will clarify the meaning of the early images or lines. Unless you give yourself the opportunity to read the entire poem, you will not have a fair chance to find out what it is saying. For example, when you begin reading the poem "since feeling is first" (1926) by the American writer e. e. cummings, you might stumble on the word *syntax* or the phrase "syntax of things" in the third line of the poem. Do not stop reading to reach for a dictionary to help you puzzle out what the poem means by "syntax." Just continue on to the end of the poem. Reach for the dictionary, if necessary, *after* you have read it all the way through the first time.

> since feeling is first
> who pays any attention
> to the syntax of things
> will never wholly kiss you;
>
> wholly to be a fool   5
> while Spring is in the world
>
> my blood approves,
> and kisses are a better fate
> than wisdom
> lady i swear by all flowers. Don't cry   10
> —the best gesture of my brain is less than
> your eyelids' flutter which says

> we are for each other:then
> laugh,leaning back in my arms
> for life's not a paragraph   15
>
> And death i think is no parenthesis

When you go back to the beginning of the poem to give it a second read-ing, you will find that the last two lines illuminate the meaning of the word *syn-tax* that might have given you trouble on your first reading. The poet is using literary terms in a playful manner to write a love poem, making the point that life is different from literature and should be lived fully and instinctively while there is still time. The speaker in the poem is urging his lady to follow the impulse of her heart, which he tells her is worth more than his poem.

In your study of poetry, you can admire the skill with which cummings employs his technical means of alliteration, rhythm, and paradox. Aware that the poem was published in 1926, before the sexual revolution of the 1960s, you might also understand that the poet has written it to persuade his "lady" not to wait for a wedding ring but to abandon her caution, urging her to acknowledge the physical attraction between them and become his lover right away. Despite cummings's use of lowercase letters and the open form of his poem, you can recognize the traditional theme of *carpe diem,* the Latin words for "seize the day," in this modern poem.

It is possible, of course, for you to pay close attention as you follow the words in a poem, read it carefully straight through to the end, reread it a second time, and still find its meaning elusive. Then you might find writing a *para-phrase* of the subject of the poem helps you to understand it as you attempt to put the poem into your own words. Your paraphrase of cummings's poem might look something like this:

> Feeling is more important than thinking. A person who thinks too much about the meaning of life will miss the pleasure of enjoying love. When you're young, you should throw caution to the winds and follow your heart. A love affair should take precedence over everything. Don't be sad thinking it won't work out. Letting yourself feel an attraction for some-one is more important than any thought you can have. Relax and enjoy being with your lover, because life is short — it isn't as long as a para-graph, it's only a sentence. And death is a full stop — it isn't a parenthe-sis, it's a period.

Usually the effort of trying to find your own words to express the subject of a poem will help you to understand it. Writing a paraphrase will force you to spend more time focusing on the poem to clarify your thoughts. This is the first step in the process of thinking critically about poetry.

Poems are "meter-making arguments," so they usually represent an idea or develop a series of ideas in a coherent discourse. Poems are also "language charged with meaning to the utmost degree," so you may have to unravel the ideas behind the words as patiently as you would unravel a ball of string after your cat has played with it. When you write a paraphrase of a poem, you take the chance that you might be mistaken about all or part of its meaning. But you also have a method of clarifying the subject that usually brings you closer to the theme or the central idea that you sense behind the poem's words.

The more skilled you become as a reader of poetry, the more readily your intuition will help you grapple with the experience of the poem. At first your study of the poet's means will give you insight into the different writers' resources as they use language to create a poem. Your increased sensitivity to meter and rhyme, diction and symbolism, and the other means used by the poet should help you to understand and enjoy the work. At the beginning of your study of poetry, it may not be possible to paraphrase the entire poem successfully, but any effort you make should help to bring you closer to the poem.

Guidelines for Reading Poetry

1. Make an entry in your notebook for each poem that is assigned in class, writing down the author's name, the title, and the date.
2. Read the poem through once in its entirety, regardless of whether you understand all the words.
3. When you read the poem a second time, use a dictionary to look up words you don't understand.
4. Copy the first lines of the poem into your notebook to scan the rhythm of the poem. Does it fall into any of the patterns you have studied?
5. Note what impresses you most about the way the poet uses language in the poem, in particular the poem's rhyme, its figurative language, and its diction.
6. Try to write a paraphrase of the subject of the poem, following the poet's argument closely as it develops throughout the lines of the poem. Does the poet use paradox, symbolism, allusion, or tribute? Summarize, if you can, the theme of the poem in a single sentence.
7. If you have difficulty understanding any parts of the poem, or the entire poem, write down specific questions about it so that you can ask them in class.
8. Review technical words about poetry that were used in class to be sure you understand them.

CRITICAL THINKING ABOUT POETRY

Paraphrasing a poem will help you to understand its subject and its theme, a necessary step in the process of thinking critically about poetry. You will also find that identifying the various means the poet has used to create the poem will help you to analyze the creative strategies behind the author's choice of form and language. For example, you might ask yourself the following questions:

1. Who is the speaker of the poem? How does identifying the speaker contribute to your understanding of the poem?
2. How closely can you identify the speaker with the author of the poem?
3. What attitude toward the subject of the poem does the speaker convey? How does the tone of the poem help you understand this attitude?
4. What use has the poet made of technical means such as imagery, alliteration, allusion, and specific figures of speech?

5. How has the poet used metaphor and simile in the poem?
6. How would you describe the diction and the syntax of the poem?
7. What is the form of the poem? Why did the poet choose this form and not another?
8. Why do you feel the poet might have written this poem?
9. What does the language of the poem tell you about the reader for whom the poem was written? Is it addressed to a person close to the poet, or to a more general reader?
10. How might different readers interpret the poem from different critical perspectives—feminist, Marxist, historical, and so forth?

It might help clarify your thinking about poetry if you take a specific poem and read it closely with these questions in mind. The answers to the questions can generate additional ideas for writing about the poem. This poem is by the modern American writer Linda Pastan.

LINDA PASTAN

To a Daughter Leaving Home   1978

When I taught you
at eight to ride
a bicycle, loping along
beside you
as you wobbled away   5
on two round wheels,
my own mouth rounding
in surprise when you pulled
ahead down the curved
path of the park,   10
I kept waiting
for the thud
of your crash as I
sprinted to catch up,
while you grew   15
smaller, more breakable
with distance,
pumping, pumping
for your life, screaming
with laughter,   20
the hair flapping
behind you like a
handkerchief waving
goodbye.

After you have carefully read a poem, you can answer the questions that were posed to help you in your understanding. Applying the questions to Pastan's poem might generate some of the following responses:

1. The speaker of the poem is clearly the writer herself. We know from this that we are reading a lyric poem, which is concerned with a moment of everyday life. Knowing that the writer is speaking in her own voice helps us to understand the tone and the context of the poem.

2. In this poem the identity of the speaker and author of the poem are the same.

3. The subject of the poem is the poet's daughter, and the emotional attitude the poet expresses is her love for her child.

4. Although the poem is written in a casual, personal tone, there is a skillful ingenuity in the use of language. Instead of writing that her daughter rode away unsteadily, Pastan uses more striking imagery: "as you wobbled away / on two round wheels." It is also useful to notice that she has written "two . . . wheels." This is an allusion to the moment when a child grows from a tricycle or training wheels to a two-wheel bicycle, which is crucial in the child's development. Also notice the writer's use of alliteration in the phrases "loping along," with its repetition of *l* sounds; "wobbled away," with its *w* sounds; and "path of the park," with its *p*s.

   There are several ways you could describe the image "my own mouth rounding / in surprise." The use of "rounding" to describe her mouth is certainly an allusion to the round wheels of the bicycle that she mentioned in the previous line. The denotative meaning of "rounding" is simply a description of the shape of her mouth, while the connotative meaning is, as she explains, that the round shape of her mouth is an expression of her surprise at what her daughter is doing.

   The phrase "more breakable with distance" is an interesting example of the use of metonymy. The writer is describing her feeling that her daughter is more vulnerable to the dangers of life as she goes further away from her mother, but Pastan uses, instead, the more poetic phrase to describe the dangers to her daughter as she travels further on the park's bicycle path.

5. The use of metaphor is very important in this poem, because the entire poem itself is a metaphor. What Pastan is describing is the moment when a daughter breaks away from her mother to become an adult. She has chosen to describe it in terms of a metaphor, that of her daughter riding away from her on the daughter's first excited trip on a two-wheel bicycle. The use of simile is very clear in the final lines, when she describes her daughter's hair "flapping . . . like a / handkerchief waving / goodbye." With the simile she has made the meaning of the poem clear. She sees her daughter's first moments on a bicycle

and her wild, runaway ride along the path as the moment when her daughter leaves her.

6. The diction of the poem is contemporary and familiar; the syntax is the conversational word order of everyday speech.

7. Since the writer does not use rhyme and the lines don't follow a regular meter we would describe this as a poem in open form, and since it is a personal poem directed to a person close to the writer we would describe it as a lyric poem. The poet chose this form because it most closely matches the style of everyday speech. Since this is a personal poem to her daughter it would strike a modern reader as unconvincing if Pastan used a more elevated and consciously "literary" form.

8. The poet clearly wrote this poem as an expression of her love for her daughter. We know by the title that it was written when her daughter had grown up and become an adult. The poem was probably written both to express the poet's emotions and to soothe her pain at their separation by comparing this moment to her daughter's first bicycle ride.

9. We can tell by the familiar, tender tone of the poem that it was written for someone close to the writer. Since the experience she is describing is familiar to so many other people, however, the poem is also meaningful for a general reader.

10. It would perhaps be a feminist critic who would be most interested in writing about the poem, since the subject of mother-daughter relationships is crucial to feminist theory. A historical critic might want to compare the relative freedom of the mother-daughter relationship that is implied in the poem with the historical past, when women had little freedom to make any choices over their own lives.

WRITING ABOUT POETRY

An assignment to write a paper about a poem will help you to focus your ideas about it and sharpen your critical thinking about what you have read. Many students find that when asked to write a paper analyzing a poem they can work more easily with the poem if they type it on a computer and print it out double-spaced or simply write it out in longhand on a piece of paper. On your copy you can underline words that strike you as significant, and you can jot down your specific feelings and thoughts about the way the poet has used language and form. You can trace the development of the poet's theme, contrast this with the poem's subject, and try to verbalize your feelings about the theme. As you read the poem, are you intrigued, sympathetic, unsympathetic, or confused? Is the subject of the poem something you feel strongly about? Is the theme of the poem something that moves you emotionally? What is your overall reaction to the poem?

If the essay you are planning to write is intended to describe your own response to the poem you could first concentrate on what it is about the poem that has triggered your response. Is it the subject, or the theme of the poem, or the various poetic means the author employed in creating the poem? Second, you could analyze what it is about you as a reader that caused this response. Perhaps you had trouble with the poem because you were uncomfortable with the subject or theme. Did the poem's diction or syntax pose problems for you in understanding the lines? Was it the poem's use of language that caused you to respond favorably or unfavorably to it?

When you are ready to begin your essay you can turn to the materials presented in the sections on reading and writing a literary essay. (See Part Four, "Writing about Literature," p. 1607.) You will find help there in planning your paper in stages, with whatever critical approach you take in writing it. You will also find suggestions about prewriting, first and final drafts, revision, and styling your essay.

All of these critical approaches depend on your close reading of the poem. The poem itself will always be the place where you begin your thinking. Recognizing the means that the poet employed in creating the poem will help you to reach deeper levels of response and will clarify your understanding of the poet's intentions. The essays by poets and critics in Chapter 16, "Commentaries on Poetry and Poets," also offer insights into how other writers respond to poetry.

RELATED SECTION   *Part Four, Writing about Literature, page 1607.*

WEB   *For writing suggestions on each poet in this anthology, visit* bedfordstmartins.com/charters/litwriters.

15.

Poems and Poets

MATTHEW ARNOLD

Matthew Arnold (1822–1888) was born in a village in the Thames Valley, just outside of London. When he was six his family moved to Rugby School where his father, a distinguished Victorian clergyman, had become headmaster. Arnold spent most of his life in an academic environment, first as a child at Rugby, then as a student at Oxford, and for thirty-five years as an inspector of schools for the British government. He traveled throughout England and Europe, studying educational systems and observing the lives of the people who were administering them.

At Oxford he had a reputation as a dandy. The novelist Charlotte Brontë, who met him at that time, wrote, "His manner displeases, from his seeming foppery." His writing, however, had a seriousness that sometimes dissatisfied even Arnold himself. His major poems—among them "The Scholar Gypsy" and "Thyrsis," an elegy on the death of his friend and fellow poet Arthur Hugh Clough—had an important influence on the attitudes and the ideals of the Victorian era. He stopped writing poetry in his thirties, and for the rest of his life he was a widely read and influential critic of English society and culture. "Dover Beach," his best-known poem, was written in 1851.

COMMENTARY Anthony Hecht, "The Dover Bitch," page 983.

WEB Research Matthew Arnold and answer questions about his work at bedfordstmartins.com/charters/litwriters.

Dover Beach   1867

The sea is calm tonight.
The tide is full, the moon lies fair
Upon the straits;—on the French coast the light
Gleams and is gone; the cliffs of England stand,
Glimmering and vast, out in the tranquil bay.   5
Come to the window, sweet is the night-air!
Only, from the long line of spray
Where the sea meets the moon-blanched land,
Listen! You hear the grating roar
Of pebbles which the waves draw back, and fling,   10

At their return, up the high strand,
Begin, and cease, and then again begin,
With tremulous cadence slow, and bring
The eternal note of sadness in.

Sophocles long ago   15
Heard it on the Aegean, and it brought
Into his mind the turbid ebb and flow
Of human misery;° we
Find also in the sound a thought,
Hearing it by this distant northern sea.   20

The Sea of Faith
Was once, too, at the full, and round earth's shore
Lay like the folds of a bright girdle furled.
But now I only hear
Its melancholy, long, withdrawing roar,   25
Retreating, to the breath
Of the night-wind, down the vast edges of drear
And naked shingles° of the world.   *pebble beaches*

Ah, love, let us be true
To one another! for the world, which seems   30
To lie before us like a land of dreams,
So various, so beautiful, so new,
Hath really neither joy, nor love, nor light,
Nor certitude, nor peace, nor help for pain;
And we are here as on a darkling plain   35
Swept with confused alarms of struggle and flight,
Where ignorant armies clash by night.

15–18. Sophocles long ago . . . misery: In *Antigone*, Sophocles compares the calamities
that afflict the house of Oedipus to a rising tide.

JOHN ASHBERY

John Ashbery (b. 1927) was born in the small city of Rochester, New York, but was raised on a farm owned by his father thirty miles east of the city on Lake Ontario, in the village of Sodus. His summers were spent working in the family cherry orchard, but he also spent many hours in the library of his grandfather, who was on the faculty of the University of Rochester. He later recalled that "when I was ten years old I tried to read Shakespeare's plays." He began publishing poetry while still an undergraduate at Harvard, and after graduation worked in New York City in the publishing industry. In 1955, after his first book of poems, Some Trees *(1956), was selected by W. H. Auden for the prestigious Yale Younger Poets series, Ashbery left for Paris on a Fulbright Fellowship. He lived in Paris for the next ten years, and his career as a poet was secured with the recognition he received for the books* Rivers and Mountains *(1966), and* The Double Dream of Spring *(1970).*

In 1975, he became one of the most widely known and discussed poets in America with the publication of Self-Portrait in a Convex Mirror, *which in an almost unprecedented sweep won the Pulitzer Prize, the National Book Critics Circle Award, and the National Book Award. After his return to the United States, he taught languages and literature for many years at Bard College. His poetry is often dense with allusion and ironic asides, and his readers have remained small in number, but faithful and enthusiastic. Ashbery's own comment on his reputation as a "difficult" poet was the laconic, "Very often people don't listen to you when you speak to them. It's only when you talk to yourself that they pick up their ears."*

"The Instruction Manual," one of his most casually spontaneous poems, was written in July 1955, somewhat in the circumstances the poem describes. He was trying to work in his office at the publishing company of McGraw-Hill, and at the same time he couldn't stop thinking about a car trip he'd just taken with friends to Mexico. "Around the Rough and Rugged Rocks the Ragged Rascal Rudely Ran," its title a classic example of the use of alliteration, was published in 1984. While it is closer in style to Ashbery's more elliptical poems, the lines "The omnipresent possibility of being interrupted / While what I stand for is still almost a bare canvas" are a poignant modern rephrasing of the opening lines of John Keats's classic sonnet "When I have fears": "When I have fears that I may cease to be / Before my pen has glean'd my teeming brain."

CONNECTION   *John Keats, "When I have fears," page 916.*

WEB   *Research John Ashbery and answer questions about his work at bedfordstmartins.com/charters/litwriters.*

The Instruction Manual   1955

As I sit looking out of a window of the building
I wish I did not have to write the instruction manual on the uses of a new
    metal.
I look down into the street and see people, each walking with an inner
    peace,

And envy them — they are so far away from me!
Not one of them has to worry about getting out this manual on
    schedule.   5
And, as my way is, I begin to dream, resting my elbows on the desk and
    leaning out of the window a little,
Of dim Guadalajara! City of rose-colored flowers!
City I wanted most to see, and most did not see, in Mexico!
But I fancy I see, under the press of having to write the instruction
    manual,
Your public square, city, with its elaborate little bandstand!   10
The band is playing *Scheherazade* by Rimsky-Korsakov.
Around stand the flower girls, handing out rose- and lemon-colored
    flowers,
Each attractive in her rose-and-blue striped dress (Oh! such shades of
    rose and blue),
And nearby is the little white booth where women in green serve you
    green and yellow fruit.
The couples are parading; everyone is in a holiday mood.   15
First, leading the parade, is a dapper fellow
Clothed in deep blue. On his head sits a white hat
And he wears a mustache, which has been trimmed for the occasion.
His dear one, his wife, is young and pretty; her shawl is rose, pink, and
    white.
Her slippers are patent leather, in the American fashion,   20
And she carries a fan, for she is modest, and does not want the crowd to
    see her face too often.
But everybody is so busy with his wife or loved one
I doubt they would notice the mustachioed man's wife.
Here come the boys! They are skipping and throwing little things on the
    sidewalk
Which is made of gray tile. One of them, a little older, has a toothpick in
    his teeth.   25
He is silenter than the rest, and affects not to notice the pretty young
    girls in white.
But his friends notice them, and shout their jeers at the laughing girls.
Yet soon all this will cease, with the deepening of their years,
And love bring each to the parade grounds for another reason.
But I have lost sight of the young fellow with the toothpick.   30
Wait — there he is — on the other side of the bandstand,
Secluded from his friends, in earnest talk with a young girl
Of fourteen or fifteen. I try to hear what they are saying
But it seems they are just mumbling something — shy words of love,
    probably.
She is slightly taller than he, and looks quietly down into his sincere
    eyes.   35
She is wearing white. The breeze ruffles her long fine black hair against
    her olive cheek.

Obviously she is in love. The boy, the young boy with the toothpick, he
    is in love too;
His eyes show it. Turning from this couple,
I see there is an intermission in the concert.
The paraders are resting and sipping drinks through straws   40
(The drinks are dispensed from a large glass crock by a lady in dark
    blue),
And the musicians mingle among them, in their creamy white uniforms,
    and talk
About the weather, perhaps, or how their kids are doing at school.

Let us take this opportunity to tiptoe into one of the side streets.
Here you may see one of those white houses with green trim   45
That are so popular here. Look — I told you!
It is cool and dim inside, but the patio is sunny.
An old woman in gray sits there, fanning herself with a palm leaf fan.
She welcomes us to her patio, and offers us a cooling drink.
"My son is in Mexico City," she says. "He would welcome you too   50
If he were here. But his job is with a bank there.
Look, here is a photograph of him."
And a dark-skinned lad with pearly teeth grins out at us from the worn
    leather frame.
We thank her for her hospitality, for it is getting late
And we must catch a view of the city, before we leave, from a good high
    place.   55
That church tower will do — the faded pink one, there against the fierce
    blue of the sky. Slowly we enter.
The caretaker, an old man dressed in brown and gray, asks us how long
    we have been in the city, and how we like it here.
His daughter is scrubbing the steps — she nods to us as we pass into the
    tower.
Soon we have reached the top, and the whole network of the city extends
    before us.
There is the rich quarter, with its houses of pink and white, and its
    crumbling, leafy terraces.   60
There is the poorer quarter, its homes a deep blue.
There is the market, where men are selling hats and swatting flies.
And there is the public library, painted several shades of pale green and
    beige.
Look! There is the square we just came from, with the promenaders.
There are fewer of them, now that the heat of the day has increased,   65
But the young boy and girl still lurk in the shadows of the bandstand.
And there is the home of the little old lady —
She is still sitting in the patio, fanning herself.
How limited, but how complete withal, has been our experience of
    Guadalajara!
We have seen young love, married love, and the love of an aged mother
    for her son.   70

We have heard the music, tasted the drinks, and looked at colored houses.
What more is there to do, except stay? And that we cannot do.
And as a last breeze freshens the top of the weathered old tower, I turn
    my gaze
Back to the instruction manual which has made me dream of Guada-
    lajara.

Around the Rough and Rugged Rocks the Ragged Rascal Rudely Ran   1984

I think a lot about it,
Think quite a lot about it—
The omnipresent possibility of being interrupted
While what I stand for is still almost a bare canvas:
A few traceries, that may be fibers, perhaps   5
Not even these but shadows, hallucinations. . . .

And it is well then to recall
That this track is the outer rim of a flat crust,
Dimensionless, except for its poor, parched surface,
The face one raises to God,   10
Not the rich dark composite
We keep to ourselves,
Carpentered together any old way,
Coffee from an old tin can, a belch of daylight,
People leaving the beach.   15
If I could write it
And also write about it—
The interruption—
Rudeness on the face of it, but who
Knows anything about our behavior?   20

Forget what it is you're coming out of,
Always into something like a landscape
Where no one has ever walked
Because they're too busy.
Excitedly you open your rhyming dictionary.   25
It has begun to snow.

W. H. AUDEN

W. H. Auden (1907–1973) was born Wystan Hugh Auden in York, a large
industrial city in northern England. He graduated from Oxford in 1930 and
taught school for five years, but he was already publishing poetry and was considered one of the most exciting of a new, young group of English poets, which
included Stephen Spender and C. Day Lewis.

In the 1930s Auden's poetry reflected his dismay at the effect of the world depression on England, and also his leftist views. In 1937 he went to Spain to take part in the Civil War, but he was disturbed by the Loyalists' hostility to organized religion and returned to England without seeing active combat. In 1939 he moved to the United States, and in 1946 he became an American citizen. He returned to England as a professor of poetry at Oxford from 1956 to 1960, but in his last years he was part of the colorful cultural life of the Lower East Side in New York City.

Auden prided himself on his literary professionalism, and he wrote plays, the libretto for Igor Stravinsky's opera The Rake's Progress, and considerable literary commentary. For many years he toured U.S. universities as an excellent reader of his own poetry.

The well-known poem "Musée des Beaux Arts" was published in 1938, shortly before Auden moved to the United States. The poem "Stop All the Clocks," sometimes also called "Funeral Blues," was untitled when it was published in 1936. It was number XXXIV in his collection Poems 1931–1936. The poem was used in a moving funeral ceremony in the film Four Weddings and a Funeral, and since then has been widely reprinted. The new titles have been added since the film. "Refugee Blues" was also published without a title. It appeared in 1940, as one of a small group of poems titled "Songs."

WEB   *Research W. H. Auden and answer questions about his work at bedfordstmartins.com/charters/litwriters.*

Musée des Beaux Arts°   1938

About suffering they were never wrong,
The Old Masters: how well they understood
Its human position; how it takes place
While someone else is eating or opening a window or just walking dully
    along;
How, when the aged are reverently, passionately waiting   5
For the miraculous birth, there always must be
Children who did not specially want it to happen, skating
On a pond at the edge of the wood:
They never forgot
That even the dreadful martyrdom must run its course   10
Anyhow in a corner, some untidy spot
Where the dogs go on with their doggy life and the torturer's horse
Scratches its innocent behind on a tree.

In Brueghel's *Icarus*,° for instance: how everything turns away
Quite leisurely from the disaster; the plowman may   15
Have heard the splash, the forsaken cry,

Musée des Beaux Arts: The Museum of Fine Arts in Brussels.   **14. Brueghel's *Icarus*:** Refers to *Landscape with the Fall of Icarus,* by Pieter Brueghel the Elder (c. 1525–1569), in the Brussels museum. The painting represents the mythical Icarus as a tiny figure, dwarfed by other characters in the painting, as he falls into the sea.

But for him it was not an important failure; the sun shown
As it had to on the white legs disappearing into the green
Water; and the expensive delicate ship that must have seen
Something amazing, a boy falling out of the sky,   20
Had somewhere to get to and sailed calmly on.

Stop All the Clocks   1936

Stop all the clocks, cut off the telephone,
Prevent the dog from barking with a juicy bone,
Silence the pianos and with muffled drum
Bring out the coffin, let the mourners come.

Let aeroplanes circle moaning overhead   5
Scribbling on the sky the message He Is Dead,
Put crêpe bows round the white necks of the public doves,
Let the traffic policemen wear black cotton gloves.

He was my North, my South, my East and West,
My working week and my Sunday rest,   10
My noon, my midnight, my talk, my song;
I thought that love would last for ever: I was wrong.

The stars are not wanted now; put out every one:
Pack up the moon and dismantle the sun;
Pour away the ocean and sweep up the woods: 15
For nothing now can ever come to any good.

Refugee Blues   1940

Say this city has ten million souls,
Some are living in mansions, some are living in holes:
Yet there's no place for us, my dear, yet there's no place for us.

Once we had a country and we thought it fair,
Look in the atlas and you'll find it there: 5
We cannot go there now, my dear, we cannot go there now.

In the village churchyard there grows an old yew,
Every spring it blossoms anew:
Old passports can't do that, my dear, old passports can't do that.

The consul banged the table and said,   10
"If you've got no passport you're officially dead":
But we are still alive, my dear, but we are still alive;

Came to a public meeting; the speaker got up and said;
"If we let them in, they will steal our daily bread":
He was talking of you and me, my dear, he was talking of you and me.   15

Thought I heard the thunder rumbling in the sky;
It was Hitler over Europe, saying, "They must die":
O we were in his mind, my dear, O we were in his mind.

Saw a poodle in a jacket fastened with a pin,
Saw a door opened and a cat let in: 20
But they weren't German Jews, my dear, but they weren't German Jews.

Went down the harbour and stood upon the quay,
Saw the fish swimming as if they were free:
Only ten feet away, my dear, only ten feet away.

Walked through a wood, saw the birds in the trees;   25
They had no politicians and sang at their ease:
They weren't the human race, my dear, they weren't the human race.

Dreamed I saw a building with a thousand floors,
A thousand windows and a thousand doors:
Not one of them was ours, my dear, not one of them was ours.   30

Stood on a great plain in the falling snow;
Ten thousand soldiers marched to and fro:
Looking for you and me, my dear, looking for you and me.

ELIZABETH BISHOP

Elizabeth Bishop (1911–1979) was the daughter of a successful Boston building contractor and his Canadian wife, but her father died when she was a baby, and when she was four her mother was placed in a mental institution. Bishop was raised by grandparents and relatives in Nova Scotia and Massachusetts. She suffered from severe asthma, and she was unable to attend school until she was sixteen. Among her friends, when she entered Vassar College in 1930, were the writers Muriel Rukeyser and Mary McCarthy.

Although Bishop grew up in a period in which talented women writers— among them Edna St. Vincent Millay, Elinor Wylie, and Louise Bogan—played a dominant role in American poetry, she found their work too traditional, and she took the modernist poet Marianne Moore as a mentor and friend. Another strong influence on her writing was her long friendship with poet Robert Lowell. A small trust fund made it possible for her to live as she wanted, and she spent several years in Key West, Florida. After reviving an old acquaintance with Lota de Macedo Soares, she moved with her to Brazil and remained there until Soares's suicide in 1977. Bishop then returned to the United States to teach at Harvard.

Bishop was a careful, selective poet, and she achieved considerable critical success. She won the Pulitzer Prize and the National Book Award, and her final collection was awarded the National Book Critics Circle Award. "The Fish," one of her best-known poems, was included in her first collection North and South, *published in 1946. (See also Bishop's "The Bight" on p. 719 and "Sestina" on p. 761.)*

COMMENTARY   Brett C. Millier, "On Elizabeth Bishop's 'One Art,'" page 992.

WEB   *Research Elizabeth Bishop and answer questions about her work at bedfordstmartins.com/charters/litwriters.*

The Fish

1946

I caught a tremendous fish
and held him beside the boat
half out of water, with my hook
fast in a corner of his mouth.
He didn't fight. 5
He hadn't fought at all.
He hung a grunting weight,
battered and venerable
and homely. Here and there
his brown skin hung in strips 10
like ancient wallpaper,
and its pattern of darker brown
was like wallpaper:
shapes like full-blown roses
stained and lost through age. 15
He was speckled with barnacles,
fine rosettes of lime,
and infested
with tiny white sea-lice,
and underneath two or three 20
rags of green weed hung down.
While his gills were breathing in
the terrible oxygen
—the frightening gills,
fresh and crisp with blood, 25
that can cut so badly—
I thought of the coarse white flesh
packed in like feathers,
the big bones and the little bones,
the dramatic reds and blacks 30
of his shiny entrails,
and the pink swim-bladder
like a big peony.
I looked into his eyes
which were far larger than mine 35
but shallower, and yellowed,
the irises backed and packed
with tarnished tinfoil
seen through the lenses
of old scratched isinglass. 40
They shifted a little, but not
to return my stare.
—It was more like the tipping
of an object toward the light.

I admired his sullen face,   45
the mechanism of his jaw,
and then I saw
that from his lower lip
—if you could call it a lip—
grim, wet, and weaponlike,   50
hung five old pieces of fish-line,
or four and a wire leader
with the swivel still attached,
with all their five big hooks
grown firmly in his mouth.   55
A green line, frayed at the end
where he broke it, two heavier lines,
and a fine black thread
still crimped from the strain and snap
when it broke and he got away.   60
Like medals with their ribbons
frayed and wavering,
a five-haired beard of wisdom
trailing from his aching jaw.
I stared and stared   65
and victory filled up
the little rented boat,
from the pool of bilge
where oil had spread a rainbow
around the rusted engine   70
to the bailer rusted orange,
the sun-cracked thwarts,
the oarlocks on their strings,
the gunnels—until everything
was rainbow, rainbow, rainbow!   75
And I let the fish go.

One Art   1976

The art of losing isn't hard to master;
so many things seem filled with the intent
to be lost that their loss is no disaster.

Lose something every day. Accept the fluster
of lost door keys, the hour badly spent.   5
The art of losing isn't hard to master.

Then practice losing farther, losing faster:
places, and names, and where it was you meant
to travel. None of these will bring disaster.

I lost my mother's watch. And look! my last, or   10
next-to-last, of three loved houses went.
The art of losing isn't hard to master.

I lost two cities, lovely ones. And, vaster,
some realms I owned, two rivers, a continent.   15
I miss them, but it wasn't a disaster.

—Even losing you (the joking voice, a gesture
I love) I shan't have lied. It's evident
the art of losing's not too hard to master
though it may look like (*Write* it!) like disaster.

WILLIAM BLAKE

William Blake (1757–1827) was born in London, one of several children of a London haberdasher. His family expected he would become a tradesman, and he was educated to be a commercial artist. He was sent to a drawing academy when he was ten, then he studied painting for a short time at the Royal Academy of Arts.

At the age of fourteen Blake was apprenticed to an engraver, and his seven-year apprenticeship provided him with enough knowledge and experience to set up his own small engraving business. At the same time he was reading on his own and beginning to write poetry. When he was twenty-four he married Catherine Boucher, whose father delivered produce to the London markets. The next year, 1783, his first book of poems, Poetical Sketches, *was published.*

Over the next ten years he produced his two most celebrated books. Songs of Innocence *appeared in 1789, and* Songs of Innocence and of Experience *in 1794. He created the books with a method of engraving that combined the illustrations and the hand-lettered poetry on the page, then he and his wife hand-painted each page with watercolors. To do a single copy was so time-consuming that only a handful of editions were produced, but they were so unusual and so beautiful that Blake attracted the attention of a small group of connoisseurs and artists.*

In 1800, with the financial assistance of a patron, the Blakes were able to move to the country, and he continued to draw and paint, to create illustrations for books by other writers and to create his own books of prophecy and mystical inspiration. To many of his contemporaries, Blake was an exasperating eccentric with radical opinions, who often described conversations he had just had with long-dead historical figures. As he said of his habit of seeing visions, "I do not distrust my corporeal or vegetative eye any more than I would distrust a window for its sight. I see through it, not with it." He died in 1827 at the age of seventy.

The selection of Blake's poetry is taken from Songs of Innocence and of Experience.

WEB *Research William Blake and answer questions about his work at* bedfordstmartins.com/charters/litwriters.

From Songs of Innocence 1789
Introduction

Piping down the valleys wild
Piping songs of pleasant glee
On a cloud I saw a child,
And he laughing said to me,

"Pipe a song about a Lamb"; 5
So I piped with merry chear;
"Piper pipe that song again" —
So I piped, he wept to hear.

"Drop thy pipe thy happy pipe
Sing thy songs of happy chear"; 10
So I sung the same again
While he wept with joy to hear.

"Piper sit thee down and write
In a book that all may read" —
So he vanish'd from my sight. 15
And I pluck'd a hollow reed,

And I made a rural pen,
And I stain'd the water clear,
And I wrote my happy songs
Every child may joy to hear. 20

The Lamb 1789

Little Lamb, who made thee?
  Dost thou know who made thee?
Gave thee life, and bid thee feed
By the stream and o'er the mead;
Gave thee clothing of delight, 5
Softest clothing, wooly, bright;
Gave thee such a tender voice,
Making all the vales rejoice?
  Little Lamb, who made thee?
  Dost thou know who made thee? 10

  Little Lamb, I'll tell thee,
  Little Lamb, I'll tell thee:
He is callèd by thy name,
For he calls himself a Lamb.
He is meek, and he is mild; 15
He became a little child.
I a child, and thou a lamb,
We are callèd by his name.

Little Lamb, God bless thee!
Little Lamb, God bless thee!   20

Holy Thursday   1789

'Twas on a Holy Thursday, their innocent faces clean,
The children walking two & two, in red & blue & green;
Grey headed beadles walkd before with wands as white as snow,
Till into the high dome of Paul's° they like Thames' waters flow.

O what a multitude they seemd, these flowers of London town!   5
Seated in companies they sit with radiance all their own.
The hum of multitudes was there, but multitudes of lambs,
Thousands of little boys & girls raising their innocent hands.

Now like a mighty wind they raise to heaven the voice of song,
Or like harmonious thunderings the seats of heaven among.   10
Beneath them sit the agèd men, wise guardians of the poor;
Then cherish pity, lest you drive an angel from your door.

The Little Boy Lost   1789

"Father, father, where are you going?
O do not walk so fast.
Speak father, speak to your little boy
Or else I shall be lost."

The night was dark, no father was there,
The child was wet with dew.
The mire was deep, & the child did weep,
And away the vapour flew.

The Little Boy Found   1789

The little boy lost in the lonely fen,
Led by the wand'ring light,
Began to cry, but God ever nigh
Appeard like his father in white.

He kissed the child & by the hand led
And to his mother brought,
Who in sorrow pale, thro' the lonely dale,
Her little boy weeping sought.

---

4. **Paul's:** St. Paul's Cathedral.

From Songs of Experience 1794

Introduction

Hear the voice of the Bard!
Who Present, Past, & Future sees;
Whose ears have heard
The Holy Word
That walk'd among the ancient trees;   5

Calling the lapsèd Soul
And weeping in the evening dew,
That might controll
The starry pole,
And fallen, fallen light renew!   10

"O Earth, O Earth, return!
Arise from out the dewy grass;
Night is worn,
And the morn
Rises from the slumberous mass.   15

"Turn away no more;
Why wilt thou turn away?
The starry floor
The watry shore
Is giv'n thee till the break of day."   20

The Sick Rose 1794

O Rose, thou art sick!
The invisible worm
That flies in the night,
In the howling storm,

Has found out thy bed
Of crimson joy,
And his dark secret love
Does thy life destroy.

The Tyger 1794

Tyger! Tyger! burning bright
In the forests of the night,
What immortal hand or eye
Could frame thy fearful symmetry?

In what distant deeps or skies   5
Burnt the fire of thine eyes?

On what wings dare he aspire?
What the hand dare seize the fire?

And what shoulder, and what art,   10
Could twist the sinews of thy heart?
And when thy heart began to beat,
What dread hand? and what dread feet?

What the hammer? what the chain?
In what furnace was thy brain?
What the anvil? what dread grasp   15
Dare its deadly terrors clasp?

When the stars threw down their spears,
And watered heaven with their tears,
Did he smile his work to see?
Did he who made the Lamb make thee?   20

Tyger! Tyger! burning bright
In the forests of the night,
What immortal hand or eye
Dare frame thy fearful symmetry?

London   1794

I wander through each chartered° street   *defined by law*
Near where the chartered Thames does flow,
And mark in every face I meet
Marks of weakness, marks of woe.

In every cry of every man,   5
In every Infant's cry of fear,
In every voice, in every ban,
The mind-forged manacles I hear.

How the Chimney-sweeper's cry
Every black'ning Church appalls;   10
And the hapless Soldier's sigh
Runs in blood down Palace walls.

But most through midnight streets I hear
How the youthful Harlot's curse°   *syphilis*
Blasts the new-born Infant's tear,   15
And blights with plagues the Marriage hearse.

A Poison Tree   1794

I was angry with my friend:
I told my wrath, my wrath did end.
I was angry with my foe:
I told it not, my wrath did grow.

And I waterd it in fears,   5
Night & morning with my tears;
And I sunnèd it with smiles,
And with soft deceitful wiles.

And it grew both day and night,
Till it bore an apple bright.   10
And my foe beheld it shine,
And he knew that it was mine,

And into my garden stole,
When the night had veild the pole;
In the morning glad I see   15
My foe outstretched beneath the tree.

The Garden of Love   1794

I went to the Garden of Love,
And saw what I never had seen:
A Chapel was built in the midst,
Where I used to play on the green.

And the gates of this Chapel were shut,   5
And "Thou shalt not" writ over the door;
So I turn'd to the Garden of Love,
That so many sweet flowers bore,

And I saw it was filled with graves,
And tomb-stones where flowers should be;   10
And Priests in black gowns were walking their rounds,
And binding with briars my joys & desires.

ANNE BRADSTREET

*Anne Bradstreet (c. 1612–1672) was born in England, the daughter of a
"well borne woman" of modest wealth and a father who was the steward of a
country estate of the Earl of Lincoln. Both the earl and Bradstreet's parents were
Puritans, and she was given a much better education than most young women of
her time. At sixteen she married Simon Bradstreet, also a Puritan, and two years
later, in 1630, she, her husband, and her parents sailed to the Massachusetts Bay
Colony. They lived first in Boston and in 1644 moved to North Andover, where
Bradstreet lived for the rest of her life.*

*As a girl she had already begun writing poems that she and her father read
with pleasure together. She continued to write, while she raised eight children and
managed the household for her husband, who, as governor of the colony, was away
for long periods.*

*In 1650, without her knowledge, her brother-in-law took a gathering of her
poems to London. The collection was the first to be published by anyone living in*

the North American colonies, and the book attracted considerable attention. Because of the constraints placed on women's lives, her brother-in-law felt obliged to assure suspicious readers, in the introduction, that Bradstreet was respectable according to the standards of the time. The poems, he wrote, were "the work of a woman, honored and esteemed where she lives, for her gracious demeanor, her eminent parts, her pious conversation, her courteous disposition, her exact diligence in her place, and discreet managing of her family occasions."

"To My Dear and Loving Husband," "Before the Birth of One of Her Children," and "In Memory of My Dear Grand-Child Elizabeth Bradstreet, Who Deceased August, 1665, Being a Year and a Half Old" were all written during Bradstreet's years in North Andover.

WEB   *Research Anne Bradstreet and answer questions about her work at bedfordstmartins.com/charters/litwriters.*

To My Dear and Loving Husband   1678

If ever two were one, then surely we.
If ever man were loved by wife, then thee;
If ever wife was happy in a man,
Compare with me, ye women, if you can.
I prize thy love more than whole mines of gold   5
Or all the riches that the East doth hold.
My love is such that rivers cannot quench,
Nor ought but love from thee, give recompense.
Thy love is such I can no way repay,
The heavens reward thee manifold, I pray.   10
Then while we live, in love let's so persevere
That when we live no more, we may live ever.

Before the Birth of One of Her Children   1678

All things within this fading world hath end,
Adversity doth still our joys attend;
No ties so strong, no friends so dear and sweet,
But with death's parting blow is sure to meet.
The sentence past is most irrevocable,   5
A common thing, yet oh, inevitable.
How soon, my Dear, death may my steps attend,
How soon't may be thy lot to lose thy friend,
We both are ignorant, yet love bids me
These farewell lines to recommend to thee,   10
That when that knot's untied that made us one,
I may seem thine, who in effect am none.
And if I see not half my days that's due,
What nature would, God grant to yours and you;

The many faults that well you know I have   15
Let be interred in my oblivious grave;
If any worth or virtue were in me,
Let that live freshly in thy memory
And when thou feel'st no grief, as I no harms,
Yet love thy dead, who long lay in thine arms.   20
And when thy loss shall be repaid with gains
Look to my little babes, my dear remains.
And if thou love thyself, or loved'st me,
These O protect from step-dame's injury.
And if chance to thine eyes shall bring this verse,   25
With some sad sighs honour my absent hearse;
And kiss this paper for thy love's dear sake,
Who with salt tears this last farewell did take.

In Memory of My Dear Grand-Child Elizabeth Bradstreet, Who Deceased August, 1665, Being a Year and a Half Old   1665

1

Farewel dear babe, my hearts too much content,
Farewel sweet babe, the pleasure of mine eye,
Farewel fair flower that for a space was lent,
Then ta'en away unto Eternity.
Blest babe why should I once bewail thy fate,   5
Or sigh thy dayes so soon were terminate;
Sith thou art setled in an Everlasting state.

2

By nature Trees do rot when they are grown.
And Plumbs and Apples thoroughly ripe do fall,
And Corn and grass are in their season mown,   10
And time brings down what is both strong and tall.
But plants new set to be eradicate,
And buds new blown, to have so short a date,
Is by his hand alone that guides nature and fate.

GWENDOLYN BROOKS

Gwendolyn Brooks (1917–2000) was born in Topeka, Kansas, but her parents moved to Chicago's South Side soon after her birth. Her father worked as a janitor, and the family was poor, but her parents encouraged her to study in school and to write poetry. She wrote her first poems when she was seven. Her childhood was so contented that she wrote later in her autobiography, "I had always felt that to be black was good."

Brooks had almost immediate success as a writer. She was already publishing her poetry when she was seventeen. Her first book, A Street in Bronzeville, *which appeared in 1945, won a series of prizes, and she was awarded a Guggenheim fellowship, which allowed her to spend a year devoted entirely to writing. In 1949 her second poetry collection,* Annie Allen, *won the Pulitzer Prize, the first time it had been given to an African American writer. She also published a novel,* Maud Martha, *in 1953, and taught at Chicago State University, where she was a Distinguished Professor.*

In 1967 Brooks took part in the Second Black Writer's Conference at Fisk University, and she was swept up in the new militancy of the younger black poets like Amiri Baraka and don l. lee. Her poetry became more specifically political, and finally she turned to alternative publishing so she could have some control over the way her poetry was presented.

"We Real Cool" is one of her shortest poems, and it is also one of her most famous. "The Mother" is an early poem in which the woman speaker projects a scarring, personal unhappiness. Brooks herself was the mother of a son and a daughter. "The Bean Eaters," with its poignant suggestion of life's vagaries in the old couple's memories of "twinklings and twinges," first appeared in 1960.

COMMENTARY *Robert Hayden, "On Negro Poetry," page 981.*

WEB *Research Gwendolyn Brooks and answer questions about her work at bedfordstmartins.com/charters/litwriters.*

We Real Cool

1960

The Pool Players.
Seven at the Golden Shovel.

We real cool. We
Left school. We

Lurk late. We   5
Strike straight. We

Sing sin. We
Thin gin. We

Jazz June. We
Die soon.   10

The Mother

1945

Abortions will not let you forget.
You remember the children you got that you did not get,
The damp small pulps with a little or with no hair,
The singers and workers that never handled the air.

You will never neglect or beat   5
Them, or silence or buy with a sweet.
You will never wind up the sucking-thumb
Or scuttle off ghosts that come.
You will never leave them, controlling your luscious sigh,
Return for a snack of them, with gobbling mother-eye.   10
I have heard in the voices of the wind the voices of my dim killed children.
I have contracted. I have eased
My dim dears at the breasts they could never suck.
I have said, Sweets, if I sinned, if I seized
Your luck   15
And your lives from your unfinished reach,
If I stole your births and your names,
Your straight baby tears and your games,
Your stilted or lovely loves, your tumults, your marriages, aches, and
    your deaths,
If I poisoned the beginnings of your breaths,   20
Believe that even in my deliberateness I was not deliberate.
Though why should I whine,
Whine that the crime was other than mine? —
Since anyhow you are dead.
Or rather, or instead,   25
You were never made.
But that too, I am afraid,
Is faulty: oh, what shall I say, how is the truth to be said?
You were born, you had body, you died.
It is just that you never giggled or planned or cried.   30
Believe me, I loved you all.
Believe me, I knew you, though faintly, and I loved, I loved you
All.

The Bean Eaters   1960

They eat beans mostly, this old yellow pair.
Dinner is a casual affair.
Plain chipware on a plain and creaking wood,
Tin flatware.

Two who are Mostly Good.   5
Two who have lived their day,
But keep on putting on their clothes
And putting things away.

And remembering . . .
Remembering, with twinklings and twinges,   10
As they lean over the beans in their rented back room that is full of beads
    and receipts and dolls and cloths, tobacco crumbs, vases and fringes.

SAMUEL TAYLOR COLERIDGE

Samuel Taylor Coleridge (1772–1834) was born in a small village in southern England, but after the death of his father he was sent to school in London. Despite his indolence, he could also be sporadically brilliant, and at nineteen he entered Cambridge University, where his lack of discipline overwhelmed him, and he was unable to complete his degree.

In 1794 Coleridge met the young poet Robert Southey and, filled with the fervor of the French Revolution, they decided to establish a utopian colony in Pennsylvania. Their plans fell apart, but Coleridge, as part of the plan, had married the sister of Southey's fiancée. The marriage was as unhappy as everything else Coleridge had attempted. The next year he met William Wordsworth and soon moved close to where the older poet and his sister Dorothy were living in England. Writing together, in a fever of excitement, he and Wordsworth completed the small collection titled Lyrical Ballads, *which was published in 1798. With their book they attempted to write a new kind of poetry, closer to ordinary speech and drawing from everyday emotions. Coleridge's contribution was the long supernatural narrative "The Rime of the Ancient Mariner" and several shorter poems.*

Coleridge by this time was addicted to opium, and his writing became chaotically uneven. "Kubla Khan" is the best known of his drug-influenced poems. When he later overcame his addiction he became one of the most important literary theorists and critics of the early nineteenth century. His lifelong friend, the writer Charles Lamb, described Coleridge as "an archangel, slightly damaged." "Frost at Midnight" is one of Coleridge's "conversation poems" in blank verse that moves back and forth between description of his surroundings and lofty meditation.

CONNECTION *Richard Leighton Green, "(Apropos Coleridge's 'Kubla Khan') When approached by a person from Porlock," page 759.*

WEB *Research Samuel Taylor Coleridge and answer questions about his work at bedfordstmartins.com/charters/litwriters.*

Kubla Khan: or, a Vision in a Dream°   1798

In Xanadu did Kubla Khan°
   A stately pleasure-dome decree:
Where Alph, the sacred river, ran
Through caverns measureless to man
    Down to a sunless sea.   5
So twice five miles of fertile ground
With walls and towers were girdled round:
And here were gardens bright with sinuous rills

Vision in a Dream: Coleridge claimed this poem came to him in a dream, but when he woke and was transcribing it, he was interrupted by a visitor and was later unable to remember the rest of the poem.   **1. Kubla Khan:** In Chinese history, Kublai Khan (1215–1294) founded the Mongol dynasty.

Where blossomed many an incense-bearing tree;
And there were forests ancient as the hills,   10
Enfolding sunny spots of greenery.

But oh! that deep romantic chasm which slanted
Down the green hill athwart a cedarn cover!°
A savage place! as holy and enchanted
As e'er beneath a waning moon was haunted   15
By woman wailing for her demon-lover!
And from this chasm, with ceaseless turmoil seething,
As if this earth in fast thick pants were breathing,
A mighty fountain momently was forced,
Amid whose swift half-intermitted burst   20
Huge fragments vaulted like rebounding hail,
Or chaffy grain beneath the thresher's flail:
And 'mid these dancing rocks at once and ever
It flung up momently the sacred river.
Five miles meandering with a mazy motion   25
Through wood and dale the sacred river ran,
Then reached the caverns measureless to man,
And sank in tumult to a lifeless ocean:
And 'mid this tumult Kubla heard from far
Ancestral voices prophesying war!   30
        The shadow of the dome of pleasure
        Floated midway on the waves;
        Where was heard the mingled measure
        From the fountain and the caves.
It was a miracle of rare device,   35
A sunny pleasure-dome with caves of ice!

        A damsel with a dulcimer
        In a vision once I saw:
        It was an Abyssinian maid,
        And on her dulcimer she played,   40
        Singing of Mount Abora.
        Could I revive within me
        Her symphony and song,
        To such a deep delight 'twould win me,
That with music loud and long,   45
I would build that dome in air,
That sunny dome! those caves of ice!
And all who heard should see them there,
And all should cry, Beware! Beware!
His flashing eyes, his floating hair!   50
Weave a circle round him thrice,

---

13. **athwart . . . cover:** Encompassing a grove of cedar trees.

And close your eyes with holy dread,
For he on honey-dew hath fed,
And drunk the milk of Paradise.

Frost at Midnight   1798

The Frost performs its secret ministry,
Unhelped by any wind. The owlet's cry
Came loud—and hark, again! loud as before.
The inmates of my cottage, all at rest,
Have left me to that solitude, which suits   5
Abstruser musings: save that at my side
My cradled infant slumbers peacefully.
'Tis calm indeed! so calm, that it disturbs
And vexes meditation with its strange
And extreme silentness. Sea, hill, and wood,   10
This populous village! Sea, and hill, and wood,
With all the numberless goings-on of life,
Inaudible as dreams! the thin blue flame
Lies on my low-burnt fire, and quivers not;
Only that film,° which fluttered on the grate,   soot   15
Still flutters there, the sole unquiet thing.
Methinks its motion in this hush of nature
Gives it dim sympathies with me who live,
Making it a companionable form,
Whose puny flaps and freaks the idling Spirit   20
By its own moods interprets, everywhere
Echo or mirror seeking of itself,
And makes a toy of Thought.
                          But O! how oft,
How oft, at school, with most believing mind,   25
Presageful, have I gazed upon the bars,
To watch that fluttering *stranger!* and as oft
With unclosed lids, already had I dreamt
Of my sweet birthplace, and the old church tower,
Whose bells, the poor man's only music, rang   30
From morn to evening, all the hot fair-day,
So sweetly, that they stirred and haunted me
With a wild pleasure, falling on mine ear
Most like articulate sounds of things to come!
So gazed I, till the soothing things, I dreamt,   35
Lulled me to sleep, and sleep prolonged my dreams!
And so I brooded all the following morn,
Awed by the stern preceptor's face, mine eye
Fixed with mock study on my swimming book:

Save if the door half opened, and I snatched   40
A hasty glance, and still my heart leaped up,
For still I hoped to see the *stranger's* face,
Townsman, or aunt, or sister more beloved,
My playmate when we both were clothed alike!

    Dear Babe,° that sleepest cradled by my side,   *Coleridge's infant son* 45
Whose gentle breathings, heard in this deep calm,
Fill up the interspersèd vacancies
And momentary pauses of the thought!
My babe so beautiful! it thrills my heart
With tender gladness, thus to look at thee,   50
And think that thou shalt learn far other lore,
And in far other scenes! For I was reared
In the great city, pent 'mid cloisters dim,
And saw nought lovely but the sky and stars.
But *thou*, my babe! shalt wander like a breeze   55
By lakes and sandy shores, beneath the crags
Of ancient mountain, and beneath the clouds,
Which image in their bulk both lakes and shores
And mountain crags: so shalt thou see and hear
The lovely shapes and sounds intelligible   60
Of that eternal language, which thy God
Utters, who from eternity doth teach
Himself in all, and all things in himself.
Great universal Teacher! he shall mold
Thy spirit, and by giving make it ask.   65

    Therefore all seasons shall be sweet to thee,
Whether the summer clothe the general earth
With greenness, or the redbreast sit and sing
Betwixt the tufts of snow on the bare branch
Of mossy apple tree, while the nigh thatch   70
Smokes in the sun-thaw; whether the eave-drops fall
Heard only in the trances of the blast,
Or if the secret ministry of frost
Shall hang them up in silent icicles,
Quietly shining to the quiet Moon.   75

BILLY COLLINS

*Billy Collins (b. 1941) was born in New York City. He studied at Holy Cross
College and at the University of California at Riverside. He returned to the East
when his degree was completed, and for many years he has been a professor of English at Lehman College (City University of New York). In the late 1990s he was
chosen for a two-year honorary position as the poet laureate of the United States.*

Collins has only in recent years emerged as one of the freshest and widely readable contemporary American poets, and behind his almost artless manner is a shrewd literary intelligence, which manages to be erudite and literary at the same time that his speech is as direct as something you might overhear on the street.

He has commented on the composition of "Tuesday, June 4th, 1991," which ends with its wonderful personification of dawn in the last verse:

> barefoot and disheveled, standing outside my window
> in one of the fragile cotton dresses of the poor.
> She will look in at me with her thin arms extended,
> offering a handful of birdsong and a small cup of light.

Collins wrote,

> I sat at the typewriter and began to describe the plain circumstances of this particular morning, and I soon found that the poem and the morning began to evolve in tandem. . . . The poem's relaxed tone and its atmosphere of domestic ease may derive loosely from Coleridge's "conversation" poems: a housebound speaker slips into a meditation that eventually leads him beyond the familiar surroundings of his room or garden. It was one of those lucky poems written without exertion, perhaps because I simply allowed into the poem whatever was happening around me. . . .

"Memento Mori," with its image of the speaker's reading lamp coming to his funeral, is another startling example of Collins's use of personification. "By a Swimming Pool Outside Siracusa" is a humorous response to the problems of speaking a foreign language. (See also Billy Collins, "American Sonnet," page 756.)

WEB *Research Billy Collins and answer questions about his work at bedfordstmartins.com/charters/litwriters.*

Tuesday, June 4th, 1991   1992

By the time I get myself out of bed, my wife has left
the house to take her botany final and the painter
has arrived in his van and is already painting
the columns of the front porch white and the decking gray.

It is early June, a breezy and sun-riddled Tuesday   5
that would quickly be forgotten were it not for my
writing these few things down as I sit here empty-headed
at the typewriter with a cup of coffee, light and sweet.

I feel like the secretary to the morning whose only
responsibility is to take down its bright, airy dictation   10
until it's time to go to lunch with the other girls,
all of us ordering the cottage cheese with half a pear.

This is what stenographers do in courtrooms,
alert at their dark contraptions catching every word.
When there is a silence they sit still as I do, waiting   15
and listening, fingers resting lightly on the keys.

This is what Samuel Pepys° did too, jotting down in
private ciphers minor events that would have otherwise
slipped into the heavy, amnesiac waters of the Thames.
His vigilance paid off finally when London caught fire   20

as mine does when the painter comes in for coffee
and says how much he likes this slow, vocal rendition
of "You Don't Know What Love Is" and I figure I will
make him a tape when he goes back to his brushes and pails.

Under the music I can hear the rush of cars and trucks   25
on the highway and every so often the new kitten, Felix,
hops into my lap and watches my fingers drumming out
a running record of this particular June Tuesday

as it unrolls before my eyes, a long intricate carpet
that I am walking on slowly with my head bowed   30
knowing that it is leading me to the quiet shrine
of the afternoon and the melancholy candles of evening.

If I look up, I see out the window the white stars
of clematis climbing a ladder of strings, a woodpile,
a stack of faded bricks, a small green garden of herbs,   35
things you would expect to find outside a window,

all written down now and placed in the setting
of a stanza as unalterably as they are seated
in their chairs in the ontological rooms of the world.
Yes, this is the kind of job I could succeed in,   40

an unpaid but contented amanuensis whose hands
are two birds fluttering on the lettered keys,
whose eyes see sunlight splashing through the leaves,
and the bright pink asterisks of honeysuckle

and the piano at the other end of this room with   45
its small vase of faded flowers and its empty bench.
So convinced am I that I have found my vocation,
tomorrow I will begin my chronicling earlier, at dawn,

a time when hangmen and farmers are up and doing,
when men holding pistols stand in a field back to back.   50
It is the time the ancients imagined in robes, as Eos°
or Aurora,° who would leave her sleeping husband in bed,

not to take her botany final, but to pull the sun,
her brother, over the horizon's brilliant rim,
her four-horse chariot aimed at the zenith of the sky.   55
But tomorrow, dawn will come the way I picture her,

---

17. Samuel Pepys: (1633–1703) English diarist whose observations of daily life are one of
the largest sources of information on the Restoration period.   **51. Eos:** Greek goddess of
dawn.   **52. Aurora:** Roman goddess of dawn.

barefoot and disheveled, standing outside my window
in one of the fragile cotton dresses of the poor.
She will look in at me with her thin arms extended,
offering a handful of birdsong and a small cup of light.   60

Memento Mori   1991

There is no need for me to keep a skull on my desk,
to stand with one foot up on the ruins of Rome,
or to wear a locket with a sliver of a saint's bone.

It is enough to realize that every common object
in this small sunny room will outlive me—   5
the mirror, radio, bookstand and rocker.

Not one of these things will attend my burial,
not even this battered goofor—
not even this battered goo6enecked lamp
with its steady, silent benediction of light,
                                                                                       10
though I could put worse things in my mind
than the image of it waddling across the cemetery
like an old servant, dragging the tail of its cord,
the small circle of mourners parting to make room.

By a Swimming Pool Outside Siracusa°   2001

All afternoon I have been struggling
to communicate in Italian
with Roberto and Giuseppe, who have begun
to resemble the two male characters
in my *Italian for Beginners,*   5
the ones who are always shopping
or inquiring about the times of trains,
and now I can hardly speak or write English.

I have made important pronouncements
in this remote limestone valley   10
with its trickle of a river,
stating that it seems hotter
today even than it was yesterday
and that swimming is very good for you,
very beneficial, you might say.   15
I also posed burning questions
about the hours of the archaeological museum
and the location of the local necropolis.

Siracusa: City and port in southeastern Sicily.

But now I am alone in the evening light
which has softened the white cliffs,   20
and I have had a little gin in a glass with ice
which has softened my mood or—
how would you say in English—
has allowed my thoughts to traverse my brain
with greater gentleness, shall we say,   25

or, to put it less literally,
this drink has extended permission
to my mind to feel—what's the word?—
a friendship with the vast sky
which is very—give me a minute—very blue   30
but with much great paleness
at this special time of day, or as we say in America, now.

COUNTEE CULLEN

Countee Cullen (1903–1946) chose not to reveal details of his early life, and when he became known as a writer he described New York City as his birthplace. It seems clear, however, from his university records, that he was born in Louisville, Kentucky, in 1903 as Counteé Le Roy Porter, and probably raised by his maternal grandmother. His grandmother died when he was fifteen, and he was adopted by Reverend Frederick Cullen, who, with his wife Carolyn, led one of Harlem's largest churches. The young poet graduated from New York University with a teaching degree in 1925 and completed his M.A. at Harvard University in 1926. He had already begun publishing poetry while he was in high school, and he attracted wide interest with his first book, Color, *which appeared in 1925, the same year as he graduated from New York University. He was twenty-two years old. The poems that made up the book, as well as most of the poetry in his next two collections,* Copper Sun *(1927) and* The Ballad of the Brown Girl, *published the same year, were written while he was still a student.*

After he completed his M.A. at Harvard, he returned to New York City as a teacher, continuing to write and publish until his death at the age of forty-three. Cullen was one of the key figures in the literary movement known as the Harlem Renaissance, but for some critics there was the troubling question of his love of English poetry, particularly the writing of John Keats, and Cullen's use of traditional English verse forms. He found himself being continually compared to his contemporary, Langston Hughes, who championed African American speech and themes for his poetry. A further complication for Cullen was his carefully concealed homosexuality, which was only later revealed in his letters. In discussing his poetry, which uses African American themes, Margaret Perry, in her A Bio-Bibliography of Counteé P. Cullen, *wrote,*

> *[Cullen] was, and probably still is, considered the least race-conscious of the Negro poets. . . . Nevertheless it was because of the color of his skin that Counteé Cullen was more aware of the racial poetry and could not be at all*

times "sheer poet." This was clearly a problem for Cullen—wanting to write lyrics on love, death, and beauty—always so consciously aware of his race. . . . For Cullen, then the racial problem was always there, even when one was thinking of odes by Keats, and he was impelled—in spite of every-thing I can do—to write about this subject. This was the cause of much weakness in his writing, as well as some strength; for there are poems about race which have an emotional intensity that most of his white peers could not have matched.

For many years "Heritage" was, with Hughes's "The Negro Speaks of Rivers" (p. 907), one of the most widely known and quoted poems of the Harlem Renaissance. It was included in Cullen's first book Color. "Incident" is his own laconic comment on his childhood experience of racism.

WEB   *Research Countee Cullen and answer questions about his work at bedfordstmartins.com/charters/litwriters.*

From "Heritage"

1925

What is Africa to me:
Copper sun or scarlet sea,
Jungle star or jungle track,
Strong bronzed men, or regal black
Women from whose loins I sprang   5
When the birds of Eden sang?
One three centuries removed
From the scenes his fathers loved,
Spicy grove, cinnamon tree,
What is Africa to me?   10

So I lie, who all day long
Want no sound except the song
Sung by wild barbaric birds
Goading massive jungle herds,
Juggernauts of flesh that pass   15
Trampling tall defiant grass
Where young forest lovers lie,
Plighting troth beneath the sky.
So I lie, who always hear,
Though I cram against my ear   20
Both my thumbs, and keep them there,
Great drums throbbing through the air.
So I lie, whose fount of pride,
Dear distress, and joy allied,
Is my somber flesh and skin,   25
With the dark blood dammed within
Like great pulsing tides of wine
That, I fear, must burst the fine

Channels of the chafing net
Where they surge and foam and fret.   30

Africa? A book one thumbs
Listlessly, till slumber comes.
Unremembered are her bats
Circling through the night, her cats
Crouching in the river reeds,   35
Stalking gentle flesh that feeds
By the river brink; no more
Does the bugle-throated roar
Cry that monarch claws have leapt
From the scabbards where they slept.   40
Silver snakes that once a year
Doff the lovely coats you wear,
Seek no covert in your fear
Lest a mortal eye should see;
What's your nakedness to me?   45
Here no leprous flowers rear
Fierce corollas in the air;
Here no bodies sleek and wet,
Dripping mingled rain and sweat,
Tread the savage measures of   50
Jungle boys and girls in love.

What is last year's snow to me,
Last year's anything? The tree
Budding yearly must forget
How its past arose or set —   55
Bough and blossom, flower, fruit,
Even what shy bird with mute
Wonder at her travail there,
Meekly labored in its hair.
One three centuries removed   60
From the scenes his fathers loved,
Spicy grove, cinnamon tree,
What is Africa to me?

Incident   1925

For Eric Walrond

Once riding in old Baltimore,
    Heart-filled, head-filled with glee,
I saw a Baltimorean
    Keep looking straight at me.

Now I was eight and very small,   5
    And he was no whit bigger,

And so I smiled, but he poked out
   His tongue, and called me, "Nigger."
I saw the whole of Baltimore
   From May until December;
Of all the things that happened there
   That's all that I remember.

10

E. E. CUMMINGS

e. e. cummings (1894–1962) was born Edward Estlin Cummings in Cambridge, Massachusetts. His father was a Unitarian minister who taught sociology at Harvard. As a Harvard undergraduate, cummings wrote conventional verse, but under the influence of the poet and critic Ezra Pound, his poetry became less sentimental and more sharply satiric.

In 1917 he went to France with a friend to join the Red Cross Ambulance Corps, but he was careless in comments he made about the French Army in letters home, forgetting that mail was censored. He was arrested by the French authorities and imprisoned for treason. His father, however, had important government connections and succeeded in getting cummings released after four months of detention. The experience became the subject of cummings's sardonic, exuberant book, The Enormous Room, *which appeared in 1922.*

When cummings's poetry began to appear in the mid-1920s, it incited considerable controversy, not only for his experimental techniques of breaking up words and punctuation, but also for his eroticism and his irreverence toward the heroism of World War I. He justified his poetic experiments by saying that he was searching for a way to express the ecstasy of life. As he described it in the introduction to his Collected Poems *(1938), "We can never be born enough." In 1933 he traveled to the Soviet Union, and, characteristically, he was bored and disappointed with the Soviet social experiment.*

Also a painter, cummings spent much of his life writing and painting in a small house in Greenwich Village. The love poem "somewhere i have never travelled" is a brilliantly free variation on the form of the sonnet. The elegy "Buffalo Bill 's" is one of his best-known poems. "In Just-" is an example of his poetic technique at its freshest and most expressive. (See also cummings's "since feeling is first" on p. 823.)

WEB   *Research e. e. cummings and answer questions about his work at bedfordstmartins.com/charters/litwriters.*

somewhere i have never travelled   1931

somewhere i have never travelled,gladly beyond
any experience,your eyes have their silence:
in your most frail gesture are things which enclose me,
or which i cannot touch because they are too near

your slightest look easily will unclose me   5
though i have closed myself as fingers,
you open always petal by petal myself as Spring opens
(touching skilfully,mysteriously)her first rose

or if your wish be to close me,i and
my life will shut very beautifully,suddenly,   10
as when the heart of this flower imagines
the snow carefully everywhere descending;

nothing which we are to perceive in this world equals
the power of your intense fragility:whose texture
compels me with the colour of its countries,   15
rendering death and forever with each breathing

(i do not know what it is about you that closes
and opens;only something in me understands
the voice of your eyes is deeper than all roses)
nobody,not even the rain,has such small hands   20

Buffalo Bill 's°   1923

Buffalo Bill 's
defunct
            who used to
            ride a watersmooth-silver
                                        stallion   5
and break onetwothreefourfive pigeonsjustlikethat
                                            Jesus
he was a handsome man
                    and what i want to know is
how do you like your blueeyed boy
Mister Death   10

in Just-   1923

in Just-
spring   when the world is mud-
luscious the little
lame balloonman

whistles   far   and wee   5

and eddieandbill come
running from marbles and

Buffalo Bill 's: William Frederick Cody (1846–1917), known as Buffalo Bill, was a frontier scout who put together a "Wild West" show that was the most popular show in America for thirty years.

piracies and it's
spring

when the world is puddle-wonderful   10

the queer
old balloonman whistles
far   and   wee
and bettyandisbel come dancing

from hop-scotch and jump-rope and   15

it's
spring
and
    the
        goat-footed   20
balloonMan   whistles
far
and
wee

EMILY DICKINSON

Emily Dickinson (1830–1886) wrote in a letter,

> *If I read a book and it makes my whole body so cold no fire can ever warm me, I know that it is poetry. If I feel physically as if the top of my head were taken off, I know that is poetry. These are the only ways I know it. Is there any other way?*

It is difficult, though, to imagine how someone whose days seemed as quiet and uneventful as hers could feel such a strong emotion. Outwardly, so little happened in her life that someone reading her poetry today could say that the one "event" of her life came a few days after her death, when her sister Lavinia opened a box she'd left at the foot of her bed and found the manuscripts of hundreds of unpublished poems — poems that had been her sister's life's work.

Dickinson, the second child of Emily and Edward Dickinson, spent her life in the small Massachusetts town of Amherst, in a house where she was born and died. For the last fourteen years of her life she lived almost entirely in one room: her large, sunny front bedroom. In her last years she dressed all in white and saw only a few friends and relatives, even though her brother and his wife lived in the house beside hers. She communicated with people through notes and lines of poems, most of them so cryptic and veiled that it was hard to know what she meant. Her niece Martha, the daughter of her brother Austin, remembered that once she came into her aunt's bedroom and Dickinson pretended to lock the door behind her, saying, "Matty, here's freedom."

The reality of Emily Dickinson's life, however, is much more complicated. In her poetry there is anger and despair as well as joy. There are many poems that hint at an unhappy love affair. One, written when she was about thirty, suggests that she thought of herself as married:

> I'm "wife" — I've finished that —
> That other state —
> I'm Czar — I'm "Woman" now —
> It's safer so —

In another, possibly written a year later, there is a burst of passion:

> Wild Nights — Wild Nights!
> Were I with thee
> Wild nights would be
> Our luxury!

In 1890, four years after she had found the box of poems, Lavinia paid to have a small selection from the manuscripts published. For help with the editing she turned to her brother's lover, Mabel Loomis Todd, and the well-known writer and literary editor Thomas Wentworth Higginson. Higginson had corresponded with Emily for more than twenty years, and even journeyed to Amherst to meet her. The public response was overwhelming — there were ten printings of the book in the first year — and immediately readers began sifting through the hints and suggestions they found in the poems to try to understand what concealed events might have inspired Dickinson to write them.

Dickinson's poetry is so oblique — so "slant" in her term — that for many years it was impossible to identify the person she loved or to guess at why the relationship ended. However, when a literary scholar reconstructed her original arrangement of the poems into small hand-sewn booklets it became clear that Dickinson had fallen deeply in love in her late twenties. Her emotional attachment to a married minister named Charles Wadsworth began in 1858 and lasted until 1863. She heard him preach on a visit to Philadelphia, and when the family needed someone to help her through an emotionally difficult period in her life she was encouraged to write him. She began sending him groups of poems and in the spring of 1858 sent him the first of a series of turbulent "master" letters, describing her love and her emotional indebtedness to him. Although his own letters to her are carefully polite he came to Amherst to visit her in 1860, and in her poetry it seems clear that their relationship was physically consummated. It is from this time that she referred to herself as "wife," and she does not seem to have considered a relationship with anyone else, although letters to a family friend, Judge Otis Lord, in 1877 hint that he had proposed to her. She continued to correspond with Wadsworth, even when she realized that they could never marry, and she saw him again when he returned to Amherst in 1880.

For many years researchers suspected that the man she loved was a close family friend named Samuel Bowles, who was often a guest in the Dickinson home. Bowles was the editor of the Springfield Republican, a daily newspaper published in nearby Springfield. Bowles, it now seems certain, was one of the two or three people she used to help her send letters to Wadsworth. He published three of her poems, but in each case they were edited to smooth out what were considered to be their "irregularities." Reading her poems as a record of her love affair makes it clear that she could never consider publishing them. They were her secret diary, *and she asked Lavinia to destroy them at her death. When she wrote her now-famous letter to Thomas Wentworth Higginson in 1862, asking if he could tell her if her verse was "alive," she was only asking for his opinion, not for help in finding a publisher for the poems.*

Other strains and tensions are also mirrored in the poetry. Dickinson had a very complicated relationship with her father, who was a lawyer and treasurer of Amherst College. As she described her family in a letter to Higginson,

> *I have a brother and sister; my mother does not care for thought, and father, too busy with his briefs to notice what we do. He buys me many books, but begs me not to read them, because he fears they joggle the mind.*

In 1856 her brother married and moved into the house next door. For several years there was a warm friendliness between Dickinson and her sister-in-law, but the marriage soured, and finally the only contact between the two households was her brother's daily visit to Emily and her sister Lavinia, who also never married. In 1881, a year after Dickinson had met Wadsworth again, a young astronomy professor named David Todd moved to Amherst with his wife, Mabel. Austin Dickinson and Mabel Todd fell passionately in love, and their affair, more or less openly acknowledged, continued until his death. Lavinia carried the messages between them, and they sometimes met in Dickinson's house.

Until she was in her thirties, Dickinson still took part in Amherst life. In 1856 her bread won second prize at the Agricultural Fair, and the next year she was on the Cattle Show Committee. As she dealt with the complex emotional tensions of her relationship, she became more and more socially withdrawn, so that by 1863 Samuel Bowles referred to her in a note to Austin as "Queen recluse." In 1862 she wrote to Higginson after he'd published an article in the April Atlantic Monthly suggesting that he might be interested in hearing from young poets. He responded to her letter with interest, but he found her poems too idiosyncratic to publish. It seems clear, however, that she had already decided that her poetry would be her "letter to the World / that never wrote to me," as she said in a poem from 1862. In 1869, when Higginson wrote and asked if she would come to Boston, she answered, "I do not cross my Father's ground to any House or Town."

Higginson, however, showed the poems to a childhood friend of Dickinson's, the successful writer Helen Hunt Jackson, and Jackson immediately recognized the genius in the work and begged her to publish. In 1876 Jackson wrote her, "You are a great poet — and it is a wrong . . . that you will not sing aloud." Jackson was able to persuade her to have a poem published anonymously, but there was never any question that Dickinson would consider further publication. The themes of the poetry of her last years were death and eternity.

Dickinson's poems seemed innocent and naive to some of her early readers, but she was conscious of other poets and their work. Unlike Elizabeth Barrett Browning, who never went to school, Dickinson went first to the Amherst Academy and then spent a year, when she was seventeen, at Mount Holyoke Female Seminary, now Mount Holyoke College. It is interesting to compare her poetry to Barrett Browning's, since she admired the English writer so much that she had a portrait of her on the wall of her bedroom. She read, but certainly was not influenced in any way by, Barrett Browning's defiant novel in verse, Aurora Leigh, with its attack on the passive role forced on women in their society. When she learned that Higginson was traveling to Europe, not long after Barrett Browning's death, Dickinson wrote him "If you touch her Grave, put one hand on the Head, for me—her unmentioned mourner."

Dickinson also read the works of John Keats, whom she admired the most of the Romantics, the Brontë sisters, and Alfred, Lord Tennyson, as well as the novels of George Eliot. But she did not let herself be influenced by the technical skill of the Victorian poets. Much of her poetry is written in simple quatrains, generally in iambic tetrameter, often with only the second and fourth lines rhyming. It is close to the style of verse that filled the hymnals she used in church. Her poetry is so startling in its imagery and its revelations that there is no real parallel to it, but it is interesting that in its form it has some similarities with the poetry of Emily Brontë. Brontë, who found literary immortality with her novel Wuthering Heights, *was one of the writers Dickinson read. Like Dickinson, Brontë was reclusive, spent her short life in her family home, and drew on the hymnal for the forms of her poetry. These lines by Brontë could also have been written by Dickinson:*

> *I'm happiest when most away*
> *I can bear my soul from its home of clay*
> *On a windy night when the moon is bright*
> *And the eye wander through worlds of light . . .*
>
> *No coward soul is mine*
> *No trembler in the world's storm-troubled sphere.*

Higginson read Brontë's poem "Last Lines" at Dickinson's funeral. Seven of Dickinson's poems were published in her lifetime, and in each case they were edited or rewritten to suit the conventions of the time. Would she have edited them herself if Helen Hunt Jackson could have finally persuaded her to publish them? Like so much else about her life, we will never know. We do know that every revision Higginson suggested in his letters to her was gently but firmly rejected. She knew what she had accomplished. What she left was a gathering of poems so unique and unexpected that we are still trying today to measure the dimensions of her achievement.

This selection from her poetry includes many of her best-known poems, in the transcriptions from her manuscripts published in 1948. The poems in the new edition were numbered, as Dickinson did not title them herself. They can be interpreted in many ways, and often they refer to some specific moment in the day they were written, like "I've nothing else—to bring, You know—," which seems to be telling Charles Wadsworth that the only things that Dickinson can bring him are poems. The poems are startling in their imagery, and behind the deceptive simplicities of their lines are subtle insights. In "I'm 'wife'—I've finished that—" Dickinson describes the passage from girl to woman as "this soft Eclipse." The sixth poem in this group begins with the unforgettable image " 'Hope' is the thing with feathers— / That perches in the soul." "I taste a liquor never brewed—" was one of the three poems that Bowles published in his newspaper, and it became one of the poems discussed by other writers when it was included in the first collection in 1890. The popular poet Thomas Bailey Aldrich was irritated by the imperfect rhyme of "pearl / alcohol" in the first stanza and quickly rewrote it. His "corrected" version was,

> *I taste a liquor never brewed*
> *In vats along the Rhine:*
> *No tankards scooped in pearl could yield*
> *An alcohol like mine.*

Nothing Aldrich ever wrote, however, could match the exuberance of the poem's last image of Dickinson herself as "the little Tippler / Leaning against the—Sun."

"I'm Nobody! Who are you?" is her sardonic comment on fame, and in "Much Madness is divinest Sense—" she could be agreeing with William Blake, with his belief that society often mistakes genius for madness. "I died for Beauty—but was scarce" is one of her many poems on the subject of death, this one agreeing with John Keats's final lines of "Ode on a Grecian Urn": " 'Beauty is truth, truth beauty'—that is all / Ye know on earth, and all ye need to know." "Love—thou art high—" and "If you were coming in the Fall," are both from the last months of Dickinson's relationship with Charles Wadsworth. "Mine—by the Right of the White Election!" was probably written when she realized they could never marry, although it is—as always—difficult to be certain of the circumstances of the poem. The phrase "White Election" probably means a wedding ceremony.

"Because I could not stop for Death—" and "The Only News I know" were written in the next years. The former, with its image of death as a gentle carriage ride, was one of the most widely quoted poems from the 1890 collection. The latter was not published until 1929. "Split the Lark—and you'll find the Music—" opens with an image as vivid as the first line of " 'Hope' is the thing with feathers—." Although "I stepped from Plank to Plank" suggests that Dickinson had lived many years to gain her "Experience," she was only thirty-four. Still, she was already feeling her life closing in around her. "A narrow Fellow in the Grass," her brilliant description of a snake and the fear she feels whenever she sees one, was published in the Springfield Republican, but she complained that it had been published without her permission. For much of her life she was troubled by her inability to accept conventional Christian dogma, but "I never saw a Moor—" is a clear statement of her religious faith. Dickinson has found her own way to eternity. (See also Dickinson's "A word is dead" on p. 692.)

CONVERSATIONS See pages 1010–1045, including Thomas Wentworth Higginson, "Emily Dickinson's Letters," page 1012; Thomas H. Johnson, "The Text of Emily Dickinson's Poetry," page 1019; Thomas Bailey Aldrich, "In Re Emily Dickinson," page 1020; Richard Wilbur, "On Emily Dickinson," page 1022; Linda Gregg, "Not Understanding Emily Dickinson," page 1024; Galway Kinnell, "The Deconstruction of Emily Dickinson," page 1027.

WEB Research Emily Dickinson and answer questions about her work at bedfordstmartins.com/charters/litwriters.

You love me—you are sure—　　　　　　　c. 1860

You love me—you are sure—
I shall not fear mistake—

I shall not *cheated* wake—
Some grinning morn—
to find the Sunrise left—   5
And Orchards—unbereft—
And Dollie—gone!

I need not start—you're sure—
That night will never be—
When frightened—home to Thee I run—   10
To find the windows dark—
And no more Dollie—mark—
Quite none?

Be sure you're sure—you know—
I'll bear it better now—   15
If you'll just tell me so—
Than when—a little dull Balm grown—
Over this pain of mine—
You sting—again!

I'm "wife"—I've finished that—   c. 1860

I'm "wife"—I've finished that—
That other state—
I'm Czar—I'm "Woman" now—
It's safer so—

How odd the Girl's life looks   5
Behind this soft Eclipse—
I think that Earth feels so
To folks in Heaven—now—

This being comfort—then
That other kind—was pain—   10
But why compare?
I'm "Wife"! Stop there!

I taste a liquor never brewed—   c. 1860

I taste a liquor never brewed—
From Tankards scooped in Pearl—
Not all the Vats upon the Rhine
Yield such an Alcohol!

Inebriate of Air—am I—   5
And Debauchee of Dew—
Reeling—thro endless summer days—
From inns of Molten Blue—

When "Landlords" turn the drunken Bee
Out of the Foxglove's door— 10
When Butterflies—renounce their "drams"—
I shall but drink the more!

Till Seraphs swing their snowy Hats—
And Saints—to windows run—
To see the little Tippler 15
Leaning against the—Sun—

I've nothing else—to bring, You know—   c. 1861

I've nothing else—to bring, You know—
So I keep bringing These—
Just as the Night keeps fetching Stars
To our familiar eyes—

Maybe, we shouldn't mind them—
Unless they didn't come—
Then—maybe, it would puzzle us
To find our way Home—

Wild Nights—Wild Nights!   c. 1861

Wild Nights—Wild Nights!
Were I with thee
Wild Nights should be
Our luxury!

Futile—the Winds— 5
To a Heart in port—
Done with the Compass—
Done with the Chart!

Rowing in Eden—
Ah, the Sea! 10
Might I but moor—Tonight—
In Thee!

"Hope" is the thing with feathers—   c. 1861

"Hope" is the thing with feathers—
That perches in the soul—
And sings the tune without the words—
And never stops—at all—

And sweetest — in the Gale — is heard —   5
And sore must be the storm —
That could abash the little Bird
That kept so many warm —

I've heard it in the chillest land —
And on the strangest Sea —   10
Yet, never, in Extremity,
It asked a crumb — of Me.

There's a certain Slant of light,   c. 1861

There's a certain Slant of light,
Winter Afternoons —
That oppresses, like the Heft
Of Cathedral Tunes —

Heavenly Hurt, it gives us —   5
We can find no scar,
But internal difference,
Where the Meanings, are —

None may teach it — Any —
'Tis the Seal Despair —   10
An imperial affliction
Sent us of the Air —

When it comes, the Landscape listens —
Shadows — hold their breath —
When it goes, 'tis like the Distance   15
On the look of Death —

I'm Nobody! Who are you?   c. 1861

I'm Nobody! Who are you?
Are you — Nobody — Too?
Then there's a pair of us!
Don't tell! they'd advertise — you know!

How dreary — to be — Somebody!
How public — like a Frog —
To tell one's name — the livelong June —
To an admiring Bog!

After great pain, a formal feeling comes —   c. 1862

After great pain, a formal feeling comes —
The Nerves sit ceremonious, like Tombs —

The stiff Heart questions was it He, that bore,
And Yesterday, or Centuries before?

The Feet, mechanical, go round— 5
Of Ground, or Air, or Ought—
A Wooden way
Regardless grown,
A Quartz contentment, like a stone—

This is the Hour of Lead— 10
Remembered, if outlived,
As Freezing persons, recollect the Snow—
First—Chill—then Stupor—then the letting go—

Much Madness is divinest Sense— c. 1862

Much Madness is divinest Sense—
To a discerning Eye—
Much Sense—the starkest Madness—
'Tis the Majority
In this, as All, prevail—
Assent—and you are sane—
Demur—you're straightway dangerous—
And handled with a Chain—

I died for Beauty—but was scarce c. 1862

I died for Beauty—but was scarce
Adjusted in the Tomb
When One who died for Truth, was lain
In an adjoining Room—

He questioned softly "Why I failed"? 5
"For Beauty," I replied—
"And I—for Truth—Themself are One—
We Brethren, are," He said—

And so, as Kinsmen, met a Night—
We talked between the Rooms— 10
Until the Moss had reached our lips—
And covered up—our names—

Love—thou art high— c. 1862

Love—thou art high—
I cannot climb thee—

But, were it Two—
Who knows but we—
Taking turns—at the Chimborazo°—   5
Ducal—at last—stand up by thee—

Love—thou art deep—
I cannot cross thee—
But, were there Two
Instead of One—   10
Rower, and Yacht—some sovereign Summer—
Who knows—but we'd reach the Sun?

Love—thou art Veiled—
A few—behold thee—
Smile—and alter—and prattle—and die—   15
Bliss—were an Oddity—without thee—
Nicknamed by God—
Eternity—

I heard a Fly buzz—when I died—   c. 1862

I heard a Fly buzz—when I died—
The Stillness in the Room
Was like the Stillness in the Air—
Between the Heaves of Storm—

The Eyes around—had wrung them dry—   5
And Breaths were gathering firm
For that last Onset—when the King
Be witnessed—in the Room—

I willed my Keepsakes—Signed away
What portion of me be   10
Assignable—and then it was
There interposed a Fly—

With Blue—uncertain stumbling Buzz—
Between the light—and me—
And then the Windows failed—and then   15
I could not see to see—

If you were coming in the Fall,   c. 1862

If you were coming in the Fall,
I'd brush the Summer by
With half a smile, and half a spurn,
As Housewives do, a Fly.

---

5. **Chimborazo:** An inactive volcano in Ecuador.

If I could see you in a year,   5
I'd wind the months in balls—
And put them each in separate Drawers,
For fear the numbers fuse—

If only Centuries, delayed,
I'd count them on my Hand,   10
Subtracting, till my fingers dropped
Into Van Dieman's Land.°

If certain, when this life was out—
That yours and mine, should be
I'd toss it yonder, like a Rind,   15
And take Eternity—

But, now, uncertain of the length
Of this, that is between,
It goads me, like the Goblin Bee—
That will not state—its sting.   20

Mine—by the Right of the White Election!   c. 1862

Mine—by the Right of the White Election!
Mine—by the Royal Seal!
Mine—by the Sign in the Scarlet prison—
Bars—cannot conceal!

Mine—here—in Vision—and in Veto!
Mine—by the Grave's Repeal—
Titled—Confirmed—
Delirious Charter!
Mine—long as Ages steal!

Because I could not stop for Death—   c. 1863

Because I could not stop for Death—
He kindly stopped for me—
The Carriage held but just Ourselves—
And Immortality.

We slowly drove—He knew no haste   5
And I had put away
My labor and my leisure too,
For His Civility—

---

12. Van Dieman's Land: The seventeenth-century Dutch navigator Abel Tasman named an island off the coast of Australia Van Diemen's Land, which Dickinson has misspelled. Today it is the Australian commonwealth of Tasmania.

We passed the School, where Children strove
At Recess—in the Ring— 10
We passed the Fields of Gazing Grain—
We passed the Setting Sun—

Or rather—He passed Us—
The Dews drew quivering and chill—
For only Gossamer, my Gown— 15
My Tippet—only Tulle—

We paused before a House that seemed
A Swelling of the Ground—
The Roof was scarcely visible—
The Cornice—in the Ground— 20

Since then—'tis Centuries—and yet
Feels shorter than the Day
I first surmised the Horses' Heads
Were toward Eternity—

The Only News I know

c. 1864

The Only News I know
Is Bulletins all Day
From Immortality.

The Only Shows I see—
Tomorrow and Today— 5
Perchance Eternity—

The Only One I meet
Is God—The Only Street—
Existence—This traversed

If Other News there be— 10
Or Admirabler Show—
I'll tell it You—

Split the Lark—and you'll find the Music—

c. 1864

Split the Lark—and you'll find the Music—
Bulb after Bulb, in Silver rolled—
Scantily dealt to the Summer Morning
Saved for your Ear when Lutes be old.

Loose the Flood—you shall find it patent—
Gush after Gush, reserved for you—
Scarlet Experiment! Sceptic Thomas!
Now, do you doubt that your Bird was true?

I stepped from Plank to Plank

c. 1864

I stepped from Plank to Plank
A slow and cautious way
The Stars about my Head I felt
About my Feet the Sea.

I knew not but the next
Would be my final inch—
This gave me that precarious Gait
Some call Experience.

A narrow Fellow in the Grass

c. 1865

A narrow Fellow in the Grass
Occasionally rides—
You may have met Him—did you not
His notice sudden is—

The Grass divides as with a Comb—   5
A spotted shaft is seen—
And then it closes at your feet
And opens further on—

He likes a Boggy Acre
A Floor too cool for Corn—   10
Yet when a Boy, and Barefoot—
I more than once at Noon

Have passed, I thought, a Whip lash
Unbraiding in the Sun
When stooping to secure it   15
It wrinkled, and was gone—

Several of Nature's People
I know, and they know me—
I feel for them a transport
Of cordiality—   20

But never met this Fellow
Attended, or alone
Without a tighter breathing
And Zero at the Bone—

I never saw a Moor—

c. 1865

I never saw a Moor—
I never saw the Sea—
Yet know I how the Heather looks
And what a Billow be.

I never spoke with God
Nor visited in Heaven —
Yet certain am I of the spot
As if the Checks were given —

JOHN DONNE

John Donne (1572–1631) was born a Roman Catholic during a period in English history when Roman Catholics were harassed by the Protestant government and were barred from advancement to most major positions of influence. His father died when he was four, and he was left with enough income to live well but not enough to purchase favor at the court of Queen Elizabeth. He studied at Oxford and Cambridge universities but earned no degrees.

In his early twenties, Donne lived like many other young, ambitious courtiers. He had many mistresses, traveled extensively in Europe, and took part in two raids against the Spanish at Cadiz and in the Azores. At the same time he read voraciously and wrote some of his most vivid erotic poetry. He had renounced his Catholicism but still hesitated to join the Church of England.

In 1598, when he was twenty-six, Donne became private secretary to Sir Thomas Egerton, one of the most powerful figures in the court of Queen Elizabeth. A brilliant future seemed certain, but three years later Donne fell deeply in love and secretly married Ann More, the seventeen-year-old niece of Lady Egerton. He was dismissed and thrown into prison, and for a dozen years he struggled against disappointment and financial difficulties. During this period his marriage was his only source of happiness.

Because of his brilliance and his early friendships, Donne was still welcome in the court, but King James, who succeeded Elizabeth, felt that Donne could be most useful to him in the church, and refused to consider granting Donne any other position. Donne finally surrendered and in 1615 became an Anglican priest. He was as talented in the church as he had been in court life, and in 1621 he became dean of St. Paul's Cathedral in London, where he delivered sermons and wrote devotional poetry and meditations until his death.

This selection of Donne's poetry includes one of his idiosyncratic love poems, "The Good-Morrow." "A Valediction: Forbidding Mourning," written earlier, was composed for his wife before he left her on a trip to France. "Batter my heart, three-personed God" is from his collection of "Holy Sonnets." (See also Donne's "Death, be not proud" on p. 753.)

CONNECTION *Wendy Cope, "The fine English poet, John Donne," page 759.*

WEB *Research John Donne and answer questions about his work at bedfordstmartins.com/charters/litwriters.*

A Valediction:° Forbidding Mourning   1611

As virtuous men pass mildly away,
   And whisper to their souls to go,
Whilst some of their sad friends do say
   The breath goes now, and some say, no;

So let us melt, and make no noise,   5
   No tear-floods, nor sigh-tempests move,
'Twere profanation of our joys
   To tell the laity° our love.

Moving of th' earth brings harms and fears,
   Men reckon what it did and meant;   10
But trepidation of the spheres,°
   Though greater far, is innocent.

Dull sublunary° lovers' love
   (Whose soul is sense) cannot admit
Absence, because it doth remove   15
   Those things which elemented° it.   *composed*

But we by a love so much refined
   That our selves know not what it is,
Inter-assurèd of the mind,
   Care less, eyes, lips, and hands to miss.   20

Our two souls therefore, which are one,
   Though I must go, endure not yet
A breach, but an expansion,
   Like gold to airy thinness beat.

If they be two, they are two so   25
   As stiff twin compasses are two;
Thy soul, the fixed foot, makes no show
   To move, but doth, if th' other do.

And though it in the center sit,
   Yet when the other far doth roam,   30
It leans and hearkens after it,
   And grows erect, as that comes home.

Such wilt thou be to me, who must
   Like th' other foot, obliquely° run.   *diagonally, aslant*
Thy firmness makes my circle° just,   35
   And makes me end where I begun.

Valediction: A departure speech or discourse; a bidding of farewell. **8. laity:** Common people. **11. trepidation of the spheres:** A trembling of the celestial spheres, hypothesized by Ptolemaic astronomers to account for unpredicted variations in the paths of the heavenly bodies. **13. sublunary:** Beneath the moon; earthly, hence, changeable. **35. circle:** The circle was a symbol of perfection; with a dot in the middle, it was also the alchemist's symbol for gold.

The Good-Morrow   1633

I wonder, by my troth, what thou and I
Did, till we loved? Were we not weaned till then,
But sucked on country pleasures, childishly?
Or snorted we in the seven sleepers' den?
'Twas so; but this, all pleasures fancies be.   5
If ever any beauty I did see,
Which I desired, and got, 'twas but a dream of thee.

And now good morrow to our waking souls,
Which watch not one another out of fear;
For love all love of other sights controls,   10
And makes one little room an everywhere.
Let sea-discoverers to new worlds have gone,
Let maps to others, worlds on worlds have shown:
Let us possess one world; each hath one, and is one.

My face in thine eye, thine in mine appears,   15
And true plain hearts do in the faces rest;
Where can we find two better hemispheres,
Without sharp North, without declining West?
Whatever dies was not mixed equally;
If our two loves be one, or thou and I   20
Love so alike that none do slacken, none can die.

Batter my heart, three-personed God   1633

Batter my heart, three-personed God; for You
As yet but knock, breathe, shine, and seek to mend;
That I may rise and stand, o'erthrow me, 'and bend
Your force to break, blow, burn, and make me new.
I, like an usurped town, to 'another due,   5
Labor to 'admit You, but O, to no end;
Reason, Your viceroy 'in me, me should defend,
But is captíved, and proves weak or untrue.
Yet dearly 'I love You, 'and would be lovéd fain,
But am betrothed unto Your enemy.   10
Divorce me, 'untie or break that knot again;
Take me to You, imprison me, for I,
Except You 'enthrall me, never shall be free,
Nor ever chaste, except You ravish me.

RITA DOVE

Rita Dove (b. 1952) was born in Akron, Ohio, in an African American family who believed that the way out of the American racial dilemma was education. As Dove later wrote, "Education was the key: that much we knew, and so I was a good student. . . . I adored learning new things and looked forward to what intellectual adventures each school day would bring; some of the luckiest magic was to open a book and to come away the wiser after having been lost in the pages."

She graduated summa cum laude from Miami University in Ohio in 1973 and traveled abroad on a Fulbright/Hayes fellowship to study modern European literature at the University of Gübingen, in Germany. After two years in Germany, she returned to the United States and completed her M.F.A. at the University of Iowa in 1977. In Iowa she met and married German novelist Fred Viebahn. Her years in Europe and her marriage have given her writing an international flavor and a broad cultural outlook. Her first poetry collection, Museum, *was published in 1983, when she was thirty-one. She was immediately recognized as an important new voice in American poetry and was awarded the Pulitzer Prize in 1986 for* Thomas and Beulah *(1986), a suite of biographical poems with her grandparents' lives as the central narrative. From 1993 to 1995, she was the poet laureate of the United States, the first African American, the first woman, and the youngest writer to be chosen for this honor. She is a professor of English, teaching creative writing at the University of Virginia.*

The writers Michael S. Harper and Anthony Walton, in their Vintage Book of African American Poetry *(2000), praised her work for its energy and elegance. "Her talent for disclosing vibrant inner images in elegant phrasing gives her lines their force and balance, ranking Dove's poems as among the finest of her era." "Singsong," "Maple Valley Branch Library, 1967," and "The Pond, Porch-View: Six P.M., Early Spring" are from her collection* On the Bus with Rosa Parks *(1999). See also "Sonnet in Primary Colors," page 755.*

COMMENTARY   *Rita Dove, "An Intact World," page 971.*

WEB   *Research Rita Dova and answer questions about her work at bedfordstmartins.com/charters/litwriters.*

Singsong   1998

When I was young, the moon spoke in riddles
and the stars rhymed. I was a new toy
waiting for my owner to pick me up.

When I was young, I ran the day to its knees.
There were trees to swing on, crickets for capture.   5

I was narrowly sweet, infinitely cruel,
tongued in honey and coddled in milk,
sunburned and silvery and scabbed like a colt.

And the world was already old.
And I was older than I am today.   10

Maple Valley Branch Library, 1967   1997

For a fifteen-year-old there was plenty
to do: Browse the magazines,
slip into the Adult Section to see
what vast *tristesse*° was born of rush-hour traffic,
décolletés,° and the plague of too much money.   5
There was so much to discover—how to
lay out a road, the language of flowers,
and the place of women in the tribe of Moost.
There were equations elegant as a French twist,
fractal geometry's unwinding maple leaf;   10

I could follow, step-by-step, the slow disclosure
of a pineapple Jell-O mold—or take
the path of Harold's purple crayon through
the bedroom window and onto a lavender
spill of stars. Oh, I could walk any aisle   15
and smell wisdom, put a hand out to touch
the rough curve of bound leather,
the harsh parchment of dreams.

As for the improbable librarian
with her salt and paprika upsweep,   20
her British accent and sweater clip
(mom of a kid I knew from school)—
I'd go up to her desk and ask for help
on bareback rodeo or binary codes,
phonics, Gestalt theory,   25
lead poisoning in the Late Roman Empire,
the play of light in Dutch Renaissance painting;
I would claim to be researching
pre-Columbian pottery or Chinese foot-binding,
but all I wanted to know was: 30
Tell me what you've read that keeps
that half smile afloat
above the collar of your impeccable blouse.

So I read *Gone with the Wind* because
it was big, and haiku because they were small.   35
I studied history for its rhapsody of dates,
lingered over Cubist art for the way
it showed all the sides of a guitar at once.
All the time in the world was there, and sometimes
all the world on a single page.   40
As much as I could hold
on my plastic card's imprint I took,

---

4. *tristesse:* Sadness.   5. **décolletés:** Low necklines.

greedily: six books, six volumes of bliss,
the stuff we humans are made of:
words and sighs and silence, 45
ink and whips, Brahma and cosine,
corsets and poetry and blood sugar levels—
I carried it home, past five blocks of aluminum siding
and the old garage where, on its boarded-up doors,
someone had scrawled: 50

I CAN EAT AN ELEPHANT
IF I TAKE SMALL BITES.

Yes, I said, to no one in particular: *That's*
what I'm gonna do!

The Pond, Porch-View: Six P.M., Early Spring 1999

I sit, and sit, and will my thoughts
the way they used to wend
when thoughts were young
(i.e., accused of wandering).
The sunset ticks another notch 5
into the pressure treated rails
of the veranda. My heart, too,
has come down to earth;
I've missed the chance
to put things in reverse, 10
recapture childhood's backseat
universe. Where I'm at now
is more like riding on a bus
through unfamiliar neighborhoods—
chair in recline, the view chopped square 15
and dimming quick. I know
I vowed I'd get off
somewhere grand; like that dear goose
come honking down
from Canada, I tried to end up 20
anyplace but here.
Who am I kidding? Here I am.

T. S. ELIOT

    T. S. Eliot (1888–1965) was born Thomas Stearns Eliot in St. Louis, Missouri. His mother was a schoolteacher who also wrote poetry, and his father was a successful businessman. Eliot was sent to finish his education at Milton Academy, south of Boston, and then attended Harvard College.

Following his graduation from Harvard in 1910, he spent a year in France studying at the Sorbonne and became intensely interested in the writing of a brilliant group of contemporary French poets who called themselves symbolists. When he returned to Harvard to earn his doctorate the next year, he began writing "The Love Song of J. Alfred Prufrock," a poem that included phrases and attitudes translated from the work of symbolist poets Jules Laforgue and Arthur Rimbaud. Conrad Aiken, a fellow student who was also a poet, encouraged him to publish it, but Eliot waited until he returned to Europe in 1914 and was studying at Oxford. He read the poem to Ezra Pound, who immediately sent it to an American magazine. It is considered by most critics to be the first modernist poem written in English.

In 1915 Eliot suddenly married Vivian Haigh-Wood, whom he had met in England, and had to find some kind of job to support them. He was first a schoolteacher, then a bank clerk, and finally a director in a London publishing house. With the publication in 1922 of his controversial long poem The Wasteland—*a work begun during a stay in a sanatorium brought about by exhaustion, marital difficulties, and depression—he became one of the world's most widely read and discussed younger poets. His writing, both as a poet and a literary critic, had a decisive effect on nearly every poetic tradition before World War II. He became a British citizen in 1927. In 1948 he won the Nobel Prize for literature.*

CONNECTION   *J. Walker, "(On T. S. Eliot's 'Prufrock') An angst-ridden amorist, Fred," page 759.*

COMMENTARIES   *Cleanth Brooks Jr. and Robert Penn Warren, "On Eliot's 'The Love Song of J. Alfred Prufrock,'" page 966; T. S. Eliot, "From 'Tradition and the Individual Talent,'" page 972.*

WEB   *Research T. S. Eliot and answer questions about his work at bedfordstmartins.com/charters/litwriters.*

The Love Song of J. Alfred Prufrock   1917

S'io credesse che mia risposta fosse
A persona che mai tornasse al mondo,
Questa fiamma staria senza piu scosse.
Ma perciocche giammai di questo fondo
Non torno vivo alcun, s'i'odo il vero,
Sensa tema d'infamia ti rispondo.°

Let us go then, you and I,
When the evening is spread out against the sky
Like a patient etherized upon a table;
Let us go, through certain half-deserted streets,

S'io . . . rispondo: In Dante's *Inferno*, these lines are spoken by one of the "false counselors" whose soul is hidden within a flame that moves as it speaks: "If I believed my reply were given / to one who might ever return to the earth, this fire would cease further movement. / But as from this chasm/none has ever come back alive—if what I have heard is true— / without fearing infamy will I respond to you."

The muttering retreats 5
Of restless nights in one-night cheap hotels
And sawdust restaurants with oyster-shells:
Streets that follow like a tedious argument
Of insidious intent
To lead you to an overwhelming question . . . 10
Oh, do not ask, "What is it?"
Let us go and make our visit.

In the room the women come and go
Talking of Michelangelo.

The yellow fog that rubs its back upon the window-panes 15
The yellow smoke that rubs its muzzle on the window-panes
Licked its tongue into the corners of the evening,
Lingered upon the pools that stand in drains,
Let fall upon its back the soot that falls from chimneys,
Slipped by the terrace, made a sudden leap, 20
And seeing that it was a soft October night,
Curled once about the house, and fell asleep.

And indeed there will be time
For the yellow smoke that slides along the street,
Rubbing its back upon the window-panes; 25
There will be time, there will be time
To prepare a face to meet the faces that you meet;
There will be time to murder and create,
And time for all the works and days of hands
That lift and drop a question on your plate; 30
Time for you and time for me,
And time yet for a hundred indecisions,
And for a hundred visions and revisions,
Before the taking of a toast and tea.

In the room the women come and go 35
Talking of Michelangelo.

And indeed there will be time
To wonder, "Do I dare?" and, "Do I dare?"
Time to turn back and descend the stair,
With a bald spot in the middle of my hair— 40
[They will say: "How his hair is growing thin!"]
My morning coat, my collar mounting firmly to the chin,
My necktie rich and modest, but asserted by a simple pin—
[They will say: "But how his arms and legs are thin!"]
Do I dare 45
Disturb the universe?
In a minute there is time
For decisions and revisions which a minute will reverse.

For I have known them all already, known them all:
Have known the evenings, mornings, afternoons, 50

I have measured out my life with coffee spoons;
I know the voices dying with a dying fall
Beneath the music from a farther room.
    So how should I presume?

And I have known the eyes already, known them all—   55
The eyes that fix you in a formulated phrase,
And when I am formulated, sprawling on a pin,
When I am pinned and wriggling on the wall,
Then how should I begin
To spit out all the butt-ends of my days and ways?   60
    And how should I presume?

And I have known the arms already, known them all—
Arms that are braceleted and white and bare
[But in the lamplight, downed with light brown hair!]
Is it perfume from a dress   65
That makes me so digress?
Arms that lie along a table, or wrap about a shawl.
    And should I then presume?
    And how should I begin?

Shall I say, I have gone at dusk through narrow streets   70
And watched the smoke that rises from the pipes
Of lonely men in shirt-sleeves, leaning out of windows? . . .

I should have been a pair of ragged claws
Scuttling across the floors of silent seas.

And the afternoon, the evening, sleeps so peacefully!   75
Smoothed by long fingers,
Asleep . . . tired . . . or it malingers,
Stretched on the floor, here beside you and me.
Should I, after tea and cakes and ices,
Have the strength to force the moment to its crisis?   80
But though I have wept and fasted, wept and prayed,
Though I have seen my head [grown slightly bald] brought in upon a
    platter,°
I am no prophet—and here's no great matter;
I have seen the moment of my greatness flicker,
And I have seen the eternal Footman hold my coat, and snicker,   85
And in short, I was afraid.

And would it have been worth it, after all,
After the cups, the marmalade, the tea,
Among the porcelain, among some talk of you and me,
Would it have been worth while,   90

---

82. **upon a platter:** A reference to the martyrdom of St. John the Baptist (Matthew 14:1–12).

To have bitten off the matter with a smile,
To have squeezed the universe into a ball
To roll it toward some overwhelming question,
To say: "I am Lazarus,° come from the dead,
Come back to tell you all, I shall tell you all" —   95
If one, settling a pillow by her head,
   Should say: "That is not what I meant at all.
   That is not it, at all."

And would it have been worth it, after all,
Would it have been worth while,   100
After the sunsets and the dooryards and the sprinkled streets,
After the novels, after the teacups, after the skirts that trail along the
   floor —
And this, and so much more? —
It is impossible to say just what I mean!
But as if a magic lantern threw the nerves in patterns on a screen: 105
Would it have been worth while
If one, settling a pillow or throwing off a shawl,
And turning toward the window, should say:
   "That is not it at all,
   That is not what I meant, at all."   110

No! I am not Prince Hamlet, nor was meant to be;
Am an attendant lord, one that will do
To swell a progress, start a scene or two,
Advise the prince; no doubt, an easy tool,
Deferential, glad to be of use,   115
Politic, cautious, and meticulous;
Full of high sentence, but a bit obtuse;
At times, indeed, almost ridiculous —
Almost, at times, the Fool.

I grow old . . . I grow old . . .   120
I shall wear the bottoms of my trousers rolled.

Shall I part my hair behind? Do I dare to eat a peach?
I shall wear white flannel trousers, and walk upon the beach.
I have heard the mermaids singing, each to each.

I do not think that they will sing to me.   125

I have seen them riding seaward on the waves
Combing the white hair of the waves blown back
When the wind blows the water white and black.

We have lingered in the chambers of the sea
By sea-girls wreathed with seaweed red and brown   130
Till human voices wake us, and we drown.

---

94. "I am Lazarus": A reference to the resurrected Lazarus (John II, 12:1–2).

ROBERT FROST

Although Walt Whitman proclaimed himself the poet of the American democracy, it is the quiet poet of the New England countryside, Robert Frost (1874–1963), who is the closest the United States has come to a "national" poet. It was fitting that when President-elect John F. Kennedy was inaugurated for a presidency that he dreamed would re-create the American spirit, he chose Robert Frost to read a new poem for the occasion. The sun shone so brightly in the poet's eyes that he could not read the new poem he had written, so he recited an old poem from memory, and it fit just as well into the solemn ceremony.

Although Robert Frost's poetry rings with the tones of New England, and the voice of his poems is that of a New England farmer, this was the result of a conscious artistic choice. His own background was more diverse. He was born in San Francisco in 1874, and lived there eleven years until his father's death. His mother then moved with Robert and his younger sister Jeanie to Lawrence, Massachusetts, where she looked for work as a schoolteacher. Frost attended high school in Lawrence and was a valedictorian at his graduation. Three years later, after a stormy and jealous courtship, he married the woman who had been the other valedictorian, Elinor White. It was a marriage with only brief moments of happiness, but Elinor gave birth to six children, two of whom died very young. After high school Frost briefly attended Dartmouth and Harvard, and for the next twenty years he struggled to support his family with a series of poorly paid jobs, writing poems at night and sending them to local newspapers. One of his failed projects was an attempt to operate a chicken farm in New Hampshire, and even though he was unsuccessful as a farmer the experience gave him the setting for his poetry.

Although Frost in later years described the family's poverty during this time in bleak terms, he was being partially supported by his grandfather. As biographer William H. Pritchard writes in Frost: A Literary Life Reconsidered *(1984),*

> Frost had tried poultry farming in Derry, New Hampshire, the farm purchased for him by his paternal grandfather, and the indifferent results probably had a good deal to do with the very qualified way he would later characterize himself as a farmer. When William Prescott Frost died in 1901, he gave his grandson free use of the farm for ten years, after which it would belong to Frost. There was, as well, an annuity of five hundred dollars for each of the first ten years; it would then become eight hundred for the rest of the grandson's life. Meanwhile, in 1906, Frost began full-time teaching at Pinkerton Academy, in Derry, and in 1911 taught for a year at the Plymouth Normal School, in Plymouth, New Hampshire. In 1911, the farm having become his to do with as he pleased, Frost sold it, and the proceeds, in addition to the enlarged annuity, which was now his, made the possibility of living away from New England for a time—with no responsibilities except literary and familial ones—real and attractive.

In 1912, despite the support from his grandfather he was so discouraged at his failure as a writer that he was close to emotional collapse, deeply depressed, and suicidal. In an effort to wrench himself free, he took the family to England, where they lived on his annuity. He formed a close friendship with Edward

Thomas, a young English literary journalist, who began writing poetry himself after he had come to know Frost. Frost said of him later that he was "the only brother I ever had." His meetings with young English poets helped him to strip his poetry of its conventional imagery, and in 1913 he was able to find a publisher for his first book, A Boy's Will. An American expatriate living in London, Ezra Pound, wrote enthusiastically to American publishers about Frost's poetry and helped him find a publisher for North of Boston, which appeared in 1914. Included in the book were many of the poems that would make Frost famous, and it was an immediate success. When he returned to the United States a year later, Frost was an established writer, and he was able to find work as a teacher. He taught for many years at several schools, among them Harvard University, Amherst College, Middlebury College, and Dartmouth College, as well at the Bread Loaf School, a summer writing program that he founded and led until his death.

Frost was free of the economic worries that had plagued him for so long, but his life was not free of tragedy. His son committed suicide, and one daughter had to be confined to a mental institution. None of his family's unhappiness was directly mirrored in his poetry, which became more and more positive in tone as he grew older. Disengaging himself from the political turmoil of the 1930s, he refused to join other poets in their struggles to achieve a more just American society. As he wrote in the introduction to his Collected Poems in 1939, "I have given up my democratic prejudices and now willingly set the lower classes free to be completely taken care of by the upper classes. Political freedom is nothing to me. I bestow it right and left." At the same time, he was fiercely jealous of other poets, and he was painfully conscious that the attention of his early audience had drifted to the more modern work of writers such as T. S. Eliot, or the more politically aware poetry of Archibald MacLeish. His attacks on their work often focused on their open poetic form. In the same introduction he wrote of their poetics, "It is painful to watch our sprung-rhythmists straining at the point of omitting one short from a foot for relief from monotony." In the emotional tides of World War II, Frost's poetry became a place of refuge and comfort for many readers, and despite the disillusionment of the 1950s, he never lost the place he had won in America's heart. There was mourning across the nation at his death in 1963.

"The Pasture" was written shortly after the family had moved to England, and its description of the cow and her new calf in the spring pasture may have been inspired by homesickness for their life in New Hampshire. Like all of Frost's poems about his experience as a farmer, "The Pasture" does not describe the reality of the farm but projects a wish that the reality might have been like that. It is this conscious presentation of idealized American experience that is at the heart of Frost's enduring popularity. Also composed in England, "Mending Wall" is unrhymed, but it is written in fluent iambic pentameter, the blank verse form that Shakespeare used for his plays. If Frost ever read Walt Whitman's poetry, with its free meter and unrhymed cadences, there is no sign of it in his own work. As he said, free verse was "like playing tennis with the net down."

In his early poetry Frost also showed a strong sense of drama, and he included several long narrative poems in his first books. The poems were stark and moody, and in them can be glimpsed some of his own unhappiness. One of the best known is "The Death of the Hired Man," a sorrowful description of an old farm *laborer who has outlived his usefulness. Although the opening line suggests a freer meter, the poem is written in blank verse.*

In "Birches" he returns to his characteristically skillful iambic pentameter. It is a poem that gives some hint of his desire to live his life more freely, even if it is only to swing on birch trees. As he writes, "Earth's the right place for love." The poem also has one of his most striking images, the description of the ice breaking loose from the frozen trees,

> *... They click upon themselves*
> *As the breeze rises, and turn many-colored*
> *As the stir cracks and crazes their enamel.*

"Fire and Ice" is only a little longer than an epigram, but in its few lines Frost manages to make a sardonic comment about the end of the world. His bitter lines can be read as an allusion to the image from the gospel song about the same moment of destruction, "no more water, fire next time." "To Earthward" describes the intense fire he felt in his early love, and now he finds that for him there is "no joy but lacks salt," and he longs to feel his old fervor again.

Frost's writing appears to be so effortless that many of his most popular poems seem as clear and as simple as someone describing the weather. At the same time they are complex examples of rhyme and diction. "Stopping by Woods on a Snowy Evening" is one of these familiar poems. The seemingly artless stanzas are actually tightly structured around a complicated rhyme scheme. Even if the reader's eye is not consciously analyzing the rhymes, the ear is hearing them.

"The Road Not Taken" is one of Frost's most popular poems, written in the United States a year after his return from England. Its metaphor of life as a journey, and the decision to make the journey down one of two roads, is a striking example of a metaphor that is the poem. Readers have sometimes noticed, however, that Frost makes it clear that the roads were actually so similar that each of them was worn "about the same." The poem was actually intended as a joke for his friend Edward Thomas. Thomas could never make up his mind about anything, and Frost teased him by saying, "No matter which road you take, you'll always sigh and wish you'd taken another." Frost sent the poem to Thomas in a letter, but his friend missed the joke entirely, thinking it was a poem about the decisions Frost had made in his own life. According to his biographer Lawrence Thompson, Frost never could bring himself to confess that the poem had not worked the way he had intended.

Written in England, "After Apple-Picking" is another poem in which Frost uses a metaphor taken from his half-imagined country life to describe his emotions at his own death, and it reflects the disappointments he and his family had endured. He was only forty when he wrote it, and he would live another forty-five years.

CONVERSATIONS *See pages 1029–1039, including Rose C. Feld, "An Interview with Robert Frost," page 1030; Robert Frost, "The Figure a Poem Makes," page 1032; Robert Lowell, "On Robert Frost," page 1034; Joseph Brodsky, "On Grief and Reason," page 1035; Philip L. Gerber, "On Frost's 'After Apple-Picking,'" page 1037.*

WEB *Research Robert Frost and answer questions about his work at bedfordstmartins.com/charters/litwriters.*

The Pasture   1913

I'm going out to clean the pasture spring;
I'll only stop to rake the leaves away
(And wait to watch the water clear, I may):
I shan't be gone long. — You come too.

I'm going out to fetch the little calf
That's standing by the mother. It's so young
It totters when she licks it with her tongue.
I shan't be gone long. — You come too.

Mending Wall   1914

Something there is that doesn't love a wall,
That sends the frozen-ground-swell under it,
And spills the upper boulders in the sun;
And makes gaps even two can pass abreast.
The work of hunters is another thing: 5
I have come after them and made repair
Where they have left not one stone on a stone,
But they would have the rabbit out of hiding,
To please the yelping dogs. The gaps I mean,
No one has seen them made or heard them made,   10
But at spring mending-time we find them there.
I let my neighbor know beyond the hill;
And on a day we meet to walk the line
And set the wall between us once again.
We keep the wall between us as we go.   15
To each the boulders that have fallen to each.
And some are loaves and some so nearly balls
We have to use a spell to make them balance:
"Stay where you are until our backs are turned!"
We wear our fingers rough with handling them.   20
Oh, just another kind of outdoor game,
One on a side. It comes to little more:
There where it is we do not need the wall:
He is all pine and I am apple orchard.
My apple trees will never get across   25
And eat the cones under his pines, I tell him.
He only says, "Good fences make good neighbors."
Spring is the mischief in me, and I wonder
If I could put a notion in his head:
"*Why* do they make good neighbors? Isn't it   30
Where there are cows? But here there are no cows.
Before I built a wall I'd ask to know
What I was walling in or walling out,

And to whom I was like to give offense.
Something there is that doesn't love a wall,   35
That wants it down." I could say "Elves" to him,
But it's not elves exactly, and I'd rather
He said it for himself. I see him there
Bringing a stone grasped firmly by the top
In each hand, like an old-stone savage armed.   40
He moves in darkness as it seems to me,
Not of woods only and the shade of trees.
He will not go behind his father's saying,
And he likes having thought of it so well
He says again, "Good fences make good neighbors."   45

The Death of the Hired Man   1914

Mary sat musing on the lamp-flame at the table
Waiting for Warren. When she heard his step,
She ran on tiptoe down the darkened passage
To meet him in the doorway with the news
And put him on his guard. "Silas is back."   5
She pushed him outward with her through the door
And shut it after her. "Be kind," she said.
She took the market things from Warren's arms
And set them on the porch, then drew him down
To sit beside her on the wooden steps.   10

    "When was I ever anything but kind to him?
But I'll not have the fellow back," he said.
"I told him so last haying, didn't I?
If he left then, I said, that ended it.
What good is he? Who else will harbor him   15
At his age for the little he can do?
What help he is there's no depending on.
Off he goes always when I need him most.
He thinks he ought to earn a little pay,
Enough at least to buy tobacco with,   20
So he won't have to beg and be beholden.
'All right,' I say, 'I can't afford to pay
Any fixed wages, though I wish I could.'
'Someone else can.' 'Then someone else will have to.'
I shouldn't mind his bettering himself   25
If that was what it was. You can be certain,
When he begins like that, there's someone at him
Trying to coax him off with pocket money, —
In haying time, when any help is scarce.
In winter he comes back to us. I'm done."   30

"Sh! not so loud: he'll hear you," Mary said.
"I want him to: he'll have to soon or late."

"He's worn out. He's asleep beside the stove.
When I came up from Rowe's I found him here,
Huddled against the barn door fast asleep,   35
A miserable sight, and frightening, too —
You needn't smile — I didn't recognize him —
I wasn't looking for him — and he's changed.
Wait till you see."

                 "Where did you say he'd been?"   40

"He didn't say. I dragged him to the house,
And gave him tea and tried to make him smoke.
I tried to make him talk about his travels.
Nothing would do: he just kept nodding off."

"What did he say? Did he say anything?"   45

"But little."

             "Anything? Mary, confess
He said he'd come to ditch the meadow for me."
"Warren!"

             "But did he? I just want to know."   50

"Of course he did. What would you have him say?
Surely you wouldn't grudge the poor old man
Some humble way to save his self-respect.
He added, if you really care to know,
He meant to clear the upper pasture, too.   55
That sounds like something you have heard before?
Warren, I wish you could have heard the way
He jumbled everything. I stopped to look
Two or three times — he made me feel so queer —
To see if he was talking in his sleep.   60
He ran on Harold Wilson — you remember —
The boy you had in haying four years since.
He's finished school, and teaching in his college.
Silas declares you'll have to get him back.
He says they two will make a team for work: 65
Between them they will lay this farm as smooth!
The way he mixed that in with other things.
He thinks young Wilson a likely lad, though daft
On education — you know how they fought
All through July under the blazing sun,   70
Silas up on the cart to build the load,
Harold along beside to pitch it on."

"Yes, I took care to keep well out of earshot."

"Well, those days trouble Silas like a dream.
You wouldn't think they would. How some things linger!   75
Harold's young college boy's assurance piqued him.
After so many years he still keeps finding
Good arguments he sees he might have used.
I sympathize. I know just how it feels
To think of the right thing to say too late.   80
Harold's associated in his mind with Latin.
He asked me what I thought of Harold's saying
He studied Latin, like the violin,
Because he liked it—that an argument!
He said he couldn't make the boy believe   85
He could find water with a hazel prong—
Which showed how much good school had ever done him.
He wanted to go over that. But most of all
He thinks if he could have another chance
To teach him how to build a load of hay—"   90

"I know, that's Silas' one accomplishment.
He bundles every forkful in its place,
And tags and numbers it for future reference,
So he can find and easily dislodge it
In the unloading. Silas does that well.   95
He takes it out in bunches like big birds' nests.
You never see him standing on the hay
He's trying to lift, straining to lift himself."

"He thinks if he could teach him that, he'd be
Some good perhaps to someone in the world.   100
He hates to see a boy the fool of books.
Poor Silas, so concerned for other folk,
And nothing to look backward to with pride,
And nothing to look forward to with hope,
So now and never any different."   105

Part of a moon was falling down the west,
Dragging the whole sky with it to the hills.
Its light poured softly in her lap. She saw it
And spread her apron to it. She put out her hand
Among the harp-like morning-glory strings,   110
Taut with the dew from garden bed to eaves,
As if she played unheard some tenderness
That wrought on him beside her in the night.
"Warren," she said, "he has come home to die:
You needn't be afraid he'll leave you this time."   115

"Home," he mocked gently.

                              "Yes, what else but home?
It all depends on what you mean by home.

Of course he's nothing to us, any more
Than was the hound that came a stranger to us   120
Out of the woods, worn out upon the trail."

"Home is the place where, when you have to go there,
They have to take you in."

                "I should have called it
Something you somehow haven't to deserve."   125

Warren leaned out and took a step or two,
Picked up a little stick, and brought it back
And broke it in his hand and tossed it by.
"Silas has better claim on us you think
Than on his brother? Thirteen little miles   130
As the road winds would bring him to his door.
Silas has walked that far no doubt to-day.
Why doesn't he go there? His brother's rich,
A somebody—director in the bank."

"He never told us that."   135

                "We know it though."

"I think his brother ought to help, of course.
I'll see to that if there is need. He ought of right
To take him in, and might be willing to—
He may be better than appearances.   140
But have some pity on Silas. Do you think
If he had any pride in claiming kin
Or anything he looked for from his brother,
He'd keep so still about him all this time?"

"I wonder what's between them."   145

                "I can tell you.
Silas is what he is—we wouldn't mind him—
But just the kind that kinfolk can't abide.
He never did a thing so very bad.
He don't know why he isn't quite as good   150
As anybody. Worthless though he is,
He won't be made ashamed to please his brother."

"*I* can't think Si ever hurt anyone."

"No, but he hurt my heart the way he lay
And rolled his old head on that sharp-edged chair-back.   155
He wouldn't let me put him on the lounge.
You must go in and see what you can do.
I made the bed up for him there tonight.
You'll be surprised at him—how much he's broken.
His working days are done; I'm sure of it."   160

"I'd not be in a hurry to say that."

I haven't been. Go, look, see for yourself.
But, Warren, please remember how it is:
He's come to help you ditch the meadow.
He has a plan. You mustn't laugh at him.   165
He may not speak of it, and then he may.
I'll sit and see if that small sailing cloud
Will hit or miss the moon."

                It hit the moon.
Then there were three there, making a dim row,   170
The moon, the little silver cloud, and she.

Warren returned—too soon, it seemed to her,
Slipped to her side, caught up her hand and waited.
"Warren?" she questioned.

                    "Dead," was all he answered.   175

Birches   1916

When I see birches bend to left and right
Across the lines of straighter darker trees,
I like to think some boy's been swinging them.
But swinging doesn't bend them down to stay
As ice-storms do. Often you must have seen them   5
Loaded with ice a sunny winter morning
After a rain. They click upon themselves
As the breeze rises, and turn many-colored
As the stir cracks and crazes their enamel.
Soon the sun's warmth makes them shed crystal shells   10
Shattering and avalanching on the snow-crust—
Such heaps of broken glass to sweep away
You'd think the inner dome of heaven had fallen.
They are dragged to the withered bracken by the load,
And they seem not to break; though once they are bowed   15
So low for long, they never right themselves:
You may see their trunks arching in the woods
Years afterwards, trailing their leaves on the ground
Like girls on hands and knees that throw their hair
Before them over their heads to dry in the sun.   20
But I was going to say when Truth broke in
With all her matter-of-fact about the ice-storm,
I should prefer to have some boy bend them
As he went out and in to fetch the cows—
Some boy too far from town to learn baseball,   25
Whose only play was what he found himself,
Summer or winter, and could play alone.

One by one he subdued his father's trees
By riding them down over and over again
Until he took the stiffness out of them,   30
And not one but hung limp, not one was left
For him to conquer. He learned all there was
To learn about not launching out too soon
And so not carrying the tree away
Clear to the ground. He always kept his poise   35
To the top branches, climbing carefully
With the same pains you use to fill a cup
Up to the brim, and even above the brim.
Then he flung outward, feet first, with a swish,
Kicking his way down through the air to the ground.   40
So was I once myself a swinger of birches.
And so I dream of going back to be.
It's when I'm weary of considerations,
And life is too much like a pathless wood
Where your face burns and tickles with the cobwebs   45
Broken across it, and one eye is weeping
From a twig's having lashed across it open.
I'd like to get away from earth awhile
And then come back to it and begin over.
May no fate willfully misunderstand me   50
And half grant what I wish and snatch me away
Not to return. Earth's the right place for love:
I don't know where it's likely to go better.
I'd like to go by climbing a birch tree,
And climb black branches up a snow-white trunk,   55
Toward heaven, till the tree could bear no more,
But dipped its top and set me down again.
That would be good both going and coming back.
One could do worse than be a swinger of birches.

Fire and Ice   1923

Some say the world will end in fire,
Some say in ice.
From what I've tasted of desire
I hold with those who favor fire.
But if it had to perish twice,
I think I know enough of hate
To say that for destruction ice
Is also great
And would suffice.

To Earthward   1923

Love at the lips was touch
As sweet as I could bear;
And once that seemed too much;
I lived on air

That crossed me from sweet things   5
The flow of — was it musk
From hidden grapevine springs
Down hill at dusk?

I had the swirl and ache
From sprays of honeysuckle   10
That when they're gathered shake
Dew on the knuckle.

I craved strong sweets, but those
Seemed strong when I was young;
The petal of the rose   15
It was that stung.

Now no joy but lacks salt
That is not dashed with pain
And weariness and fault;
I crave the stain   20

Of tears, the aftermark
Of almost too much love,
The sweet of bitter bark
And burning clove.

When stiff and sore and scarred   25
I take away my hand
From leaning on it hard
In grass and sand,

The hurt is not enough:
I long for weight and strength   30
To feel the earth as rough
To all my length.

Stopping by Woods on a Snowy Evening   1923

Whose woods these are I think I know.
His house is in the village, though;
He will not see me stopping here
To watch his woods fill up with snow.

My little horse must think it queer   5
To stop without a farmhouse near
Between the woods and frozen lake
The darkest evening of the year.

He gives his harness bells a shake
To ask if there is some mistake.   10
The only other sound's the sweep
Of easy wind and downy flake.

The woods are lovely, dark and deep,
But I have promises to keep,
And miles to go before I sleep,   15
And miles to go before I sleep.

The Road Not Taken   1916

Two roads diverged in a yellow wood,
And sorry I could not travel both
And be one traveler, long I stood
And looked down one as far as I could
To where it bent in the undergrowth;   5

Then took the other, as just as fair,
And having perhaps the better claim,
Because it was grassy and wanted wear;
Though as for that the passing there
Had worn them really about the same,   10

And both that morning equally lay
In leaves no step had trodden black.
Oh, I kept the first for another day!
Yet knowing how way leads on to way,
I doubted if I should ever come back.   15

I shall be telling this with a sigh
Somewhere ages and ages hence:
Two roads diverged in a wood, and I—
I took the one less traveled by,
And that has made all the difference.   20

After Apple-Picking   1914

My long two-pointed ladder's sticking through a tree
Toward heaven still,
And there's a barrel that I didn't fill
Beside it, and there may be two or three
Apples I didn't pick upon some bough.   5
But I am done with apple-picking now.
Essence of winter sleep is on the night,
The scent of apples: I am drowsing off.
I cannot rub the strangeness from my sight
I got from looking through a pane of glass   10
I skimmed this morning from the drinking trough

And held against the world of hoary grass.
It melted, and I let it fall and break.
But I was well
Upon my way to sleep before it fell,   15
And I could tell
What form my dreaming was about to take.
Magnified apples appear and disappear,
Stem end and blossom end,
And every fleck of russet showing clear.   20
My instep arch not only keeps the ache,
It keeps the pressure of a ladder-round.
I feel the ladder sway as the boughs bend.
And I keep hearing from the cellar bin
The rumbling sound   25
Of load on load of apples coming in.
For I have had too much
Of apple-picking: I am overtired
Of the great harvest I myself desired.
There were ten thousand thousand fruit to touch,   30
Cherish in hand, lift down, and not let fall.
For all
That struck the earth,
No matter if not bruised or spiked with stubble,
Went surely to the cider-apple heap   35
As of no worth.
One can see what will trouble
This sleep of mine, whatever sleep it is.
Were he not gone,
The woodchuck could say whether it's like his   40
Long sleep, as I describe its coming on,
Or just some human sleep.

ROBERT HAYDEN

*Robert Hayden (1913–1980) was born in Detroit. When he was three his
mother, Asa Sheffey, decided that she wanted to live her own life, and although
she never lost contact with her son, she gave him to a working couple named Hayden to raise. His adoptive father worked when he could as a day laborer, and Hayden grew up in poverty in the Detroit ghetto. As a boy, Hayden was small and
extremely nearsighted, and he spent many hours alone reading.*

*By his teens, he was already absorbed by literature, and Hayden's was a gen-
eration of African Americans who no longer felt excluded from mainstream American intellectual culture. His early poetic models were the African American writer
Countee Cullen and the white poet Elinor Wylie. When Hayden graduated from
high school, America was entering the Depression. He attended Detroit City College until 1936, then was employed by the WPA Federal Writer's Project until the*

war. He married in 1940 and entered the University of Michigan, where he stud-ied under the English poet W. H. Auden, who had recently moved to the United States.

From 1946 until 1969 Hayden taught at Fisk University in Nashville while also writing and publishing steadily. An early book had been published in 1940, but Hayden did not achieve wide recognition until 1966, when he was awarded the Grand Prize for Poetry for A Ballad of Remembrance *at the First World Festival of Negro Arts in Senegal. At the same time he had become reluctantly involved in the debate over political consciousness that was shaking the black literary world. Younger African American writers accused him of accommodating his writing to the white culture and refused to listen to his argument that he considered himself part of a literary culture that had no racial boundaries. The angry disagreement was one of his reasons for leaving Fisk.*

Hayden was awarded many literary prizes and honors. For four years he was Consultant in Poetry to the Library of Congress, a position that now has the title of poet laureate. In January 1980, a month before his death, he took part in a reading at the White House.

"Those Winter Sundays" is Hayden's best-known poem, describing his father in Detroit. "A Letter from Phillis Wheatley," from his last book, is an evocative por-trait of the first published African American writer. His "Night, Death, Missis-sippi" is a disturbing poem that describes the murder of African Americans in Mississippi through the thoughts of one of the white men responsible for these deaths.

RELATED POEMS *Sterling A. Brown, "Frankie and Johnny" (p. 737); Langston Hughes, "Song for a Dark Girl" (p. 909).*

COMMENTARY *Robert Hayden, "On Negro Poetry," page 981.*

WEB *Research Robert Hayden and answer questions about his work at bedfordst-martins.com/charters/litwriters.*

Those Winter Sundays

1962

Sundays too my father got up early
and put his clothes on in the blueblack cold,
then with cracked hands that ached
from labor in the weekday weather made
banked fires blaze. No one ever thanked him.   5

I'd wake and hear the cold splintering, breaking.
When the rooms were warm, he'd call,
and slowly I would rise and dress,
fearing the chronic angers of that house,

Speaking indifferently to him,   10
who had driven out the cold
and polished my good shoes as well.
What did I know, what did I know
of love's austere and lonely offices?

A Letter from Phillis Wheatley

1978

London, 1773

Dear Obour°
      Our crossing was without
event. I could not help, at times,
reflecting on that first — my Destined —
voyage long ago (I yet   5
have some remembrance of its Horrors)
and marvelling at God's Ways.
      Last evening, her Ladyship presented me
to her illustrious Friends.
I scarce could tell them anything   10
of Africa, though much of Boston
and my hope of Heaven. I read
my latest Elegies to them.
"O Sable Muse!" the Countess cried,
embracing me, when I had done.   15
I held back tears, as is my wont,
and there were tears in Dear
Nathaniel's eyes.
      At supper — I dined apart
like captive Royalty —   20
the Countess and her Guests promised
signatures affirming me
True Poetess, albeit once a slave.
Indeed, they were most kind, and spoke,
moreover, of presenting me   25
at Court (I thought of Pocahontas) —
an Honor, to be sure, but one,
I should, no doubt, as Patriot decline.
      My health is much improved;
I feel I may, if God so Wills,   30
entirely recover here.

---

1. **Obour:** Obour Tanner, a former slave who was one of Wheatley's friends.

Night, Death, Mississippi

1966

I

A quavering cry. Screech-owl?
Or one of them?
The old man in his reek
and gauntness laughs—

One of them, I bet—   5
and turns out the kitchen lamp,
limping to the porch to listen
in the windowless night.

Be there with Boy and the rest
if I was well again.   10
Time was. Time was.
White robes like moonlight

In the sweetgum dark.
Unbucked that one then
and him squealing bloody Jesus   15
as we cut it off.

Time was. A cry?
A cry all right.
He hawks and spits,
fevered as by groinfire.   20

Have us a bottle,
Boy and me—
he's earned him a bottle—
when he gets home.

II

Then we beat them, he said,   25
beat them till our arms was tired
and the big old chains
messy and red.

O Jesus burning on the lily cross

Christ, it was better   30
than hunting bear
which don't know why
you want him dead.

O night, rawhead and bloodybones night

You kids fetch Paw   35
some water now so's he
can wash that blood
off him, she said.

O night betrayed by darkness not its own

SEAMUS HEANEY

Seamus Heaney (b. 1939) was born in Ireland, in Castledown in County Kerry. He grew up in a small farming community, and this has shaped his writing and his outlook on the world. He trained as a teacher and after teaching in a secondary school for a year he returned to the university and completed his studies in English at Queen's College in Belfast. Belfast is the capital of Northern Ireland, and Heaney has spent his life in the midst of the violent struggle for political power between the province's Catholic minority and Protestant majority. He became a lecturer at Queen's College and in 1966 his first collection, Death of a Naturalist, *appeared.*

In the years since then, Heaney has continued to teach, to study the work of other poets, and to write. He has won nearly every major literary prize in England and Ireland and was awarded the Nobel Prize in 1995. For extended periods he has been a guest lecturer at Harvard University and Oxford University. As an Irish writer who is also a Catholic he has felt considerable pressure to become engaged in the effort of the Irish minority in the north to end the ties between the Protestant majority, which is largely of Scottish descent, and England, which maintains the status quo with a large military force. Although he is sympathetic to the Catholic minority's aims, he is deeply disturbed by the use of violence by the IRA, the underground Irish Republican Army. He has written poems that lament the present situation, but he has also insisted that this is not the role of poetry. As he wrote in his essay "The Redress of Poetry," "Poetry cannot afford to lose its fundamentally self-delighting inventiveness, its joy in being a process of language as well as a representation of things in the world."

"Digging," from Death of a Naturalist, *is one of his most frequently anthologized poems. "The Harvest Bow," with its evocation of Ireland's old folk beliefs, was published in 1990.*

WEB *Research Seamus Heaney and answer questions about his work at bedfordstmartins.com/charters/litwriters.*

Digging

1966

Between my finger and my thumb
The squat pen rests; snug as a gun.

Under my window, a clean rasping sound
When the spade sinks into gravelly ground:
My father, digging. I look down
Till his straining rump among the flowerbeds
Bends low, comes up twenty years away
Stooping in rhythm through potato drills°
Where he was digging.

5

---

8. **drills:** Furrows in which seeds are sown.

The coarse boot nestled on the lug, the shaft   10
Against the inside knee was levered firmly.
He rooted out tall tops, buried the bright edge deep
To scatter new potatoes that we picked
Loving their cool hardness in our hands.

By god, the old man could handle a spade.   15
Just like his old man.

My grandfather cut more turf° in a day
Than any other man on Toner's bog.
Once I carried him milk in a bottle
Corked sloppily with paper. He straightened up   20
To drink it, then fell to right away
Nicking and slicing neatly, heaving sods
Over his shoulder, going down and down
For the good turf. Digging.

The cold smell of potato mould, the squelch and slap   25
Of soggy peat, the curt cuts of an edge
Through living roots awaken in my head.
But I've no spade to follow men like them.

Between my finger and my thumb
The squat pen rests.   30
I'll dig with it.

The Harvest Bow   1990

As you plaited the harvest bow
You implicated the mellowed silence in you
In wheat that does not rust
But brightens as it tightens twist by twist
Into a knowable corona,   5
A throwaway love-knot of straw.

Hands that aged round ashplants and cane sticks
And lapped the spurs on a lifetime of game cocks
Harked to their gift and worked with fine intent
Until your fingers moved somnambulant: 10
I tell and finger it like braille,
Gleaning the unsaid off the palpable.

And if I spy into its golden loops
I see us walk between the railway slopes
Into an evening of long grass and midges,   15
Blue smoke straight up, old beds and ploughs in hedges,

---

17. turf: Bricks of peat used for fuel.

An auction notice on an outhouse wall—
You with a harvest bow in your lapel,

Me with the fishing rod, already homesick
For the big lift of these evenings, as your stick   20
Whacking the tips off weeds and bushes
Beats out of time, and beats, but flushes
Nothing: that original townland
Still tongue-tied in the straw tied by your hand.

The end of art is peace   25
Could be the motto of this frail device
That I have pinned up on our deal dresser—
Like a drawn snare

LANGSTON HUGHES

Langston Hughes (1902–1967), who was to become America's best-known African American writer, was one of the first American poets to reach a wide audience with a direct, personal poetic style created from the rhythms and language of everyday black speech. When we read him today we see only the depth of his accomplishment, but it was achieved by a lifetime of dedication to his goal, which was to create a voice for the African American community. He lived for many years alone in his small Harlem apartment, and there were years of discouraging poverty. His determination, however—and his optimism—never wavered. As his biographer Arnold Rampersad wrote, the greatest truth of Hughes's life was that "in his chronic loneliness, true satisfaction came only from the love and regard of the black race, which he earned by placing his finest gift, his skill with language, in its service."

He was born in Joplin, Missouri, but his parents separated, and he spent most of his childhood with his maternal grandmother in Lawrence, Kansas. His father, angry at racial intolerance but prejudiced himself against darker-skinned blacks, moved to Mexico. His mother settled in Cleveland. His grandmother was emotionally reserved, and he yearned for more contact with his mother, but his grandmother gave him a strong sense of racial pride that never left him. She was the widow of one of the men killed in the battle at Harpers Ferry, Virginia, in 1859, when a small group under the leadership of abolitionist John Brown attempted to ignite a rebellion in the South by capturing the federal arsenal there and seizing weapons to arm southern slaves. Hughes heard the story from her many times, and sometimes she covered him in bed with her husband's bullet-torn shawl.

Hughes's grandmother died when he was thirteen, and he went to live with his mother in Cleveland, Ohio. He was already writing poetry. He once humorously described how he was chosen to be class poet for his graduation from Central High School, where he and a girl were the only black class members.

My classmates, knowing that a poem had to have rhythm, elected me unanimously—thinking, no doubt, that I had some, being a Negro. . . . In the first half of the poem, I said that our school had the finest teachers that there ever were. And in the latter half, I said our class was the greatest class ever graduated. Naturally everybody applauded loudly. That was the way I began to write poetry.

He was elected, however, because he was popular with other students, competed on the track team, and, as his English teacher told an interviewer when his first book appeared, he was one of the most gifted members of his class.

Following his graduation he went to live in Mexico with his father, who was impatient with his literary ambitions. In Mexico, where he stayed for several months, Hughes learned Spanish and wrote the poem "The Negro Speaks of Rivers," which was published in 1921 in The Crisis, an intellectual journal edited by the Harlem writer and activist W. E. B. Du Bois. Uncomfortable with his father, who wanted him to study to be an engineer, Hughes returned to the United States, lived in Harlem, and attended Columbia University for a year. Restless again, he drifted for several years while he struggled to find a way to write the poetry and prose he dreamed of, and to support himself doing it. He worked as a seaman, traveling to Africa and northern Europe. For some months in 1924 he shared a small apartment in Paris with a Russian ballet dancer, then after a trip to Italy he returned to the United States, painting and scrubbing the decks on a tramp steamer to earn his fare. He spent most of the next year in Washington, D.C., working first for the Association for the Study of Negro Life and History, then as a busboy in the dining room of the Wardman Park Hotel.

Although still in his early twenties Hughes was considered one of the most promising members of the cultural movement called the Harlem Renaissance, a talented gathering of writers, artists, and musicians, who were creating a new African American consciousness. A bohemian white writer, photographer, and active supporter of the movement named Carl Van Vechten became interested in Hughes's poetry and recommended him to his own publisher. Van Vechten also chose the title, The Weary Blues, for Hughes's first poetry collection. Hughes was waiting for the book to appear at the time he was working in Washington. His breakthrough as a writer came through his job. The popular poet Vachel Lindsay stayed over at the hotel on one of his reading tours, and Hughes left some of his poems at Lindsay's place in the dining room. Lindsay read them with interest and at his reading announced to his audience that he had found a poet right there at the hotel, and a Negro poet at that. The next morning reporters from several white newspapers were waiting to interview the "busboy poet."

In 1925 Hughes won his first prize as a poet, and after some months back in Harlem he returned to school, this time at Lincoln University, in Pennsylvania. He also continued to write poetry, attempted an unsuccessful collaboration on a play with Zora Neale Hurston, and he was encouraged to begin his first novel, Not without Laughter, by a wealthy white woman who had become the financial patron of several Harlem writers. In 1931 he traveled through the southern states, reading his poetry to schools and private gatherings and using his poems to encourage his audiences to live their lives as fully as they could, despite the harsh reality of racial segregation. The racism he encountered affected him so deeply that the next year he traveled to Moscow with a group of Harlem writers and actors, and when the project collapsed he stayed in the Soviet Union for almost a year. When he came back to the United States he became politically active in several groups connected to the Communist Party, although he was never a party member. Many of his poems in the 1930s reflected his emotional response to these early years of the Soviet experiment. In the late 1930s he supported the Loyalist government during the Spanish Civil War, and he spent months as a war correspondent in Madrid during the siege of the city, sharing quarters with other sympathetic writers like Ernest Hemingway and John Steinbeck. When it was clear that the struggle was hopeless, he returned to the United States.

Back in Harlem, Hughes became a public figure, working as a journalist, founding black theater groups, editing anthologies of black writing, and writing poetry, plays, and essays. He actively supported the U.S. war effort when the nation entered World War II in 1941. In 1943 he created the character of Jesse B. Semple, a Harlem Everyman called "Simple" by his friends, who commented with shrewd intelligence on the world of Harlem and its place in the larger world of American society. The "Simple Stories" were first published in a Harlem newspaper, then gathered into four very successful collections. After the war Hughes was questioned about his Communist sympathies by the House Un-American Activities Committee, but he was not blacklisted, as were many Americans involved in the arts during the McCarthy era. He continued to write poetry and create works for the theater and to support the work of other African American creative artists, among them young writers, painters, and jazz musicians, until his death in 1967.

In this selection from Langston Hughes's poetry you will find many of his recurring themes. "The Negro Speaks of Rivers," written while he was still a teenager and strongly influenced by the midwestern poet Carl Sandburg, is a haunting expression of the rich sense of history in his poetry, even though the language is direct and uncomplicated. "Mother to Son" explores the theme of family and the difficulties of everyday life. "I, Too," which borrows some of its language and style from Walt Whitman, is an expression of Hughes's consciousness of his blackness and his certainty of the worth of his blackness, even if now he is forced to "eat in the kitchen." "Bound No'th Blues" is one of the many poems he wrote in the blues form. In a blues verse the first two lines are repeated, often with small variations, and a third line concludes the idea of the first two lines and rhymes with them. The first two lines of Hughes's poem represent the first line of a blues verse; then he repeats the words, with slight variations; and the last two lines of his verse represent the third line of the blues, concluding his thought and completing the rhyme. He was the first poet to use the blues form successfully, and he used it with continued skill for many years.

The tragedy of lynching is the subject of "Song for a Dark Girl," which quotes a line from the song "Dixie" as a sardonic comment on southern racism. Hughes is becoming much more engaged politically in poems like "Song for a Dark Girl," "House in the World," and "Florida Road Workers," although he is still writing in a language that is deceptively simple and immediate in its appeal. The speaker in "House in the World" despairs that he and his "dark brothers" will never be free of white domination, and the poor worker who is building the road in Florida cheers himself up by proclaiming proudly that even if it is only rich people who will get to "sweep over" his road he will "get to see 'em ride." Hughes's turn *away from this kind of public poetry can be marked in the simple but enigmatic poem "Personal." "Little Lyric (Of Great Importance)" reflects his response to Harlem and his neighbors' worries.*

　　Although there was a consciousness in America in the 1960s that the problem of racism had to be faced, Hughes lived through the violence of the voter registration drives in the southern states, and the turbulence of the efforts of the "Freedom Riders," northern students who came by the busload into the South, to challenge the legality of segregated public facilities. In poems like "Merry-Go-Round" and the well-known "Theme for English B" he continues to protest against racism, though in these poems the protest is expressed in wry, half-amused terms. The protest in "Down Where I Am" is presented wearily by someone who has been fighting prejudice for a long time and insists now that if anyone wants to see them, they'll have to, as the poem says in its closing line, "come down." In his famous poem "Dream Deferred"—the source of the phrase "raisin in the sun" that Lorraine Hansberry later used as the title of her well-known play—the speaker's patience is worn thin. The "dream deferred" is the dream of racial equality, and the speaker suggests that if the dream does not come true soon, there might be an explosion. It was a prophecy that was fulfilled in the months before his death, as in one city after another the ghettoes exploded into violence and rioting.

COMMENTARY　*Robert Hayden, "On Negro Poetry," page 981.*

CONVERSATIONS　*See pages 1039–1045, including Langston Hughes, "A Toast to Harlem," page 1040; Jessie Fauset, "Meeting Langston Hughes," page 1041; Richard Wright, "A Review of* The Big Sea," *page 1043; Arnold Rampersad, "Langston Hughes as Folk Poet," page 1045.*

WEB　*Research Langston Hughes and answer questions about his work at bedfordstmartins.com/charters/litwriters.*

The Negro Speaks of Rivers

1921

I've known rivers:
I've known rivers ancient as the world and older than the
　　flow of human blood in human veins.

My soul has grown deep like the rivers.

I bathed in the Euphrates when dawns were young.　　　　　　　　5
I built my hut near the Congo and it lulled me to sleep.
I looked upon the Nile and raised the Pyramids above it.
I heard the singing of the Mississippi when Abe Lincoln
　　　　went down to New Orleans, and I've seen its muddy
　　　　bosom turn all golden in the sunset.　　　　　　　　　　10

I've known rivers:
Ancient, dusky rivers.

My soul has grown deep like the rivers.

Mother to Son

1926

Well, son, I'll tell you:
Life for me ain't been no crystal stair.
It's had tacks in it,
And splinters,
And boards torn up,   5
And places with no carpet on the floor —
Bare.
But all the time
I'se been a-climbin' on,
And reachin' landin's,   10
And turnin' corners,
And sometimes goin' in the dark
Where there ain't been no light.
So boy, don't you turn back.
Don't you set down on the steps   15
'Cause you finds it's kinder hard.
Don't you fall now —
For I'se still goin', honey,
I'se still climbin',
And life for me ain't been no crystal stair.   20

I, Too

1926

I, too, sing America.

I am the darker brother.
They send me to eat in the kitchen
When company comes,
But I laugh,   5
And eat well,
And grow strong.

Tomorrow,
I'll be at the table
When company comes.   10
Nobody'll dare
Say to me,
"Eat in the kitchen,"
Then.

Besides,   15
They'll see how beautiful I am
And be ashamed —

I, too, am America.

Bound No'th Blues

1927

Goin' down the road, Lawd,
Goin' down the road.
Down the road, Lawd,
Way, way down the road.
Got to find somebody   5
To help me carry this load.

Road's in front o' me,
Nothin' to do but walk.
Road's in front o' me,
Walk . . . an' walk . . . an' walk.   10
I'd like to meet a good friend
To come along an' talk.

Hates to be lonely,
Lawd, I hates to be sad.
Says I hates to be lonely,   15
Hates to be lonely an' sad,
But ever friend you finds seems
Like they try to do you bad.

Road, road, road, O!
Road, road . . . road . . . road, road!   20
Road, road, road, O!
On the no'thern road.
These Mississippi towns ain't
Fit fer a hoppin' toad.

Song for a Dark Girl

1927

Way Down South in Dixie
    (Break the heart of me)
They hung my black young lover
    To a cross roads tree.

Way Down South in Dixie   5
    (Bruised body high in air)
I asked the white Lord Jesus
    What was the use of prayer.

Way Down South in Dixie
    (Break the heart of me)   10
Love is a naked shadow
    On a gnarled and naked tree.

House in the World

1931

I'm looking for a house
In the world
Where the white shadows
Will not fall.

There is no such house,
Dark brothers,
No such house
At all.

Florida Road Workers

1931

Hey, Buddy!
Look at me!

I'm makin' a road
For the cars to fly by on,
Makin' a road
Through the palmetto thicket
For light and civilization
To travel on.   5

I'm makin' a road
For the rich to sweep over
In their big cars
And leave me standin' here.   10

Sure,
A road helps everybody.
Rich folks ride—
And I get to see 'em ride.   15
I ain't never seen nobody
Ride so fine before.

Hey, Buddy, look!
I'm makin' a road!   20

Personal

1933

In an envelope marked:
    Personal
God addressed me a letter.
In an envelope marked:
    Personal
I have given my answer.

Little Lyric *(Of Great Importance)*   1942

I wish the rent
Was heaven sent.

Merry-Go-Round   1942

Colored child at carnival

Where is the Jim Crow section
On this merry-go-round,
Mister, cause I want to ride?
Down South where I come from
White and colored   5
Can't sit side by side.
Down South on the train
There's a Jim Crow car.
On the bus we're put in the back—
But there ain't no back   10
To a merry-go-round!
Where's the horse
For a kid that's black?

Down Where I Am   1950

Too many years
Beatin' at the door—
I done beat my
Both fists sore.

Too many years   5
Tryin' to get up there—
Done broke my ankles down,
Got nowhere.

Too many years
Climbin' that hill,   10
'Bout out of breath.
I got my fill.

I'm gonna plant my feet
On solid ground.
If you want to see me,   15
Come down.

Theme for English B   1949

The instructor said,

> *Go home and write*
> *a page tonight.*
> *And let that page come out of you —*
> *Then, it will be true.*   5

I wonder if it's that simple?
I am twenty-two, colored, born in Winston-Salem.
I went to school there, then Durham, then here
to this college on the hill above Harlem.
I am the only colored student in my class.   10
The steps from the hill lead down into Harlem,
through a park, then I cross St. Nicholas,
Eighth Avenue, Seventh, and I come to the Y,
the Harlem Branch Y, where I take the elevator
up to my room, sit down, and write this page: 15

It's not easy to know what is true for you or me
at twenty-two, my age. But I guess I'm what
I feel and see and hear, Harlem, I hear you:
hear you, hear me — we two — you, me, talk on this page.
(I hear New York, too.) Me — who?   20
Well, I like to eat, sleep, drink, and be in love.
I like to work, read, learn, and understand life.
I like a pipe for a Christmas present,
or records — Bessie, bop, or Bach.
I guess being colored doesn't make me *not* like   25
the same things other folks like who are other races.
So will my page be colored that I write?
Being me, it will not be white.
But it will be
a part of you, instructor.   30
You are white —
yet a part of me, as I am a part of you.
That's American.
Sometimes perhaps you don't want to be a part of me.
Nor do I often want to be a part of you.   35
But we are, that's true!
As I learn from you,
I guess you learn from me —
although you're older — and white —
and somewhat more free.   40

This is my page for English B.

Dream Deferred

What happens to a dream deferred?

    Does it dry up
    like a raisin in the sun?
    Or fester like a sore—
    And then run?   5
    Does it stink like rotten meat?
    Or crust and sugar over—
    like a syrupy sweet?

    Maybe it just sags   10
    like a heavy load.

    Or does it explode?

JOHN KEATS

John Keats (1795–1821) was the oldest of five children. His mother was the wife of the head stableman in a London livery stable. In his brief school years, Keats, despite his small stature, was mostly distinguished for his numerous fist fights. He also developed a passion for reading, under the fortunate tutelage of Charles Cowden Clarke, but after the deaths of his parents he was apprenticed at age fifteen to an apothecary surgeon. When he completed a year of studies at Guy's College, he was licensed to continue his trade, but he quickly abandoned it to become a poet.

Little of the poetry Keats had written up to this time showed any sign of genius, although he received ample encouragement from a number of older writers, including Leigh Hunt, who introduced him to Percy Bysshe Shelley. The sonnet "On First Looking into Chapman's Homer" (p. 813), written when he was twenty-one, first hinted at what he would accomplish in the short time that was left to him. His language and ideas were an important influence on nineteenth-century English poetry.

His mother had died of tuberculosis, and Keats nursed a tubercular younger brother through his dying months in 1818. Keats contracted the disease and at the same time fell hopelessly in love with an eighteen-year-old girl named Fanny Brawne. Too poor and too ill to marry, he poured his emotions into poems and letters that were suffused with his despair, his love for Brawne, and his consciousness that his life was already running out.

Keats tried to fight his illness by traveling to Italy, but he was weakened by a series of hemorrhages and died in Rome at the age of twenty-six. In his last letter he apologized to a friend for writing such a clumsy good-bye. He wrote, "I always made an awkward bow."

"Ode to a Nightingale" was one of several poems Keats wrote in his remarkable year of 1819, when he composed several of his major works, including "To Autumn" (p. 718) and "Ode on a Grecian Urn" (p. 743). "When I have fears," with its tone of tragic prophecy, was written in January of the year before.

RELATED POEM   *John Ashbery, "Around the Rough and Rugged Rocks the Ragged Rascal Rudely Ran," page 835.*

COMMENTARY   *Philip Levine, "From 'Keats in Detroit,' " page 987.*

WEB   *Research John Keats and answer questions about his work at bedfordstmartins.com/charters/litwriters.*

Ode to a Nightingale   1819

I

My heart aches, and a drowsy numbness pains
   My sense, as though of hemlock° I had drunk,   *a poison*
Or emptied some dull opiate to the drains
   One minute past, and Lethe-wards° had sunk:
'Tis not through envy of thy happy lot,   5
   But being too happy in thine happiness —
      That thou, light-wingèd Dryad° of the trees,   *wood nymph*
        In some melodious plot
   Of beechen green, and shadows numberless,
      Singest of summer in full-throated ease.   10

II

O, for a draught of vintage! that hath been
   Cooled a long age in the deep-delvèd earth,
Tasting of Flora° and the country green,   *goddess of flowers*
   Dance, and Provençal song,° and sunburnt mirth!
O for a beaker full of the warm South,   15
   Full of the true, the blushful Hippocrene,°
      With beaded bubbles winking at the brim,
        And purple-stainèd mouth;
That I might drink, and leave the world unseen,
      And with thee fade away into the forest dim.   20

III

Fade far away, dissolve, and quite forget
   What thou among the leaves hast never known,
The weariness, the fever, and the fret
   Here, where men sit and hear each other groan;
Where palsy shakes a few, sad, last gray hairs,   25

---

4. Lethe-wards: Lethe is the river of forgetfulness in Greek mythology.   **14. Provençal song:** Provence, in medieval France, was famous for its troubadors.   **16. Hippocrene:** Hippocrene is the fountain of the Muses, the goddesses of artistic inspiration.

Where youth grows pale, and specter-thin, and dies,
    Where but to think is to be full of sorrow
      And leaden-eyed despairs,
    Where Beauty cannot keep her lustrous eyes;
      Or new Love pine at them beyond tomorrow.   30

IV

Away! away! for I will fly to thee,
    Not charioted by Bacchus and his pards,°
But on the viewless wings of Poesy,
    Though the dull brain perplexes and retards:
Already with thee! tender is the night,   35
    And haply the Queen-Moon is on her throne,
      Clustered around by all her starry Fays;°   *fairies*
        But here there is no light,
Save what from heaven is with the breezes blown
    Through verdurous glooms and winding mossy ways.   40

V

I cannot see what flowers are at my feet,
    Nor what soft incense hangs upon the boughs,
But, in embalmèd° darkness, guess each sweet   *perfumed*
    Wherewith the seasonable month endows
The grass, the thicket, and the fruit-tree wild;   45
    What hawthorn, and the pastoral eglantine;
      Fast fading violets covered up in leaves;
      And mid-May's eldest child,
The coming musk-rose, full of dewy wine,
    The murmurous haunt of flies on summer eves.   50

VI

Darkling° I listen; and for many a time   *in the dark*
    I have been half in love with easeful Death,
Called him soft names in many a musèd rhyme,
    To take into the air my quiet breath;
Now more than ever seems it rich to die,   55
    To cease upon the midnight with no pain,
      While thou art pouring forth thy soul abroad
        In such an ecstasy!
Still wouldst thou sing, and I have ears in vain —
    To thy high requiem become a sod.   60

---

32. Bacchus and his pards: Bacchus, the god of wine, supposedly traveled in a chariot drawn by leopards.

VII

Thou wast not born for death, immortal Bird!
　　No hungry generations tread thee down;
The voice I hear this passing night was heard
　　In ancient days by emperor and clown:
Perhaps the selfsame song that found a path　　　　　　　　　65
　　　　Through the sad heart of Ruth,° when, sick for home,
　　　　　　She stood in tears amid the alien corn:
　　　　　　　　The same that oft-times hath
　　　　Charmed magic casements, opening on the foam
　　　　　　Of perilous seas, in faery lands forlorn.　　　　　70

VIII

Forlorn! the very word is like a bell
　　To toll me back from thee to my sole self!
Adieu! the fancy cannot cheat so well
　　As she is famed to do, deceiving elf.
Adieu! adieu! thy plaintive anthem fades　　　　　　　　　75
　　　　Past the near meadows, over the still stream,
　　　　　　Up the hill side; and now 'tis buried deep
　　　　　　　　In the next valley-glades:
　　　　Was it a vision, or a waking dream?
　　　　　　Fled is that music: — Do I wake or sleep?　　　　80

When I have fears   1818

When I have fears that I may cease to be
　　Before my pen has gleaned my teeming brain,
Before high-pilèd books, in charact'ry,
　　Hold like rich garners the full-ripen'd grain;
When I behold, upon the night's starr'd face,　　　　　　　5
　　Huge cloudy symbols of a high romance,
And think that I may never live to trace
　　Their shadows, with the magic hand of chance;
And when I feel, fair creature of an hour!
　　That I shall never look upon thee more,　　　　　　　　10
Never have relish in the faery power
　　Of unreflecting love! — then on the shore
Of the wide world I stand alone, and think,
Till Love and Fame to nothingness do sink.

---

66. the sad heart of Ruth: Reference to the young widow in the biblical Book of Ruth.

ROBERT LOWELL

Robert Lowell (1917–1977) was born in Boston to a distinguished New England family that had already produced two major poets, James Russell Lowell (1819–1891) and Amy Lowell (1874–1925), one of the leaders of the imagist movement (p. 769). After two years at Harvard University, Lowell left in 1937 for Kenyon College in Ohio to join a group of young poets who had gathered around teacher and poet John Crowe Ransom. Although his father had been a Navy officer, Lowell became a conscientious objector during World War II and was imprisoned for five months in 1943. He continued to write poetry through his personal crises, and his second book, Lord Weary's Castle, won the Pulitzer Prize in 1946.

Lowell published steadily, and his books were well received, but he was beginning to suffer from acute attacks of depression. Two of his three marriages were to novelists—first to Jean Stafford in 1940 and then to Elizabeth Hardwick in 1949. He was also drinking heavily and when he was drunk he was emotionally abusive. In the 1950s he visited San Francisco and experienced the excitement of the Beat Generation, the new literary movement that had sprung up there. After seeing the effect of Beat writer Allen Ginsberg's poetry on audiences and reading an emotional poem titled "Heart's Needle" by a former student named W. D. Snodgrass, he changed his way of writing. His poems became freer and more personal. His collection Life Studies, written in the new "confessional" style, was one of the most influential books published after the war, winning the National Book Award in 1959. At this same time he was teaching a poetry course at Boston University, and among his students were Sylvia Plath and Anne Sexton, who adopted the new style in their own writing.

Finally diagnosed as manic-depressive, Lowell was able to avoid with medication some of the psychotic episodes that had periodically caused him to be hospitalized. With novelist Norman Mailer, he was involved in the struggle against the Vietnam War, and in 1972 he married for the third time and settled in England. He had written plays and literary criticism and won the Bollingen Prize for his translations. In 1977 he returned to the United States planning to teach at Harvard, but he died of a heart attack a short time later.

One of his closest friends was poet Elizabeth Bishop—in emotional moments he asked her to marry him—and "Skunk Hour" is dedicated to her. His poem is a response to her "Armadillo." It reads almost like a letter, describing a scene that is familiar to both of them. "For the Union Dead" is also a description, this time of the Boston Common and the memorial statue by Augustus Saint-Gaudens to the Civil War regiment of African American soldiers that was destroyed with its young commander, Boston's Colonel Shaw. "Epilogue" was written in 1977, shortly before Lowell's death.

COMMENTARIES Robert Lowell, "An Explication of 'Skunk Hour,'" page 989; Robert Lowell, "Foreword to Plath's Ariel," page 990; Robert Lowell, "On Robert Frost," page 1034.

WEB Research Robert Lowell and answer questions about his work at bedfordstmartins.com/charters/litwriters.

Skunk Hour

1959

For Elizabeth Bishop

Nautilus Island's hermit
heiress still lives through winters in her Spartan cottage;
her sheep still graze above the sea.
Her son's a bishop. Her farmer
is first selectman in our village;   5
she's in her dotage.

Thirsting for
the hierarchic privacy
of Queen Victoria's century,
she buys up all   10
the eyesores facing her shore,
and lets them fall.

The season's ill—
we've lost our summer millionaire,
who seemed to leap from an L. L. Bean°   15
catalogue. His nine-knot yawl
was auctioned off to lobstermen.
A red fox stain covers Blue Hill.

And now our fairy
decorator brightens his shop for fall;   20
his fishnet's filled with orange cork,
orange, his cobbler's bench and awl;
there is no money in his work,
he'd rather marry.

One dark night,
my Tudor Ford climbed the hill's skull;   25
I watched for love-cars. Lights turned down,
they lay together, hull to hull,
where the graveyard shelves on the town. . . .
My mind's not right.

A car radio bleats,   30
"Love, O careless Love. . . ." I hear
my ill-spirit sob in each blood cell,
as if my hand were at its throat. . . .
I myself am hell;
nobody's here—   35

only skunks, that search
in the moonlight for a bite to eat.

---

15. L. L. Bean: A Maine mail-order store known for its sporting goods and outdoor
equipment.

They march on their soles up Main Street:
white stripes, moonstruck eyes' red fire   40
under the chalk-dry and spar spire
of the Trinitarian Church.

I stand on top
of our back steps and breathe the rich air—
a mother skunk with her column of kittens swills the garbage pail.   45
She jabs her wedge-head in a cup
of sour cream, drops her ostrich tail,
and will not scare.

For the Union Dead   1964

"Relinquunt Omnia Servare Rem Publican."°

The old South Boston Aquarium stands
in a Sahara of snow now. Its broken windows are boarded.
The bronze weathervane cod has lost half its scales.
The airy tanks are dry.

Once my nose crawled like a snail on the glass;   5
my hand tingled
to burst the bubbles
drifting from the noses of the cowed, compliant fish.

My hand draws back. I often sigh still
for the dark downward and vegetating kingdom   10
of the fish and reptile. One morning last March,
I pressed against the new barbed and galvanized

fence on the Boston Common. Behind their cage,
yellow dinosaur steamshovels were grunting
as they cropped up tons of mush and grass   15
to gouge their underworld garage.

Parking spaces luxuriate like civic
sandpiles in the heart of Boston.
A girdle of orange, Puritan-pumpkin colored girders
braces the tingling Statehouse,   20

shaking over the excavations, as it faces Colonel Shaw
and his bell-cheeked Negro infantry
on St. Gaudens' shaking Civil War relief,
propped by a plank splint against the garage's earthquake.

Two months after marching through Boston,   25
half the regiment was dead;

Relinquunt . . . Publican: "They gave up all to serve the republic."

at the dedication,
William James° could almost hear the bronze Negroes breathe.

Their monument sticks like a fishbone
in the city's throat.   30
Its Colonel is as lean
as a compass-needle.

He has an angry wrenlike vigilance,
a greyhound's gentle tautness;
he seems to wince at pleasure,   35
and suffocate for privacy.

He is out of bounds now. He rejoices in man's lovely,
peculiar power to choose life and die —
when he leads his black soldiers to death,
he cannot bend his back.   40

On a thousand small town New England greens,
the old white churches hold their air
of sparse, sincere rebellion; frayed flags
quilt the graveyards of the Grand Army of the Republic.

The stone statues of the abstract Union Soldier   45
grow slimmer and younger each year —
wasp-waisted, they doze over muskets
and muse through their sideburns . . .

Shaw's father wanted no monument
except the ditch,   50
where his son's body was thrown
and lost with his "niggers."

The ditch is nearer.
There are no statues for the last war here;
on Boylston Street, a commercial photograph   55
shows Hiroshima boiling

over a Mosler Safe, the "Rock of Ages"
that survived the blast. Space is nearer.
When I crouch to my television set,
the drained faces of Negro school-children rise like balloons.   60

Colonel Shaw
is riding on his bubble,
he waits
for the blessèd break.

The Aquarium is gone. Everywhere,   65
giant finned cars nose forward like fish;
a savage servility
slides by on grease.

---

28. William James: Harvard psychologist and philosopher (1842–1910).

Epilogue

1977

Those blessèd structures, plot and rhyme —
why are they no help to me now
I want to make
something imagined, not recalled?
I hear the noise of my own voice: 5
The painter's vision is not a lens,
it trembles to caress the light.
But sometimes everything I write
with the threadbare art of my eye
seems a snapshot,   10
lurid, rapid, garish, grouped,
heightened from life,
yet paralyzed by fact.
All's misalliance.
Yet why not say what happened?   15
Pray for the grace of accuracy
Vermeer° gave to the sun's illumination
stealing like the tide across a map
to his girl solid with yearning.
We are poor passing facts,   20
warned by that to give
each figure in the photograph
his living name.

MARIANNE MOORE

*Marianne Moore (1887–1972) was born in St. Louis, Missouri, but her
father chose not to remain with his family, and eventually Moore and her mother
moved to Carlisle, Pennsylvania. She graduated from Bryn Mawr College in
1909. Following her graduation, she and her mother traveled to France and England, then for five years she taught courses in office skills at the U.S. Indian
School for Native Americans in Carlisle. In 1918 she and her mother moved to
New York with her brother, who was a Presbyterian minister.*

*She had already begun writing poetry in college, and she began submitting
her work to several small experimental magazines. Her poetry immediately
attracted the attention of other writers, including William Carlos Williams and
Wallace Stevens. Williams included her work in a small mimeographed magazine
he published in the early 1920s. From 1925 to 1929 she was editor of* The Dial, *a
New York literary journal.*

*Moore's life was quiet. She lived with her mother in Brooklyn and worked on
her poetry. The poet Elizabeth Bishop, who was close to her for thirty-five years,*

---

17. Vermeer: Dutch painter Jan Vermeer (1632–1675).

remembered her conversation as "entertaining, enlightening, fascinating, and memorable; her talk, like her poetry, was quite different from anyone else in the world."

In 1951 Moore's Collected Poems won almost every major American literary award, and her work found new audiences who were charmed by her enthusiasm for oddly named animals, racehorses, and the Brooklyn Dodgers. "The Fish" is an early poem that attracted immediate attention and may have inspired the poem with the same title by Elizabeth Bishop. "In the Public Garden" is from O to Be a Dragon, published in 1959. (See also Moore's "Poetry" on p. 685 and "What Are Years?" on p. 699.)

COMMENTARY   *Marianne Moore, "Some Answers to Questions Posed by Howard Nemerov," page 994.*

WEB   *Research Marianne Moore and answer questions about her work at bedfordstmartins.com/charters/litwriters.*

The Fish

1921

wade
through black jade.
   Of the crow-blue mussel shells, one keeps
   adjusting the ash heaps;
      opening and shutting itself like

an
injured fan.
   The barnacles which encrust the side
   of the wave, cannot hide
      there for the submerged shafts of the

sun,
split like spun
   glass, move themselves with spotlight swiftness
   into the crevices —
      in and out, illuminating

the
turquoise sea
   of bodies. The water drives a wedge
   of iron through the iron edge
      of the cliff; whereupon the stars,

pink
rice-grains, ink-
   bespattered jellyfish, crabs like green
   lilies, and submarine
      toadstools, slide each on the other.

All
external
   marks of abuse are present on this

5
10
15
20
25

defiant edifice—
    all the physical features of   30
ac-
cident—lack
    of cornice, dynamite grooves, burns, and
    hatchet strokes, these things stand
        out on it; the chasm side is   35
dead.
Repeated
    evidence has proved that it can live
    on what can not revive
        its youth. The sea grows old in it.   40

In the Public Garden   1959

    Boston has a festival—
    compositely for all—
and nearby, cupolas of learning
(crimson, blue, and gold) that
    have made education individual.   5

    My first—an exceptional,
    an almost scriptural—
taxi driver to Cambridge from Back Bay
said, as we went along, "They
    make some fine young men at Harvard." I recall   10

    the summer when Faneuil Hall
    had its weathervane with gold ball
and grasshopper, gilded again by
a -leafer and -jack
    till it glittered. Spring can be a miracle   15

    there—a more than usual
    bouquet of what is vernal—
"pear blossoms whiter than the clouds," pin-
oak leaves that barely show
    when other trees are making shade, besides small   20

    fairy iris suitable
    for Dulcinea del
Toboso;° O yes, and snowdrops
in the snow, that smell like
    violets. Despite secular bustle,   25

    let me enter King's Chapel
    to hear them sing: "My work be praise while

22–23. Dulcinea del Toboso: Beloved of Don Quixote.

others go and come. No more a stranger
or a guest but like a child
    at home." A chapel or a festival   30

    means giving what is mutual,
    even if irrational:
black sturgeon eggs—a camel
from Hamadan, Iran;
    a jewel, or, what is more unusual,   35

    silence—after a word-waterfall of the banal—
    as unattainable
as freedom. And what is freedom for?
For "self-discipline," as our
    hardest-working citizen has said—a school;   40

    it is for "freedom to toil"
    with a feel for the tool.
Those in the trans-shipment camp must have
a skill. With hope of freedom hanging
    by a thread—some gather medicinal   45

    herbs which they can sell.
    Ineligible if they ail.
                Well?

There are those who will talk for an hour
without telling you why they have   50
    come. And I? This is no madrigal—
    no medieval gradual.
    It is a grateful tale—
without that radiance which poets
are supposed to have—   55
    unofficial, unprofessional. But still one need not fail

    to wish poetry well
    where intellect is habitual—
    glad that the Muses have a home and swans—
    that legend can be factual;   60
        happy that Art, admired in general,
        is always actually personal.

SHARON OLDS

Sharon Olds (b. 1942) was born in San Francisco and grew up in Berkeley. She has consistently refused to answer questions about her family and her personal life, feeling that the people she describes in her poetry have a right to privacy. As she told an interviewer for the New York Times, *"I promised I'd keep them out of this." She went on, "I never thought anyone would read anything I'd written. If I'd* known the number of readers I would have, I would have used a pseudonym." Her critics and interviewers have generally respected her wishes, and there have been no published interviews or reminiscences by people who have been part of her life.

The other side of Olds's reticence has been to create a body of poetry that is the most explicitly personal record any woman has ever given us about her body, her sexuality, and her complex relationships with her lovers, her father, her children, her sister, and her husband. She writes in the confessional mode of Robert Lowell, Anne Sexton, and Sylvia Plath, but without the verbal defenses that often make their poetry more ambiguous. As the interviewer Dinitia Smith wrote, "Her work has a robust sensuality, a delight in the physical that is almost Whitmanesque. She has made the minutiae of a woman's everyday life as valid a subject for poetry as the grand abstract themes that have preoccupied other poets." The literary critic Helen Vendler termed her poetry "pornographic," but there is no pornographic intent in anything Olds writes, even though a few of the poems would have caused difficulties for her publishers before the legal decisions that cleared the way for the work of writers such as D. H. Lawrence, Vladimir Nabokov, and Allen Ginsberg in the 1950s.

What Olds has allowed interviewers to learn about her life is that she grew up in a middle-class home that was deeply religious. Her parents were Episcopalians, and the family attended church twice weekly. As she has written in the poem "The Elder Sister," she had an older sibling, who she felt helped open the way for her own development. Olds's relationship with her father, as she described it in her book The Father, was difficult. He is presented as a physically bullying figure who dominated her life. In newer poems she has softened the portrait, but he is still a troubling presence.

Olds was sent to the Dana Hall School in Wellesley, Massachusetts, but returned to California for her university years. She graduated from Stanford and moved to New York City to study for her Ph.D. at Columbia University. She married in the late 1960s and is the mother of a son and a daughter. The painful breakup of her marriage has also caused her to shield herself from personal questions.

Although Olds has preferred to present a low personal profile, her life in New York is a rush of public activity. She has taught creative writing at New York University since the mid-1980s, and from 1989 to 1991 she was director of the Graduate Creative Writing Program. In 1984 she founded a poetry workshop for the severely disabled in New York's Goldwater Hospital. Adding to her already crammed schedule, in the spring of 1998 she was selected as the official New York state poet, which involves two years of presentations and appearances across the state. When one interviewer asked her about fitting all of these things into her life, she confessed that she has given up reading newspapers and watching television. She agreed that this has its disadvantages, but cheerfully defended herself by saying, "I try to look at the front page whenever I'm walking by a newsstand."

Olds also manages to fit a demanding line-up of readings into her schedule, and she is one of a handful of poets in the United States whose books sell in large quantities. The Father was reprinted several times within a few months of its publication, and her 1984 collection The Dead and the Living, which won the National Book Critics Circle Award, has sold more than 50,000 copies. The demands of her life, however, mean that each book is a gathering of work that was written *years before. She writes continuously, and it is only after considerable time has passed that she feels the need to put together the poems that make up a book. She doesn't conceive of her books as following a specific theme, but with* The Father *she made the decision to include only poems that created a loose narrative sequence. "At first I thought it would not be a good idea to have a book all on one theme. I also didn't know if I had enough poems on the subject that I liked well enough to make a book of them. But it turned out that I did. And it just seemed true to make a story that was all of itself. It pleased me to do so, and it still does."*

Her poetry is composed in her head as she is busy with her other responsibilities, and the actual writing of a poem goes quickly. She joked with an interviewer that she could write a poem in half an hour. When the response to this was surprise, Olds laughed and agreed, "Forty-five minutes is much better."

This selection of Olds's work includes many of her continuing themes. "The Elder Sister" suggests the tensions in her family; "Summer Solstice, New York City" deals with a person whose life has reached a breaking point, the would-be suicide on the New York rooftop saved by the police. There is perhaps no poem that better reflects the current uncertainty about sexual mores in our society than her "Sex without Love."

COMMENTARY *Sharon Olds, "From the* Salon *Interview," page 995.*

WEB *Research Sharon Olds and answer questions about her work at bedfordstmartins.com/charters/litwriters.*

The Elder Sister   1984

When I look at my elder sister now
I think how she had to go first, down through the
birth canal, to force her way
head-first through the tiny channel,
the pressure of Mother's muscles on her brain,   5
the tight walls scraping her skin.
Her face is still narrow from it, the long
hollow cheeks of a Crusader on a tomb,
and her inky eyes have the look of someone who has
been in prison a long time and   10
knows they can send her back. I look at her
body and think how her breasts were the first to
rise, slowly, like swans on a pond.
By the time mine came along, they were just
two more birds in the flock, and when the hair   15
rose on the white mound of her flesh, like
threads of water out of the ground, it was the
first time, but when mine came
they knew about it. I used to think
only in terms of her harshness, sitting and   20
pissing on me in bed, but now I

see I had her before me always
like a shield. I look at her wrinkles, her clenched
jaws, her frown-lines — I see they are
the dents on my shield, the blows that did not reach me.   25
She protected me, not as a mother
protects a child, with love, but as a
hostage protects the one who makes her
escape as I made my escape, with my sister's
body held in front of me.   30

Summer Solstice, New York City   1987

By the end of the longest day of the year he could not stand it,
he went up the iron stairs through the roof of the building
and over the soft, tarry surface
to the edge, put one leg over the complex green tin cornice
and said if they came a step closer that was it.   5
Then the huge machinery of the earth began to work for his life,
the cops came in their suits blue-grey as the sky on a cloudy evening,
and one put on a bullet-proof vest,
a black shell around his own life,
life of his children's father, in case   10
the man was armed, and one, slung with a
rope like the sign of his bounden duty,
came up out of a hole in the top of the neighbouring building
like the gold hole they say is in the top of the head,
and began to lurk toward the man who wanted to die.   15
The tallest cop approached him directly,
softly, slowly, talking to him, talking, talking,
while the man's leg hung over the lip of the next world
and the crowd gathered in the street, silent, and the
hairy net with its implacable grid was   20
unfolded near the curb and spread out and
stretched as the sheet is prepared to receive at a birth.
Then they all came a little closer
where he squatted next to his death, his shirt
glowing its milky glow like something   25
growing in a dish at night in the dark in a lab and then
everything stopped
as his body jerked and he
stepped down from the parapet and went toward them
and they closed on him, I thought they were going to   30
beat him up, as a mother whose child has been
lost will scream at the child when it's found, they
took him by the arms and held him up and
leaned him against the wall of the chimney and the

tall cop lit a cigarette   35
in his own mouth, and gave it to him, and
then they all lit cigarettes, and the
red, glowing ends burned like the
tiny campfires we lit at night
back at the beginning of the world.   40

Sex without Love   1983

How do they do it, the ones who make love
without love? Beautiful as dancers,
gliding over each other like ice-skaters
over the ice, fingers hooked
inside each other's bodies, faces   5
red as steak, wine, wet as the
children at birth whose mothers are going to
give them away. How do they come to the
come to the   come to the   God   come to the
still waters, and not love   10
the one who came there with them, light
rising slowly as steam off their joined
skin? These are the true religious,
the purists, the pros, the ones who will not
accept a false Messiah, love the   15
priest instead of the God. They do not
mistake the lover for their own pleasure,
they are like great runners: they know they are alone
with the road surface, the cold, the wind,
the fit of their shoes, their over-all cardio-   20
vascular health — just factors, like the partner
in the bed, and not the truth, which is the
single body alone in the universe
against its own best time.

MARGE PIERCY

Marge Piercy (b. 1936) was born in Detroit, where her father was employed as an installation worker by Westinghouse. Her mother was the daughter of a union activist who was murdered for his efforts to organize workers. Piercy had an emotionally difficult adolescence, and a severe attack of rheumatic fever left her physically weakened. She also began writing as a teenager, however, and with the help of scholarships and prizes she graduated from the University of Michigan in 1957 and received her M.A. a year later.

Briefly married, Piercy was divorced by the time she was twenty-three. In the 1960s she married again, and with her husband became committed to a communal lifestyle and to the protest movement against the Vietnam War and U.S. involvement in Latin America. In 1980 she married for a third time, and since then she has lived in Wellfleet, Massachusetts, on Cape Cod. Although Piercy is one of the more popular feminist poets, she is still much better known as a novelist. Her long, fictionalized accounts of her family background and her life as a radical in the 1960s have been best-sellers, and she has been able to live comfortably on the income from her fiction and her readings.

"The woman in the ordinary" was written in 1973. "In which she begs (like everybody else) that love may last" is from her 1983 collection Stone, Paper, Knife. "It ain't heavy, it's my purse," with its humorous allusion to a well-known sentimental drawing of a small boy carrying a much larger, older boy on his shoulders with the caption, "He ain't heavy, he's my brother," was published in 1992.

COMMENTARY   Marge Piercy, "Imagery Can't Really Be Taught," page 997.

WEB   Research Marge Piercy and answer questions about her work at bedfordstmartins.com/charters/litwriters.

The woman in the ordinary   1973

The woman in the ordinary pudgy downcast girl
is crouching with eyes and muscles clenched.
Round and pebble smooth she effaces herself
under ripples of conversation and debate.
The woman in the block of ivory soap   5
has massive thighs that neigh,
great breasts that blare and strong arms that trumpet.
The woman of the golden fleece
laughs uproariously from the belly
inside the girl who imitates   10
a Christmas card virgin with glued hands,
who fishes for herself in other's eyes,
who stoops and creeps to make herself smaller.
In her bottled up is a woman peppery as curry,
a yam of a woman of butter and brass,   15
compounded of acid and sweet like a pineapple,
like a handgrenade set to explode,
like goldenrod ready to bloom.

In which she begs (like everybody
else) that love may last   1983

The lilac blooms now in May,
our bed awash with its fragrance,

while beside the drive, buds
of peony and poppy swell
toward cracking, slivers of color   5
bulging like a flash of eye
from someone pretending to sleep.
Each in its garden slot, each
in its season, crocus gives way
to daffodil, through to fall   10
monkshood and chrysanthemum.
Only I am the wicked rose
that wants to bloom all year.
I am never replete with loving
you. Satisfaction   15
makes me greedy. I want
to blossom out with my joy of you
in March, in July, in October.
I want to drop my red red
petals on the hard black ice.   20

It ain't heavy, it's my purse   1992

We have marsupial instincts, women
who lug purses as big as garbage igloos,
women who hang leather hippos from their shoulders:

we are hiding the helpless greedy naked worms
of our intentions shivering in chaos.   5
In bags the size of Manhattan studio apartments,

we carry not merely the apparatus of neatness
and legality, cards, licenses, combs,
mirrors, spare glasses, lens fluid,

but hex signs against disaster and loss.   10
Antihistamines — if we should sneeze.
Painkillers — suppose the back goes out.

Snake bite medicine — a copperhead
may lurk in the next subway car.
Extra shoes — I may have to ford a stream.   15

On my keyring, flats I used to stay in,
a Volvo I traded in 1985, two unknown doors
opening on what I might sometime direly need.

Ten pens, because the ink may run out.
Band-Aids, safety pins, rubber bands, glue,   20
maps, a notebook in case, addresses of friends

estranged. So we go hopping lopsided, women
like kangaroos with huge purses bearing hidden
our own helplessness and its fancied cures.

SYLVIA PLATH

Sylvia Plath (1932–1963) was born in Boston. Her father, who had emigrated from a German area of Poland as a boy, taught entomology at Boston University. Their relationship, as she described it in her poetry, was complicated, but he died when she was eight, and her mother, a high-school language teacher, encouraged her to write. Plath attended Smith College and graduated summa cum laude, but between her junior and senior years she suffered a nervous breakdown and attempted suicide.

In 1955, after her graduation, she received a Fulbright grant to study at Cambridge University, where she met one of the most promising young English poets, Ted Hughes. They were married in 1956 and came to the United States, where Plath had a job teaching at Smith College and Hughes later took a job at Amherst College. After two years Hughes returned to England, and despite strains in their marriage Plath joined him there in December 1959. They had two children, a daughter born in 1960 and a son in 1962, and they settled in a cottage in Devon.

On the surface Plath's life seemed ideal, with a house in the English countryside, a husband who respected her writing, and the publication of her first book the same year her first child was born. The poems she was writing, however, depict her despair at her isolation and the tensions of marriage to someone who was also a gifted writer and who was attractive to other women. Hughes began a relationship with someone else and left the cottage in Devon in October 1962. Several weeks later Plath moved with her children into a bleak London flat. She had been writing at a frantic pace through the autumn months and, despite near poverty and a deepening sense of isolation, she continued to compose the poems that Hughes later collected in his edited version of the manuscript she had titled Ariel. By February she could no longer see any way out of her emotional turmoil and ended her life. As Robert Lowell wrote in an introduction to the poems, "Her art's immortality is life's disintegration."

"Morning Song" is the first poem in Ariel. It describes the birth of Plath's second child and their first night together. Plath completed "Daddy" on October 12, 1962, the day after Hughes left her, and she continued to write raging poems over the next weeks. "Event" is from these last Ariel poems.

COMMENTARY Robert Lowell, "Foreword to Plath's Ariel," page 990.

WEB Research Sylvia Plath and answer questions about her work at bedfordstmartins.com/charters/litwriters.

Morning Song   1961

Love set you going like a fat gold watch.
The midwife slapped your footsoles, and your bald cry
Took its place among the elements.

Our voices echo, magnifying your arrival. New statue.
In a drafty museum, your nakedness
Shadows our safety. We stand round blankly as walls.

5

I'm no more your mother
Than the cloud that distils a mirror to reflect its own slow
Effacement at the wind's hand.

All night your moth-breath   10
Flickers among the flat pink roses. I wake to listen:
A far sea moves in my ear.

One cry, and I stumble from bed, cow-heavy and floral
In my Victorian nightgown.
Your mouth opens clean as a cat's. The window square   15

Whitens and swallows its dull stars. And now you try
Your handful of notes;
The clear vowels rise like balloons.

Daddy   1962

You do not do, you do not do
Any more, black shoe
In which I have lived like a foot
For thirty years, poor and white,
Barely daring to breathe or Achoo.   5

Daddy, I have had to kill you.
You died before I had time——
Marble-heavy, a bag full of God,
Ghastly statue with one gray toe
Big as a Frisco seal   10

And a head in the freakish Atlantic
Where it pours bean green over blue
In the waters off beautiful Nauset.
I used to pray to recover you.
Ach, du.°   *Oh, you*   15

In the German tongue, in the Polish Town°
Scraped flat by the roller
Of wars, wars, wars.
But the name of the town is common.
My Polack friend   20

Says there are a dozen or two.
So I never could tell where you
Put your foot, your root,
I never could talk to you.
The tongue stuck in my jaw.   25

---

16. **Polish Town:** Refers to Otto Plath's birthplace, Granbow.

It stuck in a barb wire snare.
Ich, ich, ich, ich,°   *I, I, I, I*
I could hardly speak.
I thought every German was you.
And the language obscene   30

An engine, an engine
Chuffing me off like a Jew.
A Jew to Dachau, Auschwitz, Belsen.°
I began to talk like a Jew.
I think I may well be a Jew.   35

The snows of the Tyrol, the clear beer of Vienna
Are not very pure or true.
With my gypsy-ancestress and my weird luck
And my Taroc° pack and my Taroc pack
I may be a bit of a Jew.   40

I have always been scared of *you,*
With your Luftwaffe,° your gobbledygoo.
And your neat mustache
And your Aryan eye, bright blue.
Panzer-man, panzer-man,° O You—   45

Not God but a swastika
So black no sky could squeak through.
Every woman adores a Fascist,
The boot in the face, the brute
Brute heart of a brute like you.   50

You stand at the blackboard, daddy,
In the picture I have of you,
A cleft in your chin instead of your foot
But no less a devil for that, no not
Any less the black man who   55

Bit my pretty red heart in two.
I was ten when they buried you.
At twenty I tried to die
And get back, back, back to you.
I thought even the bones would do   60

But they pulled me out of the sack,
And they stuck me together with glue.
And then I knew what to do.
I made a model of you,
A man in black with a Meinkampf° look   65

---

33. Dachau . . . Belsen: Nazi death camps in World War II.   **39. Taroc:** Pack of fortune-telling (tarot) cards.   **42. Luftwaffe:** World War II German aircorps.   **45. Panzer-man:** In World War II, the German panzer division was that made up of armored vehicles. **65. Meinkampf:** Adolf Hitler's autobiography was titled *Mein kampf,* or "My Struggle."

And a love of the rack and the screw.
And I said I do, I do.
So daddy, I'm finally through.
The black telephone's off at the root,
The voices just can't worm through.   70

If I've killed one man, I've killed two——
The vampire who said he was you
And drank my blood for a year,
Seven years, if you want to know.
Daddy, you can lie back now.   75

There's a stake in your fat black heart
And the villagers never liked you.
They are dancing and stamping on you.
They always *knew* it was you.
Daddy, daddy, you bastard, I'm through.   80

Event   1962

How the elements solidify!——
The moonlight, that chalk cliff
In whose rift we lie

Back to back. I hear an owl cry
From its cold indigo.
Intolerable vowels enter my heart.   5

The child in the white crib revolves and sighs,
Opens its mouth now, demanding.
His little face is carved in pained, red wood.

Then there are the stars—ineradicable, hard.
One touch: it burns and sickens.   10
I cannot see your eyes.

Where apple bloom ices the night
I walk in a ring,
A groove of old faults, deep and bitter.

Love cannot come here.   15
A black gap discloses itself.
On the opposite lip

A small white soul is waving, a small white maggot.
My limbs, also, have left me.
Who has dismembered us?   20

The dark is melting. We touch like cripples.

ADRIENNE RICH

Adrienne Rich was born in Baltimore, Maryland, in 1929. She graduated from Radcliffe College in 1951, the year her first book, A Change of World, *was published as one of the Yale Series of Younger Poets, which immediately brought her to the attention of a large reading audience. For many years she lived in New York City, one of many writers and intellectuals living in close contact on New York's Upper West Side. She was married, and in addition to her writing she actively raised her children. Several years after her husband's death in 1970, she entered a long-term lesbian relationship.*

In a 1967 review, the poet Hayden Carruth wrote of her work:

> *The dominating quality in Adrienne Rich's work, the quality which knits all, sound, syntax, and sense, into a marvelous unitary structure, is what she herself calls "fierce attention." . . . Other words have been used for it — compression, concern, concentration — and none is exactly right; but the poetry shows what it is: a need not simply to confront experience . . . but to solve it; to make it come right.*

In 1973 her book Diving into the Wreck *won the National Book Award. In 1984 she moved to California. She continues to write and publish today.*

"Aunt Jennifer's Tigers" is one of the most popular poems from her early collections. "To the Days" is included in a group titled What Kind of Times Are These, *published in her book* Dark Fields of the Republic. *In her own comment on the poem she quoted from a 1916 letter of the German/Jewish revolutionary Rosa Luxemburg:*

> *Then see to it that you stay human. . . . Being human means joyfully throwing your whole life "on the scales of destiny" when need be, but all the while rejoicing in every sunny day and every beautiful cloud, Ach, I know of no formula to write you for being human. . . .*

WEB   *Research Adrienne Rich and answer questions about her work at bedfordstmartins.com/charters/litwriters.*

Aunt Jennifer's Tigers   1952

Aunt Jennifer's tigers prance across a screen,
Bright topaz denizens of a world of green.
They do not fear the men beneath the tree;
They pace in sleek chivalric certainty.

Aunt Jennifer's fingers fluttering through her wool   5
Find even the ivory needle hard to pull.
The massive weight of Uncle's wedding band
Sits heavily upon Aunt Jennifer's hand.

When Aunt is dead, her terrified hands will lie
Still ringed with ordeals she was mastered by.   10
The tigers in the panel that she made
Will go on prancing, proud and unafraid.

Diving into the Wreck   1971

First having read the book of myths,
and loaded the camera,
and checked the edge of the knife-blade,
I put on
the body-armor of black rubber   5
the absurd flippers
the grave and awkward mask.
I am having to do this
not like Cousteau° with his
assiduous team   10
aboard the sun-flooded schooner
but here alone.

There is a ladder.
The ladder is always there
hanging innocently   15
close to the side of the schooner.
We know what it is for,
we who have used it.
Otherwise
it is a piece of maritime floss   20
some sundry equipment.
I go down.
Rung after rung and still
the oxygen immerses me
the blue light   25
the clear atoms
of our human air.
I go down.
My flippers cripple me,
I crawl like an insect down the ladder   30
and there is no one
to tell me when the ocean
will begin.

First the air is blue and then
it is bluer and then green and then   35
black I am blacking out and yet
my mask is powerful
it pumps my blood with power
the sea is another story

---

9. **Cousteau:** Jacques Cousteau (1910–1997), French underwater explorer, photographer, and author.

the sea is not a question of power   40
I have to learn alone
to turn my body without force
in the deep element.

And now: it is easy to forget
what I came for   45
among so many who have always
lived here
swaying their crenellated° fans
between the reefs
and besides   50
you breathe differently down here.

I came to explore the wreck.
The words are purposes.
The words are maps.
I came to see the damage that was done   55
and the treasures that prevail.
I stroke the beam of my lamp
slowly along the flank
of something more permanent
than fish or weed   60

the thing I came for:
the wreck and not the story of the wreck
the thing itself and not the myth
the drowned face always staring
toward the sun   65
the evidence of damage
worn by salt and sway into this threadbare beauty
the ribs of the disaster
curving their assertion
among the tentative haunters.   70

This is the place.
And I am here, the mermaid whose dark hair
streams black, the merman in his armored body
We circle silently
about the wreck   75
we dive into the hold.
I am she: I am he

whose drowned face sleeps with open eyes
whose breasts still bear the stress

---

48. crenellated: Notched with rounded or scalloped projections.

whose silver, copper, vermeil° cargo lies   80
obscurely inside barrels
half-wedged and left to rot
we are the half-destroyed instruments
that once held to a course
the water-eaten log   85
the fouled compass

We are, I am, you are
by cowardice or courage
the one who find our way
back to this scene   90
carrying a knife, a camera
a book of myths
in which
our names do not appear.

To the Days   1993

From you I want more than I've ever asked,
all of it — the newscasts' terrible stories
of life in my time, the knowing it's worse than that,
much worse — the knowing what it means to be lied to.

Fog in the mornings, hunger for clarity,   5
coffee and bread with sour plum jam.
Numbness of soul in placid neighborhoods.
Lives ticking on as if.

A typewriter's torrent, suddenly still.
Blue soaking through fog, two dragonflies wheeling.   10
Acceptable levels of cruelty, steadily rising.
Whatever you bring in your hands, I need to see it.

Suddenly I understand the verb without tenses.
To smell another woman's hair, to taste her skin.
To know the bodies drifting underwater.   15
To be human, said Rosa — I can't teach you that.

A cat drinks from a bowl of marigold — his moment.
Surely the love of life is neverending,
the failure of nerve, a charred fuse?
I want more from you than I ever knew to ask.   20

Wild pink lilies erupting, tasselled stalks of corn
in the Mexican gardens, corn and roses.
Shortening days, strawberry fields in ferment
with tossed-aside, bruised fruit.

---

80. vermeil: Gilded silver or bronze.

THEODORE ROETHKE

Theodore Roethke (1908–1963) was born in Saginaw, Michigan, the son of a successful operator of commercial greenhouses. Already writing poetry as an undergraduate at the University of Michigan, he began publishing his work during his graduate studies at Michigan and Harvard. His first full-time teaching position was at Lafayette College in Pennsylvania in 1931. He later taught at several other universities before going in 1947 to the University of Washington, where he taught for the rest of his life. His book Words for the Wind: The Collected Verse, *in 1958, established his reputation.*

Roethke was a prolific writer and had a successful career as a poet, but he struggled against alcoholism and manic-depressive illness. On more than one occasion he had to be taken in handcuffs from his classroom and was hospitalized for long periods. The poet Robert Lowell, a close friend, described him as "a ponderous, coarse, fattish, fortyish man, well read, likes the same things I do, and is quite a competent poet."

"My Papa's Waltz" recounts a painful childhood memory; "Night Journey" describes a night journey by train through the American West. (See also Roethke's "The Waking" on p. 762.)

WEB   *Research Theodore Roethke and answer questions about his work at bedfordstmartins.com/charters/litwriters.*

My Papa's Waltz   1948

The whiskey on your breath
Could make a small boy dizzy;
But I hung on like death:
Such waltzing was not easy.

We romped until the pans   5
Slid from the kitchen shelf;
My mother's countenance
Could not unfrown itself.

The hand that held my wrist
Was battered on one knuckle;   10
At every step you missed
My right ear scraped a buckle.

You beat time on my head
With a palm caked hard by dirt,
Then waltzed me off to bed   15
Still clinging to your shirt.

Night Journey

1954

Now as the train bears west,
Its rhythm rocks the earth,
And from my Pullman berth
I stare into the night
While others take their rest.   5
Bridges of iron lace,
A suddenness of trees,
A lap of mountain mist
All cross my line of sight,
Then a bleak wasted place,   10
And a lake below my knees.
Full on my neck I feel
The straining at a curve;
My muscles move with steel,
I wake in every nerve.   15
I watch a beacon swing
From dark to blazing bright;
We thunder through ravines
And gullies washed with light.
Beyond the mountain pass   20
Mist deepens on the pane;
We rush into a rain
That rattles double glass.
Wheels shake the roadbed stone,
The pistons jerk and shove,   25
I stay up half the night
To see the land I love.

ANNE SEXTON

Anne Sexton (1928–1974), the youngest of three daughters, was born in Newton, Massachusetts, a suburb of Boston, and grew up in Wellesley. She was from a well-off New England family, spending her winters in the city and her summers on Squirrel Island in Maine. When she was nineteen she eloped with a man who was, like her father, successful in the woolen industry.

Although outwardly she conformed to her family's expectations, Sexton was unable to resolve her inner conflicts. After the birth of each of her daughters, in 1953 and 1955, she was hospitalized for psychiatric treatment. When she first attempted suicide in 1956, her doctor suggested she begin writing poetry as therapy. She enrolled in her first writing workshop the next year, where she met the writer Maxine Kumin, who would become a close friend. The following year she enrolled in Robert Lowell's poetry class at Boston University. Another young poet, Sylvia Plath, was in the same class.

Sexton's first book, To Bedlam and Part Way Back, *published in 1960, only a year after her class with Lowell, attracted considerable attention for its powerful confessional style. She received awards and grants, and in 1967 she won the Pulitzer Prize for her book* Live or Die. *She taught at Harvard and Colgate universities, and was appointed a professor at Boston University in 1972. Despite her recognition, however, she was unable to free herself from her emotional torment. She finally succeeded in a suicide attempt in 1974.*

"The Starry Night" is her response to a painting by Vincent van Gogh. It is interesting, as an example of how artists and writers relate to each other's work, that in a letter to his sister van Gogh wrote that his painting had been inspired by a poem of Walt Whitman's. "For My Lover, Returning to His Wife," published after her death, is a harsh example of Sexton's cruel self-revelation, with its bitter image of her lover's wife as "as real as a cast-iron pot."

WEB *Research Anne Sexton and answer questions about her work at bedfordstmartins.com/charters/litwriters.*

The Starry Night

1962

That does not keep me from having a terrible need of—shall I say the
word—religion. Then I go out at night to paint the stars.
> —VINCENT VAN GOGH in a letter to his brother°

The town does not exist
except where one black-haired tree slips
up like a drowned woman into the hot sky.
The town is silent. The night boils with eleven stars
Oh starry starry night! This is how   5
I want to die.

It moves. They are all alive.
Even the moon bulges in its orange irons
to push children, like a god, from its eye.
The old unseen serpent swallows up the stars.   10
Oh starry starry night! This is how
I want to die:

into that rushing beast of the night,
sucked up by that great dragon, to split
from my life with no flag,   15
no belly,
no cry.

Vincent van Gogh . . . to his brother: Sexton's title echoes *Starry Night on the Rhône,* a painting by the Dutch artist Vincent van Gogh (1853–1890), who eventually went mad and committed suicide; the epigraph is taken from a letter van Gogh wrote to his brother, Theo, in 1888—at about the time he was painting *Starry Night.*

For My Lover, Returning to His Wife   1991

She is all there.
She was melted carefully down for you
and cast up from your childhood,
cast up from your one hundred favorite aggies.

She has always been there, my darling.   5
She is, in fact, exquisite.
Fireworks in the dull middle of February
and as real as a cast-iron pot.

Let's face it, I have been momentary.
A luxury. A bright red sloop in the harbor.   10
My hair rising like smoke from the car window.
Littleneck clams out of season.
She is more than that. She is your have to have,
has grown you your practical your tropical growth.
This is not an experiment. She is all harmony.   15
She sees to oars and oarlocks for the dinghy,

has placed wild flowers at the window at breakfast,
sat by the potter's wheel at midday,
set forth three children under the moon,
three cherubs drawn by Michelangelo,   20

done this with her legs spread out
in the terrible months in the chapel.
If you glance up, the children are there
like delicate balloons resting on the ceiling.

She has also carried each one down the hall   25
after supper, their heads privately bent,
two legs protesting, person to person,
her face flushed with a song and their little sleep.

I give you back your heart.
I give you permission—   30
for the fuse inside her, throbbing
angrily in the dirt, for the bitch in her
and the burying of her wound—
for the burying of her small red wound alive—

for the pale flickering flare under her ribs,   35
for the drunken sailor who waits in her left pulse,
for the mother's knee, for the stockings,
for the garter belt, for the call—

the curious call
when you will burrow in arms and breasts   40
and tug at the orange ribbon in her hair
and answer the call, the curious call.

She is so naked and singular.
She is the sum of yourself and your dream.
Climb her like a monument, step after step.   45
She is solid.

As for me, I am a watercolor.
I wash off.

WILLIAM SHAKESPEARE

William Shakespeare (1564–1616) is best known as a playwright, and his life and career are presented in the drama section in this book. Almost as honored is the sequence of sonnets he wrote during the latter part of his career. A contemporary of Shakespeare's wrote in 1598 that in addition to his plays, he was known "among his private friends" for "his sugared sonnets." They were published in 1609, the year before he retired from the theater, and since then they have been the standard against which all other sonnets in the English language are measured.

The 154 sonnets in the sequence seem to tell the story of an unhappy love affair, but, like so much else about Shakespeare's work, there is considerable confusion and continual scholarly wrangling over interpretation of the poems themselves and the story they may tell us. There is even uncertainty about the order of the sonnets. A "Dark Lady" is the central figure in many of them, and in some there is a suggestion of a love triangle involving two men and a woman. Some of the early sonnets are written to a young man of great beauty, urging him to marry.

More important than these details of the possible "story" of the sequence are the sonnets themselves, many lines and phrases from which have entered into the English language. The small gathering that follows reprints some of Shakespeare's most often anthologized sonnets. (The Shakespearean sonnet form is also discussed on pp. 750–756.)

COMMENTARY   *Erica Jong, "Devouring Time: Shakespeare's Sonnets," page 984.*

WEB   *Research William Shakespeare and answer questions about his work at bedfordstmartins.com/charters/litwriters.*

Shall I compare thee to a summer's day?   1609

Shall I compare thee to a summer's day?
Thou art more lovely and more temperate;
Rough winds do shake the darling buds of May,
And summer's lease hath all too short a date.
Sometime too hot the eye of heaven shines,   5
And often is his gold complexion dimmed;
And every fair from fair sometime declines,
By chance, or nature's changing course untrimmed.
But thy eternal summer shall not fade

Nor lose possession of that fair thou owest;   10
Nor shall Death brag thou wander'st in his shade,
When in eternal lines to time thou growest.
So long as men can breathe or eyes can see,
So long lives this and this gives life to thee.

When to the sessions of sweet silent thought   1609

When to the sessions of sweet silent thought
I summon up remembrance of things past,
I sigh the lack of many a thing I sought,
And with old woes new wail my dear time's waste:
Then can I drown an eye, unused to flow,   5
For precious friends hid in death's dateless night,
And weep afresh love's long since canceled woe,
And moan the expense of many a vanished sight:
Then can I grieve at grievances foregone,
And heavily from woe to woe tell o'er   10
The sad account of fore-bemoanèd moan,
Which I new pay as if not paid before.
But if the while I think on thee, dear friend,
All losses are restored and sorrows end.

Let me not to the marriage of true minds   1609

Let me not to the marriage of true minds
Admit impediments. Love is not love
Which alters when it alteration finds,
Or bends with the remover to remove:
O, no! it is an ever-fixèd mark   5
That looks on tempests and is never shaken;
It is the star to every wandering bark,
Whose worth's unknown, although his height be taken.
Love's not Time's fool, though rosy lips and cheeks
Within his bending sickle's compass come;   10
Love alters not with his brief hours and weeks,
But bears it out even to the edge of doom.
If this be error and upon me proved,
I never writ, nor no man ever loved.

My mistress' eyes are nothing like the sun   1609

My mistress' eyes are nothing like the sun;
Coral is far more red than her lips' red:
If snow be white, why then her breasts are dun;

If hairs be wires, black wires grow on her head.
I have seen roses damasked, red and white,   5
But no such roses see I in her cheeks;
And in some perfumes is there more delight
Than in the breath that from my mistress reeks.
I love to hear her speak, yet well I know
That music hath a far more pleasing sound;   10
I grant I never saw a goddess go;
My mistress, when she walks, treads on the ground:
And yet, by heaven, I think my love as rare
As any she belied with false compare.

GARY SOTO

Gary Soto (b. 1952) was born to Mexican American parents in Fresno, an agricultural town in California's Central Valley. He worked in the fields in the summers and in the Fresno factories. After his graduation from high school, he entered California State University at Fresno, planning to study urban planning, but classes with poet Philip Levine turned his interest to literature and writing. After graduation he went on to the University of California at Irvine for an M.F.A.

Soto's first poems appeared when he was still a senior in college, and his first collection, The Elements of San Joaquin, *was published in 1977. He began teaching literature and Chicano studies at the University of California campus at Berkeley the same year. His work has won many awards, and he has been granted a Guggenheim fellowship. Although Soto is perhaps the best known of the new Chicano poets, his writing has a personal identity that places it directly in the American mainstream.*

"Mexicans Begin Jogging" is a wryly humorous memory from his youth; "Teaching English from an Old Composition Book," written in the same tone, describes an experience from his years as a young teacher.

WEB   *Research Gary Soto and answer questions about his work at bedfordstmartins.com/charters/litwriters.*

Mexicans Begin Jogging   1981

At the factory I worked
In the fleck of rubber, under the press
Of an oven yellow with flame,
Until the border patrol opened
Their vans and my boss waved for us to run.   5
"Over the fence, Soto," he shouted,
And I shouted that I was American.
"No time for lies," he said, and pressed
A dollar in my palm, hurrying me
Through the back door.   10

Since I was on his time, I ran
And became the wag to a short tail of Mexicans—
Ran past the amazed crowds that lined
The street and blurred like photographs, in rain.
I ran from that industrial road to the soft   15
Houses where people paled at the turn of an autumn sky.
What could I do but yell *vivas*
To baseball, milkshakes, and those sociologists
Who would clock me
As I jog into the next century   20
On the power of a great, silly grin.

Teaching English from an Old Composition Book

1996

My chalk is no larger than a chip of fingernail,
Chip by which I must explain this Monday
Night the verbs "to get," "to wear," "to cut."
I'm not given much, these tired students,
Knuckle-wrapped from work as roofers,   5
Sour from scrubbing toilets and pedestal sinks.
I'm given this room with five windows,
A coffee machine, a piano with busted strings,
The music of how we feel as the sun falls,
Exhausted from keeping up.   10
                                I stand at
The blackboard. The chip is worn to a hangnail,
Nearly gone, the dust of some educational bone.
By and by I'm Cantinflas, the comic
Busy body in front. I say, "I want the coffee."
I pick up a coffee cup and sip.   15
I clip my heels and say, "I wear my shoes."
I bring an invisible fork to my mouth
And say, "I eat the chicken."
Suddenly the class is alive—
Each one putting on hats and shoes,   20
Drinking sodas and beers, cutting flowers
And steaks—a pantomime of sumptuous living.

At break I pass out cookies.
Augustine, the Guatemalan, asks in Spanish,
"Teacher, what is 'tally-ho'?"   25
I look at the word in the composition book.
I raise my face to the bare bulb for a blind answer.
I stutter, then say, "It's like *adelante*."°

---

29. *adelante:* Move.

Augustine smiles, then nudges a friend   30
In the next desk, now smarter by one word.
After the cookies are eaten,
We move ahead to prepositions—
"Under," "over," and "between,"
Useful words when *la migra*° opens the doors   35
Of their idling vans.
At ten to nine, I'm tired of acting,
And they're tired of their roles.
When class ends, I clap my hands of chalk dust,
And two students applaud, thinking it's a new verb.   40
I tell them *adelante,*
And they pick up their old books.
They smile and, in return, cry, "Tally-ho"
As they head for the door.

WALT WHITMAN

Walt Whitman (1819–1892) was born on Long Island, close to New York City. When he was three his father moved the family to Brooklyn. Whitman went to work as an errand boy when he was eleven and the next year took a job in a newspaper office. He educated himself by reading novels and soon was contributing poems to a Manhattan newspaper. For five years, beginning when he was sixteen, he worked mostly as a country schoolmaster on Long Island, boarding with the families of his students.

When Whitman gave up teaching, he went back to New York and Brooklyn, and for the next fifteen years he held a series of newspaper jobs, wrote a temperance novel, and published several short stories in a national magazine. By his mid-thirties he was living at home again, crowded into a shabby house in Brooklyn with his parents and his brothers and sisters. He had lost his newspaper job and was working—when he did work—as a carpenter. He spent his days walking the streets or sitting in local libraries. He was emotionally dependent on his mother, but he was careless about missing family meals, came and went as he pleased, and hid himself for hours writing poetry in the room he shared with his brother.

In the spring of 1855 Whitman arranged with a small Brooklyn print shop to bring out a book of the poems he had been writing. He titled it Leaves of Grass. *He printed enough sheets for three hundred copies, had one hundred bound in green cloth with gold stamping, and sent copies to many important American writers. Some threw their copies in the fire, but Ralph Waldo Emerson, then the leading American intellectual figure, recognized the book's genius and sent Whitman a letter that began, "I greet you at the beginning of a great career . . ."*

Emerson's praise meant that the book received some attention, but Whitman's poetry confused most readers. It was unrhymed, the rhythms were so irregular that

---

35. *la migra:* Border Patrol.

there was no way to determine the meter of the lines, and the language was as free and direct as someone shouting in the street. Readers were also confused because the only subject of the poems seemed to be Whitman himself. It was not only the form of his poems that opened the path to modern poetry. His use of himself as the persona of the poems was an important source for the tone of confession and self-examination of much twentieth-century American poetry.

Whitman spent the rest of his life trying to organize the writing that poured into his book. Each subsequent edition of Leaves of Grass *contained new poems, and he also rewrote and retitled older poems. By the end of his life he was a revered literary figure whose work was read as enthusiastically in Europe as it was in the United States. Support from friends made it possible for him to buy a small house in Camden, New Jersey, where he died in 1892.*

The first edition of Leaves of Grass *opened with the poem "Song of Myself," though it was at that point still untitled. Through all the revisions of his book, Whitman continued to place "Song of Myself" close to the book's opening pages. Among the poem's sections, including 1 and 6, and the concluding sections, are some of his best-known and best-loved lines. "A Noiseless Patient Spider," one of Whitman's most explicitly spiritual poems, was included in the 1868 edition of his book.*

COMMENTARY   *Ezra Pound, "What I Feel about Walt Whitman," page 1001.*

WEB   *Research Walt Whitman and answer questions about his work at bedfordstmartins.com/charters/litwriters.*

From "Song of Myself"   1855

1

I celebrate myself, and sing myself,
And what I assume you shall assume,
For every atom belonging to me as good belongs to you.

I loafe and invite my soul,
I lean and loafe at my ease observing a spear of summer grass.   5

My tongue, every atom of my blood, form'd from this soil, this air,
Born here of parents born here from parents the same, and their parents
     the same,
I, now thirty-seven years old in perfect health begin,
Hoping to cease not till death.

Creeds and schools in abeyance,   10
Retiring back a while sufficed at what they are, but never forgotten,
I harbor for good or bad, I permit to speak at every hazard,
Nature without check with original energy.

6

A child said *What is the grass?* fetching it to me with full hands;
How could I answer the child? I do not know what it is any more than he. 15

I guess it must be the flag of my disposition, out of hopeful green stuff
    woven.

Or I guess it is the handkerchief of the Lord,
A scented gift and remembrancer designedly dropt,
Bearing the owner's name someway in the corners, that we may see and
    remark, and say *Whose?*

Or I guess the grass is itself a child, the produced babe of the vegetation.   20

Or I guess it is a uniform hieroglyphic,
And it means, Sprouting alike in broad zones and narrow zones,
Growing among black folks as among white,
Kanuck, Tuckahoe, Congressman, Cuff, I give them the same, I receive
    them the same.

And now it seems to me the beautiful uncut hair of graves.   25

Tenderly will I use you curling grass,
It may be you transpire from the breasts of young men,
It may be if I had known them I would have loved them,
It may be you are from old people, or from offspring taken soon out of
    their mothers' laps,
And here you are the mothers' laps.   30

This grass is very dark to be from the white heads of old mothers,
Darker than the colorless beards of old men,
Dark to come from under the faint red roofs of mouths.

O I perceive after all so many uttering tongues,
And I perceive they do not come from the roofs of mouths for nothing.   35

I wish I could translate the hints about the dead young men and
    women,
And the hints about old men and mothers, and the offspring taken soon
    out of their laps.

What do you think has become of the young and old men?
And what do you think has become of the women and children?

They are alive and well somewhere,   40
The smallest sprout shows there is really no death,
And if ever there was it led forward life, and does not wait at the end to
    arrest it,
And ceas'd the moment life appear'd.

All goes onward and outward, nothing collapses,
And to die is different from what anyone supposed, and luckier.   45

50

There is that in me—I do not know what it is—but I know it is in me.

Wrench'd and sweaty—calm and cool then my body becomes,
I sleep—I sleep long.

I do not know it—it is without name—it is a word unsaid,
It is not in any dictionary, utterance, symbol.   50

Sometimes it swings on more than the earth I swing on,
To it the creation is the friend whose embracing awakes me.

Perhaps I might tell more. Outlines! I plead for my brothers and sisters.

Do you see O my brothers and sisters?
It is not chaos or death — it is form, union, plan — it is eternal life — it is
    Happiness.   55

51

The past and present wilt — I have fill'd them, emptied them.
And proceed to fill my next fold of the future.

Listener up there! what have you to confide to me?
Look in my face while I snuff the sidle of evening,
(Talk honestly, no one else hears you, and I stay only a minute longer.)   60

Do I contradict myself?
Very well then I contradict myself.
(I am large, I contain multitudes.)

I concentrate toward them that are nigh, I wait on the door-slab.

Who has done his day's work? who will soonest be through with his
    supper?
Who wishes to walk with me?   65

Will you speak before I am gone? will you prove already too late?

52

The spotted hawk swoops by and accuses me, he complains of my gab
    and my loitering.

I too am not a bit tamed, I too am untranslatable,
I sound my barbaric yawp over the roofs of the world.   70

The last scud of day holds back for me,
It flings my likeness after the rest and true as any on the shadowed wilds,
It coaxes me to the vapor and the dusk.

I depart as air, I shake my white locks at the runaway sun,
I effuse my flesh in eddies, and drift it in lacy jags.   75

I bequeath myself to the dirt to grow from the grass I love,
If you want me again look for me under your boot-soles.

You will hardly know who I am or what I mean,
But I shall be good health to you nevertheless,
And filter and fibre your blood.   80

Failing to fetch me at first keep encouraged,
Missing me one place search another,
I stop somewhere waiting for you.

A Noiseless Patient Spider

1868

A noiseless patient spider,
I mark'd where on a little promontory it stood isolated,
Mark'd how to explore the vacant vast surrounding,
It launch'd forth filament, filament, filament, out of itself,
Ever unreeling them, ever tirelessly speeding them.   5

And you O my soul where you stand,
Surrounded, detached, in measureless oceans of space,
Ceaselessly musing, venturing, throwing, seeking the spheres to
    connect them,
Till the bridge you will need be form'd, till the ductile anchor hold,
Till the gossamer thread you fling catch somewhere, O my soul.   10

WILLIAM CARLOS WILLIAMS

William Carlos Williams (1883–1963) was born in Rutherford, New Jersey, where he lived and practiced medicine all his life. His mother was Puerto Rican; his father was English. Although he spent his life as a pediatrician, when he was a student at the University of Pennsylvania he was friends with Hilda Doolittle, who became the poet H.D., and the poet Ezra Pound. His encounter with them encouraged his own ambitions to be a poet, and he managed to lead a double life — as a doctor and a writer — until a series of strokes forced him to give up medicine in the 1950s.

Williams felt himself isolated in his small town medical practice, but he was part of the avant-garde poetry movements of his time, and it was as an imagist (see imagism on pp. 769–773) that he was best known when be began publishing after World War I. During his long career he founded small magazines; contributed essays, poems, and stories to literary journals; and also found time to write novels, plays, and an autobiography.

Many of Williams's poems are short. In his autobiography he remembers that some of them were written on his office typewriter between patients, and some first versions of his poems were written on prescription blanks. He was the last of the modernist poets to achieve recognition, but his work became an important influence on younger poets like Allen Ginsberg, who brought Jack Kerouac, among others, to visit Williams in the 1950s.

"Spring and All" was published as an untitled entry in an experimental collection of writing with the title Spring and All, *and the poem has assumed the book's name. Poems like this one, as well as "This Is Just to Say," and "The Widow's Lament in Springtime," have the same directness of speech, the personal vocabulary, and the spontaneous poetic form that Williams termed "the American idiom." (See also Williams's "The Red Wheelbarrow" on p. 771.)*

WEB *Research William Carlos Williams and answer questions about his work at bedfordstmartins.com/charters/litwriters.*

Spring and All   1923

By the road to the contagious hospital,
under the surge of the blue
mottled clouds driven from the
northeast—cold wind. Beyond, the
waste of broad, muddy fields,   5
brown with dried weeds, standing and fallen,

patches of standing water,
the scattering of tall trees.

All along the road the reddish,
purplish, forked, upstanding, twiggy   10
stuff of brushes and small trees
with dead, brown leaves under them
leafless vines—

Lifeless in appearance, sluggish,
dazed spring approaches—   15

They enter the new world naked,
cold, uncertain of all
save that they enter. All about them
the cold, familiar wind—

Now the grass, tomorrow   20
the stiff curl of wild-carrot leaf.

One by one objects are defined—
It quickens: clarity, outline of leaf,

But now the stark dignity of
entrance—Still, the profound change   25
has come upon them; rooted, they
grip down and begin to awaken.

This Is Just to Say   1934

I have eaten
the plums
that were in
the icebox

and which   5
you were probably
saving
for breakfast

Forgive me
they were delicious   10
so sweet
and so cold

The Widow's° Lament in Springtime

1921

Sorrow is my own yard
where the new grass
flames as it has flamed
often before but not
with the cold fire   5
that closes round me this year.
Thirtyfive years
I lived with my husband.
The plumtree is white today
with masses of flowers.   10
Masses of flowers
loaded the cherry branches
and color some bushes
yellow and some red
but the grief in my heart   15
is stronger than they
for though they were my joy
formerly, today I notice them
and turned away forgetting.
Today my son told me   20
that in the meadows,
at the edge of the heavy woods
in the distance, he saw
trees of white flowers.
I feel that I would like   25
to go there
and fall into those flowers
and sink into the marsh near them.

WILLIAM WORDSWORTH

William Wordsworth (1770–1850) was born in the north of England, close to the Lake District. After the death of his mother when he was eight, he and his three brothers were raised in the countryside and often left free to roam. He also read hungrily and was encouraged to think of becoming a poet by his schoolmaster.

Wordsworth had a turbulent youth. In 1790, during his summer break from St. John's College in Cambridge, he went on a long walking trip through France and Switzerland, then returned to France after his graduation the next year, hoping to improve his French language skills enough to qualify as a teacher. He remained in France during the period of the wildest triumphs and fervors of the French Revolution. He fell in love with Annette Vallon, daughter of a family of

---

Widow's: The widow of the poem is Williams's mother.

Royalist sympathizers. She gave birth to Wordsworth's child, but the political tur-moil forced him to return to England, and Annette was unable to follow him.

In England, Wordsworth was torn between the love he had left behind him and his disillusionment with the Revolution, which was becoming increasingly vio-lent and despotic. At this moment, when he was struggling against a complete emo-tional collapse, a friend died and left Wordsworth enough money to enable the poet to devote himself entirely to his art. With his sister Dorothy, and a new friend, the young poet and critic Samuel Taylor Coleridge, Wordsworth began a new life.

Wordsworth and Coleridge set out to create a new style of poetry — poetry that would be closer to the language of ordinary people and would deal with gen-uine emotions. In 1798 they published a slim book, Lyrical Ballads, *with poems by each of them. This book is considered the beginning of the romantic movement in English poetry.*

In the course of his long life, Wordsworth lost the creative fire of his early years, but at his death he was hailed as one of the most significant literary figures England had ever produced. He began "Ode: Intimations of Immortality" in his mid thirties, and it took him two years after he wrote the first four stanzas to com-plete the poem. He wrote to an admirer about its subject, "Nothing was more diffi-cult for me in childhood than to admit the notion of death as a state applicable to my own being." The sonnet "The world is too much with us" was published the same year. (See also Wordsworth's "I Wandered Lonely as a Cloud" on p. 727.)

COMMENTARY *William Wordsworth, "From the Introduction to* Lyrical Ballads," *page 1006.*

WEB *Research William Wordsworth and answer questions about his work at bedfordstmartins.com/charters/litwriters.*

Ode
1807

Intimations of Immortality
from Recollections of Early Childhood

The Child is Father of the Man;
And I could wish my days to be
Bound each to each by natural piety.

1

There was a time when meadow, grove, and stream,
The earth, and every common sight,
    To me did seem
    Apparelled in celestial light,
The glory and the freshness of a dream.
It is not now as it hath been of yore; —
    Turn wheresoe'er I may,
      By night or day,
The things which I have seen I now can see no more.   5

2

      The Rainbow comes and goes, 10
      And lovely is the Rose,
      The Moon doth with delight
Look round her when the heavens are bare,
      Waters on a starry night
      Are beautiful and fair; 15
    The sunshine is a glorious birth;
    But yet I know, where'er I go,
That there hath past away a glory from the earth.

3

Now, while the birds thus sing a joyous song,
    And while the young lambs bound 20
      As to the tabor's sound,
To me alone there came a thought of grief:
A timely utterance gave that thought relief,
      And I again am strong:
The cataracts blow their trumpets from the steep; 25
No more shall grief of mine the season wrong;
I hear the Echoes through the mountains throng,
The Winds come to me from the fields of sleep,
      And all the earth is gay;
        Land and sea 30
    Give themselves up to jollity,
      And with the heart of May
    Doth every Beast keep holiday; —
        Thou Child of Joy,
Shout round me, let me hear thy shouts, thou happy Shepherd-boy! 35

4

Ye blessed Creatures, I have heard the call
      Ye to each other make; I see
The heavens laugh with you in your jubilee;
      My heart is at your festival,
      My head hath its coronal,° 40
The fulness of your bliss, I feel — I feel it all.
      Oh evil day! if I were sullen
      While Earth herself is adorning,
        This sweet May-morning,
      And the Children are culling 45
        On every side,
    In a thousand valleys far and wide,
    Fresh flowers; while the sun shines warm,

---

40. coronal: Crown of flowers worn by young shepherds in May.

And the Babe leaps up on his Mother's arm: —
      I hear, I hear, with joy I hear!   50
      —But there's a Tree, of many, one,
A single Field which I have looked upon,
Both of them speak of something that is gone:
      The Pansy at my feet
      Doth the same tale repeat: 55
Whither is fled the visionary gleam?
Where is it now, the glory and the dream?

5

Our birth is but a sleep and a forgetting:
The Soul that rises with us, our life's Star,
      Hath had elsewhere its setting,   60
        And cometh from afar:
      Not in entire forgetfulness,
      And not in utter nakedness,
But trailing clouds of glory do we come
      From God, who is our home: 65
Heaven lies about us in our infancy!
Shades of the prison-house begin to close
      Upon the growing Boy,
But He beholds the light, and whence it flows,
      He sees it in his joy;   70
The Youth, who daily farther from the east
      Must travel, still is Nature's Priest,
      And by the vision splendid
      Is on his way attended;
At length the Man perceives it die away,   75
And fade into the light of common day.

6

Earth fills her lap with pleasures of her own;
Yearnings she hath in her own natural kind,
And, even with something of a Mother's mind,
      And no unworthy aim,   80
      The homely Nurse doth all she can
To make her Foster-child, her Inmate Man,
      Forget the glories he hath known,
And that imperial palace whence he came.

7

Behold the Child among his new-born blisses,   85
A six years' Darling of a pigmy size!
See, where 'mid work of his own hand he lies,
Fretted by sallies of his mother's kisses,

With light upon him from his father's eyes!
See, at his feet, some little plan or chart,   90
Some fragment from his dream of human life,
Shaped by himself with newly-learnèd art;
    A wedding or a festival,
    A mourning or a funeral;
      And this hath now his heart,   95
    And unto this he frames his song:
      Then will he fit his tongue
To dialogues of business, love, or strife;
    But it will not be long
    Ere this be thrown aside,   100
    And with new joy and pride
The little Actor cons another part;
Filling from time to time his "humorous stage"°
With all the Persons, down to palsied Age,
That Life brings with her in her equipage;   105
    As if his whole vocation
    Were endless imitation.

8

Thou, whose exterior semblance doth belie
    Thy Soul's immensity;
Thou best Philosopher, who yet dost keep   110
Thy heritage, thou Eye among the blind,
That, deaf and silent, read'st the eternal deep,
Haunted for ever by the eternal mind, —
    Mighty Prophet! Seer blest!
    On whom those truths do rest,   115
Which we are toiling all our lives to find,
In darkness lost, the darkness of the grave;
Thou, over whom thy Immortality
Broods like the Day, a Master o'er a Slave,
A Presence which is not to be put by;   120
Thou little Child, yet glorious in the might
Of heaven-born freedom on thy being's height,
Why with such earnest pains dost thou provoke
The years to bring the inevitable yoke,
Thus blindly with thy blessedness at strife?   125
Full soon thy Soul shall have her earthly freight,
And custom lie upon thee with a weight,
Heavy as frost, and deep almost as life!

---

103. **"humorous stage"**: Capriciousness, but also carries the sense of the classical temperaments ("humors").

9

O joy! that in our embers
Is something that doth live,   130
That nature yet remembers
What was so fugitive!
The thought of our past years in me doth breed
Perpetual benediction: not indeed
For that which is most worthy to be blest;   135
Delight and liberty, the simple creed
Of Childhood, whether busy or at rest,
With new-fledged hope still fluttering in his breast—
    Not for these I raise
    The song of thanks and praise;   140
    But for those obstinate questionings
    Of sense and outward things,
    Fallings from us, vanishings;
    Blank misgivings of a Creature
Moving about in worlds not realised,   145
High instincts before which our mortal Nature
Did tremble like a guilty Thing surprised:
    But for those first affections,
    Those shadowy recollections,
    Which, be they what they may,   150
Are yet the fountain light of all our day,
Are yet a master light of all our seeing;
    Uphold us, cherish, and have power to make
Our noisy years seem moments in the being
Of the eternal Silence: truths that wake,   155
    To perish never;
Which neither listlessness, nor mad endeavour,
    Nor Man nor Boy,
Nor all that is at enmity with joy,
Can utterly abolish or destroy!   160
    Hence in a season of calm weather
    Though inland far we be,
Our Souls have sight of that immortal sea
    Which brought us hither,
    Can in a moment travel thither,   165
And see the Children sport upon the shore,
And hear the mighty waters rolling evermore.

10

Then sing, ye Birds, sing, sing a joyous song!
    And let the young Lambs bound
    As to the tabor's sound!   170
We in thought will join your throng,

Ye that pipe and ye that play,
Ye that through your hearts to-day
Feel the gladness of the May!
What though the radiance which was once so bright   175
Be now for ever taken from my sight,
  Though nothing can bring back the hour
Of splendour in the grass, of glory in the flower;
   We will grieve not, rather find
   Strength in what remains behind;   180
   In the primal sympathy
   Which having been must ever be;
   In the soothing thoughts that spring
   Out of human suffering;
   In the faith that looks through death,   185
In years that bring the philosophic mind.

11

And O, ye Fountains, Meadows, Hills, and Groves,
Forebode not any severing of our loves!
Yet in my heart of hearts I feel your might;
I only have relinquished one delight   190
To live beneath your more habitual sway.
I love the Brooks which down their channels fret,
Even more than when I tripped lightly as they;
The innocent brightness of a new-born Day
   Is lovely yet;   195
The Clouds that gather round the setting sun
Do take a sober colouring from an eye
That hath kept watch o'er man's mortality;
Another race hath been, and other palms are won.
Thanks to the human heart by which we live,   200
Thanks to its tenderness, its joys, and fears,
To me the meanest flower that blows can give
Thoughts that do often lie too deep for tears.

The world is too much with us   1807

The world is too much with us; late and soon,
Getting and spending, we lay waste our powers:
Little we see in nature that is ours;
We have given our hearts away, a sordid boon!
This Sea that bares her bosom to the moon;   5
The Winds that will be howling at all hours
And are up-gathered now like sleeping flowers;
For this, for every thing, we are out of tune;

It moves us not—Great God! I'd rather be
A Pagan suckled in a creed outworn;　　　　　　　　　　10
So might I, standing on this pleasant lea,
Have glimpses that would make me less forlorn;
Have sight of Proteus coming from the sea;
Or hear old Triton blow his wreathed horn.

JAMES WRIGHT

James Wright (1927–1980) was born in Martin's Ferry, Ohio, and although he spent much of his life in New York City he returned again and again to images of his rural childhood for the inspiration for his poetry. He graduated from Kenyon College and completed his Ph.D. at the University of Washington. After he received his doctorate he lived for some time in Austria and then returned to the United States and a career as a teacher. He taught first at the University of Minnesota, then moved to Hunter College in New York City and remained there for the final years of his troubled life. In addition to his own poetry, he translated writing by important European and South American poets in conjunction with Robert Bly's Fifties Press. *With Bly he translated George Trakl and Pablo Neruda, and he translated César Vallejo with Bly and John Knoeple.*

In his introduction to the collection of essays he edited, Clear Word: Essays on the Poetry of James Wright, *Dave Smith wrote,*

> *Wright continuously praised writers for telling the truth boldly and powerfully but shied away from such claims for himself. The irony . . . is that the more he brought his life into his poems, his emotional and ethical and biographical and mythical life, the more he made us feel in ourselves, the more courage he gave us.*

"Evening," with its evocation of a father's search for his son in the garden when he's been called in to dinner, demonstrates Wright's sensitivity to the magic of ordinary moments. In the other poems, "A Blessing," "Milkweed," and "Lying in a Hammock at William Duffy's Farm in Pine Island, Minnesota," each of them often anthologized, a simple country setting is again a cause for introspection and wonder.

WEB　*Research James Wright and answer questions about his work at bedfordstmartins.com/charters/litwriters.*

Evening　　　　　　　　　　　　　　　　　　　　　　　　　1959

I called him to come in,
The wide lawn darkened so.
Laughing, he held his chin
And hid beside a bush.
The light gave him a push,　　　　　　　　　　　　　　　5

Shadowy grass moved slow.
He crept on agile toes
Under a sheltering rose.

His mother, still beyond
The bare porch and the door,
Called faintly out of sound,
And vanished with her voice.
I caught his curious eyes
Measuring me, and more —
The light dancing behind
My shoulder in the wind.

Then, struck beyond belief
By the child's voice I heard,
I saw his hair turn leaf,
His dancing toes divide
To hooves on either side,
One hand become a bird.
Startled, I held my tongue
To hear what note he sang.

Where was the boy gone now?
I stood on the grass, alone.
Swung from the apple bough
The bees ignored my cry.
A dog roved past, and I
Turned up a sinking stone,
But found beneath no more
Than grasses dead last year.

Suddenly lost and cold,
I knew the yard lay bare.
I longed to touch and hold
My child, my talking child,
Laughing or tame or wild —
Solid in light and air,
The supple hands, the face
To fill that barren place.

Slowly, the leaves descended,
The birds resolved to hands;
Laugh, and the charm was ended,
The hungry boy stepped forth.
He stood on the hard earth,
Like one who understands
Fairy and ghost — but less
Our human loneliness.

Then, on the withering lawn,
He walked beside my arm.
Trees and the sun were gone,

10

15

20

25

30

35

40

45

50

Everything gone but us.
His mother sang in the house,
And kept our supper warm,
And loved us, God knows how,   55
The wide earth darkened so.

A Blessing   1963

Just off the highway to Rochester, Minnesota,
Twilight bounds softly forth on the grass.
And the eyes of those two Indian ponies
Darken with kindness.
They have come gladly out of the willows   5
To welcome my friend and me.
We step over the barbed wire into the pasture
Where they have been grazing all day, alone.
They ripple tensely, they can hardly contain their happiness
That we have come.   10
They bow shyly as wet swans. They love each other.
There is no loneliness like theirs.
At home once more,
They begin munching the young tufts of spring in the darkness.
I would like to hold the slenderer one in my arms,   15
For she has walked over to me
And nuzzled my left hand.
She is black and white,
Her mane falls wild on her forehead,
And the light breeze moves me to caress her long ear   20
That is delicate as the skin over a girl's wrist.
Suddenly I realize
That if I stepped out of my body I would break
Into blossom.

Milkweed   1963

While I stood here, in the open, lost in myself,
I must have looked a long time
Down the corn rows, beyond grass,
The small house,
White walls, animals lumbering toward the barn.   5
I look down now. It is all changed.
Whatever it was I lost, whatever I wept for
Was a wild, gentle thing, the small dark eyes
Loving me in secret.
It is here. At a touch of my hand,   10
The air fills with delicate creatures
From the other world.

Lying in a Hammock at William Duffy's Farm in Pine Island, Minnesota

1963

Over my head, I see the bronze butterfly,
Asleep on the black trunk,
Blowing like a leaf in green shadow.
Down the ravine behind the empty house,
The cowbells follow one another   5
Into the distances of the afternoon.
To my right,
In a field of sunlight between two pines,
The droppings of last year's horses
Blaze up into golden stones.   10
I lean back, as the evening darkens and comes on.
A chicken hawk floats over, looking for home.
I have wasted my life.

WILLIAM BUTLER YEATS

William Butler Yeats (1865–1939) was born in Dublin, but his parents were of English descent, and he spent much of his youth in London. His father, Jack Yeats, was a gifted but struggling artist. Yeats first decided to follow his father and become a painter. He changed his mind, however, after beginning his art studies. His first published poems appeared in the Dublin University Review *when he was twenty.*

For most of his life Yeats journeyed between England and Ireland, where he lived some of the time in Dublin and at other times with his mother's family in County Sligo, a rural area in northwest Ireland. All three of these very different environments had an effect on his writing. His early poetry often presented a soft mood of reverie, influenced by younger poets he met in London. He also drew from his Irish background in verse dramas based on Irish legends and myths. The rough countryside of County Sligo lent his poetry a sharper, less romantic tone than that of the London poets' verse.

In 1899 Yeats helped found the Irish National Theatre, but bitter struggles with the conservative middle-class audiences eventually drove him to London. The Irish Rebellion of 1916, however, when a group of Irish idealists attempted to seize power from the British occupying forces, brought him back, and when Ireland achieved partial independence in 1922 he was appointed a senator and served in the government for six years.

Yeats had a long and successful career as a writer, and he won the Nobel Prize for literature in 1923. "The Lake Isle of Innisfree" and "When You Are Old" were written almost thirty years earlier. "The Second Coming" is one of his most impassioned visionary poems.

WEB *Research William Butler Yeats and answer questions about his work at bedfordstmartins.com/charters/litwriters.*

The Lake Isle of Innisfree   1890

I will arise and go now, and go to Innisfree,
And a small cabin build there, of clay and wattles made;
Nine bean rows will I have there, a hive for the honey bee,
      And live alone in the bee-loud glade.

And I shall have some peace there, for peace comes dropping slow,   5
Dropping from the veils of the morning to where the cricket sings;
There midnight's all a glimmer, and noon a purple glow,
      And evening full of the linnet's wings.

I will arise and go now, for always night and day
I hear lake water lapping with low sounds by the shore;   10
While I stand on the roadway, or on the pavements gray,
      I hear it in the deep heart's core.

When You Are Old   1892

When you are old and grey and full of sleep,
And nodding by the fire, take down this book,
And slowly read, and dream of the soft look
Your eyes had once, and of their shadows deep;

How many loved your moments of glad grace,   5
And loved your beauty with love false or true,
But one man loved the pilgrim soul in you,
And loved the sorrows of your changing face;

And bending down beside the glowing bars,
Murmur, a little sadly, how Love fled   10
And paced upon the mountains overhead
And hid his face amid a crowd of stars.

The Second Coming   1919

Turning and turning in the widening gyre
The falcon cannot hear the falconer;
Things fall apart; the centre cannot hold;
Mere anarchy is loosed upon the world,
The blood-dimmed tide is loosed, and everywhere   5
The ceremony of innocence is drowned;
The best lack all conviction, while the worst
Are full of passionate intensity.

Surely some revelation is at hand;
Surely the Second Coming is at hand.   10
The Second Coming! Hardly are those words out

When a vast image out of *Spiritus Mundi*°
Troubles my sight: somewhere in sands of the desert
A shape with lion body and the head of a man,
A gaze blank and pitiless as the sun,   15
Is moving its slow thighs, while all about it

Reel shadows of the indignant desert birds.
The darkness drops again; but now I know
That twenty centuries of stony sleep
Were vexed to nightmare by a rocking cradle,   20
And what rough beast, its hour come round at last,
Slouches towards Bethlehem to be born?

---

12. *Spiritus Mundi:* Spirit of the universe.

16.

Commentaries on Poetry and Poets

CLEANTH BROOKS JR. AND ROBERT PENN WARREN

Cleanth Brooks Jr. and Robert Penn Warren (the literary critic and the American poet) discussed in their groundbreaking textbook Understanding Poetry *(1938) T. S. Eliot's major early poem from the perspective of New Criticism, an approach that emphasizes close reading of the formal properties of literary works.*

On Eliot's "The Love Song of J. Alfred Prufrock"   1938

The character of Prufrock, as we shall see, is really very much like that of Hamlet — a man who is apparently betrayed by his possession of such qualities as intellect and imagination. But it is particularly dangerous to attempt to portray, and make the audience believe in and take seriously, such a person as Prufrock. We are inclined to laugh at the person who is really so painfully self-conscious that he is inhibited from all action. Moreover, in so far as the poet is using Prufrock as a character typical of our age, he must in fairness to truth avoid treating him quite so heroically as a Hamlet. At the very beginning, therefore, the poet faces a difficult problem. In using the materials of the present, the desire to be accurate, to be thoroughly truthful, forces him to exhibit the character as not purely romantic or tragic. And yet there is in such a person as he describes a very real tragedy. How shall he treat him? To attempt to treat Prufrock in full seriousness is doomed to failure; on the other hand, to make him purely comic is to falsify matters too.

Faced with this problem, the poet resorts to irony, and by employing varying shades of irony he is able to do justice to the ludicrous elements in the situation and yet do justice to the serious ones also. The casual and careless reader will probably see only the comic aspects: he will be likely to fail to appreciate the underlying seriousness of the whole poem.

The title itself gives us the first clue to the fact that the poem is ironical. We think of a love song as simple and full of warm emotion. But this poem opens on a scene where the streets

> . . . follow like a tedious argument
> Of insidious intent
> To lead you to an overwhelming question. . . .

One notices also that the character Prufrock is continually interested in stating that "there will be time" to make up his mind. But in saying that there will be time for this, he is so hopelessly unable to act that he continues in a sort of abstracted and unconscious patter to state that there will be time

> For the yellow smoke that slides along the street,
> Rubbing its back upon the window-panes;
> There will be time, there will be time
> To prepare a face to meet the faces that you meet;
> There will be time to murder and create,
> And time for all the works and days of hands
> That lift and drop a question on your plate.

Then, caught up by the irrelevance of his patter, he goes on to say that there will be time — not for decisions — but, ironically, for a "hundred indecisions," and for a "hundred visions and revisions."

The first part of the poem, then, can be imagined as the monologue of Prufrock himself as he finds his indecisiveness reflected in the apparently aimless streets of the city and in the fog which hangs over the city. It is filled with a rather bitter self-irony, a self-irony which is reflected in some of the abrupt transitions. But in observing this ironical monologue which illuminates the character, one has missed the point entirely if he has failed to see the psychological penetration in it. Take, for example, the tone and associations of the comparison of the evening to a "patient etherized upon a table." This comparison is "in character." It is an appropriate observation for Prufrock, being what he is, though it might not be very appropriate for an entirely different character or in a poem of entirely different tone. The evening — not any evening, but this particular evening, as seen by this particular observer — does seem to have the hushed quiet of the perfectly, and yet fatally relaxed, body of a person under ether.

Or notice also the psychological penetration of the remark, "To prepare a face to meet the faces that you meet." Again, the remark must be taken in character. Yet it is possible to observe, as a general truth, that we do prepare a face, an expression, a look, to meet the various "faces" that we meet — faces which have duly undergone a like preparation. A poorer poet would have written "To put on a mask to meet the people that you meet." Eliot's line with its concentration and its slight ironical shock is far superior. . . .

After the opening sections in which the character of the speaker is to some extent established for the reader, Prufrock describes a scene in which overcultured, bored women sip tea and discuss art. It is as though he had just stepped inside after wandering alone in the streets. Here are the people of whose criticism Prufrock is most afraid, and yet, as his characterization of them abundantly shows, he sees their shallowness. But Prufrock does not attempt to treat romantically or heroically his own character: he is able to see the ludicrous aspect of himself, his timid preciseness and vanity.

> With a bald spot in the middle of my hair —
> [They will say: "How his hair is growing thin!"]
> My necktie rich and modest, but asserted by a simple pin.

But what is the function of a statement so abrupt as "I have measured out my life with coffee spoons"? Here again, the line must be taken in character. But if we are willing to take it in character, we shall be able to see that it is brilliantly ironical. It would mean literally, one supposes, that he has measured out his life in little driblets, coffee spoons being tiny in size. But it carries another and more concrete meaning: namely, that he has spent his life in just such an environment as this drawing room which he is describing. The comparison makes the same ironical point, therefore, as the lines

> And time yet for a hundred indecisions,
> And for a hundred visions and revisions,
> Before the taking of a toast and tea.

The poem's sense of fidelity to the whole situation — its willingness to take into account so many apparently discordant views and points of view — is shown in the lines

> Arms that are braceleted and white and bare
> [But in the lamplight, downed with light brown hair!]

These lines give us a contrast between what might be termed loosely the romantic and the realistic attitude. The ironical comment here parallels exactly the reference to his own bald head.

The structure of the poem is, as we have noticed, that of a sort of monologue in which the poet describes this scene or that and comments on them, and, by means of them, on himself. The irrelevance, or apparent irrelevance, is exactly the sort of irrelevance and abrupt transition which is often admired in a personal essay by a writer like Charles Lamb. The structure is essentially the same here (though of course with an entirely different tone and for a different effect). But having seen what the structure is — not a logical structure, or one following the lines of a narrative, or one based on the description of a scene, but the structure of the flow of ideas — the reader is not puzzled at the rather abrupt transition from the stanza about the arms to

> Shall I say, I have gone at dusk through narrow streets,

etc. It is a scene from the beginning of the poem — or perhaps it is a scene viewed earlier and brought back to memory by the statement about the streets and the smoke in the opening lines of the poem. It is the sort of scene which has a very real poignance about it. Prufrock feels that it meant something. But he is utterly incapable of stating the meaning before the bored and sophisticated audience of the world to which he belongs. He would be laughed at as a fool. And then comes the thought — apparently irrelevant, but the sort of thought which might easily occur in such a monologue:

> I should have been a pair of ragged claws
> Scuttling across the floors of silent seas.

A crab is about as vivid a symbol as one might find, for a person who is completely self-sufficing and cannot be, and does not need to be, sociable. And there is, moreover, a secondary implication of irony here growing out of Prufrock's disgust with these people about him and with himself: the crab is at least "alive" and has, as Prufrock does not have, a meaning and a place in its world. (Observe that the poet does not use the word *crab*. Why? Because in mentioning the most prominent feature of the crab, the claws, and with the vivid description of the effect of the crab's swimming, "scuttling," he makes the point more sharply.)

There are several literary allusions in the latter part of the poem, allusions which we must know in order to understand the poem. . . . Can they be justified? And if so, how? In the first place, they are fairly commonly known: an allusion to John the Baptist's head having been cut off at Herod's orders and brought in on a platter; an allusion to the raising of Lazarus from the dead; and a reference to Shakespeare's *Hamlet*. The poet has not imposed a very heavy burden on us, therefore, in expecting that we shall know these references. But what can be said by way of justification? In the first place, all the allusions are "in character." They are comparisons which would normally occur to such a person as Prufrock, and they would naturally occur in the sort of meditation in which he indulges in this poem. In the second place, they do a great deal to sharpen the irony in the poem. Prufrock is vividly conscious of the sorry figure which he cuts in comparison with the various great figures from the past or from literature whom, in a far-off sense, he resembles. He has seen his reputation picked to pieces — his head, a slightly bald head, brought in on a platter like that of John the Baptist. But *he* is no prophet — nothing is lost. Death itself in this society can be regarded as nothing more than a liveried footman, putting on the coats of the departing, and death, like the knowing and insolent footman, is quite capable, he believes, of snickering behind his back.

MARILYN CHIN

Marilyn Chin, a Chinese American poet, responded to a question about "the canon" in a 1995 interview. In recent years much discussion has centered on the canon, the long tradition of literature that has served as the American educational standard. Some people believe the canon defines U.S. culture; others consider it a fence that has kept out writing by women and members of cultural minorities.

On the Canon   1995

My personal psychology regarding "the canon" is this: To the outer world I say in a devil-may-care manner "to hell with it." It's a fixed endgame: There will always be an imperialist, Eurocentric bias. The powers-that-be who lord over the selection process are and forevermore will be privileged white male critics. They will decide who will be validated along with Shakespeare and Milton and the latter-day saints of the like of Keats, Yeats, and Eliot. They will guard that "canon" jealously with their elaborate "critical" apparatus; and driven by their own Darwinian instinct to "survive," they will do the best they can to "exclude" us and to promote their own monolithic vision.

But deep inside me another voice rings resolute. I am a serious poet with a rich palette and important missive and I shall fight for the survival of my poetry. What I learned from my youth as a marginalized and isolated west coast Asian American poet is this: It's no fun to be "excluded" . . . as a matter of fact, it feels like hell. What is the purpose of spending most of your adult life hunched in a dark corner perfecting your poems, if your oeuvre will be buried and forgotten anyway? I don't believe any poet who tells me, "No, baby, I don't give a damn about the canon." I am certain that the very same poet has his little poems all dressed up, organized and alphabetized and locked in a vault to be opened in the next century.

The poet's mission on earth is to inspire and to illuminate; and to leave behind to our glorious descendents an intricate and varied map of humanity. One way to survive is to be like Milton, who sits aloft in the great pantheon in the sky and only a very few self-flagellating geeky scholar/poets could indulge into his knotty points. Another way to survive is to be like Gwendolyn Brooks; I predict that her poem "We Real Cool" will be warm on schoolchildren's lips forever. To survive is to be like Langston Hughes, whose poem "A Raisin in the Sun" inspired the young playwright Lorraine Hansberry to write a masterpiece bearing that same name. The true test of "validation" is when one's poems can serve as inspirational models and guiding spirits for a younger generation. We must survive! We must fight to be included in "the canon," so that our voices will sing through history and the global consciousness in eternal echoes. And I'll be damned if I'm going to miss out on THAT out-of-the-body experience!

RITA DOVE

Rita Dove, whose collection Mother Love *(1995) is written mostly in sonnet form, discusses the traditional verse form in the following excerpt from her introduction.*

An Intact World   1995

"Sonnet" literally means "little song." The sonnet is a *heile Welt,* an intact world where everything is in sync, from the stars down to the tiniest mite on a blade of grass. And if the "true" sonnet reflects the music of the spheres, it then follows that any variation from the strictly Petrarchan or Shakespearean forms represents a world gone awry.

Or does it? Can't form also be a talisman against disintegration? The sonnet defends itself against the vicissitudes of fortune by its charmed structure, its beautiful bubble. All the while, though, chaos is lurking outside the gate.

The ancient story of Demeter and Persephone is just such a tale of a violated world. It is a modern dilemma as well — there comes a point when a mother can no longer protect her child, when the daughter must go her own way into womanhood. Persephone, out picking flowers with her girlfriends, wanders off from the group. She has just stooped to pluck a golden narcissus, when the earth opens and Hades emerges, dragging her down with him into the Underworld. Inconsolable in her grief, Demeter neglects her duties as goddess of agriculture, and the crops wither. The Olympians disapprove of the abduction but are more shaken by Demeter's reaction, her refusal to return to her godly work in defiance of the laws of nature; she's even left her throne in Olympus and taken to wandering about on earth disguised as a mortal. In varying degrees she is admonished or pitied by the other gods for the depth of her grief. She refuses to accept her fate, however; she strikes out against the Law, forcing Zeus to ask his brother Hades to return Persephone to her mother. Hades agrees.

But ah, can we ever really go back home, as if nothing had happened? Before returning to the surface, the girl eats a few pomegranate seeds, not realizing that anyone who partakes of the food of the dead cannot be wholly restored to the living. So she must spend half of each year at Hades' side, as Queen of the Underworld, and her mother must acquiesce: Every fall and winter Demeter is permitted to grieve for the loss of her daughter, letting vegetation wilt and die, but she is obliged to act cheerful in spring and summer, making the earth blossom and bear fruit.

Sonnets seemed the proper mode for most of [the poems in *Mother Love*] — and not only in homage and as counterpoint to Rilke's° *Sonnets to Orpheus.* Much has been said about the many ways to "violate" the sonnet in the service of American speech or modern love or whatever; I will simply say that I like how the sonnet comforts even while its prim borders (but what a

---

Rilke's: I.e., the German poet Rainer Maria Rilke (1875–1926).

pretty fence!) are stultifying; one is constantly bumping up against Order. The Demeter/Persephone cycle of betrayal and regeneration is ideally suited for this form since all three — mother-goddess, daughter-consort, and poet — are struggling to sing in their chains.

T. S. ELIOT

T. S. Eliot first published his essay discussing literary tradition in the London magazine The Egoist *in 1919. He included it in his collection* The Sacred Wood *the following year.*

From "Tradition and the Individual Talent"   1919

I

In English writing we seldom speak of tradition, though we occasionally apply its name in deploring its absence. We cannot refer to "the tradition" or to "a tradition"; at most, we employ the adjective in saying that the poetry of so-and-so is "traditional" or even "too traditional." Seldom, perhaps, does the word appear except in a phrase of censure. If otherwise, it is vaguely approbative, with the implication, as to the work approved, of some pleasing archaeological reconstruction. You can hardly make the word agreeable to English ears without this comfortable reference to the reassuring science of archaeology.

Certainly the word is not likely to appear in our appreciations of living or dead writers. Every nation, every race, has not only its own creative, but its own critical turn of mind; and is even more oblivious of the shortcomings and limitations of its critical habits than of those of its creative genius. We know, or think we know, from the enormous mass of critical writing that has appeared in the French language the critical method or habit of the French; we only conclude (we are such unconscious people) that the French are "more critical" than we, and sometimes even plume ourselves a little with the fact, as if the French were the less spontaneous. Perhaps they are; but we might remind ourselves that criticism is as inevitable as breathing, and that we should be none the worse for articulating what passes in our minds when we read a book and feel an emotion about it, for criticizing our own minds in their work of criticism. One of the facts that might come to light in this process is our tendency to insist, when we praise a poet, upon those aspects of his work in which he least resembles any one else. In these aspects or parts of his work we pretend to find what is individual, what is the peculiar essence of the man. We dwell with satisfaction upon the poet's difference from his predecessors, especially his immediate predecessors; we endeavour to find something that can be isolated in order to be enjoyed. Whereas if we approach a poet without this prejudice we shall often find that not only the best, but the most individual parts of his work may be those in which the dead poets, his ancestors, assert their immortality most vigorously. And I do not mean the impressionable period of adolescence, but the period of full maturity.

Yet if the only form of tradition, of handing down, consisted in following the ways of the immediate generation before us in a blind or timid adherence to its successes, "tradition" should positively be discouraged. We have seen many such simple currents soon lost in the sand; and novelty is better than repetition. Tradition is a matter of much wider significance. It cannot be inherited, and if you want it you must obtain it by great labour. It involves, in the first place, the historical sense, which we may call nearly indispensable to any one who would continue to be a poet beyond his twenty-fifth year; and the historical sense involves a perception, not only of the pastness of the past, but of its presence; the historical sense compels a man to write not merely with his own generation in his bones, but with a feeling that the whole of the literature of Europe from Homer and within it the whole of the literature of his own country has a simultaneous existence and composes a simultaneous order. This historical sense, which is a sense of the timeless as well as of the temporal and of the timeless and of the temporal together, is what makes a writer traditional. And it is at the same time what makes a writer most acutely conscious of his place in time, of his own contemporaneity.

No poet, no artist of any art, has his complete meaning alone. His significance, his appreciation is the appreciation of his relation to the dead poets and artists. You cannot value him alone; you must set him, for contrast and comparison, among the dead. I mean this as a principle of aesthetic, not merely historical, criticism. The necessity that he shall conform, that he shall cohere, is not one-sided; what happens when a new work of art is created is something that happens simultaneously to all the works of art which preceded it. The existing monuments form an ideal order among themselves, which is modified by the introduction of the new (the really new) work of art among them. The existing order is complete before the new work arrives; for order to persist after the supervention of novelty, the *whole* existing order must be, if ever so slightly, altered; and so the relations, proportions, values of each work of art toward the whole are readjusted; and this is conformity between the old and the new. Whoever has approved this idea of order, of the form of European, of English literature will not find it preposterous that the past should be altered by the present as much as the present is directed by the past. And the poet who is aware of this will be aware of great difficulties and responsibilities.

In a peculiar sense he will be aware also that he must inevitably be judged by the standards of the past. I say judged, not amputated, by them; not judged to be as good as, or worse or better than, the dead; and certainly not judged by the canons of dead critics. It is a judgment, a comparison, in which two things are measured by each other. To conform merely would be for the new work not really to conform at all; it would not be new, and would therefore not be a work of art. And we do not quite say that the new is more valuable because it fits in; but its fitting in is a test of its value—a test, it is true, which can only be slowly and cautiously applied, for we are none of us infallible judges of conformity. We say: it appears to conform, and is perhaps individual, or it appears individual, and may conform; but we are hardly likely to find that it is one and not the other.

To proceed to a more intelligible exposition of the relation of the poet to the past: he can neither take the past as a lump, an indiscriminate bolus,° nor can he form himself wholly on one or two private admirations, nor can he form himself wholly upon one preferred period. The first course is inadmissible, the second is an important experience of youth, and the third is a pleasant and highly desirable supplement. The poet must be very conscious of the main current, which does not at all flow invariably through the most distinguished reputations. He must be quite aware of the obvious fact that art never improves, but that the material of art is never quite the same. He must be aware that the mind of Europe—the mind of his own country—a mind which he learns in time to be much more important than his own private mind—is a mind which changes, and that this change is a development which abandons nothing *en route*, which does not superannuate either Shakespeare, or Homer, or the rock drawing of the Magdalenian draughtsmen.° That this development, refinement perhaps, complication certainly, is not, from the point of view of the artist, any improvement. Perhaps not even an improvement from the point of view of the psychologist or not to the extent which we imagine; perhaps only in the end based upon a complication in economics and machinery. But the difference between the present and the past is that the conscious present is an awareness of the past in a way and to an extent which the past's awareness of itself cannot show.

Some one said: "The dead writers are remote from us because we *know* so much more than they did." Precisely, and they are that which we know.

I am alive to a usual objection to what is clearly part of my programme for the *métier*° of poetry. The objection is that the doctrine requires a ridiculous amount of erudition (pedantry), a claim which can be rejected by appeal to the lives of poets in any pantheon. It will even be affirmed that much learning deadens or perverts poetic sensibility. While, however, we persist in believing that a poet ought to know as much as will not encroach upon his necessary receptivity and necessary laziness, it is not desirable to confine knowledge to whatever can be put into a useful shape for examinations, drawing-rooms, or the still more pretentious modes of publicity. Some can absorb knowledge, the more tardy must sweat for it. Shakespeare acquired more essential history from Plutarch° than most men could from the whole British Museum. What is to be insisted upon is that the poet must develop or procure the consciousness of the past and that he should continue to develop this consciousness throughout his career.

What happens is a continual surrender of himself as he is at the moment to something which is more valuable. The progress of an artist is a continual self-sacrifice, a continual extinction of personality.

---

bolus: A large pill.   **Magdalenian draughtsmen:** The artists of the Paleolithic period who drew on cave walls in La Madeleine, in the south of France.   **métier:** French for "art" or "craft."   **Plutarch:** Greek writer (c. 46–119?) whose work was used by Shakespeare as a source for his plays.

ALLEN GINSBERG

*Allen Ginsberg discusses and expands on the concepts in his writing in this
1987 interview in the* New York Quarterly.

On His Poetic Craft   1987

Interviewer: You have talked about this before, but would you begin this
interview by describing the early influences on your work, or the influences on
your early work?

Ginsberg: Emily Dickinson. Poe's "Bells" — "Hear the sledges with the
bells — Silver Bells! . . ." Milton's long line breath in *Paradise Lost* —

> Him the almighty power
> Hurled headlong flaming from the ethereal sky
> With hideous ruin and combustion down
> To bottomless perdition, there to dwell
> In adamantine chains and penal fire,
> Who durst defy the omnipotent to arms.

Shelley's "Epipsychidion" — "one life, one death, / One Heaven, one
Hell, one immortality, / And one annihilation. Woe is me! . . ." The end of
Shelley's "Adonais"; and Shelley's "Ode to the West Wind" exhibits continu-
ous breath leading to ecstatic climax.

Wordsworth's "Intimations of Immortality" —

> Our birth is but a sleep and a forgetting:
> The soul that rises with us, our life's Star,
> Hath had elsewhere its setting,

— also Wordsworth's "Tintern Abbey" exhortation, or whatever you call it:

> a sense sublime
> Of something far more deeply interfused,
> Whose dwelling is the light of setting suns,
> And the round ocean and the living air,
> And the blue sky, and in the mind of man;

That kind of poetry influenced me: a long breath poetry that has a sort of
ecstatic climax.

Interviewer: What about Whitman?

Ginsberg: No, I replied very specifically. You asked me about my *first*
poetry. Whitman and Blake, yes, but in terms of the *early* poems I replied
specifically. When I began writing I was writing rhymed verse, stanzaic forms
that I derived from my father's practice. As I progressed into that, I got more
involved with Andrew Marvell.

Interviewer: Did you used to go to the Poetry Society of America meetings?

Ginsberg: Yes, I used to go with my father. It was a horrifying experience — mostly old ladies and second-rate poets.

Interviewer: Would you elaborate?

Ginsberg: That's the PSA I'm talking about. At the time it was mainly people who were enemies of, and denounced, William Carlos Williams and Ezra Pound and T. S. Eliot.

Interviewer: How long did it take you to realize they were enemies?

Ginsberg: Oh, I knew right away. I meant enemies of poetry, very specifically. Or enemies of that poetry which now by hindsight is considered sincere poetry of the time. *Their* highwater mark was, I guess, Edwin Arlington Robinson; "Eros Tyrranos" was considered, I guess, the great highwater mark of twentieth-century poetry.

Interviewer: Where did you first hear long lines in momentum?

Ginsberg: The texts I was citing were things my father taught me when I was prepubescent.

Interviewer: Did he teach them to you as beautiful words, or as the craft of poetry?

Ginsberg: I don't think people used that word "craft" in those days. It's sort of like a word that has only come into use in the last few decades. There were texts of great poetry around the house, and he would recite from memory. He never sat down and said now I am going to teach you: Capital C-R-A-F-T. Actually I don't like the use of the word craft applied to poetry, because generally along with it comes a defense of stressed iambic prosody, which I find uncraftsmanly and pedantical in its use. There are very few people in whose mouths that word makes any sense. I think Marianne Moore may have used it a few times. Pound has used it a couple of times in very specific circumstances — more often as a verb than as a general noun: "This or that poet has crafted a sestina."

Interviewer: Would you talk about later influences on your work? William Blake? Walt Whitman?

Ginsberg: Later on for open verse I was interested in Kerouac's poetry. I think that turned me on more than anyone else. I think he is a very great poet and much underrated. He hadn't been read yet by poets.

Interviewer: Most people associate Kerouac with prose, with *On the Road,* and not so much with *Mexico City Blues.* Or maybe they differentiate too strictly between prose and poetry.

Ginsberg: I think it's because people are so preoccupied with the use of the word craft and its meaning that they can't see poetry in front of them on the page. Kerouac's poetry looks like the most "uncrafted stuff" in the world. He's got a different idea of craft from most people who use the word "craft." I would say Kerouac's poetry is the craftiest of all. And as far as having the most craft of anyone, though those who talk about craft have not yet discovered it, his craft is spontaneity; his craft is having the instantaneous recall of the unconscious; his craft is the perfect executive conjunction of archetypal memorial images articulating present observation of detail and childhood epiphany fact.

Interviewer: In *Howl,* at the end of Section One, you came close to a definition of poetry, when you wrote:

who dreamt and made incarnate gaps in Time & Space through images
    juxtaposed, and trapped the archangel of the soul between 2 visual

images and joined the elemental verbs and set the noun and dash of
consciousness together jumping with sensation of Pater Omnipotens
Aeterne Deus

Ginsberg: I reparaphrased that when I was talking about Kerouac. If you
heard the structure of the sentence I was composing, it was about putting present observed detail into epiphany, or catching the archangel of the soul between
two visual images. I was thinking then about what Kerouac and I thought about
haiku—two visual images, opposite poles, which are connected by a lightning
in the mind. In other words "Today's been a good day; let another fly come on
the rice." Two disparate images, unconnected, which the mind connects.

Interviewer: Chinese poets do that. Is that what you are talking about?

Ginsberg: This is characteristic of Chinese poetry as Ezra Pound pointed
out in his essay "The Chinese Written Character as a Medium for Poetry"
nearly fifty years ago. Do you know that work? Well, way back when, Ezra
Pound proposed Chinese hieroglyphic language as more fit for poetry, considering that it was primarily visual, than generalized language-abstraction
English, with visionless words like Truth, Beauty, Craft, etc. Pound then translated some Chinese poetry and translated (from Professor Fenellossa's papers)
this philosophic essay pointing to Chinese language as pictorial. There is no
concrete in English, and poets could learn from Chinese to present image-
detail: and out of that Pound hieroglyph rose the whole practice of imagism,
the school which is referred to as "Imagism." So what you are referring to is an
old history in twentieth-century poetry. My own thing about two visual images
is just from that tradition, actually drawing from Pound's discovery and interpretation of Chinese as later practiced by Williams and everybody who studied
with Pound or who understood Pound. What I'm trying to point out is that this
tradition in American poetry in the twentieth century is not something *just* discovered. It was done by Pound and Williams, precisely the people that are
anathema to the PSA mediocrities who were attacking Pound and Williams for
not having "craft."

Interviewer: In that same section of *Howl,* in the next line, you wrote:

> to recreate the syntax and measure of poor human prose and stand before
> you speechless and intelligent and shaking with shame, rejected yet
> confessing out the soul to conform to the rhythm of thought in his
> naked and endless head.

Ginsberg: Description of aesthetic method. Key phrases that I picked up
around that time and was using when I wrote the book. I meant again that if
you place two visual images side by side and let the mind connect them, the gap
between the two images, the lightning in the mind illuminates. It's the *sunyata*
(Buddhist term for blissful empty void) which can only be known by living
creatures. So, the emptiness to which the Zen finger classically points—the
ellipse—is the unspoken hair-raising awareness in between two mental visual
images. I should try to make my answers a little more succinct.

Interviewer: Despite your feeling about craft, poets have developed an
attitude towards your work, they have discovered certain principles of breath
division in your lines—

Ginsberg: Primary fact of my writing is that I don't have any craft and don't know what I'm doing. There is absolutely no art involved, in the context of the general use of the words "art" and "craft." Such craft or art as there is, is in illuminating mental formations, and trying to observe the naked activity of my own mind. Then transcribing that activity down on paper. So the craft is being shrewd at flash lighting mental activity. Trapping the archangel of the soul, by accident, so to speak. The subject matter is the action of my mind. To put it on the most vulgar level, like on the psychoanalyst's couch is supposed to be. Now if you are thinking of "form" or even the "well-made poem" or a sonnet when you're lying on the couch, you'll never say what you have on your mind. You'd be babbling about corset styles or something *else* all the time instead of saying, "I want to fuck my mother," or whatever it is you want. So my problem is to get down the fact that I want to fuck my mother or whatever. I'm taking the most hideous image possible, so there will be no misunderstanding about what area of mind you are dealing with: what is socially unspoken, what is prophetic from the unconscious, what is universal to all men, what's the main subject of poetry, what's underneath, *inside* the mind. So, how do you get that out on the page? You observe your own mind during the time of composition and write down whatever goes through the ticker tape of mentality, or whatever you hear in the echo of your inner ear, or what flashes in picture on the eyeball while you're writing. So the subject is constantly interrupting because the mind is constantly going on vagaries—so whenever it changes I have a dash. The dashes are a function of this method of transcription of unconscious data. Now you can't write down *everything* that you've got going on—half-conscious data. You can't write down everything, you can only write down what the hand can carry. Your hand can't carry more than a twentieth of what the mind flashes, and the very fact of writing interrupts the mind's flashes and redirects attention to writing. So that the observation (for writing) impedes the function of the mind. You might say "Observation impedes Function." I get down as much as I can of genuine material, interrupting the flow of material as I get it down and when I look, I turn to the center of my brain to see the next thought, but it's probably about thirty thoughts later. So I make a dash to indicate a break, sometimes a dash plus dots. Am I making sense?— ...

Interviewer: How much do you revise your work?

Ginsberg: As little revision as possible. The craft, the art consists in paying attention on the actual movie of the mind. Writing it down is like a byproduct of that. If you can actually keep track of your own head movie, then the writing it down is just like a secretarial job, and who gets crafty about that? Use dashes instead of semicolons. Knowing the difference between a dash—and a hyphen -. Long lines are useful at certain times, and short lines at other times. But a big notebook with lines is a helpful thing, and three pens—you have to be shrewd about that. The actual materials are important. A book at the nightstand is important—a light you can get at—or a flashlight, as Kerouac had a brakeman's lantern. That's the craft. Having the brakeman's lantern and knowing where to use the ampersand "&" for swiftness in writing. If your attention is focused all the time—as my attention was in writing "Sunflower Sutra,"

"TV Baby" poem later ("Wichita Vortex Sutra" later, in a book called *Planet News*)—when attention is focused, there is no likelihood there will be much need for blue penciling revision because there'll be a sensuous continuum in the composition. So when I look over something that I've written down, I find that if my attention has lapsed from the subject, I begin to talk about myself writing about the subject or talking about my irrelevant left foot itch instead of about the giant smog factory I'm observing in Linden, New Jersey. Then I'll have to do some blue penciling, excising whatever is irrelevant: whatever I inserted self-consciously, instead of conscious of the Subject. Where self-consciousness intervenes on attention, blue pencil excision means getting rid of the dross of self-consciousness. Since the subject matter is really the opera-tion of the mind, as in Gertrude Stein, anything that the mind passes through is proper and shouldn't be revised out, almost anything that passes through mind, anything with the exception of self-consciousness. Anything that occurs to the mind is the proper subject. So if you are making a graph of the move-ments of the mind, there is no point in revising it. Because then you would obliterate the actual markings of the graph. So if you're interested in writing as a form of meditation or introspective yoga, which I am, then there's no revision possible.

LOUISE GLÜCK

Louise Glück wrote these comments as part of her introduction to The Best American Poems *of 1993, of which she was the editor.*

Poems *Are* Autobiography   1993

The world is complete without us. Intolerable fact. To which the poet responds by rebelling, wanting to prove otherwise. Out of wounded vanity or stubborn pride or desolate need, the poet lives in chronic dispute with fact, and an astonishment occurs: another fact is created, like a new element, in partial contradiction of the intolerable. Indelible voice, though it has no impact on the nonhuman universe, profoundly alters our experience of that universe as well as of the world of human relations; to all that is most solitary in our natures, it is the sustaining companion.

We know this happens: literature is its record or testament. A chilling word, literature. It lacks all sense of the voice's adamant vitality. As an abstrac-tion, it converts the poem into something equally disembodied, a resolved thing, inert and distant. Whereas the voice that rises from the page is weirdly restless: seductive, demanding, embittered, witty. Speaking not from the past but in the present. And it still occurs: voices emerge from which, in Robinson Jeffers's phrase, fire cannot be leached, whether because cultural shifts create them or because they enact the ancient dispute with new emphasis or because there is in them some quality or force not yet identified.

It would be interesting to know something about that quality, because the poem, no matter how charged its content, survives not through content but through voice. By *voice* I mean style of thought, for which a style of speech — the clever grafts and borrowings, the habitual gestures scattered like clues in the lines — never convincingly substitutes. We fall back on that term, *voice*, for all its insufficiencies; it suggests, at least, the sound of an authentic being. Although such sound may draw on the poet's actual manner of speech, it is not, on the page, transcription. The voice is at liberty to excerpt, to exaggerate, to bypass what it chooses, to issue from conditions the real world will never exactly reproduce; unlike speech, it bears no immediate social pressure, since the other to whom it strives to make itself clear may not yet exist. The poem means to create that person, first in the poet, then in the reader. Meanwhile, its fidelity is not to external reality: it need not provide a replica of the outward, or of social relations. This is why time confers more readily on the apolitical novel political significance: nineteenth-century romantic novels, for example, were not necessarily conceived as political statements; they become such statements in light of a contemporary readiness to politicize gender relations. The novel seems oddly easier on many readers, who are puzzled by the poem's independence, puzzled, even, by the voice's unnerving authenticity. The conviction that poems must be autobiography (since they are not description) begins here; in the reader's belief that the actual and the true are synonyms.

Poems *are* autobiography, but divested of the trappings of chronology and comment, the metronomic alternation of anecdote and response. Moreover, a body of work may change and develop less in reaction to the lived life than in reaction to the poet's prior discoveries, or the discoveries of others. If a poem remains so selectively amplified, so casual with fact, as to seem elusive, we must remember its agenda: not, or not simply, to record the actual but to continuously create the sensation of immersion in the actual. And if, in its striving to be free of the imprisoning self, the poet's gaze trains itself outward, it rests nevertheless on what compels or arrests it. Such choices constitute a portrait. Where the gaze is held, voice, or response, begins. Always in what follows the poet is alert, resistant, resisting dogma and fashion, resisting the greater danger of personal conviction, which must be held suspect, given its resemblance to dogma.

Still, for poems to touch us, we have to be magnetically drawn, we have to want to read these things. What makes this possible, what are the characteristics of those voices that, even as they become epigraphs or inscriptions on stone, mock the stone and the page with their vitality? Not, I think, that they sound beautiful or speak truth. Of these claims, the second seems at once grander and more accessible because of the ease with which truth identifies itself with sincerity as opposed to insight. Art's truth is as different from sincerity's honest disclosure as it is different from the truth administered in the doctor's office, that sequence of knowns which the doctor, newly trained to respect the patient's dignity, makes wholly available, affording, in the process, glimpses into a world of probabilities and strategies, the world of action transposed to conditions in which action can do only so much. The poem may embody perception so luminous it seems truth, but what keeps it alive is not fixed discovery but the means to discovery; what keeps it alive is intelligence.

ROBERT HAYDEN

Robert Hayden's introduction to his anthology of African American poetry discusses the tradition of "Negro poetry," which, like American poetry generally, was concerned with developing a distinctive language and form.

On Negro Poetry   1967

The question whether we can speak with any real justification of "Negro poetry" arises often today. Some object to the term because it has been used disparagingly to indicate a kind of pseudo-poetry concerned with the race problem to the exclusion of almost everything else. Others hold that Negro poetry *per se* could only be produced in black Africa. Seen from this point of view, the poetry of the American Negro, its "specialized" content notwithstanding, is obviously not to be thought of as existing apart from the rest of our literature, but as having been shaped over some three centuries by social, moral, and literary forces essentially American.

Those who presently avow themselves "poets of the Negro revolution" argue that they do indeed constitute a separate group or school, since the purpose of their writing is to give Negroes a sense of human dignity and provide them with ideological weapons. A belligerent race pride moves these celebrants of Black Power to declare themselves not simply "poets," but "Negro poets." However, Countee Cullen, the brilliant lyricist of the Harlem Renaissance in the 1920s, insisted that he be considered a "poet," not a "Negro poet," for he did not want to be restricted to racial themes nor have his poetry judged solely on the basis of its relevance to the Negro struggle.

Cullen was aware of a peculiar risk Negro poets have had to face. The tendency of American critics has been to label the established Negro writer a "spokesman for his race." There are, as we have seen, poets who think of themselves in that role. But the effect of such labeling is to place any Negro author in a kind of literary ghetto where the standards applied to other writers are not likely to be applied to him, since he, being a "spokesman for his race," is not considered primarily a writer but a species of race-relations man, the leader of a cause, the voice of protest.

Protest has been a recurring element in the writing of American Negroes, a fact hardly to be wondered at, given the social conditions under which they have been forced to live. And the Negro poet's devotion to the cause of freedom is not in any way reprehensible, for throughout history poets have often been champions of human liberty. But bad poetry is another matter, and there is no denying that a great deal of "race poetry" is poor, because its content seems ready-made and art is displaced by argument.

Phillis Wheatley (c. 1750–1784), the first poet of African descent to win some measure of recognition, had almost nothing to say about the plight of her people. And if she resented her own ambiguous position in society, she did not express her resentment. One reason for her silence is that, although brought to Boston as a slave, she never lived as one. Another is that as a neoclassical poet she would scarcely have thought it proper to reveal much of herself in her poetry, although we do get brief glimpses of her in the poem addressed to the Earl of Dartmouth and in "On Being Brought from Africa to America." Neoclassicism emphasized reason rather than emotion and favored elegance and formality. The English poet Alexander Pope was the acknowledged master of this style, and in submitting to his influence Phillis Wheatley produced poetry that was as good as that of her American contemporaries. She actually wrote better than some of them.

But the poetry of Phillis Wheatley and her fellow poet, Jupiter Hammon, has historical and not literary interest for us now. The same can be said of much of eighteenth-century American poetry in general. Not until the nineteenth century did the United States begin to have literature of unqualified merit and originality. There were no Negro poets of stature in the period before the Civil War, but there were several with talent, among them George Moses Horton (1797–c. 1883) and Frances E. W. Harper (1825–1911). Didactic and sentimental, they wrote with competence and moral fervor in the manner of their times. Their poetry is remembered chiefly because it contributed to the anti-slavery struggle, and because it testifies to the creative efforts of Negroes under disheartening conditions. . . .

In the twentieth century Negro poets have abandoned dialect for an idiom truer to folk speech. The change has been due not only to differences in social outlook on their part but also to revolutionary developments in American poetry. The New Poetry movement, which began before the First World War and reached its definitive point in the 1920s, represented a break with the past. Free verse, diction close to everyday speech, a realistic approach to life, and the use of material once considered unpoetic — these were the goals of the movement. The Negro poet-critic, William Stanley Braithwaite, encouraged the "new" poetry through his articles in the *Boston Evening Transcript* and his yearly anthologies of magazine verse.

The New Negro movement or Negro Renaissance, resulting from the social, political, and artistic awakening of Negroes in the twenties, brought into prominence poets whose work showed the influence of the poetic revolution. Protest became more defiant, racial bitterness and racial pride more outspoken than ever before. Negro history and folklore were explored as new sources of inspiration. Spirituals, blues, and jazz suggested themes and verse patterns to young poets like Jean Toomer and Langston Hughes. Certain conventions, notably what has been called "literary Garveyism," grew out of a fervent Negro nationalism. Marcus Garvey, leader of the United Negro Improvement Association, advocated a "return" to Africa, the lost homeland, and nearly all the Renaissance poets wrote poems about their spiritual ties to Africa, about the dormant fires of African paganism in the Negro soul that the white man's civilization could never extinguish. Countee Cullen's "Heritage" is one of the best of these poems, even though the Africa it presents is artificial, romanticized, and it reiterates exotic clichés in vogue during the period when it was written.

Harlem was the center of the Negro Renaissance, which for that reason is also referred to as the Harlem Renaissance. Two magazines, *The Crisis* and *Opportunity,* gave aid and encouragement to Negro writers by publishing their work and by awarding literary prizes.

In the decades since the New Negro movement, which ended with the twenties, protest and race consciousness have continued to find expression in the poetry of the American Negro. But other motivating forces are also in evidence. There are Negro poets who believe that any poet's most clearly defined task is to create with honesty and sincerity poems that will illuminate human experience — not exclusively "Negro experience." They reject the idea of poetry as racial propaganda, of poetry that functions as a kind of sociology. Their attitude is not wholly new, of course, being substantially that of Dunbar and Cullen. In counterpoise to it is the "Beat" or "nonacademic" view held by poets who are not only in rebellion against middle-class ideals and the older poetic traditions but who also advocate a militant racism in a definitely "Negro" poetry.

It has come to be expected of Negro poets that they will address themselves to the race question — and that they will all say nearly the same things about it. Such "group unity" is more apparent than real. Differences in vision and emphasis, fundamental differences in approach to the art of poetry itself, modify and give diversity to the writing of these poets, even when they employ similar themes. And certainly there is no agreement among them as to what the much debated role of the Negro poet should be.

ANTHONY HECHT

Anthony Hecht's 1968 parody of Matthew Arnold's "Dover Beach" (p. 831) is not meant as an attack on the earlier poem. It is, rather, a deliberately amusing way of looking at a familiar masterpiece from another point of view.

The Dover Bitch   1968
A Criticism of Life

So there stood Matthew Arnold and this girl
With the cliffs of England crumbling away behind them,
And he said to her, "Try to be true to me,
And I'll do the same for you, for things are bad
All over, etc., etc."   5
Well now, I knew this girl. It's true she had read
Sophocles in a fairly good translation
And caught that bitter allusion to the sea,

But all the time he was talking she had in mind
The notion of what his whiskers would feel like   10
On the back of her neck. She told me later on
That after a while she got to looking out
At the lights across the channel, and really felt sad,
Thinking of all the wine and enormous beds
And blandishments in French and the perfumes.   15
And then she got really angry. To have been brought
All the way down from London, and then be addressed
As a sort of mournful cosmic last resort
Is really tough on a girl, and she was pretty.
Anyway, she watched him pace the room   20
And finger his watch-chain and seem to sweat a bit,
And then she said one or two unprintable things.
But you mustn't judge her by that. What I mean to say is,
She's really all right. I still see her once in a while
And she always treats me right. We have a drink   25
And I give her a good time, and perhaps it's a year
Before I see her again, but there she is,
Running to fat, but dependable as they come.
And sometimes I bring her a bottle of *Nuit d'Amour*.

ERICA JONG

Erica Jong first became known for her feminist novel Fear of Flying *(1973),
but she has also published several collections of poetry and a recent memoir,* Any
Woman's Blues *(1991). Her essay describes her discovery of Shakespeare's sonnets when she was a college student.*

Devouring Time: Shakespeare's Sonnets   1996

My love affair with Shakespeare's sonnets began when I was in college. Looking back, it seems to me that at every stage of my adult life, the
sonnets have meant something different to me—always deepening, always
inexhaustible.

The most daunting challenge is to choose a favorite out of the 152 best
poems in our language, since there are so many that move me deeply. I begin
this impossible task by reading through the sonnets to myself silently, and then
by listening to Sir John Gielgud's astonishing rendition of them, recorded in
1963, Shakespeare's quatercentenary. (I deliberately do not turn to my groaning bookshelves of Shakespeare criticism with their pointless, and ultimately
snobbish, debates about the identity of "Mr. W. H." or whether or not our
"Top Poet," as Auden called him, could really be a mere middle-class man of
Stratford rather than the Earl of Oxford—or perhaps even the Virgin Queen

herself. I want to return to the sonnets freshly—as a common reader, responding to them as a person first, a poet second.) As Gielgud's great actor's voice reawakens these dazzling poems for me, I hear again the toll of mortality in the sonnets, the elaboration of the themes of love and death and the stark repetition of their central word: "time."

Devouring time, the wastes of Time, Time's scythe, Wasteful time, in war with time, this bloody tyrant time, time's pencil, time's furrows, dear time's waste, Time's injurious hand, Time's spoils, Time's fool, a hell of time, Time's fickle glass. . . . It seems I cannot read or hear the sonnets without being reminded of how little time is left—which sends me to my desk to write with frenzied hand.

Time is the all-powerful, wrathful God of the sonnets. And to this awesome power, the poet opposes procreation, love, and poetry.

The first thirteen sonnets urge begetting a child to oppose death:

> Th'ou art thy mother's glass, and she in thee
> Calls back the lovely April of her prime.
> 　　　　　　　(Sonnet 3)

Then the theme shifts, and by Sonnet 15 the poet is comparing his own craft to procreation as a way of winning the war with time:

> And all in war with Time for love of you,
> As he takes from you, I ingraft you new.

But poetry is fired by love, so these two forms of redemption are really the same. Children redeem us from time, poetry redeems us from time, and love is the force that drives them both. As the sonnets go on to tell their twisted tale of rival loves, rival poets, love, passion, parting, obsessional sexuality, wrath, reunion, forgiveness, self-love, self-loathing, and self-forgiveness, time never ceases to be the poet's alpha and omega, the deity he both worships and despises.

And so I find myself coming back again and again to Sonnet 19, a poet's credo if ever there were one.

> Devouring Time, blunt thou the lion's paws,
> And make the earth devour her own sweet brood;
> Pluck the keen teeth from the fierce tiger's yaws,
> And burn the long-liv'd phoenix in her blood;
> Make glad and sorry seasons as thou fleet'st,
> And do whate'er thou wilt, swift-footed Time,
> To the wide world and all her fading sweets;
> But I forbid thee one most heinous crime:
> O, carve not with thy hours my love's fair brow,
> Nor draw no lines there with thine antique pen;
> Him in thy course untained do allow
> For beauty's pattern to succeeding men.
> 　　Yet do thy worst, old Time: despite thy wrong,
> 　　My love shall in my verse ever live young.

Sonnet 19 is hardly the most complex of Shakespeare's sonnets, nor the most tortured. The sonnets that recount obsessional love, jealousy, and lust are far darker and more fretted. But Sonnet 19 calls me back again and again because it is one of the few in which the poet addresses time directly and takes him on—David against Goliath.

The simplicity of the sonnet's "statement" delights me: "Time, you big bully, you think you're so great. You can make people die and tigers lose their teeth and change the seasons so fast it makes us dizzy. But spare my love. Don't scribble on him with your antique pen. On second thought, do whatever the hell you like. You have the power to destroy, but I have an even greater power: I create. And by capturing my love in poetry, I can keep my love young forever, whatever you may do to destroy him!"

There is a fluidity to this sonnet that seems to me a triumph of this difficult form. The three quatrains flow into one another and become one exhortation. The couplet argues with them all, changing the direction swiftly and ironically. The poet is standing up to the bully. Suddenly "Devouring Time" becomes "old Time," as if in the course of fourteen lines he had withered like a vampire thrown into a raging inferno. The poem itself has subdued time, made him old before his time, vanquished him. The force of poetry alone defeats time.

This theme is elaborated often in the sonnets, but seldom with such simplicity, the simplicity of a person addressing a fearsome deity without fear: the poet speaking to the gods. Throughout the sonnets, the poet addresses his love, his siren, his lust, even himself, but only in this sonnet (and once more in Sonnet 123) does he address Time directly. He throws down the gauntlet and takes Time on as if one might defeat a powerful foe simply with the force of language.

And, of course, one *can*, as Shakespeare's sonnets prove. We go back to them again and again, discovering new depths in them as time carves new depths in our hearts.

In youth, we tend to love the love poems, the poems of obsessional lust, jealousy, and rage. "Th'expense of spirit in a waste of shame" (129) reminds us of our own struggles to master lust. "So are you to my thoughts as food to life" (75) reminds us of the yearning of first love. As we age, we increasingly see Time shadowing love and the bliss of creation as the only redemption. Shakespeare's sonnets are a fugue on the theme of time. They can be read together or separately, line by line, quatrain by quatrain, or as a narrative of the power of art against decay. They prove the poet's point by their very durability.

Each time I go back to the sonnets, I find something that seemed not to be there before. Perhaps I have changed and my vision is less clouded, or else the sonnets metamorphose on the shelf. The sonnets I love best are those with sustained voices, those that sound like a person speaking. I think I hear Shakespeare's private voice in these sonnets, as if he were whispering directly in my ear.

That Shakespeare's sonnets have defeated death comforts me—for what is great poetry, after all, but the continuation of the human voice after death?

PHILIP LEVINE

Philip Levine wrote this reminiscence of his youthful discovery of the poetry of Keats for the New York Times.

From "Keats in Detroit"   1995

We were twelve young and not-so-young men and women from Detroit. The class, Prof. A. D. Wooly's introduction to the Romantic poets, met in the late afternoon, and some hurried to it after finishing the day shift at one of the local factories. Even our clothing revealed that.

With one month left in the semester, we arrived at young John Keats— who was born two hundred years ago this week and is hardly more fashionable now than he was when I sat in that classroom forty-seven years ago. With Keats there was an immediate affinity we had not felt before. Shelley and Byron were exotic aristocrats, who rode far above the clouds of industrial garbage that hovered over our university campus. Keats was one of us: young, uncertain, determined, decently educated at mediocre schools, struggling to survive. He was what one of us might have been, had one of us been phenomenal John Keats.

From the moment I read "On First Looking into Chapman's Homer," I was hooked. It expressed perfectly my own response to the great Romantic poetry I was reading for the first time and—to use Keats's expression—feeling on my pulse as I had felt no poetry before:

> Much have I travell'd in the realms of gold,
> And many goodly states and kingdoms seen;
> Round many western islands have I been
> Which bards in fealty to Apollo hold.
> Oft of one wide expanse had I been told
> That deep-brow'd Homer ruled as his demesne;
> Yet did I never breathe its pure serene
> Till I heard Chapman speak out loud and bold:
> Then felt I like some watcher of the skies
> When a new planet swims into his ken;
> Or like stout Cortez when with eagle eyes
> He star'd at the Pacific—and all his men
> Look'd at each other with a wild surmise—
> Silent, upon a peak in Darien.

I do not know if Professor Wooly knew that my ambition was to become a poet. Detroit was not Greenwich Village or even Berkeley; it taught you not to advertise all of your ambitions. Its stance was ferociously masculine, and most of its citizens seemed to have little tolerance for the arts or for what might be described as "artistic behavior." Even half the women I went to school with carried themselves as though they yearned to become professional bowlers.

My guess is that Professor Wooly divined certain needs in me. One afternoon, as the last of daylight faded across his desk, he handed me a volume of Keats's letters opened to the page concerned with what the poet called "the vale of Soul-making." In what I read, a man barely older than I was attempting to account for the function of pain and suffering in the creation of the human spirit. I found, to use Keats's words, "the use of the world" for probably the first time in my life.

"I will call the world a School," Keats had written, "instituted for the purpose of teaching little children to read." He went on, "Do you not see how necessary a World of Pains and troubles is to school an Intelligence and make it a Soul?" For a moment I saw. Nothing I had read before had so potently lifted the gloom that hovered over my small portion of Detroit.

This was some ten years before Americans of my generation would set about the creation of a body of poetry that would later be labeled "confessional" and even longer before those poets' acts of self-destruction, but the models were already there. That year, Detroit itself would welcome the besotted Dylan Thomas. My mentor-to-be, John Berryman, would later claim that what the poet required above all else was a wounding so terrible that he or she could only barely survive it.

Imagine my relief and surprise when Professor Wooly pointed to the following passage: "Whenever I find myself growing vaporish I rouse myself, wash, and put on a clean shirt, brush my hair and clothes, tie my shoestrings neatly, and in fact adonize as I were going out—then all clean and comfortable I sit down to write. This I find the greatest relief." A poet writing out of his joy in the world and in himself, out of what Coleridge had called his "genial spirits."

It seemed quite suddenly I could be both a poet and a person, even in a world like ours—that is, if I were able to create such a person out of what I'd been given. By this time, even at age twenty, certain things were clear to me. One was that Keats was a genius and I was not, so I would have to apply myself with even greater dedication than he. Another was that his early poems gave not the least hint of what was to come. Yet he had made himself a poet and he had done this while living "in uncertainties, Mysteries, doubts, without any irritable reaching after fact and reason."

According to Keats, my ability to write in a world I did not understand and from which I did not demand final answers might prove to be an asset rather than a defect of character. Like Keats, I was descended from ordinary people, in my case with extraordinary minds and imaginations. I realized that this, too, could prove to be a virtue, for it meant that I could not live apart from the daily difficulties of the world. I could regard these circumstances as the Alps that stood between me and the poetry I might write, or like Keats I could regard them as part of the material out of which I might build my character and, later, my poetry.

ROBERT LOWELL

Robert Lowell's comments on "Skunk Hour" were a response to a discussion of the poem by fellow poets Richard Wilbur, John Frederick Nims, and John Berryman. The comments were included in the book The Contemporary Artist as Artist and Critic *(1964), edited by Anthony Ostroff.*

An Explication of "Skunk Hour"   1964

I. THE MEANING

The author of a poem is not necessarily the ideal person to explain its meaning. He is as liable as anyone else to muddle, dishonesty, and reticence. Nor is it his purpose to provide a peg for a prose essay. Meaning varies in importance from poem to poem, and from style to style, but always it is only a strand and an element in the brute flow of composition. Other elements are pictures that please or thrill for themselves, phrases that ring for their music or carry some buried suggestion. For all this the author is an opportunist, throwing whatever comes to hand into his feeling for start, continuity, contrast, climax, and completion. It is imbecile for him not to know his intentions, and unsophisticated for him to know too explicitly and fully. . . .

I am not sure whether I can distinguish between intention and interpretation. I think this is what I more or less intended. The first four stanzas are meant to give a dawdling more or less amiable picture of a declining Maine sea town. I move from the ocean inland. Sterility howls through the scenery, but I try to give a tone of tolerance, humor, and randomness to the sad prospect. The composition drifts, its direction sinks out of sight into the casual, chancy arrangements of nature and decay. Then all comes alive in stanzas V and VI. This is the dark night. I hoped my readers would remember John of the Cross's° poem. My night is not gracious, but secular, puritan, and agnostical. An Existentialist night. Somewhere in my mind was a passage from Sartre or Camus° about reaching some point of final darkness where the one free act is suicide. Out of this comes the march and affirmation, an ambiguous one, of my skunks in the last two stanzas. The skunks are both quixotic and barbarously absurd, hence the tone of amusement and defiance. "Skunk Hour" is not entirely independent, but the anchor poem in its sequence. . . .

"Skunk Hour" was begun in mid-August 1957, and finished about a month later. In March of the same year, I had been giving readings on the West Coast, often reading six days a week and sometimes twice on a single day. I was in San Francisco, the era and setting of Allen Ginsberg, and all about very modest poets were waking up prophets. I became sorely aware of how few poems I had written, and that these few had been finished at the latest three or four years earlier. Their style seemed distant, symbol-ridden and willfully difficult. I began to paraphrase my Latin quotations, and to add extra syllables to a line to make it clearer and more colloquial. I felt my old poems hid what they were really about, and many times offered a stiff, humorless, and even impenetrable surface. I am no convert to the "beats." I know well too that the best poems are not necessarily poems that read aloud. Many of the greatest poems can only be read to one's self, for inspiration is no substitute for humor, shock, narrative, and a hypnotic voice, the four musts for oral performance. Still, my

---

John of the Cross's: Reference to Juan de Yepes y Alvarez (1542–1591), Spanish mystic and poet. **Sartre or Camus:** Jean-Paul Sartre (1905–1980) and Albert Camus (1913–1960) were important modern French writers.

own poems seemed like prehistoric monsters dragged down into the bog and death by their ponderous armor. I was reciting what I no longer felt. What influenced me more than San Francisco and reading aloud was that for some time I had been writing prose. I felt that the best style for poetry was none of the many poetic styles in English, but something like the prose of Chekhov or Flaubert.

When I returned to my home, I began writing lines in a new style. No poem, however, got finished and soon I left off and tried to forget the whole headache. Suddenly, in August, I was struck by the sadness of writing nothing, and having nothing to write, of having, at least, no language. When I began writing "Skunk Hour," I felt that most of what I knew about writing was a hindrance.

The dedication is to Elizabeth Bishop, because rereading her suggested a way of breaking through the shell of my old manner. Her rhythms, idiom, images, and stanza structure seemed to belong to a later century. "Skunk Hour" is modeled on Miss Bishop's "The Armadillo," a much better poem and one I had heard her read and had later carried around with me. Both "Skunk Hour" and "The Armadillo" use short line stanzas, start with drifting description, and end with a single animal. . . .

"Skunk Hour" was written backwards, first the last two stanzas, I think, and then the next to last two. Anyway, there was a time when I had the last four stanzas much as they now are and nothing before them. I found the bleak personal violence repellent. All was too close, though watching the lovers was not mine, but from an anecdote about Walt Whitman in his old age. I began to feel that real poetry came, not from fierce confessions, but from something almost meaningless but imagined. I was haunted by an image of a blue china doorknob. I never used the doorknob, or knew what it meant, yet somehow it started the current of images in my opening stanzas. They were written in reverse order, and at last gave my poem an earth to stand on, and space to breathe.

Robert Lowell, as both poet and teacher, was an important influence on the work of Sylvia Plath. As he describes in his introduction to the collection of her final poems published after her death, he remembered her from his class, without knowing then the poetry she would create in those last months.

Foreword to Plath's *Ariel*   1966

In these poems, written in the last months of her life and often rushed out at the rate of two or three a day, Sylvia Plath becomes herself, becomes something imaginary, newly, wildly and subtly created — hardly a person at all, or a woman, certainly not another "poetess," but one of those super-real, hypnotic, great classical heroines. This character is feminine, rather than female, though almost everything we customarily think of as feminine is turned on its head.

The voice is now coolly amused, witty, now sour, now fanciful, girlish, charming, now sinking to the strident rasp of the vampire—a Dido,° Phaedra,° or Medea,° who can laugh at herself as "cow-heavy and floral in my Victorian nightgown." Though lines get repeated, and sometimes the plot is lost, language never dies in her mouth.

Everything in these poems is personal, confessional, felt, but the manner of feeling is controlled hallucination, the autobiography of a fever. She burns to be on the move, a walk, a ride, a journey, the flight of the queen bee. She is driven forward by the pounding pistons of her heart. The title *Ariel* summons up Shakespeare's lovely, though slightly chilling and androgenous spirit, but the truth is that this *Ariel* is the author's horse. Dangerous, more powerful than man, machinelike from hard training, she herself is a little like a racehorse, galloping relentlessly with risked, outstretched neck, death hurdle after death hurdle topped. She cries out for that rapid life of starting pistols, snapping tapes, and new world records broken. What is most heroic in her, though, is not her force, but the desperate practicality of her control, her hand of metal with its modest, womanish touch. Almost pure motion, she can endure "God, the great stasis in his vacuous night," hospitals, fever, paralysis, the iron lung, being stripped like a girl in the booth of a circus sideshow, dressed like a mannequin, tied down like Gulliver by the Lilliputians . . . apartments, babies, prim English landscapes, beehives, yew trees, gardens, the moon, hooks, the black boot, wounds, flowers with mouths like wounds, Belsen's lampshades° made of human skin, Hitler's homicidal iron tanks clanking over Russia. Suicide, father-hatred, self-loathing—nothing is too much for the macabre gaiety of her control. Yet it is too much; her art's immortality is life's disintegration. The surprise, the shimmering, unwrapped birthday present, the transcendence "into the red eye, the cauldron of morning," and the lover, who are always waiting for her, are Death, her own abrupt and defiant death.

> He tells me how badly I photograph.
> He tells me how sweet
> The babies look in their hospital
> Icebox, a simple
>
> Frill at the neck,
> Then the flutings of their Ionian
> Death gowns,
> Then two little feet.

There is a peculiar, haunting challenge to these poems. Probably many, after reading *Ariel*, will recoil from their first overawed shock, and painfully wonder why so much of it leaves them feeling empty, evasive and inarticulate.

Dido: In Virgil's *Aeneid*, queen of Carthage who commits suicide when Aeneas abandons her. **Phaedra:** In Greek mythology, daughter of Minos who falls tragically in love with her stepson Hippolytus and hangs herself. **Medea:** A sorceress in Greek mythology who helps Jason obtain the Golden Fleece and who commits murder to achieve her purposes. **Belsen's lampshades:** Reference to Bergen-Belsen, a Nazi concentration camp during World War II.

In her lines, I often hear the serpent whisper, "Come, if only you had the courage, you too could have my rightness, audacity and ease of inspiration." But most of us will turn back. These poems are playing Russian roulette with six cartridges in the cylinder, a game of "chicken," the wheels of both cars locked and unable to swerve. Oh, for that heaven of the humble copyist, those millennia of Egyptian artists repeating their lofty set patterns! And yet Sylvia Plath's poems are not the celebration of some savage and debauched existence, that of the "damned" poet, glad to burn out his body for a few years of continuous intensity. This poetry and life are not a career; they tell that life, even when disciplined, is simply not worth it.

It is poignant, looking back, to realize that the secret of Sylvia Plath's last irresistible blaze lies lost somewhere in the checks and courtesies of her early laborious shyness. She was never a student of mine, but for a couple of months seven years ago, she used to drop in on my poetry seminar at Boston University. I see her dim against the bright sky of a high window, viewless unless one cared to look down on the city outskirts' defeated yellow brick and square concrete pillbox filling stations. She was willowy, long-waisted, sharp-elbowed, nervous, giggly, gracious—a brilliant tense presence embarrassed by restraint. Her humility and willingness to accept what was admired seemed at times to give her an air of maddening docility that hid her unfashionable patience and boldness. She showed us poems that later, more or less unchanged, went into her first book, *The Colossus*. They were somber, formidably expert in stanza structure, and had a flair for alliteration and Massachusetts' low-tide dolor.

> A mongrel working his legs to a gallop
> Hustles the gull flock to flap off the sand-spit.

Other lines showed her wit and directness.

> The pears fatten like little Buddhas.

Somehow none of it sank very deep into my awareness. I sensed her abashment and distinction, and never guessed her later appalling and triumphant fulfillment.

BRETT C. MILLIER

Brett C. Millier described the biographical context of the composition of the poem "One Art" in Elizabeth Bishop: Life and the Memory of It. *This study was published by the University of California Press in 1993.*

On Elizabeth Bishop's "One Art"   1993

Elizabeth Bishop left seventeen drafts of the poem "One Art" among her papers. In the first draft, she lists all the things she's lost in her life—keys, pens, glasses, cities—and then she writes "One might think this would have prepared me / for losing one average-sized not exceptionally / beautiful or dazzlingly intelligent person . . . / But it doesn't seem to have at all. . . ." By the seventeenth draft, nearly every word has been transformed, but most importantly, Bishop discovered along the way that there might be a way to master this loss.

One way to read Bishop's modulation between the first and last drafts from "the loss of you is impossible to master" to something like "I am still the master of losing even though losing you looks like a disaster" is that in the writing of such a disciplined, demanding poem as this villanelle ("[*Write* it!]") lies the potential mastery of the loss. Working through each of her losses—from the bold, painful catalog of the first draft to the finely honed and privately meaningful final version—is the way to overcome them or, if not to overcome them, then to see the way in which she might possibly master herself in the face of loss. It is all, perhaps, "one art"—writing elegy, mastering loss, mastering grief, self-mastery. Bishop had a precocious familiarity with loss. Her father died before her first birthday, and four years later her mother disappeared into a sanitarium, never to be seen by her daughter again. The losses in the poem are real: time in the form of the "hour badly spent" and, more tellingly for the orphaned Bishop "my mother's watch": the lost houses, in Key West, Petrópolis, and Ouro Prêto, Brazil. The city of Rio de Janeiro and the whole South American continent (where she had lived for nearly two decades) were lost to her with the suicide of her Brazilian companion. And currently, in the fall of 1975, she seemed to have lost her dearest friend and lover, who was trying to end their relationship. But each version of the poem distanced the pain a little more, depersonalized it, moved it away from the tawdry self-pity and "confession" that Bishop disliked in so many of her contemporaries.

Bishop's friends remained for a long time protective of her personal reputation, and unwilling to have her grouped among lesbian poets or even among the other great poets of her generation—Robert Lowell, John Berryman, Theodore Roethke—as they seemed to self-destruct before their readers' eyes. Bishop herself taught them this reticence by keeping her private life to herself, and by investing what "confession" there was in her poems deeply in objects and places, thus deflecting biographical inquiry. In the development of this poem, discretion is both a poetic method, and a part of a process of self-understanding, the seeing of a pattern in her own life.

MARIANNE MOORE

Marianne Moore was one of the most skillful commentators on her own poetry and poetics. Her answers to these questions presented by poet Howard Nemerov were published in 1966.

Some Answers to Questions Posed
by Howard Nemerov
1966

Nemerov: Do you see your work as having essentially changed in character or style since you began?

Moore: No, except that rhythm was my prime objective. If I succeeded in embodying a rhythm that preoccupied me, I was satisfied.

Uniform line length seemed to me essential as accrediting the satisfactory model stanza and I sometimes ended a line with a hyphen, expecting the reader to maintain the line unbroken (disregarding the hyphen). I have found readers misled by the hyphen, mistaking it as an arcane form of emphasis, so I seldom use it today.

I am today much aware of the world's dilemma. People's effect on other people results, it seems to me, in an enforced sense of responsibility—a compulsory obligation to participate in others' problems.

Nemerov: Is there, has there been, was there ever, a "revolution" in poetry, or is all that a matter of a few sleazy technical tricks? What is the relation of your work to this question, if there is a relation? Otherwise put: do you respond to such notions as The New Poetry, An American Language Distinct from English, The Collapse of Prosody, No Thoughts but in Things, The Battle between Academics and—What?—Others (A Fair Field Full of Mostly Corpses)?

Moore: The individuality and emotions of the writer should transcend modes. I recall feeling oversolitary occasionally (say in 1912)—in reflecting no "influences"; in not being able to be called an "Imagist"—but determined to put the emphasis on what mattered most to me, in a manner natural to me. I like end-stopped lines and depend on rhyme, but my rhymes are often hidden and, in being inconspicuous, escape detection. When I began writing verse, I regarded flowing continuity as indispensable.

A Jellyfish

Visible, invisible,
    a fluctuating charm
an amber-tinctured amethyst
    inhabits it, your arm
approaches and it opens
    and it closes; you had meant
to catch it and it quivers;
    you abandon your intent.

Then when I came on Charles Sorley's "The Idea" (probably in *The Egoist,* London)—

It was all my own;
    I have guarded it well from
the winds that have blown
    too bitterly

—I recognized the unaccented syllable (the light rhyme) as means for me, as in "The Jerboa":

. . . one would not be he
who has nothing but plenty.

. . . closed upper paws seeming one with the fur
in its flight from a danger.

Having written the last stanza first, I had to duplicate it, progressing backward.

Its leaps should be set
to the flageolet;
pillar body erect
on a three-cornered smooth-working Chippendale
claw — propped on hind legs, and tail as third toe
between leaps to its burrow.

In "Occasionem Cognosce," the light rhyme is upside down:

. . . "Atlas"
(pressed glass)

looks best
embossed.

Poetry is a magic of pauses, as a dog-valentine contrasting "pawses" and "pauses" — sent me from Harvard where I had been discussing pauses — reminded me. I do not know what syllabic verse is. I find no appropriate application for it.

Might I say of the light rhyme that T. S. Eliot's phrase, "the greatest living master of the light rhyme," in his Introduction to my *Selected Poems* — suggesting conscious proficiency or at most a regulator art on my part, hardly deserves the term. Conscious writing can be the death of poetry.

SHARON OLDS

Sharon Olds is a writer whose work has attracted a wide readership. In this excerpt from the online magazine Salon, *the poet is interviewed by academic critic Jonathan Holden. Holden was one of the first to discuss Olds's poetry in terms of the differences between masculine and feminine sensibilities.*

From the *Salon* Interview   1999

Interviewer: Thanks for the tea. Which reminds me that I once read somewhere that you don't smoke or drink coffee, and that you consume very little alcohol. Why is that?

Olds: Well, one thing I'm really interested in, when I'm writing, is being accurate. If I am trying to describe something, I'd like to be able to get it right. Of course, what's "right" is different for every person. Sometimes what's accurate might be kind of mysterious. So I don't just mean mathematically accurate. But to get it right according to my vision. I think this is true for all artists. My senses are very important to me. I want to be able to describe accurately what I see and hear and smell. And what they say about those things not being good for one's longevity makes an impression on me also. So I did quit coffee and I did quit smoking. But I haven't managed that with drinking!

Interviewer: So many poets are associated with alcohol and other kinds of excess.

Olds: There are some fine books and essays about that. Lewis Hyde has written about alcoholism and poets and the role that society gives its writers— encouraging them to die [laughs]. And Donald Hall has wonderful, sobering stories about many of these poets. But I don't think anyone believes anymore that drugs and alcohol are good for writing, do they? I'm probably so out of it at my age that I don't know what people think. But I think that exercise and as much good health as one can enjoy is the best thing for writing.

Interviewer: I was even more surprised to read that you don't take a newspaper or watch television.

Olds: It's true, but it's kind of a different issue. At one point I took on a new job, and I just didn't have time to do anything but work. [Olds was the director of the Graduate Creative Writing Program at NYU from 1989 to 1991.] So I figured that for a year, just for the first year of this job, I would not watch TV, I wouldn't read a newspaper, I wouldn't read a book, I wouldn't go hear any music, I wouldn't do any of that kind of thing. Just so I'd have enough time. I was very afraid that I wouldn't be able to do this job well. And the time never came back. But there are problems connected with this—with keeping informed about what's happening in the world. So I try to look at the front page whenever I'm walking by a newsstand. And people talk about what's happening, so I get a certain amount of information that way. It might be a bad thing, not to know what's going on in the world. I can't say I really approve of it. . . .

Interviewer: People who know your work well might be surprised to know that you have such a vigorous public life. Because your work is very focused and often kind of quiet. It's hard to imagine the narrator of one of your poems fending off multiple phone calls.

Olds: But don't you think that every single one of us is leading a harried life? We're all taking on too much, we're all asking too much of ourselves. We're all wishing we could do more, and therefore just doing more. So I don't think my life is different from anybody else's. Every poet I know—although there may be some I don't know who lead very different lives, who maybe live in the country and don't teach—tends to be just like the rest of us: just really busy, really overcommitted. We wouldn't necessarily see it in their poems. Because a poem is not written while running or while answering the phone. It's written in whatever minutes one has. Sometimes you have half an hour.

Interviewer: Can you write a poem in half an hour?

Olds: Forty-five minutes is much better [laughs] . . .

Interviewer: As accessible as your poetry can seem to be, there also seems to be an almost brutally direct emotional quality sometimes. There are some tough images.

Olds: I think that I am slowly improving in my ability to not be too melo-dramatic, to help the images have the right tenor. My first book came out when I was thirty-seven, so when I was finally able to speak as a writer my wish to not be silent was, in my early work, extreme. It's like someone, in baseball, who thinks that the ball is being thrown by a very strong arm from the outfield, and so she can't just land on home, she has to try to run way past it, practically into the dugout. Reading some of my earlier work, I get that sense of the need for too big a head of steam to be built up. It seems extreme to me at times, some of the imagery. That's part of why I'm not so sorry I'm a little behind in putting books together, because some of those rather crude images I can now maybe correct. It also might be that maybe I've used an image that is too mild, and I'll correct in the other direction. I don't want to imply that it's always going the other way. But my tendency was to be a little over the mark. And so I just really love now the possibility of getting it right.

Interviewer: Your new book contains several poems that are quite realistic in terms of their descriptions of sex. Is it difficult writing poetry about sex, not to fall into language that might seem clichéd?

Olds: I don't think that sex has been written about a lot in poetry. And I want to be able to write about any subject. There is a failure rate—there are subjects that are probably a lot harder to write about than others. I think that love is almost the hardest thing to write about. Not a general state of being in love, but a particular love for a particular person. Just one's taste for that one. And if you look at all the love poetry in our tradition, there isn't much that helps us know why that one. I'm just interested in human stuff like hate, love, sexual love, and sex. I don't see why not. It just seems to me if writers can assemble, in language, something that bears any relation to experience—espe-cially important experience, experience we care about, moving and powerful experience—then it is worth trying. The opportunities for offense and failure are always aplenty. They lie all around us.

MARGE PIERCY

Marge Piercy answered a question by interviewer Bill Moyers with this com-ment about one of the most distinctive features of a poet's craft.

Imagery Can't Really Be Taught   1999

I am an intensely curious person, nosy, insatiable, as a poet, everything you experience, whether personally or vicariously, or virtuously or virtually, for that matter, is your stuff. Imagery can't really be taught. You can lecture about the different kinds of imagery in different sorts of poems, but the truth is, imagery is the most personal core of a poet. The more you actually see— how carefully you look at an opossum or a wildflower or the way light strikes water or hair; the more you actually listen to the natural and manufactured sounds of our world; the more you know about what the shape of a bird's beak means about what it eats, or what the weeds growing in a field tell you about the soil and its history — then the more stuff you will have within you that will rise and suggest itself as imagery. You have to stay open and curious and keep learn-ing as you go. Poems come from a whole variety of sources. When you're younger, you believe in inspiration. As you get older, you believe most in receptivity and work.

EZRA POUND

Ezra Pound was one of the founders of the short-lived but influential move-ment called imagism, which stressed clarity and economy of language. In this 1918 statement, which was later published under the title "A Retrospect" in a 1954 col-lection of his literary essays, Pound describes the imagists' aims.

On the Principles of Imagism   1918

There has been so much scribbling about a new fashion in poetry, that I may perhaps be pardoned this brief recapitulation and retrospect.

In the spring or early summer of 1912, "H.D.," Richard Aldington, and myself decided that we were agreed upon the three principles following:

1. Direct treatment of the "thing" whether subjective or objective.
2. To use absolutely no word that does not contribute to the presentation.
3. As regarding rhythm: to compose in the sequence of the musical phrase, not in sequence of a metronome.

Upon many points of taste and of predilection we differed, but agreeing upon these three positions we thought we had as much right to a group name, at least as much right, as a number of French "schools" proclaimed by Mr Flint in the August number of Harold Monro's magazine for 1911.

This school has since been "joined" or "followed" by numerous people who, whatever their merits, do not show any signs of agreeing with the second specification. Indeed *vers libre* has become as prolix and as verbose as any of the flaccid varieties that preceded it. It has brought faults of its own. The actual language and phrasing is often as bad as that of our elders without even the excuse that the words are shovelled in to fill a metric pattern or to complete the noise of a rhyme-sound. Whether or no the phrases followed by the followers are musical must be left to the reader's decision. At times I can find a marked metre in "vers libres," as stale and hackneyed as any pseudo-Swinburnian,° at times the writers seem to follow no musical structure whatever. But it is, on the

---

pseudo-Swinburnian: I.e., one who mimics the work of Algernon Charles Swinburne (1837–1909), the English poet whose poetry was noted for its romantic exaggeration.

whole, good that the field should be ploughed. Perhaps a few good poems have come from the new method, and if so it is justified.

Criticism is not a circumscription or a set of prohibitions. It provides fixed points of departure. It may startle a dull reader into alertness. That little of it which is good is mostly in stray phrases; or if it be an older artist helping a younger it is in great measure but rules of thumb, cautions gained by experience.

I set together a few phrases on practical working about the time the first remarks on imagism were published. The first use of the word "Imagiste" was in my note to T. E. Hulme's five poems, printed at the end of my "Ripostes" in the autumn of 1912. I reprint my cautions from *Poetry* for March, 1913.

A FEW DON'TS

An "Image" is that which presents an intellectual and emotional complex in an instant of time. I use the term "complex" rather in the technical sense employed by the newer psychologists, such as Hart, though we might not agree absolutely in our application.

It is the presentation of such a "complex" instantaneously which gives that sense of sudden liberation; that sense of freedom from time limits and space limits; that sense of sudden growth, which we experience in the presence of the greatest works of art.

It is better to present one Image in a lifetime than to produce voluminous works.

All this, however, some may consider open to debate. The immediate necessity is to tabulate A LIST OF DON'TS for those beginning to write verses. I can not put all of them into Mosaic negative.

To begin with, consider the three propositions (demanding direct treatment, economy of words, and the sequence of the musical phrase), not as dogma—never consider anything as dogma—but as the result of long contemplation, which, even if it is some one else's contemplation, may be worth consideration.

Pay no attention to the criticism of men who have never themselves written a notable work. Consider the discrepancies between the actual writing of the Greek poets and dramatists, and the theories of the Graeco-Roman grammarians, concocted to explain their metres.

LANGUAGE

Use no superfluous word, no adjective which does not reveal something.

Don't use such an expression as "dim lands *of peace.*" It dulls the image. It mixes an abstraction with the concrete. It comes from the writer's not realizing that the natural object is always the *adequate* symbol.

Go in fear of abstractions. Do not retell in mediocre verse what has already been done in good prose. Don't think any intelligent person is going to be deceived when you try to shirk all the difficulties of the unspeakably difficult art of good prose by chopping your composition into line lengths.

What the expert is tired of today the public will be tired of to-morrow.

Don't imagine that the art of poetry is any simpler than the art of music, or that you can please the expert before you have spent at least as much effort on the art of verse as the average piano teacher spends on the art of music.

Be influenced by as many great artists as you can, but have the decency either to acknowledge the debt outright, or to try to conceal it.

Don't allow "influence" to mean merely that you mop up the particular decorative vocabulary of some one or two poets whom you happen to admire. A Turkish war correspondent was recently caught red-handed babbling in his despatches of "dove-grey" hills, or else it was "pearl-pale," I can not remember.

Use either no ornament or good ornament.

RHYTHM AND RHYME

Let the candidate fill his mind with the finest cadences he can discover, preferably in a foreign language,[1] so that the meaning of the words may be less likely to divert his attention from the movement; e.g. Saxon charms, Hebridean Folk Songs, the verse of Dante, and the lyrics of Shakespeare—if he can dissociate the vocabulary from the cadence. Let him dissect the lyrics of Goethe coldly into their component sound values, syllables long and short, stressed and unstressed, into vowels and consonants.

It is not necessary that a poem should rely on its music, but if it does rely on its music that music must be such as will delight the expert.

Let the neophyte know assonance and alliteration, rhyme immediate and delayed, simple and polyphonic, as a musician would expect to know harmony and counterpoint and all the minutiae of his craft. No time is too great to give to these matters or to any one of them, even if the artist seldom have need of them.

Don't imagine that a thing will "go" in verse just because it's too dull to go in prose.

Don't be "viewy"—leave that to the writers of pretty little philosophic essays. Don't be descriptive; remember that the painter can describe a landscape much better than you can, and that he has to know a deal more about it.

When Shakespeare talks of the "Dawn in russet mantle clad" he presents something which the painter does not present. There is in this line of his nothing that one can call description; he presents.

Consider the way of the scientists rather than the way of an advertising agent for a new soap.

The scientist does not expect to be acclaimed as a great scientist until he has *discovered* something. He begins by learning what has been discovered already. He goes from that point onward. He does not bank on being a charming fellow personally. He does not expect his friends to applaud the results of his freshman class work. Freshmen in poetry are unfortunately not confined to a definite and recognizable class room. They are "all over the shop." Is it any wonder "the public is indifferent to poetry"?

---

[1] This is for rhythm, his vocabulary must of course be found in his native tongue. [Pound's note]

Don't chop your stuff into separate *iambs*. Don't make each line stop dead at the end, and then begin every next line with a heave. Let the beginning of the next line catch the rise of the rhythm wave, unless you want a definite longish pause.

In short, behave as a musician, a good musician, when dealing with that phase of your art which has exact parallels in music. The same laws govern, and you are bound by no others.

Ezra Pound wrote this essay on Walt Whitman in 1909, only a year after he had left the United States to live permanently in Europe.

What I Feel about Walt Whitman   1909

From this side of the Atlantic I am for the first time able to read Whitman, and from the vantage of my education and — if it be permitted a man of my scant years — my world citizenship: I see him America's poet. The only Poet before the artists of the Carmen-Hovey° period, or better, the only one of the conventionally recognised "American Poets" who is worth reading.

He *is* America. His crudity is an exceeding great stench, but it *is* America. He is the hollow place in the rock that echoes with his time. He *does* "chant the crucial stage" and he is the "voice triumphant." He is disgusting. He is an exceedingly nauseating pill, but he accomplishes his mission.

Entirely free from the renaissance humanist ideal of the complete man or from the Greek idealism, he is content to be what he is, and he is his time and his people. He is a genius because he has vision of what he is and of his function. He knows that he is a beginning and not a classically finished work.

I honour him for he prophesied me while I can only recognise him as a forebear of whom I ought to be proud.

In America there is much for the healing of the nations, but woe unto him of the cultured palate who attempts the dose.

As for Whitman, I read him (in many parts) with acute pain, but when I write of certain things I find myself using his rhythms. The expression of certain things related to cosmic consciousness seems tainted with this maramis.°

I am (in common with every educated man) an heir of the ages and I demand my birthright. Yet if Whitman represented his time in language acceptable to one accustomed to my standard of intellectual-artistic living he would belie his time and nation. And yet I am but one of his "ages and ages' encrustations" or to be exact an encrustation of the next age. The vital part of my message, taken from the sap and fibre of America, is the same as his.

Carmen-Hovey: Canadian poet William Bliss Carman (1861–1929) and American poet Richard Hovey (1864–1900) collaborated on three books of verse in their *Songs of Vagabondia* series (1894, 1896, 1901).   **maramis:** Likely "marasmus," wasting away.

Mentally I am a Walt Whitman who has learned to wear a collar and a dress shirt (although at times inimical to both). Personally I might be very glad to conceal my relationship to my spiritual father and brag about my more congenial ancestry—Dante, Shakespeare, Theocritus, Villon, but the descent is a bit difficult to establish. And, to be frank, Whitman is to my fatherland (*Patriam quam odi et amo°* for no uncertain reasons) what Dante is to Italy and I at my best can only be a strife for a renaissance in America of all the lost or temporarily mislaid beauty, truth, valour, glory of Greece, Italy, England, and all the rest of it.

And yet if a man has written lines like Whitman's to *Sunset Breeze* one has to love him. I think we have not yet paid enough attention to the deliberate artistry of the man, not in details but in the large.

I am immortal even as he is, yet with a lesser vitality as I am the more in love with beauty (If I really do love it more than he did). Like Dante he wrote in the "vulgar tongue," in a new metric. The first great man to write in the language of his people.

Et ego Petrarca in lingua vetera scribo,° and in a tongue my people understand not.

It seems to me I should like to drive Whitman into the old world. I sledge, he drill—and to scourge America with all the old beauty. (For Beauty *is* an accusation) and with a thousand thongs from Homer to Yeats, from Theocritus to Marcel Schwob. This desire is because I am young and impatient, were I old and wise I should content myself in seeing and saying that these things will come. But now, since I am by no means sure it would be true prophecy, I am fain set my own hand to the labour.

It is a great thing, reading a man to know, not "His Tricks are not as yet my Tricks, but I can easily make them mine" but "His message is my message. We will see that men hear it."

PERCY BYSSHE SHELLEY

Percy Bysshe Shelley's lyrical, impassioned defense of the poet and his art is an expression of the romantic attitude toward art and literature. In part, Shelley is defending poetry against Plato's idea that poets should be banished from the ideal city, but he is also presenting the poet and the artist as an individual who should be free of the society's constrictions.

From "A Defence of Poetry"   1821

A poem is the very image of life expressed in its eternal truth. There is this difference between a story and a poem, that a story is a catalogue of

---

Patriam quam odi et amo: Latin for "Country that I hate and love." *Et ego Petrarca in lingua vetera scribo:* "And I, Petrarca, write in the old language." The Italian poet and scholar Francesco Petrarca (1304–1374) chose to write in Latin rather than Italian.

detached facts, which have no other bond of connexion than time, place, circumstance, cause and effect; the other is the creation of actions according to the
unchangeable forms of human nature, as existing in the mind of the creator,
which is itself the image of all other minds. The one is partial, and applies only
to a definite period of time, and a certain combination of events which can
never again recur; the other is universal, and contains within itself the germ of a
relation to whatever motives or actions have place in the possible varieties of
human nature. Time, which destroys the beauty and the use of the story of particular facts, stript of the poetry which should invest them, augments that of
Poetry, and for ever develops new and wonderful applications of the eternal
truth which it contains. Hence epitomes have been called the moths of just history; they eat out the poetry of it. The story of particular facts is as a mirror
which obscures and distorts that which should be beautiful: Poetry is a mirror
which makes beautiful that which is distorted.

The parts of a composition may be poetical, without the composition as a
whole being a poem. A single sentence may be considered as a whole though it
be found in a series of unassimilated portions; a single word even may be a
spark of inextinguishable thought. And thus all the great historians, Herodotus, Plutarch, Livy, were poets; and although the plan of these writers, especially that of Livy, restrained them from developing this faculty in its highest
degree, they make copious and ample amends for their subjection, by filling all
the interstices of their subjects with living images.

Having determined what is poetry, and who are poets, let us proceed to
estimate its effects upon society.

Poetry is ever accompanied with pleasure: all spirits on which it falls,
open themselves to receive the wisdom which is mingled with its delight. In the
infancy of the world, neither poets themselves nor their auditors are fully aware
of the excellence of poetry: for it acts in a divine and unapprehended manner,
beyond and above consciousness; and it is reserved for future generations to
contemplate and measure the mighty cause and effect in all the strength and
splendour of their union. Even in modern times, no living poet ever arrived at
the fulness of his fame; the jury which sits in judgement upon a poet, belonging
as he does to all time, must be composed of his peers: it must be impanelled by
Time from the selectest of the wise of many generations. A Poet is a nightingale, who sits in darkness and sings to cheer its own solitude with sweet sounds;
his auditors are as men entranced by the melody of an unseen musician, who
feel that they are moved and softened, yet know not whence or why. The poems
of Homer and his contemporaries were the delight of infant Greece; they were
the elements of that social system which is the column upon which all succeeding civilization has reposed. Homer embodied the ideal perfection of his age in
human character; nor can we doubt that those who read his verses were awakened to an ambition of becoming like to Achilles, Hector and Ulysses: the truth
and beauty of friendship, patriotism and persevering devotion to an object,
were unveiled to the depths in these immortal creations: the sentiments of the
auditors must have been refined and enlarged by a sympathy with such great
and lovely impersonations, until from admiring they imitated, and from imitation they identified themselves with the objects of their admiration. Nor let it

be objected, that these characters are remote from moral perfection, and that they can by no means be considered as edifying patterns for general imitation. Every epoch under names more or less specious has deified its peculiar errors; Revenge is the naked Idol of the worship of a semi-barbarous age; and Self-deceit is the veiled Image of unknown evil before which luxury and satiety lie prostrate. But a poet considers the vices of his contemporaries as the temporary dress in which his creations must be arrayed, and which cover without concealing the eternal proportions of their beauty. An epic or dramatic personage is understood to wear them around his soul, as he may the antient armour or the modern uniform around his body; whilst it is easy to conceive a dress more graceful than either. The beauty of the internal nature cannot be so far concealed by its accidental vesture, but that the spirit of its form shall communicate itself to the very disguise, and indicate the shape it hides from the manner in which it is worn. A majestic form and graceful motions will express themselves through the most barbarous and tasteless costume. Few poets of the highest class have chosen to exhibit the beauty of their conceptions in its naked truth and splendour; and it is doubtful whether the alloy of costume, habit, etc., be not necessary to temper this planetary music for mortal ears. . . .

Poetry is indeed something divine. It is at once the centre and circumference of knowledge; it is that which comprehends all science, and that to which all science must be referred. It is at the same time the root and blossom of all other systems of thought; it is that from which all spring, and that which adorns all; and that which, if blighted, denies the fruit and the seed, and withholds from the barren world the nourishment and the succession of the scions of the tree of life. It is the perfect and consummate surface and bloom of things; it is as the odour and the colour of the rose to the texture of the elements which compose it, as the form and the splendour of unfaded beauty to the secrets of anatomy and corruption. What were Virtue, Love, Patriotism, Friendship etc.—what were the scenery of this beautiful Universe which we inhabit—what were our consolations on this side of the grave—and what were our aspirations beyond it—if Poetry did not ascend to bring light and fire from those eternal regions where the owl-winged faculty of calculation dare not ever soar? Poetry is not like reasoning, a power to be exerted according to the determination of the will. A man cannot say, "I will compose poetry." The greatest poet even cannot say it: for the mind in creation is as a fading coal which some invisible influence, like an inconstant wind, awakens to transitory brightness: this power arises from within, like the colour of a flower which fades and changes as it is developed, and the conscious portions of our natures are unprophetic either of its approach or its departure. Could this influence be durable in its original purity and force, it is impossible to predict the greatness of the results; but when composition begins, inspiration is already on the decline, and the most glorious poetry that has ever been communicated to the world is probably a feeble shadow of the original conception of the poet. I appeal to the greatest Poets of the present day, whether it be not an error to assert that the finest passages of poetry are produced by labour and study. The toil and the delay recommended by critics can be justly interpreted to mean no more than a careful observation of the inspired moments, and an artificial connexion of the spaces between their suggestions by the intertexture of conventional expressions; a necessity only imposed by the limitedness of the poetical faculty itself. For Milton conceived the Paradise Lost as a whole before he executed it in portions. We have his own authority also for the Muse having "dictated" to him the "unpremeditated song," and let this be an answer to those who would allege the fifty-six various readings of the first line of the Orlando Furioso. Compositions so produced are to poetry what mosaic is to painting. This instinct and intuition of the poetical faculty is still more observable in the plastic and pictorial arts: a great statue or picture grows under the power of the artist as a child in the mother's womb; and the very mind which directs the hands in formation is incapable of accounting to itself for the origin, the gradations, or the media of the process.

Poetry is the record of the best and happiest moments of the happiest and best minds. We are aware of evanescent visitations of thought and feeling sometimes associated with place or person, sometimes regarding our own mind alone, and always arising unforeseen and departing unbidden, but elevating and delightful beyond all expression: so that even in the desire and the regret they leave, there cannot but be pleasure, participating as it does in the nature of its object. It is as it were the interpenetration of a diviner nature through our own; but its footsteps are like those of a wind over a sea, where the coming calm erases, and whose traces remain only as on the wrinkled sand which paves it. These and corresponding conditions of being are experienced principally by those of the most delicate sensibility and the most enlarged imagination; and the state of mind produced by them is at war with every base desire. The enthusiasm of virtue, love, patriotism, and friendship is essentially linked with these emotions; and whilst they last, self appears as what it is, an atom to a Universe. Poets are not only subject to these experiences as spirits of the most refined organization, but they can colour all that they combine with the evanescent hues of this etherial world; a word, or a trait in the representation of a sense or a passion, will touch the enchanted chord, and reanimate, in those who have ever experienced these emotions, the sleeping, the cold, the buried image of the past. Poetry thus makes immortal all that is best and most beautiful in the world; it arrests the vanishing apparitions which haunt the interlunations of life, and veiling them or in language or in form sends them forth among mankind, bearing sweet news of kindred joy to those with whom their sisters abide—abide, because there is no portal of expression from the caverns of the spirit which they inhabit into the universe of things. Poetry redeems from decay the visitations of the divinity in man.

Poetry turns all things to loveliness; it exalts the beauty of that which is most beautiful, and it adds beauty to that which is most deformed; it marries exultation and horror, grief and pleasure, eternity and change; it subdues to union under its light yoke all irreconcilable things. It transmutes all that it touches, and every form moving within the radiance of its presence is changed by wondrous sympathy to an incarnation of the spirit which it breathes; its secret alchemy turns to potable gold the poisonous waters which flow from death through life; it strips the veil of familiarity from the world, and lays bare the naked and sleeping beauty which is the spirit of its forms. . . .

. . . The most unfailing herald, companion, and follower of the awakening of a great people to work a beneficial change in opinion or institution, is Poetry. At such periods there is an accumulation of the power of communicating and receiving intense and impassioned conceptions respecting man and nature. The persons in whom this power resides, may often, as far as regards many portions of their nature, have little apparent correspondence with that spirit of good of which they are the ministers. But even whilst they deny and abjure, they are yet compelled to serve, the Power which is seated upon the throne of their own soul. It is impossible to read the compositions of the most celebrated writers of the present day without being startled with the electric life which burns within their words. They measure the circumference and sound the depths of human nature with a comprehensive and all-penetrating spirit, and they are themselves perhaps the most sincerely astonished at its manifestations, for it is less their spirit than the spirit of the age. Poets are the hierophants of an unapprehended inspiration, the mirrors of the gigantic shadows which futurity casts upon the present, the words which express what they understand not; the trumpets which sing to battle, and feel not what they inspire: the influence which is moved not, but moves. Poets are the unacknowledged legislators of the World.

WILLIAM WORDSWORTH

William Wordsworth wrote two introductions to the collection of poems titled Lyrical Ballads. *This is the second introduction, to the edition of 1802, which expanded and explained ideas that he had presented in the introduction to the first edition of the work in 1798.*

From the Introduction to
Lyrical Ballads

1802

It is supposed, that by the act of writing in verse an author makes a formal engagement that he will gratify certain known habits of association; that he not only thus apprizes the reader that certain classes of ideas and expressions will be found in his book, but that others will be carefully excluded. This exponent or symbol held forth by metrical language must in different eras of literature have excited very different expectations: for example, in the age of Catullus, Terence, and Lucretius and that of Statius or Claudian,° and in our own country, in the age of Shakespeare and Beaumont and Fletcher, and that of Donne and Cowley, or Dryden, or Pope. I will not take upon me to determine the exact import of the promise which by the act of writing in verse an author, in the

---

Catullus . . . Claudian: Catullus (84–54 B.C.), Terence (186–159 B.C.), and Lucretius (96–55 B.C.) were Roman poets who wrote simply, in contrast to Statius (45–96) and Claudian (370?–410?), whose work was more elaborate.

present day, makes to his reader; but I am certain, it will appear to many persons that I have not fulfilled the terms of an engagement thus voluntarily contracted. They who have been accustomed to the gaudiness and inane phraseology of many modern writers, if they persist in reading this book to its conclusion, will, no doubt, frequently have to struggle with feelings of strangeness and awkwardness: they will look round for poetry, and will be induced to inquire by what species of courtesy these attempts can be permitted to assume that title. I hope therefore the reader will not censure me, if I attempt to state what I have proposed to myself to perform; and also (as far as the limits of a preface will permit) to explain some of the chief reasons which have determined me in the choice of my purpose: that at least he may be spared any unpleasant feeling of disappointment, and that I myself may be protected from the most dishonorable accusation which can be brought against an author, namely, that of an indolence which prevents him from endeavouring to ascertain what is his duty, or, when this duty is ascertained, prevents him from performing it.

The principal object, then, which I proposed to myself in these poems was to choose incidents and situations from common life, and to relate or describe them, throughout, as far as was possible, in a selection of language really used by men; and, at the same time, to throw over them a certain colouring of imagination, whereby ordinary things should be presented to the mind in an unusual way; and, further, and above all, to make these incidents and situations interesting by tracing in them, truly though not ostentatiously, the primary laws of our nature: chiefly, as far as regards the manner in which we associate ideas in a state of excitement. Low and rustic life was generally chosen, because in that condition, the essential passions of the heart find a better soil in which they can attain their maturity, are less under restraint, and speak a plainer and more emphatic language; because in that condition of life our elementary feelings co-exist in a state of greater simplicity, and, consequently, may be more accurately contemplated, and more forcibly communicated; because the manners of rural life germinate from those elementary feelings; and, from the necessary character of rural occupations, are more easily comprehended; and are more durable; and lastly, because in that condition the passions of men are incorporated with the beautiful and permanent forms of nature. The language, too, of these men is adopted (purified indeed from what appear to be its real defects, from all lasting and rational causes of dislike or disgust) because such men hourly communicate with the best objects from which the best part of language is originally derived; and because, from their rank in society and the sameness and narrow circle of their intercourse, being less under the influence of social vanity they convey their feelings and notions in simple and unelaborated expressions. Accordingly, such a language, arising out of repeated experience and regular feelings, is a more permanent, and a far more philosophical language, than that which is frequently substituted for it by poets, who think that they are conferring honour upon themselves and their art, in proportion as they separate themselves from the sympathies of men, and indulge in arbitrary and capricious habits of expression, in order to furnish food for fickle tastes, and fickle appetites, of their own creation.

I cannot, however, be insensible of the present outcry against the triviality and meanness both of thought and language, which some of my contemporaries have occasionally introduced into their metrical compositions; and I acknowledge, that this defect, where it exists, is more dishonorable to the writer's own character than false refinement or arbitrary innovation, though I should contend at the same time that it is far less pernicious in the sum of its consequences. From such verses the poems in these volumes will be found distinguished at least by one mark of difference, that each of them has a worthy *purpose*. Not that I mean to say, that I always began to write with a distinct purpose formally conceived; but I believe that my habits of meditation have so formed my feelings, as that my descriptions of such objects as strongly excite those feelings, will be found to carry along with them a *purpose*. If in this opinion I am mistaken, I can have little right to the name of a poet. For all good poetry is the spontaneous overflow of powerful feelings: but though this be true, poems to which any value can be attached, were never produced on any variety of subjects but by a man who, being possessed of more than usual organic sensibility, had also thought long and deeply. For our continued influxes of feeling are modified and directed by our thoughts, which are indeed the representatives of all our past feelings; and, as by contemplating the relation of these general representatives to each other we discover what is really important to men, so, by the repetition and continuance of this act, our feelings will be connected with important subjects, till at length, if we be originally possessed of much sensibility, such habits of mind will be produced, that, by obeying blindly and mechanically the impulses of those habits, we shall describe objects, and utter sentiments, of such a nature and in such connection with each other, that the understanding of the being to whom we address ourselves, if he be in a healthful state of association, must necessarily be in some degree enlightened, and his affections ameliorated. . . .

I have said that poetry is the spontaneous overflow of powerful feelings: it takes its origin from emotion recollected in tranquillity: the emotion is contemplated till by a species of reaction the tranquillity gradually disappears, and an emotion, kindred to that which was before the subject of contemplation, is gradually produced, and does itself actually exist in the mind. In this mood successful composition generally begins, and in a mood similar to this it is carried on; but the emotion, of whatever kind and in whatever degree, from various causes is qualified by various pleasures, so that in describing any passions whatsoever, which are voluntarily described, the mind will upon the whole be in a state of enjoyment. Now, if nature be thus cautious in preserving in a state of enjoyment a being thus employed, the poet ought to profit by the lesson thus held forth to him, and ought especially to take care, that whatever passions he communicates to his reader, those passions, if his reader's mind be sound and vigorous, should always be accompanied with an overbalance of pleasure. Now the music of harmonious metrical language, the sense of difficulty overcome, and the blind association of pleasure which has been previously received from works of rhyme or metre of the same or similar construction, an indistinct perception perpetually renewed of language closely resembling that of real life, and yet, in the circumstance of metre, differing from it so widely, all these imperceptibly make up a complex feeling of delight, which is of the most important use in tempering the painful feeling which will always be found intermingled with powerful descriptions of the deeper passions. This effect is always produced in pathetic and impassioned poetry; while, in lighter compositions, the ease and gracefulness with which the poet manages his numbers are themselves confessedly a principal source of the gratification of the reader. I might perhaps include all which it is *necessary* to say upon this subject by affirming, what few persons will deny, that, of two descriptions, either of passions, manners, or characters, each of them equally well executed, the one in prose and the other in verse, the verse will be read a hundred times where the prose is read once.

17.

Conversations on Poetry and Poets

EMILY DICKINSON

LANGSTON HUGHES

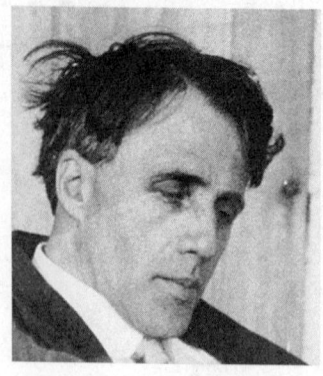

ROBERT FROST

Conversations on Interpreting Emily Dickinson

*This section on Emily Dickinson opens with material from her most impor-
tant editors. Thomas Wentworth Higginson was approached by her in 1862 as a
possible mentor and advisor for her writing, but Higginson found her as evasive
and puzzling as she was fascinating. Higginson's description of their meeting is the
only one we have of Dickinson by a contemporary who was involved in the world of
literature and publishing. Following Higginson's selection is one from Thomas H.
Johnson, who edited the manuscripts for the first collected edition of her poetry in
1955. The dismissive remarks by a poet who was a contemporary of Dickinson's,
Thomas Bailey Aldrich, reflect some of the confusion that greeted the appearance
of the first collection of her work. Commentaries by three poets of our day follow.
Richard Wilbur discusses some of the emotions he detects behind the brilliant surfaces
of Dickinson's poetry. Then Linda Gregg, a California poet who first encountered*

A seventeen-year-old Emily Dickinson in a daguerreotype, the only authenticated likeness of
her. (Reprinted by permission of the Robert Frost Library, Amherst College.)

Dickinson's poetry when she was in grammar school, writes about Dickinson in an essay that introduced her own poetry in the anthology 19 New American Poets of the Golden Gate, *published in 1984. Finally, a poem by Galway Kinnell describes with dismay his encounter with a deconstructed Emily Dickinson in a modern classroom.*

THOMAS WENTWORTH HIGGINSON

Emily Dickinson's Letters   1891

On April 16, 1862, I took from the post office in Worcester, Mass., where I was then living, the following letter: —

MR. HIGGINSON, — Are you too deeply occupied to say if my verse is alive?

The mind is so near itself it cannot see distinctly, and I have none to ask.

Should you think it breathed, and had you the leisure to tell me, I should feel quick gratitude.

If I make the mistake, that you dared to tell me would give me sincerer honor toward you.

I inclose my name, asking you, if you please, sir, to tell me what is true?

That you will not betray me it is needless to ask, since honor is its own pawn.

The letter was postmarked "Amherst," and it was in a handwriting so peculiar that it seemed as if the writer might have taken her first lessons by studying the famous fossil bird-tracks in the museum of that college town. Yet it was not in the slightest degree illiterate, but cultivated, quaint, and wholly unique. Of punctuation there was little; she used chiefly dashes, and it has been thought better, in printing these letters, as with her poems, to give them the benefit in this respect of the ordinary usages; and so with her habit as to capitalization, as the printers call it, in which she followed the Old English and present German method of thus distinguishing every noun substantive. But the most curious thing about the letter was the total absence of a signature. It proved, however, that she had written her name on a card, and put it under the shelter of a smaller envelope inclosed in the larger; and even this name was written — as if the shy writer wished to recede as far as possible from view — in pencil, not in ink. The name was Emily Dickinson. Inclosed with the letter were four poems, two of which have been already printed, — "Safe in their alabaster chambers" and "I'll tell you how the sun rose," together with the two that here follow. The first comprises in its eight lines a truth so searching that it seems a condensed summary of the whole experience of a long life: —

> We play at paste
> Till qualified for pearl;
> Then drop the paste
> And deem ourself a fool.

The shapes, though, were similar
And our new hands
Learned gem-tactics,
Practicing sands.

Then came one which I have always classed among the most exquisite of her productions, with a singular felicity of phrase and an aerial lift that bears the ear upward with the bee it traces:—

The nearest dream recedes unrealized.
The heaven we chase,
Like the June bee
Before the schoolboy,
Invites the race,
Stoops to an easy clover,
Dips—evades—teases—deploys—
Then to the royal clouds
Lifts his light pinnace,
Heedless of the boy
Staring, bewildered, at the mocking sky

Homesick for steadfast honey,—
Ah! the bee flies not
Which brews that rare variety.

The impression of a wholly new and original poetic genius was as distinct on my mind at the first reading of these four poems as it is now, after thirty years of further knowledge; and with it came the problem never yet solved, what place ought to be assigned in literature to what is so remarkable, yet so elusive of criticism. The bee himself did not evade the schoolboy more than she evaded me; and even at this day I still stand somewhat bewildered, like the boy.

Circumstances, however, soon brought me in contact with an uncle of Emily Dickinson, a gentleman not now living; a prominent citizen of Worcester, a man of integrity and character, who shared her abruptness and impulsiveness but certainly not her poetic temperament, from which he was indeed singularly remote. He could tell but little of her, she being evidently an enigma to him, as to me. It is hard to tell what answer was made by me, under these circumstances, to this letter. It is probable that the adviser sought to gain time a little and find out with what strange creature he was dealing. I remember to have ventured on some criticism which she afterwards called "surgery," and on some questions, part of which she evaded, as will be seen, with a naïve skill such as the most experienced and worldly coquette might envy. Her second letter (received April 26, 1862), was as follows:—

Mr. Higginson,—Your kindness claimed earlier gratitude, but I was ill, and write to-day from my pillow.

Thank you for the surgery; it was not so painful as I supposed. I bring you others, as you ask, though they might not differ. While my thought is undressed, I can make the distinction; but when I put them in the gown, they look alike and numb.

You asked how old I was? I made no verse, but one or two, until this winter, sir.

I had a terror since September, I could tell to none; and so I sing, as the boy does of the burying ground, because I am afraid.

You inquire my books. For poets, I have Keats, and Mr. and Mrs. Browning. For prose, Mr. Ruskin, Sir Thomas Browne, and the Revelations. I went to school, but in your manner of the phrase had no education. When a little girl, I had a friend who taught me Immortality; but venturing too near, himself, he never returned. Soon after my tutor died, and for several years my lexicon was my only companion. Then I found one more, but he was not contented I be his scholar, so he left the land.

You ask of my companions. Hills, sir, and the sundown, and a dog large as myself, that my father bought me. They are better than beings because they know, but do not tell; and the noise in the pool at noon excels my piano.

I have a brother and sister; my mother does not care for thought, and father, too busy with his briefs to notice what we do. He buys me many books, but begs me not to read them, because he fears they joggle the mind. They are religious, except me, and address an eclipse, every morning, whom they call their "Father."

But I fear my story fatigues you. I would like to learn. Could you tell me how to grow, or is it unconveyed, like melody or witchcraft?

You speak of Mr. Whitman. I never read his book, but was told that it was disgraceful.

I read Miss Prescott's Circumstance, but it followed me in the dark, so I avoided her.

Two editors of journals came to my father's house this winter, and asked me for my mind, and when I asked them "why" they said I was penurious, and they would use it for the world.

I could not weigh myself, myself. My size felt small to me. I read your chapters in the Atlantic, and experienced honor for you. I was sure you would not reject a confiding question.

Is this, sir, what you asked me to tell you? Your friend,

E. DICKINSON.

It will be seen that she had now drawn a step nearer, signing her name, and as my "friend." It will also be noticed that I had sounded her about certain American authors, then much read; and that she knew how to put her own criticisms in a very trenchant way. With this letter came some more verses, still in the same birdlike script, as for instance the following:—

Your riches taught me poverty,
　　Myself a millionaire
In little wealths, as girls could boast,
　　Till, broad as Buenos Ayre,
You drifted your dominions
　　A different Peru,

And I esteemed all poverty
  For life's estate, with you.
Of mines, I little know, myself,
  But just the names of gems,
The colors of the commonest,
  And scarce of diadems
So much that, did I meet the queen
  Her glory I should know;
But this must be a different wealth,
  To miss it, beggars so.

I'm sure 't is India, all day,
  To those who look on you
Without a stint, without a blame,
  Might I but be the Jew!
I'm sure it is Golconda
  Beyond my power to deem,
To have a smile for mine, each day,
  How better than a gem!

At least, it solaces to know
  That there exists a gold
Although I prove it just in time
  Its distance to behold;
Its far, far treasure to surmise
  And estimate the pearl
That slipped my simple fingers through
  While just a girl at school!

Here was already manifest that defiance of form, never through carelessness, and never precisely from whimsy which so marked her. The slightest change in the order of words — the "While yet at school, a girl" — would have given her a rhyme for this last line but no; she was intent upon her thought and it would not have satisfied her to make the change. . . .

It is possible that in a second letter I gave more of distinct praise or encouragement, for her third is in a different mood. This was received June 8, 1862. There is something startling in its opening image: and in the yet stranger phrase that follows, where she apparently uses "mob" in the sense of chaos or bewilderment: —

DEAR FRIEND, — Your letter gave no drunkenness, because I tasted rum before. Domingo comes but once; yet I have had few pleasures so deep as your opinion, and if I tried to thank you, my tears would block my tongue.

My dying tutor told me that he would like to live till I had been a poet, but Death was much of mob as I could master, then. And when, far afterward, a sudden light on orchards, or a new fashion in the wind troubled my attention, I felt a palsy, here, the verses just relieve.

Your second letter surprised me, and for a moment, swung. I had not supposed it. Your first gave no dishonor, because the true are not ashamed. I thanked you for your justice, but could not drop the bells whose jingling cooled my tramp. Perhaps the balm seemed better, because you bled me first. I smile when you suggest that I delay "to publish," that being foreign to my thought as firmament to fin.

If fame belonged to me, I could not escape her; if she did not, the longest day would pass me on the chase, and the approbation of my dog would forsake me then. My barefoot rank is better.

You think my gait "spasmodic." I am in danger, sir. You think me "uncontrolled." I have no tribunal.

Would you have time to be the "friend" you should think I need? I have a little shape: it would not crowd your desk, nor make much racket as the mouse that dents your galleries.

If I might bring you what I do — not so frequent to trouble you — and ask you if I told it clear, 't would be control to me. The sailor cannot see the North, but knows the needle can. The "hand you stretch me in the dark" I put mine in, and turn away. I have no Saxon now: —

> As if I asked a common alms,
> And in my wondering hand
> A stranger pressed a kingdom,
> And I, bewildered, stand;
> As if I asked the Orient
> Had it for me a morn,
> And it should lift its purple dikes
> And shatter me with dawn!

But, will you be my preceptor, Mr. Higginson?

With this came the poem already published in her volume and entitled Renunciation; and also that beginning "Of all the sounds dispatched abroad," thus fixing approximately the date of those two. I must soon have written to ask her for her picture, that I might form some impression of my enigmatical correspondent. To this came the following reply, in July, 1862: —

Could you believe me without? I had no portrait, now, but am small, like the wren; and my hair is bold, like the chestnut bur; and my eyes, like the sherry in the glass, that the guest leaves. Would this do just as well?

It often alarms father. He says death might occur, and he has moulds of all the rest, but has no mould of me; but I noticed the quick wore off those things, in a few days, and forestall the dishonor. You will think no caprice of me.

You said "Dark." I know the butterfly, and the lizard, and the orchis. Are not those *your* countrymen?

I am happy to be your scholar, and will deserve the kindness I cannot repay.

If you truly consent, I recite now. Will you tell me my fault, frankly as to yourself, for I had rather wince than die. Men do not call the surgeon to commend the bone, but to set it, sir, and fracture within is more critical. And for this, preceptor, I shall bring you obedience, the blossom from my garden, and every gratitude I know.

Perhaps you smile at me. I could not stop for that. My business is circumference. An ignorance, not of customs, but if caught with the dawn, or the sunset see me, myself the only kangaroo among the beauty, sir, if you please, it afflicts me, and I thought that instruction would take it away.

Because you have much business, beside the growth of me, you will appoint, yourself, how often I shall come, without your inconvenience.

And if at any time you regret you received me, or I prove a different fabric to that you supposed, you must banish me.

When I state myself, as the representative of the verse, it does not mean me, but a supposed person.

You are true about the "perfection." To-day makes Yesterday mean.

You spoke of Pippa Passes. I never heard anybody speak of Pippa Passes before. You see my posture is benighted.

To thank you baffles me. Are you perfectly powerful? Had I a pleasure you had not, I could delight to bring it.

YOUR SCHOLAR. . . .

At last, after many postponements, on August 16, 1870, I found myself face to face with my hitherto unseen correspondent. It was at her father's house, one of those large, square, brick mansions so familiar in our older New England towns, surrounded by trees and blossoming shrubs without, and within exquisitely neat, cool, spacious, and fragrant with flowers. After a little delay, I heard an extremely faint and pattering footstep like that of a child, in the hall, and in glided, almost noiselessly, a plain, shy little person, the face without a single good feature, but with eyes, as she herself said, "like the sherry the guest leaves in the glass," and with smooth bands of reddish chestnut hair. She had a quaint and nun-like look, as if she might be a German canoness of some religious order, whose prescribed garb was white piqué, with a blue net worsted shawl. She came toward me with two day-lilies, which she put in a childlike way into my hand, saying softly, under her breath, "These are my introduction," and adding, also under her breath, in childlike fashion, "Forgive me if I am frightened; I never see strangers, and hardly know what I say." But soon she began to talk, and thenceforward continued almost constantly; pausing sometimes to beg that I would talk instead, but readily recommencing when I evaded. There was not a trace of affectation in all this; she seemed to speak absolutely for her own relief, and wholly without watching its effect on her hearer. Led on by me, she told much about her early life, in which her father was always the chief figure, —evidently a man of the old type, *la vielle roche* of Puritanism—a man who, as she said, read on Sunday "lonely and rigorous books"; and who had from childhood inspired her with such awe, that she never learned to tell time by the clock till she was fifteen, simply because he had tried to explain it to her when she was a little child, and she had been afraid to tell him that she did not understand, and also afraid to ask any one else lest he should hear of it. Yet she had never heard him speak a harsh word, and it needed only a glance at his photograph to see how truly the Puritan tradition was preserved in him. He did not wish his children, when little, to read any-thing but the Bible; and when, one day, her brother brought her home Longfel-low's Kavanagh, he put it secretly under the pianoforte cover, made signs to her, and they both afterwards read it. It may have been before this, however, that a student of her father's was amazed to find that she and her brother had never heard of Lydia Maria Child, then much read, and he brought Letters from New York, and hid it in the great bush of old-fashioned tree-box beside the front door. After the first book she thought in ecstasy, "This, then, is a book, and there are more of them." But she did not find so many as she expected, for she afterwards said to me, "When I lost the use of my eyes, it was a comfort to think that there were so few real books that I could easily find one to read me all of them." Afterwards, when she regained her eyes, she read Shakespeare, and thought to herself, "Why is any other book needed?"

She went on talking constantly and saying, in the midst of narrative, things quaint and aphoristic. "Is it oblivion or absorption when things pass from our minds?" "Truth is such a rare thing, it is delightful to tell it." "I find ecstacy in living; the mere sense of living is joy enough." When I asked her if she never felt any want of employment, not going off the grounds and rarely seeing a visitor, she answered, "I never thought of conceiving that I could ever have the slightest approach to such a want in all future time"; and then added, after a pause, "I feel that I have not expressed myself strongly enough," although it seemed to me that she had. She told me of her household occupa-tions, that she made all their bread, because her father liked only hers; then saying shyly, "And people must have puddings," this very timidly and sugges-tively, as if they were meteors or comets. Interspersed with these confidences came phrases so emphasized as to seem the very wantonness of over-statement, as if she pleased herself with putting into words what the most extravagant might possibly think without saying, as thus: "How do most people live with-out any thoughts? There are many people in the world, — you must have noticed them in the street, — how do they live? How do they get strength to put on their clothes in the morning?" Or this crowning extravaganza: "If I read a book and it makes my whole body so cold no fire can ever warm me, I know that is poetry. If I feel physically as if the top of my head were taken off, I know that is poetry. These are the only ways I know it. Is there any other way?"

I have tried to describe her just as she was, with the aid of notes taken at the time; but this interview left our relation very much what it was before; — on my side an interest that was strong and even affectionate, but not based on any thorough comprehension; and on her side a hope, always rather baffled, that I should afford some aid in solving her abstruse problem of life. . . .

When I said, at parting, that I would come again some time, she replied, "Say, in a long time; that will be nearer. Some time is no time."

THOMAS H. JOHNSON

The Text of Emily Dickinson's Poetry   1960

At the time of her death in 1886, Emily Dickinson left in manuscript a body of verse far more extensive than anyone imagined. Cared for by a servant, Emily and her sister Lavinia had been living together in the Amherst house built by their grandfather Dickinson, alone after their mother's death in 1882. On going through her sister's effects, Lavinia discovered a small box containing about 900 poems. These were the sixty little "volumes," as Lavinia called them, "tied together with twine," that constitute the packets. Determined that she must find a publisher for them, she persuaded Mabel Loomis Todd, the wife of an Amherst professor, to undertake the task of transcribing them. Mrs. Todd enlisted the aid of Thomas Wentworth Higginson, and together they made a selection of 115 poems for publication. But Colonel Higginson was apprehensive about the willingness of the public to accept the poems as they stood. Therefore in preparing copy for the printer he undertook to smooth rhymes, regularize the meter, delete provincialisms, and substitute "sensible" metaphors. Thus "folks" became "those," "heft" became "weight," and occasionally line arrangement was altered.

The publication of *Poems by Emily Dickinson* by Roberts Brothers of Boston nevertheless proved to be one of the literary events of 1890, and the reception of the slender volume encouraged the editors to select 166 more verses, issued a year later as *Poems, Second Series*. These likewise were warmly received. In 1896 Mrs. Todd alone edited *Poems, Third Series*, bringing the total number published to 449, and together with 102 additional poems and parts of poems included in Mrs. Todd's edition of *Letters of Emily Dickinson* (1894), they constituted the Dickinson canon until 1914, when Emily Dickinson's niece and literary heir, Martha Dickinson Bianchi, issued *The Single Hound*.

By now the public had come to appreciate the quality of Dickinson's originalities, and alterations in the text of *The Single Hound* are refreshingly few. But Mrs. Bianchi sometimes had trouble reading the manuscripts, and on occasion words or phrases were misread, in that volume and in the two later ones which completed publication of all the verses in Mrs. Bianchi's possession: *Further Poems* (1929) and *Unpublished Poems* (1935). The appearance of *Bolts of Melody* (1945), from texts prepared by Mrs. Todd and her daughter, Millicent Todd Bingham, virtually completed publication of all the Dickinson poetry, and marked a new era in textual fidelity. It presented 668 poems and fragments, deriving from transcripts made by Mrs. Todd, or from manuscripts which had remained among her papers.

Clearly the time had come to present the Dickinson poetry in an unreconstructed text with some degree of chronological arrangement, and that opportunity was presented in 1950 when ownership of Emily Dickinson's literary estate was transferred to Harvard University. Editing then began on the variorum text of *The Poems of Emily Dickinson*, which I prepared for the Belknap Press of Harvard University Press (3 vols., 1955), comprising a total of 1775 poems and fragments.

The text for this edition of *The Complete Poems of Emily Dickinson* reproduces solely and completely that of the 1955 variorum edition, but intended as a reading text, it selects but one form of each poem. Inevitably therefore one is forced to make some editorial decisions about a text which never was prepared by the author as copy for the printer. Rare instances exist, notably in the poem "Blazing in gold" (228), where no text can be called "final." That poem describes a sunset which in one version stoops as low as "the kitchen window"; in another, as low as an "oriel windoe"; in a third, as low as "the Otter's Window." These copies were made over a period of five years from 1861 to 1866, and one text is apparently as "final" as another. The reader may make the choice.

Selection becomes mandatory for the semifinal drafts. Though by far the largest number of packet copies exist in but a single fair-copy version, several exist in semifinal form: those for which marginally the poet suggested an alternate reading for one word or more. In order to keep editorial construction to a bare minimum, I have followed the policy of adopting such suggestions only when they are underlined, presumably Emily Dickinson's method of indicating her own preference.

Rough drafts, of which there are relatively few, are allowed to stand as such, with no editorial tinkering.

I have silently corrected obvious misspelling (*witheld, visiter,* etc.), and misplaced apostrophes (*does'nt*). Punctuation and capitalization remain unaltered. Dickinson used dashes as a musical device, and though some may be elongated end stops, any "correction" would be gratuitous. Capitalization, though often capricious, is likewise untouched.

THOMAS BAILEY ALDRICH

Thomas Bailey Aldrich, at the time he wrote this slighting comment on Emily Dickinson, was one of America's best-known poets. Although he suggests in his final sentence that her work will soon be forgotten, the irony is that his own reputation has failed to survive into the present.

In Re Emily Dickinson   1892

The English critic who said of Miss Emily Dickinson that she might have become a fifth-rate poet "if she had only mastered the rudiments of grammar and gone into metrical training for about fifteen years," — the rather candid English critic who said this somewhat overstated his case. He had, however, a fairly good case. If Miss Dickinson had undergone the austere curriculum indicated, she would, I am sure, have become an admirable lyric poet of the second magnitude. In the first volume of her poetical chaos is a little poem which needs only slight revision in the initial stanza in order to make it worthy of ranking with some of the odd swallow flights in Heine's° lyrical *intermezzo*. I have ven-

---

Heine's: Heinrich Heine (1797–1856), German poet and critic.

tured to desecrate this stanza by tossing a rhyme into it, as the other stanzas happened to rhyme, and here print the lyric, hoping the reader will not accuse me of overvaluing it: —

I taste a liquor never brewed
In vats upon the Rhine;
No tankard ever held a draught
Of alcohol like mine.

Inebriate of air am I,
And debauchee of dew,
Reeling, through endless summer days,
From inns of molten blue.

When landlords turn the drunken bee
Out of the Foxglove's door,
When butterflies renounce their drams,
I shall but drink the more!

Till seraphs swing their snowy caps
And saints to windows run,
To see the little tippler
Leaning against the sun!

Certainly those inns of molten blue, and that disreputable honey-gatherer who got himself turned out-of-doors at the sign of the Foxglove, are very taking matters. I know of more important things that interest me less. There are three or four bits in this kind in Miss Dickinson's book; but for the most part the ideas totter and toddle, not having learned to walk. In spite of this, several of the quatrains are curiously touching, they have such a pathetic air of yearning to be poems.

It is plain that Miss Dickinson possessed an extremely unconventional and grotesque fancy. She was deeply tinged by the mysticism of Blake, and strongly influenced by the mannerism of Emerson. The very way she tied her bonnet-strings, preparatory to one of her nunlike walks in her claustral garden, must have been Emersonian. She had much fancy of a queer sort, but only, as it appears to me, intermittent flashes of imagination. I fail to detect in her work any of that profound thought which her editor professes to discover in it. The phenomenal insight, I am inclined to believe, exists only in his partiality; for whenever a woman poet is in question Mr. Higginson always puts on his rose-colored spectacles. This is being chivalrous; but the invariable result is not clear vision. That Miss Dickinson's whimsical memoranda have a certain something which, for want of a more precise name, we term *quality* is not to be denied except by the unconvertible heathen who are not worth conversion. But the incoherence and formlessness of her — I don't know how to designate them — versicles are fatal. Sydney Smith, or some other humorist, mentions a person whose bump of veneration was so inadequately developed as to permit him to damn the equator if he wanted to. This certainly established a precedent for independence; but an eccentric, dreamy, half-educated recluse in an out-of-the-way New England village (or anywhere else) cannot with impunity set at defiance the laws of gravitation and grammar. In his charming preface to

Miss Dickinson's collection, Mr. Higginson insidiously remarks: "After all, when a thought takes one's breath away, a lesson on grammar seems an impertinence." But an ungrammatical thought does not, as a general thing, take one's breath away, except in a sense the reverse of flattering. Touching this matter of mere technique Mr. Ruskin° has a word to say (it appears that he said it "in his earlier and better days"), and Mr. Higginson quotes it: "No weight, nor mass, nor beauty of execution can outweigh one grain or fragment of thought." This is a proposition to which one would cordially subscribe, if it were not so intemperately stated. A suggestive commentary on Mr. Ruskin's impressive dictum is furnished by the fact that Mr. Ruskin has lately published a volume of the most tedious verse that has been printed in this century. The substance of it is weighty enough, but the workmanship lacks just that touch which distinguishes the artist from the bungler, — the touch which Mr. Ruskin seems not to have much regarded either in his later or "in his earlier and better days."

If Miss Dickinson's *disjecta membra* are poems, then Shakespeare's prolonged imposition should be exposed without further loss of time, and Lord Tennyson ought to be advised of the error of his ways before it is too late. But I do not hold the situation to be so desperate. Miss Dickinson's versicles have a queerness and a quaintness that have stirred a momentary curiosity in emotional bosoms. Oblivion lingers in the immediate neighborhood.

RICHARD WILBUR

On Emily Dickinson   1963

Emily Dickinson never lets us forget for very long that in some respects life gave her short measure; and indeed it is possible to see the greater part of her poetry as an effort to cope with her sense of privation. I think that for her there were three major privations: she was deprived of an orthodox and steady religious faith; she was deprived of love; she was deprived of literary recognition.

At the age of seventeen, after a series of revival meetings at Mount Holyoke Seminary, Emily Dickinson found that she must refuse to become a professing Christian. To some modern minds this may seem to have been a sensible and necessary step; and surely it was a step toward becoming such a poet as she became. But for her, no pleasure in her own integrity could then eradicate the feeling that she had betrayed a deficiency, a want of grace. In her letters to Abiah Root she tells of the enhancing effect of conversion on her fellow-students, and says of herself in a famous passage:

> *I am one of the lingering bad ones, and so do I slink away, and pause and ponder, and ponder and pause, and do work without knowing why, not surely, for this brief world, and more sure it is not for heaven, and I*

Ruskin: John Ruskin (1819–1900), English essayist, critic, and reformer.

ask what this message *means* that they ask for so very eagerly: *you* know of this depth and fulness, will you try to tell me about it?

There is humor in that, and stubbornness, and a bit of characteristic lurking pride: but there is also an anguished sense of having separated herself, through some dry incapacity, from spiritual community, from purpose, and from magnitude of life. As a child of evangelical Amherst, she inevitably thought of purposive, heroic life as requiring a vigorous faith. Out of such a thought she later wrote:

> The abdication of Belief
> Makes the Behavior small —
> Better an ingis fatuus
> Than no illume at all — (1551)

That hers *was* a species of religious personality goes without saying; but by her refusal of such ideas as original sin, redemption, hell, and election, she made it impossible for herself — as Professor Whicher observed — "to share the religious life of her generation." She became an unsteady congregation of one.

Her second privation, the privation of love, is one with which her poems and her biographies have made us exceedingly familiar, though some biographical facts remain conjectural. She had the good fortune, at least once, to bestow her heart on another; but she seems to have found her life, in great part, a history of loneliness, separation, and bereavement.

As for literary fame, some will deny that Emily Dickinson ever greatly desired it, and certainly there is evidence, mostly from her latter years, to support such a view. She *did* write that "Publication is the auction / Of the mind of man." And she *did* say to Helen Hunt Jackson, "How can you print a piece of your soul?" But earlier, in 1861, she had frankly expressed to Sue Dickinson the hope that "sometime" she might make her kinfolk proud of her. The truth is, I think, that Emily Dickinson knew she was good, and began her career with a normal appetite for recognition. I think that she later came, with some reason, to despair of being understood or properly valued, and so directed against her hopes of fame what was by then a well-developed disposition to renounce. That she wrote a good number of poems about fame supports my view: the subjects to which a poet returns are those which vex him.

What did Emily Dickinson do, as a poet, with her sense of privation? One thing she quite often did was to pose as the laureate and attorney of the empty-handed, and question God about the economy of His creation. Why, she asked, is a fatherly God so sparing of His presence? Why is there never a sign that prayers are heard? Why does Nature tell us no comforting news of its Maker? Why do some receive a whole loaf, while others must starve on a crumb? Where is the benevolence in shipwreck and earthquake? By asking such questions as these, she turned complaint into critique, and used her own sufferings as experiential evidence about the nature of the deity. The God who emerges from these poems is a God who does not answer, an unrevealed God whom one cannot confidently approach through Nature or through doctrine.

But there was another way in which Emily Dickinson dealt with her sentiment of lack — another emotional strategy which was both more frequent and more fruitful. I refer to her repeated assertion of the paradox that privation is more plentiful than plenty; that to renounce is to possess the more; that "The Banquet of abstemiousness / Defaces that of wine." We all know how the poet illustrated this ascetic paradox in her behavior—how in her latter years she chose to live in relative retirement, keeping the world, even in its dearest aspects, at a physical remove. She would write her friends, telling them how she missed them, then flee upstairs when they came to see her; afterward, she might send a note of apology, offering the odd explanation that "We shun because we prize." Any reader of Dickinson biographies can furnish other examples, dramatic or homely, of this prizing and shunning, this yearning and renouncing: in my own mind's eye is a picture of Emily Dickinson watching a gay circus caravan from the distance of her chamber window.

LINDA GREGG

Not Understanding Emily Dickinson   1984

Emily Dickinson was the first poet I really read. I was in the fifth or sixth grade and she seemed such a secret thing to me that I always read her in bed. I remember clearly the amazement, respect, and something maybe like horror when I read her. I still react to her that way.

I felt then and feel now that she halts me at the border of her poetry while she uses the space beyond like a landscape with many birds in it feeding on the trees after snow has fallen and now it is morning and there is a steady small rain. I didn't understand that when I was little. She was different from those I knew. For me there has always been that something in her which wanted to remain separate. I have never felt let in. Not as I feel let in by [Theodore] Roethke or [D. H.] Lawrence or Sappho or Catullus or Shakespeare. I respect it. I do not wish to approach closer than she wishes. I think of how she would stand on the upstairs landing to listen when there were guests talking downstairs in the living room. Out of respect, I do not go up those stairs after her. She called her poems her letter to the world, not her meeting or her embrace. When I went to her grave, I kept wondering what she would want me to do. I listened to the silence between us of earth and air, and of time, and to the natural silence around us. I listened for her there, and what she gave me was that silence and that distance. I accepted it gratefully, as a gift. And stayed still to be more closely where she was. I did not touch the stone.

There are still a lot of things I don't understand. The wind that seems to be in her poetry, for example. Is it her breath? I don't think so. There is very little natural breathing in her poems. I think it is something other than herself, something which halts her breath. I think she has let something like God's will into her poetry. It halts her, adds much, pushes her, even works against her feelings and body, yet is a great strength in her poems. It blows through and the words do not blow down. This doubleness in her work creates power.

One of the important ways of understanding the poetry of Emily Dickinson may be *not* understanding her. Not, at least, understanding her in the rational way. In the way we understand prose, for example. When I was a young girl, I often did not know what the poems meant. To be honest, that happened more than often. It happened almost all the time when I read her that I did not understand in the usual way. But I did understand nevertheless. Even now, I think many of her poems are successful without being understandable in a logical sense.

I want to be careful to make clear that I am not *against* understanding or explaining the poems. It gives me great pleasure when the poems suddenly yield themselves to me and become clear. I delight in people who help that to happen. I delight in the poetry whose meanings *are* clear, instantly. Lines like:

> There's a certain Slant of light
> Winter Afternoons —
> That oppresses, like the Heft
> Of Cathedral tunes —

For all of us who grew up in the country, there is a special pleasure when she speaks of a snake in the grass *wrinkling*. But one of the most important things about her poetry for the young girl I was *was* the other kind of poetry she wrote, the kind which made no logical sense to me but worked wonderfully. Lines like the ones which end that very poem about the wrinkling snake (called "A narrow fellow in the grass"):

> . . . never met this Fellow
> Attended, or alone
> Without a tighter breathing
> And Zero at the Bone —

I still don't know what "Zero at the Bone" means, not in a logical way, but it seems clear to me in another and equally important sense. This is also true for lines like:

> The deer attracts no further
> Than it resists the hound
> (979)

Or poem 690, which begins: "Victory comes late" and ends with the fine lines:

> God keep His oath to Sparrows
> Who of little Love know how to starve.

Sometimes whole poems have this quality for me, such as poem 512:

> The Soul has Bandaged moments —
> When too appalled to stir —
> She feels some ghastly Fright come up
> And stop to look at her —
>
> Salute her — with long fingers —
> Caress her freezing hair —
> Sip, Goblin, from the very lips
> The lover — hovered — o'er —
> Unworthy, that a thought so mean
> Accost a Theme — so — fair —

> The Soul has moments of Escape —
> When bursting all the doors —
> She dances like a Bomb, abroad,
> And swings upon the Hours,
>
> As do the Bee — delirious borne —
> Long Dungeoned from his Rose —
> Touch Liberty — then know no more,
> But Noon, and Paradise —
>
> The Soul's retaken moments —
> When, Felon led along,
> With shackles on the plumed feet,
> And staples, in the Song,
>
> The Horror welcomes her, again,
> These, are not brayed of Tongue —

This could be explained. I can glimpse bits of meaning in among the dazzle; but to tell the truth, I am content (in this poem) not to track the meaning down by those clues. I really don't care what the exact meaning is when she speaks of:

> The Soul's retaken moments —
> When, Felon led along,
> With shackles on the plumed feet,
> And staples, in the Song, . . .

I liked it even when I thought *plumed* was *plummed*. And I secretly hope *staples* means what we use it to mean now. Stapled Songs! It is a successful poem for me without the other kind of understanding. However, I'm not saying that I like to ride the energy, or the images. What I *am* trying to say is that there's an important way of getting to the *true* meaning which may elude analysis. I *do* understand what *the soul's bandaged moments means*. It *means* the soul's bandaged moments.

I am *not* choosing between understanding and not understanding in these poems. But I *am* trying to suggest that *sometimes* there is a legitimate way her poems communicate without needing to be decoded into logic. It is important to me and to my own work to remember that in even the greatest poetry there is often the other kind of meaning.

Anyhow, this was true for me when I read Emily Dickinson at the very beginning of my knowing about poetry. It helped me to know there is a magic at the center of poetry, a way of meaning that is different from logic. So that from the first I had the encouragement to trust my instinct in preferring metaphor to simile, image to abstractions, to trust the intuitive more than the rational in my poetry.

Of course, I am not saying this should be true for all poets. Not even for all *her* poetry, but it has *always* been how I work. Or part of how I work. And it is so partly because of Emily Dickinson. She taught me there is a difficult, hard-to-understand, hard-to-translate, hard-to-write-about-or-explain place. I knew I had that in me also. But at the same time, I learned that the difficulty or obscurity in her poetry is not because she uses images to hide a secret. Rather, it is an attempt to say something that cannot be said in a simple or direct way.

One of the amazing things about Emily Dickinson for me, when I first read her and also now, is the presence of thought in her poetry which thinks like a poem does. I remember how as a child I could almost easily understand those thoughts without understanding. Or maybe I should say understanding it *before* understanding. I remember clearly saying at that early time: "then I will have to write my own poetry. A poetry of a kind I cannot understand in the same way I cannot understand *hers.*"

Understanding before understanding led me and led me toward what is magical in poetry. Maybe that is one of the most valuable things about the poetry of Emily Dickinson: to teach that there is something in poetry which cannot be handled, cannot be studied scientifically. Can only be approached, can only be honored. We can go up to the border. Can name what is there. Can know a lot. But we must remember that it is still country on the other side of the border and there are things there which we do not have good names for. We must remember there is a kind of safety in trusting the unknown. There are things beyond the border which are invisible, but if we are patient and listen hard, we can sometimes hear them.

GALWAY KINNELL

The Deconstruction of Emily Dickinson   1994

The lecture had ended when I came in,
and the professor was answering questions.
I do not know what he had been doing with her
poetry, but now he was speaking of her
as a victim of reluctant male publishers.   5
When the questions dwindled, I put up my hand.
I said the ignorant meddling of the Springfield *Daily Republican*
and the hidebound response of literary men,
and the gulf between the poetic wishfulness
then admired and her own harsh knowledge,   10
had let her see that her poems
would not be understood in her time;
and therefore, passionate to publish,
she vowed not to publish again. I said
I would recite a version of her vow,   15

    Publication—is the Auction
    Of the mind of Man—

But before I could, the professor broke in.
"Yes," he said, " 'the Auction'—'auction,' from *augere, auctum,* to
    augment, to author . . ."
"Let's hear the poem!" "The poem!" several women,   20
who at such a moment are more outspoken than men, shouted,
but I kept still and he kept going.

"In *auctum* the economy of the signifier is split, revealing an unconscious
    collusion in the bourgeois commodification of consciousness. While
    our author says 'no,' the unreified text says 'yes,' yes?"
He kissed his lips together and turned to me
saying, "Now, may we hear the poem?"   25
I waited a moment for full effect.
Without rising to my feet, I said,
"Professor, to understand Dickinson
it may not always be necessary to uproot her words.
Why not, first, try *listening* to her?   30
Loyalty forbids me to recite her poem now."
No, I didn't say that—I realized
she would want me to finish him off with one wallop.
So I said, "Professor, I thought you
would welcome the words of your author.   35
I see you prefer to hear yourself speak."
No, I held back—for I could hear her
urging me to put outrage into my voice
and substance into my argument.
I stood up so that everyone might see   40
the derision in my smile. "Professor," I said,
"you live in Amherst at the end of the twentieth century.
For you 'auction' means a quaint event
where somebody coaxes out the bids
on butter churns on a summer Saturday.   45
Forget etymology, this is history.
In Amherst in 1860 'auction' meant
the slave auction, you dope!"
Well, I didn't say that either,
although I have said them all,   50
many times, in the middle of the night.
In reality, I stood up and recited
like a schoolboy called upon in class.
My voice gradually weakened, and the women
who had called out for the poem   55
now looked as though they were thinking
of errands to be done on the way home.
When I finished, the professor smiled.
"Thank you. So, what at first some of us may have taken as a simple
    outcry, we all now see is an ambivalent, self-subversive text."
As people got up to go, I moved   60
into that sanctum within me where Emily
sometimes speaks a verse, and listened
for a sign of how she felt, such as,
"Thanks—Sweet—countryman—
for wanting—to Sing out—of Me—   65
after all that Humbug." But she was silent.

Conversations on Robert Frost's Poetics

This section on Robert Frost begins with a perceptive interview with the poet by Rose C. Feld that appeared in the New York Times Book Review in 1923. The next commentary is Frost's introduction to his Selected Poems of 1939; although he did not consider himself a critic, he did express opinions about his poetic methods in the introductions to his collections. Fellow poet Robert Lowell's sonnet suggests the more complicated reality behind the figure of the genial, wise New England bard Frost presented to his public. The Nobel Prize–winning poet Joseph Brodsky's discerning response to the profoundly American poetry of Frost is from the perspective of someone who grew up in the Soviet Union and moved to the United States as an adult. Finally, Philip L. Gerber looks at Frost's "After Apple-Picking" (p. 897) as an example of the poet's "honest duplicity," a characteristic he finds essential to all poetry.

Robert Frost at his writing desk. (Reprinted by permission of Dartmouth College Library.)

ROSE C. FELD

An Interview with Robert Frost   1923

Have you ever seen a sensitive child enter a dark room, fearful of the enveloping blackness, yet more than half ashamed of the fear? That is the way Robert Frost, poet, approached the interview arranged for him with the writer. He didn't want to come, he was half afraid of coming, and he was ashamed of the fear of meeting questions.

He was met at his publisher's office at the request of his friends there. "Come and get him, please," they said. "He is a shy person—a gentle and a sensitive person—and the idea of knocking at your doors, saying, 'Here I am, come to be interviewed,' will make him run and hide." The writer came and got him.

All the way down Fifth Avenue for ten or fifteen blocks he smiled often and talked rapidly to show that he was at ease and confident. But he was not. One could see the child telling itself not to be afraid.

Arrived at the house, he took the chair offered him and sat down rigidly. Still he smiled.

"Go ahead," he said. "Ask me the questions. Let's get at it."

"There are no questions—no specific questions. Suppose you just ramble on about American poetry, about poets, about men of the past and men of the present, about where we are drifting or where we are marching. Just talk."

He looked nonplused. The rigid smile gave way to one of relief and relaxation.

"You mean to say that you're not going to fire machine-gun questions at me and expect me to answer with skyrocketing repartee. Well, I wish I'd known. Well."

The brown hand opened up on the arms of the chair and the graying head leaned back. Robert Frost began to talk. He talked of some of the poets of the past, and in his quiet, gentle manner exploded the first bombshell. He exploded many others.

"One of the real American poets of yesterday," he said, "was Longfellow. No, I am not being sarcastic. I mean it. It is the fashion nowadays to make fun of him. I come across this pose and attitude with people I meet socially, with men and women I meet in the classrooms of colleges where I teach. They laugh at his gentleness, at his lack of worldliness, at his detachment from the world and the meaning thereof.

"When and where has it been written that a poet must be a club-swinging warrior, a teller of barroom tales, a participant of unspeakable experiences? That, today, apparently is the stamp of poetic integrity. I hear people speak of men who are writing today, and their eyes light up with a deep glow of satisfaction when they can mention some putrid bit of gossip about them. 'He writes such lovely things,' they say, and in the next breath add, half worshipfully, 'He lives such a terrible life.'

"I can't see it. I can't see that a man must needs have his feet plowing through unhealthy mud in order to appreciate more fully the glowing splendor of the clouds. I can't see that a man must fill his soul with sick and miserable experiences, self-imposed and self-inflicted, and greatly enjoyed, before he can sit down and write a lyric of strange and compelling beauty. Inspiration doesn't lie in the mud; it lies in the clean and wholesome life of the ordinary man.

"Maybe I am wrong. Maybe there is something wrong with me. Maybe I haven't the power to feel, to appreciate and live the extremes of dank living and beautiful inspiration.

"Men have told me, and perhaps they are right, that I have no 'straddle.' That is the term they use: I have no straddle. That means that I cannot spread out far enough to live in filth and write in the treetops. I can't. Perhaps it is because I am so ordinary. I like the middle way, as I like to talk to the man who walks the middle way with me.

"I have given thought to this business of straddling, and there's always seemed to me to be something wrong with it, something tricky. I see a man riding two horses, one foot on the back of one horse, one foot on the other. One horse pulls one way, the other a second. His straddle is wide, Heaven help him, but it seems to me that before long it's going to hurt him. It isn't the natural way, the normal way, the powerful way to ride. It's a trick." . . .

"People do me the honor to say that I am truly a poet of America. They point to my New England background, to the fact that my paternal ancestor came here some time in the sixteen hundreds. So much is true, but what they either do not know or do not say is that my mother was an immigrant. She came to these shores from Edinburgh in an old vessel that docked at Philadelphia. But she felt the spirit of America and became part of it before she even set her foot off the boat.

"She used to tell about it when I was a child. She was sitting on the deck of the boat waiting for orders to come ashore. Near her some workmen were loading Delaware peaches on to the ship. One of them picked out one of them and dropped it into her lap.

" 'Here, take that,' he said. The way he said it and the spirit in which he gave it left an indelible impression on her mind.

" 'It was a bonny peach,' she used to say, 'and I didn't eat it. I kept it to show my friends.'

"Looking back would I say that she was less the American than my father? No. America meant something live and real and virile to her. He took it for granted. He was a Fourth-of-July American, by which I mean that he rarely failed to celebrate in the way considered proper and appropriate. She, however, was a year-around American.

"I had an aunt in New England who used to talk long and loud about the foreigners who were taking over this country. Across the way from her house stood a French Catholic church which the new people of the village had put up. Every Sunday my aunt would stand at her window, behind the curtain, and watch the steady stream of men and women pouring into church. Her mouth would twist in the way that seems peculiar to dried-up New Englanders, and she would say, 'My soul!' Just that: 'My soul!'

"All the disapproval and indignation and disgust were concentrated in these two words. She never could see why I laughed at her, but it did strike me very funny for her to be calling upon her soul for help when this mass of industrious people were going to church to save theirs." . . .

"Today almost every man who writes poetry confesses his debt to Whitman. Many have gone very much further than Whitman would have traveled with them. They are the people who believe in wide straddling.

"I, myself, as I said before, don't like it for myself. I do not write free verse; I write blank verse. I must have the pulse beat of rhythm, I like to hear it beating under the things I write.

"That doesn't mean I do not like to read a bit of free verse occasionally. I do. It sometimes succeeds in painting a picture that is very clear and startling. It's good as something created momentarily for its sudden startling effect; it hasn't the qualities, however, of something lastingly beautiful.

"And sometimes my objection to it is that it's a pose. It's not honest. When a man sets out consciously to tear up forms and rhythms and measures, then he is not interested in giving you poetry. He just wants to perform; he wants to show you his tricks. He will get an effect; nobody will deny that, but it is not a harmonious effect.

"Sometimes it strikes me that the free-verse people got their idea from incorrect proof sheets. I have had stuff come from the printers with lines half left out or positions changed about. I read the poems as they stood, distorted and half finished, and I confess I get a rather pleasant sensation from them. They make a sort of nightmarish half-sense."

As he rose to go, he said, "I am an ordinary man, I guess. That's what's the trouble with me. I like my school and I like my farm and I like people. Just ordinary, you see."

ROBERT FROST

The Figure a Poem Makes   1939

Abstraction is an old story with the philosophers, but it has been like a new toy in the hands of the artists of our day. Why can't we have any one quality of poetry we choose by itself? We can have in thought. Then it will go hard if we can't in practice. Our lives for it.

Granted no one but a humanist much cares how sound a poem is if it is only *a* sound. The sound is the gold in the ore. Then we will have the sound out alone and dispense with the inessential. We do till we make the discovery that the object in writing poetry is to make all poems sound as different as possible from each other, and the resources for that of vowels, consonants, punctuation, syntax, words, sentences, meter are not enough. We need the help of context—meaning—subject matter. That is the greatest help towards variety. All that

we told him Merrill Moore° would come to treat him,
he said, 'I'll kill him first.' One of my daughters thought things,
knew every male she met was out to make her; 10
the way she dresses, she couldn't make a whorehouse."
And I, "Sometimes I'm so happy I can't stand myself."
And he, "When I am too full of joy, I think
how little good my health did anyone near me."

JOSEPH BRODSKY

On Grief and Reason   1994

I should tell you that what follows is a spinoff of a seminar given four
years ago at the Collège International de Philosophie, in Paris. Hence a certain
breeziness to the pace; hence, too, the paucity of biographical material—irrelevant, in my view, to the analysis of a work of art in general, and particularly
where a foreign audience is concerned. In any case, the pronoun "you" in these
pages stands for those ignorant of or poorly acquainted with the lyrical and
narrative strengths of the poetry of Robert Frost. But, first, some basics.

Robert Frost was born in 1874 and died in 1963, at the age of eighty-
eight. One marriage, six children; fairly strapped when young; farming, and,
later, teaching jobs in various schools. Not much travelling until late in his life;
he mostly resided on the East Coast, in New England. If biography accounts
for poetry, this one should have resulted in none. Yet he published nine books
of poems; the second one, "North of Boston," which came out when he was
forty, made him famous. This was in 1914.

After that, his sailing was a bit smoother. But literary fame is not exactly
popularity. As it happens, it took the Second World War to bring Frost's work
to the general public's notice. In 1943, the Council on Books in Wartime distributed fifty thousand copies of Frost's "Come In" to United States troops
stationed overseas, as a morale-builder. By 1955, his "Selected Poems" was in
its fourth edition, and one could speak of his poetry's having acquired national
standing.

It did. In the course of nearly five decades following the publication of
"North of Boston," Frost reaped every possible reward and honor an American
poet can get; shortly before Frost's death, John Kennedy invited him to read a
poem at the Inauguration ceremony. Along with recognition naturally came a
great deal of envy and resentment, a substantial contribution to which emerged
from the pen of Frost's own biographer. And yet both the adulation and resentment had one thing in common: a nearly total misconception of what Frost was
all about.

He is generally regarded as the poet of the countryside, of rural
settings—as a folksy, crusty, wisecracking old gentleman farmer, generally of

---

Merrill Moore: Poet and psychiatrist. Frost's son later committed suicide.

positive disposition. In short, as American as apple pie. To be fair, he greatly enhanced this notion by projecting precisely this image of himself in numerous public appearances and interviews throughout his career. I suppose it wasn't that difficult for him to do, for he had those qualities in him as well. He was indeed a quintessential American poet; it is up to us, however, to find out what that quintessence is made of, and what the term "American" means as applied to poetry and, perhaps, in general.

In 1959, at a banquet thrown in New York on the occasion of Robert Frost's eighty-fifth birthday, the most prominent literary critic at that time, Lionel Trilling, rose and declared that Robert Frost was "a terrifying poet." That, of course, caused a certain stir, but the epithet was well chosen.

Now, I want you to make the distinction here between terrifying and tragic. Tragedy, as you know, is always a fait accompli, whereas terror always has to do with anticipation, with man's recognition of his own negative potential—with his sense of what he is capable of. And it is the latter that was Frost's forte, not the former. In other words, his posture is radically different from the Continental tradition of the poet as tragic hero. And that difference alone makes him—for want of a better term—American.

On the surface, he looks very positively predisposed toward his surroundings—particularly toward nature. His fluency, his "being versed in country things" alone can produce this impression. However, there is a difference between the way a European perceives nature and the way an American does. Addressing this difference, W. H. Auden, in his short essay on Frost, suggests something to the effect that when a European conceives of confronting nature, he walks out of his cottage or a little inn, filled with either friends or family, and goes for an evening stroll. If he encounters a tree, it's a tree made familiar by history, to which it's been a witness. This or that king sat underneath it, laying down this or that law—something of that sort. A tree stands there rustling, as it were, with allusions. Pleased and somewhat pensive, our man, refreshed but unchanged by that encounter, returns to his inn or cottage, finds his friends or family absolutely intact, and proceeds to have a good, merry time. Whereas when an American walks out of his house and encounters a tree it is a meeting of equals. Man and tree face each other in their respective primal power, free of references: neither has a past, and as to whose future is greater, it is a toss-up. Basically, it's epidermis meeting bark. Our man returns to his cabin in a state of bewilderment, to say the least, if not in actual shock or terror.

Now, this is obviously a romantic caricature, but it accentuates the features, and that's what I am after here. In any case, the second point could be safely billed as the gist of Robert Frost's nature poetry. Nature for this poet is neither friend nor foe, nor is it the backdrop for human drama; it is this poet's terrifying self-portrait.

that the original goal will not be reached without compromise forced by circumstance. Surprisingly, it no longer seems so very critical to finish. Finally comes the letting-go, first with the hands, then with the mind, but never with the heart. The apple-picker, a sadder but wiser man, relinquishes his task altogether. Now is the time to rest from toil, to accept the verdict on his performance, to listen to himself harshly judging himself.

This harvest action, complete in itself, slips so neatly into the convenient circle created by the natural symbolism, and the whole tallies so comfortably with the surface events of the poem, that the reader arrives at the final period in a euphoria of "rightness." Surface and symbol coincide neatly.

How fortunate that Frost resisted any impulse he may have felt to press his poem into the didactic mold. A phrase or two would have shaped the verse into a substantiation of the orthodox religious view—and would have done untold violence to the lyrical purity so far sustained. But he fortuitously elected instead to suggest, to hint. Whatever sleep it is, only a woodchuck, he says fancifully, could tell for sure. The poem thus ends in deliberate ambiguity. But if a reader chooses to see "After Apple-Picking" as an allegory of man's life ascending from the eager grasping of youth to the letting-go of age, Frost will not object. Nor will he frown upon his poem viewed as a moral tale of the world having its inevitable way with human ambition. Let there be no mistake; all poetry is hinting—is metaphor. Poetry is the legitimate means of saying one thing and meaning another, an "honest duplicity."

Conversations on Langston Hughes and the African American Poetic Tradition

This section begins with a tribute by Hughes to his beloved Harlem. The excerpt is from one of the Simple stories Hughes wrote for a Harlem newspaper in which he used the character of a Harlem Everyman, Jessie Semple—nicknamed "Simple"—as a foil for his own attitudes and opinions. The next selection is a reminiscence published in The Crisis, *an African American journal, in 1926 by the writer Jessie Fauset, a contemporary of Hughes and like him a member of the generation of writers, artists, musicians, and critics identified as the Harlem Renaissance. There follows a review of Hughes's autobiography,* The Big Sea *(1940), by Richard Wright, the most successful and controversial African American writer of the 1930s. A savagely realistic novelist and poet, Wright might have been expected to be critical of Hughes's deceptively softer and more accommodating style. Wright, however, was perceptive enough to see that in his writing Hughes "bends, but he never breaks." Finally, Arnold Rampersad, author of the first extended biography of Hughes, comments in his introduction to the collected poems about Hughes's role as a folk poet.*

Langston Hughes as photographed by photojournalist Gordon Parks in 1943. (Reproduced from the collections of the Library of Congress.)

LANGSTON HUGHES

A Toast to Harlem   1950

Quiet can seem unduly loud at times. Since nobody at the bar was saying a word during a lull in the bright blues-blare of the Wishing Well's usually overworked juke box, I addressed my friend Simple.

"Since you told me last night you are an Indian, explain to me how it is you find yourself living in a furnished room in Harlem, my brave buck, instead of on a reservation?"

"I am a colored Indian," said Simple.

"In other words, a Negro."

"A Black Foot Indian, daddy-o, not a red one. Anyhow, Harlem is the place I always did want to be. And if it wasn't for landladies, I would be happy. That's a fact! I love Harlem."

"What is it you love about Harlem?"

"It's so full of Negroes," said Simple. "I feel like I got protection."

"From what?"

"From white folks," said Simple. "Furthermore, I like Harlem because it belongs to me."

"Harlem does not belong to you. You don't own the houses in Harlem. They belong to white folks."

"I might not own 'em," said Simple, "but I live in 'em. It would take an atom bomb to get me out."

"Or a depression," I said.

"I would not move for no depression. No, I would not go back down South, not even to Baltimore. I am in Harlem to stay! You say the houses ain't mine. Well, the sidewalk is — and don't nobody push me off. The cops don't even say, 'Move on,' hardly no more. They learned something from them Harlem riots. They used to beat your head right in public, but now they only beat it after they get you down to the stationhouse. And they don't beat it then if they think you know a colored congressman."

"Harlem has a few Negro leaders," I said.

"Elected by my *own* vote," said Simple. "Here I ain't scared to vote — that's another thing I like about Harlem. I also like it because we've got subways and it does not take all day to get downtown, neither are you Jim Crowed° on the way. Why, Negroes is running some of these subway trains. This morning I rode the A Train down to 34th Street. There were a Negro driving it, making ninety miles a hour. That cat *were really driving* that train! Every time he flew by one of them local stations looks like he was saying, 'Look at me! This train is mine!' That cat were gone, ole man. Which is another reason why I like Harlem! Sometimes I run into Duke Ellington on 125th Street and I say, 'What you know there, Duke?' Duke says, 'Solid, ole man.' He does not know me from Adam, but he speaks. One day I saw Lena Horne coming out of the Hotel Theresa and I said, 'Huba! Huba!' Lena smiled. Folks is friendly in Harlem. I feel like I got the world in a jug and the stopper in my hand! So drink a toast to Harlem!"

Simple lifted his glass of beer:

> "*Here's to Harlem!*
> *They say Heaven is Paradise.*
> *If Harlem ain't Heaven,*
> *Then a mouse ain't mice!*"

JESSIE FAUSET

Meeting Langston Hughes   1926

Very perfect is the memory of my first literary acquaintance with Langston Hughes. In the unforgettable days when we were publishing *The Brownies' Book* we had already appreciated a charming fragile conceit which read:

Jim Crowed: Jim Crow laws were the "legal" foundation for racial discrimination in the southern states.

Out of the dust of dreams,
Fairies weave their garments;
Out of the purple and rose of old memories,
They make purple wings.
No wonder we find them such marvelous things.

Then one day came "The Negro Speaks of Rivers." I took the beautiful dignified creation to Dr. Du Bois and said: "What colored person is there, do you suppose, in the United States who writes like that and yet is unknown to us?" And I wrote and found him to be a Cleveland high school graduate who had just gone to live in Mexico. Already he had begun to assume that remote, so elusive quality which permeates most of his work. Before long we had the pleasure of seeing the work of the boy, whom we had sponsored, copied, and recopied in journals far and wide. "The Negro Speaks of Rivers" even appeared in translation in a paper printed in Germany.

Not very long after Hughes came to New York and not long after that he began to travel and to set down the impressions, the pictures, which his sensitive mind had registered of new forms of life and living in Holland, in France, in Spain, in Italy, and in Africa.

His poems are warm, exotic, and shot through with color. Never is he preoccupied with form. But this fault, if it is one, has its corresponding virtue, for it gives his verse, which almost always is imbued with the essence of poetry, the perfection of spontaneity. And one characteristic which makes for this bubbling-like charm is the remarkable objectivity which he occasionally achieves, remarkable for one so young, and a first step toward philosophy. Hughes has seen a great deal of the world, and this has taught him that nothing matters much but life. Its forms and aspects may vary, but living is the essential thing. Therefore make no bones about it, — "make the most of what you may spend."

Some consciousness of this must have been in him even before he began to wander for he sent us as far back as 1921:

"Shake your brown feet, honey,
Shake your brown feet, chile,
Shake your brown feet, honey,
Shake 'em swift and wil'— . . .
Sun's going down this evening—
Might never rise no mo'.
The sun's going down this very night—
Might never rise no mo'—
So dance with swift feet, honey,
(The banjo's sobbing low . . .
The sun's going down this very night—
Might never rise no mo'."

Now this is very significant, combining as it does the doctrine of the old Biblical exhortation, "eat, drink, and be merry for tomorrow ye die," Horace's "Carpe diem," the German "Freut euch des Lebens," and [Robert] Herrick's

"Gather ye rosebuds while ye may." This is indeed a universal subject served Negro-style and though I am no great lover of any dialect I hope heartily that Mr. Hughes will give us many more such combinations.

Mr. Hughes is not always the calm philosopher; he has feeling a-plenty and is not ashamed to show it. He "loved his friend" who left him and so taken up is he with the sorrow of it all that he has no room for anger or resentment. While I do not think of him as a protagonist of color, — he is too much the citizen of the world for that — , I doubt if any one will ever write more tenderly, more understandingly, more humorously of the life of Harlem shot through as it is with mirth, abandon and pain. Hughes comprehends this life, has studied it and loved it. In one poem he has epitomized its essence:

> Does a jazz-band ever sob?
> They say a jazz-band's gay.
> Yet as the vulgar dancers whirled
> And the wan night wore away,
> One said she heard the jazz-band sob
> When the little dawn was grey.

Harlem is undoubtedly one of his great loves; the sea is another. Indeed all life is his love and his work a brilliant, sensitive interpretation of its numerous facets.

RICHARD WRIGHT

A Review of *The Big Sea*   1940

The double role that Langston Hughes has played in the rise of a realistic literature among the Negro people resembles in one phase the role that Theodore Dreiser° played in freeing American literary expression from the restrictions of Puritanism. Not that Negro literature was ever Puritanical, but it was timid and vaguely lyrical and folkish. Hughes's early poems, "The Weary Blues" and "Fine Clothes to the Jew," full of irony and urban imagery, were greeted by a large section of the Negro reading public with suspicion and shock when they first appeared in the middle twenties. Since then the realistic position assumed by Hughes has become the dominant outlook of all those Negro writers who have something to say.

The other phase of Hughes's role has been, for the lack of a better term, that of a cultural ambassador. Performing his task quietly and almost casually, he has represented the Negroes' case, in his poems, plays, short stories and novels, at the court of world opinion. On the other hand he has brought the experiences of other nations within the orbit of the Negro writer by his translations from the French, Russian and Spanish.

Theodore Dreiser: American realistic novelist (1871–1945).

How Hughes became this forerunner and ambassador can best be understood in the cameo sequences of his own life that he gives us in his sixth and latest book, *The Big Sea.* Out of his experiences as a seaman, cook, laundry worker, farm helper, bus boy, doorman, unemployed worker, have come his writings dealing with black gals who wore red stockings and black men who sang the blues all night and slept like rocks all day.

Unlike the sons and daughters of Negro "society," Hughes was not ashamed of those of his race who had to scuffle for their bread. The jerky transitions of his own life did not admit of his remaining in one place long enough to become a slave of prevailing Negro middle-class prejudices. So beneficial does this ceaseless movement seem to Hughes that he has made it one of his life principles: six months in one place, he says, is long enough to make one's life complicated. The result has been a range of artistic interest and expression possessed by no other Negro writer of his time.

Born in Joplin, Missouri, in 1902, Hughes lived in half a dozen Midwestern towns until he entered high school in Cleveland, Ohio, where he began to write poetry. His father, succumbing to that fit of disgust which overtakes so many self-willed Negroes in the face of American restrictions, went off to Mexico to make money and proceeded to treat the Mexicans just as the whites in America had treated him. The father yearned to educate Hughes and establish him in business. His favorite phrase was "hurry up," and it irritated Hughes so much that he fled his father's home.

Later he entered Columbia University, only to find it dull. He got a job on a merchant ship, threw his books into the sea and sailed for Africa. But for all his work, he arrived home with only a monkey and a few dollars, much to his mother's bewilderment. Again he sailed, this time for Rotterdam, where he left the ship and made his way to Paris. After an interval of hunger he found a job as a doorman, then as second cook in a night club, which closed later because of bad business. He went to Italy to visit friends and had his passport stolen. Jobless in an alien land, he became a beachcomber until he found a ship on which he could work his way back to New York.

The poems he had written off and on had attracted the attention of some of his relatives in Washington and, at their invitation, he went to live with them. What Hughes has to say about Negro "society" in Washington, relatives and hunger are bitter poems in themselves. While living in Washington, he won his first poetry prize; shortly afterwards Carl Van Vechten submitted a batch of his poems to a publisher.

The rest of *The Big Sea* is literary history, most of it dealing with the Negro renaissance, that astonishing period of prolific productivity among Negro artists that coincided with America's "golden age" of prosperity. Hughes writes of it with humor, urbanity and objectivity; one has the feeling that never for a moment was his sense of solidarity with those who had known hunger shaken by it. Even when a Park Avenue patron was having him driven about the streets of New York in her town car, he "felt bad because he could not share his new-found comfort with his mother and relatives." When the bubble burst in 1929, Hughes returned to the mood that seems to fit him best. He wrote of the opening of the Waldorf-Astoria:

Now, won't that be charming when the last flophouse
    has turned you down this winter?

Hughes is tough; he bends but he never breaks, and he has carried on a manly tradition in literary expression when many of his fellow writers have gone to sleep at their posts.

ARNOLD RAMPERSAD

Langston Hughes as Folk Poet   1994

Hughes was often called, and sometimes called himself, a folk poet. To some people, this means that his work is almost artless and thus possibly beneath criticism. The truth indeed is that Hughes published many poems that are doggerel. To reach his primary audience — the black masses — he was prepared to write "down" to them. Some of the pieces in this volume were intended for public recitation mainly; some started as song lyrics. Like many democratic poets, such as William Carlos Williams, he believed that the full range of his poetry should reach print as soon as possible; poetry is a form of social action. However, for Hughes, as for all serious poets, the writing of poetry was virtually a sacred commitment. And while he wished to write no verse that was beyond the ability of the masses of people to understand, his poetry, in common with that of other committed writers, is replete with allusions that must be respected and understood if it is to be properly appreciated. To respect Hughes's work, above all one must respect the African American people and their culture, as well as the American people in general and their national culture.

If Hughes kept at the center of his art the hopes and dreams, as well as the actual lived conditions, of African Americans, he almost always saw these factors in the context of the eternally embattled but eternally inspiring American democratic tradition, even as changes in the world order, notably the collapse of colonialism in Africa, redefined the experiences of African peoples around the world. Almost always, too, Hughes attempted to preserve a sense of himself as a poet beyond race and other corrosive social pressures. By his absolute dedication to his art and to his social vision, as well as to his central audience, he fused his unique vision of himself as a poet to his production of art.

"What is poetry?" Langston Hughes asked near his death. He answered, "It is the human soul entire, squeezed like a lemon or a lime, drop by drop, into atomic words." He wanted no definition of the poet that divorced his art from the immediacy of life. "A poet is a human being," he declared. "Each human being must live within his time, with and for his people, and within the boundaries of his country." Hughes constantly called upon himself for the courage and the endurance necessary to write according to these beliefs. "Hang yourself, poet, in your own words," he urged all those who would take up the mantle of the poet and dare to speak to the world. "Otherwise, you are dead."

PART THREE

Drama

. . . the lasting appeal of tragedy is due
to our need to face the fact of death in
order to strengthen ourselves for life. . . .

— ARTHUR MILLER

I don't think you should frighten them
[the audience], I think you should terrify
them.

— EDWARD ALBEE

The great and only possible dignity of
man lies in his power deliberately to
choose certain moral values by which
to live as steadfastly as if he, too, like
a character in a play, were immured
against the corrupting rush of time.

— TENNESSEE WILLIAMS

18.

What Is a Play?

Suit the action to the word, the word to the action; with this special observance, that you o'erstep not the modesty of nature: for any thing so o'erdone is from the purpose of playing, whose end, both at the first and now, was and is, to hold, as 't were, the mirror up to nature.

—HAMLET TO THE PLAYERS

Of all the literary genres, drama has the greatest potential to reach the emotions of an audience. The American dramatist Tennessee Williams understood how easy it is for us to disguise "from ourselves the intensity of our own feelings, the sensibility of our own hearts" as we are inexorably caught up in the ceaseless rush of events in our everyday lives. In "The Timeless World of a Play," an essay included in Williams's collection *Where I Live* (1978), he wrote that

> In a play, time is arrested in the sense of being confined. By a sort of legerdemain, events are made to remain *events,* rather than being reduced so quickly to mere *occurrences.* The audience can sit back in a comforting dusk to watch a world which is flooded with light and in which emotion and action have a dimension and dignity that they would likewise have in real existence, if only the shattering intrusion of time could be locked out.
>
> About their lives, people ought to remember that when they are finished, everything in them will be contained in a marvelous state of repose which is the same as that which they unconsciously admired in drama. The rush is temporary. The great and only possible dignity of man lies in his power deliberately to choose certain moral values by which to live as steadfastly as if he, too, like a character in a play, were immured against the corrupting rush of time. Snatching the eternal out of the desperately fleeting is the great magic trick of human existence.

Williams believed that what he called "the created world of a play" gives spectators the opportunity to escape from time's inevitable sense of impermanence. Sitting in a theater, we experience a "special kind of repose which allows contemplation and produces the climate in which tragic importance is a possible thing," because plays in the tragic tradition offer us a view of certain moral values in violent juxtaposition. Because we do not participate, except as spectators, we can view them clearly, within the limits of our emotional equipment. These people on the stage do not return our looks. We do not have to answer their questions nor make any sign of being in company with them, nor do we have to compete with their virtues nor resist their offenses. All at once, for this reason, we are able to *see* them! Our hearts are wrung by recognition and pity, so that the dusky shell of the auditorium where we are gathered anonymously together is flooded with an almost liquid warmth of unchecked human sympathies, relieved of self-consciousness, allowed to function. . . .

After poetry, drama is our second oldest literary form. To define **drama** as a play written to be performed in a theater is true only for the earliest plays. Later works known as "closet dramas," written in the nineteenth century by such poets as Percy Bysshe Shelley and such playwrights as Henrik Ibsen, were meant to be performed in the solitary theater of the reader's mind. A play can be considered a story told in dialogue, but even here there are exceptions: The modern playwright Samuel Beckett wrote stories without dialogue for the stage intended to be mimed by a single performer. Today millions of viewers watch works of drama — television sitcoms, prime-time soap operas, and weekly network dramatic series — that were never intended to be performed in a theater. But for centuries *drama* meant a stage play, and it is this meaning of the word that we primarily have in mind when we speak of drama as a literary genre.

As Aristotle understood, action is the essence of drama. This is suggested in the origin of the word *drama*, which is the Greek verb *dran*, "to perform." A century after drama flourished in Greece, Aristotle wrote the *Poetics* (c. 340 B.C.), a work in which he analyzed the literary form used by Sophocles and other Greek dramatists. For Aristotle, a play was the process of imitating a significant action complete unto itself by means of language "made sensuously attractive" and spoken by the persons involved in the action, not presented through narrative. Aristotle's definition of tragedy contained six important elements: (1) plot or action, the basic principle of drama; (2) characterization, an almost equally important element; (3) the thought or theme of the play; (4) verbal expression or dialogue; (5) visual adornment or stage decoration and costumes and masks for the actors; and (6) song or music to accompany the performers' words and movement.

Because most plays are literary works meant to give an illusion of reality through their performance onstage, a playwright who has set actors in motion to tell a story cannot interrupt the action, as in a work of fiction, to offer background information about the characters or summarize events taking place over a period of time, unless he introduces a narrator at the beginning of the play. Usually, the playwright gives the audience information about the story through dialogue. Playwrights can also suggest the development of their story by the physical behavior of the actors onstage and by changes in lighting, sets, or costumes.

When we think of the word *drama* we have in mind an illusion of reality invented for a striking effect. To illustrate the relationship between the everyday life we live and the life we see portrayed in the theater, the director Peter Brook described a simple exercise in *The Open Door* (1993):

> Ask any volunteer to walk from one side of a space to another. Anyone can do this. The clumsiest idiot cannot fail; he just has to walk. He makes no effort and deserves no reward.
>
> Now ask him to try to imagine that he is holding a precious bowl in his hands and to walk carefully so as not to spill a drop of its contents. Here again anyone can accomplish the act of imagination that this requires and can move in a more or less convincing manner. Yet your volunteer has made a special effort, so perhaps he deserves thanks and a five-penny piece as a reward for trying.
>
> Next ask him to imagine that as he walks the bowl slips from his fingers and crashes to the ground, spilling its contents. Now he's in trouble. He tries to act and the worst kind of artificial, amateur acting will take over his body, making the expression on his face "acted"—in other words, woefully unreal.
>
> To execute this apparently simple action so that it will appear as natural as just walking demands all the skills of a highly professional artist—an idea has to be given flesh and blood and emotional reality; it must go beyond imitation, so that an invented life is also a parallel life, which at no level can be distinguished from the real thing. Now we can see why a true actor is worth the enormous daily rate that film companies pay him for giving a plausible impression of everyday life.
>
> One goes to the theatre to find life, but if there is no difference between life outside the theatre and life inside, then theatre makes no sense. There's no point doing it. But if we accept that life in the theatre is more visible, more vivid than on the outside, then we can see that it is simultaneously the same thing and somewhat different.

Plays are acts of make-believe—acts in which the author, actors, stage technicians, and audience are united in their participation in an imaginary world. This world onstage can mimic "real life" in such plays as Lorraine Hansberry's *A Raisin in the Sun* (1959) with actors and sets representing contemporary everyday reality, or it can project a view of our potential experience as in a dream, in such poetic plays as William Shakespeare's *Hamlet* (c. 1600) or Tennessee Williams's *The Glass Menagerie* (1945).

As a story primarily told in dialogue, each play in this anthology falls into one of three conventional categories: tragedy, comedy, and tragicomedy. Broadly speaking, in **tragedy** the story ends unhappily, usually in the death of the main character, as in Sophocles' *Antigone* (c. 441 B.C.). In **comedy** the story ends happily, often with a marriage symbolizing the continuation of life and the resolution of the conflict, as in Shakespeare's *The Tempest* (1611). In **tragicomedy,** a mixture of sad and happy events, the story's resolution can take different forms, but the audience usually experiences the play as a positive statement, an affirmation of life. This category can be further subdivided in modern plays into dark comedy, where the playwright's sardonic humor offers a frightening glimpse of the futility of life, and farce, a short play that depends for its comic effect on exaggerated, improbable situations and slapstick action.

Drama has experienced many innovations in form and staging in the twentieth century, even while such practitioners as the contemporary English playwright Tom Stoppard make fun of the increasing pace of our lives and the trivialization of our most cherished institutions, including the theater. In *Dogg's Hamlet* (1979), Stoppard created two short versions of Shakespeare's *Hamlet*—one that would take fifteen minutes to perform and a second, even briefer "encore" version of the play—streamlined for a production on a double-decker London bus. As short as it is, Stoppard's "encore" version of *Hamlet* as a farce (see "Conversations on *Hamlet* as Text and Performance," p. 1588) still satisfies our definition of a play—a performance by actors of a story told in dialogue. Stoppard has edited Shakespeare's words so drastically that our familiarity with the original *Hamlet*—one of the most famous plays in the European tradition—is essential to our understanding the cut version.

If the text of *Hamlet* were performed in its complete version, it would take almost six hours onstage. Every director makes some cuts in the script, but Stoppard's version is so short that he seems to be implying that contemporary audiences are so busy watching television that they have practically no time at all to sit through the long classic plays. But he also assumes that the tradition of European theater is still relevant today. The people who bought tickets when Stoppard's play was performed on the bus probably studied Shakespeare in school, where they might have become familiar with the complicated plot of *Hamlet* through reading the play or a summary of it for an English class.

If you are familiar with Shakespeare's play, Stoppard's collapsed version will remind you of what has been cut. The "encore" version of *Hamlet* conveys none of the complexity of the hero's passionate character, none of the poetry of his unforgettable soliloquies, and none of the tragedy of his dilemma. This bizarre version is meant to be only a faint, funny echo of the original.

Stoppard wrote his farce for a specific theater company in England, intending it to be seen and heard as well as read. This adds another dimension to our experience of drama. When performed in front of an audience, the text of a play is transmitted by the theatrical director, the costume and set designers, the technical staff responsible for sound and lighting, and the actors who make the play come alive. All these people work together to shape a play's meaning for the audience.

Even on a red double-decker London bus, an actor interpreting Hamlet as an aristocrat dressed in luxurious black velvet and silk ruffles will elicit a different response to the hero's personality and emotional situation than an actor who depicts Hamlet as a clown in a silly wig and circus tights or as a scruffy, leather-jacketed, metal-studded biker or as a pajama-clad patient recently escaped from a psychiatric hospital. Actors have performed the role in all these costumes, and they are all—at least in name—Hamlet. Every time an actor "plays" him, or any other character in a drama, there is the potential for interpreting the role differently.

Because drama is a collaborative effort that results in a work performed on a stage in front of an audience, we call a writer who creates plays a play-*wright*, suggesting a highly skilled craftsperson or artisan who makes something tangible. But the basic text of a play—the author's creation of dialogue and stage action and the description on the page of the setting and the characters—has a special significance. The text is the only aspect of the theater in which the writer has the last word. When we read a play, following the dialogue and the stage directions makes us conscious of how the story might take on another life when performed on a stage or in a film, but we are also aware as we follow the words on the page that reading a play puts us into a special relationship with the playwright. Like the writer, we have only words to fire our imaginations; there are no actors, costumes, or sets.

What endures is the play on the page. As Aristotle wrote about the primacy of the text in *The Poetics,* "The visual adornment of the dramatic persons can have a strong emotional effect but is the least artistic element, the least connected with the poetic art; in fact the force of tragedy can be felt even without benefit of public performance and actors, while for the production of the visual effect the property man's art is even more decisive than that of the poet's."

If a play is to survive beyond its ephemeral stage or film presentations, it depends on its text and the response of generations of readers to its story, language, structure, and deeper meaning or theme. If a play exists only in performance, it will probably not survive as literature. Reading a play in addition to seeing it performed can help you understand the work better, especially if its language or meaning is difficult to follow in the action onstage. From your seat in the theater you cannot stop a play in the middle of a scene to tell the actor, "Wait, I didn't understand that line. Please repeat it." As a reader, however, you have the luxury of being able to stop in the midst of your reading to ponder the meaning of a line or to go over an entire scene that is not immediately clear to you.

COMMENTARY   *Aristotle, "On the Elements and General Principles of Tragedy," page 1528.*

19.

The Elements of Drama: A Playwright's Means

INTERVIEWER: Which playwrights did you most admire when you were young?

ARTHUR MILLER: Well, first the Greeks, for their magnificent form, the symmetry. Half the time I couldn't really repeat the story because the characters in the mythology were completely blank to me. I had no background at that time to know really what was involved in these plays, but the architecture was clear. One looks at some building of the past whose use one is ignorant of, and yet it has a modernity. It had its own specific gravity. That form has never left me; I suppose it just got burned in.

—ARTHUR MILLER, *Paris Review* interview (1967)

Like short story writers and poets, playwrights have several important means or elements at their disposal in creating dramatic works for the stage. Familiarizing yourself with these elements will help you appreciate the artistry of these creations and understand them better. Some terms used to analyze drama (for instance, *plot, characterizations,* and *theme*) are also used in discussing short fiction; others (*dialogue* and *staging*) refer exclusively to theater.

Even the most basic form of drama, the **monologue**—words meant to be spoken by one actor—suggests the resources available to the playwright. Consider, for example, the following fragment by Anton Chekhov. Found in his handwriting among his papers after his death, it appears to be a page that survived from one of his early attempts to rewrite his play *Uncle Vanya* (1896):

SOLOMON (*alone*): Oh! how dark is life! No night, when I was a child, so terrified me by its darkness as does my invisible existence. Lord, to David my father thou gavest only the gift of harmonizing words and songs, to sing and praise thee on strings, to lament sweetly, to make people weep or admire beauty; but why hast thou given me a meditative, sleepless, hungry mind? Like an insect born of the dust, I hide in darkness; and in fear and despair, all shaking and shivering, I see and hear in everything an invisible mystery. Why this morning? Why does the sun come out from behind the temple and gild the palm tree? Why this beauty of women? Where does the bird hurry, what is the meaning of its flight, if it and its young and the place to which it hastens will like myself, turn to dust? It were better I had never been born or were a stone, to which God has given neither eyes nor thoughts. In order to tire out my body by nightfall, all day yesterday, like a mere workman, I carried marble to the temple; but now the night has come and I cannot sleep. . . . I'll go and lie down. Phorses told me that if one imagines a flock of sheep running and fixes one's attention upon it, the mind gets confused and one falls asleep. I'll do it. . . . (*Exit.*)

Chekhov suggests several elements of drama in this monologue. The first word gives us the name of the character speaking the lines, Solomon, the son of King David, the great Hebrew poet whose psalms are included in the Old Testament. Solomon himself is a judge, not a poet, renowned throughout his kingdom for his wisdom. His first words ("Oh! how dark is life!") suggest the poetic language of his speech in his use of a metaphor. His next words ("No night, when I was a child, so terrified me by its darkness as does my invisible existence") suggest the subject or theme of his monologue, a philosophical contemplation of his own mortality. His words take on the element of dramatic irony, because the reader assumes that a man as wise as King Solomon would not be troubled by doubts or uncertainties.

Chekhov uses an elegant structure to present the progression of Solomon's thoughts, beginning with his statement or exposition of the theme. Solomon's situation is then developed in the rising action of the monologue, when he compares himself to his father and states the conflict within his personality: Unlike David, he is not content to praise the Lord; he has a "sleepless, hungry mind." Next, Solomon gives specific examples of his dilemma—first his awareness of the darkness and mystery in the world, then his observation of the same mystery in sunlight and beauty. Finally, at the climax of his thought, when he recognizes his own mortality and the evidence all around him of the futility of all existence ("turn to dust"), he admits, "It were better I had never been born or were a stone, to which God has given neither eyes nor thoughts." In the falling action he reminds himself about the advice he's heard from Phorses, about a method of counting sheep to put himself to sleep, and he leaves the stage determined to try it.

This monologue is a fragment, with no resolution other than Solomon's exit from the stage. It also lacks any physical action other than the speech itself, wherein Solomon meditates on mortality and attempts to fill the time before he tries to sleep. His words suggest a plot, telling us about what he did the previous day, trying to shake off his depression by carrying blocks of heavy marble in order to exhaust himself for sleep. Movement or staging of the monologue would depend on the actor saying the words onstage. We would not actually see Solomon pick up the marble slabs, but he could suggest his heavy labor—or his fatigue—by his physical stance and gestures. Each of us can imagine an appropriate staging for the monologue of a great Hebrew king, as ornate or as simple as we wish—a room in a realistic set that suggests a palace filled with silver and gold objects, or a symbolic bare stage furnished only with a classic plain-cloth backdrop. These choices, of course, affect how the viewer perceives the scene and the actor speaking his lines.

Plot, characterization, dialogue, and theme are the four main elements that you analyze when you think about plays as literary texts. Naturally, in plays with more than one character, playwrights can develop these elements in more complex ways. As you read the short play *Tender Offer* by the contemporary

American playwright Wendy Wasserstein, be aware of how she uses plot, characterization, dialogue, and theme, as well as various physical elements of staging (for instance, the stage set and the two performers' song and dance routine), to tell a story in the words exchanged by two actors on a stage.

WENDY WASSERSTEIN

Tender Offer   1991

A girl of around nine is alone in a dance studio. She is dressed in traditional leotards and tights. She begins singing to herself, "Nothing Could Be Finer Than to Be in Carolina." She maps out a dance routine, including parts for the chorus. She builds to a finale. A man, Paul, around thirty-five, walks in. He has a sweet, though distant, demeanor. As he walks in, Lisa notices him and stops.

PAUL: You don't have to stop, sweetheart.

LISA: That's okay.

PAUL: Looked very good.

LISA: Thanks.

PAUL: Don't I get a kiss hello?

LISA: Sure.

PAUL (*embraces her*): Hi, Tiger.

LISA: Hi, Dad.

PAUL: I'm sorry I'm late.

LISA: That's okay.

PAUL: How'd it go?

LISA: Good.

PAUL: Just good?

LISA: Pretty good.

PAUL: "Pretty good." You mean you got a lot of applause or "pretty good" you could have done better?

LISA: Well, Courtney Palumbo's mother thought I was pretty good. But you know the part in the middle when everybody's supposed to freeze and the big girl comes out. Well, I think I moved a little bit.

PAUL: I thought what you were doing looked very good.

LISA: Daddy, that's not what I was doing. That was tap-dancing. I made that up.

PAUL: Oh. Well it looked good. Kind of sexy.

LISA: Yuch!

PAUL: What do you mean "yuch"?

LISA: Just yuch!

PAUL: You don't want to be sexy?

LISA: I don't care.

PAUL: Let's go, Tiger. I promised your mother I'd get you home in time for dinner.

LISA: I can't find my leg warmers.

PAUL: You can't find your what?

LISA: Leg warmers. I can't go home till I find my leg warmers.

PAUL: I don't see you looking for them.

LISA: I was waiting for you.

PAUL: Oh.

LISA: Daddy.

PAUL: What?

LISA: Nothing.

PAUL: Where do you think you left them?

LISA: Somewhere around here. I can't remember.

PAUL: Well, try to remember, Lisa. We don't have all night.

LISA: I told you. I think somewhere around here.

PAUL: I don't see them. Let's go home now. You'll call the dancing school tomorrow.

LISA: Daddy, I can't go home till I find them. Miss Judy says it's not professional to leave things.

PAUL: Who's Miss Judy?

LISA: She's my ballet teacher. She once danced the lead in *Swan Lake,* and she
was a June Taylor dancer.

PAUL: Well, then, I'm sure she'll understand about the leg warmers.

LISA: Daddy, Miss Judy wanted to know why you were late today.

PAUL: Hmmmmmmmm?

LISA: Why were you late?

PAUL: I was in a meeting. Business. I'm sorry.

LISA: Why did you tell Mommy you'd come instead of her if you knew you had
business?

PAUL: Honey, something just came up. I thought I'd be able to be here. I was
looking forward to it.

LISA: I wish you wouldn't make appointments to see me.

PAUL: Hmmmmmmm.

LISA: You shouldn't make appointments to see me unless you know you're
going to come.

PAUL: Of course I'm going to come.

LISA: No, you're not. Talia Robbins told me she's much happier living without her father in the house. Her father used to come home late and go to
sleep early.

PAUL: Lisa, stop it. Let's go.

LISA: I can't find my leg warmers.

PAUL: Forget your leg warmers.

LISA: Daddy.

PAUL: What is it?

LISA: I saw this show on television, I think it was WPIX Channel 11. Well, the
father was crying about his daughter.

PAUL: Why was he crying? Was she sick?

LISA: No. She was at school. And he was at business. And he just missed her, so
he started to cry.

PAUL: What was the name of this show?

LISA: I don't know. I came in in the middle.

PAUL: Well, Lisa, I certainly would cry if you were sick or far away, but I know that you're well and you're home. So no reason to get maudlin.

LISA: What's maudlin?

PAUL: Sentimental, soppy. Frequently used by children who make things up to get attention.

LISA: I am sick! I am sick! I have Hodgkin's disease and a bad itch on my leg.

PAUL: What do you mean you have Hodgkin's disease? Don't say things like that.

LISA: Swoosie Kurtz, she had Hodgkin's disease on a TV movie last year, but she got better and now she's on *Love, Sidney*.

PAUL: Who is Swoosie Kurtz?

LISA: She's an actress named after an airplane. I saw her on *Live at Five*.

PAUL: You watch too much television; you should do your homework. Now, put your coat on.

LISA: Daddy, I really do have a bad itch on my leg. Would you scratch it?

PAUL: Lisa, you're procrastinating.

LISA: Why do you use words I don't understand? I hate it. You're like Daria Feldman's mother. She always talks in Yiddish to her husband so Daria won't understand.

PAUL: Procrastinating is not Yiddish.

LISA: Well, I don't know what it is.

PAUL: Procrastinating means you don't want to go about your business.

LISA: I don't go to business. I go to school.

PAUL: What I mean is you want to hang around here until you and I are late for dinner and your mother's angry and it's too late for you to do your homework.

LISA: I do not.

PAUL: Well, it sure looks that way. Now put your coat on and let's go.

LISA: Daddy.

PAUL: Honey, I'm tired. Really, later.

LISA: Why don't you want to talk to me?

PAUL: I do want to talk to you. I promise when we get home we'll have a nice talk.

LISA: No, we won't. You'll read the paper and fall asleep in front of the news.

PAUL: Honey, we'll talk on the weekend, I promise. Aren't I taking you to the theater this weekend? Let me look. (*He takes out appointment book.*) Yes. Sunday. *Joseph and the Amazing Technicolor Raincoat* with Lisa. Okay, Tiger?

LISA: Sure. It's Dreamcoat.

PAUL: What?

LISA: Nothing. I think I see my leg warmers. (*She goes to pick them up, and an odd-looking trophy.*)

PAUL: What's that?

LISA: It's stupid. I was second best at the dance recital, so they gave me this thing. It's stupid.

PAUL: Lisa.

LISA: What?

PAUL: What did you want to talk about?

LISA: Nothing.

PAUL: Was it about my missing your recital? I'm really sorry, Tiger. I would have liked to have been here.

LISA: That's okay.

PAUL: Honest?

LISA: Daddy, you're prostrastinating.

PAUL: I'm procrastinating. Sit down. Let's talk. So. How's school?

LISA: Fine.

PAUL: You like it?

LISA: Yup.

PAUL: You looking forward to camp this summer?

LISA: Yup.

PAUL: Is Daria Feldman going back?

LISA: Nope.

PAUL: Why not?

LISA: I don't know. We can go home now. Honest, my foot doesn't itch anymore.

PAUL: Lisa, you know what you do in business when it seems like there's nothing left to say? That's when you really start talking. Put a bid on the table.

LISA: What's a bid?

PAUL: You tell me what you want and I'll tell you what I've got to offer. Like Monopoly. You want Boardwalk, but I'm only willing to give you the Railroads. Now, because you are my daughter I'd throw in Water Works and Electricity. Understand, Tiger?

LISA: No. I don't like board games. You know, Daddy, we could get Space Invaders for our home for thirty-five dollars. In fact, we could get an Osborne System for two thousand. Daria Feldman's parents . . .

PAUL: Daria Feldman's parents refuse to talk to Daria, so they bought a computer to keep Daria busy so they won't have to speak in Yiddish. Daria will probably grow up to be a homicidal maniac lesbian prostitute.

LISA: I know what that word prostitute means.

PAUL: Good. (*Pause.*) You still haven't told me about school. Do you still like your teacher?

LISA: She's okay.

PAUL: Lisa, if we're talking try to answer me.

LISA: I am answering you. Can we go home now, please?

PAUL: Damn it, Lisa, if you want to talk to me . . . Talk to me!

LISA: I can't wait till I'm old enough so I can make my own money and never have to see you again. Maybe I'll become a prostitute.

PAUL: Young lady, that's enough.

LISA: I hate you, Daddy! I hate you! (*She throws her trophy into the trash bin.*)

PAUL: What'd you do that for?

LISA: It's stupid.

PAUL: Maybe I wanted it.

LISA: What for?

PAUL: Maybe I wanted to put it where I keep your dinosaur and the picture you made of Mrs. Kimbel with the chicken pox.

LISA: You got mad at me when I made that picture. You told me I had to respect Mrs. Kimbel because she was my teacher.

PAUL: That's true. But she wasn't my teacher. I liked her better with the chicken pox. (*Pause.*) Lisa, I'm sorry. I was very wrong to miss your recital, and you don't have to become a prostitute. That's not the type of profession Miss Judy has in mind for you.

LISA (*mumbles*): No.

PAUL: No. (*Pause.*) So Talia Robbins is really happy her father moved out?

LISA: Talia Robbins picks open the eighth-grade lockers during gym period. But she did that before her father moved out.

PAUL: You can't always judge someone by what they do or what they don't do. Sometimes you come home from dancing school and run upstairs and shut the door, and when I finally get to talk to you, everything is "okay" or "fine." Yup or nope?

LISA: Yup.

PAUL: Sometimes, a lot of times, I come home and fall asleep in front of the television. So you and I spend a lot of time being a little scared of each other. Maybe?

LISA: Maybe.

PAUL: Tell you what. I'll make you a tender offer.

LISA: What?

PAUL: I'll make you a tender offer. That's when one company publishes in the newspaper that they want to buy another company. And the company that publishes is called the Black Knight because they want to gobble up the poor little company. So the poor little company needs to be rescued. And then a White Knight comes along and makes a bigger and better offer so the shareholders won't have to tender shares to the Big Black Knight. You with me?

LISA: Sort of.

PAUL: I'll make you a tender offer like the White Knight. But I don't want to own you. I just want to make a much better offer. Okay?

LISA (*sort of understanding*): Okay. (*Pause. They sit for a moment.*) Sort of, Daddy, what do you think about? I mean, like when you're quiet what do you think about?

PAUL: Oh, business usually. If I think I made a mistake or if I think I'm doing okay. Sometimes I think about what I'll be doing five years from now and if it's what I hoped it would be five years ago. Sometimes I think about what your life will be like, if Mount Saint Helens will erupt again. What you'll become if you'll study penmanship or word processing. If you speak kindly of me to your psychiatrist when you are in graduate school. And how the hell I'll pay for your graduate school. And sometimes I try and think what it was I thought about when I was your age.

LISA: Do you ever look out your window at the clouds and try to see which kinds of shapes they are? Like one time, honest, I saw the head of Walter Cronkite in a flower vase. Really! Like look don't those kinda look like if you turn it upside down, two big elbows or two elephant trunks dancing?

PAUL: Actually still looks like Walter Cronkite in a flower vase to me. But look up a little. See the one that's still moving? That sorta looks like a whale on a thimble.

LISA: Where?

PAUL: Look up. To your right.

LISA: I don't see it. Where?

PAUL: The other way.

LISA: Oh, yeah! There's the head and there's the stomach. Yeah! (*Lisa picks up her trophy.*) Hey, Daddy.

PAUL: Hey, Lisa.

LISA: You can have this thing if you want it. But you have to put it like this, because if you put it like that it is gross.

PAUL: You know what I'd like? So I can tell people who come into my office why I have this gross stupid thing on my shelf, I'd like it if you could show me your dance recital.

LISA: Now?

PAUL: We've got time. Mother said she won't be home till late.

LISA: Well, Daddy, during a lot of it I freeze and the big girl in front dances.

PAUL: Well, how 'bout the number you were doing when I walked in?

LISA: Well, see, I have parts for a lot of people in that one, too.

PAUL: I'll dance the other parts.

LISA: You can't dance.

PAUL: Young lady, I played Yvette Mimimieux in a *Hasty Pudding Show.*°

LISA: Who's Yvette Mimimieux?

PAUL: Watch more television. You'll find out. (*Paul stands up.*) So I'm ready. (*He begins singing.*) "Nothing could be finer than to be in Carolina."

LISA: Now I go. In the morning. And now you go. Dum-da.

PAUL (*obviously not a tap dancer*): Da-da-dum.

LISA (*whines*): Daddy!

PAUL (*mimics her*): Lisa! Nothing could be finer . . .

LISA: That looks dumb.

PAUL: Oh, yeah? You think they do this better in *The Amazing Minkcoat*? No way! Now you go—da da da dum.

LISA: Da da da dum.

PAUL: If I had Aladdin's lamp for only a day, I'd make a wish . . .

LISA: Daddy, that's maudlin!

PAUL: I know it's maudlin. And here's what I'd say:

LISA AND PAUL: I'd say that "nothing could be finer than to be in Carolina in the mooooooooooornin'."

Hasty Pudding Show: An all-male revue, written and staged by Harvard students and renowned for its zany humor, men in drag, and parodies of cultural icons (e.g., the mock-reference to Yvette Mimieux, a '60s movie star).

PLOT

Plot is the structuring of the events in a play. Also called the story, plot is the essential element with which a dramatist works. If "to play," according to the dictionary definition, is to engage in mimicry, acting, or make believe, then "a play" is a literary work that mimics or imitates a complete action onstage.

The plot of *Tender Offer* is the story of how a father and his young daughter resolve their differences during a quarrel and grow closer. When Paul and Lisa finish their tap routine in the dance studio, we sense that something has been resolved between them and that the stage action is complete. The exposition of the plot begins with Lisa's solitary dance as the play starts and continues with the entrance of Paul, who has arrived too late to see Lisa's recital. The development of the quarrel between them is the plot's rising action. Paul's attempts to evade the issue of Lisa's disappointment with him and Lisa's expression of her anger lead to the climax of the action, when she throws her trophy away. The father's "tender offer" to his daughter is the turning point of the plot. Their game together finding shapes in the clouds is the falling action, and their final song and dance duet constitutes the resolution or denouement of the drama. This progression of events develops a story with a beginning, a middle, and an end.

What drives the plot is usually conflict, and drama can be defined most simply as a progression of events that develop and resolve conflicts. Wasserstein's play continues a tradition of drama begun in the fifth century B.C. by such Greek playwrights as Sophocles and analyzed by Aristotle in *The Poetics*. Aristotle emphasized that the plot or story of a play should be unified and complete, with all aspects of the conflict resolved by the end. Suspense is created for the audience before the resolution of the conflict in the plot. We can see both conflict and suspense in this play.

We do not know that there is a problem between Paul and Lisa at the beginning of *Tender Offer*: All we know is that the father is so late picking up his young daughter at the dance studio that he has missed her performance at the recital. This is the dramatic situation that suggests the conflict between them. Suspense begins to build during the events of the rising action, as Wasserstein keeps us in the dark about whether Paul and Lisa will be able to resolve their differences. Lisa procrastinates about going home and suggests indirectly that she is angry with Paul by responding flatly to his opening remarks and baiting him in lines like "Talia Robbins told me she's much happier living without her father in the house." At first Paul is an authoritarian father ("Lisa, stop it. Let's go"); then, as this has no effect, he tries a softer approach ("Honey, I'm tired. Really, later").

Both characters are gentle, "tender" people, so their quarrel does not escalate to physical violence or a life-or-death struggle, but Wasserstein increases the tension between them when Lisa cuts through their skirmishing to confront Paul directly. She asks her father, "Why don't you want to talk to me?" When Paul responds in his customary role as the emotionally reserved parent ("I promise when we get home we'll have a nice talk"), his daughter seems to give up, delaying the resolution of the plot.

Halfway into the story, a complication in the plot occurs when Lisa picks up the trophy she won at the recital, and Paul begins to understand how important the afternoon has been for her. In the second half of the play, he begins to build the bridge between them that allows him to share her feelings, beginning with his next action ("Sit down. Let's talk"). Wasserstein continues to delay the resolution of the conflict and build suspense. Lisa may act calmly, but she is furious with her father. She expresses her anger in words, trying to rile him ("Can we go home now, please?," "Maybe I'll become a prostitute").

Then Wasserstein heightens the suspense: Lisa expresses her frustration by a physical action, throwing her trophy into the trash bin. Her act of hostility is the most violent event in the play, the climax or high point. It is also, of course, an act of hostility toward her father. He reacts as a concerned adult by accepting her action; he is honest enough to admit they have a problem and explains their quarrel in terms that a nine-year-old can understand ("So you and I spend a lot of time being a little scared of each other"). He defuses the tension by surprising her with his "tender offer." Taking her seriously, he shares his feelings with her, and gradually they move closer into a reconciliation symbolized by their song and dance together at the end of the play.

The action of Wasserstein's short play is very tightly constructed, exhibiting what Aristotle would call the unity of time and place. Its action takes less than an hour, and it occurs in one place, the dance studio. In defining the elements of classic drama, Aristotle stipulated that the action of a well-made play should be contained within a restricted period of time and a single physical place. In Sophocles' *Oedipus the King* (p. 1083), for example, the action occurs within one day, and the setting represents one place, the exterior of Oedipus's palace. For centuries theater critics judged playwrights according to their fidelity to Aristotle's rules about these unities, even though such brilliant writers as Shakespeare broke the rules constantly, writing plays like *Hamlet* that have complicated **subplots** with action occurring in different locations over extended periods of time.

Finally, in the eighteenth century, the great English critic Samuel Johnson brought some common sense to the debate. In *The Preface to Shakespeare*, Johnson wrote that Aristotle's analysis was not "an unquestionable principle":

> The truth is that the spectators [of a play in the theater] are always in their senses, and know, from the first act to the last, that the stage is only a stage, and that the players are only players. They came to hear a certain number of lines recited with just gesture and elegant modulation. The lines related to some action, and an action must be in some place; but the different actions that complete a story may be in places very remote from each other. . . . [A] lapse of years is as easily conceived as a passage of hours. In contemplation we easily contract the time of real actions, and therefore willingly permit it to be contracted when we only see their imitation.

Johnson understood that all literature, including drama, is an imitation of life. The actions we watch onstage in *Tender Offer* by the actors portraying Paul and Lisa are only imitations of what happens in a real-life relationship between father and daughter. In the play, as Johnson would have put it, these "imitations produce pain or pleasure, not because they are mistaken for realities, but because they bring realities to mind."

CHARACTERIZATION

Another important means of the playwright is characterization, which, as in a short story, can be the presentation of characters who play either major or minor roles in the action. Both characters in *Tender Offer* play major roles. They are also **round characters,** or fully developed human beings, a father and a daughter who are "tender" toward each other. They work through their quarrel step by step, changing their attitudes as each moves toward a better understanding of the other. In the conflict between parent and child, neither one could be called a hero or a villain. Paul was late to the recital, but he was kept busy at his office. Lisa tries to hurt him by what she says, but she enters into the spirit of his "tender offer" and invites him to look at cloud shapes outside the studio window as a prelude to joining him in their final tap dance.

In classic drama, where conflict between the characters is a confrontation between clearly delineated moral good and moral evil, the terms **protagonist** and **antagonist** are used for the hero (the central character, man or woman) and the villain, respectively. We can consider Lisa the protagonist of *Tender Offer* in that she is present on stage when the play begins, waiting for her father's arrival at the dance studio, and that the ensuing action focuses on her anger toward him. Paul could be called the antagonist because he provokes Lisa's anger, first by being late and then by not noticing she is upset. Both characters have leading roles in the short play, and both are equally complex psychological beings. When the stage directions state that Lisa "mumbles" her line and that there's a "pause" before Paul asks her a question about her friend Talia Robbins, Wasserstein is giving us subtle clues to suggest the growing tension between them.

Like short stories, plays depend on characterization to motivate the action or plot. The events occurring on stage are set in motion by the characters' personalities, and the more we understand their psychological behavior, the closer we come to understanding the play. We assume that the actions that we see on stage are plausible and consistent, within our "reading" of the different characters. We understand, for example, from the play's setting in a dance studio and from what the characters say to each other, that Lisa comes from an affluent family and seems to have a secure economic background. We factor these details into our reading of the play. As a realistic depiction of a father-daughter relationship, the characters in *Tender Offer* are solidly believable. In this short play, unlike many longer plays, there are no minor characters who exist on stage primarily to advance the action of the story or introduce subplots that complicate the main action. Minor characters usually are presented with fewer dimensions to their personalities.

The actors playing the characters can also shape our response to them. Wasserstein tells us at the beginning of *Tender Offer* that Paul has "a sweet, though distant, demeanor," but she does not give any indication of why he is "distant." It could be that while he is temperamentally reserved, he is basically honest in his dealings with his family and just happens to be so caught up in his business that he has neglected his daughter. Or we can imagine that he is "distant" because he has something to hide—for example, perhaps he missed Lisa's dance recital not because he worked late at his office but because he is having an extramarital affair. At the beginning of the play we can decide from the way the actor playing Paul speaks his lines whether we want to believe him. By the end of the play, Paul has reacted so sensitively to Lisa's feelings that we probably trust him and judge him an honest person, at least on the basis of what we have seen of his behavior onstage.

Aristotle maintained in the *Poetics* that characterization in a play was second to the element of plot or action, yet he emphasized the importance of the characters. In his ranking of the elements of drama, Aristotle was apparently as much a pragmatist as he was a theorist, judging the relative importance of plot, character, dialogue, theme, and the other elements on the basis of the literature he had actually seen and read. As evidence for his belief that structuring a good plot was the most essential element in drama, Aristotle said he noticed that beginning writers "manage to hit the mark in verbal expression and character portrayal sooner than they do in plot construction." Other critics have argued that dialogue, not characterization or plot action, is the most important element in drama. You can reach your own conclusion in this matter after you have read more plays.

DIALOGUE

Dialogue is the exchange of words between the characters in a play. In short fiction and poetry, dialogue is often set emotionally for us by the descriptive words that authors use to introduce it. They write, "He shouted," to show strong emotion, for example, or "She wailed," to show extreme unhappiness. Wasserstein tells us that Lisa "mumbles," but playwrights rely primarily on the dialogue to tell their stories.

Most critics agree that dialogue has three main functions in a play: to advance the plot, to establish the setting, and to reveal character. When we say that plot is *dialogue driven* in drama, we mean that the words of the actors advance the plot. In the exposition at the start of the play, the actors' words can also reveal important information about what has gone on before the stage action commences; dialogue continues to introduce new complications throughout the development of the plot. When Lisa greets Paul by saying "Hi, Dad," her words establish their relationship with great economy and precision. When he says, "I'm sorry I'm late" and "How'd it go?," her flat replies suggest her disappointment with him. Their exchange establishes the setting and tells what happened before the play began. In her choice of words, Lisa also hints that something is wrong.

Paul's opening dialogue presents him as a loving, if breezy, parent: "You don't have to stop, sweetheart." He's also a stickler for information, holding his daughter accountable for her actions (" 'Pretty good.' You mean you got a lot of applause or 'pretty good' you could have done better?"). He puts off her question about why he's late with a noncommittal "hmmmmmmmmm," which he repeats evasively when she attempts to give him an order by saying "I wish you wouldn't make appointments to see me." Paul introduces words that Lisa doesn't understand—*maudlin* and *procrastinating*—but she is responsive to him, asking him for definitions and then deliberately misunderstanding him ("I don't go to business. I go to school"). In response, he simplifies his language as if he thinks she is stupid ("What I mean is you want to hang around here until you and I are late for dinner and your mother's angry and it's too late for you to do your homework"). This is the height of the misunderstanding between them.

When we say that Wasserstein has written realistic dialogue between the two characters in *Tender Offer* we mean that the words they speak onstage strike us as the way people could actually have a conversation. With a little thought, you realize that this is not true. Where are the pauses, incomplete sentences, rushes of words, and fillers like "like," "uh," and "you know" that creep into our usual attempts at verbal communication with another human being? We may think we are having a dialogue when we exchange words with another person, but usually it is nothing like the dialogue we hear onstage. Wasserstein has ironed out all the wrinkles in the words that Lisa and Paul exchange. Every word has been chosen for its effect on the listener. This does not mean that Wasserstein's dialogue strikes our ears as false or badly written. It is a tribute to her skill as a playwright that we believe Lisa and Paul talk in the way that people *could* have this conversation—if they were both speaking their lines onstage.

Taking Chekhov as an example, the director Peter Brook has described in *The Open Door* the way that playwrights must go beyond an imitation of life in order to create effective dialogue:

> Life in the theatre is more readable and intense because it is more concentrated. The act of reducing space and compressing time creates a concentrate.
>
> In life we speak in a chattering tumble of repetitive words, yet this quite natural way of expressing ourselves always takes a great deal of time in relation to the actual content of what one wants to say. . . . The [dramatist's] compression consists of removing everything that is not strictly necessary and intensifying what is there, such as putting a strong adjective in the place of a bland one, whilst preserving the impression of spontaneity. If this impression is maintained, we reach the point where if in life it takes two people three hours to say something, onstage it should take three minutes. . . .
>
> With Chekhov, the text gives the impression of having been recorded on tape, of taking its sentences from daily life. But there is not a phrase of Chekhov's that has not been chiseled, polished, modified, with great skill and artistry so as to give the impression that the actor is really speaking "like in daily life."
>
> However, if one tries to speak and behave just like in daily life, one cannot play Chekhov. The actor and the director must follow the same process as the author, which is to be aware that each word, even if it appears to be innocent, is not so. It contains in itself, and in the silence that precedes and follows it, an entire unspoken complexity of energies

between the characters. If one can manage to find that, and if, further-more, one looks for the art needed to conceal it, then one succeeds in say-ing these simple words and giving the impression of life.

In *Tender Offer* Wasserstein also uses dialogue to be funny and lighten up the situation. As a running joke, Paul keeps giving an incorrect title (*raincoat*, *minkcoat*) to the musical he is going to see with his daughter, *Joseph and the Amazing Technicolor Dreamcoat*. Lisa uses colloquialisms like "kinda" and "gross," which Paul adapts into his speech to sustain their fragile bonding near the end of the play ("That sorta looks like a whale on a thimble" and "So I can tell people who come into my office why I have this gross stupid thing on my shelf"). The different levels of diction in each character's choice of words helps to enliven the dialogue, which tends to be matter of fact. This is a characteristic of realistic plays written in recent years, as opposed to the heights of poetic fancy expressed in Shakespearean dialogue. Paul tries to heighten his choice of words when he tells Lisa, "Young lady, I played Yvette Mimimieux in a *Hasty Pudding Show,*" revealing in the process that he has been educated at Harvard by his casual reference to the university's drama club. Their verbal exchange is light years away from the poetry of Hamlet's words pledging obedience to his father's ghost in Act I, Scene V, of *Hamlet:*

> Remember thee!
> Yea, from the table of my memory
> I'll wipe away all trivial fond records,
> All saws of books, all forms, all pressures past
> That youth and observation copied there,
> And thy commandment all alone shall live
> Within the book and volume of my brain,
> Unmix'd with baser matter . . .

The poetic dialogues Shakespeare created in *Hamlet* (p. 1132) are a treasury of words, not only in Hamlet's speeches to the other characters in the play but also in his **soliloquies** (speeches spoken when he is alone onstage). Wasserstein has written her dialogue in *Tender Offer* to mirror the flatter expectations of her characters: Not for them is the poetry in the lines of *Hamlet*.

STAGING

The staging of a play refers to the physical spectacle it presents to the audience in a performance by the actors. It takes into account such elements as the stage set, the different props and costumes used by the actors, their move-ment onstage, and the lighting and sound effects. *Tender Offer* is a one-set play, with its stripped-down dance-studio setting contributing to the spectator's sense of listening in on an intimate family quarrel. By entering his daughter's practice room, the father can become emotionally accessible to her in ways that he probably would not be in his office. We can read the description of the set-ting at the beginning of the play to locate ourselves in the world of the drama, even if the playwright gives only sparse directions (*"A girl of around nine is alone in a dance studio"*) to help us place ourselves in Lisa's story.

The transformation of a play from the page to the stage is usually a collaboration among the director; the actors; and the costume, light, and set designers. Their creativity can help the audience interpret what the dialogue reveals to them as the drama proceeds. Costumes signal aspects of character that the actors are trying to project. The lighting of the sets (now often controlled by technicians with computers transmitting hundreds of cues during a performance) helps to give the stage composition a focus. Light also casts shadows, suggesting a mood and a sense of dimensionality to the actors. The designers' work enables the viewer to *feel* a scene rather than just see it.

In most productions the director has a vision of the play that he or she communicates to the actors and the set, costume, and light designers. In the 1949 staging of Arthur Miller's *Death of a Salesman* (p. 1351), for example, the set designer Jo Mielziner collaborated with the author and director Elia Kazan to create a design concept centered on what he considered "the most important visual symbol in the play," the salesman's house. With great ingenuity, Mielziner constructed his set to harmonize with the effect Miller was trying to achieve in the way he told his story. Mielziner explained,

> Why should that house not be the main set, with all the other scenes—the corner of a graveyard, a hotel room in Boston, the corner of a business office, a lawyer's consultation room, and so on—played on a forestage? If I designed these little scenes in segments and fragments, with easily moved props and fluid lighting effects, I might be able, without ever lowering the curtain, to achieve the easy flow that the author clearly wanted.

The actors' movement onstage during their delivery of the dialogue is called **blocking.** Their nonverbal gestures are known as stage business. At times the playwright can combine the elements of movement and music to create very effective stage business, as with the tap dance symbolizing the harmony between parent and child at the end of *Tender Offer.*

A director can suggest ways for the actors to move on the set and give them stage business to further the action of the plot or support the desired illusion. When the Swedish film director Ingmar Bergman staged Henrik Ibsen's *A Doll House* (p. 1237) in 1992, he began his production by raising the curtain to reveal the woman playing the main character Nora wearing a wine-red dress and seated on a red plush sofa. Surrounded by a clutter of toys, dolls, and doll furniture, she waited motionless for a few moments, staring out into empty space like a human doll ready to be played with.

As readers of plays we become the director, actors, designers, and musicians all in one. We may not be able to visualize Paul and Lisa's tap dance, but reading the text of plays is a challenge to our imaginations to simulate the experience of seeing and hearing them brought to life in a theater.

THEME

As with short fiction and poetry, **theme** is the underlying meaning of a dramatic work, suggested through the dialogue spoken by the characters as they move through the action of the play. Theme must also take into account the overall effect of the different elements of drama, including the way we imagine the play staged in a theater. The theme of Wasserstein's *Tender Offer* could be expressed as the importance of a parent and child's communication with each other to build trust for their future relationship. This acknowledges the playwright's careful structure of her plot and dialogue, so that both Paul and Lisa are held accountable for the breach of good feeling between them, with Paul as a parent who has not kept his promise to attend the recital, and Lisa as a child who is acting out her disappointment. Other interpretations of the theme of *Tender Offer* are possible, of course, just as long as they do not contradict the facts in the play. For example, citing a theme of child abuse or juvenile delinquency would be to disregard what the characters do and say. Only a careless or perverse reader would come up with these faulty statements of the theme.

Awareness of the genre of a play can also help you to express its theme. Reading early plays like Sophocles' *Oedipus the King* and Shakespeare's *Hamlet,* you might find it easier to summarize the theme if you remember that these are examples of *tragedy.* Both of the title characters have a tragic flaw, or defect of character, that brings about the end of their lives as if inevitably decreed by fate. In Tom Stoppard's play *Rosencrantz and Guildenstern Are Dead* (1967), which — like his farcical *Dogg's Hamlet* — is based on Shakespeare's classic, the character of the Player gives this definition of tragedy: "We're tragedians, you see. We follow directions — there is no *choice* involved. The bad end unhappily, the good unluckily. That is what tragedy means."

Willy Russell, a contemporary of Stoppard, explored the definition of tragedy in a funny scene from his play *Educating Rita.* Here the title character, a young woman from a working-class background employed as a hairdresser who is taking classes at an English university, is so excited after seeing her first production of a Shakespeare play that she rushes back to the office of her tutor, Frank, to talk to him about it.

WILLY RUSSELL

From Educating Rita   1983

Frank enters carrying a briefcase and a pile of essays. He goes to the filing cabinet, takes his lecture notes from the briefcase and puts them in a drawer. He takes the sandwiches and apple from his briefcase and puts them on his desk and then goes to the window desk and dumps the essays and briefcase. He switches on the radio and then sits in the swivel chair. He opens the packet of sandwiches, takes a bite, and then picks up a book and starts reading.

Rita bursts through the door out of breath.

FRANK: What are you doing here? (*He looks at his watch.*) It's Thursday, you . . .

RITA (*moving over to the desk; quickly*): I know I shouldn't be here, it's me dinner hour, but listen, I've gorra tell someone, have y' git a few minutes, can y' spare . . . ?

FRANK (*alarmed*): My God, what is it?

RITA: I had to come an' tell y', Frank, last night, I went to the theatre! A proper one, a professional theatre.

Frank gets up and switches off the radio and then returns to the swivel chair.

FRANK (*sighing*): For God's sake, you had me worried, I thought it was something serious.

RITA: No, listen, it was. I went out an' got me ticket, it was Shakespeare, I thought it was gonna be dead borin' . . .

FRANK: Then why did you go in the first place?

RITA: I wanted to find out. But listen, it wasn't borin', it was bleedin' great, honest, ogh, it done me in, it was fantastic. I'm gonna do an essay on it.

FRANK (*smiling*): Come on, which one was it?

Rita moves upper right centre.

RITA: ". . . Out, out, brief candle!
Life's but a walking shadow, a poor player
That struts and frets his hour upon the stage
And then is heard no more. It is a tale
Told by an idiot, full of sound and fury
Signifying nothing."

FRANK (*deliberately*): Ah, *Romeo and Juliet*.

RITA (*moving towards Frank*): Tch. Frank! Be serious. I learnt that today from the book. (*She produces a copy of* Macbeth.) Look, I went out an' bought the book. Isn't it great? What I couldn't get over is how excitin' it was.

Frank puts his feet up on the desk.

RITA: Wasn't his wife a cow, eh? An' that fantastic bit where he meets Macduff an' he thinks he's all invincible. I was on the edge of me seat at that bit. I wanted to shout out an' tell Macbeth, warn him.

FRANK: You didn't, did you?

RITA: Nah. Y' can't do that in a theatre, can y'? It was dead good. It was like a thriller.

FRANK: Yes. You'll have to go and see more.

RITA: I'm goin' to. *Macbeth*'s a tragedy, isn't it?

Frank nods.

RITA: Right.

Rita smiles at Frank and he smiles back at her.

Well I just—I just had to tell someone who'd understand.

FRANK: I'm honoured that you chose me.

RITA (*moving towards the door*): Well, I better get back. I've left a customer with a perm lotion. If I don't get a move on there'll be another tragedy.

FRANK: No. There won't be a tragedy.

RITA: There will, y' know. I know this woman; she's dead fussy. If her perm doesn't come out right there'll be blood an' guts everywhere.

FRANK: Which might be quite tragic—(*He throws her the apple from his desk which she catches.*)—but it won't be a tragedy.

RITA: What?

FRANK: Well—erm—look; the tragedy of the drama has nothing to do with the sort of tragic event you're talking about. Macbeth is flawed by his ambition—yes?

RITA (*going and sitting in the chair by the desk*): Yeh. Go on. (*She starts to eat the apple.*)

FRANK: Erm—it's that flaw which forces him to take the inevitable steps towards his own doom. You see?

Rita offers him the can of soft drink. He takes it and looks at it.

FRANK (*putting the can down on the desk*): No thanks. Whereas, Rita, a woman's hair being reduced to an inch of stubble, or—or the sort of thing you read in the paper that's reported as being tragic, "Man Killed By Falling Tree," is not a tragedy.

RITA: It is for the poor sod under the tree.

FRANK: Yes, it's tragic, absolutely tragic. But it's not a tragedy in the way that *Macbeth* is a tragedy. Tragedy in dramatic terms is inevitable, preordained. Look, now, even without ever having heard the story of *Macbeth* you wanted to shout out, to warn him and prevent him going on, didn't you? But you wouldn't have been able to stop him would you?

RITA: No.

FRANK: Why?

RITA: They would have thrown me out the theatre.

FRANK: But what I mean is that your warning would have been ignored. He's warned in the play. But he can't go back. He still treads the path to doom. But the poor old fellow under the tree hasn't arrived there by following any inevitable steps has he?

RITA: No.

FRANK: There's no particular flaw in his character that has dictated his end. If he'd been warned of the consequences of standing beneath that particular tree he wouldn't have done it, would he? Understand?

RITA: So—so Macbeth brings it on himself?

FRANK: Yes. You see he goes blindly on and on and with every step he's spinning one more piece of thread which will eventually make up the network of his own tragedy. Do you see?

RITA: I think so. I'm not used to thinkin' like this.

FRANK: It's quite easy, Rita.

RITA: It is for you. I just thought it was a dead excitin' story. But the way you tell it you make me see all sorts of things in it. (*After a pause.*) It's fun, tragedy, isn't it?

Frank's explanation of why the death of "the poor old sod under the tree" is not an example of tragedy suggests the difference between tragedy and pathos. Pathos, according to the playwright Arthur Miller, arouses our feelings of "sadness, sympathy, identification, and even fear," while tragedy "brings us knowledge or enlightenment" about the "right way of living in the world." As

Miller observed, "The reason we confuse the tragic with the pathetic, as well as why we create so few [new] tragedies, is twofold: in the first place many of our writers have given up trying to search out the right way of living, and secondly, there is not among us any commonly accepted faith in a way of life that will give us not only material gain but satisfaction."

Another category of drama is the **didactic** play, which teaches a lesson. Although presented within the context of a comedy, Frank's explanation of tragedy in *Educating Rita* is a didactic scene. Didactic plays often teach a lesson about the best way to live or lecture the audience about serious matters.

Modern plays by such authors as Henrik Ibsen, Susan Glaspell, Tennessee Williams, and Lorraine Hansberry are realistic dramas in which the characters seem to exhibit free will in regard to their choices for future action. They are usually a mixture of comic and tragic elements. There is no end to the ways in which plays can be classified (recall Hamlet's troupe of touring actors who are proficient in acting "tragedy, comedy, history, pastoral, pastoral-comical, historical-pastoral, tragical-historical, tragical-comical-historical-pastoral, scene individable, or poem unlimited"). In each case, the way you classify the play can help you to clarify the dramatist's underlying theme.

COMMENTARY *Leonard Mustazza, "Generic Translation and Thematic Shift in Glaspell's* Trifles *and 'A Jury of Her Peers,'" page 1560.*

20.

Reading, Thinking, and Writing about Drama

If my tragedy makes a tragic impression on people, they have only themselves to blame.
— AUGUST STRINDBERG, preface to *Miss Julie*

READING DRAMA

Reading a play allows you to have it both ways: you can stop the action at any time to think about the words on the page, and you can envision what is happening in a make-believe performance in the theater of your mind. Whether you follow a play as a passive spectator or an imaginative reader, you understand that its author is engaged in more than an act of "let's pretend." Most playwrights are attempting to make a serious statement about how we live—both as individuals and as members of society. Like other forms of literature, drama takes us out of our lives and allows us access to a wider range of human thoughts and feelings, showing us our vast potential as individuals for both good and evil.

Having drama available as texts on the page has another advantage. Like other writers, playwrights are conscious of themselves as contributing to an ongoing tradition. It is possible to see many of the plays in this anthology produced onstage or as film, but they are immediately accessible within the covers of this book. Furthermore, in Part One of this anthology, you can read the story by Susan Glaspell that has a counterpart in her play *Trifles*. Glaspell wrote her story "A Jury of Her Peers" (p. 194) after the success of *Trifles* at the Provincetown Playhouse. Comparing the story with the play, you will gain a deeper appreciation of the differences in the two literary genres and the different resources of playwrights and short story writers. You can also appreciate the scope of William Shakespeare's extraordinary achievement as a playwright and a poet by reading his selections in the different parts of this anthology.

Even in such short, relatively simple plays as *Tender Offer* you probably need two readings of the text in order to be able to discuss it in class. On the first reading, let your imagination expand and try to see the play enacted onstage. On the second reading, be more detached from the text and try to analyze it as a work of literature by thinking about how the playwright has used the elements of drama.

For example, Wendy Wasserstein has a double meaning in mind when she uses the term *tender offer* as the title of her play. Its use in business may not be clear to every reader, but she explains it in the conversation between the father and his daughter. In your first reading you will get to understand the literal meaning of the term in business negotiations. As you follow the action on stage to its conclusion, you also see the meaning of the term enacted in the relationship between the two characters. On your second reading, you might allow the literal meaning of the play's title to take on connotative associations, symbolizing the fragile relationship between father and daughter. Then you can go on to consider how this theme is dramatized in the play's other structural elements.

Sometimes you will still have questions about the meaning of a play even after your second reading. Close the book and give yourself some time to think about it. Your effort to understand the work is a necessary part of the learning process. Remember Peter Brook's direction: "In order for something of quality to take place, an empty space needs to be created. An empty space makes it possible for a new phenomenon to come to life, for anything that touches on content, meaning, expression, language, and music can exist only if the experience is fresh and new. However, no fresh and new experience is possible if there isn't a pure, virgin space ready to receive it." If you are still confused after you have thought about the play, write down your questions and bring them to the next class discussion.

In a sense, reading drama is easier than reading poetry and short fiction because playwrights introduce you in a more leisurely fashion to the imaginative world they create on the page. For one thing, plays begin with a description of the characters who perform the action. For example, opening to the first page of Sophocles' *Oedipus the King* (p. 1083), you encounter a list of characters right after the title of the play. The setting or "scene" of the play is also described before you start to read the dialogue between the various characters. In *Oedipus the King* you are told that the Greek stage is meant to suggest the front of the royal house of Thebes. This is a neutral description, but then you learn that "many years have passed since Oedipus solved the riddle of the Sphinx and ascended the throne of Thebes, and now a plague has struck the city. A procession of priests enters; suppliants, broken and despondent, they carry branches wound in wool and lay them on the altar." The editor of the text of *Oedipus the King* is giving you a clue about the serious mood in which the play begins. You do not know what has caused the priests to become so unhappy, but as Oedipus comes forward with a "telltale limp" and the play starts, you read his speech in the prologue with more information to help you understand his words than you have when you begin a poem or a short story.

The opening dialogue between Oedipus and the Priest who speaks for the suppliants is an admirable illustration of the drama at the heart of a great play. There is no physical action as such between the two characters—no brawny fisticuffs, no spectacular duel, no surprising exchange of weapons. Standing side by side, the two actors exchange only words. But the dialogue allows the reader of the play to create a personality for Oedipus and get a first sense of the conflict—or mystery—within his situation that will evoke a sense of pity and terror for him as the play unfolds.

Guidelines for Reading Drama

1. Make an entry in your notebook for each play assigned in class, writing down the author's name and the title and date of the play.
2. Use a dictionary to look up words in the headnote or in the play that you do not understand.
3. Remember that the type of theater—Greek, Elizabethan, realistic, contemporary—prevalent at the time the playwright is working can influence his or her plays.
4. When you start to read a play, note the list of characters and the playwright's description of them. Try to envision the set, if it is described at the beginning of the various scenes and acts.
5. As you read the dialogue, imagine the gestures and the costumes of the actors specified in the stage directions or suggested by what the characters say.
6. Notice what the characters *don't* say in the dialogue—their pauses and silences. Remember that their words, like those of real people, are not always to be trusted.

CRITICAL THINKING ABOUT DRAMA

As in your study of short fiction and poetry, your critical thinking about a play depends on your first having formulated an interpretation of it after reading and perhaps rereading the text. Then you can begin asking yourself questions about different aspects of the work's structure, depending on the topic you are writing about. The various elements of drama are often the focus of a critical inquiry. The questions to help you think critically about drama are similar to those asked of short fiction. You might consider the following topics as you read.

Plot. What is the conflict of the play? Is it developed in separate stages of rising action, complication, climax, falling action, and resolution? Can you find examples of foreshadowing? Does the play have a subplot or second plot? How is it related to the main plot? Is there any repetition of significant action? If so, what do you think the playwright intended?

Characters. Is there a protagonist and an antagonist in the play? Do you think that they are presented as round or flat, static or dynamic characters? Are they realistic or symbolic? Often in drama it helps you to think critically about characterization if you select one character for your analysis. How is this character described in stage directions? How do other characters in the play see him or her? How does the character view himself or herself? What words or actions given to this character help to define his or her personality?

Dialogue. Which is given more emphasis in the play, dialogue or physical action? Is the dialogue realistic or symbolic? To what effect does the author use poetic, colloquial, or dialect English? What is the tone of the speeches? Does the playwright use consistent patterns of imagery or metaphor in the speeches of different characters in order to suggest something important about them?

Stage Setting. How does the setting help establish the time and place of the play? Is the setting realistic or symbolic? What objects onstage are particularly important in suggesting the mood of the characters or their values? What does the setting suggest about the theme of the play? How would a different staging of the play affect your interpretation?

Irony and Symbolism. Can you find any instances of dramatic irony in the play when you (as a reader or spectator) know more about the situation than do the onstage characters? Does this make you more or less sympathetic toward the characters? What aspects of the play and its staging seem symbolic? What do they symbolize? Is the symbolism extensive enough to form an allegorical system? If so, what is the meaning implied by the allegory?

Theme. What ideas explored by the play seem most significant to you? Which of the preceding elements of the play conveys the theme most effectively? Does the playwright give a clear statement of the theme to any one of the characters? If there is no resolution of the theme in the action of the play, what emotional effect does this have on you? Is the conflict between the characters a struggle between moral good and moral evil? Is the playwright attempting to *explain* or to *explore* the issues?

It will also help you to understand drama if you remember that playwrights, like all other writers, create their plays within a tradition. The genius of Sophocles, Shakespeare, and Henrik Ibsen is inimitable, but their plays have inspired later playwrights to give their own interpretation of similar themes or develop their own approach based on an awareness of the earlier writers' dramatic techniques. Writing their plays during periods when the theater flourished in ancient Greece and Renaissance England, Sophocles and Shakespeare borrowed or appropriated the plots of *Oedipus the King* and *Hamlet* from legend, history, and earlier plays — a standard practice among playwrights in their historical periods. Appropriation, or creating a new work by taking something from a previous work, continues today as part of the legacy of our cultural heritage of literature, music, and art. As a technique or method of working, appropriation can become a new vehicle for playwrights to express their view of the human condition.

Sophocles' and Shakespeare's versions of earlier material survive because their dramatic works reveal the fullest dimensions of their sources. Their brilliant exploration of the characters of Oedipus and Hamlet have kept their plays alive in theater repertoires throughout the world, whereas the literature that gave them the ideas for their plays is now known only to specialists. The essay by Francis Fergusson on *Oedipus the King* in the Commentaries section

(p. 1536) and that by Geoffrey Bullough on *Hamlet* in Chapter 23, "Conversations on *Hamlet* as Text and Performance" (p. 1589), will help you to understand how Sophocles and Shakespeare transformed their sources into great works of literature.

The influence of Greek dramatists such as Sophocles has continued to the present day. When Arthur Miller was interviewed by Leonard Moss in 1980, Miller said that he "would have liked to live in Greece with the tragedies." He went on to explain the influence of earlier writers on him: "I attach myself to Ibsen because I saw him as a contemporary Greek, and I suppose it's because there was a terrific reliance in him as there was in the Greeks on the idea of the continuity between the distant past and the present. 'The birds come home to roost' — they always did; your character was your fate. I like that immensely."

Playwrights are often willing to discuss how they were influenced by earlier writers. A few years after the debut of *Death of a Salesman,* when Miller adapted Ibsen's play *An Enemy of the People* for American audiences in 1951, he wrote a preface to the published version of the play to explain the strong influence of Ibsen's work on him:

> There is one quality in Ibsen that no serious writer can afford to overlook. It lies at the very center of his force, and I found in it — as I hope others will — a profound source of strength. It is his insistence, his utter conviction, that he is going to say what he has to say, and that the audience, by God, is going to listen. It is the very same quality that makes a star actor, a great public speaker, and a lunatic. Every Ibsen play begins with the unwritten words: "Now listen here!" And these words have shown me a path through the wall of "entertainment," a path that leads beyond the formulas and dried-up precepts, the pretense and fraud, of the business of the stage. Whatever else Ibsen has to teach, this is his first and greatest contribution.

As the critic Seymour L. Flaxman observed, "The realistic drama reached the peak of its development with Ibsen, and in many ways this style continues to dominate the drama today." Ibsen extended the use of discussion and debate in the dialogues between his characters to probe their mental states, and his method of analytic exposition survives in the structure of later work by Miller and Tennessee Williams as well as Lorraine Hansberry and Paula Vogel, to name only a few recent American dramatists. All of these playwrights have gone beyond Ibsen's realism to incorporate symbolic and expressionistic elements in their work, as Ibsen himself did in his later plays.

Sometimes the actors who interpret a play onstage are in a special position to perceive affinities between playwrights. Geraldine Page, an actress with a special affinity for Williams's work, has sensed the influence of Chekhov's plays on Williams. She told an interviewer that Chekhov "gives so much of the drama out of the surface noise of life. I mean in a lot of the Chekhov plays, people are sitting around talking about tea or going fishing or things that are not to do with the central drama, but to do with the way human beings express themselves and convey these things. And Tennessee uses that too."

The contemporary playwright Edward Albee often gives provocative interviews about both the positive and negative influence of earlier playwrights on him. Albee acknowledged a negative influence in Eugene O'Neill, who argued in his plays that people needed deceptions or dreams in their lives in order to live. Albee confessed that he "probably became a playwright as much as anything to refute that whole argument of O'Neill." Like the great German playwright Bertolt Brecht, Albee has what the editor Philip Kolin describes as a "combative" view of the theater, believing that it "must disturb in order to reform society." Albee explained, "I don't think you should frighten them [the audience], I think you should terrify them."

Albee has also been outspoken in his advice to aspiring playwrights. Discussing his craft in *Dramatics* magazine, he cautioned young writers about the harmful influence of reading too many great plays:

> But let me tell you one thing, if you are going to learn from other writers, don't only read the great ones, because if you do that you'll get so filled with despair and the fear that you'll never be able to do anywhere near as well as they did that you'll stop writing. I recommend that you read a lot of bad stuff, too. It's very encouraging. "Hey, I can do so much better than this." Read the greatest stuff but read the stuff that isn't so great, too. Great stuff is very discouraging. If you read only Beckett and Chekhov you'll go away and only deliver telegrams at Western Union.

Reading widely in the history of drama, you become aware that talented writers often come of age in clusters or groups, sometimes influenced by specific theaters or directors. The cluster of playwrights in Athens who created the great tragedies for the stage during the Golden Age of Greece is well known and includes Aeschylus, Euripides, and Sophocles. The Provincetown Players, an experimental theater that flourished in the early years of this century in the bohemian enclaves of Provincetown, Massachusetts, and Greenwich Village in New York City, supported another group of writers whose plays have stood the test of time—Susan Glaspell, Eugene O'Neill, and Edna St. Vincent Millay, among scores of others. The creative work of these playwrights helped establish the modern American theater, preparing the way for the gifted playwrights of the next generation.

WRITING ABOUT DRAMA

An assignment to write an essay about a specific play or aspect of drama will give you the opportunity to bring your ideas about what you have read into focus. The process of writing about drama will sharpen your critical analysis of the text you have chosen to discuss and will clarify your understanding of the ideas dramatized by the playwright. Because every reader's background is different, your reading of the plays will reflect the life experience that you bring to them. Using the vocabulary of the elements of drama to help you express your thoughts about the plays, you have the opportunity to articulate your interpretations clearly and forcibly to another reader.

Finally, remember that while you can always compare and contrast the literary texts in this anthology, you can also get additional ideas for your papers by seeing a play produced on film or in the theater. In your essay, you will be expected to analyze your impressions beyond summarizing the plot. The questions about drama earlier in this chapter can help you think critically about the play.

Often, choosing a specific critical approach in your paper—biographical, historical, or reader-response, for example—can give you a perspective from which to take useful notes during your second close reading of the play. Taking such an approach will clarify your understanding of how the playwright has developed dialogue, images, and patterns of action. In the Commentaries section that starts on page 1528, you will find material that illustrates different critical perspectives and suggests background information for your essays.

COMMENTARIES *Geoffrey Bullough, "Sources of Shakespeare's* Hamlet*," page 1589; Francis Fergusson, "Oedipus, Myth and Play," page 1536; Leonard Mustazza, "Generic Translation and Thematic Shift in Glaspell's* Trifles *and 'A Jury of Her Peers,'" page 1560; Helge Normann Nilsen, "Marxism and the Early Plays of Arthur Miller," page 1569; Joan Templeton, "Is* A Doll House *a Feminist Text?" page 1575.*

WEB *For writing suggestions on each playwright in this anthology, visit bedfordstmartins.com/charters/litwriters.*

21.

Plays and Playwrights

SOPHOCLES

Sophocles (495–406 B.C.), along with Aeschylus and Euripides, was one of the three major authors of Greek tragedy. He lived for nearly ninety years through most of the turbulent events of his country during the fifth century B.C. He was only five when the Greek army turned back the invading Persians at Marathon, but he probably heard that after the battle a messenger brought word of the victory back to Athens, running the twenty-six miles between Marathon and Athens and dying of exhaustion while delivering the news. Ten years later, in 480 B.C., the Greeks won another major battle against the Persian navy at Salamis. At the victory celebration Sophocles, a teenager trained in dance, is said to have made his first public appearance dancing nude to his own lyre accompaniment.

The period in which the Greek playwrights flourished is known as the Golden Age. Athens became rich as the city's allies paid its statesmen tribute money, and statesmen honored the gifted poets, playwrights, philosophers, architects, and scientists who thrived in the city. This great period lasted barely to the last years of the century, starting its decline when the armed forces of the Greek city-state were defeated in Sicily in 413 B.C. Six years later, just before the death of Sophocles, the Spartans destroyed the Greek navy at Aegospotami and imposed their own government in Athens, bringing the Golden Age to an end.

The earliest extant Greek play for two actors, Aeschylus's The Persians, *dates from 472 B.C. Thirty years younger than Aeschylus, Sophocles won his first prize for one of his plays in 468 B.C. at the Great Dionysia during the competition for playwrights in Athens. The Great Dionysia was the name given to the important holiday each year when the Greek plays were produced. Occurring just before the arrival of spring, the festival honored Dionysus, the god of fertility and growth, who was mysteriously linked to Hades, the lord of the underworld and death. The celebration began in Athens with a procession carrying a statue of Dionysus from his temple to the theater at the Acropolis. It included the ritual slaying of a sacrificial bull and much drunken revelry, as Dionysus was also the god of wine in Greece.*

The high point of the annual festival was the three-day competition among the playwrights, each of whom submitted four plays: three tragedies (tragedy was considered the highest form of drama by the Greeks) and a brief satyr play, which combined slapstick and erotic comedy. A comic play was also included in the performances, so although the plays were relatively short, the audience was expected to have sufficient stamina and interest to sit through several plays each day. As the British playwright Tony Harrison has observed, the Greek dramatists were "open-eyed about suffering but with a heart still open to celebration and physical affirmation." Traditionally during the Great Dionysia, a comic play began the program each day, and the tragic plays were followed by a satyr play to maintain "a kind of celebratory route in the sensual and everyday to follow the tragedy."

The dramatic performances at the Acropolis were part of a religious celebration, a public holiday rather than a commercial theater, with the entire population of the city marching in the procession and thousands of people filling the amphitheater on the slopes of the Acropolis to watch the plays. Originally the audience sat on the ground, then on wooden seats. When the weight of the crowd caused the wooden seats to collapse, they were replaced with concentric tiers of stone seats designed on the hillside to surround the stage almost completely. The high priest of Dionysus sat at the place of honor at the center of the first tier of this theater-in-the-round in Athens.

To keep order among the huge crowd, there were strict laws—apparently even the penalty of death—against taking another person's seat or engaging in fights. Tickets were expensive (almost the price of a laborer's daily wage), but funds were available so that poor people and slaves could attend. To underscore the religious importance of the event, prisoners were released from jail so they could also participate. Evidence suggests that women weren't admitted into the audience to watch Greek plays, but this is a contentious point argued by archeologists and historians.

During the three days of theater in Athens each year, it was customary for playwrights to act in their own plays. Apparently Sophocles could dance better than he could project his voice onstage (contemporary viewers describe him as having a "small voice"), and this would explain why he did not perform the leading role in his plays. Sophocles originated the practice of giving parts to a third actor onstage and introduced such innovations as painted scenery and a larger tragic chorus (increasing it from twelve men to fifteen). Active as a playwright in Athens for over half a century, he wrote more than a hundred plays and won first prize at the Great Dionysia eighteen times, more than any other playwright. Today only seven complete Sophoclean tragedies survive (the Oedipus trilogy and the plays Philoctetes, Ajax, Trachiniae, and Elektra) as well as a satyr play about the childhood of the god Hermes and nearly a thousand fragments of his other plays.

Sophocles and other playwrights who introduced their work during the Great Dionysia sought to arouse pity and fear among the spectators with their tragic plays about death and suffering; they sought to instill a sense of religious awe at the mysterious power of the gods, whose perfect knowledge of events stands in contrast to the imperfect knowledge of mortal beings. In classical Greek theater, only men were actors. They wore shoes with high heels to increase their stature and masks to help amplify their voices and simulate their appearance as mythical heroes or gods. The masks and costumes also enabled them to assume the roles of women, who were often central characters in the plays that dramatized mythical stories and legends made famous by earlier poets and historians. Actors were trained in singing and dancing as well as speaking, but in the large amphitheaters they were judged by how effectively they projected their voices to suggest the emotional states of their characters. The design of the outdoor theater and the costuming and masks of the actors contributed to the audience's sense of participation in a religious ritual. The importance of respecting the oracles—and of accepting the gods' prophecy, which is often fulfilled in ways that humans do not expect—is frequently mentioned in Oedipus the King. At the end of the play Oedipus has learned to his sorrow that the gods are omnipotent and that he cannot escape his fate.

Audiences watching Oedipus the King would have known the legendary story before they came to the theater. At the beginning of the play they were aware of the tragic flaw of pride in Oedipus's character and understood the mysterious circumstances of his birth far better than he did. In the theater, the spectators' pleasure would derive from recognizing the dramatic irony in the poetic dialogue and the elegant way Sophocles structured the events of the story as Oedipus gradually uncovers the truth about his past. Unlike Aeschylian tragedy, which is essentially static, Sophocles unfolded the incidents of Oedipus's past like a detective story, linking events by cause and effect and motivating them plausibly. In the process Sophocles also revealed different dimensions of his protagonist's character, his strong as well as his weak points. Oedipus exhibits a high moral character as king. He is genuinely concerned about his subjects and eager to help them during the plague that has descended on the city. Yet he is quick to suspect his loyal brother-in-law Creon of a plot to usurp his power and ready to taunt his heartbroken wife, Jocasta, when he thinks she is glorying in her "noble blood."

Sophocles was nicknamed "the Attic Bee" because he relied on such earlier works as Homer's Iliad and Odyssey for material for his plays, but he always developed his characterizations far beyond his sources and created dialogue marked by eloquence and vigor. He also gave active roles to the chorus of citizens and the messenger, who function as important characters in the play. When Sophocles began Oedipus the King by having the king promise the chorus of citizens to help fight the plague, the playwright knew that this detail would arouse sympathy in the Athenian audience, because plague had ravaged their city only five years before. This addition also deepens our sense of foreboding at the beginning of the play, because Sophocles was suggesting a further irony about Oedipus's character. It was believed at the time that the well-being of the state was a reflection of the health of its ruler. The Greek audience would know that, according to legend, Oedipus was a descendent of Cadmus, the founder of Thebes. The city had a disputed leadership because of a fraternal rivalry that the gods had decreed would wipe out Cadmus's entire family. Oedipus the King is the first of the trilogy of plays Sophocles wrote about this tragic situation. When the three plays are produced together, they are usually presented in the order that follows the chronology of events in the plot: Oedipus the King (first produced between 430 and 427 B.C.),

Oedipus at Colonus *(posthumously produced in 401 B.C.), and* Antigone *(first produced in 441 B.C.).*

Oedipus the King *was considered such a masterpiece a century after its creation that the philosopher and critic Aristotle used it in the* Poetics *as the example on which to base his aesthetic theory of drama. Aristotle understood that Sophocles structured the story of* Oedipus the King *so that the rising action that revealed the complications of the plot led to Oedipus's moment of recognition in the second half of the play, precisely at the time the falling action began. In Aristotle's analysis, this combination of a serious character defect combined with the destiny ordained by the implacable gods constitutes a "tragic flaw." Sophocles structured his play so as to first arouse pity and fear in the spectators watching the proud and headstrong Oedipus gradually unravel the truth about his past, and then allow them to experience a purging or catharsis of their emotions at the sight of Oedipus broken by the gods' prophecy at the end of the play. Yet, paradoxically, the blinded figure of Oedipus remains heroic, because his determination to discover the truth about his own identity remains a moral victory despite the tragic outcome of his search. This dramatic illustration of the gods' power over human frailty must have been a transcendent religious experience for the audience during the festival of Dionysus.*

COMMENTARIES *Aristotle, "On the Elements and General Principles of Tragedy," page 1528; Francis Fergusson, "Oedipus, Myth and Play," page 1536; Sigmund Freud, "The Oedipus Complex," page 1543.*

WEB *Research Sophocles and answer questions about his work at bedfordstmartins.com/charters/litwriters.*

Oedipus the King

c. 430 B.C.

TRANSLATED BY ROBERT FAGLES

CHARACTERS

OEDIPUS, king of Thebes
A PRIEST of Zeus
CREON, brother of Jocasta
A CHORUS of Theban citizens and
    their LEADER
TIRESIAS, a blind prophet
JOCASTA, the queen, wife of
    Oedipus

A MESSENGER from Corinth
A SHEPHERD
A MESSENGER from inside the palace
ANTIGONE, ISMENE, daughters
    of Oedipus and Jocasta
GUARDS AND ATTENDANTS
PRIESTS OF THEBES

TIME AND SCENE: *The royal house of Thebes. Double doors dominate the facade; a stone altar stands at the center of the stage.*

    Many years have passed since Oedipus solved the riddle of the Sphinx°and ascended the throne of Thebes, and now a plague has struck the city. A procession

---

s.d. the riddle of the Sphinx: The Sphinx asked, "What walks on four legs in the morning, two at noon, and three in the evening?" Oedipus replied, "Man."

of priests enters; suppliants, broken and despondent, they carry branches wound in wool° *and lay them on the altar.*

    The doors open. Guards assemble. Oedipus comes forward, majestic but for a telltale limp, and slowly views the condition of his people.

OEDIPUS: Oh my children, the new blood of ancient Thebes,
    why are you here? Huddling at my altar,
    praying before me, your branches wound in wool.
    Our city reeks with the smoke of burning incense,
    rings with cries for the Healer and wailing for the dead.   5
    I thought it wrong, my children, to hear the truth
    from others, messengers. Here I am myself—
    you all know me, the world knows my fame:
    I am Oedipus.

Helping a Priest to his feet.

                Speak up, old man. Your years,
    your dignity—you should speak for the others.   10
    Why here and kneeling, what preys upon you so?
    Some sudden fear? some strong desire?
    You can trust me; I am ready to help,
    I'll do anything. I would be blind to misery
    not to pity my people kneeling at my feet.   15
PRIEST: Oh Oedipus, king of the land, our greatest power!
    You see us before you, men of all ages
    clinging to your altars. Here are boys,
    still too weak to fly from the nest,
    and here the old, bowed down with the years,   20
    the holy ones—a priest of Zeus° myself—and here
    the picked, unmarried men, the young hope of Thebes.
    And all the rest, your great family gathers now,
    branches wreathed, massing in the squares,
    kneeling before the two temples of queen Athena°   25
    or the river-shrine where the embers glow and die
    and Apollo sees the future in the ashes.
                      Our city—
    look around you, see with your own eyes—
    our ship pitches wildly, cannot lift her head
    from the depths, the red waves of death . . .   30
    Thebes is dying. A blight on the fresh crops
    and the rich pastures, cattle sicken and die,
    and the women die in labor, children stillborn,
    and the plague, the fiery god of fever hurls down

---

s.d. wool: Wool was used in offerings to Apollo, the god of poetry, sun, prophecy, and healing.   **21. Zeus:** The highest Olympian deity and father of Apollo.   **25. Athena:** The goddess of wisdom and protector of Greek cities.

on the city, his lightning slashing through us—   35
raging plague in all its vengeance, devastating
the house of Cadmus!° And Black Death luxuriates
in the raw, wailing miseries of Thebes.

Now we pray to you. You cannot equal the gods,
your children know that, bending at your altar.   40
But we do rate you first of men,
both in the common crises of our lives
and face-to-face encounters with the gods.
You freed us from the Sphinx; you came to Thebes
and cut us loose from the bloody tribute we had paid   45
that harsh, brutal singer. We taught you nothing,
no skill, no extra knowledge, still you triumphed.
A god was with you, so they say, and we believe it—
you lifted up our lives.
                              So now again,
Oedipus, king, we bend to you, your power—   50
we implore you, all of us on our knees:
find us strength, rescue! Perhaps you've heard
the voice of a god or something from other men,
Oedipus . . . what do you know?
The man of experience—you see it every day—   55
his plans will work in a crisis, his first of all.
Act now—we beg you, best of men, raise up our city!
Act, defend yourself, your former glory!
Your country calls you savior now
for your zeal, your action years ago.   60
Never let us remember of your reign:
you helped us stand, only to fall once more.
Oh raise up our city, set us on our feet.
The omens were good that day you brought us joy—
be the same man today!   65
Rule our land, you know you have the power,
but rule a land of the living, not a wasteland.
Ship and towered city are nothing, stripped of men
alive within it, living all as one.

OEDIPUS: My children,
I pity you. I see—how could I fail to see   70
what longings bring you here? Well I know
you are sick to death, all of you,
but sick as you are, not one is sick as I.
Your pain strikes each of you alone, each
in the confines of himself, no other. But my spirit   75

---

37. Cadmus: The legendary founder of Thebes.

grieves for the city, for myself and all of you.
I wasn't asleep, dreaming. You haven't wakened me—
I've wept through the nights, you must know that,
groping, laboring over many paths of thought.
After a painful search I found one cure: 80
I acted at once. I sent Creon,
my wife's own brother, to Delphi°—
Apollo the Prophet's oracle—to learn
what I might do or say to save our city.

Today's the day. When I count the days gone by   85
it torments me . . . what is he doing?
Strange, he's late, he's gone too long.
But once he returns, then, then I'll be a traitor
if I do not do all the god makes clear.

PRIEST: Timely words. The men over there   90
are signaling—Creon's just arriving.

OEDIPUS:

Sighting Creon, then turning to the altar.

                                       Lord Apollo,
let him come with a lucky word of rescue,
shining like his eyes!

PRIEST: Welcome news, I think—he's crowned, look,
and the laurel wreath is bright with berries.   95

OEDIPUS: We'll soon see. He's close enough to hear—

Enter Creon from the side; his face is shaded with a wreath.

Creon, prince, my kinsman, what do you bring us?
What message from the god?

CREON: Good news.
I tell you even the hardest things to bear,
if they should turn out well, all would be well.   100

OEDIPUS: Of course, but what were the god's *words?* There's no hope
and nothing to fear in what you've said so far.

CREON: If you want my report in the presence of these . . .

Pointing to the priests while drawing Oedipus toward the palace.

I'm ready now, or we might go inside.

OEDIPUS: Speak out,
speak to us all. I grieve for these, my people,   105
far more than I fear for my own life.

CREON: Very well,
I will tell you what I heard from the god.
Apollo commands us—he was quite clear—
"Drive the corruption from the land,

---

82. **Delphi:** The shrine where the oracle of Apollo held forth.

don't harbor it any longer, past all cure,   110
don't nurse it in your soil—root it out!"
OEDIPUS: How can we cleanse ourselves—what rites?
    What's the source of the trouble?
CREON: Banish the man, or pay back blood with blood.
    Murder sets the plague-storm on the city.
OEDIPUS: Whose murder?   115
    Whose fate does Apollo bring to light?
CREON: Our leader,
    my lord, was once a man named Laius,
    before you came and put us straight on course.
OEDIPUS: I know—
    or so I've heard. I never saw the man myself.
CREON: Well, he was killed, and Apollo commands us now—   120
    he could not be more clear,
    "Pay the killers back—whoever is responsible."
OEDIPUS: Where on earth are they? Where to find it now,
    the trail of the ancient guilt so hard to trace?
CREON: "Here in Thebes," he said.   125
    Whatever is sought for can be caught, you know,
    whatever is neglected slips away.
OEDIPUS: But where,
    in the palace, the fields or foreign soil,
    where did Laius meet his bloody death?
CREON: He went to consult an oracle, he said,   130
    and he set out and never came home again.
OEDIPUS: No messenger, no fellow-traveler saw what happened?
    Someone to cross-examine?
CREON: No,
    they were all killed but one. He escaped,
    terrified, he could tell us nothing clearly,   135
    nothing of what he saw—just one thing.
OEDIPUS: What's that?
    One thing could hold the key to it all,
    a small beginning gives us grounds for hope.
CREON: He said thieves attacked them—a whole band,
    not single-handed, cut King Laius down.
OEDIPUS: A thief,   140
    so daring, wild, he'd kill a king? Impossible,
    unless conspirators paid him off in Thebes.
CREON: We suspected as much. But with Laius dead
    no leader appeared to help us in our troubles.
OEDIPUS: Trouble? Your *king* was murdered—royal blood!   145
    What stopped you from tracking down the killer
    then and there?
CREON: The singing, riddling Sphinx.

She . . . persuaded us to let the mystery go
and concentrate on what lay at our feet.

OEDIPUS: No,
I'll start again—I'll bring it all to light myself!   150
Apollo is right, and so are you, Creon,
to turn our attention back to the murdered man.
Now you have *me* to fight for you, you'll see:
I am the land's avenger by all rights
and Apollo's champion too.   155
But not to assist some distant kinsman, no,
for my own sake I'll rid us of this corruption.
Whoever killed the king may decide to kill me too,
with the same violent hand—by avenging Laius
I defend myself.

To the priests.

                              Quickly, my children.   160
Up from the steps, take up your branches now.

To the guards.

One of you summon the city here before us,
tell them I'll do everything. God help us,
we will see our triumph—or our fall.

Oedipus and Creon enter the palace, followed by the guards.

PRIEST: Rise, my sons. The kindness we came for   165
Oedipus volunteers himself.
Apollo has sent his word, his oracle—
Come down, Apollo, save us, stop the plague.

*The priests rise, remove their branches, and exit to the side. Enter a Chorus, the cit-
izens of Thebes, who have not heard the news that Creon brings. They march around
the altar, chanting.*

CHORUS: Zeus!
Great welcome voice of Zeus, what do you bring?
What word from the gold vaults of Delphi   170
comes to brilliant Thebes? I'm racked with terror—
                              terror shakes my heart
and I cry your wild cries, Apollo, Healer of Delos°
I worship you in dread . . . what now, what is your price?
some new sacrifice? some ancient rite from the past   175
come round again each spring?—
                              what will you bring to birth?
Tell me, child of golden Hope
        warm voice that never dies!
You are the first I call, daughter of Zeus   180

---

173. Delos: Apollo was born on this sacred island.

deathless Athena — I call your sister Artemis,°
heart of the market place enthroned in glory,
        guardian of our earth —
I call Apollo astride the thunderheads of heaven —
O triple shield against death, shine before me now!   185
If ever, once in the past, you stopped some ruin
launched against our walls
      you hurled the flame of pain
far, far from Thebes — you gods
  come now, come down once more!
           No, no   190
the miseries numberless, grief on grief, no end —
too much to bear, we are all dying
O my people . . .
   Thebes like a great army dying
and there is no sword of thought to save us, no   195
and the fruits of our famous earth, they will not ripen
no and the women cannot scream their pangs to birth —
screams for the Healer, children dead in the womb
    and life on life goes down
       you can watch them go   200
  like seabirds winging west, outracing the day's fire
down the horizon, irresistibly
    streaking on to the shores of Evening
           Death
so many deaths, numberless deaths on deaths, no end —
Thebes is dying, look, her children   205
stripped of pity . . .
   generations strewn on the ground
unburied, unwept, the dead spreading death
and the young wives and gray-haired mothers with them
cling to the altars, trailing in from all over the city —   210
Thebes, city of death, one long cortege
    and the suffering rises
       wails for mercy rise
    and the wild hymn for the Healer blazes out
clashing with our sobs our cries of mourning —   215
  O golden daughter of god, send rescue
  radiant as the kindness in your eyes!
Drive him back! — the fever, the god of death
      that raging god of war
not armored in bronze, not shielded now, he burns me,   220
battle cries in the onslaught burning on —
O rout him from our borders!

---

181. Artemis: Apollo's sister, the goddess of hunting, the moon, and chastity.

Sail him, blast him out to the Sea-queen's chamber
the black Atlantic gulfs
or the northern harbor, death to all   225
where the Thracian surf comes crashing.
Now what the night spares he comes by day and kills—
the god of death.
O lord of the stormcloud,
you who twirl the lightning, Zeus, Father,
thunder Death to nothing!   230

Apollo, lord of the light, I beg you—
whip your longbow's golden cord
showering arrows on our enemies—shafts of power
champions strong before us rushing on!

Artemis, Huntress,   235
torches flaring over the eastern ridges—
ride Death down in pain!

God of the headdress gleaming gold, I cry to you—
your name and ours are one, Dionysus°—
come with your face aflame with wine   240
your raving women's cries°
your army on the march! Come with the lightning
come with torches blazing, eyes ablaze with glory!
Burn that god of death that all gods hate!

*Oedipus enters from the palace to address the Chorus, as if addressing the entire
city of Thebes.*

OEDIPUS: You pray to the gods? Let me grant your prayers.   245
Come, listen to me—do what the plague demands:
you'll find relief and lift your head from the depths.

I will speak out now as a stranger to the story,
a stranger to the crime. If I'd been present then,
there would have been no mystery, no long hunt   250
without a clue in hand. So now, counted
a native Theban years after the murder,
to all of Thebes I make this proclamation:
if any one of you knows who murdered Laius,
the son of Labdacus, I order him to reveal   255
the whole truth to me. Nothing to fear,
even if he must denounce himself,
let him speak up
and so escape the brunt of the charge—

---

239. Dionysus: The god of fertility and wine. **241. your . . . cries:** Dionysus was
attended by female celebrants.

he will suffer no unbearable punishment,   260
nothing worse than exile, totally unharmed.

Oedipus pauses, waiting for a reply.

                                            Next,
if anyone knows the murderer is a stranger,
a man from alien soil, come, speak up.
I will give him a handsome reward, and lay up
gratitude in my heart for him besides.   265

Silence again, no reply.

But if you keep silent, if anyone panicking,
trying to shield himself or friend or kin,
rejects my offer, then hear what I will do.
I order you, every citizen of the state
where I hold throne and power: banish this man —   270
whoever he may be — never shelter him, never
speak a word to him, never make him partner
to your prayers, your victims burned to the gods.
Never let the holy water touch his hands.
Drive him out, each of you, from every home.   275
He is the plague, the heart of our corruption,
as Apollo's oracle has revealed to me
just now. So I honor my obligations:
I fight for the god and for the murdered man.

Now my curse on the murderer. Whoever he is,   280
a lone man unknown in his crime
or one among many, let that man drag out
his life in agony, step by painful step —
I curse myself as well . . . if by any chance
he proves to be an intimate of our house,   285
here at my hearth, with my full knowledge,
may the curse I just called down on him strike me!

These are your orders: perform them to the last.
I command you, for my sake, for Apollo's, for this country
blasted root and branch by the angry heavens.   290
Even if god had never urged you on to act,
how could you leave the crime uncleansed so long?
A man so noble — your king, brought down in blood —
you should have searched. But I am the king now,
I hold the throne that he held then, possess his bed   295
and a wife who shares our seed . . . why, our seed
might be the same, children born of the same mother
might have created blood-bonds between us
if his hope of offspring hadn't met disaster —
but fate swooped at his head and cut him short.   300
So I will fight for him as if he were my father,

stop at nothing, search the world
to lay my hands on the man who shed his blood,
the son of Labdacus descended of Polydorus,
Cadmus of old and Agenor, founder of the line: 305
their power and mine are one.
                            Oh dear gods,
my curse on those who disobey these orders!
Let no crops grow out of the earth for them —
shrivel their women, kill their sons,
burn them to nothing in this plague   310
that hits us now, or something even worse.
But you, loyal men of Thebes who approve my actions,
may our champion, Justice, may all the gods
be with us, fight beside us to the end!

LEADER: In the grip of your curse, my king, I swear   315
    I'm not the murderer, cannot point him out.
    As for the search, Apollo pressed it on us —
    he should name the killer.

OEDIPUS: Quite right,
    but to force the gods to act against their will —
    no man has the power.

LEADER: Then if I might mention   320
    the next best thing . . .

OEDIPUS: The third best too —
    don't hold back, say it.

LEADER: I still believe . . .
    Lord Tiresias sees with the eyes of Lord Apollo.
    Anyone searching for the truth, my king,
    might learn it from the prophet, clear as day.   325

OEDIPUS: I've not been slow with that. On Creon's cue
    I sent the escorts, twice, within the hour.
    I'm surprised he isn't here.

LEADER: We need him —
    without him we have nothing but old, useless rumors.

OEDIPUS: Which rumors? I'll search out every word.   330

LEADER: Laius was killed, they say, by certain travelers.

OEDIPUS: I know — but no one can find the murderer.

LEADER: If the man has a trace of fear in him
    he won't stay silent long,
    not with your curses ringing in his ears.   335

OEDIPUS: He didn't flinch at murder,
    he'll never flinch at words.

Enter Tiresias, the blind prophet, led by a boy with escorts in attendance. He remains at a distance.

LEADER: Here is the one who will convict him, look,
    they bring him on at last, the seer, the man of god.
    The truth lives inside him, him alone.

OEDIPUS: O Tiresias,   340
  master of all the mysteries of our life,
  all you teach and all you dare not tell,
  signs in the heavens, signs that walk the earth!
  Blind as you are, you can feel all the more
  what sickness haunts our city. You, my lord,   345
  are the one shield, the one savior we can find.

  We asked Apollo — perhaps the messengers
  haven't told you — he sent his answer back:
  "Relief from the plague can only come one way.
  Uncover the murderers of Laius,   350
  put them to death or drive them into exile."
  So I beg you, grudge us nothing now, no voice,
  no message plucked from the birds, the embers
  or the other mantic ways within your grasp.
  Rescue yourself, your city, rescue me —   355
  rescue everything infected by the dead.
  We are in your hands. For a man to help others
  with all his gifts and native strength:
  that is the noblest work.
TIRESIAS: How terrible — to see the truth
  when the truth is only pain to him who sees!   360
  I knew it well, but I put it from my mind,
  else I never would have come.
OEDIPUS: What's this? Why so grim, so dire?
TIRESIAS: Just send me home. You bear your burdens,
  I'll bear mine. It's better that way,   365
  please believe me.
OEDIPUS: Strange response — unlawful,
  unfriendly too to the state that bred and raised you;
  you're withholding the word of god.
TIRESIAS: I fail to see
  that your own words are so well-timed.
  I'd rather not have the same thing said of me . . .   370
OEDIPUS: For the love of god, don't turn away,
  not if you know something. We beg you,
  all of us on our knees.
TIRESIAS: None of you knows —
  and I will never reveal my dreadful secrets,
  not to say your own.   375
OEDIPUS: What? You know and you won't tell?
  You're bent on betraying us, destroying Thebes?
TIRESIAS: I'd rather not cause pain for you or me.
  So why this . . . useless interrogation?
  You'll get nothing from me.
OEDIPUS: Nothing! You,   380
  you scum of the earth, you'd enrage a heart of stone!

You won't talk? Nothing moves you?
Out with it, once and for all!
TIRESIAS: You criticize my temper . . . unaware
 of the one *you* live with, you revile me.   385
OEDIPUS: Who could restrain his anger hearing you?
 What outrage—you spurn the city!
TIRESIAS: What will come will come.
 Even if I shroud it all in silence.
OEDIPUS: What will come? You're bound to *tell* me that.   390
TIRESIAS: I'll say no more. Do as you like, build your anger
 to whatever pitch you please, rage your worst—
OEDIPUS: Oh I'll let loose, I have such fury in me—
 now I see it all. You helped hatch the plot,
 you did the work, yes, short of killing him   395
 with your own hands—and given eyes I'd say
 you did the killing single-handed!
TIRESIAS: Is that so!
 I charge you, then, submit to that decree
 you just laid down: from this day onward
 speak to no one, not these citizens, not myself.   400
 You are the curse, the corruption of the land!
OEDIPUS: You, shameless—
 aren't you appalled to start up such a story?
 You think you can get away with this?
TIRESIAS: I have already.
 The truth with all its power lives inside me.   405
OEDIPUS: Who primed you for this? Not your prophet's trade.
TIRESIAS: You did, you forced me, twisted it out of me.
OEDIPUS: What? Say it again—I'll understand it better.
TIRESIAS: Didn't you understand, just now?
 Or are you tempting me to talk?   410
OEDIPUS: No, I can't say I grasped your meaning.
 Out with it, again!
TIRESIAS: I say you are the murderer you hunt.
OEDIPUS: That obscenity, twice—by god, you'll pay.
TIRESIAS: Shall I say more, so you can really rage?   415
OEDIPUS: Much as you want. Your words are nothing—
 futile.
TIRESIAS: You cannot imagine . . . I tell you,
 you and your loved ones live together in infamy,
 you cannot see how far you've gone in guilt.
OEDIPUS: You think you can keep this up and never suffer? 420
TIRESIAS: Indeed, if the truth has any power.
OEDIPUS: It does
 but not for you, old man. You've lost your power,
 stone-blind, stone-deaf—senses, eyes blind as stone!

TIRESIAS: I pity you, flinging at me the very insults
 each man here will fling at you so soon.
OEDIPUS: Blind,   425
 lost in the night, endless night that nursed you!
 You can't hurt me or anyone else who sees the light —
 you can never touch me.
TIRESIAS: True, it is not your fate
 to fall at my hands. Apollo is quite enough,
 and he will take some pains to work this out.   430
OEDIPUS: Creon! Is this conspiracy his or yours?
TIRESIAS: Creon is not your downfall, no, you are your own.
OEDIPUS: O power—
 wealth and empire, skill outstripping skill
 in the heady rivalries of life,
 what envy lurks inside you! Just for this,   435
 the crown the city gave me — I never sought it,
 they laid it in my hands — for this alone, Creon,
 the soul of trust, my loyal friend from the start
 steals against me . . . so hungry to overthrow me
 he sets this wizard on me, this scheming quack,   440
 this fortune-teller peddling lies, eyes peeled
 for his own profit — seer blind in his craft!

 Come here, you pious fraud. Tell me,
 when did you ever prove yourself a prophet?
 When the Sphinx, that chanting Fury kept her deathwatch here,   445
 why silent then, not a word to set our people free?
 There was a riddle, not for some passer-by to solve —
 it cried out for a prophet. Where were you?
 Did you rise to the crisis? Not a word,
 you and your birds, your gods — nothing.   450
 No, but I came by, Oedipus the ignorant,
 I stopped the Sphinx! With no help from the birds,
 the flight of my own intelligence hit the mark.
 And this is the man you'd try to overthrow?
 You think you'll stand by Creon when he's king?   455
 You and the great mastermind —
 you'll pay in tears, I promise you, for this,
 this witch-hunt. If you didn't look so senile
 the lash would teach you what your scheming means!
LEADER: I'd suggest his words were spoken in anger,   460
 Oedipus . . . yours too, and it isn't what we need.
 The best solution to the oracle, the riddle
 posed by god — we should look for that.
TIRESIAS: You are the king no doubt, but in one respect,
 at least, I am your equal: the right to reply.   465

I claim that privilege too.
I am not your slave. I serve Apollo.
I don't need Creon to speak for me in public.
                                        So,
you mock my blindness? Let me tell you this.
You with your precious eyes,   470
you're blind to the corruption of your life,
to the house you live in, those you live with—
who *are* your parents? Do you know? All unknowing
you are the scourge of your own flesh and blood,
the dead below the earth and the living here above,   475
and the double lash of your mother and your father's curse
will whip you from this land one day, their footfall
treading you down in terror, darkness shrouding
your eyes that now can see the light!
                                        Soon, soon
you'll scream aloud—what haven won't reverberate?   480
What rock of Cithaeron° won't scream back in echo?
That day you learn the truth about your marriage,
the wedding-march that sang you into your halls,
the lusty voyage home to the fatal harbor!
And a load of other horrors you'd never dream   485
will level you with yourself and all your children.

There. Now smear us with insults—Creon, myself
and every word I've said. No man will ever
be rooted from the earth as brutally as you.
OEDIPUS: Enough! Such filth from him? Insufferable—   490
what, still alive? Get out—
faster, back where you came from—vanish!
TIRESIAS: I'd never have come if you hadn't called me here.
OEDIPUS: If I thought you'd blurt out such absurdities,
you'd have died waiting before I'd had you summoned.   495
TIRESIAS: Absurd, am I? To you, not to your parents:
the ones who bore you found me sane enough.
OEDIPUS: Parents—who? Wait . . . who is my father?
TIRESIAS: This day will bring your birth and your destruction.
OEDIPUS: Riddles—all you can say are riddles, murk and darkness.   500
TIRESIAS: Ah, but aren't you the best man alive at solving riddles?
OEDIPUS: Mock me for that, go on, and you'll reveal my greatness.
TIRESIAS: Your great good fortune, true, it was your ruin.
OEDIPUS: Not if I saved the city—what do I care?
TIRESIAS: Well then, I'll be going.

---

481. Cithaeron: The mountains where Oedipus was abandoned as an infant.

To his attendant.

TIRESIAS: Take me home, boy.   505
OEDIPUS: Yes, take him away. You're a nuisance here.
      Out of the way, the irritation's gone.

Turning his back on Tiresias, moving toward the palace.

TIRESIAS: I will go,
      once I have said what I came here to say.
      I'll never shrink from the anger in your eyes—
      you can't destroy me. Listen to me closely: 510
      the man you've sought so long, proclaiming,
      cursing up and down, the murderer of Laius—
      he is here. A stranger,
      you may think, who lives among you,
      he soon will be revealed a native Theban   515
      but he will take no joy in the revelation.
      Blind who now has eyes, beggar who now is rich,
      he will grope his way toward a foreign soil,
      a stick tapping before him step by step.

Oedipus enters the palace.

      Revealed at last, brother and father both   520
      to the children he embraces, to his mother
      son and husband both—he sowed the loins
      his father sowed, he spilled his father's blood!

      Go in and reflect on that, solve that.
      And if you find I've lied   525
      from this day onward call the prophet blind.

Tiresias and the boy exit to the side.

CHORUS: Who—
      who is the man the voice of god denounces
      resounding out of the rocky gorge of Delphi?
            The horror too dark to tell,
      whose ruthless bloody hands have done the work?   530
      His time has come to fly
            to outrace the stallions of the storm
                        his feet a streak of speed—
      Cased in armor, Apollo son of the Father
      lunges on him, lightning-bolts afire!   535
      And the grim unerring Furies°
                  closing for the kill.
                        Look,

---

536. Furies: Three spirits who avenged evildoers.

the word of god has just come blazing
flashing off Parnassus'° snowy heights!
  That man who left no trace— 540
after him, hunt him down with all our strength!
Now under bristling timber
   up through rocks and caves he stalks
     like the wild mountain bull—
cut off from men, each step an agony, frenzied, racing blind 545
but he cannot outrace the dread voices of Delphi
ringing out of the heart of Earth,
  the dark wings beating around him shrieking doom
    the doom that never dies, the terror—

The skilled prophet scans the birds and shatters me with terror! 550
I can't accept him, can't deny him, don't know what to say,
I'm lost, and the wings of dark foreboding beating—
I cannot see what's come, what's still to come . . .
and what could breed a blood feud between
  Laius' house and the son of Polybus?° 555
I know of nothing, not in the past and not now,
no charge to bring against our king, no cause
to attack his fame that rings throughout Thebes—
  not without proof—not for the ghost of Laius,
  not to avenge a murder gone without a trace. 560

Zeus and Apollo know, they know, the great masters
  of all the dark and depth of human life.
But whether a mere man can know the truth,
whether a seer can fathom more than I—
there is no test, no certain proof 565
  though matching skill for skill
a man can outstrip a rival. No, not till I see
these charges proved will I side with his accusers.
We saw him then, when the she-hawk° swept against him,
saw with our own eyes his skill, his brilliant triumph— 570
  there was the test—he was the joy of Thebes!
  Never will I convict my king, never in my heart.

Enter Creon from the side.

CREON: My fellow-citizens, I hear King Oedipus
levels terrible charges at me. I had to come.
I resent it deeply. If, in the present crisis, 575
he thinks he suffers any abuse from me,
anything I've done or said that offers him
the slightest injury, why, I've no desire

---

539. Parnassus: A mountain in Greece associated with Apollo. **555. Polybus:** The King of Corinth, who is thought to be Oedipus's father. **569. she-hawk:** The Sphinx.

to linger out this life, my reputation a shambles.
The damage I'd face from such an accusation   580
is nothing simple. No, there's nothing worse:
branded a traitor in the city, a traitor
to all of you and my good friends.

LEADER: True,
but a slur might have been forced out of him,
by anger perhaps, not any firm conviction.   585

CREON: The charge was made in public, wasn't it?
I put the prophet up to spreading lies?

LEADER: Such things were said . . .
I don't know with what intent, if any.

CREON: Was his glance steady, his mind right   590
when the charge was brought against me?

LEADER: I really couldn't say. I never look
to judge the ones in power.

The doors open. Oedipus enters.

                                        Wait,
here's Oedipus now.

OEDIPUS: You—here? You have the gall
to show your face before the palace gates?   595
You, plotting to kill me, kill the king—
I see it all, the marauding thief himself
scheming to steal my crown and power!

                                        Tell me,
in god's name, what did you take me for,
coward or fool, when you spun out your plot?   600
Your treachery—you think I'd never detect it
creeping against me in the dark? Or sensing it,
not defend myself? Aren't you the fool,
you and your high adventure. Lacking numbers,
powerful friends, out for the big game of empire—   605
you need riches, armies to bring that quarry down!

CREON: Are you quite finished? It's your turn to listen
for just as long as you've . . . instructed me.
Hear me out, then judge me on the facts.

OEDIPUS: You've a wicked way with words, Creon,   610
but I'll be slow to learn—from you.
I find you a menace, a great burden to me.

CREON: Just one thing, hear me out in this.

OEDIPUS: Just one thing,
don't tell me you're not the enemy, the traitor.

CREON: Look, if you think crude, mindless stubbornness   615
such a gift, you've lost your sense of balance.

OEDIPUS: If you think you can abuse a kinsman,
then escape the penalty, you're insane.

CREON: Fair enough, I grant you. But this injury
    you say I've done you, what is it?   620
OEDIPUS: Did you induce me, yes or no,
    to send for that sanctimonious prophet?
CREON: I did. And I'd do the same again.
OEDIPUS: All right then, tell me, how long is it now
    since Laius . . .
CREON: Laius — what did *he* do?
OEDIPUS: Vanished,   625
    swept from sight, murdered in his tracks.
CREON: The count of the years would run you far back . . .
OEDIPUS: And that far back, was the prophet at his trade?
CREON: Skilled as he is today, and just as honored.
OEDIPUS: Did he ever refer to me then, at that time?
CREON: No,   630
    never, at least, when I was in his presence.
OEDIPUS: But you did investigate the murder, didn't you?
CREON: We did our best, of course, discovered nothing.
OEDIPUS: But the great seer never accused me then — why not?
CREON: I don't know. And when I don't, *I* keep quiet.   635
OEDIPUS: You do know this, you'd tell it too —
    if you had a shred of decency.
CREON: What?
    If I know, I won't hold back.
OEDIPUS: Simply this:
    if the two of you had never put heads together,
    we'd never have heard about *my* killing Laius.   640
CREON: If that's what he says . . . well, you know best.
    But now I have a right to learn from you
    as you just learned from me.
OEDIPUS: Learn your fill,
    you never will convict me of the murder.
CREON: Tell me, you're married to my sister, aren't you?   645
OEDIPUS: A genuine discovery — there's no denying that.
CREON: And you rule the land with her, with equal power?
OEDIPUS: She receives from me whatever she desires.
CREON: And I am the third, all of us are equals?
OEDIPUS: Yes, and it's there you show your stripes —   650
    you betray a kinsman.
CREON: Not at all.
    Not if you see things calmly, rationally,
    as I do. Look at it this way first:
    who in his right mind would rather rule
    and live in anxiety than sleep in peace?   655
    Particularly if he enjoys the same authority.
    Not I, I'm not the man to yearn for kingship,
    not with a king's power in my hands. Who would?

No one with any sense of self-control.
Now, as it is, you offer me all I need,   660
not a fear in the world. But if I wore the crown . . .
there'd be many painful duties to perform,
hardly to my taste.
       How could kingship
please me more than influence, power
without a qualm? I'm not that deluded yet,   665
to reach for anything but privilege outright,
profit free and clear.
Now all men sing my praises, all salute me,
now all who request your favors curry mine.
I'm their best hope: success rests in me.   670
Why give up that, I ask you, and borrow trouble?
A man of sense, someone who sees things clearly
would never resort to treason.
No, I've no lust for conspiracy in me,
nor could I ever suffer one who does.   675

Do you want proof? Go to Delphi yourself,
examine the oracle and see if I've reported
the message word-for-word. This too:
if you detect that I and the clairvoyant
have plotted anything in common, arrest me,   680
execute me. Not on the strength of one vote,
two in this case, mine as well as yours.
But don't convict me on sheer unverified surmise.

How wrong it is to take the good for bad,
purely at random, or take the bad for good.   685
But reject a friend, a kinsman? I would as soon
tear out the life within us, priceless life itself.
You'll learn this well, without fail, in time.
Time alone can bring the just man to light;
the criminal you can spot in one short day.

LEADER: Good advice,   690
  my lord, for anyone who wants to avoid disaster.
  Those who jump to conclusions may be wrong.

OEDIPUS: When my enemy moves against me quickly,
  plots in secret, I move quickly too, I must,
  I plot and pay him back. Relax my guard a moment,   695
  waiting his next move—he wins his objective,
  I lose mine.

CREON: What do you want?
  You want me banished?

OEDIPUS: No, I want you dead.

CREON: Just to show how ugly a grudge can . . .

OEDIPUS: So,
    still stubborn? you don't think I'm serious?   700
CREON: I think you're insane.
OEDIPUS: Quite sane — in my behalf.
CREON: Not just as much in mine?
OEDIPUS: You — my mortal enemy?
CREON: What if you're wholly wrong?
OEDIPUS: No matter — I must rule.
CREON: Not if you rule unjustly.
OEDIPUS: Hear him, Thebes, my city!
CREON: My city too, not yours alone!   705
LEADER: Please, my lords.

Enter Jocasta from the palace.

                Look, Jocasta's coming,
    and just in time too. With her help
    you must put this fighting of yours to rest.
JOCASTA: Have you no sense? Poor misguided men,
    such shouting — why this public outburst?   710
    Aren't you ashamed, with the land so sick,
    to stir up private quarrels?

To Oedipus.

    Into the palace now. And Creon, you go home.
    Why make such a furor over nothing?
CREON: My sister, it's dreadful . . . Oedipus, your husband,   715
    he's bent on a choice of punishments for me,
    banishment from the fatherland or death.
OEDIPUS: Precisely. I caught him in the act, Jocasta,
    plotting, about to stab me in the back.
CREON: Never — curse me, let me die and be damned   720
    if I've done you any wrong you charge me with.
JOCASTA: Oh god, believe it, Oedipus,
    honor the solemn oath he swears to heaven.
    Do it for me, for the sake of all your people.

The Chorus begins to chant.

CHORUS: Believe it, be sensible   725
            give way, my king, I beg you!
OEDIPUS: What do you want from me, concessions?
CHORUS: Respect him — he's been no fool in the past
    and now he's strong with the oath he swears to god.
OEDIPUS: You know what you're asking?
CHORUS: I do.
OEDIPUS: Then out with it!   730
CHORUS: The man's your friend, your kin, he's under oath —
    don't cast him out, disgraced
    branded with guilt on the strength of hearsay only.

OEDIPUS: Know full well, if that's what you want
    you want me dead or banished from the land.
CHORUS: Never—   735
    no, by the blazing Sun, first god of the heavens!
        Stripped of the gods, stripped of loved ones,
    let me die by inches if that ever crossed my mind.
    But the heart inside me sickens, dies as the land dies
    and now on top of the old griefs you pile this,   740
    your fury—both of you!
OEDIPUS: Then let him go,
    even if it does lead to my ruin, my death
    or my disgrace, driven from Thebes for life.
    It's you, not him I pity—your words move me.
    He, wherever he goes, my hate goes with him.   745
CREON: Look at you, sullen in yielding, brutal in your rage—
    you'll go too far. It's perfect justice:
    natures like yours are hardest on themselves.
OEDIPUS: Then leave me alone—get out!
CREON: I'm going.
    You're wrong, so wrong. These men know I'm right.   750

Exit to the side. The Chorus turns to Jocasta.

CHORUS: Why do you hesitate, my lady
        why not help him in?
JOCASTA: Tell me what's happened first.
CHORUS: Loose, ignorant talk started dark suspicions
    and a sense of injustice cut deeply too.   755
JOCASTA: On both sides?
CHORUS: Oh yes.
JOCASTA: What did they say?
CHORUS: Enough, please, enough! The land's so racked already
    or so it seems to me . . .
    End the trouble here, just where they left it.
OEDIPUS: You see what comes of your good intentions now?   760
    And all because you tried to blunt my anger.
CHORUS: My king,
    I've said it once, I'll say it time and again—
        I'd be insane, you know it,
    senseless, ever to turn my back on you.
    You who set our beloved land—storm-tossed, shattered—   765
    straight on course. Now again, good helmsman,
    steer us through the storm!

The Chorus draws away, leaving Oedipus and Jocasta side by side.

JOCASTA: For the love of god,
    Oedipus, tell me too, what is it?
    Why this rage? You're so unbending.

OEDIPUS: I will tell you. I respect you, Jocasta,   770
    much more than these . . .

Glancing at the Chorus.

    Creon's to blame, Creon schemes against me.
JOCASTA: Tell me clearly, how did the quarrel start?
OEDIPUS: He says *I* murdered Laius — I am guilty.
JOCASTA: How does he know? Some secret knowledge   775
    or simple hearsay?
OEDIPUS: Oh, he sent his prophet in
    to do his dirty work. You know Creon,
    Creon keeps his own lips clean.
JOCASTA: A prophet?
    Well then, free yourself of every charge!
    Listen to me and learn some peace of mind: 780
    no skill in the world,
    nothing human can penetrate the future.
    Here is proof, quick and to the point.
    An oracle came to Laius one fine day
    (I won't say from Apollo himself   785
    but his underlings, his priests) and it said
    that doom would strike him down at the hands of a son,
    our son, to be born of our own flesh and blood. But Laius,
    so the report goes at least, was killed by strangers,
    thieves, at a place where three roads meet . . . my son —   790
    he wasn't three days old and the boy's father
    fastened his ankles, had a henchman fling him away
    on a barren, trackless mountain.
            There, you see?
    Apollo brought neither thing to pass. My baby
    no more murdered his father than Laius suffered —   795
    his wildest fear — death at his own son's hands.
    That's how the seers and their revelations
    mapped out the future. Brush them from your mind.
    Whatever the god needs and seeks
    he'll bring to light himself, with ease.
OEDIPUS: Strange,   800
    hearing you just now . . . my mind wandered,
    my thoughts racing back and forth.
JOCASTA: What do you mean? Why so anxious, startled?
OEDIPUS: I thought I heard you say that Laius
    was cut down at a place where three roads meet.   805
JOCASTA: That was the story. It hasn't died out yet.
OEDIPUS: Where did this thing happen? Be precise.
JOCASTA: A place called Phocis, where two branching roads,
    one from Daulia, one from Delphi,
    come together — a crossroads.   810
OEDIPUS: When? How long ago?

JOCASTA: The heralds no sooner reported Laius dead
    than you appeared and they hailed you king of Thebes.
OEDIPUS: My god, my god—what have you planned to do to me?
JOCASTA: What, Oedipus? What haunts you so?
OEDIPUS: Not yet.   815
    Laius—how did he look? Describe him.
    Had he reached his prime?
JOCASTA: He was swarthy,
    and the gray had just begun to streak his temples,
    and his build . . . wasn't far from yours.
OEDIPUS: Oh no no,
    I think I've just called down a dreadful curse   820
    upon myself—I simply didn't know!
JOCASTA: What are you saying? I shudder to look at you.
OEDIPUS: I have a terrible fear the blind seer can see.
    I'll know in a moment. One thing more—
JOCASTA: Anything,
    afraid as I am—ask, I'll answer, all I can.   825
OEDIPUS: Did he go with a light or heavy escort,
    several men-at-arms, like a lord, a king?
JOCASTA: There were five in the party, a herald among them,
    and a single wagon carrying Laius.
OEDIPUS: Ai—
    now I can see it all, clear as day.   830
    Who told you all this at the time, Jocasta?
JOCASTA: A servant who reached home, the lone survivor.
OEDIPUS: So, could he still be in the palace—even now?
JOCASTA: No indeed. Soon as he returned from the scene
    and saw you on the throne with Laius dead and gone,   835
    he knelt and clutched my hand, pleading with me
    to send him into the hinterlands, to pasture,
    far as possible, out of sight of Thebes.
    I sent him away. Slave though he was,
    he'd earned that favor—and much more.   840
OEDIPUS: Can we bring him back, quickly?
JOCASTA: Easily. Why do you want him so?
OEDIPUS: I'm afraid,
    Jocasta, I have said too much already.
    That man—I've got to see him.
JOCASTA: Then he'll come.
    But even I have a right, I'd like to think,   845
    to know what's torturing you, my lord.
OEDIPUS: And so you shall—I can hold nothing back from you,
    now I've reached this pitch of dark foreboding.
    Who means more to me than you? Tell me,
    whom would I turn toward but you   850
    as I go through all this?

My father was Polybus, king of Corinth.
My mother, a Dorian, Merope. And I was held
the prince of the realm among the people there,
till something struck me out of nowhere,   855
something strange . . . worth remarking perhaps,
hardly worth the anxiety I gave it.
Some man at a banquet who had drunk too much
shouted out — he was far gone, mind you —
that I am not my father's son. Fighting words!   860
I barely restrained myself that day
but early the next I went to mother and father,
questioned them closely, and they were enraged
at the accusation and the fool who let it fly.
So as for my parents I was satisfied,   865
but still this thing kept gnawing at me,
the slander spread — I had to make my move.
                                                            And so,
unknown to mother and father I set out for Delphi,
and the god Apollo spurned me, sent me away
denied the facts I came for,   870
but first he flashed before my eyes a future
great with pain, terror, disaster — I can hear him cry,
"You are fated to couple with your mother, you will bring
a breed of children into the light no man can bear to see —
you will kill your father, the one who gave you life!"   875
I heard all that and ran. I abandoned Corinth,
from that day on I gauged its landfall only
by the stars, running, always running
toward some place where I would never see
the shame of all those oracles come true.   880
And as I fled I reached that very spot
where the great king, you say, met his death.
Now, Jocasta, I will tell you all.
Making my way toward this triple crossroad
I began to see a herald, then a brace of colts   885
drawing a wagon, and mounted on the bench . . . a man,
just as you've described him, coming face-to-face,
and the one in the lead and the old man himself
were about to thrust me off the road — brute force —
and the one shouldering me aside, the driver,   890
I strike him in anger! — and the old man, watching me
coming up along his wheels — he brings down
his prod, two prongs straight at my head!
I paid him back with interest!
Short work, by god — with one blow of the staff   895
in this right hand I knock him out of his high seat,

roll him out of the wagon, sprawling headlong—
I killed them all—every mother's son!

Oh, but if there is any blood-tie
between Laius and this stranger . . .   900
what man alive more miserable than I?
More hated by the gods? *I* am the man
no alien, no citizen welcomes to his house,
law forbids it—not a word to me in public,
driven out of every hearth and home.   905
And all these curses I—no one but I
brought down these piling curses on myself!
And you, his wife, I've touched your body with these,
the hands that killed your husband cover you with blood.

Wasn't I born for torment? Look me in the eyes!   910
I am abomination—heart and soul!
I must be exiled, and even in exile
never see my parents, never set foot
on native earth again. Else I'm doomed
to couple with my mother and cut my father down . . .   915
Polybus who reared me, gave me life.

                                    But why, why?
Wouldn't a man of judgment say—and wouldn't he be right—
some savage power has brought this down upon my head?
Oh no, not that, you pure and awesome gods,
never let me see that day! Let me slip   920
from the world of men, vanish without a trace
before I see myself stained with such corruption,
stained to the heart.

LEADER: My lord, you fill our hearts with fear.
But at least until you question the witness,   925
do take hope.

OEDIPUS: Exactly. He is my last hope—
I'm waiting for the shepherd. He is crucial.

JOCASTA: And once he appears, what then? Why so urgent?

OEDIPUS: I'll tell you. If it turns out that his story
matches yours, I've escaped the worst.   930

JOCASTA: What did I say? What struck you so?

OEDIPUS: You said *thieves*—
he told you a whole band of them murdered Laius.
So, if he still holds to the same number,
I cannot be the killer. One can't equal many.
But if he refers to one man, one alone,   935
clearly the scales come down on me:
I am guilty.

JOCASTA: Impossible. Trust me,

I told you precisely what he said,
and he can't retract it now;
the whole city heard it, not just I.   940
And even if he should vary his first report
by one man more or less, still, my lord,
he could never make the murder of Laius
truly fit the prophecy. Apollo was explicit:
my son was doomed to kill my husband . . . my son,   945
poor defenseless thing, he never had a chance
to kill his father. They destroyed him first.

So much for prophecy. It's neither here nor there.
From this day on, I wouldn't look right or left.
OEDIPUS: True, true. Still, that shepherd,   950
someone fetch him—now!
JOCASTA: I'll send at once. But do let's go inside.
I'd never displease you, least of all in this.

Oedipus and Jocasta enter the palace.

CHORUS: Destiny guide me always
Destiny find me filled with reverence   955
              pure in word and deed.
Great laws tower above us, reared on high
born for the brilliant vault of heaven—
        Olympian sky their only father,
nothing mortal, no man gave them birth,   960
their memory deathless, never lost in sleep:
within them lives a mighty god, the god does not grow old.

Pride breeds the tyrant
violent pride, gorging, crammed to bursting
        with all that is overripe and rich with ruin—   965
clawing up to the heights, headlong pride
crashes down the abyss—sheer doom!
        No footing helps, all foothold lost and gone,
But the healthy strife that makes the city strong—
I pray that god will never end that wrestling: 970
god, my champion, I will never let you go.

But if any man comes striding, high and mighty
        in all he says and does,
no fear of justice, no reverence
for the temples of the gods—   975
        let a rough doom tear him down,
repay his pride, breakneck, ruinous pride!
If he cannot reap his profits fairly
        cannot restrain himself from outrage—
mad, laying hands on the holy things untouchable!   980

Can such a man, so desperate, still boast
he can save his life from the flashing bolts of god?
If all such violence goes with honor now
why join the sacred dance?

Never again will I go reverent to Delphi,   985
        the inviolate heart of Earth
or Apollo's ancient oracle at Abae
or Olympia of the fires —
        unless these prophecies all come true
for all mankind to point toward in wonder.   990
King of kings, if you deserve your titles
        Zeus, remember, never forget!
You and your deathless, everlasting reign.

        They are dying, the old oracles sent to Laius,
        now our masters strike them off the rolls.   995
            Nowhere Apollo's golden glory now —
                the gods, the gods go down.

Enter Jocasta from the palace, carrying a suppliant's branch wound in wool.

JOCASTA: Lords of the realm, it occurred to me,
        just now, to visit the temples of the gods,
        so I have my branch in hand and incense too.   1000

Oedipus is beside himself. Racked with anguish,
no longer a man of sense, he won't admit
the latest prophecies are hollow as the old —
he's at the mercy of every passing voice
if the voice tells of terror.   1005
I urge him gently, nothing seems to help,
so I turn to you, Apollo, you are nearest.

Placing her branch on the altar, while an old herdsman enters from the side, not the one just summoned by the king but an unexpected messenger from Corinth.

I come with prayers and offerings . . . I beg you,
cleanse us, set us free of defilement!
Look at us, passengers in the grip of fear,   1010
watching the pilot of the vessel go to pieces.
MESSENGER:

Approaching Jocasta and the Chorus.

Strangers, please, I wonder if you could lead us
to the palace of the king . . . I think it's Oedipus.
Better, the man himself—you know where he is?
LEADER: This is his palace, stranger. He's inside.   1015
But here is his queen, his wife and mother
of his children.

MESSENGER: Blessings on you, noble queen,
     queen of Oedipus crowned with all your family—
     blessings on you always!

JOCASTA: And the same to you, stranger, you deserve it . . .   1020
     such a greeting. But what have you come for?
     Have you brought us news?

MESSENGER: Wonderful news—
     for the house, my lady, for your husband too.

JOCASTA: Really, what? Who sent you?

MESSENGER: Corinth.
     I'll give you the message in a moment.   1025
     You'll be glad of it—how could you help it?—
     though it costs a little sorrow in the bargain.

JOCASTA: What can it be, with such a double edge?

MESSENGER: The people there, they want to make your Oedipus
     king of Corinth, so they're saying now.   1030

JOCASTA: Why? Isn't old Polybus still in power?

MESSENGER: No more. Death has got him in the tomb.

JOCASTA: What are you saying? Polybus, dead?—dead?

MESSENGER: If not,
     if I'm not telling the truth, strike me dead too.

JOCASTA:

To a servant.

     Quickly, go to your master, tell him this!   1035

     You prophecies of the gods, where are you now?
     This is the man that Oedipus feared for years,
     he fled him, not to kill him—and now he's dead,
     quite by chance, a normal, natural death,
     not murdered by his son.

OEDIPUS:

Emerging from the palace.

                     Dearest,   1040
     what now? Why call me from the palace?

JOCASTA:

Bringing the Messenger closer.

     Listen to *him,* see for yourself what all
     those awful prophecies of god have come to.

OEDIPUS: And who is he? What can he have for me?

JOCASTA: He's from Corinth, he's come to tell you   1045
     your father is no more—Polybus—he's dead!

OEDIPUS:

Wheeling on the Messenger.

     What? Let me have it from your lips.

MESSENGER: Well,
     if that's what you want first, then here it is:

make no mistake, Polybus is dead and gone.

OEDIPUS: How — murder? sickness? — what? what killed him? 1050

MESSENGER: A light tip of the scales can put old bones to rest.

OEDIPUS: Sickness then — poor man, it wore him down.

MESSENGER: That,
and the long count of years he'd measured out.

OEDIPUS: So!
Jocasta, why, why look to the Prophet's hearth,
the fires of the future? Why scan the birds 1055
that scream above our heads? They winged me on
to the murder of my father, did they? That was my doom?
Well look, he's dead and buried, hidden under the earth,
and here I am in Thebes, I never put hand to sword —
unless some longing for me wasted him away, 1060
then in a sense you'd say I caused his death.
But now, all those prophecies I feared — Polybus
packs them off to sleep with him in hell!
They're nothing, worthless.

JOCASTA: There.
Didn't I tell you from the start? 1065

OEDIPUS: So you did. I was lost in fear.

JOCASTA: No more, sweep it from your mind forever.

OEDIPUS: But my mother's bed, surely I must fear —

JOCASTA: Fear?
What should a man fear? It's all chance,
chance rules our lives. Not a man on earth 1070
can see a day ahead, groping through the dark.
Better to live at random, best we can.
And as for this marriage with your mother —
have no fear. Many a man before you,
in his dreams, has shared his mother's bed. 1075
Take such things for shadows, nothing at all —
Live, Oedipus,
as if there's no tomorrow!

OEDIPUS: Brave words,
and you'd persuade me if mother weren't alive.
But mother lives, so for all your reassurances 1080
I live in fear, I must.

JOCASTA: But your father's death,
that, at least, is a great blessing, joy to the eyes!

OEDIPUS: Great, I know . . . but I fear *her* — she's still alive.

MESSENGER: Wait, who is this woman, makes you so afraid?

OEDIPUS: Merope, old man. The wife of Polybus. 1085

MESSENGER: The queen? What's there to fear in her?

OEDIPUS: A dreadful prophecy, stranger, sent by the gods.

MESSENGER: Tell me, could you? Unless it's forbidden
other ears to hear.

OEDIPUS: Not at all.
    Apollo told me once—it is my fate—   1090
    I must make love with my own mother,
    shed my father's blood with my own hands.
    So for years I've given Corinth a wide berth,
    and it's been my good fortune too. But still,
    to see one's parents and look into their eyes   1095
    is the greatest joy I know.
MESSENGER: You're afraid of that?
    That kept you out of Corinth?
OEDIPUS: My *father*, old man—
    so I wouldn't kill my father.
MESSENGER: So that's it.
    Well then, seeing I came with such good will, my king,
    why don't I rid you of that old worry now?   1100
OEDIPUS: What a rich reward you'd have for that.
MESSENGER: What do you think I came for, majesty?
    So you'd come home and I'd be better off.
OEDIPUS: Never, I will never go near my parents.
MESSENGER: My boy, it's clear, you don't know what you're doing.   1105
OEDIPUS: What do you mean, old man? For god's sake, explain.
MESSENGER: If you ran from *them,* always dodging home . . .
OEDIPUS: Always, terrified Apollo's oracle might come true—
MESSENGER: And you'd be covered with guilt, from both your parents.
OEDIPUS: That's right, old man, that fear is always with me.   1110
MESSENGER: Don't you know? You've really nothing to fear.
OEDIPUS: But why? If I'm their son—Merope, Polybus?
MESSENGER: Polybus was nothing to you, that's why, not in blood.
OEDIPUS: What are you saying—Polybus was not my father?
MESSENGER: No more than I am. He and I are equals.
OEDIPUS: My father—   1115
    how can my father equal nothing? You're nothing to me!
MESSENGER: Neither was he, no more your father than I am.
OEDIPUS: Then why did he call me his son?
MESSENGER: You were a gift,
    years ago—know for a fact he took you
    from my hands.
OEDIPUS: No, from another's hands?   1120
    Then how could he love me so? He loved me, deeply . . .
MESSENGER: True, and his early years without a child
    made him love you all the more.
OEDIPUS: And you, did you . . .
    buy me? find me by accident?
MESSENGER: I stumbled on you,
    down the woody flanks of Mount Cithaeron.
OEDIPUS: So close,   1125
    what were you doing here, just passing through?

MESSENGER: Watching over my flocks, grazing them on the slopes.

OEDIPUS: A herdsman, were you? A vagabond, scraping for wages?

MESSENGER: Your savior too, my son, in your worst hour.

OEDIPUS: Oh—
    when you picked me up, was I in pain? What exactly?   1130

MESSENGER: Your ankles . . . they tell the story. Look at them.

OEDIPUS: Why remind me of that, that old affliction?

MESSENGER: Your ankles were pinned together; I set you free.

OEDIPUS: That dreadful mark—I've had it from the cradle.

MESSENGER: And you got your name from that misfortune too,   1135
    the name's still with you.

OEDIPUS: Dear god, who did it?—
    mother? father? Tell me.

MESSENGER: I don't know.
    The one who gave you to me, he'd know more.

OEDIPUS: What? You took me from someone else?
    You didn't find me yourself?

MESSENGER: No sir,   1140
    another shepherd passed you on to me.

OEDIPUS: Who? Do you know? Describe him.

MESSENGER: He called himself a servant of . . .
    if I remember rightly—Laius.

Jocasta turns sharply.

OEDIPUS: The king of the land who ruled here long ago?   1145

MESSENGER: That's the one. That herdsman was *his* man.

OEDIPUS: Is he still alive? Can I see him?

MESSENGER: They'd know best, the people of these parts.

Oedipus and the Messenger turn to the Chorus.

OEDIPUS: Does anyone know that herdsman,
    the one he mentioned? Anyone seen him   1150
    in the fields, in town? Out with it!
    The time has come to reveal this once for all.

LEADER: I think he's the very shepherd you wanted to see,
    a moment ago. But the queen, Jocasta,
    she's the one to say.

OEDIPUS: Jocasta,   1155
    you remember the man we just sent for?
    Is *that* the one he means?

JOCASTA: That man . . .
    why ask? Old shepherd, talk, empty nonsense,
    don't give it another thought, don't even think—

OEDIPUS: What—give up now, with a clue like this?   1160
    Fail to solve the mystery of my birth?
    Not for all the world!

JOCASTA: Stop—in the name of god,

if you love your own life, call off this search!
My suffering is enough.

OEDIPUS: Courage!
Even if my mother turns out to be a slave,   1165
and I a slave, three generations back,
you would not seem common.

JOCASTA: Oh no,
listen to me, I beg you, don't do this.

OEDIPUS: Listen to you? No more. I must know it all,
see the truth at last.

JOCASTA: No, please—   1170
for your sake—I want the best for you!

OEDIPUS: Your best is more than I can bear.

JOCASTA: You're doomed—
may you never fathom who you are!

OEDIPUS:

To a servant.

Hurry, fetch me the herdsman, now!
Leave her to glory in her royal birth.   1175

JOCASTA: Aieeeeee—
                    man of agony—
that is the only name I have for you,
that, no other—ever, ever, ever!

Flinging [herself] through the palace doors. A long, tense silence follows.

LEADER: Where's she gone, Oedipus?
Rushing off, such wild grief . . .   1180
I'm afraid that from this silence
something monstrous may come bursting forth.

OEDIPUS: Let it burst! Whatever will, whatever must!
I must know my birth, no matter how common
it may be—must see my origins face-to-face.   1185
She perhaps, she with her woman's pride
may well be mortified by my birth,
but I, I count myself the son of Chance,
the great goddess, giver of all good things—
I'll never see myself disgraced. She is my mother!   1190
And the moons have marked me out, my blood-brothers,
one moon on the wane, the next moon great with power.
That is my blood, my nature—I will never betray it,
never fail to search and learn my birth!

CHORUS: Yes—if I am a true prophet   1195
          if I can grasp the truth,
               by the boundless skies of Olympus,
at the full moon of tomorrow, Mount Cithaeron
you will know how Oedipus glories in you—
you, his birthplace, nurse, his mountain-mother!   1200

And we will sing you, dancing out your praise—
you lift our monarch's heart!
      Apollo, Apollo, god of the wild cry
          may our dancing please you!
                    Oedipus—
          son, dear child, who bore you?   1205
Who of the nymphs who seem to live forever
mated with Pan,° the mountain-striding Father?
Who was your mother? who, some bride of Apollo
the god who loves the pastures spreading toward the sun?
      Or was it Hermes, king of the lightning ridges?   1210
Or Dionysus, lord of frenzy, lord of the barren peaks—
did he seize you in his hands, dearest of all his lucky finds?—
      found by the nymphs, their warm eyes dancing, gift
to the lord who loves them dancing out his joy!

Oedipus strains to see a figure coming from the distance. Attended by palace guards,
an old Shepherd enters slowly, reluctant to approach the King.

OEDIPUS: I never met the man, my friends . . . still,   1215
if I had to guess, I'd say that's the shepherd,
the very one we've looked for all along.
Brothers in old age, two of a kind,
he and our guest here. At any rate
the ones who bring him in are my own men,   1220
I recognize them.

Turning to the Leader.

             But you know more than I,
you should, you've seen the man before.
LEADER: I know him, definitely. One of Laius' men,
a trusty shepherd, if there ever was one.
OEDIPUS: You, I ask you first, stranger,   1225
you from Corinth—is this the one you mean?
MESSENGER: You're looking at him. He's your man.
OEDIPUS:

To the Shepherd.

You, old man, come over here—
look at me. Answer all my questions.
Did you ever serve King Laius?
SHEPHERD: So I did . . .   1230
a slave, not bought on the block though,
born and reared in the palace.
OEDIPUS: Your duties, your kind of work?
SHEPHERD: Herding the flocks, the better part of my life.

1207. Pan: The god of shepherds, who was, like Hermes and Dionysus, associated with
the wilderness.

OEDIPUS: Where, mostly? Where did you do your grazing?

SHEPHERD: Well,   1235
      Cithaeron sometimes, or the foothills round about.

OEDIPUS: This man — you know him? ever see him there?

SHEPHERD:

Confused, glancing from the Messenger to the King.

      Doing what — what man do you mean?

OEDIPUS:

Pointing to the Messenger.

      This one here — ever have dealings with him?

SHEPHERD: Not so I could say, but give me a chance,   1240
      my memory's bad . . .

MESSENGER: No wonder he doesn't know me, master.
      But let me refresh his memory for him.
      I'm sure he recalls old times we had
      on the slopes of Mount Cithaeron;   1245
      he and I, grazing our flocks, he with two
      and I with one — we both struck up together,
      three whole seasons, six months at a stretch
      from spring to the rising of Arcturus° in the fall,
      then with winter coming on I'd drive my herds   1250
      to my own pens, and back he'd go with his
      to Laius' folds.

To the Shepherd.

               Now that's how it was,
      wasn't it — yes or no?

SHEPHERD: Yes, I suppose . . .
      it's all so long ago.

MESSENGER: Come, tell me,
      you gave me a child back then, a boy, remember?   1255
      A little fellow to rear, my very own.

SHEPHERD: What? Why rake up that again?

MESSENGER: Look, here he is, my fine old friend —
      the same man who was just a baby then.

SHEPHERD: Damn you, shut your mouth — quiet!   1260

OEDIPUS: Don't lash out at him, old man —
      you need lashing more than he does.

SHEPHERD: Why,
      master, majesty — what have I done wrong?

OEDIPUS: You won't answer his question about the boy.

SHEPHERD: He's talking nonsense, wasting his breath.   1265

OEDIPUS: So, you won't talk willingly —
      then you'll talk with pain.

1249. **Arcturus:** A star whose rising marked the end of summer.

The guards seize the Shepherd.

SHEPHERD: No, dear god, don't torture an old man!

OEDIPUS: Twist his arms back, quickly!

SHEPHERD: God help us, why? —
    what more do you need to know?   1270

OEDIPUS: Did you give him that child? He's asking.

SHEPHERD: I did . . . I wish to god I'd died that day.

OEDIPUS: You've got your wish if you don't tell the truth.

SHEPHERD: The more I tell, the worse the death I'll die.

OEDIPUS: Our friend here wants to stretch things out, does he?   1275

Motioning to his men for torture.

SHEPHERD: No, no, I gave it to him — I just said so.

OEDIPUS: Where did you get it? Your house? Someone else's?

SHEPHERD: It wasn't mine, no, I got it from . . . someone.

OEDIPUS: Which one of them?

Looking at the citizens.

                      Whose house?

SHEPHERD: No —
    god's sake, master, no more questions!   1280

OEDIPUS: You're a dead man if I have to ask again.

SHEPHERD: Then — the child came from the house . . .
    of Laius.

OEDIPUS: A slave? or born of his own blood?

SHEPHERD: Oh no,
    I'm right at the edge, the horrible truth — I've got to say it!

OEDIPUS: And I'm at the edge of hearing horrors, yes, but I must hear!   1285

SHEPHERD: All right! His son, they said it was — his son!
    But the one inside, your wife,
    she'd tell it best.

OEDIPUS: My wife —
    she gave it to you?   1290

SHEPHERD: Yes, yes, my king.

OEDIPUS: Why, what for?

SHEPHERD: To kill it.

OEDIPUS: Her own child,
    how could she?   1295

SHEPHERD: She was afraid —
    frightening prophecies.

OEDIPUS: What?

SHEPHERD: They said —
    he'd kill his parents.

OEDIPUS: But you gave him to this old man — why?   1300

SHEPHERD: I pitied the little baby, master,
    hoped he'd take him off to his own country,
    far away, but he saved him for this, this fate.
    If you are the man he says you are, believe me,

you were born for pain.

OEDIPUS: O god —   1305
all come true, all burst to light!
O light — now let me look my last on you!
I stand revealed at last —
cursed in my birth, cursed in marriage,
cursed in the lives I cut down with these hands!   1310

Rushing through the doors with a great cry. The Corinthian Messenger, the Shepherd, and attendants exit slowly to the side.

CHORUS: O the generations of men
            the dying generations — adding the total
of all your lives I find they come to nothing . . .
                        does there exist, is there a man on earth
who seizes more joy than just a dream, a vision?   1315
And the vision no sooner dawns than dies
blazing into oblivion.

You are my great example, you, your life,
your destiny, Oedipus, man of misery —
I count no man blest.

                        You outranged all men!   1320
            Bending your bow to the breaking-point
you captured priceless glory, O dear god,
and the Sphinx came crashing down,
                        the virgin, claws hooked
like a bird of omen singing, shrieking death —   1325
like a fortress reared in the face of death
you rose and saved our land.

From that day on we called you king
we crowned you with honors, Oedipus, towering over all —
mighty king of the seven gates of Thebes.   1330

But now to hear your story — is there a man more agonized?
More wed to pain and frenzy? Not a man on earth,
the joy of your life ground down to nothing
O Oedipus, name for the ages —
            one and the same wide harbor served you   1335
                        son and father both
son and father came to rest in the same bridal chamber.
How, how could the furrows your father plowed
bear you, your agony, harrowing on
in silence O so long?
                        But now for all your power   1340
Time, all-seeing Time has dragged you to the light,
judged your marriage monstrous from the start —

the son and the father tangling, both one—
O child of Laius, would to god
    I'd never seen you, never never!   1345
        Now I weep like a man who wails the dead
and the dirge comes pouring forth with all my heart!
I tell you the truth, you gave me life
my breath leapt up in you
and now you bring down night upon my eyes.   1350

Enter a Messenger from the palace.

MESSENGER: Men of Thebes, always the first in honor,
    what horrors you will hear, what you will see,
    what a heavy weight of sorrow you will shoulder . . .
    if you are true to your birth, if you still have
    some feeling for the royal house of Thebes.   1355
    I tell you neither the waters of the Danube
    nor the Nile can wash this palace clean.
    Such things it hides, it soon will bring to light—
    terrible things, and none done blindly now,
    all done with a will. The pains   1360
    we inflict upon ourselves hurt most of all.
LEADER: God knows we have pains enough already.
    What can you add to them?
MESSENGER: The queen is dead.
LEADER: Poor lady—how?
MESSENGER: By her own hand. But you are spared the worst,   1365
    you never had to watch . . . I saw it all,
    and with all the memory that's in me
    you will learn what that poor woman suffered.

    Once she'd broken in through the gates,
    dashing past us, frantic, whipped to fury,   1370
    ripping her hair out with both hands—
    straight to her rooms she rushed, flinging herself
    across the bridal-bed, doors slamming behind her—
    once inside, she wailed for Laius, dead so long,
    remembering how she bore his child long ago,   1375
    the life that rose up to destroy him, leaving
    its mother to mother living creatures
    with the very son she'd borne.
    Oh how she wept, mourning the marriage-bed
    where she let loose that double brood—monsters—   1380
    husband by her husband, children by her child.
                     And then—
    but how she died is more than I can say. Suddenly
    Oedipus burst in, screaming, he stunned us so
    we couldn't watch her agony to the end,

our eyes were fixed on him. Circling   1385
like a maddened beast, stalking, here, there
crying out to us—
                    Give him a sword! His wife,
no wife, his mother, where can he find the mother earth
that cropped two crops at once, himself and all his children?
He was raging—one of the dark powers pointing the way,   1390
none of us mortals crowding around him, no,
with a great shattering cry—someone, something leading him on—
he hurled at the twin doors and bending the bolts back
out of their sockets, crashed through the chamber.
And there we saw the woman hanging by the neck,   1395
cradled high in a woven noose, spinning,
swinging back and forth. And when he saw her,
giving a low, wrenching sob that broke our hearts,
slipping the halter from her throat, he eased her down,
in a slow embrace he laid her down, poor thing . . .   1400
then, what came next, what horror we beheld!
He rips off her brooches, the long gold pins
holding her robes—and lifting them high,
looking straight up into the points,
he digs them down the sockets of his eyes, crying, "You,   1405
you'll see no more the pain I suffered, all the pain I caused!
Too long you looked on the ones you never should have seen,
blind to the ones you longed to see, to know! Blind
from this hour on! Blind in the darkness—blind!"
His voice like a dirge, rising, over and over   1410
raising the pins, raking them down his eyes.
And at each stroke blood spurts from the roots,
splashing his beard, a swirl of it, nerves and clots—
black hail of blood pulsing, gushing down.

These are the griefs that burst upon them both,   1415
coupling man and woman. The joy they had so lately,
the fortune of their old ancestral house
was deep joy indeed. Now, in this one day,
wailing, madness and doom, death, disgrace,
all the griefs in the world that you can name,   1420
all are theirs forever.
LEADER: Oh poor man, the misery—
has he any rest from pain now?

A voice within, in torment.

MESSENGER: He's shouting,
"Loose the bolts, someone, show me to all of Thebes!
My father's murderer, my mother's—"
No, I can't repeat it, it's unholy.   1425
Now he'll tear himself from his native earth,

not linger, curse the house with his own curse.
But he needs strength, and a guide to lead him on.
This is sickness more than he can bear.

The palace doors open.

                                               Look,
he'll show you himself. The great doors are opening—   1430
you are about to see a sight, a horror
even his mortal enemy would pity.

Enter Oedipus, blinded, led by a boy. He stands at the palace steps, as if surveying his people once again.

CHORUS: O the terror—
the suffering, for all the world to see,
the worst terror that ever met my eyes.
What madness swept over you? What god,   1435
what dark power leapt beyond all bounds,
beyond belief, to crush your wretched life?—
godforsaken, cursed by the gods!
I pity you but I can't bear to look.
I've much to ask, so much to learn,   1440
so much fascinates my eyes,
but you . . . I shudder at the sight.

OEDIPUS: Oh, Ohhh—
the agony! I am agony—
where am I going? where on earth?
               where does all this agony hurl me?   1445
where's my voice?—
             winging, swept away on a dark tide—
         My destiny, my dark power, what a leap you made!

CHORUS: To the depths of terror, too dark to hear, to see.

OEDIPUS: Dark, horror of darkness   1450
      my darkness, drowning, swirling around me
      crashing wave on wave—unspeakable, irresistible
          headwind, fatal harbor! Oh again,
      the misery, all at once, over and over
      the stabbing daggers, stab of memory   1455
raking me insane.

CHORUS: No wonder you suffer
twice over, the pain of your wounds,
the lasting grief of pain.

OEDIPUS: Dear friend, still here?
      Standing by me, still with a care for me,
      the blind man? Such compassion,   1460
          loyal to the last. Oh it's you,
      I know you're here, dark as it is
      I'd know you anywhere, your voice—
it's yours, clearly yours.

CHORUS: Dreadful, what you've done . . .
    how could you bear it, gouging out your eyes?   1465
    What superhuman power drove you on?
OEDIPUS: Apollo, friends, Apollo—
    he ordained my agonies—these, my pains on pains!
        But the hand that struck my eyes was mine,
        mine alone—no one else—   1470
            I did it all myself!
    What good were eyes to me?
    Nothing I could see could bring me joy.
CHORUS: No, no, exactly as you say.
OEDIPUS: What can I ever see?
        What love, what call of the heart   1475
    can touch my ears with joy? Nothing, friends.
        Take me away, far, far from Thebes,
        quickly, cast me away, my friends—
    this great murderous ruin, this man cursed to heaven,
        the man the deathless gods hate most of all!   1480
CHORUS: Pitiful, you suffer so, you understand so much . . .
    I wish you'd never known.
OEDIPUS: Die, die—
    whoever he was that day in the wilds
  who cut my ankles free of the ruthless pins,
        he pulled me clear of death, he saved my life   1485
    for this, this kindness—
        Curse him, kill him!
    If I'd died then, I'd never have dragged myself,
    my loved ones through such hell.
CHORUS: Oh if only . . . would to god.
OEDIPUS: I'd never have come to this,   1490
    my father's murderer—never been branded
  mother's husband, all men see me now! Now,
        loathed by the gods, son of the mother I defiled
        coupling in my father's bed, spawning lives in the loins
  that spawned my wretched life. What grief can crown this grief?   1495
        It's mine alone, my destiny—I am Oedipus!
CHORUS: How can I say you've chosen for the best?
    Better to die than be alive and blind.
OEDIPUS: What I did was best—don't lecture me,
    no more advice. I, with *my* eyes,   1500
    how could I look my father in the eyes
    when I go down to death? Or mother, so abused . . .
    I've done such things to the two of them,
    crimes too huge for hanging.
        Worse yet,
    the sight of my children, born as they were born,   1505
    how could I long to look into their eyes?

No, not with these eyes of mine, never.
Not this city either, her high towers,
the sacred glittering images of her gods—
I am misery! I, her best son, reared   1510
as no other son of Thebes was ever reared,
I've stripped myself, I gave the command myself.
All men must cast away the great blasphemer,
the curse now brought to light by the gods,
the son of Laius—I, my father's son!   1515

Now I've exposed my guilt, horrendous guilt,
could I train a level glance on you, my countrymen?
Impossible! No, if I could just block off my ears,
the springs of hearing, I would stop at nothing—
I'd wall up my loathsome body like a prison,   1520
blind to the sound of life, not just the sight.
Oblivion—what a blessing . . .
for the mind to dwell a world away from pain.
O Cithaeron, why did you give me shelter?
Why didn't you take me, crush my life out on the spot?   1525
I'd never have revealed my birth to all mankind.

O Polybus, Corinth, the old house of my fathers,
so I believed—what a handsome prince you raised—
under the skin, what sickness to the core.
Look at me! Born of outrage, outrage to the core.   1530

O triple roads—it all comes back, the secret,
dark ravine, and the oaks closing in
where the three roads join . . .
You drank my father's blood, my own blood
spilled by my own hands—you still remember me?   1535
What things you saw me do? Then I came here
and did them all once more!
           Marriages! O marriage,
you gave me birth, and once you brought me into the world
you brought my sperm rising back, springing to light
fathers, brothers, sons—one deadly breed—   1540
brides, wives, mothers. The blackest things
a man can do, I have done them all!
                No more—
it's wrong to name what's wrong to do. Quickly,
for the love of god, hide me somewhere,
kill me, hurl me into the sea   1545
where you can never look on me again.

Beckoning to the Chorus as they shrink away.

                    Closer,
it's all right. Touch the man of sorrow.

Do. Don't be afraid. My troubles are mine
and I am the only man alive who can sustain them.

Enter Creon from the palace, attended by palace guards.

LEADER: Put your requests to Creon. Here he is,   1550
    just when we need him. He'll have a plan, he'll act.
    Now that he's the sole defense of the country
    in your place.
OEDIPUS: Oh no, what can I say to him?
    How can I ever hope to win his trust?
    I wronged him so, just now, in every way.   1555
    You must see that—I was so wrong, so wrong.
CREON: I haven't come to mock you, Oedipus,
    or to criticize your former failings.

Turning to the guards.

                          You there,
    have you lost all respect for human feeling?
    At least revere the Sun, the holy fire   1560
    that keeps us all alive. Never expose a thing
    of guilt and holy dread so great it appalls
    the earth, the rain from heaven, the light of day!
    Get him into the halls—quickly as you can.
    Piety demands no less. Kindred alone   1565
    should see a kinsman's shame. This is obscene.
OEDIPUS: Please, in god's name . . . you wipe my fears away,
    coming so generously to me, the worst of men.
    Do one thing more, for your sake, not mine.
CREON: What do you want? Why so insistent?   1570
OEDIPUS: Drive me out of the land at once, far from sight,
    where I can never hear a human voice.
CREON: I'd have done that already, I promise you.
    First I wanted the god to clarify my duties.
OEDIPUS: The god? His command was clear, every word: 1575
    death for the father-killer, the curse—
    he said destroy me!
CREON: So he did. Still, in such a crisis
    it's better to ask precisely what to do.
OEDIPUS: You'd ask the oracle about a man like me?   1580
CREON: By all means. And this time, I assume,
    even you will obey the god's decrees.
OEDIPUS: I will,
    I will. And you, I command you—I beg you . . .
    the woman inside, bury her as you see fit.
    It's the only decent thing,   1585
    to give your own last rites. As for me,
    never condemn the city of my fathers

to house my body, not while I'm alive, no,
let me live on the mountains, on Cithaeron,
my favorite haunt, I have made it famous. 1590
Mother and father marked out that rock
to be my everlasting tomb—buried alive.
Let me die there, where they tried to kill me.
Oh but this I know: no sickness can destroy me,
nothing can. I would never have been saved 1595
from death—I have been saved
for something great and terrible, something strange.
Well let my destiny come and take me on its way!

About my children, Creon, the boys at least,
don't burden yourself. They're men; 1600
wherever they go, they'll find the means to live.
But my two daughters, my poor helpless girls,
clustering at our table, never without me
hovering near them . . . whatever I touched,
they always had their share. Take care of them, 1605
I beg you. Wait, better—permit me, would you?
Just to touch them with my hands and take
our fill of tears. Please . . . my king.
Grant it, with all your noble heart.
If I could hold them, just once, I'd think 1610
I had them with me, like the early days
when I could see their eyes.

Antigone and Ismene, two small children, are led in from the palace by a nurse.

What's that?
O god! Do I really hear you sobbing?—
my two children. Creon, you've pitied me?
Sent me my darling girls, my own flesh and blood! 1615
Am I right?

CREON: Yes, it's my doing.
I know the joy they gave you all these years,
the joy you must feel now.

OEDIPUS: Bless you, Creon!
May god watch over you for this kindness,
better than he ever guarded me.
Children, where are you? 1620
Here, come quickly—

Groping for Antigone and Ismene, who approach their father cautiously, then embrace him.

Come to these hands of mine,
your brother's hands, your own father's hands
that served his once bright eyes so well—
that made them blind. Seeing nothing, children,

knowing nothing, I became your father, 1625
I fathered you in the soil that gave me life.

How I weep for you — I cannot see you now . . .
just thinking of all your days to come, the bitterness,
the life that rough mankind will thrust upon you.
Where are the public gatherings you can join, 1630
the banquets of the clans? Home you'll come,
in tears, cut off from the sight of it all,
the brilliant rites unfinished.
And when you reach perfection, ripe for marriage,
who will he be, my dear ones? Risking all 1635
to shoulder the curse that weighs down my parents,
yes and you too — that wounds us all together.
What more misery could you want?
Your father killed his father, sowed his mother,
one, one and the selfsame womb sprang you — 1640
he cropped the very roots of his existence.
Such disgrace, and you must bear it all!
Who will marry you then? Not a man on earth.
Your doom is clear: you'll wither away to nothing,
single, without a child.

Turning to Creon.

Oh Creon, 1645
you are the only father they have now . . .
we who brought them into the world
are gone, both gone at a stroke —
Don't let them go begging, abandoned,
women without men. Your own flesh and blood! 1650
Never bring them down to the level of my pains.
Pity them. Look at them, so young, so vulnerable,
shorn of everything — you're their only hope.
Promise me, noble Creon, touch my hand.

Reaching toward Creon, who draws back.

You, little ones, if you were old enough 1655
to understand, there is much I'd tell you.
Now, as it is, I'd have you say a prayer.
Pray for life, my children,
live where you are free to grow and season.
Pray god you find a better life than mine, 1660
the father who begot you.

CREON: Enough.
You've wept enough. Into the palace now.
OEDIPUS: I must, but I find it very hard.
CREON: Time is the great healer, you will see.
OEDIPUS: I am going — you know on what condition? 1665
CREON: Tell me. I'm listening.

OEDIPUS: Drive me out of Thebes, in exile.
CREON: Not I. Only the gods can give you that.
OEDIPUS: Surely the gods hate me so much —
CREON: You'll get your wish at once.
OEDIPUS: You consent?   1670
CREON: I try to say what I mean; it's my habit.
OEDIPUS: Then take me away. It's time.
CREON: Come along, let go of the children.
OEDIPUS: No —
        don't take them away from me, not now! No no no!

*Clutching his daughters as the guards wrench them loose and take them through
the palace doors.*

CREON: Still the king, the master of all things?   1675
        No more: here your power ends.
        None of your power follows you through life.

*Exit Oedipus and Creon to the palace. The Chorus comes forward to address the
audience directly.*

CHORUS: People of Thebes, my countrymen, look on Oedipus.
        He solved the famous riddle with his brilliance,
        he rose to power, a man beyond all power.   1680
        Who could behold his greatness without envy?
        Now what a black sea of terror has overwhelmed him.
        Now as we keep our watch and wait the final day,
        count no man happy till he dies, free of pain at last.

Exit in procession.

WILLIAM SHAKESPEARE

*William Shakespeare (1564–1616), the great English playwright and poet,
was born in Stratford, the third of eight children of Mary Arden, daughter of a
prosperous landowner, and John Shakespeare, a glovemaker. We know a little more
about Shakespeare's personal life than we know about Sophocles' life two thousand years before. Some forty documents of Shakespeare's time offer details about
him, commensurate with his station in life and professional activities. The register
of the Stratford parish church documents Shakespeare's baptism and burial, along
with the baptisms of his daughter Susanna and his twins, Judith and Hamnet. We
also know that in 1582, at the age of eighteen, he married Anne Hathaway in
Stratford (she was twenty-six), and that before his death he made a will leaving
most of his considerable property to his two daughters (his son, Hamnet, had died
at age eleven). Shakespeare willed only his "second best bed" to his wife, whom he
apparently left in Stratford with his children when he went off to London to make
his fortune in the theater.*

*As a young man in London, Shakespeare worked as an actor and playwright,
but his first publications were two books of poetry. In 1593, after an outbreak of the*

plague had closed the London theaters, he published his first poem, Venus and Adonis, *dedicated to his wealthy patron the Earl of Southampton. A year later he published another long narrative poem,* The Rape of Lucrece. *(A third book, his collection of sonnets, was published in 1609.) When the theaters reopened in London at the end of 1594, Shakespeare joined the new Lord Chamberlain's Company, for whom he continued to act and write plays until 1613. The literary historian François Laroque has described the astute way Shakespeare managed his career before his retirement as a wealthy man in Stratford:*

> *The Chamberlain's Men were organized in an unusual manner: the six main actors [including Shakespeare] formed an association in which each was a shareholder, directly receiving part of the takings from performances. The actors were financially independent, paying only rent to the theatre proprietor James Burbage. . . . Shakespeare never changed company, a fact rare enough to be worthy of note. From now on he worked to strengthen his position as both player and playwright. In addition to his acting he wrote an average of two plays a year until 1608, when the pace of theatrical production slackened. The decision early in his career to remain in one place, with one company, enabled him quickly to consolidate his first successes as a writer and to become in his lifetime the most highly sought after dramatist of the Elizabethan and Jacobean stage.*

The exact number of plays written by Shakespeare is unknown, as the practice of his time was for playwrights to collaborate on scripts, often reworking and adapting older material, but thirty-seven plays currently make up the Shakespeare canon. Seven years after his death, thirty-six of his plays were collected by actors in his theater company desirous to honor his memory and to protect his work from unscrupulous publishers. The table of contents in this First Folio edition of 1623 reads, "A Catalogue of the several Comedies, Histories, and Tragedies contained in this Volume." This way of organizing the plays has continued to the present day.

The comedies included, among other plays, The Tempest, The Comedy of Errors, A Midsummer Night's Dream, As You Like It, The Taming of the Shrew, *and* The Merchant of Venice. *The history plays — most of which Shakespeare wrote early in his career, between 1590 and 1597 — included* Richard II; Henry IV, Parts 1 and 2; Henry V; Henry VI, Parts 1–3; *and* Richard III. *The tragedies included* Romeo and Juliet, Macbeth, King Lear, Othello, *and* Hamlet. *Although eighteen of Shakespeare's plays were published in his lifetime as small books called* quartos, *no play manuscript used by a printer in this time has survived, so we depend on the work of scholars for the editing of his texts.*

The Elizabethan theater flourished during the reign of Elizabeth I and her successor, James I, having its origins in fifteenth-century religious pageants and plays such as The Second Shepherd's Play *and* Everyman, *which were performed by actors who were part of traveling companies. The first permanent theater in England was not built until 1576, only about fifteen years before Shakespeare came to London to begin his career. Toward the end of the sixteenth century, playwrights began to glorify English history, turning to secular material for their subjects. National patriotism was stirred by the defeat of the Spanish Armada, which had failed spectacularly in its attempt to conquer England in 1588. When Shakespeare began to write plays, there were several professional acting companies in*

London, and we have a good idea of the design of their theaters from the foundations of the Rose Playhouse, excavated in 1988. A reconstruction of the Globe Playhouse, in which Shakespeare once held a one-tenth interest as a partner in the company of the Chamberlain's Men, opened in London in 1997. The original structure's thatched roof sported a globe with the Latin inscription totus mundus agit histrionem— "All the world's a stage."

Elizabethan theaters such as the Rose and the Globe, the two largest public theaters in London, were tall buildings, usually round or octagonal, with three tiers of galleries for the spectators. The Globe was located south of the Thames River in a neighborhood famous for its bearbaiting pits, gambling houses, brothels, and theaters. The Globe was the finest playhouse in London, yet its raised, covered stage, which projected into the audience, was so small that no more than a dozen

Interior of the first Globe Playhouse. (Drawing by C. Walter Hodges. Reprinted from *The Third Globe: Symposium for the Reconstruction of the Globe Playhouse,* edited by C. Walter Hodges, S. Schoenbaum, and Leonard Leone. © 1981 Wayne State University Press. Reprinted by permission of the publisher.)

The reconstructed Globe Theatre. Southwark, London, 1999. (Photo: © Nik Wheeler/CORBIS)

actors could appear at a time. The gallery directly behind the stage was used by musicians or actors (as for the balcony scene in Romeo and Juliet). *In the front section of the stage was a trapdoor used for the entrance and disappearance of devils and ghosts, or for burial scenes, as in* Hamlet. *Actors could also stand under the stage, as in the mention in* Hamlet *that the "ghost cries under the stage."*

Audiences of up to eight hundred people paid a penny each to stand in the uncovered pit to watch the play, with ticket prices increasing up to six pence for a seat in the galleries, which held an additional fifteen hundred spectators. Plays were performed in these public theaters only in daylight, without artificial illumination. As in Greek and classical Japanese Nō theater, only men were trained as actors, including boys who played women's roles until their voices broke. Shakespeare wrote complex parts for specific actors in his company, such as Richard Burbage, who first played the role of Hamlet. As an actor Shakespeare was not a star performer; probably he played the ghost of the murdered king in productions of Hamlet. *In theater records he was designated a "principal comedian" in 1598, a "principle tragedian" in 1603, and one of the "man players" in 1608.*

On June 29, 1613, soon after Shakespeare's retirement to Stratford, the Globe Playhouse burned to the ground during a performance of his play Henry VIII. *A volley of blank shots fired by an actor onstage set fire to the thatched roof of the galleries. Everyone in the audience escaped unharmed, with the exception of a man whose trousers caught fire in the blaze; according to spectators, he doused the fire in his clothes with a bottle of ale. Thirty years later, all the theaters in England would be torn down by order of Parliament in 1642 and 1644 under Puritan rule.*

While Shakespeare and his generation of gifted contemporaries—Christopher Marlowe, Thomas Kyd, and Ben Jonson, to name only a few—were creating their plays, audiences crammed into the theaters six days a week, eager to witness stage spectacles and listen to the players' grandiloquence. Plays such as Hamlet, which included a ghost, stabbings, suicide, and duels, in addition to rich and complex lines of poetry, were the regular fare of the patrons of the Globe Playhouse. Shakespeare and his company of actors were so successful that they enjoyed royal patronage. They performed for Queen Elizabeth I on the average of three times a year, and it is recorded that King James I was in attendance at the first performance of Macbeth in 1604.

Just as Shakespeare depended on the contemporary historian Raphael Holinshed's chronicles for the material of his English history plays, he used earlier sources as the basis for Hamlet. He was also influenced by Kyd's Spanish Tragedy (c. 1587), which set the standard for a new genre of English plays called "revenge tragedies." In addition, writings by Shakespeare's contemporaries indicate that a "lost play" of Hamlet was known to Shakespeare before he wrote his version of the play. In creating their **revenge tragedies** (plays in which the plot typically centers on a spectacular attempt to avenge the murder of a family member), Shakespeare and other popular English dramatists took the early Roman playwrights as their models. The Greek playwrights were not popular at the time, but a contemporary account credited Shakespeare with being as polished a writer of comedy and tragedy as the Romans Plautus and Seneca, respectively.

The extraordinary richness of Shakespeare's theatrical world is made evident in Hamlet. Unlike other avengers in the revenge tragedies of his time, Hamlet is a complex figure. He plays the multiple roles of son, lover, philosopher, actor, and prince. He questions the reality of his experience, procrastinates in carrying out his promise to avenge his father's death, considers his own failure of will and emotional paralysis, and contemplates suicide. Because most of us can sympathize with his difficult situation, Hamlet is the best known and most often performed of Shakespeare's plays. Actors have offered different interpretations of the role as diverse as Sir John Gielgud's aristocratic, disillusioned Hamlet in 1934 to the young actor Mark Rylance's recent performance of a psychotic Hamlet dressed in striped pajamas, inhabiting the Danish court as if it were a psychiatric hospital. As the critic Edward Hubler recognized, "Tragedy of the first order is a rare phenomenon. It came into being in Greece in the fifth century B.C., where it flourished for a while, and it did not appear again until some two thousand years later when Shakespeare wrote Hamlet in 1600."

CONNECTION   Margaret Atwood, "Gertrude Talks Back," page 33.

CONVERSATIONS   See pages 1587–1605, including Geoffrey Bullough, "Sources of Shakespeare's Hamlet," page 1589; H. D. F. Kitto, "Hamlet and the Oedipus," page 1592; John Keats, "From a Letter to George and Thomas Keats, 21 December 1817," page 1594; Virginia Woolf, "What If Shakespeare Had Had a Sister?" page 1594; Tom Stoppard, Dogg's Hamlet: The Encore, page 1596; Sir John Gielgud, "On Playing Hamlet," page 1598; photographs of Hamlet in performance, pages 1600–1602; John Lahr, "Review of Hamlet," page 1602.

WEB   Research William Shakespeare and answer questions about his work at bedfordstmartins.com/charters/litwriters.

Hamlet, Prince of Denmark

[DRAMATIS PERSONAE

CLAUDIUS, King of Denmark

HAMLET, son to the late and nephew
   to the present king

POLONIUS, lord chamberlain

HORATIO, friend to Hamlet

LAERTES, son to Polonius

VOLTIMAND ⎫
CORNELIUS ⎪
ROSENCRANTZ ⎬ courtiers
GUILDENSTERN ⎪
OSRIC ⎭

A GENTLEMAN

A PRIEST

MARCELLUS ⎫
         ⎬ officers
BERNARDO ⎭

FRANCISCO, a soldier

REYNALDO, servant to Polonius

PLAYERS

TWO CLOWNS, grave-diggers

FORTINBRAS, Prince of Norway

A CAPTAIN

ENGLISH AMBASSADORS

GERTRUDE, Queen of Denmark,
   and mother to Hamlet

OPHELIA, daughter to Polonius

LORDS, LADIES, OFFICERS,
   SOLDIERS, SAILORS, MESSENGERS,
   and other ATTENDANTS

GHOST of Hamlet's father

SCENE: *Denmark.*]

   [ACT I

SCENE I: *Elsinore. A platform° before the castle.*]

Enter Bernardo and Francisco, two sentinels.

BERNARDO: Who's there?

FRANCISCO: Nay, answer me:° stand, and unfold yourself.

BERNARDO: Long live the king!°

FRANCISCO: Bernardo?

BERNARDO: He.   5

FRANCISCO: You come most carefully upon your hour.

BERNARDO: 'Tis now struck twelve; get thee to bed, Francisco.

FRANCISCO: For this relief much thanks: 'tis bitter cold,
   And I am sick at heart.

BERNARDO: Have you had quiet guard?

FRANCISCO: Not a mouse stirring.   10

BERNARDO: Well, good night.
   If you do meet Horatio and Marcellus,
   The rivals° of my watch, bid them make haste.

Enter Horatio and Marcellus.

FRANCISCO: I think I hear them. Stand, ho! Who is there?

HORATIO: Friends to this ground.

ACT I, SCENE I.   **s.d. platform:** A level space on the battlements of the royal castle at Elsinore, a Danish seaport; now Helsingör.   **2. me:** This is emphatic, since Francisco is the sentry.   **3. Long live the king:** Either a password or greeting; Horatio and Marcellus use a different one in line 15.   **13. rivals:** Partners.

MARCELLUS: And liegemen to the Dane.   15
FRANCISCO: Give you° good night.
MARCELLUS: O, farewell, honest soldier:
    Who hath reliev'd you?
FRANCISCO: Bernardo hath my place.
    Give you good night.   *Exit Francisco.*
MARCELLUS: Holla! Bernardo!
BERNARDO: Say,
    What, is Horatio there?
HORATIO: A piece of him.
BERNARDO: Welcome, Horatio: welcome, good Marcellus.   20
MARCELLUS: What, has this thing appear'd again to-night?
BERNARDO: I have seen nothing.
MARCELLUS: Horatio says 'tis but our fantasy,
    And will not let belief take hold of him
    Touching this dreaded sight, twice seen of us: 25
    Therefore I have entreated him along
    With us to watch the minutes of this night;
    That if again this apparition come,
    He may approve° our eyes and speak to it.
HORATIO: Tush, tush, 'twill not appear.
BERNARDO: Sit down awhile;   30
    And let us once again assail your ears,
    That are so fortified against our story
    What we have two nights seen.
HORATIO: Well, sit we down,
    And let us hear Bernardo speak of this.
BERNARDO: Last night of all,   35
    When yond same star that's westward from the pole°
    Had made his course t' illume that part of heaven
    Where now it burns, Marcellus and myself,
    The bell then beating one, —

Enter Ghost.

MARCELLUS: Peace, break thee off; look, where it comes again!   40
BERNARDO: In the same figure, like the king that's dead.
MARCELLUS: Thou art a scholar;° speak to it, Horatio.
BERNARDO: Looks 'a not like the king? mark it, Horatio.
HORATIO: Most like: it harrows° me with fear and wonder.
BERNARDO: It would be spoke to.°
MARCELLUS: Speak to it, Horatio.   45

---

16. Give you: God give you. **29. approve:** Corroborate. **36. pole:** Polestar.
42. scholar: Exorcisms were performed in Latin, which Horatio, as an educated man,
would be able to speak. **44. harrows:** Lacerates the feelings. **45. It . . . to:** A ghost
could not speak until spoken to.

HORATIO: What art thou that usurp'st this time of night,
　　　Together with that fair and warlike form
　　　In which the majesty of buried Denmark°
　　　Did sometimes march? by heaven I charge thee, speak!
MARCELLUS: It is offended.
BERNARDO:　　　　　　See it stalks away!　　　　　　　　50
HORATIO: Stay! speak, speak! I charge thee, speak!　　　*Exit Ghost.*
MARCELLUS: 'Tis gone, and will not answer.
BERNARDO: How now, Horatio! you tremble and look pale:
　　　Is not this something more than fantasy?
　　　What think you on 't?　　　　　　　　　　　　　55
HORATIO: Before my God, I might not this believe
　　　Without the sensible and true avouch
　　　Of mine own eyes.
MARCELLUS:　　　　　Is it not like the king?
HORATIO: As thou art to thyself:
　　　Such was the very armour he had on　　　　　　　60
　　　When he the ambitious Norway combated;
　　　So frown'd he once, when, in an angry parle,
　　　He smote° the sledded Polacks° on the ice.
　　　'Tis strange.
MARCELLUS: Thus twice before, and jump° at this dead hour,　　65
　　　With martial stalk hath he gone by our watch.
HORATIO: In what particular thought to work I know not;
　　　But in the gross and scope° of my opinion,
　　　This bodes some strange eruption to our state.
MARCELLUS: Good now,° sit down, and tell me, he that knows,　　70
　　　Why this same strict and most observant watch
　　　So nightly toils° the subject° of the land,
　　　And why such daily cast° of brazen cannon,
　　　And foreign mart° for implements of war;
　　　Why such impress° of shipwrights, whose sore task　　75
　　　Does not divide the Sunday from the week;
　　　What might be toward, that this sweaty haste
　　　Doth make the night joint-labourer with the day:
　　　Who is 't that can inform me?
HORATIO:　　　　　　　That can I;
　　　At least, the whisper goes so. Our last king,　　　　80
　　　Whose image even but now appear'd to us,

---

48. buried Denmark: The buried king of Denmark.　**63. smote:** Defeated; **sledded Polacks:** Polanders using sledges.　**65. jump:** Exactly.　**68. gross and scope:** General drift.　**70. Good now:** An expression denoting entreaty or expostulation.　**72. toils:** Causes or makes to toil; **subject:** People, subjects.　**73. cast:** Casting, founding. **74. mart:** Buying and selling, traffic.　**75. impress:** Impressment.

Was, as you know, by Fortinbras of Norway,
Thereto prick'd on° by a most emulate° pride,
Dar'd to the combat; in which our valiant Hamlet—
For so this side of our known world esteem'd him—   85
Did slay this Fortinbras; who, by a seal'd compact,
Well ratified by law and heraldry,°
Did forfeit, with his life, all those his lands
Which he stood seiz'd° of, to the conqueror:
Against the which, a moiety competent°   90
Was gaged by our king; which had return'd
To the inheritance of Fortinbras,
Had he been vanquisher; as, by the same comart,°
And carriage° of the article design'd,
His fell to Hamlet. Now, sir, young Fortinbras,   95
Of unimproved° mettle hot and full,°
Hath in the skirts of Norway here and there
Shark'd up° a list of lawless resolutes,°
For food and diet,° to some enterprise
That hath a stomach in't; which is no other—   100
As it doth well appear unto our state—
But to recover of us, by strong hand
And terms compulsatory, those foresaid lands
So by his father lost: and this, I take it,
Is the main motive of our preparations,   105
The source of this our watch and the chief head
Of this post-haste and romage° in the land.
BERNARDO: I think it be no other but e'en so:
Well may it sort° that this portentous figure
Comes armed through our watch; so like the king   110
That was and is the question of these wars.
HORATIO: A mote° it is to trouble the mind's eye.
In the most high and palmy state° of Rome,
A little ere the mightiest Julius fell,
The graves stood tenantless and the sheeted dead   115
Did squeak and gibber in the Roman streets:
As stars with trains of fire° and dews of blood,
Disasters° in the sun; and the moist star°

---

83. prick'd on: Incited; **emulate:** Rivaling.   **87. law and heraldry:** Heraldic law, governing combat.   **89. seiz'd:** Possessed.   **90. moiety competent:** Adequate or sufficient portion.   **93. comart:** Joint bargain.   **94. carriage:** Import, bearing.   **96. unimproved:** Not turned to account; **hot and full:** Full of fight.   **98. Shark'd up:** Got together in haphazard fashion; **resolutes:** Desperadoes.   **99. food and diet:** No pay but their keep.   **107. romage:** Bustle, commotion.   **109. sort:** Suit.   **112. mote:** Speck of dust.   **113. palmy state:** Triumphant sovereignty.   **117. stars . . . fire:** I.e., comets.   **118. Disasters:** Unfavorable aspects; **moist star:** The moon, governing tides.

Upon whose influence Neptune's empire° stands
Was sick almost to doomsday with eclipse: 120
And even the like precurse° of fear'd events,
As harbingers preceding still the fates
And prologue to the omen coming on,
Have heaven and earth together demonstrated
Unto our climatures and countrymen. —   125

Enter Ghost.

But soft, behold! lo, where it comes again!
I'll cross° it, though it blast me. Stay, illusion!
If thou hast any sound, or use of voice,
Speak to me!   *It° spreads his arms.*
If there be any good thing to be done,   130
That may to thee do ease and grace to me,
Speak to me!
If thou art privy to thy country's fate,
Which, happily, foreknowing may avoid,
O, speak!   135
Or if thou hast uphoarded in thy life
Extorted treasure in the womb of earth,
For which, they say, you spirits oft walk in death,   *The cock crows.*
Speak of it:° stay, and speak! Stop it, Marcellus.
MARCELLUS: Shall I strike at it with my partisan?°   140
HORATIO: Do, if it will not stand.
BERNARDO: 'Tis here!
HORATIO: 'Tis here!
MARCELLUS: 'Tis gone!   *[Exit Ghost.]*
We do it wrong, being so majestical,
To offer it the show of violence;
For it is, as the air, invulnerable,   145
And our vain blows malicious mockery.
BERNARDO: It was about to speak, when the cock crew.°
HORATIO: And then it started like a guilty thing
Upon a fearful summons. I have heard,
The cock, that is the trumpet to the morn,   150
Doth with his lofty and shrill-sounding throat
Awake the god of day; and, at his warning,
Whether in sea or fire, in earth or air,

---

119. **Neptune's empire:** The sea.   121. **precurse:** Heralding.   127. **cross:** Meet, face, thus bringing down the evil influence on the person who crosses it.   129. **It:** The Ghost, or perhaps Horatio.   133–139. **If . . . it:** Horatio recites the traditional reasons why ghosts might walk.   140. **partisan:** Long-handled spear with a blade having lateral projections.   147. **cock crew:** According to traditional ghost lore, spirits returned to their confines at cockcrow.

Th' extravagant and erring° spirit hies
To his confine:° and of the truth herein   155
This present object made probation.°
MARCELLUS: It faded on the crowing of the cock.
    Some say that ever 'gainst° that season comes
    Wherein our Saviour's birth is celebrated,
    The bird of dawning singeth all night long: 160
    And then, they say, no spirit dare stir abroad;
    The nights are wholesome; then no planets strike,°
    No fairy takes, nor witch hath power to charm,
    So hallow'd and so gracious° is that time.
HORATIO: So have I heard and do in part believe it.   165
    But, look, the morn, in russet mantle clad,
    Walks o'er the dew of yon high eastward hill:
    Break we our watch up; and by my advice,
    Let us impart what we have seen to-night
    Unto young Hamlet; for, upon my life,   170
    This spirit, dumb to us, will speak to him.
    Do you consent we shall acquaint him with it,
    As needful in our loves, fitting our duty?
MARCELLUS: Let's do 't, I pray; and I this morning know
    Where we shall find him most conveniently.   *Exeunt.* 175

[SCENE II: *A room of state in the castle.*]

*Flourish. Enter Claudius, King of Denmark, Gertrude the Queen, Councilors,
Polonius and his Son Laertes, Hamlet, cum aliis*° [*including Voltimand and Cornelius*].

KING: Though yet of Hamlet our dear brother's death
    The memory be green, and that it us befitted
    To bear our hearts in grief and our whole kingdom
    To be contracted in one brow of woe,
    Yet so far hath discretion fought with nature   5
    That we with wisest sorrow think on him,
    Together with remembrance of ourselves.
    Therefore our sometime sister, now our queen,
    Th' imperial jointress° to this warlike state,
    Have we, as 'twere with a defeated joy, —   10
    With an auspicious and a dropping eye,
    With mirth in funeral and with dirge in marriage,

---

154. extravagant and erring: Wandering. Both words mean the same thing. **155. confine:** Place of confinement. **156. probation:** Proof, trial. **158. 'gainst:** Just before.
162. planets strike: It was thought that planets were malignant and might strike travelers
by night. **164. gracious:** Full of goodness. SCENE II. **s.d. cum aliis:** With others.
9. jointress: Woman possessed of a jointure, or, joint tenancy of an estate.

In equal scale weighing delight and dole, —
Taken to wife: nor have we herein barr'd
Your better wisdoms, which have freely gone   15
With this affair along. For all, our thanks.
Now follows, that° you know, young Fortinbras,
Holding a weak supposal° of our worth,
Or thinking by our late dear brother's death
Our state to be disjoint° and out of frame,°   20
Colleagued° with this dream of his advantage,°
He hath not fail'd to pester us with message,
Importing° the surrender of those lands
Lost by his father, with all bands of law,
To our most valiant brother. So much for him.   25
Now for ourself and for this time of meeting:
Thus much the business is: we have here writ
To Norway, uncle of young Fortinbras, —
Who, impotent and bed-rid, scarcely hears
Of this his nephew's purpose, — to suppress   30
His further gait° herein; in that the levies,
The lists and full proportions, are all made
Out of his subject:° and we here dispatch
You, good Cornelius, and you, Voltimand,
For bearers of this greeting to old Norway;   35
Giving to you no further personal power
To business with the king, more than the scope
Of these delated° articles allow.
Farewell, and let your haste commend your duty.

CORNELIUS: ⎫
                ⎬ In that and all things will we show our duty.   40
VOLTIMAND: ⎭

KING: We doubt it nothing: heartily farewell.

                    [Exeunt Voltimand and Cornelius.]

And now, Laertes, what's the news with you?
You told us of some suit; what is't, Laertes?
You cannot speak of reason to the Dane,°
And lose your voice:° what wouldst thou beg, Laertes,   45
That shall not be my offer, not thy asking?
The head is not more native° to the heart,
The hand more instrumental° to the mouth,
Than is the throne of Denmark to thy father.
What wouldst thou have, Laertes?

---

17. that: That which.   **18. weak supposal:** Low estimate.   **20. disjoint:** Distracted, out of joint; **frame:** Order.   **21. Colleagued:** added to; **dream . . . advantage:** Visionary hope of success.   **23. Importing:** Purporting, pertaining to.   **31. gait:** Proceeding. **33. Out of his subject:** At the expense of Norway's subjects (collectively).   **38. delated:** Expressly stated.   **44. the Dane:** Danish king.   **45. lose your voice:** Speak in vain. **47. native:** Closely connected, related.   **48. instrumental:** Serviceable.

LAERTES: My dread lord,   50
    Your leave and favour to return to France;
    From whence though willingly I came to Denmark,
    To show my duty in your coronation,
    Yet now, I must confess, that duty done,
    My thoughts and wishes bend again toward France   55
    And bow them to your gracious leave and pardon.°
KING: Have you your father's leave? What says Polonius?
POLONIUS: He hath, my lord, wrung from me my slow leave
    By laboursome petition, and at last
    Upon his will I seal'd my hard consent: 60
    I do beseech you, give him leave to go.
KING: Take thy fair hour, Laertes; time be thine,
    And thy best graces spend it at thy will!
    But now, my cousin° Hamlet, and my son, —
HAMLET [*aside*]: A little more than kin, and less than kind!°   65
KING: How is it that the clouds still hang on you?
HAMLET: Not so, my lord; I am too much in the sun.°
QUEEN: Good Hamlet, cast thy nighted colour off,
    And let thine eye look like a friend on Denmark.
    Do not for ever with thy vailed lids   70
    Seek for thy noble father in the dust:
    Thou know'st 'tis common; all that lives must die,
    Passing through nature to eternity.
HAMLET: Ay, madam, it is common.°
QUEEN: If it be,
    Why seems it so particular with thee?   75
HAMLET: Seems, madam! nay, it is; I know not "seems."
    'Tis not alone my inky cloak, good mother,
    Nor customary suits° of solemn black,
    Nor windy suspiration° of forc'd breath,
    No, nor the fruitful river in the eye,   80
    Nor the dejected 'haviour of the visage,
    Together with all forms, moods, shapes of grief,
    That can denote me truly: these indeed seem,
    For they are actions that a man might play:

---

56. leave and pardon: Permission to depart.   **64. cousin:** Any kin not of the immediate family.   **65. A little . . . kind:** My relation to you has become more than kinship warrants; it has also become unnatural.   **67. I am . . . sun:** The senses seem to be: I am too much out of doors, I am too much in the sun of your grace (ironical), I am too much of a son to you. Possibly an allusion to the proverb "Out of heaven's blessing into the warm sun"; i.e., Hamlet is out of house and home in being deprived of the kingship.   **74. Ay . . . common:** It is common, but it hurts nevertheless; possibly a reference to the commonplace quality of the queen's remark.   **78. customary suits:** Suits prescribed by custom for mourning.   **79. windy suspiration:** Heavy sighing.

But I have that within which passeth show;   85
These but the trappings and the suits of woe.
KING: 'Tis sweet and commendable in your nature, Hamlet,
To give these mourning duties to your father:
But, you must know, your father lost a father;
That father lost, lost his, and the survivor bound   90
In filial obligation for some term
To do obsequious° sorrow: but to persever
In obstinate condolement° is a course
Of impious stubbornness; 'tis unmanly grief;
It shows a will most incorrect° to heaven,   95
A heart unfortified, a mind impatient,
An understanding simple and unschool'd:
For what we know must be and is as common
As any the most vulgar thing° to sense,
Why should we in our peevish opposition   100
Take it to heart? Fie! 'tis a fault to heaven,
A fault against the dead, a fault to nature,
To reason most absurd; whose common theme
Is death of fathers, and who still hath cried,
From the first corse till he that died to-day,   105
"This must be so." We pray you, throw to earth
This unprevailing° woe, and think of us
As of a father: for let the world take note,
You are the most immediate° to our throne;
And with no less nobility° of love   110
Than that which dearest father bears his son,
Do I impart° toward you. For your intent
In going back to school in Wittenberg,°
It is most retrograde° to our desire:
And we beseech you, bend you° to remain   115
Here, in the cheer and comfort of our eye,
Our chiefest courtier, cousin, and our son.
QUEEN: Let not thy mother lose her prayers, Hamlet:
I pray thee, stay with us; go not to Wittenberg.
HAMLET: I shall in all my best obey you, madam.   120
KING: Why, 'tis a loving and a fair reply:
Be as ourself in Denmark. Madam, come;
This gentle and unforc'd accord of Hamlet
Sits smiling to my heart: in grace whereof,

---

92. obsequious: Dutiful.   **93. condolement:** Sorrowing.   **95. incorrect:** Untrained,
uncorrected.   **99. vulgar thing:** Common experience.   **107. unprevailing:** Unavail-
ing.   **109. most immediate:** Next in succession.   **110. nobility:** High degree.   **112.
impart:** The object is apparently *love* (line 110).   **113. Wittenberg:** Famous German
university founded in 1502.   **114. retrograde:** Contrary.   **115. bend you:** Incline
yourself; imperative.

No jocund health that Denmark drinks to-day,   125
But the great cannon to the clouds shall tell,
And the king's rouse° the heaven shall bruit again,°
Re-speaking earthly thunder. Come away.

Flourish. Exeunt all but Hamlet.

HAMLET: O, that this too too sullied flesh would melt,
    Thaw and resolve itself into a dew!   130
    Or that the Everlasting had not fix'd
    His canon 'gainst self-slaughter! O God! God!
    How weary, stale, flat and unprofitable,
    Seem to me all the uses of this world!
    Fie on't! ah fie! 'tis an unweeded garden,   135
    That grows to seed; things rank and gross in nature
    Possess it merely.° That it should come to this!
    But two months dead: nay, not so much, not two:
    So excellent a king; that was, to this,
    Hyperion° to a satyr; so loving to my mother   140
    That he might not beteem° the winds of heaven
    Visit her face too roughly. Heaven and earth!
    Must I remember? why, she would hang on him,
    As if increase of appetite had grown
    By what it fed on: and yet, within a month —   145
    Let me not think on't — Frailty, thy name is woman! —
    A little month, or ere those shoes were old
    With which she followed my poor father's body,
    Like Niobe,° all tears: — why she, even she —
    O God! a beast, that wants discourse of reason,°   150
    Would have mourn'd longer — married with my uncle,
    My father's brother, but no more like my father
    Than I to Hercules: within a month:
    Ere yet the salt of most unrighteous tears
    Had left the flushing in her galled° eyes,   155
    She married. O, most wicked speed, to post
    With such dexterity° to incestuous sheets!
    It is not nor it cannot come to good:
    But break, my heart; for I must hold my tongue.

Enter Horatio, Marcellus, and Bernardo.

HORATIO: Hail to your lordship!
HAMLET: I am glad to see you well: 160
    Horatio! — or I do forget myself.

---

127. rouse: Draft of liquor; **bruit again:** Echo.   **137. merely:** Completely, entirely.
140. Hyperion: God of the sun in the older regime of ancient gods.   **141. beteem:**
Allow.   **149. Niobe:** Tantalus's daughter, who boasted that she had more sons and
daughters than Leto; for this Apollo and Artemis slew her children. She was turned into
stone by Zeus on Mount Sipylus.   **150. discourse of reason:** Process or faculty of reason.   **155. galled:** Irritated.   **157. dexterity:** Facility.

HORATIO: The same, my lord, and your poor servant ever.

HAMLET: Sir, my good friend; I'll change that name with you:°
> And what make you from Wittenberg, Horatio?
> Marcellus?   165

MARCELLUS: My good lord—

HAMLET: I am very glad to see you. Good even, sir.
> But what, in faith, make you from Wittenberg?

HORATIO: A truant disposition, good my lord.

HAMLET: I would not hear your enemy say so,   170
> Nor shall you do my ear that violence,
> To make it truster of your own report
> Against yourself: I know you are no truant.
> But what is your affair in Elsinore?
> We'll teach you to drink deep ere you depart.   175

HORATIO: My lord, I came to see your father's funeral.

HAMLET: I prithee, do not mock me, fellow-student;
> I think it was to see my mother's wedding.

HORATIO: Indeed, my lord, it follow'd hard° upon.

HAMLET: Thrift, thrift, Horatio! the funeral bak'd meats°   180
> Did coldly furnish forth the marriage tables.
> Would I had met my dearest° foe in heaven
> Or ever I had seen that day, Horatio!
> My father!—methinks I see my father.

HORATIO: Where, my lord!

HAMLET: In my mind's eye, Horatio.   185

HORATIO: I saw him once; 'a° was a goodly king.

HAMLET: 'A was a man, take him for all in all,
> I shall not look upon his like again.

HORATIO: My lord, I think I saw him yesternight.

HAMLET: Saw? who?   190

HORATIO: My lord, the king your father.

HAMLET: The king my father!

HORATIO: Season your admiration° for a while
> With an attent ear, till I may deliver,
> Upon the witness of these gentlemen,
> This marvel to you.

HAMLET: For God's love, let me hear.   195

HORATIO: Two nights together had these gentlemen,
> Marcellus and Bernardo, on their watch,
> In the dead waste and middle of the night,
> Been thus encount'red. A figure like your father,

---

163. I'll . . . you: I'll be your servant; you shall be my friend; also explained as "I'll exchange the name of friend with you."   **179. hard:** Close.   **180. bak'd meats:** Meat pies.   **182. dearest:** Direst. The adjective *dear* in Shakespeare has two different origins: O.E. *deore*, "beloved," and O.E. *deor*, "fierce." *Dearest* is the superlative of the second.   **186. 'a:** He.   **192. Season your admiration:** Restrain your astonishment.

Armed at point exactly, cap-a-pe,°   200
Appears before them, and with solemn march
Goes slow and stately by them: thrice he walk'd
By their oppress'd° and fear-surprised eyes,
Within his truncheon's° length; whilst they, distill'd°
Almost to jelly with the act° of fear,   205
Stand dumb and speak not to him. This to me
In dreadful secrecy impart they did;
And I with them the third night kept the watch:
Where, as they had deliver'd, both in time,
Form of the thing, each word made true and good,   210
The apparition comes: I knew your father;
These hands are not more like.

HAMLET: But where was this?
MARCELLUS: My lord, upon the platform where we watch'd.
HAMLET: Did you not speak to it?
HORATIO: My lord, I did;
But answer made it none: yet once methought   215
It lifted up it° head and did address
Itself to motion, like as it would speak;
But even then the morning cock crew loud,
And at the sound it shrunk in haste away,
And vanish'd from our sight.
HAMLET: 'Tis very strange.   220
HORATIO: As I do live, my honour'd lord, 'tis true;
And we did think it writ down in our duty
To let you know of it.
HAMLET: Indeed, indeed, sirs, but this troubles me.
Hold you the watch to-night?
MARCELLUS: ⎫
BERNARDO: ⎭   We do, my lord.   225
HAMLET: Arm'd, say you?
MARCELLUS: ⎫
BERNARDO: ⎭ Arm'd, my lord.
HAMLET: From top to toe?
MARCELLUS: ⎫
BERNARDO: ⎭   My lord, from head to foot.
HAMLET: Then saw you not his face?
HORATIO: O, yes, my lord; he wore his beaver° up.   230
HAMLET: What, look'd he frowningly?
HORATIO: A countenance more
In sorrow than in anger.

---

200. cap-a-pe: From head to foot.   **203. oppress'd:** Distressed.   **204. truncheon:** Officer's staff; **distill'd:** Softened, weakened.   **205. act:** Action.   **216. it:** Its.   **230. beaver:**
Visor on the helmet.

HAMLET: Pale or red?

HORATIO: Nay, very pale.

HAMLET: And fix'd his eyes upon you?

HORATIO: Most constantly.

HAMLET: I would I had been there.

HORATIO: It would have much amaz'd you.   235

HAMLET: Very like, very like. Stay'd it long?

HORATIO: While one with moderate haste might tell a hundred.

MARCELLUS: ⎤
BERNARDO: ⎦ Longer, longer.

HORATIO: Not when I saw't.

HAMLET: His beard was grizzled, — no?

HORATIO: It was, as I have seen it in his life,   240
          A sable° silver'd.

HAMLET: I will watch to-night;
          Perchance 'twill walk again.

HORATIO: I warr'nt it will.

HAMLET: If it assume my noble father's person,
          I'll speak to it, though hell itself should gape
          And bid me hold my peace. I pray you all,   245
          If you have hitherto conceal'd this sight,
          Let it be tenable in your silence still;
          And whatsoever else shall hap to-night,
          Give it an understanding, but no tongue:
          I will requite your loves. So, fare you well: 250
          Upon the platform, 'twixt eleven and twelve,
          I'll visit you.

ALL: Our duty to your honour.

HAMLET: Your loves, as mine to you: farewell.   *Exeunt [all but Hamlet].*
          My father's spirit in arms! all is not well;
          I doubt° some foul play: would the night were come!   255
          Till then sit still, my soul: foul deeds will rise,
          Though all the earth o'erwhelm them, to men's eyes.   *Exit.*

[SCENE III: *A room in Polonius's house.*]

Enter Laertes and Ophelia, his Sister.

LAERTES: My necessaries are embark'd: farewell:
          And, sister, as the winds give benefit
          And convoy is assistant,° do not sleep,
          But let me hear from you.

OPHELIA: Do you doubt that?

LAERTES: For Hamlet and the trifling of his favour,   5

---

241. sable: Black color.   **255. doubt:** Fear.   SCENE III.   **3. convoy is assistant:** Means
of conveyance are available.

Hold it a fashion° and a toy in blood,°
A violet in the youth of primy° nature,
Forward,° not permanent, sweet, not lasting,
The perfume and suppliance of a minute;°
No more.

OPHELIA: No more but so?

LAERTES: Think it no more: 10
For nature, crescent,° does not grow alone
In thews° and bulk, but, as this temple° waxes,
The inward service of the mind and soul
Grows wide withal. Perhaps he loves you now,
And now no soil° nor cautel° doth besmirch   15
The virtue of his will: but you must fear,
His greatness weigh'd,° his will is not his own;
For he himself is subject to his birth:
He may not, as unvalued persons do,
Carve for himself; for on his choice depends   20
The safety and health of this whole state;
And therefore must his choice be circumscrib'd
Unto the voice and yielding° of that body
Whereof he is the head. Then if he says he loves you,
It fits your wisdom so far to believe it   25
As he in his particular act and place
May give his saying deed;° which is no further
Than the main voice of Denmark goes withal.
Then weigh what loss your honour may sustain,
If with too credent° ear you list his songs,   30
Or lose your heart, or your chaste treasure open
To his unmast'red° importunity.
Fear it, Ophelia, fear it, my dear sister,
And keep you in the rear of your affection,
Out of the shot and danger of desire.   35
The chariest° maid is prodigal enough,
If she unmask her beauty to the moon:
Virtue itself 'scapes not calumnious strokes:
The canker galls the infants of the spring,°
Too oft before their buttons° be disclos'd,°   40

---

6. fashion: Custom, prevailing usage; **toy in blood:** Passing amorous fancy.   **7. primy:** In its prime.   **8. Forward:** Precocious.   **9. suppliance of a minute:** Diversion to fill up a minute.   **11. crescent:** Growing, waxing.   **12. thews:** Bodily strength; **temple:** Body. **15. soil:** blemish; **cautel:** Crafty device.   **17. greatness weigh'd:** High position considered.   **23. voice and yielding:** Assent, approval.   **27. deed:** Effect.   **30. credent:** Credulous.   **32. unmast'red:** Unrestrained.   **36. chariest:** Most scrupulously modest. **39. The canker . . . spring:** The cankerworm destroys the young plants of spring. **40. buttons:** Buds; **disclos'd:** Opened.

And in the morn and liquid dew° of youth
Contagious blastments° are most imminent.
Be wary then; best safety lies in fear:
Youth to itself rebels, though none else near.

OPHELIA: I shall the effect of this good lesson keep, 45
As watchman to my heart. But, good my brother,
Do not, as some ungracious° pastors do,
Show me the steep and thorny way to heaven;
Whiles, like a puff'd° and reckless libertine,
Himself the primrose path of dalliance treads, 50
And recks° not his own rede.°

Enter Polonius.

LAERTES: O, fear me not.
I stay too long: but here my father comes.
A double° blessing is a double grace;
Occasion° smiles upon a second leave.

POLONIUS: Yet here, Laertes? aboard, aboard, for shame! 55
The wind sits in the shoulder of your sail,
And you are stay'd for. There; my blessing with thee!
And these few precepts° in thy memory
Look thou character.° Give thy thoughts no tongue,
Nor any unproportion'd° thought his act. 60
Be thou familiar, but by no means vulgar.°
Those friends thou hast, and their adoption tried,
Grapple them to thy soul with hoops of steel;
But do not dull thy palm with entertainment
Of each new-hatch'd, unfledg'd° comrade. Beware 65
Of entrance to a quarrel, but being in,
Bear't that th' opposed may beware of thee.
Give every man thy ear, but few thy voice;
Take each man's censure, but reserve thy judgement.
Costly thy habit as thy purse can buy, 70
But not express'd in fancy;° rich, not gaudy,
For the apparel oft proclaims the man,
And they in France of the best rank and station
Are of a most select and generous chief in that.°
Neither a borrower nor a lender be; 75
For loan oft loses both itself and friend,

---

41. **liquid dew:** I.e., time when dew is fresh.   42. **blastments:** Blights.   47. **ungracious:** Graceless.   49. **puff'd:** Bloated.   51. **recks:** Heeds; **rede:** Counsel.   53. **double:** I.e., Laertes has already bade his father good-by.   54. **Occasion:** Opportunity.   58. **precepts:** Many parallels have been found to the series of maxims which follows, one of the closer being that in Lyly's *Euphues*.   59. **character:** Inscribe.   60. **unproportion'd:** Inordinate.   61. **vulgar:** Common.   65. **unfledg'd:** Immature.   71. **express'd in fancy:** Fantastical in design.   74. **Are . . . that:** *Chief* is usually taken as a substantive meaning "head," "eminence."

And borrowing dulleth edge of husbandry.°
This above all: to thine own self be true,
And it must follow, as the night the day,
Thou canst not then be false to any man.   80
Farewell: my blessing season° this in thee!
LAERTES: Most humbly do I take my leave, my lord.
POLONIUS: The time invites you; go; your servants tend.
LAERTES: Farewell, Ophelia; and remember well
  What I have said to you.
OPHELIA: 'Tis in my memory lock'd,   85
  And you yourself shall keep the key of it.
LAERTES: Farewell.   *Exit Laertes.*
POLONIUS: What is 't, Ophelia, he hath said to you?
OPHELIA: So please you, something touching the Lord Hamlet.
POLONIUS: Marry, well bethought: 90
  'Tis told me, he hath very oft of late
  Given private time to you; and you yourself
  Have of your audience been most free and bounteous:
  If it be so, as so 't is put on° me,
  And that in way of caution, I must tell you,   95
  You do not understand yourself so clearly
  As it behooves my daughter and your honour.
  What is between you? give me up the truth.
OPHELIA: He hath, my lord, of late made many tenders°
  Of his affection to me.   100
POLONIUS: Affection! pooh! you speak like a green girl,
  Unsifted° in such perilous circumstance.
  Do you believe his tenders, as you call them?
OPHELIA: I do not know, my lord, what I should think.
POLONIUS: Marry, I will teach you: think yourself a baby;   105
  That you have ta'en these tenders° for true pay,
  Which are not sterling.° Tender° yourself more dearly;
  Or—not to crack the wind° of the poor phrase,
  Running it thus—you'll tender me a fool.°
OPHELIA: My lord, he hath importun'd me with love   110
  In honourable fashion.
POLONIUS: Ay, fashion° you may call it; go to, go to.
OPHELIA: And hath given countenance° to his speech, my lord,
  With almost all the holy vows of heaven.
POLONIUS: Ay, springes° to catch woodcocks.° I do know,   115

---

77. **husbandry:** Thrift.   81. **season:** Mature.   94. **put on:** Impressed on.   99, 103. **tenders:** Offers.   102. **Unsifted:** Untried.   106. **tenders:** Promises to pay.   107. **sterling:** Legal currency; **Tender:** Hold.   108. **crack the wind:** I.e., run it until it is broken-winded.   109. **tender . . . fool:** Show me a fool (for a daughter).   112. **fashion:** Mere form, pretense.   113. **countenance:** Credit, support.   115. **springes:** Snares; **woodcocks:** Birds easily caught, type of stupidity.

When the blood burns, how prodigal the soul
Lends the tongue vows: these blazes, daughter,
Giving more light than heat, extinct in both,
Even in their promise, as it is a-making,
You must not take for fire. From this time   120
Be somewhat scanter of your maiden presence;
Set your entreatments° at a higher rate
Than a command to parley.° For Lord Hamlet,
Believe so much in him,° that he is young,
And with a larger tether may he walk   125
Than may be given you: in few,° Ophelia,
Do not believe his vows; for they are brokers;°
Not of that dye° which their investments° show,
But mere implorators of° unholy suits,
Breathing° like sanctified and pious bawds,   130
The better to beguile. This is for all:
I would not, in plain terms, from this time forth,
Have you so slander° any moment leisure,
As to give words or talk with the Lord Hamlet.
Look to 't, I charge you: come your ways.   135

OPHELIA: I shall obey, my lord.   *Exeunt.*

[SCENE IV: *The platform.*]

Enter Hamlet, Horatio, and Marcellus.

HAMLET: The air bites shrewdly; it is very cold.
HORATIO: It is a nipping and an eager air.
HAMLET: What hour now?
HORATIO: I think it lacks of twelve.
MARCELLUS: No, it is struck.
HORATIO: Indeed? I heard it not: then it draws near the season   5
  Wherein the spirit held his wont to walk.

A flourish of trumpets, and two pieces go off.

  What does this mean, my lord?
HAMLET: The king doth wake° to-night and takes his rouse,°
  Keeps wassail,° and the swagg'ring up-spring° reels;°
  And, as he drains his draughts of Rhenish° down,   10
  The kettle-drum and trumpet thus bray out
  The triumph of his pledge.°

---

122. entreatments: Conversations, interviews.   **123. command to parley:** Mere invitation to talk.   **124. so . . . him:** This much concerning him.   **126. in few:** Briefly.
127. brokers: Go-betweens, procurers.   **128. dye:** Color or sort; **investments:** Clothes.
129. implorators of: Solicitors of.   **130. Breathing:** Speaking.   **133. slander:** Bring disgrace or reproach upon.   SCENE IV.   **8. wake:** Stay awake, hold revel; **rouse:** Carouse, drinking bout.   **9. wassail:** Carousal; **up-spring:** Last and wildest dance at German merry-makings; **reels:** Reels through.   **10. Rhenish:** Rhine wine.   **12. triumph . . . pledge:** His glorious achievement as a drinker.

HORATIO: Is it a custom?

HAMLET: Ay, marry, is 't:
    But to my mind, though I am native here
    And to the manner born,° it is a custom   15
    More honour'd in the breach than the observance.
    This heavy-headed revel east and west
    Makes us traduc'd and tax'd of other nations:
    They clepe° us drunkards, and with swinish phrase°
    Soil our addition;° and indeed it takes   20
    From our achievements, though perform'd at height,
    The pith and marrow of our attribute.°
    So, oft it chances in particular men,
    That for some vicious mole of nature° in them,
    As, in their birth—wherein they are not guilty,   25
    Since nature cannot choose his origin—
    By the o'ergrowth of some complexion,
    Oft breaking down the pales° and forts of reason,
    Or by some habit that too much o'er-leavens°
    The form of plausive° manners, that these men,   30
    Carrying, I say, the stamp of one defect,
    Being nature's livery,° or fortune's star,°—
    Their virtues else—be they as pure as grace,
    As infinite as man may undergo—
    Shall in the general censure take corruption   35
    From that particular fault: the dram of eale
    Doth all the noble substance of a doubt
    To his own scandal.°

Enter Ghost.

HORATIO: Look, my lord, it comes!

HAMLET: Angels and ministers of grace° defend us!
    Be thou a spirit of health or goblin damn'd,   40
    Bring with thee airs from heaven or blasts from hell,
    Be thy intents wicked or charitable,
    Thou com'st in such a questionable° shape
    That I will speak to thee: I'll call thee Hamlet,
    King, father, royal Dane: O, answer me!   45

---

15. to ... born: Destined by birth to be subject to the custom in question.   **19. clepe:** Call; **with swinish phrase:** By calling us swine.   **20. addition:** Reputation.   **22. attribute:** Reputation.   **24. mole of nature:** Natural blemish in one's constitution.   **28. pales:** Palings (as of a fortification).   **29. o'er-leavens:** Induces a change throughout (as yeast works in bread).   **30. plausive:** Pleasing.   **32. nature's livery:** Endowment from nature; **fortune's star:** The position in which one is placed by fortune, a reference to astrology. The two phrases are aspects of the same thing.   **36–38. the dram ... scandal:** A famous crux: *dram of eale* has had various interpretations, the preferred one being probably, "a dram of evil."   **39. ministers of grace:** Messengers of God.   **43. questionable:** Inviting question or conversation.

Let me not burst in ignorance; but tell
Why thy canoniz'd° bones, hearsed° in death,
Have burst their cerements;° why the sepulchre,
Wherein we saw thee quietly interr'd,
Hath op'd his ponderous and marble jaws,   50
To cast thee up again. What may this mean,
That thou, dead corse, again in complete steel
Revisits thus the glimpses of the moon,°
Making night hideous; and we fools of nature°
So horridly to shake our disposition   55
With thoughts beyond the reaches of our souls?
Say, why is this? wherefore? what should we do?

[Ghost] beckons [Hamlet].

HORATIO: It beckons you to go away with it,
        As if it some impartment° did desire
        To you alone.
MARCELLUS: Look, with what courteous action   60
        It waves you to a more removed° ground:
        But do not go with it.
HORATIO: No, by no means.
HAMLET: It will not speak; then I will follow it.
HORATIO: Do not, my lord!
HAMLET: Why, what should be the fear?
        I do not set my life at a pin's fee;   65
        And for my soul, what can it do to that,
        Being a thing immortal as itself?
        It waves me forth again: I'll follow it.
HORATIO: What if it tempt you toward the flood, my lord,
        Or to the dreadful summit of the cliff   70
        That beetles o'er° his base into the sea,
        And there assume some other horrible form,
        Which might deprive your sovereignty of reason°
        And draw you into madness? think of it:
        The very place puts toys of desperation,°   75
        Without more motive, into every brain
        That looks so many fathoms to the sea
        And hears it roar beneath.
HAMLET: It waves me still.
        Go on; I'll follow thee.

---

47. canoniz'd: Buried according to the canons of the church; **hearsed:** Coffined.   **48. cerements:** Grave-clothes.   **53. glimpses of the moon:** The earth by night.   **54. fools of nature:** Mere men, limited to natural knowledge.   **59. impartment:** Communication.   **61. removed:** Remote.   **71. beetles o'er:** Overhangs threateningly.   **73. deprive . . . reason:** Take away the sovereignty of your reason. It was thought that evil spirits would sometimes assume the form of departed spirits in order to work madness in a human creature.   **75. toys of desperation:** Freakish notions of suicide.

MARCELLUS: You shall not go, my lord.
HAMLET: Hold off your hands!   80
HORATIO: Be rul'd; you shall not go.
HAMLET: My fate cries out,
   And makes each petty artere° in this body
   As hardy as the Nemean lion's° nerve.°
   Still am I call'd. Unhand me, gentlemen.
   By heaven, I'll make a ghost of him that lets° me!   85
   I say, away! Go on; I'll follow thee.   *Exeunt Ghost and Hamlet.*
HORATIO: He waxes desperate with imagination.
MARCELLUS: Let's follow; 'tis not fit thus to obey him.
HORATIO: Have after. To what issue° will this come?
MARCELLUS: Something is rotten in the state of Denmark.   90
HORATIO: Heaven will direct it.°
MARCELLUS: Nay, let's follow him.   *Exeunt.*

[SCENE V: *Another part of the platform.*]

Enter Ghost and Hamlet.

HAMLET: Whither wilt thou lead me? speak; I'll go no further.
GHOST: Mark me.
HAMLET: I will.
GHOST: My hour is almost come,
   When I to sulphurous and tormenting flames
   Must render up myself.
HAMLET: Alas, poor ghost!
GHOST: Pity me not, but lend thy serious hearing   5
   To what I shall unfold.
HAMLET: Speak; I am bound to hear.
GHOST: So art thou to revenge, when thou shalt hear.
HAMLET: What?
GHOST: I am thy father's spirit,
   Doom'd for a certain term to walk the night,   10
   And for the day confin'd to fast° in fires,
   Till the foul crimes done in my days of nature
   Are burnt and purg'd away. But that I am forbid
   To tell the secrets of my prison-house,
   I could a tale unfold whose lightest word   15
   Would harrow up thy soul, freeze thy young blood,
   Make thy two eyes, like stars, start from their spheres,°

---

82. artere: Artery.   **83. Nemean lion's:** The Nemean lion was one of the monsters slain by Hercules; **nerve:** Sinew, tendon. The point is that the arteries which were carrying the spirits out into the body were functioning and were as stiff and hard as the sinews of the lion.   **85. lets:** Hinders.   **89. issue:** Outcome.   **91. it:** I.e., the outcome.   SCENE V. **11. fast:** Probably, do without food. It has been sometimes taken in the sense of doing general penance.   **17. spheres:** Orbits.

Thy knotted° and combined° locks to part
And each particular hair to stand an end,
Like quills upon the fretful porpentine:° 20
But this eternal blazon° must not be
To ears of flesh and blood. List, list, O, list!
If thou didst ever thy dear father love—

HAMLET: O God!

GHOST: Revenge his foul and most unnatural° murder. 25

HAMLET: Murder!

GHOST: Murder most foul, as in the best it is;
But this most foul, strange and unnatural.

HAMLET: Haste me to know't, that I, with wings as swift
As meditation or the thoughts of love, 30
May sweep to my revenge.

GHOST: I find thee apt;
And duller shouldst thou be than the fat weed°
That roots itself in ease on Lethe wharf,°
Wouldst thou not stir in this. Now, Hamlet, hear:
'Tis given out that, sleeping in my orchard, 35
A serpent stung me; so the whole ear of Denmark
Is by a forged process of my death
Rankly abus'd: but know, thou noble youth,
The serpent that did sting thy father's life
Now wears his crown.

HAMLET: O my prophetic soul! 40
My uncle!

GHOST: Ay, that incestuous, that adulterate° beast,
With witchcraft of his wit, with traitorous gifts,—
O wicked wit and gifts, that have the power
So to seduce!—won to his shameful lust 45
The will of my most seeming-virtuous queen:
O Hamlet, what a falling-off was there!
From me, whose love was of that dignity
That it went hand in hand even with the vow
I made to her in marriage, and to decline 50
Upon a wretch whose natural gifts were poor
To those of mine!
But virtue, as it never will be moved,
Though lewdness court it in a shape of heaven,

---

18. knotted: Perhaps intricately arranged; **combined:** Tied, bound.   **20. porpentine:** Porcupine.   **21. eternal blazon:** Promulgation or proclamation of eternity, revelation of the hereafter.   **25. unnatural:** I.e., pertaining to fratricide.   **32. fat weed:** Many suggestions have been offered as to the particular plant intended, including asphodel; probably a general figure for plants growing along rotting wharves and piles.   **33. Lethe wharf:** Bank of the river of forgetfulness in Hades.   **42. adulterate:** Adulterous.

So lust, though to a radiant angel link'd,   55
Will sate itself in a celestial bed,
And prey on garbage.
But, soft! methinks I scent the morning air;
Brief let me be. Sleeping within my orchard,
My custom always of the afternoon,   60
Upon my secure° hour thy uncle stole,
With juice of cursed hebona° in a vial,
And in the porches of my ears did pour
The leperous° distilment; whose effect
Holds such an enmity with blood of man   65
That swift as quicksilver it courses through
The natural gates and alleys of the body,
And with a sudden vigour it doth posset°
And curd, like eager° droppings into milk,
The thin and wholesome blood: so did it mine;   70
And a most instant tetter bark'd about,
Most lazar-like,° with vile and loathsome crust,
All my smooth body.
Thus was I, sleeping, by a brother's hand
Of life, of crown, of queen, at once dispatch'd:°   75
Cut off even in the blossoms of my sin,
Unhous'led,° disappointed,° unanel'd,°
No reck'ning made, but sent to my account
With all my imperfections on my head:
O, horrible! O, horrible! most horrible!°   80
If thou hast nature in thee, bear it not;
Let not the royal bed of Denmark be
A couch for luxury° and damned incest.
But, howsomever thou pursues this act,
Taint not thy mind,° nor let thy soul contrive   85
Against thy mother aught: leave her to heaven
And to those thorns that in her bosom lodge,
To prick and sting her. Fare thee well at once!
The glow-worm shows the matin° to be near,
And 'gins to pale his uneffectual fire:°   90
Adieu, adieu, adieu! remember me.   [*Exit.*]

---

61. secure: Confident, unsuspicious.   **62. hebona:** Generally supposed to mean henbane, conjectured *hemlock; ebenus,* meaning "yew."   **64. leperous:** Causing leprosy.   **68. posset:** Coagulate, curdle.   **69. eager:** Sour, acid.   **72. lazar-like:** Leperlike.   **75. dispatch'd:** Suddenly bereft.   **77. Unhous'led:** Without having received the sacrament; **disappointed:** Unready, without equipment for the last journey; **unanel'd:** Without having received extreme unction.   **80. O . . . horrible:** Many editors give this line to Hamlet; Garrick and Sir Henry Irving spoke it in that part.   **83. luxury:** Lechery. **85. Taint . . . mind:** Probably, deprave not thy character, do nothing except in the pursuit of a natural revenge.   **89. matin:** Morning.   **90. uneffectual fire:** Cold light.

HAMLET: O all you host of heaven! O earth! what else?
    And shall I couple° hell? O, fie! Hold, hold, my heart;
    And you, my sinews, grow not instant old,
    But bear me stiffly up. Remember thee!   95
    Ay, thou poor ghost, whiles memory holds a seat
    In this distracted globe.° Remember thee!
    Yea, from the table of my memory
    I'll wipe away all trivial fond records,
    All saws° of books, all forms, all pressures° past,   100
    That youth and observation copied there;
    And thy commandment all alone shall live
    Within the book and volume of my brain,
    Unmix'd with baser matter: yes, by heaven!
    O most pernicious woman!   105
    O villain, villain, smiling, damned villain!
    My tables,° — meet it is I set it down,
    That one may smile, and smile, and be a villain;
    At least I am sure it may be so in Denmark: [*Writing.*]
    So, uncle, there you are. Now to my word;°   110
    It is "Adieu, adieu! remember me,"
    I have sworn't.

Enter Horatio and Marcellus.

HORATIO: My lord, my lord —
MARCELLUS: Lord Hamlet, —
HORATIO: Heavens secure him!
HAMLET: So be it!
MARCELLUS: Hillo, ho, ho,° my lord!   115
HAMLET: Hillo, ho, ho, boy! come, bird, come.
MARCELLUS: How is't, my noble lord?
HORATIO: What news, my lord?
HAMLET: O, wonderful!
HORATIO: Good my lord, tell it.
HAMLET: No; you will reveal it.
HORATIO: Not I, my lord, by heaven.
MARCELLUS: Nor I, my lord.   120
HAMLET: How say you, then; would heart of man once think it?
    But you'll be secret?
HORATIO: ⎱
MARCELLUS: ⎰   Ay, by heaven, my lord.
HAMLET: There's ne'er a villain dwelling in all Denmark
    But he's an arrant° knave.

---

93. **couple:** Add.   **97. distracted globe:** Confused head.   **100. saws:** Wise sayings;
pressures: Impressions stamped.   **107. tables:** Probably a small portable writing tablet
carried at the belt.   **110. word:** Watchword.   **115. Hillo, ho, ho:** A falconer's call to a
hawk in air.   **124. arrant:** Thoroughgoing.

HORATIO: There needs no ghost, my lord, come from the grave 125
    To tell us this.

HAMLET: Why, right; you are in the right;
    And so, without more circumstance at all,
    I hold it fit that we shake hands and part:
    You, as your business and desire shall point you;
    For every man has business and desire, 130
    Such as it is; and for my own poor part,
    Look you, I'll go pray.

HORATIO: These are but wild and whirling words, my lord.

HAMLET: I am sorry they offend you, heartily;
    Yes, 'faith, heartily.

HORATIO: There's no offence, my lord. 135

HAMLET: Yes, by Saint Patrick,° but there is, Horatio,
    And much offence too. Touching this vision here,
    It is an honest° ghost, that let me tell you:
    For your desire to know what is between us,
    O'ermaster 't as you may. And now, good friends, 140
    As you are friends, scholars and soldiers,
    Give me one poor request.

HORATIO: What is 't, my lord? we will.

HAMLET: Never make known what you have seen to-night.

HORATIO: }
MARCELLUS: } My lord, we will not.

HAMLET: Nay, but swear 't.

HORATIO: In faith, 145
    My lord, not I.

MARCELLUS: Nor I, my lord, in faith.

HAMLET: Upon my sword.°

MARCELLUS: We have sworn, my lord, already.

HAMLET: Indeed, upon my sword, indeed.   *Ghost cries under the stage.*

GHOST: Swear.

HAMLET: Ah, ha, boy! say'st thou so? art thou there, truepenny?° 150
    Come on — you hear this fellow in the cellarage —
    Consent to swear.

HORATIO: Propose the oath, my lord.

HAMLET: Never to speak of this that you have seen,
    Swear by my sword.

GHOST [*beneath*]: Swear. 155

HAMLET: Hic et ubique?° then we'll shift our ground.
    Come hither, gentlemen,
    And lay your hands again upon my sword:

---

136. Saint Patrick: St. Patrick was keeper of Purgatory and patron saint of all blunders and confusion.   **138. honest:** I.e., a real ghost and not an evil spirit.   **147. sword:** I.e., the hilt in the form of a cross.   **150. truepenny:** Good old boy, or the like.   **156. Hic et ubique?:** Here and everywhere?

> Swear by my sword,
> Never to speak of this that you have heard. 160
> GHOST [*beneath*]: Swear by his sword.
> HAMLET: Well said, old mole! canst work i' th' earth so fast?
> A worthy pioner!° Once more remove, good friends.
> HORATIO: O day and night, but this is wondrous strange!
> HAMLET: And therefore as a stranger give it welcome. 165
> There are more things in heaven and earth, Horatio,
> Than are dreamt of in your philosophy.
> But come;
> Here, as before, never, so help you mercy,
> How strange or odd soe'er I bear myself, 170
> As I perchance hereafter shall think meet
> To put an antic° disposition on,
> That you, at such times seeing me, never shall,
> With arms encumb'red° thus, or this head-shake,
> Or by pronouncing of some doubtful phrase, 175
> As "Well, well, we know," or "We could, an if we would,"
> Or "If we list to speak," or "There be, an if they might,"
> Or such ambiguous giving out,° to note°
> That you know aught of me: this not to do,
> So grace and mercy at your most need help you, 180
> Swear.
> GHOST [*beneath*]: Swear.
> HAMLET: Rest, rest, perturbed spirit! [*They swear.*] So, gentlemen,
> With all my love I do commend me to you:
> And what so poor a man as Hamlet is 185
> May do, t' express his love and friending° to you,
> God willing, shall not lack. Let us go in together;
> And still your fingers on your lips, I pray.
> The time is out of joint: O cursed spite,
> That ever I was born to set it right! 190
> Nay, come, let's go together. *Exeunt.*

[ACT II

SCENE I: *A room in Polonius's house.*]

Enter old Polonius with his man [Reynaldo].

POLONIUS: Give him this money and these notes, Reynaldo.
REYNALDO: I will, my lord.
POLONIUS: You shall do marvellous wisely, good Reynaldo,
> Before you visit him, to make inquire
> Of his behaviour.

---

163. pioner: Digger, miner. **172. antic:** Fantastic. **174. encumb'red:** Folded or entwined. **178. giving out:** Profession of knowledge; **to note:** To give a sign. **186. friend-
ing:** Friendliness.

REYNALDO: My lord, I did intend it.   5
POLONIUS: Marry, well said; very well said. Look you, sir,
    Inquire me first what Danskers° are in Paris;
    And how, and who, what means, and where they keep,°
    What company, at what expense; and finding
    By this encompassment° and drift° of question   10
    That they do know my son, come you more nearer
    Than your particular demands will touch it:°
    Take° you as 'twere, some distant knowledge of him;
    As thus, "I know his father and his friends,
    And in part him": do you mark this, Reynaldo?   15
REYNALDO: Ay, very well, my lord.
POLONIUS: "And in part him; but" you may say "not well:
    But, if 't be he I mean, he's very wild;
    Addicted so and so": and there put on° him
    What forgeries° you please; marry, none so rank   20
    As may dishonour him; take heed of that;
    But, sir, such wanton,° wild and usual slips
    As are companions noted and most known
    To youth and liberty.
REYNALDO: As gaming, my lord.
POLONIUS: Ay, or drinking, fencing,° swearing, quarrelling,   25
    Drabbing;° you may go so far.
REYNALDO: My lord, that would dishonour him.
POLONIUS: 'Faith, no; as you may season it in the charge.
    You must not put another scandal on him,
    That he is open to incontinency;°   30
    That's not my meaning: but breathe his faults so quaintly°
    That they may seem the taints of liberty°
    The flash and outbreak of a fiery mind,
    A savageness in unreclaimed° blood,
    Of general assault.°
REYNALDO: But, my good lord, —   35
POLONIUS: Wherefore should you do this?
REYNALDO: Ay, my lord,
    I would know that.
POLONIUS: Marry, sir, here's my drift;
    And, I believe, it is a fetch of wit:°

ACT II, SCENE I.   **7. Danskers:** Danke was a common variant for "Denmark"; hence "Dane."   **8. keep:** Dwell.   **10. encompassment:** Roundabout talking; **drift:** Gradual approach or course.   **11–12. come . . . it:** I.e., you will find out more this way than by asking pointed questions.   **13. Take:** Assume, pretend.   **19. put on:** Impute to.   **20. forgeries:** Invented tales.   **22. wanton:** Sportive, unrestrained.   **25. fencing:** Indicative of the ill repute of professional fencers and fencing schools in Elizabethan times.   **26. Drabbing:** Associating with immoral women.   **30. incontinency:** Habitual loose behavior.   **31. quaintly:** Delicately, ingeniously.   **32. taints of liberty:** Blemishes due to freedom.   **34. unreclaimed:** Untamed.   **35. general assault:** Tendency that assails all untrained youth.   **38. fetch of wit:** Clever trick.

You laying these slight sullies on my son,
As 'twere a thing a little soil'd i' th' working,
Mark you, 40
Your party in converse, him you would sound,
Having ever° seen in the prenominate° crimes
The youth you breathe of guilty, be assur'd
He closes with you in this consequence;° 45
"Good sir," or so, or "friend," or "gentleman,"
According to the phrase or the addition
Of man and country.

REYNALDO: Very good, my lord.
POLONIUS: And then, sir, does 'a this—'a does—what was I about to say? By
    the mass, I was about to say something: where did I leave? 50
REYNALDO: At "closes in the consequence," at "friend or so," and "gentleman."
POLONIUS: At "closes in the consequence," ay, marry;
    He closes thus: "I know the gentleman;
    I saw him yesterday, or t' other day,
    Or then, or then; with such, or such; and, as you say, 55
    There was 'a gaming; there o'ertook in 's rouse°
    There falling out at tennis": or perchance,
    "I saw him enter such a house of sale,"
    Videlicet,° a brothel, or so forth.
    See you now; 60
    Your bait of falsehood takes this carp of truth:
    And thus do we of wisdom and of reach,°
    With windlasses° and with assays of bias,°
    By indirections° find directions° out:
    So by my former lecture° and advice, 65
    Shall you my son. You have me, have you not?

REYNALDO: My lord, I have.
POLONIUS: God bye ye;° fare ye well.
REYNALDO: Good my lord!
POLONIUS: Observe his inclination in yourself.°
REYNALDO: I shall, my lord. 70
POLONIUS: And let him ply his music.°
REYNALDO: Well, my lord.
POLONIUS: Farewell!   *Exit Reynaldo.*

---

43. ever: At any time; **prenominate:** Before-mentioned.   **45. closes . . . consequence:**
Agrees with you in this conclusion.   **56. o'ertook in 's rouse:** Overcome by drink.
59. Videlicet: Namely.   **62. reach:** Capacity, ability.   **63. windlasses:** I.e., circuitous
paths; **assays of bias:** Attempts that resemble the course of the bowl, which, being
weighted on one side, has a curving motion.   **64. indirections:** Devious courses; **directions:** Straight courses, i.e., the truth.   **65. lecture:** Admonition.   **67. bye ye:** Be with
you.   **69. Observe . . . yourself:** In your own person, not by spies; or conform your own
conduct to his inclination; or test him by studying yourself.   **71. ply his music:** Probably
to be taken literally.

Enter Ophelia.

                         How now, Ophelia! what's the matter?

OPHELIA: O, my lord, my lord, I have been so affrighted!

POLONIUS: With what, i' th' name of God?

OPHELIA: My lord, as I was sewing in my closet,°   75
    Lord Hamlet, with his doublet° all unbrac'd;°
    No hat upon his head; his stockings foul'd,
    Ungart'red, and down-gyved° to his ankle;
    Pale as his shirt; his knees knocking each other;
    And with a look so piteous in purport   80
    As if he had been loosed out of hell
    To speak of horrors,—he comes before me.

POLONIUS: Mad for thy love?

OPHELIA: My lord, I do not know;
    But truly, I do fear it.

POLONIUS: What said he?

OPHELIA: He took me by the wrist and held me hard;   85
    Then goes he to the length of all his arm;
    And, with his other hand thus o'er his brow,
    He falls to such perusal of my face
    As 'a would draw it. Long stay'd he so;
    At last, a little shaking of mine arm   90
    And thrice his head thus waving up and down,
    He rais'd a sigh so piteous and profound
    As it did seem to shatter all his bulk°
    And end his being: that done, he lets me go:
    And, with his head over his shoulder turn'd,   95
    He seem'd to find his way without his eyes;
    For out o' doors he went without their helps,
    And, to the last, bended their light on me.

POLONIUS: Come, go with me: I will go seek the king.
    This is the very ecstasy of love,   100
    Whose violent property° fordoes° itself
    And leads the will to desperate undertakings
    As oft as any passion under heaven
    That does afflict our natures. I am sorry.
    What, have you given him any hard words of late?   105

OPHELIA: No, my good lord, but, as you did command,
    I did repel his letters and denied
    His access to me.

POLONIUS: That hath made him mad.
    I am sorry that with better heed and judgement

---

75. closet: Private chamber.   **76. doublet:** Close-fitting coat; **unbrac'd:** Unfastened.
78. down-gyved: Fallen to the ankles (like gyves or fetters).   **93. bulk:** Body.
101. property: Nature; **fordoes:** Destroys.

I had not quoted° him: I fear'd he did but trifle,   110
And meant to wrack thee; but, beshrew my jealousy!°
By heaven, it is as proper to our age
To cast beyond° ourselves in our opinions
As it is common for the younger sort
To lack discretion. Come, go we to the king: 115
This must be known; which, being kept close, might move
More grief to hide than hate to utter love.°
Come.   *Exeunt.*

[SCENE II: *A room in the castle.*]

Flourish. Enter King and Queen, Rosencrantz, and Guildenstern [with others].

KING: Welcome, dear Rosencrantz and Guildenstern!
     Moreover that° we much did long to see you,
     The need we have to use you did provoke
     Our hasty sending. Something have you heard
     Of Hamlet's transformation; so call it,   5
     Sith° nor th' exterior nor the inward man
     Resembles that it was. What it should be,
     More than his father's death, that thus hath put him
     So much from th' understanding of himself,
     I cannot dream of: I entreat you both,   10
     That, being of so young days° brought up with him,
     And sith so neighbour'd to his youth and haviour,
     That you vouchsafe your rest° here in our court
     Some little time: so by your companies
     To draw him on to pleasures, and to gather,   15
     So much as from occasion you may glean,
     Whether aught, to us unknown, afflicts him thus,
     That, open'd, lies within our remedy.
QUEEN: Good gentlemen, he hath much talk'd of you;
     And sure I am two men there are not living   20
     To whom he more adheres. If it will please you
     To show us so much gentry° and good will
     As to expend your time with us awhile,
     For the supply and profit° of our hope,
     Your visitation shall receive such thanks   25
     As fits a king's remembrance.
ROSENCRANTZ: Both your majesties
     Might, by the sovereign power you have of us,

---

110. **quoted:** Observed.   111. **beshrew my jealousy:** Curse my suspicions.   113. **cast beyond:** Overshoot, miscalculate.   116–117. **might . . . love:** I.e., I might cause more grief to others by hiding the knowledge of Hamlet's love to Ophelia than hatred to me and mine by telling of it.   SCENE II.   2. **Moreover that:** Besides the fact that.   6. **Sith:** Since.   11. **of . . . days:** From such early youth.   13. **vouchsafe your rest:** Please to stay.   22. **gentry:** Courtesy.   24. **supply and profit:** Aid and successful outcome.

Put your dread pleasures more into command
Than to entreaty.

GUILDENSTERN: But we both obey,
And here give up ourselves, in the full bent°   30
To lay our service freely at your feet,
To be commanded.

KING: Thanks, Rosencrantz and gentle Guildenstern.

QUEEN: Thanks, Guildenstern and gentle Rosencrantz:
And I beseech you instantly to visit   35
My too much changed son. Go, some of you,
And bring these gentlemen where Hamlet is.

GUILDENSTERN: Heavens make our presence and our practices
Pleasant and helpful to him!

QUEEN: Ay, amen!

Exeunt Rosencrantz and Guildenstern [with some Attendants].

Enter Polonius.

POLONIUS: Th' ambassadors from Norway, my good lord,   40
Are joyfully return'd.

KING: Thou still hast been the father of good news.

POLONIUS: Have I, my lord? I assure my good liege,
I hold my duty, as I hold my soul,
Both to my God and to my gracious king: 45
And I do think, or else this brain of mine
Hunts not the trail of policy so sure
As it hath us'd to do, that I have found
The very cause of Hamlet's lunacy.

KING: O, speak of that; that do I long to hear.   50

POLONIUS: Give first admittance to th' ambassadors;
My news shall be the fruit to that great feast.

KING: Thyself do grace to them, and bring them in.   *[Exit Polonius.]*
He tells me, my dear Gertrude, he hath found
The head and source of all your son's distemper.   55

QUEEN: I doubt° it is no other but the main;°
His father's death, and our o'erhasty marriage.

KING: Well, we shall sift him.

Enter Ambassadors [Voltimand and Cornelius, with Polonius.]

                        Welcome, my good friends!
Say, Voltimand, what from our brother Norway?

VOLTIMAND: Most fair return of greetings and desires.   60
Upon our first, he sent out to suppress
His nephew's levies; which to him appear'd
To be a preparation 'gainst the Polack;
But, better look'd into, he truly found

---

30. in . . . bent: To the utmost degree of our mental capacity.   **56. doubt:** Fear; **main:**
Chief point, principal concern.

It was against your highness: whereat griev'd,   65
That so his sickness, age and impotence
Was falsely borne in hand,° sends out arrests
On Fortinbras; which he, in brief, obeys;
Receives rebuke from Norway, and in fine°
Makes vow before his uncle never more   70
To give th' assay° of arms against your majesty.
Whereon old Norway, overcome with joy,
Gives him three score thousand crowns in annual fee,
And his commission to employ those soldiers,
So levied as before, against the Polack: 75
With an entreaty, herein further shown, [*giving a paper.*]
That it might please you to give quiet pass
Through your dominions for this enterprise,
On such regards of safety and allowance°
As therein are set down.

KING: It likes° us well;   80
And at our more consider'd° time we'll read,
Answer, and think upon this business.
Meantime we thank you for your well-took labour:
Go to your rest; at night we'll feast together:
Most welcome home!   *Exeunt Ambassadors.*

POLONIUS: This business is well ended.   85
My liege, and madam, to expostulate
What majesty should be, what duty is,
Why day is day, night night, and time is time,
Were nothing but to waste night, day and time.
Therefore, since brevity is the soul of wit,°   90
And tediousness the limbs and outward flourishes,°
I will be brief: your noble son is mad:
Mad call I it; for, to define true madness
What is 't but to be nothing else but mad?
But let that go.

QUEEN: More matter, with less art.   95

POLONIUS: Madam, I swear I use no art at all.
That he is mad, 'tis true: 'tis true 'tis pity;
And pity 'tis 'tis true: a foolish figure;°
But farewell it, for I will use no art.
Mad let us grant him, then: and now remains   100
That we find out the cause of this effect,
Or rather say, the cause of this defect,
For this effect defective comes by cause:

---

67. borne in hand: Deluded.   **69. in fine:** In the end.   **71. assay:** Assault, trial (of
arms).   **79. safety and allowance:** Pledges of safety to the country and terms of permission for the troops to pass.   **80. likes:** Pleases.   **81. consider'd:** Suitable for delibera-
tion.   **90. wit:** Sound sense or judgment.   **91. flourishes:** Ostentation, embellishments.
98. figure: Figure of speech.

Thus it remains, and the remainder thus.
Perpend.° 105
I have a daughter — have while she is mine —
Who, in her duty and obedience, mark,
Hath given me this: now gather, and surmise. [*Reads the letter.*] "To the
celestial and my soul's idol,
the most beautified Ophelia," — 110
That's an ill phrase, a vile phrase; "beautified" is a vile phrase: but you
shall hear. Thus: [*Reads.*]
"In her excellent white bosom, these, & c."
QUEEN: Came this from Hamlet to her?
POLONIUS: Good madam, stay awhile; I will be faithful. [*Reads.*] 115
    "Doubt thou the stars are fire;
      Doubt that the sun doth move;
      Doubt truth to be a liar;
      But never doubt I love.
"O dear Ophelia, I am ill at these numbers;° I have not art to reckon° my 120
groans: but that I love thee best, O most best, believe it. Adieu.
    "Thine evermore, most dear lady, whilst this machine° is to him,
                      HAMLET."

This, in obedience, hath my daughter shown me,
And more above,° hath his solicitings, 125
As they fell out° by time, by means° and place,
All given to mine ear.
KING: But how hath she
Receiv'd his love?
POLONIUS: What do you think of me?
KING: As of a man faithful and honourable.
POLONIUS: I would fain prove so. But what might you think, 130
When I had seen this hot love on the wing —
As I perceiv'd it, I must tell you that,
Before my daughter told me — what might you,
Or my dear majesty your queen here, think,
If I had play'd the desk or table-book,° 135
Or given my heart a winking,° mute and dumb,
Or look'd upon this love with idle sight;
What might you think? No, I went round to work,
And my young mistress thus I did bespeak:°
"Lord Hamlet is a prince, out of thy star;° 140
This must not be": and then I prescripts gave her,

---

105. Perpend: Consider.   **120. ill . . . numbers:** Unskilled at writing verses; **reckon:**
Number metrically, scan.   **122. machine:** Bodily frame.   **125. more above:** Moreover.
126. fell out: Occurred; **means:** Opportunities (of access).   **135. play'd . . . table-book:**
I.e., remained shut up, concealed this information.   **136. given . . . winking:** Given my
heart a signal to keep silent.   **139. bespeak:** Address.   **140. out . . . star:** Above thee in
position.

That she should lock herself from his resort,
Admit no messengers, receive no tokens.
Which done, she took the fruits of my advice;
And he, repelled—a short tale to make—   145
Fell into a sadness, then into a fast,
Thence to a watch,° thence into a weakness,
Thence to a lightness,° and, by this declension,°
Into the madness wherein now he raves,
And all we mourn for.

KING: Do you think 'tis this?   150
QUEEN: It may be, very like.
POLONIUS: Hath there been such a time—I would fain know that—
That I have positively said "'Tis so,"
When it prov'd otherwise?
KING: Not that I know.
POLONIUS [*pointing to his head and shoulder*]: Take this from this, if this be
    otherwise: 155
If circumstances lead me, I will find
Where truth is hid, though it were hid indeed
Within the centre.°
KING: How may we try it further?
POLONIUS: You know, sometimes he walks four hours together
Here in the lobby.
QUEEN: So he does indeed.   160
POLONIUS: At such a time I'll loose my daughter to him:
Be you and I behind an arras° then;
Mark the encounter: if he love her not
And be not from his reason fall'n thereon,°
Let me be no assistant for a state,   165
But keep a farm and carters.
KING: We will try it.

Enter Hamlet [reading on a book].

QUEEN: But, look, where sadly the poor wretch comes reading.
POLONIUS: Away, I do beseech you both, away:
                      Exeunt King and Queen [with Attendants].
I'll board° him presently. O, give me leave.
How does my good Lord Hamlet?   170
HAMLET: Well, God-a-mercy.
POLONIUS: Do you know me, my lord?
HAMLET: Excellent well; you are a fishmonger.°
POLONIUS: Not I, my lord.
HAMLET: Then I would you were so honest a man.   175

---

147. **watch:** State of sleeplessness.   148. **lightness:** Lightheadedness; **declension:**
Decline, deterioration.   158. **centre:** Middle point of the earth.   162. **arras:** Hanging,
tapestry.   164. **thereon:** On that account.   169. **board:** Accost.   173. **fishmonger:**
An opprobrious expression meaning "bawd," "procurer."

POLONIUS: Honest, my lord!

HAMLET: Ay, sir; to be honest, as this world goes, is to be one man picked out of ten thousand.

POLONIUS: That's very true, my lord.

HAMLET: For if the sun breed maggots in a dead dog, being a good kissing car- 180
rion,° — Have you a daughter?

POLONIUS: I have, my lord.

HAMLET: Let her not walk i' the sun:° conception° is a blessing: but as your daughter may conceive — Friend, look to 't.

POLONIUS [*aside*]: How say you by° that? Still harping on my daughter: yet he 185
knew me not at first; 'a said I was a fishmonger: 'a is far gone, far gone:
and truly in my youth I suffered much extremity for love; very near this.
I'll speak to him again. What do you read, my lord?

HAMLET: Words, words, words.

POLONIUS: What is the matter,° my lord? 190

HAMLET: Between who?°

POLONIUS: I mean, the matter that you read, my lord.

HAMLET: Slanders, sir: for the satirical rogue says here that old men have grey beards, that their faces are wrinkled, their eyes purging° thick amber and plum-tree gum and that they have a plentiful lack of wit, together with 195
most weak hams: all which, sir, though I most powerfully and potently believe, yet I hold it not honesty° to have it thus set down, for yourself, sir, should be old as I am, if like a crab you could go backward.

POLONIUS [*aside*]: Though this be madness, yet there is method in 't. — Will you walk out of the air, my lord? 200

HAMLET: Into my grave.

POLONIUS: Indeed, that's out of the air. (*Aside.*) How pregnant sometimes his replies are! a happiness° that often madness hits on, which reason and sanity could not so prosperously° be delivered of. I will leave him, and suddenly contrive the means of meeting between him and my daugh- 205
ter. — My honourable lord, I will most humbly take my leave of you.

HAMLET: You cannot, sir, take from me any thing that I will more willingly part withal: except my life, except my life, except my life.

Enter Guildenstern and Rosencrantz.

POLONIUS: Fare you well, my lord.

HAMLET: These tedious old fools! 210

POLONIUS: You go to seek the Lord Hamlet; there he is.

ROSENCRANTZ [*to Polonius*]: God save you, sir!   [*Exit Polonius.*]

GUILDENSTERN: My honoured lord!

ROSENCRANTZ: My most dear lord!

180–181. good kissing carrion: I.e., a good piece of flesh for kissing (?). **183. i' the sun:** In the sunshine of princely favors; **conception:** Quibble on "understanding" and "preg-nancy." **185. by:** Concerning. **190. matter:** Substance. **191. Between who:** Ham-let deliberately takes *matter* as meaning "basis of dispute." **194. purging:** discharging. **197. honesty:** Decency. **203. happiness:** Felicity of expression. **204. prosperously:** Successfully.

HAMLET: My excellent good friends! How dost thou, Guildenstern? Ah, 215
Rosencrantz! Good lads, how do ye both?

ROSENCRANTZ: As the indifferent° children of the earth.

GUILDENSTERN: Happy, in that we are not over-happy;
On Fortune's cap we are not the very button.

HAMLET: Nor the soles of her shoe? 220

ROSENCRANTZ: Neither, my lord.

HAMLET: Then you live about her waist, or in the middle of her favours?

GUILDENSTERN: 'Faith, her privates° we.

HAMLET: In the secret parts of Fortune? O, most true; she is a strumpet. What's
the news? 225

ROSENCRANTZ: None, my lord, but that the world's grown honest.

HAMLET: Then is doomsday near: but your news is not true. Let me question
more in particular: what have you, my good friends, deserved at the
hands of Fortune, that she sends you to prison hither?

GUILDENSTERN: Prison, my lord! 230

HAMLET: Denmark's a prison.

ROSENCRANTZ: Then is the world one.

HAMLET: A goodly one; in which there are many confines,° wards and dun-
geons, Denmark being one o' the worst.

ROSENCRANTZ: We think not so, my lord. 235

HAMLET: Why, then, 'tis none to you; for there is nothing either good or bad,
but thinking makes it so: to me it is a prison.

ROSENCRANTZ: Why then, your ambition makes it one; 'tis too narrow for your
mind.

HAMLET: O God, I could be bounded in a nutshell and count myself a king of 240
infinite space, were it not that I have bad dreams.

GUILDENSTERN: Which dreams indeed are ambition, for the very substance of
the ambitious° is merely the shadow of a dream.

HAMLET: A dream itself is but a shadow.

ROSENCRANTZ: Truly, and I hold ambition of so airy and light a quality that it is 245
but a shadow's shadow.

HAMLET: Then are our beggars bodies, and our monarchs and outstretched
heroes the beggars' shadows. Shall we to the court? for, by my fay,° I
cannot reason.°

ROSENCRANTZ: ⎱
GUILDENSTERN: ⎰ We'll wait upon° you. 250

HAMLET: No such matter: I will not sort° you with the rest of my servants, for,
to speak to you like an honest man, I am most dreadfully attended.° But,
in the beaten way of friendship,° what make you at Elsinore?

ROSENCRANTZ: To visit you, my lord: no other occasion.

---

217. indifferent: Ordinary.   **223. privates:** I.e., ordinary men (sexual pun on *private parts*).   **233. confines:** Places of confinement.   **242–243. very . . . ambitious:**
That seemingly most substantial thing which the ambitious pursue.   **248. fay:** Faith.
249. reason: Argue.   **250. wait upon:** Accompany.   **251. sort:** Class.   **252. dreadfully attended:** Poorly provided with servants.   **253. in the . . . friendship:** As a matter
of course among friends.

HAMLET: Beggar that I am, I am ever poor in thanks; but I thank you: and sure, 255
dear friends, my thanks are too dear a° halfpenny. Were you not sent for?
Is it your own inclining? Is it a free visitation? Come, come, deal justly
with me: come, come; nay, speak.

GUILDENSTERN: What should we say, my lord?

HAMLET: Why, any thing, but to the purpose. You were sent for; and there is a 260
kind of confession in your looks which your modesties have not craft
enough to colour: I know the good king and queen have sent for you.

ROSENCRANTZ: To what end, my lord?

HAMLET: That you must teach me. But let me conjure° you, by the rights of our
fellowship, by the consonancy of our youth,° by the obligation of our 265
ever-preserved love, and by what more dear a better proposer° could
charge you withal, be even and direct with me, whether you were sent for,
or no?

ROSENCRANTZ [*aside to Guildenstern*]: What say you?

HAMLET [*aside*]: Nay, then, I have an eye of you. — If you love me, hold not 270
off.

GUILDENSTERN: My lord, we were sent for.

HAMLET: I will tell you why; so shall my anticipation prevent your discovery,°
and your secrecy to the king and queen moult no feather. I have of late —
but wherefore I know not — lost all my mirth, forgone all custom of exer- 275
cises; and indeed it goes so heavily with my disposition that this goodly
frame, the earth, seems to me a sterile promontory, this most excellent canopy, the air, look you, this brave o'erhanging firmament, this majestical roof fretted° with golden fire, why, it appeareth nothing to me
but a foul and pestilent congregation of vapours. What a piece of work 280
is a man! how noble in reason! how infinite in faculties° in form and
moving how express° and admirable! in action how like an angel! in
apprehension° how like a god! the beauty of the world! the paragon
of animals! And yet, to me, what is this quintessence° of dust? man delights not me: no, nor woman neither, though by your smiling you seem 285
to say so.

ROSENCRANTZ: My lord, there was no such stuff in my thoughts.

HAMLET: Why did you laugh then, when I said "man delights not me"?

ROSENCRANTZ: To think, my lord, if you delight not in man, what lenten° entertainment the players shall receive from you: we coted° them on the way; 290
and hither are they coming, to offer you service.

HAMLET: He that plays the king shall be welcome; his majesty shall have tribute
of me; the adventurous knight shall use his foil and target;° the lover

---

256. a: I.e., at a.   **264. conjure:** Adjure, entreat.   **265. consonancy of our youth:** The
fact that we are of the same age.   **266. better proposer:** One more skillful in finding pro-
posals.   **273. prevent your discovery:** Forestall your disclosure.   **279. fretted:** Adorned.
281. faculties: Capacity.   **282. express:** Well-framed(?), exact(?).   **283. apprehension:**
Understanding.   **284. quintessence:** The fifth essence of ancient philosophy, supposed
to be the substance of the heavenly bodies and to be latent in all things.   **289. lenten:**
Meager.   **290. coted:** Overtook and passed beyond.   **293. foil and target:** Sword and
shield.

shall not sigh gratis; the humorous man° shall end his part in peace; the
clown shall make those laugh whose lungs are tickle o' the sere;° and the   295
lady shall say her mind freely, or the blank verse shall halt for 't.° What
players are they?

ROSENCRANTZ: Even those you were wont to take delight in, the tragedians of
the city.

HAMLET: How chances it they travel? their residence,° both in reputation and   300
profit, was better both ways.

ROSENCRANTZ: I think their inhibition° comes by the means of the late innovation.°

HAMLET: Do they hold the same estimation they did when I was in the city? are
they so followed?   305

ROSENCRANTZ: No, indeed, are they not.

HAMLET: How° comes it? do they grow rusty?

ROSENCRANTZ: Nay, their endeavour keeps in the wonted pace: but there is, sir,
an aery° of children, little eyases,° that cry out on the top of question,°
and are most tyrannically° clapped for 't: these are now the fashion, and   310
so berattle° the common stages° — so they call them — that many wearing rapiers° are afraid of goose-quills° and dare scarce come thither.

HAMLET: What, are they children? who maintains 'em? how are they escoted?°
Will they pursue the quality° no longer than they can sing?° will they
not say afterwards, if they should grow themselves to common°   315
players — as it is most like, if their means are no better — their writers do
them wrong, to make them exclaim against their own succession?°

ROSENCRANTZ: 'Faith, there has been much to do on both sides; and the nation
holds it no sin to tarre° them to controversy: there was, for a while, no
money bid for argument,° unless the poet and the player went to cuffs° in   320
the question.°

HAMLET: Is't possible?

GUILDENSTERN: O, there has been much throwing about of brains.

HAMLET: Do the boys carry it away?°

---

294. humorous man: Actor who takes the part of the humor characters.   **295. tickle o'
the sere:** Easy on the trigger.   **295–296. the lady . . . for 't:** The lady (fond of talking)
shall have opportunity to talk, blank verse or no blank verse.   **300. residence:** Remaining in one place.   **302. inhibition:** Formal prohibition (from acting plays in the city or,
possibly, at court).   **302–303. innovation:** The new fashion in satirical plays performed
by boy actors in the "private" theaters.   **307–325. How . . . load too:** The passage is the
famous one dealing with the War of the Theatres (1599–1602); namely, the rivalry
between the children's companies and the adult actors.   **309. aery:** Nest; **eyases:** Young
hawks; **cry . . . question:** Speak in a high key dominating conversation; clamor forth the
height of controversy; probably "excel" (cf. line 462); perhaps intended to decry leaders of
the dramatic profession.   **310. tyrannically:** Outrageously.   **311. berattle:** Berate;
common stages: Public theaters.   **311–312. many wearing rapiers:** Many men of
fashion, who were afraid to patronize the common players for fear of being satirized by
the poets who wrote for the children.   **312. goose-quills:** I.e., pens of satirists.   **313. escoted:** Maintained.   **314. quality:** Acting profession; **no longer . . . sing:** I.e., until
their voices change.   **315. common:** Regular, adult.   **317. succession:** future careers.
319. tarre: Set on (as dogs).   **320. argument:** Probably, plot for a play; **went to cuffs:**
Came to blows.   **321. question:** Controversy.   **324. carry it away:** Win the day.

ROSENCRANTZ: Ay, that they do, my lord; Hercules and his load° too. 325

HAMLET: It is not very strange; for my uncle is king of Denmark, and those that would make mows° at him while my father lived, give twenty, forty, fifty, a hundred ducats° a-piece for his picture in little.° 'Sblood, there is something in this more than natural, if philosophy could find it out.

A flourish [of trumpets within].

GUILDENSTERN: There are the players. 330

HAMLET: Gentlemen, you are welcome to Elsinore. Your hands, come then: the appurtenance of welcome is fashion and ceremony: let me comply° with you in this garb,° lest my extent° to the players, which, I tell you, must show fairly outwards, should more appear like entertainment than yours. You are welcome: but my uncle-father and aunt-mother are de- 335 ceived.

GUILDENSTERN: In what, my dear lord?

HAMLET: I am but mad north-north-west:° when the wind is southerly I know a hawk from a handsaw.°

Enter Polonius.

POLONIUS: Well be with you, gentlemen! 340

HAMLET: Hark you, Guildenstern; and you too: at each ear a hearer: that great baby you see there is not yet out of his swaddling-clouts.°

ROSENCRANTZ: Happily he is the second time come to them; for they say an old man is twice a child.

HAMLET: I will prophesy he comes to tell me of the players; mark it. — You say 345 right, sir: o' Monday morning;° 'twas then indeed.

POLONIUS: My lord, I have news to tell you.

HAMLET: My lord, I have news to tell you. When Roscius° was an actor in Rome, —

POLONIUS: The actors are come hither, my lord. 350

HAMLET: Buz, buz!°

POLONIUS: Upon my honour, —

HAMLET: Then came each actor on his ass, —

POLONIUS: The best actors in the world, either for tragedy, comedy, history, pastoral, pastoral-comical, historical-pastoral, tragical-historical, tragical- 355 comical-historical-pastoral, scene individable,° or poem unlimited:°

---

325. **Hercules . . . load:** Regarded as an allusion to the sign of the Globe Theatre, which was Hercules bearing the world on his shoulder. 327. **mows:** Grimaces. 328. **ducats:** Gold coins worth 9s. 4d; **in little:** In miniature. 332. **comply:** Observe the formalities of courtesy. 333. **garb:** Manner; **extent:** Showing of kindness. 338. **I am . . . north-north-west:** I am only partly mad, i.e., in only one point of the compass. 339. **handsaw:** A proposed reading of *hernshaw* would mean "heron"; *handsaw* may be an early corruption of *hernshaw.* Another view regards *hawk* as the variant of *hack,* a tool of the pickax type, and *handsaw* as a saw operated by hand. 342. **swaddling-clouts:** Cloths in which to wrap a newborn baby. 346. **o' Monday morning:** Said to mislead Polonius. 348. **Roscius:** A famous Roman actor. 351. **Buz, buz:** An interjection used at Oxford to denote stale news. 356. **scene individable:** A play observing the unity of place; **poem unlimited:** A play disregarding the unities of time and place.

Seneca° cannot be too heavy, nor Plautus° too light. For the law of writ
and the liberty,° these are the only men.

HAMLET: O Jephthah, judge of Israel,° what a treasure hadst thou!

POLONIUS: What a treasure had he, my lord?   360

HAMLET: Why,

"One fair daughter, and no more,
     The which he loved passing well."

POLONIUS [*aside*]: Still on my daughter.

HAMLET: Am I not i' the right, old Jephthah?   365

POLONIUS: If you call me Jephthah, my lord, I have a daughter that I love pass-
ing° well.

HAMLET: Nay, that follows not.

POLONIUS: What follows, then, my lord?

HAMLET: Why,   370

"As by lot, God wot,"
and then, you know,
     "It came to pass, as most like° it was," —
the first row° of the pious chanson° will show you more; for look, where
my abridgement comes.°   375

Enter the Players.

You are welcome, masters; welcome, all. I am glad to see thee well. Welcome, good friends. O, old friend! why, thy face is valanced° since I saw
thee last: comest thou to beard me in Denmark? What, my young lady
and mistress! By'r lady, your ladyship is nearer to heaven than when I saw
you last, by the altitude of a chopine.° Pray God, your voice, like a piece   380
of uncurrent° gold, be not cracked within the ring.° Masters, you are all
welcome. We'll e'en to 't like French falconers, fly at any thing we see:
we'll have a speech straight: come, give us a taste of your quality; come, a
passionate speech.

FIRST PLAYER: What speech, my good lord?   385

HAMLET: I heard thee speak me a speech once, but it was never acted; or, if it
was, not above once; for the play, I remember, pleased not the million;
'twas caviary to the general:° but it was — as I received it, and others,
whose judgements in such matters cried in the top of° mine — an excellent play, well digested in the scenes, set down with as much modesty as   390

---

357. Seneca: Writer of Latin tragedies, model of early Elizabethan writers of tragedy;
Plautus: Writer of Latin comedy.   **357–358. law . . . liberty:** Pieces written according
to rules and without rules, i.e., "classical" and "romantic" dramas.   **359. Jephthah . . .
Israel:** Jephthah had to sacrifice his daughter; see Judges 11.   **366–367. passing:** Surpassingly.   **373. like:** Probable.   **374. row:** Stanza; **chanson:** Ballad.   **375. abridgement comes:** Opportunity comes for cutting short the conversation.   **377. valanced:**
Fringed (with a beard).   **380. chopine:** Kind of shoe raised by the thickness of the heel;
worn in Italy, particularly at Venice.   **381. uncurrent:** Not passable as lawful coinage;
cracked within the ring: In the center of coins were rings enclosing the sovereign's head;
if the coin was cracked within this ring, it was unfit for currency.   **388. caviary to the
general:** Not relished by the multitude.   **389. cried in the top of:** Spoke with greater
authority than.

cunning.° I remember, one said there were no sallets° in the lines to
make the matter savoury, nor no matter in the phrase that might indict°
the author of affectation; but called it an honest method, as wholesome as
sweet, and by very much more handsome than fine.° One speech in 't I
chiefly loved: 'twas Æneas' tale to Dido;° and thereabout of it especially,   395
where he speaks of Priam's slaughter: if it live in your memory, begin at
this line: let me see, let me see—
"The rugged Pyrrhus,° like th' Hyrcanian beast,"°—
'tis not so:—it begins with Pyrrhus:—
"The rugged Pyrrhus, he whose sable arms,   400
Black as his purpose, did the night resemble
When he lay couched in the ominous horse,°
Hath now this dread and black complexion smear'd
With heraldry more dismal; head to foot
Now is he total gules;° horridly trick'd°   405
With blood of fathers, mothers, daughters, sons,
Bak'd and impasted° with the parching streets,
That lend a tyrannous and a damned light
To their lord's murder: roasted in wrath and fire,
And thus o'er-sized° with coagulate gore,   410
With eyes like carbuncles, the hellish Pyrrhus
Old grandsire Priam seeks."
So, proceed you.

POLONIUS: 'Fore God, my lord, well spoken, with good accent and good discretion.   415

FIRST PLAYER: "Anon he finds him
Striking too short at Greeks; his antique sword,
Rebellious to his arm, lies where it falls,
Repugnant° to command: unequal match'd,
Pyrrhus at Priam drives; in rage strikes wide;   420
But with the whiff and wind of his fell sword
Th' unnerved father falls. Then senseless Ilium,°
Seeming to feel this blow, with flaming top
Stoops to his base, and with a hideous crash
Takes prisoner Pyrrhus' ear: for, lo! his sword   425
Which was declining on the milky head
Of reverend Priam, seem'd i' th' air to stick:

---

391. **cunning:** Skill; **sallets:** Salads: here, spicy improprieties.   392. **indict:** Convict.
393–394. **as wholesome . . . fine:** Its beauty was not that of elaborate ornament, but that
of order and proportion.   395. **Æneas' tale to Dido:** The lines recited by the player
are imitated from Marlowe and Nashe's *Dido Queen of Carthage* (II.i.214ff.). They are
written in such a way that the conventionality of the play within a play is raised above
that of ordinary drama.   398. **Pyrrhus:** A Greek hero in the Trojan War; **Hyrcanian
beast:** The tiger; see Virgil, *Aeneid*, IV.266.   402. **ominous horse:** Trojan horse.
405. **gules:** Red, a heraldic term; **trick'd:** Spotted, smeared.   407. **impasted:** Made into
a paste.   410. **o'er-sized:** Covered as with size or glue.   419. **Repugnant:** Disobedient.
422. **Then senseless Ilium:** Insensate Troy.

So, as a painted tyrant,° Pyrrhus stood,
And like a neutral to his will and matter,°
Did nothing.   430
But, as we often see, against° some storm,
A silence in the heavens, the rack° stand still,
The bold winds speechless and the orb below
As hush as death, anon the dreadful thunder
Doth rend the region,° so, after Pyrrhus' pause,   435
Aroused vengeance sets him new a-work;
And never did the Cyclops' hammers fall
On Mars's armour forg'd for proof eterne°
With less remorse than Pyrrhus' bleeding sword
Now falls on Priam.   440
Out, out, thou strumpet, Fortune! All you gods,
In general synod,° take away her power;
Break all the spokes and fellies° from her wheel,
And bowl the round nave° down the hill of heaven,
As low as to the fiends!"   445

POLONIUS: This is too long.

HAMLET: It shall to the barber's, with your beard. Prithee, say on: he's for a jig°
or a tale of bawdry,° or he sleeps: say on: come to Hecuba.°

FIRST PLAYER: "But who, ah woe! had seen the mobled° queen—"

HAMLET: "The mobled queen?"   450

POLONIUS: That's good; "mobled queen" is good.

FIRST PLAYER: "Run barefoot up and down, threat'ning the flames
With bisson rheum;° a clout° upon that head
Where late the diadem stood, and for a robe,
About her lank and all o'er-teemed° loins,   455
A blanket, in the alarm of fear caught up;
Who this had seen, with tongue in venom steep'd,
'Gainst Fortune's state would treason have pronounc'd:°
But if the gods themselves did see her then
When she saw Pyrrhus make malicious sport   460
In mincing with his sword her husband's limbs,
The instant burst of clamour that she made,
Unless things mortal move them not at all,
Would have made milch° the burning eyes of heaven,
And passion in the gods."   465

---

428. painted tyrant: Tyrant in a picture.   **429. matter:** Task.   **431. against:** Before.
432. rack: Mass of clouds.   **435. region:** Assembly.   **438. proof eterne:** External
resistance to assault.   **442. synod:** Assembly.   **443. fellies:** Pieces of wood forming the
rim of a wheel.   **444. nave:** Hub.   **447. jig:** Comic performance given at the end or in an
interval of a play.   **448. bawdry:** Indecency; **Hecuba:** Wife of Priam, king of Troy.
449. mobled: Muffled.   **453. bisson rheum:** Blinding tears; **clout:** Piece of cloth.
455. o'er-teemed: Worn out with bearing children.   **458. pronounc'd:** Proclaimed.
464. milch: Moist with tears.

POLONIUS: Look, whe'r he has not turned° his colour and has tears in 's eyes.
    Prithee, no more.
HAMLET: 'Tis well; I'll have thee speak out the rest soon. Good my lord, will
    you see the players well bestowed? Do you hear, let them be well used; for
    they are the abstract° and brief chronicles of the time: after your death 470
    you were better have a bad epitaph than their ill report while you live.
POLONIUS: My lord, I will use them according to their desert.
HAMLET: God's bodykins,° man, much better: use every man after his desert,
    and who shall 'scape whipping? Use them after your own honour and
    dignity: the less they deserve, the more merit is in your bounty. Take 475
    them in.
POLONIUS: Come, sirs.
HAMLET: Follow him, friends: we'll hear a play tomorrow. [*Aside to First Player.*]
    Dost thou hear me, old friend; can you play the Murder of Gonzago?
FIRST PLAYER: Ay, my lord.   480
HAMLET: We'll ha 't to-morrow night. You could, for a need, study a speech of
    some dozen or sixteen lines,° which I would set down and insert in 't,
    could you not?
FIRST PLAYER: Ay, my lord.
HAMLET: Very well. Follow that lord; and look you mock him not. — My good 485
    friends, I'll leave you till night: you are welcome to Elsinore.
                                            Exeunt Polonius and Players.
ROSENCRANTZ: Good my lord!   *Exeunt* [*Rosencrantz and Guildenstern.*]
HAMLET: Ay, so, God bye to you. — Now I am alone.
    O, what a rogue and peasant° slave am I!
    Is it not monstrous that this player here,   490
    But in a fiction, in a dream of passion,
    Could force his soul so to his own conceit
    That from her working all his visage wann'd,°
    Tears in his eyes, distraction in 's aspect,
    A broken voice, and his whole function suiting   495
    With forms to his conceit?° and all for nothing!
    For Hecuba!
    What's Hecuba to him, or he to Hecuba,
    That he should weep for her? What would he do,
    Had he the motive and the cue for passion   500
    That I have? He would drown the stage with tears
    And cleave the general ear with horrid speech,
    Make mad the guilty and appall the free,
    Confound the ignorant, and amaze indeed
    The very faculties of eyes and ears.   505

---

466. turned: Changed. **470. abstract:** Summary account. **473. bodykins:** Diminutive form of the oath "by God's body." **482. dozen or sixteen lines:** Critics have amused themselves by trying to locate Hamlet's lines. Lucianus's speech III.ii.226–231 is the best guess. **489. peasant:** Base. **493. wann'd:** Grew pale. **495–496. his whole . . . conceit:** His whole being responded with forms to suit his thought.

Yet I,
A dull and muddy-mettled° rascal, peak,°
Like John-a-dreams,° unpregnant of° my cause,
And can say nothing; no, not for a king.
Upon whose property° and most dear life   510
A damn'd defeat was made. Am I a coward?
Who calls me villain? breaks my pate across?
Plucks off my beard, and blows it in my face?
Tweaks me by the nose? gives me the lie i' th' throat,
As deep as to the lungs? who does me this?   515
Ha!
'Swounds, I should take it: for it cannot be
But I am pigeon-liver'd° and lack gall
To make oppression bitter, or ere this
I should have fatted all the region kites°   520
With this slave's offal: bloody, bawdy villain!
Remorseless, treacherous, lecherous, kindless° villain!
O, vengeance!
Why, what an ass am I! This is most brave,
That I, the son of a dear father murder'd,   525
Prompted to my revenge by heaven and hell,
Must, like a whore, unpack my heart with words,
And fall a-cursing, like a very drab,°
A stallion!°
Fie upon 't! foh! About,° my brains! Hum, I have heard   530
That guilty creatures sitting at a play
Have by the very cunning of the scene
Been struck so to the soul that presently
They have proclaim'd their malefactions;
For murder, though it have no tongue, will speak   535
With most miraculous organ. I'll have these players
Play something like the murder of my father
Before mine uncle: I'll observe his looks:
I'll tent° him to the quick: if 'a do blench,°
I know my course. The spirit that I have seen   540
May be the devil:° and the devil hath power
T' assume a pleasing shape; yea, and perhaps

---

507. **muddy-mettled:** Dull-spirited; **peak:** Mope, pine.   508. **John-a-dreams:** An
expression occurring elsewhere in Elizabethan literature to indicate a dreamer; **unpregnant of:** Not quickened by.   510. **property:** Proprietorship (of crown and life).   518.
pigeon-liver'd: The pigeon was supposed to secrete no gall; if Hamlet, so he says, had had
gall, he would have felt the bitterness of oppression, and avenged it.   520. **region kites:**
Kites of the air.   522. **kindless:** Unnatural.   528. **drab:** Prostitute.   529. **stallion:**
Prostitute (male or female).   530. **About:** About it, or turn thou right about.   539. **tent:**
Probe; **blench:** Quail, flinch.   541. **May be the devil:** Hamlet's suspicion is properly
grounded in the belief of the time.

Out of my weakness and my melancholy,
As he is very potent with such spirits,°
Abuses me to damn me: I'll have grounds   545
More relative° than this:° the play's the thing
Wherein I'll catch the conscience of the king.   *Exit.*

[ACT III

SCENE I: *A room in the castle.*]

Enter King, Queen, Polonius, Ophelia, Rosencrantz, Guildenstern, Lords.

KING: And can you, by no drift of conference,°
      Get from him why he puts on this confusion,
      Grating so harshly all his days of quiet
      With turbulent and dangerous lunacy?
ROSENCRANTZ: He does confess he feels himself distracted;   5
      But from what cause 'a will by no means speak.
GUILDENSTERN: Nor do we find him forward° to be sounded,
      But, with a crafty madness, keeps aloof,
      When we would bring him on to some confession
      Of his true state.
QUEEN: Did he receive you well?   10
ROSENCRANTZ: Most like a gentleman.
GUILDENSTERN: But with much forcing of his disposition.°
ROSENCRANTZ: Niggard of question;° but, of our demands,
      Most free in his reply.
QUEEN: Did you assay° him
      To any pastime?   15
ROSENCRANTZ: Madam, it so fell out, that certain players
      We o'er-raught° on the way: of these we told him;
      And there did seem in him a kind of joy
      To hear of it: they are here about the court,
      And, as I think, they have already order   20
      This night to play before him.
POLONIUS: 'Tis most true:
      And he beseech'd me to entreat your majesties
      To hear and see the matter.
KING: With all my heart; and it doth much content me
      To hear him so inclin'd.   25
      Good gentlemen, give him a further edge,°
      And drive his purpose into these delights.
ROSENCRANTZ: We shall, my lord.   *Exeunt Rosencrantz and Guildenstern.*

---

544. spirits: Humors.   **546. relative:** Closely related, definite; **this:** I.e., the ghost's
story.   ACT III, SCENE I.   **1. drift of conference:** Device of conversation.   **7. for-**
ward: Willing.   **12. forcing of his disposition:** I.e., against his will.   **13. Niggard of**
question: Sparing of conversation.   **14. assay:** Try to win.   **17. o'er-raught:** Overtook.
26. edge: Incitement.

KING: Sweet Gertrude, leave us too;
    For we have closely° sent for Hamlet hither,
    That he, as 'twere by accident, may here   30
    Affront° Ophelia:
    Her father and myself, lawful espials,°
    Will so bestow ourselves that, seeing, unseen,
    We may of their encounter frankly judge,
    And gather by him, as he is behav'd,   35
    If 't be th' affliction of his love or no
    That thus he suffers for.
QUEEN: I shall obey you.
    And for your part, Ophelia, I do wish
    That your good beauties be the happy cause
    Of Hamlet's wildness:° so shall I hope your virtues   40
    Will bring him to his wonted way again,
    To both your honours.
OPHELIA: Madam, I wish it may.   *[Exit Queen.]*
POLONIUS: Ophelia, walk you here. Gracious,° so please you,
    We will bestow ourselves. [*To Ophelia.*] Read on this book;
    That show of such an exercise° may colour°   45
    Your loneliness. We are oft to blame in this, —
    'Tis too much prov'd — that with devotion's visage
    And pious action we do sugar o'er
    The devil himself.
KING: [*aside*] O, 'tis too true!
    How smart a lash that speech doth give my conscience!   50
    The harlot's cheek, beautied with plast'ring art,
    Is not more ugly to° the thing° that helps it
    Than is my deed to my most painted word:
    O heavy burthen!
POLONIUS: I hear him coming: let's withdraw, my lord.   55
                            [Exeunt King and Polonius.]
Enter Hamlet.

HAMLET: To be, or not to be: that is the question:
    Whether 'tis nobler in the mind to suffer
    The slings and arrows of outrageous fortune,
    Or to take arms against a sea° of troubles,
    And by opposing end them? To die: to sleep;   60
    No more; and by a sleep to say we end
    The heart-ache and the thousand natural shocks

---

29. closely: Secretly.   **31. Affront:** Confront.   **32. lawful espials:** Legitimate spies.
40. wildness: Madness.   **43. Gracious:** Your grace (addressed to the king).   **45. exercise:** Act of devotion (the book she reads is one of devotion); **colour:** Give a plausible appearance to.   **52. to:** Compared to; **thing:** I.e., the cosmetic.   **59. sea:** The mixed metaphor of this speech has often been commented on; a later emendation *siege* has sometimes been spoken on the stage.

That flesh is heir to, 'tis a consummation
Devoutly to be wish'd. To die, to sleep;
To sleep: perchance to dream: ay, there's the rub;   65
For in that sleep of death what dreams may come
When we have shuffled° off this mortal coil,°
Must give us pause: there's the respect°
That makes calamity of so long life;°
For who would bear the whips and scorns of time,°   70
Th' oppressor's wrong, the proud man's contumely,
The pangs of despis'd° love, the law's delay,
The insolence of office° and the spurns°
That patient merit of th' unworthy takes,
When he himself might his quietus° make   75
With a bare bodkin?° who would fardels° bear,
To grunt and sweat under a weary life,
But that the dread of something after death,
The undiscover'd country from whose bourn°
No traveller returns, puzzles the will   80
And makes us rather bear those ills we have
Than fly to others that we know not of?
Thus conscience° does make cowards of us all;
And thus the native hue° of resolution
Is sicklied o'er° with the pale cast° of thought,   85
And enterprises of great pitch° and moment°
With this regard° their currents° turn awry,
And lose the name of action—Soft you now!
The fair Ophelia! Nymph, in thy orisons°
Be all my sins rememb'red.

OPHELIA: Good my lord,   90
How does your honour for this many a day?
HAMLET: I humbly thank you; well, well, well.
OPHELIA: My lord, I have remembrances of yours,
That I have longed long to re-deliver;
I pray you, now receive them.
HAMLET: No, not I;   95
I never gave you aught.

---

67. shuffled: Sloughed, cast; **coil:** Usually means "turmoil"; here, possibly "body" (conceived of as wound about the soul like rope); *clay, soil, veil,* have been suggested as emendations.   **68. respect:** Consideration.   **69. of . . . life:** So long-lived.   **70. time:** The world.   **72. despis'd:** Rejected.   **73. office:** Office-holders; **spurns:** Insults.   **75. quietus:** Acquittance; here, death.   **76. bare bodkin:** Mere dagger; *bare* is sometimes understood as "unsheathed"; **fardels:** Burdens.   **79. bourn:** Boundary.   **83. conscience:** Probably, inhibition by the faculty of reason restraining the will from doing wrong.   **84. native hue:** Natural color; metaphor derived from the color of the face.   **85. sicklied o'er:** Given a sickly tinge; **cast:** Shade of color.   **86. pitch:** Height (as of a falcon's flight); **moment:** Importance.   **87. regard:** Respect, consideration; **currents:** Courses.   **89. orisons:** Prayers.

OPHELIA: My honour'd lord, you know right well you did;
    And, with them, words of so sweet breath compos'd
    As made the things more rich: their perfume lost,
    Take these again; for to the noble mind   100
    Rich gifts wax poor when givers prove unkind.
    There, my lord.

HAMLET: Ha, ha! are you honest?°

OPHELIA: My lord?

HAMLET: Are you fair?   105

OPHELIA: What means your lordship?

HAMLET: That if you be honest and fair, your honesty° should admit no dis-
    course to° your beauty.

OPHELIA: Could beauty, my lord, have better commerce° than with honesty?

HAMLET: Ay, truly; for the power of beauty will sooner transform honesty from 110
    what it is to a bawd than the force of honesty can translate beauty into his
    likeness: this was sometime a paradox, but now the time° gives it proof. I
    did love you once.

OPHELIA: Indeed, my lord, you made me believe so.

HAMLET: You should not have believed me; for virtue cannot so inoculate° our 115
    old stock but we shall relish of it:° I loved you not.

OPHELIA: I was the more deceived.

HAMLET: Get thee to a nunnery: why wouldst thou be a breeder of sinners? I am
    myself indifferent honest;° but yet I could accuse me of such things that
    it were better my mother had not borne me: I am very proud, revengeful,   120
    ambitious, with more offences at my beck° than I have thoughts to put
    them in, imagination to give them shape, or time to act them in. What
    should such fellows as I do crawling between earth and heaven? We are
    arrant knaves, all; believe none of us. Go thy ways to a nunnery. Where's
    your father?   125

OPHELIA: At home, my lord.

HAMLET: Let the doors be shut upon him, that he may play the fool no where
    but in 's own house. Farewell.

OPHELIA: O, help him, you sweet heavens!

HAMLET: If thou dost marry, I'll give thee this plague for thy dowry: be thou as 130
    chaste as ice, as pure as snow, thou shalt not escape calumny. Get thee to a
    nunnery, go: farewell. Or, if thou wilt needs marry, marry a fool; for wise
    men know well enough what monsters° you make of them. To a nunnery,
    go, and quickly too. Farewell.

103–108. are you honest . . . beauty: *Honest* meaning "truthful" and "chaste" and *fair*
meaning "just, honorable" (line 105) and "beautiful" (line 107) are not mere quibbles;
the speech has the irony of a *double entendre.*   **107. your honesty:** Your chastity.
107–108. discourse to: Familiar intercourse with.   **109. commerce:** Intercourse.
112. the time: The present age.   **115. inoculate:** Graft (metaphorical).   **116. but . . .
it:** I.e., that we do not still have about us a taste of the old stock; i.e., retain our sinfulness.
119. indifferent honest: Moderately virtuous.   **121. beck:** Command.   **133. monsters:** An allusion to the horns of a cuckold.

OPHELIA: O heavenly powers, restore him! 135

HAMLET: I have heard of your° paintings too, well enough; God hath given you
 one face, and you make yourselves another: you jig,° you amble, and you
 lisp; you nick-name God's creatures, and make your wantonness your
 ignorance.° Go to, I'll no more on 't; it hath made me mad. I say, we will
 have no moe marriage: those that are married already, all but one,° shall 140
 live; the rest shall keep as they are. To a nunnery, go.   *Exit.*

OPHELIA: O, what a noble mind is here o'er-thrown!
 The courtier's, soldier's, scholar's, eye, tongue, sword;
 Th' expectancy and rose° of the fair state,
 The glass of fashion and the mould of form,° 145
 Th' observ'd of all observers,° quite, quite down!
 And I, of ladies most deject and wretched,
 That suck'd the honey of his music vows,
 Now see that noble and most sovereign reason,
 Like sweet bells jangled, out of time and harsh; 150
 That unmatch'd form and feature of blown° youth
 Blasted with ecstasy:° O, woe is me,
 T' have seen what I have seen, see what I see!

Enter King and Polonius.

KING: Love! his affections do not that way tend;
 Nor what he spake, though it lack'd form a little, 155
 Was not like madness. There's something in his soul,
 O'er which his melancholy sits on brood;
 And I do doubt° the hatch and the disclose°
 Will be some danger: which for to prevent,
 I have in quick determination 160
 Thus set it down: he shall with speed to England,
 For the demand of our neglected tribute:
 Haply the seas and countries different
 With variable° objects shall expel
 This something-settled° matter in his heart, 165
 Whereon his brains still beating puts him thus
 From fashion of himself.° What think you on 't?

POLONIUS: It shall do well: but yet do I believe
 The origin and commencement of his grief
 Sprung from neglected love. How now, Ophelia! 170

---

136. your: Indefinite use. **137. jig:** Move with jerky motion; probably allusion to the *jig*,
or song and dance, of the current stage. **138–139. make . . . ignorance:** I.e., excuse
your wantonness on the ground of your ignorance. **140. one:** I.e., the king. **144. expectancy and rose:** Source of hope. **145. The glass . . . form:** The mirror of fashion
and the pattern of courtly behavior. **146. observ'd . . . observers:** I.e., the center of
attention in the court. **151. blown:** Blooming. **152. ecstasy:** Madness. **158. doubt:**
Fear; **disclose:** Disclosure or revelation (by chipping of the shell). **164. variable:** Various. **165. something-settled:** Somewhat settled. **167. From . . . himself:** Out of his
natural manner.

You need not tell us what Lord Hamlet said;
We heard it all. My lord, do as you please;
But, if you hold it fit, after the play
Let his queen mother all alone entreat him
To show his grief: let her be round° with him;   175
And I'll be plac'd, so please you, in the ear
Of all their conference. If she find him not,
To England send him, or confine him where
Your wisdom best shall think.

KING: It shall be so:
Madness in great ones must not unwatch'd go.   *Exeunt.* 180

[SCENE II: *A hall in the castle.*]

Enter Hamlet and three of the Players.

HAMLET: Speak the speech, I pray you, as I pronounced it to you, trippingly on
the tongue: but if you mouth it, as many of your° players do, I had as lief
the town-crier spoke my lines. Nor do not saw the air too much with your
hand, thus, but use all gently; for in the very torrent, tempest, and, as I
may say, whirlwind of your passion, you must acquire and beget a tem-   5
perance that may give it smoothness. O, it offends me to the soul to hear a
robustious° periwig-pated° fellow tear a passion to tatters, to very rags,
to split the ears of the groundlings,° who for the most part are capable of°
nothing but inexplicable° dumb-shows and noise: I would have such a
fellow whipped for o'er-doing Termagant;° it out-herods Herod:° pray   10
you, avoid it.

FIRST PLAYER: I warrant your honour.

HAMLET: Be not too tame neither, but let your own discretion be your tutor: suit
the action to the word, the word to the action; with this special observance, that you o'er-step not the modesty of nature: for any thing so   15
overdone is from the purpose of playing, whose end, both at the first and
now, was and is, to hold, as 't were, the mirror up to nature; to show
virtue her own feature, scorn her own image, and the very age and body
of the time his form and pressure.° Now this overdone, or come tardy
off,° though it make the unskilful laugh, cannot but make the judicious   20
grieve; the censure of the which one° must in your allowance o'erweigh a
whole theatre of others. O, there be players that I have seen play, and
heard others praise, and that highly, not to speak it profanely, that, neither having the accent of Christians nor the gait of Christian, pagan, nor

---

175. round: Blunt. SCENE II. **2. your:** Indefinite use. **7. robustious:** Violent, boisterous; **periwig-pated:** Wearing a wig. **8. groundlings:** Those who stood in the yard of
the theater; **capable of:** Susceptible of being influenced by. **9. inexplicable:** Of no significance worth explaining. **10. Termagant:** A god of the Saracens; a character in the
St. Nicholas play, where one of his worshipers, leaving him in charge of goods, returns to
find them stolen; whereupon he beats the god (or idol), which howls vociferously; **Herod:**
Herod of Jewry; a character in *The Slaughter of the Innocents* and other cycle plays. The
part was played with great noise and fury. **19. pressure:** Stamp, impressed character.
19–20. come tardy off: Inadequately done. **21. the censure . . . one:** The judgment of
even one of whom.

man, have so strutted and bellowed that I have thought some of nature's 25
journeymen° had made men and not made them well, they imitated
humanity so abominably.

FIRST PLAYER: I hope we have reformed that indifferently° with us, sir.

HAMLET: O, reform it altogether. And let those that play your clowns speak no
more than is set down for them; for there be of° them that will them- 30
selves laugh, to set on some quantity of barren° spectators to laugh too;
though, in the mean time, some necessary question of the play be then to
be considered: that's villanous, and shows a most pitiful ambition in the
fool that uses it. Go, make you ready.   [*Exeunt Players.*]

Enter Polonius, Guildenstern, and Rosencrantz.

How now, my lord! will the king hear this piece of work?   35

POLONIUS: And the queen too, and that presently.

HAMLET: Bid the players make haste.   [*Exit Polonius.*]
Will you two help to hasten them?

ROSENCRANTZ: } We will, my lord.
GUILDENSTERN: *Exeunt they two.*

HAMLET: What ho! Horatio!

Enter Horatio.

HORATIO: Here, sweet lord, at your service.   40

HAMLET: Horatio, thou art e'en as just° a man
As e'er my conversation cop'd withal.

HORATIO: O, my dear lord, —

HAMLET: Nay, do not think I flatter;
For what advancement may I hope from thee
That no revenue hast but thy good spirits,   45
To feed and clothe thee? Why should the poor be flatter'd?
No, let the candied tongue lick absurd pomp,
And crook the pregnant° hinges of the knee
Where thrift° may follow fawning. Dost thou hear?
Since my dear soul was mistress of her choice   50
And could of men distinguish her election,
S' hath seal'd thee for herself; for thou hast been
As one, in suff'ring all, that suffers nothing,
A man that fortune's buffets and rewards
Hast ta'en with equal thanks: and blest are those   55
Whose blood and judgement are so well commeddled,
That they are not a pipe for fortune's finger
To sound what stop° she please. Give me that man
That is not passion's slave, and I will wear him
In my heart's core, ay, in my heart of heart,   60

---

26. journeymen: Laborers not yet masters in their trade.   **28. indifferently:** Fairly, tol-
erably.   **30. of:** I.e., some among them.   **31. barren:** I.e., of wit.   **41. just:** Honest,
honorable.   **48. pregnant:** Pliant.   **49. thrift:** Profit.   **58. stop:** Hole in a wind instrument for controlling the sound.

As I do thee. — Something too much of this. —
There is a play to-night before the king;
One scene of it comes near the circumstance
Which I have told thee of my father's death:
I prithee, when thou seest that act afoot,   65
Even with the very comment of thy soul°
Observe my uncle: if his occulted° guilt
Do not itself unkennel in one speech,
It is a damned° ghost that we have seen,
And my imaginations are as foul   70
As Vulcan's stithy.° Give him heedful note;
For I mine eyes will rivet to his face,
And after we will both our judgements join
In censure of his seeming.°
HORATIO: Well, my lord:
If 'a steal aught the whilst this play is playing,   75
And 'scape detecting, I will pay the theft.

Enter trumpets and kettledrums, King, Queen, Polonius, Ophelia, [Rosencrantz,
Guildenstern, and others].

HAMLET: They are coming to the play; I must be idle:° Get you a place.
KING: How fares our cousin Hamlet?
HAMLET: Excellent, i' faith; of the chameleon's dish:° I eat the air, promise-
crammed: you cannot feed capons so.   80
KING: I have nothing with° this answer, Hamlet; these words are not mine.°
HAMLET: No, nor mine now. [*To Polonius.*] My lord, you played once i' the uni-
versity, you say?
POLONIUS: That did I, my lord; and was accounted a good actor.
HAMLET: What did you enact?   85
POLONIUS: I did enact Julius Cæsar: I was killed i' the Capitol; Brutus killed
me.
HAMLET: It was a brute part of him to kill so capital a calf there. Be the players
ready?
ROSENCRANTZ: Ay, my lord; they stay upon your patience.   90
QUEEN: Come hither, my dear Hamlet, sit by me.
HAMLET: No, good mother, here's metal more attractive.
POLONIUS [*to the king*]: O, ho! do you mark that?
HAMLET: Lady, shall I lie in your lap?   [*Lying down at Ophelia's feet.*]
OPHELIA: No, my lord.   95
HAMLET: I mean, my head upon your lap?
OPHELIA: Ay, my lord.

---

66. very . . . soul: Inward and sagacious criticism.   **67. occulted:** Hidden.   **69. damned:**
In league with Satan.   **71. stithy:** Smithy, place of *stiths* (anvils).   **74. censure . . .**
seeming: Judgment of his appearance or behavior.   **77. idle:** Crazy, or not attending to
anything serious.   **79. chameleon's dish:** Chameleons were supposed to feed on air.
(Hamlet deliberately misinterprets the king's "fares" as "feeds.")   **81. have . . . with:**
Make nothing of; **are not mine:** Do not respond to what I ask.

HAMLET: Do you think I meant country° matters?

OPHELIA: I think nothing, my lord.

HAMLET: That's a fair thought to lie between maids' legs. 100

OPHELIA: What is, my lord?

HAMLET: Nothing.

OPHELIA: You are merry, my lord.

HAMLET: Who, I?

OPHELIA: Ay, my lord. 105

HAMLET: O God, your only° jig-maker.° What should a man do but be merry? for, look you, how cheerfully my mother looks, and my father died within's two hours.

OPHELIA: Nay, 'tis twice two months, my lord.

HAMLET: So long? Nay then, let the devil wear black, for I'll have a suit of 110 sables.° O heavens! die two months ago, and not forgotten yet? Then there's hope a great man's memory may outlive his life half a year: but, by 'r lady, 'a must build churches, then; or else shall 'a suffer not thinking on,° with the hobbyhorse, whose epitaph is "For, O, for, O, the hobby-horse is forgot."° 115

The trumpets sound. Dumb show follows.

Enter a King and a Queen [very lovingly]; the Queen embracing him, and he her. [She kneels, and makes show of protestation unto him.] He takes her up, and declines his head upon her neck: he lies him down upon a bank of flowers: she, seeing him asleep, leaves him. Anon comes in another man, takes off his crown, kisses it, pours poison in the sleeper's ears, and leaves him. The Queen returns; finds the King dead, makes passionate action. The Poisoner, with some three or four come in again, seem to condole with her. The dead body is carried away. The Poisoner woos the Queen with gifts: she seems harsh awhile, but in the end accepts love. [Exeunt.]

OPHELIA: What means this, my lord?

HAMLET: Marry, this is miching mallecho;° it means mischief.

OPHELIA: Belike this show imports the argument of the play.

Enter Prologue.

HAMLET: We shall know by this fellow: the players cannot keep counsel; they'll tell all. 120

OPHELIA: Will 'a tell us what this show meant?

HAMLET: Ay, or any show that you'll show him: be not you ashamed to show, he'll not shame to tell you what it means.

OPHELIA: You are naught, you are naught:° I'll mark the play.

PROLOGUE: For us, and for our tragedy, 125
    Here stooping° to your clemency,
    We beg your hearing patiently.   *[Exit.]*

---

98. country: With a bawdy pun.   **106. your only:** Only your; **jig-maker:** Composer of jigs (song and dance).   **110–111. suit of sables:** Garments trimmed with the fur of the sable, with a quibble on *sable* meaning "black."   **113–114. suffer . . . on:** Undergo oblivion.   **114–115. "For . . . forgot":** Verse of a song occurring also in *Love's Labour's Lost*, III.i.30. The hobbyhorse was a character in the Morris Dance.   **117. miching mallecho:** Sneaking mischief.   **124. naught:** Indecent.   **126. stooping:** Bowing.

HAMLET: Is this a prologue, or the posy° of a ring?
OPHELIA: 'Tis brief, my lord.
HAMLET: As woman's love.   130

Enter [two Players as] King and Queen.

PLAYER KING: Full thirty times hath Phoebus' cart gone round
    Neptune's salt wash° and Tellus'° orbed ground,
    And thirty dozen moons with borrowed° sheen
    About the world have times twelve thirties been,
    Since love our hearts and Hymen° did our hands   135
    Unite commutual° in most sacred bands.
PLAYER QUEEN: So many journeys may the sun and moon
    Make us again count o'er ere love be done!
    But, woe is me, you are so sick of late,
    So far from cheer and from your former state,   140
    That I distrust° you. Yet, though I distrust,
    Discomfort you, my lord, it nothing must:
    For women's fear and love holds quantity;°
    In neither aught, or in extremity.
    Now, what my love is, proof hath made you know;   145
    And as my love is siz'd, my fear is so:
    Where love is great, the littlest doubts are fear;
    Where little fears grow great, great love grows there.
PLAYER KING: 'Faith, I must leave thee, love, and shortly too;
    My operant° powers their functions leave° to do: 150
    And thou shalt live in this fair world behind,
    Honour'd, belov'd; and haply one as kind
    For husband shalt thou—
PLAYER QUEEN: O, confound the rest!
    Such love must needs be treason in my breast:
    In second husband let me be accurst!   155
    None wed the second but who kill'd the first.
HAMLET (*aside*): Wormwood, wormwood.
PLAYER QUEEN: The instances that second marriage move
    Are base respects of thrift, but none of love:
    A second time I kill my husband dead,   160
    When second husband kisses me in bed.
PLAYER KING: I do believe you think what now you speak;
    But what we do determine oft we break.
    Purpose is but the slave to memory,
    Of violent birth, but poor validity: 165
    Which now, like fruit unripe, sticks on the tree;

---

128. posy: Motto.   **132. salt wash:** The sea; **Tellus:** Goddess of the earth (*orbed ground*).
133. borrowed: I.e., reflected.   **135. Hymen:** God of matrimony.   **136. commutual:**
Mutually.   **141. distrust:** Am anxious about.   **143. holds quantity:** Keeps proportion
between.   **150. operant:** Active; **leave:** Cease.

But fall, unshaken, when they mellow be.
Most necessary 'tis that we forget
To pay ourselves what to ourselves is debt:
What to ourselves in passion we propose, 170
The passion ending, doth the purpose lose.
The violence of either grief or joy
Their own enactures° with themselves destroy:
Where joy most revels, grief doth most lament;
Grief joys, joy grieves, on slender accident. 175
This world is not for aye,° nor 'tis not strange
That even our loves should with our fortunes change;
For 'tis a question left us yet to prove,
Whether love lead fortune, or else fortune love.
The great man down, you mark his favourite flies; 180
The poor advanc'd makes friends of enemies.
And hitherto doth love on fortune tend;
For who° not needs shall never lack a friend,
And who in want a hollow friend doth try,
Directly seasons° him his enemy. 185
But, orderly to end where I begun,
Our wills and fates do so contrary run
That our devices still are overthrown;
Our thoughts are ours, their ends° none of our own:
So think thou wilt no second husband wed; 190
But die thy thoughts when thy first lord is dead.
PLAYER QUEEN: Nor earth to me give food, nor heaven light!
Sport and repose lock from me day and night!
To desperation turn my trust and hope!
An anchor's° cheer° in prison be my scope! 195
Each opposite° that blanks° the face of joy
Meet what I would have well and it destroy!
Both here and hence pursue me lasting strife,
If, once a widow, ever I be wife!
HAMLET: If she should break it now! 200
PLAYER KING: 'Tis deeply sworn. Sweet, leave me here awhile;
My spirits grow dull, and fain I would beguile
The tedious day with sleep. [*Sleeps.*]
PLAYER QUEEN: Sleep rock thy brain;
And never come mischance between us twain! *Exit.*
HAMLET: Madam, how like you this play? 205
QUEEN: The lady doth protest too much, methinks.
HAMLET: O, but she'll keep her word.

---

173. enactures: Fulfillments.   **176. aye:** Ever.   **183. who:** Whoever.   **185. seasons:**
Matures, ripens.   **189. ends:** Results.   **195. An anchor's:** An anchorite's; **cheer:** Fare;
sometimes printed as *chair.*   **196. opposite:** Adverse thing; **blanks:** Causes to *blanch* or
grow pale.

KING: Have you heard the argument? Is there no offence in 't?

HAMLET: No, no, they do but jest, poison in jest; no offence i' the world.

KING: What do you call the play?   210

HAMLET: The Mouse-trap. Marry, how? Tropically.° This play is the image of a
murder done in Vienna: Gonzago° is the duke's name; his wife, Baptista:
you shall see anon; 't is a knavish piece of work: but what o' that? your
majesty and we that have free souls, it touches us not: let the galled jade°
winch,° our withers° are unwrung.°   215

Enter Lucianus.

This is one Lucianus, nephew to the king.

OPHELIA: You are as good as a chorus,° my lord.

HAMLET: I could interpret between you and your love, if I could see the puppets
dallying.°

OPHELIA: You are keen, my lord, you are keen.   220

HAMLET: It would cost you a groaning to take off my edge.

OPHELIA: Still better, and worse.°

HAMLET: So you mistake° your husbands. Begin, murderer; pox,° leave thy
damnable faces, and begin. Come: the croaking raven doth bellow for
revenge.   225

LUCIANUS: Thoughts black, hands apt, drugs fit, and time agreeing;
Confederate° season, else no creature seeing;
Thou mixture rank, of midnight weeds collected,
With Hecate's° ban° thrice blasted, thrice infected,
Thy natural magic and dire property,   230
On wholesome life usurp immediately.

                                         [Pours the poison into the sleeper's ears.]

HAMLET: 'A poisons him i' the garden for his estate. His name's Gonzago: the
story is extant, and written in very choice Italian: you shall see anon how
the murderer gets the love of Gonzago's wife.

OPHELIA: The king rises.   235

HAMLET: What, frighted with false fire!°

QUEEN: How fares my lord?

POLONIUS: Give o'er the play.

KING: Give me some light: away!

POLONIUS: Lights, lights, lights!   *Exeunt all but Hamlet and Horatio.* 240

---

211. Tropically: Figuratively, *trapically* suggests a pun on *trap* in *Mouse-trap* (line 211).
212. Gonzago: In 1538 Luigi Gonzago murdered the Duke of Urbano by pouring poisoned lotion in his ears.   **214. galled jade:** Horse whose hide is rubbed by saddle or harness.   **215. winch:** Wince; **withers:** The part between the horse's shoulder blades;
unwrung: Not wrung or twisted.   **217. chorus:** In many Elizabethan plays the action
was explained by an actor known as the "chorus"; at a puppet show the actor who
explained the action was known as an "interpreter," as indicated by the lines following.
219. dallying: With sexual suggestion, continued in *keen* (sexually aroused), *groaning*
(i.e., in pregnancy), and *edge* (i.e., sexual desire or impetuosity).   **222. Still . . . worse:**
More keen, less decorous.   **223. mistake:** Err in taking; **pox:** An imprecation.   **227. Con-**
federate: Conspiring (to assist the murderer).   **229. Hecate:** The goddess of witchcraft;
ban: Curse.   **236. false fire:** Fireworks, or a blank discharge.

HAMLET: Why, let the strucken deer go weep,
    The hart ungalled play;
For some must watch, while some must sleep:
    Thus runs the world away.°
Would not this,° sir, and a forest of feathers° — if the rest of my fortunes 245
turn Turk with° me — with two Provincial roses° on my razed° shoes,
get me a fellowship in a cry° of players,° sir?
HORATIO: Half a share.°
HAMLET: A whole one, I.
    For thou dost know, O Damon dear, 250
      This realm dismantled° was
    Of Jove himself; and now reigns here
      A very, very° — pajock.°
HORATIO: You might have rhymed.
HAMLET: O good Horatio, I'll take the ghost's word for a thousand pound. 255
    Didst perceive?
HORATIO: Very well, my lord.
HAMLET: Upon the talk of the poisoning?
HORATIO: I did very well note him.
HAMLET: Ah, ha! Come, some music! come, the recorders!° 260
    For if the king like not the comedy,
    Why then, belike, he likes it not, perdy.°
    Come, some music!

Enter Rosencrantz and Guildenstern.

GUILDENSTERN: Good my lord, vouchsafe me a word with you.
HAMLET: Sir, a whole history. 265
GUILDENSTERN: The king, sir, —
HAMLET: Ay, sir, what of him?
GUILDENSTERN: Is in his retirement marvellous distempered.
HAMLET: With drink, sir?
GUILDENSTERN: No, my lord, rather with choler.° 270
HAMLET: Your wisdom should show itself more richer to signify this to his doc-
    tor; for, for me to put him to his purgation would perhaps plunge him
    into far more choler.

241–244. Why . . . away: Probably from an old ballad, with allusion to the popular belief that a wounded deer retires to weep and die. Cf. *As You Like It,* II.i.66.   **245. this:** I.e., the play; **feathers:** Allusion to the plumes which Elizabethan actors were fond of wearing. **246. turn Turk with:** Go back on; **two Provincial roses:** Rosettes of ribbon like the roses of Provins near Paris, or else the roses of Provence; **razed:** Cut, slashed (by way of ornament).   **247. cry:** Pack (as of hounds); **fellowship . . . players:** Partnership in a theatrical company.   **248. Half a share:** Allusion to the custom in dramatic companies of dividing the ownership into a number of shares among the householders.   **251. dismantled:** Stripped, divested.   **250–253. For . . . very:** Probably from an old ballad having to do with Damon and Pythias.   **253. pajock:** Peacock (a bird with a bad reputation). Possibly the word was *patchock,* diminutive of *patch,* clown.   **260. recorders:** Wind instruments of the flute kind.   **262. perdy:** Corruption of *par dieu.*   **270. choler:** Bilious disorder, with quibble on the sense "anger."

GUILDENSTERN: Good my lord, put your discourse into some frame° and start   275
not so wildly from my affair.

HAMLET: I am tame, sir: pronounce.

GUILDENSTERN: The queen, your mother, in most great affliction of spirit, hath
sent me to you.

HAMLET: You are welcome.

GUILDENSTERN: Nay, good my lord, this courtesy is not of the right breed. If it   280
shall please you to make me a wholesome° answer, I will do your
mother's commandment; if not, your pardon and my return shall be the
end of my business.

HAMLET: Sir, I cannot.

GUILDENSTERN: What, my lord?   285

HAMLET: Make you a wholesome answer; my wit's diseased: but, sir, such
answer as I can make, you shall command; or, rather, as you say, my
mother: therefore no more, but to the matter:° my mother, you say,—

ROSENCRANTZ: Then thus she says; your behaviour hath struck her into amazement and admiration.   290

HAMLET: O wonderful son, that can so 'stonish a mother! But is there no sequel
at the heels of this mother's admiration? Impart.

ROSENCRANTZ: She desires to speak with you in her closet, ere you go to bed.

HAMLET: We shall obey, were she ten times our mother. Have you any further
trade with us?   295

ROSENCRANTZ: My lord, you once did love me.

HAMLET: And do still, by these pickers and stealers.°

ROSENCRANTZ: Good my lord, what is your cause of distemper? you do, surely,
bar the door upon your own liberty, if you deny your griefs to your friend.

HAMLET: Sir, I lack advancement.   300

ROSENCRANTZ: How can that be, when you have the voice° of the king himself
for your succession in Denmark?

HAMLET: Ay, sir, but "While the grass grows,"°—the proverb is something
musty.

Enter the Players with recorders.

O, the recorders! let me see one. To withdraw° with you:—why do you   305
go about to recover the wind° of me, as if you would drive me into a toil?°

GUILDENSTERN: O, my lord, if my duty be too bold, my love is too unmannerly.°

HAMLET: I do not well understand that. Will you play upon this pipe?

GUILDENSTERN: My lord, I cannot.

HAMLET: I pray you.   310

GUILDENSTERN: Believe me, I cannot.

---

274. frame: Order.   **281. wholesome:** Sensible.   **288. matter:** Matter in hand.
297. pickers and stealers: Hands, so called from the catechism "to keep my hands from
picking and stealing."   **301. voice:** Support.   **303. "While . . . grows":** The rest of the
proverb is "the silly horse starves." Hamlet may be destroyed while he is waiting for the
succession to the kingdom.   **305. withdraw:** Speak in private.   **306. recover the wind:**
Get to the windward side; **toil:** Snare.   **307. if . . . unmannerly:** If I am using an unmannerly boldness, it is my love which occasions it.

HAMLET: I beseech you.

GUILDENSTERN: I know no touch of it, my lord.

HAMLET: 'Tis as easy as lying: govern these ventages° with your fingers and thumb, give it breath with your mouth, and it will discourse most elo- 315 quent music. Look you, these are the stops.

GUILDENSTERN: But these cannot I command to any utterance of harmony; I have not the skill.

HAMLET: Why, look you now, how unworthy a thing you make of me! You would play upon me; you would seem to know my stops; you would 320 pluck out the heart of my mystery; you would sound me from my lowest note to the top of my compass:° and there is much music, excellent voice, in this little organ;° yet cannot you make it speak. 'Sblood, do you think I am easier to be played on than a pipe? Call me what instrument you will, though you can fret° me, you cannot play upon me. 325

Enter Polonius.

God bless you, sir!

POLONIUS: My lord, the queen would speak with you, and presently.

HAMLET: Do you see yonder cloud that 's almost in shape of a camel?

POLONIUS: By the mass, and 'tis like a camel, indeed.

HAMLET: Methinks it is like a weasel. 330

POLONIUS: It is backed like a weasel.

HAMLET: Or like a whale?

POLONIUS: Very like a whale.

HAMLET: Then I will come to my mother by and by. [*Aside.*] They fool me to the top of my bent.° — I will come by and by.° 335

POLONIUS: I will say so. [*Exit.*]

HAMLET: By and by is easily said.

 Leave me, friends. [*Exeunt all but Hamlet.*]
 'Tis now the very witching time° of night,
 When churchyards yawn and hell itself breathes out 340
 Contagion to this world: now could I drink hot blood,
 And do such bitter business as the day
 Would quake to look on. Soft! now to my mother.
 O heart, lose not thy nature; let not ever
 The soul of Nero° enter this firm bosom: 345
 Let me be cruel, not unnatural:
 I will speak daggers to her, but use none;
 My tongue and soul in this be hypocrites;
 How in my words somever she be shent,°
 To give them seals° never, my soul, consent! *Exit.* 350

---

314. **ventages:** Stops of the recorders. 322. **compass:** Range of voice. 323. **organ:** Musical instrument, i.e., the pipe. 325. **fret:** Quibble on meaning "irritate" and the piece of wood, gut, or metal which regulates the fingering. 335. **top of my bent:** Limit of endurance, i.e., extent to which a bow may be bent; **by and by:** Immediately. 339. **witching time:** I.e., time when spells are cast. 345. **Nero:** Murderer of his mother, Agrippina. 349. **shent:** Rebuked. 350. **give them seals:** Confirm with deeds.

[SCENE III: *A room in the castle.*]

Enter King, Rosencrantz, and Guildenstern.

KING: I like him not, nor stands it safe with us
    To let his madness range. Therefore prepare you;
    I your commission will forthwith dispatch,°
    And he to England shall along with you:
    The terms° of our estate° may not endure   5
    Hazard so near us as doth hourly grow
    Out of his brows.°

GUILDENSTERN: We will ourselves provide:
    Most holy and religious fear it is
    To keep those many many bodies safe
    That live and feed upon your majesty.   10

ROSENCRANTZ: The single and peculiar° life is bound,
    With all the strength and armour of the mind,
    To keep itself from noyance;° but much more
    That spirit upon whose weal depend and rest
    The lives of many. The cess° of majesty   15
    Dies not alone; but, like a gulf,° doth draw
    What's near it with it: it is a massy wheel,
    Fix'd on the summit of the highest mount,
    To whose huge spokes ten thousand lesser things
    Are mortis'd and adjoin'd; which, when it falls,   20
    Each small annexment, petty consequence,
    Attends° the boist'rous ruin. Never alone
    Did the king sigh, but with a general groan.

KING: Arm° you, I pray you, to this speedy voyage;
    For we will fetters put about this fear,   25
    Which now goes too free-footed.

ROSENCRANTZ: We will haste us.

        Exeunt Gentlemen [Rosencrantz and Guildenstern].

Enter Polonius.

POLONIUS: My lord, he's going to his mother's closet:
    Behind the arras° I'll convey° myself,
    To hear the process;° I'll warrant she'll tax him home:°
    And, as you said, and wisely was it said,   30
    'Tis meet that some more audience than a mother,
    Since nature makes them partial, should o'erhear
    The speech, of vantage.° Fare you well, my liege:

SCENE III. **3. dispatch:** Prepare. **5. terms:** Condition, circumstances; **estate:** State. **7. brows:** Effronteries. **11. single and peculiar:** Individual and private. **13. noyance:** Harm. **15. cess:** Decease. **16. gulf:** Whirlpool. **22. Attends:** Participates in. **24. Arm:** Prepare. **28. arras:** Screen of tapestry placed around the walls of household apartments; **convey:** Implication of secrecy, *convey* was often used to mean "steal." **29. process:** Proceedings; **tax him home:** Reprove him severely. **33. of vantage:** From an advantageous place.

I'll call upon you ere you go to bed,
And tell you what I know.

KING: Thanks, dear my lord.   *Exit [Polonius].* 35
          O, my offence is rank, it smells to heaven;
          It hath the primal eldest curse° upon't,
          A brother's murder. Pray can I not,
          Though inclination be as sharp as will:°
          My stronger guilt defeats my strong intent;   40
          And, like a man to double business bound,
          I stand in pause where I shall first begin,
          And both neglect. What if this cursed hand
          Were thicker than itself with brother's blood,
          Is there not rain enough in the sweet heavens   45
          To wash it white as snow? Whereto serves mercy
          But to confront° the visage of offence?
          And what's in prayer but this two-fold force,
          To be forestalled° ere we come to fall,
          Or pardon'd being down? Then I'll look up;   50
          My fault is past. But, O, what form of prayer
          Can serve my turn? "Forgive me my foul murder"?
          That cannot be; since I am still possess'd
          Of those effects for which I did the murder,
          My crown, mine own ambition° and my queen.   55
          May one be pardon'd and retain th' offence?°
          In the corrupted currents° of this world
          Offence's gilded hand° may shove by justice,
          And oft 'tis seen the wicked prize° itself
          Buys out the law: but 'tis not so above;   60
          There is no shuffling,° there the action lies°
          In his true nature; and we ourselves compell'd,
          Even to the teeth and forehead° of our faults,
          To give in evidence. What then? what rests?°
          Try what repentance can: what can it not?   65
          Yet what can it when one can not repent?
          O wretched state! O bosom black as death!
          O limed° soul, that, struggling to be free,
          Art more engag'd!° Help, angels! Make assay!°
          Bow, stubborn knees; and, heart with strings of steel,   70
          Be soft as sinews of the new-born babe!
          All may be well.   *[He kneels.]*

---

37. primal eldest curse: The curse of Cain, the first to kill his brother.   **39. sharp as will:** I.e., his desire is as strong as his determination.   **47. confront:** Oppose directly.   **49. forestalled:** Prevented.   **55. ambition:** I.e., realization of ambition.   **56. offence:** Benefit accruing from offense.   **57. currents:** Courses.   **58. gilded hand:** Hand offering gold as a bribe.   **59. wicked prize:** Prize won by wickedness.   **61. shuffling:** Escape by trickery; **lies:** Is sustainable.   **63. teeth and forehead:** Very face.   **64. rests:** Remains.   **68. limed:** Caught as with birdlime.   **69. engag'd:** Embedded; **assay:** Trial.

Enter Hamlet.

HAMLET: Now might I do it pat,° now he is praying;
And now I'll do't. And so 'a goes to heaven;
And so am I reveng'd. That would be scann'd:° 75
A villain kills my father; and for that,
I, his sole son, do this same villain send
To heaven.
Why, this is hire and salary, not revenge.
'A took my father grossly, full of bread;° 80
With all his crimes broad blown,° as flush° as May;
And how his audit stands who knows save heaven?
But in our circumstance and course° of thought,
'Tis heavy with him: and am I then reveng'd,
To take him in the purging of his soul, 85
When he is fit and season'd for his passage?°
No!
Up, sword; and know thou a more horrid hent:°
When he is drunk asleep,° or in his rage,
Or in th' incestuous pleasure of his bed; 90
At game, a-swearing, or about some act
That has no relish of salvation in't;
Then trip him, that his heels may kick at heaven,
And that his soul may be as damn'd and black
As hell, whereto it goes. My mother stays: 95
This physic° but prolongs thy sickly days. *Exit.*
KING: [*Rising*] My words fly up, my thoughts remain below:
Words without thoughts never to heaven go. *Exit.*

[SCENE IV: *The Queen's closet.*]

Enter [Queen] Gertrude and Polonius.

POLONIUS: 'A will come straight. Look you lay° home to him:
Tell him his pranks have been too broad° to bear with,
And that your grace hath screen'd and stood between
Much heat° and him. I'll sconce° me even here.
Pray you, be round° with him. 5
HAMLET (*within*): Mother, mother, mother!
QUEEN: I'll warrant you,
Fear me not: withdraw, I hear him coming.

[*Polonius hides behind the arras.*]

---

73. pat: Opportunely.   **75. would be scann'd:** Needs to be looked into.   **80. full of bread:** Enjoying his worldly pleasures (see Ezekiel 16:49).   **81. broad blown:** In full bloom; **flush:** Lusty.   **83. in . . . course:** As we see it in our mortal situation.   **86. fit . . . passage:** I.e., reconciled to heaven by forgiveness of his sins.   **88. hent:** Seizing; or more probably, occasion of seizure.   **89. drunk asleep:** In a drunken sleep.   **96. physic:** Purging (by prayer).   SCENE IV.   **1. lay:** Thrust.   **2. broad:** Unrestrained.   **4. Much heat:** I.e., the king's anger; **sconce:** Hide.   **5. round:** Blunt.

Enter Hamlet.

HAMLET: Now, mother, what's the matter?

QUEEN: Hamlet, thou hast thy father much offended.

HAMLET: Mother, you have my father° much offended.   10

QUEEN: Come, come, you answer with an idle tongue.

HAMLET: Go, go, you question with a wicked tongue.

QUEEN: Why, how now, Hamlet!

HAMLET: What's the matter now?

QUEEN: Have you forgot me?

HAMLET: No, by the rood,° not so:

  You are the queen, your husband's brother's wife;   15

  And—would it were not so!—you are my mother.

QUEEN: Nay, then, I'll set those to you that can speak.

HAMLET: Come, come, and sit you down; you shall not budge;

  You go not till I set you up a glass

  Where you may see the inmost part of you.   20

QUEEN: What wilt thou do? thou wilt not murder me?

  Help, help, ho!

POLONIUS [*behind*]: What, ho! help, help; help!

HAMLET [*drawing*]: How now! a rat? Dead, for a ducat, dead!

                              [*Makes a pass through the arras.*]

POLONIUS [*behind*]: O, I am slain!   [*Falls and dies.*] 25

QUEEN: O me, what hast thou done?

HAMLET: Nay, I know not:

  Is it the king?

QUEEN: O, what a rash and bloody deed is this!

HAMLET: A bloody deed! almost as bad, good mother,

  As kill a king, and marry with his brother.   30

QUEEN: As kill a king!

HAMLET: Ay, lady, it was my word.

              [*Lifts up the arras and discovers Polonius.*]

  Thou wretched, rash, intruding fool, farewell!

  I took thee for thy better: take thy fortune;

  Thou find'st to be too busy is some danger.

  Leave wringing of your hands: peace! sit you down,   35

  And let me wring your heart; for so I shall,

  If it be made of penetrable stuff,

  If damned custom have not braz'd° it so

  That it be proof and bulwark against sense.

QUEEN: What have I done, that thou dar'st wag thy tongue   40

  In noise so rude against me?

HAMLET: Such an act

  That blurs the grace and blush of modesty,

  Calls virtue hypocrite, takes off the rose

9–10. thy father, my father: I.e., Claudius, the elder Hamlet. **14. rood:** Cross.
38. braz'd: Brazened, hardened.

From the fair forehead of an innocent love
And sets a blister° there, makes marriage-vows 45
As false as dicers' oaths: O, such a deed
As from the body of contraction° plucks
The very soul, and sweet religion° makes
A rhapsody° of words: heaven's face does glow
O'er this solidity and compound mass 50
With heated visage, as against the doom
Is thought-sick at the act.°

QUEEN: Ay me, what act,
That roars so loud, and thunders in the index?°

HAMLET: Look here, upon this picture, and on this.
The counterfeit presentment° of two brothers. 55
See, what grace was seated on this brow;
Hyperion's° curls; the front° of Jove himself;
An eye like Mars, to threaten and command;
A station° like the herald Mercury
New-lighted on a heaven-kissing hill; 60
A combination and a form indeed,
Where every god did seem to set his seal,
To give the world assurance° of a man:
This was your husband. Look you now, what follows:
Here is your husband; like a mildew'd ear,° 65
Blasting his wholesome brother. Have you eyes?
Could you on this fair mountain leave to feed,
And batten° on this moor?° Ha! have you eyes?
You cannot call it love; for at your age
The hey-day° in the blood is tame, it's humble, 70
And waits upon the judgement: and what judgement
Would step from this to this? Sense, sure, you have,
Else could you not have motion;° but sure, that sense
Is apoplex'd;° for madness would not err,
Nor sense to ecstasy was ne'er so thrall'd° 75
But it reserv'd some quantity of choice,°

---

45. sets a blister: Brands as a harlot. **47. contraction:** The marriage contract. **48. religion:** Religious vows. **49. rhapsody:** Senseless string. **49–52. heaven's . . . act:** Heaven's face blushes to look down upon this world, compounded of the four elements, with hot face as though the day of doom were near, and thought-sick at the deed (i.e., Gertrude's marriage). **53. index:** Prelude or preface. **55. counterfeit presentment:** Portrayed representation. **57. Hyperion's:** The sun god's; **front:** Brow. **59. station:** Manner of standing. **63. assurance:** Pledge, guarantee. **65. mildew'd ear:** See Genesis 41:5–7. **68. batten:** Grow fat; **moor:** Barren upland. **70. hey-day:** State of excitement. **72–73. Sense . . . motion:** Sense and motion are functions of the middle or sensible soul, the possession of sense being the basis of motion. **74. apoplex'd:** Paralyzed. Mental derangement was thus of three sorts: apoplexy, ectasy, and diabolic possession. **75. thrall'd:** Enslaved. **76. quantity of choice:** Fragment of the power to choose.

To serve in such a difference. What devil was't
That thus hath cozen'd° you at hoodman-blind?°
Eyes without feeling, feeling without sight,
Ears without hands or eyes, smelling sans° all,   80
Or but a sickly part of one true sense
Could not so mope.°
O shame! where is thy blush? Rebellious hell,
If thou canst mutine° in a matron's bones,
To flaming youth let virtue be as wax,   85
And melt in her own fire: proclaim no shame
When the compulsive ardour gives the charge,°
Since frost itself as actively doth burn
And reason pandars will.°

QUEEN: O Hamlet, speak no more:
Thou turn'st mine eyes into my very soul;   90
And there I see such black and grained° spots
As will not leave their tinct.

HAMLET: Nay, but to live
In the rank sweat of an enseamed° bed,
Stew'd in corruption, honeying and making love
Over the nasty sty, —

QUEEN: O, speak to me no more;   95
These words, like daggers, enter in mine ears;
No more, sweet Hamlet!

HAMLET: A murderer and a villain;
A slave that is not twentieth part the tithe
Of your precedent lord;° a vice of kings;°
A cutpurse of the empire and the rule,   100
That from a shelf the precious diadem stole,
And put it in his pocket!

QUEEN: No more!

Enter Ghost.

HAMLET: A king of shreds and patches,° —
Save me, and hover o'er me with your wings,
You heavenly guards! What would your gracious figure?   105

QUEEN: Alas, he's mad!

---

78. cozen'd: Tricked, cheated; **hoodman-blind:** Blindman's buff.   **80. sans:** Without.
82. mope: Be in a depressed, spiritless state, act aimlessly.   **84. mutine:** Mutiny, rebel.
87. gives the charge: Delivers the attack.   **89. reason pandars will:** The normal and
proper situation was one in which reason guided the will in the direction of good;
here, reason is perverted and leads in the direction of evil.   **91. grained:** Dyed in grain.
93. enseamed: Loaded with grease, greased.   **99. precedent lord:** I.e., the elder Hamlet; **vice of kings:** Buffoon of kings; a reference to the Vice, or clown, of the morality plays
and interludes.   **103. shreds and patches:** I.e., motley, the traditional costume of the
Vice.

HAMLET: Do you not come your tardy son to chide,
    That, laps'd in time and passion,° lets go by
    Th' important° acting of your dread command?
    O, say!   110
GHOST: Do not forget: this visitation
    Is but to whet thy almost blunted purpose.
    But, look, amazement° on thy mother sits:
    O, step between her and her fighting soul:
    Conceit in weakest bodies strongest works: 115
    Speak to her, Hamlet.
HAMLET: How is it with you, lady?
QUEEN: Alas, how is 't with you,
    That you do bend your eye on vacancy
    And with th' incorporal° air do hold discourse?
    Forth at your eyes your spirits wildly peep;   120
    And, as the sleeping soldiers in th' alarm,
    Your bedded° hair, like life in excrements,°
    Start up, and stand an° end. O gentle son,
    Upon the heat and flame of thy distemper
    Sprinkle cool patience. Whereon do you look?   125
HAMLET: On him, on him! Look you, how pale he glares!
    His form and cause conjoin'd,° preaching to stones,
    Would make them capable. — Do not look upon me;
    Lest with this piteous action you convert
    My stern effects:° then what I have to do   130
    Will want true colour;° tears perchance for blood.
QUEEN: To whom do you speak this?
HAMLET: Do you see nothing there?
QUEEN: Nothing at all; yet all that is I see.
HAMLET: Nor did you nothing hear?
QUEEN: No, nothing but ourselves.
HAMLET: Why, look you there! look, how it steals away!   135
    My father, in his habit as he liv'd!
    Look, where he goes, even now, out at the portal!   *Exit Ghost.*
QUEEN: This is the very coinage of your brain:
    This bodiless creation ecstasy
    Is very cunning in.

---

108. laps'd . . . passion: Having suffered time to slip and passion to cool; also explained as "engrossed in casual events and lapsed into mere fruitless passion, so that he no longer entertains a rational purpose."   **109. important:** Urgent.   **113. amazement:** Frenzy, distraction.   **119. incorporal:** Immaterial.   **122. bedded:** Laid in smooth layers; **excrements:** The hair was considered an excrement or voided part of the body.   **123. an:** On.   **127. conjoin'd:** United.   **129–130. convert . . . effects:** Divert me from my stern duty. For *effects,* possibly *affects* (affections of the mind).   **131. want true colour:** Lack good reason so that (with a play on the normal sense of *colour*) I shall shed tears instead of blood.

HAMLET: Ecstasy!   140
   My pulse, as yours, doth temperately keep time,
   And makes as healthful music: it is not madness
   That I have utt'red: bring me to the test,
   And I the matter will re-word,° which madness
   Would gambol° from. Mother, for love of grace,   145
   Lay not that flattering unction° to your soul,
   That not your trespass, but my madness speaks:
   It will but skin and film the ulcerous place,
   Whiles rank corruption, mining° all within,
   Infects unseen. Confess yourself to heaven;   150
   Repent what's past; avoid what is to come;°
   And do not spread the compost° on the weeds,
   To make them ranker. Forgive me this my virtue;°
   For in the fatness° of these pursy° times
   Virtue itself of vice must pardon beg,   155
   Yea, curb° and woo for leave to do him good.
QUEEN: O Hamlet, thou hast cleft my heart in twain.
HAMLET: O, throw away the worser part of it,
   And live the purer with the other half.
   Good night: but go not to my uncle's bed;   160
   Assume a virtue, if you have it not.
   That monster, custom, who all sense doth eat,
   Of habits devil, is angel yet in this,
   That to the use of actions fair and good
   He likewise gives a frock or livery,   165
   That aptly is put on. Refrain to-night,
   And that shall lend a kind of easiness
   To the next abstinence: the next more easy;
   For use almost can change the stamp of nature,
   And either . . . the devil, or throw him out°   170
   With wondrous potency. Once more, good night:
   And when you are desirous to be bless'd,°
   I'll blessing beg of you. For this same lord,   [*Pointing to Polonius.*]
   I do repent: but heaven hath pleas'd it so,
   To punish me with this and this with me,   175
   That I must be their scourge and minister.
   I will bestow him, and will answer well
   The death I gave him. So, again, good night.

---

144. re-word: Repeat in words.   **145. gambol:** Skip away.   **146. unction:** Ointment
used medicinally or as a rite; suggestion that forgiveness for sin may not be so easily
achieved.   **149. mining:** Working under the surface.   **151. what is to come:** I.e., the
sins of the future.   **152. compost:** Manure.   **153. this my virtue:** My virtuous talk in
reproving you.   **154. fatness:** Grossness; **pursy:** Short-winded, corpulent.   **156. curb:**
Bow, bend the knee.   **170.** Defective line usually emended by inserting *master* after
either.   **172. be bless'd:** Become blessed, i.e., repentant.

I must be cruel, only to be kind:
Thus bad begins and worse remains behind.   180
One word more, good lady.
QUEEN: What shall I do?
HAMLET: Not this, by no means, that I bid you do:
Let the bloat° king tempt you again to bed;
Pinch wanton on your cheek; call you his mouse;
And let him, for a pair of reechy° kisses,   185
Or paddling in your neck with his damn'd fingers,
Make you to ravel all this matter out,
That I essentially° am not in madness,
But mad in craft. 'Twere good you let him know;
For who, that's but a queen, fair, sober, wise,   190
Would from a paddock,° from a bat, a gib,°
Such dear concernings° hide? who would do so?
No, in despite of sense and secrecy,
Unpeg the basket on the house's top,
Let the birds fly, and, like the famous ape.°   195
To try conclusions,° in the basket creep,
And break your own neck down.
QUEEN: Be thou assur'd, if words be made of breath,
And breath of life, I have no life to breathe
What thou hast said to me.   200
HAMLET: I must to England; you know that?
QUEEN: Alack,
I had forgot: 'tis so concluded on.
HAMLET: There's letters seal'd: and my two schoolfellows,
Whom I will trust as I will adders fang'd,
They bear the mandate; they must sweep my way,°   205
And marshal me to knavery. Let it work;
For 'tis the sport to have the enginer°
Hoist° with his own petar:° and 't shall go hard
But I will delve one yard below their mines,
And blow them at the moon: O, 'tis most sweet,   210
When in one line two crafts° directly meet.
This man shall set me packing:°

---

183. **bloat:** Bloated.   185. **reechy:** Dirty, filthy.   188. **essentially:** In my essential nature.   191. **paddock:** Toad; **gib:** Tomcat.   192. **dear concernings:** Important affairs.   195. **the famous ape:** A letter from Sir John Suckling seems to supply other details of the story, otherwise not identified: "It is the story of the jackanapes and the partridges; thou starest after a beauty till it be lost to thee, then let'st out another, and starest after that till it is gone too."   196. **conclusions:** Experiments.   205. **sweep my way:** Clear my path.   207. **enginer:** Constructor of military works, or possibly, artilleryman.   208. **Hoist:** Blown up; **petar:** Defined as a small engine of war used to blow in a door or make a breach, and as a case filled with explosive materials.   211. **two crafts:** Two acts of guile, with quibble on the sense of "two ships."   212. **set me packing:** Set me to making schemes, and set me to lugging (him), and, also, send me off in a hurry.

I'll lug the guts into the neighbour room.
Mother, good night. Indeed this counsellor
Is now most still, most secret and most grave,   215
Who was in life a foolish prating knave.
Come, sir, to draw° toward an end with you.
Good night, mother.   *Exeunt [severally; Hamlet dragging in Polonius.]*

[ACT IV

SCENE I: *A room in the castle.*]

Enter King and Queen, with Rosencrantz and Guildenstern.

KING: There's matter in these sighs, these profound heaves:
You must translate: 'tis fit we understand them.
Where is your son?
QUEEN: Bestow this place on us a little while.
                           [Exeunt Rosencrantz and Guildenstern.]
Ah, mine own lord, what have I seen to-night!   5
KING: What, Gertrude? How does Hamlet?
QUEEN: Mad as the sea and wind, when both contend
Which is the mightier: in his lawless fit,
Behind the arras hearing something stir,
Whips out his rapier, cries, "A rat, a rat!"   10
And, in this brainish° apprehension,° kills
The unseen good old man.
KING: O heavy deed!
It had been so with us, had we been there:
His liberty is full of threats to all;
To you yourself, to us, to every one.   15
Alas, how shall this bloody deed be answer'd?
It will be laid to us, whose providence°
Should have kept short,° restrain'd and out of haunt,°
This mad young man: but so much was our love,
We would not understand what was most fit;   20
But, like the owner of a foul disease,
To keep it from divulging,° let it feed
Even on the pith of life. Where is he gone?
QUEEN: To draw apart the body he hath kill'd:
O'er whom his very madness, like some ore   25
Among a mineral° of metals base,
Shows itself pure; 'a weeps for what is done.
KING: O Gertrude, come away!
The sun no sooner shall the mountains touch,

---

217. draw: Come, with quibble on literal sense.   ACT IV, SCENE I.   **11. brainish:** Head-strong, passionate; **apprehension:** Conception, imagination.   **17. providence:** Foresight. **18. short:** I.e., on a short tether; **out of haunt:** Secluded.   **22. divulging:** Becoming evident.   **26. mineral:** Mine.

But we will ship him hence: and this vile deed   30
We must, with all our majesty and skill,
Both countenance and excuse. Ho, Guildenstern!

Enter Rosencrantz and Guildenstern.

Friends both, go join you with some further aid:
Hamlet in madness hath Polonius slain,
And from his mother's closet hath he dragg'd him: 35
Go seek him out; speak fair, and bring the body
Into the chapel. I pray you, haste in this.
                    [*Exeunt Rosencrantz and Guildenstern.*]
Come, Gertrude, we'll call up our wisest friends;
And let them know, both what we mean to do,
And what's untimely done . . . °   40
Whose whisper o'er the world's diameter,°
As level° as the cannon to his blank,°
Transports his pois'ned shot, may miss our name,
And hit the woundless° air. O, come away!
My soul is full of discord and dismay.   *Exeunt.* 45

[SCENE II: *Another room in the castle.*]

Enter Hamlet.

HAMLET: Safely stowed.
ROSENCRANTZ:
             } (*within*) Hamlet! Lord Hamlet!
GUILDENSTERN:
HAMLET: But soft, what noise? who calls on Hamlet? O, here they come.

Enter Rosencrantz and Guildenstern.

ROSENCRANTZ: What have you done, my lord, with the dead body?
HAMLET: Compounded it with dust, whereto 'tis kin.
ROSENCRANTZ: Tell us where 'tis, that we may take it thence   5
    And bear it to the chapel.
HAMLET: Do not believe it.
ROSENCRANTZ: Believe what?
HAMLET: That I can keep your counsel° and not mine own. Besides, to be de-
    manded of a sponge! what replication° should be made by the son of a 10
    king?
ROSENCRANTZ: Take you me for a sponge, my lord?
HAMLET: Ay, sir, that soaks up the king's countenance, his rewards, his authori-
    ties.° But such officers do the king best service in the end: he keeps them,
    like an ape an apple, in the corner of his jaw; first mouthed, to be last 15

---

40. Defective line; some editors add: *so, haply, slander;* others add: *for, haply, slander;*
other conjectures.　**41. diameter:** Extent from side to side.　**42. level:** Straight; **blank:**
White spot in the center of a target.　**44. woundless:** Invulnerable.　SCENE II.　**9. keep
your counsel:** Hamlet is aware of their treachery but says nothing about it.　**10. replica-
tion:** Reply.　**13–14. authorities:** Authoritative backing.

swallowed: when he needs what you have gleaned, it is but squeezing you, and, sponge, you shall be dry again.

ROSENCRANTZ: I understand you not, my lord.

HAMLET: I am glad of it: a knavish speech sleeps in a foolish ear.

ROSENCRANTZ: My lord, you must tell us where the body is, and go with us to   20
    the king.

HAMLET: The body is with the king, but the king is not with the body.° The
    king is a thing—

GUILDENSTERN: A thing, my lord!

HAMLET: Of nothing: bring me to him. Hide fox, and all after.°   *Exeunt.* 25

[SCENE III: *Another room in the castle.*]

Enter King, and two or three.

KING: I have sent to seek him, and to find the body.
    How dangerous is it that this man goes loose!
    Yet must not we put the strong law on him:
    He's lov'd of the distracted° multitude,
    Who like not in their judgement, but their eyes;   5
    And where 'tis so, th' offender's scourge° is weigh'd,°
    But never the offence. To bear all smooth and even,
    This sudden sending him away must seem
    Deliberate pause:° diseases desperate grown
    By desperate appliance are reliev'd,   10
    Or not at all.

Enter Rosencrantz, [Guildenstern,] and all the rest.

              How now! what hath befall'n?

ROSENCRANTZ: Where the dead body is bestow'd, my lord,
    We cannot get from him.

KING: But where is he?

ROSENCRANTZ: Without, my lord; guarded, to know your pleasure.

KING: Bring him before us.   15

ROSENCRANTZ: Ho! bring in the lord.

They enter [with Hamlet].

KING: Now, Hamlet, where's Polonius?

HAMLET: At supper.

KING: At supper! where?

HAMLET: Not where he eats, but where 'a is eaten: a certain convocation of   20
    politic° worms° are e'en at him. Your worm is your only emperor for diet:

---

22. The body . . . body: There are many interpretations; possibly, "The body lies in
death with the king, my father; but my father walks disembodied"; or "Claudius has
the bodily possession of kingship, but kingliness, or justice of inheritance, is not with
him."   **25. Hide . . . after:** An old signal cry in the game of hide-and-seek.   SCENE III.
4. distracted: I.e., without power of forming logical judgments.   **6. scourge:** Punishment; **weigh'd:** Taken into consideration.   **9. Deliberate pause:** Considered action.
20–21. convocation . . . worms: Allusion to the Diet of Worms (1521); **politic:** Crafty.

we fat all creatures else to fat us, and we fat ourselves for maggots: your
fat king and your lean beggar is but variable service,° two dishes, but to
one table: that's the end.

KING: Alas, alas! 25

HAMLET: A man may fish with the worm that hath eat of a king, and eat of the
fish that hath fed of that worm.

KING: What dost thou mean by this?

HAMLET: Nothing but to show you how a king may go a progress° through the
guts of a beggar. 30

KING: Where is Polonius?

HAMLET: In heaven; send thither to see: if your messenger find him not there,
seek him i' the other place yourself. But if indeed you find him not within
this month, you shall nose him as you go up the stairs into the lobby.

KING [*to some Attendants*]: Go seek him there. 35

HAMLET: 'A will stay till you come. [*Exeunt Attendants.*]

KING: Hamlet, this deed, for thine especial safety, —
Which we do tender,° as we dearly grieve
For that which thou hast done, — must send thee hence
With fiery quickness: therefore prepare thyself; 40
The bark is ready, and the wind at help,
Th' associates tend, and everything is bent
For England.

HAMLET: For England!

KING: Ay, Hamlet.

HAMLET: Good.

KING: So is it, if thou knew'st our purposes.

HAMLET: I see a cherub° that sees them. But, come; for England! Farewell, dear 45
mother.

KING: Thy loving father, Hamlet.

HAMLET: My mother: father and mother is man and wife; man and wife is one
flesh; and so, my mother. Come, for England!   *Exit.*

KING: Follow him at foot;° tempt him with speed aboard; 50
Delay it not; I'll have him hence to-night:
Away! for every thing is seal'd and done
That else leans on th' affair: pray you, make haste.

                                        [*Exeunt all but the King.*]
And, England, if my love thou hold'st at aught —
As my great power thereof may give thee sense, 55
Since yet thy cicatrice° looks raw and red
After the Danish sword, and thy free awe°
Pays homage to us — thou mayst not coldly set
Our sovereign process; which imports at full,

---

23. **variable service:** A variety of dishes.   29. **progress:** Royal journey of state.
38. **tender:** Regard, hold dear.   45. **cherub:** Cherubim are angels of knowledge.
50. **at foot:** Close behind, at heel.   56. **cicatrice:** Scar.   57. **free awe:** Voluntary show of
respect.

By letters congruing to that effect,   60
The present death of Hamlet. Do it, England;
For like the hectic° in my blood he rages,
And thou must cure me: till I know 'tis done,
Howe'er my haps,° my joys were ne'er begun.   *Exit.*

[SCENE IV: *A plain in Denmark.*]

Enter Fortinbras with his Army over the stage.

FORTINBRAS: Go, captain, from me greet the Danish king;
    Tell him that, by his license,° Fortinbras
    Craves the conveyance° of a promis'd march
    Over his kingdom. You know the rendezvous.
    If that his majesty would aught with us,   5
    We shall express our duty in his eye;°
    And let him know so.
CAPTAIN: I will do't, my lord.
FORTINBRAS: Go softly° on.   [*Exeunt all but Captain.*]

Enter Hamlet, Rosencrantz, [Guildenstern,] &c.

HAMLET: Good sir, whose powers are these?
CAPTAIN: They are of Norway, sir.   10
HAMLET: How purpos'd, sir, I pray you?
CAPTAIN: Against some part of Poland.
HAMLET: Who commands them, sir?
CAPTAIN: The nephew to old Norway, Fortinbras.
HAMLET: Goes it against the main° of Poland, sir,   15
    Or for some frontier?
CAPTAIN: Truly to speak, and with no addition,
    We go to gain a little patch of ground
    That hath in it no profit but the name.
    To pay five ducats, five, I would not farm it;°   20
    Nor will it yield to Norway or the Pole
    A ranker rate, should it be sold in fee.°
HAMLET: Why, then the Polack never will defend it.
CAPTAIN: Yes, it is already garrison'd.
HAMLET: Two thousand souls and twenty thousand ducats   25
    Will not debate the question of this straw:°
    This is th' imposthume° of much wealth and peace,
    That inward breaks, and shows no cause without
    Why the man dies. I humbly thank you, sir.
CAPTAIN: God be wi' you, sir.   [*Exit.*]
ROSENCRANTZ: Will 't please you go, my lord?   30

---

62. **hectic:** Fever.   64. **haps:** Fortunes.   SCENE IV.   2. **license:** Leave.   3. **conveyance:** Escort, convoy.   6. **in his eye:** In his presence.   8. **softly:** Slowly.   15. **main:**
Country itself.   20. **farm it:** Take a lease of it.   22. **fee:** Fee simple.   26. **debate . . .
straw:** Settle this trifling matter.   27. **imposthume:** Purulent abscess or swelling.

HAMLET: I'll be with you straight. Go a little before.

[Exeunt all except Hamlet.]

How all occasions° do inform against° me,
And spur my dull revenge! What is a man,
If his chief good and market of his time°
Be but to sleep and feed? a beast, no more.   35
Sure, he that made us with such large discourse,
Looking before and after, gave us not
That capability and god-like reason
To fust° in us unus'd. Now, whether it be
Bestial oblivion, or some craven scruple   40
Of thinking too precisely on th' event,
A thought which, quarter'd, hath but one part wisdom
And ever three parts coward, I do not know
Why yet I live to say "This thing 's to do";
Sith I have cause and will and strength and means   45
To do 't. Examples gross as earth exhort me:
Witness this army of such mass and charge
Led by a delicate and tender prince,
Whose spirit with divine ambition puff'd
Makes mouths at the invisible event,   50
Exposing what is mortal and unsure
To all that fortune, death and danger dare,
Even for an egg-shell. Rightly to be great
Is not to stir without great argument,
But greatly to find quarrel in a straw   55
When honour's at the stake. How stand I then,
That have a father kill'd, a mother stain'd,
Excitements of° my reason and my blood,
And let all sleep? while, to my shame, I see
The imminent death of twenty thousand men,   60
That, for a fantasy and trick° of fame,
Go to their graves like beds, fight for a plot°
Whereon the numbers cannot try the cause,
Which is not tomb enough and continent
To hide the slain? O, from this time forth,   65
My thoughts be bloody, or be nothing worth!   *Exit.*

[SCENE V: *Elsinore. A room in the castle.*]

Enter Horatio, [Queen] Gertrude, and a Gentleman.

QUEEN: I will not speak with her.

---

32. occasions: Incidents, events; **inform against:** Generally defined as "show," "betray"
(i.e., his tardiness); more probably *inform* means "take shape," as in *Macbeth,* II.i.48.
34. market of his time: The best use he makes of his time, or, that for which he sells his
time. **39. fust:** Grow moldy. **58. Excitements of:** Incentives to. **61. trick:** Toy,
trifle. **62. plot:** I.e., of ground.

GENTLEMAN: She is importunate, indeed distract:
  Her mood will needs be pitied.
QUEEN: What would she have?
GENTLEMAN: She speaks much of her father; says she hears
  There's tricks° i' th' world; and hems, and beats her heart;°   5
  Spurns enviously at straws;° speaks things in doubt,
  That carry but half sense: her speech is nothing,
  Yet the unshaped° use of it doth move
  The hearers to collection;° they yawn° at it,
  And botch° the words up fit to their own thoughts;   10
  Which, as her winks, and nods, and gestures yield° them,
  Indeed would make one think there might be thought,
  Though nothing sure, yet much unhappily.°
HORATIO: 'Twere good she were spoken with: for she may strew
  Dangerous conjectures in ill-breeding minds.°   15
QUEEN: Let her come in.   [*Exit Gentleman.*]
  [*Aside.*] To my sick soul, as sin's true nature is,
  Each toy seems prologue to some great amiss:°
  So full of artless jealousy is guilt,
  It spills itself in fearing to be spilt.°   20

Enter Ophelia [distracted].

OPHELIA: Where is the beauteous majesty of Denmark?
QUEEN: How now, Ophelia!
OPHELIA (*she sings*): How should I your true love know
      From another one?
  By his cockle hat° and staff,   25
      And his sandal shoon.°
QUEEN: Alas, sweet lady, what imports this song?
OPHELIA: Say you? nay, pray you mark.
  (*Song*) He is dead and gone, lady,
      He is dead and gone;   30
  At his head a grass-green turf,
      At his heels a stone.
  O, ho!
QUEEN: Nay, but, Ophelia —
OPHELIA: Pray you, mark   35
  [*Sings.*] White his shroud as the mountain snow, —

SCENE V. **5. tricks:** Deceptions; **heart:** I.e., breast. **6. Spurns . . . straws:** Kicks spite-
fully at small objects in her path. **8. unshaped:** Unformed, artless. **9. collection:**
Inference, a guess at some sort of meaning; **yawn:** Wonder. **10. botch:** Patch. **11. yield:**
Deliver, bring forth (her words). **13. much unhappily:** Expressive of much unhappiness. **15. ill-breeding minds:** Minds bent on mischief. **18. great amiss:** Calamity,
disaster. **19–20. So . . . spilt:** Guilt is so full of suspicion that it unskillfully betrays itself
in fearing to be betrayed. **25. cockle hat:** Hat with cockleshell stuck in it as a sign that
the wearer has been a pilgrim to the shrine of St. James of Compostella. The pilgrim's garb
was a conventional disguise for lovers. **26. shoon:** Shoes.

Enter King.

QUEEN: Alas, look here, my lord.

OPHELIA (*Song*): Larded° all with flowers;
    Which bewept to the grave did not go
        With true-love showers.   40

KING: How do you, pretty lady?

OPHELIA: Well, God 'ild° you! They say the owl° was a baker's daughter. Lord,
    we know what we are, but know not what we may be. God be at your
    table!

KING: Conceit upon her father.   45

OPHELIA: Pray let's have no words of this; but when they ask you what it means,
    say you this:

    (*Song*) To-morrow is Saint Valentine's day,
        All in the morning betime,
    And I a maid at your window,   50
        To be your Valentine.°
    Then up he rose, and donn'd his clothes,
        And dupp'd° the chamber-door;
    Let in the maid, that out a maid
        Never departed more.   55

KING: Pretty Ophelia!

OPHELIA: Indeed, la, without an oath, I'll make an end on 't:
    [*Sings.*] By Gis° and by Saint Charity,
        Alack, and fie for shame!
    Young men will do 't, if they come to 't;   60
        By cock,° they are to blame.
    Quoth she, before you tumbled me,
        You promis'd me to wed.
    So would I ha' done, by yonder sun,
        An thou hadst not come to my bed.   65

KING: How long hath she been thus?

OPHELIA: I hope all will be well. We must be patient: but I cannot choose but
    weep, to think they would lay him i' the cold ground. My brother shall
    know of it: and so I thank you for your good counsel. Come, my coach!
    Good night, ladies; good night, sweet ladies; good night, good night. 70

                                                              [*Exit.*]

KING: Follow her close; give her good watch, I pray you.   [*Exit Horatio.*]
    O, this is the poison of deep grief; it springs
    All from her father's death. O Gertrude, Gertrude,
    When sorrows come, they come not single spies,

---

38. Larded: Decorated.   **42. God 'ild:** God yield or reward; **owl:** Reference to a monk-
ish legend that a baker's daughter was turned into an owl for refusing bread to the Savior.
51. Valentine: This song alludes to the belief that the first girl seen by a man on the morning of this day was his valentine or true love.   **53. dupp'd:** Opened.   **58. Gis:** Jesus.
61. cock: Perversion of "God" in oaths.

But in battalions. First, her father slain: 75
Next your son gone; and he most violent author
Of his own just remove: the people muddied,
Thick and unwholesome in their thoughts and whispers,
For good Polonius' death; and we have done but greenly,°
In hugger-mugger° to inter him: poor Ophelia   80
Divided from herself and her fair judgement,
Without the which we are pictures, or mere beasts:
Last, and as much containing as all these,
Her brother is in secret come from France;
Feeds on his wonder, keeps himself in clouds,°   85
And wants not buzzers° to infect his ear
With pestilent speeches of his father's death;
Wherein necessity, of matter beggar'd,°
Will nothing stick° our person to arraign
In ear and ear.° O my dear Gertrude, this,   90
Like to a murd'ring-piece,° in many places
Gives me superfluous death.   *A noise within.*

QUEEN: Alack, what noise is this?

KING: Where are my Switzers?° Let them guard the door.

Enter a Messenger.

What is the matter?

MESSENGER: Save yourself, my lord:
The ocean, overpeering° of his list,°   95
Eats not the flats with more impiteous haste
Than young Laertes, in a riotous head,
O'erbears your officers. The rabble call him lord;
And, as the world were now but to begin,
Antiquity forgot, custom not known,   100
The ratifiers and props of every word,°
They cry "Choose we: Laertes shall be king":
Caps, hands, and tongues, applaud it to the clouds:
"Laertes shall be king, Laertes king!"   *A noise within.*

QUEEN: How cheerfully on the false trail they cry!   105
O, this is counter,° you false Danish dogs!

KING: The doors are broke.

Enter Laertes with others.

---

79. greenly: Foolishly.   **80. hugger-mugger:** Secret haste.   **85. in clouds:** Invisible.
86. buzzers: Gossipers.   **88. of matter beggar'd:** Unprovided with facts.   **89. nothing stick:** Not hesitate.   **90. In ear and ear:** In everybody's ears.   **91. murd'ring-piece:** Small cannon or mortar; suggestion of numerous missiles fired.   **93. Switzers:** Swiss guards, mercenaries.   **95. overpeering:** Overflowing; **list:** Shore.   **101. word:** Promise.   **106. counter:** A hunting term meaning to follow the trail in a direction opposite to that which the game has taken.

LAERTES: Where is this king? Sirs, stand you all without.
DANES: No, let's come in.
LAERTES: I pray you, give me leave.
DANES: We will, we will.   [*They retire without the door.*] 110
LAERTES: I thank you: keep the door. O thou vile king,
     Give me my father!
QUEEN: Calmly, good Laertes.
LAERTES: That drop of blood that's calm proclaims me bastard,
     Cries cuckold to my father, brands the harlot
     Even here, between the chaste unsmirched brow   115
     Of my true mother.
KING: What is the cause, Laertes,
     That thy rebellion looks so giant-like?
     Let him go, Gertrude; do not fear our person:
     There's such divinity doth hedge a king,
     That treason can but peep to° what it would°   120
     Acts little of his will. Tell me, Laertes,
     Why thou art thus incens'd. Let him go, Gertrude.
     Speak, man.
LAERTES: Where is my father?
KING: Dead.
QUEEN: But not by him.
KING: Let him demand his fill.   125
LAERTES: How came he dead? I'll not be juggled with:
     To hell, allegiance! vows, to the blackest devil!
     Conscience and grace, to the profoundest pit!
     I dare damnation. To this point I stand,
     That both the worlds I give to negligence,°   130
     Let come what comes; only I'll be reveng'd
     Most throughly° for my father.
KING: Who shall stay you?
LAERTES: My will,° not all the world's:
     And for my means, I'll husband them so well,
     They shall go far with little.
KING: Good Laertes,   135
     If you desire to know the certainty
     Of your dear father, is 't writ in your revenge,
     That, swoopstake,° you will draw both friend and foe,
     Winner and loser?
LAERTES: None but his enemies.
KING: Will you know them then?   140
LAERTES: To his good friends thus wide I'll ope my arms;

---

120. **peep to:** I.e., look at from afar off; **would:** Wishes to do.   130. **give to negligence:**
He despises both the here and the hereafter.   132. **throughly:** thoroughly.   133. **My
will:** He will not be stopped except by his own will.   138. **swoopstake:** Literally, drawing the whole stake at once, i.e., indiscriminately.

And like the kind life-rend'ring pelican,°
Repast° them with my blood.
KING: Why, now you speak
Like a good child and a true gentleman.
That I am guiltless of your father's death,   145
And am most sensibly in grief for it,
It shall as level to your judgement 'pear
As day does to your eye.   *A noise within: "Let her come in."*
LAERTES: How now! what noise is that?

Enter Ophelia.

O heat,° dry up my brains! tears seven times salt,   150
Burn out the sense and virtue of mine eye!
By heaven, thy madness shall be paid with weight,
Till our scale turn the beam. O rose of May!
Dear maid, kind sister, sweet Ophelia!
O heavens! is 't possible, a young maid's wits   155
Should be as mortal as an old man's life?
Nature is fine in love, and where 'tis fine,
It sends some precious instance of itself
After the thing it loves.
OPHELIA (*Song*): They bore him barefac'd on the bier;   160
Hey non nonny, nonny, hey nonny;
And in his grave rain'd many a tear: —
Fare you well, my dove!
LAERTES: Hadst thou thy wits, and didst persuade revenge,
It could not move thus.   165
OPHELIA [*sings*]: You must sing a-down a-down,
An you call him a-down-a.
O, how the wheel° becomes it! It is the false steward,° that stole his mas-
ter's daughter.
LAERTES: This nothing's more than matter.   170
OPHELIA: There's rosemary,° that's for remembrance; pray you, love, remem-
ber: and there is pansies,° that's for thoughts.
LAERTES: A document° in madness, thoughts and remembrance fitted.
OPHELIA: There's fennel° for you, and columbines:° there's rue° for you; and
here's some for me: we may call it herb of grace o' Sundays: O, you must 175

---

142. pelican: Reference to the belief that the pelican feeds its young with its own blood.
143. Repast: Feed.   **150. heat:** Probably the heat generated by the passion of grief.
168. wheel: Spinning wheel as accompaniment to the song refrain; **false steward:** The
story is unknown.   **171. rosemary:** Used as a symbol of remembrance both at weddings
and at funerals.   **172. pansies:** Emblems of love and courtship. Cf. French *pensées.*
173. document: Piece of instruction or lesson.   **174. fennel:** Emblem of flattery;
columbines: Emblem of unchastity (?) or ingratitude(?); **rue:** Emblem of repentance. It
was usually mingled with holy water and then known as *herb of grace.* Ophelia is probably
playing on the two meanings of *rue,* "repentant" and "even for ruth (pity)"; the former
signification is for the queen, the latter for herself.

wear your rue with a difference. There's a daisy:° I would give you some
violets,° but they withered all when my father died: they say 'a made a
good end, —

[*Sings.*] For bonny sweet Robin is all my joy.°

LAERTES: Thought° and affliction, passion, hell itself,   180
She turns to favour and to prettiness.

OPHELIA (*Song*): And will 'a not come again?°
And will 'a not come again?
   No, no, he is dead:
   Go to thy death-bed: 185
He never will come again.

His beard was as white as snow,
All flaxen was his poll:°
   He is gone, he is gone,
   And we cast away° moan: 190
God ha' mercy on his soul!
And of all Christian souls, I pray God. God be wi' you.   [*Exit.*]

LAERTES: Do you see this, O God?

KING: Laertes, I must commune with your grief,
Or you deny me right.° Go but apart,   195
Make choice of whom your wisest friends you will,
And they shall hear and judge 'twixt you and me:
If by direct or by collateral° hand
They find us touch'd,° we will our kingdom give,
Our crown, our life, and all that we call ours,   200
To you in satisfaction; but if not,
Be you content to lend your patience to us,
And we shall jointly labour with your soul
To give it due content.

LAERTES: Let this be so;
His means of death, his obscure funeral —   205
No trophy, sword, nor hatchment° o'er his bones,
No noble rite nor formal ostentation —
Cry to be heard, as 'twere from heaven to earth,
That I must call 't in question.

KING: So you shall;
And where th' offence is let the great axe fall.   210
I pray you, go with me.   *Exeunt.*

---

176. **daisy:** Emblem of dissembling, faithlessness.   177. **violets:** Emblems of faithful-
ness.   179. **For . . . joy:** Probably a line from a Robin Hood ballad.   180. **Thought:**
Melancholy thought.   182. **And . . . again:** This song appeared in the songbooks as
"The Merry Milkmaids' Dumps."   188. **poll:** Head.   190. **cast away:** Shipwrecked.
195. **right:** My rights.   198. **collateral:** Indirect.   199. **touch'd:** Implicated.   206.
hatchment: Tablet displaying the armorial bearings of a deceased person.

[SCENE VI: *Another room in the castle.*]

Enter Horatio and others.

HORATIO: What are they that would speak with me?

GENTLEMAN: Sea-faring men, sir: they say they have letters for you.

HORATIO: Let them come in.   [*Exit Gentleman.*]
    I do not know from what part of the world
    I should be greeted, if not from lord Hamlet.   5

Enter Sailors.

FIRST SAILOR: God bless you, sir.

HORATIO: Let him bless thee too.

FIRST SAILOR: 'A shall sir, an 't please him. There's a letter for you, sir; it comes
    from the ambassador that was bound for England; if your name be Hora-
    tio, as I am let to know it is.   10

HORATIO [*reads*]: "Horatio, when thou shalt have overlooked this, give these
    fellows some means° to the king: they have letters for him. Ere we were
    two days old at sea, a pirate of very warlike appointment gave us chase.
    Finding ourselves too slow of sail, we put on a compelled valour, and in
    the grapple I boarded them: on the instant they got clear of our ship; so I   15
    alone became their prisoner. They have dealt with me like thieves of
    mercy:° but they knew what they did; I am to do a good turn for them.
    Let the king have the letters I have sent; and repair thou to me with as
    much speed as thou wouldest fly death. I have words to speak in thine ear
    will make thee dumb; yet are they much too light for the bore° of the   20
    matter. These good fellows will bring thee where I am. Rosencrantz and
    Guildenstern hold their course for England: of them I have much to tell
    thee. Farewell.

                                  "He that thou knowest thine, HAMLET."

Come, I will give you way for these your letters;   25
And do 't the speedier, that you may direct me
To him from whom you brought them.   *Exeunt.*

[SCENE VII: *Another room in the castle.*]

Enter King and Laertes.

KING: Now must your conscience° my acquittance seal,
    And you must put me in your heart for friend,
    Sith you have heard, and with a knowing ear,
    That he which hath your noble father slain
    Pursued my life.

LAERTES: It well appears: but tell me   5
    Why you proceeded not against these feats,
    So criminal and so capital° in nature,

SCENE VI.   **12. means:** Means of access.   **16–17. thieves of mercy:** Merciful thieves.
20. bore: Caliber, importance.   SCENE VII.   **1. conscience:** Knowledge that this is
true.   **7. capital:** Punishable by death.

As by your safety, wisdom, all things else,
You mainly° were stirr'd up.

KING: O, for two special reasons;
Which may to you, perhaps, seem much unsinew'd,°   10
But yet to me th' are strong. The queen his mother
Lives almost by his looks; and for myself—
My virtue or my plague, be it either which—
She's so conjunctive° to my life and soul,
That, as the star moves not but in his sphere,°   15
I could not but by her. The other motive,
Why to a public count° I might not go,
Is the great love the general gender° bear him;
Who, dipping all his faults in their affection,
Would, like the spring° that turneth wood to stone,   20
Convert his gyves° to graces; so that my arrows,
Too slightly timber'd° for so loud° a wind,
Would have reverted to my bow again,
And not where I had aim'd them.

LAERTES: And so have I a noble father lost;   25
A sister driven into desp'rate terms,°
Whose worth, if praises may go back° again,
Stood challenger on mount° of all the age°
For her perfections: but my revenge will come.

KING: Break not your sleeps for that: you must not think 30
That we are made of stuff so flat and dull
That we can let our beard be shook with danger
And think it pastime. You shortly shall hear more:
I lov'd your father, and we love ourself;
And that, I hope, will teach you to imagine—   35

Enter a Messenger with letters.

How now! what news?

MESSENGER: Letters, my lord, from Hamlet:
These to your majesty; this to the queen.°

KING: From Hamlet! who brought them?

MESSENGER: Sailors, my lord, they say; I saw them not:
They were given me by Claudio;° he receiv'd them   40
Of him that brought them.

---

9. mainly: Greatly. **10. unsinew'd:** Weak. **14. conjunctive:** Conformable (the next line suggesting planetary conjunction). **15. sphere:** The hollow sphere in which, according to Ptolemaic astronomy, the planets were supposed to move. **17. count:** Account, reckoning. **18. general gender:** Common people. **20. spring:** I.e., one heavily charged with lime. **21. gyves:** Fetters; here, faults, or possibly, punishments inflicted (on him). **22. slightly timber'd:** Light; **loud:** Strong. **26. terms:** State, condition. **27. go back:** I.e., to Ophelia's former virtues. **28. on mount:** Set up on high, *mounted* (on horseback); **of all the age:** Qualifies *challenger* and not *mount*. **37. to the queen:** One hears no more of the letter to the queen. **40. Claudio:** This character does not appear in the play.

KING: Laertes, you shall hear them.
 Leave us.   [*Exit Messenger.*]
 [*Reads.*] "High and mighty, You shall know I am set naked° on your
 kingdom. To-morrow shall I beg leave to see your kingly eyes: when I
 shall, first asking your pardon thereunto, recount the occasion of my sud- 45
 den and more strange return.   "HAMLET."
 What should this mean? Are all the rest come back?
 Or is it some abuse, and no such thing?
LAERTES: Know you the hand?
KING: 'Tis Hamlet's character. "Naked!"
 And in a postscript here, he says "alone."   50
 Can you devise° me?
LAERTES: I'm lost in it, my lord. But let him come;
 It warms the very sickness in my heart,
 That I shall live and tell him to his teeth,
 "Thus didst thou."
KING: If it be so, Laertes —   55
 As how should it be so? how otherwise?° —
 Will you be rul'd by me?
LAERTES: Ay, my lord;
 So you will not o'errule me to a peace.
KING: To thine own peace. If he be now return'd,
 As checking at° his voyage, and that he means   60
 No more to undertake it, I will work him
 To an exploit, now ripe in my device,
 Under the which he shall not choose but fall:
 And for his death no wind of blame shall breathe,
 But even his mother shall uncharge the practice°   65
 And call it accident.
LAERTES: My lord, I will be rul'd;
 The rather, if you could devise it so
 That I might be the organ.°
KING: It falls right.
 You have been talk'd of since your travel much,
 And that in Hamlet's hearing, for a quality   70
 Wherein, they say, you shine: your sum of parts
 Did not together pluck such envy from him
 As did that one, and that, in my regard,
 Of the unworthiest siege.°
LAERTES: What part is that, my lord?

---

43. naked: Unprovided (with retinue).   **51. devise:** Explain to.   **56. As . . . otherwise?**
How can this (Hamlet's return) be true? (yet) how otherwise than true (since we have the
evidence of his letter)? Some editors read *How should it not be so*, etc., making the words
refer to Laertes' desire to meet with Hamlet.   **60. checking at:** Used in falconry of a
hawk's leaving the quarry to fly at a chance bird, turn aside.   **65. uncharge the practice:**
Acquit the stratagem of being a plot.   **68. organ:** Agent, instrument.   **74. siege:** Rank.

KING: A very riband in the cap of youth,   75
    Yet needful too; for youth no less becomes
    The light and careless livery that it wears
    Than settled age his sables° and his weeds,
    Importing health and graveness. Two months since,
    Here was a gentleman of Normandy: —   80
    I have seen myself, and serv'd against, the French,
    And they can well° on horseback: but this gallant
    Had witchcraft in 't; he grew unto his seat;
    And to such wondrous doing brought his horse,
    As had he been incorps'd and demi-natur'd°   85
    With the brave beast: so far he topp'd° my thought,
    That I, in forgery° of shapes and tricks,
    Come short of what he did.
LAERTES: A Norman was 't?
KING: A Norman.
LAERTES: Upon my life, Lamord.°
KING: The very same.   90
LAERTES: I know him well: he is the brooch indeed
    And gem of all the nation.
KING: He made confession° of you,
    And gave you such a masterly report
    For art and exercise° in your defence°   95
    And for your rapier most especial,
    That he cried out, 'twould be a sight indeed,
    If one could match you: the scrimers° of their nation,
    He swore, had neither motion, guard, nor eye,
    If you oppos'd them. Sir, this report of his   100
    Did Hamlet so envenom with his envy
    That he could nothing do but wish and beg
    Your sudden coming o'er, to play° with you.
    Now, out of this, —
LAERTES: What out of this, my lord?
KING: Laertes, was your father dear to you?   105
    Or are you like the painting of a sorrow,
    A face without a heart?
LAERTES: Why ask you this?
KING: Not that I think you did not love your father;
    But that I know love is begun by time;
    And that I see, in passages of proof,°   110

---

78. **sables:** Rich garments.   82. **can well:** Are skilled.   85. **incorps'd and demi-natur'd:** Of one body and nearly of one nature (like the centaur). 86. **topp'd:** Surpassed. 87. **forgery:** Invention.   90. **Lamord:** This refers possibly to Pietro Monte, instructor to Louis XII's master of the horse.   93. **confession:** Grudging admission of superiority. 95. **art and exercise:** Skillful exercise; **defence:** Science of defense in sword practice. 98. **scrimers:** Fencers.   103. **play:** Fence.   110. **passages of proof:** Proved instances.

Time qualifies the spark and fire of it.
There lives within the very flame of love
A kind of wick or snuff that will abate it;
And nothing is at a like goodness still;
For goodness, growing to a plurisy,°   115
Dies in his own too much:° that we would do,
We should do when we would; for this "would" changes
And hath abatements° and delays as many
As there are tongues, are hands, are accidents;°
And then this "should" is like a spendthrift° sigh,   120
That hurts by easing. But, to the quick o' th' ulcer:° —
Hamlet comes back: what would you undertake,
To show yourself your father's son in deed
More than in words?
LAERTES: To cut his throat i' th' church.
KING: No place, indeed, should murder sanctuarize;°   125
Revenge should have no bounds. But, good Laertes,
Will you do this, keep close within your chamber.
Hamlet return'd shall know you are come home:
We'll put on those shall praise your excellence
And set a double varnish on the fame   130
The Frenchman gave you, bring you in fine together
And wager on your heads: he, being remiss,
Most generous and free from all contriving,
Will not peruse the foils; so that, with ease,
Or with a little shuffling, you may choose   135
A sword unbated,° and in a pass of practice°
Requite him for your father.
LAERTES: I will do 't:
And, for that purpose, I'll anoint my sword.
I bought an unction of a mountebank,°
So mortal that, but dip a knife in it,   140
Where it draws blood no cataplasm° so rare,
Collected from all simples° that have virtue
Under the moon,° can save the thing from death
That is but scratch'd withal: I'll touch my point
With this contagion, that, if I gall° him slightly,   145
It may be death.

---

115. plurisy: Excess, plethora.   **116. in his own too much:** Of its own excess.
118. abatements: Diminutions.   **119. accidents:** Occurrences, incidents.   **120. spend-thrift:** An allusion to the belief that each sigh cost the heart a drop of blood.   **121. quick o' th' ulcer:** Heart of the difficulty.   **125. sanctuarize:** Protect from punishment; allusion to the right of sanctuary with which certain religious places were invested.   **136. unbated:** Not blunted, having no button; **pass of practice:** Treacherous thrust.   **139. mountebank:** Quack doctor.   **141. cataplasm:** Plaster or poultice.   **142. simples:** Herbs.   **143. Under the moon:** I.e., when collected by moonlight to add to their medicinal value.   **145. gall:** Graze, wound.

KING: Let's further think of this;
    Weigh what convenience both of time and means
    May fit us to our shape:° if this should fail,
    And that our drift look through our bad performance,°
    'Twere better not assay'd: therefore this project   150
    Should have a back or second, that might hold,
    If this should blast in proof.° Soft! let me see:
    We'll make a solemn wager on your cunnings:°
    I ha 't:
    When in your motion you are hot and dry—   155
    As make your bouts more violent to that end—
    And that he calls for drink, I'll have prepar'd him
    A chalice° for the nonce, whereon but sipping,
    If he by chance escape your venom'd stuck,°
    Our purpose may hold there. But stay, what noise?   160

Enter Queen.

QUEEN: One woe doth tread upon another's heel,
    So fast they follow: your sister's drown'd, Laertes.
LAERTES: Drown'd! O, where?
QUEEN: There is a willow° grows askant° the brook,
    That shows his hoar° leaves in the glassy stream;   165
    There with fantastic garlands did she make
    Of crow-flowers,° nettles, daisies, and long purples°
    That liberal° shepherds give a grosser name,
    But our cold maids do dead men's fingers call them:
    There, on the pendent boughs her crownet° weeds   170
    Clamb'ring to hang, an envious sliver° broke;
    When down her weedy° trophies and herself
    Fell in the weeping brook. Her clothes spread wide;
    And, mermaid-like, awhile they bore her up:
    Which time she chanted snatches of old lauds;°   175
    As one incapable° of her own distress,
    Or like a creature native and indued°
    Upon that element: but long it could not be
    Till that her garments, heavy with their drink,
    Pull'd the poor wretch from her melodious lay   180
    To muddy death.

---

148. **shape:** Part we propose to act.   149. **drift . . . performance:** Intention be disclosed by our bungling.   152. **blast in proof:** Burst in the test (like a cannon).   153. **cunnings:** Skills.   158. **chalice:** Cup.   159. **stuck:** Thrust (from *stoccado*).   164. **willow:** For its significance of forsaken love; **askant:** Aslant.   165. **hoar:** White (i.e., on the underside).   167. **crow-flowers:** Buttercups; **long purples:** Early purple orchids.   168. **liberal:** Probably, free-spoken.   170. **crownet:** Coronet; made into a chaplet.   171. **sliver:** Branch.   172. **weedy:** I.e., of plants.   175. **lauds:** Hymns.   176. **incapable:** Lacking capacity to apprehend.   177. **indued:** Endowed with qualities fitting her for living in water.

LAERTES: Alas, then, she is drown'd?

QUEEN: Drown'd, drown'd.

LAERTES: Too much of water hast thou, poor Ophelia,
  And therefore I forbid my tears: but yet
  It is our trick;° nature her custom holds,   185
  Let shame say what it will: when these are gone,
  The woman will be out.° Adieu, my lord:
  I have a speech of fire, that fain would blaze,
  But that this folly drowns it.   *Exit.*

KING: Let's follow, Gertrude:
  How much I had to do to calm his rage!   190
  Now fear I this will give it start again;
  Therefore let 's follow.   *Exeunt.*

[ACT V

SCENE I: *A churchyard.*]

Enter two Clowns° [*with spades, &c.*].

FIRST CLOWN: Is she to be buried in Christian burial when she wilfully seeks her
  own salvation?

SECOND CLOWN: I tell thee she is; therefore make her grave straight:° the
  crowner° hath sat on her, and finds it Christian burial.

FIRST CLOWN: How can that be, unless she drowned herself in her own defence?   5

SECOND CLOWN: Why, 'tis found so.

FIRST CLOWN: It must be "se offendendo";° it cannot be else. For here lies the
  point: if I drown myself wittingly,° it argues an act: and an act hath three
  branches;° it is, to act, to do, and to perform: argal,° she drowned herself
  wittingly.   10

SECOND CLOWN: Nay, but hear you, goodman delver,° —

FIRST CLOWN: Give me leave. Here lies the water; good: here stands the man;
  good: if the man go to this water, and drown himself, it is, will he, nill he,
  he goes, — mark you that; but if the water come to him and drown him,
  he drowns not himself: argal, he that is not guilty of his own death short-   15
  ens not his own life.

SECOND CLOWN: But is this law?

FIRST CLOWN: Ay, marry, is 't; crowner's quest° law.

SECOND CLOWN: Will you ha' the truth on 't? If this had not been a
  gentlewoman, she should have been buried out o' Christian burial.   20

---

185. **trick:** Way.   186–187. **when . . . out:** When my tears are all shed, the woman in
me will be satisfied.   ACT V, SCENE I.   **s.d. Clowns:** The word *clown* was used to
denote peasants as well as humorous characters; here applied to the rustic type of clown.
3. straight: Straightway, immediately; some interpret "from east to west in a direct
line, parallel with the church."   **4. crowner:** Coroner.   **7. "se offendendo":** For *se
defendendo,* term used in verdicts of justifiable homicide.   **8. wittingly:** Intentionally.
8–9. three branches: Parody of legal phraseology; **argal:** Corruption of *ergo,* therefore.
11. delver: Digger.   **18. quest:** Inquest.

FIRST CLOWN: Why, there thou say'st:° and the more pity that great folk should have countenance° in this world to drown or hang themselves, more than their even° Christian. Come, my spade. There is no ancient gentlemen but gardeners, ditchers, and grave-makers: they hold up° Adam's profession.   25

SECOND CLOWN: Was he a gentleman?

FIRST CLOWN: 'A was the first that ever bore arms.

SECOND CLOWN: Why, he had none.

FIRST CLOWN: What, art a heathen? How dost thou understand the Scripture? The Scripture says "Adam digged": could he dig without arms? I'll put 30 another question to thee: if thou answerest me not to the purpose, confess thyself° —

SECOND CLOWN: Go to.°

FIRST CLOWN: What is he that builds stronger than either the mason, the shipwright, or the carpenter?   35

SECOND CLOWN: The gallows-maker; for that frame outlives a thousand tenants.

FIRST CLOWN: I like thy wit well, in good faith: the gallows does well; but how does it well? it does well to those that do ill: now thou dost ill to say the gallows is built stronger than the church: argal, the gallows may do well 40 to thee. To 't again, come.

SECOND CLOWN: "Who builds stronger than a mason, a shipwright, or a carpenter?"

FIRST CLOWN: Ay, tell me that, and unyoke.°

SECOND CLOWN: Marry, now I can tell.   45

FIRST CLOWN: To 't.

SECOND CLOWN: Mass,° I cannot tell.

Enter Hamlet and Horatio [at a distance].

FIRST CLOWN: Cudgel thy brains no more about it, for your dull ass will not mend his pace with beating; and, when you are asked this question next, say "a grave-maker": the houses he makes lasts till doomsday. Go, get 50 thee in, and fetch me a stoup° of liquor.

[Exit Second Clown.] Song. [He digs.]

In youth, when I did love, did love,
  Methought it was very sweet,
To contract — O — the time, for — a — my behove,°
O, methought, there — a — was nothing — a — meet.   55

HAMLET: Has this fellow no feeling of his business, that 'a sings at grave-making?

HORATIO: Custom hath made it in him a property of easiness.°

---

21. there thou say'st: That's right.   22. countenance: Privilege.   23. even: Fellow.
24. hold up: Maintain, continue.   31–32. confess thyself: "And be hanged" completes
the proverb.   33. Go to: Perhaps, "begin," or some other form of concession.   44. unyoke: After this great effort you may unharness the team of your wits.   47. Mass: By the
Mass.   51. stoup: Two-quart measure.   54. behove: Benefit.   58. property of easiness: A peculiarity that now is easy.

HAMLET: 'Tis e'en so: the hand of little employment hath the daintier sense.

FIRST CLOWN: (*Song.*) But age, with his stealing steps,   60
>   Hath claw'd me in his clutch,
>   And hath shipped me into the land
>   As if I had never been such.   [*Throws up a skull.*]

HAMLET: That skull had a tongue in it, and could sing once: how the knave jowls° it to the ground, as if 'twere Cain's jaw-bone,° that did the first   65
murder! This might be the pate of a politician,° which this ass now o'er-reaches;° one that would circumvent God, might it not?

HORATIO: It might, my lord.

HAMLET: Or of a courtier; which could say "Good morrow, sweet lord! How dost thou, sweet lord?" This might be my lord such-a-one, that praised   70
my lord such-a-one's horse, when he meant to beg it; might it not?

HORATIO: Ay, my lord.

HAMLET: Why, e'en so: and now my Lady Worm's; chapless,° and knocked about the mazzard° with a sexton's spade: here's fine revolution, an we had the trick to see 't. Did these bones cost no more the breeding, but to   75
play at loggats° with 'em? mine ache to think on 't.

FIRST CLOWN: (*Song.*) A pick-axe, and a spade, a spade,
>   For and° a shrouding sheet:
>   O, a pit of clay for to be made
>   For such a guest is meet.   [*Throws up another skull.*]   80

HAMLET: There's another: why may not that be the skull of a lawyer? Where be his quiddities° now, his quillities,° his cases, his tenures,° and his tricks? why does he suffer this mad knave now to knock him about the sconce° with a dirty shovel, and will not tell him of his action of battery? Hum! This fellow might be in 's time a great buyer of land, with his statutes, his   85
recognizances,° his fines, his double vouchers,° his recoveries:° is this the fine° of his fines, and the recovery of his recoveries, to have his fine pate full of fine dirt? will his vouchers vouch him no more of his purchases, and double ones too, than the length and breadth of a pair of inden-tures?° The very conveyances of his lands will scarcely lie in this box; and   90
must the inheritor° himself have no more, ha?

HORATIO: Not a jot more, my lord.

HAMLET: Is not parchment made of sheep-skins?

---

65. **jowls:** Dashes; **Cain's jaw-bone:** Allusion to the old tradition that Cain slew Abel with the jawbone of an ass.   66. **politician:** Schemer, plotter.   66–67. **o'er-reaches:** Quibble on the literal sense and the sense "circumvent."   73. **chapless:** Having no lower jaw.   74. **mazzard:** Head.   76. **loggats:** A game in which six sticks are thrown to lie as near as possible to a stake fixed in the ground, or block of wood on a floor.   78. **For and:** And moreover.   82. **quiddities:** Subtleties, quibbles; **quillities:** Verbal niceties, subtle distinctions; **tenures:** The holding of a piece of property or office or the conditions or period of such holding.   83. **sconce:** Head.   85–86. **statutes, recognizances:** Legal terms connected with the transfer of land; **vouchers:** Persons called on to warrant a ten-ant's title; **recoveries:** Process for transfer of entailed estate.   87. **fine:** The four uses of this word are as follows: (1) end, (2) legal process, (3) elegant, (4) small.   90. **indentures:** Conveyances or contracts.   91. **inheritor:** Possessor, owner.

HORATIO: Ay, my lord, and of calf-skins° too.

HAMLET: They are sheep and calves which seek out assurance in that.° I will   95
speak to this fellow. Whose grave's this, sirrah?

FIRST CLOWN: Mine, sir.

[*Sings.*] O, a pit of clay for to be made
For such a guest is meet.

HAMLET: I think it be thine, indeed; for thou liest in 't.   100

FIRST CLOWN: You lie out on 't, sir, and therefore 't is not yours: for my part, I do
not lie in 't, yet it is mine.

HAMLET: Thou dost lie in 't, to be in 't and say it is thine: 'tis for the dead, not
for the quick; therefore thou liest.

FIRST CLOWN: 'Tis a quick lie, sir; 'twill away again, from me to you.   105

HAMLET: What man dost thou dig it for?

FIRST CLOWN: For no man, sir.

HAMLET: What woman, then?

FIRST CLOWN: For none, neither.

HAMLET: Who is to be buried in 't?   110

FIRST CLOWN: One that was a woman, sir; but, rest her soul, she's dead.

HAMLET: How absolute° the knave is! we must speak by the card,° or equivoca-
tion° will undo us. By the Lord, Horatio, these three years I have taken
note of it; the age is grown so picked° that the toe of the peasant comes so
near the heel of the courtier, he galls° his kibe.° How long hast thou been   115
a grave-maker?

FIRST CLOWN: Of all the day i' the year, I came to 't that day that our last king
Hamlet overcame Fortinbras.

HAMLET: How long is that since?

FIRST CLOWN: Cannot you tell that? every fool can tell that: it was the very day   120
that young Hamlet was born; he that is mad, and sent into England.

HAMLET: Ay, marry, why was he sent into England?

FIRST CLOWN: Why, because 'a was mad: 'a shall recover his wits there; or, if 'a
do not, 'tis no great matter there.

HAMLET: Why?   125

FIRST CLOWN: 'Twill not be seen in him there; there the men are as mad as he.

HAMLET: How came he mad?

FIRST CLOWN: Very strangely, they say.

HAMLET: How strangely?

FIRST CLOWN: Faith, e'en with losing his wits.   130

HAMLET: Upon what ground?

FIRST CLOWN: Why, here in Denmark: I have been sexton here, man and boy,
thirty years.°

---

94. **calf-skins:** Parchments.   95. **assurance in that:** Safety in legal parchments.
112. **absolute:** Positive, decided; **by the card:** With precision, i.e., by the mariner's card
on which the points of the compass were marked.   112–113. **equivocation:** Ambiguity
in the use of terms.   114. **picked:** Refined, fastidious.   115. **galls:** Chafes; **kibe:** Chil-
blain.   133. **thirty years:** This statement with that in lines 120–121 shows Hamlet's age
to be thirty years.

HAMLET: How long will a man lie i' the earth ere he rot?

FIRST CLOWN: Faith, if 'a be not rotten before 'a die—as we have many pocky° 135
corses now-a-days, that will scarce hold the laying in—'a will last you
some eight year or nine year: a tanner will last you nine year.

HAMLET: Why he more than another?

FIRST CLOWN: Why, sir, his hide is so tanned with his trade, that 'a will keep out
water a great while; and your water is a sore decayer of your whoreson 140
dead body. Here's a skull now hath lain you i' th' earth three and twenty
years.

HAMLET: Whose was it?

FIRST CLOWN: A whoreson mad fellow's it was: whose do you think it was?

HAMLET: Nay, I know not. 145

FIRST CLOWN: A pestilence on him for a mad rogue! 'a poured a flagon of Rhenish on my head once. This same skull, sir, was Yorick's skull, the king's
jester.

HAMLET: This?

FIRST CLOWN: E'en that. 150

HAMLET: Let me see. [*Takes the skull.*] Alas, poor Yorick! I knew him, Horatio: a
fellow of infinite jest, of most excellent fancy: he hath borne me on his
back a thousand times; and now, how abhorred in my imagination it is!
my gorge rises at it. Here hung those lips that I have kissed I know not
how oft. Where be your gibes now? your gambols? your songs? your 155
flashes of merriment, that were wont to set the table on a roar? Not one
now, to mock your own grinning? quite chap-fallen? Now get you to my
lady's chamber, and tell her, let her paint an inch thick, to this favour she
must come; make her laugh at that. Prithee, Horatio, tell me one thing.

HORATIO: What's that, my lord? 160

HAMLET: Dost thou think Alexander looked o' this fashion i' the earth?

HORATIO: E'en so.

HAMLET: And smelt so? pah!   [*Puts down the skull.*]

HORATIO: E'en so, my lord.

HAMLET: To what base uses we may return, Horatio! Why may not imagination 165
trace the noble dust of Alexander, till 'a find it stopping a bunghole?

HORATIO: 'Twere to consider too curiously,° to consider so.

HAMLET: No, faith, not a jot; but to follow him thither with modesty enough,
and likelihood to lead it: as thus: Alexander died, Alexander was buried,
Alexander returneth into dust; the dust is earth; of earth we make loam;° 170
and why of that loam, whereto he was converted, might they not stop a
beer-barrel?

> Imperious° Cæsar, dead and turn'd to clay,
> Might stop a hole to keep the wind away:
> O, that that earth, which kept the world in awe, 175
> Should patch a wall t'expel the winter's flaw!°
> But soft! but soft awhile! here comes the king,

---

135. **pocky:** Rotten, diseased.   167. **curiously:** Minutely.   170. **loam:** Clay paste for
brickmaking.   173. **Imperious:** Imperial.   176. **flaw:** Gust of wind.

*Enter King, Queen, Laertes, and the Corse of [Ophelia, in procession, with Priest,
Lords, etc.].*

	The queen, the courtiers: who is this they follow?	
	And with such maimed rites? This doth betoken	
	The corse they follow did with desp'rate hand	180
	Fordo° it° own life: 'twas of some estate.	
	Couch° we awhile, and mark. [*Retiring with Horatio.*]	

LAERTES: What ceremony else?

HAMLET: That is Laertes,
    A very noble youth: mark.

LAERTES: What ceremony else?   185

FIRST PRIEST: Her obsequies have been as far enlarg'd°
    As we have warranty: her death was doubtful;
    And, but that great command o'ersways the order,
    She should in ground unsanctified have lodg'd
    Till the last trumpet; for charitable prayers,   190
    Shards,° flints and pebbles should be thrown on her:
    Yet here she is allow'd her virgin crants,°
    Her maiden strewments° and the bringing home
    Of bell and burial.°

LAERTES: Must there no more be done?

FIRST PRIEST: No more be done: 195
    We should profane the service of the dead
    To sing a requiem and such rest to her
    As to peace-parted° souls.

LAERTES: Lay her i' th' earth:
    And from her fair and unpolluted flesh
    May violets spring! I tell thee, churlish priest,   200
    A minist'ring angel shall my sister be,
    When thou liest howling.°

HAMLET: What, the fair Ophelia!

QUEEN: Sweets to the sweet: farewell!   [*Scattering flowers.*]
    I hop'd thou shouldst have been my Hamlet's wife;
    I thought thy bride-bed to have deck'd, sweet maid,   205
    And not have strew'd thy grave.

LAERTES: O, treble woe
    Fall ten times treble on that cursed head,
    Whose wicked deed thy most ingenious sense°
    Depriv'd thee of! Hold off the earth awhile,

---

181. Fordo: Destroy; **it:** Its.   **182. Couch:** Hide, lurk.   **186. enlarg'd:** Extended, referring to the fact that suicides are not given full burial rites.   **191. Shards:** Broken bits of
pottery.   **192. crants:** Garlands customarily hung upon the biers of unmarried women.
193. strewments: Traditional strewing of flowers.   **193–194. bringing . . . burial:** The
laying to rest of the body, to the sound of the bell.   **198. peace-parted:** Allusion to the
text "Lord, now lettest thou thy servant depart in peace."   **202. howling:** I.e., in hell.
208. ingenious sense: Mind endowed with finest qualities.

Till I have caught her once more in mine arms: [*Leaps into the grave.*] 210
Now pile your dust upon the quick and dead,
Till of this flat a mountain you have made,
T' o'ertop old Pelion,° or the skyish head
Of blue Olympus.

HAMLET: [*Advancing*] What is he whose grief
Bears such an emphasis? whose phrase of sorrow   215
Conjures the wand'ring stars,° and makes them stand
Like wonder-wounded hearers? This is I,
Hamlet the Dane.   [*Leaps into the grave.*]

LAERTES: The devil take thy soul!   [*Grappling with him.*]

HAMLET: Thou pray'st not well.
I prithee, take thy fingers from my throat;   220
For, though I am not splenitive° and rash,
Yet have I in me something dangerous,
Which let thy wisdom fear: hold off thy hand.

KING: Pluck them asunder.

QUEEN: Hamlet, Hamlet!

ALL: Gentlemen, —

HORATIO: Good my lord, be quiet.   225
                    [*The Attendants part them, and they come out of the grave.*]

HAMLET: Why, I will fight with him upon this theme
Until my eyelids will no longer wag.°

QUEEN: O my son, what theme?

HAMLET: I lov'd Ophelia: forty thousand brothers
Could not, with all their quantity° of love,   230
Make up my sum. What wilt thou do for her?

KING: O, he is mad, Laertes.

QUEEN: For love of God, forbear° him.

HAMLET: 'Swounds,° show me what thou 'lt do:
Woo 't° weep? woo 't fight? woo 't fast? woo 't tear thyself?   235
Woo 't drink up eisel?° eat a crocodile?
I'll do 't. Dost thou come here to whine?
To outface me with leaping in her grave?
Be buried quick with her, and so will I:
And, if thou prate of mountains, let them throw   240
Millions of acres on us, till our ground,
Singeing his pate against the burning zone,°
Make Ossa like a wart! Nay, an thou 'lt mouth,
I'll rant as well as thou.

---

213. Pelion: Olympus, Pelion, and Ossa are mountains in the north of Thessaly.
216. wand'ring stars: Planets.   **221. splenitive:** Quick-tempered.   **227. wag:** Move
(not used ludicrously).   **230. quantity:** Some suggest that the word is used in a depre-
catory sense (little bits, fragments).   **233. forbear:** Leave alone.   **234. 'Swounds:**
Oath, "God's wounds."   **235. Woo 't:** Wilt thou.   **236. eisel:** Vinegar. Some editors
have taken this to be the name of a river, such as the Yssel, the Weissel, and the Nile.
242. burning zone: Sun's orbit.

QUEEN: This is mere madness:
    And thus awhile the fit will work on him;   245
    Anon, as patient as the female dove,
    When that her golden couplets° are disclos'd,
    His silence will sit drooping.
HAMLET: Hear you, sir;
    What is the reason that you use me thus?
    I lov'd you ever: but it is no matter;   250
    Let Hercules himself do what he may,
    The cat will mew and dog will have his day.
KING: I pray thee, good Horatio, wait upon him.   *Exit Hamlet and Horatio.*
    [*To Laertes.*] Strengthen your patience in° our last night's speech;
    We'll put the matter to the present push.°   255
    Good Gertrude, set some watch over your son.
    This grave shall have a living° monument:
    An hour of quiet shortly shall we see;
    Till then, in patience our proceeding be.   *Exeunt.*

[SCENE II: *A hall in the castle.*]

Enter Hamlet and Horatio.

HAMLET: So much for this, sir: now shall you see the other;
    You do remember all the circumstance?
HORATIO: Remember it, my lord!
HAMLET: Sir, in my heart there was a kind of fighting,
    That would not let me sleep: methought I lay   5
    Worse than the mutines° in the bilboes.° Rashly°
    And prais'd be rashness for it, let us know,
    Our indiscretion sometime serves us well,
    When our deep plots do pall:° and that should learn us
    There's a divinity that shapes our ends,   10
    Rough-hew° them how we will, —
HORATIO: That is most certain.
HAMLET: Up from my cabin,
    My sea-gown° scarf'd about me, in the dark
    Grop'd I to find out them; had my desire,
    Finger'd° their packet, and in fine° withdrew   15
    To mine own room again; making so bold,
    My fears forgetting manners, to unseal

---

247. **golden couplets:** The pigeon lays two eggs; the young when hatched are covered with golden down.   254. **in:** By recalling.   255. **present push:** Immediate test.   257. **living:** Lasting; also refers (for Laertes' benefit) to the plot against Hamlet.   SCENE II. 6. **mutines:** Mutineers; **bilboes:** Shackles; **Rashly:** Goes with line 12.   9. **pall:** Fail. 11. **Rough-hew:** Shape roughly; it may mean "bungle."   13. **sea-gown:** "A sea-gown, or a coarse, high-collered, and short-sleeved gowne, reaching down to the mid-leg, and used most by seamen and saylors" (Cotgrave, quoted by Singer).   15. **Finger'd:** Pilfered, filched; **in fine:** Finally.

Their grand commission; where I found, Horatio, —
O royal knavery! — an exact command,
Larded° with many several sorts of reasons   20
Importing Denmark's health and England's too,
With, ho! such bugs° and goblins in my life,°
That, on the supervise,° no leisure bated,°
No, not to stay the grinding of the axe,
My head should be struck off.

HORATIO: Is 't possible?   25

HAMLET: Here's the commission: read it at more leisure.
    But wilt thou hear me how I did proceed?

HORATIO: I beseech you.

HAMLET: Being thus be-netted round with villanies, —
    Ere I could make a prologue to my brains,   30
    They had begun the play° — I sat me down,
    Devis'd a new commission, wrote it fair:
    I once did hold it, as our statists° do,
    A baseness to write fair° and labour'd much
    How to forget that learning, but, sir, now   35
    It did me yeoman's° service: wilt thou know
    Th' effect of what I wrote?

HORATIO: Ay, good my lord.

HAMLET: An earnest conjuration from the king,
    As England was his faithful tributary,
    As love between them like the palm might flourish,   40
    As peace should still her wheaten garland° wear
    And stand a comma° 'tween their amities,
    And many such-like 'As'es° of great charge,°
    That, on the view and knowing of these contents,
    Without debatement further, more or less,   45
    He should the bearers put to sudden death,
    Not shriving-time° allow'd.

HORATIO: How was this seal'd?

HAMLET: Why, even in that was heaven ordinant.°
    I had my father's signet in my purse,
    Which was the model of that Danish seal;   50
    Folded the writ up in the form of th' other,
    Subscrib'd it, gave 't th' impression, plac'd it safely,

---

20. Larded: Enriched. **22. bugs:** Bugbears; **such . . . life:** Such imaginary dangers
if I were allowed to live. **23. supervise:** Perusal; **leisure bated:** Delay allowed.
30–31. prologue . . . play: I.e., before I could begin to think, my mind had made its decision. **33. statists:** Statesmen. **34. fair:** In a clear hand. **36. yeoman's:** I.e., faithful.
41. wheaten garland: Symbol of peace. **42. comma:** Smallest break or separation.
Here *amity* begins and *amity* end the period, and *peace* stands between like a dependent
clause. The comma indicates continuity, link. **43. 'As'es:** The "whereases" of a formal
document, with play on the word *ass;* **charge:** Import, and burden. **47. shriving-time:**
Time for absolution. **48. ordinant:** Directing.

The changeling never known. Now, the next day
Was our sea-fight; and what to this was sequent°
Thou know'st already.   55

HORATIO: So Guildenstern and Rosencrantz go to 't.

HAMLET: Why, man, they did make love to this employment;
They are not near my conscience; their defeat
Does by their own insinuation° grow:
'Tis dangerous when the baser nature comes   60
Between the pass° and fell incensed° points
Of mighty opposites.

HORATIO: Why, what a king is this!

HAMLET: Does it not, think thee, stand° me now upon —
He that hath kill'd my king and whor'd my mother,
Popp'd in between th' election° and my hopes,   65
Thrown out his angle° for my proper life,
And with such coz'nage° — is 't not perfect conscience,
To quit° him with this arm? and is 't not to be damn'd,
To let this canker° of our nature come
In further evil?   70

HORATIO: It must be shortly known to him from England
What is the issue of the business there.

HAMLET: It will be short: the interim is mine;
And a man's life's no more than to say "One."
But I am very sorry, good Horatio,   75
That to Laertes I forgot myself;
For, by the image of my cause, I see
The portraiture of his: I'll court his favours:
But, sure, the bravery° of his grief did put me
Into a tow'ring passion.

HORATIO: Peace! who comes here?   80

Enter a Courtier [Osric].

OSRIC: Your lordship is right welcome back to Denmark.

HAMLET: I humbly thank you, sir. [*To Horatio.*] Dost know this water-fly?°

HORATIO: No, my good lord.

HAMLET: Thy state is the more gracious; for 'tis a vice to know him. He hath
much land, and fertile: let a beast be lord of beasts,° and his crib shall   85
stand at the king's mess:° 'tis a chough;° but, as I say, spacious in the
possession of dirt.

---

54. sequent: Subsequent. **59. insinuation:** Interference. **61. pass:** Thrust; **fell
incensed:** Fiercely angered. **63. stand:** Become incumbent. **65. election:** The Danish
throne was filled by election. **66. angle:** Fishing line. **67. coz'nage:** Trickery. **68. quit:**
Repay. **69. canker:** Ulcer, or possibly the worm which destroys buds and leaves.
79. bravery: Bravado. **82. water-fly:** Vain or busily idle person. **85. lord of beasts:**
Cf. Genesis 1:26, 28. **85–86. his crib . . . mess:** He shall eat at the king's table, i.e., be
one of the group of persons (usually four) constituting a *mess* at a banquet. **86. chough:**
Probably, chattering jackdaw; also explained as *chuff,* provincial boor or churl.

OSRIC: Sweet lord, if your lordship were at leisure, I should impart a thing to
   you from his majesty.

HAMLET: I will receive it, sir, with all diligence of spirit. Put your bonnet to his   90
   right use; 'tis for the head.

OSRIC: I thank you lordship, it is very hot.

HAMLET: No, believe me, 'tis very cold; the wind is northerly.

OSRIC: It is indifferent° cold, my lord, indeed.

HAMLET: But yet methinks it is very sultry and hot for my complexion.   95

OSRIC: Exceedingly, my lord; it is very sultry, — as 'twere, — I cannot tell how.
   But, my lord, his majesty bade me signify to you that 'a has laid a great
   wager on your head: sir, this is the matter, —

HAMLET: I beseech you, remember° —[*Hamlet moves him to put on his hat.*]

OSRIC: Nay, good my lord; for mine ease,° in good faith. Sir, here is newly come   100
   to court Laertes; believe me, an absolute gentleman, full of most excellent differences, of very soft° society and great showing:° indeed, to
   speak feelingly° of him, he is the card° or calendar of gentry,° for you
   shall find in him the continent of what part a gentleman would see.

HAMLET: Sir, his definement° suffers no perdition° in you; though, I know, to   105
   divide him inventorially° would dozy° the arithmetic of memory, and
   yet but yaw° neither, in respect of his quick sail. But, in the verity of
   extolment, I take him to be a soul of great article;° and his infusion° of
   such dearth and rareness,° as, to make true diction of him, his semblable°
   is his mirror; and who else would trace° him, his umbrage,° nothing   110
   more.

OSRIC: Your lordship speaks most infallibly of him.

HAMLET: The concernancy,° sir? why do we wrap the gentleman in our more
   rawer breath?°

OSRIC: Sir?   115

HORATIO [*aside to Hamlet*]: Is 't not possible to understand in another tongue?°
   You will do 't, sir, really.

HAMLET: What imports the nomination° of this gentleman?

OSRIC: Of Laertes?

HORATIO [*aside to Hamlet*]: His purse is empty already; all 's golden words are   120
   spent.

HAMLET: Of him, sir.

OSRIC: I know you are not ignorant—

---

94. indifferent: Somewhat.   **99. remember:** I.e., remember thy courtesy; conventional
phrase for "Be covered."   **100. mine ease:** Conventional reply declining the invitation of "Remember thy courtesy." **102. soft:** Gentle; **showing:** Distinguished appearance.
103. feelingly: With just perception; **card:** Chart, map; **gentry:** Good breeding.
105. definement: Definition; **perdition:** Loss, diminution.   **106. divide him inven-
torially:** I.e., enumerate his graces; **dozy:** Dizzy.   **107. yaw:** To move unsteadily (of a
ship).   **108. article:** Moment or importance; **infusion:** Infused temperament, character
imparted by nature.   **109. dearth and rareness:** Rarity; **semblable:** True likeness.
110. trace: Follow; **umbrage:** Shadow.   **113. concernancy:** Import.   **114. breath:**
Speech.   **116. Is 't . . . tongue?:** I.e., can one converse with Osric only in this outlandish
jargon?   **118. nomination:** Naming.

HAMLET: I would you did, sir; yet, in faith, if you did, it would not much
approve° me. Well, sir?   125

OSRIC: You are not ignorant of what excellence Laertes is —

HAMLET: I dare not confess that, lest I should compare with him in excellence;
but, to know a man well, were to know himself.°

OSRIC: I mean, sir, for his weapon; but in the imputation° laid on him by them,
in his meed° he's unfellowed.   130

HAMLET: What's his weapon?

OSRIC: Rapier and dagger.

HAMLET: That's two of his weapons: but, well.

OSRIC: The king, sir, hath wagered with him six Barbary horses: against the
which he has impawned,° as I take it, six French rapiers and poniards,   135
with their assigns, as girdle, hangers,° and so: three of the carriages, in
faith, are very dear to fancy,° very responsive° to the hilts, most delicate°
carriages, and of very liberal conceit.°

HAMLET: What call you the carriages?

HORATIO [*aside to Hamlet*]: I knew you must be edified by the margent° ere   140
you had done.

OSRIC: The carriages, sir, are the hangers.

HAMLET: The phrase would be more german° to the matter, if we could carry
cannon by our sides: I would it might be hangers till then. But, on: six
Barbary horses against six French swords, their assigns, and three lib-   145
eral-conceited carriages; that's the French bet against the Danish. Why is
this "impawned," as you call it?

OSRIC: The king, sir, hath laid, that in a dozen passes between yourself and him,
he shall not exceed you three hits: he hath laid on twelve for nine; and it
would come to immediate trial, if your lordship would vouchsafe the   150
answer.

HAMLET: How if I answer "no"?

OSRIC: I mean, my lord, the opposition of your person in trial.

HAMLET: Sir, I will walk here in the hall: if it please his majesty, it is the breathing time° of day with me; let the foils be brought, the gentleman willing,   155
and the king hold his purpose, I will win for him as I can; if not, I will gain
nothing but my shame and the odd hits.

OSRIC: Shall I re-deliver you e'en so?

HAMLET: To this effect, sir; after what flourish your nature will.

OSRIC: I commend my duty to your lordship.   160

HAMLET: Yours, yours. [*Exit Osric.*] He does well to commend it himself; there
are no tongues else for 's turn.

---

125. **approve:** Command.   128. **but . . . himself:** But to know a man as excellent were
to know Laertes.   129. **imputation:** Reputation.   130. **meed:** Merit.   135. **he has impawned:** He has wagered.   136. **hangers:** Straps on the sword belt from which the sword
hung.   137. **dear to fancy:** Fancifully made; **responsive:** Probably, well balanced, corresponding closely; **delicate:** I.e., in workmanship.   138. **liberal conceit:** Elaborate
design.   140. **margent:** Margin of a book, place for explanatory notes.   143. **german:**
Germane, appropriate.   154–155. **breathing time:** Exercise period.

HAMLET: This likes me well. These foils have all a length?

                                  [*They prepare to play.*]

OSRIC: Ay, my good lord.   235

KING: Set me the stoups of wine upon that table.

    If Hamlet give the first or second hit,

    Or quit in answer of the third exchange,

    Let all the battlements their ordnance fire;

    The king shall drink to Hamlet's better breath;   240

    And in the cup an union° shall he throw,

    Richer than that which four successive kings

    In Denmark's crown have worn. Give me the cups;

    And let the kettle° to the trumpet speak,

    The trumpet to the cannoneer without,   245

    The cannons to the heavens, the heavens to earth,

    "Now the king drinks to Hamlet." Come begin: *Trumpets the while.*

    And you, the judges, bear a wary eye.

HAMLET: Come on, sir.

LAERTES: Come, my lord.   [*They play.*]

HAMLET: One.

LAERTES: No.

HAMLET: Judgement.

OSRIC: A hit, a very palpable hit.

                Drum, trumpets, and shot. Flourish. A piece goes off.

LAERTES: Well; again.   250

KING: Stay; give me drink. Hamlet, this pearl° is thine;

    Here's to thy health. Give him the cup.

HAMLET: I'll play this bout first; set it by awhile.

    Come. [*They play.*] Another hit; what say you?

LAERTES: A touch, a touch, I do confess 't.   255

KING: Our son shall win.

QUEEN: He's fat,° and scant of breath.

    Here, Hamlet, take my napkin, rub thy brows:

    The queen carouses° to thy fortune, Hamlet.

HAMLET: Good madam!

KING: Gertrude, do not drink.

QUEEN: I will, my lord; I pray you, pardon me. [*Drinks.*]   260

KING [*aside*]: It is the poison'd cup: it is too late.

HAMLET: I dare not drink yet, madam; by and by.

QUEEN: Come, let me wipe thy face.

LAERTES: My lord, I'll hit him now.

KING: I do not think 't.

LAERTES [*aside*]: And yet 'tis almost 'gainst my conscience.   265

---

241. union: Pearl.   **244. kettle:** Kettledrum.   **251. pearl:** I.e., the poison.   **256. fat:** Not physically fit, out of training. Some earlier editors speculated that the term applied to the corpulence of Richard Burbage, who originally played the part, but the allusion now appears unlikely. *Fat* may also suggest "sweaty."   **258. carouses:** Drinks a toast.

HAMLET: Come, for the third, Laertes: you but dally;
    I pray you, pass with your best violence;
    I am afeard you make a wanton° of me.
LAERTES: Say you so? come on.   [*They play.*]
OSRIC: Nothing, neither way.   270
LAERTES: Have at you now!
            [*Laertes wounds Hamlet; then, in scuffling, they change rapiers°*
                           and Hamlet wounds Laertes.]
KING: Part them; they are incens'd.
HAMLET: Nay, come again.   [*The Queen falls.*]
OSRIC: Look to the queen there, ho!
HORATIO: They bleed on both sides. How is it, my lord?
OSRIC: How is 't, Laertes?
LAERTES: Why, as a woodcock° to mine own springe,° Osric;   275
    I am justly kill'd with mine own treachery.
HAMLET: How does the queen?
KING: She swounds° to see them bleed.
QUEEN: No, no, the drink, the drink, — O my dear Hamlet, —
    The drink, the drink! I am poison'd.   [*Dies.*]
HAMLET: O villany! Ho! let the door be lock'd: 280
    Treachery! Seek it out.   [*Laertes falls.*]
LAERTES: It is here, Hamlet: Hamlet, thou art slain;
    No med'cine in the world can do thee good;
    In thee there is not half an hour of life;
    The treacherous instrument is in thy hand,   285
    Unbated° and envenom'd: the foul practice
    Hath turn'd itself on me; lo, here I lie,
    Never to rise again: thy mother's poison'd:
    I can no more: the king, the king's to blame.
HAMLET: The point envenom'd too!   290
    Then, venom, to thy work.   [*Stabs the King.*]
ALL: Treason! treason!
KING: O, yet defend me, friends; I am but hurt.
HAMLET: Here, thou incestuous, murd'rous, damned Dane,
    Drink off this potion. Is thy union here?   295
    Follow my mother.   [*King dies.*]
LAERTES: He is justly serv'd;
    It is a poison temper'd° by himself.
    Exchange forgiveness with me, noble Hamlet:
    Mine and my father's death come not upon thee,
    Nor thine on me!   [*Dies.*] 300

---

268. wanton: Spoiled child.   **271. s.d. in scuffling, they change rapiers:** According to a widespread stage tradition, Hamlet receives a scratch, realizes that Laertes' sword is unbated, and accordingly forces an exchange.   **275. woodcock:** As type of stupidity or as decoy; **springe:** Trap, snare.   **277. swounds:** Swoons.   **286. Unbated:** Not blunted with a button.   **297. temper'd:** Mixed.

HAMLET: Heaven make thee free of it! I follow thee.
    I am dead, Horatio. Wretched queen, adieu!
    You that look pale and tremble at this chance,
    That are but mutes° or audience to this act,
    Had I but time — as this fell sergeant,° Death,   305
    Is strict in his arrest — O, I could tell you —
    But let it be. Horatio, I am dead;
    Thou livest; report me and my cause aright
    To the unsatisfied.
HORATIO: Never believe it:
    I am more an antique Roman° than a Dane: 310
    Here 's yet some liquor left.
HAMLET: As th' art a man,
    Give me the cup: let go, by heaven, I'll ha 't.
    O God! Horatio, what a wounded name,
    Things standing thus unknown, shall live behind me!
    If thou didst ever hold me in thy heart,   315
    Absent thee from felicity awhile,
    And in this harsh world draw thy breath in pain,
    To tell my story.   *A march afar off.*
            What warlike noise is this?
OSRIC: Young Fortinbras, with conquest come from Poland,
    To the ambassadors of England gives   320
    This warlike volley.
HAMLET: O, I die, Horatio;
    The potent poison quite o'er-crows° my spirit:
    I cannot live to hear the news from England;
    But I do prophesy th' election lights
    On Fortinbras: he has my dying voice;   325
    So tell him, with th' occurrents,° more and less,
    Which have solicited.° The rest is silence.   *[Dies.]*
HORATIO: Now cracks a noble heart. Good night, sweet prince;
    And flights of angels sing thee to thy rest!
    Why does the drum come hither?   *[March within.]* 330

Enter Fortinbras, with the [English] Ambassadors [and others].

FORTINBRAS: Where is this sight?
HORATIO: What is it you would see?
    If aught of woe or wonder, cease your search.
FORTINBRAS: This quarry° cries on havoc.° O proud Death,
    What feast is toward in thine eternal cell,
    That thou so many princes at a shot   335
    So bloodily hast struck?

---

304. mutes: Performers in a play who speak no words.   **305. sergeant:** Sheriff's officer.
310. Roman: It was the Roman custom to follow masters in death.   **322. o'er-crows:**
Triumphs over.   **326. occurrents:** Events, incidents.   **327. solicited:** Moved, urged.
333. quarry: Heap of dead; **cries on havoc:** Proclaims a general slaughter.

FIRST AMBASSADOR: The sight is dismal;
    And our affairs from England come too late:
    The ears are senseless that should give us hearing,
    To tell him his commandment is fulfill'd,
    That Rosencrantz and Guildenstern are dead: 340
    Where should we have our thanks?
HORATIO: Not from his mouth,°
    Had it th' ability of life to thank you:
    He never gave commandment for their death.
    But since, so jump° upon this bloody question,°
    You from the Polack wars, and you from England,   345
    Are here arriv'd, give order that these bodies
    High on a stage° be placed to the view;
    And let me speak to th' yet unknowing world
    How these things came about: so shall you hear
    Of carnal, bloody, and unnatural acts,   350
    Of accidental judgements, casual slaughters,
    Of deaths put on by cunning and forc'd cause,
    And, in this upshot, purposes mistook
    Fall'n on th' inventors' heads: all this can I
    Truly deliver.
FORTINBRAS: Let us haste to hear it,   355
    And call the noblest to the audience.
    For me, with sorrow I embrace my fortune:
    I have some rights of memory° in this kingdom,
    Which now to claim my vantage doth invite me.
HORATIO: Of that I shall have also cause to speak,   360
    And from his mouth whose voice will draw on more:°
    But let this same be presently perform'd,
    Even while men's minds are wild; lest more mischance,
    On° plots and errors, happen.
FORTINBRAS: Let four captains
    Bear Hamlet, like a soldier, to the stage;   365
    For he was likely, had he been put on,
    To have prov'd most royal: and, for his passage,°
    The soldiers' music and the rites of war
    Speak loudly for him.
    Take up the bodies: such a sight as this   370
    Becomes the field,° but here shows much amiss.
    Go, bid the soldiers shoot.

Exeunt [marching, bearing off the dead bodies; after which a peal of ordnance is heard].

---

341. **his mouth:** I.e., the king's.   344. **jump:** Precisely; **question:** Dispute.   347. **stage:**
Platform.   **358. of memory:** Traditional, remembered.   **361. voice . . . more:** Vote
will influence still others.   **364. On:** On account of, or possibly, on top of, in addition to.
367. passage: Death.   **371. field:** I.e., of battle.

HENRIK IBSEN

Henrik Ibsen (1828–1906), dramatist and poet, was born the second child of a merchant in a small town in southeast Norway. After the ruin of his father's business, Ibsen was raised in extreme poverty. His familiarity with economic hardship and his long struggle to make ends meet were later reflected in his realistic dramas. As a teenager Ibsen intended to study medicine, and he helped support his family by working for six years in an apothecary shop in the seaport town of Grimstad. Self-educated, he wrote his first play, Catilina, in verse when he was twenty-one. A year later he left Grimstad to become a student in Oslo, and then in 1851 he became active in the newly formed National Theatre at Bergen, the first theater in Norway to use Norwegian actors (Danish actors had previously dominated the stage). There Ibsen gained practical experience designing costumes, keeping the accounts, directing, and writing. After the theater went bankrupt, he left Norway with his wife and young son in 1864 and settled in Rome. Living abroad, he wrote the historical plays Brand (1866) and Peer Gynt (1867) as closet dramas, intended to be read, not acted. These plays' brilliant vision of human vocation and self-realization made Ibsen famous throughout Scandinavia when they were published, and Ibsen was awarded a government pension, although the two plays were not staged for many years.

In 1875 Ibsen moved to Munich, where he began to experiment with a different kind of drama in The Pillars of Society (1877), the first of his twelve realistic prose plays addressing social issues. Four years later, living in Rome and Amalfi, he wrote A Doll House. Its portrayal of a marriage in crisis aroused so much controversy that the play caused an immediate sensation when it was performed. His next play, Ghosts (1881), was also attacked for its subject matter (syphilis passed on from father to son within a respected, upper-class family), although it was staged the following year by a small experimental theater company in Chicago. In the 1880s Ibsen's plays—An Enemy of the People (1882) and The Wild Duck (1884) among them—were regarded as obscure and unconventional. The earliest major English-language production of any of his plays was in 1889 when A Doll House was performed in London. In 1891, after writing Hedda Gabler in Munich, Ibsen returned to live for the remainder of his life in Norway, where he wrote four last plays about spiritual conflicts in a new symbolic style.

Ibsen based the plot of A Doll House on a true story. In 1871 a young Norwegian woman named Laura Petersen sent him a sequel that she had written to his play Brand. Ibsen encouraged her to continue writing, calling her his "skylark." The following year she married a Danish schoolmaster who, suffering from tuberculosis, learned that he had to live in a warmer climate. The couple was poor, so Laura secretly arranged a loan to finance their trip to Italy. In 1878, after her creditor demanded repayment of the loan, she wrote a novel and sent it to Ibsen, asking him to recommend it to his publisher. Ibsen refused to endorse her book, and acting in panic, she forged a check to repay the debt. When the bank refused payment, Laura confessed to her husband what she had done. Instead of being sympathetic because she had been so concerned about his health, he accused her of being a criminal and an unfit mother for their children. Laura had a nervous breakdown, and her husband had her committed to a psychiatric hospital. After a month in the *institution, she begged her husband to let her come back home for their children's sake, which he did, making it clear to her that it was against his higher moral principles. As Ibsen's biographer Michael Meyer understood, "The incident must have seemed to Ibsen to crystallize not merely woman's, but mankind's fight against conventional morality and prejudice."*

Three months after hearing that Laura Petersen had been institutionalized, Ibsen composed his "Notes for a Modern Tragedy," in which he stated the germ of the idea that he developed in A Doll House: "There are two kinds of moral laws, two kinds of conscience, one for men and one, quite different, for women. They don't understand each other; but in practical life, woman is judged by masculine law, as though she weren't a woman but a man." Ibsen had been interested for some time in what was then called the problem of women's rights. His wife, Suzannah, championed the cause, and his friend the Norwegian novelist Camilla Collett had criticized what she considered his old-fashioned ideas about women's place in society.

The English writer John Stuart Mill's The Subjection of Women had been translated into Norwegian in 1869, the same year that Ibsen wrote his comedy The League of Youth. In this play one of the minor characters, a young wife, tells her husband, "You dressed me up like a doll; you played with me as one plays with a child." The Danish theater critic and champion of modernism Georg Brandes told Ibsen that a strong woman character like her might be a good subject for a play. In The Pillars of Society, which Ibsen completed just before A Doll House, he created two roles for women who rebel against the subordinate position dictated to them by their uncompromising patriarchal society. Yet he later insisted that in A Doll House he had not "worked for the Women's Rights movement. I am not even very sure what Women's Rights really are." What he really wanted to show in creating the character of Nora, he told Brandes, was a revolution of the human spirit.

By 1879, when A Doll House premiered at the Royal Theatre in Copenhagen, stage production had developed into the realistic theater familiar to us today. In his printed stage directions Ibsen had described the set in minute detail as a middle-class apartment, and the Danes followed his floor plan closely, adding flowering plants and a reproduction of Raphael's painting of the Madonna and child on the wall above the piano. The Royal Theatre even envisioned how to furnish Torvald's study offstage authentically with a paperweight and two candlesticks, although this view of his desk would be seen by very few people in the audience. Betty Hennings, the beautiful twenty-nine-year-old Danish actress playing Nora, was an accomplished dancer, and she was so attractive in the role that she became established as an international star. One reviewer who had come under Hennings's spell declared that in the first two acts she presented such a charming "picture of the young, inexperienced, naive, and carefree wife and mother that one truly envied" her husband for "the treasure which he possessed," thus completely missing the point of the play.

By the end of A Doll House, nineteenth-century audiences were nearly unanimous in their sympathy for Nora's husband, Torvald. Theater historians Frederick Marker and Lise-Lone Marker point out that in 1879, all the reviewers of this first production agreed that "the spiritual metamorphosis" that Nora undergoes in the third act of A Doll House from a naive wife and mother to a self-possessed independent woman was totally unconvincing. Attacked for being im-

moral, the play aroused so much controversy in Copenhagen that a placard read-ing Her tales ikke Dukkehjem *("No Doll House discussions here") was sold for Danes to put in their parlors to keep the peace at home.*

Two months after the Danish premier, Ibsen rewrote the play for a German actress who refused to appear on stage unless there was a happy ending—an end-ing in which Nora (as a so-called normal mother) agrees to stay home to continue her marriage. This version of the play was not a success, and Ibsen restored the original ending. Later critics understood that in A Doll House *Ibsen had gone beyond the conventional idea of a "well-made play" in realistic drama to create a new type of "discussion play." Where the carefully plotted well-made play ends in a denouement or a closed ending that resolves all the aspects of the conflict between the characters, Ibsen's discussion play culminates in an open ending without a clear resolution of the issues dramatized onstage, because the debate itself is intended to be an integral part of the dramatic action. Contemporary audiences accept Ibsen's open ending in the play, but a century ago most people were shocked by Nora's decision to leave her children and go off on her own. When she slammed the door of her husband's house at the end of the play, the sound reverberated round the world.*

COMMENTARIES   *Henrik Ibsen, "Notes for* A Doll House*," page 1553; George Bernard Shaw, "On* A Doll House*," page 1573; Joan Templeton, "Is* A Doll House *a Feminist Text?," page 1575.*

WEB   *Research Henrik Ibsen and answer questions about his work at bedfordstmartins.com/charters/litwriters.*

A Doll House   1879

TRANSLATED BY ROLF FJELDE

THE CHARACTERS

TORVALD HELMER, a lawyer	The Helmers' three small children
NORA, his wife	ANNE-MARIE, their nurse
DR. RANK	HELENE, a maid
MRS. LINDE	A Delivery Boy
NILS KROGSTAD, a bank clerk	

SCENE: *The action takes place in Helmer's residence.*

ACT I

A comfortable room, tastefully but not expensively furnished. A door to the right in the back wall leads to the entryway; another to the left leads to Helmer's study. Between these doors, a piano. Midway in the left-hand wall a door, and further back a window. Near the window a round table with an armchair and a small sofa. In the right-hand wall, toward the rear, a door, and nearer the foreground a porcelain stove with two armchairs and a rocking chair beside it. Between the stove and the side door, a small table. Engravings on the walls. A set of shelves with china figures and other small art objects; a small bookcase with richly bound books; the floor carpeted; a fire burning in the stove. It is a winter day.

A bell rings in the entryway; shortly after we hear the door being unlocked. Nora comes into the room, humming happily to herself; she is wearing street clothes and carries an armload of packages, which she puts down on the table to the right. She has left the hall door open; and through it a Delivery Boy is seen, holding a Christmas tree and a basket, which he gives to the Maid who let them in.

NORA: Hide the tree well, Helene. The children mustn't get a glimpse of it till this evening, after it's trimmed. (*To the Delivery Boy, taking out her purse.*) How much?

DELIVERY BOY: Fifty, ma'am.

NORA: There's a crown. No, keep the change. (*The Boy thanks her and leaves. Nora shuts the door. She laughs softly to herself while taking off her street things. Drawing a bag of macaroons from her pocket, she eats a couple, then steals over and listens at her husband's study door.*) Yes, he's home. (*Hums again as she moves to the table right.*)

HELMER (*from the study*): Is that my little lark twittering out there?

NORA (*busy opening some packages*): Yes, it is.

HELMER: Is that my squirrel rummaging around?

NORA: Yes!

HELMER: When did my squirrel get in?

NORA: Just now. (*Putting the macaroon bag in her pocket and wiping her mouth.*) Do come in, Torvald, and see what I've bought.

HELMER: Can't be disturbed. (*After a moment he opens the door and peers in, pen in hand.*) Bought, you say? All that there? Has the little spendthrift been out throwing money around again?

NORA: Oh, but Torvald, this year we really should let ourselves go a bit. It's the first Christmas we haven't had to economize.

HELMER: But you know we can't go squandering.

NORA: Oh yes, Torvald, we can squander a little now. Can't we? Just a tiny, wee bit. Now that you've got a big salary and are going to make piles and piles of money.

HELMER: Yes—starting New Year's. But then it's a full three months till the raise comes through.

NORA: Pooh! We can borrow that long.

HELMER: Nora! (*Goes over and playfully takes her by the ear.*) Are your scatter-brains off again? What if today I borrowed a thousand crowns, and you squandered them over Christmas week, and then on New Year's Eve a roof tile fell on my head and I lay there—

NORA (*putting her hand on his mouth*): Oh! Don't say such things!

HELMER: Yes, but what if it happened—then what?

NORA: If anything so awful happened, then it just wouldn't matter if I had debts or not.

HELMER: Well, but the people I'd borrowed from?

NORA: Them? Who cares about them! They're strangers.

HELMER: Nora, Nora, how like a woman! No, but seriously, Nora, you know what I think about that. No debts! Never borrow! Something of freedom's lost—and something of beauty, too—from a home that's founded on borrowing and debt. We've made a brave stand up to now, the two of us; and we'll go right on like that the little while we have to.

NORA (*going toward the stove*): Yes, whatever you say, Torvald.

HELMER (*following her*): Now, now, the little lark's wings mustn't droop. Come on, don't be a sulky squirrel. (*Taking out his wallet.*) Nora, guess what I have here.

NORA (*turning quickly*): Money!

HELMER: There, see. (*Hands her some notes.*) Good grief, I know how costs go up in a house at Christmastime.

NORA: Ten—twenty—thirty—forty. Oh, thank you, Torvald; I can manage no end on this.

HELMER: You really will have to.

NORA: Oh yes, I promise I will! But come here so I can show you everything I bought. And so cheap! Look, new clothes for Ivar here—and a sword. Here a horse and a trumpet for Bob. And a doll and a doll's bed here for Emmy; they're nothing much, but she'll tear them to bits in no time anyway. And here I have dress material and handkerchiefs for the maids. Old Anne-Marie really deserves something more.

HELMER: And what's in that package there?

NORA (*with a cry*): Torvald, no! You can't see that till tonight!

HELMER: I see. But tell me now, you little prodigal, what have you thought of for yourself?

NORA: For myself? Oh, I don't want anything at all.

HELMER: Of course you do. Tell me just what—within reason—you'd most like to have.

NORA: I honestly don't know. Oh, listen, Torvald—

HELMER: Well?

NORA (*fumbling at his coat buttons, without looking at him*): If you want to give me something, then maybe you could—you could—

HELMER: Come on, out with it.

NORA (*hurriedly*): You could give me money, Torvald. No more than you think you can spare; then one of these days I'll buy something with it.

HELMER: But Nora—

NORA: Oh please, Torvald darling, do that! I beg you, please. Then I could hang the bills in pretty gilt paper on the Christmas tree. Wouldn't that be fun?

HELMER: What are those little birds called that always fly through their fortunes?

NORA: Oh yes, spendthrifts: I know all that. But let's do as I say, Torvald; then I'll have time to decide what I really need most. That's very sensible, isn't it?

HELMER (*smiling*): Yes, very—that is, if you actually hung onto the money I give you, and you actually used it to buy yourself something. But it goes for the house and for all sorts of foolish things, and then I only have to lay out some more.

NORA: Oh, but Torvald—

HELMER: Don't deny it, my dear little Nora. (*Putting his arm around her waist.*) Spendthrifts are sweet, but they use up a frightful amount of money. It's incredible what it costs a man to feed such birds.

NORA: Oh, how can you say that! Really, I save everything I can.

HELMER (*laughing*): Yes, that's the truth. Everything you can. But that's nothing at all.

NORA (*humming, with a smile of quiet satisfaction*): Hm, if you only knew what expenses we larks and squirrels have, Torvald.

HELMER: You're an odd little one. Exactly the way your father was. You're never at a loss for scaring up money; but the moment you have it, it runs right out through your fingers; you never know what you've done with it. Well, one takes you as you are. It's deep in your blood. Yes, these things are hereditary, Nora.

NORA: Ah, I could wish I'd inherited many of Papa's qualities.

HELMER: And I couldn't wish you anything but just what you are, my sweet little lark. But wait; it seems to me you have a very—what should I call it?—a very suspicious look today—

NORA: I do?

HELMER: You certainly do. Look me straight in the eye.

NORA (*looking at him*): Well?

HELMER (*shaking an admonitory finger*): Surely my sweet tooth hasn't been running riot in town today, has she?

NORA: No. Why do you imagine that?

HELMER: My sweet tooth really didn't make a little detour through the confectioner's?

NORA: No, I assure you, Torvald—

HELMER: Hasn't nibbled some pastry?

NORA: No, not at all.

HELMER: Not even munched a macaroon or two?

NORA: No, Torvald, I assure you, really—

HELMER: There, there now. Of course I'm only joking.

NORA (*going to the table, right*): You know I could never think of going against you.

HELMER: No, I understand that; and you *have* given me your word. (*Going over to her.*) Well, you keep your little Christmas secrets to yourself, Nora darling. I expect they'll come to light this evening, when the tree is lit.

NORA: Did you remember to ask Dr. Rank?

HELMER: No. But there's no need for that: it's assumed he'll be dining with us. All the same, I'll ask him when he stops by here this morning. I've ordered some fine wine. Nora, you can't imagine how I'm looking forward to this evening.

NORA: So am I. And what fun for the children, Torvald!

HELMER: Ah, it's so gratifying to know that one's gotten a safe, secure job, and with a comfortable salary. It's a great satisfaction, isn't it?

NORA: Oh, it's wonderful!

HELMER: Remember last Christmas? Three whole weeks before, you shut yourself in every evening till long after midnight, making flowers for the Christmas tree, and all the other decorations to surprise us. Ugh, that was the dullest time I've ever lived through.

NORA: It wasn't at all dull for me.

HELMER (*smiling*): But the outcome *was* pretty sorry, Nora.

NORA: Oh, don't tease me with that again. How could I help it that the cat came in and tore everything to shreds.

HELMER: No, poor thing, you certainly couldn't. You wanted so much to please us all, and that's what counts. But it's just as well that the hard times are past.

NORA: Yes, it's really wonderful.

HELMER: Now I don't have to sit here alone, boring myself, and you don't have to tire your precious eyes and your fair little delicate hands—

NORA (*clapping her hands*): No, is it really true, Torvald, I don't have to? Oh, how wonderfully lovely to hear! (*Taking his arm.*) Now I'll tell you just how I've thought we should plan things. Right after Christmas—(*The doorbell rings.*) Oh, the bell. (*Straightening the room up a bit.*) Somebody would have to come. What a bore!

HELMER: I'm not home to visitors, don't forget.

MAID (*from the hall doorway*): Ma'am, a lady to see you—

NORA: All right, let her come in.

MAID (*to Helmer*): And the doctor's just come too.

HELMER: Did he go right to my study?

MAID: Yes, he did.

Helmer goes into his room. The Maid shows in Mrs. Linde, dressed in traveling clothes, and shuts the door after her.

MRS. LINDE (*in a dispirited and somewhat hesitant voice*): Hello, Nora.

NORA (*uncertain*): Hello—

MRS. LINDE: You don't recognize me.

NORA: No, I don't know—but wait, I think—(*Exclaiming.*) What! Kristine! Is it really you?

MRS. LINDE: Yes, it's me.

NORA: Kristine! To think I didn't recognize you. But then, how could I? (*More quietly.*) How you've changed, Kristine!

MRS. LINDE: Yes, no doubt I have. In nine—ten long years.

NORA: Is it so long since we met! Yes, it's all of that. Oh, these last eight years have been a happy time, believe me. And so now you've come in to town, too. Made the long trip in the winter. That took courage.

MRS. LINDE: I just got here by ship this morning.

NORA: To enjoy yourself over Christmas, of course. Oh, how lovely! Yes, enjoy ourselves, we'll do that. But take your coat off. You're not still cold? (*Helping her.*) There now, let's get cozy here by the stove. No, the easy chair there! I'll take the rocker here. (*Seizing her hands.*) Yes, now you have your old look again; it was only in that first moment. You're a bit more pale, Kristine—and maybe a bit thinner.

MRS. LINDE: And much, much older, Nora.

NORA: Yes, perhaps a bit older: a tiny, tiny bit; not much at all. (*Stopping short; suddenly serious.*) Oh, but thoughtless me, to sit here, chattering away. Sweet, good Kristine, can you forgive me?

MRS. LINDE: What do you mean, Nora?

NORA (*softly*): Poor Kristine, you've become a widow.

MRS. LINDE: Yes, three years ago.

NORA: Oh, I knew it, of course: I read it in the papers. Oh, Kristine, you must believe me; I often thought of writing you then, but I kept postponing it, and something always interfered.

MRS. LINDE: Nora dear, I understand completely.

NORA: No, it was awful of me, Kristine. You poor thing, how much you must have gone through. And he left you nothing?

MRS. LINDE: No.

NORA: And no children?

MRS. LINDE: No.

NORA: Nothing at all, then?

MRS. LINDE: Not even a sense of loss to feed on.

NORA (*looking incredulously at her*): But Kristine, how could that be?

MRS. LINDE (*smiling wearily and smoothing her hair*): Oh, sometimes it happens, Nora.

NORA: So completely alone. How terribly hard that must be for you. I have three lovely children. You can't see them now; they're out with the maid. But now you must tell me everything—

MRS. LINDE: No, no, no, tell me about yourself.

NORA: No, you begin. Today I don't want to be selfish. I want to think only of you today. But there *is* something I must tell you. Did you hear of the wonderful luck we had recently?

MRS. LINDE: No, what's that?

NORA: My husband's been made manager in the bank, just think!

MRS. LINDE: Your husband? How marvelous!

NORA: Isn't it? Being a lawyer is such an uncertain living, you know, especially if one won't touch any cases that aren't clean and decent. And of course Torvald would never do that, and I'm with him completely there. Oh, we're simply delighted, believe me! He'll join the bank right after New Year's and start getting a huge salary and lots of commissions. From now on we can live quite differently—just as we want. Oh, Kristine, I feel so light and happy! Won't it be lovely to have stacks of money and not a care in the world?

MRS. LINDE: Well, anyway, it would be lovely to have enough for necessities.

NORA: No, not just for necessities, but stacks and stacks of money!

MRS. LINDE (*smiling*): Nora, Nora, aren't you sensible yet? Back in school you were such a free spender.

NORA (*with a quiet laugh*): Yes, that's what Torvald still says. (*Shaking her finger.*) But "Nora, Nora" isn't as silly as you all think. Really, we've been in no position for me to go squandering. We've had to work, both of us.

MRS. LINDE: You too?

NORA: Yes, at odd jobs—needlework, crocheting, embroidery, and such—(*Casually.*) and other things too. You remember that Torvald left the department when we were married? There was no chance of promotion in his office, and of course he needed to earn more money. But that first year he drove himself terribly. He took on all kinds of extra work that kept him going morning and night. It wore him down, and then he fell deathly ill. The doctors said it was essential for him to travel south.

MRS. LINDE: Yes, didn't you spend a whole year in Italy?

NORA: That's right. It wasn't easy to get away, you know. Ivar had just been born. But of course we had to go. Oh, that was a beautiful trip, and it saved Torvald's life. But it cost a frightful sum, Kristine.

MRS. LINDE: I can well imagine.

NORA: Four thousand, eight hundred crowns it cost. That's really a lot of money.

MRS. LINDE: But it's lucky you had it when you needed it.

NORA: Well, as it was, we got it from Papa.

MRS. LINDE: I see. It was just about the time your father died.

NORA: Yes, just about then. And, you know, I couldn't make that trip out to nurse him. I had to stay here, expecting Ivar any moment, and with my poor sick Torvald to care for. Dearest Papa, I never saw him again, Kristine. Oh, that was the worst time I've known in all my marriage.

MRS. LINDE: I know how you loved him. And then you went off to Italy?

NORA: Yes. We had the means now, and the doctors urged us. So we left a month after.

MRS. LINDE: And your husband came back completely cured?

NORA: Sound as a drum!

MRS. LINDE: But—the doctor?

NORA: Who?

MRS. LINDE: I thought the maid said he was a doctor, the man who came in with me.

NORA: Yes, that was Dr. Rank—but he's not making a sick call. He's our closest friend, and he stops by at least once a day. No, Torvald hasn't had a sick moment since, and the children are fit and strong, and I am, too. (*Jumping up and clapping her hands.*) Oh, dear God, Kristine, what a lovely thing to live and be happy! But how disgusting of me—I'm talking of nothing but my own affairs. (*Sits on a stool close by Kristine, arms resting across her knees.*) Oh, don't be angry with me! Tell me, is it really true that you weren't in love with your husband? Why did you marry him, then?

MRS. LINDE: My mother was still alive, but bedridden and helpless—and I had my two younger brothers to look after. In all conscience, I didn't think I could turn him down.

NORA: No, you were right there. But was he rich at the time?

MRS. LINDE: He was very well off, I'd say. But the business was shaky, Nora. When he died, it all fell apart, and nothing was left.

NORA: And then—?

MRS. LINDE: Yes, so I had to scrape up a living with a little shop and a little teaching and whatever else I could find. The last three years have been like one endless workday without a rest for me. Now it's over, Nora. My poor mother doesn't need me, for she's passed on. Nor the boys, either; they're working now and can take care of themselves.

NORA: How free you must feel—

MRS. LINDE: No—only unspeakably empty. Nothing to live for now. (*Standing up anxiously.*) That's why I couldn't take it any longer out in that desolate hole. Maybe here it'll be easier to find something to do and keep my mind occupied. If I could only be lucky enough to get a steady job, some office work—

NORA: Oh, but Kristine, that's so dreadfully tiring, and you already look so tired. It would be much better for you if you could go off to a bathing resort.

MRS. LINDE (*going toward the window*): I have no father to give me travel money, Nora.

NORA (*rising*): Oh, don't be angry with me.

MRS. LINDE (*going to her*): Nora dear, don't you be angry with me. The worst of my kind of situation is all the bitterness that's stored away. No one to work for, and yet you're always having to snap up your opportunities. You have to live; and so you grow selfish. When you told me the happy change in your lot, do you know I was delighted less for your sakes than for mine?

NORA: How so? Oh, I see. You think maybe Torvald could do something for you.

MRS. LINDE: Yes, that's what I thought.

NORA: And he will, Kristine! Just leave it to me; I'll bring it up so delicately— find something attractive to humor him with. Oh, I'm so eager to help you.

MRS. LINDE: How very kind of you, Nora, to be so concerned over me—doubly kind, considering you really know so little of life's burdens yourself.

NORA: I—? I know so little—?

MRS. LINDE (*smiling*): Well, my heavens—a little needlework and such—Nora, you're just a child.

NORA (*tossing her head and pacing the floor*): You don't have to act so superior.

MRS. LINDE: Oh?

NORA: You're just like the others. You all think I'm incapable of anything serious—

MRS. LINDE: Come now—

NORA: That I've never had to face the raw world.

MRS. LINDE: Nora dear, you've just been telling me all your troubles.

NORA: Hm! Trivia! (*Quietly.*) I haven't told you the big thing.

MRS. LINDE: Big thing? What do you mean?

NORA: You look down on me so, Kristine, but you shouldn't. You're proud that you worked so long and hard for your mother.

MRS. LINDE: I don't look down on a soul. But it *is* true: I'm proud—and happy, too—to think it was given to me to make my mother's last days almost free of care.

NORA: And you're also proud thinking of what you've done for your brothers.

MRS. LINDE: I feel I've a right to be.

NORA: I agree. But listen to this, Kristine—I've also got something to be proud and happy for.

MRS. LINDE: I don't doubt it. But whatever do you mean?

NORA: Not so loud. What if Torvald heard! He mustn't, not for anything in the world. Nobody must know, Kristine. No one but you.

MRS. LINDE: But what is it, then?

NORA: Come here. (*Drawing her down beside her on the sofa.*) It's true—I've also got something to be proud and happy for. I'm the one who saved Torvald's life.

MRS. LINDE: Saved—? Saved how?

NORA: I told you about the trip to Italy. Torvald never would have lived if he hadn't gone south—

MRS. LINDE: Of course; your father gave you the means—

NORA (*smiling*): That's what Torvald and all the rest think, but—

MRS. LINDE: But—?

NORA: Papa didn't give us a pin. I was the one who raised the money.

MRS. LINDE: You? That whole amount?

NORA: Four thousand, eight hundred crowns. What do you say to that?

MRS. LINDE: But Nora, how was it possible? Did you win the lottery?

NORA (*disdainfully*): The lottery? Pooh! No art to that.

MRS. LINDE: But where did you get it from then?

NORA (*humming, with a mysterious smile*): Hmm, tra-la-la-la.

MRS. LINDE: Because you couldn't have borrowed it.

NORA: No? Why not?

MRS. LINDE: A wife can't borrow without her husband's consent.

NORA (*tossing her head*): Oh, but a wife with a little business sense, a wife who knows how to manage—

MRS. LINDE: Nora, I simply don't understand—

NORA: You don't have to. Whoever said I *borrowed* the money? I could have gotten it other ways. (*Throwing herself back on the sofa.*) I could have gotten it from some admirer or other. After all, a girl with my ravishing appeal—

MRS. LINDE: You lunatic.

NORA: I'll bet you're eaten up with curiosity, Kristine.

MRS. LINDE: Now listen here, Nora—you haven't done something indiscreet?

NORA (*sitting up again*): Is it indiscreet to save your husband's life?

MRS. LINDE: I think it's indiscreet that without his knowledge you—

NORA: But that's the point: he mustn't know! My Lord, can't you understand? He mustn't ever know the close call he had. It was to *me* the doctors came to say his life was in danger—that nothing could save him but a stay in the south. Didn't I try strategy then! I began talking about how lovely it would be for me to travel abroad like other young wives; I begged and I cried; I told him please to remember my condition, to be kind and indulge me; and then I dropped a hint that he could easily take out a loan. But at that, Kristine, he nearly exploded. He said I was frivolous, and it was his duty as man of the house not to indulge me in whims and fancies—as I think he called them. Aha, I thought, now you'll just have to be saved—and that's when I saw my chance.

MRS. LINDE: And your father never told Torvald the money wasn't from him?

NORA: No, never. Papa died right about then. I'd considered bringing him into my secret and begging him never to tell. But he was too sick at the time— and then, sadly, it didn't matter.

MRS. LINDE: And you've never confided in your husband since?

NORA: For heaven's sake, no! Are you serious? He's so strict on that subject. Besides—Torvald, with all his masculine pride—how painfully humiliating for him if he ever found out he was in debt to me. That would just ruin our relationship. Our beautiful, happy home would never be the same.

MRS. LINDE: Won't you ever tell him?

NORA (*thoughtfully, half smiling*): Yes—maybe sometime, years from now, when I'm no longer so attractive. Don't laugh! I only mean when Torvald loves me less than now, when he stops enjoying my dancing and dressing up and reciting for him. Then it might be wise to have something in reserve—(*Breaking off.*) How ridiculous! That'll never happen—Well, Kristine, what do you think of my big secret? I'm capable of something too, hm? You can imagine, of course, how this thing hangs over me. It really hasn't been easy meeting the payments on time. In the business world there's what they call quarterly interest and what they call amortization, and these are always so terribly hard to manage. I've had to skimp a little here and there, wherever I could, you know. I could hardly spare anything from my house allowance, because Torvald has to live well. I couldn't let the children go poorly dressed; whatever I got for them, I felt I had to use up completely—the darlings!

MRS. LINDE: Poor Nora, so it had to come out of your own budget, then?

NORA: Yes, of course. But I was the one most responsible, too. Every time Torvald gave me money for new clothes and such, I never used more than half; always bought the simplest, cheapest outfits. It was a godsend that everything looks so well on me that Torvald never noticed. But it did weigh me down at times, Kristine. It *is* such a joy to wear fine things. You understand.

MRS. LINDE: Oh, of course.

NORA: And then I found other ways of making money. Last winter I was lucky enough to get a lot of copying to do. I locked myself in and sat writing every evening till late in the night. Ah, I was tired so often, dead tired. But still it was wonderful fun, sitting and working like that, earning money. It was almost like being a man.

MRS. LINDE: But how much have you paid off this way so far?

NORA: That's hard to say, exactly. These accounts, you know, aren't easy to figure. I only know that I've paid out all I could scrape together. Time and again I haven't known where to turn. (*Smiling.*) Then I'd sit here dreaming of a rich old gentleman who had fallen in love with me—

MRS. LINDE: What! Who is he?

NORA: Oh, really! And that he'd died, and when his will was opened, there in big letters it said, "All my fortune shall be paid over in cash, immediately, to that enchanting Mrs. Nora Helmer."

MRS. LINDE: But Nora dear — who *was* this gentleman?

NORA: Good grief, can't you understand? The old man never existed; that was only something I'd dream up time and again whenever I was at my wits' end for money. But it makes no difference now; the old fossil can go where he pleases for all I care; I don't need him or his will — because now I'm free. (*Jumping up.*) Oh, how lovely to think of that, Kristine! Carefree! To know you're carefree, utterly carefree; to be able to romp and play with the children, and to keep up a beautiful, charming home — everything just the way Torvald likes it! And think, spring is coming, with big blue skies. Maybe we can travel a little then. Maybe I'll see the ocean again. Oh yes, it *is* so marvelous to live and be happy!

The front doorbell rings.

MRS. LINDE (*rising*): There's the bell. It's probably best that I go.

NORA: No, stay. No one's expected. It must be for Torvald.

MAID (*from the hall doorway*): Excuse me, ma'am — there's a gentleman here to see Mr. Helmer, but I didn't know — since the doctor's with him —

NORA: Who is the gentleman?

KROGSTAD (*from the doorway*): It's me, Mrs. Helmer.

Mrs. Linde starts and turns away toward the window.

NORA (*stepping toward him, tense, her voice a whisper*): You? What is it? Why do you want to speak to my husband?

KROGSTAD: Bank business — after a fashion. I have a small job in the investment bank, and I hear now your husband is going to be our chief —

NORA: In other words, it's —

KROGSTAD: Just dry business, Mrs. Helmer. Nothing but that.

NORA: Yes, then please be good enough to step into the study. (*She nods indifferently as she sees him out by the hall door, then returns and begins stirring up the stove.*)

MRS. LINDE: Nora — who was that man?

NORA: That was a Mr. Krogstad — a lawyer.

MRS. LINDE: Then it really was him.

NORA: Do you know that person?

MRS. LINDE: I did once — many years ago. For a time he was a law clerk in our town.

NORA: Yes, he's been that.

MRS. LINDE: How he's changed.

NORA: I understand he had a very unhappy marriage.

MRS. LINDE: He's a widower now.

NORA: With a number of children. There now, it's burning. (*She closes the stove door and moves the rocker a bit to one side.*)

MRS. LINDE: They say he has a hand in all kinds of business.

NORA: Oh? That may be true; I wouldn't know. But let's not think about business. It's so dull.

Dr. Rank enters from Helmer's study.

RANK (*still in the doorway*): No, no really — I don't want to intrude, I'd just as soon talk a little while with your wife. (*Shuts the door, then notices Mrs. Linde.*) Oh, beg pardon. I'm intruding here too.

NORA: No, not at all. (*Introducing him.*) Dr. Rank, Mrs. Linde.

RANK: Well now, that's a name much heard in this house. I believe I passed the lady on the stairs as I came.

MRS. LINDE: Yes, I take the stairs very slowly. They're rather hard on me.

RANK: Uh-hm, some touch of internal weakness?

MRS. LINDE: More overexertion, I'd say.

RANK: Nothing else? Then you're probably here in town to rest up in a round of parties?

MRS. LINDE: I'm here to look for work.

RANK: Is that the best cure for overexertion?

MRS. LINDE: One has to live, Doctor.

RANK: Yes, there's a common prejudice to that effect.

NORA: Oh, come on, Dr. Rank — you really do want to live yourself.

RANK: Yes, I really do. Wretched as I am, I'll gladly prolong my torment indefinitely. All my patients feel like that. And it's quite the same, too, with the morally sick. Right at this moment there's one of those moral invalids in there with Helmer —

MRS. LINDE (*softly*): Ah!

NORA: Who do you mean?

RANK: Oh, it's a lawyer, Krogstad, a type you wouldn't know. His character is rotten to the root — but even he began chattering all-importantly about how he had to *live.*

NORA: Oh? What did he want to talk to Torvald about?

RANK: I really don't know. I only heard something about the bank.

NORA: I didn't know that Krog — that this man Krogstad had anything to do with the bank.

RANK: Yes, he's gotten some kind of berth down there. (*To Mrs. Linde.*) I don't know if you also have, in your neck of the woods, a type of person who scuttles about breathlessly, sniffing out hints of moral corruption, and then maneuvers his victim into some sort of key position where he can keep an eye on him. It's the healthy these days that are out in the cold.

MRS. LINDE: All the same, it's the sick who most need to be taken in.

RANK (*with a shrug*): Yes, there we have it. That's the concept that's turning society into a sanatorium.

Nora, lost in her thoughts, breaks out into quiet laughter and claps her hands.

RANK: Why do you laugh at that? Do you have any real idea of what society is?

NORA: What do I care about dreary old society? I was laughing at something quite different — something terribly funny. Tell me, Doctor — is everyone who works in the bank dependent now on Torvald?

RANK: Is that what you find so terribly funny?

NORA (*smiling and humming*): Never mind, never mind! (*Pacing the floor.*) Yes, that's really immensely amusing: that we — that Torvald has so much power now over all those people. (*Taking the bag out of her pocket.*) Dr. Rank, a little macaroon on that?

RANK: See here, macaroons! I thought they were contraband here.

NORA: Yes, but these are some that Kristine gave me.

MRS. LINDE: What? I—?

NORA: Now, now, don't be afraid. You couldn't possibly know that Torvald had forbidden them. You see, he's worried they'll ruin my teeth. But hmp! Just this once! Isn't that so, Dr. Rank? Help yourself! (*Puts a macaroon in his mouth.*) And you too, Kristine. And I'll also have one, only a little one—or two, at the most. (*Walking about again.*) Now I'm really tremendously happy. Now there's just one last thing in the world that I have an enormous desire to do.

RANK: Well! And what's that?

NORA: It's something I have such a consuming desire to say so Torvald could hear.

RANK: And why can't you say it?

NORA: I don't dare. It's quite shocking.

MRS. LINDE: Shocking?

RANK: Well, then it isn't advisable. But in front of us you certainly can. What do you have such a desire to say so Torvald could hear?

NORA: I have such a huge desire to say—to hell and be damned!

RANK: Are you crazy?

MRS. LINDE: My goodness, Nora!

RANK: Go on, say it. Here he is.

NORA (*hiding the macaroon bag*): Shh, shh, shh!

Helmer comes in from his study, hat in hand, overcoat over his arm.

NORA (*going toward him*): Well, Torvald dear, are you through with him?

HELMER: Yes, he just left.

NORA: Let me introduce you—this is Kristine, who's arrived here in town.

HELMER: Kristine—? I'm sorry, but I don't know—

NORA: Mrs. Linde, Torvald dear. Mrs. Kristine Linde.

HELMER: Of course. A childhood friend of my wife's, no doubt?

MRS. LINDE: Yes, we knew each other in those days.

NORA: And just think, she made the long trip down here in order to talk with you.

HELMER: What's this?

MRS. LINDE: Well, not exactly—

NORA: You see, Kristine is remarkably clever in office work, and so she's terribly eager to come under a capable man's supervision and add more to what she already knows—

HELMER: Very wise, Mrs. Linde.

NORA: And then when she heard that you'd become a bank manager—the story was wired out to the papers—then she came in as fast as she could and—Really, Torvald, for my sake you can do a little something for Kristine, can't you?

HELMER: Yes, it's not at all impossible. Mrs. Linde, I suppose you're a widow?

MRS. LINDE: Yes.

HELMER: Any experience in office work?

MRS. LINDE: Yes, a good deal.

HELMER: Well, it's quite likely that I can make an opening for you—

NORA (*clapping her hands*): You see, you see!

HELMER: You've come at a lucky moment, Mrs. Linde.

MRS. LINDE: Oh, how can I thank you?

HELMER: Not necessary. (*Putting his overcoat on.*) But today you'll have to excuse me—

RANK: Wait, I'll go with you. (*He fetches his coat from the hall and warms it at the stove.*)

NORA: Don't stay out long, dear.

HELMER: An hour; no more.

NORA: Are you going too, Kristine?

MRS. LINDE (*putting on her winter garments*): Yes, I have to see about a room now.

HELMER: Then perhaps we can all walk together.

NORA (*helping her*): What a shame we're so cramped here, but it's quite impossible for us to—

MRS. LINDE: Oh, don't even think of it! Good-bye, Nora dear, and thanks for everything.

NORA: Good-bye for now. Of course you'll be back this evening. And you too, Dr. Rank. What? If you're well enough? Oh, you've got to be! Wrap up tight now.

In a ripple of small talk the company moves out into the hall; children's voices are heard outside on the steps.

NORA: There they are! There they are! (*She runs to open the door. The children come in with their nurse, Anne-Marie.*) Come in, come in! (*Bends down and kisses them.*) Oh, you darlings—! Look at them, Kristine. Aren't they lovely!

RANK: No loitering in the draft here.

HELMER: Come, Mrs. Linde—this place is unbearable now for anyone but mothers.

Dr. Rank, Helmer, and Mrs. Linde go down the stairs. Anne-Marie goes into the living room with the children. Nora follows, after closing the hall door.

NORA: How fresh and strong you look. Oh, such red cheeks you have! Like apples and roses. (*The children interrupt her throughout the following.*) And it was so much fun? That's wonderful. Really? You pulled both Emmy and Bob on the sled? Imagine, all together! Yes, you're a clever boy, Ivar. Oh, let me hold her a bit, Anne-Marie. My sweet little doll baby! (*Takes the smallest from the nurse and dances with her.*) Yes, yes, Mama will dance with Bob as well. What? Did you throw snowballs? Oh, if I'd only been there! No, don't bother, Anne-Marie—I'll undress them myself. Oh yes, let me. It's such fun. Go in and rest; you look half frozen. There's hot coffee waiting for you on the stove. (*The nurse goes into the room to the left. Nora takes the children's winter things off, throwing them about, while the children talk to her all at once.*) Is that so? A big dog chased you? But it didn't bite? No, dogs never bite little, lovely doll babies. Don't peek in the packages, Ivar! What is it? Yes, wouldn't you like to know. No, no, it's an ugly something. Well? Shall we play? What shall we play? Hide-and-seek? Yes, let's play hide-and-seek. Bob must hide first. I must? Yes, let me hide first. (*Laughing and shouting, she and the children play in and out of the living room and the adjoining room to the right. At last Nora hides under the table. The children come storming in, search, but cannot find her, then hear her muffled laughter, dash over to the table, lift the cloth up and find her. Wild shouting. She creeps forward as if to scare them. More shouts. Meanwhile, a knock at the hall door; no one has noticed it. Now the door half opens, and Krogstad appears. He waits a moment; the game goes on.*)

KROGSTAD: Beg pardon, Mrs. Helmer—

NORA (*with a strangled cry, turning and scrambling to her knees*): Oh! What do you want?

KROGSTAD: Excuse me. The outer door was ajar; it must be someone forgot to shut it—

NORA (*rising*): My husband isn't home, Mr. Krogstad.

KROGSTAD: I know that.

NORA: Yes—then what do you want here?

KROGSTAD: A word with you.

NORA: With—? (*To the children, quietly.*) Go in to Anne-Marie. What? No, the strange man won't hurt Mama. When he's gone, we'll play some more. (*She leads the children into the room to the left and shuts the door after them. Then, tense and nervous:*) You want to speak to me?

KROGSTAD: Yes, I want to.

NORA: Today? But it's not yet the first of the month—

KROGSTAD: No, it's Christmas Eve. It's going to be up to you how merry a Christmas you have.

NORA: What is it you want? Today I absolutely can't—

KROGSTAD: We won't talk about that till later. This is something else. You do have a moment to spare, I suppose?

NORA: Oh yes, of course—I do, except—

KROGSTAD: Good. I was sitting over at Olsen's Restaurant when I saw your husband go down the street—

NORA: Yes?

KROGSTAD: With a lady.

NORA: Yes. So?

KROGSTAD: If you'll pardon my asking: wasn't that lady a Mrs. Linde?

NORA: Yes.

KROGSTAD: Just now come into town?

NORA: Yes, today.

KROGSTAD: She's a good friend of yours?

NORA: Yes, she is. But I don't see—

KROGSTAD: I also knew her once.

NORA: I'm aware of that.

KROGSTAD: Oh? You know all about it. I thought so. Well, then let me ask you short and sweet: is Mrs. Linde getting a job in the bank?

NORA: What makes you think you can cross-examine me, Mr. Krogstad—you, one of my husband's employees? But since you ask, you might as well know—yes, Mrs. Linde's going to be taken on at the bank. And I'm the one who spoke for her, Mr. Krogstad. Now you know.

KROGSTAD: So I guessed right.

NORA (*pacing up and down*): Oh, one does have a tiny bit of influence, I should hope. Just because I am a woman, don't think it means that—When one has a subordinate position, Mr. Krogstad, one really ought to be careful about pushing somebody who—hm—

KROGSTAD: Who has influence?

NORA: That's right.

KROGSTAD (*in a different tone*): Mrs. Helmer, would you be good enough to use your influence on my behalf?

NORA: What? What do you mean?

KROGSTAD: Would you please make sure that I keep my subordinate position in the bank?

NORA: What does that mean? Who's thinking of taking away your position?

KROGSTAD: Oh, don't play the innocent with me. I'm quite aware that your friend would hardly relish the chance of running into me again; and I'm also aware now whom I can thank for being turned out.

NORA: But I promise you—

KROGSTAD: Yes, yes, yes, to the point: there's still time, and I'm advising you to use your influence to prevent it.

NORA: But Mr. Krogstad, I have absolutely no influence.

KROGSTAD: You haven't? I thought you were just saying—

NORA: You shouldn't take me so literally. I! How can you believe that I have any such influence over my husband?

KROGSTAD: Oh, I've known your husband from our student days. I don't think the great bank manager's more steadfast than any other married man.

NORA: You speak insolently about my husband, and I'll show you the door.

KROGSTAD: The lady has spirit.

NORA: I'm not afraid of you any longer. After New Year's, I'll soon be done with the whole business.

KROGSTAD (*restraining himself*): Now listen to me, Mrs. Helmer. If necessary, I'll fight for my little job in the bank as if it were life itself.

NORA: Yes, so it seems.

KROGSTAD: It's not just a matter of income; that's the least of it. It's something else—All right, out with it! Look, this is the thing. You know, just like all the others, of course, that once, a good many years ago, I did something rather rash.

NORA: I've heard rumors to that effect.

KROGSTAD: The case never got into court; but all the same, every door was closed in my face from then on. So I took up those various activities you know about. I had to grab hold somewhere; and I dare say I haven't been among the worst. But now I want to drop all that. My boys are growing up. For their sakes, I'll have to win back as much respect as possible here in town. That job in the bank was like the first rung in my ladder. And now your husband wants to kick me right back down in the mud again.

NORA: But for heaven's sake, Mr. Krogstad, it's simply not in my power to help you.

KROGSTAD: That's because you haven't the will to—but I have the means to make you.

NORA: You certainly won't tell my husband that I owe you money?

KROGSTAD: Hm—what if I told him that?

NORA: That would be shameful of you. (*Nearly in tears.*) This secret—my joy and my pride—that he should learn it in such a crude and disgusting way—learn it from you. You'd expose me to the most horrible unpleasantness—

KROGSTAD: Only unpleasantness?

NORA (*vehemently*): But go on and try. It'll turn out the worse for you, because then my husband will really see what a crook you are, and then you'll *never* be able to hold your job.

KROGSTAD: I asked if it was just domestic unpleasantness you were afraid of?

NORA: If my husband finds out, then of course he'll pay what I owe at once, and then we'd be through with you for good.

KROGSTAD (*a step closer*): Listen, Mrs. Helmer—you've either got a very bad memory, or else no head at all for business. I'd better put you a little more in touch with the facts.

NORA: What do you mean?

KROGSTAD: When your husband was sick, you came to me for a loan of four thousand, eight hundred crowns.

NORA: Where else could I go?

KROGSTAD: I promised to get you that sum—

NORA: And you got it.

KROGSTAD: I promised to get you that sum, on certain conditions. You were so involved in your husband's illness, and so eager to finance your trip, that I guess you didn't think out all the details. It might just be a good idea to remind you. I promised you the money on the strength of a note I drew up.

NORA: Yes, and that I signed.

KROGSTAD: Right. But at the bottom I added some lines for your father to guarantee the loan. He was supposed to sign down there.

NORA: Supposed to? He did sign.

KROGSTAD: I left the date blank. In other words, your father would have dated his signature himself. Do you remember that?

NORA: Yes, I think—

KROGSTAD: Then I gave you the note for you to mail to your father. Isn't that so?

NORA: Yes.

KROGSTAD: And naturally you sent it at once—because only some five, six days later you brought me the note, properly signed. And with that, the money was yours.

NORA: Well, then; I've made my payments regularly, haven't I?

KROGSTAD: More or less. But—getting back to the point—those were hard times for you then, Mrs. Helmer.

NORA: Yes, they were.

KROGSTAD: Your father was very ill, I believe.

NORA: He was near the end.

KROGSTAD: He died soon after?

NORA: Yes.

KROGSTAD: Tell me, Mrs. Helmer, do you happen to recall the date of your father's death? The day of the month, I mean.

NORA: Papa died the twenty-ninth of September.

KROGSTAD: That's quite correct; I've already looked into that. And now we come to a curious thing—(*Taking out a paper.*) which I simply cannot comprehend.

NORA: Curious thing? I don't know—

KROGSTAD: This is the curious thing: that your father co-signed the note for your loan three days after his death.

NORA: How—? I don't understand.

KROGSTAD: Your father died the twenty-ninth of September. But look. Here your father dated his signature October second. Isn't that curious, Mrs. Helmer? (*Nora is silent.*) Can you explain it to me? (*Nora remains silent.*) It's also remarkable that the words "October second" and the year aren't written in your father's hand, but rather in one that I think I know. Well, it's easy to understand. Your father forgot perhaps to date his signature, and then someone or other added it, a bit sloppily, before anyone knew of his death. There's nothing wrong in that. It all comes down to the signature. And there's no question about *that*, Mrs. Helmer. It really *was* your father who signed his own name here, wasn't it?

NORA (*after a short silence, throwing her head back and looking squarely at him*): No, it wasn't. *I* signed Papa's name.

KROGSTAD: Wait, now—are you fully aware that this is a dangerous confession?

NORA: Why? You'll soon get your money.

KROGSTAD: Let me ask you a question—why didn't you send the paper to your father?

NORA: That was impossible. Papa was so sick. If I'd asked him for his signature, I also would have had to tell him what the money was for. But I couldn't tell him, sick as he was, that my husband's life was in danger. That was just impossible.

KROGSTAD: Then it would have been better if you'd given up the trip abroad.

NORA: I couldn't possibly. The trip was to save my husband's life. I couldn't give that up.

KROGSTAD: But didn't you ever consider that this was a fraud against me?

NORA: I couldn't let myself be bothered by that. You weren't any concern of mine. I couldn't stand you, with all those cold complications you made, even though you knew how badly off my husband was.

KROGSTAD: Mrs. Helmer, obviously you haven't the vaguest idea of what you've involved yourself in. But I can tell you this: it was nothing more and nothing worse that I once did—and it wrecked my whole reputation.

NORA: You? Do you expect me to believe that you ever acted bravely to save your wife's life?

KROGSTAD: Laws don't inquire into motives.

NORA: Then they must be very poor laws.

KROGSTAD: Poor or not—if I introduce this paper in court, you'll be judged according to law.

NORA: This I refuse to believe. A daughter hasn't a right to protect her dying father from anxiety and care? A wife hasn't a right to save her husband's life? I don't know much about laws, but I'm sure that somewhere in the books these things are allowed. And you don't know anything about it— you who practice the law? You must be an awful lawyer, Mr. Krogstad.

KROGSTAD: Could be. But business—the kind of business we two are mixed up in—don't you think I know about that? All right. Do what you want now. But I'm telling you *this:* if I get shoved down a second time, you're going to keep me company. (*He bows and goes out through the hall.*)

NORA (*pensive for a moment, then tossing her head*): Oh, really! Trying to frighten me! I'm not so silly as all that. (*Begins gathering up the children's clothes, but soon stops.*) But—? No, but that's impossible! I did it out of love.

THE CHILDREN (*in the doorway, left*): Mama, that strange man's gone out the door.

NORA: Yes, yes, I know it. But don't tell anyone about the strange man. Do you hear? Not even Papa!

THE CHILDREN: No, Mama. But now will you play again?

NORA: No, not now.

THE CHILDREN: Oh, but Mama, you promised.

NORA: Yes, but I can't now. Go inside; I have too much to do. Go in, go in, my sweet darlings. (*She herds them gently back in the room and shuts the door after them. Settling on the sofa, she takes up a piece of embroidery and makes some stitches, but soon stops abruptly.*) No! (*Throws the work aside, rises, goes to the hall door and calls out.*) Helene! Let me have the tree in here. (*Goes to the table, left, opens the table drawer, and stops again.*) No, but that's utterly impossible!

MAID (*with the Christmas tree*): Where should I put it, ma'am?

NORA: There. The middle of the floor.

MAID: Should I bring anything else?

NORA: No, thanks. I have what I need.

The Maid, who has set the tree down, goes out.

NORA (*absorbed in trimming the tree*): Candles here—and flowers here. That terrible creature! Talk, talk, talk! There's nothing to it at all. The tree's going to be lovely. I'll do anything to please you, Torvald. I'll sing for you, dance for you—

Helmer comes in from the hall, with a sheaf of papers under his arm.

NORA: Oh! You're back so soon?

HELMER: Yes. Has anyone been here?

NORA: Here? No.

HELMER: That's odd. I saw Krogstad leaving the front door.

NORA: So? Oh yes, that's true. Krogstad was here a moment.

HELMER: Nora, I can see by your face that he's been here, begging you to put in a good word for him.

NORA: Yes.

HELMER: And it was supposed to seem like your own idea? You were to hide it from me that he'd been here. He asked you that, too, didn't he?

NORA: Yes, Torvald, but—

HELMER: Nora, Nora, and you could fall for that? Talk with that sort of person and promise him anything? And then in the bargain, tell me an untruth.

NORA: An untruth—?

HELMER: Didn't you say that no one had been here? (*Wagging his finger.*) My little songbird must never do that again. A songbird needs a clean beak to warble with. No false notes. (*Putting his arm about her waist.*) That's the way it should be, isn't it? Yes, I'm sure of it. (*Releasing her.*) And so, enough of that. (*Sitting by the stove.*) Ah, how snug and cozy it is here. (*Leafing among his papers.*)

NORA (*busy with the tree, after a short pause*): Torvald!

HELMER: Yes.

NORA: I'm so much looking forward to the Stenborgs' costume party, day after tomorrow.

HELMER: And I can't wait to see what you'll surprise me with.

NORA: Oh, that stupid business!

HELMER: What?

NORA: I can't find anything that's right. Everything seems so ridiculous, so inane.

HELMER: So my little Nora's come to *that* recognition?

NORA (*going behind his chair, her arms resting on its back*): Are you very busy, Torvald?

HELMER: Oh—

NORA: What papers are those?

HELMER: Bank matters.

NORA: Already?

HELMER: I've gotten full authority from the retiring management to make all necessary changes in personnel and procedure. I'll need Christmas week for that. I want to have everything in order by New Year's.

NORA: So that was the reason this poor Krogstad—

HELMER: Hm.

NORA (*still leaning on the chair and slowly stroking the nape of his neck*): If you weren't so very busy, I would have asked you an enormous favor, Torvald.

HELMER: Let's hear. What is it?

NORA: You know, there isn't anyone who has your good taste—and I want so much to look well at the costume party. Torvald, couldn't you take over and decide what I should be and plan my costume?

HELMER: Ah, is my stubborn little creature calling for a lifeguard?

NORA: Yes, Torvald, I can't get anywhere without your help.

HELMER: All right—I'll think it over. We'll hit on something.

NORA: Oh, how sweet of you. (*Goes to the tree again. Pause.*) Aren't the red flowers pretty—? But tell me, was it really such a crime that this Krogstad committed?

HELMER: Forgery. Do you have any idea what that means?

NORA: Couldn't he have done it out of need?

HELMER: Yes, or thoughtlessness, like so many others. I'm not so heartless that I'd condemn a man categorically for just one mistake.

NORA: No, of course not, Torvald!

HELMER: Plenty of men have redeemed themselves by openly confessing their crimes and taking their punishment.

NORA: Punishment—?

HELMER: But now Krogstad didn't go that way. He got himself out by sharp practices, and that's the real cause of his moral breakdown.

NORA: Do you really think that would—?

HELMER: Just imagine how a man with that sort of guilt in him has to lie and cheat and deceive on all sides, has to wear a mask even with the nearest and dearest he has, even with his own wife and children. And with the children, Nora—that's where it's most horrible.

NORA: Why?

HELMER: Because that kind of atmosphere of lies infects the whole life of a home. Every breath the children take in is filled with the germs of something degenerate.

NORA (*coming closer behind him*): Are you sure of that?

HELMER: Oh, I've seen it often enough as a lawyer. Almost everyone who goes bad early in life has a mother who's a chronic liar.

NORA: Why just—the mother?

HELMER: It's usually the mother's influence that's dominant, but the father's works in the same way, of course. Every lawyer is quite familiar with it. And still this Krogstad's been going home year in, year out, poisoning his own children with lies and pretense; that's why I call him morally lost. (*Reaching his hands out toward her.*) So my sweet little Nora must promise me never to plead his cause. Your hand on it. Come, come, what's this? Give me your hand. There, now. All settled. I can tell you it'd be impossible for me to work alongside of him. I literally feel physically revolted when I'm anywhere near such a person.

NORA (*withdraws her hand and goes to the other side of the Christmas tree*): How hot it is here! And I've got so much to do.

HELMER (*getting up and gathering his papers*): Yes, and I have to think about getting some of these read through before dinner. I'll think about your costume, too. And something to hang on the tree in gilt paper, I may even see about that. (*Putting his hand on her head.*) Oh you, my darling little songbird. (*He goes into his study and closes the door after him.*)

NORA (*softly, after a silence*): Oh, really! It isn't so. It's impossible. It must be impossible.

ANNE-MARIE (*in the doorway, left*): The children are begging so hard to come in to Mama.

NORA: No, no, no, don't let them in to me! You stay with them, Anne-Marie.

ANNE-MARIE: Of course, ma'am. (*Closes the door.*)

NORA (*pale with terror*): Hurt my children—! Poison my home? (*A moment's pause; then she tosses her head.*) That's not true. Never. Never in all the world.

ACT II

Same room. Beside the piano the Christmas tree now stands stripped of ornament, burned-down candle stubs on its ragged branches. Nora's street clothes lie on the sofa. Nora, alone in the room, moves restlessly about; at last she stops at the sofa and picks up her coat.

NORA (*dropping the coat again*): Someone's coming! (*Goes toward the door, listens.*) No—there's no one. Of course—nobody's coming today, Christmas Day—or tomorrow, either. But maybe—(*Opens the door and looks out.*) No, nothing in the mailbox. Quite empty. (*Coming forward.*) What nonsense! He won't do anything serious. Nothing terrible could happen. It's impossible. Why, I have three small children.

Anne-Marie, with a large carton, comes in from the room to the left.

ANNE-MARIE: Well, at last I found the box with the masquerade clothes.

NORA: Thanks. Put it on the table.

ANNE-MARIE (*does so*): But they're all pretty much of a mess.

NORA: Ahh! I'd love to rip them in a million pieces!

ANNE-MARIE: Oh, mercy, they can be fixed right up. Just a little patience.

NORA: Yes, I'll go get Mrs. Linde to help me.

ANNE-MARIE: Out again now? In this nasty weather? Miss Nora will catch cold—get sick.

NORA: Oh, worse things could happen. How are the children?

ANNE-MARIE: The poor mites are playing with their Christmas presents, but—

NORA: Do they ask for me much?

ANNE-MARIE: They're so used to having Mama around, you know.

NORA: Yes, but Anne-Marie, I *can't* be together with them as much as I was.

ANNE-MARIE: Well, small children get used to anything.

NORA: You think so? Do you think they'd forget their mother if she was gone for good?

ANNE-MARIE: Oh, mercy—gone for good!

NORA: Wait, tell me, Anne-Marie—I've wondered so often—how could you ever have the heart to give your child over to strangers?

ANNE-MARIE: But I had to, you know, to become little Nora's nurse.

NORA: Yes, but how could you *do* it?

ANNE-MARIE: When I could get such a good place? A girl who's poor and who's gotten in trouble is glad enough for that. Because that slippery fish, he didn't do a thing for me, you know.

NORA: But your daughter's surely forgotten you.

ANNE-MARIE: Oh, she certainly has not. She's written to me, both when she was confirmed and when she was married.

NORA (*clasping her about the neck*): You old Anne-Marie, you were a good mother for me when I was little.

ANNE-MARIE: Poor little Nora, with no other mother but me.

NORA: And if the babies didn't have one, then I know that you'd—What silly talk! (*Opening the carton.*) Go in to them. Now I'll have to—Tomorrow you can see how lovely I'll look.

ANNE-MARIE: Oh, there won't be anyone at the party as lovely as Miss Nora. (*She goes off into the room, left.*)

NORA (*begins unpacking the box, but soon throws it aside*): Oh, if I dared to go out. If only nobody would come. If only nothing would happen here while I'm out. What craziness—nobody's coming. Just don't think. This muff—needs a brushing. Beautiful gloves, beautiful gloves. Let it go. Let it go! One, two, three, four, five, six—(*With a cry.*) Oh, there they are! (*Poises to move toward the door, but remains irresolutely standing. Mrs. Linde enters from the hall, where she has removed her street clothes.*)

NORA: Oh, it's you, Kristine. There's no one else out there? How good that you've come.

MRS. LINDE: I hear you were up asking for me.

NORA: Yes, I just stopped by. There's something you really can help me with. Let's get settled on the sofa. Look, there's going to be a costume party tomorrow evening at the Stenborgs' right above us, and now Torvald wants me to go as a Neapolitan peasant girl and dance the tarantella that I learned in Capri.

MRS. LINDE: Really, are you giving a whole performance?

NORA: Torvald says yes, I should. See, here's the dress. Torvald had it made for me down there; but now it's all so tattered that I just don't know—

MRS. LINDE: Oh, we'll fix that up in no time. It's nothing more than the trimmings—they're a bit loose here and there. Needle and thread? Good, now we have what we need.

NORA: Oh, how sweet of you!

MRS. LINDE (*sewing*): So you'll be in disguise tomorrow, Nora. You know what? I'll stop by then for a moment and have a look at you all dressed up. But listen, I've absolutely forgotten to thank you for that pleasant evening yesterday.

NORA (*getting up and walking about*): I don't think it was as pleasant as usual yesterday. You should have come to town a bit sooner, Kristine—Yes, Torvald really knows how to give a home elegance and charm.

MRS. LINDE: And you do, too, if you ask me. You're not your father's daughter for nothing. But tell me, is Dr. Rank always so down in the mouth as yesterday?

NORA: No, that was quite an exception. But he goes around critically ill all the time—tuberculosis of the spine, poor man. You know, his father was a disgusting thing who kept mistresses and so on—and that's why the son's been sickly from birth.

MRS. LINDE (*lets her sewing fall to her lap*): But my dearest Nora, how do you know about such things?

NORA (*walking more jauntily*): Hmp! When you've had three children, then you've had a few visits from—from women who know something of medicine, and they tell you this and that.

MRS. LINDE (*resumes sewing; a short pause*): Does Dr. Rank come here every day?

NORA: Every blessed day. He's Torvald's best friend from childhood, and *my* good friend, too. Dr. Rank almost belongs to this house.

MRS. LINDE: But tell me—is he quite sincere? I mean, doesn't he rather enjoy flattering people?

NORA: Just the opposite. Why do you think that?

MRS. LINDE: When you introduced us yesterday, he was proclaiming that he'd often heard my name in this house; but later I noticed that your husband hadn't the slightest idea who I really was. So how could Dr. Rank—?

NORA: But it's all true, Kristine. You see, Torvald loves me beyond words, and, as he puts it, he'd like to keep me all to himself. For a long time he'd almost be jealous if I even mentioned any of my old friends back home. So of course I dropped that. But with Dr. Rank I talk a lot about such things, because he likes hearing about them.

MRS. LINDE: Now listen, Nora; in many ways you're still like a child. I'm a good deal older than you, with a little more experience. I'll tell you something: you ought to put an end to all this with Dr. Rank.

NORA: What should I put an end to?

MRS. LINDE: Both parts of it, I think. Yesterday you said something about a rich admirer who'd provide you with money—

NORA: Yes, one who doesn't exist—worse luck. So?

MRS. LINDE: Is Dr. Rank well off?

NORA: Yes, he is.

MRS. LINDE: With no dependents?

NORA: No, no one. But—

MRS. LINDE: And he's over here every day?

NORA: Yes, I told you that.

MRS. LINDE: How can a man of such refinement be so grasping?

NORA: I don't follow you at all.

MRS. LINDE: Now don't try to hide it, Nora. You think I can't guess who loaned you the forty-eight hundred crowns?

NORA: Are you out of your mind? How could you think such a thing! A friend of ours, who comes here every single day. What an intolerable situation that would have been!

MRS. LINDE: Then it really wasn't him.

NORA: No, absolutely not. It never even crossed my mind for a moment—And he had nothing to lend in those days; his inheritance came later.

MRS. LINDE: Well, I think that was a stroke of luck for you, Nora dear.

NORA: No, it never would have occurred to me to ask Dr. Rank—Still, I'm quite sure that if I had asked him—

MRS. LINDE: Which you won't, of course.

NORA: No, of course not. I can't see that I'd ever need to. But I'm quite positive that if I talked to Dr. Rank—

MRS. LINDE: Behind your husband's back?

NORA: I've got to clear up this other thing; *that's* also behind his back. I've *got* to clear it all up.

MRS. LINDE: Yes, I was saying that yesterday, but—

NORA (*pacing up and down*): A man handles these problems so much better than a woman—

MRS. LINDE: One's husband does, yes.

NORA: Nonsense. (*Stopping.*) When you pay everything you owe, then you get your note back, right?

MRS. LINDE: Yes, naturally.

NORA: And can rip it into a million pieces and burn it up — that filthy scrap of paper!

MRS. LINDE (*looking hard at her, laying her sewing aside, and rising slowly*): Nora, you're hiding something from me.

NORA: You can see it in my face?

MRS. LINDE: Something's happened to you since yesterday morning. Nora, what is it?

NORA (*hurrying toward her*): Kristine! (*Listening.*) Shh! Torvald's home. Look, go in with the children a while. Torvald can't bear all this snipping and stitching. Let Anne-Marie help you.

MRS. LINDE (*gathering up some of the things*): All right, but I'm not leaving here until we've talked this out. (*She disappears into the room, left, as Torvald enters from the hall.*)

NORA: Oh, how I've been waiting for you, Torvald dear.

HELMER: Was that the dressmaker?

NORA: No, that was Kristine. She's helping me fix up my costume. You know, it's going to be quite attractive.

HELMER: Yes, wasn't that a bright idea I had?

NORA: Brilliant! But then wasn't I good as well to give in to you?

HELMER: Good — because you give in to your husband's judgment? All right, you little goose, I know you didn't mean it like that. But I won't disturb you. You'll want to have a fitting, I suppose.

NORA: And you'll be working?

HELMER: Yes. (*Indicating a bundle of papers.*) See. I've been down to the bank. (*Starts toward his study.*)

NORA: Torvald.

HELMER (*stops*): Yes.

NORA: If your little squirrel begged you, with all her heart and soul, for something — ?

HELMER: What's that?

NORA: Then would you do it?

HELMER: First, naturally, I'd have to know what it was.

NORA: Your squirrel would scamper about and do tricks, if you'd only be sweet and give in.

HELMER: Out with it.

NORA: Your lark would be singing high and low in every room —

HELMER: Come on, she does that anyway.

NORA: I'd be a wood nymph and dance for you in the moonlight.

HELMER: Nora — don't tell me it's that same business from this morning?

NORA (*coming closer*): Yes, Torvald, I beg you, please!

HELMER: And you actually have the nerve to drag that up again?

NORA: Yes, yes, you've got to give in to me; you *have* to let Krogstad keep his job in the bank.

HELMER: My dear Nora, I've slated his job for Mrs. Linde.

NORA: That's awfully kind of you. But you could just fire another clerk instead of Krogstad.

HELMER: This is the most incredible stubbornness! Because you go and give an impulsive promise to speak up for him, I'm expected to—

NORA: That's not the reason, Torvald. It's for your own sake. That man does writing for the worst papers; you said it yourself. He could do you any amount of harm. I'm scared to death of him—

HELMER: Ah, I understand. It's the old memories haunting you.

NORA: What do you mean by that?

HELMER: Of course, you're thinking about your father.

NORA: Yes, all right. Just remember how those nasty gossips wrote in the papers about Papa and slandered him so cruelly. I think they'd have had him dismissed if the department hadn't sent you up to investigate, and if you hadn't been so kind and open-minded toward him.

HELMER: My dear Nora, there's a notable difference between your father and me. Your father's official career was hardly above reproach. But mine is; and I hope it'll stay that way as long as I hold my position.

NORA: Oh, who can ever tell what vicious minds can invent? We could be so snug and happy now in our quiet, carefree home—you and I and the children, Torvald! That's why I'm pleading with you so—

HELMER: And just by pleading for him you make it impossible for me to keep him on. It's already known at the bank that I'm firing Krogstad. What if it's rumored around now that the new bank manager was vetoed by his wife—

NORA: Yes, what then—?

HELMER: Oh yes—as long as our little bundle of stubbornness gets her way—! I should go and make myself ridiculous in front of the whole office— give people the idea I can be swayed by all kinds of outside pressure. Oh, you can bet I'd feel the effects of that soon enough! Besides—there's something that rules Krogstad right out at the bank as long as I'm the manager.

NORA: What's that?

HELMER: His moral failings I could maybe overlook if I had to—

NORA: Yes, Torvald, why not?

HELMER: And I hear he's quite efficient on the job. But he was a crony of mine back in my teens—one of those rash friendships that crop up again and again to embarrass you later in life. Well, I might as well say it straight out: we're on a first-name basis. And that tactless fool makes no effort at all to hide it in front of others. Quite the contrary—he thinks that entitles him to take a familiar air around me, and so every other second he comes booming out with his "Yes, Torvald!" and "Sure thing, Torvald!" I tell you, it's been excruciating for me. He's out to make my place in the bank unbearable.

NORA: Torvald, you can't be serious about all this.

HELMER: Oh no? Why not?

NORA: Because these are such petty considerations.

HELMER: What are you saying? Petty? You think I'm petty!

NORA: No, just the opposite, Torvald dear. That's exactly why —

HELMER: Never mind. You call my motives petty; then I might as well be just that. Petty! All right! We'll put a stop to this for good. (*Goes to the hall door and calls.*) Helene!

NORA: What do you want?

HELMER (*searching among his papers*): A decision. (*The Maid comes in.*) Look here; take this letter; go out with it at once. Get hold of a messenger and have him deliver it. Quick now. It's already addressed. Wait, here's some money.

MAID: Yes, sir. (*She leaves with the letter.*)

HELMER (*straightening his papers*): There, now, little Miss Willful.

NORA (*breathlessly*): Torvald, what was that letter?

HELMER: Krogstad's notice.

NORA: Call it back, Torvald! There's still time. Oh, Torvald, call it back! Do it for my sake — for your sake, for the children's sake! Do you hear, Torvald; do it! You don't know how this can harm us.

HELMER: Too late.

NORA: Yes, too late.

HELMER: Nora dear, I can forgive you this panic, even though basically you're insulting me. Yes, you are! Or isn't it an insult to think that *I* should be afraid of a courtroom hack's revenge? But I forgive you anyway, because this shows so beautifully how much you love me. (*Takes her in his arms.*) This is the way it should be, my darling Nora. Whatever comes, you'll see; when it really counts, I have strength and courage enough as a man to take on the whole weight myself.

NORA (*terrified*): What do you mean by that?

HELMER: The whole weight, I said.

NORA (*resolutely*): No, never in all the world.

HELMER: Good. So we'll share it, Nora, as man and wife. That's as it should be. (*Fondling her.*) Are you happy now? There, there, there — not these frightened dove's eyes. It's nothing at all but empty fantasies — Now you should run through your tarantella and practice your tambourine. I'll go to the inner office and shut both doors, so I won't hear a thing; you can make all the noise you like. (*Turning in the doorway.*) And when Rank comes, just tell him where he can find me. (*He nods to her and goes with his papers into the study, closing the door.*)

NORA (*standing as though rooted, dazed with fright, in a whisper*): He really could do it. He will do it. He'll do it in spite of everything. No, not that, never, never! Anything but that! Escape! A way out — (*The doorbell rings.*) Dr. Rank! Anything but that! *Anything*, whatever it is! (*Her hands pass over her face, smoothing it; she pulls herself together, goes over and opens the hall door. Dr. Rank stands outside, hanging his fur coat up. During the following scene, it begins getting dark.*)

NORA: Hello, Dr. Rank. I recognized your ring. But you mustn't go in to Torvald yet; I believe he's working.

RANK: And you?

NORA: For you, I always have an hour to spare—you know that. (*He has entered, and she shuts the door after him.*)

RANK: Many thanks. I'll make use of these hours while I can.

NORA: What do you mean by that? While you can?

RANK: Does that disturb you?

NORA: Well, it's such an odd phrase. Is anything going to happen?

RANK: What's going to happen is what I've been expecting so long—but I honestly didn't think it would come so soon.

NORA (*gripping his arm*): What is it you've found out? Dr. Rank, you have to tell me!

RANK (*sitting by the stove*): It's all over for me. There's nothing to be done about it.

NORA (*breathing easier*): Is it you—then—?

RANK: Who else? There's no point in lying to one's self. I'm the most miserable of all my patients, Mrs. Helmer. These past few days I've been auditing my internal accounts. Bankrupt! Within a month I'll probably be laid out and rotting in the churchyard.

NORA: Oh, what a horrible thing to say.

RANK: The thing itself is horrible. But the worst of it is all the other horror before it's over. There's only one final examination left; when I'm finished with that, I'll know about when my disintegration will begin. There's something I want to say. Helmer with his sensitivity has such a sharp distaste for anything ugly. I don't want him near my sickroom.

NORA: Oh, but Dr. Rank—

RANK: I won't have him in there. Under no condition. I'll lock my door to him—As soon as I'm completely sure of the worst, I'll send you my calling card marked with a black cross, and you'll know then the wreck has started to come apart.

NORA: No, today you're completely unreasonable. And I wanted you so much to be in a really good humor.

RANK: With death up my sleeve? And then to suffer this way for somebody else's sins. Is there any justice in that? And in every single family, in some way or another, this inevitable retribution of nature goes on—

NORA (*her hands pressed over her ears*): Oh, stuff! Cheer up! Please—be gay!

RANK: Yes, I'd just as soon laugh at it all. My poor, innocent spine, serving time for my father's gay army days.

NORA (*by the table, left*): He was so infatuated with asparagus tips and pâté de foie gras, wasn't that it?

RANK: Yes—and with truffles.

NORA: Truffles, yes. And then with oysters, I suppose?

RANK: Yes, tons of oysters, naturally.

NORA: And then the port and champagne to go with it. It's so sad that all these delectable things have to strike at our bones.

RANK: Especially when they strike at the unhappy bones that never shared in the fun.

NORA: Ah, that's the saddest of all.

RANK (*looks searchingly at her*): Hm.

NORA (*after a moment*): Why did you smile?

RANK: No, it was you who laughed.

NORA: No, it was you who smiled, Dr. Rank!

RANK (*getting up*): You're even a bigger tease than I'd thought.

NORA: I'm full of wild ideas today.

RANK: That's obvious.

NORA (*putting both hands on his shoulders*): Dear, dear Dr. Rank, you'll never die for Torvald and me.

RANK: Oh, that loss you'll easily get over. Those who go away are soon forgotten.

NORA (*looks fearfully at him*): You believe that?

RANK: One makes new connections, and then—

NORA: Who makes new connections?

RANK: Both you and Torvald will when I'm gone. I'd say you're well under way already. What was that Mrs. Linde doing here last evening?

NORA: Oh, come—you can't be jealous of poor Kristine?

RANK: Oh yes, I am. She'll be my successor here in the house. When I'm down under, that woman will probably—

NORA: Shh! Not so loud. She's right in there.

RANK: Today as well. So you see.

NORA: Only to sew on my dress. Good gracious, how unreasonable you are. (*Sitting on the sofa.*) Be nice now, Dr. Rank. Tomorrow you'll see how beautifully I'll dance; and you can imagine then that I'm dancing only for you—yes, and of course for Torvald, too—that's understood. (*Takes various items out of the carton.*) Dr. Rank, sit over here and I'll show you something.

RANK (*sitting*): What's that?

NORA: Look here. Look.

RANK: Silk stockings.

NORA: Flesh-colored. Aren't they lovely? Now it's so dark here, but tomorrow—No, no, no, just look at the feet. Oh well, you might as well look at the rest.

RANK: Hm—

NORA: Why do you look so critical? Don't you believe they'll fit?

RANK: I've never had any chance to form an opinion on that.

NORA (*glancing at him a moment*): Shame on you. (*Hits him lightly on the ear with the stockings.*) That's for you. (*Puts them away again.*)

RANK: And what other splendors am I going to see now?

NORA: Not the least bit more, because you've been naughty. (*She hums a little and rummages among her things.*)

RANK (*after a short silence*): When I sit here together with you like this, completely easy and open, then I don't know—I simply can't imagine—whatever would have become of me if I'd never come into this house.

NORA (*smiling*): Yes, I really think you feel completely at ease with us.

RANK (*more quietly, staring straight ahead*): And then to have to go away from it all—

NORA: Nonsense, you're not going away.

RANK (*his voice unchanged*): — and not even be able to leave some poor show of gratitude behind, scarcely a fleeting regret — no more than a vacant place that anyone can fill.

NORA: And if I asked you now for —? No —

RANK: For what?

NORA: For a great proof of your friendship —

RANK: Yes, yes?

NORA: No, I mean — for an exceptionally big favor —

RANK: Would you really, for once, make me so happy?

NORA: Oh, you haven't the vaguest idea what it is.

RANK: All right, then tell me.

NORA: No, but I can't, Dr. Rank — it's all out of reason. It's advice and help, too — and a favor —

RANK: So much the better. I can't fathom what you're hinting at. Just speak out. Don't you trust me?

NORA: Of course. More than anyone else. You're my best and truest friend, I'm sure. That's why I want to talk to you. All right, then, Dr. Rank: there's something you can help me prevent. You know how deeply, how inexpressibly dearly Torvald loves me; he'd never hesitate a second to give up his life for me.

RANK (*leaning close to her*): Nora — do you think he's the only one —

NORA (*with a slight start*): Who —?

RANK: Who'd gladly give up his life for you.

NORA (*heavily*): I see.

RANK: I swore to myself you should know this before I'm gone. I'll never find a better chance. Yes, Nora, now you know. And also you know now that you can trust me beyond anyone else.

NORA (*rising, natural and calm*): Let me by.

RANK (*making room for her, but still sitting*): Nora —

NORA (*in the hall doorway*): Helene, bring the lamp in. (*Goes over to the stove.*) Ah, dear Dr. Rank, that was really mean of you.

RANK (*getting up*): That I've loved you just as deeply as somebody else? Was *that* mean?

NORA: No, but that you came out and told me. That was quite unnecessary —

RANK: What do you mean? Have you known —?

The Maid comes in with the lamp, sets it on the table, and goes out again.

RANK: Nora — Mrs. Helmer — I'm asking you: have you known about it?

NORA: Oh, how can I tell what I know or don't know? Really, I don't know what to say — Why did you have to be so clumsy, Dr. Rank! Everything was so good.

RANK: Well, in any case, you now have the knowledge that my body and soul are at your command. So won't you speak out?

NORA (*looking at him*): After that?

RANK: Please, just let me know what it is.

NORA: You can't know anything now.

RANK: I have to. You mustn't punish me like this. Give me the chance to do whatever is humanly possible for you.

NORA: Now there's nothing you can do for me. Besides, actually, I don't need any help. You'll see — it's only my fantasies. That's what it is. Of course! (*Sits in the rocker, looks at him, and smiles.*) What a nice one you are, Dr. Rank. Aren't you a little bit ashamed, now that the lamp is here?

RANK: No, not exactly. But perhaps I'd better go — for good?

NORA: No, you certainly can't do that. You must come here just as you always have. You know Torvald can't do without you.

RANK: Yes, but *you?*

NORA: You know how much I enjoy it when you're here.

RANK: That's precisely what threw me off. You're a mystery to me. So many times I've felt you'd almost rather be with me than with Helmer.

NORA: Yes — you see, there are some people that one loves most and other people that one would almost prefer being with.

RANK: Yes, there's something to that.

NORA: When I was back home, of course I loved Papa most. But I always thought it was so much fun when I could sneak down to the maids' quarters, because they never tried to improve me, and it was always so amusing, the way they talked to each other.

RANK: Aha, so it's *their* place that I've filled.

NORA (*jumping up and going to him*): Oh, dear, sweet Dr. Rank, that's not what I meant at all. But you can understand that with Torvald it's just the same as with Papa —

The Maid enters from the hall.

MAID: Ma'am — please! (*She whispers to Nora and hands her a calling card.*)

NORA (*glancing at the card*): Ah! (*Slips it into her pocket.*)

RANK: Anything wrong?

NORA: No, no, not at all. It's only some — it's my new dress —

RANK: Really? But — there's your dress.

NORA: Oh, that. But this is another one — I ordered it — Torvald mustn't know —

RANK: Ah, now we have the big secret.

NORA: That's right. Just go in with him — he's back in the inner study. Keep him there as long as —

RANK: Don't worry. He won't get away. (*Goes into the study.*)

NORA (*to the Maid*): And he's standing waiting in the kitchen?

MAID: Yes, he came up by the back stairs.

NORA: But didn't you tell him somebody was here?

MAID: Yes, but that didn't do any good.

NORA: He won't leave?

MAID: No, he won't go till he's talked with you, ma'am.

NORA: Let him come in, then — but quietly. Helene, don't breathe a word about this. It's a surprise for my husband.

MAID: Yes, yes, I understand — (*Goes out.*)

NORA: This horror — it's going to happen. No, no, no, it can't happen, it mustn't. (*She goes and bolts Helmer's door. The Maid opens the hall door for Krogstad and shuts it behind him. He is dressed for travel in a fur coat, boots, and a fur cap.*)

NORA (*going toward him*): Talk softly. My husband's home.

KROGSTAD: Well, good for him.

NORA: What do you want?

KROGSTAD: Some information.

NORA: Hurry up, then. What is it?

KROGSTAD: You know, of course, that I got my notice.

NORA: I couldn't prevent it, Mr. Krogstad. I fought for you to the bitter end, but nothing worked.

KROGSTAD: Does your husband's love for you run so thin? He knows everything I can expose you to, and all the same he dares to —

NORA: How can you imagine he knows anything about this?

KROGSTAD: Ah, no — I can't imagine it either, now. It's not at all like my fine Torvald Helmer to have so much guts —

NORA: Mr. Krogstad, I demand respect for my husband!

KROGSTAD: Why, of course — all due respect. But since the lady's keeping it so carefully hidden, may I presume to ask if you're also a bit better informed than yesterday about what you've actually done?

NORA: More than you could ever teach me.

KROGSTAD: Yes, I *am* such an awful lawyer.

NORA: What is it you want from me?

KROGSTAD: Just a glimpse of how you are, Mrs. Helmer. I've been thinking about you all day long. A cashier, a night-court scribbler, a — well, a type like me also has a little of what they call a heart, you know.

NORA: Then show it. Think of my children.

KROGSTAD: Did you or your husband ever think of mine? But never mind. I simply wanted to tell you that you don't need to take this thing too seriously. For the present, I'm not proceeding with any action.

NORA: Oh no, really! Well — I knew that.

KROGSTAD: Everything can be settled in a friendly spirit. It doesn't have to get around town at all; it can stay just among us three.

NORA: My husband must never know anything of this.

KROGSTAD: How can you manage that? Perhaps you can pay me the balance?

NORA: No, not right now.

KROGSTAD: Or you know some way of raising the money in a day or two?

NORA: No way that I'm willing to use.

KROGSTAD: Well, it wouldn't have done you any good, anyway. If you stood in front of me with a fistful of bills, you still couldn't buy your signature back.

NORA: Then tell me what you're going to do with it.

KROGSTAD: I'll just hold onto it — keep it on file. There's no outsider who'll even get wind of it. So if you've been thinking of taking some desperate step —

NORA: I have.

KROGSTAD: Been thinking of running away from home—

NORA: I have!

KROGSTAD: Or even of something worse—

NORA: How could you guess that?

KROGSTAD: You can drop those thoughts.

NORA: How could you guess I was thinking of *that?*

KROGSTAD: Most of us think about *that* at first. I thought about it too, but I discovered I hadn't the courage—

NORA (*lifelessly*): I don't either.

KROGSTAD (*relieved*): That's true, you haven't the courage? You too?

NORA: I don't have it—I don't have it.

KROGSTAD: It would be terribly stupid, anyway. After that first storm at home blows out, why, then—I have here in my pocket a letter for your husband—

NORA: Telling everything?

KROGSTAD: As charitably as possible.

NORA (*quickly*): He mustn't ever get that letter. Tear it up. I'll find some way to get money.

KROGSTAD: Beg pardon, Mrs. Helmer, but I think I just told you—

NORA: Oh, I don't mean the money I owe you. Let me know how much you want from my husband, and I'll manage it.

KROGSTAD: I don't want money from your husband.

NORA: What do you want, then?

KROGSTAD: I'll tell you what. I want to recoup, Mrs. Helmer; I want to get on in the world—and there's where your husband can help me. For a year and a half I've kept myself clean of anything disreputable—all that time struggling with the worst conditions; but I was satisfied, working my way up step by step. Now I've been written right off, and I'm just not in the mood to come crawling back. I tell you, I want to move on. I want to get back in the bank—in a better position. Your husband can set up a job for me—

NORA: He'll never do that!

KROGSTAD: He'll do it. I know him. He won't dare breathe a word of protest. And once I'm in there together with him, you just wait and see! Inside of a year, I'll be the manager's right-hand man. It'll be Nils Krogstad, not Torvald Helmer, who runs the bank.

NORA: You'll never see the day!

KROGSTAD: Maybe you think you can—

NORA: I have the courage now—for *that.*

KROGSTAD: Oh, you don't scare me. A smart, spoiled lady like you—

NORA: You'll see; you'll see!

KROGSTAD: Under the ice, maybe? Down in the freezing coal-black water? There, till you float up in the spring, ugly, unrecognizable, with your hair falling out—

NORA: You don't frighten me.

KROGSTAD: Nor do you frighten me. One doesn't do these things, Mrs. Helmer. Besides, what good would it be? I'd still have him safe in my pocket.

NORA: Afterwards? When I'm no longer—?

KROGSTAD: Are you forgetting that *I'll* be in control then over your final reputation? (*Nora stands speechless, staring at him.*) Good; now I've warned you. Don't do anything stupid. When Helmer's read my letter, I'll be waiting for his reply. And bear in mind that it's your husband himself who's forced me back to my old ways. I'll never forgive him for that. Good-bye, Mrs. Helmer. (*He goes out through the hall.*)

NORA (*goes to the hall door, opens it a crack, and listens*): He's gone. Didn't leave the letter. Oh no, no, that's impossible too! (*Opening the door more and more.*) What's that? He's standing outside—not going downstairs. He's thinking it over? Maybe he'll—? (*A letter falls in the mailbox; then Krogstad's footsteps are heard, dying away down a flight of stairs. Nora gives a muffled cry and runs over toward the sofa table. A short pause.*) In the mailbox. (*Slips warily over to the hall door.*) It's lying there. Torvald, Torvald—now we're lost!

MRS. LINDE (*entering with costume from the room, left*): There now, I can't see anything else to mend. Perhaps you'd like to try—

NORA (*in a hoarse whisper*): Kristine, come here.

MRS. LINDE (*tossing the dress on the sofa*): What's wrong? You look upset.

NORA: Come here. See that letter? *There!* Look—through the glass in the mailbox.

MRS. LINDE: Yes, yes, I see it.

NORA: That letter's from Krogstad—

MRS. LINDE: Nora—it's Krogstad who loaned you the money!

NORA: Yes, and now Torvald will find out everything.

MRS. LINDE: Believe me, Nora, it's best for both of you.

NORA: There's more you don't know. I forged a name.

MRS. LINDE: But for heaven's sake—?

NORA: I only want to tell you that, Kristine, so that you can be my witness.

MRS. LINDE: Witness? Why should I—?

NORA: If I should go out of my mind—it could easily happen—

MRS. LINDE: Nora!

NORA: Or anything else occurred—so I couldn't be present here—

MRS. LINDE: Nora, Nora, you aren't yourself at all!

NORA: And someone should try to take on the whole weight, all of the guilt, you follow me—

MRS. LINDE: Yes, of course, but why do you think—?

NORA: Then you're the witness that it isn't true, Kristine. I'm very much myself; my mind right now is perfectly clear; and I'm telling you: nobody else has known about this; I alone did everything. Remember that.

MRS. LINDE: I will. But I don't understand all this.

NORA: Oh, how could you ever understand it? It's the miracle now that's going to take place.

MRS. LINDE: The miracle?

NORA: Yes, the miracle. But it's so awful, Kristine. It mustn't take place, not for anything in the world.

MRS. LINDE: I'm going right over and talk with Krogstad.

NORA: Don't go near him; he'll do you some terrible harm!

MRS. LINDE: There was a time once when he'd gladly have done anything for me.

NORA: He?

MRS. LINDE: Where does he live?

NORA: Oh, how do I know? Yes. (*Searches in her pocket.*) Here's his card. But the letter, the letter—!

HELMER (*from the study, knocking on the door*): Nora!

NORA (*with a cry of fear*): Oh! What is it? What do you want?

HELMER: Now, now, don't be so frightened. We're not coming in. You locked the door—are you trying on the dress?

NORA: Yes, I'm trying it. I'll look just beautiful, Torvald.

MRS. LINDE (*who has read the card*): He's living right around the corner.

NORA: Yes, but what's the use? We're lost. The letter's in the box.

MRS. LINDE: And your husband has the key?

NORA: Yes, always.

MRS. LINDE: Krogstad can ask for his letter back unread; he can find some excuse—

NORA: But it's just this time that Torvald usually—

MRS. LINDE: Stall him. Keep him in there. I'll be back as quick as I can. (*She hurries out through the hall entrance.*)

NORA (*goes to Helmer's door, opens it, and peers in*): Torvald!

HELMER (*from the inner study*): Well—does one dare set foot in one's own living room at last? Come on, Rank, now we'll get a look—(*In the doorway.*) But what's this?

NORA: What, Torvald dear?

HELMER: Rank had me expecting some grand masquerade.

RANK (*in the doorway*): That was my impression, but I must have been wrong.

NORA: No one can admire me in my splendor—not till tomorrow.

HELMER: But Nora dear, you look so exhausted. Have you practiced too hard?

NORA: No, I haven't practiced at all yet.

HELMER: You know, it's necessary—

NORA: Oh, it's absolutely necessary, Torvald. But I can't get anywhere without your help. I've forgotten the whole thing completely.

HELMER: Ah, we'll soon take care of that.

NORA: Yes, take care of me, Torvald, please! Promise me that? Oh, I'm so nervous. That big party—You must give up everything this evening for me. No business—don't even touch your pen. Yes? Dear Torvald, promise?

HELMER: It's a promise. Tonight I'm totally at your service—you little helpless thing. Hm—but first there's one thing I want to—(*Goes toward the hall door.*)

NORA: What are you looking for?

HELMER: Just to see if there's any mail.

NORA: No, no, don't do that, Torvald!

HELMER: Now what?

NORA: Torvald, please. There isn't any.

HELMER: Let me look, though. (*Starts out. Nora, at the piano, strikes the first notes of the tarantella. Helmer, at the door, stops.*) Aha!

NORA: I can't dance tomorrow if I don't practice with you.

HELMER (*going over to her*): Nora dear, are you really so frightened?

NORA: Yes, so terribly frightened. Let me practice right now; there's still time before dinner. Oh, sit down and play for me, Torvald. Direct me. Teach me, the way you always have.

HELMER: Gladly, if it's what you want. (*Sits at the piano.*)

NORA (*snatches the tambourine up from the box, then a long, varicolored shawl, which she throws around herself, whereupon she springs forward and cries out*): Play for me now! Now I'll dance!

Helmer plays and Nora dances. Rank stands behind Helmer at the piano and looks on.

HELMER (*as he plays*): Slower. Slow down.

NORA: Can't change it.

HELMER: Not so violent, Nora!

NORA: Has to be just like this.

HELMER (*stopping*): No, no, that won't do at all.

NORA (*laughing and swinging her tambourine*): Isn't that what I told you?

RANK: Let me play for her.

HELMER (*getting up*): Yes, go on. I can teach her more easily then.

Rank sits at the piano and plays; Nora dances more and more wildly. Helmer has stationed himself by the stove and repeatedly gives her directions; she seems not to hear them; her hair loosens and falls over her shoulders; she does not notice, but goes on dancing. Mrs. Linde enters.

MRS. LINDE (*standing dumbfounded at the door*): Ah—!

NORA (*still dancing*): See what fun, Kristine!

HELMER: But Nora darling, you dance as if your life were at stake.

NORA: And it is.

HELMER: Rank, stop! This is pure madness. Stop it, I say!

Rank breaks off playing, and Nora halts abruptly.

HELMER (*going over to her*): I never would have believed it. You've forgotten everything I taught you.

NORA (*throwing away the tambourine*): You see for yourself.

HELMER: Well, there's certainly room for instruction here.

NORA: Yes, you see how important it is. You've got to teach me to the very last minute. Promise me that, Torvald?

HELMER: You can bet on it.

NORA: You mustn't, either today or tomorrow, think about anything else but me; you mustn't open any letters—or the mailbox—

HELMER: Ah, it's still the fear of that man—

NORA: Oh yes, yes, that too.

HELMER: Nora, it's written all over you—there's already a letter from him out there.

NORA: I don't know. I guess so. But you mustn't read such things now; there mustn't be anything ugly between us before it's all over.

RANK (*quietly to Helmer*): You shouldn't deny her.

HELMER (*putting his arms around her*): The child can have her way. But tomorrow night, after you've danced—

NORA: Then you'll be free.

MAID (*in the doorway, right*): Ma'am, dinner is served.

NORA: We'll be wanting champagne, Helene.

MAID: Very good, ma'am. (*Goes out.*)

HELMER: So—a regular banquet, hm?

NORA: Yes, a banquet—champagne till daybreak! (*Calling out.*) And some macaroons, Helene. Heaps of them—just this once.

HELMER (*taking her hands*): Now, now, now—no hysterics. Be my own little lark again.

NORA: Oh, I will soon enough. But go on in—and you, Dr. Rank. Kristine, help me put up my hair.

RANK (*whispering, as they go*): There's nothing wrong—really wrong, is there?

HELMER: Oh, of course not. It's nothing more than this childish anxiety I was telling you about. (*They go out, right.*)

NORA: Well?

MRS. LINDE: Left town.

NORA: I could see by your face.

MRS. LINDE: He'll be home tomorrow evening. I wrote him a note.

NORA: You shouldn't have. Don't try to stop anything now. After all, it's a wonderful joy, this waiting here for the miracle.

MRS. LINDE: What is it you're waiting for?

NORA: Oh, you can't understand that. Go in to them; I'll be along in a moment.

Mrs. Linde goes into the dining room. Nora stands a short while as if composing herself; then she looks at her watch.

NORA: Five. Seven hours to midnight. Twenty-four hours to the midnight after, and then the tarantella's done. Seven and twenty-four? Thirty-one hours to live.

HELMER (*in the doorway, right*): What's become of the little lark?

NORA (*going toward him with open arms*): Here's your lark!

ACT III

Same scene. The table, with chairs around it, has been moved to the center of the room. A lamp on the table is lit. The hall door stands open. Dance music drifts down from the floor above. Mrs. Linde sits at the table, absently paging through a book, trying to read, but apparently unable to focus her thoughts. Once or twice she pauses, tensely listening for a sound at the outer entrance.

MRS. LINDE (*glancing at her watch*): Not yet—and there's hardly any time left. If only he's not—(*Listening again.*) Ah, there he is. (*She goes out in the hall and cautiously opens the outer door. Quiet footsteps are heard on the stairs. She whispers:*) Come in. Nobody's here.

KROGSTAD (*in the doorway*): I found a note from you at home. What's back of all this?

MRS. LINDE: I just *had* to talk to you.

KROGSTAD: Oh? And it just *had* to be here in this house?

MRS. LINDE: At my place it was impossible; my room hasn't a private entrance. Come in; we're all alone. The maid's asleep, and the Helmers are at the dance upstairs.

KROGSTAD (*entering the room*): Well, well, the Helmers are dancing tonight? Really?

MRS. LINDE: Yes, why not?

KROGSTAD: How true—why not?

MRS. LINDE: All right, Krogstad, let's talk.

KROGSTAD: Do we two have anything more to talk about?

MRS. LINDE: We have a great deal to talk about.

KROGSTAD: I wouldn't have thought so.

MRS. LINDE: No, because you've never understood me, really.

KROGSTAD: Was there anything more to understand—except what's all too common in life? A calculating woman throws over a man the moment a better catch comes by.

MRS. LINDE: You think I'm so thoroughly calculating? You think I broke it off lightly?

KROGSTAD: Didn't you?

MRS. LINDE: Nils—is that what you really thought?

KROGSTAD: If you cared, then why did you write me the way you did?

MRS. LINDE: What else could I do? If I had to break off with you, then it was my job as well to root out everything you felt for me.

KROGSTAD (*wringing his hands*): So that was it. And this—all this, simply for money!

MRS. LINDE: Don't forget I had a helpless mother and two small brothers. We couldn't wait for you, Nils; you had such a long road ahead of you then.

KROGSTAD: That may be; but you still hadn't the right to abandon me for somebody else's sake.

MRS. LINDE: Yes—I don't know. So many, many times I've asked myself if I did have that right.

KROGSTAD (*more softly*): When I lost you, it was as if all the solid ground dissolved from under my feet. Look at me; I'm a half-drowned man now, hanging onto a wreck.

MRS. LINDE: Help may be near.

KROGSTAD: It was near—but then you came and blocked it off.

MRS. LINDE: Without my knowing it, Nils. Today for the first time I learned that it's you I'm replacing at the bank.

KROGSTAD: All right—I believe you. But now that you know, will you step aside?

MRS. LINDE: No, because that wouldn't benefit you in the slightest.

KROGSTAD: Not "benefit" me, hm! I'd step aside anyway.

MRS. LINDE: I've learned to be realistic. Life and hard, bitter necessity have taught me that.

KROGSTAD: And life's taught me never to trust fine phrases.

MRS. LINDE: Then life's taught you a very sound thing. But you do have to trust in actions, don't you?

KROGSTAD: What does that mean?

MRS. LINDE: You said you were hanging on like a half-drowned man to a wreck.

KROGSTAD: I've good reason to say that.

MRS. LINDE: I'm also like a half-drowned woman on a wreck. No one to suffer with; no one to care for.

KROGSTAD: You made your choice.

MRS. LINDE: There wasn't any choice then.

KROGSTAD: So—what of it?

MRS. LINDE: Nils, if only we two shipwrecked people could reach across to each other.

KROGSTAD: What are you saying?

MRS. LINDE: Two on one wreck are at least better off than each on his own.

KROGSTAD: Kristine!

MRS. LINDE: Why do you think I came into town?

KROGSTAD: Did you really have some thought of me?

MRS. LINDE: I have to work to go on living. All my born days, as long as I can remember, I've worked, and it's been my best and my only joy. But now I'm completely alone in the world; it frightens me to be so empty and lost. To work for yourself—there's no joy in that. Nils, give me something—someone to work for.

KROGSTAD: I don't believe all this. It's just some hysterical feminine urge to go out and make a noble sacrifice.

MRS. LINDE: Have you ever found me to be hysterical?

KROGSTAD: Can you honestly mean this? Tell me—do you know everything about my past?

MRS. LINDE: Yes.

KROGSTAD: And you know what they think I'm worth around here.

MRS. LINDE: From what you were saying before, it would seem that with me you could have been another person.

KROGSTAD: I'm positive of that.

MRS. LINDE: Couldn't it happen still?

KROGSTAD: Kristine—you're saying this in all seriousness? Yes, you are! I can see it in you. And do you really have the courage, then—?

MRS. LINDE: I need to have someone to care for; and your children need a mother. We both need each other. Nils, I have faith that you're good at heart—I'll risk everything together with you.

KROGSTAD (*gripping her hands*): Kristine, thank you, thank you—Now I know I can win back a place in their eyes. Yes—but I forgot—

MRS. LINDE (*listening*): Shh! The tarantella. Go now! Go on!

KROGSTAD: Why? What is it?

MRS. LINDE: Hear the dance up there? When that's over, they'll be coming down.

KROGSTAD: Oh, then I'll go. But—it's all pointless. Of course, you don't know the move I made against the Helmers.

MRS. LINDE: Yes, Nils, I know.

KROGSTAD: And all the same, you have the courage to—?

MRS. LINDE: I know how far despair can drive a man like you.

KROGSTAD: Oh, if I only could take it all back.

MRS. LINDE: You easily could—your letter's still lying in the mailbox.

KROGSTAD: Are you sure of that?

MRS. LINDE: Positive. But—

KROGSTAD (*looks at her searchingly*): Is that the meaning of it, then? You'll save your friend at any price. Tell me straight out. Is that it?

MRS. LINDE: Nils—anyone who's sold herself for somebody else once isn't going to do it again.

KROGSTAD: I'll demand my letter back.

MRS. LINDE: No, no.

KROGSTAD: Yes, of course. I'll stay here till Helmer comes down; I'll tell him to give me my letter again—that it only involves my dismissal—that he shouldn't read it—

MRS. LINDE: No, Nils, don't call the letter back.

KROGSTAD: But wasn't that exactly why you wrote me to come here?

MRS. LINDE: Yes, in that first panic. But it's been a whole day and night since then, and in that time I've seen such incredible things in this house. Helmer's got to learn everything; this dreadful secret has to be aired; those two have to come to a full understanding; all these lies and evasions can't go on.

KROGSTAD: Well, then, if you want to chance it. But at least there's one thing I can do, and do right away—

MRS. LINDE (*listening*): Go now, go quick! The dance is over. We're not safe another second.

KROGSTAD: I'll wait for you downstairs.

MRS. LINDE: Yes, please do; take me home.

KROGSTAD: I can't believe it; I've never been so happy. (*He leaves by way of the outer door; the door between the room and the hall stays open.*)

MRS. LINDE (*straightening up a bit and getting together her street clothes*): How different now! How different! Someone to work for, to live for—a home to build. Well, it is worth the try! Oh, if they'd only come! (*Listening.*) Ah, there they are. Bundle up. (*She picks up her hat and coat. Nora's and Helmer's voices can be heard outside; a key turns in the lock, and Helmer brings Nora into the hall almost by force. She is wearing the Italian costume with a large black shawl about her; he has on evening dress, with a black domino open over it.*)

NORA (*struggling in the doorway*): No, no, no, not inside! I'm going up again. I don't want to leave so soon.

HELMER: But Nora dear—

NORA: Oh, I beg you, please, Torvald. From the bottom of my heart, please— only an hour more!

HELMER: Not a single minute, Nora darling. You know our agreement. Come on, in we go; you'll catch cold out here. (*In spite of her resistance, he gently draws her into the room.*)

MRS. LINDE: Good evening.

NORA: Kristine!

HELMER: Why, Mrs. Linde—are you here so late?

MRS. LINDE: Yes, I'm sorry, but I did want to see Nora in costume.

NORA: Have you been sitting here, waiting for me?

MRS. LINDE: Yes. I didn't come early enough; you were all upstairs; and then I thought I really couldn't leave without seeing you.

HELMER (*removing Nora's shawl*): Yes, take a good look. She's worth looking at, I can tell you that, Mrs. Linde. Isn't she lovely?

MRS. LINDE: Yes, I should say —

HELMER: A dream of loveliness, isn't she? That's what everyone thought at the party, too. But she's horribly stubborn — this sweet little thing. What's to be done with her? Can you imagine, I almost had to use force to pry her away.

NORA: Oh, Torvald, you're going to regret you didn't indulge me, even for just a half hour more.

HELMER: There, you see. She danced her tarantella and got a tumultuous hand — which was well earned, although the performance may have been a bit too naturalistic — I mean it rather overstepped the proprieties of art. But never mind — what's important is, she made a success, an over- whelming success. You think I could let her stay on after that and spoil the effect? Oh no; I took my lovely little Capri girl — my capricious little Capri girl, I should say — took her under my arm; one quick tour of the ballroom, a curtsy to every side, and then — as they say in novels — the beautiful vision disappeared. An exit should always be effective, Mrs. Linde, but that's what I can't get Nora to grasp. Phew, it's hot in here. (*Flings the domino on a chair and opens the door to his room.*) Why's it dark in here? Oh yes, of course. Excuse me. (*He goes in and lights a couple of candles.*)

NORA (*in a sharp, breathless whisper*): So?

MRS. LINDE (*quietly*): I talked with him.

NORA: And —?

MRS. LINDE: Nora — you must tell your husband everything.

NORA (*dully*): I knew it.

MRS. LINDE: You've got nothing to fear from Krogstad, but you have to speak out.

NORA: I won't tell.

MRS. LINDE: Then the letter will.

NORA: Thanks, Kristine. I know now what's to be done. Shh!

HELMER (*reentering*): Well, then, Mrs. Linde — have you admired her?

MRS. LINDE: Yes, and now I'll say good night.

HELMER: Oh, come, so soon? Is this yours, this knitting?

MRS. LINDE: Yes, thanks. I nearly forgot it.

HELMER: Do you knit, then?

MRS. LINDE: Oh yes.

HELMER: You know what? You should embroider instead.

MRS. LINDE: Really? Why?

HELMER: Yes, because it's a lot prettier. See here, one holds the embroidery so, in the left hand, and then one guides the needle with the right — so — in an easy, sweeping curve — right?

MRS. LINDE: Yes, I guess that's —

HELMER: But, on the other hand, knitting — it can never be anything but ugly. Look, see here, the arms tucked in, the knitting needles going up and down—there's something Chinese about it. Ah, that was really a glorious champagne they served.

MRS. LINDE: Yes, good night, Nora, and don't be stubborn anymore.

HELMER: Well put, Mrs. Linde!

MRS. LINDE: Good night, Mr. Helmer.

HELMER (*accompanying her to the door*): Good night, good night. I hope you get home all right. I'd be very happy to—but you don't have far to go. Good night, good night. (*She leaves. He shuts the door after her and returns.*) There, now, at last we got her out the door. She's a deadly bore, that creature.

NORA: Aren't you pretty tired, Torvald?

HELMER: No, not a bit.

NORA: You're not sleepy?

HELMER: Not at all. On the contrary, I'm feeling quite exhilarated. But you? Yes, you really look tired and sleepy.

NORA: Yes, I'm very tired. Soon now I'll sleep.

HELMER: See! You see! I was right all along that we shouldn't stay longer.

NORA: Whatever you do is always right.

HELMER (*kissing her brow*): Now my little lark talks sense. Say, did you notice what a time Rank was having tonight?

NORA: Oh, was he? I didn't get to speak with him.

HELMER: I scarcely did either, but it's a long time since I've seen him in such high spirits. (*Gazes at her a moment, then comes nearer her.*) Hm—it's marvelous, though, to be back home again—to be completely alone with you. Oh, you bewitchingly lovely young woman!

NORA: Torvald, don't look at me like that!

HELMER: Can't I look at my richest treasure? At all that beauty that's mine, mine alone—completely and utterly.

NORA (*moving around to the other side of the table*): You mustn't talk to me that way tonight.

HELMER (*following her*): The tarantella is still in your blood, I can see—and it makes you even more enticing. Listen. The guests are beginning to go. (*Dropping his voice.*) Nora—it'll soon be quiet through this whole house.

NORA: Yes, I hope so.

HELMER: You do, don't you, my love? Do you realize—when I'm out at a party like this with you—do you know why I talk to you so little, and keep such a distance away; just send you a stolen look now and then—you know why I do it? It's because I'm imagining then that you're my secret darling, my secret bride-to-be, and that no one suspects there's anything between us.

NORA: Yes, yes; oh, yes, I know you're always thinking of me.

HELMER: And then when we leave and I place the shawl over those fine young rounded shoulders—over that wonderful curving neck—then I pretend that you're my young bride, that we're just coming from the wedding, that for the first time I'm bringing you into my house—that for the first time I'm alone with you—completely alone with you, your trembling young beauty! All this evening I've longed for nothing but you. When I saw you turn and sway in the tarantella — my blood was pounding till I couldn't stand it — that's why I brought you down here so early —

NORA: Go away, Torvald! Leave me alone. I don't want all this.

HELMER: What do you mean? Nora, you're teasing me. You will, won't you? Aren't I your husband — ?

A knock at the outside door.

NORA (*startled*): What's that?

HELMER (*going toward the hall*): Who is it?

RANK (*outside*): It's me. May I come in a moment?

HELMER (*with quiet irritation*): Oh, what does he want now? (*Aloud.*) Hold on. (*Goes and opens the door.*) Oh, how nice that you didn't just pass us by!

RANK: I thought I heard your voice, and then I wanted so badly to have a look in. (*Lightly glancing about.*) Ah, me, these old familiar haunts. You have it snug and cozy in here, you two.

HELMER: You seemed to be having it pretty cozy upstairs, too.

RANK: Absolutely. Why shouldn't I? Why not take in everything in life? As much as you can, anyway, and as long as you can. The wine was superb —

HELMER: The champagne especially.

RANK: You noticed that too? It's amazing how much I could guzzle down.

NORA: Torvald also drank a lot of champagne this evening.

RANK: Oh?

NORA: Yes, and that always makes him so entertaining.

RANK: Well, why shouldn't one have a pleasant evening after a well-spent day?

HELMER: Well spent? I'm afraid I can't claim that.

RANK (*slapping him on the back*): But I can, you see!

NORA: Dr. Rank, you must have done some scientific research today.

RANK: Quite so.

HELMER: Come now — little Nora talking about scientific research!

NORA: And can I congratulate you on the results?

RANK: Indeed you may.

NORA: Then they were good?

RANK: The best possible for both doctor and patient — certainty.

NORA (*quickly and searchingly*): Certainty?

RANK: Complete certainty. So don't I owe myself a gay evening afterwards?

NORA: Yes, you're right, Dr. Rank.

HELMER: I'm with you — just so long as you don't have to suffer for it in the morning.

RANK: Well, one never gets something for nothing in life.

NORA: Dr. Rank — are you very fond of masquerade parties?

RANK: Yes, if there's a good array of odd disguises —

NORA: Tell me, what should we two go as at the next masquerade?

HELMER: You little featherhead — already thinking of the next!

RANK: We two? I'll tell you what: you must go as Charmed Life —

HELMER: Yes, but find a costume for *that!*

RANK: Your wife can appear just as she looks every day.

HELMER: That was nicely put. But don't you know what you're going to be?

RANK: Yes, Helmer, I've made up my mind.

HELMER: Well?

RANK: At the next masquerade I'm going to be invisible.

HELMER: That's a funny idea.

RANK: They say there's a hat—black, huge—have you never heard of the hat that makes you invisible? You put it on, and then no one on earth can see you.

HELMER (*suppressing a smile*): Ah, of course.

RANK: But I'm quite forgetting what I came for. Helmer, give me a cigar, one of the dark Havanas.

HELMER: With the greatest pleasure. (*Holds out his case.*)

RANK: Thanks. (*Takes one and cuts off the tip.*)

NORA (*striking a match*): Let me give you a light.

RANK: Thank you. (*She holds the match for him; he lights the cigar.*) And now good-bye.

HELMER: Good-bye, good-bye, old friend.

NORA: Sleep well, Doctor.

RANK: Thanks for that wish.

NORA: Wish me the same.

RANK: You? All right, if you like—Sleep well. And thanks for the light. (*He nods to them both and leaves.*)

HELMER (*his voice subdued*): He's been drinking heavily.

NORA (*absently*): Could be. (*Helmer takes his keys from his pocket and goes out in the hall.*) Torvald—what are you after?

HELMER: Got to empty the mailbox; it's nearly full. There won't be room for the morning papers.

NORA: Are you working tonight?

HELMER: You know I'm not. Why—what's this? Someone's been at the lock.

NORA: At the lock—?

HELMER: Yes, I'm positive. What do you suppose—? I can't imagine one of the maids—? Here's a broken hairpin. Nora, it's yours—

NORA (*quickly*): Then it must be the children—

HELMER: You'd better break them of that. Hm, hm—well, opened it after all. (*Takes the contents out and calls into the kitchen.*) Helene! Helene, would you put out the lamp in the hall. (*He returns to the room shutting the hall door, then displays the handful of mail.*) Look how it's piled up. (*Sorting through them.*) Now what's this?

NORA (*at the window*): The letter! Oh, Torvald, no!

HELMER: Two calling cards—from Rank.

NORA: From Dr. Rank?

HELMER (*examining them*): "Dr. Rank, Consulting Physician." They were on top. He must have dropped them in as he left.

NORA: Is there anything on them?

HELMER: There's a black cross over the name. See? That's a gruesome notion. He could almost be announcing his own death.

NORA: That's just what he's doing.

HELMER: What! You've heard something? Something he's told you?

NORA: Yes. That when those cards came, he'd be taking his leave of us. He'll shut himself in now and die.

HELMER: Ah, my poor friend! Of course I knew he wouldn't be here much longer. But so soon—And then to hide himself away like a wounded animal.

NORA: If it has to happen, then it's best it happens in silence—don't you think so, Torvald?

HELMER (*pacing up and down*): He'd grown right into our lives. I simply can't imagine him gone. He with his suffering and loneliness—like a dark cloud setting off our sunlit happiness. Well, maybe it's best this way. For him, at least. (*Standing still.*) And maybe for us too, Nora. Now we're thrown back on each other, completely. (*Embracing her.*) Oh you, my darling wife, how can I hold you close enough? You know what, Nora—time and again I've wished you were in some terrible danger, just so I could stake my life and soul and everything, for your sake.

NORA (*tearing herself away, her voice firm and decisive*): Now you must read your mail, Torvald.

HELMER: No, no, not tonight. I want to stay with you, dearest.

NORA: With a dying friend on your mind?

HELMER: You're right. We've both had a shock. There's ugliness between us—these thoughts of death and corruption. We'll have to get free of them first. Until then—we'll stay apart.

NORA (*clinging about his neck*): Torvald—good night! Good night!

HELMER (*kissing her on the cheek*): Good night, little songbird. Sleep well, Nora. I'll be reading my mail now. (*He takes the letters into his room and shuts the door after him.*)

NORA (*with bewildered glances, groping about, seizing Helmer's domino, throwing it around her, and speaking in short, hoarse, broken whispers*): Never see him again. Never, never. (*Putting her shawl over her head.*) Never see the children either—them, too. Never, never. Oh, the freezing black water! The depths—down—Oh, I wish it were over—He has it now; he's reading it—now. Oh no, no, not yet. Torvald, good-bye, you and the children—(*She starts for the hall; as she does, Helmer throws open his door and stands with an open letter in his hand.*)

HELMER: Nora!

NORA (*screams*): Oh—!

HELMER: What is this? You know what's in this letter?

NORA: Yes, I know. Let me go! Let me out!

HELMER (*holding her back*): Where are you going?

NORA (*struggling to break loose*): You can't save me, Torvald!

HELMER (*slumping back*): True! Then it's true what he writes? How horrible! No, no, it's impossible—it can't be true.

NORA: It *is* true. I've loved you more than all this world.

HELMER: Ah, none of your slippery tricks.

NORA (*taking one step toward him*): Torvald—!

HELMER: What *is* this you've blundered into!

NORA: Just let me loose. You're not going to suffer for my sake. You're not going to take on my guilt.

HELMER: No more play-acting. (*Locks the hall door.*) You stay right here and give me a reckoning. You understand what you've done? Answer! You understand?

NORA (*looking squarely at him, her face hardening*): Yes. I'm beginning to understand everything now.

HELMER (*striding about*): Oh, what an awful awakening! In all these eight years—she who was my pride and joy—a hypocrite, a liar—worse, worse—a criminal! How infinitely disgusting it all is! The shame! (*Nora says nothing and goes on looking straight at him. He stops in front of her.*) I should have suspected something of the kind. I should have known. All your father's flimsy values—Be still! All your father's flimsy values have come out in you. No religion, no morals, no sense of duty—Oh, how I'm punished for letting him off! I did it for your sake, and you repay me like this.

NORA: Yes, like this.

HELMER: Now you've wrecked all my happiness—ruined my whole future. Oh, it's awful to think of. I'm in a cheap little grafter's hands; he can do anything he wants with me, ask for anything, play with me like a puppet—and I can't breathe a word. I'll be swept down miserably into the depths on account of a featherbrained woman.

NORA: When I'm gone from this world, you'll be free.

HELMER: Oh, quit posing. Your father had a mess of those speeches too. What good would that ever do me if you were gone from this world, as you say? Not the slightest. He can still make the whole thing known; and if he does, I could be falsely suspected as your accomplice. They might even think that I was behind it—that I put you up to it. And all that I can thank you for—you that I've coddled the whole of our marriage. Can you see now what you've done to me?

NORA (*icily calm*): Yes.

HELMER: It's so incredible, I just can't grasp it. But we'll have to patch up whatever we can. Take off the shawl. I said, take it off! I've got to appease him somehow or other. The thing has to be hushed up at any cost. And as for you and me, it's got to seem like everything between us is just as it was—to the outside world, that is. You'll go right on living in this house, of course. But you can't be allowed to bring up the children; I don't dare trust you with them—Oh, to have to say this to someone I've loved so much! Well, that's done with. From now on happiness doesn't matter; all that matters is saving the bits and pieces, the appearance—(*The doorbell rings. Helmer starts.*) What's that? And so late. Maybe the worst—? You think he'd—? Hide, Nora! Say you're sick. (*Nora remains standing motionless. Helmer goes and opens the door.*)

MAID (*half dressed, in the hall*): A letter for Mrs. Helmer.

HELMER: I'll take it. (*Snatches the letter and shuts the door.*) Yes, it's from him. You don't get it; I'm reading it myself.

NORA: Then read it.

HELMER (*by the lamp*): I hardly dare. We may be ruined, you and I. But—I've got to know. (*Rips open the letter, skims through a few lines, glances at an enclosure, then cries out joyfully.*) Nora! (*Nora looks inquiringly at him.*) Nora! Wait—better check it again—Yes, yes, it's true. I'm saved. Nora, I'm saved!

NORA: And I?

HELMER: You too, of course. We're both saved, both of us. Look. He's sent back your note. He says he's sorry and ashamed—that a happy development in his life—oh, who cares what he says! Nora, we're saved! No one can hurt you. Oh, Nora, Nora—but first, this ugliness all has to go. Let me see—(*Takes a look at the note.*) No, I don't want to see it; I want the whole thing to fade like a dream. (*Tears the note and both letters to pieces, throws them into the stove and watches them burn.*) There—now there's nothing left—He wrote that since Christmas Eve you—Oh, they must have been three terrible days for you, Nora.

NORA: I fought a hard fight.

HELMER: And suffered pain and saw no escape but—No, we're not going to dwell on anything unpleasant. We'll just be grateful and keep on repeating: it's over now, it's over! You hear me, Nora? You don't seem to realize—it's over. What's it mean—that frozen look? Oh, poor little Nora, I under-stand. You can't believe I've forgiven you. But I have, Nora; I swear I have. I know that what you did, you did out of love for me.

NORA: That's true.

HELMER: You loved me the way a wife ought to love her husband. It's simply the means that you couldn't judge. But you think I love you any the less for not knowing how to handle your affairs? No, no—just lean on me; I'll guide you and teach you. I wouldn't be a man if this feminine helpless-ness didn't make you twice as attractive to me. You mustn't mind those sharp words I said—that was all in the first confusion of thinking my world had collapsed. I've forgiven you, Nora; I swear I've forgiven you.

NORA: My thanks for your forgiveness. (*She goes out through the door, right.*)

HELMER: No, wait—(*Peers in.*) What are you doing in there?

NORA (*inside*): Getting out of my costume.

HELMER (*by the open door*): Yes, do that. Try to calm yourself and collect your thoughts again, my frightened little songbird. You can rest easy now; I've got wide wings to shelter you with. (*Walking about close by the door.*) How snug and nice our home is, Nora. You're safe here; I'll keep you like a hunted dove I've rescued out of a hawk's claws. I'll bring peace to your poor, shuddering heart. Gradually it'll happen, Nora; you'll see. Tomor-row all this will look different to you; then everything will be as it was. I won't have to go on repeating I forgive you; you'll feel it for yourself. How can you imagine I'd ever conceivably want to disown you—or even blame you in any way? Ah, you don't know a man's heart, Nora. For a man there's something indescribably sweet and satisfying in knowing he's forgiven his wife—and forgiven her out of a full and open heart. It's as if she belongs to him in two ways now: in a sense he's given her fresh into the world again, and she's become his wife and his child as well. From now on that's what you'll be to me—you little, bewildered, help-less thing. Don't be afraid of anything, Nora; just open your heart to me, and I'll be conscience and will to you both——(*Nora enters in her regular clothes.*) What's this? Not in bed? You've changed your dress?

NORA: Yes, Torvald, I've changed my dress.

HELMER: But why now, so late?

NORA: Tonight I'm not sleeping.

HELMER: But Nora dear—

NORA (*looking at her watch*): It's still not so very late. Sit down, Torvald; we have a lot to talk over. (*She sits at one side of the table.*)

HELMER: Nora—what is this? That hard expression—

NORA: Sit down. This'll take some time. I have a lot to say.

HELMER (*sitting at the table directly opposite her*): You worry me, Nora. And I don't understand you.

NORA: No, that's exactly it. You don't understand me. And I've never understood you either—until tonight. No, don't interrupt. You can just listen to what I say. We're closing out accounts, Torvald.

HELMER: How do you mean that?

NORA (*after a short pause*): Doesn't anything strike you about our sitting here like this?

HELMER: What's that?

NORA: We've been married now eight years. Doesn't it occur to you that this is the first time we two, you and I, man and wife, have ever talked seriously together?

HELMER: What do you mean—seriously?

NORA: In eight whole years—longer even—right from our first acquaintance, we've never exchanged a serious word on any serious thing.

HELMER: You mean I should constantly go and involve you in problems you couldn't possibly help me with?

NORA: I'm not talking of problems. I'm saying that we've never sat down seriously together and tried to get to the bottom of anything.

HELMER: But dearest, what good would that ever do you?

NORA: That's the point right there: you've never understood me. I've been wronged greatly, Torvald—first by Papa, and then by you.

HELMER: What! By us—the two people who've loved you more than anyone else?

NORA (*shaking her head*): You never loved me. You've thought it fun to be in love with me, that's all.

HELMER: Nora, what a thing to say!

NORA: Yes, it's true now, Torvald. When I lived at home with Papa, he told me all his opinions, so I had the same ones too; or if they were different I hid them, since he wouldn't have cared for that. He used to call me his doll-child, and he played with me the way I played with my dolls. Then I came into your house—

HELMER: How can you speak of our marriage like that?

NORA (*unperturbed*): I mean, then I went from Papa's hands into yours. You arranged everything to your own taste, and so I got the same taste as you—or I pretended to; I can't remember. I guess a little of both, first one, then the other. Now when I look back, it seems as if I'd lived here like a beggar—just from hand to mouth. I've lived by doing tricks for you, Torvald. But that's the way you wanted it. It's a great sin what you and Papa did to me. You're to blame that nothing's become of me.

HELMER: Nora, how unfair and ungrateful you are! Haven't you been happy here?

NORA: No, never. I thought so—but I never have.

HELMER: Not—not happy!

NORA: No, only lighthearted. And you've always been so kind to me. But our home's been nothing but a playpen. I've been your doll-wife here, just as at home I was Papa's doll-child. And in turn the children have been my dolls. I thought it was fun when you played with me, just as they thought it fun when I played with them. That's been our marriage, Torvald.

HELMER: There's some truth in what you're saying—under all the raving exaggeration. But it'll all be different after this. Playtime's over; now for the schooling.

NORA: Whose schooling—mine or the children's?

HELMER: Both yours and the children's, dearest.

NORA: Oh, Torvald, you're not the man to teach me to be a good wife to you.

HELMER: And you can say that?

NORA: And I—how am I equipped to bring up children?

HELMER: Nora!

NORA: Didn't you say a moment ago that that was no job to trust me with?

HELMER: In a flare of temper! Why fasten on that?

NORA: Yes, but you were so very right. I'm not up to the job. There's another job I have to do first. I have to try to educate myself. You can't help me with that. I've got to do it alone. And that's why I'm leaving you now.

HELMER (*jumping up*): What's that?

NORA: I have to stand completely alone, if I'm ever going to discover myself and the world out there. So I can't go on living with you.

HELMER: Nora, Nora!

NORA: I want to leave right away. Kristine should put me up for the night—

HELMER: You're insane! You've no right! I forbid you!

NORA: From here on, there's no use forbidding me anything. I'll take with me whatever is mine. I don't want a thing from you, either now or later.

HELMER: What kind of madness is this!

NORA: Tomorrow I'm going home—I mean, home where I came from. It'll be easier up there to find something to do.

HELMER: Oh, you blind, incompetent child!

NORA: I must learn to be competent, Torvald.

HELMER: Abandon your home, your husband, your children! And you're not even thinking what people will say.

NORA: I can't be concerned about that. I only know how essential this is.

HELMER: Oh, it's outrageous. So you'll run out like this on your most sacred vows.

NORA: What do you think are my most sacred vows?

HELMER: And I have to tell you that! Aren't they your duties to your husband and children?

NORA: I have other duties equally sacred.

HELMER: That isn't true. What duties are they?

NORA: Duties to myself.

HELMER: Before all else, you're a wife and mother.

NORA: I don't believe in that anymore. I believe that, before all else, I'm a human being, no less than you—or anyway, I ought to try to become one. I know the majority thinks you're right, Torvald, and plenty of books agree with you, too. But I can't go on believing what the majority says, or what's written in books. I have to think over these things myself and try to understand them.

HELMER: Why can't you understand your place in your own home? On a point like that, isn't there one everlasting guide you can turn to? Where's your religion?

NORA: Oh, Torvald, I'm really not sure what religion is.

HELMER: What—?

NORA: I only know what the minister said when I was confirmed. He told me religion was this thing and that. When I get clear and away by myself, I'll go into that problem too. I'll see if what the minister said was right, or, in any case, if it's right for me.

HELMER: A young woman your age shouldn't talk like that. If religion can't move you, I can try to rouse your conscience. You do have some moral feeling? Or, tell me—has that gone too?

NORA: It's not easy to answer that, Torvald. I simply don't know. I'm all confused about these things. I just know I see them so differently from you. I find out, for one thing, that the law's not at all what I'd thought—but I can't get it through my head that the law is fair. A woman hasn't a right to protect her dying father or save her husband's life! I can't believe that.

HELMER: You talk like a child. You don't know anything of the world you live in.

NORA: No, I don't. But now I'll begin to learn for myself. I'll try to discover who's right, the world or I.

HELMER: Nora, you're sick; you've got a fever. I almost think you're out of your head.

NORA: I've never felt more clearheaded and sure in my life.

HELMER: And—clearheaded and sure—you're leaving your husband and children?

NORA: Yes.

HELMER: Then there's only one possible reason.

NORA: What?

HELMER: You no longer love me.

NORA: No. That's exactly it.

HELMER: Nora! You can't be serious!

NORA: Oh, this is so hard, Torvald—you've been so kind to me always. But I can't help it. I don't love you anymore.

HELMER (*struggling for composure*): Are you also clearheaded and sure about that?

NORA: Yes, completely. That's why I can't go on staying here.

HELMER: Can you tell me what I did to lose your love?

NORA: Yes, I can tell you. It was this evening when the miraculous thing didn't come—then I knew you weren't the man I'd imagined.

HELMER: Be more explicit; I don't follow you.

NORA: I've waited now so patiently eight long years—for, my Lord, I know miracles don't come every day. Then this crisis broke over me, and such a certainty filled me: *now* the miraculous event would occur. While Krogstad's letter was lying out there, I never for an instant dreamed that you could give in to his terms. I was so utterly sure you'd say to him: go on, tell your tale to the whole wide world. And when he'd done that—

HELMER: Yes, what then? When I'd delivered my own wife into shame and disgrace—

NORA: When he'd done that, I was so utterly sure that you'd step forward, take the blame on yourself and say: I am the guilty one.

HELMER: Nora—!

NORA: You're thinking I'd never accept such a sacrifice from you? No, of course not. But what good would my protests be against you? That was the miracle I was waiting for, in terror and hope. And to stave that off, I would have taken my life.

HELMER: I'd gladly work for you day and night, Nora—and take on pain and deprivation. But there's no one who gives up honor for love.

NORA: Millions of women have done just that.

HELMER: Oh, you think and talk like a silly child.

NORA: Perhaps. But you neither think nor talk like the man I could join myself to. When your big fright was over—and it wasn't from any threat against me, only for what might damage you—when all the danger was past, for you it was just as if nothing had happened. I was exactly the same, your little lark, your doll, that you'd have to handle with double care now that I'd turned out so brittle and frail. (*Gets up.*) Torvald—in that instant it dawned on me that for eight years I've been living here with a stranger, and that I've even conceived three children—oh, I can't stand the thought of it! I could tear myself to bits.

HELMER (*heavily*): I see. There a gulf that's opened between us—that's clear. Oh, but Nora, can't we bridge it somehow?

NORA: The way I am now, I'm no wife for you.

HELMER: I have the strength to make myself over.

NORA: Maybe—if your doll gets taken away.

HELMER: But to part! To part from you! No, Nora no—I can't imagine it.

NORA (*going out, right*): All the more reason why it has to be. (*She reenters with her coat and a small overnight bag, which she puts on a chair by the table.*)

HELMER: Nora, Nora, not now! Wait till tomorrow.

NORA: I can't spend the night in a strange man's room.

HELMER: But couldn't we live here like brother and sister—

NORA: You know very well how long that would last. (*Throws her shawl about her.*) Good-bye, Torvald. I won't look in on the children. I know they're in better hands than mine. The way I am now, I'm no use to them.

HELMER: But someday, Nora—someday—?

NORA: How can I tell? I haven't the least idea what'll become of me.

HELMER: But you're my wife, now and wherever you go.

NORA: Listen, Torvald—I've heard that when a wife deserts her husband's house just as I'm doing, then the law frees him from all responsibility. In any case, I'm freeing you from being responsible. Don't feel yourself bound, any more than I will. There has to be absolute freedom for us both. Here, take your ring back. Give me mine.

HELMER: That too?

NORA: That too.

HELMER: There it is.

NORA: Good. Well, now it's all over. I'm putting the keys here. The maids know all about keeping up the house—better than I do. Tomorrow, after I've left town, Kristine will stop by to pack up everything that's mine from home. I'd like those things shipped up to me.

HELMER: Over! All over! Nora, won't you ever think about me?

NORA: I'm sure I'll think of you often, and about the children and the house here.

HELMER: May I write you?

NORA: No—never. You're not to do that.

HELMER: Oh, but let me send you—

NORA: Nothing. Nothing.

HELMER: Or help you if you need it.

NORA: No. I accept nothing from strangers.

HELMER: Nora—can I never be more than a stranger to you?

NORA (*picking up her overnight bag*): Ah, Torvald—it would take the greatest miracle of all—

HELMER: Tell me the greatest miracle!

NORA: You and I both would have to transform ourselves to the point that— Oh, Torvald, I've stopped believing in miracles.

HELMER: But I'll believe. Tell me! Transform ourselves to the point that—?

NORA: That our living together could be a true marriage. (*She goes out down the hall.*)

HELMER (*sinks down on a chair by the door, face buried in his hands*): Nora! Nora! (*Looking about and rising.*) Empty. She's gone. (*A sudden hope leaps in him.*) The greatest miracle—?

From below, the sound of a door slamming shut.

SUSAN GLASPELL

Susan Glaspell (1876–1948) was born in Davenport, Iowa, into a family that had been among the state's first settlers a generation before. After her graduation from high school, she worked as a reporter and society editor for various newspapers before enrolling at Drake University in Des Moines, where she studied literature, philosophy, and history. She also edited the college newspaper and began to write short stories. In 1899 she took a job as statehouse reporter for the

Des Moines Daily News. *Years later she claimed that the discipline of newspaper work helped her to become a creative writer.*

At the age of twenty-five, Glaspell returned to Davenport to live with her family, "boldly" determined, as she said, to quit journalism and "give all my time to my own writing. I say 'boldly,' because I had to earn my living." Slowly she began to publish her own work, mostly sentimental magazine stories and an undistinguished first novel—fiction that, as her biographer C. W. E. Bigsby has noted, "suggested little of the originality and power which were to mark her work in the theater." In 1909 Glaspell met George Cram Cook, a novelist and utopian socialist from a wealthy family who divorced his second wife and left his two children to marry her.

Glaspell and Cook moved to Greenwich Village in New York City and collaborated on a short play for the experimental Washington Square Players in 1915, Suppressed Desires, a comedy about psychoanalysis and its founder, Sigmund Freud, whom they sarcastically referred to as "the new Messiah." The simple sets and amateur performances in this off-Broadway theater company contrasted with the ostentation then prevailing on Broadway. There producers such as David Belasco went to extreme lengths in the lavishness of their sets and costumes, transferring to the stage every detail of an actual Child's Restaurant, for example, in the popular play The Governor's Lady in 1912. After the Players left Greenwich Village to relocate in Provincetown on Cape Cod in 1916, Cook urged Glaspell to write a new play for their fledgling theater company, renamed the Provincetown Players. When she protested that she did not know how to write plays, he told her, "Nonsense. You've got a stage, haven't you?"

Glaspell's memory of a murder trial in Iowa that she'd covered as a newspaper reporter served as the inspiration for the short play Trifles (1916). A decade later, in her biography of her husband, The Road to the Temple (1927), Glaspell recalled how she visualized the play while sitting in a ramshackle fish house at the end of a wharf in Provincetown where she and Cook were establishing a theater:

> So I went out on the wharf, sat alone on one of our wooden benches without a back, and looked a long time at that bare little stage. After a time the stage became a kitchen—a kitchen there all by itself. I saw just where the stove was, the table, and the steps going upstairs. Then the door at the back opened, and people all bundled up came in—two or three men, I wasn't sure which, but sure enough about the two women, who hung back, reluctant to enter that kitchen. When I was a newspaper reporter out in Iowa, I was sent down-state to do a murder trial, and I never forgot going into the kitchen of a woman locked up in town. I had meant to do it as a short story, but the stage took it for its own, so I hurried in from the wharf to write down what I had seen. Whenever I got stuck, I would run across the street to the old wharf, sit in that leaning little theater under which the sea sounded, until the play was ready to continue. Sometimes things written in my room would not form on the stage, and I must go home and cross them out.

Glaspell finished Trifles in ten days. It opened on August 8, 1916, with Glaspell and Cook in the cast. Glaspell went on to write ten more plays for the Provincetown Players, but Trifles is the one play of hers that is continually reprinted. She also published a short story version of the play, titled "A Jury of Her

Peers," in 1917. *During the six years of Cook's visionary leadership, the Provincetown Players produced one hundred plays by fifty-two authors. The company's promotion of American playwrights was an important landmark in the history of theater in the United States. As the historian Barbara Ozieblo realized, the Provincetown Players "constituted a laboratory for their two stars, Eugene O'Neill and Susan Glaspell; they triumphed both in the United States and in England; they broke the hegemony of Broadway, proving the value of little theatres and their experimental work and so seeding the mature drama of America."*

CONNECTION   *Susan Glaspell, "A Jury of Her Peers," page 194.*

COMMENTARY   *Leonard Mustazza, "Generic Translation and Thematic Shift in Susan Glaspell's* Trifles *and 'A Jury of Her Peers,'" page 1560.*

WEB   *Research Susan Glaspell and answer questions about her work at bedfordstmartins.com/charters/litwriters.*

Trifles   1916

CHARACTERS

GEORGE HENDERSON,
   county attorney
HENRY PETERS, sheriff

LEWIS HALE, a neighboring farmer
MRS. PETERS
MRS. HALE

SCENE: *The kitchen in the now abandoned farmhouse of John Wright, a gloomy kitchen, and left without having been put in order — the walls covered with a faded wall paper. Down right is a door leading to the parlor. On the right wall above this door is a built-in kitchen cupboard with shelves in the upper portion and drawers below. In the rear wall at right, up two steps is a door opening onto stairs leading to the second floor. In the rear wall at left is a door to the shed and from there to the outside. Between these two doors is an old-fashioned black iron stove. Running along the left wall from the shed door is an old iron sink and sink shelf, in which is set a hand pump. Downstage of the sink is an uncurtained window. Near the window is an old wooden rocker. Center stage is an unpainted wooden kitchen table with straight chairs on either side. There is a small chair down right. Unwashed pans under the sink, a loaf of bread outside the breadbox, a dish towel on the table — other signs of incompleted work. At the rear the shed door opens and the Sheriff comes in followed by the County Attorney and Hale. The Sheriff and Hale are men in middle life, the County Attorney is a young man; all are much bundled up and go at once to the stove. They are followed by the two women — the Sheriff's wife, Mrs. Peters, first; she is a slight wiry woman, a thin nervous face. Mrs. Hale is larger and would ordinarily be called more comfortable looking, but she is disturbed now and looks fearfully about as she enters. The women have come in slowly, and stand close together near the door.*

COUNTY ATTORNEY (*at stove rubbing his hands*): This feels good. Come up to the
   fire, ladies.

MRS. PETERS (*after taking a step forward*): I'm not—cold.

SHERIFF (*unbuttoning his overcoat and stepping away from the stove to right of table as if to mark the beginning of official business*): Now, Mr. Hale, before we move things about, you explain to Mr. Henderson just what you saw when you came here yesterday morning.

COUNTY ATTORNEY (*crossing down to left of the table*): By the way, has anything been moved? Are things just as you left them yesterday?

SHERIFF (*looking about*): It's just about the same. When it dropped below zero last night I thought I'd better send Frank out this morning to make a fire for us—(*sits right of center table*) no use getting pneumonia with a big case on, but I told him not to touch anything except the stove—and you know Frank.

COUNTY ATTORNEY: Somebody should have been left here yesterday.

SHERIFF: Oh—yesterday. When I had to send Frank to Morris Center for that man who went crazy—I want you to know I had my hands full yesterday. I knew you could get back from Omaha by today and as long as I went over everything here myself———

COUNTY ATTORNEY: Well, Mr. Hale, tell just what happened when you came here yesterday morning.

HALE (*crossing down to above table*): Harry and I had started to town with a load of potatoes. We came along the road from my place and as I got here I said, "I'm going to see if I can't get John Wright to go in with me on a party telephone." I spoke to Wright about it once before and he put me off, saying folks talked too much anyway, and all he asked was peace and quiet—I guess you know about how much he talked himself; but I thought maybe if I went to the house and talked about it before his wife, though I said to Harry that I didn't know as what his wife wanted made much difference to John———

COUNTY ATTORNEY: Let's talk about that later, Mr. Hale. I do want to talk about that, but tell now just what happened when you got to the house.

HALE: I didn't hear or see anything; I knocked at the door, and still it was all quiet inside. I knew they must be up, it was past eight o'clock. So I knocked again, and I thought I heard somebody say, "Come in." I wasn't sure, I'm not sure yet, but I opened the door—this door (*indicating the door by which the two women are still standing*) and there in that rocker—(*pointing to it*) sat Mrs. Wright. (*They all look at the rocker down left.*)

COUNTY ATTORNEY: What—was she doing?

HALE: She was rockin' back and forth. She had her apron in her hand and was kind of—pleating it.

COUNTY ATTORNEY: And how did she—look?

HALE: Well, she looked queer.

COUNTY ATTORNEY: How do you mean—queer?

HALE: Well, as if she didn't know what she was going to do next. And kind of done up.

COUNTY ATTORNEY (*takes out notebook and pencil and sits left of center table*): How did she seem to feel about your coming?

HALE: Why, I don't think she minded—one way or other. She didn't pay much attention. I said, "How do, Mrs. Wright, it's cold, ain't it?" And she said, "Is it?"—and went on kind of pleating at her apron. Well, I was surprised; she didn't ask me to come up to the stove, or to set down, but just sat there, not even looking at me, so I said, "I want to see John." And then she—laughed. I guess you would call it a laugh. I thought of Harry and the team outside, so I said a little sharp: "Can't I see John?" "No," she says, kind o' dull like. "Ain't he home?" says I. "Yes," says she, "he's home." "Then why can't I see him?" I asked her, out of patience. "'Cause he's dead," says she. *"Dead?"* says I. She just nodded her head, not getting a bit excited, but rockin' back and forth. "Why—where is he?" says I, not knowing what to say. She just pointed upstairs—like that. (*Himself pointing to the room above.*) I started for the stairs, with the idea of going up there. I walked from there to here—then I says, "Why, what did he die of?" "He died of a rope round his neck," says she, and just went on pleatin' at her apron. Well, I went out and called Harry. I thought I might—need help. We went upstairs and there he was lyin' ——

COUNTY ATTORNEY: I think I'd rather have you go into that upstairs, where you can point it all out. Just go on now with the rest of the story.

HALE: Well, my first thought was to get that rope off. It looked . . . (*stops; his face twitches*) . . . but Harry, he went up to him, and he said, "No, he's dead all right, and we'd better not touch anything." So we went back downstairs. She was still sitting that same way. "Has anybody been notified?" I asked. "No," says she, unconcerned. "Who did this, Mrs. Wright?" said Harry. He said it businesslike—and she stopped pleatin' of her apron. "I don't know," she says. "You don't *know?*" says Harry. "No," says she. "Weren't you sleepin' in the bed with him?" says Harry. "Yes," says she, "but I was on the inside." "Somebody slipped a rope round his neck and strangled him and you didn't wake up?" says Harry. "I didn't wake up," she said after him. We must 'a' looked as if we didn't see how that could be, for after a minute she said, "I sleep sound." Harry was going to ask her more questions but I said maybe we ought to let her tell her story first to the coroner, or the sheriff, so Harry went fast as he could to Rivers' place, where there's a telephone.

COUNTY ATTORNEY: And what did Mrs. Wright do when she knew that you had gone for the coroner?

HALE: She moved from the rocker to that chair over there (*pointing to a small chair in the down right corner*) and just sat there with her hands held together and looking down. I got a feeling that I ought to make some conversation, so I said I had come in to see if John wanted to put in a telephone, and at that she started to laugh, and then she stopped and looked at me—scared. (*The County Attorney, who has had his notebook out, makes a note.*) I dunno, maybe it wasn't scared. I wouldn't like to say it was. Soon Harry got back, and then Dr. Lloyd came and you, Mr. Peters, and so I guess that's all I know that you don't.

COUNTY ATTORNEY (*rising and looking around*): I guess we'll go upstairs first—and then out to the barn and around there. (*To the Sheriff.*) You're convinced that there was nothing important here—nothing that would point to any motive?

SHERIFF: Nothing here but kitchen things. (*The County Attorney, after again looking around the kitchen, opens the door of a cupboard closet in right wall. He brings a small chair from right—gets on it and looks on a shelf. Pulls his hand away, sticky.*)

COUNTY ATTORNEY: Here's a nice mess. (*The women draw nearer up center.*)

MRS. PETERS (*to the other woman*): Oh, her fruit; it did freeze. (*To the Lawyer.*) She worried about that when it turned so cold. She said the fire'd go out and her jars would break.

SHERIFF (*rises*): Well, can you beat the woman! Held for murder and worryin' about her preserves.

COUNTY ATTORNEY (*getting down from chair*): I guess before we're through she may have something more serious than preserves to worry about. (*Crosses down right center.*)

HALE: Well, women are used to worrying over trifles. (*The two women move a little closer together.*)

COUNTY ATTORNEY (*with the gallantry of a young politician*): And yet, for all their worries, what would we do without the ladies? (*The women do not unbend. He goes below the center table to the sink, takes a dipperful of water from the pail, and pouring it into a basin, washes his hands. While he is doing this the Sheriff and Hale cross to cupboard, which they inspect. The County Attorney starts to wipe his hands on the roller towel, turns it for a cleaner place.*) Dirty towels! (*Kicks his foot against the pans under the sink.*) Not much of a housekeeper, would you say, ladies?

MRS. HALE (*stiffly*): There's a great deal of work to be done on a farm.

COUNTY ATTORNEY: To be sure. And yet (*with a little bow to her*) I know there are some Dickson County farmhouses which do not have such roller towels. (*He gives it a pull to expose its full-length again.*)

MRS. HALE: Those towels get dirty awful quick. Men's hands aren't always as clean as they might be.

COUNTY ATTORNEY: Ah, loyal to your sex, I see. But you and Mrs. Wright were neighbors. I suppose you were friends, too.

MRS. HALE (*shaking her head*): I've not seen much of her of late years. I've not been in this house—it's more than a year.

COUNTY ATTORNEY (*crossing to women up center*): And why was that? You didn't like her?

MRS. HALE: I liked her all well enough. Farmers' wives have their hands full, Mr. Henderson. And then——

COUNTY ATTORNEY: Yes——?

MRS. HALE (*looking about*): It never seemed a very cheerful place.

COUNTY ATTORNEY: No—it's not cheerful. I shouldn't say she had the home-making instinct.

MRS. HALE: Well, I don't know as Wright had, either.

COUNTY ATTORNEY: You mean that they didn't get on very well?

MRS. HALE: No, I don't mean anything. But I don't think a place'd be any cheer-fuller for John Wright's being in it.

COUNTY ATTORNEY: I'd like to talk more of that a little later. I want to get the lay of things upstairs now. (*He goes past the women to up right where steps lead to a stair door.*)

SHERIFF: I suppose anything Mrs. Peters does'll be all right. She was to take in some clothes for her, you know, and a few little things. We left in such a hurry yesterday.

COUNTY ATTORNEY: Yes, but I would like to see what you take, Mrs. Peters, and keep an eye out for anything that might be of use to us.

MRS. PETERS: Yes, Mr. Henderson. (*The men leave by up right door to stairs. The women listen to the men's steps on the stairs, then look about the kitchen.*)

MRS. HALE (*crossing left to sink*): I'd hate to have men coming into my kitchen, snooping around and criticizing. (*She arranges the pans under sink which the lawyer had shoved out of place.*)

MRS. PETERS: Of course it's no more than their duty. (*Crosses to cupboard up right.*)

MRS. HALE: Duty's all right, but I guess that deputy sheriff that came out to make the fire might have got a little of this on. (*Gives the roller towel a pull.*) Wish I'd thought of that sooner. Seems mean to talk about her for not having things slicked up when she had to come away in such a hurry. (*Crosses right to Mrs. Peters at cupboard.*)

MRS. PETERS (*who has been looking through cupboard, lifts one end of towel that covers a pan*): She had bread set. (*Stands still.*)

MRS. HALE (*eyes fixed on a loaf of bread beside the breadbox, which is on a low shelf of the cupboard*): She was going to put this in there. (*Picks up loaf, abruptly drops it. In a manner of returning to familiar things.*) It's a shame about her fruit. I wonder if it's all gone. (*Gets up on the chair and looks.*) I think there's some here that's all right, Mrs. Peters. Yes—here; (*holding it toward the window*) this is cherries, too. (*Looking again.*) I declare I believe that's the only one. (*Gets down, jar in her hand. Goes to the sink and wipes it off on the outside.*) She'll feel awful bad after all her hard work in the hot weather. I remember the afternoon I put up my cherries last summer. (*She puts the jar on the big kitchen table, center of the room. With a sigh, is about to sit down in the rocking chair. Before she is seated realizes what chair it is; with a slow look at it, steps back. The chair which she has touched rocks back and forth. Mrs. Peters moves to center table and they both watch the chair rock for a moment or two.*)

MRS. PETERS (*shaking off the mood which the empty rocking chair has evoked. Now in a businesslike manner she speaks*): Well I must get those things from the front room closet. (*She goes to the door at the right but, after looking into the other room, steps back.*) You coming with me, Mrs. Hale? You could help me carry them. (*They go in the other room; reappear, Mrs. Peters carrying a dress, petticoat, and skirt, Mrs. Hale following with a pair of shoes.*) My, it's cold in there. (*She puts the clothes on the big table and hurries to the stove.*)

MRS. HALE (*right of center table examining the skirt*): Wright was close. I think maybe that's why she kept so much to herself. She didn't even belong to the Ladies' Aid. I suppose she felt she couldn't do her part, and then you don't enjoy things when you feel shabby. I heard she used to wear pretty clothes and be lively, when she was Minnie Foster, one of the town girls singing in the choir. But that—oh, that was thirty years ago. This all you want to take in?

MRS. PETERS: She said she wanted an apron. Funny thing to want, for there isn't much to get you dirty in jail, goodness knows. But I suppose just to make her feel more natural. (*Crosses to cupboard.*) She said they was in the top drawer in this cupboard. Yes, here. And then her little shawl that always hung behind the door. (*Opens stair door and looks.*) Yes, here it is. (*Quickly shuts door leading upstairs.*)

MRS. HALE (*abruptly moving toward her*): Mrs. Peters?

MRS. PETERS: Yes, Mrs. Hale? (*At up right door.*)

MRS. HALE: Do you think she did it?

MRS. PETERS (*in a frightened voice*): Oh, I don't know.

MRS. HALE: Well, I don't think she did. Asking for an apron and her little shawl. Worrying about her fruit.

MRS. PETERS (*starts to speak, glances up, where footsteps are heard in the room above. In a low voice*): Mr. Peters says it looks bad for her. Mr. Henderson is awful sarcastic in a speech and he'll make fun of her sayin' she didn't wake up.

MRS. HALE: Well, I guess John Wright didn't wake when they was slipping that rope under his neck.

MRS. PETERS (*crossing slowly to table and placing shawl and apron on table with other clothing*): No, it's strange. It must have been done awful crafty and still. They say it was such a—funny way to kill a man, rigging it all up like that.

MRS. HALE (*crossing to left of Mrs. Peters at table*): That's just what Mr. Hale said. There was a gun in the house. He says that's what he can't understand.

MRS. PETERS: Mr. Henderson said coming out that what was needed for the case was a motive; something to show anger, or—sudden feeling.

MRS. HALE (*who is standing by the table*): Well, I don't see any signs of anger around here. (*She puts her hand on the dish towel, which lies on the table, stands looking down at table, one-half of which is clean, the other half messy.*) It's wiped to here. (*Makes a move as if to finish work, then turns and looks at loaf of bread outside the breadbox. Drops towel. In that voice of coming back to familiar things.*) Wonder how they are finding things upstairs. (*Crossing below table to down right.*) I hope she had it a little more redd up° up there. You know, it seems kind of *sneaking*. Locking her up in town and then coming out here and trying to get her own house to turn against her!

MRS. PETERS: But, Mrs. Hale, the law is the law.

MRS. HALE: I s'pose 'tis. (*Unbuttoning her coat.*) Better loosen up your things, Mrs. Peters. You won't feel them when you go out. (*Mrs. Peters takes off her fur tippet, goes to hang it on chair back left of table, stands looking at the work basket on floor near down left window.*)

---

redd up: Neat.

MRS. PETERS: She was piecing a quilt. (*She brings the large sewing basket to the center table and they look at the bright pieces, Mrs. Hale above the table and Mrs. Peters left of it.*)

MRS. HALE: It's a log cabin pattern. Pretty, isn't it? I wonder if she was goin' to quilt it or just knot it? (*Footsteps have been heard coming down the stairs. The Sheriff enters followed by Hale and the County Attorney.*)

SHERIFF: They wonder if she was going to quilt it or just knot it! (*The men laugh, the women look abashed.*)

COUNTY ATTORNEY (*rubbing his hands over the stove*): Frank's fire didn't do much up there, did it? Well, let's go out to the barn and get that cleared up. (*The men go outside by up left door.*)

MRS. HALE (*resentfully*): I don't know as there's anything so strange, our takin' up our time with little things while we're waiting for them to get the evidence. (*She sits in chair right of table smoothing out a block with decision.*) I don't see as it's anything to laugh about.

MRS. PETERS (*apologetically*): Of course they've got awful important things on their minds. (*Pulls up a chair and joins Mrs. Hale at the left of the table.*)

MRS. HALE (*examining another block*): Mrs. Peters, look at this one. Here, this is the one she was working on, and look at the sewing! All the rest of it has been so nice and even. And look at this! It's all over the place! Why, it looks as if she didn't know what she was about! (*After she has said this they look at each other, then start to glance back at the door. After an instant Mrs. Hale has pulled at a knot and ripped the sewing.*)

MRS. PETERS: Oh, what are you doing, Mrs. Hale?

MRS. HALE (*mildly*): Just pulling out a stitch or two that's not sewed very good. (*Threading a needle.*) Bad sewing always made me fidgety.

MRS. PETERS (*with a glance at door, nervously*): I don't think we ought to touch things.

MRS. HALE: I'll just finish up this end. (*Suddenly stopping and leaning forward.*) Mrs. Peters?

MRS. PETERS: Yes, Mrs. Hale?

MRS. HALE: What do you suppose she was so nervous about?

MRS. PETERS: Oh—I don't know. I don't know as she was nervous. I sometimes sew awful queer when I'm just tired. (*Mrs. Hale starts to say something, looks at Mrs. Peters, then goes on sewing.*) Well, I must get these things wrapped up. They may be through sooner than we think. (*Putting apron and other things together.*) I wonder where I can find a piece of paper, and string. (*Rises.*)

MRS. HALE: In that cupboard, maybe.

MRS. PETERS (*crosses right looking in cupboard*): Why, here's a bird-cage. (*Holds it up.*) Did she have a bird, Mrs. Hale?

MRS. HALE: Why, I don't know whether she did or not—I've not been here for so long. There was a man around last year selling canaries cheap, but I don't know as she took one; maybe she did. She used to sing real pretty herself.

MRS. PETERS (*glancing around*): Seems funny to think of a bird here. But she must have had one, or why would she have a cage? I wonder what happened to it?

MRS. HALE: I s'pose maybe the cat got it.

MRS. PETERS: No, she didn't have a cat. She's got that feeling some people have about cats—being afraid of them. My cat got in her room and she was real upset and asked me to take it out.

MRS. HALE: My sister Bessie was like that. Queer, ain't it?

MRS. PETERS (*examining the cage*): Why, look at this door. It's broke. One hinge is pulled apart. (*Takes a step down to Mrs. Hale's right.*)

MRS. HALE (*looking too*): Looks as if someone must have been rough with it.

MRS. PETERS: Why, yes. (*She brings the cage forward and puts it on the table.*)

MRS. HALE (*glancing toward up left door*): I wish if they're going to find any evidence they'd be about it. I don't like this place.

MRS. PETERS: But I'm awful glad you came with me, Mrs. Hale. It would be lonesome for me sitting here alone.

MRS. HALE: It would, wouldn't it? (*Dropping her sewing.*) But I tell you what I do wish, Mrs. Peters. I wish I had come over sometimes when *she* was here. I—(*looking around the room*)—wish I had.

MRS. PETERS: But of course you were awful busy, Mrs. Hale—your house and your children.

MRS. HALE (*rises and crosses left*): I could've come. I stayed away because it weren't cheerful—and that's why I ought to have come. I—(*looking out left window*)—I've never liked this place. Maybe because it's down in a hollow and you don't see the road. I dunno what it is, but it's a lonesome place and always was. I wish I had come over to see Minnie Foster sometimes. I can see now—(*Shakes her head.*)

MRS. PETERS (*left of table and above it*): Well, you mustn't reproach yourself, Mrs. Hale. Somehow we just don't see how it is with other folks until—something turns up.

MRS. HALE: Not having children makes less work—but it makes a quiet house, and Wright out to work all day, and no company when he did come in. (*Turning from window.*) Did you know John Wright, Mrs. Peters?

MRS. PETERS: Not to know him; I've seen him in town. They say he was a good man.

MRS. HALE: Yes—good; he didn't drink, and kept his word as well as most, I guess, and paid his debts. But he was a hard man, Mrs. Peters. Just to pass the time of day with him—(*Shivers.*) Like a raw wind that gets to the bone. (*Pauses, her eye falling on the cage.*) I should think she would 'a' wanted a bird. But what do you suppose went with it?

MRS. PETERS: I don't know, unless it got sick and died. (*She reaches over and swings the broken door, swings it again, both women watch it.*)

MRS. HALE: You weren't raised round here, were you? (*Mrs. Peters shakes her head.*) You didn't know—her?

MRS. PETERS: Not till they brought her yesterday.

MRS. HALE: She—come to think of it, she was kind of like a bird herself—real sweet and pretty, but kind of timid and—fluttery. How—she—did—change. (*Silence: then as if struck by a happy thought and relieved to get back to everyday things. Crosses right above Mrs. Peters to cupboard, replaces small chair used to stand on to its original place down right.*) Tell you what, Mrs. Peters, why don't you take the quilt in with you? It might take up her mind.

MRS. PETERS: Why, I think that's a real nice idea, Mrs. Hale. There couldn't possibly be any objection to it could there? Now, just what would I take? I wonder if her patches are in here—and her things. (*They look in the sewing basket.*)

MRS. HALE (*crosses to right of table*): Here's some red. I expect this has got sewing things in it. (*Brings out a fancy box.*) What a pretty box. Looks like something somebody would give you. Maybe her scissors are in here. (*Opens box. Suddenly puts her hand to her nose.*) Why ———— (*Mrs. Peters bends nearer, then turns her face away.*) There's something wrapped up in this piece of silk.

MRS. PETERS: Why, this isn't her scissors.

MRS. HALE (*lifting the silk*): Oh, Mrs. Peters—it's ———— (*Mrs. Peters bends closer.*)

MRS. PETERS: It's the bird.

MRS. HALE: But, Mrs. Peters—look at it! Its neck! Look at its neck! It's all—other side *to*.

MRS. PETERS: Somebody—wrung—its—neck. (*Their eyes meet. A look of growing comprehension, of horror. Steps are heard outside. Mrs. Hale slips box under quilt pieces, and sinks into her chair. Enter Sheriff and County Attorney. Mrs. Peters steps down left and stands looking out of window.*)

COUNTY ATTORNEY (*as one turning from serious things to little pleasantries*): Well, ladies, have you decided whether she was going to quilt it or knot it? (*Crosses to center above table.*)

MRS. PETERS: We think she was going to—knot it. (*Sheriff crosses to right of stove, lifts stove lid, and glances at fire, then stands warming hands at stove.*)

COUNTY ATTORNEY: Well, that's interesting, I'm sure. (*Seeing the bird-cage.*) Has the bird flown?

MRS. HALE (*putting more quilt pieces over the box*): We think the—cat got it.

COUNTY ATTORNEY (*preoccupied*): Is there a cat? (*Mrs. Hale glances in a quick covert way at Mrs. Peters.*)

MRS. PETERS (*turning from window takes a step in*): Well, not now. They're superstitious, you know. They leave.

COUNTY ATTORNEY (*to Sheriff Peters, continuing an interrupted conversation*): No sign at all of anyone having come from the outside. Their own rope. Now let's go up again and go over it piece by piece. (*They start upstairs.*) It would have to have been someone who knew just the ———— (*Mrs. Peters sits down left of table. The two women sit there not looking at one another, but as if peering into something and at the same time holding back. When they talk now it is in the manner of feeling their way over strange ground, as if afraid of what they are saying, but as if they cannot help saying it.*)

MRS. HALE (*hesitatively and in hushed voice*): She liked the bird. She was going to bury it in that pretty box.

MRS. PETERS (*in a whisper*): When I was a girl—my kitten—there was a boy took a hatchet, and before my eyes—and before I could get there————

(*Covers her face an instant.*) If they hadn't held me back I would have—(*catches herself, looks upstairs where steps are heard, falters weakly*)—hurt him.

MRS. HALE (*with a slow look around her*): I wonder how it would seem never to have had any children around. (*Pause.*) No, Wright wouldn't like the bird—a thing that sang. She used to sing. He killed that, too.

MRS. PETERS (*moving uneasily*): We don't know who killed the bird.

MRS. HALE: I knew John Wright.

MRS. PETERS: It was an awful thing was done in this house that night, Mrs. Hale. Killing a man while he slept, slipping a rope around his neck that choked the life out of him.

MRS. HALE: His neck. Choked the life out of him. (*Her hand goes out and rests on the bird-cage.*)

MRS. PETERS (*with rising voice*): We don't know who killed him. We don't *know*.

MRS. HALE (*her own feeling not interrupted*): If there'd been years and years of nothing, then a bird to sing to you, it would be awful—still, after the bird was still.

MRS. PETERS (*something within her speaking*): I know what stillness is. When we homesteaded in Dakota, and my first baby died—after he was two years old, and me with no other then———

MRS. HALE (*moving*): How soon do you suppose they'll be through looking for the evidence?

MRS. PETERS: I know what stillness is. (*Pulling herself back.*) The law has got to punish crime, Mrs. Hale.

MRS. HALE (*not as if answering that*): I wish you'd seen Minnie Foster when she wore a white dress with blue ribbons and stood up there in the choir and sang. (*A look around the room.*) Oh, I *wish* I'd come over here once in a while! That was a crime! That was a crime! Who's going to punish that?

MRS. PETERS (*looking upstairs*): We mustn't—take on.

MRS. HALE: I might have known she needed help! I know how things can be—for women. I tell you, it's queer, Mrs. Peters. We live close together and we live far apart. We all go through the same things—it's all just a different kind of the same thing. (*Brushes her eyes, noticing the jar of fruit, reaches out for it.*) If I was you I wouldn't tell her her fruit was gone. Tell her it *ain't*. Tell her it's all right. Take this in to prove it to her. She—she may never know whether it was broke or not.

MRS. PETERS (*takes the jar, looks about for something to wrap it in; takes petticoat from the clothes brought from the other room, very nervously begins winding this around the jar. In a false voice*): My, it's a good thing the men couldn't hear us. Wouldn't they just laugh! Getting all stirred up over a little thing like a—dead canary. As if that could have anything to do with—with—wouldn't they *laugh*! (*The men are heard coming downstairs.*)

MRS. HALE (*under her breath*): Maybe they would—maybe they wouldn't.

COUNTY ATTORNEY: No, Peters, it's all perfectly clear except a reason for doing it. But you know juries when it comes to women. If there was some definite thing. (*Crosses slowly to above table. Sheriff crosses down right. Mrs. Hale and Mrs. Peters remain seated at either side of table.*) Something to show—something to make a story about—a thing that would connect up with this strange way of doing it ——— (*The women's eyes meet for an instant. Enter Hale from outer door.*)

HALE (*remaining by door*): Well, I've got the team around. Pretty cold out there.

COUNTY ATTORNEY: I'm going to stay awhile by myself. (*To the Sheriff.*) You can send Frank out for me, can't you? I want to go over everything. I'm not satisfied that we can't do better.

SHERIFF: Do you want to see what Mrs. Peters is going to take in? (*The Lawyer picks up the apron, laughs.*)

COUNTY ATTORNEY: Oh, I guess they're not very dangerous things the ladies have picked out. (*Moves a few things about, disturbing the quilt pieces which cover the box. Steps back.*) No, Mrs. Peters doesn't need supervising. For that matter a sheriff's wife is married to the law. Ever think of it that way, Mrs. Peters?

MRS. PETERS: Not—just that way.

SHERIFF (*chuckling*): Married to the law. (*Moves to down right door to the other room.*) I just want you to come in here a minute, George. We ought to take a look at these windows.

COUNTY ATTORNEY (*scoffingly*): Oh, windows!

SHERIFF: We'll be right out, Mr. Hale. (*Hale goes outside. The Sheriff follows the County Attorney into the room. Then Mrs. Hale rises, hands tight together, looking intensely at Mrs. Peters, whose eyes make a slow turn, finally meeting Mrs. Hale's. A moment Mrs. Hale holds her, then her own eyes point the way to where the box is concealed. Suddenly Mrs. Peters throws back quilt pieces and tries to put the box in the bag she is carrying. It is too big. She opens box, starts to take bird out, cannot touch it, goes to pieces, stands there helpless. Sound of a knob turning in the other room. Mrs. Hale snatches the box and puts it in the pocket of her big coat. Enter County Attorney and Sheriff, who remains down right.*)

COUNTY ATTORNEY (*crosses to up left door facetiously*): Well, Henry, at least we found out that she was not going to quilt it. She was going to—what is it you call it, ladies?

MRS. HALE (*standing center below table facing front, her hand against her pocket*): We call it—knot it, Mr. Henderson.

Curtain.

TENNESSEE WILLIAMS

Tennessee Williams (1911–1983) was born Thomas Lanier Williams in Columbus, Mississippi, the second child of Edwina Dakin Williams, the daughter of an Episcopal clergyman, and Cornelius Coffin Williams, a traveling salesman. Williams spent the first fifteen years of his life living with his mother and older sister, Rose, in more than sixteen homes until his father took a permanent job in St. Louis. Williams was an indifferent high school student, but he began to publish stories in school newspapers as a teenager. An English major in college, his favorite authors were dramatists—Chekhov, Ibsen, and Strindberg—and he decided to become a playwright. After attending two other universities, he enrolled at the University of Iowa in 1937, where he saw his first full-length plays produced onstage. After graduation he held different jobs to support himself while he worked on his plays, poetry, and short fiction.

Williams wrote the story "Portrait of a Girl in Glass" in 1943. He turned the story into a play, The Gentleman Caller, while he was under contract with M-G-M to write a script for a movie starring Lana Turner. (Williams had a cataract in one eye, so he was exempt from military service during World War II.) The script was turned down, and Williams left Hollywood soon after. He then re-wrote the script as The Glass Menagerie, which opened in Chicago in December 1944. After a shaky start, the play ran for 561 performances in New York City and won the Drama Critics Circle Award as the best American play of the year.

In the introduction to Williams's Collected Stories, the writer Gore Vidal analyzed how Williams used his life as the basis of his art:

> Like most natural writers, Tennessee could not possess his own life until he had written about it. This is common. But what is not common was the way that he went about not only recapturing lost time but then regaining it in a way that far surpassed the original experience. . . . [First he turned his memories into stories, then] he would make a play of the story and then— and this is why he was so compulsive a working playwright— he would have the play produced so that he could, like God, rearrange his original experi- ence into something that was no longer God's and unpossessable but his. The frantic lifelong desire for play-productions was not just ambition or a need to be busy, it was the only way that he ever had of being entirely alive.

In Williams's production notes to The Glass Menagerie, he calls it a "mem- ory play" and describes his vision of a revitalized, lyrical theater of feelings. Both the play and "Portrait of a Girl in Glass" are based on Williams's memories of his close relationship with his sister, Rose, who was institutionalized after a lobotomy authorized by Williams's parents while he was a student at the University of Iowa. In his autobiographical play, he portrayed his sister and himself as victims and outsiders in the family. He used his own name for himself as the character Tom and called his sister Laura, as well as punning on her name in the phrase "Blue Roses" later in her dialogue with the gentleman caller.

When Williams turned the original short story into a play, he gave a much larger role to the figure of the mother, Amanda, who tries to dominate the lives of her son and daughter. The young playwright William Inge, who met Williams just before The Glass Menagerie was produced, recalled that the play was exciting because "it enabled me to see the true dynamics between life and art. . . . I don't think any of his plays is quite as personal as the Menagerie, although Menagerie, when you see it, does not strike you as a too personal play in any way at all. It's a real work of art . . . it's not self-indulgent, is what I'm trying to say. It is out of self, but it is conceived in terms of universality."

The Glass Menagerie introduces several themes that recur in later Williams plays, including the fear of isolation and the need for understanding by the dispos- sessed. The most successful American playwright of his generation, Williams wrote several other prize-winning plays, including A Streetcar Named Desire (1948),

The Rose Tattoo *(1951),* Cat on a Hot Tin Roof *(1955),* Suddenly Last Summer *(1958),* Sweet Bird of Youth *(1959), and* The Night of the Iguana *(1961). All of them, like* The Glass Menagerie, *were made into motion pictures.*

COMMENTARIES   *Benjamin Nelson, "Problems in* The Glass Menagerie*," page 1566; Tennessee Williams, "Production Notes to* The Glass Menagerie*," page 1577; Tennessee Williams, "Portrait of a Girl in Glass," page 1579.*

WEB   *Research Tennessee Williams and answer questions about his work at bedfordstmartins.com/charters/litwriters.*

The Glass Menagerie   1945

nobody,not even the rain,has such small hands
                                        — E. E. CUMMINGS

LIST OF CHARACTERS

AMANDA WINGFIELD, the mother. A little woman of great but confused vitality clinging frantically to another time and place. Her characterization must be carefully created, not copied from type. She is not paranoiac, but her life is paranoia. There is much to admire in Amanda, and as much to love and pity as there is to laugh at. Certainly she has endurance and a kind of heroism, and though her foolishness makes her unwittingly cruel at times, there is tenderness in her slight person.

LAURA WINGFIELD, her daughter. Amanda, having failed to establish contact with reality, continues to live vitally in her illusions, but Laura's situation is even graver. A childhood illness has left her crippled, one leg slightly shorter than the other, and held in a brace. This defect need not be more than suggested on the stage. Stemming from this, Laura's separation increases till she is like a piece of her own glass collection, too exquisitely fragile to move from the shelf.

TOM WINGFIELD, her son. And the narrator of the play. A poet with a job in a warehouse. His nature is not remorseless, but to escape from a trap he has to act without pity.

JIM O'CONNOR, the gentleman caller. A nice, ordinary, young man.

SCENE: *An alley in St. Louis.*

PART I: *Preparation for a Gentleman Caller.*

PART II: *The Gentleman Calls.*

TIME: *Now and the Past.*

SCENE I

The Wingfield apartment is in the rear of the building, one of those vast hivelike conglomerations of cellular living-units that flower as warty growths in overcrowded urban centers of lower middle-class population and are symptomatic of the impulse of this largest and fundamentally enslaved section of American society to avoid fluidity and differentiation and to exist and function as one interfused mass of automatism.

The apartment faces an alley and is entered by a fire-escape, a structure whose name is a touch of accidental poetic truth, for all of these huge buildings are always burning with the slow and implacable fires of human desperation. The fire-escape is included in the set—that is, the landing of it and steps descending from it.

The scene is memory and is therefore nonrealistic. Memory takes a lot of poetic license. It omits some details; others are exaggerated, according to the emotional value of the articles it touches, for memory is seated predominantly in the heart. The interior is therefore rather dim and poetic.

At the rise of the curtain, the audience is faced with the dark, grim rear wall of the Wingfield tenement. This building, which runs parallel to the footlights, is flanked on both sides by dark, narrow alleys which run into murky canyons of tangled clotheslines, garbage cans, and the sinister latticework of neighboring fire-escapes. It is up and down these side alleys that exterior entrances and exits are made, during the play. At the end of Tom's opening commentary, the dark tenement wall slowly reveals (by means of a transparency) the interior of the ground floor Wingfield apartment.

Downstage is the living room, which also serves as a sleeping room for Laura, the sofa unfolding to make her bed. Upstage, center, and divided by a wide arch or second proscenium with transparent faded portieres (or second curtain), is the dining room. In an old-fashioned what-not in the living room are seen scores of transparent glass animals. A blown-up photograph of the father hangs on the wall of the living room, facing the audience, to the left of the archway. It is the face of a very handsome young man in a doughboy's First World War cap. He is gallantly smiling, ineluctably smiling, as if to say, "I will be smiling forever."

The audience hears and sees the opening scene in the dining room through both the transparent fourth wall of the building and the transparent gauze portieres of the dining-room arch. It is during this revealing scene that the fourth wall slowly ascends, out of sight. This transparent exterior wall is not brought down again until the very end of the play, during Tom's final speech.

The narrator is an undisguised convention of the play. He takes whatever license with dramatic convention as is convenient to his purposes.

Tom enters dressed as a merchant sailor from alley, stage left, and strolls across the front of the stage to the fire-escape. There he stops and lights a cigarette. He addresses the audience.

TOM: Yes, I have tricks in my pocket, I have things up my sleeve. But I am the opposite of a stage magician. He gives you illusion that has the appearance of truth. I give you truth in the pleasant disguise of illusion. To begin with, I turn back time. I reverse it to that quaint period, the thirties, when the huge middle class of America was matriculating in a school for the blind. Their eyes had failed them, or they had failed their eyes, and so they were having their fingers pressed forcibly down on the fiery Braille alphabet of a dissolving economy. In Spain there was revolution. Here there was only shouting and confusion. In Spain there was Guernica.° Here there were disturbances of labor, sometimes pretty violent, in otherwise peaceful cities such as Chicago, Cleveland, Saint Louis. . . . This is the social background of the play.

(*Music.*)

The play is memory. Being a memory play, it is dimly lighted, it is sentimental, it is not realistic. In memory everything seems to happen to music. That explains the fiddle in the wings. I am the narrator of the play, and also a character in it. The other characters are my mother, Amanda, my sister, Laura, and a gentleman caller who appears in the final scenes. He is the most realistic character in the play, being an emissary from a world of reality that we were somehow set apart from. But since I have a poet's weakness for symbols, I am using this character also as a symbol; he is the long delayed but always expected something that we live for. There is a fifth character in the play who doesn't appear except in this larger-than-life photograph over the mantel. This is our father who left us a long time ago. He was a telephone man who fell in love with long distances; he gave up his job with the telephone company and skipped the light fantastic out of town. . . . The last we heard of him was a picture post-card from Mazatlán, on the Pacific coast of Mexico, containing a message of two words—"Hello—Good-bye!" and no address. I think the rest of the play will explain itself. . . .

Amanda's voice becomes audible through the portieres.

(*Legend on screen: "Où sont les neiges."°*)

He divides the portieres and enters the upstage area.

Amanda and Laura are seated at a drop-leaf table. Eating is indicated by gestures without food or utensils. Amanda faces the audience.

Tom and Laura are seated in profile.

The interior has lit up softly and through the scrim we see Amanda and Laura seated at the table in the upstage area.

AMANDA (*calling*): Tom?

TOM: Yes, Mother.

AMANDA: We can't say grace until you come to the table!

TOM: Coming, Mother. (*He bows slightly and withdraws, reappearing a few moments later in his place at the table.*)

AMANDA (*to her son*): Honey, don't *push* with your *fingers*. If you have to push with something, the thing to push with is a crust of bread. And chew— chew! Animals have sections in their stomachs which enable them to digest food without mastication, but human beings are supposed to chew their food before they swallow it down. Eat food leisurely, son, and really enjoy it. A well-cooked meal has lots of delicate flavors that have to be

---

Guernica: A town in Spain annihilated by German bombers in 1937.
Où sont les neiges: Part of a line by the French poet François Villon; the complete line translates, "But where are the snows of Yesteryear?"

held in the mouth for appreciation. So chew your food and give your salivary glands a chance to function!

Tom deliberately lays his imaginary fork down and pushes his chair back from the table.

TOM: I haven't enjoyed one bite of this dinner because of your constant directions on how to eat it. It's you that makes me rush through meals with your hawklike attention to every bite I take. Sickening—spoils my appetite—all this discussion of animals' secretion—salivary glands—mastication!

AMANDA (*lightly*): Temperament like a Metropolitan star! (*He rises and crosses downstage.*) You're not excused from the table.

TOM: I am getting a cigarette.

AMANDA: You smoke too much.

Laura rises.

LAURA: I'll bring in the blanc mange.

He remains standing with his cigarette by the portieres during the following.

AMANDA (*rising*): No, sister, no, sister—you be the lady this time and I'll be the darky.

LAURA: I'm already up.

AMANDA: Resume your seat, little sister—I want you to stay fresh and pretty—for gentlemen callers!

LAURA: I'm not expecting any gentlemen callers.

AMANDA (*crossing out to kitchenette. Airily*): Sometimes they come when they are least expected! Why, I remember one Sunday afternoon in Blue Mountain—(*Enters kitchenette.*)

TOM: I know what's coming!

LAURA: Yes. But let her tell it.

TOM: Again?

LAURA: She loves to tell it.

Amanda returns with bowl of dessert.

AMANDA: One Sunday afternoon in Blue Mountain—your mother received—seventeen!—gentlemen callers! Why, sometimes there weren't chairs enough to accommodate them all. We had to send the nigger over to bring in folding chairs from the parish house.

TOM (*remaining at portieres*): How did you entertain those gentlemen callers?

AMANDA: I understood the art of conversation!

TOM: I bet you could talk.

AMANDA: Girls in those days *knew* how to talk, I can tell you.

TOM: Yes?

(*Image: Amanda as a girl on a porch greeting callers.*)

AMANDA: They knew how to entertain their gentlemen callers. It wasn't enough for a girl to be possessed of a pretty face and a graceful figure—although I wasn't slighted in either respect. She also needed to have a nimble wit and a tongue to meet all occasions.

TOM: What did you talk about?

AMANDA: Things of importance going on in the world! Never anything coarse or common or vulgar. (*She addresses Tom as though he were seated in the vacant chair at the table though he remains by portieres. He plays this scene as though he held the book.*) My callers were gentlemen—all! Among my callers were some of the most prominent young planters of the Mississippi Delta—planters and sons of planters!

Tom motions for music and a spot of light on Amanda.

Her eyes lift, her face glows, her voice becomes rich and elegiac.

(*Screen legend: "Où sont les neiges."*)

There was young Champ Laughlin who later became vice-president of the Delta Planters Bank. Hadley Stevenson who was drowned in Moon Lake and left his widow one hundred and fifty thousand in Government bonds. There were the Cutrere brothers, Wesley and Bates. Bates was one of my bright particular beaux! He got in a quarrel with that wild Wainright boy. They shot it out on the floor of Moon Lake Casino. Bates was shot through the stomach. Died in the ambulance on his way to Memphis. His widow was also well-provided for, came into eight or ten thousand acres, that's all. She married him on the rebound—never loved her—carried my picture on him the night he died! And there was that boy that every girl in the Delta had set her cap for! That beautiful, brilliant young Fitzhugh boy from Green County!

TOM: What did he leave his widow?

AMANDA: He never married! Gracious, you talk as though all of my old admirers had turned up their toes to the daisies!

TOM: Isn't this the first you mentioned that still survives?

AMANDA: That Fitzhugh boy went North and made a fortune—came to be known as the Wolf of Wall Street! He had the Midas touch, whatever he touched turned to gold! And I could have been Mrs. Duncan J. Fitzhugh, mind you! But—I picked your *father*!

LAURA (*rising*): Mother, let me clear the table.

AMANDA: No dear, you go in front and study your typewriter chart. Or practice your shorthand a little. Stay fresh and pretty!—It's almost time for our gentlemen callers to start arriving. (*She flounces girlishly toward the kitchenette.*) How many do you suppose we're going to entertain this afternoon?

Tom throws down the paper and jumps up with a groan.

LAURA (*alone in the dining room*): I don't believe we're going to receive any, Mother.

AMANDA (*reappearing, airily*): What? No one—not one? You must be joking! (*Laura nervously echoes her laugh. She slips in a fugitive manner through the half-open portieres and draws them gently behind her. A shaft of very clear light is thrown on her face against the faded tapestry of the curtains.*) (*Music: "The Glass Menagerie" under faintly.*) (*Lightly.*) Not one gentleman caller? It can't be true! There must be a flood, there must have been a tornado!

LAURA: It isn't a flood, it's not a tornado, Mother. I'm just not popular like you were in Blue Mountain. . . . (*Tom utters another groan. Laura glances at him with a faint, apologetic smile. Her voice catching a little.*) Mother's afraid I'm going to be an old maid.

(*The scene dims out with "Glass Menagerie" music.*)

SCENE II

"Laura, Haven't You Ever Liked Some Boy?"

On the dark stage the screen is lighted with the image of blue roses.

    Gradually Laura's figure becomes apparent and the screen goes out.

    The music subsides.

    Laura is seated in the delicate ivory chair at the small clawfoot table.

    She wears a dress of soft violet material for a kimono—her hair tied back from her forehead with a ribbon.

    She is washing and polishing her collection of glass.

    Amanda appears on the fire-escape steps. At the sound of her ascent, Laura catches her breath, thrusts the bowl of ornaments away, and seats herself stiffly before the diagram of the typewriter keyboard as though it held her spellbound. Something has happened to Amanda. It is written in her face as she climbs to the landing: a look that is grim and hopeless and a little absurd.

    She has on one of those cheap or imitation velvety-looking cloth coats with imitation fur collar. Her hat is five or six years old, one of those dreadful cloche hats that were worn in the late twenties, and she is clasping an enormous black patent-leather pocketbook with nickel clasp and initials. This is her full-dress out-fit, the one she usually wears to the D.A.R. °

    Before entering she looks through the door.

    She purses her lips, opens her eyes wide, rolls them upward, and shakes her head.

    Then she slowly lets herself in the door. Seeing her mother's expression Laura touches her lips with a nervous gesture.

LAURA: Hello, Mother, I was—(*She makes a nervous gesture toward the chart on the wall. Amanda leans against the shut door and stares at Laura with a martyred look.*)

AMANDA: Deception? Deception? (*She slowly removes her hat and gloves, continuing the swift suffering stare. She lets the hat and gloves fall on the floor—a bit of acting.*)

LAURA (*shakily*): How was the D.A.R. meeting? (*Amanda slowly opens her purse and removes a dainty white handkerchief, which she shakes out delicately and delicately touches to her lips and nostrils.*) Didn't you go to the D.A.R. meeting, Mother?

AMANDA (*faintly, almost inaudibly*): —No. —No. (*Then more forcibly.*) I did not have the strength—to go to the D.A.R. In fact, I did not have the courage! I wanted to find a hole in the ground and hide myself in it forever! (*She*

D.A.R.: Daughters of the American Revolution, whose ancestors served the patriots' cause in the Revolutionary War.

crosses slowly to the wall and removes the diagram of the typewriter key-board. She holds it in front of her for a second, staring at it sweetly and sor-rowfully—then bites her lips and tears it in two pieces.)

LAURA (*faintly*): Why did you do that, Mother? (*Amanda repeats the same proce-dure with the chart of the Gregg Alphabet.*°) Why are you—

AMANDA: Why? Why? How old are you, Laura?

LAURA: Mother, you know my age.

AMANDA: I thought that you were an adult; it seems that I was mistaken. (*She crosses slowly to the sofa and sinks down and stares at Laura.*)

LAURA: Please don't stare at me, Mother.

Amanda closes her eyes and lowers her head. Count ten.

AMANDA: What are we going to do, what is going to become of us, what is the future?

Count ten.

LAURA: Has something happened, Mother? (*Amanda draws a long breath and takes out the handkerchief again. Dabbing process.*) Mother, has—some-thing happened?

AMANDA: I'll be all right in a minute. I'm just bewildered—(*count five*)—by life. . . .

LAURA: Mother, I wish that you would tell me what's happened.

AMANDA: As you know, I was supposed to be inducted into my office at the D.A.R. this afternoon. (*Image: A swarm of typewriters.*) But I stopped off at Rubicam's Business College to speak to your teachers about your hav-ing a cold and ask them what progress they thought you were making down there.

LAURA: Oh. . . .

AMANDA: I went to the typing instructor and introduced myself as your mother. She didn't know who you were. Wingfield, she said. We don't have any such student enrolled at the school! I assured her she did, that you had been going to classes since early in January. "I wonder," she said, "if you could be talking about that terribly shy little girl who dropped out of school after only a few days' attendance?" "No," I said, "Laura, my daughter, has been going to school every day for the past six weeks!" "Excuse me," she said. She took the attendance book out and there was your name, unmistakably printed, and all the dates you were absent until they decided that you had dropped out of school. I still said, "No, there must have been some mistake! There must have been some mix-up in the records!" And she said, "No—I remember her perfectly now. Her hand shook so that she couldn't hit the right keys! The first time we gave a speed-test, she broke down completely—was sick at the stomach and almost had to be carried into the wash-room! After that morning she never showed up any more. We phoned the house but never got any answer"—while I was working at Famous and Barr, I suppose, demon-strating those—Oh! I felt so weak I could barely keep on my feet. I had

---

Gregg Alphabet: Shorthand system invented by John Robert Gregg.

to sit down while they got me a glass of water! Fifty dollars' tuition, all of our plans—my hopes and ambitions for you—just gone up the spout, just gone up the spout like that. (*Laura draws a long breath and gets awkwardly to her feet. She crosses to the Victrola, and winds it up.*) What are you doing?

LAURA: Oh! (*She releases the handle and returns to her seat.*)

AMANDA: Laura, where have you been going when you've gone out pretending that you were going to business college?

LAURA: I've just been going out walking.

AMANDA: That's not true.

LAURA: It is. I just went walking.

AMANDA: Walking? Walking? In winter? Deliberately courting pneumonia in that light coat? Where did you walk to, Laura?

LAURA: It was the lesser of two evils, Mother. (*Image: Winter scene in park.*) I couldn't go back up. I—threw up—on the floor!

AMANDA: From half past seven till after five every day you mean to tell me you walked around in the park, because you wanted to make me think that you were still going to Rubicam's Business College?

LAURA: It wasn't as bad as it sounds. I went inside places to get warmed up.

AMANDA: Inside where?

LAURA: I went in the art museum and the bird-houses at the Zoo. I visited the penguins every day! Sometimes I did without lunch and went to the movies. Lately I've been spending most of my afternoons in the Jewel-box, that big glass house where they raise the tropical flowers.

AMANDA: You did all this to deceive me, just for the deception? (*Laura looks down.*) Why?

LAURA: Mother, when you're disappointed, you get that awful suffering look on your face, like the picture of Jesus' mother in the museum!

AMANDA: Hush!

LAURA: I couldn't face it.

Pause. A whisper of strings.
  (*Legend: "The Crust of Humility."*)

AMANDA (*hopelessly fingering the huge pocketbook*): So what are we going to do the rest of our lives? Stay home and watch the parades go by? Amuse ourselves with the glass menagerie, darling? Eternally play those worn-out phonograph records your father left as a painful reminder of him? We won't have a business career—we've given that up because it gave us nervous indigestion! (*Laughs wearily.*) What is there left but dependency all our lives? I know so well what becomes of unmarried women who aren't prepared to occupy a position. I've seen such pitiful cases in the South—barely tolerated spinsters living upon the grudging patronage of sister's husband or brother's wife!—stuck away in some little mousetrap of a room—encouraged by one in-law to visit another—little birdlike women without any nest—eating the crust of humility all their life! Is that the future that we've mapped out for ourselves? I swear it's the only alternative I can think of! It isn't a very pleasant alternative, is it? Of course—some girls *do marry*. (*Laura twists her hands nervously.*) Haven't you ever liked some boy?

LAURA: Yes. I liked one once. (*Rises.*) I came across his picture a while ago.

AMANDA (*with some interest*): He gave you his picture?

LAURA: No, it's in the year-book.

AMANDA (*disappointed*): Oh—a high-school boy.

(*Screen image: Jim as a high-school hero bearing a silver cup.*)

LAURA: Yes. His name was Jim. (*Laura lifts the heavy annual from the clawfoot table.*) Here he is in *The Pirates of Penzance*.

AMANDA (*absently*): The what?

LAURA: The operetta the senior class put on. He had a wonderful voice and we sat across the aisle from each other Mondays, Wednesdays, and Fridays in the Aud. Here he is with the silver cup for debating! See his grin?

AMANDA (*absently*): He must have had a jolly disposition.

LAURA: He used to call me—Blue Roses.

(*Image: Blue roses.*)

AMANDA: Why did he call you such a name as that?

LAURA: When I had that attack of pleurosis—he asked me what was the matter when I came back. I said pleurosis—he thought that I said Blue Roses! So that's what he always called me after that. Whenever he saw me, he'd holler, "Hello, Blue Roses!" I didn't care for the girl that he went out with. Emily Meisenbach. Emily was the best-dressed girl at Soldan. She never struck me, though, as being sincere. . . . It says in the Personal Section— they're engaged. That's—six years ago! They must be married by now.

AMANDA: Girls that aren't cut out for business careers usually wind up married to some nice man. (*Gets up with a spark of revival.*) Sister, that's what you'll do!

Laura utters a startled, doubtful laugh. She reaches quickly for a piece of glass.

LAURA: But, Mother—

AMANDA: Yes? (*Crossing to photograph.*)

LAURA (*in a tone of frightened apology*): I'm—crippled!

(*Image: Screen.*)

AMANDA: Nonsense! Laura, I've told you never, never to use that word. Why, you're not crippled, you just have a little defect—hardly noticeable, even! When people have some slight disadvantage like that, they culti- vate other things to make up for it—develop charm—and vivacity— and—*charm!* That's all you have to do! (*She turns again to the photo- graph.*) One thing your father had *plenty* of—was *charm!*

Tom motions to the fiddle in the wings.

(*The scene fades out with music.*)

SCENE III

(*Legend on the screen: "After the Fiasco—"*)
  Tom speaks from the fire-escape landing.

TOM: After the fiasco at Rubicam's Business College, the idea of getting a gentleman caller for Laura began to play a more important part in Mother's calculations. It became an obsession. Like some archetype of the universal unconscious, the image of the gentleman caller haunted our small apartment. . . . (*Image: Young man at door with flowers.*) An evening at home rarely passed without some allusion to this image, this specter, this hope. . . . Even when he wasn't mentioned, his presence hung in Mother's preoccupied look and in my sister's frightened, apologetic manner—hung like a sentence passed upon the Wingfields! Mother was a woman of action as well as words. She began to take logical steps in the planned direction. Late that winter and in the early spring—realizing that extra money would be needed to properly feather the nest and plume the bird—she conducted a vigorous campaign on the telephone, roping in subscribers to one of those magazines for matrons called *The Home-maker's Companion*, the type of journal that features the serialized subli-mations of ladies of letters who think in terms of delicate cuplike breasts, slim, tapering waists, rich, creamy thighs, eyes like wood-smoke in autumn, fingers that soothe and caress like strains of music, bodies as powerful as Etruscan sculpture.

(*Screen image:* Glamour *magazine cover.*)

Amanda enters with phone on long extension cord. She is spotted in the dim
stage.

AMANDA: Ida Scott? This is Amanda Wingfield! We *missed* you at the D.A.R. last Monday! I said to myself: She's probably suffering with that sinus condition! How is that sinus condition? Horrors! Heaven have mercy!—You're a Christian martyr, yes, that's what you are, a Christian martyr! Well, I just now happened to notice that your subscription to the *Com-panion's* about to expire! Yes, it expires with the next issue, honey!—just when that wonderful new serial by Bessie Mae Hopper is getting off to such an exciting start. Oh, honey, it's something that you can't miss! You remember how *Gone with the Wind* took everybody by storm? You simply couldn't go out if you hadn't read it. All everybody *talked* was Scarlett O'Hara. Well, this is a book that critics already compare to *Gone with the Wind*. It's the *Gone with the Wind* of the post–World War gener-ation!—What?—Burning?—Oh, honey, don't let them burn, go take a look in the oven and I'll hold the wire! Heavens—I think she's hung up!

(*Dim out.*)

(*Legend on screen: "You think I'm in love with Continental Shoemakers?"*)

Before the stage is lighted, the violent voices of Tom and Amanda are heard. They are quarreling behind the portieres. In front of them stands Laura with clenched hands and panicky expression.

A clear pool of light on her figure throughout this scene.

TOM: What in Christ's name am I—

AMANDA (*shrilly*): Don't you use that—

TOM: Supposed to do!

AMANDA: Expression! Not in my—

TOM: Ohhh!

AMANDA: Presence! Have you gone out of your senses?

TOM: I have, that's true, *driven* out!

AMANDA: What is the matter with you, you—big—big—IDIOT!

TOM: Look—I've got *no thing,* no single thing—

AMANDA: Lower your voice!

TOM: In my life here that I can call my own! Everything is—

AMANDA: Stop that shouting!

TOM: Yesterday you confiscated my books! You had the nerve to—

AMANDA: I took that horrible novel back to the library—yes! That hideous book by that insane Mr. Lawrence.° (*Tom laughs wildly.*) I cannot control the output of diseased minds or people who cater to them—(*Tom laughs still more wildly.*) BUT I WON'T ALLOW SUCH FILTH BROUGHT INTO MY HOUSE! No, no, no, no, no!

TOM: House, house! Who pays rent on it, who makes a slave of himself to—

AMANDA (*fairly screeching*): Don't you DARE to—

TOM: No, no, I mustn't say things! *I've* got to just—

AMANDA: Let me tell you—

TOM: I don't want to hear any more! (*He tears the portieres open. The upstage area is lit with a turgid smoky red glow.*)

Amanda's hair is in metal curlers and she wears a very old bathrobe, much too large for her slight figure, a relic of the faithless Mr. Wingfield.

An upright typewriter and a wild disarray of manuscripts are on the drop-leaf table. The quarrel was probably precipitated by Amanda's interruption of his creative labor. A chair lying overthrown on the floor.

Their gesticulating shadows are cast on the ceiling by the fiery glow.

AMANDA: You *will* hear more, you—

TOM: No, I won't hear more, I'm going out!

AMANDA: You come right back in—

TOM: Out, out, out! Because I'm—

AMANDA: Come back here, Tom Wingfield! I'm not through talking to you!

TOM: Oh, go—

LAURA (*desperately*): Tom!

AMANDA: You're going to listen, and no more insolence from you! I'm at the end of my patience! (*He comes back toward her.*)

TOM: What do you think I'm at? Aren't I supposed to have any patience to reach the end of, Mother? I know, I know. It seems unimportant to you, what I'm *doing*—what I *want* to do—having a little *difference* between them! You don't think that—

AMANDA: I think you've been doing things that you're ashamed of. That's why you act like this. I don't believe that you go every night to the movies. Nobody goes to the movies night after night. Nobody in their right minds goes to the movies as often as you pretend to. People don't go to

---

Mr. Lawrence: D. H. Lawrence (1885–1930), English writer who propounded free sexuality.

the movies at nearly midnight, and movies don't let out at two A.M. Come in stumbling. Muttering to yourself like a maniac! You get three hours' sleep and then go to work. Oh, I can picture the way you're doing down there. Moping, doping, because you're in no condition.

TOM (*wildly*): No, I'm in no condition!

AMANDA: What right have you got to jeopardize your job? Jeopardize the security of us all? How do you think we'd manage if you were—

TOM: Listen! You think I'm crazy *about* the *warehouse!* (*He bends fiercely toward her slight figure.*) You think I'm in love with the Continental Shoemakers? You think I want to spend fifty-five *years* down there in that—*celotex interior!* with—*fluorescent—tubes!* Look! I'd rather somebody picked up a crowbar and battered out my brains—than go back mornings! I *go!* Every time you come in yelling that God damn *"Rise and Shine!" "Rise and Shine!"* I say to myself "How *lucky dead* people are!" But I get up. I *go!* For sixty-five dollars a month I give up all that I dream of doing and being *ever!* And you say self—*self*'s all I ever think of. Why, listen, if self is what I thought of, Mother, I'd be where he is—! (*Pointing to father's picture.*) As far as the system of transportation reaches! (*He starts past her. She grabs his arm.*) Don't grab at me, Mother!

AMANDA: Where are you going?

TOM: I'm going to the *movies!*

AMANDA: I don't believe that lie!

TOM (*crouching toward her, overtowering her tiny figure. She backs away, gasping*): I'm going to opium dens! Yes, opium dens, dens of vice and criminals' hang-outs, Mother. I've joined the Hogan gang, I'm a hired assassin, I carry a tommy-gun in a violin case! I run a string of cat-houses in the Valley! They call me Killer, Killer Wingfield, I'm leading a double-life, a simple, honest warehouse worker by day, by night a dynamic *czar* of the *underworld, Mother.* I go to gambling casinos, I spin away fortunes on the roulette table! I wear a patch over one eye and a false mustache, sometimes I put on green whiskers. On those occasions they call me—*El Diablo!*° Oh, I could tell you things to make you sleepless! My enemies plan to dynamite this place. They're going to blow us all sky-high some night! I'll be glad, very happy, and so will you! You'll go up, up on a broomstick, over Blue Mountain with seventeen gentlemen callers! You ugly—babbling old—*witch.* . . . (*He goes through a series of violent, clumsy movements, seizing his overcoat, lunging to the door, pulling it fiercely open. The women watch him, aghast. His arm catches in the sleeve of the coat as he struggles to pull it on. For a moment he is pinioned by the bulky garment. With an outraged groan he tears the coat off again, splitting the shoulders of it, and hurls it across the room. It strikes against the shelf of Laura's glass collection, there is a tinkle of shattering glass. Laura cries out as if wounded.*)

(*Music legend: "The Glass Menagerie."*)

El Diablo: The devil (Spanish).

LAURA (*shrilly*): *My glass!*—menagerie. . . . (*She covers her face and turns away.*)

But Amanda is still stunned and stupefied by the "ugly witch" so that she barely notices this occurrence. Now she recovers her speech.

AMANDA (*in an awful voice*): I won't speak to you—until you apologize! (*She crosses through portieres and draws them together behind her. Tom is left with Laura. Laura clings weakly to the mantel with her face averted. Tom stares at her stupidly for a moment. Then he crosses to shelf. Drops awkwardly to his knees to collect the fallen glass, glancing at Laura as if he would speak but couldn't.*)

"The Glass Menagerie" steals in as

(*The scene dims out.*)

SCENE IV

The interior is dark. Faint light in the alley.

A deep-voiced bell in a church is tolling the hour of five as the scene commences.

Tom appears at the top of the alley. After each solemn boom of the bell in the tower, he shakes a little noise-maker or rattle as if to express the tiny spasm of man in contrast to the sustained power and dignity of the Almighty. This and the unsteadiness of his advance make it evident that he has been drinking.

As he climbs the few steps to the fire-escape landing light steals up inside. Laura appears in night-dress, observing Tom's empty bed in the front room.

Tom fishes in his pockets for the door-key, removing a motley assortment of articles in the search, including a perfect shower of movie-ticket stubs and an empty bottle. At last he finds the key, but just as he is about to insert it, it slips from his fingers. He strikes a match and crouches below the door.

TOM (*bitterly*): One crack—and it falls through!

Laura opens the door.

LAURA: Tom! Tom, what are you doing?

TOM: Looking for a door-key.

LAURA: Where have you been all this time?

TOM: I have been to the movies.

LAURA: All this time at the movies?

TOM: There was a very long program. There was a Garbo picture and a Mickey Mouse and a travelogue and a newsreel and a preview of coming attractions. And there was an organ solo and a collection for the milk-fund—simultaneously—which ended up in a terrible fight between a fat lady and an usher!

LAURA (*innocently*): Did you have to stay through everything?

TOM: Of course! And, oh, I forgot! There was a big stage show! The headliner on this stage show was Malvolio the Magician. He performed wonderful tricks, many of them, such as pouring water back and forth between pitchers. First it turned to wine and then it turned to beer and then it turned to whiskey. I know it was whiskey it finally turned into because he needed somebody to come up out of the audience to help him, and I came up—both shows! It was Kentucky Straight Bourbon. A very generous fellow, he gave souvenirs. (*He pulls from his back pocket a shimmering rainbow-colored scarf.*) He gave me this. This is his magic scarf. You can have it, Laura. You wave it over a canary cage and you get a bowl of gold-fish. You wave it over the gold-fish bowl and they fly away canaries. . . . But the wonderfullest trick of all was the coffin trick. We nailed him into a coffin and he got out of the coffin without removing one nail. (*He has come inside.*) There is a trick that would come in handy for me—get me out of this 2 by 4 situation! (*Flops onto bed and starts removing shoes.*)

LAURA: Tom—Shhh!

TOM: What you shushing me for?

LAURA: You'll wake up Mother.

TOM: Goody, goody! Pay 'er back for all those "Rise an' Shines." (*Lies down, groaning.*) You know it don't take much intelligence to get yourself into a nailed-up coffin, Laura. But who in hell ever got himself out of one without removing one nail?

As if in answer, the father's grinning photograph lights up.
    (*Scene dims out.*)
    Immediately following: The church bell is heard striking six. At the sixth stroke the alarm clock goes off in Amanda's room, and after a few moments we hear her calling: "Rise and Shine! Rise and Shine! Laura, go tell your brother to rise and shine!"

TOM (*sitting up slowly*): I'll rise—but I won't shine.

The light increases.

AMANDA: Laura, tell your brother his coffee is ready.

Laura slips into front room.

LAURA: Tom! it's nearly seven. Don't make Mother nervous. (*He stares at her stupidly. Beseechingly.*) Tom, speak to Mother this morning. Make up with her, apologize, speak to her!

TOM: She won't to me. It's her that started not speaking.

LAURA: If you just say you're sorry she'll start speaking.

TOM: Her not speaking—is that such a tragedy?

LAURA: Please—please!

AMANDA (*calling from kitchenette*): Laura, are you going to do what I asked you to do, or do I have to get dressed and go out myself?

LAURA: Going, going—soon as I get on my coat! (*She pulls on a shapeless felt hat with nervous, jerky movement, pleadingly glancing at Tom. Rushes awkwardly for coat. The coat is one of Amanda's, inaccurately made-over, the sleeves too short for Laura.*) Butter and what else?

AMANDA (*entering upstage*): Just butter. Tell them to charge it.

LAURA: Mother, they make such faces when I do that.

AMANDA: Sticks and stones may break my bones, but the expression on Mr. Garfinkel's face won't harm us! Tell your brother his coffee is getting cold.

LAURA (*at door*): Do what I asked you, will you, will you, Tom?

He looks sullenly away.

AMANDA: Laura, go now or just don't go at all!

LAURA (*rushing out*): Going — going! (*A second later she cries out. Tom springs up and crosses to the door. Amanda rushes anxiously in. Tom opens the door.*)

TOM: Laura?

LAURA: I'm all right. I slipped, but I'm all right.

AMANDA (*peering anxiously after her*): If anyone breaks a leg on those fire-escape steps, the landlord ought to be sued for every cent he possesses! (*She shuts door. Remembers she isn't speaking and returns to other room.*)

As Tom enters listlessly for his coffee, she turns her back to him and stands rigidly facing the window on the gloomy gray vault of the areaway. Its light on her face with its aged but childish features is cruelly sharp, satirical as a Daumier° print. (Music under: "Ave Maria.")

Tom glances sheepishly but sullenly at her averted figure and slumps at the table. The coffee is scalding hot; he sips it and gasps and spits it back in the cup. At his gasp, Amanda catches her breath and half turns. Then catches herself and turns back to window.

Tom blows on his coffee, glancing sidewise at his mother. She clears her throat. Tom clears his. He starts to rise. Sinks back down again, scratches his head, clears his throat again. Amanda coughs. Tom raises his cup in both hands to blow on it, his eyes staring over the rim of it at his mother for several moments. Then he slowly sets the cup down and awkwardly and hesitantly rises from the chair.

TOM (*hoarsely*): Mother. I — I apologize. Mother. (*Amanda draws a quick, shuddering breath. Her face works grotesquely. She breaks into childlike tears.*) I'm sorry for what I said, for everything that I said, I didn't mean it.

AMANDA (*sobbingly*): My devotion has made me a witch and so I make myself hateful to my children!

TOM: No, you *don't*.

AMANDA: I worry so much, don't sleep, it makes me nervous!

TOM (*gently*): I understand that.

AMANDA: I've had to put up a solitary battle all these years. But you're my right-hand bower! Don't fall down, don't fail!

TOM (*gently*): I try, Mother.

AMANDA (*with great enthusiasm*): Try and you will SUCCEED! (*The notion makes her breathless.*) Why, you — you're just *full* of natural endowments! Both of my children — they're *unusual* children! Don't you think I know it? I'm so — proud! Happy and — feel I've — so much to be thankful for but — Promise me one thing, son!

TOM: What, Mother?

AMANDA: Promise, son, you'll — never be a drunkard!

TOM (*turns to her grinning*): I will never be a drunkard, Mother.

AMANDA: That's what frightened me so, that you'd be drinking! Eat a bowl of Purina!

Daumier: Honoré Daumier (1808–1879) was a French caricaturist, lithographer, and painter.

TOM: Just coffee, Mother.

AMANDA: Shredded wheat biscuit?

TOM: No. No, Mother, just coffee.

AMANDA: You can't put in a day's work on an empty stomach. You've got ten minutes — don't gulp! Drinking too-hot liquids makes cancer of the stomach. . . . Put cream in.

TOM: No, thank you.

AMANDA: To cool it.

TOM: No! No, thank you, I want it black.

AMANDA: I know, but it's not good for you. We have to do all that we can to build ourselves up. In these trying times we live in, all that we have to cling to is — each other. . . . That's why it's so important to — Tom, I — I sent out your sister so I could discuss something with you. If you hadn't spoken I would have spoken to you. (*Sits down.*)

TOM (*gently*): What is it, Mother, that you want to discuss?

AMANDA: Laura!

Tom puts his cup down slowly.
(*Legend on screen: "Laura."*)
(*Music: "The Glass Menagerie."*)

TOM: — Oh. — Laura . . .

AMANDA (*touching his sleeve*): You know how Laura is. So quiet but — still water runs deep! She notices things and I think she — broods about them. (*Tom looks up.*) A few days ago I came in and she was crying.

TOM: What about?

AMANDA: You.

TOM: Me?

AMANDA: She has an idea that you're not happy here.

TOM: What gave her that idea?

AMANDA: What gives her any idea? However, you do act strangely. I — I'm not criticizing, understand *that!* I know your ambitions do not lie in the warehouse, that like everybody in the whole wide world — you've had to — make sacrifices, but — Tom — Tom — life's not easy, it calls for — Spartan endurance! There's so many things in my heart that I cannot describe to you! I've never told you but I — *loved* your father. . . .

TOM (*gently*): I know that, Mother.

AMANDA: And you — when I see you taking after his ways! Staying out late — and — well, you *had* been drinking the night you were in that — terrifying condition! Laura says that you hate the apartment and that you go out nights to get away from it! Is that true, Tom?

TOM: No. You say there's so much in your heart that you can't describe to me. That's true of me, too. There's so much in my heart that I can't describe to *you!* So let's respect each other's —

AMANDA: But, why — *why*, Tom — are you always so *restless?* Where do you go to, nights?

TOM: I — go to the movies.

AMANDA: Why do you go to the movies so much, Tom?

TOM: I go to the movies because—I like adventure. Adventure is something I don't have much of at work, so I go to the movies.

AMANDA: But, Tom, you go to the movies *entirely too much!*

TOM: I like a lot of adventure.

Amanda looks baffled, then hurt. As the familiar inquisition resumes he becomes hard and impatient again. Amanda slips back into her querulous attitude toward him.

> *(Image on screen: Sailing vessel with Jolly Roger.)*

AMANDA: Most young men find adventure in their careers.

TOM: Then most young men are not employed in a warehouse.

AMANDA: The world is full of young men employed in warehouses and offices and factories.

TOM: Do all of them find adventure in their careers?

AMANDA: They do or they do without it! Not everybody has a craze for adventure.

TOM: Man is by instinct a lover, a hunter, a fighter, and none of those instincts are given much play at the warehouse!

AMANDA: Man is by instinct! Don't quote instinct to me! Instinct is something that people have got away from! It belongs to animals! Christian adults don't want it!

TOM: What do Christian adults want, then, Mother?

AMANDA: Superior things! Things of the mind and the spirit! Only animals have to satisfy instincts! Surely your aims are somewhat higher than theirs! Than monkeys—pigs—

TOM: I reckon they're not.

AMANDA: You're joking. However, that isn't what I wanted to discuss.

TOM (*rising*): I haven't much time.

AMANDA (*pushing his shoulders*): Sit down.

TOM: You want me to punch in red° at the warehouse, Mother?

AMANDA: You have five minutes. I want to talk about Laura.

(Legend: "Plans and Provisions.")

TOM: All right! What about Laura?

AMANDA: We have to be making plans and provisions for her. She's older than you, two years, and nothing has happened. She just drifts along doing nothing. It frightens me terribly how she just drifts along.

TOM: I guess she's the type that people call home girls.

AMANDA: There's no such type, and if there is, it's a pity! That is unless the home is hers, with a husband!

TOM: What?

AMANDA: Oh, I can see the handwriting on the wall as plain as I see the nose in front of my face! It's terrifying! More and more you remind me of your father! He was out all hours without explanation—Then *left! Good-bye!* And me with the bag to hold. I saw that letter you got from the Merchant Marine. I know what you're dreaming of. I'm not standing here blind-

---

punch in red: Show up late for work.

folded. Very well, then. Then *do* it! But not till there's somebody to take your place.

TOM: What do you mean?

AMANDA: I mean that as soon as Laura has got somebody to take care of her, married, a home of her own, independent — why, then you'll be free to go wherever you please, on land, on sea, whichever way the wind blows! But until that time you've got to look out for your sister. I don't say me because I'm old and don't matter! I say for your sister because she's young and dependent. I put her in business college — a dismal failure! Frightened her so it made her sick to her stomach. I took her over to the Young People's League at the church. Another fiasco. She spoke to nobody, nobody spoke to her. Now all she does is fool with those pieces of glass and play those worn-out records. What kind of a life is that for a girl to lead!

TOM: What can I do about it?

AMANDA: Overcome selfishness! Self, self, self is all that you ever think of! (*Tom springs up and crosses to get his coat. It is ugly and bulky. He pulls on a cap with earmuffs.*) Where is your muffler? Put your wool muffler on! (*He snatches it angrily from the closet and tosses it around his neck and pulls both ends tight.*) Tom! I haven't said what I had in mind to ask you.

TOM: I'm too late to —

AMANDA (*catching his arms — very importunately. Then shyly.*): Down at the warehouse, aren't there some — nice young men?

TOM: No!

AMANDA: There *must* be — *some.*

TOM: Mother —

Gesture.

AMANDA: Find out one that's clean-living — doesn't drink and — ask him out for sister!

TOM: What?

AMANDA: For *sister!* To *meet!* Get *acquainted!*

TOM (*stamping to door*): Oh, my go-osh!

AMANDA: Will you? (*He opens door. Imploringly.*) Will you? (*He starts down.*) Will you? *Will* you, dear?

TOM (*calling back*): YES!

Amanda closes the door hesitantly and with a troubled but faintly hopeful expression.
(*Screen image:* Glamour *magazine cover.*)
Spot Amanda at phone.

AMANDA: Ella Cartwright? This is Amanda Wingfield! How are you, honey? How is that kidney condition? (*Count five.*) Horrors! (*Count five.*) You're a Christian martyr, yes, honey, that's what you are, a Christian martyr! Well, I just happened to notice in my little red book that your subscription to the *Companion* has just run out! I knew that you wouldn't want to miss out on the wonderful serial starting in this new issue. It's by Bessie Mae Hopper, the first thing she's written since *Honeymoon for Three.* Wasn't that a strange and interesting story? Well, this one is even lovelier, I believe. It has a sophisticated society background. It's all about the horsey set on Long Island!

(*Fade out.*)

SCENE V

(*Legend on screen: "Annunciation."*) *Fade with music.*

It is early dusk of a spring evening. Supper has just been finished in the Wing-field apartment. Amanda and Laura in light-colored dresses are removing dishes from the table, in the upstage area, which is shadowy, their movements formalized almost as a dance or ritual, their moving forms as pale and silent as moths.

Tom, in white shirt and trousers, rises from the table and crosses toward the fire-escape.

AMANDA (*as he passes her*): Son, will you do me a favor?

TOM: What?

AMANDA: Comb your hair! You look so pretty when your hair is combed! (*Tom slouches on sofa with evening paper. Enormous caption "Franco Tri-umphs."*°) There is only one respect in which I would like you to emulate your father.

TOM: What respect is that?

AMANDA: The care he always took of his appearance. He never allowed himself to look untidy. (*He throws down the paper and crosses to fire-escape.*) Where are you going?

TOM: I'm going out to smoke.

AMANDA: You smoke too much. A pack a day at fifteen cents a pack. How much would that amount to in a month? Thirty times fifteen is how much, Tom? Figure it out and you will be astounded at what you could save. Enough to give you a night-school course in accounting at Washington U! Just think what a wonderful thing that would be for you, son!

Tom is unmoved by the thought.

TOM: I'd rather smoke. (*He steps out on landing, letting the screen door slam.*)

AMANDA (*sharply*): I know! That's the tragedy of it. . . . (*Alone, she turns to look at her husband's picture.*)

(*Dance music: "All the World Is Waiting for the Sunrise!"*)

TOM (*to the audience*): Across the alley from us was the Paradise Dance Hall. On evenings in spring the windows and doors were open and the music came outdoors. Sometimes the lights were turned out except for a large glass sphere that hung from the ceiling. It would turn slowly about and filter the dusk with delicate rainbow colors. Then the orchestra played a waltz or a tango, something that had a slow and sensuous rhythm. Couples would come outside, to the relative privacy of the alley. You could see them kissing behind ash-pits and telephone poles. This was the compensation for lives that passed like mine, without any change or ad-

---

"Franco Triumphs": In January 1939 Francisco Franco's (1892–1975) victory over the Loyalists ended the Spanish Civil War.

venture. Adventure and change were imminent in this year. They were waiting around the corner for all these kids. Suspended in the mist over the Berchtesgaden,° caught in the folds of Chamberlain's° umbrella— In Spain there was Guernica! But here there was only hot swing music and liquor, dance halls, bars, and movies, and sex that hung in the gloom like a chandelier and flooded the world with brief, deceptive rainbows. . . . All the world was waiting for bombardments!

Amanda turns from the picture and comes outside.

AMANDA (*sighing*): A fire-escape landing's a poor excuse for a porch. (*She spreads a newspaper on a step and sits down, gracefully and demurely as if she were settling into a swing on a Mississippi veranda.*) What are you looking at?

TOM: The moon.

AMANDA: Is there a moon this evening?

TOM: It's rising over Garfinkel's Delicatessen.

AMANDA: So it is! A little silver slipper of a moon. Have you made a wish on it yet?

TOM: Um-hum.

AMANDA: What did you wish for?

TOM: That's a secret.

AMANDA: A secret, huh? Well, I won't tell mine either. I will be just as mysterious as you.

TOM: I bet I can guess what yours is.

AMANDA: Is my head so transparent?

TOM: You're not a sphinx.

AMANDA: No, I don't have secrets. I'll tell you what I wished for on the moon. Success and happiness for my precious children! I wish for that whenever there's a moon, and when there isn't a moon, I wish for it, too.

TOM: I thought perhaps you wished for a gentleman caller.

AMANDA: Why do you say that?

TOM: Don't you remember asking me to fetch one?

AMANDA: I remember suggesting that it would be nice for your sister if you brought home some nice young man from the warehouse. I think I've made that suggestion more than once.

TOM: Yes, you have made it repeatedly.

AMANDA: Well?

TOM: We are going to have one.

AMANDA: *What?*

TOM: A gentleman caller!

(*The Annunciation is celebrated with music.*)
    Amanda rises.
    (*Image on screen: Caller with bouquet.*)

Berchtesgaden: A resort in the German Alps where Adolf Hitler had a heavily protected villa. **Chamberlain:** Neville Chamberlain (1869–1940) was the British prime minister who sought to avoid war with Hitler through a policy of appeasement.

AMANDA: You mean you have asked some nice young man to come over?

TOM: Yep. I've asked him to dinner.

AMANDA: You really did?

TOM: I did!

AMANDA: You did, and did he—*accept?*

TOM: He did!

AMANDA: Well, well—well, well! That's—lovely!

TOM: I thought that you would be pleased.

AMANDA: It's definite, then?

TOM: Very definite.

AMANDA: Soon?

TOM: Very soon.

AMANDA: For heaven's sake, stop putting on and tell me some things, will you?

TOM: What things do you want me to tell you?

AMANDA: Naturally I would like to know when he's *coming!*

TOM: He's coming tomorrow.

AMANDA: *Tomorrow?*

TOM: Yep. Tomorrow.

AMANDA: But, Tom!

TOM: Yes, Mother?

AMANDA: Tomorrow gives me no time!

TOM: Time for what?

AMANDA: Preparations! Why didn't you phone me at once, as soon as you asked him, the minute that he accepted? Then, don't you see, I could have been getting ready!

TOM: You don't have to make any fuss.

AMANDA: Oh, Tom, Tom, Tom, of course I have to make a fuss! I want things nice, not sloppy! Not thrown together. I'll certainly have to do some fast thinking, won't I?

TOM: I don't see why you have to think at all.

AMANDA: You just don't know. We can't have a gentleman caller in a pig-sty! All my wedding silver has to be polished, the monogrammed table linen ought to be laundered! The windows have to be washed and fresh curtains put up. And how about clothes? We have to *wear* something, don't we?

TOM: Mother, this boy is no one to make a fuss over!

AMANDA: Do you realize he's the first young man we've introduced to your sister? It's terrible, dreadful, disgraceful that poor little sister has never received a single gentleman caller! Tom, come inside! (*She opens the screen door.*)

TOM: What for?

AMANDA: I want to ask you some things.

TOM: If you're going to make such a fuss, I'll call it off, I'll tell him not to come.

AMANDA: You certainly won't do anything of the kind. Nothing offends people worse than broken engagements. It simply means I'll have to work like a Turk! We won't be brilliant, but we'll pass inspection. Come on inside. (*Tom follows, groaning.*) Sit down.

TOM: Any particular place you would like me to sit?

AMANDA: Thank heavens I've got that new sofa! I'm also making payments on a floor lamp I'll have sent out! And put the chintz covers on, they'll brighten things up! Of course I'd hoped to have these walls re-papered. . . . What is the young man's name?

TOM: His name is O'Connor.

AMANDA: That, of course, means fish—tomorrow is Friday! I'll have that salmon loaf—with Durkee's dressing! What does he do? He works at the warehouse?

TOM: Of course! How else would I—

AMANDA: Tom, he—doesn't drink?

TOM: Why do you ask me that?

AMANDA: Your father *did*!

TOM: Don't get started on that!

AMANDA: He *does* drink, then?

TOM: Not that I know of!

AMANDA: Make sure, be certain! The last thing I want for my daughter's a boy who drinks!

TOM: Aren't you being a little premature? Mr. O'Connor has not yet appeared on the scene!

AMANDA: But will tomorrow. To meet your sister, and what do I know about his character? Nothing! Old maids are better off than wives of drunkards!

TOM: Oh, my God!

AMANDA: Be still!

TOM (*leaning forward to whisper*): Lots of fellows meet girls whom they don't marry!

AMANDA: Oh, talk sensibly, Tom—and don't be sarcastic! (*She has gotten a hairbrush.*)

TOM: What are you doing?

AMANDA: I'm brushing that cow-lick down! What is this young man's position at the warehouse?

TOM (*submitting grimly to the brush and the interrogation*): This young man's position is that of a shipping clerk, Mother.

AMANDA: Sounds to me like a fairly responsible job, the sort of a job *you* would be in if you just had more *get-up*. What is his salary? Have you got any idea?

TOM: I would judge it to be approximately eighty-five dollars a month.

AMANDA: Well—not princely, but—

TOM: Twenty more than I make.

AMANDA: Yes, how well I know! But for a family man, eighty-five dollars a month is not much more than you can just get by on. . . .

TOM: Yes, but Mr. O'Connor is not a family man.

AMANDA: He might be, mightn't he? Some time in the future?

TOM: I see. Plans and provisions.

AMANDA: You are the only young man that I know of who ignores the fact that the future becomes the present, the present the past, and the past turns into everlasting regret if you don't plan for it!

TOM: I will think that over and see what I can make of it.

AMANDA: Don't be supercilious with your mother! Tell me some more about this—what do you call him?

TOM: James D. O'Connor. The D. is for Delaney.

AMANDA: Irish on *both* sides! *Gracious!* And doesn't drink?

TOM: Shall I call him up and ask him right this minute?

AMANDA: The only way to find out about those things is to make discreet inquiries at the proper moment. When I was a girl in Blue Mountain and it was suspected that a young man drank, the girl whose attentions he had been receiving, if any girl *was,* would sometimes speak to the minister of his church, or rather her father would if her father was living, and sort of feel him out on the young man's character. That is the way such things are discreetly handled to keep a young woman from making a tragic mistake!

TOM: Then how did you happen to make a tragic mistake?

AMANDA: That innocent look of your father's had everyone fooled! He *smiled*— the world was *enchanted!* No girl can do worse than put herself at the mercy of a handsome appearance! I hope that Mr. O'Connor is not too good-looking.

TOM: No, he's not too good-looking. He's covered with freckles and hasn't too much of a nose.

AMANDA: He's not right-down homely, though?

TOM: Not right-down homely. Just medium homely, I'd say.

AMANDA: Character's what to look for in a man.

TOM: That's what I've always said, Mother.

AMANDA: You've never said anything of the kind and I suspect you would never give it a thought.

TOM: Don't be suspicious of me.

AMANDA: At least I hope he's the type that's up and coming.

TOM: I think he really goes in for self-improvement.

AMANDA: What reason have you to think so?

TOM: He goes to night school.

AMANDA (*beaming*): Splendid! What does he do, I mean study?

TOM: Radio engineering and public speaking!

AMANDA: Then he has visions of being advanced in the world! Any young man who studies public speaking is aiming to have an executive job some day! And radio engineering? A thing for the future! Both of these facts are very illuminating. Those are the sort of things that a mother should know concerning any young man who comes to call on her daughter. Seriously or—not.

TOM: One little warning. He doesn't know about Laura. I didn't let on that we had dark ulterior motives. I just said, why don't you come have dinner with us? He said okay and that was the whole conversation.

AMANDA: I bet it was! You're eloquent as an oyster. However, he'll know about Laura when he gets here. When he sees how lovely and sweet and pretty she is, he'll thank his lucky stars he was asked to dinner.

TOM: Mother, you mustn't expect too much of Laura.

AMANDA: What do you mean?

TOM: Laura seems all those things to you and me because she's ours and we love her. We don't even notice she's crippled any more.

AMANDA: Don't say crippled! You know that I never allow that word to be used!

TOM: But face facts, Mother. She is and—that's not all—

AMANDA: What do you mean "not all"?

TOM: Laura is very different from other girls.

AMANDA: I think the difference is all to her advantage.

TOM: Not quite all—in the eyes of others—strangers—she's terribly shy and lives in a world of her own and those things make her seem a little peculiar to people outside the house.

AMANDA: Don't say peculiar.

TOM: Face the facts. She is.

(*The dance-hall music changes to a tango that has a minor and somewhat ominous tone.*)

AMANDA: In what way is she peculiar—may I ask?

TOM (*gently*): She lives in a world of her own—a world of—little glass ornaments, Mother. . . . (*Gets up. Amanda remains holding brush, looking at him, troubled.*) She plays old phonograph records and—that's about all—(*He glances at himself in the mirror and crosses to door.*)

AMANDA (*sharply*): Where are you going?

TOM: I'm going to the movies. (*Out screen door.*)

AMANDA: Not to the movies, every night to the movies! (*Follows quickly to screen door.*) I don't believe you always go to the movies! (*He is gone. Amanda looks worriedly after him for a moment. Then vitality and optimism return and she turns from the door. Crossing to portieres.*) Laura! Laura! (*Laura answers from kitchenette.*)

LAURA: Yes, Mother.

AMANDA: Let those dishes go and come in front! (*Laura appears with dish towel. Gaily.*) Laura, come here and make a wish on the moon!

LAURA (*entering*): Moon—moon?

AMANDA: A little silver slipper of a moon. Look over your left shoulder, Laura, and make a wish! (*Laura looks faintly puzzled as if called out of sleep. Amanda seizes her shoulders and turns her at angle by the door.*) Now! Now, darling, wish!

LAURA: What shall I wish for, Mother?

AMANDA (*her voice trembling and her eyes suddenly filling with tears*): Happiness! Good Fortune!

The violin rises and the stage dims out.

SCENE VI

(*Image: High-school hero.*)

TOM: And so the following evening I brought Jim home to dinner. I had known Jim slightly in high school. In high school Jim was a hero. He had tremendous Irish good nature and vitality with the scrubbed and polished look of white chinaware. He seemed to move in a continual spotlight. He was a star in basketball, captain of the debating club, president of the senior class and the glee club and he sang the male lead in the annual light operas. He was always running or bounding, never just walking. He seemed always at the point of defeating the law of gravity. He was shooting with such velocity through his adolescence that you would logically expect him to arrive at nothing short of the White House by the time he was thirty. But Jim apparently ran into more interference after his graduation from Soldan. His speed had definitely slowed. Six years after he left high school he was holding a job that wasn't much better than mine.

(Image: Clerk.)

He was the only one at the warehouse with whom I was on friendly terms. I was valuable to him as someone who could remember his former glory, who had seen him win basketball games and the silver cup in debating. He knew of my secret practice of retiring to a cabinet of the washroom to work on poems when business was slack in the warehouse. He called me Shakespeare. And while the other boys in the warehouse regarded me with suspicious hostility, Jim took a humorous attitude toward me. Gradually his attitude affected the others, their hostility wore off, and they also began to smile at me as people smile at an oddly fashioned dog who trots across their paths at some distance.

I knew that Jim and Laura had known each other at Soldan, and I had heard Laura speak admiringly of his voice. I didn't know if Jim remembered her or not. In high school Laura had been as unobtrusive as Jim had been astonishing. If he did remember Laura, it was not as my sister, for when I asked him to dinner, he grinned and said, "You know, Shakespeare, I never thought of you as having folks!"

He was about to discover that I did. . . .

(Light upstage.)

(Legend on screen: "The Accent of a Coming Foot.")

Friday evening. It is about five o'clock of a late spring evening which comes "scattering poems in the sky."

A delicate lemony light is in the Wingfield apartment.

Amanda has worked like a Turk in preparation for the gentleman caller. The results are astonishing. The new floor lamp with its rose-silk shade is in place, a colored paper lantern conceals the broken light fixture in the ceiling, new billowing white curtains are at the windows, chintz covers are on chairs and sofa, a pair of new sofa pillows make their initial appearance.

Open boxes and tissue paper are scattered on the floor.

Laura stands in the middle with lifted arms while Amanda crouches before her, adjusting the hem of the new dress, devout and ritualistic. The dress is colored and designed by memory. The arrangement of Laura's hair is changed; it is softer and more becoming. A fragile, unearthly prettiness has come out in Laura: she is like a piece of translucent glass touched by light, given a momentary radiance, not actual, not lasting.

AMANDA (*impatiently*): Why are you trembling?

LAURA: Mother, you've made me so nervous!

AMANDA: How have I made you nervous?

LAURA: By all this fuss! You make it seem so important!

AMANDA: I don't understand you, Laura. You couldn't be satisfied with just sitting home, and yet whenever I try to arrange something for you, you seem to resist it. (*She gets up.*) Now take a look at yourself. No, wait! Wait just a moment — I have an idea!

LAURA: What is it now?

Amanda produces two powder puffs which she wraps in handkerchiefs and stuffs in Laura's bosom.

LAURA: Mother, what are you doing?

AMANDA: They call them "Gay Deceivers"!

LAURA: I won't wear them!

AMANDA: You will!

LAURA: Why should I?

AMANDA: Because, to be painfully honest, your chest is flat.

LAURA: You make it seem like we were setting a trap.

AMANDA: All pretty girls are a trap, a pretty trap, and men expect them to be. (*Legend: "A Pretty Trap."*) Now look at yourself, young lady. This is the prettiest you will ever be! I've got to fix myself now! You're going to be surprised by your mother's appearance! (*She crosses through portieres, humming gaily.*)

Laura moves slowly to the long mirror and stares solemnly at herself.

A wind blows the white curtains inward in a slow, graceful motion and with a faint, sorrowful sighing.

AMANDA (*offstage*): It isn't dark enough yet. (*She turns slowly before the mirror with a troubled look*).

(*Legend on screen: "This Is My Sister: Celebrate Her with Strings!" Music.*)

AMANDA (*laughing, off*): I'm going to show you something. I'm going to make a spectacular appearance!

LAURA: What is it, Mother?

AMANDA: Possess your soul in patience — you will see! Something I've resurrected from that old trunk! Styles haven't changed so terribly much after all. . . . (*She parts the portieres.*) Now just look at your mother! (*She wears a girlish frock of yellowed voile with a blue silk sash. She carries a bunch of jonquils — the legend of her youth is nearly revived. Feverishly.*) This is the dress in which I led the cotillion. Won the cakewalk twice at Sunset Hill, wore one spring to the Governor's ball in Jackson! See how I sashayed around the ballroom, Laura? (*She raises her skirt and does a mincing step around the room.*) I wore it on Sundays for my gentlemen callers! I had it on the day I met your father — I had malaria fever all that spring. The change of climate from East Tennessee to the Delta — weakened resistance — I had a little temperature all the time — not enough to be serious—just enough to make me restless and giddy! Invitations poured in—parties all over the Delta!—"Stay in bed," said Mother, "you have fever!"—but I just wouldn't.—I took quinine but kept on going, going!—Evenings, dances!—Afternoons, long, long rides! Picnics—lovely!—So lovely, that country in May.—All lacy with dogwood, literally flooded with jonquils!—That was the spring I had the craze for jonquils. Jonquils became an absolute obsession. Mother said, "Honey, there's no more room for jonquils." And still I kept bringing in more jonquils. Whenever, wherever I saw them, I'd say, "Stop! Stop! I see jonquils!" I made the young men help me gather the jonquils! It was a joke, Amanda and her jonquils! Finally there were no more vases to hold them, every available space was filled with jonquils. No vases to hold them? All right, I'll hold them myself! And then I—(*She stops in front of the picture.*) (*Music.*) met your father! Malaria fever and jonquils and then—this—boy. . . . (*She switches on the rose-colored lamp.*) I hope they get here before it starts to rain. (*She crosses upstage and places the jonquils in bowl on table.*) I gave your brother a little extra change so he and Mr. O'Connor could take the service car home.

LAURA (*with altered look*): What did you say his name was?

AMANDA: O'Connor.

LAURA: What is his first name?

AMANDA: I don't remember. Oh, yes, I do. It was—Jim!

Laura sways slightly and catches hold of a chair.

> (*Legend on screen: "Not Jim!"*)

LAURA (*faintly*): Not—Jim!

AMANDA: Yes, that was it, it was Jim! I've never known a Jim that wasn't nice!

(*Music: Ominous.*)

LAURA: Are you sure his name is Jim O'Connor?

AMANDA: Yes. Why?

LAURA: Is he the one that Tom used to know in high school?

AMANDA: He didn't say so. I think he just got to know him at the warehouse.

LAURA: There was a Jim O'Connor we both knew in high school—(*Then, with effort.*) If that is the one that Tom is bringing to dinner—you'll have to excuse me, I won't come to the table.

AMANDA: What sort of nonsense is this?

LAURA: You asked me once if I'd ever liked a boy. Don't you remember I showed you this boy's picture?

AMANDA: You mean the boy you showed me in the year-book?

LAURA: Yes, that boy.

AMANDA: Laura, Laura, were you in love with that boy?

LAURA: I don't know, Mother. All I know is I couldn't sit at the table if it was him!

AMANDA: It won't be him! It isn't the least bit likely. But whether it is or not, you will come to the table. You will not be excused.

LAURA: I'll have to be, Mother.

AMANDA: I don't intend to humor your silliness, Laura. I've had too much from you and your brother, both! So just sit down and compose yourself till they come. Tom has forgotten his key so you'll have to let them in, when they arrive.

LAURA (*panicky*): Oh, Mother—*you* answer the door!

AMANDA (*lightly*): I'll be in the kitchen—busy!

LAURA: Oh, Mother, please answer the door, don't make me do it!

AMANDA (*crossing into kitchenette*): I've got to fix the dressing for the salmon. Fuss, fuss—silliness!—over a gentleman caller!

Door swings shut. Laura is left alone.

(Legend: "Terror!")

She utters a low moan and turns off the lamp—sits stiffly on the edge of the sofa, knotting her fingers together.

(Legend on screen: "The Opening of a Door!")

Tom and Jim appear on the fire-escape steps and climb to landing. Hearing their approach, Laura rises with a panicky gesture. She retreats to the portieres.

The doorbell. Laura catches her breath and touches her throat. Low drums.

AMANDA (*calling*): Laura, sweetheart! The door!

Laura stares at it without moving.

JIM: I think we just beat the rain.

TOM: Uh-huh. (*He rings again, nervously. Jim whistles and fishes for a cigarette.*)

AMANDA (*very, very gaily*): Laura, that is your brother and Mr. O'Connor! Will you let them in, darling?

Laura crosses toward kitchenette door.

LAURA (*breathlessly*): Mother—you go to the door!

Amanda steps out of kitchenette and stares furiously at Laura. She points imperiously at the door.

LAURA: Please, please!

AMANDA (*in a fierce whisper*): What is the matter with you, you silly thing?

LAURA (*desperately*): Please, you answer it, *please!*

AMANDA: I told you I wasn't going to humor you, Laura. Why have you chosen this moment to lose your mind?

LAURA: Please, please, please, you go!

AMANDA: You'll have to go to the door because I can't!

LAURA (*despairingly*): I can't either!

AMANDA: Why?

LAURA: I'm *sick!*

AMANDA: I'm sick, too—of your nonsense! Why can't you and your brother be normal people? Fantastic whims and behavior! (*Tom gives a long ring.*) Preposterous goings on! Can you give me one reason—(*Calls out lyrically.*) COMING! JUST ONE SECOND!—why should you be afraid to open a door? Now you answer it, Laura!

LAURA: Oh, oh, oh . . . (*She returns through the portieres. Darts to the Victrola and winds it frantically and turns it on.*)

AMANDA: Laura Wingfield, you march right to that door!

LAURA: Yes — yes, Mother!

A faraway, scratchy rendition of "Dardanella" softens the air and gives her strength to move through it. She slips to the door and draws it cautiously open.
Tom enters with the caller, Jim O'Connor.

TOM: Laura, this is Jim. Jim, this is my sister, Laura.

JIM (*stepping inside*): I didn't know that Shakespeare had a sister!

LAURA (*retreating stiff and trembling from the door*): How — how do you do?

JIM (*heartily extending his hand*): Okay!

Laura touches it hesitantly with hers.

JIM: Your hand's *cold*, Laura!

LAURA: Yes, well — I've been playing the Victrola . . .

JIM: Must have been playing classical music on it! You ought to play a little hot swing music to warm you up!

LAURA: Excuse me — I haven't finished playing the Victrola . . .

She turns awkwardly and hurries into the front room. She pauses a second by the Victrola. Then catches her breath and darts through the portieres like a frightened deer.

JIM (*grinning*): What was the matter?

TOM: Oh — with Laura? Laura is — terribly shy.

JIM: Shy, huh? It's unusual to meet a shy girl nowadays. I don't believe you ever mentioned you had a sister.

TOM: Well, now you know. I have one. Here is the *Post Dispatch*. You want a piece of it?

JIM: Uh-huh.

TOM: What piece? The comics?

JIM: Sports! (*Glances at it.*) Ole Dizzy Dean is on his bad behavior.

TOM (*disinterest*): Yeah? (*Lights cigarette and crosses back to fire-escape door.*)

JIM: Where are *you* going?

TOM: I'm going out on the terrace.

JIM (*goes after him*): You know, Shakespeare — I'm going to sell you a bill of goods!

TOM: What goods?

JIM: A course I'm taking.

TOM: Huh?

JIM: In public speaking! You and me, we're not the warehouse type.

TOM: Thanks — that's good news. But what has public speaking got to do with it?

JIM: It fits you for — executive positions!

TOM: Awww.

JIM: I tell you it's done a helluva lot for me.

(*Image: Executive at desk.*)

TOM: In what respect?

JIM: In every! Ask yourself what is the difference between you an' me and men in the office down front? Brains? — No! — Ability? — No! Then what? Just one little thing —

TOM: What is that one little thing?

JIM: Primarily it amounts to — social poise! Being able to square up to people and hold your own on any social level!

AMANDA (*offstage*): Tom?

TOM: Yes, Mother?

AMANDA: Is that you and Mr. O'Connor?

TOM: Yes, Mother.

AMANDA: Well, you just make yourselves comfortable in there.

TOM: Yes, Mother.

AMANDA: Ask Mr. O'Connor if he would like to wash his hands.

JIM: Aw — no — no — thank you — I took care of that at the warehouse. Tom —

TOM: Yes?

JIM: Mr. Mendoza was speaking to me about you.

TOM: Favorably?

JIM: What do you think?

TOM: Well —

JIM: You're going to be out of a job if you don't wake up.

TOM: I am waking up —

JIM: You show no signs.

TOM: The signs are interior.

(*Image on screen: The sailing vessel with Jolly Roger again.*)

TOM: I'm planning to change. (*He leans over the rail speaking with quiet exhilaration. The incandescent marquees and signs of the first-run movie houses light his face from across the alley. He looks like a voyager.*) I'm right at the point of committing myself to a future that doesn't include the warehouse and Mr. Mendoza or even a night-school course in public speaking.

JIM: What are you gassing about?

TOM: I'm tired of the movies.

JIM: Movies!

TOM: Yes, movies! Look at them — (*A wave toward the marvels of Grand Avenue.*) All of those glamorous people — having adventures — hogging it all, gobbling the whole thing up! You know what happens? People go to the *movies* instead of *moving!* Hollywood characters are supposed to have all the adventures for everybody in America, while everybody in America sits in a dark room and watches them have them! Yes, until there's a war. That's when adventure becomes available to the masses! *Everyone's* dish, not only Gable's! Then the people in the dark room come out of the dark room to have some adventures themselves — Goody, goody — It's our turn now, to go to the South Sea Island — to make a safari — to be exotic, far-off — But I'm not patient. I don't want to wait till then. I'm tired of the *movies* and I am *about* to *move!*

JIM (*incredulously*): Move?

TOM: Yes.

JIM: When?

TOM: Soon!

JIM: Where? Where?

(*Theme three: Music seems to answer the question, while Tom thinks it over. He searches among his pockets.*)

TOM: I'm starting to boil inside. I know I seem dreamy, but inside—well, I'm boiling! Whenever I pick up a shoe, I shudder a little thinking how short life is and what I am doing!—Whatever that means. I know it doesn't mean shoes—except as something to wear on a traveler's feet! (*Finds paper.*) Look—

JIM: What?

TOM: I'm a member.

JIM (*reading*): The Union of Merchant Seamen.

TOM: I paid my dues this month, instead of the light bill.

JIM: You will regret it when they turn the lights off.

TOM: I won't be here.

JIM: How about your mother?

TOM: I'm like my father. The bastard son of a bastard! See how he grins? And he's been absent going on sixteen years!

JIM: You're just talking, you drip. How does your mother feel about it?

TOM: Shhh—Here comes Mother! Mother is not acquainted with my plans!

AMANDA (*enters portieres*): Where are you all?

TOM: On the terrace, Mother.

They start inside. She advances to them. Tom is distinctly shocked at her appearance. Even Jim blinks a little. He is making his first contact with girlish Southern vivacity and in spite of the night-school course in public speaking is somewhat thrown off the beam by the unexpected outlay of social charm.

Certain responses are attempted by Jim but are swept aside by Amanda's gay laughter and chatter. Tom is embarrassed but after the first shock Jim reacts very warmly. Grins and chuckles, is altogether won over.

(*Image: Amanda as a girl.*)

AMANDA (*coyly smiling, shaking her girlish ringlets*): Well, well, well, so this is Mr. O'Connor. Introductions entirely unnecessary. I've heard so much about you from my boy. I finally said to him, Tom—good gracious!— why don't you bring this paragon to supper? I'd like to meet this nice young man at the warehouse!—Instead of just hearing him sing your praises so much! I don't know why my son is so stand-offish—that's not Southern behavior! Let's sit down and—I think we could stand a little more air in here! Tom, leave the door open. I felt a nice fresh breeze a moment ago. Where has it gone? Mmm, so warm already! And not quite summer, even. We're going to burn up when summer really gets started. However, we're having—we're having a very light supper. I think light things are better fo' this time of year. The same as light clothes are. Light clothes an' light food are what warm weather calls fo'. You know our blood gets so thick during th' winter—it takes a while fo' us to *adjust* ou'selves!—when the season changes. . . . It's come so quick this year. I wasn't prepared. All of a sudden—heavens! Already summer!—I ran to the trunk an' pulled out this light dress—Terribly old! Historical almost! But feels so good—so good an' co-ol, y'know. . . .

TOM: Mother—

AMANDA: Yes, honey?

TOM: How about—supper?

AMANDA: Honey, you go ask Sister if supper is ready! You know that Sister is in full charge of supper! Tell her you hungry boys are waiting for it. (*To Jim.*) Have you met Laura?

JIM: She—

AMANDA: Let you in? Oh, good, you've met already! It's rare for a girl as sweet an' pretty as Laura to be domestic! But Laura is, thank heavens, not only pretty but also very domestic. I'm not at all. I never was a bit. I never could make a thing but angel-food cake. Well, in the South we had so many servants. Gone, gone, gone. All vestiges of gracious living! Gone completely! I wasn't prepared for what the future brought me. All of my gentlemen callers were sons of planters and so of course I assumed that I would be married to one and raise my family on a large piece of land with plenty of servants. But man proposes—and woman accepts the proposal!—To vary that old, old saying a little bit—I married no planter! I married a man who worked for the telephone company!—that gallantly smiling gentleman over there! (*Points to the picture.*) A telephone man who—fell in love with long distance!—Now he travels and I don't even know where!—But what am I going on for about my—tribulations! Tell me yours—I hope you don't have any! Tom?

TOM (*returning*): Yes, Mother?

AMANDA: Is supper nearly ready?

TOM: It looks to me like supper is on the table.

AMANDA: Let me look—(*She rises prettily and looks through portieres.*) Oh, lovely—But where is Sister?

TOM: Laura is not feeling well and she says that she thinks she'd better not come to the table.

AMANDA: What?—Nonsense!—Laura? Oh, Laura!

LAURA (*offstage, faintly*): Yes, Mother.

AMANDA: You really must come to the table. We won't be seated until you come to the table! Come in, Mr. O'Connor. You sit over there and I'll—Laura? Laura Wingfield! You're keeping us waiting, honey! We can't say grace until you come to the table!

The back door is pushed weakly open and Laura comes in. She is obviously quite faint, her lips trembling, her eyes wide and staring. She moves unsteadily toward the table.

(*Legend: "Terror!"*)

Outside a summer storm is coming abruptly. The white curtains billow inward at the windows and there is a sorrowful murmur and deep blue dusk.

Laura suddenly stumbles—She catches at a chair with a faint moan.

TOM: Laura!

AMANDA: Laura! (*There is a clap of thunder.*) (*Legend: "Ah!"*) (*Despairingly.*) Why, Laura, you *are* sick, darling! Tom, help your sister into the living room, dear! Sit in the living room, Laura — rest on the sofa. Well! (*To the gentleman caller.*) Standing over the hot stove made her ill! — I told her that it was just too warm this evening, but — (*Tom comes back in. Laura is on the sofa.*) Is Laura all right now?

TOM: Yes.

AMANDA: What *is* that? Rain? A nice cool rain has come up! (*She gives the gentleman caller a frightened look.*) I think we may — have grace — now . . . (*Tom looks at her stupidly.*) Tom, honey — you say grace!

TOM: Oh . . . "For these and all thy mercies —" (*They bow their heads, Amanda stealing a nervous glance at Jim. In the living room Laura, stretched on the sofa, clenches her hand to her lips, to hold back a shuddering sob.*) God's Holy Name be praised —

(*The scene dims out.*)

SCENE VII

A Souvenir

 Half an hour later. Dinner is just being finished in the upstage area, which is concealed by the drawn portieres.

 As the curtain rises Laura is still huddled upon the sofa, her feet drawn under her, her head resting on a pale blue pillow, her eyes wide and mysteriously watchful. The new floor lamp with its shade of rose-colored silk gives a soft, becoming light to her face, bringing out the fragile, unearthly prettiness which usually escapes attention. There is a steady murmur of rain, but it is slackening and stops soon after the scene begins; the air outside becomes pale and luminous as the moon breaks out.

 A moment after the curtain rises, the lights in both rooms flicker and go out.

JIM: Hey, there, Mr. Light Bulb!

Amanda laughs nervously.

 (*Legend: "Suspension of a Public Service."*)

AMANDA: Where was Moses when the lights went out? Ha-ha. Do you know the answer to that one, Mr. O'Connor?

JIM: No, Ma'am, what's the answer?

AMANDA: In the dark! (*Jim laughs appreciatively.*) Everybody sit still. I'll light the candles. Isn't it lucky we have them on the table? Where's a match? Which of you gentlemen can provide a match?

JIM: Here.

AMANDA: Thank you, sir.

JIM: Not at all, Ma'am!

AMANDA: I guess the fuse has burnt out. Mr. O'Connor, can you tell a burnt-out fuse? I know I can't and Tom is a total loss when it comes to mechanics. (*Sound: Getting up: Voices recede a little to kitchenette.*) Oh, be careful you don't bump into something. We don't want our gentleman caller to break his neck. Now wouldn't that be a fine howdy-do?

JIM: Ha-ha! Where is the fuse-box?

AMANDA: Right here next to the stove. Can you see anything?

JIM: Just a minute.

AMANDA: Isn't electricity a mysterious thing? Wasn't it Benjamin Franklin who tied a key to a kite? We live in such a mysterious universe, don't we? Some people say that science clears up all the mysteries for us. In my opinion it only creates more! Have you found it yet?

JIM: No, Ma'am. All these fuses look okay to me.

AMANDA: Tom!

TOM: Yes, Mother?

AMANDA: That light bill I gave you several days ago. The one I told you we got the notices about?

TOM: Oh. — Yeah.

(*Legend: "Ha!"*)

AMANDA: You didn't neglect to pay it by any chance?

TOM: Why, I —

AMANDA: Didn't! I might have known it!

JIM: Shakespeare probably wrote a poem on that light bill, Mrs. Wingfield.

AMANDA: I might have known better than to trust him with it! There's such a high price for negligence in this world!

JIM: Maybe the poem will win a ten-dollar prize.

AMANDA: We'll just have to spend the remainder of the evening in the nineteenth century, before Mr. Edison made the Mazda lamp!

JIM: Candlelight is my favorite kind of light.

AMANDA: That shows you're romantic! But that's no excuse for Tom. Well, we got through dinner. Very considerate of them to let us get through dinner before they plunged us into everlasting darkness, wasn't it, Mr. O'Connor?

JIM: Ha-ha!

AMANDA: Tom, as a penalty for your carelessness you can help me with the dishes.

JIM: Let me give you a hand.

AMANDA: Indeed you will not!

JIM: I ought to be good for something.

AMANDA: Good for something? (*Her tone is rhapsodic.*) You? Why, Mr. O'Connor, nobody, *nobody's* given me this much entertainment in years — as you have!

JIM: Aw, now, Mrs. Wingfield!

AMANDA: I'm not exaggerating, not one bit! But Sister is all by her lonesome. You go keep her company in the parlor! I'll give you this lovely old candelabrum that used to be on the altar at the church of the Heavenly Rest. It was melted a little out of shape when the church burnt down. Lightning struck it one spring. Gypsy Jones was holding a revival at the time and he intimated that the church was destroyed because the Episcopalians gave card parties.

JIM: Ha-ha.

AMANDA: And how about coaxing Sister to drink a little wine? I think it would be good for her! Can you carry both at once?

JIM: Sure. I'm Superman!

AMANDA: Now, Thomas, get into this apron!

The door of kitchenette swings closed on Amanda's gay laughter; the flickering light approaches the portieres.

    Laura sits up nervously as he enters. Her speech at first is low and breathless from the almost intolerable strain of being alone with a stranger.

    (*Legend: "I Don't Suppose You Remember Me at All!"*)

    In her first speeches in this scene, before Jim's warmth overcomes her paralyzing shyness, Laura's voice is thin and breathless as though she has run up a steep flight of stairs.

    Jim's attitude is gently humorous. In playing this scene it should be stressed that while the incident is apparently unimportant, it is to Laura the climax of her secret life.

JIM: Hello, there, Laura.

LAURA (*faintly*): Hello. (*She clears her throat.*)

JIM: How are you feeling now? Better?

LAURA: Yes. Yes, thank you.

JIM: This is for you. A little dandelion wine. (*He extends it toward her with extravagant gallantry.*)

LAURA: Thank you.

JIM: Drink it—but don't get drunk! (*He laughs heartily. Laura takes the glass uncertainly; laughs shyly.*) Where shall I set the candles?

LAURA: Oh—oh, anywhere . . .

JIM: How about here on the floor? Any objections?

LAURA: No.

JIM: I'll spread a newspaper under to catch the drippings. I like to sit on the floor. Mind if I do?

LAURA: Oh, no.

JIM: Give me a pillow?

LAURA: What?

JIM: A pillow!

LAURA: Oh . . . (*Hands him one quickly.*)

JIM: How about you? Don't you like to sit on the floor?

LAURA: Oh—yes.

JIM: Why don't you, then?

LAURA: I—will.

JIM: Take a pillow! (*Laura does. Sits on the other side of the candelabrum. Jim crosses his legs and smiles engagingly at her.*) I can't hardly see you sitting way over there.

LAURA: I can—see you.

JIM: I know, but that's not fair, I'm in the limelight. (*Laura moves her pillow closer.*) Good! Now I can see you! Comfortable?

LAURA: Yes.

JIM: So am I. Comfortable as a cow. Will you have some gum?

LAURA: No, thank you.

JIM: I think that I will indulge, with your permission. (*Musingly unwraps it and holds it up.*) Think of the fortune made by the guy that invented the first piece of chewing gum. Amazing, huh? The Wrigley Building is one of the sights of Chicago. —I saw it summer before last when I went up to the Century of Progress. Did you take in the Century of Progress?

LAURA: No, I didn't.

JIM: Well, it was quite a wonderful exposition. What impressed me most was the Hall of Science. Gives you an idea of what the future will be in America, even more wonderful than the present time is! (*Pause. Smiling at her.*) Your brother tells me you're shy. Is that right, Laura?

LAURA: I—don't know.

JIM: I judge you to be an old-fashioned type of girl. Well, I think that's a pretty good type to be. Hope you don't think I'm being too personal—do you?

LAURA (*hastily, out of embarrassment*): I believe I *will* take a piece of gum, if you—don't mind. (*Clearing her throat.*) Mr. O'Connor, have you— kept up with your singing?

JIM: Singing? Me?

LAURA: Yes. I remember what a beautiful voice you had.

JIM: When did you hear me sing?

(*Voice offstage in the pause.*)

VOICE (*offstage*): O blow, ye winds, heigh-ho,
         A-roving I will go!
         I'm off to my love
         With a boxing glove—
         Ten thousand miles away!

JIM: You say you've heard me sing?

LAURA: Oh, yes! Yes, very often ... I—don't suppose you remember me— at all?

JIM (*smiling doubtfully*): You know I have an idea I've seen you before. I had that idea soon as you opened the door. It seemed almost like I was about to remember your name. But the name that I started to call you—wasn't a name! And so I stopped myself before I said it.

LAURA: Wasn't it—Blue Roses?

JIM (*springs up, grinning*): Blue Roses! My gosh, yes—Blue Roses! That's what I had on my tongue when you opened the door! Isn't it funny what tricks your memory plays? I didn't connect you with the high school somehow or other. But that's where it was; it was high school. I didn't even know you were Shakespeare's sister! Gosh, I'm sorry.

LAURA: I didn't expect you to. You—barely knew me!

JIM: But we did have a speaking acquaintance, huh?

LAURA: Yes, we—spoke to each other.

JIM: When did you recognize me?

LAURA: Oh, right away!

JIM: Soon as I came in the door?

LAURA: When I heard your name I thought it was probably you. I knew that Tom used to know you a little in high school. So when you came in the door—Well, then I was—sure.

JIM: Why didn't you *say* something, then?

LAURA (*breathlessly*): I didn't know what to say, I was—too surprised!

JIM: For goodness' sakes! You know, this sure is funny!

LAURA: Yes! Yes, isn't it, though . . .

JIM: Didn't we have a class in something together?

LAURA: Yes, we did.

JIM: What class was that?

LAURA: It was — singing — Chorus!

JIM: Aw!

LAURA: I sat across the aisle from you in the Aud.

JIM: Aw.

LAURA: Mondays, Wednesdays, and Fridays.

JIM: Now I remember — you always came in late.

LAURA: Yes, it was so hard for me, getting upstairs. I had that brace on my leg — it clumped so loud!

JIM: I never heard any clumping.

LAURA (*wincing in the recollection*): To me it sounded like — thunder!

JIM: Well, well, well. I never even noticed.

LAURA: And everybody was seated before I came in. I had to walk in front of all those people. My seat was in the back row. I had to go clumping all the way up the aisle with everyone watching!

JIM: You shouldn't have been self-conscious.

LAURA: I know, but I was. It was always such a relief when the singing started.

JIM: Aw, yes, I've placed you now! I used to call you Blue Roses. How was it that I got started calling you that?

LAURA: I was out of school a little while with pleurosis. When I came back you asked me what was the matter. I said I had pleurosis — you thought I said Blue Roses. That's what you always called me after that!

JIM: I hope you didn't mind.

LAURA: Oh, no — I liked it. You see, I wasn't acquainted with many — people. . . .

JIM: As I remember you sort of stuck by yourself.

LAURA: I — I — never had much luck at — making friends.

JIM: I don't see why you wouldn't.

LAURA: Well, I — started out badly.

JIM: You mean being —

LAURA: Yes, it sort of — stood between me —

JIM: You shouldn't have let it!

LAURA: I know, but it did, and —

JIM: You were shy with people!

LAURA: I tried not to be but never could —

JIM: Overcome it?

LAURA: No, I — I never could!

JIM: I guess being shy is something you have to work out of kind of gradually.

LAURA (*sorrowfully*): Yes — I guess it —

JIM: Takes time!

LAURA: Yes —

JIM: People are not so dreadful when you know them. That's what you have to remember! And everybody has problems, not just you, but practically everybody has got some problems. You think of yourself as having the only problems, as being the only one who is disappointed. But just look around you and you will see lots of people as disappointed as you are. For instance, I hoped when I was going to high school that I would be further along at this time, six years later, than I am now — You remember that wonderful write-up I had in *The Torch?*

LAURA: Yes! (*She rises and crosses to table.*)

JIM: It said I was bound to succeed in anything I went into! (*Laura returns with the annual.*) Holy Jeez! *The Torch!* (*He accepts it reverently. They smile across it with mutual wonder. Laura crouches beside him and they begin to turn through it. Laura's shyness is dissolving in his warmth.*)

LAURA: Here you are in *Pirates of Penzance!*

JIM (*wistfully*): I sang the baritone lead in that operetta.

LAURA (*rapidly*): So — *beautifully!*

JIM (*protesting*): Aw —

LAURA: Yes, yes — beautifully — beautifully!

JIM: You heard me?

LAURA: All three times!

JIM: No!

LAURA: Yes!

JIM: All three performances?

LAURA (*looking down*): Yes.

JIM: Why?

LAURA: I — wanted to ask you to — autograph my program.

JIM: Why didn't you ask me to?

LAURA: You were always surrounded by your own friends so much that I never had a chance to.

JIM: You should have just —

LAURA: Well, I — thought you might think I was —

JIM: Thought I might think you was — what?

LAURA: Oh —

JIM (*with reflective relish*): I was beleaguered by females in those days.

LAURA: You were terribly popular!

JIM: Yeah —

LAURA: You had such a — friendly way —

JIM: I was spoiled in high school.

LAURA: Everybody — liked you!

JIM: Including you?

LAURA: I — yes, I — I did, too — (*She gently closes the book in her lap.*)

JIM: Well, well, well! — Give me that program, Laura. (*She hands it to him. He signs it with a flourish.*) There you are — better late than never!

LAURA: Oh, I — what a — surprise!

JIM: My signature isn't worth very much right now. But some day — maybe — it will increase in value! Being disappointed is one thing and being discouraged is something else. I am disappointed but I'm not discouraged. I'm twenty-three years old. How old are you?

LAURA: I'll be twenty-four in June.

JIM: That's not old age.

LAURA: No, but—

JIM: You finished high school?

LAURA (*with difficulty*): I didn't go back.

JIM: You mean you dropped out?

LAURA: I made bad grades in my final examinations. (*She rises and replaces the book and the program. Her voice strained.*) How is—Emily Meisenbach getting along?

JIM: Oh, that kraut-head!

LAURA: Why do you call her that?

JIM: That's what she was.

LAURA: You're not still—going with her?

JIM: I never see her.

LAURA: It said in the Personal Section that you were—engaged!

JIM: I know, but I wasn't impressed by that—propaganda!

LAURA: It wasn't—the truth?

JIM: Only in Emily's optimistic opinion!

LAURA: Oh—

(*Legend: "What Have You Done since High School?"*)

Jim lights a cigarette and leans indolently back on his elbows smiling at Laura with a warmth and charm which light her inwardly with altar candles. She remains by the table and turns in her hands a piece of glass to cover her tumult.

JIM (*after several reflective puffs on a cigarette*): What have you done since high school? (*She seems not to hear him.*) Huh? (*Laura looks up.*) I said what have you done since high school, Laura?

LAURA: Nothing much.

JIM: You must have been doing something these six long years.

LAURA: Yes.

JIM: Well, then, such as what?

LAURA: I took a business course at business college—

JIM: How did that work out?

LAURA: Well, not very—well—I had to drop out, it gave me—indigestion—

Jim laughs gently.

JIM: What are you doing now?

LAURA: I don't do anything—much. Oh, please don't think I sit around doing nothing! My glass collection takes up a good deal of my time. Glass is something you have to take good care of.

JIM: What did you say—about glass?

LAURA: Collection I said—I have one—(*She clears her throat and turns away again, acutely shy.*)

JIM (*abruptly*): You know what I judge to be the trouble with you? Inferiority complex! Know what that is? That's what they call it when someone low-rates himself! I understand it because I had it, too. Although my case was not so aggravated as yours seems to be. I had it until I took up public speaking, developed my voice, and learned that I had an aptitude for science. Before that time I never thought of myself as being outstanding in any way whatsoever! Now I've never made a regular study of it, but I have a friend who says I can analyze people better than doctors that make a profession of it. I don't claim that to be necessarily true, but I can sure guess a person's psychology, Laura! (*Takes out his gum.*) Excuse me, Laura. I always take it out when the flavor is gone. I'll use this scrap of paper to wrap it in. I know how it is to get it stuck on a shoe. Yep—that's what I judge to be your principal trouble. A lack of confidence in yourself as a person. You don't have the proper amount of faith in yourself. I'm basing that fact on a number of your remarks and also on certain observations I've made. For instance that clumping you thought was so awful in high school. You say that you even dreaded to walk into class. You see what you did? You dropped out of school, you gave up an education because of a clump, which as far as I know was practically nonexistent! A little physical defect is what you have. Hardly noticeable even! Magnified thousands of times by imagination! You know what my strong advice to you is? Think of yourself as *superior* in some way!

LAURA: In what way would I think?

JIM: Why, man alive, Laura! Just look about you a little. What do you see? A world full of common people! All of 'em born and all of 'em going to die! Which of them has one-tenth of your good points! Or mine! Or anyone else's, as far as that goes—Gosh! Everybody excels in some one thing. Some in many! (*Unconsciously glances at himself in the mirror.*) All you've got to do is discover in *what!* Take me, for instance. (*He adjusts his tie at the mirror.*) My interest happened to lie in electrodynamics. I'm taking a course in radio engineering at night school, Laura, on top of a fairly responsible job at the warehouse. I'm taking that course and studying public speaking.

LAURA: Ohhhh.

JIM: Because I believe in the future of television! (*Turning back to her.*) I wish to be ready to go up right along with it. Therefore I'm planning to get in on the ground floor. In fact, I've already made the right connections and all that remains is for the industry itself to get under way! Full steam— (*His eyes are starry.*) Knowledge—Zzzzzp! Money—Zzzzzzp!—Power! That's the cycle democracy is built on! (*His attitude is convincingly dynamic. Laura stares at him, even her shyness eclipsed in her absolute wonder. He suddenly grins.*) I guess you think I think a lot of myself!

LAURA: No—o-o-o, I—

JIM: Now how about you? Isn't there something you take more interest in than anything else?

LAURA: Well, I do—as I said—have my—glass collection—

A peal of girlish laughter from the kitchen.

JIM: I'm not right sure I know what you're talking about. What kind of glass is it?

LAURA: Little articles of it, they're ornaments mostly! Most of them are little animals made out of glass, the tiniest little animals in the world. Mother calls them a glass menagerie! Here's an example of one, if you'd like to see it! This one is one of the oldest. It's nearly thirteen. (*He stretches out his hand.*) (*Music: "The Glass Menagerie."*) Oh, be careful — if you breathe, it breaks!

JIM: I'd better not take it. I'm pretty clumsy with things.

LAURA: Go on, I trust you with him! (*Places it in his palm.*) There now — you're holding him gently! Hold him over the light, he loves the light! You see how the light shines through him?

JIM: It sure does shine!

LAURA: I shouldn't be partial, but he is my favorite one.

JIM: What kind of thing is this one supposed to be?

LAURA: Haven't you noticed the single horn on his forehead?

JIM: A unicorn, huh?

LAURA: Mmm-hmmm!

JIM: Unicorns, aren't they extinct in the modern world?

LAURA: I know!

JIM: Poor little fellow, he must feel sort of lonesome.

LAURA (*smiling*): Well, if he does he doesn't complain about it. He stays on a shelf with some horses that don't have horns and all of them seem to get along nicely together.

JIM: How do you know?

LAURA (*lightly*): I haven't heard any arguments among them!

JIM (*grinning*): No arguments, huh? Well, that's a pretty good sign! Where shall I set him?

LAURA: Put him on the table. They all like a change of scenery once in a while!

JIM (*stretching*): Well, well, well, well — Look how big my shadow is when I stretch!

LAURA: Oh, oh, yes — it stretches across the ceiling!

JIM (*crossing to door*): I think it's stopped raining. (*Opens fire-escape door.*) Where does the music come from?

LAURA: From the Paradise Dance Hall across the alley.

JIM: How about cutting the rug a little, Miss Wingfield?

LAURA: Oh, I —

JIM: Or is your program filled up? Let me have a look at it. (*Grasps imaginary card.*) Why, every dance is taken! I'll have to scratch some out. (*Waltz music: "La Golondrina."*) Ahhh, a waltz! (*He executes some sweeping turns by himself then holds his arms toward Laura.*)

LAURA (*breathlessly*): I — can't dance!

JIM: There you go, that inferiority stuff!

LAURA: I've never danced in my life!

JIM: Come on, try!

LAURA: Oh, but I'd step on you!

JIM: I'm not made out of glass.

LAURA: How — how — how do we start?

JIM: Just leave it to me. You hold your arms out a little.

LAURA: Like this?

JIM: A little bit higher. Right. Now don't tighten up, that's the main thing about it—relax.

LAURA (*laughing breathlessly*): It's hard not to.

JIM: Okay.

LAURA: I'm afraid you can't budge me.

JIM: What do you bet I can't? (*He swings her into motion.*)

LAURA: Goodness, yes, you can!

JIM: Let yourself go, now, Laura, just let yourself go.

LAURA: I'm—

JIM: Come on!

LAURA: Trying.

JIM: Not so stiff—Easy does it!

LAURA: I know but I'm—

JIM: Loosen th' backbone! There now, that's a lot better.

LAURA: Am I?

JIM: Lots, lots better! (*He moves her about the room in a clumsy waltz.*)

LAURA: Oh, my!

JIM: Ha-ha!

LAURA: Goodness, yes you can!

JIM: Ha-ha-ha! (*They suddenly bump into the table. Jim stops.*) What did we hit on?

LAURA: Table.

JIM: Did something fall off it? I think—

LAURA: Yes.

JIM: I hope it wasn't the little glass horse with the horn!

LAURA: Yes.

JIM: Aw, aw, aw. Is it broken?

LAURA: Now it is just like all the other horses.

JIM: It's lost its—

LAURA: Horn! It doesn't matter. Maybe it's a blessing in disguise.

JIM: You'll never forgive me. I bet that that was your favorite piece of glass.

LAURA: I don't have favorites much. It's no tragedy, Freckles. Glass breaks so easily. No matter how careful you are. The traffic jars the shelves and things fall off them.

JIM: Still I'm awfully sorry that I was the cause.

LAURA (*smiling*): I'll just imagine he had an operation. The horn was removed to make him feel less—freakish! (*They both laugh.*) Now he will feel more at home with the other horses, the ones that don't have horns . . .

JIM: Ha-ha, that's very funny! (*Suddenly serious.*) I'm glad to see that you have a sense of humor. You know—you're—well—very different! Surprisingly different from anyone else I know! (*His voice becomes soft and hesitant with a genuine feeling.*) Do you mind me telling you that? (*Laura is abashed beyond speech.*) You make me feel sort of—I don't know how to put it! I'm usually pretty good at expressing things, but—This is something that I don't know how to say! (*Laura touches her throat and clears it—turns the broken unicorn in her hands.*) (*Even softer.*) Has anyone ever told you that you were pretty?

Pause: Music.

> (*Laura looks up slowly, with wonder, and shakes her head.*) Well, you are! In a very different way from anyone else. And all the nicer because of the difference, too. (*His voice becomes low and husky. Laura turns away, nearly faint with the novelty of her emotions.*) I wish that you were my sister. I'd teach you to have some confidence in yourself. The different people are not like other people, but being different is nothing to be ashamed of. Because other people are not such wonderful people. They're one hundred times one thousand. You're one times one! They walk all over the earth. You just stay here. They're common as—weeds, but—you—well, you're—*Blue Roses!*

(*Image on screen: Blue Roses.*)
(*Music changes.*)

LAURA: But blue is wrong for—roses . . .

JIM: It's right for you—You're—pretty!

LAURA: In what respect am I pretty?

JIM: In all respects—believe me! Your eyes—your hair—are pretty! Your hands are pretty! (*He catches hold of her hand.*) You think I'm making this up because I'm invited to dinner and have to be nice. Oh, I could do that! I could put on an act for you, Laura, and say lots of things without being very sincere. But this time I am. I'm talking to you sincerely. I happened to notice you had this inferiority complex that keeps you from feeling comfortable with people. Somebody needs to build your confidence up and make you proud instead of shy and turning away and—blushing—Somebody ought to—ought to—*kiss you, Laura!* (*His hand slips slowly up her arm to her shoulder.*) (*Music swells tumultuously.*) (*He suddenly turns her about and kisses her on the lips. When he releases her Laura sinks on the sofa with a bright, dazed look. Jim backs away and fishes in his pocket for a cigarette.*) (*Legend on screen: "Souvenir."*) Stumble-john! (*He lights the cigarette, avoiding her look. There is a peal of girlish laughter from Amanda in the kitchen. Laura slowly raises and opens her hand. It still contains the little broken glass animal. She looks at it with a tender, bewildered expression.*) Stumble-john! I shouldn't have done that—That was way off the beam. You don't smoke, do you? (*She looks up, smiling, not hearing the question. He sits beside her a little gingerly. She looks at him speechlessly—waiting. He coughs decorously and moves a little farther aside as he considers the situation and senses her feelings, dimly, with perturbation. Gently.*) Would you—care for a—mint? (*She doesn't seem to hear him but her look grows brighter even.*) Peppermint—Life Saver? My pocket's a regular drug store—wherever I go . . . (*He pops a mint in his mouth. Then gulps and decides to make a clean breast of it. He speaks slowly and gingerly.*) Laura, you know, if I had a sister like you, I'd do the same thing as Tom. I'd bring out fellows—introduce her to them. The right type of boys of a type to—appreciate her. Only—well—he made a mistake about me. Maybe I've got no call to be saying this. That may not have been the idea in having me over. But what if it was? There's nothing wrong about that. The only trouble is that in my case — I'm not in a situation to — do the right thing. I can't take down your number and say I'll phone. I can't call up next week and — ask for a date. I thought I had better explain the situation in case you misunderstood it and — hurt your feelings. . . . (*Pause. Slowly, very slowly, Laura's look changes, her eyes returning slowly from his to the ornament in her palm.*)

Amanda utters another gay laugh in the kitchen.

LAURA (*faintly*): You — won't — call again?

JIM: No, Laura, I can't. (*He rises from the sofa.*) As I was just explaining, I've — got strings on me, Laura, I've — been going steady! I go out all the time with a girl named Betty. She's a home-girl like you, and Catholic, and Irish, and in a great many ways we — get along fine. I met her last summer on a moonlight boat trip up the river to Alton, on the *Majestic*. Well — right away from the start it was — love! (*Legend: Love!*) (*Laura sways slightly forward and grips the arm of the sofa. He fails to notice, now enrapt in his own comfortable being.*) Being in love has made a new man of me! (*Leaning stiffly forward, clutching the arm of the sofa, Laura struggles visibly with her storm. But Jim is oblivious, she is a long way off.*) The power of love is really pretty tremendous! Love is something that — changes the whole world, Laura! (*The storm abates a little and Laura leans back. He notices her again.*) It happened that Betty's aunt took sick, she got a wire and had to go to Centralia. So Tom — when he asked me to dinner — I naturally just accepted the invitation, not knowing that you — that he — that I — (*He stops awkwardly.*) Huh — I'm a stumble-john! (*He flops back on the sofa. The holy candles in the altar of Laura's face have been snuffed out! There is a look of almost infinite desolation. Jim glances at her uneasily.*) I wish that you would — say something. (*She bites her lip which was trembling and then bravely smiles. She opens her hand again on the broken glass ornament. Then she gently takes his hand and raises it level with her own. She carefully places the unicorn in the palm of his hand, then pushes his fingers closed upon it.*) What are you — doing that for? You want me to have him? — Laura? (*She nods.*) What for?

LAURA: A — souvenir . . .

She rises unsteadily and crouches beside the Victrola to wind it up.

(*Legend on screen: "Things Have a Way of Turning Out So Badly."*)

(*Or image: "Gentleman caller waving good-bye! — Gaily."*)

At this moment Amanda rushes brightly back in the front room. She bears a pitcher of fruit punch in an old-fashioned cut-glass pitcher and a plate of macaroons. The plate has a gold border and poppies painted on it.

AMANDA: Well, well, well! Isn't the air delightful after the shower? I've made you children a little liquid refreshment. (*Turns gaily to the gentleman caller.*) Jim, do you know that song about lemonade?

"Lemonade, lemonade
Made in the shade and stirred with a spade —
Good enough for any old maid!"

JIM (*uneasily*): Ha-ha! No—I never heard it.

AMANDA: Why, Laura! You look so serious!

JIM: We were having a serious conversation.

AMANDA: Good! Now you're better acquainted!

JIM (*uncertainly*): Ha-ha! Yes.

AMANDA: You modern young people are much more serious-minded than my generation. I was so gay as a girl!

JIM: You haven't changed, Mrs. Wingfield.

AMANDA: Tonight I'm rejuvenated! The gaiety of the occasion, Mr. O'Connor! (*She tosses her head with a peal of laughter. Spills lemonade.*) Oooo! I'm baptizing myself!

JIM: Here—let me—

AMANDA (*setting the pitcher down*): There now. I discovered we had some maraschino cherries. I dumped them in, juice and all!

JIM: You shouldn't have gone to that trouble, Mrs. Wingfield.

AMANDA: Trouble, trouble? Why it was loads of fun! Didn't you hear me cutting up in the kitchen? I bet your ears were burning! I told Tom how outdone with him I was for keeping you to himself so long a time! He should have brought you over much, much sooner! Well, now that you've found your way, I want you to be a very frequent caller! Not just occasional but all the time. Oh, we're going to have a lot of gay times together! I see them coming! Mmm, just breathe that air! So fresh, and the moon's so pretty! I'll skip back out—I know where my place is when young folks are having a—serious conversation!

JIM: Oh, don't go out, Mrs. Wingfield. The fact of the matter is I've got to be going.

AMANDA: Going, now? You're joking! Why, it's only the shank of the evening, Mr. O'Connor!

JIM: Well, you know how it is.

AMANDA: You mean you're a young workingman and have to keep workingmen's hours. We'll let you off early tonight. But only on the condition that next time you stay later. What's the best night for you? Isn't Saturday night the best night for you workingmen?

JIM: I have a couple of time-clocks to punch, Mrs. Wingfield. One at morning, another one at night!

AMANDA: My, but you *are* ambitious! You work at night, too?

JIM: No, Ma'am, not work but—Betty! (*He crosses deliberately to pick up his hat. The band at the Paradise Dance Hall goes into a tender waltz.*)

AMANDA: Betty? Betty? Who's—Betty! (*There is an ominous cracking sound in the sky.*)

JIM: Oh, just a girl. The girl I go steady with! (*He smiles charmingly. The sky falls.*)

(*Legend: "The Sky Falls."*)

AMANDA (*a long-drawn exhalation*): Ohhhh . . . Is it a serious romance, Mr. O'Connor?

JIM: We're going to be married the second Sunday in June.

AMANDA: Ohhhh—how nice! Tom didn't mention that you were engaged to be married.

JIM: The cat's not out of the bag at the warehouse yet. You know how they are. They call you Romeo and stuff like that. (*He stops at the oval mirror to put on his hat. He carefully shapes the brim and the crown to give a discreetly dashing effect.*) It's been a wonderful evening, Mrs. Wingfield. I guess this is what they mean by Southern hospitality.

AMANDA: It really wasn't anything at all.

JIM: I hope it don't seem like I'm rushing off. But I promised Betty I'd pick her up at the Wabash depot, an' by the time I get my jalopy down there her train'll be in. Some women are pretty upset if you keep 'em waiting.

AMANDA: Yes, I know — The tyranny of women! (*Extends her hand.*) Good-bye, Mr. O'Connor. I wish you luck — and happiness — and success! All three of them, and so does Laura — Don't you, Laura?

LAURA: Yes!

JIM (*taking her hand*): Good-bye, Laura. I'm certainly going to treasure that souvenir. And don't you forget the good advice I gave you. (*Raises his voice to a cheery shout.*) So long, Shakespeare! Thanks again, ladies — Good night!

He grins and ducks jauntily out.

Still bravely grimacing, Amanda closes the door on the gentleman caller. Then she turns back to the room with a puzzled expression. She and Laura don't dare to face each other. Laura crouches beside the Victrola to wind it.

AMANDA (*faintly*): Things have a way of turning out so badly. I don't believe that I would play the Victrola. Well, well — well — Our gentleman caller was engaged to be married! Tom!

TOM (*from back*): Yes, Mother?

AMANDA: Come in here a minute. I want to tell you something awfully funny.

TOM (*enters with macaroon and a glass of the lemonade*): Has the gentleman caller gotten away already?

AMANDA: The gentleman caller has made an early departure. What a wonderful joke you played on us!

TOM: How do you mean?

AMANDA: You didn't mention that he was engaged to be married.

TOM: Jim? Engaged?

AMANDA: That's what he just informed us.

TOM: I'll be jiggered! I didn't know about that.

AMANDA: That seems very peculiar.

TOM: What's peculiar about it?

AMANDA: Didn't you call him your best friend down at the warehouse?

TOM: He is, but how did I know?

AMANDA: It seems extremely peculiar that you wouldn't know your best friend was going to be married!

TOM: The warehouse is where I work, not where I know things about people!

AMANDA: You don't know things anywhere! You live in a dream; you manufacture illusions! (*He crosses to door.*) Where are you going?

TOM: I'm going to the movies.

AMANDA: That's right, now that you've had us make such fools of ourselves. The effort, the preparations, all the expense! The new floor lamp, the rug, the clothes for Laura! All for what? To entertain some other girl's fiancé! Go to the movies, go! Don't think about us, a mother deserted, an unmarried sister who's crippled and has no job! Don't let anything interfere with your selfish pleasure! Just go, go, go — to the movies!

TOM: All right, I will! The more you shout about my selfishness to me the quicker I'll go, and I won't go to the movies!

AMANDA: Go, then! Then go to the moon — you selfish dreamer!

Tom smashes his glass on the floor. He plunges out on the fire-escape, slamming the door. Laura screams — cut by door.

Dance-hall music up. Tom goes to the rail and grips it desperately, lifting his face in the chill white moonlight penetrating the narrow abyss of the alley.

(Legend on screen: "And So Good-Bye . . .")

Tom's closing speech is timed with the interior pantomime. The interior scene is played as though viewed through sound-proof glass. Amanda appears to be making a comforting speech to Laura who is huddled upon the sofa. Now that we cannot hear the mother's speech, her silliness is gone and she has dignity and tragic beauty. Laura's dark hair hides her face until at the end of the speech she lifts it to smile at her mother. Amanda's gestures are slow and graceful, almost dancelike, as she comforts the daughter. At the end of her speech she glances a moment at the father's picture — then withdraws through the portieres. At close of Tom's speech, Laura blows out the candles, ending the play.

TOM: I didn't go to the moon, I went much further — for time is the longest distance between two places — Not long after that I was fired for writing a poem on the lid of a shoe-box. I left Saint Louis. I descended the steps of this fire-escape for a last time and followed, from then on, in my father's footsteps, attempting to find in motion what was lost in space — I traveled around a great deal. The cities swept about me like dead leaves, leaves that were brightly colored but torn away from the branches. I would have stopped, but I was pursued by something. It always came upon me unawares, taking me altogether by surprise. Perhaps it was a familiar bit of music. Perhaps it was only a piece of transparent glass — Perhaps I am walking along a street at night, in some strange city, before I have found companions. I pass the lighted window of a shop where perfume is sold. The window is filled with pieces of colored glass, tiny transparent bottles in delicate colors, like bits of a shattered rainbow. Then all at once my sister touches my shoulder. I turn around and look into her eyes. . . . Oh, Laura, Laura, I tried to leave you behind me, but I am more faithful than I intended to be! I reach for a cigarette, I cross the street, I run into the movies or a bar, I buy a drink, I speak to the nearest stranger — anything that can blow your candles out! (*Laura bends over the candles*) — for nowadays the world is lit by lightning! Blow out your candles, Laura — and so good-bye . . .

She blows the candles out.

(The Scene Dissolves.)

ARTHUR MILLER

Arthur Miller (b. 1915), the son of a clothing manufacturer, was born in Manhattan but moved to Brooklyn as a teenager when his father's business collapsed during the Depression. After high school he worked for two years in an automobile parts warehouse to save money for his college tuition. He wrote his first play in 1935 as a journalism student at the University of Michigan, later recalling for a Paris Review *interviewer that*

> *it was written on a spring vacation in six days. I was so young that I dared do such things, begin it and finish it in a week. I'd seen about two plays in my life, so I didn't know how long an act was supposed to be, but across the hall there was a fellow who did the costumes for the University theater and he said, "Well, it's roughly forty minutes." I had written an enormous amount of material and I got an alarm clock. It was all a lark to me, and not to be taken too seriously . . . that's what I told myself. As it turned out, the acts were longer than that, but the sense of timing was in me even from the beginning, and the play had a form right from the start.*

Miller's early plays won prizes at the University of Michigan, and he went on after graduation to write plays for radio and work for the Federal Theater Project. After failing with The Man Who Had All the Luck *in 1944, Miller had his first successful play in 1947 with* All My Sons.

In Boston during the pre-Broadway preview of this play, Miller had a chance meeting outside the Colonial Theater with his uncle Manny Newman, a traveling salesman. Their encounter suggested the idea of Death of a Salesman *to Miller a short time later. Miller recalled, "I could see his grim hotel room behind him, the long trip up from New York in his little car, the hopeless hope of the day's business. Without so much as acknowledging my greeting, he said, 'Buddy is doing very well.'" Miller understood that his uncle was a competitor at all times, and that he had taken the Colonial Theater marquee advertising Miller's new play as an irresistible challenge to assert that his own son, Buddy, was also a success. To Miller, his uncle was an absurd yet unforgettable figure, "so completely isolated from the ordinary laws of gravity, so elaborate in his fantastic inventions, and despite his ugliness so lyrically in love with fame and fortune and their inevitable descent on his family, that he possessed my imagination until I knew more or less precisely how he would react to any sign or word or idea."*

*Yet Miller was also aware that his uncle's unexpected appearance outside the Boston theater had another effect on him, cutting "through time like a knife through a layer cake." In the encounter Miller had felt himself reduced from an accomplished thirty-year-old playwright (*All My Sons *went on to win the year's Pulitzer Prize and a Drama Critics Circle Award) to an emotionally vulnerable adolescent. He decided to write a play about his uncle "without any transitions at all, dialogue that would simply leap from bone to bone of a skeleton that would not for an instant cease being added to, an organism as strictly economic as a leaf, as trim as an ant."*

In six weeks during the spring of 1948, Miller wrote the first draft of Death of a Salesman. *He credits a production of Tennessee Williams's* A Streetcar

Named Desire *the previous November as another important influence that shaped his play: Williams's "words and their liberation, the joy of the writer in writing them, the radiant eloquence of its composition." The theater historian Brenda Murphy sees a link between Williams's poetic language in that play and "the poetry of the mundane that infuses* Salesman." *Elia Kazan, who directed both* Streetcar *and* Salesman, *recalled that Miller was also greatly impressed with the staging of Williams's play, appearing to be "full of wonder at the theatre's expressive possibilities. [Miller] told me he was amazed at how simply and successfully the non-realistic elements in the play . . . blended with the realistic ones."*

Collaborating with Kazan and set designer Jo Mielziner, Miller extensively revised his preproduction script of Death of a Salesman. *It was the hit of the 1948–49 Broadway season, running for 742 performances and winning the Pulitzer Prize, the Drama Critics Circle Award, the Donaldson Award, and Tony Awards for best play, best direction, best scene design, and best supporting actor. Published as a script, the play became a best-seller, and it was the only play ever to be a Book-of-the-Month Club selection. Perhaps the drama critic Brooks Atkinson summarized its appeal for audiences in his* New York Times *review after the premier of the play: "Mr. Miller has looked with compassion into the hearts of some ordinary Americans and quietly transferred their hope and anguish to the theatre." In the essay "Tragedy and the Common Man," Miller interpreted Willy Loman's tragedy as that of Everyman: "The Chinese reaction to my Beijing production of* Salesman *would confirm what had become more and more obvious over the decades in the play's hundreds of productions throughout the world: Willy was representative everywhere, in every kind of system, of ourselves in this time."*

Miller has continued to write plays, most notably in The Crucible *(1953) and* A View from the Bridge *(1956). He also wrote the screenplay of the film* The Misfits *for his second wife, Marilyn Monroe, from whom he was divorced in 1961. Among his later plays are* After the Fall *(1964),* The Archbishop's Ceiling *(1977),* Danger: Memory! *(1986), and* The Last Yankee *(1993). Miller has also written a memoir,* Timebends *(1987), and excellent essays on the theater and the craft of playwriting, many of them collected in 1978 in* The Theatre Essays of Arthur Miller, *edited by Robert A. Martin.*

COMMENTARIES Arthur Miller, *"On* Death of a Salesman *as an American Tragedy," page 1554; Arthur Miller, "From the* Paris Review *Interview," page 1557; Helge Normann Nilsen, "Marxism and the Early Plays of Arthur Miller," page 1569.*

WEB *Research Arthur Miller and answer questions about his work at bedfordstmartins.com/charters/litwriters.*

Death of a Salesman

1949

Certain Private Conversations in Two Acts and a Requiem

CAST

WILLY LOMAN	UNCLE BEN
LINDA	HOWARD WAGNER
BIFF	JENNY
HAPPY	STANLEY
BERNARD	MISS FORSYTHE
THE WOMAN	LETTA
CHARLEY	

SCENE: *The action takes place in Willy Loman's house and yard and in various places he visits in the New York and Boston of today.*

Throughout the play, in the stage directions, left and right mean stage left and stage right.

ACT I

A melody is heard, played upon a flute. It is small and fine, telling of grass and trees and the horizon. The curtain rises.

Before us is the Salesman's house. We are aware of towering, angular shapes behind it, surrounding it on all sides. Only the blue light of the sky falls upon the house and forestage; the surrounding area shows an angry glow of orange. As more light appears, we see a solid vault of apartment houses around the small, fragile-seeming home. An air of the dream clings to the place, a dream rising out of reality. The kitchen at center seems actual enough, for there is a kitchen table with three chairs, and a refrigerator. But no other fixtures are seen. At the back of the kitchen there is a draped entrance, which leads to the living-room. To the right of the kitchen, on a level raised two feet, is a bedroom furnished only with a brass bedstead and a straight chair. On a shelf over the bed a silver athletic trophy stands. A window opens onto the apartment house at the side.

Behind the kitchen, on a level raised six and a half feet, is the boys' bedroom, at present barely visible. Two beds are dimly seen, and at the back of the room a dormer window. (This bedroom is above the unseen living-room.) At the left a stairway curves up to it from the kitchen.

The entire setting is wholly or, in some places, partially transparent. The roof-line of the house is one-dimensional; under and over it we see the apartment buildings. Before the house lies an apron, curving beyond the forestage into the orchestra. This forward area serves as the back yard as well as the locale of all Willy's imaginings and of his city scenes. Whenever the action is in the present the actors observe the imaginary wall-lines, entering the house only through its door at the left. But in the scenes of the past these boundaries are broken, and characters enter or leave a room by stepping "through" a wall onto the forestage.

From the right, Willy Loman, the Salesman, enters, carrying two large sample cases. The flute plays on. He hears but is not aware of it. He is past sixty years of age, dressed quietly. Even as he crosses the stage to the doorway of the house, his exhaustion is apparent. He unlocks the door, comes into the kitchen, and thankfully lets his burden down, feeling the soreness of his palms. A word-sigh escapes his lips—it might be "Oh, boy, oh, boy." He closes the door, then carries his cases out into the living-room, through the draped kitchen doorway.

Linda, his wife, has stirred in her bed at the right. She gets out and puts on a robe, listening. Most often jovial, she has developed an iron repression of her exceptions to Willy's behavior—she more than loves him, she admires him, as though his mercurial nature, his temper, his massive dreams and little cruelties, served her only as sharp reminders of the turbulent longings within him, longings which she shares but lacks the temperament to utter and follow to their end.

LINDA (*hearing Willy outside the bedroom, calls with some trepidation*): Willy!

WILLY: It's all right. I came back.

LINDA: Why? What happened? (*Slight pause.*) Did something happen, Willy?

WILLY: No, nothing happened.

LINDA: You didn't smash the car, did you?

WILLY (*with casual irritation*): I said nothing happened. Didn't you hear me?

LINDA: Don't you feel well?

WILLY: I'm tired to the death. (*The flute has faded away. He sits on the bed beside her, a little numb.*) I couldn't make it. I just couldn't make it, Linda.

LINDA (*very carefully, delicately*): Where were you all day? You look terrible.

WILLY: I got as far as a little above Yonkers. I stopped for a cup of coffee. Maybe it was the coffee.

LINDA: What?

WILLY (*after a pause*): I suddenly couldn't drive any more. The car kept going off onto the shoulder, y'know?

LINDA (*helpfully*): Oh. Maybe it was the steering again. I don't think Angelo knows the Studebaker.

WILLY: No, it's me, it's me. Suddenly I realize I'm goin' sixty miles an hour and I don't remember the last five minutes. I'm—I can't seem to—keep my mind to it.

LINDA: Maybe it's your glasses. You never went for your new glasses.

WILLY: No, I see everything. I came back ten miles an hour. It took me nearly four hours from Yonkers.

LINDA (*resigned*): Well, you'll just have to take a rest, Willy, you can't continue this way.

WILLY: I just got back from Florida.

LINDA: But you didn't rest your mind. Your mind is overactive, and the mind is what counts, dear.

WILLY: I'll start out in the morning. Maybe I'll feel better in the morning. (*She is taking off his shoes.*) These goddam arch supports are killing me.

LINDA: Take an aspirin. Should I get you an aspirin? It'll soothe you.

WILLY (*with wonder*): I was driving along, you understand? And I was fine. I was even observing the scenery. You can imagine, me looking at scenery, on the road every week of my life. But it's so beautiful up there, Linda, the trees are so thick, and the sun is warm. I opened the windshield and just let the warm air bathe over me. And then all of a sudden I'm goin' off the road! I'm tellin' ya, I absolutely forgot I was driving. If I'd've gone the other way over the white line I might've killed somebody. So I went on again—and five minutes later I'm dreamin' again, and I nearly—(*He presses two fingers against his eyes.*) I have such thoughts, I have such strange thoughts.

LINDA: Willy, dear. Talk to them again. There's no reason why you can't work in New York.

WILLY: They don't need me in New York. I'm the New England man. I'm vital in New England.

LINDA: But you're sixty years old. They can't expect you to keep traveling every week.

WILLY: I'll have to send a wire to Portland. I'm supposed to see Brown and Morrison tomorrow morning at ten o'clock to show the line. Goddammit, I could sell them! (*He starts putting on his jacket.*)

LINDA (*taking the jacket from him*): Why don't you go down to the place tomorrow and tell Howard you've simply got to work in New York? You're too accommodating, dear.

WILLY: If old man Wagner was alive I'd a been in charge of New York now! That man was a prince, he was a masterful man. But that boy of his, that Howard, he don't appreciate. When I went north the first time, the Wagner Company didn't know where New England was!

LINDA: Why don't you tell those things to Howard, dear?

WILLY (*encouraged*): I will, I definitely will. Is there any cheese?

LINDA: I'll make you a sandwich.

WILLY: No, go to sleep. I'll take some milk. I'll be up right away. The boys in?

LINDA: They're sleeping. Happy took Biff on a date tonight.

WILLY (*interested*): That so?

LINDA: It was so nice to see them shaving together, one behind the other, in the bathroom. And going out together. You notice? The whole house smells of shaving lotion.

WILLY: Figure it out. Work a lifetime to pay off a house. You finally own it, and there's nobody to live in it.

LINDA: Well, dear, life is a casting off. It's always that way.

WILLY: No, no, some people—some people accomplish something. Did Biff say anything after I went this morning?

LINDA: You shouldn't have criticized him, Willy, especially after he just got off the train. You mustn't lose your temper with him.

WILLY: When the hell did I lose my temper? I simply asked him if he was making any money. Is that a criticism?

LINDA: But, dear, how could he make any money?

WILLY (*worried and angered*): There's such an undercurrent in him. He became a moody man. Did he apologize when I left this morning?

LINDA: He was crestfallen, Willy. You know how he admires you. I think if he finds himself, then you'll both be happier and not fight any more.

WILLY: How can he find himself on a farm? Is that a life? A farmhand? In the beginning, when he was young, I thought, well, a young man, it's good for him to tramp around, take a lot of different jobs. But it's more than ten years now and he has yet to make thirty-five dollars a week!

LINDA: He's finding himself, Willy.

WILLY: Not finding yourself at the age of thirty-four is a disgrace!

LINDA: Shh!

WILLY: The trouble is he's lazy, goddammit!

LINDA: Willy, please!

WILLY: Biff is a lazy bum!

LINDA: They're sleeping. Get something to eat. Go on down.

WILLY: Why did he come home? I would like to know what brought him home.

LINDA: I don't know. I think he's still lost, Willy. I think he's very lost.

WILLY: Biff Loman is lost. In the greatest country in the world a young man
 with such — personal attractiveness, gets lost. And such a hard worker.
 There's one thing about Biff — he's not lazy.

LINDA: Never.

WILLY (*with pity and resolve*): I'll see him in the morning; I'll have a nice talk
 with him. I'll get him a job selling. He could be big in no time. My God!
 Remember how they used to follow him around in high school? When he
 smiled at one of them their faces lit up. When he walked down the
 street . . . (*He loses himself in reminiscences.*)

LINDA (*trying to bring him out of it*): Willy, dear, I got a new kind of American-
 type cheese today. It's whipped.

WILLY: Why do you get American when I like Swiss?

LINDA: I just thought you'd like a change —

WILLY: I don't want a change! I want Swiss cheese. Why am I always being contradicted?

LINDA (*with a covering laugh*): I thought it would be a surprise.

WILLY: Why don't you open a window in here, for God's sake?

LINDA (*with infinite patience*): They're all open, dear.

WILLY: The way they boxed us in here. Bricks and windows, windows and
 bricks.

LINDA: We should've bought the land next door.

WILLY: The street is lined with cars. There's not a breath of fresh air in the
 neighborhood. The grass don't grow any more, you can't raise a carrot in
 the back yard. They should've had a law against apartment houses.
 Remember those two beautiful elm trees out there? When I and Biff
 hung the swing between them?

LINDA: Yeah, like being a million miles from the city.

WILLY: They should've arrested the builder for cutting those down. They mas-
 sacred the neighborhood. (*Lost.*) More and more I think of those days,
 Linda. This time of year it was lilac and wisteria. And then the peonies
 would come out, and the daffodils. What fragrance in this room!

LINDA: Well, after all, people had to move somewhere.

WILLY: No, there's more people now.

LINDA: I don't think there's more people. I think —

WILLY: There's more people! That's what's ruining this country! Population is
 getting out of control. The competition is maddening! Smell the stink
 from that apartment house! And another one on the other side . . . How
 can they whip cheese?

On Willy's last line, Biff and Happy raise themselves up in their beds, listening.

LINDA: Go down, try it. And be quiet.

WILLY (*turning to Linda, guiltily*): You're not worried about me, are you, sweetheart?

BIFF: What's the matter?

HAPPY: Listen!

LINDA: You've got too much on the ball to worry about.

WILLY: You're my foundation and my support, Linda.

LINDA: Just try to relax, dear. You make mountains out of molehills.

WILLY: I won't fight with him any more. If he wants to go back to Texas, let him go.

LINDA: He'll find his way.

WILLY: Sure. Certain men just don't get started till later in life. Like Thomas Edison, I think. Or B. F. Goodrich. One of them was deaf. (*He starts for the bedroom doorway.*) I'll put my money on Biff.

LINDA: And Willy—if it's warm Sunday we'll drive in the country. And we'll open the windshield, and take lunch.

WILLY: No, the windshields don't open on the new cars.

LINDA: But you opened it today.

WILLY: Me? I didn't. (*He stops.*) Now isn't that peculiar! Isn't that a remarkable—(*He breaks off in amazement and fright as the flute is heard distantly.*)

LINDA: What, darling?

WILLY: That is the most remarkable thing.

LINDA: What, dear?

WILLY: I was thinking of the Chevy. (*Slight pause.*) Nineteen twenty-eight . . . when I had that red Chevy—(*Breaks off.*) That funny? I coulda sworn I was driving that Chevy today.

LINDA: Well, that's nothing. Something must've reminded you.

WILLY: Remarkable. Ts. Remember those days? The way Biff used to simonize that car? The dealer refused to believe there was eighty thousand miles on it. (*He shakes his head.*) Heh! (*To Linda.*) Close your eyes, I'll be right up. (*He walks out of the bedroom.*)

HAPPY (*to Biff*): Jesus, maybe he smashed up the car again!

LINDA (*calling after Willy*): Be careful on the stairs, dear! The cheese is on the middle shelf! (*She turns, goes over to the bed, takes his jacket, and goes out of the bedroom.*)

Light has risen on the boys' room. Unseen, Willy is heard talking to himself, "Eighty thousand miles," and a little laugh. Biff gets out of bed, comes downstage a bit, and stands attentively. Biff is two years older than his brother Happy, well built, but in these days bears a worn air and seems less self-assured. He has succeeded less, and his dreams are stronger and less acceptable than Happy's. Happy is tall, powerfully made. Sexuality is like a visible color on him, or a scent that many women have discovered. He, like his brother, is lost, but in a different way, for he has never allowed himself to turn his face toward defeat and is thus more confused and hard-skinned, although seemingly more content.

HAPPY (*getting out of bed*): He's going to get his license taken away if he keeps that up. I'm getting nervous about him, y'know, Biff?

BIFF: His eyes are going.

HAPPY: No, I've driven with him. He sees all right. He just doesn't keep his mind on it. I drove into the city with him last week. He stops at a green light and then it turns red and he goes. (*He laughs.*)

BIFF: Maybe he's color-blind.

HAPPY: Pop? Why he's got the finest eye for color in the business. You know that.

BIFF (*sitting down on his bed*): I'm going to sleep.

HAPPY: You're not still sour on Dad, are you, Biff?

BIFF: He's all right, I guess.

WILLY (*underneath them, in the living-room*): Yes, sir, eighty thousand miles—eighty-two thousand!

BIFF: You smoking?

HAPPY (*holding out a pack of cigarettes*): Want one?

BIFF (*taking a cigarette*): I can never sleep when I smell it.

WILLY: What a simonizing job, heh!

HAPPY (*with deep sentiment*): Funny, Biff, y'know? Us sleeping in here again? The old beds. (*He pats his bed affectionately.*) All the talk that went across those two beds, huh? Our whole lives.

BIFF: Yeah. Lotta dreams and plans.

HAPPY (*with a deep and masculine laugh*): About five hundred women would like to know what was said in this room.

They share a soft laugh.

BIFF: Remember that big Betsy something—what the hell was her name—over on Bushwick Avenue?

HAPPY (*combing his hair*): With the collie dog!

BIFF: That's the one. I got you in there, remember?

HAPPY: Yeah, that was my first time—I think. Boy, there was a pig! (*They laugh, almost crudely.*) You taught me everything I know about women. Don't forget that.

BIFF: I bet you forgot how bashful you used to be. Especially with girls.

HAPPY: Oh, I still am, Biff.

BIFF: Oh, go on.

HAPPY: I just control it, that's all. I think I got less bashful and you got more so. What happened, Biff? Where's the old humor, the old confidence? (*He shakes Biff's knee. Biff gets up and moves restlessly about the room.*) What's the matter?

BIFF: Why does Dad mock me all the time?

HAPPY: He's not mocking you, he—

BIFF: Everything I say there's a twist of mockery on his face. I can't get near him.

HAPPY: He just wants you to make good, that's all. I wanted to talk to you about Dad for a long time, Biff. Something's—happening to him. He—talks to himself.

BIFF: I noticed that this morning. But he always mumbled.

HAPPY: But not so noticeable. It got so embarrassing I sent him to Florida. And you know something? Most of the time he's talking to you.

BIFF: What's he say about me?

HAPPY: I can't make it out.

BIFF: What's he say about me?

HAPPY: I think the fact that you're not settled, that you're still kind of up in the air . . .

BIFF: There's one or two other things depressing him, Happy.

HAPPY: What do you mean?

BIFF: Never mind. Just don't lay it all to me.

HAPPY: But I think if you just got started — I mean — is there any future for you out there?

BIFF: I tell ya, Hap, I don't know what the future is. I don't know — what I'm supposed to want.

HAPPY: What do you mean?

BIFF: Well, I spent six or seven years after high school trying to work myself up. Shipping clerk, salesman, business of one kind or another. And it's a measly manner of existence. To get on that subway on the hot mornings in summer. To devote your whole life to keeping stock, or making phone calls, or selling or buying. To suffer fifty weeks of the year for the sake of a two-week vacation, when all you really desire is to be outdoors, with your shirt off. And always to have to get ahead of the next fella. And still — that's how you build a future.

HAPPY: Well, you really enjoy it on a farm? Are you content out there?

BIFF (*with rising agitation*): Hap, I've had twenty or thirty different kinds of jobs since I left home before the war, and it always turns out the same. I just realized it lately. In Nebraska when I herded cattle, and the Dakotas, and Arizona, and now in Texas. It's why I came home now, I guess, because I realized it. This farm I work on, it's spring there now, see? And they've got about fifteen new colts. There's nothing more inspiring or — beautiful than the sight of a mare and a new colt. And it's cool there now, see? Texas is cool now, and it's spring. And whenever spring comes to where I am, I suddenly get the feeling, my God, I'm not gettin' anywhere! What the hell am I doing, playing around with horses, twenty-eight dollars a week! I'm thirty-four years old, I oughta be makin' my future. That's when I come running home. And now, I get here, and I don't know what to do with myself. (*After a pause.*) I've always made a point of not wasting my life, and everytime I come back here I know that all I've done is to waste my life.

HAPPY: You're a poet, you know that, Biff? You're a — you're an idealist!

BIFF: No, I'm mixed up very bad. Maybe I oughta get married. Maybe I oughta get stuck into something. Maybe that's my trouble. I'm like a boy. I'm not married. I'm not in business, I just — I'm like a boy. Are you content, Hap? You're a success, aren't you? Are you content?

HAPPY: Hell, no!

BIFF: Why? You're making money, aren't you?

HAPPY (*moving about with energy, expressiveness*): All I can do now is wait for the merchandise manager to die. And suppose I get to be merchandise manager? He's a good friend of mine, and he just built a terrific estate on Long Island. And he lived there about two months and sold it, and now he's building another one. He can't enjoy it once it's finished. And I know that's just what I would do. I don't know what the hell I'm workin' for. Sometimes I sit in my apartment—all alone. And I think of the rent I'm paying. And it's crazy. But then, it's what I always wanted. My own apartment, a car, and plenty of women. And still, goddammit, I'm lonely.

BIFF (*with enthusiasm*): Listen, why don't you come out West with me?

HAPPY: You and I, heh?

BIFF: Sure, maybe we could buy a ranch. Raise cattle, use our muscles. Men built like we are should be working out in the open.

HAPPY (*avidly*): The Loman Brothers, heh?

BIFF (*with vast affection*): Sure, we'd be known all over the counties!

HAPPY (*enthralled*): That's what I dream about, Biff. Sometimes I want to just rip my clothes off in the middle of the store and outbox that goddam merchandise manager. I mean I can outbox, outrun, and outlift anybody in that store, and I have to take orders from those common, petty sons-of-bitches till I can't stand it any more.

BIFF: I'm tellin' you, kid, if you were with me I'd be happy out there.

HAPPY (*enthused*): See, Biff, everybody around me is so false that I'm constantly lowering my ideals . . .

BIFF: Baby, together we'd stand up for one another, we'd have someone to trust.

HAPPY: If I were around you—

BIFF: Hap, the trouble is we weren't brought up to grub for money. I don't know how to do it.

HAPPY: Neither can I!

BIFF: Then let's go!

HAPPY: The only thing is—what can you make out there?

BIFF: But look at your friend. Builds an estate and then hasn't the peace of mind to live in it.

HAPPY: Yeah, but when he walks into the store the waves part in front of him. That's fifty-two thousand dollars a year coming through the revolving door, and I got more in my pinky finger than he's got in his head.

BIFF: Yeah, but you just said—

HAPPY: I gotta show some of those pompous, self-important executives over there that Hap Loman can make the grade. I want to walk into the store the way he walks in. Then I'll go with you, Biff. We'll be together yet, I swear. But take those two we had tonight. Now weren't they gorgeous creatures?

BIFF: Yeah, yeah, most gorgeous I've had in years.

HAPPY: I get that any time I want, Biff. Whenever I feel disgusted. The trouble is, it gets like bowling or something. I just keep knockin' them over and it doesn't mean anything. You still run around a lot?

BIFF: Naa. I'd like to find a girl—steady, somebody with substance.

HAPPY: That's what I long for.

BIFF: Go on! You'd never come home.

HAPPY: I would! Somebody with character, with resistance! Like Mom, y'know? You're gonna call me a bastard when I tell you this. That girl Charlotte I was with tonight is engaged to be married in five weeks. (*He tries on his new hat.*)

BIFF: No kiddin'!

HAPPY: Sure, the guy's in line for the vice-presidency of the store. I don't know what gets into me, maybe I just have an overdeveloped sense of competition or something, but I went and ruined her, and furthermore I can't get rid of her. And he's the third executive I've done that to. Isn't that a crummy characteristic? And to top it all, I go to their weddings! (*Indignantly, but laughing.*) Like I'm not supposed to take bribes. Manufacturers offer me a hundred-dollar bill now and then to throw an order their way. You know how honest I am, but it's like this girl, see. I hate myself for it. Because I don't want the girl, and, still, I take it and — I love it!

BIFF: Let's go to sleep.

HAPPY: I guess we didn't settle anything, heh?

BIFF: I just got one idea that I think I'm going to try.

HAPPY: What's that?

BIFF: Remember Bill Oliver?

HAPPY: Sure, Oliver is very big now. You want to work for him again?

BIFF: No, but when I quit he said something to me. He put his arm on my shoulder, and he said, "Biff, if you ever need anything, come to me."

HAPPY: I remember that. That sounds good.

BIFF: I think I'll go to see him. If I could get ten thousand or even seven or eight thousand dollars I could buy a beautiful ranch.

HAPPY: I bet he'd back you. 'Cause he thought highly of you, Biff. I mean, they all do. You're well liked, Biff. That's why I say to come back here, and we both have the apartment. And I'm tellin' you, Biff, any babe you want . . .

BIFF: No, with a ranch I could do the work I like and still be something. I just wonder though. I wonder if Oliver still thinks I stole that carton of basketballs.

HAPPY: Oh, he probably forgot that long ago. It's almost ten years. You're too sensitive. Anyway, he didn't really fire you.

BIFF: Well, I think he was going to. I think that's why I quit. I was never sure whether he knew or not. I know he thought the world of me, though. I was the only one he'd let lock up the place.

WILLY (*below*): You gonna wash the engine, Biff?

HAPPY: Shh!

Biff looks at Happy, who is gazing down, listening. Willy is mumbling in the parlor.

HAPPY: You hear that?

They listen. Willy laughs warmly.

BIFF (*growing angry*): Doesn't he know Mom can hear that?

WILLY: Don't get your sweater dirty, Biff!

A look of pain crosses Biff's face.

HAPPY: Isn't that terrible? Don't leave again, will you? You'll find a job here. You
  gotta stick around. I don't know what to do about him, it's getting embarrassing.

WILLY: What a simonizing job!

BIFF: Mom's hearing that!

WILLY: No kiddin', Biff, you got a date? Wonderful!

HAPPY: Go on to sleep. But talk to him in the morning, will you?

BIFF (*reluctantly getting into bed*): With her in the house. Brother!

HAPPY (*getting into bed*): I wish you'd have a good talk with him.

The light on their room begins to fade.

BIFF (*to himself in bed*): That selfish, stupid . . .

HAPPY: Sh . . . Sleep, Biff.

*Their light is out. Well before they have finished speaking, Willy's form is dimly
seen below in the darkened kitchen. He opens the refrigerator, searches in there,
and takes out a bottle of milk. The apartment houses are fading out, and the entire
house and surroundings become covered with leaves. Music insinuates itself as the
leaves appear.*

WILLY: Just wanna be careful with those girls, Biff, that's all. Don't make any
  promises. No promises of any kind. Because a girl, y'know, they always
  believe what you tell 'em, and you're very young, Biff, you're too young
  to be talking seriously to girls.

*Light rises on the kitchen. Willy, talking, shuts the refrigerator door and comes
downstage to the kitchen table. He pours milk into a glass. He is totally immersed
in himself, smiling faintly.*

WILLY: Too young entirely, Biff. You want to watch your schooling first. Then
  when you're all set, there'll be plenty of girls for a boy like you. (*He smiles
  broadly at a kitchen chair.*) That so? The girls pay for you? (*He laughs.*)
  Boy, you must really be makin' a hit.

*Willy is gradually addressing—physically—a point offstage, speaking through
the wall of the kitchen, and his voice has been rising in volume to that of a normal
conversation.*

WILLY: I been wondering why you polish the car so careful. Ha! Don't leave the
  hubcaps, boys. Get the chamois to the hubcaps. Happy, use newspaper
  on the windows, it's the easiest thing. Show him how to do it, Biff! You
  see, Happy? Pad it up, use it like a pad. That's it, that's it, good work.
  You're doin' all right, Hap. (*He pauses, then nods in approbation for a few
  seconds, then looks upward.*) Biff, first thing we gotta do when we get time
  is clip that big branch over the house. Afraid it's gonna fall in a storm and
  hit the roof. Tell you what. We get a rope and sling her around, and then
  we climb up there with a couple of saws and take her down. Soon as you
  finish the car, boys, I wanna see ya. I got a surprise for you, boys.

BIFF (*offstage*): Whatta ya got, Dad?

WILLY: No, you finish first. Never leave a job till you're finished—remember that. (*Looking toward the "big trees."*) Biff, up in Albany I saw a beautiful hammock. I think I'll buy it next trip, and we'll hang it right between those two elms. Wouldn't that be something? Just swingin' there under those branches. Boy, that would be . . .

Young Biff and Young Happy appear from the direction Willy was addressing. Happy carries rags and a pail of water. Biff, wearing a sweater with a block "S," carries a football.

BIFF (*pointing in the direction of the car offstage*): How's that, Pop, professional?

WILLY: Terrific. Terrific job, boys. Good work, Biff.

HAPPY: Where's the surprise, Pop?

WILLY: In the back seat of the car.

HAPPY: Boy! (*He runs off.*)

BIFF: What is it, Dad? Tell me, what'd you buy?

WILLY (*laughing, cuffs him*): Never mind, something I want you to have.

BIFF (*turns and starts off*): What is it, Hap?

HAPPY (*offstage*): It's a punching bag!

BIFF: Oh, Pop!

WILLY: It's got Gene Tunney's signature on it!

Happy runs onstage with a punching bag.

BIFF: Gee, how'd you know we wanted a punching bag?

WILLY: Well, it's the finest thing for the timing.

HAPPY (*lies down on his back and pedals with his feet*): I'm losing weight, you notice, Pop?

WILLY (*to Happy*): Jumping rope is good too.

BIFF: Did you see the new football I got?

WILLY (*examining the ball*): Where'd you get a new ball?

BIFF: The coach told me to practice my passing.

WILLY: That so? And he gave you the ball, heh?

BIFF: Well, I borrowed it from the locker room. (*He laughs confidentially.*)

WILLY (*laughing with him at the theft*): I want you to return that.

HAPPY: I told you he wouldn't like it!

BIFF (*angrily*): Well, I'm bringing it back!

WILLY (*stopping the incipient argument, to Happy*): Sure, he's gotta practice with a regulation ball, doesn't he? (*To Biff.*) Coach'll probably congratulate you on your initiative!

BIFF: Oh, he keeps congratulating my initiative all the time, Pop.

WILLY: That's because he likes you. If somebody else took that ball there'd be an uproar. So what's the report, boys, what's the report?

BIFF: Where'd you go this time, Dad? Gee we were lonesome for you.

WILLY (*pleased, puts an arm around each boy and they come down to the apron*): Lonesome, heh?

BIFF: Missed you every minute.

WILLY: Don't say? Tell you a secret, boys. Don't breathe it to a soul. Someday I'll have my own business, and I'll never have to leave home any more.

HAPPY: Like Uncle Charley, heh?

WILLY: Bigger than Uncle Charley! Because Charley is not—liked. He's liked, but he's not—well liked.

BIFF: Where'd you go this time, Dad?

WILLY: Well, I got on the road, and I went north to Providence. Met the Mayor.

BIFF: The Mayor of Providence!

WILLY: He was sitting in the hotel lobby.

BIFF: What'd he say?

WILLY: He said, "Morning!" And I said, "You got a fine city here, Mayor." And then he had coffee with me. And then I went to Waterbury. Waterbury is a fine city. Big clock city, the famous Waterbury clock. Sold a nice bill there. And then Boston—Boston is the cradle of the Revolution. A fine city. And a couple of other towns in Mass., and on to Portland and Bangor and straight home!

BIFF: Gee, I'd love to go with you sometime, Dad.

WILLY: Soon as summer comes.

HAPPY: Promise?

WILLY: You and Hap and I, and I'll show you all the towns. America is full of beautiful towns and fine, upstanding people. And they know me, boys, they know me up and down New England. The finest people. And when I bring you fellas up, there'll be open sesame for all of us, 'cause one thing, boys: I have friends. I can park my car in any street in New England, and the cops protect it like their own. This summer, heh?

BIFF AND HAPPY (*together*): Yeah! You bet!

WILLY: We'll take our bathing suits.

HAPPY: We'll carry your bags, Pop!

WILLY: Oh, won't that be something! Me comin' into the Boston stores with you boys carryin' my bags. What a sensation!

Biff is prancing around, practicing passing the ball.

WILLY: You nervous, Biff, about the game?

BIFF: Not if you're gonna be there.

WILLY: What do they say about you in school, now that they made you captain?

HAPPY: There's a crowd of girls behind him everytime the classes change.

BIFF (*taking Willy's hand*): This Saturday, Pop, this Saturday—just for you, I'm going to break through for a touchdown.

HAPPY: You're supposed to pass.

BIFF: I'm takin' one play for Pop. You watch me, Pop, and when I take off my helmet, that means I'm breakin' out. Then you watch me crash through that line!

WILLY (*kisses Biff*): Oh, wait'll I tell this in Boston!

Bernard enters in knickers. He is younger than Biff, earnest and loyal, a worried boy.

BERNARD: Biff, where are you? You're supposed to study with me today.

WILLY: Hey, looka Bernard. What're you lookin' so anemic about, Bernard?

BERNARD: He's gotta study, Uncle Willy. He's got Regents next week.

HAPPY (*tauntingly, spinning Bernard around*): Let's box, Bernard!

BERNARD: Biff! (*He gets away from Happy.*) Listen, Biff, I heard Mr. Birnbaum say that if you don't start studyin' math, he's gonna flunk you, and you won't graduate. I heard him!

WILLY: You better study with him, Biff. Go ahead now.

BERNARD: I heard him!

BIFF: Oh, Pop, you didn't see my sneakers! (*He holds up a foot for Willy to look at.*)

WILLY: Hey, that's a beautiful job of printing!

BERNARD (*wiping his glasses*): Just because he printed University of Virginia on his sneakers doesn't mean they've got to graduate him, Uncle Willy!

WILLY (*angrily*): What're you talking about? With scholarships to three universities they're gonna flunk him?

BERNARD: But I heard Mr. Birnbaum say —

WILLY: Don't be a pest, Bernard! (*To his boys.*) What an anemic!

BERNARD: Okay, I'm waiting for you in my house, Biff.

Bernard goes off. The Lomans laugh.

WILLY: Bernard is not well liked, is he?

BIFF: He's liked, but he's not well liked.

HAPPY: That's right, Pop.

WILLY: That's just what I mean. Bernard can get the best marks in school, y'understand, but when he gets out in the business world, y'understand, you are going to be five times ahead of him. That's why I thank Almighty God you're both built like Adonises.° Because the man who makes an appearance in the business world, the man who creates personal interest, is the man who gets ahead. Be liked and you will never want. You take me, for instance. I never have to wait in line to see a buyer. "Willy Loman is here!" That's all they have to know, and I go right through.

BIFF: Did you knock them dead, Pop?

WILLY: Knocked 'em cold in Providence, slaughtered 'em in Boston.

HAPPY (*on his back, pedaling again*): I'm losing weight, you notice, Pop?

Linda enters, as of old, a ribbon in her hair, carrying a basket of washing.

LINDA (*with youthful energy*): Hello, dear!

WILLY: Sweetheart!

LINDA: How'd the Chevy run?

WILLY: Chevrolet, Linda, is the greatest car ever built. (*To the boys.*) Since when do you let your mother carry wash up the stairs?

BIFF: Grab hold there, boy!

HAPPY: Where to, Mom?

LINDA: Hang them up on the line. And you better go down to your friends, Biff. The cellar is full of boys. They don't know what to do with themselves.

BIFF: Ah, when Pop comes home they can wait!

WILLY (*laughs appreciatively*): You better go down and tell them what to do, Biff.

Adonises: In Greek Mythology Adonis is a youth known for his good looks and favored by Aphrodite, the goddess of love and beauty.

BIFF: I think I'll have them sweep out the furnace room.

WILLY: Good work, Biff.

BIFF (*goes through wall-line of kitchen to doorway at back and calls down*): Fellas! Everybody sweep out the furnace room! I'll be right down!

VOICES: All right! Okay, Biff.

BIFF: George and Sam and Frank, come out back! We're hangin' up the wash! Come on, Hap, on the double! (*He and Happy carry out the basket.*)

LINDA: The way they obey him!

WILLY: Well, that's training, the training. I'm tellin' you, I was sellin' thousands and thousands, but I had to come home.

LINDA: Oh, the whole block'll be at that game. Did you sell anything?

WILLY: I did five hundred gross in Providence and seven hundred gross in Boston.

LINDA: No! Wait a minute, I've got a pencil. (*She pulls pencil and paper out of her apron pocket.*) That makes your commission . . . Two hundred—my God! Two hundred and twelve dollars!

WILLY: Well, I didn't figure it yet, but . . .

LINDA: How much did you do?

WILLY: Well, I—I did—about a hundred and eighty gross in Providence. Well, no—it came to—roughly two hundred gross on the whole trip.

LINDA (*without hesitation*): Two hundred gross. That's . . . (*She figures.*)

WILLY: The trouble was that three of the stores were half closed for inventory in Boston. Otherwise I woulda broke records.

LINDA: Well, it makes seventy dollars and some pennies. That's very good.

WILLY: What do we owe?

LINDA: Well, on the first there's sixteen dollars on the refrigerator—

WILLY: Why sixteen?

LINDA: Well, the fan belt broke, so it was a dollar eighty.

WILLY: But it's brand new.

LINDA: Well, the man said that's the way it is. Till they work themselves in, y'know.

They move through the wall-line into the kitchen.

WILLY: I hope we didn't get stuck on that machine.

LINDA: They got the biggest ads of any of them!

WILLY: I know, it's a fine machine. What else?

LINDA: Well, there's nine-sixty for the washing machine. And for the vacuum cleaner there's three and a half due on the fifteenth. Then the roof, you got twenty-one dollars remaining.

WILLY: It don't leak, does it?

LINDA: No, they did a wonderful job. Then you owe Frank for the carburetor.

WILLY: I'm not going to pay that man! That goddam Chevrolet, they ought to prohibit the manufacture of that car!

LINDA: Well, you owe him three and a half. And odds and ends, comes to around a hundred and twenty dollars by the fifteenth.

WILLY: A hundred and twenty dollars! My God, if business don't pick up I don't know what I'm gonna do!

LINDA: Well, next week you'll do better.

WILLY: Oh, I'll knock 'em dead next week. I'll go to Hartford. I'm very well liked in Hartford. You know, the trouble is, Linda, people don't seem to take to me.

They move onto the forestage.

LINDA: Oh, don't be foolish.

WILLY: I know it when I walk in. They seem to laugh at me.

LINDA: Why? Why would they laugh at you? Don't talk that way, Willy.

Willy moves to the edge of the stage. Linda goes into the kitchen and starts to darn stockings.

WILLY: I don't know the reason for it, but they just pass me by. I'm not noticed.

LINDA: But you're doing wonderful, dear. You're making seventy to a hundred dollars a week.

WILLY: But I gotta be at it ten, twelve hours a day. Other men — I don't know — they do it easier. I don't know why — I can't stop myself — I talk too much. A man oughta come in with a few words. One thing about Charley. He's a man of few words, and they respect him.

LINDA: You don't talk too much, you're just lively.

WILLY (*smiling*): Well, I figure, what the hell, life is short, a couple of jokes. (*To himself.*) I joke too much! (*The smile goes.*)

LINDA: Why? You're —

WILLY: I'm fat. I'm very — foolish to look at, Linda. I didn't tell you, but Christmas time I happened to be calling on F. H. Stewarts, and a salesman I know, as I was going in to see the buyer I heard him say something about — walrus. And I — I cracked him right across the face. I won't take that. I simply will not take that. But they do laugh at me. I know that.

LINDA: Darling . . .

WILLY: I gotta overcome it. I know I gotta overcome it. I'm not dressing to advantage, maybe.

LINDA: Willy, darling, you're the handsomest man in the world —

WILLY: Oh, no, Linda.

LINDA: To me you are. (*Slight pause.*) The handsomest.

From the darkness is heard the laughter of a woman. Willy doesn't turn to it, but it continues through Linda's lines.

LINDA: And the boys, Willy. Few men are idolized by their children the way you are.

Music is heard as behind a scrim, to the left of the house, The Woman, dimly seen, is dressing.

WILLY (*with great feeling*): You're the best there is, Linda, you're a pal, you know that? On the road — on the road I want to grab you sometimes and just kiss the life outa you.

The laughter is loud now, and he moves into a brightening area at the left, where The Woman has come from behind the scrim and is standing, putting on her hat, looking into a "mirror" and laughing.

WILLY: 'Cause I get so lonely—especially when business is bad and there's nobody to talk to. I get the feeling that I'll never sell anything again, that I won't make a living for you, or a business, a business for the boys. (*He talks through The Woman's subsiding laughter; The Woman primps at the "mirror."*) There's so much I want to make for—

THE WOMAN: Me? You didn't make me, Willy. I picked you.

WILLY (*pleased*): You picked me?

THE WOMAN (*who is quite proper-looking, Willy's age*): I did. I've been sitting at that desk watching all the salesmen go by, day in, day out. But you've got such a sense of humor, and we do have such a good time together, don't we?

WILLY: Sure, sure. (*He takes her in his arms.*) Why do you have to go now?

THE WOMAN: It's two o'clock . . .

WILLY: No, come on in! (*He pulls her.*)

THE WOMAN: . . . my sisters'll be scandalized. When'll you be back?

WILLY: Oh, two weeks about. Will you come up again?

THE WOMAN: Sure thing. You do make me laugh. It's good for me. (*She squeezes his arm, kisses him.*) And I think you're a wonderful man.

WILLY: You picked me, heh?

THE WOMAN: Sure. Because you're so sweet. And such a kidder.

WILLY: Well, I'll see you next time I'm in Boston.

THE WOMAN: I'll put you right through to the buyers.

WILLY (*slapping her bottom*): Right. Well, bottoms up!

THE WOMAN (*slaps him gently and laughs*): You just kill me, Willy. (*He suddenly grabs her and kisses her roughly.*) You kill me. And thanks for the stockings. I love a lot of stockings. Well, good night.

WILLY: Good night. And keep your pores open!

THE WOMAN: Oh, Willy!

The Woman bursts out laughing, and Linda's laughter blends in. The Woman disappears into the dark. Now the area at the kitchen table brightens. Linda is sitting where she was at the kitchen table, but now is mending a pair of her silk stockings.

LINDA: You are, Willy. The handsomest man. You've got no reason to feel that—

WILLY (*coming out of The Woman's dimming area and going over to Linda*): I'll make it all up to you, Linda, I'll—

LINDA: There's nothing to make up, dear. You're doing fine, better than—

WILLY (*noticing her mending*): What's that?

LINDA: Just mending my stockings. They're so expensive—

WILLY (*angrily, taking them from her*): I won't have you mending stockings in this house! Now throw them out!

Linda puts the stockings in her pocket.

BERNARD (*entering on the run*): Where is he? If he doesn't study!

WILLY (*moving to the forestage, with great agitation*): You'll give him the answers!

BERNARD: I do, but I can't on a Regents! That's a state exam! They're liable to arrest me!

WILLY: Where is he? I'll whip him, I'll whip him!

LINDA: And he'd better give back that football, Willy, it's not nice.

WILLY: Biff! Where is he? Why is he taking everything?

LINDA: He's too rough with the girls, Willy. All the mothers are afraid of him!

WILLY: I'll whip him!

BERNARD: He's driving the car without a license!

The Woman's laugh is heard.

WILLY: Shut up!

LINDA: All the mothers—

WILLY: Shut up!

BERNARD (*backing quietly away and out*): Mr. Birnbaum says he's stuck up.

WILLY: Get outa here!

BERNARD: If he doesn't buckle down he'll flunk math! (*He goes off.*)

LINDA: He's right, Willy, you've gotta—

WILLY (*exploding at her*): There's nothing the matter with him! You want him to be a worm like Bernard? He's got spirit, personality . . .

As he speaks, Linda, almost in tears, exits into the living-room. Willy is alone in the kitchen, wilting and staring. The leaves are gone. It is night again, and the apartment houses look down from behind.

WILLY: Loaded with it. Loaded! What is he stealing? He's giving it back, isn't he? Why is he stealing? What did I tell him? I never in my life told him anything but decent things.

Happy in pajamas has come down the stairs; Willy suddenly becomes aware of Happy's presence.

HAPPY: Let's go now, come on.

WILLY (*sitting down at the kitchen table*): Huh! Why did she have to wax the floors herself? Everytime she waxes the floors she keels over. She knows that!

HAPPY: Shh! Take it easy. What brought you back tonight?

WILLY: I got an awful scare. Nearly hit a kid in Yonkers. God! Why didn't I go to Alaska with my brother Ben that time! Ben! That man was a genius, that man was success incarnate! What a mistake! He begged me to go.

HAPPY: Well, there's no use in—

WILLY: You guys! There was a man started with the clothes on his back and ended up with diamond mines!

HAPPY: Boy, someday I'd like to know how he did it.

WILLY: What's the mystery? The man knew what he wanted and went out and got it! Walked into a jungle, and comes out, the age of twenty-one, and he's rich! The world is an oyster, but you don't crack it open on a mattress!

HAPPY: Pop, I told you I'm gonna retire you for life.

WILLY: You'll retire me for life on seventy goddam dollars a week? And your women and your car and your apartment, and you'll retire me for life! Christ's sake, I couldn't get past Yonkers today! Where are you guys, where are you? The woods are burning! I can't drive a car!

Charley has appeared in the doorway. He is a large man, slow of speech, laconic, immovable. In all he says, despite what he says, there is pity, and, now, trepidation. He has a robe over pajamas, slippers on his feet. He enters the kitchen.

CHARLEY: Everything all right?

HAPPY: Yeah, Charley, everything's . . .

WILLY: What's the matter?

CHARLEY: I heard some noise. I thought something happened. Can't we do something about the walls? You sneeze in here, and in my house hats blow off.

HAPPY: Let's go to bed, Dad. Come on.

Charley signals to Happy to go.

WILLY: You go ahead, I'm not tired at the moment.

HAPPY (*to Willy*): Take it easy, huh? (*He exits.*)

WILLY: What're you doin' up?

CHARLEY (*sitting down at the kitchen table opposite Willy*): Couldn't sleep good. I had a heartburn.

WILLY: Well, you don't know how to eat.

CHARLEY: I eat with my mouth.

WILLY: No, you're ignorant. You gotta know about vitamins and things like that.

CHARLEY: Come on, let's shoot. Tire you out a little.

WILLY (*hesitantly*): All right. You got cards?

CHARLEY (*taking a deck from his pocket*): Yeah, I got them. Someplace. What is it with those vitamins?

WILLY (*dealing*): They build up your bones. Chemistry.

CHARLEY: Yeah, but there's no bones in a heartburn.

WILLY: What are you talkin' about? Do you know the first thing about it?

CHARLEY: Don't get insulted.

WILLY: Don't talk about something you don't know anything about.

They are playing. Pause.

CHARLEY: What're you doin' home?

WILLY: A little trouble with the car.

CHARLEY: Oh. (*Pause.*) I'd like to take a trip to California.

WILLY: Don't say.

CHARLEY: You want a job?

WILLY: I got a job, I told you that. (*After a slight pause.*) What the hell are you offering me a job for?

CHARLEY: Don't get insulted.

WILLY: Don't insult me.

CHARLEY: I don't see no sense in it. You don't have to go on this way.

WILLY: I got a good job. (*Slight pause.*) What do you keep comin' in here for?

CHARLEY: You want me to go?

WILLY (*after a pause, withering*): I can't understand it. He's going back to Texas again. What the hell is that?

CHARLEY: Let him go.

WILLY: I got nothin' to give him, Charley, I'm clean, I'm clean.

CHARLEY: He won't starve. None a them starve. Forget about him.

WILLY: Then what have I got to remember?

CHARLEY: You take it too hard. To hell with it. When a deposit bottle is broken you don't get your nickel back.

WILLY: That's easy enough for you to say.

CHARLEY: That ain't easy for me to say.

WILLY: Did you see the ceiling I put up in the living-room?

CHARLEY: Yeah, that's a piece of work. To put up a ceiling is a mystery to me. How do you do it?

WILLY: What's the difference?

CHARLEY: Well, talk about it.

WILLY: You gonna put up a ceiling?

CHARLEY: How could I put up a ceiling?

WILLY: Then what the hell are you bothering me for?

CHARLEY: You're insulted again.

WILLY: A man who can't handle tools is not a man. You're disgusting.

CHARLEY: Don't call me disgusting, Willy.

Uncle Ben, carrying a valise and an umbrella, enters the forestage from around the right corner of the house. He is a stolid man, in his sixties, with a mustache and an authoritative air. He is utterly certain of his destiny, and there is an aura of far places about him. He enters exactly as Willy speaks.

WILLY: I'm getting awfully tired, Ben.

Ben's music is heard. Ben looks around at everything.

CHARLEY: Good, keep playing; you'll sleep better. Did you call me Ben?

Ben looks at his watch.

WILLY: That's funny. For a second there you reminded me of my brother Ben.

BEN: I only have a few minutes. (*He strolls, inspecting the place. Willy and Charley continue playing.*)

CHARLEY: You never heard from him again, heh? Since that time?

WILLY: Didn't Linda tell you? Couple of weeks ago we got a letter from his wife in Africa. He died.

CHARLEY: That so.

BEN (*chuckling*): So this is Brooklyn, eh?

CHARLEY: Maybe you're in for some of his money.

WILLY: Naa, he had seven sons. There's just one opportunity I had with that man . . .

BEN: I must make a train, William. There are several properties I'm looking at in Alaska.

WILLY: Sure, sure! If I'd gone with him to Alaska that time, everything would've been totally different.

CHARLEY: Go on, you'd froze to death up there.

WILLY: What're you talking about?

BEN: Opportunity is tremendous in Alaska, William. Surprised you're not up there.

WILLY: Sure, tremendous.

CHARLEY: Heh?

WILLY: There was the only man I ever met who knew the answers.

CHARLEY: Who?

BEN: How are you all?

WILLY (*taking a pot, smiling*): Fine, fine.

CHARLEY: Pretty sharp tonight.

BEN: Is mother living with you?

WILLY: No, she died a long time ago.

CHARLEY: Who?

BEN: That's too bad. Fine specimen of a lady, Mother.

WILLY (*to Charley*): Heh?

BEN: I'd hoped to see the old girl.

CHARLEY: Who died?

BEN: Heard anything from Father, have you?

WILLY (*unnerved*): What do you mean, who died?

CHARLEY (*taking a pot*): What're you talkin' about?

BEN (*looking at his watch*): William, it's half-past eight!

WILLY (*as though to dispel his confusion he angrily stops Charley's hand*): That's my build!

CHARLEY: I put the ace—

WILLY: If you don't know how to play the game I'm not gonna throw my money away on you!

CHARLEY (*rising*): It was my ace, for God's sake!

WILLY: I'm through, I'm through!

BEN: When did Mother die?

WILLY: Long ago. Since the beginning you never knew how to play cards.

CHARLEY (*picks up the cards and goes to the door*): All right! Next time I'll bring a deck with five aces.

WILLY: I don't play that kind of game!

CHARLEY (*turning to him*): You ought to be ashamed of yourself!

WILLY: Yeah?

CHARLEY: Yeah! (*He goes out.*)

WILLY (*slamming the door after him*): Ignoramus!

BEN (*as Willy comes toward him through the wall-line of the kitchen*): So you're William.

WILLY (*shaking Ben's hand*): Ben! I've been waiting for you so long! What's the answer? How did you do it?

BEN: Oh, there's a story in that.

Linda enters the forestage, as of old, carrying the wash basket.

LINDA: Is this Ben?

BEN (*gallantly*): How do you do, my dear.

LINDA: Where've you been all these years? Willy's always wondered why you—

WILLY (*pulling Ben away from her impatiently*): Where is Dad? Didn't you follow him? How did you get started?

BEN: Well, I don't know how much you remember.

WILLY: Well, I was just a baby, of course, only three or four years old —

BEN: Three years and eleven months.

WILLY: What a memory, Ben!

BEN: I have many enterprises, William, and I have never kept books.

WILLY: I remember I was sitting under the wagon in — was it Nebraska?

BEN: It was South Dakota, and I gave you a bunch of wild flowers.

WILLY: I remember you walking away down some open road.

BEN (*laughing*): I was going to find Father in Alaska.

WILLY: Where is he?

BEN: At that age I had a very faulty view of geography, William. I discovered after a few days that I was heading due south, so instead of Alaska, I ended up in Africa.

LINDA: Africa!

WILLY: The Gold Coast!

BEN: Principally diamond mines.

LINDA: Diamond mines!

BEN: Yes, my dear. But I've only a few minutes —

WILLY: No! Boys! Boys! (*Young Biff and Happy appear.*) Listen to this. This is your Uncle Ben, a great man! Tell my boys, Ben!

BEN: Why, boys, when I was seventeen I walked into the jungle, and when I was twenty-one I walked out. (*He laughs.*) And by God I was rich.

WILLY (*to the boys*): You see what I been talking about? The greatest things can happen!

BEN (*glancing at his watch*): I have an appointment in Ketchikan Tuesday week.

WILLY: No, Ben! Please tell about Dad. I want my boys to hear. I want them to know the kind of stock they spring from. All I remember is a man with a big beard, and I was in Mamma's lap, sitting around a fire, and some kind of high music.

BEN: His flute. He played the flute.

WILLY: Sure, the flute, that's right!

New music is heard, a high, rollicking tune.

BEN: Father was a very great and a very wild-hearted man. We would start in Boston, and he'd toss the whole family into the wagon, and then he'd drive the team right across the country; through Ohio, and Indiana, Michigan, Illinois, and all the Western states. And we'd stop in the towns and sell the flutes that he'd made on the way. Great inventor, Father. With one gadget he made more in a week than a man like you could make in a lifetime.

WILLY: That's just the way I'm bringing them up, Ben — rugged, well liked, all-around.

BEN: Yeah? (*To Biff.*) Hit that, boy — hard as you can. (*He pounds his stomach.*)

BIFF: Oh, no, sir!

BEN (*taking boxing stance*): Come on, get to me. (*He laughs.*)

WILLY: Go to it, Biff! Go ahead, show him!

BIFF: Okay! (*He cocks his fists and starts in.*)

LINDA (*to Willy*): Why must he fight, dear?

BEN (*sparring with Biff*): Good boy! Good boy!

WILLY: How's that, Ben, heh?

HAPPY: Give him the left, Biff!

LINDA: Why are you fighting?

BEN: Good boy! (*Suddenly comes in, trips Biff, and stands over him, the point of his umbrella poised over Biff's eye.*)

LINDA: Look out, Biff!

BIFF: Gee!

BEN (*patting Biff's knee*): Never fight fair with a stranger, boy. You'll never get out of the jungle that way. (*Taking Linda's hand and bowing*): It was an honor and a pleasure to meet you, Linda.

LINDA (*withdrawing her hand coldly, frightened*): Have a nice—trip.

BEN (*to Willy*): And good luck with your—what do you do?

WILLY: Selling.

BEN: Yes. Well . . . (*He raises his hand in farewell to all.*)

WILLY: No, Ben, I don't want you to think . . . (*He takes Ben's arm to show him.*) It's Brooklyn, I know, but we hunt too.

BEN: Really, now.

WILLY: Oh, sure, there's snakes and rabbits and—that's why I moved out here. Why, Biff can fell any one of these trees in no time! Boys! Go right over to where they're building the apartment house and get some sand. We're gonna rebuild the entire front stoop now! Watch this, Ben!

BIFF: Yes, sir! On the double, Hap!

HAPPY (*as he and Biff run off*): I lost weight, Pop, you notice?

Charley enters in knickers, even before the boys are gone.

CHARLEY: Listen, if they steal any more from that building the watchman'll put the cops on them!

LINDA (*to Willy*): Don't let Biff . . .

Ben laughs lustily.

WILLY: You shoulda seen the lumber they brought home last week. At least a dozen six-by-tens worth all kinds a money.

CHARLEY: Listen, if that watchman—

WILLY: I gave them hell, understand. But I got a couple of fearless characters there.

CHARLEY: Willy, the jails are full of fearless characters.

BEN (*clapping Willy on the back, with a laugh at Charley*): And the stock exchange, friend!

WILLY (*joining in Ben's laughter*): Where are the rest of your pants?

CHARLEY: My wife bought them.

WILLY: Now all you need is a golf club and you can go upstairs and go to sleep. (*To Ben*). Great athlete! Between him and his son Bernard they can't hammer a nail!

BERNARD (*rushing in*): The watchman's chasing Biff!

WILLY (*angrily*): Shut up! He's not stealing anything!

LINDA (*alarmed, hurrying off left*): Where is he? Biff, dear! (*She exits.*)

WILLY (*moving toward the left, away from Ben*): There's nothing wrong. What's the matter with you?

BEN: Nervy boy. Good!

WILLY (*laughing*): Oh, nerves of iron, that Biff!

CHARLEY: Don't know what it is. My New England man comes back and he's bleedin', they murdered him up there.

WILLY: It's contacts, Charley, I got important contacts!

CHARLEY (*sarcastically*): Glad to hear it, Willy. Come in later, we'll shoot a little casino. I'll take some of your Portland money. (*He laughs at Willy and exits.*)

WILLY (*turning to Ben*): Business is bad, it's murderous. But not for me, of course.

BEN: I'll stop by on my way back to Africa.

WILLY (*longingly*): Can't you stay a few days? You're just what I need, Ben, because I — I have a fine position here, but I — well, Dad left when I was such a baby and I never had a chance to talk to him and I still feel — kind of temporary about myself.

BEN: I'll be late for my train.

They are at opposite ends of the stage.

WILLY: Ben, my boys — can't we talk? They'd go into the jaws of hell for me, see, but I —

BEN: William, you're being first-rate with your boys. Outstanding, manly chaps!

WILLY (*hanging on to his words*): Oh, Ben, that's good to hear! Because sometimes I'm afraid that I'm not teaching them the right kind of — Ben, how should I teach them?

BEN (*giving great weight to each word, and with a certain vicious audacity*): William, when I walked into the jungle, I was seventeen. When I walked out I was twenty-one. And, by God, I was rich! (*He goes off into darkness around the right corner of the house.*)

WILLY: . . . was rich! That's just the spirit I want to imbue them with! To walk into a jungle! I was right! I was right! I was right!

Ben is gone, but Willy is still speaking to him as Linda, in nightgown and robe, enters the kitchen, glances around for Willy, then goes to the door of the house, looks out, and sees him. Comes down to his left. He looks at her.

LINDA: Willy, dear? Willy?

WILLY: I was right!

LINDA: Did you have some cheese? (*He can't answer.*) It's very late, darling. Come to bed, heh?

WILLY (*looking straight up*): Gotta break your neck to see a star in this yard.

LINDA: You coming in?

WILLY: Whatever happened to that diamond watch fob? Remember? When Ben came from Africa that time? Didn't he give me a watch fob with a diamond in it?

LINDA: You pawned it, dear. Twelve, thirteen years ago. For Biff's radio correspondence course.

WILLY: Gee, that was a beautiful thing. I'll take a walk.

LINDA: But you're in your slippers.

WILLY (*starting to go around the house at the left*): I was right! I was! (*Half to Linda, as he goes, shaking his head.*) What a man! There was a man worth talking to. I was right!

LINDA (*calling after Willy*): But in your slippers, Willy!

Willy is almost gone when Biff, in his pajamas, comes down the stairs and enters the kitchen.

BIFF: What is he doing out there?

LINDA: Sh!

BIFF: God Almighty, Mom, how long has he been doing this?

LINDA: Don't, he'll hear you.

BIFF: What the hell is the matter with him?

LINDA: It'll pass by morning.

BIFF: Shouldn't we do anything?

LINDA: Oh, my dear, you should do a lot of things, but there's nothing to do, so go to sleep.

Happy comes down the stairs and sits on the steps.

HAPPY: I never heard him so loud, Mom.

LINDA: Well, come around more often; you'll hear him. (*She sits down at the table and mends the lining of Willy's jacket.*)

BIFF: Why didn't you ever write me about this, Mom?

LINDA: How would I write to you? For over three months you had no address.

BIFF: I was on the move. But you know I thought of you all the time. You know that, don't you, pal?

LINDA: I know, dear, I know. But he likes to have a letter. Just to know that there's still a possibility for better things.

BIFF: He's not like this all the time, is he?

LINDA: It's when you come home he's always the worst.

BIFF: When I come home?

LINDA: When you write you're coming, he's all smiles, and talks about the future, and—he's just wonderful. And then the closer you seem to come, the more shaky he gets, and then, by the time you get here, he's arguing, and he seems angry at you. I think it's just that maybe he can't bring himself to—to open up to you. Why are you so hateful to each other? Why is that?

BIFF (*evasively*): I'm not hateful, Mom.

LINDA: But you no sooner come in the door than you're fighting!

BIFF: I don't know why. I mean to change. I'm tryin', Mom, you understand?

LINDA: Are you home to stay now?

BIFF: I don't know. I want to look around, see what's doin'.

LINDA: Biff, you can't look around all your life, can you?

BIFF: I just can't take hold, Mom. I can't take hold of some kind of a life.

LINDA: Biff, a man is not a bird, to come and go with the springtime.

BIFF: Your hair . . . (*He touches her hair.*) Your hair got so gray.

LINDA: Oh, it's been gray since you were in high school. I just stopped dyeing it, that's all.

BIFF: Dye it again, will ya? I don't want my pal looking old. (*He smiles.*)

LINDA: You're such a boy! You think you can go away for a year and . . . You've
   got to get it into your head now that one day you'll knock on this door and
   there'll be strange people here —

BIFF: What are you talking about? You're not even sixty, Mom.

LINDA: But what about your father?

BIFF (*lamely*): Well, I meant him too.

HAPPY: He admires Pop.

LINDA: Biff, dear, if you don't have any feeling for him, then you can't have any
   feeling for me.

BIFF: Sure I can, Mom.

LINDA: No. You can't just come to see me, because I love him. (*With a threat,
   but only a threat, of tears.*) He's the dearest man in the world to me, and I
   won't have anyone making him feel unwanted and low and blue. You've
   got to make up your mind now, darling, there's no leeway any more.
   Either he's your father and you pay him that respect, or else you're not to
   come here. I know he's not easy to get along with — nobody knows that
   better than me — but . . .

WILLY (*from the left, with a laugh*): Hey, hey, Biffo!

BIFF (*starting to go out after Willy*): What the hell is the matter with him?
   (*Happy stops him.*)

LINDA: Don't — don't go near him!

BIFF: Stop making excuses for him! He always, always wiped the floor with you.
   Never had an ounce of respect for you.

HAPPY: He's always had respect for —

BIFF: What the hell do you know about it?

HAPPY (*surlily*): Just don't call him crazy!

BIFF: He's got no character — Charley wouldn't do this. Not in his own
   house — spewing out that vomit from his mind.

HAPPY: Charley never had to cope with what he's got to.

BIFF: People are worse off than Willy Loman. Believe me, I've seen them!

LINDA: Then make Charley your father, Biff. You can't do that, can you? I don't
   say he's a great man. Willy Loman never made a lot of money. His name
   was never in the paper. He's not the finest character that ever lived. But
   he's a human being, and a terrible thing is happening to him. So attention
   must be paid. He's not to be allowed to fall into his grave like an old dog.
   Attention, attention must be finally paid to such a person. You called him
   crazy —

BIFF: I didn't mean —

LINDA: No, a lot of people think he's lost his — balance. But you don't have to
   be very smart to know what his trouble is. The man is exhausted.

HAPPY: Sure!

LINDA: A small man can be just as exhausted as a great man. He works for a
   company thirty-six years this March, opens up unheard-of territories to
   their trademark, and now in his old age they take his salary away.

HAPPY (*indignantly*): I didn't know that, Mom.

LINDA: You never asked, my dear! Now that you get your spending money
   someplace else you don't trouble your mind with him.

HAPPY: But I gave you money last —

LINDA: Christmas time, fifty dollars! To fix the hot water it cost ninety-seven fifty! For five weeks he's been on straight commission, like a beginner, an unknown!

BIFF: Those ungrateful bastards!

LINDA: Are they any worse than his sons? When he brought them business, when he was young, they were glad to see him. But now his old friends, the old buyers that loved him so and always found some order to hand him in a pinch — they're all dead, retired. He used to be able to make six, seven calls a day in Boston. Now he takes his valises out of the car and puts them back and takes them out again and he's exhausted. Instead of walking he talks now. He drives seven hundred miles, and when he gets there no one knows him any more, no one welcomes him. And what goes through a man's mind, driving seven hundred miles home without having earned a cent? Why shouldn't he talk to himself? Why? When he has to go to Charley and borrow fifty dollars a week and pretend to me that it's his pay? How long can that go on? How long? You see what I'm sitting here and waiting for? And you tell me he has no character? The man who never worked a day but for your benefit? When does he get the medal for that? Is this his reward — to turn around at the age of sixty-three and find his sons, who he loved better than his life, one a philandering bum —

HAPPY: Mom!

LINDA: That's all you are, my baby! (*To Biff.*) And you! What happened to the love you had for him? You were such pals! How you used to talk to him on the phone every night! How lonely he was till he could come home to you!

BIFF: All right, Mom. I'll live here in my room, and I'll get a job. I'll keep away from him, that's all.

LINDA: No, Biff. You can't stay here and fight all the time.

BIFF: He threw me out of this house, remember that.

LINDA: Why did he do that? I never knew why.

BIFF: Because I know he's a fake and he doesn't like anybody around who knows!

LINDA: Why a fake? In what way? What do you mean?

BIFF: Just don't lay it all at my feet. It's between me and him — that's all I have to say. I'll chip in from now on. He'll settle for half my pay check. He'll be all right. I'm going to bed. (*He starts for the stairs.*)

LINDA: He won't be all right.

BIFF (*turning on the stairs, furiously*): I hate this city and I'll stay here. Now what do you want?

LINDA: He's dying, Biff.

Happy turns quickly to her, shocked.

BIFF (*after a pause*): Why is he dying?

LINDA: He's been trying to kill himself.

BIFF (*with great horror*): How?

LINDA: I live from day to day.

BIFF: What're you talking about?

LINDA: Remember I wrote you that he smashed up the car again? In February?

BIFF: Well?

LINDA: The insurance inspector came. He said that they have evidence. That all these accidents in the last year—weren't—weren't—accidents.

HAPPY: How can they tell that? That's a lie.

LINDA: It seems there's a woman . . . (*She takes a breath as*):

BIFF (*sharply but contained*): What woman?

LINDA (*simultaneously*): . . . and this woman . . .

LINDA: What?

BIFF: Nothing. Go ahead.

LINDA: What did you say?

BIFF: Nothing. I just said what woman?

HAPPY: What about her?

LINDA: Well, it seems she was walking down the road and saw his car. She says that he wasn't driving fast at all, and that he didn't skid. She says he came to that little bridge, and then deliberately smashed into the railing, and it was only the shallowness of the water that saved him.

BIFF: Oh, no, he probably just fell asleep again.

LINDA: I don't think he fell asleep.

BIFF: Why not?

LINDA: Last month . . . (*With great difficulty.*) Oh, boys, it's so hard to say a thing like this! He's just a big stupid man to you, but I tell you there's more good in him than in many other people. (*She chokes, wipes her eyes.*) I was looking for a fuse. The lights blew out, and I went down the cellar. And behind the fuse box—it happened to fall out—was a length of rubber pipe—just short.

HAPPY: No kidding?

LINDA: There's a little attachment on the end of it. I knew right away. And sure enough, on the bottom of the water heater there's a new little nipple on the gas pipe.

HAPPY (*angrily*): That—jerk.

BIFF: Did you have it taken off?

LINDA: I'm—I'm ashamed to. How can I mention it to him? Every day I go down and take away that little rubber pipe. But, when he comes home, I put it back where it was. How can I insult him that way? I don't know what to do. I live from day to day, boys. I tell you, I know every thought in his mind. It sounds so old-fashioned and silly, but I tell you he put his whole life into you and you've turned your backs on him. (*She is bent over in chair, weeping, her face in her hands.*) Biff, I swear to God! Biff, his life is in your hands!

HAPPY (*to Biff*): How do you like that damned fool!

BIFF (*kissing her*): All right, pal, all right. It's all settled now. I've been remiss. I know that, Mom. But now I'll stay, and I swear to you, I'll apply myself. (*Kneeling in front of her, in a fever of self-reproach.*) It's just—you see, Mom, I don't fit in business. Not that I won't try. I'll try, and I'll make good.

HAPPY: Sure you will. The trouble with you in business was you never tried to please people.

BIFF: I know, I —

HAPPY: Like when you worked for Harrison's. Bob Harrison said you were tops, and then you go and do some damn fool thing like whistling whole songs in the elevator like a comedian.

BIFF (*against Happy*): So what? I like to whistle sometimes.

HAPPY: You don't raise a guy to a responsible job who whistles in the elevator!

LINDA: Well, don't argue about it now.

HAPPY: Like when you'd go off and swim in the middle of the day instead of taking the line around.

BIFF (*his resentment rising*): Well, don't you run off? You take off sometimes, don't you? On a nice summer day?

HAPPY: Yeah, but I cover myself!

LINDA: Boys!

HAPPY: If I'm going to take a fade the boss can call any number where I'm supposed to be and they'll swear to him that I just left. I'll tell you something that I hate to say, Biff, but in the business world some of them think you're crazy.

BIFF (*angered*): Screw the business world!

HAPPY: All right, screw it! Great, but cover yourself!

LINDA: Hap, Hap!

BIFF: I don't care what they think! They've laughed at Dad for years, and you know why? Because we don't belong in this nuthouse of a city! We should be mixing cement on some open plain, or — or carpenters. A carpenter is allowed to whistle!

Willy walks in from the entrance of the house, at left.

WILLY: Even your grandfather was better than a carpenter. (*Pause. They watch him.*) You never grew up. Bernard does not whistle in the elevator, I assure you.

BIFF (*as though to laugh Willy out of it*): Yeah, but you do, Pop.

WILLY: I never in my life whistled in an elevator! And who in the business world thinks I'm crazy?

BIFF: I didn't mean it like that, Pop. Now don't make a whole thing out of it, will ya?

WILLY: Go back to the West! Be a carpenter, a cowboy, enjoy yourself!

LINDA: Willy, he was just saying —

WILLY: I heard what he said!

HAPPY (*trying to quiet Willy*): Hey, Pop, come on now . . .

WILLY (*continuing over Happy's line*): They laugh at me, heh? Go to Filene's, go to the Hub, go to Slattery's, Boston. Call out the name Willy Loman and see what happens! Big shot!

BIFF: All right, Pop.

WILLY: Big!

BIFF: All right!

WILLY: Why do you always insult me?

BIFF: I didn't say a word. (*To Linda.*) Did I say a word?

LINDA: He didn't say anything, Willy.

WILLY (*going to the doorway of the living-room*): All right, good night, good night.

LINDA: Willy, dear, he just decided . . .

WILLY (*to Biff*): If you get tired hanging around tomorrow, paint the ceiling I put up in the living-room.

BIFF: I'm leaving early tomorrow.

HAPPY: He's going to see Bill Oliver, Pop.

WILLY (*interestedly*): Oliver? For what?

BIFF (*with reserve, but trying, trying*): He always said he'd stake me. I'd like to go into business, so maybe I can take him up on it.

LINDA: Isn't that wonderful?

WILLY: Don't interrupt. What's wonderful about it? There's fifty men in the City of New York who'd stake him. (*To Biff.*) Sporting goods?

BIFF: I guess so. I know something about it and —

WILLY: He knows something about it! You know sporting goods better than Spalding, for God's sake! How much is he giving you?

BIFF: I don't know, I didn't even see him yet, but —

WILLY: Then what're you talkin' about?

BIFF (*getting angry*): Well, all I said was I'm gonna see him, that's all!

WILLY (*turning away*): Ah, you're counting your chickens again.

BIFF (*starting left for the stairs*): Oh, Jesus, I'm going to sleep!

WILLY (*calling after him*): Don't curse in this house!

BIFF (*turning*): Since when did you get so clean?

HAPPY (*trying to stop them*): Wait a . . .

WILLY: Don't use that language to me! I won't have it!

HAPPY (*grabbing Biff, shouts*): Wait a minute! I got an idea. I got a feasible idea. Come here, Biff, let's talk this over now, let's talk some sense here. When I was down in Florida last time, I thought of a great idea to sell sporting goods. It just came back to me. You and I, Biff — we have a line, the Loman Line. We train a couple of weeks, and put on a couple of exhibitions, see?

WILLY: That's an idea!

HAPPY: Wait! We form two basketball teams, see? Two water-polo teams. We play each other. It's a million dollars' worth of publicity. Two brothers, see? The Loman Brothers. Displays in the Royal Palms — all the hotels. And banners over the ring and the basketball court: "Loman Brothers." Baby, we could sell sporting goods!

WILLY: That is a one-million-dollar idea!

LINDA: Marvelous!

BIFF: I'm in great shape as far as that's concerned.

HAPPY: And the beauty of it is, Biff, it wouldn't be like a business. We'd be out playin' ball again . . .

BIFF (*enthused*): Yeah, that's . . .

WILLY: Million-dollar . . .

HAPPY: And you wouldn't get fed up with it, Biff. It'd be the family again. There'd be the old honor, and comradeship, and if you wanted to go off for a swim or somethin'—well, you'd do it! Without some smart cooky gettin' up ahead of you!

WILLY: Lick the world! You guys together could absolutely lick the civilized world.

BIFF: I'll see Oliver tomorrow. Hap, if we could work that out . . .

LINDA: Maybe things are beginning to—

WILLY (*wildly enthused, to Linda*): Stop interrupting! (*To Biff.*) But don't wear sport jacket and slacks when you see Oliver.

BIFF: No, I'll—

WILLY: A business suit, and talk as little as possible, and don't crack any jokes.

BIFF: He did like me. Always liked me.

LINDA: He loved you!

WILLY (*to Linda*): Will you stop! (*To Biff.*) Walk in very serious. You are not applying for a boy's job. Money is to pass. Be quiet, fine, and serious. Everybody likes a kidder, but nobody lends him money.

HAPPY: I'll try to get some myself, Biff. I'm sure I can.

WILLY: I see great things for you kids, I think your troubles are over. But remember, start big and you'll end big. Ask for fifteen. How much you gonna ask for?

BIFF: Gee, I don't know—

WILLY: And don't say "Gee." "Gee" is a boy's word. A man walking in for fifteen thousand dollars does not say "Gee!"

BIFF: Ten, I think, would be top though.

WILLY: Don't be so modest. You always started too low. Walk in with a big laugh. Don't look worried. Start off with a couple of your good stories to lighten things up. It's not what you say, it's how you say it—because personality always wins the day.

LINDA: Oliver always thought the highest of him—

WILLY: Will you let me talk?

BIFF: Don't yell at her, Pop, will ya?

WILLY (*angrily*): I was talking, wasn't I?

BIFF: I don't like you yelling at her all the time, and I'm tellin' you, that's all.

WILLY: What're you, takin' over this house?

LINDA: Willy—

WILLY (*turning on her*): Don't take his side all the time, goddammit!

BIFF (*furiously*): Stop yelling at her!

WILLY (*suddenly pulling on his cheek, beaten down, guilt ridden*): Give my best to Bill Oliver—he may remember me. (*He exits through the living-room doorway.*)

LINDA (*her voice subdued*): What'd you have to start that for? (*Biff turns away.*) You see how sweet he was as soon as you talked hopefully? (*She goes over to Biff.*) Come up and say good night to him. Don't let him go to bed that way.

HAPPY: Come on, Biff, let's buck him up.

LINDA: Please, dear. Just say good night. It takes so little to make him happy. Come. (*She goes through the living-room doorway, calling upstairs from within the living-room.*) Your pajamas are hanging in the bathroom, Willy!

HAPPY (*looking toward where Linda went out*): What a woman! They broke the mold when they made her. You know that, Biff?

BIFF: He's off salary. My God, working on commission!

HAPPY: Well, let's face it: he's no hot-shot selling man. Except that sometimes, you have to admit, he's a sweet personality.

BIFF (*deciding*): Lend me ten bucks, will ya? I want to buy some new ties.

HAPPY: I'll take you to a place I know. Beautiful stuff. Wear one of my striped shirts tomorrow.

BIFF: She got gray. Mom got awful old. Gee, I'm gonna go in to Oliver tomorrow and knock him for a—

HAPPY: Come on up. Tell that to Dad. Let's give him a whirl. Come on.

BIFF (*steamed up*): You know, with ten thousand bucks, boy!

HAPPY (*as they go into the living-room*): That's the talk, Biff, that's the first time I've heard the old confidence out of you! (*From within the living-room, fading off.*) You're gonna live with me, kid, and any babe you want just say the word . . . (*The last lines are hardly heard. They are mounting the stairs to their parents' bedroom.*)

LINDA (*entering her bedroom and addressing Willy, who is in the bathroom. She is straightening the bed for him*): Can you do anything about the shower? It drips.

WILLY (*from the bathroom*): All of a sudden everything falls to pieces! Goddam plumbing, oughta be sued, those people. I hardly finished putting it in and the thing . . . (*His words rumble off.*)

LINDA: I'm just wondering if Oliver will remember him. You think he might?

WILLY (*coming out of the bathroom in his pajamas*): Remember him? What's the matter with you, you crazy? If he'd've stayed with Oliver he'd be on top by now! Wait'll Oliver gets a look at him. You don't know the average caliber any more. The average young man today—(*he is getting into bed*)—is got a caliber of zero. Greatest thing in the world for him was to bum around.

Biff and Happy enter the bedroom. Slight pause.

WILLY (*stops short, looking at Biff*): Glad to hear it, boy.

HAPPY: He wanted to say good night to you, sport.

WILLY (*to Biff*): Yeah. Knock him dead, boy. What'd you want to tell me?

BIFF: Just take it easy, Pop. Good night. (*He turns to go.*)

WILLY (*unable to resist*): And if anything falls off the desk while you're talking to him—like a package or something—don't you pick it up. They have office boys for that.

LINDA: I'll make a big breakfast—

WILLY: Will you let me finish? (*To Biff.*) Tell him you were in the business in the West. Not farm work.

BIFF: All right, Dad.

LINDA: I think everything—

WILLY (*going right through her speech*): And don't undersell yourself. No less than fifteen thousand dollars.

BIFF (*unable to bear him*): Okay. Good night, Mom. (*He starts moving.*)

WILLY: Because you got a greatness in you, Biff, remember that. You got all kinds a greatness . . . (*He lies back, exhausted. Biff walks out.*)

LINDA (*calling after Biff*): Sleep well, darling!

HAPPY: I'm gonna get married, Mom. I wanted to tell you.

LINDA: Go to sleep, dear.

HAPPY (*going*): I just wanted to tell you.

WILLY: Keep up the good work. (*Happy exits.*) God . . . remember that Ebbets Field game? The championship of the city?

LINDA: Just rest. Should I sing to you?

WILLY: Yeah. Sing to me. (*Linda hums a soft lullaby.*) When that team came out — he was the tallest, remember?

LINDA: Oh, yes. And in gold.

Biff enters the darkened kitchen, takes a cigarette, and leaves the house. He comes downstage into a golden pool of light. He smokes, staring at the night.

WILLY: Like a young god. Hercules — something like that. And the sun, the sun all around him. Remember how he waved to me? Right up from the field, with the representatives of three colleges standing by? And the buyers I brought, and the cheers when he came out — Loman, Loman, Loman! God Almighty, he'll be great yet. A star like that, magnificent, can never really fade away!

The light on Willy is fading. The gas heater begins to glow through the kitchen wall, near the stairs, a blue flame beneath red coils.

LINDA (*timidly*): Willy dear, what has he got against you?

WILLY: I'm so tired. Don't talk any more.

Biff slowly returns to the kitchen. He stops, stares toward the heater.

LINDA: Will you ask Howard to let you work in New York?

WILLY: First thing in the morning. Everything'll be all right.

Biff reaches behind the heater and draws out a length of rubber tubing. He is horrified and turns his head toward Willy's room, still dimly lit, from which the strains of Linda's desperate but monotonous humming rise.

WILLY (*staring through the window into the moonlight*): Gee, look at the moon moving between the buildings!

Biff wraps the tubing around his hand and quickly goes up the stairs.

Curtain

ACT II

Music is heard, gay and bright. The curtain rises as the music fades away. Willy, in shirt sleeves, is sitting at the kitchen table, sipping coffee, his hat in his lap. Linda is filling his cup when she can.

WILLY: Wonderful coffee. Meal in itself.

LINDA: Can I make you some eggs?

WILLY: No. Take a breath.

LINDA: You look so rested, dear.

WILLY: I slept like a dead one. First time in months. Imagine, sleeping till ten on a Tuesday morning. Boys left nice and early, heh?

LINDA: They were out of here by eight o'clock.

WILLY: Good work!

LINDA: It was so thrilling to see them leaving together. I can't get over the shaving lotion in this house!

WILLY (*smiling*): Mmm —

LINDA: Biff was very changed this morning. His whole attitude seemed to be hopeful. He couldn't wait to get downtown to see Oliver.

WILLY: He's heading for a change. There's no question, there simply are certain men that take longer to get — solidified. How did he dress?

LINDA: His blue suit. He's so handsome in that suit. He could be a — anything in that suit!

Willy gets up from the table. Linda holds his jacket for him.

WILLY: There's no question, no question at all. Gee, on the way home tonight I'd like to buy some seeds.

LINDA (*laughing*): That'd be wonderful. But not enough sun gets back there. Nothing'll grow any more.

WILLY: You wait, kid, before it's all over we're gonna get a little place out in the country, and I'll raise some vegetables, a couple of chickens . . .

LINDA: You'll do it yet, dear.

Willy walks out of his jacket. Linda follows him.

WILLY: And they'll get married, and come for a weekend. I'd build a little guest house. 'Cause I got so many fine tools, all I'd need would be a little lumber and some peace of mind.

LINDA (*joyfully*): I sewed the lining . . .

WILLY: I could build two guest houses, so they'd both come. Did he decide how much he's going to ask Oliver for?

LINDA (*getting him into the jacket*): He didn't mention it, but I imagine ten or fifteen thousand. You going to talk to Howard today?

WILLY: Yeah. I'll put it to him straight and simple. He'll just have to take me off the road.

LINDA: And Willy, don't forget to ask for a little advance, because we've got the insurance premium. It's the grace period now.

WILLY: That's a hundred . . . ?

LINDA: A hundred and eight, sixty-eight. Because we're a little short again.

WILLY: Why are we short?

LINDA: Well, you had the motor job on the car . . .

WILLY: That goddam Studebaker!

LINDA: And you got one more payment on the refrigerator . . .

WILLY: But it just broke again!

LINDA: Well, it's old, dear.

WILLY: I told you we should've bought a well-advertised machine. Charley bought a General Electric and it's twenty years old and it's still good, that son-of-a-bitch.

LINDA: But, Willy—

WILLY: Whoever heard of a Hastings refrigerator? Once in my life I would like to own something outright before it's broken! I'm always in a race with the junkyard! I just finished paying for the car and it's on its last legs. The refrigerator consumes belts like a goddam maniac. They time those things. They time them so when you finally paid for them, they're used up.

LINDA (*buttoning up his jacket as he unbuttons it*): All told, about two hundred dollars would carry us, dear. But that includes the last payment on the mortgage. After this payment, Willy, the house belongs to us.

WILLY: It's twenty-five years!

LINDA: Biff was nine years old when we bought it.

WILLY: Well, that's a great thing. To weather a twenty-five year mortgage is—

LINDA: It's an accomplishment.

WILLY: All the cement, the lumber, the reconstruction I put in this house! There ain't a crack to be found in it any more.

LINDA: Well, it served its purpose.

WILLY: What purpose? Some stranger'll come along, move in, and that's that. If only Biff would take this house, and raise a family . . . (*He starts to go.*) Good-by, I'm late.

LINDA (*suddenly remembering*): Oh, I forgot! You're supposed to meet them for dinner.

WILLY: Me?

LINDA: At Frank's Chop House on Forty-eighth near Sixth Avenue.

WILLY: Is that so! How about you?

LINDA: No, just the three of you. They're gonna blow you to a big meal!

WILLY: Don't say! Who thought of that?

LINDA: Biff came to me this morning, Willy, and he said, "Tell Dad, we want to blow him to a big meal." Be there six o'clock. You and your two boys are going to have dinner.

WILLY: Gee whiz! That's really somethin'. I'm gonna knock Howard for a loop, kid. I'll get an advance, and I'll come home with a New York job. God-dammit, now I'm gonna do it!

LINDA: Oh, that's the spirit, Willy!

WILLY: I will never get behind a wheel the rest of my life!

LINDA: It's changing, Willy, I can feel it changing!

WILLY: Beyond a question. G'by, I'm late. (*He starts to go again.*)

LINDA (*calling after him as she runs to the kitchen table for a handkerchief*): You got your glasses?

WILLY (*feels for them, then comes back in*): Yeah, yeah, got my glasses.

LINDA (*giving him the handkerchief*): And a handkerchief.

WILLY: Yeah, handkerchief.

LINDA: And your saccharine?

WILLY: Yeah, my saccharine.

LINDA: Be careful on the subway stairs.

She kisses him, and a silk stocking is seen hanging from her hand. Willy notices it.

WILLY: Will you stop mending stockings? At least while I'm in the house. It gets me nervous. I can't tell you. Please.

Linda hides the stocking in her hand as she follows Willy across the forestage in front of the house.

LINDA: Remember, Frank's Chop House.

WILLY (*passing the apron*): Maybe beets would grow out there.

LINDA (*laughing*): But you tried so many times.

WILLY: Yeah. Well, don't work hard today. (*He disappears around the right corner of the house.*)

LINDA: Be careful!

As Willy vanishes, Linda waves to him. Suddenly the phone rings. She runs across the stage and into the kitchen and lifts it.

LINDA: Hello? Oh, Biff! I'm so glad you called, I just . . . Yes, sure, I just told him. Yes, he'll be there for dinner at six o'clock, I didn't forget. Listen, I was just dying to tell you. You know that little rubber pipe I told you about? That he connected to the gas heater? I finally decided to go down the cellar this morning and take it away and destroy it. But it's gone! Imagine? He took it away himself, it isn't there! (*She listens.*) When? Oh, then you took it. Oh — nothing, it's just that I'd hoped he'd taken it away himself. Oh, I'm not worried, darling, because this morning he left in such high spirits, it was like the old days! I'm not afraid any more. Did Mr. Oliver see you? . . . Well, you wait there then. And make a nice impression on him, darling. Just don't perspire too much before you see him. And have a nice time with Dad. He may have big news too! . . . That's right, a New York job. And be sweet to him tonight, dear. Be loving to him. Because he's only a little boat looking for a harbor. (*She is trembling with sorrow and joy.*) Oh, that's wonderful, Biff, you'll save his life. Thanks, darling. Just put your arm around him when he comes into the restaurant. Give him a smile. That's the boy . . . Good-by, dear . . . You got your comb? . . . That's fine. Good-by, Biff dear.

In the middle of her speech, Howard Wagner, thirty-six, wheels in a small typewriter table on which is a wire-recording machine and proceeds to plug it in. This is on the left forestage. Light slowly fades on Linda as it rises on Howard. Howard is intent on threading the machine and only glances over his shoulder as Willy appears.

WILLY: Pst! Pst!

HOWARD: Hello, Willy, come in.

WILLY: Like to have a little talk with you, Howard.

HOWARD: Sorry to keep you waiting. I'll be with you in a minute.

WILLY: What's that, Howard?

HOWARD: Didn't you ever see one of these? Wire recorder.

WILLY: Oh. Can we talk a minute?

HOWARD: Records things. Just got delivery yesterday. Been driving me crazy, the most terrific machine I ever saw in my life. I was up all night with it.

WILLY: What do you do with it?

HOWARD: I bought it for dictation, but you can do anything with it. Listen to this. I had it home last night. Listen to what I picked up. The first one is my daughter. Get this. (*He flicks the switch and "Roll Out the Barrel" is heard being whistled.*) Listen to that kid whistle.

WILLY: That is lifelike, isn't it?

HOWARD: Seven years old. Get that tone.

WILLY: Ts, ts. Like to ask a little favor if you . . .

The whistling breaks off, and the voice of Howard's daughter is heard.

HIS DAUGHTER: "Now you, Daddy."

HOWARD: She's crazy for me! (*Again the same song is whistled.*) That's me! Ha! (*He winks.*)

WILLY: You're very good!

The whistling breaks off again. The machine runs silent for a moment.

HOWARD: Sh! Get this now, this is my son.

HIS SON: "The capital of Alabama is Montgomery; the capital of Arizona is Phoenix; the capital of Arkansas is Little Rock; the capital of California is Sacramento . . ." (*and on, and on*).

HOWARD (*holding up five fingers*): Five years old, Willy!

WILLY: He'll make an announcer some day!

HIS SON (*continuing*): "The capital . . ."

HOWARD: Get that—alphabetical order! (*The machine breaks off suddenly.*) Wait a minute. The maid kicked the plug out.

WILLY: It certainly is a—

HOWARD: Sh, for God's sake!

HIS SON: "It's nine o'clock, Bulova watch time. So I have to go to sleep."

WILLY: That really is—

HOWARD: Wait a minute! The next is my wife.

They wait.

HOWARD'S VOICE: "Go on, say something." (*Pause.*) "Well, you gonna talk?"

HIS WIFE: "I can't think of anything."

HOWARD'S VOICE: "Well, talk—it's turning."

HIS WIFE (*shyly, beaten*): "Hello." (*Silence.*) "Oh, Howard, I can't talk into this . . ."

HOWARD (*snapping the machine off*): That was my wife.

WILLY: That is a wonderful machine. Can we—

HOWARD: I tell you, Willy, I'm gonna take my camera, and my bandsaw, and all my hobbies, and out they go. This is the most fascinating relaxation I ever found.

WILLY: I think I'll get one myself.

HOWARD: Sure, they're only a hundred and a half. You can't do without it. Supposing you wanna hear Jack Benny, see? But you can't be at home at that hour. So you tell the maid to turn the radio on when Jack Benny comes on, and this automatically goes on with the radio . . .

WILLY: And when you come home you . . .

HOWARD: You can come home twelve o'clock, one o'clock, any time you like, and you get yourself a Coke and sit yourself down, throw the switch, and there's Jack Benny's program in the middle of the night!

WILLY: I'm definitely going to get one. Because lots of time I'm on the road, and I think to myself, what I must be missing on the radio!

HOWARD: Don't you have a radio in the car?

WILLY: Well, yeah, but who ever thinks of turning it on?

HOWARD: Say, aren't you supposed to be in Boston?

WILLY: That's what I want to talk to you about, Howard. You got a minute? (*He draws a chair in from the wing.*)

HOWARD: What happened? What're you doing here?

WILLY: Well . . .

HOWARD: You didn't crack up again, did you?

WILLY: Oh, no. No . . .

HOWARD: Geez, you had me worried there for a minute. What's the trouble?

WILLY: Well, tell you the truth, Howard. I've come to the decision that I'd rather not travel any more.

HOWARD: Not travel! Well, what'll you do?

WILLY: Remember, Christmas time, when you had the party here? You said you'd try to think of some spot for me here in town.

HOWARD: With us?

WILLY: Well, sure.

HOWARD: Oh, yeah, yeah. I remember. Well, I couldn't think of anything for you, Willy.

WILLY: I tell ya, Howard. The kids are all grown up, y'know. I don't need much any more. If I could take home—well, sixty-five dollars a week, I could swing it.

HOWARD: Yeah, but Willy, see I—

WILLY: I tell ya why, Howard. Speaking frankly and between the two of us, y'know—I'm just a little tired.

HOWARD: Oh, I could understand that, Willy. But you're a road man, Willy, and we do a road business. We've only got a half-dozen salesmen on the floor here.

WILLY: God knows, Howard, I never asked a favor of any man. But I was with the firm when your father used to carry you in here in his arms.

HOWARD: I know that, Willy, but—

WILLY: Your father came to me the day you were born and asked me what I thought of the name of Howard, may he rest in peace.

HOWARD: I appreciate that, Willy, but there just is no spot here for you. If I had a spot I'd slam you right in, but I just don't have a single solitary spot.

He looks for his lighter. Willy has picked it up and gives it to him. Pause.

WILLY (*with increasing anger*): Howard, all I need to set my table is fifty dollars a week.

HOWARD: But where am I going to put you, kid?

WILLY: Look, it isn't a question of whether I can sell merchandise, is it?

HOWARD: No, but it's a business, kid, and everybody's gotta pull his own weight.

WILLY (*desperately*): Just let me tell you a story, Howard—

HOWARD: 'Cause you gotta admit, business is business.

WILLY (*angrily*): Business is definitely business, but just listen for a minute. You don't understand this. When I was a boy—eighteen, nineteen—I was already on the road. And there was a question in my mind as to whether selling had a future for me. Because in those days I had a yearning to go to Alaska. See, there were three gold strikes in one month in Alaska, and I felt like going out. Just for the ride, you might say.

HOWARD (*barely interested*): Don't say.

WILLY: Oh, yeah, my father lived many years in Alaska. He was an adventurous man. We've got quite a little streak of self-reliance in our family. I thought I'd go out with my older brother and try to locate him, and maybe settle in the North with the old man. And I was almost decided to go, when I met a salesman in the Parker House. His name was Dave Singleman. And he was eighty-four years old, and he'd drummed merchandise in thirty-one states. And old Dave, he'd go up to his room, y'understand, put on his green velvet slippers—I'll never forget—and pick up his phone and call the buyers, and without ever leaving his room, at the age of eighty-four, he made his living. And when I saw that, I realized that selling was the greatest career a man could want. 'Cause what could be more satisfying than to be able to go, at the age of eighty-four, into twenty or thirty different cities, and pick up a phone, and be remembered and loved and helped by so many different people? Do you know? when he died—and by the way he died the death of a salesman, in his green velvet slippers in the smoker of the New York, New Haven, and Hartford, going into Boston—when he died, hundreds of salesmen and buyers were at his funeral. Things were sad on a lotta trains for months after that. (*He stands up. Howard has not looked at him.*) In those days there was personality in it, Howard. There was respect, and comradeship, and gratitude in it. Today, it's all cut and dried, and there's no chance for bringing friendship to bear—or personality. You see what I mean? They don't know me any more.

HOWARD (*moving away, to the right*): That's just the thing, Willy.

WILLY: If I had forty dollars a week—that's all I'd need. Forty dollars, Howard.

HOWARD: Kid, I can't take blood from a stone, I—

WILLY (*desperation is on him now*): Howard, the year Al Smith° was nominated, your father came to me and—

HOWARD (*starting to go off*): I've got to see some people, kid.

WILLY (*stopping him*): I'm talking about your father! There were promises made across this desk! You mustn't tell me you've got people to see—I put thirty-four years into this firm, Howard, and now I can't pay my insurance! You can't eat the orange and throw the peel away—a man is not a

---

Al Smith: The Democratic candidate for president of the United States in 1928, Smith lost the election to Herbert Hoover.

piece of fruit! (*After a pause.*) Now pay attention. Your father—in 1928 I had a big year. I averaged a hundred and seventy dollars a week in commissions.

HOWARD (*impatiently*): Now, Willy, you never averaged—

WILLY (*banging his hand on the desk*): I averaged a hundred and seventy dollars a week in the year of 1928! And your father came to me—or rather, I was in the office here—it was right over this desk—and he put his hand on my shoulder—

HOWARD (*getting up*): You'll have to excuse me, Willy, I gotta see some people. Pull yourself together. (*Going out.*) I'll be back in a little while.

On Howard's exit, the light on his chair grows very bright and strange.

WILLY: Pull myself together! What the hell did I say to him? My God, I was yelling at him! How could I! (*Willy breaks off, staring at the light, which occupies the chair, animating it. He approaches this chair, standing across the desk from it.*) Frank, Frank, don't you remember what you told me that time? How you put your hand on my shoulder, and Frank . . . (*He leans on the desk and as he speaks the dead man's name he accidentally switches on the recorder, and instantly:*)

HOWARD'S SON: ". . . of New York is Albany. The capital of Ohio is Cincinnati, the capital of Rhode Island is . . ." (*The recitation continues.*)

WILLY (*leaping away with fright, shouting*): Ha! Howard! Howard! Howard!

HOWARD (*rushing in*): What happened?

WILLY (*pointing at the machine, which continues nasally, childishly, with the capital cities*): Shut it off! Shut it off!

HOWARD (*pulling the plug out*): Look, Willy . . .

WILLY (*pressing his hands to his eyes*): I gotta get myself some coffee. I'll get some coffee . . .

Willy starts to walk out. Howard stops him.

HOWARD (*rolling up the cord*): Willy, look . . .

WILLY: I'll go to Boston.

HOWARD: Willy, you can't go to Boston for us.

WILLY: Why can't I go?

HOWARD: I don't want you to represent us. I've been meaning to tell you for a long time now.

WILLY: Howard, are you firing me?

HOWARD: I think you need a good long rest, Willy.

WILLY: Howard—

HOWARD: And when you feel better, come back, and we'll see if we can work something out.

WILLY: But I gotta earn money, Howard. I'm in no position to—

HOWARD: Where are your sons? Why don't your sons give you a hand?

WILLY: They're working on a very big deal.

HOWARD: This is no time for false pride, Willy. You go to your sons and you tell them that you're tired. You've got two great boys, haven't you?

WILLY: Oh, no question, no question, but in the meantime . . .

HOWARD: Then that's that, heh?

WILLY: All right, I'll go to Boston tomorrow.

HOWARD: No, no.

WILLY: I can't throw myself on my sons. I'm not a cripple!

HOWARD: Look, kid, I'm busy this morning.

WILLY (*grasping Howard's arm*): Howard, you've got to let me go to Boston!

HOWARD (*hard, keeping himself under control*): I've got a line of people to see this morning. Sit down, take five minutes, and pull yourself together, and then go home, will ya? I need the office, Willy. (*He starts to go, turns, remembering the recorder, starts to push off the table holding the recorder.*) Oh, yeah. Whenever you can this week, stop by and drop off the samples. You'll feel better, Willy, and then come back and we'll talk. Pull yourself together, kid, there's people outside.

Howard exits, pushing the table off left. Willy stares into space, exhausted. Now the music is heard—Ben's music—first distantly, then closer, closer. As Willy speaks, Ben enters from the right. He carries valise and umbrella.

WILLY: Oh, Ben, how did you do it? What is the answer? Did you wind up the Alaska deal already?

BEN: Doesn't take much time if you know what you're doing. Just a short business trip. Boarding ship in an hour. Wanted to say good-by.

WILLY: Ben, I've got to talk to you.

BEN (*glancing at his watch*): Haven't the time, William.

WILLY (*crossing the apron to Ben*): Ben, nothing's working out. I don't know what to do.

BEN: Now, look here, William. I've bought timberland in Alaska and I need a man to look after things for me.

WILLY: God, timberland! Me and my boys in those grand outdoors!

BEN: You've a new continent at your doorstep, William. Get out of these cities, they're full of talk and time payments and courts of law. Screw on your fists and you can fight for a fortune up there.

WILLY: Yes, yes! Linda, Linda!

Linda enters as of old, with the wash.

LINDA: Oh, you're back?

BEN: I haven't much time.

WILLY: No, wait! Linda, he's got a proposition for me in Alaska.

LINDA: But you've got—(*To Ben.*) He's got a beautiful job here.

WILLY: But in Alaska, kid, I could—

LINDA: You're doing well enough, Willy!

BEN (*to Linda*): Enough for what, my dear?

LINDA (*frightened of Ben and angry at him*): Don't say those things to him! Enough to be happy right here, right now. (*To Willy, while Ben laughs.*) Why must everybody conquer the world? You're well liked, and the boys love you, and someday—(*to Ben*)—why, old man Wagner told him just the other day that if he keeps it up he'll be a member of the firm, didn't he, Willy?

WILLY: Sure, sure. I am building something with this firm, Ben, and if a man is building something he must be on the right track, mustn't he?

BEN: What are you building? Lay your hand on it. Where is it?

WILLY (*hesitantly*): That's true, Linda, there's nothing.

LINDA: Why? (*To Ben.*) There's a man eighty-four years old —

WILLY: That's right, Ben, that's right. When I look at that man I say, what is there to worry about?

BEN: Bah!

WILLY: It's true, Ben. All he has to do is go into any city, pick up the phone, and he's making his living and you know why?

BEN (*picking up his valise*): I've got to go.

WILLY (*holding Ben back*): Look at this boy!

Biff, in his high school sweater, enters carrying suitcase. Happy carries Biff's shoulder guards, gold helmet, and football pants.

WILLY: Without a penny to his name, three great universities are begging for him, and from there the sky's the limit, because it's not what you do, Ben. It's who you know and the smile on your face! It's contacts, Ben, contacts! The whole wealth of Alaska passes over the lunch table at the Commodore Hotel, and that's the wonder, the wonder of this country, that a man can end with diamonds here on the basis of being liked! (*He turns to Biff.*) And that's why when you get out on that field today it's important. Because thousands of people will be rooting for you and loving you. (*To Ben, who has again begun to leave.*) And Ben! when he walks into a business office his name will sound out like a bell and all the doors will open to him! I've seen it, Ben, I've seen it a thousand times! You can't feel it with your hand like timber, but it's there!

BEN: Good-by, William.

WILLY: Ben, am I right? Don't you think I'm right? I value your advice.

BEN: There's a new continent at your doorstep, William. You could walk out rich. Rich! (*He is gone.*)

WILLY: We'll do it here, Ben! You hear me? We're gonna do it here!

Young Bernard rushes in. The gay music of the Boys is heard.

BERNARD: Oh, gee, I was afraid you left already!

WILLY: Why? What time is it?

BERNARD: It's half-past one!

WILLY: Well, come on, everybody! Ebbets Field next stop! Where's the pennants? (*He rushes through the wall-line of the kitchen and out into the living-room.*)

LINDA (*to Biff*): Did you pack fresh underwear?

BIFF (*who has been limbering up*): I want to go!

BERNARD: Biff, I'm carrying your helmet, ain't I?

HAPPY: I'm carrying the helmet.

BERNARD: How am I going to get in the locker room?

LINDA: Let him carry the shoulder guards. (*She puts her coat and hat on in the kitchen.*)

BERNARD: Can I, Biff? 'Cause I told everybody I'm going to be in the locker room.

HAPPY: In Ebbets Field it's the clubhouse.

BERNARD: I meant the clubhouse. Biff!

HAPPY: Biff!

BIFF (*grandly, after a slight pause*): Let him carry the shoulder guards.

HAPPY (*as he gives Bernard the shoulder guards*): Stay close to us now.

Willy rushes in with the pennants.

WILLY (*handing them out*): Everybody wave when Biff comes out on the field.
     (*Happy and Bernard run off.*) You set now, boy?

The music has died away.

BIFF: Ready to go, Pop. Every muscle is ready.

WILLY (*at the edge of the apron*): You realize what this means?

BIFF: That's right, Pop.

WILLY (*feeling Biff's muscles*): You're comin' home this afternoon captain of the
     All-Scholastic Championship Team of the City of New York.

BIFF: I got it, Pop. And remember, pal, when I take off my helmet, that touch-
     down is for you.

WILLY: Let's go! (*He is starting out, with his arm around Biff, when Charley
     enters, as of old, in knickers.*) I got no room for you, Charley.

CHARLEY: Room? For what?

WILLY: In the car.

CHARLEY: You goin' for a ride? I wanted to shoot some casino.

WILLY (*furiously*): Casino! (*Incredulously.*) Don't you realize what today is?

LINDA: Oh, he knows, Willy. He's just kidding you.

WILLY: That's nothing to kid about!

CHARLEY: No, Linda, what's goin' on?

LINDA: He's playing in Ebbets Field.

CHARLEY: Baseball in this weather?

WILLY: Don't talk to him. Come on, come on! (*He is pushing them out.*)

CHARLEY: Wait a minute, didn't you hear the news?

WILLY: What?

CHARLEY: Don't you listen to the radio? Ebbets Field just blew up.

WILLY: You go to hell! (*Charley laughs. Pushing them out.*) Come on, come on!
     We're late.

CHARLEY (*as they go*): Knock a homer, Biff, knock a homer!

WILLY (*the last to leave, turning to Charley*): I don't think that was funny,
     Charley. This is the greatest day of his life.

CHARLEY: Willy, when are you going to grow up?

WILLY: Yeah, heh? When this game is over, Charley, you'll be laughing out of
     the other side of your face. They'll be calling him another Red Grange.
     Twenty-five thousand a year.

CHARLEY (*kidding*): Is that so?

WILLY: Yeah, that's so.

CHARLEY: Well, then, I'm sorry, Willy. But tell me something.

WILLY: What?

CHARLEY: Who is Red Grange?

WILLY: Put up your hands. Goddam you, put up your hands!

Charley, chuckling, shakes his head and walks away, around the left corner of the stage. Willy follows him. The music rises to a mocking frenzy.

WILLY: Who the hell do you think you are, better than everybody else? You don't know everything, you big, ignorant, stupid . . . Put up your hands!

Light rises, on the right side of the forestage, on a small table in the reception room of Charley's office. Traffic sounds are heard. Bernard, now mature, sits whistling to himself. A pair of tennis rackets and an overnight bag are on the floor beside him.

WILLY (*offstage*): What are you walking away for? Don't walk away! If you're going to say something say it to my face! I know you laugh at me behind my back. You'll laugh out of the other side of your goddam face after this game. Touchdown! Touchdown! Eighty thousand people! Touchdown! Right between the goal posts.

Bernard is a quiet, earnest, but self-assured young man. Willy's voice is coming from right upstage now. Bernard lowers his feet off the table and listens. Jenny, his father's secretary, enters.

JENNY (*distressed*): Say, Bernard, will you go out in the hall?

BERNARD: What is that noise? Who is it?

JENNY: Mr. Loman. He just got off the elevator.

BERNARD (*getting up*): Who's he arguing with?

JENNY: Nobody. There's nobody with him. I can't deal with him any more, and your father gets all upset everytime he comes. I've got a lot of typing to do, and your father's waiting to sign it. Will you see him?

WILLY (*entering*): Touchdown! Touch—(*He sees Jenny.*) Jenny, Jenny, good to see you. How're ya? Workin'? Or still honest?

JENNY: Fine. How've you been feeling?

WILLY: Not much any more, Jenny. Ha, ha! (*He is surprised to see the rackets.*)

BERNARD: Hello, Uncle Willy.

WILLY (*almost shocked*): Bernard! Well, look who's here! (*He comes quickly, guiltily, to Bernard and warmly shakes his hand.*)

BERNARD: How are you? Good to see you.

WILLY: What are you doing here?

BERNARD: Oh, just stopped by to see Pop. Get off my feet till my train leaves. I'm going to Washington in a few minutes.

WILLY: Is he in?

BERNARD: Yes, he's in his office with the accountant. Sit down.

WILLY (*sitting down*): What're you going to do in Washington?

BERNARD: Oh, just a case I've got there, Willy.

WILLY: That so? (*Indicating the rackets.*) You going to play tennis there?

BERNARD: I'm staying with a friend who's got a court.

WILLY: Don't say. His own tennis court. Must be fine people, I bet.

BERNARD: They are, very nice. Dad tells me Biff's in town.

WILLY (*with a big smile*): Yeah, Biff's in. Working on a very big deal, Bernard.

BERNARD: What's Biff doing?

WILLY: Well, he's been doing very big things in the West. But he decided to establish himself here. Very big. We're having dinner. Did I hear your wife had a boy?

BERNARD: That's right. Our second.

WILLY: Two boys! What do you know!

BERNARD: What kind of a deal has Biff got?

WILLY: Well, Bill Oliver — very big sporting-goods man — he wants Biff very badly. Called him in from the West. Long distance, carte blanche, special deliveries. Your friends have their own private tennis court?

BERNARD: You still with the old firm, Willy?

WILLY (*after a pause*): I'm — I'm overjoyed to see how you made the grade, Bernard, overjoyed. It's an encouraging thing to see a young man really — really — Looks very good for Biff — very — (*He breaks off, then.*) Bernard — (*He is so full of emotion, he breaks off again.*)

BERNARD: What is it, Willy?

WILLY (*small and alone*): What — what's the secret?

BERNARD: What secret?

WILLY: How — how did you? Why didn't he ever catch on?

BERNARD: I wouldn't know that, Willy.

WILLY (*confidentially, desperately*): You were his friend, his boyhood friend. There's something I don't understand about it. His life ended after that Ebbets Field game. From the age of seventeen nothing good ever happened to him.

BERNARD: He never trained himself for anything.

WILLY: But he did, he did. After high school he took so many correspondence courses. Radio mechanics; television; God knows what, and never made the slightest mark.

BERNARD (*taking off his glasses*): Willy, do you want to talk candidly?

WILLY (*rising, faces Bernard*): I regard you as a very brilliant man, Bernard. I value your advice.

BERNARD: Oh, the hell with the advice, Willy. I couldn't advise you. There's just one thing I've always wanted to ask you. When he was supposed to graduate, and the math teacher flunked him —

WILLY: Oh, that son-of-a-bitch ruined his life.

BERNARD: Yeah, but, Willy, all he had to do was go to summer school and make up that subject.

WILLY: That's right, that's right.

BERNARD: Did you tell him not to go to summer school?

WILLY: Me? I begged him to go. I ordered him to go!

BERNARD: Then why wouldn't he go?

WILLY: Why? Why! Bernard, that question has been trailing me like a ghost for the last fifteen years. He flunked the subject, and laid down and died like a hammer hit him!

BERNARD: Take it easy, kid.

WILLY: Let me talk to you — I got nobody to talk to. Bernard, Bernard, was it my fault? Y'see? It keeps going around in my mind, maybe I did something to him. I got nothing to give him.

BERNARD: Don't take it so hard.

WILLY: Why did he lay down? What is the story there? You were his friend!

BERNARD: Willy, I remember, it was June, and our grades came out. And he'd flunked math.

WILLY: That son-of-a-bitch!

BERNARD: No, it wasn't right then. Biff just got very angry, I remember, and he was ready to enroll in summer school.

WILLY (*surprised*): He was?

BERNARD: He wasn't beaten by it at all. But then, Willy, he disappeared from the block for almost a month. And I got the idea that he'd gone up to New England to see you. Did he have a talk with you then?

Willy stares in silence.

BERNARD: Willy?

WILLY (*with a strong edge of resentment in his voice*): Yeah, he came to Boston. What about it?

BERNARD: Well, just that when he came back — I'll never forget this, it always mystifies me. Because I'd thought so well of Biff, even though he'd always taken advantage of me. I loved him, Willy, y'know? And he came back after that month and took his sneakers — remember those sneakers with "University of Virginia" printed on them? He was so proud of those, wore them every day. And he took them down in the cellar, and burned them up in the furnace. We had a fist fight. It lasted at least half an hour. Just the two of us, punching each other down the cellar, and crying right through it. I've often thought of how strange it was that I knew he'd given up his life. What happened in Boston, Willy?

Willy looks at him as at an intruder.

BERNARD: I just bring it up because you asked me.

WILLY (*angrily*): Nothing. What do you mean, "What happened?" What's that got to do with anything?

BERNARD: Well, don't get sore.

WILLY: What are you trying to do, blame it on me? If a boy lays down is that my fault?

BERNARD: Now, Willy, don't get —

WILLY: Well, don't — don't talk to me that way! What does that mean, "What happened?"

Charley enters. He is in his vest, and he carries a bottle of bourbon.

CHARLEY: Hey, you're going to miss that train. (*He waves the bottle.*)

BERNARD: Yeah, I'm going. (*He takes the bottle.*) Thanks, Pop. (*He picks up his rackets and bag.*) Good-by, Willy, and don't worry about it. You know. "If at first you don't succeed . . ."

WILLY: Yes, I believe in that.

BERNARD: But sometimes, Willy, it's better for a man just to walk away.

WILLY: Walk away?

BERNARD: That's right.

WILLY: But if you can't walk away?

BERNARD (*after a slight pause*): I guess that's when it's tough. (*Extending his hand.*) Good-by, Willy.

WILLY (*shaking Bernard's hand*): Good-by, boy.

CHARLEY (*an arm on Bernard's shoulder*): How do you like this kid? Gonna argue a case in front of the Supreme Court.

BERNARD (*protesting*): Pop!

WILLY (*genuinely shocked, pained, and happy*): No! The Supreme Court!

BERNARD: I gotta run. 'By, Dad!

CHARLEY: Knock 'em dead, Bernard!

Bernard goes off.

WILLY (*as Charley takes out his wallet*): The Supreme Court! And he didn't even mention it!

CHARLEY (*counting out money on the desk*): He don't have to—he's gonna do it.

WILLY: And you never told him what to do, did you? You never took any interest in him.

CHARLEY: My salvation is that I never took any interest in any thing. There's some money—fifty dollars. I got an accountant inside.

WILLY: Charley, look . . . (*With difficulty.*) I got my insurance to pay. If you can manage it—I need a hundred and ten dollars.

Charley doesn't reply for a moment; merely stops moving.

WILLY: I'd draw it from my bank but Linda would know, and I . . .

CHARLEY: Sit down, Willy.

WILLY (*moving toward the chair*): I'm keeping an account of everything, remember. I'll pay every penny back. (*He sits.*)

CHARLEY: Now listen to me, Willy.

WILLY: I want you to know I appreciate . . .

CHARLEY (*sitting down on the table*): Willy, what're you doin'? What the hell is goin' on in your head?

WILLY: Why? I'm simply . . .

CHARLEY: I offered you a job. You can make fifty dollars a week. And I won't send you on the road.

WILLY: I've got a job.

CHARLEY: Without pay? What kind of a job is a job without pay? (*He rises.*) Now, look, kid, enough is enough. I'm no genius but I know when I'm being insulted.

WILLY: Insulted!

CHARLEY: Why don't you want to work for me?

WILLY: What's the matter with you? I've got a job.

CHARLEY: Then what're you walkin' in here every week for?

WILLY (*getting up*): Well, if you don't want me to walk in here—

CHARLEY: I am offering you a job.

WILLY: I don't want your goddam job!

CHARLEY: When the hell are you going to grow up?

WILLY (*furiously*): You big ignoramus, if you say that to me again I'll rap you one! I don't care how big you are! (*He's ready to fight.*)

Pause.

CHARLEY (*kindly, going to him*): How much do you need, Willy?

WILLY: Charley, I'm strapped. I'm strapped. I don't know what to do. I was just fired.

CHARLEY: Howard fired you?

WILLY: That snotnose. Imagine that? I named him. I named him Howard.

CHARLEY: Willy, when're you gonna realize that them things don't mean anything? You named him Howard, but you can't sell that. The only thing you got in this world is what you can sell. And the funny thing is that you're a salesman, and you don't know that.

WILLY: I've always tried to think otherwise, I guess. I always felt that if a man was impressive, and well liked, that nothing—

CHARLEY: Why must everybody like you? Who liked J. P. Morgan? Was he impressive? In a Turkish bath he'd look like a butcher. But with his pockets on he was very well liked. Now listen, Willy, I know you don't like me, and nobody can say I'm in love with you, but I'll give you a job because—just for the hell of it, put it that way. Now what do you say?

WILLY: I—I just can't work for you, Charley.

CHARLEY: What're you, jealous of me?

WILLY: I can't work for you, that's all, don't ask me why.

CHARLEY (*angered, takes out more bills*): You been jealous of me all your life, you damned fool! Here, pay your insurance. (*He puts the money in Willy's hand.*)

WILLY: I'm keeping strict accounts.

CHARLEY: I've got some work to do. Take care of yourself. And pay your insurance.

WILLY (*moving to the right*): Funny, y'know? After all the highways, and the trains, and the appointments, and the years, you end up worth more dead than alive.

CHARLEY: Willy, nobody's worth nothin' dead. (*After a slight pause.*) Did you hear what I said?

Willy stands still, dreaming.

CHARLEY: Willy!

WILLY: Apologize to Bernard for me when you see him. I didn't mean to argue with him. He's a fine boy. They're all fine boys, and they'll end up big— all of them. Someday they'll all play tennis together. Wish me luck, Charley. He saw Bill Oliver today.

CHARLEY: Good luck.

WILLY (*on the verge of tears*): Charley, you're the only friend I got. Isn't that a remarkable thing? (*He goes out.*)

CHARLEY: Jesus!

Charley stares after him a moment and follows. All light blacks out. Suddenly raucous music is heard, and a red glow rises behind the screen at right. Stanley, a young waiter, appears, carrying a table, followed by Happy, who is carrying two chairs.

STANLEY (*putting the table down*): That's all right, Mr. Loman, I can handle it myself. (*He turns and takes the chairs from Happy and places them at the table.*)

HAPPY (*glancing around*): Oh, this is better.

STANLEY: Sure, in the front there you're in the middle of all kinds a noise. Whenever you got a party, Mr. Loman, you just tell me and I'll put you back here. Y'know, there's a lotta people they don't like it private, because when they go out they like to see a lotta action around them because they're sick and tired to stay in the house by theirself. But I know you, you ain't from Hackensack. You know what I mean?

HAPPY (*sitting down*): So how's it coming, Stanley?

STANLEY: Ah, it's a dog's life. I only wish during the war they'd a took me in the Army. I coulda been dead by now.

HAPPY: My brother's back, Stanley.

STANLEY: Oh, he come back, heh? From the Far West.

HAPPY: Yeah, big cattle man, my brother, so treat him right. And my father's coming too.

STANLEY: Oh, your father too!

HAPPY: You got a couple of nice lobsters?

STANLEY: Hundred per cent, big.

HAPPY: I want them with the claws.

STANLEY: Don't worry, I don't give you no mice. (*Happy laughs.*) How about some wine? It'll put a head on the meal.

HAPPY: No. You remember, Stanley, that recipe I brought you from overseas? With the champagne in it?

STANLEY: Oh, yeah, sure. I still got it tacked up yet in the kitchen. But that'll have to cost a buck apiece anyways.

HAPPY: That's all right.

STANLEY: What'd you, hit a number or somethin'?

HAPPY: No, it's a little celebration. My brother is—I think he pulled off a big deal today. I think we're going into business together.

STANLEY: Great! That's the best for you. Because a family business, you know what I mean?—that's the best.

HAPPY: That's what I think.

STANLEY: 'Cause what's the difference? Somebody steals? It's in the family. Know what I mean? (*Sotto voce.°*) Like this bartender here. The boss is goin' crazy what kinda leak he's got in the cash register. You put it in but it don't come out.

HAPPY (*raising his head*): Sh!

STANLEY: What?

HAPPY: You notice I wasn't lookin' right or left, was I?

STANLEY: No.

HAPPY: And my eyes are closed.

STANLEY: So what's the—?

HAPPY: Strudel's comin'.

Sotto voce: Softly, "under the breath" (Italian).

STANLEY (*catching on, looks around*): Ah, no, there's no—

He breaks off as a furred, lavishly dressed girl enters and sits at the next table. Both follow her with their eyes.

STANLEY: Geez, how'd ya know?

HAPPY: I got radar or something. (*Staring directly at her profile.*) Oooooooo . . . Stanley.

STANLEY: I think that's for you, Mr. Loman.

HAPPY: Look at that mouth. Oh, God. And the binoculars.

STANLEY: Geez, you got a life, Mr. Loman.

HAPPY: Wait on her.

STANLEY (*going to the girl's table*): Would you like a menu, ma'am?

GIRL: I'm expecting someone, but I'd like a—

HAPPY: Why don't you bring her—excuse me, miss, do you mind? I sell champagne, and I'd like you to try my brand. Bring her a champagne, Stanley.

GIRL: That's awfully nice of you.

HAPPY: Don't mention it. It's all company money. (*He laughs.*)

GIRL: That's a charming product to be selling, isn't it?

HAPPY: Oh, gets to be like everything else. Selling is selling, y'know.

GIRL: I suppose.

HAPPY: You don't happen to sell, do you?

GIRL: No, I don't sell.

HAPPY: Would you object to a compliment from a stranger? You ought to be on a magazine cover.

GIRL (*looking at him a little archly*): I have been.

Stanley comes in with a glass of champagne.

HAPPY: What'd I say before, Stanley? You see? She's a cover girl.

STANLEY: Oh, I could see, I could see.

HAPPY (*to the Girl*): What magazine?

GIRL: Oh, a lot of them. (*She takes the drink.*) Thank you.

HAPPY: You know what they say in France, don't you? "Champagne is the drink of the complexion"—Hya, Biff!

Biff has entered and sits with Happy.

BIFF: Hello, kid. Sorry I'm late.

HAPPY: I just got here. Uh, Miss—?

GIRL: Forsythe.

HAPPY: Miss Forsythe, this is my brother.

BIFF: Is Dad here?

HAPPY: His name is Biff. You might've heard of him. Great football player.

GIRL: Really? What team?

HAPPY: Are you familiar with football?

GIRL: No, I'm afraid I'm not.

HAPPY: Biff is quarterback with the New York Giants.

GIRL: Well, that is nice, isn't it? (*She drinks.*)

HAPPY: Good health.

GIRL: I'm happy to meet you.

HAPPY: That's my name. Hap. It's really Harold, but at West Point they called me Happy.

GIRL (*now really impressed*): Oh, I see. How do you do? (*She turns her profile.*)

BIFF: Isn't Dad coming?

HAPPY: You want her?

BIFF: Oh, I could never make that.

HAPPY: I remember the time that idea would never come into your head. Where's the old confidence, Biff?

BIFF: I just saw Oliver—

HAPPY: Wait a minute. I've got to see that old confidence again. Do you want her? She's on call.

BIFF: Oh, no. (*He turns to look at the Girl.*)

HAPPY: I'm telling you. Watch this. (*Turning to the Girl.*) Honey? (*She turns to him.*) Are you busy?

GIRL: Well, I am . . . but I could make a phone call.

HAPPY: Do that, will you, honey? And see if you can get a friend. We'll be here for a while. Biff is one of the greatest football players in the country.

GIRL (*standing up*): Well, I'm certainly happy to meet you.

HAPPY: Come back soon.

GIRL: I'll try.

HAPPY: Don't try, honey, try hard.

The Girl exits. Stanley follows, shaking his head in bewildered admiration.

HAPPY: Isn't that a shame now? A beautiful girl like that? That's why I can't get married. There's not a good woman in a thousand. New York is loaded with them, kid!

BIFF: Hap, look—

HAPPY: I told you she was on call!

BIFF (*strangely unnerved*): Cut it out, will ya? I want to say something to you.

HAPPY: Did you see Oliver?

BIFF: I saw him all right. Now look, I want to tell Dad a couple of things and I want you to help me.

HAPPY: What? Is he going to back you?

BIFF: Are you crazy? You're out of your goddam head, you know that?

HAPPY: Why? What happened?

BIFF (*breathlessly*): I did a terrible thing today, Hap. It's been the strangest day I ever went through. I'm all numb, I swear.

HAPPY: You mean he wouldn't see you?

BIFF: Well, I waited six hours for him, see? All day. Kept sending my name in. Even tried to date his secretary so she'd get me to him, but no soap.

HAPPY: Because you're not showin' the old confidence, Biff. He remembered you, didn't he?

BIFF (*stopping Happy with a gesture*): Finally, about five o'clock, he comes out. Didn't remember who I was or anything. I felt like such an idiot, Hap.

HAPPY: Did you tell him my Florida idea?

BIFF: He walked away. I saw him for one minute. I got so mad I could've torn the walls down! How the hell did I ever get the idea I was a salesman there? I even believed myself that I'd been a salesman for him! And then he gave me one look and — I realized what a ridiculous lie my whole life has been! We've been talking in a dream for fifteen years. I was a shipping clerk.

HAPPY: What'd you do?

BIFF (*with great tension and wonder*): Well, he left, see. And the secretary went out. I was all alone in the waiting-room. I don't know what came over me, Hap. The next thing I know I'm in his office — paneled walls, everything. I can't explain it. I — Hap, I took his fountain pen.

HAPPY: Geez, did he catch you?

BIFF: I ran out. I ran down all eleven flights. I ran and ran and ran.

HAPPY: That was an awful dumb — what'd you do that for?

BIFF (*agonized*): I don't know, I just — wanted to take something, I don't know. You gotta help me, Hap, I'm gonna tell Pop.

HAPPY: You crazy? What for?

BIFF: Hap, he's got to understand that I'm not the man somebody lends that kind of money to. He thinks I've been spiting him all these years and it's eating him up.

HAPPY: That's just it. You tell him something nice.

BIFF: I can't.

HAPPY: Say you got a lunch date with Oliver tomorrow.

BIFF: So what do I do tomorrow?

HAPPY: You leave the house tomorrow and come back at night and say Oliver is thinking it over. And he thinks it over for a couple of weeks, and gradually it fades away and nobody's the worse.

BIFF: But it'll go on forever!

HAPPY: Dad is never so happy as when he's looking forward to something!

Willy enters.

HAPPY: Hello, scout!

WILLY: Gee, I haven't been here in years!

Stanley has followed Willy in and sets a chair for him. Stanley starts off but Happy stops him.

HAPPY: Stanley!

Stanley stands by, waiting for an order.

BIFF (*going to Willy with guilt, as to an invalid*): Sit down, Pop. You want a drink?

WILLY: Sure, I don't mind.

BIFF: Let's get a load on.

WILLY: You look worried.

BIFF: N-no. (*To Stanley.*) Scotch all around. Make it doubles.

STANLEY: Doubles, right. (*He goes.*)

WILLY: You had a couple already, didn't you?

BIFF: Just a couple, yeah.

WILLY: Well, what happened, boy? (*Nodding affirmatively, with a smile.*) Everything go all right?

BIFF (*takes a breath, then reaches out and grasps Willy's hand.*) Pal . . . (*He is smiling bravely, and Willy is smiling too.*) I had an experience today.

HAPPY: Terrific, Pop.

WILLY: That so? What happened?

BIFF (*high, slightly alcoholic, above the earth*): I'm going to tell you everything
from first to last. It's been a strange day. (*Silence. He looks around, composes himself as best he can, but his breath keeps breaking the rhythm of his
voice.*) I had to wait quite a while for him, and —

WILLY: Oliver.

BIFF: Yeah, Oliver. All day, as a matter of cold fact. And a lot of — instances —
facts, Pop, facts about my life came back to me. Who was it, Pop? Who
ever said I was a salesman with Oliver?

WILLY: Well, you were.

BIFF: No, Dad, I was a shipping clerk.

WILLY: But you were practically —

BIFF (*with determination*): Dad, I don't know who said it first, but I was never a
salesman for Bill Oliver.

WILLY: What're you talking about?

BIFF: Let's hold on to the facts tonight, Pop. We're not going to get anywhere
bullin' around. I was a shipping clerk.

WILLY (*angrily*): All right, now listen to me —

BIFF: Why don't you let me finish?

WILLY: I'm not interested in stories about the past or any crap of that kind
because the woods are burning, boys, you understand? There's a big
blaze going on all around. I was fired today.

BIFF (*shocked*): How could you be?

WILLY: I was fired, and I'm looking for a little good news to tell your mother,
because the woman has waited and the woman has suffered. The gist of it
is that I haven't got a story left in my head, Biff. So don't give me a lecture
about facts and aspects. I am not interested. Now what've you got to say
to me?

Stanley enters with three drinks. They wait until he leaves.

WILLY: Did you see Oliver?

BIFF: Jesus, Dad!

WILLY: You mean you didn't go up there?

HAPPY: Sure he went up there.

BIFF: I did. I — saw him. How could they fire you?

WILLY (*on the edge of his chair*): What kind of a welcome did he give you?

BIFF: He won't even let you work on commission?

WILLY: I'm out! (*Driving.*) So tell me, he gave you a warm welcome?

HAPPY: Sure, Pop, sure!

BIFF (*driven*): Well, it was kind of —

WILLY: I was wondering if he'd remember you. (*To Happy.*) Imagine, man
doesn't see him for ten, twelve years and gives him that kind of a welcome!

HAPPY: Damn right!

BIFF (*trying to return to the offensive*): Pop, look —

WILLY: You know why he remembered you, don't you? Because you impressed
him in those days.

BIFF: Let's talk quietly and get this down to the facts, huh?

WILLY (*as though Biff had been interrupting*): Well, what happened? It's great news, Biff. Did he take you into his office or'd you talk in the waiting-room?

BIFF: Well, he came in, see, and—

WILLY (*with a big smile*): What'd he say? Betcha he threw his arm around you.

BIFF: Well, he kinda—

WILLY: He's a fine man. (*To Happy.*) Very hard man to see, y'know.

HAPPY (*agreeing*): Oh, I know.

WILLY (*to Biff*): Is that where you had the drinks?

BIFF: Yeah, he gave me a couple of—no, no!

HAPPY (*cutting in*): He told him my Florida idea.

WILLY: Don't interrupt. (*To Biff.*) How'd he react to the Florida idea?

BIFF: Dad, will you give me a minute to explain?

WILLY: I've been waiting for you to explain since I sat down here! What happened? He took you into his office and what?

BIFF: Well—I talked. And—and he listened, see.

WILLY: Famous for the way he listens, y'know. What was his answer?

BIFF: His answer was—(*He breaks off, suddenly angry.*) Dad, you're not letting me tell you what I want to tell you!

WILLY (*accusing, angered*): You didn't see him, did you?

BIFF: I did see him!

WILLY: What'd you insult him or something? You insulted him, didn't you?

BIFF: Listen, will you let me out of it, will you just let me out of it!

HAPPY: What the hell!

WILLY: Tell me what happened!

BIFF (*to Happy*): I can't talk to him!

A single trumpet note jars the ear. The light of green leaves stains the house, which holds the air of night and a dream. Young Bernard enters and knocks on the door of the house.

YOUNG BERNARD (*frantically*): Mrs. Loman, Mrs. Loman!

HAPPY: Tell him what happened!

BIFF (*to Happy*): Shut up and leave me alone!

WILLY: No, no! You had to go and flunk math!

BIFF: What math? What're you talking about?

YOUNG BERNARD: Mrs. Loman, Mrs. Loman!

Linda appears in the house, as of old.

WILLY (*wildly*): Math, math, math!

BIFF: Take it easy, Pop!

YOUNG BERNARD: Mrs. Loman!

WILLY (*furiously*): If you hadn't flunked you'd've been set by now!

BIFF: Now, look, I'm gonna tell you what happened, and you're going to listen to me.

YOUNG BERNARD: Mrs. Loman!

BIFF: I waited six hours—

HAPPY: What the hell are you saying?

BIFF: I kept sending in my name but he wouldn't see me. So finally he . . . (*He continues unheard as light fades low on the restaurant.*)

YOUNG BERNARD: Biff flunked math!

LINDA: No!

YOUNG BERNARD: Birnbaum flunked him! They won't graduate him!

LINDA: But they have to. He's gotta go to the university. Where is he? Biff! Biff!

YOUNG BERNARD: No, he left. He went to Grand Central.

LINDA: Grand— You mean he went to Boston!

YOUNG BERNARD: Is Uncle Willy in Boston?

LINDA: Oh, maybe Willy can talk to the teacher. Oh, the poor, poor boy!

Light on house area snaps out.

BIFF (*at the table, now audible, holding up a gold fountain pen*): . . . so I'm washed up with Oliver, you understand? Are you listening to me?

WILLY (*at a loss*): Yeah, sure. If you hadn't flunked—

BIFF: Flunked what? What're you talking about?

WILLY: Don't blame everything on me! I didn't flunk math—you did! What pen?

HAPPY: That was awful dumb, Biff, a pen like that is worth—

WILLY (*seeing the pen for the first time*): You took Oliver's pen?

BIFF (*weakening*): Dad, I just explained it to you.

WILLY: You stole Bill Oliver's fountain pen!

BIFF: I didn't exactly steal it! That's just what I've been explaining to you!

HAPPY: He had it in his hand and just then Oliver walked in, so he got nervous and stuck it in his pocket!

WILLY: My God, Biff!

BIFF: I never intended to do it, Dad!

OPERATOR'S VOICE: Standish Arms, good evening!

WILLY (*shouting*): I'm not in my room!

BIFF (*frightened*): Dad, what's the matter? (*He and Happy stand up.*)

OPERATOR: Ringing Mr. Loman for you!

WILLY: I'm not there, stop it!

BIFF (*horrified, gets down on one knee before Willy*): Dad, I'll make good, I'll make good. (*Willy tries to get to his feet. Biff holds him down.*) Sit down now.

WILLY: No, you're no good, you're no good for anything.

BIFF: I am, Dad, I'll find something else, you understand? Now don't worry about anything. (*He holds up Willy's face.*) Talk to me, Dad.

OPERATOR: Mr. Loman does not answer. Shall I page him?

WILLY (*attempting to stand, as though to rush and silence the Operator*): No, no, no!

HAPPY: He'll strike something, Pop.

WILLY: No, no . . .

BIFF (*desperately, standing over Willy*): Pop, listen! Listen to me! I'm telling you something good. Oliver talked to his partner about the Florida idea. You listening? He—he talked to his partner, and he came to me . . . I'm going to be all right, you hear? Dad, listen to me, he said it was just a question of the amount!

WILLY: Then you . . . got it?

HAPPY: He's gonna be terrific, Pop!

WILLY (*trying to stand*): Then you got it, haven't you? You got it! You got it!

BIFF (*agonized, holds Willy down*): No, no. Look, Pop. I'm supposed to have lunch with them tomorrow. I'm just telling you this so you'll know that I can still make an impression, Pop. And I'll make good somewhere, but I can't go tomorrow, see?

WILLY: Why not? You simply—

BIFF: But the pen, Pop!

WILLY: You give it to him and tell him it was an oversight!

HAPPY: Sure, have lunch tomorrow!

BIFF: I can't say that—

WILLY: You were doing a crossword puzzle and accidentally used his pen!

BIFF: Listen, kid, I took those balls years ago, now I walk in with his fountain pen? That clinches it, don't you see? I can't face him like that! I'll try elsewhere.

PAGE'S VOICE: Paging Mr. Loman!

WILLY: Don't you want to be anything?

BIFF: Pop, how can I go back?

WILLY: You don't want to be anything, is that what's behind it?

BIFF (*now angry at Willy for not crediting his sympathy*): Don't take it that way! You think it was easy walking into that office after what I'd done to him? A team of horses couldn't have dragged me back to Bill Oliver!

WILLY: Then why'd you go?

BIFF: Why did I go? Why did I go! Look at you! Look at what's become of you!

Off left, The Woman laughs.

WILLY: Biff, you're going to lunch tomorrow, or—

BIFF: I can't go. I've got no appointment!

HAPPY: Biff, for . . . !

WILLY: Are you spiting me?

BIFF: Don't take it that way! Goddammit!

WILLY (*strikes Biff and falters away from the table*): You rotten little louse! Are you spiting me?

THE WOMAN: Someone's at the door, Willy!

BIFF: I'm no good, can't you see what I am?

HAPPY (*separating them*): Hey, you're in a restaurant! Now cut it out, both of you! (*The girls enter.*) Hello, girls, sit down.

The Woman laughs, off left.

MISS FORSYTHE: I guess we might as well. This is Letta.

THE WOMAN: Willy, are you going to wake up?

BIFF (*ignoring Willy*): How're ya, miss, sit down. What do you drink?

MISS FORSYTHE: Letta might not be able to stay long.

LETTA: I gotta get up very early tomorrow. I got jury duty. I'm so excited! Were you fellows ever on a jury?

BIFF: No, but I been in front of them! (*The girls laugh.*) This is my father.

LETTA: Isn't he cute? Sit down with us, Pop.

HAPPY: Sit him down, Biff!

BIFF (*going to him*): Come on, slugger, drink us under the table. To hell with it! Come on, sit down, pal.

On Biff's last insistence, Willy is about to sit.

THE WOMAN (*now urgently*): Willy, are you going to answer the door!

The Woman's call pulls Willy back. He starts right, befuddled.

BIFF: Hey, where are you going?

WILLY: Open the door.

BIFF: The door?

WILLY: The washroom . . . the door . . . where's the door?

BIFF (*leading Willy to the left*): Just go straight down.

Willy moves left.

THE WOMAN: Willy, Willy, are you going to get up, get up, get up, get up?

Willy exits left.

LETTA: I think it's sweet you bring your daddy along.

MISS FORSYTHE: Oh, he isn't really your father!

BIFF (*at left, turning to her resentfully*): Miss Forsythe, you've just seen a prince walk by. A fine, troubled prince. A hard-working, unappreciated prince. A pal, you understand? A good companion. Always for his boys.

LETTA: That's so sweet.

HAPPY: Well, girls, what's the program? We're wasting time. Come on, Biff. Gather round. Where would you like to go?

BIFF: Why don't you do something for him?

HAPPY: Me!

BIFF: Don't you give a damn for him, Hap?

HAPPY: What're you talking about? I'm the one who—

BIFF: I sense it, you don't give a good goddamn about him. (*He takes the rolled-up hose from his pocket and puts it on the table in front of Happy.*) Look what I found in the cellar, for Christ's sake. How can you bear to let it go on?

HAPPY: Me? Who goes away? Who runs off and—

BIFF: Yeah, but he doesn't mean anything to you. You could help him—I can't! Don't you understand what I'm talking about? He's going to kill himself, don't you know that?

HAPPY: Don't I know it! Me!

BIFF: Hap, help him! Jesus . . . help him . . . Help me, help me, I can't bear to look at his face! (*Ready to weep, he hurries out, up right.*)

HAPPY (*starting after him*): Where are you going?

MISS FORSYTHE: What's he so mad about?

HAPPY: Come on, girls, we'll catch up with him.

MISS FORSYTHE (*as Happy pushes her out*): Say, I don't like that temper of his!

HAPPY: He's just a little overstrung, he'll be all right!

WILLY (*off left, as The Woman laughs*): Don't answer! Don't answer!

LETTA: Don't you want to tell your father—

HAPPY: No, that's not my father. He's just a guy. Come on, we'll catch Biff, and, honey, we're going to paint this town! Stanley, where's the check! Hey, Stanley!

They exit. Stanley looks toward left.

STANLEY (*calling to Happy indignantly*): Mr. Loman! Mr. Loman!

Stanley picks up a chair and follows them off. Knocking is heard off left. The Woman enters, laughing. Willy follows her. She is in a black slip; he is buttoning his shirt. Raw, sensuous music accompanies their speech.

WILLY: Will you stop laughing? Will you stop?

THE WOMAN: Aren't you going to answer the door? He'll wake the whole hotel.

WILLY: I'm not expecting anybody.

THE WOMAN: Whyn't you have another drink, honey, and stop being so damn self-centered?

WILLY: I'm so lonely.

THE WOMAN: You know you ruined me, Willy? From now on, whenever you come to the office, I'll see that you go right through to the buyers. No waiting at my desk any more, Willy. You ruined me.

WILLY: That's nice of you to say that.

THE WOMAN: Gee, you are self-centered! Why so sad? You are the saddest, self-centeredest soul I ever did see-saw. (*She laughs. He kisses her.*) Come on inside, drummer boy. It's silly to be dressing in the middle of the night. (*As knocking is heard.*) Aren't you going to answer the door?

WILLY: They're knocking on the wrong door.

THE WOMAN: But I felt the knocking. And he heard us talking in here. Maybe the hotel's on fire!

WILLY (*his terror rising*): It's a mistake.

THE WOMAN: Then tell him to go away!

WILLY: There's nobody there.

THE WOMAN: It's getting on my nerves, Willy. There's somebody standing out there and it's getting on my nerves!

WILLY (*pushing her away from him*): All right, stay in the bathroom here, and don't come out. I think there's a law in Massachusetts about it, so don't come out. It may be that new room clerk. He looked very mean. So don't come out. It's a mistake, there's no fire.

The knocking is heard again. He takes a few steps away from her, and she vanishes into the wing. The light follows him, and now he is facing Young Biff, who carries a suitcase. Biff steps toward him. The music is gone.

BIFF: Why didn't you answer?

WILLY: Biff! What are you doing in Boston?

BIFF: Why didn't you answer? I've been knocking for five minutes, I called you on the phone—

WILLY: I just heard you. I was in the bathroom and had the door shut. Did anything happen home?

BIFF: Dad—I let you down.

WILLY: What do you mean?

BIFF: Dad . . .

WILLY: Biffo, what's this about? (*Putting his arm around Biff.*) Come on, let's go downstairs and get you a malted.

BIFF: Dad, I flunked math.

WILLY: Not for the term?

BIFF: The term. I haven't got enough credits to graduate.

WILLY: You mean to say Bernard wouldn't give you the answers?

BIFF: He did, he tried, but I only got a sixty-one.

WILLY: And they wouldn't give you four points?

BIFF: Birnbaum refused absolutely. I begged him, Pop, but he won't give me those points. You gotta talk to him before they close the school. Because if he saw the kind of man you are, and you just talked to him in your way, I'm sure he'd come through for me. The class came right before practice, see, and I didn't go enough. Would you talk to him? He'd like you, Pop. You know the way you could talk.

WILLY: You're on. We'll drive right back.

BIFF: Oh, Dad, good work! I'm sure he'll change it for you!

WILLY: Go downstairs and tell the clerk I'm checkin' out. Go right down.

BIFF: Yes, sir! See, the reason he hates me, Pop—one day he was late for class so I got up at the blackboard and imitated him. I crossed my eyes and talked with a lithp.

WILLY (*laughing*): You did? The kids like it?

BIFF: They nearly died laughing!

WILLY: Yeah? What'd you do?

BIFF: The thquare root of thixthy twee is . . . (*Willy bursts out laughing; Biff joins him.*) And in the middle of it he walked in!

Willy laughs and The Woman joins in offstage.

WILLY (*without hesitation*): Hurry downstairs and—

BIFF: Somebody in there?

WILLY: No, that was next door.

The Woman laughs offstage.

BIFF: Somebody got in your bathroom!

WILLY: No, it's the next room, there's a party—

THE WOMAN (*enters, laughing. She lisps this*): Can I come in? There's something in the bathtub, Willy, and it's moving!

Willy looks at Biff, who is staring open-mouthed and horrified at The Woman.

WILLY: Ah—you better go back to your room. They must be finished painting by now. They're painting her room so I let her take a shower here. Go back, go back . . . (*He pushes her.*)

THE WOMAN (*resisting*): But I've got to get dressed, Willy, I can't—

WILLY: Get out of here! Go back, go back . . . (*Suddenly striving for the ordinary*): This is Miss Francis, Biff, she's a buyer. They're painting her room. Go back, Miss Francis, go back . . .

THE WOMAN: But my clothes, I can't go out naked in the hall!

WILLY (*pushing her offstage*): Get outa here! Go back, go back!

Biff slowly sits down on his suitcase as the argument continues offstage.

THE WOMAN: Where's my stockings? You promised me stockings, Willy!

WILLY: I have no stockings here!

THE WOMAN: You had two boxes of size nine sheers for me, and I want them!

WILLY: Here, for God's sake, will you get outa here!

THE WOMAN (*enters holding a box of stockings*): I just hope there's nobody in the hall. That's all I hope. (*To Biff.*) Are you football or baseball?

BIFF: Football.

THE WOMAN (*angry, humiliated*): That's me too. G'night. (*She snatches her clothes from Willy, and walks out.*)

WILLY (*after a pause*): Well, better get going. I want to get to the school first thing in the morning. Get my suits out of the closet. I'll get my valise. (*Biff doesn't move.*) What's the matter? (*Biff remains motionless, tears falling.*) She's a buyer. Buys for J. H. Simmons. She lives down the hall — they're painting. You don't imagine — (*He breaks off. After a pause.*) Now listen, pal, she's just a buyer. She sees merchandise in her room and they have to keep it looking just so . . . (*Pause. Assuming command.*) All right, get my suits. (*Biff doesn't move.*) Now stop crying and do as I say. I gave you an order. Biff, I gave you an order! Is that what you do when I give you an order? How dare you cry! (*Putting his arm around Biff.*) Now look, Biff, when you grow up you'll understand about these things. You mustn't — you mustn't overemphasize a thing like this. I'll see Birnbaum first thing in the morning.

BIFF: Never mind.

WILLY (*getting down beside Biff*): Never mind! He's going to give you those points. I'll see to it.

BIFF: He wouldn't listen to you.

WILLY: He certainly will listen to me. You need those points for the U. of Virginia.

BIFF: I'm not going there.

WILLY: Heh? If I can't get him to change that mark you'll make it up in summer school. You've got all summer to —

BIFF (*his weeping breaking from him*): Dad . . .

WILLY (*infected by it*): Oh, my boy . . .

BIFF: Dad . . .

WILLY: She's nothing to me, Biff. I was lonely, I was terribly lonely.

BIFF: You — you gave her Mama's stockings! (*His tears break through and he rises to go.*)

WILLY (*grabbing for Biff*): I gave you an order!

BIFF: Don't touch me, you — liar!

WILLY: Apologize for that!

BIFF: You fake! You phony little fake! You fake! (*Overcome, he turns quickly and weeping fully goes out with his suitcase. Willy is left on the floor on his knees.*)

WILLY: I gave you an order! Biff, come back here or I'll beat you! Come back here! I'll whip you!

Stanley comes quickly in from the right and stands in front of Willy.

WILLY (*shouts at Stanley*): I gave you an order . . .

STANLEY: Hey, let's pick it up, pick it up, Mr. Loman. (*He helps Willy to his feet.*) Your boys left with the chippies. They said they'll see you home.

A second waiter watches some distance away.

WILLY: But we were supposed to have dinner together.

Music is heard, Willy's theme.

STANLEY: Can you make it?

WILLY: I'll—sure, I can make it. (*Suddenly concerned about his clothes.*) Do I— I look all right?

STANLEY: Sure, you look all right. (*He flicks a speck off Willy's lapel.*)

WILLY: Here—here's a dollar.

STANLEY: Oh, your son paid me. It's all right.

WILLY (*putting it in Stanley's hand*): No, take it. You're a good boy.

STANLEY: Oh, no, you don't have to . . .

WILLY: Here—here's some more, I don't need it any more. (*After a slight pause.*) Tell me—is there a seed store in the neighborhood?

STANLEY: Seeds? You mean like to plant?

As Willy turns, Stanley slips the money back into his jacket pocket.

WILLY: Yes. Carrots, peas . . .

STANLEY: Well, there's hardware stores on Sixth Avenue, but it may be too late now.

WILLY (*anxiously*): Oh, I'd better hurry. I've got to get some seeds. (*He starts off to the right.*) I've got to get some seeds, right away. Nothing's planted. I don't have a thing in the ground.

Willy hurries out as the light goes down. Stanley moves over to the right after him, watches him off. The other waiter has been staring at Willy.

STANLEY (*to the waiter*): Well, whatta you looking at?

The waiter picks up the chairs and moves off right. Stanley takes the table and follows him. The light fades on this area. There is a long pause, the sound of the flute coming over. The light gradually rises on the kitchen, which is empty. Happy appears at the door of the house, followed by Biff. Happy is carrying a large bunch of long-stemmed roses. He enters the kitchen, looks around for Linda. Not seeing her, he turns to Biff, who is just outside the house door, and makes a gesture with his hands, indicating "Not here, I guess." He looks into the living-room and freezes. Inside, Linda, unseen, is seated, Willy's coat on her lap. She rises ominously and quietly and moves toward Happy, who backs up into the kitchen, afraid.

HAPPY: Hey, what're you doing up? (*Linda says nothing but moves toward him implacably.*) Where's Pop? (*He keeps backing to the right, and now Linda is in full view in the doorway to the living-room.*) Is he sleeping?

LINDA: Where were you?

HAPPY (*trying to laugh it off*): We met two girls, Mom, very fine types. Here, we brought you some flowers. (*Offering them to her.*) Put them in your room, Ma.

She knocks them to the floor at Biff's feet. He has now come inside and closed the door behind him. She stares at Biff, silent.

HAPPY: Now what'd you do that for? Mom, I want you to have some flowers—

LINDA (*cutting Happy off, violently to Biff*): Don't you care whether he lives or dies?

HAPPY (*going to the stairs*): Come upstairs, Biff.

BIFF (*with a flare of disgust, to Happy*): Go away from me! (*To Linda.*) What do you mean, lives or dies? Nobody's dying around here, pal.

LINDA: Get out of my sight! Get out of here!

BIFF: I wanna see the boss.

LINDA: You're not going near him!

BIFF: Where is he? (*He moves into the living-room and Linda follows.*)

LINDA (*shouting after Biff*): You invite him for dinner. He looks forward to it all day — (*Biff appears in his parents' bedroom, looks around, and exits.*) — and then you desert him there. There's no stranger you'd do that to!

HAPPY: Why? He had a swell time with us. Listen, when I — (*Linda comes back into the kitchen*) — desert him I hope I don't outlive the day!

LINDA: Get out of here!

HAPPY: Now look, Mom . . .

LINDA: Did you have to go to women tonight? You and your lousy rotten whores!

Biff re-enters the kitchen.

HAPPY: Mom, all we did was follow Biff around trying to cheer him up! (*To Biff.*) Boy, what a night you gave me!

LINDA: Get out of here, both of you, and don't come back! I don't want you tormenting him any more. Go on now, get your things together! (*To Biff.*) You can sleep in his apartment. (*She starts to pick up the flowers and stops herself.*) Pick up this stuff, I'm not your maid any more. Pick it up, you bum, you!

Happy turns his back to her in refusal. Biff slowly moves over and gets down on his knees, picking up the flowers.

LINDA: You're a pair of animals! Not one, not another living soul would have had the cruelty to walk out on that man in a restaurant!

BIFF (*not looking at her*): Is that what he said?

LINDA: He didn't have to say anything. He was so humiliated he nearly limped when he came in.

HAPPY: But, Mom, he had a great time with us —

BIFF (*cutting him off violently*): Shut up!

Without another word, Happy goes upstairs.

LINDA: You! You didn't even go in to see if he was all right!

BIFF (*still on the floor in front of Linda, the flowers in his hand; with self-loathing*): No. Didn't. Didn't do a damned thing. How do you like that, heh? Left him babbling in a toilet.

LINDA: You louse. You . . .

BIFF: Now you hit it on the nose! (*He gets up, throws the flowers in the wastebasket.*) The scum of the earth, and you're looking at him!

LINDA: Get out of here!

BIFF: I gotta talk to the boss, Mom. Where is he?

LINDA: You're not going near him. Get out of this house!

BIFF (*with absolute assurance, determination*): No. We're gonna have an abrupt conversation, him and me.

LINDA: You're not talking to him!

Hammering is heard from outside the house, off right. Biff turns toward the noise.

LINDA (*suddenly pleading*): Will you please leave him alone?

BIFF: What's he doing out there?

LINDA: He's planting the garden!

BIFF (*quietly*): Now? Oh, my God!

Biff moves outside, Linda following. The light dies down on them and comes up on the center of the apron as Willy walks into it. He is carrying a flashlight, a hoe, and handful of seed packets. He raps the top of the hoe sharply to fix it firmly, and then moves to the left, measuring off the distance with his foot. He holds the flashlight to look at the seed packets, reading off the instructions. He is in the blue of night.

WILLY: Carrots . . . quarter-inch apart. Rows . . . one-foot rows. (*He measures it off.*) One foot. (*He puts down a package and measures off.*) Beets. (*He puts down another package and measures again.*) Lettuce. (*He reads the package, puts it down.*) One foot—(*He breaks off as Ben appears at the right and moves slowly down to him.*) What a proposition, ts, ts. Terrific, terrific. 'Cause she's suffered, Ben, the woman has suffered. You understand me? A man can't go out the way he came in, Ben, a man has got to add up to something. You can't, you can't—(*Ben moves toward him as though to interrupt.*) You gotta consider, now. Don't answer so quick. Remember, it's a guaranteed twenty-thousand-dollar proposition. Now look, Ben, I want you to go through the ins and outs of this thing with me. I've got nobody to talk to, Ben, and the woman has suffered, you hear me?

BEN (*standing still, considering*): What's the proposition?

WILLY: It's twenty thousand dollars on the barrelhead. Guaranteed, gilt-edged, you understand?

BEN: You don't want to make a fool of yourself. They might not honor the policy.

WILLY: How can they dare refuse? Didn't I work like a coolie to meet every premium on the nose? And now they don't pay off? Impossible!

BEN: It's called a cowardly thing, William.

WILLY: Why? Does it take more guts to stand here the rest of my life ringing up a zero?

BEN (*yielding*): That's a point, William. (*He moves, thinking, turns.*) And twenty thousand—that *is* something one can feel with the hand, it is there.

WILLY (*now assured, with rising power*): Oh, Ben, that's the whole beauty of it! I see it like a diamond, shining in the dark, hard and rough, that I can pick up and touch in my hand. Not like—like an appointment! This would not be another damned-fool appointment, Ben, and it changes all the aspects. Because he thinks I'm nothing, see, and so he spites me. But the funeral—(*Straightening up.*) Ben, that funeral will be massive! They'll come from Maine, Massachusetts, Vermont, New Hampshire! All the old-timers with the strange license plates—that boy will be thunderstruck, Ben, because he never realized—I am known! Rhode Island,

New York, New Jersey — I am known, Ben, and he'll see it with his eyes once and for all. He'll see what I am, Ben! He's in for a shock, that boy!

BEN (*coming to the edge of the garden*): He'll call you a coward.

WILLY (*suddenly fearful*): No, that would be terrible.

BEN: Yes. And a damned fool.

WILLY: No, no, he mustn't, I won't have that! (*He is broken and desperate.*)

BEN: He'll hate you William.

The gay music of the Boys is heard.

WILLY: Oh, Ben, how do we get back to all the great times? Used to be so full of light, and comradeship, the sleigh-riding in winter, and the ruddiness on his cheeks. And always some kind of good news coming up, always something nice coming up ahead. And never even let me carry the valises in the house, and simonizing, simonizing that little red car! Why, why can't I give him something and not have him hate me?

BEN: Let me think about it. (*He glances at his watch.*) I still have a little time. Remarkable proposition, but you've got to be sure you're not making a fool of yourself.

Ben drifts off upstage and goes out of sight. Biff comes down from the left.

WILLY (*suddenly conscious of Biff, turns and looks up at him, then begins picking up the packages of seeds in confusion*): Where the hell is that seed? (*Indignantly.*) You can't see nothing out here! They boxed in the whole goddamn neighborhood!

BIFF: There are people all around here. Don't you realize that?

WILLY: I'm busy. Don't bother me.

BIFF (*taking the hoe from Willy*): I'm saying good-by to you, Pop. (*Willy looks at him, silent, unable to move.*) I'm not coming back any more.

WILLY: You're not going to see Oliver tomorrow?

BIFF: I've got no appointment, Dad.

WILLY: He put his arm around you, and you've got no appointment?

BIFF: Pop, get this now, will you? Everytime I've left it's been a fight that sent me out of here. Today I realized something about myself and I tried to explain it to you and I — I think I'm just not smart enough to make any sense out of it for you. To hell with whose fault it is or anything like that. (*He takes Willy's arm.*) Let's just wrap it up, heh? Come on in, we'll tell Mom. (*He gently tries to pull Willy to left.*)

WILLY (*frozen, immobile, with guilt in his voice*): No, I don't want to see her.

BIFF: Come on! (*He pulls again, and Willy tries to pull away.*)

WILLY (*highly nervous*): No, no, I don't want to see her.

BIFF (*tries to look into Willy's face, as if to find the answer there*): Why don't you want to see her?

WILLY (*more harshly now*): Don't bother me, will you?

BIFF: What do you mean, you don't want to see her? You don't want them calling you yellow, do you? This isn't your fault; it's me, I'm a bum. Now come inside! (*Willy strains to get away.*) Did you hear what I said to you?

Willy pulls away and quickly goes by himself into the house. Biff follows.

LINDA (*to Willy*): Did you plant, dear?

BIFF (*at the door, to Linda*): All right, we had it out. I'm going and I'm not writing any more.

LINDA (*going to Willy in the kitchen*): I think that's the best way, dear. 'Cause there's no use drawing it out, you'll just never get along.

Willy doesn't respond.

BIFF: People ask where I am and what I'm doing, you don't know, and you don't care. That way it'll be off your mind and you can start brightening up again. All right? That clears it, doesn't it? (*Willy is silent, and Biff goes to him.*) You gonna wish me luck, scout? (*He extends his hand.*) What do you say?

LINDA: Shake his hand, Willy.

WILLY (*turning to her, seething with hurt*): There's no necessity to mention the pen at all, y'know.

BIFF (*gently*): I've got no appointment, Dad.

WILLY (*erupting fiercely*): He put his arm around . . . ?

BIFF: Dad, you're never going to see what I am, so what's the use of arguing? If I strike oil I'll send you a check. Meantime forget I'm alive.

WILLY (*to Linda*): Spite, see?

BIFF: Shake hands, Dad.

WILLY: Not my hand.

BIFF: I was hoping not to go this way.

WILLY: Well, this is the way you're going. Good-by.

Biff looks at him a moment, then turns sharply and goes to the stairs.

WILLY (*stops him with*): May you rot in hell if you leave this house!

BIFF (*turning*): Exactly what is it that you want from me?

WILLY: I want you to know, on the train, in the mountains, in the valleys, wherever you go, that you cut down your life for spite!

BIFF: No, no.

WILLY: Spite, spite, is the word of your undoing! And when you're down and out, remember what did it. When you're rotting somewhere beside the railroad tracks, remember, and don't you dare blame it on me!

BIFF: I'm not blaming it on you!

WILLY: I won't take the rap for this, you hear?

Happy comes down the stairs and stands on the bottom step, watching.

BIFF: That's just what I'm telling you!

WILLY (*sinking into a chair at the table, with full accusation*): You're trying to put a knife in me — don't think I don't know what you're doing!

BIFF: All right, phony! Then let's lay it on the line. (*He whips the rubber tube out of his pocket and puts it on the table.*)

HAPPY: You crazy —

LINDA: Biff! (*She moves to grab the hose, but Biff holds it down with his hand.*)

BIFF: Leave it there! Don't move it!

WILLY (*not looking at it*): What is that?

BIFF: You know goddam well what that is.

WILLY (*caged, wanting to escape*): I never saw that.

BIFF: You saw it. The mice didn't bring it into the cellar! What is this supposed to do, make a hero out of you? This supposed to make me sorry for you?

WILLY: Never heard of it.

BIFF: There'll be no pity for you, you hear it? No pity!

WILLY (*to Linda*): You hear the spite!

BIFF: No, you're going to hear the truth — what you are and what I am!

LINDA: Stop it!

WILLY: Spite!

HAPPY (*coming down toward Biff*): You cut it now!

BIFF (*to Happy*): The man don't know who we are! The man is gonna know! (*To Willy.*) We never told the truth for ten minutes in this house!

HAPPY: We always told the truth!

BIFF (*turning on him*): You big blow, are you the assistant buyer? You're one of the two assistants to the assistant, aren't you?

HAPPY: Well, I'm practically —

BIFF: You're practically full of it! We all are! And I'm through with it. (*To Willy.*) Now hear this, Willy, this is me.

WILLY: I know you!

BIFF: You know why I had no address for three months? I stole a suit in Kansas City and I was in jail. (*To Linda, who is sobbing.*) Stop crying. I'm through with it.

Linda turns away from them, her hands covering her face.

WILLY: I suppose that's my fault!

BIFF: I stole myself out of every good job since high school!

WILLY: And whose fault is that?

BIFF: And I never got anywhere because you blew me so full of hot air I could never stand taking orders from anybody! That's whose fault it is!

WILLY: I hear that!

LINDA: Don't, Biff!

BIFF: It's goddam time you heard that! I had to be boss big shot in two weeks, and I'm through with it!

WILLY: Then hang yourself! For spite, hang yourself!

BIFF: No! Nobody's hanging himself, Willy! I ran down eleven flights with a pen in my hand today. And suddenly I stopped, you hear me? And in the middle of that office building, do you hear this? I stopped in the middle of that building and I saw — the sky. I saw the things that I love in this world. The work and the food and time to sit and smoke. And I looked at the pen and said to myself, what the hell am I grabbing this for? Why am I trying to become what I don't want to be? What am I doing in an office, making a contemptuous, begging fool of myself, when all I want is out there, waiting for me the minute I say I know who I am! Why can't I say that, Willy? (*He tries to make Willy face him, but Willy pulls away and moves to the left.*)

WILLY (*with hatred, threateningly*): The door of your life is wide open!

BIFF: Pop! I'm a dime a dozen, and so are you!

WILLY (*turning on him now in an uncontrolled outburst*): I am not a dime a dozen! I am Willy Loman, and you are Biff Loman!

Biff starts for Willy, but is blocked by Happy. In his fury, Biff seems on the verge of attacking his father.

BIFF: I am not a leader of men, Willy, and neither are you. You were never anything but a hard-working drummer who landed in the ash can like all the rest of them! I'm one dollar an hour, Willy! I tried seven states and couldn't raise it. A buck an hour! Do you gather my meaning? I'm not bringing home any prizes any more, and you're going to stop waiting for me to bring them home!

WILLY (*directly to Biff*): You vengeful, spiteful mutt!

Biff breaks from Happy. Willy, in fright, starts up the stairs. Biff grabs him.

BIFF (*at the peak of his fury*): Pop, I'm nothing! I'm nothing, Pop. Can't you understand that? There's no spite in it any more. I'm just what I am, that's all.

Biff's fury has spent itself, and he breaks down, sobbing, holding on to Willy, who dumbly fumbles for Biff's face.

WILLY (*astonished*): What're you doing? What're you doing? (*To Linda.*) Why is he crying?

BIFF (*crying, broken*): Will you let me go, for Christ's sake? Will you take that phony dream and burn it before something happens? (*Struggling to contain himself, he pulls away and moves to the stairs.*) I'll go in the morning. Put him—put him to bed. (*Exhausted, Biff moves up the stairs to his room.*)

WILLY (*after a long pause, astonished, elevated*): Isn't that—isn't that remarkable? Biff—he likes me!

LINDA: He loves you, Willy!

HAPPY (*deeply moved*): Always did, Pop.

WILLY: Oh, Biff! (*Staring wildly.*) He cried! Cried to me. (*He is choking with his love, and now cries out his promise.*) That boy—that boy is going to be magnificent!

Ben appears in the light just outside the kitchen.

BEN: Yes, outstanding, with twenty thousand behind him.

LINDA (*sensing the racing of his mind, fearfully, carefully*): Now come to bed, Willy. It's all settled now.

WILLY (*finding it difficult not to rush out of the house*): Yes, we'll sleep. Come on. Go to sleep, Hap.

BEN: And it does take a great kind of a man to crack the jungle.

In accents of dread, Ben's idyllic music starts up.

HAPPY (*his arm around Linda*): I'm getting married, Pop, don't forget it. I'm changing everything. I'm gonna run that department before the year is up. You'll see, Mom. (*He kisses her.*)

BEN: The jungle is dark but full of diamonds, Willy.

Willy turns, moves, listening to Ben.

LINDA: Be good. You're both good boys, just act that way, that's all.

HAPPY: 'Night, Pop. (*He goes upstairs.*)

LINDA (*to Willy*): Come, dear.

BEN (*with greater force*): One must go in to fetch a diamond out.

WILLY (*to Linda, as he moves slowly along the edge of the kitchen, toward the door*): I just want to get settled down, Linda. Let me sit alone for a little.

LINDA (*almost uttering her fear*): I want you upstairs.

WILLY (*taking her in his arms*): In a few minutes, Linda. I couldn't sleep right now. Go on, you look awful tired. (*He kisses her.*)

BEN: Not like an appointment at all. A diamond is rough and hard to the touch.

WILLY: Go on now. I'll be right up.

LINDA: I think this is the only way, Willy.

WILLY: Sure, it's the best thing.

BEN: Best thing!

WILLY: The only way. Everything is gonna be — go on, kid, get to bed. You look so tired.

LINDA: Come right up.

WILLY: Two minutes.

Linda goes into the living-room, then reappears in her bedroom. Willy moves just outside the kitchen door.

WILLY: Loves me. (*Wonderingly.*) Always loved me. Isn't that a remarkable thing? Ben, he'll worship me for it!

BEN (*with promise*): It's dark there, but full of diamonds.

WILLY: Can you imagine that magnificence with twenty thousand dollars in his pocket?

LINDA (*calling from her room*): Willy! Come up!

WILLY (*calling into the kitchen*): Yes! Yes. Coming! It's very smart, you realize that, don't you, sweetheart? Even Ben sees it. I gotta go, baby. 'By! 'By! (*Going over to Ben, almost dancing.*) Imagine? When the mail comes he'll be ahead of Bernard again!

BEN: A perfect proposition all around.

WILLY: Did you see how he cried to me? Oh, if I could kiss him, Ben!

BEN: Time, William, time!

WILLY: Oh, Ben, I always knew one way or another we were gonna make it, Biff and I!

BEN (*looking at his watch*): The boat. We'll be late. (*He moves slowly off into the darkness.*)

WILLY (*elegiacally, turning to the house*): Now when you kick off, boy, I want a seventy-yard boot, and get right down the field under the ball, and when you hit, hit low and hit hard, because it's important, boy. (*He swings around and faces the audience.*) There's all kinds of important people in the stands, and the first thing you know . . . (*Suddenly realizing he is alone.*) Ben! Ben, where do I . . . ? (*He makes a sudden movement of search.*) Ben, how do I . . . ?

LINDA (*calling*): Willy, you coming up?

WILLY (*uttering a gasp of fear, whirling about as if to quiet her*): Sh! (*He turns around as if to find his way; sounds, faces, voices, seem to be swarming in upon him and he flicks at them, crying.)* Sh! Sh! *(Suddenly music, faint and high, stops him. It rises in intensity, almost to an unbearable scream. He goes up and down on his toes, and rushes off around the house.)* Shhh!

LINDA: Willy?

There is no answer. Linda waits. Biff gets up off his bed. He is still in his clothes. Happy sits up. Biff stands listening.

LINDA *(with real fear)*: Willy, answer me! Willy!

There is the sound of a car starting and moving away at full speed.

LINDA: No!

BIFF *(rushing down the stairs)*: Pop!

As the car speeds off, the music crashes down in a frenzy of sound, which becomes the soft pulsation of a single cello string. Biff slowly returns to his bedroom. He and Happy gravely don their jackets. Linda slowly walks out of her room. The music has developed into a dead march. The leaves of day are appearing over everything. Charley and Bernard, somberly dressed, appear and knock on the kitchen door. Biff and Happy slowly descend the stairs to the kitchen as Charley and Bernard enter. All stop a moment when Linda, in clothes of mourning, bearing a little bunch of roses, comes through the draped doorway into the kitchen. She goes to Charley and takes his arm. Now all move toward the audience, through the wall-line of the kitchen. At the limit of the apron, Linda lays down the flowers, kneels, and sits back on her heels. All stare down at the grave.

REQUIEM

CHARLEY: It's getting dark, Linda.

Linda doesn't react. She stares at the grave.

BIFF: How about it, Mom? Better get some rest, heh? They'll be closing the gate soon.

Linda makes no move. Pause.

HAPPY *(deeply angered)*: He had no right to do that. There was no necessity for it. We would've helped him.

CHARLEY *(grunting)*: Hmmm.

BIFF: Come along, Mom.

LINDA: Why didn't anybody come?

CHARLEY: It was a very nice funeral.

LINDA: But where are all the people he knew? Maybe they blame him.

CHARLEY: Naa. It's a rough world, Linda. They wouldn't blame him.

LINDA: I can't understand it. At this time especially. First time in thirty-five years we were just about free and clear. He only needed a little salary. He was even finished with the dentist.

CHARLEY: No man only needs a little salary.

LINDA: I can't understand it.

BIFF: There were a lot of nice days. When he'd come home from a trip; or on Sundays, making the stoop; finishing the cellar; putting on the new porch; when he built the extra bathroom; and put up the garage. You know something, Charley, there's more of him in that front stoop than in all the sales he ever made.

CHARLEY: Yeah. He was a happy man with a batch of cement.

LINDA: He was so wonderful with his hands.

BIFF: He had the wrong dreams. All, all, wrong.

HAPPY (*almost ready to fight Biff*): Don't say that!

BIFF: He never knew who he was.

CHARLEY (*stopping Happy's movement and reply. To Biff*): Nobody dast blame this man. You don't understand: Willy was a salesman. And for a salesman, there is no rock bottom to the life. He don't put a bolt to a nut, he don't tell you the law or give you medicine. He's a man way out there in the blue, riding on a smile and a shoeshine. And when they start not smiling back—that's an earthquake. And then you get yourself a couple of spots on your hat, and you're finished. Nobody dast blame this man. A salesman is got to dream, boy. It comes with the territory.

BIFF: Charley, the man didn't know who he was.

HAPPY (*infuriated*): Don't say that!

BIFF: Why don't you come with me, Happy?

HAPPY: I'm not licked that easily. I'm staying right in this city, and I'm gonna beat this racket! (*He looks at Biff, his chin set.*) The Loman Brothers!

BIFF: I know who I am, kid.

HAPPY: All right, boy. I'm gonna show you and everybody else that Willy Loman did not die in vain. He had a good dream. It's the only dream you can have—to come out number-one man. He fought it out here, and this is where I'm gonna win it for him.

BIFF (*with a hopeless glance at Happy, bends toward his mother*): Let's go, Mom.

LINDA: I'll be with you in a minute. Go on, Charley. (*He hesitates.*) I want to, just for a minute. I never had a chance to say good-by.

Charley moves away, followed by Happy. Biff remains a slight distance up and left of Linda. She sits there, summoning herself. The flute begins, not far away, playing behind her speech.

LINDA: Forgive me, dear. I can't cry. I don't know what it is, but I can't cry. I don't understand it. Why did you ever do that? Help me, Willy, I can't cry. It seems to me that you're just on another trip. I keep expecting you. Willy, dear, I can't cry. Why did you do it? I search and search and I search, and I can't understand it, Willy. I made the last payment on the house today. Today, dear. And there'll be nobody home. (*A sob rises in her throat.*) We're free and clear. (*Sobbing more fully, released.*) We're free. (*Biff comes slowly toward her.*) We're free . . . We're free . . .

Biff lifts her to her feet and moves out up right with her in his arms. Linda sobs quietly. Bernard and Charley come together and follow them, followed by Happy. Only the music of the flute is left on the darkening stage as over the house the hard towers of the apartment buildings rise into sharp focus, and

The Curtain Falls

LORRAINE HANSBERRY

Lorraine Hansberry (1930–1965) was born in Chicago, the youngest of four children of Carl Hansberry, a successful real estate agent who founded one of the first African American banks in that city. Despite her parents' wealth, the family was forced by Chicago law to live in the ghetto on the South Side. When Hansberry was eight years old, her father bought a home in a white neighborhood. After the family moved into their new house, a mob threw a brick through the window, barely missing her. Carl Hansberry decided to stay in the house, although he had not been given clear title to it, and he began a civil rights suit to test the restrictive law. After he lost his case in the Illinois courts, he was supported by the National Association for the Advancement of Colored People (NAACP) to appeal the decision in the United States Supreme Court. The ruling was reversed, and the family continued to live in the house.

In To Be Young, Gifted and Black *(1971), a posthumous collection of Hansberry's writing, she described how she became involved in a race riot in high school that radicalized her still further when she was seventeen. She attended officially integrated Englewood High School, but in 1947 the white students went on a strike against the blacks. Hansberry described how "the well-dressed, colored students like herself had stood amusedly around the parapet, staring, simply staring at the mob of several hundred striking whites, trading taunts and insults — but showing not the least inclination to further assert racial pride." Word about the riot at the high school spread from the affluent neighborhood to the South Side ghetto schools: "The ofays [whites] are out on strike and beating up and raping colored girls under the viaduct." Carloads of poor black students, "waving baseball bats and shouting slogans of the charge," drove up to Englewood High School. Hansberry watched them "come, pouring out of the bowels of the ghetto, the children of the unqualified oppressed: the black working class in their costumes of pegged pants and conked heads and tight skirts and almost knee-length sweaters and — worst of all — colored anklets, held up by rubber bands! Yes, they had come and they had fought . . . She never could forget one thing:* They had fought back!"

Hansberry's ambition in high school was to become a journalist. After two years at the University of Wisconsin, she transferred to the New School for Social Research in New York City. In New York she began working as a reporter and editor for Freedom, *a monthly magazine owned by the black actor Paul Robeson. After her marriage to the playwright Robert Nemiroff in 1953, she began to write plays full-time.* A Raisin in the Sun, *her first completed work, was produced on Broadway in 1959 with money raised by her friends. Starring the then little-known Sidney Poitier as Walter Lee Younger, the play was immediately successful. Hansberry became the first black playwright to win the New York Drama Critics Circle Award, a landmark achievement in American theater in view of both her gender and race.*

Hansberry took the title of A Raisin in the Sun *from a poem by Langston Hughes, "Harlem (A Dream Deferred)." In her play she looked beneath what Hughes called "the surface of Negro color" to dramatize the human situation of her characters, fulfilling Hughes's vision in his essay "Writers: Black and White" that an African American writer would succeed by becoming a "writer first, colored second. This means losing nothing of your racial identity. It is just that in the great sense of the word, anytime, any place, good art transcends land, race, or nationality, and color drops away. If you are a good writer, in the end neither blackness nor whiteness makes a difference to readers."*

In the early 1960s Hansberry used her prominence as a successful playwright to champion civil rights causes, as in The Movement: Documentary of a Struggle for Equality *(1964), a book of photographs in support of the Student Nonviolent Coordinating Committee (SNCC). Suffering from cancer, she completed only one other full-length play,* The Sign in Sidney Brustein's Window, *produced in 1964, three months before her death. In 1972 Nemiroff edited a volume of her short plays,* Les Blancs: The Collected Last Plays of Lorraine Hansberry, *and produced a musical version of* A Raisin in the Sun *that won a Tony Award.*

COMMENTARIES *Lorraine Hansberry, "An Author's Reflections: Willy Loman, Walter Younger, and He Who Must Live," page 1546; Lorraine Hansberry, "My Shakespearean Experience," page 1551.*

WEB *Research Lorraine Hansberry and answer questions about her work at bedfordstmartins.com/charters/litwriters.*

A Raisin in the Sun   1959

Harlem (A Dream Deferred)

What happens to a dream deferred?

Does it dry up
Like a raisin in the sun?
Or fester like a sore —
And then run?
Does it stink like rotten meat?
Or crust and sugar over —
Like a syrupy sweet?

Maybe it just sags
Like a heavy load.

Or does it explode?
          —LANGSTON HUGHES

CHARACTERS (IN ORDER OF APPEARANCE)

RUTH YOUNGER	GEORGE MURCHISON
TRAVIS YOUNGER	MRS. JOHNSON
WALTER LEE YOUNGER, brother	KARL LINDNER
BENEATHA YOUNGER	BOBO
LENA YOUNGER, Mama	MOVING MEN
JOSEPH ASAGAI	

The action of the play is set in Chicago's Southside, sometime between World War II and the present.

ACT I

SCENE I. [*Friday morning.*]

The Younger living room would be a comfortable and well-ordered room if it were not for a number of indestructible contradictions to this state of being. Its furnishings are typical and undistinguished and their primary feature now is that they have clearly had to accommodate the living of too many people for too many years — and they are tired. Still, we can see that at some time, a time probably no longer remembered by the family (except perhaps for Mama), the furnishings of this room were actually selected with care and love and even hope — and brought to this apartment and arranged with taste and pride.

That was a long time ago. Now the once-loved pattern of the couch upholstery has to fight to show itself from under acres of crocheted doilies and couch covers which have themselves finally come to be more important than the upholstery. And here a table or a chair has been moved to disguise the worn places in the carpet; but the carpet has fought back by showing its weariness, with depressing uniformity, elsewhere on its surface.

Weariness has, in fact, won in this room. Everything has been polished, washed, sat on, used, scrubbed too often. All pretenses but living itself have long since vanished from the very atmosphere of this room.

Moreover, a section of this room, for it is not really a room unto itself, though the landlord's lease would make it seem so, slopes backward to provide a small kitchen area, where the family prepares the meals that are eaten in the living room proper, which must also serve as dining room. The single window that has been provided for these "two" rooms is located in this kitchen area. The sole natural light the family may enjoy in the course of a day is only that which fights its way through this little window.

At left, a door leads to a bedroom which is shared by Mama and her daughter, Beneatha. At right, opposite, is a second room (which in the beginning of the life of this apartment was probably a breakfast room) which serves as a bedroom for Walter and his wife, Ruth.

Time: Sometime between World War II and the present.

Place: Chicago's Southside.

At Rise: It is morning dark in the living room. Travis is asleep on the make-down bed at center. An alarm clock sounds from within the bedroom at right, and presently Ruth enters from that room and closes the door behind her. She crosses sleepily toward the window. As she passes her sleeping son she reaches down and shakes him a little. At the window she raises the shade and a dusky Southside morning light comes in feebly. She fills a pot with water and puts it on to boil. She calls to the boy, between yawns, in a slightly muffled voice.

Ruth is about thirty. We can see that she was a pretty girl, even exceptionally so, but now it is apparent that life has been little that she expected, and disappointment has already begun to hang in her face. In a few years, before thirty-five even, she will be known among her people as a "settled woman."

She crosses to her son and gives him a good, final, rousing shake.

RUTH: Come on now, boy, it's seven thirty! (*Her son sits up at last, in a stupor of sleepiness.*) I say hurry up, Travis! You ain't the only person in the world got to use a bathroom! (*The child, a sturdy, handsome little boy of ten or eleven, drags himself out of the bed and almost blindly takes his towels and "today's clothes" from drawers and a closet and goes out to the bathroom, which is in an outside hall and which is shared by another family or families on the same floor. Ruth crosses to the bedroom door at right and opens it and calls in to her husband.*) Walter Lee! . . . It's after seven thirty! Lemme see you do some waking up in there now! (*She waits.*) You better get up from there, man! It's after seven thirty I tell you. (*She waits again.*) All right, you just go ahead and lay there and next thing you know Travis be finished and Mr. Johnson'll be in there and you'll be fussing and cussing round here like a madman! And be late too! (*She waits, at the end of patience.*) Walter Lee — it's time for you to GET UP!

She waits another second and then starts to go into the bedroom, but is apparently satisfied that her husband has begun to get up. She stops, pulls the door to, and returns to the kitchen area. She wipes her face with a moist cloth and runs her fingers through her sleep-disheveled hair in a vain effort and ties an apron around her housecoat. The bedroom door at right opens and her husband stands in the doorway in his pajamas, which are rumpled and mismated. He is a lean, intense young man in his middle thirties, inclined to quick nervous movements and erratic speech habits — and always in his voice there is a quality of indictment.

WALTER: Is he out yet?

RUTH: What you mean *out*? He ain't hardly got in there good yet.

WALTER (*wandering in, still more oriented to sleep than to a new day*): Well, what was you doing all that yelling for if I can't even get in there yet? (*Stopping and thinking.*) Check coming today?

RUTH: They *said* Saturday and this is just Friday and I hopes to God you ain't going to get up here first thing this morning and start talking to me 'bout no money — 'cause I 'bout don't want to hear it.

WALTER: Something the matter with you this morning?

RUTH: No — I'm just sleepy as the devil. What kind of eggs you want?

WALTER: Not scrambled. (*Ruth starts to scramble eggs.*) Paper come? (*Ruth points impatiently to the rolled up* Tribune *on the table, and he gets it and spreads it out and vaguely reads the front page.*) Set off another bomb yesterday.

RUTH (*maximum indifference*): Did they?

WALTER (*looking up*): What's the matter with you?

RUTH: Ain't nothing the matter with me. And don't keep asking me that this morning.

WALTER: Ain't nobody bothering you. (*Reading the news of the day absently again.*) Say Colonel McCormick is sick.

RUTH (*affecting tea-party interest*): Is he now? Poor thing.

WALTER (*sighing and looking at his watch*): Oh, me. (*He waits.*) Now what is that boy doing in that bathroom all this time? He just going to have to start getting up earlier. I can't be being late to work on account of him fooling around in there.

RUTH (*turning on him*): Oh, no he ain't going to be getting up no earlier no such thing! It ain't his fault that he can't get to bed no earlier nights 'cause he got a bunch of crazy good-for-nothing clowns sitting up running their mouths in what is supposed to be his bedroom after ten o'clock at night . . .

WALTER: That's what you mad about, ain't it? The things I want to talk about with my friends just couldn't be important in your mind, could they?

He rises and finds a cigarette in her handbag on the table and crosses to the little window and looks out, smoking and deeply enjoying this first one.

RUTH (*almost matter of factly, a complaint too automatic to deserve emphasis*): Why you always got to smoke before you eat in the morning?

WALTER (*at the window*): Just look at 'em down there . . . Running and racing to work . . . (*He turns and faces his wife and watches her a moment at the stove, and then, suddenly.*) You look young this morning, baby.

RUTH (*indifferently*): Yeah?

WALTER: Just for a second—stirring them eggs. Just for a second it was—you looked real young again. (*He reaches for her; she crosses away. Then, drily.*) It's gone now—you look like yourself again!

RUTH: Man, if you don't shut up and leave me alone.

WALTER (*looking out to the street again*): First thing a man ought to learn in life is not to make love to no colored woman first thing in the morning. You all some eeeevil people at eight o'clock in the morning.

Travis appears in the hall doorway, almost fully dressed and quite wide awake now, his towels and pajamas across his shoulders. He opens the door and signals for his father to make the bathroom in a hurry.

TRAVIS (*watching the bathroom*): Daddy, come on!

Walter gets his bathroom utensils and flies out to the bathroom.

RUTH: Sit down and have your breakfast, Travis.

TRAVIS: Mama, this is Friday. (*Gleefully.*) Check coming tomorrow, huh?

RUTH: You get your mind off money and eat your breakfast.

TRAVIS (*eating*): This is the morning we supposed to bring the fifty cents to school.

RUTH: Well, I ain't got no fifty cents this morning.

TRAVIS: Teacher say we have to.

RUTH: I don't care what teacher say. I ain't got it. Eat your breakfast, Travis.

TRAVIS: I *am* eating.

RUTH: Hush up now and just eat!

The boy gives her an exasperated look for her lack of understanding, and eats grudgingly.

TRAVIS: You think Grandmama would have it?

RUTH: No! And I want you to stop asking your grandmother for money, you hear me?

TRAVIS (*outraged*): Gaaaleee! I don't ask her, she just gimme it sometimes!

RUTH: Travis Willard Younger—I got too much on me this morning to be—

TRAVIS: Maybe Daddy—

RUTH: *Travis!*

The boy hushes abruptly. They are both quiet and tense for several seconds.

TRAVIS (*presently*): Could I maybe go carry some groceries in front of the super-market for a little while after school then?

RUTH: Just hush, I said. (*Travis jabs his spoon into his cereal bowl viciously, and rests his head in anger upon his fists.*) If you through eating, you can get over there and make up your bed.

The boy obeys stiffly and crosses the room, almost mechanically, to the bed and more or less folds the bedding into a heap, then angrily gets his books and cap.

TRAVIS (*sulking and standing apart from her unnaturally*): I'm gone.

RUTH (*looking up from the stove to inspect him automatically*): Come here. (*He crosses to her and she studies his head.*) If you don't take this comb and fix this here head, you better! (*Travis puts down his books with a great sigh of oppression, and crosses to the mirror. His mother mutters under her breath about his "slubbornness."*) 'Bout to march out of here with that head look-ing just like chickens slept in it! I just don't know where you get your slubborn ways . . . And get your jacket, too. Looks chilly out this morning.

TRAVIS (*with conspicuously brushed hair and jacket*): I'm gone.

RUTH: Get carfare and milk money—(*Waving one finger.*)—and not a single penny for no caps, you hear me?

TRAVIS (*with sullen politeness*): Yes'm.

He turns in outrage to leave. His mother watches after him as in his frustration he approaches the door almost comically. When she speaks to him, her voice has become a very gentle tease.

RUTH (*mocking; as she thinks he would say it*): Oh, Mama makes me so mad sometimes, I don't know what to do! (*She waits and continues to his back as he stands stock-still in front of the door.*) I wouldn't kiss that woman good-bye for nothing in this world this morning! (*The boy finally turns around and rolls his eyes at her, knowing the mood has changed and he is vindicated; he does not, however, move toward her yet.*) Not for nothing in this world! (*She finally laughs aloud at him and holds out her arms to him and we see that it is a way between them, very old and practiced. He crosses to her and allows her to embrace him warmly but keeps his face fixed with masculine rigidity. She holds him back from her presently and looks at him and runs her fingers over the features of his face. With utter gentleness—.*) Now—whose little old angry man are you?

TRAVIS (*the masculinity and gruffness start to fade at last*): Aw gaalee—Mama . . .

RUTH (*mimicking*): Aw—gaaaaalleeeee, Mama! (*She pushes him, with rough playfulness and finality, toward the door.*) Get on out of here or you going to be late.

TRAVIS (*in the face of love, new aggressiveness*): Mama, could I *please* go carry groceries?

RUTH: Honey, it's starting to get so cold evenings.

WALTER (*coming in from the bathroom and drawing a make-believe gun from a make-believe holster and shooting at his son*): What is it he wants to do?

RUTH: Go carry groceries after school at the supermarket.

WALTER: Well, let him go . . .

TRAVIS (*quickly, to the ally*): I have to—she won't gimme the fifty cents . . .

WALTER (*to his wife only*): Why not?

RUTH (*simply, and with flavor*): 'Cause we don't have it.

WALTER (*to Ruth only*): What you tell the boy things like that for? (*Reaching down into his pants with a rather important gesture.*) Here, son —

He hands the boy the coin, but his eyes are directed to his wife's. Travis takes the money happily.

TRAVIS: Thanks, Daddy.

He starts out. Ruth watches both of them with murder in her eyes. Walter stands and stares back at her with defiance, and suddenly reaches into his pocket again on an afterthought.

WALTER (*without even looking at his son, still staring hard at his wife*): In fact, here's another fifty cents . . . Buy yourself some fruit today — or take a taxicab to school or something!

TRAVIS: Whoopee —

He leaps up and clasps his father around the middle with his legs, and they face each other in mutual appreciation; slowly Walter Lee peeks around the boy to catch the violent rays from his wife's eyes and draws his head back as if shot.

WALTER: You better get down now — and get to school, man.

TRAVIS (*at the door*): O.K. Good-bye.

He exits.

WALTER (*after him, pointing with pride*): That's *my* boy. (*She looks at him in disgust and turns back to her work.*) You know what I was thinking 'bout in the bathroom this morning?

RUTH: No.

WALTER: How come you always try to be so pleasant!

RUTH: What is there to be pleasant 'bout!

WALTER: You want to know what I was thinking 'bout in the bathroom or not!

RUTH: I know what you thinking 'bout.

WALTER (*ignoring her*): 'Bout what me and Willy Harris was talking about last night.

RUTH (*immediately — a refrain*): Willy Harris is a good-for-nothing loudmouth.

WALTER: Anybody who talks to me has got to be a good-for-nothing loudmouth, ain't he? And what you know about who is just a good-for-nothing loudmouth? Charlie Atkins was just a "good-for-nothing loudmouth" too, wasn't he! When he wanted me to go in the dry-cleaning business with him. And now — he's grossing a hundred thousand a year. A hundred thousand dollars a year! You still call *him* a loudmouth!

RUTH (*bitterly*): Oh, Walter Lee . . .

She folds her head on her arms over the table.

WALTER (*rising and coming to her and standing over her*): You tired, ain't you? Tired of everything. Me, the boy, the way we live — this beat-up hole — everything. Ain't you? (*She doesn't look up, doesn't answer.*) So tired — moaning and groaning all the time, but you wouldn't do nothing to help, would you? You couldn't be on my side that long for nothing, could you?

RUTH: Walter, please leave me alone.

WALTER: A man needs for a woman to back him up . . .

RUTH: Walter—

WALTER: Mama would listen to you. You know she listen to you more than she do me and Bennie. She think more of you. All you have to do is just sit down with her when you drinking your coffee one morning and talking 'bout things like you do and—(*He sits down beside her and demonstrates graphically what he thinks her methods and tone should be.*)—you just sip your coffee, see, and say easy like that you been thinking 'bout that deal Walter Lee is so interested in, 'bout the store and all, and sip some more coffee, like what you saying ain't really that important to you—And the next thing you know, she be listening good and asking you questions and when I come home—I can tell her the details. This ain't no fly-by-night proposition, baby. I mean we figured it out, me and Willy and Bobo.

RUTH (*with a frown*): Bobo?

WALTER: Yeah. You see, this little liquor store we got in mind cost seventy-five thousand and we figured the initial investment on the place be 'bout thirty thousand, see. That be ten thousand each. Course, there's a couple of hundred you got to pay so's you don't spend your life just waiting for them clowns to let your license get approved—

RUTH: You mean graft?

WALTER (*frowning impatiently*): Don't call it that. See there, that just goes to show you what women understand about the world. Baby, don't *nothing* happen for you in the world 'less you pay *somebody* off!

RUTH: Walter, leave me alone! (*She raises her head and stares at him vigorously—then says, more quietly.*) *Eat* your eggs, they gonna be cold.

WALTER (*straightening up from her and looking off*): That's it. There you are. Man say to his woman: I got me a dream. His woman say: Eat your eggs. (*Sadly, but gaining in power.*) Man say: I got to take hold of this here world, baby! And a woman will say: Eat your eggs and go to work. (*Passionately now.*) Man say: I got to change my life, I'm choking to death, baby! And his woman say—(*In utter anguish as he brings his fists down on his thighs.*)—Your eggs is getting cold!

RUTH (*softly*): Walter, that ain't none of our money.

WALTER (*not listening at all or even looking at her*): This morning, I was lookin' in the mirror and thinking about it . . . I'm thirty-five years old; I been married eleven years and I got a boy who sleeps in the living room—(*Very, very quietly.*)—and all I got to give him is stories about how rich white people live . . .

RUTH: Eat your eggs, Walter.

WALTER (*slams the table and jumps up*): —DAMN MY EGGS—DAMN ALL THE EGGS THAT EVER WAS!

RUTH: Then go to work.

WALTER (*looking up at her*): See—I'm trying to talk to you 'bout myself—(*Shaking his head with the repetition.*)—and all you can say is eat them eggs and go to work.

RUTH (*wearily*): Honey, you never say nothing new. I listen to you every day, every night and every morning, and you never say nothing new. (*Shrug-*

ging.) So you would rather *be* Mr. Arnold than be his chauffeur. So — I would *rather* be living in Buckingham Palace.

WALTER: That is just what is wrong with the colored woman in this world . . . Don't understand about building their men up and making 'em feel like they somebody. Like they can do something.

RUTH (*drily, but to hurt*): There *are* colored men who do things.

WALTER: No thanks to the colored woman.

RUTH: Well, being a colored woman, I guess I can't help myself none.

She rises and gets the ironing board and sets it up and attacks a huge pile of rough-dried clothes, sprinkling them in preparation for the ironing and then rolling them into tight fat balls.

WALTER (*mumbling*): We one group of men tied to a race of women with small minds!

His sister Beneatha enters. She is about twenty, as slim and intense as her brother. She is not as pretty as her sister-in-law, but her lean, almost intellectual face has a handsomeness of its own. She wears a bright-red flannel nightie, and her thick hair stands wildly about her head. Her speech is a mixture of many things; it is different from the rest of the family's insofar as education has permeated her sense of English — and perhaps the Midwest rather than the South has finally — at last — won out in her inflection; but not altogether, because over all of it is a soft slurring and transformed use of vowels which is the decided influence of the Southside. She passes through the room without looking at either Ruth or Walter and goes to the outside door and looks, a little blindly, out to the bathroom. She sees that it has been lost to the Johnsons. She closes the door with a sleepy vengeance and crosses to the table and sits down a little defeated.

BENEATHA: I am going to start timing those people.

WALTER: You should get up earlier.

BENEATHA (*her face in her hands. She is still fighting the urge to go back to bed*): Really — would you suggest dawn? Where's the paper?

WALTER (*pushing the paper across the table to her as he studies her almost clinically, as though he has never seen her before*): You a horrible-looking chick at this hour.

BENEATHA (*drily*): Good morning, everybody.

WALTER (*senselessly*): How is school coming?

BENEATHA (*in the same spirit*): Lovely. Lovely. And you know, biology is the greatest. (*Looking up at him.*) I dissected something that looked just like you yesterday.

WALTER: I just wondered if you've made up your mind and everything.

BENEATHA (*gaining in sharpness and impatience*): And what did I answer yesterday morning — and the day before that?

RUTH (*from the ironing board, like someone disinterested and old*): Don't be so nasty, Bennie.

BENEATHA (*still to her brother*): And the day before that and the day before that!

WALTER (*defensively*): I'm interested in you. Something wrong with that? Ain't many girls who decide —

WALTER AND BENEATHA (*in unison*): — "to be a doctor."

MAMA (*seeing the make-down bed as Travis has left it*): Lord have mercy, look at that poor bed. Bless his heart — he tries, don't he?

She moves to the bed Travis has sloppily made up.

RUTH: No — he don't half try at all 'cause he knows you going to come along behind him and fix everything. That's just how come he don't know how to do nothing right now — you done spoiled that boy so.

MAMA (*folding bedding*): Well — he's a little boy. Ain't supposed to know 'bout housekeeping. My baby, that's what he is. What you fix for his breakfast this morning?

RUTH (*angrily*): I feed my son, Lena!

MAMA: I ain't meddling — (*Under breath; busy-bodyish.*) I just noticed all last week he had cold cereal, and when it starts getting this chilly in the fall a child ought to have some hot grits or something when he goes out in the cold —

RUTH (*furious*): I gave him hot oats — is that all right!

MAMA: I ain't meddling. (*Pause.*) Put a lot of nice butter on it? (*Ruth shoots her an angry look and does not reply.*) He likes lots of butter.

RUTH (*exasperated*): Lena —

MAMA (*to Beneatha. Mama is inclined to wander conversationally sometimes*): What was you and your brother fussing 'bout this morning?

BENEATHA: It's not important, Mama.

She gets up and goes to look out at the bathroom, which is apparently free, and she picks up her towels and rushes out.

MAMA: What was they fighting about?

RUTH: Now you know as well as I do.

MAMA (*shaking her head*): Brother still worrying hisself sick about that money?

RUTH: You know he is.

MAMA: You had breakfast?

RUTH: Some coffee.

MAMA: Girl, you better start eating and looking after yourself better. You almost thin as Travis.

RUTH: Lena —

MAMA: Un-hunh?

RUTH: What are you going to do with it?

MAMA: Now don't you start, child. It's too early in the morning to be talking about money. It ain't Christian.

RUTH: It's just that he got his heart set on that store —

MAMA: You mean that liquor store that Willy Harris want him to invest in?

RUTH: Yes —

MAMA: We ain't no business people, Ruth. We just plain working folks.

RUTH: Ain't nobody business people till they go into business. Walter Lee say colored people ain't never going to start getting ahead till they start gambling on some different kinds of things in the world — investments and things.

MAMA: What done got into you, girl? Walter Lee done finally sold you on investing.

RUTH: No. Mama, something is happening between Walter and me. I don't know what it is—but he needs something—something I can't give him any more. He needs this chance, Lena.

MAMA (*frowning deeply*): But liquor, honey—

RUTH: Well—like Walter say—I spec people going to always be drinking themselves some liquor.

MAMA: Well—whether they drinks it or not ain't none of my business. But whether I go into business selling it to 'em *is,* and I don't want that on my ledger this late in life. (*Stopping suddenly and studying her daughter-in-law.*) Ruth Younger, what's the matter with you today? You look like you could fall over right there.

RUTH: I'm tired.

MAMA: Then you better stay home from work today.

RUTH: I can't stay home. She'd be calling up the agency and screaming at them, "My girl didn't come in today—send me somebody! My girl didn't come in!" Oh, she just have a fit . . .

MAMA: Well, let her have it. I'll just call her up and say you got the flu—

RUTH (*laughing*): Why the flu?

MAMA: 'Cause it sounds respectable to 'em. Something white people get, too. They know 'bout the flu. Otherwise they think you been cut up or something when you tell 'em you sick.

RUTH: I got to go in. We need the money.

MAMA: Somebody would of thought my children done all but starved to death the way they talk about money here late. Child, we got a great big old check coming tomorrow.

RUTH (*sincerely, but also self-righteously*): Now that's your money. It ain't got nothing to do with me. We all feel like that—Walter and Bennie and me—even Travis.

MAMA (*thoughtfully, and suddenly very far away*): Ten thousand dollars—

RUTH: Sure is wonderful.

MAMA: Ten thousand dollars.

RUTH: You know what you should do, Miss Lena? You should take yourself a trip somewhere. To Europe or South America or someplace—

MAMA (*throwing up her hands at the thought*): Oh, child!

RUTH: I'm serious. Just pack up and leave! Go on away and enjoy yourself some. Forget about the family and have yourself a ball for once in your life—

MAMA (*drily*): You sound like I'm just about ready to die. Who'd go with me? What I look like wandering 'round Europe by myself?

RUTH: Shoot—these here rich white women do it all the time. They don't think nothing of packing up they suitcases and piling on one of them big steamships and—swoosh!—they gone, child.

MAMA: Something always told me I wasn't no rich white woman.

RUTH: Well—what are you going to do with it then?

MAMA: I ain't rightly decided. (*Thinking. She speaks now with emphasis.*) Some of it got to be put away for Beneatha and her schoolin'—and ain't nothing going to touch that part of it. Nothing. (*She waits several seconds, trying to make up her mind about something, and looks at Ruth a little tentatively before going on.*) Been thinking that we maybe could meet the notes on a little old two-story somewhere, with a yard where Travis could play in the summertime, if we use part of the insurance for a down payment and everybody kind of pitch in. I could maybe take on a little day work again, few days a week—

RUTH (*studying her mother-in-law furtively and concentrating on her ironing, anxious to encourage without seeming to*): Well, Lord knows, we've put enough rent into this here rat trap to pay for four houses by now . . .

MAMA (*looking up at the words "rat trap" and then looking around and leaning back and sighing—in a suddenly reflective mood—*): "Rat trap"—yes, that's all it is. (*Smiling.*) I remember just as well the day me and Big Walter moved in here. Hadn't been married but two weeks and wasn't planning on living here no more than a year. (*She shakes her head at the dissolved dream.*) We was going to set away, little by little, don't you know, and buy a little place out in Morgan Park. We had even picked out the house. (*Chuckling a little.*) Looks right dumpy today. But Lord, child, you should know all the dreams I had 'bout buying that house and fixing it up and making me a little garden in the back—(*She waits and stops smiling.*) And didn't none of it happen.

Dropping her hands in a futile gesture.

RUTH (*keeps her head down, ironing*): Yes, life can be a barrel of disappointments, sometimes.

MAMA: Honey, Big Walter would come in here some nights back then and slump down on that couch there and just look at the rug, and look at me and look at the rug and then back at me—and I'd know he was down then . . . really down. (*After a second very long and thoughtful pause; she is seeing back to times that only she can see.*) And then, Lord, when I lost that baby—little Claude—I almost thought I was going to lose Big Walter too. Oh, that man grieved hisself! He was one man to love his children.

RUTH: Ain't nothin' can tear at you like losin' your baby.

MAMA: I guess that's how come that man finally worked hisself to death like he done. Like he was fighting his own war with this here world that took his baby from him.

RUTH: He sure was a fine man, all right. I always liked Mr. Younger.

MAMA: Crazy 'bout his children! God knows there was plenty wrong with Walter Younger—hard-headed, mean, kind of wild with women—plenty wrong with him. But he sure loved his children. Always wanted them to have something—be something. That's where Brother gets all these notions, I reckon. Big Walter used to say, he'd get right wet in the eyes sometimes, lean his head back with the water standing in his eyes and say, "Seem like God didn't see fit to give the black man nothing but dreams—but He did give us children to make them dreams seem worthwhile." (*She smiles.*) He could talk like that, don't you know.

RUTH: Yes, he sure could. He was a good man, Mr. Younger.

MAMA: Yes, a fine man—just couldn't never catch up with his dreams, that's all.

Beneatha comes in, brushing her hair and looking up to the ceiling, where the sound of a vacuum cleaner has started up.

BENEATHA: What could be so dirty on that woman's rugs that she has to vacuum them every single day?

RUTH: I wish certain young women 'round here who I could name would take inspiration about certain rugs in a certain apartment I could also mention.

BENEATHA (*shrugging*): How much cleaning can a house need, for Christ's sakes.

MAMA (*not liking the Lord's name used thus*): Bennie!

RUTH: Just listen to her—just listen!

BENEATHA: Oh, God!

MAMA: If you use the Lord's name just one more time—

BENEATHA (*a bit of a whine*): Oh, Mama—

RUTH: Fresh—just fresh as salt, this girl!

BENEATHA (*drily*): Well—if the salt loses its savor—

MAMA: Now that will do. I just ain't going to have you 'round here reciting the scriptures in vain—you hear me?

BENEATHA: How did I manage to get on everybody's wrong side by just walking into a room?

RUTH: If you weren't so fresh—

BENEATHA: Ruth, I'm twenty years old.

MAMA: What time you be home from school today?

BENEATHA: Kind of late. (*With enthusiasm.*) Madeline is going to start my guitar lessons today.

Mama and Ruth look up with the same expression.

MAMA: Your *what* kind of lessons?

BENEATHA: Guitar.

RUTH: Oh, Father!

MAMA: How come you done taken it in your mind to learn to play the guitar?

BENEATHA: I just want to, that's all.

MAMA (*smiling*): Lord, child, don't you know what to do with yourself? How long it going to be before you get tired of this now—like you got tired of that little play-acting group you joined last year? (*Looking at Ruth.*) And what was it the year before that?

RUTH: The horseback-riding club for which she bought that fifty-five-dollar riding habit that's been hanging in the closet ever since!

MAMA (*to Beneatha*): Why you got to flit so from one thing to another, baby?

BENEATHA (*sharply*): I just want to learn to play the guitar. Is there anything wrong with that?

MAMA: Ain't nobody trying to stop you. I just wonders sometimes why you has to flit so from one thing to another all the time. You ain't never done nothing with all that camera equipment you brought home—

BENEATHA: I don't flit! I—I experiment with different forms of expression—

RUTH: Like riding a horse?

BENEATHA: —People have to express themselves one way or another.

MAMA: What is it you want to express?

BENEATHA (*angrily*): Me! (*Mama and Ruth look at each other and burst into raucous laughter.*) Don't worry — I don't expect you to understand.

MAMA (*to change the subject*): Who you going out with tomorrow night?

BENEATHA (*with displeasure*): George Murchison again.

MAMA (*pleased*): Oh — you getting a little sweet on him?

RUTH: You ask me, this child ain't sweet on nobody but herself — (*Under breath.*) Express herself!

They laugh.

BENEATHA: Oh — I like George all right, Mama. I mean I like him enough to go out with him and stuff, but —

RUTH (*for devilment*): What does *and stuff* mean?

BENEATHA: Mind your own business.

MAMA: Stop picking at her now, Ruth. (*She chuckles — then a suspicious sudden look at her daughter as she turns in her chair for emphasis.*) What DOES it mean?

BENEATHA (*wearily*): Oh, I just mean I couldn't ever really be serious about George. He's — he's so shallow.

RUTH: Shallow — what do you mean he's shallow? He's *Rich!*

MAMA: Hush, Ruth.

BENEATHA: I know he's rich. He knows he's rich, too.

RUTH: Well — what other qualities a man got to have to satisfy you, little girl?

BENEATHA: You wouldn't even begin to understand. Anybody who married Walter could not possibly understand.

MAMA (*outraged*): What kind of way is that to talk about your brother?

BENEATHA: Brother is a flip — let's face it.

MAMA (*to Ruth, helplessly*): What's a flip?

RUTH (*glad to add kindling*): She's saying he's crazy.

BENEATHA: Not crazy. Brother isn't really crazy yet — he — he's an elaborate neurotic.

MAMA: Hush your mouth!

BENEATHA: As for George. Well. George looks good — he's got a beautiful car and he takes me to nice places and, as my sister-in-law says, he is probably the richest boy I will ever get to know and I even like him sometimes — but if the Youngers are sitting around waiting to see if their little Bennie is going to tie up the family with the Murchisons, they are wasting their time.

RUTH: You mean you wouldn't marry George Murchison if he asked you someday? That pretty, rich thing? Honey, I knew you was odd —

BENEATHA: No I would not marry him if all I felt for him was what I feel now. Besides, George's family wouldn't really like it.

MAMA: Why not?

BENEATHA: Oh, Mama — The Murchisons are honest-to-God-real-*live*-rich colored people, and the only people in the world who are more snobbish than rich white people are rich colored people. I thought everybody knew that. I've met Mrs. Murchison. She's a scene!

MAMA: You must not dislike people 'cause they well off, honey.

BENEATHA: Why not? It makes just as much sense as disliking people 'cause they are poor, and lots of people do that.

RUTH (*a wisdom-of-the-ages manner. To Mama*): Well, she'll get over some of this—

BENEATHA: Get over it? What are you talking about, Ruth? Listen, I'm going to be a doctor. I'm not worried about who I'm going to marry yet—if I ever get married.

MAMA AND RUTH: *If!*

MAMA: Now, Bennie—

BENEATHA: Oh, I probably will . . . but first I'm going to be a doctor, and George, for one, still thinks that's pretty funny. I couldn't be bothered with that. I am going to be a doctor and everybody around here better understand that!

MAMA (*kindly*): 'Course you going to be a doctor, honey, God willing.

BENEATHA (*drily*): God hasn't got a thing to do with it.

MAMA: Beneatha—that just wasn't necessary.

BENEATHA: Well—neither is God. I get sick of hearing about God.

MAMA: Beneatha!

BENEATHA: I mean it! I'm just tired of hearing about God all the time. What has He got to do with anything? Does He pay tuition?

MAMA: You 'bout to get your fresh little jaw slapped!

RUTH: That's just what she needs, all right!

BENEATHA: Why? Why can't I say what I want to around here, like everybody else?

MAMA: It don't sound nice for a young girl to say things like that—you wasn't brought up that way. Me and your father went to trouble to get you and Brother to church every Sunday.

BENEATHA: Mama, you don't understand. It's all a matter of ideas, and God is just one idea I don't accept. It's not important. I am not going out and be immoral or commit crimes because I don't believe in God. I don't even think about it. It's just that I get tired of Him getting credit for all the things the human race achieves through its own stubborn effort. There simply is no blasted God—there is only man and it is *He* who makes miracles!

Mama absorbs this speech, studies her daughter, and rises slowly and crosses to Beneatha and slaps her powerfully across the face. After, there is only silence and the daughter drops her eyes from her mother's face, and Mama is very tall before her.

MAMA: Now—you say after me, in my mother's house there is still God. (*There is a long pause and Beneatha stares at the floor wordlessly. Mama repeats the phrase with precision and cool emotion.*) In my mother's house there is still God.

BENEATHA: In my mother's house there is still God.

A long pause.

MAMA (*walking away from Beneatha, too disturbed for triumphant posture. Stopping and turning back to her daughter*): There are some ideas we ain't going to have in this house. Not long as I am at the head of this family.

BENEATHA: Yes, ma'am.

Mama walks out of the room.

RUTH (*almost gently, with profound understanding*): You think you a woman, Bennie — but you still a little girl. What you did was childish — so you got treated like a child.

BENEATHA: I see. (*Quietly.*) I also see that everybody thinks it's all right for Mama to be a tyrant. But all the tyranny in the world will never put a God in the heavens!

She picks up her books and goes out. Pause.

RUTH (*goes to Mama's door*): She said she was sorry.

MAMA (*coming out, going to her plant*): They frightens me, Ruth. My children.

RUTH: You got good children, Lena. They just a little off sometimes — but they're good.

MAMA: No — there's something come down between me and them that don't let us understand each other and I don't know what it is. One done almost lost his mind thinking 'bout money all the time and the other done commence to talk about things I can't seem to understand in no form or fashion. What is it that's changing, Ruth.

RUTH (*soothingly, older than her years*): Now . . . you taking it all too seriously. You just got strong-willed children and it takes a strong woman like you to keep 'em in hand.

MAMA (*looking at her plant and sprinkling a little water on it*): They spirited all right, my children. Got to admit they got spirit — Bennie and Walter. Like this little old plant that ain't never had enough sunshine or nothing — and look at it . . .

She has her back to Ruth, who has had to stop ironing and lean against something and put the back of her hand to her forehead.

RUTH (*trying to keep Mama from noticing*): You . . . sure . . . loves that little old thing, don't you? . . .

MAMA: Well, I always wanted me a garden like I used to see sometimes at the back of the houses down home. This plant is close as I ever got to having one. (*She looks out of the window as she replaces the plant.*) Lord, ain't nothing as dreary as the view from this window on a dreary day, is there? Why ain't you singing this morning, Ruth? Sing that "No Ways Tired." That song always lifts me up so — (*She turns at last to see that Ruth has slipped quietly to the floor, in a state of semiconsciousness.*) Ruth! Ruth honey — what's the matter with you . . . Ruth!

Curtain.

SCENE II: [*The following morning.*]

It is the following morning; a Saturday morning, and house cleaning is in progress at the Youngers'. Furniture has been shoved hither and yon and Mama is giving the kitchen-area walls a washing down. Beneatha, in dungarees, with a handkerchief tied around her face, is spraying insecticide into the cracks in the walls. As they work, the radio is on and a Southside disk-jockey program is inappropriately filling the house with a rather exotic saxophone blues. Travis, the sole idle one, is leaning on his arms, looking out of the window.

TRAVIS: Grandmama, that stuff Bennie is using smells awful. Can I go downstairs, please?

MAMA: Did you get all them chores done already? I ain't seen you doing much.

TRAVIS: Yes'm — finished early. Where did Mama go this morning?

MAMA (*looking at Beneatha*): She had to go on a little errand.

The phone rings. Beneatha runs to answer it and reaches it before Walter, who has entered from bedroom.

TRAVIS: Where?

MAMA: To tend to her business.

BENEATHA: Haylo . . . (*Disappointed.*) Yes, he is. (*She tosses the phone to Walter, who barely catches it.*) It's Willie Harris again.

WALTER (*as privately as possible under Mama's gaze*): Hello, Willie. Did you get the papers from the lawyer? . . . No, not yet. I told you the mailman doesn't get here till ten-thirty . . . No, I'll come there . . . Yeah! Right away. (*He hangs up and goes for his coat.*)

BENEATHA: Brother, where did Ruth go?

WALTER (*as he exits*): How should I know!

TRAVIS: Aw come on, Grandma. Can I go outside?

MAMA: Oh, I guess so. You stay right in front of the house, though, and keep a good lookout for the postman.

TRAVIS: Yes'm. (*He darts into bedroom for stickball and bat, reenters, and sees Beneatha on her knees spraying under sofa with behind upraised. He edges closer to the target, takes aim, and lets her have it. She screams.*) Leave them poor little cockroaches alone, they ain't bothering you none! (*He runs as she swings the spraygun at him viciously and playfully.*) Grandma! Grandma!

MAMA: Look out there, girl, before you be spilling some of that stuff on that child!

TRAVIS (*safely behind the bastion of Mama*): That's right — look out, now! (*He exits.*)

BENEATHA (*drily*): I can't imagine that it would hurt him — it has never hurt the roaches.

MAMA: Well, little boys' hides ain't as tough as Southside roaches. You better get over there behind the bureau. I seen one marching out of there like Napoleon yesterday.

BENEATHA: There's really only one way to get rid of them, Mama —

MAMA: How?

BENEATHA: Set fire to this building! Mama, where did Ruth go?

MAMA (*looking at her with meaning*): To the doctor, I think.

BENEATHA: The doctor? What's the matter? (*They exchange glances.*) You don't think —

MAMA (*with her sense of drama*): Now I ain't saying what I think. But I ain't never been wrong 'bout a woman neither.

The phone rings.

BENEATHA (*at the phone*): Hay-lo . . . (*Pause, and a moment of recognition.*)
Well—when did you get back! . . . And how was it? . . . Of course I've
missed you—in my way . . . This morning? No . . . house cleaning and
all that and Mama hates it if I let people come over when the house is like
this . . . You *have?* Well, that's different . . . What is it—Oh, what the
hell, come on over . . . Right, see you then. *Arrividerci.*

She hangs up.

MAMA (*who has listened vigorously, as is her habit*): Who is that you inviting over
here with this house looking like this? You ain't got the pride you was
born with!

BENEATHA: Asagai doesn't care how houses look, Mama—he's an intellectual.

MAMA: *Who?*

BENEATHA: Asagai—Joseph Asagai. He's an African boy I met on campus.
He's been studying in Canada all summer.

MAMA: What's his name?

BENEATHA: Asagai, Joseph. Ah-sah-guy . . . He's from Nigeria.

MAMA: Oh, that's the little country that was founded by slaves way back . . .

BENEATHA: No, Mama—that's Liberia.

MAMA: I don't think I never met no African before.

BENEATHA: Well, do me a favor and don't ask him a whole lot of ignorant questions about Africans. I mean, do they wear clothes and all that—

MAMA: Well, now, I guess if you think we so ignorant 'round here maybe you
shouldn't bring your friends here—

BENEATHA: It's just that people ask such crazy things. All anyone seems to know
about when it comes to Africa is Tarzan—

MAMA (*indignantly*): Why should I know anything about Africa?

BENEATHA: Why do you give money at church for the missionary work?

MAMA: Well, that's to help save people.

BENEATHA: You mean save them from *heathenism*—

MAMA (*innocently*): Yes.

BENEATHA: I'm afraid they need more salvation from the British and the
French.

*Ruth comes in forlornly and pulls off her coat with dejection. They both turn to
look at her.*

RUTH (*dispiritedly*): Well, I guess from all the happy faces—everybody knows.

BENEATHA: You pregnant?

MAMA: Lord have mercy, I sure hope it's a little old girl. Travis ought to have a
sister.

Beneatha and Ruth give her a hopeless look for this grandmotherly enthusiasm.

BENEATHA: How far along are you?

RUTH: Two months.

BENEATHA: Did you mean to? I mean did you plan it or was it an accident?

MAMA: What do you know about planning or not planning?

BENEATHA: Oh, Mama.

RUTH (*wearily*): She's twenty years old, Lena.

BENEATHA: Did you plan it, Ruth?

RUTH: Mind your own business.

BENEATHA: It is my business—where is he going to live, on the *roof*? (*There is silence following the remark as the three women react to the sense of it.*) Gee—I didn't mean that, Ruth, honest. Gee, I don't feel like that at all. I—I think it is wonderful.

RUTH (*dully*): Wonderful.

BENEATHA: Yes—really.

MAMA (*looking at Ruth, worried*): Doctor say everything going to be all right?

RUTH (*far away*): Yes—she says everything is going to be fine . . .

MAMA (*immediately suspicious*): "She"—What doctor you went to?

Ruth folds over, near hysteria.

MAMA (*worriedly hovering over Ruth*): Ruth honey—what's the matter with you—you sick?

Ruth has her fists clenched on her thighs and is fighting hard to suppress a scream that seems to be rising in her.

BENEATHA: What's the matter with her, Mama?

MAMA (*working her fingers in Ruth's shoulders to relax her*): She be all right. Women gets right depressed sometimes when they get her way. (*Speaking softly, expertly, rapidly.*) Now you just relax. That's right . . . just lean back, don't think 'bout nothing at all . . . nothing at all—

RUTH: I'm all right . . .

The glassy-eyed look melts and then she collapses into a fit of heavy sobbing. The bell rings.

BENEATHA: Oh, my God—that must be Asagai.

MAMA (*to Ruth*): Come on now, honey. You need to lie down and rest awhile . . . then have some nice hot food.

They exit, Ruth's weight on her mother-in-law. Beneatha, herself profoundly disturbed, opens the door to admit a rather dramatic-looking young man with a large package.

ASAGAI: Hello, Alaiyo—

BENEATHA (*holding the door open and regarding him with pleasure*): Hello . . . (*Long pause.*) Well—come in. And please excuse everything. My mother was very upset about my letting anyone come here with the place like this.

ASAGAI (*coming into the room*): You look disturbed too . . . Is something wrong?

BENEATHA (*still at the door, absently*): Yes . . . we've all got acute ghetto-itus. (*She smiles and comes toward him, finding a cigarette and sitting.*) So—sit down! No! Wait! (*She whips the spraygun off sofa where she had left it and puts the cushions back. At last perches on arm of sofa. He sits.*) So, how was Canada?

ASAGAI (*a sophisticate*): Canadian.

BENEATHA (*looking at him*): Asagai, I'm very glad you are back.

ASAGAI (*looking back at her in turn*): Are you really?

BENEATHA: Yes—very.

ASAGAI: Why? — you were quite glad when I went away. What happened?

BENEATHA: You went away.

ASAGAI: Ahhhhhhhh.

BENEATHA: Before — you wanted to be so serious before there was time.

ASAGAI: How much time must there be before one knows what one feels?

BENEATHA (*stalling this particular conversation. Her hands pressed together, in a deliberately childish gesture*): What did you bring me?

ASAGAI (*handing her the package*): Open it and see.

BENEATHA (*eagerly opening the package and drawing out some records and the colorful robes of a Nigerian woman*): Oh Asagai! . . . You got them for me! . . . How beautiful . . . and the records too! (*She lifts out the robes and runs to the mirror with them and holds the drapery up in front of herself.*)

ASAGAI (*coming to her at the mirror*): I shall have to teach you how to drape it properly. (*He flings the material about her for the moment and stands back to look at her.*) Ah — Oh-pay-gay-day, oh-gbah-mu-shay. (*A Yoruba exclamation for admiration.*) You wear it well . . . very well . . . mutilated hair and all.

BENEATHA (*turning suddenly*): My hair — what's wrong with my hair?

ASAGAI (*shrugging*): Were you born with it like that?

BENEATHA (*reaching up to touch it*): No . . . of course not.

She looks back to the mirror, disturbed.

ASAGAI (*smiling*): How then?

BENEATHA: You know perfectly well how . . . as crinkly as yours . . . that's how.

ASAGAI: And it is ugly to you that way?

BENEATHA (*quickly*): Oh, no — not ugly . . . (*More slowly, apologetically.*) But it's so hard to manage when it's, well — raw.

ASAGAI: And so to accommodate that — you mutilate it every week?

BENEATHA: It's not mutilation!

ASAGAI (*laughing aloud at her seriousness*): Oh . . . please! I am only teasing you because you are so very serious about these things. (*He stands back from her and folds his arms across his chest as he watches her pulling at her hair and frowning in the mirror.*) Do you remember the first time you met me at school? . . . (*He laughs.*) You came up to me and you said — and I thought you were the most serious little thing I had ever seen — you said: (*He imitates her.*) "Mr. Asagai — I want very much to talk with you. About Africa. You see, Mr. Asagai, I am looking for my *identity!*"

He laughs.

BENEATHA (*turning to him, not laughing*): Yes —

Her face is quizzical, profoundly disturbed.

ASAGAI (*still teasing and reaching out and taking her face in his hands and turning her profile to him*): Well . . . it is true that this is not so much a profile of a Hollywood queen as perhaps a queen of the Nile — (*A mock dismissal of the importance of the question.*) But what does it matter? Assimilationism is so popular in your country.

BENEATHA (*wheeling, passionately, sharply*): I am not an assimilationist!

ASAGAI (*the protest hangs in the room for a moment and Asagai studies her, his laughter fading*): Such a serious one. (*There is a pause.*) So—you like the robes? You must take excellent care of them—they are from my sister's personal wardrobe.

BENEATHA (*with incredulity*): You—you sent all the way home—for me?

ASAGAI (*with charm*): For you—I would do much more . . . Well, that is what I came for. I must go.

BENEATHA: Will you call me Monday?

ASAGAI: Yes . . . We have a great deal to talk about. I mean about identity and time and all that.

BENEATHA: Time?

ASAGAI: Yes. About how much time one needs to know what one feels.

BENEATHA: You see! You never understood that there is more than one kind of feeling which can exist between a man and a woman—or, at least, there should be.

ASAGAI (*shaking his head negatively but gently*): No. Between a man and a woman there need be only one kind of feeling. I have that for you . . . Now even . . . right this moment . . .

BENEATHA: I know—and by itself—it won't do. I can find that anywhere.

ASAGAI: For a woman it should be enough.

BENEATHA: I know—because that's what it says in all the novels that men write. But it isn't. Go ahead and laugh—but I'm not interested in being someone's little episode in America or—(*With feminine vengeance.*)—one of them! (*Asagai has burst into laughter again.*) That's funny as hell, huh!

ASAGAI: It's just that every American girl I have known has said that to me. White—black—in this you are all the same. And the same speech, too!

BENEATHA (*angrily*): Yuk, yuk, yuk!

ASAGAI: It's how you can be sure that the world's most liberated women are not liberated at all. You all talk about it too much!

Mama enters and is immediately all social charm because of the presence of a guest.

BENEATHA: Oh—Mama—this is Mr. Asagai.

MAMA: How do you do?

ASAGAI (*total politeness to an elder*): How do you do, Mrs. Younger. Please forgive me for coming at such an outrageous hour on a Saturday.

MAMA: Well, you are quite welcome. I just hope you understand that our house don't always look like this. (*Chatterish.*) You must come again. I would love to hear all about—(*Not sure of the name.*)—your country. I think it's so sad the way our American Negroes don't know nothing about Africa 'cept Tarzan and all that. And all that money they pour into these churches when they ought to be helping you people over there drive out them French and Englishmen done taken away your land.

The mother flashes a slightly superior look at her daughter upon completion of the recitation.

ASAGAI (*taken aback by this sudden and acutely unrelated expression of sympathy*): Yes . . . yes . . .

MAMA (*smiling at him suddenly and relaxing and looking him over*): How many miles is it from here to where you come from?

ASAGAI: Many thousands.

MAMA (*looking at him as she would Walter*): I bet you don't half look after yourself, being away from your mama either. I spec you better come 'round here from time to time to get yourself some decent homecooked meals . . .

ASAGAI (*moved*): Thank you. Thank you very much. (*They are all quiet, then—*) Well . . . I must go. I will call you Monday, Alaiyo.

MAMA: What's that he call you?

ASAGAI: Oh—"Alaiyo." I hope you don't mind. It is what you would call a nickname, I think. It is a Yoruba word. I am a Yoruba.

MAMA (*looking at Beneatha*): I—I thought he was from—(*Uncertain.*)

ASAGAI (*understanding*): Nigeria is my country. Yoruba is my tribal origin—

BENEATHA: You didn't tell us what Alaiyo means . . . for all I know, you might be calling me Little Idiot or something . . .

ASAGAI: Well . . . let me see . . . I do not know how just to explain it . . . The sense of a thing can be so different when it changes languages.

BENEATHA: You're evading.

ASAGAI: No—really it is difficult . . . (*Thinking.*) It means . . . it means One for Whom Bread—Food—Is Not Enough. (*He looks at her.*) Is that all right?

BENEATHA (*understanding, softly*): Thank you.

MAMA (*looking from one to the other and not understanding any of it*): Well . . . that's nice . . . You must come see us again—Mr.—

ASAGAI: Ah-sah-guy . . .

MAMA: Yes . . . Do come again.

ASAGAI: Good-bye.

He exits.

MAMA (*after him*): Lord, that's a pretty thing just went out here! (*Insinuatingly, to her daughter.*) Yes, I guess I see why we done commence to get so interested in Africa 'round here. Missionaries my aunt Jenny!

She exits.

BENEATHA: Oh, Mama! . . .

She picks up the Nigerian dress and holds it up to her in front of the mirror again. She sets the headdress on haphazardly and then notices her hair again and clutches at it and then replaces the headdress and frowns at herself. Then she starts to wriggle in front of the mirror as she thinks a Nigerian woman might. Travis enters and stands regarding her.

TRAVIS: What's the matter, girl, you cracking up?

BENEATHA: Shut up.

She pulls the headdress off and looks at herself in the mirror and clutches at her hair again and squinches her eyes as if trying to imagine something. Then, suddenly, she gets her raincoat and kerchief and hurriedly prepares for going out.

MAMA (*coming back into the room*): She's resting now. Travis, baby, run next door and ask Miss Johnson to please let me have a little kitchen cleanser. This here can is empty as Jacob's kettle.

TRAVIS: I just came in.

MAMA: Do as you told. (*He exits and she looks at her daughter.*) Where you going?

BENEATHA (*halting at the door*): To become a queen of the Nile!

She exits in a breathless blaze of glory. Ruth appears in the bedroom doorway.

MAMA: Who told you to get up?

RUTH: Ain't nothing wrong with me to be lying in no bed for. Where did Bennie go?

MAMA (*drumming her fingers*): Far as I could make out—to Egypt. (*Ruth just looks at her.*) What time is it getting to?

RUTH: Ten twenty. And the mailman going to ring that bell this morning just like he done every morning for the last umpteen years.

Travis comes in with the cleanser can.

TRAVIS: She say to tell you that she don't have much.

MAMA (*angrily*): Lord, some people I could name sure is tight-fisted! (*Directing her grandson.*) Mark two cans of cleanser on the list there. If she that hard up for kitchen cleanser, I sure don't want to forget to get her none!

RUTH: Lena—maybe the woman is just short on cleanser—

MAMA (*not listening*): —Much baking powder as she done borrowed from me all these years, she could of done gone into the baking business!

The bell sounds suddenly and sharply and all three are stunned—serious and silent—midspeech. In spite of all the other conversations and distractions of the morning, this is what they have been waiting for, even Travis, who looks helplessly from his mother to his grandmother. Ruth is the first to come to life again.

RUTH (*to Travis*): Get down them steps, boy!

Travis snaps to life and flies out to get the mail.

MAMA (*her eyes wide, her hand to her breast*): You mean it done really come?

RUTH (*excited*): Oh, Miss Lena!

MAMA (*collecting herself*): Well . . . I don't know what we all so excited about 'round here for. We known it was coming for months.

RUTH: That's a whole lot different from having it come and being able to hold it in your hands . . . a piece of paper worth ten thousand dollars . . . (*Travis bursts back into the room. He holds the envelope high above his head, like a little dancer, his face is radiant and he is breathless. He moves to his grandmother with sudden slow ceremony and puts the envelope into her hands. She accepts it, and then merely holds it and looks at it.*) Come on! Open it . . . Lord have mercy, I wish Walter Lee was here!

TRAVIS: Open it, Grandmama!

MAMA (*staring at it*): Now you all be quiet. It's just a check.

RUTH: Open it . . .

MAMA (*still staring at it*): Now don't act silly . . . We ain't never been no people to act silly 'bout no money—

RUTH (*swiftly*): We ain't never had none before — OPEN IT!

Mama finally makes a good strong tear and pulls out the thin blue slice of paper and inspects it closely. The boy and his mother study it raptly over Mama's shoulders.

MAMA: Travis! (*She is counting off with doubt.*) Is that the right number of zeros?

TRAVIS: Yes'm . . . ten thousand dollars. Gaalee, grandmama, you rich.

MAMA (*She holds the check away from her, still looking at it. Slowly her face sobers into a mask of unhappiness*): Ten thousand dollars. (*She hands it to Ruth.*) Put it away somewhere, Ruth. (*She does not look at Ruth; her eyes seem to be seeing something somewhere very far off.*) Ten thousand dollars they give you. Ten thousand dollars.

TRAVIS (*to his mother, sincerely*): What's the matter with Grandmama — don't she want to be rich?

RUTH (*distractedly*): You go on out and play now, baby. (*Travis exits. Mama starts wiping dishes absently, humming intently to herself. Ruth turns to her, with kind exasperation.*) You've gone and got yourself upset.

MAMA (*not looking at her*): I spec if it wasn't for you all . . . I would just put that money away or give it to the church or something.

RUTH: Now what kind of talk is that. Mr. Younger would just be plain mad if he could hear you talking foolish like that.

MAMA (*stopping and staring off*): Yes . . . he sure would. (*Sighing.*) We got enough to do with that money, all right. (*She halts then, and turns and looks at her daughter-in-law hard; Ruth avoids her eyes and Mama wipes her hands with finality and starts to speak firmly to Ruth.*) Where did you go today, girl?

RUTH: To the doctor.

MAMA (*impatiently*): Now, Ruth . . . you know better than that. Old Doctor Jones is strange enough in his way but there ain't nothing 'bout him make somebody slip and call him "she" — like you done this morning.

RUTH: Well, that's what happened — my tongue slipped.

MAMA: You went to see that woman, didn't you?

RUTH (*defensively, giving herself away*): What woman you talking about?

MAMA (*angrily*): That woman who —

Walter enters in great excitement.

WALTER: Did it come?

MAMA (*quietly*): Can't you give people a Christian greeting before you start asking about money?

WALTER (*to Ruth*): Did it come? (*Ruth unfolds the check and lays it quietly before him, watching him intently with thoughts of her own. Walter sits down and grasps it close and counts off the zeros.*) Ten thousand dollars — (*He turns suddenly, frantically to his mother and draws some papers out of his breast pocket.*) Mama — look. Old Willy Harris put everything on paper —

MAMA: Son — I think you ought to talk to your wife . . . I'll go on out and leave you alone if you want —

WALTER: I can talk to her later — Mama, look —

MAMA: Son —

WALTER: WILL SOMEBODY PLEASE LISTEN TO ME TODAY!

MAMA (*quietly*): I don't 'low no yellin' in this house, Walter Lee, and you know it—(*Walter stares at them in frustration and starts to speak several times.*) And there ain't going to be no investing in no liquor stores.

WALTER: But, Mama, you ain't even looked at it.

MAMA: I don't aim to have to speak on that again.

A long pause.

WALTER: You ain't looked at it and you don't aim to have to speak on that again? You ain't even looked at it and *you* have decided—(*Crumpling his papers.*) Well, *you* tell that to my boy tonight when you put him to sleep on the living-room couch . . . (*Turning to Mama and speaking directly to her.*) Yeah—and tell it to my wife, Mama, tomorrow when she has to go out of here to look after somebody else's kids. And tell it to *me*, Mama, every time we need a new pair of curtains and I have to watch *you* go out and work in somebody's kitchen. Yeah, you tell me then!

Walter starts out.

RUTH: Where you going?

WALTER: I'm going out!

RUTH: Where?

WALTER: Just out of this house somewhere—

RUTH (*getting her coat*): I'll come too.

WALTER: I don't want you to come!

RUTH: I got something to talk to you about, Walter.

WALTER: That's too bad.

MAMA (*still quietly*): Walter Lee—(*She waits and he finally turns and looks at her.*) Sit down.

WALTER: I'm a grown man, Mama.

MAMA: Ain't nobody said you wasn't grown. But you still in my house and my presence. And as long as you are—you'll talk to your wife civil. Now sit down.

RUTH (*suddenly*): Oh, let him go on out and drink himself to death! He makes me sick to my stomach! (*She flings her coat against him and exits to bedroom.*)

WALTER (*violently flinging the coat after her*): And you turn mine too, baby! (*The door slams behind her.*) That was my biggest mistake—

MAMA (*still quietly*): Walter, what is the matter with you?

WALTER: Matter with me? Ain't nothing the matter with *me*!

MAMA: Yes there is. Something eating you up like a crazy man. Something more than me not giving you this money. The past few years I been watching it happen to you. You get all nervous acting and kind of wild in the eyes—(*Walter jumps up impatiently at her words.*) I said sit there now, I'm talking to you!

WALTER: Mama—I don't need no nagging at me today.

MAMA: Seem like you getting to a place where you always tied up in some kind of knot about something. But if anybody ask you 'bout it you just yell at 'em and bust out the house and go out and drink somewheres. Walter

Lee, people can't live with that. Ruth's a good, patient girl in her way—
but you getting to be too much. Boy, don't make the mistake of driving
that girl away from you.

WALTER: Why—what she do for me?

MAMA: She loves you.

WALTER: Mama—I'm going out. I want to go off somewhere and be by myself
for a while.

MAMA: I'm sorry 'bout your liquor store, son. It just wasn't the thing for us to
do. That's what I want to tell you about—

WALTER: I got to go out, Mama—

He rises.

MAMA: It's dangerous, son.

WALTER: What's dangerous?

MAMA: When a man goes outside his home to look for peace.

WALTER (*beseechingly*): Then why can't there never be no peace in this house
then?

MAMA: You done found it in some other house?

WALTER: No—there ain't no woman! Why do women always think there's a
woman somewhere when a man gets restless. (*Picks up the check.*) Do you
know what this money means to me? Do you know what this money can
do for us? (*Puts it back.*) Mama—Mama—I want so many things . . .

MAMA: Yes, son—

WALTER: I want so many things that they are driving me kind of crazy . . .
Mama—look at me.

MAMA: I'm looking at you. You a good-looking boy. You got a job, a nice wife, a
fine boy, and—

WALTER: A job. (*Looks at her.*) Mama, a job? I open and close car doors all day
long. I drive a man around in his limousine and I say, "Yes, sir; no, sir; very
good, sir; shall I take the Drive, sir?" Mama, that ain't no kind of job . . .
that ain't nothing at all. (*Very quietly.*) Mama, I don't know if I can make
you understand.

MAMA: Understand what, baby?

WALTER (*quietly*): Sometimes it's like I can see the future stretched out in front
of me—just plain as day. The future, Mama. Hanging over there at the
edge of my days. Just waiting for me—a big, looming blank space—full
of *nothing.* Just waiting for *me.* But it don't have to be. (*Pause. Kneeling
beside her chair.*) Mama—sometimes when I'm downtown and I pass them
cool, quiet-looking restaurants where them white boys are sitting back
and talking 'bout things . . . sitting there turning deals worth millions of
dollars . . . sometimes I see guys don't look much older than me—

MAMA: Son—how come you talk so much 'bout money?

WALTER (*with immense passion*): Because it is life, Mama!

MAMA (*quietly*): Oh—(*Very quietly.*) So now it's life. Money is life. Once upon a
time freedom used to be life—now it's money. I guess the world really do
change . . .

WALTER: No—it was always money, Mama. We just didn't know about it.

MAMA: No . . . something has changed. (*She looks at him.*) You something new, boy. In my time we was worried about not being lynched and getting to the North if we could and how to stay alive and still have a pinch of dignity too . . . Now here come you and Beneatha—talking 'bout things we ain't never even thought about hardly, me and your daddy. You ain't satisfied or proud of nothing we done. I mean that you had a home; that we kept you out of trouble till you was grown; that you don't have to ride to work on the back of nobody's streetcar—You my children—but how different we done become.

WALTER (*a long beat. He pats her hand and gets up*): You just don't understand, Mama, you just don't understand.

MAMA: Son—do you know your wife is expecting another baby? (*Walter stands, stunned, and absorbs what his mother has said.*) That's what she wanted to talk to you about. (*Walter sinks down into a chair.*) This ain't for me to be telling—but you ought to know. (*She waits.*) I think Ruth is thinking 'bout getting rid of that child.

WALTER (*slowly understanding*): —No—no—Ruth wouldn't do that.

MAMA: When the world gets ugly enough—a woman will do anything for her family. *The part that's already living.*

WALTER: You don't know Ruth, Mama, if you think she would do that.

Ruth opens the bedroom door and stands there a little limp.

RUTH (*beaten*): Yes I would too, Walter. (*Pause.*) I gave her a five-dollar down payment.

There is total silence as the man stares at his wife and the mother stares at her son.

MAMA (*presently*): Well—(*Tightly.*) Well—son, I'm waiting to hear you say something . . . (*She waits.*) I'm waiting to hear how you be your father's son. Be the man he was . . . (*Pause. The silence shouts.*) Your wife say she going to destroy your child. And I'm waiting to hear you talk like him and say we a people who give children life, not who destroys them—(*She rises.*) I'm waiting to see you stand up and look like your daddy and say we done give up one baby to poverty and that we ain't going to give up nary another one . . . I'm waiting.

WALTER: Ruth—(*He can say nothing.*)

MAMA: If you a son of mine, tell her! (*Walter picks up his keys and his coat and walks out. She continues, bitterly.*) You . . . you are a disgrace to your father's memory. Somebody get me my hat!

Curtain.

ACT II

SCENE I

Time: Later the same day.

At rise: Ruth is ironing again. She has the radio going. Presently Beneatha's bedroom door opens and Ruth's mouth falls and she puts down the iron in fascination.

RUTH: What have we got on tonight!

BENEATHA (*emerging grandly from the doorway so that we can see her thoroughly robed in the costume Asagai brought*): You are looking at what a well-dressed Nigerian woman wears—(*She parades for Ruth, her hair completely hidden by the headdress; she is coquettishly fanning herself with an ornate oriental fan, mistakenly more like Butterfly than any Nigerian that ever was.*) Isn't it beautiful? (*She promenades to the radio and, with an arrogant flourish, turns off the good loud blues that is playing.*) Enough of this assimilationist junk! (*Ruth follows her with her eyes as she goes to the phonograph and puts on a record and turns and waits ceremoniously for the music to come up. Then, with a shout—*) OCOMOGOSIAY!

Ruth jumps. The music comes up, a lovely Nigerian melody. Beneatha listens, enraptured, her eyes far away— "back to the past." She begins to dance. Ruth is dumfounded.

RUTH: What kind of dance is that?

BENEATHA: A folk dance.

RUTH (*Pearl Bailey°*): What kind of folks do that, honey?

BENEATHA: It's from Nigeria. It's a dance of welcome.

RUTH: Who you welcoming?

BENEATHA: The men back to the village.

RUTH: Where they been?

BENEATHA: How should I know—out hunting or something. Anyway, they are coming back now . . .

RUTH: Well, that's good.

BENEATHA (*with the record*):

> Alundi, alundi
> Alundi alunya
> Jop pu a jeepua
> Ang gu soooooooooo
> Ai yai yae . . .
> Ayehaye—alundi . . .

Walter comes in during this performance; he has obviously been drinking. He leans against the door heavily and watches his sister, at first with distaste. Then his eyes look off— "back to the past"—as he lifts both his fists to the roof, screaming.

WALTER: YEAH . . . AND ETHIOPIA STRETCH FORTH HER HANDS AGAIN! . . .

RUTH (*drily, looking at him*): Yes—and Africa sure is claiming her own tonight. (*She gives them both up and starts ironing again.*)

WALTER (*all in a drunken, dramatic shout*): Shut up! . . . I'm diggin them drums . . . them drums move me! . . . (*He makes his weaving way to his wife's face and leans in close to her.*) In my *heart of hearts*—(*He thumps his chest.*)—I am much warrior!

RUTH (*without even looking up*): In your heart of hearts you are much drunkard.

Pearl Bailey: A popular African American singer (1918–1990).

WALTER (*coming away from her and starting to wander around the room, shouting*): Me and Jomo . . . (*Intently, in his sister's face. She has stopped dancing to watch him in this unknown mood.*) That's my man, Kenyatta.° (*Shouting and thumping his chest.*) FLAMING SPEAR! HOT DAMN! (*He is suddenly in possession of an imaginary spear and actively spearing enemies all over the room.*) OCOMOGOSIAY . . .

BENEATHA (*to encourage Walter, thoroughly caught up with this side of him*): OCOMOGOSIAY, FLAMING SPEAR!

WALTER: THE LION IS WAKING . . . OWIMOWEH!

He pulls his shirt open and leaps up on the table and gestures with his spear.

BENEATHA: OWIMOWEH!

WALTER (*on the table, very far gone, his eyes pure glass sheets. He sees what we cannot, that he is a leader of his people, a great chief, a descendant of Chaka,° and that the hour to march has come*): Listen, my black brothers—

BENEATHA: OCOMOGOSIAY!

WALTER: —Do you hear the waters rushing against the shores of the coastlands—

BENEATHA: OCOMOGOSIAY!

WALTER: —Do you hear the screeching of the cocks in yonder hills beyond where the chiefs meet in council for the coming of the mighty war—

BENEATHA: OCOMOGOSIAY!

And now the lighting shifts subtly to suggest the world of Walter's imagination, and the mood shifts from pure comedy. It is the inner Walter speaking: the Southside chauffeur has assumed an unexpected majesty.

WALTER: —Do you hear the beating of the wings of the birds flying low over the mountains and the low places of our land—

BENEATHA: OCOMOGOSIAY!

WALTER: —Do you hear the singing of the women, singing the war songs of our fathers to the babies in the great houses? Singing the sweet war songs! (*The doorbell rings.*) OH, DO YOU HEAR, MY *BLACK* BROTHERS!

BENEATHA (*completely gone*): We hear you, Flaming Spear—

Ruth shuts off the phonograph and opens the door. George Murchison enters.

WALTER: Telling us to prepare for the GREATNESS OF THE TIME! (*Lights back to normal. He turns and sees George.*) Black Brother!

He extends his hand for the fraternal clasp.

GEORGE: Black Brother, hell!

RUTH (*having had enough, and embarrassed for the family*): Beneatha, you got company—what's the matter with you? Walter Lee Younger, get down off that table and stop acting like a fool . . .

Kenyatta: Jomo Kenyatta (c. 1894–1978), a Kenyan politician involved in the country's nationalist movement. **Chaka:** Also spelled Shaka (c. 1787–1828), he became chief of the Zulu clan in 1816 and founded the great Zulu empire by conquering most of southern Africa.

Walter comes down off the table suddenly and makes a quick exit to the bathroom.

RUTH: He's had a little to drink . . . I don't know what her excuse is.

GEORGE (*to Beneatha*): Look honey, we're going to the theater—we're not going to be *in* it . . . so go change, huh?

Beneatha looks at him and slowly, ceremoniously, lifts her hands and pulls off the headdress. Her hair is close-cropped and unstraightened. George freezes midsentence and Ruth's eyes all but fall out of her head.

GEORGE: What in the name of—

RUTH (*touching Beneatha's hair*): Girl, you done lost your natural mind? Look at your head!

GEORGE: What have you done to your head—I mean your hair!

BENEATHA: Nothing—except cut it off.

RUTH: Now that's the truth—it's what ain't been done to it! You expect this boy to go out with you with your head all nappy like that?

BENEATHA (*looking at George*): That's up to George. If he's ashamed of his heritage—

GEORGE: Oh, don't be so proud of yourself, Bennie—just because you look eccentric.

BENEATHA: How can something that's natural be eccentric?

GEORGE: That's what being eccentric means—being natural. Get dressed.

BENEATHA: I don't like that, George.

RUTH: Why must you and your brother make an argument out of everything people say?

BENEATHA: Because I hate assimilationist Negroes!

RUTH: Will somebody please tell me what assimila-whoever means!

GEORGE: Oh, it's just a college girl's way of calling people Uncle Toms—but that isn't what it means at all.

RUTH: Well, what does it mean?

BENEATHA (*cutting George off and staring at him as she replies to Ruth*): It means someone who is willing to give up his own culture and submerge himself completely in the dominant, and in this case *oppressive* culture!

GEORGE: Oh, dear, dear, dear! Here we go! A lecture on the African past! On our Great West African Heritage! In one second we will hear all about the great Ashanti empires; the great Songhay civilizations; and the great sculpture of Bénin—and then some poetry in the Bantu—and the whole monologue will end with the word *heritage!* (*Nastily.*) Let's face it, baby, your heritage is nothing but a bunch of raggedy-assed spirituals and some grass huts!

BENEATHA: GRASS HUTS! (*Ruth crosses to her and forcibly pushes her toward the bedroom.*) See there . . . you are standing there in your splendid ignorance talking about people who were the first to smelt iron on the face of the earth! (*Ruth is pushing her through the door.*) The Ashanti were performing surgical operations when the English—(*Ruth pulls the door to, with Beneatha on the other side, and smiles graciously at George. Beneatha opens the door and shouts the end of the sentence defiantly at George.*)—were still tatooing themselves with blue dragons! (*She goes back inside.*)

RUTH: Have a seat, George. (*They both sit. Ruth folds her hands rather primly on her lap, determined to demonstrate the civilization of the family.*) Warm, ain't it? I mean for September. (*Pause.*) Just like they always say about Chicago weather: if it's too hot or cold for you, just wait a minute and it'll change. (*She smiles happily at this cliché of clichés.*) Everybody say it's got to do with them bombs and things they keep setting off. (*Pause.*) Would you like a nice cold beer?

GEORGE: No, thank you. I don't care for beer. (*He looks at his watch.*) I hope she hurries up.

RUTH: What time is the show?

GEORGE: It's an eight-thirty curtain. That's just Chicago, though. In New York standard curtain time is eight forty.

He is rather proud of this knowledge.

RUTH (*properly appreciating it*): You get to New York a lot?

GEORGE (*offhand*): Few times a year.

RUTH: Oh—that's nice. I've never been to New York.

Walter enters. We feel he has relieved himself, but the edge of unreality is still with him.

WALTER: New York ain't got nothing Chicago ain't. Just a bunch of hustling people all squeezed up together—being "Eastern."

He turns his face into a screw of displeasure.

GEORGE: Oh—you've been?

WALTER: *Plenty* of times.

RUTH (*shocked at the lie*): Walter Lee Younger!

WALTER (*staring her down*): Plenty! (*Pause.*) What we got to drink in this house? Why don't you offer this man some refreshment. (*To George.*) They don't know how to entertain people in this house, man.

GEORGE: Thank you—I don't really care for anything.

WALTER (*feeling his head; sobriety coming*): Where's Mama?

RUTH: She ain't come back yet.

WALTER (*looking Murchison over from head to toe, scrutinizing his carefully casual tweed sports jacket over cashmere V-neck sweater over soft eyelet shirt and tie, and soft slacks, finished off with white buckskin shoes*): Why all you college boys wear them faggoty-looking white shoes?

RUTH: Walter Lee!

George Murchison ignores the remark.

WALTER (*to Ruth*): Well, they look crazy as hell—white shoes, cold as it is.

RUTH (*crushed*): You have to excuse him—

WALTER: No he don't! Excuse me for what? What you always excusing me for! I'll excuse myself when I needs to be excused! (*A pause.*) They look as funny as them black knee socks Beneatha wears out of here all the time.

RUTH: It's the college *style*, Walter.

WALTER: Style, hell. She looks like she got burnt legs or something!

RUTH: Oh, Walter—

WALTER (*an irritable mimic*): Oh, Walter! Oh, Walter! (*To Murchison.*) How's your old man making out? I understand you all going to buy that big hotel on the Drive? (*He finds a beer in the refrigerator, wanders over to Murchison, sipping and wiping his lips with the back of his hand, and strad-dling a chair backwards to talk to the other man.*) Shrewd move. Your old man is all right, man. (*Tapping his head and half winking for emphasis.*) I mean he knows how to operate. I mean he thinks *big*, you know what I mean, I mean for a *home*, you know? But I think he's kind of running out of ideas now. I'd like to talk to him. Listen, man, I got some plans that could turn this city upside down. I mean think like he does. *Big.* Invest big, gamble big, hell, lose *big* if you have to, you know what I mean. It's hard to find a man on this whole Southside who understands my kind of thinking—you dig? (*He scrutinizes Murchison again, drinks his beer, squints his eyes and leans in close, confidential, man to man.*) Me and you ought to sit down and talk sometimes, man. Man, I got me some ideas . . .

MURCHISON (*with boredom*): Yeah—sometimes we'll have to do that, Walter.

WALTER (*understanding the indifference, and offended*): Yeah—well, when you get the time, man. I know you a busy little boy.

RUTH: Walter, please—

WALTER (*bitterly, hurt*): I know ain't nothing in this world as busy as you col-ored college boys with your fraternity pins and white shoes . . .

RUTH (*covering her face with humiliation*): Oh, Walter Lee—

WALTER: I see you all all the time—with the books tucked under your arms—going to your (*British A—a mimic.*) "clahsses." And for what! What the hell you learning over there? Filling up your heads—(*Counting off on his fingers.*)—with the sociology and the psychology—but they teaching you how to be a man? How to take over and run the world? They teaching you how to run a rubber plantation or a steel mill? Naw—just to talk proper and read books and wear them faggoty-looking white shoes . . .

GEORGE (*looking at him with distaste, a little above it all*): You're all wacked up with bitterness, man.

WALTER (*intently, almost quietly, between the teeth, glaring at the boy*): And you—ain't you bitter, man? Ain't you just about had it yet? Don't you see no stars gleaming that you can't reach out and grab? You happy?—You contented son-of-a-bitch—you happy? You got it made? Bitter? Man, I'm a volcano. Bitter? Here I am a giant—surrounded by ants! Ants who can't even understand what it is the giant is talking about.

RUTH (*passionately and suddenly*): Oh, Walter—ain't you with nobody!

WALTER (*violently*): No! 'Cause ain't nobody with me! Not even my own mother!

RUTH: Walter, that's a terrible thing to say!

Beneatha enters, dressed for the evening in a cocktail dress and earrings, hair natural.

GEORGE: Well—hey—(*Crosses to Beneatha; thoughtful, with emphasis, since this is a reversal.*) You look great!

WALTER (*seeing his sister's hair for the first time*): What's the matter with your head?

BENEATHA (*tired of the jokes now*): I cut it off, Brother.

WALTER (*coming close to inspect it and walking around her*): Well, I'll be damned. So that's what they mean by the African bush . . .

BENEATHA: Ha ha. Let's go, George.

GEORGE (*looking at her*): You know something? I like it. It's sharp. I mean it really is. (*Helps her into her wrap.*)

RUTH: Yes—I think so, too. (*She goes to the mirror and starts to clutch at her hair.*)

WALTER: Oh no! You leave yours alone, baby. You might turn out to have a pin-shaped head or something!

BENEATHA: See you all later.

RUTH: Have a nice time.

GEORGE: Thanks. Good night. (*Half out the door, he reopens it. To Walter.*) Good night, Prometheus!°

Beneatha and George exit.

WALTER (*to Ruth*): Who is Prometheus?

RUTH: I don't know. Don't worry about it.

WALTER (*in fury, pointing after George*): See there—they get to a point where they can't insult you man to man—they got to go talk about something ain't nobody never heard of!

RUTH: How do you know it was an insult? (*To humor him.*) Maybe Prometheus is a nice fellow.

WALTER: Prometheus! I bet there ain't even no such thing! I bet that simple-minded clown—

RUTH: Walter—

She stops what she is doing and looks at him.

WALTER (*yelling*): Don't start!

RUTH: Start what?

WALTER: Your nagging! Where was I? Who was I with? How much money did I spend?

RUTH (*plaintively*): Walter Lee—why don't we just try to talk about it . . .

WALTER (*not listening*): I been out talking with people who understand me. People who care about the things I got on my mind.

RUTH (*wearily*): I guess that means people like Willy Harris.

WALTER: Yes, people like Willy Harris.

RUTH (*with a sudden flash of impatience*): Why don't you all just hurry up and go into the banking business and stop talking about it!

WALTER: Why? You want to know why? 'Cause we all tied up in a race of people that don't know how to do nothing but moan, pray, and have babies!

The line is too bitter even for him and he looks at her and sits down.

Prometheus: In Greek myth, a Titan who was punished by Zeus for stealing fire from the gods and giving it to humankind.

RUTH: Oh, Walter . . . (*Softly.*) Honey, why can't you stop fighting me?

WALTER (*without thinking*): Who's fighting you? Who even cares about you?

This line begins the retardation of his mood.

RUTH: Well — (*She waits a long time, and then with resignation starts to put away her things.*) I guess I might as well go on to bed . . . (*More or less to herself.*) I don't know where we lost it . . . but we have . . . (*Then, to him.*) I — I'm sorry about this new baby, Walter. I guess maybe I better go on and do what I started . . . I guess I just didn't realize how bad things was with us . . . I guess I just didn't really realize — (*She starts out to the bedroom and stops.*) You want some hot milk?

WALTER: Hot milk?

RUTH: Yes — hot milk.

WALTER: Why hot milk?

RUTH: 'Cause after all that liquor you come home with you ought to have something hot in your stomach.

WALTER: I don't want no milk.

RUTH: You want some coffee then?

WALTER: No, I don't want no coffee. I don't want nothing hot to drink. (*Almost plaintively.*) Why you always trying to give me something to eat?

RUTH (*standing and looking at him helplessly*): What *else* can I give you, Walter Lee Younger?

She stands and looks at him and presently turns to go out again. He lifts his head and watches her going away from him in a new mood which began to emerge when he asked her "Who cares about you?"

WALTER: It's been rough, ain't it, baby? (*She hears and stops but does not turn around and he continues to her back.*) I guess between two people there ain't never as much understood as folks generally thinks there is. I mean like between me and you — (*She turns to face him.*) How we gets to the place where we scared to talk softness to each other. (*He waits, thinking hard himself.*) Why you think it got to be like that? (*He is thoughtful, almost as a child would be.*) Ruth, what is it gets into people ought to be close?

RUTH: I don't know, honey. I think about it a lot.

WALTER: On account of you and me, you mean? The way things are with us. The way something done come down between us.

RUTH: There ain't so much between us, Walter . . . Not when you come to me and try to talk to me. Try to be with me . . . a little even.

WALTER (*total honesty*): Sometimes . . . sometimes . . . I don't even know how to try.

RUTH: Walter —

WALTER: Yes?

RUTH (*coming to him, gently and with misgiving, but coming to him*): Honey . . . life don't have to be like this. I mean sometimes people can do things so that things are better . . . You remember how we used to talk when Travis was born . . . about the way we were going to live . . . the kind of house . . . (*She is stroking his head.*) Well, it's all starting to slip away from us . . .

He turns her to him and they look at each other and kiss, tenderly and hungrily. The door opens and Mama enters—Walter breaks away and jumps up. A beat.

WALTER: Mama, where have you been?

MAMA: My—them steps is longer than they used to be. Whew! (*She sits down and ignores him.*) How you feeling this evening, Ruth?

Ruth shrugs, disturbed at having been interrupted and watching her husband knowingly.

WALTER: Mama, where have you been all day?

MAMA (*still ignoring him and leaning on the table and changing to more comfortable shoes*): Where's Travis?

RUTH: I let him go out earlier and he ain't come back yet. Boy, is he going to get it!

WALTER: Mama!

MAMA (*as if she has heard him for the first time*): Yes, son?

WALTER: Where did you go this afternoon?

MAMA: I went downtown to tend to some business that I had to tend to.

WALTER: What kind of business?

MAMA: You know better than to question me like a child, Brother.

WALTER (*rising and bending over the table*): Where were you, Mama? (*Bringing his fists down and shouting.*) Mama, you didn't go do something with that insurance money, something crazy?

The front door opens slowly, interrupting him, and Travis peeks his head in, less than hopefully.

TRAVIS (*to his mother*): Mama, I—

RUTH: "Mama I" nothing! You're going to get it, boy! Get on in that bedroom and get yourself ready!

TRAVIS: But I—

MAMA: Why don't you all never let the child explain hisself.

RUTH: Keep out of it now, Lena.

Mama clamps her lips together, and Ruth advances toward her son menacingly.

RUTH: A thousand times I have told you not to go off like that—

MAMA (*holding out her arms to her grandson*): Well—at least let me tell him something. I want him to be the first one to hear . . . Come here, Travis (*The boy obeys, gladly.*) Travis—(*She takes him by the shoulder and looks into his face.*)—you know that money we got in the mail this morning?

TRAVIS: Yes'm—

MAMA: Well—what you think your grandmama gone and done with that money?

TRAVIS: I don't know, Grandmama.

MAMA (*putting her finger on his nose for emphasis*): She went out and she bought you a house! (*The explosion comes from Walter at the end of the revelation and he jumps up and turns away from all of them in a fury. Mama continues, to Travis.*) You glad about the house? It's going to be yours when you get to be a man.

TRAVIS: Yeah—I always wanted to live in a house.

MAMA: All right, gimme some sugar then—(*Travis puts his arms around her neck as she watches her son over the boy's shoulder. Then, to Travis, after the embrace.*) Now when you say your prayers tonight, you thank God and your grandfather—'cause it was him who give you the house—in his way.

RUTH (*taking the boy from Mama and pushing him toward the bedroom*): Now you get out of here and get ready for your beating.

TRAVIS: Aw, Mama—

RUTH: Get on in there—(*Closing the door behind him and turning radiantly to her mother-in-law.*) So you went and did it!

MAMA (*quietly, looking at her son with pain*): Yes, I did.

RUTH (*raising both arms classically*): PRAISE GOD! (*Looks at Walter a moment, who says nothing. She crosses rapidly to her husband.*) Please, honey—let me be glad . . . you be glad too. (*She has laid her hands on his shoulders, but he shakes himself free of her roughly, without turning to face her.*) Oh, Walter . . . a home . . . a home. (*She comes back to Mama.*) Well—where is it? How big is it? How much it going to cost?

MAMA: Well—

RUTH: When we moving?

MAMA (*smiling at her*): First of the month.

RUTH (*throwing back her head with jubilance*): Praise God!

MAMA (*tentatively, still looking at her son's back turned against her and Ruth*): It's—it's a nice house too . . . (*She cannot help speaking directly to him. An imploring quality in her voice, her manner, makes her almost like a girl now.*) Three bedrooms—nice big one for you and Ruth . . . Me and Beneatha still have to share our room, but Travis have one of his own—and (*With difficulty.*) I figure if the—new baby—is a boy, we could get one of them double-decker outfits . . . And there's a yard with a little patch of dirt where I could maybe get to grow me a few flowers . . . And a nice big basement . . .

RUTH: Walter honey, be glad—

MAMA (*still to his back, fingering things on the table*): 'Course I don't want to make it sound fancier than it is . . . It's just a plain little old house—but it's made good and solid—and it will be *ours*. Walter Lee—it makes a difference in a man when he can walk on floors that belong to *him* . . .

RUTH: Where is it?

MAMA (*frightened at this telling*): Well—well—it's out there in Clybourne Park—

Ruth's radiance fades abruptly, and Walter finally turns slowly to face his mother with incredulity and hostility.

RUTH: Where?

MAMA (*matter-of-factly*): Four o six Clybourne Street, Clybourne Park.

RUTH: Clybourne Park? Mama, there ain't no colored people living in Clybourne Park.

MAMA (*almost idiotically*): Well, I guess there's going to be some now.

WALTER (*bitterly*): So that's the peace and comfort you went out and bought for us today!

MAMA (*raising her eyes to meet his finally*): Son—I just tried to find the nicest place for the least amount of money for my family.

RUTH (*trying to recover from the shock*): Well—well—'course I ain't one never been 'fraid of no crackers, mind you—but—well, wasn't there no other houses nowhere?

MAMA: Them houses they put up for colored in them areas way out all seem to cost twice as much as other houses. I did the best I could.

RUTH (*struck senseless with the news, in its various degrees of goodness and trouble, she sits a moment, her fists propping her chin in thought, and then she starts to rise, bringing her fists down with vigor, the radiance spreading from cheek to cheek again*): Well—well—All I can say is—if this is my time in life—MY TIME—to say good-bye—(*And she builds with momentum as she starts to circle the room with an exuberant, almost tearfully happy release.*)—to these Goddamned cracking walls!—(*She pounds the walls.*)—and these marching roaches!—(*She wipes at an imaginary army of marching roaches.*)—and this cramped little closet which ain't now or never was no kitchen!... then I say it loud and good, HAL-LELUJAH! AND GOOD-BYE MISERY...I DON'T NEVER WANT TO SEE YOUR UGLY FACE AGAIN! (*She laughs joyously, having practically destroyed the apartment, and flings her arms up and lets them come down happily, slowly, reflectively, over her abdomen, aware for the first time perhaps that the life therein pulses with happiness and not despair.*) Lena?

MAMA (*moved, watching her happiness*): Yes, honey?

RUTH (*looking off*): Is there—is there a whole lot of sunlight?

MAMA (*understanding*): Yes, child, there's a whole lot of sunlight.

Long pause.

RUTH (*collecting herself and going to the door of the room Travis is in*): Well—I guess I better see 'bout Travis. (*To Mama.*) Lord, I sure don't feel like whipping nobody today!

She exits.

MAMA (*the mother and son are left alone now and the mother waits a long time, considering deeply, before she speaks*): Son—you—you understand what I done, don't you? (*Walter is silent and sullen.*) I—I just seen my family falling apart today...just falling to pieces in front of my eyes...We couldn't of gone on like we was today. We was going backwards 'stead of forwards—talking 'bout killing babies and wishing each other was dead...When it gets like that in life—you just got to do something different, push on out and do something bigger...(*She waits.*) I wish you say something, son...I wish you'd say how deep inside you you think I done the right thing—

WALTER (*crossing slowly to his bedroom door and finally turning there and speaking measuredly*): What you need me to say you done right for? *You* the head of this family. You run our lives like you want to. It was your money and you did what you wanted with it. So what you need for me to say it was all right for? (*Bitterly, to hurt her as deeply as he knows is possible.*) So you butchered up a dream of mine — you — who always talking 'bout your children's dreams . . .

MAMA: Walter Lee —

He just closes the door behind him. Mama sits alone, thinking heavily.

Curtain.

SCENE II

Time: Friday night, a few weeks later.

> *At rise: Packing crates mark the intention of the family to move. Beneatha and George come in, presumably from an evening out again.*

GEORGE: O.K. . . . O.K., whatever you say . . . (*They both sit on the couch. He tries to kiss her. She moves away.*) Look, we've had a nice evening; let's not spoil it, huh? . . .

He again turns her head and tries to nuzzle in and she turns away from him, not with distaste but with momentary lack of interest; in a mood to pursue what they were talking about.

BENEATHA: I'm *trying* to talk to you.

GEORGE: We always talk.

BENEATHA: Yes — and I love to talk.

GEORGE (*exasperated; rising*): I know it and I don't mind it sometimes . . . I want you to cut it out, see — The moody stuff, I mean. I don't like it. You're a nice-looking girl . . . all over. That's all you need, honey, forget the atmosphere. Guys aren't going to go for the atmosphere — they're going to go for what they see. Be glad for that. Drop the Garbo routine. It doesn't go with you. As for myself, I want a nice — (*Groping.*) — simple (*Thoughtfully.*) — sophisticated girl . . . not a poet — O.K.?

He starts to kiss her, she rebuffs him again and he jumps up.

BENEATHA: Why are you angry, George?

GEORGE: Because this is stupid! I don't go out with you to discuss the nature of "quiet desperation" or to hear all about your thoughts — because the world will go on thinking what it thinks regardless —

BENEATHA: Then why read books? Why go to school?

GEORGE (*with artificial patience, counting on his fingers*): It's simple. You read books — to learn facts — to get grades — to pass the course — to get a degree. That's all — it has nothing to do with thoughts.

A long pause.

BENEATHA: I see. (*He starts to sit.*) Good night, George.

George looks at her a little oddly, and starts to exit. He meets Mama coming in.

GEORGE: Oh — hello, Mrs. Younger.

MAMA: Hello, George, how you feeling?

GEORGE: Fine — fine, how are you?

MAMA: Oh, a little tired. You know them steps can get you after a day's work. You all have a nice time tonight?

GEORGE: Yes — a fine time. A fine time.

MAMA: Well, good night.

GEORGE: Good night. (*He exits. Mama closes the door behind her.*)

MAMA: Hello, honey. What you sitting like that for?

BENEATHA: I'm just sitting.

MAMA: Didn't you have a nice time?

BENEATHA: No.

MAMA: No? What's the matter?

BENEATHA: Mama, George is a fool—honest. (*She rises.*)

MAMA (*hustling around unloading the packages she has entered with. She stops*): Is he, baby?

BENEATHA: Yes.

Beneatha makes up Travis's bed as she talks.

MAMA: You sure?

BENEATHA: Yes.

MAMA: Well—I guess you better not waste your time with no fools.

Beneatha looks up at her mother, watching her put groceries in the refrigerator. Finally she gathers up her things and starts into the bedroom. At the door she stops and looks back at her mother.

BENEATHA: Mama—

MAMA: Yes, baby—

BENEATHA: Thank you.

MAMA: For what?

BENEATHA: For understanding me this time.

She exits quickly and the mother stands, smiling a little, looking at the place where Beneatha just stood. Ruth enters.

RUTH: Now don't you fool with any of this stuff, Lena—

MAMA: Oh, I just thought I'd sort a few things out. Is Brother here?

RUTH: Yes.

MAMA (*with concern*): Is he—

RUTH (*reading her eyes*): Yes.

Mama is silent and someone knocks on the door. Mama and Ruth exchange weary and knowing glances and Ruth opens it to admit the neighbor, Mrs. Johnson,° who is a rather squeaky wide-eyed lady of no particular age, with a newspaper under her arm.

MAMA (*changing her expression to acute delight and a ringing cheerful greeting*): Oh—hello there, Johnson.

JOHNSON (*this is a woman who decided long ago to be enthusiastic about EVERY- THING in life and she is inclined to wave her wrist vigorously at the height of her exclamatory comments*): Hello there, yourself! H'you this evening, Ruth?

RUTH (*not much of a deceptive type*): Fine, Mis' Johnson, h'you?

Mrs. Johnson: This character and the scene of her visit were cut from the original pro- duction and early editions of the play.

JOHNSON: Fine. (*Reaching out quickly, playfully, and patting Ruth's stomach.*) Ain't you starting to poke out none yet! (*She mugs with delight at the over familiar remark and her eyes dart around looking at the crates and packing preparation; Mama's face is a cold sheet of endurance.*) Oh, ain't we getting ready round here, though! Yessir! Lookathere! I'm telling you the Youngers is really getting ready to "move on up a little higher!" — Bless God!

MAMA (*a little drily, doubting the total sincerity of the Blesser*): Bless God.

JOHNSON: He's good, ain't He?

MAMA: Oh yes, He's good.

JOHNSON: I mean sometimes He works in mysterious ways . . . but He works, don't He!

MAMA (*the same*): Yes, he does.

JOHNSON: I'm just soooooo happy for y'all. And this here child — (*about Ruth*) looks like she could just pop open with happiness, don't she. Where's all the rest of the family?

MAMA: Bennie's gone to bed —

JOHNSON: Ain't no . . . (*the implication is pregnancy*) sickness done hit you — I hope . . . ?

MAMA: No — she just tired. She was out this evening.

JOHNSON (*all is a coo, an emphatic coo*): Aw — ain't that lovely. She still going out with the little Murchison boy?

MAMA (*drily*): Ummmm huh.

JOHNSON: That's lovely. You sure got lovely children, Younger. Me and Isaiah talks all the time 'bout what fine children you was blessed with. We sure do.

MAMA: Ruth, give Mis' Johnson a piece of sweet potato pie and some milk.

JOHNSON: Oh honey, I can't stay hardly a minute — I just dropped in to see if there was anything I could do. (*Accepting the food easily.*) I guess y'all seen the news what's all over the colored paper this week . . .

MAMA: No — didn't get mine yet this week.

JOHNSON (*lifting her head and blinking with the spirit of catastrophe*): You mean you ain't read 'bout them colored people that was bombed out their place out there?

Ruth straightens with concern and takes the paper and reads it. Johnson notices her and feeds commentary.

JOHNSON: Ain't it something how bad these here white folks is getting here in Chicago! Lord, getting so you think you right down in Mississippi! (*With a tremendous and rather insincere sense of melodrama.*) 'Course I thinks it's wonderful how our folk keeps on pushing out. You hear some of these Negroes round here talking 'bout how they don't go where they ain't wanted and all that — but not me, honey! (*This is a lie.*) Wilhemenia Othella Johnson goes anywhere, any time she feels like it! (*With head movement for emphasis.*) Yes I do! Why if we left it up to these here crackers, the poor niggers wouldn't have nothing — (*She clasps her hand over her mouth.*) Oh, I always forgets you don't 'low that word in your house.

MAMA (*quietly, looking at her*): No — I don't 'low it.

JOHNSON (*vigorously again*): Me neither! I was just telling Isaiah yesterday when he come using it in front of me—I said, "Isaiah, it's just like Mis' Younger says all the time—"

MAMA: Don't you want some more pie?

JOHNSON: No—no thank you; this was lovely. I got to get on over home and have my midnight coffee. I hear some people say it don't let them sleep but I finds I can't close my eyes right lessen I done had that laaaast cup of coffee . . . (*She waits. A beat. Undaunted.*) My Goodnight coffee, I calls it!

MAMA (*with much eye-rolling and communication between herself and Ruth*): Ruth, why don't you give Mis' Johnson some coffee.

Ruth gives Mama an unpleasant look for her kindness.

JOHNSON (*accepting the coffee*): Where's Brother tonight?

MAMA: He's lying down.

JOHNSON: MMmmmmm, he sure gets his beauty rest, don't he? Good-looking man. Sure is a good-looking man! (*Reaching out to pat Ruth's stomach again.*) I guess that's how come we keep on having babies around here. (*She winks at Mama.*) One thing 'bout Brother, he always know how to have a *good* time. And soooooo ambitious! I bet it was his idea y'all moving out to Clybourne Park. Lord—I bet this time next month y'all's names will have been in the papers plenty—(*Holding up her hands to mark off each word of the headline she can see in front of her.*) "NEGROES INVADE CLYBOURNE PARK—BOMBED!"

MAMA (*she and Ruth look at the woman in amazement*): We ain't exactly moving out there to get bombed.

JOHNSON: Oh honey—you know I'm praying to God every day that don't nothing like that happen! But you have to think of life like it is—and these here Chicago peckerwoods is some baaaad peckerwoods.

MAMA (*wearily*): We done thought about all that Mis' Johnson.

Beneatha comes out of the bedroom in her robe and passes through to the bathroom. Mrs. Johnson turns.

JOHNSON: Hello there, Bennie!

BENEATHA (*crisply*): Hello, Mrs. Johnson.

JOHNSON: How is school?

BENEATHA (*crisply*): Fine, thank you. (*She goes out.*)

JOHNSON (*insulted*): Getting so she don't have much to say to nobody.

MAMA: The child was on her way to the bathroom.

JOHNSON: I know—but sometimes she act like ain't got time to pass the time of day with nobody ain't been to college. Oh—I ain't criticizing her none. It's just—you know how some of our young people gets when they get a little education. (*Mama and Ruth say nothing, just look at her.*) Yes—well. Well, I guess I better get on home. (*Unmoving.*) 'Course I can understand how she must be proud and everything—being the only one in the family to make something of herself. I know just being a chauffeur ain't never satisfied Brother none. He shouldn't feel like that, though. Ain't nothing wrong with being a chauffeur.

MAMA: There's plenty wrong with it.

JOHNSON: What?

MAMA: Plenty. My husband always said being any kind of a servant wasn't a fit thing for a man to have to be. He always said a man's hands was made to make things, or to turn the earth with—not to drive nobody's car for 'em—or—(*she looks at her own hands*) carry they slop jars. And my boy is just like him—he wasn't meant to wait on nobody.

JOHNSON (*rising, somewhat offended*): Mmmmmmmmm. The Youngers is too much for me! (*She looks around.*) You sure one proud-acting bunch of colored folks. Well—I always thinks like Booker T. Washington said that time—"Education has spoiled many a good plow hand"—

MAMA: Is that what old Booker T. said?

JOHNSON: He sure did.

MAMA: Well, it sounds just like him. The fool.

JOHNSON (*indignantly*): Well—he was one of our great men.

MAMA: Who said so?

JOHNSON (*nonplussed*): You know, me and you ain't never agreed about some things, Lena Younger. I guess I better be going—

RUTH (*quickly*): Good night.

JOHNSON: Good night. Oh—(*Thrusting it at her.*) You can keep the paper! (*With a trill.*) 'Night.

MAMA: Good night, Mis' Johnson.

Mrs. Johnson exits.

RUTH: If ignorance was gold . . .

MAMA: Shush. Don't talk about folks behind their backs.

RUTH: You do.

MAMA: I'm old and corrupted. (*Beneatha enters.*) You was rude to Mis' Johnson, Beneatha, and I don't like it at all.

BENEATHA (*at her door*): Mama, if there are two things we, as a people, have got to overcome, one is the Klu Klux Klan—and the other is Mrs. Johnson. (*She exits.*)

MAMA: Smart aleck.

The phone rings.

RUTH: I'll get it.

MAMA: Lord, ain't this a popular place tonight.

RUTH (*at the phone*): Hello—Just a minute. (*Goes to door.*) Walter, it's Mrs. Arnold. (*Waits. Goes back to the phone. Tense.*) Hello. Yes, this is his wife speaking . . . He's lying down now. Yes . . . well, he'll be in tomorrow. He's been very sick. Yes—I know we should have called, but we were so sure he'd be able to come in today. Yes—yes, I'm very sorry. Yes . . . Thank you very much. (*She hangs up. Walter is standing in the doorway of the bedroom behind her.*) That was Mrs. Arnold.

WALTER (*indifferently*): Was it?

RUTH: She said if you don't come in tomorrow that they are getting a new man . . .

WALTER: Ain't that sad — ain't that crying sad.

RUTH: She said Mr. Arnold has had to take a cab for three days . . . Walter, you ain't been to work for three days! (*This is a revelation to her.*) Where you been, Walter Lee Younger? (*Walter looks at her and starts to laugh.*) You're going to lose your job.

WALTER: That's right . . . (*He turns on the radio.*)

RUTH: Oh, Walter, and with your mother working like a dog every day —

A steamy, deep blues pours into the room.

WALTER: That's sad too — Everything is sad.

MAMA: What you been doing for these three days, son?

WALTER: Mama — you don't know all the things a man what got leisure can find to do in this city . . . What's this — Friday night? Well — Wednesday I borrowed Willy Harris' car and I went for a drive . . . just me and myself and I drove and drove . . . Way out . . . way past South Chicago, and I parked the car and I sat and looked at the steel mills all day long. I just sat in the car and looked at them big black chimneys for hours. Then I drove back and I went to the Green Hat. (*Pause.*) And Thursday — Thursday I borrowed the car again and I got in it and I pointed it the other way and I drove the other way — for hours — way, way up to Wisconsin, and I looked at the farms. I just drove and looked at the farms. Then I drove back and I went to the Green Hat. (*Pause.*) And today — today I didn't get the car. Today I just walked. All over the Southside. And I looked at the Negroes and they looked at me and finally I just sat down on the curb at Thirty-ninth and South Parkway and I just sat there and watched the Negroes go by. And then I went to the Green Hat. You all sad? You all depressed? And you know where I am going right now —

Ruth goes out quietly.

MAMA: Oh, Big Walter, is this the harvest of our days?

WALTER: You know what I like about the Green Hat? I like this little cat they got there who blows a sax . . . He blows. He talks to me. He ain't but 'bout five feet tall and he's got a conked head and his eyes is always closed and he's all music —

MAMA (*rising and getting some papers out of her handbag*): Walter —

WALTER: And there's this other guy who plays the piano . . . and they got a sound. I mean they can work on some music . . . They got the best little combo in the world in the Green Hat . . . You can just sit there and drink and listen to them three men play and you realize that don't nothing matter worth a damn, but just being there —

MAMA: I've helped do it to you, haven't I, son? Walter, I been wrong.

WALTER: Naw — you ain't never been wrong about nothing, Mama.

MAMA: Listen to me, now. I say I been wrong, son. That I been doing to you what the rest of the world been doing to you. (*She turns off the radio.*) Walter — (*She stops and he looks up slowly at her and she meets his eyes pleadingly.*) What you ain't never understood is that I ain't got nothing, don't own nothing, ain't never really wanted nothing that wasn't for you. There ain't nothing as precious to me . . . There ain't nothing worth holding on to, money, dreams, nothing else—if it means—if it means it's going to destroy my boy. (*She takes an envelope out of her handbag and puts it in front of him and he watches her without speaking or moving.*) I paid the man thirty-five hundred dollars down on the house. That leaves sixty-five hundred dollars. Monday morning I want you to take this money and take three thousand dollars and put it in a savings account for Beneatha's medical schooling. The rest you put in a checking account—with your name on it. And from now on any penny that come out of it or that go in it is for you to look after. For you to decide. (*She drops her hands a little helplessly.*) It ain't much, but it's all I got in the world and I'm putting it in your hands. I'm telling you to be the head of this family from now on like you supposed to be.

WALTER (*stares at the money*): You trust me like that, Mama?

MAMA: I ain't never stop trusting you. Like I ain't never stop loving you.

She goes out, and Walter sits looking at the money on the table. Finally, in a decisive gesture, he gets up, and, in mingled joy and desperation, picks up the money. At the same moment, Travis enters for bed.

TRAVIS: What's the matter, Daddy? You drunk?

WALTER (*sweetly, more sweetly than we have ever known him*): No, Daddy ain't drunk. Daddy ain't going to never be drunk again . . .

TRAVIS: Well, good night, Daddy.

The father has come from behind the couch and leans over, embracing his son.

WALTER: Son, I feel like talking to you tonight.

TRAVIS: About what?

WALTER: Oh, about a lot of things. About you and what kind of man you going to be when you grow up . . . Son—son, what do you want to be when you grow up?

TRAVIS: A bus driver.

WALTER (*laughing a little*): A what? Man, that ain't nothing to want to be!

TRAVIS: Why not?

WALTER: 'Cause, man—it ain't big enough—you know what I mean.

TRAVIS: I don't know then. I can't make up my mind. Sometimes Mama asks me that too. And sometimes when I tell her I just want to be like you—she says she don't want me to be like that and sometimes she says she does. . . .

WALTER (*gathering him up in his arms*): You know what, Travis? In seven years you going to be seventeen years old. And things is going to be very different with us in seven years, Travis. . . . One day when you are seventeen I'll come home—home from my office downtown somewhere—

TRAVIS: You don't work in no office, Daddy.

WALTER: No—but after tonight. After what your daddy gonna do tonight, there's going to be offices—a whole lot of offices. . . .

TRAVIS: What you gonna do tonight, Daddy?

WALTER: You wouldn't understand yet, son, but your daddy's gonna make a transaction . . . a business transaction that's going to change our lives. . . . That's how come one day when you 'bout seventeen years old I'll come home and I'll be pretty tired, you know what I mean, after a day of conferences and secretaries getting things wrong the way they do . . . 'cause an executive's life is hell, man—(*The more he talks the farther away he gets.*) And I'll pull the car up on the driveway . . . just a plain black Chrysler, I think, with white walls—no—black tires. More elegant. Rich people don't have to be flashy . . . though I'll have to get something a little sportier for Ruth—maybe a Cadillac convertible to do her shopping in. . . . And I'll come up the steps to the house and the gardener will be clipping away at the hedges and he'll say, "Good evening, Mr. Younger." And I'll say, "Hello, Jefferson, how are you this evening?" And I'll go inside and Ruth will come downstairs and meet me at the door and we'll kiss each other and she'll take my arm and we'll go up to your room to see you sitting on the floor with the catalogues of all the great schools in America around you. . . . All the great schools in the world! And—and I'll say, all right son—it's your seventeenth birthday, what is it you've decided? . . . Just tell me where you want to go to school and you'll go. Just tell me, what it is you want to be—and you'll *be* it. . . . Whatever you want to be—Yessir! (*He holds his arms open for Travis.*) You just name it, son . . . (*Travis leaps into them.*) and I hand you the world!

Walter's voice has risen in pitch and hysterical promise and on the last line he lifts Travis high.

Blackout.

SCENE III

Time: Saturday, moving day, one week later.
Before the curtain rises, Ruth's voice, a strident, dramatic church alto, cuts through the silence.
It is, in the darkness, a triumphant surge, a penetrating statement of expectation: "Oh, Lord, I don't feel no ways tired! Children, oh, glory hallelujah!"
As the curtain rises we see that Ruth is alone in the living room, finishing up the family's packing. It is moving day. She is nailing crates and tying cartons. Beneatha enters, carrying a guitar case, and watches her exuberant sister-in-law.

RUTH: Hey!

BENEATHA (*putting away the case*): Hi.

RUTH (*pointing at a package*): Honey—look in that package there and see what I found on sale this morning at the South Center. (*Ruth gets up and moves to the package and draws out some curtains.*) Lookahere—hand-turned hems!

BENEATHA: How do you know the window size out there?

RUTH (*who hadn't thought of that*): Oh—Well, they bound to fit something in the whole house. Anyhow, they was too good a bargain to pass up. (*Ruth slaps her head, suddenly remembering something.*) Oh, Bennie—I meant to put a special note on that carton over there. That's your mama's good china and she wants 'em to be very careful with it.

BENEATHA: I'll do it.

Beneatha finds a piece of paper and starts to draw large letters on it.

RUTH: You know what I'm going to do soon as I get in that new house?

BENEATHA: What?

RUTH: Honey—I'm going to run me a tub of water up to here . . . (*With her fingers practically up to her nostrils.*) And I'm going to get in it—and I am going to sit . . . and sit . . . and sit in that hot water and the first person who knocks to tell *me* to hurry up and come out—

BENEATHA: Gets shot at sunrise.

RUTH (*laughing happily*): You said it, sister! (*Noticing how large Beneatha is absent-mindedly making the note*): Honey, they ain't going to read that from no airplane.

BENEATHA (*laughing herself*): I guess I always think things have more emphasis if they are big, somehow.

RUTH (*looking up at her and smiling*): You and your brother seem to have that as a philosophy of life. Lord, that man—done changed so 'round here. You know—you know what we did last night? Me and Walter Lee?

BENEATHA: What?

RUTH (*smiling to herself*): We went to the movies. (*Looking at Beneatha to see if she understands.*) We went to the movies. You know the last time me and Walter went to the movies together?

BENEATHA: No.

RUTH: Me neither. That's how long it been. (*Smiling again.*) But we went last night. The picture wasn't much good, but that didn't seem to matter. We went—and we held hands.

BENEATHA: Oh, Lord!

RUTH: We held hands—and you know what?

BENEATHA: What?

RUTH: When we come out of the show it was late and dark and all the stores and things was closed up . . . and it was kind of chilly and there wasn't many people on the streets . . . and we was still holding hands, me and Walter.

BENEATHA: You're killing me.

Walter enters with a large package. His happiness is deep in him; he cannot keep still with his newfound exuberance. He is singing and wiggling and snapping his fingers. He puts his package in a corner and puts a phonograph record, which he has brought in with him, on the record player. As the music, soulful and sensuous, comes up he dances over to Ruth and tries to get her to dance with him. She gives in at last to his raunchiness and in a fit of giggling allows herself to be drawn into his mood. They dip and she melts into his arms in a classic, body-melting "slow drag."

BENEATHA (*regarding them a long time as they dance, then drawing in her breath for a deeply exaggerated comment which she does not particularly mean*): Talk about—oldddddddddd-fashioneddddddddd—Negroes!

WALTER (*stopping momentarily*): What kind of Negroes?

He says this in fun. He is not angry with her today, nor with anyone. He starts to dance with his wife again.

BENEATHA: Old-fashioned.

WALTER (*as he dances with Ruth*): You know, when these *New Negroes* have their convention—(*Pointing at his sister.*)—that is going to be the chairman of the Committee on Unending Agitation. (*He goes on dancing, then stops.*) Race, race, race! . . . Girl, I do believe you are the first person in the history of the entire human race to successfully brainwash yourself. (*Beneatha breaks up and he goes on dancing. He stops again, enjoying his tease.*) Damn, even the N double A C P takes a holiday sometimes! (*Beneatha and Ruth laugh. He dances with Ruth some more and starts to laugh and stops and pantomimes someone over an operating table.*) I can just see that chick someday looking down at some poor cat on an operating table and before she starts to slice him, she says . . . (*Pulling his sleeves back maliciously.*) "By the way, what are your views on civil rights down there? . . ."

He laughs at her again and starts to dance happily. The bell sounds.

BENEATHA: Sticks and stones may break my bones but . . . words will never hurt me!

Beneatha goes to the door and opens it as Walter and Ruth go on with the clowning. Beneatha is somewhat surprised to see a quiet-looking middle-aged white man in a business suit holding his hat and a briefcase in his hand and consulting a small piece of paper.

MAN: Uh—how do you do, miss. I am looking for a Mrs. —(*He looks at the slip of paper.*) Mrs. Lena Younger? (*He stops short, struck dumb at the sight of the oblivious Walter and Ruth.*)

BENEATHA (*smoothing her hair with slight embarrassment*): Oh—yes, that's my mother. Excuse me. (*She closes the door and turns to quiet the other two.*) Ruth! Brother! (*Enunciating precisely but soundlessly: "There's a white man at the door!" They stop dancing, Ruth cuts off the phonograph, Beneatha opens the door. The man casts a curious quick glance at all of them.*) Uh—come in please.

MAN (*coming in*): Thank you.

BENEATHA: My mother isn't here just now. Is it business?

MAN: Yes . . . well, of a sort.

WALTER (*freely, the Man of the House*): Have a seat. I'm Mrs. Younger's son. I look after most of her business matters.

Ruth and Beneatha exchange amused glances.

MAN (*regarding Walter, and sitting*): Well—My name is Karl Lindner . . .

WALTER (*stretching out his hand*): Walter Younger. This is my wife—(*Ruth nods politely.*)—and my sister.

LINDNER: How do you do.

WALTER (*amiably, as he sits himself easily on a chair, leaning forward on his knees with interest and looking expectantly into the newcomer's face*): What can we do for you, Mr. Lindner!

LINDNER (*some minor shuffling of the hat and briefcase on his knees*): Well—I am a representative of the Clybourne Park Improvement Association—

WALTER (*pointing*): Why don't you sit your things on the floor?

LINDNER: Oh—yes. Thank you. (*He slides the briefcase and hat under the chair.*) And as I was saying—I am from the Clybourne Park Improvement Association and we have had it brought to our attention at the last meeting that you people—or at least your mother—has bought a piece of residential property at—(*He digs for the slip of paper again.*)—four o six Clybourne Street . . .

WALTER: That's right. Care for something to drink? Ruth, get Mr. Lindner a beer.

LINDNER (*upset for some reason*): Oh—no, really. I mean thank you very much, but no thank you.

RUTH (*innocently*): Some coffee?

LINDNER: Thank you, nothing at all.

Beneatha is watching the man carefully.

LINDNER: Well, I don't know how much you folks know about our organization. (*He is a gentle man; thoughtful and somewhat labored in his manner.*) It is one of these community organizations set up to look after—oh, you know, things like block upkeep and special projects and we also have what we call our New Neighbors Orientation Committee . . .

BENEATHA (*drily*): Yes—and what do they do?

LINDNER (*turning a little to her and then returning the main force to Walter*): Well—it's what you might call a sort of welcoming committee, I guess. I mean they, we—I'm the chairman of the committee—go around and see the new people who move into the neighborhood and sort of give them the lowdown on the way we do things out in Clybourne Park.

BENEATHA (*with appreciation of the two meanings, which escape Ruth and Walter*): Un-huh.

LINDNER: And we also have the category of what the association calls—(*he looks elsewhere*)—uh—special community problems . . .

BENEATHA: Yes—and what are some of those?

WALTER: Girl, let the man talk.

LINDNER (*with understated relief*): Thank you. I would sort of like to explain this thing in my own way. I mean I want to explain to you in a certain way.

WALTER: Go ahead.

LINDNER: Yes. Well. I'm going to try to get right to the point. I'm sure we'll all appreciate that in the long run.

BENEATHA: Yes.

WALTER: Be still now!

LINDNER: Well—

RUTH (*still innocently*): Would you like another chair—you don't look comfortable.

LINDNER (*more frustrated than annoyed*): No, thank you very much. Please. Well—to get right to the point, I—(*A great breath, and he is off at last.*) I am sure you people must be aware of some of the incidents which have happened in various parts of the city when colored people have moved into certain areas—(*Beneatha exhales heavily and starts tossing a piece of fruit up and down in the air.*) Well—because we have what I think is going to be a unique type of organization in American community life—not only do we deplore that kind of thing—but we are trying to do something about it. (*Beneatha stops tossing and turns with a new and quizzical interest to the man.*) We feel—(*gaining confidence in his mission because of the interest in the faces of the people he is talking to*)—we feel that most of the trouble in this world, when you come right down to it—(*he hits his knee for emphasis*)—most of the trouble exists because people just don't sit down and talk to each other.

RUTH (*nodding as she might in church, pleased with the remark*): You can say that again, mister.

LINDNER (*more encouraged by such affirmation*): That we don't try hard enough in this world to understand the other fellow's problem. The other guy's point of view.

RUTH: Now that's right.

Beneatha and Walter merely watch and listen with genuine interest.

LINDNER: Yes—that's the way we feel out in Clybourne Park. And that's why I was elected to come here this afternoon and talk to you people. Friendly like, you know, the way people should talk to each other and see if we couldn't find some way to work this thing out. As I say, the whole business is a matter of *caring* about the other fellow. Anybody can see that you are a nice family of folks, hard working and honest I'm sure. (*Beneatha frowns slightly, quizzically, her head tilted regarding him.*) Today everybody knows what it means to be on the outside of *something*. And of course, there is always somebody who is out to take advantage of people who don't always understand.

WALTER: What do you mean?

LINDNER: Well—you see our community is made up of people who've worked hard as the dickens for years to build up that little community. They're not rich and fancy people; just hard-working, honest people who don't really have much but those little homes and a dream of the kind of community they want to raise their children in. Now, I don't say we are perfect and there is a lot wrong in some of the things they want. But you've got to admit that a man, right or wrong, has the right to want to have the neighborhood he lives in a certain kind of way. And at the moment the overwhelming majority of our people out there feel that people get along better, take more of a common interest in the life of the community, when they share a common background. I want you to believe me when I tell you that race prejudice simply doesn't enter into it. It is a matter of the people of Clybourne Park believing, rightly or wrongly, as I say, that for the happiness of all concerned that our Negro families are happier when they live in their *own* communities.

BENEATHA (*with a grand and bitter gesture*): This, friends, is the Welcoming Committee!

WALTER (*dumfounded, looking at Lindner*): Is this what you came marching all the way over here to tell us?

LINDNER: Well, now we've been having a fine conversation. I hope you'll hear me all the way through.

WALTER (*tightly*): Go ahead, man.

LINDNER: You see—in the face of all the things I have said, we are prepared to make your family a very generous offer . . .

BENEATHA: Thirty pieces and not a coin less!

WALTER: Yeah?

LINDNER (*putting on his glasses and drawing a form out of the briefcase*): Our association is prepared, through the collective effort of our people, to buy the house from you at a financial gain to your family.

RUTH: Lord have mercy, ain't this the living gall!

WALTER: All right, you through?

LINDNER: Well, I want to give you the exact terms of the financial arrangement—

WALTER: We don't want to hear no exact terms of no arrangements. I want to know if you got any more to tell us 'bout getting together?

LINDNER (*taking off his glasses*): Well—I don't suppose that you feel . . .

WALTER: Never mind how I feel—you got any more to say 'bout how people ought to sit down and talk to each other? . . . Get out of my house, man.

He turns his back and walks to the door.

LINDNER (*looking around at the hostile faces and reaching and assembling his hat and briefcase*): Well—I don't understand why you people are reacting this way. What do you think you are going to gain by moving into a neighborhood where you just aren't wanted and where some elements—well—people can get awful worked up when they feel that their whole way of life and everything they've ever worked for is threatened.

WALTER: Get out.

LINDNER (*at the door, holding a small card*): Well—I'm sorry it went like this.

WALTER: Get out.

LINDNER (*almost sadly regarding Walter*): You just can't force people to change their hearts, son.

He turns and puts his card on a table and exits. Walter pushes the door to with stinging hatred, and stands looking at it. Ruth just sits and Beneatha just stands. They say nothing. Mama and Travis enter.

MAMA: Well—this all the packing got done since I left out of here this morning. I testify before God that my children got all the energy of the *dead!* What time the moving men due?

BENEATHA: Four o'clock. You had a caller, Mama.

She is smiling, teasingly.

MAMA: Sure enough—who?

BENEATHA (*her arms folded saucily*): The Welcoming Committee.

Walter and Ruth giggle.

MAMA (*innocently*): Who?

BENEATHA: The Welcoming Committee. They said they're sure going to be glad to see you when you get there.

WALTER (*devilishly*): Yeah, they said they can't hardly wait to see your face.

Laughter.

MAMA (*sensing their facetiousness*): What's the matter with you all?

WALTER: Ain't nothing the matter with us. We just telling you 'bout the gentleman who came to see you this afternoon. From the Clybourne Park Improvement Association.

MAMA: What he want?

RUTH (*in the same mood as Beneatha and Walter*): To welcome you, honey.

WALTER: He said they can't hardly wait. He said the one thing they don't have, that they just *dying* to have out there is a fine family of fine colored people! (*To Ruth and Beneatha.*) Ain't that right!

RUTH (*mockingly*): Yeah! He left his card —

BENEATHA (*handing card to Mama*): In case.

Mama reads and throws it on the floor—understanding and looking off as she draws her chair up to the table on which she has put her plant and some sticks and some cord.

MAMA: Father, give us strength. (*Knowingly—and without fun.*) Did he threaten us?

BENEATHA: Oh—Mama—they don't do it like that any more. He talked Brotherhood. He said everybody ought to learn how to sit down and hate each other with good Christian fellowship.

She and Walter shake hands to ridicule the remark.

MAMA (*sadly*): Lord, protect us . . .

RUTH: You should hear the money those folks raised to buy the house from us. All we paid and then some.

BENEATHA: What they think we going to do—eat 'em?

RUTH: No, honey, marry 'em.

MAMA (*shaking her head*): Lord, Lord, Lord . . .

RUTH: Well—that's the way the crackers crumble. (*A beat.*) Joke.

BENEATHA (*laughingly noticing what her mother is doing*): Mama, what are you doing?

MAMA: Fixing my plant so it won't get hurt none on the way . . .

BENEATHA: Mama, you going to take *that* to the new house?

MAMA: Un-huh—

BENEATHA: That raggedy-looking old thing?

MAMA (*stopping and looking at her*): It expresses ME!

RUTH (*with delight, to Beneatha*): So there, Miss Thing!

Walter comes to Mama suddenly and bends down behind her and squeezes her in his arms with all his strength. She is overwhelmed by the suddenness of it and, though delighted, her manner is like that of Ruth and Travis.

MAMA: Look out now, boy! You make me mess up my thing here!

WALTER (*his face lit, he slips down on his knees beside her, his arms still about her*): Mama . . . you know what it means to climb up in the chariot?

MAMA (*gruffly, very happy*): Get on away from me now . . .

RUTH (*near the gift-wrapped package, trying to catch Walter's eye*): Psst—

WALTER: What the old song say, Mama . . .

RUTH: Walter—Now?

She is pointing at the package.

WALTER (*speaking the lines, sweetly, playfully, in his mother's face*):
> *I got wings . . . you got wings . . .*
> *All God's Children got wings . . .*

MAMA: Boy — get out of my face and do some work . . .

WALTER:
> *When I get to heaven gonna put on my wings,*
> *Gonna fly all over God's heaven . . .*

BENEATHA (*teasingly, from across the room*): Everybody talking 'bout heaven ain't going there!

WALTER (*to Ruth, who is carrying the box across to them*): I don't know, you think we ought to give her that . . . Seems to me she ain't been very appreciative around here.

MAMA (*eying the box, which is obviously a gift*): What is that?

WALTER (*taking it from Ruth and putting it on the table in front of Mama*): Well — what you all think? Should we give it to her?

RUTH: Oh — she was pretty good today.

MAMA: I'll good you —

She turns her eyes to the box again.

BENEATHA: Open it, Mama.

She stands up, looks at it, turns and looks at all of them, and then presses her hands together and does not open the package.

WALTER (*sweetly*): Open it, Mama. It's for you. (*Mama looks in his eyes. It is the first present in her life without its being Christmas. Slowly she opens her package and lifts out, one by one, a brand-new sparkling set of gardening tools. Walter continues, prodding.*) Ruth made up the note — read it . . .

MAMA (*picking up the card and adjusting her glasses*): "To our own Mrs. Mini-ver° — Love from Brother, Ruth, and Beneatha." Ain't that lovely . . .

TRAVIS (*tugging at his father's sleeve*): Daddy, can I give her mine now?

WALTER: All right, son. (*Travis flies to get his gift.*)

MAMA: Now I don't have to use my knives and forks no more . . .

WALTER: Travis didn't want to go in with the rest of us, Mama. He got his own. (*Somewhat amused.*) We don't know what it is . . .

TRAVIS (*racing back in the room with a large hatbox and putting it in front of his grandmother*): Here!

MAMA: Lord have mercy, baby. You done gone and bought your grandmother a hat?

TRAVIS (*very proud*): Open it!

She does and lifts out an elaborate, but very elaborate, wide gardening hat, and all the adults break up at the sight of it.

RUTH: Travis, honey, what is that?

TRAVIS (*who thinks it is beautiful and appropriate*): It's a gardening hat! Like the ladies always have on in the magazines when they work in their gardens.

Mrs. Miniver: Title character of the 1942 film about a middle-class family's struggle to survive in wartorn Britain.

BENEATHA (*giggling fiercely*): Travis—we were trying to make Mama Mrs. Miniver—not Scarlett O'Hara!

MAMA (*indignantly*): What's the matter with you all! This here is a beautiful hat! (*Absurdly.*) I always wanted me one just like it!

She pops it on her head to prove it to her grandson, and the hat is ludicrous and considerably oversized.

RUTH: Hot dog! Go, Mama!

WALTER (*doubled over with laughter*): I'm sorry, Mama—but you look like you ready to go out and chop you some cotton sure enough!

They all laugh except Mama, out of deference to Travis's feelings.

MAMA (*gathering the boy up to her*): Bless your heart—this is the prettiest hat I ever owned—(*Walter, Ruth, and Beneatha chime in—noisily, festively, and insincerely congratulating Travis on his gift.*) What are we all standing around here for? We ain't finished packin' yet. Bennie, you ain't packed one book.

The bell rings.

BENEATHA: That couldn't be the movers . . . it's not hardly two good yet—

Beneatha goes into her room. Mama starts for door.

WALTER (*turning, stiffening*): Wait—wait—I'll get it.

He stands and looks at the door.

MAMA: You expecting company, son?

WALTER (*just looking at the door*): Yeah—yeah . . .

Mama looks at Ruth, and they exchange innocent and unfrightened glances.

MAMA (*not understanding*): Well, let them in, son.

BENEATHA (*from her room*): We need some more string.

MAMA: Travis—you run to the hardware and get me some string cord.

Mama goes out and Walter turns and looks at Ruth. Travis goes to a dish for money.

RUTH: Why don't you answer the door, man?

WALTER (*suddenly bounding across the floor to embrace her*): 'Cause sometimes it hard to let the future begin! (*Stooping down in her face.*)

I got wings! You got wings!
All God's children got wings!

He crosses to the door and throws it open. Standing there is a very slight little man in a not-too-prosperous business suit and with haunted frightened eyes and a hat pulled down tightly, brim up, around his forehead. Travis passes between the men and exits. Walter leans deep in the man's face, still in his jubilance.

When I get to heaven gonna put on my wings,
Gonna fly all over God's heaven . . .

The little man just stares at him.

Heaven—

Suddenly he stops and looks past the little man into the empty hallway.

Where's Willy, man?

BOBO: He ain't with me.

WALTER (*not disturbed*): Oh—come on in. You know my wife.

BOBO (*dumbly, taking off his hat*): Yes—h'you, Miss Ruth.

RUTH (*quietly, a mood apart from her husband already, seeing Bobo*): Hello, Bobo.

WALTER: You right on time today . . . Right on time. That's the way! (*He slaps Bobo on his back.*) Sit down . . . lemme hear.

Ruth stands stiffly and quietly in back of them, as though somehow she senses death, her eyes fixed on her husband.

BOBO (*his frightened eyes on the floor, his hat in his hands*): Could I please get a drink of water, before I tell you about it, Walter Lee?

Walter does not take his eyes off the man. Ruth goes blindly to the tap and gets a glass of water and brings it to Bobo.

WALTER: There ain't nothing wrong, is there?

BOBO: Lemme tell you—

WALTER: Man—didn't nothing go wrong?

BOBO: Lemme tell you—Walter Lee. (*Looking at Ruth and talking to her more than to Walter.*) You know how it was. I got to tell you how it was. I mean first I got to tell you how it was all the way . . . I mean about the money I put in, Walter Lee . . .

WALTER (*with taut agitation now*): What about the money you put in?

BOBO: Well—it wasn't much as we told you—me and Willy—(*He stops.*) I'm sorry, Walter. I got a bad feeling about it. I got a real bad feeling about it . . .

WALTER: Man, what you telling me about all this for? . . . Tell me what happened in Springfield . . .

BOBO: Springfield.

RUTH (*like a dead woman*): What was supposed to happen in Springfield?

BOBO (*to her*): This deal that me and Walter went into with Willy—Me and Willy was going to go down to Springfield and spread some money 'round so's we wouldn't have to wait so long for the liquor license . . . That's what we were going to do. Everybody said that was the way you had to do, you understand, Miss Ruth?

WALTER: Man—what happened down there?

BOBO (*a pitiful man, near tears*): I'm trying to tell you, Walter.

WALTER (*screaming at him suddenly*): THEN TELL ME, GODDAMMIT . . . WHAT'S THE MATTER WITH YOU?

BOBO: Man . . . I didn't go to no Springfield, yesterday.

WALTER (*halted, life hanging in the moment*): Why not?

BOBO (*the long way, the hard way to tell*): 'Cause I didn't have no reasons to . . .

WALTER: Man, what are you talking about!

BOBO: I'm talking about the fact that when I got to the train station yesterday morning—eight o'clock like we planned . . . Man—*Willy didn't never show up.*

WALTER: Why . . . where was he . . . where is he?

BOBO: That's what I'm trying to tell you ... I don't know ... I waited six hours ... I called his house ... and I waited ... six hours ... I waited in that train station six hours ... (*Breaking into tears.*) That was all the extra money I had in the world ... (*Looking up at Walter with the tears running down his face.*) Man, *Willy is gone.*

WALTER: Gone, what you mean Willy is gone? Gone where? You mean he went by himself. You mean he went off to Springfield by himself—to take care of getting the license—(*Turns and looks anxiously at Ruth.*) You mean maybe he didn't want too many people in on the business down there? (*Looks to Ruth again, as before.*) You know Willy got his own ways. (*Looks back to Bobo.*) Maybe you was late yesterday and he just went on down there without you. Maybe—maybe—he's been callin' you at home tryin' to tell you what happened or something. Maybe—maybe—he just got sick. He's somewhere—he's got to be somewhere. We just got to find him—me and you got to find him. (*Grabs Bobo senselessly by the collar and starts to shake him.*) We got to!

BOBO (*in sudden angry, frightened agony*): What's the matter with you, Walter! *When a cat take off with your money he don't leave you no road maps!*

WALTER (*turning madly, as though he is looking for Willy in the very room*): Willy! ... Willy ... don't do it ... Please don't do it ... Man, not with that money ... Man, please, not with that money ... Oh, God ... Don't let it be true ... (*He is wandering around, crying out for Willy and looking for him or perhaps for help from God.*) Man ... I trusted you ... Man, I put my life in your hands ... (*He starts to crumple down on the floor as Ruth just covers her face in horror. Mama opens the door and comes into the room, with Beneatha behind her.*) Man ... (*He starts to pound the floor with his fists, sobbing wildly.*) THAT MONEY IS MADE OUT OF MY FATHER'S FLESH—

BOBO (*standing over him helplessly*): I'm sorry, Walter ... (*Only Walter's sobs reply. Bobo puts on his hat.*) I had my life staked on this deal, too ...

He exits.

MAMA (*to Walter*): Son—(*She goes to him, bends down to him, talks to his bent head.*) Son ... Is it gone? Son, I gave you sixty-five hundred dollars. Is it gone? All of it? Beneatha's money too?

WALTER (*lifting his head slowly*): Mama ... I never ... went to the bank at all ...

MAMA (*not wanting to believe him*): You mean ... your sister's school money ... you used that too ... Walter? ...

WALTER: Yessss! All of it ... It's all gone ...

There is total silence. Ruth stands with her face covered with her hands; Beneatha leans forlornly against a wall, fingering a piece of red ribbon from the mother's gift. Mama stops and looks at her son without recognition and then, quite without thinking about it, starts to beat him senselessly in the face. Beneatha goes to them and stops it.

BENEATHA: Mama!

Mama stops and looks at both of her children and rises slowly and wanders vaguely, aimlessly away from them.

MAMA: I seen . . . him . . . night after night . . . come in . . . and look at that rug . . . and then look at me . . . the red showing in his eyes . . . the veins moving in his head . . . I seen him grow thin and old before he was forty . . . working and working and working like somebody's old horse . . . killing himself . . . and you—you give it all away in a day— (*She raises her arms to strike him again.*)

BENEATHA: Mama—

MAMA: Oh, God . . . (*She looks up to Him.*) Look down here—and show me the strength.

BENEATHA: Mama—

MAMA (*folding over*): Strength . . .

BENEATHA (*plaintively*): Mama . . .

MAMA: Strength!

Curtain.

ACT III

Time: An hour later.

At curtain, there is a sullen light of gloom in the living room, gray light not unlike that which began the first scene of Act I. At left we can see Walter within his room, alone with himself. He is stretched out on the bed, his shirt out and open, his arms under his head. He does not smoke, he does not cry out, he merely lies there, looking up at the ceiling, much as if he were alone in the world.

In the living room Beneatha sits at the table, still surrounded by the now almost ominous packing crates. She sits looking off. We feel that this is a mood struck perhaps an hour before, and it lingers now, full of the empty sound of profound disappointment. We see on a line from her brother's bedroom the sameness of their attitudes. Presently the bell rings and Beneatha rises without ambition or interest in answering. It is Asagai, smiling broadly, striding into the room with energy and happy expectation and conversation.

ASAGAI: I came over . . . I had some free time. I thought I might help with the packing. Ah, I like the look of packing crates! A household in preparation for a journey! It depresses some people . . . but for me . . . it is another feeling. Something full of the flow of life, do you understand? Movement, progress . . . It makes me think of Africa.

BENEATHA: Africa!

ASAGAI: What kind of a mood is this? Have I told you how deeply you move me?

BENEATHA: He gave away the money, Asagai . . .

ASAGAI: Who gave away what money?

BENEATHA: The insurance money. My brother gave it away.

ASAGAI: Gave it away?

BENEATHA: He made an investment! With a man even Travis wouldn't have trusted with his most worn-out marbles.

ASAGAI: And it's gone?

BENEATHA: Gone!

ASAGAI: I'm very sorry . . . And you, now?

BENEATHA: Me? . . . Me? . . . Me, I'm nothing . . . Me. When I was very small . . . we used to take our sleds out in the wintertime and the only hills we had were the ice-covered stone steps of some houses down the street. And we used to fill them in with snow and make them smooth and slide down them all day . . . and it was very dangerous, you know . . . far too steep . . . and sure enough one day a kid named Rufus came down too fast and hit the sidewalk and we saw his face just split open right there in front of us . . . And I remember standing there looking at his bloody open face thinking that was the end of Rufus. But the ambulance came and they took him to the hospital and they fixed the broken bones and they sewed it all up . . . and the next time I saw Rufus he just had a little line down the middle of his face . . . I never got over that . . .

ASAGAI: What?

BENEATHA: That that was what one person could do for another, fix him up — sew up the problem, make him all right again. That was the most marvelous thing in the world . . . I wanted to do that. I always thought it was the one concrete thing in the world that a human being could do. Fix up the sick, you know — and make them whole again. This was truly being God . . .

ASAGAI: You wanted to be God?

BENEATHA: No — I wanted to cure. It used to be so important to me. I wanted to cure. It used to matter. I used to care. I mean about people and how their bodies hurt . . .

ASAGAI: And you've stopped caring?

BENEATHA: Yes — I think so.

ASAGAI: Why?

BENEATHA (*bitterly*): Because it doesn't seem deep enough, close enough to what ails mankind! It was a child's way of seeing things — or an idealist's.

ASAGAI: Children see things very well sometimes — and idealists even better.

BENEATHA: I know that's what you think. Because you are still where I left off. You with all your talk and dreams about Africa! You still think you can patch up the world. Cure the Great Sore of Colonialism — (*loftily, mocking it*) with the Penicillin of Independence —!

ASAGAI: Yes!

BENEATHA: Independence *and then what?* What about all the crooks and thieves and just plain idiots who will come into power and steal and plunder the same as before — only now they will be black and do it in the name of the new Independence — WHAT ABOUT THEM?!

ASAGAI: That will be the problem for another time. First we must get there.

BENEATHA: And where does it end?

ASAGAI: End? Who even spoke of an end? To life? To living?

BENEATHA: An end to misery! To stupidity! Don't you see there isn't any real progress, Asagai, there is only one large circle that we march in, around and around, each of us with our own little picture in front of us — our own little mirage that we think is the future.

ASAGAI: That is the mistake.

BENEATHA: What?

ASAGAI: What you just said—about the circle. It isn't a circle—it is simply a long line—as in geometry, you know, one that reaches into infinity. And because we cannot see the end—we also cannot see how it changes. And it is very odd but those who see the changes—who dream, who will not give up—are called idealists . . . and those who see only the circle—we call *them* the "realists"!

BENEATHA: Asagai, while I was sleeping in that bed in there, people went out and took the future right out of my hands! And nobody asked me, nobody consulted me—they just went out and changed my life!

ASAGAI: Was it your money?

BENEATHA: What?

ASAGAI: Was it your money he gave away?

BENEATHA: It belonged to all of us.

ASAGAI: But did you earn it? Would you have had it at all if your father had not died?

BENEATHA: No.

ASAGAI: Then isn't there something wrong in a house—in a world—where all dreams, good or bad, must depend on the death of a man? I never thought to see *you* like this, Alaiyo. You! Your brother made a mistake and you are grateful to him so that now you can give up the ailing human race on account of it! You talk about what good is struggle, what good is anything! Where are we all going and why are we bothering!

BENEATHA: AND YOU CANNOT ANSWER IT!

ASAGAI (*shouting over her*): I LIVE THE ANSWER! (*Pause.*) In my village at home it is the exceptional man who can even read a newspaper . . . or who ever sees a book at all. I will go home and much of what I will have to say will seem strange to the people of my village. But I will teach and work and things will happen, slowly and swiftly. At times it will seem that nothing changes at all . . . and then again the sudden dramatic events which make history leap into the future. And then quiet again. Retrogression even. Guns, murder, revolution. And I even will have moments when I wonder if the quiet was not better than all that death and hatred. But I will look about my village at the illiteracy and disease and ignorance and I will not wonder long. And perhaps . . . perhaps I will be a great man . . . I mean perhaps I will hold on to the substance of truth and find my way always with the right course . . . and perhaps for it I will be butchered in my bed some night by the servants of empire . . .

BENEATHA: *The martyr!*

ASAGAI (*he smiles*): . . . or perhaps I shall live to be a very old man, respected and esteemed in my new nation . . . And perhaps I shall hold office and this is what I'm trying to tell you, Alaiyo: perhaps the things I believe now for my country will be wrong and outmoded, and I will not understand and do terrible things to have things my way or merely to keep my power. Don't you see that there will be young men and women—not British soldiers then, but my own black countrymen—to step out of the shadows some evening and slit my then useless throat? Don't you see they have always been there . . . that they always will be. And that such a thing as

my own death will be an advance? They who might kill me even . . . actually replenish all that I was.

BENEATHA: Oh, Asagai, I know all that.

ASAGAI: Good! Then stop moaning and groaning and tell me what you plan
to do.

BENEATHA: Do?

ASAGAI: I have a bit of a suggestion.

BENEATHA: What?

ASAGAI (*rather quietly for him*): That when it is all over—that you come home
with me—

BENEATHA (*staring at him and crossing away with exasperation*): Oh—Asagai—
at this moment you decide to be romantic!

ASAGAI (*quickly understanding the misunderstanding*): My dear, young creature
of the New World—I do not mean across the city—I mean across the
ocean: home—to Africa.

BENEATHA (*slowly understanding and turning to him with murmured amazement*):
To Africa?

ASAGAI: Yes! . . . (*Smiling and lifting his arms playfully.*) Three hundred years
later the African Prince rose up out of the seas and swept the maiden back
across the middle passage over which her ancestors had come—

BENEATHA (*unable to play*): To—to Nigeria?

ASAGAI: Nigeria. Home. (*Coming to her with genuine romantic flippancy.*) I will
show you our mountains and our stars; and give you cool drinks from
gourds and teach you the old songs and the ways of our people—and, in
time, we will pretend that—(*very softly*)—you have only been away for a
day. Say that you'll come—(*He swings her around and takes her full in his
arms in a kiss which proceeds to passion.*)

BENEATHA (*pulling away suddenly*): You're getting me all mixed up—

ASAGAI: Why?

BENEATHA: Too many things—too many things have happened today. I must
sit down and think. I don't know what I feel about anything right this
minute.

She promptly sits down and props her chin on her fist.

ASAGAI (*charmed*): All right, I shall leave you. No—don't get up. (*Touching her,
gently, sweetly.*) Just sit awhile and think . . . Never be afraid to sit awhile
and think. (*He goes to door and looks at her.*) How often I have looked
at you and said, "Ah—so this is what the New World hath finally
wrought . . ."

*He exits. Beneatha sits on alone. Presently Walter enters from his room and starts
to rummage through things, feverishly looking for something. She looks up and
turns in her seat.*

BENEATHA (*hissingly*): Yes—just look at what the New World hath wrought! . . .
Just look! (*She gestures with bitter disgust.*) There he is! *Monsieur le petit
bourgeois noir*—himself! There he is—Symbol of a Rising Class! Entrepreneur! Titan of the system! (*Walter ignores her completely and continues*

frantically and destructively looking for something and hurling things to floor and tearing things out of their place in his search. Beneatha ignores the eccentricity of his actions and goes on with the monologue of insult.) Did you dream of yachts on Lake Michigan, Brother? Did you see yourself on that Great Day sitting down at the Conference Table, surrounded by all the mighty bald-headed men in America? All halted, waiting, breathless, waiting for your pronouncements on industry? Waiting for you—Chairman of the Board! (*Walter finds what he is looking for—a small piece of white paper—and pushes it in his pocket and puts on his coat and rushes out without ever having looked at her. She shouts after him.*) I look at you and I see the final triumph of stupidity in the world!

The door slams and she returns to just sitting again. Ruth comes quickly out of Mama's room.

RUTH: Who was that?

BENEATHA: Your husband.

RUTH: Where did he go?

BENEATHA: Who knows—maybe he has an appointment at U.S. Steel.

RUTH (*anxiously, with frightened eyes*): You didn't say nothing bad to him, did you?

BENEATHA: Bad? Say anything bad to him? No—I told him he was a sweet boy and full of dreams and everything is strictly peachy keen, as the ofay kids say!

Mama enters from her bedroom. She is lost, vague, trying to catch hold, to make some sense of her former command of the world, but it still eludes her. A sense of waste overwhelms her gait; a measure of apology rides on her shoulders. She goes to her plant, which has remained on the table, looks at it, picks it up and takes it to the window sill and sits it outside, and she stands and looks at it a long moment. Then she closes the window, straightens her body with effort and turns around to her children.

MAMA: Well—ain't it a mess in here, though? (*A false cheerfulness, a beginning of something.*) I guess we all better stop moping around and get some work done. All this unpacking and everything we got to do. (*Ruth raises her head slowly in response to the sense of the line; and Beneatha in similar manner turns very slowly to look at her mother.*) One of you all better call the moving people and tell 'em not to come.

RUTH: Tell 'em not to come?

MAMA: Of course, baby. Ain't no need in 'em coming all the way here and having to go back. They charges for that too. (*She sits down, fingers to her brow, thinking.*) Lord, ever since I was a little girl, I always remembers people saying, "Lena—Lena Eggleston, you aims too high all the time. You needs to slow down and see life a little more like it is. Just slow down some." That's what they always used to say down home—"Lord, that Lena Eggleston is a high-minded thing. She'll get her due one day!"

RUTH: No, Lena . . .

MAMA: Me and Big Walter just didn't never learn right.

RUTH: Lena, no! We gotta go. Bennie—tell her . . .

She rises and crosses to Beneatha with her arms outstretched. Beneatha doesn't respond.

> Tell her we can still move . . . the notes ain't but a hundred and twenty-five a month. We got four grown people in this house—we can work . . .

MAMA (*to herself*): Just aimed too high all the time—

RUTH (*turning and going to Mama fast—the words pouring out with urgency and desperation*): Lena—I'll work . . . I'll work twenty hours a day in all the kitchens in Chicago . . . I'll strap my baby on my back if I have to and scrub all the floors in America and wash all the sheets in America if I have to—but we got to MOVE! We got to get OUT OF HERE!!

Mama reaches out absently and pats Ruth's hand.

MAMA: No—I sees things differently now. Been thinking 'bout some of the things we could do to fix this place up some. I seen a second-hand bureau over on Maxwell Street just the other day that could fit right there. (*She points to where the new furniture might go. Ruth wanders away from her.*) Would need some new handles on it and then a little varnish and it look like something brand-new. And—we can put up them new curtains in the kitchen . . . Why this place be looking fine. Cheer us all up so that we forget trouble ever come . . . (*To Ruth.*) And you could get some nice screens to put up in your room round the baby's bassinet . . . (*She looks at both of them pleadingly.*) Sometimes you just got to know when to give up some things . . . and hold on to what you got . . .

Walter enters from the outside, looking spent and leaning against the door, his coat hanging from him.

MAMA: Where you been, son?

WALTER (*breathing hard*): Made a call.

MAMA: To who, son?

WALTER: To The Man. (*He heads for his room.*)

MAMA: What man, baby?

WALTER (*stops in the door*): The Man, Mama. Don't you know who The Man is?

RUTH: Walter Lee?

WALTER: *The Man.* Like the guys in the streets say—The Man. Captain Boss—Mistuh Charley . . . Old Cap'n Please Mr. Bossman . . .

BENEATHA (*suddenly*): Lindner!

WALTER: That's right! That's good. I told him to come right over.

BENEATHA (*fiercely, understanding*): For what? What do you want to see him for!

WALTER (*looking at his sister*): We going to do business with him.

MAMA: What you talking 'bout, son?

WALTER: Talking 'bout life, Mama. You all always telling me to see life like it is. Well—I laid in there on my back today . . . and I figured it out. Life just like it is. Who gets and who don't get. (*He sits down with his coat on and laughs.*) Mama, you know it's all divided up. Life is. Sure enough. Between the takers and the "tooken." (*He laughs.*) I've figured it out finally. (*He looks around at them.*) Yeah. Some of us always getting "tooken." (*He laughs.*) People like Willy Harris, they don't never get "tooken." And you know why the rest of us do? 'Cause we all mixed up. Mixed up bad. We get to looking 'round for the right and the wrong; and we worry about it and cry about it and stay up nights trying to figure out 'bout the wrong and the right of things all the time . . . And all the time, man, them takers is out there operating, just taking and taking. Willy Harris? Shoot — Willy Harris don't even count. He don't even count in the big scheme of things. But I'll say one thing for old Willy Harris . . . he's taught me something. He's taught me to keep my eye on what counts in this world. Yeah — (*Shouting out a little.*) Thanks, Willy!

RUTH: What did you call that man for, Walter Lee?

WALTER: Called him to tell him to come on over to the show. Gonna put on a show for the man. Just what he wants to see. You see, Mama, the man came here today and he told us that them people out there where you want us to move — well they so upset they willing to pay us *not* to move! (*He laughs again.*) And — and oh, Mama — you would of been proud of the way me and Ruth and Bennie acted. We told him to get out . . . Lord have mercy! We told the man to get out! Oh, we was some proud folks this afternoon, yeah. (*He lights a cigarette.*) We were still full of that old-time stuff . . . .

RUTH (*coming toward him slowly*): You talking 'bout taking them people's money to keep us from moving in that house?

WALTER: I ain't just talking 'bout it, baby — I'm telling you that's what's going to happen!

BENEATHA: Oh, God! Where is the bottom! Where is the real honest-to-God bottom so he can't go any farther!

WALTER: See — that's the old stuff. You and that boy that was here today. You all want everybody to carry a flag and a spear and sing some marching songs, huh? You wanna spend your life looking into things and trying to find the right and the wrong part, huh? Yeah. You know what's going to happen to that boy someday — he'll find himself sitting in a dungeon, locked in forever — and the takers will have the key! Forget it, baby! There ain't no causes — there ain't nothing but taking in this world, and he who takes most is smartest — and it don't make a damn bit of difference *how*.

MAMA: You making something inside me cry, son. Some awful pain inside me.

WALTER: Don't cry, Mama. Understand. That white man is going to walk in that door able to write checks for more money than we ever had. It's important to him and I'm going to help him . . . I'm going to put on the show, Mama.

MAMA: Son — I come from five generations of people who was slaves and share-croppers — but ain't nobody in my family never let nobody pay 'em no money that was a way of telling us we wasn't fit to walk the earth. We ain't never been that poor. (*Raising her eyes and looking at him.*) We ain't never been that — dead inside.

BENEATHA: Well — we are dead now. All the talk about dreams and sunlight that goes on in this house. It's all dead now.

WALTER: What's the matter with you all! I didn't make this world! It was give to me this way! Hell, yes, I want me some yachts someday! Yes, I want to hang some real pearls 'round my wife's neck. Ain't she supposed to wear no pearls? Somebody tell me—tell me, who decides which women is suppose to wear pearls in this world. I tell you I am a *man*—and I think my wife should wear some pearls in this world!

This last line hangs a good while and Walter begins to move about the room. The word "Man" has penetrated his consciousness; he mumbles it to himself repeatedly between strange agitated pauses as he moves about.

MAMA: Baby, how you going to feel on the inside?

WALTER: Fine! . . . Going to feel fine . . . a man . . .

MAMA: You won't have nothing left then, Walter Lee.

WALTER (*coming to her*): I'm going to feel fine, Mama. I'm going to look that son-of-a-bitch in the eyes and say—(*he falters*)—and say, "All right, Mr. Lindner—(*he falters even more*)—that's *your* neighborhood out there! You got the right to keep it like you want! You got the right to have it like you want! Just write the check and—the house is yours." And—and I am going to say—(*his voice almost breaks*) "And you—you people just put the money in my hand and you won't have to live next to this bunch of stinking niggers! . . ." (*He straightens up and moves away from his mother, walking around the room.*) And maybe—maybe I'll just get down on my black knees . . . (*He does so; Ruth and Bennie and Mama watch him in frozen horror.*) "Captain, Mistuh, Bossman—(*Groveling and grinning and wringing his hands in profoundly anguished imitation of the slow-witted movie stereotype.*) A-hee-hee-hee! Oh, yassuh boss! Yasssssuh! Great white—(*voice breaking, he forces himself to go on*)— Father, just gi' ussen de money, fo' God's sake, and we's—we's ain't gwine come out deh and dirty up yo' white folks neighborhood..." (*He breaks down completely.*) And I'll feel fine! Fine! FINE! (*He gets up and goes into the bedroom.*)

BENEATHA: That is not a man. That is nothing but a toothless rat.

MAMA: Yes—death done come in this here house. (*She is nodding, slowly, reflectively.*) Done come walking in my house on the lips of my children. You what supposed to be my beginning again. You—what supposed to be my harvest. (*To Beneatha.*) You—you mourning your brother?

BENEATHA: He's no brother of mine.

MAMA: What you say?

BENEATHA: I said that that individual in that room is no brother of mine.

MAMA: That's what I thought you said. You feeling like you better than he is today? (*Beneatha does not answer.*) Yes? What you tell him a minute ago? That he wasn't a man? Yes? You give him up for me? You done wrote his epitaph too—like the rest of the world? Well, who give you the privilege?

BENEATHA: Be on my side for once! You saw what he just did, Mama! You saw him—down on his knees. Wasn't it you who taught me to despise any man who would do that? Do what he's going to do?

MAMA: Yes—I taught you that. Me and your daddy. But I thought I taught you something else too . . . I thought I taught you to love him.

BENEATHA: Love him? There is nothing left to love.

MAMA: There is *always* something left to love. And if you ain't learned that, you ain't learned nothing. (*Looking at her.*) Have you cried for that boy today? I don't mean for yourself and for the family 'cause we lost the money. I mean for him: what he been through and what it done to him. Child, when do you think is the time to love somebody the most? When they done good and made things easy for everybody? Well then, you ain't through learning—because that ain't the time at all. It's when he's at his lowest and can't believe in hisself 'cause the world done whipped him so! When you starts measuring somebody, measure him right, child, measure him right. Make sure you done taken into account what hills and valleys he come through before he got to wherever he is.

Travis bursts into the room at the end of the speech, leaving the door open.

TRAVIS: Grandmama—the moving men are downstairs! The truck just pulled up.

MAMA (*turning and looking at him*): Are they, baby? They downstairs?

She sighs and sits. Lindner appears in the doorway. He peers in and knocks lightly, to gain attention, and comes in. All turn to look at him.

LINDNER (*hat and briefcase in hand*): Uh—hello . . .

Ruth crosses mechanically to the bedroom door and opens it and lets it swing open freely and slowly as the lights come up on Walter within, still in his coat, sitting at the far corner of the room. He looks up and out through the room to Lindner.

RUTH: He's here.

A long minute passes and Walter slowly gets up.

LINDNER (*coming to the table with efficiency, putting his briefcase on the table and starting to unfold papers and unscrew fountain pens*): Well, I certainly was glad to hear from you people. (*Walter has begun the trek out of the room, slowly and awkwardly, rather like a small boy, passing the back of his sleeve across his mouth from time to time.*) Life can really be so much simpler than people let it be most of the time. Well—with whom do I negotiate? You, Mrs. Younger, or your son here? (*Mama sits with her hands folded on her lap and her eyes closed as Walter advances. Travis goes closer to Lindner and looks at the papers curiously.*) Just some official papers, sonny.

RUTH: Travis, you go downstairs—

MAMA (*opening her eyes and looking into Walter's*): No. Travis, you stay right here. And you make him understand what you doing, Walter Lee. You teach him good. Like Willy Harris taught you. You show where our five generations done come to. (*Walter looks from her to the boy, who grins at him innocently.*) Go ahead, son—(*She folds her hands and closes her eyes.*) Go ahead.

WALTER (*at last crosses to Lindner, who is reviewing the contract*): Well, Mr. Lindner. (*Beneatha turns away.*) We called you—(*there is a profound, simple groping quality in his speech*)—because, well, me and my family (*He looks around and shifts from one foot to the other.*) Well—we are very plain people . . .

LINDNER: Yes—

WALTER: I mean—I have worked as a chauffeur most of my life—and my wife here, she does domestic work in people's kitchens. So does my mother. I mean—we are plain people . . .

LINDNER: Yes, Mr. Younger—

WALTER (*really like a small boy, looking down at his shoes and then up at the man*): And—uh—well, my father, well, he was a laborer most of his life. . . .

LINDNER (*absolutely confused*): Uh, yes—yes, I understand. (*He turns back to the contract.*)

WALTER (*a beat; staring at him*): And my father—(*With sudden intensity.*) My father almost *beat a man to death* once because this man called him a bad name or something, you know what I mean?

LINDNER (*looking up, frozen*): No, no, I'm afraid I don't—

WALTER (*a beat. The tension hangs; then Walter steps back from it*): Yeah. Well— what I mean is that we come from people who had a lot of *pride*. I mean— we are very proud people. And that's my sister over there and she's going to be a doctor—and we are very proud—

LINDNER: Well—I am sure that is very nice, but—

WALTER: What I am telling you is that we called you over here to tell you that we are very proud and that this—(*Signaling to Travis.*) Travis, come here. (*Travis crosses and Walter draws him before him facing the man.*) This is my son, and he makes the sixth generation of our family in this country. And we have all thought about your offer—

LINDNER: Well, good . . . good—

WALTER: And we have decided to move into our house because my father—my father—he earned it for us brick by brick. (*Mama has her eyes closed and is rocking back and forth as though she were in church, with her head nodding the Amen yes.*) We don't want to make no trouble for nobody or fight no causes, and we will try to be good neighbors. And that's *all* we got to say about that. (*He looks the man absolutely in the eyes.*) We don't want your money. (*He turns and walks away.*)

LINDNER (*looking around at all of them*): I take it then—that you have decided to occupy . . .

BENEATHA: That's what the man said.

LINDNER (*to Mama in her reverie*): Then I would like to appeal to you, Mrs. Younger. You are older and wiser and understand things better I am sure . . .

MAMA: I am afraid you don't understand. My son said we was going to move and there ain't nothing left for me to say. (*Briskly.*) You know how these young folks is nowadays, mister. Can't do a thing with 'em! (*As he opens his mouth, she rises.*) Good-bye.

LINDNER (*folding up his materials*): Well—if you are that final about it . . . there is nothing left for me to say. (*He finishes, almost ignored by the family, who are concentrating on Walter Lee. At the door Lindner halts and looks around.*) I sure hope you people know what you're getting into.

He shakes his head and exits.

RUTH (*looking around and coming to life*): Well, for God's sake—if the moving men are here—LET'S GET THE HELL OUT OF HERE!

MAMA (*into action*): Ain't it the truth! Look at all this here mess. Ruth, put Travis' good jacket on him . . . Walter Lee, fix your tie and tuck your shirt in, you look like somebody's hoodlum! Lord have mercy, where is my plant? (*She flies to get it amid the general bustling of the family, who are deliberately trying to ignore the nobility of the past moment.*) You all start on down . . . Travis child, don't go empty-handed . . . Ruth, where did I put that box with my skillets in it? I want to be in charge of it myself . . . I'm going to make us the biggest dinner we ever ate tonight . . . Beneatha, what's the matter with them stockings? Pull them things up, girl . . .

The family starts to file out as two moving men appear and begin to carry out the heavier pieces of furniture, bumping into the family as they move about.

BENEATHA: Mama, Asagai asked me to marry him today and go to Africa—

MAMA (*in the middle of her getting-ready activity*): He did? You ain't old enough to marry nobody—(*Seeing the moving men lifting one of her chairs precariously.*) Darling, that ain't no bale of cotton, please handle it so we can sit in it again! I had that chair twenty-five years . . .

The movers sigh with exasperation and go on with their work.

BENEATHA (*girlishly and unreasonably trying to pursue the conversation*): To go to Africa, Mama—be a doctor in Africa . . .

MAMA (*distracted*): Yes, baby—

WALTER: *Africa!* What he want you to go to Africa for?

BENEATHA: To practice there . . .

WALTER: Girl, if you don't get all them silly ideas out your head! You better marry yourself a man with some loot . . .

BENEATHA (*angrily, precisely as in the first scene of the play*): What have you got to do with who I marry!

WALTER: Plenty. Now I think George Murchison—

BENEATHA: *George Murchison!* I wouldn't marry him if he was Adam and I was Eve!

Walter and Beneatha go out yelling at each other vigorously and the anger is loud and real till their voices diminish. Ruth stands at the door and turns to Mama and smiles knowingly.

MAMA (*fixing her hat at last*): Yeah—they something all right, my children . . .

RUTH: Yeah—they're something. Let's go, Lena.

MAMA (*stalling, starting to look around at the house*): Yes—I'm coming. Ruth—

RUTH: Yes?

MAMA (*quietly, woman to woman*): He finally come into his manhood today, didn't he? Kind of like a rainbow after the rain . . .

RUTH (*biting her lip lest her own pride explode in front of Mama*): Yes, Lena.

Walter's voice calls for them raucously.

WALTER (*off stage*): Y'all come on! These people charges by the hour, you know!

MAMA (*waving Ruth out vaguely*): All right, honey—go on down. I be down directly.

Ruth hesitates, then exits. Mama stands, at last alone in the living room, her plant on the table before her as the lights start to come down. She looks around at all the walls and ceilings and suddenly, despite herself, while the children call below, a great heaving thing rises in her and she puts her fist to her mouth to stifle it, takes a final desperate look, pulls her coat about her, pats her hat, and goes out. The lights dim down. The door opens and she comes back in, grabs her plant, and goes out for the last time.

Curtain.

PAULA VOGEL

Paula Vogel (b. 1951) was born in Washington, D.C. After earning her B.A. degree from the Catholic University of America in 1974, she entered the doctoral program at Cornell University, which she left before completing her degree. In 1976 her play Meg was produced at Cornell; the production went on to the Kennedy Center in Washington and was published in 1981 by Samuel French. In 1979–80 Vogel was the recipient of a playwriting fellowship from the National Endowment for the Arts. Since 1985 she has been directing and teaching playwriting in the M.F.A. writing program at Brown University.

After creating a number of one-act plays, including Apple-Brown Betty and The Oldest Profession, Vogel began writing longer works such as The Last Pat Epstein Show before the Reruns and Desdemona: A Play about a Handkerchief. In 1996, the Theatre Communications Group published a collection of her work, The Baltimore Waltz and Other Plays. A year later her play How I Learned to Drive was first produced off-Broadway in New York City. It won the New York Drama Critics Circle, Drama Desk, and Obie awards for the best play of the year, as well as the 1998 Pulitzer Prize for Drama. That year Vogel's play had twenty-six regional productions, the most produced play in the United States.

In his book The Playwright's Voice, the interviewer David Savran, one of Vogel's colleagues in the writing program at Brown University, noted that:

> In her playwriting classes, Paula Vogel always asks her students to write the impossible: a play with a dog as protagonist, a play that cannot be staged, a play that dramatizes the end of the world in five pages. And while these provocative exercises stretch students' imaginations in remarkable ways, they also inadvertently reveal much about Vogel's own playwriting. For all her plays endeavor to stage the impossible. . . .
>
> For a Vogel play is never simply a politely dramatized fiction, it is always a meditation on the theatre itself—on role-playing, on the socially sanctioned scripts from which characters diverge at their peril, and on a theatrical tradition that has punished women who don't remain quiet, passive and demure. . . . [Her Pulitzer Prize–winning How I Learned to Drive] does far more than explain the effects of sexual predation on a young girl; it literally splits her into two—a body and a voice—in order to represent the radical alienation from Self that results from having been molested.

How I Learned to Drive is also about many other things, such as families, growing up, and becoming a survivor. Vogel has said, "My play dramatizes the *gifts we receive from people who hurt us," explaining that in her opinion, the young girl Li'l Bit "received the gift of how to survive" from the experience of being seduced by her Uncle Peck. For Li'l Bit, "learning to drive" is a complex metaphor for sexual initiation. In Vogel's interpretation, the play explores how Li'l Bit grows into an adult and becomes able to look at and understand her complicity in the seduction, and then forgive herself.*

COMMENTARY   *Jill Dolan, "Review of* How I Learned to Drive," *page 1534.*

WEB   *Research Paula Vogel and answer questions about her work at bedfordstmartins.com/charters/litwriters.*

How I Learned to Drive   1997

CHARACTERS

LI'L BIT, A woman who ages forty-something to eleven years old.

PECK, Attractive man in his forties. Despite a few problems, he should be
played by an actor one might cast in the role of Atticus in To KILL A
MOCKINGBIRD.

THE GREEK CHORUS, If possible, these three members should be able to
sing three-part harmony.

> MALE GREEK CHORUS, Plays Grandfather, Waiter, High School
> Boys. Thirties–forties.
>
> FEMALE GREEK CHORUS, Plays Mother, Aunt Mary, High School
> Girls. Thirty–fifty.
>
> TEENAGE GREEK CHORUS, Plays Grandmother, high school girls,
> and the voice of eleven-year-old Li'l Bit. Note on the casting of this
> actor: I would strongly recommend casting a young woman who is
> "of legal age," that is, twenty-one to twenty-five years old, who can
> look as close to eleven as possible. The contrast with the other cast
> members will help. If the actor is too young, the audience may feel
> uncomfortable.

As the house lights dim, a Voice announces:

Safety first — You and Driver Education.

Then the sound of a key turning the ignition of a car. Li'l Bit steps into a spotlight on the stage; "well-endowed," she is a softer-looking woman in the present time than she was at seventeen.

LI'L BIT: Sometimes to tell a secret, you first have to teach a lesson. We're going
to start our lesson tonight on an early, warm summer evening.

   In a parking lot overlooking the Beltsville Agricultural Farms in
suburban Maryland.

   Less than a mile away, the crumbling concrete of U.S. One wends
its way past one-room revival churches, the porno drive-in, and boarded
up motels with For Sale signs tumbling down.

   Like I said, it's a warm summer evening.

Here on the land the Department of Agriculture owns, the smell of sleeping farm animal is thick on the air. The smells of clover and hay mix in with the smells of the leather dashboard. You can still imagine how Maryland used to be, before the malls took over. This countryside was once dotted with farmhouses — from their porches you could have witnessed the Civil War raging in the front fields.

Oh yes. There's a moon over Maryland tonight, that spills into the car where I sit beside a man old enough to be — did I mention how still the night is? Damp soil and tranquil air. It's the kind of night that makes a middle-aged man with a mortgage feel like a country boy again.

It's 1969. And I am very old, very cynical of the world, and I know it all. In short, I am seventeen years old, parking off a dark lane with a married man on an early summer night.

(*Lights up on two chairs facing front — or a Buick Riviera, if you will. Waiting patiently, with a smile on his face, Peck sits sniffing the night air. Li'l Bit climbs in beside him, seventeen years old and tense. Throughout the following, the two sit facing directly front. They do not touch. Their bodies remain passive. Only their facial expressions emote.*)

PECK: Ummm. I love the smell of your hair.

LI'L BIT: Uh-huh.

PECK: Oh, Lord. Ummmm. (*Beat*) A man could die happy like this.

LI'L BIT: Well, *don't.*

PECK: What shampoo is this?

LI'L BIT: Herbal Essence.

PECK: Herbal Essence. I'm gonna buy me some. Herbal Essence. And when I'm all alone in the house, I'm going to get into the bathtub, and uncap the bottle and —

LI'L BIT: — Be good.

PECK: What?

LI'L BIT: Stop being . . . bad.

PECK: What did you think I was going to say? What do you think I'm going to do with the shampoo?

LI'L BIT: I don't want to know. I don't want to hear it.

PECK: I'm going to wash my hair. That's all.

LI'L BIT: Oh.

PECK: What did you think I was going to do?

LI'L BIT: Nothing . . . I don't know. Something . . . nasty.

PECK: With shampoo? Lord, gal — your mind!

LI'L BIT: And whose fault is it?

PECK: Not mine. I've got the mind of a boy scout.

LI'L BIT: Right. A horny boy scout.

PECK: Boy scouts are always horny. What do you think the first Merit Badge is for?

LI'L BIT: There. You're going to be nasty again.

PECK: Oh, no. I'm good. Very good.

LI'L BIT: It's getting late.

PECK: Don't change the subject. I was talking about how good I am. (*Beat*) Are you ever gonna let me show you how good I am?

LI'L BIT: Don't go over the line now.

PECK: I won't. I'm not gonna do anything you don't want me to do.

LI'L BIT: That's right.

PECK: And I've been good all week.

LI'L BIT: You have?

PECK: Yes. All week. Not a single drink.

LI'L BIT: Good boy.

PECK: Do I get a reward? For not drinking?

LI'L BIT: A small one. It's getting late.

PECK: Just let me undo you. I'll do you back up.

LI'L BIT: All right. But be quick about it. (*Peck pantomimes undoing Li'l Bit's brassiere with one hand*) You know, that's amazing. The way you can undo the hooks through my blouse with one hand.

PECK: Years of practice.

LI'L BIT: You would make an incredible brain surgeon with that dexterity.

PECK: I'll bet Clyde—what's the name of the boy taking you to the prom?

LI'L BIT: Claude Souders.

PECK: Claude Souders. I'll bet it takes him two hands, lights on, and you helping him on to get to first base.

LI'L BIT: Maybe.

(*Beat.*)

PECK: Can I . . . kiss them? Please?

LI'L BIT: I don't know.

PECK: Don't make a grown man beg.

LI'L BIT: Just one kiss.

PECK: I'm going to lift your blouse.

LI'L BIT: It's a little cold.

(*Peck laughs gently.*)

PECK: That's not why you're shivering. (*They sit, perfectly still, for a long moment of silence. Peck makes gentle, concentric circles with his thumbs in the air in front of him*) How does that feel?

(*Li'l Bit closes her eyes, carefully keeps her voice calm:*)

LI'L BIT: It's . . . okay.

(*Sacred music, organ music or a boy's choir swells beneath the following.*)

PECK: I tell you, you can keep all the cathedrals of Europe. Just give me a second with these—these celestial orbs—

(*Peck bows his head as if praying. But he is kissing her nipple. Li'l Bit, eyes still closed, rears back her head on the leather Buick car seat.*)

LI'L BIT: Uncle Peck—we've got to go. I've got graduation rehearsal at school tomorrow morning. And you should get on home to Aunt Mary—

PECK: —All right, Li'l Bit.

LI'L BIT: —*Don't* call me that no more. (*Calmer*) Any more. I'm a big girl now, Uncle Peck. As you know.

(*Li'l Bit pantomimes refastening her bra behind her back.*)

PECK: That you are. Going on eighteen. Kittens will turn into cats. (*Sighs*) I live all week long for these few minutes with you — you know that?

LI'L BIT: I'll drive.

(*A Voice cuts in with:*)

Idling in the Neutral Gear.

(*Sound of car revving cuts off the sacred music; Li'l Bit, now an adult, rises out of the car and comes to us.*)

LI'L BIT: In most families, relatives get names like "Junior," or "Brother," or "Bubba." In my family, if we call someone "Big Papa," it's not because he's tall. In my family, folks tend to get nicknamed for their genitalia. Uncle Peck, for example. My mama's adage was "the titless wonder," and my cousin Bobby got branded for life as "B.B."

(*In unison with Greek Chorus:*)

LI'L BIT: For blue balls.   GREEK CHORUS: For blue balls.

FEMALE GREEK CHORUS (*As Mother*): And of course, we were so excited to have a baby girl that when the nurse brought you in and said, "It's a girl! It's a baby girl!" I just had to see for myself. So we whipped your diapers down and parted your chubby little legs — and right between your legs there was —

(*Peck has come over during the above and chimes along:*)

PECK: Just a little bit.   GREEK CHORUS: Just a little bit.

FEMALE GREEK CHORUS (*As Mother*): And when you were born, you were so tiny that you fit in Uncle Peck's outstretched hand.

(*Peck stretches his hand out.*)

PECK: Now that's a fact. I held you, one day old, right in this hand.

(*A traffic signal is projected of a bicycle in a circle with a diagonal red slash.*)

LI'L BIT: Even with my family background, I was sixteen or so before I realized that pedophilia did not mean people who loved to bicycle. . . .

(*A Voice intrudes:*)

Driving in First Gear.

LI'L BIT: 1969. A typical family dinner.

FEMALE GREEK CHORUS (*As Mother*): Look, Grandma. Li'l Bit's getting to be as big in the bust as you are.

LI'L BIT: Mother! Could we please change the subject?

TEENAGE GREEK CHORUS (*As Grandmother*): Well, I hope you are buying her some decent bras. I never had a decent bra, growing up in the Depression, and now my shoulders are just crippled — crippled from the weight hanging on my shoulders — the dents from my bra straps are big enough to put your finger in. — Here, let me show you —

(*As Grandmother starts to open her blouse:*)

LI'L BIT: Grandma! Please don't undress at the dinner table.

PECK: I thought the entertainment came *after* the dinner.

LI'L BIT (*To the audience*): This is how it always starts. My grandfather, Big Papa, will chime in next with—

MALE GREEK CHORUS (*As Grandfather*): Yup. If Li'l Bit gets any bigger, we're gonna haveta buy her a wheelbarrow to carry in front of her—

LI'L BIT: —Damn it—

PECK: —How about those Redskins on Sunday, Big Papa?

LI'L BIT (*To the audience*): The only sport Big Papa followed was chasing Grandma around the house—

MALE GREEK CHORUS (*As Grandfather*): —Or we could write to Kate Smith. Ask her for somma her used brassieres she don't want anymore—she could maybe give to Li'l Bit here—

LI'L BIT: —I can't stand it. I can't.

PECK: Now, honey, that's just their way—

FEMALE GREEK CHORUS (*As Mother*): I tell you, Grandma, Li'l Bit's at that age. She's so sensitive, you can't say boo—

LI'L BIT: I'd like some privacy, that's all. Okay? Some goddamn privacy—

PECK: —Well, at least she didn't use the savior's name—

LI'L BIT (*To the audience*): And Big Papa wouldn't let a dead dog lie. No sirree.

MALE GREEK CHORUS (*As Grandfather*): Well, she'd better stop being so sensitive. 'Cause five minutes before Li'l Bit turns the corner, her tits turn first—

LI'L BIT (*Starting to rise from the table*): —That's it. That's it.

PECK: Li'l Bit, you can't let him get to you. Then he wins.

LI'L BIT: I hate him. *Hate* him.

PECK: That's fine. But hate him and eat a good dinner at the same time.

(*Li'l Bit calms down and sits with perfect dignity.*)

LI'L BIT: The gumbo is really good, Grandma.

MALE GREEK CHORUS (*As Grandfather*): A'course, Li'l Bit's got a big surprise coming for her when she goes to that fancy college this fall—

PECK: Big Papa—let it go.

MALE GREEK CHORUS (*As Grandfather*): What does she need a college degree for? She's got all the credentials she'll need on her chest—

LI'L BIT: —Maybe I want to learn things. Read. Rise above my cracker background—

PECK: —Whoa, now, Li'l Bit—

MALE GREEK CHORUS (*As Grandfather*): What kind of things do you want to read?

LI'L BIT: There's a whole semester course, for example, on Shakespeare—

(*Greek Chorus, as Grandfather, laughs until he weeps.*)

MALE GREEK CHORUS (*As Grandfather*): Shakespeare. That's a good one. Shakespeare is really going to help you in life.

PECK: I think it's wonderful. And on scholarship!

MALE GREEK CHORUS (*As Grandfather*): How is Shakespeare going to help her lie on her back in the dark?

(*Li'l Bit is on her feet.*)

LI'L BIT: You're getting old, Big Papa. You are going to die—very very soon. Maybe even *tonight*. And when you get to heaven, God's going to be a beautiful black woman in a long white robe. She's gonna look at your chart and say: Uh-oh. Fornication. Dog-ugly mean with blood relatives. Oh. Uh-oh. Voted for George Wallace. Well, one last chance: If you can name the play, all will be forgiven. And then she'll quote: "The quality of mercy is not strained." Your answer? Oh, too bad—*Merchant of Venice:* Act IV, Scene iii. And then she'll send your ass to fry in hell with all the other crackers. Excuse me, please.

    (*To the audience*) And as I left the house, I would always hear Big Papa say:

MALE GREEK CHORUS (*As Grandfather*): Lucy, your daughter's got a mouth on her. Well, no sense in wasting good gumbo. Pass me her plate, Mama.

LI'L BIT: And Aunt Mary would come up to Uncle Peck:

FEMALE GREEK CHORUS (*As Aunt Mary*): Peck, go after her, will you? You're the only one she'll listen to when she gets like this.

PECK: She just needs to cool off.

FEMALE GREEK CHORUS (*As Aunt Mary*): Please, honey—Grandma's been on her feet cooking all day.

PECK: All right.

LI'L BIT: And as he left the room, Aunt Mary would say:

FEMALE GREEK CHORUS (*As Aunt Mary*): Peck's so good with them when they get to be this age.

(*Li'l Bit has stormed to another part of the stage, her back turned, weeping with a teenage fury. Peck, cautiously, as if stalking a deer, comes to her. She turns away even more. He waits a bit.*)

PECK: I don't suppose you're talking to family. (*No response*) Does it help that I'm in-law?

LI'L BIT: Don't you dare make fun of this.

PECK: I'm not. There's nothing funny about this. (*Beat*) Although I'll bet when Big Papa is about to meet his maker, he'll remember *The Merchant of Venice*.

LI'L BIT: I've got to get away from here.

PECK: You're going away. Soon. Here, take this.

(*Peck hands her his folded handkerchief. Li'l Bit uses it, noisily. Hands it back. Without her seeing, he reverently puts it back.*)

LI'L BIT: I hate this family.

PECK: Your grandfather's ignorant. And you're right—he's going to die soon. But he's family. Family is . . . family.

LI'L BIT: Grown-ups are always saying that. Family.

PECK: Well, when you get a little older, you'll see what we're saying.

LI'L BIT: Uh-huh. So family is another acquired taste, like French kissing?

PECK: Come again?

LI'L BIT: You know, at first it really grosses you out, but in time you grow to like it?

PECK: Girl, you are . . . a handful.

LI'L BIT: Uncle Peck — you have the keys to your car?

PECK: Where do you want to go?

LI'L BIT: Just up the road.

PECK: I'll come with you.

LI'L BIT: No — please? I just need to . . . to drive for a little bit. Alone.

(*Peck tosses her the keys.*)

PECK: When can I see you alone again?

LI'L BIT: Tonight.

(*Li'l Bit crosses to center stage while the lights dim around her. A Voice directs:*)

Shifting Forward from First to Second Gear.

LI'L BIT: There were a lot of rumors about why I got kicked out of that fancy school in 1970. Some say I got caught with a man in my room. Some say as a kid on scholarship I fooled around with a rich man's daughter.

(*Li'l Bit smiles innocently at the audience*) I'm not talking.

But the real truth was I had a constant companion in my dorm room — who was less than discreet. Canadian V.O. A fifth a day.

1970. A Nixon recession. I slept on the floors of friends who were out of work themselves. Took factory work when I could find it. A string of dead-end jobs that didn't last very long.

What I did, most nights, was cruise the Beltway and the back roads of Maryland, where there was still country, past the battlefields and farm houses. Racing in a 1965 Mustang — and as long as I had gasoline for my car and whiskey for me, the nights would pass. Fully tanked, I would speed past the churches and the trees on the bend, thinking just one notch of the steering wheel would be all it would take, and yet some . . . reflex took over. My hands on the wheel in the nine and three o'clock position — I never so much as got a ticket. He taught me well.

(*A Voice announces:*)

You and the Reverse Gear.

LI'L BIT: Back up. 1968. On the Eastern Shore. A celebration dinner.

(*Li'l Bit joins Peck at a table in a restaurant.*)

PECK: Feeling better, missy?

LI'L BIT: The bathroom's really amazing here, Uncle Peck! They have these little soaps — instead of borax or something — and they're in the shape of shells.

PECK: I'll have to take a trip to the gentleman's room just to see.

LI'L BIT: How did you know about this place?

PECK: This inn is famous on the Eastern Shore — it's been open since the seventeenth century. And I know how you like history. . . .

(*Li'l Bit is shy and pleased.*)

LI'L BIT: It's great.

PECK: And you've just done your first, legal, long-distance drive. You must be hungry.

LI'L BIT: I'm starved.

PECK: I would suggest a dozen oysters to start, and the crab imperial . . . (*Li'l Bit is genuinely agog*) You might be interested to know the town history. When the British sailed up this very river in the dead of night—see outside where I'm pointing?—they were going to bombard the heck out of this town. But the town fathers were ready for them. They crept up all the trees with lanterns so that the British would think they saw the town lights and they aimed their cannons too high. And that's why the inn is still here for business today.

LI'L BIT: That's a great story.

PECK (*Casually*): Would you like to start with a cocktail?

LI'L BIT: You're not . . . you're not going to start drinking, are you, Uncle Peck?

PECK: Not me. I told you, as long as you're with me, I'll never drink. I asked you if *you'd* like a cocktail before dinner. It's nice to have a little something with the oysters.

LI'L BIT: But . . . I'm not . . . legal. We could get arrested. Uncle Peck, they'll never believe I'm twenty-one!

PECK: So? Today we celebrate your driver's license—on the first try. This establishment reminds me a lot of places back home.

LI'L BIT: What does that mean?

PECK: In South Carolina, like here on the Eastern Shore, they're . . . (*Searches for the right euphemism*) . . . "European." Not so puritanical. And very understanding if gentlemen wish to escort very attractive young ladies who might want a before-dinner cocktail. If you want one, I'll order one.

LI'L BIT: Well—sure. Just . . . one.

(*The Female Greek Chorus appears in a spot.*)

FEMALE GREEK CHORUS (*As Mother*): A Mother's Guide to Social Drinking:

A lady never gets sloppy—she may, however, get tipsy and a little gay.

Never drink on an empty stomach. Avail yourself of the bread basket and generous portions of butter. *Slather* the butter on your bread.

Sip your drink, slowly, let the beverage linger in your mouth—interspersed with interesting, fascinating conversation. Sip, never . . . slurp or gulp. Your glass should always be three-quarters full when his glass is empty.

Stay away from *ladies'* drinks: drinks like pink ladies, slow gin fizzes, daiquiris, gold cadillacs, Long Island iced teas, margaritas, piña coladas, mai tais, planters punch, white Russians, black Russians, red Russians, melon balls, blue balls, hummingbirds, hemorrhages and hurricanes. In short, avoid anything with sugar, or anything with an umbrella. Get your vitamin C from *fruit*. Don't order anything with Voodoo or Vixen in the title or sexual positions in the name like Dead Man Screw or the Missionary. (*She sort of titters*)

Believe me, they are lethal. . . . I think you were conceived after one of those.

Drink, instead, like a man: straight up or on the rocks, with plenty of water in between.

Oh, yes. And never mix your drinks. Stay with one all night long, like the man you came in with: bourbon, gin, or tequila till dawn, damn the torpedoes, full speed ahead!

(*As the Female Greek Chorus retreats, the Male Greek Chorus approaches the table as a Waiter.*)

MALE GREEK CHORUS (*As Waiter*): I hope you all are having a pleasant evening. Is there something I can bring you, sir, before you order?

(*Li'l Bit waits in anxious fear. Carefully, Uncle Peck says with command:*)

PECK: I'll have a plain iced tea. The lady would like a drink, I believe.

(*The Male Greek Chorus does a double take; there is a moment when Uncle Peck and he are in silent communication.*)

MALE GREEK CHORUS (*As Waiter*): Very good. What would the . . . lady like?
LI'L BIT (*A bit flushed*): Is there . . . is there any sugar in a martini?
PECK: None that I know of.
LI'L BIT: That's what I'd like then—a dry martini. And could we maybe have some bread?
PECK: A drink fit for a woman of the world. —Please bring the lady a dry martini, be generous with the olives, straight up.

(*The Male Greek Chorus anticipates a large tip.*)

MALE GREEK CHORUS (*As Waiter*): Right away. Very good, sir.

(*The Male Greek Chorus returns with an empty martini glass which he puts in front of Li'l Bit.*)

PECK: Your glass is empty. Another martini, madam?
LI'L BIT: Yes, thank you.
          (*Peck signals the Male Greek Chorus, who nods*) So why did you leave South Carolina, Uncle Peck?
PECK: I was stationed in D.C. after the war, and decided to stay. Go North, Young Man, someone might have said.
LI'L BIT: What did you do in the service anyway?
PECK (*Suddenly taciturn*): I . . . I did just this and that. Nothing heroic or spectacular.
LI'L BIT: But did you see fighting? Or go to Europe?
PECK: I served in the Pacific Theater. It's really nothing interesting to talk about.
LI'L BIT: It is to me. (*The Waiter has brought another empty glass*) Oh, goody. I love the color of the swizzle sticks. What were we talking about?
PECK: Swizzle sticks.
LI'L BIT: Do you ever think of going back?
PECK: To the Marines?
LI'L BIT: No—to South Carolina.

PECK: Well, we do go back. To visit.

LI'L BIT: No, I mean to live.

PECK: Not very likely. I think it's better if my mother doesn't have a daily reminder of her disappointment.

LI'L BIT: Are these floorboards slanted?

PECK: Yes, the floor is very slanted. I think this is the original floor.

LI'L BIT: Oh, good.

(*The Female Greek Chorus as Mother enters swaying a little, a little past tipsy.*)

FEMALE GREEK CHORUS (*As Mother*): Don't leave your drink unattended when you visit the ladies' room. There is such a thing as white slavery; the modus operandi is to spike an unsuspecting young girl's drink with a "mickey" when she's left the room to powder her nose.

But if you feel you have had more than your sufficiency in liquor, do go to the ladies' room — often. Pop your head out of doors for a refreshing breath of the night air. If you must, wet your face and head with tap water. Don't be afraid to dunk your head if necessary. A wet woman is still less conspicuous than a drunk woman.

(*The Female Greek Chorus stumbles a little; conspiratorially*) When in the course of human events it becomes necessary, go to a corner stall and insert the index and middle finger down the throat almost to the epiglottis. Divulge your stomach contents by such persuasion, and then wait a few moments before rejoining your beau waiting for you at your table.

Oh, no. Don't be shy or embarrassed. In the very best of establishments, there's always one or two debutantes crouched in the corner stalls, their beaded purses tossed willy-nilly, sounding like cats in heat, heaving up the contents of their stomachs.

(*The Female Greek Chorus begins to wander off*) I wonder what it is they do in the men's rooms. . . .

LI'L BIT: So why is your mother disappointed in you, Uncle Peck?

PECK: Every mother in Horry County has Great Expectations.

LI'L BIT: — Could I have another mar-ti-ni, please?

PECK: I think this is your last one.

(*Peck signals the Waiter. The Waiter looks at Li'l Bit and shakes his head no. Peck raises his eyebrow, raises his finger to indicate one more, and then rubs his fingers together. It looks like a secret code. The Waiter sighs, shakes his head sadly, and brings over another empty martini glass. He glares at Peck.*)

LI'L BIT: The name of the county where you grew up is "Horry"? (*Li'l Bit, plastered, begins to laugh. Then she stops*) I think your mother should be proud of you.

(*Peck signals for the check.*)

PECK: Well, missy, she wanted me to do — to be everything my father was not. She wanted me to amount to something.

LI'L BIT: But you have! You've amounted a lot. . . .

PECK: I'm just a very ordinary man.

(*The Waiter has brought the check and waits. Peck draws out a large bill and hands it to the Waiter. Li'l Bit is in the soppy stage.*)

LI'L BIT: I'll bet your mother loves you, Uncle Peck.

(*Peck freezes a bit. To Male Greek Chorus as Waiter:*)

PECK: Thank you. The service was exceptional. Please keep the change.

MALE GREEK CHORUS (*As Waiter, in a tone that could freeze*): Thank you, sir. Will you be needing any help?

PECK: I think we can manage, thank you.

(*Just then, the Female Greek Chorus as Mother lurches on stage; the Male Greek Chorus as Waiter escorts her off as she delivers:*)

FEMALE GREEK CHORUS (*As Mother*): Thanks to judicious planning and several trips to the ladies' loo, your mother once out-drank an entire regiment of British officers on a good-will visit to Washington! Every last man of them! Milquetoasts! How'd they ever kick Hitler's cahones, huh? No match for an American lady—I could drink every man in here under the table.

> (*She delivers one last crucial hint before she is gently "bounced"*) As a last resort, when going out for an evening on the town, be sure to wear a skin-tight girdle—so tight that only a surgical knife or acetylene torch can get it off you—so that if you do pass out in the arms of your escort, he'll end up with rubber burns on his fingers before he can steal your virtue—

(*A Voice punctures the interlude with:*)

> **Vehicle Failure.**
> **Even with careful maintenance and preventive operation of your automobile, it is all too common for us to experience an unexpected breakdown. If you are driving at any speed when a breakdown occurs, you must slow down and guide the automobile to the side of the road.**

(*Peck is slowly propping up Li'l Bit as they work their way to his car in the parking lot of the inn.*)

PECK: How are you doing, missy?

LI'L BIT: It's so far to the car, Uncle Peck. Like the lanterns in the trees the British fired on. . . .

(*Li'l Bit stumbles. Peck swoops her up in his arms.*)

PECK: Okay, I think we're going to take a more direct route.

> (*Li'l Bit closes her eyes*) Dizzy? (*She nods her head*) Don't look at the ground. Almost there—do you feel sick to your stomach? (*Li'l Bit nods. They reach the "car." Peck gently deposits her on the front seat*) Just settle here a little while until things stop spinning. (*Li'l Bit opens her eyes*)

LI'L BIT: What are we doing?

PECK: We're just going to sit here until your tummy settles down.

LI'L BIT: It's such nice upholst'ry—

PECK: Think you can go for a ride, now?

LI'L BIT: Where are you taking me?

PECK: Home.

LI'L BIT: You're not taking me—upstairs? There's no room at the inn? (*Li'l Bit giggles*)

PECK: Do you want to go upstairs? (*Li'l Bit doesn't answer*) Or home?

LI'L BIT: —This isn't right, Uncle Peck.

PECK: What isn't right?

LI'L BIT: What we're doing. It's wrong. It's very wrong.

PECK: What are we doing? (*Li'l Bit does not answer*) We're just going out to dinner.

LI'L BIT: You know. It's not nice to Aunt Mary.

PECK: You let me be the judge of what's nice and not nice to my wife.

(*Beat.*)

LI'L BIT: Now you're mad.

PECK: I'm not mad. It's just that I thought you . . . understood me, Li'l Bit. I think you're the only one who does.

LI'L BIT: Someone will get hurt.

PECK: Have I forced you to do anything?

(*There is a long pause as Li'l Bit tries to get sober enough to think this through.*)

LI'L BIT: . . . I guess not.

PECK: We are just enjoying each other's company. I've told you, nothing is going to happen between us until you want it to. Do you know that?

LI'L BIT: Yes.

PECK: Nothing is going to happen until you want it to. (*A second more, with Peck staring ahead at the river while seated at the wheel of his car. Then, softly:*) Do you want something to happen?

(*Peck reaches over and strokes her face, very gently. Li'l Bit softens, reaches for him, and buries her head in his neck. Then she kisses him. Then she moves away, dizzy again.*)

LI'L BIT: . . . I don't know.

(*Peck smiles; this has been good news for him—it hasn't been a "no."*)

PECK: Then I'll wait. I'm a very patient man. I've been waiting for a long time. I don't mind waiting.

LI'L BIT: Someone is going to get hurt.

PECK: No one is going to get hurt. (*Li'l Bit closes her eyes*) Are you feeling sick?

LI'L BIT: Sleepy.

(*Carefully, Peck props Li'l Bit up on the seat.*)

PECK: Stay here a second.

LI'L BIT: Where're you going?

PECK: I'm getting something from the back seat.

LI'L BIT (*Scared; too loud*): What? What are you going to do?

(*Peck reappears in the front seat with a lap rug.*)

PECK: Shhhh. (*Peck covers Li'l Bit. She calms down*) There. Think you can sleep?

(*Li'l Bit nods. She slides over to rest on his shoulder. With a look of happiness, Peck turns the ignition key. Beat. Peck leaves Li'l Bit sleeping in the car and strolls down to the audience. Wagner's* Flying Dutchman *comes up faintly.*)

(*A Voice interjects:*)

Idling in the Neutral Gear.

TEENAGE GREEK CHORUS: Uncle Peck Teaches Cousin Bobby How to Fish.

PECK: I get back once or twice a year—supposedly to visit Mama and the family, but the real truth is to fish. I miss this the most of all. There's a smell in the Low Country—where the swamp and fresh inlet join the saltwater—a scent of sand and cypress, that I haven't found anywhere yet.

    I don't say this very often up North because it will just play into the stereotype everyone has, but I will tell you: I didn't wear shoes in the summertime until I was sixteen. It's unnatural down here to pen up your feet in leather. Go ahead—take 'em off. Let yourself breathe—it really will make you feel better.

    We're going to aim for some pompano today—and I have to tell you, they're a very shy, mercurial fish. Takes patience, and psychology. You have to believe it doesn't matter if you catch one or not.

    Sky's pretty spectacular—there's some beer in the cooler next to the crab salad I packed, so help yourself if you get hungry. Are you hungry? Thirsty? Holler if you are.

    Okay. You don't want to lean over the bridge like that—pompano feed in shallow water, and you don't want to get too close—they're frisky and shy little things—wait, check your line. Yep, something's been munching while we were talking.

    Okay, look: We take the sand flea and you take the hook like this—right through his little sand flea rump. Sand fleas should always keep their backs to the wall. Okay. Cast it in, like I showed you. That's great! I can taste that pompano now, sautéed with some pecans and butter, a little bourbon—now—let it lie on the bottom—now, reel, jerk, reel, jerk—

    Look—look at your line. There's something calling, all right. Okay, tip the rod up—not too sharp—hook it—all right, now easy, reel and then rest—let it play. And reel—play it out, that's right—really good! I can't believe it! It's a pompano. —Good work! Way to go! You are an official fisherman now. Pompano are hard to catch. We are going to have a delicious little—

    What? Well, I don't know how much pain a fish feels—you can't think of that. Oh, no, don't cry, come on now, it's just a fish—the other guys are going to see you. —No, no, you're just real sensitive, and I think that's wonderful at your age—look, do you want me to cut it free? You do?

    Okay, hand me those pliers—look—I'm cutting the hook—okay? And we're just going to drop it in—no I'm not mad. It's just for fun, okay? There—it's going to swim back to its lady friend and tell her what a terrible day it had and she's going to stroke him with her fins until he feels better, and then they'll do something alone together that will make them both feel good and sleepy. . . .

(*Peck bends down, very earnest*) I don't want you to feel ashamed about crying. I'm not going to tell anyone, okay? I can keep secrets. You know, men cry all the time. They just don't tell anybody, and they don't let anybody catch them. There's nothing you could do that would make me feel ashamed of you. Do you know that? Okay. (*Peck straightens up, smiles*)

Do you want to pack up and call it a day? I tell you what—I think I can still remember—there's a really neat tree house where I used to stay for days. I think it's still here—it was the last time I looked. But it's a secret place—you can't tell anybody we've gone there—least of all your mom or your sisters. — This is something special just between you and me. Sound good? We'll climb up there and have a beer and some crab salad—okay, B.B.? Bobby? Robert . . .

(*Li'l Bit sits at a kitchen table with the two Female Greek Chorus members.*)

LI'L BIT (*To the audience*): Three women, three generations, sit at the kitchen table.

On Men, Sex, and Women: Part I:

FEMALE GREEK CHORUS (*As Mother*): Men only want one thing.

LI'L BIT (*Wide-eyed*): But what? What is it they want?

FEMALE GREEK CHORUS (*As Mother*): And once they have it, they lose all interest. So Don't Give It to Them.

TEENAGE GREEK CHORUS (*As Grandmother*): I never had the luxury of the rhythm method. Your grandfather is just a big bull. A big bull. Every morning, every evening.

FEMALE GREEK CHORUS (*As Mother, whispers to Li'l Bit*): And he used to come home for lunch every day.

LI'L BIT: My god, Grandma!

TEENAGE GREEK CHORUS (*As Grandmother*): Your grandfather only cares that I do two things: have the table set and the bed turned down.

FEMALE GREEK CHORUS (*As Mother*): And in all that time, Mother, you never have experienced—?

LI'L BIT (*To the audience*): —Now my grandmother believed in all the sacraments of the church, to the day she died. She believed in Santa Claus and the Easter Bunny until she was fifteen. But she didn't believe in—

TEENAGE GREEK CHORUS (*As Grandmother*): —Orgasm! That's just something you and Mary have made up! I don't believe you.

FEMALE GREEK CHORUS (*As Mother*): Mother, it happens to women all the time—

TEENAGE GREEK CHORUS (*As Grandmother*): —Oh, now you're going to tell me about the G force!

LI'L BIT: No, Grandma, I think that's astronauts—

FEMALE GREEK CHORUS (*As Mother*): Well, Mama, after all, you were a child bride when Big Papa came and got you—you were a married woman and you still believed in Santa Claus.

TEENAGE GREEK CHORUS (*As Grandmother*): It was legal, what Daddy and I did! I was fourteen and in those days, fourteen was a grown-up woman—

(*Big Papa shuffles in the kitchen for a cookie.*)

MALE GREEK CHORUS (*As Grandfather*): —Oh, now we're off on Grandma and the Rape of the Sa-bean Women!

TEENAGE GREEK CHORUS (*As Grandmother*): Well, you were the one in such a big hurry—

MALE GREEK CHORUS (*As Grandfather to Li'l Bit*): —I picked your grandmother out of that herd of sisters just like a lion chooses the gazelle—the plump, slow, flaky gazelle dawdling at the edge of the herd—your sisters were too smart and too fast and too scrawny—

LI'L BIT (*To the audience*): —The family story is that when Big Papa came for Grandma, my Aunt Lily was waiting for him with a broom—and she beat him over the head all the way down the stairs as he was carrying out Grandma's hope chest—

MALE GREEK CHORUS (*As Grandfather*): —And they were *mean*. 'Specially Lily.

FEMALE GREEK CHORUS (*As Mother*): Well, you were robbing the baby of the family!

TEENAGE GREEK CHORUS (*As Grandmother*): I still keep a broom handy in the kitchen! And I know how to use it! So get your hand out of the cookie jar and don't you spoil your appetite for dinner—out of the kitchen!

(*Male Greek Chorus as Grandfather leaves chuckling with a cookie.*)

FEMALE GREEK CHORUS (*As Mother*): Just one thing a married woman needs to know how to use—the rolling pin or the broom. I prefer a heavy, cast-iron fry pan—they're great on a man's head, no matter how thick the skull is.

TEENAGE GREEK CHORUS (*As Grandmother*): Yes, sir, your father is ruled by only two bosses! Mr. Gut and Mr. Peter! And sometimes, first thing in the morning, Mr. Sphincter Muscle!

FEMALE GREEK CHORUS (*As Mother*): It's true. Men are like children. Just like little boys.

TEENAGE GREEK CHORUS (*As Grandmother*): Men are bulls! Big bulls!

(*The Greek Chorus is getting aroused.*)

FEMALE GREEK CHORUS (*As Mother*): They'd still be crouched on their haunches over a fire in a cave if we hadn't cleaned them up!

TEENAGE GREEK CHORUS (*As Grandmother, flushed*): Coming in smelling of sweat—

FEMALE GREEK CHORUS (*As Mother*): —Looking at those naughty pictures like boys in a dime store with a dollar in their pockets!

TEENAGE GREEK CHORUS (*As Grandmother; raucous*): No matter to them what they smell like! They've got to have it, right then, on the spot, right there! Nasty!—

FEMALE GREEK CHORUS (*As Mother*): —Vulgar!

TEENAGE GREEK CHORUS (*As Grandmother*): Primitive!—

FEMALE GREEK CHORUS (*As Mother*): —Hot!—

LI'L BIT: And just about then, Big Papa would shuffle in with—

MALE GREEK CHORUS (*As Grandfather*): —What are you all cackling about in here?

TEENAGE GREEK CHORUS (*As Grandmother*): Stay out of the kitchen! This is just for girls!

(*As Grandfather leaves:*)

MALE GREEK CHORUS (*As Grandfather*): Lucy, you'd better not be filling Mama's head with sex! Every time you and Mary come over and start in about sex, when I ask a simple question like, "What time is dinner going to be ready?," Mama snaps my head off!

TEENAGE GREEK CHORUS (*As Grandmother*): Dinner will be ready when I'm good and ready! Stay out of this kitchen!

(*Li'l Bit steps out.*
A Voice directs:)

When Making a Left Turn, You Must Downshift While Going Forward.

LI'L BIT: 1979. A long bus trip to Upstate New York. I settled in to read, when a young man sat beside me.

MALE GREEK CHORUS (*As Young Man; voice cracking*): "What are you reading?"

LI'L BIT: He asked. His voice broke into that miserable equivalent of vocal acne, not quite falsetto and not tenor, either. I glanced a side view. He was appealing in an odd way, huge ears at a defiant angle springing forward at ninety degrees. He must have been shaving, because his face, with a peach sheen, was speckled with nicks and styptic. "I have a class tomorrow," I told him.

MALE GREEK CHORUS (*As Young Man*): "You're taking a class?"

LI'L BIT: "I'm teaching a class." He concentrated on lowering his voice.

MALE GREEK CHORUS (*As Young Man*): "I'm a senior. Walt Whitman High."

LI'L BIT: The light was fading outside, so perhaps he was—with a very high voice.

I felt his "interest" quicken. Five steps ahead of the hopes in his head, I slowed down, waited, pretended surprise, acted at listening, all the while knowing we would get off the bus, he would just then seem to think to ask me to dinner, he would chivalrously insist on walking me home, he would continue to converse in the street until I would casually invite him up to my room—and—I was only into the second moment of conversation and I could see the whole evening before me.

And dramaturgically speaking, after the faltering and slightly comical "first act," there was the very briefest of intermissions, and an extremely capable and forceful and *sustained* second act. And after the second act climax and a gentle denouement—before the post-play discussion—I lay on my back in the dark and I thought about you, Uncle Peck. Oh. Oh—this is the allure. Being older. Being the first. Being the translator, the teacher, the epicure, the already jaded. This is how the giver gets taken.

(*Li'l Bit changes her tone*) On Men, Sex, and Women: Part II:

(*Li'l Bit steps back into the scene as a fifteen-year-old, gawky and quiet, as the gazelle at the edge of the herd.*)

TEENAGE GREEK CHORUS (*As Grandmother, to Li'l Bit*): You're being mighty quiet, missy. Cat Got Your Tongue?

LI'L BIT: I'm just listening. Just thinking.

TEENAGE GREEK CHORUS (*As Grandmother*): Oh, yes, Little Miss Radar Ears? Soaking it all in? Little Miss Sponge? Penny for your thoughts?

(*Li'l Bit hesitates to ask but she really wants to know.*)

LI'L BIT: Does it — when you do it — you know, theoretically when I do it and I haven't done it before — I mean — does it hurt?

FEMALE GREEK CHORUS (*As Mother*): Does what hurt, honey?

LI'L BIT: When a . . . when a girl does it for the first time — with a man — does it hurt?

TEENAGE GREEK CHORUS (*As Grandmother; horrified*): *That's* what you're thinking about?

FEMALE GREEK CHORUS (*As Mother, calm*): Well, just a little bit. Like a pinch. And there's a little blood.

TEENAGE GREEK CHORUS (*As Grandmother*): Don't tell her that! She's too young to be thinking those things!

FEMALE GREEK CHORUS (*As Mother*): Well, if she doesn't find out from me, where is she going to find out? In the street?

TEENAGE GREEK CHORUS (*As Grandmother*): Tell her it hurts! It's agony! You think you're going to die! Especially if you do it before marriage!

FEMALE GREEK CHORUS (*As Mother*): Mama! I'm going to tell her the truth! Unlike you, you left me and Mary completely in the dark with fairy tales and told us to go to the priest! What does an eighty-year-old priest know about lovemaking with girls!

LI'L BIT (*Getting upset*): It's not fair!

FEMALE GREEK CHORUS (*As Mother*): Now, see, she's getting upset — you're scaring her.

TEENAGE GREEK CHORUS (*As Grandmother*): Good! Let her be good and scared! It hurts! You bleed like a stuck pig! And you lay there and say, "Why, O Lord, have you forsaken me?!"

LI'L BIT: It's not fair! Why does everything have to hurt for girls? Why is there always blood?

FEMALE GREEK CHORUS (*As Mother*): It's not a lot of blood — and it feels wonderful after the pain subsides . . .

TEENAGE GREEK CHORUS (*As Grandmother*): You're encouraging her to just go out and find out with the first drugstore joe who buys her a milkshake!

FEMALE GREEK CHORUS (*As Mother*): Don't be scared. It won't hurt you — if the man you go to bed with really loves you. It's important that he loves you.

TEENAGE GREEK CHORUS (*As Grandmother*): — Why don't you just go out and rent a motel room for her, Lucy?

FEMALE GREEK CHORUS (*As Mother*): I believe in telling my daughter the truth! We have a very close relationship! I want her to be able to ask me anything — I'm not scaring her with stories about Eve's sin and snakes crawling on their bellies for eternity and women bearing children in mortal pain—

TEENAGE GREEK CHORUS (*As Grandmother*): —If she stops and thinks before she takes her knickers off, maybe someone in this family will finish high school!

(*Li'l Bit knows what is about to happen and starts to retreat from the scene at this point.*)

FEMALE GREEK CHORUS (*As Mother*): Mother! If you and Daddy had helped me—I wouldn't have had to marry that—that no-good-son-of-a—

TEENAGE GREEK CHORUS (*As Grandmother*): —He was good enough for you on a full moon! I hold you responsible!

FEMALE GREEK CHORUS (*As Mother*): —You could have helped me! You could have told me something about the facts of life!

TEENAGE GREEK CHORUS (*As Grandmother*): —I told you what my mother told me! A girl with her skirt up can outrun a man with his pants down!

(*The Male Greek Chorus enters the fray; Li'l Bit edges further downstage.*)

FEMALE GREEK CHORUS (*As Mother*): And when I turned to you for a little help, all I got afterwards was—

MALE GREEK CHORUS (*As Grandfather*): You Made Your Bed; Now Lie On It!

(*The Greek Chorus freezes, mouths open, argumentatively.*)

LI'L BIT (*To the audience*): Oh, please! I still can't bear to listen to it, after all these years—

(*The Male Greek Chorus "unfreezes," but out of his open mouth, as if to his surprise, comes a bass refrain from a Motown song.*)

MALE GREEK CHORUS: "Do-Bee-Do-Wah!"

(*The Female Greek Chorus member is also surprised; but she, too, unfreezes.*)

FEMALE GREEK CHORUS: "Shoo-doo-be-doo-be-doo; shoo-doo-be-doo-be-doo."

(*The Male and Female Greek Chorus members continue with their harmony, until the Teenage member of the Chorus starts in with Motown lyrics such as "Dedicated to the One I Love," or "In the Still of the Night," or "Hold Me"—any Sam Cooke will do. The three modulate down into three-part harmony, softly, until they are submerged by the actual recording playing over the radio in the car in which Uncle Peck sits in the driver's seat, waiting. Li'l Bit sits in the passenger's seat.*)

LI'L BIT: Ahh. That's better.

(*Uncle Peck reaches over and turns the volume down; to Li'l Bit:*)

PECK: How can you hear yourself think?

(*Li'l Bit does not answer.*

A Voice insinuates itself in the pause:)

Before You Drive.
Always check under your car for obstructions—broken bottles, fallen tree branches, and the bodies of small children. Each year hundreds of children are crushed beneath the wheels of unwary

drivers in their own driveways. Children depend on *you* to watch them.

(*Pause.*

The Voice continues:)

You and the Reverse Gear.

(*In the following section, it would be nice to have slides of erotic photographs of women and cars: women posed over the hood; women draped along the sideboards; women with water hoses spraying the car; and the actress playing Li'l Bit with a Bel Air or any 1950s car one can find for the finale.*)

LI'L BIT: 1967. In a parking lot of the Beltsville Agricultural Farms. The Initiation into a Boy's First Love.

PECK (*With a soft look on his face*): Of course, my favorite car will always be the '56 Bel Air Sports Coupe. Chevy sold more '55s, but the '56!—a V-8 with Corvette option, 225 horsepower; went from zero to sixty miles per hour in 8.9 seconds.

LI'L BIT (*To the audience*): Long after a mother's tits, but before a woman's breasts:

PECK: Super-Turbo-Fire! What a Power Pack—mechanical lifters, twin four-barrel carbs, lightweight valves, dual exhausts—

LI'L BIT (*To the audience*): After the milk but before the beer:

PECK: A specific intake manifold, higher-lift camshaft, and the tightest squeeze Chevy had ever made—

LI'L BIT (*To the audience*): Long after he's squeezed down the birth canal but before he's pushed his way back in: The boy falls in love with the thing that bears his weight with speed.

PECK: I want you to know your automobile inside and out. —Are you there? Li'l Bit?

(*Slides end here.*)

LI'L BIT: —What?

PECK: You're drifting. I need you to concentrate.

LI'L BIT: Sorry.

PECK: Okay. Get into the driver's seat. (*Li'l Bit does*) Okay. Now. Show me what you're going to do before you start the car.

(*Li'l Bit sits, with her hands in her lap. She starts to giggle.*)

LI'L BIT: I don't know, Uncle Peck.

PECK: Now, come on. What's the first thing you're going to adjust?

LI'L BIT: My bra strap?—

PECK: —Li'l Bit. What's the most important thing to have control of on the inside of the car?

LI'L BIT: That's easy. The radio. I tune the radio from Mama's old fart tunes to—

(*Li'l Bit turns the radio up so we can hear a 1960s tune. With surprising firmness, Peck commands:*)

PECK: —Radio off. Right now. (*Li'l Bit turns the radio off*) When you are driving your car, with your license, you can fiddle with the stations all you want. But when you are driving with a learner's permit in my car, I want all your attention to be on the road.

LI'L BIT: Yes, sir.

PECK: Okay. Now the seat — forward and up. (*Li'l Bit pushes it forward*) Do you want a cushion?

LI'L BIT: No — I'm good.

PECK: You should be able to reach all the switches and controls. Your feet should be able to push the accelerator, brake and clutch all the way down. Can you do that?

LI'L BIT: Yes.

PECK: Okay, the side mirrors. You want to be able to see just a bit of the right side of the car in the right mirror — can you?

LI'L BIT: Turn it out more.

PECK: Okay. How's that?

LI'L BIT: A little more. . . . Okay, that's good.

PECK: Now the left — again, you want to be able to see behind you — but the left lane — adjust it until you feel comfortable. (*Li'l Bit does so*) Next. I want you to check the rearview mirror. Angle it so you have a clear vision of the back. (*Li'l Bit does so*) Okay. Lock your door. Make sure all the doors are locked.

LI'L BIT (*Making a joke of it*): But then I'm locked in with you.

PECK: Don't fool.

LI'L BIT: All right. We're locked in.

PECK: We'll deal with the air vents and defroster later. I'm teaching you on a manual — once you learn manual, you can drive anything. I want you to be able to drive any car, any machine. Manual gives you *control*. In ice, if your brakes fail, if you need more power — okay? It's a little harder at first, but then it becomes like breathing. Now. Put your hands on the wheel. I never want to see you driving with one hand. Always two hands. (*Li'l Bit hesitates*) What? What is it now?

LI'L BIT: If I put my hands on the wheel — how do I defend myself?

PECK (*Softly*): Now listen. Listen up close. We're not going to fool around with this. This is serious business. I will never touch you when you are driving a car. Understand?

LI'L BIT: Okay.

PECK: Hands on the nine o'clock and three o'clock position gives you maximum control and turn.

(*Peck goes silent for a while. Li'l Bit waits for more instruction.*)

Okay. Just relax and listen to me, Li'l Bit, okay? I want you to lift your hands for a second and look at them. (*Li'l Bit feels a bit silly, but does it*)

Those are your two hands. When you are driving, your life is in your own two hands. Understand? (*Li'l Bit nods*)

I don't have any sons. You're the nearest to a son I'll ever have — and I want to give you something. Something that really matters to me.

There's something about driving — when you're in control of the car, just you and the machine and the road — that nobody can take from you. A power. I feel more myself in my car than anywhere else. And that's what I want to give to you.

There's a lot of assholes out there. Crazy men, arrogant idiots, drunks, angry kids, geezers who are blind—and you have to be ready for them. I want to teach you to drive like a man.

LI'L BIT: What does that mean?

PECK: Men are taught to drive with confidence—with aggression. The road belongs to them. They drive defensively—always looking out for the other guy. Women tend to be polite—to hesitate. And that can be fatal.

You're going to learn to think what the other guy is going to do before he does it. If there's an accident, and ten cars pile up, and people get killed, you're the one who's gonna steer through it, put your foot on the gas if you have to, and be the only one to walk away. I don't know how long you or I are going to live, but we're for damned sure not going to die in a car.

So if you're going to drive with me, I want you to take this very seriously.

LI'L BIT: I will, Uncle Peck. I want you to teach me to drive.

PECK: Good. You're going to pass your test on the first try. Perfect score. Before the next four weeks are over, you're going to know this baby inside and out. Treat her with respect.

LI'L BIT: Why is it a "she"?

PECK: Good question. It doesn't have to be a "she"—but when you close your eyes and think of someone who responds to your touch—someone who performs just for you and gives you what you ask for—I guess I always see a "she." You can call her what you like.

LI'L BIT (*To the audience*): I closed my eyes—and decided not to change the gender.

(*A Voice:*)

Defensive driving involves defending yourself from hazardous and sudden changes in your automotive environment. By thinking ahead, the defensive driver can adjust to weather, road conditions, and road kill. Good defensive driving involves mental and physical preparation. Are you prepared?

(*Another Voice chimes in:*)

You and the Reverse Gear.

LI'L BIT: 1966. The Anthropology of the Female Body in Ninth Grade—Or A Walk Down Mammary Lane.

(*Throughout the following, there is occasional rhythmic beeping, like a transmitter signaling. Li'l Bit is aware of it, but can't figure out where it is coming from. No one else seems to hear it.*)

MALE GREEK CHORUS: In the hallway of Francis Scott Key Middle School.

(*A bell rings; the Greek Chorus is changing classes and meets in the hall, conspiratorially.*)

TEENAGE GREEK CHORUS: She's coming!

(*Li'l Bit enters the scene; the Male Greek Chorus member has a sudden, violent sneezing and lethal allergy attack.*)

FEMALE GREEK CHORUS: Jerome? Jerome? Are you all right?

MALE GREEK CHORUS: I — don't — know. I can't breathe — get Li'l Bit —

TEENAGE GREEK CHORUS: — He needs oxygen! —

FEMALE GREEK CHORUS: — Can you help us here?

LI'L BIT: What's wrong? Do you want me to get the school nurse —

(*The Male Greek Chorus member wheezes, grabs his throat and sniffs at Li'l Bit's chest, which is beeping away.*)

MALE GREEK CHORUS: No — it's okay — I only get this way when I'm around an allergy trigger —

LI'L BIT: Golly. What are you allergic to?

MALE GREEK CHORUS (*with a sudden grab of her breast*): Foam rubber.

(*The Greek Chorus members break up with hilarity; Jerome leaps away from Li'l Bit's kicking rage with agility; as he retreats:*)

LI'L BIT: Jerome! Creep! Cretin! Cro-Magnon!

TEENAGE GREEK CHORUS: Rage is not attractive in a girl.

FEMALE GREEK CHORUS: Really. Get a Sense of Humor.

(*A Voice echoes:*)

> **Good defensive driving involves mental and physical preparation. Were You Prepared?**

FEMALE GREEK CHORUS: Gym Class: In the showers.

(*The sudden sound of water; the Female Greek Chorus members and Li'l Bit, while fully clothed, drape towels across their fronts, miming nudity. They stand, hesitate, at an imaginary shower's edge.*)

LI'L BIT: Water looks hot.

FEMALE GREEK CHORUS: Yesss. . . .

(*Female Greek Chorus members are not going to make the first move. One dips a tentative toe under the water, clutching the towel around her.*)

LI'L BIT: Well, I guess we'd better shower and get out of here.

FEMALE GREEK CHORUS: Yep. You go ahead. I'm still cooling off.

LI'L BIT: Okay. —Sally? Are you gonna shower?

TEENAGE GREEK CHORUS: After you —

(*Li'l Bit takes a deep breath for courage, drops the towel and plunges in: The two Female Greek Chorus members look at Li'l Bit in the all together, laugh, gasp and high-five each other.*)

TEENAGE GREEK CHORUS: Oh my god! Can you believe —

FEMALE GREEK CHORUS: Told you! It's not foam rubber! I win! Jerome owes me fifty cents!

(*A Voice editorializes:*)

> **Were You Prepared?**

(*Li'l Bit tries to cover up; she is exposed, as suddenly 1960s Motown fills the room and we segue into:*)

FEMALE GREEK CHORUS: The Sock Hop.

(*Li'l Bit stands up against the wall with her female classmates. Teenage Greek Chorus is mesmerized by the music and just sways alone, lip-synching the lyrics.*)

LI'L BIT: I don't know. Maybe it's just me — but — do you ever feel like you're just a walking Mary Jane joke?

FEMALE GREEK CHORUS: I don't know what you mean.

LI'L BIT: You haven't heard the Mary Jane jokes? (*Female Greek Chorus member shakes her head no*) Okay. "Little Mary Jane is walking through the woods, when all of a sudden this man who was hiding behind a tree *jumps* out, *rips* open Mary Jane's blouse, and *plunges* his hands on her breasts. And Little Mary Jane just laughed and laughed because she knew her money was in her shoes."

(*Li'l Bit laughs; the Female Greek Chorus does not.*)

FEMALE GREEK CHORUS: You're weird.

(*In another space, in a strange light, Uncle Peck stands and stares at Li'l Bit's body. He is setting up a tripod, but he just stands, appreciative, watching her.*)

LI'L BIT: Well, don't you ever feel . . . self-conscious? Like you're being looked at all the time?

FEMALE GREEK CHORUS: That's not a problem for me. — Oh — look — Greg's coming over to ask you to dance.

(*Teenage Greek Chorus becomes attentive, flustered. Male Greek Chorus member, as Greg, bends slightly as a very short young man, whose head is at Li'l Bit's chest level. Ardent, sincere, and socially inept, Greg will become a successful gynecologist.*)

TEENAGE GREEK CHORUS (*softly*): Hi, Greg.

(*Greg does not hear. He is intent on only one thing.*)

MALE GREEK CHORUS (*As Greg, to Li'l Bit*): Good Evening. Would you care to dance?

LI'L BIT (*Gently*): Thank you very much, Greg — but I'm going to sit this one out.

MALE GREEK CHORUS (*As Greg*): Oh. Okay. I'll try my luck later.

(*He disappears.*)

TEENAGE GREEK CHORUS: Oohhh.

(*Li'l Bit relaxes. Then she tenses, aware of Peck's gaze.*)

FEMALE GREEK CHORUS: Take pity on him. Someone should.

LI'L BIT: But he's so short.

TEENAGE GREEK CHORUS: He can't help it.

LI'L BIT: But his head comes up to (*Li'l Bit gestures*) here. And I think he asks me on the fast dances so he can watch me — you know — jiggle.

FEMALE GREEK CHORUS: I wish I had your problems.

(*The tune changes; Greg is across the room in a flash.*)

MALE GREEK CHORUS (*As Greg*): Evening again. May I ask you for the honor of a spin on the floor?

LI'L BIT: I'm . . . very complimented, Greg. But I . . . I just don't do fast dances.

MALE GREEK CHORUS (*As Greg*): Oh. No problem. That's okay.

(*He disappears. Teenage Greek Chorus watches him go.*)

TEENAGE GREEK CHORUS: That is just so—*sad*.

(*Li'l Bit becomes aware of Peck waiting.*)

FEMALE GREEK CHORUS: You know, you should take it as a compliment that the guys want to watch you jiggle. They're guys. That's what they're supposed to do.

LI'L BIT: I guess you're right. But sometimes I feel like these alien life forces, these two mounds of flesh have grafted themselves onto my chest, and they're using me until they can "propagate" and take over the world and they'll just keep growing, with a mind of their own until I collapse under their weight and they suck all the nourishment out of my body and I finally just waste away while they get bigger and bigger and— (*Li'l Bit's classmates are just staring at her in disbelief*)

FEMALE GREEK CHORUS: —You are the strangest girl I have ever met.

(*Li'l Bit's trying to joke but feels on the verge of tears.*)

LI'L BIT: Or maybe someone's implanted radio transmitters in my chest at a frequency I can't hear, that girls can't detect, but they're sending out these signals to men who get mesmerized, like sirens, calling them to dash themselves on these "rocks"—

(*Just then, the music segues into a slow dance, perhaps a Beach Boys tune like "Little Surfer," but over the music there's a rhythmic, hypnotic beeping transmitted, which both Greg and Peck hear. Li'l Bit hears it too, and in horror she stares at her chest. She, too, is almost hypnotized. In a trance, Greg responds to the signals and is called to her side—actually, her front. Like a zombie, he stands in front of her, his eyes planted on her two orbs.*)

MALE GREEK CHORUS (*As Greg*): This one's a slow dance. I hope your dance card isn't . . . filled?

(*Li'l Bit is aware of Peck; but the signals are calling her to him. The signals are no longer transmitters, but an electromagnetic force, pulling Li'l Bit to his side, where he again waits for her to join him. She must get away from the dance floor.*)

LI'L BIT: Greg—you really are a nice boy. But I don't like to dance.

MALE GREEK CHORUS (*As Greg*): That's okay. We don't have to move or anything. I could just hold you and we could just *sway* a little—

LI'L BIT: —No! I'm sorry—but I think I have to leave; I hear someone calling me—

(*Li'l Bit starts across the dance floor, leaving Greg behind. The beeping stops. The lights change, although the music does not. As Li'l Bit talks to the audience, she continues to change and prepare for the coming session. She should be wearing a tight tank top or a sheer blouse and very tight pants. To the audience:*)

In every man's home some small room, some zone in his house, is set aside. It might be the attic, or the study, or a den. And there's an invisible sign as if from the old treehouse: Girls Keep Out.

Here, away from female eyes, lace doilies and crochet, he keeps his manly toys: the Vargas pinups, the tackle. A scent of tobacco and WD-40. (*She inhales deeply.*) A dash of his Bay Rum. Ahhh . . . (*Li'l Bit savors it for just a moment more*)

Here he keeps his secrets: a violin or saxophone, drum set or darkroom, and the stacks of *Playboy*. (*In a whisper*) Here, in my aunt's home, it was the basement. Uncle Peck's turf.

(*A Voice commands:*)

You and the Reverse Gear.

LI'L BIT: 1965. The Photo Shoot.

(*Li'l Bit steps into the scene as a nervous but curious thirteen-year-old. Music, from the previous scene, continues to play, changing into something like Roy Orbison later—something seductive with a beat. Peck fiddles, all business, with his camera. As in the driving lesson, he is all competency and concentration. Li'l Bit stands awkwardly. He looks through the Leica camera on the tripod, adjusts the back lighting, etc.*)

PECK: Are you cold? The lights should heat up some in a few minutes—

LI'L BIT: —Aunt Mary is?

PECK: At the National Theatre matinee. With your mother. We have time.

LI'L BIT: But—what if—

PECK: —And so what if they return? I told them you and I were going to be working with my camera. They won't come down. (*Li'l Bit is quiet, apprehensive*) Look, are you sure you want to do this?

LI'L BIT: I said I'd do it. But—

PECK: —I know. You've drawn the line.

LI'L BIT (*Reassured*): That's right. No frontal nudity.

PECK: Good heavens, girl, where did you pick that up?

LI'L BIT (*Defensive*): I read.

(*Peck tries not to laugh.*)

PECK: And I read *Playboy* for the interviews. Okay. Let's try some different music.

(*Peck goes to an expensive reel-to-reel and forwards. Something like "Sweet Dreams" begins to play.*)

LI'L BIT: I didn't know you listened to this.

PECK: I'm not dead, you know. I try to keep up. Do you like this song? (*Li'l Bit nods with pleasure*) Good. Now listen—at professional photo shoots, they always play music for the models. Okay? I want you to just enjoy the music. Listen to it with your body, and just—respond.

LI'L BIT: Respond to the music with my . . . body?

PECK: Right. Almost like dancing. Here—let's get you on the stool, first. (*Peck comes over and helps her up*)

LI'L BIT: But nothing showing—

(*Peck firmly, with his large capable hands, brushes back her hair, angles her face. Li'l Bit turns to him like a plant to the sun.*)

PECK: Nothing showing. Just a peek.

> (*He holds her by the shoulders, looking at her critically. Then he unbuttons her blouse to the midpoint, and runs his hands over the flesh of her exposed sternum, arranging the fabric, just touching her. Deliberately, calmly. Asexually. Li'l Bit quiets, sits perfectly still, and closes her eyes*)
> Okay?

LI'L BIT: Yes.

(*Peck goes back to his camera.*)

PECK: I'm going to keep talking to you. Listen without responding to what I'm saying; you want to *listen* to the music. Sway, move just your torso or your head—I've got to check the light meter.

LI'L BIT: But—you'll be watching.

PECK: No—I'm not here—just my voice. Pretend you're in your room all alone on a Friday night with your mirror—and the music feels good— just move for me, Li'l Bit—

> (*Li'l Bit closes her eyes. At first self-conscious; then she gets more into the music and begins to sway. We hear the camera start to whir. Throughout the shoot, there can be a slide montage of actual shots of the actor playing Li'l Bit—interspersed with other models à la* Playboy, *Calvin Klein, and Victoriana/Lewis Carroll's Alice Liddell*)
> That's it. That looks great. Okay. Just keep doing that. Lift your head up a bit more, good, good, just keep moving, that a girl—you're a very beautiful young woman. Do you know that? (*Li'l Bit looks up, blushes. Peck shoots the camera. The audience should see this shot on the screen*)

LI'L BIT: No. I don't know that.

PECK: Listen to the music. (*Li'l Bit closes her eyes again*) Well you are. For a thirteen-year-old, you have a body a twenty-year-old woman would die for.

LI'L BIT: The boys in school don't think so.

PECK: The boys in school are little Neanderthals in short pants. You're ten years ahead of them in maturity; it's gonna take a while for them to catch up.

> (*Peck clicks another shot; we see a faint smile on Li'l Bit on the screen*)
> Girls turn into women long before boys turn into men.

LI'L BIT: Why is that?

PECK: I don't know, Li'l Bit. But it's a blessing for men.

> (*Li'l Bit turns silent*) Keep moving. Try arching your back on the stool, hands behind you, and throw your head back. (*The slide shows a* Playboy *model in this pose*) Oohh, great. That one was great. Turn your head away, same position. (*Whir*) Beautiful.

(*Li'l Bit looks at him a bit defiantly.*)

LI'L BIT: I think Aunt Mary is beautiful.

(*Peck stands still.*)

PECK: My wife is a very beautiful woman. Her beauty doesn't cancel yours out. (*More casually; he returns to the camera*) All the women in your family are beautiful. In fact, I think all women are. You're not listening to the music. (*Peck shoots some more film in silence*) All right, turn your head to the left. Good. Now take the back of your right hand and put it on your right cheek — your elbow angled up — now slowly, slowly, stroke your cheek, draw back your hair with the back of your hand. (*Another classic* Playboy *or* Vargas) Good. One hand above and behind your head; stretch your body; smile. (*Another pose*)

    Li'l Bit. I want you to think of something that makes you laugh —

LI'L BIT: I can't think of anything.

PECK: Okay. Think of Big Papa chasing Grandma around the living room. (*Li'l Bit lifts her head and laughs. Click. We should see this shot*) Good. Both hands behind your head. Great! Hold that. (*From behind his camera*) You're doing great work. If we keep this up, in five years we'll have a really professional portfolio.

(*Li'l Bit stops.*)

LI'L BIT: What do you mean in five years?

PECK: You can't submit work to *Playboy* until you're eighteen. —

(*Peck continues to shoot; he knows he's made a mistake.*)

LI'L BIT: — Wait a minute. You're joking, aren't you, Uncle Peck?

PECK: Heck, no. You can't get into *Playboy* unless you're the very best. And you are the very best.

LI'L BIT: I would never do that!

(*Peck stops shooting. He turns off the music.*)

PECK: Why? There's nothing wrong with *Playboy* — it's a very classy maga —

LI'L BIT (*More upset*): But I thought you said I should go to college!

PECK: Wait — Li'l Bit — it's nothing like that. Very respectable women model for *Playboy* — actresses with major careers — women in college — there's an Ivy League issue every —

LI'L BIT: — I'm never doing anything like that! You'd show other people these — other *men* — what I'm doing. — Why would you do that?! Any *boy* around here could just pick up, just go into The Stop & Go and *buy* — Why would you ever want to — to share —

PECK: — Whoa, whoa. Just stop a second and listen to me. Li'l Bit. Listen. There's nothing wrong in what we're doing. I'm very proud of you. I think you have a wonderful body and an even more wonderful mind. And of course I want other people to *appreciate* it. It's not anything shameful.

LI'L BIT (*Hurt*): But this is something — that I'm only doing for you. This is something — that you said was just between us.

PECK: It is. And if that's how you feel, five years from now, it will remain that way. Okay? I know you're not going to do anything you don't feel like doing.

(*He walks back to the camera.*) Do you want to stop now? I've got just a few more shots on this roll—

LI'L BIT: I don't want anyone seeing this.

PECK: I swear to you. No one will. I'll treasure this—that you're doing this only for me.

(*Li'l Bit, still shaken, sits on the stool. She closes her eyes*) Li'l Bit? Open your eyes and look at me. (*Li'l Bit shakes her head no*) Come on. Just open your eyes, honey.

LI'L BIT: If I look at you—if I look at the camera: You're gonna know what I'm thinking. You'll see right through me—

PECK: —No, I won't. I want you to look at me. All right, then. I just want you to listen. Li'l Bit. (*She waits*) I love you. (*Li'l Bit opens her eyes; she is startled. Peck captures the shot. On the screen we see right through her. Peck says softly*) Do you know that? (*Li'l Bit nods her head yes*) I have loved you every day since the day you were born.

LI'L BIT: Yes.

(*Li'l Bit and Peck just look at each other. Beat. Beneath the shot of herself on the screen, Li'l Bit, still looking at her uncle, begins to unbutton her blouse.*

A neutral Voice cuts off the above scene with:)

Implied Consent.

As an individual operating a motor vehicle in the state of Maryland, you must abide by "Implied Consent." If you do not consent to take the blood alcohol content test, there may be severe penalties: a suspension of license, a fine, community service and a possible *jail* sentence.

(*The Voice shifts tone:*)

Idling in the Neutral Gear.

MALE GREEK CHORUS (*Announcing*): Aunt Mary on behalf of her husband.

(*Female Greek Chorus checks her appearance, and with dignity comes to the front of the stage and sits down to talk to the audience.*)

FEMALE GREEK CHORUS (*As Aunt Mary*): My husband was such a good man—is. Is such a good man. Every night, he does the dishes. The second he comes home, he's taking out the garbage, or doing yard work, lifting the heavy things I can't. Everyone in the neighborhood borrows Peck—it's true—women with husbands of their own, men who just don't have Peck's abilities—there's always a knock on our door for a jump start on cold mornings, when anyone needs a ride, or help shoveling the sidewalk—I look out, and there Peck is, without a coat, pitching in.

I know I'm lucky. The man works from dawn to dusk. And the overtime he does every year—my poor sister. She sits every Christmas when I come to dinner with a new stole, or diamonds, or with the tickets to Bermuda.

I know he has troubles. And we don't talk about them. I wonder, sometimes, what happened to him during the war. The men who fought World War II didn't have "rap sessions" to talk about their feelings. Men in his generation were expected to be quiet about it and get on with their lives. And sometimes I can feel him just fighting the trouble—whatever has burrowed deeper than the scar tissue—and we don't talk about it. I know he's having a bad spell because he comes looking for me in the house, and just hangs around me until it passes. And I keep my banter light—I discuss a new recipe, or sales, or gossip—because I think domesticity can be a balm for men when they're lost. We sit in the house and listen to the peace of the clock ticking in his well-ordered living room, until it passes.

(*Sharply*) I'm not a fool. I know what's going on. I wish you could feel how hard Peck fights against it—he's swimming against the tide, and what he needs is to see me on the shore, believing in him, knowing he won't go under, he won't give up—

And I want to say this about my niece. She's a sly one, that one is. She knows exactly what she's doing; she's twisted Peck around her little finger and thinks it's all a big secret. Yet another one who's borrowing my husband until it doesn't suit her anymore.

Well. I'm counting the days until she goes away to school. And she manipulates someone else. And then he'll come back again, and sit in the kitchen while I bake, or beside me on the sofa when I sew in the evenings. I'm a very patient woman. But I'd like my husband back.

I am counting the days.

(*A Voice repeats:*)

You and the Reverse Gear.

MALE GREEK CHORUS: Li'l Bit's Thirteenth Christmas. Uncle Peck Does the Dishes. Christmas 1964.

(*Peck stands in a dress shirt and tie, nice pants, with an apron. He is washing dishes. He's in a mood we haven't seen. Quiet, brooding. Li'l Bit watches him a moment before seeking him out.*)

LI'L BIT: Uncle Peck? (*He does not answer. He continues to work on the pots*) I didn't know where you'd gone to. (*He nods. She takes this as a sign to come in*) Don't you want to sit with us for a while?

PECK: No. I'd rather do the dishes.

(*Pause. Li'l Bit watches him.*)

LI'L BIT: You're the only man I know who does dishes. (*Peck says nothing*) I think it's really nice.

PECK: My wife has been on her feet all day. So's your grandmother and your mother.

LI'L BIT: I know. (*Beat*) Do you want some help?

PECK: No. (*He softens a bit towards her*) You can help by just talking to me.

LI'L BIT: Big Papa never does the dishes. I think it's nice.

PECK: I think men should be nice to women. Women are always working for us. There's nothing particularly manly in wolfing down food and then sitting around in a stupor while the women clean up.

LI'L BIT: That looks like a really neat camera that Aunt Mary got you.

PECK: It is. It's a very nice one.

(*Pause, as Peck works on the dishes and some demon that Li'l Bit intuits.*)

LI'L BIT: Did Big Papa hurt your feelings?

PECK (*Tired*): What? Oh, no—it doesn't hurt me. Family is family. I'd rather have him picking on me than—I don't pay him any mind, Li'l Bit.

LI'L BIT: Are you angry with us?

PECK: No, Li'l Bit. I'm not angry.

(*Another pause.*)

LI'L BIT: We missed you at Thanksgiving. . . . I did. I missed you.

PECK: Well, there were . . . "things" going on. I didn't want to spoil anyone's Thanksgiving.

LI'L BIT: Uncle Peck? (*Very carefully*) Please don't drink anymore tonight.

PECK: I'm not . . . overdoing it.

LI'L BIT: I know. (*Beat*) Why do you drink so much?

(*Peck stops and thinks, carefully.*)

PECK: Well, Li'l Bit—let me explain it this way. There are some people who have a . . . a "fire" in the belly. I think they go to work on Wall Street or they run for office. And then there are people who have a "fire" in their heads—and they become writers or scientists or historians. (*He smiles a little at her*) You. You've got a "fire" in the head. And then there are people like me.

LI'L BIT: Where do you have . . . a fire?

PECK: I have a fire in my heart. And sometimes the drinking helps.

LI'L BIT: There's got to be other things that can help.

PECK: I suppose there are.

LI'L BIT: Does it help—to talk to me?

PECK: Yes. It does. (*Quiet*) I don't get to see you very much.

LI'L BIT: I know. (*Li'l Bit thinks*) You could talk to me more.

PECK: Oh?

LI'L BIT: I could make a deal with you, Uncle Peck.

PECK: I'm listening.

LI'L BIT: We could meet and talk—once a week. You could just store up whatever's bothering you during the week—and then we could talk.

PECK: Would you like that?

LI'L BIT: As long as you don't drink. I'd meet you somewhere for lunch or for a walk—on the weekends—as long as you stop drinking. And we could talk about whatever you want.

PECK: You would do that for me?

LI'L BIT: I don't think I'd want Mom to know. Or Aunt Mary. I wouldn't want them to think—

PECK: —No. It would just be us talking.

LI'L BIT: I'll tell Mom I'm going to a girlfriend's. To study. Mom doesn't get home until six, so you can call me after school and tell me where to meet you.

PECK: You get home at four?

LI'L BIT: We can meet once a week. But only in public. You've got to let me—draw the line. And once it's drawn, you mustn't cross it.

PECK: Understood.

LI'L BIT: Would that help?

(*Peck is very moved.*)

PECK: Yes. Very much.

LI'L BIT: I'm going to join the others in the living room now. (*Li'l Bit turns to go*)

PECK: Merry Christmas, Li'l Bit.

(*Li'l Bit bestows a very warm smile on him.*)

LI'L BIT: Merry Christmas, Uncle Peck.

(*A Voice dictates:*)

Shifting Forward from Second to Third Gear.

(*The Male and Female Greek Chorus members come forward.*)

MALE GREEK CHORUS: 1969. Days and Gifts: A Countdown:

FEMALE GREEK CHORUS: A note. "September 3, 1969. Li'l Bit: You've only been away two days and it feels like months. Hope your dorm room is cozy. I'm sending you this tape cassette—it's a new model—so you'll have some music in your room. Also that music you're reading about for class—*Carmina Burana*. Hope you enjoy. Only ninety days to go! —Peck."

MALE GREEK CHORUS: September 22. A bouquet of roses. A note: "Miss you like crazy. Sixty-nine days..."

TEENAGE GREEK CHORUS: September 25. A box of chocolates. A card: "Don't worry about the weight gain. You still look great. Got a post office box—write to me there. Sixty-six days. —Love, your candy man."

MALE GREEK CHORUS: October 16. A note: "Am trying to get through the Jane Austen you're reading—*Emma*—here's a book in return: *Liaisons Dangereuses*. Hope you're saving time for me." Scrawled in the margin the number: "47."

FEMALE GREEK CHORUS: November 16. "Sixteen days to go! —Hope you like the perfume. —Having a hard time reaching you on the dorm phone. You must be in the library a lot. Won't you think about me getting you your own phone so we can talk?"

TEENAGE GREEK CHORUS: November 18. "Li'l Bit—got a package returned to the P.O. Box. Have you changed dorms? Call me at work or write to the P.O. Am still on the wagon. Waiting to see you. Only two weeks more!"

MALE GREEK CHORUS: November 23. A letter. "Li'l Bit. So disappointed you couldn't come home for the turkey. Sending you some money for a nice dinner out—nine days and counting!"

GREEK CHORUS (*In unison*): November 25th. A letter:

LI'L BIT: "Dear Uncle Peck: I am sending this to you at work. Don't come up next weekend for my birthday. I will not be here—"

(A Voice directs:)

Shifting Forward from Third to Fourth Gear.

MALE GREEK CHORUS: December 10, 1969. A hotel room. Philadelphia. There is no moon tonight.

(Peck sits on the side of the bed while Li'l Bit paces. He can't believe she's in his room, but there's a desperate edge to his happiness. Li'l Bit is furious, edgy. There is a bottle of champagne in an ice bucket in a very nice hotel room.)

PECK: Why don't you sit?

LI'L BIT: I don't want to. — What's the champagne for?

PECK: I thought we might toast your birthday —

LI'L BIT: — I am so pissed off at you, Uncle Peck.

PECK: Why?

LI'L BIT: I mean, are you crazy?

PECK: What did I do?

LI'L BIT: You scared the holy crap out of me — sending me that stuff in the mail —

PECK: — They were gifts! I just wanted to give you some little perks your first semester —

LI'L BIT: — Well, what the hell were those numbers all about! Forty-four days to go — only two more weeks. — And then just numbers — 69 — 68 — 67 — like some serial killer!

PECK: Li'l Bit! Whoa! This is me you're talking to — I was just trying to pick up your spirits, trying to celebrate your birthday.

LI'L BIT: My *eighteenth* birthday. I'm not a child, Uncle Peck. You were counting down to my eighteenth birthday.

PECK: So?

LI'L BIT: So? So statutory rape is not in effect when a young woman turns eighteen. And you and I both know it.

(Peck is walking on ice.)

PECK: I think you misunderstand.

LI'L BIT: I think I understand all too well. I know what you want to do five steps ahead of you doing it. Defensive Driving 101.

PECK: Then why did you suggest we meet here instead of the restaurant?

LI'L BIT: I don't want to have this conversation in public.

PECK: Fine. Fine. We have a lot to talk about.

LI'L BIT: Yeah. We do.

    (Li'l Bit doesn't want to do what she has to do) Could I . . . have some of that champagne?

PECK: Of course, madam! *(Peck makes a big show of it)* Let me do the honors. I wasn't sure which you might prefer — Taittingers or Veuve Clicquot — so I thought we'd start out with an old standard — Perrier Jouet. *(The bottle is popped.)*

    Quick — Li'l Bit — your glass! *(Uncle Peck fills Li'l Bit's glass. He puts the bottle back in the ice and goes for a can of ginger ale)* Let me get some of this ginger ale — my bubbly — and toast you.

(*He turns and sees that Li'l Bit has not waited for him.*)

LI'L BIT: Oh—sorry, Uncle Peck. Let me have another. (*Peck fills her glass and reaches for his ginger ale; she stops him*) Uncle Peck—maybe you should join me in the champagne.

PECK: You want me—to drink?

LI'L BIT: It's not polite to let a lady drink alone.

PECK: Well, missy, if you insist. . . . (*Peck hesitates*)—Just one. It's been a while. (*Peck fills another flute for himself*) There. I'd like to propose a toast to you and your birthday! (*Peck sips it tentatively*) I'm not used to this anymore.

LI'L BIT: You don't have anywhere to go tonight, do you?

(*Peck hopes this is a good sign.*)

PECK: I'm all yours. —God, it's good to see you! I've gotten so used to . . . to . . . talking to you in my head. I'm used to seeing you every week—there's so much—I don't quite know where to begin. How's school, Li'l Bit?

LI'L BIT: I—it's hard. Uncle Peck. Harder than I thought it would be. I'm in the middle of exams and papers and—I don't know.

PECK: You'll pull through. You always do.

LI'L BIT: Maybe. I . . . might be flunking out.

PECK: You always think the worst, Li'l Bit, but when the going gets tough— (*Li'l Bit shrugs and pours herself another glass*)—Hey, honey, go easy on that stuff, okay?

LI'L BIT: Is it very expensive?

PECK: Only the best for you. But the cost doesn't matter—champagne should be "sipped." (*Li'l Bit is quiet*) Look—if you're in trouble in school—you can always come back home for a while.

LI'L BIT: *No*— (*Li'l Bit tries not to be so harsh*) —Thanks, Uncle Peck, but I'll figure some way out of this.

PECK: You're supposed to get in scrapes, your first year away from home.

LI'L BIT: Right. How's Aunt Mary?

PECK: She's fine. (*Pause*) Well—how about the new car?

LI'L BIT: It's real nice. What is it, again?

PECK: It's a Cadillac El Dorado.

LI'L BIT: Oh. Well, I'm real happy for you, Uncle Peck.

PECK: I got it for you.

LI'L BIT: What?

PECK: I always wanted to get a Cadillac—but I thought, Peck, wait until Li'l Bit's old enough—and thought maybe you'd like to drive it, too.

LI'L BIT (*Confused*): Why would I want to drive your car?

PECK: Just because it's the best—I want you to have the best.

(*They are running out of "gas"; small talk.*)

LI'L BIT: Listen, Uncle Peck, I don't know how to begin this, but—	PECK: I have been thinking of how to say this in my head, over and over—

PECK: Sorry

LI'L BIT: You first.

PECK: Well, your going away—has just made me realize how much I miss you. Talking to you and being alone with you. I've really come to depend on you, Li'l Bit. And it's been so hard to get in touch with you lately—the distance and—and you're never in when I call—I guess you've been living in the library—

LI'L BIT: —No—the problem is, I haven't been in the library—

PECK: —Well, it doesn't matter—I hope you've been missing me as much.

LI'L BIT: Uncle Peck—I've been thinking a lot about this—and I came here tonight to tell you that—I'm not doing very well. I'm getting very confused—I can't concentrate on my work—and now that I'm away—I've been going over and over it in my mind—and I don't want us to "see" each other anymore. Other than with the rest of the family.

PECK (*Quiet*): Are you seeing other men?

LI'L BIT (*Getting agitated*): I—no, that's not the reason—I—well, yes, I am seeing other—listen, it's not really anybody's business!

PECK: Are you in love with anyone else?

LI'L BIT: That's not what this is about.

PECK: Li'l Bit—you're scared. Your mother and your grandparents have filled your head with all kinds of nonsense about men—I hear them working on you all the time—and you're scared. It won't hurt you—if the man you go to bed with really loves you. (*Li'l Bit is scared. She starts to tremble*) And I have loved you since the day I held you in my hand. And I think everyone's just gotten you frightened to death about something that is just like breathing—

LI'L BIT: Oh, my god— (*She takes a breath*) I can't see you anymore, Uncle Peck.

(*Peck downs the rest of his champagne.*)

PECK: Li'l Bit. Listen. Listen. Open your eyes and look at me. Come on. Just open your eyes, honey. (*Li'l Bit, eyes squeezed shut, refuses*) All right then. I just want you to listen. Li'l Bit—I'm going to ask you just this once. Of your own free will. Just lie down on the bed with me—our clothes on—just lie down with me, a man and a woman . . . and let's . . . hold one another. Nothing else. Before you say anything else. I want the chance to . . . hold you. Because sometimes the body knows things that the mind isn't listening to . . . and after I've held you, then I want you to tell me what you feel.

LI'L BIT: You'll just . . . hold me?

PECK: Yes. And then you can tell me what you're feeling.

(*Li'l Bit—half wanting to run, half wanting to get it over with, half wanting to be held by him:*)

LI'L BIT: Yes. All right. Just hold. Nothing else.

(*Peck lies down on the bed and holds his arms out to her. Li'l Bit lies beside him, putting her head on his chest. He looks as if he's trying to soak her into his pores by osmosis. He strokes her hair, and she lies very still. The Male Greek Chorus member and the Female Greek Chorus member as Aunt Mary come into the room.*)

MALE GREEK CHORUS: Recipe for a Southern Boy:

FEMALE GREEK CHORUS (*As Aunt Mary*): A drawl of molasses in the way he speaks.

MALE GREEK CHORUS: A gumbo of red and brown mixed in the cream of his skin.

(*While Peck lies, his eyes closed, Li'l Bit rises in the bed and responds to her aunt.*)

LI'L BIT: Warm brown eyes —

FEMALE GREEK CHORUS (*As Aunt Mary*): Bedroom eyes —

MALE GREEK CHORUS: A dash of Southern Baptist Fire and Brimstone —

LI'L BIT: A curl of Elvis on his forehead —

FEMALE GREEK CHORUS (*As Aunt Mary*): A splash of Bay Rum —

MALE GREEK CHORUS: A closely shaven beard that he razors just for you —

FEMALE GREEK CHORUS (*As Aunt Mary*): Large hands — rough hands —

LI'L BIT: Warm hands —

MALE GREEK CHORUS: The steel of the military in his walk —

LI'L BIT: The slouch of the fishing skiff in his walk —

MALE GREEK CHORUS: Neatly pressed khakis —

FEMALE GREEK CHORUS (*As Aunt Mary*): And under the wide leather of the belt —

LI'L BIT: Sweat of cypress and sand —

MALE GREEK CHORUS: Neatly pressed khakis —

LI'L BIT: His heart beating Dixie —

FEMALE GREEK CHORUS (*As Aunt Mary*): The whisper of the zipper — you could reach out with your hand and —

LI'L BIT: His mouth —

FEMALE GREEK CHORUS (*As Aunt Mary*): You could just reach out and —

LI'L BIT: Hold him in your hand —

FEMALE GREEK CHORUS (*As Aunt Mary*): And his mouth —

(*Li'l Bit rises above her uncle and looks at his mouth; she starts to lower herself to kiss him — and wrenches herself free. She gets up from the bed.*)

LI'L BIT: — I've got to get back.

PECK: Wait — Li'l Bit. Did you . . . feel nothing?

LI'L BIT (*Lying*): No. Nothing.

PECK: Do you — do you think of me?

(*The Greek Chorus whispers:*)

FEMALE GREEK CHORUS: Khakis —

MALE GREEK CHORUS: Bay Rum —

FEMALE GREEK CHORUS: The whisper of the —

LI'L BIT: — No.

(*Peck, in a rush, trembling, gets something out of his pocket.*)

PECK: I'm forty-five. That's not old for a man. And I haven't been able to do anything else but think of you. I can't concentrate on my work — Li'l Bit. You've got to — I want you to think about what I am about to ask you.

LI'L BIT: I'm listening.

(*Peck opens a small ring box.*)

PECK: I want you to be my wife.

LI'L BIT: This isn't happening.

PECK: I'll tell Mary I want a divorce. We're not blood-related. It would be legal —

LI'L BIT: — What have you been thinking! You are married to my aunt, Uncle Peck. She's my family. You have — you have gone way over the line. Family is family.

(*Quickly, Li'l Bit flies through the room, gets her coat*) I'm leaving. Now. I am not seeing you. Again.

(*Peck lies down on the bed for a moment, trying to absorb the terrible news. For a moment, he almost curls into a fetal position.*)

I'm not coming home for Christmas. You should go home to Aunt Mary. Go home now, Uncle Peck.

(*Peck gets control, and sits, rigid.*)

Uncle Peck? — I'm sorry but I have to go.

(*Pause.*)

Are you all right.

(*With a discipline that comes from being told that boys don't cry, Peck stands upright.*)

PECK: I'm fine. I just think — I need a real drink.

(*The Male Greek Chorus has become a bartender. At a small counter, he is lining up shots for Peck. As Li'l Bit narrates, we see Peck sitting, carefully and calmly downing shot glasses.*)

LI'L BIT (*To the audience*): I never saw him again. I stayed away from Christmas and Thanksgiving for years after.

It took my uncle seven years to drink himself to death. First he lost his job, then his wife, and finally his driver's license. He retreated to his house, and had his bottles delivered.

(*Peck stands, and puts his hands in front of him — almost like Superman flying*)

One night he tried to go downstairs to the basement — and he flew down the steep basement stairs. My aunt came by weekly to put food on the porch, and she noticed the mail and the papers stacked up, uncollected.

They found him at the bottom of the stairs. Just steps away from his dark room.

Now that I'm old enough, there are some questions I would have liked to have asked him. Who did it to you, Uncle Peck? How old were you? Were you eleven?

(*Peck moves to the driver's seat of the car and waits*)

Sometimes I think of my uncle as a kind of Flying Dutchman. In the opera, the Dutchman is doomed to wander the sea; but every seven years he can come ashore, and if he finds a maiden who will love him of her own free will — he will be released.

And I see Uncle Peck in my mind, in his Chevy '56, a spirit driving up and down the back roads of Carolina — looking for a young girl who, of her own free will, will love him. Release him.

(*A Voice states:*)

You and the Reverse Gear.

LI'L BIT: The summer of 1962. On Men, Sex, and Women: Part III:

(*Li'l Bit steps, as an eleven-year-old, into:*)

FEMALE GREEK CHORUS (*As Mother*): It is out of the question. End of Discussion.

LI'L BIT: But why?

FEMALE GREEK CHORUS (*As Mother*): Li'l Bit—we are not discussing this. I said no.

LI'L BIT: But I could spend an extra week at the beach! You're not telling me why!

FEMALE GREEK CHORUS (*As Mother*): Your uncle pays entirely too much attention to you.

LI'L BIT: He listens to me when I talk. And—and he talks to me. He teaches me about things. Mama—he knows an awful lot.

FEMALE GREEK CHORUS (*As Mother*): He's a small town hick who's learned how to mix drinks from Hugh Hefner.

LI'L BIT: Who's Hugh Hefner?

(*Beat.*)

FEMALE GREEK CHORUS (*As Mother*): I am not letting an eleven-year-old girl spend seven hours alone in the car with a man. . . . I don't like the way your uncle looks at you.

LI'L BIT: For god's sake, mother! Just because you've gone through a bad time with my father—you think every man is evil!

FEMALE GREEK CHORUS (*As Mother*): Oh no, Li'l Bit—not all men. . . . We . . . we just haven't been very lucky with the men in our family.

LI'L BIT: Just because you lost your husband—I still deserve a chance at having a father! Someone! A man who will look out for me! Don't I get a chance?

FEMALE GREEK CHORUS (*As Mother*): I will feel terrible if something happens.

LI'L BIT: Mother! It's in your head! Nothing will happen! I can take care of myself. And I can certainly handle Uncle Peck.

FEMALE GREEK CHORUS (*As Mother*): All right. But I'm warning you—if anything happens, I hold you responsible.

(*Li'l Bit moves out of this scene and toward the car.*)

LI'L BIT: 1962. On the Back Roads of Carolina: The First Driving Lesson.

(*The Teenage Greek Chorus member stands apart on stage. She will speak all of Li'l Bit's lines. Li'l Bit sits beside Peck in the front seat. She looks at him closely, remembering.*)

PECK: Li'l Bit? Are you getting tired?

TEENAGE GREEK CHORUS: A little.

PECK: It's a long drive. But we're making really good time. We can take the back road from here and see . . . a little scenery. Say—I've got an idea—(*Peck checks his rearview mirror*)

TEENAGE GREEK CHORUS: Are we stopping, Uncle Peck?

PECK: There's no traffic here. Do you want to drive?

TEENAGE GREEK CHORUS: I can't drive.

PECK: It's easy. I'll show you how. I started driving when I was your age. Don't you want to? —

TEENAGE GREEK CHORUS: — But it's against the law at my age!

PECK: And that's why you can't tell anyone I'm letting you do this —

TEENAGE GREEK CHORUS: — But — I can't reach the pedals.

PECK: You can sit in my lap and steer. I'll push the pedals for you. Did your father ever let you drive his car?

TEENAGE GREEK CHORUS: No way.

PECK: Want to try?

TEENAGE GREEK CHORUS: Okay. (*Li'l Bit moves into Peck's lap. She leans against him, closing her eyes*)

PECK: You're just a little thing, aren't you? Okay — now think of the wheel as a big clock — I want you to put your right hand on the clock where three o'clock would be; and your left hand on the nine —

(*Li'l Bit puts one hand to Peck's face, to stroke him. Then, she takes the wheel.*)

TEENAGE GREEK CHORUS: Am I doing it right?

PECK: That's right. Now, whatever you do, don't let go of the wheel. You tell me whether to go faster or slower —

TEENAGE GREEK CHORUS: Not so fast, Uncle Peck!

PECK: Li'l Bit — I need you to watch the road —

(*Peck puts his hands on Li'l Bit's breasts. She relaxes against him, silent, accepting his touch.*)

TEENAGE GREEK CHORUS: Uncle Peck — what are you doing?

PECK: Keep driving. (*He slips his hands under her blouse*)

TEENAGE GREEK CHORUS: Uncle Peck — please don't do this —

PECK: — Just a moment longer . . . (*Peck tenses against Li'l Bit*)

TEENAGE GREEK CHORUS (*trying not to cry*): This isn't happening.

(*Peck tenses more, sharply. He buries his face in Li'l Bit's neck, and moans softly. The Teenage Greek Chorus exits, and Li'l Bit steps out of the car. Peck, too, disappears.*

A Voice reflects:)

Driving in Today's World.

LI'L BIT: That day was the last day I lived in my body. I retreated above the neck, and I've lived inside the "fire" in my head ever since.

   And now that seems like a long, long time ago. When we were both very young.

   And before you know it, I'll be thirty-five. That's getting up there for a woman. And I find myself believing in things that a younger self vowed never to believe in. Things like family and forgiveness.

   I know I'm lucky. Although I still have never known what it feels like to jog or dance. Any thing that . . . "jiggles." I do like to watch people on the dance floor, or out on the running paths, just jiggling away. And I say — good for them. (*Li'l Bit moves to the car with pleasure*)

The nearest sensation I feel—of flight in the body—I guess I feel when I'm driving. On a day like today. It's five A.M. The radio says it's going to be clear and crisp. I've got five hundred miles of highway ahead of me—and some back roads too. I filled the tank last night, and had the oil checked. Checked the tires, too. You've got to treat her . . . with respect.

First thing I do is: Check under the car. To see if any two year olds or household cats have crawled beneath, and strategically placed their skulls behind my back tires. (*Li'l Bit crouches*)

Nope. Then I get in the car. (*Li'l Bit does so*)

I lock the doors. And turn the key. Then I adjust the most important control on the dashboard—the radio— (*Li'l Bit turns the radio on: We hear all of the Greek Chorus overlapping, and static:*)

FEMALE GREEK CHORUS (*Overlapping*): — "You were so tiny you fit in his hand—"

MALE GREEK CHORUS (*Overlapping*): — "How is Shakespeare gonna help her lie on her back in the—"

TEENAGE GREEK CHORUS (*Overlapping*): — "Am I doing it right?"

(*Li'l Bit fine-tunes the radio station. A song like "Dedicated to the One I Love" or Orbison's "Sweet Dreams" comes on, and cuts off the Greek Chorus.*)

LI'L BIT: Ahh . . . (*Beat*) I adjust my seat. Fasten my seat belt. Then I check the right side mirror—check the left side. (*She does*) Finally, I adjust the rearview mirror. (*As Li'l Bit adjusts the rearview mirror, a faint light strikes the spirit of Uncle Peck, who is sitting in the back seat of the car. She sees him in the mirror. She smiles at him, and he nods at her. They are happy to be going for a long drive together. Li'l Bit slips the car into first gear; to the audience:*) And then—I floor it. (*Sound of a car taking off. Blackout*)

22.

Commentaries on Plays and Playwrights

ARISTOTLE

Aristotle (384–322 B.C.), the Greek philosopher, included an analysis of tragedy in his Poetics *a century after Sophocles' plays were performed during the Great Dionysia in Athens. A student of Plato, Aristotle founded his own school, called the Lyceum, where he lectured on philosophy, science, and the arts. His lectures or treatises were so insightful that they were preserved by his students, and nearly two thousand years later, they form the basis of literary criticism. As the critic Lee Jacobus points out, Aristotle's work not only provides insight into the theoretical basis of the work of the Greek playwrights, but it also "helps us see that the drama was significant enough in Greek intellectual life to warrant an examination by the most influential Greek minds."*

On the Elements and General Principles of Tragedy
c. 340 B.C.

TRANSLATED BY GERALD F. ELSE

TRAGEDY AND ITS SIX CONSTITUENT ELEMENTS

. . . At present let us deal with tragedy, recovering from what has been said so far the definition of its essential nature, as it was in development. Tragedy, then, is a process of imitating an action which has serious implications, is complete, and possesses magnitude; by means of language which has been made sensuously attractive, with each of its varieties found separately in

1528

the parts; enacted by the persons themselves and not presented through narrative; through a course of pity and fear completing the purification of tragic acts which have those emotional characteristics. By "language made sensuously attractive" I mean language that has rhythm and melody, and by "its varieties found separately" I mean the fact that certain parts of the play are carried on through spoken verses alone and others the other way around, through song.

Now first of all, since they perform the imitation through action (by acting it), the adornment of their visual appearance will perforce constitute some part of the making of tragedy; and song-composition and verbal expression also, for those are the media in which they perform the imitation. By "verbal expression" I mean the actual composition of the verses, and by "song-composition" something whose meaning is entirely clear.

Next, since it is an imitation of an action and is enacted by certain people who are performing the action, and since those people must necessarily have certain traits both of character and thought (for it is thanks to these two factors that we speak of people's actions also as having a defined character, and it is in accordance with their actions that all either succeed or fail); and since the imitation of the action is the plot, for by "plot" I mean here the structuring of the events, and by the "characters" that in accordance with which we say that the persons who are acting have a defined moral character, and by "thought" all the passages in which they attempt to prove some thesis or set forth an opinion — it follows of necessity, then, that tragedy as a whole has just six constituent elements, in relation to the essence that makes it a distinct species; and they are plot, characters, verbal expression, thought, visual adornment, and song-composition. For the elements by which they imitate are two (i.e., verbal expression and song-composition), the manner in which they imitate is one (visual adornment), the things they imitate are three (plot, characters, thought), and there is nothing more beyond these. These then are the constituent forms they use.

THE RELATIVE IMPORTANCE OF THE SIX ELEMENTS

The greatest of these elements is the structuring of the incidents. For tragedy is an imitation not of men but of a life, an action, and they have moral quality in accordance with their characters but are happy or unhappy in accordance with their actions; hence they are not active in order to imitate their characters, but they include the characters along with the actions for the sake of the latter. Thus the structure of events, the plot, is the goal of tragedy, and the goal is the greatest thing of all. . . .

Again: if one strings end to end speeches that are expressive of character and carefully worked in thought and expression, he still will not achieve the result which we said was the aim of tragedy; the job will be done much better by a tragedy that is more deficient in these other respects but has a plot, a structure of events. It is much the same case as with painting: the most beautiful pigments smeared on at random will not give as much pleasure as a black-and-white outline picture. Besides, the most powerful means tragedy has for swaying our feelings, namely the peripeties and recognitions,° are elements of plot.

Again: an indicative sign is that those who are beginning a poetic career manage to hit the mark in verbal expression and character portrayal sooner than they do in plot construction; and the same is true of practically all the earliest poets.

So plot is the basic principle, the heart and soul, as it were, of tragedy, and the characters come second: . . . it is the imitation of an action and imitates the persons primarily for the sake of their action.

Third in rank is thought. This is the ability to state the issues and appropriate points pertaining to a given topic, an ability which springs from the arts of politics and rhetoric; in fact the earliest poets made their characters talk "politically," the present-day poets rhetorically. But "character" is that kind of utterance which clearly reveals the bent of a man's moral choice (hence there is no character in that class of utterances in which there is nothing at all that the speaker is choosing or rejecting), while "thought" is the passages in which they try to prove that something is so or not so, or state some general principle.

Fourth is the verbal expression of the speeches. I mean by this the same thing that was said earlier, that the "verbal expression" is the conveyance of thought through language: a statement which has the same meaning whether one says "verses" or "speeches."

The song-composition of the remaining parts is the greatest of the sensuous attractions, and the visual adornment of the dramatic persons can have a strong emotional effect but is the least artistic element, the least connected with the poetic art; in fact the force of tragedy can be felt even without benefit of public performance and actors, while for the production of the visual effect the property man's art is even more decisive than that of the poets.

GENERAL PRINCIPLES OF THE TRAGIC PLOT

With these distinctions out of the way, let us next discuss what the structuring of the events should be like, since this is both the basic and the most important element in the tragic art. We have established, then, that tragedy is an imitation of an action which is complete and whole and has some magnitude (for there is also such a thing as a whole that has no magnitude). "Whole" is that which has beginning, middle, and end. "Beginning" is that which does not necessarily follow on something else, but after it something else naturally is or happens; "end," the other way around, is that which naturally follows on something else, either necessarily or for the most part, but nothing else after it; and "middle" that which naturally follows on something else and something else on it. So, then, well-constructed plots should neither begin nor end at any chance point but follow the guidelines just laid down.

---

peripeties and recognitions: The turning-about of fortune and the recognition on the part of the tragic hero of the truth. This is, for Aristotle, a critical moment in the drama, especially if both events happen simultaneously, as they do in *Oedipus the King.* It is quite possible for these moments to happen apart from one another. [All notes are the translator's.]

Furthermore, since the beautiful, whether a living creature or anything that is composed of parts, should not only have these in a fixed order to one another but also possess a definite size which does not depend on chance—for beauty depends on size and order; hence neither can a very tiny creature turn out to be beautiful (since our perception of it grows blurred as it approaches the period of imperceptibility) nor an excessively huge one (for then it cannot all be perceived at once and so its unity and wholeness are lost), if for example there were a creature a thousand miles long—so, just as in the case of living creatures they must have some size, but one that can be taken in a single view, so with plots: they should have length, but such that they are easy to remember. As to a limit of the length, the one is determined by the tragic competitions and the ordinary span of attention. (If they had to compete with a hundred tragedies they would compete by the water clock, as they say used to be done [?].) But the limit fixed by the very nature of the case is: the longer the plot, up to the point of still being perspicuous as a whole, the finer it is so far as size is concerned; or to put it in general terms, the length in which, with things happening in unbroken sequence, a shift takes place either probably or necessarily from bad to good fortune or from good to bad—that is an acceptable norm of length.

But a plot is not unified, as some people think, simply because it has to do with a single person. A large, indeed an indefinite number of things can happen to a given individual, some of which go to constitute no unified event; and in the same way there can be many acts of a given individual from which no single action emerges. Hence it seems clear that those poets are wrong who have composed *Heracleïds, Theseïds,* and the like. They think that since Heracles was a single person it follows that the plot will be single too. But Homer, superior as he is in all other respects, appears to have grasped this point well also, thanks either to art or nature, for in composing an *Odyssey* he did not incorporate into it everything that happened to the hero, for example how he was wounded on Mt. Parnassus° or how he feigned madness at the muster, neither of which events, by happening, made it at all necessary or probable that the other should happen. Instead, he composed the *Odyssey*—and the *Iliad* similarly—around a unified action of the kind we have been talking about.

A poetic imitation, then, ought to be unified in the same way as a single imitation in any other mimetic field, by having a single object: since the plot is an imitation of an action, the latter ought to be both unified and complete, and the component events ought to be so firmly compacted that if any one of them is shifted to another place, or removed, the whole is loosened up and dislocated; for an element whose addition or subtraction makes no perceptible extra difference is not really a part of the whole.

From what has been said it is also clear that the poet's job is not to report what has happened but what is likely to happen: that is, what is capable of

---

Mt. Parnassus: A mountain in central Greece traditionally sacred to Apollo. In legend, Odysseus was wounded there, but the point Aristotle is making is that the writer of epics need not include every detail of his hero's life in a given work. Homer, in writing the *Odyssey*, was working with a hero, Odysseus, whose story had been legendary long before he began writing.

happening according to the rule of probability or necessity. Thus the difference between the historian and the poet is not in their utterances being in verse or prose (it would be quite possible for Herodotus' work to be translated into verse, and it would not be any the less a history with verse than it is without it); the difference lies in the fact that the historian speaks of what has happened, the poet of the kind of thing that *can* happen. Hence also poetry is a more philosophical and serious business than history; for poetry speaks more of universals, history of particulars. "Universal" in this case is what kind of person is likely to do or say certain kinds of things, according to probability or necessity; that is what poetry aims at, although it gives its persons particular names afterward; while the "particular" is what Alcibiades did or what happened to him.

In the field of comedy this point has been grasped: our comic poets construct their plots on the basis of general probabilities and then assign names to the persons quite arbitrarily, instead of dealing with individuals as the old iambic poets° did. But in tragedy they still cling to the historically given names. The reason is that what is possible is persuasive; so what has not happened we are not yet ready to believe is possible, while what has happened is, we feel, obviously possible: for it would not have happened if it were impossible. Nevertheless, it is a fact that even in our tragedies, in some cases only one or two of the names are traditional, the rest being invented, and in some others none at all. It is so, for example, in Agathon's *Antheus* — the names in it are as fictional as the events — and it gives no less pleasure because of that. Hence the poets ought not to cling at all costs to the traditional plots, around which our tragedies are constructed. And in fact it is absurd to go searching for this kind of authentication, since even the familiar names are familiar to only a few in the audience and yet give the same kind of pleasure to all.

So from these considerations it is evident that the poet should be a maker of his plots more than of his verses, insofar as he is a poet by virtue of his imitations and what he imitates is actions. Hence even if it happens that he puts something that has actually taken place into poetry, he is none the less a poet; for there is nothing to prevent some of the things that have happened from being the kind of things that can happen, and that is the sense in which he is their maker.

SIMPLE AND COMPLEX PLOTS

Among simple plots and actions the episodic are the worst. By "episodic" plot I mean one in which there is no probability or necessity for the order in which the episodes follow one another. Such structures are composed by the bad poets because they are bad poets, but by the good poets because of the actors: in composing contest pieces for them, and stretching out the plot beyond its capacity, they are forced frequently to dislocate the sequence.

---

old iambic poets: Aristotle may be referring to Archilochus (fl. 650 B.C.) and the iambic style he developed. The iamb is a metrical foot of two syllables, a short and a long syllable, and was the most popular metrical style before the time of Aristotle. "Dealing with individuals" implies using figures already known to the audience rather than figures whose names can be arbitrarily assigned because no one knows who they are.

Furthermore, since the tragic imitation is not only of a complete action but also of events that are fearful and pathetic,° and these come about best when they come about contrary to one's expectation yet logically, one following from the other; that way they will be more productive of wonder than if they happen merely at random, by chance—because even among chance occurrences the ones people consider most marvelous are those that seem to have come about as if on purpose: for example the way the statue of Mitys at Argos killed the man who had been the cause of Mitys' death, by falling on him while he was attending the festival; it stands to reason, people think, that such things don't happen by chance—so plots of that sort cannot fail to be artistically superior.

Some plots are simple, others are complex; indeed the actions of which the plots are imitations already fall into these two categories. By "simple" action I mean one the development of which being continuous and unified in the manner stated above, the reversal comes without peripety or recognition, and by "complex" action one in which the reversal is continuous but with recognition or peripety or both. And these developments must grow out of the very structure of the plot itself, in such a way that on the basis of what has happened previously this particular outcome follows either by necessity or in accordance with probability; for there is a greater difference in whether these events happen because of those or merely after them.

"Peripety" is a shift of what is being undertaken to the opposite in the way previously stated, and that in accordance with probability or necessity as we have just been saying; as for example in the *Oedipus* the man who has come, thinking that he will reassure Oedipus, that is, relieve him of his fear with respect to his mother, by revealing who he once was, brings about the opposite; and in the *Lynceus*, as he (Lynceus) is being led away with every prospect of being executed, and Danaus pursuing him with every prospect of doing the executing, it comes about as a result of the other things that have happened in the play that *he* is executed and Lynceus is saved. And "recognition" is, as indeed the name indicates, a shift from ignorance to awareness, pointing in the direction either of close blood ties or of hostility, of people who have previously been in a clearly marked state of happiness or unhappiness.

The finest recognition is one that happens at the same time as a peripety, as is the case with the one in the *Oedipus*. Naturally, there are also other kinds of recognition: it is possible for one to take place in the prescribed manner in relation to inanimate objects and chance occurrences, and it is possible to recognize whether a person has acted or not acted. But the form that is most integrally a part of the plot, the action, is the one aforesaid; for that kind of recognition combined with peripety will excite either pity or fear (and these are the kinds of action of which tragedy is an imitation according to our definition), because

---

fearful and pathetic: Aristotle said that tragedy should evoke two emotions: terror and pity. The terror results from our realizing that what is happening to the hero might just as easily happen to us; the pity results from our human sympathy with a fellow sufferer. Therefore, the fearful and pathetic represent significant emotions appropriate to our witnessing drama.

both good and bad fortune will also be most likely to follow that kind of event. Since, further, the recognition is a recognition of persons, some are of one person by the other one only (when it is already known who the "other one" is), but sometimes it is necessary for both persons to go through a recognition, as for example Iphigenia is recognized by her brother through the sending of the letter, but of him by Iphigenia another recognition is required.

These then are two elements of plot: peripety and recognition; third is the *pathos*. Of these, peripety and recognition have been discussed; a *pathos* is a destructive or painful act, such as deaths on stage, paroxysms of pain, woundings, and all that sort of thing.

JILL DOLAN

Jill Dolan reviewed How I Learned to Drive *after Paula Vogel's play was produced in February 1997 at The Vineyard Theatre in New York City. Dolan's sympathetic review, along with other positive reviews, helped to launch the play, which was moved to a larger theater in New York City two months later.* How I Learned to Drive *also won the Pulitzer Prize for drama for 1997.*

Review of *How I Learned to Drive* 1997

Playwright Paula Vogel tends to select sensitive, difficult, fraught issues to theatricalize, and to spin them with a dramaturgy that's at once creative, highly imaginative, and brutally honest. In *How I Learned to Drive*—which won the 1997 Drama Desk Award for Best Play and several Obie Awards— Vogel's conceits remain personal, political, and highly theatrical. In a nonlinear narrative, Li'l Bit (Mary Louise Parker) tries to understand her relationship with her Uncle Peck (David Morse), whose driving lessons taught her as much about gender relations and her own sexuality as they did about the proper use of rearview mirrors, gearshifts, and turn signals.

Driving becomes the action that evokes Li'l Bit's memories; driving metaphors chart Li'l Bit's growth into automotive mastery and sexual mystery, punctuating the play's movement back and forth in time. Sitting in straight-backed chairs on a nearly bare set, Morse and Parker evoke the car rides that shape and intertwine their lives. Mark Brokaw's crisp, unsparing direction allows them to craft the scene with gesture and light, leaving the production unencumbered by more than minimal props and set pieces. The sparse set is framed by a map of Baltimore in the 1950s and 1960s, when the play's first memories occur. The geographical snippets, covered with interstates, route numbers, town names, and zip codes that move in and out of sight, remind spectators how difficult it is to truly map the territory of relationships, sexuality, and desire.

Vogel's choice to remember Li'l Bit and Peck's relationship nonchronologically illustrates its complexity, and allows the playwright to build sympathy for a man who might otherwise be despised and dismissed as a child molester. As played with affable gentility and gentleness by Morse, Peck is charming, kind, and sympathetic, a man driven toward children by his own demons but attentive to Li'l Bit's adolescent needs in ways that are never violent, paternalistic, or condescending. Peck takes the young woman seriously, and she takes great pleasure from believing that she helps him emotionally. Vogel paints their relationship as flirtatious and sexual, but also as a careful balance of power between Peck's adult desires and Li'l Bit's inchoate, exploratory impulses. Parker's lithe, erotic performance captures in subtle gestures and in postures weighted with ambivalence and desire the pleasure Li'l Bit takes in the power of saying no while her body urges her to say yes. The attraction between them becomes more urgent and mutual as the play progresses, along with Li'l Bit's knowledge that the relationship is not right. Li'l Bit's isolation in the face of strong emotions she can not understand is palpable; Parker's virtuosic performance illustrates the nuances of Li'l Bit's desire and loathing for a man who taught her so much and could finally give her so little.

Vogel builds the relationship in scenes sculpted with spare efficiency by Brokaw that crystallize moments of trust, disappointment, longing, and desire. When Peck's loneliness grips him, a very young Li'l Bit offers solace with weekly outings that are as much about companionship as they come to be about sex or driving lessons. Later, Peck photographs Li'l Bit in his basement studio, and although it's clear his motives are not pure, the experience instills in Li'l Bit a sense of her own allure, a glimpse of a budding sexuality that's powerful to her in a family life in which she is otherwise naive and powerless. Peck takes her to dinner at a sophisticated restaurant out of town when she passes her driving test. Under the disapproving eye of a sanctimonious waiter, Li'l Bit drinks martinis while one of the female chorus relates how to stay safe sexually while leaving the shores of sobriety in masculine company.

These interventions are delivered with wry and empathetic clarity directly to the audience by a three-actor chorus that shifts agilely through roles as family members and other commentators. The actors transform precisely and pointedly, with help from iconic costume pieces like glasses or scarves, into those who either deny or judge the relationship. Brokaw directs them on a nearly empty set, using chairs and the occasional table to evoke the car, the restaurant, the basement photo studio. The physical performances his actors achieve imaginatively flesh out the edges of this searing portrait.

How I Learned to Drive is only "about" incest after the scene of Li'l Bit's first molestation scene, when Li'l Bit asks the audience rhetorically, "How old were you when someone did this to you?" The moment is startling, because although the audience has witnessed Peck in an early scene prepare to molest a little boy (the boy is imagined and Morse elegantly, chillingly mimes the actions), the play has been about more than incest. Through Parker's and Morse's multilayered performances, power and danger are always present, but so are moments of understanding and mutuality.

Parker and Morse are empathetic and moving, and Johanna Day, Kerry O'Malley, and Michael Showalter, as the chorus, present tight economical sketches of Li'l Bit's family and the social characters with whom Bit and Peck interact. Vogel's wry, insightful humor captures the pain and awkward pleasure of growing into social awareness and understanding. Vogel's play is about forgiveness and family, about the instability of sexuality, about the unpredictable ways in which we learn who we are, how we desire, and how our growth is built on loss.

FRANCIS FERGUSSON

Francis Fergusson, the eminent theater critic, discussed the way Sophocles reimagined his source of the traditional myth of Oedipus in this essay from The Idea of a Theater *(1949). Fergusson also analyzed how Sophocles developed the important role of the chorus to help the spectators of this drama form "a new perception of the immediate situation."*

Oedipus, Myth and Play   1949

When Sophocles came to write his play he had the myth of Oedipus to start with. Laius and Jocasta, King and Queen of Thebes, are told by the oracle that their son will grow up to kill his father and marry his mother. The infant, his feet pierced, is left on Mount Kitharon to die. But a shepherd finds him and takes care of him; at last gives him to another shepherd, who takes him to Corinth, and there the King and Queen bring him up as their own son. But Oedipus — "Clubfoot" — is plagued in his turn by the oracle; he hears that he is fated to kill his father and marry his mother; and to escape that fate he leaves Corinth never to return. On his journey he meets an old man with his servants; gets into a dispute with him, and kills him and all his followers. He comes to Thebes at the time when the Sphinx is preying upon that City; solves the riddle which the Sphinx propounds, and saves the City. He marries the widowed Queen, Jocasta; has several children by her; rules prosperously for many years. But, when Thebes is suffering under a plague and a drought, the oracle reports that the gods are angry because Laius' slayer is unpunished. Oedipus, as King, undertakes to find him; discovers that he is himself the culprit and that Jocasta is his own mother. He blinds himself and goes into exile. From this time forth he becomes a sort of sacred relic, like the bones of a saint; perilous, but "good medicine" for the community that possesses him. He dies, at last, at Athens, in a grove sacred to the Eumenides, female spirits of fertility and night.

It is obvious, even from this sketch, that the myth, which covers several generations, has as much narrative material as *Gone with the Wind.* We do not know what versions of the story Sophocles used. It is the way of myths that they generate whole progenies of elaborations and varying versions. They are so suggestive, seem to say so much, yet so mysteriously, that the mind cannot rest content with any single form, but must add, or interpret, or simplify — reduce to terms which the reason can accept. Mr. William Troy suggests that "what is possibly most in order at the moment is a thoroughgoing refurbishment of the medieval fourfold method of interpretation, which was first developed, it will be recalled, for just such a purpose — to make at least partially available to the reason that complex of human problems which are embedded, deep and imponderable, in the Myth."[1] It appears that Sophocles, in his play, succeeded in preserving the suggestive mystery of the Oedipus myth, while presenting it in a wonderfully unified dramatic form; and this drama has all the dimensions which the fourfold method was intended to explore.

Everyone knows that when Sophocles planned the plot of the play itself, he started almost at the end of the story, when the plague descends upon the City of Thebes which Oedipus and Jocasta had been ruling with great success for a number of years. The action of the play takes less than a day, and consists of Oedipus' quest for Laius' slayer — his consulting the Oracle of Apollo, his examination of the Prophet, Tiresias, and of a series of witnesses, ending with the old Shepherd who gave him to the King and Queen of Corinth. The play ends when Oedipus is unmistakably revealed as himself the culprit.

At this literal level, the play is intelligible as a murder mystery. Oedipus takes the role of District Attorney; and when he at last convicts himself, we have a twist, a *coup de théâtre*, of unparalleled excitement. But no one who sees or reads the play can rest content with its literal coherence. Questions as to its meaning arise at once: Is Oedipus really guilty, or simply a victim of the gods, or his famous complex, of fate, of original sin? How much did he know, all along? How much did Jocasta know? The first, and most deeply instinctive effort of the mind, when confronted with this play, is to endeavor to reduce its meanings to some set of rational categories.

The critics of the Age of Reason tried to understand it as a fable of the enlightened moral will, in accordance with the philosophy of that time. Voltaire's version of the play, following Corneille, and his comments upon it, may be taken as typical. He sees it as essentially a struggle between a strong and righteous Oedipus, and the malicious and very human gods, aided and abetted by the corrupt priest Tiresias; he makes it an antireligious tract, with an unmistakable moral to satisfy the needs of the discursive intellect. In order to make Oedipus "sympathetic" to his audience, he elides, as much as possible, the incest motif; and he adds an irrelevant love story. He was aware that his version and interpretation were not those of Sophocles but, with the complacent provinciality of his period, he attributes the difference to the darkness of the age in which *Sophocles* lived.

Other attempts to rationalize *Oedipus Rex* are subtler than Voltaire's, and take us further toward an understanding of the play. Freud's reduction of the play to the concepts of his psychology reveals a great deal, opens up perspectives which we are still exploring. If one reads *Oedipus* in the light of Fustel de Coulanges's *The Ancient City*, one may see it as the expression of the ancient

---

[1] "Myth, Method and the Future," by William Troy. *Chimera*, Spring 1946.

patriarchal religion of the Greeks. And other interpretations of the play, theological, philosophical, historical, are available, none of them wrong, but all partial, all reductions of Sophocles' masterpiece to an alien set of categories. For the peculiar virtue of Sophocles' presentation of the myth is that it preserves the ultimate mystery by focusing upon the tragic human at a level beneath, or prior to any rationalization whatever. The plot is so arranged that we see the action, as it were, illumined from many sides at once.

By starting the play at the end of the story, and showing on stage only the last crucial episode in Oedipus' life, the past and present action of the protagonist are revealed together; and, in each other's light, are at last felt as one. Oedipus' quest for the slayer of Laius becomes a quest for the hidden reality of his own past; and as that slowly comes into focus, like repressed material under psychoanalysis—with sensory and emotional immediacy, yet in the light of acceptance and understanding—his immediate quest also reaches its end: he comes to see himself (the Savior of the City) and the guilty one, the plague of Thebes, at once and at one.

This presentation of the myth of Oedipus constitutes, in one sense, an "interpretation" of it. What Sophocles saw as the essence of Oedipus' nature and destiny is not what Seneca or Dryden or Cocteau saw; and one may grant that even Sophocles did not exhaust the possibilities in the materials of the myth. But Sophocles' version of the myth does not constitute a "reduction" in the same sense as the rest.

I have said that the action which Sophocles shows is a quest, the quest for Laius' slayer; and that as Oedipus' past is unrolled before us his whole life is seen as a kind of quest for his true nature and destiny. But since the object of this quest is not clear until the end, the seeking action takes many forms, as its object appears in different lights. The object, indeed, the final perception, the "truth," looks so different at the end from what it did at the beginning that Oedipus' action itself may seem not a quest, but its opposite, a flight. Thus it would be hard to say, simply, that Oedipus either succeeds or fails. He succeeds; but his success is his undoing. He fails to find what, in one way, he sought; yet from another point of view his search is brilliantly successful. The same ambiguities surround his effort to discover who and what he is. He seems to find that he is nothing; yet thereby finds himself. And what of his relation to the gods? His quest may be regarded as a heroic attempt to escape their decrees, or as an attempt, based upon some deep natural faith, to discover what their wishes are, and what true obedience would be. In one sense Oedipus suffers forces he can neither control nor understand, the puppet of fate; yet at the same time he wills and intelligently intends his every move.

The meaning, or spiritual content of the play, is not to be sought by trying to resolve such ambiguities as these. The spiritual content of the play is the tragic action which Sophocles directly presents; and this action is in its essence *zweideutig:* triumph and destruction, darkness and enlightenment, mourning and rejoicing, at any moment we care to consider it. But this action has also a shape: a beginning, middle, and end, in time. It starts with the reasoned purpose of finding Laius' slayer. But this aim meets unforeseen difficulties, evidences which do not fit, and therefore shake the purpose as it was first understood; and so the characters suffer the piteous and terrible sense of the mystery of the human situation. From this suffering or passion, with its shifting visions, a new perception of the situation emerges; and on that basis the purpose of the action is redefined, and a new movement starts. This movement, or *tragic rhythm of action,* constitutes the shape of the play as a whole; it is also the shape of each episode, each discussion between principals with the chorus following. Mr. Kenneth Burke has studied the tragic rhythm in his *Philosophy of Literary Form,* and also in *A Grammar of Motives,* where he gives the three moments traditional designations which are very suggestive: *Poiema, Pathema, Mathema.* They may also be called, for convenience, Purpose, Passion (or Suffering) and Perception. It is this tragic rhythm of action which is the substance or spiritual content of the play, and the clue to its extraordinarily comprehensive form.

In order to illustrate these points in more detail, it is convenient to examine the scene between Oedipus and Tiresias with the chorus following it. This episode, being early in the play (the first big agon), presents, as it were, a preview of the whole action and constitutes a clear and complete example of action in the tragic rhythm. . . .

The Cambridge School of Classical Anthropologists has shown in great detail that the form of Greek tragedy follows the form of a very ancient ritual, that of the *Enniautos-Daimon,* or seasonal god.[2] This was one of the most influential discoveries of the last few generations, and it gives us new insights into *Oedipus* which I think are not yet completely explored. The clue to Sophocles' dramatizing of the myth of Oedipus is to be found in this ancient ritual, which had a similar form and meaning — that is, it also moved in the "tragic rhythm."

Experts in classical anthropology, like experts in other fields, dispute innumerable questions of fact and of interpretation which the layman can only pass over in respectful silence. One of the thornier questions seems to be whether myth or ritual came first. Is the ancient ceremony merely an enactment of the Ur-Myth of the year-god—Attis, or Adonis, or Osiris, or the "Fisher-King"—in any case that Hero-King-Father-High-Priest who fights with his rival, is slain and dismembered, then rises anew with the spring season? Or did the innumerable myths of this kind arise to "explain" a ritual which was perhaps mimed or danced or sung to celebrate the annual change of seasons?

For the purpose of understanding the form and meaning of *Oedipus,* it is not necessary to worry about the answer to this question of historic fact. The figure of Oedipus himself fulfills all the requirements of the scapegoat, the dismembered king or god-figure. The situation in which Thebes is presented at the beginning of the play—in peril of its life; its crops, its herds, its women mysteriously infertile, signs of a mortal disease of the City, and the disfavor of the gods—is like the withering which winter brings, and calls, in the same way,

---

[2]See especially Jane Ellen Harrison's *Ancient Art and Ritual,* and her *Themis* which contains an "Excursus on the ritual forms preserved in Greek Tragedy" by Professor Gilbert Murray.

for struggle, dismemberment, death, and renewal. And this tragic sequence is the substance of the play. It is enough to know that myth and ritual are close together in their genesis, two direct imitations of the perennial experience of the race.

But when one considers *Oedipus* as a ritual one understands it in ways which one cannot by thinking of it merely as a dramatization of a story, even that story. Harrison has shown that the Festival of Dionysos, based ultimately upon the yearly vegetation ceremonies, included *rites de passage,* like that celebrating the assumption of adulthood — celebrations of the mystery of individual growth and development. At the same time, it was a prayer for the welfare of the whole City; and this welfare was understood not only as material prosperity, but also as the natural order of the family, the ancestors, the present members, and the generations still to come, and, by the same token, obedience to the gods who were jealous, each in his own province, of this natural and divinely sanctioned order and proportion.

We must suppose that Sophocles' audience (the whole population of the City) came early, prepared to spend the day in the bleachers. At their feet was the semicircular dancing-ground for the chorus, and the thrones for the priests, and the altar. Behind that was the raised platform for the principal actors, backed by the all-purpose, emblematic façade, which would presently be taken to represent Oedipus' palace in Thebes. The actors were not professionals in our sense, but citizens selected for a religious office, and Sophocles himself had trained them and the chorus.

This crowd must have had as much appetite for thrills and diversion as the crowds who assemble in our day for football games and musical comedies, and Sophocles certainly holds the attention with an exciting show. At the same time his audience must have been alert for the fine points of poetry and dramaturgy, for *Oedipus* is being offered in competition with other plays on the same bill. But the element which distinguishes this theater, giving it its unique directness and depth, is the *ritual expectancy* which Sophocles assumed in his audience. The nearest thing we have to this ritual sense of theater is, I suppose, to be found at an Easter performance of the *Mattias Passion.* We also can observe something similar in the dances and ritual mummery of the Pueblo Indians. Sophocles' audience must have been prepared, like the Indians standing around their plaza, to consider the playing, the make-believe it was about to see — the choral invocations, with dancing and chanting; the reasoned discourses and the terrible combats of the protagonists; the mourning, the rejoicing, and the contemplation of the final stage-picture of epiphany — as imitating and celebrating the mystery of human nature and destiny. And this mystery was at once that of individual growth and development, and that of the precarious life of the human City.

I have indicated how Sophocles presents the life of the mythic Oedipus in the tragic rhythm, the mysterious quest of life. Oedipus is shown seeking his own true being; but at the same time and by the same token, the welfare of the City. When one considers the ritual form of the whole play, it becomes evident that it presents the tragic but perennial, even normal, quest of the whole City for its well-being. In this larger action, Oedipus is only the protagonist, the first and most important champion. This tragic quest is realized by all the characters in their various ways; but in the development of the action as a whole it is the chorus alone that plays a part as important as that of Oedipus; its counterpart, in fact. The chorus holds the balance between Oedipus and his antagonists, marks the progress of their struggles, and restates the main theme, and its new variation, after each dialogue or agon. The ancient ritual was probably performed by a chorus alone without individual developments and variations, and the chorus, in *Oedipus,* is still the element that throws most light on the ritual form of the play as a whole.

The chorus consists of twelve or fifteen "Elders of Thebes." This group is not intended to represent literally all of the citizens either of Thebes or of Athens. The play opens with a large delegation of Theban citizens before Oedipus' palace, and the chorus proper does not enter until after the prologue. Nor does the chorus speak directly for the Athenian audience; we are asked throughout to make-believe that the theater is the agora at Thebes; and at the same time Sophocles' audience is witnessing a ritual. It would, I think, be more accurate to say that the chorus represents the point of view and the faith of Thebes as a whole, and, by analogy, of the Athenian audience. Their errand before Oedipus' palace is like that of Sophocles' audience in the theater: they are watching a sacred combat, in the issue of which they have an all-important and official stake. Thus they represent the audience and the citizens in a particular way—not as a mob formed in response to some momentary feeling, but rather as an organ of a highly self-conscious community: something closer to the "conscience of the race" than to the overheated affectivity of a mob.

According to Aristotle, a Sophoclean chorus is a character that takes an important role in the action of the play, instead of merely making incidental music between the scenes, as in the plays of Euripides. The chorus may be described as a group personality, like an old Parliament. It has its own traditions, habits of thought and feeling, and mode of being. It exists, in a sense, as a living entity, but not with the sharp actuality of an individual. It perceives; but its perception is at once wider and vaguer than that of a single man. It shares, in its way, the seeking action of the play as a whole; but it cannot act in all the modes; it depends upon the chief agonists to invent and try out the detail of policy, just as a rather helpless but critical Parliament depends upon the Prime Minister to act but, in its less specific form of life, survives his destruction.

When the chorus enters after the prologue, with its questions, its invocation of the various gods, and its focus upon the hidden and jeopardized welfare of the City—Athens or Thebes—the list of essential *dramatis personae,* as well as the elements needed to celebrate the ritual, is complete, and the main action can begin. It is the function of the chorus to mark the stages of this action, and to perform the suffering and perceiving part of the tragic rhythm. The protagonist and his antagonists develop the "purpose" with which the tragic sequence begins; the chorus, with its less than individual being, broods over the agons, marks their stages with a word (like that of the chorus leader in the middle of the Tiresias scene), and (expressing its emotions and visions in song and dance) suffers the results, and the new perception at the end of the fight.

The choral odes are lyrics but they are not to be understood as poetry, the art of words, only, for they are intended also to be danced and sung. And though each chorus has its own shape, like that of a discrete lyric—its beginning, middle, and end—it represents also one passion or pathos in the changing action of the whole. This passion, like the other moments in the tragic rhythm, is felt at so general or, rather, so deep a level that it seems to contain both the mob ferocity that Nietzsche felt in it and, at the other extreme, the patience of prayer. It is informed by faith in the unseen order of nature and the gods, and moves through a sequence of modes of suffering. This may be illustrated from the chorus I have quoted at the end of the Tiresias scene.

It begins (close to the savage emotion of the end of the fight) with images suggesting that cruel "Bacchic frenzy" which is supposed to be the common root of tragedy and of the "old" comedy: "In panoply of fire and lightning / The son of Zeus now springs upon him." In the first antistrophe these images come together more clearly as we relish the chase; and the fleeing culprit, as we imagine him, begins to resemble Oedipus, who is lame, and always associated with the rough wilderness of Kitharon. But in the second strophe, as though appalled by its ambivalent feelings and the imagined possibilities, the chorus sinks back into a more dark and patient posture of suffering, "in awe," "hovering in hope." In the second antistrophe this is developed into something like the orthodox Christian attitude of prayer, based on faith, and assuming the possibility of a hitherto unimaginable truth and answer: "Zeus and Apollo are wise," etc. The whole chorus then ends with a new vision of Oedipus, of the culprit, and of the direction in which the welfare of the City is to be sought. This vision is still colored by the chorus's human love of Oedipus as Hero, for the chorus has still its own purgation to complete, cannot as yet accept completely either the suffering in store for it, or Oedipus as scapegoat. But it marks the end of the first complete "purpose-passion-perception" unit, and lays the basis for the new purpose which will begin the next unit.

It is also to be noted that the chorus changes the scene which we, as audience, are to imagine. During the agon between Oedipus and Tiresias, our attention is fixed upon their clash, and the scene is literal, close, and immediate: before Oedipus' palace. When the fighters depart and the choral music starts, the focus suddenly widens, as though we had been removed to a distance. We become aware of the interested City around the bright arena; and beyond that, still more dimly, of Nature, sacred to the hidden gods. Mr. Burke has expounded the fertile notion that human action may be understood in terms of the scene in which it occurs, and vice versa: the scene is defined by the mode of action. The chorus's action is not limited by the sharp, rationalized purposes of the protagonist; its mode of action, more patient, less sharply realized, is cognate with a wider, if less accurate, awareness of the scene of human life. But the chorus's action, as I have remarked, is not that of passion itself (Nietzsche's cosmic void of night) but suffering informed by the faith of the tribe in a human and a divinely sanctioned natural order: "If such deeds as these are honored," the chorus asks after Jocasta's impiety, "why should I dance and sing?" Thus it is one of the most important functions of the chorus to reveal, in its widest and most mysterious extent, the theater of human life which the play, and indeed the whole Festival of Dionysos, assumed. Even when the chorus does not speak, but only watches, it maintains this theme and this perspective — ready to take the whole stage when the fighters depart.

If one thinks of the movements of the play, it appears that the tragic rhythm analyzes human action temporally into successive modes, as a crystal analyzes a white beam of light spatially into the colored bands of the spectrum. The chorus, always present, represents one of these modes, and at the recurrent moments when reasoned purpose is gone, it takes the stage with its faith-informed passion, moving through an ordered succession of modes of suffering, to a new perception of the immediate situation.

SIGMUND FREUD

Sigmund Freud (1856–1939) used Sophocles' play in The Interpretation of Dreams *(1900) to derive the term* Oedipus complex, *which is central to his explanation of neurosis in his theory of psychoanalysis. Freud sought to explain the drama's enduring psychological appeal for audiences despite its lack of a contemporary religious context. He hypothesized that audiences respond to Sophocles' tragedy because they recognize that Oedipus's relationship to his parents "might have been ours" as children. According to Freud's interpretation, the incest theme is dramatized so forcefully in* Oedipus the King *that it enables us to recognize our own "primeval wishes," suppressed in our later psychological development as individuals.*

The Oedipus Complex   1900

In my experience, which is already extensive, the chief part in the mental lives of all children who later become psychoneurotics is played by their parents. Being in love with the one parent and hating the other are among the essential constituents of the stock of psychical impulses which is formed at that time and which is of such importance in determining the symptoms of the later neurosis. It is not my belief, however, that psychoneurotics differ sharply in this respect from other human beings who remain normal — that they are able, that is, to create something absolutely new and peculiar to themselves. It is far more probable — and this is confirmed by occasional observations on normal children — that they are only distinguished by exhibiting on a magnified scale feelings of love and hatred to their parents which occur less obviously and less intensely in the minds of most children.

This discovery is confirmed by a legend that has come down to us from classical antiquity: a legend whose profound and universal power to move can only be understood if the hypothesis I have put forward in regard to the psychology of children has an equally universal validity. What I have in mind is the legend of King Oedipus and Sophocles' drama which bears his name.

Oedipus, son of Laius, King of Thebes, and of Jocasta, was exposed as an infant because an oracle had warned Laius that the still unborn child would be his father's murderer. The child was rescued and grew up as a prince in an alien court, until, in doubts as to his origin, he too questioned the oracle and was warned to avoid his home since he was destined to murder his father and take his mother in marriage. On the road leading away from what he believed was his home, he met King Laius and slew him in a sudden quarrel. He came next to Thebes and solved the riddle set him by the Sphinx who barred his way. Out of gratitude the Thebans made him their king and gave him Jocasta's hand in marriage. He reigned long in peace and honor, and she who, unknown to him, was his mother bore him two sons and two daughters. Then at last a plague broke out and the Thebans made inquiry once more of the oracle. It is at this point that Sophocles' tragedy opens. The messengers bring back the reply that the plague will cease when the murderer of Laius has been driven from the land.

> But he, where is he? Where shall now be read
> The fading record of this ancient guilt?[1]

The action of the play consists in nothing other than the process of revealing, with cunning delays and ever-mounting excitement — a process that can be likened to the work of a psychoanalysis — that Oedipus himself is the murderer of Laius, but further that he is the son of the murdered man and of Jocasta. Appalled at the abomination which he has unwittingly perpetrated, Oedipus blinds himself and forsakes his home. The oracle has been fulfilled.

Oedipus Rex is what is known as a tragedy of destiny. Its tragic effect is said to lie in the contrast between the supreme will of the gods and the vain attempts of mankind to escape the evil that threatens them. The lesson which, it is said, the deeply moved spectator should learn from the tragedy is submission to the divine will and realization of his own impotence. Modern dramatists have accordingly tried to achieve a similar tragic effect by weaving the same contrast into a plot invented by themselves. But the spectators have looked on unmoved while a curse or an oracle was fulfilled in spite of all the efforts of some innocent man: later tragedies of destiny have failed in their effect.

If *Oedipus Rex* moves a modern audience no less than it did the contemporary Greek one, the explanation can only be that its effect does not lie in the contrast between destiny and human will, but is to be looked for in the particular nature of the material on which that contrast is exemplified. There must be something which makes a voice within us ready to recognize the compelling force of destiny in the *Oedipus*, while we can dismiss as merely arbitrary such dispositions as are laid down in [Grillparzer's] *Die Ahnfrau* or other modern tragedies of destiny. And a factor of this kind is in fact involved in the story of King Oedipus. His destiny moves us only because it might have been ours — because the oracle laid the same curse upon us before our birth as upon him. It is the fate of all of us, perhaps, to direct our first sexual impulse toward our

---

[1]Lewis Campbell's translation (1883), lines 108ff. [Cf. lines 123–124 of the Fagles translation in this volume. — Editors' note]

mother and our first hatred and our first murderous wish against our father. Our dreams convince us that that is so. King Oedipus, who slew his father Laius and married his mother Jocasta, merely shows us the fulfillment of our own childhood wishes. But, more fortunate than he, we have meanwhile succeeded, in so far as we have not become psychoneurotics, in detaching our sexual impulses from our mothers and in forgetting our jealousy of our fathers. Here is one in whom these primeval wishes of our childhood have been fulfilled, and we shrink back from him with the whole force of the repression by which those wishes have since that time been held down within us. While the poet, as he unravels the past, brings to light the guilt of Oedipus, he is at the same time compelling us to recognize our own inner minds, in which those same impulses, though suppressed, are still to be found. The contrast with which the closing Chorus leaves us confronted —

> . . . Fix on Oedipus your eyes,
> Who resolved the dark enigma, noblest champion and most wise.
> Like a star his envied fortune mounted beaming far and wide:
> Now he sinks in seas of anguish, whelmed beneath a raging tide . . . [2]

— strikes as a warning at ourselves and our pride, at us who since our childhood have grown so wise and so mighty in our own eyes. Like Oedipus, we live in ignorance of these wishes, repugnant to morality, which have been forced upon us by Nature, and after their revelation we may all of us well seek to close our eyes to the scenes of our childhood. [3]

There is an unmistakable indication in the text of Sophocles' tragedy itself that the legend of Oedipus sprang from some primeval dream material which had as its content the distressing disturbance of a child's relation to his parents owing to the first stirrings of sexuality. At a point when Oedipus, though he is not yet enlightened, has begun to feel troubled by his recollection of the oracle, Jocasta consoles him by referring to a dream which many people dream, though, as she thinks, it has no meaning:

> Many a man ere now in dreams hath lain
> With her who bare him. He hath least annoy
> Who with such omens troubleth not his mind. [4]

---

[2] Lewis Campbell's translation, lines 1524ff. [Cf. lines 1678–1682 in the Fagles translation in this volume. — Editors' note]

[3] [*Footnote added by Freud in 1914 edition.*] None of the findings of psychoanalytic research has provoked such embittered denials, such fierce opposition — or such amusing contortions — on the part of critics as this indication of the childhood impulses toward incest which persist in the unconscious. An attempt has even been made recently to make out, in the face of all experience, that the incest should only be taken as "symbolic." — Ferenczi (1912) has proposed an ingenious "overinterpretation" of the Oedipus myth, based on a passage in one of Schopenhauer's letters. [*Added 1919.*] Later studies have shown that the "Oedipus complex," which was touched upon for the first time in the above paragraphs in the *Interpretation of Dreams*, throws a light of undreamt-of importance on the history of the human race and the evolution of religion and morality.

[4] Lewis Campbell's translation, lines 982ff. [Cf. lines 1074–1078 in the Fagles translation in this volume. — Editors' note]

Today, just as then, many men dream of having sexual relations with their mothers, and speak of the fact with indignation and astonishment. It is clearly the key to the tragedy and the complement to the dream of the dreamer's father being dead. The story of Oedipus is the reaction of the imagination to these two typical dreams. And just as these dreams, when dreamt by adults, are accompanied by feelings of repulsion, so too the legend must include horror and self-punishment. Its further modification originates once again in a misconceived secondary revision of the material, which has sought to exploit it for theological purposes. . . . The attempt to harmonize divine omnipotence with human responsibility must naturally fail in connection with this subject matter just as with any other.

LORRAINE HANSBERRY

Lorraine Hansberry reflected on the relationship between Walter Lee in A Raisin in the Sun *and Willy Loman in* Death of a Salesman *in an article published in* The Village Voice Reader *in 1962.*

An Author's Reflections: Willy Loman, Walter Younger, and He Who Must Live   1962

A man can't go out the way he came in . . . Ben, that funeral will be massive!

                 —WILLY LOMAN, 1946

We have all thought about your offer and we have decided to move into our house.

                 —WALTER LEE YOUNGER, 1958

Some of the acute partisanship revolving around *A Raisin in the Sun* is amusing. Those who announce that they find the piece less than fine are regarded in some quarters with dramatic hostility, as though such admission automatically implied the meanest of racist reservations. On the other hand, the ultra-sophisticates have hardly acquitted themselves less ludicrously, gazing coolly down their noses at those who are moved by the play, and going on at length about "melodrama" and/or "soap opera" as if these were not completely definable terms which cannot simply be tacked onto any play and all plays we do not like.

Personally, I find no pain whatever—at least of the traditional ego type—in saying that *Raisin* is a play which contains dramaturgical incompletions. Fine plays tend to utilize one big fat character who runs right through the middle of the structure, by action or implication, with whom we rise or fall. A central character as such is certainly lacking from *Raisin*. I should be delighted to pretend that it was *inventiveness,* as some suggest for me, but it is, also, craft inadequacy and creative indecision. The result is that neither Walter Lee nor Mama Younger loom large enough to monumentally command the play. I consider it an enormous dramatic fault if no one else does. (Nor am I less critical of the production which, by and large, performance and direction alike, is splendid. Yet I should have preferred that the second-act curtain, for instance, be performed with quiet assertion rather than the apparently popular declamatory opulence which prevails.)

All in all, however, I believe that, for the most part, the play has been magnificently understood. In some cases it was not only thematically absorbed but attention was actually paid to the tender treacherousness of its craft-imposed "simplicity." Some, it is true, quite missed that part of the overt intent and went on to harangue the bones of the play with rather useless observations of the terribly clear fact that they are old bones indeed. More meaningful discussions tended to delve into the flesh which hangs from those bones and its implications in mid-century American drama and life.

In that connection it is interesting to note that while the names of Chekhov, O'Casey, and the early Odets were introduced for comparative purposes in some of the reviews, almost no one—with the exception of Gerald Weales in *Commentary*—discovered a simple line of descent between Walter Lee Younger and the last great hero in American drama to also *accept* the values of his culture, Willy Loman. I am sure that the already mentioned primary fault of the play must account in part for this. The family so overwhelms the play that Walter Lee necessarily fails as the true symbol he should be, even though *his* ambitions, *his* frustrations, and *his* decisions are those which decisively drive the play on. But however recognizable he proves to be, he fails to dominate our imagination and finally emerges as a reasonably interesting study, but not, like Arthur Miller's great character—and like Hamlet, of course—a summation of an immense (though not crucial) portion of his culture.

Then too, in fairness to the author and to Sidney Poitier's basically brilliant portrayal of Walter Lee, we must not completely omit reference to some of the prior attitudes which were brought into the theatre from the world outside. For in the minds of many, Walter remains, despite the play, despite performance, what American radical traditions *wish* him to be: an exotic. Some writers have been astonishingly incapable of discussing his purely *class* aspirations and have persistently confounded them with what they consider to be an exotic being's longing to "wheel and deal" in what they further consider to be (and what Walter never can) "the white man's world." Very few people today must consider the ownership of a liquor store as an expression of extraordinary affluence, and yet, as joined to a dream of Walter Younger, it takes on, for some, aspects of the fantastic. We have grown accustomed to the dynamics of "Negro" personality as expressed by white authors. Thus, de Emperor, de Lawd, and, of course, Porgy still haunt our frame of reference when a new character emerges. We have become romantically jealous of the great image of a prototype whom we believe is summarized by the wishfulness of a self-assumed opposite. Presumably there is a quality in human beings that makes us *wish* that we *were* capable of primitive contentments; the *universality* of ambition and its anguish can escape us only if we construct elaborate legends about the rudimentary simplicity of *other* men.

America, for this reason, long ago fell in love with the image of the simple, lovable, and glandular "Negro." We all know that Catfish Row was never intended to slander anyone; it was intended as a mental haven for readers and audiences who could bask in the unleashed passions of those "lucky ones" for whom abandonment was apparently permissible. In an almost paradoxical fashion, it disturbs the soul of man to truly understand what he invariably senses: that *nobody* really finds oppression and/or poverty tolerable. If we ever destroy the image of the black people who supposedly do find those things tolerable in America, then that much-touted "guilt" which allegedly haunts most middle-class white Americans with regard to the Negro question would really become unendurable. It would also mean the death of a dubious literary tradition, but it would undoubtedly and more significantly help toward the more rapid transformation of the status of a people who have never found their imposed misery very charming.

My colleagues and I were reduced to mirth and tears by that gentleman writing his review of our play in a Connecticut paper who remarked of his pleasure at seeing how "our dusky brethren" could "come up with a song and hum their troubles away." It did not disturb the writer in the least that there is no such implication in the entire three acts. He did not need it in the play; he had it in his head.

For all these reasons, then, I imagine that the ordinary impulse to compare Willy Loman and Walter Younger was remote. Walter Lee Younger jumped out at us from a play about a largely unknown world. We knew who Willy Loman was instantaneously; we recognized his milieu. We also knew at once that he represented that curious paradox in what the *English* character in that *English* play could call, though dismally, "The American Age." Willy Loman was a product of a nation of great military strength, indescribable material wealth, and incredible mastery of the physical realm, which nonetheless was unable, in 1946, to produce a *typical* hero who was capable of an affirmative view of life.

I believe it is a testament to Miller's brilliance that it is hardly a misstatement of the case, as some preferred to believe. Something has indeed gone wrong with at least part of the American dream, and Willy Loman is the victim of the detour. Willy had to be overwhelmed on the stage as, in fact, his prototypes are in everyday life. Coming out of his section of our great sprawling middle class, preoccupied with its own restlessness and displaying its obsession for the possession of trivia, Willy was indeed trapped. His predicament in a New World where there just aren't any more forests to clear or virgin railroads to lay or native American empires to first steal and then build upon left him with nothing but some left-over values which had forgotten how to prize industriousness over cunning, usefulness over mere acquisition, and, above all, humanism over "success." The potency of the great tale of a salesman's

death was in our familiar recognition of his entrapment which, suicide or no,
is *deathly.*

What then of this new figure who appears in American drama in 1958;
from what source is he drawn so that, upon inspection, and despite class differences, so much of his encirclement must still remind us of that of Willy
Loman? Why, finally, is it possible that when his third-act will is brought to
bear, *his* typicality is capable of a choice which *affirms* life? After all, Walter
Younger is an American more than he is anything else. His ordeal, give or take
his personal expression of it, is not extraordinary but intensely familiar like
Willy's. The two of them have virtually no values which have not come out of
their culture, and to a significant point, no view of the possible solutions to
their problems which do not also come out of the self-same culture. Walter can
find no peace with that part of society which seems to permit him entry and no
entry into that which has willfully excluded him. He shares with Willy Loman
the acute awareness that *something* is obstructing some abstract progress that
he feels he *should* be making; that *something* is in the way of his ascendancy. It
does not occur to either of them to question the nature of this desired "ascendancy." Walter accepts, he believes in the "world" as it has been presented to
him. When we first meet him, he does not wish to alter *it;* merely to change *his*
position in it. His mentors and his associates all take the view that the institutions which frustrate him are somehow impeccable, or, at best, "unfortunate."
"Things being as they are," he must look to *himself* as the only source of any
rewards he may expect. Within himself, he is encouraged to believe, are the
only seeds of defeat or victory within the universe. And Walter believes this
and when opportunity, haphazard and rooted in death, prevails, he acts.

But the obstacles which are introduced are gigantic; the weight of the loss
of the money is in fact the weight of death. In Walter Lee Younger's life, somebody *has* to die for ten thousand bucks to pile up—if then. Elsewhere in the
world, in the face of catastrophe, he might be tempted to don the saffron robes
of acceptance and sit on a mountain top all day contemplating the divine justice
of his misery. Or, history being what it is turning out to be, he might wander
down to his first Communist Party meeting. But here in the dynamic and confusing post-war years on the South Side of Chicago, his choices of action are
equal to those gestures only in symbolic terms. The American ghetto hero may
give up and contemplate his misery in rose-colored bars to the melodies of hypnotic saxophones, but revolution seems alien to him in his circumstances
(America), and it is easier to dream of personal wealth than of a communal state
wherein universal dignity is supposed to be a corollary. Yet his position in time
and space does allow for one other alternative: he may take his place on any one
of a number of frontiers of challenge. Challenges (such as helping to break
down restricted neighborhoods) which are admittedly limited because they
most certainly do not threaten the basic social order.

But why is even this final choice possible, considering the ever-present
(and ever-so-popular) vogue of despair? Well, that is where Walter departs
from Willy Loman; there is a second pulse in his still dual culture. His people

have had "somewhere" they have been trying to get for so long that more sophisticated confusions do not yet bind them. *Thus the weight and power of their current social temperament intrudes and affects him, and it is, at the moment, at least, gloriously and rigidly affirmative.* In the course of *their* brutally difficult ascent, they have dismissed the ostrich and still sing, *"Went to the rock to hide my face, but the rock cried out: 'No hidin' place down here!' "* Walter is, despite his lack of consciousness of it, inextricably as much wedded to his special mass as Willy was to his, and the moods of each are able to decisively determine the dramatic typicality. Furthermore, the very nature of the situation of American Negroes can force their representative hero to recognize that for his *true* ascendancy he must ultimately be at cross-purposes with at least certain of his culture's values. It is to the pathos of Willy Loman that his section of American life seems to have momentarily lost that urgency; that he cannot, like Walter, draw on the strength of an incredible people who, historically, have simply refused to give up.

In other words, the symbolism of moving into the new house is quite as small as it seems and quite as significant. For if there are no waving flags and marching songs at the barricades as Walter marches out with his little battalion, it is not because the battle lacks nobility. On the contrary, he has picked up in his way, still imperfect and wobbly in his small view of human destiny, what I believe Arthur Miller once called "the golden thread of history." He becomes, in spite of those who are too intrigued with despair and hatred of man to see it, King Oedipus refusing to tear out his eyes, but attacking the Oracle instead. He is that last Jewish patriot manning his rifle in the burning ghetto at Warsaw; he is that young girl who swam into sharks to save a friend a few weeks ago; he is Anne Frank,° still believing in people; he is the nine small heroes of Little Rock;° he is Michelangelo creating David and Beethoven bursting forth with the Ninth Symphony. He is all those things because he has finally reached out in his tiny moment and caught that sweet essence which is human dignity, and it shines like the old star-touched dream that it is in his eyes. We see, in the moment, I think, what becomes, and not for Negroes alone, but for Willy and all of us, entirely an American responsibility.

Out in the darkness where we watch, most of us are not afraid to cry.

Anne Frank: A German Jewish teenager (1929–1945) who, during World War II, hid from the Nazis with her family for twenty-five months in an annex of rooms in Amsterdam. She recorded the experience in her diary which was published in 1947, two years after her death from typhus in a Nazi concentration camp.
nine small heroes of Little Rock: Following the U.S. Supreme Court's ruling that racial segregation in U.S. schools was unconstitutional, nine black teenagers defied white mobs and a hostile governor and marched into Little Rock, Arkansas's Central High School on September 25, 1957. They were supported by the federal government.

Lorraine Hansberry wrote about her "Shakespearean Experience" in high school in To Be Young, Gifted and Black, *which was published four years after her death in 1965. In this piece, Hansberry began to shape her memoir of her high school English teacher nicknamed "Pale Hecate" as an essay, but within a few paragraphs she was so deeply involved in her memories of adolescence that she dramatized them in dialogue form as a series of imaginary exchanges between the teacher and her students.*

My Shakespearean Experience   1969

1

My High School Yearbook bears the dedication: "Englewood High trains for citizenship in a world of many different peoples. Who could better appreciate this wonderful country than our forefathers who traveled hundreds of miles from every known nation, seeking a land of freedom from discrimination of race, color, or creed." And in illustration, there is this:

> *The Great Branches of Man at Englewood High:* in front, Mangolia Ali of East Indian Mohammedan descent; second couple, Nancy Diagre and Harold Bradley, Negroid; middle couple, Rosalind Sherr and William Krugman, Jewish religion, not a racial stock; next, Eleanor Trester and Theodore Flood, Caucasoid; extreme right, Lois Lee and Barbara Nomura, Mongoloid; rear, left, Mr. Thompson, principal.

2

I was reminded of Englewood by a questionnaire which came from *Show* magazine the other day. . . .

THE SHAKESPEAREAN EXPERIENCE
SHOW POLL #5, February 1964
Some Questions Answered by: Robert Bolt, Jean Cocteau, T. S. Eliot, Tyrone Guthrie, Lorraine Hansberry, Joan Littlewood, Harold Pinter, Alain Robbe-Grillet, Igor Stravinsky, Harry S Truman

QUESTION: *What was your first contact with Shakespeare?*

High School. English literature classwork. We had to read and memorize speeches from *Macbeth* and *Julius Caesar* all under the auspices of a strange and bewigged teacher who we, after this induction, naturally and cruelly christened "Pale Hecate" — God rest her gentle, enraptured, and igniting soul!

Pale Hecate enters, ruler in hand, and takes her place in the classroom. She surveys the class. They come to attention as her eye falls on each in turn.

PALE HECATE: Y'do not read, nor speak, nor write the English language! I suspect that y'do not even *think* in it! God only knows in what language y'do think, or if you think at all. 'Tis true the *English* have done little enough with the tongue, but being the English I expect it was the best they could do. (*They giggle.*) In any case, I'll have it learned properly before a living one of y'll pass out of this class. That I will! (*Waving a composition book and indicating the grade marked in red at the top.*) As for *you*, Miss — as for you, indeed, surely you will recognize the third letter of the alphabet when y'have seen it?

STUDENT: "C."

PALE HECATE: Aye, a "C" it 'tis! You're a bright and clever one now after all, aren't y'lass? (*The class snickers.*) And now, my brilliance, would you also be informing us as to what a grade signifies when it is thus put upon the page?

STUDENT: Average.

PALE HECATE: "Average." Yes, yes — and what else in your case, my iridescence? Well then, I'll be tellin' you in fine order. It stands for "cheat," my luminous one! (*The class sobers.*) For them that will do *half* when *all* is called for; for them that will slip and slide through life at the edge of their minds, never once pushing into the interior to see what wonders are hiding there — content to drift along on whatever gets them by, *cheating* themselves, *cheating* the world, *cheating* Nature! That is what the "C" means, my dear child — (*she smiles*) — my pet (*they giggle; in rapid order she raps each on the head with her ruler*) — my laziest *Queen of the Ethiopes!*

She exits or dims out.

QUESTION: *Which is your favorite Shakespeare play and why?*

Favorite? It is like choosing the "superiority" of autumn days; mingling titles permits a reply: *Othello* and *Hamlet*. Why? There is a sweetness in the former that lingers long after the tragedy is done. A kind of possibility that we suspect in man wherein even its flaw is a tribute. The latter because there remains a depth in the Prince that, as we all know, constantly re-engages as we mature. And it does seem that the wit remains the brightest and most instructive in all dramatic literature.

QUESTION: *What is the most important result of your familiarity with Shakespeare? What has he given you?*

Comfort and agitation so bound together that they are inseparable. Man, as set down in the plays, is large. Enormous. Capable of anything at all. And yet fragile, too, this view of the human spirit; one feels it ought be respected and protected and loved rather fiercely.

Rollicking times, Shakespeare has given me. I love to laugh and his humor is that of everyday; of every man's foible at no man's expense. Language. At thirteen a difficult and alien tedium, those Elizabethan cadences; but soon a balm, a thrilling source of contact with life.

HENRIK IBSEN

Henrik Ibsen wrote his first notes for the play that would become A Doll House *on October 19, 1878. At first he conceived of the drama essentially as a marital conflict that would lead to Nora's destruction because of what he saw as her entrapment in a patriarchal society. This excerpt from Ibsen's notes is from the translator A. G. Chater's* From Ibsen's Workshop *(1978).*

Notes for *A Doll House*   1878

There are two kinds of spiritual law, two kinds of conscience, one in man and another, altogether different, in woman. They do not understand each other; but in practical life the woman is judged by man's law, as though she were not a woman but a man.

The wife in the play ends by having no idea of what is right or wrong; natural feeling on the one hand and belief in authority on the other have altogether bewildered her.

A woman cannot be herself in the society of the present day, which is an exclusively masculine society, with laws framed by men and with a judicial system that judges feminine conduct from a masculine point of view.

She has committed forgery, and she is proud of it; for she did it out of love for her husband, to save his life. But this husband with his commonplace principles of honor is on the side of the law and looks at the question from the masculine point of view.

Spiritual conflicts. Oppressed and bewildered by the belief in authority, she loses faith in her moral right and ability to bring up her children. Bitterness. A mother in modern society, like certain insects who go away and die when she has done her duty in the propagation of the race. Love of life, of home, of husband and children and family. Now and then a womanly shaking off of her thoughts. Sudden return of anxiety and terror. She must bear it all alone. The catastrophe approaches, inexorably, inevitably. Despair, conflict, and destruction.

ARTHUR MILLER

Arthur Miller analyzed what he considered the tragic dimension in Willy Loman's character when Death of a Salesman *was published by Viking Press in 1957. In his introduction to the play, Miller discussed how his view of a tragic hero differed from Aristotle's formulation in the* Poetics. *Miller then went on to describe his dramatic method of calling Willy Loman's values into question by presenting what Miller called "an opposing system" of love within the family to counter American society's false ideals of power and success. As Miller remarked during a symposium on his play the following year, "The trouble with Willy Loman is that he has tremendously powerful ideas. . . . [If] Willy Loman, for instance, had not had a very profound sense that his life as lived had left him hollow, he would have died contentedly polishing his car on some Sunday afternoon at a ripe old age. The fact is he has values. The fact that they cannot be realized is what is driving him mad."*

On *Death of a Salesman* as an American Tragedy

I set out not to "write a tragedy" in this play, but to show the truth as I saw it. However, some of the attacks upon it as a pseudo-tragedy contain ideas so misleading, and in some cases so laughable, that it might be in place here to deal with a few of them.

Aristotle having spoken of a fall from the heights, it goes without saying that someone of the common mold cannot be a fit tragic hero. It is now many centuries since Aristotle lived. There is no more reason for falling down in a faint before his *Poetics* than before Euclid's geometry, which has been amended numerous times by men with new insights; nor, for that matter, would I choose to have my illness diagnosed by Hippocrates rather than the most ordinary graduate of an American medical school, despite the Greek's genius. Things do change, and even a genius is limited by his time and the nature of his society.

I would deny, on grounds of simple logic, this one of Aristotle's contentions if only because he lived in a slave society. When a vast number of people are divested of alternatives, as slaves are, it is rather inevitable that one will not be able to imagine drama, let alone tragedy, as being possible for any but the higher ranks of society. There is a legitimate question of stature here, but none of rank, which is so often confused with it. So long as the hero may be said to have had alternatives of a magnitude to have materially changed the course of his life, it seems to me that in this respect at least, he cannot be debarred from the heroic role.

The question of rank is significant to me only as it reflects the question of the social application of the hero's career. There is no doubt that if a character is shown on the stage who goes through the most ordinary actions, and is suddenly revealed to be the President of the United States, his actions immediately assume a much greater magnitude, and pose the possibilities of much greater meaning, than if he is the corner grocer. But at the same time, his stature as a hero is not so utterly dependent upon his rank that the corner grocer cannot outdistance him as a tragic figure — providing, of course, that the grocer's career engages the issues of, for instance, the survival of the race, the relationships of man to God — the questions, in short, whose answers define humanity and the right way to live so that the world is a home, instead of a battleground or a fog in which disembodied spirits pass each other in an endless twilight.

In this respect *Death of a Salesman* is a slippery play to categorize because nobody in it stops to make a speech objectively stating the great issues which I believe it embodies. If it were a worse play, less closely articulating its meanings with its actions, I think it would have more quickly satisfied a certain kind of criticism. But it was meant to be less a play than a fact; it refused admission to its author's opinions and opened itself to a revelation of process and the operations of an ethic, of social laws of action no less powerful in their effects upon individuals than any tribal law administered by gods with names. I need not claim that this play is a genuine solid gold tragedy for my opinions on tragedy to be held valid. My purpose here is simply to point out a historical fact which must be taken into account in any consideration of tragedy, and it is the sharp alteration in the meaning of rank in society between the present time and the distant past. More important to me is the fact that this particular kind of argument obscures much more relevant considerations.

One of these is the question of intensity. It matters not at all whether a modern play concerns itself with a grocer or a president if the intensity of the hero's commitment to his course is less than the maximum possible. It matters not at all whether the hero falls from a great height or a small one, whether he is highly conscious or only dimly aware of what is happening, whether his pride brings the fall or an unseen pattern written behind clouds; if the intensity, the human passion to surpass his given bounds, the fanatic insistence upon his self-conceived role — if these are not present there can only be an outline of tragedy but no living thing. I believe, for myself, that the lasting appeal of tragedy is due to our need to face the fact of death in order to strengthen ourselves for life, and that over and above this function of the tragic viewpoint there are and will be a great number of formal variations which no single definition will ever embrace.

Another issue worth considering is the so-called tragic victory, a question closely related to the consciousness of the hero. One makes nonsense of this if a "victory" means that the hero makes us feel some certain joy when, for instance, he sacrifices himself for a "cause," and unhappy and morose because he dies without one. To begin at the bottom, a man's death is and ought to be an essentially terrifying thing and ought to make nobody happy. But in a great variety of ways even death, the ultimate negative, can be, and appear to be, an assertion of bravery, and can serve to separate the death of man from the death of animals; and I think it is this distinction which underlies any conceptions of a victory in death. For a society of faith, the nature of the death can prove the existence of the spirit, and posit its immortality. For a secular society it is perhaps more difficult for such a victory to document itself and to make itself felt, but, conversely, the need to offer greater proofs of the humanity of man can make that victory more real. It goes without saying that in a society where there is basic disagreement as to the right way to live, there can hardly be agreement as to the right way to die, and both life and death must be heavily weighted with meaningless futility.

It was not out of any deference to a tragic definition that Willy Loman is filled with a joy, however broken-hearted, as he approaches his end, but simply that my sense of his character dictated his joy, and even what I felt was an exultation. In terms of his character, he has achieved a very powerful piece of knowledge, which is that he is loved by his son and has been embraced by him and forgiven. In this he is given his existence, so to speak — his fatherhood, for which he has always striven and which until now he could not achieve. That he is unable to take this victory thoroughly to his heart, that it closes the circle for him and propels him to his death, is the wage of his sin, which was to have committed himself so completely to the counterfeits of dignity and the false coinage embodied in his idea of success that he can prove his existence only by bestowing "power" on his posterity, a power deriving from the sale of his last asset, himself, for the price of his insurance policy.

I must confess here to a miscalculation, however. I did not realize while writing the play that so many people in the world do not see as clearly, or would not admit, as I thought they must, how futile most lives are; so there could be no hope of consoling the audience for the death of this man. I did not realize either how few would be impressed by the fact that this man is actually a very brave spirit who cannot settle for half but must pursue his dream of himself to the end. Finally, I thought it must be clear, even obvious, that this was no dumb brute heading mindlessly to his catastrophe.

I have no need to be Willy's advocate before the jury which decides who is and who is not a tragic hero. I am merely noting that the lingering ponderousness of so many ancient definitions has blinded students and critics to the facts before them, and not only in regard to this play. Had Willy been unaware of his separation from values that endure he would have died contentedly while polishing his car, probably on a Sunday afternoon with the ball game coming over the radio. But he was agonized by his awareness of being in a false position, so constantly haunted by the hollowness of all he had placed his faith in, so aware, in short, that he must somehow be filled in his spirit or fly apart, that he staked his very life on the ultimate assertion. That he had not the intellectual fluency to verbalize his situation is not the same thing as saying that he lacked awareness, even an overly intensified consciousness that the life he had made was without form and inner meaning.

To be sure, had he been able to know that he was as much the victim of his beliefs as their defeated exemplar, had he known how much of guilt he ought to bear and how much to shed from his soul, he would be more conscious. But it seems to me that there is of necessity a severe limitation of self-awareness in any character, even the most knowing, which serves to define him as a character, and more, that this very limit serves to complete the tragedy and, indeed, to make it at all possible. Complete consciousness is possible only in a play about forces, like *Prometheus*, ° but not in a play about people. I think that the point is whether there is a sufficient awareness in the hero's career to make the audience supply the rest. Had Oedipus, for instance, been more conscious and more aware of the forces at work upon him he must surely have said that he was not really to blame for having cohabited with his mother since neither he nor anyone else knew she was his mother. He must surely decide to divorce her, provide for their children, firmly resolve to investigate the family background of his next wife, and thus deprive us of a very fine play and the name for a famous neurosis. But he is conscious only up to a point, the point at which guilt begins. Now he is inconsolable and must tear out his eyes. What is tragic about this? Why is it not even ridiculous? How can we respect a man who

---

Prometheus: *Prometheus Bound* by the Greek tragedian Aeschylus (c. 525–456 B.C.).

Miller: It's aware, but it will not admit into itself any moral universe at all. Another thing that's missing is the positioning of the author in relation to power. I always assumed that underlying any story is the question of who should wield power. See, in *Death of a Salesman* you have two viewpoints. They show what would happen if we all took Willy's viewpoint toward the world, or if we all took Biff's. And took it seriously, as almost a political fact. I'm debating really which way the world ought to be run; I'm speaking of psychology and the spirit, too. For example, a play that isn't usually linked with this kind of problem is Tennessee Williams's *Cat on a Hot Tin Roof.* It struck me sharply that what is at stake there is the father's great power. He's the owner, literally, of an empire of land and farms. And he wants to immortalize that power, he wants to hand it on, because he's dying. The son has a much finer appreciation of justice and human relations than the father. The father is rougher, more Philistine; he's cruder; and when we speak of the fineness of emotions, we would probably say the son has them and the father lacks them. When I saw the play I thought, This is going to be simply marvelous because the person with the sensitivity will be presented with power and what is he going to do about it? But it never gets to that. It gets deflected onto a question of personal neurosis. It comes to a dead end. If we're talking about tragedy, the Greeks would have done something miraculous with that idea. They would have stuck the son with the power, and faced him with the racking conflicts of the sensitive man having to rule. And then you would throw light on what the tragedy of power is.

Interviewer: Which is what you were getting at in *Incident at Vichy.*

Miller: That's exactly what I was after. But I feel today's stage turns away from any consideration of power, which always lies at the heart of tragedy. I use Williams's play as an example because he's that excellent that his problems are symptomatic of the time—*Cat* ultimately came down to the mendacity of human relations. It was a most accurate personalization but it bypasses the issue which the play seems to me to raise, namely the mendacity in social relations. I still believe that when a play questions, even threatens, our social arrangement, that is when it really shakes us profoundly and dangerously, and that is when you've got to be great; good isn't enough.

Interviewer: Do you think that people in general now rationalize so, and have so many euphemisms for death, that they can't face tragedy?

Miller: I wonder whether there isn't a certain—I'm speaking now of all classes of people—you could call it a softness, or else a genuine inability to face the tough decisions and the dreadful results of error.

LEONARD MUSTAZZA

Leonard Mustazza considers the similarities and differences between Glaspell's play and short story. This essay was published in the literary journal Studies in Short Fiction.

Generic Translation and Thematic Shift in Glaspell's *Trifles* and "A Jury of Her Peers" 1989

Commentators on Susan Glaspell's classic feminist short story, "A Jury of Her Peers" (1917), and the one-act play from which it derives, *Trifles* (1916), have tended to regard the two works as essentially alike. And even those few who have noticed the changes that Glaspell made in the process of generic translation have done so only in passing. In his monograph on Glaspell, Arthur Waterman, who seems to have a higher regard for the story than for the play, suggests that the story is a "moving fictional experience" because of the progressive honing of the author's skills, the story's vivid realism owing to her work as a local-color writer for the *Des Moines Daily News,* and its unified plot due to its dramatic origin.[1] More specifically, Elaine Hedges appropriately notes the significance of Glaspell's change in titles from *Trifles,* which emphasizes the supposedly trivial household items with which the women "acquit" their accused peer, to "A Jury of Her Peers," which emphasizes the question of legality. In 1917, Hedges observes, women were engaged in the final years of their fight for the vote, and Glaspell's change in titles thus "emphasizes the story's contemporaneity, by calling attention to its references to the issue of women's legal place in American society."[2] Apart from these and a few other passing remarks, however, critics have chosen to focus on one work or the other. Indeed, thematic criticisms of the respective pieces are virtually indistinguishable, most of these commentaries focusing on the question of assumed "roles" in the works.[3]

---

[1] Arthur E. Waterman, *Susan Glaspell* (New York: Twayne, 1966), pp. 29–30.

[2] Elaine Hedges, "Small Things Reconsidered: Susan Glaspell's 'A Jury of Her Peers,'" *Women's Studies,* 12, No. 1 (1986), 106.

[3] Rachel France notes that *Trifles* reveals "the dichotomy between men and women in rural life," an important feature of that dichotomy being the men's "proclivity for the letter of the law" as opposed to the women's more humane understanding of justice ("Apropos of Women and the Folk Play," in *Women in American Theatre: Careers, Images, Movements,* ed. Helen Krich Chinoy and Linda Walsh Jenkins [New York: Crown, 1981], p. 151). Karen Alkalay-Gut observes three polarities in "Jury": the opposition between the large external male world and the women's more circumscribed place within the home; the attitudes of men and women generally; and the distinction between *law,* which is identified with "the imposition of abstractions on individual circumstances," and *justice,* "the extrapolation of judgment from individual circumstances" ("Jury of Her Peers: The Importance of *Trifles,*" *Studies in Short Fiction,* 21 [Winter 1984], 2). Karen Stein calls the play "an anomaly in the murder mystery genre, which is predominantly a male tour de force." By bonding together, she goes on, the women act in a manner that is "diametrically opposed to the solo virtuosity usually displayed by male detectives" ("The Women's World of Glaspell's *Trifles,*" in *Women in American Theatre,* ed. Helen Krich Chinoy and Linda Walsh Jenkins [New York: Crown, 1981], p. 254). Judith Fetterly also advances an interesting and imaginative interpretation. She sees the characters in "Jury" as readers and the trivial household items as their text. The men fail to read the same meanings in that text that the women do because they are committed to "the equation of textuality with masculine subject matter and masculine point of view" ("Reading about Reading: 'A Jury of Her Peers,' 'The Murders in the Rue Morgue,' and 'The Yellow Wallpaper,'" in *Gender and Reading: Essays on Readers, Texts and Contexts,* ed. Elizabeth A. Flynn and Patrocinio P. Schweickart [Baltimore: Johns Hopkins Univ. Press, 1986], pp. 147–48).

a different situation altogether, for any emotional closeness we might infer from their act is undercut by our knowledge of Mrs. Hale's lack of respect for Mrs. Peters, particularly by comparison with her predecessor, Mrs. Gorman.

Ironically, however, despite her seeming mismatch with her husband, her lack of corporal "presence," Mrs. Peters turns out to be more suited to her assumed public role than Mrs. Hale had suspected—all too suited, in fact, since she perfectly assumes her male-approved role. "Of course Mrs. Peters is one of us," the county attorney asserts prior to getting on with his investigation of the house, and that statement turns out to be laden with meaning in the story. In *Trifles,* when the men leave to go about their investigative business, the women, we are told, "listen to the men's steps, then look about the kitchen." In "Jury," however, we get much more. Again here, the women stand motionless, listening to the men's footsteps, but this momentary stasis is followed by a significant gesture: "Then, *as if releasing herself from something strange,* Mrs. Hale began to arrange the dirty pans under the sink, which the county attorney's disdainful push of the foot had deranged" (emphasis added). One is prompted here to ask: what is this "something strange" from which she releases herself? Though the actions described in the play and the story are the same, why does Glaspell not include in the stage directions to the play an indication of Mrs. Hale's facial expression?

The answer, I think, lies again in the expanded and altered context of "Jury," where the author continually stresses the distance between the women. If Mrs. Peters is, as the county attorney has suggested, one of "them," Mrs. Hale certainly is not, and she distances herself from her male-approved peer in word and deed. The something strange from which she releases herself is, in this context, her reflexive movement towards Mrs. Peters. Mrs. Hale is, in fact, both extricating herself from the male strictures placed upon all of the women and asserting her intellectual independence. Karen Alkalay-Gut has correctly observed that, to the men, the disorder of Mrs. Wright's kitchen implies her "potential homicidal tendencies, inconceivable in a good wife."[8] For her part, Mrs. Hale is rejecting the men's specious reasoning, complaining about the lawyer's disdainful treatment of the kitchen things and asserting, "I'd hate to have men comin' into my kitchen, snoopin' round and criticizin'," obviously recalling the disorder in her kitchen and resenting the conclusions about her that could be drawn. Lacking that opening scene, the play simply does not resonate so profoundly.

Even more telling is a subtle but important change that Glaspell made following Mrs. Hale's testy assertion. In both the play and the story, Mrs. Peters offers the meek defense, "Of course it's no more than their duty," and then the two works diverge. In *Trifles,* Mrs. Peters manages to change the subject. Noticing some dough that Mrs. Wright had been preparing the day before, she says flatly, "she had set bread," and that statement directs Mrs. Hale's attention to the half-done and ruined kitchen chores. In effect, the flow of conversation is mutually directed in the play, and the distance between the

---

[8]"Jury of Her Peers: The Importance of *Trifles,*" p. 3.

women is thus minimized. When she wrote the play, however, Glaspell omitted mention of the bread and instead took us into Mrs. Hale's thoughts, as she does at the beginning of the story:

> She thought of the flour in her kitchen at home — half sifted, half not sifted. She had been interrupted, and had left things half done. What had interrupted Minnie Foster? Why had that work been left half done? She made a move as if to finish it, — unfinished things always bothered her, — and then she glanced around and saw that Mrs. Peters was watching her — and she didn't want Mrs. Peters to get that feeling she got of work begun and then — for some reason — not finished.
>   "It's a shame about her fruit," she said. . . .

Although mention of the ruined fruit preserves is included in the play as well, two significant additions are made in the above passage. First, there is the continual comparison between Mrs. Hale's life and Mrs. Wright's. Second, and more important, we get the clear sense here of Mrs. Hale's suspicion of Mrs. Peters, her not wanting to call attention to the unfinished job for fear that the sheriff's wife will get the wrong idea — or, in this case, the right idea, for the evidence of disturbance, however circumstantial, is something the men may be able to use against Mrs. Wright. In other words, unlike the play, the story posits a different set of polarities, with Mrs. Peters presumably occupying a place within the official party and Mrs. Hale taking the side of the accused against all of them.

We come at this point to a crossroads in the story. Mrs. Hale can leave things as they are and keep information to herself, or she can recruit Mrs. Peters as a fellow "juror" in the case, moving the sheriff's wife away from her sympathy for her husband's position and towards identification with the accused woman. Mrs. Hale chooses the latter course and sets about persuading Mrs. Peters to emerge, in Alkalay-Gut's words, "as an individual distinct from her role as sheriff's wife." Once that happens, "her identification with Minnie is rapid and becomes complete."[9]

The persuasive process begins easily but effectively, with Mrs. Hale reflecting upon the change in Minnie Foster Wright over the thirty or so years she has known her — the change, to use the metaphor that Glaspell will develop, from singing bird to muted caged bird. She follows this reminiscence with a direct question to Mrs. Peters about whether the latter thinks that Minnie killed her husband. "Oh, I don't know," is the frightened response in both works, but, as always, the story provides more insight and tension than does the drama. Still emphasizing in her revision the distance between the women, Glaspell has Mrs. Hale believe that her talk of the youthful Minnie has fallen on deaf ears: "Much difference it makes to her whether Minnie Foster had pretty clothes when she was a girl." This sense of the other woman's indifference to such irrelevant trivialities is occasioned not only by Mrs. Hale's persistent belief in the other woman's official role but also by an odd look that crosses Mrs. Peters's face. At second glance, however, Mrs. Hale notices something

---

[9]"Jury of Her Peers: The Importance of *Trifles*," p. 6.

else that melts her annoyance and undercuts her suspicions about the sheriff's wife: "Then she looked again, and she wasn't so sure; in fact, she hadn't at any time been perfectly sure about Mrs. Peters. She had that shrinking manner, and yet her eyes looked as if they could see a long way into things." Whereas the play shows the women meandering towards concurrence, the short story is here seen to evolve—and part of that evolution, we must conclude, is due to Mrs. Hale's ability to persuade her peer to regard the case from her perspective. The look that she sees in Mrs. Peters's eyes suggests to her that she might be able to persuade her, that the potential for identification is there. Hence, when she asks whether Mrs. Peters thinks Minnie is guilty, the question resonates here in ways the play does not.

Accordingly, Mrs. Hale will become much more aggressive in her arguments hereafter, taking on something of the persuader's hopeful hostility, which, in the case of the story, stands in marked contrast to the hostility she felt for Mrs. Peters's official role earlier. Thus, when Mrs. Peters tries to retreat into a male argument, weakly asserting that "the law is the law," the Mrs. Hale of the short story does not let the remark pass, as the one in *Trifles* does: "the law is the law—and a bad stove is a bad stove. How'd you like to cook on this?" Even she, however, is startled by Mrs. Peters's immediate response to her homey analogy and *ad hominem* attack: "A person gets discouraged—and loses heart," Mrs. Peters says—"That look of seeing . . . through a thing to something else" back on her face.

As far as I am concerned, the addition of this passage is the most important change that Glaspell made in her generic translation. Having used this direct personal attack and having noted the ambivalence that Mrs. Peters feels for her role as sheriff's wife, Mrs. Hale will now proceed to effect closure of the gap between them—again, a gap that is never this widely opened in *Trifles*. Now Mrs. Hale will change her entire mode of attack, pushing the limits, doing things she hesitated doing earlier, assailing Mrs. Peters whenever she lapses into her easy conventional attitudes. For instance, when Mrs. Peters objects to Mrs. Hale's repair of a badly knitted quilt block—in effect, tampering with circumstantial evidence of Minnie's mental disturbance of the day before—Mrs. Hale proceeds to do it anyway. As a measure of how much she has changed, we have only to compare this act with her earlier hesitation to finish another chore for fear of what Mrs. Peters might think. She has no reason to be distrustful of Mrs. Peters any longer, for the process of identification is now well underway.

That identification becomes quite evident by the time the women find the most compelling piece of circumstantial evidence against Mrs. Wright— the broken bird cage and the dead bird, its neck wrung and its body placed in a pretty box in Mrs. Wright's sewing basket. When the men notice the cage and Mrs. Hale misleadingly speculates that a cat may have been at it, it is Mrs. Peters who confirms the matter. Asked by the county attorney whether a cat was on the premises, Mrs. Peters—fully aware that there is no cat and never has been—quickly and evasively replies, "Well, not *now.* . . . They're superstitious, you know; they leave." Not only is Mrs. Peters deliberately lying here, but, more important, she is assuming quite another role from the one she played earlier. Uttering a banality, she plays at being the shallow woman who believes in superstitions, thus consciously playing one of the roles the men expect her to assume and concealing her keen intellect from them, her ability to extrapolate facts from small details.

From this point forward, the play and the short story are essentially the same. Mrs. Hale will continue her persuasive assault, and Mrs. Peters will continue to struggle inwardly. The culmination of this struggle occurs when, late in the story, the county attorney says that "a sheriff's wife is married to the law," and she responds, "Not — just that way." In "Jury," however, this protest carries much greater force than it does in *Trifles* for the simple reason that it is a measure of how far Mrs. Peters has come in the course of the short story.

Appropriately enough, too, Mrs. Hale has the final word in both narratives. Asked derisively by the county attorney what stitch Mrs. Wright had been using to make her quilt, Mrs. Hale responds with false sincerity, "We call it — knot it, Mr. Henderson." Most critics have read this line as an ironic reference to the women's solidarity at this point.[10] That is quite true, but, as I have been suggesting here, the progress towards this solidarity varies subtly but unmistakably in the two narratives. Whereas *Trifles,* opening as it does with the women's close physical proximity, reveals the dichotomy between male and female concepts of justice and social roles, "A Jury of Her Peers" is much more concerned with the separateness of the women themselves and their self-injurious acquiescence in male-defined roles. Hence, in her reworking of the narrative, Glaspell did much more than translate the material from one genre to another. Rather, she subtly changed its theme, and, in so doing, she wrote a story that is much more interesting, resonant, and disturbing than the slighter drama from which it derives.

BENJAMIN NELSON

Benjamin Nelson discussed what he considered the strengths and weaknesses of The Glass Menagerie *in his critical study* Tennessee Williams: The Man and His Work *(1961). Nelson asked himself whether or not the play can be defined as a tragedy, and drew his conclusion after referring to Williams's short fiction.*

Problems in *The Glass Menagerie*   1961

The Glass Menagerie exhibits several of Williams's weaknesses as well as his strengths as a playwright. The great strength of the play is of course the delicate, sympathetic, yet objective creation of meaningful people in a meaningful

---

[10]Beverly Smith sees "the bond among women [as] the essential knot" ("Women's Work," p. 179). Cynthia Sutherland regards the reference to knotting as "a subdued, ironic, and grisly reminder of the manner in which a stifled wife has enacted her desperate retaliation" ("American Women Playwrights," p. 323). And Elaine Hedges argues that the reference has three meanings: the rope that Minnie knotted around her husband's neck; the bond among the women; and the fact that the women have tied the men in knots ("Small Things Reconsidered," p. 107).

situation. Williams has caught a decisive and desperate moment in the lives of four individuals and given it illumination and a sense of deep meaning—no small feat for any writer.

His characterizations are not equally realized. He has been unable to create Laura on more than a single dimension, while Amanda is overwhelming in her multi-faceted delineation. On a more technical level the play manifests a doubt on the part of its author toward the power of the written word. As a backdrop for *The Glass Menagerie,* Williams originally wished to use a screen to register emotions and present images from the past, present, and future. For example, when Jim O'Connor confesses to the family that he is going steady with another girl, the legend on the screen is to read, "The Sky Falls." Fortunately, [actor-director] Eddie Dowling deleted these touches of the poet from his production, but the play still abounds with a number of pretentious statements on the part of Tom as Narrator.

I assume that the final scene between Amanda and Laura is played in pantomime because Williams wished to portray Amanda's dignity through her gestures and her daughter's reaction, rather than through the mother's speech, which during the course of the drama has been either shrill, simpering, or saucy. But in relegating this scene to background silence while Tom makes a self-conscious statement about drifting like a dead leaf "attempting to find in motion what was lost in space," he has substituted a painfully pretentious narration for what could have been an intense and luminous moment between the two women.

Again, on the credit side of the author, his play presents genuine situation, motivation, and, as Joseph Wood Krutch has noted, "a hard substantial core of shrewd observation and deft, economical characterization." But Mr. Krutch also noted that "this hard core is enveloped in a fuzzy haze of pretentious, sentimental, pseudo-poetic verbiage."[1] In *The Glass Menagerie,* the strained lyricism runs parallel with dialogue that is fresh, alive, and highly characteristic, particularly in the speech of Amanda. This dialogue fortunately dominates the proceedings, but the excess of self-conscious "poetical" passages is quite apparent and is a fault of which Williams is to be guilty in much of his later work.

But the great weakness of *The Glass Menagerie* does not lie in its author's artistic or technical deficiencies. The weakness lies at the core of the play and evolves out of what is to become the playwright's hardening philosophical commitment. We can begin to comprehend this when we ask ourselves whether or not *The Glass Menagerie* is a tragedy. It presents a tragic situation and characters who, despite their moodiness and foolishness and self-deception, possess a sense of the tragic. With the possible exception of Laura, they are intensely genuine and the destruction of their dreams and aspirations bears the illusion of great importance. But the play is not a tragedy. The universe of *The Glass Menagerie* does not allow tragedy.

Everyone in the play is a failure and in the course of their drama they all perish a little. Amanda, the most heroic of the quartet, is pitiful but not tragic

---

[1] Joseph Wood Krutch, *The Nation* 14 April 1945: 24.

because from the outset she is doomed to failure despite her desperate struggle to right things. None of these people are given the opportunity to triumph against a fate which is as malignant as it is implacable. Their struggle is a rear-guard action against life, a continuous retreat. This retreat may be moving, pathetic, melodramatic, or boisterous, but it is always a withdrawal. After all, what is the world outside the glass menagerie?

> There was only hot swing music and liquor, dance halls, bars, and movies, and sex that hung in the gloom like a chandelier and flooded the world with brief, deceptive rainbows. . . . All the world was waiting for bombardments!

The world outside the Wingfield apartment is a world of illusions, also, even more deceptive and destructive than those held by Amanda and Laura. It is the world of *Stairs to the Roof* and this time the escape is not to a new star but into the individual and personal illusions fostered by each of the characters as his private defense against destruction. Jim waits for the day when his "zzzzzp!" will at last disperse his fear and uncertainty; Laura creates her own sparkling, cold world which gives the illusion of warmth but is as eternal in its unreality as the glass from which it is composed; Amanda strikes out with all her power against her fate by clinging to the past as to a shield; and Tom, recognizing the plight of his family, can do no more than drift away from them, rudderless, frightened, and never really as far from Amanda and Laura as he knows he should be.

Not one of these individuals can cope with his situation. They struggle and their hopes and the destruction of these hopes possess a sense of great importance because Williams has created genuine people in an intensely genuine situation, but they lack the completeness to truly cope with their dilemma. They are not responsible for what has happened to them and they are much too helpless to do more than delay the inevitable. And destruction is inevitable because it is implicit in the universe of Tennessee Williams.

> For the sins of the world are really only its partialities, and these are what sufferings must atone for. . . . The nature of man is full of such makeshift arrangements, devised by himself to cover his incompletion. He feels a part of himself to be like a missing wall or a room left unfurnished and he tries as well as he can to make up for it. The use of imagination, resorting to dreams or the loftier purpose of art, is a mask he devises to cover his incompletion. Or violence such as a war, between two men or among a number of nations, is also a blind and senseless compensation for that which is not yet formed in human nature. Then there is still another compensation. This one is found in the principle of atonement, the surrender of self to violent treatment by others with the idea of thereby cleansing one's self of his guilt.[2]

This statement emanates from the core of Williams's thought and is perhaps his most illuminating commentary about himself and his work. It represents a philosophy, or let us say an attitude toward man in his universe, which is

---

[2]Tennessee Williams, "Desire and the Black Masseur," *One Arm and Other Stories* (New York, 1948), 85.

to manifest itself in all his work. It is taken from his short story, "Desire and the Black Masseur," which deals with the final compensation cited in the above quotation: purification through violence. In this tale, a man atones for what the author feels is cosmic fragmentation and guilt by allowing — and actually furthering — his destruction by a cannibal. In *Battle of Angels* and *The Purification,* we find this same kind of violent cleansing.

The Glass Menagerie is a far cry from any of these works; it is the most nonviolent drama written by Williams. Nevertheless it adheres to the belief set forth in the short story. The underlying belief in *The Glass Menagerie* is that there is very little, if any, reason for living. Man is by nature incomplete because his universe is fragmented. There is nothing to be done about this condition because nothing *can* be done about it. Human guilt becomes a corollary of universal guilt and man's life is an atonement for the human condition. In each character in *The Glass Menagerie* there is a part "like a missing wall or a room left unfurnished and he tries as well as he can to make up for it." The mask devised by Laura and Amanda and Tom and Jim is "the use of imagination, resorting to dreams." The Wingfields are broken, fragmented people because "the sins of the world are really only its partialities." They are really not at all responsible for their condition, and thus are in no way able to cope with it. They are trapped in a determined universe. Without some kind of responsibility on the part of the protagonist there is opportunity neither for tragic elevation nor tragic fall. The Wingfields were doomed the moment they were born. At best their struggles will allow them to survive . . . for a time. They will never be allowed to triumph. Thus their struggles, their hopes, and even their eventual destruction can never move far beyond pathos. The beauty and magic of *The Glass Menagerie* is that this pathos is genuine, objective, and deeply moving.

HELGE NORMANN NILSEN

Helge Normann Nilsen examines the influence of Marxist theory on Miller's Death of a Salesman. *This commentary is excerpted from an essay that appeared in the journal* English Studies.

Marxism and the Early Plays of Arthur Miller   1994

During the period from the nineteen-thirties through the forties Marxism exercised a controlling influence on Arthur Miller's work. This is evident in several of his earliest, unpublished plays, propaganda pieces advocating the overthrow of capitalism and the establishment of a socialist system.[1] The

---

[1]Miller has described his own and his friends' early adoption of Marxism in his autobiography: "We enjoyed a certain unity within ourselves by virtue of a higher consciousness bestowed by our expectation of a socialist evolution of the planet," *Timebends: A Life* (New York, 1987), p. 70.

political tendency of these plays is too obvious to be ignored, but it has escaped the attention of most readers that the same message is embodied in the first three plays that Miller published. These are *The Man Who Had All the Luck* (1944), *All My Sons* (1947) and *Death of a Salesman* (1949), his most famous work.

If one compares the unpublished plays with the published ones, the common features emerge. American capitalism is criticized and rejected, and an alternative, socialist community and system of values are pointed to. The message is implicit rather than explicit in the printed works, but the political agenda remains the same. The most important reason behind Miller's commitment to radicalism is that the Great Depression created in him a lasting and traumatic impression of the devastating power of economic forces in the shaping of people's lives. This also meant that, in the early plays, he portrayed and analyzed his major characters as products of the American capitalist society and its influence.[2] At the same time he managed to give them individuality and persuasiveness as characters.

Miller's political attitudes at the time emerge mainly in the plays in question, but are also described in his autobiography. They fall within the tradition of analysis and criticism of capitalism established by Marx and the movements building on his theories. Miller's critique can be summed up as follows: capitalism is inhuman in its glorification of private property and its exclusive orientation toward profitmaking. Human beings are sacrificed to economic interests in ways that are not only immoral, but even criminal in nature. In business, ruthless competition is the norm. People's moral character is threatened. They may become scoundrels, or rendered insane and suicidal. Egocentric individualism reigns supreme, and society fosters no sense of responsibility to anyone beyond self and family. There is an unjust concentration of financial power into a few hands, making all others powerless and bereft of economic security. The capitalists also control most of the cultural life of society and the media, spreading their conservative political views. No institution or aspect of society can escape this influence. The false values of materialism and the cult of success threaten to extinguish human love and caring. Conformism rules, turning people into mere cogs in the machine of production, and genuine individualism and even enjoyment of life become hard to obtain. The coming socialist society, on the other hand, will be built on solidarity, human brotherhood, and the ownership of the workers and citizens of the means of production.[3] . . .

---

[2]In the early forties Miller attended a Marxist study group and was proposed for membership in the American Communist Party. In the *New York Times*, May 25, 1947, his name appeared on a list of sponsors of the World Youth Festival, organized by the communist World Federation of Democratic Youth. See J. Schlueter and J. K. Flanagan, *Arthur Miller* (New York, 1987), pp. 6, 146.

[3]Interpreting Marx, R. W. Miller states that: "under socialism and communism, most people are less dominated, more in possession of their lives, since they are better able to develop their capacities in light of their own assessments of their needs. Moreover, their interactions will be governed to a greater extent than now by mutual well-wishing and concern," "Marx and Morality," in *Marxism*, ed. J. R. Pennock and J. W. Chapman (New York, 1983), p. 60.

Death of a Salesman is . . . rooted in the playwright's early, agonized reactions to the Depression. Marxism had taught him that this disaster was one of the vagaries of capitalism, and his early, militant stance is suggested in an observation recorded in a notebook containing an early version of the play: "The restrictions, like all tyrannies, exist by default of revolutionary resistance."[4] The reference is to formal conventions in drama, but the choice of words reveals a political radicalism also.

As in the other plays, victimization by the free play of economic forces is the main theme of *Death of a Salesman*. It is suggested in the initial stage direction: "A melody is heard, played upon a flute. It is small and fine, telling of grass and trees and the horizon. Before us is the salesman's house. We are aware of towering, angular shapes behind it, surrounding it on all sides." The people in the house are threatened and overwhelmed by the tall buildings, symbols of the crushing power of those who win out in a capitalist struggle that has no room for failures and losers.

Willy Loman, the aging salesman, is worn out to the point of breakdown by his many years on the road. But he remains a firm believer in capitalist values and has transferred his hope of success to his son Biff. Willy is a dreamer, and the play contrasts his dreams with the harsh realities of failure and mediocrity that he tries to shut out of his mind. Corrupted, or brainwashed by the system, Willy is blind to its destructiveness and is obsessed by his plans for Biff.

Biff, however, has begun to rebel against his father's ideas and to feel his way towards different standards, meaning those that Miller associates with the socialist society. Unlike his brother Happy, he has "allowed himself to turn his face toward defeat," and even this becomes a possible source of strength for him. His lack of conventional success is slowly teaching him, not that he is worthless, but that he may not be cut out for a business career and may actually be better off without it. He is trying to understand himself and discover his real identity, this also being an aim of socialism as Miller understood it. But Biff is not yet sure of himself, in the first part of the play, and still feels guilty for not being a success. He has returned to his parents in a last attempt to fulfill his father's dreams.

Happy, who has a good job and wants to get further ahead, also has doubts about his own careerism but cannot find anything to put in its place. Biff struggles with this issue, searching for and finally finding another path for himself. However, his father remains a man whose self-respect depends entirely on his role as a breadwinner and useful cog in the production machine. He worships the memory of Ben, the youth who walked into the jungle of Africa at the age of seventeen and came out rich at twenty-one, a powerful *entrepreneur*. What Willy fails to realize is that only a very few can hope to be that successful. His greatest illusion is his belief in the capitalist myth that every man can succeed in business if he only uses his opportunities. Willy is also haunted by the equally superhuman success ideal embodied in his grand-

---

[4]Notebook, in longhand, undated, in the Harry Ransom Humanities Research Center.

father, a heroic pioneer figure who drove across America with his family, supporting them all by selling flutes that he made himself.

The scene in which Willy is fired by his young boss Howard is a perfect illustration of the logic of the capitalist economic mechanism. Willy has been with the firm since before Howard was born, but the almost familiar relationship between these two still counts for nothing. Mortally afraid of ruin, like Keller, Willy appeals to Howard's conscience, reminding him how long and faithfully he has worked for the company, but to no avail. Howard is not evil, however; he is even able to sympathize with Willy's plight, but this in no way interferes with his decision to fire an aging employee who can no longer ring up any sales. Howard, like Ben or Charley, a businessman who is Willy's friend and neighbor, abides by the law of profitability first that is supreme in the world of capitalist business. He is impersonal about it, again like Charley or Ben, regarding it as a law of nature.[5]

Wanting to help Willy, Charley offers him a job, but the former refuses to take it, feeling that it would be a kind of charity and would violate the image he has of himself as a self-reliant, honorable individual who does not depend on others. Rugged individualism is the ideology of the *laissez-faire* capitalism that he believes in so deeply. But the facts are that Willy's failure is destroying him and that Biff's similar fate makes his father reject him. The all-important success ideal prevents Willy from perceiving Biff as a person and an individual. Capitalist values distort and destroy what should have been a rewarding human relationship between father and son.

The horrifying consequences of a blind adherence to these values emerge in Willy's decision to commit suicide so that his life insurance payment will enable Biff to rise in the world. But Biff, like Chris Keller, instead becomes the vehicle through which Miller subtly introduces his alternative socialist perceptions and values into his work. Biff thus becomes the only character in the drama who really understands the destructive nature of capitalist priorities and feels pity and concern for his father, exclaiming: "I can't bear to look at his face!" He tries to make Willy understand the realities of their situation, which is that their lives have been dominated by a dream that is no better than a lie. Biff has realized that the whole family are victims, in various ways and like most people, of capitalist oppression and false standards. They are basically downtrodden people, "a dime a dozen." But this, of course, is the very thing that Willy refuses to admit, and he denies it furiously. Biff tries to impress upon him that they ought to lower their expectations and rely on the comforts of love and human caring. Willy, however, is not willing to correct his capitalist hierarchy of values and accuses Biff of betrayal. His son, he says, is "vengeful" and "spiteful." But Biff continues his attempt to break through to his father's feelings and establish a genuine connection and respect between them. Hence his plaintive cry: "Pop, I'm nothing . . . I'm just what I am, that's all."

---

[5]Brian Parker argues that because Howard and Charley, both capitalists, are ordinary men and not evil, *Death of a Salesman* cannot be an anti-capitalist play. But the fact that these are not bad men does not change the workings of the system that they represent. See "Point of View in Arthur Miller's *Death of a Salesman*," *Arthur Miller: A Collection of Critical Essays* (Englewood Cliffs, 1969), p. 99.

In this central scene, Willy does perceive that his son wants to show him his love, but is unable to respond to this in a simple way. Instead, and in keeping with his blinkered vision, he grotesquely interprets Biff's love as yet another sign of his potentially glorious future, or as a part of the fine personality that will help make him rich: "That boy—that boy is going to be magnificent!" The insurance money will yet secure Biff's success, he thinks, and is deluded enough to assume that his son will be thankful for the sacrifice he is making.

But at Willy Loman's grave it is capitalism and the dreams it is responsible for that are indicted. Looking back on his father's life, Biff firmly declares: "He had the wrong dreams. All, all wrong." *Death of a Salesman* suggests that the right dreams are opposed to rapacious capitalism and that they are about justice, love, and genuine selfhood as envisaged by Marxism.

. . . In *Death of a Salesman* the jobless Willy Loman has become mentally disturbed, his suicide for the sake of money an eloquent testimony to the corrosive effects of the tyrannical success ideal extolled by his society. Willy is a victim, both directly and indirectly, of the logic of a capitalism which says that human worth is proportional to economic achievement. Taken as a whole, these dramas build a powerful indictment against the American capitalist system that Miller knew, but they do not stop at that point. Whether openly or more discreetly, they suggest the possibility of another, just and humane society. This new, socialist world will be built on the principles of love, mutual concern, and sharing rather than competition.

GEORGE BERNARD SHAW

George Bernard Shaw (1856–1950), the British playwright, was one of the first authors to recognize the importance of Ibsen's work in the theater. In The Quintessence of Ibsenism *(1891; rev. ed. 1913) Shaw summarized the plot of the play and analyzed Nora's character with great sensitivity to the social issues that Ibsen had raised in the drama.*

On A Doll House   1891

In the famous [*Doll*] *House,* the pillar of society who owns the doll is a model husband, father, and citizen. In his little household, with the three darling children and the affectionate little wife, all on the most loving terms with one another, we have the sweet home, the womanly woman, the happy family life of the idealist's dream. Mrs. Nora Helmer is happy in the belief that she has attained a valid realization of all these illusions; that she is an ideal wife and mother; and that Helmer is an ideal husband who would, if the necessity arose, give his life to save her reputation. A few simply contrived incidents disabuse her effectually on all these points. One of her earliest acts of devotion to her husband has been the secret raising of a sum of money to enable him to make a tour which was necessary to restore his health. As he would have broken down sooner than go into debt, she has had to persuade him that the money was a gift from her father. It was really obtained from a moneylender, who refused to make her the loan unless she induced her father to endorse the promissory note. This being impossible, as her father was dying at the time, she took the shortest way out of the difficulty by writing the name herself, to the entire satisfaction of the moneylender, who, though not at all duped, knew that forged bills are often the surest to be paid. Since then she has slaved in secret at scrivener's work until she has nearly paid off the debt.

At this point Helmer is made manager of the bank in which he is employed; and the moneylender, wishing to obtain a post there, uses the forged bill to force Nora to exert her influence with Helmer on his behalf. But she, having a hearty contempt for the man, cannot be persuaded by him that there was any harm in putting her father's name on the bill, and ridicules the suggestion that the law would not recognize that she was right under the circumstances. It is her husband's own contemptuous denunciation of a forgery formerly committed by the moneylender himself that destroys her self-satisfaction and opens her eyes to her ignorance of the serious business of the world to which her husband belongs: the world outside the home he shares with her. When he goes on to tell her that commercial dishonesty is generally to be traced to the influence of bad mothers, she begins to perceive that the happy way in which she plays with the children, and the care she takes to dress them nicely, are not sufficient to constitute her a fit person to train them. To redeem the forged bill, she resolves to borrow the balance due upon it from an intimate friend of the family. She has learnt to coax her husband into giving her what she asks by appealing to his affection for her: that is, by playing all sorts of pretty tricks until he is wheedled into an amorous humor. This plan she has adopted without thinking about it, instinctively taking the line of least resistance with him. And now she naturally takes the same line with her husband's friend. An unexpected declaration of love from him is the result; and it at once explains to her the real nature of the domestic influence she has been so proud of.

All her illusions about herself are now shatterd. She sees herself as an ignorant and silly woman, a dangerous mother, and a wife kept for her husband's pleasure merely; but she clings all the harder to her illusion about him: He is still the ideal husband who would make any sacrifice to rescue her from ruin. She resolves to kill herself rather than allow him to destroy his own career by taking the forgery on himself to save her reputation. The final disillusion comes when he, instead of at once proposing to pursue this ideal line of conduct when he hears of the forgery, naturally enough flies into a vulgar rage and heaps invective on her for disgracing him. Then she sees that their whole family life has been a fiction: their home a mere doll's house in which they have been playing at ideal husband and father, wife and mother. So she leaves him then and there and goes out into the real world to find out its reality for herself, and to gain some position not fundamentally false, refusing to see her children again until she is fit to be in charge of them, or to live with him until she and he become capable of a more honorable relation to one another. He at first cannot understand what has happened, and flourishes the shattered ideals over her as if they were as potent as ever. He presents the course most agreeable to him —

that of her staying at home and avoiding a scandal — as her duty to her husband, to her children, and to her religion; but the magic of these disguises is gone; and at last even he understands what has really happened, and sits down alone to wonder whether that more honorable relation can ever come to pass between them.

JOAN TEMPLETON

Joan Templeton prepared her ironic summary of the responses of a dozen critics writing about Ibsen's theme in his famous play for the Publication of the Modern Language Association. *After reading the critics, you may find Templeton's conclusion surprises you in its uncompromising statement of uncommon sense.*

Is *A Doll House* a Feminist Text?   1989

A Doll House *is no more about women's rights than Shakespeare's*
Richard II *is about the divine right of kings, or* Ghosts *about syphilis. . . .
Its theme is the need of every individual to find out the kind of person he or she is and to strive to become that person.*[1]

Ibsen has been resoundingly saved from feminism, or, as it was called in his day, "the woman question." His rescuers customarily cite a statement the dramatist made on 26 May 1898 at a seventieth-birthday banquet given in his honor by the Norwegian Women's Rights League:

> I thank you for the toast, but must disclaim the honor of having consciously worked for the women's rights movement. . . . True enough, it is desirable to solve the woman problem, along with all the others; but that has not been the whole purpose. My task has been the description of humanity.[2]

Ibsen's champions like to take this disavowal as a precise reference to his purpose in writing *A Doll House* twenty years earlier, his "original intention," according to Maurice Valency.[3] Ibsen's biographer Michael Meyer urges all reviewers of *Doll House* revivals to learn Ibsen's speech by heart,[4] and James McFarlane, editor of *The Oxford Ibsen,* includes it in his explanatory material on *A Doll House,* under "Some Pronouncements of the Author," as though Ibsen had been speaking of the play.[5] Whatever propaganda feminists may

---

[1]Michael Meyer, *Ibsen* (Garden City: Doubleday, 1971), 457.

[2]Henrik Ibsen, *Letters and Speeches,* ed. and trans. Evert Sprinchorn (New York: Hill, 1964), 337.

[3]Maurice Valency, *The Flower and the Castle: An Introduction to Modern Drama* (New York: Schocken, 1982), 151.

[4]Meyer, 774.

[5]James McFarlane, *"A Doll's House:* Commentary" in *The Oxford Ibsen,* ed. McFarlane (Oxford UP, 1961), V, 456.

have made of *A Doll House*, Ibsen, it is argued, never meant to write a play about the highly topical subject of women's rights; Nora's conflict represents something other than, or something more than, woman's. In an article commemorating the half century of Ibsen's death, R. M. Adams explains, "*A Doll House* represents a woman imbued with the idea of becoming a person, but it proposes nothing categorical about women becoming people; in fact, its real theme has nothing to do with the sexes."[6] Over twenty years later, after feminism had resurfaced as an international movement, Einar Haugen, the doyen of American Scandinavian studies, insisted that "Ibsen's Nora is not just a woman arguing for female liberation; she is much more. She embodies the comedy as well as the tragedy of modern life."[7] In the Modern Language Association's *Approaches to Teaching* A Doll House, the editor speaks disparagingly of "reductionist views of [*A Doll House*] as a feminist drama." Summarizing a "major theme" in the volume as "the need for a broad view of the play and a condemnation of a static approach," she warns that discussions of the play's "connection with feminism" have value only if they are monitored, "properly channeled and kept firmly linked to Ibsen's text."[8]

Removing the woman question from *A Doll House* is presented as part of a corrective effort to free Ibsen from his erroneous reputation as a writer of thesis plays, a wrongheaded notion usually blamed on Shaw, who, it is claimed, mistakenly saw Ibsen as the nineteenth century's greatest iconoclast and offered that misreading to the public as *The Quintessence of Ibsenism.* Ibsen, it is now de rigueur to explain, did not stoop to "issues." He was a poet of the truth of the human soul. That Nora's exit from her dollhouse has long been the principal international symbol for women's issues, including many that far exceed the confines of her small world, is irrelevant to the essential meaning of *A Doll House*, a play, in Richard Gilman's phrase, "pitched beyond sexual difference."[9] Ibsen, explains Robert Brustein, "was completely indifferent to (the woman question) except as a metaphor for individual freedom."[10] Discussing the relation of *A Doll House* to feminism, Halvdan Koht, author of the definitive Norwegian Ibsen life, says in summary, "Little by little the topical controversy died away; what remained was the work of art, with its demand for truth in every human relation."[11]

Thus, it turns out, the *Uncle Tom's Cabin* of the women's rights movement is not really about women at all. "Fiddle-faddle," pronounced R. M. Adams, dismissing feminist claims for the play.[12] Like angels, Nora has no sex. Ibsen meant her to be Everyman.

---

[6]R. M. Adams, "The Fifty-First Anniversary," *Hudson Review* 10 (1957), 416.

[7]Einar Haugen, *Ibsen's Drama: Author to Audience* (Minneapolis: U of Minnesota P, 1979), vii.

[8]Yvonne Shafer, ed., *Approaches to Teaching Ibsen's* A Doll House (New York: MLA, 1985), 32.

[9]Richard Gilman, *The Making of Modern Drama* (New York: Farrar, 1972), 65.

[10]Robert Brustein, *The Theatre of Revolt* (New York: Little, 1962), 105.

[11]Halvdan Koht, *Life of Ibsen* (New York: Blom, 1971), 323.

[12]Adams, 416.

TENNESSEE WILLIAMS

Tennessee Williams published his notes describing how he envisioned an ideal production of The Glass Menagerie *on the stage in 1945, soon after the play had survived its shaky premiere at the Civic Theatre in Chicago. Jo Mielziner designed the sets and Paul Bowles composed the music for the original production. The play caught on with audiences because in the first three weeks of its run it was championed almost daily in laudatory articles by the* Chicago Tribune *theater critic Claudia Cassidy. As Donald Spoto wrote in* The Kindness of Strangers: The Life of Tennessee Williams *(1985), "In an unusual example of journalistic salvation, a play was for once not lost but kept alive because of critical support."*

Production Notes
to *The Glass Menagerie*   1945

Being a "memory play," *The Glass Menagerie* can be presented with unusual freedom of convention. Because of its considerably delicate or tenuous material, atmospheric touches and subtleties of direction play a particularly important part. Expressionism and all other unconventional techniques in drama have only one valid aim, and that is a closer approach to truth. When a play employs unconventional techniques, it is not, or certainly shouldn't be, trying to escape its responsibility of dealing with reality, or interpreting experience, but is actually or should be attempting to find a closer approach, a more penetrating and vivid expression of things as they are. The straight realistic play with its genuine Frigidaire and authentic ice cubes, its characters that speak exactly as its audience speaks, corresponds to the academic landscape and has the same virtue of a photographic likeness. Everyone should know nowadays the unimportance of the photographic in art: that truth, life, or reality is an organic thing which the poetic imagination can represent or suggest, in essence, only through transformation, through changing into other forms than those which were merely present in appearance.

These remarks are not meant as a preface only to this particular play. They have to do with a conception of a new, plastic theater which must take the place of the exhausted theater of realistic conventions if the theater is to resume vitality as a part of our culture.

The Screen Device. There is *only one important difference between the original and acting version of the play* and that is the *omission* in the latter of the device which I tentatively included in my *original* script. This device was the use of a screen on which were projected magic-lantern slides bearing images or titles. I do not regret the omission of this device from the present Broadway production. The extraordinary power of Miss Taylor's° performance made it suitable to have the utmost simplicity in the physical production. But I

Miss Taylor's: Laurette Taylor (1884–1946) played the role of Amanda in the original Broadway production.

think it may be interesting to some readers to see how this device was conceived. So I am putting it into the published manuscript. These images and legends, projected from behind, were cast on a section of wall between the front-room and dining-room areas, which should be indistinguishable from the rest when not in use.

The purpose of this will probably be apparent. It is to give accent to certain values in each scene. Each scene contains a particular point (or several) which is structurally the most important. In an episodic play, such as this, the basic structure or narrative line may be obscured from the audience; the effect may seem fragmentary rather than architectural. This may not be the fault of the play so much as a lack of attention in the audience. The legend or image upon the screen will strengthen the effect of what is merely allusion in the writing and allow the primary point to be made more simply and lightly than if the entire responsibility were on the spoken lines. Aside from this structural value, I think the screen will have a definite emotional appeal, less definable but just as important. An imaginative producer or director may invent many other uses for this device than those indicated in the present script. In fact the possibilities of the device seem much larger to me than the instance of this play can possibly utilize.

The Music. Another extra-literary accent in this play is provided by the use of music. A single recurring tune, "The Glass Menagerie," is used to give emotional emphasis to suitable passages. This tune is like circus music, not when you are on the grounds or in the immediate vicinity of the parade, but when you are at some distance and very likely thinking of something else. It seems under those circumstances to continue almost interminably and it weaves in and out of your preoccupied consciousness; then it is the lightest, most delicate music in the world and perhaps the saddest. It expresses the surface vivacity of life with the underlying strain of immutable and inexpressible sorrow. When you look at a piece of delicately spun glass you think of two things: how beautiful it is and how easily it can be broken. Both of those ideas should be woven into the recurring tune, which dips in and out of the play as if it were carried on a wind that changes. It serves as a thread of connection and allusion between the narrator with his separate point in time and space and the subject of his story. Between each episode it returns as reference to the emotion, nostalgia, which is the first condition of the play. It is primarily Laura's music and therefore comes out most clearly when the play focuses upon her and the lovely fragility of glass which is her image.

The Lighting. The lighting in the play is not realistic. In keeping with the atmosphere of memory, the stage is dim. Shafts of light are focused on selected areas or actors, sometimes in contradistinction to what is the apparent center. For instance, in the quarrel scene between Tom and Amanda, in which Laura has no active part, the clearest pool of light is on her figure. This is also true of the supper scene, when her silent figure on the sofa should remain the visual center. The light upon Laura should be distinct from the others, having a peculiar pristine clarity such as light used in early religious portraits of female saints or madonnas. A certain correspondence to light in religious paintings, such as El Greco's,° where the figures are radiant in atmosphere that is relatively dusky, could be effectively used throughout the play. (It will also permit a more effective use of the screen.) A free, imaginative use of light can be of enormous value in giving a mobile, plastic quality to plays of a more or less static nature.

Tennessee Williams wrote the story "Portrait of a Girl in Glass" in 1943. He turned the story into a play, The Gentleman Caller, *while he was under contract with M-G-M and then rewrote the script as* The Glass Menagerie, *which opened in Chicago in December 1944.*

Williams continued writing short stories in addition to plays for most of his life. "Portrait of a Girl in Glass" was published in 1948 in his first collection of short fiction, One Arm and Other Stories. *An autobiographical story, it is based on Williams's close relationship with his sister, Rose, who was institutionalized after her prefrontal lobotomy in 1937. Williams used his own name Tom for himself as one of the characters in the story, and he called the character based on his sister Laura. The story takes place in St. Louis in the early 1930s, during the Depression, at a time when Williams had been taken out of college by his father to work at the International Shoe Company, where his father had found a job fifteen years before.*

Portrait of a Girl in Glass   1948

We lived in a third floor apartment on Maple Street in Saint Louis, on a block which also contained the Ever-ready Garage, a Chinese laundry, and a bookie shop disguised as a cigar store.

Mine was an anomalous character, one that appeared to be slated for radical change or disaster, for I was a poet who had a job in a warehouse. As for my sister Laura, she could be classified even less readily than I. She made no positive motion toward the world but stood at the edge of the water, so to speak, with feet that anticipated too much cold to move. She'd never have budged an inch, I'm pretty sure, if my mother who was a relatively aggressive sort of woman had not shoved her roughly forward, when Laura was twenty years old, by enrolling her as a student in a nearby business college. Out of her "magazine money" (she sold subscriptions to women's magazines), Mother had paid my sister's tuition for a term of six months. It did not work out. Laura tried to memorize the typewriter keyboard, she had a chart at home, she used to sit silently in front of it for hours, staring at it while she cleaned and polished her infinite number of little glass ornaments. She did this every evening after dinner. Mother would caution me to be very quiet. "Sister is looking at her typewriter chart!" I felt somehow that it would do her no good, and I was

---

El Greco: Painter (1541–1614) known for the uncanny lighting in his large canvases.

right. She would seem to know the positions of the keys until the weekly speed drill got underway, and then they would fly from her mind like a bunch of startled birds.

At last she couldn't bring herself to enter the school any more. She kept this failure a secret for a while. She left the house each morning as before and spent six hours walking around the park. This was in February, and all the walking outdoors regardless of weather brought on influenza. She was in bed for a couple of weeks with a curiously happy little smile on her face. Of course Mother phoned the business college to let them know she was ill. Whoever was talking on the other end of the line had some trouble, it seems, in remembering who Laura was, which annoyed my mother and she spoke up pretty sharply. "Laura has been attending that school of yours for two months, you certainly ought to recognize her name!" Then came the stunning disclosure. The person sharply retorted, after a moment or two, that now she *did* remember the Wing-field girl, and that she had not been at the business college *once* in about a month. Mother's voice became strident. Another person was brought to the phone to verify the statement of the first. Mother hung up and went to Laura's bedroom where she lay with a tense and frightened look in place of the faint little smile. Yes, admitted my sister, what they said was true. "I couldn't go any longer, it scared me too much, it made me sick at the stomach!"

After this fiasco, my sister stayed at home and kept in her bedroom mostly. This was a narrow room that had two windows on a dusky areaway between two wings of the building. We called this areaway Death Valley for a reason that seems worth telling. There were a great many alley cats in the neighborhood and one particularly vicious dirty white Chow who stalked them continually. In the open or on the fire escapes they could usually elude him but now and again he cleverly contrived to run some youngster among them into the cul-de-sac of this narrow areaway at the far end of which, directly beneath my sister's bedroom windows, they made the blinding discovery that what had appeared to be an avenue of escape was really a locked arena, a gloomy vault of concrete and brick with walls too high for any cat to spring, in which they must suddenly turn to spit at their death until it was hurled upon them. Hardly a week went by without a repetition of this violent drama. The areaway had grown to be hateful to Laura because she could not look out on it with-out recalling the screams and the snarls of killing. She kept the shades drawn down, and as Mother would not permit the use of electric current except when needed, her days were spent almost in perpetual twilight. There were three pieces of dingy ivory furniture in the room, a bed, a bureau, a chair. Over the bed was a remarkably bad religious painting, a very effeminate head of Christ with teardrops visible just below the eyes. The charm of the room was pro-duced by my sister's collection of glass. She loved colored glass and had covered the walls with shelves of little glass articles, all of them light and delicate in color. These she washed and polished with endless care. When you entered the room there was always this soft, transparent radiance in it which came from the glass absorbing whatever faint light came through the shades on Death Valley. I have no idea how many articles there were of this delicate glass. There must have been hundreds of them. But Laura could tell you exactly. She loved each one.

She lived in a world of glass and also a world of music. The music came from a 1920 victrola and a bunch of records that dated from about the same period, pieces such as "Whispering" or "The Love Nest" or "Dardanella." These records were souvenirs of our father, a man whom we barely remembered, whose name was spoken rarely. Before his sudden and unexplained disappearance from our lives, he had made this gift to the household, the phonograph and the records, whose music remained as a sort of apology for him. Once in a while, on payday at the warehouse, I would bring home a new record. But Laura seldom cared for these new records, maybe because they reminded her too much of the noisy tragedies in Death Valley or the speed drills at the business college. The tunes she loved were the ones she had always heard. Often she sang to herself at night in her bedroom. Her voice was thin, it usually wandered off-key. Yet it had a curious child-like sweetness. At eight o'clock in the evening I sat down to write in my own mousetrap of a room. Through the closed doors, through the walls, I would hear my sister singing to herself, a piece like "Whispering" or "I Love You" or "Sleepy Time Gal," losing the tune now and then but always preserving the minor atmosphere of the music. I think that was why I always wrote such strange and sorrowful poems in those days. Because I had in my ears the wispy sound of my sister serenading her pieces of colored glass, washing them while she sang or merely looking down at them with her vague blue eyes until the points of gem-like radiance in them gently drew the arching particles of reality from her mind and finally produced a state of hypnotic calm in which she even stopped singing or washing the glass and merely sat without motion until my mother knocked at the door and warned her against the waste of electric current.

I don't believe that my sister was actually foolish. I think the petals of her mind had simply closed through fear, and it's no telling how much they had closed upon in the way of secret wisdom. She never talked very much, not even to me, but once in a while she did pop out with something that took you by surprise.

After work at the warehouse or after I'd finished my writing in the evening, I'd drop in her room for a little visit because she had a restful and soothing effect on nerves that were worn rather thin from trying to ride two horses simultaneously in two opposite directions.

I usually found her seated in the straight-back ivory chair with a piece of glass cupped tenderly in her palm.

"What are you doing? Talking to it?" I asked.

"No," she answered gravely, "I was just looking at it."

On the bureau were two pieces of fiction which she had received as Christmas or birthday presents. One was a novel called the *Rose-Garden Husband* by someone whose name escapes me. The other was *Freckles* by Gene Stratton Porter. I never saw her reading the *Rose-Garden Husband,* but the other book was one that she actually lived with. It had probably never occurred to Laura that a book was something you read straight through and then laid aside as finished. The character Freckles, a one-armed orphan youth who worked in a lumber camp, was someone that she invited into her bedroom now and then for a friendly visit just as she did me. When I came in and found this novel open upon her lap, she would gravely remark that Freckles was having some trouble with the foreman of the lumber camp or that he had just received an injury to his spine when a tree fell on him. She frowned with genuine sorrow when she reported these misadventures of her story-book hero, possibly not recalling how successfully he came through them all, that the injury to the spine fortuitously resulted in the discovery of rich parents and that the bad-tempered foreman had a heart of gold at the end of the book. Freckles became involved in romance with a girl he called The Angel, but my sister usually stopped reading when this girl became too prominent in the story. She closed the book or turned back to the lonelier periods in the orphan's story. I only remember her making one reference to this heroine of the novel. "The Angel is nice," she said, "but seems to be kind of conceited about her looks."

Then one time at Christmas, while she was trimming the artificial tree, she picked up the Star of Bethlehem that went on the topmost branch and held it gravely toward the chandelier.

"Do stars have five points really?" she enquired.

This was the sort of thing that you didn't believe and that made you stare at Laura with sorrow and confusion.

"No," I told her, seeing she really meant it, "they're round like the earth and most of them much bigger."

She was gently surprised by this new information. She went to the window to look up at the sky which was, as usual during Saint Louis winters, completely shrouded by smoke.

"It's hard to tell," she said, and returned to the tree.

So time passed on till my sister was twenty-three. Old enough to be married, but the fact of the matter was she had never even had a date with a boy. I don't believe this seemed as awful to her as it did to Mother.

At breakfast one morning Mother said to me, "Why don't you cultivate some nice young friends? How about down at the warehouse? Aren't there some young men down there you could ask to dinner?"

This suggestion surprised me because there was seldom quite enough food on her table to satisfy three people. My mother was a terribly stringent housekeeper, God knows we were poor enough in actuality, but my mother had an almost obsessive dread of becoming even poorer. A not unreasonable fear since the man of the house was a poet who worked in a warehouse, but one which I thought played too important a part in all her calculations.

Almost immediately Mother explained herself.

"I think it might be nice," she said, "for your sister."

I brought Jim home to dinner a few nights later. Jim was a big red-haired Irishman who had the scrubbed and polished look of well-kept chinaware. His big square hands seemed to have a direct and very innocent hunger for touching his friends. He was always clapping them on your arms or shoulders and they burned through the cloth of your shirt like plates taken out of an oven. He was the best-liked man in the warehouse and oddly enough he was the only one that I was on good terms with. He found me agreeably ridiculous, I think. He knew of my secret practice of retiring to a cabinet in the lavatory and working on rhyme schemes when work was slack in the warehouse, and of sneaking up on the roof now and then to smoke my cigarette with a view across the river at the undulant open country of Illinois. No doubt I was classified as screwy in Jim's mind as much as in the others', but while their attitude was suspicious and hostile when they first knew me, Jim's was warmly tolerant from the beginning. He called me Slim, and gradually his cordial acceptance drew the others around, and while he remained the only one who actually had anything to do with me, the others had now begun to smile when they saw me as people smile at an oddly fashioned dog who crosses their path at some distance.

Nevertheless it took some courage for me to invite Jim to dinner. I thought about it all week and delayed the action till Friday noon, the last possible moment, as the dinner was set for that evening.

"What are you doing tonight?" I finally asked him.

"Not a God damn thing," said Jim. "I had a date but her Aunt took sick and she's hauled her freight to Centralia!"

"Well," I said, "why don't you come over for dinner?"

"Sure!" said Jim. He grinned with astonishing brightness.

I went outside to phone the news to Mother.

Her voice that was never tired responded with an energy that made the wires crackle.

"I suppose he's Catholic?" she said.

"Yes," I told her, remembering the tiny silver cross on his freckled chest.

"Good!" she said. "I'll bake a salmon loaf!"

And so we rode home together in his jalopy.

I had a curious feeling of guilt and apprehension as I led the lamb-like Irishman up three flights of cracked marble steps to the door of Apartment F, which was not thick enough to hold inside it the odor of baking salmon.

Never having a key, I pressed the bell.

"Laura!" came Mother's voice. "That's Tom and Mr. Delaney! Let them in!"

There was a long, long pause.

"Laura?" she called again. "I'm busy in the kitchen, you answer the door!"

Then at last I heard my sister's footsteps. They went right past the door at which we were standing and into the parlor. I heard the creaking noise of the phonograph crank. Music commenced. One of the oldest records, a march of Sousa's, put on to give her the courage to let in a stranger.

The door came timidly open and there she stood in a dress from Mother's wardrobe, a black chiffon ankle-length and high-heeled slippers on which she balanced uncertainly like a tipsy crane of melancholy plumage. Her eyes stared back at us with a glassy brightness and her delicate wing-like shoulders were hunched with nervousness.

"Hello!" said Jim, before I could introduce him.

He stretched out his hand. My sister touched it only for a second.

"Excuse me!" she whispered, and turned with a breathless rustle back to her bedroom door, the sanctuary beyond it briefly revealing itself with the tinkling, muted radiance of glass before the door closed rapidly but gently on her wraith-like figure.

Jim seemed to be incapable of surprise.

"Your sister?" he asked.

"Yes, that was her," I admitted. "She's terribly shy with strangers."

"She looks like you," said Jim, "except she's pretty."

Laura did not reappear till called to dinner. Her place was next to Jim at the drop-leaf table and all through the meal her figure was slightly tilted away from his. Her face was feverishly bright and one eyelid, the one on the side toward Jim, had developed a nervous wink. Three times in the course of the dinner she dropped her fork on her plate with a terrible clatter and she was continually raising the water glass to her lips for hasty little gulps. She went on doing this even after the water was gone from the glass. And her handling of the silver became more awkward and hurried all the time.

I thought of nothing to say.

To Mother belonged the conversational honors, such as they were. She asked the caller about his home and family. She was delighted to learn that his father had a business of his own, a retail shoe store somewhere in Wyoming. The news that he went to night school to study accounting was still more edifying. What was his heart set on beside the warehouse? Radio-engineering? My, my, my! It was easy to see that here was a very up-and-coming young man who was certainly going to make his place in the world!

Then she started to talk about her children. Laura, she said, was not cut out for business. She was domestic, however, and making a home was really a girl's best bet.

Jim agreed with all this and seemed not to sense the ghost of an implication. I suffered through it dumbly, trying not to see Laura trembling more and more beneath the incredible unawareness of Mother.

And bad as it was, excruciating in fact, I thought with dread of the moment when dinner was going to be over, for then the diversion of food would be taken away, we would have to go into the little steam-heated parlor. I fancied the four of us having run out of talk, even Mother's seemingly endless store of questions about Jim's home and his job all used up finally — the four of us, then, just sitting there in the parlor, listening to the hiss of the radiator and nervously clearing our throats in the kind of self-consciousness that gets to be suffocating.

But when the blancmange was finished, a miracle happened.

Mother got up to clear the dishes away. Jim gave me a clap on the shoulders and said, "Hey, Slim, let's go have a look at those old records in there!"

He sauntered carelessly into the front room and flopped down on the floor beside the victrola. He began sorting through the collection of worn-out records and reading their titles aloud in a voice so hearty that it shot like beams of sunlight through the vapors of self-consciousness engulfing my sister and me.

He was sitting directly under the floor-lamp and all at once my sister jumped up and said to him, "Oh — you have freckles!"

Jim grinned. "Sure that's what my folks call me — Freckles!"

23.

Conversations on Plays and Playwrights

WILLIAM SHAKESPEARE

Conversations on *Hamlet* as Text and Performance

These Conversations on Shakespeare's Hamlet *contain several items to help you understand the play. The section begins with a commentary by Geoffrey Bullough, who discusses two early treatments of this basic plot closer to Shakespeare's time, one by the French historian François de Belleforest (1530–1583) and the other by the Elizabethan playwright Thomas Kyd (1558–1594), whose play* The Spanish Tragedy *was the most popular revenge tragedy in the London theater before Shakespeare's* Hamlet. *Bullough speculates that one of the plays Kyd wrote shortly before Shakespeare created his version of the popular story might have been the original* Hamlet. *The text of this play (nicknamed "the Ur-Hamlet" by modern historians) unfortunately has not survived. Bullough's discussion of the role of the ghost in* Hamlet *is continued by the critic H. D. F. Kitto, whose reading analyzes the similarities between Shakespeare's play and Sophocles'* Oedipus the King.*

Next, the excerpt from the letter by the English Romantic poet John Keats to his brothers on December 21, 1817, contains his comments on what he calls Shakespeare's "negative capability." This term has been widely discussed by generations of critics since the publication of Keats's letter. Some interpret it as Shakespeare's ability as a dramatist to lose his identity in the creation of a wide range of characters. Others believe that Keats meant that as a poet Shakespeare was able to deal with uncertainty, that he did not adhere (as did Milton in Paradise Lost, *for example) to the strict tenets of religion or moral philosophy, trusting his "sense of Beauty" instead.*

Virginia Woolf's speculation about what would have happened if Shakespeare had a sister is from her book A Room of One's Own *(1929). Woolf's description of how a woman's life differed from a man's life in Elizabethan England helps us understand how this brilliant playwright, possibly the most articulate person ever to create works of literature in English, could be the father of two daughters who signed legal documents with an "X" and probably were illiterate. (See historian S. Schoenbaum's* William Shakespeare: A Compact Documentary Life *[1977].)*

The final commentaries by a contemporary playwright, an actor, and a theater critic are some responses to Hamlet *inspired by the idea of the play in performance. Photographs of actual performances accompany them. In 1979, the English playwright Tom Stoppard wrote a two-part play,* Dogg's Hamlet, Cahoot's Macbeth, *in which* Dogg's Hamlet *was meant to be a farcical version of Shakespeare's play. Stoppard intended it as an encore to a performance of* Hamlet *enacted on top of a double-decker London bus. The eminent English actor John Gielgud describes in his autobiography,* Early Stages *(1939), how he prepared for the demanding role of Hamlet on the stage. The American theater critic John Lahr reviews the performance of actor Ralph Fiennes as Hamlet in a landmark 1995 production of the play that created what Lahr describes as a melodramatic and highly effective "climate of delirium" on Broadway. Lahr also discusses the costumes and stage settings of the production, which the play's director, Jonathan Kent, set in Edwardian England.*

An image of William Shakespeare included on the First Folio, a collected edition of Shakespeare plays published seven years after his death. (Reprinted by permission of The Folger Shakespeare Library.)

GEOFFREY BULLOUGH

Sources of Shakespeare's *Hamlet*   1973

There was no Ghost in Saxo [Grammaticus] or [François de] Belleforest, but it was the feature of the *Ur-Hamlet* which most affected spectators and lingered on in public memory, so that in 1596 Thomas Lodge (in *Wits Miserie*) described a devil looking "as pale as the Visard of the ghost which cried so miserably at the Theatre, like an oister-wife, Hamlet, revenge."

When [Thomas] Kyd, or whoever else wrote it, adapted Belleforest's tale in terms of Senecan drama,° he dealt only with the first part of Amleth's life until his triumph over Feng, and changed the climax of that to make it tragic and (no doubt) easier to stage. The main factors shaping the altered plot were the secrecy of Amleth's father's murder and the introduction of his Ghost to incite the hero to revenge. Whereas in *The Spanish Tragedy* the Ghost of Andrea (killed before the play opens) accompanies Revenge to watch the action and "serve for Chorus in this tragedie," taking no part in the action save to express impatience at the slowness with which punishment falls on the wicked, in the *Ur-Hamlet* the father's Ghost really had some reason for demanding vengeance, and presumably started off the action by revealing it. This was a new departure in ghostly behaviour,[1] and it makes me believe that *Hamlet* was written after *The Spanish Tragedy*.

Seneca's dramas lacked the religious attitude of Greek tragedy and the theme of personal revenge superseded divine retribution; horror became a dominant effect, and the Senecan Chorus contributed to this.[2] Thus at the beginning of *Agamemnon*, Thyestes' Ghost rises from Hell to describe his own adultery with his brother Atreus' wife, and how Atreus took revenge by feasting him on the flesh of his own son; tells too how he raped his own daughter Pelopea (who later married Atreus) and had by her a son, Aegysthus, who is now Clytemnestra's paramour and will shortly help her murder Thyestes' nephew, her husband Agamemnon. The Ghost does not interfere in the action; it expounds the past and prepares the atmosphere of horror. The *Agamemnon* also has a scene in which Electra accuses her mother of adultery and murder — a striking anticipation of the closet-scene in *Hamlet*. The Amleth saga was in this tradition of fraternal hate and incest; hence no doubt its appeal to Elizabethan Senecan playwrights.

In *Troades* Talthybius tells how the Ghost of Achilles demanded the sacrifice of Polyxena (whom he had loved while living) before the Greek fleet could sail from Troy. In the Latin play this ghost did not appear in person, but Jasper Heywood introduced it in Act II of his translation, craving revenge on the Trojans.[3] Ignoring this proof of survival after death, Seneca's Chorus later doubts whether the soul lives on. There is a resemblance here to the apparent inconsistency in *Hamlet* where, soon after accepting the Ghost as his "father's spirit," the hero speaks of "the undiscover'd country from whose bourn / No traveller returns."

Professor Eleanor Prosser's study of the ghosts in Elizabethan drama shows that many act as Chorus or Prologue, or as the retributory voices of conscience, and that these are almost all pagan ghosts risen from Hades.[4] Few

---

Senecan drama: Tragedies by the Roman playwright and Stoic philosopher Seneca (4 B.C.–A.D. 65).

[1]Cf. F. T. Bowers, *Elizabethan Revenge Tragedy*, Gloucester, Mass., 1940; E. Prosser, *Hamlet and Revenge*, Stanford, 1967.

[2]H. B. Charlton, *The Senecan Tradition in Renaissance Tragedy*, 1946.

[3]Cf. G. Ll. Evans, "Shakespeare, Seneca and the Kingdom of Violence," in *Roman Drama*, ed. T. A. Dorey and D. R. Dudley, 1965.

[4]E. Prosser, *op. cit.* Appendix A.

ghosts show Christian characteristics. After *Hamlet* three or four mingle Christian and pagan qualities. Only Andrugio in *Antonio's Revenge* (probably derived from the *Ur-Hamlet*) and the Ghost in *Hamlet* "appear to a protagonist to command blood revenge." (This occasionally occurred in Italian Senecan tragedies.) Andrugio's Ghost comes from his coffin to demand that his son

> Invent some stratagem of vengeance
> Which, but to think on, may like lightning glide
> With horror through thy breast.

He combines delight in the most awful tortures with assurances that he is in league with Heaven. But the play is so confused in tone that some critics have regarded it as a parody. Old Hamlet's Ghost is unique in the problems it posits, and "Shakespeare may well have intended to jolt his audience into a fresh response to what had become a hackneyed convention."[5] It is extremely unlikely that the inventor of Andrea in *The Spanish Tragedy* also created a spirit so complex as that in *Hamlet* Q2.

This is not a suitable place in which to enter the debate about the nature of this ghost. W. W. Greg's suggestion that it is a figment of Hamlet's imagination was countered by E. Stoll who thought it an objectivation of Elizabethan popular lore. For J. D. Wilson it was an occasion for Shakespeare to present three different attitudes to ghosts: the Catholic view (of Marcellus and Bernardo) that a soul could come from Purgatory; the sceptical view of Horatio (like Reginald Scot's) but soon changed to belief; and Hamlet's Protestant view (held by L. Lavater and James VI) that ghosts were probably devils but might be angels, never the souls of men. Another school of thought, including Roy W. Battenhouse and Miss Prosser, argues that the Ghost is a damned spirit come to mislead Hamlet into offending against the divine injunction against revenge.

My own view is nearer to that of I. J. Semper who saw the Ghost as a visitant from Purgatory and that of Sister Miriam who sees Hamlet as justifiably doubting and testing it. But we should not exaggerate the doctrinal strictness of Shakespeare's approach or assume that he was a Catholic because he used the idea of Purgatory. P. N. Siegel was right to insist: "The Hamlet Ghost is a compound of the Senecan revenge ghost, the Catholic purgatorial spirit and the popular graveyard spook, created for an audience prepared by theatrical tradition, by what Cardinal Newman called "floating religious opinions" (as against official dogma) and by current folklore to give it dramatic credence."[6] The pagan element appears in the Ghost's insistence on quasi-physical horrors unspeakable and the reference to "Lethe wharf"; its purgatorial quality in [act 1, scene 5]. It has an almost Miltonic apprehension of virtue and vice; it loves the Sacraments and deeply regrets having died. "Unhousel'd, disappointed, unaneal'd." Its folklore features include the hour when it walks and when it disappears, and its knocking underground.

---

[5]Prosser, *op. cit.* pp. 101–102.
[6]P. N. Siegel, "Discerning the Ghost in *Hamlet,*" *PMLA*, lxxviii, 1963, p. 148.

H. D. F. KITTO

Hamlet and the *Oedipus* 1956

The *Oedipus Tyrannus*° begins by describing twice, once in dialogue and once in lyrics, the plague which is afflicting Thebes. The cause of the plague is the presence in the city of a man who has done two things foul and unnatural above all others: he has killed his own father, and he is living incestuously with his own mother. The details of the plague are so described that we can see how its nature is strictly proportioned to its cause: to death is added sterility; the soil of Thebes, the animals, and the human kind are all barren. The meaning is obvious—unless we make it invisible by reducing the play to the stature of Tragedy of Character: what Oedipus has done is an affront to what we should call Nature, to what Sophocles calls Dikê; and since it is the first law of Nature, or Dikê, that she cannot indefinitely tolerate what is . . . contrary to Nature, she rises at last against these unpurged affronts. The plague of sterility is the outcome of the unnatural things which Oedipus has done to his parents.

Hamlet begins in the same way. The two soldiers Marcellus and Bernardo, and Horatio, who is both a soldier and a scholar, are almost terrified out of their wits by something so clean contrary to the natural order that

> I might not this believe
> Without the sensible and true avouch
> Of mine own eyes.

Professor Dover Wilson, learned in sixteenth-century demonology, has explained that the eschatology of Horatio and Hamlet is Protestant, that the Ghost is a Catholic ghost, and that Bernardo and Marcellus are plain untheological Elizabethans. On this it would be impertinent for an ignoramus to express an opinion, but it does seem that if the "statists" in Shakespeare's audience, and scholars from the Inns of Court, saw and savoured theological *expertise* in this scene, they would be in danger of missing the main point: that the repeated appearances of the Ghost are something quite outside ordinary experience. Horatio the scholar has heard of something similar, in ancient history, "a little ere the mightiest Julius fell." So perhaps this present unnatural terror "bodes some strange eruption to our state"; or—a less disturbing thought— perhaps the ghost is concerned for some uphoarded treasure hidden in the womb of the Earth.

But at this point Shakespeare decides to write some poetry—and he is never so dangerous as when he is writing poetry:

> It faded on the crowing of the cock.
> Some say that ever 'gainst that season comes
> Wherein our Saviour's birth is celebrated,
> The bird of dawning singeth all night long:
> And then, they say, no spirit dare stir abroad,
> The nights are wholesome; then no planets strike,

Oedipus Tyrannus: "Oedipus the Tyrant," another name for Sophocles' play.

> No fairy takes, nor witch hath power to charm,
> So hallowed and so gracious is the time.

Pretty good, for a simple soldier. The intense and solemn beauty of these verses lifts us, and was designed to lift us, high above the level of Horatio's conjectures. The night "wherein our Saviour's birth is celebrated" is holy and pure beyond all others; therefore these nights which the Ghost makes hideous by rising so incredibly from the grave, are impure beyond most. Unless Greek Tragedy has bemused me, this passage does more than "give a religious background to the supernatural happenings" of the scene;[1] they give the "background," that is, the logical and dynamic centre, of the whole play. We are in the presence of evil. Hamlet's own prophetic soul recognises this as soon as he hears of the Ghost:

> Foul deeds will rise,
> Though all the earth o'erwhelm them, to men's eyes.

If we may assume that Shakespeare had not read Sophocles — and that Hamlet had not read him, at Wittenberg, behind Shakespeare's back — the parallel with the *Oedipus* becomes the more interesting; for when Oedipus has at last discovered the truth the Chorus observes:

> Time sees all, and it has found you out, in your own despite. It exacts
> Dikê from you for that unnatural marriage that united mother with son.

"Foul deeds will rise": there are evils so great that Nature will not allow them to lie unpurged. So, returning to the battlements with Hamlet, and enquiring with him

> Why thy canonized bones, hearsed in death,
> Have burst their cerements; why the sepulchre
> Wherein we saw thee quietly inurned
> Hath o'ped his ponderous and marble jaws
> To cast thee up again —

we learn the cause: fratricide, incest, "Murder most foul, strange and unnatural."

Here, most emphatically stated, are the very foundations and framework of the tragedy. We can, of course, neglect these, and erect a framework of our own which we find more interesting or more congenial to us. We can say, with Dr. Gregg, that the Ghost is all my eye; or, with Professor Dover Wilson, that the first act, "a little play of itself," is "an epitome of the ghost-lore of the age" — in which case it becomes something of a learned Prologue to the real play;[2] or, like Dr. de Madariaga, we can neglect this encircling presence of evil, and substitute what we know of sixteenth-century Court manners; or, again without constant reference to the background which Shakespeare himself

---

[1]Dover Wilson, *What Happens in "Hamlet,"* p. 67.

[2]Or, if it is not this, let it be shown what its organic function is. Shakespeare, having a capacious mind, may well have been keenly interested in contemporary ghost-lore, but our first question is: what has he done with it as a creative artist? Or has he done nothing with it?

erected, we can subtly anatomise the soul and mind of Hamlet, on the assumption that Hamlet is the whole play. But if we do these things, let us not then complain that Shakespeare attempted a task too difficult for him, or conclude that the play is an ineffable mystery. Turning it into "secular" tragedy we shall be using the wrong focus. The correct focus is one which will set the whole action against a background of Nature and Heaven; for this is the background which the dramatist himself has provided.

JOHN KEATS

From a Letter to George and Thomas Keats, 21 December 1817

Hampstead Sunday

My dear Brothers,

I must crave your pardon for not having written ere this. . . .

. . . Brown and Dilke walked with me and back from the Christmas pantomime. I had not a dispute but a disquisition, with Dilke on various subjects; several things dove-tailed in my mind, and at once it struck me what quality went to form a Man of Achievement, especially in Literature and which Shakespeare possessed so enormously — I mean *Negative Capability*, that is, when a man is capable of being in uncertainties, mysteries, doubts, without any irritable reaching after fact and reason — [Samuel Taylor] Coleridge, for instance, would let go by a fine isolated verisimilitude caught from the Penetralium of mystery, from being incapable of remaining content with half-knowledge. This pursued through volumes would perhaps take us no further than this, that with a great poet the sense of Beauty overcomes every other consideration, or rather obliterates all consideration.

[Percy Bysshe] Shelley's poem is out, and there are words about its being objected to as much as "Queen Mab" was. Poor Shelley, I think he has his Quota of good qualities, in sooth la!! Write soon to your most sincere friend and affectionate Brother

John.

VIRGINIA WOOLF

What If Shakespeare Had Had a Sister?   1929

Let me imagine, since facts are so hard to come by, what would have happened had Shakespeare had a wonderfully gifted sister, called Judith, let us say. Shakespeare himself went, very probably — his mother was an heiress — to the grammar school, where he may have learnt Latin — Ovid, Virgil and Horace — and the elements of grammar and logic. He was, it is well known, a wild boy who poached rabbits, perhaps shot a deer, and had, rather sooner than he should have done, to marry a woman in the neighborhood, who bore him a child rather quicker than was right. That escapade sent him to seek his fortune in London. He had, it seemed, a taste for the theater; he began by holding horses at the stage door. Very soon he got work in the theater, became a successful actor, and lived at the hub of the universe, meeting everybody, knowing everybody, practicing his art on the boards, exercising his wits in the streets, and even getting access to the palace of the queen. Meanwhile his extraordinarily gifted sister, let us suppose, remained at home. She was as adventurous, as imaginative, as agog to see the world as he was. But she was not sent to school. She had no chance of learning grammar and logic, let alone of reading Horace and Virgil. She picked up a book now and then, one of her brother's perhaps, and read a few pages. But then her parents came in and told her to mend the stockings or mind the stew and not moon about with books and papers. They would have spoken sharply but kindly, for they were substantial people who knew the conditions of life for a woman and loved their daughter—indeed, more likely than not she was the apple of her father's eye. Perhaps she scribbled some pages up in an apple loft on the sly, but was careful to hide them or set fire to them. Soon, however, before she was out of her teens, she was to be betrothed to the son of a neighboring wool-stapler. She cried out that marriage was hateful to her, and for that she was severely beaten by her father. Then he ceased to scold her. He begged her instead not to hurt him, not to shame him in this matter of her marriage. He would give her a chain of beads or a fine petticoat, he said; and there were tears in his eyes. How could she disobey him? How could she break his heart? The force of her own gift alone drove her to it. She made up a small parcel of her belongings, let herself down by a rope one summer's night, and took the road to London. She was not seventeen. The birds that sang in the hedge were not more musical than she was. She had the quickest fancy, a gift like her brother's, for the tune of words. Like him, she had a taste for the theater. She stood at the stage door; she wanted to act, she said. Men laughed in her face. The manager—a fat, loose-lipped man—guffawed. He bellowed something about poodles dancing and women acting—no woman, he said, could possibly be an actress. He hinted—you can imagine what. She could get no training in her craft. Could she even seek her dinner in a tavern or roam the streets at midnight? Yet her genius was for fiction and lusted to feed abundantly upon the lives of men and women and the study of their ways. At last—for she was very young, oddly like Shakespeare the poet in her face, with the same grey eyes and rounded brows—at last Nick Greene the actor-manager took pity on her; she found herself with child by that gentleman and so—who shall measure the heat and violence of the poet's heart when caught and tangled in a woman's body?—killed herself one winter's night and lies buried at some cross-roads where the omnibuses now stop outside the Elephant and Castle.

That, more or less, is how the story would run, I think, if a woman in Shakespeare's day had had Shakespeare's genius. . . . Any woman born with a great gift in the sixteenth century would certainly have gone crazed, shot herself, or ended her days in some lonely cottage outside the village, half witch, half wizard, feared and mocked at. . . . To have lived a free life in London in the sixteenth century would have meant for a woman who was poet and playwright a nervous stress and dilemma which might well have killed her. Had she survived, whatever she had written would have been twisted and deformed, issuing from a strained and morbid imagination. And undoubtedly, I thought, looking at the shelf where there are no plays by women, her work would have gone unsigned.

TOM STOPPARD

Dogg's Hamlet: The Encore   1979

SCENE: *Staging the play on a double-decker London bus, Stoppard gave directions for two folding screens to be placed left and right at the back of the playing area. The screen on the left had a bolt through the top for a cut-out sun, moon, and crown on hinges to be swung in and out of sight. The other screen had a two-dimensional grave for Ophelia.*

Flourish of trumpets, crown hinges up. Enter Claudius and Gertrude.

CLAUDIUS: Our sometime sister, now our Queen,
  (*Enter Hamlet.*)
  Have we taken to wife.
  (*Crown hinges down.*)
HAMLET: That it should come to this!
  (*Exit Claudius and Gertrude. Wind noise. Moon hinges up. Enter Horatio above.*)
HORATIO: My lord, I saw him yesternight—
  The King, your father.
HAMLET: Angels and ministers of grace defend us!
  (*Exit, running, through rest of speech.*)
  Something is rotten in the state of Denmark.
  (*Enter Ghost above.*)
GHOST: I am thy father's spirit.
  The serpent that did sting thy father's life
  (*Enter Hamlet above.*)
  Now wears his crown.
HAMLET: O my prophetic soul!
  Hereafter I shall think meet
  To put an antic disposition on.
  (*Moon hinges down. Exeunt. Short flourish of trumpets. Enter Polonius below, running. Crown hinges up.*)
POLONIUS: Look where sadly the poor wretch comes.
  (*Exit Polonius, running, Enter Hamlet.*)
HAMLET: I have heard that guilty creatures sitting at a play
  Have by the very cunning of the scene been struck.

(*Enter Claudius, Gertrude, Ophelia, Marcellus, and Horatio joking. All sit to watch imaginary play, puppets appear above screen.*)
If he but blench, I know my course.
(*Masque music. Claudius rises.*)
The King rises!

ALL: Give o'er the play!

(*Exeunt all except Gertrude and Hamlet. Crown hinges down.*)

HAMLET: I'll take the ghost's word for a thousand pounds.
(*Enter Polonius, goes behind arras. Short flourish of trumpets.*)
Mother, you have my father much offended.

GERTRUDE: Help!

POLONIUS: Help, Ho!

HAMLET: (*Stabs Polonius.*) Dead for a ducat, dead!
(*Polonius falls dead offstage. Exit Gertrude and Hamlet. Short flourish of trumpets. Enter Claudius followed by Hamlet.*)

CLAUDIUS: Hamlet, this deed must send thee hence.
(*Exit Hamlet.*)
Do it, England.
(*Exit Claudius. Enter Ophelia, falls to ground. Rises and pulls gravestone to cover herself. Bell tolls twice. Enter Gravedigger and Hamlet.*)

HAMLET: A pirate gave us chase. I alone became their prisoner.
(*Takes skull from Gravedigger.*)
Alas poor Yorick — but soft (*Returns skull to Gravedigger.*)
— This is I,
Hamlet the Dane!
(*Exit Gravedigger. Enter Laertes.*)

LAERTES: The devil take thy soul!
(*They grapple, then break. Enter Osric between them with swords. They draw. Crown hinges up. Enter Claudius and Gertrude with goblets.*)

HAMLET: Come on, Sir!
(*Laertes and Hamlet fight.*)

OSRIC: A hit, a very palpable hit!

CLAUDIUS: Give him the cup. Gertrude, do not drink!

GERTRUDE: I am poisoned! (*Dies.*)

LAERTES: Hamlet, thou art slain! (*Dies.*)

HAMLET: Then venom to thy work! (*Kills Claudius. Crown hinges down.*)
The rest is silence. (*Dies.*)

(*Two shots offstage. End.*)

SIR JOHN GIELGUD

On Playing Hamlet   1939

The last production of my first Old Vic season was *Hamlet*. It was exciting to have the chance of playing it after all, but I did not think it likely that I should give an interesting performance. I had not made a success of Romeo, though I had played the part before, and I considered Richard and Macbeth, in which I had done better work, were both character parts. From my childhood I had had some sort of picture in my mind of these two personages. I could imagine myself at once dressed in their clothes and I tried, in rehearsing and acting them, to forget myself completely, to keep the imagined image fresh and vivid, and to some extent I had succeeded. Hamlet was different. How could I seem great enough, simple enough to say those hackneyed, wonderful lines as if I was thinking of them for the first time? How could I avoid certain passages in the manner of other actors I had seen, how could I put into the part my own personal feelings—many of which fitted the feelings of Hamlet—and yet lift them to a high classical style worthy of the character?

We began to rehearse. Some of the scenes came to me more easily than others; the first appearance of Hamlet particularly—one of my favorite scenes of all the plays I have ever read or acted—sincerity, real emotion, and marvellously simple words to express them in. The second scene, when Hamlet first sees the Ghost, difficult, sudden, technically hard to speak, the following Ghost scene terribly difficult, intensely tiring to act, nothing to say, then, after the Ghost disappears, too many words. Impossible to convey, even with Shakespeare's help, the horror and madness of the situation, the changing tenderness and weary resignation.

The mad scenes. How mad should Hamlet be? So easy to score off Polonius, to get laughs, so important not to clown, to keep the story true—then the intricate scene with Rosencrantz and Guildenstern, and my favorite prose speech in the play, "What a piece of work is a man! . . ." The arrival of the players, easier again, natural, true feeling, but the big soliloquy is coming in a minute, one must concentrate, take care not to anticipate, not begin worrying beforehand how one is going to say it, take time, but don't lose time, don't break the verse up, don't succumb to the temptation of a big melodramatic effect for the sake of gaining applause at the curtain—Nunnery scene. Shall it be a love scene? How much emotion? When should Hamlet see the King? I feel so much that I convey nothing. This scene never ceases to baffle me.

Interval—The Advice to the Players. Dreadful little pill to open the second part, all the people coming back to their seats, slamming them down, somehow try to connect the speech with the rest of the play, not just a set piece—Tender for the tiny scene with Horatio, a moment's relief—then into the Play Scene. Relax if possible, enjoy the scene, watch the Gonzago Play, watch the King, forget that this is the most famous of famous scenes, remember that Hamlet is not yet sure of Claudius, delay the climax, then carry it (and it needs all the control and breath in the world to keep the pitch at the right level). No pause before the Recorders scene begins, and this cannot make the effect it should unless Rosencrantz and Guildenstern pull their weight and share the scene with Hamlet. Half a minute to collect oneself, and on again to the praying King, such a difficult unsatisfactory scene, and how important to the play—but the closet scene is more grateful, and a woman's voice helps to make a contrast in tone and pitch. The scene starts at terrific emotional tension, though, and only slows up for a minute in the middle for the beautiful passage with the Ghost. The "hiding of Polonius's body" scene . . . and then grab a cloak and hat in the wings and rush on to speak the Fortinbras soliloquy as if it wasn't the last hundred yards in a relay race.

Now the one long interval for Hamlet, while Ophelia is doing her mad scene, and Claudius and Laertes are laying their plot, and the Queen is saying her willow speech. Last lap. Graveyard scene, with the lovely philosophizing, and the lines about Yorick, and that hellish shouting fight and the "Ossa" speech at the end, which takes the last ounce of remaining breath. Now for Osric, and a struggle to hold one's own with the scene-shifters banging about behind the front cloth, and a careful ear for the first coughs and fidgets in the audience, which must somehow be silenced before the "fall of a sparrow" (I remember one night a gentleman in the front row took out a large watch in this scene, and wound it resignedly). And so to the apology to Laertes, with half one's mind occupied trying to remember the fight, which has been so carefully rehearsed but always goes wrong at least once a week, and on to the poisoning of the Queen and Claudius's death, and, if all has gone well, a still, attentive audience to the very end. . . .

. . . In rehearsing Hamlet I found it at first impossible to characterize. I could not "imagine" the part, and live in it, forgetting myself in the words and adventures of the character, as I had tried to do in other plays. This difficulty surprised and alarmed me. Although I knew the theatrical effect that should be produced by each scene, I could only act the part if I felt that I really experienced every word of it as I spoke. The need to "make an effort" or "force a climax" paralyzed my imagination immediately, and destroyed any reality which I had begun to feel. I knew that I must act in a broad style, that I must be grander, more dignified and noble, more tender and gracious, more bitter and scathing, than was absolutely natural—that I must not be as slow as I should be if I were really thinking aloud, that I must drive the dialogue along at a regular moving pace, and, above all, that every shade of thought must be arranged, behind the lines, so that nothing should be left to chance in presenting them to the audience correctly and clearly in the pattern which I had conceived. All through rehearsals I was dismayed by my utter inability to forget myself while I was acting. It was not until I stood before an audience that I seemed to find the breadth and voice which enabled me suddenly to shake off my self-consciousness and live the part in my imagination, while I executed the technical difficulties with another part of my consciousness at the same time.

Tim Woodward as Claudius and Mark Rylance as Hamlet in a March 2000 performance directed by Giles Block at the restored Globe Theatre in London. (Photo: Colin Willoughby/ArenaPAL)

Foreground: Yoshisada Sakaguchi as Polonius and Hiroyuki Sanada as Hamlet in the Ninagawa Theatre Company's August 1998 production at the Barbican Theatre, London, directed by Yukio Ninagawa. (Photo: Colin Willoughby/ArenaPAL)

Ralph Fiennes as Hamlet and Tara Fitzgerald as Ophelia in the Almeida Theatre/Hackney Empire's 1995 performance. (Photo: Ben Christopher/ArenaPAL)

Paul Freeman as Claudius, Diana Quick as Gertrude, and Alex Jennings as Hamlet in the Royal Shakespeare Company's 1997 production in Stratford, directed by Matthew Warchus. (Photo: Clive Barda/PAL)

JOHN LAHR

Review of *Hamlet* 1994

Hamlet is a play that tests the best actors of each generation, and also each generation's sense of itself. Over the last thirty years, in England, no fewer than three *Hamlet*s have served as such cultural bellwethers. In 1965, during the Vietnam War, David Warner gave us an untidy undergraduate Hamlet who was frustrated by Denmark's military-industrial complex. In 1980, as Britain's economy went into a weird free fall, Jonathan Pryce's *Hamlet* was possessed by the ghost of his father, who spoke through him in a frightening supernatural flirtation with madness. And now, in the neutral, post-Thatcher nineties, Ralph Fiennes has pitched his drop-dead matinee-idol profile and the modesty of his sensitive soul into a postmodern *Hamlet* whose refusal to risk interpretation reflects Britain's current bland and winded times.

Fiennes, an intelligent, reticent player, seems almost as unwilling to enter the vortex of Hamlet's torment as Hamlet himself is to take action. Fiennes radiates an elegance of spirit that rivets the audience with its sense of unspoken mystery. His performance is a stylish event, much more the "mould of form" than the "glass of fashion." He has a mellow, reedy voice that filters Shakespeare's gorgeous complexity and gives the language an accessible colloquial ring. Fiennes is not one for grand histrionic gestures. His personality doesn't take up a lot of space. He compels attention by his decency, not by his declaiming. Fiennes, who has limpid green eyes and tousled chestnut hair, and who is a laid-back, brooding, romantic star, is catnip to the public and oxygen at the box office. (The Almeida Theatre Company's production, which began its much ballyhooed life at the Hackney Empire, the wonderful old music-hall venue in London's East End, has arrived at the Belasco for a fourteen-week Broadway engagement.) This *Hamlet* has been designed to be a people's *Hamlet,* which is to say a *Hamlet* in which the plot, not the psychology, is complicated, and in which the cast works the room instead of working for meaning. Inevitably, therefore, Fiennes's Hamlet is not a navel-gazing scholar or an alienated adolescent or a demented psychological case study. His Hamlet turns out to be the guy Horatio always said he was: a "sweet prince," a sort of rogue and *pleasant* slave.

The director, Jonathan Kent, who last year transferred the Almeida's *Medea,* with Diana Rigg, to Broadway with great success, has set the play in Edwardian England and has lopped an hour off the playing time. The speed favors breadth over depth; the streamlining suits the cut of Fiennes's jib, and he wears James Acheson's period clothes well. What we have here is a ripping Shakespearean yarn that shows off the thrills and chills of the story's melodramatic elements: the ghost of a murdered king, a mother's hasty marriage to her husband's murderer, a prince driven to near-madness and revenge, a lovelorn suicide, a lot of ghoulish high jinks around graves, a terrific sword fight, and a quadruple poisoning. The result is lucid without being moving: a kind of aerobic *Hamlet,* which works hard to keep up the pace while going nowhere.

The lights come up on a bare, raked stage, and the sound of crashing waves fills the auditorium. In the background, the environs of Elsinore are suggested by faint, blurred beams of light projected through a murky scrim on which the outlines of rocks are just visible. A sentinel climbs up through a trapdoor — more for effect than for sense, it seems, like many things in this production. "Who's there?" he calls. That's the play; the whole existential ball of wax. Hamlet's entire dramatic journey is foreshadowed in these first words. He, too, must penetrate the surrounding darkness and tease out the reality of his parents, of the corrupt court, and of himself. By finally taking action — which means accepting loss, including the loss of his own life, Hamlet sees clear into the heart of things and achieves his adulthood. In this sense, *Hamlet* is both a detective story and a metaphysical investigation. The practical and the philosophical aspects of the tale need time to build properly, as the saying goes, "No delay, no play." But here, with the proceedings speeded up, the text is not so much examined as *done.* It's significant that Fiennes attacks the "To be, or not to be" soliloquy, which sets out Hamlet's spiritual quandary, by coming toward us in manic stutter steps and turning the famous meditation into yapping thought. He skirts the issue of interpretation by turning talk into behavior. The image is novel but little nuance comes across the footlights. In this ranting mode, dissembling a madness that is really giddy grief, the barefoot Fiennes grabs Ophelia's crotch and insolently shoves Claudius's shoulder. But Fiennes can't really get up a convincingly antic head of steam. He is slow to kindle and never really burns. He's not so much tormented as pissed off.

Fiennes has his best moment with the grave-digger (the excellent grizzled Terence Rigby, who also plays Hamlet's father's ghost and the Player King). Listening to the Gravedigger expound matter-of-factly on how a body decomposes, and learning that a skull he has unearthed belonged to Yorick, the former King's jester, Hamlet gently takes this relic of his old acquaintance from the grave-digger. "This?" Fiennes says, uttering the word with a huge sense of recognition, wonder, and sadness. His sensitivity and the mournfulness of the moment coalesce. "Where be your gibes now? your gambols? your songs? your flashes of merriment, that were wont to set the table on a roar?" Fiennes says, with a delicacy that delivers Shakespeare's observations about mortality like a punch to the heart.

The production's obsession with surface has its most effective expression in Peter J. Davison's sets. He creates a dark, lugubrious officialdom of behemoth ceilings, heavy brown-stained doors, and large shuttered windows that turn the actors into scuttling Lilliputians. Hamlet is first seen framed by one of these gigantic windows, standing upstage with his back turned away from the bustle of power, whose aggrandizement is reflected in the monumentality that surrounds it. Still, Davison, too, succumbs to the production's impulse to startle rather than compel. The ghost is conjured up on a high platform behind the scrim. There, lit from above by the white glare of a halogen lamp and announced by a jolt of electronic sound, Hamlet's dead father appears twice, in his carapace of armor: a "Star Wars" effect that is a projection of commercial instincts more than of Hamlet's unconscious. Similarly, Jonathan Kent's eye for business is sometimes shrewder than his eye for detail. When Laertes and Hamlet take turns leaping into Ophelia's grave and embracing her body, each trying to outdo the remorse of the other, the poor dead girl bobs up and down like a hand puppet. And at the finale, when Fortinbras (Rupert Penry-Jones, who is also Fiennes's understudy) arrives to take over the kingdom that Hamlet has died to save, his Aryan good looks and the gray capes of his lieutenants make it seem as if the Luftwaffe had invaded Denmark.

In American theatrical circles, the definition of a genius is anybody from England. But the prestige of this production can't hide the unevenness of its seasoned supporting cast, who prove the adage that British actors are either tours de force or forced to tour. Besides Terence Rigby, only the lanky, bearded Peter Eyre, as Polonius, breathes distinctive life into his role. Eyre plays the meddling bureaucrat as a long drink of cold water: cleaning his pince-nez as he counsels his hotheaded son to "neither a borrower, nor a lender be," and withholding his hand from Laertes when he goes, Eyre misses no opportunity to have fun with the old blowhard's pedantry. Polonius rushes to the Queen with a letter that Hamlet has sent his daughter, and reads it to her as a presenting symptom of Hamlet's lunacy. Reciting "To the celestial and my soul's idol, the most beautified Ophelia," Eyre's Polonius bristles with dopey patrician disdain. "That's an ill phrase, a vile phrase, 'beautified' is a vile phrase," he says, and gets one of the evening's best laughs.

Others are not so much at home in Shakespeare's climate of delirium. Tara Fitzgerald, a talented young actress with a bright future, flounders as Ophelia. There is nothing fractured or vulnerable about her, and when Ophelia goes mad Fitzgerald won't let her rip. Fitzgerald's behavior—the compulsive walking back and forth, the sexual taunts directed at Claudius—feels tame and glib: a trick of the mind, not a journey of the heart. Often, when English actors are nowhere near the center of their parts they rely on the power of their articulate voices; James Laurenson's Claudius falls into the trap of such posturing. Claudius is John Gotti with a pedigree—carnal, vicious, power-hungry, ruthless—but Laurenson gives us chicanery on the half shell. He does a lot of Urgent Shakespeare Acting. A few wheeling turns upstage, some nips at the top of his hand, a little booming oratory, and—presto!—you have a villain. This stock rep stuff is also dished up by the beautiful Francesca Annis, as a Gertrude who can't manage much grief at the sight of Ophelia's dementia but does manage a long, lingering kiss with Hamlet. It's a bit of business that has become the theatrical baggage of the role in this century, but the incestuous overtone seems inappropriate, especially in such an unanalytic production.

A word about Hamlet's duel. Jonathan Kent and the fight director, William Hobbs, have built up this face-off between idealism and treachery into a scintillating contest that takes excellent advantage of the story's melodrama. A cream-colored tarp is rolled downstage for the match, and the court sits watching upstage right, in gray upholstered chairs. Hamlet fights with graceful, playful enthusiasm, unaware that he's up against the double whammy of Laertes' poisoned sword and Claudius's poisoned chalice. Hamlet gets the first couple of touches; then Laertes' temper flares, and he cuts Hamlet. They scuffle, and in the hurly-burly their swords get mixed up. Hamlet chases Laertes around the room, sending chairs flying and courtiers scurrying for safety. It's exciting and well-staged hokom, in which Laertes ends up hoist with his own petard. At that point, the Queen, who has drunk from the chalice, collapses; then the Grand Guignol of Shakespeare's ending quickly plays itself out. At the finale, Fortinbras's men lift Hamlet's corpse on their shoulders and, swaying, carry him slowly upstage and toward the light beyond. Fiennes's head falls back, giving the audience one last glimpse of the star. Even backward, upside down, and dead, Fiennes exits looking good.

PART FOUR

Writing about Literature

. . . a combination of the artistic and scientific [temperament]. The enthusiastic artist alone is apt to be too subjective in his attitude toward a book, and so a scientific coolness of judgment will temper the intuitive heat.

> —VLADIMIR NABOKOV (on the
> qualities of the ideal reader)

A story writer is more than happy to be read by students; the fact that these serious readers think and feel something in response to his work he finds life-giving.

> —EUDORA WELTY (on her readers'
> response to "A Worn Path")

I now know and trust completely that writing happens long before I ever type a word; that my best thinking and writing will happen before and after the first draft but not necessarily during it.

> —ALEX JOHNSON

24.

Critical Perspectives and Literary Theory

Literature is what gets taught.
— ROLAND BARTHES

In the opening pages of his book *Literary Theory*, the contemporary English critic Terry Eagleton wrote that "Hostility to theory usually means an opposition to other people's theories and an oblivion of one's own." You may feel that literary theory is formidable, but as you begin to explore the various commentaries by short story writers, poets, dramatists, and critics in this anthology, you will discover that they make available many different approaches to the study of literature. In the Commentaries on Stories and Storytellers, for example, Sandra M. Gilbert and Susan Gubar give a feminist reading of Charlotte Perkins Gilman's "The Yellow Wallpaper" (p. 564) and J. Hillis Miller develops a deconstructive reading of Herman Melville's "Bartleby, the Scrivener" (p. 577), to list only two selections in the anthology. You may also read a student essay adapting a reader-response perspective (the paper on Eudora Welty's "A Worn Path" in Chapter 25, p. 1630). Reading different critical interpretations may also make you become more aware of the assumptions that underlie your own thoughts about literature.

Literary theory is the term used in academic criticism to characterize particular methods of inquiry into the nature and value of literature. Formulating general critical principles — rather than analyzing particular literary texts — is the job of theorists like Terry Eagleton, whereas your assignment is usually to analyze a specific story, poem, or play. The following ten critical approaches to literary texts are the ones you will encounter most frequently in your reading of the commentaries, or secondary sources. They offer some useful perspectives to consider in your critical thinking and writing about literature.

FORMALIST CRITICISM

Formalist criticism is probably the most basic approach to the analysis of literature. Along with other theoretical perspectives, critics often use it to develop their interpretation of literary texts. René Wellek and Austin Warren, the pioneering practitioners of formalism in the United States, wrote in their *Theory of Literature* (1942) that "the natural and sensible starting point for work in literary scholarship is the interpretation and analysis of the works of literature themselves."

Formalists regard a work of fiction, poetry, or drama as a world in itself that can be understood by its intrinsic nature—focusing on form over content. There is an implicit formalist approach inherent in the organization of this textbook into chapters featuring a discussion of the elements of the short story, the poem, and the play. However, a pure formalist would not include headnotes about the authors, considering facts about the author's life and historical times irrelevant to the appreciation of a text. Instead, a formalist would concentrate on analyzing how the various elements of a literary work are integrated into the complex and unique structure of a self-contained aesthetic work.

For example, the academic critic Cleanth Brooks Jr. and the poet Robert Penn Warren give a formalist analysis of T. S. Eliot's "The Love Song of J. Alfred Prufrock" on page 966. Their discussion was included in *Understanding Poetry* (1938), a college textbook that introduced generations of teachers and students to the formalist techniques of what was then called "New Criticism" based on a close reading of the text. In Brooks and Warren's discussion of Eliot's poem, they emphasize the irony implicit in its tone. They compare Prufrock's character to that of Hamlet, but for the most part their references remain inside the text, explicating the poem line by line to unravel the complexity of Eliot's linguistic and cultural erudition.

BIOGRAPHICAL CRITICISM

In "The Formalist Critic," Cleanth Brooks Jr. stated that

> the formalist critic is concerned primarily with the work itself. Speculation on the mental processes of the author takes the critic away from the work into biography and psychology. There is no reason, of course, why he should not turn away into biography and psychology. Such explorations are very much worth making. But they should not be confused with an account of the work. Such studies describe the process of composition, not the structure of the thing composed. . . .

Unlike formalist criticism, **biographical criticism** starts with the premise that stories, poems, and plays are written by human beings, and that important facts about the life of an author can shed light on literary texts. Usually this kind of critical approach develops the thesis of an essay by suggesting the connection of *cause and effect*. That is, you maintain that the imaginative world of the text has characteristics that originate from causes or sources in the author's background.

You have probably written papers about literature in a biographical context. A favorite high-school English term paper project is to assign an author as a topic, requiring research into the details about his or her life. If you ever wrote this kind of paper, you may have organized your material chronologically, tracing the life of your author and listing his or her most important literary works, often with no clearly defined thesis in mind. In writing essays for college English classes based on a unified central idea, on the other hand, you must ask yourself how knowing the facts of an author's life can help you to understand a specific text. Usually you do not attempt to survey an author's complete works in a short paper.

A biographical approach to literature requires at least as much care as formalist criticism—care in presenting only the relevant facts of an author's life and in using a sensitive interpretation of them to show clear connections between the writer's experience or personality and the work. Brett C. Millier's discussion of Elizabeth Bishop's poem "One Art" (p. 992) is an exemplary use of the biographical approach to literature. Millier has focused this account of Bishop's revision of the poem through a careful examination of the seventeen drafts of the manuscript. In the long middle paragraph of the analysis, Millier introduces Bishop's biographical information, a summary of the poet's losses beginning with the disappearance and death of her parents when she was still a child. The biographical critic then concludes that the list of these personal losses encoded into the poem is an example of Bishop's method of "reticence" as a confessional poet, part of her lifelong process of acquiring self-discipline.

PSYCHOLOGICAL CRITICISM

Psychological criticism is indebted to modern psychology, which began with the psychoanalytic theories of its founder, the Austrian psychoanalyst Sigmund Freud (1856–1939). Freud wrote that he learned nearly as much about psychology from reading authors such as Sophocles and Shakespeare as he did from his clinical work with his patients in Vienna as an analyst and physician. Freud's writing about psychology, along with books by his disciples including Carl Jung, Marie Bonaparte, and Bruno Bettelheim, modified our understanding of human behavior, introducing such concepts as the unconscious forces of the id and the superego active within every individual.

Three approaches are most often taken by critics interested in exploring the psychological aspect of literature. First is the investigation of the creative process and the nature of literary genius. This field of investigation can also include other forms of genius—musical, mathematical, and so forth. The second is the study of an individual writer (or artist or musician or scientist), particularly appropriate if, like the American poets Anne Sexton, Sylvia Plath, and Robert Lowell, the individual was deeply involved in psychological therapy or analysis. The third is the analysis of fictional characters, which began with Freud's study of the character of Oedipus when he analyzed Sophocles' play in his book *The Interpretation of Dreams* (1900).

An excerpt from Freud's discussion of "The Oedipus Complex" is on page 1543 of this anthology. Freud begins his analysis by referring to the childhood of his neurotic patients, many of whom he observed possessing on "a magnified scale feelings of love and hatred to their parents." The psychoanalyst then summarizes the plot of *Oedipus the King,* observing that Sophocles has dramatized "a legend whose profound and universal power to move can only be understood if the hypothesis I have put forward in regard to the psychology of children has an equally universal validity." Freud argues that the destiny of the fictional king of Thebes "moves us only because it might have been ours—because the oracle laid the same curse upon us before our birth as upon him." Moving from literary analysis to psychological generalizations, Freud used literature to formulate universal theories about human psychology that have continued to influence our ideas for over a century.

MYTHOLOGICAL CRITICISM

Mythological criticism developed out of psychoanalytic theory in the work of Freud's younger disciple, the Swiss psychiatrist Carl G. Jung. A man of vast reading in anthropology and comparative religion as well as literature, Jung formulated the theory of the archetype. Derived from the experience of the human race in different cultures, **archetypes** consist of images present in the unconscious mind of every individual, which Jung called the "collective unconscious." Archetypal images of the sun, for example, are inherent in every culture and give rise to storytelling that results in tribal myths. The critic Northrop Frye defined the archetype in strictly literary terms as "a symbol, usually an image, which recurs often enough in literature to be recognizable as an element of one's literary experience as a whole."

When critics characterize archetypal images in specific works of literature, they usually refer to several texts beyond the one being scrutinized in order to establish an underlying pattern of similarity. On page 1536 the theater critic Francis Fergusson's discussion of "Oedipus, Myth and Play" from *The Idea of a Theater* (1949) moves from a summary of the plot of the play to a paragraph speculating on the different versions of the Oedipus myth possibly known by the playwright. Fergusson then suggests how later authors like Pierre Corneille, Voltaire, and Fustel de Coulanges interpreted Oedipus after Sophocles. The erudition of this mythological approach to reading Oedipus as a universal scapegoat figure leads Fergusson to conclude his analysis with a lively description of what he calls "the ritual expectancy" of the rowdy crowd in the Greek theater assembled to watch Sophocles' play.

HISTORICAL CRITICISM

Historical criticism approaches a literary work through its historical context, the events that were occurring in the world during the time the author wrote a particular story, poem, or play. This method is often combined with the biographical approach, if the historical events contributed to the author's thought process and resulted in the creation of a work of literature. Historical critics may also explain the meaning that the work had for its original readers, especially if the text includes words that had different connotations in the past.

The critic Sally Fitzgerald, who was a close friend of the writer Flannery O'Connor, takes a historical approach in her discussion of the 1953 short story "A Good Man Is Hard to Find" (p. 641). During the years of their friendship, O'Connor sent Fitzgerald clippings of articles with "lurid headlines" from local newspapers of her hometown, Milledgeville, Georgia. Although O'Connor was merely trying to amuse Fitzgerald, the critic saved the clippings and used them in an article about O'Connor titled "Happy Endings," published in *Image* in 1997. The newspaper clippings from the early 1950s included accounts of a prize-winning child singer "decked out in ribbons and tutu and sausage curls," whose winning song was titled "A Good Man Is Hard to Find," as well as a series of articles about a criminal "aloose" in the region who totaled up a record of twenty-six kidnappings and ten car thefts, among other high jinks, in what Fitzgerald described in her essay as "two fun-filled weeks." The critic suggests how these documents may have influenced O'Connor when she created the fictional character of The Misfit. Fitzgerald concludes by using the newspaper articles to shed light on the theme of redemption dramatized in the story.

SOCIOLOGICAL CRITICISM

Sociological criticism is written by critics interested in exploring the economic, racial, and political context in which works of literature are created and read. Examining the relationships between writers and their society, these critics focus on the ideological aspects inherent in stories, poems, and plays. As the critic Wilbur Scott understood, "Art is not created in a vacuum; it is the work not simply of a person, but of an author fixed in time and space, answering a community of which he is an important, because articulate, part." The novelist Joseph Conrad went even further in making a connection between literature and society when he wrote in *Notes on Life and Letters* that

> Fiction is history, human history, or it is nothing. But it is also more than that; it stands on firmer ground, being based on the reality of forms and the observation of social phenomena, whereas history is based on documents, and the reading of print and handwriting—on second-hand impression. Thus fiction is nearer truth.

Perhaps the most controversial type of sociological criticism is **Marxist criticism.** Marxist critics, including the Hungarian philosopher Georg Lukács, believe that all art is political. This approach can become highly theoretical, as in Mikhail Bakhtin and V. N. Voloshinov's 1929 study *Marxism and the Philosophy of Language,* which argues that language is fundamentally "dialogic," a focus of social struggle and contradiction. As Eagleton explained in *Literary Theory,* for these critics, "It was not simply a matter of asking 'what the sign [word] meant,' but of investigating its varied history, as conflicting social groups, classes, individuals, and discourses sought to appropriate it and imbue it with their own meanings. Language, in short, was a field of ideological contention, not a monolithic system."

In this anthology, Helge Normann Nilsen examines the influence of Marxist theory on *Death of a Salesman* in her essay "Marxism and the Early Plays of Arthur Miller" on page 1569. Nilsen bases her analysis of Miller's political attitudes on his statements about the destructive aspects of capitalism in his autobiography, bolstering her argument with footnotes from the playwright's *Timebends: A Life* (1987).

READER-RESPONSE CRITICISM

For much of the twentieth century, the formalist approach to "close reading" of stories, poems, and plays was the most popular method of analysis in American college classrooms. After the turbulent social changes of the 1960s, literary critics in the United States became receptive to many new approaches to the text. The critic Ross Murfin has summarized the reaction against the "New Critical" practices:

> About 1970, the New Criticism came under attack by reader-response critics (who believe that the meaning of a work is not inherent in its internal form but rather is cooperatively produced by the reader and the text) and poststructuralists (who, following the philosophy of Jacques Derrida, argue that texts are inevitably self-contradictory and that we can find form in them only by ignoring or suppressing conflicting details or elements). In retrospect it is clear that, in their outspoken opposition to the New Criticism notwithstanding, the reader-response critics and poststructuralists of the 1970s were very much *like* their formalist predecessors in two important respects: for the most part, they ignored the world beyond the text and its reader, and, for the most part, they ignored the historical contexts within which literary works are written and read.

Reader-response criticism postulates that reading is as much a creative act as the writing of a text, because both involve the play of imagination and intelligence. Some reader-response critics even go so far as to say that a literary text has no existence outside of a reader's mind. Recognizing that different readers can find different meaning in works of literature, reader-response critics also emphasize the fact that the same reader can, at different periods of his or her life, find the experience of reading a book changes with maturity. If you keep the notes you take on reading *Hamlet* as a college freshman, for example, you will probably find that in twenty years or so, your interpretation of the play will change if you read it again or see a new production in the theater.

On page 595 of this anthology, the literary critic Cheryl B. Torsney gives a reader-response interpretation of Alice Walker's "Everyday Use" based on an experience at Parchman Farm, the Mississippi state penitentiary, meeting a prisoner who was a skilled quilter. This encounter taught Torsney a great deal about the life of many poverty-stricken southern blacks, and caused her to revise her reading of Walker's short story.

POSTSTRUCTURALIST AND DECONSTRUCTIONIST CRITICISM

Poststructuralist and **deconstructionist criticism** are two modern approaches to critical theory that, like reader-response criticism, focus on the multiple, sometimes self-contradictory meanings that exist in a literary work — meanings that resist a final interpretation. Critics who practice these approaches believe in a basic logical syllogism:

A. Human language is fundamentally unstable, as its meaning is dependent on changing but omnipresent social and historical factors.

B. Literary texts are composed of human language.

C. Therefore, literary texts are fundamentally unstable. Q.E.D.

Arguing that the literary text is unstable, deconstructionist critics like the French authorities Roland Barthes and Michel Foucault have called for "the death of literature" and "the death of the author." In 1968 Barthes explained in his essay "The Death of the Author" that

> Once the Author is removed, the claim to decipher a text becomes quite futile. To give a text an Author is to impose a limit on that text, to furnish it with a final signified, to close the writing. Such a conception suits criticism very well, the latter then allotting itself the important task of discovering the Author (or its hypostases: society, history, psyche, liberty) beneath the work: when the Author has been found, the text is "explained" — victory to the critic. . . . In the multiplicity of writing, everything is to be *disentangled*, nothing *deciphered;* the structure can be followed, "run" (like the thread of a stocking) at every point and at every level, but there is nothing beneath. . . . writing ceaselessly posits meaning ceaselessly to evaporate it, carrying out a systematic exemption of meaning.

While formalists find coherence in the different elements of a text, deconstructionists show how the author's language can be broken or "deconstructed" into irreconcilable meanings. Their efforts have influenced many contemporary critics, and their theories are worth investigating if you continue your study of literature in upper-division courses and graduate school.

You can sample their approach in the list of books at the end of this section, as well as in J. Hillis Miller's deconstructive reading of Herman Melville's "Bartleby, the Scrivener" on page 577 of this anthology. Miller takes a mythological approach (analyzing versions of the Pygmalion myth) in his deconstruction of Melville's text. The critic illuminates how Melville "disables reading" any one particular interpretation into the story by selecting the lawyer, Bartleby's employer, as his narrator.

GENDER CRITICISM

Gender criticism emerged in the wake of the development of feminist criticism on American college campuses in the 1970s, gradually evolving into gender criticism with the inclusion of gay and lesbian critics. This branch of critical theory is indebted to early works such as the French critic Simone de Beauvoir's *The Second Sex* (1949) as well as the American feminists Betty Friedan's *The Feminine Mystique* (1963) and Kate Millett's *Sexual Politics* (1970).

Gender critics are concerned with the gender and sexual orientation of both writers and readers of literature. They argue that our patriarchal culture is so imbued with assumptions of heterosexual male superiority that we must continuously correct the imbalance by identifying and analyzing its components and negative influences. Explaining how gender has influenced both an author's work and a reader's response to a literary text, this approach often contains aspects of reader-response criticism.

On page 564 of this anthology you can read the feminist commentary of the eminent critics Sandra M. Gilbert and Susan Gubar on Charlotte Perkins Gilman's "The Yellow Wallpaper." This excerpt is taken from their book *The Madwoman in the Attic: The Woman Writer and the Nineteenth-Century Literary Imagination* (1979). Gilbert and Gubar place the story within the context of what they call the "literature of confinement," where a woman trapped by the patriarchal society attempts to free herself "through strategic re-definitions of self, art, and society."

CULTURAL CRITICISM

Cultural criticism, like gender criticism, can be viewed as an important contemporary development in literary studies erected upon the sturdy but limited foundation of formalist practice. Cultural critics, including New Historicists, do not advocate any one particular approach to literary study. Frequently they participate in interdisciplinary approaches, combining more than one field of academic study due to their assumption that individual works of literature should be approached as part of a larger cultural context. For example, if you investigated the changes in 1960s popular music as reflected in Joyce Carol Oates's "Where Are You Going, Where Have You Been?" (p. 396), incorporating musical history into your essay, you have been practicing cultural criticism.

As the poet X. J. Kennedy realizes,

> In theory, a cultural studies critic might employ any methodology. In practice, however, he or she will most often borrow concepts from deconstruction, Marxism analysis, gender criticism, race theory, and psychology. . . . Whereas traditional critical approaches often sought to demonstrate the unity of a literary work, cultural studies often seeks to portray social, political, and psychological conflicts it masks.

Leslie Marmon Silko uses the methodology of a cultural critic in her essay analyzing "Language and Literature from a Pueblo Indian Perspective" on page 586 of this anthology.

SELECTED BIBLIOGRAPHY

GENERAL OVERVIEW

Eagleton, Terry. *Literary Theory: An Introduction.* 2nd ed. Minneapolis: U of Minnesota P, 1996.

Selden, Raman. *Theory of Criticism.* New York: Addison Wesley, 1988.

THE CHANGING LITERARY CANON

Lauter, Paul. *Canons and Contexts.* New York: Oxford UP, 1991.

FORMALIST CRITICISM

Brooks, Cleanth. *The Well Wrought Urn: Studies in the Structure of Poetry.* New York: Reynal and Hitchcock, 1947.

Eliot, T. S. *The Sacred Wood: Essays in Poetry and Criticism.* London: Methuen, 1920.

Ransom, John Crowe. *The New Criticism.* Norfolk, CT: New Directions, 1941.

Wellek, René, and Austin Warren. *Theory of Literature.* New York: Harcourt, Brace and World, 1949.

BIOGRAPHICAL AND PSYCHOLOGICAL CRITICISM

Bloom, Harold. *The Anxiety of Influence.* New York: Oxford UP, 1978.

Crews, Frederick. *Out of My System: Psychoanalysis, Ideology, and Critical Method.* New York: Oxford UP, 1975.

Freud, Sigmund. *The Standard Edition of the Complete Psychological Works.* 24 vols. Ed. James Strachey. London: Hogarth Press and the Institute of Psychoanalysis, 1940–68.

Lesser, Simon O. *Fiction and the Unconscious.* Chicago: U of Chicago P, 1957.

Skura, Meredith Anne. *The Literary Use of the Psychoanalytic Process.* New Haven: Yale UP, 1981.

MYTHOLOGICAL CRITICISM

Bodkin, Maud. *Archetypal Patterns in Poetry.* London: Oxford UP, 1934.

Frye, Northrop. *Anatomy of Criticism: Four Essays.* Princeton: Princeton UP, 1957.

Jung, Carl Gustav. *Collected Works.* Ed. Herbert Read, Michael Fordham, and Gerhard Adler. 17 vols. New York: Pantheon, 1953.

HISTORICAL AND SOCIOLOGICAL CRITICISM

Escarpit, Robert. *Sociology of Literature.* Painesville, OH: Lake Erie College P, 1965.

Frow, John. *Marxist and Literary History.* Cambridge: Harvard UP, 1986.

Lindenberger, Herbert. *Historical Drama: The Relation of Literature and Reality.* Chicago: U of Chicago P, 1985.

Williams, Raymond. *Marxism and Literature.* Oxford: Oxford UP, 1977.

READER-RESPONSE CRITICISM

Booth, Wayne C. *The Rhetoric of Fiction.* Chicago: U of Chicago P, 1983.

Eco, Umberto. *The Role of the Reader: Explorations in the Semiotics of Texts.* Bloomington: Indiana UP, 1979.

Fish, Stanley. *Is There a Text in This Class? The Authority of Interpretive Communities.* Cambridge: Harvard UP, 1980.

Freund, Elizabeth. *The Return of the Reader: Reader-Response Criticism.* London: Methuen, 1987.

Tompkins, Jane P., ed. *Reader-Response Criticism: From Formalism to Post-Structuralism.* Baltimore: Johns Hopkins UP, 1980.

POSTSTRUCTURALIST AND DECONSTRUCTIONIST CRITICISM

Barthes, Roland. *The Rustle of Language.* New York: Hill and Wang, 1986.

Culler, Jonathan. *On Deconstruction: Theory and Criticism after Structuralism.* Ithaca: Cornell UP, 1982.

Derrida, Jacques. *Of Grammatology.* Baltimore: Johns Hopkins UP, 1976.

Foucault, Michel. *Language, Counter-Memory, Practice.* Ithaca: Cornell UP, 1977.

Smith, Barbara Herrnstein. *On the Margins of Discourse: The Relation of Literature to Language.* Chicago: U of Chicago P, 1979.

GENDER CRITICISM

Baym, Nina. *Feminism and American Literary History.* New Brunswick: Rutgers UP, 1992.

Edelman, Lee. *Homographesis: Essays in Gay Literary and Cultural Theory.* New York: Routledge, 1994.

Fetterley, Judith. *The Resisting Reader: A Feminist Approach to American Fiction.* Bloomington: Indiana UP, 1978.

Jagose, Annamarie. *Queer Theory.* Victoria: Melbourne UP, 1996.

Sedgwick, Eve Kosofsky. *Between Men: English Literature and Male Homosocial Desire.* New York: Columbia UP, 1985.

Showalter, Elaine. *A Literature of Their Own.* Princeton: Princeton UP, 1977.

Smith, Barbara. *Toward a Black Feminist Criticism.* New York: Out and Out, 1977.

CULTURAL CRITICISM

Clayton, Jay, and Eric Rothstein, eds. *Influence and Intertextuality in Literary History.* Madison: U of Wisconsin P, 1991.

Cox, Jeffrey N., and Larry J. Reynolds. *New Historical Literary Study: Essays on Reproducing Texts, Representing History.* Princeton: Princeton UP, 1993.

Geertz, Clifford. *The Interpretation of Cultures.* New York: Basic Books, 1973.

Storey, John, ed. *What Is Cultural Studies?* New York: St. Martin's, 1996.

White, Hayden. *Tropics of Discourse: Essays in Cultural Criticism.* Baltimore: Johns Hopkins UP, 1978.

WEB *Learn more about literary criticism through VirtuaLit and LitGloss at bedfordstmartins.com/charters/litwriters.*

25.

Developing Your Ideas in an Essay

Literature is our conversation between the past and present out of which we articulate ourselves.

— DANA GIOIA, "Fallen Star," *Hungry Mind Review* 52

Read literature for the pleasure of it, Ernest Hemingway once told an interviewer, adding that "whatever else you find will be the measure of what you brought to the reading." Literature expands your view of the world, by inviting you to share the perspective of gifted storytellers, poets, and dramatists who can entertain, instruct, and perhaps enchant you. An assignment to create an essay about literature gives you the opportunity to explain how you have been affected by what you have read. In your essay, you explore your connection with the text and clarify your ideas about its significance. The writing process begins as soon as you ask the smallest question about the meaning or the structure of a literary work.

Good ideas are essential to a successful essay. How do you develop your initial emotional response to a story, poem, or play into ideas for a paper? There is no magic formula that guarantees a good essay, since all writers must find their own way and learn to do it for themselves. If you understand the various steps involved, the writing process can become much easier. As the essayist Alex Johnson has observed, writing is always a challenge, but it does not always have to be a chore. In "Having a Bad Morning," she confessed uncertainty as to "how to get the thinking out."

> It took me years of trial and error to learn the obvious: writing is best and most satisfying done in stages. . . . I now know and trust completely that writing happens long before I ever type a word; that my best thinking and writing will happen before and after the first draft but not necessarily during it; that by seeing writing as a process, I now know the pleasure of making connections: ruminating on a subject, seeing patterns emerge, watching an argument evolve, evidence cohere. In short, that glorious territoriality of staking and claiming a subject as my own.

The best way to write an essay about literature is to proceed in stages, understanding that good writing is as much a process as it is an end result. When you are fully engaged in this endeavor, you will discover that the process also turns you into a better reader. Both as a reader and a writer, you will exercise your sensitivity and intelligence if you work conscientiously through the various stages toward the final draft of your paper.

Assume, for example, that your first writing assignment will be a two-to-three-page paper (500 to 750 words) on Eudora Welty's literary style in "A Worn Path" (p. 537) developing a formalist approach or a close reading of the text. You have one week to turn in your essay. Everyone works differently, but here is a description of how you might budget your time most efficiently during the week by taking the writing process in stages. This process is a lot easier than procrastinating until the day before your paper is due and then pulling a hectic all-nighter in a desperate effort to get the work finished on time.

First, before you start to write, you must read the story carefully at least twice. In "Good Readers and Good Writers," Vladimir Nabokov suggested that the ideal reader should develop "a combination of the artistic and the scientific [temperament]. The enthusiastic artist alone is apt to be too subjective in his attitude toward a book, and so a scientific coolness of judgment will temper the intuitive heat." Read Welty's story the first time for pleasure; bring out your "scientific coolness" when you study it the second time.

KEEPING A JOURNAL OR NOTEBOOK TO RECORD YOUR INITIAL RESPONSES TO THE TEXT

Often the earliest stage in responding to a literary work occurs as you read the text and feel the impulse to underline words or phrases that instinctively strike you as significant. It's relatively easy to give in to this impulse. Using a pen as a highlighter is a step in the right direction, but there's a better way that will get you started on your essay. Keeping a journal or a notebook in which you record your responses to your reading will help you to generate ideas about what you find there.

In her essay "Keeping a Notebook," the writer Joan Didion said the main reason writers keep a record of their experience is that "we forget all too soon the things we thought we could never forget. . . . Keeping in touch is what notebooks are all about." Recording your impressions right after reading the assignment helps you to remember what you thought about it.

For most students, a journal of responses to literature is an important stage in the journey of transforming themselves from readers into writers. Once you become aware of how you are reading a text, you have begun the process of using your own words to describe what you find significant about a story, play, or poem. This is the beginning of your discovery of "the measure of what you brought to the reading."

In your journal, you should note your responses after your first (or second) reading of Welty's story. Jot down short quotations from the story if they strike you as significant. Your notes might look something like this:

JOURNAL ENTRY

Eudora Welty's "A Worn Path" . . . starts right in on the story introducing a very old woman named Phoenix Jackson, who's taking a long walk by herself on a December afternoon in the country. Author knows the setting very well--lots of specific details of trees, bushes, hills, and creek--Phoenix talks to herself but she's a feisty old thing. Has trouble seeing, but she picks up and hides a nickel belonging to a hunter she meets on the trail--the old lady's conscience bothers her, but she doesn't let on--he speaks so condescendingly to her that I think she's entitled to take his money--it's just a nickel--wait--did he drop the nickel or did she just see it on the ground? yes, Welty says it fell out of his pocket--so she could have given it back to him. The old lady gets tired but she keeps going and finally arrives at Natchez. Then she goes into a building in town where "she walked up and around and around until her feet knew to stop." So she's been there often before. It seems to be a nurses' office--and she's so old and tired she forgets why she's there--then remembers that she's come to get medicine for her grandson. Horrible--the little boy swallowed lye. He lives with Phoenix, and she makes the long walk to town for his sake every year. The nurse likes Phoenix--gives her a nickel as a Christmas present. Phoenix really loves her grandson--she tells the nurse she's going to buy him a present before she starts the long walk home. I wonder, is this grandson alive or dead? Is the old woman senile? Can we trust her?

You will notice that in your journal you began by summarizing the plot in your own words. That is the first response of most students when given the assignment of writing about literature. You need not regard it as a wasted effort because you can use your notes later to review the story when studying for an exam. But your instructor has asked you to write an essay. How can your notes help you to find an idea about the story for your paper?

Notice that summarizing the events of the story has led you to ask a question about the main character's actions: Can we trust Phoenix Jackson, or is she so old that she's really senile and doesn't know whether her grandson is alive or dead? If you are an insecure reader, you may think that your question is stupid, but it isn't. Often getting the answer to a simple question that arises as you read the text will lead you to more complex ideas about its significance that you can develop in your essay.

You can bring your question about "A Worn Path" to your instructor in class. Or, working by yourself, you can find commentaries by authors and critics in this anthology that shed light on your reading. So many students asked this question about the story that Welty wrote a commentary titled "Is Phoenix Jackson's Grandson Really Dead?" (p. 604). Reading her commentary will not only show you that you have asked a good question, but it will also help you generate ideas about the story for your paper. The important thing is *your* response to the story — what makes it significant for you. Reading commentaries, such as Welty's on "A Worn Path," will help you become a more informed reader and may stimulate your critical thinking about the story.

A number of commentaries on the stories, poems, and plays in this anthology are included throughout *Literature and Its Writers* because reading commentaries can help you feel more confident when you begin to think critically about literature. While commentaries by authors and critics often clear up specific questions about a text, they always introduce you to important aspects of the significance of a story, poem, or play that you might have missed on your own. You may agree or disagree with the commentaries, but they will usually stimulate your critical thinking.

USING THE COMMENTARIES TO ASK NEW QUESTIONS ABOUT WHAT YOU HAVE READ

Reading Welty's commentary answered your first question about the story: The author tells you that the grandson is alive. After Welty answers the question, you might be struck by how seriously she takes what she calls the "fiction writer's responsibility" in the second part of her essay. Welty says that a good writer never uses tricks in order to mislead the reader; the words in a story must always "mean what they say."

Welty's commentary has caused you to look at "A Worn Path" in a new way. How does an author make her words "mean what they say"? Now you might feel a flicker of excitement as you begin to think about how Welty has selected particular words to make up her story about a solitary old woman she glimpsed walking in a country landscape. Welty states that she wanted her story to illustrate an idea she had about this woman's journey: She wanted to dramatize what she imagined as "the deep-grained habit of love."

Thinking about the commentary, you might be impressed by Welty's sympathy for her central character, Phoenix Jackson. When you scan the opening paragraphs of "A Worn Path" again, you find that this sympathy is conveyed by the words Welty has chosen to tell her story. You ask yourself, how does the author keep her subject from becoming sentimental? What words in the text suggest Welty's feelings for the woman she writes about in the story without going overboard? You remember a line from the story that you jotted down in your journal: "she walked up and around and around until her feet knew to stop." Suddenly it's clear to you that Welty has chosen words that Phoenix Jackson would use. Now your mind is full of questions about the story. You are ready for the next stage in the writing process.

GENERATING IDEAS BY BRAINSTORMING, FREEWRITING, AND LISTING

Generating ideas for the assignment can be done in a variety of ways, either as a solitary process of jotting down ideas on paper or as a communal process of talking over your ideas with a friend or classmate who has also read the story. If you follow the latter course, be sure to take notes as your conversation progresses so that your ideas do not evaporate in the general glow of good company.

Usually sufficient ideas for your paper will evolve during one of these exercises of brainstorming, freewriting, and listing. Initially you might try them all to find out which one works best for you.

Brainstorming for Ideas

Perhaps the notion that Welty has written her story in words that Phoenix Jackson might use intrigues you so much that you decide to brainstorm by yourself. Record the thoughts that occur to you while you look over the story again. Begin with Welty's first sentence and free associate about whatever comes to your mind:

> Simple language, telling the month and day and time. Welty's so logical--large
> (month) to small (morning) time units.

Now try to think more specifically about Welty's choice of words. Brainstorm further by finding adjectives to describe your impressions of the words she uses to introduce Phoenix Jackson:

> respectful, warm, sympathetic, humane, compassionate, a little funny but
> gently so--Welty never makes a joke at Phoenix's expense. She's "neat and
> tidy," but still human--her shoelaces drag and she hasn't bothered to lace her
> shoes. Is it because she's too old to bend down to lace them? Or maybe her feet
> hurt and she can't buy another pair.

At this point you might discover that brainstorming has put your imagination to work on the story. Your brief vision of the figure of Phoenix Jackson so frail with age that she is unable to bend over to tie her own shoes has made her become almost as real to you as your own grandmother. This might amuse you and cause you to realize that you have learned something about the magic of literature: Writing about it can make you a more active participant in it.

This might be a good time to review your notes. Can you find a pattern in the details Welty has given you about Phoenix Jackson? If you have been as conscious of your thoughts about the story as Phoenix was aware of the path she was following through the woods, you might begin to sense Welty building something in her careful choice of descriptive details. She seems to suggest one thing and then to continue on to its opposite. Phoenix is "an old Negro woman" (respectable), but "her head tied in a red rag" (poor, shabby). She is "neat and tidy," but her shoelaces drag. And so on. Why does Welty do this?

As you think about it, you realize that while Welty sometimes chooses words that Phoenix Jackson might use, the author is clearly in control, selecting details about her character very carefully. How do you develop this new idea? You might try another technique to help you focus your thoughts, an exercise called freewriting.

Freewriting

Like brainstorming, focused freewriting can help you develop an idea when you begin to think critically about literature. In a freewriting session, you state everything that comes to mind when you try to answer a question relating to the subject of your paper. Do not stop to think of forming complete sentences or using correct grammar or spelling. Give yourself a set time—perhaps ten or fifteen minutes or even longer if you feel inspired—to spill out all your associations about the topic. You can use a scratch pad, a notebook, or a computer—whatever you have at hand. Keep the story beside you as you write, so that you can refer to it as necessary. Then go back and underline ideas in your writing that you think could be organized into a coherent outline and developed further in an essay. Here is an example of freewriting about "A Worn Path" on the topic of Welty's style or choice of words as a storyteller.

> What does she do that makes me want to read on, one word following the next, until I'm hooked and want to know "what happens next"? First of all, her words make Phoenix into a complicated character. Simple to begin with, but more there than obviously meets the eye. Not a lot of dramatic action but a soft tone, almost as if she wanted to make you bend closer to her to hear her better. Serious, simple tone to begin the story. Then that business about the red rag. Does that do it? Or is it the choice of words, so simple and down-to-earth. Just like the character Welty's trying to describe. She's like anybody's granny in the country--even if it's Mississippi by the end of the story. Think about it. The way Welty uses alliteration, "red rag" and "path through the pinewoods," so her voice sounds good--it's very musical and rhythmic prose. Perhaps she's creating the rhythm of Phoenix's walk, "the balanced heaviness and lightness."

Focused freewriting can make you conscious of ideas you did not know you had, like the thought that Welty's prose is so musical and rhythmic that it suggests the pace of Phoenix's physical movements as she makes her slow way along the worn, familiar path to town. Brainstorming ideas and freewriting can often help you to think critically about a literary work. At this point you might want to make a list of all the things you have discovered about the story so far.

Listing

Another useful technique in the preliminary stage of the writing process is making lists. You are probably experienced at doing this whenever you try to keep several things in mind at once, especially if you are planning to use the list later on, as for grocery shopping or organizing "things to do" over the course of a busy weekend. Listing also can become a way to help you develop your thoughts about literature. Making a list is more focused than brainstorming or freewriting; first you must be clear about what you want to list.

For example, if you would like to develop the idea that what attracts you about Welty's storytelling voice is its musical quality, you could comb "A Worn Path" for more instances of memorable alliteration (like "red rag") in the words describing the protagonist. You will probably find that—strangely enough—once your brain starts to go to work analyzing literature, one idea seems to stimulate another during the writing process.

As you scan the story again, you suddenly notice the beautiful simile that Welty uses in the second paragraph to describe Phoenix's wrinkled face: "as though a whole little tree stood in the middle of her forehead." You see that Welty emphasizes the vitality and beauty of Phoenix's skin color—"golden." And this detail is followed at the end of the paragraph by another compliment, that her hair falls "in the frailest of ringlets, still black, and with an odor like copper." What is "an odor like copper"? you ask yourself. Is it a good smell or a bad one? This makes you remember an early idea when you started thinking about the assignment, that Welty blends positive and negative attributes into her description of Phoenix Jackson. Could that be how she keeps her story about the old woman from becoming sentimental?

You may feel that you have gotten a little sidetracked, but that is no matter, because your thoughts about the second paragraph have carried you further along on your idea about Welty's method of drawing you into the story by her poetic description of Phoenix Jackson's face. Return to the story to find the examples that you started looking for, of musical alliteration. They are as easy to find in the opening paragraph as ripe red strawberries in June:

> red rag
> side to side in her steps
> sugar sacks

When you begin to notice examples of assonance, like the sound of the *o*'s in "odor of copper," you could start to make another list. You could also jot down a third list of examples of inverted word order that Welty has used in her sentences to achieve musical effect, such as "On she went." And you could create a fourth list for examples of the regular rhythm of sentences she (or Phoenix) chants using the melody of parallel structure: "Up through pines. . . . Now down through oaks."

ORGANIZING YOUR NOTES INTO A PRELIMINARY THESIS SENTENCE AND OUTLINE

After you have given yourself sufficient time to think critically about the story, you are ready to organize your thoughts about what you intend to write. *This is the most crucial step in the process of creating your essay.* Many students make the mistake of beginning to write the first draft of their paper too soon, before they have taken the time to stimulate new ideas and create a strong **thesis sentence**. They string together sentences about a topic, rather than develop a clearly focused response to their assignment. If you work on a strong thesis sentence first, before you start writing your essay, you will save yourself considerable anxiety and several false starts, or—even worse—an unfocused essay that doesn't communicate clearly to your reader.

Whether you are writing an essay of only a few paragraphs or a research paper of several thousand words, the basic requirement is always the same. An essay on any subject is a type of expository writing, and *expository* means "serving to clarify, set forth, or explain in detail" a central idea about your topic. Do not start your essay until you are able to express a strong idea in a well-crafted sentence.

An effective essay always requires two things: first, a good thesis sentence or central idea about your topic to start your paper, and second, an adequate development of your thesis sentence. Often it helps you get started if you concentrate on stating your thesis as clearly as you can in your rough draft. When you revise your essay, you can make sure that you have presented sufficient evidence to support your main idea. Some useful ways of organizing longer essays about literature—by explication, analysis, and comparison and contrast—are discussed in Chapter 26. Regardless of your paper's length, you should always begin by trying to express your central idea about the topic so that it can evolve and develop in the writing process.

Which of your notes about Welty's story is the best candidate to serve as a thesis sentence? It should express the main point of your essay. Consider it a *preliminary* thesis at this point, subject to revision when you rewrite your rough draft. After some thought, you might come up with the following thesis sentences:

1. *Welty's way of telling her story is interesting.* This is a common, quick, and facile solution to the problem of formulating a thesis sentence for an essay. It is totally inadequate because it is too general. A moment's reflection will reveal that a topic is not the same as a thesis. A topic is a general subject (*"Welty's way of telling her story"*); a thesis makes a statement about a topic (*"is interesting"* is not much of a statement).

2. *Welty's way of telling her story draws the reader into "A Worn Path."* This is a much more useful thesis sentence. You have thought about the topic and narrowed it down to focus on the relationship of the topic to a specific idea. The test of a thesis sentence is whether your general subject (*"Welty's way of telling her story"*) is followed by a clearly focused predicate (*"draws the reader into 'A Worn Path'"*).

3. *Welty uses language as a storyteller the way that Phoenix Jackson would use words to express her thoughts.* This was your first insight into Welty's way of telling her story. It could serve as a useful preliminary thesis. You have narrowed the topic even further. Your general subject (*"Welty uses language as a storyteller"*) is followed by a very specific predicate (*"the way that Phoenix Jackson would use words to express her thoughts"*). This thesis sentence unmistakably points the way to how you could begin to develop your rough draft. You might suspect that this idea is too narrowly focused for your entire paper, but you will discover whether this is true as you write.

4. *Welty uses language the way a poet does to keep readers interested in her story.* This idea came out of the listing exercise, where you found

examples of Welty's use of alliteration, assonance, and rhetorical structure. Like the previous two ideas, this could also serve as a useful preliminary thesis sentence to get you started on your rough draft.

Assume you take the third choice, because this was your original insight about the story and you like the idea best. Working on an essay is always more enjoyable when you are enthusiastic about the assignment. Before you sit down at the computer, you will find that making a brief outline will help you see the direction to take more clearly. It does not have to be a traditional outline. Shape it in any way that will help you remember the points you intend to make if you are interrupted. Start by writing down your preliminary thesis sentence. Then assemble the evidence you have found to support it.

> As a storyteller, Welty uses language the way that Phoenix Jackson uses words to express her thoughts.
>
> 1. Simple, down-to-earth vocabulary.
> 2. Poetic and musical phrases.

Because your assignment is a short paper, this initial thesis sentence and outline will get you started on your first draft. Don't worry about making the thesis perfect at this stage. You will bring your thesis into even sharper focus as you develop what you have to say about your topic in your essay. As Alex Johnson understood, the object of a first draft is to shape the thesis sentence into what she called a "controlling idea":

> The most common misconception is that the first draft is about writing *per se*. It's not. It's about thinking. If you've managed to turn out felicitous phrasing, I always tell students, it's icing on the cake. The real concern is how your idea evolves and sharpens, how its deeper structure emerges. To help this process along, don't agonize over word choice. Underline a word or simply leave a space and go back in the revision stage to get it right. Use momentum. Gag your internal critic and perfectionist when they report, correctly, that the draft seems sketchy. That's why it's called a first draft.

WRITING THE ROUGH DRAFT

If you include a strong thesis sentence in the first paragraph of your rough draft, it can often jumpstart further ideas. The effort of writing itself, the act of finding the right words to express your thoughts, can suggest new ways to develop your preliminary thesis. That is the reason you should allow plenty of time to complete an essay assignment. It is an unusual first draft in which the central idea is developed coherently and fully enough to be turned in as the finished paper. Revision usually stimulates further thought, sharpening and refining your argument.

You will probably discover that, like most people, you are better at rewriting than you are at writing. More often than not, the 500 or 750 words you might think are a perfect essay when you turn in your final paper will be the end result—if you took enough time and care in writing—of winnowing many more words from your rough drafts. In your revision you can support your thesis by editing your sentences and paragraphs so that each one relates coherently to your central idea. Then your essay will express your insights about the story so clearly that they can be understood by your reader as you intended.

SAMPLE FIRST DRAFT OF AN ESSAY
ON EUDORA WELTY'S "A WORN PATH"

An author's voice   *a*   *point to consider about*
A storyteller's style is key to understanding the way she

> *Begin with broad generalization about the story.*

    From   *'s choice of words, we can hear that*
tells her story. Eudora Welty is a warm and sympathetic

she is a warm and sympathetic
narrator in "A Worn Path." She uses language so simply and

    interests us
concretely that she makes us interested immediately in the

    named Phoenix Jackson
journey of an old woman as she walks through the pinewoods

    In fact, often
to Natchez to get medicine for her grandson. Welty uses

> *Narrow your topic into a thesis sentence.*

    ,
language the way Phoenix uses it to express her thoughts/

, because when she comes to the city
At the end of the story we are told that "she walked up and

around and around until her feet knew to stop" (541).

    captures the reader's attention
This simple, down-to-earth vocabulary grounds us. It is

> *New insight in second paragraph develops out of writing the rough draft.*

Welty   *is creating*
as if the author could read the mind of the character she has

created on the page. We all would like to be able to get inside the

mind   *and*   *thoughts,*
thoughts of another person, to share their most private interior

world, so we want to read further. This could be considered a

trick, since Welty's own voice (and mind) could not be exactly

the same as the uneducated Phoenix, but Welty's sincere feeling

    fictional
for her character shines through the story. Her voice is sincere.

    use of words as a storyteller
Welty's voice interests us for another reason. She

> *Final paragraph needs further revision: repetitious vocabulary, ideas scattered, conclusion unfocused.*

         a prose story,
chooses words the way a poet would. She's writing a short

    her
story, but she chooses words like a poet. There are many

opening
examples of alliteration and assonance in the ~~first~~ para-

first   , like "red rag" and "path through
graph of her story, when she must ˄capture our interest. ˄

the pinewoods (537).   compares the pattern of wrinkles on
˄In the second paragraph, she ˄ ~~gives~~ Phoenix's ~~wrinkled~~ face to

and poetic
a "whole little tree" (538). This is a fresh ˄image to help us

visualize the old woman's appearance. The plot and characteri-

zation of Phoenix later in the story shows us how resourceful

and loving she is as a person. As a storyteller, Welty speaks of

her heroine with great affection. She blends telling and showing

in "A Worn Path."

REVISING YOUR ESSAY

Usually your first draft will be shorter than your final draft, but at this point you shouldn't worry about length. Instead, savor the feeling of satisfaction that you have made a good start on your paper. If you have the time, you should put your rough draft away for a day or so, and then read it again with fresh eyes. Before you return to it, you might want to reread the literature you are writing about, looking for more details to develop your thesis statement. In your revision, you could also try to incorporate relevant material you might be discussing in class, like the concept of an author's voice as an aspect of literary style.

Revision means exactly what it says—the opportunity to revisit your essay and take another look at it. This is the writing stage where you get the chance to do the best work on your paper. You can refine your argument by strengthening your evidence and tying together loose ends. Most students are surprised to find how rough and unfinished their first drafts appear after time away from the essay. Always go over your work with a pen or a pencil in hand so that you can continue to clarify what you have written for your reader.

If you compare the first draft of the paper on "A Worn Path" with the revised draft, you can see how the essay became more fully developed and more coherent. Two additional middle paragraphs give specific examples from the story, evidence that supports the thesis sentence. This sentence now concludes the opening paragraph, putting more emphasis on this central idea and pointing the way to its development in the following paragraphs. In the final version, the essay begins with a general sentence based on information from class discussions of short fiction about an author's voice as an aspect of literary style. This concept ties together several ideas about the story that had emerged from brainstorming, freewriting, and listing and also provides a title for the paper. The argument is further strengthened by the specific reference to Welty's commentary "Is Phoenix Jackson's Grandson Really Dead?"

SAMPLE REVISED DRAFT

The Voice of the Storyteller

in Eudora Welty's "A Worn Path"

An author's voice is a key point to consider about the
effect of literary style on a reader. From Eudora Welty's choice
of words in "A Worn Path," we can tell she's a warm and sympathetic narrator. She uses language so simply and concretely
that she makes us interested in the journey of an old woman
named Phoenix Jackson as she walks through the pinewoods
to Natchez to get medicine for her grandson. In fact, Welty
often uses language the way that Phoenix would use it to
express her thoughts.

At the beginning of the story, Welty introduces Phoenix
by describing her as "an old Negro woman with her head tied
in a red rag" (537). This description, so clear and direct, gives
us a vivid image of the central character. In the second paragraph, Welty tells us what she is wearing, a dark dress covered
by a "long apron of bleached sugar sacks" (537). This old
woman may be poor, but she is also clean and thrifty. We
respect her even before we learn that she cares enough about
her sick grandson to walk many miles along a rugged country
path from her home to the clinic for a bottle of medicine.

When the old woman comes to the city sidewalks, we are
told that "she walked up and around and around until her feet
knew to stop" (541). Phoenix has gotten tired after her long
trek through the woods, over the hills, across a creek, through
a field of dead cornstalks, along a wagon track, and across a
swamp on her way to Natchez. These are the words that she
herself would use, and the sentence is structured the way she
would talk.

This lively colloquial vocabulary captures the reader's
attention. It is as if the author could read the mind of her
character. We all would like to be able to get inside the mind of
another person, to share his or her private thoughts and feelings, so we want to read further. Welty has revealed in her
commentary on "A Worn Path" that "the story is told through
Phoenix's mind" (604). This could be considered a trick, since
Welty's own voice (and mind) could not be exactly the same as
uneducated, unsophisticated Phoenix. But Welty shows her
deep respect for what she calls "the deep-grained habit of love"

in Phoenix's actions (605). The sound of the author's voice is sincere, so we trust her.

Welty's voice attracts us for another reason. She is writing prose, but she chooses words like a poet. There are many examples of alliteration and assonance in the opening paragraph of her story, like "red rag" and "path through the pinewoods" (537), when the author must first capture our interest. In the second paragraph, Welty uses a poetic simile to compare the pattern of wrinkles on Phoenix's face to a "whole little tree" (538). This comparison helps us visualize the old woman's appearance. It is also so down-to-earth that it could even have occurred to Phoenix herself if we imagine her seeing her reflection in the water of a spring or in a Natchez shop window. We are irresistibly drawn into the story by the skillful voice of the storyteller in "A Worn Path."

MAKING A FINAL CHECK OF YOUR FINISHED ESSAY

Before you turn in your essay, you should check the quotations you have used to make sure that you have copied them accurately. If you have used a computer to write your paper, you should also run a spell-check. The following guide can help you in the final preparation of your essay:

1. Be sure to include your name, date, and class section on the paper.
2. Check your title. Ideally, it should suggest an idea of your approach to the assigned topic. If you include the author's name or title of the work here, be sure you have spelled it correctly and have used quotation marks or underlining appropriately.
3. Include the name of the author and title of the work you are writing about in your opening paragraph so that the reader knows what you plan to discuss. Often, at least in short essays, the reader expects you to state your thesis sentence in the first paragraph.
4. Review your organization. Does your essay offer solid evidence to support your thesis statement? Does it develop ideas clearly and coherently? For effective emphasis, do your paragraphs proceed from the least important to the most important point? Can some of the longer paragraphs be divided into shorter units to clarify your main points? Are your short paragraphs adequately developed? Does each sentence relate to the one before? Have you supplied transitional sentences between paragraphs? Do you need to write shorter sentences so that your ideas come through more clearly?
5. Include quotations from the work you are discussing to add variety to the vocabulary you customarily use. Such a practice also offers a change of

pace to the reader of your paper, as well as a reminder of the pleasures of the original text.

6. Check that your punctuation and grammar are correct throughout your essay, and that you have written varied and complete sentences, not sentence fragments. If you spot unintentional verbal repetitions, find fresh words to replace them or revise the sentence to eliminate wordiness.

7. Look for the conclusion to your essay. If it is a short paper, you can phrase your conclusion as a sentence or two in the final paragraph. In a longer paper, you could devote at least an entire final paragraph to a statement of your conclusion.

Peer Review

Before turning in your essay, you could exchange papers with another student to check each other's work. Your instructor might also include a peer review of rough drafts or finished papers during class time, allowing you to benefit from other readers' suggestions for improvement. This could help you clarify your ideas and strengthen your argument. If you are given another student's paper, read it twice. The first time, read it straight through for enjoyment and illumination; the second time, read it critically.

If you think your classmate can improve the paper, put a question mark in the margin close to any places where the sentences are unclear or you don't understand what the writer is trying to say. Put a check mark in the margin where you would like to see a quotation from the text to illustrate and strengthen the writer's interpretation of the material. Can you identify the thesis statement? Would it be more effective if placed earlier in the essay? Underline it and, if necessary, suggest how it could be repositioned or rewritten more clearly and forcefully. Does the writer adequately discuss the specific quotations from the text so that you understand why they are in the paper? Finally, comment on the writer's conclusion: Have you learned something from the paper? Does the conclusion relate back to the thesis statement and sum up the essay?

COMMON PROBLEMS IN WRITING ABOUT LITERATURE

Interpret, don't summarize. Summarizing the contents of a story, poem, or play in an essay is not the same as giving insights into the work's pattern and meaning. Occasionally you can summarize the plot in a sentence if you are making a transition from one part of your paper to another, but keep in mind that the reader of your paper is usually your instructor, who has already read the work and will get the impression that you do not know much about what you are doing if you merely summarize it.

Write about how you read the story, poem, or play. Try to express your own ideas through the text. If you find yourself summarizing it in more than a couple of sentences, it is probably because you did not organize your essay around a strong thesis. Your impressions and ideas are the measure of your encounter with literature. Writing encourages your clarification of these ideas. Be sure to state your central idea in a sentence in your paper. It does not matter where it appears, although if you include it in your opening paragraph it will help you keep your discussion focused.

Avoid long personal anecdotes. Writing on the basis of your personal experience can result in a fine memoir, but such an essay is usually not about the literature you were asked to discuss. You may want to introduce an analysis of D. H. Lawrence's "The Rocking-Horse Winner" (p. 322) with a short anecdote about a relevant experience you had as a child with a rocking horse, but make sure your anecdote goes on for only a few sentences before you connect it explicitly with your central idea about Lawrence's story.

Use the text to check your interpretation. Opinions about literature can be wrong. Do not insist on ideas that will not fit the details of the work. You may stumble on a central idea for your paper with an intuitive leap or a hunch about a story's meaning, but be sure the specific details of the text support your interpretation. "Whatever I discover in the work is right for me," you may say, but that will not take you very far when writing a paper for an English class. Works of literature are tough, tangible constructions of language, not shifting tea leaves in the bottom of an empty cup onto which you can project whatever meaning you like.

Make good use of quotations. You must quote from the text to give evidence of your interpretation. Usually a sentence should introduce and follow each quotation, linking it to the idea being developed in your paper. Never drop quotations into the body of your essay without a comment.

Be careful not to quote too much. Use only those passages that are relevant to your discussion. Overquoting can weaken an essay, easily turning it into a string of short quotations choppily connected by a few insufficient words from you. Be sure to make it clear to the reader why the passage you are quoting is important.

When the quotation is short (four lines or less), it should be enclosed in quotation marks and included within the regular text, as you have seen in the sample essay. When typing a quotation longer than four lines, separate it from the preceding typewritten line with double space. Then indent ten spaces, *omit quotation marks,* and type with a double spacing (unless your instructor tells you differently). If you include the opening paragraph of "Young Goodman Brown" (p. 219) in a research paper, for example, you would indent it like this:

> Young Goodman Brown came forth at sunset into the street at Salem village; but put his head back, after crossing the threshold, to exchange a parting kiss with his young wife. And Faith, as the wife was aptly named, thrust her own pretty head into the street, letting the wind play with the pink ribbons of her cap while she called to Goodman Brown.

In a shorter passage in which you use a quotation within a quotation, such as a line of dialogue inside an excerpt from a story, use double and single quotation marks: "The echoes of the forest mocked him, crying, 'Faith! Faith!' as if bewildered wretches were seeking her all through the wilderness."

If you wish to leave out words in a quoted passage, use ellipsis points, that is, three periods (or four periods if the omitted material includes the end of a sentence) in brackets: "And Faith [. . .] thrust her own pretty head into the street [. . .]."

Always quote the exact wording, punctuation, and capitalization of the original text. If you underline words in a quotation for emphasis, say that you have done so.

If you find an error, for example a misspelled word in a quotation, indicate that the error is in the original by inserting *sic,* a Latin word meaning "thus," in brackets after the error itself.

Last but not least, punctuate sentences that appear in quotation marks correctly. Commas and periods always belong *inside* the quotation marks, whether or not they appeared in the original text. Semicolons, question marks, colons, and exclamation points, however, belong *outside* the quotation marks, unless they are part of the quoted material.

Avoid plagiarism. Any material you borrow from other sources and include in your paper must be documented. If you present someone else's material (other than factual information) as if it were your own, you may be open to the charge of plagiarism. Even with factual information, if you use the exact wording of a source, you must indicate that it is a quotation. To be on the safe side, it is always better to footnote your original source, or give credit by working into your essay the name of the author and the title of the work in which you found the material you cited.

The one exception to this principle is information that is considered *common knowledge*. Common knowledge is material that is repeated in a number of sources, so that it is difficult to tell what the original source might have been. Such items as the basic biographical facts about an author or information about the publication of literary works do not need footnoting, unless you quote someone's exact words at length in your essay.

Know when and how to document the sources in your bibliography. Include the name of the author and the page number in a parenthetical citation or in the text itself when you use references other than this textbook:

> In Richard J. Jacobson's study, we learn that Hawthorne feared the artist might become "insulated from the common business of life" (27).

If you cite from more than one book by an author, mention the title in the text or include a shortened form of the title in the citation:

> We learn that Hawthorne feared the artist might become "insulated from the common business of life" (Jacobson, <u>Hawthorne's Conception</u> 27).

If your instructor asks you to use footnotes or endnotes, instead of parenthetical citation, you may place notes at the bottom of the page on which the reference appears, or they may be gathered together on a separate *notes* page at the end of your essay. When you footnote a source, indent the first line of each footnote five spaces before listing the author's first and last name; the title of the book; the city of publication, publisher, and date in parentheses; and the page number cited:

[1]Richard J. Jacobson, Hawthorne's Conception of the Creative Process (Cambridge, MA: Harvard UP, 1965) 27.

A separate bibliography of sources is handled differently than a list of notes or footnotes. When you gather several sources together on a separate page at the end of your essay as a bibliography, you list them alphabetically, starting with the *last* name of the author.

Welty, Eudora. "Is Phoenix Jackson's Grandson Really Dead?" Literature and Its Writers. 3rd ed. Ed. Ann Charters and Samuel Charters. Boston: Bedford/St. Martin's, 2003. 604-06.

Instructions for basic documentation form for different sources — books, magazines, encyclopedias, and so on — appear in every handbook and guide to writing college papers. They may also be found in various manuals of style and style sheets that should be available in the reference section of your college library. You will find a guide to the most frequently used types of citation in the chapter on the research paper that concludes this textbook.

GUIDELINES FOR WRITING AN ESSAY ABOUT LITERATURE

1. *Do not wait until the last minute to start.* Allow plenty of time to write and revise.
2. *Be sure you have a clear idea of what you want to say about the work.* Can you state this idea as a sharply focused thesis sentence? Remember that all expository writing serves to clarify, set forth, or explain in detail an idea about a topic.
3. *Read the work over again.* Check the notes in your journal and take notes that will help you amplify your central idea. If necessary, try to generate ideas by brainstorming, freewriting, and listing. Use the commentaries to ask new questions about the text. It might help at this point to assemble a short outline, to stake out the ground you intend your essay to cover. Look for an approach that is distinctive enough to be worth your time and effort yet manageable enough to be handled in a paper of the length you are assigned.
4. *Develop a strong thesis sentence.* It should express your central idea about your topic.

5. *Write a rough draft of your essay.* Be sure to state your central idea as a thesis sentence somewhere—preferably at the beginning of your essay. If you are using an outline, try to follow it, but allow yourself the possibility of discovering something new that you did not know you had to say while you are writing. If you have taken notes or jotted down quotations from your reading, try to introduce such material smoothly into your discussion. Remember that the heart of literary criticism is good quotation. Brief, accurate examples from the text that illustrate the points you are trying to make about your thesis are essential in writing about literature.

6. *Allow some time to pass before you look over your rough draft—at least a day. Then make at least one thorough revision before you copy or type a finished draft of your paper.* Some students find they need several revisions before they are satisfied with what they have written. When you review your rough draft, concentrate and read critically. Let your words stimulate a flow of ideas about your topic; this will lead you to find more ways to develop your train of thought. Fill out paragraphs that seem thin. Be sure transitions between paragraphs are smooth and quotations are integrated into the discussion. If you sense that your sentences are wordy, try to be more concise. Eliminate repetition. Be sure your general organization is coherent and your discussion proceeds in a clear, logical order.

7. *Check over your paper one last time.* Make sure you have always used complete sentences and correct spelling and punctuation. Avoid sentence fragments and exclamation points, unless they are part of a quotation.

8. *Type the paper or write it neatly in its final form.* If your instructor requires some particular style for class papers, such as extra-wide margins or triple spacing, follow those instructions. Use 8½-by-11-inch paper. Type if you can, double spacing between lines. If you write by hand, use ink and write on only one side of each piece of paper. Leave generous margins at the top, bottom, and sides. Number the pages, beginning with the number 2 (not the word *two*) in the upper-right-hand corner of the second page. (Your title on the first page will indicate that it is the first page.) Clip or staple your pages together in the upper-left-hand corner. Be sure your name, your instructor's name, your class and section number, and the date appear on your paper.

9. *Read your essay over one last time for typographical errors.* Make legible corrections in ink. Have you put quotation marks around titles of short stories ("A Rose for Emily") and underlined or used italics for the titles of books (A Room of One's Own)? Have you placed commas and periods *within* quotation marks in the titles and quotations that appear in your essay? Have you inadvertently left out any words or sentences when you went from the rough draft to the final version of your essay?

10. *Finally, make a copy of your paper.* If you have written the paper by hand, make a photocopy of it before handing it in; if you wrote it on a computer, be sure to save a copy of it on disk. It is a good idea to save your notes and rough drafts as well, in case the accuracy of a quotation or the originality of your work is called into question.

What do you do after you hand in your paper? You have probably spent so much time on it — thinking, organizing, writing, and rewriting — that you feel you may never want to look at it again. The act of writing the essay will have clarified your thinking and brought you closer to the literary work, so you carry with you the intangible benefit of something learned in the writing process. Returning to your essay in the future might have one final benefit: Your paper will refresh your memory, reminding you of what you did not know you knew, about both yourself and literature.

WEB *For more information on drafting a literary essay, visit VirtuaLit at bedfordstmartins.com/charters/litwriters.*

26.

Basic Types
of Literary Papers

Regardless of the critical perspective that you choose to formulate your ideas about literature, you will probably be using one of the three basic ways to develop your thinking in your essays. Here are examples of these useful rhetorical strategies along with student essays incorporating them.

EXPLICATION

The word **explication** is derived from a Latin word that means "unfolding." When you explicate a text, you unfold its meaning in an essay, proceeding carefully to interpret it passage by passage, sometimes even line by line or word by word. A good explication concentrates on details, quoting the text of the story, poem, or play to bring the details to the attention of a reader who might have missed them approaching the text from a different perspective.

An entire story, poem, or play is usually too long to explicate completely—the explication would be far longer than the original work. You usually select a short passage or section that relates to the idea you are developing. If a poem is brief, you can explicate all of it, as in the following student essay on Langston Hughes's poem "The Negro Speaks of Rivers" (p. 907). In a play, you could choose to explicate a key scene or a crucial dialogue. In a story, you could concentrate on the opening or closing paragraph, where you might suggest the implications of the text to develop the central idea of your essay.

Explication does not usually concern itself with the author's life or times, but his or her historical period may determine the definitions of words or the meaning of concepts that appear in the passage you are interpreting. If the literary work is a century or more old, the meanings of some words may have changed. The explication is supposed to reveal what the author might have meant when he or she wrote the poem, story, or play (not assuming conscious intentions but explicating possibilities).

For older literature, you will have to do a little research if the passage you choose for explication contains words whose meanings have changed. The *Oxford English Dictionary,* available in the reference section of your college library, will give you the meaning of a word in a particular era. The philosophical, religious, scientific, or political beliefs of the author or of his or her historical time may also enter into your interpretation of the text. The main emphasis in explication, however, is on the meaning of the words—both *denotative* and *connotative*—and the way those words affect you.

STUDENT ESSAY

An Interpretation of Langston Hughes's

"The Negro Speaks of Rivers"

In the poem "The Negro Speaks of Rivers," Langston Hughes uses elements of the blues to suggest the history of blacks from ancient Egypt to the twentieth century through the extended metaphor of the river. He explores the cultural identity and endurance of his people, emphasizing his racial uniqueness by his rejection of traditional European writing styles.

At the beginning of "The Negro Speaks of Rivers," Hughes is searching for his cultural identity. The poem is written in plain-spoken free verse, with an emphasis on spoken rhythm and an intimate, blues-like tone as opposed to a structured rhyme and formal rhythmic scheme. A statement of his situation in the first line ("I've known rivers") is repeated in the second, as in a blues lyric, but extended so it can be followed with a third line that stands alone as well as comments on the first two. With this third line ("My soul has grown deep like the rivers"), Hughes begins a brief historical account as the voice of the African American race.

This history celebrates the transition from slavery to freedom, suggesting the strength of his race by connecting it to the image of the river. The representation of rivers and pyramids in the next lines of the poem suggests the endurance of the human spirit through time, mystically connecting his heritage to something "older than the flow of human blood in human veins." As the rivers continue to flow, so do his people continue to thrive through the changing times and the slow acceptance of racial differences.

Hughes then moves from this portrayal of his race in the bondage of slavery from the old world to the new, where Abraham Lincoln symbolizes the progressive movement from slavery to freedom. Hughes's pride and love for his race can be seen as the water of the Mississippi turns "all golden in the sunset." The last three lines of the poem suggest the sadness and complexity of the racial situation in Hughes's somber conclusion. As in a blues lyric, he ends by repeating the line that introduced his historical panorama of African American history: "My soul has grown deep like the rivers."

ANALYSIS

An analysis of a literary work is the result of the process of separating it into its parts in order to study the whole. Analysis is commonly applied in thinking about almost any complex subject. When you are asked to analyze literature, you must break it down into various parts and then usually select a single aspect for close study. Often what you are analyzing is one of the elements of fiction, poetry, or drama—an aspect of style, characterization, dialogue, setting, or symbolism, for example.

Whereas explication deals with a specific section of the text, analysis can range further, discussing details through the story, poem, or play that are related to your thesis. You cannot possibly analyze every word of a literary work any more than you would attempt to explicate all of it. You might begin with a general idea, or arrive at one by thinking about some smaller detail that catches your attention, as the student did by analyzing the storyteller's voice as an aspect of literary style in Eudora Welty's "A Worn Path" (see pp. 1630–1631).

Most students find that when they are asked to write an essay analyzing a poem, they can come closer to the poem by copying it out double-spaced into a computer or writing it in longhand on paper. Then you can scribble your observations about the poem in the margins of your paper, brainstorming alongside the text itself. To analyze Robert Frost's poem "Mending Wall" (p. 889), for example, you could write a list of adjectives and uses for a wall—*to hide, block out, a barrier, protection, a blockade, safety, security, separation,* and so on—to familiarize yourself with the "walled" metaphor of the poem. You could also annotate Frost's use of language and the technical means of poetry. You could consider the title, weighing its various connotations in your mind after you've studied the poem. When one student tried freewriting about her response to the poem, she was reminded of a photograph of Ireland on a travel poster. This memory inspired her opening paragraph in the following essay, "Nature and Neighbors in Robert Frost's 'Mending Wall.'"

STUDENT ESSAY

Nature and Neighbors

in Robert Frost's "Mending Wall"

Ireland is known for its rolling green countryside. Without forests, the land appears to be a sea of green stretching to a sea of blue. The land, however, is not uninterrupted; there are a few roads and homes floating in that green sea, and they are even further outnumbered by Ireland's stone walls. They streak across every grazing field, surround the family farmhouses, and never seem to be in need of repair. The reason these walls remain has little to do with the skill of their original builders. Years of maintenance keep them strong. Why the walls are maintained, despite the fact that few sheep graze within their boundaries, can be explained by examining Robert Frost's poem "Mending Wall."

Funnel paragraph, narrows down to focus on assigned topic of paper.

The wall is in need of repair as the narrator and his neighbor meet to fill in the gaps a cold winter has made. As the two walk along the wall at "spring mending time" one on each side, they replace the fallen stones and rebuild the tumbled-down boundaries. As the stones are restored to their places in the wall, the chaos of nature is replaced by a man-made sense of order.

Summary of poem's subject.

The neighbors "set the wall between [them] once again," and in doing so, they strengthen the order a year of freedom has weakened. As they repair the wall, they are restoring order to the natural world in which they live and work and to their emotional worlds, where the relationships they have with one another reside. In both cases, the wall symbolizes the control the two men wish to possess over unpredictable forces in their lives.

Summary of poem's theme.

As a control over nature, the wall has many weaknesses. When nature does not work against the wall in New England, sending "the frozen ground swell under it," hunters come through, leaving "not one stone on a stone." Each year in an annual ritual, the two neighbors must meet again to repair the damage not because they enjoy the endless process of rebuilding the wall, but because the wall's presence gives them some sense of control over the chaos of nature. The wall divides the wilderness into manageable segments that are far easier to maintain than an endless expanse of farmland.

Beginning of analysis—ritual as a sense of control over nature.

In a visible and tangible way, the wall reminds the two that, despite nature's awesome power, they can in some, though impermanent, way check that power.

The borders the wall forms also indicate where the responsibility of one person ends and the duty of another begins. It is in this way that the wall crosses from control over nature to a controlling factor in the neighbors' relationship. Despite the fact that the wall separates two plots of trees, and the "apple trees will never get across and eat the cones under [the] pines," the wall is necessary in maintaining their friendly and mutually beneficial relationship. As the neighbor states, in the most memorable line of the poem, "Good fences make good neighbors." And in answer to the narrator's question of "Why do they make good neighbors?," one can look to the final image of the poem, a comparison of the neighbor to "an old stone savage armed."

Ritual as a statement of the neighbors' relationship— use of quotations.

In addition to illustrating the idea of ancient property rights, this image turns the neighbor into a threatening creature; revealing anything to him could prove dangerous. "He moves in darkness"--not the darkness caused by the shade a tree casts on a sunny day but a deeper darkness that holds the power to damage emotions that the wall symbolically protects. Therefore, the wall is a wise protection against a potentially hostile invader. It is for this reason that a wall, in this case a mental wall or symbolic sense of limits, is essential in the relationship.

Analysis of poetic imagery as it relates to the theme of the poem.

Below the surface of any human being is the potential to do harm, just as in the distance, on a clear day, a storm may be brewing. Though it is not the trusting thing to do, both neighbors understand the necessity of the wall in separating their properties and respecting personal space. The narrator begins to question his faith in the wall and the distrust it perpetuates, but in the end, as is evident by his repetition of the line "Good fences make good neighbors," he realizes the truth in such a motto. For the symbolic protection it affords and its ability to give some order to chaos, the wall has become a part of their lives.

Fresh comparison to a natural phenomenon.

Beginning of conclusion.

In Ireland, as in New England, the old stone walls remain, climbing to the tops of mountains and disappearing over the ridge. They seem to hold the green sea of grasses down as a row of stones might hold down a blanket on a breezy day. In

Conclusion refers back to opening paragraph and restates thesis sentence.

the walls the neighbors find a sense of control over their wild land, restraining the endless landscape in manageable squares and rectangles, keeping each neighbor's overgrown field of nettles within the walls and allowing responsibility to begin and end with the stone borders. In a way the good relations between neighbors are maintained with as much devotion as the walls have been maintained over the years.

COMPARISON AND CONTRAST

If you were to write about two works of literature in this anthology, you would probably use the technique of comparison and contrast. When making a comparison, you place the two works side by side and comment on their similarities. When contrasting them, you point out their differences. It is always more meaningful to compare and contrast two literary works that have something in common than two that are unrelated. As you work on your essay you will find that if there are not important similarities between the two works, your discussion will be as strained and pointless as an attempt to link closely any two dissimilar objects, like elephants and oranges.

If you decide to use the method of comparison and contrast to develop the ideas in your essay, it is usually smoother to mingle them as you go along, rather than using contrast in the first half of your paper and comparison in the second half. The result of such a fifty-fifty split is rarely a unified essay. Rather, it tends to give the impression of two separate analyses linked together at the last minute.

Here is an example of a student essay comparing works in two literary genres. After reading Susan Glaspell's *Trifles* (p. 1290) and Leonard Mustazza's commentary on Glaspell's transformation of the play into a story (p. 1560), the student decided to present his own ideas about why the author might have chosen to rewrite the play a year later as "A Jury of Her Peers" (p. 194).

STUDENT ESSAY

On the Differences between Susan Glaspell's

Trifles and "A Jury of Her Peers"

What is the difference between a play and a short story? Why should an author choose to write one over the other? An essential difference between a short story and a play lies in how each expresses emotion and thought to the audience. A short story allows the reader to enter a character's thoughts much more easily than a play would. In drama, a thought that could be said in a sentence in a short story requires a soliloquy or dialogue with another character that the audience can trust. On the other hand, a simple action or gesture in drama could require a great amount of narration in a short story. Each type of literature has its strengths and weaknesses.

Given the differences between the two genres, why did Susan Glaspell choose to turn her play Trifles into the short story "A Jury of Her Peers," instead of reworking the play? The answer to this question lies in what her goal with each work was, and how she wanted to achieve that goal. Both works have exactly the same dialogue, but "A Jury of Her Peers" is much longer, and has a different and more complex theme. It is the variances in theme, and the manner in which those variances are achieved, that illustrate why Glaspell might have been tempted to change genres when she transformed Trifles into a short story.

Transforming Trifles means narrating the story from the point of view of one of the main characters, even though by doing so Glaspell loses two of the themes she developed in her play. One of those is the diminution of wives by their husbands over "trifles." Another theme is the importance of the little things or "trifles" in life. The main theme in "A Jury of Her Peers," however, is much more complex. As the title suggests, the theme of the story is based on how two women, Mrs. Hale and Mrs. Peters, come to one opinion in judging another woman, Mrs. Wright. Illustrating their coming together necessitates a change in the point of view of the narratives. Trifles is presented, as most drama is, in the third-person objective while "A Jury of Her Peers" is presented in the third-person limited: The reader sees into the mind of Mrs. Hale.

In "A Jury of Her Peers," dramatizing the difference in the minds of the two women and watching them reach a consensus is the main action of the story. Glaspell makes it evident early in the narrative that Mrs. Hale and Mrs. Peters think differently. Mrs. Hale says, "I'd hate to have men comin' into my kitchen, . . . snoopin' round and criticizin'." Here Mrs. Hale is testing Mrs. Peters's response to see if Mrs. Peters will follow the letter of the law. Initially, Mrs. Peters believes in the letter of the law: "'Of course it's no more than their duty,' said the sheriff's wife, in her manner of timid acquiescence." Mrs. Peters's "acquiescence" refers to the fact that she feels she must remind Mrs. Hale of the law. But her manner is "timid," suggesting that there might be room for change in Mrs. Peters's mind.

The evolution of Mrs. Peters's attitude is evident when she says, "A person gets discouraged--and loses heart." Here Mrs. Peters shows that she understands why Mrs. Wright might have murdered her husband, given that she now knows that Mr. Wright was not the kind of person who made life enjoyable for his wife. Nevertheless, as the sheriff's wife, Mrs. Peters still struggles with the concept that "the law is the law."

Mrs. Peters's real transformation comes when Mrs. Hale starts to restitch the bad sewing. When Mrs. Peters says, "I don't think that we ought to touch things," the narrator describes her comment as being said "a little helplessly." At this point she realizes that she has lost the battle to follow the letter of the law; she starts to see things as Mrs. Hale does, in the spirit of the law. Thus, when the topic of how still the house was after the death of the bird arises, Mrs. Peters remembers the death of her baby in Dakota. She now understands the life that Mrs. Wright led and feels compassion for her. Mrs. Peters now discerns the position of Mrs. Hale. They come to an unspoken agreement to tamper with the evidence in the kitchen.

On the stage in Trifles, there is no need for the women to come to agreement over the issue of withholding evidence. When the bad sewing and the bird are found in the play, it is almost as if both women know that it must be hidden. Both seem to realize that the other knows as well. This mutual sharing of each other's feelings shows an underdevelopment of characterization in Trifles, making it seem flat in comparison to "A Jury of Her Peers." The use of a narrator to develop characterization is what gives the story a more complex theme.

Character revelation aside, the conclusion of both the play and the story is the same. The women come to agree that even though Mrs. Wright is guilty of murder, she does not deserve the punishment that the county attorney seeks. Both women feel compassion for Mrs. Wright because they can relate to her. Mrs. Hale relates the unfinished work in the Wright house to the unfinished work in her own house. Mrs. Peters relates to the stillness that was in the house. The understanding that both women have of Mrs. Wright causes them to tamper with the evidence.

Changes in the theme reflect the genre change, but they don't explain why Glaspell changed genres. A little biographical background is relevant here. Writing in the early twentieth century, Glaspell often emphasized feminist issues. Trifles tells men that women are capable of noticing details and that they have sharp minds. "A Jury of Her Peers" tells men that one of the strengths of women is their compassion. While both works tell about compassion, only the story shows men the path to feeling compassion for others.

"A Jury of Her Peers" argues that in the case of Mrs. Wright, the full weight of the law is not a just punishment for murder, because Mrs. Wright's personality and lifestyle were adversely altered by her husband. Before her marriage, she was Minnie Foster. As Mrs. Hale says, "She used to wear pretty clothes and be lively--when she was Minnie Foster, one of the town girls, singing in the choir." The key word in that passage is "when." It means that Mrs. Wright used to be like that, before her marriage. Mr. Wright is described as "a hard man. . . . Just to pass the time of day with him--. . . . Like a raw wind that gets to the bone." Mr. Wright liked none of the "trifles" that make life enjoyable. Mrs. Wright lived with him for twenty years, meaning that she did not enjoy life for twenty years. From this perspective, she could have committed murder to save her own sanity. If this was the case, then the harsh punishment that the county attorney seeks would be excessive. Though murder is wrong, seeking an excessive punishment is worse. It is akin to the saying "two wrongs don't make a right." Compassionately paying attention to the spirit of the law is what men can learn from women.

Teaching men what women have to offer society seems to be one of the reasons that Glaspell changed Trifles from a play into a short story in "A Jury of Her Peers." The story illustrates a change from thinking to feeling compassion, a transition particularly necessary for men at a time when women were still denied the right to vote or serve on juries. The evolution of the characters gives "A Jury of Her Peers" a feeling of completeness lacking in Trifles. New themes, descriptions, and lessons to be taught are all aspects of "A Jury of Her Peers." Together they form an answer to the question of why Susan Glaspell chose to change her play Trifles into a short story.

This student began to think critically about Glaspell's play and short story after reading a commentary. The method of comparison and contrast works especially well when you are thinking about two or more works by a single writer. You can also use this method when you analyze two works by different authors that are closely related.

WRITING ABOUT THE CONTEXT OF LITERATURE

In addition to developing an idea by explication, analysis, or comparison and contrast—all methods primarily involving a close reading of the text—there are other ways to write about literature. The *context* of stories, poems, and plays is important to our understanding and appreciation of the text, as you have learned from reading the headnotes to each author's work in this anthology. The context of literature is usually defined as the biographical and historical background of the work. Literature does not exist in a vacuum. Created by a human being at some particular time in history, it is intended to speak to other human beings about ideas that have human relevance. Any critical method that clarifies the meaning and the pattern of literature is valuable, and often literary critics use more than one method in their approach to a text.

A paper on the context of literature is also an expository essay based on the development of a central idea or thesis statement. A critic creating this kind of essay, as for example in biographical criticism, develops the thesis of the paper by suggesting the connection of *cause and effect*. That is, you maintain that the story, poem, or play has characteristics that originate from causes or sources in the author's background—personal life, historical period, or literary influences. For example, you can use Kate Chopin's statement on her discovery of Maupassant's stories (p. 556) to show something about her own method of writing short fiction. To establish this connection between the life and work of a writer, you could also analyze or explicate a Chopin story, or compare one of her stories with one of Maupassant's.

Material from other classes can also be used in papers about literature. If you major in history or psychology, for example, you can investigate the way stories, poems, or plays are sometimes read to give valuable historical or psychological information about the world they describe. You are not limited to writing about remote times when considering essays that take this approach. Joyce Carol Oates's story "Where Are You Going, Where Have You Been?" (p. 396) is about modern teenage life. A paper about it could investigate the connection between Oates's fantasy and psychological theories about adolescence in contemporary America. Characters in literature are often used in psychological and sociological textbooks to illustrate pathological symptoms or complexes. Sociology textbooks, for example, cite Oates's fictional characters as representing current tendencies toward *anomie,* a condition in which normative standards of conduct have weakened or disappeared. It is possible in writing about literature to illustrate philosophical, historical, sociological, or psychological material you are familiar with through your work in other college courses.

At times the background of the author can suggest an ideological approach: Richard Wright was a communist, Tillie Olsen is a feminist, Flannery O'Connor was a Catholic, and so forth. At other times an ideology held by the student but not necessarily by the author can lead to a fresh reading of a story. Depending on what you as a reader bring to "The Metamorphosis" (p. 262), for example, there is a "Freudian Kafka, an existentialist Kafka, a Catholic Kafka, a Marxist Kafka, a Zionist Kafka," and so forth, as suggested by the critic Hans Eichner.

Proceed with your literary analysis according to your ideology with great care, realizing that you might become insensitive to nuances of meaning other than those you are predisposed to find in a doctrinaire interpretation of the text. At the same time an ideological approach can illuminate aspects of literature that are particularly valid and relevant for contemporary readers. A feminist interpretation of "Young Goodman Brown" (p. 219), for example, must not take the story literally, because Hawthorne wrote it as a moral allegory, but a feminist could use the story to argue provocatively about implied sexual stereotyping in Hawthorne's characterization of women.

If you possess fluency in a foreign language, you can also bring your own special knowledge to your papers about literature. One student who could read Russian went back to the original version of Anton Chekhov's "The Darling" (p. 108). She read the story in Russian and compared the English translation in this anthology with the original text. In the opening paragraph of her essay, she wrote personally as a reader-response critic, but in the next paragraph she gave a detailed analysis of the Russian words she found in the story.

STUDENT ESSAY

Anton Chekhov's "The Darling"

in Russian and English Translation

The Russian version of Anton Chekhov's "The Darling" was clearer to me than the translated version. Because I grew up in Russia before immigrating to the United States, I could relate to the description of the streets and the house in the provincial town where Olenka lived. This was clear in both the English and the Russian versions of the story. But the original version gave me a better understanding of the character of Olenka. She appeared as a genuinely religious person in the Russian version, not only because she went to church and used expressions like "May the Mother of God give you health," but also because Chekhov's choice of words for the title of the story made you understand how religious Olenka truly is.

In the Russian version, the title of the story is "Duschechka," a word that comes from the word soul--duscha. The direct translation would be "the dear little soul," meaning a spiritual person with a good heart. This description perfectly suits Olenka. She is affectionate but naive in her relationships with men, falling in love with each of her two husbands out of pity. Introducing her in the first paragraph, Chekhov calls her by her nickname "Olenka" instead of her Christian name "Olga," to suggest that her character is childish and foolish: "Olenka, the daughter of the retired collegiate assessor, Plemyanniakov, was sitting in her back porch, lost in thought."

Later in the story we learn that Olenka completely identifies with all of the men in her life, including her lover the veterinary surgeon and his young son, Sasha. She thinks like each of them and talks about what they talk about. She does not have her own opinion about anything; just like a child she needs to depend upon someone. Chekhov successfully emphasized her complete emotional dependency on others throughout the story. Just as the soul needs the body for completion, so Olenka needs to be in love to feel alive. Chekhov wrote realistic stories, not religious parables, but as Tolstoy once noted in an essay on "The Darling," there seems to be a religious subtext here. I believe I came closer to understanding Chekhov's story about "The Dear Little Soul" when I read it in Russian.

You misread literature if you think of it as absolute, perfect, final statements far removed from the commonplaces of life. It needs the reader's involvement to come alive. Through their aesthetic patterns, stories, poems, and plays show us what life is like. What they are ultimately saying, in their affirmation of life and human creativity, is — in the words of Henry James — "Live! Live!"

27.

Writing Research Papers

THREE KEYS TO LITERARY RESEARCH

The first key to doing good research is to understand its purpose. In a literature class using this anthology, research writing is really an extension of the other sorts of writing you will do, such as explication, analysis, or comparison and contrast. As with these other sorts of writing, the purpose is for you to learn more about one or more pieces of literature, and perhaps about the context in which it was written, and to pass what you learn on to a reader.

The second key to doing effective literary research is understanding that a good research paper is not a dull collection of facts and quotations. Rather, a research paper is a type of essay. As with any other essay, a research paper should have a strong and compelling thesis, maintain a focus on a particular question or issue, and clearly be a product of serious, original thinking on the part of its author.

The third key to literary research is simple and practical: Do not wait. Get moving with the process of your paper as soon as you get the assignment, and never put off working on it under the assumption that you'll have plenty of time later. Sometimes the best research materials may be difficult to find, and they may take longer to read and understand than you anticipate. Organizing thoughts provoked by many sources and presenting them in a clear manner may take quite a bit of time too. Finally, you will probably need extra editing and proofreading time to make sure you get the details of citation and documentation just right.

FINDING AND FOCUSING A TOPIC

The topic of your research paper may be assigned by your teacher, or you may have free choice as to what you will write about. Either way, you will need to do some thinking and focusing before you dive into the research. Regardless of the form of your assignment, try to bring something of yourself, your personality and interests, to your research.

Once you have chosen a topic or found an approach to an assigned topic, try to stick with it. It can be tempting to drop your topic or change directions if the first stages of the research don't go as smoothly as you had hoped. Students cause themselves many wasted hours and a great deal of anguish by changing topics before giving their original ideas the real chance they deserve.

Assigned Topics

Even if the topic is assigned, it is still your job to make it your own and to find an angle which will allow you to write an original essay on the subject. Consider for example the two following topics:

1. What is the function of the literary allusions in Eliot's "The Love Song of J. Alfred Prufrock"?
2. The nineteenth century was a time of great upheaval in norms regarding marriage and family. How does Ibsen's *A Doll House* reflect this upheaval?

In both of these topics, the questions are broad, and given enough time and energy you would probably end up with far more to say than you could comfortably fit into a single, well-focused paper. In other words, you need to narrow and focus the topics so that your paper takes on a clear purpose and you have the chance to develop fully whatever ideas you choose to pursue.

For the first question, you would probably need to begin by doing some library research in literary criticism and history in order to develop a sense of what the possibilities are and how these might fit in with your own initial response to Eliot's poem. Only after this stage could you proceed to narrowing the topic and focusing your research on those aspects of the poem most interesting to you. For the second question, you might be able to find an initial direction for your research right away and frame some questions you would like to answer. You could then proceed with your research knowing from the start what to look for.

Choosing Your Own Topic

If you are given free, or relatively free, choice of a topic for your paper, your initial job is both harder and easier than if you are given a specific assignment. It can be difficult, when faced with the almost limitless possibilities of such a project, to focus your thoughts and get down to work. Still, you have the opportunity to begin with a writer or a piece of literature that you find especially exciting and choose to investigate an issue in which you have some personal investment.

The best place to begin finding your topic is by choosing a piece of literature which had a strong effect on you. Read through the work and its headnote again, making note of those things you find most worth thinking more about, especially any unanswered questions you may have.

Then take some time to brainstorm a list of questions about the work, the author, and the context. Write down all your questions, even those which you think you won't be pursuing. Try to move quickly beyond the sorts of questions which can be answered with a *yes* or *no* or which can be answered by a simple piece of information—*who, when,* and *where* questions. Think instead of meaty *how, what,* and *why* questions. What are the major themes and issues in the literature? How does the literature relate to other writings (by the same author or others)? What impact did the author's life have on his or her work? How did social and historical conditions shape the literature? What did previous critics and researchers—experts on this author, perhaps—have to say about the work?

Once you have a substantial list, check it for the two or three questions that most interest you. Would one of these make a good focus for your paper? If you can find enough information about the issues the question raises, could you write a paper of the appropriate length and type? Is the question narrow enough in its scope that you can investigate it thoroughly? If so, you are just about ready to begin researching. If not, look over your list again and try talking to your instructor or fellow students to see if they can offer some further refinements of your ideas. If you are concerned that the information you need will not be out there, have a backup question ready. In any case, it's important to be flexible in the early stages of your research and allow your questions to evolve and grow more complex as you become more of an expert on the topic you have chosen.

FINDING AND USING SOURCES

There are as many ways of proceeding with research as there are researchers. In working on previous projects, you may have developed your own perfect method for keeping track of sources, taking notes, and organizing your ideas. If, on the other hand, you haven't done a great deal of research (or if you have had less than satisfactory experiences with research), you might benefit from trying out the method outlined in the next section, which has worked for many researchers over the years. The system involves taking two different kinds of notes: bibliographic notes to find and acknowledge your sources, and content notes to keep track of the information you find in these sources. As you become a more practiced researcher, you will probably find yourself adapting the method to fit your own working style. The only solid rule is to be precise with your notes and references. Nothing is more frustrating than finding a gap or mistake in your notes and having to go back to the library to check a page number or the spelling of a name.

Begin your research by thinking about what sources you will need to complete your project. Plan a strategy to find those sources—the section on library research will suggest some approaches—and start a working bibliography of the books, articles, and other resources that will help you answer your research questions.

Library Research

Once you have reread the primary source (the literature about which you are writing), the headnote on the writer, and any related information in the commentaries or casebook sections of this textbook, continue your search in the college or university library. How you proceed will depend upon your topic and focus, so consider some questions before you start your search. Is your topic primarily literary, leading you to books and articles that focus on a writer's life and works? Or will you be delving into questions about history or religion or philosophy or other fields outside literary criticism? Are you researching a well-established author or one who has recently emerged and hasn't yet attracted much attention? Do you have some specific questions in mind at this point, or do you want to browse around and see how other researchers have approached your primary source? At any time during your research, you can ask a reference librarian for help, either while using one of the tools described below or simply to discuss where to look next.

The most complete listing of publications in the field of literature is the Modern Language Association's *MLA International Bibliography.* Published annually and available in some libraries in electronic format, this bibliography can provide the most thorough list of sources if what you are looking for is scholarly books and articles about writers and their work. It also covers linguistics, folklore, and to some extent, film criticism.

The print version of this bibliography covers a year at a time and is in two volumes, one that lists works by nationality, period, author, and work and another volume that is an alphabetical subject index. If, for example, you wanted to see what had been published recently on D. H. Lawrence's story "The Rocking-Horse Winner" you could look in the first volume of the most recent year, find the section for English literature, then the subsection for the twentieth century (labeled *1900–99*), and then the listing for Lawrence, which would be further subdivided for general studies and for each of his major works. If you are using an electronic version, which may be available through your library's Web site or at a CD-ROM station in the library, you can type in the name of an author or the title of a work to see what has been published on that topic. You can also search by a theme or subject or combine a topic and author (such as *Lawrence and childhood*). As with all unfamiliar electronic databases, spending ten minutes skimming through the help screens or asking a librarian how to get started is a wise investment of time.

The *MLA International Bibliography* is a good place to get a sense of how literary scholars have approached a primary source. However, because it strives for completeness, it can provide an overwhelming amount of sources when the work is well known and frequently analyzed by critics. On the other hand, you may not find enough information. If you are researching a contemporary writer, you may find few sources because there usually is a time lag before a writer gains scholarly attention. And the *MLA International Bibliography* doesn't cover publications in other fields, such as history. If, for example, you are writing about a story by Helena María Viramontes, you may have questions about the Chicana experience in California in the middle decades of the twentieth century. For these needs, most libraries provide access to an inter-disciplinary database of articles covering the major journals in various fields, including history, urban affairs, and ethnic studies. Many also index some popular publications that may include book reviews of contemporary fiction or interviews with writers. Ask your reference librarians which interdisciplinary databases are available locally and whether they might work for your topic.

Your library's online catalog is another resource. An excellent first step is to find a basic critical study of a writer and his or her works. Look for recently published, general studies that will give you background knowledge of your author's life and work to ground your research. As with all scholarly writing, these texts will provide useful bibliographies that will point you to the most significant books and articles about your topic.

The reference section of your library is a rich source of background and factual information. A series such as *Contemporary Literary Criticism* or *American Writers* can provide a quick and thorough overview of a writer's life and work. The *Encyclopedia of the American Religious Experience* might give you insight into the spiritual world of Emily Dickinson; the *Encyclopedia of African American History and Culture* may answer questions raised in reading a play by Lorraine Hansberry. The reference section is full of such specialized resources. A librarian will be able to take you straight to the sources that will provide answers.

Finally, don't expect to gather all of your sources in one or two visits to the library. As you find resources, scan through them to evaluate how they might be useful, what issues they raise, and what publications they cite as criti-cal evidence. Read as you research and let that reading help you refine the ques-tions you are asking.

Using the Web for Research

The World Wide Web is an increasingly popular place to conduct research. For some topics, such as public affairs, politics, and popular culture, it is an excellent source of information; for others, including many topics in lit-erature, it is less useful. Most literary scholars are more likely to publish their work in the form of journal articles and books than they are to put it on the Web to mingle indiscriminately with a sixth grader's term paper or a hobbyist's fan page. However, you might find interesting sites devoted to the culture of a period or digitized primary-source collections at sites such as the *Electronic Text Center* at the University of Virginia or the *American Memory* project at the Library of Congress, where you can find old film clips, recordings of speeches, and such treasures as Orson Welles's hand-annotated working script for a pro-duction of *Macbeth* that he directed in Harlem in 1936.

General search engines are of limited use for the literary scholar. Search engines work by mining the Web mechanically, pulling together sites based on words used on pages and in URLs, regardless of quality or depth. Relevance ratings are assigned not by actually reading the sites but by counting the num-ber of uses of a word or by some other automated mechanism. And even the most thorough search engines currently index less than 20 percent of the Web.

If you use a search engine, try to focus your search. For example, a search for "Shakespeare" will retrieve tens of thousands of sites, many of them of limited usefulness. But a search that uses the terms *Hamlet, Branagh,* and *film* will narrow your search to sites about the 1996 Kenneth Branagh film version of *Hamlet.* An alternative to using general search engines is to use subject-oriented selective Web directories such as the Argus Clearinghouse or Scout Signpost. These have been compiled by researchers who have attempted to find and organize by subject the best sites on the Web. Another option is to seek out valuable digital collections such as the *American Memory* project and use the search capabilities of that site to find useful resources. Finally, reference librarians pay attention to quality Web sites and may be able to point you to helpful sites. If you are researching a particular author or literary period, be sure to visit the companion Web site for this book at bedfordstmartins.com where LitLinks provides clear, concise annotations and links to over 500 literature sites. Each critical annotation will help you choose the best Web sources for your research.

In addition to sites available to anyone on the Web, many subscription information sources are now available from libraries through the Web. Library catalogs and indexes are frequently accessible through Web browsers. If your library has an electronic version of the *MLA International Bibliography,* it may be Web-based. Your library may also subscribe to full-text journal collections such as Project Muse or JSTOR, which reproduce the contents of hundreds of scholarly journals in Web format. And they may have access to general resources such as Lexis/Nexis Universe, which provides newspaper and magazine coverage as well as political and legal information. These sites are not part of the "free" Web and are not indexed by general search engines. They are generally available to a campus community either through the campus network or by modem, but may not be accessible if you connect to the Internet through a service provider other than your college or university.

Your research will most likely require you to use a combination of electronic and print resources. Above all, bear in mind that you want to find the best sources you can, regardless of how they are packaged.

Evaluating Print and Online Sources

Not all information is created equal, and just because an item has found its way into print (or has a place on a flashy Web site), you should not necessarily believe it. You should evaluate every potential source you identify in at least two ways before you include it in your paper, first to determine if the source is respectable (that is, likely to be accurate) and second to find out if it is really appropriate to your purpose.

The first and most obvious question to ask is, Who wrote and published the information? For an academic paper, the best and most reliable sources are usually scholarly journals and books published by university presses. This is not to say that a paperback book, an article from a popular magazine, or a Web site can never be an appropriate source in an academic paper. Depending on the topic of your paper, these may prove to be valuable and even vital sources.

But don't forget in compiling your bibliography that in general your paper will carry more weight if it derives its substance from scholarly sources.

Dates are also worth being aware of. Not all literary research needs to be absolutely up to date; sometimes historical research is the key to a successful paper. But if you have a choice between two critical studies, one written in 1954 and one written in 1994, use the more recent one unless you have a compelling reason to choose the other. Not only will the recent work be based on more up-to-date theories and utilize recently discovered information, but it is also likely to incorporate the ideas of earlier researchers as well.

Special caution is needed when evaluating online sources. The Internet is a vast and largely uncensored place, and much of the information available on it is incomplete, misleading, or just plain wrong. If you can't tell whether a Robert Frost Web page was posted by a professor of American literature or a middle-school student doing a project for English class, be sure to confirm any doubtful information. Sometimes the author of a Web site will include a link to a personal home page at the bottom of the page, where you might learn more about the author's credentials. If an organization has sponsored a Web project, look for links to information about the purpose and nature of the organization. URLs can offer clues as to whether the site is running on a university server (*.edu*), a commercial server (*.com*), a federal government server (*.gov*), a school (*.k12*), or the site of a nonprofit organization (*.org*). Country abbreviations such as *.ca* for Canada or *.uk* for United Kingdom may also be useful clues. If you delete the part of the URL after the first slash, you can sometimes learn something useful. It may reveal that your author has posted a page at a particular university (which doesn't necessarily tell you about its academic quality — most universities allow the members of its community to post just about anything on their sites) or at a federal government agency such as the Library of Congress (which is particular about its content). Apply to Web sites the same criteria of accuracy and relevance that you use in evaluating printed information.

Once you have established the general respectability of your sources, you need to be sure that they are actually pertinent to your research question. Including information tangential to your point just because it is interesting or comes from a strong source will not improve your paper. Your first priority should be to make the paper as sharp and well focused as possible, even if it means leaving out some fascinating ideas or facts you encounter.

Your Working Bibliography

Each time you identify a potential source of information, you will add a reference to your working bibliography. More and more these days, researchers keep bibliographies as computer files that can later be adapted into a list of works cited. If you like to work on a computer, and especially if you have a laptop model you can take to the library with you, by all means keep your working bibliography this way. The traditional way of keeping bibliographic notes, however, is on 3″ × 5″ note cards, one reference to a card, and even many computer-savvy researchers still prefer this method because they can take notes anywhere without worrying about booting up a computer.

Complete instructions on the information you will need to turn your working bibliography into a list of works cited can be found in the section on MLA format (p. 1666). The rule of thumb: If you think there is any chance the information may be needed, write it down. Copy source information from the title and copyright pages of a book (or the pages of an article or other short work).

It will save you time and trouble in preparing your list of works cited if you put the correct format for capitalization and punctuation in your bibliographic references. All titles and publication information should appear in capital and lowercase letters, even when the original is in all capitals. Subtitles are separated from titles by a colon. The titles of long works should be either underlined or italicized (not both); these works include books, plays, newspapers, magazines, journals, CDs, films, and radio and television programs. Titles of short works are put in quotation marks, not underlined or italicized; these works include stories, poems, essays, articles, chapters of books, songs, and single episodes of radio or television programs.

For a book, your bibliographic references should always present the full name of the author or editor; the full title of the book (underlined or italicized); the city, publisher, and date of publication. In addition, if the book is an edition other than the first, a volume in a series, a translation, or a work in more than one volume, provide that information too. The example shows a useful format for writing down this information and one easily adaptable for your list of works cited.

BIBLIOGRAPHY ENTRY FOR A BOOK

Danticat, Edwidge. <u>Breath, Eyes, Memory</u>. New York: Random House, 1998.

If your source is an article in a journal, magazine, or newspaper, the information will be slightly different. You will still begin with the name of the author and the title of the article (in quotation marks), followed by the title of the periodical in which the article appeared (underlined or italicized). For an academic journal, next comes the volume number and year of publication. For a magazine or newspaper, note the date (or month for a monthly publication) and year and the edition if one is given. For all types of periodicals, be sure to note the inclusive pages on which the article appeared.

BIBLIOGRAPHY ENTRY FOR A PERIODICAL

Thompson, Deborah. "Keeping Up with the Joneses: The Naming of Radical Identities in the Autobiographical Writings of LeRoi Jones/Amiri Baraka, Hetti Jones and Lisa Jones." <u>College Literature</u> 29.1 (2002):83-101.

Many academic books are collections of short works or essays written by a number of different authors on a certain topic. If you include such sources, make note of the author of the essay or chapter, the title of the chapter, the title and editor of the book, and the same publication information as for a book by a single author. The same format is used for works (including poems, stories, plays, and nonfiction essays and articles) in anthologies.

WORK IN A COLLECTION OR ANTHOLOGY

Davis, Tracy C. "Shotgun Wedlock: Annie Oakley's Power Politics in the Wild West." Gender in Performance: The Presentation of Difference in the Performing Arts. Ed. Laurence Senelick. Hanover, NH: UP of New England, 1992. 141-57.

If you intend to use online or other electronic sources, you will need to collect bibliographic information similar to that for traditional print sources, with a few notable additions. Full citation formats to use in your list of works cited are shown in the section on MLA format (p. 1666), but the following brief guidelines should help you proceed at the information-gathering stage of your research. It is not always possible to find all of the information called for, especially for Internet sources. If any of the information you need from any source — electronic or traditional — is missing, simply skip it and keep the format of the rest of your citation exactly the same.

For full-text articles published in both print and electronic formats, give the print source (if there is one) followed by the date of access and the electronic address.

Harper, Michael S. "Mary Kinzie's Talk on Milton." Callaloo 24.1 (2001): 1033-34. 4 Oct. 2002 <http://muse.jhu.edu/journals/callaloo/toc/cal24.4harper02.html>.

Some electronic addresses for articles retrieved through a database can be extremely long. In such a case, provide the name of the database and its electronic address.

Vonnegut, Kurt. "Despite Tough Guys, Life Is Not the Only School for Real Novelists." New York Times 24 May 1999, E1. 14 Nov. 1999 Lexis/Nexis Universe. <http://web.lexis-nexis.com/universe>.

There are several kinds of Internet sources you might use in your research beyond the Web-accessible databases your library provides. These include Web sites, e-mail messages, and postings to newsgroups and e-mail lists. Full documentation styles for each may be found in the section on MLA format. For Web sites, give as much of the following information as you can find: author, title of the section of the site (in quotation marks), title of the site itself (underlined), the name of any institution or organization associated with the site, the date of access, and (in angle brackets) the URL.

"The New Deal Stage: Selections from the Federal Theatre Project,

1935-1939." <u>American Memory</u>. Library of Congress. 14 Nov. 2000

<http://memory.loc.gov/ammem/fedtp/fthome.html>.

When citing communications through e-mail, newsgroups, or e-mail discussion lists, include the author of the message; the subject line (in quotation marks); the description *Online posting;* the date; the name of the forum, if relevant; the date of access; and the URL in angle brackets or, if no URL is available, the e-mail address of the list's moderator.

Downs, Jerry. "Re: Joseph Pequigney's 'Such Is My Love--A Study of

Shakespeare's Sonnets.'" Online posting. 3 Oct. 2002. 4 Oct. 2002

<news:humanities.lit.authors.shakespeare>.

When is your working bibliography complete? There is no easy answer to that question because the number and types of sources you need will depend upon the sort of paper you are writing. Also, as your research proceeds, you will likely come across additional references you will want to follow up, so in theory the bibliography is in flux until the paper is completed. Realistically, though, at some point you need to stop looking for leads and begin working with the sources themselves.

WORKING WITH SOURCES AND TAKING NOTES

So far, we have discussed how to find the information sources you will need for your research. This detective work is what many people think of when they hear the word "research." But it is only now—when the sources are in your hands—that the real research begins, as you start the intellectual work of reading, assimilating, and working with your sources.

Careful note taking is crucial to this phase of the process. No matter how sharp your memory or your organizational skills, as you work with a growing number of sources, it is easy to forget who wrote what, or even if an idea was original to you or came from another author. So it is especially important to keep yourself well organized at this point. You should have a stack of cards or a computer file with your bibliographic notes, but now you will begin to take the second kind of notes for your project—content notes. Most researchers prefer to take content notes on larger (generally 4" × 6") cards, that serve the dual purpose of making them instantly distinguishable from bibliographic cards and allow more room to make comments on the notes. Once again, if you work with a computer, you can take notes directly into a word-processing file.

As you begin to read each source, start a new note card with a heading indicating the author's last name and perhaps a shortened version of the source's title. If you are using more than one source by the same author, noting the source on each card will save you a lot of trouble should your cards get shuffled later on. Also be sure to include on all notes the page numbers from which the note is taken. When the time comes to write your paper and document your sources, you will need to provide page references for every fact, opinion, or idea you get from an outside source, whether you use the author's words or your own to record the idea.

A good way to begin note taking is with a brief summary (perhaps a few sentences) of the author's main point or idea. Try to phrase this summary in your own words. This will not only help you to be sure that you have understood your reading, it will also help you compose your essay later on because you will already have had to think through the ideas and produce some prose of your own. Remember that just changing the order of the author's words or substituting a few words of your own is not the same as writing notes in your own voice.

After you have the main idea down, your notes can grow more specific, homing in on those elements of your reading that most relate to the research question you have set for yourself. If a section of one of your sources seems especially important or speaks directly to your question, devote a separate card to it. Remember that you might disagree with an author and still find his or her ideas important, if only as points to argue against in your paper. When you are comfortably familiar with your authors and their arguments, you will almost certainly want to pull out some direct quotations from your sources. It is best to reserve quoting for times when the author has written something in memorable and effective language or when he or she expresses an idea so succinctly and clearly that you really can't imagine saying it any better. If you find yourself wanting to note more than a few short quotations from each source, you may not be focusing on what's important. When you transcribe a quotation, put the material in quotation marks; always double check to make sure that your transcription is scrupulously accurate. Remember to note the page number from which the quotation was taken. If the quotation spans two pages in the original, mark the spot in your note at which the new page begins.

Imagine, for example, you were focusing your research on the ways gender roles are portrayed in Charlotte Perkins Gilman's "The Yellow Wallpaper." Sandra M. Gilbert and Susan Gubar's commentary on the story, reprinted in this anthology, directly relates to this issue and would be a good place to start your research. Here are examples of how you might write three note cards—a summary, a paraphrase, and a quotation—from this source. The numbers in parentheses are page numbers in the original. These cards would, of course, be keyed to bibliographic cards giving the authors' full names, the article's complete title, and the necessary publication information.

SUMMARY

> The authors focus on the ways in which women--in literature and in real life--are made to feel trapped and imprisoned, in actual rooms and houses as well as in social roles. The wallpaper symbolically imprisons the narrator, and her madness allows her a sort of freedom.

PARAPHRASE

> The woman trapped behind the wallpaper represents how the narrator herself is trapped in circumstances beyond her control. In freeing the woman, she frees herself through her madness. (682)

QUOTATION

> "[. . .] even when a supposedly 'mad' woman has been sentenced to imprisonment in the 'infected' house of her own body, she may discover that, as Sylvia Plath was to put it seventy years later, she has 'a self to recover, a queen.'" (683)

Of course, as you work with your sources and take notes from them, don't let yourself be so swept up in other people's words and arguments that you forget your own purpose and ideas in writing the paper. Write your own responses and opinions directly on your note cards—but be sure to distinguish them from the author's ideas, perhaps by using a different color ink. If your reading sparks any major new ideas from you (which ideally it will), make note of these on separate cards, indicating your own name as a heading and treating these cards for now as you would the material from outside sources.

DRAFTING YOUR RESEARCH PAPER

By the time you have read and assimilated your preliminary research materials, you should basically know the direction of your paper and what you want it to say. Now is the time to write a tentative thesis statement and to begin drafting your paper. A thesis statement does not just name your topic or state a fact; it asserts what the rest of your paper will argue. It should be clearly focused and guide the reader as to the general direction of your paper. Consider these two potential theses:

1. Kate Chopin's writing was very controversial in its day.
2. By developing characters like Mrs. Mallard from "The Story of an Hour," Kate Chopin proved that she was interested more in portraying emotional truth than in the social norms of her day.

The first of these is too vague, merely stating a fact that can be easily verified. The second is more specific, more interesting, and gives its writer a real assertion to defend. The tentative thesis as you initially draft it may or may not find its way into your final paper, but it should help you set a single, manageable task for yourself and keep you on track as you begin organizing your notes and ideas.

After you have drafted your tentative thesis, you must impose some order on the pile of notes and ideas you have amassed. (If you have taken your notes on a computer, this is a good time to print out a hard copy. You may wish to cut the printout into individual notes so that you can shuffle them around.)

Whatever method you normally use to begin writing can probably be adapted to deal with including outside sources as well. But if you are having trouble getting all your thoughts in order, one way to start is by arranging smaller stacks of related notes on subtopics. Don't worry if the stacks are very uneven or if some notes seem to be unrelated to the others; you can deal with these anomalies later. And don't forget to include the notes that contain your own original ideas; they are the most important notes you have.

Now look over the cards again and put aside any that no longer seem relevant to your thesis. At this point you may discover that ideas are represented in your research about which you do not have enough information, and you will want to follow these up with more reading. You can continue with your research now, or you can proceed with writing the paper, leaving a space to be filled in later.

Start drafting your paper by whatever process has worked for you in the past for other types of writing. Some students find it helpful to begin with an outline (formal or not) or a list of key points. Others prefer to jump right into the writing itself, knowing that they will probably have to substantially reorganize the draft work at a later stage. Chapter 25 of this anthology provides several ideas, beginning on page 1622, for how to use brainstorming, freewriting, listing, and questioning to start drafting.

The following sections suggest how to develop your research materials as you write. Don't forget, though, that this is *your* paper, not a mere presentation of other people's ideas, however compelling they may be. Each time you mention an idea from an outside source, comment on it thoroughly. You may agree, dispute, analyze, or explain, but never let a quote or thought from someone else stand on its own.

Summarizing, Paraphrasing, and Quoting

You can integrate the material you have found in your research sources into your paper in three ways—as summaries, paraphrases, or quotations. Each of these techniques is useful, and you will probably end up using all three in your paper. Each time you write from a source, consider your purpose in using this source.

Integrating summaries. To help your readers understand the background and the important questions within your topic, you will sometimes want to provide a quick overview of an author's main ideas or major contributions to scholarship. In these cases, rather than give an exhaustive account of all an author has to say, you should provide brief summaries. In some cases, the summary may be as simple as rephrasing a part of your summary note card for a source. For instance, the example of a summary note from the feminist reading of "The Yellow Wallpaper" (p. 564) might appear in your paper as follows.

> Gilbert and Gubar focus on the ways in which women--in literature and in real
> life--are made to feel trapped and imprisoned, in actual rooms and houses as
> well as in social roles.

Note that such a summary gives direct credit to the authors whose ideas you are discussing and presents those ideas succinctly, without getting bogged down in the article's supporting details.

Integrating paraphrases.   You will sometimes want to focus on a more specific point made by one of your sources, and in these cases you will need either to paraphrase or to quote. As a general rule, think about paraphrasing first and save quoting for especially important points. As it did at the note-taking stage, paraphrasing makes clear that you understand the material with which you are working. It also keeps the ideas in your own words so that they fit in better with your own prose style. The example shows a paraphrase of part of the Gilbert and Gubar essay just summarized.

> Gilbert and Gubar consider the narrator's madness--and women's madness
> in general--a sort of triumph which allows her to be free of her oppressive
> surroundings.

Although the words of this paraphrase do not appear in the original essay, the idea it expresses is Gilbert and Gubar's. A paraphrase of this sort acknowledges the source of the idea while setting up the expectation that you will offer further comment on the critics' reading.

Integrating quotations.   When you want your readers to pay special attention to the material you are using, the time has come for quoting. Many students worry about how to integrate quotations into their research papers, but with practice it eventually becomes much easier and more natural. Keep in mind a few formatting features and helpful tips as you begin working with quotations from both primary and secondary sources. First, quotations should be short, using as few words as you can while conveying what you need to. Long quotations are distracting, can be difficult to integrate with your own prose, and may suggest (unjustifiably or not) that you are trying to pad your paper.

Quotations of four lines of prose (from a literary or a critical source) or three lines of poetry should be integrated into your paragraph and enclosed within quotation marks. For longer quotations, set off the quoted material from your paragraph by beginning a new line and indenting an inch from the left margin only. It will be clear to your readers that any material thus set off is a quotation, so do not use quotation marks and do not switch to single spacing. The examples show the formats for integrating a short and a long quotation.

> Melville begins "Bartleby, the Scrivener" with the narrator's description of his
> qualifications as a storyteller. Melville's narrator begins by telling us the fol-
> lowing information about himself:
>
> > I am a rather elderly man. The nature of my avocations, for the last
> > thirty years, has brought me into more than ordinary contact with
> > what would seem an interesting and somewhat singular set of men,

> of whom, as yet, nothing, that I know of, has ever been written--I mean,
> the law-copyists, or scriveners. (352)

Indicate deletions with an ellipsis.   A few special situations deserve note. In some cases, you might wish to change a quotation slightly to make it fit the grammar of your sentence, or you may choose to delete part of a quotation in the interest of being succinct. Any additions or changes in wording that you make should be placed within brackets. Short deletions that you make should be indicated with an ellipsis within brackets. For deletions of more than a sentence, use four periods for the ellipsis (the first period is closed up; a space then follows each one). The example shows changes and a short deletion from the Melville passage quoted.

> The narrator says that "the nature of [his] avocations [. . .] has brought [him]
> into more than ordinary contact with what would seem an interesting and
> somewhat singular set of men" (352).

Of course, it is dishonest to put words into someone else's mouth, so it is important that any changes you make do not affect the basic content or meaning of the passage you quote.

Indicate line breaks in a short quotation from a poem.   When a short quotation is from a poem, you need to indicate any line breaks that occur within the quotation. This is done with a slash mark, with single spaces before and after.

> Langston Hughes declares, "They'll see how beautiful I am / And be ashamed--
> I, too, am America" (16-18).

Indicate a quotation within a quotation.   When part of the material you need to put in quotation marks is already in quotation marks in the original use single quotation marks to indicate the marks which appear in the original and double quotation marks to indicate what you are quoting.

> The narrator calls, "'Bartleby! quick, I am waiting'" (358).
>
> In his essay "The Origin of 'Cathedral,'" Tom Jenks recalls the first time he
> met Raymond Carver.

In addition to understanding the correct format for presenting and punctuating quotations, you will need to integrate them smoothly into your paper so that they do not interrupt or distract from your original prose. Three ways of integrating quotations are explained, from the least to the most effective.

Avoid the floating quotation.   First, try to avoid the *floating quotation,* which is simply a sentence or phrase lifted out of the original and put in quotation marks with the attribution of the source and any commentary coming in another sentence (if at all).

> "Rage, rage against the dying of the light" (3). These words show Dylan
> Thomas's passionate sorrow at his father's impending death.

This method creates two problems. First, because the quotation is self-contained, it leaves a reader (albeit momentarily) to ponder its source and wonder why it has been presented at this point. Also, it makes for choppy reading; it presents an awkward transition from the poet's voice to that of the commentator.

Use an attributed quotation.　When possible, then, you should always use at least an *attributed quotation,* which identifies the author with a lead-in to the quotation.

> Thomas writes, "Rage, rage against the dying of the light" (3). In doing so he
> demonstrates his passionate sorrow at his father's impending death.

With this type of quotation, the reader sees immediately where the quoted text comes from and knows (or at least expects) that your commentary will follow.

Use an integrated quotation.　Even more effective is the *integrated quotation;* it not only attributes the quoted material to its author but smoothly makes the quotation a part of your own sentence.

> Thomas demonstrates his passionate sorrow when he begs his father to "rage
> against the dying of the light" (3).

This is the hardest sort of integration to achieve because you have to make the quotation fit in grammatically with your own sentence. Usually, though, the payoff in sharp prose is well worth a little time spent in revising.

DOCUMENTING YOUR SOURCES

Beginning researchers often find frustrating the precise format they must follow in giving credit to sources. Once again, understanding why documentation format exists as it does will help you to learn how to do it right. Documentation serves two purposes: It protects you from charges of plagiarism, and it allows your readers to find the source of any quoted or cited material.

Nearly all students know that copying the words of an author and turning them in as their own work is plagiarism. What many do not realize, however, is that plagiarism can take more subtle forms. In fact, because they don't fully understand the concept, students often plagiarize unintentionally. Plagiarism occurs any time a writer uses another person's words or *ideas* without giving full credit to the original source. So even if you paraphrase another writer's thoughts entirely in your own words, you must document fully where those thoughts originated. Your readers will assume that everything not credited in your paper is either your original idea or that you are trying to take credit for it.

The only exception to the rule on crediting sources is that you need not document common knowledge, which might be defined as anything that a reasonably well-educated person should be expected to know. The name of the U.S. president or the fact that William Shakespeare was an English playwright, for instance, would not need to be attributed. If you are unsure whether or not something counts as common knowledge, document it.

MLA Format

Several systems of documentation are used in academic disciplines, and while these systems vary, they all serve the same purpose. For papers in literature and some of the humanities, the format is the one developed by the Modern Language Association, or MLA. The system breaks down into two parts. First are brief in-text parenthetical citations that occur in the body of a paper to indicate an author and page number for each summary, paraphrase, or quotation. Second is a works cited list (a bibliography) that provides complete information about the sources for those citations. When readers come across a reference to an author in the body of your paper, they can then turn to the list of works cited, look up the name, and find out more about the source. Check the *MLA Handbook* for complete instructions on citing all types of sources.

In-Text or Parenthetical Citations

MLA style presents two types of in-text citations: when the author's name appears in a signal phrase, or when the name is not included or there is no signal phrase. In the first, you signal the author's name in the lead-in to your citation (see instructions for attributed and integrated quotations, p. 1665) and provide a page reference in parentheses following the citation. The examples demonstrate the method using both a short and long quotation from literature.

SHORT QUOTATION WITH AUTHOR'S NAME IN TEXT

In Lorraine Hansberry's A Raisin in the Sun, Walter says, "Rich people don't have to be flashy" (1466).

LONG QUOTATION WITH AUTHOR'S NAME IN TEXT

In his poem "Mexicans Begin Jogging," Gary Soto asks,

> What could I do but yell vivas
> To baseball, milkshakes, and those sociologists
> Who would clock me
> As I jog into the next century
> On the power of a great, silly grin. (17-21)

For circumstances such as works by more than one author, multiple works by the same author, anonymous works, and works by corporate authors, the system for in-text citations is essentially the same, with a few notable differences.

WORK WITH TWO OR THREE AUTHORS

According to Gates and Appiah, . . .

WORK WITH MORE THAN THREE AUTHORS

Berger et al. claim . . .

If your paper refers to more than one work by the same author or to an anonymous work, it is especially important to include the name of the work in your signal phrase.

MORE THAN ONE WORK BY THE SAME AUTHOR

In "Technique in Writing the Short Story," Chekhov argues . . .

ANONYMOUS WORK

A U.S. News and World Report article titled "Barbour Gets a Comeuppance" states that . . .

If the author is an organization rather than an individual, use the organization name.

ORGANIZATION AS AUTHOR

The American Psychological Association reports that . . .

The second type of MLA in-text citation is used when the author is not named in a signal phrase. In this case, both the author's last name and the page number appear in the parentheses.

CITATION WITH AUTHOR'S NAME IN REFERENCE

The authors explain that "a setting may be either a simple backdrop to the action or it may be crucial in itself" (DeMarr and Bekerman 109).

The citation consists of only the last name (or names) and page number with no additional punctuation or information. The exception to this is when your paper cites more than one work by the same author; in this case your citation should include the author's name followed by a comma, the title (or a shortened version of it) of the work being cited, and the page number.

CITATION WITH AUTHOR'S NAME AND TITLE OF WORK IN REFERENCE

The author feels that words must mean what they say (Welty, "Is Phoenix Jackson's Grandson Really Dead?" 604).

List of Works Cited

Start your list of works cited on a new page in your paper, with the words "Works Cited" centered at the top. Continue double-spacing throughout, but do not add additional spaces between entries. Use hanging indentation in your list of works cited; this means that all lines *except* the first of each entry are indented. All entries are alphabetized by author's last name (or in the event of an anonymous work, by the first word of the title, disregarding *a, an,* or *the*).

Citing information from books. An entry for a book should contain as much of the following information as is applicable, in the following order and format, with periods between groups of elements. For most books you will use, details on editor, translator, volume, or series will not be needed.

1. The name of the author (or editor, if no author is listed), last name first
2. The title (underlined or in italics), including any subtitle (separate the title from subtitle by a colon)
3. The name of the editor (for a book with both author and editor), translator, or compiler (with the abbreviation "ed.," "trans.," or "comp.")
4. The edition, if it is not the first
5. Volume used if the book is part of a multivolume set
6. Series name if the book is part of a series
7. City of publication (followed by a colon), name of the publisher (comma), and year of publication

The most basic entry would be for a book by a single author or editor.

BOOK BY A SINGLE AUTHOR OR EDITOR

Moody, Anthony David. Thomas Stearns Eliot, Poet. 2nd ed. Cambridge: Cambridge UP, 1994.

Adams, Hazard, ed. Critical Essays on William Blake. Boston: Hall, 1991.

Citing works in anthologies. When you are citing an article, story, poem, or other shorter work that appears as a part of a book, include as much of the following information as you can.

1. The name of the author of the short work
2. The title of the short work, enclosed in quotation marks
3. The name of the anthology's editor
4. All relevant publication information just as it would appear in a book citation
5. The inclusive page numbers for the shorter work

To cite a work of literature in an anthology or an article or chapter in a compilation:

WORK IN AN ANTHOLOGY

Ellison, Ralph. "Battle Royal." Literature and Its Writers: A Compact Introduction to Fiction, Poetry, and Drama. 3rd ed. Ed. Ann Charters and Samuel Charters. Boston: Bedford/St. Martin's, 2003. 150-60.

Citing works in periodicals. When you cite sources from journals, magazines, or newspapers, include the following information.

1. The name of the author of the short work
2. The title of the short work, enclosed in quotation marks
3. The title of the periodical, underlined or italicized
4. All relevant publication information (specified in the examples)
5. The inclusive page numbers for the shorter work

For a work in a scholarly journal with continuous pagination (that is, a journal that numbers the pages straight through a volume year, as if each issue were a part of a single work), publication information should include the volume number and the year of publication (in parentheses), followed by a colon and the page numbers.

ARTICLE IN A SCHOLARLY JOURNAL

Montgomery, Thomas. "The Presence of a Text: The Poema de Cid." MLN 108
(1993): 199-213.

Citing newspaper articles. To cite an article in a newspaper, include the date (day, month, then year) and an edition if one is listed on the masthead, followed by a colon and the page number. Remember that many papers paginate each section separately, so you may need to include a section number or letter as part of the page number.

ARTICLE IN A NEWSPAPER

Swarns, Rachel. "Zimbabwe's Novels of Reckoning." New York Times 7 Oct.
2002: B1.

Citing other sources. You may want to cite a review, a television or radio program, a video or sound recording, a letter, e-mail communication, or interview. The following models demonstrate the basic format to follow.

REVIEW

Brantley, Ben. "A Pedophile Even a Mother Could Love." Rev. of How I Learned
to Drive by Paula Vogel. New York Times 17 Mar. 1997, late ed.: C11.

TELEVISION OR RADIO PROGRAM

Elie Wiesel: First Person Singular. PBS. WGBH, Boston. 25 Oct. 2002.

VIDEO OR SOUND RECORDING

Brook, Peter, dir. William Shakespeare's King Lear. Orion, 1970.

Kinnell, Galway. "In the Hotel of Lost Light." The Poetry and Voice of Galway
Kinnell. Caedmon Cassette, 1971.

LETTER, E-MAIL COMMUNICATION, OR INTERVIEW

Crane, Carolyn. Letter to the author. 8 Feb. 1997.

Higgins, Andrew J. E-mail to the author. 4 June 1997.

Smith, Melanie. Personal interview [or Telephone interview]. 12 Apr. 1997.

Citing CD-ROMs, the Internet, and other electronic sources. Cite information from a CD-ROM, the Internet, and other electronic sources using these formats. If any of the required information is missing from an electronic source, skip it and keep the format for the rest of the citation exactly the same.

NONPERIODICAL PUBLICATION ON CD-ROM

"Brontë, Emily." Discovering Authors. Vers. 1.0. CD-ROM. Detroit: Gale, 1992.

PERIODICALLY PUBLISHED DATABASE ON CD-ROM

Gauch, Patricia Lee. "A Quest for the Heart of Fantasy." New Advocate 7.3

(1994): 159-67. Abstract. ERIC. CD-ROM. Silverplatter, 1999.

WEB SITE

"Iranian Women Poets." Art Arena. 4 Oct. 2002 <http://www.art-arena.com/
womenp.htm>.

NEWSGROUP POSTING

Karg, Moritz. "New Web Directory for Human Rights." Online posting. 11 Oct.

1999. 14 Nov. 1999 <news:soc.rights.human>.

The instructions and examples above will cover the vast majority of the sources you encounter. Complete information for how to cite these and any other type of source as well as additional information on conducting research and the mechanics of writing and formatting a research paper can be found in:

> Gibaldi, Joseph. *MLA Handbook for Writers of Research Papers.* 5th ed. New York: MLA, 1999.

Footnotes and Endnotes

You will have noticed that the MLA format, with its in-text citations and list of works cited, does not require footnotes or endnotes to refer to sources. However, the format does allow for the use of notes in two specific circumstances. The first instance is for *bibliographic notes* in which the writer of the research paper, in addition to referring the reader to one or more sources, makes specific comment on the sources themselves. The second is for *content notes,* in which the writer makes a comment that is related to the research topic but does not fit easily within the text of the paper itself. Both types of notes should be used only when you cannot find another way to integrate the information, and for most research papers such notes will probably not be necessary.

Unless your instructor specifically asks for footnotes, always use endnotes instead. As the name implies, endnotes appear at the end of the paper — on a separate page, after the text but before the Works Cited list. To signal a note in your paper, use a superscript numeral in the text matching the numeral that precedes the note. Notes should be in the same type font and size as the rest of your paper and should maintain double spacing. For examples of both sorts of notes, see the sample research paper that begins on page 1673.

REVISING YOUR RESEARCH PAPER

Once your research paper is completely drafted, with all sources fully integrated and documented, the time has come to revise it, just as you would any other paper. The following six-part checklist provides a systematic method for approaching revision. You might also ask a classmate, or even your instructor, to look over the draft and offer advice.

1. First, look again at your tentative thesis statement. Now that you have written the paper, does the thesis still seem exactly right? It is possible, even likely, that in the process of writing you may have refined or changed your ideas about your topic. If so, reword the thesis to accurately reflect your new thinking.
2. Now look again at the supporting evidence you offer in each body paragraph. Do all of the ideas directly relate to and uphold the thesis? If any of them do not, you should cut these sections from your paper, regardless of the intrinsic interest of the ideas or the strength of the writing.
3. Are there any portions of the paper where you worry that the argument may be thin or underdeveloped or where the connection to your thesis may not be entirely clear? If so, you should try to explain your ideas more fully. You may even need to do some additional research to fill in the gaps.
4. After any necessary cuts and additions have been made, you may need to slightly reorganize the paper. Is your argument presented in the most logical order and are all related ideas kept together? Rearrange and revise any awkwardly placed paragraphs or sentences.
5. Does the style and voice sound at all like your usual writing? It is easy when reading the thoughts and words of other authors to begin adopting the style of these authors and losing your own voice. Check to make sure that the vocabulary and tone reflect your personality and your attitude toward the subject. By writing in your own voice, you make the material and the project your own.
6. Finally, carefully review the assignment and make sure that your essay conforms to your instructor's guidelines in all respects. In the event of disagreement, his or her guidelines should always take precedence over those offered here or anywhere else.

Your essay should now be ready for the final polish before you turn it in. Print out a clean copy and review it twice more. The first time, edit and proofread for word choice, grammar, spelling, and punctuation as well as any other small changes that will improve style and readability. If you are in doubt about anything, look it up. Even small mistakes can have a large negative effect on a reader. The second time, go over the format of all quotations, parenthetical references, and your works cited page to make sure that they are consistent and conform exactly to guidelines. You are now ready to make your last changes, print out a final copy, and turn in a research paper you can be proud of.

WEB *For more information on writing a research paper, see Research and Documentation Online at bedfordstmartins.com/charters/litwriters.*

STUDENT RESEARCH PAPER

The student research paper that follows puts into practice the instructions and suggestions we have been discussing. You can also use it as a guide to proper manuscript format. Unless your teacher calls for some other format (such as a cover page), you should begin in the upper left corner of page 1 with your name, your instructor's name, the course for which you are writing the paper, and the date you turn it in. Double-space and center the title of your paper in capitals and lowercase letters without underlining or quotation marks (unless, of course, a quotation or title appears within your own title). Then begin the paper itself, with regular one-inch margins and double-spacing throughout (including for quotations and the list of works cited). A running head with your last name and the page number should appear in the upper right corner of each page. All word-processing programs make it easy to include such headings.

Silva 1

Jennifer Silva

Professor Gardner

English 102

7 November ----

Emily Dickinson and Religion

Upon a cursory examination of her biography, it could be easy to dismiss religion as playing an insignificant role in Emily Dickinson's life and work. At the time of the Second Great Awakening, when most of New England was swept along by the fervent religious revival movement, Dickinson resisted. Even after the rest of her family formally joined the church, she refused since she just could not accept all aspects of church doctrine (Benet 19). Even in her poems, because "most have predictable rhyme schemes" and are "easy to memorize," it is easy to overlook the religious value (Schmidt 31). Many readers and critics have, in fact, drawn attention to her unconventional views, claiming that "she was deprived of an orthodox and steady religious faith" (Wilbur 955) or that "she fought against God" (Tanter). But in overlooking or dismissing the important role that religion played in her life, we miss an important element of Emily Dickinson's poetry.

Even though she never felt able to fully accept all aspects of Christian doctrine, it would be wrong to assume that religion did not influence Dickinson's life and work. In fact, religion and her faith in God seems to have played a large role. Emily Dickinson was raised in a deeply religious household. As a child, she was discouraged from reading anything except the Bible (Higginson 949). In her childhood, adolescence, and early twenties, she attended church with her family twice every Sunday, hearing at least 1,500 sermons during this period. From the letters she wrote, it is clear that she was "capable of being transported by a good sermon" and "the effect on her of these weekly [. . .] invasions of her spirit [. . .] was profound" (Doriani 45). While she still didn't accept all of the conventions of the church, Dickinson wrote to her brother Austin that the preachings of Professor Edwards Amasa Park of Andover Theological Seminary, Reverend Edward S. Dwight, and especially Reverend Charles Wadsworth, among others, greatly inspired her (Doriani 46).

Silva 2

The influence of religion on her life spills over into her
poetry, which reveals her strong belief in God and heaven.
Dickinson discloses her great faith, her ability to believe without the assurance of concrete proof, in the poem "I never saw
a Moor--." She writes,

> I never spoke with God
>
> Nor visited in Heaven--
>
> Yet certain am I of the spot
>
> As if the Checks were given-- (5-8)

Indent quotation of three or more lines of poetry, four or more lines of prose.

She does not have to see God or heaven to know that they
exist, just as she has never seen "a Moor" or "the Sea" but still
knows "how the Heather looks / And what a Billow be" (3-4).
For her, the existence of heaven is as real and certain as the
existence of the heather and billow. How can she be so sure of
the existence of these things she cannot see? Presumably, she
has learned about the heather and billows through the written
and spoken accounts of others. In the same way, she accepts
the existence of God and heaven probably as a result of the
influence of the Bible, the words of the many preachers she
has heard in her life, and the teachings of her family. Surrounded by these testimonies since early childhood, Dickinson
feels she can faithfully commit herself to believing in God and
heaven's existence. Many avid readers of her poetry agree that
"she never forsook her strong beliefs in God" (Nelson).

Page number only; author cited in text.

Her faith and religion are such a significant part of her
life that words with religious connotations even appear in her
poems about other subjects, as if her immersion in religion is
so great that she cannot separate it from other parts of her
life. Even in her poetry about secular subjects, Dickinson's
"Puritan heritage persistently provided her with a vocabulary,
with metaphors, for experience that she and her world understood" (Juhasz 124). In poems about love and death (such as
"Love--thou art high--," "If you were coming in the Fall," and
"Because I could not stop for Death--") appear the words "eternity" and "Eden," words with significant religious meaning and
implications which affect the connotations of the poems. "I
taste a liquor never brewed--" includes the religious words
"seraphs" and "saints": "[. . .] Seraphs swing their snowy
Hats-- / And Saints--to windows run--" (13-14). Religion has a

Slash indicates line break in poetry.

Silva 3

place in all parts of her life, and consequently in all of her poetry. We can read these poems without focusing on their religious content, but to do so deprives us of an important layer of their meaning.

Even the formal style of her poetry reflects the influence of religion, for the hymns she learned in church and psalms she read in the Bible shaped her work. Many of her poems, "written in simple quatrains, generally in iambic tetrameter [. . .] with only the second and fourth lines rhyming," follow the same basic pattern as church hymns (Charters and Charters 866).[1] Poems written in this hymn-like form--with approximate rhyme of the second and fourth lines, written in primarily iambic tetrameter and trimeter in simple quatrains-- include "Because I could not stop for Death--," "If you were coming in the Fall," and "I heard a Fly buzz--when I died--." Once again, while these poems do not focus on explicitly religious subjects, the impact of religion on their form and content is evident.

Superscript numeral for endnote.

Because of the hymn-like quality of Dickinson's poetry, readers can be swept along quickly by the rhythm and miss some of the meaning of a poem. To alleviate this problem, Dickinson uses dashes as pauses to slow fast-moving lines, similar to the pausing technique she observed preachers using to emphasize a thought or hold the audience's attention (Doriani 48). For example, to place emphasis on the word "Nobody" in line 2 of the poem "I'm Nobody! Who are you?," she surrounds the word with dashes: "Are you--Nobody--Too?" Similarly, in "I died for Beauty--but was scarce" Dickinson uses dashes to slow down the reading of line 7 and emphasize the word "Truth": "And I--for Truth--Themself are One--." By adopting a convention used by the preachers who impressed her, Dickinson not only indicates the influence of religion in her life but also enhances the quality of her poetry for readers.

Another preaching technique that Dickinson adopted for her poetry concerns the use of natural speech. In addition to pausing for emphasis, "the practice of the preachers of the Puritan legacy [. . . was] to reject an affected style or an eloquence not characteristic of ordinary speech" (Doriani 16). This style is mirrored in much of Dickinson's poetry. Even

Brackets for addition or change to citation.

when attempting to capture a complex concept like hope in her poetry, she skillfully expresses her thoughts with refreshingly simple, yet elegant language without compromising the elevated content. In "'Hope' is the thing with feathers--" she describes the complicated feeling of hope with very simple words and metaphors: "the thing with feathers-- / That perches in the soul-- / [. . .] sweetest--in the Gale [. . .]" (1-2, 5). At times, Dickinson even seems to be conversing with the reader through her poems. The poem "I'm Nobody! Who are you?" addresses the reader directly in a conversational tone. The many preachers that she heard using this type of language in speeches and sermons must surely have influenced her poetry style.

Much has been made of the fact that the young Emily Dickinson "found that she must refuse to become a professing Christian" (Wilbur 955).[2] But even though Dickinson's religion has no church, her faith in God should not be doubted. A distinction must be made between nonconformist religious views and an outright rejection of God or religious values. Throughout her life, Dickinson strongly believed, "God's residence is next to mine, / His furniture is love" ("Who has" 197). Her God resides with her always--a guiding force touching all aspects of her life. Her faith is strong and unwavering. And if we read her work carefully and with an open mind, we can see that Dickinson's religious faith did not die with her in her Amherst house in 1886. Its fervor and vitality are still alive in her elegant poetry, preserved in simple verse to inspire generations for all time.

Silva 5

Notes

¹ A number of interesting studies--including Morris and
Wolosky--discuss the ways in which Dickinson adapted and
reshaped the hymn form in her poems.

*Bibliographic
endnote commenting
on sources.*

² Nearly all biographies of the poet stress her resistance
to the doctrine preached during her brief time at Mount
Holyoke Seminary.

Content endnote.

Silva 6

Works Cited

Benet, Laura. <u>The Mystery of Emily Dickinson</u>. New York:
Dodd, 1974.

Book by a single author.

Charters, Ann, and Samuel Charters, eds. <u>Literature and Its</u>
<u>Writers: A Compact Introduction to Fiction, Poetry, and</u>
<u>Drama</u>. 3rd ed. Boston: Bedford/St. Martin's, 2003.

Anthology cited by editors' names.

Dickinson, Emily. "'Hope' is the thing with feathers--." Charters
and Charters 869-70.

---. "I died for Beauty--but was scarce." Charters and Charters
871.

More than one work by an author.

---. "I'm Nobody! Who are you?" Charters and Charters 870.

---. "I never saw a Moor--." Charters and Charters 875-76.

---. "I taste a liquor never brewed--." Charters and Charters 868-
69.

---. "Who has not found the heaven below." <u>Selected Poems and</u>
<u>Letters of Emily Dickinson</u>. Ed. Robert N. Linscott.
Garden City, NY: Anchor, 1959. 197.

Doriani, Beth Maclay. <u>Emily Dickinson, Daughter of Prophecy</u>.
Amherst: U of Massachusetts P, 1996.

Higginson, Thomas Wentworth. "Emily Dickinson's Letters."
Charters and Charters 1012-18.

Cross-reference to another citation in an anthology.

Juhasz, Suzanne. <u>The Undiscovered Continent: Emily Dickinson</u>
<u>and the Space of the Mind</u>. Bloomington: Indiana UP,
1983.

Morris, Timothy. "The Development of Dickinson's Style."
<u>American Literature</u> 60 (1988): 256-41. 14 Nov. 2002.
JSTOR. <http://wwwjstor.org>.

Article in a scholarly journal.

Nelson, Perry L. "Re: Dashes and Meter." Online posting. 29 July
1996. EMWEB. 14 Nov. 2002 <http://lal.cs.byu.edu/
mlists/emweb/199607/19960729-12.html>.

Internet source.

Schmidt, Elizabeth. "Imagining Emily." <u>New York Times Book</u>
<u>Review</u> 2 Mar. 1997: 31.

Article in a newspaper.

Tanter, Marcy. "ED as War Poet." Online posting. 9 Jan. 1997.
EMWEB. 14 Nov. 2002 <http://lal.cs.byu.edu/mlists/
emweb/199701/19970109-1.html>.

Wilbur, Richard. "On Emily Dickinson." Charters and Charters
1022-24.

Wolosky, Shira. "Rhetoric or Not: Hymnal Tropes in Emily
Dickinson and Isaac Watts." <u>New England Quarterly</u> 61
(1988): 214-32.

Glossary of Literary Terms

The boldfaced page references indicate where a key term is highlighted in the text.

Abstraction Language that describes ideas or qualities rather than tangible, observable people, places, and things, which are described in concrete language. **717**

Accent The strong syllable, or syllables, in a word; the emphasis, or stress, given a syllable in pronunciation. All words with more than one syllable will have at least one *strong* accent. The other syllables are called *weak* accents. **697,** 705

Action At its simplest, the events or things that happen in a PLOT — what the CHARACTERS do and what is done to them. 1055

Alexandrine A line of poetry with six stressed accents. **760**

Allegory A NARRATIVE usually restricted to a single meaning or general truth, in which characters, places, things, and events represent abstract qualities. Such characters, places, things, and events thus often function as SYMBOLS of the concepts or ideas referred to. See also PARABLE. 218

Alliteration The repetition of the same consonant sounds beginning each word in a sequence of words. **692**

Allusion An implied or indirect reference to something with which the reader is supposed to be familiar. **818**

Anacrusis An unstressed syllable at the beginning of a line that does not affect the overall poetic meter. **707**

Anapest See FOOT.

Anapestic meter See FOOT.

Antagonist   The character in a short story or play who is in real or imagined opposition to the PROTAGONIST. The conflict between these characters makes up the action, or plot, of the story. It is usually resolved in some way, but it need not be.   **1064**

Aphorism   A short, concise statement of a principle or a sentiment.   **757**

Apostrophe   A figure of speech in which the poet addresses something that is inanimate or abstract as a personified thing.   **719,** 725

Archetypes   The characters, images, and themes that symbolically embody universal human meanings and experiences.   1612

Assonance   The repetition of internal vowel sounds without the repetition of consonant sounds used as an alternative to rhyme in verse to create an aural unity within a poetic line or sequence of lines.   **693**

Ballad   A narrative poem, often a song, that tells a story.   **734**

Biographical criticism   A critical approach that uses important facts about the life of an author to shed light on literary texts.   **1610**

Blank verse   Unrhymed iambic pentameter. It was used by Shakespeare and other Elizabethan dramatists because iambic meter was closest to the natural rhythms of English speech.   **708**

Blocking   The actors' movement onstage during the duration of the play. **1068**

Caesura   A break or pause within a line of poetry that contributes to the rhythm of the line.   **707**

Character   Any person who plays a part in a narrative work. Characters may be *flat*—simple and one-dimensional, or *static*—unsurprising and unchanging; or *round*—complex, full, described in detail, or *dynamic*—often contradictory and changing in some way during the story. The main character can usually be labeled the PROTAGONIST or hero; he or she is often in conflict with some other character, an ANTAGONIST. Other characters who affect the ACTION slightly or only indirectly are called *minor* characters; but, depending on the intention or the skill of the author, the main characters need not be round, nor the minor characters flat.   **10**–11, 19, 1055, **1064,** 1065, 1075

Climax   The turning point or point of highest interest in a narrative; the point at which the most important part of the ACTION takes place and the final outcome or RESOLUTION of the PLOT becomes inevitable. Leading up to the climax is the RISING ACTION of the story; after the climax, the FALLING ACTION takes the reader to the conclusion or *denouement*, in which the resolution of the climactic action is presented.   **8,** 1055

Close reading   Reading works of literature analytically in order to understand the author's creation of design and pattern in the text.   **xlii**

Closed form   Traditional verse forms, as opposed to OPEN FORM or FREE VERSE. **705**

Comedy   A literary work, often written in a light and amusing style, in which the plot ends happily. See also TRAGEDY.   **1051**

Connotative meaning   The associated meanings that have built up around a word, or what a word connotes. These implications go beyond the literal meaning of a word. See also DENOTATIVE MEANING.   **714**

Convention   A traditional or commonly accepted technique of writing or device used in writing, sometimes an unbelievable device that the reader agrees to believe — such as, for example, the fact that a FIRST-PERSON NARRATOR is addressing the reader in a friendly and intimate manner.

Couplet   Two consecutive lines of poetry with the same meter that end in a perfect rhyme. See also RHYME.   **732**

Cultural criticism   A critical method that advocates an interdisciplinary approach, often using history, sociology, or philosophy, to study literary works in a cultural context.   **1616**

Dactyl   See FOOT.

Dactylic meter   See FOOT.

Deconstructionist criticism   An approach to literature that emphasizes a close reading guided not so much by a search for surface meaning as by an exploration of the text's internal contradictions, the places where meaning does not remain stable.   **1615**

Denotative meaning   The direct, specific meaning of a word, as distinct from an implied or associated meaning. See also CONNOTATIVE MEANING.   **714**

Dialogue   The exchange of words between characters in a story, poem, or play. Do not confuse with *dialect*, which is a type of non-standard English diction spoken by people from a particular geographic region, economic group, or social class.   **1065,** 1076

Diction   A writer's choice of language — including words, phrases, and sentence structure. A writer's diction is an important element of STYLE. The same idea will leave a different impression on the reader when it is narrated in street slang, in the precise language of an old schoolteacher, or in the professional jargon of a social worker. **Poetic diction** refers to the way poets can employ an elevated diction that is different from common speech, using so-called poetic language.   **715**

Didactic   Literature that attempts to instruct or teach a lesson, convey a moral, or inspire and provide a model for proper behavior.   **1072**

Drama   Originating in the Greek verb *dran*, "to perform," drama may refer to a single play or to a group of plays ("Elizabethan drama"). Usually drama is designed to be performed in a theater where actors take on the roles of the characters. A *play* is the general term for a work of dramatic literature; it is created by a *playwright*, a writer who makes plays.   **1050**

Dramatic monologue   A poem written in the form of a speech or extended narration that the person who is the speaker in the poem delivers to someone else. This kind of lyric poetry often describes a dramatic situation while also indirectly suggesting an important aspect of the speaker's personality.   **774**

Dramatic poetry   The use of poetry in the writing of drama.   **773**

Dynamic character   See CHARACTER.

Elegy   A serious, contemplative lyric poem written to lament someone's death and memorialize his or her life. See also LYRIC POETRY.   **746**

End orientation   The suggestion of the outcome of the action or the conclusion of the plot contained in the opening paragraphs of a short story.   **8**

End rhyme   See RHYME.

End-stopped line   A poetic line that comes to a definite stop or pause at the end.   **698**

Enjambed/enjambment   A poetic line whose meaning is not complete at the end but continues on without pause to the next line. This is also called a *run-on line*.   **698**

Epic   The oldest form of narrative poetry, usually written in an elevated style, that chronicles important heroic deeds and events in a nation's history. See also NARRATIVE POETRY.   **733**

Epigram   Short poems, often rhymed, that are usually funny or wryly satirical. They are intended to make a sharp comment or witty observation.   **756**

Epiphany   A "showing forth" or sudden revelation of the true nature of a CHARACTER or situation through a specific event — a word, gesture, or other action — that causes the reader to see the significance of that character or situation in a new light. The term was first associated with modern literature in the writing of James Joyce.   250

Explication   The act of explaining or interpreting the meaning of a text.   **1638**

Exposition   The presentation of background information, usually early in a story, that a reader or a theatrical audience must be aware of, especially about situations that exist and events that have occurred before the ACTION of a NARRATIVE begins.   **8**, 1055

Eye rhyme   See RHYME.

Falling action   The events of a NARRATIVE that follow the CLIMAX and resolve the conflict before the story is brought to its conclusion.   **8**, 1055

Falling meter   See METER.

Feminine rhyme   See RHYME.

Feminist criticism   See GENDER CRITICISM.

Figurative language   The use of a word or a group of words that is literally inaccurate but is used to describe or define a person, event, or thing more vividly by calling forth the sensations or responses that person, event, or thing evokes. Such language often takes the form of METAPHORS, in which one thing is equated with another, or of SIMILES, in which one thing is compared to another by using *like, as,* or some other such connecting word.   **724**

First-person narration   The telling of a story by a person who was involved in or directly observed the action narrated. Such a narrator refers to himself as *I* and becomes a CHARACTER in the story, with his or her understanding shaping the reader's perception of the events and the other characters. The first-person narrator can be either a major or a minor character in the story. **13**

Flat character See CHARACTER.

Foot The unit of the rhythmic pattern that makes up the meter, usually consisting of one stressed and one or two unstressed syllables. An *iambic foot* or *iambic meter* consists of one unstressed syllable followed by one stressed syllable ("invok'd"). A *trochaic foot* consists of one stressed syllable followed by an unstressed syllable ("wonder"). An *anapestic foot* is two unstressed syllables followed by one stressed syllable ("by the sea"). A *dactylic foot* is one stressed syllable followed by two unstressed syllables ("beautiful"). A *spondee* is a foot consisting of two stressed syllables ("drop dead"). A *pyrrhus* is a foot with two unstressed syllables. **706–8**

Foreshadowing The introduction of specific words into a NARRATIVE to suggest or anticipate later events that are central to the ACTION and its RESOLUTION. **9**

Formalist criticism An approach to literature that focuses on the formal elements of the work. Formalist critics concentrate on analyzing how the various elements of a literary work — especially such elements of style as irony, metaphor, and symbol — are integrated into the unique structure of a literary work. Anything outside of the work, such as biographical information or the work's historical context, is usually not discussed. See also NEW CRITICISM. **1610**

Free verse Poetry written by poets who felt that they had to break free of traditional poetic forms. Often free verse uses colloquial speech patterns and breath pauses to shape the poetic line, and it usually is unrhymed. See also OPEN FORM. **705**

Gender criticism An approach to literature that considers the gender and sexual orientation of both writers and readers of literature. Gender criticism developed from *feminist criticism,* which sought to correct or supplement a predominantly male-dominated critical perspective with a woman's point of view, often showing how women's writing strategies were related to their social conditions. **1615**

Genre A type of literary work, such as SHORT STORY, novel, essay, play, or poem. The term may also be used to classify literature within a type, such as science-fiction stories or detective novels. In film, the term refers to a recognizable type of movie, such as a western or a thriller, that follows familiar NARRATIVE or visual conventions.

Haiku A short lyric poetic form found in Japanese poetry that suggests a world of allusion and response. The traditional haiku form is three lines, with five syllables in the two outer lines and seven syllables in the middle line. **766**

Historical criticism An approach to literature that investigates the historical background of the text. Historical critics may also explain the meaning that the work had for its original readers, especially if the text includes words that had different connotations in the past. **1612**

Hyperbole   Exaggerated statements that are not intended to be taken for the truth. Often called *overstatement,* hyperbole is often used for comic or ironic effect.   **726**

Iamb   See FOOT.

Iambic meter   See FOOT.

Iambic pentameter   A metrical pattern in poetry that consists of five iambic feet per line, each foot consisting of one unstressed syllable followed by a stressed syllable. See also BLANK VERSE.   **706**

Imagery   A word, phrase, or figure of speech such as a simile or a metaphor that suggests mental pictures of sensory impressions, such as *visual images* (things we see), *aural images* (things we hear), and *tactile images* (things we touch).   717, **718**

Imagism   A term invented by the American poet Ezra Pound as the name for a group of poets experimenting with the language of common speech before World War I. As an imagist poet, Pound believed that poems should "present an image. Poetry should render particulars exactly, and not deal in vague generalities, however magnificent and sonorous."   **769**

Internal rhyme   See RHYME.

Irony   A literary device that uses words to express something other than what is meant by the speaker. *Verbal irony* is a figure of speech that occurs when the speaker says one thing but means the opposite. If the intention of the speaker is to hurt someone else, then this form of verbal irony verges on *sarcasm. Dramatic irony* occurs when the reader (or the audience of a play) knows more about a situation than the imaginary characters.   **15,** 1076

Limerick   A short, humorous poem consisting of five lines with the rhyme scheme *aabba.* Since the characteristic anapestic meter of limericks makes them easy to remember, they are one of the most widespread types of folk poetry.   **758**

Line   A sequence of words printed on the page. Poetic lines are often measured by the number of feet they contain, such as:

> *monometer*: one foot   *pentameter*: five feet
> *dimeter*: two feet   *hexameter*: six feet
> *trimeter*: three feet   *heptameter*: seven feet
> *tetrameter*: four feet   *octameter*: eight feet

The number of feet in a line, along with the name of the foot, describes the metrical qualities of that line. See also END-STOPPED LINE, ENJAMBMENT, FOOT, METER.

Literal language   Words used in their denotative sense, the opposite of FIGURATIVE LANGUAGE.   **724**

Literary theory   The term used by academic critics to characterize a method of inquiry into the nature and value of literature.   **1609**

Lyric poetry   The word *lyric* comes from *lyre,* the small harp played by the Greek poets to accompany their songs. A lyric is a type of poem that is highly suggestive, deeply personal, and often intensely emotional. Among the types of lyric poetry are the ELEGY, the ODE, and the SONNET.   740

Lyrics   The text of a song.

Marxist criticism   An approach to literature based on the writings of Karl Marx that emphasizes the political and socioeconomic aspects and contexts of literary works. See also SOCIOLOGICAL CRITICISM.   **1613**

Masculine rhyme   See RHYME.

Metaphor   A figure of speech or type of FIGURATIVE SPEECH in which one thing is equated with another in an indirect comparison without using the word *like* or *as*. Writers use metaphors in order not to define the first terms mentioned, but to attribute certain qualities to the thing being discussed, such as "Love is a rose" or "The exam was a killer." See also METONYMY, PERSONIFICATION, SYNECDOCHE.   **721**

Meter   The pattern set up by the regular rhythm of words in a poem. *Rising meter* refers to metrical feet moving from unstressed to stressed sounds, such as the iambic foot. *Falling meter* refers to metrical feet moving from stressed to unstressed sounds, such as the dactylic foot. See also ACCENT, FOOT, LINE.   **706–8**

Metonymy   A type of metaphor in which the writer uses the name of one thing in place of the name of something closely related to it, such as saying "I knew him in his cradle" to mean "I knew him when he was young." See also METAPHOR.   **725**

Minimalism   A literary styled exemplifying economy and restraint, as seen in the early stories of Raymond Carver. Some of Ernest Hemingway's stories, such as "Hills Like White Elephants," are considered pioneering works of minimalism.   74

Monologue   A play meant to be spoken or performed by one actor appearing alone on stage.   **1054**

Mythological criticism   An approach to literature that developed out of Jungian psychoanalytic theory about the importance of archetypal human behavior. Mythological critics attempt to identify and analyze the psychological elements of recurrent patterns in literary works that create deep universal responses in readers. See also ARCHETYPES.   **1612**

Narrative   An example of discourse designed to represent a connected succession of events or happenings, usually involving CHARACTERS, PLOT, and SETTING.   3

Narrative poetry   A long or short poem that tells a story. See also EPIC.   **733**

Narrator   The dramatic voice of the person telling the story, not to be confused with the author's voice. With FIRST-PERSON NARRATION, the *I* in the story presents the viewpoint of only one character, who may play either a major or a minor role in the action. An UNRELIABLE NARRATOR gives an interpretation of events that the reader cannot trust to represent the view of the author. A *naive narrator* is usually too innocent or inexperienced to understand the deeper meaning of the action. An OMNISCIENT NARRATOR is an all-knowing narrator, usually the author, who is not a character in the story. *Limited omniscience* occurs when the author restricts a story in THIRD-PERSON NARRATION to the single perspective of either a major or a minor character. See also OBJECTIVE NARRATION, PERSONA, POINT OF VIEW. 13–14

Near rhyme   See RHYME.

New criticism   An approach to literature developed after World War II that evolved out of FORMALIST CRITICISM. New critics emphasize close reading of literary texts rather than inquiring into their biographical or historical backgrounds.   1610

Objective narration   A way of telling a story from a third-person point of view without revealing the thoughts or feelings of any character. The detached and impersonal narrator reports action and dialogue directly, without analysis or interpretation, relying on the dialogue, actions, and physical descriptions to reveal the meaning of the story to the reader. See also NARRATOR, POINT OF VIEW, THIRD-PERSON NARRATION.   13–14

Octave   A poetic stanza of eight lines, often forming one part of a SONNET. **733**

Ode   One of the oldest forms of poetry, a lyric that serves as a formal, serious poem of praise, often presenting philosophic ideas and moral concerns. See also LYRIC POETRY.   **742**

Omniscient narrator   Literally "all-knowingness"; the ability of an author or narrator (usually in THIRD-PERSON NARRATION) to tell the reader directly about any events that have occurred, are occurring, or will occur in the PLOT of a story, and about the thoughts and feelings of any CHARACTER. 13, 14

Onomatopoeia   A term referring to the use of a word that resembles the sound it denotes, for example, *buzz*. Writers may also create lines or entire paragraphs using onomatopoeia, where the sound of the words helps to convey the meaning of the passage.   **694**

Open form   Earlier called FREE VERSE, open form poetry breaks from traditional use of METER and RHYME. Instead, the poet depends upon the arrangement of words on the printed page, or grammatical structure, or other means to produce the concentration and technical virtuosity of poetry written in closed forms.   705, **764**

Ottava rima   An eight-line stanza with a rhyme scheme of *ababahcc*.   **760**

Oxymoron   A statement that contradicts itself, such as "jumbo shrimp."   **726**

Parable   A short narrative used to answer a difficult moral question or teach a moral truth. Often a form of ALLEGORY, because each person, event, or thing in the parable represents a literally unrelated person, event, thing, or quality that is involved in the moral dilemma being examined.   **765**

Paradox   A statement that on the surface seems that it cannot possibly be true, but that turns out to be true after all. To solve a paradox, the reader must uncover a meaning that is not evident at first sight. Poets often use paradox to capture a reader's attention by suggesting an idea that appears to be nonsense, as in John Donne's statement "Death, thou shalt die." 723, **725**

Paraphrase A device used by poets as a response to poetic tradition, where writers find their own words to express their sense of an earlier literary work they consider important. **816,** 824–25

Parody A humorous imitation of another, usually serious, work or type of work, in which the parodist adopts the quirks of STYLE or the CONVENTIONS of the work or works being imitated and uses them in extreme and ridiculous ways, or applies them to a comically inappropriate subject matter. **817**

Perfect rhyme See RHYME.

Persona An imaginary person through whom the poet can speak. Literally, a persona is a mask, behind which an author speaks or narrates a story. A persona is always a separate self, neither a character in the narrative, nor the author's personal voice. **740**

Personification A form of metaphor in which human characteristics are given to something inanimate, animal, or abstract. For example, in Keats's "Ode on a Grecian Urn," the urn is called an "unravished bride of quietness." See also METAPHOR. **724**

Plot The sequence of events in a short story or a play and their relation to one another. Authors select and arrange the incidents to give their stories a particular focus or emphasis. The series of events in the narrative form the ACTION, in which a CHARACTER or characters face an internal or external conflict that propels the plot to a CLIMAX and an ultimate RESOLUTION. The conclusion or *denouement* of the plot may have a *closed ending,* in which the major issues are resolved, or an *open ending,* in which the future actions of the characters are undetermined. Literary works concluding with the death of the protagonist are considered to have *closed endings.* See also WELL-MADE PLAY. **6, 7**–10, 19, 1055, **1062,** 1075

Poetic diction See DICTION.

Point of view The author's choice of a narrator for the story to shape what the reader knows and how the reader feels about the events of a story. See also FIRST-PERSON NARRATION, NARRATOR, OBJECTIVE NARRATION, THIRD-PERSON NARRATION. **6, 13,** 19

Poststructuralist criticism Similar to DECONSTRUCTIONIST CRITICISM, this is a modern approach to critical theory that focuses on the multiple, sometimes self-contradictory meanings that exist in a literary work. **1615**

Prose poem A lyric poem that has all the characteristics of a lyric but is written in densely compact prose. It presents one image or, like a lyric poem in open form, a response to a single emotion. See also LYRIC POETRY. **765**

Protagonist The main CHARACTER of a narrative, who engages the reader's interest and empathy. The ACTION of a story is usually the presentation and RESOLUTION of some internal or external conflict of the protagonist; if the conflict is with another major character, that character may be called the ANTAGONIST.   **10, 1064**

Psychological criticism   An approach to literature indebted to modern psychological theories, including those of Sigmund Freud, that explores the unconscious motivations of characters and the symbolic meaning of events, as well as the reader's personal responses to the text.   **1611**

Pyrrhus   See FOOT.

Quatrain   A four-line stanza, usually rhymed, that for centuries has continued to be one of the most widely used poetic means in English and American poetry.   **733**

Reader-response criticism   An approach to literature that suggests that reading is as much a creative act as the writing of a text, because both involve the play of imagination and intelligence. The consciousness of the reader as he or she reads the literary work is the subject of this type of criticism, investigating the possibility of multiple readings and analyzing what our readings tell us about ourselves.   **1614**

Realism   The telling of a story or a drama in a manner that is faithful to the reader's experience of real life, limiting events in the PLOT to things that might actually happen and CHARACTERS to people who might actually exist.

Refrain   The repeated line that ends the verses in a BALLAD.   **734**

Resolution   The conclusion of a plot's conflicts and complications. The resolution follows the CLIMAX and the FALLING ACTION in the PLOT.   1055, 1062

Revenge tragedies   Plays in which the plot typically centers on a spectacular attempt to avenge the murder of a family member.   **1130**

Rhyme   The repetition of similar or identical terminal sounds of concluding syllables in different words, usually at the ends of lines. *Eye rhyme* is when two words look as though they would sound alike, but their sound, if spoken aloud, is different, such as *bough* and *cough*. Words can rhyme even if they aren't spelled the same way or look as if they rhyme, such as *day, weigh,* and *bouquet*. *End rhyme* is when the words at the end of the line rhyme. The *rhyme scheme* of a poem is the pattern of end rhymes. *Internal rhyme* places at least one of the rhymed words in the middle of the line. *Masculine rhyme* means that the accent on the rhyming words is on a final stressed syllable (*betray* and *away*) or the rhyming consists of one-syllable words (*milk* and *silk*). *Feminine rhyme* consists of a rhymed stressed syllable followed by one or more identical unstressed syllables (*season* and *reason*). *Exact* or *perfect rhymes* (such as the examples above) exist between words that share the same stressed vowel sounds as well as the sounds that follow the vowel. In *near rhyme* or *slant rhyme*, the sound of the rhyming words is close but not exact, such as *read* and *red, ball* and *bell. Consonance* is a common form of near rhyme, in which identical consonant sounds are preceded by different vowel sounds, such as *home* and *same, worth* and *breath*. **694**–98

Rhyme royal   A seven-line stanza in iambic pentameter with a rhyme scheme of *ababbcc*.   **760**

Rhythm   A term used to refer to the recurrence of stressed and unstressed sounds in poetry. The pattern of words in LINES and STANZAS, and the repetitions of sounds within the poem create different rhythmic effects that add to the pleasure of reading, reciting, and listening to poetry.   705

Rising action   See PLOT.

Rising meter   See METER.

Romanticism   A literary movement that flourished in the nineteenth century, valuing individuality, imagination, and the truth revealed in nature.   954

Round (characters)   See CHARACTER.

Satire   A work that ridicules some aspect of human behavior by portraying it at its most extreme; distinguished from PARODY, which burlesques the STYLE or content of a work.

Scansion   The reader's analysis of the arrangement of ACCENTS or STRESSED SYLLABLES in a LINE of poetry in an attempt to understand its pattern. **706**

Sentimentality   A negative term in literary criticism, suggesting that the author of a literary work has engaged in emotional overindulgence, trying to force emotional responses in the reader that are not justified by the situation or characters' behavior.   **11**

Sestet   A six-line stanza. See also STANZA.   **733**

Sestina   A verse form composed of six stanzas, each six lines long, with a concluding verse of three lines called the *envoy*.   **761**

Setting   The physical details of the place, the time, and the social context that influence the actions of the CHARACTERS. Often setting also evokes a mood or atmosphere, FORESHADOWING events to come for the attentive reader. **7, 11,** 19

Short story   A short fictional prose narrative, usually consisting of one unified episode or a sequence of related events. Fables, sketches, and tales are included in this genre. The term is often applied to any work of narrative prose fiction shorter than a novel. Edgar Allan Poe said the tale or story's distinguishing feature was that it was a prose form possessing aesthetic unity that could be read in one sitting. The trouble with that definition, as writer William Saroyan later pointed out, is that some people can sit longer than others.   **3**

Simile   A figure of speech that makes an explicit comparison between two things by using words such as *like* or *as*. "My love is like a red, red rose" is a simile. "My love is a red rose" is a metaphor. "My love smells like a red rose because she is wearing perfume tonight" is a sentence that uses *like*, but it is not a simile; it is a statement of fact.   **721**

Sketch   A relaxed, predominantly descriptive prose composition that usually includes some action. Typically, however, a sketch doesn't develop characterization or dramatize complex, causally related actions that resolve a conflict.

Slant rhyme See RHYME.

Sociological criticism An approach to literature by critics interested in exploring the economic, racial, and political context in which fiction, poetry, and drama are created and read. Sociological critics treat literature as either a document reflecting social conditions, or a literary work produced by those conditions. MARXIST CRITICISM and *feminist criticism* are two forms of sociological criticism. See also GENDER CRITICISM. **1613**

Soliloquy A dramatic convention by means of which a character speaks his or her thoughts aloud when alone onstage, conveniently informing the audience about his or her state of mind so that we can understand the character's motivation for subsequent acts. Hamlet's soliloquy beginning "To be or not to be" is the most famous soliloquy in English. **1067**

Sonnet A fourteen-line lyric poem written in a regular rhyme sequence, often in iambic pentameter. The two basic types are the *Italian sonnet,* perfected in Italy in the early fourteenth century, and the *English sonnet.* The Italian sonnet, also known as the Petrarchan sonnet, is divided into an OCTAVE and a SESTET. The English sonnet is organized into three QUATRAINS and a concluding COUPLET, typically rhyming *abab cdcd efef gg.* This rhyme scheme is more suited to the English language, which has fewer rhyming words than Italian. **750**

Spenserian stanza Eight lines of iambic pentameter and a last line of six stressed feet (an ALEXANDRINE). This nine-line stanza is named after the English poet Edmund Spenser, who used it for his epic poem *The Faerie Queen,* written at the end of the sixteenth century. **760**

Spondee See FOOT.

Stanza A grouping of lines, set off by a space on the page, that usually has a set pattern of METER and RHYME. **732**

Static character See CHARACTER.

Stereotyping Characters who are oversimplified and generalized into stock types in a literary work, whose thoughts and actions are easily predictable because they are used so frequently that they have become conventional. **11**

Stressed syllables Syllables given heavier emphasis when reading a line of poetry. See also ACCENT. **705**

Style The distinctive and recognizable way an author uses language to create a work of literature. This can involve the writer's DICTION, sentence length and SYNTAX, TONE, use of figures of speech, IRONY, and THEME. **7, 15,** 19

Subplot A minor PLOT, often involving one or more secondary CHARACTERS, that may add a complication to the ACTION of a SHORT STORY or DRAMA. A subplot may also reinforce the major plot or provide an enlightening contrast to it or a welcome relief from its tension. **1063**

Symbol   A word (or person, object, image, or event) that evokes a range of additional meanings that are usually more abstract than its literal significance. *Conventional symbols* such as the American flag have so much meaning attached to them that we cannot see them without immediately thinking about something else at the same time. Writers use conventional symbols to reinforce meanings or suggest FORESHADOWING, as when Edgar Allan Poe mentions the mound of bones in the crypt into which Montresor has lured Fortunato to suggest Fortunato's imminent death. *Literary* or *contextual symbols* are settings, characters, actions, or things in a work of fiction, poetry, or drama that keep their literal significance but also suggest symbolic interpretation.   **15,** 724

Synecdoche   A type of metaphor in which the writer uses part of something to stand for the whole thing, such as saying "He has a heavy bat" to mean "He hits the ball well." See also METAPHOR.   **725**

Syntax   A reference to the order of the words in writing of any kind. Syntax usually implies a word order that results in meaningful verbal patterns in the author's choice of words, phrases, and sentence structure. These verbal choices allow authors to emphasize any word of their choice as they manipulate syntax.   **716**

Tale   An early form of the SHORT STORY, usually involving remote places and times, and often events that lead to a dramatic, conclusive ending. Early tales were told in either poetry or prose.

Tercet   A three-line STANZA.   **733**

Terza rima   A TERCET in IAMBIC PENTAMETER with an interlocking three-line rhyme scheme: *aba, bcb, cdc, ded,* etc.   **744,** 760

Theme   A generalization about the meaning of a story, poem, or play. It is an abstract concept that is made concrete through the other means available to the writer, such as PLOT, CHARACTERIZATION, and SYMBOL. This underlying central idea serves as a unifying point around which the literary work is created and/or understood.   **7, 15**–16, 20, **686,** 1055, **1068,** 1076

Thesis sentence   The central idea of an essay expressed in a complete sentence (or group of sentences, if the central idea to be developed in the essay is a complex one).   **1625**

Third-person narration   A way of telling a story using the third person "he" or "she," in which the narrator is a nonparticipant in the story. There are many varieties of third-person narration, including OMNISCIENT, limited omniscient, and OBJECTIVE. See also NARRATOR and POINT OF VIEW.   **14**

Tone   The way authors convey their unstated attitudes toward their subjects as revealed in their literary STYLE. Tone can be described as serious or comic, ironic or naive, angry or funny, or any other emotional states that human beings can experience and find words to express.   **15,** 710–11

Tragedy   A drama typically describing the downfall of a human being, often a conflict between the PROTAGONIST and a superior force (such as fate or a powerful ANTAGONIST), leading to a disastrous conclusion that excites pity or terror. A *tragic flaw* is a defect in the tragic hero that precipitates his or her downfall, such as ambition or pride.   **1051**

Tragicomedy   A mixture of sad and happy events in a DRAMA. Often the PLOT of a tragicomedy is fast moving, dealing with love, jealousy, intrigue, and surprises, but at the end of the story, as in Paula Vogel's *How I Learned to Drive,* the audience usually experiences the play as a positive statement, an affirmation of life.   **1051**

Triplet   A TERCET in which all three lines rhyme.

Trochaic meter   See FOOT.

Trochee   See FOOT.

Understatement   Describing something, often for comic effect, in terms that suggest it is much smaller or less important than we know it really is. Understatement is the opposite of HYPERBOLE.   **726**

Unity   The relation of all parts of a work to one central or organizing principle that forms them into a complete and coherent whole.   6

Unreliable narrator   A fictional CHARACTER telling the story whose knowledge or judgment about events and other characters is so flawed or so limited as to make him or her a misleading guide to the reader.   13

Unstressed syllables   Syllables given less emphasis when reading a line of poetry. See also ACCENT.   **705**

Verse   A term used generically to mean poetry or a specific unit within a poem. The term can also be used to describe metrical writing distinguished from poetry by its lower level of intensity.   **732**

Villanelle   A fixed form of poetry in nineteen lines composed of five TERCETS and a final QUATRAIN, written in IAMBIC PENTAMETER. The rhyme scheme for the tercets is *aba,* and the quatrain repeats the final rhyme, *abaa.* Like the SESTINA, the villanelle is an elaborate word game in which entire lines appear again and again. Dylan Thomas's "Do not go gentle into that good night" is a villanelle.   **762**

Voice   A term referring to the specific manner chosen by the author to create a story or poem. Voice encompasses elements of literary STYLE such as TONE and DICTION. It is usually difficult to get a sense of the original author's voice in a text that has been translated from a foreign language into English.   **15**

Well-made play   A nineteenth-century realistic play that was so carefully and logically constructed that its plot led unfailingly to a final scene resolving all the dramatic conflicts. Henrik Ibsen challenged the *closed ending* convention of a well-made play when *A Doll House* culminated in an *open ending* without a clear resolution of the complex moral and gender issues dramatized onstage. See also PLOT.   **1237**

Acknowledgments (continued from p. iv)

Margaret Atwood. "Gertrude Talks Back" and "Happy Endings" from *Good Bones and Simple Murders* by Margaret Atwood. Copyright © 1983, 1992, 1994 by O. W. Toad Ltd. A Nan A. Talese Book. Reprinted by permission of Doubleday, a division of Random House, Inc., and McClelland & Stewart Ltd., The Canadian Publishers.

James Baldwin. "Sonny's Blues," copyright © 1965 by James Baldwin, was originally published in the *Partisan Review.* Copyright renewed. Collected into *Going to Meet the Man,* published by Vintage Books, reprinted by arrangement with the James Baldwin Estate.

Toni Cade Bambara. "The Lesson" from *Gorilla, My Love* by Toni Cade Bambara. Copyright © 1972 by Toni Cade Bambara. Reprinted by permission of Random House, Inc.

Russell Banks. "Black Man and White Woman in Dark Green Rowboat" from *The Angel on the Roof: Stories* by Russell Banks. Copyright © 2000 by Russell Banks. Reprinted by permission of HarperCollins Publishers Inc.

Raymond Carver. "The Bath" from *What We Talk About When We Talk About Love* by Raymond Carver. Copyright © 1981 by Raymond Carver. "Cathedral" and "A Small, Good Thing" from *Cathedral* by Raymond Carver. Copyright © 1983 by Raymond Carver. Reprinted by permission of Alfred A. Knopf, a division of Random House, Inc.

Anton Chekhov. "The Lady with the Pet Dog" translated by Avrahm Yarmolinsky, from *The Portable Chekhov* by Anton Chekhov, edited by Avrahm Yarmolinsky, copyright 1947, © 1968 by Viking Penguin, Inc. Renewed © 1975 by Avrahm Yarmolinsky. Used by permission of Viking Penguin, a division of Penguin Group (USA) Inc.

Edwidge Danticat. "Seven" first appeared in *The New Yorker.* Reprinted by permission of Edwidge Danticat and Aragi, Inc.

Ralph Ellison. "Battle Royal" from *Invisible Man* by Ralph Ellison. Copyright © 1948 by Ralph Ellison. Reprinted by permission of Random House, Inc.

Louise Erdrich. "The Red Convertible" from *Love Medicine, New and Expanded Version.* Copyright © 1984, 1993 by Louise Erdrich. Reprinted by permission of Henry Holt and Company

William Faulkner. "A Rose for Emily" from *Collected Stories of William Faulkner.* Copyright 1930 and renewed 1958 by William Faulkner. Reprinted by permission of Random House, Inc.

Gabriel García Márquez. "A Very Old Man with Enormous Wings" from *Leaf Storm and Other Stories* by Gabriel García Márquez. Copyright © 1971 by Gabriel García Márquez. Reprinted by permission of HarperCollins Publishers, Inc.

Nadine Gordimer. "The Ultimate Safari" from *Jump and Other Stories.* Copyright Felix Licensing B. V., 1991. Reprinted by permission of Farrar, Straus & Giroux, LLC.

Ernest Hemingway. "Hills Like White Elephants" from *The Short Stories of Ernest Hemingway.* Copyright 1927 by Charles Scribner's Sons, renewed © 1955 by Ernest Hemingway. Reprinted by permission of Scribner, an imprint of Simon & Schuster, Inc.

Shirley Jackson. "The Lottery" from *The Lottery and Other Stories.* Copyright 1948, 1949 by Shirley Jackson, renewed © 1976, 1977 by Lawrence Hyman, Barry Hyman, Mrs. Sarah Webster, and Mrs. Joanne Schnurer. Reprinted by permission of Farrar, Straus & Giroux, LLC.

Franz Kafka. "The Metamorphosis" and "A Hunger Artist" by Franz Kafka, translated by Ann Charters. Copyright © 2002 by Ann Charters. Reprinted by permission of the translator.

Jamaica Kincaid. "Girl" from *At the Bottom of the River.* Copyright © 1978, 1983 by Jamaica Kincaid. Reprinted by permission of Farrar, Straus & Giroux, LLC.

Jhumpa Lahiri. "Interpreter of Maladies" from *Interpreter of Maladies* by Jhumpa Lahiri. Copyright © 1999 by Jhumpa Lahiri. Reprinted by permission of Houghton Mifflin Company. All rights reserved.

Mary Lavin. "The Widow's Son" from *A Café: Selected Stories* by Mary Lavin. Copyright © 1999 by Mary Lavin. Reprinted by permission of Anthony Sheil Associates.

D. H. Lawrence. "The Rocking-Horse Winner" copyright 1933 by the Estate of D. H. Lawrence, renewed © 1961 by Angelo Ravagli and C. M. Weekley, Executors of the Estate of Frieda Lawrence, from *Complete Short Stories of D. H. Lawrence* by D. H. Lawrence. Used by permission of Viking Penguin, a division of Penguin Group (USA) Inc.

Guy de Maupassant. "The Necklace," translated by Marjorie Laurie from *Short Stories of Guy de Maupassant* (New York: E. P. Dutton, 1934). Reprinted by permission of Everyman's Library/David Campbell Publishers.

Rick Moody. "Boys" from *Demonology* by Rick Moody. Copyright © 2001 by Rick Moody. Reprinted by permission of Little, Brown and Company.

Joyce Carol Oates. "Where Are You Going, Where Have You Been?" from *The Wheel of Love and Other Stories*. (New York: Vanguard, 1970). Copyright © 1970 by Joyce Carol Oates. "The Lady with the Pet Dog" from *Marriages and Infidelities* by Joyce Carol Oates. Copyright © 1972 by Joyce Carol Oates. Reprinted by permission of John Hawkins Associates, Inc.

Tim O'Brien. "The Things They Carried" from *The Things They Carried*. Originally published in the August 1986 issue of *Esquire*. Copyright © 1989 by Tim O'Brien. Reprinted by permission of Houghton Mifflin Company.

Flannery O'Connor. "Everything That Rises Must Converge" from *The Complete Stories*. Copyright © 1971 by the Estate of Mary Flannery O'Connor. Reprinted by permission of Farrar, Straus and Giroux, LLC. "A Good Man Is Hard to Find," copyright © 1953 by Flannery O'Connor and renewed © 1981 by Regina O'Connor, and "Good Country People," copyright 1955 by Flannery O'Connor and renewed © 1983 by Regina O'Connor, from *A Good Man Is Hard to Find and Other Stories*. Reprinted by permission of Harcourt, Inc.

Tillie Olsen. "I Stand Here Ironing" from *Tell Me a Riddle*. Copyright © 1956, 1957, 1960, 1961 by Tillie Olsen. Reprinted by permission of Dell Publishing, a division of Random House, Inc.

Grace Paley. "A Conversation with My Father" from *Enormous Changes at the Last Minute*. Copyright 1971, 1974 by Grace Paley. Reprinted by permission of Farrar, Straus and Giroux, LLC.

Annie Proulx. "The Blood Bay" reprinted with permission of Scribner, an imprint of Simon & Schuster Adult Publishing Group, from *Close Range: Wyoming Stories* by Annie Proulx. Copyright © 1999 by Dead Line, Ltd.

Leslie Marmon Silko. "The Man to Send Rain Clouds" from *Storyteller* by Leslie Marmon Silko. Copyright © 1981 by Leslie Marmon Silko. Reprinted by permission of Seaver Books, New York, New York.

John Steinbeck. "Chrysanthemums" copyright 1937, renewed © 1965 by John Steinbeck, from *The Long Valley* by John Steinbeck. Reprinted by permission of Viking Penguin, a division of Penguin Group (USA) Inc.

Amy Tan. "Two Kinds" from *The Joy Luck Club*. Copyright © 1989 by Amy Tan. Reprinted by permission of G. P. Putnam's Sons, a division of Penguin Group (USA) Inc.

John Updike. "A & P" from *Pigeon Feathers and Other Stories* by John Updike. Copyright © 1962 and renewed 1990 by John Updike. Reprinted by permission of Alfred A. Knopf, a division of Random House, Inc.

Helena María Viramontes. "Miss Clairol" from *Chicana Creativity and Criticism: Charting New Frontiers in American Literature*, 2nd ed., edited by Maria Herrera-Sobek and Helena María Viramontes. Copyright © 1988 by Helena María Viramontes and Maria Herrera-Sobek. Copyright © 1996 by University of New Mexico Press. Reprinted by permission of the publisher.

Alice Walker. "Everyday Use" from *In Love & Trouble: Stories of Black Women*. Copyright © 1973 by Alice Walker. Reprinted by permission of Harcourt, Inc.

Eudora Welty. "A Worn Path" from *A Curtain of Green and Other Stories*. Copyright 1941 and renewed 1969 by Eudora Welty. Reprinted by permission of Harcourt, Inc.

William Carlos Williams. "The Use of Force" from *The Collected Stories of William Carlos Williams*. Copyright © 1938 by William Carlos Williams. Reprinted by permission of New Directions Publishing Corp.

FICTION COMMENTARIES

James Baldwin. Excerpt from *Notes of a Native Son* by James Baldwin. Copyright © 1955, renewed 1983 by James Baldwin. Reprinted by permission of Beacon Press, Boston.

Wayne C. Booth. "A Rhetorical Reading of O'Connor's 'Everything That Rises Must Converge'" from *A Rhetoric of Irony.* Copyright © 1974 by the University of Chicago Press. Reprinted by permission of the author and the University of Chicago Press.

Robert H. Brinkmeyer Jr. "Flannery O'Connor and Her Readers" is reprinted by permission of Louisiana State University Press from *The Art and Vision of Flannery O'Connor* by Robert H. Brinkmeyer Jr. Copyright © 1989 by Louisiana State University Press.

Cleanth Brooks and Robert Penn Warren. "A New Critical Reading of 'The Fall of the House of Usher'" from *Understanding Fiction* by Cleanth Brooks and Robert Penn Warren (New York: Appleton-Century-Crofts, 1943). Copyright 1943 by F. S. Crofts and Co., Inc.

Raymond Carver. "On Writing" from the *New York Times,* February 15, 1981. Copyright © 1981 by the New York Times Company. Reprinted by permission. "Creative Writing 101" from the Foreword to *On Being a Novelist* by John Gardner. Foreword copyright © 1983 by Raymond Carver. Reprinted by permission of HarperCollins Publishers, Inc.

Anton Chekhov. "Technique in Writing the Short Story" excerpted from *Letters on the Short Story, the Drama, and Other Literary Topics* by Anton Chekhov, translated by Constance Garnett. Copyright by Constance Garnett. Reprinted by permission.

Kate Chopin. "How I Stumbled upon Maupassant" reprinted by permission of Louisiana State University Press from *The Complete Works of Kate Chopin,* edited by Per Seyersted. Copyright © 1969 by Louisiana State University Press.

Joan Dayan. "Amorous Bondage: Poe, Ladies, and Slaves" from *The American Face of Edgar Allan Poe,* edited by Rosenheim, Shawn, and Rachman, pp. 179–209. Copyright © 1995. Reprinted by permission of the Johns Hopkins University Press.

Ralph Ellison. "The Influence of Folklore on 'Battle Royal'" from *Shadow and Act* by Ralph Ellison. Copyright © 1953, 1964 and renewed 1981, 1992 by Ralph Ellison. Reprinted by permission of Random House, Inc.

William Faulkner. "The Meaning of 'A Rose for Emily'" by William Faulkner from *Faulkner in the University,* edited by Frederick Gwynn and Joseph Blotner (Charlottesville: Virginia, 1959). Reprinted by permission of the University of Virginia Press.

Sally Fitzgerald. "Southern Sources of 'A Good Man Is Hard To Find'" from "Happy Endings" by Sally Fitzgerald in *Image* (Summer 1997). Reprinted by permission of *Image.*

Richard Ford. "On Chekhov's 'Lady with the Pet Dog'" (originally titled "Why We Like Chekhov") from *The Essential Tales of Chekhov,* edited and with an Introduction by Richard Ford and translations by Constance Garnett. Copyright 1919, © 1972 by Macmillan Co. Introduction copyright © 1998 by Richard Ford. Reprinted by permission of Harper-Collins Publishers.

James W. Gargano. "The Question of Poe's Narrators in 'The Tell-Tale Heart' and 'The Cask of Amontillado'" reprinted from *College English* (December 1963). Copyright © 1963 by the National Council of Teachers of English.

Sandra M. Gilbert and Susan Gubar. "A Feminist Reading of 'The Yellow Wallpaper'" from *Madwoman in the Attic.* Copyright © 1979 by Yale University. Reprinted by permission of Yale University Press.

Zora Neale Hurston. "How It Feels to Be Colored Me" from *I Love Myself When I Am Laughing.* Reprinted by permission of the Estate of Zora Neale Hurston and the Victoria Sanders Agency.

Shirley Jackson. "The Morning of June 28, 1948, and 'The Lottery'" (editors' title; originally titled "Biography of a Story") from *Come Along with Me,* edited by Stanley Edgar Hyman. Copyright 1948, 1952 © 1960 by Shirley Jackson. Reprinted by permission of Viking Penguin, a division of Penguin Group (USA) Inc.

Tom Jenks. "The Origin of 'Cathedral'" from *Remembering Ray: A Composite Biography of Raymond Carver,* edited by William L. Stull and Maureen P. Carroll. Copyright © 1993 by William L. Stull and Maureen P. Carroll. Reprinted by permission of Capra Press, Santa Barbara.

J. Gerald Kennedy. "On 'The Fall of the House of Usher'" from *Death and the Life of Writing.* Reprinted by permission of Yale University Press.

D. H. Lawrence. "On 'The Fall of the House of Usher' and 'The Cask of Amontillado'—Edgar Allan Poe" from *Studies in Classic American Literature* by D. H. Lawrence. Copyright

1923 by Thomas Seltzer, Inc., renewed 1950 by Frieda Lawrence. © 1961 by The Estate of the late Mrs. Frieda Lawrence.

Bobbie Ann Mason. "On Tim O'Brien's 'The Things They Carried'" from *Esquire* (August 1986). Reprinted by permission of International Creative Management, Inc.

Dorothy Tuck McFarland. "On 'Good Country People'" from *Flannery O'Connor*. Copyright © 1976 by Frederick Unger. Reprinted by permission of The Continuum Publishing Group.

J. Hillis Miller. "A Deconstructive Reading of Melville's 'Bartleby, the Scrivener'" from *Versions of Pygmalion*. Copyright © 1990 by the President and Fellows of Harvard College. Reprinted by permission of Harvard University Press.

Jim Naughton. "As Raymond Carver Muses, His Stature Grows" from the *Post-Standard* (Syracuse, New York), November 23, 1982. Reprinted by permission of the author.

Flannery O'Connor. "Letters 1954–55" from *The Habit of Being*, selected and edited by Sally Fitzgerald. Copyright © 1979 by Regina O'Connor. "The Element of Surprise in 'A Good Man Is Hard to Find'" (excerpted from "On Her Own Work") and "Writing Short Stories" from *Mystery and Manners: Occasional Prose*, selected and edited by Sally Fitzgerald and Robert Fitzgerald. Copyright © 1969 by The Estate of Mary Flannery O'Connor. All reprinted by permission of Farrar, Straus and Giroux, LLC.

Grace Paley. "A Conversation with Ann Charters" reprinted by permission of Ann Charters.

David S. Reynolds. "Poe's Art of Transformation in 'The Cask of Amontillado'" excerpted from *New Essays on Poe's Major Tales*, edited by Kenneth Silverman. Copyright © 1993. Reprinted with permission of Cambridge University Press.

A. O. Scott. "Looking for Raymond Carver" from *The New York Review*, August 12, 1999. Copyright © 1999 NYREV, Inc. Reprinted by permission of *The New York Review of Books*.

Kathleen Westfall Shute. "On 'The Bath' and 'A Small Good Thing'" from "Finding the Words: The Struggle for Salvation in the Fiction of Raymond Carver," *Hollins Critic* 24.5 (1987). Reprinted by permission of the publisher.

Leslie Marmon Silko. "Language and Literature from a Pueblo Indian Perspective" from *English Literature: Opening Up the Canon*, edited by Leslie A. Fiedler and Houston A. Baker Jr., Selected Papers from the English Institute, 1979, pp. 54–72. Copyright © 1981 by Leslie Marmon Silko. Reprinted by permission of Johns Hopkins University Press.

Amy Tan. "In the Canon for All the Wrong Reasons" from *The Threepenny Review* (Fall, 1996). Copyright © 1996. Reprinted by permission of the Sandra Dijkstra Agency.

Cheryl B. Torsney. "'Everyday Use': My Sojourn at Parchman Farm" from *The Intimate Critique: Autobiographical Literary Criticism*, edited by Diane P. Freedman, Olivia Frey, and Frances Murphy Zauhar. Copyright © 1993. Reprinted by permission of Duke University Press.

John Updike. "Kafka and 'The Metamorphosis'" from *Odd Jobs* by John Updike. Copyright © 1991 by John Updike. Reprinted by permission of Alfred A. Knopf, a division of Random House, Inc.

Alice Walker. "Zora Neale Hurston: A Cautionary Tale and a Partisan View" from the Foreword to *Zora Neale Hurston: A Literary Biography* by Robert E. Hemenway. Copyright © 1977 by the Board of Trustees of the University of Illinois. Reprinted by permission of the University of Illinois Press.

Eudora Welty. "Is Phoenix Jackson's Grandson Really Dead?" and "Reality in Chekhov's Stories" from *The Eye of the Story: Selected Essays and Reviews* by Eudora Welty. Copyright © 1978 by Eudora Welty. Reprinted by permission of Random House, Inc.

POETRY

Rolf Aggestam. "Lightning Bolt," translated by Sam Charters from *Att Fla En Blixt* (*To Skin a Bolt of Lightning*), published by Wahlstrom and Wistrand (Sweden). Reprinted by permission of the author.

Anna Akhmatova. "Instead of a Preface," translated by Richard M. Kane from *Selected Poems*. Copyright © 1967 by Richard McKane. Reprinted by permission of Bloodaxe Books Ltd. Also from *Poem without a Hero and Selected Poems* by Anna Akhmatova, translated by Lenore Mayhew and William McNaughton, *Field* Translation Series #14, Oberlin College Press, 1989.

John Ashbery. "The Instruction Manual" from *Some Trees* by John Ashbery. Copyright © 1956 by John Ashbery. "Around the Rough and Rugged Rocks the Ragged Rascal Rudely

Ran" from *A Wave* by John Ashbery. Copyright © 1981, 1982, 1983, 1984 by John Ashbery. Reprinted with permission of Georges Borchardt, Inc., for the author.

Margaret Atwood. "Siren Song" from *You Are Happy, Selected Poems 1965–1975*. Copyright © 1976 by Margaret Atwood. Reprinted by permission of Houghton Mifflin Co. and Oxford University Press, Canada. All rights reserved.

W. H. Auden. "Musée des Beaux Arts" from *W. H. Auden: Collected Poems* by W. H. Auden, edited by Edward Mendelson. Copyright © 1940 and renewed 1968 by W. H. Auden. "Refugee Blues," "Stop All the Clocks," and five epigrams from *Collected Poems* by W. H. Auden. Copyright © 1976 by Edward Mendelson, William Meredith, and Monroe K. Spears, Executors of the Estate of W. H. Auden. Reprinted by permission of Random House, Inc.

Amiri Baraka. "Legacy" from *Black Magic* by Amiri Baraka. Copyright by Amiri Baraka. Reprinted by permission of Sterling Lord Literistic, Inc.

Bashō. "Day by day," "Having no talent," "Ripening barley —," and "A crow is perched" from *The Essential Haiku: Versions of Bashō, Buson, and Issa*, edited and with an Introduction by Robert Hass. Introduction and Selection copyright 1994 by Robert Hass. Translations copyright 1994 by Robert Hass. Reprinted by permission of HarperCollins Publishers, Inc.

Elizabeth Bishop. "One Art," "The Bight," "Sestina," and "The Fish" from *The Complete Poems 1927–1979*. Copyright © 1979, 1983 by Alice Helen Methfessel. Reprinted by permission of Farrar, Straus and Giroux, LLC.

Robert Bly. "August Rain" from *Eating the Honey of Words*. Copyright © 1999 by Robert Bly. Reprinted by permission of HarperCollins Publishers.

Gwendolyn Brooks. "We Real Cool," "The Mother," and "The Bean Eaters" from *Blacks* by Gwendolyn Brooks. Copyright © 1991 by Gwendolyn Brooks Blakely. Reprinted by consent of Brooks Permissions.

Sterling A. Brown. "Frankie and Johnny" from *The Collected Poems of Sterling A. Brown*, edited by Michael S. Harper. Copyright © 1939, 1980 by Sterling A. Brown. Reprinted with permission of HarperCollins Publishers, Inc.

Samuel Charters. "Hopi Corn," copyright © by Samuel Charters. Reprinted by permission of Samuel Charters.

Marilyn Chin. "How I Got That Name" from *The Phoenix Gone, The Terrace Empty* by Marilyn Chin. Copyright © 1994 by Marilyn Chin. Reprinted by permission of Milkweed Editions, www.milkweed.org.

A. Cinna. "Did Ophelia ask Hamlet to bed?" from *The Penguin Book of Limericks*, edited by E. O. Parrott (New York: Viking Penguin, 1983). Reprinted by permission.

Amy Clampitt. "Fog" and "Real Estate" from *The Collected Poems of Amy Clampitt* by Amy Clampitt. Copyright © 1997 by the Estate of Amy Clampitt. Introduction by Mary Jo Salter. Reprinted by permission of Alfred A. Knopf, a division of Random House, Inc.

Lucille Clifton. "to ms. ann" from *Good Woman: Poems and a Memoir 1969–1980*. Copyright © 1987 by Lucille Clifton. "why some people be mad at me sometimes" from *Next*. Copyright © 1987 by Lucille Clifton. Reprinted by permission of BOA Editions Ltd.

Billy Collins. "American Sonnet" and "Memento Mori" from *Questions about Angels* by Billy Collins. Copyright © 1999. "Tuesday, June 4, 1991" from *The Art of Drowning* by Billy Collins. Copyright © 1995. Reprinted by permission of the University of Pittsburgh Press. "By a Swimming Pool Outside Siracusa" from *Pushcart* 2002. First appeared in *The Gettysburg Review*. Reprinted by permission.

Wendy Cope. "Two Cures for Love" from *Serious Concerns*. Copyright © 1992. Reprinted by permission of Sterling Lord Literistic. "The fine English poet, John Donne" from *The Penguin Book of Limericks*, edited by E. O. Parrott. Reprinted by permission of the author.

Hart Crane. "Forgetfulness" from *The Complete Poems of Hart Crane*, edited by Marc Simon. Copyright © 1933, 1958, 1966 by Liveright Publishing Corporation. Copyright © 1986 by Marc Simon. Reprinted with the permission of Liveright Publishing Corporation.

Countee Cullen. "Yet Do I Marvel," "Heritage," and "Incident" from *Color*. Copyright 1925 by Harper & Brothers, renewed 1953 by Ida M. Cullen. Reprinted by permission of Thompson & Thompson, New York.

e. e. cummings. "since feeling is first," "somewhere i have never travelled,gladly beyond," "Buffalo Bill 's," and "in Just-" from *Complete Poems: 1904–1962* by e. e. cummings, edited by George J. Firmage. Copyright 1923, 1925, 1926, 1931, 1935, 1938, 1939, 1940, 1944, 1945, 1946, 1947, 1948, 1949, 1950, 1951, 1952, 1953, 1954, © 1955, 1956, 1957, 1958, 1959, 1960, 1961, 1962, 1963, 1966, 1967, 1968, 1972, 1973, 1974, 1975, 1976, 1977, 1978, 1979, 1980, 1981, 1982, 1983, 1984, 1985, 1986, 1987, 1988, 1989, 1990, 1991 by the Trustees for the E. E. Cummings Trust. Copyright © 1973, 1976, 1978, 1979, 1981, 1983, 1985, 1991 by George James Firmage. Reprinted by permission of Liveright Publishing Corporation.

H. D. (Hilda Doolittle). "Mid-day" and "Oread" from *Collected Poems, 1912–1944*. Copyright © 1982 by The Estate of Hilda Doolittle. Reprinted by permission of New Directions Publishing Corp.

James Dickey. "The Dusk of Horses" from *Helmets: Poems* by James Dickey. Copyright © 1962, 1963, 1964. Wesleyan University Press. Reprinted by permission.

Emily Dickinson. #199 / "I'm 'wife'—I've finished that—," #214 / "I taste a liquor never brewed—," #224 / "I've nothing else—to bring, You know—," #249 / "Wild Nights—Wild Nights!," #254 / "Hope is the thing with feathers," #258 / "There's a certain Slant of light," #288 / "I'm Nobody! Who are you?," #341 / "After great pain, a formal feeling comes," #435 / "Much Madness is divinest Sense," #449 / "I died for Beauty—but was scarce," #453 / "Love—thou are high—," #465 / "I heard a Fly buzz—when I died," #511 / "If you were coming in the Fall," #528 / "Mine—by the right of the White Election!," #712 / "Because I could not stop for Death," #827 / "The Only News I know," #861 / "Split the Lark—and you'll find the Music—," #875 / "I stepped from Plank to Plank," and #986 / "a narrow Fellow in the Grass" from *The Poems of Emily Dickinson*, edited by Ralph W. Franklin (Cambridge, Mass.: The Belknap Press of Harvard University Press). Copyright © 1951, 1955, 1979, 1983, 1998 by the President and Fellows of Harvard College.

Rita Dove. "Sonnet in Primary Colors" from *Mother Love* by Rita Dove. Copyright © 1995 by Rita Dove. "Singsong," "Maple Valley Branch Library, 1967," and "The Pond, Porch-View: Six P.M., Early Spring" from *On the Bus with Rosa Parks* by Rita Dove. Copyright © 1999 by Rita Dove. Reprinted by permission of W. W. Norton & Company, Inc.

Robert Duncan. "The Ballad of Mrs. Noah" from *The Opening of the Field* by Robert Duncan. New Directions Publishing Corp. Copyright © 1960 by Robert Duncan. Reprinted by permission.

T. S. Eliot. "The Love Song of J. Alfred Prufrock" from *T. S. Eliot: The Complete Poems and Plays 1909–1950*. Copyright 1917 by T. S. Eliot. Reprinted by permission of Faber and Faber Ltd.

Lawrence Ferlinghetti. "Constantly Risking Absurdity" from *A Coney Island of the Mind*. Copyright © 1958 by Lawrence Ferlinghetti. Reprinted by permission of New Directions Publishing Corp.

Carolyn Forché. "The Colonel" from *The Country Between Us*. Copyright © 1981 by Carolyn Forché. Reprinted by permission of HarperCollins Publishers, Inc.

Robert Frost. "The Pasture," "Fire and Ice," "To Earthward," and "Stopping by Woods on a Snowy Evening" from *The Poetry of Robert Frost*, edited by Edward Connery Lathem. Copyright 1923, 1939, © 1967, 1969 by Henry Holt and Co. Copyright 1951 by Robert Frost. All reprinted by permission of Henry Holt and Company, LLC.

Allen Ginsberg. "A Supermarket in California" and "America" from *Collected Poems 1947–1980*. Copyright © 1955, 1958 and renewed 1983, 1986 by Allen Ginsberg. Reprinted by permission of HarperCollins Publishers, Inc.

Louise Glück. "First Memory" from *Ararat* (Ecco Press). Copyright © 1990 by Louise Glück. Reprinted by permission of HarperCollins Publishers, Inc.

Richard Leighton Green. "(Apropos Coleridge's 'Kubla Khan') When approached by a person from Porlock" from *The Penguin Book of Limericks*, edited by E. O. Parrott (New York: Viking Penguin, 1983).

Jim Harrison. "Northern Michigan" from *The Shape of the Journey: New and Collected Poems*. Copyright © 1998 by Jim Harrison. Copper Canyon Press. Reprinted by permission.

Robert Hass. "A Story about the Body" from *Human Wishes* by Robert Hass. Copyright © 1989 by Robert Hass. First published by the Ecco Press in 1989. Reprinted by permission of HarperCollins Publishers, Inc.

Robert Hayden. "Those Winter Sundays" and "A Letter from Phillis Wheatley" from *Collected Poems of Robert Hayden*, edited by Frederick Glaysher. Copyright © 1966, 1978 by Robert Hayden. "Night, Death, Mississippi" from *Angle of Ascent: New and Selected Poems* by Robert Hayden. Copyright © 1975, 1972, 1966 by Robert Hayden. Reprinted by permission of Liveright Publishing Corporation.

Seamus Heaney. "Digging" from *Poems 1965–1975* by Seamus Heaney. Copyright © 1980 by Seamus Heaney. "The Harvest Bow" from *Field Work* by Seamus Heaney. Copyright © 1976, 1979 by Seamus Heaney. Reprinted by permission of Farrar, Straus & Giroux, LLC, and Faber and Faber Ltd.

Tobey Hiller. "The Poem (or, Alice's Remarks on Reading the Fine Print on the Bottle's Label)" from *Certain Weathers* (Berkeley, CA: Oyez, 1987). Copyright © 1987 by Tobey Hiller. "the closing of the south park road," copyright © 1996 by Toby Hiller. Reprinted by permission of the author.

Langston Hughes. "Mother to Son," "Bound No'th Blues," "Song for a Dark Girl," "House in the World," "Florida Road Workers," "I, Too," "Down Where I Am," "Personal," "Little Lyric *(Of Great Importance),*" "Merry-Go-Round," "Dream Deferred," and "Theme for English B" from *The Collected Poems of Langston Hughes* by Langston Hughes. Copyright © 1994 by the Estate of Langston Hughes. Reprinted by permission of Alfred A. Knopf, a division of Random House, Inc.

Randall Jarrell. "The Death of the Ball Turret Gunner" from *The Complete Poems* by Randall Jarrell. Copyright © 1969 by Mrs. Randall Jarrell. Reprinted by permission of Farrar, Straus & Giroux, LLC.

Jack Kerouac. "Birds singing," "The summer chair," and "In my medicine cabinet" from *Scattered Poems,* compiled by Ann Charters (San Francisco: City Lights Books, 1971). Copyright © 1971 by the Estate of Jack Kerouac. Reprinted by permission of Sterling Lord Literistic, Inc.

Hugh Kingsmill. "What, Still Alive at Twenty-Two?" from *The Best of Hugh Kingsmill.* Copyright © 1970 by Brook Kingsmill-Lunn. Reprinted by permission of The Revd. Brook Kingsmill-Lunn.

Galway Kinnell. "Oatmeal" from *When One Has Lived a Long Time Alone* by Galway Kinnell. Copyright © 1990 by Galway Kinnell. Reprinted by permission of Alfred A. Knopf, a division of Random House, Inc. "The Man Splitting Wood in the Daybreak" from *Three Books* by Galway Kinnell. Copyright © 1993 by Galway Kinnell. Previously published in *The Past* (1985). Reprinted by permission of Houghton Mifflin Company. All rights reserved.

Etheridge Knight. "The Idea of Ancestry" from *The Essential Etheridge Knight* by Etheridge Knight. Copyright © 1986 by Etheridge Knight. Reprinted by permission of the University of Pittsburgh Press.

Yusef Komunyakaa. "Facing It" from *Dien Cai Dau.* Copyright © 1988 by Yusef Komunyakaa. Reprinted by permission of Wesleyan University Press.

Denise Levertov. "The Mutes" from *Poems 1960–1967* by Denise Levertov. Copyright © 1966 by Denise Levertov. Reprinted by permission of New Directions Publishing Corporation.

Primo Levi. "Almanac" from *Collected Poems.* Copyright © 1988. Reprinted by permission of Faber and Faber Ltd.

Audre Lorde. "Hanging Fire" from *The Black Unicorn* by Audre Lorde. Copyright © 1978 by Audre Lorde. Reprinted by permission of W. W. Norton & Co.

Robert Lowell. "Skunk Hour" from *Life Studies.* "For the Union Dead" from *For the Union Dead.* Copyright © 1959 by Robert Lowell, renewed © 1987 by Harriet W. Lowell, Sheridan Lowell, and Caroline Lowell. "Epilogue" from *Day by Day.* Copyright © 1977 by Robert Lowell. All reprinted with permission of Farrar, Straus and Giroux LLC.

Mina Loy. "One O'Clock at Night" from *The Last Lunar Baedeker/Mina Loy* edited by Roger L. Conover. Highlands (N.C.): Jargon Society, 1982. Reprinted by permission of the author.

Archibald MacLeish. "Ars Poetica" from *Collected Poems 1917–1982* by Archibald MacLeish. Copyright © 1985 by The Estate of Archibald MacLeish. Reprinted by permission of Houghton Mifflin Company. All rights reserved.

W. S. Merwin. "Birds Waking" from *The First Four Books of Poems: A Mask for Janus, The Dancing Bears, Green with Beasts, The Drunk in the Furnace.* Copyright © 1975. Atheneum.

Marianne Moore. "The Fish," copyright 1935 by Marianne Moore and renewed 1963 by Marianne Moore, and "What Are Years?" copyright 1941 by Marianne Moore and renewed 1969 by Marianne Moore, reprinted with the permission of Scribner, a division of Simon & Schuster, from *The Complete Poems of Marianne Moore.* "In the Public Garden" from *The Complete Poems of Marianne Moore.* Copyright © 1959 by Marianne Moore. Reprinted by permission of Viking Penguin, a division of Penguin Group (USA) Inc.

Edwin Morgan. "Siesta of a Hungarian Snake" from *Selected Poems* by Edwin Morgan. Copyright © 1985. Reprinted by permission of Carcanet Press Ltd.

Andrew Motion. "Anne Frank Huis" from *The Pleasure Steamers.* Copyright © 1974. Reprinted by permission of Carcanet Press Ltd..

Ogden Nash. "Reflections on Ice Breaking" from *Verses from 1929 On* by Ogden Nash. Copyright © 1930 by Ogden Nash. First appeared in *The New Yorker.* Reprinted by permission of Little, Brown and Company.

Lorine Niedecker. "Poet's Work" from *Collected Works,* edited by Jenny Lynn Pemberthy. Reprinted by permission of the University of California Press.

Frank O'Hara. "The Day Lady Died" from *Lunch Poems* by Frank O'Hara. Copyright © 1964 by Frank O'Hara. Reprinted by permission of City Light Books.

Sharon Olds. "Sex Without Love" and "The Elder Sister" from *The Dead and the Living* by Sharon Olds. Copyright © 1987 by Sharon Olds. "Summer Solstice, New York City" from *The Gold Cell* by Sharon Olds. Copyright © 1987 by Sharon Olds. All reprinted by permission of Alfred A. Knopf, a division of Random House, Inc.

Alicia Susan Ostriker. "Wrinkly Lady Dancer" and "The Change" from *The Little Space: Poems Selected and New 1968–1998* by Alicia Susan Ostriker. Copyright © 1998. Reprinted by permission of the University of Pittsburgh Press.

Wilfred Owen. "Dulce et Decorum Est" from *The Collected Poems of Wilfred Owen.* Copyright © 1963 by Chatto & Windus, Ltd. Reprinted by permission of New Directions Publishing Corp.

Dorothy Parker. "Indian Summer" copyright 1926, renewed © 1954 by Dorothy Parker, from *The Portable Dorothy Parker* by Dorothy Parker, edited by Brendan Gill. Reprinted by permission of Viking Penguin, a division of Penguin Group (USA) Inc.

Linda Pastan. "To a Daughter Leaving Home" from *The Imperfect Paradise.* Copyright © 1978 by Linda Pastan. Reprinted by permission of W. W. Norton & Co.

Marge Piercy. "In which she begs (like everybody else) that love may last" from *Stone, Paper, Knife* by Marge Piercy. Copyright © 1983 by Marge Piercy. "The woman in the ordinary" from *Circles on the Water* by Marge Piercy. Copyright © 1982 by Marge Piercy. "It ain't heavy, it's my purse" from *Mars and Her Children* by Marge Piercy. Copyright © 1992 by Middlemarsh, Inc. All reprinted by permission of Alfred A. Knopf, a division of Random House, Inc.

Sylvia Plath. "Morning Song" and "Daddy" from *Ariel* by Sylvia Plath. Copyright © 1961, 1963, 1966 by Ted Hughes. "Event" from *Winter Trees* by Sylvia Plath. Copyright © 1972 by Ted Hughes. All reprinted by permission of HarperCollins Publishers and Faber and Faber Ltd.

Allen Polite. "Song" from *Poems* by Allen Polite. Copyright © 1966. Reprinted by permission of Helene Polite Etzelsdorfer.

Ezra Pound. "A Pact" from *Personae.* Copyright 1926 by Ezra Pound. Reprinted by permission of New Directions Publishing Corp.

Dudley Randall. "Ballad of Birmingham" from *Cities Burning* (Broadside Press). Reprinted by permission of the author.

John Crowe Ransom. "Bells for John Whiteside's Daughter" from *Selected Poems* by John Crowe Ransom. Copyright 1924 by Alfred A. Knopf, Inc., and renewed 1952 by John Crowe Ransom. Reprinted by permission of Alfred A. Knopf, a division of Random House, Inc.

Ishmael Reed. "The Reactionary Poet" from *New and Collected Poems* by Ishmael Reed. Copyright © 1988. Atheneum. Reprinted by permission of the author.

Lou Reed. "Chelsea Girls" from *Pass Thru Fire: The Collected Lyrics* by Lou Reed. © 2000 by Lou Reed. NY: Hyperion. Reprinted by permission.

Adrienne Rich. "Diving into the Wreck," copyright © 2002 by Adrienne Rich, copyright © 1973 by W. W. Norton & Company, Inc. "Aunt Jennifer's Tigers," copyright © 2002, 1951 by Adrienne Rich. Both from *The Fact of a Doorframe: Selected Poems 1950–2001* by Adrienne Rich. "To the Days" from *Dark Fields of the Republic: Poems 1991–1995.* Copyright © 1995 by Adrienne Rich. All reprinted by permission of the author and W. W. Norton & Company, Inc.

Theodore Roethke. "My Papa's Waltz," copyright 1942 by Hearst Magazines, Inc. "The Waking," copyright 1953 by Theodore Roethke. "Night Journey," copyright © 1940 by Theodore Roethke. From *Collected Poems of Theodore Roethke* by Theodore Roethke. Reprinted by permission of Doubleday, a division of Random House, Inc.

Norman Rosten. "Who Killed Norma Jean" from "For Marilyn Monroe" in *Selected Poems* by Norman Rosten. Copyright © 1979. George Braziller.

Anne Sexton. "The Starry Night" from *All My Pretty Ones.* Copyright © 1962 by Anne Sexton, renewed 1990 by Linda Sexton. "For My Lover, Returning to His Wife" from *Love Poems.* Copyright © 1967, 1968, 1969 by Anne Sexton. Reprinted by permission of Houghton Mifflin Company.

Stevie Smith. "Not Waving but Drowning" from *The Collected Poems of Stevie Smith.* Copyright © 1972 by Stevie Smith. Reprinted by permission of New Directions Publishing Corp.

Gary Snyder. "Ripples on the Surface" from *No Nature.* Copyright © 1992 by Gary Snyder. Reprinted by permission of North Point Press, a division of Farrar, Straus and Giroux, LLC.

Gary Soto. "Mexicans Begin Jogging" from *New and Selected Poems* by Gary Soto. Copyright © 1995. "Teaching English from an Old Composition Book" from *A Natural Man* by Gary Soto. Copyright © 1999 by Gary Soto. Published in the U.S. by Chronicle Books LLC, San Francisco. Reprinted by permission.

Wallace Stevens. "The Emperor of Ice-Cream" and "Thirteen Ways of Looking at a Blackbird" from *The Collected Poems of Wallace Stevens* by Wallace Stevens. Copyright 1954 by Wallace Stevens and renewed 1982 by Holly Stevens. Reprinted by permission of Alfred A. Knopf, a division of Random House, Inc.

Anne Stevenson. "The Spirit is too Blunt an Instrument" from *The Collected Poems, 1955–1995.* Bloodaxe Books, 2000. Reprinted by permission of the author and the publisher.

Wislawa Szymborska. "True Love" from *View with a Grain of Sand.* Copyright © 1993 by Wislawa Szymborska. English translation by Stanislaw Baranczak and Clare Cavanagh. Copyright © 1995 by Harcourt, Inc. Reprinted by permission of the publisher.

Dylan Thomas. "The Last Time I Slept with the Queen," reprinted by permission of Harold Ober Associates, Inc., from *The Silver Treasury of Light Verse.* Copyright © 1956 by New Directions. "Do Not Go Gentle into That Good Night" from *The Poems of Dylan Thomas.* Copyright 1952 by New Directions Publishing Corporation. Reprinted by permission of New Directions Publishing Corp.

Alice Walker. "I Said to Poetry" from *Horses Make a Landscape Look More Beautiful: Poetry* by Alice Walker. Copyright © 1984 by Alice Walker. Reprinted by permission of Harcourt, Inc.

Robert Penn Warren. "What Voice at Moth Hour" from *The Collected Poems of Robert Penn Warren,* edited by John Burt. Copyright © 1998. Reprinted by permission of the William Morris Agency.

Richard Wilbur. "My Father Paints the Summer," copyright 1947 from *The Poems of Richard Wilbur.* Reprinted by permission of Harcourt, Inc.

Big Joe Williams. "Levee Break Blues," copyright © 1975. Stainless Music Corp. All rights reserved. Used with permission.

Miller Williams. "Thinking about Bill, Dead of AIDS" from *Living on the Surface: New and Selected Poems* by Miller Williams. Copyright © 1989 by Miller Williams. Reprinted by permission of Louisiana State University Press.

William Carlos Williams. "This Is Just to Say," "The Widow's Lament in Springtime," "The Red Wheelbarrow," and "Spring and All" (section I) from *Collected Poems: 1909–1939,* Volume I. Copyright © 1938 by New Directions Publishing Corp. Reprinted by permission of New Directions Publishing Corp.

POETRY COMMENTARIES

Simple. Copyright 1950, © 1961 by Langston Hughes, renewed 1978, 1991 by George Houston Bass. Reprinted by permission of Hill & Wang, a division of Farrar, Straus & Giroux, LLC.

Thomas J. Johnson. "The Text of Emily Dickinson's Poetry" (editors' title) from the Introduction to *The Complete Poems of Emily Dickinson*, edited by Thomas H. Johnson. Copyright © 1960 by Thomas H. Johnson, renewed 1988 by Catherine R. Johnson. Reprinted by permission of Harvard University Press.

Erica Jong. "Devouring Time: Shakespeare's Sonnets" from *Touchstones: American Poets on a Favorite Poem*, edited by Robert Pack and Jay Parini. Copyright © 1996 by the President and Fellows of Middlebury College. Reprinted by permission of the University Press of New England.

Galway Kinnell. "The Deconstruction of Emily Dickinson" from *Imperfect Thirst*. Originally published in *The American Poetry Review*. Copyright © 1994 by Galway Kinnell. Reprinted by permission of Houghton Mifflin Co. All rights reserved.

Philip Levine. Excerpt from "Keats in Detroit" by Philip Levine. Copyright © 1995 by The New York Times Company. Reprinted by permission.

Robert Lowell. "An Explication of 'Skunk Hour' " (editors' title) from *The Contemporary Poet as Artist and Critic*, edited by Anthony Ostroff. Copyright © 1964 by Little, Brown and Company. Reprinted by permission of the publishers. Foreword to Sylvia Plath's *Ariel*, copyright © 1963 and renewed 1991 by Ted Hughes. Reprinted by permission of Harper-Collins Publishers, Inc. "On Robert Frost" from *Notebook*, Revised and Expanded Edition. Copyright © 1967, 1968, 1969, 1970 by Robert Lowell, copyright renewed 1998 by Harriet Lowell. Reprinted by permission of Farrar, Straus and Giroux, LLC.

Brett C. Millier. "On Elizabeth Bishop's 'One Art,' " copyright © 1993 by Brett C. Millier. Reprinted by permission of the author. A fuller treatment of the subject appears in *Elizabeth Bishop: Life and the Memory of It* by Brett C. Millier. Lines from the first draft of "One Art" by Elizabeth Bishop are quoted by permission of the Special Collections of the Vassar College Libraries and Elizabeth Bishop's literary executor, Alice H. Methfessell.

Marianne Moore. "Some Answers to Questions Posed by Howard Nemerov" from *Poets on Poetry*, edited by Howard Nemerov. Copyright © 1966 by Howard Nemerov. Reprinted by permission of Basic Books, a member of Perseus Books LLC.

Sharon Olds. Excerpt from the *Salon* interview by Dwight Garner. This article first appeared in *Salon.com*, at www.Salon.com. An online version remains in the *Salon* archives. Reprinted with permission.

Marge Piercy. "Imagery Can't Really Be Taught" (editors' title) quoted in *Fooling with Words* by Bill Morrow. Copyright © 1999. Reprinted by permission of William Morrow.

Ezra Pound. "On the Principles of Imagism" (excerpted from "A Retrospect") from *Literary Essays of Ezra Pound*, edited by T. S. Eliot. Copyright 1935 by Ezra Pound. "What I Feel about Walt Whitman" from *Selected Prose 1909–1965*, edited by William Cookson. Copyright © 1955 by Ezra Pound. Copyright © 1973 by The Estate of Ezra Pound. Reprinted by permission of New Directions Publishing Corp.

Richard Wilbur. "On Emily Dickinson" (excerpted from "Sumptuous Destitution") from *Emily Dickinson: Three Views* by Richard Wilbur, Louise Bogan, and Archibald MacLeish (Amherst, Mass: Amherst College Press, 1960). This piece was later reprinted in *Responses* (New York: Harcourt Brace, 1976). Copyright © 1960 by Richard Wilbur. Reprinted by permission of the author.

Richard Wright. "A Review of *The Big Sea*" by Richard Wright. Published in *Langston Hughes: Critical Perspectives* (Gates & Appiah) and in *The New Republic*, October 18, 1940. Copyright © 1940 by Richard Wright. Reprinted by permission of John Hawkins Associates, Inc.

DRAMA

Lorraine Hansberry. *A Raisin in the Sun*. Copyright © 1958 by Robert Nemiroff as an unpublished work. Copyright © 1959, 1966, 1984, by Robert Nemiroff. Reprinted by permission of Random House, Inc.

Henrik Ibsen. *A Doll House* from *The Complete Major Prose Plays of Henrik Ibsen*, translated by Rolf Fjelde. Copyright © 1965, 1970, 1978 by Rolf Fjelde. Reprinted by permission of Dutton Signet, a division of Penguin Group (USA) Inc.

Arthur Miller. *Death of a Salesman* from *Death of a Salesman* by Arthur Miller. Copyright 1949, renewed © 1977 by Arthur Miller. Reprinted by permission of Viking Penguin, a division of Penguin Group (USA) Inc.

Willy Russell. Excerpt from Act 1, Scene 6 of *Educating Rita* (New York: Samuel French, 1981). Copyright © 1981 by Willy Russell. Reprinted by permission of Methuen Publishing Ltd.

William Shakespeare. *Hamlet, Prince of Denmark* from *An Introduction to Shakespeare*, revised edition (Craig & Bevington). Reprinted by permission of Addison Wesley Educational Publishers.

Sophocles. *Oedipus the King* from *Three Theban Plays* by Sophocles, translated by Robert Fagles. Copyright © 1982 by Robert Fagles. Reprinted by permission of Viking Penguin, a division of Penguin Group (USA) Inc.

Paula Vogel. *How I Learned to Drive* from *The Mammary Plays* by Paula Vogel. Copyright © 1997, 1998 by Paula Vogel. Published by Theatre Communications Group. Used by permission of the publisher.

Wendy Wasserstein. *Tender Offer*, copyright © 1991 by Wendy Wasserstein. First published in *Antaeus* #66, Plays in One Act, Spring 1991. No part of this material may be reproduced in whole or in part without the express written permission of the author or her agent. Reprinted by permission of Rosenstone/Wender.

Tennessee Williams. *The Glass Menagerie* from *The Glass Menagerie* by Tennessee Williams. Copyright © 1945 by Tennessee Williams and Edwina D. Williams and renewed 1973 by Tennessee Williams. Reprinted by permission of Random House, Inc.

DRAMA COMMENTARIES

Aristotle. "On the Elements and General Principles of Tragedy" (editors' title) translated by Gerald F. Else, from *Poetics*. Copyright © 1967. Reprinted by permission of the University of Michigan Press.

Geoffrey Bullough. "Sources of Shakespeare's *Hamlet*" (editors' title) from *Narrative and Dramatic Sources of Shakespeare*, 8 vols. Copyright © 1964 and renewed 1992 by Geoffrey Bullough. Reprinted by permission of Columbia University Press.

Jill Dolan. Review of *How I Learned to Drive* from *Theatre Journal* 50:1 (March 1998), pp. 127–28. Copyright © 1998 by the Johns Hopkins University Press. Reprinted by permission.

Francis Fergusson. "Oedipus, Myth and Play" from *The Idea of Theater*. Copyright 1949 by Princeton University Press. Reprinted by permission of the publishers.

Sigmund Freud. "The Oedipus Complex," © copyrights, The Institute of Psychoanalysis and the Hogarth Press for permission to quote from *The Standard Edition of the Complete Psychological Works of Sigmund Freud*, translated and edited by James Strachey. Reprinted by permission of The Random House Group.

Sir John Gielgud. "On Playing Hamlet" from *Early Stages* by Sir John Gielgud (New York: Macmillan, 1939). Copyright 1939.

Lorraine Hansberry. "An Author's Reflections: Willy Loman, Walter Younger, and He Who Must Live" from *The Village Voice Reader*, edited by Daniel Wolf and Edwin Fancher (New York: Doubleday, 1962). "My Shakespearean Experience" from *To Be Young, Gifted, and Black: Lorraine Hansberry in Her Own Words*. Copyright © 1960 by Robert Nemiroff. Reprinted by permission of Simon & Schuster.

H. D. F. Kitto. "*Hamlet* and the *Oedipus*" from *Form and Meaning in Drama*. Copyright © 1956. Reprinted by permission of Methuen Publishing Ltd.

John Lahr. "Review of *Hamlet*" from "Matinee Idolatry" in *Light Fantastic* by John Lahr. Copyright © 1996 by John Lahr. Reprinted by permission of The Dial Press/Dell Publishing, a division of Random House, Inc.

Arthur Miller. Excerpt from an interview in *The Paris Review* #38. Copyright © 1967 by The Paris Review, Inc. Reprinted by permission of *The Paris Review*. "Introduction" from

Arthur Miller's Collected Plays by Arthur Miller, copyright © 1957 by Arthur Miller. Used by permission of Viking Penguin, a division of Penguin Group (USA) Inc.

Leonard Mustazza. "Generic Translation and Thematic Shift in Susan Glaspell's *Trifles* and 'A Jury of Her Peers'" from *Studies in Short Fiction* 26 (1989), 489–96. Copyright © 1989 by Newbury College. Reprinted by permission of *Studies in Short Fiction*, Newbury College, Newbury, SC.

Benjamin Nelson. "Problems in *The Glass Menagerie*" from *Tennessee Williams: The Man and His Work* (New York: I. Obolensky, 1961). Copyright 1961 by Benjamin Nelson. Reprinted by permission of the author.

Helge Normann Nilsen. "Marxism and the Early Plays of Arthur Miller" from *"Honors at Dawn* to *Death of a Salesman:* Marxism and the Early Plays of Arthur Miller" in *English Studies* 75.2 (1994). Copyright © 1994 by Swets & Zeitlinger. Reprinted by permission of Swets Publishing Service, Lisse, The Netherlands.

Bernard Shaw. "On *A Doll House*" from *The Quintessence of Ibsenism, Now Completed to the Death of Ibsen* (New York: Brentano, 1919). Originally published in London by W. Scott in 1891. Reprinted by permission of the Society of Authors.

Tom Stoppard. *The Encore* from *Dogg's Hamlet, Cahoot's Macbeth.* Copyright © 1979 by Tom Stoppard. Reprinted by permission of Faber & Faber Ltd.

Joan Templeton. "Is *A Doll House* a Feminist Text?" excerpted from "The *Doll House* Backlash: Criticism, Feminism and Ibsen" in *Proceedings of the Modern Language Association* (January, 1989). Copyright © 1989 by The Modern Language Association. Reprinted by permission of The Modern Language Association.

Tennessee Williams. Production Notes to *The Glass Menagerie* from *The Theatre of Tennessee Williams*, Vol. 1. Copyright 1945 by Tennessee Williams and Edwina D. Williams. "Portrait of a Girl in Glass" from *The Collected Stories of Tennessee Williams.* Copyright 1948 by The University of the South. Renewed 1976 by The University of the South. Reprinted by permission of New Directions Publishing Corp.

Virginia Woolf. "What If Shakespeare Had Had a Sister?" (editors' title) excerpted from *A Room of One's Own* by Virginia Woolf. Copyright 1929 by Harcourt, Inc. and renewed 1957 by Leonard Woolf. Reprinted by permission of the publisher.

Index of First Lines

Index of Authors and Titles

"Enemies tend to utilize the one big fat character who runs right through the middle of the structure, by action or implication with whom we rise or fall."
— Lorraine Hansberry

"My task has been the description of humanity."
— Henrik Ibsen

"I still believe that when a play questions, even threatens, our social arrangement, that's when it really shakes us profoundly and dangerously."
— Arthur Miller

"The one and only possible salvation lies in his power to disbelieve those certain..."
— Tennessee Williams

"I don't think you should frighten them (the audience), I think you should terrify them."
— Edward Albee

drama

"Fine plays tend to utilize the one big fat character who runs right through the middle of the structure, by action or implication, with whom we rise or fall."
– Lorraine Hansberry

"My task has been the description of humanity."
– Henrik Ibsen

"I still believe that when a play questions, even threatens, our social arrangement, that is when it really shakes us profoundly and dangerously."
– Arthur Miller

"The great and only possible dignity of man lies in his power to deliberately choose certain moral values by which to live as steadfastly as if he too, like a character in a play, were immured against the corrupting rush of time."
– Tennessee Williams

"I don't think you should frighten them [the audience], I think you should terrify them."
– Edward Albee